EARL BLACKWELL'S CELEBRITY REGISTER 1990

EARL BLACKWELL'S CELEBRITY REGISTER 1990

Compiled by Celebrity Service International, Inc.

Gale Research Inc.

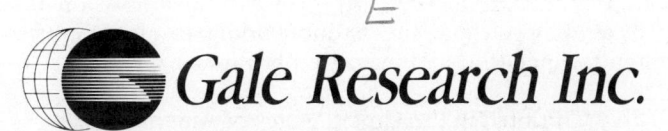

DETROIT · NEW YORK · FORT LAUDERDALE · LONDON

Published by Gale Research Inc.

Production Manager: Mary Beth Trimper
Assistant Production Manager: Evi Seoud
Art Director: Arthur Chartow
Graphic Designer: Bernadette M. Gornie
Keyliner: C.J. Jonik
Production Supervisor: Laura Bryant
Internal Production Associate: Louise Gagné
Internal Production Assistants: Kelly L. Krust and Sharana M. Wier

While every effort has been made to ensure the reliability of the information presented in this publication, Gale Research Inc. does not guarantee the accuracy of the data contained herein. Gale accepts no payment for listing; and inclusion in the publication of any organization, agency, institution, publication, service, or individual does not imply endorsement of the publisher. Errors brought to the attention of the publisher and verified to the satisfaction of the publisher will be corrected in future editions.

Copyright © 1990 by Celebrity Register, Inc.
1780 Broadway, New York, NY 10019
Vicki Bagley, President

Library of Congress Catalog Card Number: 85-51472
ISBN 0-8103-6875-7

No part of this book may be reproduced in any form without permission in writing from the publisher, except by a reviewer who wishes to quote brief passages or entries in connection with a review written for inclusion in a magazine or newspaper.

Printed in the United States of America

Celebrity Service International, Inc.

PRESIDENT:	Vicki Bagley
CHAIRMAN:	Earl Blackwell
MANAGING EDITOR & SENIOR WRITER:	Patsy Maharam
STAFF WRITERS:	Frank Gehrecke
	Joan Schilling
	Dina Pitenis
	Evangeline Rapess
	Davida Lynne
ASSISTANT TO THE EDITOR:	Joan Schilling
TECHNICAL ASSISTANT:	Sirpaul Sundown
CSI RESEARCHERS:	Nancy Preiser
	Frances Van
	Carol Schiff
	Bill Murray
	Jeff Kormos

PAST CONTRIBUTORS: Barbara McGurn, Elizabeth Pierce, Barbara Sansone, William Norwich, Tony Chapelle, Michael Halberstadt, Elizabeth Kramer, Susan O'Meara, Warren Strugatch, Tammy Tanaka

A Note From the President of Celebrity Service International, Inc.

I would like to acknowledge the many individuals and organizations who have aided us in the acquisition of both information and photographs. My particular thanks to the New York and California staffs of Celebrity Service International, as well as the past contributors to Volumes I, II, III, and IV of the *Celebrity Register*. I extend my appreciation to Gale Research Inc. for the publication of this book, and to Patsy Maharam (Managing Editor) for a job well done. Most of all, my sincere congratulations and gratitude to Earl Blackwell.

Vicki Bagley
President
Celebrity Service International, Inc.

A Tribute To Mr. Celebrity

"Earl and I are perfect examples of the belief that durability is the thing. Above all else, be durable,"

writes Helen Hayes on 21 April 1989 in a letter to me about Earl Blackwell. I have chosen her most wonderful quote to be the impetus which sets this foreword in motion. In these pages are faces surrounded by landscapes sketching the lives of famous people. What Is a Celebrity—Who Is a Celebrity—and the definition of celebrity have served as the forewords of past *Celebrity Registers*. In 1963, Cleveland Amory defined celebrity as ". . . a name which, once made by news, now makes news by itself." Putting together this 1990 edition, it struck me to change the flavor of the foreword and focus the attention on a man who is as familiar to the theatrical world as the theatrical world is familiar to him. Celebrating his 50th Anniversary in the business (as Founder and Chairman of Celebrity Service International), Earl Blackwell is not only a confidant to the industry, but a friend to the stars. With contributions from legendary performers in theatre and film, here is a toast to our Mr. Celebrity.

"Celebrities move around madly. Earl Blackwell has contributed to the peace and pleasantness of my life by putting me in touch with my famous friends who are never where one hopes them to be."

HELEN HAYES

"*The Celebrity Register* was an idea as necessary and obvious as the original *Who's Who*, but it took someone with imagination, energy, ability and knowledge of the needs of the media and the theatrical industry to bring it into being. Earl Blackwell was that special man."

DOUGLAS FAIRBANKS, JR.

"I understand this volume of *The Celebrity Register* is dedicated to Mr. Earl Blackwell. A celebration in effect of his 50 years in the celebrity firmament. Mr. Blackwell has known, worked with, and helped many stars in that heaven. No one that I can think of has shown a greater fidelity to those stars. A Southern Gentleman of charm and discretion; a star in his own right."

CLIFF ROBERTSON

"Earl's 'staying power' shows not only in his dedication to his work, but also in his friendship—after 35 years of being a happy recipient I know what I'm talking about!"

AUDREY HEPBURN

A reflective cogitation from a member of the new fame generation details the timeless respect presented to Earl Blackwell.

"50 years ago, my grandparents loved *The Celebrity Register;* for the past 25 years my parents have loved *The Celebrity Register.* I love *The Celebrity Register* today, and tomorrow my children will delight in its splendor."

BROOKE SHIELDS

There is an unspoken internal weave procreated between generations that becomes clearer as we compare the accomplishments of various eras. The guidelines molded by Earl Blackwell can be appreciated for years to come. I know they have been useful to me as I compiled this Volume V, with love. . . .

Patsy Maharam

Managing Editor

Photo Credits

Andre Agassi: Russ Adams/International Management Group
Alvin Ailey: Eric N. Hong
Edward Albee: Alix Jeffry
Alan Alda: Arlene Alda
Muhammad Ali: Karsh
Marcus Allen: Los Angeles Raiders
Herb Alpert: A&M Records
Loni Anderson: Harry Langdon Photography
Richard Dean Anderson: Paramount Pictures Corporation
Julie Andrews: Zoe Dominic
Ann-Margret: E. J. Camp/Paramount Pictures Corporation
Claudio Arrau: Sophie Baker/ICM Artists Ltd.
Peggy Ashcroft: Granada TV
Vladimir Ashkenazy: Christina Burton/ICM Artists Ltd.
Isaac Asimov: Kurt Muller
Edward Asner: Dana Gluckstein
Rick Astley: RCA
Chet Atkins: Melodie Gimple
Louis Auchincloss: Inge Morath
Arnold "Red" Auerbach: Boston Celtics
Richard Avedon: Gideon Lewin
Emanuel Ax: Nick Sangiamo/ICM Artists Ltd.
Dan Aykroyd: Universal City Studios

Pearl Bailey: Bachrach
Anita Baker: Buckmaster/Elektra
Janet Baker: Zoe Dominic
Russell Baker: Thomas Victor
Severiano Ballesteros: PGA Tour
Daniel Barenboim: Columbia Artists Management Inc.
Roseanne Barr: Capital Cities/ABC
Donald Barthelme: Jerry Bauer
Mikhail Baryshnikov: Kenn Duncan Ltd.
Kim Basinger: Greg Gorman/Weintraub Entertainment Group
Jason Bateman: Lorimar Television
Justine Bateman: Paramount Pictures Corp.
Kathleen Battle: Christian Steiner
Ann Beattie: Thomas Victor
Samuel Beckett: Jerry Bauer
Hildegard Behrens: Columbia Artists Management Inc.
Barbara Bel Geddes: Lorimar
Pat Benatar: Moshe Brakha/Chrysalis
Tony Bennett: Annie Leibovitz
George Benson: Robert Hakalski/Warner Bros. Records
Tom Berenger: Suzanne Tenner
Candice Bergen: Universal City Studios, Inc.
Corbin Bernsen: Timothy White/Morgan Creek Productions
Leonard Bernstein: Andrey's Studio/Deutsche Grammophon
Yogi Berra: Houston Astros
Bernardo Bertolucci: Columbia Pictures
Stephen Birmingham: Bachrach
Shirley Temple Black: Curt Gunther
Betsy Bloomingdale: Robert R. Bloomingdale
Brian Boitano: Roy Blakey
Erma Bombeck: Rod Moyer
Bon Jovi: Mercury/Polygram
Bjorn Borg: International Management Group
Victor Borge: Martin Reichenthal
Brian Bosworth: Seattle Seahawks
Pierre Boulez: Fee Schlapper
Boy George: Paul Gobel/Virgin
James Brady: Jade Albert
Marlon Brando: David James/Metro-Goldwyn-Mayer Pictures, Inc.
George Brett: Kansas City Royals
Tom Brokaw: NBC
David Brown: Etienne George
Tina Brown: Martin Seymour
Jackson Browne: Henry Diltz/Asylum
John Browning: Kenn Duncan
Susan Brownmiller: Jill Krementz
Robert Brustein: Jeffrey Melvoin
Art Buchwald: Donal Holway
Jimmy Buffett: MCA Records
Fernando Bujones: Kenn Duncan
Anthony Burgess: Jerry Bauer
David Byrne: Cori Wells Braun

Paul Cadmus: Robert Le Strange Rose
Herb Caen: San Francisco Chronicle
Sammy Cahn: Kenneth Johansson
Sarah Caldwell: Jack Mitchell
Cab Calloway: International Creative Management, Inc.
Kirk Cameron: Greg Gorman
Glen Campbell: Peter Nash/MCA Records Nashville
John Candy: Paramount Pictures Corporation
Jose Canseco: Oakland A's
Eric Carmen: Roxy Rifken
Kim Carnes: Henry Diltz/MCA Records
John Carpenter: Columbia Pictures
Jose Carreras: Columbia Artists Management Inc.
Diahann Carroll: Harry Langdon
Pat Cash: International Management Group
Peter Cetera: Andrew Kent/Warner Bros. Records
Wilt Chamberlain: NBC
Anne Cox Chambers: Mikel Yeakle
John Chancellor: NBC
Ray Charles: Howard Morehead/CBS Records Inc.
Cher: Greg Gorman
Marian Christy: Mark Babushkin
Connie Chung: NBC
Craig Claiborne: William E. Sauro
Eric Clapton: Warner Bros. Records
Mary Higgins Clark: Sigrid Estrada
Arthur C. Clarke: Charles Adams
James Clavell: Frank Carroll/NBC
Jill Clayburgh: Universal City Studios, Inc.
Alexander H. Cohen: Frederic Ohringer
Natalie Cole: EMI-Manhattan Records
Dabney Coleman: Universal City Studios, Inc.
Ornette Coleman: Steven Needham/Antilles
Robert Coles: Robert Emmet Coles
Jackie Collins: Brian Aris
Judy Collins: Gary Heery/Elektra
Phil Collins: Atlantic Records
Jimmy Connors: Beverly Schaefer/ProServ
Alistair Cooke: Eric Roth
Aaron Copland: Bill Malone
Francis Ford Coppola: Adger W. Cowans
Bob Costas: NBC
Jacques Cousteau: The Cousteau Society
Michael Crawford: Simon Fowler/CBS Records Inc.
Michael Crichton: United Artists Corp.
Hume Cronyn: Zoe Dominic
Tom Cruise: United Artists Pictures, Inc.
Merce Cunningham: Minagawa
Jamie Lee Curtis: Capital Cities/ABC

Jacques D'Amboise: Swope
Timothy Dalton: United Artists Pictures, Inc.
Ron Darling: New York Mets
Al Davis: Los Angeles Raiders
Miles Davis: Ebet Roberts/Warner Bros. Records
Sammy Davis, Jr.: Tri-Star Pictures
Mary Decker Slaney: Steve Sutton/Duomo/International Management Group
Willem de Kooning: Martin Koeniges
Alicia De Larrocha: Christian Steiner/London Records
Agnes de Mille: Jack Mitchell
Philippe de Montebello: Christopher Little
Robert DeNiro: Universal City Studios, Inc.
Brian De Palma: Columbia Pictures Industries, Inc.
William Devane: Lorimar Television
Danny De Vito: Touchstone Pictures
Eric Dickerson: Mark Husmann
James Dickey: Terry Parke
Joe Di Maggio: Jerry Engel
Kevin Dobson: Lorimar Television
E. L. Doctorow: Nancy Crampton
Sam Donaldson: Capital Cities/ABC
Michael Douglas: Twentieth Century Fox
Robert Downey, Jr.: Tri-Star Pictures, Inc.
Hugh Downs: Capital Cities/ABC
Allen Drury: Alex Gotfryd
Patrick Duffy: Lorimar Television

Michael Dukakis: Richard Sobol
Angier Biddle Duke: Fabian Bachrach
David Dukes: ICM
Dominick Dunne: Jerry Bauer
Duran Duran: Denis O'Regan/Capitol Records
Bob Dylan: Ken Regan/Camera 5

Sheena Easton: Randee St. Nicholas/MCA Records
Clint Eastwood: Warner Brothers
Blake Edwards: Columbia Pictures Industries, Inc.
Nora Ephron: Thomas Victor
Julius Erving: Philadelphia 76ers
Gloria Estefan: Randee St. Nicholas/Epic
Emilio Estevez: Nancy Ellison/Morgan Creek Productions, Inc.

John Fairchild: Bachrach
Suzanne Farrell: Steven Caras
Michael Feinstein: Greg Gorman
Harvey Fierstein: William Garrett
Albert Finney: Francois Duhamel-Mega
Bobby Fischer: Wide World Photos
Avery Fisher: Lincoln Center for the Perfoming Arts/William E. Sauro/NY Times
Carrie Fisher: Universal City Studios
Eileen & Jerry Ford: Mr. James Moore
Betty Ford: Russell Ohlson
Harrison Ford: Twentieth Century Fox
Milos Forman: Los Angeles Time/Michael Edwards
Jodie Foster: Paramount Pictures Corporation/Rob McEwan
Dick Francis: Mary Francis
Helen Frankenthaler: Andre Emmerich
Aretha Franklin: Norman Parkinson/Arista
Antonia Fraser: Sophie Baker
Mirella Freni: Christian Steiner/Columbia Artists Management Inc.
Betty Friedan: Susan Wood
David Frost: Snowdon
Athol Fugard: Martha Swope

Kenny G: Arista
Peter Gabriel: Robert Mapplethorpe/Geffen Records
John Kenneth Galbraith: Jim Kalett
James Galway: Brian Davis/ICM Artists Ltd.
Joe Garagiola: NBC
Gabriel Garcia Marquez: Sophie Baker
Ava Gardner: Seawell
Art Garfunkel: Caroline Greyshock/CBS Records Inc.
Phyllis George: Harry Langdon Photography
Vitas Gerulaitis: International Management Group
Charles Gibson: Capital Cities/ABC
Frank Gifford: Capital Cities/ABC
Kathie Lee Gifford: The Walt Disney Co.
Dizzy Gillesepie: Martin Cohen
Allen Ginsberg: Elsa Dorfman
Philip Glass: Jack Mitchell
Whoopi Goldberg: Warner Bros. Inc.
Jeff Goldblum: Vestron Pictures
William Golding: Caroline Forbes
Martha Graham: Hiro
Amy Grant: Eika Aoshima/A&M Records
Günter Grass: foto-studio-rama
Barry Gray: Rita Katz
Linda Gray: Lorimar Television
Andrew Greeley: H. Darr Beiser
Cynthia Gregory: Gregory Heisler
Wayne Gretzky: Los Angeles Kings
Jennifer Grey: Vestron Pictures
Tammy Grimes: James Radiches
Charles Grodin: Universal City Studios, Inc.
John Guare: Martha Swope
Aldo Gucci: Alan Berliner
Alec Guinness: Twentieth Century-Fox Film Corporation

Gene Hackman: David Appleby
Merle Haggard: Randee St. Nicholas/CBS Records Inc.
Larry Hagman: Lorimar Television
David Halberstam: Andy Oates
Daryl Hall and John Oates: Arista
Arsenio Hall: Bonnie Schiffman/Paramount Pictures
George Hamilton: Harry Langdon
Pete Hamill: Steve Friedman
Marvin Hamlisch: Francesco Scavullo/ICM Artists Ltd.
Tom Hanks: Brian Hamill
Daryl Hannah: Twentieth Century Fox Film/Andy Schwartz
Keith Haring: Tseng Kwong Chi

Sheldon Harnick: Margery Gray Harnick
Michael Harrington: Gretchen Donart
George Harrison: Warner Bros. Records
Rickey Henderson: New York Yankees
Jim Henson: Henson Associates, Inc.
Audrey Hepburn: Roddy McDowall
Katharine Hepburn: John Seakwood/Cannon Films, Inc.
John Hersey: Alison Shaw
Charlton Heston: Lydia Heston
Gregory Hines: Tri-Star Pictures
David Hockney: Andre Emmerich
Dustin Hoffman: Greg Gorman
Marilyn Horne: Robert Cahen/Columbia Artists Management Inc.
Vladimir Horowitz: Christian Steiner
Whitney Houston: Arista

Billy Idol: Albert Sanchez/Chrysalis
INXS: Atlantic Records
Eugene Ionesco: Jerry Bauer
Amy Irving: Patrick Demarchelier
John Irving: Shyla Irving

Janet Jackson: Eddie Wolfl/A&M Records
Kate Jackson: Maria Conti
Michael Jackson: Matthew Rolston/MJJ Productions
Reggie Jackson: California Angels
Mick Jagger: Bill King/Rolling Stones Records
Byron Janis: ICM Artists Ltd.
Tama Janowitz: Michel Delsol
Waylon Jennings: Wayne Williams/MCA Records Nashville
Norman Jewison: Columbia Pictures
Billy Joel: The Walt Disney Co.
Elton John: MCA Records
Jasper Johns: Judy Tomkins
Don Johnson: Randee St. Nicholas/CBS Records Inc.
Lady Bird Johnson: Frank Wolfe
Erica Jong: Tom Victor
Michael Jordon: Chicago Bulls
The Judds: RCA

Pauline Kael: Deborah Feingold
Diane Keaton: United Artists Corporation
Michael Keaton: DC Comics Inc.
Ruby Keeler: Charles Caron
Edward M. Kennedy: DeSilva/STUDIO 7
Rose Kennedy: Jerry Engel/New York Post
William Kennedy: Thomas Victor
Deborah Kerr: Christy/Kerr Cutline
Billie Jean King: International Management Group
Larry King: F. Guthrie/Mutual Broadcasting
Nastassja Kinski: Twentieth Century-Fox Film Corp.
Gelsey Kirkland: Kenn Duncan
Darci Kistler: Paul Kolnik/New York City Ballet
Kevin Kline: Metro-Goldwyn-Mayer Pictures, Inc.
Edward I. Koch: Thomas Victor
Michael Korda: Milton H. Greene
Judith Krantz: Harry Langdon
Kris Kristofferson: Mercury/PolyGram
Elisabeth Kübler-Ross: Ken Ross
Stanley Kubrick: Warner Bros., Inc.

Patti LaBelle: Marc Raboy/MCA Records
Karl Lagerfeld: De Lucia
Lester Lanin: Bachrach
Lewis Lapham: Cynthia B. Matthews
Estee Lauder: Victor Skrebneski
Cyndi Lauper: Epic Records
David Lean: Columbia Pictures Industries, Inc.
Norman Lear: Embassy Television
Timothy Leary: Alice Springs
Fran Lebowitz: John Bean
John Le Carré: Stephen Cornwell
Spike Lee: Universal City Studios Inc.
Ursula Le Guin: Thomas Victor
Greg LeMond: International Management Group
Ivan Lendl: Jerry Wachter/ProServ, Inc.
James Levine: Jack Mitchell
Huey Lewis (Huey Lewis and the News): Jock McDonald/Chrysalis
Roy Lichtenstein: Richard Leslie Schulman
Hal Linden: E. J. Camp/Paramount Pictures Corporation
Little Richard: Larry Williams
Nancy Lopez: International Management Group
Shirley Lord: Peter Pouridas
Iris Love: Holland Taylor

Rob Lowe: Columbia Pictures Industries, Inc.
Myrna Loy: James Radiches
George Lucas: Lucasfilm Ltd.
Robert Ludlum: Michelle Ryder
Sidney Lumet: United Artists Corporation
Joan Lunden: Capital Cities/ABC, Inc.
Alison Lurie: Jim Kalett

Yo-Yo Ma: Dorothea V. Haeften/ICM Artists Ltd.
Andie MacDowell: Miramax Films
Madonna: Herb Ritts/Sire Records Company
Norman Mailer: Nancy Crampton
John Malkovich: Tri-Star Pictures
David Mamet: Nobby Clark
Barbara Mandrell: Ric Boyer/Capitol Records
Manhattan Transfer: Atlantic
Barry Manilow: Arista Records
Branford Marsalis: Chris Cuffaro/CBS Record Inc.
Wynton Marsalis: Marcus DeVoe
Penny Marshall: Eugene Pinkowski/Twentieth Century Fox Film Corporation
Thurgood Marshall: Library of Congress
Billy Martin: New York Yankees
Mary Martin: Seawell
Richard Marx: Elisa Casas/EMI-Manhattan Records
Masters & Johnson: Scott F. Johnson
Marlee Matlin: Greg Gorman
Don Mattingly: New York Yankees
Paul Mazursky: Warner Bros. Inc.
Andrew McCarthy: Twentieth Century Fox Film
Mary McCarthy: Jerry Bauer
Paul McCartney: Richard Haughton/MPL Communications Ltd.
Alec McCowen: Metro-Goldwyn-Mayer, Inc.
Mary McFadden: Alex Chatelain
Bobby McFerrin: Carol Friedman/EMI-Manhattan Records
Kelly McGillis: Rob McEwan/Paramount Pictures Corporation
Elizabeth McGovern: The Ladd Company
Maureen McGovern: Nancy Moran/CBS Records Inc.
Jay McInerney: Annie Leibovitz
Jim McKay: ABC
Rod McKuen: Hy Fujita
Richard Meier: Irving Penn/Courtesy Vogue/Conde Nast Publications, Inc.
John Cougar Mellencamp: Mercury/PolyGram
Melina Mercouri: Greek Press and Information Service
George Michael: Chris Cuffaro/CBS Records Inc.
James Michener: John Kings
Julia Migenes: Barbra Walz/Columbia Pictures Industries, Inc.
Arthur Miller: Inge Morath/Magnum
Jonathan Miller: Ken Howard
Mitch Miller: Dennis Wile
Sherrill Milnes: Waring Abbott
Ronnie Milsap: RCA
Joni Mitchell: Geffen Records
Monaco Royal Family: Tony Franck/Sygma
Meredith Monk: Jack Mitchell
Joe Montana: San Francisco 49ers
Moody Blues: Terry O'Neill
Dudley Moore: Universal City Studios, Inc.
Robert Morley: Monitor Press Features Ltd.
Gary Morris: Randee St. Nicholas/Warner Bros. Records
Toni Morrison: Maria Mulas
Robert Motherwell: Renate Ponsold
Richard Mulligan: NBC
Eddie Murphy: Enrique Badulescu
Ricardo Muti: Henry Grossman

Ralph Nader: Judith Conrad/Conrad Studios
Martina Navratilova: Carol L. Newsom
Willie Nelson: Beth Gwinn/CBS Records Inc.
Peter Nero: Martha Swope
Olivia Newton-John: Herb Ritts/MCA Records
Jack Nicholson: Elliott Marks/Paramount Pictures Corporation
Alwin Nikolais: Spencer Snyder
Richard Nixon: Benjamin Rush Martin III
Jessye Norman: Christian Steiner
Marsha Norman: Stokley Towles, The Patriot Ledger
Chuck Norris: Cannon Films

Oak Ridge Boys: MCA Records
Joyce Carol Oates: Jerry Bauer
Billy Ocean: International Creative Management, Inc.
Claes Oldenburg: Richard Leslie Schulman
Richard Oldenburg: Jonathan Wenk
Ryan O'Neal: Tri-Star Pictures, Inc.
Thomas P. O'Neill: Benno Friedman

Donny Osmond: Dean Freeman/Capitol Records
Peter O'Toole: DC Comics Inc.

Al Pacino: Universal City Studios, Inc.
Nam June Paik: Ken Regan/Camera 5
Alan Pakula: Universal City Studios, Inc.
Joseph Papp: Jean-Marie Guyaux
Mandy Patinkin: Peter Cunningham
Luciano Pavarotti: Allen Malschick
I. M. Pei: Evelyn Hofer
Sean Penn: Marc Raboy
Anthony Perkins: Columbia Pictures Industries, Inc.
Itzhak Perlman: Christian Steiner/ICM Artists Ltd.
Roberta Peters: ICM Artists Ltd.
Regis Philbin: The Walt Disney Company
T. Boone Pickens: Dagmar Fabricius
Amanda Plummer: Mike Tighe
Sidney Poitier: Columbia Pictures Corporation
Roman Polanski: Long Road Productions
Maury Povich: Ken Korsh
Priscilla Presley: Harry Langdon Photography
Frances Preston: BMI/Randi St. Nicholas
Leontyne Price: Jack Mitchell
Prince: Jeff Katz/D. C. Comics, Inc.

Dan Quayle: David Valdez

Raffi: David Street
Regine: Gerard Barnier
Rob Reiner: Castle Rock Entertainment
Debbie Reynolds: Harry Langdon Photography
Lionel Richie: Matthew Rolston/Motown
Molly Ringwald: Patrick Demarchelier/Twentieth Century Fox Film Corp.
Harold Robbins: INI
Jerome Robbins: Frederic Ohringer
James D. Robinson, III: Cheryl Rossum
Kenny Rogers: Matthew Rolston
Rosemary Rogers: Francesco Scavullo
Felix Rohatyn: Bachrach
Linda Ronstadt: William Coupon
Ned Rorem: The Bettman Archive, Inc.
Pete Rose: Cincinnati Reds
Diana Ross: Motown/Ross Records
Philip Roth: Nancy Crampton
Mike Royko: Chicago Tribune
Run-DMC: Janette Beckman
Meg Ryan: Castle Rock Entertainment

Sade: Chris Roberts/CBS Records Inc.
Carole Bayer Sager: Harry Langdon Photography
J. D. Salinger: Lotte Jacobi
Harrison E. Salisbury: Gene Maggio/The New York Times
Susan Sarandon: MGM/UA Entertainment, Co.
Vidal Sassoon: Vidal Sassoon, Inc.
Arnold Schwarzenegger: Harry Langdon Photography
Willard Scott: NBC
Pete Seeger: Emilio Rodriguez
Dr. Seuss: Antony Di Gesu
Gene Shalit: NBC
George Shearing: Christian Steiner
Charlie Sheen: Timothy White/Morgan Creek Productions
Sidney Sheldon: Jerry Bauer
Sam Shepard: Paul Schumach
Nicollette Sheridan: Lorimar Television
Brooke Shields: Patrick Demarchelier
Bobby Short: Anthony Edgeworth
Phil Simms: New York Giants
Carly Simon: Arista Records
Neil Simon: Jay Thompson, L.A.
Paul Simon: Maria Robledos/Warner Bros. Records
Siskel & Ebert: Buena Vista Television
Steven Soderbergh: Amy Etra/Miramax Films
Alexandr Solzhenitsyn: AP Laserphoto
Suzanne Somers: Stephen Hamel
Stephen Sondheim: Nick Sanglamo
Sissy Spacek: Greg Gorman/Universal City Studios, Inc.
James Spader: Miramax Films
Aaron Spelling: Harry Langdon Photography
Steven Spielberg: Lucasfilm Ltd.
Bruce Springsteen: Todd Kaplan
Maureen Stapleton: International Creative Management
Ringo Starr: Bill Bernstein/Quality Family Entertainment, Inc.
Danielle Steel: Russ Fischella
Gloria Steinem: Thomas Victor

Isaac Stern: ICM Artists, Ltd.
Shadoe Stevens: Greg Gorman
Sting: A&M Records
George Strait: MCA Records
Roger W. Straus, Jr.: Thomas Victor
Darryl Strawberry: New York Mets
Barbra Streisand: CBS Records Inc.
William Styron: Nancy Crampton
Arthur Ochs Sulzberger: Duane Michals
Donna Summer: Atlantic Records
Patrick Swayze: Vestron Pictures

Jessica Tandy: Zoe Dominic
Elizabeth Taylor: Gary Bernstein
James Taylor: Raul Vega/CBS Records Inc.
Paul Taylor: Jack Mitchell
Kiri Te Kanawa: Christian Steiner
Studs Terkel: Patrick E. Girouard
Twyla Tharp: Kenn Duncan
Isiah Thomas: Einstein Photo
Randy Travis: Jeff Katz
John Travolta: Patrick DeMarchelier
Calvin Trillin: San Diego Tribune/Thane McIntosh
Tatiana Troyanos: Christian Steiner
Margaret Truman: Francesco Scavullo
Tanya Tucker: Alan Messer/Capitol Records
Tina Turner: Henry Diltz/Capitol Records
Twiggy: Simon Mein
Conway Twitty: Dennis Carney/Warner Bros. Records

U2: Anton Corbijn
Leslie Uggams: Harry Langdon Photography
John Updike: Hana Hamplova/Knopf
Leon and Jill Uris: Alex Gotfryd

Jack Valenti: Bachrach
Valentino: Richard Gummere/New York Post
Joan Van Ark: Dick Zimmerman

Gloria Vanderbilt: Cris Alexander
Van Halen: Mark Weiss/Warner Bros. Records
Gore Vidal: Alain Le Garsmeur
Jon Voight: CBS, Inc.
Nicholas Von Hoffman: Jerry Bauer

The Prince and Princess of Wales: London Press Service
Alice Walker: Wide World Photos
Barbara Walters: Capital Cities/ABC, Inc.
Dionne Warwick: Arista
Lew Wasserman: John Engstead/Universal City Studios, Inc.
Wendy Wasserstein: Peter Cunningham
André Watts: Columbia Pictures
Sigourney Weaver: Twentieth Century Fox Film Corp.
Raquel Welch: Claude Mougin/Sygma
Betty White: Wayne Williams
Marylou and Cornelius Vanderbilt Whitney: Bert and Richard Morgan
Tom Wicker: Gene Maggio/NY Times Studio
Mats Wilander: International Management Group
Billy Wilder: Metro-Goldwyn-Mayer Film Co.
Gene Wilder: Columbia Pictures Industries, Inc.
John Williams: Samantha Winslow
Vanessa Williams: International Creative Management, Inc.
Bruce Willis: MCA Records
Lanford Wilson: Diane Gorodnitzki
Dave Winfield: New York Yankees
Shelley Winters: James Haspiel
Steve Winwood: Herb Ritts/Virgin
Tom Wolfe: Nancy Crampton
Stevie Wonder: Motown/Black Bull
Joanne Woodward: Harry Langdon Photography
Herman Wouk: Jill Krementz
Tammy Wynette: Randee St. Nicholas/CBS Records Inc.

Cale Yarborough: Dorsey Patrick Photography
Dwight Yoakam: Graham Hughes/Warner Bros. Records
The Duke and Duchess of York: British Information Services

Pinchas Zukerman: Christian Steiner/ICM Artists Ltd.

EARL BLACKWELL'S
CELEBRITY REGISTER 1990

Hank Aaron

Baseball's all-time home run king has stayed close to the game following his retirement in 1976. "I wouldn't want to be doing something away from baseball. I was in the majors by the time I was 20. I've never had time to think about anything else." He challenged the czars of the game when he protested the exclusion of black ex-ballplayers from management jobs; later he suggested himself as a candidate for commissioner. A Hall of Famer, he's now farm director for his old team, the Atlanta Braves. Aaron says he doesn't miss the crushing attention (including frequent death threats by prejudiced fans) of the days when he chased and finally passed Babe Ruth's homer record of 715. Hank passed the record in 1974 by hitting 716.

Born Henry Louis Aaron, 5 February 1934 in Mobile, Alabama he entered pro baseball in 1951 with the Negro League's Indianapolis Clowns. He began his National League career with the then Milwaukee Braves in 1954; by 1957 he was league MVP and a World Series team winner. At the plate his style was far from orthodox. He had incredibly strong wrists, and though a notorious bad-ball hitter, he hit many outside the strike zone. "If it's near the plate I'm gonna swing at it," said Hammering Hank. That philosophy earned him dozens of major league records, including the astounding 755 career homers he totalled in his 23 seasons.

Aaron has four children by his first wife from whom he is divorced. He and his second wife and daughter, Ceci, now live in Atlanta. His son Lary was a minor league outfielder for the Braves.

George Abbott

"I must confess," he said in his 1963 autobiography, *Mr. Abbott*, "that one of my major defects as a director is an incurable impatience. I have always been very sure of myself as a director, perhaps even conceited. What's more, I have usually felt when seeing other people's direcfon that I could improve on it." As author, actor, director, and producer, George Abbott has had more shows hit the 500-performance mark than any other person in theatrical history and has restaged or re-written more shows than he can remember. In 1983, in his mid-90's, he rewrote and directed a highly successful revival of *On Your Toes* (for which he wrote the original book in 1936).

He was born in Forestville, N.Y., on 25 June 1887. For a long time his father was the town drunk. He attended Harvard and began his career as an actor in 1913. He wrote plays, often in collaboration, and directed and produced many of his own and others on Broadway. He moved to Hollywood during the switch to sound, collaborated on the script of *All Quiet on the Western Front* ('30) and directed several films between 1929 and 1931, usually supplying his own scripts. In 1931 Abbott returned to the stage where his numerous hits (as author and/or director) include: *Three Men On the Horse; On Your Toes; Room Service; The Boys From Syracuse; Pal Joey; On The Town; Call Me Madam; Fiorello!; A Funny Thing Happened on the Way to the Forum; The Pajama Game* and *Damn Yankees*. With Stanley Donen, he co-directed the film versions of the last two.

He was married first to Edna Levis (one daughter), and has revealed in his frank autobiography that after her death, while on a train back to N.Y. he heard "the click, clack of the wheels saying, 'You're free, you're free, you're free.'" He was later married to actress Mary Sinclair for three years, taught her to play chess, and "was surprised and very shocked" when she once beat him 13 to 2. "I thought that I either ought to give up chess or get a divorce." He explains that "Many great minds have made a botch of matters because their emotions fettered their thinking. That is why I may be smarter when it comes to assessing life than some other fellow who can beat the hell out of me at chess or a crossword puzzle."

In June, 1987, Mr. Abbott celebrated his 100th birthday with an event at New York City's Palace Theatre.

Joey and Cindy Adams

One of the nicer things about New York life is its institutions. There's the Macy's Thanksgiving Day parade, Circle Line cruises around Manhattan, Yankee games, Broadway openings and Ma and Pa Adams— Joey and Cindy—a touch of the '50s every day in his-and-her kissing columns published in the New York *Post*. His is comedy, hers is gossip, and often the two overlap.

"Marriage to a comedian," says New-York born Cindy (née Heller), "isn't easy. I wake-up. I say 'Good morning', and he says, 'What's funny about that?'" Soon as the punchline's worked out, the female half of the indefatigable twosome is at her desk in their Fifth Avenue apartment writing about last night's opening or reporting her side of some hot piece of gossip written in a style that just whistles over, and sometimes under, the belt. "Take David Bowie," she wrote during the summer of 1984 in her space in the *Post* she seized when Earl Wilson retired, "put a slightly longer wig on him, and who've you got? Geraldine Ferraro." Or this: "Now for that other theatrical personality Adam Khashoggi. He's up to his bullion in show business. He tells me he loves it, although his last was some B'way floppola which lasted an hour."

Once a model and actress who won 57 beauty titles, Cindy has written for numerous magazines and newspapers, among them *Good Housekeeping* and *Parade*. Something of an expert on Southeast Asian "affairs" ever since Joey headed President Kennedy's first cultural exchange there, she is the author of *My Friend the Dictator* and an as-told-to autobiography of Indonesia's President Sukarno. She co-wrote another as-told-to with Zsa Zsa and Eva Gabor's mother Jolie.

Cindy's fourth book was about the late Actor's Studio founder Lee Strasberg. For two years she was a newscaster on New York City's ABC affiliate and in one of many characteristic moments of bravery and chutzpah she was the only journalist left in Indonesia after all the others were expelled in 1965. Armed, we presume, with her famous gold pen, she was able to inverview Sukarno. For 17 years she was heard every weekend on NBC Radio's "Monitor." The super achiever is even the model for a "Cindy Doll," made in her image and likeness wearing only red white and black as does the original. In 1989 she became a reporter on the syndicated "A Current Affair."

Husband Joey, author of numerous humor books, was born Joe Abramowitz in Brooklyn, 6 January 1911. Clowning his way through school he went from Borscht belt to his big break at Leon and Eddie's talent free-for-alls. The former protégé of Mayor Fiorello LaGuardia, he's an internationally known comedian, toastmaster and goodwill ambassador. His daily column "Strictly for Laughs" appears in dozens of papers coast to coast and abroad.

The couple met in 1951 when Cindy was trying to become a comedienne. Joey let her get the comedy out of her system before he married her on Valentine's Day in 1952. "One of the conditions of the marriage," Joey said right after the wedding, "was that I get custody of all the material."

Adolfo

"A vote for Ronald Reagan is a vote for Adolfo," is how one society observer explained Adolfo's ever-rising popularity, and Nancy Reagan would be president of the Adolfo fan club if there were such a thing. She has worn his little Chanel-like suits around the world. Born Adolfo Sardina to a titled family in Cardones, Cuba, 15 February 1933, he was introduced to Mrs. Reagan by Betsy Bloomingdale over a seafood salad in 1967. One Californian explains that the designer appeals to his customer's "love of security, one of their stronger emotions." And the designer (known as Fito to his friends) says: "My women want to be well put together, to have snap, to look fashionable, to never look foolish." Harriet Deutsch, Lee Annenberg, Jean Tailer, and Marietta Tree are just a few of his devoted followers, most of whom couldn't care less when they all arrive at parties in the same Adolfo suit or gown. "If it works perfectly for me, why shouldn't it work perfectly for someone else too?" says one fan. Harriet Deutsch adds: "I'm just proud it's an Adolfo."

I wasn't one of those boys who played with dolls or read *Vogue*," he recalls. "I didn't want to go into law either. I dreamed of making dresses, something the Jesuits wouldn't have liked, so I never told them." An aunt who bought her clothes in Paris took Adolfo away from his Jesuit education, and on a French shopping spree in 1948. Balenciaga took a shining to the 16-year-old child and offered him a job. Six months later Adolfo was in New York designing hats that were worn by all the most fashionable ladies of the time such as Babe Paley and Jackie Kennedy. The swooping Adolfo brim became a signature piece and in 1955 he won a Coty award for his millinery.

Inspired by Gloria Vanderbilt, who asked him to whip up a few evening skirts using some of her patchwork quilts, he began dressing not just the heads, but the bodies of the ladies of his club. By reviving the Chanel-style suit he became the man-of-the-decade.

Is it bad to copy? Is it wrong to become rich? Adolfo explains: "I first started making Chanel-like dresses in 1967. Well, in 1967 nobody was interested in Chanel, not even in Paris. It was all Saint Laurent, Courreges and Cardin. But I did it, and I called it the Chanel look and when the Chanel people saw how successful it was they started to do it themselves. People always insist I copy Chanel, but they got the idea from me. And if you look carefully, you can see that they *still* sometimes get their ideas from me."

"I don't copy," says the loner who does not socialize with his clients, preferring the comforts of his pugs and his books. "I accept inspiration, and that's nothing to be ashamed of. People who write, people who make movies, they're all inspired by the artists that came before them. It's a natural progression."

Andre Agassi

As soon as Andre could open his eyes, his father took a tennis racquet, attached it to the ceiling, and tied a ball to it with a string so it could hang down above his infant son's crib. Now, 18 years later, Andre Agassi has rocketed to the top ranks of the tennis world, becoming the youngest player to be ranked number 4, and threatening those who stand in his way from becoming number 1. In just two and a half years since he joined the pro tour on May 1, 1986—two days before his 16th birthday—the 5'6", 150-lb. Andre has become known for his devastating forehand, two-handed backhand, pumped-up serve, natural talent and mental toughness; all of which account for his consistent climb through the rankings and explains why the editors of *Tennis* named Agassi as "male most improved pro of 1988." In 1988, Andre won six tournaments, holding the record with number 2 seeded Mats Wilander, advanced to the semifinals of the French Open (losing a 5-set match to Wilander), became the youngest man to ever reach the semifinal round in the U.S. Open, and was a Davis Cup hero after he and John McEnroe beat Argentina to put the U.S. back into the World Group, eligible for the 1989 Davis Cup. When asked about his partner, McEnroe told *Sports Illustrated*, "Andre's timing—his eye, picking up the ball—is incredible. His mixed shots, the drops and lobs, the way he clocks the forehand—phenomenal. He's still a kid, but he has that confidence, the attitude, the feeling of a champion."

Born 29 April 1970 in Las Vegas, Nevada, Andre was one of four children. His father, Emmanuel "Mike" Agassi, nurtured a dream that one of his children would become a great tennis champion. At the age of 13, Andre dropped out of junior high school and was taken, by his father, to Bollettieri Tennis Academy in Bradenton, Florida. During his years at the Academy, he performed bursts of spectacular tennis and showed glimpses of his rare physical skills, but he was moody, erratic, nervous and verbally abusive to his opponents. He also had a tendency to destroy his racquets by smashing them into the wall or grinding them into the ground. Even with these antics, Andre had an impressive junior career: he holds five national junior titles.

Today, Andre Agassi is still setting records. In October, 1988, he beat Stefan Edberg, the 1988 Wimbledon champion, in the first professional tennis match ever played in Beijing, China. Andre's on-court bravura—bowing, waving, throwing kisses, applauding opponents good points, and cracking jokes—his wide-eyed youthfulness, cute smile, frosted shoulder-length hair and fresh, unconventional manner have helped to label him as a heartthrob, especially for the teenage girls who throw flowers on the court after his matches. "It's the people in the audience that make you or break you," Andre said in an interview with "Vis a Vis." When not playing, the recent born-again Christian spends time reading the Bible. Andre feels "I am blessed with a talent and I have an obligation to the Lord to make the most of it."

Alvin Ailey

Called by *Dance Magazine* (in its 1975 Award citation) one "who has fused black and white dance into a brilliant chiaroscuro," this dance legend presides over a virtual empire, which includes two dance companies and a dance school encompassing 4,000 active dancers. But his real labor of love (and the focus of his energy since a breakdown in the early 1980's forced him to slow down) is the Alvin Ailey American Dance Theater, the company he founded in 1958 with seven members and which now boasts a roster of 30 dancers and a repertory of 150 works. Since its inception, the company has been seen by an estimated 15 million people in 43 states and 44 countries on six continents, including a 1970 tour as the first modern American dance company to visit the Soviet Union. In Leningrad, Ailey recalls, "the people would not go home. I signed people's arms, calendars and programs. It was beautiful!"

Leningrad was a distant place—geographically and sociologically—from the Rogers, Texas, birthplace (5 January 1931) of Alvin Ailey, who spent his early years "just involved in trying to be alive." He moved with his mother to Los Angeles, where at 12 he "first saw the (Katherine) Dunham Company . . . and there were . . . black dancers!" Dancing held no great interest for Ailey until his junior year in high school when "it was all the vogue to take tap dancing lessons, so we used to all go over and tap dance on this lady's shellacked living room floor for twenty-five cents a lesson." It was curiosity more than anything else that compelled him to follow classmate Carmen DeLavallade to her ballet classes, run by choreographer Lester Horton, who gave his young dancers "a chance to learn, to create and to grow as people, not just dancers," Ailey recalls. He joined the Horton Theater as a member of the stage crew, but soon made his debut as a dancer ("I was terrified . . . it was a horrible experience . . . but I enjoyed it"), and when Horton died in 1953, Ailey became the company's choreographer, the role that made him famous.

In 1954 he and DeLavallade were the leading dancers in Broadway's *House of Flowers*, and he saw his works premiere at Jacob's Pillow dance festival that same year. The move to New York marked the real beginning of his protean creative and performing careers (he stopped dancing in the early 60's). Broadway appearances include *The Carefree Tree, Sing Man Sing, Showboat* and *Jamaica* (as a dancer/actor); *Call Me By My Rightful Name;*

Tiger, Tiger, Burning Bright and *Ding Dong Bell* (acting only), and *Carmen Jones, Dark of the Moon* and *African Holiday* (choreography). Among the operatic works he has staged and/or choreographed are Virgil Thomson's *Four Saints in Three Acts;* Samuel Barber's *Antony and Cleopatra* (which opened the Met's 88th season) and Leonard Bernstein's *Mass* (which opened the Kennedy Center for Performing Arts in Washington, D.C.). In addition to the 50 works he has created for his own company (*Revelations, Cry, Love Songs, Night Creature, The River, Memoria, Landscape* and *Pas de 'Duke,'* among others), he has made works for such distinctive dancers as Judith Jameson (who began with the Ailey company), Mikhail Baryshnikov and Patrick Dupond, and for such companies as the Joffrey Ballet, American Ballet Theatre, the Royal Danish Ballet, the Paris Opera Ballet and the Bat-Dor Company of Israel.

Holder of a raft of honorary degrees, Ailey received the NAACP's Spingarn Medal in 1976 and the Capezio Award in 1979, in recognition, as he puts it, of "just a man who is involved in trying to make something out of the fabric of life as it is predicted through the dance." Alvin's award collection continues to grow; he was honored on December 4, 1988, at the Kennedy Center.

Alabama

"The hottest country band to ever hit the charts," is, according to one critic, Alabama. Randy Owen (born 13 December 1949), Teddy Gentry (born 22 January 1952), Jeff Cook (born 27 August 1949), and Mark Herndon (born 11 May 1955) rose quickly from obscurity to fame to become "country music's undisputed success story of the 80s," according to *Country Song Roundup*. In 1985 Alabama was the recipient of one of the Record Industry Association of America's (RIAA) first multi-platinum awards, leading the country music division with four multi-platinum awards for total album sales exceeding ten million. At the prestigious American Music Awards, televised nationally in January, 1986, the band was named "Top Group—Country" for the fourth year in a row. They have also won several Grammy Awards. Their smash hit album "Forty Hour Week" reached the top of the country music charts in the spring of 1985. In 1986 they were Top Overall Album Artist/Group for both singles and albums. Taking advantage of the entertainment medium of the eighties, Alabama has produced videos of several hit songs and continues to hit gold with such singles as "Forty Hour Week," "There's No Way," "Touch Me When We're Dancing" and "Face To Face." More popular albums released include 1987's "Just Us" and 1988's "Live."

Randy Owen (lead vocals and rhythm guitar), Teddy Gentry (vocals and electric bass and Jeff Cook (vocals, lead guitar, keyboards and fiddle) are cousins and grew up in Ft. Payne, Alabama, where they still make their home. In late 1969, the three got together to jam for the first time. They began making music on the weekends while continuing regular jobs during the week. (Randy and Teddy worked as carpet layers; Jeff held a government job.) It was all or nothing in March, 1973, when they quit their jobs and moved to Myrtle Beach, S.C., where they worked in clubs playing six nights a week. In 1979 Mark Herndon (drummer, born in Springfield, Mass.) joined the band and the following year Alabama's single "My Home's in Alabama" was in the top 20 nationally. They signed a recording contract with RCA Records in the spring of 1980 and their records have since soared to the top of the national charts. The four musicians are also songwriters and have penned many chart-toppers. (Credits include title songs from their first three albums, "Feels So Right," "Mountain Music" and the song that has become the band's theme, "My Home's in Alabama.") The group has an extensive road schedule and plays to standing-room-only crowds across the country. Founders of the "June Jam" in Alabama, an annual day-long festival that features top-notch performers, Alabama generously donates the proceeds to charities. In 1985 they recorded "All Together Now" for the first film featuring Big Bird and his friends from "Sesame Street." A CBS-TV special, "My Home In Alabama," aired in 1986 and the group drew rave reviews for the Marlboro Music Concert in 1987. The superstars of country music are humble about their success and remain "The boys from Fort Payne, Alabama."

Edward Albee

Drama critic John Simon feels he is preposterously overrated, a result of having been hailed by the critics at too young an age. Harold Clurman, on the other hand, said of him: "He is frozen fire. . . . No one else in our theatre writes in this particular way." Albee says that his plays are "really not going to present any problems to anybody who is willing to be receptive and fairly objective." No box-office has been either of late. "The truth is that in this country we just do not have a theatre culture," America's foremost bruised playwright said after the shellacking the critics gave his "minuet of death," *All Over* in 1971. He had more evidence for America's lack of theatre savvy when later works *Listening, Counting the Ways, The Lady from Dubuque, Lolita* (adopted from the Nabokov novel), *The Man Who Had Three Arms, Another Part of the Zoo, Finding the Sun and Walking* also failed to make box office cash registers sing. *Seascape*, 1975, did win the Pulitzer Prize (his second; the first was for *A Delicate Balance* in 1967), but it closed after just 65 performances.

Born 12 March 1928 in Washington, D.C., he was adopted at age two by the Reid Albees of the Keith-Albee theatre chain, and became "the richest boy in Greenwich Village," with one Larchmont estate, three prep schools, a discharge from Trinity College, and a trust fund of $100,000. He gave his age in 1963 as four. "I am four-years-old, because I have only been writing plays for four years." His pre-*Zoo Story* days, he says, were "pudding years. . . . One year was the same as another. I remember the whole decade in a haze." (Much was. One alcoholic night he wrote a play about a lonely boy who had to deal "WITH A GOD WHO IS A COLORED QUEEN WHO WEARS A KIMONO AND PICKS HIS (SIC) EYEBROWS.") Some years later came *Zoo Story*, first produced in Berlin and then in New York in 1958, and three one-act plays. In 1962, *Who's Afraid of Virginia Woolf?* was produced ("I made $800,000 on the movie and paid $900,000 in taxes"), followed by *Tiny Alice, A Delicate Balance, Everything in the Garden* and *The Ballad of the Sad Cafe.*

"The critics set somebody up," Albee mourned several years ago, "maybe too soon, and then they take great pleasure, the only pleasure critics *do* take—except possibly with their wives and mistresses—in knocking them down." A frequent lecturer, he splits his time between a loft in Manhattan and a house in Montauk where he has established a small summer colony for young, unknown artists and writers. He was elected to the Theatre Hall of Fame in 1984.

Eddie Albert

"Man has carbon monoxide in his brain, DDT and synthetic nitrate in his liver, asbestos in his lungs, mercury poisoning in his cells and strontium 90 in his bones. We have a serious problem about survival," says this veteran stage-screen-TV actor who, in recent seasons, has spent almost as much time sharing with audiences his concerns about poverty, pollution and other problems of the planet as he has in performance. He was welcomed back to Broadway in 1983 in the revival of Kaufman and Hart's 1938 Pulitzer Prize winning comedy *You Can't Take It With You.*

Albert made his debut into the world on 22 April 1908 in Rock Island, Ill., billed originally as Edward Albert Heimberger. When radio announcers

Alan Alda

with whom he sang, danced and pattered after leaving the U. of Minnesota habitually announced him as "Eddie Hamburger," he decided to simplify his name. Albert first earned critical acclaim on B'way as the light-comedian lead of *Brother Rat* in 1936, a role he repeated in Hollywood co-starring with a young newcomer named Ronald Reagan. He's now made some 60 films, including *Roman Holiday* (for which he received his first Academy Award nomination in 1955), *Oklahoma!, The Teahouse of the August Moon, I'll Cry Tomorrow* and *The Heartbreak Kid* (for which he received a second Oscar bid in 1972). In between films were Broadway appearances in *The Boys from Syracuse, Miss Liberty, The Music Man, The Seven Year Itch* and others. He also had a seven-year run playing a city-slicker lawyer transplanted to the country in the TV sitcom "Green Acres" (1964-71), a three-year run playing a private eye on "Switch" (1975-78), a role as a "Falcon Crest" scoundrel (1987) and one as Breckinridge Long in the made-for-TV 30-hour miniseries "War and Remembrance" (1988).

After World War II and Navy duty in the Pacific, he married Mexican-American actress Margo (best remembered as the Shangri La dweller who ages dramatically when she leaves her Himalayan paradise in *Lost Horizon*) in 1945. (She died in 1985.) They had an actor son, Edward Albert (who made his debut in the film *Butterflies Are Free*) and a daughter, Maria.

Alan Alda

After 15 years of relative obscurity as a stage and screen actor, he finally gained stardom as Capt. Benjamin Franklin "Hawkeye" Pierce on "M*A*S*H." The long-running TV comedy sensation began in 1972 and earned Alda several Emmy Awards for his role as the insubordinate and skirt-chasing, but skilled and dedicated combat surgeon. At Alda's insistence, "M*A*S*H" creator Larry Gelbart agreed to insert into each episode at least one operating room sequence. "I was worried the show would become a 30-minute commercial for the Army," says the actor. "On the other hand, the opportunity to make a humane statement was so great.... It's the only comedy show on TV that shows the results of war. It's humor with feeling."

The son of actor Robert Alda, Alan was born in N.Y.C. on 28 January 1936. The younger Alda occasionally teamed with his father to entertain soldiers at the Hollywood Canteen and in the early 50's they appeared together in a summer stock production of *3 Men on a Horse*. After graduating at 20 from Fordham U., Alda appeared again with his father onstage in Rome and on TV in Amsterdam. He served in the Army Reserve, studied acting at the Cleveland Playhouse on a 3-year Ford Foundation grant, performed off-Broadway and did TV guest shots. *The Owl and the Pussycat* ('64) was his first Broadway success, followed two years later by the musical *The Apple Tree*, for which he received a Tony nomination. His pre-"M*A*S*H" films were forgettable, but he starred in Truman Capote's memorable 1972 TV prison drama, "The Glass House."

Married since 1957 to classical clarinetist and photographer Arlene Weiss, Alda and his wife raised their three daughters in Leonia, N.J. (they presently live in Long Island). A non-materialist, he prefers "small-town living" and cherishes his privacy. Influenced by his spouse, he is an ardent feminist and member of Men for ERA. "I never wanted to be famous," he says. "What I wanted was to be very, very good at what I do and though I realized that if I was, then I'd be famous, that always seemed a little absurd." A compulsive worker, he adds, "To me, work is love. Work is at the heart of health." Alda wrote and directed some "M*A*S*H" episodes before its '83 demise. He also starred in the successful films *The Seduction of Joe Tynan* ('79), and *The Four Seasons* ('81). He wrote both ("Since I was a little boy, I've wanted to be accepted as a writer") and directed the latter. In 1985

CELEBRITY REGISTER 1990

he produced, co-scripted, directed and acted in the film, *Sweet Liberty*. Wearing three hats, Alan wrote the screenplay, directed and appeared with co-star Ann-Margret in *A New Life*, released in 1988.

Jane Alexander

Vitriolic theatre critic John Simon once described her with uncharacteristic warmth: "a strangulated charm and tragic sweetness, a slightly nasal melancholy and deep rooted womanliness." Of her own talents she has said: "I grew up thinking I was never very pretty and so I was attracted to parts that weren't physically glamourous; I could identify with them because they seemed to fit my own emotional past. I go at a part like an athlete. It's like working towards the Olympics. I gear myself to give my best and my most.... I'm not a person who sees life as a comedy. If you gave me a Rorschach, I'd probably see dark images."

Born Jane Quigley in Boston, Massachusetts, on 28 October 1939 she was encouraged from the age of 6 to become an actress by her father, a prominent Boston surgeon. As a 9-to-5 secretary by day and drama student of Mira Rostova by night, Alexander devised an innovative strategy for breaking into show business. On nighttime visits to the theatre district in New York she sought out the stage managers of hit plays and asked them to keep her in mind in case any actress suddenly departed, and so she was picked to be Sandy Dennis' stand-by in "A Thousand Clowns." She originated the role of the white mistress of the black heavyweight champion in *The Great White Hope* at Washington's Arena Stage, directed by her husband Edwin Sherin. Later, on Broadway, she won a Tony and was nominated for an Academy Award for her performance in the film version. She was nominated again for her part as the frightened bookkeeper entangled in the Watergate conspiracy in "All The President's Men," and a third nomination came for her part as the mother in the 1984 film about nuclear holocaust, "Testament." Alexander became known to television audiences as Eleanor Roosevelt in the 1976 adaptation of Joseph P. Lash's bestseller *Eleanor and Franklin*, and revived her critically acclaimed characterization in the show's sequel, "The White House Years." She won an Emmy for her work in the controversial TV drama "Playing for Time," about the tortures of a group of female musicians in a Nazi concentration camp. In 1985 Jane appeared in the CBS miniseries "Blood and Orchids." On the lighter side, she teamed with Elizabeth Taylor in the 1985 TV movie, "Malice in Wonderland," in which she portrayed acidulous Hollywood gossip Hedda Hopper to Taylor's Louella Parsons. As an actress she has a knack for finding classy parts. "Things come up suddenly these days, but that's all right because I work better under pressure." She dives into her parts "like a chameleon looking for food," becoming the outrageous "Calamity Jane," or Annie Sullivan in William Gibson's "Monday After the Miracle." Taking another creative turn, Jane was the co-executive producer and star of the 1986 film "Square Dance."

Shana Alexander

"It takes a Shana Alexander, one of the finest reporters of our day in America, to shape this horror into literature.... It rivals Capote's *In Cold Blood*," raved writer Willie Morris about the critically acclaimed *Nutcracker: Money, Madness and Murder: A Family Album*, Alexander's brilliant piece of reportage about a wealthy New York arts patron who persuaded her son to kill her multimillionaire father because she feared he might disinherit her. Journalist, lecturer, TV personality, and one of the foremost non-fiction writers in this country, Shana Alexander wrote her previous book, *Very Much a Lady*, about convicted murderer Jean Harris; it was a bestseller, while her

4

1979 book about the Patty Hearst case, *Anyone's Daughter,* was critically well-received.

Born 6 October 1925, the daughter of Milton and Cecelia Ager, she attended Vassar College from 1942 to 1945. Her early journalistic career began as a staff member of *PM,* followed by several years at *Harper's Bazaar.* After a brief time at *Flair,* in 1951 she became a reporter on *Life* magazine then a staff writer from 1961 through 1964. She wrote a semimonthly column "The Feminine Eye" from 1965 to 1969. That same year she became the editor of *McCall's* magazine, a position she held until 1971. From 1971 to 1972 she was vice-president of Norton Simon Communications, Inc., and a radio and TV commentator for Spectrum CBS News during the same years. She served as a columnist and contributing editor to *Newsweek* from 1972 to 1975. Alexander became known to millions of television viewers for her heated debates with James J. Kilpatrick on "60 Minutes" from 1975 to 1979. Alexander's other books include: *The Feminine Eye* (1970), *Shana Alexander's State-by-State Guide to Women's Legal Rights* (1975), *Talking Woman* (1976), and *Dangerous Games* (1988). She is the recipient of many journalism awards including the Sigma Delta Chi and University of Southern California National Journalism Award, the Los Angeles *Times* Woman of the Year Award, Golden Pen Award American Newspaper Women's Club, Front Page Award, Newswoman's Club of New York, the Matrix Award, New York Woman in Communications, Spirit of Achievement Award, Albert Einstein College of Medicine, Creative Arts Award, National Women's Division, American Jewish Congress.

Divorced from Stephen Alexander, she has one daughter, Katherine.

Kim Alexis

"If a model doesn't make it in *Sports Illustrated,* she won't be known to men and men are almost half the population." Good advice to any young model trying to make it in the business from a supermodel who really knows her stuff. Adorning the pages of the notorious swimsuit issue of *Sports Illustrated,* Kim Alexis is the very epitome of what a young beauty should look like on the beach, so natural looking surrounded by the sand and surf that she reminds you of a Beach Boys tune.

Although she has that California-native look, Ms. Alexis was born 15 July 1960 in Lockport, a suburb of Buffalo, New York. An athletic young woman, she enjoyed playing basketball and participating in competitive swimming. Kim was not just another gorgeous face; she was an excellent student. Upon graduating from high school, she planned to enter the University of Rhode Island's prestigious five-year pharmacy program; to prepare herself financially for her first year of college she modeled in Lockport during the summer she turned eighteen. The president of a prominent New York City modeling agency saw Kim's work, loved her look, and convinced Kim to put college on "hold" in order to pursue a modeling career. In 1979 the Italian edition of *Harper's Bazaar* was the first publication to display Kim's talents, and the rest is history. Kim's great looks propelled her to the status of one of the top models in the industry! Indicative of the point when a model "makes it" is when she finds herself adorning the cover of a top-rated fashion magazine. For Kim, it was her first cover assignment for *Glamour* magazine. Since her first cover she has graced the covers of over four hundred magazines in the U.S. and abroad. "One of those creatures who likes to get my fingers in many different areas and do them all as well as I can," Kim has proven herself in the world of broadcasting as well. She started off as a fitness reporter for a morning news program at WTLV-TV in Jacksonville, Florida. This move into broadcasting enabled Kim to implement her fashion sense in an even broader medium. In September, 1987, Kim was named fashion editor for ABC-TV's national morning show "Good Morning America." With an eagerness to learn Kim has excelled in this position, which enables her to convey ideas on topics from holiday dressings for women to fall fashion for men. Renowned photographer Francesco Scavullo labels her one of the six most beautiful women on television. A sports enthusiast, Kim has concentrated these past few years on running. Although she is kept quite busy with her flourishing career, she has found the time to compete in marathons: the famous L'Eggs and New York City marathons.

Marrying real estate developer James Stockton III in 1983 has added two dimensions to Kim's life. She was blessed with motherhood when their son James Stockton IV (nicknamed Jamie) was born 1 April 1986. When she opened two health clubs in Jacksonville, Florida, she assumed the title of entrepreneur. The multifaceted Alexis, husband James and sons Jamie and Robert (born 22 May 1989) live in Jacksonville with a wide array of animals: a cougar, a pig, two peacocks, goats, ducks, and a Jack Russell terrier.

Muhammad Ali

The energetic voice once insisted, "I am The Greatest," and an enthralled world came to believe it. He took on boxing's best heavyweights, the U.S. government, and a critical public, and was almost always victorious (his ring record, 56-4). But he tried to come back once too often and was humiliated by new champion Larry Holmes in his pathetic last fight. While he tarnished his image of invincibility, his legacy of temerity had already influenced a generation of outspoken athletes.

Born Cassius Marcellus Clay, Jr., in Louisville, Kentucky, 18 January 1942, a pampered first-born whose great-grandfather was an Irishman named Grady, he first hefted the gloves at 12. At 18 he was the Olympic champion. His distracting habit of taunting opponents became as much a part of his style as did his "rope-a-dope," "Ali Shuffle," and "float like a butterfly, sting like a bee" ring tactics. As an 8-1 betting underdog, at six-feet-three and 200 pounds of unbeatable arrogance ("Ain't I beautiful?"), the black Adonis won the world title in 1964 by dethroning the fierce Sonny Liston in a clouded finish. The next year Ali scored a first-round knockout with what many observers considered to be a phantom punch in a return bout with Liston. But the fistic controversies were mild compared with Ali's sudden allegiance to the Black Muslim faith and his break with the group of Louisville businessmen who had guided his early career. When he defied the draft on the grounds that he was a minister of the Nation of Islam ("I got no quarrel with them Viet Cong") and then fought and embarrassed Floyd Patterson, whom he called a "white puppet," he alienated much of his public. But after the New York State Athletic Commission and the World Boxing Association stripped him of his title in 1967 for not serving in the Armed Forces he developed into a hero of the black revolution, and became much-beloved by Third World peoples, many of whom weren't even sports fans.

He made a successful comeback after 3 years. Ali's reign as arguably the best heavyweight ever included immortal bouts against Joe Frazier (2-1), and memorable fights against Ken Norton (also 2-1), Sonny Liston, Leon Spinks and George Cooper. He was three-time world champ and his style was immediately visible in another young Olympic champion, welterweight Sugar Ray Leonard, who came along at a time when Ali *was* boxing.

Although he'd vowed to retire with more dignity (and money) than former champ Joe Louis, Ali's first two marriages cost him dearly in alimony and child support. In addition to maintaining a large entourage, and homes in Pennsylvania and California, he is also quite benevolent, once giving more than $100,000 to Atlantans victimized by a mass murderer of children. But Ali's financial straits may have forced him to return for one last, ill-advised big-money bout, the 1980 Las Vegas debacle with Holmes in which trainer Angelo Dundee threw in the towel in the 13th. The pounding of the pugilistic profession has left him with a bad speech slur, and he is far from the days when he could excitedly proclaim, "I'm young, I'm fast, I'm pretty, and I can't possibly be beat!" (His physiological difficulties stem in part from a mild Parkinson's Syndrome.) Ali still speaks of his many "blessings from Allah," however, and lives in a Los Angeles-area manse. He and third wife Veronica separated in 1985.

Muhammad Ali takes the time to champion causes and participate in charitable events. He married his fourth wife, Lonnie Williams, in November, 1986.

Marcus Allen

This agile-hipped young pigskin-packer was the college game's all-time most productive single-season rusher after scampering for 2,342 yards in 1981. Maybe USC's best-ever running back (which includes company like O.J. Simpson, Mike Garrett, Charles White and Anthony Davis), he took his Heisman Trophy to Oakland to begin a pro career with the Raiders. But after his 1982 AFC Rookie of the Year season in the Bay Area, the restless Raiders moved to the L.A. Coliseum, and Allen returned to the site of his old college gallopings to show the fans what he'd learned in a year. He'd discovered how to catch more tosses than any other running back in the American Football Conference. Still, ground-gaining was his bread and butter, and he earned MVP honors for setting Super Bowl yardage records for one day's work (191 yds.) and longest run (a 74-yd. TD) in the Raiders' 1983 season finale win over the Redskins.

The first collegian ever to run for 2,000 yards in a season had the requisite background to become a Southern Cal tailback. Born 22 March 1960 in San Diego, he was among the best high school ball-movers and tackle-shakers in the Golden State, and led Lincoln High of San Diego to the county championship by scoring all five of its touchdowns in the title game. But the young quarterback was converted to a fullback at USC, and had to learn to block for 1979 Heisman-winner Charles White. In his first day of practice at fullback he broke his nose, "I looked down and saw blood all over my jersey, and I said, 'Hey, did I hurt somebody?'" But "Young Juice," as teammates called him (a comparison to O.J. himself) got his chance to cut loose as a junior and was second in the nation in rushing. While taking weekly speech tutoring sessions to improve his already-good communicative ability for future interaction with white corporate types, he left school needing but one semester to obtain his public administration degree. He was unable to complete the degree because of extensive travel during his last semester, after winning the Heisman Award. Allen fairly ran away with that award by *averaging* over 200 yards a game in his senior year. In the 20 games in which he started at tailback he romped for 100 yards 19 times! The catquick, six-feet-two, 205-pounder, in addition to giving the Raiders their first true game-breaking runner, may be football's most versatile back—he's an expert blocker (thanks to the broken nose) and even throws touchdown passes. The broad-smiling nice guy is a Brentwood, Calif., bachelor who says his prime commitment is to help his family achieve their goals since they all made sure he achieved his. His parents, Harold and Gwendolyn, drive up from San Diego to see most of his home games.

Peter Allen

"I was born in Australia [1944] and live in California, but I think of myself as a New Yorker," says Peter Allen, whose career has been as eclectic as his places of residence. Discovered in Hong Kong by Judy Garland in 1964, he was hired as her opening act, then married her daughter, Liza Minnelli, in 1967. Allen's teenage experience performing in piano bars in his native land and in the Orient (he had left school at 14) eventually led to his dancing with the Rockettes in highly successful Radio City Music Hall engagements, recording albums of his own compositions (beginning in 1971), acting in Gilbert and Sullivan for British TV and writing songs for Hollywood films (including *Arthur*, for which he shared an Oscar).

While others turned Allen's songs into hits, including Olivia Newton-John's "I Honestly Love You" (1974) and Melissa Manchester's "Don't Cry Out Loud" (1978), he performed in relative obscurity for years in small, chic New York clubs, becoming a cult entertainer. The mocking sexual ambivalence of his cabaret style earned him an early following among gay audiences. This was accentuated by such outlandish costumes as red-sequined suits and silver lame shirts. Allen is one of the few male performers in the U.S. to use nightclubs as his launching pad to stardom.

Crediting Garland as an inspiration, her former son-in-law (he separated from Minnelli in '70 and they divorced in '74) says, "She was brilliant. The first time I saw her work was when I realized that's what being in show business was really like." Allen's poignant ballad, "Quiet Please, There's a Lady Onstage," is a tribute to her. Despite such N.Y. triumphs as a 1977 Central Park concert—which drew 8000—and his 1979 Broadway act, *Up in One*, he returns annually to Australia for several months. In 1988, he hit the Broadway lights again, this time collaborating with playwright Harvey Fierstein in a new musical "Legs Diamond." Peter wrote the music and lyrics, and starred in this critically mixed-up musical. Although, the show was not hailed a huge success, advance box-office sales by faithful fans kept "Legs Diamond" on the boards.

Regarding his image as an entertainer, Allen told *Newsweek:* "I think he's a very different person from me, a much more interesting person than me. I think that's why I'm in show business—to get to be that other person."

Steve Allen

Destined one day to bear the sobriquet "TV's Man for All Seasons" because he has "never been off television in 35 years for more than a few weeks at a time," the multi-talented Steve Allen told an interviewer in 1984 he considers the 24 one-hour PBS shows "Meeting of the Minds" his most significant television work, for "they'll certainly long outlast me. That series . . . is the only thing that has any lasting, social importance." Described by friend Andy Williams as "the only man I know who's listed in every one of the Yellow Pages," the actor-host-musician fits into many categories from A to Z—comedian-composer-clarinetist-columnist, pianist-playwright-poet-philosopher-publisher or satirist-singer-songwriter-scholar.

Certainly born with more talents "all natural to me" than first names, Stephen Valentine Patrick William Allen made his debut on 26 December 1921 in New York City into a family of vaudevillians and toured some 18 schools as class clown before landing his first job in radio. By 1950, with established credentials as an ad-lib comedian with a highly successful Los Angeles radio show described as having an "anything-goes structure," he switched to New York television. That year, he hosted the half-hour "Steve Allen Show" and made the guest circuit. "The Tonight Show" first aired in 1954, with Allen developing and using virtually all the elements now familiar to talk-show viewers. For a number of months in 1956, he was doing 90 minutes of "Tonight" (1954-1956), 60 minutes of "The Steve Allen Show" (1956-1959) on Sunday night opposite Ed Sullivan, and filming the title role in "The Benny Goodman Story" for Universal-International. Dropping out of the nightly position for other endeavors, he followed with: "The Steve Allen Playhouse" (1961-1964), "I've Got a Secret" (1964-1966), "Meeting of Minds" (1977-1978), "Comedy Zone" (CBS), "Life's Most Embarrassing Moments" (ABC) and music and comedy series for the Disney Channel. Known to work on dozens of different projects at the same time, he has written 26 books, including two novels, two volumes of short stories and two of poetry, as well as humorous and political works. In 1986 his book *How To Be Funny*, written with Jane Wollman, was published. He's written over 4,000 songs, including "The Theme from Picnic," "This Could Be the Start of Something Big" and "Impossible," and made some 40 record albums. In addition to his current "works in motion" and an ongoing lecture tour, he appears as a pianist on the concert stage, in his own musical comedy revue "Seymour Glick is Alive But Sick," and as a performer in jazz clubs throughout the land.

Allen's first marriage, to Dorothy Goodman, ended after eight years in 1952 (three sons). In 1954, he married actress Jayne Meadows (one son), whose Broadway credits include "Kiss Them for Me." Meadows has also been active on the TV guest spot circuit and starred in a majority of the "Meeting of Minds" series. Allen believes that "the raw material of most jokes, funny plays, funny essays, or whatever, is bad news," so, as millions watched a $250,000 fire consume parts of his San Fernando Valley home in October, 1984, he gamely told an inane TV reporter that, although homes in the neighborhood do sell for upwards of a million dollars, "I don't think we'll be trying to sell ours this week."

In 1986, Mr. Allen was named to the TV Hall of Fame.

Woody Allen

He calls himself a "latent heterosexual" and says he has an intense desire to return to the womb—"anybody's.". "I'm a compulsive worker. What I really like to do best is whatever I'm not doing at the moment," he claims. "When I'm writing jokes I wish I was directing movies. And when I'm writing a play, I wish I was performing in a nightclub." The versatile, philosophical comedian's understated wit has been dominating American humor since the mid '60s in print, on recordings, and on the stage and screen.

Born Allen Stewart Konigsberg ("When the other kids learned my name they'd beat me up. So I'd tell them my name was Frank, but they'd still beat me up") in Brooklyn, 1 December 1935, he says he was "a fearful student. . . . I went to both NYU and CCNY but I was always a freshman, year after year, never even a sophomore. I was a motion picture major, I wanted to be a cowboy. But when I was in high school I used to mail jokes to columnists. They were terrible jokes." His special brand of cynical parody and devastating understatement was soon in demand on TV talk shows and in top nightclubs. He entered films in 1965 as both screenwriter and performer in *What's New, Pussycat?* He directed his first film, *Take the Money and Run*, in 1969, the year he divorced his second wife, Louise Lasser. (She subsequently appeared in two of his films.) He achieved a peak of success in the '70s, with a string of highly successful comedies, six starring his longtime lover (before Mia Farrow), Diane Keaton. Until *Annie Hall* ('77), his films were typically disjointed but contained a comic brilliance, highlighted by self-effacing parody, inside jokes, and spoofing of great filmmakers (Antonioni, Bergman, Eisenstein), authors and philosophers. *Annie Hall,* with its balanced structure and high seriousness underlying its humor, was his most acclaimed film—critically and commercially. It earned him two Oscars, as director and co-screenwriter. He didn't collect them in person, however, because the award ceremony conflicted with his firm Monday night date playing jazz clarinet at Michael's Pub in Manhattan.

For his next film he received another Academy Award nomination as director, but *Interiors* ('78) was a departure for him on two counts: it was a straight, gloomy, Bergmanesque drama, and Allen didn't appear in it. *Manhattan* ('79) was a brilliant comic romance, with a Gershwin soundtrack (it won him his second Best Director award from the N.Y. Film Critics, complementing the one he'd received for *Annie Hall*), but response to his early '80s films (*Zelig, Broadway Danny Rose*, etc.) was mixed. Then in 1985 he scored with *The Purple Rose of Cairo*, with *New York Times* film critic Vincent Canby going so far as to declare that the "sweet, lyrically funny, multilayered work . . . again demonstrates that Woody Allen is our premier film maker who, standing something over five feet tall in his sneakers, towers above all others." His third full-length play, *The Floating Light Bulb*, which premiered at Lincoln Center in 1981, was less successful than its predecessors: *Don't Drink the Water* and *Play it Again, Sam. Getting Even, Without Feathers* and *Side Effects* are book collections of his *New Yorker* pieces.

Presently, Woody Allen appears active in all areas of life. His recent films include: *Radio Days* (1987), *September* (1987) and *Another Woman* (1988). Perhaps his dearest accomplishment arrived in December, 1987, when he and his longtime lady, Mia Farrow, announced the birth of their son, Satchel.

Herb Alpert

Recalling his days with the Tijuana Brass, he says, "The seven who made up the TJB sound were not of Spanish-American descent. We were four salamis, two bagels, and an American cheese." Their sound, called Ameriachi and Dixiachi, rumbled into jukeboxes on the horns of "The Lonely Bull" in 1962, heralding a new era of instrumental music. "There is no exact TJB sound," Alpert once said. "As in all music, there is a pulse and a groove." Imitations sprang up ubiquitously during the group's heyday (1960's) but Alpert didn't sweat it. "A lot of good musicians are too clinical. Like the groups who copied us. They copied us by note and lost the human element." The trumpet whiz reassembled the band (four of the original members plus four more) for an Olympic '84 gig in L.A. and followed up with play dates around the country, plus a new record, "Bullish." Alpert last hit #1 on the charts with 1979's moody "marvelously arranged" disco single "Rise."

Born in Los Angeles, 31 March 1935, the son of a Hungarian mother and a Russian Jew from Kiev ("My father wanted me to be a tailor"), he began trumpet lessons at eight and garnered much of his early experience in the Army where he sometimes played taps for as many as 19 funerals a day. After leaving the service, Alpert attended the University of Southern California for a while, and eventually teamed up with Jerry Moss, each putting up $100 to form A&M Records. They took time off to check out the Tijuana bullfights when they needed a breather. ("That's where it hit me. Something in the excitement of the crowd, the traditional mariachi music, it all clicked.") He married and divorced high school sweetheart Sharon Lubin (two children) and has one child with second wife Lani Hall.

Herb Alpert's album "Under a Spanish Moon" (1988) explored the adventurous spirit of the talented player, mixing orchestral music with the heat of Latin jazz. Alpert's A&M Records celebrated its 25th Anniversary in the summer of 1987 and like many other celebrity entrepreneurs, Herb launched a new perfume in 1988; his is called "Listen."

Robert Altman

"When I make films like *Nashville* and *Buffalo Bill and the Indians,*" the iconoclastic director told an interviewer in the late '70s, "it's not to say we're the worst country in the world. I'm just saying we're at this point and it's sad." In the 1970's Hollywood's preeminent "philosopher and commentator on social mores" was among the world's most honored filmmakers: his M*A*S*H (1970) had won the Grand Prize at the Cannes Film Festival and *Nashville* (1975) the Best Film and Best Director Awards of both the New York Film Critics Circle and The National Board of Review. And in 1979, when 20 of the world's leading critics were asked to name the decade's best films, Robert Altman was the only director with two on the final list; *Nashville* and *McCabe and Mrs. Miller* (the latter an exploration of the contributions prostitutes made toward the taming of the American West).

That same year, however, the director's career suddenly cooled with the failures of *A Wedding* ("irritatingly cynical," wrote the *Daily News*) and *Quintet*, which, to one critic, demonstrated that Altman "has developed a profound grasp of the obvious. He has really made a '50's Bergman movie." His *Popeye* (1980) was a commercial success, but the money men were now skittish about bankrolling this brilliant and strikingly original but unpredictable maverick. In 1981 he sold his Lion's Gate Films studio, saying "I feel my time has run out. Every studio wants *Raiders of the Lost Ark*," and at 56 began, for the first time in his life, to direct plays. He staged, first in Los Angeles and then off Broadway, two one-act plays by novice playwright Frank South, and Ed Graczyk's *Come Back to the 5 & Dime, Jimmy Dean, Jimmy Dean*. After this "sabbatical" Altman went back to making movies, including film versions of *Jimmy Dean* and David Rabe's play *Streamers* (Golden Lion Award for Best Acting—to Matthew Modine—at the 1983 Venice Film Festival), and *O.C. and Stiggs*, "an adult exploitation film." In 1985 he directed *Secret Honor* and *Fool For Love*, and in 1986 he wrote the screenplay for and directed *Beyond Therapy*. Touching television, Altman directed *The Caine Mutiny Court-Martial*, which aired in May, 1988, and in collaboration with cartoonist Garry Trudeau made an eleven-part television series about a fictional presidential candidate, *Tanner '88*.

Born 20 February 1925 in Kansas City, Mo., Robert Altman was a bomber pilot in the Pacific in World War II. Following three years at the University of Missouri he worked in industrial films and finally landed TV work with Alfred Hitchcock. After that he was hired and fired by a host of producers, eventually learning to "get comfortable in my own failure." As for his prospects with the major studios, he says he will continue to show them projects, but "they don't want to make the same pictures I do and I'm too old to change," which simply means that some of his future films will be independently financed, as *Nashville* was.

Hardy Amies

It was Somerset Maugham who said, "Well-dressed men's clothes should be appropriate but unobtrusive." Edith Sitwell's "Vulgarity never wears a simple frock," is not without significance. And Queen Elizabeth II's Royal Dressmaker (he began designing for her, then Princess, in 1951 and received the Royal Warrant in 1955), Hardy Amies, whose name is also identified with impeccable men's apparel throughout the world, adds a further observation: "A man should look as if he had bought his clothes with intelligence, put them on with care, and then forgotten all about them." A member of the Faculty of Royal Designers for Industry and the recipient of myriad fashion awards, he has popularized the idea that the "Whole Man" should have one sartorial shape, an identifiable silhouette, and that all his garments should be harmoniously coordinated. Furthermore, he has helped give us the British Royal family, one of the most delightful fashion anachronisms in contemporary life, excepting of course the pacesetting Princess Diana.

Born in Maida Vale, London, 17 July 1909, the son of an architect and a court dressmaking establishment vendeuse, he was educated at Brentwood, Essex, and on the Continent. He became a business analyst for the House of Lachasse, a London couturier, and eventually became its managing designer. Joining the British Army in 1939, he held a commission in the Intelligence Corps and subsequently was decorated by the Belgian government for his services as head of the Special Forces Mission. He opened his establishment at 14 Saville Row on 1 January 1945 and thanks to help from the modern royals and a contract to Hepworth's, one of Britian's leading multiple tailors, he became the first English "name" designer in the fashion field. In 1966 he became a consultant to Genesco, Inc., which brought his designs for men to the United States. The author of 1964's *ABC of Men's Fashions*, he also includes among his credits the clothes worn in Stanley Kubrick's *2001*. Current international sales of goodies with the Amies label exceed $160 million sales annually. Enough loot so that in the early 1980s he was able to repurchase his own company from the British conglomerate Debenham's Ltd. Then, at an age when most would be longing to retire, Amies signed a contract with Dae-wo in 1984 for a line of menswear that will afford the Britisher his biggest American promotion to date. As green a thumb as he is a stitch, he divides his time between homes in London, the Cotswolds and New York.

Cleveland Amory

"I used to write about Mrs. Astor and her pet horse, now I just write about the horse," says Cleveland Amory, whose Swiftian pen has in recent years been wielded against a whole new breed of adversary—the hunters and trappers and even wearers of animals. Whether he's throttling a Central Park horse-drawn carriage driver for kicking his beast, or spraying harmless red dye on 1000 baby harp seals off the coast of Canada to render their pelts worthless, Amory has emerged as one of the world's most visible crusaders against cruelty to animals. His Fund for Animals, founded in 1967 and for which he takes no salary as president, has more than 200,000 members and is regarded as one of the most effective anti-cruelty societies in the world. His new foes are no more immune from his biting observations than past targets: "Statistics show that it is more dangerous to take a bath than it is to fight a bull." His proposed Hunt-the-Hunters Hunt Club has among its rules: "Hunters who shoot with a bow and arrow will themselves be shot with a bow and arrow.... Trappers will be trapped—humanely, of course—and if they're too small, they'll be thrown back to live to play another day."

Born 2 September 1917 in the Boston resort community of Nahant ("a place which, if you were not born there, you are mispronouncing") into a long line of Boston merchants and Harvard men, Amory actually defied his own father by writing away for catalogues to "other colleges" before he came to his senses. He became president of the Harvard *Crimson*, a job which he described as "meaning so much that, while life afterward does go on, it's never quite the same thing." After graduation, he became the youngest editor ever at the *Saturday Evening Post*, but it was in 1947 with *The Proper Bostonians*, in which he penetrated the fussy and fusty facade of the denizens of his home town (and earned him the title "Boston's Benedict Arnold") that he emerged on the national literary scene. *Home Town*, a satirical novel, followed in 1950, and 1952 saw *The Last Resorts*, a social history of America's great watering places from Newport to Palm Springs. *Who Killed Society* (1960), for months the number 2 bestseller, contained such epigrammatic gems as: "A good family is one that used to be better," and "The New England conscience doesn't stop you from doing what you shouldn't—it just stops you from enjoying it." Amory has written regularly for a variety of magazines, including *TV Guide, This Week, Saturday Review, Cosmopolitan* and *Town & Country*. He edited the popular *Vanity Fair Anthology* as well as the first two editions of *Celebrity Register*. A collection of his newspaper columns, *Animail*, was published in book form in 1976, two years after his fifth book, *Man Kind?* (1974), had the unusual distinction of inspiring an editorial in *The New York Times*. It is a withering indictment of cruelty to animals, providing as he says, "a voice for the voiceless." His deeply felt concern has its roots in a bullfight he witnessed in Mexico as a young reporter, which "changed my life." His former adversaries felt his barbs once more in 1979 with the publication of *The Trouble With Nowadays*, "the accumulated wisdom of a charter member of The Society to Put Things Back the Way They Were," including such trenchant observations as "Some of my best friends are Unitarians," "Say what you will about the Children's Crusade, you must admit it got rid of the more militant ones" and "The only difference between the Republicans and the Democrats is that the Republicans are socialists and the Democrats are communists."

On a more popular scale, Amory's book *The Cat Who Came For Christmas* (published October, 1987) reached the bestseller list. Plans are in progress for a TV film based on the book.

Jack Anderson

"To expose and oppose. To be an ombudsman to the oppressed, the minority groups, people who are calling out and not being heard." That's the goal of the relentlessly probing Washington columnist who, in 1972, collected a Pulitzer Prize for his public airing of secret government documents outlining the U.S. role in the India-Pakistan war. "The public wants someone behind the scenes telling it like it really is," says Jack Anderson. "That's us." The chunky, sandy-thatched Mormon who took over the "Washington Merry-Go-Round" column after the death of Drew Pearson in 1968 now reigns as one of the most widely read and listened to newspaper, radio and TV columnists in the nation's capital. His regularly served-up exposés are all part of Anderson's theory that "Sunlight is the best disinfectant." Mr. Anderson produces documentaries for the Public Broadcasting Service, docudramas for Home Box Office and television specials for the Group W network. In addition, he publishes a twice-a-month newsletter.

Born 19 October 1922 in Long Beach, Calif., Jack Northman Anderson was taken at two by his Mormon parents to live in Salt Lake City, the sect's capital. At 19 he served as a Mormon missionary in the South; then, during World War II, he wound up as a China-based reporter for *Stars and Stripes*. After the war he headed for Washington and a job with Drew Pearson. Anderson helped reveal the scoops that led to the resignation of Eisenhower aide Sherman Adams and the discreditation of the late Senator Thomas J. Dodd for mixing private and public funds. Now syndicated widely all across the U.S., Anderson sees his present column of muck-raking personal opinion as "a court of last resort for the voiceless, the little people," and a colleague describes him as "kind of a little man's lobby in Washington, forever pointing out how the average guy is getting screwed." Still a regular churchgoer, Anderson is married to the former Olivia Farley and the father of nine children. He eschews Washington night life, alcohol, and tobacco with equal fervor. His tips, for the most part, come from carefully nurtured "sources" inside government, but every day several hundred come from readers, and others are the result of long, tedious digging on the part of young, eager staff members. But careless reporting occurred in the case of Senator Thomas Eagleton, then Senator McGovern's 1972 running mate, when Anderson reported a series of drunken driving convictions against the Senator that were later proved untrue. Ultimately, he made a public apology on "Meet the Press" and retracted the charges. Later President Carter labelled him a liar for a story that later proved true—the military attempt to rescue the American hostages in Iran. The sometimes risky revelations prompted one newspaper editor to say, "We have never refused to publish one of Anderson's columns but I have pondered several of them before publishing."

Loni Anderson

"I was thought of as being sexy, but I was never thought of as being a sex symbol until I became blond," says the not-so-dumb blonder-than-life star of TV's "WKRP in Cincinnati" (1978-82).

Born 5 August 1950 into a comfortable upper-middle class family in Minneapolis, Loni was married at 17 after a whirlwind courtship of exactly two weeks with the 26-year-old brother of a friend. She soon realized the marriage was doomed to fail and so she and her husband split after three months, when she discovered she was pregnant. Moving back home with her parents, Loni raised her daughter while attending college. By the time she auditioned for the part of "WKRP's" va-va-voom receptionist in 1977, she had behind her a college degree plus "more than ten years of stage experience." Since her sitcom debut, she has appeared on screen in *Sizzle* (1981), *Stand On It* (1983), *Stroke R Ace* (1983) and *Fast Eddie* (1984), did a voice over for the film *All Dogs Go To Heaven,* (1989), and appeared in numerous made-for-TV movies, including *Stranded, Easy Street, Necessity* and *Too Good To Be True.* Co-starring with Lynda Carter in "Partners in Crime," an NBC series that aired fall, 1984 (presently in syndication), Anderson is far from relaxed about her success. Insecure about her looks, she says she wouldn't dream of setting foot outside the front door of her California abode without being thoroughly made up and ready to face her public.

She and second husband Ross Bickell divorced in 1981 and she married long-time boyfriend Burt Reynolds in Jupiter, Florida, on 29 April 1988. They have a son, Quinton Anderson Reynolds (August 1988). A collector of Snow White memorabilia, Loni lives with her happy new family in Holmby Hills, California.

Richard Dean Anderson

Since 1976 TV audiences have been gazing into the penetrating dark brown eyes of the tall (6'2"), dark and rugged Richard Dean Anderson. From his five years as Dr. Jeff Webber on ABC-TV's popular daytime soap, "General Hospital" (1976-1981), the talented actor went on to star as the eldest brother in the TV series "Seven Brides for Seven Brothers" (1982) before doing two seasons on "Emerald Point, N.A.S." (1983-1984). Starring in the title role of ABC-TV's action-adventure series "MacGyver" since 1985, Anderson took time out to make his film debut in "Ordinary Hereos" (1986), a remake of "Pride of the Marines."

Born 23 January 1950 in Minneapolis, Anderson was raised in a creative environment. His mother was an artist and his father, Stuart, was a jazz bassist. Anderson's first career goal was to become a professional hockey player. This goal soon changed when, playing on his high school varsity team, Anderson broke both arms in separate incidents on the ice. Seeking a less violent profession, he developed an interest in performing. He studied drama at St. Cloud State College and at Ohio State University before moving to Los Angeles to pursue a professional acting career. Anderson paid his dues while trying to break into the business; sometimes working as a street mime or juggler or as a jester-singer at a Renaissance-style cabaret. He even landed a job as a writer/director/performer of shows at Marineland. Getting closer to his chosen field, Anderson worked as a stage manager for the Improvisational Theatre Company. Finally, the determined actor got a break when he landed a role in "Superman of the Bones" at the Pilgrimage Theatre in Los Angeles.

As a youth, Anderson crossed the country by hopping freight trains. The natural athlete who also completed a 5600-mile solo bicycle tour from Minnesota to Alaska and back, no longer has the free time to pursue his favorite outdoor sports: sky-diving, scuba diving and snow skiing. Even with his busy schedule, Anderson tries to keep up with his first love by playing hockey on a regular basis.

Mario Andretti

"Who d'ya think you are . . . Mario Andretti?" Recreational drivers who try to exceed their limitations are likely to hear that taunt from wives, children and assorted fellow occupants of the nation's highways and byways—most

Julie Andrews

of whom wouldn't know a crank shaft from a piston ring. People who think the Indianapolis 500 are the principals in a mass Hoosier protest movement still know the name Mario Andretti. But all Mario the Magnificent could think about on the winner's stand in July of 1984 after he had triumphed in the inaugural Meadowlands (NJ) Grand Prix was his elder son Michael, another participant in the race who had crashed his vehicle (and emerged uninjured). "I tell him not to race with me," his father despairs, "but he won't listen. I always worry." A year later, Mario missed winning at Indy by four seconds, thereby having to make do for another year with his brace of victories in 1968 and 1981. With 40-plus triumphs in Indy-type cars, Andretti ranks second only to A.J. Foyt, whose racing career preceded Mario's by almost a decade. A member of the Automobile Hall of Fame, ABC-TV's Athlete of the Year (1969), three-time National USAC Champ ('65, '66 and '69) and World Champion in 1978, Mario Andretti stands out in a sport of specialists for his extraordinary versatility—seemingly at home in a grand prix event, a drag race or a 100-mile championship race. "I've always wanted to be an all-around driver, to be able to handle any car on any surface."

Born 28 February 1940 in Montona, Trieste, Andretti came to America in 1955 (naturalized in 1959), and learned an almost accentless English while working in his uncle's gas station in Nazareth, Pa., where he still lives with his wife DeeAnn and younger children Jeffrey and Barbara Dee. His boyhood idol was the late racing car champion Alberto Ascari. "The race I remember best of all was the 1954 Grand Prix of Monza. It was Ascari versus Fangio, wheel to wheel in those big front-engine giants. That race at Monza crystallized my thinking. Before that race I wanted to be a racing driver. After that race I had to be a driver."

Julie Andrews

"Does Mary Poppins have an orgasm? Does she go to the bathroom? I assure you she does," declares the actress once pegged as the biggest goody-goody in Hollywood. "You're always remembered best for the things that are successful," she says, referring to her perky parts in *The Sound of Music* and *Mary Poppins*. (Actually her early attempts to squeeze out of her virginal mold like *Darling Lili* and *Star* were box office bombs.) "I think of part of myself as a very passionate person, but I don't think that comes across. I don't know where it comes from, that reserve or veneer of British niceness. But it doesn't bother me if people don't spot the passion. I know it's there," and she adds, smiling, "as long as Blake knows," referring to her movie-maker husband Blake Edwards whom she married in 1969. (She has one daughter from her first marriage to childhood sweetheart Tony Walton, the set and costume designer; she and Edwards have adopted two Vietnamese orphans.)

Two of Edwards films helped changed people's view of Julie Andrews. In *S.O.B.*, a sticky sweet American actress is forced by her director-husband to bare her breasts in one scene; in *Victor/Victoria* Andrews plays a woman impersonating a homosexual Polish count who, in turn, plays a celebrated Parisian female impersonator.

"Most people think I'm ten years older than I am because I've been around so long," says Andrews. Born Julia Elizabeth Wells in Walton-on-Thames, England, 1 October 1935, she began in show business when her divorced mother remarried and formed a vaudeville team with her new husband, who gave Julie vocal lessons. At the age of 12 she was singing arias at the London Hippodrome; at age 13 she gave a special command performance for the Queen of England and was her family's main source of financial support. While portraying Cinderella in 1953 she was signed to star in the New York production of *The Boyfriend*. Anticipating homesickness, she sailed for America and recalls, "I was green as grass. I was immensely impressed and I thought, 'My God, this is bigger than anything I'd expected. Better pull my socks up a bit." She became famous on opening night of *The Boyfriend*, which was also her 19th birthday. At 21 she played Eliza Doolittle in *My Fair Lady*; next she starred opposite Richard Burton in *Camelot*. Snubbed by the producers of the film version of *My Fair Lady* (Audrey Hepburn got the part) she won an Academy Award for her performance as P. L. Travers' steel-and-sugar British nanny Mary Poppins. Andrews has also appeared in such non-musical films as *Hawaii*, *The Americanization of Emily*, "*10*," *The Tamarind Seed*, *Torn Curtain*, *Little Miss Marker*, *The Man Who Loved Women*, *That's Life*, and *Duet for One*. A veteran of television, Andrews' first series, "The Julie Andrews Hour" on ABC, won a total of eight Emmy Awards and her first Christmas special, "Julie Andrews . . . The Sound of Christmas" (aired December 1987), won 5 Emmys. A recent one-woman concert tour was applauded by reviewers and a new record album "Love, Julie" was released in 1987 with a collection of standard & contemporary ballads. Her literary endeavors began with her first children's book, *Mandy*, published in 1971, followed by another book *The Last of the Really Great Whangdoodles*. (Her pen name is Julie Edwards). The Andrews-Edwards family live year round in Gstaad, Switzerland.

Years ago writer Helen Lawrenson wrote that she wasn't deceived by the "lie-die goo" of Andrews' Mary Poppins-on-the-cross image. She wrote: "When you've fought your way up the ladder as she has done, baby, you're *tough*."

Paul Anka

With 20 hit songs to his credit by age 20, he has continued in the entertainment forefront for three decades. A tireless performer packing houses in Las Vegas, Paul Anka is still a noted songwriter penning hits for other singing greats. Anka wrote "My Way" for Frank Sinatra, "Jubilation," for Barbra Streisand, as well as the theme for the "Tonight Show."

Paul Albert Anka was born 30 July 1941 in Ottawa, Canada. By age 15, he had sold his first hit, "Diana," and was signed to a lucrative contract with ABC-Paramount. On the road for concert tours, Anka found himself mobbed by throngs of teenage girls. He recalls, "Pop music was in its infancy, and The Platters and I were the new wave, evolving out of the Forties and setting the stage for the Sixties. All the countries that loved everything that was American were suddenly hit with this new music. And there I was, with that high-pitched, sincere, adolescent voice, and young people everywhere just embraced it."

Anka appeared in the film *Girls Town* in 1959 and *The Longest Day*, for which he wrote the score, in 1962. The machinations behind making Anka a superstar were the subject of a 1963 prize-winning film short, "Lonely Boy." His performances on film, though respectable, failed to set hearts aflutter with the intensity of his love ballads, so he remained primarily a singer/composer. His popularity grew, as did his business smarts, and the young singer formed Paul Anka Records, using his own funds to reclaim the rights to his earlier hits for republishing.

Other Anka songs include, "You're Having My Baby," "One-Man Woman," "Puppy Love," and "Put Your Head on My Shoulder." Paul continues to "pack the house" in Las Vegas and at other engagements around the U.S. The 1980's brought a resurge of his song "Diana" whenever news reporters covered the whereabouts of Britain's Princess Diana.

Anka has his own storybook marriage. He married Lebanese model Anne de Zogheb in 1963 and their sturdy marriage produced five daughters.

Walter Annenberg

"My personal view of life is that it is constant warfare with occasional pleasant interludes," says this media tycoon, philanthropist, former ambassador to Great Britain (under Richard Nixon) and friend of the powerful.

His guarded observations, spoken in 1984 during a pleasant interlude at the peak of a long career, reflect the many battles he's fought to win both his goals and respectability. Son of the wealthy, virulent Republican publisher M.L. ("Moe") Annenberg, who made enemies among New Deal Democrats and was indicted for income tax evasion of $9.5 million, Walter took over his father's Triangle Publications and vowed to restore honor to the family name. This he did, though he still has his detractors. On every desk he uses sits a plaque with the motto: "Cause my works on earth to reflect honor on my father's memory." Annenberg's performance as U.S. Ambassador to the Court of St. James lifted him to the ranks of respected statesman, he became close to the British Royal Family and earned the rare distinction among U.S. Ambassadors to Britain of being knighted. Annenberg counts among his friends many of the world's most influential leaders, including Ronald Reagan. Named in the *Forbes 400* list of wealthiest Americans, Annenberg is also one of the most generous, according to *Town & Country* magazine, having given away more than $100 million. "Everyone must be something of a missionary," he says. "For every advantage you have, you have at least a corresponding responsibility. Otherwise you're nothing more than a well-fed house dog."

Born in Milwaukee on 13 March 1908, Walter Hubert Annenberg attended Peddie School (his classmates voted him Most Likely To Succeed) and the University of Pennsylvania's Wharton School. After his father's death in 1942, he took over Triangle Publication (which included such diverse outlets as *Philadelphia Inquirer* and *Daily Racing Form*), and later started *Seventeen* magazine and *TV Guide* (1953). He also owned TV and radio stations and cable-TV franchises. Lacking a male heir (his only son committed suicide), Annenberg sold most of his property except for *Seventeen* and *TV Guide* and channeled the proceeds into a variety of charitable causes. He built and endowed the Annenberg School of Communication at his alma mater, U. of Pennsylvania, and is the sole donor of the Annenberg Fund, which in a recent typical year dispensed $3 million in 168 grants. His future philanthropies may well dwarf those thus far, predicts *Town & Country*. In 1981, Annenberg announced he would give $150 million over the next 15 years to the Corporation for Public Broadcasting.

His first marriage to Veronica Dunkelman (one daughter) ended in divorce. His current wife is Lenore ("Lee") Cohn. They live on a 250-acre Palm Springs, Calif., estate called Sunnylands, an idyllic isolated haven frequented by Annenberg's famous friends. Guests have included members of the British Royal Family, Nelson Rockefeller, and Gerald Ford. Nixon, a friend of Annenberg's since 1952, received solace at Sunnylands after Watergate, and the Shah of Iran's family was offered sanctuary there when things got too hot elsewhere. Annenberg's home contains a collection of masterpieces that rivals most museums. Sunnylands is also host to one of the world's most exclusive New Year's Eve parties, to which the Reagans have been regular guests for a decade.

Ann-Margret

She worked with top veterans for her 1961 film debut, playing Bette Davis' sheltered daughter in Frank Capra's *Pocketful of Miracles*. Her second movie was the last remake of Rodgers and Hammerstein's *State Fair* and her third, *Bye Bye Birdie*, launched her to stardom. Throughout the sixties she was typecast, both in musicals and dramas, as a teen-market sex kitten, a sort of female counterpart to Elvis Presley (the co-star of her fourth film, *Viva Las Vegas!*). Except for *The Cincinnati Kid* and the *Stagecoach* remake (in which she played Clair Trevor's role), she made no noteworthy films until, in 1971, her poignant performance in Jules Feiffer and Mike Nichols' *Carnal Knowledge* surprised many and earned her a supporting Oscar nomination. She received another Academy Award nomination for years later, for her lead role as the mother in *Tommy*.

Born Ann-Margret Olsson in Valsjobyn, Sweden, on 28 April 1941, she came to the U.S. as a child and was raised in various Illinois towns. She first entered the TV spotlight at 16 on "Ted Mack's Amateur Hour," and sang with a band at Northwestern U., which she attended for a year. Her film career has been augmented by appearances on TV specials and in nightclubs. She wrote *Exercises for the Tired Businessman*.

In 1967 she married Roger Smith, who gave up his successful acting career to become her personal manager. While rehearsing her nightclub act in late summer of 1972, she fell 22 feet from a high scaffold. The accident almost ended her career, but after extensive reconstructive facial surgery she resumed work and solidified her superstar status.

The 1980's have been very productive for Ann-Margret. In 1983 she played Blanche duBois in a TV version of *A Streetcar Named Desire* and in 1985 filmed *Twice in A Lifetime*. She starred in the telefilms "Who Will Love My Children?" (1983), and "The Two Mrs. Grenvilles" (1986-87) and several motion pictures, including, *The Return of The Soldier* (1983), *52-Pick-up* (1987), and *A New Life* (with Alan Alda in 1987). She also returned to the stage again, doing what she does extraordinarily well—dancing and singing up a storm at Caesar's Palace.

Anne Archer

For her role as the resilient wife and mother whose very existence is threatened in "Fatal Attraction," Anne Archer again received widespread acclaim, with Golden Globe and Academy Award nominations for Best Supporting Actress. Since her film debut in "The All American Boy" (1970) opposite Jon Voight, the talented beauty has starred with a wide variety of Hollywood's dynamic and glamorous leading men, including Roger Moore ("The Naked Face"), Sylvester Stallone ("Paradise Alley"), Sam Elliott ("Lifeguard"), John Ritter ("Hero at Large"), and Ryan O'Neal ("Green Ice"). Even with that list of credits, Anne claims that her most demanding film experience was "Waltz Across Texas," a 1982 film that she co-produced and in which she co-starred with her husband, Emmy-Award-winning sports producer/director Terry Jastrow, under their own Aster Corporation banner. Fortunately, Anne has not limited herself to the big screen. National TV audiences had the opportunity to watch her opposite William Holden in the original telefilm "The Blue Knight," the miniseries "Seventh Avenue," and "The Pirate," with Franco Nero. Also drawn to the stage, in 1981 she made her New York debut as Maude Mix in the acclaimed Off-Broadway production of "A Coupla White Chicks Sitting Around Talking" and reprised the role in 1985 in Los Angeles. The 1988 season saw Anne star as Tourvel in the Williamstown production of "Les Liaisons Dangereuse."

Born 25 of August 1947 in Los Angeles, Anne was surrounded by show business. Her mother, Marjorie Lord, played opposite Danny Thomas on the popular TV series "Make Room for Daddy." Her father, John Archer, was also an actor. In 1954 her parents divorced and four years later Anne and brother Gregg had another show business person in their lives, stepfather/producer Randolph Hale. Always drawn to the business, Anne received a theatre arts degree from Claremont College.

When not busy with one of her many projects, Anne devotes her time to issues and concerns of Planned Parenthood Federation of America, which appointed her National Public Advocacy Chairperson. In recognition of her commitment, *Ms* magazine named Anne as one of 1988's six "Women of the Year." A mother of two, Anne resides with second husband Jastrow, son Thomas (son of first husband William Davis, born August, 1972) and son Jeffrey (born 18 October 1984), in her native Los Angeles.

Roone Arledge

When he was president of ABC News and Sports he had been accused of introducing "jazzed up" technology to television news productions, sometimes to the detriment of journalistic integrity. But the husky, red-haired dynamo believes "the image that ultimately appears on the tube is what TV is all about. The most rewarding and exciting part of my job is making pictures and words that move people." Shows such as "NFL Monday Night Football," "Wide World of Sports," and "Nightline" have emanated from his supervision, and the innovations he has helped popularize include the instant replay, isolated cameras, and split screens. "We started using television to make you see it better on television than in person," Arledge says.

Born on 8 July 1931 in Forest Hills, N.Y., Roone Pinckney Arledge, Jr., lived what he calls "a typical Long Island childhood, affluence masquerading as the middle class." After getting his degree from Columbia in 1952 he found an entry-level job at the Dumont TV network, was later drafted into the Army where he produced radio spots. Afterwards, he produced an Emmy-winning children's show for NBC starring Shari Lewis, and handled news, special events, and entertainment chores as well. In 1960 he took on field producing college football at ABC, and later persuaded the web to begin the "Wide World of Sports" program that roamed the world in search of competition in over 100 sports. His crafty business sense a boon to his exceptional production skills, he has successfully negotiated for rights to telecast the Olympics, major league baseball and pro football. What's the key to Arledge's three Peabody Awards and scores of Emmys? He gets involved in small details of broadcasts and is called a workaholic of the first order. In 1977 ABC handed him the dismally-rated news division which he promptly gave a faster-paced feel with back-to-back reports delivered by younger correspondents and aided by graphics and special effects. With no luminary anchor on ABC's evening newcast, Arledge put in three (including network TV's first black nightly anchor, the late Max Robinson). The refreshing change from traditional news shows drew younger, formerly nonnews viewers, which sparked a spurt in higher ratings. The triumverate concept was scrapped when Frank Reynolds died. Peter Jennings came home from London to act as solo anchor, with Robinson leaving for other assignments. ABC usurped a huge chunk of otherwise uncommitted late night viewers with the 1980-launched "Nightline." Unable to lure Dan Rather from the watchful eye of CBS, Arledge swiped several of other webs' correspondents with his open checkbook. When Capital Cities came in and took over ABC, Roone lost his dual title, but still remains President of ABC News.

The flashy-dressing Arledge filed for divorce from his second wife in 1983. His first marriage, which held for 18 years, produced four children. An outdoor sports lover, he's found that "it's disturbing when your hobby—sports—is also your business. You find yourself not being as well-informed in other areas."

Giorgio Armani

Milan's top designer was born in July, 1934, in pastoral Piacenza, in Northern Italy. Unaware of the fortunes that just a few stitches in time would reap, he wanted to grow up and become a simple country doctor. Given this tidbit, *Women's Wear Daily* commented: "Like a simple country doctor, Armani's manner and personality are devoid of affectation. There are no stereotyped fashion mannerisms." He prides himself on his ability to minimalize which is his way of striking perfection. "He has taught women how to dress with the slouchy ease of a man ... men's inspired classics with a feminine edge," describes *WWD*. Complementing this, his men's wear has a feminine edge that makes even the most roughly-cut diamond look smoothly elegant, as Richard Gere did in the Armani-costumed film *American Gigolo*. (Perhaps the movie's most memorable scene was when Gere picked up selections from his completely Armani closet before hustling off to Palm Springs.)

Disenchanted with studying, Armani dropped out of medicine, enjoyed a short romance with photography and then became an assistant buyer for a large chain of Italian department stores. He disliked the way men dressed, feeling the stiff, formal, uniformed look served only to camouflage individuality. Hired by Cerruti, the menswear manufacturer, Armani was able to develop the style that gave him the reputation of being "the master tailor," and that eventually led to his revolutionary fashion concept: the unconstructed blazer, which was heralded and copied across the world. In 1974 he created his first collection under his own label and did the same for women the following year. Of the many who sing Armani praises, Bill Blass zeroes right in when he stated: "Armani did for the 80s what Pierre Cardin did for the 60s."

The movie-star-handsome designer with Mediterranean blue eyes is reverential when he discusses his simple beginnings. "My tastes are simple," he says. "I have always worked hard. My success hopefully hasn't changed me. You don't see things like 17th, 18th or 19th century antiques in my house because its not part of my life and never was. As I wasn't born an aristocrat, it's useless to try to become one through fashion. I don't want to be too distant from my roots. It's only important to be modern in my work and honest."

"In everything from the design of his Mediterranean getaway—a compound of houses on the island of Pantelleria," observed *WWD* "to the cut of a mannequin's hair and makeup, he insists on having absolute control . . . the sheer force of his personal vision continues to keep him at the top of the totem pole."

Expanding the Armani style, five Emporio Armani boutiques are scheduled to open in the spring of 1989, adding to Armani's worldwide chain of retail stores. Up to ten Armani stores are planned for opening in the U.K. through 1992. Not only are the boutiques growing, but a full Emporio line of products (including Emporio stationery, papergoods, and sachets) will be available to consumers.

James Arness

To a full TV generation of "Gunsmoke"-ophiles, he is known as the durable Dodge City defender, Matt Dillon. Few associate his face with the restless young Minneapolis dreamer who, "on days when the wind was blowing," would "almost go crazy sitting in school." Or the six-foot-six WW II G.I. who, as the tallest man in his company, was sent to test the depth of the water at Anzio. Not even the promising young comer from *Battleground* whom the producers picked in lieu of the man the role was written for, John Wayne. And certainly not the actor who played the title role in *The Thing*. After a phenomenal eighteen seasons (through 1975), Jim Arness is Matt Dillon, and that's that.

This strong character identification notwithstanding, the facts are that Arness is actually a Minnesota boy (born 26 May 1923), a World War II vet (hospitalized after a year from wounds suffered two weeks after the Anzio landing), and a veteran also of Hollywood ups and downs. (He shares the latter status with his brother, actor Peter "Mission Impossible" Graves.) Following his discharge from the army he headed for the West Coast ("I just wanted to see California. I wasn't thinking of acting."), and joined up with a little-theatre group. He was spotted by an agent, and wound up with a part in Loretta Young's Oscar winner *Farmer's Daughter*. Later he peddled real estate, beachcombed ("I still have this feeling about the ocean. The greatest spiritual cleansing I can imagine is to dive into a big surf."), appeared in *Candida* at the Pasadena Playhouse, married his leading lady, Virginia Chapman (they had three children, the youngest of whom committed suicide in 1975; Chapman committed suicide in 1977; Arness married Janet Surtees in 1978), and had a relatively successful "meat and potatoes" career in films before "Gunsmoke." In 1977 he appeared in ABC's "How the West Was Won." A multimillionaire from income for his years on "Gunsmoke," he divides his time between homes in Los Angeles and a 100-acre "ranchette" in the hills near Santa Barbara. Although he is famous for the many pranks he pulled while on the "Gunsmoke" set, his fellow cast members found him reclusive off the set, a man overshadowed by the larger-than-life character he'd created. Recent projects include the NBC-TV movie "The Alamo: 13 Days To Glory" (1986-87) and the CBS-TV film "Red River" (1988).

Eddy Arnold

He refers to himself simply as a "singer." A drawlin', cleft-chinned Country Music Monument, he has sold more than 80,000,000 records. He is listed among the top recording artists of all time, among artists such as Elvis Presley, the Beatles and Bing Crosby. His stampede of fans has grown alongside the rising popularity of country music in general since the mid-'70s. The 180-pound, six food "succais" has hosted more than twenty TV specials, including guest-hosting "The Tonight Show."

Anytime someone refers to the "Ambassador of Country Music" you can bet they're talking about Eddy Arnold, who is by now so rich he'd be hard pressed to want to "Make The World Go Away." What with lovely wife Sally, whom he met when she was working at a 5 & 10 in Kentucky, you can also bet that he gets more than "Just a Little Lovin'" and needn't fear being "Lonely Again" since his family life (two grown children) continues to be as stalwart as his music. A sharp investor (principally real estate and land development), he is on the Board of Directors of many leading business establishments, and would enjoy a staggering annual income should he choose never to sing again.

Born in Henderson, Tenn., 15 May 1918, Eddy dropped out of high school after his first year and got a job warbling on a radio station in Jackson, Tenn., while moonlighting in a funeral parlor. From there he joined Pee Wee King and The Golden West Cowboys. The rest is all chronicled in his 1969 book, *It's a Long Way From Chester County*. This share-cropper's son is so well respected on his home turf in Tennessee that both political parties have asked him to run for governor of that state. Although "honored by these overtures," Eddy sighs, "If I won, I wouldn't be able to sing anymore and then I just wouldn't be me." Keeping in tune with his musical fans, Eddy appears continually at Harrah's in Reno and Caesar's Palace in Las Vegas.

Rosanna Arquette

"Creativity doesn't come from some stupid white powder, it comes from God," explains this reed-thin actress who has been described as a cross between Audrey Hepburn and Jane Fonda. A drug rehabilitation program has brought her sobriety and stardom in such films as John Sayles' *Baby It's You* and *Desperately Seeking Susan*.

Rosanna was born in 1960; her grandfather was Cliff Arquette (Charlie Weaver on the old Jack Paar Show) and her parents were both political activists. (Pop was a member of Chicago's innovative theatre group The Committee; her mother, Mardi, is a well-respected poet.) The eldest of five children, Rosanna spent her childhood swinging from one peace march to another. She lived for three years at the Virginian commune of a guru named Bapak. At age 14, with her boyfriend, she hitchhiked to San Francisco. Later, in Los Angeles, she became the platonic roommate of her idol, actor John Heard. By the time she was 18 she was a veteran of TV specials and several films.

In 1984 she was voted the Best Actress of the year by the persnickity Boston Society of Film Critics for her performance in *Baby, It's You*. (Her competition had been Meryl Streep, Shirley MacLaine and Debra Winger, certainly not a wayward lot.) In an utterly different role that same year she played Gary Gilmore's young girlfriend in the TV version of Norman Mailer's *The Executioner's Song*. She also was the bare-breasted hitchhiker in Blake Edward's *S.O.B.*, the valiant "Johnny Belinda" in a TV remake of that classic and her other credits include *Silverado*, *The Aviator*, *After Hours*, *Eight Million Ways to Die*. *Nobody's Fool*, *Amazon Women on the Moon*, and *The Big Blue*. In 1988 she starred in the CBS-TV movie "Promised a Miracle."

"As an actress I suck," she sighed in a 1985 interview with Guy Flatley for the *New York Daily News*. "I have an awful lot to learn.... I have instinct, but now I need technique." If she sounds self-reproachful she isn't. She's a winner whose only regret is "dropping out of school in the eleventh grade. I feel stupid—even though I *can* balance my checkbook." So stay tuned, Rosanna fans, there's much more to come.

"By the time I'm 40 I want to raise money for incredible causes. I'm not doing movies just to have a Jacuzzi, you know."

Rosanna married James Newton Howard in September, 1986, but their relationship faltered and they separated in May, 1988.

Claudio Arrau

"Music, if it's great, brings people together and I wanted to do that," he said in 1984, returning to his native Chile after a 17-year absence that was due to the prevailing local political conditions. On the occasion of his homecoming, the 81-year-old piano great was (wrote the *New York Times*) "accorded the national attention normally reserved for heads of state and rock stars." "Chileans," responded the pianist modestly, "appreciate art, which rises above any social or political differences."

The active concert performer is esteemed by critics as "the dean and master," especially of 19th century romantic composers, notably Beethoven. (In Beethoven's native Germany, Arrau is headlined on the music pages as "King of the Pianists.") He has recorded all 32 Beethoven piano sonatas as well as the five Beethoven piano concerti and frequently performs all-Beethoven evenings in the concert hall. Explaining why he never tires of the German master, Arrau asks, "Does one ever get tired of the beating of the heart?"

Like most of history's legendary musicians, Claudio Arrau was a child prodigy. Born in Chillan, Chile, 6 February 1903, he gave his first recital in Santiago at five and two years later sailed off on a special government scholarship to study abroad. He made his Berlin Philharmonic and London debuts at 17 and won the famed Liszt Prize twice before turning 20.

The master pianist came to the U.S. for the first time in 1923 at the age of 20 and has made his home here since leaving Nazi Germany in 1941. He was married in 1937 to German-born Ruth Schneider and the couple have two grown children. In a typical season, Arrau (who "still looks and plays like a man many years younger") regularly performs some 80 concerts in all the music centers of the world, often on three and sometimes on four continents. His sixth tour of Japan in May, 1987, was his most acclaimed to date. "Only if, as in creation, it involves the whole of one's being and calls up from the depths of intuition and feeling an answering response, can music be meaningful," he says. "Without that power of renewal to which one must literally give oneself with entire body and soul, so much concert giving would be impossible."

Bea Arthur

Cast as a liberal foil to "All in the Family's" Archie Bunker during the 1971 television season, Bea Arthur displayed a formidable comic command in the two-part guest shot that caused such a rating sensation she was back the following season (and six more) as "Maude," TV's favorite "liberal, libertarian and libber." Through Maude, an upper-middle-class matron with a WASP background and a quartet of husbands, the show delved deftly into such provocative issues as abortion, alcoholism, cosmetic surgery (Arthur herself had a face-lift during the course of the show), marijuana, pornography and pre-marital sex. Said Walter Kerr of Bea Arthur, "She has a very firm, haughty way of informing you that the next line—no matter what it says—is going to be funny." She returned to the tube in the fall of 1985 in the NBC series, "The Golden Girls." Sharing the set with a talented ensemble (Rue McClanahan, Betty White, Estelle Getty), her portrayal of the level-headed "Dorothy" earned Bea an Emmy (1988) for Best Leading Actress in a Comedy.

Born Bernice Frankel, 13 May 1924 in New York City, she grew up and was educated in Cambridge, Md., before returning to New York and embarking on an acting career. Arthur was extremely active in the early heyday of Off Broadway (*Threepenny Opera*—1954), and was cited for an "impressive portrayal of the dominating brothel madam, Bella" in *Ulysses in Nighttown* (1958). She was dubbed "the devine Beatrice" by Tallulah Bankhead when they worked together in the ill-fated *Ziegfeld Follies* (1956). Other notable roles include Yente, (*Fiddler on the Roof*, 1964) and Vera Charles, *Mame*'s severest friend (1966—winning her a Tony). (Arthur recreated the role for the 1974 film and has appeared in a number of other movies.) For a change of pace, she played the romantic attraction to Richard Kiley in the ABC-TV film "One More Time." (1988)

Arthur married fellow New School actor (now director) Gene Saks in 1950. The couple raised two adopted sons before divorcing. Although she relaxes at her California home by gardening and cooking gourmet specialties, Bea has shed much of the Earth Mother image of "Maude" by streamlining her statuesque (5'9") figure. As she once told a reporter, "my training has been total; I've done everything except stag movies and rodeos."

Mary Kay Ash

Contests, pageant nights, trips to glamourous resorts, gifts of jewels, pink Cadillacs and cream-colored Oldsmobiles. A beauty contest? Far from it (though the business is beauty)—it's part of the corporate "structure" of Mary Kay Cosmetics. "Our P&L statement doesn't stand for 'Profit and Loss,' it stands for 'People and Love,'" says Mary Kay Ash, the founder, chairman of the board, and mentor of the company whose motto is "praise people to success" (from her 1984 book, *Mary Kay on People Management*). Founded on the Golden Rule and tailor-made to fit a homemaker's lifestyle, Ash's corporate philosophy reflects her desire to give women an unlimited opportunity for success. Her product line has expanded from a face cream based on a tanning concoction (that's hide-tanning, not sun-tanning; Ash bought the rights to the formula in the 1960s) to include hair and body care, four fragrances and a men's grooming line.

Born in Hot Wells, Texas (circa 1915), Mary Kathlyn Wagner had, like many of the members of her "fold," her own share of heartbreak and hard times. As a child, she cared for her father who was bedridden with tuberculosis, while her mother worked 14-hour days. Ash rose above these hardships, outshining her classmates at school and, later, her colleagues in business. Twice married (her second husband died before she started her empire) and "sweet as a magnolia blossom" (said *People* magazine), Mary Kay Ash inspires her sales force to reach "the highest level of achievement and enjoy a successful Mary Kay career," through her successful incentive program. "I feel like I'm doing something far more important than just selling cosmetics. I think we're building lives." In 1984, she was listed among the 25 most influential women in America in the *World Almanac and Book of Facts*. The next year, according to the *Wall Street Journal*, the directors of Mary Kay Cosmetics Inc "approved a sweetened leveraged buyout offer from an investor group led by Mary Kay Ash, founder and chairman, and her son, Richard R. Rogers, president and chief executive officer." As the company continues to boom, Mary Kay's National Sales Directors are hitting record highs. In 1987, the sales force included over 150,000 women, and by 1988, Directors achieved millionaire status—earning from $1 million to $3 million.

Peggy Ashcroft

"She can be enchantingly feminine," says Sir John Gielgud of Dame Peggy Ashcroft, whom he has both directed and played opposite in the theatre, "yet turn and play monstrous, villainous people, parts you wouldn't think her right for." Although she admits she loves performing "bitches," she explains her standards as an actress in a role: "you show people in all their weakness and beastliness, yes, but you have to put yourself in their position, too. I don't think artists should make judgments on the characters they play." Although the senior theatrical "dame" in the English theatre has had scores of personal theatrical triumphs in Britain for decades, she won a host of new ardent American admirers (awards, as well) with her magnificently moving performances in film and television in *Passage to India* and "The Jewel in the Crown," respectively. In 1988 she appeared with Shirley MacLaine in the movie *Madame Sousatzka* and could be heard via voice-over in *When The Wind Blows*.

Born Edith Margaret Emily Ashcroft 22 December 1907, she was educated at Woodford School, Croydon (the Ashcroft Theatre there was named in her honor in 1962) and the Central School of Dramatic Arts. Since her first appearance on stage in *Dear Brutus* (1926) she literally hasn't stopped trodding the boards, playing all the classics, all the works of major playwrights of yesterday and today. She has said the role of Winnie in Beckett's *Happy Days* is "the greatest part ever written—nearer to Everywoman than any other I can think of, and like climbing Everest to play." Although theatre is definitely her first and great love, she has commented on her recent film and television work. "I do think I'm very fortunate that just at the age when playing a stage role night after night is becoming difficult, I've had these opportunities.... Acting is the same whatever you do. But that long sustaining of energy is not demanded of you." Ashcroft is the mother of two children and has been thrice divorced.

Arthur Ashe, Jr.

In 1968, competing as an amateur at the Forest Hills (the tennis club that had denied membership to U.N. Undersecretary Ralph Bunche), Arthur Ashe swept top honors in the first U.S. Open tournament. His victory was called the most notable achievement by a black man in the history of one of the nation's most restricted sports. Seven years later he was Wimbledon's first black Men's Singles winner. But when he suffered three minor heart attacks at age 36 he retired from playing, gave up his number 7 world ranking, and became the official captain of the U.S. Davis

Cup team. Once possessed of a deadly serve ("the fastest since my own," allowed Pancho Gonzalez) an unflappable cool ("What I like best about myself is my demeanor"), Ashe was dubbed "The Shadow" for his ubiquitous coverage of his side of the net. At exclusive clubs he was more than once mistaken for a busboy or a waiter. "I guess I'm just a sociological phenomenon," observed the man whose childhood idol was Pancho Gonzalez because of all tennis greats his skin color was closest to Arthur's.

The son of a parks department guard, Ashe was born 10 April 1943 in Richmond, Va. He first served a ball across the net at age seven, playing with a borrowed racket on a segregated court. By his teens Ashe demonstrated skills that attracted the attention of Dr. R. Walter Johnson, a physician who encouraged promising black tennis players (including Althea Gibson). Under his tutelage, Arthur won the national junior championship. He attended UCLA on a tennis scholarship and, despite occasionally erratic play ("A lot of people said he lacked competitive desire," said a former champion; "I lacked a sense of identity," said Arthur), collected a number of trophies and was the first black to make the American Davis Cup team. As a result of his travels he became well aware of the black condition and is still outspoken in condemning the apartheid government of South Africa, and the athletes and performers who are paid to entertain segregated audiences there.

A good communicator, he has had a syndicated column in the *Washington Post*. He also contributes articles to several sports magazines as well as doing analysis for televised tennis matches. He is married to photographer Jeanne Moutoussamy with whom he lives in New York City. He says his playing is now confined to "hit-and-giggle" tennis with her and friends. In 1970, he published the candid *Arthur Ashe: An Autobiography*, and in 1981 *Off the Court*. His three-volume work *A Hard Road to Glory: The History of the African-American Athlete* was published in 1988. He was inducted into the International Tennis Hall of Fame in 1985.

Following the bouncing ball to the instructional video craze, Ashe teamed up with Stan Smith and Vic Braden in 1986 to create "Tennis Our Way."

Vladimir Ashkenazy

Since he walked away with first prize in Moscow's Tchaikovsky Competition in 1962 Vladimir Ashkenazy has been a household name ... at least in households where the playing of piano is prized. Most recently the noted pianist (whose playing says *Grove*, "combines intellectual probity with warm and sincere feeling" has proven himself as a conductor as well. In the 1984 Adelaide Festival, Ashkenazy conducted and played all the Beethoven Piano Concertos and Symphonies before an ecstatic audience. He has also worked closely with the Philharmonia Orchestra of London (he lived in England from 1963-68), the Cleveland Orchestra (with whom he made a digital recording of *Cinderella*, 1984) and the Concertgebouw of Amsterdam.

Born 6 July 1937 in Gorky, Ashkenazy studied at the Moscow Conservatory under Oborin. At nineteen he won first prize at the Brussels International Competition (under the auspices of Queen Elisabeth of Belgium, 1956). The brilliant technician was the first major figure to leave the Soviet Union in the 1960's, leading a wave of talented artists taking flight from their homeland. The renowned keyboard artist has built up an enormous catalogue of recordings covering almost all the major works for piano by Mozart, Beethoven, Chopin, Rachmaninov and Scriabin. As a conductor, his list of recordings encompasses the Rachmaninov Symphonies with the Concertgebouw, Sibelius (completing a "uniformly excellent," according to critics, digital survey), Beethoven Symphonies and Mozart Piano Concertos with the Philharmonia, and works by Prokofiev and Strauss with the Cleveland Orchestra. He is also extremely active as a chamber musician, notably in partnership with Itzhak Perlman and Lynn Harrell, with whom he has performed and recorded many of the great works of the Classical and Romantic repertoire.

In addition to being a guest conductor for such orchestras as the Los Angeles Philharmonic Orchestra and the Berlin Philharmonic Orchestra, Ashkenazy was the Principal Guest Conductor of the Cleveland Orchestra for the 1987-1988 season, and continued this position for the 1988-1989 season. He was also appointed Chief Conductor of the Radio Symphony Orchestra Berlin for a three-year period, beginning with the 1988-90 season.

Vladimir Ashkenazy lives with his wife and five children in Lucerne, Switzerland.

Merrill Ashley

"You know, you're *not* so charming out there. You're not so fun to watch! *You* know you're doing wonderful steps, but they don't know it." Merrill Ashley's husband, the provider of this harsh appraisal "helped [her] more than anybody else" to transcend her reputation as the dancer with "the fastest feet in the West" and to become a ballerina who shines as one of the brightest stars in the ostensibly "no star" New York City Ballet, where formerly she had been "merely" their most brilliant technician. "I was a whiz and maybe that was the problem. I was all legs and feet. From the waist up, though, I wasn't every exciting," she admits, adding that she felt she had to be technically secure enough in order to be free enough to bring out her artistic qualities. "I couldn't see trying to show what I felt but be falling all over the place," she told *Ballet News'* Robert Jacobson in 1984. "I had to get strong first, then the other would come."

Speed and athleticism are the identifying features of the New York City Ballet, and these qualities came easily to the sports-loving Linda Merrill (born 2 December 1950 in St. Paul, Minnesota), who grew up in Rutland, Vermont, revelling in gymnastics, ice-skating, swimming and horseback riding. But the moment she saw her older sister's ballet class, she thought, 'That's what I want to do, and I never changed my mind. I just had me.'" Her once-a-week lessons soon progressed to intensive classes in New York City, where she was awarded a Ford Foundation scholarship in 1964 to the School of American Ballet, the New York City Ballet's official school. In 1967, Linda received her high school diploma, an invitation from NYCB's director George Balanchine to join the corps de ballet, and a new name (there was already a Linda Merrill among the company's dancers). Promoted to soloist in 1974 and to principal in 1977, Ashley became one of the last ballerinas towards whom Balanchine turned his special attention. (He died in 1983.) To display her quicksilver speed and unparalleled allegro technique, he created *Ballo della Regina* in 1977. Then, in an attempt to stretch his young dancer, he choreographed the serene *Ballade* in 1980 to show off a completely different Ashley. Citing her initial difficulties with the latter ballet, she recalls, "It was like Balanchine saying, 'Come on, I'll pull it out of you.'" Married since 1980 to UN translator Kibbe Fitzpatrick ("I like it that he's not a dancer"), Merrill Ashley is determined to carry on the tradition of the other man in her life. In the fall of 1984, her book *Dancing for Balanchine* was published, and she joined the teaching staff of the School of American Ballet (while still carrying her full performance schedule), because "there should be no gap between the dancers who knew what Balanchine wanted and the new ones."

Merrill has remained in the spotlight, sharing her talents abroad; in 1987 she guest-starred with the Royal Ballet in London. As an added honor, Ashley received the *Dance Magazine* Award in 1987 for her outstanding abilities.

Isaac Asimov

"There is no one future; human beings make the future out of a vast array of possibilities," says famed writer Isaac Asimov, "I prefer to consider the future in terms of the ideal, wherein all people act sanely and with judgement and decency." Known for the variety and volume of his books, which number about 300, he has written forty-odd science fiction novels (including the best seller *Foundation's Edge*), fifty nonfiction books on various aspects of science, a two-volume guide to Shakespeare, an annotated *Paradise Lost*, an annotated *Don Juan*, and five volumes of Lecherous Limericks. He is called the "great explainer" for his articulate, accessible writing style.

Born 2 January 1920 in Petrovichi, Russia, Asimov arrived in the United States with his family at the age of three (he considers himself "Brooklyn bred"). His early years were occupied in his parents candy store reading all the magazines "as well as supplementary matter from every public library within ten miles." Asimov received his B. S. from Columbia University in 1939, an M. A. in 1941 (his doctoral studies were interrupted for a time while Asimov served as a chemist in the U. S. Navy until 1946), and a Ph.D. in Chemistry in 1948. While at Columbia he began writing science fiction and as a biochemistry professor at Boston University he produced such textbooks as *Biochemistry* and *Human Metabolism*.

Asimov has been busy during the 1980's. Some recent titles include *Beginnings: The Story of Origins . . .* (1987), *Prelude to Foundation* (1988), and *Azazel* (1988). He prepared for the animated screen "Light Years" (1988) and created with Michael Wagner an ABC-TV series "Probe" (1988).

Asimov resides in New York City with his wife, Gertrude Blugerman (married in 1942; one son, one daughter). Convinced that science fiction frequently precedes reality Asimov says, "It is unlikely that science and technology in their great sweeps will outstrip science fiction in many small and unexpected ways; however, there will undoubtedly continue to be surprises that no science fiction writer or scientist, for that matter, has thought of. It is these surprises that are the excitement and glory of the human intellectual adventure."

Edward Asner

The burly actor was first embraced by audiences as the gruff, irascible newsman Lou Grant, boss of a Minneapolis television newsroom in "The Mary Tyler Moore Show" and then as City Editor of a Los Angeles newspaper in the gritty drama "Lou Grant." After assuming the presidency of the Screen Actors Guild following a crippling strike in 1981, his outspoken politics caused a bitter rift within SAG, but the union, and Asner, survived. "The entertainer is designed to please and as soon as he takes a political stand, he's immediately going to alienate a certain number of people. In my case, I still regard myself as a viable performer who is quite bankable," he has said. Yet Asner blamed the controversy over his politics for contributing to the demise of "Lou Grant." He entered the lists once again in 1985 with a new TV series, "Off the Rack."

Edward Asner was born on 15 November 1929 in Kansas City. In addition to theatre and occasional film appearances, his mainstay was episodic television until he won, by audition, his role on "The Mary Tyler Moore Show" in 1970. The ensemble sitcom remained a top rated program for seven years, earning Asner three Emmy awards and the chance to expand his character in an evolving storyline. A master of comic timing, he created a character who made perfect foils out of the star's peppy Mary Richards and the pompous Ted Baxter, played by the late Ted Knight. When Lou Grant was transposed into a serious, hour-long format, Asner replaced that delightful sarcasm with depth and authenticity. The critically acclaimed drama about a hard-as-nails editor who shepherds a group of ambitious reporters earned mixed ratings and was cancelled by CBS in 1981, but was revived in reruns in 1984.

An active member of Common Cause, SANE, and other liberally oriented groups, Asner was swept into the union office after leading strike activities. But he soon found himself in hot water over his criticism of U.S. involvement in El Salvador. Also under heated debate was Asner's support of a SAG merger with two other performers' unions, a move opposed by a conservative SAG faction. Said Asner, "I want the Guild to be identified with the labor movement. The rollback in unionism in this country is a dangerous thing. It spells disaster for workers—and actors are definitely workers." He resigned as SAG president in 1985.

Full swing into his acting career, Asner starred in the brief NBC-TV series "Bronx Zoo" (1986-87), as the principal of an inner city high school. After touring the country in the play "Born Yesterday" he opened as Harry Brock on Broadway (with Madeline Kahn) in January 1989.

Asner is divorced from Nancy Lou Sykes, whom he married in 1959. They have three children.

Rick Astley

He promises: "Never gonna give you up. . . . Never gonna let you down." He insists: "And don't you know I would move heaven and earth, to be together, forever with you." Rick Astley is a girl's dream—a peaches and cream, freckle-faced complexion, topped with red hair. His debut album *Whenever You Need Somebody* was filled with uplifting, positive, heart-beating tunes, backed by smooth-looking videos of Rick in action. Dressed in a beige trenchcoat for his video of the hit single "Never Gonna Give You Up," his style became a symbol for men's fashion. Where did this new idol come from?

Richard Paul Astley was born 2 June 1966 in Newton-le-Willows, Lancashire. He was hit by the performing bug while singing in a local Manchester church choir. Experimenting with instruments, Rick began on piano, shifted to drums, and then relied on his vocal abilities to lead a local band "FBI". The group won numerous competitions, and during one of their gigs at the Pier Casino, he discovered a type of music he likes to blend with his own style. He says; "Soul music can be a bit difficult to get into at first, especially if you've been listening to other things. But once you're hooked on it, well—that's it."

Definitely a contender to be filling the airwaves and clubs for years to come, Astley has already developed a solid footing on several continents. A number 1 bestseller in England, Germany, Holland, Belgium, Sweden, Norway, Finland and Denmark with top-ten hits in Switzerland, Italy, Australia and Austria, Rick also remains a chart-buster in America. He received a Grammy and American Music Award nomination for Best New Artist and *Billboard* magazine cited him as the Number 1 Top Dance Sales Artist in 1988. His second album *Hold Me In Your Arms* continued his success with the hot single "She Wants to Dance With Me." Astley is philosophical about his success and flattered by his popularity. He insists "I really can't handle the 'getting recognized' bit at all. I don't understand what's going on. I was dropping someone off in the street the other night when someone pulled alongside my car. It was, 'It's him, it's him, it's him!' But I still find it hard to relate to. . . . I just don't think I'm one of the devastating ones." Rick remains single and lives in a two-bedroom flat in London.

Brooke Astor

Although she may effuse, "It's fun to give money away," Brooke Astor sees for herself how it will be spent. The millionaire-socialite "sniffs and feels to get an impression not only of the projects but of the people running them." When Vincent Astor died in 1959, he left his widow (Brooke, to almost everyone) wealthy in her own right and entrusted her with the direction of the $60-million Astor Foundation, mandating that its monies be used for

"the alleviation of human misery." In the 25-plus years since, she has overseen the distribution of about $150 million principally directed into New York philanthropies, since she feels money made in New York should be spent there. Astor largesse flows into such expected channels as Carnegie Hall, The Bronx Zoo, the South Street Seaport, rebuilding Brooklyn's Bedford-Stuyvesant, and the Charlotte Gardens and industrial projects in the Bronx. But the Foundation also counts among its beneficiaries an animal medical center for aging pets of aging owners, youth projects and nursing homes in need of protective grillwork. Acknowledged for her homework and imagination, when Brooke turns her attention to a specific project, "she gives it a special imprimatur and attracts interest and additional support from other philanthropists concerned with New York." The New York Public Library has been an Astor family project since John Jacob Astor, founder of the fortune, left $400,000 and his personal collection of books to the institution in 1848. In 1983, jolted by an Orwellian vision of a world without books, Brooke undertook the rejuvenation of the NYPL in a two-pronged fashion. Pledging $5 million of the Foundation's money contingent on the Library's raising $10 million, she then turned her personal energies, fortune and considerable influence toward seeing that task completed.

Born Brooke Russell circa 1903, she grew up the daughter of a future Marine commandant. Pushed into marriage at 16 to J. Dryden Kuser, whose riches "dazzled" her mother, she endured his physical abuse, gambling, womanizing and alcoholism for ten years. Her subsequent marriage to stockbroker Charles (Buddie) Marshall was idyllic and her only child, Anthony, son of the Kuser years, took the Marshall name. Marshall died in 1952 and she was still wearing black when Vincent Astor began his courtship. Inundated by his witty letters, she married him in October 1953 and shared his solitary life for the next five and one-half years until his death.

Although the Astor social clout is there, when needed, she has been called "more of an example to her class than an arbiter of it." Her personal philanthropies tend to Republican politics and her small dinner parties usually include the working rich. Although she flirts unmercifully and has been courted by the very accomplished, she explains that "I want to go at my own speed, and it's a lot faster than theirs." Relaxing weekends at Holly Hill, her Westchester estate, Brooke reads, "daydreams" and occasionally writes. Two autobiographical works, *Patchwork Child* (1962) and *Footprints* (1980) perhaps helped to resolve past conflicts but it was Astor's death that allowed her to "re-create myself. Now I feel I've become a public monument."

Mrs. Vincent Astor has been the recipient of many awards and commendations recognizing her various contributions to society. She received "The Governor's Arts Award" in May, 1985, "The Gold Medal Merit" awarded for her support and encouragement of the arts in New York City on December 4, 1987, and was honored with two awards by President Reagan in 1988 ("Presidential Citizen's Medal" and "The National Medal of Arts Award"). Brooke Astor continues to be a consulting editor for *House and Garden* magazine.

Chet Atkins

"I can't play fast like a lot of guys. . . . I always thought I was just a *warm* player," says the versatile guitar-picker from Nashville who may well be the most recorded solo instrumentalist in American music. As of 1984, he had a career total of 115 albums, and has done memorable rockabilly back-up picking behind the Everly Brothers and Elvis Presley, down-home country licks behind Hank Snow, pop with Andy Williams and gospel with Martha Carson. He's been nominated "Instrumentalist of the Year" (three-time winner) by the Country Music Association every year of its existence. In 1973, he became the youngest person ever elected to the Country Music Hall of Fame. By 1988, Chet had recorded 118 albums and earned six Grammy Awards.

Chester Atkins was a Depression kid, born in the Tennessee hill town of Luttrell on 20 June 1924. ("I was from so far back in the sticks, I didn't know *anything* of the world. I didn't know how to dress. I didn't know if green went with blue.") What he did know was how to play the guitar and he spent most of the 1940s strumming on radio stints throughout the South and Midwest. ("I was always getting fired. I was a loser constantly until I came to the 'Grand Ole Opry.' My mother used to tell me, 'You'll never hold down a job. You're always telling everybody what to do.' And I was. The reason was usually that I'd know four chords, but the group leader usually only knew three.") Starting in the 1950s, in addition to picking, Atkins became an important figure behind the scenes, keeping an eye on the Nashville operations of RCA Victor, first as a producer and eventually as company vice-president. As such, he was the principle architect of what came to be known as "the Nashville Sound."

Chet and his wife Leona (since 1946) saluted another country music great, Merle Travis, when they named their only daughter Merle. Another friend, Johnny Cash, once summed up the secret of Atkins' enormous popularity: "The downtrodden flock to him because he is a human anchor. He has been a helper of the underdog, and I believe one reason he has been that is because he remembers what it was like to be in a cornfield on the side of a hill."

Chet Atkins chooses to be known as a "C.G.P.—a certified guitar player."

Richard Attenborough

After seeing him at a London auction bidding for the bust of Prime Minister Nehru, a civil servant from India tried to interest this British actor-director in making a movie based on a book about the life of Mohandas Gandhi. "I took the book with me on a holiday to the south of France," says Richard Attenborough, "and before I was halfway through it, I knew I had to make the film." And although he also had to go to India more than 50 times, became ensnarled in red tape there, and was villified by the indigenous press and filmmakers for receiving government funds ("Can you imagine the British government giving [us] money to make a movie about Winston Churchill?") he was rewarded for his 20 years of producing (and months of directing) with a film in which Ben Kingsley, who portrayed Gandhi, won an Oscar. "I wanted to tell the story of Gandhi the man," Attenborough said, "and all the connotations and premises and peripheral matters didn't matter to me." *Gandhi* also heralded a renewed interest in the world's most populous democracy, as demonstrated in such films as *A Passage to India*, *The Far Pavillions* and the 14-part television miniseries, *The Jewel in the Crown*.

During the 1940s, the future Sir Richard Attenborough (knighted in 1976) was one of the most saccharine "tennis anyone?" juveniles on the British screen. Sick of his image, he donned a false nose and was soon hamming it up as a competent character actor in many films including *Seance on a Wet Afternoon*, *Dr. Dolittle*, *A Severed Head*, and *The Great Escape*. A seasoned vet in all areas of the cinema, he also directed *Oh What a Lovely War*, *Young Winston*, and *A Bridge Too Far*, and produced *The L-Shaped Room*.

Born in Cambridge, England, 29 August 1923 (to an Anglo-Saxon scholar and educator; his naturalist brother, David, is well known to television viewers), Attenborough was determined at the age of 12 to become an actor after seeing a Charlie Chaplin film. While studying at London's Royal Academy of Dramatic Art, he met fellow student Sheila Sim, whom he married in 1945 (three children), and with whom he lives in West London. His first post-*Gandhi* film was a complete change of pace—*A Chorus Line* (1985). His most recent project is *Cry Freedom*, a film he directed and co-produced about South African anti-Apartheid martyr Steve Biko.

Louis Auchincloss

A lawyer by day, at night he writes first class fiction about the well-to-do. Like his 1984 novel *The Book Class,* his other works revolve around the monied and well-bred, their upper class attitudes and postures. The tiny social stratum that Auchincloss has dissected is insular and snobbish, and is, says one critic, "acutely tribal in its rituals and intensely status conscious, a class that defines 'comfortable' as owning a brownstone on the Upper East Side—maintained by half a dozen servants—several cars and maybe a yacht or two." He easily blends the literary world of his mother and the legal world of his father. "The transition from law to writing is like a vacation. I never need to get away from writing. Writing makes me feel alive."

Born 27 September 1917 in Lawrence, New York, he is married to Adele Lawrence. They have three sons—John, Blake, and Andrew. Once telling an interviewer, "One will lead a better life if one does one's duty," he was asked what was the nature of that duty. "At the risk of being rude," he replied, "I cannot answer that question because it has no thought content."

Auchincloss has written over 30 books in the past 30 years; they include *The Injustice Collectors, Portrait in Brownstone, The Rector of Justin, The Embezzler, A World of Profit, Edith Wharton: A Woman in Her Time, Richlieu, Watchfires, False Dawn* (a collaborative effort with Jacqueline Onassis, Auchincloss' relative by marriage), his autobiography, *A Writer's Capital, Honorable Men, Diary of a Yuppie, Skinny Island* and *The Golden Curves.*

The lawyer/author, who was once described as a "tall, thin, patrician Valentino," resides in a cozy Park Avenue apartment and country house in Bedford, New York. He will most likely hold on to his two professions: "If a person really has the gift to be a novelist, he should give it 100% of his time. But, you never know if you have the talent. You risk wasting your life."

Arnold "Red" Auerbach

Of the variety of incendiary devices used over the ages to signal victory, few were more familiar than the glowing cigar that protruded from the mouth of Red Auerbach when his Boston Celtics had another game in the bag. The backbone and driving force behind the most successful sports franchise in history, Auerbach saw his Celtics capture their 15th National Basketball Association championship in June of 1984, and stepped down as general manager that same year (he had retired from coaching in 1966). By retaining the title of president, however, Red was still around Boston Garden when the super-deals and cobra-quick decisions needed to be made. This to insure that the Celtics continue to play, according to Los Angeles *Times* Jim Murray, "a different game from anyone else in the sport. They have so many so good players that Auerbach keeps shuttling them in until the opposition begins to feel like General Custer."

Arnold Jacob Auerbach was born 20 September 1917 into a Russian Jewish family in the Williamsburg section of Brooklyn ("which was not exactly genteel in those days"). An athletic scholarship enabled him to attend George Washington University in the nation's capital, where he played guard while earning his B.S. (phys. ed.) and M.A. (education). His first professional coaching job was with the old Washington Capitols, and in 1950 he became coach of the Boston Celtics, then stagnating at the bottom of the NBA's Eastern Division. Such sterling acquisitions as Bob Cousy, Ed Macauley and Chuck Cooper (the first black player drafted into professional basketball) could not get the team any higher than second place for his first six seasons, but with the arrival in 1956 of Bill Russell, the game's premier defensive center, it was on its way. As a mentor and disciplinarian, Auerbach was, by his own description, a "dictator." By drilling his players relentlessly for speed, finesse and defense press, and instilling in them a "championship" attitude (inspired by the New York Yankees of Joe McCarthy), his teams went on to win 11 championships in the next 13 seasons, establishing their unchallenged superiority in the league. His career coaching record of 1,037 victories exceeds his closest competitor's score by more than 300. Under his general managership, the Celtics won NBA championships in 1974 and 1978 (under coach Bill Russell) and, led by the brilliant Larry Bird at forward, in 1981 and 1984.

Married since 1941 to the former Dorothy Lewis (two daughters), Auerbach's coaching wizardry has been rewarded by membership (1968) in the Basketball Hall of Fame. When the NBA selected the best players of its first 25 years as its Silver Anniversary team, Red Auerbach was the inevitable choice for best coach. (That cigar, incidentally, has another purpose. Says Celtic guard, M.L. Carr, "After a game Red always comes in [to the locker room]. He'll go up to each man. . . . If you really played well, he'll flick the ashes from his cigar on you.") In January of 1985, this semi-retired legend was given not a day, but a weekend—during which a banner bearing the number "2" was raised to the Boston Garden rafters ("1" belongs to the club's original owner); an oldtimers game was played for the Red Auerbach Foundation, which also benefited from a $500-a-plate dinner; and finally an announcement that in the fall of 1985 a sculpture of Red would be placed in Boston's Quincy Market area. A friendly face to television viewers, Red is featured in the popular Miller Lite beer commercials.

Richard Avedon

"My photographs don't go below the surface," he says. "They don't go below anything. They're readings of what's in the surface. I have great faith in surfaces. A good one is full of clues." Born 15 May 1923 in New York City, he remembers photography when he was a child as "a real event in the house. The knowledge that you could *make* a photograph instead of just discover it—that was in me very early. . . . We didn't own a dog but for some reason it was essential to have one in the photographs. We used to borrow them from people on the street. We'd pose in our English clothes with borrowed dogs in front of some magnificent Packard that didn't belong to us. Every one of the photographs in the family album was built around . . . some sort of lie about who we all were." At 19 he received his first camera from his father when he joined the merchant marine. "I must have taken pictures of maybe 100,000 baffled faces before it ever occurred to me I was becoming a photographer."

After the war, still in uniform, Avedon raced to Bonwit Teller and offered to take pictures of their fashion models free of charge. Soon hired by *Harper's Bazaar*, he helped bring fame and fortune to such models as Dovima, Dorian Leigh, and Suzy Parker, and, in the process, found considerable fame and fortune himself. His celebrity portraits, gathered into two books, *Observations* (with Truman Capote, in 1959) and *Nothing Personal* (with James Baldwin, 1964), are now classics. ("I'm drawn to photographs in which the light is raw and the defenses are down. I find passport pictures beautiful.") He's been named by his peers as one of the ten greatest photographers in the world. In 1966 he became staff photographer for *Vogue*. In 1969 Avedon photographed the anti-war movement across America; in 1971, Vietnam. He's exhibited at the Museum of Modern Art ("Jacob Israel Avedon," 1974) and the Metropolitan Museum of Art ("Avedon: Photographs 1947-1978"). His published works include *Portraits* (1976), and *Avedon: Photographs 1947-1977* (1978). In 1979 he began working on *In the American West*, a project exhibited at the Amon Carter Museum in Fort Worth, Texas in 1985. In January, 1989, he received the Lifetime Achievement Award from the Council of Fashion Designers.

Avedon has been married twice; first to actress Doe Avedon née Dorcas Norwell, then to Evelyn Franklin, and is the father of one son, John. "If a day goes by without my doing something related to photography, it's as though I've neglected something essential to my existence."

Emanuel Ax

"Emanuel Ax can often be counted on to provide the best music-making of an evening and, just as equally, to be reluctant to accept the accolades of his success," a music critic once wrote about the prize-winning young artist as renowned for his engaging personality and lack of affectation as for his keyboard mastery. Says Ax: "I'm having a wonderful time. Maybe later on I'll get tired of making planes and trains and so on, but right now I'm very happy about it. It's always an adventure." A highlight of that odyssey for Ax, whose idol was Arthur Rubinstein ("the most complete pianism . . . the most powerful, the most emotional, the most aristocratic"), was winning the first prize in the Arthur Rubenstein International Piano Competition in Israel in 1974. This earned him enough prestige to last many pianists a lifetime, but he saw it chiefly as an opportunity to bid farewell to competitions, which he sees as "really lotteries. . . . I would stake as much on a bingo game as on a piano competition . . . but that's our only means of getting attention." Competitions behind him (his prestigious Avery Fisher Prize in 1979 is noncompetitive), his goal now is to achieve not so much note-perfect performances but the act of "making music", preferring the concert hall to the recording studio. "The problem," he once told the *New York Times* writer Donal Henahan, "is how you make people understand what you understand, making 3,000 people love music the way you love it."

Born 8 June 1949 in the Polish (now USSR) city of Lvov (he considers himself "Polish more than anything else"), to Joachim and Hellen Ax (Nazi concentration camp survivors, both of whose first spouses perished in the Holocaust), Ax heard a Rubinstein recording of Chopin when he was six and immediately decided to become a concert pianist. His father, a singer who also coached singers at the Lvov Opera House, became his son's first piano teacher, but those duties were turned over to the distinguished pianist and teacher Miecyslaw Munz at Juilliard when Emanuel was 12 (the family having moved to New York under the sponsorship of Earl Blackwell in 1961). In 1970 Ax became a citizen, received a Bachelor of Arts degree in French from Columbia University, and began entering competitions, culminating in his 1974 triumph. The Boys Clubs of America (which supported his Juilliard studies) sponsored his New York recital debut in 1973 at Alice Tully Hall. A year later his performance as part of the Young Concert Artists Series at Hunter brought forth this *New York Times* accolade: "The sweep is there, along with complete technical control, but there is also emphasis on a round, singing piano tone, on graceful shaping of phrase and line." A decade later he was hailed (in the *New York Post*) as a performer "blessed with such unfailing elegance and good taste that one often takes for granted his sterling technique, partly because he does not flaunt it as blatantly as many other young pianists do." Ax has earned kudos as well for his performances with chamber groups, most notably the trio he, violinist Young-Uck Kim and cellist Yo-Yo Ma have formed. A joint appearance with Ma in 1982 was hailed by the music critic of the Boston *Globe* as "the performance of a lifetime," calling both "among the rarest kind of performer, the kind whose transcendental technique is completely matched by transcendental musical instinct and insight." The possessor, according to Ma, of "one of the greatest repertoires of jokes since Mel Brooks," is an opera lover, a tennis enthusiast ("my game is mostly picking up the ball") and doting father of Joseph and Sarah. His wife, the former Yoko Nozaki, whom he met when they were students at Juilliard, is also a pianist, and they occasionally perform in joint recitals.

Emanuel Ax does not limit his musical mind to playing the classics. During an interview with the *New York Times* in 1988, he insisted, "When you read the letters of Mozart and Beethoven, it makes you realize that they were people, that they were alive and writing for a purpose—for success, for money, to get audiences to love them, whatever. And when you see them not as icons but as real human beings, you begin to think, 'Well, after all, there are composers living today, and am I not being incredibly narrow-minded by having no contact with their work?' It's wrong not to. It was wrong 200 years ago, 100 years ago, and it's wrong now. Certainly for me, it's a way of life now to look forward to learning a new piece by someone." Of course, Ax's roots remain with the classics, but he maintains a resolve "to learn a new 20th-century concerto every year . . . even though most of what I play is Beethoven, Brahms, Mozart, Liszt. And of course I still do want to learn older repertory as well."

Dan Aykroyd

"I have friends who don't care what I do, who have never seen "Saturday Night Live" and with whom I associate on a totally different scale. The entertainment business is not the be-all and end-all for me," says the comic-actor-writer, whose friends must have been on Mars between 1975 and 1979, when he was an integral part of SNL's phenomenally successful early years. He received a 1977 Emmy Award for his memorable comedic contributions, both as one of SNL's seven original cast members and as one of its stable of writers. One of his recurring routines, performed with the flamboyant John Belushi, was the Blues Brothers, a dead-pan singing duo bedecked in dark suits, fedoras and sunglasses. Aykroyd calls his late partner "my wife. The only man I could ever dance with. . . . His loss is so tremendous." If he'd known of Belushi's drug habit, which caused the comedian's death, "I would have slapped all this stuff out of his hands."

A Canadian, born in Ottawa, Ontario, on 1 July 1952, Aykroyd was a rebellious youth who left Ottawa's Carlton College at 20 to join the Toronto branch of the Second City improvisational troupe, where he was spotted by SNL producer Lorne Michaels. Arriving in the U.S. in 1975, the year of the show's debut, he became popular with his Cone-head family skits and his varied impressions of Nixon, Carter, Tom Snyder, et al. His film debut was in 1979's *1941*, and the following year he wrote the film version of *The Blues Brothers*, in which he starred with Belushi. His other films include: *Neighbors* ('81, also with Belushi), *Twilight Zone—The Movie* (83), *Trading Places* ('83) and—also as co-writer—*Ghostbusters* ('84). Aykroyd has co-starred with a variety of talented people including Chevy Chase in *Spies Like Us* (1985), Charles Grodin in *The Couch Trip* (1987), Tom Hanks in *Dragnet 1987*, Kim Basinger in *My Stepmother Is An Alien* (1988), Gene Hackman in *The Von Metz Incident* (1988), and he reunited with Bill Murray and Sigourney Weaver for *Ghostbusters II* (1989).

His wife (married 29 April 1983) is actress Donna Dixon. He has three sons by an earlier marriage. He's a part-owner of Crooks—a Toronto bar—and the popular Hard Rock Cafe. He claims, "I have this kind of mild nice-guy exterior, but inside, my heart is like a steel trap. I'm really quite robotic."

Lauren Bacall

Of her early film career, which spanned hardly a dozen years, she has said she arrived in Tinsel Town knowing "they would never have one goddam bit of respect for me as an actress, a talent, a potential, whatever, and of course, I was right. I was a commodity, a piece of meat." The cut was, of course, choice. "Baby" Bacall left behind a nascent Broadway career and a full-fledged modeling career at *Harper's Bazaar* under the tutelage of Diana Vreeland to make her film debut in *To Have and Have Not* (1944). Although she captured the eye of the movie-going public and the heart (and hand) of the legendary actor Humphrey Bogart all before the age of 21, the sloe-eyed beauty has confessed: "I was not a woman of the world. I'd lived with Mother all my life." Her sleek, sultry look and whiskey voice sustained her for the next five years. By then, she had *The Big*

Sleep, Dark Passage, Key Largo and *Young Man With a Horn* under her cinch belt. "What I learned from Mr. Bogart, I learned from a master, and that, God knows, has stood me in very good stead." Indeed she was doing well in sophisticated comedy and her cutting delivery seemed more than natural in such efforts as *How to Marry a Millionaire* (1953), *Woman's World* (1954), *Written on the Wind* (1956) and *Designing Woman* (1957). To be sure, much of the cynicism must have come form the daily disparity of being mother of two (Stephen and Leslie) and chatelaine of a drunk tank affectionately known in Hollywood lore as the Holmby Hills Rat Pack which had her husband as the cheese. "I knew I couldn't last with that bunch if I didn't keep up."

Shortly after Bogey's death in 1957, she fled back to New York, where on 16 September 1924 she was born Betty (and to intimates remains) Joan Perske in Greenwich Village. A graduate of Julia Richman High School, she had also studied acting at the American Academy of Dramatic Arts. From the security of the famous Dakota apartments, she again essayed Broadway with *Goodbye Charlie* (1959), married actor Jason Robards, and had a second son, Sam. The Robards divorced eight years later. "Well, there is nothing to say about *that* except that it's over. *Period.*" Her first big success on Broadway was a two-year run in *Cactus Flower* (1966), but Broadway bitchery has proved to be her strong suit, although her own backstage behavior has not always been what becomes a legend most. She was awarded a Tony for her portrayal of Margo Channing in *Applause* (1970, the musical version of *All About Eve*), which ran for two years before a national tour, an appearance on London's West End and a televised adaptation. A second Tony followed for her characterization of Tess Harding in *Woman of the Year* (1981), which also ran for two years before a national tour. A mannequin for Blackglama advertisements, she also looks to commercials for a Long Island jeweler and a decaffinated coffee miller as her "source" of television revenues.

Successful films from Bacall's mature career include *Murder on the Orient Express* (1974), Robert Altman's *Health* (1980) and *The Fan* (1981), based on the best-selling novel. She also appeared in *Mr North* (1987), *Appointment With Death* (1987) and touched television with the PBS special *Bacall on Bogart* (1988). Her autobiography *By Myself* (1978) was a bestseller in both hardcover and paperback editions. Casting her mind over the past, she once reflected, "The harshness you might feel is bound to be reflected in your face—and I have enough things coming out on my face."

Burt Bacharach

A legend in the same Songwriters Hall of Fame league as Lennon and McCartney, Bob Dylan, and Paul Simon, Burt Bacharach revolutionized the music of the '60s. A product of his age, he has demonstrated the ability to write material that runs the gamut from rock and soul to the highly polished Broadway show score, and his phenomenally successful music continues to make the hit charts and win Emmys and Oscars. He was ecstatic that the critics called his 1969 show *Promises, Promises* a musical breakthrough, because "before this show the quality of sound in the theater was really rotten."

Born in Kansas City, 12 May 1929, he is the son of the late columnist Bert Bacharach. After graduating from high school, Bacharach went on to study at McGill University, the New School for Social Research in New York and Mannes School of Music. He also won a scholarship to the Music Academy of the West in Santa Barbara. He studied music composition from such famous teachers as Darius Milhaud, Boguslav Martinu and Henry Cowell. In the Army during the Korean War, he toured the bases as a "concert pianist" ("It was the put-on of all time. I had nothing to play, man, it was all improvisation.") After the war he worked as an accompanist for Vic Damone, who fired him. Later he played with Polly Bergen, Imogene Coca, and the Ames Brothers. He also played piano for Paula Stewart, to whom he was married for three years. After a stint in New York playing for Joel Grey in the Catskills, he met Marlene Dietrich. Asked to fill in for her regular conductor, he was soon touring the world with her. Leaving a London theatre with Bacharach, Dietrich was surrounded by autograph hounds. "Ask *him* for *his* autograph," she said waving them to him, "He's the person you'll be after some day." Bacharach was her conductor and arranger when she made her triumphant Broadway debut in 1968. ("Marlene taught me a lot about never settling for less. I just watched her—what she went after she got.") Another singer in his life was Dionne Warwick, for whom many of his songs were written, and who starred in several of his popular TV specials. (She later sued Bacharach and his partner Hal David for millions over a contractual dispute; she settled out of court.) His hits in partnership with David include: "Alfie," "What the World Needs Now is Love," "What's New, Pussycat?," "Do You Know the Way to San Jose?" and "Walk on By." He won two Academy Awards in 1970—for scoring *Butch Cassidy and the Sundance Kid* and for the movie's smash song, "Raindrops Keep Fallin' on My Head."

Bacharach and his second wife, actress Angie Dickinson (1 daughter, Nikki) were divorced after 16 years of marriage, and in 1982 he married his latest collaborator, lyricist Carole Bayer Sager. The couple have a son, Christopher Elton, born in December ,1985. "I always thought you shouldn't mix business with pleasure," declared Bacharach (apparently he did some rethinking). Glowing with pride, he says, "I think Carole is the best lyric writer in the country." He won another Oscar in 1981 for Best Song—"Arthur's Theme" which he co-wrote with Sager, Peter Allen, and Christopher Cross. "Heartlight," a Neil Diamond hit, was written by Bacharach, Sager and Diamond (the Bacharachs named one of their horses "Heartlight No. One" in the hopes the filly would do as well as the hit record and album; the horse is a consistent winner, attributed to the fact the Bacharachs and Diamond sing the song to her before she races.) Horseracing is Bacharach's escape valve (he owns about 20 thoroughbreds), and he plays an "energetic" game of tennis. He continues working with his glamourous new collaborator, co-producing her album, *Sometimes Late at Night* and collaborating on the Pointer Sisters hits "Too Good To Last" "Where Did the Time Go?" and "On My Own." Bacharach added another Grammy to his shelf in February, 1987, when he and Sager won "1986 Song of the Year" for their timeless anthem "That's What Friends Are For."

Joan Baez

"I'm obsessed with one thing: stopping people from blowing their brains out. I've been obsessed with that since I was ten," says this charismatic folksinger-activist whose dedication to non-violence in the tradition of Gandhi has taken her everywhere from Hanoi (where, in 1972, she spent two weeks witnessing what's been called "the most intense aerial bombardment in the history of warfare") to Latin America (where official pressure prevented her from performing in Argentina, Chile and Brazil) to the U.S.S.R. (where she met with various Soviet dissidents, including Nobel Peace Prize winner Andrei Sakharov but didn't get a chance to sing in public). In the 1980s, through her human rights group Humanitas International, Joan Baez continued to combine her gift of song with a personal commitment to a more peaceful world.

Born 9 January 1941 on Staten Island of English-Scots and Mexican parentage, she made her professional debut at the Newport Folk Festival in 1958. Often barefoot on stage, her long hair flowing, she was apotheosized as a virtual goddess by "troubled intellectuals with the Bomb on their minds." ("When I started singing," she once said, "I felt as if we just had so long to live.") She made the cover of *Time* in 1962 after her no-discrimination policy on Southern campuses helped to successfully integrate audiences and she has continued to combine concertizing with causes all over the globe. One of the outspoken activists against the Vietnam War and a prime supporter of Amnesty International, she has turned her energies to opposing the use of nuclear power and in 1979 formed the Humanitas International Human Rights Committee to address global human rights violations. The publication of a controversial Open Letter to the Socialist Republic of Vietnam that same year catapulted Joan and her group into the head-lines—and established her as a peacemaker who cut across political lines to attack human rights violations wherever she saw them. She remained a headline figure during the Indochina refugee crisis, urging the U.S. President to send the Seventh Fleet to rescue boat people in the South China Sea (he did) and helping to organize the Cambodia Emergency Relief Fund which raised $1 million. In 1979, she received the American Civil Liberties Union's Earl Warren Award for her long commitment to civil liberties and human rights. Active in the 1980s nuclear disarmament movement, she appeared with Paul Simon in a benefit concert for the National Nuclear Weapons Freeze Campaign in 1982. During a 60-concert tour of Europe and the U.S. in 1983, she sang for free in Paris before a crowd of 120,000 the day after Bastille Day, in a concert dedicated to nonviolence. She divorced former student leader David Harris in 1973; they have a son, Gabriel, born 1969.

Still an important voice of the 80's, Joan continues to record her music and appear in concert. 1987 saw the release of an album *Recently* and a revealing autobiography, *And A Voice To Sing With: My Story*. She was also active in the widely publicized "Human Rights Now" concert in 1988.

F. Lee Bailey

"He is a throwback," said one lawyer who'd drawn against him. "In the old days he would have dashed up to the courthouse on the best horse in town, with his cape trailing behind him." One of the top defense attorneys, comparable to great defenders like Clarence Darrow and Lloyd Paul Stryker, he was born 10 June 1933 in Waltham, MA. A Harvard dropout, Bailey joined the Marines to become a jet fighter pilot, and still spends considerable time in the cockpit. Admitted to Boston University after his discharge, he scored one of the highest academic averages in the Law School's history. Yet he also found time to do some extracurricular scoring in a tough hockey league and manage his own detective agency. When the dismembered body of George Edgerly's wife was fished out of the Merrimac River, Bailey, fresh out of law school, lucked into the case as defense counsel. He won an acquittal, and extensive publicity as well. His subsequent clients read like a Who's Who of American crime, including Albert DeSalvo (The Boston Strangler), Charles Schmid, Jr. (The Pied Piper of Tucson), Dr. Sam Sheppard, Captain Ernest Medina (of the My Lai Massacre), and Patty Hearst (who later asked for a new trial on grounds that Bailey was incompetent).

Bailey, who's written some 16 books, recounted many of his early cases in *The Defense Never Rests*, published in 1972. He showed a flair for fiction in *Secrets*, a 1979 novel about a lawyer who is charged with murder. The well-known jurist has been a regular legal expert for the "Good Morning, America" television show, and even had a short-lived program of his own on which he tested novices' knowledge of the law in drummed-up situations.

The high-living Bailey's toys—a couple of planes, a helicopter, a 35-foot oceangoing speed boat—necessitate a heavy lecture schedule in order to maintain his collection. Miss Hearst maintained that Bailey lost her case because his obligations and alleged hangovers prevented him from defending her adequately. For the most part, he has a reputation for thoroughly investigated and carefully reasoned cases. Says Bailey, "If you put in good solid evidence and make the jury reason and listen and come up to it, they will—as opposed to the old theory where you block all the evidence, cause confusion and say, 'People, please be stupid enough to do what I want.'" Thrice-divorced, he lives near his Boston offices in Marshfield, Mass., and has a Bahamas townhouse, which he shares with his fourth wife, Patricia Shiers, whom he wed in June, 1985.

Pearl Bailey

"Oh! Life is so full and rich." Pearl Mae Bailey has unquestionably provided life with part of that richness, entertaining two generations with her records, her performances on Broadway, in night clubs and vaudeville (still her favorite form of show business), in films, on television, and in five popular books. "Papa was a preacher. Holy Roller, I suppose you'd call it. From him I got the wisdom, the philosophizing, the soul."

Bailey was born in Newport News, VA, 29 March 1918, and first sang at religious services led by her father. "In his church you've got to have a lot of rhythm," she says. "Folks sway, and sometimes they shout." Following her famous tap-dancing brother, Bill Bailey, she started singing in small clubs in Washington at 13, and starred with Count Basie and Cootie Williams. Johnny Mercer and Harold Arlen signed her for the Broadway production of *St. Louis Woman* in 1946 for which she received the Donaldson Award as best newcomer on Broadway. Her other Broadway shows include *Bless You All* (1950), *House of Flowers* (1954) and the all-black production of *Hello, Dolly!*, which in 1967 won her Entertainer of the Year award from *Cue* magazine. But Pearl Bailey is best known for her recordings—songs such as "Tired," "Legalize My Name," and "Takes Two to Tango," and albums like "The Bad Old Days" and "For Adult Listening." Her autobiography, *The Raw Pearl*, came out in 1968.

In 1975 and 1976, Bailey was appointed by President Gerald R. Ford as Special Advisor to the U.S. Mission to the United Nations. She traveled to the Middle East and Africa, including Jordan, Egypt, Kuwait, Liberia, Senegal and the United Arab Emirates. When she departed, U.S. Ambassador Jamil Baroody of Saudi Arabia thanked the U.S. for "having retained as a representative . . . a Pearl not cultured by Mimimoto, but cultured in the art of the theatre and in her genuine humanitarian attitude towards all those who know her."

Bailey and her husband, French jazz drummer Louis Bellson, were married in 1952 and have two children. She has been honored in the Middle East with such awards as King Hussein of Jordan's Ben-Ali Freedom Medal, and Egypt's First Order of Arts and Science of Egypt. In 1978, Bailey received an Honorary Degree from Georgetown University and soon after enrolled as a freshman. Earning a place on the Dean's List was one of her proudest achievements. Graduating in 1985 with a B.A. in Theology, she wrote a song to mark the happy occasion.

Pearl presented a wonderful Christmas gift to the public with her performance in the PBS television special "Miss Ruby's Southern Holiday Dinner," which aired in 1988.

Anita Baker

Entrusted with the creative control on production of her first album for a major record company, sultry-voiced Anita Baker showed that she was not just a singer possessed with a pure vocal ability, but that she also possessed the technical understanding of recording. She executive-produced *Rapture*, the 1986 album that sold 5 million copies and skyrocketed Baker into public acclaim. For her efforts, Anita won the 1987 Grammy for R&B Female Vocalist, while her song "Sweet Love" was awarded the honors as R&B Song of the Year. *Rolling Stone*'s critical poll designated Baker as the "best female singer," while the magazine's fan poll chose her as the "best new female singer." Securing her spot in the limelight, Baker walked away with two Grammys in 1989; Best R&B Vocal Female and as co-writer of "Giving You the Best That I've Got"—Best R&B Song.

This "new" singer began her musical career at age 12 in Detroit, Michigan, singing in church with her traveling minister grandfather. Although born in Toledo, Ohio, on 26 January 1958, Anita was raised in Detroit and obtained some of the inspiration for her style from Detroit's WJZZ radio. Baker then started singing with "basement bands" formed by classmates and choir members. After high school she spent two years moving from band to band until she was invited to audition for one of Detroit's top club bands, "Chapter 8," which led to her recording debut with the band in 1980. She sang the lead in a minor hit "I Just Wanna Be Your Girl," then later separated from the group to become a legal secretary. Fortunately, this career was cut short and she entered the music world again with the album *Songstress*. The album spawned a Top-Ten single on the Black charts, "Angel," and made people aware of Anita's jazz/R&B synthesis. This eventually prompted a major label to sign Baker and soon she was executive-producing her second album, *Giving You the Best That I've Got*.

Not leaving her roots behind, Anita recorded a duet with the Detroit group, The Winans. Titled "Ain't No Need To Worry," the record won a Grammy for Best Gospel Performance by Duo or Group. A committed performer, Baker says, "I have to personalize a song: I have to fit it in me." It's for that reason she's been called one of the most distinctive voices of the decade.

New Year's Eve, 1988, was especially romantic for Anita Baker, when she married Detroit businessman Walter Bridgeforth.

James A. Baker III

A "completely apolitical" Texas plutocrat until he was 40, James Addison Baker III has such "an instinct for politics on the hoof" that he was able to use his quick-study intellect and organizational talent to engineer two Presidential election victories for Ronald Reagan and serve through RR's first Administration as "the best manager who's ever run the White House." As Chief of Staff, he successfully side-stepped political quagmires and sublimated his own more-moderate political ideology rather than challenge the President's policies, pointing out "my job is not to go into the Oval Office and advocate a view because I happen to believe it strongly. My job is to let the President know what I think is best politically." Nonetheless, archconservative Reagan factotums were pleased in early 1985, before the second term began, by Reagan's announcement that Baker and the more-conservative Secretary of the Treasury Donald Regan were exchanging jobs. Earlier, Baker had actively sought a post that would give him experience in foreign affairs, but he pronounced himself "dedicated to the Administration," Treasury and his seat on the National Security Council. His followers were even more pleased when President Bush appointed Baker as Secretary of State in 1989.

The scion of a prominent Houston family of attorneys, he was born there 28 April 1930 and graduated from Princeton (1952) before serving in the Marines and earning his law degree at the University of Texas. Barred from joining the highly successful family firm by antinepotism rules, he began practicing corporate law at another firm in 1957 and, with his diligence to detail, became managing partner. Like most local aristocrats at that time, he was a conservative Democrat, but assiduously avoided politics, as had all of his family. Then, in 1970, grieving over the loss of his first wife, he was cajoled by a country-club buddy, Congressman George Bush, into helping Bush in a bid for the U.S. Senate. Transformed by that experience into an "absolutely, totally, pure Republican," he subsequently worked on the Nixon re-election campaign, served briefly as Under Secretary of Commerce during the Ford Administration, helped Ford defeat Reagan for the Republican nomination in 1976 and campaigned aggressively against Carter. After securing Bush's victory in the Iowa primary in 1980, he proved strategist enough at the nominating convention to assure Bush's slot as Vice Presidential pick. Although he was an outsider to the Reagan camp, the confident candidate opted for ability over long-term loyalty in choosing Baker as campaign manager and then Chief of Staff. Known for an uncommon ability to form coalitions across ideological lines, Baker is popular with the press; his finesse was credited with the quiet sway of public opinion to Reagan's position on many issues.

It has been said that Baker's stamina for politics was forged in his weathering of the death of his first wife, Mary Stuart Baker, the mother of his four sons. In 1973, he married the former Susan Garrett, the mother of three and a close family friend. In 1978 the couple added a daughter of their own, Mary Bonner Baker.

Janet Baker

"All my life I'd seen my voice, my art as a burden, a God-given gift that has to be shared with others, so I had this terrific sense of duty, of obligation," says the British-born performer often called a "thinker-singer" for the piercing interpretations she gives to her music. Dame Janet Baker (named a Commander of the British Empire in 1970) has shared her blessings with countless patrons of music throughout the world. She is equally comfortable singing opera (primarily in England), lieder and oratorio. Her 1982 journal *Full Circle* gave a detailed account of the constant pressures and stress inherent in the role of public figure. In 1982 the operatic portion of her career came to a close and Baker gave numerous farewell performances. But the mezzo-soprano continues as a recitalist and once a year performs at New York City's Carnegie Hall where according to Baker, she will give her final performance: "New York audiences have a total, warmhearted response unlike any other." Said one Baker admirer, "Janet Baker's New York recitals are rather like state visits from some distantly regal monarch, occasions for automatic genuflection."

Born Janet Abbott Baker, 21 August 1933, in York, England, she "soaked in" the surrounding English church music as a young girl. While in her teens Baker practiced singing while working at a coin-sorting machine at the bank where she was employed. In 1956 she won the *Daily Mail* Kathleen Ferrier Prize giving her publicity and the opportunity to study at the Mozarteum in Salzburg. In 1959 Baker was awarded the Queen's Prize from the Royal College of Music and in 1960 she received an Arts Council grant to continue her studies. Baker's reputation steadily grew as did her operatic repertory. It has been noted that she is at her best with Mahler, yet (according to *New York Times* writer Howard Klein) "she can do just about anything vocally and dramatically in a variety of contexts, and she does it all with a communicative radiance and personal warmth that borders on magic." It may come as a surprise to many that for much of her career, Baker suffered from a severe case of stagefright and underwent counselling to overcome it and discover the joy and pleasures of her music. And though singing comes almost as naturally as breathing ("Singing is a natural function. You clear away the debris to let what's there come through") she was constantly aware of the emotional and physical strain inherent in the more passionate roles. Prima donna in status but not in temperament, Baker is down-to-earth and known for the warmth and intelligence she brings to her music, putting the song first, not her voice: "There's always somebody as good as you are or better.... I try not to bother myself about it.... I believe I'm employed to deliver my own thing. I'm Janet Baker and no one else." The blue-eyed, auburn-haired singer lives with her husband and business manager, James Keith Shelley, outside of London. Relaxation includes walking, playing tennis and reading—mostly history and philosophy.

Making the transition "Full Circle" from book to video, Baker recorded a documentary of the same title for home audiences. The cassette shows Dame Janet's activities during her 1981-1982 farewell season. According to the *New York Times* (1987), "this is an important, well-conceived documentary about an artist who has long considered her gift 'a responsibility to be given to other people' and has now come to realize that 'it is a joy to me' as well."

Russell Baker

In his "Sunday Observer" column early in 1985, he mourned the decade's trend toward celebrity proliferation, pointing out that "a single weekly magazine like *People* ... uses up approximately 2,000 stars per year." It wasn't like that in the old days, he reminded readers. "In terms of star mega-tonnage, if Gable was the H-bomb, these fellows in *People*, talented though they may be, are a box of Fourth of July sparklers.... You can see the catastrophic trend. A great star—Gable, Rossevelt, Flynn, Mae West, dies out, and three dozen tiny stars are created. Result: the American star arsenal is becoming all quantity and no bang." Ruminating on topics such as this, the Pulitzer Prizewinning former police and political reporter is today one of journalism's wittiest observers of life and a deflater of the pompous. And something of a star himself. His "Observer" columns have appeared in the *New York Times* since 1962 and are now syndicated to more than 100 other papers. A prolific writer, Baker's proud of the fact that he's never had a column in reserve. ("I figure that if I write one and then I died, the *Times* will get something free."). Baker revealed a new dimension of his talents—and himself—in his bestselling autobiography *Growing Up* (Pulitzer Prize, 1983), which reviewer Harrison Salisbury described as "the saddest, funniest, most tragical, most comical picture of coming of age in the USA in the Depression years and World War II that has ever been written. He also served as editor of *The Norton Book of Light Verse* in 1986.

Born 14 August 1925 in Morrisonville, Va., the son of an easy-going stonemason who loved booze and a domineering former schoolteacher who admired "gumption," Russell Baker "slumbered through the bliss of infancy, feeling no impulse whatever to make something of myself," he writes in *Growing Up*. His blissful childhood was shattered when his father died, whereupon his mother took Russell and his sister to live in Newark, N.J., and later Baltimore, determined that her son would make something of himself. When he was eight, she tried to launch him on a business career selling *The Saturday Evening Post*; he hated it. Three years later, after he brought home an A in composition she got another idea: "Buddy, maybe you could be a writer."

Baker said he "clasped the idea to my heart.... So far as I could make out, what writers did couldn't even be classified as work. I was enchanted. Writers didn't have to have any gumption at all." He did, of course, become a writer, beginning his newspaper career in 1947 with the *Baltimore Sun* after serving in the Navy and graduating from Johns Hopkins University. In 1954, he joined the *Times*, for which he covered Congress, the White House, and national politics, before turning to his "Observer" column. In 1979, he won the George Polk Award for Commentary and the Pulitzer Prize for Distinguished Commentary. His columns have been collected in *So This is Depravity*. He's also author of *Poor Russell's Almanac*. Married to Miriam (Mimi) Emily Nash since 1950, the father of three children and now a grandfather, Baker said he got interested in "life's circularity" writing his autobiography. "We all come from the past," he says, "and children ought to know what it was that went into their making, to know that life is a braided cord of humanity stretching up from time long gone, and that it cannot be defined by the span of a single journey from diaper to shroud."

Severiano Ballesteros

"He hits every obstacle on the course," said a golf spectator of the young spray-hitting Spaniard. "He plays the way we play," replied his friend. "That's why everybody likes to watch him." Ballesteros' all-out drives are probably easy for non-professionals to identify with because he, as they in many cases, had no formal training at the game. But it's impossible for bewildered, or resentful, opponents on the tour to continue calling his phenomenal winning "lucky" as he's now nabbed a pair each of British Opens and Masters victories to add to his throng of other international tourney wins.

Severiano Ballesteros, born 9 April 1957 in the Spanish fishing village of Pedrena, still lives in the farmhouse that borders the royally-commissioned golf course where he learned the game. As a fifth son, he grew up with an internationally-competing uncle and four brothers who were pro competitors. Young caddies weren't allowed to play on the Real Pedrena course, so nine-year-old Seve (pronounced Sevvy) sneaked around at night with other little aspirants to play. Other times they would play with a lone club on the beach, possibly accounting for Ballesteros' remarkable bunker-extricating shots today. He was a pro who had left school by 16, and three years later played more tourneys than any other player in the world to earn $100,000 in 1976. At 19 he made the golf world sit up and notice as he smacked his way to a second-place tie at the British Open with Jack Nicklaus, behind Johnny Miller. He found he preferred the European circuit and committed himself to play there, even though the PGA tour commissioner offered him an unprecedented free card after winning his second World Cup for Spain. In 1979 he became the youngest golfer in over a hundred years to win the British Open as the 22-year-old beat Nicklaus as well as Ben Crenshaw. The long years of practice may have taken their toll on Ballesteros' back which is bothered by chronic pain. Quite an eligible bachelor, the athlete lives almost incognito with his parents and dog in Pedrena, near the course where it all began for him.

Anne Bancroft

"Who would have thought that when I left California, I would wind up sleeping in Golda Meir's bed?" In preparation for *Golda* ('77-'78), William Gibson's dramatization of Golda Meir's autobiography, *My Life*, Anne Bancroft did just that—travelling to Israel, accompanying Meir to religious, political and social events. "Golda was a legend to me. She was out of my realm," said Bancroft before meeting Meir. In search of a personal link to aid her in her portrayal, Bancroft jetted to Israel—as soon as they met that bond was established; "I was suddenly calm. My anxiety was gone. I looked into her eyes and I knew. I knew I would be OK.... When I work I have to find a personal image that is similar to the person I'm relating to in the play. If you don't lock into something extremely personal within yourself the play will have gone by without your having felt anything." An Oscar winner (*The Miracle Worker*—1962), Bancroft has been visible on the screen in *Garbo Talks*, in hubby Mel Brooks' mordant comedy *To Be or Not To Be*, *Agnes of God*, *'night, mother*, and *84 Charing Cross Road*.

Born Anne Marie Italiano, 17 September 1931, in the Bronx, she breezed through a Hollywood screen test at age 18, was then becalmed for the next six years in a series of B and lower movies. "Everybody drank beer for breakfast," she recalls hazily of those years. "We had a ball." Hung over from the California merry-go-round and her four-year marriage to Texan Martin May, she returned to New York in 1955, lived at home, and enrolled in Herbert Berghof's acting classes. "It was the beginning of a whole new approach to acting, a deeper, more fulfilling and more thinking approach. I learned to think a little to set certain tasks for myself. My work became much more exciting." Bancroft first reached Broadway star status in 1958 opposite Henry Fonda in *Two for the Seesaw*. She stayed with the highly acclaimed show for a year and half, and recalls, "For the first time in my life I was a star, an honest-to-gosh star, in an important production. There was a tremendous sense of achievement in me and I really felt like an actress." The down-to-earth luminary received Oscar nominations for *The Pumpkin Eater* (1963), *The Graduate* (1968) and *The Turning Point* (1977). Other standout Bancroft appearances include Neil Simon's *Prisoner of Second Avenue*, *The Elephant Man* (1980) and *Torch Song Trilogy* (1988).

The hard-driving actress has mellowed considerably since her 1964 marriage to writer/director Mel Brooks (one son). "Oh, I still get deeply involved in the roles I take. Mel gets totally involved when he's writing, too, and I am shut out, alone. But life is not all work now. Work is just part of life."

Daniel Barenboim

"So many people," sighs this Israeli pianist-conductor, "regard music as a matter of ability." To Daniel Barenboim what counts more is "musicianship," and, according to at least one professional observer, he has more of it "than many musicians twice his age."

"Unless I feel the totality of the thing," Barenboim explains, "I can't understand what's going on. And if I can't, what must it sound like to the audience? Chaos," he concludes. His quest for that "totality" has led him from the keyboard to the conductor's podium, which now accounts for a quarter of his more than 100 annual bookings.

Barenboim's career parallels that of many prodigies. He was born in Buenos Aires 15 November 1942, began studying with his piano-teaching parents when he was five, and gave his first recital at seven. After his parents resettled in Tel Aviv, he studied in Europe (Igor Markevitch's conducting classes in Salzburg at age 10; with Nadia Boulanger in Paris as the recipient of a grant from the American Israel Foundation, age 11), becoming at 13 the youngest student ever to win a master's degree at Rome's Academy of Santa Cecilia. Although most pianists refrain from tackling Beethoven's 32 sonatas until their ripest years, Barenboim, who had learned them at 14, challenged the peak of piano repertory and performed them all in a series of concerts in 1966. He has been heard as piano soloist with virtually every major orchestra in the world. He made his conducting debut in '68 leading the English Chamber Orchestra in N.Y., had his European debut with the Berlin Philharmonic the next year and has subsequently led almost all the major orchestras with whom he previously was heard as soloist. In '75 he was named Music Director of the Orchestre de Paris.

When the six-day Arab-Israeli war of June '67 broke out, Barenboim and his fiancee, British cellist Jacqueline du Pre, cancelled all engagements and flew to Israel to perform. They were married in Jerusalem on 18 June of that year and performed frequently together in public and on recordings until her tragic retirement in the early '70s due to multiple sclerosis. She died in 1987.

Christiaan Barnard

An obscure South African doctor until he performed the first human heart transplant in history, replacing grocer Louis Washkansky's stricken heart with that of young Denise Darvall in December, 1967, he instantly became the most famous surgeon in the world—and the most resented. While Barnard dazzled the world at large with his medical accomplishment, many physicians saw him as an opportunist and publicity hound who "had rushed prematurely into a risky procedure" and then succeeded in keeping the spotlight on himself. Barnard became an overnight sensation, making much-sought-after appearances throughout the world. Between speaking engagements he always found time to pose alongside popes, heads of state and movie stars. Shortly after he first made headlines, Barnard began to make the gossip columns with a series of torrid love affairs, including one with Italian bombshell Gina Lollobrigida. Amidst the hoopla, he was divorced by his wife of 21 years Aletta (two children, one of whom, son Andre, died at the age of 32 in 1984 of a drug over-dose) so he could marry a voluptuous 19-year-old blond heiress from Johannesburg, Barbara Zoellner, in 1970. The couple, with their expensive, flashy style, became, as one British columnist put it, "South Africa's only 'Beautiful People.'"

Born in Beaufort West, South Africa, 8 October 1922, the son of an impoverished Dutch Reformed minister, Barnard attended the University of Cape Town, nearly fainting at an appendectomy but reassured when a scrub nurse told him, "It's the ones with the most imagination who get the worst." His taste for the lavish was already present—ducking out of classes to watch affluent people alight from first-class Pullman cars was his favorite pastime.

In time, Barnard derived a drug treatment for tubercular meningitis while at Cape Town's City Hospital. He was subsequently appointed to Groote Schuur Hospital where he distinguished himself again, showing for the first time that intestinal atresia, a congenital gap in the small bowel, is caused by insufficient blood supply. Soon he was taking advanced training at the University of Minnesota. Observing pioneer open-heart surgeon Dr. Walton Lillehei use a heart-lung machine, he decided finally on his own surgical specialty. Winning his Ph.D. in the two-year limit (a six-year course), Barnard set out for himself and returned to Cape Town's Groote Schuur.

"I could see little sense in continuing the further sacrifice of animals," he said while performing dog heart transplants, a method inspired by the work of Drs. Norman E. Shumway of Stanford and Richard Lower of the Medical College of Virginia. "I'm ready to go ahead," announced 54-year-old Louis Washkansky after Groote Schuur's chief of cardiology referred the incurably ill patient to Barnard. The surgeon's reputation as a publicity addict escalated with the 1970 appearance of his autobiography (co-authored with former *Newsweek* Rome bureau chief, Curtis Bill Pepper), several novels (all ghost-written) and the 1972 *Heart Attack: You Don't Have to Die.*

"The bubble burst," however, in the early 1980's when Barnard's second wife left him for a young nightclub owner. (They divorced in 1982.) Downtrodden and suffering from anorexia, Barnard hibernated in a hotel room, rarely emerging. Later, after an attempted reconciliation floundered, Barnard began his enthusiastic womanizing anew. In 1982, after 25 years as head of the cardiac unit in Cape Town, Barnard retired to his farm in southeastern Africa to raise cattle, write and overlook management of his Italian restaurant chain. He blamed rheumatoid arthritis, a crippling affliction which impaired the use of his hands, for this move. "The first thing I shall probably do is look for a new wife," Barnard joked at his farewell press conference. This bit of humor turned into reality when on 24 January 1988 Barnard married his third wife, Karin Setzkorn. Inspired to work again, he became involved launching a new skin care line: Glycel. Although he has given up his surgical gloves, Christiaan's cardiac accomplishments remain an inspiration for a worldwide research effort. "He is a thinking, creative surgeon," a colleague once said. "No one who ever saw him at work will ever forget him."

Clive Barnes

Once described as "a short, pudgy man, with a rugged head and jutting brow," Clive Barnes is a self-proclaimed "sucker" for all kinds of plays. "I probably get more out of a bad performance," he says, "than most people get out of a good one," adding that "my ideal criticism is to write a notice about a play that I didn't like, and yet send people to see it." Frequently, therein lies the rub. "To stimulate thought and opinion" as "sort of a catalyst . . . between the artist and the audience," he couches his critiques in what he calls a "chatty" style that often leaves the reader on the periphery of a dialogue between Barnes and his muse/mentor of whatever art(s) concerned. One may then be faced with the decision: is he writing of artistically presented trash or trashily done art, or are his paragraphs "uncomprehending non-sense," as sometimes charged, or is the whole simply autistic criticism? When he abdicated his undisputed power as the Theatrical Editor of the *New York Times* in 1978 to occupy the lesser slot at Rupert Murdoch's *New York Post*, many felt that Barnes was trading cachet for cash. Eleven years before, however, on the occasion of becoming the *Times* "man on the aisle," Barnes told his readers "we are prepared to break the power of the *Times* critic. We want influence, not power. I'm terrified by the idea of the critic as a racing tipster."

Barnes, who calls himself a "typical working class overachiever," was born 13 May 1927 in a London slum. The precocious Cockney youngster aspired to the Ballet Club at Oxford and won a scholarship to the university, where he achieved editorship of the Club's publication *Arabesque* in 1950. Barnes and his fellow members wanted every paper in London to have a specialist dance critic. "We were terribly mean to the established dance critics, who were all music critics, really, and didn't know a thing about dance. We were kind of young Turks, obnoxious as hell, but it worked.... Now they all do." While writing music and dance criticism for the London *Times*, he served as London correspondant for *Dance* magazine and, by 1963, was contributing London pieces to the *Times* in New York. In 1965, he moved to the U.S. to become the *Times* dance critic and, two years later, replaced Walter Kerr as drama critic. At that time, Barnes declared "on no account will I give up dance. An overwhelming passion!" In 1974, in yet another alignment of duties, he became Theatrical Editor of the *Times*. In his *Post* position, he has been drama and dance critic since 1978.

After divorcing his first wife of ten years, Barnes married dancer/dance commentator and writer Patricia Amy Evelyn Winckley in 1958 (one son, one daughter); they later divorced. In 1985 he married *Post* reporter Amy Pagnozzi. An adjacent associate professor in the Department of Journalism at New York University, Barnes' prolific personal output has included the books *Dance Scene, U.S.A.* (1967) and *Inside American Ballet Theatre* (1977).

Roseanne Barr

"Hi I'm a housewife, domestic goddess."

"We're all married to the same guy.... You may marry the man of your dreams, ladies, but 15 years later you are married to a reclining chair that burps."

"Mom, where's my English book?" "I sold it."

"The 'Terrible Twos' last until your kids move out of the house."

"Mom, I've got a knot in my shoe." "Wear loafers."

"It's OK to be fat. So you're fat. Just be fat and shut up about it."

Her one-liners have people doubled-up with laughter. Her television series "Roseanne" won the People's Choice Award (1989) as Favorite Comedy Show and Roseanne Barr is thrilled with her success. She jokes, "As long as I bitch and get paid for it, I'm the luckiest person in the world."

Born in Salt Lake City, Utah, circa 1953 to a working-class Jewish family, she told *USA Weekend*, "Mormon country was not the best place for Jews. I survived by never saying I was Jewish. I was very quiet. I'd sit in the back of the classroom and had very few friends." She had to drop out of high school at 18, when she was hit by a car. She admitted during a Barbara Walters interview that she was institutionalized as a teenager for her rebellious behavior (she recently visited the hospital to give the patients a Barr-boost talk.) After a slow recovery, Roseanne moved to Colorado Springs where she met her future husband, Bill Pentland (a mail sorter at a local post office). Without appropriate funds to live in "style", the newlyweds set up house in a 9-by-36-foot trailer. Three children later (Jessica, Jennifer, Jacob) the family moved into a "larger" 600-square-foot house in Denver. She claims, "It wasn't 'Dynasty,' but it was cool. We thought we were artsy folks." Discouraged from showing her standup routines in the 70's because of her down-to-earth, sometimes brash bits, Roseanne only performed at private parties, biker bars and punk clubs. It wasn't until she appeared on "The Tonight Show" that all hell broke loose. With her sitcom scoring high in the ratings, she's assured of theatrical longevity. Her autobiography *Stand Up: My Life As a Woman* (1989) is a frank tell-all of her struggles—a serious side to the funny lady.

With obstacles in the past and now a huge jump from her grassroot beginnings, Roseanne lives in California; she and Bill split in 1989 and she is seen about town with comedian/writer Tom Arnold. Roseanne has her life mapped out: "I went into standup so I could do television and movies. Right now, I'm in the seventh year of a 10-year plan. In year 10, I become Woody Allen. I write and direct $3-million films. I wear glasses. I move to New York."

Donald Barthelme

"Oh, there's brain damage in the east, and brain damage in the west, and upstair's there's brain damage, and downstairs there's brain damage, and in my lady's parlor . . . there's brain damage on the horizon, a great big blubbery cloud of it coming this way." So writes this *New Yorker* author of unconventional short stories. He has been known to write a complete story using only one sentence, or using exactly 100 numbered ones, or entirely by question and answer form. The editors of the *New Yorker* have said that they get more mail objecting to his work than any other writer. The critics and his fans consider Barthelme to be one of the more interesting writers around.

The son of a well-known architect (and the brother of author Frederick), he was born 7 April 1931 in Philadelphia, but grew up and spent his early working and writing years in Houston. He was a reporter on a Houston paper, served with the Army in Korea, and thought for a while about becoming an artist. Instead, he became a surrealist collagist of the written word. Barthelme's books include: *Come Back, Dr. Caligari* (1964), *Unspeakable Practices, Unnatural Acts* (1968), *City Life* (1970), *Sadness* (1972), *Guilty Pleasures* (1974), *The Dead Father* (1975), *Great Days* (1979), *Sixty Stories* (1982), *Paradise* (1986), *Forty Stories* (1987) and *Sam's Bar: An American Landscape* (1987). In 1972 he was the recipient of the National Book Award for his children's book *The Slightly Irregular Fire Engine*. His novel *Snow White* (1967) typifies the Barthelme point of view. (The title character is an East Village nymphomaniac living with seven roommates, all of whom like to take showers together.) A reluctant celebrity, he is married to his third wife and they have one daughter. Friends say he's moody and "one of the great despairers of all time." Critics praise him for his inventiveness but even they sometimes admit to not knowing what he is up to. In the summer of 1983 he adapted for the stage seven of his short stories and they were presented under the title of *Great Days*. It is "the principle of collage [that] is the central principle of all art in the twentieth century in all media," he has said. Among the writers who have influenced him are the poets John Ashbery and Kenneth Koch. When Barthelme fulfilled his dream of becoming "a *New Yorker* writer" a pal back in Houston read his stories and commented about their absurdities: "God, what's happened to old Don? It was not what one expected from the F. Scott Fitzgerald of Houston."

Mikhail Baryshnikov

"He's a combination of Nureyev, Erik Bruhn and what one has heard about Nijinsky," was the word out of Leningrad in 1972 about the new principal dancer at the Kirov Ballet. Two years later, after Mikhail Baryshnikov followed Nureyev and Makarova in their leaps to the West, American audiences were able to see for themselves what all the fuss was about, as they witnessed Misha and Makarova in a performance of *Giselle* at the New York State Theatre at Lincoln Center. "Thunder broke in the theatre at Baryshnikov's entrance," according to *Dance Magazine*. "It rolled in peal after peal of applause through the ballet and for twenty-seven minutes after." Ten years later, the "new Nijinsky" seemingly had it all. As a dancer, he'd won unparalleled acclaim in America and Europe for his complete mastery of the classical repertory as well as his virtuoso command of contemporary works. He'd followed up his hit movie *The Turning Point* (1976) with the semi-autobiographical *White Nights* (1985). He'd been the star of a series of hit television specials. He choreographed a new *Nutcracker* that has become a holiday television staple, a smashing *Don Quixote* and a popular *Cinderella* (which received mixed critical response). In 1980 he was made artistic director of American Ballet Theatre, one of the world's great dance companies. One has to wonder if Baryshnikov's extraordinary achievements have relieved the melancholy suggested by his words of 1974—"No other country in the world will be my home but Russia. You can be a citizen anywhere, but my soul will always be Russian."

It was to Russian parents that Mikhail Baryshnikov was born in Riga, Latvia, 27 January 1948, and he recalls being "a very normal schoolboy. It was only *after* I began my ballet training that I became 'abnormal.' I became obsessed with dancing." At the relatively advanced age of 12, he entered the Latvian Opera Ballet School, and three years later passed the rigorous examination required for entrance into the Kirov's training institute. After three years of study under the legendary Aleksandr Pushkin (who had unleashed the marvels of Nureyev), he joined the parent company as a soloist, where he performed brilliantly—as a character dancer. "I did not have the look of a *premier dânseur*," he recalled to John Gruen in *The Private World of Ballet*. "I was short (five foot five), I was very young, and I looked it.... I did not have that princely look." He did, however, have awards—the gold medal at the 1966 international ballet competition in Varna (Bulgaria); in 1968 the Nijinsky Award and the gold in the first international ballet competition in Moscow; the State Award of Merit; and in line for "People's Artist" designation. Of his 1970 debut in the West, with the Kirov in London, Clive Barnes wrote in the *New York Times*, "Mr. Baryshnikov, already a legend as a student, smilingly lived up to his reputation. This young man ... is technically the most gifted and the most stylish male dancer in the world today." By the time he was made a principal dancer in 1972, and thus able to perform all the princely roles he desired, it was too late—for the Kirov. "I was dancing the same things over and over again. I seldom had a suitable partner to dance with ... a great handicap. Furthermore, the Kirov would not permit me to be a guest artist [with the great international companies]. In short, I began to feel I had no identity—no *true* identity," he told John Gruen. When in 1974 he was sent to Toronto to add some high voltage to a touring Bolshoi troupe, he successfully eluded the K.G.B. and made his escape with the help of friends he'd met in London in 1970.

"In Russia he went through everyone, why not here?" says a friend about Baryshnikov's reputation as a womanizer. His headline romances include a whirl with Gelsey Kirkland (who left George Balanchine's New York City Ballet to become his partner at ABT), Liza Minnelli and Oscar-winning actress Jessica Lange, with whom he has a daughter, Alexandra ("Shura"), born 5 March 1981.

Under the direction of Steven Berkoff, Baryshnikov appeared on Broadway in "Metamorphosis" (1989).

Kim Basinger

In a very short period of time Kim Basinger has gone from a successful New York model/covergirl to one of Hollywood's leading ladies, starring opposite such leading men as Sean Connery, Burt Reynolds, Robert Redford, Sam Shepard and Dan Aykroyd. Her film role, as Domino in James Bond's *Never Say Never Again*, brought her widespread attention and led to other roles, including the temptress opposite Robert Redford in *The Natural*, the nymphomaniac opposite Burt Reynolds in *The Man Who Loved Women*, the experimenting lover, Elizabeth, opposite Mickey Rourke in *9 Weeks*, and the alien opposite Dan Aykroyd in *My Stepmother Is an Alien*.

Born 8 December 1953, one of five children, Kim grew up in Athens, Georgia. She inherited her father's love for music and became accomplished on the piano and guitar. Kim, dedicated to become a well-rounded talent, took ballet training for 15 years and practiced to perfect her singing voice. The next step was moving to New York, where Basinger's good looks, talent and winning personality helped to make her a sought-after model. After five years Kim left her career and drove cross-country to Los Angeles to become an actress. Success was hers when she landed the lead in the TV movie "Katie: Portrait of a Centerfold." Basinger made her feature film debut opposite Jan-Michael Vincent in *Hard Country*, followed by *Mother Lode* with Charlon Heston. In the midst of her screen successes, her 1980 marriage to Ron Britton fizzled, and they filed for divorce in December, 1988.

Basinger is enjoying her rise to stardom and the diversity of roles. Hoping to add to her comedy credits, she was chosen to appear in the 1989 film *Batman* with Michael Keaton. She insists, "I love comedy and think it's the most powerful thing we have in the entertainment industry. I think people don't laugh enough and good humor is very seldom written. So I love it once I get something good. I love the ride along the way."

Jason Bateman

He's the type of guy that any young girl would want to bring home. His innocent, friendly smile has brought him admirers of all ages—grandmothers, mothers, and daughters all adore jovial Jason. Handsome, clean-cut looks might have opened a few doors for him, but Bateman's acting gift is securing his standing in Hollywood.

Born in Rye, New York, 14 January 1969, Jason was destined for show biz. Jason's father, producer/theatrical manager Kent Bateman, was already deeply involved in the industry, and it seemed only natural that his offspring would follow in his footsteps. Jason began his career at ten years old, when he accompanied a friend to an audition for an educational film, and instead he got the lead role. Bateman became popular in television commercials and then landed a role at age 12 on the Michael Landon series "Little House on the Prairie." It's been a steady rise ever since, with other roles rolling his way, including guest appearances on the Ricky Schroder series "Silver Spoons," a lead on the comedy series, "It's Your Move," a major motion picture, *Teen Wolf* (1987—produced by his father), and a made-for-television film "Moving Target" (1988). His claim to fame was a continuation of the former "Valerie" (1985-88) show starring Valerie Harper.

Rather than wasting time on sibling rivalry, Jason and his actress/sister Justine are creatively intertwined. Along with their father they formed a Hollywood repertory stage company and produced a telefilm, "Can You Hear Me Dancing?" Brother and sister also starred together in this family venture. Bateman can plan on being busy for quite some time; his latest is a 1989 release, *Philly Boy*. Always active, Jason likes sports (skiing, basketball, surfing) and is an outstanding driver (won the 1987 Long Beach Grand Prix) on the Celebrity circuit. At such a young age, his race has just begun.

Justine Bateman

Nominated for a Golden Globe Award in 1987 for Best Supporting Actress in a TV series, miniseries, telefilm, Justine Bateman was very close to fulfilling her motto: "Anything I want to do, I will do." Since 1982 Justine has portrayed "Mallory Keaton", the eldest daughter of the Keaton family on the prime-time show "Family Ties." Playing opposite Michael J. Fox, she has acquired her own fans with her smooth acting ability. As the straight-faced, zany sister of "Alex," "Mallory" flips over clothes sales, mall trips, dress shops and her "Hey Pops" boyfriend, Nick.

Justine Bateman was born in Rye, New York, on 19 February 1966 to a film producer father and a flight attendant mother. Along with her younger brother, actor Jason Bateman, she began her acting career at an early age. She performed in various theatrical productions, including "Up the Down Staircase," "Barefoot in the Park," and "Midsummer's Night Dream." Her favorite role to date was a family production, as well as her professional stage debut. She starred as "Katherine," a suicidal young woman who is sent to a mental institution. The play was directed by her father, Kent Bateman; her mother assisted behind-the-scenes and Jason co-starred with his sister. She also worked with Jason in a made-for-TV-movie "Can You Feel Me Dancing?" (1986) in which she played the role of a blind girl fighting to overcome her handicap. On the big screen, Justine starred in a trite teen movie *Satisfaction* (1988).

Although 1989 proved the last season for "Family Ties," Justine is confident her career will move forward; she wants to direct and act in upcoming features for both film and television. The young actress remains single and lives in California. She enjoys writing poetry and experimenting with photography.

Alan Bates

Without any of the usual Hollywood hype, this Britisher has risen on Cupid's wings to become the "International Reluctant Heartthrob." The *New York Times'* Judy Klemesrud asked him what his secret was and he answered, "I haven't a clue," later adding, "I think I've played a lot of parts which in themselves are attractive, such as Birkin in *Women in Love* (he wrestled nude with Oliver Reed in front of a raging amber fire in the 1970 film), the tenant farmer in *The Go Between*, and Saul Kaplan, the Soho artist in *An Unmarried Woman*. They are all very different, but they somehow have a mysterious quality." To this list of rugged yet sensitive brooders and broad-shouldered teddy bears add *Whistle Down The Wind* playing a fugitive murderer mistaken for Jesus Christ, *King of Hearts* as the soldier crowned king in a French loony bin, the prisoner in *The Fixer*, the father in *Joe Egg*, Diaghilev in the movie about the life of *Nijinsky*, and an amnesiac (1985) desired by Glenda Jackson, Ann-Margret and Julie Christie in the *The Return of the Soldier*.

The oldest of three brothers, Alan Bates was born 17 February 1934 and studied acting at London's Royal Academy of Dramatic Art on scholarship. A Royal Air Force veteran, he made his stage debut in 1955 at Coventry with the Midland Theatre Company in *You and Your Wife*. Soon afterward he joined the English Stage Company where his most notable role was as "the other man" in John Osborne's *Look Back in Anger* (which he encored in his Broadway debut in 1957). As one of the two eccentric brothers in Harold Pinter's *The Caretaker*, he repeated his London performance on Broadway in 1961, and did the same with *Poor Richard* and *Butley* for which he won a Tony in 1973. Clive Barnes exulted, "Bates gives one of the greatest performance I've ever seen." He has appeared in many BBC made-for-TV dramas, including John Mortimer's "Voyage Around My Father," with Sir Laurence Olivier. His other movie roles have included *Zorba the Greek*, *Georgy Girl*, *The Rose*, *Duet for One*, *A Prayer for the Dying*, and *We Think the World of You*.

The 5-foot-11 inch actor remained a bachelor until he was 36, and now lives happily in England with his wife ("she's British, but we met in New York") Victoria Ward, a former actress, and their twin sons Tristan and Benedick.

Kathleen Battle

"With every performance, the young soprano seems to develop a greater range of expression, a more vibrant voice over her entire range and a new dimension in personality." That's how *New York Times* writer Donal Henahan appraised the lyric talents of soprano Kathleen Battle who is considered (according to at least one critic) "the greatest young soprano of our time." Though Mozart is Battle's first love ("Mozart is perfect . . . he suits me,") her greatest critical triumphs were for two performances in works by Handel: in a 1984 production of *Solomon*, a *New Yorker* writer called Battle's interpretation "the most ravishing performance of a Handel air I have ever heard;" the following year in *Semele* the *New York Times* said Battle's portrayal of the "self-adoring but adorable" title character "had to be *the* performance of her young and still-blossoming career.*" The former elementary music teacher from the Midwest has become a star. Under the tutelage of James Levine (music director of the Metropolitan Opera) for the past decade, Battle has opted to concentrate on her recital repertory, developing her voice with music "that's right for me" (building on her reputation for sacred music with an emphasis on Mozart), rather than the heavier operatic parts. "I won't stretch or pull my voice beyond its capacity and capability. . . . In this business you have to be careful about scheduling or you pay an awful price—your voice."

The youngest of seven children, Kathleen Deanne Battle was born on 13 August 1948, in Portsmouth, Ohio. Piano lessons began at the age of twelve though the idea of a career in music came much later. "When I was growing up . . . my idea of music was the Temptations, and whatever else I knew that wasn't right for me. . . . With time however, I discovered that I had this consistently high voice and decided to study singing." Battle studied at the College-Conservatory of Music at the University of Cincinnati on a National Achievement Scholarship and put her musical knowledge to work teaching fifth and sixth-graders in Cincinnati's inner city. She kept up with her voice studies and debuted in 1972 at the Spoleto (Italy) Festival of Two Worlds. "That night was very magical for me. After that experience I knew I wanted to be a singer and that somehow I would find a way to pursue music as a career." There have been few battles for recognition since, though (on a more personal level) the beautiful black singer has a reputation for being "difficult," "grand" and "arrogant"—among female colleagues, anyway.

Acknowledged by the recording industry, Kathleen is the recipient of Grammy Awards in both 1987 and 1988. In 1986 she recorded an album for the holiday season, *A Christmas Celebration*.

The diva with the "gleaming high notes" and "ravishing trill" has an apartment near Manhattan's Lincoln Center and a Long Island beach house.

Meredith Baxter-Birney

One can't help but think of the word "family" when discussing this 5'7" blonde-haired blue-eyed actress. Three of her television series roles revolved around family—as a young Catholic in "Bridget Loves Bernie" (1972), where argumentative relatives played a key role in a mixed-religion marriage; as the eldest daughter of Kate and Doug Lawrence in the long-running "Family" (1976-1980); and as the radical 60's hippie, Elyse Keaton, mother of money-conscious, pro-republican, Alex, in the NBC hit "Family Ties" (1982-1989). Perhaps being raised in a theatrical household added to Meredith's choice to become involved in the industry, but through the years she has collected an impressive array of distinguished roles.

Born in Los Angeles, 21 June 1947, Meredith is the daughter of Tom and Whitney (Blake) Baxter. Her mother, Whitney Blake, played "Dorothy Baxter," wife of "George" on the timeless "Hazel" show. Showing an interest in singing, Meredith started with lessons in her early teens. She expanded her artistic drive by performing in school while attending Hollywood High School. She then went on to continue her studies at Michigan's Interlochen Arts Academy. Taken a bit off course, Meredith had to put her plans on hold when she married in her teens and became a young mother before she was 20 (son, Ted). Her career stayed on hold until after the birth of her second child (daughter Eva) and an eventual divorce.

It didn't take long for Meredith to focus her energies in the right direction; her career zoomed. Motion pictures included *Ben* (1972), *Bittersweet Love* (1976) and *All The President's Men* (1976). Stints on stage include roles in "Vanities," "Butterflies Are Free," "Guys And Dolls," "Tally's Folly," and "The Diaries of Adam and Eve," which was also presented on PBS in 1988.

The Beach Boys

In addition to her well-known television series, Meredith has starred in a variety of juicy made-for-TV movies, such as "The Night That Panicked America" (1975), "The Rape of Richard Beck" (1985), "The Long Journey Home" (1987), "Kate's Secret" (1987) and in the much-acclaimed uplifting story about an institutionalized woman who overcame her mental retardation, "Winnie" (1989).

Meredith married her co-star David Birney, of "Bridget Loves Bernie," in 1974. The couple have three children; Kate (1975) and twins Mollie and Peter (1984). The couple filed for divorce in February, 1989.

The Beach Boys

Ronald Reagan stood up for them when his Interior Secretary, James Watt, tried to ban the Boys from their scheduled 1983 Fourth of July concert on The Mall. The Reagans, who are fans, may have asked, "Watt do you mean their fans are an 'unwholesome element'?" The Presidential Connection expedited a hasty turnabout, and on Independence Day the Beach came to the grassy expanse in the nation's capital, to the delight of a half million celebrants.

Nearly 30 years after they began, similar throngs still greet them in beach concerts in Atlantic City and Daytona Beach but, less predictably, they're a hit also in limited-audience shows for corporate execs. "We're the perfect group for them," explains lead singer Mike Love, "white Anglo-Saxon, middle-class." But whether for small corporate concerts, or big beach bashes, "Beach Boy music has taken on a life of its own. It's bigger than any of us," Love says. This despite the 1983 drowning of their drummer, Dennis Wilson, whom doctors had warned to seek help for alcoholism. The other members are apparently hale. Brother Brian Wilson, the songwriter, is making a comeback from drugs and nerves with the vigilant aid of a tour-accompanying psychiatrist. Mike Love is peppy and enthusiastic with help from transcendental mediation and healthy habits. Their bio wasn't a book, but a two-hour video piece done in 1984, "The Complete Beach Boys," complete with shots of them teaching then Vice President George Bush how to harmonize.

The longest-running rock 'n' roll group in history got its start in Hawthorne, Calif., in 1961. Of the six original members, three were Wilson boys, who, with their frustrated songwriter father and organ-playing mom, harmonized at home just for fun. When cousin Mike Love and buddies Al Jardine and Bruce Johnston first joined the Wilson three, they concentrated on imitations of songs by The Four Freshmen and Chuck Berry, but when Dennis asked the group to write about his hobby, surfing, their identity was born. In a year they had a national hit, "Surfin' Safari," and later with records like "Surfin' U.S.A.," "Surfer Girls," and "Good Vibrations" (their first million-seller) they were hailed as "America's Greatest Rock 'n' Roll Band." Their popularity waned in the days of acid rock and heavy metal, although they still recorded.

Seeking to top the pop charts again, The Beach Boys released a single with video "Getcha Back" in 1985. On the right track, but not quite on course, the group made a slight dent into the Pop market. Longing for a personal debut, Brian Wilson took a hiatus and released a self-titled solo album (1988). The LP faired well with critics, but it stalled at #54 on *Billboard's* Top 100. In a twist of fate, members Mike Love, Al Jardine and Bruce Johnston recorded the song "Kokomo" for the film *Cocktail* and the tune topped the *Billboard* Hot 100; their first number 1 record in nearly 22 years! Coinciding with a 1988 "Heartbeat of America" concert tour, The Beach Boys proved that they still rank as one of music's biggest attractions. Obviously, when it comes to the sun-and-surf singers of Southern California, fans still associate them with "Fun, Fun, Fun."

Ann Beattie

The players who move in and out of affairs, arrangements and relationships in Ann Beattie's short stories and novels do so with an air of isolation and alienation so typical of the youths of the Sixties and Seventies (they are the adults of the Eighties). Often affluent and well-educated (yuppies abound), they seem neither impressed nor impassioned by anything or anyone. "Miss Beattie's power and influence," explained John Updike in a 1985 issue of *The New Yorker,* "arise from her seemingly resistless immersion in the stoic bewilderment of a generation without a cause, a generation for whom love as well as politics is a consumer item too long on the shelves and whose deflationary mood is but dimly brightened by the background chirping of nostalgia-inducing pop tunes and the faithful attendance of personable pet dogs; in the now swollen chorus of minimalist fiction, it was she who first found the tone for the post-Vietnam, post-engage mood, much as Hemingway found the tone for his own generation's disenchantment with all brands of officially promoted importance." So deftly and accurately does Beattie depict these characters and their lifestyles that she's called "a high priestess of the Baby Boomer's generation."

Born 8 September 1947 in Washington, D.C., Beattie attended American University (she gave the commencement address at her *alma mater* in 1983) and received her master's degree from the University of Connecticut. Beattie has served as visiting professor and writer at the University of Virginia and at Harvard, respectively. Boosted early in her career by the publication of her short stories in *The New Yorker* magazine (they now appear frequently), Beattie has continued to explore that literary form. Her books include *Chilly Scenes of Winter* (1976; Beattie made a cameo appearance in its film adaptation), *Distortions* (1976), *Secrets and Surprises* (1979), *Falling in Place* (1980), *Jacklighting* (1981), *The Burning House* (1982), *Love Always* (1985), and *Where You'll Find Me* (1987). One of her short stories, "Weekend," was adapted for television.

Beattie is married to David Gates; they have one son and live in Charlottesville, Virginia.

Warren Beatty

It's hard to talk about him without mentioning *something* about sex, unless, of course you're referring to him as Shirley MacLaine's brother. Joan Collins had the same problem when she wrote about him in her autobiography. "He loved the telephone," she said of her ex-amoroso. "He made twenty to thirty calls a day, often to the same people three or four times. . . . Telephoning, however, was secondary to his main passion, which was making love—and he was also able to accept phone calls at the same time."

Elia Kazan's *Splendor in the Grass* (1961) first shot him to fame in a starring role opposite amour-of-the-moment, Natalie Wood. A series of film flops (*Lilith, The Roman Spring of Mrs. Stone*) and headline-making "relationships" (with Jean Seberg, Leslie Caron, the earlier-mentioned Collins and Julie Christie) followed. ("I think a very short relationship where you tell the truth to somebody is in many ways more satisfying than a longer relationship when the truth becomes more painful. . . . And I've always been antagonized by the Freudian Victorian assumption that a hyperactive life with women was necessarily a manifestation of misogynistic feelings or latent homosexuality. I've always felt that was a stupid generalization, that sometimes it might be the case, but as often as not it isn't."

Born in Richmond 30 March 1937 and raised in Arlington, Va., in what he describes as a "a very middle class atmosphere with all its rigidities," he was the high school football star, class president ("I was a cheerful hypocrite"), and American Legion Boys Stater. He was offered ten football scholarships from as many major colleges and universities, all of which he turned down because he decided to study acting at Northwestern University. He dropped out, moved to New York and studied acting with Stella Adler; there he supported himself by working as a bricklayer and as a sandhog on the third tube of the Lincoln Tunnel under the Hudson River. Beginning with small parts in television, he also worked in summer stock. Between jobs he supported himself by playing piano at night so he could audition by day. In a winter stock production of *Compulsion*, he was discovered by playwright William Inge and director Joshua Logan and shipped to Hollywood (after the critics went wild over his Broadway debut in Inge's *A Loss of Roses*). "This boy," said Logan, "is the sexiest thing around." The winner of the Hollywood press ladies' Sour Apple Award for the Most Uncooperative Actor in Movies when he made *Splendor in the Grass*, he returned from a two-year absence from acting to triumph both as an actor and producer, functioning in this dual role on such box office bonanzas as *Bonnie and Clyde*, *Shampoo*, *Heaven Can Wait* and *Reds*, the cinematic saga of John Reed, radical journalist of the World War I era. Beatty has also starred in *McCabe and Mrs. Miller*, *$*, *The Parallax View*, and *Ishtar*. He was the Executive Producer for the 1987 Molly Ringwald vehicle, *Pickup Artist*.

"He plays so much on what the audience responds to in him—the all-American combination of innocence and earnestness," wrote one critic, "—that he's in danger of turning into Li'l Abner." Well, "Abner's" also an activist and a supporter of a variety of liberal causes. "Anyone who says an artist should stay out of politics is a *fool*," he decrees. "I'm talking about an artist who is able to say what truth is. The real artist—the person who is able to perceive and clarify the truth—if that person is activated, then that artist is what Solzhenitsyn says he is: 'An alternative government.' And you know he's right." Sharing his Hollywood experiences, he released an autobiography, *Warren Beatty and Desert Eyes: A Life and a Story*, in 1987.

Never married, but constantly dating, we weren't able to confirm if the song "You're So Vain"—by yet another ex, Carly Simon,—is really about him or not.

Boris Becker

By the time he was three years old—when most toddlers were caressing toy bears and perfecting their walk—Boris Becker was swinging a racquet on the clay court his father had designed. Fourteen years and innumerable serves later (in 1985), Boris Becker became the youngest champion in the history of the men's singles at the most prestigious tournament in the world—Wimbledon—and an overnight celebrity. With his searing serve (which earned him the nickname Boom-Boom) and tremendous court agility he wowed a crowd of 15,000 to defeat 27 year-old Kevin Curren (6-3, 6-7, 7-6, 6-4). In his hometown of Leimen, West Germany, his fans and fellow countrymen rejoiced at Becker's good fortune. Among the well-wishers was West German Chancellor Helmut Kohl who sent Becker a congratulatory note. Becker is the first unseeded player to capture the men's singles title and the first German male Wimbledon champion. Duplicating his expertise on the court, Becker became the Wimbledon champion in 1986 and 1989, too. His winning streak took a slide in 1987 when he won only two major tournaments and dropped to number 4 in the world ratings. Though it appeared to be a slight setback, Boris has very little to worry about. His lucrative promotional deals will keep his ball rolling for a long time. He has a six-year, $24-million contract with Puma, plus additional tie-ins with Phillips (electronics conglomerate), Deutsche Bank, and a German watch manufacturer.

Born 22 November 1967 in Leimen, Becker began playing competitive tennis at the age of 8. By the time he was 11 he was playing in adult divisions and at 12 began to take the game very seriously. He dropped out of school when he was 16 because he didn't have the time to devote to both tennis and an education. Becker was schooled in the West German Tennis Federation where his principal coach was Gunther Bosch. The flamboyant Romanian Ion Tiriac took over as Becker's manager, planning his tournament and practice schedules. Said Tiriac of the boy wonder, "He's the most stubborn human being I ever met," but admitted to being impressed by Becker's "determination and guts."

Becker's training regimen involves about five hours a day of practice. The 6'2" 175-pounder with "thighs like tree trunks and a bullying style on the tennis court"—according to the *New York Times*—also plays basketball to stay in condition.

Becker lives part of the time in Monaco, joining his tennis idol Bjorn Borg for the tax benefits. He spends most of his free time viewing films and listening to pop music.

Samuel Beckett

"I can't go on like this." "That's what you think." That exchange from Beckett's play, *Waiting for Godot*, epitomizes the ethic of 1979 Nobel laureate Samuel Beckett: perseverance in the face of pointlessness. Beckett's novels and plays have delighted, and often bewildered, both critics and audiences since the mid-50's when Godot brought him out of obscurity. His "grim, exquisite art" depicts characters and situations that have little to do with the realities of everyday life: humanoids crawling through primeval slime (*How It Is*); bums living in ash cans (*Endgame*); a trio spending the entire play in funeral urns (*Play*); a woman buried up to her neck in sand (*Happy Days*). "Long ago," wrote Benedict Nightingale in the *New York Times* in 1984 "[Beckett] looked four-square at the vast, uncaring cosmos that he supposes to be our momentary habitat, and long ago he faced out the logic of that dour supposition. . . . [He is] a secular monk of austere integrity, picking through his runes and piecing together threnody after threnody, all adding up to a litany of pain and grief which rebukes God for not existing or, if existing, for allowing *this*."

Samuel Barclay Beckett committed "the major sin . . . being born" on Good Friday the 13th of April 1906 in Dublin, Ireland, and was brought up "in the Protestant religion and the rhythms of the English prayer book of 1547." After taking his B.A. degree from Trinity in 1927, he spent two years teaching in Paris, where he met fellow Irish expatriate James Joyce (who, Beckett once remarked, tended in his writing toward omniscience and omnipresence, "whereas I work with impotence and ignorance"). After returning to Trinity for his M.A. in 1931, he left Ireland forever ("theocracy, censorship . . . that kind of thing"), except for annual visits to his mother which ended with her death in 1950. He settled permanently in Paris in 1937, fled south with his French wife, pianist Suzanne Dechevaus-Dumesnil, to unoccupied France when the Nazis invaded, and wrote his last work in English in 1942 (*Watt*, a novel). After completing his narrative masterpiece, the *Molloy* trilogy (in which may be found the famous line, "Nothing is more real than nothing"), he turned to the theatre with *Waiting for Godot*. Other plays include *Krapp's Last Tape*, *Breath*, *Footfalls*, *Ohio Impromptu*, *What Where*, *Catastrophe* and *Rockaby*. He has also written short stories, two volumes of verse and critical studies of Proust and Joyce. His latest work, *Arikha*, was published in 1986. Beckett has said that with each work his writing becomes more rather then less difficult, each word seeming to him "an unnecessary stain on silence and nothingness." In Nightingale's view, "Beckett, alone of contemporary dramatists, continues to keep us mindful of the big, brain-splintering questions . . . with a care, love and unaffected dignity that, paradoxically, seem almost to amount to an affirmation of the human value he denies."

Geoffrey Beene

Eugenia Sheppard called him a "think designer," and Kennedy Fraser has said that the distinctive quality of his clothes "must be characterized as a variety of intellectualism." Another observer described his designs as being

Hildegard Behrens

"not the ones that blind you when you enter a room, but rather they operate at the slow, sensual speed of good loving." The winner of at least eight Coty Awards, the most ever given to a single designer, says in his genteel Southern voice, "My clothes are precious and expensive because they endure, not because they are trendy. You don't put them in a corner and look at them—you use them, abuse them, whatever, and they still last."

Born 30 August 1927, in Haynesville, Louisiana, he enrolled at Tulane University as a premed student after graduating from high school at age 16. "In the South, if you were not a doctor, a lawyer, merchant or thief, everything else was a hobby.... The first two years weren't bad, [then] every disease we studied, I got." His disappointed parents sent him West to complete his schooling at the University of Southern California. But before classes began, he found a job as an assistant in the display department of I. Magnin, the fashionable department store. An executive there encouraged Beene's flair for design. In the mid-40's, Beene moved to New York (a friend of the period remembers the fledgling designer as a "shy, hard-working Southern boy who still loved chicken and cornbread"), studied at the Traphagen School, and went on to Paris for two years of intensive training in sketching and design. He learned the fine art of fabric cutting on-the-bias from a tailor at Molyneux. Back in Manhattan, he toiled in relative obscurity until he set out on his own in the early 1960s. With quite remarkable swiftness, the Beene label began cropping up on best-dressed backs. And by 1967 the designer had reached so dizzying a peak on the fashion scene that he was summoned to the nation's capital to design Lynda Bird Johnson's wedding gown when she married Charles Robb.

Beene believes that the choice of fabric is of the essence, and is the core of every one of his collections. He feels that weightlessness should play a major role in the way clothes are conceived and made. Besides his opulent high-priced line, he also designs cleancut, casually elegant clothing under the Beenebag label. His empire sports 23 licensees, including men's wear. He divides his time between his art deco-style Manhattan apartment and an estate on Long Island's North Shore, where he rises weekend mornings at 5:30 to tend his flower and vegetable gardens.

Hildegard Behrens

"When I do something, I do it. Either I do it all, or I don't do it." What Hildegard Behrens is, is a formidable soprano. What she does is rule the dramatic opera repertory with her "light and bright [voice], a laser beam that can knife through an orchestra to reach the top balcony with its candescence," noted one impressed critic. Behrens is noted for her acting ability as well as her redoubtable voice—a *New York Times* writer praised a 1984 performance in a production of *Wozzeck*—"she was riveting in rage, fear, remorse, tenderness, and abandon. She knows how to shape a scene." The passionate temperament is a Behrens' trait and it reaches beyond her professional career and into her private life—"I live very intensely, both onstage and off." One result: two children born out of wedlock to two different fathers. "I am liberated but on an individual basis," states Behrens. "I don't believe in programs or ideologies." Behrens is actively engaged in an attempt "to push out to the limits," both professionally and personally. Compared to the legendary Birgit Nilsson, Behrens is flattered—"If I should be so considered I am very honored. I feel absolutely ready."

Born in 1940 in Oldenberg, Germany, Hildegard was the youngest of seven children and it was one of her brothers—not she—who was singled out as the musical star of the family. "Nobody cared for me and I had no expectations." It was not until the age of twenty-six, after studying law (and barely passing her bar exams) that she decided on singing as a career. After six years of study her voice and temperament were ready. "I consider my career to have had fantastic logic. At the time I couldn't understand what was happening. Now I realize that all that time I spent at the Conservatory allowed me to evolve as a musician." Behrens' professional career began in Dusseldorf and in 1976 she debuted at the Royal Opera House at Covent Garden and at the Metropolitan Opera House in Puccini's "Tabarro." After her appearance the following year in Strauss' *Salome* at the Salzburg Easter Festival it was clear she was fated for stardom. "I knew right from the beginning that I would be a dramatic soprano.... I wonder who could technically or physically do better." In 1984 she participated in Robert Wilson's "CIVIL warS" as part of the Los Angeles Olympic Arts Festival. In 1985 at the Met she sang the role of Marie in Berg's *Wozzeck* (to universal acclaim) and the title role of the new Franco Zefirelli production of *Tosca* (to mixed reviews). Behrens excels in Wagnerian roles but has a repertoire of enormous breadth. "I can think through a part and my throat will subconsciously assume all the correct positions without my actually having to sing."

Home is in Manhattan, where she lives with her husband and two children. Behrens performs an average of 50 concerts a year and is choosy about the productions she participates in. Always aiming higher, Behrens still struggles to enrich her work and life—"I have a curiosity to find out how the present expresses itself in art. I'm trying to expand my emotional panorama, from the most tender to the most violent. I take my ideas of interpretation from the complexity of my life experiences." An article in the *New York Times* (October, 1988) talked of Hildegard's talent: "Miss Behrens must be counted the finest Wagnerian actress of our time.... She can put a flash of emotion into the most offhand phrase."

Harry Belafonte

This entertainment giant, like fellow contemporary folk singer Pete Seeger, has often used his stage as a forum for musical messages against injustice. "We gave birth to Joan Baez, and Bob Dylan and James Taylor and all those other great people," says Harry Belafonte, "and they began to write in the folk tradition of the day.... I fully believed in the civil rights movement. I had a personal commitment to it and I had my personal breakthroughs. I felt that if we could just turn the nation around, things would fall into place. And it actually happened."

That his own career fell into place is almost as amazing as the eventual firsts he was to engineer. Belafonte was born 1 March 1927 in Harlem. He moved with his parents to Jamaica when he was eight, but returned in time to go to high school in New York before joining the Navy in 1944. Later, as a Harlem janitor, he was given a pair of tickets that were to change his life: the passes enabled him to see the American Negro Theater, and he was hooked. Although he meant to be an actor, when he was heard singing in a sketch he was hired by a Greenwich Village nightclub. After buying into his own restaurant he discovered folk music, and in short order became The Calypso King. After turning out hit records, he returned to acting, both in films and on Broadway, and, true to his West Indian entrepreneurial spirit, was again in charge when he produced his own films starting with 1958's *The World, the Flesh and the Devil*. Carrying with him a commitment to more opportunities for blacks, he created an apprenticeship program to train black and Puerto Rican technicians for his 1970 film *The Angel Levine*. Then he joined forces (and dollars) with Sidney Poitier to make the *Uptown Saturday Night* trilogy, as well as *Buck and the Preacher*. He landed the hip-hop culture in 1984's *Beat Street*. This singer of work and chain-gang songs won Emmys for his TV music specials, awards for his civil rights works with Dr. Martin Luther King (1982's MLK Nonviolent Peace Prize), and introduced South African singers Letta Mbulu and Miriam Makeba and Greece's Nana Mouskouri to the U.S. He is also committed to the struggle of black South Africans and has been active in Athletes & Artists Against Apartheid. Belafonte was also a major force behind the making of the record, "We Are the World," which garnered millions for African famine relief.

Mixing his music with his beliefs, he recorded "Paradise in Gazankulu" (1988), filled with beautiful, haunting poetry and songs of South Africa. Ironically, Belafonte was not allowed to go to South Africa and the musical tracks for the album were laid down in Johannesburg, then shipped back to Belafonte in the United States to complete. In February, 1988, he traveled to Harare, Zimbabwe, in his role as UNICEF Goodwill Ambassador and performed a concert that was recorded on video.

Belafonte is married to Julia Robinson, once the only white dancer in the Katherine Dunham Company. They have two children, Gina and David. He has two other children from his first marriage: Shari (actress/model) and Adrienne (the mother of his two grandchildren). In 1989 Belafonte was scheduled to produce a television mini-series for ABC-TV "The Mandelas—a South African Saga" with guest stars Sidney Poitier, Jane Fonda, and Marlon Brando. "In the future," says Belafonte, "I'll be doing exactly what I'm doing now and have been doing for 20 years, only better. And I'll still be trying to use my life wisely."

Shari Belafonte

People are quick to point out that children of celebrities can ride on the crest of parental success and cash in on the strength of their names. Not the case with Shari Belafonte. Before her name became a household word, her face was the focus of attention. Shari's dark brown eyes, brown hair, and well-built 5'5" body saturated the television screens with the much-talked-about Calvin Klein commercials. It was not until Shari was a familiar model, making it on her own, that the public learned she was the daughter of legendary entertainer Harry Belafonte.

Born in New York City, 22 September 1954, Shari spent most of her young years with her mother, Frances. She later attended a Massachusetts boarding school and then graduated from Buxton in Williamstown. She enrolled in Hampshire College and one year later transferred to Carnegie-Mellon University where she graduated with a Bachelor of Fine Arts degree in drama. At college, Belafonte met and fell in love with Robert Harper and the two were married in 1977. The couple moved to Washington, DC, followed by Los Angeles, where Shari landed a job as a publicist's assistant at Hanna-Barbera. Simultaneously, she was submitting photos and resumes around town to casting agents, and struck lucky when she was picked up by famous agent Nina Blanchard. Television commercials and print ads brought exposure; she made her acting debut in the feature film *If You Could See What I Hear* (1982). She says: "I'd been studying acting since grade school and been around the business ever since I can remember.... Consciously, I always said I would never get into show business but, subconsciously, I knew that entertaining was my life."

Shari's career has expanded to encompass various aspects of show biz. She had a continuing role as Julie Gillette in the ABC-TV series "Hotel," guest roles on such series as "Hart to Hart," "The Love Boat," "Trapper John M.D.," and "Code Red." She has reported on-air for "Good Morning America," hosted "AM Los Angeles," and filmed the 1989 feature film *Speed Zone*. She has appeared on over 300 magazine covers; sharing her beauty expertise, Shari released a home video, "Massage for Health" (1988), and developed a new line of cosmetics, "Montaj... For a World of Color."

Belafonte is now adjusting to the single life; she and Robert split in 1988.

Barbara Bel Geddes

The matriarch of the Ewing family in the top-rated television series "Dallas," Eleanor Southward Ewing ("Miss Ellie"), also known as Barbara Bel Geddes, returned to the series in the 1985 season and the family was mighty glad to see her back. And so were the hordes of fans who were devastated when "Miss Ellie" underwent bypass surgery in 1983 and was to leave the show permanently. The rate of her recovery plus the urgency of her many fans restored her health, courage, and determination, so she was back to holding the Ewings together. The series, which had its beginning in 1978 and for which Bel Geddes won an Emmy award, had opened a new frontier for her, after an earlier brilliant career of the Broadway stage in addition to a parcel of Hollywood movies and television specials.

Born in New York City 31 October 1922, the daughter of celebrated scenic designer Norman Bel Geddes, she was raised in a creative household. Her first stage role was in *School for Scandal* at the Clinton (Conn.) Playhouse in 1939. She made her Broadway debut in *Out of the Frying Pan* (1940), and appeared in *Little Darling* (1942), *Nine Girls* (1943), *Mrs. January and Mr. X* (1944). In 1945 she appeared in the controversial *Deep Are the Roots* for which she won the Clarence Derwent Award. She was the recipient of a Theatre World Award in 1946. A series of memorable stage appearances followed, including *The Moon Is Blue* (1952), *The Living Room* (1954), Tennessee Williams' *Cat on a Hot Tin Roof* (1955), *The Sleeping Prince* (1956), *Silent Night, Lonely Night* (1959), Jean Kerr's *Mary, Mary* (1961), *The Porcelain Years* (1965), *Everything in the Garden* (1967), *Finishing Touches* (1973) and *Ah, Wilderness,* (1975). Her movies, spanning a time period of 1946 through 1971, included *The Long Night, I Remember Mama, Blood on the Moon, Caught, Panic in the Streets, Fourteen Hours, The Five Pennies, Five Branded Women, By Love Possessed, The Todd Killings,* and *Summertree*. As an author and illustrator Bel Geddes has produced several books, among them *I Like To Be Me* (1963) and *So Do I* (1972); she has also designed greeting cards. Bel Geddes's first marriage was to Carl Schreuer in 1944 (one child, daughter Susan); it ended in divorce. Her second marriage was to the late Windsor Lewis in 1951 (a second daughter, Betsy).

Melvin Belli

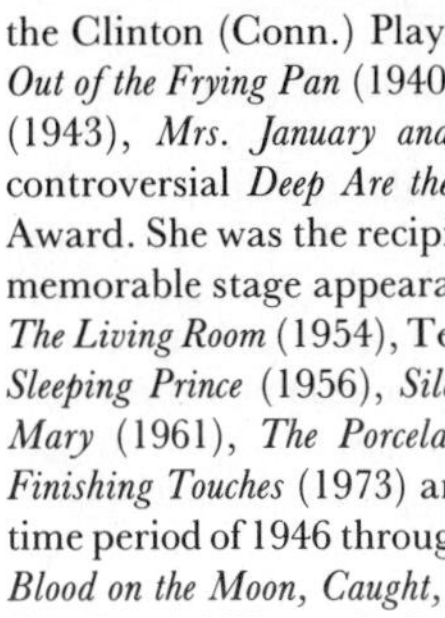

Perhaps this "King of Torts" (as *Life* magazine dubbed him in 1954) is best at enunciating his professional philosophy when he says, "For every injury and injustice, there is a remedy in the law. Or ought to be." Still one of America's most active attorneys after more than 50 years of trying cases, he's been counsel to more than 2500 clients, and has garnered a whopping $600 million-plus for them, drawing down in excess of $100,000 each for well over 100 of his clients. The white-maned Belli specializes in malpractice and negligence cases, and believes that "jurors learn through all their senses ... if you can tell them and show them, too, let them see and feel and even taste or smell the evidence, then you will reach the jury." He's dropped a client's artifical leg into a juror's lap and used similar "demonstrative evidence" to extract pathos from panels. Belli has been in the forefront of making manufacturers liable for warranties (and defects) and credits himself with setting legal precedents that have made Ralph Nader's consumer class-action suits possible. In 1985 he was in the vanguard of the swarm of lawyers suing Union Carbide on behalf of the victims of India's Bohpal disaster.

This prodigious writer of over 62 books was born into a pioneer family 29 July 1907 at Sonora, Calif., and took his law degree at Berkeley's Boalt Hall in 1933. Among his clients: Jack Ruby, for whom he unsuccessfully used the insanity plea; trunk murderer Winnie Ruth Judd; Mae West; the Catholic priest at San Quentin; topless waitresses; Berkeley free speech activists; Errol Flynn; and the "Death Angel" nurse for whom he won a dismissal on a murder rap. The Belli Society and Belli Seminars were set up to promote legal research and give grants to law students. He's also been on a protracted crusade against cigarette makers since the 1960's and wants to hold them liable for their "lethal" products.

Belli has himself faced the judge for four divorces in five tries and in 1988 it looked like his fifth attempt at marriage was ending up in court. Familiar with this ever-expanding topic, Belli wrote the book *Divorcing* with Mel Krantzler in 1988.

Quoting Justice Oliver Wendell Holmes, he says, "A man must share the passion and the action of his times—or run the risk of not having lived." Then Belli adds, "I have shared, I have lived." This tailor-made fashion plate (all his suits include red satin or silk linings) shared his life in his 1976 autobiography, *Melvin Belli: My Life On Trial*.

Saul Bellow

"Every writer draws on an innate sense of what being is. Ultimately, his judgment depends on it," asserts this novelist and social critic who won the Nobel Prize for Literature in 1976 and was presented with the National Medal of Arts by President Ronald Reagan in 1987. Bellow's novels (including *Henderson the Rain King, Herzog, Mr. Samler's Planet*) address profound, often gloomy truths of modern life—but with humor and hope. Once dubbed "the most rigorous naysayer to nihilism of his era," he is also one of the most learned of living American fiction writers. His 1984 collection of short fiction, *Him With His Foot in His Month and Other Stories*, was hailed as capturing the best Bellow. Said one critic, "The short format suits him well. Trot out an idea of Marx or Hegel onstage, fool with it a sentence or two, and then—because this is, after all, a short story—move on." Said Bellow of his new direction: "All my axes are hanging on the wall now, unground, and I have no desire to take them down.... The mood is lighter, more at ease. I suppose I am getting rid of the melioristic and reforming side of myself." But grinding axes aside, he continues prodding people to think for themselves. "How could I be anything but a dissenter?... We have no mind control yet, but we do have received opinion. It comes from universities, journalism, television, psychiatry.... The whole thing is a crowd phenomenon and very American."

Saul Bellow was born 10 July 1915 in Lachine, Quebec, of Russian parents. He grew up in Chicago, attended the University of Chicago during the heyday of Robert Hutchins' Great Books era, and transferred after two years to the more relaxed atmosphere of Northwestern, where he majored in anthropology and sociology. Asked if the "American Jewish writer" label fit him, he replied, "It is accurate only insofar as it is true that I am an American, a Jew and a writer. But I don't clearly see the value of running all three of these items together." His first novel, *Dangling Man*, was published in the 1940s. Among his nine novels are several National Book Award winners, including the autobiographical *The Adventures of Augie March* (1953). Plays include *The Last Analysis* and *Under the Weather*. His characters are drawn from real people, including relatives. The stories in his 1984 collection contain affectionate portraits of characters drawn from life-long friendships and 60-plus years of memories.

Bellow has been married four times, all unions resulting in divorce. He lives alone in Hyde Park, Chicago, and also has a summer home in Vermont. He is a professor at the University of Chicago, teaching in the Committee of Social Thought. His novels published in the 1980's include *The Dean's December* (1982), *More Die of Heartbreak* (1987), and *A Theft* (1989).

Jean-Paul Belmondo

"New blood, new looks, new vitality new *fluidum*, new eroticism, new normality for that malady-ridden strain of today's neurotic actors"—from Marlene Dietrich's "ABC" under B for Belmondo. Called by film-maker Jean-Pierre Melville the most accomplished actor of his generation and considered France's coolest film sigh, he popped upon the scene in 1960 as the irresistible hoodlum in Jean-Luc Godard's New Wave *Breathless*, after he fluttered many a heart throughout the world (from Bangor to Bangkok, femme college students plastered his broken-nosed image to their bedroom ceilings) in such films as *The Man from Rio, Up to His Ears* (opposite Ursula Andress, for whom he later left his wife Elodie, a son and two daughters; he left *her* in 1972), *The Thief of Paris, Borsalino, L'Incorrigible, Le Voleur* and *Stavisky*. Preferring to play sympathetic characters, Belmondo is also attached to—and has made a success of—the theme of "virile friendship" between men. Having worked with a stellar cast of French directors—Truffaut, Malle, Godard and de Broca among them—and international beauties—including Jean Seberg and Catherine Deneuve—Belmondo served as executive producer on many of his films, but with many of them dubbed, his films in later years often did not catch on overseas. Sticking primarily to French soil seems to suit his fancy; he refused the lure of Hollywood until 1986 when he starred in *Hold-Up*. For a change of scene, he spent most of 1988 filming in various locales (Africa, Singapore, San Francisco, Paris) for the 1989 film *L'Itineraire d'un Enfant Gate*.

Born in Neuilly-sur-Seine, France, 9 April 1933, the son of sculptor Paul Belmondo (president of the Academie des Beaux-Arts) young Belmondo's main achievements as a boy were in sports. At 16 he was a "walking disaster, a school flunk-out and brawler." When he announced one day that he wanted to become an actor, his distinguished papa grudgingly arranged an audition with a friend from the Comedie Francaise, from whom he received the following verdict: "He has no talent, and no voice. Besides, he's ugly." This did not deplete our hero. Four years later, with an education at the Conservatoire d'Art Dramatique behind him, he once again called at the Comedie Francaise and much to everyone's surprise but his own, was accepted. After playing Moliere with his hands in his pockets ("You imbecile," snapped a director. "Do you call yourself an actor?") his brief tenure with the illustrious company came to an end and he was soon playing the back rooms of Paris cafes ("where the boss grudgingly moves out the beer-stained tables and would rather watch television anyway"). After several months in France's chaotic drama wasteland ("I love a good scrap, but now I can't afford it any more"), he was caught up *in nouvelle vague*, some stage work and then made his sensational film debut as a leading man in *Breathless*. ("Hell, everyone knows that an ugly guy with a good line gets the chicks," he said at the time. There seems to be a style now for ugly men. Look at Lee Marvin. Look at Quinn. Mean guys.")

Noted for his pranks, he was booted out of a Spanish town for throwing furniture out of the window. In Hong Kong he and his sidekick rode up and down an elevator naked as trees in a March wind. Sports preoccupy him completely. He is an ex-welterweight, does his own film stunts, and is part owner of a soccer team, Les Polymuscles. "He's an animal," says director Daniel Boulander. "In a way, he's the image of the modern world. He represents ease, but a little bit lost. He's always a little mocking, there's always a little wink in his eye. He even walks with humor. Wrong or right, I suppose he represents France."

Pat Benatar

"A lot of women singers today seem to be saying, 'If you love and then hurt me, I'll die.' I say, 'If you love and then hurt me, I'll kick your ass.'" The diminutive powerhouse put more than a little kick into her act, to challenge rock's male bastions.

She was born Pat Andrzejewski in Brooklyn in 1952, and raised on Long Island, where she enjoyed, "a real Catholic upbringing—cheerleader, the beach, Gidget." She abandoned plans for serious music study to marry an army enlistee, Dennis Benatar. Energetic and impulsive by nature, Benatar felt stifled by her job as a bank teller, and ditched it on a whim to become a singing waitress in a "sleazy" bar. With frequent performances at the talent showcase Catch A Rising Star in New York, she developed her individual style and caught the notice of Chrysalis Records. "I stopped trying to emulate Diana Ross and Barbra Streisand. I just stopped listening to anybody I liked because I so desperately wanted to find my own voice." After the 1978 release of her debut album, *In the Heat of the Night*, she created considerable fire touring the country topping her act with hard-driving rock hits such as "Treat Me Right," and "Hit Me With Your Best Shot." "Onstage, your power comes from an absolutely different place from the stuff that would happen in a boardroom. You're controlling people's emotions. You're captivating them." Generally an apolitical performer, Benatar penned the single, "Hell is for Children," about the agonies of child abuse. But she got the best response from upbeat rock tunes that implied, as rock forerunner Janis Joplin said, "that a woman can be tough." Benatar's popular albums include *Crimes of Passion, I Get Nervous,* and *Seven the Hard Way*.

Divorced in 1979, Benatar mixed business with pleasure by marrying band member Neil Geraldo on 16 February 1985. Three days later their daughter, Haley, was born. Benatar's outspoken video "Sex As a Weapon" won the American Music Video Award in January, 1986. After a brief hiatus Benatar released a new album, *Wide Awake in Dreamland*, in 1988; its lyrics focus on the need for love in honest rockers. On the first single from the album, entitled "All Fired Up," Benatar shares her beliefs: "I believe there comes a time/When everything just falls in line/We live and learn from our mistakes/The deepest cuts are healed by faith."

Johnny Bench

"When I first came up here," said baseball's most prolific homer-hitting catcher, "I thought I'd play until I was 35, and I did. I wanted to be a millionaire when I was 30; I was. I knew those things were possible if I lived up to how good I felt I could be. If you plan your life right, get on the right track . . . save your money . . . work hard in the off-season, you prepare yourself for (retirement), knowing it has to come."

The man who realized those ambitions is Johnny Bench, formerly of the Cincinnati Reds. "So many people from my hometown of Binger, Oklahoma [born 7 December 1947] were (behind) me when I left. . . . I didn't want to let them down. I had enormous confidence to succeed." The success came quickly. By age 20 he was a starter and 1968 Rookie of the Year in the National League. "I can throw out any runner alive," he boasted, and he could. His actions, too, communicated a certain cockiness. He once told a headstrong pitcher to throw curves: when the pitcher insisted on serving up his weak fastball, Bench embarrassed him by catching the pitcher bare-handed. The opposing team fell down with laughter. In 1970 he hit .293 and smacked a league-leading 45 homers to become the N.L.'s MVP. By the time he won it again in 1972 he'd helped the "Big Red Machine" to a pennant. The Reds won the Series in 1975 and '76. "I lived for home runs," he said, and his 325 career four-baggers is the most by a catcher. He developed arthritis in all his major joints in 1981, so he came out of the crouch and played wherever else the Reds needed him: third base, first, pinch hitter. Since Bench's retirement there have been Johnny Bench Day celebrations at eight N.L. ballparks coinciding with his visits to them. His gifts from the various teams have been legion. In his 16th and last season (1983) he basked in the fans' accolades. It was a new feeling for him. "I played every game with my head on the field, not in the stands. I played hard. You didn't really have a lot of fun. Catching, I was so mentally involved in the game . . . but I never took it home. I knew how to turn it on and off." In 1975 Bench married model Vickie (Ultra Brite, etc.) Chesser (they separated in 1976) and in 1979 he published *Catch You Later: The Autobiography of Johnny Bench*.

In January, 1989, he was elected into the Baseball Hall of Fame.

Richard Benjamin

Discriminating filmgoers will long remember his erotic grunts as Philip Roth's onanistic anti-hero in *Portnoy's Complaint* back in 1972. Prior to becoming a different Roth character in the earlier *Goodbye, Columbus* (1968), this New York City-born (22 May 1938) actor had been known best as "Paula Prentiss's husband." ("If you are married to an actress and your wife is getting all the calls . . . it is very hard on the ego. But Paula solidified things for me. I married this gorgeous long-legged girl who wasn't Jewish and became a man.") By the 1970s Richard Benjamin was getting the calls even more often than his wife and being cast in such big-screen offerings as the sardonic comedy classic *Catch-22* (1970). *Diary of a Mad Housewife (1970)*, and *The Last of Sheila* (1973). During a subsequent dry period, he bummed around (mostly playing tennis) with fellow actor George Segal ("When one of us would get a job, the other would say, 'Oh, no, what am I going to do now?'") but soon began turning up again in the likes of *The Sunshine Boys* with George Burns and Walter Matthau in 1975, with Matthau and Glenda Jackson in *House Calls* in 1977, and with George Hamilton in 1978 in another comedy classic, *Love At First Bite*.

Taking seriously some wifely advice ("Take [the chance] or shut up and stop complaining when other directors do something you don't like") he applied his proven comedic talents to directing Peter O'Toole in 1982's high-laugh-quotient exploration of early television, *My Favorite Year*. In 1984, he had another hit on his hands with *City Heat* in which he directed Burt Reynolds and Clint Eastwood. Leaving his director's hat on, Benjamin followed with *The Money Pit* (1986), *Little Nikita* (1987), and the Dan Aykroyd/Kim Basinger comedy *My Stepmother is an Alien* (1988).

A joint production (with Paula Prentiss) away from the cameras was son Ross Thomas, born in 1974.

Tony Bennett

He started out wanting to be either a jazz singer or a painter. Today he is both. "My first public appearance was on July 11, 1936, when the Triborough Bridge was opened. It was a parade. My mother put me next to Mayor LaGuardia cutting a ribbon on the bridge. You talk about Carnival in Rio, that was nothing compared to that day. Everybody was singing. I saw everybody feeling so good, I just said, 'I'd like to do this the rest of my life, make people feel that way.'" With over 90 albums of songs by legendary composers like Kern, Rodgers, and Gershwin, Bennett ought to be pleased.

Born Antonio Dominick Benedetto, 3 August 1926, into the Astoria, Queens, family of an Italian immigrant grocer, Tony launched his performing career singing weekends at local pasta restaurants. He was discovered and renamed by Bob Hope in a Greenwich Village Club in 1949. Best known back in the '50s as a purveyor of sentimental standards (e.g. "Boulevard of Broken Dreams"), Bennett has through the years, moved into the front ranks of pop. ("He's my man, this cat," said Frank Sinatra, "Tony's the greatest singer in the world.") A hardy perennial in the night-blooming gardens of Nevada, Bennett is most often asked to perform his 1962 superhit, "I Left My Heart in San Francisco." Originally trained as a commercial artist at New York's High School of Industrial Art, Tony returned to painting in 1960. Under his "nom de brush" of Anthony Benedetto, he made

George Benson

his professional debut at a one man show in Chicago in 1977. His paintings now sell for thousands of dollars a canvas.

A long-awaited first studio album in ten years, *The Art of Excellence* was released in 1986, followed by his 90th record for Columbia, *Bennett/Berlin*. These days, Tony's heart has been involved performing to SRO audiences throughout the world. He has given five British Royal Command performances, highlighted by a 1983 concert in San Francisco for Britain's Queen Elizabeth and Prince Phillip.

"A swinging homebody," Bennett has two grown sons from his first marriage and two daughters from his second marriage. Both marriages ended in divorce.

George Benson

When rhythm & blues and jazz lovers first heard the song "This Masquerade" in 1977, many thought Stevie Wonder had gone into the studios and crafted another thoughtful ballad. But the sound-alike was guitarist George Benson. He was, to be sure, no newcomer to the music world, (he'd been nominated for a Grammy for his instrumental "White Rabbit"), but he didn't find real commercial success until he changed his style from mainstream to pop. Some purists then changed their opinion of him, accusing him of selling out; undaunted, he luxuriated in the success of *Breezin'*, the album from which the hit single was taken. It became the biggest jazz seller of all time, and three subsequent albums went platinum as well.

Pittsburgh-born George Benson (22 March 1943) started out as a crooner when he was four and won $7 in a street-fair singing contest. At eight, he was singing on street corners with ukelele accompaniment and raking in up to $40 a night. It was some time after his step-father had made him a guitar from his mom's oak chest and he'd cut his first RCA single (at ten), that he heard a Charlie Parker record and fled headlong into jazz. As he eked out a living as a bandleader playing this poorly-supported "black classical music," he was reminded of his youth and the times when his family didn't have enough to eat. Having survived Pittsburgh's Hill District neighborhood gangs and reform schools as a kid, he finally managed to make ends meet with his playing even though he'd never had lessons. He sat in with and used the best jazz musicians of the day in his own albums but he remained significant in only a small sphere. Then he joined other jazzmen like Herbie Hancock and Donald Byrd in playing more accessible sounds for larger audiences, and suddenly his scat-singing and Wes Montgomery—inspired guitar-picking got wide play.

Teaming up with creative jazz artist Earl Klugh, Benson performed on their *Collaboration* album, which became a gold-seller. A follow-up tour in 1987 for the duo in the U.S. and Japan met with enthusiastic crowds. Benson's next album, *Twice the Love* (1988), featured guest performances by Siedah Garrett, Paul Jackson Jr., and Marcus Miller. George hoped to record with the London Symphony Orchestra in 1989.

The father of four, and now in his second marriage, he lives in a ten-room house, in Englewood Cliffs, N.J. with wife Johnny, and two sons. A Jehovah's Witness, he says, "Once you start generating money in this system, people pay attention to you. Before this, I couldn't get anybody to listen to me. Now they're all ears."

Tom Berenger

It's always interesting when a talented actor who has been around for some time is suddenly thrust into stardom with one role. Such is the case with Tom Berenger, who was first seen on the big screen in the 1975 film *Beyond the Door*, and twelve years later, after playing such characters as the psychotic killer in *Looking for Mr. Goodbar* (1977), a TV private eye in *The Big Chill* (1983), a piano player and writer in *Eddie and the Cruisers* (1983), and a cowboy hero in the comedy *Rustlers Rapsody* (1985), he finally reached stardom in the role of the ruthless Sargeant Barnes in the critically acclaimed 1987 film *Platoon*, which won Berenger a Golden Globe Award and an Academy Award nomination for Best Actor. Since that film's phenomenal success, Berenger has been more in demand, displaying his remarkable talents in a vivid range of roles such as a policeman in *Someone To Watch Over Me* (1987), an unfriendly mountain man in *Shoot To Kill* (1987), a farmer leading a double life in *Betrayed* (1988) and a priest in *Last Rites* (1988). The rugged actor's latest film, *Major League*, was released in 1989.

Born 31 May 1950 in Chicago, Berenger had originally intended to go into journalism. After enrolling in the University of Missouri, however, his interests changed to drama. In college Berenger starred in a production of *Who's Afraid of Virginia Woolf*. After moving to New York, Berenger studied acting at H.B. Studios in Manhattan and performed in a number of stage productions. His theatrical credits include the roles of Jocko in *End as a Man*, a Circle Repertory production, Orestes in *Electra*, Jack in *The Rose Tattoo*, a Long Wharf Theatre production, and Stanley Kowalski in *A Streetcar Named Desire*, which toured Japan after it was staged at home by the Milwaukee Repertory Company. Moving over to TV, Berenger acted in the daytime soap "One Life To Live" and made TV movies "Johnny We Hardly Knew Ye" (1977) and "Flesh and Blood" (1979) before acting in the CBS-TV seven-hour version of Sidney Sheldon's *If Tomorrow Comes* (1985).

With scripts to choose from, Berenger decided to take time off from the big screen to return to the stage in the Long Wharf Theatre's production of *National Anthems*, performed in New Haven, Connecticut, through the beginning of 1989. Berenger, father of two children (Allison, born in 1977, and Patrick, born in 1979) by his first marriage to Barbara, currently resides in South Carolina with his second wife, Lisa (married 29 July 1986) and their two daughters, Chelsea and Chloe.

Candice Bergen

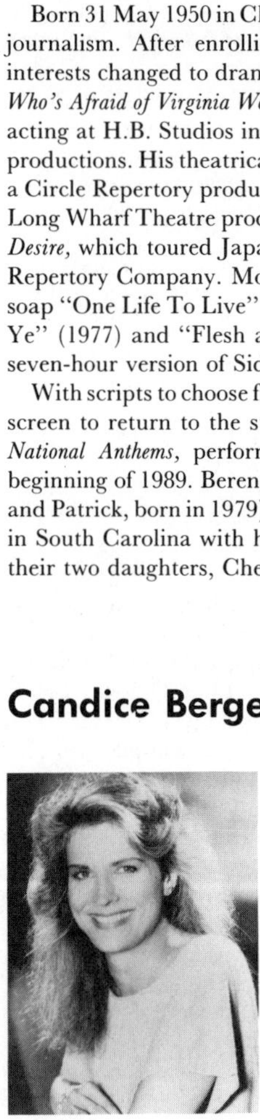

"It takes a long time to grow up. Longer than they tell you," she says. The beautiful blonde daughter of ventriloquist Edgar Bergen ("a complicated and original figure of a father") grew up in the shadow of her "big brother"—Bergen's glib, wise-cracking, smartly-attired dummy, Charlie McCarthy. Only after her father's death, she feels, did she come into her own as actress, wife, person. "His death ('78) left a space for me. I was much more able to live according to my own expectations. I always felt my fame was ill-gotten, sort of borrowed from his, and that perhaps I tried to keep some kind of rein on it. Even when he was in retirement I felt I was poaching on his territory."

Born in Beverly Hills, 9 May 1946, she attended posh schools in Washington, D.C., and Switzerland. "My parents were smart. They let me go. They'd always been smarter than other parents, I guess. When other fathers gave their kids automobiles, mine gave me a horse, that kind of thing. But still there were those awful vacations back in Beverly Hills. I'd return from Switzerland after a vacation worn out by the ordeal." After dropping out of the University of Pennsylvania ("I was tired of sorority houses, tired of beer"), she became a model. ("I suppose it's 'in' to say modeling is boring. But I did find it completely dehumanizing. A model treats her face like a computer. You keep it oiled up and greased and use it like an instrument.") About that time—age 19—she landed her first movie role, in *The Group* ('66). ("They kept calling me. When I couldn't think of a good enough excuse, I saw them and got the part.") In Sidney Lumet's adaptation of Mary McCarthy's bestselling novel, she played an enigmatic Lesbian.

Except for the 1971 Mike Nicholas-Jules Feiffer *Carnal Knowledge,* her film career was, charitably speaking, lackluster for nearly a decade-and-a-half. But in *Starting Over* ('79) she revealed a hitherto untapped flair for comedy and her performance was nominated for a best supporting actress Academy Award. *Rich and Famous* ('81; George Cukor's last film) confirmed her talent for comedy. Her own sense of humor is often self-deprecating, especially when she talks of her glamorous image and her film career. "It's one of my few acknowledged strong suits—my sense of irony about myself and others." An accomplished photographer and a writer for leading national magazines and newspapers, she appropriately played photo-journalist Margaret Bourke-White in the celebrated 1982 film *Gandhi.*

The 1980's have been particularly rewarding for her; an Oscar nomination in February, 1980; marriage later that year at age 34 to director Louis Malle; publication in 1984 of her acclaimed autobiography, *Knock Wood;* her Broadway debut under Nichols' direction as Sigourney Weaver's replacement in the hit play *Hurlyburly;* starring roles in made-for-television movies "Hollywood Wives" (1984) and "Mayflower Madam" (1987). A perfect match came along in 1988 when she was signed to play the title role in "Murphy Brown", a television hit that showcases her comedic talents. She impressed the critics, delighted her fans, and won the 1988 Golden Globe Award for Best Actress in a Comedy Series.

Candice shares her duplex apartment on Manhattan's Central Park South with husband Louis Malle and their daughter, Chloe (born 8 November 1985). They also spend time at his 18th-century chateau in southern France. She says, "My marriage is the keystone of my life.... I was really at the point where I had given up (on the idea of marrying). I had spent a lot of my life waiting for my prince, and I made some terrible mistakes in the process. It wasn't until I gave up that I found him."

Polly Bergen

"I'm one of those people who always needs a mountain to climb. When I get as far up a mountain as I think I'm going to get, I try to find another mountain." So says this singer, actress, lecturer and businesswoman whose business venture in 1984 was designing shoes. She started in show business as a country singer, turned to pop music and movies, then branched out into TV, torching her way to an Emmy in "The Helen Morgan Story" (1957). In the late 1960s, she promoted her own cosmetic company and at one time also owned three dress shops and served on boards of corporations. Despite the demands of her business (Polly Bergen Shoes) she says she doesn't plan to give up any of her other careers, admitting that she's something of a workaholic. "I'm not good at being idle. I suppose it comes from an early work ethic background where work is what you did." Since 1975, she's also been on the lecture circuit, talking about "The Psychology of Being a Woman" and promoting the ERA. In 1983 she made a TV dramatic "comeback" as a Navy wife on the high-rated miniseries, "Winds of War." She continued in the limelight, appearing in the film *Making Mr. Right* (1986), a TV-movie "Addicted to His Love" (1988) and then reprising her role as Pug's wife in "War & Rememberance" (1988).

Born Nellie Paulina Burgin, 14 July 1930, in Knoxville, Tenn., she was the daughter of a construction engineer and raised a Southern Baptist. She remembers growing up in "one-room apartments" and attending 45 schools in 28 states before she was 18 as the family moved around the country to road and bridge construction sites. "I was determined to be a singer," she says, and her father, who liked singing hillbilly songs almost as much as engineering, had no objections. She was a professional singer by age 13. Discovered singing hillbilly tunes in a Hollywood cafe, she was hired as the heart-shaped interest in some early Martin-Lewis films, and went on to make it big on records, in supper clubs, and on TV (her own show, plus "To Tell the Truth").

Starting in 1965, she and a partner marketed a line of turtle oil cosmetics, selling out eight years later to Faberge, and serving as a director for three years. She was the first woman appointed to the board by the Singer Company.

Her first marriage to actor Jerome Courtland ended in divorce in 1955. After marrying agent Freddie Fields in 1956, Polly retired briefly to raise their three children (his daughter by a previous marriage and two the couple adopted). They were divorced in 1975 and she married attorney Jeffrey Endervelt in 1982.

Ingmar Bergman

A poet of the joy and pain of human existence, this Swedish film maker has long been ranked as one of the foremost creative forces in world cinema. "His films are Munch paintings come to life," wrote one critic, "offering the highest happiness and the deepest misery. Offering all that being alive can bring." Others suggest he is "a poet with the camera," who has "a mesmeric ability to extract hidden resources from his cast." Because he has used film as a medium of personal expression, his body of work has a rare cohesiveness around one major theme—and a well-known one for any Bergman devotee: "mankind's search for love in a universe where God remains inexplicably silent." Some of his major films include *The Seventh Seal, The Magician, Wild Strawberries* (the film many consider his finest), *Through a Glass Darkly, Virgin Spring, Persona, The Silence, Hour of the Wolf, The Passion of Anna,* the multi-part *Scenes from A Marriage, Cries and Whispers,* and *Fanny and Alexander,* which he has announced as his last film (and which won an Oscar as Best Foreign Language Film of 1983).

Born Ernst Ingmar Bergman 14 July 1918 in the Swedish University town of Uppsala, he experienced an early upbringing as the son of a clergyman that was characterized by rigid punishments of the cane and the closet. Early on he learned to escape through movies, and managed ways to see them. His childhood profoundly influenced his themes: "When you are born and brought up in a vicarage," he once said, "you are bound at an early stage to peep behind the scenes of life and death." Among his earliest toys were a magic lantern and a puppet theater, foreshadowing his present dual commitment to the screen and the stage. It was in 1937, when Bergman entered the University of Stockholm to study art history and literature, that he got his first chance to direct a play. He later dropped out of school to be a glorified errand boy at the Royal Opera House, where he began "to learn my craft." In 1940, he got a job as a scriptwriter, but his name never came to light until his first attempt at an original screenplay *Hets* (*Torment* in the American version) won eight "Charlies" (the Swedish equivalent of the Oscar), and the Grand Prix at the 1946 Cannes Film Festival. But it was not until his 1956 *Smiles of a Summer Night* that he began to gain substantial acclaim as author and director. Hollywood honored him in 1970 with the Irving Thalberg Award.

He has been credited for the development of a number of best known Swedish stars, among them Ingrid Thulin, Liv Ullmann, Bibi Andersson, and Harriet Andersson, and is known for having wooed or married most of them. At least six marriages are known of, though his most famous relationship was with his mistress Liv Ullmann (the mother of his daughter) until in 1971 he married Ingrid von Rosen, his second wife. He has fathered nine children and is said to remain cordial with all of his ex-wives and ex-mistresses. He returned from exile (caused by tax troubles) to his homeland in 1977 to receive the Swedish Academy of Letters Great Gold Medal, one of only seventeen persons to receive it in this century. In 1978 he resumed his directorship of Stockholm's Royal Dramatic Theatre, and in the same year, the Swedish Film Institute established a prize for excellence in filmmaking in his name. Letting the public share in some of his secrets and escapades, his autobiography *The Magic Lantern* was released in fall, 1988.

As one critic summed it up, "He has made forty-three films in forty years; he has had six wives and nine children; he has lived in exile, been sick unto death, fearful unto loathing, as well as having had the strength and charm to find life 'rich and entertaining.'" He is often found at his beloved retreat on the remote Baltic island of Faro.

Milton Berle

"In my day, we did everything live. It was real; it was fun. You screwed up, tough; you had egg on your face. Now, it's all tape and retakes and canned laughter. That robs TV of its spontaneity." Such a fixture was he during the years 1948 to 1956 that Tuesdays, when his "Texaco Star Theatre" was telecast, became known as "Berlesday." Rubber-faced "Uncle Miltie" leaned heavily on props like false noses and frenetic costume changes, and in addition to usurping his own guests stars' spots he took an active part in directing, producing, and overseeing the musicians, stagehands, and sound men on his weekly show, all with unshakable confidence. In his more recent incarnations on the tube he's been a bit more subdued and has on a number of occasions performed as a straight actor in serious dramas. But in the TV history books, the man with "the Bugs Bunny smile" will be remembered mainly as "The Thief of Badgags," "Public Energy No. 1," and the medium's first master of "brash and boisterous bombast." In 1984, in tribute to his pioneering contributions to the small screen, Berle was one of the first seven people inducted into the newly formed Television Academy Hall of Fame.

Born Milton Berlinger on 12 July 1908 in New York City, he was the son of a painter (his father) and a store detective (his mother, who later took the name of Sandra and became a renowned stage mother whose "piercing, compelling laugh cued audiences in almost every city in America"). Little Miltie started winning Charlie Chaplin contests at age six and peddled the $2 loving cups he won for 25 cents for pocket money. In his early vaudeville days, it is recorded, "he developed a stage practice that was to become a hallmark of his career—he began to collect his colleagues' jokes, songs, and bits of comedy business in the belief that all jokes are public property." At the height of his career, he had a repertoire of well over 50,000 gags.

And those gags have grown right into the 80's. In 1987, Berle's memoir *B.S. I Love You* became a bestseller ("I've been saving up these stories since I was about 14.") At the start of 1988, Berle celebrated his 40th year in television with some new bags of tricks. First he starred with fellow friends Sid Caesar and Danny Thomas in a CBS TV-movie "Side-By-Side," which featured three men who "will not be called too old." During an interview with *People*, Berle proclaimed, "A whole new generation is beginning to appreciate me." Then, in typical Uncle Miltie tradition, he graced the cover of *Spy* magazine (March, 1988) with an unforgettable pose—"That Filofax Girl." Clad in a businesswoman's attire, Milton portrays a yuppie complete with portfolio, filofax, "good legs" and sneakers.

Twice married and twice divorced from actress Joyce Matthews (who later was also twice married and divorced from the late Billy Rose), he married Ruth Cosgrove in 1953 (she died in April 1989). They have one adopted son.

Irving Berlin

Although he could play piano in only one key—F sharp—and never learned to read music, or to transcribe it, Irving Berlin published some 900 songs, dozens of them part of the enduring body of Broadway lore. A prolific combination of genius and schmaltz, he was dubbed "America's Franz Schubert" by George Gershwin, but another contemporary, Jerome Kern, was more definitive: "Irving Berlin has no place in American music. He is American music." Indeed, this "Jewish" composer commemorated America's principal Christian holidays with "White Christmas" (1942) and "Easter Parade" (1933) and celebrated the nation itself with "God Bless America" (1939), a hymn so popular that it has become virtually a second national anthem.

The youngest of eight children, Isidore Baline was born in Temum, Russia, on 11 May 1888, four years before the family emigrated to America and settled on New York's Lower East Side. He was a desultory student who idolized George M. Cohan, whom every Jewish boy of the era simply assumed was a Jewish composer and performer. When Izzy hit his teenage years, the flamboyantly disreputable Bowery bars were the popular diversion of slumming uptowners and he earned a living there as a busker—a free-lance entertainer. Later, working as a singing waiter at Nigger Mike's on the Bowery and in Chinatown's Pelham Cafe, he laboriously picked out new songs, but had no means to transcribe them. He published his first song, "Marie from Sunny Italy" with pianist M. Nicholson and began writing his own music and lyrics in 1911; that year, he published "Alexander's Ragtime Band." In 1919, he celebrated forming his own music-publishing firm with "A Pretty Girl Is Like a Melody." Irrepressible classics which followed include: "Let's Have Another Cup of Coffee" (1932), "Cheek to Cheek" (1935), "This Is the Army, Mr. Jones" (1941), "There's No Business Like Show Business" and "They Say that Falling in Love is Wonderful" (1946). These and many more were part of his output for both Hollywood and Broadway. Berlin's Hollywood credits include three Fred Astaire-Ginger Rogers romps, *Top Hat* (1935), *Follow the Fleet* (1936) and *Carefree* (1938). His Broadway shows included: *As Thousands Cheer* (1935), *Louisiana Purchase* (1940), *This Is The Army* (1942), *Annie Get Your Gun* (1946), and *Call Me Madam* (1950). He was last represented on the Great White Way by *Mr. President* (1962).

In 1913 Berlin married Dorothy Goetz, who died five months after their wedding of typhoid fever. His second marriage, in 1926 was to heiress Ellin Mackay, with whom he had three daughters and a son, Irving, who died in infancy.

Corbin Bernsen

Corbin Bernsen is a player. Whether he's male-chauvinist divorce attorney Arnie Becker in the long-playing series TV "L.A. Law," or third baseman Roger Dorn in the film *Major League*, he's always acting in top form. This 6-foot, 175-lb, blond-haired, blue-eyed hunk is the subject of many women's fantasies, and the male spokesperson for a brassiere company.

Born 7 September, the son of a popular daytime-television actress Jeanne Cooper "The Young and The Restless", Bernsen was destined for a theatrical career. Not satisfied as a philosophy student at Humboldt State College, he transferred to the UCLA Theatre Arts Department and earned a Masters Degree in Playwriting. Migrating to New York City, he landed roles Off-Broadway in such plays as *Lone Star*, and in the touring company of *Plaza Suite*. Following in his mom's footsteps, he was cast in a continuing part in the soap "Ryan's Hope." His role on "L.A. Law" brought him back to the West Coast and has earned him two Emmy nominations plus a Golden Globe nomination.

Bernsen's good looks and proven acting ability have paved the way for motion picture offers. He has appeared in *The Sofia Conspiracy* (1986), *Hello Again* (with Shelley Long in 1987), *Bert Rigby, You're a Fool* (1989), *Major League* (1989), and *Disorganized Crime* (with Lou Diamond Phillips in 1989). Divorced from his first wife, Corbin married actress Amanda Pays 19 November 1988. The couple have a son Oliver born 14 March 1989.

Leonard Bernstein

Few serious musicians have ever been as popular or as versatile. "Who," New York's multifaceted maestro of the concert hall once demanded, "do I think I am—everybody?" His self-confessed early ambition was "to do at least one of everything in the field of music." If Leonard Bernstein falls short of the mark, it won't be for lack of trying. Born 25 August 1918 in Lawrence,

Mass., raised in Boston, a Harvard graduate, and protege of Koussevitzky, "Lenny" exploded onto the musical firmament with characteristic sensation in 1943 at age 25, as a substitute for ailing conductor Bruno Walter. His pinch-hit, nationally broadcast performance was, the *Daily News* declared, "like a shoestring catch in center field. Make it and you're a hero. Muff it and you're a dope. Bernstein made it."

In the opinion of many, he has been making it ever since as pianist, conductor and musical director ('56–'69, and thereafter Laureate Conductor) of the N.Y. Philharmonic; the first American-born, American-trained musician to hold the post, composer of opera, song cycles, symphonies, Broadway musicals *(On the Town, Wonderful Town, Candide, West Side Story)*, the film score for *On the Waterfront*, ballets *(Fancy Free)*, and incidental *(Peter Pan)* and sacred *(Mass)* music, author (the '59 bestseller *The Joy of Music* and—based on his six Norton lectures at Harvard in '72–'73—*The Unanswered Question)*, guest conductor (the first American invited to take the baton at La Scala), and, by virtue of his televised commentaries on the Emmy-winning "Young People's Concerts" over 14 seasons ("I spend weeks . . . on a single script!"), music teacher to the nation. Critics carp, citing him as an expert interpreter of romantic and contemporary music but less adept with the classics. "There is something about me the critics don't trust," he suggests. But a Bernstein appearance generally means a sell-out crowd, for whom not the least of the attractions is the maestro's repertory of podium pyrotechnics. "He shagged, shimmied, and, believe it or not, bumped!" critic Virgil Thomson once wrote.

He married the late Chilean actress Felicia Montealegre Cohn (deceased) in 1951 (three children). Becoming Laureate Conductor ("less a disconnection from the orchestra," one critic observed, "than an elevation over it") allowed him to devote more time to composing. Does this role mean the graying *Wunderkind* is slipping into obscurity? Hardly, "All music," he says, "gives me goose pimples. . . . I wish I could sing."

April, 1977, saw the first retrospective of his compositions when Israel held a two-week nationwide Bernstein festival to celebrate the 30th anniversary of his first concert in that country. The following year his 60th birthday was commemorated on national public TV and, in '83 to honor his 65th birthday homecoming after many years' absence, a street was named for him in Lawrence. Other recent highlights of his career: N.Y.C. Opera's hit '82 (and '84) revival of *Candide* and, the same year, PBS's Beethoven symphony series with Bernstein conducting the Vienna Philharmonic, Houston Grand Opera's '83 world premiere of *A Quiet Place*, the operatic sequel to *Trouble in Tahiti*—the first trans-Atlantic triple commission in history (with D.C.'s Kennedy Center for the Performing Arts and La Scala, Milan), and the '85 recording—for the first time with opera singers—of *West Side Story*.

He has received numerous honors and awards over the years, including the Lifetime Achievement Grammy and 11 Emmys and he was recently given honorary citzenship and the Dvorak Medal by Czechoslovakia. Bernstein's seventieth birthday was celebrated on 25 August 1988 with a formal celebration conducted at Tanglewood, a gala occasion for this acclaimed musician.

Yogi Berra

This Hall of Famer (1972) and three-time American League Most Valuable Player (1951, 1954 and 1955) is one of only three men to manage pennant-winning teams in both leagues. The Yankees unceremoniously fired him as manager after the club lost the 1964 World Series. Going to crosstown rivals, the Mets, the next year as first base coach, he was named Mets' skipper in 1972 after the untimely death of Gil Hodges. His '73 Mets team lost to the Oakland A's in that year's World Series. He returned to the Yanks, and after almost a decade as coach, he was offered the manager's job by owner George Steinbrenner, but after the team got off to a slow start in 1985, Steinbrenner fired Yogi and rehired . . . Billy Martin (for the fourth time!). In 1987 he became the coach of the Houston Astros.

Lovable, and "dumb like a fox," Lawrence Peter Berra, son of an Italian immigrant brickmaker, was born 12 May 1925 in St. Louis. He worked in a coalyard and shoe factory while playing YMCA ball, before the Yanks brought him up from the farm to the Stadium in 1946, where he hit a home run his first time at bat.

Famed for his malapropisms "Mickey Mantle hits right-handed and left-handed . . . he's naturally amphibious," on "Yogi Berra Day" at Yankee Stadium he emotionally thanked all the people "who made this day necessary." Perhaps his most famous and most frequently quoted line is, "It ain't over til it's over." Yogi produced nary a smile in opposing pitchers, however, during a career that earned him the record for most homers hit by a catcher until topped by Johnny Bench. His World Series records include most games played (74), most hits (71), most runs scored (41) and most RBI's (39)—achievements topped only by his calling the pitches in Don Larsen's perfect game (the only one in Series history) in 1965.

Yogi, who got his name when friends compared him to a fakir, is married to the former Carmen Short (three sons, one of whom, Dale, became a Yankee infielder in 1984) and has co-written two autobiographies, *Yogi* (1961), and *It Ain't Over*, published in 1989.

Bernardo Bertolucci

"I don't follow a script," asserts the Italian film director whose 1972 film—*Last Tango in Paris*—earned him a conviction for obscenity. "I write one, mostly for producers, and then close it. I prefer to go on the memory of what I've written rather than film an illustration of words. All film for me is cinema *verité*, and that means capturing what happens naturally between two actors in from of the camera, unrehearsed and unprepared." Though this may be so, the director of the well-received *Before the Revolution* (1964) and *The Conformist* (1969) carefully crafts his films to shock bourgeois sensibilities by flouting social taboos and touting Marxism.

This aging enfant terrible has long been obsessed by the theme of intergenerational conflict, and he regularly sets his highly personal screen dramas in and around his native Parma, in the Po Valley. His monumental *1900*, released here in 1977, covers 45 years of Italian history in slightly over four hours. It is, wrote Vincent Canby, "essentially a Marxist romance," and "an anthology of various kinds of indecision." ("It is a great film," *Newsweek* concluded, "but it is also a great 'Yes, but' film.") *Luna* (1979), about an American singer and her heroin-addict teen-age son, is a "no-holds-barred probe of mother-son incest" *(Women's Wear Daily)*. Andrew Sarris noted that the director "has shown once more that he is not afraid to take chances," but Donald Barthelme *(The New Yorker)* felt that he "slips badly here" and called the film "near-ludicrous."

In *Tragedy of a Ridiculous Man* (1982), a "cerebrally tantalizing" story of the kidnapping by terrorists of the wealthy "Ridiculous Man's" son, the director for the first time sided with the father. But the fact that the viewer never learns who perpetrated the kidnapping caused an impatient Pauline Kael to brand it "a dopey movie—complex yet undramatic . . . like an old man's movie."

Bertolucci traveled to China to film 1987's *The Last Emperor*. He was fascinated with the story of Pu Yi, "an extraordinary anti-hero of modern times. He had been kidnapped on a gust of wind by history and at the age of 3 set on the throne of China." Bernardo's intense interest in seeing this story on the screen ensured that this film would be a huge success. *The Last Emperor* won the Golden Globe Awards across the board—Best Dramatic Picture,

Best Director, Best Screenplay and Best Original Score. The 1987 Academy Awards honored the film with two Oscars: Best Director and Best Screenplay Adaptation.

Born 16 March 1940, the son of a respected poet and film critic, Bertolucci won early fame for his poetry but then switched to film-making. His mentor was Pier Paolo Pasolini, and he completed his first film, *The Grim Reaper*, at 21. He is married to Clare Peptoe, and—oddly, for one so concerned about generation gaps—has no children.

Bruno Bettelheim

"Much of modern psychology," he says, "seeks to know about others; too much of it, in my opinion, without an equal commitment to knowing the self." That's why this tireless explorer of the intricacies of the human mind so often draws upon his own experience in his work. His months as a prisoner in Dachau and Buchenwald inspired his pioneering studies on "Individual and Mass Behavior in Extreme Situations;" his work as principal of the Sonia Shankman Orthogenic School of the University of Chicago gave him the insights he published in such books as *Love Is Not Enough—Treatment of Emotionally Disturbed Children* (1950), *Truants from Life* (1955), and his classic 1967 study of infantile autism, *The Empty Fortress*. "But," he concludes, "I believe that knowing the other—which is different from knowing the about the other—can only be a function of knowing oneself."

Born 28 August 1903 in Vienna and educated in Austria and Germany, Bruno Bettelheim spent a tumultuous adolescence in the social and economic chaos of post–World War I Europe and eventually turned to psychoanalysis. Impelled by the experience to make a career of the study of the human mind, he specialized in psychology and philosophy at the University of Vienna (Ph.D., 1938), but his work was cut short when he became a concentration camp prisoner after the Germans annexed Austria. After his 1939 release he moved to th U.S., where he began compiling his notes on his firsthand observations of totalitarian terrorism. ("I felt subject to near total manipulation by an environment that seemed focused on destroying my independent existence, if not my life.") The resulting article, published in 1943, became required reading for all U.S. military government officers in Europe and it afterward served as the nucleus for a book on concentration camp life, *The Informed Heart* (1960). A later book dealing with communal child rearing on an Israel kibbutz, was *Children of the Dream* (1969). His 1976 *The Uses of Enchantment*, addressing the importance of children's fairy tales won Bettelheim both the National Book Award and the National Book Critic's Circle Award. His most recent books include *On Learning to Read* (with Karen Zelan, 1982); *Freud and Man's Soul* (1983), in which Bettelheim suggests that much of Freud's work has been mistranslated and therefore, misunderstood; and *A Good Enough Parent* (1987). Bettelheim is married to Gertrud Weinfeld and is the father of three children.

Bijan

"Please, I do not want to sound snobby," a phrase which punctuates much of Bijan's speech, "but I have power, I have connections with all those people." He is referring to his customers, among them prime ministers, presidents, royalty, business tycoons and Hollywood celebrities. "I have homes all over the world," he boasts, "all you want for a 45 year-old man. I am a multimillionaire myself." Bijan (named for the hero of a classic Persian romantic poem), who has been dubbed the world's most outrageously expensive designer of men's apparel, has parlayed his passion for clothing into a multimillion-dollar enterprise. With stores in Beverly Hills, New York, Rome and Paris and factories and workshops in Italy, he has become "the Bernard Berenson of the fine art of excess," noted Washington columnist George F. Will. His New York showplace, replete with Baccarat crystal chandelier and 17th-century furniture, bears a tiny gold sign outside, "By Appointment Only," and a locked front door. The white-gloved doorman wards off what Bijan calls "untasty people"—those without the wherewithal for $150 ties and $2,000 suits, not to mention $94,000 chinchilla bedspreads or $1,500 bottles of cologne. Bijan is wholly consumed by his work-designing, choosing fabrics and colors and catering to his clients. "I will bring my collection to them," he says. Bijan makes about six trips ("house calls") a year to Europe and the Middle East to his customers who are unable to visit the stores.

Born in Teheran, Iran (4 April 1940), to a well-to-do merchant family, Bijan Pakzad attended a Swiss boarding school and traveled extensively in Europe. Although his parents wanted him to become an engineer. Bijan had his mind set on fashion and studied in Northern Italy and Switzerland. He moved to the United States and opened (along with partner Daryoush Mahboubi) his Beverly Hills showplace and in 1984 his Fifth Avenue shop. At the request of his clients Bijan introduced a line of bullet-proof clothes.

As of 1989 Bijan maintains four boutiques, including 2 shops on Rodeo Drive in Beverly Hills and 1 on Fifth Avenue in New York. Hopping on his successful women's perfume, Bijan introduced a new men's fragrance collection in 1988 that earned awards from the Fragrance Foundation.

Bijan's penchant for the luxurious extends to his personal lifestyle; Bijan owns a penthouse in New York and estate in Bel Air. He jets between coasts in his private plane and owns a fleet of cars (two Rolls Royces, a Ferrari and, his favorite, an Aston Martin). He is devoted to his eldest daughter, Daniela, 26, who lives in Beverly Hills and is an executive in the Bijan enterprises. Bijan and his wife Tracy have a lovely baby daughter, Alexandra.

Very much consumed by his work—"When I jog, I'm thinking about my designs. In the middle of the night I wake up and I design. When I'm traveling—I think and draw. If I'm taking a bath or showering I'm designing"—he displays a workaholic tendency, the "vice" that has made him a celebrated tastemaker.

Matt Biondi

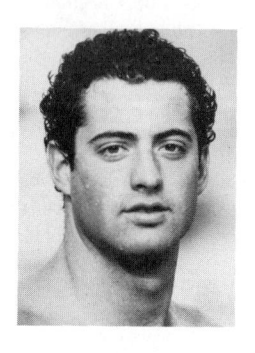

One of the highlights of the 1988 Summer Olympic Games in Seoul, South Korea, was the performance of U.S. swimmer Matt Biondi. Biondi swam away with seven medals (five gold, one silver and one bronze) and set four world records in the process. His 6'6", 210-pound frame and dark good looks inspired a fan following as he became a media darling and sex symbol. But more than anything, it was Biondi's speed that inspired awe. His time of 1:46.44 as the anchor leg in the gold-medal-winning 4 x 200-meter freestyle relay (world record) was the fastest ever in this relay. His 7-foot wing span also set world records while winning gold medals in the 50-meter freestyle, 4 x 100-meter freestyle relay and 4 x 100-meter medley relay in Seoul. His fifth gold medal set an Olympic record time of 48.63 seconds in the 100-meter freestyle. He just missed the gold in the 100-meter butterfly (earning a silver) and won the bronze in the 200-meter freestyle.

Matt Biondi was born 8 October 1965 in Palo Alto, California, the second child and oldest son of Nick and Lucille Biondi. He was a four-sport star (football, basketball, swimming and water polo) at Campolindo High School in Moraga, Ca. A four-time All-American at the University of California at Berkeley (where he majored in political economics of industrial societies), Biondi became the first swimmer in fifty-six years to sweep the 50-yard, 100-yard and 200-yard freestyles at the NCAA Championships in 1986. He duplicated the feat at the '87 NCAA Championships, the only swimmer in history to do so. Biondi's achievements earned him the NCAA

Swimmer of the Year award for three consecutive years (1985-87). While swimming competitively, Biondi also found time to be a four-time All-American in water polo for the Golden Bears at Cal. A co-captain for the 1987 squad, Biondi played on three NCAA championship teams ('83, '84, '87) and has indicated his intention to play for the U.S. national water polo team in the future. Biondi's performance in Seoul was not surprising to followers of his career. In 1984 at the Los Angeles Summer Olympics he swam the fastest leg for the U.S. gold-medal-winning 400-meter freestyle relay squad. Two years later at the World Championships in Madrid, he captured an unprecedented seven medals. It foreshadowed his 1988 Olympic performance.

Biondi continues training in water polo for future Olympics. He hopes to contribute to the sport of swimming either as a coach or as a spokesperson. Single, he resides in Moraga, California, where his hobbies include all sports, especially basketball. He enjoys music, camping, the great outdoors, and animals, especially dolphins.

Stephen Birmingham

Described in *The Atlantic* as "a persistent explorer of ethnic byways provided they are paved with gold," he's a best-selling author of novels and books about wealthy and distinguished American families. Because of his highly successful trilogy on notable American Jews (*Our Crowd: The Great Jewish Families of New York*, 1967; *The Grandees: America's Sephardic Jews*, 1971; and *The Rest of Us: The Rise of America's East European Jews*, 1984), he's often mistaken for a Jew, which amuses him. He's an Irish-American Episcopalian (who wrote a stinging study of WASP society in the U.S., *The Right People*) and readily admits that it seemed "all my best friends were Jewish—not just some, all." He's also written about the famous in his own heritage (*Real Lace: America's Irish Rich*, 1973) and among U.S. blacks (*Certain People: America's Black Elite*, 1977). "I think rich people are more interesting than poor people," he says of his subject preference. But "it's not just money.... I think it's how they achieved a place and recognition and a name for themselves. They had flair, and guts and courage. It's a gambling instinct; gamblers call it 'heart;' you stay in the game, even though all the chips are stacked against you."

Born 28 May 1931, the son of a prosperous "but by no means rich" lawyer in Hartford, Conn., Stephen Birmingham had an "intellectually snobbish mother" who sent her two children to all the fanciest boarding schools and colleges, where they mingled and became friends with society's upper crust. At Hotchkiss, "a very snobbish boys' school," Stephen's schoolmates included "Fords, Mellons, Pillsburys, all these rich people. I felt like a little fly on the wall, just sort of observing them." Thus, at an early age, he became an alert observer of the rich and powerful, though he didn't focus on writing about them until he had several novels under his belt and years of experience as a New York adman, writing, among other things, the celebrated series of ads for the *Ladies Home Journal* under the theme, "Never Underestimate the Power of a Woman."

A tall, slim, dark-haired man who looks like one of the upper elite, Birmingham graduated cum laude from Williams College, married, spent a year at Oxford and served in the Korean War. By the time he left the ad agency in 1967 for full-time writing, he had published five novels. He partly attributes his eventual divorce from his wife Nan Tillson to the pressures of working at home and trying to support a family with three children on a writer's budget. His recent works include *The Auerbach Will* (1983), *The Rest of Us* (1984), *The LeBaron Secret* (1986) which became his fourth consecutive best-seller, and *Shades of Fortune*, which was published in May, 1989. Discussing his prolific writing ability, he says, "I write compulsively because I cannot stand to see a blank sheet of paper. I have to begin filling it up with words."

Jacqueline Bisset

She always seems a bit put out by being beautiful. When writers refer to her "luminous" gray-green eyes, mane of copper-gold brown hair, her "classic cheekbones" and "sensuous" mouth. Bisset pooh-pooh's her image. "Producers aren't necessarily interested in beautiful women but those who are pleasant-looking, and I just happen to fall into that category along with dozens of other actresses.... I'm just an average woman who has worked hard all her life. My folks weren't rich, and I never made any conscious effort to be glamourous. I avoided Hollywood parties. They are absysmal.... I happen to like good quality, and never wore cheap cloths even in those days when I worked as a waitress."

Born Jacqueline Fraser Bisset in Weybridge, England, 13 September 1944, she wanted to be a ballet dancer, but had to give up her ambition because she was "too tall and had too many bones." She left her home, a centuries-old thatched-roof cottage where she was the only daughter of a general practioner and a mother who had been a barrister in Paris. After attending a private girl's school, Bisset began modeling. She posed for famed British photographer David Bailey in British *Vogue* and *Queen* layouts, and appeared in many TV commercials. When she was broke, she toiled as a waitress in a less-than-fancy London coffee shop.

Her first film was a bit part in *The Knack*, followed by several more small parts, including a featured role in Roman Polanski's *Cul-de-Sac*, Then, by landing a slithering part in *Casino Royale*, playing "Giovanna Goodthighs," a sexy spy whose mission was to seduce and then do away with a secret agent played by Peter Sellers, she won the attention of Twentieth Century-Fox, which signed her for a long-term contract. Her first Fox film was *Two for the Road*. She replaced Mia Farrow as Frank Sinatra's co-star in *The Detective* when Farrow and Sinatra announced the end of their short-lived marriage. This sparked much publicity heat and set Bisset on the path of overnight, spontaneous celebrity.

Her other films include *Bullitt*, *Airport*, *The Mephisto Waltz*, and Francois Truffaut's *Day for Night*, a performance critic Vincent Canby called "hugely funny" and "hugely affecting." The part allowed her to be taken seriously by Hollywood as an actress. She has since starred in *The Deep* (that shot of her in her wet T-shirt was a sexy lucky-fluke nobody had planned on), *The Greek Tycoon*, *Who is Killing the Great Chefs of Europe?*, *Under the Volcano*, *Class*, *Rich and Famous* (an MGM release with Candice Bergen), plus the TV movies "Forbidden" and a remake of "Anna Karenina." In 1987 she played Josephine to Armand Assante's Napoleon in ABC's historical three-part miniseries "Napoleon and Josephine: The Love Story." Movies in 1989 include *L'Amoureuse* and *Scenes From the Class Struggle in Beverly Hills*.

Switching to real life, Bisset remains in a continual struggle with her main squeeze, ballet dancer Alexander Godunov. Their on-again, off-again romance attracts tabloid headlines, but Bisset maintains, "I'm fascinated by a man with a twinkle in his eye, someone with irony and humor. A certain kind of chutzpah or cheekiness is also very appealing—a daring or courage in their manner."

Karen Black

She was the acid-tripping whore of *Easy Rider* in 1969, the warm and unforgettable waitress in *Five Easy Pieces* (for which she was nominated for an Oscar in 1970), and a nymphomaniac in 1972's *Portnoy's Complaint*. After several uneven box office flicks she again drew important roles in such cinematic trailblazers as *The Day of the Locust* (1975) and Robert Altman's *Nashville* (1975). She has even added a cabaret performance to her talents. The woman once said to have a "lopsided caricature of a pretty face" because of her close-set eyes is the attractive, one-time Karen Blanche Ziegler, born near Chicago in Park Ridge, Ill., on 1 July 1942. Although she decided to become a movie star at age seven, she dropped out of high school to marry. Soon divorced, she attended Northwestern for two years before at last taking steps to "get on with it" by going for broke as an actress in New York. She found herself performing in two off-Broadway revues and she studied with Lee Strasberg at Actor's Studio. ("I'm pretty impatient with all these acting teachers who can't act themselves and therefore don't have the slightest idea of what you're going through.") She was a night clerk, a waitress, then got a role in the thriller, *The Playroom*, called "one of the best and least attended Broadway productions of 1965." Next? Hollywood and a part in a film, many TV dramas, and finally a call from Dennis Hopper concerning something or other called *Easy Rider* he wanted to do. In 1982 she returned to Broadway as a Texan transsexual in *Come Back to the Five and Dime, Jimmy Dean, Jimmy Dean*, with Cher and Sandy Dennis.

A glance at some Karen Black film titles from the 80's alerts the audience to an interesting viewing experience. They include: *Invaders From Mars* (1986), *Night Angel* (1988), *Home and Eddie* (1988), *Out of the Dark* (1988) and *The Invisible Kid* (1988). She branched out in a different direction in 1988, making her cabaret debut at the Los Angeles Cinegrill.

Thrice divorced, she married her fourth husband, Steven Eckelbery (film editor), in 1987. The couple live in California with their daughter, Celine (1987). Karen also has a son, Hunter Minor Norman (1975) from a previous marriage. She says: "A lot of love now occurs in this business: people helping each other to do good work, getting high on each other's success. Isn't that great?"

Shirley Temple Black

Responding on cue when mother said, "Sparkle, Shirley," she became the movie miracle of the Depression years, the most successful child star in Hollywood history, and the biggest box-office draw of her day. "I stopped believing in Santa Claus at an early age," she recalled later. "Mother took me to see Santa Claus in a Hollywood department store and he asked for my autograph." Unlike many other toddler stars, she emerged from her Hollywood years with both psyche and bankroll intact and became the model of a modern suburban woman, dedicated to home, family, good works, and conservative politics. Credited with raising almost $1 million for the Republican Party, she made an unsuccessful bid for Congress in 1967, was named Ambassador to Ghana (1974-76) by President Nixon and was chief of protocol at the Ford White House 1976-77.

Born 23 April 1928 in Santa Monica, the daughter of a bank clerk (her earnings were later to total half the bank's total assets), she was spotted by a talent scout in dancing school and was firmly entrenched as a superstar by the time she was five—relentlessly adorable in such films as *Little Miss Marker, The Little Colonel,* and *The Littlest Rebel*. She still avows it was a "perfect childhood" marred only by the shock of discovering her 12th birthday was really her 13th. (Her parents had cooperated with the studio press department in lopping off a year from her real age.) After a few modest junior miss roles, she retired from the screen, married actor John Agar (one daughter), and then the wealthy Socially-Registered Charles A. Black, whom she met while recuperating from her divorce in Honolulu. Their children (two) are now grown. While Black went to work as a $1-a-year man in the administration of then-Governor Ronald Reagan, Shirley became more and more interested in civic affairs.

She needed an extra measure of determination when in late 1972 she not only underwent surgery for breast cancer, but publicly announced the operation so that "women will not be afraid to go to their doctors for diagnosis when they have unusual symptoms," adding that she was "grateful to God, my family, and my doctors for the successful outcome, because I have much more to accomplish before I am through."

Shirley published her appropriately titled autobiography, *Child Star*, in 1988. The book was a national bestseller, bringing back highlights of that little girl who encouraged everyone to join her "On the Good Ship Lollipop."

Harry A. Blackmun

"Must our law be so rigid and . . . inflexible that we render ourselves helpless when the existing methods and traditional concepts do not quite fit and do not prove to be entirely adequate for new issues?" asked Justice Harry A. Blackmun not long after taking his set on the Supreme Court. Blackmun immediately added to the confusion of Washingtonians who thought they knew the Court. He refused to be typecast as a judicial twin to his fellow Minnesotan, Chief Justice Burger. (The two were sandbox cronies many years before, in Minneapolis.) Justice Blackmun has demonstrated an independence of spirit, a mind and philosophy of his own that often places him squarely on the liberal side of issues facing the court. Blackmun spoke for the Court in one of its most controversial decisions when he explained why women had the right to choose abortion. When a critic contended that the women plaintiffs had already given birth, and so the question was moot. Blackmun endeared himself to feminists by pointing out that the pregnancy period was far shorter than the time needed to bring an issue through the courts.

Harry Andrew Blackmun was born 12 November 1908 in Nashville, Ill. He was a Harvard Phi Beta and summa cum laude and, before becoming a federal judge, spent many years in the quiet practice tax law and estate management in Minneapolis. He then was hired by the Mayo Clinic, and his years of experience there make him the Court's expert on medical questions. The judicial phase of his career began in 1959 when President Eisenhower appointed him to the U.S. Court of Appeals for the Eighth Circuit in St. Louis, Blackmun shuns the Washington social scene, preferring to relax in the privacy of his family for his favorite pastimes: watching pro football and major league baseball TV broadcasts. The judge's life seems happily occupied with his court duties and with his family, which includes three grown daughters. When the FBI ran a check on him, an agent later confided to Mrs. Blackmun, the only dirt was that "he works too hard."

Earl Blackwell

He has been called the present-day Ward McAllister (by columnist Suzy). "The Celebrity pied piper" by Palm Beach's Shiny Sheet, "The Ringmaster" by *Women's Wear Daily* and "Mr. Celebrity" throughout Europe and the United States. Each of those designations is correct . . . yet incomplete. For in addition to Earl's friendship with some of the 20th century's most celebrated movers and shakers—from Winston Churchill to President and Mrs. Reagan, from Brooke Shields to Lillian Gish—and his chairmanship of the world's foremost information bureau on celebrities (with offices in New York, Hollywood, London, Paris and Rome), the peripatetic courtly southern gentleman is also actively involved on a number of other fronts. Co-author of *Crystal Clear* and *Skyrocket*, he and longtime friend and companion Eugenia Sheppard completed their third novel—*All About Love*—shortly before her death in 1984. In 1975 Blackwell endowed a scholarship at his alma mater, Oglethorpe University in Atlanta for deserving journalism students. Each year he supervises the induction ceremonies for the Theater Hall of Fame (honoring Broadway notables)

which he originated in 1971 and of which he is chairman. He is also founder and president of Gotham's exclusive social club the Nine O'Clocks of New York. Each day he dictates a few more pages of his autobiography, which he expects to complete within the next few years. He served as editor-in-chief of the previous edition of *Celebrity Register*. The breakneck pace is maintained in spite of the fact that in 1988 Earl celebrated his 75 birthday and has been waging a spirited battle against Parkinson's disease since 1981. A product of southern gentility, Earl Blackwell was born 3 May 1913 in Atlanta, the son of cotton broker Samuel Earl Blackwell and the former Carrie Lagomarsino into whose Roman Catholic faith he was baptized (he was made a Knight of Malta in the early 1980's). After graduating from Oglethorpe, which he entered at 16, he made his way to Hollywood, was offered a contract by Louis B. Mayer, but had more success making friends—among them Joan Crawford, Tyrone Power, Merle Oberon and Ginger Rogers—than in achieving film stardom.

In 1938 Earl came to New York with a play he had written, *Aries is Rising*. It opened at the John Golden Theatre in November, 1939, starring Constance Collier, and closed two weeks later. In a *Cosmopolitan* profile (1985) he recalled, "I had failed on Broadway and I hadn't set the woods on fire in Hollywood either. Then along came a journalist from Atlanta who mentioned she had to contact a celebrity. I immediately furnished her with the star's telephone number." After this was repeated several times Earl realized he had always been interested in famous people, ever since childhood when he caddied for Bobby Jones. That's how Celebrity Service was born. Today, celebrating his 50th Anniversary in the business, Earl is Chairman of the company owned by Vicki Bagley (purchased in 1985). Celebrity Service's international network knows how to locate a half million celebrities—stars of stage, screen and TV, ballplayers, ballerinas, writers, wrestlers, opera singers, Olympians, politicians and pedagogues, heart surgeons and historians-throughout the world.

Earl Blackwell's fame rests as well with his memorable—and newsworthy—special events. When the organizers of JFK's 1962 birthday party at Madison Square Garden wanted someone to sing "Happy Birthday Mr. President" they turned to Earl, and he produced Marilyn Monroe. Earl organized the opening of the art museum in Oslo (1968) for Sonja Henie, the legendary Norwegian queen of the ice. When Israel celebrated its 25th anniversary in 1973, he staged a cast of a thousand at the Tower of David for his friend, Golda Meier. He is also well known as a host. The stately London *Times* dubbed his fabulous costume ball in Venice (1967) "the party of the century".

Bill Blass

"Self-made, strapping and somehow a dandified man (although you will never see any of the mauve and lavender peril in his deportment)," wrote Andre Leon Talley in *Interview*. "With a leathery veneer, the best of Bill Blass . . . is yet to come. Impeccable in manners, grooming and social credentials, and blessed with a sense of control over his life . . . Blass known by many as Mr. Right, is the only man who can drag on his favorite cigarette, Carlton, and turn a mean twist of tongue at the same time." As another observer observed: "Bill Blass' most successful design is his business— a growing empire that generated over $330 million dollars in sales" (in 1984).

William Ralph Blass was born 22 June 1922 in Fort Wayne, Ind. His father, who was "in hardware," committed suicide when Blass was five. He sold sketches for $35 through the mail to Seventh Avenue manufacturers, then moved from Indiana and made his mark in New York in the late 1950s working at films of Anna Miller and Maurice Rentner. The Coty award winner travels all over the U.S. to get to know the women who will wear his designs. "When I design for the American woman, I'm designing for someone who is independent in her choice and taste. I don't consider my women as clothes horses and they aren't necessarily blonde Anglo-Saxons either." (A popular Blass ad listed his nine "dislikes" and ten "likes" under the heading: "What I like and don't like so much in a woman." Among the dislikes: "A woman who jogs and tells, who won't admit she reads cheap novels," and "who wouldn't spend her last few bucks on perfume." Blass' likes include: "A woman who seems to be listening, even if she isn't, who can cuss in five languages, who's a big eater.") He was one of the first to venture afield from dress designing into such profitable licenses as men's clothes and grooming aids, linens (which comprise 15 percent of his sales), shoes, scarves, the Lincoln Continental and even chocolates, a venture which didn't quite work out. ("I've been guilty of over-licensing myself sometimes," he has confessed, "Let's face it, food products aren't for designers,") Blass was the first president and the organizer of the Council of Fashion Designers of America. A favorite of movie stars, business leaders and Nancy Reagan, his concession to success is a home in Connecticut to which he retreats every weekend he can. "I think I am fortunate," he told Andre Leon Talley, "as I was born without envy. I do not envy the success of others. You must remember, I have not been an overnight success. I was already in my forties when I bought my own business with my own name. What I have learned about life is patience, to maintain a certain patience about success. It takes time to develop and be sure of one's craft. The only thing I long for is time. Time to do what I choose to do."

Earning recognition for his winning style, Blass has won numerous awards throughout the years. He holds 3 Coty American Fashion Critics' awards, the *Gentlemen Quarterly* "Manstyle" Award, and the Lifetime Achievement Award from the Council of Fashion Designers of America and in 1987 President Ronald Reagan appointed Blass to the President's Committee on the Arts and the Humanities.

Claire Bloom

"I think that few professions-from the beginning of a career until the end-have so much to do with chance and so little to do with the calculation of will," wrote this actress in her memoir *Limelight and After* (1982). Throughout her career, chance has complemented the considerable talent of this British-born actress who (in the words of critic Walter Kerr) "could not be more beautiful without upsetting the balance of nature." She made her Old Vic debut as Shakespeare's Juliet at age 21 and a few weeks later was catapulated to international fame co-starring with Charlie Chaplin in his 1952 film *Limelight*. Since then, she's become a regular Atlantic-hopper, appearing in classics on stage, film and TV with a veritable Who's Who of the British and American theater. She's also one of the foremost Shakespearean actresses, gaining her reputation playing opposite the three great "Sirs" of the British theater: John Gielgud, Ralph Richardson, and Laurence Olivier.

Born in London, 15 February 1931, Claire Bloom is the product of the great tradition of British acting—with a disordered childhood thrown in. Her family was constantly on the move, due mainly to her irresponsible father. With the coming of the World War II blitz, Claire, her mother and brother, moved to Florida and it was there that she began to perform—first in Miami resort hotels to raise money for British War Relief, and then on radio in New York. But already pointed toward a stage career ("I wanted to be an actress ever since I was three"), and homesick for London, she returned to England to study despite the buzz bombs, and soon became a teenaged regular on the BBC, debuting as a prostitute ("I hardly knew what the word meant") in *Diary of an Opium Eater*. After her stage debut at age 16 with the Oxford Repertory Company, her first major role came a year later—as Ophelia at Stratford-upon-Avon. Her first London appearance was in Gielgud's production of *The Lady's Not for Burning*.

Among her notable stage roles at the Old Vic was Cordelia to Gielgud's *Lear*. She's appeared in such films as *Richard III* (with Olivier) and *The Spy Who Came in from the Cold* (with Richard Burton). In New York, she's had leading roles in *A Doll's House* and *Hedda Gabler* among others. She and Olivier starred as Lord and Lady Marchmain in the 1982 TV series "Brideshead Revisited"; and in 1983 she was in theatres with her one-woman show, *These Are Women: A Portrait of Shakespeare's Heroines*. Says Bloom of the Bard: "Shakespeare is really our contemporary. His works are extremely personal, depending on your stage of life. When you're in first love, there is the glory and poetry of *Romeo and Juliet*. In confusion, you can find rhyme and reason in *Hamlet*. And what better touches the problems of rejection and loneliness in old age than *King Lear?*"

Married first to actor Rod Steiger after appearing with him on Broadway in *Rashomon* (one daughter), she wed producer Hillard Eikins in 1969. That marriage, too, ended in divorce. She now lives, partly in the U.S., partly in London, with novelist Philip Roth.

Betsy Bloomingdale

A California original, a native who made her mark in international society. Betsy Bloomingdale gets on the Concorde as easily as she turns her snappy Mercedes onto the San Diego Freeway. Known to most as Nancy Reagan's best friend, Betsy is a survivor. In speaking of her late husband, Alfred Bloomingdale (founder of the Diner's Club) after his liaison with the late Vicki Morgan was revealed when Vicki tried to lay claim to part of his estate, Betsy steadfastly maintained her ground of silence. Her only comment being, "I can just say Alfred was the most wonderful husband and father to our children. We had 35 happy years together."

The daughter of a dental surgeon who taught dentistry and medicine at the University of Southern California, she was born Betty Lee Newling in Los Angeles 2 August circa 1926. She attended the Marlborough School and later Bennett College in Milbrook, N.Y. After a whirlwind courtship she married Alfred Bloomingdale in 1946 (three children). "My husband wanted his wife to run his house and to dress well, to do everything as well as one could." Betsy was elected to the Best Dressed list in 1964 and to the Fashion Hall of Fame five years later. A friend recently commented, "Although Betsy dines at Buckingham Palace and often spends the night in the Lincoln bedroom at the White House, she is dedicated to the California lifestyle and would never want to live anywhere else."

Dirk Bogarde

Number-one box-office draw in postwar pre-Beatles Britain (as the star of light comic films), Dirk Bogarde emerged in the 1960s as a serious actor *(The Servant, Darling*, then later in the 1970s in *Justine* and *Death in Venice)*. The turning point, as he sees it, came with his appearance in the film *Victim*. Until then, he reflected, "all the British ever did" about his success was call up and ask "'How did it happen?'" But after *Victim* the press was "wonderful." "They accepted the film as a thriller hung on a serious theme," he told the *New York Times*. "It was a tremendous departure, playing my first queer . . . the fanatics who had been sending me 4,000 letters a week stopped overnight . . . not because I was playing a homosexual, but because I was playing a middle-aged man."

Born Dirk Niven van de Bogaerde, 29 March 1921 in London, he made his film debut in *Esther Waters*, over which he thinks it best to "draw a cool veil" ("I was billed as Burke Gocarte"), played in the stage version of *The Power and the Glory* ("I had a great scene in the third act where I screamed my head off. That's where I got notices"), and later came to harbor great admiration for the plays of Harold Pinter ("Harold has said I am one of the best players of his work"). Though cast in serious roles, Bogarde does not see the cinema as an educational force. "You're never going to change anything by making a film, saying 'Look, this is what you shouldn't do, dears!'. . . . People like being bad. If you learn anything from a movie, it's up to you." Audiences may or may not have learned anything from *Despair* (1977) or *A Bridge Too Far* (1976). Bogarde has also written three highly-praised books, generally autobiographical: *A Postillion Struck by Lightning* (1977), *Snakes and Ladders* (1979), and *A Gentle Occupation* (1980). He appeared in *The Vision* in 1988.

Peter Bogdanovich

The son of an immigrant Yugoslavian father and an Austrian mother, he'd become one of Hollywood's best and brightest with such films as *The Last Picture Show* (1971), *What's Up, Doc?* (1972), and *Paper Moon* (1973) when a couple of bombs, *Daisy Miller* (1974) and *At Long Last Love* (1975) cast their dark smoke over his spectacular 1960's and early 1970's ascendancy. Then his mother died. His second wife, the actress-model Cybill Shepherd left him (as his first wife Polly Platt had in 1972 with their two daughters in tow). Then he met the now infamous deceased 1980 *Playboy* Playmate of the Year, Dorothy Stratten, a former Dairy Queen waitress from Vancouver, British Columbia. Two weeks before the wedding she was savagely murdered by her ex-husband, a small time hustler named Paul Snider, the man who originally sent her nude photos to a receptive *Playboy*. Infuriated by her affair with Bogdanovich he brutally killed her with a 12-gauge shotgun before turning the gun upon himself. A month before the fatal bloodbath, Dorothy had finished shooting *They All Laughed* and Bogdanovich retreated behind the walls of his Bel Air estate to edit the film, clinging to her every image. Then, having written her story in *The Killing of the Unicorn: Dorothy Stratten* published in 1984, he re-emerged to direct the films *Mask* and *Illegally Yours*.

"I'm sure I had preconceived ideas about Hef's Playmates," says the writer-director born 30 June 1939 in Kingston, New York and educated at Manhattan's prestigious Collegiate School for boys, "but Dorothy was very spiritual, very deep. I was arrogant, but she showed me a different way."

Once a young actor with the New York Shakespeare Festival, Bogdanovich produced plays Off-Broadway in the early 1960's and was a successful film feature-writer for many magazines and newspapers including the *Village Voice*, *Variety*, the *Los Angeles Times* and *Esquire*, for which he wrote a monthly column. He also wrote several books on film including *The Cinema of Howard Hawks* (1962) and *Fritz Lang in America* (1969). His directing career came about as a result of wish fullfillment—Roger Corman, whom he knew via his journalism connections, hired him as a second unit director on *The Wild Angels* and later recommended Bogdanovich to direct the quickie thriller *Targets* with Boris Karloff, which Bogdanovich did as a sort of homage to Hitchcock. Expressing his own views on cinema, he wrote *Pieces of Time: Peter Bogdanovich on the Movies* (1985).

In 1982 he said: "I'm a widower and I don't do much of anything. I don't know if I can ever love as totally as I loved Dorothy, but I'm still a hopeless romantic." Those words took on a unique change of fate when Peter surprised the world by marrying Louise Hoogstratten (Dorothy Stratten's younger sister) on 30 December 1988.

Wade Boggs

To baseball fans consistency is a word most often associated with All Star Red Sox third baseman Wade Boggs. He has been called a hitting machine, having won the American League (AL) batting title four straight years and five out of the last six years. He became the first player since 1900 to have six straight 200-hit seasons and joined Lou Gehrig as the only other player to have three consecutive 200-hit, 100-walk seasons. His lifetime average reached .356 by the end of the 1988 season.

Wade Anthony Boggs was born 15 June 1958 in Omaha, Nebraska. A shortstop in Little League and Legion Ball, He was MVP and won All-Conference, All-State and All-American honors at H.B. Plant High School in Tampa, Florida as a shortstop. He was All-State as a three-year letterman kicker in football. Through seven years of major league service, Boggs has continued to amass awards and honors. He has been voted to the UPI American League Team ('83, '86, '87), Baseball America AL Team ('87), Associated Press AL Team ('87), the *Sporting News* AL Team ('83, '85, '86, '87) and the *Sporting News* Silver Slugger Team ('86, '87). Boggs was selected for the 1985 All-Star game and has been voted the starting third baseman by the fans for three consecutive years, beginning in 1986. He has earned AL Player of the Month and AL Player of the Week Honors. Boggs reached the milestone of 1,000 hits on April 30, 1987, and belongs to an exclusive group of thirty-six players since 1901 who reached base 300 times by hits, walks, and hit-by-pitches. Eleven players have achieved this three or more times; Boggs is among them, having done it five times to date.

Boggs resides with his wife Deborah and their two children, daughter Meagann and son Brett Anthony in Tampa, Florida, during the off season. In 1985 Boggs was chosen Boston Red Sox Club Man of the Year for cooperation in community endeavors and contributions to the team. He is very involved in fund-raising for the Multiple Sclerosis organization.

Brian Boitano

"All I wanted to do was to skate my best. . . . Whatever happened after that didn't really matter. It didn't make any difference to me if I won the gold or the silver medal." Brian Boitano's flawless performance earned him the gold medal in a dramatic showdown with Canada's Brian Orser at the 1988 Winter Olympics in Calgary and propelled him to stardom beyond the skating arena.

Brian was born in Sunnyvale, California, 22 October 1963, the youngest of Donna and Lew Boitano's four children. The family moved to San Francisco a year later where Brian grew up. Boitano began his figure-skating career at age eight, inspired by an Ice Follies performance. Group lessons from coach Linda Leaver sooned turned into private lessons, and together they have achieved over 50 titles and 12 gold medals, including four national titles, two World titles and the Olympic gold medal.

At 5'11" and 160 pounds, Boitano combines his athletic strength and precision with an elegant, passionate romantic style of skating. He created the Tano triple, a jump never attempted by another skater. At the 1988 Novarat Trophy competition in Budapest Boitano was awarded an unprecedented seven perfect marks. His honors and accomplishments in 1988 include being nominated for ABC's Athlete of the Year, receiving the Victor Award (voted by U.S. sportswriters for special contributions to sports), being honored by the National Italian-American Foundation, undertaking a skating tour with other world and Olympic champions, and starring in his own ABC television special, "Brian Boitano: Canvas of Ice". With the special's broadcast Brian made the transition from amateur to professional.

Off the ice, Boitano devoted time to charities like the Jimmy Fund, a fund-raising organization for children suffering from cancer. He also served as national spokesperson for the Starlight Foundation, an organization that grants wishes to terminally ill children. Boitano appeared on television as a presenter on "The People's Choice Awards" and the "Sports Emmys" and as part of four "American Treasury" spots. His uncanny resemblance to actor Bronson Pinchot prompted an invitation to guest star on the ABC series "Perfect Strangers" as Pinchot's relative.

Currently single, Boitano resides in San Francisco where he plans to someday open an Italian restaurant. Future plans also include another world and Olympic skating tour throughout the United States in 1989. Pursuing a variety of innovative ideas to showcase his talent through television, motion pictures, theatre and other arenas, Boitano seems head for a future that's golden indeed.

Derek Bok

"Education is always imperfect, and however we may appear to be succeeding, there are vast unrealized opportunities in the future for us and serious flaws in our present," says the lean, 6'1" pragmatist who reigns as "the biggest man on campus" at what many feel is the world's foremost university. Stanford-grad Derek Bok became Harvard's 25th president in June, 1971, the first who had not attended the university as an undergraduate. Spot-lighting him in 1984, after 12 years on the job, *M* found him "still bounding with energy" and "impatient with tradition," but nevertheless "imperiously protective of his status as Boston's first citizen." Uncomfortable with the suggestion that his school might be elitist, Bok concedes that *some* Harvard grads may manifest a superior air. "But that is a hateful characteristic," he says, "and they have done so to our great embarassment."

Born in Bryn Mawr, PA, 22 March 1930, Bok is the son of Curtis Bok, the late Pennsylvania Supreme Court judge, grandson of Edward Bok, the first editor of *Ladies Home Journal* and great-grandson of Cyrus Curtis, founder of the Curtis Publishing Company. Majoring in political science at Stanford, he first touched base in Cambridge as a student at Harvard Law, then went off on a Fulbright Scholarship to the Sorbonne where he met and married Sissela Ann Myrdal, daughter of the Swedish sociologist Gunnar Myrdal (three children). He returned to Harvard (with a master's degree in economics from George Washington University) as an assistant professor and was Dean of Law School when he succeeded Nathan M. Pusey in the presidency.

The 350-year-old university sometimes dubbed "the Rolls Royce of education" (endowment: $2.2 billion) has, under Bok, more than 15,000 full-time students and 3000 professors in Harvard College and 10 graduate schools. The no-nonsense chief refuses to compare his institution with others, but concedes that "we do exert influence through the people we train, who . . . then disperse themselves around the world and leave a mark on society in different ways. In that way we're powerful." As for the charge of elitism, he has this to say: "Are we dedicated to finding the most talented people, regardless of income, background, political beliefs or nationality? Absolutely!"

Erma Bombeck

"My second favorite household chore is ironing, my first being hitting my head on the top bunk until I faint," says the pen-wielding champion of the suburban housewife. Erma Bombeck's thrice weekly column is syndicated in over 1,000 newspapers and read by nearly 30 million people throughout the world. By exposing, via side-splitting satire, the foibles of the middle class lifestyle, Erma Bombeck has endeared herself to many. "A housewife reads my column and says, 'But that happened to me! I know just what she's talking about!'" The titles of her books aptly illustrate her particular brand of wit: *The Grass Is Always Greener Over the Septic Tank; If Life Is a Bowl Of Cherries, What Am I Doing in the Pits?; Aunt Erma's Cope Book; I Lost Everything in the Post Natal*

Depression; Motherhood, the Second Oldest Profession; and *Family: The Ties that Bind . . . and Gag.*

Erma Fiste was born 21 February 1927 in Dayton, Ohio. After graduating from the University of Dayton she wrote obituaries, the weather forecast ("my first bit of fiction") and bits for the women's section of the Dayton *Journal Herald*. Then she retired to marriage and motherhood. ("I didn't do anything except blow up sterlizers for ten or eleven years.") She began writing her column in 1965. "I was 37," she recalls, "too old for a paper route, too young for social security and too tired for an affair." The column was an instant success and Bombeck's popularity spread through her regular appearances on ABC's "Good Morning America." Describing herself as having "green eyes and light brown hair subject to change," Bombeck lives in a nine-room ranch-style house in a suburb of Phoenix, Arizona, with her husband William, an educator. Her three children, Betsy, Andrew and Matthew are fully grown and on their own. They are pursuing their own domestic dilemmas, we trust, with mum's gift for finding a giggle in the soup.

Bon Jovi

Crowned with the reputation as "the hardest working band in the world," these five guys from New Jersey have created a group with staying power. From their debut LP *Bon Jovi* (1984) through 1988's *New Jersey*, they have branded their mark on the pop charts and earned respect from critics, peers, and fans. Winner of both American Music and People's Choice awards, Bon Jovi is undoubtedly a favorite band of young America. Expanding their artistry to the video world, they even won MTV's award for "Best Performance in a Video" for "Livin' On a Prayer." Comprised of top-notch musicians, the group includes: Jon Bon Jovi (vocals), Richie Sambora (guitar), Alec John Such (bass), Tico Tones (drums), and David Bryan (keyboards). With instinct for forming a winning combination, the band was actually the brainchild of the group's lead singer.

Jon Bon Jovi was born 2 March 1962 in Sayreville, New Jersey, to John and Carol Bongiovi. The young boy had a natural ability for performing and nurtured his talent with various local bands. Some names included: "The Rest," "The Wild Ones," "Johnny and the Lechers," "The Raze," and "Atlantic City Expressway." In the midst of experimenting with his original material, Jon clicked on the radio airwaves with a single, "Runaway," which appeared on a local radio compilation LP of local artists from the metropolitan area. The strength of this song opened the door for a club tour, so in a quick turn of events, the group Bon Jovi was created in 1983.

Bon Jovi's first two albums, *Bon Jovi* (1984) and *7800 Farenheit* (1985), both passed the platinum point in sales. The ever popular *Slippery When Wet* (1986) is certified nine-times-platinum, selling more than 14 million copies around the world. Their tours are events; musicians from major rock bands (such as Van Halen, Journey, Kiss, Cheap Trick, Ted Nugent) have held surprise encore jam sessions on stage with the group, adding to the live excitement. Jon and guitarist Richie Sambora have written and produced songs for other artists: Cher (hit comeback single "We All Sleep Alone"), Loverboy ("Notorious"), Ted Nugent and Witness. With proceeds going to the Special Olympics, Bon Jovi recorded a Christmas song "Back Door Santa" (1987) for a benefit album. Sales totaled over four million. In November, 1988, they went to the USSR in support of the Make A Difference Foundation for anti-substance abuse. During the summer of 1989 they held a concert in the Soviet Union. These New Jersey boys have come a long way from their 1983 "Station Wagon Tour," during which their motto was "We'd play a pay toilet and pay with our own change."

Sonny Bono

"He was tough/he was hard/but he was kind. And he was loved/'cause guys like him were hard to find." Sonny sang his song "A Cowboy's Work Is Never Done" with his ex-wife and partner Cher in 1971, never realizing that over 18 years later he would be running a city. Elected Mayor of Palm Springs, California, on 12 April 1988, Sonny's slogan could quote his other original composition, "United We Stand." He cheers: "Palm Springs has earned and maintained its status as a premier resort destination for decades. We must continue to grow and offer the services and facilities visitors expect in a glamorous resort—and to promote our assets—so we can retain that reputation of excellence."

On 16 February 1935, Salvatore Bono debuted into the world in Detroit, Michigan, as the son of Santo and Jean Bono. His family had very little money but they tried to make ends meet during the early years. When Sonny was seven, the Bonos moved to Los Angeles and his parents eventually divorced. Finding his forte was writing songs, not doing his homework, young Bono dropped out of high school. While songplugging, he worked such odd jobs as grocery store delivery boy, waiter, construction worker, butcher's helper, and even truck driver. His demos finally hit pay dirt when he landed a job in 1957 as a songwriter/producer for Sam Cooke, Little Richard and Larry Williams. His first minor hit was "Koko Joe", performed by the Righteous Brothers in 1964. His first big success was the popular "Needles and Pins," for Jackie de Shannon. Moving onward and upward, Bono switched over to work as an A&R man at Phillies Records (associated with Phil Spector's "wall of sound" techniques) and used the job as a learning experience. Bono received the chance to write, sing and play with such artists as Darlene Love and the Ronettes. While maturing musically at Phillies, he met his future wife, Cherilyn Sarkisian LaPiere, a teenager trying to launch her own singing career. The couple were married within a year, on 27 October 1964. In an interview with the *New York Times* Bono said, "I thought Cher was a natural star immediately. She was a real generator for me." Originally billed as "Caesar and Cleo," they decided to use the nicknames "Sonny & Cher" on recordings. Their life together was a blast; the duo's debut single "The Letter" fared well and their next record "Baby Don't Go" zoomed to the top of the pop charts, followed by the classics "I Got You Babe," "Bang Bang (My Baby Shot Me Down)", and "All I Really Want To Do." They had sold over 40,000,000 records by 1967. Rock stars sometimes don't last forever, and the singers stumbled out of popularity in 1968. Investing in a campy film, *Good Times*, in which husband and wife played themselves—an affluent pair of singing stars—they lost money. By 1969 they were broke. but Bono had the insight to reshape their image, forming a nightclub act to attract an adult audience. CBS television executive Fred Silverman flipped over their new act and signed them to do a summer replacement show.

The "Sonny and Cher Show" was a ratings success, propelling a pick-up as a continuing weekly variety hour. Everything seemed sensational, until the couple's personal and professional split in 1974. Their divorce became final in 1975. Going forward, Sonny had a short-lived solo television show, "The Sonny Comedy Revue," and many special-guest spot appearances, including an episode of "Love Boat." As an actor he appeared in such films as *Airplane II, Troll, Escape to Athena, Wipeout* and *Hairspray*. Searching for his new niche, Sonny went into the restaurant business and opened the "Bono" restaurant in Hollywood, followed by one in Houston. He eventually sold those two and opened the "Bono" restaurant in Palm Springs, serving Sicilian-style Italian cuisine. He insists, "This is not California nouvelle cuisine; it's real, hearty peasant food." As everyone knows, his other specialty lies in pleasing people. Hence, Bono's role as Mayor.

There is a soft side to Sonny; in his song "You'd Better Sit Down Kids" he tells a heart-tugging story about divorce. Married four times, Sonny's teenage first marriage produced one child, Christine. Sonny and Cher's union produced a daughter, Chastity. He married model/actress Susie Coelho in 1981; they split in 1984. Finding stability, Sonny married model/champion gymnast Mary Whitaker of Pasadena in March

Debby Boone

"I don't think people think I'm normal. They think I'm some strange, overly disciplined, restricted, stilted girl who's happy being that way. That I believe going to church on Sunday and getting married and having my little family and singing my sweet songs is my life. If that's all I was doing I'd feel sorry for myself too," Debby Boone told *People* Magazine in a featured interview. Letting her gift of music outweigh the skeptics, Debby proved she is a celebrity. Her debut solo single "You Light Up My Life" (1977) sold more than 4 million copies, held as the number 1 song on the *Billboard* charts for over ten weeks and became one of the most popular records of the past decade. She's received 3 Grammys (1977-Best New Artist, 1980-Best Inspirational Performance, 1984-Best Gospel Performance for "Keep the Flame Burning"), Dove and American Music Awards plus was named Best New Country Artist (1977), Singing Star of the Year by AGVA (1978), and Working Mother of the Year (1982).

Deborah Ann Boone was born 22 September 1956 in Hackensack, New Jersey, to singers Pat and Shirley Boone. Thrust in the limelight at an early age, Debby sang with her three sisters: Cherry, Lindy and Laury, as "The Boone Girls" on recordings and on the road with Pat Boone. Debby stood out from her sisters (she says she "sang the loudest"), so when a solo vehicle came along, it was understood that Debby could follow her own direction. History was made when the young blond-haired girl recorded the Joseph Brooks-penned "You Light Up My Life," which was honored with an Academy Award. On a whirlwind, Debby released the *You Light Up My LIfe* album, followed by pop LP's (*Midstream*, 1978; *Debby Boone*, 1979, country LP's *Love Has No Reason*, 1980; *Savin' It Up*, 1980 and gospel LP's *With My Song. . .*, 1980; *Surrender*, 1983; *Choose Life*, 1985; *Friends for Life*, 1987; and *Reflections*, 1989. In between recordings, she appeared in concert on national and international tours. Crossing her credits to television, Debby hosted two specials (1980 and 1982), in which, *Hollywood Reporter* stated, she "proves she's actually a vivacious, polished professional." Debby burst on Broadway in *Seven Brides for Seven Brothers* (1982), toured in a much-acclaimed version of *The Sound of Music* (1987), appeared in a Christmas TV story, "The Gift of the Maji" (1978), a made-for-TV film, "Sins of the Past" (1984), and graced the covers of *USA Today*, *Ladies Home Journal*, *Good Housekeeping*, *Saturday Evening Post*, and *People*. An autobiographical book *Debby Boone . . . So Far* "is the story of a strong-willed child with more than her share of foolishness bound up in her heart, who was determined to make her mark by her own might and main." Debby Boone has hurdled over obstacles, understanding the path she follows, admitting: "The unprencendented popularity of 'You Light Up My Life' was, I knew from the first, impossible to duplicate. Yet for a while, I felt pressure from within and without to try, somehow, to top it." She goes on to say, "Careers may be marked by occasional spectacular success, but those successes are not the substance of their careers. Lying beneath is a solid, steady flow of good music—winter, spring, summer, and fall, year in and year out. These are the entertainers who become known to the public as a person, rather than a name. That's what I want."

Assuring the theatrical bloodline in the next generation, Debby married Gabriel Ferrer (son of Rosemary Clooney and Jose Ferrer) 1 September 1979 at the First Presbyterian Church of Hollywood. Although Gabri studied to be an art major and attended Pepperdine, he dropped out to work full-time as coordinator of his wife's affairs. The couple live in California with their four children: Jordan Alexander, Gabrielle Monserrate and Dustin Boone (twins) and Tessa Rose. Her most recent endeavor was an offshoot of parenthood; Debby wrote a children's book, *Bedtime Hugs for Little Ones* (1988), professionally illustrated by her husband Gabri and featuring drawings of their children.

1986. They have a son, Chesaré Elan (born 25 April 1988). "And the beat goes on. . . ."

Pat Boone

"I think my life is a vindication of what Middle America wants," he says proudly, "the traditional things—God, love, togetherness." The kid from Nashville with white bucks has grown up, survived the temptation to stray from the path of the Lamb in glitzy Hollywood, and now tries to help others "see the way" (he is now an elder in the Church on the Way). Through a series of books (his latest, *PRAY TO WIN: God Wants You To Succeed*) Boone counsels on his personal approach to prayer and spiritual awareness. His career—records, singing engagements, TV appearances and commercials—is still going strong. He is the author of a 1958 best seller *'Twixt Twelve and Twenty* and his autobiography, *A New Song*, has sold over a million copies.

Born in Jacksonville, Florida, 1 June 1934, Charles Eugene Boone made an impact worthy of frontiersman ancestor Daniel Boone (18 million records sold when he was 24) but he lost out to rock 'n' roll as teenage fans and Booner-swooners by the million defected to hip-swinging nemesis Elvis Presley or opted for the Beatles, Pat himself firmly declined to gyrate anything, least of all his hips, and his record sales plunged, "The Pat Boone Chevy Showroom"—his ABC-TV stint for Chevrolet—was dropped by the sponsor in the wake of audience apathy and his movie career sagged following the death of 20th Century-Fox production chief Buddy Adler, who once predicted Pat would be the biggest star "since Jimmy Stewart." Having previously refused to kiss Shirley Jones on screen because his religion forbade physical contact with females other than his wife, he took a fling at sexy roles and nightclub entertainment, bounding on stage in Las Vegas "looking like a choirboy imitating Liberace," as columnist Herb Caen put it. "But I suffered for it," Pat explained. "I was trying to round myself out as an actor."

He is married to his high school sweetheart Shirley Foley (daughter of country-music legend Red). The third and most rebellious of their four daughters, Debby, has joined her father in show business. Her hit single, "You Light Up My Life" topped the music charts for twelve weeks in 1978. His youngest daughter, Laury, is also a gospel recording artist.

Boone's always bust. 1986 saw the release of an exercise video for mature adults, "Take Time With Pat Boone." For a complete change of pace, Pat played the "new David" on the popular TV series "Moonlighting" in 1988. Crossing over to cable, Pat is one of three hosts on the Shop Television Network (STN), and appears with his wife, Shirley, on the Nashville Network as "RV travelers" on the "Wish You Were Here RV Show."

These past several years, he has been national chairman and host of the Easter Seal Society telephon. His "Pat Boone Radio Show" continues successfully on over 300 stations around the country and the world; it's the only Christian contemporary radio show with secular sponsors, in addition to Christian sponsors. A longtime dream was fulfilled for Pat Boone during the summer of 1988, when he performed with Deniece Williams, The Imperials, Kim Boyce and Johnnie Wilder in the first "Gospel America Tour '88."

Perhaps the most exciting aspect of Pat's life centers around his grandchildren; current count totals a joyous combination of 13 young boys and girls.

Bjorn Borg

World Tennis magazine compared his retirement to that of his most famous countrywoman. "(When) Bjorn began to echo the xenophobic sentiments of another famous Swede, Greta Garbo—I want to be alone—(it was a) classic example of a world-renowned star abdicating the throne at the peak of (his) profession." The 26-year-old, five-time Wimbledon champion and six-time French Open victor decided to take several months' rest in 1982, and afterwards said, "During my break, I had plenty of time to discover how nice life was without tennis, and that there were other things in life." The discovery moved him to take a permanent break from the pro tour, but the business-like player whom opponents called "The Iceman" left a legacy as possibly the best player ever to whoosh a racket at a tennis ball. Since his lamented departure, this long-legged, long-maned, multi-millionaire high-school dropout (at age 14 to pursue the game) has continued to reap riches from product endorsements and an occasional tournament.

Bjorn Borg was born in Sodertalje, Sweden, a suburb of Stockholm, on 6 June 1956; an only child, he wholeheartedly embraced tennis at the age of nine by swatting balls against the family garage with his father's new racket. The rather awkward boy pleaded for more play, and so started with a tennis teacher. By 14 Bjorn was the best junior player in the world. "I recognized his mental toughness at an early age," said one coach. "He is a nice chap but so tough mentally." By age 17, Borg was beating the top-ranked players. One big confidence-builder occurred in 1973 when he played at Wimbledon while most male members of the Association of Tennis Pros boycotted. The teenager did well, and his murderous forehand and youthful looks made him a globally recognized, groupie-hounded star. But while he became the youngest man to win a major tourney, beating Ilie Nastase in the Italian Open at age 17, and while he had a five-year winning streak at Wimbledon (before John McEnroe ended it in the '81 final), Borg never won a U.S. Open. Otherwise he was one of the most dominant players in any sport—ever. After circling the world countless times, he and his Roumanian wife Mariana, a former tennis pro, made Monte Carlo the most permanent of their four intercontinental seaside homes. In 1984 Mariana ended the match when Borg took up with Swedish model Jannike Bjorling, who bore him a son in 1985.

Victor Borge

This unmelancholy Dane, a past master of music depreciation, claims, "I know two numbers. One is 'Clair de Lune' and the other isn't." Actually, he was a concert pianist at ten, but now prefers to meld his brilliant musicianship with comedy. Audiences seem to like it that way. His 1953 one man show on Broadway, *Comedy in Music,* wound up three years later with the longest solo run in the history of American theatre. Twenty years later, with a somewhat straighter face, he guest conducted with numerous symphony orchestras. He made a comeback on Broadway in 1977 and in 1980 wrote *My Favorite Comedies in Music.*

Born 3 January 1909 in Copenhagen ("There is a bit of Hans Christian Anderson in every Dane—this gloomy Hamlet stuff is strictly for the bards") young Victor Borge started making himself at home at the piano keyboard when he was three. (His father was first violinist with the Royal Danish Symphony.) Borge was a stage and screen idol in Denmark in the 1930's, but his career came to a smashing halt with the Nazi invasion. Celebrated for his satiric attacks on Hitler and his goose-steppers, Borge was forced to flee and arrived in America in 1940, almost penniless and unable to speak English. He somehow managed a spot on Bing Crosby's radio show which made such an impact that he was invited back for the next 56 weeks. He's been in the star category ever since, and made the complexities of the English language part of his act before going into semi-retirement. Married to Sarahbelle Scraper Roach, he has five heirs—two by a previous marriage. Once, when a stuffy critic reported, "Borge is a good pianist but he's no Horowitz," Borge replied, deadpan, "That should come as a relief to the parents of Horowitz." In 1981 Borge was knighted by Denmark, Sweden and Norway into the Order of the White Rose. The winter of 1984 saw a 10-day 75th birthday celebration engagement at Carnegie Hall.

To encourage young artists, Borge has set up scholarships at universities and colleges, in addition to the "Thanks to Scandinavia" scholarship fund created in 1963 with his lawyer, Richard Netter. The multi-million-dollar fund has brought hundreds of students and scientists from Scandinaian countries to America for studies and research. He also created a home videotape, "Victor Borge on Stage with Audience Favorites."

Frank Borman

"I didn't want to ride for the rest of my life on the publicity I had achieved from NASA and become a dancing bear. I knew (Eastern) had some problems, and I thought I could contribute. I wanted to work." Having flown two successful space missions, Borman faced perhaps his biggest challenge: to steer debt-ridden Eastern Air Lines out of the red.

Frank Borman was born 14 March 1928 in Gary, Indiana. After his family relocated to Phoenix because of his ailing health, he grew strong and became an adept sportsman and aviator. He funded flying lessons with money earned on a paper route. After graduating eighth in a class of 670 at West Point, he excelled as an Air Force fighter pilot and instructor. With his sights on NASA, he earned an M.S. degree in aeronautical engineering in 1957, and worked as an experimental test pilot at Edwards Air Force Base. Drafted into NASA's training program in 1962, he commanded the Gemini 7 in its two-week earth orbital flight in 1965, and piloted the Apollo 8 in the first manned circumnavigation of the moon three years later.

Retired from the Air Force with the rank of Colonel, he accepted a position as senior vice-president of operations at Eastern, and rose quickly in the corporate structure, to become president and chief executive officer in 1975. Borman, affectionately called, "the Colonel," ran a tight ship. Facing a gloomy scenario of declining passenger traffic and skyrocketing fuel costs, he streamlined the carrier's top-heavy management, revamped Eastern's route structure, and replaced inefficient aircraft. He gave the industry its first wage freeze in 1976, and initiated a hefty profit-sharing program for all employees. "Labor is faced with a difficult decision. . . . They're going to have to decide whether a substantial part of the cake is better than no cake at all."

Borman often used his persuasive personality to influence employees during Eastern's frequent labor disputes, while he lent his image for airline promotions, appearing in numerous television and magazine ads, bolstering the company's image of courtesy and efficiency. A conservative, personally and politically, he neither smokes nor drinks. He married Susan Bugbee in 1950 and they have two sons. He resigned from Eastern in 1986 and applied his expertise in the business world, as Chairman and Chief Executive Officer of the Patlex Corporation in Chatsworth, California.

Brian Bosworth

See the earring that reads "BOZ," view the blond mohawk haircut, and you know you're looking at the big linebacker Brian Bosworth. At the young age of 23, he reached celebrity status not only by signing the most profitable deal for a rookie in pro football history, but also by appearing on the cover of national magazines. As a member of NFL's Seattle Seahawks, Brian has contributed a popularity that has propelled the team to national television—competing with the Dallas Cowboys as "America's Team."

Born 9 March 1965 in Irving, Texas, he attended Oklahoma University. Unlike other athletes, Brian excelled equally in the classroom and on the field. He graduated with a 3.25 GPA, majoring in business. As a linebaker with the Oklahoma University Sooners he was the Big 8 Defensive Player of the Week five times in his 3-year career and was nominated for the award 17i times. He was a Butkus-Award winner and first team All-American. Such a good standing made him a top draft pick, and his contract with the Seattle Seahawks recognizes that.

Combining his literary skills with his athletic prowess, Bosworth wrote his much-talked-about autobiography, *The Boz,* with Rick Reilly in 1988. The future looks bright for Brian; still single, he lives in the state of Washington.

Pierre Boulez

"Music moved out of the world of Newton and into the world of Einstein," said Pierre Boulez (boo-lez) the firebrand of French modernists, when he first encountered the atonal system of musical composition originated by Arnold Schoenberg. Boulez' own compositions helped establish a grammar for that new language, but there he parted company with Schoenberg, rebelling against Germanic "expressionism" in favor of the path carved out by fellow Frenchman Claude Debussy. Then, to ensure the competent interpretation and performance of his highly original and esoteric music (Oliver Messiaen has placed Boulez among the two or three most talented composers of the century), he turned to conducting. And if as a composer he is in tune with the revolutionary spirit of his age (one of the sessions of the International Assembly of Revolutionary Students which met at Columbia University in 1968 was opened by Boulez' "Sonatine for Flute and Piano"), he is, according to Lloyd Schwarts in *Vanity Fair* in 1984, "among living conductors, the most complete embodiment of his time. He understands it and, without condescension show us its ideals: flexibility, clarity in the midst of complexity, individuality without mannerism or self-promotion, beauty without prettification, deep feeling without sentimental or melodramatic display." As musical director of the New York Philharmonic 1971-1977, he ruffled a few traditionalist feather, but he also succeeded in introducing into the standard repertoire much of the body of work in the serial idiom, leaving behind an audience that is probably the most knowledgeable in America about radical composers of the 20th century.

Born 26 March 1925 in Montbrison, France, to a steel manufacturer who wanted his son to become an engineer, Pierre combined musical studies with a rigorous mathematical and scientific curriculum, mostly in Lyons. (Some critics believe his knowledge of mathematics has influenced his musical composition, just as it has affected the vocabulary of his musical criticism.) Arriving in Paris during the war years to continue his musical studies at the Paris Conservatory, he found the city under German occupation restrictive in entertainment, but amenable to approved "culture," which resulted in filled concert halls. Graduating in 1945 with a first prize in harmony, he spent a decade as music director of the theatre company of Jean-Louis Barrault and Madeleine Renaud, touring the Orient, Europe and North and South America. During the early '50s, Boulez and other avant-garde composers tried to gain control over music. "What we were doing, by total serialization, was to annihilate the will of the composer in favor of a predetermining system," he told Alan Rich in the *New York Times* in 1963. He established his reputation as a brilliant conductor through the "Domaine Musicale," a series of concerts whose purpose was to educate the French in 20th century music, and through the annual summer festivals of contemporary music at Darmstadt, Germany. His recorded repertory includes his own large body of work as well as that of such 20th century composers as Berg, Debussy, Berlioz, Messaien, Bartok and Stravinsky. Passed over in 1966 by then Minister of Culture Andre Malraux for the post of the ministry's musical director (in favor of a "neoromantic!"), Boulez declared that he could never again live in Paris "where music was put in the hands of incompetent men." In 1972, French President Georges Pompidou convinced him to reconsider, by naming him to the post of founder and director of IRCAM (Institut de Recherche et de Coordination Acoutique/Musique), one of the four departments of the Pompidou Centre which opened in 1977. In 1976, commemorating the century of Wagner's *Ring* cycle at Bayreuth, he conducted the controversial (Patrice) Chereau/Boulez production of the *Ring*—with the Rhine Maidens as whores and Wotan as the Daddy Warbucks of Valhalla—which was repeated from 1977 to 1980 and which U.S. audiences watched over PBS in 1983. He returned to Bayreuth in 1983 to conduct the memorial concert of the centenary of Wagner's death, and later that year organized the international Webern Festival in Paris, London and Vienna.

David Bowie

"One of the reasons I've never been in analysis," says the rock singer-actor, "is that I've always been afraid of what I would find out. Most of my family is either nutty or dead." He has been a commanding presence on the music scene since he first surfaced from the English art underground in 1970. "I'm an actor. My whole professional life is an act." Observed Anne Rice in *Vogue:* "In a time when both men and women are becoming more androgynous to meet the demands of career and family, Bowie is jumbling all our safe ideas about gender. Through the alchemy of his subtle strength and yielding beauty he is giving androgyny a good name."

He was born 8 January 1947 in Brixton, England, a rough area south of London. "My father was a gambler, a drinker, a layabout," Bowie says. "I have one brother and one sister I know about. We are all illegitimate." He went to commercial art school and tried a brief stint in advertising, but reading the Beat writers changed him. He learned to play the saxophone, studied mime for two and a half years, and decided to give rock a try, living out of dustbins on the back streets of Carnaby. In 1969, his first song "Space Oddity" about an astronaut named Major "Tom," and his much-publicized bisexuality propelled Bowie into the public's eye. As the leading character in what *People* called "his shifting, ever improving brand of rock 'n' roll space drama," he journeyed from the hard rock of his Ziggy Stardust days to soul to synthesized disco and beyond. He is one of the few rock stars to successfully make the transition from jukebox to screen and stage. His credits include the sublimely gentle extraterrestial in Nicholas Roeg's *The Man Who Fell to Earth* (1976), *The Hunger* (1983), *Merry Christmas Mr. Lawrence* (1983), *Absolute Beginners* (1985), *Labyrinth* (1986), *The Last Temptation of Christ* (1988), and *The Delinquents* (1989). He played a season on Broadway in the title role of *The Elephant Man* (1980). His latest albums include *Tonight* (1984) and *Never Let Me Down* (1987). Throughout 1987 he and his band toured the country in the "Glass Spider Tour."

From his 1970 marriage to wife Angela, the singer has a son named Zowie born in 1971. David Bowie, whose real name is David Jones, says he chose the name Bowie for a stage name because it was "the ultimate American Knife." He also said, "I don't want to be stationary. I want to make myself a vehicle, a video newspaper."

Boy George

What's all this talk about androgyny? It was such a hot topic in the summer of 1984 that "Face the Nation" devoted an entire segment to the subject with comments from Jerry Falwell, Gore Vidal and this sparkler. "But I *am* like other people," he has said, "the way I differ is that I didn't believe I should do what I was cut out to do. It's very difficult to explain why you suddenly decide not to look like everyone else. People can't understand that I dress up because I want to. They think that my image is a professional thing. I want to look like this. I sewed it up years ago. I resent explaining, I resent everything about it. What frightens people the most is that I'm not confused about my sexuality. I've said I'm bisexual and that's enough of an explanation. It's 1984, people shouldn't be bothered by this stuff," declared Boy George. Born George O'Dowd 14 June 1962, he emerged from London working-class roots to become the lead singer of the video and rock and roll phenomenon Culture Club, whose sound combined Jamaican reggae with American soul and British New Wave.

By the time the group was formed in 1981, Boy George was already a minor celebrity in London's Club scene because of his Carmen Miranda-goes-Geisha flair for unique costumes and make-up, including long hair done up in strips of colorful ribbon and beads. The group happened as a part of England's New Romanticism—a working-class response against recession and unemployment. The kids were bored so everybody started painting their faces and getting into outrageous dressing. Boy George is the most famous of the lot. Princess Margaret refused to have her picture taken with him and called him an "over made-up tart." Joan Rivers claims he's one of her greatest friends and notes that he was one of the best interviews she's ever done as host of the "Tonight Show." George tries to keep things simple. "I'm overanxious, obnoxious, careless, careful, considerate, selfish, aggressive and gentle at the same time. Optimistic. My situation has changed but I'm pretty much the same as I was—a normal person." The man who admits to reading just one book in his entire life (Tallulah Bankhead's autobiography) confessed his surprise over his reign as King/Queen of the Charts: "God . . . I never thought I'd get it together to even be able to sign a check."

Boy George had trouble getting it together when the pressures of fame piled up on him. Tabloids spread news of his drug addiction and overwhelming personal problems. Then 1987 became a bounce-back year for the velvet-voiced vocalist. He released his first solo album, *Sold*, which featured a reggae remake of the classic Bread song "Everything I Own." The single hit number 1 in England and reinstated him as a contender in the music business. Renewing his success in the U.S., Boy George went one-on-one on the "Donahue" show, talking with Phil about his love of life and music. A second solo album recorded in London was released with the single "Don't Cry" hitting the airwaves.

As his unforgettable "Karma Chameleon" song says, he might ". . . come and go . . .", but Boy George will always remain a musical innovator.

Ray Bradbury

"We can't be good unless we know what bad is," says the master wizard of science fiction. "What I do is something called magic realism. I'm a poetic maker of metaphors and trapper of ideas." Ray Bradbury has written well over 1,000 stories, several books (among them *The Martian Chronicle*, which NBC adapted for a TV movie; *The Illustrated Man* and *Farenheit 451*, both of which were translated to film), twenty-five plays and eight volumes of poetry. In the midst of it all he found time to write the Oscar-winning script for the film version of *Moby Dick*. Bradbury served as consultant to a new advanced technology center (the Spaceship Earth Building) at Walt Disney's Epcot Center in Florida. (Bradbury provided a dramatic outline-blueprint-scenario.) Other projects include a screenplay, an opera, a book on Ireland (where he once lived for six months, and two novels, *Death Is a Lonely Business* (1985), and *The Toynbee Convector* (1988). In 1984 "Bradbury 13," a radio drama series based on many of his short stories, was presented on National Public Radio's "NPR Playhouse." "It's easy to juggle projects," quips the indefatigable Bradbury; "you borrow energy from one and give to another."

Ray Douglas Bradbury was born 22 August 1920 in Waukegan, Illinois. His early influences were Edgar Allen Poe, Wilkie Collins, the Wizard of Oz, and Buck Rogers. He first saw his name in print as an author at twenty-one, and graduated from *Weird Tales* to *The American Mercury* in 1945. Married to Marguerite McClure (whom he met in a bookstore) in 1947, he is the father of four daughters. Bradbury never drives (quite a feat for an L.A. resident) and took his first plane trip just recently. Weekends are spent in Palm Springs where Bradbury swims for relaxation. Concerned about city planning, Bradbury has ideas to revitalize the small towns of America with public malls and entertainment centers. Advice for would-be creators? "Don't think! Thinking is the enemy of Creativity. It's self-conscious and anything self-conscious is lousy. You can't try to do things. You simply must do things . . . time runs out very soon. If you don't hurry and get your work done, you die leaving nothing behind to show you were here."

Barbara Taylor Bradford

"I like women who are achievers and doers rather than victims," she said, describing the characters in her novels. This description is much more, however; it's a description of the novelist herself. Barbara Taylor Bradford is a strong woman who writes stories of strong women. "I'm not really a feminist, but I do resent the implication that women are the weaker sex and have a weaker brain." No one could ever say such things about Bradford. Her first novel, *A Woman of Substance*, which thrust her into prominence in the publishing world, was made into a TV miniseries in 1984 and earned two Emmy nominations. Her next three novels enhanced her reputation in the thirty-two countries and eighteen languages in which she is read. Her current sales top twenty-five million copies of the English-language editions alone. To date she has published five novels; three of which relate the saga of a young Yorkshire servant girl Emma Harte and her descendants. Barbara's writing credits go back long before her novels. She wrote bestselling books on decorating and had a syndicated column, "Decorating Woman," which ran three times a week in one hundred eighty-five American newspapers for twelve years. At age eighteen Bradford was the youngest women's-page editor in all of England.

As determined and talented as her Yorkshire-bred heroines, Bradford was born in a suburb of Leeds, England, the only child of a former nanny/nurse and an engineer. At age seven Barbara began writing and sold her first story to a children's magazine for ten shillings and sixpence at the age of twelve. She left the Northcote Private School for Girls at age sixteen, and against her parents wishes took a typing job instead of continuing her education. Within six months Bradford was promoted to cub reporter at the *Yorkshire Evening Post*. After four years in Leeds, Barbara left for London, and at twenty became the fashion editor of *Woman's Own*. But the fashion scene was too limiting for Barbara, so she took jobs with the *London Evening News* and other Fleet Street newspapers and covered everything from crime to show business. An avid lover of the works of the Brontes, Bradford finds her manuscripts are now requested by Brotherton Library at the University of Leeds and housed alongside the world's most extensive Bronte Collection.

Bradford and her film-producer husband, Robert Bradford, live in New York City with their Bichon Frise dog, Gemmy. Although here in the States since their marriage in 1963, the couple still maintain a home in Mayfair, London. Currently working on the research for her next novel, Bradford takes time out to consult with her husband, who is preparing miniseries versions of two of her novels scheduled to air in 1989.

Ben Bradlee

This history-making editor led the ultimate plundering of the Nixon Administration by releasing two eager newshounds onto the scent of what was being down-played as "a third-rate burglary." Only when television's

Walter Cronkite (whom Bradlee warmly refers to as "the Great White Father") aired whiffs about Watergate did the country become hungry for meatier news of Nixon's nasty doings. In 1973 his *Washington Post* received a Pulitzer for public service, and in 1975 Bradlee and his doggedly-determined diggers, Bob Woodward and Carl Bernstein, were lionized through Jason Robards, Robert Redford and Dustin Hoffman portrayals in the film, *All The President's Men*. Of the White House's personal criticism of Bradlee before the eventual congressional intervention, he said, "I kept asking . . . how could their contempt be so great as to think that Ben Bradlee would publicly destroy himself and the paper he loved by printing something not true? . . . They had to attack us for their own survival, . . . which led to the conviction that we were right."

Benjamin Crowninshield Bradlee, born 26 August 1921 in Boston, has a long history of scooping the journalistic competition. The Harvard grad earned his Greek and English lit degree in just three years' time so he could serve in World War II. A year after he got out of the Navy, he and friends began a newspaper in New Hampshire; upon selling it two years later, in 1948, he began his first stint at the *Washington Post* as a reporter. From there, he turned out copy at the U.S. Embassy in Paris, and then for *Newsweek*. With that magazine he transferred conversations with his Georgetown neighbor, U.S. Sen. John F. Kennedy, into timely stories about upcoming federal plans, and, in 1975, into the book, *Conversations With Kennedy*.

Bradlee was more tight-lipped about the identity of the tattling "Deep Throat" of Watergate infamy, and one story he wishes the *Post* hadn't printed was the Janet Cooke-fabricated piece about a child drug addict; it won a Pulitzer that Cooke, later fired, was forced to return. Aware that he is forever in competition with the other national journal, the *New York Times*, he strives to avert losing out to *Times*' blockbusters like the early Pentagon Papers' stories.

Thrice-married, the journalist who jokingly calls himself "mean, triple-spaced, (with) graying hair, (who is) nervous and (a user of) bad language," tied the knot with *Post* writer Sally Quinn in 1978 (one son, Josiah; three children by previous marriages).

Bill Bradley

Having already been raised "to become a successful gentleman" by his well-heeled parents, this gifted scholar and athlete picked politics as his future career. "I think the experience of ten years on the road, seeing America, living with a group of people (the New York Knicks) like I did made me more conscious of the contribution of public service and gave me some different perspectives. In one sense it was (being) in a black environment, in another I was on the road constantly, in yet another I was an active union member. It was living with a group of people who were different from each other." Since 1979 he's been the Democratic U.S. Senator from New Jersey.

This solon who advocates a neoliberal line, helped create the toxic waste "Superfund" by taxing polluters, and favors free choice on abortion, was born 29 July 1943 in Crystal City, Mo. The bank president's son rewrote the Ivy League record books as a Princeton basketball brain. He postponed his entry into the pro ranks by taking a Rhodes Scholarship to Oxford, where he practiced his shooting alone in a medieval gym better suited for falconry. The former U.S. Olympian, once his chosen sport's best amateur, finally capitulated and joined the New York Knicks' special brand of ball—intelligent, savvy, and demonic on defense. They called the frugal Bradley "Dollar Bill;" he refused commercial endorsements and, offcourt as well as on, was patently un-flamboyant. But busy. While teammates ribbed him about preparing for his future (unannounced) presidential campaign, Bradley spent off-seasons working in a Harlem reading program, and at the Office of Economic Opportunity in Washington. After ten seasons and two NBA championships, he stepped off Madison Square Garden's hardwood and was offered positions by President Carter, Senator Edward Kennedy, and New Jersey's Governor Byrne.

Bradley told Kennedy he preferred a job on the order of the Senator's; one year later he had it. He won, by a wide margin despite the early opposition of the state's Democratic machine, and six years later he won by an even greater landslide. As a superbly informed legislator, he is especially knowledgeable about energy issues, and went to Moscow to participate in arms limitation talks. He's also an articulate proponent of a flat income tax. Married to a German-born literature professor, Dr. Ernestine Schlant, he is the father of one and stepfather of another. "If we fail to provide (federal) assistance (for education) we are essentially saying to a whole class that we don't care about you, that you are stuck and the ladder of upward mobility is now removed from your grasp. I don't think we want to say that."

Ed Bradley

"I worked for nothing, then $1 an hour," says this gruff and independent correspondent of TV's all-time favorite news show, "60 Minutes," about his entry into broadcasting. "I did the news, the sports, even play-by-play. At WCBS in New York I worked a regular shift from 6 a.m. to 2 p.m. and then did more stories on my own. Hours meant nothing to me." But eventually living in Paris meant everything. After Bradley, born in Philadelphia in 1941, made the transition from college football player to sixth grade teacher to radio reporter, he moved to Paris in 1971 "to write the Great American Novel" and work as a network TV stringer. Another correspondent tattles that "when he first came over he spoke not a word of French. When he left, about eight months later, he spoke four works." But his strong reporting in English was what moved CBS to give him a year's assignment in Vietnam. He ended up spending two years there, was flung air-borne by mortar shrapnel that tore a piece from his left arm, and later found himself one of the last American correspondents evacuated from Phnom Penh, Cambodia, when the Khmer Rouge captured it in 1975.

His next action was far less exciting or dangerous, but his reporting on the 1976 Presidential campaigns when he ended up covering future President Carter garnered him a White House correspondent's slot. Then came the anchor job on the CBS "Sunday Night News," a 15-minute wrapup. He was thus the first black anchorman, in the strict sense, and indisputably "60 Minutes"'s first black correspondent. The report that got him the plum role as one of the news-exposing "tigers" on the highly rated show was his documentary on "The Boat People." Acclaimed for his journalistic style, Bradley has received numerous awards, including the Pioneers of Excellence Award (1987) and the 1988 YMCA "Service to Youth Award."

Bradley made the news himself in 1981 when he married Priscilla Coolidge. The couple divorced in 1984.

Tom Bradley

"His facial expression seldom varies, but his eyes twinkle, he laughs easily, and he is not 'stolid' as some of his critics describe him, but a self-contained cool cat." That's how one journalist sized up Los Angeles Mayor Tom Bradley. This "cool cat's" moderate views and reserved demeanor, combined with his law enforcement background, earned him nearly half the white vote in the 1973 majoral race. His victory made him the first black mayor of a mostly white U.S. city.

Born 29 December 1917 to an East Texas sharecropping family with seven children, Bradley experienced lean early years. The family relocated to Los Angeles, where his father found work at odd jobs and his mother toiled as a domestic. A serious student, Bradley disregarded advice that blacks should not seek higher education and used his athletic skills to win a scholarship to the University of California at Los Angeles, where he ran track. He quit college to join the police force but later earned a law degree at night from Southwestern University. Retiring from the force in 1961, he established a private law practice in L.A.

His entrance into politics came with the 1963 City Council race. Running as an independent, he became the first black councilman, and was reelected by his district in 1967 and 1971. But Bradley wanted more. He ran in the 1969 mayoral race but was easily defeated by incumbent Sam Yorty in a run-off election. Yorty scared the white voters by claiming Bradley was controlled by "black militants and left-wing radicals." In a slicker campaign four years later, Bradley defeated Yorty with 56 percent of the vote. He lost the 1982 Gubernatorial race to GOPer George Deukmejian, and in 1984 presided over the brilliant L.A. Olympic Games and was easily reelected mayor in 1985.

As Mayor, Bradley has stressed public transit construction to help overcome the city's severe smog problem, crime reduction programs, and a moratorium on off-shore oil drilling. Arguably the most powerful black politician in the country precisely because he's not viewed as "a black politician," it's Bradley's contention that for today's blacks economic development is what civil right was in the 1960's. Respected by many for his fashion sense, he received an award in 1985 from the American Image/Men's Fashion. Married since 1941 to his teenage sweetheart, Ethel Arnold, Bradley and his wife are the parents of two daughters.

Terry Bradshaw

He was tough and he got the job done. After a pro debut in which he was so nervous he reportedly vomited on a teammate in the huddle, he led the team by his example and came back each time from a fractured nose, broken collarbone and ribs, and torn hip muscle, among other injuries. But in his last season he tried to come back too fast from an elbow tear. Maybe, unwisely, he pushed himself and his Pittsburgh team too "Win one for the thumb," or a fifth Super Bowl championship ring, a goal he fell short of.

Born 2 September 1948, Terry Paxton Bradshaw set all school passing and total offense marks at little-known Louisiana Tech, made several All-American teams, and played in his senior year in two college all-star games before becoming the NFL's number 1 draft pick in 1970. As a rookie he was still convinced that passing was the name of the game, but in just eight games he led the NFL in interceptions. He acquired a "dumb quarterback" label early on. But by his third year the Steelers had gone from being a five-game winner to eleven and three and the American Football Conference title. They were contenders from then on, and when Bradshaw finally won his job at the helm in 1974, they were on their way to 6 Superbowls under him. He divorced former Miss Teenage America of 1969, Melissa Babish, in 1974, however, and he went into a personal tailspin. "I'm a Baptist, a Christian. I'd failed. I didn't become an alcoholic or a whoremonger, but I was moody and depressed and I drank and hustled women in bars—a total jerk having a ball . . . (but) I have never enjoyed those things . . . (and) . . . the guilt brought me to my knees." Two years later he married pro ice skater Jo Jo Starbuck, another Christian with whom he prayed daily by telephone when away from home. Unfortunately, sharing the same religion and prayer did not hold their union together. The couple divorced; Terry married his third wife, Charla Hopkins, in 1987.

James Brady

"A professional writer," declares this hardworking Irish-American columnist, novelist, TV commentator and overall trend-zapper, "does it when everything has gone wrong. His wife has just left him, his kids are on dope, he's broke, his salary is being garnisheed and the editor has just warned him that he is about to be canned. In these dire circumstances he will still turn out 1,500 beautiful words." Once called the "Spencer Tracy of writing," he's also noted for his infectious sense of humor.

Born 15 November 1928 in Brooklyn, Brady prepared himself at Manhattan College ("But," wrote Julie Baumgold in *New York* magazine, "he always seemed to have gone to Yale.") After a stint in the Marines, he ventured into the garment jungle as a copywriter at Macy's. Later, for Fairchild Publications, he covered a variety of beats, including London and Paris for *Women's Wear Daily*. As that paper's publisher in 1964, he made the international shiny sheet of the fashion biz a household name. The 60s were *it* for wild style, fashion and social revolutions and Brady was there covering it all. "Clothes never turned me on," he said, "people do." Innately curious, Brady helped bring gossip to the forefront of the technological age. In 1971, seven years after *WWD*, he took over *Harper's Bazaar*, but 14 months at the glossy were *basta* for both the editor and the magazine. He went to work gossiping in Rupert Murdoch's *Star* and when, in 1977, the Australian publisher acquired *New York* magazine, Brady became its Editor-in-Chief. Preferring writing to editing, he was recruited to pen "Page Six," a daily compendium of delectable scoops and scandals in the Murdoch-owned *New York Post*. His high horsepowered pen moved, in the 1980s, to *Advertising Age*. He also appears on New York City's WCBS-TV's afternoon news program. (He won an Emmy for his "New York Live.") He is the author of several books including the novels *Paris One*, *The Press Lord* (Murdoch-inspired?) and *Holy Wars;* two non-fiction works, *Superchic* and *Neilsen's Children*. His well-received book *Designs* was published in 1986, and Brady set up office writing for *Ad Ag* in 1988. Married once and now divorced, he has grown daughters, Fiona and Susan. He divides his time between Manhattan and seaside Bridgehampton, Long Island.

Marlon Brando

"You see that," he said to a companion when two fans wanted to shake his hand, "they are preconditioned. I'm just another S.O.B. sitting in a motor home and they come looking for Zeus. I could have been a Malaysian orangutan. . . . You know. I don't mind what people think about me; they can write whatever they want. I've been devotedly indifferent, I don't even bother suing them. . . . Personally, I'm not interested in making an assessment of myself and stripping myself for the general public to view. We put to sleep our notions about ourselves that are real and dream others."

Born 3 April 1924 in Omaha, he moved with his family to Evanston, then Libertyville, Ill., attending and getting expelled from schools in each town. When he finally turned to ditch digging, his father offered to finance training in any field he chose, so Brando followed older sisters Frances (an art student) and Jocelyn (an actress) to New York, where he enrolled first in Erwin Piscator's Dramatic Workshop and then in the Actor's Studio. His Broadway debut was in *I Remember Mama* (1944) and then he was directed by Elia Kazan for the first time in *Truckline Cafe*, which he followed with a much discussed Marchbanks to Katharine Cornell's 1946 *Candida*.

He was directed again by Kazan as Stanley Kowalski in *Streetcar Named Desire*, a performance that continues to influence subsequent generations of actors. He went to Hollywood after *Streetcar* in 1950 to play a paraplegic in

The Men, followed by the film version of the Tennessee Williams classic. For a long time it seemed he was brilliant under Kazan's direction (e.g., *Streetcar, Viva Zapata*, and *On the Waterfront*) and bad to mediocre when directed by almost anyone else *(Desire, Guys and Dolls, The Ugly American, Julius Caesar, A Countess from Hong Kong, Morituri, Bedtime Story, Sayonara, Teahouse of the August Moon, Nightcomers, The Missouri Breaks* and *Superman;* exception: *The Wild Ones.)*

Said colleague Rod Steiger: "Marlon was in a unique position. He could have done anything. But he didn't choose to." He insisted that his role in *The Young Lions* be rewritten as more sympathetic, which weakened the film; he took over as director of *One-Eyed Jacks*, bringing the film in late and over budget. *Mutiny on the Bounty* was renamed "The Mutiny of Marlon Brando" as he battled several directors, most of the actors, and the scriptwriter.

Brando married and divorced Anna Kashfi and then Motiva Castenada and was involved in a well-publicized custody fight for his three children—Christian Devi, Miko and Rebecca. He fathered Simon (Tehotu) and a daughter Cheyenne with his third wife Tarita who played his lady-love in *Mutiny on the Bounty*. He settled with her on Tetiaroa, a South Sea atoll of 13 islands that he bought in 1966. Brando's career seemed in serious decline until his stunning performance as Don Corleone in *The Godfather*. Next he shocked the world in the controversial *Last Tango in Paris*, but his performance as a grief-stricken widower who plunges into a bizarre, sexually complicated affair with a young woman about whom he knows nothing (played by Maria Schneider) won him a whole new generation of international fans. (Brando exposed more than his body in *Last Tango*—the sex may be staged but the dialogue is real; director Bernardo Bertolucci insisted not only on improvisation but on Brando making himself the character Paul.) Awarded the Oscar in 1972 for his role in *The Godfather*, Brando asked a young American Indian actress to appear at the award ceremony on his behalf and refuse the award as a protest against America's and Hollywood's treatment of the American Indian. In 1979 Brando gave what some critics consider his finest performance in Francis Coppola's *Apocalypse Now*.

Recent films include *A Dry White Season* (1989), *The Freshman* (1989), and *Jericho* (1989); he was the narrator for a 1986 film titled *Raoni*.

William J. Brennan, Jr.

William Joseph Brennan, Jr., was President Eisenhower's choice for Associate Justice of the Supreme Court in 1956, at a time when the liberal bent of the Court was at odds with a more conservative tone in both the White House and the nation's Main Streets. By the 1980s, however, the cycle had been completed: Justice Brennan now found himself in consistent opposition to a Supreme Court dominated by conservatives. He became the voice of dissent in a Court that put the Conservative imprimatur on a string of major cases in the area of civil rights, religion, Federal regulatory authority and criminal law. At one point, "Brennan started to get shrill" about his opinions, one critic claimed. When his brethren on the bench decided that if police acted "in good faith" evidence obtained illegally can be admitted in court, Brennan threw up his hands and declared the Fourth Ammendment was dead.

Born in Newark, 25 April 1906, and a lifelong Democrat, Brennan is the fourth New Jerseyan on the Court. He was nominated by President Eisenhower while he was sitting in the New Jersey Supreme Court. He came to the attention of court-watchers when he led a successful nationwide campaign to clear up court congestion. He married Marjorie Leonard in 1928. They had three children. After her death, Brennan married Mary Fowler of Arlington, Virginia, 9 March 1983.

Eleanor Brenner

"I design clothes that will make women look young, tall, thin and sexy," says petite and attractive Eleanor P. Brenner, the name and power behind the Eleanor P. Brenner Ltd. label. Feeling that there were revolutionary changes taking place in the lifestyles of contemporary women in the early 1980's, Brenner developed her own concept of sportswear dressing—clothes that were versatile and stylish—and in March 1983 she opened her own company with designs that reflected her fashion philosophy. "I want my clothes to help woman say, 'I like who I am.'" The industry approved. In 1985, Brenner was awarded the annual Chicago Apparel Center Fashion Award for outstanding designer sportswear. With such market approval and her drive, Brenner expanded her business, launching EPB Easy—her weekend sportswear division—in spring, 1986 and opening TPR—her knit division—in spring, 1987. Whether it's designing in New York, shopping for fabrics in Europe and Japan, overseeing production in the Orient, or meeting with clients all over the United States, Brenner is a woman on the move.

After graduating Phi Beta Kappa from New York University, Brenner began her fashion career with the training squad at Bloomingdale's. At the store she met, and eventually married, Richard Brenner, a vice-president. While pregnant with their two children, Tony and Pat, Brenner attended design school. Setting out to conquer Seventh Avenue, Brenner ran into a stone wall; she was told her designs and fabrics weren't "commercial." Knowing that she had the talent as well as the drive to succeed Brenner opened her own small studio to sell couture clothes. Her first collection was seen and loved by Henri Bendel. Soon her clothes were selling in specialty stores all over America. Convinced by her husband Richard that her designs would do well in the dress market, Brenner and her husband launched Brenner Couture, which branched out into several divisions, including Brenner Bees. With Eleanor as designing partner and Richard as business partner the business thrived until 1979 when Richard gave up Seventh Avenue for Wall Street. Opting to close the business instead of contining without her husband, Brenner took a four year sabbatical from fashion. With extra time for her other roles, Brenner wrote *Gourmet Cooking Without Salt* (Doubleday, 1987) before developing her concept for sportswear "dressing." Today, the fashion-designing wife and mother (who's also a gourmet cook, an art collector, and a political activist) also finds time for her commitment to raise funds for abused or battered women and children. Also an astrology devotee, Brenner believes she is in her ninth life. Those who know and admire her think she's crowded all those nine lives into this one.

Jimmy Breslin

This tough-guy chronicler of New York City lowlife has himself often been grist for the news mill. From his most visible hey-days as outrageous City Council president candidate on Norman Mailer's gag 51st State Party ticket, to outspoken commentator on a local newscast, to the novelist and columnist he continues to be, Breslin has always reflected on the city of his birth (17 October 1930) with streetwise common sense. "This is a lovely way to make a living. It it works, you've bought total liberty. If it doesn't work, you're another welfare statistic."

The 1969 primary was the first time Breslin actually ran for political office, but as a reporter the tough little Irishman once described as a "police station genius" has been covering the New York political scene most of his working life. After 20 years of newswriting and raising hell with the help of the *Tribune* and *Post*, Breslin gave up his three-time-weekly column because he felt his stuff "got lost between the girdle ads." He supported himself, his wife and six children by writing magazine articles and spinning novels on his busy typewriter. *The Gang That Couldn't Shoot Straight*, and *World Without End, Amen* were best-sellers that went to the movies. He and sportscaster Dick Schaap collaborated on *.44*, inspired by the "Son of Sam" killings. (Before the case was solved, Breslin was the

George Brett

recipient of several letters from the "Son of Sam" killer David Berkowitz.) His *Forsaking All Others* was a Puerto Rican-Italian Mafia version of "Romeo and Juliet."

Called "a New Yorker's New Yorker . . . brash, arrogant, and often irreverent," Breslin returned to the newsroom wars in 1976. During the early 1980's he wrote for the *New York Daily News* and in 1988 switched to write his column in *New York Newsday*. Two recent books, *Table Money* (1986) and *He Got Hungry and Forgot His Manners* (1988) showed off Breslin's biting creative writing.

A soft side to Jimmy appears every now and then. At one time, he became personally involved in getting the city to free an evicted vet from Bellevue (mental) Hospital. Breslin smacked the institution with a writ of habeus corpus to oppose the man's lockup for setting up housekeeping—bed, chair, etc.—on a traffic island after his VA check was stopped and his rent money dried up. Breslin made headlines again in early 1985 when New York's Mayor Koch accused him (and two black journalists) of writing racist columns, a charge Breslin refuted in his customary style.

The father of six by his marriage to Rosemary Dattolico, who died of cancer in 1981, he married Manhattan political activist Ronnie Eldridge in 1982.

George Brett

In 1980 he tore through American League pitching to come within a few hits of the elusive .400 batting average season. Three years later, he was at the heart of one of the game's most laughable controversies when a home run was nullified because his bat barrel had pine tar on it. (Later, the league office reinstated the four bagger.) This tobacco-chewing blue-eyed, 200 pounder continued to be a perennial All-Star and a favorite with fans.

George Howard Brett, born in Glendale, W. Va., on 15 May 1953 is the youngest of four brothers, all of whom played baseball. Older brother Ken became a teammate on the Kansas City Royals. Their father, a car finance officer "backed us all the way," George said, buying them the best gloves and telling them to enjoy their summers instead of working. Drafted as a power-hitting shortstop out of junior college by the Royals, he was an all-league third baseman in his two full minor league seasons. At Kansas City in 1974, hitting coach Charlie Lau changed his stance and bat release, and Brett evolved into a high-average spray hitter. He started running harder, too, saying, "It makes you feel great inside when you're standing on second or third base knowing you've just stretched a hit."

He won the A.L. batting crown and was first chosen an All-Star in 1976 (he was still manning third base in 1985's All-Star game). Brett led K.C. to Western Division titles in '76-78 and in '80. The Yankees frustrated the midwesterners in the playoffs the first three years. Then came "The Year." In 1980 Brett went on a 30-game hitting streak. Going to bat saying to himself, "I'm going to get a hit," he peaked at .407 in late August. When his fall to earth came, it wasn't far; his season's .390 average was baseball's best since Ted Williams' 39 years before. Debates ensued over which was the more remarkable feat: Williams' .406 average was achieved when gloves were smaller and pitching was in shorter supply compared to the present era of the designated hitter, whereas Brett's was earned in a home stadium with artificial turf, which makes grounders harder to field. Although K.C. finally beat the Yanks that year and went to the World Series they were beaten by the Phillies. Brett was chosen 1980's A.L. Most Valuable Player. Teammates say he remains easygoing despite his possibly head-swelling million dollar-a-year 1980 contract. Brett switched bases in the late 1980's and was playing first base in '89. He lives in a lakeside home outside Kansas City, and golfs, hunts, fishes, and photographs.

Jeff Bridges

Once upon a time he was known as Hollywood's playboy hippie, a reputation that came from his widely publicized experiments with est, marijuana and LSD—not to mention Candy Clark, Valerie Perrine and Cybil Shepherd. He'd become a star in 1971 via his appealing portrayal of a troubled Texas youth in *The Last Picture Show* and was nominated for the first of three Oscar nominations. (The others were *Thunderbolt and Lightfoot* in 1974 and *Starman* in 1985.) But by playing the first beefcake extraterrestrial in the history of Hollywood flicks in 1984's *Starman*, Jeff Bridges emerged from past critically-appreciated, quirky, but oftentimes noncommercial parts to become as well-beloved and desired as the Teddy Bear (who also enjoyed a wide-spread revival in 1984-85.)

The son of actor Lloyd and kid brother of actor Beau, Jeff Bridges was born in Los Angeles 4 December 1949. He made his acting debut at age eight on his father's popular TV series "Sea Hunt" and at age 14 toured in summer stock with his dad. As a teenager he recalls improvising scenes from J.D. Salinger's *Catcher in the Rye* with brother Beau on the platform of a flatbed truck which they would rent and park in different L.A. grocery store lots, their audience made up of shoppers and children. "If the cops came," Bridges says, "we'd just jump into the cab of the truck and zip off to the next one." After studying acting at N.Y.'s Hagen-Berghof Studio and a stint in the Coast Guard, he made his film debut in *Halls of Anger* (1970). After his success in *The Last Picture Show* he appeared in *Fat City*, *Bad Company* (both 1972), *The Iceman Cometh* (1973), *Rancho Deluxe* and *Hearts of the West* (1975). He was also in a couple of celebrated fiascos: the remake of *King Kong* in 1976 and *Heaven's Gate* in 1980. In 1976 he was in *Stay Hungry* and in 1984 the sexy *Against All Odds*. In 1985 he filmed *The Jagged Edge* and *Eight Million Ways to Die*. More movies followed: *The Morning After* (1986), *Nadine* (1987), *Tucker: The Man and His Dream* (1988), *See You In The Morning* (1988) and *The Fabulous Baker Boys* (1989).

Bridges is married to the photographer Susan Gaston, and with their two daughters, they live in Santa Monica and on a ranch in Montana where the actor relaxes between movies and composes music, paints and writes. He is involved in several social causes; foremost among them is the End Hunger Network, an organization he helped to found that intends, via the media, to end hunger on the planet.

Lloyd Bridges

Playing a patriarchal tycoon on the 1984 series "Paper Dolls" was just his latest tube adventure. "Damp good," said one critic dryly of his performance as "Sea Hunt's" skin-diving Mike Nelson, a million-dollar role in which he submerged himself for 156 watery TV weeks in the late '50s and early '60s. Later, waterlogged but not weary, he surfaced for his own TV anthology show, a western series called "The Loner," a Broadway run in *Cactus Flower* and such films as *The Happy Ending* ('69) and the hit *Airplane!* ('80). The younger generation knows him best as the father of actors Beau and Jeff.

A native Californian, born 15 January 1913 in San Leandro, he arrived before the cameras of Hollywood and Marineland via Broadway. After studying dramatics a UCLA, he met and married his leading lady, Dorothy Simpson. They taught drama briefly on the East Coast and he made his Broadway debut in *Othello*. During the W.W.II years he appeared in over two dozen 'B' films for Columbia. His tall, blond, rugged good looks suited him for westerns and action movies, sometimes as a heavy. After leaving his studio in 1945, he began freelancing and his roles improved. His better films include: *A Walk in the Sun* ('45), *Canyon Passage* ('46), *Home of the Brave* ('49), *The Sound of Fury* (aka *Try and Get Me*, '51), *High Noon* ('52), *The Rainmaker* ('56) and *The Goddess* ('58). Occasionally he has returned to the stage, including a two-week stint in *Man of La Mancha* ("What a ball I had singing"). Recent roles include appearances in "North and South Book II" (1986 TV movie) and films *The Devil's Odds* (1987) and *Winter People* (1989). In 1988, he played the bad guy opposite his son Jeff in the film *Tucker*.

Lloyd Bridges lives with his wife near UCLA, where they first met, as well as in the High Sierra Mountains and at Malibu Beach. Besides Beau and Jeff, they have a daughter, Lucinda. He enjoys traveling and playing tennis for charities. In the early '50s he had been a key witness before the House Un-American Activities Committee after affirming his past membership in the Communist Party. His career suffered no setback after his testimony. Like his son Beau (Lloyd 3rd), he doesn't much like his given name. His father call him Bud.

Christie Brinkley

It wasn't until after high school that this model-with-the-mostest (millions, that is) was given the chance to prove herself. After spending a brief spell in a junior college in Los Angeles, she decided to follow a career as an artist in Paris. "I was just leaving my puppy's vet after being told that the dog was very ill, and I was very upset over that. As I walked with my head hung in despair, I literally bumped into a young photographer, who asked if I'd model for him. It seemed like an easy way to make some extra money, so I said YES." The magic of Paris—within months Christie Brinkley was the rage in the modeling world. When she returned to the United States she was carrying an armload of French magazine covers on which she was the star attraction. Was Eileen Ford really waiting at customs for Christie to get off the plane so she could sign her right up? We don't know, but a Ford model Brinkley became, and the rest is fashion history at its highest gloss.

Born 2 February 1954 the daughter of television writer-producer Don Brinkley, Christie grew up in the posh Pacific Palisades. As a young girl, she considered herself a little "chubby . . . not quite an ugly duckling," she recalls, "I just wanted to be like everyone else." After being on the cover of magazines as different as *Vogue*, *Harper's Bazaar*, *Rolling Stone*, *Sports Illustrated* (three years straight on the cover of their annual bathing suit issue—no wonder she unveiled her own swimwear line) and *Life* magazine's largest selling issue ever, Christie Brinkley *is just not like everyone else*. ("God divides," as Joan Rivers says when explaining the differences between super-beauties and the rest of the world.) Even when her live-in, handsome boyfriend Olivier Chandon, the champagne heir, died in a racing car crash, she rebounded with Billy Joel, the superstar pop singer. If you're Christie Brinkley you don't have to worry about the 2 women-for-every-1 single man ratio. Joel's no French playboy, but he certainly isn't any kind of a schlepp either. The engagement ring he gave her was very large, thank you, a nice diamond solitaire from Harry Winston; they were married in 1985. Their daughter, Alexa Ray, was born in December, 1985, and her growing years seem surrounded with publicity. She traveled with her family to the USSR to watch Daddy perform with his band and she appeared with Mommy Christie in the 1989 famous *Sports Illustrated* swimsuit edition (without a bathing suit!)

Besides time spent as a super-face cover girl, Brinkley has lent her body and soul to such self-help books as *Beauty and the Beach*, *Christie Brinkley's Outdoor Fitness and Beauty Book* and *Thirty Days to Get Into a Bathing Suit*. She's appeared on many variety and interview shows and was triumphantly titillating in the 1983 film *National Lampoon's Vacation*.

David Brinkley

For almost 14 years he was half of "the biggest team in broadcasting history since Amos 'n' Andy." This former Washington anchorman, "the other half of the hyphen" of the "Huntley-Brinkley Report" established a whole new style in newscasting with his dry and vaguely cynical approach to the news. After 38 years at NBC, he migrated over to ABC in 1981 and a Sunday morning interview show, "This Week with David Brinkley." "It's at least shown that those Sunday morning programs don't have to go on forever doing the same thing over and over," he says—"30 minute interviews with one person, with four interviewers sitting at a table—it looks like an airline ticket counter—and the guest set up in a chair like a witness in a courtroom to be grilled."

One of television news's pioneers, Brinkley began at NBC in 1943, and it was in 1956 that he got to cover the national political conventions. Brinkley described it: "They said, 'We think that whoever does the convention . . . is going to become famous, and so we want somebody who is young enough that we can get some years out of him, and so we want you (Brinkley) and Huntley to do it.'" They were made into a nightly news team shortly thereafter. Born David McClure Brinkley in Wilmington, N.C., 10 July 1920, the former newspaper reporter had a wry, irreverent style that, coupled with Huntley's sobriety, caught on. Their "Good night, Chet" and "Good night, David" became a TV institution. Married first to Ann Fischer (three sons), the newsman was remarried in 1972 to divorcee Susan Adolph. Now a dean of electronic journalism, Brinkley doesn't wax nostalgic over the glories of past network newscasts. "They've become much, much more substantial, more serious, better staffed, better financed. Management's approach is more serious. I think at that time they didn't have a whole lot of confidence in the news staff to play it straight or to be accurate or to be fair."

A veteran of broadcast news, Brinkley won the George Foster Peabody Award in 1987.

David S. Broder

In 1980 an American University survey of the Washington press corps concluded, "David Broder's integrity and hard work have led him to be anointed the unofficial 'chairman of the board' by national political writers. . . . He heads an elite clan whose articles are carefully watched by the public, politicians, and most important, other reporters." The national political correspondent for the *Washington Post* whose twice-syndicated column is carried by 275 newspapers across the nation won journalism's most coveted award in 1973 when he was voted a Pulitzer Prize for distinguished commentary. This influential reporter is not a D.C.-bound pundit, having covered every national and major state political campaign and convention since 1960, traveling up to 100,000 miles a year to report on the candidates and interview voters.

Born 11 September 1929 in Chicago Heights, Ill., a precocious Broder received his B.A. in 1947 and an M.A. in 1951 from the University of Chicago. He began his career in journalism in 1953 as a reporter on *The Daily Pantagraph* in Bloomington, Ill., and began his career in the nation's capital in 1955 covering national politics for *Congressional Quarterly*, then for *The Washington Star* from 1960 to 1965 and *The New York Times* from 1965 to 1966, when he joined the *Post*, of which he was named an associate editor in 1975. A frequent radio and television panelist and commentator, Broder is the co-author with Stephen Hess of *The Republican Establishment: The Present and Future of the G.O.P.* (1967), author of *The Party's Over: The Failure of Politics in America* (1972), *Changing of the Guard: Power and Leadership in America* (1980) and *Behind the Front Page* (1987). He has been a fellow of the Institute of

Politics at the John F. Kennedy School of Government at Harvard and a fellow of the Institute of Policy Sciences and Public Affairs at Duke University. Married since 1951 to the former Ann Creighton Collar, he is the father of four sons.

Matthew Broderick

"At times I wanted to be a fireman, a baseball player and a veterinarian, but never an actor. Actually, between the time I was 3 until the age of 13, acting was the last thing I ever wanted to do." But the only son of the late James Broderick (best remembered as the gentle, thoughtful father on the award-winning "Family" TV series) changed his mind in time to become a star, at 21, of both stage and screen. In *War Games,* one of the biggest box office draws of 1983, he played a 16-year-old computer whiz who unwittingly taps into a Defense Department computer and brings the world to the brink of nuclear disaster; in his Broadway debut in Neil Simon's *Brighton Beach Memoirs,* he collected a Tony as the playwright's boyhood alter-ego. He essayed the same role in 1985 in Simon's *Biloxi Blues.*

Matthew Broderick was born in New York City on 21 August 1962. When he was 5, his dad wanted him to do a small role in a play, but "it really scared me," he recalls. "I remember kicking and screaming. I just couldn't do it." Later, he spent a number of school vacations touring with his father on the summer stock circuit and got hooked. "My sisters would be bored, but I would just hang around and watch rehearsals. I just liked being backstage and I loved watching my father work." His decision to take up acting himself came during his final years at NYC's Walden School and, just prior to graduation in 1979, he made his professional debut appearing with his father in an Off-Off-Broadway production of Horton Foote's *Valentine's Day.* He was first spotted as an actor "with a distinctive presence that augurs a bright future" in the original Off-Off-Broadway incarnation of Harvey Fierstein's *Torch Song Trilogy* and made his film debut in a not-so-successful Neil Simon film, *Max Dugan Returns.*

Broderick has appeared in a steady stream of films throughout the '80's: *Ladyhawke* (1984), *Ferris Bueller's Day Off* (1986), *Project X* (1986), *Biloxi Blues* (1987), *Torch Song Trilogy* (1988), *Family Business* (1989), *The Freshman* (1989) and *Lay This Laurel* (1989). He starred Off-Broadway in *The Widow Claire* (1986) and was seen in Athol Fugard's drama "Master Harold . . . and the Boys" (1985) on PBS television. While on a visit to Ireland, Broderick was involved in a car accident that landed him in a hospital in Belfast (August, 1987). He was later charged with reckless driving.

Once a steady date with actress Jennifer Grey, Broderick is presently single; he maintains apartments in Los Angeles and New York City.

Tom Brokaw

"One of the advantages of a South Dakota childhood is that there is so little around you intellectually that you reach out for broader sources of material," says the boyishly handsome NBC Nightly Newscaster. "I was always aware of what was happening in New York, or other power centers. I was known as the town talker. I was always involved in whatever arguments were going, agitating things constantly, always had an opinion for everything."

His fondness for Chet Huntley and David Brinkley, co-hosts then of NBC's Nightly News, prompted him to pursue a career in broadcast journalism. He began at the age of 15 as an announcer after school on KYNT in his hometown of Yankton, South Dakota (where he was born 6 February 1940). After graduating from the University of South Dakota, he went to work for the NBC affiliate in Omaha, Nebraska. From there he rolled to other jobs in other cities—Atlanta and Los Angeles among them—and then, due to his on-the-mark reporting of the assassination of Robert Kennedy and the Reagan-Brown gubernatorial campaign, Brokaw was picked to anchor NBC's national "First Tuesday," a monthly prime-time newsmagazine. In 1973 he became their man at the White House and in 1974, as co-host with Barbara Walters on the "Today Show," he found doing commercials on air so "repulsive" he returned to the White House beat. When the network no longer required hosts of the show do commercials, Brokaw returned to replace Barbara Walters when she made her million-dollar move to ABC. He quickly won acclaim with the TV-watching morning set so that network executives, "suits," as they are called, put him in the "Nightly News" chair in 1982.

An avid mountain climber, Brokaw is faithful to his home state. He married a former Miss South Dakota, Meredith Auld, in 1962. She is the co-owner of a successful Manhattan toy shop called Penny Whistle. The Brokaws have three daughters—Jennifer, Andrea and Sarah.

James Brolin

Known best for many seasons as the eager young associate of Robert Young on the doctor-knows-best-series, "Marcus Welby, M.D.," James Brolin has been by choice one of Hollywood's underemployed actors. After hanging up his stethoscope, he bided his time with occasional film and TV roles, until he was lured back to series television in 1983 to play the swinging, laidback manager of the St. Gregory on ABC's glossy "Hotel."

The son of a Los Angeles builder, Brolin, born 18 July 1940, had early ambitions as an aviator but was sidetracked by the lure of Hollywood. "I was also a big moviegoer. One day I got a tour through a studio and I was hooked." After leaving UCLA in 1958 to pursue auditions, he landed a contract with 20th Century-Fox, and later with Universal. "I never really starved." He appeared in the 1964 ABC series "The Monroes" before being cast as Dr. Steven Kiley on "Marcus Welby" in 1969. For six years he argued medical ethics, rode a tame motorcycle, and fell in love with women patients who invariably succumbed to disease before the hour was up, leaving him free to love once more.

Brolin's film credits include the generally panned *Gable and Lombard* (in which he played the screen idol), the supernatural thriller *The Amityville Horror,* and *Capricorn One.* Brolin and his wife, Jane Agee, a wildlife enthusiast whom he married in 1967, dissolved their marriage in 1985 (two sons: Josh James, Jess). He took up with "WKRP" actress Jan Smithers and married her in a nonlegal ceremony (June, 1986) in Novia Scotia. The couple actually made their union legal later that year when they remarried in Carmel, California. They have one daughter, Molly Elizabeth, born 28 November 1987.

Charles Bronson

"I'm not making pictures for messages, nor do I do parts where I would get some self-satisfaction," says this actor who's been likened to "a college wrestler with the face of an Inca mask," "It's the quality of the work that I strive for. And when I say quality, I mean quality that satisfies me, not some fat-ass critic in New York in a swivel chair." Never the conventional Hollywood matinee idol, he became a world-wide superstar at fifty after nearly twenty years of playing bit parts, heavies or the hero's friend. It wasn't until he transferred operations to Europe that the magic happened and, in 1972, a poll of Hollywood's Foreign Press Association showed him to be the actor with the biggest box-office appeal outside U.S. borders. He was the number one sex symbol in Spain, *Le Sacre Monstre* in France, *Il Brutto* ("the ugly one") in Italy, and in 1979, he received the Gold Star Award as the film industry's top international star, renowned the world over for his screen image of "strength and determination." Actually, these qualities are much more than mere image, for they are the very roots of his early life.

Born in the scrubby Pennsylvania coal town of Ehrenfield (in a section known as Scooptown) on 3 November 1921. Charlie Buchinsky followed his dad and two elder brothers into the mines helping to support twelve younger siblings and their mother after their father's death. He worked underground until he was drafted into the Army during World War II and didn't hit on the notion of becoming an actor until he was 27. Enrolling in the Pasadena Playhouse in 1950, he was soon spotted on stage by director Henry Hathaway and offered a small role in the 1951 Gary Cooper film, *You're In the Navy Now*, in which his one big scene involved belching on cue. He made a number of films in Hollywood but didn't become a bona fide star until 1968 when he began making pictures in France and Italy, most notably Sergio Leone's "spaghetti western" *Once Upon a Time in the West*. He finally was accepted as a U.S. star after the hit *Death Wish* (in which he played an architect-turned-vigilante) in 1974. Subsequent films (he'd made a total of 63 by 1984) include *Hard Times* (1976), *St. Ives* (1976), TV's "Raid on Entebbe" (1977) and sequels to *Death Wish* in 1981, 1986, and 1987. More Bronson movies include *Murphy's Law* (1986), *Messenger of Death* (1988), *Kinjite* (1989) and *The Golem* (1989). He also appeared in the HBO presentation "Act of Vengeance" (1986).

It was in 1963, during the filming of *The Great Escape*, that Bronson met future wife Jill Ireland (his first wife was Harriet Tendler, Jill's first husband was actor David McCallum). Since their marriage in 1969, they have appeared together frequently on the big screen (e.g. *The Valachi Papers*, 1972.) "After being in five pictures with him," Ireland once said, "I'm prepared to have him come home still playing the role. It's like making love to five different guys." The parents of five children make their home in a Bel Air mansion.

Peter Brook

At the age of five, according to one story, Peter Brook staged his first production, in a miniature theatre given him by his father: *HAMLET, by Peter Brook and William Shakespeare*. The billing is significant. As a director, the grown-up Brook "is not interested in interpreting material, but in converting it to his own use," observed an American critic in the late 1960s. A leader of the transatlantic avant-garde, Brook has called for a "holy theatre" of the type envisioned by French theorist-visionary Antonin Artaud: "a theatre working like the plague, by intoxication, by infection, by analogy, by magic; a theatre in which the play, the event itself stands in place of a text."

Peter Stephen Paul Brook was born in London 21 March 1925, of Russian parents. He streaked through Oxford as a kind of odd-man out theatrical prodigy. Graduating at 19, the "small, sausage-shaped man" (as Kenneth Tynan described the young Brook) began his professional career with a production of *Man and Superman*, and quickly established himself as London's directorial boy wonder. He joined the Royal Shakespeare Company and, during his quarter-century with the group, produced some of its most famous works, including *Marat/Sade* and the Paul Scofield *King Lear* (both later made into films).

In 1970 he left London for Paris where, together with Micheline Rozan, he founded the International Centre of Theatre Research, devoted to "exploring the sources of dramatic expression." For ten years the company toured the world with productions of well-known works (*Measure for Measure, Timon of Athens*) and some more obscure (*The Ilk, Conference of the Birds*). Though the group disbanded (voluntarily) in 1980, Brook continues to direct in Les Bouffes du Nord, the Paris theatre that was the Centre's home.

His most recent work has included productions of *The Cherry Orchard* and a radical reworking of Bizet's *Carmen* (retitled *La Tragedie de Carmen*) which cut the work to 90 minutes and eliminated the bulk of its cast. Theatre critics responded enthusiastically, opera critics somewhat less so; nonetheless, the work was honored with a special Tony award in 1984 for its New York run. He also directed and co-adapted *The Mahabharata* (1987) for a unique stage event.

"In a sense," he suggests, "the director is always an impostor, a guide at night who does not know the territory, and yet . . . has no choice—he must guide, learning the route as he goes." Some have criticized Brook on his overwhelmingly intellectual approach to his craft ("Isn't interested in people," complained one unhappy collaborator) and a "maddening" tendency to overexplain ("London is full of actors who will tell you they never understand a word he says"). But despite the criticism, Tynan's early assessment—"an almost perfect director"—still finds wide agreement. In 1971, Clive Barnes of the *New York Times* described Brook's *Midsummer Night's Dream* as "without any equivocation whatsoever the greatest production of Shakespeare I have ever seen in my life." Thirteen years later the *Times*, in the person of Frank Rich, was still rhapsodizing. "This director has found the way to put savagery back into tragedy—utter simplicity" he wrote of Brook's *Carmen*. Brook's secret? He never settles for "the adequate," says a colleague, "when the extraordinary is within reach." Brook is married to actress Natasha Perry, and they have two children, a son and a daughter. His films include *Marat/Sade, King Lear, Vacant, The Sailor Who Fell from Grace with the Sea*, and *Meetings with Remarkable Men*. Providing an inside look at Brook's life, his autobiography *The Shifting Point: Forty Years of Theatrical Exploration, 1946-1987* was published in 1988.

Donald Brooks

This designer gets around, from New York (where his designs range from casual sportswear to dramatic evening gowns worn by such fans as Claudette Colbert, Judy Peabody, Lee Radziwell and Lady "Slim" Keith) to Hollywood where he received a 1983 Emmy for "The Letter," with Lee Remick. Besides television, Brooks has made his mark on Broadway by designing the costumes for Diahann Carroll in *No Strings*, for Barbara Harris in *On a Clear Day You Can See Forever*, Linda Lavin in *Last of the Red Hot Lovers*, Jane Powell in *Irene* and for the ladies in *Promises, Promises*. His film credits include *The Cardinal, Star* and *Darling Lili* all of which received Academy Award nominations. His guiding tenet: clothes are less important than the woman wearing them. "The lines of the Brooks look," according to one aficionado, "are simple, uncluttered; the colors pure; the detailing masterly."

Born 10 January 1928 in New Haven, the three-time Coty Award winner studied fine arts and English at Syracuse University, and art history and design at the Parsons School in New York. He developed his affection for understated elegance, he says, as a reaction against the "hopped-up, jazzy sportswear" that he had to design as a beginner—"the kind," he recalls painfully, "where they put rhinestones on Irish linen and the sales staff called it raindrops."

Gwendolyn Brooks

Called an "objective" poet, Gwendolyn Brooks was awarded the Pulitzer Prize for her second volume of verse (*Annie Allen*, 1950), was named poet laureate of the state of Illinois in 1968 (succeeding Carl Sandberg) and was appointed to the prestigious National Institute Arts and Letters in 1976. Once hailed for her work's universality, rather than its raciality, she has now changed her tune about integration after giving lifelong support to interracial cooperation. "The glorious thing about today [is] we aren't concerned about what whites think of our work. . . . Whites are not going to understand what is happening in black literature today. Even those who want to sympathize with it still are not equipped to be proper critics." Formerly lionized in national literary circles, she has said of her integration days, "The [whites] thought I was lovely. I was a real pet for them. They thought I was nice, and I was nice. I believed in integration and so did they. But now, I rarely see these people, though a couple still call themselves my friends."

Born 7 June 1917 in Topeka, she completed her formal education in 1936 when she graduated from Wilson Junior College in Chicago. She then worked at jobs ranging from maid to secretary to spiritual advisor, collecting the experiences she later versified in *A Street in Bronzeville*, *Bronzeville Boys and Girls*, and *The Bean Eaters*. Her 1968 book of poems *In the Mecca* reflects her heightened black consciousness. Other poems such as "Malcolm X" and "The Wall" were even more militant. Married to Henry Blakely (two children) in 1939, she asserts women's lib "is not for black women at the time being, because black men need their women beside them, supporting them in these very tempestuous times." She has, as she explains, "rediscovered her blackness."

Mel Brooks

Named one of "the official satirists of a world that badly needs a hot needle in the posterior," by writer Arthur Cooper, born sometime in 1926, 27, or 28, with the real name of Mel Kaminsky, he remembers his childhood this way: "My father died when he was 34. I was 2. I think that unconsciously, there's an outrage there. I may be angry at God, or at the world, for that. And I'm sure a lot of my comedy is based on anger and hostility. Growing up in Williamsburg, Brooklyn. I learned to clothe it in comedy to spare myself problems—like a punch in the face." On the Borscht Belt, he met fellow comedian Sid Caesar who asked him to help write material for a TV show called "Broadway Revue" (on which Caesar debuted in one of his most famous roles—the daffy German professor).

When Caesar launched "Your Show of Shows," Brooks was hired as one of the writers and sometimes appeared on camera.

By all descriptions this was a wonderful, madcap period in his life. "For 18 months after the show went off, I'd wake up at 6:30 every morning and bang my head against the bathroom wall." In 1960, with pal Carl Reiner, Brooks launched his ad-lib interviews with the hilarious "2,000 Year Old Man"—a guy who'd been around and around, seeing it all. He said when asked if he'd known Christ: "Yes, thin, nervous, wore sandals. Came into the store a lot. Never bought anything."

Broadway shows, TV commercials for Ballantine Beer ("My tongue just threw a party for my mouth") the TV show "Get Smart," and hit comedy films *The Producers* and *The Twelve Chairs* all made him the master of intelligent farce with a decidedly oy vey twist. His 1974 hit *Blazing Saddles*, a jaundiced, giggly view of westerns, won him America's funnybone for life. More movies, more laughs, even a controversial rap video in which he played Hitler, and his own production company, (*Frances*, *My Favorite Year*, *History of the World Part I,*) make him one of Hollywood's most formidable figures. The year 1986 saw the release of *84 Charing Cross Road*, with his wife in the leading role. Keeping ahead of the times, Mel's recent movies were *Solarbabies* (1986) and *Spaceballs* (1987).

To his wife, Anne Bancroft (married 1964), and kids, Maxmillian and (from his first marriage to Florence Baum) Stefanie, Nicky and Edward, he is just the 2,000-year-old love of their lives.

Pierce Brosnan

"I don't see myself as a hunk of the month." he says modestly. "I don't think anyone is going to ask me to take off my shirt. My chest is rather pale." But this dark, 6'1" Irishman became a TV heartthrob of the first rank in 1982 as the sexy shamus, "Remington Steele," and was soon heralded (by *People*) as a "new Cary Grant—sexy but suave, funny with subtlety instead of slapstick, manly but mannered." He and co-star Stephanie Zimbalist, alternating between on-screen flirting and fighting, approximated "a modern Nick and Nora Charles," in the sophisticated tradition of William Powell and Myrna Loy in the old *Thin Man* movies of the 1930s.

Born 16 May 1952 in Limerick, Ireland, he was an altar boy taught by nononsense nuns in a school where the slightest deviation from the straight and narrow got one "strapped with a paddybat." Moving at eleven to the lessrestricted atmosphere of London, he had his first taste of acting at a theatre club and joyfully felt "the veils lifting off all those years of inhibitions." After studies at London's Drama Centre, he made his on-stage debut in 1976 in a local production of *Wait Until Dark* and later played numerous roles in repertory. American TV audiences first saw him in the 1981 series "The Mansions of America."

Caught in a commitment to continue as "Remington Steele," Brosnan was unable to pursue an offer to become the new James Bond. His pledge to remain as Remington proved disappointing and a short-season resurge ended with cancellation. Major films followed, including *Nomads* (1986), *The Fourth Protocol* (1987), *The Deceivers* (1988) and *Taffin* (1988), along with TV miniseries roles in "Noble House" (NBC, 1988) and "Around the World in Eighty Days" (NBC, 1989).

He and his English actress wife Cassandra Harris (nominated by photographer Lord Patrick Litchfield as one of "the world's most beautiful women"), have three children: Charlotte, Christopher and Sean William. How close is he in real life to the insouciant Remington Steele? "I panic more than he does," says Brosnan. "He doesn't take a lot of things seriously. I do."

Joyce Brothers

She's had the hottest career as a psychologist since B.F. Skinner plugged a little white rat into a lamp socket. A petite blonde, she has been a college teacher, boxing buff, quiz show contestant, author and a psychologist-at-large to anyone who doesn't object to mass advice. Dr. (in psychology) Joyce first came to public attention in 1955 when, to raise cash to help her husband, Dr. (of medicine) Milton Brothers (one daughter) start his practice, she boned up on boxing and quiz-kidded her way to a total of $134,000 on the 64,000 Question and Challenge." Three years later she had her own TV show, and a grateful nation had what one reviewer called "a sort of soap-opera Emily Post."

Born in New York City, 20 October 1928, the former Joyce Bauer graduated from Cornell, went on to earn a Ph.D. in psychology at Columbia. An overnight celebrity after her quiz show wins, she was offered a 25-minute show every afternoon on a New York station—for four weeks. When she began pulling tear-stained letters signed "Anxious Mother" and "Half-

Crocked," the station kept her on and eventually added an evening program in which she explored such subjects as frigidity and impotence. ("I'm kind of a middleman between the viewer and psychological literature.") Her "chicken-soup Freud" has been squawked at by her fellow competitors in the mind-candy biz, but her continued success (she has a column in more than 350 newspapers, appears on radio, and has written popular books such as *What Every Woman Should Know About Marriage*, *What Every Woman Should Know About Men*, *How to Get What You Want Out of Life* and *The Successful Woman: How You Can Have . . .*) would seem to be a clear sign that there are plenty of people around who like playing doctor with Joyce Brothers.

Dr. Joyce Brothers became a widow when her long-time husband, Dr. Milton Brothers, died in 1989.

David Brown

"Film-making, like drilling for oil, is a big gamble," says David Brown, who, partnered with Richard D. Zanuck, made up one-half of the successful producing organization The Zanuck/Brown Company. "The only difference is that they don't review dry holes!" Over the years they haven't had to worry much about "the dry hole syndrome." Their films together included *Jaws*, *The Sting*, *The Sugarland Express*, *Jaws 2*, *MacArthur*, *The Verdict*, *Cocoon* and *Target*. During their years as executives at 20th Century-Fox their regime garnered 159 Academy Award nominations, with a record 22 nominations in 1971. Three of their films, *The Sound of Music*, *Patton* and *The French Connection* won Oscars as Best Picture of the Year. Other smash successes included *The Planet of the Apes* films, *Butch Cassidy and the Sundance Kid* and *M*A*S*H*.

Brown was born in New York City on 28 July 1916, and is a graduate of Stanford University and the Columbia School of Journalism. After working in San Francisco as a newspaper copy editor he became a critic with Fairchild Publications (publishers of *Women's Wear Daily*, etc.) back in New York. Brown spent the war years in the U.S. Army and when mustered out in 1943 was appointed editor-in-chief of *Liberty* magazine and later became managing editor of *Cosmopolitan*, where he met Helen Gurley, whom he married in 1959. (He was married twice before, and has a son from his first marriage.) Early in 1952, Brown heeded the call of Darryl F. Zanuck who wanted the "best editor in New York" to head up his creative operations at the Fox studios. In 1963 he returned to publishing as head of the hardcover division of New American Library where he was responsible for the first hardcover James Bond novels by Ian Fleming. Brown, himself, is the author of numerous books, including *Brown's Guide to Growing Gray* (1988) and has contributed stories and humorous material for all media.

Brown made a break in the late 1980's from Zanuck and opened his own company in Manhattan. Recent credits are: *Blue Lightning* (1988), *Cocoon II* (1988) and *Driving Miss Daisy* (1989).

Helen Gurley Brown

She is, according to onetime *Cosmo* cohort Liz Smith, "a demanding editor but an easy friend: predictable yet unique, tough, fragile, candid but unknowable." The woman who masterminded *Cosmopolitan*'s renaissance from a circulation-limping service magazine for ladies into an up-to-the-second how-to-do-it monthly for swinging singles ladled out an additional savory serving of how-to-do-it advice in 1982 in her bestseller, *Having It All*. Billed as "the ultimate self-help guide" in the ways of money, work, success, love, marriage and other female concerns of the late twentieth century, its well-thumbed Chapter Seven (on the general subject of sex—"magic sex; intimate, comfortable sex; friendly sex; casual sex; scruffy sex"—with many colorful specifics including a much-discussed section on oral techniques) was one of the prime conversation topics of the season, primarily because of the publisher's printed guarantee that "everything Helen Gurley Brown recommends, she has done herself."

The writer-editor and self-described former "mouseburger" (her term for "a young woman who is not very prepossessing") was born Helen Gurley on 18 February 1922 in Green Forest, Arkansas, in the Ozarks, the daughter of two schoolteachers. ("I'm not beautiful nor bosomy—33 inches when I inhale. I'm not even pretty. I once had the world's worse case of acne. I grew up in a small town and didn't go to college.") She began her working career in Los Angeles, sweating it out as a secretary for 13 years in 17 different companies before landing a copywriter's job at an ad agency and becoming one of the best. Unmarried until she was 37 (to movie producer David Brown), she had ample first-hand experience with the pains and pleasures of the single life prior to composing her 1962 bestseller *Sex and Single Girl*, which led to her being invited to take over *Cosmo* in 1965. The self-help guru thinks of herself as a feminist but "also a realist' and Liz Smith (who spent eleven years as *Cosmo*'s film reviewer) calls her old boss "the Princess of Pragmatism." Though she has revitalized her magazine into a publishing success read by some 2,860,000 women a month (compared with 850,000 before she took over), Brown confesses that, despite all her impressive career triumphs, "there are areas where I find myself acting like a mouseburger more than I'd wish." In 1982, when *Having It All* was first wending its way to the bestseller lists, Brown told the *New York Times*'s Glenn Collins: "I'm terrified *not* to have a big job, because it's having a big job that makes me popular. If I didn't have it, then no one would be interested in inviting me to lunch. I always feel so ordinary. I guess having that nose-pressed-to-the-glass feeling never altogether leaves you."

In 1988 Brown was inducted into the Publisher's Hall of Fame, an honor previously bestowed upon such publishing originals as Henry Luce, Norman Cousins, and the founders of Simon & Schuster. Recently she was voted one of the Top Achievers by Women Achievers Association of America.

J. Carter Brown

He made art news headlines in 1969 when, at 34, he was appointed the director of Washington's prestigious National Gallery, becoming the youngest major museum director in the country. He continues to make the papers as one of the most enthusiastic proponents of "international blockbuster exhibition," the lavish touring museum shows like "The Treasures of Tutankhamen" and "The Search for Alexander." Both exhibitions attracted an unprecedented number of people to museums nationwide. In 1984, he announced the Gallery's richest show yet, slated for 1984-85: "The Treasure Houses of Britain: Five Hundred Years of Private Patronage and Art Collecting." Cost: "in the seven figures."

John Carter Brown III was born on 8 October 1934 in Providence, R.I., a descendant of both the state's founder Roger Williams and the manufacturer/philanthropist who endowed Brown University. It is not true, as one legend has it, that the first time he saw the National Gallery from a limousine window at age 12 he announced, "Someday I'll be its director." The fact is, according to his music-critic mother, he made the resolve a year earlier when he regularly sailed at Fishers Island with the Gallery's then-director, John Walker. By the time he replaced Walker, twenty-three years later, he had acquired some impressive credentials: a summa cum laude, Phi Beta Kappa key and M.B.A. degree from Harvard, studies with Bernard Berenson in Italy, and an M.A. at the Institute of Fine Arts at N.Y.U. His first real museum job was as Walker's assistant, a position he would keep for nine years before taking over. Now, as Washington's biggest star, he is (according to *Art News*) "articulate, a top notch public speaker, charming, witty and diplomatic," and his affluent background ("It's so much easier for Carter to wine and dine prospective donors") doesn't hurt one bit. After a divorce from his first wife, Constance Mellon, Brown married socialite Pamela Braga Drexel in 1976 in Westminster Abbey. They have two children, John Carter Brown IV (born 1977) and Elissa Lucinda Brown (born 1983). The director famous for his "patrician chutzpah" had this to say (to Russell Lynes) about the crowds who flock to the National Gallery with or without the bait of a big exhibit. "I'm not as interested in the 'visitation,' as Congress calls the number of bodies who come here, as in what they get from coming. The point is to get them to take something away with them, to have their eyes opened."

Jim Brown

"If Franco Harris is going to creep to my record, I may as well come back and creep too," said football's former ground-gaining king in the face of inevitable second placedom. In 1983 Brown accused the likeliest challenger to his statistical crown of playing at half-speed toward the end of his career, and of taking safety by running out of bounds rather than butting tacklers for the extra yard. He succeeded in not only attracting the sports spotlight again, but he voiced what he and other former players deemed was a just denunciation of the present crop of prideless, money-crazy NFL stars. However, of eventual yardage champ Walter Payton, Brown said, "He's a gladiator." Brown had made headlines when, as president of comedian Richard Pryor's Indio Productions movie company, he helped the funnyman sign a $40-million deal with Columbia Pictures. Soon, after, he was fired. Some felt Columbia prompted Brown's dismissal.

Born on St. Simeon's Island, Ga., 17 February 1936 and raised partly in Georgia and in Manhasset, N.Y., Brown (known then as Jimmy) starred at Syracuse University in track and basketball, and was All-American in football and lacrosse. He was the other Brown at Cleveland, the first being coach Paul (no relation), after whom the NFL Browns were named. Those who eclipse his long-standing record of 12,312 career yards achieved their marks in an age of 16-game seasons. Brown's came in 12-and 14-game seasons, and in two to three fewer of *those* seasons than the elongated versions his pursuers enjoyed. In his brilliant nine-year career he never missed a game.

Athletics aside, he's the veteran of some 20 acting roles, including some for former footballer-turned producer Fred Williamson. The circles around Brown's eyes are now rather pronounced on his medium brown, ruggedly handsome face, but the no-nonsense embodiment of athletic prowess is only five pounds heavier than when he boasted of his fearsome six-feet-two, 230-pound playing physique. After retiring, he organized a Small Business Administration fund, the Black Economic Union, that went under in the early '70's, and he's also managed soul singing groups and the United Athletic Association. Now fortunately in the past are the court cases for kicking a girlfriend off a balcony, forearming a policeman, and tossing a Hollywood businessman onto a street. Today he's living in the Hollywood Hills with girlfriend Kim Jones, who's the mother of his daughter (his ex-wife had three children by him), and who's 27 years his junior. One area he refuses to tread in is politics. "I believe we need certain black people that aren't under the umbrella of anybody," Brown once said. "Money and power make me free. I got to get it clear to the brothers that I can do plenty for them because I'm free."

Tina Brown

At 22 this whiz kid was given her own column in *Punch* and at 26 became editor of *Tatler* (the slick monthly that chronicles Britain's highlife), giving it a face-lift, making it "smarter, cooler and more witty." Before coming to *Tatler*, Brown was known around England for her deft writings in publications like the *New Statesman* et al. (In one of her pieces describing an acquaintance of Princess Margaret's she wrote, "Arch self-publicist Roddy Llewellyn veers between press conferences in the VIP lounge and wan statements about invasion of privacy." She quotes Llewellyn as having said, "I'll murder you if you write this down, but what's the name of that ghastly fellow who wants to ban fox-hunting? It's just another dreary Socialist plot to stop us from having fun.") Her ear for dialogue was instrumental in her having written two award-winning plays: *Under the Bamboo Tree*, produced at the Edinburgh Festival in 1973 and *Happy Yellow*, produced at the Bush Theatre in London in 1977. She was introduced to America via her "Today Show" running commentary on the June 1981 wedding of Prince Charles to Lady Diana Spencer.

Born 21 November 1953, she sailed through middle and high school with honors, finally receiving an M.A. in English from Oxford University. In 1975 she was named Most Promising Female Journalist of the Year and was awarded the Katherine Pakenham prize. She has had two books published: *Loose Talk* and *Life as a Party* ("I think parties are absolutely riveting. Jane Austin said that everything happens at parties, and she was right.") Brown, by 1984, held the august title of editor in chief of *Vanity Fair* which had its share of editorial pilots, trying to keep it a-wing after its take-off in the early 80s. She is married to Harold Evans, author and former editor of the London *Times* whose battles with owner Rupert Murdoch were recounted in his book *Good Times Bad Times*. They have a son, George Frederick.

Tony Brown

The civil rights crusader of national television uses the medium to expound his belief that mass communications can help liberate blacks from the misappropriation of their self-image. "Blacks must stop allowing themselves to be defined," Brown asserts. He also admonishes those who inadvertently bandy about concepts that perpetuate blacks' "social psychosis," saying, "We are not a minority. We are the largest segment of this pluralistic society.... We pay taxes and the portion we pay entitles us to television coverage and programming that is relevant to us and our needs." His show, now called "Tony Brown's Journal," and now back on the Public Broadcasting System, has been television's longest-running (since 1970) and more often than not the only national black public affairs program.

Brown also sweeps the country lecturing on the critical questions facing blacks today, including declaring his belief in the superiority of education at traditionally black colleges ("Every Prairie View engineering grad gets an average of 17 job offers"), and emphasizing to young blacks the importance of developing tomorrow's skills. "If we are a spiritual people, as we claim, we must put some flesh on that spirit and the flesh of American society is technology." Brown was also in the forefront in the successful effort to spur congressional legislation making Martin Luther King, Jr.'s birthday a national holiday.

Growing up in Charleston, W.Va. (born 11 April 1933), he says, "All my economic, social, educational, spiritual and pure needs were solved by black people." It wasn't until he went to Detroit, and Wayne State University, that he realized what it meant to live in a predominantly white society. Although he trained as a psychiatric social worker, he wrote a weekly newspaper column, and became "excited to find that a column . . . could cause such a stir." Brown began doing public affairs broadcasting in Detroit, and in 1970 joined PBS's "Black Journal," a magazine show resulting from the 1968 Kerner Report that singled out the media as a major agent fostering segregation. The Emmy-winning program nearly died because of cutbacks but black and white viewers lobbied for its continuation in 1972, and again in '74. The show was the focus of an FCC license revocation investigation into an Alabama public station that wouldn't air the show on racist grounds. Brown got Pepsico to sponsor the program's switch to commercial syndication in 1978, but later moved it back to PBS. In between, he's been the dean (in 1971-72) of Howard University's School of Communications where he started a yearly jobs conference to get more blacks in the industry. The whirlwind producer-publisher-lecturer-columnist also hosted D.C.'s "Daybreak" on the NBC affiliate. Between stops the father of one says, "I'm interested in what I'm doing. . . . When people get involved in what they're doing, time takes on a different meaning."

Jackson Browne

"Writing for me is always something to do when there's nothing else. Not out of boredom—but to continue the inner dialogues." In an interview in *People*, Browne talks about his music. "People always want to say what I think my songs are all about. But I don't even think about it. I think I'll become a man of mystery." Browne, with his own inimitable style, has been an intriguing recording artist to observe during the past decade.

The good-looking, generation gap crossover guitarist was born 9 October 1948. His father, Dixieland pianist Clyde Browne, established his son's musical roots. Jackson received his first folk guitar in high school and soon he was playing in clubs around California. He migrated to New York's Greenwich Village for a brief stay, then returned to the West Coast rock scene. Word of Browne's creative writing style, along with his guitar playing, attracted the right musical circles. He was back-up guitarist for the late night singer Nico and composed original songs for her *Chelsea Girl* album. He had songs recorded by The Nitty Gritty Dirt Band, Tom Rush and Linda Rondstadt while working on his own albums, whose titles include *Jackson Browne* (1972), *For Everyman* (1973), *Running on Empty* (1978), *No Nukes* (1980), *Lawyers in Love* (1983) and *Lives in the Balance* (1986).

Tragedy struck Browne when his wife Phyllis, a former fashion model, committed suicide in 1976. This sudden event left Browne a single father to their young son, Ethan (born August, 1974). Determined to stick with a pre-scheduled concert tour, Browne brought Ethan along with him on the road. Proving too much to handle (bus trips, night tours, hotel rooms), Ethan was eventually sent home to Hollywood with a nanny to continue nursery school. A deep love developed between father and son; Jackson writes in his song "The Only Child": "Let the disappointment pass. . . . Let the laughter fill your glass."

Jackson Browne has always been active in lending his talents to good causes—he raised funds for California politicians Tom Hayden and Jerry Brown, he's played benefits to oppose nuclear power, and was involved with the Nelson Mandela tribute in June, 1987. He has remained unmarried; his steady companion is actress Daryl Hannah.

John Browning

Inspired, insightful and gifted, he "can come close to perfection as one would hope to hear in this world." In addition, he is a workhorse at the keyboard, keeping himself fit for a grueling schedule of concerts, averaging more than one out of every four days year round. A member of the jet-set generation of pianists, John Browning is as much at home in European concert halls as those of the U.S. and once played both—at the Lewisohn Stadium in New York and at the Festival of Two Worlds in Spoleto, Italy—within a span of 36 hours.

Born in Denver, 23 May 1933, in his early years Browning was described as "a golden boy in a golden age of pianists," and he comes by his brilliance naturally. Both of his parents were professional musicians—his father a violinist, his mother a pianist. Browning began to show an interest in the piano when he was three and made his debut in his hometown playing a Mozart concerto at the age of ten. He was spared the stresses and strains of life as a prodigy, however, for his parents insisted on a "normal" childhood, with music just one of many interests. He spent two years majoring in English literature and music at Occidental College and only then did a scholarship lead to study with the famous Rosina Lhevinne at Juilliard. While there, he won the $2,000 Steinway Centennial Award in a nationwide contest in 1954. In 1955 the Leventritt Award entitled him to solo engagements with several major American orchestras, including the New York Philharmonic—with which he also made his Carnegie Hall debut in 1956. He subsequently captured second prize in Belgium's prestigious Queen Elizabeth International Piano Competition and received many other honors in the U.S. A gold medal in the Brussels International Piano Competition opened more doors to the virtuoso. He was also signed to a recording contract and his music appears on RCA and Capitol among other labels—testament to his versatility. In the era of piano specialists, he is one artist who refuses to confine his playing within any particular stylistic boundaries. Because of Browning, the piano repertoire has been enriched by the Samuel Barber concerto (written especially for him). Beginning with his performance of the world premiere of this piece in 1962, it has since become the most frequently performed concerto of the second part of the 20th century, winning the Pulitzer Prize for music in 1963.

On foreign tours, Browning has become a champion recitalist; he belongs to that select group of American pianists who are equally successful in the U.S., Europe, Mexico and Russia. His repertory is a wide one though Browning is especially inclined towards contemporary music, demonstrating a "virtuoso scope." A highlight of the 1982-83 television season was Browning's appearance in the special, "Mikhail Baryshnikov, the Dancer and the Dance," which concentrated on a new ballet set to the music of the Barber piano concerto.

Called "one of the most sensitive and poetic artists America has produced" *(Los Angeles Times)*, Browning resides in a luxurious sound-proof penthouse overlooking the East River. "Whenever I'm away from the piano," he says, "I'm itching and nervous. Not working makes me feel useless—as if nobody loved or needed me—as if my purpose in life wasn't being carried out."

Susan Brownmiller

A self-described "radical" feminist, she raised the hackles of some and the consciousness of many with her probing analysis of rape in her 1975 bestseller *Against Our Will*. Described by *Time* magazine as "a kind of Whole Earth Catalogue of man's inhumanity to women," the book bluntly asserts that rape "is nothing more or less than a conscious intimidation by which all men keep all women in fear." Nearly a decade later she turned her exacting eye on the ways of women and wrote *Feminity*. The term itself she refers to as "a strategy of appeasement." She wrote, "It is in order to appeal to men that the yielded autonomy and contrived manifestations of helplessness become second nature as expressions of good manners and sexual good will."

Susan Brownmiller was born in Brooklyn on 15 February 1935. She attended Cornell University and pursued an early career as an actress in Manhattan before embarking on an ambitious and often controversial career as a freelance writer. She held staff positions on publications as well, including the *Village Voice*. Her interest in the burgeoning women's movement produced a feminist slant in much of her work, and led her to undertake a profile of Congresswoman Shirley Chisholm, which she developed into a 1971 biography. A passionate activist and piercingly intelligent spokeswoman for feminist causes, she became a familiar face in the front lines of demonstrations and displays of female unity. She was the driving force behind the formation of Women Against Pornography, a group that sees definite connection between the spread of pornography and the proliferation of violence against women. WAP frequently takes its message to the heart of red-light districts in cities across the country, drawing media attention and provoking much debate.

Brownmiller's first novel, *Waverly Place* (1989), deals with the frightening topic of child abuse. As she says in her forward, "Early one morning in November, 1987, the silence was broken on a quiet residential street in Greenwich Village. In response to an emergency call, police and paramedics entered a dark apartment and found an unconscious six-year-old girl. Three days later she died."

Dave Brubeck

"I know Dave Brubeck can swing," admits one jazz critic who never took the pianist's career seriously. "I'm sure of that because most of the times I've heard him he's *not* swinging." The pianist, who has composed over 250 songs and copped nearly every award a jazz or popular musician can claim, learned years ago to ignore carping critics and to play music people can tap their toes to. That's not to say toe-tapping to Brubeck's catchy tunes is easily done. Brubeck's claim to fame, indeed, is the fact that his quartet helped introduce esoteric time signatures to jazz public. His *Time Out* album in 1960 became the first modern jazz gold record, fulfilling a destiny *Time* had anticipated six years earlier, when it placed Brubeck on its cover.

Ironically, the California-born musician (6 December 1920) is perhaps most closely associated with a song written by the late, longtime saxophonist in his band, Paul Desmond. That song—"Take Five"—featured an enthusiastic romp through a number based on a five-beat meter. Nevertheless, the success of that song launched the quartet on a globe-trotting tour that lasted from 1960 until December, 1967—virtually a millenium in jazz's world of impromptu jam sessions and one-night stands.

The next several years represented a period of transition for the composer-performer. He continued to tour with a new saxophonist, baritone man Gerry Mulligan, and occasionally Desmond returned in a cameo role, inevitably honoring requests for "Take Five." Brubeck began to devote more time to composing, and his output now includes a body of compositions that blend classical formats (including oratorios) with jazz. He performs with symphonies and takes the piano chair, and frequently tours with a quartet made up entirely of Brubecks: son Chris plays trombone and bass, son Danny plays drums, and son Darius (named for composer Darius Milhaud) is a chip off the old block at the keyboard. Married to the former Iola Whitlock, Brubeck homesteads in Connecticut not far from Yale, where he occasionally teaches as the Duke Ellington fellow.

Robert Brustein

Once reputed to be "the most important drama critic in America," he founded repertory theaters at Yale and later Harvard. His Harvard-affiliated American Repertory Theater, started in the late 1970s, took root in the Boston area, attracting high-caliber artists and producing some plays that moved quickly to Broadway (Jules Feiffer's *Grown Ups,* Marsha Norman's Pulitzer Prize-winning *Night Mother*). But success posed some integrity problems for this former dean of Yale School of Drama, whose ambition was to create a resident professional acting ensemble performing new plays and classics in rotating repertory. A longtime critic of the commercial theater establishment, he feels uneasy about his theater being used as a tryout house for Broadway. Marsha Norman (who took her second play, *Traveler in the Dark,* to A.R.T.) scoffed at Brustein's fears. "Anyone who comes here has raging battles with Bob about this. It's impossible to do new work commercially. It has to be done through the energies of the resident theaters." To maintain his ideal of high-quality resident acting company, Brustein admits he needs lots more money. "Every single cultural institution in this country has a deficit of some amount and has to raise money every year—a function of the fact that our government does not support the arts the way most civilized nations do, and the private sector has not yet picked up the baton. The amazing thing is we're all alive, and we in particular are very healthy."

Born in New York City, 21 April 1927, Robert Brustein collected degrees from Amherst (B.A.). Yale (M.A.) and Columbia (Ph.D.) and then, as a teacher, ventured into the academic groves of Cornell, Vassar, and Columbia before becoming dean at Yale. He transformed Yale's graduate drama school into a conservatory, founded the Yale Repertory Theater—and moved on to Cambridge, Mass.

As a drama critic, his observations on the contemporary theater ruffled more than a few feathers. But his books *(The Theater of Revolt: Studies in the Modern Drama,* 1964; *Seasons of Discontent: Dramatic Opinions,* 1959-65; and *Who Needs Theatre,* (1987) are now classroom classics. He took off against campus and Broadway radicals in his much-debated 1971 *Revolution as Theater,* declaring, "I am skeptical about the radical theater's power to affect anybody except those who are already converted.... Many of today's 'revolutionaries' are play-acting without knowing it. I do not think any significant change can come about in America until we can develop a much greater sense of reality." His A.R.T., one of a shrinking handful of resident acting companies performing in rotating repertory, has performed new contemporary plays and also classics in experimental, often controversial productions (Chekov's *Three Sisters,* Gogol's *Inspector General*).

Art Buchwald

Needler of the mighty in the Washington establishment, this roundish cigar-smoking pixie has been called "a one-man conglomerate." His column appears in more than 530 newspapers, he has published more than two dozen books, written a political satire for Broadway called *Sheep on the Runway,* and is a popular lecturer. One of the most widely read columnists in official Washington, he has one big advantage over other reporters of the capital scene. "I never talk to anybody," he says, puffing on one of his daily six to eight cigars. "Facts just get in my way." It usually takes him less than an hour to bang out a column, but his quick work earned him a Pulitzer in 1982 for "Outstanding Commentary."

Born in Mount Vernon, N.Y., 20 October 1925. Art Buchwald (pronounced *Buck-wald*) was raised in six foster homes as a child and dropped out of high school at 16 to join the Marine Corps in World War II. After the war he spent some time at the University of Southern California but dropped out to go to France because he'd heard that "in Paris, the streets are lined with beds." He began newspaper work in 1948 as a $25-a-week movie reviewer on the Paris edition of the New York *Harold Tribune* and achieved celebrity status when he began a column called "Paris After Dark." Switching from Paris to Washington in 1962, he quickly attracted a new following by delivering such deadpan scoops as the one that J. Edgar Hoover was "a mythical person first thought up by the *Reader's Digest."* Married to Pennsylvanian Ann McGarry, whom he met in Paris ("We both had the same black market money changer"), he's the father of three adopted children, Joel, Connie and Jennifer. Buchwald, who lives in northwest Washington, prefers recreation not requiring "physical exercise. I think exercise is dangerous. People should stay in the horizontal position as much as possible."

William F. Buckley, Jr.

"I don't think it's correct to say that conservatives have taken over America. . . . The thing we take considerable satisfaction from is that the avenues of thought have opened up a great deal," declares this master of the refined riposte who has used his pen (in his column, more than 20 books, and hundreds of articles) and television show (the Emmy-winning "Firing Line") to articulate with polysyllabic assurance the principles that helped elect his friend Ronald Reagan President of the United States, an historic event for which William Frank Buckley, Jr., deserves considerable credit. The indefatigable "classic patrician," a style that *Newsweek* observes "has seldom revealed itself in this country since the election of Andrew Jackson in 1828," is the most visible of the media stars of the right (George Will, William Safire, etc.) who have successfully challenged the notion that "the conservative is someone who spends his leisure time at baseball games or in front of a television set, whereas the liberal is thought to spend his time going to the ballet or the library." Founder and president of America's foremost conservative journal of opinion, *National Review*, author of scores of articles for such publications as *The Atlantic, Harper's, Esquire* and *Playboy,* "On the Right" columnist (syndicated in more than 300 newspapers), Buckley has achieved his greatest visibility via the tube with "Firing Line," which first aired in 1966 and has been a PBS fixture since 1971. Among the guests who have voluntarily submitted to Buckley's well-honed barbs are Reagan, Margaret Thatcher, Edward Heath, Jimmy Carter, Valery Giscard d'Estaing and Gerald Ford (mostly when out of office; it's Buckley's conviction that sitting heads of state "are the poorest guests . . . they're much too guarded"). Apolitical viewers may remember him as the host of the prize-winning PBS miniseries "Brideshead Revisited," written by one of his literary heroes and fellow "old-fashioned" Catholic Evelyn Waugh. (Buckley has used as a proof of God's existence the fastidious Waugh's death of a heart attack just before the Church adopted the shake-hands-with-your-neighbor part of the Mass—"an instance of divine mercy.") The Bach-lover (his sumptuous Manhattan apartment was the site in 1985 of one of the official musicales commemorating the baroque master's tricentennial), schooner skipper (a memorable voyage was chronicled in 1982 in *Atlantic High*) and avid skier (when at his Swiss home), found a brand new audience in 1976 when his handsome and sexy gentleman spy (and alter ego?) Blackford Oakes made his debut in *Saving the Queen* (Elizabeth II and a friend of Blackie, who knows everyone), followed by a string of bestselling thrillers: *Stained Glass; Who's On First; Marco Polo, If You Can; The Story of Henri Tod* and 1985's *See You Later, Alligator* (supposedly Che Guevera's parting words to Blackie).

It was to William Frank Buckley, Sr., who struck oil in Mexico, and Aloise Buckley, a southern belle (the inspiration for her son's purring drawl), that young Bill was born 24 November 1925 in New York. After early schooling in France and England, Buckley returned to America for prep school, the army, and—much to its later chagrin—Yale (chairman of the *Yale Daily News*, Class Day Orator, Skull & Bones—the works). Then in 1951 came youthful notoriety and bestsellerdom with *God & Man at Yale*, a polemic against his *alma mater* which a fellow Eli called "dishonest in its use of fact . . . and a discredit to the author." No less controversial was *McCarthy and His Enemies* (1954), a spirited defense of the late Wisconsin red-hunting senator. Other books include *Up From Liberalism, Rumbles Left and Right, The Unmaking of a Mayor* (about his 1966 run for Mayor of New York, the most memorable aspect of which was his reply to a reporter who asked what he would have done if he'd won: "Demand a recount."), *The Jeweler's Eye, Inveighing We Will Go, A Hymnal: The Controversial Arts, Right Reason, High Jinx, Racing Through Paradise* and *Moongoose.* Buckley is married to the former Patricia Taylor, the tall, striking and witty giver of some of NYC's best parties and the most sought-after benefit chairman in town. The couple have a married son, Christopher, also a writer.

Jimmy Buffet

"One night they put a price on the sunset and that got the whole world shakin'," writes Jimmy Buffet in his song "Prince of the Tides." This tropical rocker, known for his Caribbean soul shirts, salt-water music, environmental interests and populist philosophies is actually a well-rounded man.

Born on Christmas 1946, in Pascagoula, Mississippi, to James Delaney and Loraine Peets, Jimmy's early years were mixed with education and adventure. He graduated from the University of Southern Mississippi in 1969 with a BS in History and Journalism. Also developing his own style on guitar, Buffet traveled to Key West, Florida, to get his sea legs wet while performing in local bars, such as The Green Parrot and Sloppy Joe's (Ernest Hemingway's old hangout.) His first album *A White Sport Coat and a Pink Crustacean*, was released in 1973, introducing his Nashville-meets-Caribbean sound. Rumor has it that Buffet's friend Tony introduced him to his first margarita, and after jotting down the drink's name on a coctail napkin, it's been one happy hour after another.

Popular gold and platinum albums followed: *Changes in Latitudes, Changes in Attitudes* (1977), *Son of a Son of a Sailor* (1978), *You Had To Be There* (1978), *Volcano* (1979), plus more song twists of sea expressions included on *Coconut Telegraph* (1981), *One Particular Harbour* (1983), *Riddles in the Sand* (1984), *Floridays* (1986) and *Hot Water* (1988). On a wonderful wave of success, Buffet continues expanding his career. He wrote a children's book *The Jolly Mon* (1988), with his young daughter Savannah. He's the editor of his own "Coconut Telegraph Newsletter," wrote a screenplay for the long-awaited "Margaritaville" project, and opened a clothing store and restaurant, both aptly titled "Margaritaville." Buffet has been married to the same woman, Jane Slagsvol, since August, 1977; the couple have one daughter, Savannah Jane (born 1979). An environmentalist, the sailor/singer is active raising funds to save the Key West Salt Ponds and he is chairman of the Save the Manatee Committee.

Genevieve Bujold

"Her hair is shiny and gleaming as a stallion's mane," wrote Rex Reed in 1976. "Her eyes big and brown as chocolate jawbreakers, her tiny mouth a rosebud of surprise. Packed into her 5-foot, 4-inch doll's frame is an intriguing mixture of purloined innocence, succulent sexuality and guerilla warfare." Also, for many recent years, a resistance to work before the cameras. After enchanting audiences in such well-received films of the 60's as *Anne of a Thousand Days* (for which she was nominated for an Oscar in 1969) and *King of Hearts* (the antiwar parable starring Alan Bates, set in a French insane asylum, which has become a cult favorite), she opted during the early '80s for motherhood over movies. She told Joanne Mattera of *Women's Wear Daily* in 1984, "I'm an actress—I'm good at it—but I'm also a mother. Being at home with the kids is what I'm most comfortable doing." Result: rather slim pickings in the way of movie-making, limited to a TV version of *Caesar and Cleopatra* (in which she played the African queen to Alec Guinness's noblest Roman of them all), *Coma*, and such turkeys as *Monsignor* and the low-budget *Choose Me*.

A busdriver's daughter, born in Montreal, 1 July 1942, Genevieve Bujold was reared in the French-Canadian tradition. ("For twelve years I was in convent school. Everything was very *comme il faut*, very strict, but I remained myself.") Encouraged by the sisters to depart after she was caught reading an outlawed volume of Marcel Pagnol's *Fanny*, she studied at the Province of Quebec Conservatory of Drama but dropped out before graduation when she was offered a job touring with the Green Curtain theater company. While performing in France, she was "discovered" by the mother of director Alain Resnais who promptly cast her in *La Guerre Est Finie*, the 1966 film that launched her screen career.

Ever the rebel, she married (in 1967) a divorced Protestant English-Canadian, Paul Almond, who directed her in *Isabel* and *The Act of the Heart*. Later, after spending three months filming near Malibu following their divorce, Bujold decided to settle and build there. Recent movies include *The Suspect* (1987), *Dead Ringers r(1988)*, *The Moderns* (1988) and *Thank You Satan* (1988).

Fernando Bujones

When teenager Fernando Bujones returned to America in July of 1974 as the first and only American to win the gold medal at the Varna (Bulgaria) International Ballet Competition, he found that his triumph was all but eclipsed by the excitement surrounding the defection a month earlier of Mikhail Baryshnikov. "Baryshnikov has the publicity, but I have the talent!" he pouted to Anna Kisselgoff in the *New York Times*. Verbal sass coupled with a swaggering cockiness made him "ballet's bad boy" in the mid '70s, a title he began to shed only around 1980, at the time of his marriage to Marcia Kubitschek (the daughter of a former president of Brazil; a daughter, Alejandra, was born in 1983; two stepdaughters via her prior marriage). He took a more reflective tone then (to John Gruen in the *Times*): "You see, I am no longer the teenager living with his mom and his cousin, but a man who has come to realize that there are certain nuances in life which are perhaps even more important than ballet dancing."

Generally acknowledged to be America's greatest native-born classical dancer, Bujones was born in Miami, Fla., 9 March 1955 ("My birthday is between Nijinsky's and Nureyev's . . . I've always believed I had something special working for me.") to Cuban parents who divorced a year later. At five, he went with his mother to Cuba, and three years later was enrolled at the Academia de Ballet Alicia Alonso in a desperate attempt by his dancer mother to build up his frail frame and encourage a virtually non-existent appetite. In 1965 the family returned to Miami, where ten-year old Fernando was spotted by New York City Ballet principal dancer Jacques D'Amboise, who enthusiastically recommended him to his company's School of American Ballet. In his fifth year as a full scholarship student. 15-year-old Bujones inspired Clive Barnes to comment on his "remarkable promise" in the school's annual workshop production, adding, "He has a style that is unmistakable. His feet are perfect and his manner has the authority of a born classicist." After graduation, he declined George Balanchine's invitation to join NYCB and opted instead to sign with the American Ballet Theatre, whose classical repertory of full-length ballets he preferred. In 1972, just a few months after joining ABT's corps de ballet, Natalia Makarova requested the 17-year old as her partner in a *Don Quixote*, but the company vetoed the proposition, citing his youth and inexperience. In less than a year, however, he was performing solos to enthusiastic public and critical response. In May of 1973 he was the youngest dancer ever to partner Dame Margot Fonteyn, in the romantic one-act ballet *Les Sylphides*, and in 1974 he made his long-awaited European debut in an all-star benefit performance in London, where he was hailed by usually reserved British critics. In Varna that July he chose to compete in the senior division (against 20 to 28-year olds), and ABT rewarded his gold medal performance by raising him to principal dancer status ("probably the youngest principal in the world"). He also got to partner Makarova in the *Don Quixote pas de deux* and scored successes in a series of demanding roles such as Balanchine's *Theme and Variations*. Still, the spotlight shone on Baryshnikov, prompting another petulant observation from Bujones: "I do consider myself just as good . . . and since I am seven years younger . . . I am in that fact better than him." The two have since formed a professional alliance, but that has not prevented Bujones from voicing his opinions as to the relative merits of American *versus* Russian dancers: "I think these Russians will have to learn form *us*. We are no longer the Pilgrims, but are beginning to teach the rest of the world what ballet dancing is all about." Future projects include more books (*Fernando Bujones* came out in the fall of 1984), more videotapes (a big seller), and more ballets. His first major choreographic work, *Grand Pas Romantique*, entered ABT's repertory in spring 1985.

Grace Bumbry

"I realize I have a great gift that I just can't put aside. I know it sounds lofty and corny, but I believe that each of us is put here for a reason, a purpose—to perform a service for humanity." Mezzo-soprano turned soprano Grace Bumbry, who skyrocketed to international fame in the 1960s as "the Black Venus of Bayreuth," makes good use of her God-given gift in concerts the world over. (In Europe, according to Bumbry, she is "the number one lady singer.") Bumbry has captivated audiences in her performances of the most famous operas—*Tosca*, *Norma*, *Medea* and in her New York City Opera debut, in Verdi's *Nabucco*, which Bumbry called "the hardest opera I have ever done." Critics have likened her to Maria Callas, which flatters the diva "to no end; I'm her greatest fan." The tall, regal beauty gives over 80 performances each year noting that "the older and more famous you are the more you have to come through for yourself, for your audience. The responsibility is enormous." A mainstay of the Metropolitan Opera House since 1972, Bumbry starred in the Met's historic 1985 production of *Porgy and Bess*.

The daughter of a railway clerk in St. Louis (born 4 January 1937), Grace Bumbry was drawn to a career in music by her girlhood admiration for the black contralto Marian Anderson. She started voice training at 15 and won her first recognition from the outside world when, at 17, she won a radio talent contest. Because of her race, however, she was denied entry into the all-white St. Louis Institute of Music. When a TV show publicized her plight, offers of college scholarships came flooding in. While Bumbry was at Boston University the legendary Lotte Lehmann heard her sing and whisked her off to the Music Academy of the West in Santa Barbara. It was there that Bumbry began her operatic training. With Lehmann's encouragement, Grace made her operatic debut at the Paris Opera in 1960 in a performance that was so impressive that she was invited to star in the famed Bayreuth Festival in a new production of Wagner's *Tannhouser*. Debuts the world over followed, including her New York recital debut at Carnegie Hall in the fall of 1962, for which she was praised by the *New York Times* as a "superbly gifted artist with a gorgeous clear ringing voice." Home is Lugano, Switzerland, where the diva has lived for the last 25 years. She also keeps a Manhattan pied-a-terre. Bumbry jogs four miles three times a week and swims in her indoor pool each day. Her social life revolves around friends outside the cliqueish opera world and her slightly arrogant attitude towards colleagues ahs earned her such derogatory epithets as "Her Grace" and "La Bumbarina." Her nine-year marriage to a German tenor ended in the 70s (she blames the breakup on his wanting her to remain a mezzo-soprano). The super-successful Bumbry admits she is not as driven as she once was—"I used to be terribly ambitious—I mean *really* ambitious—I kind of miss that drive. I wonder whether it's because of my age or because I don't need to be ambitious? Perhaps I'm just mellowing." Grace entered a new phase of her career when she joined Frank Sinatra in a Gala Benefit and sang the pop ballad "Natalie." She followed this appearance with a concert at the Ford's Theatre Gala for the President. This event was recorded, adding to the growing collection of Bumbry classical recordings, including the first stereo LP of *Carmen* (in the original 1975 Opera Comique version) and the complete Bayreuth *Tannhauser*.

Warren E. Burger

When President Nixon designated Warren Earl Burger as the successor to retiring chief Justice Earl Warren, he was hoping—as were conservatives everywhere—that the liberal direction of the Warren Court would be reversed. No such U-turn occurred, however. Most Court-watchers point to the central, "swing" votes as the reason that the Burger court has been decidedly unpredictable in ideology. One Washington wag said Burger has done more for dog food than for ideology, referring to Burger's celebrated jibes at lawyers who advertise: "lawyers (are) advertising in newspapers, on radio and on television in much the same way that automobiles, dog food, cosmetics and hair tonic are touted." Under Burger's gavel, the Court has been viewed as "more umpire than ideological player"—a scenario that has pleased some and irritated others. Says Professor G. Edward White of the University of Virginia Law School: "It is a floating court, with no Justices continually carrying the balance of power." Adds a journalist: "The court is pulled first thisaway, then thataway in a shifting tug-of-war as the Justices align themselves differently on almost every case."

Burger—a rock-solid Midwesterner (born 17 September 1907 of Swiss-German descent in St. Paul, Minn.)—could be Central Casting's dream choice for the chair. Elevated to the Court while an obscure federal Court of Appeals judge, Burger's background as an Eisenhower supporter gave cheer to conservatives; he had headed Ike's Department of Justice's Civil Division in the mid-1950s. On the other hand, his credentials also included hands-on work in his home state's civil rights struggle. Then an attorney and law professor, Burger was in the forefront of efforts to improve relations between St. Paul's black and Hispanic minorities.

If Burger emerged as ideologically unwavering on any issue, it was law and order: "The seeming anxiety of judges to protect every accused person from every consequence of his voluntary utterances [via the Mallory and Miranda decisions] is giving rise to myriad rules, subrules, variations, and exceptions, which even the most sophisticated lawyers and judges are taxed to follow . . . guilt or innocence becomes irrelevant in the criminal trial as we founder in a morass of artificial rules poorly conceived and often impossible of application." Burger's opinions are, of course, required reading for attorneys and law students across the land, but his own early reading consisted of Horatio Alger stories. He himself fits the success-story mold. Born to a railroad cargo inspector-traveling salesman father and an old fashioned German mother, Burger started earning pocket money by delivering newspapers at the age of nine. He had to turn down an offer from Princeton because of family financial strains. Instead he took extension courses at the University of Minnesota (he married former classmate Elvera Stromberg in 1933; one son, one daughter) and received his LL.B. magna cum laude in 1931 from the St. Paul College of Law. (He paid his way selling insurance.) A gourmet and connoisseur of fine wines, Burger was described at the time of his appointment (by *New York Times* columnist James Reston) as "experienced, industrious, middle-class, middle-aged, middle-of-the-road, Middle-Western, Presbyterian, and handsome."

Anthony Burgess

Easily one of Britain's most prolific writers (some two dozen books in half as many years, plus a constant stream of articles, essays, and reviews), he's been described as "an Elizabethan character: an unrefined Englishman, running over with creative energy, enjoying his own vitality without concern about being vulgar." "He eats and drinks as he writes," wrote American reporter Anthony Lewis, "with unfinicky pleasure." Says Burgess himself: "I'm a pub man. I like pubs best because people don't talk about your work. . . . I don't like literary people . . . they're jealous . . . they want to know how much you're earning."

For many years John Anthony Burgess (who has also published under the pen name Joseph Kell) earned precious little. Manchester born (15 February 1917), he enjoyed, by his own account, "very little love" as a child. Local schools provided "no intellectual companionship," he remembers, "no intellectual stimulants." Music in those days was his first love ("I regret that no one ever refers to me as a composer. I am always called a writer who happens to compose music, never a composer who happens to write."), but he wound up studying literature at Manchester University and eventually became a schoolteacher. Then, "raging, fed up" with attempts to exist on less than $1,500 a year in a Branbury grammar school, in 1954 Burgess took a teaching post with the Colonial Service in Malaya and there began to write. "Maybe it was the climate," he suggests. "I sweated the words out." He also fell ill and returned to England where he was told he had a brain tumor and would not live a year. That, he now recalls, was "rather exhilarating;" at once "I decided to write as many books as I could so there would be something for my widow." In one year he turned out five novels. ("Rather a lot," one Burgess critic sniffed. "The sneer of the impotent," Burgess shot back.) In any case, the mysterious tumor apparently vanished and Burgess went on writing. Subsequent books (*A Clockwork Orange, Tremor of Intent, One-Hand Clapping* and *Enderby*) won favor for their black humor, their "insight into the disorientation of modern man," and their display of high-level linguistic pyrotechnics.

"I see myself as a creature of gloom and sobriety," Burgess says, "but my books reflect a sort of clown." Reflecting not at all clownishly but very publicly on the inequities of English taxation, and his conclusions that Britain "does not like her writers very much," Burgess and his second wife Liliana Macellari (his first wife died in 1968) removed themselves in the late '60s to a residence on Malta. Burgess has much to say about the evolution of the novel in the list he compiled of 99 best. "The popular novel of our day provides much technical information; it often depends on research more than insight; its clashes are physical; its character interest is minimal." Although his own writings aren't on the list, he says by way of self assessment, "I think I know my own aims. . . . We want to entertain, surprise and present the preoccupations of real human beings." Apparently, those endeavors are very much in sync with today's readers. Recent works include *The Pianoplayers* (1986), *But Do Blondes Prefer Gentlemen?* (1986), *Little Wilson and Big God* (1987) and *Any Old Iron* (1989).

Carol Burnett

"How many people do you know who earn a lot of money by crossing their eyes and taking pratfalls?" asked Carol Burnett, who was born on 26 April 1933 in San Antonio, Texas, where her father managed a movie theater. ("I was almost born during the matinee of *Rasputin and the Empress*.") Because her parents were chronically alcoholic, she was sent at age eight to L.A., where she and her younger sister were reared by their grandmother. After Hollywood H.S. she enrolled in a theater arts course at UCLA and was briefly married to fellow actor Don Saroyan.

Later, living at the Rehearsal club in N.Y. and scrounging for jobs, she organized *The Rehearsal Club Revue of 1955*, which resulted in 13 weeks as the girlfriend of Jerry Mahoney, the dummy on ventriloquist Paul Winchell's TV show. In 1957 she appeared on the Jack Parr show singing, "I Made a Fool of Myself over John Foster Dulles," which led to an engagement on the Garry Moore show, on which she appeared regularly from 1959-1962. In 1959 she was cast as Princess Winifred the Woebegone in the off-Broadway musical *Once Upon a Mattress*, which moved to Broadway, where it ran for a year. When she left Moore, CBS-TV signed her to a ten-year million-dollar contract, which resulted in the tremendously successful "Julie (Andrews) and Carol at Carnegie Hall" and "Calamity Jane," the first TV special to try out before a live audience.

In 1963 (the year of her film debut in *Who's Been Sleeping in My Bed?*) she married Moore's executive producer, Joe Hamilton. They have three daughters: Carrie, Jody and Erin. There were also eight step-children from Hamilton's previous marriage, all of whom she took in her stride, calling herself "activity director of Camp Hamilton." The Hamiltons divorced in the early '80s.

In 1964 she returned to Broadway in the musical *Fade Out-Fade In*, while simultaneously taping the TV series "The Entertainers." Both projects were plagued with injuries, ill health, lawsuits, and breach-of-contract charges, all of which were dropped when she announced that she was pregnant. Burnett bounced back in 1965-66 with the special "Carol and 2" with Lucille Ball and Zero Mostel. From 1966-77 she was hostess-star of "The Carol Burnett Show," the longest-running musical-comedy series in TV history and the winner of 22 Emmys. Her other TV specials include "Carol and Company" with Rock Hudson, "Julie and Carol at the Palace" and, in 1972, a 90-minute version of *Once Upon a Mattress*. In a change of image, she starred in the dramatic Vietnam-theme TV film, "Friendly Fire" ('79). For HBO she co-starred with Elizabeth Taylor in "Best Friends" ('83). That year she played Miss Hannigan in the film version of the musical *Annie*, was named by *Good Houskeeping* magazine as one of the world's ten most admired women, and successfully sued the *National Enquirer* for libel. Her other theatrical films include: *Pete 'n' Tillie* ('72), *The Front Page* ('74), *A Wedding* ('77), *HEALTH* ('79-release delayed) and *The Four Seasons* ('81). She played opposite her daughter Carrie Hamilton in a television movie, "Hostage" (1987), and published her autobiography, *One More Time*, in 1986.

She's frank; about her parents' fatal alcoholism, her daughter Carries' successful battle with drugs, and her early '80s osteotomy—a surgical operation she (and her daughter Jody) had to relieve headaches and improve her recessed chin and overbite ("what my family used to call the Burnett lower lip"). The physical results were remarkable. "And you know what's the greatest thing of all?" she marvels. "Feeling the rain on my chin for the first time."

On being a celebrity: "I certainly like it, (but) I don't really think about it. It was a long time in coming; it will go away. Everything goes away. So I don't dwell on it." In 1985 she was inducted into the Television Academy Hall of Fame.

George Burns

"I've got all these age jokes," he deadpans, "and I've got to use them—they're funny. Like when I talk about becoming a country singer and I say, 'Why shouldn't I be a country singer? I'm older than most countries.'" After 85 years in show business, the comic with the cigar, toupee and often risqué jokes is still at the top of his form. In his debut as a dramatic actor in *The Sunshine Boys* at the age of 79, he won an Oscar. At 81, he played God for the first time on screen; at 84, he launched a career as a country singer; at 87, he published his "ultimate diet, sex and exercise book," *How to Live to be 100-Or More*.

Born Nathan Birnbaum, one of 13 children, on 20 January 1896, George Burns launched his career at the age of seven in the PeeWee Quartet, a foursome of Lower East Side youngsters who sang on street corners, in saloons, in front of theaters, and wherever a passed hat would bring a few pennies. Before he was 20 he had been a trick roller skater, dance teacher, and vaudeville comedian. ("In those days, a 'switch' was when you took a gag out of *College Humor* and said you got it out of *Whiz Bang*. Even the suit I wore was stolen from another comic.") He met Gracie Allen in 1923 and the two were partners on the vaudeville circuit for three years before deciding to become partners for life (two adopted children, Sandra and Ronnie). As the team of Burns and Allen, they broke virtually every record in the business until Gracie retired in 1958. (She died in 1964.) George made funny as a single for a season on NBC-TV and since then has worked busily in guestshots and clubs as well as films. (He's made, so far, three *Oh, God* comedies.)

Burns admits that he *is* slowing down in a few respects. "My cuticles," he confesses, "are not what they used to be." And when he smokes a cigar, "the smoke rings are smaller." But over-all, things are fine. In 1982 *Harper's Bazaar* ranked him as one of six of "America's Sexiest Bachelors"—a step up from being a mere "sex symbol," which is what the *New York Times* called him when he was 86. In 1985 he returned to television as the host of the anthology series, "George Burns' Comedy Week," in 1987 he starred in the film, *Eighteen Again*, and in 1988 he published his touching story *Gracie: A Love Letter;* a special home video, *George Burns: His Wit and Wisdom* was scheduled for 1989 distribution.

James MacGregor Burns

Political leadership, particularly at the highest level, is the subject of analysis for this professor of political science, who believes "that Presidents—all Presidents—should be held to account." He was first acclaimed as a perspicacious student of the presidency with the publication of his study of F.D.R. entitled *The Lion and the Fox* (1956), which was followed with *Roosevelt: The Solider of Freedom* (1970). In 1971, he received the Pulitzer Prize and the National Book Award for history and was awarded the Woodrow Wilson Prize for his Roosevelt biographies. Other presidents who have come under his scrutiny are John F. Kennedy (*A Political Profile*, 1960) and Lyndon Johnson (*To Heal and to Build*, 1968). Examination has also fallen on those following political footpaths: *Edward Kennedy and The Camelot Legacy* (1976), *Leadership* (1978) and *The Power to Lead* (1984). Volume I in a prospective trilogy entitled *The American Experiment* was *The Vineyard of Liberty* (1982), which lucidly explicated the political and intellectual history of the United States from the Constitutional Convention in 1787 to the Emancipation Proclamation in 1863. This effort was accorded the Christopher Award in 1983.

Born 3 August 1918, James MacGregor Burns has served in the Democratic Party since F.D.R's second presidential campaign in 1936. A delegate to the 1952, 1956, 1960 and 1964 Democratic national conventions, he unsuccessfully ran for a Congressional seat in 1958 ("It was probably the least satisfying experience in my life. My education was complete the night I lost"). A combat historian (1943-46), he participated in the invasions of Saipan, Guam and Okinawa and returned to teach political science at Williams College in Massachusetts, his alma mater.

First married to Janet Thompson Dismorr (four children), he married the former Joan Simpson Meyers in 1969 (two children). Presently the Woodrow Wilson Professor of Political Science at Williams, he is a prolific contributor to scholarly periodicals, as well as the book review and magazine sections of the *New York Times*, and the author of numerous other books on politics, political parties and government. His allied activities have included the presidencies of the American Political Science Association (1975-76) and The International Society of Political Psychology (1982-83). His follow-up to *The American Experiment*, entitled *The Workship of Democracy*, was published in 1985.

Ellen Burstyn

"Acting feels like a congenital condition to me—it's in my genes," says Ellen Burstyn. "I can't ever remember not having that idea. I didn't decide to do it till I was 24, but it had been kinds in the back of my mind. I always felt like an actress." The year 1975 was an exciting one for Burstyn; she had the distinction of winning both the Tony (*Same Time, Next Year*) and the Oscar (*Alice Doesn't Live Here Anymore*) in the same year. In 1982 she became the first female president of Actor's Equity in its 69-year history, "the most overwhelming job I've ever taken on." (Too overwhelming, apparently; she resigned the post in 1985.) Also in 1982 Burstyn was named co-artistic director (with Al Pacino) of the Actors Studio, succeeding the late Lee Strasberg, the father of Method Acting in the U.S. "We want to keep the Actors Studio a safe place where actors can stretch and grow and take risks they can't take in the commercial world. I've used it like that for 17 years—as a gymnasium." In December of '82, continuing to pursue her first live, acting, Burstyn opened on Broadway in *84 Charing Cross Road*. ("When rehearsals started for the play, I locked the Studio and the union out of my mind and concentrated on the play. It's the only way I can do three things at once. . . . I think there's a time in your life when you've got to be of service to other people. I've been very lucky in life and feel I should start giving back.")

Born Edna Rae Gillooly in Detroit, Michigan, 7 December 1932, the daughter of middle-class Irish Catholic parents who divorced when she was quite young, Burstyn grew up hopelessly movie-struck ("I wrote my first Academy Award acceptance speech at the age of 7"). Flunking most courses at Cass Technical High School (cheerleading and student council took up most of her time), she dropped out of school and got married in 1950 ("to a poet"). She eventually worked her way to New York where she had as many different jobs (model, soda jerk, short-order cook, fashion coordinator) as names (Keri Flynn to Erica Dean to Edna Rae). After a year as a "Ziegfeld-type" show girl on the Jackie Gleason television show, she made her Broadway debut in *Fair Game* (1957) with Sam Levene ("I got the part because I sparkled, and I smiled good, but I didn't know how to act, and the rest of the company resented it"). She went to Hollywood (as Ellen McRae) and in 1969 appeared in the film of Henry Miller's *Tropic of Cancer* as Ellen Burstyn (her married name). Subsequent movies include *Alex in Wonderland* (1970), *The Last Picture Show* (1973), *The King of Marvin Gardens* (1972), *The Exorcist* (1973), *Harry and Tonto* (1974), *Alice Doesn't Live Here Anymore* (1975), and *Same Time, Next Year* (1978). More recent movies include: *Resurrection* (1980), *Silence of the North* (1980), *The Ambassador* (1984), *Twice in a Lifetime* 1985), and *Innocent Heroes* (1987). She starred in her own television show for ABC, *The Ellen Burstyn Show* (1986); a HBO presentation, *Act of Vengeance* (1986); and a CBS TV-film, "Pack of Lies" (1987). Burstyn also played the title role in the television drama "Jean Harris" (about the headmistress convicted of killing her lover, Scarsdale Diet doctor Herman Tarnower).

Each of Burstyn's three marriages ended in divorce (#2, director Paul Roberts); (#3, actor Neil Burstyn). ("It's not one of the things I'm, good at.") She lives in a house near the Hudson River in New York's Rockland County with her son, Jefferson Burstyn. "I love my age," smiles Burstyn, "I enjoy my son thoroughly. I am as happy now as I have ever been. I think not becoming famous until I was past 40 helped a lot; fame was easier to accept."

Barbara Bush

"The person a pillow away from the presidency is held up to an undefined ideal; she bears all America's conflicting notions about women as wives, mothers, lovers, colleagues and friends. A First Lady should be charming but not all fluff, gracious but not a doormat, substansive but not co-president. She must defend her husband and smile bravely when he says stupid things. . . . She has both a day and a night job, but is not allowed a profession of her own. Hardest of all, she has to appear to love every minute of it." This definition, according to *Time* magazine, leaves no room for error, no space for kicking off one's shoes, and no free time to unwind. Without too much fanfare, Barbara Bush is bending the stereotype and has become a respected, relaxed First Lady. Nicknamed by her children "The Silver Fox," Barbara has made it fashionable to do her own hair, state her real age, and pick her own wardrobe for her size 14 figure.

Barbara Pierce was born in Rye, New York, on 8 June 1925 to Marvin and Pauline (Robinson) Pierce. Her father was the president of McCall Corporation (owning *McCalls* magazine among other properties) and her mother a suburban housewife. Barbara attended both public and private schools; she graduated from Ashley Hall (a South Carolina prep school) and attended Smith College from 1943-1944. It was love at first sight when she met George Bush at a party in Greenwich, Connecticut. She claims, "I married the first man I kissed." They kept their engagement secret until George returned home from service after being shot down over the Pacific. Finally hitched on 6 January 1945, the young couple moved to Texas. Beginning with a "one-bedroom apartment where they shared a bathroom with a mother-daughter team of prostitutes," Mr. Bush finally struck it rich in the oil business and sold his stake in Zapata Off-Shore for $1 million. In the midst of their fortunes, tragedy struck. Barbara's mother passed away in a car accident and the Bush's second child, Robin, was diagnosed as having leukemia in 1953; the three-year-old died eight months later. Barbara told *Time*, "George held me tight and wouldn't let me go. You know, 70% of the people who lose children get divorced because one doesn't talk to the other. He did not allow that." Planning ahead for a large family, the Bushs raised five children: George Walker, John Ellis (Jeb), Neil, Mallon, Marvin Pierce, and Dorothy Walker. (In addition the Bushs are proud grandparents of a delightful bunch of youngsters).

Mrs. Bush had practice before assuming the role as the 38th First Lady of the country in 1989. As the wife of a Senator, she developed her public image. Later, as the wife of the Vice-President, she became accustomed to her upcoming responsibilities. Thrust into learning about dyslexia due to her son Neil's reading problem, she continues her battle against the nation's illiteracy. In 1984 she combined her sense of humor and literary sense to write a book, *C. Fred's Story*, a glimpse at Washington life from a dog's point of view. All proceeds from the book were donated to the Laubach Action and Literacy volunteers of America, Inc. As part of her White House affairs, Barbara will be involved with various charities. She supports such groups as Business Council for Effective Literacy, Reading Is Fundamental, the Sloan Kettering Cancer Center, Atlanta's Morehouse School of Medicine (on the board since 1983), Children's Oncology Services of Metropolitian Washington, the Leukemia Society of America, the Hispanic American Family of the Year Award Programs and the National School Association of Partners in Education. In 1986 Mrs. Bush was named "Outstanding Mother of the Year." Perhaps George's wife was summed up best by Margaret Carlson (senior writer of *Time*) when she asserted, "Mrs. Bush is so sure of herself, she has no need to prove anything." When Barbara just wants to relax she likes reading and needlepoint.

George Bush

"Use power to help. . . . We are not the sum of our possessions. . . . We cannot hope only to leave our children a bigger car, a bigger bank account. We must hope to give them a sense of what it means to be a loyal friend, a loving parent, a citizen who leaves his home, his neighborhood and town better than he found it." George Bush, the nation's 41st President, used such simple language at his inaugural speech to express his beliefs. As William Greider wrote in *Rolling Stone*, "Introducing the post-Hollywood presidency. For better or worse, it's going to be very different from the campy melodrama that has entertained the nation for the last eight years." *Time* magazine states: "The prescription has already taken hold: Bush is more sensitive and caring than Ronald Reagan, more of a hands-on administrator." A new breeze is blowing and George Bush is the leader.

Born in Milton, Mass., 12 June 1924, the son of a former Connecticut

Senator, Prescott Bush, he flew in combat in the Pacific for three years from the carrier U.S.S. *San Jacinto* and was shot down over Chichi Jima. Bush won the Distinguished Flying Cross and was discharged in 1945 with the rank of Lieutenant (j.g.). While still in the Navy he wed nineteen-year-old socialite Barbara Pierce, daughter of the late publisher of *McCall's* (five children). A civvie once again, Bush went to his father for a job with Dresser Industries (Bush senior was director) during the boom days of the Texas oil fields. Six years later he became president of the multi-million-dollar Zapata Off-Shore Co. The floundering local GOP drew the young world-beater into their party, and convinced him to stage a dark-horse candidacy for the Senate in 1964. To no one's surprise, he lost. But two years later he ran for Congress and won so convincingly that he was unopposed in 1968.

As Vice-President, George Bush established an excellent working relationship with the President and on his behalf travelled over 350,000 miles during his first three years in office, addressing 189 Republican gatherings in 48 states. In 1983 he made a seven-nation tour of Europe to reinforce the commitments of the governments in the North Atlantic Treaty Organization.

Standing six feet two inches tall, and weighing approximately 195 pounds, Bush keeps trim by jogging several miles before beginning his work day. Along with his Vice-President, Dan Quayle, he is steadfast in maintaining a compassionate and family-oriented America. He revealed to White House correspondents Michael Duffy and Dan Goodgame his various viewpoints in a *Time* magazine interview. On fiscal constraints, he says: "Those who want to measure your concern or compassion purely by federal money may find some disappointment." On taxes: "I'm going to hold the line on taxes." On the Gorbachev challenge: "I think if we make the mistake of assessing our relationship with the Soviet Union in terms of a personality, we'll live to regret it. . . . I don't think you can shape the foreign policy of the United States based on the leader of the moment."

Melinda Bush

Being responsible for the quarterly publication of "the Bible" is a big job. But Melinda Bush has shown that she can more than handle it. Since 1976 when Bush took over the publication of *Hotel & Travel Index*, a multimillion-dollar quarterly publication considered "the Bible" of the hotel industry, revenues and profits have climbed 900 percent. As the Senior V.P. and Publisher, Bush has total profit and budget responsibility for the 3,200 page index, directing the marketing, advertising sales, editorial and research of a major profit generator. Other responsibilities include the supervision of a staff of 165, including a sales organization inside and out of the U.S., with affiliated representatives in 12 countries in Latin America and in Asia/Pacific. Called an expert on the development of total marketing "positioning" programs, Bush developed and directs innovative marketing, advertising and research programs. She's winner of the 1980 "Travel Women of the Year" Award.

Bush, a cum laude graduate from the University of Colorado with a Bachelor of Science degree in Marketing, also attended the London School of Economics and Political Science, NYU Graduate School of Business and Harvard School of Advanced Management. The first woman to hold a position as publishing executive in the mulitmillion-dollar division of Murdoch finds time to chair the Cornell University/Hotel & Travel Index work studies program, to serve on numerous committees of The American Hotel & Motel Association, The Hotel Sales Management Association International, The Culinary Institute of America, The New School for Social Research Travel & Tourism Program and to be a Trustee of the Institute of Certified Travel Agents. She also serves on the Boards of Sun Resorts, Master-Media, Inc., and as a member of The National Advisory Board of the American University in Washington, D.C. Bush is a resident of New Jersey.

Robert Byrd

When most people hear the name of Robert Byrd, they think: "Oh, he's the Senator who plays the fiddle." True, this self-made scrambler from the hills and hollows of West Virginia's coal-mining wastelands has made the country fiddle an integral part of his campaign style since 1944 when he called on every voter in his district to win a seat in the West Virginia House of Delegates. For a fiddler, he hasn't done badly in the Capitol, playing major league politics with the best of them: an ally to liberals and conservatives depending on the moment, Byrd remains enigmatic even to his closest colleagues. "I want to be a part of making the Senate the institution it was meant to be," he explains. "The Senate has an independent role. This doesn't mean that it can't cooperate, or won't cooperate with the executive, but the role of the Senate is not to be a rubber stamp for any President."

Hardly a rubber stamp, and certainly not an ideologue, this man who in his youth was a KKK kleagle (organizer) nevertheless gave his backing to LBJ's Great Society legislation and, under President Carter, served as a rather unenthusiastic "point man" in the Senate. His unwavering attention to the needs of his constituents routinely garners him 80% of the vote. And after years of his methodically looking after the interests of other Senators, and reminding them of this fact, in the Capital *everyone* owes Byrd *something*. His detailed knowledge of bills under consideration as well as his encyclopedic knowledge of parliamentary procedure is widely respected. It all paid off in 1977 when he unseated Ted Kennedy as Majority Whip, then went on to become Minority Leader. Under his auspices the Democratic Steering Committee grew in stature and influence, and his presence is also felt on the Democratic Policy Committee and the Senate Democratic Conference.

Born in North Wilkesboro, N.C., on 20 November 1917, he grew up in abject poverty. His mother died in a flu epidemic and his father sent him to live with his aunt and uncle in Stotesbury, a coal-mining town in the Appalachian mountains of West Virginia. He remembers Christmases "without a present in the house, not even a stick of candy." His skill as a spellbinding fundamentalist preacher gained him local renown and eventually a weekly radio broadcast. This he forged into a political constituency that he has suckled for some four decades. His education was obtained after his youth, through night classes—ending with a J.D. degree *cum laude* from American University in Washington, D.C. in 1963. A reserved, private man, he shuns the Washington social circuit for the pleasures of home and health. He and the former Erma Ora James (m. 1937) have two daughters.

David Byrne

Pauline Kael, reviewing the 1984 rock documentary *Stop Making Sense*, a concert film with the New York-based new wave group The Talking Heads, wrote: "a continuous rock experience that keeps building, becoming ever more intense and euphoric . . . David Byrne is a stupefying performer who gives the group its modernism—the undertone of repressed hysteria, which he somehow blends with freshness and adventurousness and a driving beat." The aesthetic David Byrne applies no glitter, no sleaze to his performing, and that, in part, is why he has been called "The New Wave Nijinsky." Born in Dumbarton, Scotland, 14 May 1952, Byrne moved with his family to America in 1958. An artist as well as a musician and a composer, with drummer Chris Frantzx and bassist Tina Weymouth Byrne formed The Talking Heads in 1975, shortly after the threesome arrived in Manhattan after all having attended the prestigious Providence art school, The Rhode Island School of Design. "We felt there was this big hole," Byrne recalls. "Very little we were hearing appealed directly to us. It appealed to kids younger than us or to other people. We felt nobody's doing anything for our crowd—we'll have to do it ourselves." With its early appearances at clubs like CBGB in the Village, along with the Ramones and Blondie, The Talking Heads became the vanguard of what was known, then, as "punk rock" or "new wave." With producer Brian Eno, The Talking Heads released three LPs. Their first album included the FM hit "Psycho Killer." 1983's album *Speaking in Tongues*, included the superhit "Burning Down the House." Before *Stop Making Sense* was released, Byrne received critical acclaim for the music he composed for Twyla Tharp's "The Catherine Wheel." He has also composed music and helped design the staging for Robert Wilson's *CIVIL warS* and he played an actor on PBS television's "Survival Guides."

Expanding his artistic talents to the fullest, Byrne became active in motion pictures. He co-wrote the screenplay and directed *True Stories* (1986), appeared in *Checking Out* (1988) and composed the film scores for *The Last Emperor* (co-recipient Academy Award for best original score, 1987) and *Married to the Mob* (1988). David took on the role as husband in 1987 when he married Adelle Lutz.

James Caan

"Give the cowboy a big hand!" the barker chants at California's Antelope Valley Fair and Alfalfa Festival. The cowboy is blond, blue-eyed, tough-guy star James Caan Hollywood's Sonny Corleone of *The Godfather*, who has just roped a running steer around both hind legs. "This ain't my hobby; the other is my hobby," says Caan in a Sunnyside Queens accent. (His family moved to Queens soon after he was born in the Bronx, the son of a now-retired kosher meat dealer.) "I have to do that acting to pay for this."

Born 26 March 1939, Caan came to films by way of the theater and TV, having studied at the Neighborhood Playhouse while variously employed as a bouncer, waiter, and carrier of hindquarters of beef at a meat market. His first role in the Off-Broadway *La Ronde* paid him $37.50 a week, supplemented by odd jobs at the poolroom and Friday night poker, which parlayed his take to about $600. Married at 21 (divorced four years and one daughter later), Caan moved to Hollywood in 1962. In 1971 his portrayal of pro-football player Brian Piccolo in ABC-TV's movie *Brian's Song* made him hot property, but it wasn't until his performance in Coppola's *Godfather* (1972) that he achieved the sure-fire status of superstar. Caan is not the big bruiser he is often type-cast as. Just a shade over 5'10" and a slight 162 pounds, his celluloid aura of strength makes up for what he lacks in actual physical size. (By the time he was eleven, he had learned how to defend himself with his fists so well that he was known as Killer Caan. "I was the toughest guy at P.S. 106," he told a reporter for *Time*.) He has, however, played many a sensitive male role, as in *Cinderella Liberty* (1974), *The Rain People* (1969 and *Chapter Two* (1979). Other films include *Comes a Horseman* (1977), *Thief* (1980), *Hide in Plain Sight* (which also marked his directing debut), *Kiss Me Goodbye* (1983), *The Holcroft Covenant* (1985), *Alien Nation* (1988) and *Dad* (1989). Caan's two marriages produced a daughter Tara (1964) and a son, Scott Andrew (1976). Both mergers only temporarily interrupted his philosophy of life. "I'm the kind of guy when work is done I've got to be with my friends. I've got to blow it off like going to the rodeo, drinking or whoring."

Montserrat Caballé

A supreme soprano, she has been described as a singing actress "who can express high emotional voltage with great dignity, keeping a smooth exterior while giving the impression she is seething within." Since her entrance on the American scene in 1965, she has had several successful seasons at the Metropolitan, playing the dynamic likes of Desdemona (*Otello*), Liu (*Turandot*), Elisabetta (*Don Carlo*), Violetta in *La Traviata* and the challenging role of *Norma* in which she triumphed in 1973 to the audience's rapture. Throughout the U.S., she has been hailed for her performances as Mimi, Salome, and as Pamina in *The Magic Flute*. By the 1970s, Caballé also had triumphant debuts as the Salzburg Festival as Donna Elvira and at La Scala in the title role of *Luisa Miller*. She has performed in most of the leading houses of Europe, including the Vienna State Opera, Covent Garden, La Scala, the Bolshoi Opera in Moscow and in the renowned festivals at Edinburgh, Aix-en-Provence, and Florence. She sang *Tosca* with Luciano Pavorotti as Cavaradossi at the Met's 1985-86 season opener.

Caballé was born in Barcelona on 12 April 1933 into a family with no history of musicians, but they had a strong appreciation for music and despite being poor, owned a phonograph. Thus, recordings by opera singers provided Caballe with her first musical experiences and she sang along with gusto. "My parents loved music and when they could, they went to concerts or an opera." She heard her first opera (*Aida*) at the age of four, when the spark to study music was further fanned. She attended convent school and managed ballet lessons for several years, but Caballe's love of singing was in the forefront. At nine she was accepted into the Conservatorio del Liceo. Later, an affluent Barcelona family came to her rescue as patrons and helped Caballé continue at the Liceo where she studied with such notables as Eugenie Keminy, Conchita Badia and Maestro Annovazzi. In 1953 she received the conservatory's gold medal, the highest award given to a Spanish singer. After graduation, Caballé obtained a contract in Basel, Switzerland and she filled small roles for a time, finally receiving a stroke of luck in November 1957 when the singer pegged for Mimi in *La Boheme* took ill. Caballé was received with enthusiasm and riding on this success; the Basel Opera offered her leading roles through the next three years: Tosca, Aida, Violetta, Salome. Demonstrating great range and durability, Caballé had guest appearances at the Vienna State Opera and her Salome won a gold medal "as the season's finest Strauss singer." From Basel, she began an impressive tour, with an extensive and varied repertory, with the Bremen Opera and additional appearances in Germany, Austria, Spain and Mexico. Her big "international" break happened in April 1965: Marilyn Horne was supposed to sing the title soprano role in Donizetti's *Lucrezia Borgia* at Carnegie Hall in a presentation by the American Opera Society, but Caballé was recruited as a substitute when Horne became unavailable. That singular performance firmed her reputation (despite the European successes, she was still relatively unknown in the U.S.). Winthrop Sargeant noted in the *New Yorker* that "she caused a furor." The critics launched an outright horserace with their superlatives. A representative from RCA was summoned during the intermission and by the time the concert was over, Caballé had signed a recording contract. She debuted as Marguerite in *Faust* at the Met in December 1965.

In August 1964 she married Bernabe Marti, a tenor. They settled in Barcelona and have two children. An ample woman, she possesses regal bearing on and off the stage, with "the dark good looks of a Spanish lady and the comfortable figure of a prima donna." She admits to a hearty appetite for food and cigarettes and has a history of cancelled performances which she attributes to a variety of ailments. Indulgences not withstanding. Caballé has been honored in Spain with the Cross of Isabella the Catholic and given the title Most Excellent and Most Illustrious Donna.

Paul Cadmus

"People refuse to see the obvious. They need to have their noses rubbed in it, their noses and their mouths and eyes that crave only euphemisms, soda pop, bubble gum, sweetness-and-light, candied violence, anything to minimize or distract from the horrible, grotesque daily life (death)." Thus does veteran painter/draftsman/etcher Paul Cadmus offer a clue as to why, for more than forty years, he's been creating (in one critic's words) "unforgettable images of the less ideal aspects of contemporary society."

From such museum classics as his audaciously satiric representation of a "Greenwich Village Cafeteria" (1934) and "Coney Island" (1935) to 1976's "Subway Symphony," his "metaphors of moral judgment" have retained their acid bite and he has continued working through periods of both triumph and obscurity. Entering a period of triumph in the 1980s, he was the subject of both a film documentary, "Paul Cadmus: Enfant Terrible at 80," and a coffee-table book (by his brother-in-law Lincoln Kirstein) in 1984. He's been a member of the American Academy and Institute of Arts and Letters since 1974.

Paul Cadmus was born in New York City, 17 December 1904, the child of two working artists. A member of the storytelling American Scene school of artists, he became a media sensation in 1934 when his federally funded painting, "The Fleet's In," was shown at the first organized exhibit of New Deal art. Its carnal depiction of sailors and floosies carousing in a New York park so shocked Navy brass that the picture was hastily removed from the Corcoran Gallery and onto the news pages. (Observed the artist: "Everybody knows what sailors do. If there's vice and sordidness in life, I don't see why it shouldn't be painted.") But, as able to enchant as to shock, Cadmus is also admired for his sensitive ballet studies, among them a group illustrating Lincoln Kirstein's *Ballet Alphabet*. Called "a virtuoso of the classical, freehand sketch," Cadmus is also known for his lovingly rendered male nudes. ("Generally, men are much better models," says Cadmus. "They work harder on their posing, perhaps because they're so much vainer than women.") Long before the closet-opening influence of Gay Liberation, he was dealing straightforwardly in his work with the subject of homosexuality. The painter sometimes referred to as "our 20th century Breugel" now lives and works in an isolated Connecticut home off a dirt road with no signpost. Cutting down drastically on his output in past decades, he has produced fewer than seventy works since 1941. "The characteristic vice of the modern artist," says Cadmus, "is overproduction."

Herb Caen

"Isn't it nice," an admirer of the Golden Gate once mused, "that the kind of people who prefer Los Angeles to San Francisco live there?" This Caliph of Baghdad-by-the-Bay royally agrees and says to LA lovers: "I wouldn't say we're smug. It's more like the humble pride of natural superiority." To many, Citizen Caen of the *Chronicle* and his coastal city are one and the same. "Mr. San Francisco" openly adores his town in print six days a week and thousands of readers have returned the compliment.

Born 3 April 1916 not in San Francisco but in Sacramento, he wrote his first column in the school paper in 1931 as "Raisin" Caen. He signed on with the *Chronicle* in 1938 and, with the exception of an interlude at the rival *Examiner* (1950-58), has been there ever since. "I still don't know what makes a good item," he says, but an envious rival offers this theory: "The secret of Caen's success is his outstanding ability to take a wisp of fog, a chance phrase overheard in an elevator, a happy child on a cable car, a deb in a tizzy over a social reversal, a family in distress, and give each circumstance the magic touch that makes a reader an understanding eyewitness of the day's happenings."

Divorced from his third wife in 1983, the columnist now lives in an apartment on Telegraph Hill with one of the finest jazz record collections in the Bay Area. He is the father of one son, Christopher, born in 1965. He is also the author of ten books about his favorite city.

Sid Caesar

Rendering unto Caesar what is Caesar's, audiences have paid him tribute with everything from genial giggles to gargantuan guffaws, plus roars, raves, rants, rails and mixed ratings. One of the rare comedians without a joke file, he emerged in 1949 as one of TV's first and finest satiric talents on the "Admiral Broadway Revue" and made "Your Show of Shows" and "Caesar's Hour" a Saturday night viewing habit in the 1950's. Critics saluted him as the "funniest man in America." However, behind his classic satiric comedy were real tears of rage and despair: He was an alcoholic and barbiturate addict skidding into disaster. During his self-described "20-year blackout" on booze and pills, he continued working. "But I wasn't really there," recalled Caesar in his 1982 autobiography, *Where Have I Been*, which describes his harrowing experience and recovery. He relates his gradual awakening to the suffering he has caused people in his life, and especially himself. The hard road back to sobriety began in 1978 when he collapsed at a dinner-theater show and entered a hospital for detoxification. "A man is only a grown-up child, but if you let the child control you, you wind up like John Belushi," he said. "I finally realized there weren't going to be any more hands on the carriage. I'm in control now."

Born 8 September 1922 in Yonkers, New York, he acquired his ability to reproduce dialects and accents while toiling in his father's luncheonette, patronized chiefly by Polish, Russian and Italian laborers. He also acquired the wherewithal to invest in saxaphone lessons, after which he worked "from 9 p.m. till unconscious" swinging with a local combo. His first New York showbiz job was a $15 a week movie usher. "But I rose rapidly from the ranks," explains Caesar. "In practically no time I rocketed to doorman and $18 a week. It wasn't the money so much as the prestige—and the overcoat." He served as sax and clarinet sideman with the bands of Charlie Spivak, Claude Thornhill and then, after enlisting in the Coast Guard during World War II, wound up in the C.G. stage hit *Tars and Spars*. In 1948, in *Make Mine Manhattan*, he won a Donaldson Award "for the best debut of an authentic clown." He launched his TV career the next year, later winning five Emmy Awards as star of "Caesar's Hour" on NBC-TV. His more recent TV projects include NBC's "30 Years of Comedy," "Alice in Wonderland" (1985) and "Side By Side" (1988). On the stage, he appeared as "Frosch" in the Metropolitan Opera's performance of "Die Fledermaus" (1988). In movies, he starred in Stanley Kramer's 1963 comedy epic, *It's a Mad, Mad, Mad, Mad World*. His Broadway credits include *Little Me* (1962-63), in which he played seven different characters. He is married to the former Florence Levy; they have two sons and a daughter. In 1985 Caesar was inducted into the Television Academy Hall of Fame.

Nicolas Cage

In just a few short years, and less than a dozen movies, Nicolas Cage has flown into the limelight. Fearing he might be judged on his name, rather than his talents, he decided to hush the fact that his uncle is famous director Francis Ford Coppola. It was his consistent performances that prompted the respect he deserves. In many interviews Cage compares his craft to that of a magician and refuses to talk about his specific acting techniques. He insists, "If you give away your tricks, you lose the illusion."

Nicholas Coppola was born in Long Beach, California, on 7 January 1964. One of his first roles was in the "like-a, well, like, y'know," flighty movie *Valley Girl* (1983). Given a shot by his uncle, Nicolas was cast in Coppola's 1983 film *Rumble Fish* as a rebellious teenager, playing opposite Matt Dillon. On a roll, he was cast as a disabled Vietnam vet in Alan

Parker's powerful *Birdy* in 1984. More parts surfaced as he played Richard Gere's kid brother in *The Cotton Club* (1984), followed by Kathleen Turner's present-day middle-aged husband / back-in-time teenaged boyfriend in the comedy *Peggy Sue Got Married* (1986). He also appeared in *Racing With the Moon* (1984), *Raising Arizona* (1986), *The Boy In Blue* (1985), *Gardens of Stone* (1987), *Vampire's Kiss* (1987), and *Moonstruck* (1988). It was his role as the love-struck thirty-year-old brother of Cher's fiancé in *Moonstruck* that had the critics writing praises. Of this romantic role he says, "It could be a medicine for couples that are falling apart. They would see *Moonstruck* and say, 'See? It's alright to be angry with one another, it's alright to argue.' Love is not just holding hands."

Sammy Cahn

For many years Sammy Cahn refused to travel by plane. "Birds don't write lyrics. Cahn doesn't fly," he stated emphatically. Maybe he didn't fly (he does now), but he certainly filled the air with the sound of his inventive lyrics, including those of four Oscar-winners: "Three Coins in A Fountain" (1954), "All the Way" (1957), "High Hopes" (1959), and "Call Me Irresponsible" (1963), his personal favorite. "I want you to notice that 'irresponsible' is a five-syllable word. I stress that because I come from a one-syllable neighborhood," joked Cahn in his autobiography, *I Should Care* (1974). The song-a-minute man (he once knocked off 30 lyrics in a day just to reassure himself that he wasn't losing his grip) was born on the lowest part of NYC's Lower East Side. Cahn, the only son of restaurateur (along with a "quartet" of sisters), first saw the light of day on 18 June 1913. He was actually named Cohen, then changed it to Cohn, then Kahn and finally Cahn. He says the last change from K to C was made because, "I had a song-writing partner named Kaplan and we sounded like dress manufacturers." He grew up and studied accounting half-heartedly at Seward Park High School, played hooky and pool, worked out with orchestras, played the fiddle, wrote special material for a few performer friends, and finally hit it with composer Saul Chaplin (formerly Kaplan) and "Bei Mir Bist Du Schon" (which Sammy wrote in 10 minutes). Altogether the dapper and bespectacled Sammy has collaborated with around eight different composers, among them Jule Styne ("Let It Snow, Let It Snow," "I'll Walk Alone," "Time After Time," and the score for Broadway's *High Button Shoes*) and Jimmy Van Heusen ("The Second Time Around," the Emmy/Christopher awards-winner "Love and Marriage," "Come Fly With Me" and "My Kind of Town Chicago Is.)"

Cahn has put his lyrical stamp on a long list of Hollywood musicals and has written so many songs in the Frank Sinatra repertoire that he's earned the reputation of being th singer's personal lyricist. Cahn emerged as a Broadway singing star in his own right with his 1974 successful revue *Words and Music*, a musical reminiscence of his life and work. *The New York Times* called him "the best bad singer in the world," a great humorist who "sounds like a frog" and urged everyone not to miss it.

Married and divorced from Gloria Delson, a former Goldwyn girl (two children), Cahn decided to test his song "The Second Time Around" by marrying Tita Curtis in 1970. It was the second time for each and they picked the second (August) for their wedding day. Romantic bliss was broken; the couple divorced, then after a change of heart they remarried in 1987. This third time around proved rocky, too, and the couple were separated again in 1988.

Cahn was elected the 2nd president of the Songwriters Hall of Fame in 1975 and he was also elected to the Board of Directors of ASCAP. He continues to be active in the business; he performed for a 12-week engagement at the Duke of York Theatre in London in 1987. "If you lay still," his mother once told him, "they'll throw earth over you," Cahn says: "I'm keeping golf for my old age" and "I'm not ready to be buried."

Michael Caine

One critic put it thusly: "Like the Beatles, Caine is a product of Britain's lower class popular arts revolution," Caine says, "A Cockney used to be looked upon kindly, like Mickey Mouse, but we decided to be people instead. I just couldn't see getting up at dawn to schlep iced fish." He burst through the rigid British caste system to both fame and fortune via such vehicles as *The Ipcress File, Alfie, Sleuth, The Man Who Would Be King;* later: *Deathtrap, Dressed To Kill, Blame It On Rio, Hannah and Her Sisters* (recipient Academy Award—Best Supporting Actor, 1987), *Sweet Liberty, Half Moon Street, The Fourth Protocol* (also executive producer), *Dirty Rotten Scoundrels* and *Without a Clue.*

Caine was born Maurice Micklewhite on Old Kent Road in London, 14 March 1933; his father was a Billingate Fish Market porter, and his mother a charwoman. ("I was rich from the day I was born, I just didn't have the money.") World War II forced a breakup of his family for a year until Caine's mother was able to gather them all again under one roof. At 18 he was drafted for National Service, serving in Berlin and Korea—"a lot of very heroic-looking guys shot their toes off while cleaning their rifles," and at 20 went back to London working at the Smithfield Meat Market while taking acting classes at night. Landing a job at Lowestoft Theatre, he met and married his leading lady, Patricia Haines. "I can't remember one single moment that was happy," his ex-wife later said of their three-year marriage. There was one daughter, Dominique, born in 1956. In 1973 he married Shakira Baksh, a former Miss Guyana in a Miss World beauty pageant, and they have a daughter (Natasha, born in 1973).

While working night shift in a laundry, he got his first film part, which eventually led to an appearance in *Zulu* as—of all things—an English patrician. ("All those idiots went to Oxford just because they were lords' sons, but now their day is over. Nobody stands for that bourgeois junk any more.") From that point on, Caine was established as a film actor and continues to chalk up credits. "Money buys independence. I don't like being told what to do, especially by people who know less." 'E'as a point there, 'e' as.

Sarah Caldwell

Considered a rarity—a visual-minded musician—she believes that opera should be "an evening of theater." Inventive, persistent and courageously creative as a trooper for that cause in the U.S., she has an international reputation as one of the most adventurous producers of opera today. In 1957 she founded a home base, the still-thriving Opera Company of Boston, and the enterprising Caldwell's responsibilities extend to casting and scholarly research, stage direction, orchestra conducting and fundraising. In addition to producing innovative new versions that revitalize classics, she has been the catalyst for American premieres of such challenging works as Hindemith's *Mathis der Maler*, Luigi Non's *Intolleranza* and Schoenberg's *Moses und Aron*. Despite budgetary problems, Caldwell maintains such high standards that critics and opera lovers from all over the U.S. crowd into gyms and old movie houses, and the luminous likes of Joan Sutherland, Boris Christoff and Beverly Sills lend their services with guest appearances. With a Carnegie Hall debut in 1974 with the American Symphony Orchestra, her labors as conductor and/or director of several major opera companies (including a breakthrough as the first woman ever to wield a baton at New York's Metropolitan Opera—1976), symphonies and festivals, have established her as the indisputable maestra of American opera.

Born in Maryville, Missouri (6 March 1924), she grew up in Arkansas, her father a university professor and mother a music teacher and pianist. By the age of four, Caldwell was considered a prodigy in both mathematics and music with a special talent for the violin and was giving recitals by the age of ten. As a girl she loved theater and concerts, which explains her enthusiasm for the blend of these two ingredients in opera. Eventually beseiged with scholarships, she enrolled at the New England Conservatory of Music, concentrating on classes in opera production while studying both violin and viola. Offered a post as violinist with both the Minnesota and Indianapolis symphony orchestras, Caldwell opted instead to assist Boris Goldovsky in the direction of New England Opera Theater. For the next 11 years she operated as his right hand, as well as stage director, conducting her first opera, Mozart's *La Finta Giardiniera*, at the old Boston Opera House. Spending summers at Tanglewood, first as a student and later on as a faculty member of the Berkshire Music Center, Caldwell succeeded in staging her first operatic production before the age of twenty. Five years later she proceeded to put Boston on the musical map as head of the University's Opera Workshop Department, staging many impressive operas with her student group in the 1950s. Eventually she and her followers established the Boston Opera Group (later called the Opera Company of Boston), where Caldwell has served as artistic director and conductor since 1957. Detail-oriented and demanding, and celebrated for her rigorous rehearsal schedules, Caldwell continues to attract a fabulous array of guest stars because of her reputation and ability to create meaningful character interpretations. An admitted eclectic, she presents both popular and little-known operas, striving to blend musical quality with novel visual appeal and dramatic impact. Her mission, as Caldwell admits repeatedly, is to ward off boredom, for opera is, to her way of thinking, a form of mass entertainment. Regarded by many critics as a miracle worker for the scope and dimension of her presentations, Caldwell lends opera her "own special kind of distinction," both in the novelty of her staging and the excellence of her performance as a conductor.

Her appearance portrays a powerhouse personality. She is a monumental person, both in presence and in her powerful drive for achievement. While the lack of material resources has often plagued her company, this has only reinforced Caldwell's determination to evoke the maximum in dramatic and musical intensity. To Hubert Saal of *Newsweek*, Caldwell is living proof that imagination can go much farther in opera then mere money. The maestra's ideal is that "the acting and singing should be wedded into one beautiful performance."

Zoe Caldwell

"I was a late bloomer," says this raven-haired actress from down under. "I knew once I turned 30 I could play the Madwoman of Chaillot, Mother Courage, Cleopatra . . . all those marvelous over-thirty women. . . . I always knew that everything about me—in acting and in private life—would come to a sort of fullest bloom from my 30s on." As if to prove the point, after hitting the high side of the generation gap Miss Caldwell copped three of Broadway's much coveted Tonys: the first in 1966 for her role in Tennessee Williams' short-lived *Slapstick Tragedy*, the second, two seasons later, for her portrayal of a dowdy middle-aged school mistress in *The Prime of Miss Jean Brodie*. And shortly thereafter she married for the first time (producer Robert Whitehead; two children). "I think," Miss Caldwell concludes, wrapping up her thesis, "the later you bloom, the longer the bloom stays on." In 1970, she was drenched in huzzahs for her off-Broadway portrayal of *Colette*, was honored by Queen Elizabeth II with the Order of the British Empire, and received bravas for her portrayal of Lady Hamilton in *Bequest to the Nation* in London. She marked her directorial debut with Colleen Dewhurst in *An Almost Perfect Person*,which played on Broadway in 1977. Soon after, she directed *Richard II* at Stratford Ontario. Her third Tony was for her performance as *Medea*, directed by her husband, in 1983.

Born 14 September 1933 in Victoria, Australia, Zoe Caldwell acted first with Australian repertory companies and at 24 won a scholarship to Stratford-on-Avon. There, the late Tyrone Guthrie saw her and invited her to appear with his company in Minneapolis. Broadway took notice in 1965, when she subbed for Anne Bancroft in *The Devils*. "I think I was born an actress," Miss Caldwell once mused. "Some people are addicted to drugs. I've got a creative addiction. I could have been an appalling mother or maybe a nymphomaniac if I hadn't become an actress," she adds, "so isn't it fine that I did." In 1985 she toured with *Lillian*(based on the life of the late playwright Lillian Hellman), and brought the one-woman show to Broadway in 1986.

Cab Calloway

"Chigger Chigger Wa Wa," "Geechy Joe" and "Utt-Da-Zay," bubbles the scat-singing King of Hi-De-Ho (a soubriquet he received when he forgot his lyrics one night and substituted the cover-up words "hi-de-ho"), and fans the world over know it's Cab Calloway and no one else. Born Christmas Day, 1907, in Rochester, N.Y., as Cabell Calloway III, he dropped a potential law career to take up band leading at Harlem's Cotton Club in 1929. It was there that he first composed, sang, and made famous his "Minnie the Moocher" lament. Calloway's sounds have reached the crowned heads of Europe and the underground ears of East Berlin teenagers who covered their phonographs with blankets so as not to be discovered. A veteran of records, radio, TV, and films (e.g. *Stormy Weather*), he first performed on Broadway in *Connie's Hot Chocolates*, later touring worldwide in *Porgy and Bess* as Sportin' Life, the role originally created for him but which he couldn't assume at the time due to contract commitments. In 1971 he was heralded as "a dancing prancing delight" as the pinchpenny Yonkers merchant Horace Vandergelder in a "salt and pepper" production of *Hello Dolly*. He said he liked this role even better than the one in *Porgy* because "In that one I was portraying a guy struggling to make it big. In *Dolly* I'm already a millionaire." Father of two daughters (Camay and Constance) by an early marriage, he and his wife Nuffie (the former Zulme MacNeal) have three more (Eulalie, who has broken into the business as a singer, Chris, an actress who played in *Dolly* with Daddy, and Cabella). After his coattail-flying stint as Vandergelder, the fireball Calloway claimed he was going to retire and become an off-duty Cab permanently. But the claim was spurious; his book *Of Minnie the Moocher and Me*, a loving record of the Big Band era, was published in 1976. He performed at the Limelight (NYC-1986) for a New Year's Eve bash, sang at the "Great American Concert With Fireworks" at the Hollywood Bowl (1987), wowed 'em at Carnegie Hall (1988) and appeared on the Grammy Awards show (1988) in NYC. After a brief hospitalization in January, 1989, Calloway made a quick comeback with a dynamic performance at ASCAP's Diamond Jubilee concert in February, 1989.

Kirk Cameron

At only 18 years old, he is already a success story in the world of show business. This young actor has made the switch from popular teen idol and heartthrob, to celebrated television and film star. He has performed with such greats as Dudley Moore, Robin Williams, and Kurt Russell.

Kirk Cameron was born on 20 October 1970, in Canoga Park, California. He began acting professionally at age 9, appearing in TV commercials. Several years later he appeared in the short-lived series "Two Marriages," and the made-for-TV-movie "Goliath

Awaits." But it was his role as Mike Seaver in the popular ABC series "Growing Pains" that brought him his star status recognition. Since then he has received several awards including the Favorite Young Television Performer in both the 1987 and 1988 People's Choice Awards, the Best Actor Award presented by the Family Television and Film Awards Organization in 1988, and a Golden Globe nomination for his performance in "Growing Pains." His film credits include *Like Father Like Son* co-starring with Dudley Moore, *Mismatch*, *The Best of Times* with Robin Williams and Kurt Russell, and *Listen to Me* co-starring with Jami Gerz. Kirk is also actively involved in the "Just Say No" anti-drug campaign, using his influence as a role model to act as a spokesperson. He has appeared in several television commercials proclaiming his views against the use of drugs. "The most rewarding results of my participation is when parents stop and thank me for the positive messages I've been able to get across to their children," says Kirk. "If my positive outlook and moral values help others, that's great."

Kirk resides in California, and in his spare time he enjoys working out at the gym and playing the guitar.

Glen Campbell

Campbell's rise from obscure recording artist and studio musician to TV star ("I'm really sittin' in the high cotton now") was largely the result of two recordings in 1968: "Gentle on My Mind" and "By the Time I Get to Phoenix," both of which won Grammys. "I'm busier right now'n a three-headed woodpecker," he said at the time. "They call me an overnight success, but mah night's been 15 years long. That's just about how long I've been strugglin' in this business. I'm gettin' some of the gravy now, but it sure ain't been a picnic."

When the outdoorsy six-footer weighed in at seven pounds, two ounces (22 April 1938), first filling his lungs with Delight, Ark., air, a neighbor looked him over and said, "That boy's goin' to amount. Got to be. His paw, Wes, he's a seventh son. And Glen is the seventh son of a seventh son." "The thing I remember most about Glen," recalls a former schoolmate, "was that he was always singin' or playin' the guitar. He didn't pay any attention to us girls in the class. He weren't sweet on any of us. He was jest in love with that ol' guitar." He left school and the farm when he was 14. ("I was tired of lookin' at the north end of a southbound mule.")

TV director Roger Gimbel explains Campbell's popularity: "He's a fresh, attractive performer who fits the times.... It's almost a return to the same kind of nationalism that comes between wars; you know, when you're kind of proud of what your country's all about." Glen adds, "I'm strictly Joe American. I'm the apple-pie kinda guy." It is this kind of hokey sentiment and hillbilly dialect that has propelled Campbell to stardom. On the screen he appeared in *Any Which Way You Can* (1980) and two years later the "Glen Campbell Show" aired on prime time. Recent recordings include *It's Just a Matter Of Time* (1985), *Still Within the Sound of My Voice* (1987) and *Light Years* (1988). The latter album was produced by his long-time friend Jimmy Bowen and songwriter Jimmy Webb. "I think this album is one of the best I've ever done," claims Campbell. "The songs are consistently good—that's what I always look for. I judge a tune by the melody and what it says. That's what counts with me."

Campbell has been married four times and has nine children, the youngest a son born in 1985 to wife Kim Woollen, whom he married in 1982.

John Candy

"Working with John Candy has been one of the greatest delights of my career," remarked director Carl Reiner, who guided the young comedian in his first starring role in *Summer Rental*, the 1985 film comedy hit. "I've been very lucky in my career," continued Reiner, "I've worked with some of the best: Sid Ceasar, Mel Brooks, Dick Van Dyke, George Burns, Steve Martin, and now, John Candy."

Born in Toronto in 1951, the moon-faced Candy, an avid sports fan, played football and hockey in high school before a knee injury ended his hopes for a professional sports career. He started acting in the eleventh grade and the urge continued during his journalism studies at Centennial Community College near Toronto. Candy's first professional job was with a children's theatre group that produced such classics as *Rumpelstiltskin* and *Treasure Island*, in which the four-member cast played a lot of different roles. By 1971 he was a fixture in Toronto's underground theatre scene performing in the popular satirical revue *Creeps* at the time he met another struggling Canadian actor from Ottawa, Dan Aykroyd. He also had roles in several low-budget Canadian films, including *Faceoff*, which he describes as "a real stinker about hockey." In 1972 with Aykroyd's urging, Candy joined Chicago's famed Second City Theatre, which at the time included young comedic talents John Belushi, Shelley Long, Gilda Radner and Bill Murray. After two years there he returned to Toronto and joined the Canadian-based Second City group. This evolved into the "SCTV" television series, which was syndicated throughout the United States and Canada and finally picked up by NBC. Candy was performer/writer for the show, and garnered two Emmys for the latter. He was part of "SCTV" until 1981. His films include Steven Spielberg's *1941*, John Landis's *The Blues Brothers*, and *Stripes*, with Bill Murray. He was featured in *National Lampoon's Vacation* and was Tom Hanks's lecherous sibling in *Splash*. Other films include *Brewster's Millions* with Richard Pryor, *Volunteers*, *Spaceballs*, *Planes, Trains and Automobiles*, *Hot To Trot*, *The Great Outdoors*, *Speed Zone* and *Uncle Buck*. He starred as the bumbling private eye who "always manages to get his man" in 1989's *Who's Harry Crumb?* "I find that there's a common denominator that runs with all creative comedians," says director Reiner. "They're a pleasure to work with because they not only come in prepared but they come with creative ideas which makes everything better, easier.... Put somebody like John Candy in it and little goodies happen every day."

Dyan Cannon

She once claimed that it was almost a career unto itself having people call her "The ex-Mrs. Cary Grant." After the movie idol saw her performance in a television series, "Malibu Run," he was so impressed that he asked her to test for his next film. They married in 1965 after a four-and-a-half year courtship and had one daughter, Jennifer. Then in the best of Hollywood traditions (high drama) they divorced in 1968. She accused him of taking LSD. His shrink claimed that Cary spanked Cannon "for reasonable and adequate causes." All the while, Cannon was one of the grooviest gals in Hollywood, from Primal Screen to a three-year state of celibacy, so "California" that *People* magazine said at times "she seemed a parody of the film that was her breakthrough, 1969's *Bob & Carol & Ted & Alice*." She's much more than Cary Grant's ex, the mother of his only child. She's one of the finest comedic actresses around as her many fans will readily attest. Her films include *Deathtrap; Heaven Can Wait; Such Good Friends; Author, Author; Honeysuckle Rose*, a cult classic among puzzle lovers titled *The Last of Sheila*, and *Caddyshack II*. In 1989 she wore a triple hat when she wrote the screenplay for, directed and starred in *One Point of View*.

Born 4 January 1937, in Tacoma, Washington, her full name is Samille Diane Friesen. ("After my grandfather Sam.") Her father was a life insurance salesman and a Baptist, her mother was Jewish and "a great bowling champion." She was raised Jewish and was once Miss Seattle. She considered becoming an actress only when she was "discovered" by a producer in a Los Angeles restaurant and given an "explosive" new name. ("I thought they were putting me on.") She decided she needed a nose job and phoned home to dad and said, "I don't want that mink stole you promised me, but I want a nose job." Luckily, a Hollywood plastic surgeon realized that her slightly flat nose was one of her most distinguishing features. That was in 1957. She'd been working for a dress manufacturer, modeling and helping to run his showroom. She studied for a year with Sandy Meisner and made her professional debut in television's Playhouse 90 production of "The Ding-A-Ling Girl," which starred Art Carney, and that led to roles in "Matinee Theatre" and other TV series. She made her film debut in *The Rise and Fall of Legs Diamond*, and her Broadway debut in *The Fun Couple*, a flop that also starred Jane Fonda.

Nominated twice for Academy Awards, she won one the third time in 1976 for a 42-minute film, *Number One*, an examination of the lives of two five-year-old girls which she produced. She also was applauded for her portrayal of famed San Francisco madam Sally Stanford in a television film, and for playing a hip rock star mother in the ABC-TV movie *Rock and Roll Mom* (1988).

Cannon lives in Malibu, swims daily in her pool and begins each morning reading metaphysics. About Einstein she says, "Now there's a sexy man!" "All I know," she said in 1984, "is that I've never had as much to share or as much to express as right now, at this point in my life. I'm happy most of the time now. I'm a happy lady." She was happier still in April of 1985 when she married attorney Stanley Finberg.

Jose Canseco

When Jose Canseco stated to reporters in spring training, 1988, that he felt capable of hitting forty home runs and stealing forty bases that season, they shook their heads in disbelief. That combination had never been accomplished in major league history. Canseco, who had been unaware of that fact, remained undaunted when told of the task's impossibility. He went on to become the charter member of the so-called 40/40 club, ultimately hitting 42 homeruns and stealing 40 bases.

Jose Canseco and his identical twin brother were born 2 July 1964 in Havana, Cuba. He grew up in Florida and was obtained by the Oakland Athletics (A's) in their fifteenth-round selection of the June, 1982, free agent draft. He was named the American League Rookie of the Year in 1986. In his first three seasons with the A's, Canseco was selected twice to the American League All-Star Game, making his first appearance in the starting lineup in 1988 as he was named on more voters' ballots than any other American League player. 1988 was a brilliant season for Canseco as he set records while leading his team to the World Series, where they lost in five games to the Los Angeles Dodgers. Canseco had only one hit in the series, a grand-slam homerun (his first ever), but the disappointing performance could not eclipse his previous accomplishments. He led the major leagues in homeruns (42), runs batted in (RBIs; 124) and slugging percentage (.569). His RBI total set a new Oakland A's mark. He was the first member of the A's to lead the major leagues in RBIs and the second to lead the American League. His 42 homeruns were impressive by virtue of the fact that 27 of them either tied the game or put the A's in the lead, and he hit 16 of them with a two-strike count. It seemed fitting that the first run of the 1988 American League Championship Series came on a fourth inning-homerun in game one by Jose Canseco against the Boston Red Sox in Fenway Park; it set up his team's 2 to 1 victory. He also hit a two-run homerun off Boston's Roger Clemens to tie the score in game two, which Oakland won 4 to 3, and a solo homerun off Bruce Hurst to get the A's rolling to a 4 to 1 win in game four, enabling the A's to sweep the series in four games.

The 6'3", 220-pound outfielder broke many female hearts when he married beauty queen Esther Haddad, in a civil ceremony 25 October 1988 in Coral Gables, Florida. He won $10,000 from teammate Dave Stewart by marrying before November, 1988. The couple held a religious ceremony in Florida on 5 November 1988. The right-hand hitting and throwing slugger hopes to develop power and speed to create a 50/50 club. The multi-dimensional player (on defense, his 11 assists in rightfield topped all A's outfielders) may just be the one to do it.

Pierre Cardin

"I wash with my own soap. I wear my own perfume. I go to bed on my own sheets. I have my own food product. I can sit in my own armchair; I live on me."

No matter what state France's economy finds itself in, the nation's most peripatetic designer finds his economy a global, rather than national, issue. The Cardin empire covers more than five hundred license programs in more than seventy countries on six continents—everywhere but Antarctica. His products range from couture to towels, stereo sets, carpets, eyeglasses, wines, a partnership with Maxim's and Maxim's products, as well as the sponsorship of several hundred musical, dance, theatrical and cinema events in his Espace Cardin, a combination theater and exhibition hall he opened in 1970. He is constantly breaking with tradition, something that annoys his fellow couturiers to no end. When Cardin appeared on a cover of *Time* in 1974 wearing nothing but one of his bath towels, American designer Raymond Loewy wrote "I deeply regret that my extremely talented friend Pierre Cardin, the world's foremost clothes designer, chose to discredit a profession to which he apparently yearns to belong and to which he may eventually have to answer." Givenchy was less brutal: "Cardin tries a lot of things, but he should stick to fashion. . . . His evening gowns are excellent."

The two Cardin innovations that have influenced the world of fashion most are the concept of the boutique as opposed to the large store, and the idea that modern man should wear a more romantic, more interesting and individual uniform. In 1954, just two years after his smash-hit first showing, he opened his original Paris boutique, "Eve." In 1957 he opened a store for ready-to-wear men's clothes, "Adam." The men's shop sparked the "Peacock Revolution" in menswear during the 1960's. In 1959, Cardin did what the other couturiers found most unforgivable, although they would soon see the advantage of doing the same; he introduced a signed collection of ladies' pret-a-porter in the Paris department store *Au Printemps*.

French by nationality, Cardin was born in Venice 7 July 1922, the son of a French wine merchant who lost all his money during World War I. Shortly after he was born the family moved to Avignon and later to Grenoble. Cardin recalls that as a little boy his favorite game was wrapping himself and his playmates in yards of *tulle;* at 14 he became a tailor's apprentice. Before the Second World War he worked for a tailor in Vichy: when the war was over, he heeded the suggestion of a Vichy fortune teller, applying for and landing a job at Paquin in Paris, a prominent fashion house. A few days later he was told he would design the costumes for Jean Cocteau's film, *Beauty and the Beast*. "I was finally in the land of my dreams," he says. He went on to work for Schiaparelli and then Christian Dior. Before Dior's death in 1957 he told Cardin, "Take up the torch—it can be yours." Dior sent his clients to Cardin, who had by that time set up his own atelier.

Except for a six-year, live-in relationship with French actress Jeanne Moreau in the late '60s, Cardin has remained alone (although he enjoys a close relationship with Anouk Aimee). "After work," he says, "solitude dominates my life." A thin, ascetic man, he decrees: "It is not a dishonor to be a businessman when one is a creator too." The major threat to clothing design creativity, says Cardin, is the jean! "The jean is the destructor! It is a dictator! It is destroying creativity. The jean must be stopped!" That of course did not stop him from designing jeans.

George Carlin

Did you know that there are actually some phrases in the English language that have never been uttered? For example, nobody, in the history of speech, has ever said, "hand me that piano," or "please cut off my legs." Isn't it funny how the phrase, "military intelligence," is a contradiction in terms? And why is there no blue food? Such are the ponderings of George Carlin, a comic with a face like a Doonesbury cartoon character who has made a career out of his fascination with language, his outrage at convention, and his loathing for political doublespeak.

George Denis Patrick Carlin was born in the Bronx, N.Y. 12 May 1938. After playing the role of class clown, he dropped out of high school to observe life in the Air Force and in odd jobs before becoming a radio announcer in Shreveport, La. From his early years in broadcasting, Carlin garnered material for some of his funniest bits: the fast-talking radio DJ on "Wonderful Wino" radio; "Al Sleet, your hippy, dippy weatherman;" and the host of a TV divorce show, in which contestants spin a wheel to determine alimony and child custody rights.

Carlin came to comedy prominence in the 1960's, working Las Vegas and television, eventually becoming a regular on the "Tonight Show" in 1967, delivering mock newscasts. But in the early 1970's, tired of the restrictions placed on his imagination by the confines of TV, he grew his hair long and began a second career, gearing his routines to a younger, more politically-conscious audience, with jokes about drugs, government, and censorship. "I was just sick to my stomach of wearing the dumb tuxedo and entertaining middle-class morons."

Through the years, Carlin produced many popular comedy albums, including, *FM/AM*, (1972); *Class Clown*, (1972); *Toledo Window Box* (1974); and *What Am I Doing in New Jersey?* (1988). He recently extended his comedic talents to the big screen, starring in Disney's *Outrageous Fortune* (1987) and *Bill and Ted's Excellent Adventure* (1989).

George's famous routine, "Seven Words You Can Never Use on Television," got him arrested on a charge of public profanity in 1972. Undaunted by his arrest (the charges were dropped), Carlin continued to write material attacking censorship and government controls. Despite his outrage, audiences were warmed by the underlying message of his madness: a plea for humanity.

Eric Carmen

His Rasberries were popular way before the California Raisins. His roots were planted in rock before he branched off to become a popular solo artist. Anyone who has listened to the radio during the past twenty years knows that Eric Carmen has grown into a timeless recording artist.

Born in Cleveland, Ohio, on the 11th of August, Carmen learned the tools of his craft at an early age. During his early years, Eric studied classical piano, theory and harmony as well as guitar. In the early 70's he founded the legendary Rasberries and led them onto the charts with such Top Ten hits as: "Go All the Way," "I Wanna Be With You," "Let's Pretend," "Tonight" and "Overnight Sensation." The group's sound blended rich harmonies on top of tight arrangements. *Rolling Stone* magazine proclaimed the group's last album, *Starting Over* as "one of 1974's best."

Not afraid to take chances, Carmen then invested in a solo career. Against all odds he chose to release a long ballad, "All By Myself," in 1976; the song not only saturated the radiowaves, but also became an immediate standard, sung by entertainers throughout the country. The follow-up single, "Never Gonna Fall in Love Again," added to Carmen's popularity.

Borrowing the title of his next album, *Boats Against the Current* (1977), from the last line of a favorite book—*The Great Gatsby*—the LP produced another hit single, "She Did It." Two more albums followed—*Change of Heart* (1978) and *Tonight You're Mine* (1980), but some of Carmen's momentum was running out. Some critical successes include "Foolin' Myself" (which became a finalist in the 1980 Yamaha Music Festival in Tokyo) and his rendition of the Four Tops' classic "Baby I Need Your Loving." Next Carmen switched record labels (from Arista to Geffen). The album *Maybe My Baby* produced a single, "I Wanna Hear It From Your Lips," while the album's title song became a country hit for Louise Mandrell. A short time later Carmen made an eventful comeback by collaborating with his old Rasberries producer, Jimmy Ienner. The two men combined to create "Hungry Eyes" (1987) for the mega-hit soundtrack *Dirty Dancing;* the single was a number one smash in the United States and Europe. On the heels of this success Carmen's next single, "Make Me Lose Control," topped the charts, and a duet with Louise Mandrell featuring the theme song from the TV series "Growing Pains" climbed onto the country charts. Carmen is single and lives in his hometown of Cleveland, Ohio.

Kim Carnes

Her popular 1981 record "Bette Davis Eyes" thrust Kim Carnes into the limelight. Although a veteran of the music business for many years, it was that particular Grammy Award-winning single that set Kim up for a steady stream of subsequent hits. She is the only recording artist to have the honor of maintaining a solo, duet and trio on the National Pop Charts at the same time. In 1984 Kim's song with Kenny Rogers and James Ingram "What About Me" shared a place on the charts with "Make No Mistakes (He's Mine)"—(performed with Barbra Streisand)—and Carnes's own single "Invitation To Dance."

A famous alumni of "The Christie Minstrels," Kim Carnes was born on the 20th of July. She has been a songwriter for as long as she can remember, turning out successful tunes for herself and other artists. At the start of her career, she sang back-up with such seasoned professionals as Michael McDonald, Kenny Rogers, and David Cassidy, until she landed her own record deal. Mixing her creative abilities, Kim makes music that has "always been on the edge of rock and country." Her albums—*St. Vincent's Court* (1979), *Romance Dance* (1980), *Mistaken Identity* (1981), and *Light House* (1986), capture the adaptable Carnes sound. In 1988 she wanted to return to basics—away from the technological '80's techniques—so she recorded *View From the House*. She explains, "It was really important for me on this album to get full circle and go real non-synth. I wanted it to be an acoustic album with real instruments. Acoustic guitars, piano, mandolin—that kind of album." She insisted on heading to Tennessee: "If you want to make a rock and roll album, these days, you've got to go to Nashville."

Kim has written and co-written hundreds of songs. She composed Kenny Rogers's *Gideon* album and shared the spotlight with him on the top-five pop/country duet "Don't Fall in Love With a Dreamer." She has also written many songs with her husband, Dave Ellingson (an ex-Christie Minstrel, too), and the couple's proudest collaboration is their son Collin (born in 1975).

Art Carney

The name on his birth certificate (4 November 1918) reads Arthur William Matthew Carney, but for a generation of TV watchers, he'll always be Ed Norton, "the underground sanitation expert" of Jackie Gleason's "The Honeymooners." In reruns in the 1980s, the program was so popular that it spawned a cult of diehard devotees (The Royal Association for the Longevity and Preservation of the Honeymooners, or *RALPH*, founded in 1982 for

Ralph Kramden, the portly bus-driver played by Jackie Gleason in the 1950's television series). The many critical plums (including multitudinous Emmys) he received during his long and fruitful second-banana years make some people forget that the comic genius has also proved his mettle in tragedy. But whatever the genre the successes speak for themselves, like *Harry and Tonto* (1974), for which Carney received the Golden Globe Award as well as the Oscar for best performance by an actor. In 1985, he teamed up again with Gleason for a TV movie, "Izzy and Moe," about the legendary Prohibition agents.

The man who brought sewer-dweller Ed Norton to life started polishing his comedic craft early. The youngest of six boys, he staged his first one-man-show in the family living room in Mount Vernon, N.Y., artfully titling it "Art for Art's Sake." After touring as a $50-a-week funnyman with Horace Heidt's band, he did lighthearted second-banana duties for the likes of Fred Allen, Bert Lahr, and Edgar Bergen, but faced some rather dark days during World War II when he was wounded shortly after landing at Normandy's Omaha Beach. (His right leg is still an inch shorter than the left.) A chronic brooder ("I'm always worried about what's going to happen in the next six months"), he had another dark period in the 1960s when he departed from his highly successful Broadway run in *The Odd Couple* to enter a psychiatric hospital.

The '80's have been good to Art; he played a wonderful grandpa to Brian Bonsall in a touching Coca-Cola commercial, and guest-starred on the 1987 television series "The Cavanaughs." He played Santa Claus in a television film with Jaclyn Smith, *The Night They Saved Christmas* (1986), and received a TV award from the National Board of Review in 1989.

His marriage to Jean Meyers ended in divorce in 1966 after 26 years and three children, but was reinstated in 1977 (after an interim marriage to Barbara Isaac).

Leslie Caron

Beginning her professional career at the age of 16 as the youngest petit rat of Roland Petit's Ballet des Champs Elyseés, she so impressed David Lichine with her dancing that he gave her the leading role of the Sphinx in his ballet "La Recontre" in 1946. Her good fortune continued when Gene Kelly starred her opposite himself in the 1951 Oscar-winning film *An American in Paris,* which launched her Hollywood career. Today, however, she bears only a slight resemblance to *Lili* (1953), or *Gigi* (1958), or *Fanny* (1961), or the girl-woman who fell in love with *Daddy Long Legs* (1955).

"Most miserable period in my life," she declares. "I hate musicals. I had toe shoes on from eight thirty in the morning until six every night. I was constantly in agony.... I had bruises and sprains that couldn't heal. When I walked out of Hollywood, after years of unhappiness, Fred Astaire and Gene Kelly both told me. 'Leslie, you're so smart to quit while you can still walk.' I'm glad those days are gone forever." (An attempted dancing comeback failed when in 1984 injuries prevented her from starring in the touring company of *On Your Toes*.) She gained new status as a dramatic actress in *The L-Shaped Room* (1963) and *Is Paris Burning?* (1966). Of the latter she says, "I said hell before I did the scene and giggled right after. Dramatic scenes. I don't enjoy them." Despite her reservations regarding her movie roles, she never completely disappeared from the Hollywood scene. She appeared in *Valentino* (1977), *Goldengirl* (1979), *Dangerous Moves* (1984), *The Train* (1987), and *The Man Who Lived at the Ritz* (1989). Her book of short stories, *Vengeance*, was published in 1982. Kicking up her heels again, Leslie danced with Nureyev and Baryshnikov in a gala performance at the Met in 1986.

Born 1 July 1931 in Paris, Caron is the daughter of a French chemist and an American-born dancer. She was first married to American meat-packing heir George Hormel II and then to British producer-director Peter Hall (two children). The second marriage ended in divorce, with Warren Beatty named as correspondent. She married producer Michael Laughlin in 1967. When asked if she thought she had profited from her mistakes, she curtly replied, "What mistakes?" She divorced Laughlin in 1977. Caron is hardly reticent and speaks her mind on a myriad of subjects: "An actor I worked with ... came up and asked me to go to bed with him. If I did, he said, it would make him act better the next day. Well, I only go to bed with people I'm in love with. I'm not bragging. I haven't the slightest idea what the public thinks of me and I don't care."

John Carpenter

"The first movie [my parents] ever took me to was *The African Queen* and what I remember most is Humphrey Bogart coming out of the water covered with leeches. But my monumental experience with films was in 1953, when I was five. My parents took me to *It Came From Outer Space*, in 3-D. You had to wear special glasses. The first shot was of this meteor—it came right off the screen and exploded in my face. I couldn't believe it! It was everything I'd ever wanted! After that I was addicted to films. I made movies in my head.... I made up little stories. When I was eight, my dad gave me an 8-mm movie camera." The grown-up film addict, following several failures, eventually made—in 20 days—the hit film *Halloween* (1978), thereby carving a niche for himself as a key suspense/horror director of the '80s. "When success comes, it's a frenzy—wham! People start running; they get a fever. I remember a producer saying to me, 'You're hot!' Everybody's overreacting. I haven't changed that much; the only difference is that the film has made money. This is how you're judged."

He was born in Kentucky in 1948 and raised there in Bowling Green, the only child of a violinist/music professor. Encouraged in creative endeavors by his parents, he studied violin, piano and guitar, playing the last and singing in a 60s rock band. ("If I'd stayed in Kentucky, I'd still be playing rock and roll today. I have a tremendous love for music.") He attended Western Kentucky University and U.S.C. film school. As a youngster, "I felt I was quite a bit the outsider, a little weird. I was pretty single-minded. As a matter of fact, my movies now are pretty single-minded movies. I'm a little obsessive.... I have a great feeling for physical movies. I don't like intellectual films. I love suspense. I want the audience to laugh and cry—an emotional response. The medium *is* emotional, not so much like a book or a play really, as like music.... Movies are pieces of film stuck together in a certain rhythm, an absolute beat—like a musical composition. The rhythm you create affects the audience." The intense director also composed *Halloween's* music score. His subsequent films—most but not all in his special genre—include: *Elvis* (1979—originally for TV), *The Fog* (1980), *Escape from N.Y.* (1981), *The Thing* (1982—a remake of the classic by Howard Hawks—"My favorite director"), *Christine* (1983), *Starman* (1985), *Black Moon Rising* (1986), *Prince of Darkness* (1987) and *They Live* (1988).

He is the father of a son, John Cody, by his marriage to actress Adrienne Barbeau, who has appeared in some of his films. He has no illusions about his company town: "There's very little honor here—maybe anywhere. People lie, cheat and steal. All the clichés about Hollywood have a basis in truth. It can be very disgusting. But I live by my decision to make Hollywood films."

Allan Carr

"Caftan's Courageous," is how the *Hollywood Reporter* captioned a profile of this show-biz sybarite who has managed to move from personal manager, to producer, to entrepreneur, to renown as "the undisputed champion of quick wit and movie magic." His "La Cage au Carr" lifestyle rates a "10" for pizazz with its legendary parties (including a dinner for Truman Capote in Los Angeles' Lincoln Heights Jail), his caftans and full-length furs, his having had his jaw wired shut to keep himself from over-eating, his houses in Beverly Hills, Malibu, Waikiki ("He looks like a beach ball wearing aviator glasses," decided *Esquire*), Manhattan and London—it's all there like some frantic funhouse. Often accused of being nothing but a flit by his movie industry enemies, his accomplishments speak for themselves: his film of *Grease* with John Travolta is one of the highest earning musicals ever made in movie history and among the highest box-office grossers overall; his legit musical version of France's *La Cage Aux Folles* was Broadway's hottest ticket in 1983, 1984 and 1985. (Carr's estimated take for *La Cage* was over $100,000 a week.) He also brilliantly coordinated the promotional campaign that brought *The Deer Hunter* its five Academy Awards in 1979.

Born 27 May 1941 in Highland Park, Illinois, his days of being an overweight teenager bred dreams of show business. "I thought my life was going to be *Photoplay* and *Modern Screen*." His lifelong love affair with the theater was launched when his parents took him to a Chicago production of the Jule Styne musical, *High Button Shoes*. In his very early teens, he became the youngest angel on Broadway when he invested $750 in the Tallulah Bankhead musical *Ziegfeld Follies*, which closed, alas, out of town. He did better with a $1250 stake in *The Happiest Millionaire*, starring Walter Pidgeon, which turned out to be a hit. Carr was a full-fledged impresario by the time he was 20, with productions at Chicago's Civic Theatre of Bette Davis' *The World of Carl Sandburg*, Eva La Gallienne in the Tyrone Guthrie mounting of *Mary Stuart*, and Tennessee Williams' *Garden District*. Moving to L.A., Carr produced the West Coast premiere of Norman Krasna's *Sunday in New York* starring a then-unknown USC student named Marlo Thomas. He also doubled as Ms. Thomas's manager, a role he would later play for Ann-Margret, Marvin Hamlisch, Melina Mercouri and the late Peter Sellers, among others. His leap to millionaire status came when he ingeniously dubbed and re-edited a Mexican cheapie about a Uruguayan soccer team turned cannabalistic after a plane crash in the Andes; *Survive!* was Paramount's sleeper hit of 1976. His other films include *Can't Stop the Music, C.C. & Company, Grease 2*, a remake of *Where The Boys Are, Cloak and Dagger* and *Silence*. He is the developer for a unique theatre concept—"Goya"—and was the producer for the 1989 Academy Awards show.

Jose Carreras

"He's young, he's handsome, he's intelligent, he can sing and he's a tenor," proclaimed one repertory conductor. Jose Carreras' career has soared since his Italian debut (1971) when he walked away with a first in the Verdi Competition. Since then Carreras has sung the most celebrated roles in the most famous operas—among them, *La Boheme, Tosca, Aida* and *Carmen*. In 1984, under the baton of Leonard Bernstein, Carreras tackled a very different sort of role, that of Tony in a recording of *West Side Story*. "Struggling manfully to remove his accent," (according to a *Wall Street Journal* writer) Carreras took English lessons "whenever he [wasn't] flirting, consuming sugarless candy bars or telling jokes." Carreras has also recorded obscure music pieces, among them a little-known Puccini Mass which premiered in 1880 when Puccini was only twenty-two.

Born in Barcelona, 5 December 1946, the Spanish tenor with the "sweetness of timbre and purity of phrasing" studied piano as a youth and began vocal training at the age of seventeen. After graduating from the Barcelona Conservatory, Carreras made his operatic debut (in Barcelona) as Ismaele in Verdi's *Nabucco*. In 1971 he made a successful London debut (with two compatriots who supported Carreras' career, Montserrat Caballe and Rafael Fruhbeck de Burgos) and the following year, began a series of American performances. Carreras has, of course, made the rounds of the most famous opera houses in the world—Covent Garden, The Metropolitan Opera and La Scala. He especially enjoys American audiences. ("I must say of American audiences—normally those in New York, but generally throughout America—that they are very, very loyal. The only place similar is London. Vienna, La Scala, Hamburg—they are very dangerous. A singer can have a great night, but the next night if one tone is not 100%, they boo.") One of the most popular lyric tenors of his generation, he at times (according to critics) "essays roles heavier than ideal for his resources and follows an overtaxing schedule." Carreras himself admits his recent foray into more dramatic parts has been tough. "Heroic roles are very, very trying. One must work on them for years." Carreras played his own courageous role in 1988 when he was struck with a rare blood disease. After a life-threatening battle, Jose made a comeback and has been singing with a renewed spirit.

Diahann Carroll

"I was a big girl before I found out my name was spelled that way. I had to get a work permit and I saw my birth certificate spelled Diahann. 'Who's that?' I asked. 'That's you, Charlie,' said my mother."

Carol Diahann Johnson was born in the Bronx, N.Y., 17 July 1935, the elder daughter of a subway motorman and a nurse for retarded children. She won a Metropolitan Opera Scholarship at the age of ten and was accepted at Manahattan's prestigious High School of Music and Art. While studying sociology at N.Y.U., she auditioned for a Lou Walters black revue, *Jazz Train*. From that point her nightclub career took off; she dropped out of college and went on tour. "At first when I worked in Miami they put me in a smaller hotel down the street. I felt like garbage." She appeared on Broadway in the critically acclaimed musical *House of Flowers* (1952) and "Sleeping Bee" became her signature tune. In Hollywood she appeared in *Carmen Jones, Porgy and Bess*, and in non-singing roles in *Paris Blues, Hurry Sundown* and *Claudine*.

Richard Rodgers wrote *No Strings* to bring her back to Broadway and in 1962 she won a Tony for her portrayal in the musical of a Paris mannequin; "Sweetest Sounds" became her new signature tune. In 1968 she became the second black to star in her own TV series, "Julia" (Hattie McDaniel in "Beulah" in 1947 was the first), which ran for three seasons, with the general consensus deeming it just another sit-com. Her past husbands include TV producer Monte Kay (one daughter, Suzanne Ottilie), Freddé Glusman, and Robert DeLeon (who was found dead at the wheel of his wrecked sportscar). She was engaged to David Frost for a brief while, then married her fourth husband, Vic Damone, in January, 1987. The couple took their marriage on the road, and developed a pleasant niteclub act. Recounting her life and loves, Diahann published *Diahann: An Autobiography* in 1986. Additional television performances include: "I Know Why the Caged Bird Sings" (1978), a regular role on TV's "Dynasty" (1984/85) and a role in the NBC 4-hour miniseries "Walkers," with Lindsay Wagner. On Broadway, she played the psychiatrist in *Agnes of God* in 1982.

Diahann and Vic switch-off between 3 homes: Beverly Hills, Palm Springs and New York City. She likes cooking, entertaining and designing her own clothes.

Johnny Carson

When a reporter asked "What made you a star?" Johnny Carson replied, "I started out in a gaseous state, then cooled." Actually, he's hotter then ever since becoming television's undisputed Captain Midnight, in the host's chair (vacated by Jack Parr in 1962) on NBC-TV's "Tonight" show. His impudent on-camera activities over the years have won out in the ratings over a gaggle of rival nighttime chatterboxes, and he's now on the NBC payroll for what is rumored to be "millions" of dollars a year. "His success is due in great measure to his quick wit, his ability to seize absurdity and run with it," observed *TV Guide* in 1984. "He is Johnny-on-the-spot with an instant retort. His timing and delivery are expert. His face speaks more eloquently than his writers' scripted words. He is a master of the slow take, the mock-affronted expression, the blank stare at the camera."

John William Carson was born 23 October 1925 in Corning, Iowa ("No cracks, please"), but blossomed as a neophyte performer in the town of Norfolk, Nebraska, where he grew up. He sent away for a mail-order course in ventriloquism and magic, emerged as "The Great Carsoni" and did very well ($3 a performance) on the local Elks-Moose-Redmen circuit before heading off for the Navy. As a University of Nebraska grad after the war, he went to work on Omaha radio station WOW ("I wasn't"); when the TV era arrived, he ad-libbed his way through a local show called "The Squirrel's Nest." While working as a comedy writer for Red Skelton, he was called in on two hours' notice as a replacement when Skelton was injured. The response to that appearance put him on the road to the quiz show, "Who Do You Trust?" where Carson cavorted for five years before moving to the "Tonight" hot seat.

Always accused of being something of a Little Boy "Blue," Carson has kept pace with the enormous social changes in this country in the last 20 years. "Grown older, he has grown bolder; as sexual taboos have relaxed, he has become more permissively risqué," wrote Bill Kaufman in a 1984 *TV Guide* story. When Mr. Universe appeared on his show, he told Johnny, "Your body is your home, you know, your house." Replied Johnny: "Well, my house is a mess, but I have a woman that comes in twice a week." In response to criticism of such "off color" humor, Carson says: "If you can't talk about anything grown-up or sophisticated at midnight without being called immoral and dirty, then I think we're in trouble."

In regard to his marital-go-round, the similar names of his three ex-wives—Jody, Joanne and Joanna—have caused more than one jokester to observe that Carson has never had to change the monograms on his towels. With his first wife, Jody Wolcott (they met at the University of Nebraska), he had three boys. Wife number two was Joanne Copeland, whom he divorced in 1972. Number three was Joanna Holland, whom he married later that year. They filed for divorce in 1983 after ten years of marriage. When asked about weddings, Carson joked: "My giving advice on marriage is like the captain of the *Titanic* giving lessons on navigation.... I resolve if I ever get hit in the face again with rice; it will be because I insulted a Chinese person." Carson started from scratch again in 1987 when he married his fourth wife, Alex Maas, in Malibu. Off to a new beginning (her first name starts with an "a"), the couple reside in California.

"That he managed to survive for so long is one of the most interesting things about prankish, puckish Johnny," Bill Kaufman observed. "We have been a part of his survival; we made him, he is ours.... As long as he makes his audiences laugh at what they consider funny and dares to criticize what they would like to, he will continue to be No. 1, the King of the Talk Shows, the nice boy from Nebraska who made good, but real good, in the Big City of America."

Elliott Carter

He is, according to some creative giants, the most original, masterly, and likely-to-shake-the-world composer on the scene today. Elliott Carter's music "makes a listener glad to be living when they are eager to discover each new work, as it happens, excited to explore the new imaginative realms that each one offers," says one critic. The complexity of his works accounts for his reputation as a composer's composer. "Carter's music is difficult simply because he hears it that way in his mind and can transmit it to us in no other form," another professional observer suggests. Says Carter, "I try to write music that will appeal to an intelligent listener's ear and will be a strong enough expression so that the listener will be drawn to hear and grasp the music when it is presented to a performer who finds it gratifying enough to play it effectively."

Born in New York City, 11 December 1908, Elliott Carter attended Horace Mann High School in Manhattan. He attributes his adventurous approach to composing to the progressive philosophy of Horace Mann ("We weren't taught particular things but to deal with problems as they came up. We learned that routine was out, and we had to invent solutions for everything.... So the notion of rigid patterns in my music is out. Each piece is an adventure. Routine solution is avoided.") At Harvard, Carter minored in literature and languages. He studied piano during that time at the Longy School of Music in Cambridge, Massachusetts and by 1930 decided to devote himself exclusively to music. While studying with the legendary Nadia Boulanger in Paris at the Ecole Normale de Musique, Carter also learned Greek and mathematics. Returning to America in 1935 as music director of the Ballet Caravan, he gave courses in music, math, physics and classical Greek (at St. John's College, Annapolis). Carter held teaching posts at the Peabody Conservatory in Baltimore, Columbia University, Cornell, and Yale and in 1963 was the Composer-in-Residence at the American Academy in Rome. He is twice a Pulitzer Prize winner—for String Quartets Nos. 2 & 3 in 1960 (he also received the New York Music Critics Circle Award and the two pieces were chosen the most important work of the year by the International Rostrum of Composers) and his Second String Quartet, 1973. Stravinsky called his Double Concerto "the first true American masterpiece." The 1983 book *The Music of Elliott Carter* by David Schiff discusses Carter's role as one of the world's most important composers. In 1985 at a White House ceremony, he was one of the first recipients of the newly-created National Medal of the Arts. Carter works up to ten hours a day on a piece—"when the end is sort of in sight, I get so obsessed with the music that I sometimes become antisocial.... If a piece doesn't obsess me, I don't see any point in continuing to write it. Perhaps this is self indulgent." Carter's wife (the former Helen Frost-Jones; one son) keeps his "life in order" freeing his time for his own work and helping new composers. He sees our world as a limitless resource for music, for his own work—"Our time is... awesome, frightening, and, certainly energetic. Therefore, its greatest music must be and is more powerful than the classical masterpieces."

Carter celebrated his 80th birthday in 1988 by performing at two special concerts in London.

Hodding Carter III

Already well established with the Washington press corps thanks to his newspaper background and his willingness to give as much information as official discretion permitted over the preceding three years, Assistant Secretary of State for Public Affairs Hodding Carter III catapulted into the national limelight as the Department's official chief source of information during the 1979-80 Iranian hostage crisis. Close to his boss, Secretary of State Cyrus Vance, Carter considered himself "lucky" in the circumstances that he worked for "a guy who didn't once ask me to go out and play Joe Idiot." He resigned the post on 1 July 1980 and, in early 1981, became anchorman and chief correspondent for PBS's "Inside Story" (1981-1984), a half-hour critique of press performance that won three Emmy Awards. Carter's objective for the series was not "to 'get' the press, but to examine its performance with care. The press is an institution virtually all Americans depend on and it should be the subject for public scrutiny, as other institutions are." Carter's next institution for scrutiny was the U.S. Congress. With "Capital Journal," begun on PBS in 1985, producer-host Carter presented a weekly half hour designed to show the public how Congressional power relates to them by focusing on how Congress operates and how its power is exercised in Washington and across the country.

Born 7 April 1935, Hodding Carter III attended Phillips Exeter Academy and graduated from Greenville (Mississippi) High school and Princeton (summa cum laude, 1957). After two years in the Marines, he returned to Greenville and the family newspaper, the *Delta Democrat-Times*, in 1959. In the next 17 years, starting as a reporter, he became editorial writer (1960), managing editor (1962) and, finally, editor and associate publisher (1965), and was active politically on local, state and national levels. When President Jimmy Carter named him to the State Department in January, 1977, he turned his duties at the *Delta Democrat-Times* over to his brother Philip, and the family subsequently sold the newspaper. He quickly established an excellent rapport with the Washington press corps, accepting any hostility with equanimity, saying "If there weren't an adversary relationship between the government and the press, I'd wonder what was wrong with the press." After resigning from the Carter Administration, he "decompressed" at his vacation home in Camden, Maine, before assuming his PBS reporting duties. A regular participant on "This Week with David Brinkley" on ABC, he has also been the guest anchor for "Nightline." Since January, 1981, he has been an op-ed columnist for the *Wall Street Journal*.

In 1978 Carter divorced his wife of 21 years, the former Margaret Ainsworth Wolfe (four children) and married Patricia Murphy Derian (mother of three), a long-time political ally in Mississippi, who had served alongside him in the State Department as Assistant Secretary for Human rights. They live in a three-story townhouse in Alexandria, Virginia. The author of *The South Strikes Back* (1959), Carter has contributed to four other books and has worked on a biography of his Pulitzer Prize-winning father, Hodding Carter, Jr., known as "the conscience of the South" for his early espousal of civil rights in the *Delta Democrat-Times*, which he founded.

Jimmy Carter

It seemed fitting that the American people would elect this soft-voiced technocrat as President at the dawning of the post-industrial age of technology. What couldn't be predicted at the time was that four years later it was just as inevitable that the electorate would turn out of office the man they held responsible for a steadily escalating inflation rate and the humiliation of a year-long, almost nightly picture of blindfolded Americans being pushed around by a gang of gun-toting Khomeini-intoxicated goons during the 1979-80 hostage crises. Instead, they looked to the pre-technological soothing image of Ronald Reagan, the charmer from the West, who promised them an America where they could "stand tall." Carter's successes—the Camp David accords and the Israeli-Egyptian peace treaty, the Panama Canal treaties, the normalization of relations with China, the establishment of human rights as a prime factor in American foreign policy—meant little to a people who had made a decision that an absence of bravura performance in the highest office in the land signified a weakness that they were no longer willing to tolerate. They didn't want complexity after all—an "engineer's view of the world" where every detail of the bridge was in place. "He didn't tell the American people where it was going," recalls Mayor Andrew Young of Atlanta, one of Carter's key aides while he was President.

The route from Plains, Georgia, to Washington, D.C., began 1 October 1924, when James Earl Carter, Jr., was born, increasing the town's population to 551. A brilliant student, a fast but unspectacular basketball player, and a debater whose "delivery wasn't tops," Carter entered the U.S. Naval Academy at Annapolis in 1943, inspired by an uncle who was a career Navy man. After graduation, he gravitated towards the nuclear submarine program headed by the legendary Hyman Rickover, who became a major role model for the young officer. Forced to abandon a naval career (and his goal of someday becoming Chief of Naval Operations) when his father died in 1953, Carter returned to Plains to rescue the family's foundering seed, fertilizer and peanut-farming operations, and to assume a leadership role in the town's civic and religious communities. A member of the Georgia Senate from 1963 to 1967, he lost a bid for the Democratic gubernatorial nomination in 1966, a low point that led to "a profound religious experience." A 1970 bid was successful, and Carter, preaching racial harmony and equality, emerged as an exemplar of the "New South," a role that propelled him to the national scene—and a *Time* magazine cover. Failure to win a spot as George McGovern's running mate on the 1972 Presidential ticket did not dismay Carter or his aides, who drafted the meticulous plan that would produce success in 1976. That the success wasn't repeated in 1980 was, in the words of Tom Wicker in a July 1984, *Esquire* article, perhaps "because the people just didn't hear from him what they wanted to be told, what they wanted to believe about themselves. . . . Maybe they began to wonder, as Andy Young suggested to me, 'Is God still on our side?' And Reagan says, 'Yes God is still on our side?' He says it so well, and Carter didn't say it at all."

If Carter was not an exciting President, his family was an exciting—and colorful—First (extended) Family. Rosalynn (Married 7 July 1946) was accused of exerting undue influence on her husband. Amy (born 19 October, 1967; three sons as well) at 12 was quoted in her father's memorable debate with Reagan as a caring expert on foreign affairs (with predictable adverse results once the laughter subsided); "Miss Lillian" (who at 70 had joined the Peace Corps in India, and died in 1983 at the age of 85) was always good for a quote while disco-hopping in New York; sister Gloria Spann was a motorcyclist who had a son in the slammer; sister Ruth Carter Stapleton (who died in 1983) was a world-renowned faith healer. But it was brother Billy, everybody's idea of a "good ol' boy," whose drinkin' and dealin' (with the likes of Libya's Khaddafi) was the source of greatest embarrassment to his considerably more circumspect brother. (Billy Carter died in September, 1988.)

Active on the talk circuit and literary scene, Jimmy's recent books include: *Everything to Gain: Making the Most of Your Life* (1987) and *An Outdoor Journal* (1988).

Lynda Carter

This indefatigable "Wonder Woman" power-glided over American air-waves from 1976-70 after winning the Miss World-U.S.A. title in 1973. As amazons go, she can surely hold her own against Godzilla, but she can also score with an audience. Witness all the Lynda Carter specials and celebrations ("Body and Soul" which aired March of '81 was a typical example of a ratings clean-up) and TV movies as well: ("Born To Be Sold," 1981; "Rita Hayworth;" "The Love Goddess," 1983).

Born in Phoenix, Ariz., 24 July circa 1950 the youngest of three children, Lynda made her professional singing debut at fifteen and is as adept at singing and dancing as she is at situation comedy or realistic drama. Co-starring in the 1984 series "Partners in Crime" with Loni Anderson, the two actresses played the widow and ex-wife of the same man. After his death, they jointly inherited his detective agency. In 1987, Lynda appeared in the made-for-TV film "Stillwatch." When not doing television, the "shazam superstar" makes believers out of all who see her Vegas act, "slinking and sizzling" as one reporter puts it, her way through a battery of songs. Carter also serves as Beauty and Fashion Director of Maybelline cosmetics, appearing in the company's advertising and serving as a consultant in the development and marketing of new products. In the 18 months following her signing by Maybelline, the company's sales tripled, skyrocketing from $70 million to over $200 million.

Carter was named one of "Ten Most Exciting Women In The World" by the International Bachelors Association. That group is out of the running since she married Robert Altman (not the director) in January of 1984. Carter's Altman is a partner in a Washington, D.C., law firm. The couple are the proud parents of son, Jamie, born 14 January 1988.

Nell Carter

Although she survived as she attempted to follow that familiar trial of stardom—going to New York—it took ten years before the ironically-ill-timed pieces finally fell into place. While working as a nightclub singer at Dangerfield's, The Apartment, and even in Mayor Lindsay's campaign, she occasionally went into one production when she had the opportunity to take more fruitful offers, "I was in the original cast of *Bubbling Brown Sugar*," Carter says, "before it came to Broadway. I left it to go into *Be Kind to People Week*. Instead of *The Wiz* I chose *Miss Moffat*, which closed out of town. I chose *Duds*, which lasted one night." But, proving that where there's life there's hope, the woman the *New York Times* describes as "the short, buxom, bubbling woman with a singing voice that has the raw, penetrating quality of a steel-tipped drill" kept at it.

Born Nell Ruth Carter on 13 September 1948 in Birmingham, Ala., this frequent local radio and TV-performing teen had hightailed it north at age 19 when an NBC-TV "Today" show scout encouraged her. In New York she honed the voice that had been inspired by Dinah Washington and Dakota Staton, and studied for three years at Bill Russell's School of Drama. The persistent polishing paid premiums when she won a Tony Award in *Ain't Misbehavin'*. Her lively performance led to scads of offers, and she was soon seen in the film version of *Hair*, as a guest of Johnny Carson's and Merv Griffin's, and as a member of TV specials like the all-black Cinderella story "Cindy," and "Baryshnikov on Broadway." She picked her prized plum, to that point, when NBC-TV gave her "Gimme a Break," her own situation comedy. In 1988, Nell celebrated the tenth anniversary of *Ain't Misbehavin'* in a special new touring production of the show. She was also given the honor of performing at President George Bush's Inaugural Gala in 1989. Nell married George Krynick in 1982 and makes her home in California.

Barbara Cartland

Cited by the Guinness Book of Records as the world's top-selling author *and* its most prolific (over 370 books, some 370 million sales), this "great big beautiful pink bonbon of a woman" reigns as Britain's "First Lady of Romance." After dreaming up her first bestseller, *Jigsaw* in 1923 when she was 22, it took her nearly thirty years to write her first hundred books. Later, she speeded up her output and finished her 200th in 1978; revving up still faster to an average of 24 or more books per year, she had finished her 300th volume by the time of her 80th birthday in 1981. Highly connected in British society (her daughter Raine is Princess Diana's stepmother), it's not surprising that some of her plots touch on the doings of royalty. Some representative titles: *The Penniless Peer, The Wicked Marquis, The Elusive Earl, The Cruel Count, The Disgraceful Duke, Royal Punishment* and, most provocative of all, *The Prince and the Pekinese*. Actually, suggestive as her titles might sometimes be, and though other romance writers are getting racier ("Everyone feels they must be modern and put in some dirty bits," sniffs Cartland), Barbara Cartland heroines still manage to remain virginal until, as one critic put it, "the necessary vows have been traded in the presence of a cleric." Says the author about her works: "They're about pure love. Romeo and Juliet love, the love of the troubadours, the love of Browning and Botticelli, the love of a decent woman."

About the only thing shocking about Barbara Cartland is her favorite color of pink. Beneath her much-publicized facade of "flamboyance, fantasy and frivolity," is a hyper-energetic woman who's had more than her share of suffering. Born 9 July 1901, she was the daughter of an American major killed in Flanders during the first World War, and she and her mother and two brothers had a lean time of it. Still, she became one of London's "bright young things" in her twenties, and a prime factor in her brother Ronald's 1935 campaign to win a Parliamentary seat. (He was, in 1940, the first M.P. to be killed at Dunkirk, and her brother Anthony was also killed.) In between writing her romantic fantasies, Cartland has found time to be married and divorced, married and widowed, to give birth to a daughter and two sons, to campaign against fluoridation of Britain's water and *for* an increased diet of honey and more camps for Romany gypsies. She is also a global traveler and has recorded an album of love songs with the Royal Philharmonic Orchestra. Says her son Ian McCorquodale, who serves as her business manager: "I hold only one thing against her. Mother simply can't relax. She's never learned how." What she *has* learned is how to keep her whirlwind production schedule from being deflected by the frequent digs she gets from the London press accusing her of exploiting her link to the royals. Despite being one of the few living people ever to be immortalized with an effigy in Madame Tussaud's famed London wax museum, she is, as one reporter put it, "an American, not an English addiction." But Cartland, writing indefatigably on, manages to rise above the criticism. "Part of my philosophy of life is never to admit that you've been beaten or done down. Quite early on I learned that the best way to survive is to pretend that anything unpleasant simply hasn't happened."

Following a common trend, Cartland's stories were adapted for television movies, including "A Hazard of Hearts" (1987) and "The Lady and The Highwayman" (1989). *Barbara Cartland: An Authorized Biography* was published in 1985.

Johnny Cash

An associate analyzed this bucolic balladeer's popularity thusly: "His songs are honest and simple, and basically that's what people are. And even if they're not, they respect a man they think is. I think people pay to see him as much as they do to hear his songs. The big, rough character, thought by many to be a tough prisoner. They like to hear him talk, to hear his stories. He's the kind of person that when he talks, it always sounds as if he's got something to say." Years earlier he himself had less romantically summarized his *raison d'etre:* "I got the idea of singin' for a livin' because I was starvin' to death. You don't have to have lived in poverty to be a successful country singer, but it helps."

He's not starving anymore. In fact, he's been successful almost from the time he and his Tennessee Two graduated from playing Memphis church socials and signed, in 1955, with the same record label that Elvis Presley had just joined. When Cash toured with Elvis, the Arkansas-born (in Kingsland, on 26 February 1932) singer rocketed to popularity and tried to cash in on it all at one time. But his 200 concerts a year led to pill-popping mood changes, and divorce. (Racist white citizens' councils in the South had previously mistaken his Italian wife, Vivian, for a "Negress," and had boycotted a few concerts.) By 1968, he'd given up his self-destructive ways, and married June of the famous singing Carter Family. They honeymooned in Israel while making a movie they financed on the life of Jesus; Cash said of his half-million dollar investment in *The Gospel Road*, "This is my expression of faith. I'm not looking to make money on this. Christ is real to me."

The barrel-chested, twanging baritone at one time earned $3 million a year, and had a short-lived TV variety series. With the aid of several songs about Folsom and San Quentin prisons, he acquired a rep as "the bullet-scarred, dope-ravaged, half-breed ex-con." The only aspect of reality to this description was a 1984 near-addiction to morphine after ulcer surgery. But he has an affinity for men behind bars. "A prison audience is the most exciting in the world," he says. "The men are with you, feeding you, every second—maybe because they need you so bad." Convicts are men he understands: "I felt I was bringing them a message from home," he explained after one behind-bars concert. "Only been in jail twice, and just overnight, but you don't need much to see what it's like."

Very active in the 80's, Johnny has been recording music (*Believe in Him*—1986; *Johnny Cash Is Coming to Town*—1987) and expanding his acting career. He guest-starred in the Walt Disney television film "Davy Crocket" (1988) and the feature *Tennessee Waltz* (1989).

Pat Cash

Carrying on the tradition of great Australian tennis players, Pat Cash has evolved into Australia's favorite son. The 5'11," 170-lb right-hander's style of play—combining high energy and athleticism—join with his rugged good looks and irresistible charm to make him a spectator favorite worldwide. Adulation usually reserved for pop stars caused *Tennis* magazine to state, "If James Dean were to be incarnated as a tennis player in the 1980's, he would surely return as Cash." But it was Cash's strength, speed and skill, not his looks, that enabled him to fulfill "the one ambition in my tennis career. That was to win Wimbledon and today I've done it." By defeating Ivan Lendl that day in 1987, Cash became the first Australian to win the title since John Newcombe in 1971. In typical rebel fashion, Cash celebrated his finest two weeks of tennis by rushing off Centre Court to the "Friends Box," climbing over fans and stanchions to embrace his father—Pat Sr.—coach Ian Barclay and Aussie Davis Cup Captain Neale Fraser.

Pat Cash was born 27 May, 1965 in Melbourne, Victoria, Australia. He quickly made his presence felt in the tennis world. At sixteen years of age, in 1982, he was the Junior Champion at Wimbledon and the U.S. Open and was runner-up at the French Open Junior Championship. Moving up to the adult men's competition in 1983 he became the youngest player ever to win the deciding singles rubber in a Davis Cup final, defeating Joakim Nystrom in the match that clinched the Davis Cup for Australia. In 1984 he reached the semifinals at Wimbledon and the U.S. Open and represented Australia in the 1984 Olympic Games. Injuries plagued Cash throughout his career but he always rebounded. After a back injury in 1985 he stormed back in 1986 reaching Wimbledon quarterfinals—less than three weeks after undergoing an emergency appendectomy. Late in 1986 he again led the Australian Davis Cup team to victory by defeating both Stefan Edberg and Mikael Pernfors in the final. 1987 started off promising as Cash reached the final of the Australian Open and led his country past Yugoslavia in first-round Davis Cup play. He waltzed to the singles title in Nancy, France, without losing a set but suffered a knee injury requiring arthroscopic surgery. After being sidelined for four weeks Cash found it difficult to regain his form. It was truly an up and down year as the knee forced him to bypass semifinal singles play, allowing India an upset victory in the Davis Cup. But he prospered on grass courts, most notably at Wimbledon. He ended the year on a high note, earning his first berth with the "Elite Eight" at the Nabisco Masters. He was ranked seventh in 1987 (his highest ranking ever), earning $565,934 in prize money and pushing his career total to over $1 million. In addition to his singles prowess Cash is an excellent doubles player. He was a two-time Wimbledon doubles finalist ('84, '85) and won the 1987 Canadian Open doubles crown with Stefan Edberg.

Cash maintains two residences, one in his native Melbourne and another in London, England. Tennis experts agree he has the potential to be the world's best. "There's only one place this kid belongs" according to fellow Australian Paul McNamee. "He's not out there to be #2. A lot of guys, guys like Boris Becker and Stefan Edberg, are going to find that out, and pretty soon.

Oleg Cassini

According to major published surveys, the name Oleg Cassini is recognized internationally by 97% of the female and 80% of the male population. His name became best known when Jacqueline Kennedy designated him court dressmaker in 1961 and his thousand days in Camelot earned him his fame and helped him found his successful licensing empire.

Oleg Loiewski-Cassini was born in Paris, 11 April 1913, the son of the late Countess Marguerite Cassini (daughter of Czar Nicholas II's ambassador to the U.S.) and Alexander Loiewski, a Russian diplomatic attaché. He and his younger brother Igor (formerly society columnist Cholly Knickerbocker) were raised in Florence, where his mother opened a dress salon after the Russian revolution. He yearned for the life of a diplomat or a professional soldier, but finances forced him to follow in his mother's footsteps, and he opened a dressmaking salon in Rome in 1933. ("In those days to be a designer was almost as bad as being a tailor. I thought it was the end.") Four years later he and Igor headed for New York, taking their mother's advice to use her maiden name for its celebrity value, and Oleg gravitated to Hollywood as a movie costume designer. A U.S. citizen since 1942, he served in the Cavalry in World War II, and after the war, set up shop in New York. Early in his American career he married cough-drop heiress Merry "Madcap" Fahrney (the fourth in what was to be a series of eight husbands), then he met and married actress Gene Tierney (two daughters) in Hollywood, and since that divorce has remained a bachelor. His memoir *Pay the Price* was published in 1983, and his autobiography, *In My Own Fashion*, was released in 1987.

Dick Cavett

"Me? People say I come across as wry, subtle, Ivy League, Midwestern. Sometimes I worry about it. I don't have an image of myself," says this former Yale drama major and comedian who rose to fame in the late 1960s as the provocative TV talk show host on ABC's "Dick Cavett Show." A combination comic-raconteur, Cavett was a born talk show host and won three Emmys on his six-year ABC show. That fusion wasn't without friction, however. He was often attacked for the controversial things he said and allowed to be said, and in 1972 his show was relegated to a one-week-a-month schedule—and that only because his fans demanded he stay. He later hosted a five-year public television series, "The Dick Cavett Show," and since 1974 has hosted a number of public television specials. A man of many moods and talents (actor, comedian, writer, award-winning amateur magician, gymnast), Cavett has spread out in various directions. In 1977, he made his Broadway acting debut, starring in the comedy *Otherwise Engaged*. In 1983, he published his second book, *Eye on Cavett;* in 1986 he hosted "The Dick Cavett Show" (ABC-TV), and in 1988 he joined the cast of Sondheim's *Into the Woods* (playing the narrator). He also appeared in the movie *Moon Over Parador*.

The only child of schoolteachers, Dick Cavett was born in Gibbon, Neb., 19 November 1936. ("My mother helped out by taking in washing at night—off other people's clotheslines.") He grew up in Gibbon, Grand Island and Lincoln, Neb., where he garnered local fame as a teenage magician. At Yale, he appeared in many campus radio and stage productions, graduating in 1958 with a major in English and drama. he later spent two seasons with the Williamstown (Mass.) Summer Theater and from 1961-64 was a writer for "The Tonight Show" and "The Jerry Lewis Show." He created comedy for Johnny Carson and Jack Parr, among others. His performing career began in 1964 as a nightclub comedian in such clubs as "the hungry i" in San Francisco and Bon Soir in New York. He made guest appearances on TV shows including "The Ed Sullivan Show." His talk show debut with ABC-TV came in 1968. Beginning in 1979, he hosted "Time Was," a documentary series seen on Home Box Office cable TV, and has done several other HBO series since. During early '80s, he continued appearing on stage, including roles at Williamstown Theater. He collaborated with Christopher Porterfield in 1974 in his bestselling autobiography, *Cavett,* and also wrote his 1983 book with Porterfield.

Cavett lives in New York with his wife, Mississippi-born actress Carrie Nye, whom he met at Yale, courted for eight years and married in 1964. The two have appeared at Williamstown Theater in Noel Coward's *Nude With Violin.* Known for his nasty temper (once shouting to a heckler while on the air, "Shut up!"), Cavett insists he is really shy. His former Yale roommate describes him thus: "He has a quick, lively mind, an eager curiosity in all spheres. And he never loses his quick, light, humorous touch. He has a literate form of humor, yet it doesn't become cliquey or in-group. He'll always be somewhat of an earnest, wholesome Midwestern kid."

Peter Cetera

"The material I did with Chicago will always be part of my own musical development. They were songs I wrote and sang.... I'm very proud of those songs and I fully intend to do them in a live show. But I just don't want to go out and have people yelling up requests for old hits. I've got to have something new to offer." That's Peter Cetera talking about his career move—from lead singer of the legendary Chicago to solo recording artist. "It's a brand new beginning," he smiles. "There's no looking back."

One can't help but rewind to capture the impact Peter Cetera has on pop music. Born in the Windy City on September 13, young Peter discovered his affection for singing and writing songs at an early age. Cetera hooked up with his talented pals Bill Champlin (keyboards/guitar), Robert Lamm (keyboards), Lee Loughnane (trumpet), Walt Parazaider (woodwinds), James Pankow (trombone) and Danny Seraphine (drums) to create the group Chicago in 1968. Walt Parazaider says: "I think if you look and poll, you would find, to most of the public, Peter Cetera is the voice of Chicago." It was Cetera's contribution as bass player, vocalist and composer that produced such hits as "Baby, What a Big Surprise," "If You Leave Me Now," "Wishing You Were Here" and "Feelin' Stronger Every Day." These songs, along with other Chicago hits, have become contemporary standards, still heard on the airwaves over ten years after their initial releases.

In 1986 Cetera decided to branch out on his own with an appropriately titled solo LP *Solitude/Solitaire.* The album spawned two humongous hits: "Glory of Love" (Academy Award–nominated theme song from the movie *The Karate Kid Part II*) and the Grammy-nominated duet "The Next Time I Fall" with Amy Grant. His second solo album, *One More Story* (1988) added another plus to Cetera's musical resume. He explains the hard work that went into cutting the tracks: "I was very particular about this album and the way it sounded. But you can't make something happen just by wanting it to. It's when the music takes on a life of its own that you know you're in the zone." Definitely in the right mode, Cetera would also like to explore his talents on the big screen. He claims, "I'm very interested in films. Not just doing soundtracks but eventually, I hope, acting as well. It's an outlet for a whole other side of me that I'm just beginning to tap into."

Richard Chamberlain

He was Grand Master of the Miniseries by 1983 after "Centennial" (1978), "Shogun" (1980) and "The Thorn Birds" (1982). Chamberlain spent half a year in Japan filming "Shogun" which was based on the James Clavell bestseller. "The Thorn Birds," in which Chamberlain hypnotized his fans with his portrayal of a lust-ridden priest, focused on a pulchritudinous Australian lassie played by Rachel Ward, drew 110 million viewers. According to Chamberlain, making love to Ward in the show was easier said than done: "There's a microphone hidden in the armpit and another in the sheets. There's a wig to worry about, a shadow, an angle. Your arm is giving out because you've been sitting above her for three hours on the same elbow, and you're trying not to smear her lipstick or make slurpy sounds while you're kissing." TV being his medium, he is yet to win an Emmy despite much good work including "Cook and Peary" (1983), "Wallenberg" (1985); "Dream West (1986), "Casanova" (1986) and "The Bourne Identity" (1988). "You can't be in this business for awards," says a philosophical Chamberlain.

Born 31 March 1935 in Beverly Hills ("a few reels from the studios"), he turned to acting after an Army hitch, and became TV's Dr. Kildare at 26. After five years in the series he shook the clean-cut "apple-pie hero" image by moving to England and studying drama. Applauded there in his role as *Hamlet,* he returned to the States in a well-publicized *Richard II* and bolstered his credibility with general audiences in films like *The Last Wave* (1978) and *Allan Quatermain and the Lost City of Gold* (1986), although one could maintain his credibility had already been established in two 1971 films: *Julius Caesar,* shot on location in Spain and *The Music Lovers* (directed by Ken Russell). Recent films include: *The Return of the Three Musketeers* (1989) and *Say Goodbye To Sam* (1989). He appeared on Broadway in Noel Coward's *Blithe Spirit* in 1987, sharing the stage with the late, great Geraldine Page. In the fall of 1989 he returned to television, starring as another "Dr. K" in the series "Island Son."

Wilt Chamberlain

"The most important thing I've done," says the man who rewrote pro basketball's record books, "is to allow my life to be channelled into helping amateur athletics. I'm happier now than I've ever been before because I'm in a position to give." His "Wilt's Athletic Club" (which costs him an estimated $200,000 a year) is a top-notch track team which helped hone 1984 Olympic medal-winners like hurdler Greg Foster and woman heptathelete Jackie Joyner-Kersee. Claiming he's "very adventurous," he made his feature-length screen debut in the 1984 Arnold Schwarzenegger adventure vehicle, *Conan the Destroyer,* after allegedly turning down scripts for 15 years. He certainly didn't need acting to keep himself busy after retiring from a career of dunking, jumping and running around in nylon skivvies. He became a player-coach for the San Diego American Basketball Association entry, formed an international volleyball association, kept an eye on his nightclubs, race horses, and real estate, and worked with the Special Olympics. Chamberlain attributes his multi-talented character to his "old man." "I've never met a man smarter," he said. "There was nothing he couldn't do. I had so many different jobs when I was a kid you wouldn't believe it, and most of them I learned from him."

Born (to a pair of five-feet-eight parents) 12 August 1936 in West Philadelphia, Wilton Norman Chamberlain was already six-nine in junior high (soon to become his present seven-one, 280 pounds) and was offered 140 college scholarships. Before graduating from the University of Kansas, he signed on with the Harlem Globetrotters and a year later joined the then Philadelphia Warriors of the NBA. "Nobody loves Goliath," he allowed, to explain why fans never embraced "Wilt the Stilt," but despite their reserved affection he set the offense standards by which all big men would later be measured. Until Kareem Abdul-Jabbar passed him, Chamberlain was the pros' leading lifetime scorer, and still holds marks like most career rebounds, and minutes played. Always an extraordinary strong, all-around athlete (and always a bachelor), he was seriously considered for a bout against heavyweight champ Muhammad Ali. He was just as serious when he proposed an NBA comeback in his mid-forties. The "ceiling on how long a professional athlete can go . . . is right there within his head."

Anne Cox Chambers

"I think it's genes and good health that give you energy," says Anne Cox Chambers, former American ambassador to Belgium, chairman of Atlanta Newspapers, director of the Cox Broadcasting Corp. and a member of the Coca-Cola Co. board. Anne Chambers received international recognition in 1977 when she was appointed by President Jimmy Carter to serve as Ambassador to Belgium. During her appointment from 1977-1981 Belgium's King Baudouin accorded her his country's second highest honor, The Order of the Crown. She is only the second Ambassador to receive such an honor. "Those years changed my life," she says. "They broadened my outlook in every way. To represent the president in another country was thrilling and I always will be grateful and loyal to him for that experience."

She was born 1 December 1919 in Dayton, Ohio; her father was James M. Cox, a United States Representative from Ohio and later Governor of Ohio for three terms. He was the Democratic candidate for President in 1920 and owner and publisher of a group of newspapers. (That publishing legacy accounts for most of the $1.4 billion that make Anne and her sister Barbara among the 10 richest women in the U.S., according to *Forbes*.) Chambers believes that her concern for people and her community comes from the upbringing she had in a home where interests encompassed politics, people and news events. Chambers attended Miss Porter's School in Farmington, Conn., and Finch College in New York, with further study in Paris. Living in Atlanta since 1940, she had focused much time and energy on the growth of the city, the betterment of its citizens and preservation of its cultural and historical heritage. In 1973 she was appointed to the Board of the Fulton National Bank—the first woman in Atlanta to become a bank director. She was also elected Director of the Atlanta Chamber of Commerce—(another first for a woman). Chambers has been an active patron of a pioneer program to help inner city youth (Exodus, Inc. Cities in Schools). She has also supported legislation to improve the status of women and has a deep interest in the concerns of women. Two other areas of interest and accomplishment are the arts and conservation: Chambers is Director of the Atlanta Art Alliance and the High Museum of Art, a member of the International Sponsoring Committee of the Charles A. Lindbergh Memorial Fund (which provides fellowships and grants to further scientific progress) and a sponsor of Ducks Unlimited (a conservation organization).

"What really satisfies me? Being physical. Someone said to me, 'You're really a peasant.' I like peasant food, and being out of doors. From April to October we never have a meal inside in Provence." (Chambers owns a 16th century home and spends four months a year there.) "One of the early owners gave it to his mistress and told his wife he'd lost it gambling, and it still has such romance." There she spends her time in pursuit of her passions, books and gardening. She spends the balance of her time in Atlanta, Ga., and at her plantation in South Carolina. Divorced twice, she has three children, Katherine Johnson, Margaretta Taylor and James Chambers.

John Chancellor

NBC Nightly News' commentator (and former anchor) says, "Whatever wit I have does not translate easily . . . on the air. It's mostly insider stuff, with a kind of mordant strain. I keep it in." His on-air air has brought both praise and consternation; some consider him stuffy and ponderous, lecturing viewers in a professional manner. "I'll bet Nightly News did more stories about the European Parliament than any other news organization in history," one producer observed. Meanwhile, other NBC correspondents call Chancellor a guardian of journalistic standards who strives to communicate the straight story. The veteran political and foreign correspondent has the distinction of being the first working journalist ever given a presidential appointment as director of Voice of America (1965-67). As a TV newsman, he says, "My job is not to curry favor, not to be loved, but to tell the truth."

Born 14 July 1927 on the Near North Side of Chicago, the bespectacled TV reporter ("I'm a reporter—not a TV personality—and I like that") never finished high school but got the equivalent of a high school diploma in the Army and later spent three years at the University of Illinois, dropping out he says, "out of sheer boredom." "I have," he once observed, "the instincts of a hobo but not a bum," and his early jobs varied from deckhand on a tugboat to wrapping books at Brentano's. He entered the world of scoops and deadlines as a copy boy on the *Chicago Sun-Times* and joined NBC News in Chicago as midwestern correspondent in 1950. In his much-traveled past there was the stay-at-home assignment as host of NBC's "Today" show (serving between Dave Garroway and Hugh Downs); his TV report from Georgia's Okefenokee Swamp on 1970's solar eclipse won an Emmy. Married to the former Barbara Upshaw (they have two children whom Chancellor admits suffered from having such a globe-trotting dad), he once defined happiness as a "matter of balancing one's curiosities." The pipe-smoking expert on Mozart and urban architecture plays tennis, goes skin-diving and records the sounds of birds and whales for recreation.

Otis Chandler

"I think I'm unconventional in my personal life, but not in my business life. In terms of being known as a character, I'm used to that." This is the "silver surfer of Old Guard Los Angeles" talking. Chairman (as of January 1986) of the *Times Mirror* Executive Committee and inveterate atheete (a one-time weight-lifting champion, he claims he can still "clean-and-jerk 300 pounds over my head"), Otis Chandler often acts more the kid than the publishing magnate.

Born 23 November 1927, Chandler graduated from Stanford University, and trained on the job at the *Los Angeles Times* until he took over as publisher (a job his late father relinquished in 1960). This scion of a great and wealthy family heads a company that in 1984 was number 117 in the Fortune 500 and that in 1983 reported a record $200 million income on revenues of $2.5 billion. He also motorcycles to work on a Yamaha 495 and hunts big game. He owns three homes: "one at the beach, which takes care of my beach life; a more formal home in Hancock Park, a nice English Tudor where we entertain and live; and our home here in Keystone" (where he lives with second wife Bettina and golden retriever Turbo). "I've fought the East Coast perspective for 25 years now," he says. "There is still an Eastern snobbism, or whatever you want to call it, that's really ignorance. People who live in the East and just travel to Boston and Washington and New York don't have the slightest perception what's going on in Los Angeles, Lawrence, Kan., or Denver, Col., and it's frustrating." Chandler, who remarried in the early 80's says he has changed "radically" since then. "My father, whom I loved dearly, and admired, brought me up to appreciate hard work. The idea was, you work hard to accomplish something—then you could play a little. That's how I operated the past 30 years, raising my five children and fulfilling the responsibilities that go with my position." He now has a bit

Carol Channing

She has eyes "like baby blue baseballs," a little-girl voice that's like no other on this planet, and she's created a trio of memorable femmes—fatale or otherwise—in the Broadway pantheon. Bursting into bloom first as the Gladiola Girl of 1948's *Lend an Ear,* she metamorphised herself in 1949 into Lorelei Lee, the girl who demonstrated why *Gentlemen Prefer Blondes. Time* magazine said after she debuted in the role of Lorelei: "On Broadway, an authentic new star is almost as rare a phenomenon as it is in the heavens. Perhaps in a decade a nova explodes above the Great White Way with enough brilliance to reillumine the whole gaudy legend of show business." Then in 1964, she started the lines forming to see *Hello Dolly,* and ultimately made theatrical history by playing the role of Dolly Gallagher Levi more than 3,000 times. The kewpie-doll clown has also sparkled in clubs and concert halls with her successful one-woman shows, appeared in films and television specials, and recorded 10 gold albums.

This saucer-eyed nova was born 31 January 1921 in Seattle to George Channing, a well-known lecturer and teacher in the Christian Science Church. "At the age of four," she recalls, "I went through a black and blue period, after discovering that a funny fall was always good for a laugh." Leaving Bennington College, she sang in an ill-fated Broadway musical, *I'm Simply Fraught About You,* and the next four years were fameless and largely jobless. She left New York for California to be with her parents. ("My father dragged me home, fearful I would come down with beriberi,") As luck would have it, Gower Champion was auditioning hopefuls for a revue, *Lend an Ear.* The show was transplanted from Hollywood to Broadway success, and Carol was on her way to stardom.

She made her official nightclub debut in 1957 in Las Vegas, then took her one-woman entertainment, *Show Girl,* to Broadway in 1961. In 1970, Carol Channing and Her Ten Stout-Hearted Men invaded London's Drury Lane Theatre. She did four Command Performances for the Queen of England and was immediately elected to "Her Majesty's Royal Order of Comedians." Among her films are *Thoroughly Modern Millie* (her favorite assignment) and the award-winning *Archie and Mehitabel,* which she previously recorded on a best-selling album. Her little-girl voice has made her America's number-one best seller of children's records (including her delightful *Winnie the Pooh*). On television, she's appeared on "The Love Boat" and her own specials, including "George Burns and Carol Channing."

Wed twice before, since 1956 she's been married to producer-writer Charles F. Lowe. They have a son, Channing Lowe. Carol is almost as famous for her offstage eating habits as for her stage personality. Allergic to chemicals in food, she carries her own specially prepared dishes, even when dining at places like "21" or Buckingham Palace.

Tracy Chapman

An anachronism in 1988! Smack in the middle of metal, dance and rap music, young Tracy Chapman entered the pop field with her acoustic guitar and folk-flavored songs. Sweeping the awards scene, she garnered honors from the American Music Awards, 3 Grammy Awards and was named the number 5 Top Album Artist—Female, by *Billboard* magazine. This surprising popularity stems from the release of just one record album.

Born circa 1963 and raised in Cleveland, Ohio, Tracy received scholarships to a private school in Danbury, Connecticut and later to Tufts University in Massachusetts. While entertaining her fellow students at local coffeehouses, Tracy had the fortunate circumstance of being admired by the son of Charles Koppelman, a powerful music publishing/record mogul. Passing praises on to his father, the boy convinced Koppelman to help Tracy's direction and the rest is history. Her first album, on Elektra records and titled *Tracy Chapman,* was produced by veteran David Kershenbaum. "We tried to keep it simple," says Tracy of the album's production. Although simple to the ear, the LP was backed by light string arrangements and intricate a capella vocal flights. A critic for the *Boston Herald* wrote: "Tracy Chapman is that rare charismatic singer/songwriter in the acoustic field who can grab the attention of a listener in a moment, who can startle and amaze with a single song."

Upon accepting her Grammy for Best New Artist (February, 1989) she humbly thanked her mother for her first guitar, in addition to the growing number of music executives in her life. She recalled, "I think I remember [my mother] playing when I was very small, and maybe that influenced me when I picked up the guitar at around 11 or 12. None of my friends were into it, but I really loved the instrument." Well, today a lot of her new friends are into it (she shares the stage with seasoned professionals) and it might be hard to keep her music simple. As she notes in her hit single "You've Got a Fast Car," Tracy has traveled a swift trip to the top with her story songs. "I'm really into letting people work the songs out for themselves; let's just say there's as much fact as fiction in all these songs, in equal parts." Her second album in entitled *Crossroads* (1989).

Ray Charles

He was singing soul music long before it had a label. He had charisma long before it became a cliche. Pianist, singer, saxophonist, composer-arranger, he's taken on pop, jazz, r and b, folk and country and become a master of them all, communicating (as critic Nat Hentoff put it) "the vulnerability of a man who is aware that he has not been able to escape the demons of his past." Blind since childhood and orphaned in his teens, an admitted narcotics user since the age of 16, he's a sensitive, perhaps tortured, man who appears to live inside "concentric circles of isolation."

Born Ray Charles Robinson in Albany, Georgia, on 23 September 1930 he dropped his surname to avoid being mixed up with boxer Sugar Ray Robinson, he learned to play the piano and clarinet and memorize music—sometime as many as 2000 bars at a time—at Florida's St. Augustine School for the Blind. He formed his first trio—reminiscent of the Nat King Cole group—at 17, but gradually evolved his own special style (which he dubbed "soul music" as far back as the 1950's) and entered the ranks of the hit makers with a secular version of the old gospel tune, "My Jesus Is All the World to Me." A perfectionist with absolute pitch, he's been turning out gems ever since, including such classics as "Georgia on My Mind" (which in 1970 was approved as the Official Song of the State of Georgia), "I Can't Stop Lovin' You," "Ruby" and "Born to Love Me" his first Grammy nomination ever, in the "Best Country Vocal Performance, Male" category. His stirring rendition of "America" gave new impetus to campaigns to have it made our national anthem. As of 1984 Charles had won a total of 10 Grammy Awards. In 1979 his autobiography, *Brother Ray,* written with David Ritz, was published by Dial Press. He was honored in 1983 by the NAACP's Image Awards as recipient of its "Hall of Fame Award," and in 1975 received the first "Man of Distinction" Award from the National Association for Sickle-Cell Disease.

Martin Charnin

Shortly before Christmas of 1971, browsing in a mid-Manhattan book store, his eye chanced upon a cartoon collection titled *Little Orphan Annie*. Charnin, who'd lyricized several Broadway musicals, had been looking for several years for new material. At that moment something clicked, like the perfect rhyme. "This is it," he thought. He proceeded to recruit collaborators. Longtime friend, composer Charles Strouse, and librettist Thomas Meehan both disapproved the idea of a comic strip musical. "It wasn't a comic-strip musical I had in mind," Charnin insisted, "but merely one that happened to be based on a comic strip." For *Annie*, which opened on Broadway in 1977, he won the Tony for Best Score (with Charles Strouse) and was nominated for Best Director. Charnin celebrated his silver anniversary in show business in 1982 and with such theatrical feathers in his director's/producer's/lyricist's cap, it doesn't appear ever to have been a "Hard Knock Life" for Marty. Hopping on his success, he collaborated again with Charles Strouse for the continuation musical, *Annie 2: Miss Hannigan's Revenge*. The show is scheduled to open on Broadway in March 1990.

Born in NYC 24 November 1934, he began his career as an actor in the original Broadway production of *West Side Story* in 1957, in which he created the role of Big Deal, performing "Gee, Officer Krupke" over a thousand times. He produced and directed night club acts for Nancy Wilson, Leslie Uggams, Dionne Warwick and others. He collaborated with Richard Rodgers on *Two by Two* (1979) and conceived, produced, directed and wrote nine TV specials, among them Anne Bancroft's "Annie: The Women in the Life of a Man," which won him two Emmys, "George M" and "'S Wonderful, 'S Marvelous," for which he won two more Emmys and the Peabody Award for Broadcasting.

In 1976 he chronicled all the above for his then 12 year-old daughter, Sasha, in a book called *The Giraffe Who Sounded Like Ol' Blue Eyes*. He has one son (Randy) and lives in midtown Manhattan. In 1985 he married Vogue staffer Jade Hobson.

Chevy Chase

"I guess I just look so straight and normal nobody expects me to pick my nose and fall." He frequently did both with great gusto on NBC's irreverent late-night comedy hit "Saturday Night Live." After he left the show at the height of its popularity to become a film star, his career tumbled with the velocity of one of his spastic pratfalls, made famous as the opener of the comedy program.

He was born Cornelius Crane Chase on 8 October 1943 in New York, the son of a publishing executive and a Crane plumbing heiress. A restless student and self-described "class cutup," he was ejected from one high school and asked to leave his first college for his *Animal House*-type shenanigans, which he admits he has never outgrown. "I'm whatever I was at six, only I make more." After graduating from Bard College, he formed an off-Broadway production company in Manhattan's East Village, which created lampoons of advertisements and other TV fare. The best sketches were incorporated in the 1974 video potpourri, "Groove Tube." He appeared off-Broadway in National Lampoon's revue, *Lemmings*, while penning scripts for "National Lampoon Radio Hour." Hired as a writer by "Saturday Night Live" producer Lorne Michaels—whom he met standing on a movie line—he convinced Michaels to feature him as one of the "Not Ready for Primetime Players," the show's seven-member troupe of regular performers. With his benign manner and Joe College face, he had the perfect deadpan delivery as host of a mock newscast, "Weekend Up-date." Turning sheepishly to the camera, after being discovered involved in a steamy phone conversation with his paramour, he would intone, "Good evening, I'm Chevy Chase, and you're not," and proceed to read subversively funny stories, aided by a backdrop of doctored news photos: "President Ford pierced his left hand with a salad fork at a luncheon celebrating Tuna Salad Day at the White House today. Alert Secret Service men seized the fork and wrestled it to the ground." He earned two Emmy awards, for writing and performing, before leaving the show in 1976 to debut opposite Goldie Hawn in the 1978 movie *Foul Play*. His other film credits include: *Caddyshack* (1980), *Seems Like Old Times* (1980), *National Lampoon's Vacation* (1983), *Fletch* (1985), *National Lampoon's European Vacation* (1985), *Spies Like Us* (1986), *Three Amigos* (1986), *Memoirs of an Invisible Man* (1987), *Fletch II* (1988), *Funny Farm* (1988), *Caddyshack II* (1988), *Fletch Lives* (1989), and *National Lampoon's Christmas Vacation* (1989).

Chase entered into marriage with a model and with an actress; both unions ended in divorce. He married a production coordinator, Jayni, in 1982, and they have three children.

Cher

"Cher's identity as a famous person has been complicated by the burgeoning acceptance of her screen talent. These roles are startling departures from her earlier ones, and mark a surprising cusp in an already surprising career," wrote Bruce Weber of the *New York Times Magazine*. Earning the respect due a seasoned performer, Cher won the Academy Award and Golden Globe Award in 1988 for *Moonstruck*.

Born 20 May 1946, Cher (whose real name is Cherilyn Sarkisian LaPiere; she is of Armenian, Turkish, French and Cherokee descent) was just a teenager when she teamed up with Salvador "Sonny" Bono to play clubs in the West as "Caesar and Cleo" (their first stage name). Among the first performers to be dubbed hippies by the media in 1965, they performed their first big hit, "I Got You Babe," wearing sandals, Neanderthal-like fur vests and blue jeans. "The Sonny and Cher Comedy Hour" ran on television from 1971 to 1975, one season after her divorce from Sonny in 1974 (one daughter, Chastity). After the divorce, Cher launched her solo career as what she called "this glamorous, exotic creature." She became a frequent *Vogue* cover girl, wore Bob Mackie clothes, garnered multiple gold and platinum records, appeared in a number of TV specials and had her own "Cher Show." A second marriage to rock singer Gregg Allman (one son, Elijah Blue) also ended in divorce. "She's at the top of her act now," said an admiring Meryl Streep, who has become a close friend of Cher's since *Silkwood*. "Maybe because she's not dependent on any man." Cher made her Broadway acting debut in Robert Altman's *Come Back to the 5 & Dime, Jimmy Dean, Jimmy Dean* in 1982. Before that she'd grinded for a minimum of 20 weeks each year in Las Vegas. "I was always afraid of having no money. But I was dying in Vegas. Francis Coppola once said to me, 'You should do films, you're so talented.' I said, 'Get me a job, find anyone who'll give me a job.' I love comedy but serious is closer to who I am. I know pain, I really know it." Thanks to having Mike Nichols favor her in *Jimmy Dean* he picked her for *Silkwood* (she received an Academy Award nomination as Best Supporting Actress for her portrayal of Silkwood's lesbian coworker and housemate, Dolly Pelliker). Her third film was the Peter Bogdanovich-directed *Mask* (also well received). These days, on top of the piano in her Benedict Canyon Mansion (for sale in 1984 for a breezy $6.4 million) there is a photo of herself and Streep with an inscription from Nichols: "You are a major actress and a great human being. Love, Mike."

Involved in all aspects of showbiz, Cher continues to record and has several hit songs, accompanied by videos, including: "I Found Someone" and "After All" (duet with Peter Cetera which was the theme song of the movie *Chances Are*; 1989). Other movies with Cher, including *Witches of*

Eastwick (1987) and Suspect (1987) added to her star status. In addition, she has a hit album *Heart of Stone* (1989). Already floating on air, now Cher has become a part of it, with her fragrance, "Uninhibited," launched in 1988. Choosing to remain single at this point in her life, she continues to shine as one of America's originals—an outrageous singing star, glamorous vamp and talented actress.

Leo Cherne

This whirlwind economist, political scientist, sculptor and advisor to presidents for over 40 years is also, in the words of one White House advisor, a great humanitarian. In November, 1983, President Reagan presented Leo Cherne with the Medal of Freedom, the country's highest civilian award. Commending his "brilliance, energy and moral passion" in helping the U.S. "overcome countless challenges," the citation took special note of Cherne's work in "serving the cause of freedom, especially through his work on behalf of refugees." He has served since 1951 as the guiding light of the International Rescue Committee, which functions on four continents to assist those who flee from totalitarian governments.

Born Leo Chernetsky, 8 September 1912 in New York City, he graduated from NYU in 1931 and New York Law School in 1934. In 1935 he joined a small mail order publishing firm, and quickly became a partner in the expending enterprise which is now the Research Institute of America. The RIA provides amazingly accurate, if sometimes pessimistic, economic information to most of the nation's industrialists, as well as issuing an annual economic forecast.

Although he has never held elective office, Cherne has had more influence on government policy (via assorted advisory boards) than many members of Congress. And Cherne's influence is not restricted to government: as economic advisor to General Douglas MacArthur after World War II, he dreamed up the program which revised the Japanese tax structure and helped change the character of the Japanese economy. He is also famous for his striking bronze portraits of the mighty: Lincoln, Churchill, JFK, LBJ. Wrote Albert Schweitzer after seeing a photograph of Cherne's bust of him: "It is so vivid and accurate I can even see the uncompleted manuscripts inside the head." Divorced from his first wife (one daughter), he is now married to former Research Institute colleague Phyllis Abbott Brown. "Since her origins are in South Dakota and mine in the South Bronx, our center of intellectual gravity must be located somewhere in Ohio."

Judy Chicago

A talented Californian with the midwestern-sounding name of Judy Chicago shocked the public with "The Dinner Party" (unveiled at the San Francisco Museum of Modern Art) in 1979—and no wonder: How many sit-down dinners have you readers attended where the overriding motif graphically depicted in the place settings is that of a woman's genitalia? No many, you say—at least not lately. When two museums withdrew offers to show the "oeuvre," Chicago had to disassemble and store its component parts. "That was the closest I have ever been to despair and suicide," she says. "What was I supposed to do—simply dump the piece into the ocean?" It's best she did not; shortly thereafter, feminist groups came to her aid and raised enough money to send the work on a 10-city tour that drew crowds totaling 500,000, ending in 1983. Her mammoth "multi-media" piece is a series of dinner table place settings designed to dramatize some twenty centuries of women's history. Obviously not hankering for recognition as either a menu-planner or a cook, not a single item of food is served at her $200,000 "dinner." The "guest list" includes such well-known feminist heroines as Sacajawea, the young Indian mother who served as a guide to the Lewis and Clark expedition and suffragist Susan B. Anthony. But it also includes such lesser known lights as Tratula, an eleventh century gynecologist from Southern Italy and Caroline Herschel, the first woman to discover a comet.

Born 20 July 1939 in Chicago, Judy Cohen was the daughter of a union organizer and a doctor's secretary. She received an M.A. in Art from U.C.L.A. in 1964 after having her first bout with male chauvinism as a grad student when she had to accept a teaching assistantship in sculpture because the painting department did not award the position to women. Worse yet, she had to abandon her personal style replete with "bi-morphic" imagery (male and female anatomical parts) in order to assuage the thesis committee. In 1966 Judy Gerowitz (married name; she's now divorced) had her first solo show in L.A. where she exhibited a "rearrangeable environment" called "Sunset Squares." Ensuing shows received mixed reactions and because critics did not readily pick up the feminist tenets implied in her work, Judy Chicago ("divesting herself of all names imposed on her through male social dominance") decided to sharpen her feminist tack, looking toward a community of women as her target audience. Working with artist Mirium Shapiro, they established a Feminist Art Program at the California Institute of Arts in 1973. That same year she founded "Womanspace" and "The Woman's Building," both galleries and exhibition spaces for women's purposes. Her most recent work is "The Birth Project," another controversial idea—a collection of photographs, needlework and drawings that use the birth process to signify all creation. Chicago resides in California and uses a renovated, 19th century blacksmith shop in Benicia (along with several other artists) as her studio. Aware that there are still battles to be fought and confrontations to be reckoned with, Chicago believes that feminist artists are making headway; "At one time, no one had any idea that women could have their own point of view. There was no women's culture—it didn't exist. We created it."

Julia Child

The wacky mistress of French cuisine (who once vowed "I will never do anything but French cooking!") has transformed in the 1980s into an unabashed champion of authentic American cuisine. "We no longer have to kneel down and bow to foreigners. We can be proud of what we have here," she proclaims, joining the nationwide movement toward a redefined American style of cooking. Her switch was heralded in 1983 by a slick new California-based TV series "Dinner at Julia's," celebrating the delights of American cooking, ingredients and wines, and featuring a "gathering" sequence. (In one, dressed in a safari-like outfit, she slogged through mud in search of the wild Chanterelle mushroom.) She hasn't discarded Gallic cooking, the joys of which she zanily demonstrated to mesmerized TV audiences in the 1960's, in her Emmy Award-winning show, "The French Chef." She has become a household word with her slapdash kitchen calamities (dropped eggs, curdling hollandaise sauces, sagging apple charlottes, etc.). Her 1961 volume, *Mastering the Art of French Cooking*, remains the definitive English-language work on classic French cuisine. But, like many French chefs in the USA, she became impressed with American style cooking and the variety of increasing excellence of American raw products. "I think America is going to win," she predicts, holding that American cooking has been "nouvelle" in the best sense, based on fresh ingredients, contrasting flavors and a respect for natural tastes.

California-born (Pasadena, 15 August 1912), a graduate of Smith College, Julia could barely boil water when at the age of 34 she married Paul Child, ten years her senior. It wasn't until Paul was transferred to Paris with the USIS that, says Julia, "I really came into my own." Dusting off her fractured French, and enrolling in the Cordon Bleu course under the guidance of Master Chef Max Bugnard, she was soon soufflé-ing up a storm. She opened a cooking school in Paris with Simone Beck and Louisette Bergholle, and the three women subsequently published the classic *Mastering the Art of French Cooking*. After her husband retired in 1961 from the Foreign Service, the Childs settled in Cambridge, Mass. She was invited to appear on TV in connection with her cookbook, and the rest is history. Her 207-part "French Chef" and other TV series, five books and hundreds of magazine and newspaper articles earned her two prestigious awards from the French government. The energetic, 6 ft. 2 in., former Smith College basketball player was named "Woman of the Year" in 1979 by the Boston-New England chapter of the National Academy of Television Arts and Sciences.

Noam Chomsky

"It may be beyond the limits of human intelligence" says linguist/political activist Noam Chomsky, "to understand how human intelligence works." That possibly hasn't kept Professor Chomsky from giving it the old college try—both in the U.S.A. and Europe. Chomsky burst onto the academic scene with a notion that shocked the staid scholars of linguistics: namely, that we have the innate ability to speak at birth and do not have to "learn" it. The M.I.T. professor has been as radical in his politics as in his profession, emerging in the 1960s as an eloquent leader of the New Left. In the 1970s and '80s, he continued to make international headlines for his role in France's Faurisson Affair, thanks to his signature on a petition to insure a teaching position for the scholar whose "Holocaust studies" denied the existence of gas chambers, Nazi Germany's master plan, and so forth.

Avram Noam Chomsky, was born in Philadelphia 7 December 1928, the elder son of Russian immigrants (his father was a Hebrew Scholar). His adolescent interest in Zionist studies eventually gave way to a passion for linguistics. Hebrew, however, was the first language to which he subjected his theory of "generative grammar," or the concept of language as innate. Through such books as *Syntactic Structures* (1957) and in numerous critical reviews of the work of other linguists and psychologists (chiefly B.F. Skinner), Chomsky turned the world of linguistics on its head—and then directed his interest to anti-war activities. He joined the steering committee of the national anti-war organization, RESIST, and was idolized by the New Left. He remains active in the anti-war and free speech movement, and his influence has been felt world-wide, both through his writings and his willingness to sign petitions. He is the author of *Language & Mind* and *American Power & The New Mandarins*, and co-author of *The Political Economy of Human Rights*. His defense of those who are politically lightyears to his right is quite logical, he says: "It is precisely in the case of views that are almost universally despised and condemned that [freedom of expression] must be most vigorously defended." Much public controversy, he believes, is caused by laziness: "No rational person will condemn a book, however outlandish its conclusions may seem, without at least reading it carefully."

Married in 1949 to Carol Doris Schatz, Chomsky is father to three children: Aviva, Diane, and Harry Alan. Tongue-in-cheek acolytes honored the innovative linguist by naming the monkey they were training to "talk"—what else?—Noam Chimpsky.

Julie Christie

The winner of the New York Film Critics Award and an Oscar for *Darling* in 1965 is focusing her high-powered energy on the peace movement. The blonde, blue-eyed beauty has studied the subject, keeps files on it, quotes impressive statistics and makes a point of doing her homework before speaking. She was the narrator of the half-hour TV documentary "Taking on the Bomb." "I felt it was an important recording of the impressive, amazing activities women have organized to demonstrate for peace and I wanted to contribute. I have done far less than many, many women. There are people whose voices should certainly be heard before mine." Ironically, it's her British accent that always seems to get the publicity, particularly when she lambasted the U.S. government over its nuclear-arms policies. "I get the feeling that the U.S. doesn't really care about the annihilation of Europe and the rest of the world," she said in 1984 after meeting with American weapons negotiator Paul Nitze and other officials in Washington. "I can't believe it, but using nuclear missiles is quite clearly part of the game plan."

Born in Assam, India, 14 April 1940, the daughter of a tea planter, she was sent back to England at the age of eight for schooling. When she was 16, she went off to study art and French in Paris for a year and later attended a technical college in Brighton, before starting drama studies at the Central School of Speech Training and Dramatic Art. "I was a vagrant," she recalls of her three years there. "I used to sleep in attics, even parks. When I got some money I bought one of those air mattresses you blow up. I used to go around to friends' houses carrying my own mattress."

She first attracted real critical notice in a small role in John Schlesinger's *Billy Liar* in 1963 and then went on to play Luciana in the Royal Shakespeare Company's *A Comedy of Errors*, which toured Europe and the U.S. in 1964. After appearing in *Young Cassidy*, she was given her big chance—with Schlesinger once again—in *Darling*, a difficult role that she grew to loathe. She may be best known for her portrayal of Lara in 1965's *Dr. Zhivago*, which also starred Omar Sharif in the title role. Christie later starred in *McCabe and Mrs. Miller* (1971) and *Shampoo* (1975), both with erstwhile off-screen companion Warren Beatty. Writing of the latter, one critic, noting that the film seemed to exploit the much-publicized Beatty-Christie affair of the time, reported, "You've read about Beatty and Christie. Now you can see them screwing—almost." She appeared with Beatty again (more chastely) in *Heaven Can Wait* in 1978. She returned to India in 1983 to make the Ivory-Merchant film, *Heat and Dust*. Other films include: *The Return of the Soldier*, *Across the River and Into the Trees*, and *A Dry White Season*. She made the television mini-series "Mary, Mary" (1986) and starred in the made-for-TV film "Deadly Decision" (1988).

Marian Christy

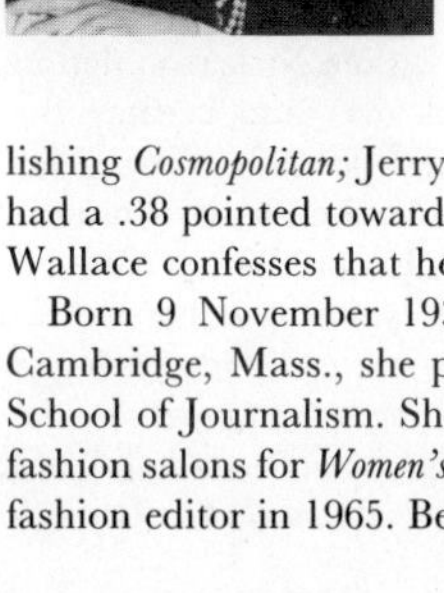

Her intimate revelations about celebrities have been a star feature in the *Boston Globe* since 1981. Now her "Conversations" column is syndicated to more than fifty papers and she's also the author of a famous-folk tell-all entitled *Invasions of Privacy* (1984). "In an ideal interview," says Marian Christy, "two people bounce feelings off each other, trading ideas, weaving them in a tapestry of a tale together." She prides herself on what she calls "a new kind of journalism which goes for the heart rather than the jugular." In this spirit of reportage Helen Gurley Brown confides that she hid under her desk on her first day publishing *Cosmopolitan;* Jerry Lewis tells why he didn't pull the trigger when he had a .38 pointed towards his mouth; ace "60 Minutes" interviewer Mike Wallace confesses that he hates giving interviews.

Born 9 November 1932 in Ridgefield, Conn., and raised mostly in Cambridge, Mass., she prepared herself for a life in print at Boston U's School of Journalism. She earned her first bylines covering the European fashion salons for *Women's Wear Daily* and signed on with the *Boston Globe* as fashion editor in 1965. Before switching to star-watching, she was the first and only three-time winner (1966, 1968 and 1970) of the University of Missouri Journalism School's prestigious J.C. Penney Tiara Award for her icon-bashing editorials about the foibles of the fashion world.

Connie Chung

She has climbed the ranks in a competitive field to become one of the most successful anchors on television today. Connie has gone from being a copy person at a local Washington, D.C., TV station to anchoring the CBS Sunday news, appearing on "West 57th Street," and filling in for Dan Rather when he is away while holding a three-year, $6-million contract with CBS.

Constance Yu-Hwa Chung was born on 20 August 1946 in Washington, D.C., into the family of an intelligence officer under Chiang Kai-shek, who later became a financial manager upon his move to the U.S. The youngest of ten children, Connie was the only one to be born in the United States, and one of only five children to survive. Connie graduated from the University of Maryland with a B.A. in journalism. She also holds an honorary doctorate in journalism from Norwich University (1974) as well as a doctorate in humane letters from Brown University (1987). Beginning her career as a copy person with WTTG-TV in Washington, she worked her way up to an on-camera reporter. From there, she joined CBS (1971) as Washington news correspondent, reporting on national politics and covering such events as Senator George McGovern's 1972 Presidential campaign, Watergate, and President Nixon's resignation. In addition, in 1974 she covered Nelson Rockefellers's Vice Presidency. From there, Connie moved to Los Angeles in 1976 to become co-anchor of the 4:30 p.m., 6 p.m. and 11 p.m. newscasts on KNXT-TV, (also a CBS affiliate) as well as to serve as the substitute anchor on the "CBS Weekend News," and "CBS Morning News." In 1983, Connie made yet another career move. This time it was to New York to join NBC News as anchor of "NBC News at Sunrise" and the Saturday edition of "NBC Nightly News." In addition, she served as NBC News political analysis correspondent for the 1988 Presidential race.

Connie's hard work and excellent reporting has not gone unrecognized. She received an Emmy for a report on a 1986 segment that was titled "Shot in Hollywood" (1987), and the George Foster Peabody Award for the series "Terra Our World" (1980). Currently holding a three-year contract with CBS, Connie will fill the Sunday Network anchor slot. Connie and husband Maury Povich (married 2 December 1984), who anchors the 7 p.m. News for Fox TV in New York and hosts Fox TV's "A Current Affair," share a Manhattan apartment as well as an 1840 manor house in New Jersey.

Craig Claiborne

He is basically a homebody whose notion of happiness involves cooking a small dinner for his friends at his East Hampton, New York, home. But "cooking" and "dinner" in the hands of this man transcend their conventional meanings and become passwords to the heavens of gustatory gods. When food editor of the *New York Times,* Jane Nickerson, left in 1957, Claiborne took over and became the first male to hold that position. During his stay at the *Times* he has been both columnist and restaurant critic. Horace Sutton credited him as "single handedly inventing honest restaurant criticism in America." He wearied of restaurant criticism, though ("It is the most punishing of assignments—the thought of dining twice a day, oftentimes seven days a week."), and resigned from the paper in 1972 in order to publish his own food newsletter. In 1974 the *Times* asked him to return and he agreed, provided he did not have to resume criticism and could work from his home kitchen. The newspaper conceded. He's been a staple since.

Born into the family of a prosperous Mississippi Delta landowner, 4 September 1920 in Sunflower, Claiborne began his love affair with good food when his mother opened up a boarding house in the neighboring town of Indianola to supplement the family's then-dwindling income. From there it was on to Casablanca, courtesy of WWII, where he first tasted exotica. His book, *A Feast Made for Laughter,* follows his trail from the chicken, spaghetti and chitterlings of his boyhood to the *quenelles de brochet* he feasted on at Henri Soule's late, lamented Pavillon in New York. The book covers his stint as a PR man for ABC in Chicago, two hitches in the Navy (WWII and Korea), and his column for *Gourmet.*

He achieved great international press when he dined with friend and collaborator Pierre Franey at the now-defunct Chez Denis restaurant in Paris in 1975—for a whopping $4000. (He'd bid on the meal several months before, during a fundraiser for Channel 13; American Express footed the bill). He has been decorated as an officer with the "Order du Merite Agricole"—one of the highest honors given to foreigners by the French government—and is the author of numerous books including: *Craig Claiborne's Kitchen Primer* (1972), *The Chinese Cookbook* (1972), *Classic French Cookery* (1970) and *The Gourmet Diet Cook Book* (1980). Claiborne travels a good deal for charity, judging "gourmet galas" in which celebs from around the country compete at "whose dish is tastiest?"

Eric Clapton

After two decades of making music and delighting millions of fans, Eric Clapton probably will never put his guitar down. "I've been on the road too long to give it up—ever. I reckon I'll play until I drop," he says. Clapton—whose role as a lead guitarist in the British rock group, Cream, caused fans to write "Clapton is God" on walls and sidewalks—concedes that he doesn't want his future career to depend on his past accomplishments. "I don't want the right to go on stage and get a standing ovation on the basis of what I've done in the past. I'd rather have a cold reception for playing badly than be applauded for what I've done in the past." Young musicians, many of whom were not yet born during Clapton's musically formative years, now look up to him in the way that Clapton regarded Muddy Waters and other greats. "Let's face it," he admits with typical candor, "I'm getting old. I can't charge around the world, or the stage, like I used to. I, and everybody else of my period, need replacing for the years to come."

Born 30 March 1945 in Surrey, Clapton's early encounter with American music came through Big Bill Broonzy blues records. In response to his enthusiasm, his parents bought him an acoustic guitar when he was 15. He taught himself how to play the blues directly from records by Blind Lemon Jefferson, Son House, Skip James and others. At 17, after getting kicked out of school for fooling around with his guitar, he started playing with such rock groups as The Roosters, Casey Jones, The Yardbirds, and John Mayall's Blues Breakers. By 1966, when at 21 he became one third of Cream, he was a British superstar. He made it big in the United States when Cream flowed through the country on a national tour in 1967.

In 1980 ulcers landed Clapton in the hospital and when he went to Seattle to recuperate, he was injured in an auto accident. Those two misfortunes sidelined Clapton for two years, but he did a major United States tour in 1982, which, along with his new album at the time, *Money and Cigarettes,* received more favorable reviews than his work had received in years. In 1982, he was in the movie *Eric Clapton's Rolling Hotel,* a film shot on the train in which the band lived during a 1978 European tour. The movie featured George Harrison, Elton John and Muddy Waters. He also appeared in the film version of *Tommy* (1974), in *The Last Waltz* (1978) and in the 1987 film *Chuck Berry Hail! Hail! Rock 'N' Roll.* Some of Clapton's popular record albums include: *Behind the Sun* (1985), *August* (1986) and *Crossroads* (1988). Eric married Patti Boyd in 1979; the couple divorced in April, 1988.

Dick Clark

Hardy television perennial Dick Clark has often been dubbed "the world's oldest teenager," thanks to his ever-boyish face. He was on a roll in the early 1980s with shows on three major networks: celebrating his 30th anniversary on the tube in 1984 as host of "American Bandstand"; the CBS daily quiz show "The New $25,000 Pyramid"; and NBC's weekly "TV's Bloopers and Practical Jokes."

Born 30 November 1929 in suburban Mount Vernon, New York, Clark was smitten as a teenager with "talk radio." He worked briefly as a news anchorman and later moved to Philadelphia where he hosted the radio version of "American Bandstand." He was made full-time host when the program went to television in 1956. Over the years he developed a long list of production companies that produce over 170 hours of television programming a year. He also supplies the networks and independent stations with dozens of award ceremonies each year. Clark says, "Too many people who produce live television lead guarded, sheltered lives in New York or Los Angeles. I get out and shake hands. I ask people on the street what they would like to see." In 1984 he scored another success for NBC with "The Most Beautiful Girl in the World," a two-hour beauty contest that permitted the television audience to vote for its favorite contestants. The show earned a 19.8 rating and a 29 share, beating or tying the programs on the other two networks.

Rising in the 1980's as a prosperous entrepreneur, he was involved in many projects. His radio roots are responsible for the success of such syndicated shows as: "Dick Clark National Music Survey" and "Dick Clark's Rock, Roll and Remember Show," airing on hundreds of stations and reaching millions of listeners. He was the co-executive producer of CBS-TV's "Promised a Miracle" (1988) and the author of a 1986 book, *Dick Clark's Easy-Going Guide to Good Grooming*. He zeroed in on the home video market and released "Dick Clark's Best of Bandstand" in 1985. Contributing his name and time to a good cause, Dick hosted the "Live Aid" Rock Concert—an internationally broadcast concert that raised money for African famine relief. In another behind-the-scenes venture, Clark was the executive producer for the ABC-TV movie "Liberace" in 1988. Dick lives in Malibu, California, with his third wife Kari, and his three children.

Mary Higgins Clark

This self-described "nice Catholic girl from the Bronx" now keeps the bookstores busy as what an admiring *New Yorker* critic called "truly a mistress of high tension." She was a fortyish widow with five young children when she moved her battered upright typewriter to her suburban New Jersey kitchen table and, working from 5 to 7 a.m. before the kids awakened, wrote her first suspense novel, *Where Are The Children?*, which became a paperback bestseller in 1975. Since then, she's hit the lists with such spinetinglers (as opposed to blood-curdlers) as 1978's *A Stranger Is Watching* (also a movie), 1980's *The Cradle Will Fall* ("an instant classic," according to the *L.A. Times*), 1983's *A Cry in the Night*, 1984's *Stillwatch*, 1986's *Murder in Manhattan*, and 1987's *Weep No More*. The secret of her success? Her talents as a natural-born storyteller, her disciplined mastery of her mystery-writer's craft and appealing leading characters—always what Mary Clark calls "nice people" and what *Newsweek's* Walter Clemons categorized as "characters to please an aunt of mine who likes to read about 'people I would invite into my own home.'" One further possible success secret might be that all Mary Higgins Clark novels have happy endings. "I love happy endings," says the author. "But only after an ordeal. Life is not 'hark, hark, the lark,' after all!"

Though young Mary Higgins (born on Christmas Eve 1929) prepared herself for the real world by attending secretarial school, she knew early on she wanted to write. After a romantic year flying the world as a Pan Am stewardess, she married her first beau, Warren Clark, and immediately began to fulfill her ambition of "having a large family." Widowed when her five youngsters (Marilyn, Warren, Jr., David, Carol and Patricia) ranged in age from five to thirteen, she decided it was time to follow through on her other ambition: becoming a successful novelist. But her "overnight success" actually came with a couple of decades of preparation. Before hitting the bestseller lists, Mary Higgins Clark had written and sold some three dozen short stories ("My first was rejected forty times"), worked as a radio writer and published a romantic biography of George Washington which sank without a trace. "I recently paid $13 for a copy from a bookhunting service," confides Clark. "When I opened it, it was the autographed copy I'd given my ex-boss."

Arthur C. Clarke

Describing himself as a "typical liberal optimist," Arthur C. Clarke writes science fiction novels that are far from ordinary: They are concerned with the struggle for survival while exploring the reaches of outer space and searching for meaning in life. The accomplished science fiction prophet (he first proposed communication satellites in 1945) refuses to make his living by "doing" science, though he holds degrees in physics and mathematics, has done advanced studies in astronomy, and is an electronics engineer. "Since I don't have any scientific reputation to lose," he remarks, "I can say what I please without giving a damn about what the professionals think of it."

Clarke was born 16 December 1917 in Minehead, England. He spent a good deal of his youth on the beaches building sand structures and exploring rock pools, and it is by the sea where he feels most at home. His imagination drifted far from the water to outer space when he discovered and came under the spell of science fiction at age twelve. In 1937, while employed with the Board of Education in London, he began publishing his stories in a journal which he and a number of like-minded amateurs printed on a mimeograph machine. More than 500 articles, books, and short stories later (his science fiction classics include, *The City and the Stars, A Fall of Moondust, 2001: A Space Odyssey*), Clarke has evolved a set of laws and principles that guide his thinking and writing. The first of the three basic Clarke Laws ("If three were enough for Newton," he remarked, "they are enough for me") states, "If an elderly but distinguished scientist says that something is possible, he is almost certainly right, but if he says that it is impossible he is very probably wrong." The second: "The only way to find the limits of the possible is to go beyond them into the impossible." The third, and most recently formulated, (he made use of it in writing the enigmatic ending to *2001*), states, "Any sufficiently advanced technology is indistinguishable from magic." Clarke's 1982 novel, *2010: Odyssey Two* followed *2001* to the box office. (The script, adapted from Clarke's book, focuses on a subtext about the politics of Russia and America.) His *Spring: A Choice of Futures* (1984), is a collection of thirty-one essays, speeches and articles in which Clarke forsees high-tech solutions to many of the world's problems, though he acknowledges that "for some people advances in communications mean a reduction in contact with others." Recent works include: *The Odyssey File* (1985), written with Peter Hyamus; *Arthur C. Clarke's July 20, 2019: Life in the 21st Century* (1986); *The Song of Distant Earth* (1986); *Cradle* (1988), written with Gentry Lee; and *2061: Odyssey Three* (1988).

An avid diver, Clarke operates underwater skin-diving safaris off the coast of Sri Lanka where he has long made his home. He serves as

James Clavell

Chancellor of the University of Moratuawa and addresses those interested in the "consciousness-expanding drug" called science fiction.

James Clavell

He's among the most widely read authors of the century, known best for his "Asian Saga," part of which (his towering 1975 best seller, *Shogun*) was translated into a twelve-hour NBC miniseries in 1980; an epic drama with a viewing audience of more than 100,000,000. Despite his enormous success, James Clavell insists he's "not a novelist," but "a storyteller.... I'm not a literary figure at all. I work very hard and try to do the best I can. I try and write for myself thinking that is what other people may like. My attitude is perhaps more romantic than psychiatric. I've never been trained as a writer either, I stumbled into it in a funny way, I do not know how it works, and I'm petrified that it will vanish as easily as it came."

James du Maresq Clavell was born 10 October 1924. He describes himself as "half-Irish Englishman with Scots overtones, born in Australia, a citizen of the U.S.A., residing in England, California and Canada or wherever." The son of a captain in the British Royal Navy, his youth led him to a succession of Commonwealth port cities including Hong Kong. Educated in England, he joined the British Royal Artillery and his World War II service was cut short when he was captured in Java. His experience in the infamous POW camp Changi was to have a tremendous influence on his life and, especially, his writing. "Changi was a school for survivors. It gave me a strength most people don't have . . . an awareness of life others lack. Changi was my university . . . [and] is the rock [on] which I put my life." Clavell returned to England, ended his military career (following a motorcycle accident and a disability discharge) and began studies at the University of Birmingham with the idea of pursuing either law or engineering. As fate would have it his career path would alter abruptly after he met his wife-to-be, April Stride, then an aspiring British ballerina and actress. After observing a "nasty little man" on the set of a movie who, "whenever he spoke or got up a hush fell over the set and people rushed to do his bidding," Clavell decided what he would do next. "I didn't know what a director did but I wanted to be one." Clavell distributed films before he landed his first Hollywood assignment. His collaboration on the box office smash *The Great Escape* (1966) won him a Screen Writers award and launched his career as writer-producer-director (*Five Gates to Hell*, 1967, *Walk Like a Dragon*, 1958, *To Sir With Love*, 1966). Idled by a Hollywood screenwriters' strike and urged by his wife to unlock his Changi experience, he began novel writing. Successes were to begin in the form of *King Rat* (1962), a catharsis for Clavell—"I started reading about Japan's history and characteristics, and then the way the Japanese treated me and my brothers became clearer to me." A stay in Hong Kong kindled the development of *Tai Pan* (1966), followed by *Shogun* and *Noble House* (1981), which later became two television miniseries. In 1986, his book *Whirlwind* was released. His editor calls Clavell "a dream to work with." Clavell has also authored a play (*Countdown to Armageddon $E = MC^2$*, 1961) and a novelette (*The Children's Story*, 1981). He has two daughters, and he and his wife share a passion for flying helicopters.

Jill Clayburgh

After appearing in a series of mediocre films during the early 70's (*Portnoy's Complaint, Gable and Lombard, Silver Streak, Semi-Tough*), Jill Clayburgh finally achieved unanimous acclaim in 1978 as Erica in Paul Mazursky's *An Unmarried Woman*. Clayburgh plays an educated, intelligent Manhattan woman whose life is shattered when her husband leaves her. The actress' straightforward, genuine performance earned her a Best-Actress award at the Cannes Film Festival, her first Oscar nomination and many fans.

The daughter of well-to-do, socially prominent parents, she was born in New York City on 30 April 1944. Her exclusive education included Sarah Lawrence College (Class of '66), where she studied philosophy, religion and literature. In college she also acted in her first film, *The Wedding Party*, which was directed by an unknown Brian De Palma and co-starred the equally obscure Robert deNiro. "I loved the fantasy of movies and theatre," says Clayburgh. By the late 60's, following summer stock, regional theatre appearances and lessons with Uta Hagen, Clayburgh was doing television. Her Broadway debut in October of 1970 was in a musical, *The Rothschilds*. This led to another musical appearance the next year in Bob Fosse's *Pippin*. In 1974 she was in the N.Y. cast of Tom Stoppard's *Jumpers*. A decade later she starred in a Broadway revival of Noel Coward's *Design for Living*. Clayburgh's role as a prostitute in the 1975 TV film "Hustling" earned an Emmy nomination. "I play this whore as funny, sensitive, childlike, and quite mad," she says, "a girl who just doesn't know how to make it, a state I know something about."

After her live-in relationship with Al Pacino ended, Clayburgh married playwright David Rabe in March 1979 (a daughter, Lily). That year she finally played a Rabe role she'd long coveted, Chrissy, a go-go dancer, *In the Boom Boom Room*. (The original Lincoln Center production had starred Madeline Kahn.) The couple have an apartment on New York's West Side and a Pennsylvania country house. "My biggest extravagance is where I live," the actress says. Like her character Erica, Clayburgh jogs regularly. "I support it so wholly," she says, "that I would never think not to talk about it."

Starting Over (1979) brought Clayburgh a second Oscar nomination. She has worked with such noted directors as Bertolucci and Costa-Gavras, but shuns the trappings of stardom, claiming, "I want to be an actress, not a personality." Clayburgh's other films include *The First Monday in October* (1981), *I'm Dancing As Fast As I Can* (1982) *Hannah K.* (1983), *Shy People* (1987) and a CBS-TV movie "Who Gets the Friends?" (1988).

Roger Clemens

Roger Clemens could easily assume the title of the American League's most dominating right-handed pitcher. Roger "Rocket" has brought the strikeout back into vogue with his 100-mile-an-hour fastball, in a league supposedly ruled by curveball and slider pitchers. In his short major league career he has established himself as a team leader on the Boston Red Sox and one of the most feared and respected pitchers today.

William Roger Clemens was born 4 August 1962 in Dayton, Ohio. The 6'4", 220-pound righthander grew up adept at several sports. He won three letters as a defensive end in football and two more as a basketball center. In high school and Legion ball he was a pitcher/first baseman who helped the Legion team win the State Championship in 1979. He was All-State in High School in baseball and All-District in football. After graduation in 1980 from Spring Woods H.S. in Houston, Clemens was the 12th pick by the N.Y. Mets in the June 1981 draft but he did not sign, electing to attend San Jacinto Junior College where he earned All-American honors in baseball. While attending the University of Texas, Clemens won All-American honors again in '82 and '83. The Red Sox made him their 1st pick in the June 1983 draft, bringing him up to the Sox in May, 1984. Injuries shortened his '84 and '85 seasons. Surgery on his right shoulder in 1985 left doubts as to whether he would ever pitch effectively again but rebounded to have an amazing season in 1986. He set a record by striking out twenty batters vs. Seattle on April 29th, 1986, erasing Tom Seaver's previous mark of nineteen. His won-loss record of 24-4 led his team to the World Series, where they lost in seven games to the New York

Mets. Despite the disappointing loss, Clemens had an incredible year, winning a multitude of awards. He was voted the All-Star Game MVP, the American League MVP, the Cy Young Award (the first of two consecutive Cy Youngs), the Sporting News Player of the Year, the Sporting News American League All-Team, the Right Handed Pitcher A.P. and U.P.I. All-Teams (he made the teams again in 1987), the Joe Cronin Award, and was voted the Red Sox MVP by Boston sportswriters in both '86 and '87. He capped it off by being voted Baseball America's American League Pitcher of the Year in 1987. Despite an 18-12 season in 1988, Clemens still managed to make the All-Star Game, break the all-time Red Sox record for strikeouts in a single season with 291 total and pitch the most shutouts by an American League pitcher (8) since Ron Guidry's nine shutouts in 1978. He was named A.L. Pitcher of the Month in July, 1988.

Clemens resides in Katy, Texas, with his wife Debbie and their sons, Koby and Kory. Off the field he devotes time to children's organizations, having established a ticket-purchasing program for youngsters under the direction of the Boys and Girls Clubs of Boston, as well as to media engagements and endorsements.

Van Cliburn

"I have been a sensation. Now I want to be a success. There's a big difference." So admitted the lanky 24-year-old Texan after being honored by New York City's first musically-oriented tickertape parade for his triumph as the first American to be awarded First Prize at the International Tchaikovsky Competition in Moscow in 1958. He also received the Medallion of the City of New York and the Scroll of the City "for exceptional and distinguished services." The mayor greeted Cliburn with: "The impact of Van Cliburn's triumph in the Moscow International Competition goes far beyond music and himself as an individual and is a dramatic testimonial to American culture.... With his two hands Van Cliburn struck a chord which has resounded around the world, raising our prestige with artists and music lovers everywhere." When he went on to be the first foreigner to play in the Kremlin's Palace of Congresses, he also demonstrated his virtuosity as a thawer of Cold War diplomacy and was credited with doing "more for Russo-American relations by playing the piano than all our diplomatic experts." In the years since his Moscow victory, he's more than met his ambition "to be a success." He now has one of the largest followings of any concert pianist on the circuit and is one of the biggest sellers in the field of classical recordings.

Born 12 July 1934 in Shreveport, Louisianna, Harvey Lavan Cliburn began playing the piano at the age of three. He gave his first public performance at four and by five, though unable to read or write, he was completely literate in music. Not until Cliburn was six did he face any major obstacles—right before a concert he knocked a tooth out of a mouth already missing many. "I can't play without any teeth," he complained to his mother, a former concert pianist and his music teacher for 14 years. Her advice was both professional and practical: "Just don't smile." After high school and several regional awards, Cliburn was off to New York in 1951 to begin his studies at Juilliard under Rosina Lhevinne, a teacher uniquely suited to his temperament and talent, and the only instruction he had besides his mother. Graduating from Juilliard with highest honors, Cliburn swept all the awards in his reach. At twenty, he attracted notice winning America's most important music prize, the Levertritt Award in 1954 which entitled him to appear as a guest artist with several major American symphony orchestras. One critic raved: "Van Cliburn is obviously going places, except that he plays like he has already been there." A lull in his promising career followed, but Cliburn hit his stride with his 1958 Moscow triumph. Winning the Tchaikovsky competition transformed him from a young artist struggling to get engagements into a solid box office attraction. Television appearances, a recording contract with RCA Victor, a Grammy Award and a stint as a conductor were all inevitable showcases. Cliburn has met the challenge of his fame and fortune with performances which place him along the great piano virtuosi of our era and he is looked upon by at least one expert as "the real and brilliant successor to Rachmaninoff," playing a heavy schedule of concerts nationwide and abroad. The Van Cliburn Competition, founded in 1962 by the late Dr. Irl Allison and named after Cliburn in honor of his achievement, represents a quest for young and inspired talent throughout the world. Says Cliburn, "The art of music, with its accent upon humanity, and its attraction for the deeper emotions of the human soul, symbolizes the universal aspect of man to his shrinking world." The author of those sentiments lives in a modest apartment near Carnegie Hall, is a man of deep religious convictions, and passes his rare leisure time reading and conversing with friends.

Rosemary Clooney

"Once upon a time," wrote Peter Reilly in *Stereo Review* in 1981, "there was a cozy, comfy Dream America presided over by an endlessly smiling, endlessly benign father figure named Ike and his cute little wife, Mamie. In those days, before Elvis and the musical Visigoths who followed him shook thing up, we all happily listened to Nice Music performed by Nice People." One of the "nicest of the nice performing stars of the time" was Rosemary Clooney. That's still the case in the 1980s with the singer's latterday performances, as often as not, being in tandem with many of the country's symphony orchestras. To more than one critic, she is "a singer at the height of her powers."

Born in Mayville, Kentucky, 23 May 1928, young "Rosie" Clooney progressed from singing in the window of her grandfather's jewelry store to station WLW in nearby Cincinnati at age 13, appearing on a musical show with her sister Betty. The sisters joined Tony Pastor's Orchestra in 1945 and toured with him until Rosemary headed for New York and a career on her own in 1949. With such Columbia recording hits as "Come-on-a-My-House" (which she resisted when Mitch Miller first showed it to her), "Tenderly," "Hey There" and "This Old House," she became (with Doris Day, Patti Page and Kay Starr) one of the top-selling female singers of the 1950s. ("It really was a *singer's* time," says Rosie.) She also had a successful film career, the culmination being her co-starring role with Bing Crosby in the December perennial *White Christmas* in 1954.

With the coming of the rock era, Clooney suffered with career pressures, plus a tempestuous marriage (3 sons, 3 daughters) and eventual divorce from actor Jose Ferrer; it led to an emotional breakdown in 1968, which she eloquently recounted in a 1978 memoir, *This for Rememberance*. (When the book was adapted for a TV biopic, "Rosie," in the 1980s, the title role was played by Sandra Locke.) Clooney had a lot of encouragement in her return to singing and she singles out old-friend Bing Crosby for special contributions above-and-beyond. ("He gave me a job every time he worked during the last year and a half of his life.") Now, both Rosie's career and her life have taken an exciting up-turn and in addition to her many live performances, she has made a much-praised series of new record albums for Concord. "I intend to go on singing and recording as long," says Rosie, "as there is anyone left to listen to me." Good news for all. In 1989 she recorded a new rendition of the standard "White Christmas" with her daughter-in-law, Debby Boone.

Glenn Close

And she sings! She's a lyric soprano who was nominated for a Tony as the feisty wife of Phineas T. in the 1980 Broadway musical *Barnum*. In 1984 she won the Tony for Best Actress playing opposite Jeremy Irons in Tom Stoppard's *The Real Thing* directed by Mike Nichols. "Twice I sang the anthem at Shea Stadium. It was when I was living with [actor] Len Cariou and he knows lots of sports people, and one day somebody said to me, 'Do you want to do it?' And I said, 'Sure.' It was terrifying. I forgot my pitchpipe and I started too low and I forgot about the echo. You go out into this field, and the mike is right behind home plate, and there are all these people. You start singing, 'oh say can you see.' and you don't hear anything for a second and a half, and then you hear, 'OH SAY CAN YOU SEE.' and You're already on the next line."

Born 19 May 1947 daughter of a Greenwich, Conn., surgeon whose family settled in that prosperous New England town sometime around 1682, she began acting while a student at a fashionable girls' boarding school, Rosemary Hall, where she organized a theater troupe called "The Fingernails—the Group with Polish." After five years of travelling with folksinging ensembles she studied drama at the College of William and Mary and graduated with a Phi Beta Kappa key. She got her first job in New York soon thereafter as understudy in a Phoenix Theatre production of *Love for Love;* she was even luckier when the leading lady backed out during dress rehearsal and Close went on although she'd never walked through the part. As she says, "it was trial by fire." She spent a very successful season at that theater before appearing on Broadway in the thriller *Crucible of Blood* and she later collected an Obie for her work in Simon Benmusa's *The Singular Life of Albert Nobbs*. "I'm a very competitive person, but I don't believe in competing with individual people because it's destructive. The best piece of advice I got on the first job I had was: 'Never compare your career with anybody else's. You'd jump out a window.'" Her screen debut was as the outspoken feminist mother in *The World According to Garp*, for which she received her first Academy Award nomination; the second came in 1984 for *The Big Chill*. That same year she played in "Something About Amelia." About incest, it was one of the most viewed TV shows of that season. She played opposite Robert Redford in the film of Bernard Malamud's *The Natural* and she jokingly lamented to *Vogue* interviewer Aimee Lee Ball that she had to play the "good woman" in the film and was allowed one very chaste kiss. "I kept saying 'This is the one man who's everyone's fantasy, and she never gets to kiss him.' But that's my image."

Close, who says that the only thing she hates about making movies is coffee "in styrofoam cups," lives in Greenwich Village. In 1984 she wed venture capitalist James Marsalis whom she met after the opening of *The Real Thing*. The couple later divorced. In 1985 she appeared off-Broadway in *Childhood*, based on the memories of French writer Nathalie Sarraute, and made the films *Maxie* and *Jagged Edge*. She returned to Broadway in the 1985-86 season in *Benefactors*. Playing the role of Alex Forrest in the 1987 film *Fatal Attraction*, Close received an Academy Award nomination, but was edged out by Cher for the highest honor. Nevertheless, Glenn received her own prize, daughter Annie Maude, born 26 April 1988. Not married to Close at the time of her baby's birth, the child's father is John Starke. Continually active, Close has taken on recent projects that include the films *Dangerous Liaisons* (Academy Award nomination—1989) and *Immediate Family* (1989).

Alexander H. Cohen

As a 21-year-old with an inheritance to spend, in 1941 Alexander Cohen was dubbed "the millionaire boy angel" when he hit the Broadway jackpot as an investor in *Angel Street*. He calls himself "the last of the big time spenders"—but all for the sake of art. Guided by the dictum "I only present what I love," he has served up such artistic indulgences as the Burton-Gielgud *Hamlet*, The Royal Shakespeare production of Harold Pinter's *The Homecoming*, the Gielgud-Richardson *Home*, the musical *Rugantino* in Italian with English subtitles, and the 1983 productions of Peter Brook's *La Tragedie de Carmen* and Ben Kingsley in *Kean*. He has also celebrated his love affair with good theatre since 1967 by producing (with wife Hildy Parks) the annual television coverage of the Antoinette Perry Awards (the Tonys) presented live from a New York theatre.

Cohen was born 24 July 1920 in New York City, the son of a financier. He attended NYU and Columbia Universities and produced his first show *Ghost for Sale* in 1941. After the successful *Angel Street* that same year, there followed a long string of flops until he came up with the notion of the Nine O'Clock Theatre in 1959 and scored with nine successive hits beginning with Michael Flanders and Donald Swann in *At the Drop of a Hat*, followed by *An Evening with Mike Nichols and Elaine May, Beyond the Fringe,* Victor Borge's long run *Comedy in Music, Maurice Chevalier at 77, An Evening with Yves Montand,* and *Lena Horne in Her Nine O'Clock Revue*. More recent Broadway productions with which he has been associated include *Ulysses in Nighttown* (1974), *Comedians* (1976), *A Day in Hollywood! A Night in the Ukraine* (1980), *84 Charing Cross Road* (1982), *Play Memory* (1984) and *Beethoven's Tenth* (1984). He received the Sam S. Shubert Award for 1962-63. His television work, in addition to the Tony presentations, includes "A World of Love" (for UNICEF), "On the Air (A Celebration of 50 Years)," "Parade of Stars," and "The Best of Everything." In 1982 Cohen and Parks produced the highly-publicized Night of 100 Stars to benefit the Actors' Fund of America, which brought out a staggering assemblage of superstars at New York's Radio City Music Hall. Hoping for another biggie bonanza, the duo spearheaded the 1985 Night of 100 Stars-II, which Cohen says is his 'Stars' swan song (his feathers were ruffled by complaints of contributors and critics alike for sacrificing his live audience entertainment for his zeal to make a TV special out of it. Liz Smith called it: "boring, sloppy, tedious, and interminable"). The benefit raised almost a million dollars for the Actors' Fund. Later, in 1987, he was the Executive Producer of the 38th Annual Emmy Awards Show.

Married first to Jocelyn Newmark (one daughter), Cohen's wife since 1966 has been actress/writer Parks. A busy Atlantic crosser, Cohen has presented many plays and musicals in London (he has a second office there).

Claudette Colbert

Hailed as "the cinema's most sparkling and deft comedienne" during Hollywood's Golden Age, her exquisite light touch and "civilized sexiness" refined and defined sophisticated comedy. "If you live long enough, everything happens to you," chirped the radiantly ageless actress who made her debut in 1923 and was still charming audiences in the 1980's. "I just tell myself I'm 60 and that I have 30 years to go," joked Colbert, an elegant 81 in 1984 when she was saluted by The Film Society of Lincoln Center for her 64-film career. Also in '84, she returned to the London stage (and a year later to Broadway) amid praise and applause, co-starring with Rex Harrison in a revival of Frederick Lonsdale's 1923 comedy of manners, *Aren't We All?* One critic noted Colbert had "kept her looks, her dimples, and her cute and cuddly naughtiness." A versatile dramatic actress, she's played a broad range of roles, through breezy comedy became her specialty. In 1934 she won a Best Actress Oscar for *It Happened One Night*, a landmark in sophisticated comedy that also won Oscars for co-star Clark Gable and director Frank Capra. She's also vamped her way seductively through serious roles such as the wicked Poppea in Cecil B. DeMille's 1933 spectacular, *The Sign of the Cross* and his 1934 epic, *Cleopatra*. Directors have found her demanding. (She was said to be bossy, stubborn, fickle about her clothes, and wanted only her left profile photographed.) However, as one actress observed, "That's why she *is* Claudette Colbert."

Born Lily Claudette Chauchoin in Paris, 13 September 1903, Colbert came to America in 1910 and grew up in New York City. She started her acting career in 1923 on the New York stage and still considers the stage her first love ("I never thought of movies, God knows, until the 1929 crash. When that came, the money seemed to dry up on Broadway.") Paramount snatched her up, and she went to Hollywood, not returning to the theater until the 1950s. During her 34 years in Hollywood, she evaded being typecast, alternating between serious drama and high comedy in a succession of film classics.

After her breakthrough year in 1934 (*Cleopatra, Imitation of Life, It Happened One Night*), she went on to such laugh classics as *Bluebeard's Eighth Wife, Tovarich,* and the wartime tearjerker, *Since You Went Away*. Her last film was *Parrish* in 1961. She's returned periodically to the stage, pleasing Broadway audiences with such light comedies as *Marriage-Go-Round* with Charles Boyer in 1958, and *The Kingfisher* with Rex Harrison in 1978. She also appeared in the 1981 suspense comedy, *A Talent for Murder*. Says Colbert of her love for the stage: "There's really nothing like that wonderful feeling of facing your audience." On television she's starred in "The Royal Family" with Helen Hayes and Fredric March, and "Blithe Spirit" with Noel Coward and Lauren Bacall. She earned a Golden Globe Award for Best Supporting Actress in 1988 for her role in the TV adaptation of "The Two Mrs. Grenvilles."

Married first to Norman Foster, but more compatibly to ear-nose-and-throat specialist Dr. Joel Pressman (who died in 1968), she once gave this secret for the success of that 35-year partnership: "A wife shouldn't bore her husband with her petty ills. He never knew what picture I was in from one year to the next." She offered some further insights into the off-screen world of Claudette Colbert to columnist Hy Gardner: "Q. What keeps you looking and feeling so young? A. Not worrying about looking and feeling so young. Q. What kind of sleep do you get? A. I don't know. I'm asleep at the time. Q. What do you worry about most? A. I devote the same amount of worry to all problems. I don't play favorites. Q. Do you take exercise? A. My dog walks me twice a day. Q. Do you use any alcohol? A. Only in my drinks. Q. Are you bitter about anything? A. No, but I'm open to suggestions. Q. Do you ever expect to retire? A. Don't call me after midnight." Colbert divides her year between her New York apartment and a house in Barbados.

Natalie Cole

"Well, the feedback from audiences, the letters I get, all say, 'We feel so much love coming from you!' ... Love's got me where I am so fast." In an interview with *TV Guide* (1978), Natalie Cole attributes her success to a whole lotta love, not only the adoration of her audiences, but God's love. She says: "I never stepped on a stage by myself. ... One concert, I was so hoarse, my voice was the pits—and it was my best show ever! God did an incredible thing that night. I could feel Him, giving love to me, and to the audience; and, honey, when He does that, we gotta give love back an' forth to each other!"

The famous daughter of a famous father was born 6 February 1950 to the legendary Nat King Cole and his wife Maria Hawkins. Growing up in Los Angeles's residental Hancock Park, she was surrounded by friends of the family who also happened to be top recording artists of the time period. One of the favorite memories was when Harry Belafonte pulled her into the family swimming pool. Inspired by her theatrical environment, she enjoyed performing around town. When she was eleven years old, she sang with Barbara McNair and her father in a stageplay, *I'm With You*, at the Greek Theatre in Los Angeles. A little later, she formed a combo with the sons of Carmen Dragon and Nelson Riddle and "it was just for fun; I never planned on being a singer back then." It wasn't until after college (majoring in psychology and sociology) that she no longer thought of singing as a hobby, and she started playing bigger clubs. After a couple of demos produced by her future husband Marvin Yancey and his partner Chuck Jackson (Reverend Jessee Jackson's half brother), Natalie was signed to Capitol Records.

Although her success happened gradually, Natalie felt her stardom came "practically overnight" as she expressed in 1978. "I feel like I've been in the business just a little over a minute." Hit albums such as: *Dangerous, Inseparable,* and *Thankful* have established Natalie Cole as a popular performer. Through the years, she has been honored with Grammy Awards, American Music Awards, Soul Train Awards and even won the Grand Prize at the 1979 Tokoyo Music Festival. Her concerts have brought acclaim from critics and she received her very own star on Hollywood's Walk of Fame in 1987.

Active in charity work, Natalie has served as chairperson for the American Cancer Society's fundraising campaigns, has performed on behalf of N.O.W. (Neighbors of Watts—raises funds for children's centers in the L.A. ghetto) and she has headlined the "Because We Care" benefit for Cambodian people. Success took a toll on Natalie and she holds a great deal of respect for the manner in which her father treated his career as she has said: "My father was as natural a man as you could ever meet. If God gives me success, I hope I can handle it with as much grace and humility as he did. That would be my greatest gift."

Overcoming obstacles in her personal life, (her husband Marvin Yancey died in 1985) Natalie Cole has come to terms with her experiences and has turned her setbacks into positive energy. Ms. Cole is a loving mother to her son Robert Adam (born 15 October 1977), while spreading her gift of music. Like her latest album, featuring the hits "Pink Cadillac" and "Jumpstart," Natalie Cole is *Everlasting*.

Cy Coleman

This Songwriters Hall of Famer is, according to critic Clive Barnes, "a permanent gem in Broadway's musical crown." But Cy Coleman's musical successes have extended far beyond the Great White Way. In 1981, he was honored at Avery Fisher Hall by the American Musical and Dramatic Academy for his work in almost every area of the entertainment world.

Born Seymour Kaufman on 14 June 1929, he came to music early in life and had performed at the piano at Steinway, Town and Carnegie Halls by the time he was nine. Popular first as the pianist in his own Cy Coleman Trio, he composed such hits as "Witchcraft" and "Why Try To Change Me Now?" Coleman went on to create the scores for such musicals as *Sweet Charity, Little Me, Wildcat* (which featured Lucille Ball belting out the Coleman classic, "Hey, Look Me Over"), *Seesaw, On the Twentieth Century* (which earned him a Tony for best Score in 1978) and *Barnum*. The hit song from the latter, "The Colors of My Life," received the Best Song Award from the National Music Publishers' Association in 1980. In 1989 his Broadway musical *Welcome to the Club* failed to stay afloat and he is working with librettist Larry Gelbart on a new musical/comedy *City of Angels* for 1990.

Cy Coleman has collaborated with many brilliant lyricists, among them Carolyn Leigh, Peggy Lee and Dorothy Fields. The composer has also had an extraordinary musical association with Shirley MacLaine. Coleman won two Emmy Awards for his work on MacLaine's 1974 TV special, "If They Could See Me Now," and a third for his contribution to her 1976 TV spectacular, "Gypsy in My Soul."

Dabney Coleman

"I've played good guys and nice guys, but the truth is that I'd rather be nasty than nice," he says. "The bad guys are always better written and more fun to play. If I do villains well, it's because I play them straight. I resist cliches. I always try to make my good guys a little bad and my bad guys a little good." A master at portraying shifty schemers, Dabney Coleman manages to turn heels into heroes by making them funnier than they are mean. After years of anonymity playing bland doctors and lawyers in TV guest stints (and a sojourn on Marlo Thomas' "That Girl"), his breakthrough came in 1976 as the lecherous, sanctimonious Rev. Merle Jeeter on "Mary Hartman, Mary Hartman," television's soap opera parody. Following a string of hit films, his own TV series, "Buffalo Bill," attracted a whole new following in 1982-83 for his character Bill Bittinger, a repungnant yet perversely bearable Buffalo talk-show host that seemed the ideal Coleman role. There was mourning in many households when the show was cancelled. Bill received another shot at his own series, "The Slap Maxwell Story," and for his work on this show was presented with a Golden Globe Award (1988) for "Best Actor in a Comedy."

He was born in 1932 in Austin, Texas, and raised in Corpus Christi, never quite losing his southern drawl. He attended Virginia Military Institute, served in the U.S. Army, and dropped out of the University of Texas Law School to study acting at N.Y.'s Neighborhood Playhouse. His caddish employer in *9 to 5* ('80) was his first important film role. He was nicer as Jane Fonda's fiance in *On Golden Pond* ('81) but the next year in *Tootsie* found him back in his exasperating image. In '83's *War Games* he was a maniacal computer expert. By the mid-'80s he was the screen's most popular comic heavy, in such films as *Dragnet* (1987), *Hot To Trot* (1987) and *Meet the Applegates* (1989). Dabney has also starred in two acclaimed real-life-stories-turned-television movies: "Guilty of Innocence: The Lenell Geter Story" (1987) and "Baby M" (1988).

"There is a lot of anger in me," he confesses. It's sublimated in his acting and also on the tennis court (sometimes up to four hours a day), where he has a reputation as a formidable opponent. He also lifts weights in his California beachfront condominium, chainsmokes, has a courtly manner and dislikes discussing himself. He's twice divorced (one marriage lasted 21 years), with three children. Wryly humorous off the set, he's a perfectionist at work. He could play heroes, he maintains, but "I just couldn't play a placid hero. Heroes are usually straight and without color. . . . I always look for something specific in a part—some rebelliousness, maybe, or eccentricity—and it usually comes in the form of a villain. That makes it fun for me to play." He excels at bringing out the best in the worst of people.

Ornette Coleman

When Duke Ellington said that there are serious artists and then there are artists who are serious about being serious artists, he unwittingly defined this gentle, but stubborn saxophonist. "In America, art has more to do with the reproductions and selling than with the art itself," says Ornette Coleman. "That's one reason why musicians are crazy and painters are crazy when it comes to what they think they're worth." When he had finally achieved a modicum of fame, he began asking for what nightclub owners and record execs thought were "crazy" sums. Those demands, and his clinging to his irregular, flat alto playing caused him to be relegated to living in cold Manhattan lofts and basements. The first jazz composer to receive a Guggenheim fellowship, he was *Down Beat's* Musician of the Year in 1966, and earned brief financial security by playing with John Coltrane. But Coleman gave most of his money away, friends say, and remains near the state he was as a kid in Niggertown, Fort Worth. "We were po'. We were so po', we couldn't afford the 'o' and the 'r'."

Born on 9 March 1930, Coleman was raised by his mother with a sister in a beat-up clapboard hovel that was built into the side of a railroad embankment. Having lost his dad when he was just seven, the new man of the house, upon graduating from high school, used the sax his mom bought him when he was 14 to earn the family's living. Touring by age 19, he was an oddity of the times; a bearded black, religious vegetarian who injected Charlie Parker-like riffs into rhythm and blues lines. He bummed around the jazz set in L.A. in the early '50's and set New York on its musical ear when he arrived there playing his white plastic sax in 1959. Miles Davis and Charlie Mingus derided the young innovator's atonal sound (others including Leonard Bernstein called him a genius), and he's remained a profoundly influential, though barely subsisting jazz maverick ever since. Of his human-voice sounding sax this "seminal jazz figure" explains, "I try and play a musical idea that is not being influenced by any previous thing I have played before. The theme you play at the start of a number is the territory, and what comes after is the adventure." His son, Denardo, a drummer ("the best thing that happened . . . in California") is the offspring of his 1954 marriage. He was the subject of a 1985 documentary film, *Ornette: Made in America*. In 1988 he was playing with a band called "Prime Time."

Robert Coles

Tabbed by *Time* as "the most influential living psychiatrist in the U.S.," he has presented his thoughtful insights to the world via some three dozen books, and received a Pulitzer Prize in 1973 for Volumes II and III of his multi-volume masterwork, the universally acclaimed *Children of Crisis*. No ivory tower theoretician, Robert Coles has traveled and worked among the people (migrant laborers, sharecroppers, children in the midst of civil rights struggles, etc.) who inhabit his in-depth studies, and has on more than one occasion invaded the consciousness, if not the conscience, of his more ideological colleagues. "My heart is with the freeze, so this has gotten me into a jam," Coles said in 1984 in the middle of a dispute over the extent of children's concerns about nuclear war. "I'm afraid this is an issue where there has been political use made of research," charged Coles, who found in *his* studies that "fears of nuclear war were largely confined to children of liberal, affluent parents, themselves concerned about nuclear war," whereas he did not find much concern among "ghetto children [or] children of working class families." It is Coles' insistence that rather than basing research "on questionnaires given to kids . . . you have to spend days and months doing interviews" that gives him clout in circles that would ignore the conclusions reached by his more dogmatic and contentious colleagues. His even-handedness in approaching with compassion the problems experienced by two totally disparate sectors of American society is exhibited in two 1978 volumes: *The Well-Off and the Rich in America* and *Women of Crisis: Lives of Struggle and Hope* (the latter in collaboration with his wife, Jane Hollowell Coles). "On the question of political socialization . . . how children in various nation's obtain their political convictions and moral values," Coles wrote the 1986 book *The Moral Life of Children*. Recent works include: *Dorothy Day: A Radical Devotion* (1987), *Simone Weil: A Modern Pilgrimage* (1987), and *Times of Surrender: Selected Essays* (1988).

Born 12 October 1929, Robert Coles grew up in the Boston suburb of Milton, attended Boston Latin School and Harvard College, and was drawn to a career in medicine after writing an undergraduate English major's thesis on the American poet and physician William Carlos Williams. It wasn't until he completed his medical studies at Columbia that he decided to become a psychiatrist—"the most philsophical of disciplines." Much influenced by another Harvard prober of the psyche, Coles published a highly regarded biography of him in 1970, *Erik H. Erikson: The Growth of His Work*. It is the example of Williams, however, that apparently led to non-medical literary excursions (besides contributing editorships at *The New Republic, Aperture, The American Poetry Review* and *The New Oxford Review*): *Irony in the Mind's Life: Essays on Novels by James Agee, Elizabeth Bowen & George Eliot* (1974); *Walker Percy: An American Search* (1978; a biography of another medic-poet-novelist) and *Flannery O'Connor's South* (1980).

His children's books include *Dead End School, Saving Face* and *Headsparks*. Essentially a solitary man whose favorite recreation is taking long country walks with his wife (they are the parents of three sons), Coles has, says *Time*, "performed one of the most difficult and important feats of all: to criticize America and yet to love it, to lament the nation's weaknesses—its 'greedy, monopolistic, avaricious and sordid sides'—while continuing to cherish its strengths."

Jackie Collins

"When it comes to the lives of the rich and famous, I wrote the book," says internationally bestselling novelist Jackie Collins, known for her chronicles on the lifestyles of the Hollywood set. From her first novel, *The World Is Full of Married Men*, originally published in 1969, to her latest blockbuster, *Rock Star* (1988), Collins' twelve novels have been translated into thirty languages and it's estimated that over one million of her books are in print worldwide. With such eye-catching titles as *The Stud* (1982), *The Bitch* (1979-England, 1984-USA), *Chances* (1982), *Lucky* (1985) and *Sinners* (1984—originally titled *Hollywood Zoo*) the Beverly Hills resident (who has the distinction of being the first author to have a billboard on the famous Sunset Boulevard in Hollywood) says, "My motto is to write about what you know." Her novels, set in Rodeo Drive Boutiques, Las Vegas nightclubs and European watering holes for the rich and famous, are frequently found on the *New York Times* bestseller list. *Hollywood Wives* (1983) spent fifteen weeks on the paperback list, including three weeks at number one. *Lucky*, sequel to *Chances*, was number one on both the hardcover and the paperback lists, staying on the hardcover list for seventeen weeks. *Rock Star*, an expose of the steamy side of the rock music world, was on the hardcover list for seventeen weeks, aside from being number one in Canada and Australia and number one on the *London Sunday Times* list for seven weeks. With the popularity of her books, it's not surprising that a number of them have been made into movies; *Hollywood Wives* (starring none other than her sister, Joan Collins) was a 1985 ABC miniseries. NBC is planning to create a miniseries out of *Lucky* and *Chances*, which follow the exploits of power and pleasure-hungry Lucky Santangelo. A miniseries is in the works for *Hollywood Husbands*, with the author making her debut as an executive producer. Collins, named as one of Americas "10 Most Beautiful Women" in 1988 by *Harpar's Bazaar* magazine, told the reporter, "Sex alone doesn't sell, believe me. A good plot and characters that you can get involved with really sell."

Born and raised in the center of London, England, Jackie states she and her sister, actress Joan Collins, had a "Bohemian upbringing." Their father, Joseph, was a theatrical agent and the house was always filled with well-known actors, singers and dancers. When Jackie was eight or nine years old she would "sneak in and hide behind the drink cabinet to watch" her father and his friends, prominent producers and theatrical agents, at their Friday night ritual card party. Jackie admits, "it was like being a fly on the wall in the world of men. The smoking, the drinking, the language—I would sit for hours, just watching and listening. I'm sure that was the first sign of my talent for observation, and it's not very different from what I do now." A rather rebellious child, Jackie would read Harold Robbins and Mickey Spillane instead of doing her homework. At eight she was copying dirty limericks into her diary and charging her schoolmates a few pence to read them. Her favorite book was *The Naughtiest Girl in the School*, by Enid Blyton. Jackie had two ambitions as a young girl: to get out of school and to go to America. At age fifteen her first came true; she was expelled from school "for truancy, for smoking and for waving at the neighborhood flasher." Her second ambition soon came true when her parents shipped Jackie off to Hollywood "to get rid of me," saying "You're not bad looking; you could be an actress like your sister Joan." But Jackie had other ideas. "I was going to be a writer." People, however, did not encourage Jackie's dream of becoming a writer, especially after she had been expelled from school. Recalling those years, the successful writer states, "I was totally discouraged, yet . . . I wanted so badly to achieve something, to show everybody I was capable. . . . I refused to let anyone destroy my dreams." Her thirteenth novel, *Lady Boss*, was scheduled for publication in the fall of 1989.

Living with her husband, Oscar Lerman, and three children, Jackie is a long-time resident of the United States and has adopted the land she was shipped off to. "I think of myself as English and American." Looking back at her childhood, Jackie states, "You won't find me or my childhood in any of my books. . . . I have so many other stories to tell."

Joan Collins

Although she acted for over 30 years—in more than 50 movies and 30 TV series—it was not until her role as the beauteous bitch Alexis Carrington Colby on television's *Dynasty*, the super-successful sentimentalization of the endless ups and downs and groin pains of the super-rich, that Collins became a Nielsen-proclaimed rhinestone icon here and abroad. Her campy numbers (escorting her episodically brain-damaged stepson Jeff via private jet to a hospital in Gstaad wearing as her skiing outfit white jodpurs, white boots, white shirt, white fox fur jacket, fox hat and fox muff; hitting husband-to-be Cecil as he was having a massive coronary attack) have dulled Joan Crawford's iceberg and shoved Liz Taylor off her "I-got-there-first" pedestal. Collins used to be referred to as "a poor man's Liz Taylor," but no longer. Her company produced and she starred in the fall 1985 miniseries "Sins," and her novel *Primetime* (1988) became a bestseller.

Jaunty Joan (a reporter once joked that she would "gussy herself up for a smog alert") was born in London 23 May 1933. She grew up surrounded by show biz sorts since her father was a theatrical agent. She left school at 15 to attend the Royal Academy of Dramatic Art, but withdrew to make her screen debut, at age 17, in *I'll Be Leaving You*, opposite Laurence Harvey. After gaining recognition as "Britain's Best Bad Girl," she headed for Hollywood where her first film was *Land of the Pharoahs*, directed by Howard Hawks. She appeared in about a dozen movies as the sultry sexpot with an impressive assortment of cinema studs, including Richard Burton, Harry Belafonte, Robert Wagner, Gregory Peck and Paul Newman. Among her later credits: *The Stud* and *The Bitch*, both based on novels written by her younger sister, Jackie Collins. Joan has spawned a cottage industry of Alexis-inspired products (from furs to jewelry to perfume and bed linen), all hot-sellers helped by her "50 is beautiful" spread in the buff for *Playboy*. According to her bestselling autobiography, *Past Imperfect*, her life has been just that: a roller coaster ride of highs and lows. Her first brief marriage, at 18 to British actor Maxwell Reed, began and ended disastrously. She claimed that on their first date, he slipped a mickey into her drink and raped her; the marriage was finished when he tried to sell her to an Arab sheik for one night for 10,000 pounds. She put her career on hold for seven years when she was married to Anthony Newley in the early 1960s and tried to be a good Hollywood wife. The Newleys had two children. Joan has a third, a daughter Katy from her marriage to American record producer Ron Kass. When Katy was eight she was hit by a car and lay in a coma for eight days. Doctors predicted that she would be permanently brain damaged, but Collins' resolve to nurse her daughter back to life effected a miraculous recovery. Joan's fourth marriage to Peter Holm fizzled fast (married November, 1985; filed for annulment in December, 1986) and their divorce trial lit up the tabloids. The courtroom antics seemed to pop right out of a soap opera, even to the introduction of Peter's "passion flower."

Thrilled but not deluded by her success in a profession where she's "been down for the count more than once," she says: "Even when you win the rat race you're still a rat." "I've had to give up certain things in my life," she adds. "One is shopping. Two is lunch with the girls. Three is cocktail parties and four is studying my lines . . . but I know Alexis so well, I know her better than I know myself."

Judy Collins

New music is what's happening, believes this balladeer and advocate of nonviolence, who sees her role as making the members of her audience "feel their common humanity." Viewing music as a means, not the end, to the communication of important messages ("It's life that is groovy, not killing and war and hypocrisy and the double standard"), she writes, sings and records in an often personal vein. "You just reach down in your experience, and who you really are . . . comes out." Collins, who once aspired to be a concert pianist and was a soloist with a local symphony in her teens, rejects the label of folksinger. ("I'm a contemporary singer, period.") From the beginning, she says, "I've had a great deal of diversity in my music," including folk/pop, country, religious, and Broadway theatre. Her songs also often make political statements. Her 20th album, *Home Again* (1983), contains a song she wrote ("Shoot First") about violence among children, an issue she feels strongly about. "People are always asking me if I'm still political," she says, "and of course the answer is that I always have been and will continue to be."

Judy (Marjorie) Collins was born in Seattle, 1 May 1939, and raised in Denver where she trained for a decade under a student of Sibelius to become a classical artist. Then, at 16, she picked up her father's old guitar, taught herself to play—and her musical career veered off in a new direction. Three years later, she got a job "in a little pub for $100 a week and all the beer I could drink." Living in the East, she became "involved with the lefties and the liberals and the activists" and "started to be fairly clear about the bad things in society." She recorded her first album, *Maid of Constant Sorrow*, in 1961. Others include *In My Life* (1966), *Wildflowers* (1968), *Judith* (1974) and *Hard Time for Lovers* (1979), which appeared with a nude cover. Collins took time from record sessions and concert appearances to become a filmmaker in 1974, producing a documentary (*Antonia: A Portrait of the Woman*) about her remarkable piano teacher, Antonia Brica, who was the first woman to conduct a major symphony orchestra. In 1969, she did Shakespeare in the Park; Joe Papp cast her as Solveig in *Peer Gynt*. She hasn't done any more theatre, but "I'm not through yet," she says.

Collins and her ex-husband, Peter A. Taylor, have one son, Clark Collins. Despite her hectic schedule (about 10 months travel per annum), she manages time for a private life. The secret to having a personal life, she says, is "by not answering too many questions about my private life." However, Judy answered alot of unanswered questions when her autobiography *Trust Your Heart* hit the bookstands in 1987. *Variety* said the book "possesses the same chilling emotional dichotomy inherent in the repertoire she has always chosen to represent her on recordings. . . . A painfully honest account of Collins' life and career, rips at the senses and strikes a series of familiar chords."

Phil Collins

"I'm a white guy from Hounslow in London," says the rocker who rocks both on his own and with the band *Genesis*. "Because of my love of R & B and the fact that I surround myself with black musicians, music critics think I'm trying to convince people that I'm half-black. I have never been under any misconception of who I am or where I come from."

Where he comes from is a comfortable middle-class suburb of London where he was born in 1950, the son of an insurance man and a stage agent for children. As reported by Rob Hoerburger in *Rolling Stone* (in 1985) Collins had his first set of drums at age 10 and was playing sessions by the time he was fourteen. Unlike other British rockers of the period who toiled in dingy, smoke-filled clubs, Collins' first performing experience was at his parents' yacht club. He attended, at the urging of his mother, a London high school for stagestruck teenagers and soon he was in demand, not as a drummer, but as an actor. But he wanted to drum his way to Nirvana and after playing for George Harrison's "All Things Must Pass" album, he heard about a group of prepsters from the chic Charterhouse School who had formed a band that was popular on the university circuit. He joined them and by 1978 *Genesis* had its first gold album, *And Then They Were Three*. The group's second album, *Abacab*, sold more than one million copies. Meanwhile, Collins, having suffered a particularly bitter divorce, got his feelings out into the airwaves with a solo album, *Face Value*, and it fared well among the top ten albums of 1981. *Genesis* released another album in 1982, *Hello . . . I Must Be Going!* and Collins's next solo album was 1985's *No Jacket Required*, which hit the number one spot on *Billboard's* chart within a mere four weeks, quicker than even Michael Jackson's album *Thriller*. The album also garnered a Grammy award in 1986. Some of Collins's songs of special note include the Academy Award Best Song nominee for the picture *Against All Odds* ("Take a Look at Me Now"); "Easy Lover" (co-written and performed with Philip Bailey), "One More Night," and "Sussudio." 1988 and 1989 were especially fruitful years for Collins; he starred in the film *Buster* and wrote the film's title song, "Two Hearts," with Lamont Dozier. The tune won a Grammy and Golden Globe award, as well as being nominated for an Academy Award.

In the summer of 1984, Collins, whose two children from his first marriage are Joely and Simon, married Jill Tavelman. The couple had a girl, Lily Jane, on 18 March 1989. "Collins has brought the music industry to its knees," wrote Hoerburger, "by being an agreeable man who makes agreeable music."

Betty Comden

A five-member group called The Revuers opened to rave reviews in 1938 at the (Greenwich) Village Vanguard. Among them were performer-writers Betty Comden and Adolph Green and young director Judy Tuvim. Almost twenty lean years later, in 1956, Comden and Green wrote the book and lyrics for the smash *Bells Are Ringing*, and Judy Tuvim (renamed Holliday) starred. Comden and Green remained a winning team; their laurels include writing the screenplay for the legendary *Singin' in the Rain* (Screen Writers Award) and, more recently, the book for *Applause* in 1970. They've performed live, in *On the Town, A Party With Betty Comden and Adolph Green* in 1959 and 1977 and then in a collection of their materials from The Revuers act and shows and films. With her Mona-Lisa smile, Comden says her long, remarkable collaboration with Green has been the result of "a kind of radar."

Betty Comden was born 3 May 1919 in Brooklyn and says she "backed into" the theater after casually deciding to take a dramatics course at NYU. With the breakup of the Revuers (when Judy accepted a movie contract), Betty and Adolph found their own fame appearing in and writing book and lyrics for Leonard Bernstein's *On the Town* (1944). Other author-lyricist credits include *Two on the Aisle* (1951), *Subways Are for Sleeping* (1961-62) and the short-lived *A Doll's Life* in 1982. They wrote lyrics only for *Wonderful Town* (1953), *Peter Pan* (1954), *Say, Darling* (1958), and *Do-Re-Mi* (1960-61). They received Oscar nominations for *The Band Wagon* and *It's Always Fair Weather* and won Screen Writers Awards for both. They collected Tonys for *Wonderful Town, Hallelujah, Baby, Applause* and *On the Twentieth Century*. A legit version of *Singin' in the Rain* opened on Broadway in 1985, and a revival of *The Band Wagon* was in the works. In 1983, Betty acted in *Isn't It Romantic* at Playwright's Horizons. Despite what many people believe, she isn't Mrs. Adolph Green. In 1942 she married Steven Kyle, who died in 1979 (two children, Susanna and Alan). In 1984, she filled the unbilled shot-from-the-back title role in Sidney Lumet's comedy about a dying movie fan, *Garbo Talks*.

Perry Como

Put someone with Italian blood down in the coal regions, and his only defense against bleakness is music. Back in Canonsburg, Pa., where his father was a millhand with 13 kids, Perry Como used to pump his trombone and sing for his family and customers in the three-chair barber-shop he owned at 14, until a friend persuaded him to audition for Freddy Carlone's band. Offered the job of vocalist, he embarked at 21 upon a career as a professional entertainer, eventually leading to a $25 million TV contract and over 50 million records in circulation.

Born Pierino Roland Como on 18 May 1912, the seventh son of a seventh son, Perry has loving memories of his parents who, he says, "raised 13 children on $35 a week and taught us we were our brothers' keepers." He married Roselle Beline, whom he met at 16 at a weenie roast. Soon after, he toured the country as a featured singer with the Ted Weems band, along with his young wife and baby son Ronnie. "I once told a writer we used to unscrew the radiator cap to warm up Ronnie's bottle at night," Como recalled. "Imagine being 21 and in love, with your own wife and a car and a baby, and making $28 a week! Hardship! I only wish it could happen to our kids!" He then graduated to the Versailles and Copacabana nightclubs in New York City and caused a traffic jam in Times Square where he played the old Paramount Theatre. His first hit record, "Till The End of Time" became one of more than a dozen million sellers. In Hollywood he made *Something for the Boys* (1944), among other pictures. The "The Perry Como Show" followed, and netted its star an Emmy in 1956. In the early 1960's Como became proprietor of the most expensive show on the air, with a multi-million-dollar contract for seven TV specials sponsored by Kraft.

An ex-choir boy with traditional values, Como has stayed with Roselle, his wife since 1933, with whom he has raised three children. He continues to record, and in '80, '82 and '84 hosted Christmas specials in the Holy Land, Paris and London respectively. A new album of enjoyable songs, *Today*, was released in 1987.

Sean Connery

"There's no question that I'm not so enamored of throwing myself around as much," he said when he returned to filming his sixth James Bond film, *Never Say Never Again* in 1983. "I'm not too mad about the underwater stuff, either, because suddenly I feel I'm out of my element. I was a bit nervous, but one ends up doing as much as is physically possible and the insurance will allow." It was his first Bond film in 12 years, and it required him to train hard in order to return his brawny body to Bond perfection. Connery, the veteran of over 35 films besides the Bond epics (including *Robin and Marian* and *The Great Train Robbery*) was showing the signs of mellow middle age. During his stunts he had to worry that his short-cropped toupee might slip. In 1985, Sean broke out of the Bond mold and starred in the film version of the bestseller *The Name of the Rose*. It's been a steady rise with continual good roles: *Presidio* (1988), *The Untouchables* (Oscar for Best Supporting Actor, 1988), *Indiana Jones and the Last Crusade* (1989), *Family Business* (1989), and *Rosencrantz and Guildenstern are Dead* (1989) with Robert Lindsay and Sting.

"I had no idea acting would be my career, but I didn't have many alternatives, mind you." Born in Edinburgh, Scotland, 25 August 1930, a truck driver's son, he dropped out of school at 13 and "took many jobs . . . it was a gradual progression before I found out what I wanted to do." He enlisted in the British Navy for three years and then worked as a milkman, trucker, cement mixer, bricklayer, and steel bender—but it was bodybuilding that eventually brought him to acting. In London in 1950, representing Scotland in the Mr. Universe contest, Connery got a part in the chorus of a West End production of *South Pacific*. Joining a small suburban London repertory company ("I learned enough to know that I didn't know enough"), he was singled out to play James Bond by producer Harry Saltzman during a London *Daily Express* reader-popularity poll. Connery first portrayed Agent 007 in the 1963 film version of Ian Fleming's *Dr. No* and repeated the role in *From Russia With Love* (1964), *Goldfinger* (1965), *Thunderball* (1965), *You Only Live Twice* (1967) and *Diamonds Are Forever* (1971).

Connery split from his first wife, actress-author Diane Cilento, in 1971 (one child). In 1975 he married French-Moroccan artist Micheline Roquebrune. In the late 1960s the pressures of being James Bond got to the actor, and he disappeared for a while in Norway under the care of famed psychiatrist, Professor Ola Raknes, to divorce the real Sean Connery from the indigestible gun-waving sex symbol. "It's very difficult for people who haven't been exposed to the public eye to appreciate what one is talking about," Connery has said by way of explaining why he chooses to live on Spain's Costa Del Sol and in the Bahamas where he is an avid golfer and tennis player. Tough, craggy-faced, a greying six-foot-two Adonis, he is atypically attached to home and hearth. On his muscular arms are two tattoos: One says, "Scotland Forever," the other, "Mum and Dad."

Jimmy Connors

Although he asserts, "I'm the only [male] world champion ever to be taught by a woman," no one has yet to describe Jimmy Connors as being lady-like, or even dignified, on court or off. One of the hardest-playing, most relentless players ever to compete in professional tennis, Connors is the most notorious precursor of ungentlemanly brats like John McEnroe. Connors applauded opponents' errors, challenged officials and antagonized heckling fans well before the practices were considered routine. "Where I was born and raised, East St. Louis [Ill.], you fight for what you get. And the tradition [of courtesy] in many places, Wimbledon included, has no place in my heart. Nobody ever gave me nothing. Anytime somebody does, I'm skeptical of it."

James Scott Connors, born 2 September 1952, learned tennis from his mother and grandmother at a downtown public court. Jimmy was a top player on the national junior circuit, thanks to his mean top-spinning volley. He was sent to a private Los Angeles high school at age 17, primarily so he could be under the tutelage of Pancho Segura. In 1971, he was across town at UCLA where, as a freshman, he took the collegiate singles title. Jimmy assaulted the international circuit in 1972, and though he joined the short-lived World Team Tennis League, he alienated his fellow players by filing a lawsuit against their union, the Association of Tennis Professionals and its president Arthur Ashe. Determined to remain the maverick, Connors refused to play on the American Davis Cup team. For years, sports pages were abuzz with news of his romance, and fickle engagement, with women's star Chris Evert. When the marriage plans were dissolved, Connors married a former *Playboy* Playmate of the Year, Patti McGuire (one son, one daughter), whom he met at Hugh Hefner's house. "If Chrissie and I had gotten married," Connors said, "she would have been playing someplace and I would have been playing someplace, and that's not my idea of being married." With Bjorn Borg's declining interest and eventual retirement from the professional tour, Connors reclaimed the top ranking in the world. Storming the courts in 1982, he beat McEnroe for the Wimbledon cup, and took the first of two consecutive titles at Forest Hills from Ivan Lendl. While he's won just about everywhere (total of 107 career singles championships; the most of any male player in tennis history-1989), he's quick to agree that his greatest moments have been before New Yorkers at the U.S. Open. Jimmy Connors wears red, white and blue court togs and says "I care about anything that says 'U.S.' in front of it."

Barbara Cook

This Broadway-ingenue-turned-*chanteuse* packs Carnegie Hall with a voice (according to the *New Yorker's* Berton Rouche) that "is generally one of good cheer, enthusiastic but also able to invest rueful ballads with charm and conviction." She immortalized both the "essentially lyric" voice and the wildly appreciative audience reception it customarily receives in the album *Barbara Cook: It's Better with a Band,* recorded at a 1981 Carnegie concert and chosen by *Stereo Review* as "Best of the Year" in the pop category. But the typical Cook *tour de force* has made many memorable stops. She's performed on eight original cast recordings, two Ben Bagley albums of Kern and Gershwin, as well as an album entitled *Songs of Perfect Propriety,* a collection of Dorothy Parker poems set to music by Seymour Barab. And her sweet-voiced evenings of "Barbara Cook in Concert" have played to SRO audiences at the Kennedy Center in Washington, the Bermuda Festival and New York's Cafe Carlyle.

Born 25 October 1927 in Atlanta, Barbara Cook headed north in 1948 and first demonstrated what one critic called her "April zing" at Tamiment, the Pocono resort that's been the spawning ground for many entertainment headliners. After her 1951 Broadway debut in *Flahooley,* she starred in a dazzling string of successes: *Plain and Fancy* (1955), *The Music Man* (in which she won a Tony in 1958 in the role of Marian the Librarian to Robert Preston's Harold Hill); *She Loves Me* (1963); and what many fans consider her *piéce de résistance,* playing Cunigonde in the original 1956 production of Leonard Bernstein's *Candide.* She also starred in revivals of *Carousel, The King and I* and *Showboat.*

In the late 1960s, Cook went into self-imposed exile from the musical theatre for nearly five years before re-emerging in her present persona of *chanteuse*—the best, in the view of some critics, in the business today.

Since the 1981 release of *It's Better With a Band,* Barbara's been performing with renewed vigor. On 6 September 1985, she sang with the New York Philharmonic as Sally in the concert version of Stephen Sondheim's *Follies* (received a Grammy Award for the live RCA album). For her one-woman show at London's Albery Theatre (1986), she was nominated for an Olivier Award and she won the Drama Desk Award (1987) for her Broadway show "A Concert for the Theatre." Striking a universal chord, Barbara released *The Disney Album* (1988) featuring her interpretations of best-loved songs from Walt Disney films. The record was arranged for the symphony orchestra by her longtime musical director, pianist and close friend Wally Harper.

Married and divorced from actor David LeGrant (one son), she has now resumed the single state. John Wilson of the *New York Times* describes feelings shared by many Barbara Cook followers: "There is currently no other voice of such magnificence in popular music."

Alistair Cooke

"I seem to be perceived in America as a benign old English gentleman, and in England as an enlightened American," says the English-born Uncle Sam-ophile who has been reporting on the U.S.A. to the folks back home since 1946. In 1983, just after his 75th birthday, the silver-haired six-footer broadcast the 1,814th edition of his popular "Letter from America" over the BBC radio, reaching over a million Britons and listeners in fifty other countries on every continent. In this country, he's best known as the erudite, stately host of "Masterpiece Theatre" on PBS.

Born 20 November 1908 in Manchester, Alistair Cooke first "fell in love with America" when he came to these shores on the first of two fellowships in drama—to both Harvard and Yale (1932-34). Back in Britain, he served as BBC drama critic, then returned to the U.S. in 1937 to cover the American scene. (He became a U.S. citizen in 1941.) Among his many work projects: serving as chief American correspondent for *The Guardian* from 1948-72; creating the PBS series "America." His books include *A Generation on Trial: U.S.A. Versus Alger Hiss* (1951), *One Man's America* (1952), *The Americans: Fifty Letters from America on Our Life and Times* (1979) and *The Patient Has the Floor* (1986). Divorced from Ruth Emerson (one son), he and his second wife, Jane, have one daughter. Famous (in the words of the late Kenneth Tynan) as a reporter who delivers "the pith as well as the husk," the gently witty broadcaster has at least one pet peeve: the misspelling of his first name. "I've had Alice Dair Cooke, also Alice The Cooke," he says. "I've even had Allstar, which I rather like. . . . Alistair is a simple Scotch name and should not be too hard to reproduce."

Denton A. Cooley

One of the world's most successful and celebrated cardiac surgeons, Cooley is surgeon-in-chief of the Texas Heart Institute and a leading practitioner of the coronary bypass operation. He's described as the world's most productive cardiac surgeon as well as one of the most skilled technicians in the field. By 1983, Cooley and his team had performed more than 50,000 open-heart operations. Cooley made headlines in 1968 with his human heart transplants, doing 22 within one year. However, confronted with legal and moral problems, as well as a low patient survival rate and lagging interest, he largely abandoned the procedure by the early 1970s. "I look upon transplants as one of those procedures we tried," says Cooley, "and for the time being, discarded." Describing Cooley's rare surgical skill, South African heart surgeon Christiaan Barnard said of his technique, "It was the most beautiful surgery I had ever seen. . . . Every movement had a purpose and achieved its aim. Where most surgeons would take three hours, he could do the same operation in one hour. It went forward like a broad river—never obvious in haste, yet never going back. . . . No one in the world, I knew, could equal it." Among Cooley's numerous awards and honors is the Medal of Freedom received from President Reagan in 1984.

Born 22 August 1920 in Houston, the son of a prosperous dentist, Denton Arthur Cooley was a basketball star at the University of Texas (B.A., honors, 1941) and took his medical degree at Johns Hopkins University School of Medicine (M.D., 1944). He became a protégé of the noted heart surgeon Alfred Blalock, assisting him in the world's first "blue baby" operation. While still an intern, Cooley distinguished himself by quickly repairing a burst aorta during an operation he was assisting, saving the patient's life. In the early 1950s, he joined fellow heart specialist Michael DeBakey at Baylor University, where he developed his new techniques for corrective heart surgery. In the 1960s, he became famous for his work with congenital heart diseases, especially in infants.

While Cooley and DeBakey worked successfully together at Baylor University College of Medicine and its affiliated Methodist Hospital, their friendly rivalry eventually grew into a feud and Cooley left Baylor in 1969. He became surgeon-in-chief of the privately funded Texas Heart Institute he founded in 1962 and is also consultant in cardiovascular surgery at St. Luke's Episcopal and Texas Children's Hospitals, and a professor at the University of Texas Medical School in Houston. He is author or coauthor of more than 800 scientific articles and several texts and belongs to more than 50 professional societies around the world.

In 1949 he married Louise Goldsborough Thomas, whom he met while she was a nurse at Johns Hopkins (five daughters). Described by his wife as a "marvelous husband and father," Cooley is also a formidable golfer, once invited to take part in the Bing Crosby Open. He plays the bass viol and in an all-physician orchestra called the Heart Beats, with which he has recorded an album. He has willed his body to the Living Bank, which he helped establish.

Joan Ganz Cooney

She is the female powerhouse responsible for the TV show Robert Redford has cited as one of his favorites, Joe Namath was eager to be a guest star on, and whose character "Big Bird" was invited by Betty Ford to a White House Christmas party. President of the multi-million-dollar Children's Television Workshop, director on the boards of Xerox, Mays, and First Pennsylvania Bank, she is best known as the midwife of "Sesame Street" whose Muppets form a "wall-less nursery school," teaching numbers and alphabets to preschoolers in 40 countries. Kudos for the show abound, ditto for its sibling "Electric Company," which was subsequently developed for kids age 7-10. The spin-offs from the shows (magazines, toys, even towels) have garnered Cooney what is, in effect, an empire. (Next she will include adult programming in her company's fare.)

Born in Phoenix, 30 November 1929, into a well-to-do Catholic family, she majored in education at the University of Arizona and legged it as a reporter on the *Arizona Republic* before coming to New York and falling under the spell of TV. At first it was as a publicist for NBC, then in 1962 she went to work as a producer for Channel 13. Her three-hour public affairs program, "Poverty, Anti-Poverty and the Poor" won an Emmy in 1966. Hired that year as a TV consultant for the Carnegie Corporation, she began a study on *The Potential Uses of Television in Preschool Education* and approached federal agencies and private foundations for funds.

Married (1964) to public relations exec Timothy Cooney (later separated) she has no children but takes care of a fatherless Harlem boy on the rare interludes when she is not working. "At times, of course, I look in the mirror and ask, 'Joan, is this a well-balanced life?' If a personal life suddenly loomed up, I might make another decision. I don't honestly know if I have built this life to keep the world away or the world is away because I have this life."

In 1989, Ms. Cooney received the prestigious James Keller Award at the 40th Anniversary of the Christopher Awards.

•Aaron Copland

"Ladies and gentlemen, I am sure you will agree that if a gifted young man can write a symphony like this at 23 . . . in five years he will be ready to commit murder!" Thus did Walter Damrosch, conductor of the New York Philharmonic, attempt to soothe with humor his conservative Sunday matinee audience after the 1925 premiere of Aaron Copland's *Symphony for Organ and Orchestra* (with the young composer's famous teacher Nadia Boulanger at the organ). The next day the open-minded critic of the *New York Herald Tribune* quipped, "Copland does not strike me as the murderous kind. . . . The real murderers of music are the unimaginative stand-patters among composers." Thus began the musical odyssey of the brash young man from Brooklyn who was destined to become, in the words of Maestro Eugene Ormandy, "the dean of American composers." William Flanagan, one of the scores of composers who were greatly influenced by Copland, said: "Aaron Copland is . . . so commanding, so vital, and so essential a figure on the American creative musical scene that it is virtually impossible to consider it even generally without his name coming immediately to mind." Virgil Thomson recently recalled that "the organ symphony of Aaron's . . . was the voice of America in our generation. . . . It spoke in the same way that Kerouac did 30 years later."

Sixty-five years after that January afternoon in 1925 Copland continues to be active as a conductor and narrator (he has led more than 100 symphony orchestras throughout the world), and continues to amass multitudes of honors, which include: a Pulitzer Prize (for his ballet score of *Appalachian Spring*, 1944); an Academy Award (the musical score for *The Heiress*, 1950); the Edward MacDowell Medal; the Handel Medallion of the City of New York; the presidency (and the Gold Medal for Music) of the American Academy of Arts and Letters; the Presidential Medal of Freedom (the nation's highest civilian honor); and in 1979, Kennedy Center Honors.

Born 14 November 1900 in Brooklyn, this child of Russian immigrants recalls, "I have often been asked why I wrote 'cowboy' music instead of 'Jewish' music. It must have been partly because I grew up in the Eastern European tradition and there was no novelty to it. Every American boy is fascinated with cowboys and Indians, and I was no exception." From piano lessons with his elder sister at 13, he steadily progressed until by his early twenties he was in Paris studying with Boulanger. On his return to America in 1924, Copland was the first composer to receive a Guggenheim Fellowship, which was renewed in 1926. Though his early career, like that of George Gershwin, was jazz-influenced, he found his metier by the mid-1930s, and his 1938 ballet, *Billy the Kid*, with its Western folk themes, has been a favorite in repertory. (Agnes DeMille's *Rodeo* in 1942 and Martha Graham's monumental *Appalachian Spring*, along with the *Clarinet Concerto*, which Jerome Robbins choreographed as *The Pied Piper*, were additional ballet scores cited in his 1979 *Dance Magazine* Award citation.) Other films scores include *Our Town*, *The Red Pony*, *Of Mice and Men* and *North Star*. *Lincoln Portrait*—for full orchestra and speaker—was given a majestic performance on the Fourth of July in 1942 on a barge in the Potomac with the Lincoln Memorial in the background and Carl Sandburg as narrator. Among other works performed throughout the world are his Piano Concerto and the Third Symphony, which *New York Times* critic Howard Taubman hailed as "one of the finest symphonies to the credit of any American" (and for which Copland received the 1946 New York Music Critics Circle Award). Books which preceded the first volume of his autobiography, *Copland: 1900 Through 1942* (in 1984 with Yale's Vivian Perlis) include *What to Listen for in Music*, *The New Music*, *Music and Imagination* and *Copland on Music*.

David Copperfield

"First I'm handcuffed and locked in the safe. Then the camera man runs for his life as the countdown to the explosion ticks away. Seconds later the camera swings around, and this huge hotel just collapses on top of me. There's not one edit in the whole sequence." That's the dean of magic describing a feat he performed on "The Magic of David Copperfield XI: The Explosive Encounter" special televised in March, 1989. This young illusionist continues to defy gravity laws and scientific calculations with his daring gift of magic.

Born in Metuchen, New Jersey, in 1957, young Copperfield had an eye for the imagination. After completing high school he enrolled at Fordham University; his education, however, was interrupted after just three weeks when he assumed the lead in a new Chicago musical *The Magic Man* (1975). He not only starred in the show, but he also created the magic. Later transporting himself to New York, he perfected his craft and shortly after was asked to host an ABC television special. This TV show brought Copperfield into the public's living rooms and became the forerunner of his popular continuing specials.

Totally in control of every situation, David relies on himself. He writes, directs and develops his own work. Audiences have watched in disbelief as Copperfield has walked through the Great Wall of China, escaped from Alcatraz and came back alive from the forbidden Bermuda Triangle. He has appeared in over ten network specials and was named "Entertainer of the Year" by the American Guild of Variety Artists and the Academy of Magical Arts. Nurturing his magical talents as a way to help the disabled, he developed "Project Magic—a rehabilitative program that utilizes simple sleight of hand magic to improve dexterity of patients. He states, "It motivates a patient's therapy and helps to build self-esteem." "Project Magic" is practiced in 500 hospitals and in 30 countries around the world. Copperfield is also the national spokesperson for the United States Organization for Disabled Athletes. A soft-spoken, dignified man, Copperfield has a home in Los Angeles. Dedicated to his profession, he is always looking ahead. He seriously says, "Every few weeks we work on developing a new illusion and try it out. It keeps me on my toes and keeps the entire show fresh."

Francis Ford Coppola

From his composer-flutist father, Carmine, he inherited a Bohemian indifference to financial stability, as well as a yearning for artistic achievement. "So what if my telephone is turned off again at home? Or my electricity is shut off? Or my credit cards cancelled? If you don't bet, you don't have a chance to win. It's so silly in life not to pursue the highest possible thing you can imagine, even if you run the risk of losing it all, because if you don't pursue it you've lost it anyway. You can't be an artist and be safe." Some of his gambles he's won, others lost. Chief among the former: 1972's *The Godfather* (his screenplay Oscar joined the one he'd won two years earlier for co-scripting *Patton*), 1974's *The Godfather, Part II* (that rare breed, a critically acclaimed sequel, it earned him Oscars for his screenplay and direction and, like its predecessor, was named Best Film by the Academy), the same year's *The Conversation* (a taut and intelligent inner view of the bugging business, which won him high critical praise as well as the Cannes Film Festival Golden Palm) and 1979's *Apocalypse Now* (which received both the Grand Prix and Best Director awards at Cannes).

Born 7 April 1939 in Detroit, raised in NYC's Queens, Coppola was bedridden and almost paralyzed for a year at age nine after contracting polio. While studying drama at Hofstra, he wrote the book and lyrics for a couple of school musicals, but returned to his first love, movies, in graduate school at UCLA. His breakthrough came via his association with Roger Corman. After helping the producer-director in various capacities in a number of films, he was awarded the opportunity to direct a low-budget horror film, *Dementia 13* (1963), made in Ireland in three days. Three years later he achieved his first artistic success with *You're A Big Boy Now*, an expanded version of his M.F.A thesis. His career over the next few years was eclectic, scripting *This Property is Condemned* (1966) and *The Great Gatsby* (1974) and directing such varied films as 1968's *Finian's Rainbow* (a big-budget flop adaptation of the Broadway musical classic) and 1969's *The Rain People* (a low-budget grim slice of Americana). In the late '60s he was in deep financial trouble and his own newly-formed San Francisco-based production company, American Zoe-trope, was on the verge of bankruptcy—not for the last time. (In 1980 it became the expanded L.A. facility, Zoetrope Studios.) In 1975 he devoted much of his energies to publishing *City* magazine (also S.F.-based), which folded the next year. Like his mentor Corman before him, Coppola has been instrumental in aiding the careers of fledgling filmmakers.

He had three children from his marriage to artist Eleanor Neil. The youngest—and only daughter—Sophia, appeared at one month old as the baby in *The Godfather*'s baptism scene. His son Gian Carlo died in a boating accident in Maryland in 1986.

Along with his even more ambitious *Apocalypse Now*, *The Godfather* saga remains the director's crowning achievement. "I feel that the Mafia is an incredible metaphor for this country," he says. Since *Apocalypse*, his movies include: *One from the Heart* (1982), *The Outsiders* (1983), *Rumblefish* (1983), *The Cotton Club* (1984), *Gardens of Stone* (1986), *Tough Guys Don't Dance* (1987), a segment in one of *New York Stories* (1988) and the critically acclaimed *Tucker: The Man and His Dream* (1988).

Angel Cordero, Jr.

"They scream at me before races and they scream at me after races. But they bet my horses. In their hearts, they know if they had two dollars left and they had to bet it on somebody, they would bet it on me." So opines the second-leading money winner in horse riding history, who, since coming to America in the early 1960s, has heard plenty of boos (more than 20,000 losing mounts) and cheers (more than 5300 winning ones). Still going strong in his forties as an especially athletic jockey, he's endured federal race-fixing investigations, and rival riders' complaints that he steers his horses into others' paths. "Winning is a feeling that wipes out all the boos and headaches," he says.

Angel Thomas Cordero, Jr., was born in Santurce, Puerto Rico, on 8 November 1942, the son of a trainer and former jockey. He began riding winners in 1960 at the island's El Commandante track; in the following year he began getting into trouble with officials and accumulated five months of suspensions. He led that meet's riders, regardless, with 124 winners. In 1962 he got to New York, where he was to settle with his wife and two children, and established himself as perennial top or runner-up jockey. With his knack for adapting himself to any track and for getting to know any horse he's hired to ride, he was trusted with some of the best steeds of the day, like 1978 Kentucky Derby winner Seattle Slew and three that he rode to Derby wins: Cannonade (1974), Bold Forbes (which he also rode to a Belmont Stakes win in 1976), and Spend A Buck (1985). He uses the whip sparingly, yet keeps total domination of his mounts with his knees held up near his elbows and his face buried in his horses' manes. Only Bill Shoemaker's $100 million plus in purses surpasses Cordero's winnings. Of the probes made into several potentially-crooked racing figures, Cordero and other big-money riders went away untouched, but the doubts remain. "There was no rap. But I know that I'll carry that curse the rest of my life."

Roger Corman

Sometimes called the "King of Schlock," he produced and/or directed an unbroken string of (financially if not critically) successful "quickies"—low budget exploitation films. The "graduates" of his unofficial film school (lending and honing their talents for a pittance before they achieved fame) include actors Jack Nicholson, Robert DeNiro, Ellen Burstyn, Bruce Dern and directors Francis Coppola, Peter Bogdanovich and Martin Scorsese. From his first critical success, 1958's *Machine Gun Kelly*, to his celebrated eight-film Edgar Allan Poe cycle of the early '60s, he savvily exploited trends and headlines, working in a variety of genres (action-adventure, monster, western) aimed chiefly at the youth market.

Born in Detroit on 5 April 1926, he moved with his family around 1940 to California and attended Beverly Hills High School. "There was no way I couldn't be interested in movies, growing up where I did," he says. "Movies just fascinated me." He was preoccupied with fantasy and horror, devouring Poe's tales and sci-fi. He enlisted in the Navy, serving for the last years of W.W. II, and graduated from Stanford in the late '40s with an engineering degree. After two years (spent partly in Europe) as a self-confessed "bum," he held a variety of Hollywood odd jobs. His stint as a script reader inspired him to write one. Using a "learn while you work" approach, he made an amazing 32 films for American International Pictures between 1955-60. In '60 he made his first color film, *House of Usher*. (*The Masque of the Red Death* and *Tomb of Ligeia* are considered his best Poe-inspired-films.) His 1960 cult classic *Little Shop of Horrors* (which Corman says was shot in only two days) inspired one of Off-Broadway's biggest musical hits of the 1980s. His 1962 *The Intruder* was an uncharacteristically grim study of racial prejudice and social injustice. Self-financed, it was his first message film and first boxoffice flop. "I was devastated," he says. "I decided, then and there, that I would never again make a movie that would be so obviously a personal statement."

Tall, slender, youthful, a tennis buff, he's been married since the early

'70s to Julie Halloran. They live with their three children in Pacific Palisades, an affluent L.A. suburb. Recent releases include: *Munchies* (1987), *Stripped to Kill* (1987), *Don't Let Go* (1987), *Matar es Morir Un Poco* (1988), and *Not of this Earth* (1988).

Bill Cosby

Born in Philadelphia, 12 July 1937, the son of an eight-dollar-a-day domestic and a father "who liked his booze," he is now Dr. William Henry Cosby, Jr. He is something of a child expert, as well as a successful actor, producer, comedian, author, tennis buff, and former bartender. He's been by Sidney Poitier's side on-screen and as co-producer in the *Uptown Saturday Night* sequels and has some half-dozen movie credits to add to those. Having received enough Grammys, Emmys, and People's Choice Awards to fill a few bookshelves, Cosby struck gold again in 1984 with the debut of the long-running NBC-TV series "The Cosby Show."

Cosby attended grammar school along with his pals Fat Albert, Old Weird Harold, Dumb Donald, and a host of others made famous by Bill in his comedy routines, as well as serving as inspiration for his Saturday animated cartoon series. During his freshman year at college he went to California to look for a summer job. ("I got some of the worst excuses for not hiring me. I got so tired of riding buses and spending money to hear some guy say, 'Well—'. Finally I just called and said over the phone, 'Do you hire Negroes?' 'No.'") Temple University was later to lose one of its finest two-year-scholarship gridders when Cosby decided he'd rather tackle show biz, although he says his dad greeted the proposition with the question, "Do you want to play for the New York Giants and be a man, or do you want to make a damned fool of yourself?" When he was singled out by a *New York Times* reporter while he was appearing at the Gaslight in Greenwich Village, his career was launched. In 1964 he married University of Maryland student Camille Hanks, by whom he has five kids whose first names all begin with the letter "E."

The first black to star in a dramatic TV series ("I Spy"), he refused to exploit his color. ("Why should I go out there and say, 'Ladies and gentlemen, I grew up in a Negro neighborhood?'") In fact, in his next series, "The Bill Cosby Show," which began in 1969, black characters were impeccably normal while the whites were stereotypical. "That's done on purpose," he said. He meant to alter other, historical prejudices when he produced, starred in and poured $350,000 of his own money into *Man and Boy*, his movie debut, about a black Wild West family and gun-slingers. Cosby is universal enough to be a sought-after commercial pitchman, however. He's an enthusiastic spokesman for Ford, Del Monte, and Jell-O.

This broad-chested funnyman who once could set hearts aflutter by taking off his shirt in his TV roles, has eased into middle aged exasperation, which only becomes a source for more mirth material. A children's television genius who's got a Ph.D. in education from the University of Massachusetts, he gave 1984 grads of Harvey Mudd College their commencement address. In addition to his role as Dr. Cliff Huxtable on "The Cosby Show," Bill's been a very busy man. His album *Cosby and the Kids* was released in 1986, two books—*Fatherhood* (1986) and *Time Flies* (1987)—hit the bookstands, and he co-produced, as well as starred in a movie *Leonard: Part VI* in 1987 with Tom Courtenay. On the heels of his sitcom success, Bill created the spin-off series "A Different World," which also became a top-rated comedy show.

Howard Cosell

"I am in my mid-60s. My father died . . . away from his family. This is not going to happen to me. I am sick of travel. Enough!" So said the most popular/unpopular sports announcer in the country (in the same poll) to the *New York Times*'s George Vecsey in 1984 about his decision to quit the ABC "Monday Night Football" broadcasting team. Two years before that he walked away from professional boxing after deploring the state into which that bloody sport had fallen, prompting some critics to accuse him of wanting it both ways: huckster and critic. Robert Lipsyte, sports essayist for the CBS "Sunday Morning" show, said, "The paradox about Howard is that he's the guy who stands outside the tent at the carnival, shouting: 'Step right in and look at the naked girls,' but when you get inside, Howard's in there too . . . saying, 'Hey, you should be ashamed to be in here.'" An opposing view (there is no unanimity of opinion concerning Howard) is taken by critic John Leonard: "In a business . . . dominated by ex-athletes . . . (who) grit their capped teeth and cough off inanities, Cosell . . . is the caustic exception. According to his enemies, who are legion, Cosell has made a career out of his insufferability. According to his admirers, including me, he tells the truth."

The object of this love/hate was born 25 March 1920 in Winston-Salem, N.C., and grew up in Brooklyn, where he recalls "having to climb a back fence and run because the kids from St. Teresa's parish were after me. My drive, in a sense, relates to being Jewish and living in an age of Hitler." Following his parents' wishes, he put aside his dream of becoming a newspaper reporter and went to law school, winding up with such clients as Willie Mays and Little League baseball. In 1953 ABC asked him to host a public service radio program in which Little League players would interrogate big leaguers, and after three years of that, he abandoned the law and signed a full-time contract with ABC. "I was restricted by the rules of evidentiary procedure—the pleadings, the depositions. There was none of the effort-into-result you get in this business. I love it, I'm a born reporter." His early years with ABC consisted of a radio show, then coverage of major boxing championships—and champions. He ran into a buzz-saw with his defense of Muhammad Ali's refusal to be inducted into the U.S. Army on the grounds of conscientious objection. "What the government did to this man was inhuman" Cosell charged. "Nobody says a damn word about the professional football players who dodged the draft . . . but Muhammad was different. . . . He was black and he was boastful." "Get that nigger-loving Jew bastard off the air," requested thousands of letters to ABC. His Olympic coverage has not been without its headlines. In 1968 he stirred the animosity of many in his audience when he interviewed sympathetically Tommie Smith, a sprinter who raised his fist in a symbolic "black power" gesture on the victory stand. In 1972, he infiltrated the cordon set up by Munich police around the Arab terrorist-invaded Olympic Village (where members of the Israeli team had been killed), and produced, as reported in *Newsweek*, "the first live, international coverage of a deadly terrorist raid." In 1970, ABC matched Cosell and pro football, and the combination proved deadly for opposing networks. "Monday Night Football" became as hot as the latest disco. People changed their lives so they could catch the game, at home or in a bar, and celebrities schemed to be glimpsed visiting the broadcast booth.

Although Howard can now stay home on Monday nights, he is still very much involved in communications. He is producer of the "Speaking of Sports" radio show and the "Speaking of Everything" television program. He spends a good deal of his time with his "beloved wife, Emmy" (Mary Edith Abrams, whom he married while in the Army during WWII), his daughters Jill and Hilary, and his grandchildren. His experiences in the broadcasting booth were told in a 1985 book *I Never Played the Game* (with Peter Benventre).

Costa-Gavras

"A camera is not a gun. In fact, a camera is the anti-weapon *par excellence*, because it can express. A gun expresses nothing." Thus does this Greek-born, French-based "*agent provocateur* of films" make a distinction between his own politically *engage* products and those of self-styled revolutionary filmmakers. While unveiling the blacker aspects of some of the major forces of our time, Costa-Gavras has shifted the political film from a genre with only sectarian appeal to one with a mass audience. His Z, about the assassination of a Greek parliament member, was a phenomenal success throughout the world, "changing the image of Greece from that of a country with colorful islands, sun-baked beaches, and evzones in pleated skirts to that of a harsh, militant state." It also won an Oscar in 1970 as Best Foreign Picture.

He was born Konstantinos Gavras in Athens in 1933, the son of a resistance leader, and shortened his name to Costa-Gavras when he moved to Paris as a 19-year-old to study comparative literature at the Sorbonne. ("All this time I was going to Latin Quarter movie houses and to the Cinematheque, where I saw the possibilities that filmmaking offered.") An insatiable movie buff from early childhood, he at last bowed to the inevitable and enrolled at the French Cinema School to prepare for a film career. After a series of jobs as assistant to some of France's leading directors, he struck out on his own in 1964, writing and directing *The Sleeping Car Murders*, a Hitchcockesque thriller which starred Yves Montand and became an instant hit. Montand also appeared in such subsequent Costa-Gavras efforts as Z and *State of Siege*, Jack Lemmon starred in 1982's *Missing*, the director's first film for a major American studio, his 1983 *Hannah K.* was a tour-de-force for Jill Clayburgh, he wrote the screenplay and directed 1987's *Family Business*, and his *Betrayed* (1988) starred Debra Winger with Tom Berenger.

Costa-Gavras was wed in 1968 to French fashion-model-turned-journalist Michele Ray who made news herself during the Viet Nam war when she was held as a prisoner for 20 days by the Viet Cong. They have a son, Alexandre, and a daughter, Julie.

Bob Costas

An expert in the field of sports, Bob Costas has crossed over to become a well-respected talk-show personality. His twinkling eyes and boyish grin lend a special dimension to his broadcast qualities. Working for over five seasons as host of NBC's pre-game show, "NFL LIVE," Costas has paid his dues along the way.

Born 22 March 1952 in Queens, New York, Bob's father was Greek and his mom was Irish. Always interested in sports and communications, Costas actually began his professional career at WSYR-TV/Radio while still an undergraduate at Syracuse University. After graduation, he move to St. Louis where he did play-by-play announcing of the ABA Spirits of St. Louis on KMOX Radio (1974). Breaking over to network, from 1976 to 1979 he had the responsibility of regional NFL and NBA assignments for CBS Sports. He was also the radio voice of the University of Missouri basketball from 1976 to 1981. Finding his niche with football broadcasts, he and Bob Trumpy were considered the most outspoken NFL announcing team from 1980 to 1983.

At the top of his field, Costas served as late-night anchor for NBC's coverage of the 1988 Olympic Games from Seoul, Korea. He has won an Emmy Award as Outstanding Sport Personality, has been twice honored as "Sportscaster of the Year" (1985 and 1987), and is frequently seen as a fill-in co-anchor of NBC's "Today" show. Presently the host of "Later With Bob Costas," a nighttime talk show, he has the savoir faire and experience to compete in this format. He is also known for his nationally syndicated sports talk show "Costas Coast-to-Coast." Married to Randi Krummenacher since 1983, Costas and his wife have one son, Keith. They recently built a house in St. Louis, in addition to a home in New York.

Kevin Costner

"Just standing there and delivering his lines Costner projects a fascinating volatility. You don't know what he might do next: grab the gun, grab the girl, or do a backflip. He is something the movies haven't seen for a while . . . a leading man." *Vanity Fair's* evaluation of Kevin Costner was right on the money (as in, box-office draw). Playing a variety of parts ranging from the free-wheeling, fun-loving cowboy Jake of *Silverado* to the incorruptible Eliot Ness of *The Untouchables*, from the duplicitous naval officer Tom Farrell in *No Way Out* to the veteran catcher Crash Davis in *Bull Durham*, Costner has been a leading man in character parts that women could swoon over and men wanted to emulate. Ironically, Costner began his career as king of the editing room floor. His roles in the films *Frances*, *Table for Five* and *Night Shift* were either edited out or cut to nothing. Cast for a key role in John Badham's *Wargames*, he was graciously released to assume the pivotal role of the suicide victim Alex in Lawrence Kasdan's *The Big Chill*, only to have his sequences (he appeared in flashback) edited out. Another character from a film made in Greece was cut before he even stepped off the plane. Undaunted, Costner prevailed.

Kevin Costner was born 18 January 1955 in Compton, California. Growing up in various Southern California communities as his utility executive father travelled the state, Costner was the class jock, lettering in high school baseball and basketball and playing on the football team. His creative side was expressed through singing in the choir, performing in church musicals and writing poetry. Enrolling in California State University, Fullerton, as a marketing major, he was halfway to a degree before acknowledging his acting interest. While continuing his college courses he enrolled at the Southcoast Actors Co-op and appeared in a number of community theatre productions. Between honing his acting skills and earning his marketing degree, he married his college sweetheart, Cindy. Landing a marketing slot with a major national firm after graduation, he resigned after 45 days, determined to break into movies. Jobless for six months, he accepted a job as a stage manager for a small independent film studio. It afforded him the opportunity to attend drama workshops, study with private coaches and perform in student films. A part in the low-budget, non-union film *Stacy's Knights* preceded his string of edited parts. Finally represented by a major agency, Costner landed a role in PBS's "Testament." Its strong reviews helped Costner nail down the lead role of the smoothly manipulative Gardner Barnes in *Fandango*. Understandably, his reaction to being in virtually every scene was, "They're going to have to stay up nights thinking how to cut me out of this one." Restitution for earlier wrongs occurred when Lawrence Kasdan—who felt he owed "this amazing young actor" a part—tapped him for Jake in *Silverado*. "I've waited all my life to do a Western," Costner exclaimed as he dedicated his performance to everyone who ever dreamed of being in a Western. John Badham then cast him as the doomed doctor in *American Flyers* and Costner was on a roll. He appeared on Steven Spielberg's television anthology series "Amazing Stories" as the Captain in "The Mission," a special hour-long segment. Voted the "Star of Tomorrow" by the National Association of Theatre Owners in 1986, Costner quickly proved their choice correct. *The Untouchables* ('87) scored with audiences and was going strong when *No Way Out* ('87) cemented his reputation as a leading man and sex symbol. It was a box office smash. His athletic ability served him well as Costner accomplished the impossible. He made a baseball film, historically box-office deadwood; *Bull Durham* was one of 1988's biggest hits. He hopes to repeat the feat with *Field of Dreams* ('89) based on W.P. Kinsella's novel about a man's devotion to "Shoeless Joe" Jackson. Other forthcoming films include *Revenge* and his directorial debut with the independent film *Dances With Wolves*.

Costner resides with his wife Cindy and their three children—daughters Annie and Lilly and son Joe—in California. With his All-American good looks, incredible acting ability and proven box-office drawing power, it seems fair to assume he's seen the last of the cutting room floor.

Norman Cousins

When he talks about his "different lives," he means in part his 35 years as editor of the *Saturday Review*, his publishing career, his diplomatic and humanitarian interests, and most recently, his role as medical guru promoting the optimistic philosophy of patient participation and "laughter" therapy. (Laughter is his metaphor for all the positive emotions.) Struck with a rare collagen disease and given a one-in-500 chance for survival, Cousins "laughed himself back to health," as one news headline said, by watching old episodes of "Candid Camera" and Marx Brothers movies and reading Bennett Cerf and other humorists. Describing his experience in his bestseller, *Anatomy of an Illness* (1979), Cousins promotes the thesis that sustained bouts of negative emotions can impair the immune system and that positive emotions can produce physical and biochemical changes toward recovery. Cousins also recovered from a heart attack, chronicling those events in *The Healing Heart* (1983), which further describes the interaction of emotions with disease and healing. "I get a kick out of challenging the odds in this way," says Cousins, now a professor of medical humanities at UCLA. "It's wonderful to be able to test yourself as a guinea pig with something you believe to be true with absolute confidence, against all odds, against the authorities."

Born in Union Hill, N.J., 24 June 1915, Norman Cousins graduated from Teacher's College at Columbia and became a reporter on the *New York Evening Post*, rising to editor of the *Saturday Review of Literature* at age 25 in 1940. Cousins expanded the *Saturday Review* to a general magazine with the strongest and largest book review section in the country, and guided it through its golden decade of the 1960s when circulation reached 650,000. "The *Saturday Review* integrated knowledge," Cousins recalled. "It was a place for the sciences, philosophy and the arts to come together." He left *SR* in 1971 when it changed corporate hands, returning briefly to help the magazine through its bankruptcy, and to begin *World* magazine, which was started as scaffolding to resurrect *SR*.

He went to California in 1977. His move from publishing to medicine wasn't as extreme as it might appear. A victim of tuberculosis in childhood, "I learned the philosophy of coping with disease," he says, and became a strong believer in the power of mind over body. *Saturday Review* was a "launching pad for change and projects," many of them medically-related. In all, he has written 17 books.

Married to Ellen Kopf (four daughters), Cousins is as much an idealist on his own time as he was with *SR* or *World* on his shoulders. He is president of the World Federalist Association, which seeks to educate Americans about nuclear weapons control. He helped arrange for the treatment in the U.S. of the atomic bomb victims known as the "Hiroshima Maidens;" later he adopted one of them.

Jacques Cousteau

"I don't think it's good to categorize human beings," says this pioneering oceanographer who's famous for talking with dolphins, playing with whales, and mingling with sharks. "But if you have to categorize me, I think I am an explorer. I want to see what is underneath." His underwater explorations, shared with the public through his books and TV and film documentaries (three Oscars), have made Cousteau and his research ship *Calypso* almost as familiar to laymen as they are to his fellow scientists. "In my films," he says, "I wish to illustrate the incredible wonders of nature. When man interferes with nature, it is catastrophic." Millions of men have gone into the sea, but few quite so far as Cousteau, whose remarkably innovative underwater exploits prompted one observer to declare, "He has opened the ocean's depths to man—and man is awed."

Jacques-Yves Cousteau ("Jeek" to friends) was born 11 June 1910 in St. André de Cubzac near Bordeaux, France, the son of a legal assistant to a Boston tycoon. Jacques attended school in France and New York City, and following his love for the sea, entered the French Naval Academy in 1930, becoming chief of the French Naval Base in Shanghai in 1935. He trained as a Navy flier until a near-fatal sports car crash stopped him. ("The doctors wanted to cut off my left arm it was so badly crushed, but I refused and turned to swimming as part of the physical therapy to regain use of it.") During World War II he worked in the underground Resistance movement, and though he doesn't like to talk about it, he earned the Legion d'Honneur and the Croix de Guerre. He had been using his spare time for diving experiments, and in 1943 he and a colleague invented the Aqua-Lung, a frogman breathing apparatus. Recalling their first test use of it, Cousteau said: "I knew now that we could swim across miles and miles of country no man had ever known before, free and level, with our flesh feeling what the fish scales know." In 1950, he acquired an American minesweeper which he converted into his oceanographic vessel, *Calypso*. He retired from the Navy in 1957 with the rank of Captain of Corvette, and turned full time to *Calypso*. His oceanographic achievements include the invention of a laboratory full of underwater exploration gear (mini-subs, Bathygraf Cinecamera, Deepsea Camera Sled).

He developed the first underwater research colonies staffed by man (Conshelf I, 1962; Conshelf II, 1963; Conshelf III, 1965) and since 1967 the *Calypso* team has journeyed from the Red Sea to the Indian Ocean, to the Atlantic and the Pacific Oceans, from the Antarctic to the Aegean—capturing its adventures on film. Cousteau has produced more than 50 films for TV and three full-length features and written more than 50 books. His "Cousteau's Amazon," was a 1984 TV series. The Mississippi River was next on his calendar.

Cousteau is married to Simone Melchoir, a granddaughter of two French admirals. Their son Jean-Michel is a *Calypso* team member; their second son, Philippe, died in an expedition accident. Simone also travels on the *Calypso*. When not exploring the seas, the ecologically-minded Cousteaus are promoting the welfare of Planet Earth and the Cousteau Society. "The aim of our society is to make waves," he says. "Those of us who love the sea, who recognize the blood relationship of all Earth's beings, who see on this water planet a growing threat to our most fundamental biological machinery, do not command the money and power of even a single major multinational corporation. But we can wield the formidable power of our numbers."

Michael Crawford

White mask, tenor tones, and tender inflections transmit a mental image of this Tony Award winning actor. *Time* magazine asserted: "As the phantom, Michael Crawford gives the most compelling performance currently to be found on any Broadway stage." He not only won the Tony Award for his riveting role, but he also took home Outer Circle Critics Award for Best Actor in a Musical, and the Drama League Award for Unique Contribution to Musical Theater. For his London rendition of the love-sick masked man, he was honored with the Laurence Olivier Award.

Born in Salisbury, Wiltshire, on 19 January 1942, Michael Crawford began his career at a young age. As a boy actor, he starred in children's films and was featured as the boy soprano in Benjamin Britten's *Let's Make an Opera*. Later, he went on to make many TV appearances and over 500 radio broadcasts. He landed a continuing role on the British TV series "Not So Much a Programme, More a Way of Life," and he won the Variety Club Award for "Most Promising Actor" (1965). The same year, he was given the British Film Academy Award as "Best Newcomer" for *The Knack*. More television parts followed, and Michael had a steady stream of work on the British tube. Some shows included: "Private

View," "Audience," "Play for Today," "Chalk and Cheese" and the long-running BBC comedy series "Some Mothers Do 'Ave 'Em." Crossing his popularity over-the-ocean, Crawford became known to American film audiences in: *Hello Dolly, A Funny Thing Happened on the Way to the Forum, The Jokers, The Games, Hello and Goodbye, How I Won the War* (with John Lennon), *The Adventures of Alice in Wonderland* and *Condorman*.

Known to theater audiences in London and New York, Michael has starred in many attractions: *Barnum* (won his first Olivier Award), *Billy, Flowers for Algernon*, and his latest claim to fame, *The Phantom of the Opera*. How does the phantom follow-up on his phenomenal success? Crawford released a wonderful record album, *Songs From the Stage and Screen*, in 1988. Divorced from his wife, Gabriella Lewis, Michael has two children: Lucy and Emma.

Ben Crenshaw

This three-time collegiate links champ has had a less-than-auspicious career since turning pro in 1973. Before winning the 1984 Master's, he had averaged less than one tourney-win a year. Although his earnings haven't exactly been paltry (he was the No. 2 money winner in his best year of 1976), he slumped as low as 83rd place on the 1982 tour, earning around half of what he made in his first red-hot six months as a pro.

Clean-cut and congenial, "Gentle Ben" was ushered into the tour with the biggest buildup and the best amateur record since Jack Nicklaus. Born in Austin, Tex., 11 January 1952, he learned golf from his lawyer dad, and one of the game's best teaching pros, Harvey Penick. He started winning tourneys as a fourth grader and was so honest he penalized himself on what would have been the winning shot to lose the USGA Junior Amateur. At the University of Texas, Crenshaw became the first frosh to win the NCAA championship, and set a record by taking it a total of three times. Golfers endlessly praised both his swing and his grip. The five-foot-nine blond got great distance on his drives from sturdy, strong legs, and developed a gallery known as "Ben's Wrens." In his first six months on the tour he won the Texas Open, and took a couple of seconds, but it would be three years before he won another victory, the Bing Crosby. "I have to learn to develop better self-control," Crenshaw has said. "I'm convinced that getting angry when a well-stroked putt didn't drop or a sand shot rolled too far past the hole . . . has cost me in terms of victories." While he didn't own the second half of the 1970's in golf, as he was expected to, he still hovers near the top. Oddly enough, Crenshaw has had to work on what many thought to be his biggest asset. "I believe my mental attitude has improved," he says. "But not pulling off an easy shot still drives me crazy and losing my temper remains my nemesis." He and his wife, Polly Speno (married in 1975) were divorced in 1984.

Michael Crichton

"Best sellers are really accidents. They're flukes. At whatever point you start taking credit for good accidents, you're loused up, because if you take credit for good accidents you've to to take credit for bad ones too." Michael Crichton had published six novels under pseudonyms before seeing his name on a book jacket and experiencing the "good accident" of hitting the bestseller charts. Since then he's added several more to the list (nonfiction as well), and been involved in both the adaptation of several of his novels to film as well as the writing and directing of several successful screenplays (*Pursuit, Westworld, Looker, Coma, The Great Train Robbery*).

Tall (six feet nine), curly-haired and boyishly charming, Crichton was born in Chicago, 23 October 1942. He spent the war years in Fort Morgan, Colorado, and then moved with his advertising executive father to Connecticut. He started writing novels while at Harvard Medical School, but used the pseudonyms Jeffrey Hudson and John Lange for fear of alienating his professors by his moonlighting activities on the typewriter. Deciding never to practice medicine, he collected his M.D. degree anyhow and later went to work as an assistant to Dr. Jonas Salk at California's prestigious Salk Institute. The multi-talented writer is probably best known for his "science-nonfiction" novel, *The Andromeda Strain*, and subsequent fictional works (*The Terminal Man, The Great Train Robbery, Eaters of the Dead* and *Congo*), but he has also deftly handled problems of a very different sort in his later nonfiction book, *The Hospital Explained*, and in his 1968 book, *A Case of Need*. He has also written a book on famed artist Jasper Johns and computers. *Electronic Life: How to Think About Computers* explains, by way of witty and entertaining discourse, that we have no reason to feel threatened by the Computer Age. To the contrary, he says, "There is a whole world of life and feeling that has nothing to do with computers. In fact, computers are really a trivial part of human experience." Always involved in a handful of writing projects, he says, "I write almost continuously, mostly in the daytime, and I resent anything that interferes with it." Crichton admits to such occasional distractions as skin diving, swimming (usually twice a day), and what he merrily describes as "a very active social life." Recent books include: *Sphere* (1987) and *Travels* (1988).

Francis Crick

"I have never seen Francis Crick in a modest mood." This is the sentence chosen by James D. Watson to launch Chapter I of *The Double Helix*, the highly personal account of his and Crick's unscrambling of the structure of DNA, a discovery which later earned both men a Nobel Prize. In 1951, when Watson and his collaborator-to-be first met at the Cavendish Laboratory of Cambridge University, Francis Harry Compton Crick was best known in the scientific community as a brash nonstop talker with an explosive laugh and a reputation for brilliance but not very solid accomplishment. Within a period of 18 months that picture radically changed. Crick talked as much as ever and laughed just as loud, but his accomplishments became very solid indeed. The work done by Crick and Watson with DNA is now looked upon as the biggest break-through in biology of the 20th century.

Born 8 June 1916, Crick grew up in the home of a solid middle class family in Northampton, England, studied physics at University College in London, and when World War II broke out, went to work as a scientist in the British Admiralty. He attracted some professional notice for his work in developing magnetic mines, but when the war ended, he found himself a bit bored by physics and decided to have a go at biology. Nothing much happened until he met James Watson at Cambridge in 1951 and the two men began trying to crack one of the most baffling problems in biology, the question of how the hereditary material duplicates itself. They announced their solution in 1953 with the help of a twisting wire contraption that looked like a piece of far-out modern sculpture, but to scientists it spelled success. In 1962 the two co-workers were awarded the Nobel Prize.

The now-celebrated "double helix" of DNA has continued to hold Crick's interest as a biologist. After a year of working in the U.S., he went back to Cambridge, devoting his attention to the nature and operation of the genetic code, a field in which, in the words of his former collaborator, "he has been the acknowledged world leader" for over a decade.

Since 1962 Crick has been a Fellow, a Ferkauf Foundation Visiting Professor, and a J.W. Kieckhefer Distinguished Research Professor, in that order, for the Salk Institute for Biological Studies in San Diego, California.

He plans to devote his remaining years to brain research after having taught himself neuroanatomy, neurobiology and psychology. In 1981 his book, *Life Itself,* was published, offering the thesis that life on earth began when an unmanned spacecraft carrying microorganisms from another planet crashed into the sea billions of years ago. Crick and his wife, Odile, whom he married in 1949, have two daughters. He has one son from an earlier marriage that ended in divorce.

Walter Cronkite

This former network anchorman with the "most trusted byline in broadcast journalism" is still an occasional video visitor (via CBS News specials) into homes where he once explained the day's news events. "But I don't miss the on-air part at all," Walter Cronkite says. "Actually, I've always thought that the anchorperson personality cult thing was awful. I don't think there should even *be* anchorpeople—except off the air. We even worked on that idea when I was at CBS, but it didn't get anywhere." That idea may have foundered but few careers have been more lauded than Cronkite's. Known as "Uncle Walter" around the industry because of Americans' trusting acceptance of his reporting, he was five times voted one of the country's ten most influential decision-makers in a poll of leaders annually conducted by *U.S. News & World Report.* He was powerful enough to prompt LBJ's quitting the presidency after he uncharacteristically opined it was time for the U.S. to get out of Vietnam, resourceful enough to get Menachem Begin and Anwar Sadat to agree on-air to meet in what became Sadat's historic visit to Jerusalem, and emotional enough to be choked up while delivering the news about President Kennedy's assassination.

He was born 4 November 1916 in St. Joseph, Mo., and by the time he was a sophomore in high school was filing junior reportorial stories for the *Houston Post.* After leaving the University of Texas to take a cub reporter spot, and marrying Mary "Betsy" Maxwell (three children), he set off to cover World War II. Cronkite flew in eight bomber missions over Germany, and crashlanded in a glider at Bastogne. After setting up United Press International bureaus in Luxembourg, Belgium, and Holland, he spent two years in Moscow for the wire service, and became a CBS regular in 1950. He was his net's answer to NBC's Huntley and Brinkley, and he promptly became one of TV's most respected figures. Winner of every conceivable major journalistic award, he was also presented with the Presidential Medal of Freedom in 1981 by President Carter for two decades of outstanding news reporting. When he was nudged out of the anchor seat upon nearing the CBS mandatory retirement age (although he was 64 when he left on his own in 1981), he was kept on for special programs. While he was gracious in avoiding the issue of his unretired 80-year old boss William S. Paley, he drew network ire when commenting on the "softness" of news reporting. An avid sailor, Cronkite takes his yawl and wife Betsy plying the waters off Martha's Vineyard and the rest of the East Coast. While no longer proclaiming, "And that's the way it is," at the conclusion of newscasts, he's busy with projects in active semi-retirement. So often the pioneer, Cronkite has one major lament. "I never achieved the hour newscast, which would not have been twice as good as the half-hour newscast, but many times as good." In 1985 he was elected to the Television Academy Hall of Fame.

Hume Cronyn

To Promenade All (1972) of his activities on the boards would take a full book. In brief, the parade of characterizations moves from a lone janitor in *Hipper's Holiday* back in 1934 through *Fourposter* in 1951 to Polonius in *Hamlet* (Tony 1964). He has graced the stage with his wife, Jessica Tandy, many times since their first Broadway outing together in 1951; including *Noel Coward in Two Keys* (1974), the Pulitzer-Prize-winning *Gin Game* (1978), followed by *Foxfire* (1982). The man who says he was "puny and lonely as a child" (born 18 July 1911 in London, Ontario) was actually nominated for the Canadian Olympic boxing team. After his pugilistic period, he wavered between law and Shaw, finally studying at the American Academy of Dramatic Arts. He has portrayed both Milquetoast-Mitty types and sadistic heavies, and has been married since 1942 to Tandy (three children). "Whenever anyone compares us with the Lunts, we're delighted. It's music and we cannot hear enough of it."

Winner in 1961 of the Barter Theatre Award for his performance in *Big Fish, Little Fish,* he is also a director, screenwriter (Hitchcock's *Rope,* 1947), and producer (*Slow Dance on the Killing Ground,* 1964) and has appeared in many films. Sean O'Casey once told him, "The theatre is no place for a man who bleeds easily," and he himself groans, "Perfectionism is a terrible burden. It's a drive I wish I didn't have." For his outstanding contribution to American theatre over a 25 year period he was inducted into the Theatre Hall of Fame in 1974. Says wife Tandy of Cronyn, "When I first met him, he was very naughty because he led me to believe, before I saw him act, that he only got jobs in plays because he would put money into them. I was in fear and trembling that this was a very bad actor, and I didn't like that at all. And then I went to see him in a play by Irwin Shaw and I was so relieved. He was the best thing in it." He and Tandy appeared in the 1985 blockbuster film, *Cocoon* and they returned to Broadway in 1986, starring in *The Petition.* Hume also appeared in the film *Batteries Not Included* (1987) plus *Cocoon II* (1988).

Tom Cruise

He's rocked in his briefs, flown through the skies, high-jinxed with a hustler and flipped jiggers in mid-air. He broke many-a-girl's heart when he married actress Mimi Rogers on 9 May 1987, but his sex appeal still stands. Labeled as one of Hollywood's "brat pack," actor Tom Cruise has proven to be more than a one-time box-office hit. His list of movie credits reads like a line-up of the leading popular movies of the 1980's. An article in *Cosmopolitan* stated, Tom "projects a potent wholesomeness . . . an optimistic air of knowing how to survive."

The only son of Thomas Cruise Mapother III (electrical engineer) and Mary Lee Mapother (teacher/actress), Thomas Cruise Mapother IV was born in Syracuse, New York, on 3 July 1962. When his parents divorced, Tom moved with his mother and sisters to Louisville, Kentucky. These were struggling years for the Mapothers; Mary Lee was attempting to make ends meet, while Tom battled to read correctly. Suffering from dyslexia (his mother and sisters did, too) he recalls the trouble he had determining "whether letters like c or d curved to the right or the left." Longing to be accepted by his peers, Tom became a sports enthusiast, participating in lacrosse, football, hockey, wrestling, skiing and tennis. After being injured during a wrestling match, Cruise sought other extracurricular activities and discovered acting. Cast as Nathan Detroit in his high school's production of *Guys and Dolls,* Cruise decided that he was destined for a theatrical career. Moving in with a friend in New York, he was cast in a local dinner theatre production of *Godspell,* followed by a small role in the Brooke Shield's film *Endless Love* (1981). With the word out on Cruise, he won the role of a psychotic cadet in *Taps* (1981) followed by *Losin' It* (1983), *The Outsiders* (1983), *All the Right Moves* (1983) and *Risky Business* (1983). The latter film shot him to stardom, as his memorable "underwear, white socks, dark sunglasses" sing-a-long to "Old Time Rock & Roll" became a favorite scene for teenagers. As Cruise says, "When their parents leave, they turn the music up." When producers Don Simpson and Jerry Bruckheimer were seeking "Tom Cruise types" for their movie *Top Gun*

(1986) they decided to approach the real person. Tom's star contribution to the film earned an incredible $8.1 million during its debut weekend at U.S. theatres. Next up, he paired with veteran actor Paul Newman in *The Color of Money* (1986). Not only did he pick up some good hustling tips, but the magic that these two actors created on the screen together touched all. Director Martin Scorese explains there was a kind of "mentor/protege relationship" between the two men. It's where "the older guy [is] passing on the torch to the younger actor." Tom was fortunate to share another artistic experience by filming the Academy Award-winning film *Rain Man* with Dustin Hoffman. Portraying Charlie Babbit, a wheeler-dealer, he turns the role into an outstanding character study. Other Tom Cruise films include: *Legend* in 1985 and *Cocktail* in 1988. In 1989, Cruise was set to star in *Born on the 4th of July*. He and his actress wife, Mimi Rogers, have homes in both New York and Los Angeles.

Billy Crystal

"I'm comfortable being old ... being black ... being Jewish," wrote Billy Crystal, the gifted mimic who feels "at home in other bodies." "And I look very good in dresses" he also admits. The comedian, sometimes described as "straight as a baseball bat" in his lifestyle, made quite a stir when he first appeared before a national TV audience in 1977 as Jodie Dallas, the first openly homosexual character in the history of television, in the prime-time ABC weekly sitcom "Soap." But the security of a successful series wasn't paramount to this energetic talent, who left "Soap" after four years because he was bored with playing the same character season after season. "It wasn't what I wanted," Crystal says in retrospect. "It wasn't me." However, the exposure was just what the 5'6", 130-pound Crystal needed. It landed him the role of Lionel, the world's first pregnant man, in the Joan Rivers film *Rabbit Test* (1978), which was followed by a number of TV movies, both comedic and dramatic. But live comedy had always been Crystal's love, and he showed his immense talents as a regular of "Saturday Night Live" during its 1984-1985 season. Writing all his own material, Crystal created the character Fernando, which helped earn him an Emmy nomination for "Best Actor in a Variety Program," and coined the expression "You look mahvelous." Crystal then parlayed his character's theme into a hit song ("Marvelous") and into the title of his slim autobiography (*Absolutely Mahvelous*, 1986). Crystal co-wrote and hosted "A Comedy Salute to Baseball" (NBC, 1985) before going on to do his own special, "On Location: Billy Crystal—Don't Get Me Started" (HBO, 1986) which garnered two Ace Awards and five nominations. Keeping busy, the multi-talented Crystal starred in such films as *Running Scared* (1986) and *Throw Momma From the Train* (1987) before writing the screenplay of *Goodnight Moon* (1987)—in which he also acted—and co-writing, producing and starring in *Memories of Me* (1988). Whether it's hosting the Grammy Awards (which also earned him an Emmy nomination), working on an new live act or preparing another edition of Comic Relief to benefit the homeless (edition III was aired in early 1989) Crystal's star is definately rising.

Born 14 March 1948 in New York City to mother Helen (who loved theatre and performed in shows at temple) and father Jack (who produced jazz concerts at a lower East Side Jewish catering hall and managed his uncle Milt Gabler's Commodore Music Shop in New York City), Crystal, the youngest of three sons, says he was "bred for show business." "My father used to bring home jazz musicians at passover. We had swinging seders." Crystal recalls meeting Billie Holiday when he was five years old ("Miss Billie called me Mister Billy") and having jazz musicians play at his bar mitzvah. Loving the musicians' "jive talk," Crystal started imitating them and doing impressions of adult visitors by donning their hats and coats. Guiding the boys' comedy viewing, Dad chose "tasty things" on TV like Laurel and Hardy movies and brought home recordings of Bill Cosby, Woody Allen, Elaine May and Jonathan Winters. After listening to Cosby's family stories, Crystal realized that he had his own "relative stories."

Encouraged by their mother, the boys (Joel, now a high school teacher and Richard, a TV producer who had the idea for Fernando's character) performed in their living room, lip-synching to Spike Jones' records or imitating Mel Brooks, Sid Caesar or Ernie Kovacs routines. Crystal was voted the wittiest student in his class at Long Beach High School where he emceed their 1964 annual variety show, contributing his own rendition of Cosby's "Noah." Starting at Marshall University on a baseball scholarship, Crystal hosted a campus call-in radio show. A year later he transferred to Nassau Community College when Marshall's baseball program was eliminated due to lack of funds. Majoring in theatre, he spent three summers acting in the school's alumni theatre group. After graduation Crystal studied television and motion picture directing with Martin Scorese at New York University. He also worked as stage manager for the Off-Broadway hit musical *You're a Good Man Charlie Brown*. In 1969, along with two Nassau alumni, Crystal formed his first improvisational comedy troupe, playing Greenwich Village, small Eastern colleges and trade shows. By then the father of an infant daughter, Crystal also worked as a part-time high school teacher to make ends meet. Turning to a solo act, Crystal played his first "gig" at a N.Y.U. fraternity party. Later, doing night solos at such places as "Catch a Rising Star" and the Playboy Clubs, Crystal spent his days watching his daughter Jennifer so that his wife Janice (whom he met at Nassau Community College, and married in 1970) could work as a secretary. After walking off the set of "Saturday Night Live" in October 1975 over a dispute about cutting his monologue from seven minutes to two minutes, Crystal finally appeared on the show April, 1976, doing "Face," his monologue of a composite of old black musicians. Even though he received good reviews, it would be eight years before he would return to the show. Moving with his wife and daughter to Los Angeles, Crystal performed at the "Comedy Store" where he was seen by Norman Lear. He was cast in a guest spot in the hit "All in the Family" before being chosen as Jodie Dallas in "Soap." After his success, NBC gave Crystal his own show, "The Billy Crystal Comedy Hour," which premiered in 1982 and was cancelled after fire airings. Reviewing the first program, which had Robin Williams as a guest, Marvin Kitman said in *Newsday*, "He [Crystal] seems to be able to do everything.... He seems to be, underneath the nice guy image, a nice guy." In 1984 and 1985 Crystal performed regularly at the Sands Hotel in Atlantic City and at the Bottom Line in New York City when not working on "Saturday Night Live."

Currently residing with his wife Janice and their two daughters, Jennifer and Lindsay, in Pacific Palisades, California, Crystal hopes to be able to move back to New York again.

Merce Cunningham

"Merce Cunningham's dance requires schooling in receptiveness which is in terms of difficulty and tedium at least comparable to the obstacles in mastering physics or engineering," says Susan Sontag about the choreographer who in 1984, more than 40 years after creating his first work, was still indefatigably searching for new frontiers and generally finding them before anyone else. From the day in 1945 when he left the Martha Graham company, dissatisfied with the literalness of modern dance that emphasized story and characterization, to produce abstract dances in which the accent was on movement itself, Cunningham has puzzled, excited, amused and infuriated audiences—and critics. Walter Terry in 1951 wrote that Cunningham's experiments were "carrying him farther and farther away from the theater and closer and closer to a sort of self-indulgent self-expressionism." Don McDonough recounts: "The historic modern dance devotee was thrown into a mild panic when he found that the usual handholds of story, character development, and musical cues were absent from Cunningham's work. The choreography became a sheer cliff face without any of the little nooks and crannies on which the dance audience could secure itself."

Born 16 April 1919 to a country lawyer of Irish descent and a mother of

Slavic extraction in the lumbering and coal-mining town of Centralia, Washington, Cunningham's first dance teacher was an oldtime vaudeville performer who taught the future avant-gardist conventional folk forms, tap and exhibition ballroom dancing. Spotted by Martha Graham at Bennington College's school of modern dance, Cunningham became the company's second male dancer (after Erick Hawkins). He created the roles of the Acrobat in *Every Soul is a Circus*, March in *Letter to the World* and the Revivalist in *Appalachian Spring*, displaying a virtuosity that admirers felt placed him second only to Graham herself. After leaving Graham, he worked independently as a dancer before forming his own company in 1953, and began the kind of work that is characteristic of him today—if anything can ever be called characteristic of a man wholly committed to chance and change. The keynote is the element of chance. Continuity is supplied by the movement of the dancers, but the interpretation of the expression is left to the individuals in the audience. Cunningham's mainstream counterpart might be the late George Balanchine. Within their different techniques both choreographers preserved an impersonal approach and each believed in the expressiveness of a single movement unimpeded by the obtrusion of other elements, such as plot or scenery, and with no feeling of compulsion towards or away from climax. (The comparison fails when it comes to sound. George Balanchine was the most musical of choreographers while Cunningham is committed to the physicality of dance independent of sound.)

So dominant a place in modern dance does Merce Cunningham hold that most of its practitioners invoke—if only in contradiction—the man with whom most of them studied or danced, who had stimulated or provoked them, whom they want to resemble, whom they want not to resemble, whom they seek to outdo and to negate. Martha Graham once observed, "Merce was made for the air." Twyla Tharp calls him *the* master teacher." "Diaghilev would have loved Cunningham," said Alexander Bland in the *London Observer*. "Besides admiring him as an artist ... his acute artistic antennae would have tingled at the sense that Cunningham was talking in the language of today." In 1985 Cunningham and Paul Taylor were the first choreographers named recipients of MacArthur Foundation "genius" awards. That same year Cunningham was on the Kennedy Center honors list.

Mario Cuomo

Arriving in San Francisco one July night to spark fellow Democrats out of their 1984 campaign lethargy, New York Governor Mario Cuomo discovered an interesting fact about himself: he was a spellbinding orator. Suddenly the Democratic talk was all about the man who *wasn't* running for president, but who certainly would be seriously considered in the future. "We must get the American public to look past the glitter, beyond the showmanship, to the reality, the hard substance of things," he exhorted to campaign delegates. "And we will do that not so much with speeches that sound good as with speeches that are good and sound. Not so much with speeches that bring people to their feet as with speeches that bring people to their senses." The son of Italian immigrants quotes Thomas More and St. Francis the way other politicans paraphrase TV commercials. Suddenly the governor's reputation was based more on his silvery words than on his deeds. "[He] has achieved enormous popularity and following for his intellectual capabilities, and that has caused people not to look at the specifics of his financial administration," charged one banker and civic leader.

Mario Cuomo first came to national attention in 1974 when he successfully mediated a housing crisis in his native Queens, one of five New York City boroughs, in which he forged a compromise between a middle-class neighborhood coalition and proponents of a Federal plan to build subsidized high-rise apartments. That same year Governor Hugh Carey appointed him Secretary of State of New York. He went up against Ed Koch in a pitched mayoralty battle in 1977 and lost, but the following year was elected lieutenant governor. Four years later he made it to the state's top job. In 1984 he published his own account of the cliff-hanging, come-from-behind victory against his old rival Koch in *Diaries of Mario M. Cuomo: The Campaign for Governor*.

Born 15 June 1932, as a boy Mario often worked in the family produce store. Later he commuted to St. John's Law School, not far from home, and eventually taught there. Cuomo was married in 1956 to the former Matilda Raffa. They have five children. Of Matilda Cuomo, Big Apple political writer Doug Ireland says: "She would make the best First Lady since Eleanor Roosevelt."

Jane Curtin

After moderate early success in showbiz, this actress-comedienne found her father singularly unimpressed. He told her, she says, that "it's a silly-ass business and that I should work in the John Hancock death claims department, something steady. But I happen to know he shows off about me to his friends on the golf course when I'm not there." If Mr. Curtin glowed with silent pride back in the early 1970's when Jane was playing in a little-known New York and Boston-area improvisational comedy production, *The Proposition*, he must be postively bursting now that she's had her very own weekly sitcom, "Kate and Allie" (with co-star Susan Saint James) on national TV. Not to mention her extended stint as one of the first-generation jokesters on NBC-TV's weekly laughfest, "Saturday Night Live." She shone as the alien Conehead housewife, in parodies of TV talkshow hosts, and as an uptight news anchorwoman.

Born 6 September 1947 in Cambridge, Mass., Jane Curtin was brought up the Catholic-reared, middle-class daughter of an insurance agency owner and "a Radcliffe graduate who ... wanted to do something worthwhile, but ... had four kids instead." Jane became the first of her siblings "who ever moved out without moving out to get married." After dropping out of Northeastern University, she spent four years with *The Proposition*, did numerous commercials and a tour with *The Last of the Red Hot Lovers* before signing on with "SNL" in 1975. Since going off on her own, she's appeared in a number of movies for both the big and small screen. She married Patrick Lynch in 1975; the couple have a daughter.

Jamie Lee Curtis

"I've worked so hard to find my identity," frets Jamie Lee Curtis. "Now all they want to know is where I got my body." The terrific body was finely tuned (which meant months of aerobic training, weight lifting and swimming) for her role in the 1985 film *Perfect*. Though serious roles are coming her way, Jamie Lee is still known as the "Scream Queen" (*Halloween*, *The Fog*, *Prom Night* and *Terror Train*), dodging knives and sadistic killers. She graduated from horror films and then played junkie-sluts on TV before landing the lead role in the made-for-TV movie "Death of a Centerfold: The Dorothy Stratten Story." Other films include *Trading Places*, *Love Letters*, *Grandview U.S.A.*, *A Fish Called Wanda*, *Amazing Grace and Chuck*, and *Blue Steel*. In 1989 she hit sitcom success playing a writer for a magazine in the ABC-TV series "Anything But Love."

The daughter of Tony Curtis and Janet Leigh (born 22 November 1958) had, by her own account "a very abnormal childhood." Says Curtis of her parents, "My father was sort of a stranger, then a real stranger, then an enemy. Now he's a friend." (She considers her stepfather to be the real father figure in her life). "My mom was very good about reminding me that if I was to be successful, it would be because I was true to myself." Yet the young

Jamie Lee is finding it very difficult to emerge from the pressures of Hollywood as a whole person. As a youngster, "I didn't want to be an individual; I just wanted to fit in and be normal," she remembers. Curtis spent most of her youth trying to conform. "I learned early to be a chameleon, to turn whatever color was needed." Her true colors are managing to surface now she's given up smoking, drinking and drugs, and trying to please all of Hollywood. Married to Chris Guest ("Saturday Night Live"), they live with their daughter, Annie, in a historic apartment in L.A. and when not pursuing stardom, Jamie Lee practices yoga and dreams of future plans to produce and direct.

Tony Curtis

His acting range covers everything from *Houdini* to *The Boston Strangler*. His lively transvestite capers (with Jack Lemmon and Marilyn Monroe) in *Some Like It Hot* (kissing Monroe, he says, "was like kissing Hitler") in 1959, uncorked his bubbly comedic talents; his gutsy portrayal of a chain gang fugitive in *The Defiant Ones* (1958) had already proven he could handle drama.

The Great Imposter came into the world as Bernard Schwartz on 3 June 1925 in the East Bronx. In his first screen appearance he was billed as Jimmy Curtis. Remembering his "hungry childhood," he suggested "Anthony Adverse" as an alternative; compromised on Anthony Curtis. He drew on his own tough Hunt's Point background when he played a juvenile gang member in *City Across the River* ("Where I come from, being good-looking was a passport out of a garbage can"), but didn't have much personal precedent for the spate of swashbuckling "Ali Baba" roles that followed. He married actress Janet Leigh (two daughters, one of whom, Jamie Lee, became a successful actress). After their 1962 divorce he married Christine Kauffman (two more daughters), and with his third wife, model Leslie Allen, became the father of a son. (He divorced Allen in 1981). The '80s saw Curtis in *Title Shot* and *The Mirror Crack'd* (both released in '80), *Where is Parsifal?* (1984), *Insignificance* (1984), the TV film "Mafia Princess" (1985), CBS's "Murder in Three Acts" (1986) and "Harry's Back" (1987), and the motion pictures *Midnight* (1988) and *Lobster Man From Mars* (1989).

Alfonse D'Amato

"He's bright, energetic, and so ambitious you can almost see the wheels in his mind spinning when he sees an opportunity," said one public official of this United States Senator who rose from the relative obscurity of local government (Hempstead, New York) to unprecedented, dramatic triumph in the 1980 elections. This pragmatic conservative Republican, skilled at the art of legislative maneuvering, quickly gained positions on several key Senate Committees, and in 1984 was rumored to have his sights set on becoming the first Italian-American President of the United States—a goal befitting a man who has been described as an "honest opportunist."

Son of an insurance broker, he was born Alfonse Marcello D'Amato 1 August 1937, in Brooklyn, New York, though he spent most of his growing-up years in Island Park on Long Island. A mischievous child, nicknamed "Tippy"—he hated "Alfonse"—preferred crabbing, fishing, and swimming to school. He must have done an about-face, for by 1961 he had received both his B.S. and J.D. degrees from Syracuse University. Though admitted to the New York State Bar in 1962, he was unsuccessful in securing a position with a major New York law firm. He began working in local Republican politics in the 1950s under the tutelage of Joseph M. Margiota, the chairman of the powerful Nassau County Republican Committee. The 1960s and 1970s saw D'Amato moving up the political ladder through a succession of positions until he was elected presiding supervisor of the Town of Hempstead and majority leader of the Nassau County Board of Supervisors. In 1979, D'Amato made a surprising and successful bid for the senate against Jacob Javits, whose declining health had become an issue. In the general election, he edged over the victory line in front of Democrat Elizabeth Holtzman, though not without problems. Accused of being involved in a kickback scheme during his senatorial campaign, he underwent a full investigation on charges of graft, nepotism, and illegal patronage in Nassau County and was cleared of all charges.

In the Senate, D'Amato aligned himself with Howard Baker, and took on three important committee assignments—Appropriations, Banking, Housing and Urban Affairs, and Small Business. In 1981, he sided with Republicans and conservative Southern Democrats in 82 percent of the roll-call votes, and was a staunch supporter of Ronald Reagan's budget cuts. Explained D'Amato, "I'm supporting the President so that when I go to the White House for help for New York, they'll receive me as a team player and maybe then they'll help." With an overall Presidential-support record of 71 percent, he supported the B-1 Bomber, the MX missile, and the neutron bomb, as well as anti-abortion legislation, but he broke this record by opposing military aid to Syria, the sale of AWACS to Saudi Arabia, cuts in student loans, mass transit operating subsidies and the provision of Reagan's 1985 tax reform package which removed the deductibility of state and local taxes.

Volatile, often abrasive, he was described by *New York* magazine (1981) as "a man whose intelligence—and he is intelligent—flows from his emotions, especially his anger. He is tightly wound, impatient, spontaneous." After eighteen-hour days, the Senator relaxes by going sailing or playing the piano. Legally separated from his wife of 23 years (four children), he still maintains a home in Island Park.

Jacques D'Amboise

After his first "Swan Lake," the durable star of the New York City Ballet for almost thirty years (until his retirement in 1984) was likened to "Jack Armstrong, the all-American boy," by the late critic John Martin. Five years later, Martin said, "He has made a romantic hero of Siegfried and transformed the role into a major one."

Born 28 July 1934 in Dedham, Mass., at age eight Jacques D'Amboise followed his older siblings into the School of American Ballet. Under the protective and demanding tutelage of dance legend George Balanchine, D'Amboise became a principal dancer with the company in 1953. He also appeared in films, most notably *Seven Brides for Seven Brothers* and *Carousel*. While his speed and buoyancy made him a star with drawing power at the New York City Ballet, D'Amboise's vanity remained remarkably unaffected, and he began to branch out into choreography and teaching. His affection for children—he enjoys a close relationship with his four children by wife Carolyn George—and his belief that dance should be a non-elitist pursuit, led him to begin a second career in the mid-70s as director of the non-profit National Dance Institute in New York. His goal is to bring dance to school children and working class people who otherwise could not afford it. D'Amboise hopes to expand the Institute to other states, and continues to teach dance. "Each class is a wonderful adventure; I'm learning something all the time. A film documentary about D'Amboise's work with children was an Academy Award winner in 1984, and in 1985 he was recipient of one of the first annual Eleanor Roosevelt Community Service Awards. Another undoubted source of pleasure for D'Amboise in 1985 was seeing his son, Christopher—a principal dancer with NYCB—as a star of Andrew Lloyd Webber's *Song and Dance* on Broadway.

Arlene Dahl

This Hollywood alumna turned beauty expert added another career notch in the 1980s based on her expertise in astrology. "Arlene Dahl's Lovescopes" became a cable TV staple in 1982 and she published a book of that title in 1983. The redheaded leading lady of such films as *Three Little Words* (with Fred Astaire, 1950) and *Here Come the Girls* (with Bob Hope, 1953) first made it as an author in 1965 with the bestseller *Always Ask a Man*, later followed by a series of beauty-advice tomes.

Women born under the sign of Leo, says Arlene, have "a flair for the dramatic and a regal bearing" and "combine authority with elegance"—a description which aptly fits the Leo-born Dahl. Born 11 August circa 1927 to a Minneapolis family of Norwegian heritage, she began performing on a local children's radio series and had her initial taste of fame as a New York Cover Girl in the 1940s.

After making her Broadway debut in the musical, *Mr. Strauss Goes to Boston,* choreographed by George Balanchine, Arlene was tapped by Jack Warner for the leading role of "Rose" in Warner Brothers' 1947 Dennis Morgan musical, *My Wild Irish Rose*. She made a total of 28 films before returning to New York and carving a niche in the fashion/beauty biz as a consultant, ad exec and designer. (Her pet invention is the patented "Dahl" boudoir cap.) In 1983 she made her soap opera debut on ABC's "One Life to Live."

The six-times-wed Arlene is pleased that all three of her children were "born under Sun signs compatible with mine." The eldest, Lorenzo Lamas (son of the late Fernando Lamas and a regular on the blockbuster TV series, "Falcon Crest") is an Aquarian; daughter Carole Christine Holmes (father: Christian R. Holmes, III) is a Leo like her mom; Sonny Schaum (father: Rounseville W. Schaum) is a Sagittarian. Other husbands include the late Lex ("Tarzan") Barker, Alexis Lichine, and, currently, cosmetics executive Marc Rosen, whom she wed in 1984 aboard the "Sea Goddess."

Jim Dale

Called the "Toast of the Town" (*N.Y. Times*) and "One of the five or six funniest comedians [he] had ever seen" (John Simon of *New York*), Jim Dale is riding the crest of Broadway's wave of popularity. From his 1974 Broadway debut performance as the swashbuckling rogue "Scapino" (which earned Dale his first Outer Critic's Circle Award for Best Actor, a Drama Desk Award and a Tony nomination) and his Tony Award-winning performance as the flamboyant Phineas T. Barnum in the musical *Barnum*, through his appearance in the revival of *Joe Egg* (which won Dale his second Outer Critics' Circle Best Actor Award and nominations for both the Tony and Drama Desk Awards), to his recent twenty-month run as the star of the number 1 musical comedy hit *Me and My Girl*, Dale has shown audiences and critics alike the talents that made and keep him a star in this, his adopted country. But the British-born singer, dancer and comedian was not new to stardom and popularity when he arrived on our shores. A pop singer in the late 1950's, Dale sang for three years on British TV's first and most popular rock and roll show, BBC's "6:05 Special," before returning to comedy with his own TV program, "The Lunchtime Show." For two years he wrote and performed comedy sketches three times a week. Switching in the 1960's to the large screen, the energetic comedian appeared in British films including a dozen of the bawdy "Carry On" films while indulging in his lyric-writing "hobby," earning an Oscar nomination for his lyrics to the title song "Georgy Girl" (1966). Always wishing to expand the showcase for his talents, Dale branched into performing Shakespeare remarking that "the laughter of a Shakespeare audience was just the same as the laughter in a music hall." Performing with the National Theatre Company, for five years, Dale took time out to host England's most popular TV variety show "Saturday Night at the Palladium" for a fifteen week season (73-74) aside from filming three movies (72-74). With these credits behind him, Dale arrived on our shores with the National Theatre Company, doing *The Taming of the Shrew* at the Brooklyn Academy of Music before moving to Broadway with *Scapino*, appearing in a variety of films, including Disney's *Pete's Dragon* and stage performances in New Haven (*Privates on Parade*, 1974) and Los Angeles (*Comedians*, 1977).

Born 15 August, 1935 in the small industrial town of Rothwell, Northamptonshire, England, Jim Smith (he changed his name when he entered show business in order to not be confused with the British entertainer Jim Smith) was not exposed to any theatre in his early years. Rothwell had neither a theatre nor a cinema. "But when I was nine," he recalls, "I went to a show at the Victoria Palace in London and saw a comic." Sitting in the audience, hearing the laughter, Dale was instantly stage struck. His first exposure to a musical, which ironically was *Me and My Girl*, changed Dale's life. He knew then and there that what he wanted to do in life was "to make people laugh." The very next day Dale started dancing lessons. For the next six years he spent most of his free time learning ballet, tap and "eccentric" dancing which Dale describes as "learning to move the body as if it has no joints, like an Indian rubber doll." Dale also studied judo and tumbling. At 16, Dale dropped out of school and took a job in a shoe factory. Fortunately, that career was cut short by the appearance of Carroll Levis and his Discoverers, a traveling vaudeville troupe. Catching the owner's attention by falling when running on stage to audition, Dale spent the next two years touring England's music halls as a comic tumbler with the troupe. After a six month disc jockey job at BBC, Dale was asked to do the warm-up comic routine on "6:05 Special." The 22-year-old picked up a guitar, did some singing and became an overnight sensation. From that point on it's been one challenging role after another for the lean comedian with the aqua eyes, weathered face and smiling disposition. "When I say challenge, I'm not talking about dangerous things," says the diversified performer. "It's the knowledge that each day, when the show begins, you and the audience are all, in a sense, starting from nothing."

Dale is the father of four children by his first wife, British born Patricia Gardine. Dale and his second wife, New York gallery owner Julie Schafler (23 March 1981), reside in New York City where he collects puppets, dolls in bell jars and antique toys when not writing or preparing for his next challenge.

Timothy Dalton

Music up . . . "My name is Bond, James Bond." The pumping underscore paves way for the unexpected happenings about to invade the screen. "What I find so appealing is that Ian Fleming tapped into a mythological figure—a 'George and the Dragon' type of hero who single-handedly takes on the forces of evil. I hope that I've captured the spirit of the man and the essence of Fleming," says the current 007, Timothy Dalton. Following in the footsteps of predecessors Sean Connery and Roger Moore, Dalton fit into his role with enough debonair to capture any Bond fan.

Born in Colwyn Bay, North Wales, 21 March 1946 to English parents, Timothy came from a theatrical heritage. His father is an advertising executive; one grandmother performed at English music halls with Charles Chaplin; and his other grandmother was a theatrical manager. At 16 years old, he debuted in an Old Vic production of *Macbeth*. After completing his studies in Manchester and Belper, he joined the National Youth Theatre in 1964 and appeared in Shakespeare's *Coriolanus*. Pursuing his career, the future James Bond trained at the Royal Academy of Dramatic Arts, joined the Birmingham Repertory Theatre Company, and appeared in many Shakespearean productions.

Not a stranger to films, Dalton has starred in an outstanding array of movies: *The Lion in Winter, Cromwell, Wuthering Heights, Mary, Queen of Scots*

Timothy Daly

(received a British Film Award nomination), *Permission To Kill*, *Sexette*, and *Agatha*. Recent releases include: *Brenda Starr* (with Brooke Shields), *Flash Gordon*, *Chanel Solitaire* and *The Doctor and the Devils*. He also appeared in a number of television roles: "Sins," "Mistral's Daughter," "The Master of Ballantrae," "Centennial," "Jane Eyre," "Candida" and "Five Finger Exercise."

Originally skeptical about signing a contract and becoming the suave screen hero, he turned down the first Bond offer: "When I was about 25, Mr. Broccoli very kindly asked me if I'd be interested in taking over the role of James Bond from Sean Connery. Frankly, I thought it would be a very stupid move—I considered myself too young and Connery too good. I was approached again several years later, but had already been asked to appear in 'Flash Gordon.' So when the schedules came back together this time, I was delighted to accept and embraced this film with a lot of joy and enthusiam." Dalton's first Bond film, *The Living Daylights* (1987), established him as this principal male character, and the sequel, *Licence to Kill* (1989), cements his position. Still single, Timothy lives in the quiet town of Chiswick in London. His best friend, actress Vanessa Redgrave, resides in the same neighborhood. When he's not filming, he likes to go fishing or relax listening to classical music and opera.

Timothy Daly

"When I was a kid, I wanted to be a brain surgeon, a plumber, an athlete, a fireman—all these things. But somehow I realized that I didn't have the stamina or the ability to be all those things at once. So I decided on the next best thing. An actor. That way, I could at least pretend to be all these things." Timothy Daly has skillfully "pretended" in theatre, film and television, embellishing the Daly family reputation that originated with his father, the late James Daly, and continued with his Emmy-award-winning sister, Tyne Daly.

Born 1 March 1956 in New York City, Daly grew up in Suffern, N.Y. Although he made his acting debut at age nine in PBS's "Enemy of the People," he truly began his career after graduating from Bennington College with a bachelor's degree in theatre. He made his screen debut in the 1982 critical and commercial success *Diner*. Initially he felt all future films had to live up to the standards set by *Diner* but he soon realized that was impossible and in the long run an unimportant task. Other films include *Made In Heaven*, *Just the Way You Are*, *Love Or Money* and *Spellbinder*. Daly found himself a home in television and on stage in between features. He was a series regular on the short-lived ABC series "Ryan's Four" during the 1982-'83 season. Television appearances followed on NBC's "Hill Street Blues", PBS/American Playhouse's "The Rise and Rise of Daniel Rocket," the NBC Movie of the Week "Mirrors" and "I Married a Centerfold" and the CBS Movie of the Week "Red Earth, White Earth". Daly received excellent notices portraying Valerie Bertinelli's blind brother on the CBS miniseries "I"ll Take Manhattan." The raves continued when Daly created the role of Norman Foley on the 1988-'89 CBS series "Almost Grown." Although the series was cancelled after a short run it showcased Daly's ability as it afforded him the opportunity to play Norman at different stages of his life. Daly aged from a clean cut high school senior to a rebellious 1960's disc jockey to a family man of the '70's who becames a fortyish divorced father of two in the 80's. Whatever the age group, Daly convinced viewers and reviewers alike that he was Norman Foley in a truly inspired performance.

Daly debuted Off-Broadway in 1984 in *Fables for Friends* followed by *Oliver Oliver*. He made his Broadway debut in 1987 with *Coastal Disturbances*. It earned him a Tony nomination and he received a Theatre World Award for the role.

Daly met his wife, actress Amy Van Nostrand, in 1981 when they performed with the Trinity Repertory Company in Providence, Rhode Island. They were married 18 September 1982, and their son, Sam, was born in 1984. The family resides in New York where Daly pursues his hobbies. Besides being a talented actor, he is an accomplished guitarist and an excellent cook.

Tyne Daly

For Tyne Daly, being the daughter of an actor and actress did not necessarily mean an automatic ticket to stardom. The brown-haired actress who has won Emmys as Outstanding Actress playing the "warm, pizazzy, tough but vulnerable" Mary Beth Lacey on the CBS series, "Cagney and Lacey," the story of two New York policewomen, went through a slow process of paying her dues with small roles in regional theater and television. "The fact that I'm an actor's kid means simply that my dad [the late James Daly] was an actor and I'm his kid. I consider myself a very privileged person. I grew up with people like Helen Hayes sitting in my living room. It was glamorous." Nevertheless, Daly is quick to remind one that privilege must not be mistaken for wealth. "My father didn't always work and we didn't always have money."

Born in Madison, Wisconsin, 21 February 1945, Tyne Daly made her performing debut in the second grade, playing the role of the Virgin Mary in a school Christmas pageant ("I was sure Mary Magdalene was the better role."). Her professional start came during her sixth, seventh and eighth grade summer vacations when she took part in productions like *H.M.S. Pinafore* with the Antrim Players at the Antrim Playhouse in New Hampshire. There followed an apprenticeship with the American Shakespeare Festival in Stratford, Conn. While still in high school, she attended a reading for an English play at Rockland Community College in Rockland, N.Y., and wound up serving as stage manager, moving scenery, working on costumes and doing whatever else had to be done. Eventually, she also had a chance to act.

After high school graduation, Tyne was sent off—under protest—to Brandeis University to major in liberal arts and humanities. She begged her parents to let her pursue an acting career and they finally agreed to her entering the American Musical and Dramatic Academy only if she continued to live at home in Suffern, N.Y. (Although her family moved around, she considered Suffern her "real home.") In her first year at the Academy, she met Georg Stanford Brown, who was working his way through classes as the institution's janitor. "We wound up scrubbing the school's dance floor together," she says. The couple was married in June 1966 and now have three children (Elizabeth, Katherine, Alyxandra). Roles on TV's "The Virginian" and a three-month stint on "General Hospital" preceded Daly's breakthrough film role in 1976 as Clint Eastwood's "Dirty Harry" Callahan's partner in *The Enforcer*. With "Cagney and Lacey" in syndication, the actress is seen daily in reruns. Breaking out of her stereotype, Tyne appeared in a television film "Kids Like These" (1987) and starred in *Come Back Little Sheba* (1987) at the Los Angeles Theatre Center. In 1989 she was Broadway-bound with the musical *Gypsy*.

Rodney Dangerfield

"I once played a club that was so far out in the sticks, the only review I got was in *Field and Stream*. I started at age 19," explains the comic, "and at age 40, I was still just a businessman going to the office during the week to support my weekend career as an entertainer. Hey, I just don't get no respect." Perhaps not, but the comedian has parlayed his tagline wail into the hearts of millions of empathetic fans, becoming the nation's most famous anti-hero.

Born 22 November 1921 in Babylon, Long Island, he went on the road as a comedian under the name of Jack Roy, a switch from his real name, Jacob Cohen. He stuck with the road for ten years but the constant travelling and not-so-constant income made it tough for a married man with responsibilities. Eventually, except for small club dates on weekends, he left show business for plain old business . . . any business. His fortune changed at age 40 when he launched a new career not only as a performer but as a comedy writer. Recognized at last, he won bookings at such New York clubs as Upstairs at the Downstairs, the Duplex and the Living Room. In 1969 he opened his own nightclub, Dangerfield's, on Second Avenue in Manhattan. Well known to audiences because of his many appearances on talk and television variety shows, including the late night chuckler "Saturday Night Live," Dangerfield's debut record was called, what else, *I Get No Respect* and won a Grammy in 1981 for best comedy album. He starred in the hit films *Easy Money, Caddyshack, Back To School,* and *The Scout,* and was one of the first comedians ever to headline his own show at the Radio City Music Hall. In 1988 he packed the Mark Hellinger Theatre with a special 2-week engagement. The icing on the sadsack cake was the tremendous success of his rap-disco song and video called "Rappin' Rodney"—which got "heavy rotation" on MTV in 1983. Dangerfield and his wife Joyce live in the kingdom of no respect itself—New York City. They have two children, Brian and Melanie.

Blythe Danner

Calling her "one of the best American actresses," *Newsweek's* Jack Kroll observed (after seeing her in repertory in 1977) that "with a face like truth, a golden intelligence and a superb stage voice, [Blythe Danner] is pure delight from the moment of her entrance." Aside from similar rave reviews, Danner has a Tony award and nominations for her Broadway efforts. However, the *New York Post* pegged her (back in 1975)as "the most underrated comedienne in American movies right now." And the *New York Times* completed the circuit by praising her role on TV in the John Updike-adapted "Too Far to Go" as helping to make it a "landmark in television programming." Having won unanimous accolades in all three acting mediums, she's still probably best described, as critic John Simon did, as "the most underrated and underused major leading lady of our screen and stage."

Tall, willowy, and interview-shy Blythe Katharine Danner was born circa 1944 and grew up in a house on Philadelphia's Main Line; she earned a B.A. in drama at upstate New York's Bard College and served her theatrical apprenticeship playing repertory in New England and New York. Her portrayal of the free-spirited young divorcee in her Broadway debut, *Butterflies Are Free,* in 1969, led to a Tony, and a stream of jobs in both movies and in TV. In addition to catching her in her own TV series in 1973, "Adam's Rib," New York theater-goers saw her in 1980 in the Lincoln Center revival of *Philadelphia Story,* and on Broadway in *Blithe Spirit* (1987). She also appeared on stage in *A Streetcar Named Desire* (1988) and in the New York Shakespeare Festival's rendition of *Much Ado About Nothing* (1988). On film, her memorable screen roles are as the singing-dancing bride of young Thomas Jefferson in *1776* (opposite Ken Howard in 1972), the wife and mother in *The Great Santini* (1980; opposite Robert Duvall), a jewish mother/housewife in Neil Simon's *Brighton Beach Memoirs* (1985) and in Woody Allen's dramatic *Another Woman* (1988). Surfacing again in her own television series, Blythe starred in the NBC-TV show "Tattinger's" (1988/89) with Stephen Collins.

Another of today's bi-coastal performers, Danner has been married to TV producer Bruce Paltrow ("The White Shadow," "St. Elsewhere") since 1969 and has two children.

Ted Danson

This square-chinned TV star holds the singular distinction of having had the male lead in both an Emmy-winning dramatic television movie, "Something About Amelia," and in an Emmy-winning comedy series, "Cheers," in the same double-barrelled TV season: 1983-84. It was well-deserved recognition for the dedicated family man whose wife, Casey, suffered a massive, left-side-paralyzing stroke while delivering their child, Kate, on Christmas Eve 1979. (Danson has another daughter, Alexis.) Told she'd be lucky ever to walk again, Danson stuck by her, sleeping on her hospital room floor for nearly the whole first month after the stroke, and using humor and their shared training in *est* (over which they met in 1976) to nurture Casey back to full health. Meanwhile, Danson's series in which he plays a slightly macho, lovable, bar-owning ex-jock, was slowly climbing to a cult-loyal status whose followers included U.S. House Speaker Tip O'Neill, who once made a personal appearance on the show. (The "Cheers" bar is based in O'Neill's hometown of Boston.) Already the star of a glamorous Aramis cologne commercial, Danson was now being widely deemed a sexy hunk, and he found himself being photographed with "all the ladies of the world." They apparently knew to separate him from his character; in the arresting "Something About Amelia" he played a father guilty of incest with his teenage daughter. Fortunately, the movie led to national discussion of the problem, and in the wake of public interest, also led to the resolution of a few pending cases.

Danson (born 29 December 1949) has been near important acting action off and on ever since he got a part in the 1979 movie *The Onion Field*. Prior to that, the Flagstaff, Arizona-reared son of an archaeologist had gone to the elite Kent School in Connecticut before flunking out of Stanford. He finished up at Carnegie-Mellon University in 1972, then went on to New York and small stage roles and commercials and eventually soaps. After he and Casey moved to L.A. in 1978, the two managed to make ends meet through his teaching at the Actors Institute while snaring TV parts on "Laverne and Shirley," and "Magnum P.I.," and movie roles in *Body Heat* and *Creepshow*. Some recent works include the films *Something in Common* (1985), *A Fine Mess* (1986), *Three Men and a Baby)* (1987), *Cousins* (1988), and *The Hard Way* (1989). He also starred in the NBC-TV movie "When the Bough Breaks" in 1986. Thus, with TV, movies and commercials he's been able to make his calling pay the bills, while finding pleasure in family. "What we like best is playing house," Danson says.

Tony Danza

"It's been 10 years since I came to Hollywood," smiles Tony Danza. "I never dreamed of such success. The best part of it all, is that I'm enjoying it." With two hit sitcoms back to back, Danza can smile. The professional boxer-turned-actor went from the hit show "Taxi," which ran for 5 seasons, to the ABC sitcom "Who's the Boss?", which, in its fifth year on the air, was the sixth highest rated show of the TV season. Branching out from his role as "Tony" (he was Tony Banta in "Taxi" and "Tony Micheli" in "Who's the Boss?"), the Brooklyn-born Danza has appeared in TV movies ("Wall of Tyranny" and "Single Bar, Single Woman") and feature films (*Hollywood Knights, Cannonball Run II* and *Going Ape*). Showing his abilities on the other side of the camera, Danza has directed episodes of "Who's the Boss?" and been the executive producer as well as the star of NBC TV movies "Freedom Fighters" and "Doing Life." The smiling, gregarious actor is also in demand as a host. Aside from hosting various TV shows and charity benefits, the 5'11" ex-middleweight also co-hosted the show "99 Ways to Attract the Right Man." "It's an exciting time. Everything is so positive. I'd like to bottle it up and share it with friends."

Born Anthony Iandanza on 21 April 1951 in Brooklyn, New York, Danza never took his education seriously. Nonetheless, he graduated from the University of Dubuque, Iowa, with a history degree. Supporting himself with such jobs as selling jeans out of the trunk of a car and tending bar, Danza had found his niche when he turned to boxing, or so he thought. As if out of a Hollywood script, a boxing match was to change young Danza's life. Like a scene from *Rocky*, the middleweight was knocked down twice in the first round, but managed to nail his opponent at the end of the round with a one-punch knockout. In the arena that night was director James Brooks, looking to cast an Irish heavyweight for his new sitcom "Taxi." After watching Danza, the director decided to use an Italian middleweight instead. With a record of 12 and 3—all decisions via knockout—Danza left the ring for Hollywood and stardom. "I thought I was going to be middleweight champion of the world and a great actor at the same time," recalls Danza. Hollywood was good to Danza so he never returned to the ring. Thinking about the old life, Danza misses the ring, "being in shape, the discipline and the guys in the locker room."

To stay trim, Danza still runs in the morning and uses an exercise bike. He plays softball on the weekends when he's not sharing the cooking honors at home with his second wife, Tracy Robinson (married 29 June 1986) or playing daddy to daughter Katherine ("Katie," born 8 May 1987) or 18-year-old son Marc Anthony (one of the two children of his first marriage to Rhonda, divorced in 1974) who has lived with his father since 1984. "My family is my life," says Danza whose latest film, *Daddy's Little Girl* was released in 1989. The successful actor is also creating and producing projects under his Katherine Anne Production banner. Daddy, who worked with son Marc on an episode of "Taxi," explains, "I'm nervous about the future. With success you have to live up to things. The levels are higher. In my case, I want to make my family proud of me."

Ron Darling

A member of the Mets all-time victory list, the right-handed pitcher had a fast ball career since joining the ball club in 1982. In 1988 he was tied for eighth in the league, with 17 wins and four shutouts, as he pitched the Mets to their fourth Eastern Division title. During the summer of 1989 he took a superstitious gamble and changed his number from 12 to 15 on his jersey. The switch paid off as he pitched numerous winning games in a row.

Ronald Maurice Darling was born in Honolulu, Hawaii, on 19 August 1960. He graduated from St. John's High School in Worcester, Massachusetts and went on to Yale University, where he excelled in baseball. With a 25-8 record, a 2.00 ERA and 256 strikeouts in 274 innings, he earned All-Ivy League and All-Eastern Intercollegiate Baseball League honors. In 1980 and 1981 he was named the EIBL Pitcher of the Year. In May 1981 he participated in the longest no-hitter in NCAA tournament history, hurling 11 innings of no-hit ball against St. John's University. Although he had plans to go on to Law School after graduating (specialized in Southeast Asian and French history), he was just short of his B.A. degree in history at Yale. (He later attended NYU during the offseason to complete credits for his undergraduate degree). On 1 April 1982, Darling was signed by Eddie Robinson of the New York Mets from Texas with pitcher Walt Terrell for outfielder Lee Mazzilli. In 1989 he re-signed a three-year contract which holds him until 1991.

In addition to baseball, Darling is co-owner (with Art Shamsky) of the Manhattan restaurant Legends. He is co-chairman of Governor Mario Cuomo's Youth Drug Prevention Campaign in New York State and was honored in 1988 at the annual Thurman Munson Awards Dinner for his charitable work. He married model Toni O'Reilly on 10 January 1986 (one child, Tyler Christien, born 18 March 1987).

Hal David

"I'm not one of those hey-look-at-me-I'm-dancing writers," says the songwriter whose spare, no-nonsense lyrics for "What the World Needs Now (Is Love More Love)" have been sung by over a hundred different recording artists. His 16-year collaboration with composer Burt Bacharach netted him an Oscar (for "Raindrops Keep Fallin' on My Head" from *Butch Cassidy and the Sundance Kid* in 1970), a Grammy (for the Broadway cast album of *Promises, Promises* in 1969) and gold records by the dozen. In 1980, he added another feather to his quiver when he was elected president of ASCAP. "I'm not a rhymester, a technical virtuoso like Lorenz Hart or Cole Porter," says David. "If I do use a rhyme, it's like paste, only to keep a line from falling over a cliff."

Born 25 May 1921 in Brooklyn, Hal David was preceded into the moon-June territory of the Brill building by his older brother Mack ("Moon Love," "On the Isle of May," "Le Vie en Rose"). After an academic interlude at NYU, Hal became an ASCAP pro by the time he was 22. Assigned during World War II to the Central Pacific Entertainment Section, he wrote lyrics for the troupe headed by Major Maurice Evans and established a postwar beachhead on Tin Pan Alley by writing special material for Sammy Kaye. His first two hits with Burt Bacharach were "The Story of My Life" and "Magic Moments" in 1957; the very fertile era of the pair's collaboration with singer Dionne Warwick began in 1962. (Among the Warwick chartbusters: "Walk On By," "Alfie," and "Do You Know the Way to San Jose?") David and Bacharach went their separate ways in 1973 after the flop of the screen musical version of *Lost Horizon*.

Hal married his childhood sweetheart, artist Anne Rauchman, in 1947; she died of lung cancer in 1987. David is the father of two grown sons, Jimmy and Craig. He remarried on 2 September 1988, taking Eunice Forester as his wife. Retired as the president of ASCAP, the softspoken lyricist believes that "The songs live, the writer doesn't. You just hope your songs outlast you."

Al Davis

This shrewd owner of pro sports' winningest team over the last two decades (the Oakland-then-Los Angeles Raiders) is the only man who's been an assistant coach, head coach, general manager, league commissioner, and owner of a team. Unlike most sports proprietors, who were wealthy industrialists first, he dreamt of building "the finest organization in sports" while he was still a kid in Brooklyn. "The primary thing," says Davis, "is winning. Outside of birth, life and death, I would rank power in a classification second to winning." Condensed, he articulates his philosophy, "Just win, baby." If, in the process of carrying out his own mandate, he is the bane of National Football League owners and its commissioner, he's none too concerned. "Not all of them are the brightest of human beings," he said regarding the team-owning enforcers of what he (and ulimately, a federal court) perceived as an unlawful restraint of trade. When the court granted him permission to move his former Oakland Raiders to new quarters in Los Angeles Coliseum, it came with a hefty $35 million thorn awarded from the flesh of the NFL. Outraged Oakland residents, angry over their two-time Super Bowl champs' departure, screamed that Davis, with his slicked-back hair worn in a 1950s "Fonzy" pompadour, and completely silver-and-black wardrobe to match his team's colors, "oozed sleaze." But Davis' Raiders won and smugly accepted two Super Bowl trophies on national TV from the chagrined commissioner during the ongoing case.

Allen Davis was born in Brockton, Mass., on Independence Day, 1929. Dad, Louis, owned several businesses in New York City, including a clothing store, but after Erasmus High, Al was off to college, and eventually played football, basketball, and baseball while majoring in English at Syracuse.

Having studied the administrative skills of Brooklyn Dodger owner Branch Rickey, Davis decided he wanted to be like him. After becoming a coach at Adelphi College in 1950 for starters, he ran through a succession of coaching and scouting positions until, while an assistant at USC, he was chosen to help Sid Gillman coach the new American Football League's San Diego Chargers in 1959. Four years later he accepted the fortunes of the loss-dizzy Oakland Raiders, and used his long-bomb offense and bump-and-run defense to transform the 1-13 club into a 10-4 powerhouse in his first season. He was chosen commissioner of the league briefly in 1966, but was mostly a figurehead while the more accommodating AFL owners forged a merger with the NFL. He was passed over as commissioner of the new NFL (which absorbed the AFL) for Rozelle, even though his plan to swipe NFL players had probably hastened the older league's willingness to bargain. While winning three out of four Super Bowl appearances between Davis' arrival and 1984, the team also amassed a winning percentage better than the Montreal Canadians, Dallas Cowboys, or Boston Celtics. Known as a players' owner, Davis relishes acquiring other teams' cast-offs, then producing a winning amalgam with the renegades. "I want them to fear us," Davis says. "to me, that's respect."

Bette Davis

In 1980 she celebrated her 50th year in show business by appearing in her eighty-fifth film, *A Watcher in the Woods*. Her career has been a mixture of setbacks and triumphs, having been the top box-office attraction in the 1930s and 1940s and then, from 1953 to 1962, living through a period when none of her films made money until *Whatever Happened to Baby Jane* spooked movie goers into lining up behind her once again.

"You've got to care," asserts Bette Davis. "Everything has to be done right. If it's worth doing at all, it's worth doing right." Describing her allure on film she says, "My eyes are basically my face, and, of course, that's very important with the camera because the camera very seldom lets you lie, you know. You can see the truth. The skeleton of your acting is in your head, your brain . . . and that comes out in your eyes. What comes out of your eyes is caring, but it's also being the person you're trying to be." (A 1983 song "Bette Davis Eyes" by singer Kim Carnes immortalized the actress' finest asset.) "You'd better be thinking every minute about *something*. Lots and lots of actors aren't thinking every minute. They're waiting for their cues. . . . I've always tried to show some reason why this person became like *that*, because nobody's all bad—or all good. Nothing is all black and nothing is all white. There are grays. But there have to be reasons."

Davis won Oscars for *Dangerous* in 1935 and *Jezebel* in 1938. Her eight Oscar nominations were for her performances in *All About Eve, Dark Victory, The Letter, The Little Foxes, Now Voyager, Mr. Skeffington, The Star* and *Whatever Happened to Baby Jane*. She won TV's Best Actress Emmy in 1979 for a TV movie "Strangers." Other noteworthy Davis films include *Of Human Bondage, The Private Lives of Elizabeth and Essex, The Man Who Came to Dinner, Pocketful of Miracles, Hush, Hush Sweet Charlotte* and *The Nanny*.

She was born Ruth Elizabeth Davis, 5 April 1908 in Lowell, Massachusetts, and after attending drama school in New York, struck out for the movies at 21. "They sent a man to meet my train," she says, "and he went back to the studio alone. He said he hadn't seen anyone at the station who could possible be a star." She was encouraged, however, by George Arliss who curtly told the studio brass, "I don't care what she looks like, this girl has the makings of a great actress." Davis began her painful Hollywood climb with the *Bad Sister* in 1931. She had four bad turns at the altar to Harmon Nelson, Art Farnsworth, William Sherry and Gary Merrill. The actress is the mother of three children, one of whom is severely retarded; another, daughter B.D. wrote a tell-all-tome in 1985, *My Mother's Keeper*.

Davis is also the author of three books, *The Lonely Life* (1962), *Mother Goddam* (1975) and *This 'n That* (1987).

In 1982, Davis moved from her home in Connecticut back to Los Angeles, where she joined the cast of TV's "Hotel" for the 1982-83 season and was replaced, due to illness, by Anne Baxter (just like in *All About Eve*). The most important thing in the world, Davis says, is liking one's work. "Apart from my children, my work has been the big romance in my life. No question about it. It really stands by you. You have your disappointments in your work and your ups and downs, but it is there when all else fails." In 1985 she teamed with Helen Hayes in a made-for-TV movie thriller, "Murder with Mirrors" and she also appeared on the big screen in two movies: *The Whales of August* (1987) and *Wicked Stepmother* (1988). Ms. Davis was honored by the Film Society of Lincoln Center in both 1988 and 1989 as well as the Kennedy Center in 1989.

Geena Davis

Equally at home in a comedy or a drama, screen actress Geena Davis won an Academy Award for Best Supporting Actress in 1989 for her role in the "comedy-drama" *The Accidental Tourist*, based on the bestselling novel of the same title by Anne Tyler. Geena plays Muriel, an unusual dog trainer who befriends Macon Leary (William Hurt), whose world is turned upside down when his wife, Sarah, leaves him.

Born 21 January 1957 in Wareham, Massachusetts, Geena Davis studied music as a child. She spent her senior year in high school in Sweden as an exchange student and switched her focus from music to theatre. Davis graduated from Boston University's Professional Actors' Training Program, and spent some time with the Mount Washington Repertory Theatre Company in New Hampshire. Once in New York, she became a model, which led to television commercials and eventually to her screen debut in *Tootsie* (1982), when she appeared as the girl in her underwear who shared a dressing room with Dustin Hoffman. Her first starring role was in 1986 when she appeared opposite Jeff Goldblum as a free-lance science reporter in the successful remake of *The Fly*.

More recently Geena Davis starred in the frightening and funny ghost story *Beetlejuice* (1988) and in *Earth Girls Are Easy* (1989). She was also in the films *Fletch* and *Transylvania 6-5000*. Davis has also appeared in her own NBC series, "Sara"; with Dabney Coleman in the much-talked-about "Buffalo Bill"; and in two memorable episodes of "Family Ties," in which she played a character hired to be the Keatons' maid although she was incompetent. After a failed marriage to Richard Emmolo, she married actor Jeff Goldblum on 1 November 1987 in Las Vegas.

Marvin Davis

This so-called "yes or no kind of guy" ("You always know when a phone conversation with Marvin is over because you hear a dial tone") is known around the oil industry as Mr. Wildcatter. The president of Davis Oil Company, he's one of the country's leaders in directing unexplored drillings for oil and gas wells. Since assuming his father's modest oil properties in the 1960s, the 300-pound Davis has parlayed profits from fossil fuels into banking and real estate investments that have made him a billionaire. While he's a news interviewer dodger, it's said he's hardly shy: Davis reportedly snatches neckties off his friends when he doesn't like the style, and hands them a box of new Dunhill cravats as a replacement. "As you get older the toys get more expensive," he once

Miles Davis

said, but he's been stymied in two bids for one such toy, the Oakland A's baseball team, because of lease entanglements A's owner Charlie Finley found himself in. Possibly still in the toy department, he fondled the idea of buying Twentieth Century-Fox Film in 1981, but withdrew his more than $700 million offer apparently because, in the words of a spokesman, he didn't "like being intimidated and manipulated as a country bumpkin." He finally wound up with 50% ownership in the company in partnership with Rupert Murdoch. Some of Denver's leadership breathed easier when another Davis deal fell through, this one of the 1980 attempted purchase of the *Denver Post* newspaper. When he pulled out because of problems with the plant's tax depreciation status, many were relieved that the man who has changed the Mile High City's skyline wasn't able to buy a conduit to change its public opinion.

New York-raised Marvin Davis (born 28 August 1925 in Newark) is the son of an English boxer turned garment manufacturer. After attending Horace Mann School and Syracuse University the Jewish youngster improved on his dad's oil holdings in Indiana and Ohio by drilling in the Big Sky country of Wyoming and Montana. Later he plunged pipes into the Rocky Mountain region and had virtually no competition. The bank of which he owns 80 percent of the stock, Metrobank of Denver, ranks in the city's top ten. In 1981 the Justice Dept. exacted penalties of $20 million on his transportation company for oil-pricing violations.

The six-feet-four Davis and wife Barbara live in "Hollywood posh" in in their Littleton, Colo., 33,000-square feet home. Among the friends of this father of three daughters and two sons are Frank Sinatra, President Gerald Ford, Henry Kissinger, and Edmund Muskie. Davis is flown in his private Gulfstream airplane; his menu is said to include caviar every night, along with home meals that include choices of fish, fowl, and meat. But when asked if he is a bona fide billionaire, the mammoth Davis answers, "I haven't checked lately."

Miles Davis

He's the embodiment of the maxim that only change is constant, and he continued his metamorphic ways when, in 1982, after nearly six years of illness-induced seclusion, he was nursed back to health by actress (and future wife) Cicely Tyson, and then returned to his adoring jazz-rock following. The most influential modern jazz trumpeter since Dizzy Gillespie, Davis and his now-electronic horn of plenty have been breaking through sound barriers since bop's early days. Says Teo Macero, Miles' producer since 1958, "You wouldn't expect Miles to go back and do something the way he did it years ago any more than you would expect Picasso to go back to what he was doing in his 'blue' or 'rose' periods."

Born in Alton, Ill., 24 May 1926, the son of a well-to-do dentist, Miles Dewey Davis III first studied trumpet in St. Louis, started sitting in with jazz bands passing through town in his teens, and in 1945 headed for studies at Julliard. Deciding he could learn more in the not-so-ivied halls of 52nd Street, he haunted the hangouts of the likes of Charlie "Bird" Parker, writing down "chords I'd heard on matchbook covers. Everybody helped me. Next day I'd play the chords at Juilliard instead of going to classes." Beginning with his own groups (which have included Max Roach, John Coltrane, and Herbie Hancock), he also participated in the *Birth of the Cool* via a now-historic series of recordings with a chamber unit, and was off to award-winning (*Down Beat, Playboy*) stardom. As much a trend-setter in his wardrobe as in his music, he's made not only the Best Trumpet, but also the Best-Dressed lists. Raspy-voiced Miles, who lost his normal speaking voice after a throat operation, is considered a "brooding loner who doesn't care whether he is regarded as an eccentric genius or a bellicose bastard." Cicely defends him, saying, "He used that facade to protect his vulnerability. Beneath that false surface you see what a sensitive, beautiful person he is. Nobody could play *that* without having a great depth of soul."

His mystique, nurtured by his pugnacious reputation off-stage and by his exasperating seeming detachment while performing, was at an all-time peak upon his return. After a stroke and other ailments, he drew down as much $100,000 per night in Japan, and his new albums were hot sellers. ("We Want Miles" won a 1983 Grammy for Best Jazz Instrumental Performance by a soloist.) Recent albums include: *Tutu* (1986), *Music From Siesta* (1987), and *Live Miles: More Music From the Legendary Carnegie Hall Concert* (1987).

Miles married actress Cicely Tyson in 1981; the couple separated in 1988. As well as owning residences in Malibu, Manhattan and Long Island, he also is owner of New York jazz club "Indigo Blues."

Ossie Davis

"There's a tremendous hunger among blacks and whites, for truth about the black experience in this country," says the author-star of the *Non-Confederate Romp Through the Cotton Patch, Purlie Victorious* (1961), and its musical version, *Purlie* (1970). "This is a way I can increasingly be part of the cultural arm of the revolution that Martin Luther King was all about. The revolution of regeneration, building a new set of values through an art that is revolutionary in that its concern is building beautiful human beings.... I'm for a moral regeneration of this country for everybody," he observed in the late 1960s.

Born in Cogdell, Ga., 18 December 1917, Ossie Davis decided to be a playwright as a child, although he had seen only a "few cowboy movies" and had never seen a stage. "We read Shakespeare in the school," he says. In New York he attended a Harlem actors' theatre by night, and worked in the garment district by day. ("If the money ran out, we slept in the park. I was young and romantic then.") He finally made good in *Jeb* in 1946. "David Merrick signed me," he says dryly "so I guess you could say he discovered me." Davis is married to his frequent co-star Ruby Dee (three grown children, three grandchildren). His Broadway credits include *The Royal Family, No Time for Sergeants*, and *Raisin in the Sun*. Screen credits include: *Let's Do It Again* (1975), *Hot Stuff* (1979) and *Nothing Personal* (1979). He appeared in and directed *Countdown at Kusinj*. His recent films include *Harry & Son* (1984), *Avenging Angel* (1985), *School Daze* (1988) and *Do the Right Thing* (1989).

Sammy Davis, Jr.

"At one time I used to think that if I didn't go fingerpoppin' until 4 A.M. I was out of it. My favorite thing when I'm not working is to charter a boat for a few weeks, go off and grow a beard and find myself not getting upset about the grey in it. I have no delusions of grandeur, I know I'm still a variety performer, but I want to de-Sammy Davis, Jr.-ize me," says the actor, singer, dancer, mimic, author, comedian, producer, director—to name but a few of the superstar's proficiencies. He has been described as "the liveliest vestige of oldtime vaudeville still working the board, not to mention today's big and small screens and recording studios," and has described himself as that "little one-eyed colored guy with the broken nose, defiant jaw and big, crooked smile."

Born in Harlem 8 December 1925, Davis was performing on the vaudeville stage by the age of four, with his mother, father, and adopted uncle in Will Mastin's "Holiday in Dixieland." Following a stint in the army during World War II, Davis returned to the nightclub circuit with the Will Mastin Trio. A car accident in 1954, while taking one of Davis' eyes and nearly his life, proved to be a spiritual and professional turning point. Davis converted to Judaism, returned to a warm and enthusiastic response from this audiences, and made his debut on Broadway with *Mr. Wonderful*, a tailor-made musical comedy which became a hit on the strength of Davis' dynamic performance. In 1964 he returned to star in *Golden Boy*, which after a rocky preview tour became a rave smash in New York, and for which *Cue* magazine named Davis Entertainer of the Year. As a screen actor his films include *Anna Lucasta, Porgy and Bess, Sweet Charity, A Man Called Adam, Ocean's Eleven, Robin and the Seven Hoods*, and 1989's uplifting *Tap* with Gregory Hines. He also appeared in the CBS-TV version of "Alice in Wonderland" (1985). As a recording artist, Davis has made some forty albums, selling more than 5 million copies, and garnering him four Gold Records with hits like "Candy Man," "Hey There," "Birth of the Blues," and "The Lady Is a Tramp." He has also written three bestselling autobiographies, *Yes I Can*, chronicling his rise to stardom as a black performer, *Hollywood in a Suitcase* and *Why Me?* In 1987 he was in the hospital for hip implant surgery. The operation was a success and Sammy can still tap up a storm. Davis lives in Beverly Hills, when he's not on the road or playing Vegas, with his wife Altovise. He has three children Tracy, Mark and Jeff.

Pam Dawber

When "Mork & Mindy" premiered on television in 1978, a nationwide audience was given its first glimpse of the bright-eyed, sweet smiling co-star. Pam Dawber has been a busy actress ever since. After four seasons opposite Robin Williams on the ABC hit series, Pam has stayed in television, acting in a TV movie every year from 1982 through 1986. These movies ran the spectrum, showing the diversity of Pam's talents: "Naked Eyes," a mystery/thriller; "Last of the Great Survivors," a romantic comedy; "Wild Horses," a Western; and "American Geisha," based upon a true story of anthropology student Liza Dalby. Returning to her first love, Pam starred in another TV series, "My Sister Sam," which was co-produced by Pam's company Pony Productions in association with Warner Brothers. Not wishing to limit herself nor lose out on one of her talents, Pam took time out to appear in musical theater productions. Her credits include such roles as Eliza in *My Fair Lady* (1980 production by Kenley Theatre) and Mabel in *The Pirates of Penzance* (1982 Broadway and 1981 L.A.). Pam also sang and danced as Marion the librarian in the 1984 three-city mid-west tour of *The Music Man*.

Born on 18 October 1954 in Detroit, Michigan, Pam admits that musical theatre was always her first love. As a teenager she performed in musicals at her high school and studied art and vocal music at Oakland Community College near her home. With her good looks, it's not surprising that modeling followed.

At the suggestion of a friend, Pam packaged her portfolio and left Michigan for the bright lights of New York City where, in 1974, she decided to devote herself to her two loves, acting and singing. Offered a part in the play *Sweet Adeline*, Pam grabbed it and went to the Tony Award-winning Goodspeed Opera House in East Haddam, Connecticut, for the production. It was there that the call came from the West Coast that changed her life. Dawber flew west, and after not being chosen for the part of "Tabitha" was seen and screen-tested by Robert Altman, which prompted ABC to give her a one-year contract.

Pam and husband, actor Mark Harmon, married 21 March 1987 and are the parents of a son, Sean, born 25 April 1988. The family resides in Los Angeles and maintains a solar home in New York.

Doris Day

In the 1950s and '60s, she was the top box-office draw in America, often voted the world's most popular actress. In such light comedies as *Pillow Talk* (1959), *Lover Come Back* (1961), and *Please Don't Eat the Daisies* (1960), her sunny on-screen personality earned her a comfortable niche as "America's Sweetheart" and everybody's favorite "girl-next-door"—as well as a *not*-so-comfortable niche as a too-pure-to-be-true perennial "Goody Two-Shoes." (The sardonic pianist Oscar Levant once remarked, "I knew her before she was a virgin.")

Doris von Kappelhoff was born 3 April 1924 in Cincinnati. Her first daydream was to be a dancer and she succeeded to the point of being en route to Hollywood when an auto accident sidelined her into singing. When she warbled "Day by Day" at a club in her hometown, the owner changed her name to Day. ("I'm glad," she said later "he didn't catch me singing *Gotterdammerung*.") Soon she was a band singer with Les Brown, then belting out the big ones on record (e.g. "Que Sera Sera" and "Secret Love"). The big Day-break on film came in 1948 when she replaced a pregnant Betty Hutton in *Romance on the High Seas* and from then on, she shone in a series of musicals (*The Pajama Game*, 1957), mysteries (*The Man Who Knew Too Much*, 1956) and the country-fresh, cider-sweet girl-who-can't-be-seduced-but-still-gets-Rock-Hudson-or-Cary-Grant-anyhow romances cited above. Married first to "the trombone player" (Al Jordan; son Terry has followed her to the music biz), second to "the saxophone player" (George Weidler), number three in 1951 was agent Marty Melcher, whom friends called "executive seeing eye dog" and she described as "my husband and best friend." She was widowed in 1968 and during the first "big black void" threw herself into work on a popular TV series which continued until 1972. Her 1976 marriage to restaurateur Barry Comden (according to friends "perhaps the most unfortunate of the lot") was later dissolved. From now on, she said in 1982, "marriage is a no-no. For some reason, it gets old. I do love seeing it work for others, and I suppose it does work for many people, but goodness knows it doesn't work for me."

In the 1980s, retiring from performing, the erstwhile superstar was occupying herself primarily with her Doris Day Pet Foundation, helping animals who are hungry, homeless or hurt. (She once reprimanded a man in Malibu who was beating to death a man-eating shark.) Her Carmel Valley home houses a family of dogs and cats (mostly strays) plus a bird. "There are things you get from the silent, devoted companionship of pets," she says, "that you can get from no other source. Perhaps there are people who don't understand my devotion. I would like them to know it is something rich and simple and beautiful. A love as soft and gentle as the summer rain."

Michael DeBakey

His colleagues in Houston call him "The Texas Tornado," and with good reason. For one thing, he's a 20-hour-a-day man who puts on his thinking cap regularly at 4 a.m. and keeps it there until close to midnight. For another thing, he makes his medical rounds at a sprint and maintains a schedule of operations so tight it's enabled him to perform more than 40,000 in his professional career. One of America's pioneer heart surgeons, DeBakey has taken his scalpel and cut where no man dared before. Patients from all over the world have come to his operating room at Methodist Hospital in Houston and he's collected numerous decorations and medals (including the Presidential Medal of Freedom with distinction) but little in the way of personal wealth. Most of his fees from operations go to the Baylor College of Medicine, where he is now chancellor and chairman of the department of surgery. He lives on his salary as an educator.

Born 7 September 1908 in Lake Charles, La., he studied at Tulane in New Orleans, went to Europe for further graduate work, and eventually settled

Mary Decker Slaney

down in 1948 at Baylor. His work in combating man's number one killer, heart disease, has many facets away from the operating room: as teacher, as writer (more than 1200 medical papers and a number of books published) and also as inventor. A pump he devised while a medical student at Tulane served as the basis for one of the essential components of the heart-lung machine now used everywhere. This master surgeon was a pioneer in the use of various synthetic materials to repair damaged tissues of the vascular system, and it is in the field of synthetics that he looks for future major breakthroughs. With the advent of more effective immunosuppressive agents, he has resumed his transplant program with enthusiasm. In February 1984, he performed his first heart transplant in 14 years, endorsing the general belief within the medical profession that the operation is now reliable.

DeBakey's entire life is dominated by his profession, even his choice of a bride. His late wife, Diana, once worked as a nurse. They were parents of four sons. He and his second wife, Katrin, have one daughter.

Mary Decker Slaney

This lean, oft-injured running machine would probably trade a few of her seven world records, and possibly even her 1982 Sullivan Award as best amateur athlete, for the prize that has eluded her four times: an Olympic gold medal. Upon finding herself in the 3,000-meter final at the Los Angeles Games in 1984, her first time in the quadrennial gathering, she thought she was finally to catch her ultimate brass ring. But it was snatched away yet again when she was tripped (purposely, she thought) by the naive and barefoot South African teenage phenomenon, Zola Budd. Afterwards, the bitter Decker angrily blamed her adoring opponent, but later vowed to vanquish her Olympic demon. "My time will come," she said. That time was 20 July 1985 in London when in a highly touted rematch, Mary easily dispatched Zola, who finished fourth.

Decker has been a fixture in international middle distance competition for all but the first 12 years of her life. Born on 4 August 1958 in Flemington, N.J., and raised in Huntington Beach, Calif., she was eleven when she entered and won, without training, a statewide meet. It became an immediate obsession with her, an outlet during her parents' divorce, and she set her first world record at 1,000 meters at age 14. As she trotted to more fame, medals, and world records, she was speeding her five-feet-six, 107-pound frame to over-training and a litany of leg injuries. "People have always described me as the perfect runner from the head to the knees—and glass from there on down," she said. Her "rabbits' feet" (very high arches with narrow heels),are the reason for her efficient, minimal surface strike, but are also responsible for transmitting an overload of shock to her heels and shins. Too young at 13 to participate in the 1972 Olympics for which she was physically ready, by the next Games in 1976 she was out for surgery because her enlarged calves were bursting out of their skin. In 1980, after opting for well-paid, condoned "shamateurism"(receiving trust fund money for competing), and after having dropped out of the University of Colorado, she was set for the Moscow Games when Pres. Carter ordered a U.S. boycott. Her Nike Shoes-sponsored training center, Athletics West, took over her coaching, and there she met and married marathoner Ron Tabb in 1981. The next year she set seven world records in the middle distances, and by the '84 Games (having lost the tab Tabb along with her husband) was confident of her first Olympic gold. But the dream that again got away may yet yield to her. Her philosophy? "I honestly think of running as an art form," Decker says. "I want to give 100 percent of myself to my sport." Divorced from Tabb, in January of 1985 Decker married British discus thrower Richard Slaney. The couple have a daughter, Ashley Lynn, Born 30 May 1986.

Midge Decter

Whether deriding the women's lib movement or issuing fervid anti-Soviet manifestos, this outspoken neoconservative writer and activist has been called "an opinion to be reckoned with." Says Decter, "Like most writers, I began with the dream of being a writer in early childhood, scribbling silly verses on all available scraps of paper. Later, it was people, not 'influences,' who helped me to find the one thing that all writers need: nerve." Demonstrating this nerve, she chose subjects bound to raise hackles. At the height of the women's liberation movement, Decter—an intellectual, twice-married mother of four—infuriated feminists by declaring that women were already liberated (by modern birth control), that women's lib was largely a fear-motivated retreat from the new freedoms, and that she didn't think "looking after a house and children is difficult." Then she zeroed in on permissive parenting and the uncritical celebration of "the young," denouncing the "love generation" as nothing but "the infinite adumbration of narcissism." She has also targeted affirmative action and the homosexual rights movement. In 1980, after attending an international conference on terrorism, she helped set up the Committee for a Free World, comprised of notables from various countries. The committee (of which she is executive director) is motivated, she says, in part by a "positive passion for insuring the survival intact of what we value"—the free society of "private rights, civil peace, and individual civil responsibility," which the committee feels is threatened by the Soviet Union and Soviet-instigated terrorism.

Born Midge Rosenthal on 25 July 1927 in St. Paul, Minn., the daughter of a sporting goods merchant, she attended the University of Minnesota and Jewish Theological Seminary but never graduated from college, (sensing, noted one reporter, that "college interfered with her education"). She married Jewish activist Moshe Decter in 1947 (two children, divorced 1954) and began her professional career as a secretary to the managing editor of *Commentary*, the intellectual journal published by the American Jewish Committee. In 1956, she married Norman Podhoretz, then associate editor of *Commentary*, who became its editor in 1980. Shaping for herself an enviable career in publishing, she held a series of editoral posts including managing editor of *Commentary* (1961-62), executive editor of *Harper's Magazine* (1969-71) and senior editor at Basic Books Inc. from 1974 to 1980. She also produced a steady stream of articles and reviews, some of which reappeared in her 1971 book, *The Liberated Woman and Other Americans*. Her other books include *The New Chastity and Other Arguments Against Women's Liberation* (1972) and *Liberal Parents, Radical Children* (1975). Though still listing her political affiliation as Democratic, she and her husband are labeled "neoconservative." A founder of the Coalition for a Democratic Majority, she serves on the board of conservative groups such as the Heritage Foundation. The Podhoretzes live in Manhattan and East Hampton and have two children.

Ruby Dee

Stereotyped for years as "the Negro June Allyson" this pretty, petite former Harlemite scored a big breakthrough as a dramatic actress Off-Broadway in 1970 in the South African-set drama *Boseman and Lena*. Asked, after the raves, if she felt she was really "on her way," she retorted, "I've been 'on my way' for the past twenty years, honey. Maybe now people will believe I've actually arrived."

Born Ruby Ann Wallace in Cleveland, 27 October circa 1924, daughter of a Pennsylvania Railroad porter, she grew up in Harlem and in 1941 got her feet wet as an actress in the American Negro Theatre, then operating in the basement of the West 135th Street branch of the New York Public

Library. (Among her classmates: Hilda Simms, Harry Belafonte, and Sidney Poitier.) One of her first important Broadway roles was in *Jeb* (1946), opposite Ossie Davis whom she later married (three children) and with whom she appeared in his hit play *Purlie Victorious* (1961). She appeared in both the stage (1959) and screen (1961) versions of *Raisin in the Sun* and in 1965, playing Kate in *The Taming of the Shrew* and Cordelia in *King Lear*, was the first black actress to appear in major roles at the American Shakespeare Festival at Stratford, Conn. In 1988 she appeared in the Broadway play *Checkmates* and was inducted into the Theatre Hall of Fame. She also appeared in the television film version of Sidney Sheldon's novel "Windmills of the Gods" that same year. Movie credits include *St. Louis Blues*, *Wedding Band*, *Cat People* and *Do the Right Thing*. A literal lightweight in frame (5'1", 108 lbs.) she's proved herself a heavy-weight in the fight for civil rights and, together with Davis, was honored in 1970 with the Frederick Douglass Award of New York's Urban League for bringing "a sense of fervor and pride to countless millions." From 1974 to 1978, she was heard on sixty-five radio stations nation-wide on the weekly series, "The Ossie Davis and Ruby Dee Story Hour" broadcast over the national Black Network. She is also a poet and a writer, with a play (*Take It From the Top*) a poetry anthology (*Glow-child*) and a column in the *New York Amsterdam News*. In 1983 she made her debut as a director in the Howard University Production *Zora Is My Name*.

Olivia De Havilland

The demure, gentle Melanie of *Gone With the Wind* never had it so tough as the torn and tattered Olivia of the 1960s. Trapped in an elevator (*Lady in a Cage*), driven crackers (*The Scream*), and crucified (*Pope Joan*), Errol Flynn's longtime light-hearted screen ladylove (*Captain Blood*, *The Adventures of Robin Hood*, et al) joined her old Warner Brothers stablemate Bette Davis in Hollywood's violent era in becoming a Grand Duchess of the Gruesomes. They actually appeared together in *Hush, Hush Sweet Charlotte*, released in 1964 and still a TV late-show favorite.

The smaller, darker half of one of the most famous sister feuds in histrionic history, Olivia by the 1970s was pooh-poohing all those nasty stories about her rivalry with Joan Fontaine as mere grindings of the publicity mill. Born 1 July 1916 in Tokyo, she preceded sister Joan to Hollywood but lagged behind her in snaring her first Academy Award (*To Each His Own*, 1946), then surged into front position again by winning a second Oscar a few years later (*The Heiress*, 1949). She broke ground for her later incarnations in the horror flicks in such epics of travail as *The Dark Mirror* and *The Snake Pit* (both 1948). After divorcing her first husband, Marcus Goodrich, in 1952 (one son), she met and married Pierre Galante, editor of *Paris-Match* (one daughter) in 1955, moved to France, and wrote a bestseller about her bilingual tribulations (*Every Frenchman Has One*; the title referred not to a mistress, but to the typical Frenchman's greatest concern, his liver.) On the loose again in 1972, she had a brief, highly publicized fling with Great Britain's bachelor prime minister, Edward Heath.

Olivia's been visible on the big screen in *Airport '77* and the horror flick *Swarm*. On the little screen, she appeared in "Roots: The Next Generation" (1978), "Charles and Diana: A Royal Romance" (1982), "North & South Book II" (1986), and received an Emmy Nomination and Golden Globe Award as Best Supporting Actress for the NBC miniseries "Anastasia: The Story of Anna" (1986). In 1989 she had the honor of accepting the People's Choice Award given to *Gone With the Wind* as the favorite film of all time.

Willem de Kooning

"The mystery of de Kooning can be pared down to a single question: How can anyone that good be that bad?" wrote Kay Larson, the art critic, in 1984 when the first generation Abstract Expressionist painter had a retrospective at the Whitney Museum. He is "a symbol of the days when American art first caught the attention of the world, one of the most sanctified painters alive. He is also a stubborn enigma and a significant source of arguments."

"Every so often," he said once, "a painter has to destroy painting. Cezanne did it. Picasso did it with cubism. Then Pollack did it. He busted our idea of a picture all to hell. Then there could be new paintings again." Thus did the shy genius who has been called "the philosopher king" of the Abstract Expressionist action painters sum up his thoughts about the creative process. He himself has been destroying and/or re-creating on canvas ever since his first one-man show in 1948 stirred up storms of controversy. He startled critics again in 1972 with a one-man show of sculpture. However, in Larson's words: "the slippery ribbon-candy confections he has turned out since moving to the Hamptons, in 1963, have by no means won unanimous praise."

Born in Rotterdam on 24 April 1904, he left school at age 12 to become an artist, and received a thorough classical training at the Rotterdam Academy before stowing away on a cattle boat at 21 and heading for the United States. Here he met and was deeply influenced by Arshile Gorky, became involved with the WPA Artists Project, and by 1950 was recognized (with Jackson Pollack) as one of the giants of the avant-garde, famous especially for his distortion of the female figure. His portraits of women (including the late Marilyn Monroe) are savage and terrifying, yet at least one critic insists that they merely "carry on with wild gusto where Franz Hals left off." Said to "abandon" paintings rather than to "finish" them, de Kooning often shuts himself away when he is at work, and, according to persistant rumor, has done many recent drawings with his eyes closed. Once married to the well-known artist Elaine de Kooning (née Fried), he says, "Art never seems to make me peaceful. I always seem to be wrapped in the melodrama of vulgarity." He has a daughter, Lisa, by Joan Ward, who in August 1989 declared him mentally incompetent. This action has given her control of de Kooning's Long Island estate, including $150 million worth of paintings.

Oscar de la Renta

"He's always been a ladies man in the courtly European tradition," notes *Women's Wear Daily*. "Both he and his stongly Parisian-flavored collections revel in feminity. For years his signature was ruffles, but recently he's forsaken them in favor of sleeker silhouettes that are utterly and unabashedly female. He knows just what his Ladies desire: short skirts, vivid colors, sensually draped jersy dresses, shapely luncheon suits, and sexy draped or shirred entrance-makers. And fans like Pat Buckley, Nancy Kissinger and Mica Ertegun find these Oscars just as irresistible as the designer himself—with his courtly good looks, pearl-toothed smile and flirtatiousness that never stops."

Born in Santo Domingo, 22 July 1932, he completed his studies in 1950 at the Escuela Normal, enrolled at Santo Domingo's National School of Art, then left for Madrid, where he completed his art studies and became interested in fashion design. It was in Madrid that the American Ambassador's wife, Mrs. John Lodge, became the first to swoon over his sketches. She immediately commissioned him to design a gown for her daughter's debut, and the dress and its wearer became a *Life* magazine cover.

From Madrid he went to Paris where he worked for Balenciaga and Antonio Castillo at Lanvin. ("He picked up the pins," the latter couturier once said.) In 1963 he visited New York and liked what he saw. Elizabeth Arden offered him a job as her top in-house designer. In 1965 he left Arden's to buy into the Seventh Avenue ready-to-wear firm of Jane Derby, Inc. and subsequently, upon Derby's retirement, became its sole owner. Then, he and his still present partner Gerald Shaw set about amassing de la Renta's kingdom of profitable licensing programs whose royalties tally hundreds of millions of dollars annually.

"Designers have become the new tycoons," said Alexander Liberman, editorial director of Condé Nast. The swiftest asset to de la Renta's empire was his wife, the former Francoise de Langlade, once the editor of French *Vogue*, who died of cancer in 1983. She was the "eminence grise of Oscar," said Marie-Helene de Rothschild. "She forged the relationships that have served him well in his career," commented Nancy, Lady Keith. Friends report that Oscar, after a period of mourning, is himself in fine fettle. That famous sparkle in his eyes can be seen at all the best parties and a de la Renta fashion show is "like old home week," according to Pat Buckley. "We all giggle and wave at each other, like a menagerie." In 1988, Oscar received the prestigious Jack Dempsey Award for his humanitarian efforts.

Alicia de Larrocha

She is widely regarded as the foremost interpreter of the Spanish repertoire for the piano and when Alicia de Larrocha plays Albeniz' *Iberia* these pieces can take on incantatory power. But she is also (according to a *New York Times* critic) "the premiere Mozart pianist of her generation" and has played each summer at the Mostly Mozart Festival in NYC's Lincoln Center. The "queen of pianists" has been performing for sixty years, yet each time she plays (says one critic) "it's always new." De Larrocha has found within herself and in her playing a balance of serenity and impetuosity (though her playing and personal life was upset by the death of her husband of thiry-two years).

Born in Barcelona (23 May 1923), de Larrocha gave her first public concert at age five. At twelve she debuted with the Madrid Symphony and in 1947 began touring outside her native land. After a 1953 British and 1955 American debut (with the Los Angeles Philharmonic) de Larrocha joined her ivories with the strings of cellist Gaspar Cassad. The "mighty little lady of the keyboard" became director of the Marshall Academy at Barcelona (where her late husband pianist Juan Torra taught). It was not until 1966 at a recital at Hunter College that New York critics took notice of her. Now there are few unaware of this tiny woman with tiny hands who "had it in her to make magical moments."

The publicity-shy de Larrocha plays approximately one hundred concerts each season. She relaxes by cooking her native Spanish dishes and is reputed to be a spectacular cook. One noted columnist expressed the feelings of many music lovers when he remarked, "We are lucky to have her in our midst."

Dino De Laurentiis

"The critics say my movies bad, but the audience is my boss. They pay me. They tell Dino what to do. I am entertainer, showman. I can always smell a good story. I read one page sometimes, think, 'is a good picture there, we make.'" Thus, in 1977, did the Italian filmmaker describe his work, spelling it out seven years later as follows: "I select the story, I select the director, I approve the script, I select the cast. I see the way the shooting is going and I see the dailies [rushes] every day. I talk to the director, I talk to the editors. I check every moment, every stage of the movie." He also somehow finances projects, juggling "private investors" and complex deals with the studios, and sells films worldwide. ("Here," actor Charles Bronson told *People*, "Dino really shines.... He can pick up the telephone and book pictures even before they're made—he has such a good reputation for success.")

Born 8 August 1919 in Torre Annunziata, Italy, the son of a Neapolitan pasta manufacturer, Dino enrolled at 17 in Rome's Centro Sperimentale di Cinematografia and at 20 produced his first film. After World War II he espoused Italian Neorealism, in 1948 producing an international hit, *Bitter Rice*, whose star, Silvana Mangano, became his wife the following year. In the '50s he and Carlo Ponti jointly made two Federico Fellini films, *La Strada* (1956) and *Nights of Cabiria* (1957), both winners of Academy Awards for Best Foreign Film, and King Vidor's *War and Peace*, anent which he recalled 20 years later that "my partner say he no believe in it, is too big. I say, 'Carlo, you no believe in "La Strada," is too small.' Then I say, 'You go your way, I go mine.'" Among the dozens of pictures he has produced solo have been such spectaculars as *The Bible* (1966), *King Kong* (1976) and *Conan the Destroyer* (1984), of which *Variety* wrote, "The sensibility is Southern California Suburban, the meat on the spit is likely to be an unfriendly barbarian." Other films include Michael Cimino's *Year of the Dragon*, *Red Sonja* and the Sissy Spacek starrer, *Marie*.

Dino, who moved to the United States with his family in 1973, is no mean cook himself. "I cook," he once said, "as Picasso paints." He also likes to eat, and out of his passion for gastronomy has come the modishly lower-cased "ddl Foodshow," a dazzling restaurant-cum-snackbar in Manhattan's superchic Trump Tower. He has three daughters, the death in 1981 of his 26-year-old son Federico was, he says, "the great tragedy of my life." But if he enjoys the give and take of family life in his rare hours of relaxation, at work he insists on sole command. "I make a movie," he says, "I want to control everything. I no see why not."

Ron Dellums

Berkeley, California's, gadfly Democratic congressman prefers to be described as a radical, and not simply a black, elected official. "If being an advocate of peace, justice and humanity toward all human beings ... [and being opposed to] the use of 70 per cent of federal monies for destruction and war [is radical] ... then I'm glad to be called a radical," says Ron Dellums. Since basing his first campaign for a job on Capitol Hill on ending the Vietnam War ("all other issues flow from that"), the nattily-dressed, six-foot-seven legislator continues to use his seat on the House Armed Services Committee to blast what he calls the "astronomical" military budget. "The problems of the world are social, political and economic. The problems are not military," Dellums believes.

Born in Oakland (part of which he now represents) on 24 November 1935 to a Pullman porter and a government clerk, Ronald V. Dellums spent his youth in the neighborhoods and ball parks of the East Bay Area, and joined the Marine Corps after high school in 1954. On his G.I. Bill he graduated from San Francisco State, then obtained a master's in social work from U. Cal Berkeley in 1962. After beginning in the field as a psychiatric social worker, he rose to become director of various Bay Area community social service agencies. In 1967, he says, "I got talked into going to a meeting to tell people why I didn't want to be a (Berkeley) city council candidate, and wound up being the candidate." Dellums won the election by pulling in a coalition of the city's left-wing blacks, Asians, and whites. Three years later he unseated the area's liberal, white congressman with the same mix of radicals, liberals, students, hippies and middle class voters. He thanked Vice President Spiro Agnew, who called him the Black Panther's choice, for being his public relations advisor. His anti-war activities included convening his own war crimes hearings against U.S. military officials, and participating in a 1971 rally on the steps of the Capitol. More than 1000 were arrested (and later were awarded individual damage judgments totalling $3 million) and Dellums was reportedly roughed up by cops. He has also been vocal about racism in the Armed Forces, forcing the government to admit that blacks in South Korea and Iceland as well as in U.S. bases were victims of prejudice. He was a nominee for Democratic presidential candidate for 15 minutes at the 1980 national convention after 400 delegates put his name up so that he could spotlight some issues they felt Jimmy Carter ignored. Dellums, whose son by his first marriage often ran afoul of the law, was himself accused in 1983 of buying cocaine and marijuana from a congressional employee. Later, the Justice Department dropped the investigation against him and two other congressmen because of insufficient admissible evidence.

The father of four has two children by his present wife, the former Leola (Roscoe) Higgs. Dellums asserts that the corrupt "old men [in Congress] wedded to the politics of the past, [have] frustrated a lot of young people wedded to the politics of the future."

Agnes De Mille

"I'm really like a playwright. That is my real value as a choreographer. I tell a story, and I tell it well." By telling a story with dance, she carved a niche for herself in the annals of American musical theatre with her dance-drama creations for *Oklahoma!* which elevated dance—theretofore an irrelevant interlude—to an integral part of the action essential to the story line of the show. And she opened up new choreographic territory in the world of classical ballet with her introduction of American folk forms and folklore—in such works as *Rodeo* and *Fall River Legend*. She's also proved herself to be very much on her toes as a writer and lecturer on the dance—and on the matter of survival. In 1975, shortly before a performance in New York City by the Heritage Dance Theatre (which she founded in 1973 to present in authentic form the native and popular dances of the United States), she suffered a massive cerebral hemorrhage that left her right side paralyzed. As she recounted in *Reprieve*, her moving 1981 account of her illness and recovery, just 14 months after her stroke she stood on the stage of the New York State Theatre acknowledging the ovation that greeted the American Ballet Theatre's world premiere of her Bicentennial celebration piece, *Texas Fourth*. A year after that, she resumed performing, as the narrator of the Joffrey Ballet's production of her lecture-demonstrations, *About the Dance*, which Walter Terry described as "an encounter with wisdom." Otherwise, as she told an interviewer for *Ballet News* in 1983, "I just sit here, and everyone treats me like some holy relic."

Agnes George De Mille, born in New York City 18 September 1905, was the granddaughter of the famous British single-tax advocate Henry George, the niece of Hollywood's "C.B.," the daughter of a driving and driven playwright-director William Churchill De Mille, and by her own account, "a spoiled, egocentric, wealthy girl." Her family moved to California in 1914, and it was there, during a performance by Anna Pavlova that she "really caught the virus." After completing undergraduate studies at UCLA, she created "character studies" for herself to present at private concerts. Encouraged, she went to New York and continued working as a concert dancer (even in third-rate nightclubs . . . all I balked at was jigging on the sidewalk with a tambourine) performing her own "realistic character sketches, dramatic rather than choreographic in form" (an acknowledgement of her limitations as a classical technician). The *New York Times*'s John Martin called her "undoubtedly one of the brightest stars now rising above our native horizon," who, like Charlie Chaplin, "sees tragedy through a lens of comedy." Her first official choreographic assignment was in 1929 when she arranged dances for the revival of the melodrama *The Black Crook* in Hoboken. After six years in Europe—during which time she acquired a "passable" classical technique and, under choreographer Antony Tudor's tutelage, came to understand "the principles behind the technique," she returned to the U.S., and in 1939 was invited to join the newly-formed ballet company now known as American Ballet Theatre. In 1942, *Rodeo*, a rousing piece of Americana set to the music of Aaron Copland for the touring Ballet Russe de Monte Carlo, received 22 curtain calls at its New York City premiere, and brought its creator to the attention of Rodgers and Hammerstein, who engaged her to stage the dances for *Oklahoma*. She went on to create the dances for *One Touch of Venus, Bloomer Girl, Carousel, Brigadoon* (Tony award), *Allegro, Out of This World, Gentlemen Prefer Blondes, Kwamina* (Tony Award) and *Paint Your Wagon*, among others. Other ballets include *Three Virgins and a Devil, Tally-Ho, The Rib of Eve, The Four Marys, The Wind in the Mountain*, and her masterpiece, the grisly dance-drama, *Fall River Legend*, recounting the celebrated case of Lizzie Bordon. Books include the autobiographical *And Promenade Home* (1956), *Speak to Me, Dance With Me* (1973), *Where the Wings Grow* (1978); *To a Young Dancer* (1962), *Lizzie Borden: A Dance of Death* (1968); and the illustrated choreographic histories, *The Book of the Dance* (1964), *Dance in America* (1971) and *America Dances* (1981).

The 1980 Kennedy Center Honors awardee, married to former artists' agent Walter F. Prude (one son, Jonathan), once described choreographing as "hell, sheer torture," but of dancing itself, she wrote, "You are out of yourself. . . larger and more potent, more beautiful. . . . You are for minutes heroic. This is power. This is glory on earth. And it is yours nightly."

Philippe de Montebello

"You have talent but no genius," was the assessment of Count Roger Lannes de Montebello, painter and art columnist, of his son's early paintings. The son accepted the critism and went on to become the next best thing—director of the museum whose holdings of works of genius are unmatched in the United States and in few museums in the world. Since he took over as the eighth director of the Metropolitan Museum of Art since its founding in 1870, Philipe de Montebello has gone about consolidating the gains it had accumulated under the dynamic leadership of his mentor, Thomas P. F. Hoving. Although conscious of the enormous benefits (not to mention revenues) of blockbuster shows like "The Treasures of Tutankhamen," which have played to SRO during his stewardship, de Montebello questioned (in *Architectual Digest* in 1979) whether such international art exchanges do not "also threaten the museum with a loss of its distinctly precious identity? Could it be that museums are starting to resemble centers for the performing arts?" Of the future, he envisions the day when the museum will again be perceived as "a place to visit repeatedly, even on a whim, and not simply when a new banner is hoisted on the facade."

"I'm not folksy, I don't slap people on the back, I don't swear, I don't walk around in shirt sleeves. But it's natural, it's me. I'm not putting on an act. . . . I have a certain formal European background." That certain background makes Guy-Philippe de Montebello, born in Paris 16 May 1936, a count by virtue of descent from Marshal Lannes, Prince de Siévers, who received the title from Napoleon following his victorious battle in the Italian town of Montebello. His mother's ancestry includes descent from the brother of the Marquis de Sade, while his grandmother, Marie-Laure de Sade, was Proust's model for the Duchesse de Guermantes in *Remembrance of Things Past*. His family moved to the U.S., where the boy continued his education at Lycée Francais before entering Harvard, from which he received a B.A. in art history *magna cum laude* in 1961 (with two years out for service as an artillery officer in the U.S. Army). Before he could complete his master's degree (which he finally claimed 15 years later), he was offered the position of curatorial assistant at the Met, advancing to the post of associate curator of European paintings. With Hoving's blessing, de Montebello accepted the directorship of the Museum of Fine Arts in Houston in 1969, acquiring more works for the museum in diverse cultures and periods during his four-year term than had been obtained during the preceding forty. Hoving called him back in early 1974, and before assuming the director's post at the Metropolitan he served as vice director for curatorial and educational affairs.

When asked by *Artnews* what he would buy, if he could, for his own collection, de Montebello stressed diversity in adding to the figurines, old

Catherine Deneuve — CELEBRITY REGISTER 1990

master drawings and modern paintings he already owns, selecting a Greek vase, a Chinese bronze, a Renaissance bronze, drawings by Picasso and Matisse, and paintings by Delacroix, Olitski, Frankenthaler and Motherwell. With his wife, the former Edith Bradford Myles (whom he married 24 June 1961) and their three children—Marc, Laure and Charles—de Montebello lives near his work on Fifth Avenue and for relaxation likes to play chess and listen to chamber music.

Catherine Deneuve

Women admire her, men desire her. Once hailed by *Esquire* as "one of the most remarkably beautiful actresses of out time," Catherine Deneuve has become for many middle-aged women the symbol of outspoken independence. Says the ageless beauty on the subject of encroaching time, "Forty is not so old anymore—not what it used to be fifteen or twenty years ago. One is old the moment she is no longer desirable. That's not to say there aren't days when I don't feel beautiful, when I don't look like the person I'm suppose to be. It's unfair, when it's expected that you're to look a certain way, you just have to work a little harder." In addition to the long list of films she's played in (among them—*Belle de Jour, The Umbrellas of Cherbourg, Mayerling, April Fools, The Last Metro, The Hunger, Fort Saganne, Scene of the Crime, Love Songs* and *Agent Trouble*) she is also into very different lines of work: jewelry design and fragrance. The "archetype of patrician grace," so dubbed by *Newsweek*, came out with her own line of jewelry complete with chic "CD" logo. In 1984, she created her own perfume, "Deneuve," which she tested for three years before a retail introduction in March, 1987. She explains, "I wanted my perfume to be a classic—to defy trends, but never bore. And it is." Deneuve has replaced Brigitte Bardot as the inspiration for the Marianne statues that adorn many town halls in France.

She was born in Paris on 22 October 1943 to a family with theater in their blood; Deneuves's father, Maurice Dorléac and mother, née Deneuve, were both actors. Her sister Francoise Dorléac, eighteen months older than Catherine, brought her into the profession, appearing with her in Deneuve's first film, *Les Petits Chats*. The volatile French actress has since appeared in over fifty films, many under the tutelage of some of the most illustrious directors in the world. ("Bunuel is a genius. His method is to explain nothing. Here, actors think too much about why a character does this or that.... Polanski is brilliant. He works by talking a great deal to the actors and analyzing emotions, yet he did not wish me to think about why the girl in the film [*Repulsion*] was crazy.... Vadim [who is the father of son Christiaan] saw me as a sex symbol. He is talented.") Roman Polanski has said of her, "When you work with an actor, you have good moments and bad moments, but at the end you remember only the pattern. With Catherine it was the best I've ever had." Though constantly besieged with and enraged by undignified questions from the press; about: (1) her illegitimate son and daughter (fathered by Vadim and Marcello Mastroianni respectively) (2) her dissolved marriage to British fashion photographer David Bailey and (3) the flaming car-crash death of her beautiful actress sister, in recent years Deneuve has softened especially on the subject of her children. She admits both kids are concerned about what people think and that, of course, is of great concern to her.

Robert De Niro

An intensely private man loath to give interviews, the brown-haired, green-eyed actor has all of this to say about the greening of his thespian inclination: "My father is a painter. My mother used to be a painter. I was lucky. They never bothered me about wanting to be an actor." And about that desire to act? "Well . . . it's complicated. Getting into it . . . it's a personal thing. Is that okay?" Having nearly filled Brando's footprints in the 1970s, a segue into doing his own thing made this renegade's talents both highly respected and dearly coveted by his celluloid peers on the silver screen.

An only child, De Niro was born 17 August 1943 on Manhattan's lower East Side. His parents (painter Robert De Niro of Irish-Italian descent and former painter Virginia Admiral, a Berkeley, California "golden girl") separated when he was just two. Nervous and rail-thin, he was a drifter and a loner, although for a while he ran with a street gang. (His mother once said her son's idea of high school "was not to show up.") At 16, he found Stella Adler and acting became his haven. For 14 years he plugged away in low budget films made by top talents like Brian De Palma and Martin Scorsese, as well as Off-Off-Broadway shows such as *One Night Stands of a Noisy Passenger*, written by his then mentor, actress Shelley Winters. The play closed after seven performances. He was catapulted into instant stardom with his heart-wrenching performance as Bruce Pearson, a crude but endearing second-string baseball catcher dying of Hodgkin's disease in the film *Bang the Drum Slowly* in 1973. Dedicated to building what he calls "a body of work," De Niro has chosen his parts with great selectivity. They include Johnny Boy in Scorsese's *Mean Streets*, the young Vito Corleone in *Godfather Part II* (the older Corleone was played by Brando), the sexual maniac Travis Bickle in *Taxi Driver*, as well as star turns in Bertolucci's *1900; The Last Tycoon; New York, New York; The Deer Hunter; Raging Bull* (1981 Academy Award as Best Actor); *King of Comedy; Falling in Love; Brazil* (1985); *The Mission* (1986), *The Untouchables* (1987), *Stanley & Iris* (1988), *Midnight Run* (nominated for a Golden Globe Award as Best Actor—1988), *Jacknife* (1988), *Stolen Flower* (1988), *Double Bang* (1989) and *We're No Angels* (1989).

In the spring of 1976, De Niro married actress and singer Diahnne Abbot and the couple divorced in 1978 (one son, Raphael). He also has a daughter, Nina Nadeja, with singer Helena Springs.

Sandy Dennis

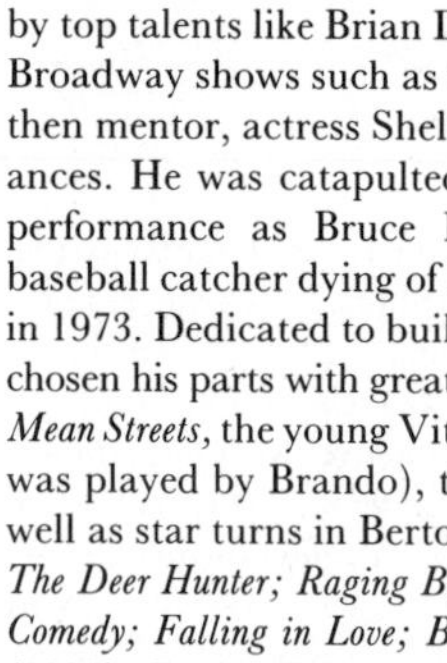

With her advancing maturity, this stage and screen actress who, uh, stutters has gotten even more flappable. She may also go down in the annals of show biz history remembered more for her spirited recitations of the names of her more than 30 cats (all of whom occupy her Connecticut house) than for her Academy Award winning performances in *Who's Afraid of Virginia Woolf*, or Tony Award performances in *Any Wednesday* and *A Thousand Clowns*.

Born 27 April 1937 in Hastings, Nebr., the daughter of a postal worker, she dropped out of Wesleyan College at 19 to become an actress in New York. For seven years she lived with actor Gerald O'Loughlin. Next she shared a place with saxman Gerry Mulligan. Her first New York appearance was in a three-week run of Ibsen's *The Lady from the Sea;* her first Broadway play was *Face of a Hero*. She made a big mark in 1962's *A Thousand Clowns* with Jason Robards, followed in 1964 in Muriel Resnik's *Any Wednesday*. Though it supposedly infuriated her co-actors and directors, her tendency to mutter, stutter, and flutter her hands about often led to highly original improvisations in the midst of a scene. Since her early days she has toned down her style. ("I think the mannerisms offended a tremendous number of people," she now confesses. "They were due to the fact that I didn't know what I was doing.") About acting she says: "It isn't like painting a picture or writing a book. When you finish an acting stint, there's nothing except money. You have to keep going, giving the best you've got, to get something intangible." Sandy has pouted, yelled, muttered, stuttered and fluttered through such other plays as Robert Altman's *Come Back to the Five & Dime Jimmy Dean, Jimmy Dean; Buried Inside*

Alive and *Absurd Person Singular* in films *The Fox, The Out-of-Towners, Thank You All Very Much, Nasty Habits,* and *The Four Seasons.*

John Denver

"I think people see themselves in me," says the singer-songwriter whose "Rocky Mountain High" appeal keeps him high on the peak of *Billboard*'s year-end listings. He explains his popularity this way: "My music is of a kind that touches people of all ages, from all different backgrounds. People are finding value in it that's more than just entertainment, more than just pretty. For a long time now it hasn't been okay to acknowledge certain things about yourself. For example that you love your old lady, that it feels good to be out in the sunshine, that every once in a while on a rainy day you feel sad. That life is good. As I have been able to communicate those things for myself and to reach a large audience, that gives them support in feeling those things . . . nobody else is singing these songs. Everybody else is talking about how hard life is, and here I am singing about how good it is to be alive."

The boyishly handsome performer was born Henry John Deutschendorf, Jr., on 31 December 1943 in Roswell, Texas. Because his father was a Lieutenant Colonel in the Air Force, the family moved around a lot. His grandmother gave him his first guitar, a 1910 Gibson, when he was in the seventh grade. After dropping out of the architecture program at Texas Tech University in Lubbock, Denver moved to Los Angeles to pursue his musical career with all of $125 in his pocket and three guitars. He changed his surname to Denver "because of the connotation of the mountains." Fittingly his 1972 album *Rocky Mountain High*, celebrating the wonders of the wide open spaces, was his first megahit, selling well over a million copies and earning him a platinum record. The composer of more than 50 songs including, "Leaving on a Jet Plane," "Annie's song," and "Take Me Home Country Road," Denver has now collected a handful of gold records. Known more recently as an actor as well as the "wholesome guru of pop music" Denver starred in *Oh God!* opposite George Burns. He has also headed up many television specials both in the U.S.A. and England. Denver often uses his concert tours as platforms for his commitment to ending world hunger. The Aspen, Colorado resident served on the Commission on World and Domestic Hunger established by then President Jimmy Carter. In 1984, Denver and his wife Ann, whom he married in 1967, and with whom he has one adopted child named Zak, were scaling and descending (mostly the latter) the mountain of matrimony. His marriage dissolved, Denver replaced his specs with contact lenses, appeared nude in a music video, and married his second wife, Cassie Delaney, on 12 August 1988 in Aspen, Colorado.

Brian De Palma

"Either I'm getting too old or they are getting worse or I've seen too many, but I rarely go to the movies. Mainly I'm disappointed." Not scary enough for his taste no doubt; Hitchcock's inheritor of fright operates on what he calls "the principle of escalating terror. My films deal with a stylized, expressionistic world that has a kind of grotesque beauty about it. I don't think you necessarily have to have blood flying across the screen and guts coming out of stomachs and stuff like that. But I think you should be able to use what you consider effective within certain limitations. There can be something very poetic about violence in film. I think movies are about action—you know, bodies falling, knives sweeping through the air. That has a lot to do with what one can do in cinema so effectively."

Brian Russell De Palma was born 11 September 1940, in Newark, New Jersey, the youngest of three sons of an orthopedic surgeon and his wife. In the mid '40s the family moved to Philadelphia where Brian attended the private Friends School. He enrolled in Columbia University's Class of 1962 intending to major in physics but instead became obsessed by movies. Becoming a filmmaker meant taking his masters degree at Sarah Lawrence, where he made a film using two then-unknown New York actors, Robert de Niro and Jill Clayburgh. After graduation he supported himself making short commercial films for corporations and cultural institutions such as the NAACP. His two independent films made at this time—*Greetings* and *Hi, Mom,* both dealing with the climate of the 60s—earned him a reputation as something of a counterculture hero. Not terribly fond of "big brother" movie studios, De Palma bolted just two weeks before completing a film for Warner Brothers starring Tommy Smothers. On his own he made *Sisters,* a tale of a Siamese twin possessed by the murderous spirit of her dead halved sister. Then came the horror classic *Obsession,* followed by Carrie, based on Stephen King's story of a high school girl with telekinetic powers of revenge. The film earned big dollars at the box office and confirmed King's career as a horror writer and De Palma's career as an independent director. He followed *Carrie* with *The Fury, Blow-Out, Dressed to Kill, Wise Guys, The Untouchables,* and *Casualties of War.* In 1979 De Palma married Nancy Allen, the actress who appeared in several of his films. They divorced in 1984. De Palma prefers New York to Hollywood. His cooperative apartment looks over gothic Washington Square Park in Greenwich Village.

Gérard Depardieu

Looking like a survivor of one too many go-arounds with Muhammad Ali, France's rugged, hefty and compellingly photogenic box office superstar is the latest of the sexy pug types French cinema has sent our way beginning with the incomparable Jean Gabin. Moreover, Gérard Depardieu's captivatingly irregular features were achieved by means not altogether genetic in origin: "I started [at 12] leading a wild life, attacking jewelry stores, stealing cars. . . . I became familiar with courtrooms, judges, detention and parole." Paradoxically, it's been in courtroom settings that he's achieved some of his major cinematic triumphs—as the titular defendants in *The Return of Martin Guerre* and *Danton,* and as a crack defense attorney in the 1984 romantic thriller *Right Bank, Left Bank.*

Born 27 December 1948 at Châteauroux ("in the heart of France"), the third of six children of an illiterate metal worker, Gérard says his occupation of convenience during his youthful days as a petty criminal was "an actor . . . I said I was playing at the Theatre National Populaire because it was the only theater I was acquainted with." Realizing that "having to confront policemen and judges is an excellent way to train your imagination. . . . In a few seconds, you have to improvise a role with talent and emotion," it was to the TNP that he turned when he decided to pursue an acting career in earnest. After studies there and private lessons, he made his motion picture debut in a short, followed by an unfinished Agnes Varda feature. A role in a television series led to a stage career in the French versions of *The Boys in the Band, A Girl in My Soup* and *Home,* among others. After a number of supporting roles, he achieved his first major film success co-starring with the late Patrick Dewaere in Bertrand Blier's *Going Places,* as "a guy who has the urge to experience all kinds of emotions at 100 miles an hour." It's that astonishing range of emotions in a wide variety of roles that sets him apart from the usual run of French heartthrobs. Of his more than 50 films, among the more popular are Blier's *Get Out Your Handkerchiefs* and *Buffet Froid;* Alain Resnais' *Mon Oncle D'Amerique;* the last Francois Truffaut's *The Last Metro* and *The Woman Next Door; The Moon in the Gutter, La Chevre* (in her 1985 review of the film's U.S. release, the *New York Times'* Janet Maslin wrote, "There appears to be nothing that Gérard Depardieu cannot do well on the screen"), *Les Comperes,* the title role in the film of a stage production of *Tartuffe* (which he also directed) and *Police* (for which he was named best actor at the 1985 Venice Film Festival). In 1987 he starred in the acclaimed *Jean de Florette,* opposite his wife, Elisabeth. He also appeared in *Sous le Soleil de Satan* that same year, followed by *Traffic Jam* in 1988. Married to Elisabeth Guignot (an actress he met at the Theatre National Populaire), Depardieu is the father of a son Guillaume and a daughter Julie. The Depardieus have a home in Bougival (near Paris) and a farm on the coast of Normandy, where Gérard raises his own livestock.

Jacqueline de Ribes

"It's not a narcissistic thing," said exotic fashion plate Jacqueline de Ribes, after the successful Paris debut of her first collection in March, 1983. "I don't just create for myself, even though I like to wear my own clothes." In summing up the motivation behind her "pre-couture" concept, she stated her desire was to create the closest possible alternative to haute couture without the frills (and fittings!)—and *only* for the American market. "I don't want to compete with the Paris designers who have been my close friends and dressed me all of my adult life."

Born in Paris, the daughter of Count Jean de Beaumont (her mother, Paule, a long-time patron of the arts, produced many of Tennessee Williams' plays in France), at the age of 17 she married Vicomte Edouard de Ribes, a wealthy banker. "At first I thought: 'God, I should have enjoyed a few years of liberty. I should have enjoyed life as a young girl.' But my husband is sophisticated and the marriage has worked." They have two children, Elizabeth, who is married and lives in Chicago, and son Jean, who lives in France. At the early age of nine, Jacqueline designed the sets and costumes for children's plays at her grandfather's home. By her late teens she created her own personality by learning the art of makeup, accenting her cheek bones and sculptured nose and enlarging her eyes with shadows and color. As the European chairman of the famous international Embassy Ball, she came to New York in 1959 with her protégé, the talented Raymundo de Larrain, who was responsible for the decor and the ballet which served as the evening's entertainment. New Yorkers had never seen anything quite so elaborate, and along with her co-chairmen C.Z. Guest and Peggy Bancroft, she filled the society pages for months. Her natural flair for making news has never stopped.

George Deukmejian

Described as "a Boy Scout in lotusland," this tough law-and-order attorney general became California's Republican governor in 1983. Though seemingly out of place in the laid-back land of hot tubs and transcendental meditation, Deukmejian ("upright, serious, middlebrow and—well, a little dull," as *Forbes* magazine put it) proved to be in tune in the growing conservative mood of most Californians. "Duke" Deukmejian, a veteran of 20 years in elected state office, set out to cut government spending, stimulate the economy, and revitalize the deteriorating public schools. The son of Armenian immigrants who fled the Turkish genocide at the turn of the century, Deukmejian and his Middle American values also struck a responsive chord among the 300,000 refugees who settled in California in recent years. He says his political goals are "that people will feel they have a better opportunity to get a higher quality of education and then find a position in a career they want to follow. I would also hope that people will feel a little safer."

Born 6 June 1928 in the village of Menands, N.Y., near Albany, he worked his way through college, receiving his law degree in 1952 from St. John's University in Brooklyn. In 1955, he moved to California where citizens of Armenian descent were becoming a politically potent group. He set up a law practice and in 1963 launched his political career by winning a seat in the state assembly. Elected to the state senate in 1966, the same year Ronald Reagan was elected governor, he carried out Reagan's crime program and tax reform bills. During his 16 years in the legislature, he authored more than 180 laws, including the death penalty statute and the community drug abuse law. He was elected senate Republican leader in 1974 and earlier served as minority whip in the assembly. In 1978, he was elected California's attorney general, serving in the post until 1983. During his term he vigorously prosecuted consumer fraud, strengthened narcotics enforcement and formed a state task force centering on youth gang problems. He and Gloria Saatjian were married in 1957. They have a son, George, and two daughters, Leslie and Andrea.

William Devane

I'm a damn good actor. . . . I only like to play roles that are good and meaty. Usually, those are character parts or villains." William Devane's matter of fact description of his acting was expressed in a 1979 press release for his role as St. Milt Warden in "From Here to Eternity: The War Years." Today, over ten years later, Devane is still playing a sleazy-type character on the nighttime soap "Knots Landing." In his role as Gregory Sumner, he divorced his first wife, ran for Senator, gave away the daughter of his late-second wife, stepped down from the Senate, ran and lost for Mayor, had an affair with his good friend's younger daughter, and then married the neighborhood manipulator for political prestige rather than love. Of his role, he explains: "Sumner is a man caught up in a struggle with power and notoriety."

William Devane was born 5 September 1939 in Albany, New York. In and out of four different high schools in four years, he eventually moved to Manhattan to seek stardom. In a 1970 interview he claimed he started out as an iron worker, but says "I decided I'd never become a millionaire that way." He studied at the New York Academy of Dramatic Arts and worked for Joseph Papp as a carpenter-electrician. Persistance paid off, and Devane would up as a mainstay of the New York Shakespeare Festival.

It's hard not to notice the physical resemblance between him and the Kennedy brothers, so it was only natural for him to be cast as President John F. Kennedy in "The Missiles of October," a part that sterotyped Devane yet brought him an Emmy Award nomination. He told Ted Morgan of the *New York Times* in 1975 how he prepared for such a demanding role. "I got me a back brace, which gave me a slight stoop. I bought me a pair of those Florsheim $60 black wing-tipped shoes, which slowed down my walk and gave me the weight of high office. I got me the record 'The Kennedy Wit,' and played it until the grooves wore out and I had that Irish attack on things that was so relaxed and so clear." More meaty roles followed, including a lead in the telefilm "Fear on Trial" and in the miniseries "From Here to Eternity" with Natalie Wood. He repeated his role as Sgt. Milt Warden in the series "From Here to Eternity: The War Years." He has also appeared in feature films; some Devane movies are: *Marathon Man, Yanks, Family Plot, The Bad News Bears in Breaking Training, Rolling Thunder, The Dark, Report to the Commissioner,* and *Testament.* In addition to his work with Joseph Papp, Devane appeared in a Broadway revival production of "One Flew Over the Cuckoo's Nest."

The sought-after actor has been married to the same woman for over 20 years. He and his wife Eugenie have two sons: Josh and Jake; the family resides in Sherman Oaks, California, and on their Arabian horse ranch in Sundance, Utah. An avid sportsman, Devane likes to relax by riding or playing a good game of polo.

Danny De Vito

"I usually try to find the redeeming qualities in the guys I play so that I can have a good sleep at night," Danny DeVito explained in a *People* magazine article. This approach could be considered a difficult task, knowing the various characters he has portrayed, both on the big and little screen. Whether he's an aluminum-siding salesman being chased by the government, a middle-aged momma's boy, a mental patient, or a cab dispatcher, DeVito becomes "one of those guys you love to hate."

He was born at Fitkin Hospital in Neptune, New Jersey, on 17 November 1944 to Julia and Daniel DeVito, Senior. He had a happy childhood in Asbury Park. He told the *Daily News* in an interview that it "was the greatest place in the world to grow up. . . . We were thirteen blocks from the beach. . . . Every woman for a five- or six-block radius was my 'aunt'. . . . In the summer everything changed. There was an incredible influx of new blood. All the city girls would come down and the place would turn these brilliant colors." After graduating from Our Lady of Mt. Carmel grammar school and Oratory Prep in Summit, Danny headed for Manhattan. He studied for two years with the Academy of Dramatic Arts. He also learned the haircutting trade at the Wilfred Academy of Hair and Beauty and at age 18 worked as a hairdresser for one year at his sister's shop to bring in money. Determined to make it as an actor, he traveled to California with hopes of appearing on the big screen. Unable to click, he was down to his last $10 in Los Angeles; he had previously purchased a round-trip plane ticket which he used to return to New York. Then the doors opened.

Landing a role in the Off-Broadway play *The Man With the Flower in His Mouth* set his career in the right direction. More offers followed, and he appeared in the stage productions of *Shrinking Bride* and *One Flew Over the Cuckoo's Nest*. As a result of his performance as Martini in the latter play, he was cast in the film version, which became the Academy Award picture of that year (1975). DeVito's been active ever since. Perhaps his most popular part was that of Louie De Palma in the ABC sitcom "Taxi." The show brought him immediate national exposure and enabled him to work with his wife, actress Rhea Perlman. A large majority of 1980's box-office smashes were DeVito's films; in addition to *Cuckoo's Nest*, he also appeared in another Academy Award Best Picture, *Terms of Endearment* (1983). Other films include: *Romancing the Stone* (1984) and its sequel, *Jewel of the Nile* (1985); *Ruthless People* (1986); *Tin Men* (1986); *Head Office* (1986); *Throw Momma From the Train* (1987); *Twins* (1988); and *The War of the Roses* (1989). Although Danny had been associated professionally with Rhea Perlman for many years (produced two short motion pictures together in their early careers: *The Sound Sleeper* and *Minestrone*), they actually tied the knot in 1982. Living in California, the couple have three children: Lucy Chet, Gracie Fan and Jake Daniel. A man of many talents, DeVito likes to unwind by playing the piano and the violin.

William DeVries

"Was Dr. Clark's head dead? Was his artificial heart working and everything else dead? Had I created a vegetable or a Frankenstein monster, something way out of control?" asked this pioneer surgeon in 1983 when a rough spot was hit by Barney Clark soon after he received the first artificial heart ever to be given to a living human being. Clark lived for 112 days after the surgery that raised extensive moral and ethical questions about life, death and superstar medicine.

The principal investigator for the Symbion artificial heart program approved by the Food and Drug Administration, DeVries, born 19 December 1943 in Brooklyn was the only surgeon authorized in 1983 to implant an artificial heart into a human being who would otherwise die from cardiovascular disease. The son of a Navy physician who was killed in WWII action just months after his son was born, DeVries was taken by his mother to her home state of Utah where he distinguished himself by his ability to take apart clocks. (He confessed in one interview to being not so swift in reconstructing them.) An athletic scholarship to the University of Utah allowed him to study medicine, and it was in Utah that he met and became the protégé of Dr. Willem Kolff, the pioneer of biomedical engineering, aka "spare parts medicine." (It was Kolff who, during WWII, built the first successful kidney dialysis machine.) After an internship at the Duke University Medical Center in North Carolina, DeVries returned to the University of Utah where he served as chairman of the division of cardiovascular and thoracic surgery from 1979 to 1984. Displeased with the University's review board, he left for the Humana Hospital in Louisville, Ky., a phenomenon of commercial medicine unto itself. "I don't like to see people die while I wait for the red tape," he explained. Interested in the proliferation of the artificial heart, Humana, one of the largest privately operated hospital chains in the United States, decided to provide free hospitalization for as many as 100 patients seeking an artificial heart as a last recourse.

Described as "gangly and with a shock of straw-colored hair that he constantly fingers out of his eyes," DeVries is more a Robert Redford than a Dr. Frankenstein lookalike. Married in 1965 to the former Karen Olsen, he and his wife have seven children. "I do the best surgery I can do," he says of his work. "You're taking a person who feels rotten, who is at death's doorstep, and you're giving him life. What could be more satisfying?"

Colleen Dewhurst

"It's a cameo role, but Miss Dewhurst, functioning as a cleanup hitter, knocks every laugh line clear out of the park," praised Frank Rich in his *New York Times* review of the 1983 revival of *You Can't Take It With You*. "Jason [Robards] and I are so used to doing heavies," beamed Dewhurst in an interview during the show's run, "that the cast broke up the other night when I said, 'Gee, it's wonderful to be in a play where the audience smiles back at you when you take the curtain call.'" Because of those "heavies" she became and remains one of the theatre's undisputed queens. Some of her memorable roles include Camille, Portia, Cleopatra, Kate, Eleanor of Aquitaine, Lady Macbeth, Medea, Miss Amelia in *Ballad of the Sad Cafe*, Sara in *More Stately Mansions*, the Albee shrikes in *Who's Afraid of Virginia Woolf* and *All Over*, Christine Mannon in *Mourning Becomes Electra*, and Josie in *The Moon for the Misbegotten*. She's won three Obies, two Tony Awards and one Emmy.

Born in Montreal, 3 June 1926, the daughter of a hockey player, she wanted to be an aviatrix at five. Years later, the dean of Milwaukee's Downer College (now Lawrence U.) wrote to her parents saying that life was an endless party to which Colleen had been the only one invited and requested her removal. There followed a $25-a-week elevator operator's job in Gary, Ind., and she later worked as a gym instructor "teaching fat old ladies how to shape up." Trekking off to New York, she enrolled at the American Academy of Dramatic Arts, made her professional acting debut in 1946 in *The Royal Family*, and in 1952 her Broadway debut in *Desire Under the Elms* by Eugene O'Neil, the playwright whose work she has so brilliantly illuminated. Varied theatrical activities have moved her on and off stage. Appearances include *An Almost Perfect Person* (1977), *The Queen and the Rebels* (1982) and as O'Neill's wife Carlotta in the 1985 Off-Broadway play, *My Gene*. She joined the ranks of women directors when she took over the reins (for a very short ride) of *Ned and Jack* (1981). Later she directed the National Theater of the Deaf's '84–'85 production of *All the Way Home* (for which she won an "actress" Tony in 1961). Elected president of Actor's Equity in 1985, she is vice-chairman of the Save The Theater movement (preservation of Broadway theatres) and is on the board of the Actor's Fund. The diversified actress continues to spread her wings across all mediums. Recent roles include: *Ah! Wilderness!* and *Long Day's Journey* on stage in 1988; the films *The Boy Who Could Fly* (1986), and *Hit & Run* (1987) and television appearances in "Moonlighting" and "Murphy Brown" (playing Candice Bergen's mother). Her mercurial marriage to George C. Scott in 1960 finally ended in 1972, *two* marriages, two divorces and two children (Campbell [the C. in George C.] and Alexander) later. She now lives in her farmhouse in South Salem, N.Y. with her two grown sons and a flock of animals and birds. She prefers the casual comfort of country life, and her passions are antiques and paintings. She once told an interviewer she'll never marry again. "Those might be famous last words," she admits, "I could live with a man without having to get married. But I have all I need—a career, children, and a house."

Susan Dey

While a "Partridge," this model-turned-actress discovered the true meaning of being a professional. She told *TV Guide* in a 1973 interview that "what I learned this year is that a set is not a home; if you're bored, too bad—get unbored in a hurry. If you're tired, wake up fast. If you're upset about something, the set is not the place to work it out." This strong sense of self and understanding of her trade have enabled Susan Dey to become one of the most popular television personalities of both the 1970's and 1980's. Her present role as Grace Van Owen in the Award-winning NBC-TV show "L.A. Law" has brought her respect, honors and a secured standing as a favorite actress of the decade.

One of four children, Susan was born 10 December 1952 in Pekin, Illinois, to Robert Smith Dey (city editor, *New Rochelle Standard-Star*) and his wife Gail. The aspiring actress grew up in Mt. Kisco, New York, and graduated in 1970 from the Fox Lane High School in Bedford. Her career began as a model, when her mother submitted pictures of her and her sister, Lesley, to a modeling agency. Dey's fresh, young look graced the covers of many magazines at the time, including *Seventeen*, *American Girl*, and *Simplicity*. Winning the role of "Laurie" in "The Partridge Family" during a New York audition, she later flew to Hollywood to make the pilot. While making the series she lived in California with a chaperon and completed her education by correspondence courses. Her fame skyrocketed and her name was popping up all over fan magazines with articles like "Susan's Popularity Secrets," "Ten Ways to Get Him to Kiss You," and "Susan Reveals All." She told *TV Guide* that she was bothered by the way her younger sisters reacted to her instant stardom. "The very first time I went home, my own little sister really surprised me by asking for my autograph—not as a joke or on a blank check or anything; she really wanted Laurie Partridge's autograph. I was very disturbed by that." Springboarding from the series to feature films, Dey's movies include *Skyjacked*, *First Love*, and *Looker*. She also starred in the telefilms "Loves Me, Loves Me Not," "The Comeback Kid," "Little Women," "Cage Without a Key," "Mary Jane Harper Cried Last Night," "The Gift of Life," and "Angel in Green," plus the 1983 TV series "Emerald Point N.A.S."

On a hiatus from acting when she gave birth to her daughter Sarah, Susan says "It was a period of change in my life, and I needed time to ground myself." Her marriage to agent Leonard Hirshan ended in divorce and her career hit a standstill. Then, as her NBC biography stated, a chance meeting became the slingshot to her current success. "Timing—and bumping into the right person—was everything for Susan Dey, whose serendipitous first meeting with 'L.A. Law' executive producer Steven Bochco at a private school function for their children paid off in a starring role just as the series was to begin its first year of production." Happily matriculated with a fine ensemble of players, Susan also finds time to branch out in other areas. She appeared in the movie *The Trouble With Dick* (1988) and the TV film "A Place at the Table" with David Morse. In 1988 she married Bernard Sofronski and the couple live, along with her daughter, in Los Angeles. During her spare time, she likes swimming or sailing, and just walking on the beach.

Neil Diamond

"When you're on a merry-go-round, you miss a lot of scenery. You have to get off every once in a while. I still need practice in enjoying the fruits of success." he once said, revealing the introspective, or perhaps, brooding nature that colors his music in serious and dramatic overtones. A bubblegum rocker in the late 1960s, with hits like "Kentucky Woman," and "Cherry, Cherry," Diamond entered the 1970s with "Cracklin' Rosie" and soon got more philosophical with "He Ain't Heavy, He's My Brother," "I Am, I Said," and "Song Sung Blue."

The descendant of Polish and Russian Jews, Neil Leslie Diamond was born 24 January 1941, in the Coney Island section of Brooklyn. Seemingly born to make music, he sang in his High School choral group, just seats away from another future singing great, Barbra Streisand. (Although they didn't know each other then, they would harmonize in 1978 for the melancholy love ballad, "You Don't Bring Me Flowers," one of the year's biggest hits.)

After attending college on a fencing scholarship, he ditched education in his senior year for a song-writing job with Sunbeam Music. Finding himself cast out by the company after only 16 weeks, Diamond rented a piano and office and began composing for himself in 1965. "It wasn't until I began to sing my own songs that I had real success." In addition to his string of soft-rock hits over the next two decades, Diamond penned two big songs that helped establish the TV pop group, The Monkees: "I'm a Believer" in 1966, and "A Little Bit Me, A Little Bit You." His score for the 1973 movie *Jonathan Livingston Seagull* earned him a Grammy award and an Oscar nomination. Exercising a long-felt itch to act, Diamond felt his ethnic roots made him a natural to star in the third remake of *The Jazz Singer*. High on sentiment and low on drama, the 1981 movie hit a sour note with most critics. *Newsweek* said of Diamond's performance as a Jewish singer torn between tradition and stardom, "One look at his conspicuously coiffed hairdo and spotlight-glazed eyes and you know this man has been assimilated years ago, probably at Caesar's Palace."

News spreads like wildfire when a Neil Diamond concert comes to town. His performances are packed with celebrity peers joining fans in the audience; almost always a sell-out crowd. In 1987, Columbia released *Hot August II* as a follow-up album to *Hot August Night* (live recording from his shows at Los Angeles' Greek Theatre in 1972), both potent reminders of why this star is one of the biggest draws in America. The long-awaited new studio LP *The Best Years Of Our Lives* came out in 1988, followed by another successful concert tour.

After an early marriage to a high school sweetheart (two daughters) Diamond married Marcia Murphy. They have two sons.

Eric Dickerson

Since it was former-halfback-turned-sportscaster O.J. Simpson who held the teetering title for most yards gained running during a pro football season, it was apt that he name his successor. "When I first saw him [as a pro]," Simpson avows, "I said on the air that he'd be the one to break the record." With a little help from the two-games-longer seasons than Simpson played, and with his team, the LA. Rams' game strategy seldom using him as a blocker, Eric Dickerson proved O.J.'s prediction true in his second year in the NFL. After, in 1984, becoming only the second turf-tallier to tick off more than 2,000 yards in a year, the 24-year-old said "Maybe sometime I'll do it in 14 games, too." (In 1985 the USFL New Jersey Generals' Herschel Walker eclipsed Eric's record.)

As a Southern Methodist University runner, the erstwhile Sealy, Texas (born 2 September 1960), high school star finished behind Herschel Walker and John Elway in the 1982 Heisman Trophy race, and remained in that third position in the pro draft, being selected after the United States Football League enticed Walker from school early, and after Elway was made the NFL's first choice. But it was the Hollywood-handsome, six-feet-three, 220-pound Dickerson whom Ram coach John Robinson had in mind when he set out to rebuild his newly-acquired team around "a man who wanted to dominate," and a runner whose "attitude is, 'Give me the ball.'" The speedster gained a record amount of yards for a rookie, despite apologizing that he was "mentally tired . . . [from] flying . . . [and from] being on the road." He symbolized his appreciation to the blockers who made it possible by presenting each of them with an expensive watch and diligently praising them. Then the slithery back, who wears a flak jacket, goggles, and heavy-duty shoulder pads, produced his record-breaking stats after discovering that "some days I do feel invincible. Some days the other team may even get into the backfield, but I still feel they can't get me. It's almost like it's me against them, myself."

Dickerson set the sports world spinning again in October, 1987, when he signed a multi-million-dollar deal with the Indianapolis Colts. This trade ended the four record-breaking seasons with the Rams for him. Thinking ahead, Eric would like to turn sportscaster, too. He's already written a book, *On the Run*, and has appeared on such shows as "Good Morning America," "Today" and "Hollywood Squares." He says: "I'm looking forward to a new creative direction that will add new dimensions and prospects for me off the field of play."

James Dickey

"Perhaps it was war," says this prolific prize-winning poet, "but I have come to look on existence from the standpoint of a survivor. I think you only know the value of life if you know death, or if you've been close to death. Then you see what a glorious thing it is to be alive." The erstwhile wartime pilot has been a striking presence on the American literary scene since the publication of his first book of poetry, *Into the Stone and Other Poems* in 1960 and now, in terms of popularity, he's the pre-eminent "people's poet" in the tradition of Robert Frost and Carl Sandberg. Interestingly, it was the 1972 film based on his first novel, *Deliverance* (1970), that popularized Dickey. He wrote the screenplay, suggested the music, and acted in the movie as the backwoods sheriff. A man whose zest for the adventure of life equals his talents for communicating it to others, Dickey is becoming a legend in his own time. His goal is to be a "poet of survival and hope."

Born in Atlanta, 2 February 1923, James Dickey was first passionate about "sports, sports, sports." He was a flashy football star at Clemson (in South Carolina) until World War II, when he became a fighter pilot flying 100 combat missions and learning to live with the threat of instant death—and delivering it. Dickey returned to civilian live with changed priorities. He would be a poet and try to "charge America and the world with a vitality of life it already had but needed explaining." Graduating from Vanderbilt University (M.A. 1950), he taught briefly and began publishing poetry in literary magazines (*The Sewanee Review*, *Harper's*). In 1956, he joined a New York advertising agency and for the next six years became "Jingle Jim," turning out commercials for Coca Cola, potato chips, and fertilizer while writing poetry at night. He began writing poetry full-time after he received a Guggenheim Fellowhsip in 1962 following the publication of his first collection. His awards include the National Book Award for Poetry in 1966 for *Buckdancer's Choice* and the Levinson Prize by *Poetry* magazine in 1981 for five poems from his book *Puella*. Dickey's ad hoc role as the "people's poet" won him assignments to cover the Apollo-7 blast-off for *Life* magazine and to write a poem for the inauguration of President Carter. He served two terms as poetry consultant to the Library of Congress.

A popular professor and poet-in-residence at several colleges over the years, Dickey has been at the University of South Carolina since 1968. He's become a familiar bardic figure on campus, dressed in blue jeans, a guitar slung over his shoulders. sometimes wearing an old buffalo hunter's hat with a pheasant feather band. His provocative, entertaining lectures teach not only about poetry but about life. "Never cower from life," he exhorts. "Live it all out." In 1976, after the death of his wife of 28 years, Maxine (two sons), Dickey married one of his students, Deborah Dobson. They have a daughter. Installed as his "muse," Deborah was the inspiration for Dickey's book of poems, *Puella*, which he says is a "kind of series of male meditations on female puberty."

Angie Dickinson

"I love hot weather," she once purred on "The Tonight Show." "I like to take my clothes off in the heat." In the next breath, she asked Johnny Carson to describe his erotic fantasies. (He just blanched and cut to a commercial.) The steamy star was certainly in her element in Brian De Palma's *Dressed to Kill* (1980) in which she played a suburban matron hungry for love in the backseat of a taxi. "I am not Doris Day," she quips. Lucky for her; *Dressed to Kill* was the biggest movie smash of her checkered career. "This is the first time I've had this instantaneous reaction, the feeling I am a hot number." (The sex and violence in the film earned the thriller $25 million and cries of exploitation from the feminist community.) Forced to retire as NBC's "Police Woman" after its abrupt cancellation in '78, she laid low until cast for *Dressed to Kill*. De Palma however, used a 23-year-old neck-to-knees stand-in for the nude scenes, and made no bones about telling the public just that. "I was shocked," says Dickinson. "Why destroy the illusion? Let them think it's Tahiti, even if it is Burbank."

Born Angeline Brown in Kulm, N.D., 30 September 1932, she became Dickinson while attending Glendale College. (Her first husband was college football star Gene Dickinson; "I was just wrong for him as wonderful as he was.") She got her first break when producer Howard Hawks spotted her, and she subsequently starred in *Rio Bravo*, *Point Blank*, and *Pretty Maids All in a Row*. A onetime Mayor of Universal City ("My community covered 408 acres, eight acres bigger than Princess Grace's Monaco"), she has, in the past, been courted by Frank Sinatra, the late David Janssen, even JFK, but at the moment her romantic involvements are being kept at bay since her split in '76 from husband Burt Bacharach (one daughter Nikki).

Joan Didion

"Yes," she would say, "I did have a happy childhood—except . . ." a cigarette lit, "for those terrible fears. I thought about the atomic bomb. A lot . . . after there was one."

She wrote that she grew up "in Sacramento Valley where a boom mentality and a sense of Chekhovian loss meet in uneasy suspension."

In uneasy suspension.

She was born twenty days before Christmas in 1934. During her childhood she typed pages from Hemingway and Conrad, "to see how the sentences worked." She won *Vogue's Prix de Paris* and went to New York to be an editor at the magazine.

In New York City, she said, "All I could do those days was talk long distance to the boy I already knew I would never marry in the spring." She wrote movie reviews for *Vogue* and freelanced elsewhere. When she published her novels (*Run River*, *Play It As It Lays*, *A Book of Common Prayer*, *Democracy*) and her nonfiction essays (*Slouching Towards Bethlehem*, *The White*

Marlene Dietrich

Album, Salvador), *Vogue* itself commented: "Joan Didion writes so tightly it cuts the flesh."

And the poet James Dickey called her "the finest woman prose stylist writing in English today."

And, wonder, were she a man rather than a woman from California, from the Sacramento Valley, where a boom mentality and a sense of Chekhovian loss meet in uneasy suspension, wouldn't she be allowed the more universal "finest prose stylist writing in English today?"

Yes. She would.

"This is Joan Didion Dunne," she would write as her caption to a self-portrait requested of herself by *Ms.* magazine, a self-portrait that was nothing other than a thumbprint. "Five-feet-two-inches, ninety-five pounds, hair red, eyes hazel. Must wear corrective lenses. Too thin. Astigmatic. Has no visual sense of her self."

In 1964 she married the author John Gregory Dunne and they moved to Malibu in California and adopted a daughter they named Quintana Roo for the amber territory of the same name in Mexico, south of the border.

Amigos.

Miss Didion drinks too much coffee and chain smokes Pall Malls. She shuns psychoanalysis. Yeats, from his tomb, would whisper to her, would say:

"Things fall apart; the center cannot hold."

Cannot hold.

With her husband she wrote films for Hollywood—*Panic in Needle Park*, the film version of her novel *Play It As It Lays* and his novel *True Confessions*.

"It's not like writing," she said of penning movies, "it's like working a puzzle."

Jigsaw. Echo. Cannot hold.

When she would compete a novel or book, she would return to her bed in her parents' home in Sacramento. Where no one would ask questions. No one would. Then, done, she would return to her husband, home to L.A., 132 rickety steps above the Pacific in Malibu. To the diminishing shore. To the cool breezes of celebrity. To the blue Catalina light.

Marlene Dietrich

Mike Todd called her "the world's greatest" entertainer. In the 1950s, as her film career waned, she became a recording star and cabaret performer, singing to packed houses internationally (including her native Berlin). Facing audiences in Paris, London, Las Vegas and New York, she could, with the measured enunciations of a single syllable, evoke a seamy Berlin honky-tonk of the 1920s. "Look me over closely," she would huskily intone while gowned in a Jean Louis dazzler, her voice ironic even in solicitation. So the legend lives; on a column in the Café de Paris against which she learned singing is a bronze plaque inscribed, "Dietrich rested here." Her legs were insured by Lloyd's of London and she had the pleasure of seeing them banned from posters in the Paris subways (too demoralizing to the customers).

She was born Maria Magdalena Von Losch, 27 December 1901, into a strict Berlin family. Aside from her basically upper-middle class conservative background, her early life is shrouded in mystery. Seriously bent on a musical career as a violinist, she was reportedly unable to perform in concert because of a chronic wrist ailment. Turning to the theatre, she coaxed Berlin's famed theatrical dictator Max Reinhardt into giving her a part in *The Taming of the Shrew*. When Josef von Sternberg brought her to America in 1930, she was regarded as Paramount's answer to MGM's Garbo. (Dietrich had appeared in a bit part five years earlier in G.W. Pabst's *The Joyless Street*, starring Garbo.) Of the two, Dietrich had vastly more theatrical experience: she had appeared in Shaw, in revues, in musical comedy, and in a dozen films. Auditioning for the 1929 UFA film that was to bring her international celebrity, she was advised by Sternberg to "learn a vulgar song"—and she walked into the sordid erotic twilight of *The Blue Angel* and film history in 1930 belting a jazzy American lunacy, "You're the cream in my coffee, You're the salt in my stew." Most of her early American films (half a dozen directed by her mentor Sternberg, whose reputation was later considerably elevated by revisionist auteurist film critics like Andrew Sarris) were criticized as so much visual rhetoric draped around a fabulous face and figure. (At the height of her fame, she was credited for starting the vogue among women for wearing slacks.) In her first, *Morocco* (1930—her sole Oscar nomination), Sternberg sent her stalking Gary Cooper across broiling Sahara sands in billowing chiffon and six-inch heels. Her subsequent films were at times even less coherent; nobody seemed to mind. Her other Sternbergs are: *Dishonored* (1931), *The Scarlet Empress* (as Catherine the Great; 1934), *Blonde Venus* (in which she sang "Hot Voodoo" while dressed in a gorilla suit; 1932), *Shanghai Express* in 1932 ("Oh, why are they always talking about those old movies of mine?") and *The Devil is a Woman* in 1935 ("I was more beautiful in that than in anything else."). Other memorable films include: *Garden of Allah* (1936), *Destry Rides Again* (1939), *A Foreign Affair* (1948), Hitchcock's *Stage Fright* (1950), *Witness for the Prosecution* (1957), Welles's *Touch of Evil* (1958) and *Judgment at Nuremberg* (1961). While filming *Knight Without Armor* in England in '37, she received a generous, personal offer from Hitler to return to German films. She refused and, as a result, her films were banned in her native country. In '39 she became an American citizen. During W.W.II she entertained U.S. troops, participated in war bond drives and made anti-Nazi propaganda broadcasts in German. She was decorated by the U.S. and France.

A longtime friend, Ernest Hemingway, said of her, "Brave, beautiful, loyal, generous . . . I value her opinion more than professors." Her only husband, Czech-born chicken farmer Rudolph Sieber (they were married in 1924 and, except for a few days each year or so, lived apart for nearly four decades until his death in 1975) said, "When I had a heart attack she flew to my bedside and nursed me to health. This is what lasts. She is basically a regular guy." She has one daughter, onetime actress Maria Riva, to whom her devotion is legendary, and four grandchildren. When Maria's first child was born, Dietrich was called "the world's most glamorous grandmother." Now she is a recluse, confined to a wheelchair in her Paris apartment. Her 1979 autobiography *My Life Story* was published in Germany. In 1984 actor-director Maximilian Schell (whose appearance with her in *Nuremberg* earned him an Oscar) filmed a documentary on her life and career. Her autobiography, translated by Salvator Attansio was published in 1989.

Phyllis Diller

She can deliver as many as 12 punchlines per minute and not all about "Fang" either ("Fang is SO-OOOO dumb that a brain operation on *him* would be minor surgery.")—in point of fact "Fang" is a dreamed-up figure and "bears no resemblance to either of my former husbands." Her hair may look as if it might have been styled by a food processor but her bankbook looks beautiful. She remains one of the busiest and most popular female comics around, headlining in six countries for over thirty years.

Born in Lima, Ohio, on 17 July 1917, as Phyllis Driver, she met her first husband Sherwood Anderson Diller at Bluffton College in Ohio. Married in 1939, she became the mother of five children, worked as an advertising copywriter, but did most of her joking at the laundromat. In 1955 her rep as a neighborhood cut-up led to a trial engagement at San Francisco's *Purple Onion;* it stretched on for 89 weeks. Since then Phyllis has been in 11 movies including a dramatic role in Elmer Rice's *The Adding Machine* and three co-starring roles with Bob Hope. ("We have an agreement," she says, "I don't make fun of his nose and he doesn't ridicule my body.") She's played Dolly Levi in a Broadway revival of *Hello Dolly* and as an accomplished pianist has appeared with some top-notch symphony orchestras in the U.S. In the early '80s she had already published four books and *The Joys of Aging and How to Avoid Them* (1981) was destined to become a bestseller if only because she looked better in '81 than she did in '61. Much better. She is a former honorary mayor of Brentwood, California, and received a Ph.D. ("Is that an abbreviation of Phyllis Diller?") from National Christian University. Divorced from Diller in 1965, she later married actor Warde Donovan whom she also divorced. Phyllis lives in a large English-style home in West Los Angeles. "The place used to be haunted," she says, "but the ghosts haven't been back since the night I tried on all my wigs."

Matt Dillon

Here's how Maura Moynihan in *Interview* gilded this teenage pistol noted for his reform-school-tough-outside and heart-of-gold inside, sort of a poor boy's knight-in-shining-armor: "The magnetism he radiates is very powerful; it is something tangible. On his taunt physique clothing falls in loose disorder. Buttons seem to come undone and fabric slackens. He is blessed with dramatic Gaelic coloring: glossy black hair, luminous skin with flushed cheeks and enormous liquid eyes. His attention is elusive but once captured, focuses with great intensity. He explores his thoughts more with instinct than intellect; often his movements convey his meaning more effectively than his words. He loves rock music and speaks with jargon comprehensible to any teenager. The qualities of maturing self-possession and ingenuousness are gracefully comingled."

In other words, he's a big heart-throbber, another one of the "sons of DeNiro." Matt Dillon, born 18 February 1964 in New Rochelle, N.Y., (where, TV trivia fans, Dick Van Dyke lived with Mary Tyler Moore), was discovered in the halls of his high school while he was cutting class one afternoon in 1979. Talent scouts were combing the area for some fresh young skin for the film *Over the Edge*. After a mere five minutes with Matt, casting director Victor Ramos pencilled in his notebook: "Should be a movie star." Soon thereafter, Ramos became Dillon's personal manager. Following *Over the Edge*, Matt appeared in *Little Darlings* and overnight became the honey to an adoring teeny-bopper population, receiving up to 7,000 pieces of fan mail a week. His subsequent films such as *My Bodyguard*, *Liar's Moon* (as the naive farmboy), *Tex* and the PBS production of Jean Shepherd's satirical "The Great American 4th of July and Other Disasters" brought him full star status and established him as an actor of depth and both dramatic and comedic versatility. Two of his best performances have been in the film adaptations of novels written by one of his favorite writers, S.E. Hinton, whose fan he was long before his film career took-off. *The Outsiders* and *Rumble Fish* were both directed by Francis Coppola, and Dillon garnered rave reviews for his starring roles in *Flamingo Kid, Target, Native Son, The Big Town, Kansas, Bloodhounds of Broadway* and *Drugstore Cowboy*.

Into astrology, reading, girls and more girls, the young actor finds it difficult "to keep a relationship together. I fall in love really hard," he says, "I get myself into trouble. For some reason I do, but I have a hard time keeping it going . . . commitment . . . my work has to be first. . . . I've had my heart smashed, stepped on, crunched, everybody has. Vice-versa, too. I know that. I don't screw anybody over, but I know that happens. It's tough."

Joe Di Maggio

Immortalized plaintively in song (Simon and Garfunkel's "Mrs. Robinson" from *The Graduate*), named Baseball's Greatest Living Player in a poll taken in 1969 by the Commissioner's office for the sport's 100th anniversary, elected to the Hall of Fame in 1955 for his flawless centerfielding and .325 lifetime batting average, Joltin' Joe remains actively retired since his 1951 farewell to the New York Yankees. He's done quite well with lucrative business deals and residuals from TV commercials, including his ever-popular Bowery Savings Bank ad.

"The greatest team player that ever lived" (as Connie Mack called him) was born Joseph Paul Di Maggio on 25 November 1914 in Martinez, Calif., the eighth of nine children of a San Francisco fisherman. Joe recalls, "We weren't poor in the sense that we were ever cold or hungry, but there never was enough money in the house for luxuries. . . . I can remember walking two miles, or maybe more, to play ball and then walking back after the game was over." While Dad expected them to follow in his footsteps, three of his boys went on to play what he called "a bum's game." The Yankee Clipper began his major league career in 1936. "I was really pea-green," he recalls. "I remember a reporter asking me for a 'quote' on something or other and I was so dumb I didn't even know what a 'quote' was. I thought it was some kind of soft drink."

The three-time MVP and first $100,000-a-year baseball player amassed 361 homers despite missing three playing years during World War II. In 1941 he performed a feat many considered the greatest of all time when he hit safely in 56 consecutive games, still a record. First married in 1939 to starlet Dorothy Arnold (one son), his 1954 marriage to Marilyn Monroe broke up little more than a year later because of conflicting career demands. It was, however, due almost entirely to him that her funeral in 1962 had what little dignity she was ever permitted. "If it hadn't been for her friends," he said at the time, "she might still be alive."

Jeane Dixon

"I don't really need my crystal ball," says America's foremost psychic, "but it helps sometimes. For me, it's like a television set. It brings in what's happening in the world." Among the things she has anticipated, with and without her crystal ball, were President Kennedy's assassination (she predicted he would be killed in the South by someone whose name began with an O), the deaths of Mahatma Gandhi and Dag Hammarskjold, the partition of India, the 1964 Alaska earthquake, and the removal of her secretary's son's adenoids. In 1984, she predicted that Geraldine Ferraro would be chosen by Walter Mondale if he put a female on the ticket and that Ferraro could face "a damaging controversy." She's also been wrong (she said Russia would land first on the moon and that the Vietnam peace terms would be settled in 1966). But she freely admits her errors, attributing them to her failure to interpret correctly her visions and psychic reactions.

Born in Medford, Wisc., in 1918, Jeane Pinckert Dixon began her life as a seer early. "When I was a little girl, an old gypsy saw my palms and gave me a crystal ball, because, she told me, I'd be able to predict future events." Her psychic gift, developed with the help of a Jesuit priest, became honed to a degree of supersensitivity by World War II. Since then, she's been in considerable demand as a consultant, as a guest on television and radio talk shows, and on the lecture circuit. Her columns are syndicated in more than 300 U.S. newspapers and 18 foreign publications. Her books, *Jeane Dixon— My Life and Prophesies* and *Reincarnation and Prayers to Live By* are brisk sellers. Her horoscopes-by-phone have become an everyday necessity for the dialing public. When she's not peering into the crystal ball and/or receiving psychic vibrations, she works as a real estate broker at James L. Dixon & Co., a Washington agency whose president is also her husband. She receives no payment for her psychic activities; all proceeds go to her pet project—the Children to Children Foundation she established in 1963 for research into birth defects.

Devoutly religious, Dixon believes her psychic ability is a gift from God. She begins each day by reciting the Twenty-Third Psalm. While she says she can get vibrations from someone over the phone, real bona fide visions are rarer. "Some years I am given three visions, some years none at all. . . . A vision can be with color or black and white. Sometimes it has music and voices. . . . One made me feel as if I were enfolded in whipped cream."

Kevin Dobson

This 6-foot, brown-haired, blue-eyed actor is perhaps one of the most sought after husbands on television. Sharing a Soap Opera Award with his co-star Michele Lee, Kevin Dobson was named as part of the "Best Couple" for playing honorable M. Patrick MacKenzie on the popular nighttime series "Knots Landing." His rugged good looks and endearing personality assure certain screen stability, but Dobson is a trained actor who has paid his dues along the way to stardom.

Born in Jackson Heights, New York, on 18 March 1944, young Dobson was initially interested in sports. While attending high school he was offered a professional baseball contract with the San Fransisco Giants. He passed on the tempting proposition in order to fulfill a military term in the U.S. Army. After his military obligation he found work as a ticket-taker for the Long Island Railroad to save enough money for college. In the interim his girlfriend (and future wife), along with his sister, prodded Kevin to try out for commercials. A short time later he appeared in his first stage play, *The Impossible Years*, which toured throughout the United States. When he returned to New York, he studied under the direction of Sanford Meisner while working odd jobs as a waiter, bartender and taxi driver. Eventually fielding offers, Dobson appeared in some off-Broadway plays and major films: *Love Story, Bananas, Klute, The Anderson Tapes, The French Connection*, and *Carnal Knowledge*. Crossing the coasts for a swing at Hollywood, he landed some guest roles on established television shows such as "Mod Squad," understudied for Jon Voight in an LA stage production of *A Streetcar Named Desire*, and then hit the bigtime hooking the recurring role as Detective Bobby Crocker on "Kojak" (1973-1978). With over 100 episodes behind him, Dobson became a popular choice in 1979 to add to the mostly female cast of "Knots Landing." As the justice-seeking Federal prosecutor, Dobson's character added bite to the soap opera. In 1989, "MacKenzie" tried it solo as an independent lawyer on the show and his relationship with his wife "Karen" (Michele Lee) was sprinkled with some teasing indiscretions. Other TV credits include the telefilms "Transplant," "Orphan Train," "Hardhat and Legs," "From Here to Eternity," "Mickey Spillane's Mike Hammer," "Reunion," and "Sweet Revenge," and the series "Shannon" (1981-1982).

Kevin and his wife, Susan, have three children. They enjoy family outings and family-oriented sports. Kevin is associated with many charities; he was the recipient of the United States Jaycees Outstanding Young Men in America Award for Professional Achievement and Community Service in 1979, and he finds time to get involved with the Retinitis Pigmentosa Foundation, Muscular Dystrophy Association, Easter Seals and the Special Olympics. An active sportsman, Dobson likes to play tennis and racquetball on his own backyard court.

E.L. Doctorow

His first three novels—*Welcome To Hard Times* (1960), *Big As Life* (1966), and *The Book Of Daniel* (1971), won him the respect of the literary set—not the bank, however. But his 1975 marvelously inventive *Ragtime*, a book that involves both real and imaginary people in the early 20th Century, took care of that and made him the author to talk about around the world. *Ragtime* was one of the most popular books of the decade. "Reading today is too much an act of will," he has said, "I don't know whose fault that is or why it is, but it is that way. I like to think that what I write does not require an act of will to read."

Edgar Laurence Doctorow was born in New York City 6 January 1931 to a Jewish immigrant family whom he describes as "old fashioned social democrats." From the third grade on he knew that he wanted to be a writer. After stints at Columbia University's graduate English department and the U.S. Army, he rose up the ranks of new York's publishing establishment, eventually becoming the vice-president and publisher of Dial Press. In his spare time he wrote his first two novels. *Welcome to Hard Times* was made into a 1967 MGM flick starring the late Henry Fonda. "The title of the book," he joked, "is what the picture gives the audience." An offer to teach at the University of California liberated him from his editing chores. Then, while teaching at Sarah Lawrence he finished *Ragtime*, a book that astounded the publishing industry with its record-breaking $1,850,000 paperback sale. Doctorow avoided the celebrity circuit. "Money is like sex," he said, "it's a private matter." In 1979, his play, *Drinks Before Dinner*, directed by Mike Nichols, received only fair reviews despite an all-star cast, elaborate sets and make-up by Way Bandy. His 1980 novel *Loon Lake* gave his patients another lit.-hit of the good doctor, but the films of *Ragtime* and *The Book of Daniel* rattled mixed notices with Hollywood's heart—the box office cash register as well as the critics. His 1989 bestseller is titled *Billy Bathgate*. He and writer Helen Setzer, married since 1954, have three children: Jenny, Caroline and Richard. "What you come to trust," says this year-round resident of peaceful Sag Harbor, Long Island, "is that writing is not quite thinking, it's an action. At the moment it occurs, it's not entirely under your control. Obviously if it were, everyone would write a masterpiece."

Christopher Dodd

When Rep. Christopher Dodd of Connecticut took on former New York Senator James Buckley in a bid for a Connecticut U.S. Senate seat, he had to outrun more than a powerful GOP opponent. His larger cross to bear may have been the soiled family reputation inherited from his father, two-term Senator Thomas Dodd, whose political career never survived a 1967 Senate censure for misuse of campaign funds. But the younger Dodd came and conquered, and is considered by political observers an up and coming force in the Democratic party.

Dodd was born 27 May 1944 in Willimantic, Conn. Raised in a politician's home, he developed interests that veered naturally toward government. After his graduation from Providence College in 1966, he earned a law degree from the University of Louisville. He served two years in the Peace Corps, and six years in the Army Reserves. Elected to the House in 1975, he served on the Judiciary Committee and the powerful Rules Committee and was active as an at-large whip. His support of gun control and lobby disclosure bills endeared him to liberals, anti-bureaucrats, and consumer groups. In 1979, when Democratic incumbent Abraham Ribicoff declared his retirement, Dodd leaped early into the Senate race, campaigning in the same vigorous and affable manner that won him votes in the Congressional race. Republican Buckley's abrasive charges that Dodd was a "big spender" and soft on defense backfired, and may have aided the young congressman in stopping Buckley in his bid to become the first senator elected from two different states. Dodd carried the unions, Catholics, liberals, and moderate suburbanites, taking the election with 56 per-cent of the vote. In the Senate, Dodd served on the Foreign Relations Committee and was a staunch supporter of human rights. Dodd is divorced from the former Susan Mooney.

Christoph von Dohnanyi

"So intense was Dohnanyi's leadership and so reponsive the orchestra's playing that the audience sat through the performance as though transfixed.... At the end, though, they stood to applaud." wrote the music critic of the *Cleveland Plain Dealer* of the Berlin-born conductor in 1983 while he was still director-designate of the world famous Cleveland Orchestra. A year later, Christoph von Dohnanyi took over as full-fledged music director of the musical organization that had been led for 24 years by the legendary George Szell (until his death in 1970), and began his stewardship with a performance that was telecast live to Europe 23 September 1984 (and taped for later showing in the U.S.) The announcement in 1981 of Dohnanyi's appointment as the sixth musical director of the Cleveland Orchestra was made shortly after his debut with the ensemble and although it came as a surprise to many, it was welcomed by the orchestra, whose members described their meeting with the conductor as "love at first sight," confirming *Newsweek*'s opinion that Dohnanyi was "tailor-made for the Cleveland." When asked in 1984 by Thor Eckert, Jr., in the *Christian Science Monitor*, if he was worried that audiences might not react well to so much new music (which he had programmed extensively), he replied, "We need most a self confidence that what we do what we really want to do, and we trust the people will be interested in getting to know something they don't already know." In a television commercial promoting the orchestra prior to his first season as musical director, he seemed especially pleased to be able to announce, "People all over the world have had to learn to pronounce my name." (It's DOCK-nan-yee.)

Born 8 September 1929 in Berlin, the grandson of Hungarian composer Ernst von Dohnanyi, the son of Hans von Dohnanyi, who was executed in 1944 for his anti-Nazi activities (as was his uncle, theologian Dietrich Bonhoeffer), young Christoph studied law after the war at the University of Munich while continuing the musical studies he'd begun at age five. A possible legal career was soon forgotten in the wake of his winning the Richard Strauss Prize for Composition and Conducting awarded by the City of Munich. After a year studying at Florida State University (where his grandfather was artist-in-residence) and participating in conducting classes by Leonard Bernstein in 1952 at Tanglewood, Dohnanyi returned to Europe to accept the position of coach and assistant conductor at the Frankfurt Opera under Sir Georg Solti, eventually becoming the principal conductor of the Frankfurt and then head of the Hamburg Opera in 1978. He jokes that he was allowed gracefully to bow out of the last post when "his brother was elected major of the city." Among the operatic world premieres he has conducted are Hans Werner Henze's "The Young Lords" and "The Bassarids" and Friedrich Cerha's "Baal." At the Metropolitan Opera House he had conducted *Falstaff* and *Der Rosenkavalier,* and among his highly regarded operatic recordings are Alban Berg's *Lulu* and *Wozzeck*.

Married to German soprano Anji Silja (three children), von Dohnanyi says, "Music is not a democracy; music is the meaning of one person.... You see it in the Cleveland Orchestra: they have a *desire* for a strong person, but that person has to give his life to them and to music, and only then will they follow."

Bob Dole

President Ford's running mate in 1976 and a presidential candidate in 1980 and 1988, this witty Republican senator from Kansas maintains his presidential ambitions. His political savvy and clout as "master of compromise" and his skill in balancing fiscal conservatism with compassion (support for food stamps, civil rights, women's equality) have earned him broad respect. The *New York Times* has called him "one of the most powerful and effective politicians in Washington." The issues that concerned him as chairman of the weighty Senate Finance Committee before he was elected Majority Leader of the Senate in 1985 (succeeding to the post when Howard Baker declined to run for re-election)—taxes, Social Security, Medicare, international trade, unemployment compensation and revenue sharing—still remain major interests of the ambitious Kansan. Once labeled an acid-tongued "hatchet man so antagonistic that he couldn't sell beer on a troop ship," he has mellowed since his marriage in 1975 to brainy North Carolina ex-May Queen, Harvard Law-grad Secretary of Transportation turned Secretary of Labor, Elizabeth Hanford Dole. They've become America's "power couple," setting a new standard for two-career marriages with their "double-Dole" punch.

Born in Russell, Kan., 22 July 1923, the son of a grain elevator manager, he left the University of Kansas to enter the Army, and in the last days of World War II was critically wounded while leading an infantry platoon in Italy. Hospitalized for 39 months, he lost the use of his right arm but regained use of the left and later taught himself to write with his left hand. While hospitalized, he met and married Phyllis Holden (one daughter; divorced 1972). She served as his "pen" while he attended the University of Arizona and earned a law degree from Washburn University in Topeka. In 1951, while still in law school, he was elected to the Kansas legislature. Two years later, he became a prosecuting attorney in Russell County, a post he held until elected to Congress in 1960, serving four terms in the House and moving up to the Senate in 1968. His personal experiences have made him a lifelong advocate of the rights of veterans, the handicapped, and disadvantaged. Says Elizabeth Dole, "I see in him concern and sensitivity for people who have suffered adversity no matter what the source of their problems."

Elizabeth Hanford Dole

Prophetically chosen as one of America's "200 faces of the future" by *Time* magazine in 1974, a decade later she was one of the GOP's most incandescent female stars. (Never mind that she's a former Democrat). In 1988 she was named by the Gallup poll as one of the world's top ten admired women. The Harvard-educated Southern belle is one of Washington's most powerful women as President Bush's Secretary of Labor and is cited most often as the Republican woman with presidential possibilities.

"We've kidded about a Dole-Dole ticket," says her husband, Senator Robert Dole, a leading presidential hopeful in the post-Reagan era. "Some people think she should head it up." When Elizabeth (known to all as "Liddy") Dole became Reagan's first woman cabinet appointee in 1983, she was asked what her credentials were to head the Transportation Department. Her response: "I know Washington." She's been scoring impressive records ever since the Johnson administration when she got her first Washington job in the Department of Health, Education and Welfare. When Nixon took over, she was one of five Federal Trade Commissioners. Before landing the cabinet post under Reagan, she was his assistant for public liaison, with the sensitive task of appeasing minorities and women who weren't pleased with the President's agenda. She's knows as a moderate with a talent for getting along with people. Says Rep. Lynn Martin (R. Ill.), "John Kennedy said 'Washington is a city of Northern efficiency and Southern charm.' The same is true of Liddy Dole."

Born Elizabeth Hanford in Salisbury, N.C., 29 July 1936, she received her B.A. in political science from Duke (1958) and was student body president. After postgraduate work at Oxford in summer 1959, she went to Harvard, getting a master's degree in education and government (1960) and law degree (1965). Moving on to Washington, she joined HEW (1966-67), specializing in educational problems of the disabled. She practiced law (1967-68) then became executive director of the President's Committee on Consumer Affairs (1968-71) and was named deputy director of the new

Office of Consumer Affairs when it was created in '71. She became a member of the FTC in 1973. In February, 1983, she was sworn in as the nation's eighth Secretary of Transportation after winning unanimous Senate approval. She maintained that position "as the longest-serving Secretary of Transportation" until October 1987.

She married Robert Dole in 1975, and they've become America's handsome, romantic "power couple." Recalling their first meeting, she says, "I don't know what love at first sight is, but I think we were really interested in each other." She has qualities of both the liberated feminist and the traditionally feminine woman. Marrying Dole at age 39, she immediately took her husband's name but noted that "my way of life by the time I met Bob was pretty well set." She became a Republican after marrying Dole, after an earlier shift from Democrat to Independent. Her husband says, "She has her career, I have my career and we have our career—whatever that is." Observers say it is a joint career that could go a great deal further, possibly to the White House. He calls her his "Southern strategy." Liddy insists that were her husband to run for President, she'd step out of the limelight and into the role of candidate's wife. "I don't have to be No. 1 all the time," she says. "I hope I've changed my priorities so that career is not the center of my life."

Placido Domingo

"God must have been in excellent spirits the day he created Placido," exulted legendary soprano Birgit Nilsson about the handsome and strapping (6'2", 225 pound) superstar who appears to be edging out Pavarotti for the title of world's foremost tenor. Born 21 January 1941 in Madrid, to professional singers who specialized in zarzuela, the uniquely Spanish lyric drama form, Domingo accompanied his family's singing troupe on the piano, made his official operatic debut in 1961 in a Mexican performance of La Traviata, and was signed shortly thereafter by the Dallas Civic Opera.

After two years with the Israel National Opera Company in Tel Aviv, he returned to the U.S. in 1965 to perform with the New York City Opera. Time magazine raved that Domingo had "the sweetest and one of the biggest lyric dramatic tenor voices . . . with a taste and elegance unmatched since the days of Jussi Bjoerling."

After gaining international success at Milan's La Scala, London's Covent Garden and the Vienna State Opera, he continues to prosper at New York's Metropolitan Opera House, commanding top fees and performing to sellout houses. Known as a driven performer, Domingo is able to sub for an absent singer at a moment's notice. "I could be performing at a different opera house every night. I have invitations . . . all over Europe, and I have to say no to many of them." His 1984-85 Met season saw him make his U.S. Wagnerian debut opening night in the title role of Lohengrin and his conducting debut later in the season in La Boheme. The charismatic tenor won praise for his Alfredo in Franco Zeffirelli's film version of La Traviata in 1983, followed up in 1984 with a passionate Don Jose in a steamy cinematic Carmen; he was seen as Verdi's tragic Moor in 1986 in Zefirelli's screen version of Otello. His pop recording of "Perhaps Love," with John Denver, was a hit in 1984, and his autobiography—My First Forty Years—was published the same year. He is married to former soprano Marta Ornelas (two children).

Phil Donahue

"What we do," he says, "is provide on daytime TV a relief from the soaps and game shows. . . . I honestly believe we have spoken more thoughtfully, more honestly, more often to more issues about which women care, than any other show." His Emmy-Award-winning program, "Donahue," which moved from Chicago to New York, is unique in tackling contemporary and often controversial (e.g., lesbian nuns; women involved with priests) topics in an innovative discussion format that encourages active audience participation. The audience is mostly female. Erma Bombeck has said, "He's every wife's replacement for the husband who doesn't talk to her. They've always got Phil who will listen and take them seriously."

Born in Cleveland on 21 December 1935, Donahue gained his initial broadcasting experience at his *alma mater,* Notre Dame, where he became an announcer on the university-owned commercial TV station. Eventually he did newscasts and phone-in talk shows. "Donahue" began as a local show in Dayton, Ohio, in 1967. From the start, it was especially popular among housewives. His first guest was atheist Madalyn Murray O'Hair, whose successful 1963 Supreme Court suit had outlawed prayer in public schools. "We were flooded with letters, calls," her host says. "Some were furious, threatening, while others were very positive. We were getting people excited, upset, thinking and expressing themselves. And this is just what we wanted." In 1969 "The Phil Donahue Show" began syndication, and in April 1974, moved to Chicago, where it had its name shortened. Today it's one of the most watched syndicated TV talk shows, with an 18-month waiting list for studio tickets.

Offscreen, Donahue says, he's a "shy, insecure, vulnerable manchild." His first wife (married 1958; divorced 1975) was his college sweetheart, Margaret Mary Cooney, by whom he has four sons and a daughter. In May 1980, he married actress/feminist Marlo Thomas. They live in New York and Connecticut. Donahue's annual salary is reported over $500,000. A "lapsed Catholic" who blames his former sexism on Roman Catholic theology, he's an ardent feminist and member of NOW. In his 1980 bestselling autobiography, *Donahue: My Own Story,* he states, "Television's problem is not controversy. It is blandness." Donahue's 1985 book *The Human Animal* explores human behavior, "the brightest and darkest corners of human nature."

Increasing his visibility, Donahue has co-hosted NBC's "Today" show (April 4-8, 1988) with Jane Pauley, and he made broadcasting history when he became the first American talk show host to tape shows inside the Soviet Union. He has received many awards, including the prestigious George Foster Peabody Broadcasting Award. Of his job, Donahue says, "Having your own talk show is an opportunity afforded very few people. It should happen to everybody. . . . This business of asking the questions and being involved in conversation they stimulate is the most personally satisfying part of all that has happened to me in my career."

Sam Donaldson

Tagged the "best television White House Correspondent in the business" by the *Washington Journal Review* in 1984, Sam Donaldson began serving as chief White House correspondent for ABC News in 1977, reporting on the actions of the President, his administration, and its policies. This included covering the President's daily activities in Washington plus traveling with the President on domestic and foreign trips. It was during one such trip that Donaldson witnessed the assassination attempt on President Reagan in March, 1981. Even with his White House schedule, Donaldson found time weekly to anchor the "World News Sunday" and serve as interviewer and roundtable participant on "This Week with David Brinkley." He turned over his White House post to ABC's Brit Hume when George Bush took office. A respected political correspondent, Donaldson has covered every national political convention since 1964, the presidential campaigns of Jimmy Carter in 1976, Senator Goldwater in 1964, the re-election campaigns of President Carter in 1980, and President

Reagan in 1984, and the campaigns of Senators McCarthy in 1986 and Humphrey in 1972. As a show of his diverse abilities, Donaldson covered such stories as the Vietnam War, the Iranian hostage crisis, and Watergate. He sub-anchored the live broadcasts of the Senate Watergate Committee in 1973 and the House judiciary Committee impeachment investigation in 1974. Recognizing Donaldson's talents outside the White House, *The Washington Journalism Review* named Donaldson "best television correspondent" in 1985, 1986 and again in 1987.

Born in El Paso, Texas, on 11 March 1934, Donaldson was educated at Texas Western College and the University of Southern California. In 1959, at the age of 25, Donaldson began his career with KRLD-TV in Dallas, Texas. Two years later he joined WTOP in Washington, where he anchored the station's weekend news program, and was the moderator and producer of a weekly interview program. He was also the station's political editor for Maryland and Virginia. From here it was not an unlikely jump to ABC for the talented and hardworking correspondent, who wrote the bestselling autobiography, *Hold on, Mr. President.*

Donaldson, twice divorced, married his third wife, Jan Smith, in April, 1983. He is the father of four children: Samuel, Jennifer, Thomas and Robert.

Nelson Doubleday

It's not easy being private about oneself when you're president of one of America's largest publishing companies and a chief executive officer of an eight-station radio group and other communications concerns. But when you pay a record amount for a major league baseball team in the nation's No. 1 market, then lead a campaign to knock off the game's commissioner, you stir up interest, even if you do tell reporters you "simply won't tell" them about the workings of your company, or your personal life." But with a background and upbringing as privileged as an American can have, personal publicity doesn't interest Doubleday.

The publishing house that's printed works from Rudyard Kipling on up to Alex Haley was founded by Nelson Doubleday, Jr.'s grandfather in 1897. And the rapidly-diversifying (though privately-held) company began its broadcasting division in the late '60s. So when the middle-aged heir, born in 1933 and Princeton-educated, took over Doubleday & Co. it was no secret he'd been given a good operation. But he was a good operator himself. Described as a sportsman, not a reader, the ink impresario became the second-largest stockholder in the New York Islanders hockey club. Then on a 1980 trip to Aruba, one of his execs talked him into buying the Mets (How could the great-grandson of Abner Doubleday—the legendary if not actual inventor the national pastime—do otherwise?). A week later Doubleday Co. owned 88 per cent of the National League East's last place team, for which it paid $21.1 million. In hopes of elevating them to the level of his puck-slappers (four straight Stanley Cups) he's attempted to build the Mets through their farm system. Forays into the free agent market have been costly and unfruitful, with disappointing performances from former stars like Tom Seaver, George Foster, and Dave Kingman. But smart TV packaging (stations carrying Mets' games must also take Islanders') has probably doubled his investment. Meanwhile the farm system's harvest, including pitching phenom Dwight Gooden, has made the Mets contenders.

Although he says he spends three times as much energy with publishing as being Mets' chairman, sports investing has made Doubleday the near household-word he is in The Big Apple. At first described as "the other baseball owner" in town, he garnered as many headlines as Yanks' owner George Steinbrenner when in 1982 he led a charge of baseball owners to block Bowie Kuhn's re-election as baseball boss. Kuhn's mistake may have been proposing to force TV revenue-rich teams like New York to share the ante with poorer brethren; publicly, Doubleday decried Kuhn's lack of business sense. Having withstood a management shakeup, Doubleday is keeping mum about the success of the paperback, hardcover, bookstore and other business arms of his empire. He's turned in year-after-profit-making-year since his ascension in the late '70s, however, and was successful in defeating a measure by his sister to turn the company public.

Kirk Douglas

"I came from the east end of Amsterdam, N.Y. and the farther east you went the tougher it got.... To mention to anybody around there you wanted to be an actor was to lay yourself open to a punch in the nose." It's no surprise, then, that the lantern-jawed actor first made his mark on screen (and collected an Oscar nomination) as a tough, wrong-side-of-the-tracks fighter in *Champion* (1949). Also, as someone his second wife once described as "a volcano... with tension spitting out of him like sparks," it's no wonder that he delivered one of his best performances as the tortured Dutch painter Vincent Van Gogh in *Lust for Life* (1955). His dimpled-chin hallmark has been on view in over 70 films including such semi-classics as *The Bad and the Beautiful, Detective Story, Gunfight at the O.K. Corral, Paths of Glory* and *Seven Days in May.*

Born Issur Danielovitch (the name was temporarily "Americanized" to Isadore Demsky) on 9 December 1916 in upstate New York, he was the only boy among six girls in the family of a Russian peddler. Working his way through St. Lawrence University and New York's American Academy of Dramatic Art, he toiled at well over 50 different jobs. ("My life is a B script," he once said. "I'd never make it as a picture—too corny.") Given a pep talk by one of Douglas' AADA classmates, Lauren Bacall, a Hollywood producer took a look at the young actor in a flop play and signed him up to play opposite Barbara Stanwyck in the 1946 drama *The Strange Love of Martha Ivers.* The not-so-wee Kirk has been a Hollywood fixture ever since, and a ranking member of the local hierarchy of actor-producers starting in 1955. His Bryna Productions (*Spartacus, The Vikings*) is named for his late mother.

Married first to drama school classmate Diana Dill (sons Michael and Joel), Douglas then wed photographer Anne Buydens (sons Peter and Eric). Michael Douglas has been a familiar face in the Tinseltown crowd since appearing on the TV series "Streets of San Francisco" and, following in his dad's footsteps as an actor-producer, put out *One Flew Over the Cuckoo's Nest* (1975) and *Romancing the Stone* (1984), among others. Kirk says now he's identified as "the father of Michael Douglas" as often as the other way around.

Michael Douglas

This green-eyed, cleft-chinned actor-producer has carved his own secure niche in the entertainment industry, but some critics and fans still try to credit a part of his remarkable success to his father, Kirk Douglas. "One never gets full credit for anything you do. Like with *One Flew Over the Cuckoo's Nest,* people will say: 'Well, it's his father's project.'"

Douglas *père has* helped him with advice and other favors Michael admits, but he will cherish the day when "I can be independent, someone more than Kirk Douglas' son. My father and I are very different." Kirk lived in poverty as a youth, Michael points out, whereas *he* attended prep school, owned a motorcycle and lived three years in a commune before deciding to work. Professionally, Douglas *fils* considers himself "a late bloomer." It wasn't until he was a senior at University of California when "they forced me to choose a major" that he decided to pursue acting.

From 1972 to 1975, Douglas starred with Karl Malden in TV's "The

Robert Downey, Jr. — CELEBRITY REGISTER 1990

Streets of San Francisco," in the role of Assistant Inspector Steve Keller, the youngest man ever to achieve that rank in the San Francisco police department. "Michael is an ambitious young man, and I used that in the best sense of the word," said Malden at the time. Douglas hit the jackpot in his film producing debut in 1975 when *One Flew Over the Cuckoo's Nest* tallied a whopping $130 million at the box office and pulled in five Academy Awards. His 1979 *China Syndrome* grossed $75 million (helped no doubt by the Three Mile Island fiasco which occurred just as filming was completed) and his 1984 romp, *Romancing The Stone* grossed $63 million in its first six months in spite of mixed reviews. One critic described *Romancing The Stone* as a "slapstick comedy" and contended that Douglas was not right for his role because he was not a comedian. "No matter how fast he moves," quipped the reviewer, "he seems to slow down whatever is going on around him." Undismayed, Douglas produced a sequel in 1985, *The Jewel of the Nile*, with his *Stone* co-star, sultry Kathleen Turner, once again along for the fun and adventure. Bouncing off from the movie bomb version of *A Chorus Line* (1985), Douglas hit it big with *Wall Street* (1987). As *Wall Street's* unscrupulous corporate raider Gordon Gekko, Michael walked away with both the Academy Award and Golden Globe Award for Best Actor in a Motion Picture. He also scored high that year with Paramount's alarming film *Fatal Attraction* (1987). Continually on the move, Michael next took on films that included *The Tender* (co-executive producer, 1988) and *The War of the Roses* (1989).

Born in New Brunswick, N.J., 25 September 1945, Michael is the elder son of Kirk and English-born actress Diana (Dill) Douglas. His parents were divorced when he was 6. In the 1960s Michael was a hippie in California, and remains active on behalf of liberal political causes, including membership in the Committee on Concern, a group of Hollywood activists involved in Central American issues. He is also part owner of the *L.A. Weekly*, an alternative newspaper. Nevertheless, his major concern is his movie career. "Finding a good script is like falling in love with a girl. You read a script like you see a girl. You flirt with her a little bit and then you're hooked." Michael got "hooked" the same way when he met Diandra Lucker, whom he married in 1977 after a courtship of just two weeks. They have one child, Cameron Morrell.

Robert Downey, Jr.

Named *Rolling Stone* magazine's Hottest Actor for 1988, Robert Downey Jr. doesn't take all the attention to heart. After an audition for "Saturday Night Live" he replied, "I was extremely nervous when I auditioned but some things are too important to take seriously." When asked what it meant to be hot, he answered, "destined to be cold." But this young, multi-talented actor is anything but cold.

Born 4 April 1965 in New York, the son of an actress/singer mother and a filmmaker/writer father (Robert Downey, Sr.), Robert was destined for show business. Although born in New York, Downey was raised in California, New Mexico and London. He debuted at the age of five in the motion picture *Pound*, which was produced by his father. Shortly after his debut, Downey starred in three more films produced by his father: *The Greasers Palace* (1972) *Up the Academy*, and *This is America the Movie, Not the Country*. Downey attended Santa Monica High School, but left in the eleventh grade to perform in the movie *Baby It's You*. Proving that he is as comfortable doing drama as he is doing comedy, Downey has tackled such diverse leading roles as a girl-crazy teenager in the comedy *Pick Up Artist* and a cocaine addict in the film *Less Than Zero*. Other films Downey has starred in include: *Firstborn, Tuff Turf, Weird Science, Back to School, Johnny B Good, Rented Lips* and his most recent *Chances Are*. His TV appearances include one season of "Saturday Night Live," and a feature role playing George C. Scott's son in the miniseries "Mussolini: The Untold Story."

Still single, Downey resides in both New York and Los Angeles.

Hugh Downs

This veteran video verbalizer has managed to remain one of the tube's most durable personalities. A long-time host (or as he says, "I'm coming into people's homes; I'm a guest") of ABC's "20/20" TV magazine, the easygoing midwesterner with the incredibly wide range of interests once said, "To be a personality is about the best thing you can be on television. Talent is freakish, but personality can't burn out or be overexposed."

Hugh Malcolm Downs, born in Akron, Ohio on 14 February 1921, had his initial broadcasting exposure in Lima, Ohio as an 18-year old radio announcer. Later, in the early days of television, he became the emcee for the Chicago-based "Kukla, Fran and Ollie" puppet show. In 1954, with his wife (the former Ruth Shauheen, whom he married in 1944) and their two children, Downs moved to New York to share TV pleasantries with Arlene Francis on NBC's "Home" show. In methodical succession, Downs introduced Sid "Caesar's Hour," "The Tonight Show" with Jack Paar, the classic "Concentration" TV game show, the "Today" show, and a PBS senior citizens entry known as "Over Easy." Having been "Barbara Walters' father figure," as he was called when they were paired on the "Today" show in the 1960s, he's again teamed with her on "20/20," ABC's weekly, prime time answer to CBS's "60 Minutes."

Although in recent years the stylish Downs has gained a reputation as a feisty advocate of aging Americans, his own lifestyle is equally as energetic. An all-around sportsman, he sails, rides, flies planes and gliders, scuba dives, and used to race cars until a partner was killed. He's written more than six books and an orchestral suite, as well as acted in summer stock. The science and astronomy buff went on an expedition to the South Pole in the early 1980s where he was given the honor of repositioning the Pole 30 inches in accordance with his readjusted calculation. Another adventure saw Mr. Downs diving in cages off the coast of Australia to film the Great White Shark (aired on "20/20" in May, 1988). "There's not the slightest doubt that I owe the opportunity to do these off-TV things to Jack Paar, and I'm grateful," Downs says of the man who once called co-host Downs, "my Sancho Panza."

Richard Dreyfuss

"I have no memory of not wanting to be an actor," says Richard Dreyfuss, whose stage and screen performances convey charm, intelligence and sensitivity. "It was emotional," he says of his chosen career. "It stemmed from my personality.... I'm an egoist.... I believe everyone is unique, everyone has within him a universe of things never adequately described. Behind all art is ego, and I am an artist and I am unique."

Born in Brooklyn on 29 October 1947, Dreyfuss was raised in Queens and L.A. His first stage experience occurred in Hebrew school productions and he began acting professionally at L.A.'s Gallery Theater. Intending to major in theatre arts at San Fernando Stage College, Dreyfuss "got kicked out of the drama department" for arguing with a professor over Marlon Brando—"the greatest actor in the world, period, bar *none*." Dreyfuss switched majors to political science, and doesn't rule out a future run for the Senate or another elective office. As a conscientious objector, he had to leave college in his sophomore year to do two years of alternative service as a file clerk on the midnight-to-morning shift at L.A. County General Hospital. TV work and a few bit parts in films followed as did stage performances in N.Y. and regional theaters. After seeing Dreyfuss in Shaw's *Major Barbara* at L.A.'s Mark Taper Forum, the screenwriters of *American Graffiti* ('73) recommended him to the film's director, George Lucas. Following *Graffiti* stardom, Dreyfuss won acclaim for *The Apprenticeship of Duddy Kravitz, Jaws, Close Encounters of the Third Kind,* earned an Academy Award for *The Goodbye Girl* ('77) and he played a paraplegic in the 1981 film *Whose Life Is It, Anyway?* More 80's films include *Down and Out in Beverly Hills* (1986), *Tin Men* (1987), *Stakeout* (1987), *Nuts* (1987), and *Moon Over Parador* (1988). Films scheduled for release in 1989 include *Fifty, Let It Ride,* and *Always*. In addition to his motion pictures, Dreyfuss created, produced, wrote, and hosted "Funny, You Don't Look 200!" on ABC-TV.

At 5'6", Dreyfuss tends toward chubbiness. Outspoken in his opinions, Dreyfuss asserts that the "motion picture business is run by corporate thieves," with "the level of corruption . . . taken for granted all over the place." Richard married Jeramie Rain (real name: Susan Davis) on 20 March 1983. They have two children: Emily and Benjamin.

Allen Drury

"Drury is very much a writer with a cause, and his cause is to expose the confusions of the liberal mind in American politics," observes a critic. "To this endeavor he brings a remarkable instinct for issues and an intimate knowledge of the political and journalistic world of Washington. Those qualities have produced a series of novels that our future historian would be wise to consult if he wants to know something about the feel and shape of mid twentieth century politics." Other critics have suggested that much of Allen Drury's writing lacks a concrete base in fact and thus a certain credibility and that the politicos portrayed on Drury's pages are little more than "ideological wind-up toys." But Drury keeps on writing and his loyal fans keep on reading. His first novel, *Advise and Consent,* not only made it to the bestseller lists and won him a Pulitzer Prize but was also adapted for film.

Born Allen Stuart Drury, 2 September 1918 in Houston, Texas, he was educated at Stanford University and began a career in journalism as editor of the *Tulare* (Calif.) *Record*. He has written, along with a collection of newspaper articles, a personal diary and a notebook on the Nixon Administration, over half a dozen novels (the list includes *Capable of Honor,* 1966; *Preserve and Protect,* 1968; *The Roads of Earth* (sequel to *The Hill of Summer,*) 1984; and his 1986 release, *Pentagon*. Their premise, according to one critic, is always the same: "the struggle between the forces of a God-fearing Americanism and hordes of journalistic, acronym-inventing, intellectual, peace at any price liberals."

Peter Duchin

"You can have lousy food, a minimum of decorations, but if you have people up and dancing all night, they'll have a wonderful time," says the bandleader/socialite whose popularity with hostesses is such that he's often booked five and six years in advance for parties. Inheritor of the dark, sophisticated good looks of his pianist father, Eddy Duchin, as well as Pop's skill at the keyboard, Peter Duchin has been a pet of the party set and a regular in the nation's better ballrooms since 1962, when he made his New York debut at the Maisonette of the St. Regis to rave reviews. He now limits his personal playing dates to around 100 a year, but also supervises all of the music at the Waldorf-Astoria Hotel. "I could play more," says Peter, "but the travel is hard and frankly I don't want to get burned out."

Son of Café Society's favorite pianist and heiress Majorie Oelrichs, Peter Duchin lost his mother only six days after his birth on 28 July 1937. Because of his father's heavy travel schedule (including a World War II stint in the Navy), Peter was raised in the home of his godparents, the W. Averell Harrimans. Eddy died of leukemia when Peter was just 13, but the musical seeds had already been sown. Peter formed his own Dixieland jazz group at Hotchkiss, his first orchestra as a freshman at Yale. Married in 1964 (and divorced in 1982) to former Cheray Zauderer, he is the father of three children, Jason, Courtnay and Colin. He married Brooke Hayward in Stowe, Vermont, in 1985. On the dance floor, he says, "the kids today are really into the music of the '40s." His most requested song among all age groups? The *Casablanca* classic, "As Time Goes By."

Patrick Duffy

"Who shot Bobby Ewing?" the cliffhanger at the close of the 1983-84 "Dallas" season, didn't set off the media fireworks of "Who shot J.R.?" in 1980, but the future career of Patrick Duffy as a leading television light nevertheless seemed secure. He was in at the start of the CBS-TV blockbuster in 1977, playing the straight-arrow "good brother" (Larry Hagman was the bad one) in the squabbling family of oil millionaires and, like the show, was an immediate hit. Says the classically-handsome 6'2" actor about his small-screen alter ego: "He is sentimental but a realist, determined but passive. He is also a happy person with a good temper and a principled set of mores and values. About 80% of Bobby is me." At Duffy's request, "Dallas" writers bumped off Bobby at the end of the 1984-85 season. Duffy returned to "Dallas" in the fall of 1986.

Born (and christened) on St. Patrick's Day, 1949, Duffy was raised by his tavern-owning folks in, first, Townsend and later Boulder, Montana, and eventually, Seattle. (Both his parents were murdered in the mid-eighties during an unexpected act of violence in their quiet tavern.) Patrick's career decision to become an actor was clinched when he was accepted into the Professional Actors Training Program at the University of Washington, one of 12 students selected out of 1200 applicants. ("I was incredibly fortunate . . . when we weren't involved in a project, we were studying with mime teachers from France, gymnasts from the Olympics, and even jugglers from Barnum and Bailey's Circus.") His first job after graduation was as "Actor in Residence" at Washington State, where he met his ballet-dancer wife, Carlyn. Later, while going through the mandatory making-the-rounds lean period in both New York and Hollywood, he supported himself with construction jobs and architectural work between acting jobs. Fittingly, he was remodeling a boat in 1976 when he was signed for his first starring TV role as "The Man from Atlantis" in which he learned to talk underwater and outswim dolphins. In addition to his long-running Bobby Ewing role on "Dallas," Duffy also directed a number of episodes and has appeared in TV movies: "Strong Medicine" (1985), "Alice in Wonderland" (1985), "Too Good To Be True" (1988). He was also seen in the big-screen release *Vamping*. He is a favorite host of the Thanksgiving Day Parade. He and his wife (two sons) are active followers of Nichiren Shoshu of America, a form of Japanese Buddhism.

Michael Dukakis

1988 was a good year, a bad year, and a tiring year combined for Michael Dukakis. After a grueling Presidential campaign trail coupled with intense media exposure, Dukakis's high hopes were flattened on Election Day. Although the Democrats kept faith till the last minute, the Dukakis/Bentsen team did not match up to the Republican's Bush/Quayle ticket. With his dream diminished, Dukakis returned home to resume his role as Governor of Massachusetts.

Born (3 November 1933) and bred in Brookline, Massachusetts, Dukakis

Olympia Dukakis

has lived in the Bay State all of his life. The son of Greek immigrant parents, Michael Stanley Dukakis spoke his first words in Greek: "monos mou," which means "by myself." Inheriting a family trait to strive for success (his grandfather Styliano Dukakis set across the Aegean Sea from Pelopi to find fortune on the Turkish mainland; first cousin Olympia Dukakis won an Academy Award for Best Supporting Actress), Dukakis enrolled at Swarthmore College, studying political science. After graduating in 1955 with high honors, he served in the U.S. Army in Korea. Immediately following the service he returned home and studied law at Harvard (graduated, 1960). Delving into politics, he became a member of the Massachusetts House of Representatives from 1963-1971. Gaining respect and political power, he was inaugurated as the 65th Governor of the Commonwealth on 2 January 1975. Looking for ways to save money, Dukakis set out to see how serious the deficit really was. "What we found was appalling.... The state was in worse financial shape than any other state in the Union. If we had not taken immediate and drastic steps, we would rapidly have become the New York City of state governments." Under his administration, the state's economy piled up, unemployment dropped to 4.3 percent by October, 1978; two hundred fifty thousand new jobs were added to the state's economy; crime between 1975-78 dropped when Dukakis left office in 1979, Massachusetts State Government had a budget surplus of $200 million. Defeated in 1978 by Democratic candidate Edward J. King, Dukakis won back his seat as Governor in 1982.

Dukakis was introduced to Katherine (Kitty) Dickson by a former girlfriend, Sandy "Peaches" Cohen; the couple were married 20 June 1963. They have three children, John, Andrea and Kara. The family have shared some hard times together, but staying close-knit has helped them to conquer the odds. Admitting to the public her drug dependency and alcohol abuse, Kitty Dukakis has been in and out of rehabilitation centers. It was a crushing blow to both husband and wife when their political aspirations were quashed in the 1988 Presidential Election. Dukakis likes to unwind by walking three or four nights a week (he finished 57th in the 1951 Boston Marathon), playing tennis, or tending to his front-yard vegetable garden at the family's Victorian row house in Brookline.

Olympia Dukakis

"People would see my name, at least at first, and assume that I must have been born in Greece and spoke English with a heavy accent. The fact was, I was born in Massachusetts and had a bit of a New England accent. Later, I was styled an 'ethnic' actor, meaning I got to play a lot of ethnics, Italians and so on. My big breakthrough in TV was that I was 'Aunt Millie' in the spaghetti sauce commercials. And for a while there, I played so many prostitutes that my resume looked like I ran a house of ill repute," Olympia Dukakis recalled during a 1988 interview with *The Record*. Her portrayal of the unsentimental mother in *Moonstruck* brought her worldwide recognition and numerous awards (L.A. Film Critics, Golden Glove, Academy Award). When talking about her performance in the movie *Moonstruck* she says: "Who is this woman to compare to some of the really challenging characters I've played on the stage? Try Hecuba [in Euripides' "The Trojan Woman"]; try Luba [Ranevskaya in "The Cherry Orchard"]; try Mother Courage [in Bertolt Brecht's "Mother Courage and Her Children"]. But then my friend Austin Pendleton tells me, 'Olympia, you're not understanding what it's all about. You're getting these awards because all those other, more challenging women you've played shine through in Rose.' And maybe that's the truth of it."

Born in Lowell, Massachusetts, on 20 June 1931, she is the cousin of Michael Dukakis, the Governor of Massachusetts and the defeated 1988 Democratic candidate for president. Centering her career on the theatre, Olympia studied for the stage. She graduated from Boston University with a Bachelor of Arts Degree. Getting started was not that easy. She told *The Washington Post*, "If your name is Olympia Dukakis, that's it, bang. The doors close, the shades come down. You play Italians.... I've been 'discovered' about six times, y'know." With her husband, actor Louis Zorich, she launched the Whole Theatre, involving some actor friends. Today, it is a well-respected Equity company. Between "discoveries," Dukakis worked as an acting teacher at NYU from 1967 to 1979, then as a master instructor from 1974 to 1983. She also taught at Yale University in 1976.

Other significant Olympia performances include, on stage: *Social Security* (Broadway), *The Marriage of Bette and Boo* (Obie Award), *Curse of the Starving Class*, *A View From the Bridge* (Theatre World Award), *Peer Gynt*, and *A Man's a Man* (Obie Award); on television: "FDR—the Last Days," "One of the Boys," "The Seagull," "King of America," and a continuing role on the daytime soap "Search for Tomorrow"; on screen: *Steel Magnolias*, *In the Spirit*, *Daddy's Home*, *Working Girl*, *Made for Each Other*, *The Idolmaker*, *Rich Kids*, *Deathwish*, and *John and Mary*.

Angier Biddle Duke

A familiar figure in the social swim, this blue-blooded former diplomat paddled into world headlines in 1966 when, as U.S. Ambassador to Spain, he took his children for a dip in the Mediterranean to prove that there were no radioactive aftereffects from an American H-bomb lost in the waters off Spain's southern coast. Then, after remaining high and dry in Madrid until 1968, he returned briefly to his old job as chief of protocol at the White House and thence on an ambassador's mission to Denmark. Departing from government service in May of 1969, he returned to the private sector until 1973 when he became New York City's commissioner of Civic Affairs and Public Events. From 1979 until 1981 he was the U.S. Ambassador to Morocco.

Born 30 November 1915 in New York, an amalgam of Durham tobacco Dukes and Philadelphia banking Biddles, "Angie" Duke was educated at St. Paul's and Yale. "During World War II," says Duke, "I found to my surprise that I had qualities of leadership"; he rose from private to major in the Air Force. Entering the Foreign Service in 1949 in the Embassy in Buenos Aires, he received his first ambassadorial assignment in 1952 when President Truman dispatched him to El Salvador as, at 36, one of the youngest ambassadors in th history of the American foreign service. After non-government work from 1954 to 1961 as president of the International Rescue Committee, Duke returned to the striped-pants set at the beginning of the Kennedy administration when JFK gave him the job of the New Frontier's chief of protocol. He arranged White House meetings for over a hundred heads of state, but his most difficult—and saddest—assignment came in 1963 when he was in charge of protocol as government leaders from all over the world gathered in Washington for Kennedy's funeral. Married and divorced twice, Duke became a widower when his third wife (the late Maria Luisa de Arana of Madrid) was killed in a plane crash. He married the fourth, Robin Chandler, in 1962, and is the father, in all, of four children and two step-children.

Doris Duke

When newspapers in 1971 headlined "The Gospel Truth About Doris Duke" they weren't spilling any X-rated beans. Rather lovely in a democratic sort of way was the story that followed, telling how the woman who had often been called "the world's richest girl" had joined the congregation of a black church in Nutley, New Jersey, and was singing in its choir every Sunday. Well, almost every Sunday, except when she's shuttling between the green-gardeny environs of her 2,500 acre Somerville, New Jersey, estate—the gardens there are open to the public (a walk through the greenhouses is the distance of one mile)—and her other residences: an apartment in Manhattan, her Newport home—"Rough Point," guarded by ferocious dogs (thanks to her and her millions, Newport has been restored)—and Shangrila, her Oriental-style home in Honolulu.

Born 22 November 1912 in New York, she was the only child of James Buchanan Duke, a later-day Horatio Alger hero who started out with two blind mules and a plug of tobacco and ended up with the American Tobacco Company. (Inside the New Jersey place, besides boasting tennis courts, a theater and an Olympic-size swimming pool, there also is a huge old sculptured bull commemorating the Bull Durham tobacco which made her father's fortune.) She was thirteen years old when he died and left her a fortune upwards of $100 million. "Dee-Dee," as she was called, was raised by her Southern-poor, Northern ambitious mother. She came out in Newport the year money came in, 1930, and started on a post-deb marry-go-round with onetime Minister to Canada, James Cromwell. When the marriage ended in 1941, he issued the statement, "A gentleman doesn't divorce his wife, even for adultery," and entered a claim for $7 million. ("He didn't get a thing," one acquaintance said happily.) Next came Dominican Ambassador (and lover) Extraordinaire, playboy Porfirio Rubirosa, in 1946. His bride presented him with a document that guaranteed him a paltry $25,000 a year—and one year later there was a divorce. She has been single ever since. Simplify, simplify seems to have been the theme. Privacy before publicity, and good for her. According to one friend "she is truly one of the great givers," which is true, and according to her Newport neighbor Noreen Drexel, "she is a remarkable woman, but it's hopeless to try to talk to her." Another friend adds: "She's just plain Jane." Her greatest luxury is "not to be known as Doris Duke."

Patty Duke

There wasn't much time for hopscotch or any other childhood diversions. From the time she was discovered at seven, Patty Duke was a working actress making the rounds. By age twelve, she had starred in more than 50 TV shows and played on stage opposite Kim Stanley, Helen Hayes and Laurence Olivier. She was 13 when she exploded as a superstar playing the young Helen Keller in *The Miracle Worker*. Wrote Walter Kerr: "She is a very great actress who only happens, at the moment, to also be a child." Duke followed it with the film version and at 16 collected an Oscar as best supporting actress. Then came her own Emmy Award winning sitcom series. "The Patty Duke Show." In her early twenties in 1968, she could sum it all up by telling writer Rex Reed, "I had days when I did nothing but cry for nine hours straight." And no wonder; her life (which began 14 December 1946) in Reed's words "reads like Elsie Dinsmore." Her cabdriver father and restaurant-cashier mother called it quits early with their marriage, and Patty's budding dramatic gifts were urged into bloom by the John Rosses, a husband-wife manager team who had no children of their own and so took in their young protégée. Diction, singing lessons and drama classes were interspersed with toothpaste commercials, TV shows and theatre appearances. (To rid her of her heavy New York accent the Rosses made her sit for hours with a tape recorder trying to learn a British accent.) Preparation for the Helen Keller role took 15 months of learning what it was like to be deaf (ear plugs), then blind (eyes closed), and then mute. The play, which opened in 1959, lasted two exhausting years. Eventually the girl beloved by tube regulars as "The All-American teenager" wound up on the big screen as a ravaged alcoholic in *Valley of the Dolls* and offscreen, on a psychiatrist's couch. She was married and divorced first from director Harry Falk, Jr., second from rock promoter Michael Tell.

She married actor John Astin in 1973 ("I inherited John's three sons") and had two children with him (Sean, born a year before their marriage, and Mackenzie, born in 1973) while continuing to act in TV movies such as: "Me, Natalie" (1969), "My Sweet Charlie" (1970), "Captains and the Kings" (1976), "Having Babies" (1978) and "The Women's Room" (1980). That marriage ended in 1985. During the filming of a television movie Patty fell in love again, and married Michael Pearce on 15 March 1986 in Lake Tahoe. They have a son, Kevin Michael Pearce. In 1983, she won "most popular actress in a new TV series" in the short-lived "It Takes Two." In 1984, she was warm and motherly Martha Washington to Barry Bostwick's George on the CBS miniseries about the Father of Our Country, and in 1985 starred as the first woman president in the TV series, "Hail to the Chief." The green-eyed snappy five-footer is charged with "positive think": "The one constant . . . is to try to keep a sense of humor about everything in life. . . . In some infinitesimal way, I would like to believe that I could leave things a little better than when I found them." Elected in 1985 to head SAG (Screen Actors Guild), she held that position through the middle of her second term. In 1987 her revealing autobiography *Call Me Anna: The Autobiography of Patty Duke* hit the bookstands.

David Dukes

Typecasting has never been a problem for actor David Dukes. He has established himself in theater, television and feature films by playing a variety of characters. From Edith Bunker's would-be rapist on the CBS series "All in the Family," to helpful diplomat Leslie Slote in the ABC miniseries "The Winds of War" and its sequel "War and Remembrance," to Dr. Frankenstein in *Frankenstein* on Broadway, Dukes has been a working actor whose face is probably better known to the public than his name.

David Dukes was born 6 June 1945 in San Francisco, California. He attended Mann College. The successes of the 6-foot, 175-pound actor with dark brown hair and hazel eyes must be attributed to his chameleon-like ability to maneuver easily between the fields of stage, television and screen, creating memorable characters along the way. Dukes made his Broadway debut in 1971 in *School for Wives*. Other theater appearances include: *Don Juan, The Play's the Thing, The Visit, Holiday,* and *Rules of the Game*. He also appeared in *Key Exchange* with Kate Jackson and Peter Riegert at the Westwood Playhouse; *Another Part of the Forest* at the Ahmanson, and *Every Boy Deserves Good Favor* at the Dorothy Chandler Pavillion. *Travesties*, in which he performed on Broadway and in Los Angeles, earned him a L.A. Drama Critics Award. Other Broadway performances were *Amadeus*, in the role of Salieri; *Dracula, Bent,* with Richard Gere; and role of the French diplomat in *M. Butterfly*.

Television has cast Dukes in different eras, from the 1700's to modern day. He appeared on the series "Beacon Hill" and in the TV movies "The Triangle Factory Fire" and "Sentimental Journey," but it is in the miniseries format that Dukes has found his niche. He co-starred with Lesley Ann Warren as the "nice guy" Michael in "79 Park Avenue" and with Barry Bostwick in "George Washington." Dukes portrayed a slick con man in "Space" co-starring Bruce Dern, played Leslie Slote in "Winds of War" and "War and Remembrance," and had roles in "Kane & Abel" with Peter Strauss and in the PBS miniseries "Strange Interlude." Dukes managed to fit in feature films between miniseries and theater roles, appearing in *The Wild Party* with James Coco and Raquel Welch, *A Little Romance, The First Deadly Sin* with Frank Sinatra, *Only When I Laugh, Without a Trace, The Men's Club, Date With an Angel, Deadly Intent* and *See You in the Morning* with Jeff Bridges.

Dukes married poet and writer Carol Muskes on 31 January 1983. They have a daughter, Annie Cameron.

Keir Dullea

He is an ancient Jon Whitcomb illustration come to life (6'1", Nordic-looking). His first two films, *The Hoodlum Priest* and *David and Lisa* cast him as an immature, repressed upper-middle class kid. ("*The Fox* was really the turning point. It was a sexual role and the women were the ones who had the problem.... And I looked older.") Other films include *Madam X, De Sade, Black Christmas, Bunny Lake is Missing, The Thin Red Line* and Stanley Kubrick's *2001, A Space Odyssey* (he also appeared in the sequel *2010* released in 1985). Of *2001* he says, "It is the only movie I have made which I grew to like better and better. It created a brand new vocabulary in film making." His Broadway credits include the Tony Award winning *Butterflies Are Free* (1969) followed by a revival of *Cat on a Hot Tin Roof* and *Doubles* (1985), and his TV films include "Law and Order," "The Hostage Tower," "No Place To Hide," and a miniseries based on Aldous Huxley's *A Brave New World*.

Although he was born in Cleveland (30 May 1936), Dullea (pronounced Delay) considers Greenwich Village his native habitat. For 25 years his Scottish-Irish parents ran a bookstore there. After attending private schools in New York, he studied briefly at Rutgers University, then hitchhiked to San Francisco, where he worked as a carpenter before enrolling at San Francisco State college in 1955. ("I had decided to be an actor, I hurried back to New York and studied with Sanford Meisner.") He seldom discusses his first wife, actress Margo Bennett. His present wife is former fashion director Susan Coe, whom he married in 1971. The pair reside in Connecticut where they run a professional workshop for actors, writers and directors, *The Theatre Artists Workshop of Westport*.

Faye Dunaway

Try to find the real woman aside from her powerfully dramatic and disparate on-screen portrayals. She's been a gangster in *Bonnie and Clyde* (for which she was nominated for an Academy award); the despotic Eva Peron in the TV drama "Evita Peron;" the silently suffering yet anxiously ambitious Wallis Simpson (on her way to becoming the Duchess of Windsor) in TV's "The Woman I Love;" the evangelist Aimee Semple McPherson in "The Disappearance of Aimee." She won her second Oscar nomination for her performance in Roman Polanski's *Chinatown*, and she won the award itself as the driven career woman in Sidney Lumet's *Network*. So who is she?

"No more..."
"Say what mommie?"
"Christina, I said—no more..."
"What *Mommie Dearest?*"

"Christina, no more wire coat hangers!" Screech, bang, wham... what a part: the ghost of Joan Crawford played to lights-camera-action perfection, the egomaniacal actress and monstrous child abuser, depicted with amphetamine alacrity by Dunaway in the 1982 film.

"I felt I needed to break into a simpler woman," she said when she accepted the lead on Broadway in 1983 of William Alfred's *The Curse of the Aching Heart*. In Alfred's *Hogan's Goat*, her first stage appearance at age 25, she earned high praises and attracted the attention of movie mogul Sam Spiegel, who launched her career in Hollywood. Born in Florida 14 January 1937, the daughter of a career Army man, Dunaway lived with her parents in such diverse places as Utah, Germany and other countries overseas. After majoring in drama at the University of Florida, she attended the Boston University School of Fine and Applied Arts, where her work led her to audition for New York's Lincoln Center Repertory and a role in Arthur Miller's *After the Fall*. Her glowing notices in *Hogan's Goat* were followed by many splendid film parts in *Hurry Sundown, The Arrangement, The Thomas Crown Affair, Little Big Man, The Wicked Lady, Barfly, Cold Sassy Tree, The Burning Secret, Crystal Or Ash, The Handmaid's Tale*, and the TV series "Ellis Island." She donned armor for her role as Queen Isabella in the 1985 miniseries "Christopher Columbus." Her most recent work is the Lina Wertmuller film *Up to Date* (1989).

Divorced from both her songwriter-composer husband Peter Wolf, and second husband Terry O'Neil (a photographer), she has one son, Liam (born 1980). Referring to her haughty reputation among Broadway and Hollywood insiders, she says: "I am a perfectionist, as you no doubt heard. The scariest thing is not the critics or the audience, but the demands I am making on myself."

Sandy Duncan

Sprightly Sandy Duncan has charmed Broadway and television audiences with her dancing, singing and dramatic talents and All-American good looks for over twenty years and shows no signs of slowing down. Her popularity helped her overcome the controversy she encountered in 1987 when she was hired to replace the fired Valerie Harper on the retitled television series "The Hogan Family." The show continues to be a hit with Duncan in the lead. Despite the demanding TV schedule, she continues to polish her singing and dancing talents performing in numerous AIDS benefits with her husband, singer/dancer/actor/choreographer Don Correia.

Sandy Duncan was born 20 February 1946 in Henderson, Texas, and raised in Tyler, Texas, where her family moved when she was nine months old. She made her theater debut at age 12 in the State Fair Music Hall production of *The King and I* in Dallas. It wasn't until 1965, however, after a year of college, that she moved to New York City intent on pursuing an entertainment career. While studying acting at the New York City Center Repertory Company she landed her first jobs as a lead dancer in its various musical productions. Performing in regional theater, summer tours, and Off-Broadway productions, Duncan got her big break in the 1969 Broadway musical *Canterbury Tales*, for which she received her first Tony Award nomination as Best Supporting Actress in a Musical. More awards followed in 1971. Her second Tony nomination came for her starring role in *The Boyfriend*. The role also garnered her a New York Drama Desk Award and the Outer Critic's Circle Award. 1971 also found Duncan starring in her first television series, "Funny Face," which earned her an Emmy nomination. To cap off the year, she was honored with the Gold Medal Photoplay and the Golden Apple Awards. Her second series, "The Sandy Duncan Show," premiered the following season in 1972. It too was short-lived but Duncan appeared on television often, guest-starring on shows, hosting two specials—"Sandy in Disneyland" and "The Sandy Duncan Special"—and "aging" from 20 to 70 years old in the miniseries "Roots" ('77), which earned her another Emmy nomination. She has also been a successful commercial spokesperson. In addition to her television work and film appearances—in Neil Simon's *Star Spangled Girl* and the Disney films *Million Dollar Duck* and *The Cat From Outer Space*—Duncan's theater career was still going strong. She won a Theatre World Award for the Off-Broadway production *Ceremony of Innocence* and a Los Angeles Drama Critics nomination for the 1976 Mark Taper Forum production of *Vanities*. Arguably, Duncan's greatest Broadway success occurred when she assumed the role made famous by Mary Martin in the 1980 production of *Peter Pan*. It brought her critical raves and her third Tony nomination. Her latest Broadway hits include *My One and Only* ('84) and *Five, Six, Seven, Eight, Dance!*, with husband Don Correia at Radio City Music Hall.

Duncan's native state of Texas honored her as she became the first female recipient of the CoCo Award, the highest honor given to those in the entertainment industry by the Dallas Communication Council. Duncan married Correia, who is her third husband, on 21 July 1980. They have two sons, Jeffrey and Michael. They currently reside on Los Angeles's west side, where in her spare time Duncan enjoys yoga, dance and time with her family.

Dominick Dunne

"Like a lot of other observers of the scene, I have been absolutely fascinated by how public the rich have gone the last seven years," said novelist Dominick Dunne, who has been on intimate terms with the powerful, the privileged and the wealthy throughout his career. "The days of the quiet rich seems to have vanished. It is in this arena that I have placed the action of *People Like Us*." A Literary Guild Selection two months before its May, 1988, publication date, Dunne's newest novel looks at "real" society and the "nouvelle" society, which explains why it was eagerly awaited by those New Yorkers who thought they might find themselves disguised amidst the pages. It's a "social history, not just gossip," says columnist Liz Smith in the *Daily News* (New York), who found herself in the book in the guise of a "dull reporter" named Mavis Jones. "In this regard," she wrote, "it is more accurate than the very columns you peruse every day, for they all pull their punches. Dunne does not." But TV audiences will get the opportunity to see for themselves. ITC plans to turn *People Like Us* into a miniseries as did NBC with Dunne's 1985 novel, *The Two Mrs. Grenvilles* (which was loosely based on a celebrated society shooting that occurred on Long Island in the 1950's). Aside from his society-based novels, Dunne's words have been found in *Vanity Fair* magazine since 1984. As a contributing editor, he was the first journalist to interview Imelda Marcos after the deposed leaders of the Philippines were forced to flee to Hawaii. This writer of the famous and the fascinating has interviewed Gloria Vanderbilt, Elizabeth Taylor, Diane Keaton and the explosive Hollywood Collins sisters (Joan and Jackie). His articles have also covered a wide variety of events, such as the Geneva auction of the late Duchess of Windsor's jewels, the trial of Claus Von Bulow, a Monte Carlo weekend of the soon-to-be-ex Mrs. Sylvester Stallone Brigitte Nielsen, and Mortimer's, New York's smart set's favorite eatery. A collection of Dunne's *Vanity Fair* pieces have been published under the title *Fatal Charms* (1987).

Born in 1926 in Hartford, Connecticut, Dunne was the second of six children. His grandfather, for whom he is named, was a philanthropist, his father, Richard, a prominent heart surgeon. Drafted out of school, young Dunne served in World War II where, during the Battle of the Bulge, he saved a soldier's life; at 18 he was awarded the Bronze Star. The war over, Dunne returned to school, graduating in 1949 with a BA in Liberal Arts from Williams College in Massachusetts. Since he had originally planned to become an actor, Dunne headed for New York City. But he abandoned that plan and took a job as a stage manager in a relatively new field: television. After working on NBC's "Howdy Doody Show," Dunne was stage manager for a number of leading dramatic and musical shows of that period. Married in 1954 to Ellen Griffin on her family's Arizona cattle ranch, Dunne decided to take his new family (which consisted of two sons: Griffin, born 8 June 1955, currently an actor and producer, and Alex) to Hollywood in 1957 where he began a career in films and TV that was to last for twenty-five years. After serving as executive producer of "Adventures in Paradise" and president of Four Star (a TV company owned by David Niven, Charles Boyer and Dick Powell) Dunne moved on to producing feature films: *Boys in the Band* (1970), *Panic in Needle Park* (1971), *Ash Wednesday* (1973) and sister-in-law Joan Didion's bestseller *Play It As It Lays* (1973). Dunne also worked with his brother, John Gregory Dunne, who wrote the screenplays for *Panic* and *Play*. After a number of attempts at screenwriting himself, in 1980 Dunne left Hollywood, moved into an Oregon cabin and began to write his first novel. Later he moved to New York to finish his novel and start another career. Keeping a journal through the trial of the man who murdered Dunne's only daughter, Dominique, Dunne transformed the piece into an article, "Justice," that appeared in *Vanity Fair* in April, 1983.

Now divorced, Dunne lives in a New York City East Side penthouse where he gathers goodies for his next expose of the rich and famous.

Duran Duran

"We jumped on the bandwagon. We got our feet in the door as quickly as we bloody well could. We needed something to give the band a sort of personality—and it worked," said lead singer Simon LeBon. But the fashion leather and frilly lace donned by members of the photogenic new wave band was only one ingredient. Along came MTV and the age of video rock, and the musicians, with their pretty-boy faces and sultry rock and roll, stirred a kind of hysteria among British and American teenagers rarely seen since the emergence of The Beatles.

Keyboardist Nick Rhodes grew up with bass guitarist John Taylor, in Birmingham, England, listening to Roxy Music and David Bowie and dreaming about being a rock star. They started the band while still teenagers, and named it after a character in the Jane Fonda movie, *Barbarella*. After several transformations in personnel, they picked up lead guitarist Andy Taylor, drummer Roger Taylor (none of the Taylors are related) and singer LeBon. With their first hit single, "Planet Earth," in 1981, followed by "Girls on Film," the band began to ease off on its fashion plate image associated with the "New Romantic" movement in British new wave. Said Roger Taylor, "After a long time of having to spend an hour to prepare for a show, it got a bit boring. It just didn't seem to make sense anymore." With Capitol Records's publicity machine in overdrive, the band toured extensively in the U.S. and abroad after the release of each album, and were always met by hordes of pubescent girls, screaming, crying, and creating mayhem in hopes of catching a glimpse of their idols, or perhaps, even a lock of hair to take to their pillows at night. In England, the band's fans (which include the Princess of Wales) are called "Durannies." Said Andy Taylor, "It's been said that we could probably go up onstage and fart and it wouldn't make any difference."

1985 was a bad year for the boys, when Simon LeBon narrowly escaped drowning in a sailing accident off the coast of England, coinciding with the decision for the group to split temporarily. John and Andy went out on their own, joining Robert Palmer and Tony Thompson for a project called "The Power Station," while Simon, Nick and Roger formed "Arcadia." It wasn't until 1988 that the group known as "Duran Duran" released another album together (*Notorious*) only this time there were only three members: Simon Le Bon (vocals), Nick Rhodes (keyboards), and John Taylor (bass).

Robert Duvall

He's risen in the Academy from nominee for Best Supporting Actor to highest Oscar honors as Best Actor and incontestable star status. One of "the most resourceful . . . technically proficient . . . remarkable actors in America today," according to the *New York Times*'s Vincent Canby, Robert Duvall is a director's dream because of the way he locks into a character, and because he demands a natural relaxed set. "The actor's the guy that's gotta be given the room, because it's his face that's going up there," he says. "The two worst things a director can say are, 'Pick up the pace,' and, 'Give me more energy.'" But the days when he physically assaults equally headstrong directors appear to be over; he's putting that tension into his roles. "I guess most of my parts have been complex, contradictory. They mostly have a hard side to them, the more interesting side."

Robert Duvall was born in San Diego in 1931 into the family of an admiral who wanted his son to go to Annapolis. The lure of the theatre, however, proved stronger than that of the sea, but he ended up making a mandatory tour of the Army anyway. With his G.I. Bill he took up studies at New York's Neighborhood Playhouse, and made his screen debut in the 1963 *To Kill a Mockingbird*. He made his first major impression on moviegoers with his portrayal of the Corleone family's *consigliere* in *The Godfather* films, for which he was first nominated for an Oscar. His other two nominations came for stunning performances as the American colonel who loved the smell of napalm in the Vietnam flashback *Apocalpse Now*, and as the Marine ace at war with the brass of his own family in *The Great Santini*. But it was his 1983 role as an ex-country music star in love with a young Texas widow in *Tender Mercies* for which he was awarded an Oscar as Best Actor. More movies followed: *The Lightship* (1986), *Let's Get Harry* (1986), *Colors* (1987), *The Handmaid's Tale* (1989) and *Convicts* (1989).

The protean film, stage, and TV actor has also been recognized as a talented director for his film, *Angelo My Love*, about modern Gypsies. On the sending end of the megaphone, Duvall instructs, "No frigging acting," to his charges; he says the true test of proficiency is not to appear to be at work. His second marriage is to actress Gail Youngs.

Bob Dylan

A prophetic friend of this songwriting performer once said, "He is not the same person he was ten or five years ago. He is unlikely to be the same five or ten years hence." Sure enough, the mid-western Jew who converted to born-again Christianity in the late '70s, had returned to Judaism in the early '80s and even had his son bar mitzvah'd in Jerusalem. Bob Dylan's music, which had tended toward rock and folk gospel, continued to prick listeners' consciences, be they politicians, enemies of the state of Israel, or the promiscuous young.

He has retained his immense popularity founded on his role in the '60s as a brilliant and original shaper of contemporary music. His present tours continue to play to large throngs around the world. He chose the name Dylan due to his awe for the poet Dylan Thomas and because, as he says, "I had a lot to run away from." He legally changed his name from Robert Allen Zimmerman, only to later legally change it back. Born in Duluth, Minn., on 24 May 1941, he would muse that, "He not busy being born is busy dying," and this refugee from small-town affluence was born many times after he stepped from a subway train in Greenwich Village in 1961. With his south-western drawl, guitar, and anti-oppression lyrics, he evolved from a proletarian revolutionary into a rock outlaw, and then, after a motorcycle accident and three-year absence, to country bard. For a while, a friend called Dylan "a man on a razor—stoned, under terrible pressure, protected and babied by The Band [his group]; [like] Hendrix, Joplin, just before they died." In 1971, the poet of protest let it all hang out with his semi-autobiographical tome, *Tarantula*, which, according to the *New York Times*, was "enough to keep ten psychiatrists busy for a month." In 1978 he was in a four-hour surrealistic flick, *Renaldo and Clara*, starring his former wife of twelve years, Shirley, and Joan Baez. And as he neared thirty years of stardom, the writer of "Mr. Tambourine Man" remained "Like a Rolling Stone;" forever being reborn. He even changed his identity in 1988 by joining a group of other celebrity musicians calling themselves "The Traveling Wilburys." Sharing the spotlight with George Harrison, Tom Petty, the late Roy Orbison and Jeff Lynne, Dylan reaped the rewards of being in a hit group. Other solo albums include: *Biograph* (1985), *Knocked Out Loaded* (1986) and *Down in the Groove* (1988).

Sheena Easton

What do James Bond and Sonny Crockett have in common? Both private eyes have been serenaded by a 5'" pop pixy, strong-voiced, two-time Grammy winner Sheena Easton. This talented Scottish import first boarded the *Billboard* pop charts with her 1981 single "Morning Train," followed by "Modern Girl" and the title song of the 007 movie *For Your Eyes Only*. Subsequent albums include: *Music Money and Madness* (1982), *Best Kept Secret* (1983), *No Sound But a Heart* (1987) and *The Lover in Me* (1988). Discussing her latest album, she says: "As you get older, you get better in a lot of ways because you have more experiences to draw on. . . . As an artist, I want to keep growing. That's my driving force."

Sheena Shirley Orr was born circa 1959 in Belshill, Scotland. Perfecting her craft at the Royal Scottish Academy of Music and Drama, she attributes most of her powerful image to her upbringing: "I believe it comes from my mother instilling a strong work ethic in me. She taught me that you can't get anything for nothing. . . . I realize that I can be somewhat abrasive when I'm trying to get my point across, but at least people know where I stand and what I mean." Jumping on her early recording success, Sheena shined in the spotlight between 1981 and 1983. Appearing on music/variety shows, talk shows and even hosting "The American Music Awards," Easton became a household name. Discovering it hard to keep the momentum, Sheena found that a brief two-year slump turned out to be a productive period. Taking the time to record new material, she released a "suggestive" single, "Sugar Walls," in 1985. The song, written by her good friend Prince, was labeled pornographic by Tipper Gore and the Parents Music Resource Center. Although there was criticism, Sheena was back on the charts again with that tune and "Strut." Teaming up with Prince, she recorded the 1987 duet "U Got The Look" and her 1988 album *The Lover In Me*. They also collaborated on a song, "Love 89," recorded by Patti LaBelle. Sheena recounts, "Basically, the song says that no matter who you are, there's a place for you with God—your love for God isn't an external thing, it comes from your heart."

Having the ability to be flexible with her career and test her talents, Sheena enjoyed playing opposite Don Johnson as his "Miami Vice" couple-of-episodes wife. She admitted to *People*: "I'm not Meryl Streep, and I'm not trying to play Lady Macbeth. . . . But I wanted something where I could draw upon my experiences. I liked the 'Miami Vice' character." Sheena, who is a daily exercise fanatic herself, acts as spokesperson for a chain of health spas and is very much involved with the "Rock Against Drugs" campaign. Her first marriage to singer-actor Sandi Easton lasted only eight months and her 2-year marriage to Rob Light also ended in divorce. She philosophizes: "I got married to the wrong person, both times." Promising to continue turning out quality product, Sheena insists: "I just don't turn up at the studio and sing. I'm there at 4:00 a.m. when the producers are cutting the drum sounds. As long as it's my name on the album cover, I want to be true to my fans and not give them anything that I'm not artistically satisfied with myself."

Clint Eastwood

He's made a big name for himself as The Man With No Name, Dirty Harry Callahan, and the aptly-named Rowdy Yates in TV's "Rawhide." He created one of the catchwords of the 80s; even President Ronald Reagan once invited a recalcitrant Congress to "make my day." Usually playing the anti-social anti-hero, this box-office lodestone now also produces and directs films that, following the hit spaghetti western *Hang 'Em High*, have grossed nearly a billion dollars. But the law-and-order-keeping actor with the screen's most famous glare says, "I really don't like to be the focus of attention. . . . Maybe being an introvert gives me, by sheer accident, a certain screen presence, a mystique. People have to come and find out what's inside me. If I threw it all out for them to see [off-screen], they might not be interested." Eastwood's tough, snarlingly-silent, gun-blasting characters have kept moviegoers interested enough, however, to support him in 40 plus movies in over 35 years of minimalist acting.

The tall (six feet four, 190 pounds) and rugged Eastwood was born in San Francisco, 31 May 1930. He grew up during the Depression, trailing a father who pumped gas in towns along the West Coast. "My family was too busy moving around, looking for work, for me to know what I wanted," he says. "Then I was drafted into the Army and was sent to work in Special Services where I met a lot of actors, so I thought I'd give that a shot." In Los Angeles, having "tripped across the movie business," he endlessly auditioned for commercials and was thrown off the Universal studios lot in the late 1950s only to land on his feet as he lassoed his cowpunching role on "Rawhide" from 1959 to 1966. Like most Western heroes, he's a political conservative, although he asserts that his acting shouldn't be taken too seriously. "When I go to the movies . . . I don't worry about social injustice." Neither have most of his characters. While Eastwood calls to mind former Holywood tight-lipped heroes like Gary Cooper and John Wayne, the German-Spanish-Italian sequels *A Fistful of Dollars*, *For a Few Dollars More*, *The Good, the Bad and the Ugly*, and *Hang 'Em High* froze him into the public consciousness as a lone gunman at odds with the law. His Dirty Harry series, about the San Francisco detective who frequently cuts procedural corners and kills aplenty, didn't tarnish the image. But Eastwood has also lightened up with comedic modern cowboy parts, and an occasional cop role in which he doesn't have all the answers, even with a .356 Magnum tucked under his jacket. He's had a reputation as an on-schedule, on-budget producer-director ever since his first try at it, *Play Misty for Me*. Now divorced from long-time wife Maggie (to the tune of a $25-million settlement), he runs the Hog's Breath Inn in Carmel, the town where he served as mayor for two years (1986-1988) and where he lives when not at his Sherman Oaks home. The physically trim and well-disciplined Eastwood believes the same qualities ought go into making movies. "With Francis Coppola's budget," he remarks, referring to the $31.5 million that went into *Apocalypse Now*, "I could have invaded some country." Son Kyle was seen in his 1982 film, *Honkytonk Man*, and ex-longtime companion Sondra Locke graced a number of Eastwood films. More popular movies include: *Pale Rider* (1985), *Heartbreak Ridge* (1986), *The Dead Pool* (1988) and *Bird* (1988). The latter film about jazz great Charlie Parker won an Academy Award for best sound in a motion picture. Eastwood's 1989 film is *Pink Cadillac*.

Blake Edwards

His first hit film, *Breakfast at Tiffany's* ('61), containing a mixture of moods ranging from slapstick to poignance, typifies his versatility. He followed this romance with the suspenseful *Experiment in Terror* and the devastating *Days of Wine and Roses* ('62). Then came his biggest success, the original *Pink Panther* ('63), which established him as a master of a kind of physical comedy seldom seen since the days of the silents. An equally popular sequel. *A Shot in the Dark* ('64) quickly followed, again featuring Peter Sellers' incomparably inept Inspector Clouseau character.

Born in Tulsa, Okla., 26 July 1922, he was raised from the age of three in California, where his stepfather was a Hollywood production manager. Much of his childhood was spent on film sets. After graduating from Beverly Hills H.S. he acted in films in the early 40s. He served in the Coast Guard during WWII, and by the late 40s was acting in his own film scripts. In 1949 he created the Dick Powell radio series, "Richard Diamond, Private Detective." Following more low-budget screenplays in the early 50s, he got to direct two Frankie Laine 'B' films. *Mister Cory*, a 1957 Tony Curtis vehicle, established him as a promising writer-director, and he fulfilled that promise directing two popular TV series: "Peter Gunn" and "Mr. Lucky." As early as this period, he was collaborating with composer Henry Mancini, who has scored most Edwards films. A temperamental man devoted to yoga, judo, mystery stories and jazz, he has a son and daughter from his first wife Patricia, whom he divorced in 1967 after 14 years of marriage. His second wife (since 1969) is Julie Andrews, who has starred in several of his films: *Darling Lili* ('69), *The Tamarind Seed* ('74), *10* ('79), *S.O.B.* ('81), *Victor/Victoria* ('82) and *The Man Who Loved Women* ('83), a Truffaut remake. Together they adopted two Vietnamese orphans, who reside with them in California and also in their Swiss chalet. His self-imposed European exile resulted from his feeling that his films of the late 60s and early 70s were sabotaged by studio executives. "I thought I was going to have a nervous breakdown," he says. "Withdrawn and very, very, angry," he revived the *Pink Panther* series to continued success in the mid-70s and—once again "bankable" after these films and *10*—made his scathing Hollywood satire, *S.O.B.* which constituted an act of revenge. He wrote and directed *A Fine Mess* (1985); directed and co-wrote the screenplay for the Bruce Willis vehicle *Blind Date* (1986); and directed, executive produced and wrote "Justin Case" for an ABC-TV movie (1988). His 1988 work includes the film *Sunset*.

Ralph Edwards

The man has an affinity for success. He took an unknown retired judge, surrounded him with a format that fit him like a glove and parlayed it into a most remarkable television success: "The People's Court," a syndicated series.

Born Ralph Livingston Edwards, 13 June 1913 in Merino, Colo., he began his radio career in Oakland, Calif., when, as a 15-year-old, he went to work as a writer on a local station for a dollar a script. Later working his way through the University of California, he was an announcer, actor, producer, writer, effects man—and janitor—at Oakland's Station KTAP. He spent a year with various San Francisco stations before heading for New York on the shaky promise of a small part in a Broadway play. He arrived and found the show closed but things picked up when he talked himself into a staff announcer's job at CBS, and by 1939 he was doing as many as 45 network shows a week. In 1940 he parlayed an old parlor game into the popular "Truth or Consequences" (1984 marked its 43rd consecutive year), thereby launching his lucrative career as a producer of such entertainment packages a "Place the Face," "It Could Be You" and the perennial favorite, "This Is Your Life" (radio debut 1948) which had a 23-year run. Married in 1939 to the former Barbara Jean Sheldon (three children), he's pleased to have made his mark not only in TV history but also on the map of the U.S.: on the tenth anniversary of his first radio success, the town of Hot Springs, N.M., officially changed its name to Truth or Consequences, the first and probably last time a radio show has ever been honored in such a way. Edwards has made substantial contributions to the Heart Association and the March of Dimes via his radio and TV shows. He is the recipient of three Emmys and the Eisenhower Award (1946).

Elaine

The records of the Internal Revenue Service list her simply as a "restaurateur," but habitués of her establishment at 1703 Second Avenue on Manhattan's Upper East Side know she's much more than that: psychiatrist, literary agent, news analyst, counselor, ticket broker, social arbiter, banker, and also excellent waitress. These are merely a few of the sub-occupations Elaine Kaufman engages in from her stand near the cash register of Elaine's, the saloon-turned-salon that is the hardest-to-get-a-good-table-at eating spot in New York. (Yes, people actually bother to eat between people-watching and being watched—the cuisine is Italian.) Under the yellow canopy that shelters the entrance come the most glittering names of stage, screen, politics, and fashion. To regulars like Woody Allen, Kurt Vonnegut, Swifty Lazar, Farrah Fawcett, Bobby Short, George Plimpton, and Jacqueline Onassis, she's the Jewish Mother Courage with 14-karat gold chicken soup. She's there protecting, keeping the lights of celebrity low, the press flacks away—although the next day, somehow, mama's special stars are named in Suzy's column.

Elaine was born on 10 February (before Dunkirk) in Manhattan. She attended Evander Childs High School in the Bronx and then started out as a breadwinner in her late teens, working in a stamp auction store on 42nd Street and later as a pitchwoman for hair products on the upstate dime-store circuit. She learned the restaurant business as a waitress-of-all-work at a Greenwich Village hangout called the Portofino, and in 1963 with a fellow waiter decided to go into business for herself. In those days Second Avenue and 88th Street was social Siberia, but after two lean years, the coterie of writers she befriended downtown followed her uptown. It became their club, for richer and poorer—when they couldn't pay their bills because their royalty checks were late or if there hadn't been a royalty check in a long time, Elaine put it on their tab. "It's a village place—it's just uptown," Elaine explains. "People don't understand that. They want to make something else out of it." For a while it was a secret, discovered at about the same time Pop Art and the Rolling Stones were discovered. It was Dorothy Killgallen who first wrote about it as *the* new watering spot. Then, like the fire of a thousand paparazzi bulbs flashing, the joint, as they say, was hopping. Elaine wears giant square horn-rimmed glasses, worries about her weight which she has managed to reduce very nicely thank-you-very-much, and hasn't uttered a dulcet tone in years. She's not exactly your "lily maid of Astolat," but Lancelot, were he in town, would surely drop by to see her nonetheless. Elaine is that sort of person, and Elaine's is that sort of place. The original one room has expanded to two. In 1980 Elaine pulled a second stool up next to hers at the bar and married Henry Ball. In 1984 the couple were estranged.

Nora Ephron

In her third collection of humorous, insightful essays *Scribble, Scribble*—the first was *Wallflower at the Orgy*, the second was *Crazy Salad*—our latter day Dorothy Parker (this pearl writes movies, too: *Silkwood, Modern Brides, The Lady Eve* and *Murder*) wrote that she'd overdosed on "star writers," on celebrity and "the first person singular pronoun." Did she realize she was being prophetic? "Journalists are interesting. They just aren't as interesting as the things they cover." *Heartburn*, her 1983 roman à clef about what soured in her marital stew when her husband, star journalist Carl Bernstein (they divorced in 1985) was discovered having an affair while she was pregnant with their second child, became the crème fraiche of the celebrity-intellectual set, eaten up and discussed bite-by-bite by the gossip-starved. The 1986 Film version of the book starred Meryl Streep as Nora and Jack Nicholson as Carl.

She was born 19 May 1941 to the successful screen-and playwriting team of Henry and Phoebe Ephron. Their 1961 Broadway hit, *Take Her She's Mine*, was inspired by their daughter's letters home from Wellesley College. "Everything is copy," Phoebe told Nora: "You're a reporter. Take notes." Her daughter remembers: "Our dinner table was like a talk show. The best way to get my parents' attention was to tell them a funny story." After five years as a reporter for the *New York Post* where she covered events from Lynda Bird Johnson's wedding to fires in Brooklyn, she decided to go freelance, and soon her by-line appeared in magazines such as *Cosmopolitan, Esquire* and *New York* magazine. She wrote about herself. Her consciousness-raising group, her rocky first marriage to writer Dan Greenburg, her 10th reunion of her Wellesley class and her small breasts—"the hang-up of my life." "Her kind of writing," comments fellow writer Joe McGinniss, "makes a reader feel as if she were calling on the phone at 10 A.M. to bounce a few impressions off you over coffee." Nora married her third husband, Nicolas Pileggi (28 March 1987), and conceived two new screenplays: *Cookie* (1989) and *Harry, This Is Sally* (1989).

Ahmet Ertegun

"I don't have a different persona for each group," says the dapper founder and chairman of Atlantic Records who with his wife Mica is part of one of the most sought-after couples in New York's social scene. "They all laugh at the same jokes and drink the same whiskey. But I will say that the conversation might be a little different. I can't for example, talk to a social type in New York about T-Bone Walker's last recording session and I don't think many of my rock and roll groups would be interested in the intricacies of the conflict between Greece and Turkey.... But on the whole it works out nicely for me because the social parties usually end at around 11 and the music people don't even begin until midnight, so I can go to both. And I don't even have to change my clothes," he told *M*, the men's monthly.

Born 31 July 1923 in Istanbul and brought to Switzerland at two when his father was appointed to the League of Nations, Ahmet Ertegun lived in Paris and London before moving to Washington at the age of 13. Although he had been collecting jazz and blues records since he was seven, it was the first opportunity for Ahmet and his older brother Nesuhi (died 1988) to hear favorites in live performances. On Sundays the brothers would invite musicians to the Embassy for brunch and "a post-meal jam session." Nesuhi began making records first, producing New Orleans archive jazz for his label, Crescent, while Ahmet studied classical philosophy for a masters' degree from Georgetown University (having graduated from St. John's College in Annapolis). He started recording Boyd Raeburn's modern jazz in 1947 and a year later, with partner Herb Abramson, created Atlantic Records.

In 1967 Atlantic was sold to Warner Communications for $17 million. From his all-white office at Atlantic he has guided the musical destinies of the likes of Ray Charles, Mabel Mercer, Ruth Brown, Crosby, Stills, Nash and Young, Emerson, Lake and Palmer, Yes, The Bee Gees, Cream, Buffalo Springfield, Sonny and Cher, The Rascals, King Crimson, Judy Collins, Aretha Franklin, Led Zepelin, Laura Branigan and the Rolling Stones, to name just a few. "Hang around Ahmet for a while," commented Michael Watts in the British trade paper *Melody Maker,* "and you get an idea where Mick Jagger got some of his style.") Ertegun, at the request of both presidents Carter and Reagan, has been an unofficial liaison between Turkey and America. He sits on the board of many charities and is a friend of Henry Kissinger and Mick Jagger. A little-known fact is that he is also a composer of songs—"Chains of Love" and "Sweet Sixteen" for Joe Turner and "Don't You Know I Love You" for the Clovers. His wife Mica and partner Chessy Rayner have a decorating company called Mac II. It was rumored in August 1989 that Ertegun would step down from his position as Chairman in the near future.

he's also affiliated with numerous charitable organizations, for whom, like his product endorsements, he does TV and print ads.

Julius Erving

Some pro athletes have changed their teams' fortunes, and thus earned the nickname, "The Franchise." But Dr. J's first league commissioner termed him "The League" for the arenas packed with fans eager to see his inimitable leaping ability, his body control and his completely-faceted game. His exciting mid-air moves spawned a generation of twisting, dunking younger players, and he's the game's most-beloved player. "I get up in the air and do whatever comes into my mind to make a play," he said. "I don't make moves for effect, although I love to hear the crowd enjoy them."

Born in Hempstead, Long Island, New York, on 22 February 1950, Julius Winfield Erving II was raised, with his sister and brother, by his mother who worked as a domestic. His father deserted the family when he was three and his mother remarried. A good student, he took up basketball at age ten and was all-league at Roosevelt High School. There, a friend named him "the Doctor" since Erving had "more moves than Carter has pills." After averaging 27 points and 20 rebounds in his sophomore junior seasons at the University of Massachusetts, he was picked for a U.S. collegiate team to tour Europe and the U.S.S.R. The new American Basketball Association was challenging the NBA for fans by luring its players away and by signing outstanding college players before their eligibility had run out, so in 1971, after three years at U Mass, Erving signed a half-million, four-year contract with the Virginia Squires. By his second year, the Afro'd six-fee-six court wizard led the circuit with a 31.9 scoring average, using his unstoppable, playground-inspired repertoire of dunks and layups to score over opponents. The struggling ABA and Erving gained wide recognition for the 1972 ABA va. NBA All-Star game. At one point, he broke loose on a one-on-one fast break against the venerable Oscar Robertson. "Big O" wisely gave ground after "the Dr." leapt from the top of the key, and, as he jetted through the lane, squeezed the ball in one of his huge hands, whipped it helicopter-like above his head, then, having been airborne for 19 or so feet, drew back his arm and jammed the ball through the rim.

Understanding his drawing power, if not binding legalities, he signed a contract with the NBA's lowly Atlanta Hawks while still with Virginia. But the NBA's Bucks had rights to him in that league, so arbitration was began to settle the quagmire. Before it had done so, the ABA's New York Nets acquired him in exchange for payment to both Virginia and Atlanta. Erving's contract was improved. The Nets, who played on Long Island, Erving's home, won the 1973-74 ABA championship behind his league-leading scoring, and they won again in the ABA's final season before it merged with the NBA in 1976-77. Erving's ability to attract fans was a factor in the NBA's assent. Although he said he thought his life was pre-destined by God ("I've tried to stay on the right side of The Man, and I've been blessed"), he once again showed initiative when it came to his contract, and demanded Nets' owner Roy Boe to renegotiate it. When Boe couldn't meet the record $3.5-million, five-year terms, the Philadelphia 76'er's obliged, and signed him. Almost immediately the Sixers were contenders; he, meanwhile, was the league's MVP in 1980-81, and made the all-time NBA's team. To insure, however, that an inadequate cast wouldn't cost Philly another championship (they had lost in the finals three times), new owner Howard Katz acquired free-agent Moses Malone before the '82-83 season. The two led Philly to its near-record wins that year and the NBA title.

Erving played his last professional game on 6 April 1987. His Philadelphia contract insures him more than $100,000 a year for his first 15 years of retirement. He owns a Philadelphia condo and a Roosevelt, Long Island, mansion with 17 rooms where he, Southern-born wife Turquoise, and their four children live. A devout Christian who attended chapel before games,

Boomer Esiason

His father explains: "Our first two children were girls. My wife's third pregnancy was so different. The baby was kicking all the time. I said, 'This can't be a girl. It's got to be a boomer because he's kicking too much.' In my day, the punter was always called the boomer. Two or three people overheard me and picked up on it. Whenever they called they'd ask, 'How's Boomer doing?' It's a real life story. He had his nickname before he was born." A southpaw quarterback, Boomer Esiason is the handsome athlete who led the Cincinnati Bengals to the American Football Conference championship, followed by Super Bowl XXIII against the San Francisco 49ers. As wide receiver Cris Collinsworth said, "There's no question, he was the main reason we were able to turn it around." The team's guard Max Montoya insists: "It was more than his stats. Boomer was definitely a force out there at every moment, every play,"

The NFL's top-ranked passer through the 16th week of the season in 1988, he was born Norman Esiason on 17 April 1961 in East Islip, Long Island. An honor roll student at East Islip High School, he was also the object of professional and college baseball scouts. A twist of fate landed Boomer on the football field rather than the diamond. He had believed he would make his career in professional baseball, but instead, he says, "I signed my letter of intent to Maryland, which was the only major school that recruited me for football, before my senior year in baseball. After my senior year in baseball, every major school in the country wanted to give me a scholarship for baseball. I even had the Seattle Mariners come to my house. I'm saying, but I've already signed a letter of intent to Maryland. What am I supposed to do? I've never been through this before. I decided to honor my decision to go to Maryland, but I thought I was going to be allowed to play baseball there, too. And I wasn't allowed. To this day that was a good decision. But I was really ticked off that I couldn't play." However, with a gut feeling his high-school coach, Sal Ciampi, knew that Esiason would end up on a football field, "I could just picture him with that white hair being the quarterback. He just has that charisma."

Boomer holds the team record for most touchdown passes in a game, he was the AFC Offensive Player of the Week three times, and he was named the Bengals' Man of the Year in 1987 for his outstanding contributions to charitable and community causes. He is a national spokesperson for the National Arthritis Foundation and an active member of Long Island Celebrity Classic Golf Tournaments. Off the field he likes to spend time with his wife, Cheryl; they live in Villa Hills, Kentucky. He enjoys listening to jazz music and playing golf. On the side, he is one of the owners of the Waterfront Restaurant in Kentucky.

Gloria Estefan (Miami Sound Machine)

Gloria Estefan—of, with, and Miami Sound Machine—is currently one of the hottest groups in the nation. The band won an American Music Award in 1989 as favorite group, in addition to being nominated for other major music awards. Their album *Let It Loose* (1987) stayed glued to the Billboard album charts for over 57 weeks. Hit singles from that album included the pretty ballad, "Anything for You" and the uplifting "One, Two, Three."

The up-up-and-away success-story of Gloria Estefan, her respected record-producer husband, Emilio, and Miami Sound Machine, began, rather logically, in the city of Miami, which is still the band's home base. The aggregation made its first big impression on the American musical Zeitgeist back in 1985 with a single called "Conga" (from the LP *Primitive Love*, 1986). Subsequent top-tenners on the pop singles chart have been "Words Get in the Way" and "Rhythm Is Gonna Get You."

Intense on bringing their "brassy, latin-flavored dance rhythms" in person to their fans, Gloria and her Sound Machine continue to tour world wide. When they performed at New York's Radio City Music Hall, in 1988, they had the whole audience standing on their feet. Not another fly-by-night group, this explosive bunch will be around to record many more singable albums. Cementing her solo power, Gloria Estefan released the album *Cuts Both Ways* in 1989 featuring the hit single "Don't Wanna Lose You."

Emilio Estevez

A member of the "Brat Pack" Emilio Estevez joins his peers Rob Lowe, Judd Nelson, and Andrew McCarthy as a rising young superstar of the screen. His early movies hinted at his appeal, paving the way for major roles in feature films. Born in Manhattan (1962) into a theatrical family, it's no wonder that talent runs in his genes. The oldest son of actor Martin Sheen and his wife Janet, Estevez was set from the start for a theatrical career. He graduated from high school in Santa Monica, California, and with his brother, actor Charlie Sheen, chose to follow in his father's footsteps. With teenage roles in the movies *The Outsiders* (1982), *Tex* (1982) and *Repo Man* (1984), Emilio became a recognizable face. *The Breakfast Club* became an even more popular film; his performance as an athletic student forced to stay for detention with fellow cast members Paul Gleason, Anthony Michael Hall, Judd Nelson, Molly Ringwald and Ally Sheedy made him the toast around the town. Not only was his next film, *St. Elmo's Fire* (1985), a hot movie ticket, but the theme song was a pop hit. Expanding his creative energies, Estevez wrote the screenplays and starred in *That Was Then This Is Now* (1985) and *Wisdom* (1986). The latter film showcased a spellbinding performance as a young man obsessed with robbing from the rich and giving to the poor. More films followed, including *Maximum Overdrive* (1986) *Stakeout* (1987) and *Young Guns* (1988). He also appeared in a couple of stage productions (*Mister Roberts, Burt Reynolds Dinner Theatre*), in addition to various television movies. Some TV works include: "Seventeen Going on Nowhere," "To Climb a Mountain," "ABC," "Making the Grade," and "In the Custody of Strangers." He filmed a special telefilm "Nightbreaker" with his dad, Martin Sheen, for the TNT network.

Estevez is the father of two children, Taylor and Paloma; his ex-companion, model Carey Salley, filed a paternity suit against him in 1986.

Evans and Novak

"The Evans and Novak of . . . " is a tag frequently applied to successful collaborative efforts in a wide variety of fields, a tribute to the high recognition factor of this journalistic duo who "traverse the shifting political sands of domestic and foreign affairs with the surefooted familiarity of camels on the Sahara run." Called by the *National Observer* "the best reporting team in Washington," Evans and Novak are noted for their rapidly moving datelines, their in-depth studies (almost miniature monographs) of key electoral constituencies during national and local political campaigns, and the utilization of sharp investigative techniques that have often yielded headline-making scoops. Whether teaming up five times a week with their "Inside Report" (syndicated in more than 200 newspapers), distributing their bi-monthly newsletter, the "Evans-Novak Political Report," or holding forth on their weekly Cable News Network "Evans & Novak" program, when Evans and Novak speak, people—and Presidents—listen.

Senior tandem member, aristocratic and urbane Rowland ("Rowley") Evans, was born 28 April 1921 in White Marsh, Pa., and prepped at the elite Kent School in Connecticut. He put in two years at Yale and four in the Marines during World War II before joining the Associated Press in 1945. Dark, brooding and tenacious Robert Novak (born 26 February 1931 in Joliet, Ill.) is a product of the University of Illinois and the U.S. Army during the Korean War. He joined the A.P. in 1954, transferred to its Washington office, and worked in the nation's capital for the *Wall Street Journal* from 1958 until he joined forces with Evans in 1963. The two newsmen have demonstrated their canny understanding of Washington's ways in such co-authored books as *Lyndon B. Johnson: The Exercise of Power* (1966); *Nixon in the White House: The Frustration of Power* (1971) and *The Reagan Revolution* (1981). Solo efforts include writing for periodicals and appearing on the major news interview programs, with Novak a regular on the "McLaughlin Group" weekly TV political roundtable. Evans, in collaboration with the former Katherine Winton, has produced two children, as has Novak in collaboration with former Geraldine Williams. Competing Washington newshounds, while conceding that "no one does more legwork" than E&N, insist as well that "It's really one of the wonders of Washington that, because of the social acceptability of the two of them, people simply let Evans and Novak get away with more than they possibly could otherwise."

Linda Evans

As Krystle Carrington in "Dynasty," television's hit series revolving around the wealthy Carrington clan of Denver, Linda Evans has become one of the most publicly applauded stars on the small screen. Not only have her devoted fans suffered with the most virtuous and patient woman on television (who gradually is getting more "claws" written into her character) but her women viewers (and men, too) have been awed by the beauty and appeal of the "over 40" actress.

Born Linda Evenstad 18 November 1943 in Hartford, Connecticut, she moved with her parents to North Hollywood when she was six months old. Her father was a decorator and painter, her mother a housewife. Painfully shy as a child ("I grew up just trying to cope"), she attended Hollywood High, and while there a friend dragged her to a casting session of a television commercial, which she got. After appearing on TV's "Bachelor Father" she signed an MGM contract. She later studied with Lee Strasberg. In 1965 she won a continuing role on ABC's "The Big Valley." She also appeared in the TV series "The Hunter." By choice her movies, in which she invariably played a glamour girl, have been few. "I'm simply not an aggressive type," she once admitted, "If I get a role that's fine. If not, that's all right, too. I've worked in show business only when I wanted to." Since the "Dynasty" success, she has taken a different approach to her career. She has formed her own production company and is negotiating to produce television movies.

Evans has been married twice. Her first well-publicized marriage to Producer John Derek began when she was in the "Big Valley" series. "It was the most wonderful life I can imagine any woman having," Evans recalls, "he cares about beauty more than anyone I've ever known. He would have made a wonderful knight of the Round Table." They separated in 1973, divorced two years later, and in 1976 Evans married real estate tycoon Stan Herman; it ended three years later. "I had marriages that didn't work," Evans says candidly. "In doing the thing that I least wanted to do—be by myself—I've discovered something really beautiful, which is I'm going to make the best partner for someone in the whole world now because I've found myself. The character Krystle is learning this, too."

Keeping busy, Evans appeared in the ABC-TV epic "North & South Book II" (1985), in CBS's "The Last Frontier" (1986), and the film *Dead Heat* (1988).

Chris Evert

She was philosophical in 1984 about the 12 consecutive losses and the abdication of her spot as top-ranked woman player in the world to Martina Navratilova. "Maybe we (athletes) need a year or two after being No. 1 to get our feet back on the ground and our heads out of the clouds. I'm not going to kill myself if I retire No. 2." Indeed, this unperturbable master of the baseline needed to take no such measures as she wound down a grand net career. Chris had been the world's No. 1 seed seven times, a winner—five times at the French Open, and six times at the U.S. Open, a three-time Wimbledon winner—and owner of the longest women's winning streak until Navratilova broke it.

Christine Marie Evert had a tennis racket placed in her hand when she was five by her father, James, a teaching pro in Fort Lauderdale who thought tennis provided a wholesome atmosphere in which to raise his five children. She first captivated national fans when, after winning 56 consecutive matches, she appeared at Forest Hills in 1971 with brightly-colored ribbons in her hair and lost a hard-fought semi-final to top-seeded Billie Jean King. Along with a superb ground stroke and devastating two-handed backhand, she had been trained by her father to be impassive and to *never* lose her temper. She admitted she became "a machine, so mechanical," which may have accounted for the loss of public affection for her. But in 1979 she married British Davis Cup player John Lloyd (after finally breaking off a tempestuous engagement to U.S. net star Jimmy Connors), an event that seemed to coincide with a slump in her play but, oddly enough, a resurgence in her popularity. As a human capable of losing, and possibly also because she was an American often playing against the Prague-born Martina, she again became fan-favorite "Chrissie."

As a player she continues "living like a gypsy" and adds to her lifetime tennis earnings of $5 million with a like income in endorsements. She's also won 14 cars as prizes, although she says among them were "none that I wanted to keep." A while after her 29th birthday on 21 December 1983, she reflected: "I still love to compete. The hatred I have of losing motivates me more, I think, than the love I have of winning." In 1985—having won at least one Grand Slam event for 12 consecutive years (a record)—she had her 17th Grand Slam victory when she bested Martina in the French Open. That year also saw publication of *Lloyd on Lloyd*, an update on her 1982 autobiography, *Chrissie*.

Although Chris was doing well career-wise, her marriage to John Lloyd went off course; the couple divorced in 1987. Finding romance again, Chris fell in love with Andy Mill and they married in Boca Raton, Florida, on 30 July 1988.

Douglas Fairbanks, Jr.

"Besides Alistair Cooke, no man is as skilled at hosting a TV series as the tanned debonair Douglas Fairbanks Jr. He has style, sophistication and knowledge, qualities that are rare in the medium," wrote Kay Gardella in the *New York Daily News* when Fairbanks began the PBS "Gilbert & Sullivan" series in 1989.

He was born in New York City 9 December 1909, son of the swashbuckling silent film star Douglas Fairbanks and Anna Beth Sully, who were divorced when he was nine (whereupon his father married Mary Pickford). He attended private school in Pasadena, and was tutored in Paris until he made his first film for Jesse Lasky, *Stephen Steps Out*, at age 14. It was not until 1927 that he came into his own as an actor, playing *Young Woodley* in Los Angeles. This led to a meeting with Joan Crawford and eventual marriage (1928). They were divorced five years later and it was not until 1939 that he married Mary Lee Hartford (she died in September, 1988). The couple had three children together, Daphne, Victoria and Melissa. In World War II Doug earned the British D.S.C. as the only U.S. officer to command a flotilla of raiding craft for Mountbatten's Commandos and in 1949 the Queen invested him with an honorary knighthood.

"One of the problems of acting today," Fairbanks says, "is that too many people want to be overnight successes." Among his many films: *Morning Glory* with Katharine Hepburn (1932), *Stella Dallas* with Barbara Stanwyck (1935), *The Joy of Living* with Irene Dunne (1940) and *Ghost Story* (1981). He lectures occasionally, divides his time between homes in Palm Beach and New York, and summers mostly in England (when not touring in the straw-hat circuit). His autobiography, *Salad Days*, was published in 1988.

John Fairchild

"People often seem to believe I'm some sort of strange wild character. I've been called everything from a Mafia Godfather to a homosexual, but I actually believe I'm an old square," says John Fairchild, chairman of the board and chief executive officer of the periodicals originated by the Fairchild family. It was John's grandfather who started the chain, strictly for clothing manufacturers, in 1905 with *Women's Wear Daily*. Upon his death the helm passed on to John's father, Louis.

Born in Newark, New Jersey, 6 March 1927, and educated at Princeton, John Fairchild met Jill Lipsky shortly after graduation and they were married at the Little Church Around the Corner in 1950 (four children: Jill, Steven, John and James). His father sent him to Paris in 1954 to head the Paris bureau, and while covering his first fashion show he found himself seated in the rear of the room, ignored in favor of the editors of *Vogue*, *Harper's Bazaar* and the *New York Times*. ("I vowed then to change that, to make them all sit up and take notice of me and *Women's Wear Daily*.") When he returned to New York, he told his father of his plan to change the character of the paper. "I had been influenced by Eugenia Sheppard's column, *Inside Fashion*, humanizing fashion by writing about the people who wear clothes as well as those who were designing and making them." However, he pushed the humanizing further by reporting gossip and scandal and making saucy comments about society. Very soon *WWD* became a must for all the beautiful people from coast to coast and appeared on the desks of executives who had never heard of it before. It wasn't long before Fairchild became the most feared man in the fashion world. John, though, didn't stop. In May, 1972, the first copy of "W" was on the newsstands with its glossy large-size format and color pictures and ads, a complete contrast to *WWD*. *M* (as in men), a monthly magazine, came out in 1983 and was snapped up by both sexes. Any social event in New York would love to have John and Jill on its guest list, but they are inclined to stay home. "If we go out what I like is dinner for six," says John. Most of their leisure time is spent in France, where they have a home in Provence that is very hard to find.

Peter Falk

"There is," says a friend of this tough talking actor, "something absolutely terrifying about the courage, the nakedness and the honesty of his work."

Suzanne Farrell

There is also something of the candid maverick about a man who has starred in dozens of films and TV shows, has twice been an Oscar nominee (*Murder, Inc.*, 1961; *A Pocketful of Miracles*, 1962), has won three Emmys (he won in 1962 for his portrayal of a truck driver in "Price of Tomatoes" and a decade later for his "Columbo" series) and who bluntly declaimed from the height of his cinematic celebrity, "You really can't be an actor unless you act on the stage." So in 1972 he won a Tony Award for his performance in Neil Simon's *Prisoner of Second Avenue*.

Born 16 September 1927 in New York City, Peter Falk grew up in Ossining, N.Y., where his parents ran a clothing and dry goods store. Despite potential handicaps—as an only child with a glass eye—he became a three-letter high school athlete, an A-B student and a member of the Merchant Marine. Also a pool shark, which he says was part of the reason he flunked out of school—"Most of my studying was done in the poolroom . . . it was a pretty classy college and I didn't fit in with the silver spoon set." He craved excitement and described it this way: "When you're a kid the real world seems dull and ordinary compared to the dream. Some of the things we do when we rebel as kids comes from a desire to put some of the dream into the real world." Armed with a B.A. from the New School and an M.B.A. from Syracuse, Falk greeted the real world scanning figures for Connecticut's Budget Bureau. Lonely, seeking companionship, he began reading scripts for local theatre groups in Hartford and in 1955 Eva Le Gallienne encouraged him to turn professional. His first work opened "at 8:45 and closed permanently two and a half hours later." But his luck changed when he landed the bartender's role in an Off-Broadway production of *The Iceman Cometh* which led to Broadway, movies and TV. The latter made his career and he was widely popular with audiences as the gruff but adorably sloppy police detective Lieutenant Columbo. Falk revives the character for television movies from time to time, and the series was back on prime-time in 1989. Falk financed and starred with his close cronies John Cassavetes and Ben Gazzara in the Cassavetes' film *Husbands*, a triumph in 1970. "I've got a weak stomach for lousy scripts," says he, so he keeps his activity down to a minimum. He and his wife of 16 years, Alyce Mayo, divorced in 1976. The couple had two daughters, Jackie and Kathryn. Falk married actress Shera Danese in 1977; they separated in 1985, then reconciled in 1987. More movie credits include: *Happy New Year* (1985), *The Princess Bride* (1987), *Vibes* (1987), *Sky Over Berlin* (1987), *In the Spirit* (1987), and *Cookie* (1989).

made visible," so it might be echoed of Farrell, of whom Clive Barnes said as early as 1965, "She is the embodiment of music." To her matchless musicality and supreme daring ("Suzanne taught me guts," admits former partner and since 1983 NYCB's co-ballet master in chief Peter Martins) add the surefire combination of regal cool and secret voluptuousness, and strength and virtuosity, and you begin to understand the citation Georgetown University attached to her honary doctorate of humane letters in 1984: "No performing artist of our time, not the greatest actors, not the greatest musicians, have done more to create an audience for their excellence than has Suzanne Farrell."

Born Roberta Sue Ficker 16 August 1945 in Cincinnati, Ohio, she was sent to ballet class at the age of eight to put an end to her tree climbing and general tomboyishness (which may account for the fearless approach she takes to her art), but because of her height it was her fate to be given only boys' roles until the age of 12, when she finally donned a tutu and danced even though "I got a splinter in my foot. I was a trooper. I was a dancer." At 15, she auditioned for Balanchine and was given a Ford Foundation scholarship to the School of American Ballet, making her first appearance with the parent company as an angel in a 1960 production of *The Nutcracker*. She joined the corps in the 1961-62 season, became a soloist in 1962 and a principal dancer in 1965. She became a star overnight that same year in the role of Dulcinea, created especialy for her by Mr. B, who essayed the role of the Don, in his full-length *Don Quixote*. "Suzanne Farrell was absolutely flawless . . . technically impeccable, light as a soap bubble, perfect in line and style. This was an exhibition of artistry which put her into the top echelon of world ballerinas," exulted Rosalyn Krakover in *High Fidelity*.

With Martins she formed one of the great ballet partnerships of the age. "As soon as Peter touched me," she recalled, "something happened—I don't know what it is . . . I don't want to analyze it; I'm afraid I might kill it." Martins: "She really challenged me. Sometimes she would fall all over the place, but she would always be exciting . . . it added a whole new aspect to my dancing." She has danced all the classical roles, but she has soared in the Balanchine canon ("Chaconne," the Diamonds section of "Jewels," "Vienna Waltzes," "Mozartiana," "Apollo," "Agon," "Walpurgisnacht," among many others). She commutes regularly to Chicago, where her husband is associate director and chief choreographer of the Chicago City Ballet (under the directorship, ironically, of Maria Tallchief, the fourth Mrs. Balanchine.) She concluded her musings (to John Gruen in *The Private World of Ballet*, 1975): "Sometimes, when I am depressed, I wonder why I am dancing. But then I hear music by Stravinsky or Tchaikovsky and I feel happy again. They give me a reason for dancing. Mostly, I dance because I have to dance in order to be happy."

Suzanne Farrell

"I love to dance so much that I almost start to hate it. I dance . . . for God, because He gave me what I have to work with. Also, I dance for Mr. B. I dance for my husband." It was not the former parochial schoolgirl's placement of her personal deity before the deity of 20th century dance that precipitated the break in 1969 between George Balanchine and Suzanne Farrell, his last muse and the embodiment of his ideal ballerina. Rather, it was Farrell's seeming indifference to Balanchine's long-held belief that "for a female dancer marriage means the end of her individuality," that led this most-favored prima ballerina of Balanchine's New York City Ballet and her husband, company soloist Paul Mejia, to leave the company and the country and settle for five years in Brussels, where they performed with Maurice Béjart's Ballet du XXme Siecle. The inevitability of her return, however, was realized in 1975, when she returned to City Ballet to continue the ascendancy to her undisputed place among the greatest ballerinas of her era, arguably the greatest America has produced. As it was said of Nijinsky that his dance was "music

Mia Farrow

"Falling in love is compulsive with me," confides Mia Farrow, who first gained wide audience recognition in 1965 as Allison MacKenzie in television's first night-time soap, "Peyton Place." "I relate to people in such a strong way." She raised eyebrows when in 1966 she eloped to Las Vegas with Frank Sinatra. She was 20; he was 50. They were divorced in 1968. Asked if she suffered a father search, she replied: "I find older men appealing. They can handle so much that I can't."

Born in Los Angeles 9 February 1945, the third eldest daughter of actress Maureen O'Sullivan and late film director John Farrow, she says: "I didn't know my parents very well, but they represent a great deal to me. My mother was a terrific mother, full of fairy tales with a soft voice and soothing manner. She was a mystical figure, and I sort of romanticized her and my father." In London, 1970, she wed conductor Andre Previn several months after making headlines with the birth of their twin sons. They subsequently adopted four Vietnamese children (and she adopted a fifth in 1985). As a film actress, she came into prominence starring in Roman Polanski's *Rosemary's Baby* (1968), and captured the plum role of Daisy Buchanan (opposite Robert Redford) in *The Great Gatsby* (1973). While

Previn toiled with the London Symphony, she performed leading roles with the Royal Shakespeare Company (in plays by Chekhov, Gorky, Lorca, Shakespeare). Filming *Hurricane* (1978) on the island of Bora Bora, she became romantically involved with Swedish cinematographer Sven Nykvist. Single again in 1979, she returned to the United States to make her Broadway debut in *Romantic Comedy* with Anthony Perkins. Her filmic association with Woody Allen began in 1982 with *A Midsummer Night's Sex Comedy*, following by *Zelig* and *Broadway Danny Rose*. "I find people who create something and live out of their own purity without fakery the most desirable to be around," she remarks. Thus, her current longtime beau—Woody Allen.

Although marriage doesn't seem to fit into the picture, the couple had a son on 19 December 1987, named Satchel. Other Farrow films, notably Allen productions: *The Purple Rose of Cairo* (1984), *Radio Days* (1987), *September* (1988), *Another Woman* (1988), and *New York Stories* (1988).

Farrah Fawcett

The tousled-haired, statuesque blonde who flew the coop of the 1976 top-rated girl detective show, "Charlie's Angels," stayed just long enough to become an overnight sensation. Farrah Fawcett, flanked by two dark-haired actresses, quickly became the focal point of the action series, described by a critic as "family-style porn, a mild erotic fantasy." Teasing and bouncing her way through nonsensical plots, Fawcett triggered a hairstyle phenomenon in the late 70s sending droves of women to the beauty parlor for "Farrah cuts." Her bathing suit poster—featuring cascading hair and blinding white teeth—rang cash registers to record profits, sparking a resurgence in personality poster sales. Farrah fever had caught. Former manager Jay Bernstein recalls, "I saw in Farrah the possibility of a real legend—baseball, apple pie and Chevrolets."

Born 2 February 1947 in Corpus Christi, and raised in a strict, working class home, Fawcett learned early to conform to traditional standards. "Catholic girls know how to take good direction," she noted. Fawcett shined as a commercial and print model, hawking Ultra-Brite toothpaste, Noxema Shaving Cream, and Wella Balsam shampoo, before landing her star-making role. Fawcett quit the series to make movies, which she did in rapid succession. *Somebody Killed Her Husband*, released in 1978, provoked one critic to quip, "To buy this film's plot, it isn't enough to suspend disbelief, you have to submit to a lobotomy." The two films that followed were similarly received.

Tiring of the star-making machinery that hyped her as more style than substance, Fawcett parted with her manager, cut her trade-mark locks, and split with husband Lee Majors (formerly TV's "Six Million Dollar Man;" of late TV's "The Fall Guy"), in 1979 (divorced 1982). Soon thereafter, she linked up with Ryan O'Neal, by whom she had a son—Redmond James—in 1985.

Against advice, Fawcett tackled a series of unglamorous roles—as a battered husband killer in TV's "The Burning Bed" (1984) and as a battered and terrorized rape victim off-Broadway in *Extremities* (1983), and received glowing reviews for both; she starred in the film version of *Extremities* in 1986. Recently, Fawcett reflected on her change in life strategies, "I never had a chance to be my own person, find out who I was, what I wanted. I was always trying to please someone else, now I want to please myself." Other works in the late 1980's include: "Between Two Women" (ABC-TV, 1986), "Poor Little Rich Girl" (NBC-TV, 1987), the movie *See You in the Morning* (1988) and a TNT special, "Margaret Bourke-White" (1989).

Michael Feinstein

Crown prince of the saloon singers, Michael Feinstein—saluted by a San Francisco critic as "surely our greatest ambassador to that golden realm in which classic American popular music dwells"—moved onward and upward from club rooms to his Broadway debut in 1988, on stage at the Lyceum Theatre. Originally planned (by producer Ron Delsener) as a two-weeks-only engagement, demand for tickets were so insistent and unremitting that the limited run was extended to four weeks. The engaging young keyboard artist was backed up by musical director David Spear and a six-piece orchestra. The program focused on the matchless melodies and lapidary lyrics of the likes of George and Ira Gershwin, Cole Porter, Irving Berlin and Jerome Kern and included a special salute to the music of Harry Warren. He returned to Broadway with "Michael Feinstein in Concert" in October that same year, this time at Booth Theatre.

Michael Jay Feinstein was born 7 September 1956 in Columbus, Ohio, the youngest child of Edward and Florence Mae Cohen. He told *Current Biography* in 1988: "From the crib I was exposed to music.... They played recordings constantly, tuned in to musical TV programs, and sang and danced around the house." Kind of out-of-sync with his own rock era, Feinstein favored the music of such standard singers as Bing Crosby, Fred Astaire, and Al Jolson, and he even liked to watch Lawrence Welk. After graduating from Exmoor High School, he worked as an accompanist for dance classes at Ohio State University. Not gaining enough satisfaction in the Midwest, he decided to head out to Los Angeles. After working as a piano salesman, young Feinstein struck it lucky when he began talking to a record store owner about his love for Gershwin's music. He then purchased a rare collector's package of Oscar Levant's recordings, which led him to contact Levant's widow. The chain of introductions continued and Michael was eventually introduced to Ira Gershwin by June Levant. A devotee, especially, of Gershwin, he became something of a surrogate son and protege of the aging Ira Gershwin and, during the lyricist's last years, worked closely with him, cataloguing lyrics, organizing memorabilia and generally soaking up all there was to know about the careers of Ira and his composer brother George. By no coincidence at all, the piano man's first recording (in 1985) was entitled, *Pure Gershwin*, and it's become a classic in its field. Equally well-received was the 1987 album *Michael Feinstein/Live at the Algonquin*, and its follow-ups *Remember: Michael Feinstein Sings Irving Berlin*, and *Isn't It Romantic*.

Although Feinstein has been audible and visable on the cabaret circuit only since 1985, his enthusiastic fan following is comprised of some of the biggest names in the music biz. (Liza Minnelli hosted his NYC debut at the Algonquin and has appeared with him several times on TV). Other numerous television appearances included a cameo in the NBC movie, "The Two Mrs. Grenvilles," a guest spot in an episode of ABC-TV's "thirty-something" (written especially for him) and on the PBS specials "George Gershwin Remembered" and "Celebrating Gershwin: 'S Wonderful." He is one of the youngest performers to be honored by ASCAP (American Society of Composers, Authors and Publishers).

Federico Fellini

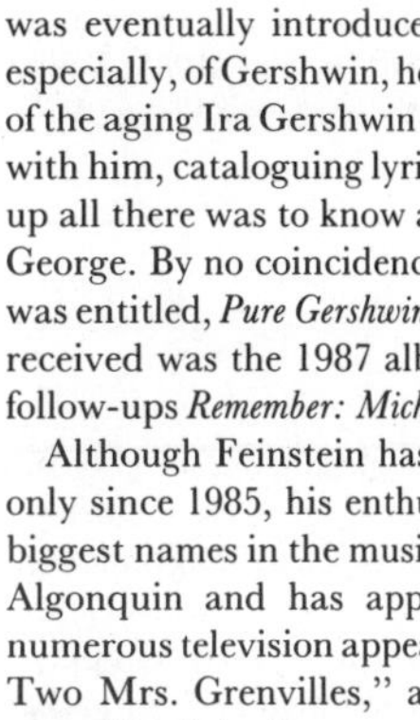

"He's a monster, a genius, a fraud, and a master, all in one," said an actress who worked for him in *La Dolce Vita* (1959). A leonine-maned burly six-footer with an expansive manner suggesting a friendly bear, he's been bewitching and startling audiences since 1946, when he scripted the Oscar-winning *Open City*. Fellini has directed more than 20 films, including four Oscar winners: *La Strada* (1954), *Nights of Cabiria* (1957), *8* (1963) which raised him to superstar status, and *Amarcord* (1974). (Nineteen years after it reached the screen the autobiographical *8* inspired the hit Broadway musical *Nine*.) Fellini's penchant for using clowns in his films reflects his lost fantasy world. His documentary *Clowns* (1970) is the study, he says, "of a world which seems inexorable destined for extinction, and therefore all the more melancholy and mysterious, made up more of rarefied memories than of concrete facts." Fellini admits he's also inexorably drawn to themes about women. After the release of his *City of Women* (1981), he observed, "I have the feeling that all my films are about women.... They represent myth, mystery, diversity, fascination, the thirst for knowledge and the search for one's own identity.... I even see the cinema itself as a woman, with its alternation of light and darkness, of appearing and disappearing images. Going to the cinema is like returning to the womb, you sit there still and meditative in the darkness, waiting for life to appear on the screen. One should go to the cinema with the innocence of a fetus."

Born 20 January 1920, the son of a salesman, in Rimini, a small resort on the Adriatic coast, Federico Fellini ran away briefly at age 12 to join the circus. After high school, he broke away from small-town life and worked as a comic-strip artist in Florence. Moving on to Rome, he worked as a cartoonist, journalist, radio scriptwriter and alternated as straight man and comic with the Fabrizzi vaudeville troupe. Hired as a gagman and scenarist for various film producers, he met Roberto Rossellini in 1944 and formed a collaboration that was to last for eight years, during which he wrote the script (in 10 days) for *Open City*. Fellini names Rossellini and Chaplin as the primary influences on his films. "Jesus, Cagliostro, St. Francis and Satan," are the historical figures he finds most interesting. When directing, Fellini becomes Cagliostro, his gift for hamming and clowning it up coming to the fore. He hurls an evenly balanced barage of jokes and insults at his actors as he prods them on into a "portrayal of the truth." Among his recent films are: *The Ship Sails On* (1983), *Ginger & Fred* (1986) and *L'Intervista* (1987). "I never know why I choose to shoot one film rather than another," he says. "I could even say that it is not I who choose a theme but the theme that chooses me, and then the film immediately takes shape and acquires images and feelings." Fellini's wife, whom he married in 1943, Giulietta Masina, an actress and the author of a column for the love lorn. In June, 1985, Fellini was honored by the Film Society of Lincoln Center at Avery Fisher Hall.

Jose Ferrer

This gifted theatrical gamut-runner (Iago to Toulouse-Lautrec to Cyrano to Charley's Aunt) has never been typecast. Flipping with ease from sober tragedy to wild farce, he's demonstrated his performing talents in plays, films and even on the nightclub circuit and as a director and producer a well. In one blockbuster season (1951-52) he was star of Broadway's *The Shrike*, Hollywood's *Moulin Rouge* and director-producer of both *Stalag 17* and *The Fourposter* on Broadway. Other noteworthy acting credits include: *Richard III*, *Volpone*, *Angel Street*, *Twentieth Century* and *Man of LaMancha* on stage, and such films as *Joan of Arc*, *The Caine Mutiny*, *Lawrence of Arabia*, *Ship of Fools*, Woody Allen's *A Midsummer Night's Sex Comedy* and *Dune*. He directed, among others, *Oh, Captain* (which he co-wrote) *My Three Angels* and *Andersonville Trial*.

Born Jose Vincente Ferrer de Otero y Cintron on 8 January 1912 in Santurce, Puerto Rico, of well-to-do parents, he was brought to the mainland United States as a child by his father ("I'm always trying to live up to him") and discovered dramatic arts at Princeton's undergraduate Triangle Club of which James Stewart and Joshua Logan were the leading lights. Married first to actress Uta Hagen (one daughter, Lauitia), he subsequently married second wife Phyllis Hill and third, singer Rosemary Clooney, with whom he had five children, Miguel Jose, Maria, Gabriel, Monsita Teresa and Rafael. They divorced in 1962, remarried in 1963 and then divorced a second time in 1966. A performer who consistently gives his all (during the run of *Charley's Aunt*, he trapezed about the stage, lost five pounds at each performance), he admits to occasional bouts of battle fatigue. "I had to do it 8 times a week," he recalls of one emotional scene, "and you should know some of the things I did in my own mind. At one point or another I think I killed every single person that I loved—and I saw them lying there bleeding before me—to work myself to the point where I was moved. I killed my father and my daughter and my best friend and his wife and my pet dog and my rabbit and my canary. I even," he concluded sorrowfully, "ran over strangers." Ferrer, who was inducted into the Theater Hall of Fame in 1980, lives in Manhattan with his fourth wife, the former Stella Daphne Magee.

Sally Field

Once upon a wave she rode her TV audiences wild with her giggly "Gidget" act, then the faithful fellows at ABC flew her up to God as Sister Bertrille, "The Flying Nun." She left the prime time box of worship and went into her own orbit as a powerfully gifted performer in such quality projects as her Emmy-award winning, made-for-TV "Sybil," the story of a woman with no less than 16 personalities, and the 1979 feature film *Norma Rae*, about a Southern textile worker, which won her an Oscar and the Best Actress Award at the Cannes Film Festival. She won her second Oscar for *Places in the Heart* (1984). In 1985 she starred with James Garner in *Murphy's Romance*, in 1986 she appeared in the telefilm "Three Minutes to Midnight", in 1988 she co-produced and starred in *Punchline* with Tom Hanks, and also starred in *Steel Magnolias* that same year.

"I grew up and didn't buckle under when they wanted me to remain cute forever," explains Sally Field, born 6 November 1946, about her unusual switch from ingenue starlet to serious actress. After high school she enrolled in Columbia Pictures Workshop, which developed new talent, and it was there that she was fished out of the talent pool to play television's "Gidget." After years of that show and the "Flying Nun," the mother of two sons, Peter and Elijah, divorced their father Steve Craig, left Hollywood and joined the Actor's Studio in New York. Before that she says: "The truth was that nobody around me had any respect for me; to them I was a joke, so I took the plunge and changed everything at once—I got rid of my agent, my business manager and my husband. For three years I dropped out and studied and did summer stock." Along with many TV and film projects of note are *Smokey and the Bandit* and its sequels, made with erstwhile lover Burt Reynolds. *Smokey* is reported to have grossed one quarter of a billion dollars. A self-described "old fashioned girl," she credits her mother, Maggie Field Mahoney, with inspiring her acting career. "She used to carry me around on her hip to acting lessons with Charles Laughton and she was always reciting Shakespeare to me. I'm sure I didn't understand any of it at that age, but what was communicated was this immense love of what she was doing." In 1985 she took Allan Griesman as her second husband. The couple have a son, Samuel H. Morian, born in 1987.

Harvey Fierstein

"I've never been secretive about being gay. Never," says Harvey Fierstein. Indeed. The actor-playwright's *Torch Song Trilogy* was the Broadway theatre's first openly homosexual successful play, and—to the happy surprise of many—earned its author-star two Tony awards in 1983. This triumph led to Fierstein's writing the book for the $5 million musical version of the French stage and film hit, *La Cage aux Folles*, which, like *Torch Song* disarmingly blended outrageous "camp" humor with relatively traditional sentiments. Fierstein is a prime example of the 1980s openly gay artist.

The gravel-voiced performer was born 6 June 1954 and raised in Brooklyn, the son of Eastern European Jewish immigrants. A "misfit" youngster, he weighted over 200 pounds at age 13. But also at this age—when most nice Jewish boys have a Bar Mitzvah—Fierstein "came out" to his parents. This disclosure of his sexual identity at an unusually early age met with acceptance: "There was no crying or screaming. It was what I was—it wasn't a family decision." With typical wit he adds, "The way I look at it, I'm a human being first and gorgeous second." Fierstein studied art at Pratt (he drew the striking eyes logo for *Torch Song*) and made his professional theatre debut in 1971 at Ellen Stewart's LaMama in an Andy Warhol production. He worked extensively Off-Off Broadway, acquiring a cult following for his transvestite act. "In drag I could completely become someone else," he says. "And guess what? I liked it. That was the kind of power I wanted. And some of us can't help it if we're ravishing."

Fierstein once considered suicide, until a therapist friend told him, "Look, you can kill yourself, or you can write a play about it." Fortunately he did the latter, resulting in *Torch Song*, which straight as well as gay audiences embraced. According to its author, "The single most important thing I'm saying is that we have to get the concept out of our minds that love and commitment and family are heterosexual rights. They're not. They're *people's* rights. Heterosexuals can adopt or reject them, gays can adopt or reject them, but everyone has the right to choose." Rather popular within the theatre world, Harvey's next work *Safe Sex* (1987) was produced as a play, published as a book, and a segment was presented on Home Box Office television. His *Torch Song Trilogy* was made into a film in 1988.

Albert Finney

"All the effort, all the struggle and sacrifice of an actor and everyone in a theatre company goes into creating a momentary illusion, it is like a dream and when it's over, it's over. Gone. Of course, what most people spend their lives doing may not add up to a hill of beans. But their love, effort, devotion goes into doing it, and it becomes worthwhile." A star at 25 in *Saturday Night and Sunday Morning*, followed by stunning successes in the films *Tom Jones* and in the plays *Luther* and *Joe Egg* on Broadway, Albert Finney asked himself, "What do you do next?" Friends advised; "Strike while the iron is hot or people will forget you." Instead, Finney lit out on a year's voyage around the world and found himself on a tiny island in the Pacific one day, a beachboy with a need to "return to the neurotic society" and decided, "I didn't find any answers, only more questions. But I came out of it more convinced than ever that I wanted to be my own man."

Finney (Albie to his friends) was born in Lancashire, England, 9 May 1936, the son of a bookie. ("We were always illegal.") He remembers a life dominated by hasty moves to avoid the police. ("No security; perfect training for the actor's life.") His North Country heritage, he says, makes him "very suspicious of success," and he turned down the lead role in *Lawrence of Arabia* because he didn't "want to become a Hollywood property or spend two years in the bloomin' desert." Of *Charlie Bubbles*, which he produced, directed and starred in, he says, "the incidents in it are not autobiographical, but the feelings are," adding that "the mood is the feeling that you are no longer living your own life, not holding your destiny in your own hands." He credits variety as the main source of inspiration in his life. This variety is best seen in the different and challenging parts he plays both on stage and in films: Daddy Warbucks in the film of the musical, *Annie;* irate husband in the film *Shoot the Moon*, playing opposite Diane Keaton; "Sir" in the *Dresser*, a movie about life in a touring stage company; the alcoholic Consul in John Huston's film of *Under the Volcano* (Oscar nomination) and "Pope John Paul II" in a television movie. More recent films include *Orphans* (1987) and *Endless Games* (1988).

At present, Finney is not married. A well publicized fling with Audrey Hepburn while making all-time favorite *Two for the Road* resulted in the fizzling of her marriage at the time. Finney was married to Anouk Aimee from 1970 until 1975, and has one grown son from his first marriage (to actress Jane Wenham from 1957-61) named Simon. One bit of Finney trivia for the road: while waiting to open Britain's new National Theatre in the Marlowe epic, *Tamburlaine*, Finney cut a record for Motown. That's variety.

Bobby Fischer

Wherever power chess is being played in the four corners of the globe there is always the specter of Bobby Fischer, who in 1972 defeated world champion Boris Spassky for the one title the Russians were thought unlikely ever to relinquish. As it was with the equally reclusive Howard Hughes, so the legends have grown around Fischer. He has been variously described as a paranoid schizophrenic, fearful of assassination by the K.G.B., who spends his time reading conspiracy novels and searching out Hitler memorabilia, or as "better than ever . . . the best in the world," studying the game only in the morning hours "when his powers of concentration are strongest." In 1985 Tim Rice acknowledged Fischer was a source of inspiration for his musical, *Chess.*

Robert James Fischer was born in Chicago, 9 March 1943, to a German physicist and his Swiss-born wife, who separated when Bobby was two. He moved to Brooklyn with his mother and sister, and from the time he was given a plastic candy store chess set at the age of six the game has been his consuming passion. His only other notable accomplishment (having dropped out of school at the age of 15) was teaching himself eight languages, and that only to enable him to read *all* the international chess journals. Mainly self-taught, by 14 Fischer was United States champion and an international grand master at 15. At about that time, he began to express his bitterness about the generally shabby treatment accorded American chess champions compared with the pampering given the top Russian players, who frequently traveled to tournaments with dozens of aides to assist them in every aspect of their game. Before competing at Reykjavik, Iceland, against Spassky in 1972, Fischer demanded and received assurances of a championship purse of $250,000 (with the winner receiving $150,000). The matches were seen on public television and a triumphant Fischer returned to America to find himself on the covers of *Sports Illustrated, Time, Life* and *Newsweek.* On the Johnny Carson and Dick Cavett Shows he told America: "Chess is like war on a board. The object is to crush the other man's mind. . . . I like to see 'em squirm." America, used to more circumspect and decorous language from chess players, ate it up. Chess was "in." Clubs proliferated. Children put down their gloves and bats and took up chess. For one brief shining moment, shy, introspective chess players were lionized like rock stars. And in the ultimate tribute, chess groupies arrived on the scene. "They seduced the most ascetic grand masters," recalled Bruce Pandolfini, manager of the Manhattan Chess Club. "They all wanted Fischer." Those heady days were to be short-lived, however. In 1978 Fischer refused to defend his world title against Anatoly Karpov and retired to Pasadena, Calif., where he gave his prize money and royalties from two successful books to the Worldwide Church of God. He turned down, as too low an offer, $250,000 to play one game at Caesars Palace in Las Vegas. He declined Ferdinand Marcos's offer to sponsor a $3 million championship match in the Philippines, and ignored a reported $10 million in commercial offers. His tantalizing shadow existence may be what *New York* magazine called in 1984 "Fischer's most enduring and original chess creation . . . a kind of life gambit. In the fantasies of American chess fans, Fischer's game grows more unbeatable with every unplayed tournament and every spurned offer of millions."

Avery Fisher

This New Yorker (born circa 1910) is not only the name of a building (Lincoln Center's Philharmonic Hall was renamed Avery Fisher Hall after he presented the arts complex with a $10 million gift), he is the pathfinder of

Carrie Fisher — **CELEBRITY REGISTER 1990**

high-fidelity sound. With a reverence for music and an inventor's imagination, he pioneered the concepts and the products that allowed hi-fi's to become commonplace in every home. He entered the field in a rather roundabout fashion, having majored in English and biology as a New York University student. His first job in the early 1930s was at the publishing house of Dodd, Mead and Company, where, he recalls, "I held two jobs in order to earn a salary [$18 a week] equal to half a job." Music had been prominent in his home as a child, and in his publishing days, he became more and more determined to improve the sound then available from traditional home audio equipment. He scouted Radio Row (a downtown district in Manhattan that sold outsize electronic and audio equipment) and began creating his own home-grown system. Eventually he capitalized on the interest people took in his inventions and opened his first company, Philharmonic Radio, in 1937. In 1945, Fisher resigned as president to start Fisher Radio. His innovations weren't just technical; Fisher also insisted that audio components should sport ample control features but still present an attractive look for home appeal. Eventually the "pioneer" in home entertainment became "the Establishment." For the wealthy Mr. Fisher, music is the sweet-sounding mainstay of his life. He's an "enthusiastic amateur," and his retirement from business and full involvement in Lincoln Center and the Marlboro Music Festival allow him to enjoy chamber music sessions in his home, besides regularly attending concerts at Avery Fisher Hall where getting a last minute seat is never a problem. He is the founder of the Avery Fisher Prize, which is awarded every year to an outstanding American instrumentalist and carries with it a $5,000 cash stipend and engagements with the Great Performers Series in Avery Fisher Hall, the New York Philharmonic, the Chamber Music Society of Lincoln Center, and the Mostly Mozart Festival.

Carrie Fisher

"You are not allowed to grow up with parents who are famous and then get into one of the biggest movies of all time and run around with famous people—it's resented after a while. And I would always try to emphasize something really wrong with me, so that people wouldn't be put off." More confident now, the daughter of Debbie Reynolds and Eddie Fisher—a self-declared Hollywood brat with "high-velocity-verbiage"—gained her own fame as Princess Leia in the phenomenally successful *Star Wars* ('77) and its equally popular sequels: *The Empire Strikes Back* ('80) and *Return of the Jedi* ('84) ."Who's more famous than Debbie and Eddie? C-3PO and Darth Vader, and Jesus Christ and God. There's a whole lot of freight that goes with being movie stars' kids—on the cover of *Life* when you're two minutes old. I remember the press diving through trees to get pictures of me, my brother and my mother. Poor Debbie; that bastard Eddie; and Liz. We've been the public domain all our lives. I was trained in celebrity, so I did the only thing I knew. I went into the family business. . . . My brother and I went in different directions on the Debbie and Eddie issue. He's gotten involved with Jesus, and I do active work on myself, trying to make myself better and better. It's funny."

Born in Los Angeles on 21 October 1956, Carrie Fisher began her professional career at 13 performing in her mother's Las Vegas nightclub act. She dropped out of Beverly Hills H.S. at 15 to join the chorus of *Irene*, Debbie's 1972 Broadway outing. Her film debut as a nymphet in *Shampoo* ('75) was followed by studies at London's Central School of Speech and Drama. Her other films include *The Blues Brothers* ('80), *Under the Rainbow* ('81) and *Garbo Talks* ('84). On TV she appeared in "Come Back, Little Sheba" ('77) and "Thumbelina" for Shelley Duvall's cable "Faerie Tale Theatre" ('83). She returned briefly to Broadway in 1983 in *Agnes of God*.

"There was a sort of fear of mine when I started acting that I would come off like Tammy the eternal virgin, and in fact, the opposite has happened. Because I started out with Warren Beatty, asking him 'Want to fuck?' and in *Jedi* I'm in space shooting people and saying, 'Got you, you asshole.' . . . There are a lot of people who don't like [Leia]; they think I'm some kind of space bitch." After playing such a strong character, "part of me goes, 'When does the cooking and sewing and gossiping and, you know, putting on make-up start to happen?'" She lived in a one-room Los Angeles log-cabin until her August 1983 marriage to singer-writer Paul Simon after a five-year on-again-off-again relationship. "Let's just say we had a stormy romance, and the storm's finally over." (Not quite; the couple split in 1984.) Shortly after her marriage, she scoffed, "*The National Enquirer* says I'm . . . pregnant. . . . They also say I've quit show business, so I guess that's my plan for now. . . . Yeah, I believe everything I read." The witty actress muses, "Everybody wants to be a celebrity. But you know what happens to old celebrities. They die or go to Vegas. Star-life duration is getting shorter and shorter. It could be me at the Tropicana Lounge any minute."

Securing her star status, Carrie branched out and conquered the literary field with the release of her first novel, *Postcards From the Edge* (1985). She won the PEN Award for her book and the story is being optioned for the movies by Mike Nichols. Also keeping active in films, she's starred in a variety of pictures throughout the 1980's: *Hannah and Her Sisters* (1985), *Hollywood Vice Squad* (1986), *Appointment With Death* (1987), *Amazon Women on the Moon* (1987), *Bloodshot Lightning* (1988), *The Burbs* (1989), *Harry, This Is Sally* (1989) and *Loverboy* (1989).

Ella Fitzgerald

At the age of 15, it was the "short straw" Ella Fitzgerald drew that launched her singing career "One day two girlfriends and I made a bet—a dare. We drew straws to see which of us would go on the amateur hour at the Apollo Theatre." Fitzgerald went on stage to dance, but got "cold feet" so she sang instead.

Fitzgerald later won an audition to sing with Arthur Tracy, the early king of radio known as The Street Singer. The death of her mother, however, caused that deal to collapse since she wasn't of age and she had no one to accept legal responsibility. It was back to amateur hours until finally, after many efforts, she got her big opportunity to sing with the late Chick Webb, who later adopted her, and together in 1938 they composed her first big record hit, "A-Tisket, A-Tasket." "It wasn't easy," she concedes, "but it has given me a better sense of value. . . . I've had some hard knocks and a couple of missed meals, but I don't think I'd want to change a thing."

Born 25 April 1918 in Newport News, Va., Fitzgerald has entertained the world with her ballads, swing, Dixieland, Calypso, pop, jazz, scat and whatever else she chooses to sing. A critic once said she "could sing the Van Nuys telephone directory with a broken jaw and make it sound good." Among her many Grammy Awards was s special Bing Crosby Award in 1967, honoring her "superb musicianship and consistent musical integrity." In 1979, with President Jimmy Carter leading the applause, Fitzgerald was awarded Kennedy Center Honors for Lifetime Achievement in the Arts. In 1985 she was inducted into the Jazz Hall of Fame.

Geraldine Fitzgerald

She's been called "an enchantingly free spirit who roams . . . fast and far on her facile intellect and voluble Irish charm." Indeed for over forty-five years she has roamed from theatre to screen and back again capturing both audiences with her artistry. In the last decades not only has she had the opportunity to secure her place as one of the most luminous stars of the American stage, but has become a concert singer of "street songs," a director for the stage, and, especially close to heart, has worked with young people in New York City in support of street theatre.

Geraldine Fitzgerald was born 24 November 1913 into a family notable for professional and cultural achievements. Her father was a lawyer and her aunt Stet a well-known Irish actress. After completing her early convent school education and several years of art study (her first love), and, encouraged by her aunt, she turned to the stage. She made her debut in Dublin in 1932 and after a few appearances in London, came to America in 1938 production of the newly-founded Orson Welles Mercury Theatre Company. "I looked to America when I was a girl," she says, "I read the *New Yorker* and that was considered very daring, very avant garde in those days."

Her first two Hollywood roles, *Wuthering Heights* and *Dark Victory* (both in 1939) remain among her best. Of the former Laurence Olivier said: "I saw the film on TV the other night and Geraldine Fitzgerald is the only thing that holds up in that one." Finding the commercialism of Hollywood abrasive she insisted on contracts with six months of every year to work on the stage. She continued her East Coast/West Coast shuttle and in 1969 her stage career took a decided upward swing with the revival of Eugene O'Neill's *Ah, Wilderness*, followed by an entirely different mother role in *Long Day's Journey Into Night*, (for which she won the *Variety* Critics' award in 1970-1971). *Juno and the Paycock* was a further stage triumph. At the age of 55 she started taking singing lessons, and, receiving favorable reviews in *The Threepenny Opera*, made her nightclub debut singing a program of "street songs." "I've only got about 4 tones," she says, "but it's what you do with it that counts." She has sung the songs at Lincoln Center, Circle In The Square, and elsewhere. In 1974 she received New York City's highest cultural award, the Handel Medallion for her achievement in street theatre. Geraldine Fitzgerald is the mother of Michael Lindsay-Hogg, a director of British television and films, son of her first marriage. In 1946 she married Stuart Sheftel, a business executive and chairman of the New York City Youth Board. They live in Manhattan and have a daughter, Susan. Miss Fitzgerald became one of the few American women stage directors when she presented *Mass Appeal* on Broadway in 1981. "I love to wake up in the morning looking forward to doing and experimenting and risking," she has said. "I'm delighted with it all, and I'm going to do as many things as I can and risk it all as often as I can."

In 1987, Ms. Fitzgerald appeared in a CBS-TV pilot "Mabel & Max" and she was in the Dudley Moore movie *Arthur II: On The Rocks* in 1988.

Roberta Flack

The most memorable occasion in the life of Roberta Flack was during her childhood when her father, Laron, found a piano in a junkyard and had it restored. Flack's mother, Irene, taught her how to play and, at the age of nine, she took formal lessons with Alma Blackmon in Washington, D.C. At 15, she entered Howard University on a scholarship and graduated in 1958 with a B.A. in music education. The death of her father, however, interrupted her studies for her Master's degree. Flack took a job teaching in Farmville, N.C. (1959-60), and in Washington, D.C. (1960-67). "There is nothing to compare to this life [as a musician] as opposed to my life as a schoolteacher." Flack kept up her musical interests as a church organist, a choral director, a voice coach and a pianist in clubs. "Let me tell you, it's damn tough for a black woman hanging out there [in the music business] on her own. It takes enormous strength."

In 1969, jazz pianist Les McCann heard Flack in a Washington, D.C., nightclub and arranged for her to audition with Atlantic Records. From there, it was straight up the ladder of success for Flack, who was born 10 February 1939 in Black Mountain, N.C. "To live is to suffer; to survive is to find some meaning in that suffering," she says. Flack has been cautious with her career after seeing what success does to people, especially black performers lacking the stability to deal with stardom. "All of a sudden you're thrown into a world where these things [moral principles] don't have any importance at all, like going to church on Sunday or saying grace before meals." In 1972, Flack was saluted in *Downbeat* as the nation's top female vocalist. Her smooth and silky rendering of the ballad, "The First Time Ever I Saw Your Face," garnered her two Grammy Awards as both Record of the Year and Song of the Year. That same year saw the celebration in Washington, D.C., of Roberta Flack Human Kindness Day. "Killing Me Softly with His Song" in 1973 also won her two Grammys in the categories of Record and Song of the Year. In 1988, she released a popular album *Oasis*. Her interracial marriage to jazz bassist Stephen Novosel (opposed by his family and her brother, who had forgotten, Roberta once noted, that "we had a white grandfather") lasted from 1966 to 1972, and she married briefly for the second time before becoming determined to "avoid combining marriage and the pursuit of a career."

Jane Fonda

"When you are the offspring of a celebrity it is critical to develop your own identity. You have to feel that you are your own person. And my father was such a powerful . . . figure," says Henry's daughter. "I rebelled against father because I needed my own identity, then I came close to him again. . . . He also mellowed as he got older. I think it's a universal story. . . . It's more complicated when it's played out in public." The controversial, cause-oriented actress graduated from playing sex objects (sometimes in films by her first husband, French director Roger Vadim) to earning acclaim as a serious actress. The turning point (shortly after the ebb of Vadim's *Barbarella*) came late in 1969 with *They Shoot Horses, Don't They?* Her performance as a burned-out marathon dancer brought her a N.Y. Film Critics Award and her first Academy Award nomination. Two years later she received the Oscar and another N.Y. Film Critics citation for her call-girl portrayal in *Klute*. Her second Academy Award was for *Coming Home* ('78), with additional nominations for *Julia* ('77), *The China Syndrome* ('79) and (supporting) *On Golden Pond* ('81). More memorable performances followed: *Agnes of God* (1985), *The Morning After* (1986-Academy Award nomination for Best Actress), *The Old Gringo* (produced and appeared, 1989), and *Stanley & Iris* (1989).

Born 21 December 1937 in N.Y.C., she was told at age 12 that her mother had died of a heart attack. Fonda subsequently learned the truth from a movie magazine: that her mother had actually slashed her throat in an asylum after a mental breakdown. As a child, Jane showed little interest in acting. "When I left Vassar I drifted. I went to Paris and worked for the *Paris Review*. I modeled [twice making *Vogue*'s cover]. I tried to act like a lady . . . [but] I was a slob at heart. I did all kinds of things I didn't believe in because I didn't want to disappoint my father. Then I started acting in N.Y. with Lee Strasberg and discovered because I was a Fonda everybody expected me to fall on my face. You'd think it'd be the other way around, but it wasn't. I found incredible resentment from other actors, and I remember one terrible agonizing audition when Tyrone Guthrie said to me, 'What else have you ever done besides being Henry Fonda's daughter?'" She went back to Paris and married Vadim. They had a daughter, Vanessa. Her Broadway and Hollywood debuts occurred in 1960 and despite some good films like '65's *Cat Ballou* and '67's *Barefoot in the Park*, her career floundered until the decade's end. At that point, following her return to the U.S. (and divorce from Vadim), she immediately plunged into fervent social activism, championing a variety of anti-Establishment causes and getting into trouble with the authorities over her actions on behalf of Black Panthers, American Indians and rebellious GI's. As part of her campaign to end the war in Southeast Asia, she formed with actor Donald Sutherland the Anti-War Troupe, which toured military camps in defiance of the Pentagon. She co-produced and co-wrote *F.T.A.* (*Free the Army*, '72), a filmed record of the tour. In '73 she married anitwar militant and former SDS head Tom Hayden (they separated in September, 1989). With Hayden and cinematographer Haskell Wexler, she co-directed a documentary, *Introduction to the Enemy* ('74), an account of her controversial visit to North Vietnam. Until recently she lived in California with Vanessa, Hayden and their son Troy. "I think there's this problematic tension between art and business which exists nowhere as powerfully as it does in Hollywood," she says. "It is an art form, it is a part of our culture, but the bottom line is business and you're irresponsible if you ignore it. I personally like that challenge. I think it's a healthy tension." Having formed her own production company in the '70s, she expanded her business interests in the '80s, with the staggering success of "Jane Fonda's Workout," which sold records, books and videotapes worldwide. All profits went to support Hayden's political organization, The Campaign for Economic Democracy. "I said to myself [at about age 42] . . . if you look at the history of aging actresses, it's not exactly a bright future. I intend, of course, to change that. Hollywood is not forgiving of gray hair and wrinkles on the big screen. . . . I might not be able to work as much. . . . So I realized that the only business I knew anything about beside acting was exercise." Her latest releases in the home video department are: "Jane Fonda Presents Sports Aid" and "Jane Fonda's Complete Workout."

Peter Fonda

At age ten he shot himself through the liver and kidneys with a .22 caliber pistol after he learned that his socialite mother Frances Seymour Brokaw, the second of the late Henry Fonda's wives, cut her throat. "Nobody told me the truth about my mother. I was ten years old and I didn't understand. My father won't even talk to me about it today, so he's not going to talk about yesterday," Peter Fonda said years ago before coming to terms with his famous dad just before he died. Arrested on drug possession charges in 1966, this renegade was a symbol of the alienated anti-hero in the late '60s and early '70s. His films *The Wild Angels* and especially *Easy Rider* brought the hippies battle cry to audiences across America by raising something in every sympathetic young person of those turbulent times. Also a director (*The Hired Hand*) Fonda spoke openly about his countercultural practices including his LSD trips. "After LSD, I have seen the worst and I've seen the best and I know where I am on this planet."

Born 23 February 1939, he attended the University of Omaha. "They were talking about 'art' when just the summer before I had met Picasso," he recalled. Enthusiastically received in his first Broadway part, in *Blood, Sweat and Stanley Poole,* that same year he married Susan Brewer and had two children, Brigitte and Justine. They divorced in 1974 and Fonda married Portia Crockett in 1976. The '70s brought parts in adventure flicks such as *Highballin'*, *Futureworld*, *Cannonball Run* and *Wanda Nevada*. Films in the 1980's include *Freedom Fighters* (1987), *Time of Indifference* (1987) and *The Rose Garden* (1989). Peter resides with his family in Montana. When he's not filming, he enjoys being the captain of a full crew aboard his 102' sailboat. He says "I find my time at sea and my time in the mountains of Montana rejuvenating, so that I can dive into Hollywood with increased stamina."

Joan Fontaine

Her sister, Olivia de Havilland, was 16 months older, but *she* may have been the smarter of the two. In *No Bed of Roses,* her 1978 autobiography, Joan tells of the day the two siblings were studied by the Stanford Psychologist who later developed the Stanford-Binet Intelligent Quotient tests. "Olivia, on the day of her test, had a fever. I tested higher than she—so high, as a matter of fact, the examiner called me back. The only thing I can remember was that when asked what I did at night, I answered logically, 'Wet the bed.' For goodness sake, they didn't want some obvious answer like 'sleep,' did they?"

Born Joan de Beauvoir de Havilland, 22 October 1917 in Tokyo, she adopted her stepfather's surname of Fontaine when she arrived in Hollywood so as not to be confused with her already-established sister. Up for many of the same parts, the two were often at odds, although both now say that their famous feuds were more a product of the publicity-mill than real life. Still, in her book, Fontaine tells a poignant story of the encounter that followed Olivia's winning of the 1946 Academy Award. "After Olivia delivered her acceptance speech and entered the wings, I, standing close by, went over to congratulate her. . . . She took one look at me, ignored my outstretched hand, clutched her Oscar to her bosom, and wheeled away." Earlier, in 1942, both women had been up for a Best Actress statuette (Joan for Alfred Hitchcock's *Suspicion;* Olivia for *Hold Back the Dawn*) and Joan won. Among her best-remember Hollywood efforts: 1940's *Rebecca* (in which she played the un-named "I" character of Daphne duMaurier's Gothic classic); *This Above All* (1942); *The Constant Nymph* and *Jane Eyre* (1943). On stage, she replaced Deborah Kerr in *Tea and Sympathy* in 1954. She was visible to New Yorkers in the 1980s via her own interview show on cable TV. She also appeared in the TV movies "Crossings" (1985) and "Dark Mansions" (1985).

Fontaine's autobiography tells how she swooned over romantic idol Conrad Nagel in the silent version of *Quality Street*. Years later, after she was in the sound remake, she met Nagel in a stage production of *Faust* and shortly thereafter, "you might say I was surprised out of my virginity." Nagel was old enough to be her father and Joan says they ultimately parted company because of her reluctance to "compete" with his daughter. She later married: (1) Brian Aherne; (2) William Dozier (one daughter, Deborah, and one adopted daughter, Martita); (3) Collier Young; and (4) Alfred Wright, Jr. (Multiple marriages are not unusual in the deHavilland family. Her father married for the third time at the age of 89.) As for herself, Joan credits her many marriages for the development of such extra-curricular skills as piloting a plane, ballooning, fishing for tuna and hole-in-one golfing. "If you keep marrying as I do," she once observed, "you learn everybody's hobby."

Margot Fonteyn

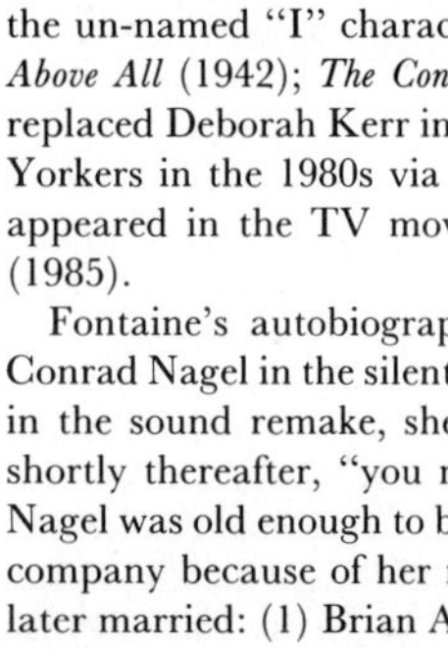

"In history there will be a Pavlova, a Karsavina, a Spessivtzeva—and there will be a Fonteyn," proclaimed George Balanchine in according to the first non-Russian the honor of being the dominant ballerina of her era. By 1962, at the age of 43, Dame Margot—the best known and most loved ballerina in the world, the individual most responsible for the emergence of British ballet as a world class power in the dance, and the model and mentor of a succession of world famous ballerinas—began gradually to reduce her schedule at Covent Garden and contemplate retirement with her husband, Dr. Roberto Arias, the Panamanian diplomat whom she had married in 1955. But out of the east came Rudolf Nureyev, a 23-year old volatile and tempestuous Tartar who would join forces with the reigning queen of the ballet establishment to set loose upon the world the phenomenon that came to be known as balletomania. From their London debut in *Giselle* (27 curtain calls) to a *Romeo and Juliet* three years later that elicited 47 curtain calls, "Margot and Rudi" rivalled the Beatles in popularity and became the darlings of the jet set. Although critics attributed the electricity of the partnership to a juxtaposition of Fonteyn's sweet radiance and classical style complementing Nureyev's turbulent physicality, Fonteyn wrote that "the young boy everyone thought so wild and spontaneous in his dancing cared desperately about technique, whereas I, the cool English ballerina, was so much more interested in the emotional aspects of the performance." Whatever it was, it lasted more than 15 years and added a daring and a dramatic intensity to the dancing of Fonteyn, whom Lincoln Kirstein had once found "wonderful but unawakened."

Born 18 May 1919, in Reigate, Surrey, England, Peggy Hookham accompanied her engineer father and coffee heiress mother (of Irish and Brazilian descent) around the world on business, including a five-year sojourn in China, where her mother found a Russian emigre to teach her dancing. The family returned to England, where Peggy was accepted at the Sadler's Wells Ballet School. She made her professional debut as a snowflake in *The Nutcracker* in 1934 (the same year she changed her name to Margot Fonteyn), and by 1935 she began to take over roles relinquished by Alicia Markova when she left the company. That same year she began her legendary association with Frederick Ashton, who created many ballets especially for her throughout her career.

While discovering herself in Ashton's ballets, she was also maturing in the classics, first with *Giselle* ("I almost died of fright, but such a lovely fright it was") at 17, then *Swan Lake*, and finally in 1938, *The Sleeping Beauty*, the ballet with which she would be associated above all others, and in which she conquered Paris *and* New York in 1949. Never a flamboyant technician, but possessed of "an effortless beauty entirely innocent of bravura," Fonteyn's "warmth and humanity" are among the intangibles that made her the greatest ballerina of her day. James Monahan said, "She has been loved, not primarily for her vituosity, but for some genuine, poignant essence of personality which is all her own."

A Dame Commander of the British Empire since 1956, Dame Margot has been president of the Royal Academy of Dancing since 1954. Although she announced her retirement in 1979, she appeared in 1981 in the supporting role of Lady Capulet in Nureyev's staging of *Romeo and Juliet* in Milan and New York's Metropolitan Opera House, to which she returned in May of 1984 to participate in the Met's final gala of its centennial year (in a duet with Sir Frederick Ashton). She was the host-narrator of BBC's "The Magic of Dance" series, which was shown on public television in the United States in 1983. She spends her rare leisure time in Panama with her husband, who was permanently paralyzed after being shot down in the streets of Panama in 1964, and who survived because of his wife's constant devotion in the aftermath of the assassination attempt. In 1984 Dame Margot authored the illustrated volume *Pavlova: Portrait of a Dancer*, thereby inextricably linking two transcendent dance legends.

Malcolm S. Forbes

This millionaire publisher, art collector, hot-air balloonist and motorcyclist likes to say that he got where he is today "through sheer ability (spelled i-n-h-e-r-i-t-a-n-c-e)," a puckish observation that happens not to be true. Malcolm S. Forbes did inherit *Forbes* magazine from his father, who founded it in 1917. But as its current publisher and head of various subsidiary enterprises, Malcolm Forbes exemplifies the aspect of capitalism that values imagination over caution, and risk-taking over balanced books. "I'm not an expert at anything," Forbes once told an interviewer who called him a Renaissance man. "I don't say that out of modesty. I think too many people don't take things up on the premise that they need to know too much about it. I outgrew that. As a youngster of 12 or 13, for instance, if you haven't been exposed to skiing or skating, you don't want to clod around with confrères who *can* do it. So you tend to shy away and say, 'I don't like it.' What you mean is, 'I can't do it.' One sign of maturity is the realization that you shouldn't be inhibited about trying something you're not good at. Enthusiasm, not expertise, is the requisite." The author of those words took up motorcycling at age 48, and four years later ballooning: in 1973 he became the first person successfully to fly from coast-to-coast in one hot-air balloon.

Malcolm Forbes joined the staff of his father's magazine in 1946, and he has been its publisher, president, editor-in-chief, and sole owner since the mid-1960s. A World War II hero (Bronze Star and Purple Heart), Forbes embarked on a career in New Jersey politics in 1949, serving as state senator from 1952 to 1958, and ran unsuccessfully as the Republican candidate for governor in 1957. Concentrating on Forbes Magazine Inc during the 1960s, he diversified his company's holdings to better reflect his own interests. He boasts of owning the Czar's celebrated Faberge objects d'art collection; a leading motorcycle dealership; various hot air balloons; and such exotic real estate items as a chateau in France, a palace in Tangiers, and a couple of cozy South Pacific retreats; he purchased Somerset Press in 1987.

Born 19 August 1919 in Brooklyn, NY, Malcolm was one of five sons born to a Scot immigrant journalist, and grew up in Englewood, NJ. He attended Princeton and launched a career as a newspaper publisher, interrupted by the war. When he returned, Pops made him his special assistant, and in 1946 he became associate publisher. In addition to a light, breezy and often irreverent editorial style, his contribution to *Forbes* includes broadly diversifying the holdings of the parent company. Separated in 1985 from his wife, Roberta, he has five children. His latest books include: *The Further Saying of Chairman Malcolm* (1986) and *What a Way To Go* (1988).

Betty Ford

"Society expects a lady to drink, but not to have a drinking problem," says the gutsy former First Lady credited by many as a pivotal figure in what *Time* headlined in 1984 as "The Getting Straight" movement: the growing number of Americans—male and female—trying to break the grip of alcohol and/or drugs. It was in 1978 that Betty Ford paved the way by announcing that she was getting hospital treatment to combat her dependency on alcohol and painkillers. Just as her candor about a mastectomy a few years earlier helped other women to cope with the trauma of breast cancer, Betty Ford's upfront acknowledgment of this problem removed much of the stigma and shame attached. Says one San Francisco drug counselor: "She has been a national treasure."

The wife of President Gerald Ford earned a reputation for never ducking hard questions soon after she moved into the White House in 1974. She shared her not-always-conventional views on smoking, psychiatry, her husband's bloopers and even answered one reporter's question about whether she and the President slept in the same bed. She also spoke out loud and clear in favor of the Equal Rights Amendment.

Christened Elizabeth Ann Bloomer when she was born in Chicago on 8 April 1918, she moved with her family to Grand Rapids, Michigan, when she was three. Her early dreams of becoming a professional dancer came at least partly to fruition when she became a member of Martha Graham's auxiliary concert troupe before coming back to Michigan and marrying. Her first husband was a local furniture dealer named William Warren (divorced after five years); her second, in 1948, was football-star-turned-aspiring-Congressman Gerald Ford. While husband Gerry rose in influence in the House, Betty held down the fort at their home, keeping the family (Susan, Michael, John, Steven) together while her husband was off politicking. (For a time, he was away making speeches an estimated 200 nights a year.)

Since going public about her own dependency problems, the former First Lady has become the mainstay of the Betty Ford Center she founded with financial support from recovered alcoholic and tire-fortune heir Leonard Firestone. The rehab center in El Rancho Mirage, California, has now attracted such superstars as Elizabeth Taylor, Johnny Cash, Robert Mitchum and Liza Minelli. Says Ford about her efforts there: "I consider it my life's work to remove the stigma from women admitting they are alcoholics." She has already (said *Time*) "made a formidable start." Her insightful book *Betty: Glad Awakening* was published in 1987.

Eileen & Jerry Ford

"Eileen is Mr. Hyde," says her #1 rival John Casablancas, "and Jerry is Dr. Jekyll. She's a sour, nasty old lady with lots of enemies." It's not surprising that she is disliked among her competitors. Year after year, the Ford Agency is tops in the business. She revolutionized modeling and made it the hard-ball business it is. It all began in 1948 when Eileen, a former model, was pregnant with her first of four children. Unable to model, she handled the bookings of a couple of friends and before she knew, she was handling six models and earning $250,000 a year. Her husband Jerry went into business with her and Ford Models was afoot. "He's the brains," she says of Jerry, "I'm the noise."

Her discoveries have included Lauren Hutton, Jean Shrimpton, Capucine, Jane Fonda, Candice Bergen, Suzy Parker, Christie Brinkley, Cheryl Tiegs, Brooke Shields, Ali MacGraw and Christine Ferrare, about whose ex-husband, car manufacturer John de Lorean, Ford made one of her many "modelling isn't for lightweights" comments. "Christine will probably lose some of her accounts now," she mourned. "I'm absolutely devoted to her. But if you were a cosmetics company what would you do? If I were John De Lorean, I'd commit suicide."

Born 25 May 1922 to a wealthy Long Island family, of whom she recalls, "my family believed I could do no wrong. That's probably why I have utter confidence in myself—even when I shouldn't have. I got everything I wanted from my parents: Brooks Brothers sweaters and Spalding saddle shoes. None of the people I grew up with had identity problems. We all had perfectly marvelous lives." She eloped with Ford who is two years her junior, after she graduated from Barnard College. Although she has written health and beauty books, the modelling business is her all-consuming $5-million-in-commissions-a-year passion. Three of her children work for the agency and models often live with the family in her comfortable Upper East Side townhouse. Every day hopeful models line up outside her office praying for her magic wand, the arbiter of America's #1 beauty look. "There's no question that I do that," she says, "I create a look and I create a style. American women mean a great deal to me. They're such lost souls, particularly the women of my generation. And women need so much help. They never have anyone to turn to. I help them understand how they can look better, how to do this, do that, get a job. And they're very trusting. Like little lost kids."

Gerald Ford

At the Gerald Ford Museum in Grand Rapids, Michigan, among 10,000 pieces of memorabilia commemorating Ford's two-year term as President, one exhibit stands out: the full-scale reproduction of the Oval Office in which Ford worked. An interesting tidbit sits atop his antique Presidential desk. It is a plaque which reads, "In August 1974 embedded microphones were removed on Ford's instructions." After pardoning his eavesdropping predecessor, President Richard Nixon, the former Grand Rapids Congressman-turned-VP (on Spiro Agnew's resignation)-turned-emergency-President went about the enormous task of assuring his nation that the Watergate era had ended. He was not re-elected into full term of his own, but he retired with his dignity and his own reputation for integrity largely intact.

Since leaving Washington in 1977 at age 63, Gerald R. Ford has remained active in business and politics. With 28 years as a member of Congress, as Vice President and as President, Ford collects an annual $100,000 pension, which he supplements with speaking fees. (At $10,000 a speech he gets more per word than nearly anyone on the rubber-chicken circuit. His memoirs and a television contract have earned him an additional $2 million.) He is part owner of two radio stations in Colorado. In 1980 he weighed pleas to enter the GOP primaries, decided against it, and then nearly joined Reagan as a running mate.

The long-time Minority Leader of the House, and ex-center of the University of Michigan gridiron Wolverines, Ford long played a conciliatroy role in national politics. "Jerry's effectiveness," explains former GOP chairman Rogers Morton, "comes from his ability to bridge all the gaps in the political spectrum—conservative, moderate, liberal, and all stops in between."

Born Gerald King 14 July 1913 in Omaha, he was the child of a marriage that ended in divorce before he was old enough to talk. His mother returned to live with her parents in Grand Rapids, Mich., and there married Gerald R. Ford, Sr., who adopted her baby, gave him his name, and in later years urged the boy to run for Congress. Working his way through the University of Michigan waiting on tables, young Ford centered the football team through two undefeated Big Ten championships (1932-33), was named Michigan's Most Valuable Player (1934) and graduated in 1935 with the idea of running for Congress already firmly in his mind. He worked as an assistant football coach at Yale while studying law there and launched his political career in 1948, taking time off from campaigning for Congress to marry divorcee Elizabeth Bloomer (four children) who, as Betty Ford, has made a name for herself apart from her husband and family. That November the voters gave him a wedding present—60.5 percent of the vote. He was routinely re-elected to represent his district, and was House minority leader until Nixon made him Vice President.

Harrison Ford

"Acting is basically like carpentry—if you know your craft, you figure out the logic of a particular job and submit yourself to it. It all comes down to detail." This is not just some weekend handyman pontificating on the mastering of hammer and nail. For nine years, as he struggled for recognition as an actor in Hollywood, he found steady employment as a "carpenter to the stars." He credits the satisfactions of his sideline business for giving him the ego strength to persist as an actor. His persistence landed him in outer space, as a swashbuckling hero of George Lucas' sci-fi thriller, *Star Wars*.

Harrison Ford was born in Chicago on 13 July 1942 the son of an Irish Catholic father and a Russian Jewish mother, and raised in the suburbs. Unable to take academia seriously, he "slept for days on end," and flunked out of Ripon College in Wisconsin three days before his class graduated. Relocated in L.A., he was signed by Columbia Pictures for $150 a week. "I did a year and a half and got kicked out on my ass for being too difficult. I was very unhappy with the process they were engaged in, which was to recreate stars the way it had been done in the fifties. They sent me to get my hair pompadoured like Elvis Presley." He repeated the experience at Universal Studios.

Then in 1977, Lucas, who had cast him in a small role in *American Graffiti*, picked him for a lead in *Star Wars*, a kind of Hardy-Boys-in-Space epic that captured the imagination of moviegoers, sparking huge profits, a merchandising campaign, and two sequels, also starring Ford, *The Empire Strikes Back*, in 1980, and the 1983 *Return of the Jedi*. His performance as adventurer Indiana Jones in the 1981 hit movie, *Raiders of the Lost Ark*, and its sequels, *Indiana Jones and the Temple of Doom,* and *Indiana Jones and the Last Crusade*, solidified his bankable image as a rugged romantic. Other popular films include *Witness* (1985), *The Mosquito Coast* (1986), *Frantic* (1987), and *Working Girl* (1988).

Resistant to publicity, he believes too much fanfare clouds an actor's vision. "The natural state for an actor is that of observer, where you can learn something. Instead, I'm a focus of attention. When you're written about you're stuck with a 'personality'—even if it's your own."

A father of two from his first marriage, which ended in divorce, he married screenwriter Melissa Mathison (*E.T.*) in 1983.

Milos Forman

His gentle comedies of contemporary life, revealing eternal truths in mundane situations, helped create the internationally celebrated mid-1960s new wave of Czech film-making, which flourished all too briefly until his country's invasion by the U.S.S.R. in 1968. Not so coincidentally, that was the year he moved to the U.S. to continue his movie career. Triumphantly, he won the 1975 Academy Award for his direction of *One Flew Over the Cuckoo's Nest*.

Born 18 February 1932 near Prague to parents (one of whom was Jewish) who died in Nazi concentration camps, he was raised with his two brothers by relatives and friends. This gypsy-like upbringing may account for his sharp eye for familial relations. "Because I wasn't emotionally involved," he says, "I became very objective. Most children aren't consciously aware of what is going on around them, but I was always following the action, trying to fit myself into the group." After study at the esteemed Prague Film Faculty, he made his first feature, *Black Peter* ('63), followed by *Loves of a Blonde* (a 1965 Oscar nominee for best foreign film) and the controversial *Fireman's Ball* ('68). His first U.S. film, *Taking Off* (made in '70 and released the following year) depicted teenage runaways and the generation gap. His adaptation of the Broadway counter-culture musical *Hair* ('79), contained similar themes. In the 70s he became co-director of the Film Division of Columbia's School of the Arts. His recent films are adaptations of huge literary and stage successes: *Ragtime* ('81) *Amadeus* ('84), which won a slew of Oscars, including Best Picture, and the multi-Academy Award-nominated *Les Liaisons Dangereuses* (1989).

His first wife was Jane Brejchova, a popular Czech film actress. He's divorced from his second, singer Vera Kresadlova, by whom he has twin sons who were raised in their native country. He enjoys skiing and basketball.

Frederick Forsyth

He exploded on the bestseller scene in 1970 with *The Day of the Jackal*, a thriller about a hired assassin on the trail of General Charles de Gaulle. "The book had such an impact," Peter Maas pointed out in the *New York Times Book Review*, "that when a real-life terrorist, Carlos Ramirez, had the good fortune to be nicknamed 'The Jackal,' it guaranteed *his* fame." Meanwhile the journalist-turned-author insured his own niche in publishing history by turning out two more bestsellers-into-movies, *The Dogs of War* and *The Odessa File*. After these first three super-successes, Frederick Forsyth resolved not to write any more novels, but in 1978, returned to the typewriter for *The Devil's Alternative* and, in 1984, hit the lists with *The Fourth Protocol* (made into a movie in 1987).

He was born in August, 1938, the son of an Ashford, Kent, shopkeeper. By his mid-teens, he had three ambitions: to be a bullfighter ("I was intoxicated by Hemingway's *Death in the Afternoon*"), to earn his wings, and to get out of school as quickly as possible. He didn't achieve the first goal, but managed the others, foregoing college to join the Royal Air Force and, at nineteen, becoming the youngest fighter pilot then in the RAF. He came to novel-writing after a decade or so as a journalist, progressing from cub reporter on a provincial newspaper to Reuters' bureau chief in spy-infested East Berlin. He also served in Paris and London and, most dramatically, in war-torn Nigeria, covering the Biafra conflict first for the BBC and then (after an indignant resignation) as a freelancer. His first book, in 1969, was *The Biafra Story*, a no-holds-barred expose of what he saw during his African stay.

By the end of 1969, he was "a journalist doing zilch and likely to do little more than zilch for the rest of my career. I had £1000, no apartment, no job, and a reputation on Fleet Street for being a bit of a rebel—the guy who told the BBC to get stuffed and walked away from a career with Reuters. So I thought I'd try my hand at novel writing." He wrote *The Day of the Jackal* in exactly thirty-five days. After a brief whirl at the life of a bestselling writer (e.g. "fast cars and changing girlfriends") Forsyth met and married his wife Carole in 1973. They and their two sons, Stuart and Shane, reside in a house in a London suburb.

John Forsythe

Some years ago his pal Gore Vidal told him, "No, I don't think you're square. Just slightly rhomboid." Now that this "sweet, avuncular, charming establishment man" has become a vintage silver fox, his sex appeal has soared. "Gray hair doesn't mean you're over the hill. It's all in your attitude," says the actor, who was type cast on TV shows such as "Bachelor Father," "The John Forsythe Show" and "To Rome With Love." In the 1980s, as the patriarch on "Dynasty," the sex, money and rage-throbbing ABC-TV nighttime soap set in oil-rich Denver, "Blake Carrington" is capitalism's most attractive symbol, a rock-hard Teddy Bear married to "Krystal" aka Linda Evans who played the pal of his niece on the sitcom "Bachelor Father." "That," smiles Forsythe who also was the disembodied voice of Charlie on ABC's "Charlie's Angels," "says a lot about hanging in."

Born in Penn's Grove, N.J., 29 January 1918, the son of a stockbroker, he worked as an announcer at Brooklyn's Ebbets Field (home of the pre-L.A. Dodgers) and as "the weak younger brother who was always killed in auto accidents" on soap operas. He joined the Air Force production of *Winged Victory* and then studied at the Actor's Studio in New York after the war. ("I was known as the Brooks Brothers bohemian.") He received attention when he replaced Arthur Kennedy on broadway in the Arthur Miller play *All My Sons* and reached star status when he replaced Henry Fonda in *Mr. Roberts;* later he originated his own starring role in *Teahouse of the August Moon*. Next came Hollywood, and all those avuncular years on TV. A devoted family man, he's been married to actress Julie Warren since 1943 (two daughters); an earlier marriage produced a son. In their Bel Air farmhouse he lives the good live, which, according to one close observer, Forsythe has managed to "elevate to a kind of art form all by itself." In 1985 he became the spokesman for a men's scent line—Carrington—inspired by his television alter ego. In 1987 he was nominated for a Golden Globe Award (Best Actor in a TV series) and in 1988 he appeared in the film *Scrooged*.

Michele Fortune

The road to success sometimes takes more than hard work and strong character. Sometimes it takes a bit of fortune. After a 19-year career in retail sales, Michele Fortune became the president and chief operating officer of AnnTaylor, the nation's leading upscale women's apparel retailer, known for its fashionable yet comfortable ready-to-wear career and casual clothes. Fortune put in her years of hard work. In 1969 she started as a trainee in Filene's Department Store in Boston, Massachusetts, working her way up to buyer before moving on. In 1976 Fortune started as a buyer in the dress department of the Manhattan branch of Lord & Taylor. Before leaving Lord & Taylor to accept the position at AnnTaylor, Fortune had moved up the success ladder from buyer to senior V.P. and general merchandising manager, with duties ranging from setting up business strategy to overseeing financial planning development and managing advertising and sales promotion. With this background, it's not surprising that Fortune is called "the force behind AnnTaylor's new, stronger, more aggressive advertising campaign." She has her job cut out for her, commanding the chain of 110 stores in 25 states with sales of $280 million in 1988.

Born in Fresno, California, Fortune swam competitively while in high school and at Idaho State University. Now, when not spending time with her financial consultant husband, Edward G. David, or her young son, Michele Fortune is either managing one of her three homes—in New York City, Long Island and Vermont—or attending a meeting of one of the committees on which she sits. The busy Fortune is a member of The Retailing Advisory Committee for the Prince Program in Retailing at Simmons College, The Fashion Group, Inc., The Committee of 200, The Round Table of Fashion Executives, The American Woman's Economic Development, The National Women's Economic Alliance, and sits on the board of The Allied Stores Corp.

Jodie Foster

Seldom does a film role earn both an Oscar nomination and result in a national scandal. But such was the case with Iris, the 12-year-old prostitute played by Jodie Foster in Martin Scorsese's *Taxi Driver*. "I knew," the deep-voiced actress said, "when the hustler part . . . came up that I had to be really perfect or it would ruin my career. That role was really risque for a child." Her portrayal was so effective that, in addition to putting Foster into the 1976 "Best Supporting Actress" competition, it allegedly inspired John W. Hinckley, Jr., to mount an assassination attempt against President Ronald Reagan 30 March 1981. The disturbed young man attributed his "historical deed" to a desire to impress Foster after becoming obsessed with Iris and the actress who portrayed her.

This unwanted notoriety plagued Foster during her freshman year at Yale, just days before she made her stage debut there as, ironically, a prison inmate in a student production of Marsha Norman's *Getting Out*. By then, Foster had been in films for nearly a decade, following a precocious childhood that saw her speaking at nine months, uttering sentences at one year, and teaching herself to read at three. Her parents divorced before her birth in L.A. 19 November 1962. "I feel lucky in a way that I never knew a father," she says, "that there was never a marital conflict in the house. I've always felt like a replacement . . . that I took the place of a husband, roommate or pal." Foster's mother has astutely managed her career, which has progressed from TV commercials (including the bare-bottom Coppertone child ad) to Disney features to an earlier Scorsese film, *Alice Doesn't Live Here Anymore*, in which she played a wine-drinking street urchin who (according to one critic) "looks like a boy and talks like a man."

At age 13, Foster had the distinction of having three of her films shown at the Cannes Film Festival: *Taxi Driver*, *Bugsy Malone* (an all-kiddie gangster musical spoof) and *The Little Girl Who Lived Down the Lane* (in which she played a murderess). An instinctive performer, Foster never studied acting. Fluent in French (the language in which she delivered her bilingual high school's valedictory), she concentrated on studying literature and creative writing at Yale, from which she was graduated in 1985. During school vacations she continued making films such as *The Hotel New Hampshire*.

Her mesmerizing portrayal of a young woman gang-raped in the movie *The Accused* brought about Jodie's popular win as Best Actress at the 1989 Academy Awards. A celebrity in demand, Foster has appeared in *Five Corners* (1987), *Siesta* (1988), *Backtrack* (1988) and *Stealing Home* (1988).

Michael J. Fox

"Call me cheap, but I wasn't ready to pay $5 to see myself on the screen," says Michael J. Fox about his smashing performance in the Steven Spielberg-produced movie *Back to the Future* which was released in 1985. "I was in London when the movie opened, and I wanted to see it when I got back to town. So I called the Cinerama Dome in L.A. and asked if I could come down. It was actually kind of cool. They even had a spot reserved for me in the parking lot." However, before all the fanfare and good reviews, Fox confided to Robert Basler of the *Washington Post* that "there's never been a Spielberg flop, and God, Lord, don't let it be my movie." He didn't have to worry; the film became the top grossing movie of 1985. The red-hot young dynamo of NBC's hit series "Family Ties" (1982-1989) works around the clock to fit both movie-making and television appearances into his schedule. In a short time span, Fox's face was seen incessantly promoting his latest features. His 1980's movies include: *Teen Wolf* (1985), *Light of Day* (with Joan Jett; 1986), *The Secret of My Success* (1986), *Bright Lights Big City* (1988), and *Casualties of War* (1989). Sticking with a good thing, Michael's next slew of films are sequels: *Back to the Future II* (1989), *Further Secrets of My Success* (1989) and *Back to the Future III* (1990).

Born in Edmonton, Alberta, Canada, on 9 June 1961, Fox was raised in a family with five children. He began working at 15 in a regional television series called "Leo and Me." After a small role in a television film with Art Carney and Maureen Stapleton, he moved to Los Angeles on his own and landed a role in a Walt Disney feature, *Midnight Madness*. He won a role in the critically acclaimed CBS series "Palmerstown, USA" by Alex Haley, and made appearances on "Trapper John," "Lou Grant" and "Family." When the part of Alex P. Keaton, the conservative "ultimate Yuppie" son of former 60's peace activists in "Family Ties" came along (he was not the producer's first choice) Fox soon became a network favorite receiving approximately 500 fan letters a week. Before "Family Ties," "I didn't have a phone, a couch or any money," says Fox. "In fact, I was getting all these great letters from collection agencies saying 'This is your last chance' in big red letters." These days he doesn't receive nasty notes from bill collectors but loving scented notes from young girls. Although Michael J. Fox was considered one of the most eligible bachelors, in true show-biz tradition, he married his ex-"Family Ties" girlfriend, "Ellen" (actress Tracy Pollan) in a private guest-list ceremony on 17 July 1988 in Arlington, Vermont. Fox's future looks bright; the long-running "Family Ties" concluded its run by sending Alex P. Keaton to work on Wall Street in Manhattan. The possibilities of spin-offs seem endless. The 5'4", 120-pound heartthrob is an avid hockey, baseball and skiing enthusiast, and resides with his wife, Tracy, in both California and Vermont.

Arlene Francis

Her lively radio interview program on New York City's WOR was, for 24 years, a mecca for prominent pilgrims from the stage, screen, literary and public life (including an occasional ex-President and/or First Lady), and when she was rudely dumped by the station in 1984, the firing became a media *cause célèbre*. But the unfazed star continued to act (as a friend once put it) "as though life were the best party she ever attended," her dance-card still filled with TV assignments such as WNBC's "The Prime of Your Life"and summer stock. She still is possessor of "one of the most infectious laughs in broadcasting" and a purveyor of what her former producer, Jean Bach, calls "vivacity under pressure."

Born Arlene Francis Kazanjian, 20 October 1908 in Boston, she was the only daughter of a successful portrait painter. After acquiring polish at Miss Finch's finishing school, she set her sights on a career in the theatre, but her father disapproved so she settled, first, for radio and eventually television. Busy on the tube since its swaddling days ("Blind Date" and NBC's daytime "Home"), she truly hit her stride as a perky regular on the hardy small-screen hit, "What's My Line?" which started in 1950 and lasted more than two decades. (She was the one everybody rooted for; co-panelist Dorothy Kilgallen was the one they loved to hate.) She also managed (father notwithstanding) to make her mark on Broadway, following up her first big hit in *The Doughgirls* (1942) with such offerings as *Once More, With Feeling* (1958), *Tchin-Tchin* (1962), *Mrs. Dally* (1965) and a 1966 revival of *Dinner at Eight*. On the big screen, she shone forth as Jimmy Cagney's wife in Billy Wilder's 1961 comedy, *One, Two, Three* and the Doris Day hit *The Thrill of it All* (1963). Married first to Neil Agnew in 1934, she met her late husband, actor Martin Gabel, in the Mercury Theatre production of *Danton's Death* in 1938. She has one son, Peter.

Dick Francis

"Having a book on the bestseller list is very nice," says this steeplechase-jockey-turned-bestselling-novelist, "but there's nothing nicer than jumping over a lovely fence on a good horse and looking through his pricked ears for the next one." Since the publication of *Dead Cert*, his first mystery with a racing setting, in 1962, he has averaged a novel a year (e.g. *Forfeit, Whip Hand, High Stakes, Banker, Proof*) and by 1984, they had sold more than 20 million copies in 20 languages. To a growing band of Francis aficionados, the books are not "just mysteries," but "splendidly readable" novels of character and manners with "gentle but stalwart morality." Observed critic John Leonard: "Not to read Dick Francis because you don't like horses is like not reading Dostoevski because you don't like God."

Born in Wales, 31 October 1920, Dick Francis grew up in Maidenhead, a city on the Thames where his father managed a hunting stable. He quit school at 15 because he liked horses better than books. After a World War II career detour to the RAF, he spent the years between 1948 and 1957 as one of England's best steeplechase jockeys, riding in 2,305 races. (He won 345; placed or showed in 525 more.) But there were bruises as well as bravos. When he married his wife, Mary, in 1947, he showed up at the wedding with his arm in a sling, having fallen from his horse and broken a collar bone. ("I've broken it 11 times since—that's six times each side," he told writer Edward Zuckerman. "You get used to it.") After a particularly nasty fall ten years later, he retired from jockeying and began his writing career with a well-received autobiography (*The Sport of Queens*) and a stint as racing correspondent for the *London Sunday Express* which lasted 16 years.

When not at work on a book, Francis is still often at the track, either in England or near his winter home in Fort Lauderdale. Though his novels often deal with horse players, he never himself bets. "I don't have any enthusiasm for it," he says. "If you have a bet, you tend to watch one horse. I like to watch the tactics of all the jockeys."

Helen Frankenthaler

"Between the possible and the impossible, you come up with something wonderful," says Helen Frankenthaler, the stylish darling of the "second generation" of Abstract Expressionists. Through her paintings she explores space (according to one critic) "walking a tightrope between spontaneity and self consciousness, improvisation and deliberation, dissolution and structure." Her artistic endeavors include print-making, sculpture, ceramic tiles and tapestry. A participant in the 1984 show "American Women Artists (Part I: 20th Century Pioneers)" at the Sidney Janis Gallery in New York, Frankenthaler produces work that lies somewhere between Abstract Expressionism and Color-Field painting. She is widely credited with the development of the so-called soak-stain technique, which begins with pouring pigments on unprimed canvas, forming what has been described as "grand gestalts of color that bob and weave, somersault and flipflop and casually loll about." The theory of Jackson Pollock, one of the first to kick over the easel traces and dribble paint on unsized, unprimed cotton duck, appealed to her "enormously," she says, "that dance-like use of arms and legs in painting, being in the center, relating to the floor." The relationships that she evolved appealed to public and critics alike. And in the late 1960s, with more than 100 shows to her credit (including a well-reviewed major retrospective at the Whitney), she was officially proclaimed, in the sententious tones of a well-known critic, "one of our best painters."

Born 12 December 1928, the youngest daughter of a New York State Supreme Court Justice, she majored in art at Bennington, which she "loved . . . because I could paint with men like Paul Feeley, listen to Eric Fromm and wait on table for W.H. Auden." She once said of former husband Robert Motherwell, a "first generation" Abstract Expressionist, "We honor each other and each other's work and each other's magic." They are now amicably divorced. Her magical work has been shown throughout the world and a book of her paintings was published in 1971. Home is a townhouse in Manhattan—the walls filled with her own paintings as well as with those of friends and favorite artists. And to satisfy her need for contact with nature, "a horizontal rather than vertical environment," Frankenthaler keeps a waterfront home in Connecticut.

Aretha Franklin

There was some talk in the mid-Seventies about a couple of female vocalists dethroning Aretha Franklin as the Queen of Soul. Franklin wasn't at the top of the charts as she had been in the late Sixties and early Seventies with such Gold tunes as "Respect," "Chain of Fools," (You Make Me Feel Like a) "Natural Woman," and many others. However, her albums *Jump to It* in 1982 and *Get It Right* in 1983—along with her hot 1985 single and video, "Freeway of Love"—reaffirmed that she is now, has been and always will be the Queen. As one newspaper put it: "Like Billie Holiday before, Aretha Franklin became the high watermark of her generation, and those after it, against which all other women singers in the R&B and soul idiom are measured." Her voice, ranging through four octaves, has been exciting listeners since her childhood when she sang in her father's church. Her late father, a minister, who has been described as a "barnstorming evangelist," frequently entertained gospel singers, from whom his daughter took her first lessons in soul music. At 14, Franklin was traveling with a revival meeting troupe and, four years later, she was recording soul music.

Franklin, born 25 March 1942 in Memphis, has numerous Gold Records and has earned 15 Grammy Awards (her latest in 1989 for "One Lord, One Faith, One Baptism"), in addition to such citations as *Billboard*'s Best Vocalist of the Year. She was raised in Detroit on the fringes of the city's black ghetto, in the neighborhood that also spawned Diana Ross, Smokey Robinson, and the Four Tops. *Quarter Notes* magazine aptly summed up Franklin's character as a "self-knowledgeable woman who had wised up in the course of a few affairs without losing any of her sensuality, who had begun to see love not just as a thrill, but as a pragmatic bargain: if you want a do-right woman, you have to be a do-right man; if you want my love and my money, give me respect; if you have 'Brain One,' think about what you're trying to do to me." First married to Ted White, in 1978 she married Glynn Turman; she is the mother of three sons. Franklin was inducted into the Rock & Roll Hall of Fame in 1987.

Antonia Fraser

When her 1969 biography *Mary Queen of Scots* hit the bestseller lists, Lady Antonia Fraser became a literary lion in America but in her native England her book was just the most recent work by the "literary Longfords," the clan (including Anthony Powell through marriage) whose volumes have filled more shelves than the Churchills and Mitfords combined. Her newfound celebrity also made the tall, beautiful, blue-eyed blonde aristocrat a trend-setter for the Beautiful People ("I had become a press creation . . . the result of a lot of friends who are journalists [and] an obliging nature.") The gossip columns had a field day again in 1975 when she left her husband of 20 years to move in with playwright Harold Pinter (at Pinter's insistence they married in 1980). "When I left my first husband and went off to live with Harold," she told Mel Gussow in a 1984 *New York Times Magazine* interview, "people said, 'How could you do such a thing?' and I said, 'I've done it!'"

The eldest (27 August 1932) of the eight children born into the Socialist-Catholic (convent) family of the seventh Earl of Longford (the title he assumed on his brother's death in 1960), Lady Antonia recalls, "Our home was knee-deep in books and the discussion that revolved around them." She was especially caught up in the story of the beautiful romantic Catholic Queen of Scotland and acted out the role at home in playlets, supported by her brothers and sisters. She followed her mother to Oxford, where among her classmates was V.S. Naipaul. ("To have known him is to have known at least one genius," adding, "I married the second.") After three years working for publisher Lord Weidenfeld (who still publishes her books, which began with juveniles and books on toys and dolls), she married handsome Scottish war hero and Conservative M.P. Hugh Fraser (six children), wearing a heart-shaped tiara and dress modeled on the ones worn by the tragic Scottish Queen. When in the '60s Antonia's mother (biographer of Queen Victoria, Wellington, Byron et al) suggested that she herself might undertake a life of Mary, the daughter secured a book contract that bound her to her ambitions task, and her efforts were rewarded by overwhelmingly favorable reviews, including Jean Stafford's: "She brings to this immense biography a vivid sense of the mores of the 16th century, [in] so lucid a manner . . . and a narrative dexterity that makes her sad tale seem told for the first time." Other biographies include lives of Cromwell and Charles II. In recent years, Fraser has become a writer of popular mystery novels, the Jemima Shore series (set in her former convent school, St. Mary's in Ascot) which have been adapted for television, creating what their author calls "a cultette." Of her 14th book, *The Weaker Vessel*, a collective biography of the suppressed women of the 17th century, Fraser admitted to Gussow that she would have had a difficult time living in that century. "The people who did well intuitively understood the system and made their way around it. Hence they were courtesans. I don't think I would have had the patience to be a courtesan, though I might have enjoyed my work." Recent books are: *Jemima Shore's First Case: And Other Stories* (1987), *Your Royal Hostage* (1988), and *The Warrior Queens* (1989).

Joe Frazier

Although it was way back in 1971 that he won the first of his memorable slugfests with Muhammad Ali, he still hasn't forgiven "The Mouth that Roared" for pre-fight insults. And while it was in 1981 that he last fought an unranked former prison con to an unimpressive draw before he hung up the gloves, he still proclaims that no heavyweight presently fighting can beat him. "But I'm having more fun now," he asserts. He's also become a successful fight trainer, having sent a gold medal winner, Meldrick Taylor, to the 1984 Olympics from his Smoking Joe Frazier, Inc., boxing gym in Philadelphia. With two of his sons and two more nephews also in the stable, he rather prematurely calls his charges "the heavyweight champs of the fight game."

Born 17 January 1944 in Beaufort, S.C., the youngest of 13 children, he was expelled from the tenth grade for flooring a schoolmate unwise enough to make a crack about Joe's mother. Wandering into a North Philadelphia gym one day out of sheer embarrassment to lose weight, he was given an indifferent once-over by former railroad welder Yancy Durham. "I thought he was just another fat kid who'd quit after a few days," recalls Durham. "But he kept coming in every day, losing that blubber. Then I saw he really had a punch." Durham started Frazier on his amateur career, which culminated in a gold medal-winning trip to the 1964 Tokyo Olympics (when the man whose alternate he was, Buster Mathis, became hurt, and Frazier won despite his own broken left hand). Back in Philly a syndicate of businessmen joined to extricate him from a low-paying slaughterhouse job by managing his boxing career, with Durham as trainer. On 8 March 1971 he pranced in the Madison Square Garden ring for his long-awaited match with arch foe Ali, whose former crown he owned after Ali was stripped of it for refusing the military draft. Frazier won the 15-round decision before 20,455 at the Garden, plus an estimated 300 million more who saw it on closed-circuit TV and via satellite.

At 206 pounds and not quite six feet, he was built like a tree stump, and was feared for his rib-rearranging hooks. He bobbed and weaved aggressively on tireless legs and used a peek-a-boo defense that hid his face but left his head exposed. He would soak his head in brine to toughen the skin. Because of the fearsome savagery of the first fight, an excited public demanded two rematches with Ali, who became his perpetual nemesis. Although Ali won both, the last, known as "The Thrilla in Manilla" prompted the winner to admit he'd never felt so close to death, which was similarly why Frazier's trainer wouldn't let him answer the bell for the 15th. But in between he was champ from 1970-73. In 1976 he was embarrassed by being knocked out in the second round by champ George Foreman, which led to his first retirement. He became a rhythm & blues singer. But he never quit some form of training, as he built a limousine service and a boxing gym business, he also battled boredom. In '81 he had his brief comeback, and in '83 he set up a fight with his son Marvis, and champ Larry Holmes. Marvis had had only ten pro fights and Holmes made a first-round KO victim of him. At home Frazier is an old-fashioned father, not allowing his two grown boxing sons or three other children to receive phone calls after 10 p.m., and harkening to his own respect for his father as a yardstick. "They can't live up to me. Your momma and daddy and the Good Man made you. How you gonna be equal to that?" Momma and daddy announced in 1985 that they were ending their 25-year marriage.

Mirella Freni

Considered "the greatest living Susanna" and the "world's foremost lyric soprano," she is an international favorite of many opera aficionados because of her clear, dynamic voice and capacity to demonstrate both mood and feeling. Distinctive in style, her singing and acting have brought a fresh dimension to such roles as Mimi (Puccini's *La Boheme*), Susanna (Mozart's *The Marriage of Figaro*), Marguerite (*Faust*), and *Madame Butterfly*. In recent years she has favored weightier roles, portraying mostly Verdi heroines. While her career has been primarily European, she has appeared with top-notch companies worldwide and is most familiar to American audiences via several excellent popular opera recordings (the works of Verdi, Puccini, and

Gounod, among other composers) and for the film versions of *La Boheme* (1965) and *Madame Butterfly* (1976).

Born 27 February 1935 in Modena, northern Italy (also supertenor Luciano Pavorotti's birthplace; his mother and Freni's were girlhood friends and co-workers), she began gathering applause at the early age of five. An uncle first noticed her unusual talent when she sang along with his opera recordings. By ten she had performed in public for the first time (a students' concert) and two years later won a national competition with her rendition of Puccini's "Un bel di," Freni (fray-nee) studied singing in Bologna for the next few years and made her professional opera debut in 1955 at Modena's Teatro Comunale in the role of Micaela (*Carmen*).

Married in June, 1955, to the accompanist of her early student concerts, Leone Magiera, who eventually became her coach and advisor, Freni temporarily relinquished her stage career to keep house. It took two years of her husband's encouragement before she resumed professional singing. in 1958, via first prize in a contest, she got the opportunity to sing Mimi at the Vercelli opera house. Appearances with various Italian opera companies followed and soon she was on tour in Germany, Holland, Spain, Austria and England. In January, 1963, she came to international attention as Mimi in the lavish Franco Zeffirelli presentation of *La Boheme* conducted by Herbert von Karajan. The controversial Austrian conductor has played something of a Svengali role in Freni's life and she credits him with challenging her to expand her range. "When I started, I thought Mozart and *La Boheme* would be the maximum for me." She has since moved beyond the definition of lyric soprano to more demanding protrayals (*Butterfly* etc.), premiering many at Karajan's seasonal Salzburg Festival.

A "reluctant diva," Freni prefers performing in the leading European opera houses to be closer to her home in Milan. The reputation she acquired overseas preceded her NYC debut in 1965 at the Metropolitan, but her performance surpassed expectation. Alan Rich of the *New York Herald Tribune* wrote: "she used voice and gesture to create a Mimi of ravishing femininity and grace . . . a standard unto herself and an artist of the highest qualities." A few enthusiastic seasons at the Met and other U.S. appearances have followed, including an enthusiastically received *Manon Lescaut* at the Met in 1984. She made her Carnegie Hall debut in 1989.

Playful, vibrant and attractive, Freni gives the impression on stage of being petite. She is a self-proclaimed homebody and soccer fan and maintains a relatively low profile in the high-strung operatic world. Her only child,, named Micaela, was born in 1956.

Betty Friedan

With battle cries such as "Women of the world, unite! You have nothing to lose but your vacuum cleaners" this talkative housewife-writer helped set off the explosion known as "women's lib." The spark that detonated this bomb, more than any other factor, was her 1963 book, *The Feminine Mystique*, which put into words the discontent and frustration so many suburban housewives had felt. Friedan took a long look at "the *Good Housekeeping* seal-of-approval American Dreamhouse" and came to the conclusion that all was not well behind the crabgrass; that for many of the female occupants the real name of the game was Rage. As speaker, writer, TV panelist, marcher, and badgerer of government officials and corporate heads, she became "Mother Superior" of the burgeoning feminist movement, which took up where the suffragettes left off. Later, Friedan became a bridge between conservative and radical elements of feminism and a leader of efforts to reconcile feminism with the American mainstream. Her 1981 book, *The Second Stage*, is an exhortation to women and men to see feminism not as a movement antagonistic to traditional female roles and values, but as a humanizing force in society at large. "Feminism is good for men," says Friedan.

Born Betty Naomi Goldstein in Peoria, Ill., 4 February 1921, in high school she was "that girl with all A's and I wanted boys worse than anything." Her father, a jewelry store owner, thought she studied too much, and allowed her to take out no more than five library books at a time. She graduated *summa cum laude* from Smith College in 1942 and gave up a graduate fellowship in psychology at Berkeley—to pursue the dream of the love, the home, and the children that were supposed to be everywoman's destiny. In 1947 she married Carl Friedan, an advertising executive; they had three children. Then came *The Feminine Mystique*, and Friedan's emancipation. In 1966, she founded the National Organization for Women (NOW), the pioneering feminist group she chaired until 1970. She was among leaders forming the National Abortion Rights Action League in 1969 and the National Women's Political Caucus in 1971. She and her husband were divorced in 1969. Never one to be out-talked, she's ruffled more than a few feathers on her trail-blazing travels. (She once startled the moderator of a TV talk show by insisting, "If you don't let me have my say, I'm going to say "orgasm" ten times.") Looking ahead to her place in history, this is how she'd like to be remembered: "She was the one who said women were people; she organized them and taught them to spell their names."

William Friedkin

His instinct for telling "a good story about a dark secret" has led him to such powerful and controversial film hits as *The Birthday Party* (1968), *The Boys in the Band* (1970), *The French Connection* (1971) and *The Exorcist* (1973)—the latter two winning him Oscars for best director. His *Deal of the Century* (1983) was a black comedy about the underworld of arms sales, a subject about which he feels deeply. "The movie is about responsibility," says Friedkin, who is known to all as Billy. "The message at the end of the movie is that people must take a stand. They cannot be apathetic." Friedkin, who began his career in the mailroom of a Chicago TV station, is pushed by an enormous enthusiasm and love for filmmaking. ("If they suddenly said all the rules are changed, you've got to pay money to direct a movie, I'd be first in line.") He maintains that the audience is always the final judge of a film's success or failure. After editing *The Exorcist*, he recalled, he told his editors "'If we get away with this, it'll be amazing. We will be laughed out of the theaters.' . . . And of course that never happened except out of nervous laughter. But the last people to know what they have, generally, are the filmmakers. You're the last to know if it's any good or if it's terrible."

Born in Chicago, 29 August 1939, he began his career in the mailroom of WGN-TV and within two years was directing live television. His first film was *The People vs. Paul Crump*, a documentary about a man on Death Row which was banned by the station for which it was made but eventually won the Golden Gate Award at the 1962 San Francisco Film Festival, attracting the attention of producer David Wolper. Friedkin was hired to make three TV documentaries for Wolper and ABC-TV. In 1967, he moved to feature films, directed *Good Times* with Sonny and Cher, and followed it with *The Night They Raided Minsky's* (1968). Among his other films are *Cruising*, *Sorcerer*, and *The Brink's Job*. His films have rung in more than $300 million at box-offices around the world. Describing his passion for filmmaking, Friedkin says it begins with huge enthusiasm during research. "During shooting, it becomes nuts and bolts, one nail at a time. Editing, I get wildly enthusiastic again; you can feel the creativity. . . . Then I put it all together and look at it and it's a piece of junk. When the fine cutting begins I begin to curse the images, the actors. Why are you smiling, you idiot? Why did I tell you to laugh? What kind of a bum director am I? Then it becomes, well, what can we do to save it? By that time it's like a patched up marriage. And by the time they release it, it's an old love affair." Additional films include *Duet for One* (1981), *Sea Trial* (1985), *Judgment Day* and *To Live and Die in L.A.*

David Frost

(both 1986), *Rampage* (1987), and *The Executioner* (1989). He returned to TV in 1984 with his first music video—for Laura Branigan—and he later was the director/writer/executive producer for an NBC-TV show, "C.A.T. Squad: Python Wolf." His two-year marriage to French film superstar Jeanne Moreau ended in 1979 and in 1985 he was involved in a heated custody battle with former wife Lesley-Anne Down (married 1982 to 1985) for their son Jack (born 1982). He married Kelly Lange on 7 June 1987.

David Frost

Author, television producer, columnist and—most formidably—an interviewer, his approach is deceptively casual, almost avuncular. Tight-lipped guests hopped aboard his departed "David Frost TV Show" and a split second later unpeeled their innermost thoughts. "It's odd to be discussing things as frankly as this with you in front of an audience," declared a foreign secretary after suddenly blurting out, "I don't want to be prime minister. I don't believe I've got what it takes to be prime minister." Frost also made television history with his revealing on-camera colloquies in 1977 with former President Richard Nixon and cites this erstwhile talk-partner in his *Book of the World's Worst Decisions*. Nixon, claims Frost, deserves the "Order of the Golden Boot" for "his decision to order voice-activated Sony tape recorders for the Oval Office in the White House," thus cinching his place in history in a much different manner than anticipated.

Frost has made his mark on both sides of the Atlantic for his efforts on the tube. Probably the smoothest, shrewdest, and most amiable interviewer around, he rocketed to the top of the slippery pole at a very early age. ("The most important thing on talk shows is to listen. And I like involving myself with the audience a lot. I like talking to people in all walks of life.") His illustrious guests have included Golda Meir, King Hussein, the Rolling Stones, Prince Charles, Jackie Gleason, Noel Coward, a fellow who sings to a tin tray, someone who blows up hot water bottles until they burst, and you-name-him-or-it. ("The thing I believe in really most of all in TV is this thing called unpredictability.") Frost has been responsible for "Headliners with David Frost" (1978), star of "The Frost Programme," joint founder of London Weekend TV and chairman/managing director of David Paradine Productions (his film-producing credits include *Charlie One-Eye*). He launched "Breakfast Television," also London-based, but the show has been a consistent also-ran behind its cozier BBC competition. He has been decorated with an Order of the British Empire, received many TV-related awards (including 2 Emmys), and been named TV Personality of the Year.

Born in Tenterden, England, 7 April 1939, the son of a Methodist minister, he attended Cambridge, where he took an honors degree in English at Gonville and Caius College ("or as I describe it to people who don't know, 'the ugly one on the right'"). Popping out of Cambridge in 1961, he found himself connected with the network called Associated Rediffusion. There he met Ned Sherrin and they cooked up "That Was the Week That Was." He was on hand for the U.S. version, which wasn't too successful. ("I think it could have been funnier and could have had a lighter touch.") Tired of satire, he created "The Frost Report" for BBC, which each week treated subjects like Frost on Money, Frost on Women, etc., then came up with "The Frost Programme," a gabfest similar to his New York show. He authored *Talking with Frost* (1967) and *The Presidential Debate* (1968). For years a confirmed and seasoned bachelor (his romantic involvements included Diahann Carroll and Carol Lynley), in 1981 he wed Peter Sellers' widow Lynne Frederick, a marriage that lasted two years. Then in 1983, this Protestant minister's son wed Lady Carina Fitzalan Howard, daughter of the Duke of Norfolk, the highest ranking Roman Catholic peer of the realm. They are the parents of three sons.

Athol Fugard

"My life's work was possibly just to witness as truthfully as I could the nameless and destitute of this one little corner of the world." That corner is South Africa, and Athol Fugard is a most sensitive witness to the plight of the black man there—a victim of apartheid. Fugard admits that being the observer is relatively easy for him because, as he explains, "I only write, finally, about what I love and what I hate."

Harold Athol Lannigan Fugard (pronounced few-gard) was born in Middleburg, in South Africa's Karoo region, 11 June 1932. The son of a father of English-Irish decent and an Afrikaans-speaking mother, Fugard is a typical South Africa hybrid. While still very young, he moved with his family to Port Elizabeth, which has (except for a brief time in London and a part-time home in Connecticut) been home ever since. Relating his kinship with his homeland he cites a line from Anna Akhmatova's poem "Requiem," "Under a foreign sky or on a strange land, I was with my people and they suffered." Three characters from Fugard's childhood were to become enormous influences in his life and on his writing—his father (a cripple who sank into a life of drink and laziness); his mother (who "paced my emancipation from prejudice and bigotry"); and Sam Semela (a black waiter from his mother's tearoom who was Fugard's childhood companion and confidant). The pivotal event and genesis of the award-winning play, *Master Harold . . . and the Boys* was an act of cruelty to Sam by a young Fugard. It was an incident for which Fugard has never forgiven himself. Trained as an auto mechanic and educated at the University of Cape Town (majored in philosophy and pursued boxing), Fugard quit school before his final examinations. He led the life of a sailor for two years (aboard a ship on which he was the only white man), returned home and made up his mind to be a writer. After a brief and unfulfilling stint as a journalist he met his future wife, writer-actress Sheila Meiring, who kindled his interest in the theatre. Before focusing on the art of playwrighting, Fugard was an actor (he still stars in many of his plays and their film adaptations), a novelist, a stage manager, a court clerk (burdened and saddened by the injustice of an oppressive court system, he wrote his first full-length play, *No Good Friday*) and, while in London, a domestic house cleaner.

Among his better known plays are *The Blood Knot* (which according to one critic altered the course of South African theatre), *The Island, Boesman and Lena* (both collaborative efforts), *A Lesson From Aloes* (winner, New York Drama Critics Circle Award, best play, 1978) and *Road to Mecca* (which, along with *Master Harold*, had their world premieres at the Yale Repertory Theatre). Inspired by Zen Buddhism, William Faulkner, Albert Camus (he relates to Camus' "courageous pessimism") and most significantly, Samuel Beckett (Fugard's idol), Fugard is obsessed with the relationship of the individual to his society, with the personal as well as the international tragedy of apartheid. Fugard and his wife have one daughter, Lisa. He divides his time between a South African and a Connecticut home. Likened in appearance to an Old Testament prophet, he shows the sorrows of his nation on his face; his deep-set, piercing brown eyes have seen and felt more than he tells. "Art," says Fugard, "is born out of conflict and not out of innocence." Amid the strife, the pain, Fugard is still able to find humanity, and to celebrate life.

Betty Furness

"If she took charge of all our money, we'd all be in better shape," observed a longtime friend in 1967 when President Lyndon B. Johnson appointed her to serve as his special assistant for consumer affairs. Skeptics wondered if a woman who'd spent eleven years as the highest paid pitchlady in television could effectively switch to the consumer point of view. But she did, and then some, making her mark in Washington via forceful (and successful) battles on behalf of such causes as federal meat inspection, truth-in-lending legislation and the use of flame retardant fabrics in children's clothing.

Following her LBJ appointment, she toiled for Governor Nelson Rockefeller as head of the New York State Consumer Protection Board and, under Mayor John Lindsay, served as Commissioner of the New York City Department of Consumer Affairs. Since 1974, she's been NBC-TV's gutsy consumer-advocate-in-residence (on "News 4 New York" and the "Today" show), famous for both her "force and charm." Among her multitudinous awards: *Ladies Home Journal*'s 1976 title of "Woman of the Year."

Consumer advocacy is really the third major career of Elizabeth Mary Furness, born 3 January 1916 in New York into the fashionable Park Avenue home of radio pioneer George C. Furness. Career No. 1, back in the 1930s and 40s, was an actress in over 30 movies and later in such stage plays as *The Doughgirls* and *My Sister Eileen*. Career No. 2, which lasted from 1949 to 1960, was as TV huckstress for Westinghouse. (At the political conventions in 1952, she spent so much television time opening refrigerator doors and bending over vacuum cleaners that "I had literally more time on air than any candidate." She was a pitchwoman also at the 1956 and 1960 conventions.) Deciding on election night, 1960, to give up commercials because "I wanted to deal with the real world," she became active in public affairs programming and, in 1964, was back at the presidential conventions as a reporter for CBS radio. She began her role as a consumer advocate after working with the Great Society programs VISTA and Head Start. Married first to music man Johnny Green, she next married, divorced and remarried radio producer Bud Ernst (died 1950) and is presently the wife of retired CBS news producer Leslie Midgley. Between them, they have four children and many grandchildren.

Diane von Furstenberg

At age 11 she told her mother "I will always get what I want." At 13 her self-made Jewish millionaire father and mother (who survived 14 months in Hitler's concentration camps) split up and Diane was off to fancy schools in Spain, England and Switzerland. "I had only one friend," she recalls of her girlhood in Brussels before the divorce (she was born there 31 December 1946) "and we used to play princesses. We both grew up and married princes." She met hers when she was 18 and a student at the University of Geneva. His name was Prince Egon von Furstenberg. "She turned me on," he recalls. Although they are divorced and he is remarried, they still remain each other's closest friend. "She was like a rich girl from upper Scarsdale. She had designer dresses. At 15, I think, she got her first mink." And Diane retorted, "I *never* had a mink. Oh, maybe it was the ocelot when I was 19 or 20."

She was already pregnant with their first child Alexander when they were married in Paris. Egon's father Prince Tassilo disapproved of Diane; he felt she was beneath the family. Egon's mother Clara Agnelli, heiress to an Italian industrial fortune (Fiat, etc.) gave her blessings. Tassilo's snub infuriated Diane. "It made me feel small," she says. "My life today is a reaction to that." Some reaction. After she and Egon had had enough dazzling New York social scene with their youth and daring, Diane managed to rock the fashion world with one simple wrap dress. That $80 dress usurped the pantsuit in fashion history and made Diane, in the words of *Newsweek* "the most marketable female in fashion since Coco Chanel." In 1984 *Savvy* magazine ranked her company among the top 10 U.S. firms run by women. The legend goes that Diane had three little dresses run up by a seamstress and showed them to Diana Vreeland, who was then editor at *Vogue*. Vreeland suggested the young princess take a room in the Gotham Hotel where lots of out-of-town dress buyers stay. Meanwhile, Vreeland ran a picture of the dresses in *Vogue*. The response was nothing less than phenomenal. Soon, she was so busy with her over-night transformation from social princess into Seventh Avenue empress that when her second child Tatiana was due to be born, she convinced her doctor to deliver the baby by Caesarean section so she could return to supervise her spring sales. Turmoil was temporary in 1977 when overproduction put her dresses into every bargain basement in the country. She was quick to save her company in a major reorganizing effort (which included cosmetics and fragrances) that, like her promise at age 11 to her mother, paid off. In 1984 she launched her first couture collection in her new shop, Diane von Furstenberg Fifth Avenue—an ultra-modern salon designed by Michael Graves. "I am a woman," she reminds us. "I create for that woman who is a product of the baby boom generation and grew up in the '60s, as I did. I understand that woman as I understand the need for comfortable shoes."

Kenny G

"I can still clearly recall sitting in the living room watching 'The Ed Sullivan Show' with my family. I was completely enthralled by a saxophonist performing on the program and after seeing his performance, I HAD to play the saxophone." Kenny G likes to reminisce about his attraction to the wind instrument. He suggests, "If you want to know where it all started I guess I can narrow it down to a particular day during my high school stage band class. I heard a funny sound coming out of the band director's room and I was mysteriously drawn to it. This mesmerizing tone was a familiar one yet it was also very obscure. What I heard was the alto saxophone sound of Grover Washington, Jr., from one of his first solo albums." Hooked on music, Kenny G studied long hours ("I became a saxophonist junkie and practiced 4 hours a day.") and perfected his craft on the road before reaching the multi-platinum successful status he maintains today. His single "Songbird" (1987) became the sixth instrumental single to crack the Top Ten in this decade and the video of the song was chosen as a top 5 video on VH-1.

Where did Kenny G come from? Born 5 June circa 1956, this musical genius was raised in Seattle, Washington. While still attending Franklin High in Seattle, he stumbled into good luck when one of the school band directors introduced him to a friend who was contracting for singer Barry White's show in Seattle. "At age 17, I got the gig as soloist (for a whole weekend) in Barry White's Love Unlimited Orchestra. This opportunity unquestionably encouraged me to continue playing and became my 'maiden voyage' as a professional musician." Looking to get in a groove, Kenny joined a local funk band Cold, Bold and Together as the token white and "That's where I got 'soul'... I witnessed music crossing the color barrier and found that people were as happy to hear my 'blue eyed soul' as they were to hear the 'real thing'." Simultaneously, he attended the University of Washington, where he majored in accounting and graduated *magna cum laude*.

As Kenny G continued to seek, he found out that his jazz band's director was responsible for booking musicians for the talent coming through town. In the right place at the right time, Kenny managed to work as a sideman with such performers as: Johnny Mathis, the Spinners, the late Liberace, and Diahann Carroll. He remembers appearing with Ringling Bros. and Barnum & Bailey Circus ("grueling gig ... and the elephants really stank"). Later, joining the Portland-based "Jeff Lorber Fusion" band, Kenny G established a strong reputation as a superb player, supporting his trademark saxophone. This relationship blossomed into a solo recording deal with Arista records, and the rest has been music to the public's ears. His albums include: *Kenny G, G-Force, Gravity, Duotones,* and *Silhouette*. Although he enjoys being in the spotlight, Kenny finds it attractive to play for other artists. He states, "I'm not trying to be a name dropper but I was flattered to receive calls for solos with: George Benson, Natalie Cole, Dionne Warwick, Aretha Franklin, Whitney Houston, Smokey Robinson, Steve Miller, Martha Davis of the Motels and many more." While making beautiful romantic music for others to hear, Kenny G remains single.

Eva Gabor

Although she allegedly once said that marriage is "too interesting an experiment to be tried once or twice," the youngest and possibly the most talented of the glamorous Hungarian sisters has tried matrimony five times.

Born 11 February circa 1924 in Budapest, she yearned early to be an actress, but was discouraged by her well-to-do parents, who viewed the theatre as too vulgar a profession for their daughters. Eva finally got her chance after a runaway marriage (1939) to Dr. Eric Drimmer landed her in Hollywood and she was signed by Paramount. Her first film, shot in ten days in 1941, was called *Forced Landing*. She said later, "It was a B picture but only to those too lazy to look down the alphabet." Divorced from Drimmer in 1942, she married millionaire realtor Charles Isaacs, appeared in a number of undistinguished films and finally found her first real success as the Hungarian housemaid in the Broadway production of *The Happy Time* (1950). She scored on Broadway again in Noel Coward's *Present Laughter* and as Vivien Leigh's replacement in *Tovarich*, acquired a third husband, surgeon John E. Williams (1956), and continued to fracture the English language on TV guest spots, cheerfully admitting. "I know four languages and misspell in them all." She wed husband No. 4, Richard Brown, in 1959 and No. 5, aeronautics tycoon Frank Jamieson, in 1973. Her long-running TV comedy "Green Acres" opposite Eddie Albert was on the tube for seven years and is still seen daily in 52 countries. In 1983 they appeared together on Broadway in a revival of *You Can't Take It With You*. Her many films include *Gigi*, *Don't Go Near the Water*, *The Last Time I Saw Paris* and two Walt Disney classics, *The Aristocats* and *The Rescuers*. In 1985 she appeared in the CBS telefilm "Bridge To Cross." Outside show business, Eva is chairman of the board of the world's largest wig company, Eva Gabor International. "We Gabors are supposed to do nothing but take bubble baths and drip with jewels, but I've worked like a demon. I didn't have time to sit in the bubbles." She is currently single; her constant companion is Merv Griffin. Eva's autobiography hit the bookstores in 1989.

Zsa Zsa Gabor

"Darling," intones the hot Hungarian beauty-at-any-age who has been married a mere eight times, "I am a wonderful house-keeper. After every divorce, I keep the house." Less famous for her acting than her jewels and her sharp-tongued barbs on television talk and game shows. She was once described by a U.S. congressman as "the most expensive courtesan since Madame de Pompadour" when she received some rather pricey gifts from General Rafael Trujillo, the former Dominican strongman.

Born Sari Gabor on 6 February in either 1921 or 1923, she received her first big boost into the International Beauty League when she was named Miss Hungary in 1936. She has since then adorned films (*Moulin Rouge* and *Lili*, 1953; *Arrivederci, Baby*, 1966; *Up the Front*, 1973), stage (*40 Carats* on Broadway in 1970 and, co-starring with her sister Eva, *Arsenic and Old Lace* in 1975), and contributed her hard-won wisdom to such tomes as *Zsa Zsa Gabor's Complete Guide to Men* (1969), *How to Catch a Man, How to Keep a Man, How to Get Rid of a Man* (1970) and her autobiography *Zsa Zsa Gabor: My Story* (1976).

"My father liked to tell me that when I was six months old, if a woman bent over my crib I cried, but if a man—I cooed," she recalls. Her first husband was Burhan Belge, press director of the Foreign Ministry of Turkey. "He was sweet but I did not like to live in Turkey." Arriving in America, she lunched her very first day at "21," and met hotel tycoon Conrad Hilton, who became husband No. 2. ("We both had one thing in common. We both wanted his money.") They had one daughter, Francesca. Hubby No. 3 was George Sanders. ("I believe in big families," she said. "Every woman should have three husbands.") But after a torrid affair and a big black eye from international playboy Porfirio Rubirosa, she had another divorce. Husband No. 4 was Herbert L. Huntner, board chairman of Struthers Wells Corp.; No. 5 was oilman Joshua Cosden, Jr.; No. 6 was Jack Ryan and No. 7 was Michael I. O'Hara from whom she was divorced in 1982. Zsa Zsa married No. 8, Prince Frederick Von Anhalt (Duke of Saxony), on 14 August 1986 in Beverly Hills.

Peter Gabriel

"Rhythm is the spine of the music, and it dictates the shape of the body that forms around it. Conventional rock rhythms tend to lead to conventional rock writing, which is why I look to other cultures for alternative inspiration." Peter Gabriel is explicit concerning his musical methods. Rather than depend on traditional structures, the former lead singer of Genesis likes to experiment with sounds from different cultures. Perhaps that is why he's been labeled one of "rock music's most original thinkers."

Born in London on 13 May 1950, Gabriel chose drums as his first instrument. At 16 years old he began writing songs; locked in a groove, he played the local rock and soul bands. Simultaneously interested in visual experiences, young Gabriel was offered a place in a film school, but chose to pursue his musical aspirations. It was this extracurricular creative interest that set Peter ahead of his peers. Utilizing his optical imagination, he created some of the most unique videos of the decade. He believes the new technology is still in its infancy and will eventually have an even greater impact in years to come. Receiving worldwide exposure in the group Genesis, Gabriel later decided to head out on his own. The decision proved profitable as his albums drew wide mainstream acceptance and increased fans. Titles include: *Peter Gabriel (I, II, III, IV)*, *Security*, *Birdy*, and *So*. His single "Sledgehammer" was acclaimed as a superb record and music video. Gabriel explains, "This is an attempt to recreate some of the spirit and style of the music that most excited me as a teenager—60s soul. . . . It is also about the use of sex as a means of getting through a breakdown in communication." Other singles include "Solsbury Hill" and "Games Without Frontiers."

Taking his knowledge to the big screen, Peter composed the film score for the controversial movie *The Last Temptation of Christ* (1988). He was the innovator of the first WOMAD Festival (World of Music Arts and Dance) in 1982, which has now become an annual event and registered charity. The multi-media event brings together musicians from over twenty-five countries for workshops, a school children's parade, film shows, and theatre and dance. Gabriel's main nonmusical activity is the development of a theme park, "Real World." His goal is to make a person an active participant in "Real World" and he would like to involve painters, psychologists, architects, musicians and filmmakers to help in the "design of experiences." Plans are in progress for a site in Sydney, Australia. Separated from his wife, Peter is frequently seen around town with actress Rosanna Arquette.

John Kenneth Galbraith

"Politics is not the art of the possible. It consists in choosing between the disastrous and the unpalatable," noted John Kenneth Galbraith, Canadian-born American economist, diplomat, writer, adviser to presidents, and political satirist. Blessed with the facility of turning the intricacies of economics into the stuff of bestsellers like *The Affluent Society*, Galbraith was called into government service by his old student at Harvard, John F. Kennedy, who made him ambassador to India. On Kennedy aide dubbed him "the non-economist's economist." A highly effective campaign volunteer and wordsmith, Galbraith was made a speechwriter for President

Johnson. His staunchly liberal policies and determined free thinking eventually made him feel more at home back at Harvard than in Washington, although he confesses to not yet "getting politics out of my system."

It is typically "Galbraithian," observed a journalist, "to never stop questioning economic policy in the United States, in the rest of the world, and in the United States in relation to the rest of the world." Once dubbed by *Time* magazine as "the philosopher of the younger generation," Galbraith has lost just a little of the radical appeal which let to comparisons with that other seminal economics philosopher, Karl Marx. Today Galbraith is predictably iconoclastic, and American tradition in irreverence informed. His lampooning of the term "conventional wisdom" has clearly survived its original coining in *The Affluent Society* (1958), and the term today suggests a raised eyebrow—a Galbraith trademark.

Preferring to be called Ken—John was an uncle he did not admire—this man whom *Time* called "a purveyor of predictions" describes himself foremost as a writer. He is a versatile one indeed, covering the literary waterfront as a novelist, a critic of letters, essayist, and in various other guises. A member of the National Institute of Arts and Letters, Galbraith has pointed out what he claimed was the real reason for his success as economic guru: his height (6'8"). "The superior confidence which people repose in the tall man is well merited. Being tall, he is more visible than other men, and being more visible, he is much more closely watched. In consequence, his behavior is far better than that of smaller men." Born 15 October 1908 in Ontario, Canada, he became a U.S. citizen in 1937. He lives with his wife, the former Catherine Atwater (three sons) in Cambridge, not far from the Harvard campus where, until his retirement in 1975, he was the James M. Warburg Professor of Economics. His books include *Money* (1975), *Annals of an Abiding Liberal* (1979), *A Life in Our Times* (1981), *A View From the Stands* (1986), *Economics in Perspective: A Critical History* (1988), *Capitalism, Communism and Coexistence* (1988), and *The Great Crash 1929* (1988).

James Galway

"The Man with the Golden Flute," as he is hailed, is equally at home performing classical and pop music, and his impish, affable manner with audiences defies the traditional notion that classical musicians must be a bit stuffy to be taken seriously.

James Galway was born 8 December 1939 in Belfast, Northern Ireland. Raised in a musical family, he picked up the tin whistle, a popular street instrument, which eventually led him to the flute. He "took up the flute like an Irishman to argument." Practicing eight hours a day, he took three solo competitions in the Irish Flute Championships at age ten. At sixteen, he won a scholarship to study at the Royal College of Music in London, under acclaimed flutist John Francis, and continued on to the prestigious Conservatoire National Superieur de Musique in Paris but dropped out before earning a degree. He played flute and piccolo with the Royal Opera House Orchestra and the BBC Symphony before touring the U.S. with the London Symphony Orchestra. Driven away from the London orchestra by backstage squabbling, he joined the Royal Philharmonic Orchestra in 1969. While in Germany, he found himself disenchanted with the formal personality of his fellow musicians and drifted into Berlin's counterculture, moved into a commune, grew a beard, and experimented with drugs. His hippie appearance prompted the conductor to ban him temporarily from televised symphony performances. But the critics were enchanted.

Galway developed a huge cult following after going solo in 1975, with classical and pop recordings. Said *Newsweek*: "Galway can break your heart with his diminuendos. His flute seems to play itself. The runs and trills arrive with remarkable clarity and fullness of tone. If Rampal's tone bubbles like French champagne, Galway's earthiness is like ale, dark and strong." He had a hit with his 1978 recording of John Denver's "Annie's Song," and with his pop album, "Sometimes When We Touch," recorded with Cleo Laine. He has won both the *Cashbox* and *Billboard* magazine Classical Album of the Year awards. His classical recordings include *James Galway Plays Mozart*, *Vivaldi—The Four Seasons*, *James Galway's Greates Hits*, and *Mercadante Concertos for Flute & Orchestra*. Galway, who stands a stocky five feet-four inches tall, has two sons and twin daughters by previous marriages. He was married for the third time in September, 1984, to fellow flutist Jeanne Cinnante.

Joe Garagiola

While he's described as having "apparently total recall for funny sports anecdotes" this former catcher-turned-self-deprecating-sportscaster downplays his success, saying, "I'm just a sweatshirt guy who's got to keep running at top speed to stay almost even." Born in St. Louis, 12 February 1926, the son of an immigrant bricklayer, he spent nine years with four big league baseball teams on his way to a respectable, if less than dazzling, .257 lifetime batting average. He retired in 1954 (following a shoulder-damaging infield collision with Jackie Robinson). But his longstanding reputation for quick-witted repartee on the sports banquet circuit (he is the past master of Yogi Berra stories) led to a spot in the broadcast booth during Yankee games, and eventually to the "Today" show. There, Garagiola applied what former "Today" host Hugh Downs termed a "direct down-to-earth approach" to subjects and persons as far afield as modern poetry and a theatre review of the musical, "Hair" ("It was hard to tell whether it was Tarzan or Jane.... If I want to see naked people, I'll go the Yankee locker room and look at the guys with the good physiques."). In 1972 he opted for a slower pace and more time with his family. NBC gave him a weekly pre-Monday night game sports show, "The Baseball World of Joe Garagiola." The intelligent insight that went into the Peabody Award-winning program (which ended in 1976 when ABC took over Monday night broadcasts) continued on the show "Game of the Week." Resigning from NBC in November, 1988, Garagiola released his book *It's Anybody's Game*.

Married (his wife once played the organ at the St. Louis ballpark), and the father of three (daughter Gina is a TV news reporter, son Steve is a sportscaster), Garagiola is a quick wit with a common touch. Describing a scary plane trip, he once admitted to landing with "rope burns from my rosary."

Greta Garbo

"The Divine," "the dream princess of eternity" and "the Sarah Bernhardt of films" are only a few of the superlatives writers have used to describe her. Mysterious, unattainable, and ever-changing,, she appealed to both male and female audiences. She has played heroines at once sensual and pure, superficial and profound, suffering and hopeful, world-weary and life-inspiring. On the screen as well as off, she represented a remote figure of loveliness—aloof, enigmatic, craving solitude. But the world did not gasp, tremble and swoon over "the face that lights from within" until, at the insistence of boy-genius Irving Thalberg, she went on a strenuous diet and had her teeth straightened and capped. It was then that the former Swedish barbershop employee became MGM's legendary Greta Garbo, "the globe's most breathtaking woman." Said one ecstatic critic: "If our century has entertained a canon of absolute beauty, this is it."

Her famous *Grand Hotel* ('32) line, "I want to be let alone" (often misquoted minus the "let"), presaged her sudden, shocking departure from movies following the failure of her last, *Two-Faced Woman*, in 1941. The aloof star renounced the blazing celebrity, which so many Americans consider the ultimate reward on earth, to a retirement so final, both public and personal, that it itself, ironically, brought a kind of celebrity. On meeting Garbo in Hollywood years ago, Lon Chaney, noted for his stand-offishness, saw something of himself in the shy recluse and advised her, "Mystery has served me well. It could do as much for you." Some say it is a pose she affects and learned from her early director, Mauritz Stiller. Yet she has said, "I was always inclined to be melancholy. Even when I was a small child, I preferred being alone. I hate crowds."

Born Greta Louisa Gustafsson, 18 September 1905, in Stockholm, she had a peasant upbringing. At 16 she entered Sweden's Royal Dramatic Academy, and at 17 was noticed by Stiller, a vain, ambitious, brutal man. She placed her career in his hands. Her mentor, a Russian Jewish immigrant, cast her in his epic *The Story of Gosta Berling* (1924). The following year she starred in G.W. Pabst's *The Joyless Street* (which featured her later "rival," Marlene Dietrich, in a bit part). In Europe on a 1924 talent hunt, Louis B. Mayer signed her, presumably because he wanted Stiller ("She's too fat," he said), but another theory claims that the shrewd Mayer really wanted Garbo and in order to get her, signed Stiller too. Stiller died in 1928, but Garbo's career soared after her first MGM film (1926's *The Torrent*) made her a superstar. "GARBO TALKS!" shrieked the ads when talkies came, and the world paused breathlessly as in *Anna Christie* (1930) she opened a door and said, immortally, "Gimme a visky." "GARBO LAUGHS!" shouted later ads, and in *Ninotchka* (1939)—(her first MGM comedy, and penultimate film) she did, though rumor has it her laughter was dubbed!

While she possessed unparalleled film magnetism and mystique, MGM spared no expense in enhancing her legend. The gowns and hats especially created for her by studio costume designer Gilbert Adrian set international fashion standards. She romanced with co-star John Gilbert ("I would rather spend an hour with her than a lifetime with any other woman."), with Leopold Stokowski ("We were destined," he told her. "It was in the stars.") and the late Gayelord Hauser ("I ain't a vegetarian," he told lecture audiences, "and Garbo does *not* have big feet."). But she never married. She won two N.Y. Film Critics Awards (for *Anna Karenina*, '35 and *Camille*, '36), but, amazingly, never the Academy Award. To rectify the oversight, she received a special Oscar in 1954 "for her unforgettable screen performances."

After her death, Simon & Schuster plans to publish a Garbo biography "in her own words," though she circulated a 1979 affidavit denying any acquaintance with the book's author. Sidney Lumet's 1984 film *Garbo Talks* depicts a woman whose dying wish is to meet the legendary recluse. The recluse spends her time in Switzerland, the Riviera and Manhattan's Upper East Side. Turn a corner onto Madison Avenue and there, always alone (immortal nose pressed to a hock-shop window), will be the "lovely wildwood animal or child" that photographer Edward Steichen saw. Periodic rumors of her return to films never materialized. Her most frequent director, Clarence Brown, said in 1963: "Today, without having made a film since 1940, she is still the greatest. She is the prototype of all stars."

Gabriel Garcia Marquez

To write what is probably his most famous book *Cien Años de Soledad* (*One Hundred Years of Solitude*), this 1982 Nobel Prize-winning Latin American author gave in to an inspiration one day in 1965. He was driving his car from Mexico City to Acapulco when the first chapter came to him. When he returned home he told his wife he was not to be disturbed for any reason, especially about their finances. For the next eighteen months he shut himself in his study for eight to ten hours everyday. "I didn't know what my wife was doing," he told the novelist William Kennedy in an interview in the *Atlantic*, "and I didn't ask questions.... We lived as if we had money. But when I was finished writing, my wife said, 'Did you really finish it? We owe twelve thousand dollars,'" The surrealistic saga of the Buendía clan was called by the Novel Prize-winning Chilean poet Pablo Neruda "perhaps the greatest revelation in the Spanish language since the *Don Quixote* of Cervantes."

Born one of 12 children on 6 March 1928 in the village of Aracataca near the northern Caribbean coast of Colombia, his family lived with his maternal grandparents in a large, falling-apart but spirited house full of history and shadows. His grandmother regaled him with stories about ghosts and dead relatives. His grandfather, a retired colonel and veteran of two civil wars and "the most important figure of my life" told him of ancient battles and the old days. In 1946 he entered the law school of the University of Bogota, but after five years did not take his degree because he disliked the law so much. "My earliest recollection is of drawing comics and I realize now that this may have been because I couldn't yet write. I've always tried to find ways of telling stories and I've stuck to literature as the most accessible." His first short story was published in 1947. For more than a decade Colombia was in a state of semi-civil war, known as *la violencia*. Quite naturally this informed the writer's experience, providing source material for three novels. He lived in Barranquilla and wrote a daily column for *El Heraldo*. During this time he began reading the authors that would influence him most, particularly Faulkner. And by working as a journalist, he was able to support himself as a fiction writer. His books include: *Leaf Storm* (his first in 1955), *The Autumn of the Patriarch*, *In Evil Hour*, *Chronicle of a Death Foretold*, the novella *The Incredible and Sad Tale of Innocent Erendira and Her Heartless Grandmother* which became the basis for his screenplay of the film *Erendira*, *Clandestine in Chile: The Adventures of Miguel Littin*, *The Story of a Shipwrecked Sailor*, and *Love in the Time of Cholera*. His *Collected Short Stories* were published in English in 1984. The father of two sons lives with wife Mercedes in Cartagena. He confesses a weakness for television soaps and popular music, admitting that one regret is having failed to write songs. "It's reactionary to scorn television or popular songs because they don't have the prestige of books or classical music. Anything that reaches people with a message, all these media, they must be recuperated instead of leaving them to those who are commercializing them and whoring them.... One can't let oneself be cowed by intellectuals."

Ava Gardner

"To me, sanity is more important than stardom," says the actress whose aloof sculptured beauty made her one of Hollywood's classic film stars. It all began when an MGM representative spotted her photograph in the window of her brother-in-law's photography studio in New York, where the then poor farm girl of 18 with misleadingly sophisticated beauty was visiting her sister. She was offered a screen test and, almost immediately, a long-term contract. "Why do writers and editors take such pleasure in picking on prominent people? I can understand a critic tearing apart a performance, but not someone's private life. My personal life is something I've always tried to keep to myself. Publicity on a personal level has never been attractive to me."

The star famous as Ava Gardner was born Lucy Johnson on Christmas Eve, 1922, in Smithfield, N.C. As an actress, she has never taken herself seriously ("I don't think I am an actress. I'm embarrassed to look at myself on the screen. If studios and producers are willing to pay me to appear in their pictures, that's their business. And I enjoy the people on the set. I like other performers.") Neither has she felt confident about being a great beauty ("Whenever I have to make a public appearance, I'm frightened to death. I've always been that way. All my life.") She is most responsive to questions concerning her career. She made her film debut as Ava Gardner in *We Were Dancing* (1942). After ten more potboilers, she established herself as more than just another starlet with *The Millers* (1946), followed by *The Hucksters, Singapore,* and *One Touch of Venus* (1948).

"I am really an uncomplicated person. I like to live simply and out of the public eye." But with three marriages ending in divorce—all to celebrated men: Mickey Rooney ("We were children. We never had a chance."); Artie Shaw; Frank Sinatra ("He is one of my best friends. We talk to each other regularly because we are two very nice people. And we like each other.")—publicity was inevitable. "All three of my husbands were extraordinary men. I found the love of my life three times. The pity is my husbands didn't also find it," she says. In the meantime she continued making an average of two films a year, some memorable, many not, including *East Side, West Side; Show Boat; Pandora and the Flying Dutchman; Snows of Kilimanjaro; Mogambo; Barefoot Contessa; Bhowani Junction; On the Beach; 55 Days at Peking; Seven Days in May; Night of the Iguana* and *Mayerling.*

In 1954, after the break-up with Sinatra, Ava Gardner abruptly turned her back on Hollywood and America, going into self-imposed exile, first in Italy, then Spain, and currently in Britain. She still abhors the clamor of fans yet is disappointed when passers-by fail to recognize her, adding: "It's lovely to have people recognize me in the street. They may not know or remember my name, but my face is familiar to them and they smile and nod their heads. That's sweet." Sweeter still was Ava's extended run on the nighttime soap "Knot's Landing" in 1985, making waves and popping bubbles, beguiling as ever. She also appeared in the steamy miniseries "A.D." (1985), and the telefilm "The Long Hot Summer" (1986). Her autobiography was published in 1989.

Art Garfunkel

The harmony of his pristine tenor voice and the pop stylings of songwriter Paul Simon made them one of the most popular folk-rock duos of the 1960s. Their reunion tour in 1982, after an eleven-year split, was sparked by the turnout of nearly half a million fans for a joint concert in New York's Central Park. Said an associate, "I think they both underestimated how many people cared about their reunion, how important it was to so many people. It was the right time, and they both sensed that."

Art Garfunkel was born 13 October 1941 in Forest Hills, N.Y. He met Simon when they appeared together in a sixth grade production of *Alice in Wonderland,* he as the Cheshire Cat, and Simon as the White Rabbit. Finding a mutual interest in music, they began singing together locally, backed by Simon's acoustic guitar. Signed by Big Records, and renamed Tom and Jerry, they produced only one mild hit, and upon the demise of the company, they split. After attending Columbia University, Garfunkel hooked up with his former partner once more to perform at popular New York clubs. Their 1964 debut album for Columbia Records, *Wednesday Morning, 3 A.M.*, netted the top single, "Sounds of Silence." Among the six popular albums that followed were *Parsley, Sage, Rosemary and Thyme,* the music to the 1969 hit movie, *The Graduate, Bookends,* and their 1970 *Bridge Over Troubled Water,* which brought them six Grammy awards. After personal and artistic friction caused their split in 1970, Garfunkel produced several pop albums with moderate success, but failed to reach the commercial heights achieved by Simon. Garfunkel's solo recording efforts include the 1973 "Angel Clare," and the albums, *Scissors Cut, Good To Go, The Animal's Christmas* (with Amy Grant), and *Lefty.* His singles include, "Second Avenue," and "I Only Have Eyes for You."

An introspective person prone to depressive moods, Garfunkel found stability through acting. "You are hired to search your soul and come up with aspects of who you are for presentation. So it behooves you to find out who you are." He debuted in films in *Catch 22,* and was favorably reviewed as a sensitive collegian evolving toward middle age in *Carnal Knowledge* (1971). After an unsuccessful marriage to Linda Marie Grossman, Garfunkel married Kim Cermak (of the Lime rock group) on 18 September 1988.

James Garner

Although he has starred in four TV series, this perpetually quizzical anti-heroic actor once said, "If you have any pride in your work, you don't go on TV. If you want to sell underarm deodorant . . . you do." Yet James Garner's multimillion dollar contract was with Polaroid Cameras, not a deodorant company, and after having won an Emmy and a People's Choice Award for "The Rockford Files" series, he's unquestionably one of the medium's most popular stars. *Esquire* characterized him as "a master at playing dumb while maintaining a sense of shrewdness and dignity. He always throws us off guard. He is the macho stud who makes fun of himself; he is the scaredy-cat who we know will not let us down in the end."

Garner, who says, "I became an actor by accident, but I'm a businessman by design," was once vice president of the Screen Actor's Guild when Ronald Reagan was its prez. "We used to tell him what to say," Garner reflects. "He can talk around a subject better than anyone in the world. He's never had an original thought that I know of." As for himself, Garner (born 7 April 1928 in Norman, Okla.) grew up as James Baumgarner before changing his moniker. Domestic troubles led him to become a high school dropout, and he arrived in Hollywood via the Army and Merchant Marines. A pesky aunt and an acquaintance turned producer helped him out of odd-job employment into a $175-a-week contract with Warner Bros. He married actress Lois Clark (two daughters) after a two-week courtship, and after a quarter-century together she says, "I think the key is that at some point Jimmy decided that he was going to stay married to me and at some point I decided that he was going to stay married to me. . . . I feel threatened all the time. I am never complacent."

Garner became an instant, though low-salaried, star on "Maverick" in 1957; while the show topped Ed Sullivan in the ratings, the actor says, "I made more money in eight weeks in summer stock than I did in three years on 'Maverick.'" Movies are more to his liking, and since buying his way out of video bondage from two of his series, he's made more than thirty-five flicks. Some have been forgettable (*Boys' Night Out, Grand Prix*) while others have been memorable (*The Americanization of Emily, The Great Escape, Victor/Victoria*); either way he prefers "clean to dirt." However, he loves real estate dirt, and owns 375 acres in Carmel with Clint Eastwood, and "one of the ten most beautiful houses in LA," to go along with other land holdings. The one-man mini-conglomerate also owns apartments, oil wells, race cars, and a production company improbably dubbed "Cherokee" after his maternal grandfather, who claimed he was, partly. He has also softened somewhat on his harsh opinion of tube-toiling. Now he says, "I'd do any script if the people were right. I am an actor. I hire out. I do commercials, television, movies, stage. I am not afraid of hurting my image." Recent films include *Murphy's Romance* (1985), *Tank* (1985), and *Sunset* (1987). He also starred in the Hallmark Hall of Fame CBS-TV movie, "My Name is Bill W" (1989) and is the commercial spokesperson for Mazda.

Crystal Gayle

The brown tresses cascading over five feet to the floor capture your attention first as they frame her beautiful face, but when she opens her mouth to sing, you understand why Crystal Gayle has had over 35 hit singles and 20 hit albums. Her soulful voice delivers the songs with all the style and emotion that have come to be her trademark. Her accomplishments have distinguished the woman previously best known as "Loretta Lynn's little sister." Crystal has successfully crossed over from the country to the pop charts with chart-toppers like her gold single "Don't It Make My Brown

Eyes Blue" (1977) and her duets with Eddie Rabbitt, "You and I" (1982) and with Gary Morris, "Another World" (1987), which became the #1 country hit theme from the NBC daytime drama of which Crystal is an avowed fan.

Crystal Gayle was born Brenda Gail Webb in Paintsville, Kentucky. The youngest of eight children, she was a child when her family moved to Wabash, Indiana. Musically, the Midwest move exposed Crystal to everyone from Leslie Gore and Patsy Cline to The Beatles and Peter, Paul and Mary. While still in school, she sang in glee clubs and school choirs, joined her brothers in a weekend country band and performed as a soloist at various local functions. She also scored with her debut single that reached the Top 25 on the country charts. A series of smash albums followed including *Crystal Gayle* (1975), *Somebody Loves You* (1975), *Crystal* (1976), the platinum—sellers *We Must Believe in Magic* (1977) and *When I Dream* (1978) and the gold certified albums *Miss the Mississippi* (1979) and *Classic Crystal* (1979). A perennial hitmaker from 1974 through 1987, she's rendered such classics as "Wrong Road Again" (1974), "I'll Get Over You" (1976; her first #1), "Talking in Your Sleep" (1978), "Half the Way" (1979), "Nobody Wants to Be Alone" (1985), "Makin' Up for Lost Time" (1985; duet with Gary Morris) and the remake of the classic song "Cry" (1986).

Crystal's popularity on the charts has translated to awards as well. She was honored as Outstanding Female Vocalist by the Academy of Country Music in 1977, 1978 and 1980, the Country Music Association in 1977 and 1978 and the Grammy Award in 1978. She also won the American Music Awards in 1979, 1980 and 1986, the AMOA Jukebox Award in 1978 and the Most Played Country Female Artist Award in 1979.

Crystal married Vassilios "Bill" Gatzimos on 3 June 1971. They have two children, Catherine Claire and Christos James. Aside from raising her two children and participating in various charities and worthy causes in and around Nashville, Crystal opened her own high-quality shop in Nashville, aptly named Crystal's for Fine Gifts & Jewelry. It's part of her continuing interest not only in fine crystal, porcelain and jewelry, but also a reflection of her interests in the healing powers of crystals, many of which are available in her store. As if her schedule were not full enough, Crystal finds the time to appear on television on a wide variety of shows, including "The Crystal Gayle Special," "Crystal," the HBO special "Crystal Gayle in Concert," and her own highly-rated holiday special, "A Crystal Christmas in Sweden," which featured many Christmas standards from her album "A Crystal Christmas." She also fulfilled a dream when she appeared for a week on the daytime drama "Another World," performing the theme with Gary Morris on air. With a professional and personal schedule that keeps her constantly on the go and a slate of future projects that include an upcoming series of shows with her sister Loretta Lynn, Crystal Gayle is more popular and productive now than at any time in her life.

David Geffen

"It's impossible to be successful without failing," says this super-successful entertainment impresario whom a 1985 New York *Times* magazine story called "the Sol Hurok of pop." "All I want is to be allowed to work in any area that I choose. I like the theatre, films, records. I like art, real estate. I don't like television. I know what I like. I like money. People who say they don't are full of it." David Geffen has made his own pile through Geffen Records sales of such artists as Elton John, Donna Summer and Neil Young, in addition to part ownership of audience-attracting Broadway hits like *Dreamgirls*, *Cats* and *Social Security*, the Off-Broadway smash (and movie) *Little Shop of Horrors*, and such movies as *Personal Best*, *Risky Business* and *Lost in America*. But what has really kept Geffen in the commmodity he likes so much is the real estate investing he did when he expected to die.

Born 21 February 1943 in Brooklyn, David Geffen has made two separate fortunes in show biz. As a youngster, his mother supported him and his unemployed father in the living room of the family's three-room apartment with her own corset business. "My parents would take me to the movies in Times Square and I could see for myself there was a better life," Geffen says. "I wanted it." He went for it by going off to the University of Texas where he flunked out, then switching to Brooklyn College where he dropped out. He was no closer to his goal after being fired from two small-time jobs at CBS. Then he managed to get a job as a mail clerk in the William Morris talent agency. From that lowly, but inside position, in 1964 he began signing up recording artists and, by age 25, was a millionaire. Using his internal "antennae" to predict with repeated accuracy which musicians would sell, he built a record company, Asylum, later bought by Warner Communications for $7 million. When, in 1975, he told Warner he "wanted to run a movie studio," he was granted his wish and was around for the production of *Oh, God!* and other flicks before realizing that decision by committee wasn't for him. Then the guy who once made all the gossip columns by living with Cher received shocking news: doctors incorrectly, but convincingly, misdiagnosed him as having a cancerous bladder tumor. Lying around for four years waiting for the end, Geffen made $23 million from smart real estate buys. By the time he came back in 1980, not dying after all, "I was a forgotten guy. I was called a flash-in-the-pan ... people ... would not answer my phone calls. I was devastated ... I am driven. But I'm not Sammy Glick. I've never killed anyone. I don't have to. I'm too talented." Geffen has now successfully "come back" with a vengeance. The bi-coastal, elfin-like entrepreneur says of his fabled talent-spotting instincts: "The record business is a disaster. Broadway is a disaster. Things are bad but I'm doing well. I'm Billy the Kid, the fastest draw. It's not arrogance ... I'm gifted at knowing what will be a success before it is."

Phyllis George

Among achievements that include being Miss America (1971), the first female network sportscaster, and anchor-person on the CBS Morning News, what ranks as her peak accomplishment? "Best of all is my family," she says. "I'm very much in love with my husband, and ... our [two] children bring the kind of joy that money or fame can't buy." While many professional women find no need to make such a revelation, glamorous Phyllis George Brown, former First Lady of Kentucky, understands that hers is a closely-scrutinized public and private life. Her husband, former fried chicken franchiser John Y. Brown, Jr., and she embarked on the well-publicized "kissing campaign" for his 1979 gubernatorial slot just months after their wedding at Norman Vincent Peale's Marble Collegiate Church. The 30-year-old newlywed was as wholesome as could be, although she scoffed at remarks that she and Brown were overly affectionate for public consumption. ("I just hope maybe some of it will rub off on other people, and they will be as full of love as we are.") While she was involved in Special Olympics for the handicapped, and women's issues, Phyllis was never quite able to shed her jet-set image in The Bluegrass State. She combined forces, therefore, opening up a shop for Kentucky artisans' and craftsmen's goods at Bloomingdale's. But she admitted, "I made a big sacrifice in my career coming down [to Kentucky], and I reminded John of that a lot. Once when I was feeling depressed, he told me he'd buy me a horse. I said, 'How good a horse?' He said, 'A very good horse.'"

This woman from Denton, Texas (born 25 June 1949), and former student at North Texas State and Texas Christian, parlayed her year as beauty queen into jobs hosting the Miss America pageant, the Super Bowl, the Tournament of Roses Parade, and a Charlie Brown special. After becoming the quintessential TV talk show guest, she joined CBS Sports in 1975, and while breaking new ground for women, won an Emmy (along with her co-hosts on "NFL Today"), and the Washington (D.C.) Football Club's 1975 Sportscaster of the Year award. Formerly married to Hollywood producer Robert Evans, she was brought onto the sunrise TV job in 1985 as star power to compete with the higher-rated ABC and NBC shows. Her agent shot down dissension over her weak journalistic background by saying, "She is absolutely a journalist. She has undertaken . . . journalist-type assignments. . . . I don't think it is necessary in this day and age for someone to have covered arson, murder, robbery and mayhem on the streets of New York and Chicago to qualify as a journalist." Her failure to raise the show's rating, however, led to her "resignation" in August of 1985, after which she returned to Kentucky.

Richard Gere

An eighties version of the traditional, darkly handsome Hollywood leading man, Richard Gere has a brooding mien than may recall James Dean. Despite his popularity with audiences, Gere shuns fame and lives out of the proverbial actor's suitcase. "The only way I can figure to keep it together," he says, "is not to accumulate materially anything and to keep people around me—my friends from way back—who still have their heads in the clouds, in the ozone; you know, who are still visionaries, poets, dope freaks, dropouts, actors, musicians. I'll be very disappointed in myself if I become just an actor."

Born 29 August 1949 in Philadelphia, Gere was one of five artistically talented children raised by their parents on a farm near Syracuse, New York. An early interest in music had him composing scores for student theatrical productions and studying piano, guitar, trumpet and banjo. He left the U. of Massachusetts following his sophomore year and, after work at the Provincetown Playhouse and Seattle Repertory Theater, joined a commune of rock musicians in Vermont in 1970. He played guitar and keyboard in a band there, but found musicians "even harder to get along with than actors." Theatrical forays in London and N.Y.—in *Grease*—preceded his film debut in 1975. Two years later he attracted much attention as the doped-up psychopath who menaced Diane Keaton in *Looking for Mr. Goodbar*. This led to starring roles in *Days of Heaven*, *Bloodbrothers*, *Yanks* and *American Gigolo*, in which he played the title role of a narcissistic male prostitute.

A bachelor, Gere, whose theatrical training includes the classics, scored a great success in December, 1979, when he ended a five-year absence from the New York stage in the controversial play, *Bent*. His performance as Max, a homosexual concentration camp inmate, earned Gere more praise than most of his movie portrayals. The subsequent *An Officer and a Gentleman* kept the Gere film career in high gear and some of the films that followed were *Breathless*, the 1984 Coppola extravaganza *Cotton Club*, the 1985 less than impressive *King David*, *Power* (1985), *No Mercy* (1986), *Farm of the Year* (1988) and *Miles From Home* (1989).

Vitas Gerulaitis

Throughout his tempestuous 12-year career on the professional circuit, Brooklyn-born Vitas Gerulaitis was counted as one of the stars of the tennis game. In his prime there was no one who could scamper from corner to corner better than the sure-footed Gerulaitis, whose remarkable quickness unnerved opponents, astonished some spectators and made watching him a pure joy. The speed at which he rushed the net helps to explain how he won 27 career single titles, including the Australian Open (1977), 2 Italian Opens (1977, 1979), a WCT Finals singles crown (1978) plus finalists' finishes in the French Open (1980), the U.S. Open (1979) and twice in the Masters (1980, 1982). Although Gerulaitis never made it to the Wimbledon singles finals, his epic semifinal match against Bjorn Borg in 1977 will long be remembered. The controversial figure both on and off the court captured the Wimbledon Doubles title with S. Mayer in 1975. As a doubles player, the 6-foot, 155-pound righthander also racked up honors. In 1985 alone he finished as a doubles runner-up with McNamee in Rotterdam, a doubles quarter-finalist with Shiras in Houston, and three tournaments as doubles semi-finalist, two with the temperamental John McEnroe in Milan and Forest Hills.

Born of Lithuanian descent on 26 July 1954, Gerulaitis, after traveling around the world, chose to maintain New York as his home and moved from his native Brooklyn to Kings Point. Always a special favorite of the home town fans, Gerulaitis repays this attention through a variety of public service activities. Each summer, since 1978, the Vitas Gerulaitis Foundation stages summer tennis camps in New York parks. With his strong dedication to children, Gerulaitis started the clinics mainly to bring the sport to under-privileged children, but welcomes all children. Although Gerulaitis sometimes became exasperated with officials on the pro tour, he never lets the children get under his skin. Personally rounding up pros such as close friends McEnroe, Borg, Billie Jean King, Ashe and Nastase, Gerulaitis is sincere about "making New York through tennis, which has been good to me, at least a slightly better place for kids to grow up in." This top-ranked athlete (ranked No. 5 in 1978 when he started the clinic) gives not only his name but his time gratis for this three-hour clinic, with each child getting personal and group instruction, as well as a tennis raquet to keep. The son of Vitas, Sr., Director of Tennis for the National Tennis Center, annually stages benefit concerts in the New York area to raise funds for a number of charitable causes, including the Special Olympics. In July, 1988, Gerulaitis, keeping his fingers in both pies, played at the United Cerebral Palsy Pro-Celebrity Tennis Tournament.

Pegged "Broadway Vitas" by those who thought the sum of his off-court life was partying in night clubs, bachelor Gerulaitis is giving something back to the town and the game that gave him so much.

Estelle Getty

"I know this lady I'm playing," Estelle Getty says about her character Sophia, the fiesty, irreverent and intractable mother of Dorothy in the hit TV sitcom "The Golden Girls." "She's partly me and partly my imagination, but she's an original and that's what I've been playing all my life, original characters." Her originality and talent were not overlooked. "The Golden Girls" first aired in the fall of 1985 and during that season Getty won the Golden Globe Award for Best Actress in a Comedy Season. Two years later, she was awarded the 1988 Emmy for Best Supporting Actress in a series. Getty, an original herself, has performed in contemporary as well as experimental theatre for over half a century.

Born on 25 July 1923 in New York City, Getty was raised near the bright lights and felt the lure of the stage. She trained at the Herbert Berghof Studio and with Gerald Russak. After a long stage career, Getty blossomed into national prominence with her much-heralded performance as Mrs. Beckhoff in the Tony Award winning show "Torch Song Trilogy," gaining her the first ever Helen Hayes Award as Best Supporting Performer in 1982. Traveling to Los Angeles with the show, Getty was "discovered" by Hollywood. While performing in the play at night, Getty was filming movies during the day. Within her first six months on the West Coast, Getty filmed the NBC pilot "No Man's Land." She went on to appear as Cher's mother in *Mask* (1984) and Barry Manilow's mother in the telefilm "Copacabana" (1986) and in *Mannequin* (1986). Even though still in demand, Getty took time out to write her book, *If I Knew Then What I Know Now . . . So What*, published in 1988. Enjoying her new-found popularity, Getty looks forward to new challenges and the release of her latest movie, *The Little Old Lady From Pasadena*.

Gordon Getty

The man whom *Fortune* magazine blared was the richest in America hasn't been consumed with attaining or maintaining that distinction. "I'm a businessman because I had to be one," Gordon Peter Getty says. As one of the three surviving sons of late oil billionaire J. Paul Getty, he became sole trustee of the trust that controls the family fortune as well as 40 percent of the stock in the U.S.'s 14th-largest petroleum company. But when he decided to take a more active hand in Getty Oil ("Gordon was just getting tired of the company taking cash flow from oil and gas, and using it to buy insurance companies and TV networks," said a confidante), he ran smack into an uncooperative board of directors. The resulting power struggle left him even more estranged from his elder half-brothers when he arranged to sell Getty Oil to Texaco in 1984 for almost $10 billion.

Secure in knowing from whence his next meal will come, Gordon Getty developed other pursuits, like opera singing (which he does in three languages), music composition and playing the piano. He's chairman of the anthropological L.S.B. Leakey Foundation, and helps the San Francisco Zoo by being a Friend. Like his father, a prolific progenitor of male children, Gordon (born 20 December 1933), was the fourth of five boys, and is himself father to four. The family tours European music festivals, and takes in occasional small performances of Getty's singing or compositions at places like the Marin (County) Symphony or New York's Lincoln Center, all enthusiastically supported by his beautiful and perennially best-dressed wife, Ann. Getty was the recipient of the Northwood Institute/IASTA Achievement in the Arts Award in 1985 in recognition of his compositions, which include *The White Election* (a song cycle utilizing the poems of Emily Dickinson) and *Plump Jack,* a cantata inspired by Shakespeare's *Jack Falstaff.*

Charles Gibson

ABC's engaging morning-man Charles Gibson is currently celebrating a significant career milestone: his third year as co-host (with Joan Lunden) of the network's popular "Good Morning America." A longtime Capitol Hill newsman, Gibson stepped in to replace the departing David Hartman on "Good Morning America" on 29 January 1987. In the course of his past busy on-camera years, he's covered such headline-making events as the economic summit from Venice and the British elections from London, has traveled to Cuba for a view of Castro's Havana and joined the Baltimore Orioles at spring training camp. His daily interviews on the show have run the gamut from politicians to starlets and bestseller-list authors to homerun hitters.

A graduate of Princeton, Gibson started his broadcasting career as Washington producer for RKO Network in 1966. He later worked as news director for WLVA-TV and radio in Lynchburg, Virginia, and WMAL-TV, the ABC affiliate in Washington. He came to the network ABC news team in 1975.

Gibson signed on with "Good Morning America" after six years serving as ABC News' chief correspondent at the House of Representatives. Prior to these Capitol Hill labors, he reported on a wide range of national news stories for ABC as a general assignment correspondent for the net. He has been seen frequently with reports on ABC's "World News Tonight" with Peter Jennings and as an occasional sub for Ted Koppel on "Nightline" and/or substitute anchor on "World News This Morning." Gibson and his wife, Arlene, a school principal, live in New Jersey with their two daughters.

Mel Gibson

The handwriting was on the wall when this "dish from Down Under" followed screen legends Clark Gable and Marlon Brando in the role of mutineer Fletcher Christian in the remake of *Mutiny on the Bounty.* Sure enough, like those predecessors, he soon exploded to supernova status—including the imprimatur of a *People* cover in 1985 certifying him as "the sexiest man alive." Plain ordinary stardom came for Mel Gibson in 1981 playing a World War I Aussie soldier in Peter Weir's *Gallipoli.* In 1983 he took a giant step toward becoming an international sex-symbol in the same director's *The Year of Living Dangerously,* a romantic adventure story set in Indonesia in which his love scenes with Sigourney Weaver (every scene they had together but one, as pointed out by sharp-eyed *New Yorker* critic Pauline Kael) were notable for what Kael called their "new-style-old-time 'dangerous' steaminess." Subsequently loving it up with Sissy Spacek (*The River*) and Diane Keaton (*Mrs Soffel*), his sizzling screen presence thrust him up front as what one critic called "the putative star of the decade." More popular films followed, including *Lethal Weapon* (1987), *Tequila Sunrise* (1988), *My Brother Jack* (1988), *Lethal Weapon II* (1989) and *Bird on a Wire* (1990).

The sixth of eleven children, born 3 January 1956 into the Catholic family of a railroad brakeman in Peekskill, N.Y., Mel Gibson first heard about Australia in stories about his paternal grandmother who'd come to the U.S. from Kangarooland to find fame and fortune as an opera singer. When Mel was 12, his dad, injured on the job, decided to use the insurance settlement to move his family back to Australia—partly so the boys in the family could avoid being drafted to fight in Vietnam. Mel was treated as an outsider at first (schoolmates sneeringly called him "Yank") and he grew into a chip-on-the-shoulder loner. Eventually, he drifted into acting via studies at the National Institute of Dramatic Arts and, in 1976, gave his first hint of sex-symboldom-to-come when he was cast as Romeo to Judy Davis's Juliet in a school production of Shakespeare's romance.

Gibson made his film debut while still a student in an Australian quickie called *Summer City* but made a bigger impact in 1980 playing a scurvy vigilante in leather in the futuristic fantasy, *Mad Max,* a $300,000 production which Gibson calls "very classy grade-B trash" but which eventually grossed $100 million. (He later appeared in the sequels, *Road Warrior* and 1985's *Mad Max Beyond Thunderdome,* in which he teamed up with Tina Turner.) Uncomfortable with his "sex object" image, Gibson ruffled reporters' feathers in 1985 with biting, negative comments about the press and the price of fame. ("I have a very bad habit of saying embarrassing, goofy things," he said later. "The next day I could kill myself.") Married to former Robyn Moore (daughter Hannah, twins Edward and Christopher, sons Will and Louis), between pictures he escapes adulatory female fans at a beachside retreat in the Sydney suburb of Coogee. Although he retains his American citizenship ("despite all the cynicism in the world today, I'm proud of it. You have to be."), he thinks of himself primarily "as an Aussie." "I think it's good to be a hybrid," he told *Interview* magazine. "You can be more objective. If you get shifted from one culture to another, you look at something unusual and say, 'What is this?'"

John Gielgud

"One of the joys of owning a TV set right now," observed James Fallon in *Women's Wear Daily* in July, 1984, "is the variety of chances to observe the elegantly active octogenarian, John Gielgud." Sir John (he was knighted in 1953) has appeared on TV in HBO's "The Far Pavilions," as the brave but bigoted Major Sir Louis Cavagnari; as the blind hermit in Showtime's "Frankenstein;" as the host-narrator of the German series on PBS, "Buddenbrooks;" as Albert Speer's father in ABC's "Inside the Third Reich;" as Pope Piux XII in CBS's "The Scarlet and the Black;" as a doge of Venice in NBC's "Marco Polo" and most wonderfully as Charles Ryder's papa in "Brideshead Revisited." Then, of course there are those TV commercials for Paul Masson wine, bits which *Time* magazine feels show how he is perceived around the world: "bright blue eyes looking condescendingly down a luxuriant nose at the unruly, almost always in-elegant world around him." In fact it seems impossible to make anything without him these days. His films include *Chariots of Fire, Priest of Love, Gandhi, Scandalous, Arthur* (Best Supporting Actor Oscar), *The Shooting Party, Plenty, The Whistle Blower, Appointment with Death, Arthur on the Rocks, Getting It Right* and *Loser Takes All*. He also appeared in the television miniseries "War & Remembrance" on ABC in 1988.

Claiming to be "a very timid, shy, cowardly man out of the theatre . . . acting has proved a great release for me," (the late Ralph Richardson contradicted Sir John's claim: "You needn't say a word with him, sometimes I will say yes or no or really? . . . afterward he will say to someone, 'I had a wonderful talk with Ralph,' and I didn't say anything . . . he's a continual firework of words."), he admits to loving junk novels and finds TV, if it is done with sufficient sincerity, skill and expertise, "Very enjoyable escapist entertainment. . . . I was born into a time when the theatre was very escapist, and I have always been an escapist in my own life and work. The romance of being in another century, in another situation, had always appealed to me because it enabled me to escape from my own emotional frustrations."

He was born in London on 14 April 1904 to Frank Gielgud and Kate Terry-Lewis, whose family, the Terrys, were the royalty of Britain's stage. Gielgud grew up in upper-middle-class comfort, and his ambition was always to become an actor. He promised his conservative stockbroker father that if he didn't make a success by 25 he'd become an architect. He went on the stage at 17 and made his first appearance at the Old Vic in 1921 as the herald in *Henry V*. With his voice, which Sir Alex Guinness says sounds like "a silver trumpet muffled in silk," Gielgud made his greatest marks in the 1920s and '30s playing Shakespeare. Many critics thought he was the best *Hamlet* of his generation. He considers his *Richard II* to be his finest performance. His contribution to Shakespearean acting was that he made it more natural and less declamatory. As the '30s came to a close, Britain's triumvirate of its finest actors were Laurence Olivier, Richardson and Gielgud, about whom British producer Derek Granger drew this distinction: "Larry is the lion, the hero who can play Oedipus, Henry V and Lear. . . . Ralph is the transmuted common man, John is the poet, the one with the finest and most aristocratic sensibility." He has had his flops, of course, but by the end of the '40s he says that he played so many Monarchs his management would say: "Just stick a crown on his head and send him onstage." In 1950 under the direction of Peter Brook, he interpreted Angelo in *Measure for Measure* not as a sensualist, but as a repressed Puritan. The role sparked his career to do the opposite of what most careers do in the golden years—glow rather than dim.

Gielgud moved from his London home behind Westminster Abbey to reside year round in a 17th Century house in Buckinghamshire more than fifteen years ago. This he says changed his life because now he goes out less. "London is too full of ghosts for me," he says. He reads avidly, watches TV and keeps an aviary of parakeets and cockatoos. "I'm a very contented man." When he turned 80 in 1984 the occasion was duly noted. Several books were published to mark his birthday, including his own *Gielgud: An Actor and His Time*. About turning 80, the star of over 50 films (including earlier in his career *The Barretts of Wimpole Street, Saint Joan, Becket, The Loved One* and *Chimes at Midnight*) and, besides the classics, such modern plays as *Home*, for which he shared the Tony award for best actor with Richardson, and Edward Albee's *Tiny Alice*, told the *London Daily Mail*, "Ideally, what I'd like to do is die on stage in the middle of a good performance—and with a full house."

Frank Gifford

This former halfback became a top-ranked TV sportscaster, first with CBS, then with ABC. In 1988 he celebrated his eighteenth consecutive season as a member of ABC's NFL "Monday Night Football" broadcast team. Possessed with an uncanny knack for predicting plays, Gifford gives an admittedly low-key, play-by-play commentary that contrasts sharply, as intended, with the mayhem both on the field and in the free-wheeling telecasts. His style hastened the departure of what one writer termed "the gee-whiz, hysterical school" of sports announcers.

Born in Santa Monica, Calif., 16 August 1930, Gifford recalls that as boys he and his brother found that athletic pre-eminence made them easy friends as they moved, sometimes up to 15 times a year, with their oilfield worker father. Gifford was an All-American at USC, went to the N.Y. Giants in 1952 as No. 1 draft choice (as a *defensive* player), and eight years later suffered a near-fatal injury when Philadelphia Eagle linebacker Chuck Bednarik hit him (after Gifford had caught a pass) with a vicious "blind-side" tackle. Gifford "retired" from the fray several times before calling it quits for good in 1965. After two failed marriages, he tied the knot for a third time with singer/talk-show hostess Kathie Lee Johnson on 18 October 1986. Gifford has three children (Jeff, Kyle, Vicki) from his first marriage. Still possessed of a glamourous, All-American image, he says his biggest disappointments were his being switched away from quarterback after high school and failing to make it as an actor. In 1958, one season after he had been voted the Most Valuable Player in the National Football League, he quit the Giants and made a TV pilot. "A friend who worked in an ad agency phoned me. He said, 'I've just seen your pilot, and it's a dog. You'd better get back with the team.' Two days later," Gifford says, "I was back taking my lumps in scrimmage."

Kathie Lee Gifford

As Regis Philbin's perky co-host on the daytime talk-show ratings champion "Live with Regis & Kathie Lee," Kathie Lee Gifford keeps up admirably on the wacky, anything-can-happen show. A professional performer since the age of 14, she's been an actress and singer as well as a television journalist and talk-show host.

Kathie Lee Gifford was born 16 August in Paris, France, where her father was stationed as the Naval attache to General Eisenhower. The family moved to Annapolis, Maryland, when she was five years old, soon relocating to Bowie, Maryland. Her parents encouraged creativity so Kathie Lee grew up putting on plays and carnivals with her older brother and younger sister. Gifford started her professional career at age 14 when she and her sister formed a folk group called Pennsylvania Next Right's. They arranged the music and even booked their own gigs at coffee houses. At the age of 17, Gifford became Maryland's Junior Miss and landed her first commercial by winning the national competition's Kraft Hostess Award. Following high school, Gifford studied communications, drama and arts in college but at age 20, a few credits shy of a degree, opted to take her chances in Los Angeles. In true Hollywood fashion, while on the set of "Days of Our Lives" she was spotted by the producer and appeared as an extra the next day. She moved up to "under fives" and voice-overs, eventually portraying the minor role of Nurse Callahan for one year, while doing a slew of commercials. Turning down a two-year contract, Kathie Lee continued to do commercials while shooting countless network pilots. In 1977 she was a featured singer on the game show "Name That Tune." That exposure launched her nightclub act as she opened for such headliners as Bill Cosby, Rich Little and Bob Hope. She also costarred on "Hee Haw Honeys," a musical sitcom spinoff of "Hee Haw." Her journalistic career began when "Good Morning, America" producers saw her gueststinting on "A.M. Los Angeles." Within five weeks of arriving on "GMA," she was substitute anchoring for Joan Lunden. As special correspondent, she logged over a quarter million air miles covering human interest stories. She continued her "GMA" work for the first year of her co-hosting duties with Philbin in 1985. Gifford has never been one to sit back and relax. In addition to "Live," she has co-hosted the "Miss America" pageant for three years, performed at the 1985 Inaugural Ball for President and Mrs. Reagan, co-hosted nightly half-hour reports with her husband, Frank Gifford, from the 1988 Winter Olympics at Calgary, and performed with Philbin in a nightclub act.

The Giffords devote a great deal of time to charitable causes like Multiple Sclerosis and the Special Olympics. She is also very involved in The Children's Charity through Variety Clubs, International, and often sings for various charity benefits. In her spare time, Gifford has supervised the interior refurbishing and decor of her historical country home. She enjoys entertaining good friends and family, cooking, searching for American pine antiques and relaxing at home with her husband and her puppy, Chardonnay.

Melissa Gilbert

At 12 years old, Melissa Gilbert stated in her NBC biography, "When I get big I'm going to be an actress. Or maybe a dancer—or a doctor, or a lawyer. But I might be a nurse." Over a decade later, it seems she stuck with her first idea. Presently a star of television, stage and screen, Melissa has matured into a stunning young woman who can tackle any role.

Born in Los Angeles on 8 May 1964, she was a product of a show-biz family. Her father was the late entertainer Paul Gilbert. Her mother Barbara Crane Gilbert was a former dancer/actress, and her grandfather, Harry Crane, was a television comedy writer. Melissa's debut in front of the camera at two-and-a-half for a Carter's baby clothes commercial provided her with the first item on her theatrical resume. Retiring until age seven, she returned to work by doing over thirty commercials. These sixty second spots led to guest appearances on such shows as "Gunsmoke," "Emergency," and "Tenafly," then eventually the reprising role as Laura Ingalls in "Little House on the Prairie" (1974-1981). Her part as an engaging nine-year-old progressed into an appealing teen-age wife and mother in weekly TV view of millions of adoring fans during her eight-year run in NBC's homespun hit. Although she is probably most widely known for her moving portrayal of young Laura on "Little House on the Prairie," she has also demonstrated her considerable talents as Helen Keller in a TV movie of "The Miracle Worker" (1979), and in the title role of a TV rendition of "The Diary of Anne Frank" (1980). Manifesting a more adult (and considerably sexier) side, she also starred in a small-screen movie of the William Inge classic, "Splendor in the Grass" (1981), playing the role originated on the big screen a generation earlier by the late Natalie Wood. On 29 October 1987, Gilbert made her official New York stage debut in a new play by Barbara Lebow called *A Shayna Maidel*. Set in Manhattan in 1946, with glimmers of Chernov, Poland, before World War II, the drama focuses on two sisters, their father and the circumstances that have torn the family apart and brought it back together. In 1987 she appeared in the telefilm "Blood Vows" and has starred in two major motion pictures: *Sylvester* (1984), and *Ice House* (1988). Other television specials include participation in "Battle of the Network Stars" (1978-1982), "Celebrity Challenge of the Sexes" (1980), and "Circus Lions, Tigers and Melissa, Too" (1977).

After a long, well-publicized affair with fellow actor Rob Lowe, Melissa married actor/director Bo Brinkman on 21 February 1988. The couple live in Manhattan and have a son, Dakota Paul (born 1 May 1989).

Dizzy Gillespie

The skin-diving, chess-playing, pipe-collecting founding father of bop was born John Birks Gillespie, 21 October 1917 in Cheraw, S.C., studied harmony and football ("They are better at the training table") and swung toward Philadelphia in 1935, horn in a paper bag. He worked with many top jazz bands (Duke Ellington, Earl Hines, Cab Calloway, Billy Eckstine), but "we couldn't really blow on our jobs—not the way we wanted to. They made us do that two-beat stuff." In 1945, together with the late Charlie "Bird" Parker and Thelonius Monk, Dizzy worked out a new nervous, fragmented sound he called "bebop"—later shortened to "bop." The forerunner of modern, "progressive" music, but not anti-oldtime jazz ("That would be like turning your back on your father"), bop brought in a new dialect ("Cool, Man!") and dress, and musicians and non-musicians alike followed Diz's costuming lead of horn-rimmed specs, beret, and goatee. The pioneer bopster's unqiuely styled trumpet, with the bell shooting upward at a 45-degree angle, was reportedly designed when someone stepped on his horn at a party, and Dizzy liked the new sound. Bandleader since 1946, composer ("Swing Low, Sweet Cadillac"), and a fine musician (said the late conductor Dimitri Mitropoulos, "That man! When I heard him, I was thrilled to death!"), the "cool man with the hot horn" was presented with New York City's Handel Award in 1972 after his enthusiastic participation in the first Newport Jazz Festival to be held in Fun City. His devoted fan club members, who called themselves the John Birks Society, several times campaigned on behalf of their hero for the job of President of the United States. Meanwhile, Diz delighted President Carter with a rendition of his '40's hit, "Salted Peanuts" at an engagement at the White House. His autobiography is called *TO BE or Not . . . to BOP*. Some of his recordings include "Closer to the Source," "Groovin' High," "The Cosmic Eye," and "Havin' a Good Time." A special film of him in concert, *A Night in Havana: Dizzy Gillespie in Cuba*, was released in 1988. He received the Lifetime Achievement Award presented by the National Academy of Recording Arts & Sciences in 1989.

Newt Gingrich

This Republican from the suburbs and rural communities around Atlanta believes, according to Steven Roberts of the *New York Times*, in helping people help themselves, "but don't give them something for nothing." Gingrich is convinced that both parties are guilty of "liberal welfare state" notions. So he came up with the Conservative Opportunity Society, and now has a cluster of fellow conservatives on Capitol Hill whose task they've made keeping Republicans on the straight and narrow, thereby obstructing liberal Democratic action. "There's a big gap in the middle for positive, dynamic conservatism," Gingrich says.

Newton Leroy Gingrich was born in Harrisburg, Pa., on 17 June 1943. The "Army brat" lived in Germany during his teens and picked up valuable lessons visiting World War I battlefields with his dad, including the realization that "societies really could collapse, and that political leadership was the key to survival for a free society." Having married (the former Jacqueline Battley) two days after his 19th birthday, he attended Emory University in Atlanta and then Tulane University where he took his Ph.D. in 1971. Gingrich became a college history professor, and in 1978 was successful in his third try for a congressional seat. He brings an academic approach to his bright assessment of solving the nation's problems. Besides espousing giving government bonuses to poor children who learn to read and tax credits to middle class families who buy home computers, he scolds fellow GOPers' poor speaking tactics, saying they "tend to have blurred and unfocused opening statements." He made the observation after poring over transcripts of Sunday morning interview shows, as is his wont. Although accused even by some Republicans of being "a pain in the fanny," Gingrich holds the right-wing line (covert aid to the Nicaraguan contras, no

International Monetary Fund loans to Communists) and draws clear lines between Democrat and Republican perspectives. "There is a deep yearning in this country for fundamental values," says the Baptist Gingrich, whose second marriage (since 1981) has been to the former Marianne Ginther. The father of two daughters was led by his values to demand censure of two Congressmen accused of sexual misconduct with House pages.

Allen Ginsberg

"Hold back the edges of your gowns, ladies, we are going through hell," wrote poet William Carlos Williams in his introduction to Allen Ginsberg's beatnik anthem, *Howl*, back in 1956. By the 1970s, the poem was being cited by a critic as one of "a small number of earth-moving angry poems of this century . . . that poems (and people) who come after have been unable to ignore," but the poet himself had mellowed. Though he was still addicted to scatological colloquialisms and an anti-establishment advocate of pansexual freedom and liberalized drug laws, his vocabulary emphasis had shifted from four-letter Anglo-Saxonisms to two-letter Far Easternisms such as "Om." By the 1980s, he had mellowed even more, shedding his full beard and ragbag tatters for conservative business attire, and even taunting his own famous epic poem. On the 25th anniversary of *Howl,* in 1981, he gave a surprise satiric reading of the poems, which had the audience howling with him in laughter, not rage. In recent verses describing himself as a failure, he confesses, "My tirades destroyed no intellectual unions of the KGB and CIA. . . . I have not yet stopped the armies of entire mankind on the way to World War III. . . . I never got to heaven, nirvana, x, whatchamacallit. I never learned to die."

He was born 3 June 1926 in Newark, raised in a "Jewish left-wing atheist Russian" household in Paterson, and his boyhood was definitely not in the pattern of WASP apple-pie America. His father, Louis, was a poet, though of a fairly conventional type. His mother, Naomi, suffered a mental breakdown when Allen was in grade school and spent most of her life in a mental hospital (The poignant *Kaddish for Naomi Ginsberg* is one of his most important works.). Following a series of mystical visions in 1948, Allen spent eight months in a mental institution, but by 1951, having collected a B.A. from Columbia, he was living the straight life as a market research consultant in San Francisco. Then, after a period of psychotherapy, a new day dawned. Relinquishing coat and tie, letting beard and hair grow, and setting up housekeeping with fellow poet Peter Orlovsky, he set out after Nirvana as a fulltime poet—a leading figure (with Jack Kerouac) in the San Francisco Renaissance of the 1950s. After becoming a national celebrity via *Howl*, Ginsberg made extended trips to the Far East, Cuba, the Soviet Union, middle Europe (on May Day 1965, 100,000 fervent admirers in Prague elected him King of the May, whereupon the Czech government promptly expelled him), worked in the U.S. on behalf of "flower power," marched on the Pentagon, and was tear-gassed in Chicago's Lincoln Park while chanting "Om" at the Yippie Life Festival at the Democratic National Convention in 1968. In the 1970s and early '80s, Ginsberg's practice of Tibetan Buddhism has injected Dharmic themes to his music and poetry and political activism. Om!

Nikki Giovanni

I really hope no white person ever has
cause to write about me
because they never understand
Black love is Black wealth and they'll
probably talk about my hard childhood
and never understand that
all the while I was quite happy.

Thus in her poem, "Nikki-Rosa," does the petite (five feet two, 100 pound) poet vehemently declare her independence from the every-black-childhood-was-tragic school of literature. In *Truth Is on the Way,* an early album on which she reads her poems to the accompaniment of gospel singing, she paints warm glowing pictures of black revolutionary poets; she has, notwithstanding, "etched her profile in . . . verse which transcends the rhetoric of revolution and forms the essence of love," says one critic.

Born in Knoxville, Tenn., 7 June 1943, Nikki Giovanni shrugs off questions about her family name. "I don't know why it causes such a scene," she told *Ebony*. "It just means that our slave masters were Italian instead of English or French." As a history major at Fisk University she helped found a campus chapter of SNCC and has written tributes to Martin Luther King and Angela Davis. She uses street talk in her speech and poems and for the last dozen years has carried the title "Princess of Black Poetry." The mother of a son, Nikki explains, "Tommy is what is fashionably known as 'an illegitimate baby.' I had a baby at 25 because I wanted to have a baby and I could afford to have a baby. I did not get married because I didn't want to get married and I could afford not to get married." She is the author of many books, among them: *Black Feeling Black Talk* (1968), *Re-Creation* (1970), *My House* (1972), *Ego Tripping and Other Poems for Young Readers* (1973), *The Women and the Men* (1975), *Cotton Candy on a Rainy Day* (1978) and *Sacred Cows . . . and Other Edibles* (1988). *Gemini* (1971) and *A Dialogue: James Baldwin and Nikki Giovannia* (1973) are conversations/essays. She also has six record albums to her credit. She's a woman full of opinions, ideas. "People are always talking about loving people but then look what they do to each other. They spank children to make them behave, they beat wives to keep them in line, they start wars to bring about peace. I don't understand it. But then I'm just a colored poet from Cincinnati . . . so I guess I'm not expected to." When asked what she is doing to help humankind, she shrugs, "I think. And I don't bite. If human beings aren't prepared to utilize this gift, life, then how do we justify our existence? Why on Earth would you take the dinosaur away and replace it with mankind if not for the betterment of Earth?"

Lillian Gish

"We didn't have unions in those days. We worked 12 hours a day seven days a week," recalled Lillian Gish who started in films in 1912, following eight years on the road barnstorming in old melodramas with her mother and sister, Dorothy. The fragile heroine of D.W. Griffith's epic film, *Birth of a Nation* (1914), *Intolerance* (1916), and *Broken Blossoms* (1918) has proven herself to be indestructible in audience appeal. On tour in the 1970s with her own one-woman show, *Lillian Gish and the Movies*, she could reminisce about a nonstop performing career on stage, screen and TV spanning nine decades, all the way back to her theatrical debut at the age of five in a drama called *In Convict Stripes*. "I was merely taught to speak clearly and loudly so the audience could understand."

The elder of the two precociously performing Gish sisters (Dorothy died in 1968) was born 14 October 1896 in Springfield, Ohio. The two moppets were allowed to go on the stage as a means of helping family finances after their father deserted them, and, in such silent film spellbinders as *Orphans of the Storm*, they became, as Brooks Atkinson put it, "as much a part of American folkore as Jack Dempsey or Harry S. Truman." In 1969, looking back with wry amusement on the old Hollywood days, Miss Gish (who never married) penned a book, *The Movies, Mr. Griffith and Me*. In 1971 she was presented with a special honorary Oscar for her "distinguished contributions to and service in making motion pictures." In 1982 she received the Kennedy Center Honors, and in 1984 the coveted Life Achievement Award from the American Film Institute. That same year she fulfilled a lifelong dream when she was partnered by Paris Opéra Ballet sensation Patrick Dupond in *Le Spectre de la Rose* on the stage of the Metropolitan Opera House during the Met's centennial celebration of the performing arts. Continuing her presence on the screen, Gish appeared in the Alan Alda film *Sweet Liberty* in 1985, followed by *The Whales of August* in 1987.

Rudolph Giuliani

Politician Rudolph Giuliani is certainly a complex and contradictory person to define. When asked in a recent interview about how he thinks the public perceives him, his reply was illuminating: "Probably as much tougher, more single-minded and rigid than I really am."

He was born in Brooklyn in 1945, and in 1952 his father moved his family to the more affluent community of Garden City, Long Island. Rudolph was impressed most by his father's innate courage. "My father was one of my heroes because he had such a tremendous ability to control—overcome—fear." His mother, still alive today, inspired him with her thirst for knowledge and tremendous interest in public affairs. He describes her as being a compulsive perfectionist and attributes his own intolerance of laziness to his mother's influence: "I don't like people who don't pay attention or slough off their work. I don't mind if people make mistakes, if they're hard working." He was a student at Catholic schools through high school and then at Manhattan College (also taught by the Christian Brothers), and during the early period of his life, he entertained the hope of becoming a priest. Eventually he opted for civil service, but attained his law degree from New York University (1965 to 1968). His first political affiliations were with the Democratic party, although he is now a staunch Republican. His first important promotion came in 1970 when he became an Assistant U.S. Attorney in the Southern District Office of New York. His star rose as a brilliant prosecuting attorney from then on. He successfully prosecuted former Bronx Democratic Boss Stanley Friedman. His office's investigation precipitated a guilty plea on tax fraud charges by Carl Capasso (Bess Meyerson's friend). Ivan Boesky and Dennis Levine, pleading guilty themselves, assisted his investigations into insider trading. And under Giuliani's instigation, Southern District Prosecutors won racketeering convictions against leaders of four of the five major New York organized-crime families. An ambitious man, he took Judge MacMahon's words to heart: "Don't be one of those guys who sits back and waits for people to give him cases. Volunteer. Get into court, overcome whatever fear you have early."

In 1989 Rudolph Giuliani undertook a new challenge. Rather than accepting the Reagan administration's offer to head the S.E.C. or take over the F.B.I., he opted for the more dangerous route of running for mayor of New York City. He won the Republican primary in September 1989 and was hoping to upset the Democratic balance by challenging David Dinkins for the job. During his campaign he promised: "All the others merely offer rhetoric. I offer experience and performance.... Most of my career has been spent in law enforcement. No one is more qualified to lead New York in the fight against crime.... As mayor I will lead the battle to take our streets, parks and subways back from the criminals.... Juvenile justice must be reformed...." Rudolph Giuliani, who had already achieved the prestigious position of Associate Attorney, abandoned this title and returned to the less influential role of a simple U.S. Attorney, and this purely by choice. This complex man, surrounded by his wife, Donna Hanover, news anchor on Channel 11 (two children: Andrew and Caroline), is an enigma to us all. But one thing is for sure, he is a man of courage who will be entirely responsible for the pattern his life will follow.

Hubert de Givenchy

Remember Audrey Hepburn during that first scene in *Breakfast at Tiffany's* when she strolls up to Tiffany's windows in the dawning hours of the day, eating a roll and drinking coffee from a styrofoam cup? Remember how divinely regal and, alternatly, childlike she was in her gown and gloves? All the clothes in that film were divine for that matter. But of course they would be. They were Givenchy.

Born 21 February 1925 into a well-to-do French Protestant Family in Beauvais (his grandfather was the director of the Gobelin tapestry works), Givenchy entered the world of *haute couture* at 17 as an apprentice-designer to Jacques Fath. His period of apprenticeship lasted for just nine years; he also studied with Robert Piguet, Lucien Lelong and Elsa Schiaparelli, for whom he created the boutique collection for four years. Encouraged both by his former employers and his mentor Balenciaga, he struck out on his own in 1951 at the age of 26. He drew his inspiration from Balenciaga and classical French art. The proportions in the very first collection were perfect; subtle details tied in to form an outfit, the fluidity of which was not contradicted by the fabric or the tailoring. One of Givenchy's first triumphs was the now-famous Bettina blouse, a white-pouf-sleeved cotton shirt worn with straight or full skirts, and named for the famous model. His other trademarks through the years have been opulent fabrics, impeccable tailoring and (in the words of fashion historian Laura Sinderbrand) his "fastidious command of color and shape." His headquarters are an elegant eighteenth century building on the Avenue George V. In 1968, to cater to his younger customers, the first Givenchy Nouvelle Boutique was opened. From the beginning the boutiques have played an integral part in the Givenchy concept for worldwide expansion, one of the richest French fashion establishments of the lot, including over 30 licensees and the highly profitable Givenchy Gentleman—men's ready-to-wear.

Says the master: "The frittery madness of new trends often leads to sensationalism, not beauty, not elegance.... My greatest pleasure is to hear a lady say 'Hubert, this coat... I've had it four years... it's like my skin, it feels so good.'" In 1984 *Givenchy: Thirty Years*, a retrospective exhibition, was mounted at New York's Fashion Institute of Technology and later toured the globe. "Elegance is harmony," says Givenchy, "and harmony is inspiring. It's what makes life bearable, beautiful. *J'adore la vie*. And I love couture." In 1988 he was honored by the state of California with a Lifetime Achievement Award.

Philip Glass

"Young man," remarked the taxicab passenger when she spotted her driver's hack license, "did you know you have the same name of a very famous composer?" He knew. Not too long after his opera *Einstein on the Beach* concluded a triumphant world tour with two sold-out performances at the Metropolitan Opera House, Philip Glass no longer had to drive a cab (or fix plumbing) to subsidize his musical career. Minimalism—the hypnotic and infectious "rebuke to three decades of over intellectualized music by the post-war avant garde" (*Time*); "putting a microscope on the sound and discerning tiny aspects of it" (choreographer Lucinda Childs); "a very naive experience... the musical equivalent of Grandma Moses" (composer Luciano Berio)—is here to stay. And to such music establishmentarians as Pulitzer Prize-winning composer Elliott Carter, who believes the "minimalists are not aware of the larger dimensions of life," adding for good measure that "one also hears constant repetition in the speeches of Hitler... it has its dangerous aspects," Philip Glass wryly responds, "What's worse than being present while a revolution is happening, and not know it?"

The innovative composer who in the late '60s broke with the classical music pattern a for which his Peabody Conservatory, Juilliard School and private classes (with Nadia Boulanger) had prepared him, was born 31 July 1937 in Baltimore, and remembers taking home from his father's record shop (where they sold "most top-40 stuff...junk)" the records that "didn't sell...a lot chamber music...what I really listened to." He began studying the flute at age eight, and later the piccolo, at his hometown Peabody Institute, and was 15 when he entered the University of Chicago to study math and philosophy (A.B., 1956). The raft of prizes he carried off for composition at his Juilliard School graduation were not enough to quell his disenchantment with his "traditionally American classical, Coplandesque" musical output. In Paris in 1965, while studying with Boulanger, he met Indian sitarist Ravi Shankar, whose music Glass was notating for a film soundtrack, and found its additive rhythmical structure "a revelation."

Back in New York in 1967, Glass was determined to create a new "world music." While fans were mesmerized by his hypnotic devices of the drone and his syncopated swinging rhythms, many critics dismissed his work as "head music...anti-intellectual, feel-good music that depends on high amplification and a glittery glassy surface." The composer's works, which have been performed at venues ranging from the Kool Jazz Festival to the stage of the Met, include the operas *Einstein at the Beach* (1976), *Satyagraha* (1980; based on Gandhi's early years) and *Akhnaten* (1984; about the hermaphrodite monotheistic Egyptian king), segments of the 12-hour Robert Wilson epic, *the CIVIL warS*, and the chamber opera, *The Photographer* (1982). Film scores include *Koyaanisqatsi* (1982), *Mishima* (1985; about the late charismatic Japanese author, *Powaqqatisi* (1988), and *The Thin Blue Line* (1988). Arlene Croce in the *New Yorker* suggested that Glass is attracted to dance because "dance is a present-tense art form...(and) Glass' hammering beat seems to drive dancers ever onward into the outer space of unanticipated movement." Jerome Robbins used music *Glassworks* and *Akhnaten* in 1983 to create *Glass Pieces* for the New York City Ballet, where it had a smashing success. Alvin Ailey, Lar Lubovitch and Lucinda Childs have all choreographed to his music. It was minimalist composer creating music for minimalist playwright in 1985 when Glass created the score for a new production of Samuel Beckett's *Endgame*.

The first composer since Aaron Copland to be offered a contract as a CBS Masterworks recording artist (he plays the electric organ with the Philip Glass Ensemble), Glass has seen much of his work recreated on discs. Twice married, he is the father of a son, Zachary, and a daughter, Juliette. He lives in a brownstone in Manhattan's East Village, an unfashionable neighborhood that gives him much longed-for privacy. "I will not exploit my life for publicity," he told Robert Jones in an interview in the *New York Daily News*, "and I refuse to discuss my personal philosophies and beliefs. My music is so very odd already, I see no need to make myself any odder." In 1987, his book *Music by Philip Glass* was published.

John Glenn

The wholesome ex-marine from Ohio was rocketed to bona fide hero status in 1962 as the first American to orbit the earth in a space capsule. Turning to politics, Glenn was elected senator of his home state in 1974. But his dewy patriotism and respected ten-year record as a legislator impressed pollsters more than voters, and Glenn bowed out of the 1984 Democratic presidential primaries. Noted a political observer at the time, "They really believed they could transfer the aura of celebrity into a political gain. It's now clear that they can't do that."

Born in Cambridge, Ohio, on 18 July 1921, Glenn compiled a school record that spoke of greater things to come. An honor student and varsity letterman in no less than three sports, Glenn took to new challenges with ease. After serving as a decorated flyer in the Marines during World War II and the Korean War, he became a military test pilot and is credited with making the first transcontinental supersonic flight. He was the perfect candidate for NASA's recruiting program in 1959. Earthbound after his historic 4-hour 55-minute orbit in the Friendship 7 capsule, Glenn tackled business, as an executive with Royal Crown Cola, before turning to politics. After two bids for Ohio's senatorial seat, in 1964 and 1970, he won the office by a sweeping victory in the first post-Watergate election. A moderate Democrat, Glenn supported the ERA, and advocated a national health insurance plan and increased funding for education and health care. Considered a viable challenger to frontrunner Walter Mondale early in the 1984 primaries, Glenn's following surprisingly seemed to dwindle, and the former astronaut's presidential high hopes came crashing to earth. "We are so far in debt, we just cannot go on," Glenn said.

Glenn married his high school sweetheart, Anna (Annie) Margaret Castor, in 1943, and they have two children.

Alexander Godunov

It was an airport scene that rivalled the one in *Casablanca* for suspense and international intrigue. For 73 hours in August of 1979 U.S. authorities delayed the departure of an Aeroflot jetliner until one of its passengers, ballerina Lyudmila Vlasova, gave firm assurances that she most assuredly did not wish to join husband Alexander Godunov as the latest member of the jeté set (and the first from the Bolshoi) to defect to the West. By April of 1980, the powerful six foot two *premier danseur*, who had been the legendary and formidable Maya Plisetskaya's preferred partner at the Bolshoi, utilized his dazzling technique and magnetic stage presence to partner Natalia Makarova to "the most passionate Giselle" of her career, according to *The New York Times*'s Anna Kisselgoff. He felt even more at home at American Ballet Theatre, the classically oriented company he joined on his arrival in America, when his old classmate Mikhail Baryshnikov took over as artistic director in 1980. So it came as a seismic shock to dancer and public alike when after the 1982 season he was fired. "He threw me away like potato peel.... I really don't know why... nobody talked to me, nobody had the guts to face me personally," he told John Gruen in *Dance* magazine, adding that it reminded him "of the Russian way of behavior," thereby decisively burning his second bridge in three years. With characteristic resilience, however, Godunov quickly lined up a series of guest appearances, formed his own touring company of dancers and a romantic alliance with actress Jacqueline Bisset (he divorced Lyudmila in 1982) and made his American motion picture debut in 1985 in *Witness* with Harrison Ford (to favorable notices), followed in 1986 with *The Money Pit* and *Die Hard* (with Bruce Willis) in 1988.

Boris Alexander ("Sasha") Godunov was born 28 November 1949 on the island of Sakhalin, and moved (after his parents' divorce) with his mother to Riga, in the republic of Latvia, where she enrolled him in the Riga State Ballet School in 1958 to keep him from becoming "a hooligan." He and classmate Mikhail Barshnikov were denied partnering classes because of their short stature, so they concentrated all the more on developing their superb techniques, while resorting to a variety of folk remedies to induce the growth that would be their ticket out of the character dancer category. (By the time he graduated in 1967 Godunov had reached his present height.) After three years touring with the Young Ballet, he auditioned for the Bolshoi and was promptly hired as a principal dancer in 1971. His debut in *Swan Lake* ("It wasn't about *pirouettes* or *cabrioles*—it was about acting," he recalled about preparing for the role) was hailed as "an evening of poetic discovery" and an accomplishment that usually results only after "years of work and many performances." He continued to expand his repertory, adding such contemporary pieces as Roland Petit's *La Rose Malade* and Plisetskaya's own *Anna Karenina*. As one of the Bolshoi headliners in a U.S. tour in 1973, he astounded audiences with his astonishing pyrotechnical display of blindingly fast multiple *pirouettes* and whiplash *tours a la seconde*. But he *captured* them with his strongest asset, a spellbinding dramatic ability. From 1974 to 1979 the rock-ribbed Bolshoi management refused to let him travel abroad, lest his affection for things American expand to include its geography. But in 1979, strapped for high-calibre *premiers danseuers* for its scheduled American tour, the company reluctantly added him to its roster, and the ever-opportunistic Godunov confirmed their worst fears by strolling out of his upper West Side of Manhattan hotel on the evening of 21 August 1979 to begin his American odyssey.

Whoopi Goldberg

"It's a Cinderella dream come true. It's a gas. . . . It's amazing. . . . Everyone should have this luck. . . . This is the last thing I expected to happen." Whoopi Goldberg—actor (as she prefers to be called), comedienne extraordinaire, was introduced to Broadway in 1984 (with the help of producer/director Mike Nichols) and met with rave reviews. Says Nichols of his "discovery," "I went backstage to . . . meet her and I burst into tears, made a complete fool of myself. . . . Her compassion and her humanity are enormously moving and quite startling in somebody that funny." Goldberg's one-woman sketches, all of her own creation, "walk a fine line between satire and pathos, stand-up comedy and acting," observed a *New York Times* critic. Midway into her act, Whoopi coaxes the audience to link hands and form a bonded chain from row to row. "They told me not to try this, said it was too risky. . . . They called it the sentimentality of the 60s. I call it the sensibility of the 80s. . . . The most wonderful thing about touching somebody is you never know who your fairy Godfather might be."

Born circa 1950, Whoopi Goldberg came by her moniker when (according to Whoopi) a burning bush with a Yiddish accent suggested that her own name (which she refuses to divulge) was boring and convinced her to change it. A native of Manhattan's Chelsea district, Whoopi attended a local Catholic school and began her theatrical career at age eight at Helena Rubinstein's Theatre at the Hudson Guild. A 60's hippie "on the fine line between the lower East side and something spiritual, I asked myself am I going to keep doing drugs or figure out what I'm going to do with my life?" She decided: straight theatre, improvisation, and chorus bits on Broadway (*Pippen, Hair, Jesus Christ Superstar*) followed. In between she supported herself with a variety of jobs—bricklayer, bank teller, cosmetician in a morgue. In California Goldberg worked with the San Diego Repertory Theatre and the Blake Street Hawkeyes. Whoopi dreams of being cast as Shaw's St. Joan. She embraces her success, yet takes it in stride. "It's not so much that my life has changed, it's that I'm now able to experience things that were not accessible to me before. . . . What I enjoy most, though, are the simple things fame provides. I can stay at interesting places when I travel. I can get lots of pants, buy groceries and pay the rent and phone bills." Whoopi shares her California home with her daughter, Alexandra, and is seen around town with cameraman Eddie Gold.

In 1985 Goldberg made her film debut as the protagonist of Alice Walker's *The Color Purple*, with Steven Spielberg in the director's chair. Her performance earned her an Oscar nomination and a Golden Globe Award. Very much in demand, Whoopi's comedic talents are frequently seen on cable and television specials such as "Whoopi Goldberg's Fontaine . . . Why Am I Straight," "Funny, You Don't Look 200," "Carol, Robin, Whoopi and Carl," and "Comic Relief." She landed a recurring role on "Star Trek: The Next Generation," playing Guinan, the alien humanoid hostess. She received an Emmy nomination in 1986 for her guest appearance on the hit television series "Moonlighting." Always returning to her stage roots, Goldberg toured with a new one-woman show *Living on the Edge of Chaos* in 1988, and was presented with the 12th annual California Theatre Award for Outstanding Achievement on stage. Her recent films include *Jumpin' Jack Flash* (1986), *The Telephone* (1987), *Fatal Beauty* (1987), *Clara's Heart* (1988), *Homer & Eddie* (1988) and the CBS-TV telefilm "Bagdad Cafe" (1989). For her contributions to charity, the comedian/actress was honored in March, 1989, by the Starlight Foundation as their Humanitarian of the Year.

Jeff Goldblum

Jeff Goldblum is both a talented and resourceful performer. He is every bit "the chameleon," his persona transforming itself for his variety of roles. Although he began his career in the theater, he is most well known for his eclectic characterizations in film.

Jeff Goldblum was born 22 October 1952 in Pittsburgh, Pennsylvania. At the age of seventeen, he left home to study acting. He landed in The Neighborhood Playhouse in New York under the tutelage of Sanford Meisner. Joseph Papp was first to spot his talent, and cast him in *The Two Gentlemen of Verona*, a resounding Broadway success. The stage gave way to the camera in Goldblum's priorities. His film career began in 1974 with both *California Split* and *Death Wish*, soon to be followed by the cult film *Nashville* (1975). He seems to have mapped out his film career very carefully. His choices of scripts were as daring as they were varied. He quickly understood the danger to typecasting, and deliberately chose to play very diverse characters in films such as Woody Allen's *Annie Hall* (1977) and Phil Kauffman's *Invasion of the Body Snatchers* (1978). He made it a point to alternate between serious and dry comedic roles. He is perhaps most remembered by the public for two performances: his participation in *The Big Chill* (1983) and the cult classic *The Fly* (1986). His most recent film appearance is in the comedy *Earth Girls Are Easy* (1989). He has temporarily resumed his theatrical stage career. He appeared at the Delacorte Theater in Shakespeare's *Twelfth Night*, produced by his old friend Joseph Papp. This 1989 produciton was not a critical success, but Goldblum will continue to persevere undaunted.

In keeping with Goldblum's wry sense of humor, however, he might agree that his greatest claim to fame just might be that of "Husband of the Year," since his wife, Geena Davis, was the surprise Academy Award winner for her performance in *The Accidental Tourist* (1989).

William Golding

"I believe man suffers from an appalling ignorance of his own nature," states the 1983 Nobel laureate in Literature. The award meant about $190,000 to this veteran British novelist and brought some outrage from the international literary establishment who felt that Golding was not as entitled as such other elder scribbers as Jorge Luis Borges, Italo Calvino and Gunter Grass, to name a few. Even the Swedish Academy which bestows the Nobel Prize noted in its lengthy statement explaining its choice that Golding's books "can be read with pleasure and profit without the need to make much effort with learning or acumen." Hardly a ringing endorsement.

Nevertheless Golding's place on the higher shelf of literature is not diminished by this sour twist of the bookworm. Born 19 September 1911 in Cornwall, he did not attain early success. He studied at Oxford, held odd jobs and enlisted in the Royal Navy at the beginning of WW II. In his early 30's, he came of age. "One had one's nose rubbed in the human condition." When he saw the sinking of the *Bismark* he decided the human race was inherently evil. "My books have been written out of a kind of delayed adolescence." Not surprisingly, his biggest fans are young people. His most popular novel, *Lord of the Flies*, was rejected by 21 publishers before it appeared in 1954. Though the book did well in England, only 3,000 copies were bought in America until it was published in paperback and became "the desired and required reading" for millions of high school and college students—7 million copies sold to date. "Mr. Golding is bound somewhere to rip through the smooth texture of social pretense with a more hideous glimpse into the pit than one had been able to anticipate," wrote Robert M.

Adams in a *New York Times Book Review* synopsis of Golding's novels, which include *The Inheritors, Pincher Martin, Free Fall, The Spire, Rites of Passage, The Paper Men* and *Close Quarters*. Each book has been markedly different in style, time, and setting. "I don't think there's much point in writing two books that are like each other," says Golding, who lives in Wiltshire, England, with his wife.

Barry Goldwater

"Every good Christian ought to kick [Jerry] Falwell right in the ass," bellowed Barry Goldwater in 1981, in response to the television evangelist and moral majoritarian's suggestion that "all good Christians" should be concerned about the appointment of Goldwater protégée Sandra Day O'Connor to the U.S. Supreme Court. It was the kind of reaction friend and foe alike have come to expect from the granite-jawed curmudgeonly conservative since he burst on the national political scene in 1952 after winning a U.S. Senate seat from the then Senate majority leader. He carried the GOP standard to defeat in the presidential election of 1964, but his message, delivered more beguilingly by Ronald Reagan in 1980, struck a more responsive chord in the American electorate. Although he reached the four score mark in 1989, and is a veteran of 14 operations ("I counted them the other day") and a variety of other ailments, he's still one of the first Washington figures reporters rush to for comment when controversies arise. He was in the GOP vanguard in asking Nixon to resign ("He lied to me.") He's privy to the most closely held national secrets as Chairman of the Senate Select Committee on Intelligence. He is a senior member on a number of powerful committees, including a seat on the Select Committee on Indian Affairs, given his lifelong interest in Indian culture.

The future GOP standard bearer was born in Phoenix, Arizona, New Year's Day 1909, to a department store merchant baron and Josephine Williams Goldwater (he the son of Michael Goldwasser, who set out from Poland to found a dry goods empire in the wild west; she a decendent of Roger Williams who nonetheless hunted with a shotgun, played winning poker and drank her whiskey neat). Senator Goldwater once quipped, "In the American tradition, I was born in a log cabin, which I had moved to Phoenix, and except for air-conditioning, a swimming pool, a shooting range and a golf course, it remains the simple log cabin it always was." After military school, he attended the University of Arizona until 1929, when his father's death forced him and his brother to take over the management of Goldwater's, then, as now, a Phoenix landmark. In an attempt to surpass his father as a merchant, young Barry introduced such novelties as undershorts printed with red ants which he called "antsy-pants" and gained national cachet by advertising in the *New Yorker*. In 1934 he married Borg-Warner heiress Margaret (Peggy) Johnson (died 1985), and their four children—Joanne (1936; a caterer), Barry, Jr. (1938; former California congressman who lost a GOP senatorial bid in 1982 amidst drug charges), Michael (1940; a building contractor) and Peggy (1944; an entrepeneur in condiments)—followed in quick succession. He pulled strings at the outset of WWII to have his age and astigmatism overlooked, thereby gaining a commission in the Army Air Force (he reached reserve status of Major General), and flew missions in every theater except the Pacific. After the war, he returned to the store—and politics. From head of the Phoenix City Council he went to the U.S. Senate, and those hallowed halls haven't been the same since his arrival in January, 1953. He was quickly taken up by the "true believers" in the GOP, who felt "their" party had been co-opted by the Eastern liberals, of which Nelson Rockefeller was the principal malefactor. After deflecting a 1960 boomlet which he feared would split the party, he appealed to his followers to "grow up. We want to take this party back, and I think some day we can." They did, and he led them—to defeat. That he kept his cool and his sense of humor amid a barrage of attacks calling him everything from a looser of atomic weapons (with appropriately ghoulish advertising accompaniment) to a new breed of neo-Nazi (the grandson of a Polish Jew variety) is a tribute not only to his grit but to his mental balance. LIke the aging gunfighters his grandfather might have encountered on the Arizona frontier, Barry Goldwater no longer enters the fray just for the combat, but picks his spots carefully and fires with an accuracy undiminished by age or ailments. His book *Goldwater* (written with Jack Casserly) was published in 1988.

Dwight Gooden

He became the all-time best rookie at baffling baseball's batters with a fastball described as "nuclear in the last three feet," an impressive arsenal of accompanying pitches, and the poise of a ten-year vet. After he destroyed the 29-year rookie strikeout record of Cleveland's Herb Score, the biggest question to settle was not whether he, New York Mets's "Dr. K." (K being baseball shorthand for strikeout), would be picked as the 1984 National League Rookie of the Year (he was), but if he'd win the Cy Young Award as well. And while Rick Sutcliffe of the East-winning Cubs won best pitcher laurels, Gooden's first outings in the bigs earned him almost unanimous predictions of greatness. Dodgers' manager Tommy Lasorda, witness to another bullet-throwing 19-year old named Sandy Koufax many years before said, "I've seen guys throw as hard as Gooden, but almost never with such accuracy, so soon. He knows where he's throwin' it all the time."

There was speculation that if Dwight continued having 276 strike-out (an average 11.4 per nine innings), 17-win, 2.6 ERA-type seasons, then to pay him, the cost of Doubleday (the Mets' owner) books would have to escalate. Born in Tampa, 16 November 1964, Dwight profited from consistent exposure to major league spring training in Florida as a kid, plus instruction from his father, a former semi-pro. He played at the young age of 14 in American Legion competition, and by the end of his noteworthy Hillsborough High pitching career the Mets made him the majors' fifth player taken in the '82 draft. After two seasons in the minors, Gooden was invited to the big club's spring camp, and his overpowering of major league hitters, plus his nonchalant attitude before crowds and opposing ace pitchers, won him the nod from reluctant Mets GM Frank Cashen. His innocent confidence was seen as durable enough to withstand the fickle winds of the New York press and fans. Speaking in careful cliches, Gooden allows, "You can't do anything about what people write and say about you. When I'm between the lines, the one and only thing on my mind is winnng. Then, comparisons and hype don't mean anything."

Ellen Gordon

In a world gone beserk over sweets, chocolate candy holds a place, if not the top place on the "most desired sweets" list. As children we each had a dream of having access to all the chocolate candy our little hands or stomachs could hold. To Ellen R. Gordon her childhood dream has come true. As President of Tootsie Roll Industries, Inc., Gordon not only has access to, but control of one of America's most well known candy companies. Gordon worked her way up the corporate management ladder of the firm, starting in 1968 with pension plans and product development. In 1970 she rose to the position of Corporate Secretary; in 1974 she became V.P. of Product Development. Gordon became Senior V.P. in 1976 and rose to the prominent position of President and Chief Operating Officer in 1978. For her endeavors she received the Dean's Award in 1978 from the National Candy Wholesalers Association and the Kettle Award in 1985 from the candy industry.

Ellen was a student at Vassar when she met her future husband, Melvin J. Gordon, the manufacturing company executive. They were married on 25 June 1950. The new Mrs. Gordon later returned to college, attending Wellesley and receiving her BA from Brandeis University in 1965. She did postgraduate study at Harvard University in 1968 at the same time she was starting at Tootsie. Gordon finds time to share her knowledge and talents by acting as Director and President of HDI Investment Corp., President and Board of Director Member of The Committee of 200, V.P. of The National Confectioners Association, as well as sitting on the Harvard University Board of Overseers Visiting Committee for its medical and dental schools. Ellen and her husband, Melvin, are the parents of four daughters. When not in their respective offices (he's Chairman of the Board of Tootsie) in Chicago, the couple resides with their children in Center Harbor, N.H.

Berry Gordy, Jr.

Berry Gordy, Jr., first made a name for himself in his Detroit hometown (born 1929) as a snappy young featherweight boxer who won seven of his fourteen pro fights by knockouts. Then he moved into the heavyweight class of the up-again-down-again music world as he built his Detroit-based "Hitsville, U.S.A." (out of a run-down row house) into Motown. The "first Negro-owned-and-operated record company in America" became a multifaceted entertainment corporation, and the country's largest black-owned company. Gordy himself, born in a Detroit slum, has become a millionaire many times over. He is the father of Terry, Berry, and Hazel Joy; the latter married one of the formerly Motown-produced Jackson Five. His singer son Kennedy, known professionally as Rockwell, recorded for Motown.

The secret of the former auto plant worker's success was an expertly brewed musical blend known as the "Motown (for Motortown) Sound," a contemporary refinement of what used to be known as "race" music or "rhythm and blues." Gordy started his company in 1959 on $700 borrowed money and collected his first gold record a year later. Although he wrote a few of his company's tunes, including Jackie Wilson's "Lonely Teardrops," he knew that the real money in music was in producing and selling it, not singing and writing. He moved his talented minions into his facility to live and work, and doggedly worked on their on-stage presence and recording polish. "We were undercapitalized. All our records had to be hits because we couldn't afford any flops." There were hits aplenty by The Temptations, The Supremes, Marvin Gaye, Smokey Robinson, and Stevie Wonder. In the early '70s, when Motown moved to Hollywood, there was even a movie hit, the Diana Ross vehicle *Lady Sings the Blues*, based on the life of singer Billie Holiday. But two other Motown-produced Ross pics, *Mahogany*, and *The Wiz*, didn't pass critical muster, and when RCA Records beckoned Ross, she decided Gordy's contract didn't either. Other artists including Michael Jackson later jumped the ship. (Singer Teena Marie did because she charged the company made more than $2 million from her music while rationing her to to $300 per week for six years.) In a profitable business move, Gordy sold Motown Records to MCA, but remains active in the music industry through The Gordy Company. The legendary hitmaker was inducted into the Rock 'n' Roll Hall of Fame in 1988.

Eydie Gormé

Born 16 August 1932 in the Bronx of Turkish parents (she loyally refused to change her name), this top of TV-nightclub-recording thrush sang with Tommy Tucker's band and Tex Beneke's Band, and in 1953 was signed as a regular on the Steve Allen Tonight show. In 1956 she headlined her own show at the Copacabana. She was married in 1957 to singer Steve Lawrence (whom she met on Steve Allen's show), and the pair have been personally and professionally linked since. Together they have set house records at clubs, theatres and concert halls throughout the U.S. and have also won the Grammy with the song "We Got Us" in 1960. Eydie's single of "If He Walked Into My Life" earned her a solo Grammy in 1966. The TV special "Steve and Eydie Celebrate Irving Berlin" collected seven Emmy Awards and "Our Love Is Here To Stay," their TV tribute to George and Ira Gershwin, won two more. They have also received the Award of Excellence from the Film Advisory Board for their tribute to Cole Porter, "From This Moment On." She and Lawrence had two sons (David and Michael). The youngest son, Michael, died in 1986 of a heart attack. Like many thespian couples, Steve and Eydie have shared the Broadway stage, starring opposite each other in *Golden Rainbow* (1968). Coincidentally Gormé is considered, just as the name implies (and is pronounced), expert at preparing haute cuisine.

Louis Gossett, Jr.

The director of *An Officer and a Gentleman* was looking for a white drill sergeant for the film when this veteran black actor tried out for the role. He got the job, made the picture, and subsequently walked off with a Best Supporting Actor Oscar in 1983. That says something about today's Hollywood, he believes, where "the racism is not conscious as much as it's an omission of thought. Black actors will look at the trade papers and if the casting list doesn't say 'black sergeant,' they won't go out for the part. And if the script doesn't say 'black sergeant,' the producers and directors won't look for one."

Born 27 May 1936 in Brooklyn, son of a porter and a maid, Louis Gossett, Jr., began acting at 17 when a leg injury temporarily sidelined the tall, lanky youngster from his first love, basketball, and he turned to the theatre. Chosen over 445 contenders for the role of a coming-of-age black youngster in *Take a Giant Step* on Broadway in 1953, he won a Donaldson Award as Best Newcomer of the Year and looked back only once. While performing in *The Desk Set* in 1958, he was drafted by the New York Knicks to play pro ball, but discovered "the others were bigger, stronger, faster and smarter," and returned to the theatre. He has appeared in more than 60 stage productions (*Lost in the Stars*, *A Raisin in the Sun*, *The Blacks*, *Murderous Angels*) and played character parts on a number of TV series ("The Nurses," "The Defenders," and "East Side, West Side") before winning an Emmy for his 1977 performance in the TV mini-series "Roots" as Fiddler, the old slave who befriends Kunta Kinte. He has also been in the cast of such films as *Skin Game* and *The Deep*, filled the title role in *Sadat* (which generated headlines when the Egyptian president banned the film because, among other things, the late Egyptian president was played by a black), and received star billing in *Firewalker* (1986), *Iron Eagle* (1986), *The Principal* (1987), *Iron Eagle II* (1988), *The Punisher* (1989) and *Gideon Oliver* (1989). Married and divorced from Hattie Glascoe and actress Christina Mangosing (one son), he favors offstage pursuits such as composing (his antiwar anthem, "Handsome Johnny" was played by Richie Havens at Woodstock), his African art collection and traveling. He tied the knot again in 1987 by marrying Cyndi James-Reese (an actress). The couple have a son, Sharron. Despite his own impressive list of credits, he believes the situation for black actors is generally "terrible—no writers are writing for us, and no producers are producing.... We should be represented in the overall fabric of America."

Elliott Gould

He refers to the period between 1971 and 1984 as "the debacle." Gould was behaving like some sort of wild man. In 1984, *TV Guide* quoted one observer: "Whether it was from drugs . . . Elliot went *crazy*. Not crazy enough to commit, but enough to think he had such unbridled power he could rule the universe. When he couldn't, he got terribly paranoid." So paranoid, in fact, that Warner Bros. was forced in 1971 to halt production of the film *A Glimpse Of the Tiger*, a decision that labelled Gould's career: on hold. Even when he was approached two years later to make *The Long Goodbye*, he was required to submit to a battery of psychiatric tests before he was given the part. "I took all the tests, and finally they put 19 needles in my head to study my brain waves," Gould explained. "At last I was certified sane. How many of us are certified by document as being sane?" Gould's "debacle" was transformed by the debut in 1984 and subsequent popularity of the TV sitcom "E/R" in which he played the cigar smoking emergency-room physician Dr. Howard Sheinfeld, a man who must work 48-hour shifts to keep up his alimony payments to his ex-wife.

Called in the 1980s "America's answer to Jean-Paul Belmondo," the beefy, brown-eyed 6-foot-3 actor was born an only child in Brooklyn, 29 August 1938, the product of a frustrated middle-class Jewish household (his real name is Elliott Goldstein). The son of a garment center employee and driving "stage mother" (it was she who changed his name to Gould without telling him, thinking it sounded better for television), he began studying drama, diction, singing and dancing at age eight. As a child he appeared in song-and-dance routines in temples and hospitals, modeled and "danced with Josh White when I was ten." On summer vacations from Manhattan's Professional Children's School, he performed in the Catskills's "borscht belt." Because he could dance, his first "real TV job was on the old 'Ernie Kovacs Show' just out of high school. I was one of 50 guys who tap-danced in the chorus as Edie Adams sang 'Lullaby of Broadway.'" Living in New York he ran up debts and pawned his father's jewelry, sold vacuum cleaners and ran a hotel elevator, among other odd jobs. He made a small name for himself playing several parts in *Irma La Douce*, which led to his lead part in the Broadway musical *I Can Get It for You Wholesale* (1962). Also in that show was a certain odd duckling with an incredible voice named Barbra Streisand. Although they were almost fired by David Merrick before it opened, the show was both a box office hit and a romantic hit as well. Streisand and Gould were married in 1963 and three years later they had a son Jason (who, at age 18 months made his first, short, non-commercial film, which starred his Pop). As Streisand's fortunes soared Gould's sunk. Known as "Mr. Streisand," he was tolerated by Hollywood to please the Mrs. He dove into deep despair and was resurrected in psychoanalysis. His stardom coincided with his separation and divorce from Streisand. The 1968 film *The Night They Raided Minsky's* led to the super-popular *Bob & Carol & Ted & Alice* (for which he won an Oscar nomination as Best Supporting Actor), *M*A*S*H* (1970), *Little Murders* (1971), *The Long Goodbye* (1973, as private eye Philip Marlowe), *California Split* (1974) and *Nashville* (1975, as himself in a cameo appearance). All of these, except for *Murders*, were directed by Robert Altman. In 1970 he was chosen by Swedish director Ingmar Bergman as his first American lead for the film *The Touch*. Gould recalls his experience after making the Bergman film: "I thought when I came home from Sweden, I'd be met with a ticker-tape parade. . . . I'd proven I was a worldclass actor— I could not accept the torch. But *oy vey* . . . I was so naive. I call it 'The Debacle' because I wasn't stable enough to take the reins of my own life." Gould has two children with his wife Jennifer Bogart, whom he has married twice, in 1974 and 1978. Recent movies include *Inside Out* (1985), *The Myth* (1986), *Joker* (1987), *The Big Picture* (1988) and *Act of Betrayal* (1988).

Robert Goulet

Judy Garland once described him as a living eight-by-ten glossy, while critics complained that he was as stiff as the cardboard backing. Nevertheless he made women swoon as Lancelot back in 1960 in Lerner and Lowe's *Camelot* and drove them crazy with his nightclub act. Not too shabby for a guy who once categorized himself as a "lousy middle-range baritone."

Robert Goulet was born 26 November 1933 in Lawrence, Mass., but grew up in Edmonton, Alberta, Canada, and prepared for a singing career at the Royal Conservatory of Music in Toronto. His first attempt at taking New York by the horns ended up benignly enough ("I wound up selling writing paper at Gimbels"). Then came *Camelot*, followed by a couple of movies (*Honeymoon Hotel* and *I'd Rather Be Rich*) and a stint on TV's "Blue Light." Notwithstanding, this beefcake baritone with the "sullenly sexual face" has fared well on TV guest stints, records, in clubs, and (together with the late Judy Garland) on the soundtrack for the 1962 filmusical *Gay Purr-ee*. Divorced from Louise Nicole (one daughter), he married singer-dancer Carol Lawrence (*West Side Story*) in 1963 and they had two sons. Vera Novak is his third wife (married 1982) and the two of them divide their time between homes in Las Vegas and Los Angeles, his L.A. quarters being his 71-foot cruiser "Roger" docked in Marina Del Rey. In 1988 he toured with the national company of *South Pacific*.

Steffi Graf

"There are many important tournaments, but this is the top one," says Steffi Graf, the top-seeded women's tennis player and reigning Wimbledon champ in a TV Guide article. In 1988, at the tender age of nineteen, she became a Grand Slam Champion, winning the titles in the Australian, French and American Opens, plus Wimbledon. Furthermore, she took all her victories on completely different surfaces; other Grand Slam Champions played predominantly on grass. The young champ's greatest competition comes from Martina Navratilova, Gabriela Sabatini and Pam Shriver; however, Graf took Wimbledon and the U.S. Open again in 1989.

She is fair-haired, blue-eyed, and is a mere 130 pounds of power. She is five-feet-nine-inches tall and is aided by unusually long, strong arms. Her rise to fame can be traced back to the single-minded devotion her parents gave to her remarkable talent. Stephanie Maria Graf was born 14 June 1969 in Mannheim, West Germany. At the tender age of four, she was playing the "tennis game" in the family living room, hitting balls off the walls. Her parents, Peter and Heidi Graf, who were semiprofessional tennis players themselves, encouraged this sport in their two children, and when they saw their daughter's gift, they devoted their lives to its development. Their loyalty paid off. When Princess Diana asked Steffi recently to give an hour's lesson sometime to Prince William, Graf replied, "Of course, I shall treat him more gently than I did Navratilova." On the other hand, her opponent, Navratilova, admits that Steffi "has arrived . . . she's not coming up, she's there!"

Billy Graham

"The Barrymore of the Bible," "the President's preacher," "Gabriel in Gabardine," and surely "the world's best-known Protestant preacher," this handsome Pied Piper of the pulpit has preached the Gospel to more millions than anyone in history. His highly publicized Billy Graham Crusades ("I'm selling the greatest product in the world. Why shouldn't it be promoted as well as soap?") have been held in almost every state of the union and more than 50 foreign countries. In 1982, ignoring the protests of White House and State Department officials, he jetted off for an unprecedented trip to the

Soviet Union to deliver his message in Moscow's Patriarchal Cathedral. "If the Gospel is not more powerful than anything I'll hear over there," he declared, "then I ought to quit preaching."

Born 7 November 1918 in Charlotte, N.C., young William Franklin Graham became a religious convert at 16 and, according to legend, groomed himself for the pulpit at Florida Bible College by practicing sermons before the bullfrogs and squirrels. Though raised a Presbyterian, he was ordained as a minister of the Southern Baptist Church, a job at which he performed so well that Wheaton College, an evangelical institution, offered him a scholarship. He graduated in 1943, the same year he married missionaries' daughter Ruth Bell (three daughters, two sons). After six increasingly successful years as a radio preacher in Chicago, he crashed into the bigtime in Los Angeles as "America's Sensational Young Evangelist" in "A Mammoth Tent Crusade." Given a generous publicity assist by the Hearst press, he attracted 10,000 people a night. He was one of the first evangelists to use extensive TV coverage; his subsequent Decision for Christ crusades had, by the 1950s, made him famous all over the globe. Read, as well as looked at and listened to, he has also spread the word via a monthly magazine (*Decision*), a syndicated newspaper column and many books. *World Aflame* was a 1965 bestseller as was 1975's *Angels: God's Secret Agents*. He published *Approaching Hoofbeats: The Four Horsemen of the Apocalypse* in 1983.

All this and the corridors of power, too. Harry Truman invited Graham to the White House for the first time in 1949 and he became, during the Nixon years, "a sort of White House chaplain on retainer," reassuringly sanctifying the status quo and allowing as how, "Nixon, I guess, is one of my ten best friends." By the 1980s, Billy Graham had been for four decades what *Newsweek* called "the symbolic leader of evangelical Christianity in the United States." But with evangelism splintering into a number of factions (including the one headed by another frequent White House visitor, Jerry Falwell), some observers felt that the Graham era might be coming to an end. Not so, in the opinion of church historian Nathan Hatch. "From the moderates to the progressives," he says, "Graham is the glue, the social cement that holds things together, He has a power that just can't be replaced."

Katharine Graham

"To love what you do and feel that it matters—how could anything be more fun?" That rhetorical question comes from Katharine Graham, who discovered her calling and her major source of fun after taking over the *Washington Post*—on very short notice. Although this Washington society fixture grew up as the publisher's daughter, she always stayed in the background. Years ago, her father had passed on the publishing empire (which includes *Newsweek*) to her husband, Philip Graham. It was in the grim aftermath of her husband's suicide that she found herself publisher.

Among the big stories of her early years as publisher was the disintegration of the Nixon White House. It might not have been a story at all if two of her more energetic reporters—Bob Woodward and Carl Bernstein—had not Deep Throated their way into the "Watergate" story. She also stood up to the White House by printing the Pentagon Papers (after the *New York Times* broke the story), despite a government injunction, thereby adding fuel to the growing anti-war feeling in the nation. She saw these developments as justification for her management policies, which are pointedly anti-bureaucratic. "You want intelligent, large-scale thinkers and writers," she likes to say, "and nobody for whom you have any respect would take an order from on high." Not even from the White House.

Born 16 June 1917 in New York City, Katharine Meyer grew up in Washington D.C. and New York suburbs. Her journalistic start was in San Francisco where she covered the waterfront before she put down her notepad and married a promising young law clerk—Philip Graham. Her husband eventually inherited the *Washington Post* from his father-in-law, while his wife raised their four children. (Daughter Lally Weymouth is a writer, son Stephen a New York theatrical producer.) Today, her piloting of her Washington-based publishing empire has made her widely respected, particularly among young women who see her as a role model. "If one is rich and one is a woman, one can be quite misunderstood," she has said. She is perhaps the greatest exception to her widely-quoted epigram: "So few grown women like their lives."

Martha Graham

"Martha, this is dreadful. How long do you expect to keep it up?" To that question asked in the '20s by an old friend from California after viewing Martha Graham's first individual work, the personification of American modern dance replied, "As long as I have an audience." Sixty years later the audiences she had educated in her personal idiom were still cheering. In February of 1984 the 90-year old Graham—who had danced the female lead in the New York premiere of Leonide Massine's *Sacre de Printemps* (choreographed in 1930)—presented her own version of Igor Stravinsky's complex and powerful masterwork, displaying once more the talent that has inspired such tributes as, "Graham, Picasso and Stravinsky have this in common—they all have an inability not to grow." Her original movement technique and her monumental body of work (173 works of which many are classics of modern American dance) have brought forth honors and tributes from the dance establishment and governments alike. She received the *Dance Magazine* Award in 1957 and the Capezio Award in 1960. More recently, in 1976 she was the first dancer and choreographer to be given our nation's highest civilian award, the Medal of Freedom, and in 1979 was a Kennedy Center Honoree. Concurrent with her company's appearance in 1984 as the first American modern dance group to appear on the stage of the Paris Opera, Graham was made a chevalier of the Legion d'Honneur.

Born 11 May 1894 in Pittsburgh, Martha moved with her mother (a direct descendant of Miles Standish) and physician father to California where she began dance lessons with Ruth St. Denis and Ted Shawn, a practice she was forced to abandon at her staunch Presbyterian father's insistence until after his death. She followed St. Denis and Shawn to New York, made her first professional appearance in Shawn's Aztec-inspired *Xochitl*, was spotted by John Murray Anderson and spent the next two years in his *Greenwich Village Follies*. Rebelling against the "tinsel" of Broadway, she quit the show and entered her "woolen period," adopting simple severe costumes and works to match, including *Baal Shem* and *Dance Languide*. She formed Martha Graham and Dance Group in 1929, a small all-woman troupe that performed such early masterworks as *Two Primitive Canticles* and *Primitive Mysteries*. She received the first-ever Guggenheim fellowship awarded to a dancer in 1932, and in 1935 helped establish the school of modern dance at Bennington College, which soon became a mecca for dance enthusiasts from all over the country.

The late '30s marked the entry into the Graham company of its first two male dancers, Erick Hawkins (to whom she was briefly married in the late '40s) and Merce Cunningham, thereby enabling her to achieve greater theatrical scope with the male-female interplay of such works as *Deaths and Entrances* and *Appalachian Spring*. By the '50s the company had evolved into a superb ensemble of individualistic dancers that began to make its presence known in Europe and Asia through highly successful State Department-sponsored tours. That decade also saw the creation of *The Triumph of St. Joan*, *Seraphic Dialogue*, *Clytemnestra*, *Embattled Garden* and, in collaboration with ballet's 20th-century genius George Balanchine, *Episodes*. Succeeding years brought forth more dances inspired by Greek drama and legend, among them *Alcesis, Phaedra* and *Phaedra's Dream, Circe, Cave of the Heart* (Media legend), *Night Journey* (Jocasta) and *Andromache's Lament.* Of the many tributes from her colleagues in 1984—designated Tribute Year to Martha Graham—Agnes DeMille's possibly comes closest to explaining this five-foot-three giant's contribution to her art: "Nothing stops Graham, age nor change of country nor condition. She no longer dances [she retired in 1969], but her stage presence still is oceanic and each year sees new works of originality and invention. Graham seems to live at the fountainhead, and what she expresses foretells our passions and our intent."

Amy Grant

She's been called "the Michael Jackson of gospel music" and "the Madonna of gospel rock," but according to Bob Millard in his biography *Amy Grant* (1986), "neither appellation is a particularly apt metaphor.... Their significance to their musical genre is minimal outside the context of their gross income." Amy says, "I see myself as sort of a combination performer and evangelist. I hope people enjoy my singing, but at the same time I hope their lives are affected by the words." Melding melodies and rhythms from rock music, she fused the two genres together to make a sound that broke the barriers between Gospel and Pop. With her album *Unguarded* (1985) and the adult/contemporary-pop smash "Find a Way," she became the first gospel artist to achieve certified sales of more than 1 million copies of a single album. The album reached #35 on the *Billboard* pop charts and rocketed her into the pop field.

Amy Lee Grant was born 25 November 1960 at St. Joseph Hospital in Augusta, Georgia, to Dr. Burton Paine Grant and his wife Gloria. When Amy was six months old, the family moved to Houston, Texas, where her father's medical training took place, and then later settled down in Nashville, Tennessee, where the Grant family were known in the society and business circles. Amy's great-grandfather was an insurance multimillionaire and a respected philanthropist, A.M. Burton. Her family was very religious and involved with the local church. In fact, it was her participation at the church's activities that set the ball rolling for Amy's career. She recalls "I was 15 years old at the time and had just made a cassette tape of the songs I had written.... Unbeknownst to me, one of my Sunday night youth group leaders (and just a good hanging out friend) Brown Bannister played my music for an old college roommate named Chris Christian.... Chris seemed to like the song enough to make a phone call from Nashville to Waco, Texas, and a company called Word.... The rest is on plastic." While pursuing her music, Amy attended both Furman (a Christian-oriented University) and Vanderbilt University. She also fell in love with singer/songwriter Gary Chapman when she heard a song he had written in 1978. Later on, her original song "I Love You" summarizes their impulsive affair. She sings: "You were pretty crazy/back when we fell in love/wanting to be everything/that I would be proud of." Amy and Gary married on 19 June 1982.

The amiable singer has come a long way from her first live performance. Not previously subjected to the rigors of the road, she remembers an incident that illustrates her innocent nature. Confused about doing an early concert for $300, she didn't realize that her hosts would *pay* her for the performance. Instead, she insisted "I only have $500 in my savings and I need it." Now a veteran of touring, Amy prepares for her extended trips in advance. She writes in the "Lead Me On" tour program, "once the 'things' are in order, then there is the thought-packing. Sections of journals . . . other pieces of illegible scrawl, soon to be songs . . . mental pictures of my family, our home, the sounds of familiar laughter . . . the memory of quiet evenings. Like an old quilt, these pieces of things I know keep my heart warm and remind me of who I am." A seasoned professional, Amy gives her all in concert. Backed by her husband, Gary Chapman, on guitar, her band is made up of the finest musicians, including writer/performer Michael Smith. Her magnetism sends the audience into a dip 'n' sway when she eases through "Everywhere I Go" and they follow in rhythm as she warns: "You better wise up/Better get smart/And use your head to guard your heart." In a quiet moment, backed by soft accompaniment and a simple spotlight, she adds a special vocal touch to "El-Shaddai," a song from her *Age to Age* (1982) album. One can hear a pin drop as the audience sits mesmerized by her rendition. Through the years Amy has won numerous Grammys (her latest in 1989 for "Lead Me On") and Dove Awards. She was named Top New Country Female Vocalist in 1983 for the single "Tennessee Christmas." She had a pop duet hit with Peter Cetera ("Last Time I Fall"), recorded "The Animal's Christmas" with Art Garfunkel and Jimmy Webb, and hosted her own television special. Some of her other albums include *Amy Grant* (1977), *My Fathers Eyes* (1979) *Never Alone* (1980), *Amy Grant in Concert I & II* (1981), and *The Collection* (1986).

Happily married, the Chapmans share a farm and a colonial mansion south of Nashville, located close to the Harpeth River. They have a son, Matthew Garrison, born 25 September 1987. Amy remains close to her family. Her brother-in-law is her personal manager and during one Christmas gathering she graciously handed each of her sisters an original song from her albums. Considering the royalties involved, this generous present will be appreciated for years to come. Sharing her thoughts, the talented writer/vocalist reflects "through a song you can see inside a person, and it doesn't matter what they both like, or what they have or haven't done. All you see is that you both feel deeply about life."

Lee Grant

The raven-haired actress, acclaimed for her portrayals of coarse, sultry women of steely dispositions, proved that she was similarly indomitable when her promising career was nearly halted by a powerful accusation. When her name, in association with that of her first husband, playwright Arnold Manoff, was added to Senator Joseph McCarthy's insidious list of suspected communists in 1952, an intimidated Hollywood slammed its doors on her. Barred from any major film work for a frustrating twelve years, she took refuge in the theatre while resisting pressure from authorities to name her husband and others as subversives. Grant returned to memorable roles in television and movies in the mid 1960s, and overcame another prejudice, of sorts, to join the elite ranks of women directors.

Born 31 October 1929, Grant is remembered by TV audiences for her long-running featured role in the popular nighttime soap opera, "Peyton Place." She was gritty and intense as the justice-hungry wife of a murder victim in *In the Heat of the Night*, (1968) the steamy detective drama of racism and murder in a Southern town. Referring to the stature of roles available during this era, she said, "At that time, women's parts were supportive of men's roles. I played ladies who just bore up when their husbands were murdered or stuck in outer space" (a reference to *Marooned*, 1970). Other film credits include *Plaza Suite, Airport '78, Damien: Omen II, Valley of the Dolls,* and *The Big Town.* She appeared in the telefilm "The Hijacking of the Achille Lauro" (1989) and the NBC miniseries "Mussolini: The Untold Story" (1985). On another level, Grant has blossomed into a well-respected director for stage and screen. She made her directorial debut with *Tell Me a Riddle,* from the Tillie Olson novel (1980). The film was well received, although sparsely released. Her directing credits include the film *A Private View* (1983); "The Willmar 8," and "A Matter of Sex" for NBC; and three documentaries—*When Women Kill, What Sex Am I? Down and Out in America* (won an Academy Award in 1987). She also directed the CBS-TV film "Nobody's Child," starring Marlo Thomas, and received the Directors Guild Award for the 1987 production. Grant directed Vaclav Haval's *A Private View* for the stage and was presented with a New York Drama Critics Award nomination. In 1989 she directed Strindberg's *Playing With Fire* for the Public Theatre.

Widowed in 1965, she is now married to independent filmmaker Joe Feury (one daughter). Her other daughter, actress Dinah Manoff, was born in 1958.

Günter Grass

One of the most perceptive political-social commentators of the postwar age and one of the most versatile writers alive, he won lasting international fame with his first novel *The Tin Drum* (1959), in which he tried to make his German compatriots come to terms with their recent Nazi past. The horrors of that era are seen in the novel through the eyes of a mischievous dwarf who had deliberately stopped growing as a protest against the infantilism of the times but whose brain develops into that of a mature man who can bring back the past by beating on his drum. *The Tin Drum* was translated into 20 languages and the film version won an Oscar for the best foreign language film of 1980. A new Renaissance man, Grass is also a poet, dramatist, graphic artist, essayist, sculptor, and political activist. Among his best-known novels are *Local Anesthetic,* 1970 (from which the play *Up Tight* was adapted) and the epic *The Flounder* (1978) which deals with culinary history and the relation of the sexes from the Stone Age to Women's Lib. In 1982, author John Irving said of Grass in *Saturday Review:* "Against the authoritative landscape of history, he creates characters so wholly larger than life, yet vivid, that they confront the authority of history with a larger authority—Grass's imagination. He does not distort history; he out-imagines it."

Born in Danzig, 16 October 1927, the son of a German grocer and a Slavonic mother, Günter Wilhelm Grass was reared "between the Holy Ghost and Hitler's photograph," he recalled in one of his poems. Günter became a Hitler "cub" at age ten, joined the Hitler Youth at 14 and was drafted into the Luftwaffe auxiliary when he was 16. Wounded during the defense of Berlin in 1945, be became a prisoner of war in a camp where he was forced to see the newly liberated Dachau death camp. That was part of his de-Nazification process. Released in 1946, he tried his hand as a farm laborer and black marketeer, spent two years as an apprentice stonemason and tombstone engraver in Düsseldorf and attended the Academy of Art there while playing with the local jazz band ("to fill my stomach."). Later, at the Berlin School of Fine Arts—which he entered in 1953—he painted, wrote poetry, and began writing plays ("to ease my soul"). Aided by a small stipend from the Hermann Luchterhand Verlag (which has since published all his novels), Grass went to Paris in 1956 to work on *The Tin Drum*—the first novel in his so-called Danzig Trilogy. The second and third volumes were *Cat and Mouse* (1963) and *Dog Years* (1965). Among his other works are his partly autobiographical *From the Diary of a Snail* (1973), *The Meeting at Telgte,* (1981) which pays tribute to the founder of Gruppe 47, a postwar association of leading authors, and *The Germans Are Dying Out* (1981). Recent works include *On Writing and Politics 1967-1983* (1985) and *The Rat* (1987). Willy Brandt's chief campaign speech writer for more than a decade, Grass switched his loyalties from the Social Democrats several years ago to the more avidly anti-nuke Green Party. First married to Swiss dancer Margareta Schwarz (four children), he married Ute Grunert in 1979; her two sons live with them. Grass commutes between his home in Berlin and a house in a village near Hamburg.

Barry Gray

His boss reports that the station (The Big Apple's WMCA) gets requests every day to throw him off the air or out of one of the building's windows. The object of the commotion is the dean of radio interviewers whose longevity on the airwaves (44 years in 1989) has not diminished the feisty, aggressive and probing style that has made him king of his domain. His studio is the traditional first stop in New York for an author with a new book or an actor with a new show—and the traditional last stop for countless politicians as they wind up their campaigns. The pre-election debates over which he presides are often the last thing a voter hears before casting his ballot. Barry Gray's guests have made more than a few headlines, including the front-page bomb-shell dropped by newsman Sidney Zion that Daniel Ellsberg was the source of the leaking of the Pentagon Papers. He's logged more than 10,000 broadcasts and interviewed more than 40,000 guests—from presidents to royalty, crooks and politicians (with its unavoidable occasional overlap), beauty queens and jocks, novelists and ballet dancers (his championing of the dance has made many a new fan for the art). He stays on top, according to the *New York Times,* "by goading his guests into what are consistently the most substantive discussions of major issues heard anywhere on the air."

Born Bernard Yaraslaw 2 July 1916 of Russian-Jewish parentage (he attributes his slightly slanted eyes to a small infusion of Tartar blood) in Atlantic City, Barry grew up in Los Angeles and, after a hitch in the Civilian Conservation Corps as a youth, served his apprenticeship by emceeing supermarket openings on the West Coast. He came East after Army service during World War II, and began broadcasting on WOR, where he "got buggy" just playing records, decided to talk a little more, and by the weekend "it was an all-talk show." He's been yakking ever since (with WMCA since 1950), seemingly impervious to a couple of close calls which almost ended his career—and his life. He incurred the wrath of powerful columnist Walter Winchell (for letting black star Josephine Baker complain over his microphone of the shabby treatment she'd received at the posh Stork Club while Winchell sat by doing nothing), and thereby became the favorite target for three years of the writer's barbs. "Once he called me a Communist, cheating with another guy's wife and 'Borey Lavender,' all in the same column." On another occasion he received a vicious beating from still unidentified assailants.

Twice divorced, Gray married his third wife, Nancy Kellog-Rice, on 5 September 1986. He is the father of a daughter, Melodie (who's in the fashion business), and a son, Michael (a California aerospace engineer). His off-mike enthusiasms include horses, skiing, travel—and buttermilk.

Linda Gray

When she tested in 1977 for CBS-TV's "Dallas," the character of Sue Ellen was a mere walk-on. "At first they did not know what to do with the part,"Linda remembers. "Sue Ellen's lines werre limited to 'More coffee, darling?' and 'I have a headache.' Gradually—I think because Larry Hagman, (who plays her ex-husband, J.R. Ewing) and I were so wonderfully evil together and had so much fun acting off each other—they expanded my part, then our parts together." Linda comments further: "I've always thought of myself as a late bloomer." For this actress who became an overnight star on the top-rated series, success came after 18 years of being just another pretty face.

Born 12 September circa 1942 in Santa Monica, she was raised a Catholic, attending Notre Dame Academy in West Los Angeles. After high-school she parlayed part time modeling work into TV commercials but it was "serious" acting that intrigued her and at the ripe age of 32, she gave it a stab. Knowing full well that youth in Hollywood is as highly prized an attribute as beauty and talent, she buttressed her efforts with a positive outlook. "If it (success) was going to happen, it would be late and therefore easier to handle. I would not have years to waste. So when the opportunity presented itself, I would give it everything I've got, knowing there might not be another chance." She studied with Charles Conrad and landed her first acting job on "Marcus Welby M.D." Norman Lear subsequently hired her to star in the unlikely role of the transsexual siren in his curious series, "All That Glitters." Since her "Dallas"debut she has co-starred with Jason Robards in "Haywire" (1979) and Lindsay Wagner in "The Two Worlds of Jenny Logan." In 1982 she starred in the CBS-TV movie "Not in Front of the Children." Linda is the recipient of Germany's "Bambi Award" and Italy's "Il Gato." She enjoys co-hosting the annual "Thanksgiving Day

Parade" on CBS and is currently writing a book, *Second Act*, for 1990 publication. Divorced from art director Ed Thrasher in 1983, she lives in Canyon Country, California, surrounded by mountains, with her two children, Jeff and Kelly.

Rocky Graziano

The former middleweight boxing champion, a crowd pleaser in the ring because of his hammerlike right, his KO ability and colorful performances, started pleasing a new kind of crowd back in the 1950's when he became a regular on TV's "Martha Raye Show." Still busy in show biz, he considers performing before the cameras tougher than boxing ever was. "If I blow a line I'm embarrassed. It's worse than being knocked out in the ring."

Born Rocco Barbella, 7 June 1922 on New York's Lower East Side, the middleweight whiz once summed up his childhood this way: "When you're in Rome, you talk Italian. When you're in Jerusalem, you talk Jewish. And when you live on the East Side, you talk tough, like everybody else talks tough, and you do the things they do." Out of public school by the seventh grade, he did time in reform school before realizing he could do better being tough in the ring than on the streets. He was champ in 1947-48. All during his boxing career, which lasted until he was 30, his answer to the question "Why do you fight?" was always "The money, of course." He figures he spent "maybe a million" in his years at the top. Despite his own acting prowess, it was Paul Newman who played the title role in the film version of his first autobiographical book, *Somebody Up There Likes Me*. In 1981 he published *Somebody Down There Likes Me Too*. But he still keeps in training in the studios. Married to the former Norma Unger in 1943 (one daughter), he now plays himself on TV commercials, complete with typical pug-like poor diction, but also with the smile that will melt your heart.

Andrew Greeley

"*The Cardinal Sins* is enough to give trash a bad name," cracked the Chicago *Sun-Times* book reviewer of the first novel by "the priest who writes dirty books," as he's called by those who are not impressed by Andrew Greeley's insistence that in his novels he's following a long biblical tradition. "Both Jesus and the early story-tellers did not try to edify with their stories," he says. "Rather their tales were about secular events-kings and generals, family feuds, passionate love affairs . . . crooked judges, women taken in adultery." And further recognizing that many people suppose him to be an embarrassment to the church (although he's never been formally rebuked or punished for anything he's written) and will eventually leave the priesthood, he states, "I'm a priest, I'm a Catholic. It's the only church I have. At times it may not be very attractive, very efficient, or very intelligent, but I won't leave it until the day after the Pope does."

From the time he was in the second grade, Chicago-born (5 February 1928) Andrew Greeley wanted to be a priest and he was ordained in 1954 ("I kept my mouth shut in the seminary. . . . I was really very docile"). He received a Doctorate in Sociology while serving in his first (and last) parish, which became the subject of his first book, *The Church in the Suburbs*, followed by other serious sociological tomes (it's been said of him that he never had an unpublished thought and that a common utterance to his secretary is "Take a book."), including *Why can't They Be Like Us?*; *That Most Distressful Nation: The Taming of the American Irish*; *The American Catholic: A Social Portrait*; *The Jesus Myth*; *The Moses Myth* and *The Making of the Popes, 1978*. Much of the raw material for his books and myriad magazine and newspaper articles is drawn from data gathered by the National Opinion Research Center, the Chicago-based organization formed by Greeley in the early 60's, which studies American life in general and American Catholic life in particular. Although Greeley had often been a thorn in the side of the Catholic hierarchy (for his support of the ordination of women, etc.), publication of *The Cardinal Sins* in 1981 opened the floodgates of criticism, less for the steaminess of the novel (reactions ranged from those who claimed, "This priest knows nothing about sex," to those who wondered, "How does this priest know so much about sex?") than for its parallel in its title character's tangled financial dealings to those of then Cardinal Cody of Chicago. Greeley's disclaimer that "I didn't become a priest to make money . . . and I didn't write books to make money" notwithstanding, the fact is that proceeds from sales of the novel exceeded by twelve times receipts from his first 63 books. He gave away the first million, endowed an $850,000 chair in Roman Catholic studies at the University of Chicago (where he taught for ten years and was denied tenure for what he calls "his blurred identity"), and underwrote a $150,000 lectureship at his former seminary. Succeeding novels, inhabited in the main by Irish Catholic priest, pols and prosperous patriarchs, include *Thy Brother's Wife*, *Ascent Into Hell*, *Lord of the Dance* and *Virgin and Martyr*.

Greeley has been extremely prolific in the 1980's and his recent works include *Confessions of a Parish Priest*, *Happy Are the Clean of Heart*, *Patience of a Saint*, *The Final Planet*, *Happy Are Those Who Thirst for Justice*, *Rite to Spring*, *Angel Fire* and *Love Song*. He lives most of the time in Arizona, where he is tenured professor of sociology at the University of Arizona at Tucson.

Adolph Green

"Looking something like Fernandel—only more so," Adolph Green has composed (with Betty Comden) the words to some of the most successful Broadway and Hollywood musicals. "Over the years," he beams, "she has had me screaming in helpless laughter." When asked how they managed to "stick" together so long, Comden once replied, "Sheer fear and terror." "Hunger!" blurted out Green.

Born 2 December 1915 in the Bronx, he attended City College "for one day" before becoming a "full-time bum." He started off as a performer in a group called the Revuers which included Comden and the late Judy Holliday, and went on to a career of writing and occasional performing with Comden as his partner and co-author. The first Broadway musical for which they wrote the book and lyrics, *On the Town* (1944) (also the first show for Leonard Bernstein and Jerome Robbins) marked their first appearance on the stage as actors. In subsequent years, they wrote book and lyrics for *Bells are Ringing* (1960), *Two on the Aisle* (1951), *Subways Are for Sleeping* (1962) and *On the Twentieth Century*, with lyrics only for *Wonderful Town* (1953), *Peter Pan* (1954), *Say Darling* (1958), and *Do, Re, Mi* (1960-61). They contributed to *Hallelujah, Baby* and *Applause* (book). They have won five Tony Awards. Their movie musicals include *Singin' in the Rain* (voted one of the ten best American films of all time by an American Film Institute poll); they wrote the book for the 1985 Broadway stage version. Other films: *Band Wagon* (also slated for a possible Broadway bow), *The Barkleys of Broadway*, *On the Town* and the non-musical screenplay of *Auntie Mame*. They have received three Screen Writers Guild Awards. In 1958 they appeared in *A Party With Comden & Green* to great acclaim; Brooks Atkinson, critic for the *New York Times* wrote "What Al Hirschfield is to the satiric line . . . they are to the satire of song and sketch." In 1977 they did a repeat of *A Party* on Broadway. Lately, Green has been appearing as an actor in films. They include *Simon*, *My Favorite Year* (with Peter O'Toole), *Playing for Keeps*, and Sidney Lumet's *Garbo Talks*. He is married to actress Phyllis Newman whom he adores ("Of course we fight. It usually focuses on some aspect of my childishness.") They have two children, Adam and Amanda (who's interested in acting). Father, mother and daughter appeared together in a 1984 production of Murray

Schisgal's *The New Yorkers*. (Unfortunately, *not* to glowing reviews.) Green enjoys both being a performer as well as a writer. "One's a thrill right then, the other's a long-term, long-playing thrill."

Cynthia Gregory

"Already she dances Odette/Odile as if she had the accumulated tradition of a young Russian or British dancer behind her... as if she had dreamed of the ballet from her cradle," reported Clive Barnes in the *New York Times* about 20-year-old Cynthia Gregory's first venture in 1967 into the treacherous waters of *Swan Lake*. Walter Terry added in the *Saturday review:* "On her entrance it was apparent that here was a ballerina. It was instinctive, this placement of arms, this extension of the legs, this tilt of the head." Those accolades might have turned the head as well had it not belonged to the supremely confident (onstage; off-stage she's painfully shy), six-foot-one (on *pointe*) *prima ballerina assoluta* (so labeled by Rudolf Nureyev) who at the age of seven had appeared on the cover of *Dance* magazine. Her prodigious technique alone—assured, sustained balances, flawlessly executed *fouettes* and graceful, slow *pirouettes en attitude*—would be enough to assure her a secure place in any ballet company in the world. "But I would have died of boredom and I would have bored the audience to death, too," she told Olga Maynard in *Dance* magazine in 1975. To add new dimensions to the characters she portrayed, then, she transformed *Giselle* from a shy (not frail; not at six-foot-one!) but vivacious peasant girl to a "yearningly spectral" and "caressingly romantic" Wili; made Odette/Odile "more a woman than a swan," a distinction that lends the character a touching vulnerability; acted *La Sylphide* more as a pixie than a sprite. Her interpretations of contemporary roles are no less impressive: Carmen in Roland Petit's *Carmen;* Caroline and The Mistress in *Jardin aux Lilas;* Hagar in *Pillar of Fire; Theme and Variations, Voluntaries* and Twyla Tharp's *Bach Parita*, among many others.

Cynthia Kathleen Gregory, of Greek and French-Canadian ancestry, was born 8 July 1946 in Los Angeles and began taking ballet lessons at five "to acquire poise." By 13, she was taking lessons from New York City Ballet principal dancer Jacques d'Amboise, who commended her to Lew Christiansen, director of the San Francisco Ballet, and after a brief period at their school, became an official member of the company in 1961. Stifled by the company's limited repertoire, she left in 1965 (with her then husband, Terry Orr, another dancer with the company who is now ballet master at ABT) and joined American Ballet Theatre in 1965, becoming a principal dancer in 1967, and beginning a love-hate relationship with the company. She "retired" in December 1975 (speculation as to the reason ranged from her disenchantment with the attention lavished on Soviet defectors Makarova and Baryshnikov, to resentment of the high fees paid guest artists, to the breakup of her marriage, in addition to her chronic complaint that the company failed to provide her with sufficiently tall partners). After two years and a new marriage to rock music manager and promotor John Hemminger (who died at 42 in 1984), she returned to the company—"better than ever"—critics agreed. She also had a small lump of her patrician nose surgically corrected. "I could have lived with my old nose," she explained, "but Giselle is happier with this one." Cynthia Gregory's 20th anniversary at ABT was celebrated at the Met, in June, 1985, with a gala evening of spectacular *pas de deux*, all starring the prima ballerina partnered by the company's leading *danseurs*. Cynthia's personal life took flight in 1985, when she married Hilary B. Miller.

Wayne Gretzky

In a tear-dripping moment, Wayne Gretzky announced during a press conference in 1988 that he was leaving his hometeam (Edmonton Oilers) to join the L.A. Kings. Due to personal changes, he chose to make the move and be close to his new wife, actress Janet Jones. "He was born to put the puck in the net," says Gordie Howe, the highest scoring player in National Hockey League history and now the most ardent supporter of his former idolater. The unspoiled, amiable and unfailingly polite Wayne Gretzky was just 23 when he led the Edmonton Oilers to the Stanley Cup in 1984, thereby breaking the New York Islanders' four-year stranglehold on that emblem of hockey supremacy. Gretzky led the Oilers to the championship again in 1985, and received the Conn Smyth Trophy as the playoffs' MVP.

Not since Bobby Orr's emergence in the 60s has one player so dominated the sport, and so energized a team that hadn't even been in the NHL when he joined them in 1978. Once in the league, the phenomenal center—known as "the Kid" and "the Great Gretzky"—proceeded to shatter the marks set by Orr, Phil Esposito and other hockey legends, including most points in a season (212), most assists in a season (120), most points per game (2.05) and the quickest accumulation of 300 points (in 159 games). He reached the 301-point plateau in one-third the time it took Gordie Howe; he was the youngest player to be voted the Hart Trophy as the league's MVP (in 1980, the year he also won the Lady Byng Memorial Trophy for gentlemanly play). The most menacing stickhandler, with an uncanny power of anticipation (stemming no doubt from his father's early exhortations to "Skate to where the puck's going to be, not to where it's been"), Gretzky likes to shoot against the flow, maintaining an unhurried grace, transcending the furious movement around him and reducing it to slow motion. His mental vantage point and a great pair of hands enable him to hold the puck the extra millisecond that upsets the rhythm of the game and opponents' reflexes. Born 26 January 1961 in Brantford, Ontario, Canada, Wayne began skating at two and a half on a rink his telephone-techician father created by flooding the backyard. His father was his first coach, and he entered organized hockey at the age of six with a team otherwise composed of ten and eleven-year olds. His advance through the Bantam League and the Juniors was rapid, and when he signed with the Oilers, they knew he was their ticket to an NHL franchise. He passed the Islanders' Mike Bossy as the highest paid hockey player in history in 1982 (15-year contract for $20 million). During the 1987-1988 season, Gretzky broke his own NHL record for assists in one playoff year with 31; he became the NHL's all-time career leader in assists (1,050) on 1 March 1988 and set an NHL record for the most consecutive—as well as the most in a career—100-or-more-point seasons. He and his wife, Janet, also scored with the birth of their first child; Paulina, on 19 December 1988.

Jennifer Grey

A third generation performer, Jennifer Grey made a name for herself with the role of "Baby" in the box office phenomenon *Dirty Dancing*. The physically demanding role required the skills of a professional dancer which Grey was not, although she had studied dance since the age of five and began her career as a dancer in a Dr. Pepper commercial. Her co-star, Patrick Swayze, cited Grey's "incredible natural talent" that allowed her to "come out with a sensuality in her dancing that has just staggered everybody". The film made the 5'4", brown-haired, grey-eyed actress a household name.

Jennifer Grey was born in 1960, the daughter of Academy Award winning actor-dancer-singer Joel Grey and singer Jo Wilder, and the granddaughter of famous Borscht Belt comedian Mickey Katz. A graduate of the Neighborhood Playhouse School of Theatre where she studied with Sanford Meisner and Wynn Handman, Grey was cast as an understudy in the Off-Broadway production of *Album* directed by Joan Micklin Silver. She followed it up with the role of Shirley in *Fifth of July* at the Portland Stage Theatre. Her brief television appearances include roles in the PBS production of "Media Probes," the ABC Afterschool Specials "The Great Love Experiment" and "Cindy Eller: A Modern Fairy Tale" and the CBS series "The Equalizer". Grey was introduced to movie audiences in James Foley's *Reckless* (1984) playing Darryl Hannah's wild Italian friend. She went on to play Nicholas Cage's wife in Francis Ford Coppola's *The Cotton Club*. She then was cast in John Milius' controversial film *Red Dawn* opposite Patrick Swayze and John Badham's *American Flyers* starring Kevin Costner. Her role as the young frustrated sister in John Hughes smash comedy *Ferris Bueller's Day Off* opposite Matthew Broderick earned her critical notice. It was followed by *Dirty Dancing*, about which David Ansen of *Newsweek* declared, "Jennifer Grey is a knockout". The independent film became a surprise international hit, spawning hit albums, concert tours, videos and even a short-lived television series (without Grey). While it seems difficult to surpass *Dirty Dancing*'s success Grey continues to work. Her latest features include a Damon-Runyonesque romantic comedy *Bloodhounds of Broadway*—with Madonna, Matt Dillon, Randy Quaid and Rutger Hauer—and *The Sixth Family*.

Romantically linked with actors Matthew Broderick and Johnny Depp, Grey is currently single.

Joel Grey

He admits he isn't Captain Nice to work with. Some actors consider him self-serving and capricious. He says "I'm impatient. I have a quick temper. I don't hold grudges though. There's no point in keeping negative stuff." This compact, 5'5" and "wispish enough to pack in a theatre trunk," crackerjack entertainer trained hard for 24 years before coming upon the resounding click that signals full-fledged stardom. The time was the decadent Berlin decade of the 1930s. The place: a soulless cellar called The Kit Kat Klub, setting for much of the action in the 1966 Broadway musical *Cabaret*. His George Grosz-inspired characterization of the red-lipped, white-faced, blue-humored MC won him critical flips, a Tony, and a follow-up role in the equally cheer-winning but totally different *George M!* ("Hooray," headlined the *Daily News*, "for the Red, White and Grey!") The Kit Kat Kaper was immortalized on film in 1972, and netted Grey an Oscar. He stayed with films for a while (*Man on a Swing, Buffalo Bill and the Indians, The Seven-Per-Cent Solution*) before returning to Broadway in 1975 as Charles VII in the musical *Goodtime Charlie*. 1979 marked a reappearance on Broadway for him as the star of *The Grand Tour*, and in 1985 he appeared off-Broadway in Larry Kramer's *The Normal Heart*.

Born in Cleveland on 11 April 1932, into the family of Yiddish comic Mickey Katz, Joel Katz (he changed his name to Grey in his teens) made his official debut at ten in a hometown production of *On Borrowed Time*, became a teen-aged protégé of Eddie Cantor on the basis of his skills as an impressionist, and was a Copa headliner at 19. Unfortunately the cabaret life "hit him below the belt" and he developed gastric as well as psychic problems. "It took many years and dollars and hours in therapy to work them out"—and a special interest in legit theatre which he "acted upon" at New York's Neighborhood Playhouse. For an extended time period, Grey began what he now refers to as his "replacement epoch"; coming to Broadway to join shows in mid-run (*Stop the World I Want To Get Off, Half a Sixpence* et al). Subsequently he developed a "benchwarmer mindset" which didn't last long, thanks to Hal Prince casting him in *Cabaret* and making him an overnight star. Showing his diversity, Grey appeared in the acclaimed ABC telefilm "Queenie" and was in the 1985 film *Remo Williams: The Adventure Begins*. Complying with a continual demand to see him "live" in *Cabaret*, Grey reprised his role in 1987 on Broadway and in a National Tour of the musical. Interviewed in *People*, he admitted, "I don't love the theatre. People ask, 'do you get a lot of pleasure when you perform?' And I say, 'Occasionally.' If I'm enjoying it, chances are the audience might not be."

Merv Griffin

"I'm afraid of becoming a huge machine." But confessions of fear do not match his ruddy cheeks and steady blue eyes. Singer/talk-show host turned mogul is now competing with such wheeler-dealers as Donald Trump in the high-stakes world of real estate. Making his millions through the ingenious creations of the game shows "Jeopardy" and "Wheel of Fortune," Merv has become financially secure enough to play his own game of Monopoly.

Griffin was the first to introduce the "theme" format to television talk programs which *de temps en temps* he taped from Cannes or Venice or even the Belmont Race Track. Although he no longer has a daily show, he occasionally hosts a nighttime special. Merv Griffin maintains his gee-whiz boyishness with whomever he happens to be interviewing and this accessibility has won him a sizeable audience and Emmy Awards. Past forays include stints as a band singer (Freddie Martin's orchestra), TV quiz-show host, nightclub performer, hit vocalist on such records as "I've Got a Lovely Bunch of Coconuts" and Hollywood contract player in such epics as *So This Is Love, The Boy From Oklahoma,* and *Cattle Town*.

Merv was born in San Mateo, California, 6 July 1925 and studied music at the University of San Francisco. His first job was singing for a San Francisco radio station: "I had a high, dreamy Irish tenor. They billed me as the Romantic Voice of America." In 1950 the slow hike to television stardom began when he hosted his own show in Miami. "I remember him hosting the Saturday-night proms," recalls Murray Schwartz, who was then Griffin's agent. "The set looked like an automobile accident." Time passed and Merv "the Good Boy" found himself pitted against Johnny "What-the-Heck's Bad Boy" in a late-night ratings war (1970). Griffin bit the bullet and survived albeit at an earlier hour. He is the author of two books: *Merv: An Autobiography* (1980) and *From Where I Sit* (1981). He married the former Julann Wright, a radio comedienne, in 1958 (they divorced in 1976; one son Anthony Patrick). Griffin's hobbies include solo piloting and tennis. He is frequently seen around Beverly Hills with actress Eva Gabor.

Andy Griffith

He is long gone from the rustic environs of Mount Airy, N.C., but his drawling Blue Ridge accent is still as thick as sow fat, and the country-boy actor is still more comfortable at an RFD address than in the glitzy spots of Hollywood and New York. Operating out of the sheriff's office of mythical Mayberry on CBS-TV's "The Andy Griffith Show," he ambled high in the ratings for five seasons during the 60s; found himself in less clovery circumstances with his short-lived stint as "Head-master" in the 70s. He served as executive producer for "Mayberry RFD" (1970), which took up where "The Andy Griffith Show" left off, but it lasted just a season. He tried again with "The New Andy Griffith Show" (1970), but that too was short-lived. Griffith, however, remained visible on the tube in such miniseries as "Centennial," "Murder in Texas," and "Fatal Vision." *Hearts of the West*, a feature with Jeff Bridges, was released in 1975. Then, the year 1986 became a comeback of sorts for Griffith. There were two NBC specials—"Diary of a Perfect Murder" and "Return to Mayberry"—and the first season of the hit series "Matlock." Playing the role of a top criminal lawyer, Griffith combines the courtroom series with a perfect blend of country sophistication. His appeal has propelled the drama to still be a ratings winner in 1989.

Born 1 June 1926, he hied himself to the University of North Carolina with the notion of becoming a Moravian minister (although he was born a Baptist), but switched to music and drama instead. After graduation he taught school, married a music teacher (Barbara Edwards whom he divorced in 1972; two adopted children), and earned his first showbiz dollars doing a "preacher act" on the Rotary circuit "in a raggedy moth-eaten split-tail coat." He landed on Broadway in 1955 as a star in *No Time for Sergeants*, then to Hollywood in *A Face in the Crowd* (1957), and back to Broadway again in *Destry Rides Again* (1959). City Slickers who discover that for seven seasons in the early part of his career (1947-54) he portrayed English-accented Sir Walter Raleigh in the famed "Lost Colony" pageant, sometimes suspect that the drawl is put on. We know better. He loves to skeet and trap-shoot and married Cindi Knight in 1983.

Melanie Griffith

Having shed the stigma of her party girl image, actress Melanie Griffith rose above the dim future most had predicted for her in triumphant "tragedy to success" movie style. Once a candidate for Hollywood fatality, Griffith, with her lilting childlike voice, vulnerable-yet-tough demeanor, has combated her way from inexperienced actress to accomplished movie star. Hers is a success story that serves as an inspiration to all who have relentlessly struggled to overcome the obstacles which sometimes make success, whether professional or personal, seem impossible.

The charming and determined Miss Griffith was born in New York 9 August 1957 to Tippi Hedron, the grand-dame of Hitchcock films, and real estate magnate Peter Griffith. A transplanted Californian at age four, Melanie spent much of her childhood attending private Catholic academies. She worked as an extra at the age of fourteen in the feature film *The Harrad Experiment* in which her mother had a leading role. On the set she became smitten with a struggling young actor by the name of Don Johnson. A rebel, Melanie lived life in the fast lane. Sixteen years old and estranged from her parents who were divorced, she moved in with Johnson, then twenty-four years old. In 1974 at age seventeen, having never gone through any professional training, she landed a role as a nymphet opposite Gene Hackman in Arthur Penn's *Night Moves*. Mitchell Ritchie's 1975 beauty pageant satire *Smile* placed her name on a billing that included Bruce Dern, followed by a role in *The Drowning Pool* (1975) opposite legendary Paul Newman and Joanne Woodward. Baby-faced Melanie seemed to be taking off at top speed professionally but her personal life was suffering; her marriage to Johnson failed and she was hooked on drinking and drugs. In 1979 Melanie began doing television work. Among her credits: a recurring role in "Carter Country" telefilms: "Steel Cowboy," "Golden Gate," "She's in the Army Now" and opposite Rock Hudson and Suzanne Pleshette in "Starmaker."

Debilitated for months after a drunk driver hit her as she was crossing a Los Angeles street in 1980, Melanie began to put her life in order. Determined to rid herself of her destructive vices, she joined Alcoholics Anonymous. She met and fell in love with actor Steven Bauer, which led to a short-lived marriage. The union produced a son, Alexander, born 22 August 1984. With her personal life in order she began to study acting with Stella Adler in New York. She landed a role as a porn queen in Brian De Palma's *Body Double* (1984) followed by her portrayal of Lulu the flamboyant seductress in Jonathan Demme's 1986 feature film *Something Wild*. In the spring of 1988 she portrayed a weary mistress in the British thriller *Stormy Monday*. That same year she was the wife of a greedy rancher in Robert Redford's *The Milagro Beanfield War*. However it was the latter part of 1988 that brought Melanie to the forefront of the Hollywood thoroughbreds. As struggling secretary Tess in Mike Nichol's *Working Girl* Griffith found herself in a role that paralleled her life in many ways. Both the character and Griffith were vulnerable yet talented and determined to rise above their present status. Tess ended up with an office with her own secretary and Melanie ended up with a Golden Globe for her portrayal and her first Oscar nomination for Best Actress.

Griffith reconciled with former husband Don Johnson; they were engaged again in 1989, expecting their first child together. The couple reside with Alexander and Jesse (Johnson's son) in Miami and California.

Tammy Grimes

"She lives," observed good friend Roddy McDowall, "on the tilt, half on the earth and half somewhere between the earth and the sky." She was *The Unsinkable Molly Brown* (1961) for which she won the Tony Award for best musical comedy actress and prompted Walter Kerr to write: "She is a genius." She was also a Tony-winning Amanda in Noel Coward's *Private Lives* (1970). It all started when McDowall once invited Noel Coward to a New York City cabaret. Tammy Grimes appeared on stage in silver sequins and proceeded to sing 18 Cole Porter songs. Mr. Coward grinned, rose above it, and offered Miss Grimes her first Broadway role—*Lulu*.

Despite her veddy British accent, she was born in Lynn, Mass., 1 January 1934. Even as a child, says her sister, "Tammy never looked like anybody else." Daughter of the manager of a swank country club, she "came out" in Boston society in 1951 ("I was quite fat and wore a dress with spangles"), served her apprenticeship as a performer at Stephens College in Missouri and at the Westport Playhouse. After the flamboyant overnight stardom she gleaned with *Molly Brown*, the 1960s proved more a career period of valleys rather than peaks (with the exception of the 1965 musical *High Spirits*). Her private life she likes to keep that way. Wed for four years to actor Christopher Plummer (daughter, actress Amanda), she had a short and stormy second marriage to Jeremy Slade, also an actor. In 1982 she married musician Richard Bell but on occasion denies the fact that they actually tied the nupital knot. She hs worked consistently in both theatre and film throughout the 1980's. Her performances include the shows *Forty-Second Street* (1980), *The Waltz of the Toreadors* (1985), *Mademoiselle Colombe* (1987) and her one-woman show *Tammy Grimes: A Concert in Words & Music* (1988). She also appeared in the films *The Last Unicorn* (1982) and *Mr. North* (1987). She describes herself as a "fake gourmet cook," likes to live in elegant surroundings, and sums up the essential Tammy this way: "If you're born an overstatement and the world sees you as one, you might as well play it that way. . . . I've always seen myself through other people's eyes, a mirror for the audience."

Charles Grodin

Who played Aardvark the navigator in the film of *Catch 22*, Mia Farrow's gynecologist in *Rosemary's Baby,* co-authored and directed Hooray! It's a Glorious Day, co-produced and directed *Unexpected Guests* and *Thieves?* Why it's *The Heartbreak Kid*, Charles Grodin, "the 1972 American Heel of the Year." Director Elaine May cast him in the film *The Heartbreak Kid* opposite her daughter Jeannie Berlin, as a three-day husband who dumps his wife while on their honeymoon. Since then Grodin has made other major stage and film appearances, e.g., as the engagingly sincere philanderer in *Same Time Next Year* at the Brooks Atkinson in 1975; as the grim and greedy oilman in *King Kong;* as the jocular divorced father in *It's My Turn* (1980) and as Goldie Hawn's husband running for attorney general of California in *Seems Like Old Times* (1980). More films followed, including *The Woman in Red* (1984), *Movers and Shakers* (1985), *Club Sandwich* (1986), *Ishtar* (1986), *Greetings From LA* (1987), *The Couch Trip* (1987) and *Midnight Run* (1988).

Born in the East Liberty section of Pittsburgh, Grodin claims to have "no idea" how old he is. (He was born 21 April 1935.) His late father used to work seven days a week selling supplies to cleaners, tailors, and dressmakers; his mother Lana, did volunteer work with disabled veterans and kids. Chuck himself is divorced from his first wife Julia (one daughter) and married Elissa in March, 1985.

A classmate of Dustin Hoffman when both were studying under Lee Strasberg, Grodin married the girl (Julia) Hoffman had been chasing. ("I got my wife and he got *The Graduate*.") Despite his success as an actor, Grodin says, "My main thrust in life is none of this. I am really more interested in educating myself, talking to people and trying to figure out what's going on, than acting, directing or writing any movie." He shifts his weight and in the next breath concludes, "I started off years ago playing bigots on television, even though I'm almost a nut in the other direction, and when someone asked me how I could do it I told them all you needed was strong feelings about these questions, and then you can apply them to the character you're playing."

John Guare

One of the most paradoxical avant garde playwrights, he writes "with a kind of lucid insanity; veal wine, Norwegian pineapples, bones that sweat, leaves budding blue in the spring," observed Ross Wetzsteon in *New York* magazine. "But the paradoxes go far deeper than such fanciful images. Decapitation and deformity and disease fill his plays ..., yet he's one of our most hilarious writers. He splatters his pages with the wild inventions and weird mutations of his imagination ... yet he's also one of our most autobiographical." Best known for his prize-winning screenplay for *Atlantic City*, Guare has become a cult figure among Off Broadway regulars since the late 1960s and his plays have been called everything from "brilliant slap-stick tragedy" to "long sick jokes." Guare watchers hailed his *Lydie Breeze* (1982) as the culmination of his career—in which chaos and despair are no longer disguised by comedy, but confronted and transcended. "It's about wounds and healing," says Guare.

Born in Manhattan 5 February 1938 and raised in Jackson Heights, John Guare attended Catholic schools until he was 21. ("For years I was berated by the priests for reading *Playboy* on the sly.") Graduating from Georgetown in 1961, he went on to get his M.F.A. in playwrighting at Yale. While there, he wrote his first one-act play, then joined the Air Force Reserve. More one-act epics were born of his typewriter. After a time as an expartiate in Europe, he created part of *The House of Blue Leaves*, shoved it in a drawer ("much too close to me at the time"), and then penned *The Loveliest Afternoon of the Year* and *A Day for Surprises*, which were performed with mild success at Caffe Cino. After licking his wounds as a result of his poorly received *Muzeeka* and *Cop-Out* (critics later rediscovered the latter as "dazzling"), he finished *The House of Blue Leaves* (opened on Broadway in 1986, which instantly established him as a top American playwright. Among his other plays are *Bosoms and Neglect, Marco Polo Sings a Solo, Landscape of the Body* and *Rich and Famous*. He has also been working on a screenplay, tentatively titled *Gershwin Story*.

"I grew up with a very small cast of characters. We had very passionate relationships," Guare says of the constant recurrence of parents in his plays. The son of possessive parents, Guare has been described as a talented "tormented soul" who released his "demons" through his fantastic stories. But since the turn of the 1980s, he's come into a happier time in his life, friends say. In 1981, he married Adele Chatfield-Taylor, director of the New York Landmarks Preservtion Foundation. "It used to be like ... like Nantucket, like fog, like living in the early morning," he told *New York* magazine. "Now ... well, now it's like living at *noon*. The light's somehow different. I mean, there's nowhere you can go. It's like all the stores are open at last."

Aldo Gucci

"The status symbol is a semi-secret," writes columnist Suzy, "shared by men and women who really care about clothes and worn like a club insignia until it becomes a fad." From upper class necessity to a sprawling enterprise of worldwide shops and franchises, the Gucci label is as necessary as a vaccination for anyone considering social climbing. And in Palm Beach, there's a rumor that those signature "G-G's" may replace the dollar signs in everyone's eyes.

Although the business was begun by his father Guccio Gucci (who started with saddle and feed bags and other equine accessories, but made his biggest hit with a pair of ladies' shoes that revolutionized women's footwear in 1920) it was Aldo, born in Florence, Italy, 26 May 1909, who consolidated the Gucci dynasty. "I had a certain role in life, to bring wealth into the family. I started to move around despite my father's conservative feelings. I began to wholesale, and I traveled to Milan, to Paris ... my New York shop has existed for 30 years," Aldo explains, recalling, also, that his father thought he was insane to try a shop in America. In 1984, he took the title of honorary chairman of Gucci, stepping down so that his nephew Maurizio Gucci could become chairman. In 1985, accusations of illegal doings divided the family. The controversy threatened to rock the Gucci empire and break the link of the golden G's. Aldo's favorite place to live in is his Palm Beach home. There he is able to spend the morning in his garden which he says "frees my mind to think of more profound matters." He is the father of three sons and one daughter.

Bob Guccione

"The girl did take her clothes off. She did sign a model release form and she signed a model registry form indicating she wanted to see these pictures published in a magazine," says America's Guru of the Guileful Groin, Bob Guccione, who founded *Penthouse*, the flesh magazine that toppled Vanessa Williams from her Miss America throne. Against attacks that he had done her wrong, he defended himself. "It was not a moral decision, it was a business decision and obviously, I made the right choice." *Penthouse*, which was the first nationally circulated men's magazine to show full frontal nudity, sold millions of copies with its July 1984 issue showing Ms. William's misadventure. The July 1985 *Penthouse* featured yawn-inducing five-year-old black and white shots of Madonna which the subject dismissed with nary a word.

Guccione was born 17 December 1930, in Brooklyn. Art was his first career and he spent three years painting in Rome before he moved to London where he began his magazine in 1965. Although he doesn't paint anymore, he has an extensive art collection housed in his Upper East Side Manhattan mansion which he shares with his companion of more than 20 years, Kathy Keeton. He has a daughter by his first wife and four children by his second. He is a self-described workaholic who puts in at least 16 hours a day editing, writing, design-directing and photographing many of the women who grace the pages of *Penthouse*. Besides *Penthouse* there is *Omni, Forum, Variations* and *Penthouse Letters*. He also publishes *Spin* Magazine. In addition to magazine publishing Guccione's many other ventures include the film *Caligula*, the controversial 1979 spectacular depicting the decadence and depravity of ancient Rome. Missing from his list of accomplishments is *Viva* magazine, his attempt to rival both Helen Gurley Brown and *Cosmopolitan*. (When *Viva* hit the newsstands in 1973 with its pictures of naked guys with flaccid fixtures, he called Ms. Brown's *Cosmo* a bunch of dirty names—

"She writes the way girls exclaim in the toilet; Women are just as interested in a graphic presentation of sex as men are.") *Viva* never could keep its heat on the newsstands and was withdrawn in the late 70s.

C.Z. Guest

"I have spent my whole life spending money and now I'm going to spend the rest of it making money," declared C.Z. Guest in 1985 when she entered the fashion business. With boundless energy that she says comes from being an athlete—"I've ridden and played tennis all my life"—she expanded her career by writing a syndicated gardening column for newspapers, including the *New York Post*.

Born Lucy Douglas Cochrane in Boston 19 February 1920, she was one of the two irresistible Cochrane girls (the other being her sister Nancy) who dazzled Back Bay stag lines when they were presented to society in 1937. Shortly thereafter the blonde beauty left for New York to appear in the chorus of the *Ziegfeld Follies* and then on to Hollywood. However, she gave up any theatrical ambitions in 1947 when she married Winston Frederick Guest, heir to the Phipps steel fortune, a renowned polo player and a very prominent in the Social Register. Very soon Mrs. Guest was being heralded as one of the best dressed women of the world. *Time* magazine put her on a cover in 1962. She is the mother of two children, Alexander and Cornelia (widely publicized in 1984 as "The Deb of the Year"), and is the author of *C.Z. Guest's Garden Planner & Date Book*. An updated edition of her *First Garden* was published by McGraw Hill in 1987.

Alec Guinness

"One became an actor," he says, "to escape oneself." Indeed, on both stage and screen, he is admired as "an actor who makes you forget that he is acting," a tribute to his characteristic, exquisite economy of technique. Playing *Hamlet* in a controversial modern dress version at the Old Vic when he was 24, he proceeded onward and upward to become an international star of films and the theatre, and, offstage, a knight of the realm. (Queen Elizabeth II added the title "Sir" to his name in 1959.) Famed for his versatility, he counts among his stage triumphs roles as startlingly dissimilar as the urbane psychiatrist in T.S. Eliot's *The Cocktail Party*, and the drink-sodden, womanizing Welsh poet in the biographical drama *Dylan*. In motion pictures, his finely detailed characterizations have ranged from a tour-de-force delineation of eight members of an eccentric English clan (including that of an elderly woman) in *Kind Hearts and Coronets* (1949) to an Oscar-winning portrayal of the priggish Colonel Nicholson in *Bridge on the River Kwai* (1957). In 1977 he won new fans among the smallfry set with his characterization of the whiskery wizard Ben (Obiwan) Kenobi in the super-successful sci-fi spectacle *Star Wars*. In the 1985 blockbuster, *A Passage to India*, he was a Brahmin professor, and he starred in the 1988 film *A Handful of Dust*. For his work in *Little Dorrit* (1988) he received an Academy Award nomination for Best Supporting Actor. His book *Blessings in Disguise* was published in 1986.

Born a banker's son in London on 2 April 1914 (no relation to the Irish brewing family), he was discouraged from participating in student theatricals at boarding school ("You're not the acting type") but eventually nabbed the part of a breathless messenger in a class production of *Macbeth*. He experienced lean years as a copywriter, layout man and acting student before landing his first theatre job in 1934—a stint with John Gielgud's repertory troupe and a later stint at the Old Vic in Shakespearean roles which really established him on the English stage as one of its most promising young actors. His depiction of Herbert Pocket in the 1946 David Lean movie version of *Great Expectations* made him an international film star. Since then the reserved, almost timid actor has turned in brilliant performances in more than a score of major pictures, among them, his deliciously adroit characterization of Fagin in Lean's *Oliver Twist* (1948); as a rogish painter in *The Horse's Mouth* (for which he wrote the screen adaptation; 1958). He also brought immense conviction to the part of Prince Feisal in Lean's 1962 epic, *Lawrence of Arabia*. While "no flesh-and-blood actor could have stolen the show from the special effects '*Star Wars*,'" by portraying a space-age sage with dignity Guinness added to the 1977 release a potent touch of class. Since *Star Wars* (and its 1980 sequel *The Empire Strikes Back* in which Guinness made a token appearance) ranks as one of the biggest-grossing motion pictures of all times, he—with his two percent of the profits and exposure to massive audiences—has acquired additional "fame and greenbacks."

Active also on the stage on both sides of the Atlantic throughout his career, he held out until recent years where television was concerned. Since September 1981, however, he's received advantageous exposure on the small screen in the U.S. as the rueful middle-aged secret agent George Smiley in the Public Television series based on John Le Carre's novel, "Tinker, Tailor, Soldier, Spy." This impressive debut spawned a sequel, "Smiley's People," in which Guinness again starred, and further TV work included underplaying the crusty but meltable Earl of Dorincourt in the classic "Little Lord Fauntleroy." Guinness believes that he possesses a "chameleon quality" that has been an asset to him as an actor "but not as a person."

Married since 1938, Guinness met his wife, the former Merula Salaman, in a London play called *Noah* in which he played a wolf and she a tigress. After departing from the ark and proceeding to the altar, Mrs. Guinness relinquished the stage but the couple's son Matthew (born during World War II) is following in his father's performing footsteps. When asked if he really enjoys acting, Guinness's reply: "Yes, I do. It's happy agony."

Bryant Gumbel

"The kinds of jobs I've held in this business and the kinds of shows I've done are not those that are given as a token measure," says network TV's first black morning show host. "It would be akin to Ronald Reagan having a black vice-president in order to have a black in his Administration. You don't put somebody at the head of the class as a token effort." At the head of his class in the broadcasting business since his start, he now holds "one of the five, six, eight most prestigious jobs in the industry," that of co-host of NBC's "Today" show.

Born in New Orleans on 29 September 1948, Bryant is the son of a probate judge who moved his family to Chicago's middle-class Hyde Park. Both of the boys in the four-sibling household were exposed to sports by their father, and both later became sportscasters. Gumbel matriculated at tiny Bates College in Maine, where he was a two-sports letterman (football and baseball) majoring in, of all things, Russian history. He became a folding carton salesman in New York after graduating in 1970, only to quit and take up writing for, and eventually the editorship of, now-defunct *Black Sports* magazine. While he was at the periodical, KNBC-TV in L.A. offered him a 1972 audition as weekend sports anchor. He got through the tryout, despite newsman and studio bystander Tom Snyder's best efforts to make Gumbel laugh while he should have been straight-faced. Then the network knocked in 1975 for the sports director Gumbel to co-host a new sports show. He accepted it, along with the L.A.-during-the-week, New York-on-weekends schedule it demanded. But his wife June, a former airline stewardess, endured until the net shelled out a half a million per year in 1980 to get his formidable journalistic-juggling live production skills all to itself. "My ability," he mused, "is to digest a lot of information, which I dispense calmly and articulately while everybody around me is going bananas."

Now ensconced in Manhattan, he works at NBC's Rockefeller Center studios beginning at 6 each morning. His competent, light handling of interviews and features adds an attractive complement to co-host Jane Pauley. Calling himself "colorless in the same sense that to most Americans O.J. Simpson has become colorless," Gumbel says, "I offer myself as a positive black image in a passive way. If you want to accept my image, fine. If not, that's fine, too. I'm a broadcaster who happens to be black. Not a black broadcaster. And that's more than a lesson in semantics." Gumbel, June, son Bradley and daughter Jillian live in an East Side brownstone in Manhattan.

Arlo Guthrie

Alice's Restaurant, the movie version of his 1967 narrative song epic LP of the same title, stands out (wrote Stephen Holden in the *New York Times*) as "a quintessential film of the late 1960s counterculture [with] the charm of a period piece evoking a world that vanished in a puff of marijuana smoke." The rambling true story of how Arlo Guthrie's arrest for littering made him unfit for military service made him an idol of the Haight-Ashbury set and, in the 1980s, was entertaining a new generation of anti-establishment types on a video cassette. Meanwhile, the balladeer himself is still mixing music and political commentary, currently singing (and speaking out) in concerts here and abroad on the Peace Movement and other assorted urgent environmental issues that characterize the final quarter of this twentieth century.

Born in the Coney Island section of Brooklyn, U.S.A., on 10 July 1947 and raised in Queens, Arlo Guthrie was influenced early by his now-legendary dad, the Oklahoma troubadour Woody Guthrie, who gave him his first guitar at the age of four. (He still has it.) Arlo's deep affection for his pop was immortalized, first, in a moving part of *Alice's Restaurant* about the elder Guthrie's losing battle with Huntingdon's Chorea and again in the 1984 film documentary *Woody Guthrie: Hard Travelin',* in which Arlo makes a journey to discover Woody's roots. Continuing the family tradition, Arlo and his wife, Jackie (wed 1969) have branched out with four young balladeers of their own. In 1987 he headlined a tribute at Carnegie hall commemorating the 20th Anniversary since the death of Woody Guthrie.

Gene Hackman

His 1971 Oscar-winning performance as tough, hard-edged narco detective Popeye Doyle in *The French Connection* rocketed him to the superstardom he had pursued since his teenage days as a movie usher. ("I had a chance to see Ethel Barrymore in *The Corn is Green.* She inspired me to want to be an actor above all else.") It wasn't easy. Enrolled at the Pasadena Playhouse, he and another student, Dustin Hoffman, were considered the two least likely to succeed. But persistence paid off. Hackman eventually made it to Broadway, playing Sandy Dennis' crude boyfriend in *Any Wednesday,* a sleeper that ran for 983 performances. His screen career began with a bit part in *Lilith*—which was big enough to attract the attention of its star, Warren Beatty, who remembered Hackman two years later when casting his 1967 classic, *Bonnie and Clyde.* Hackman's performance as Clyde Barrow's backslapping brother, Buck, earned him an Oscar nomination. Though best known for his dramatic works and tough-guy roles, Hackman is a versatile actor who has starred in sensitive dramas (*I Never Sang for My Father, Misunderstood*) and in off-beat comic roles (he was Luthor, the arch enemy of *Superman,* and the friendly blind man in *Young Frankenstein*). His performance in *Mississippi Burning* (1988) earned him an Academy Award nomination for Best Actor.

Born Eugene Alden Hackman in San Bernardino, Calif., 30 January 1931, he spent his early teens in Danville, Ill.; at sixteen, with his parents' blessing, Hackman enlisted in the Marines. He served in China, Japan, Hawaii, and Okinawa before breaking both legs in a motorcycle accident and receiving a disability discharge. His first performing stint was in China, where he worked as an announcer at his Marine unit's radio station in 1947. After returning to the states, he traveled around the country working at various small-town TV stations, then enrolled at Pasadena Playhouse. After a period of summer stock, he moved to New York and worked his way through odd jobs before landing a role in an off-Broadway revue and finally making it to Broadway.

Hackman has made more than 35 films. Some of his 1980's releases include *Uncommon Valor* (1983), *Misunderstood* (1984), *Target* (1985), *Twice in a Lifetime* 1985, *Power* (1986), *Full Moon in Blue Water* (1987), *Superman IV* (1987), *No Way Out* (1987), *Bat 21* (1988), *Another Woman* (1988), and *The Von Metz Incident* (1988). He is divorced from his first wife and has three children from the marriage. Hackman loves flying and owns three planes, races cars in events like Sebring and Riverside, and is a talented painter and avid film collector.

Merle Haggard

This self-proclaimed "Okie from Muskogee" is the first to admit that he grew up too fast. After his father, a fiddler, died when he was 9, young Merle Haggard kept running away from home because he didn't want to be a burden on his mother. "I was a pretty wild kid. I love excitement. I'm not proud of what I did. I wouldn't recommend it to anyone else, but I do believe I benefited from my experiences." At 14 Haggard was jailed on suspicion of armed robbery, and by 17 he had spent two years in reform school. He was sent to San Quentin for three years at the age of 21. "If I hadn't been knocked down, I never would have amounted to anything," he confides. Haggard now pens and chants songs about marked men, empty bars, hobos, prisoners, women, whiskey, the law, and fools and their rainbows. "Feeling is what every song is made of. But craft is what makes the difference between good ones and bad ones."

Born 6 April 1937 in Bakersfield, a Southern California tank town, Haggard is not ashamed of his past. "My folks always told me how happy they were the day I was born. They may not have had much money, but they sure had lots of love to give. My dad and I were especially close." After his release from prison, Haggard went home and worked as an electricial helper and moonlighted as a guitarist at a local country club. In 1963, after four years of living right and staying free, he was offered a recording contract with Fuzzy Owens' Tally Records. A year later, he was making discs with Tally, and his third release, "All of My Friends Are Gonna Be Strangers," made the Top Ten. Haggard signed a contract with Capitol Records. From there it was no looking back.

In 1970, he was named Nashville Songwriters Association's Songwriter of the Year and the Country Music Association Entertainer of the Year. His recent records include "Amber Waves of Grain" (1985), "A Friend in California" (1986), "Seashores of Old Mexico" (with Willie Nelson; 1987), and "Chill Factor" (1987). Haggard also is the author of the book *Sing Me Back Home,* published in 1981. He is married to singer Leona Williams. (With former wife Bonnie Owens, ex-wife of country singer Buck, he had four children.) "When I sing about believing in our country," he says in answer to those who consider his patriotism square, "I hope I'm saying it for a lot of people. I know I have to say it for myself."

Larry Hagman

". . . hssssssssss." Watch out for your toes, America, watch out for your fingers. Don't pick-up any stray ten-gallon hats, there's a snake in there and his name is J.R. Ewing, America's Lone Star viper with a honeycured tongue. "The time is right for a real bad guy and, well, I guess I'm it," says the son of Mary Martin who, as the star villain of the TV super-soap "Dallas" is watched weekly and worldwide by over 40 million viewers, endeared to them, no doubt, by *that* smile: as rapid as a rattlesnake's, as flashy as a silver bullet bucking from a pistol called sweet revenge. On the air as J.R. since 1977, Hagman is still pulling in awards as "Best Villian." He won the Soap Opera Award in 1988.

Larry Hagman was born 21 September 1934 in Weatherford, Texas. He says he bases his money-making character J.R. on some of the "oil rich boys" who employed his lawyer father, the late Benjamin Hagman, in the Texas of his youth. "They had such a nice, sweet smile but when you finished meeting with them your socks were missing and you hadn't even noticed they'd taken your boots." After his parents' divorce, he moved to Los Angeles with his mother. Many schools later he turned to New York to pursue an acting career, making his stage debut in a City Center production of *The Taming of the Shrew*. He spent five years with the Air Force in Europe as the director of USO shows, then returned again to New York where he starred on the soap opera "Edge of Night." He appeared in the films *Fail Safe*, *The Group*, and *Harry and Tonto* before his five-year orbit as an amiable astronaut visited by the curvaceous Barbara Eden on TV's "I Dream of Jeannie." Married since 1954 to wife Maj (whom he met when they were both appearing in a production of *South Pacific*), they enjoy a quiet lifestyle in Malibu with their two children Heidi and Preston.

In Dallas, on location, Hagman spends his off-camera time shooing around the streets in his "Texas taxi," a white Cadillac convertible with steer-horn adorned grille, waving a can of Lone Star beer, tipping his hat to everyone, and hooting out howdy-do's, sort of a J.R. for president do-si-do on the range. And why not J.R. for president; he's got the smile and the ratings.

David Halberstam

This Pulitzer Prize-winning journalist, who has been called the father of modern investigative reporting, first achieved fame as the New York *Times'* Vietnam War correspondent. Since then, he has produced a stream of blockbuster books including several "landmarks"—*The Best and the Brightest* (1972), which tells how the Kennedy-Johnson people took us to war in Vietnam; and *The Powers That Be* (1979), the story of the rise of the power of modern media, particularly television, culminating in the struggle between the media and the government in Watergate. Called "a legend in American journalism" by *Harper's* magazine, Halberstam has become known as a powerful journalist who selects large and crucial subjects and then masters them in a way laymen can understand. Says Halberstam, "I'm not a writer like John Cheever or Dostoevski, but a reporter-dramatist-storyteller who tries to make complicated trends more understandable. A good book always begins with your own curiosity, with a question you feel you've *got* to go out and find the answer to . . . and as you go out and learn, in the end, your readers join you on that journey."

Born 10 April 1934 in New York City, David Halberstam got his first journalism experience on the Harvard Crimson (B.A. 1955), then set forth to cover the civil rights struggle for the smallest daily in Mississippi and then for the Nashville *Tennessean*. In the early 1960s he was part of the small handful of American reporters who, much to the irritation of the Kennedy administration, refused to accept the official optimism about Vietnam and who reported that the war was being lost. At age 30, Halberstam received the Pulitzer Prize and several other journalistic awards for his Vietnam coverage. His first major Vietnam book, *The Making of a Quagmire* (1965), proved to be as prophetic as it was pessimistic. His six overseas years with the *Times* (1961-67) also took him to the Congo and eastern Europe. In 1965, in Warsaw, he met and married actress Elizbeta Tchizevska (divorced 1977), then settled in New York to become a contributing editor at *Harper's* until 1971. He married Jean Sandness Butler in 1979; they have one daughter, Julia Sandness. Recent works include *The Amateurs* (1985), *The Reckoning* (1986), and *Summer of '49* (1989).

Daryl Hall and John Oates

"We've been together for over ten years now and it's funny, but it really seems as though we're just starting out. Like we've been preparing for ten years and now we're gonna do it," Daryl Hall said in 1981, just after the versatile pop duo bolstered their popularity by adapting a "hotter," more danceable sound, and a more rock-and-roll image. Daryl Hall, born 11 October 1949, and John Oates, born 7 April 1948, met at a teen dance in their native Philadelphia when they escaped an erupting gang fight in the same elevator. Kindred spirits from the start, they became singing/songwriting partners and moved to New York City in 1971 in search of a recording contract. From the 1972 release of their first album, *Whole Oates*, they placed slick pop tunes high on the charts, including, "Sara Smile," "Rich Girl," and "She's Gone." Following a three-year commercial slump in the late 1970s, they debuted their new sound with the 1980 album, *Voices*, containing four hit singles, including the rocking "Kiss on My List." They followed that success with *Private Eyes*, which netted another four hit singles including "I Can't Go for That," a cross-over tune that made it to the top of four charts. It featured a driving, contagious beat duplicated in "Maneater," a smash hit single off their H^2O album.

With three gold albums and more than ten hit singles in three years, Hall and Oates shined as a top recording act in the early 1980s, bested, perhaps, only by Michael Jackson. In 1983, they hit the charts with two new singles, "Say It Isn't So" and "Adult Education." Although simpatico musically and personally, standing side-by-side the duo is a bit of an odd couple. Oates, short and stocky with sensual, dark features, stands a whole head shorter than his blond, sleek partner. Their relationship has never been rocky but rather filled with mutual respect. Each artist has tried solo projects for "new sources of information." Hall says: "When we work together, we just deal with reality as it exists to us, our point of view at that moment of time. We have this strange ability that, even after we've been apart and get together, we seem to be thinking about the same things." The duo's album *Ooh Yeah!* (1988) is the result of their typical creative process. "Ooh Yeah is what you say when the groove feels right. . . . Ooh Yeah is what you say when the music moves you."

Arsenio Hall

The 12-year-old Arsenio Hall told his mother he wanted "to do what Johnny Carson does." At age 30, with the 3 January 1989 premiere of "The Arsenio Hall Show," that dream was fulfilled. But Hall was more than just another talking head. By the time his show (of which he is also executive producer) hit the airwaves he was already known as a talented comedian and actor. With a comedic style he has described as "'brown bread' on the edge,'" he has succeeded in clubs, film, and television.

Born circa 1958 Hall grew up in Cleveland, Ohio, the son of a Baptist preacher. He inherited his father's ability to work a crowd, starting at age 7 performing magic at wedding receptions while working birthday parties and local talent shows. The young magician was fascinated by "The Tonight Show," especially the Mighty Carson Art Players, and began to switch his focus from magic to comedy. A high school promotional visit by comedian Franklin Ajaye convinced Hall to try stand-up comedy after completing his education. In high school, Hall explored other areas of his talent. He was a drummer in the marching band and orchestra and had his own music group. While at Kent State University, he became involved in theatre arts and was a deejay for the campus radio station.

After graduation Hall embarked on an advertising career but began doing stand-up comedy on a dare in 1979. He quit his job, relocating to Chicago where he was discovered in a nightclub by singer Nancy Wilson. She funded his move to Los Angeles. Hall opened for dozens of top name performers including Aretha Franklin, Tom Jones, Wayne Newton, and Tina Turner. Making the transition from clubs to television in 1983, Hall co-hosted the ABC summer series "The Hour Comedy Hour." The following year he was a regular on "Thicke of the Night" and went on to co-host the music/variety series "Solid Gold". He hit his stride when he signed as an interim guest host on Fox Broadcasting's "The Late Show." The show enjoyed some of its highest ratings ever during his tenure, and he eventually hosted it for 13 weeks. Following the "Late Show" stint, Hall signed an exclusive 2-year, multi-film agreement with Paramount Pictures, leading to his acclaimed performance in the box office blockbuster *Coming to America*. Returning to television, Hall was the sole host of the 1988 "MTV Awards." While promoting *Coming to America*, Hall decided to return to the talk show circuit. Preferring the immediacy of television to film, Hall explains: "A talk show is a blessing for a stand-up. It's the perfect vehicle." Hall wrote his own monologues while hosting "The Late Show" commenting on a wide variety of subjects. His role as the executive producer of his current show fills another need. "I've worked very hard all my life to educate myself, and now I get a chance not only to show the funny side of my personality, but the businessman locked inside me as well. . . . If this show succeeds, there will be nothing greater than hearing someone say, 'Arsenio Hall is a great businessman.'"

With all the success he's achieved, Hall still sets goals for himself. "I want to be an artist respected by other artists, which I don't think I've achieved yet. . . . I want a person to look at me and be affected by my work. . . . And I'm going to keep working until I do it right."

Jerry Hall

The story is one we have come to associate with the Hollywood big screen . . . small-town girl does good. No matter what the obstacles, she nurtures her dreams with determination and turns them into reality. For Jerry Hall, life imitates art.

The pride and joy of Mesquite, Texas was born Jerry Faye Hall on 2 July 1956. Accompanied by her twin sister, Terry, on her journey into the world, they were raised in a small pink house with three other sisters. Their father had the dangerous job of hauling explosive chemicals; a tragic accident left him burned by acid, which transformed him into a bitter man who often beat his daughters. It was Jerry's patient, loving and caring mother who kept the family together despite her husband's violent nature. While Jerry's home life was not ideal, her activities were that of any other small-town girl. Chores included shoveling out the stables for money, and she was employed as a cashier at a local Dairy Queen. For exercise she swam in the cow trough. All the while Jerry longed for the day when she could venture out into the world. That dream became a reality due to, ironically, an automobile accident which put her in the hospital. Ignorant of the fact that she was allergic to penicillin, she convulsed after the doctor had given the antibiotic. Eager to conceal the doctors' negligence, the hospital offered Jerry eight hundred dollars. The extra money afforded Jerry's big break. With her mom's assistance, Jerry sewed creations copied from the Fredricks of Hollywood catalogue. At sixteen years of age, the leggy five-foot-eleven beauty made her way to Paris in 1973, placing her homemade fashions in her knapsack. One of the first people Jerry met in Paris was world-renowned photographer Helmut Newton. Before long her work with Newton became the springboard for her meteoric rise on the famous Paris fashion runways. In 1974 she launched what was to be an 8-year campaign for Yves Saint Laurent Opium perfume. She campaigned for Charles of the Ritz make-up in 1976 and Revlon products ranging from mascara to nail polish in the '80s, among other well-known beauty products. Her face adorned the covers of over one hundred magazines, and she has been seen on the small screen promoting such products as Dr. Pepper soda, Clairol curling irons, Michelob beer and Calvin Klein jeans.

Not just another pretty face, Jerry penned a book, *Tall Tales* (1984), which was on the *LA Times* best-seller list and a Literary Guild Book of the Month choice for December 1984. Small parts in feature films include *St. Germain des Pres Apres la Guerre* (1974), *Willie and Phil* (1978), *Urban Cowboy* (1979) and *Running Out of Luck* (1984). In 1976 and 1977, she appeared in two Bryan Ferry videos, "Let's Stick Together" and "The Price of Love." She even sang with Bryan Ferry live at the Bottom Line in New York City in 1976. Her television appearances include hosting "Saturday Night Live" (1986), an NBC pilot, "She's With Me" (1986), and at least two appearances on "David Letterman" (1985). While she has been a favorite for talk show and guest-host TV appearances, her talent as an actress has been recognized through another medium. August of 1988 brought Jerry to the stage of the Whole Theatre, where she starred as Cherie in *Bus Stop*, and in 1987 she appeared in *Batman*.

True to her warm and loving Cancerian nature, Jerry has made a wonderful home for her live-in lover since 1977, rocker Mick Jagger, and their two young children: Elizabeth Scarlett, born on 1 March 1984, and James Leroy Augustice, born on 28 August 1985. Jerry considers her children to be the greatest accomplishments of her life. The happy family has homes in London, Paris and New York.

Halston

"You're only as good as the people you dress," says the former Roy Halston Frowick, who in his heyday dressed Lauren Bacall, Katherine Graham, Liza Minnelli, Candice Bergen, Jacqueline Onassis, Baronne Guy de Rothschild, Doris Duke, Babe Paley, and Catherine Deneuve and became the star designer of the 1970s in New York. "The 1970s belong to Halston," wrote Patrick McCarthy in *WWD*. "Whether it was cashmere sweater sets, Ultrasuede shirt dresses, buttonless jackets, tie-dye caftans or simply cardigans tied loosely around the shoulders, Halston's clothes were, in the words of one critic, 'distinguished by their utter lack of contrivance.'" In 1973 he sold his business to Norton Simon and compared the deal to "having a Renaissance patron."

Born 23 April 1932, the second of four children of an accountant and a housewife for whom Halston made his design debut in 1945 (a homemade red Easter hat), he moved to Evansville, Ind., with his family after World War II and attended the University of Indiana for two years before enrolling at the Chicago Art Institute. In his spare time he made women's hats on a secondhand sewing machine and convinced an Ambassador Hotel hairdresser to display them. At 21 he opened a millinery shop in the hotel. Four years later he came to New York and, after a brief spell working for a Lily Dache, he moved to Bergdorf Goodman's custom millinery salon where one of his first customers was Jacqueline Kennedy who needed hats for her husband's presidential campaign. Halston designed the famous beige pillbox hat that Mrs. Kennedy wore to the 1961 inaguration. He received the first of his many Coty awards in 1962 and, in 1968, went on his own, first signing a millinery contract and soon afterwards finding backing for a clothing line.

"I calmed fashion down," he once observed. "When I started [my] house on East 68th street, it was the end of the youthquake; everything was steeped in mad, far-out fashion—being Indians and ethnic and gypsies.... We made it possible for a fashionable woman to wear a sweater and a pair of pants or a skirt and shirt.... I didn't invent the sweater. I just put it on lots of expensive backs."

Mark Hamill

He's recognized by his fans as anyone from Luke Skywalker, the doe-eyed goody in the 1976 superhit-flic *Star Wars* (and its sequels *The Return of the Jedi* and *The Empire Strikes Back*,) to *The Elephant Man* (where he made his Broadway debut) and Mozart (for his role as Wolfgang Amadeus in Peter Shaffer's award-winning play *Amadeus* on Broadway).

Born 25 September 1951 in Oakland, Cal., into the family of a U.S. Navy officer, Mark Hamill spent a peripatetic childhood moving with his parents and two brothers and six sisters to posts as far afield as Yokosuka, Japan. As a child he was mildly interested in acting, but when he accompanied his father on a visit to New York City for a marathon of live theatre, he was bitten by the show-biz bug. "After seeing eight plays in six days," he says, "I was hooked." He majored in Theatre Arts at Los Angeles City College and began his professional career with a nine-month stint on the daytime TV soap "General Hospital." He later starred in the MTM series "The Texas Wheelers" and a number of television movies, including "Sarah T.," "Eric," "In Circumstantial Evidence," and "Delancey Street." Besides the *Star Wars* trilogy, his other films include *Britannia Hospital*, *Corvette Summer* (also known as *Dantley and Vanessa*), *The Big Red One*, *Avalon Awakening*, and *Slipstream*.

Married and the father of one son, he returned to Broadway in the ill-fated musical *Harrigan 'N Hart* in 1985 (playing the 19th-century American actor Tony Hart). In his next show, *The Nerd* (1987), Hamill played a beleaguered architect whose ordered existence turns to chaos when he begins to share his home with a man who once saved his life. The walking, talking human catastrophe known as "the Nerd" was played by Robert Joy, and the production was directed by Charles Nelson Reilly.

Pete Hamill

That fretful phrasemaker, Spiro Agnew, described Hamill's New York *Post* account of the 1970 Kent State killings as "irrational ravings." So in 1971, when the journalist gathered his columns into a book, that's what he chose as his title. Included in it were some impassioned words against the Vietnam War (having opposed it as far back as 1965), appraisals of "coming of age in Nueva York," miscellaneous politics, and a plea urging parole for bank robber Willie Sutton (who was granted it the day after Hamill's column appeared). His observations and musings have also graced the *Village Voice*, *Playboy*, and *Saturday Evening Post*, as well as six novels and numerous "Tales of New York" in the New York *Daily News*.

He was born 24 June 1935 in Brooklyn, the eldest of seven children of a family of poor Irish immigrants. ("I had my first steak when I was 17.") Enraptured by the work of cartoonist Milton Caniff, his first tentative tries at writing were comic books. He quit Xavier High School at 16, went to work in the Brooklyn Navy Yard, joined the Navy a year later, and discovered "literature" through the base library. ("My letters home started getting literary in the worst way, as I tried to use words to explain what was happening to me, and I started filling notebooks with fragments of prose, words I had never heard before, poems, epigrams, character sketches....") After his discharge he worked in an advertising agency by day, studied at Pratt Institute by night, and later opened up his own commercial art studio. He was hired as a reporter by the *Post* after he wrote "a long, impassioned letter" to then-editor James Wechsler about the state of the world in general and American journalism in particular. With time out as a roving magazine writer in Europe, later a screenwriter, he returned to the *Post* when "the bodies started coming home from Asia in rubber bags." Hamill, the divorced father of two daughters, says he grew up with "a kind of rude sympathy for underdogs, for the damaged and the lost." He married again in 1987, when he took Fukiko Aoki (New York Bureau Chief of *Newsweek*, Japanese Edition) as his wife.

George Hamilton

"If," suggested Pauline Kael in *The New Yorker* in 1981, "you could combine the screen images of Douglas Fairbanks, Sr. and Peter Sellers, the result might be pretty close to the slinky, self-mocking George Hamilton" in his on-screen guise of *Zorro, the Gay Blade*—a satire of the swashbuckler of the 1930s. A far cry from his early years as a Cary Grant look-alike emoting in a series of mostly forgettable films to generally lukewarm reviews, the erstwhile glamorboy first showed his "joyously silly" *farceur* side in the 1979 comedy, *Love at First Bite*, playing a modern-day Dracula driven from Communist Transylvania to put down new roots in New York City. To many critics (perspicacious Pauline among them), his "gleaming-eyed Zorro with his idiotic leering grin and his idiosyncratic Spanish accent" was even funnier.

The actor once nicknamed "Gorgeous George" was born George Hamilton IV (no relation to the country singer of the same name) in Memphis (12 August 1939) but spent most of his boyhood bouncing around to 25 different schools while his social, much-married mom followed the sun and party circuit. It was a longtime family friend, the silent screen star Mae Murray, who first pointed him in the direction of Hollywood, and he made his debut in the quickie *Crime and Punishment, USA*, in 1958. Always suavely polite and impeccably dressed, he cut a wide Tinseltown swath with his 1939 white Rolls Royce ("The car got more publicity than I did"), which sometimes earned as much money as he for he often rented the car to his studio for $100 a day. He also earned publicity points as one of "Hollywood's most eligible bachelors," his most headlined romantic fling being with Lynda Bird Johnson when her dad, LBJ, was in the White House. He married Alana Collins in 1972 (one son, Ashley Steven, born 1974), divorced her in 1976 (after which she went on to marry rocker Rod Stewart), and has been back in the bachelor ranks ever since. Among Hamilton's most noteworthy screen credits during the first phase of his career were *The Light in the Piazza* (1962), as Moss Hart in *Act One* (1963), and in the title role of *Evil Knievel*, a film bio of the motorcycle stuntman which he produced for himself in 1972. He appeared on television's "Dynasty" during the 1985 season.

Linda Hamilton

It seems ironic that Linda Hamilton, the "Beauty" of CBS-TV's "Beauty and the Beast," insists "glamour is hardly my style," but her previous roles support her claim. Prior to portraying the beautiful lawyer Catherine

Chandler on "Beast," Linda had played a rape victim on "Hill Street Blues," a battered wife in the CBS-TV movie "Rape and Marriage: The Rideout Case" with Mickey Rourke, and usually ended up getting killed in her action adventure films. Her image began to change with the role of heart surgeon Amy Franklin in Dino DeLaurentiis' *King Kong Lives*. She wore a designer wardrobe and got the guy. Then came "Catherine." "The show wouldn't work as well if Catherine didn't have some beauty. It is the extremes in the characters' looks that help make the story work. But I never thought Vincent wouldn't love Catherine if she weren't beautiful." She added she's always found "Vincent" attractive—"leonine and magnificently proud and with a great voice."

Linda was born 26 September 1957 in Salisbury, Maryland, along with her identical twin sister, Leslie, a registered nurse. She grew up there with her older sister and younger brother. Her father, who died when she was five years old, was a physician. Her stepfather, now retired, was the police chief of Salisbury. Hamilton began acting as a child with children's theater groups. Acting became her career choice at Washington College in Maryland, where she studied for two years and appeared in school productions of *Story Theatre*, *Prometheus Bound* and *The Adding Machine*. She then went to New York where she attended workshops at the Lee Strasberg Theatre Institute and also studied with Nicholas Ray. Student productions of *Richard III* and *A View from the Bridge* were followed by her professional debut with an appearance on the daytime drama "Search for Tomorrow." In 1979, Hamilton reluctantly moved to Hollywood. She landed movie-of-the-week appearances, including "Secrets of a Mother and Daughter," "Secret Weapons," and "Club Med." Hamilton also appeared in the pilot "Wishman" and was a series regular on "Secrets of Midland Heights" and "Kings Crossing." Her movie career blossomed as well. Starting out with low budget features *Nightflowers* and *TAG* (where she met her husband, actor Bruce Abbott), Hamilton moved on to *The Stone Boy* and *Children Of The Corn*. Her co-starring role opposite Arnold Schwarzenegger in *The Terminator* gained her recognition and led to other starring roles in *Black Moon Rising* with Tommy Lee Jones and *King Kong Lives*. The role of Catherine has earned Hamilton two Golden Globe nominations for Best Actress (1988 and 1989) and a People's Choice Award nomination as Favorite Female Performer in a New Television Program in 1988.

Hamilton relaxes by reading, interior decorating, and playing Scrabble. She's a Los Angeles Dodgers fan and a lifelong lover of horses. The 5'5", 115-pound Hamilton has light brown hair and green eyes like "Catherine" but lives "a much shaggier lifestyle" than her television counterpart. She resides in Marina del Rey with husband Bruce Abbott and their 115-pound German Shephard-St. Bernard mix, Bosco. Children are in the future. "They're the real legacy we leave in this world—not your face on film."

Marvin Hamlisch

On April 2, 1974, upon receiving his third record-breaking Academy Award in the same evening (two for *The Way We Were*, one for *The Sting*), Marvin Hamlisch told the audience, "I think now we can talk to each other as friends." The following year the composer won four Grammys as his Broadway musical *A Chorus Line* earned the Pulitzer Prize and nine Tony Awards. Not bad for a self-described "square" (doesn't smoke or drink; attends weekly Sabbath services) who calls writing "such a lonely life."

Marvin Hamlisch was born 2 June 1944 in New York City and raised on the Upper West Side. The son of an accordionist/bandleader and "a real Jewish, terrific mother," he was, at age five, reproducing on the piano music he heard on the radio, he began piano lessons at six, and at seven became the youngest student ever admitted to Juilliard. Hamlisch attended Professional Children's School and Queen's College (B.A. in music cum laude). Before his teens he was giving piano recitals in Manhattan (including Town Hall), but soon gave up the idea of a concert career. "The nerves got to me. Before every recital, I would violently throw up, lose weight, the veins in my hands would stand out. By the time I was 13 or 14 it became obvious it was going to kill me."

Meanwhile, he constantly wrote music, mostly imitation show tunes. "I had no style of my own. Whatever I heard, I imitated." He worked as accompanist on *Funny Girl* and other Broadway musicals and in three days wrote the theme for *The Swimmer*, his first of fourteen film scores before his Oscar sweep. Other film scores include *Ordinary People*, *Sophie's Choice* and the film version of *A Chorus Line* (the new song "Surprise, Surprise" was nominated for an Academy Award). His semi-autobiographical musical, *They're Playing Our Song*, enjoyed a healthy Broadway run, but his next musical *Smile* didn't give the critics any reason to grin and bear it! In 1989, Hamlisch was the musical conductor of the Academy Awards show produced by Allan Carr. He married Terre Blair on 29 May 1989.

Armand Hammer

"I think when I work 14 hours a day, I get lucky," says this brash maverick businessman/art collector who transformed a floundering oil company called Occidental Petroleum into the multibillion dollar, multinational empire which now ranks as the 12th mightiest in the U.S. Famous for his capitalistic wheeling and dealing behind the Iron Curtain, the indefatigable octogenarian confides, "I've always found a way to achieve what I was after. I've been quite resourceful. I've never admitted defeat in anything."

Born in New York City on 21 May 1898, he was the eldest son of Julian Hammer—a doctor, owner of a pharmaceutical company, and a founder of the American Communist Party who sold supplies to the fledgling Soviet Union when other countries were blockading it. After earning an M.D. from Columbia University, Armand Hammer (named for the lover in Dumas' *La Dame aux Camelias*) went to Russia in 1921 to help with relief work and on a business mission for his father. His arrival in Moscow turned out to be perfect timing. Lenin had decided on his New Economic Policy, which allowed limited capitalism and foreign capital to rebuild Russia's devastated industries. Hammer credits Lenin with convincing him to drop his medical career and become a capitalist. Quickly negotiating deals for grain and an asbestos mine in the Ural Mountains, Hammer returned to the U.S. and formed the Allied American Company, which, according to author Joseph Finder, became the Soviet agent for 37 other American firms in the early 1920s. As the Russian's favorite capitalist over the years, Hammer is the industrialist most closely identified with East-West trade. His acquaintance with Lenin was a legend in the West by the 1970s and assured him of a hero's welcome behind the Iron Curtain, opening doors closed to most others. In 1976, Brezhnev gave him an apartment in Moscow, overlooking Red Square.

Hammer left the Soviet Union in the early 1930s after Stalin decided all foreign businessmen should leave. But he was allowed to take with him a vast collection of art treasures of the Czarist aristocracy appraised at $1 million—launching him in his art business. Items for the Hammer Collection continued to flow from Moscow through the 1930s. Hammer's dealings with the USSR stopped after World War II. In 1955, he bought Occidental, an unprofitable company until 1961 when it found the second largest natural gas field in California. He entered the fertilizer business and returned to the Soviet Union in 1961, finally negotiating a $20 million fertilizer contract for Occidental in 1972, once again becoming the Kremlin's most favored American businessman. In 1985, after five years of negotiations, he closed a $500 million deal with China to help them increase their coal production.

Hammer first married Olga von Root, a Russian, in 1927 (one son), and then Angela Zevely in 1943. He married his current wife, Frances Barrett, in

1956. Known as extremely generous as well as industrious, he's donated millions to educational institutions and cancer research. (In 1985 he donated $1 million to New York City's Metropolitan Museum of Art to refurbish their Arms and Armory department, and in 1988 he was chairman for a huge gala raising money for the American Cancer Society). "I like to make money in order to give it away," says Hammer, whose wealth is estimated at more than $200 million. To keep in touch with his various international interest, he travels a half-million miles a year in his N1 OXY, a Boeing 727 jet transformed into a personal salon. His autobiography *Hammer: Witness to History* was released in 1987.

Lionel Hampton

"That nun was little, but she sure had hard hands!" he says about his first instructor on the snare drum, a Dominican sister who rapped him on the knuckles if he used his left hand to set the beat. The frenetic jazz showman has worn out a good many pair of drumsticks since those days, not to mention mallets for the vibraharp ("vibes") the instrument that brought him fame. Associated with Louis Armstrong and Benny Goodman during the golden days of the big bands, he has in the years since toured the world with his own jazz ensembles and riffed his way to the top of many music polls. He's also the only male ever saluted with an honorary membership in Hadassah.

Lionel Leo Hampton was born 20 April 1913 in Birmingham Ala., and raised by his grandparents in Chicago. He made his public performing debut banging the big drum with the Chicago *Defender's* Newsboys Marching Band and at 15 had a job on the West Coast with Reb Spike's Sharps and Flats. He helped break the color barrier and made jazz history in 1936 when he joined the Benny Goodman Quartet and toured and recorded with it for four years before launching his own group. The Hamp has appeared in many movies (starting with Bing Crosby's *Pennies from Heaven* in 1938), invented his own two-finger piano style, and written many jazz classics, most notably the jumping "Flyin' Home." Considering himself more agile with his fingers than with his vocal cords, he let his wife, Gladys Riddle, do all his business talking for him from the time of their marriage in 1936 until her death in 1971. Though he is now a committed Christian Scientist, Hamp has found "a spiritual home" in Israel and even has the nickname "The Great Rabbi of Jazz."

In the 1980s, in a White House celebration saluting Hampton's more than fifty years in music, Ronald Reagan lauded his "courage" and "decency" and observed that "his talent and hard work have made him one of the most respected musicians in America." Invited to the White House by a total of six presidents and the recipient of six honorary degrees, he's also proud of the Harlem housing development which bears his name. In 1986 his album *Sentimental Journey* was released, and in 1987 he played Carnegie Hall with Frank Sinatra.

Tom Hanks

With the face of a teasing little boy who just put a whoopie cushion on a chair, Tom Hanks displays playful, dry, quick-witted comic sense that has helped skyrocket him to the forefront of the new generation of comic actors. Since the premiere of the sitcom "Bosom Buddies" in 1980, Hanks has been in demand. Although the show about two struggling advertising men who dress in drag to live in a low-budget women's hotel only lasted two seasons, it proved to be a showcase for his comedic talents. "I enjoyed working in television," he said. "Sure, the pace is hectic, but the work has substance as long as you keep mentally stimulated." After the release of the TV movie "Mazes and Monsters" in 1982, Hanks made the transition to movies. His first film was 1980's *He Knows You're Alone*, and his first box office smash was as a young man in love with a mermaid in the 1984 Ron Howard film *Splash*. Howard sees Hanks as "a terrific leading man, like Jack Lemmon or James Stewart . . . funny guys who make you care." Joe Dante, director of Hanks' film *The 'Burbs*, also says Hanks is "definitely in the mold of Jimmy Stewart or Jack Lemmon."

Since *Splash* Hanks has appeared in *Bachelor Party* (1984), *The Man with One Red Shoe* (for which Hanks learned to play the violin; 1985), *Volunteers*, (with John Candy; 1985), *The Money Pit*, a Speilberg production directed by Richard Benjamin and co-starring Shelley Long (1986), *Nothing in Common* (where Hanks had to deal with his mother divorcing his father, played by Jackie Gleason; 1986), *Every Time We Say Goodbye* (1986), and opposite Dan Aykroyd in *Dragnet* (1987). His next movie, the 1987 Penny Marshall box office hit *Big* (1988 Golden Globe Award, Best Actor), could have been written for the star. His role as a thirteen-year-old boy who makes a wish and wakes up the next morning in a man's body won Hanks widespread acclaim. After playing a stand-up comic opposite Sally Field in David Seltzer's *Punchline*, the indefatiguable Hanks completed two films for 1989 release: *The 'Burbs* (a suspense-comedy directed by Joe Dante) and *Turner and Hooch* (a Disney production). "Hanks is an actor capable of acting funny, rather than funny acting," says producer Larry Brezner. "He's now proving himself as one of the country's most versatile actors." His latest film is *Joe Versus the Volcano* (1990) with Meg Ryan.

Born 2 July 1956 in Oakland, California, Hanks started acting in high school. Even though he was bitten by the comedy bug ("I was always trying to stuff myself into lockers—crazy things like that"), Hanks was inspired to pursue serious acting after seeing a production of *The Iceman Cometh* while attending college in San Francisco. Studying acting at California State University in Sacramento, Hanks performed in *The Cherry Orchard*, directed by Vincent Dowling. As luck would have it, Dowling was also the resident director of the Great Lakes Shakespeare Festival in Cleveland and invited Hanks to intern with the classical company. In his first season, Hanks made his professional debut as Grunico in *The Taming of the Shrew*, followed the next season by *The Two Gentlemen from Verona*, which earned him The Cleveland Critics Award for Best Actor. At the end of the second season Hanks moved to New York where he appeared in *The Mandrake* at the Riverside Shakespeare Co. Following his third and final season in Cleveland, Hanks returned to New York to make his first feature film, *He Knows You're Alone*, before returning to the stage in *Taming of the Shrew* in New York and *The Dollmaker* in Los Angeles. It was during one of his stints in New York that he learned of the auditions for a new sitcom. Impressing the producers, the classically trained Hanks landed the role on "Bosom Buddies," left the stage for the little screen, and returned to his first love, comedy.

Tom has two children from previous marriages; he married Rita Wilson in 1988. They live in his native California.

Bill Hanna and Joe Barbera

"The Sultans of Saturday Morning," as the *Hollywood Reporter* calls them, comprise one of America's biggest exports, for one cartoon or another of their 200 series is broadcast every hour of every day in some part of the world. "The most important thing to keep in mind is never to play down to kids," says Joseph Barbera. "That's the worst thing you can do in this business. . . . Do you think Yogi Bear (one of the H-B team's creations) would have been successful if he played down to kids?" Barbera then cites Yogi's upbeat respect for young TV viewers' vocabularies. "When the ranger says, 'Please don't make trouble,' Yogi responds with, 'I'm sorry but I'm a non-conformist type of bear.'"

The cartoon studio team that disdains saccharine characters has been a producing unit since 1937 when at Metro-Goldwyn-Mayer the two men developed an ongoing cartoon feud between a cat and mouse for between-movies entertainment. "Tom and Jerry" (winners of seven Academy Awards) launched the successful union of William Denby Hanna (born in Melrose, N.M., in 1910) and Joseph Roland Barbera (born in New York City in 1916) when they came up with the idea of creating comedic conflict between natural enemies. (Recalls Hanna: "We almost decided on a dog and a fox before we hit on the idea of using a cat and mouse.") Since striking out on their own when the major film studios dropped animated shorts in 1957, the duo has gathered the artists, producers, directors, camerapersons, soundpersons, etc., who've given the TV world "The Flintstones," "Casper the Ghost," "The Jetsons," "The Smurfs," and "Huckleberry Hound." Despite Barbera's assertions that "the name Hanna-Barbera will not guarantee" that networks will buy their shows, children's television critics find H-B's Saturday morning stranglehold far too monopolistic. More of a problem to "the cartoonists who own Saturday morning" are the critics who have complained of too much violence in the H-B products. Unfortunately, the statistical tally of violent acts makes no distinction between Fred Flintstone stumbling over a dinosaur bone and Superman blowing up an alien spaceship, a situation that frustrates the partners. Barbera looks back to the good old/bad old "Tom and Jerry" days when Tom might get zonked with an anvil "and the mouse would peel him off the ground, and you'd hear it like a Band-Aid, right? But the cat was in perfect condition in the next sequence. We can't do that stuff anymore. They tell me it's not good for kids to see. I don't understand what they're talking about."

Daryl Hannah

She is as versatile as she is talented. She has assumed a variety of roles ranging from a mermaid in the hit comedy *Splash,* to a lovestruck astronomer in *Roxanne* to an upwardly mobile interior decorator lacking in scruples in *Wall Street.* Her talent goes beyond the big screen. Daryl has studied extensively in theatre, and has appeared on television as well.

Daryl Hannah was born in 1960 in Chicago, Illinois, and began studying acting at the Goodman Theatre. In 1978, before she even graduated from high school, she made her film debut with a small part in *The Fury.* Upon finishing high school, Daryl moved to Los Angeles where she attended U.C.L.A., and studied under Stella Adler. Within a few short years, she was being cast in starring roles in feature films such as *The Final Terror* (1981), *Summer Lovers* (1982), *Blade Runners* (1982), *Reckless* (1984), *Splash* (1984), *The Pope of Greenwich Village* (1984), *The Clan of the Cave Bear* (1986), *Legal Eagles* (1986), *Roxanne* (1987), *Wall Street* (1988), *High Spirits* (1988), and *Steel Magnolias* (1989). Her television appearances include a role in the successful telefilm *Paper Dolls* (1982).

Tall, lean and physically fit, in her spare time Daryl enjoys dancing, swimming, and diving. Currently single, she has frequently been seen around New York City with John F. Kennedy, Jr.

Keith Haring

"It seemed obvious to me when I saw the first empty subway panel that this was the perfect situation. . . . I remember noticing a panel in the Times Square station and immediately going above-ground and buying chalk. After the first drawing, things just fell into place." Thus does Keith Haring, "the clown prince of the graffiti scene," explain the launching of his career as New York's most prolific and celebrated underground artist. Since the early 1980s, his on-the-run drawings of radiant babies, barking dogs, and zapping spacecraft have been a familiar sight to riders on the IRT, BMT and IND and, above-ground, his dancing creations of "goofy cheerfulness" have been star attractions in galleries from SoHo to Los Angeles and Amsterdam to Australia, as well as on an eighteen-foot-high wall at the 1983 Whitney Biennial. He has also made his mark on magazine covers (*Vanity Fair, The Paris Review*), a David Bowie album, and stage sets (*Interrupted River Ballet,* 1987). He was honored in April 1989 at the Night of 100 Parties, hosted by FAIRPAC (Friends & Associates of Individual Rights). In 1986, he opened the Pop Shop, a retail outlet in Manhattan with many products bearing his imagery. Due to this store's success, another Pop Shop opened in Tokyo in 1988.

Born in Kutztown, Pennsylvania in 1959, Keith Haring has been drawing since the age of four—encouraged by his dad who "would entertain me by inventing cartoon animals." After a brief stint at a commercial art school in Pittsburgh, he headed, at twenty, for New York to enroll in the School of Visual Arts. It was, he says, "a time when the most beautiful paintings being shown were on wheels—on trains—paintings that traveled to you instead of vice versa." Immediately attracted to this moveable art, he was impressed by "the obvious mastery of drawing and color, the scale, the pop imagery, the commitment to drawing worthy of risk, and the direct relationship between artist and audience." He began his own down-under labors of love a year or so later and although his career on the outside has skyrocketed, the subway is still his favorite place to draw. Among the risks he himself has experienced in executing literally thousands of drawings: "I have been caught many times. Some cops have given me a $10 ticket, some have handcuffed me and taken me in." But his relationship with the NYPD hasn't been all bad. "More than once," Haring says, "I've been taken to a station handcuffed by a cop who realized, much to his dismay, that the other cops in the precinct are my fans and were anxious to meet me and shake my hand."

Mark Harmon

He was dubbed "The Sexiest Man Alive (1986)" by *People* Magazine and thrust into the national spotlight. After years of toiling on television and in films, Mark Harmon was suddenly a hot household name. The 6 foot, 170-lb. actor with brown hair and blue eyes adorned magazine covers along with television and movie screens. His easygoing style coupled with his "All-American" good looks sold America on him as he pitched beer-making in a series of Coors Beer commercials. Although his fame may have seemed sudden, it was not unexpected. Rather, with Harmon's background, it seemed preordained.

Mark Harmon was born 2 September 1951 in Burbank, California, the son of football player/broadcaster Tom Harmon and actress Elyse Knox. The family also includes Mark's sister, Kelly Harmon, a top spokesmodel, and Mark's niece, actress Tracy Nelson. Harmon's first brush with stardom came during his college days as an All-American quarterback at UCLA, where he graduated with a degree in communications in 1974. From 1975 through 1977, Harmon appeared in numerous guest shots on shows like "Adam-12," "Laverne & Shirley," and "Police Story." Television has always favored Harmon, casting him as a regular on four different series: the forgettable "Sam" (1978) and "240-Robert" (1979-1980), the romantic lead Fielding Carlyle on NBC's nighttime soap "Flamingo Road" (1980-1982), and the plum role of playboy Dr. Caldwell who eventually contracts AIDS on the acclaimed NBC series "St. Elsewhere" (1983-1986). Harmon also portrayed Sam the astronaut, on part of the controversial "Moonlighting" romantic triangle during the 1986-1987 season.

The industry recognized his potential as he earned an Emmy nomination for his performance in the 1977 movie-of-the-week "Eleanor and Franklin:

The White House Years." A variety of film and television roles were interwoven between his series committments, including "Comes a Horseman" (1978), "Little Mo" (1978), "Beyond The Poseidon Adventure" (1979), "Goliath Awaits" (1981), "Intimate Agony" (1983), the charming lead in "The Prince of Bel Air" (1986), and the Depression era farmer fighting for custody of his children in "After the Promise" (1987-1988). Harmon was featured in the miniseries "Centennial" (1978-1979) and "The Dream Merchants" (1980), but arguably his best role to date has been that of the executed serial killer Ted Bundy in the NBC miniseries "The Deliberate Stranger" (1986). Bundy was a definite departure from Harmon's usual good guy roles. His chilling portrayal of this real-life figure drew critical raves and excellent ratings. Its success helped Harmon secure the lead in three distinctly different feature films. He segued from the California cool teacher wooing Kirstie Alley in the comedy *Summer School* (1987), to the aging ballplayer returning home for his best friend Jodie Foster's funeral in the dramatic *Stealing Home* (1988), to the cop going up against Sean Connery in the police action adventure *The Presidio* (1988), and *Worth Winning* (1989).

Harmon married actress Pam Dawber on 21 March 1987 in Los Angeles. Their son, Sean Thomas, was born 25 April 1988. They reside in California while both pursue individual acting projects. Harmon's hobbies include carpentry; his most ambitious project was building his own home. With his devotion to family and the exciting direction that his career has been taking, it appears that Harmon won't have much time for crafting anything else.

Sheldon Harnick

Back in the early 1950s, shortly after his graduation from Northwestern University, Sheldon Harnick made a fairly comfortable living in his hometown of Chicago playing his violin in dance orchestras. One night he and his fiddle showed up for a gig with bandleader Xavier Cugat and, after an altercation, the cause of which has grown cloudy with the years, Harnick found himself without a job. He renounced fiddle-playing on the spot, headed for New York, and set out to make a career for himself as a songwriter. Not until a dozen years later did he re-establish professional connections with his old instrument, and this time he wasn't playing it but writing songs about it. The year was 1964. The occasion was the opening of a smash hit musical for which he wrote the lyrics. Its title was *Fiddler on the Roof*.

The trail from Chicago to Broadway had only one minor detour—to the upstate resort of Green Mansions, where Harnick spent some time polishing his craft writing musical revues for the summer visitors. He got his feet wet on Broadway with the song "The Boston Beguine" in *New Faces of 1952* and provided material for *Two's Company* and the *Shoestring Revues*. Then in 1956 he met composer Jerry Bock and a new chapter began. The two men decided to become a team—Bock on music, Harnick on words—and they hit the jackpot their second time out with *Fiorello!*, which in 1960 won them a Pulitzer. In 1960 they served up *Tenderloin*, in 1963 *She Loves Me*, in 1964 *Fiddler*, their biggest hit to date, which played all over the world, and in 1970, *The Rothschilds*. Harnick later collaborated with Leonard Bernstein in *Rex* (1976) and with Peter Brooks in *Carmen*.

Born 30 April 1924, Harnick has been married three times, the second time in 1962 to the performer Elaine May (they divorced a year later), the third time to Margery Grey in 1965. He was honored by the Northwood Institute for Advanced Studies in Theatrical Arts with the "Achievement of the Arts Award" in 1986.

Valerie Harper

Best known for the irrepressible character "Rhoda Morganstern," Valerie Harper has enjoyed a long and varied career in show business spanning the worlds of dance, theater, television, and film.

Born 22 August 1940 in Suffern, New York, Harper made her professional debut in the corps de ballet at Radio City Music Hall. Musical comedy captured her interest while performing on Broadway in *Li'l Abner*, leading her to study acting with Marcy Tarcai and John Cassavetes' workshop. She continued her dancing while studying, appearing in major stage productions of *Take Me Along* with Jackie Gleason, *Wildcat* with Lucille Ball, and *Subways Are for Sleeping* with Orson Bean and Carol Lawrence. Eventually she became involved with Paul Sills' Second City Troupe and developed her skills by performing in nightclubs, summer stock, and regional theater, including the prestigious Seattle Repertory Company. Live performances included roles in Carl Reiner's *Something Different* and Paul Sills' productions of Ovid's *Metamorphosis* and the Tony Award-winning *Story Theatre*.

Television has given Harper her greatest recognition as "Rhoda" and brought her popularity and awards for her efforts. The character debuted on "The Mary Tyler Moore Show" in 1970 and earned her three consecutive Emmy Awards for Outstanding Performance by an Actress in a Supporting Role (in 1970/1971, 1971/1972, 1972/1973). Supporting turned to lead as "Rhoda" premiered as an "MTM" spinoff in 1974. The hit show lasted five years, earning Harper another Emmy—this time as Best Television Actress in a Comedy or Musical (1974/1975). Harper has also been honored with a Golden Globe Award in 1975, the Golden Apple Award from the Hollywood Women's Press Club, Harvard's Hasty Pudding "Woman of the Year" Award, and the Photoplay Gold Medal Award. After "Rhoda's" departure, television continued to welcome Harper's presence. She starred in movie-of-the-weeks for all three networks, ranging from light comedy to serious drama. They included "Drop Out Mother," "Strange Voices," "The Execution," "Farrell for the People," "Don't Go to Sleep" with Ruth Gordon, "Invasion of Privacy," "When The Loving Stops," and the Paul Newman-directed "The Shadow Box." Harper also starred in the Jim Brooks'-scripted "Thursday's Game" with Gene Wilder and Ellen Burstyn and the special "The Night of 100 Stars." Feature films explored Harper's comedic side with roles in *Blame It on Rio*, *Chapter Two*, *The Last Married Couple in America*, and *Freebie and the Bean*. Returning to her theater background, Harper toured in *Agnes of God* and still occasionally returns to the Paul Sills' Co. in Los Angeles to perfect her improvisational skills.

Attuned to the needs of less fortunate people, Harper devotes much of her time to the Hunger Project, whose goal is to end world hunger in this century. She is one of the founders of LIFE (Love Is Feeding Everyone), dedicated to ending hunger in Los Angeles, and works with the End Hunger Network, Save the Children, Africare, Oxfam, and the Santa Monica Rape treatment center as well as actively supporting women's rights issues.

Harper marked her return to situation comedy in 1985 with "Valerie," a show she helped create. Her success was marred when Lorimar Telepictures abruptly fired her. A legal battle ensued, and she eventually won a substantial monetary award in court.

Divorced from first husband Dick Schaal, the 5'6" brown-haired, green-eyed actress married Tony Cacciotti 8 April 1987. They adopted a daughter, Christine, and the three reside in California. Future plans include a comedy series pilot for MTM Productions.

Michael Harrington

"Tens of millions of Americans are, at this very moment, maimed in body and spirit existing at levels beneath those necessary for human decency." In his 1963 book, *The Other America: Poverty in the United States*, this ardent Socialist expressed his moral outrage at what he described as America's "invisible poor"—the blighted underside of the affluent society. Credited with being the prime impetus behind President Lyndon Johnson's war on poverty, the book helped make poverty a major priority of national concern in the 1960s and transformed its "nuts-and-bolts activist" author into one of the best known political evangelists in the U.S. "America is a class society," he observed in *Harper's* in 1981. "Though an enormous advance over medieval caste structures, our class structure has a similar consequence, namely an unconscionable disparity of wealth and power." In the decline of smokestack industries—which formerly provided a pathway from lower to middle class status—he sees a permanently locked in poverty class.

Born 24 February 1928 into an "Irish New Dealer" family in St. Louis, Michael Harrington was, by his own description, "a Taft conservative" until he signed on for a summer job project working with Arkansas sharecroppers. Cutting short his law studies at Yale, he headed for the Robert Hutchins-guided campus of the University of Chicago (M.A. 1949), and started on a social worker's career back in his hometown. In 1951, switching his base of operations to the Bowery, he joined Dorothy Day's *Catholic Worker* and began a schedule of "compulsive 16-hour days"—writing articles and speaking on civil rights, unionism, poverty and politics—which he still maintains. He has also toiled as an organizer for the Young Socialist League and as a researcher for the Fund for the Republic. He is married to *Village Voice* writer Stephanie Gervis (their son Alexander is named for their late friend, Alexander Calder). His books now include *The Accidental Century* (1965), *Toward a Democratic Left* (1968), *The Politics at God's Funeral, Taking Sides, The Next Left: The History of a Future*, and *The Long Distance Runner: An Autobiography*. He also serves as national co-chairman of the Democratic Socialists of America and is a professor of political science at Queens College in New York City.

Julie Harris

As a girl, Julie Harris once recalled, "I was very plain, all knobby knees." Despite her mother's intense ambition, Julie was not a glossy deb type. "I had some dates," she says, "but never the ones I wanted . . . the school heroes. . . ." And so she "escaped into acting." "The movies became almost a sickness to me," Julie has said. Sometimes she sat staring at the silver screen of Vivien Leigh and Joan Crawford "all day Saturday and all day Sunday." And at night she lived in the fantasy of becoming "a great star like Bernhardt." Years later, though she lacked the flamboyant life style of Madame Sarah, her special brand of stage magic made her one of the most versatile and widely acclaimed actresses in the American theatre, which is precisely why she was inducted into the Theatre Hall of Fame.

Julie Ann Harris was born 2 December 1925 in Grosse Point, Mich., the daughter of an investment banker. She arrived on Broadway via circuitous routing, which included the finishing schools of Miss Wheeler and Miss Hewitt, as well as Yale Drama School and the Actors Studio. She made her debut in *It's a Gift*, and went on to win more than 20 awards (including two Emmys, five Tonys) for performances in such diverse stage, film, and TV vehicles as *A Member of the Wedding*, *I Am a Camera* (her first Tony), *The Lark* (five top awards, including a Tony), *Victoria Regina*, *East of Eden*, *Little Moon of Alban*, *The Power and the Glory*, *Forty Carats* (Tony), *And Miss Reardon Drinks a Little*, *The Last of Mr. Lincoln* (1973 Tony), and *The Belle of Amherst* (1976 Tony). Beginning in the 1981-1982 television season, she became a regular on the CBS primetime series "Knots Landing." Her character married (actor Red Buttons) and she departed the show in 1988, with the possibility of returning at any time. She also appeared in two telefilms "The Woman He Loved" (1988) and "Too Good to Be True" (1988) in addition to the Sigourney Weaver film *Gorillas in The Mist* (1988).

Mount Holyoke College awarded Harris an honorary Doctor of Fine Arts degree in 1976. She had earlier received honorary degrees from Smith, LaSalle, Ithaca, and Wayne State, among other institutions. Harris was brought up an Episcopalian, but after her confirmation she did not attend formal church services. "I don't hesitate to say that I found God in the theatre," she told an interviewer for *The Christian Science Monitor* in 1975. In 1977 Julie Harris married William Carroll, a writer. She had two earlier marriages, in 1946 to Jay Julien, a lawyer and producer whom she divorced in 1954, and to stage manager Manning Gurian from 1954 to 1967 (one son, Peter Allen Gurian). Reading 19th-century American literature is one of Harris' favorite pastimes, as well as tennis and cooking.

Richard Harris

"Why should a man know exactly who he is?" asks Richard Harris. "I've no idea who I am. I'm five people, and each of them is fighting the other four." He is so aggressively professional, with the tongue (and capacity) of a Behan and the talent of a latter-day Olivier, that his offstage antics have brought him precipitously close to being tagged as that most loathsome of Gaels, "a professional Irishman." But by sheer force of personality and staggering versatility, he manages to disarm his critics and fortify his friends. Born 1 October 1930 in Limerick ("When I'm in trouble, I'm an Irishman. When I turn in a good performance I'm an Englishman"), he rejected a job with his family's flour mill business to pursue acting studies at London Academy (having been turned down by the August Royal Academy of Dramatic Art). While still in school he produced and acted in a production of Brendan Behan's *The Quare Fellow*, and lost every penny of his investment.

Following appearances with Joan Littlewood's Theater Workshop in *A View from the Bridge* and *Macbeth*, he turned to the screen; his first part was in *Shake Hands with the Devil*, a film starring Jimmy Cagney about the IRA, followed by *The Guns of Navarone* and *Mutiny on the Bounty*. But it wasn't until his stunning performance in 1963 as an inarticulate rugby player in *This Sporting Life* (Oscar nomination) that he reached the pinnacle as a dramatic actor. He turned to musicals in 1967 as King Arthur in *Camelot*, and that in turn led to a singing career ("no Irishman need be taught to sing"), resulting in, among others, a haunting version of "MacArthur Park." He has mixed a film career (*Cromwell, The Hero, A Man Called Horse*) with a successful concert career, combining songs and poetry. (In 1988 he appeared on stage at Carnegie Hall, performing with The Chieftains). "Poetry is bred in my loins," admits Harris. "I can't remember when I first started writing it, maybe when I was 5 or 6, but I only began writing it down recently." His book of poetry, *In the Membership of My Days* (1974), was recorded with his sons assisting in the reading. Although he continues his devotion to poetry, he received good notices from the literary reviewers for his 1982 thriller, *Honor Bound*.

Originally taking over the role of King Arthur for his ailing friend, Richard Burton, Harris' triumphant national tour in *Camelot* (climaxing in Broadway and television productions) was received with glowing notices. When Frank Rich did not feed the flame in his 1981 New York *Times* review, Harris snorted: "He doesn't deserve a job. He couldn't even get a job with the Liverpool *Legend*. Send him off to the Cardiff *Courier*." He reprised his role in *Camelot* in 1988 for another stage production.

"I want to do *Hamlet* before I'm too old, to do *Coriolanus, Macbeth, Oedipus*, Marlowe's *Edward II*. I'm going to spend the rest of my acting career basically in the theatre now," admitted Harris in a 1982 interview. "I don't know what's ahead but the night and the fog. When I was coming along in the mid-50s, I used to steal sugar lumps to live on. Remember I never quit. They haven't heard the last of Richard Harris, and neither have you." In 1989 he filmed *The Three Penny Opera* with Raul Julia.

George Harrison

When you next get the card in "Trivial Pursuit" asking which of the Beatles is the youngest, don't just answer George. Tell your competition that in 1960, when the group was just a wee thing playing at Liverpool's Cavern

Club (first as the Moondogs, then the Silver Beatles) and they left for a season at Hamburg, Germany's Indra Club (they were required to play eight hours a night), George, still only 17, was deported for being underage.

Born 25 February 1943 in Liverpool, a bus driver's son, he says he "bought a guitar from a schoolmate—I was 12 or 13, I think, but the trouble was I couldn't play it. Then I started fooling around with one of the screws and it fell apart and I put the thing in the closet." He quit the Liverpool Art Institute in his mid-teens to become an electrician's assistant. His illustrious electrical career soon came to a halt; he was in the habit of blowing everything up. Of the Beatles and their earliest days he says: "Oh, we never starved. The fact is, we were all working class, all the families. We never had a lot of things, any of the Beatles, but I can't stand all those stories about us all as scruffs with no clothes on our backs." (Harrison bristles easily. When Sir Noel Coward attempted the putdown "Delightful lads, absolutely no talent," George sucked in an outraged breath and retorted, "He's just jealous because he never wrote anything that ever lived.") He was the first of the Beatles to turn to the East for inspiration (yoga, Maharishi Mahesh Yogi, etc.) and he flipped not only over the philosophy ("Once you've seen the truth, life becomes so simple") but over the music. He studied sitar with Ravi Shankar and introduced the first sitar riff into the Beatle's sounds on the 1965 recording of "Norwegian Wood." A top performer in his own right, his solo work includes the 1970 triple album *All Things Must Pass*, the single "My Sweet Lord," *Bangladesh* (with Ravi Shankar he organized top rock performers to play at benefits for the relief of poverty stricken Bangladesh), *Dark Horse, Somewhere in England, Gone Troppo, Cloud 9* and the single/video smash "Got My Mind Set On You."

Before the Liverpool wonders called it quits in 1971, their records sold more than 250 million copies. They made three films—*Hard Day's Night, Help* and *Let It Be*—and lent their names and voices to a fourth, *Yellow Submarine*. Divorced from his first wife, Patti Boyd, in 1977 (they were married in 1966), in 1978 he married Oliva Arias (one son Dhani born that same year). He has been involved in the production of several films including *Time Bandits, Monty Python Live at the Hollywood Bowl, The Missionary, The Life of Brian, Mona Lisa, How To Get Ahead in Advertising,* and *The Raggedy Rawney*. In 1988 he was inducted into the Rock 'n' Roll Hall of Fame. Harrison lives in seclusion on a 35-acre estate near Henley-on-Thames in England. In addition to his solo endeavors, he was instrumental in forming the band "The Traveling Wilburys" with fellow rock legends Tom Petty, Bob Dylan, Jeff Lynne, and the late Roy Orbison. The group spawned the hit single/video "End of the line."

Rex Harrison

"When legendary performers like Rex Harrison . . . take command of the stage, they seem to do so by divine right," says one critic. A passion for theatre which began at age seven (after seeing a Christmas pantomime, he rushed home to perform it again and again) developed into a brilliant career. Harrison is known as "the greatest actor of light comedy in the world." His 1984 performance as Captain Shotover in Shaw's *Heartbreak House* was considered by many critics as his finest work. And no one can forget the caustic elocution professor Henry Higgins (*My Fair Lady*) whom Harrison brought to life first on Broadway in 1957 (Tony Award), on the screen in 1964 (Academy Award), and back on Broadway in 1981. He returned to Broadway in 1985 with Claudette Colbert in Frederick Lonsdale's light comedy, *Aren't We All*, and appeared on the London stage in *The Admirable Crichton* in 1988. Trying his hand at a television miniseries, he starred with Amy Irving in "Anastasia: The Story of Anna Anderson" for the 1986-1987 season.

Named Reginald Cary Harrison when he was born in Huyton, England, 5 March 1908, the actor changed his name to Rex in the 1920s when be began impressing audiences in London's West End in such sophisticated comedies as Noel Coward's *Design for Living* and Terence Rattigan's *French Without Tears*. He first appeared on the New York stage in *Sweet Aloes* in 1936 and subsequently starred in John Van Druten's *Bell, Book and Candle* and as Henry VIII in Maxwell Anderson's *Anne of the Thousand Days*, a role which earned him his first Tony Award. Film credits include *Cleopatra* (Oscar nomination), *Major Barbara, Blithe Spirit,* and *Dr. Dolittle*. For years he feuded with the press because he did not like interviews—"I am not a shy man, but I prefer to be a private man." Harrison has now mellowed and has even sanctioned photographs. His second wife, Lilli Palmer, once remarked, "Of course he was selfish . . . but he was always absolutely devoted to learning his trade." And Harrison himself, who finally admitted he just wasn't suited to Shakespeare ("I think Shakespeare's comedies are absolutely abominable"), has quipped, "I find it less difficult than some actors to be irascible without being unpleasant." Now married to his sixth wife Mercia Tinker (past wives include the late actresses Kay Kendall and Rachel Roberts), he seems finally happy; he has dedicated a book of poetry to her—" . . . (she) has taught me the art of living and loving at last."The Gentleman Actor says that what keeps him fresh is "concentration, total concentration, creating another detail. Good acting is an accumulation of details. But I usually give only one or two performances a week that come up to my standards. I'm a chronically dissatisfied perfectionist."

Kitty Carlisle Hart

Best known to generations of television views as the soignee but "always overdressed" imposter-spotter on "To Tell the Truth" (broadcast from 1956 through 1977), she was appointed to her second five-year term as Chairman of the New York State Council on the Arts in 1982. Once admonished by her mother to marry a prince or learn to play one on the stage, she spotted her prince among men in Pulitzer Prize-winning playwright-director Moss Hart, whom she married 10 August 1946. Active on the ladies' club lecture circuit since 1959, Kitty relates "I tell them that, with a soupcon of courage and a dash of self-discipline, one can make a small talent go a long way." Her "poise and polish," as well as her contralto, first cited in her Broadway debut (1933), were still very much in evidence in her 1983 stint as a replacement for Dina Merrill in the Broadway revival of Rodgers' and Hart's *On Your Toes*.

Born Catherine Conn on 3 September 1914 in New Orleans, she was educated in Switzerland and Paris before beginning two seasons as a debutante in Rome at age 15, thrust on the marriage market early by the Depression. With no prince in the offing, she went on to study at the London School of Economics and Royal Academy of Dramatic Arts. In New York, Kitty Carlisle (the surname selected from the N.Y. telephone directory) debuted on Broadway portraying Prince Orlofsky in *Champagne, Sec* (1933), an English-language concoction based on Strauss' *Die Fledermaus*. Moving to Hollywood, she appeared with Bing Crosby in two pictures at Paramount, then the Marx Brothers classic *A Night at the Opera* (1936) at M-G-M, and *Hollywood Canteen* (1944) for Warners. After her marriage, her performing duties were as wife, mother (Cathy and Christopher), and secretary-companion in the Hart household until an NBC panel show "Who Said That?" in the early 1950s. There followed "To Tell the Truth," lecture tours and moderating "Women on the Move" in 1964. Widowed in 1961, in December, 1966, she was back rehearsing Prince Orlofsky, this time for her debut in the Metropolitan Opera's 1967 production of *Die Fledermaus*. She also appeared in the Met's series of Operas in the Park during the summer of 1973. Kitty directs her very social life and her duties in the arts from her East Side residence and her West Side office. In her wide range of public service activities, she has taken particular interest in the role of women in society, chairing New York's Statewide Conference on Women and serving as the appointed Special Consultant to the Governor on Women's Opportunities. Most appropriately, she was designated Woman of the Year by the United Service Organizations in 1975. In 1988 her inner most secrets were revealed when she released her book *Kitty: An Autobiography*.

Mary Hart

She's perky, pretty, wholesome and ambitious. Possessing an All-American, Doris Day kind of attitude, Mary confesses, "Sometimes I must seem like the world's biggest cornball, but that's who I am, and what I do." Well, corny or not, this acclaimed singer, dancer, actress and former beauty queen—with the 2 million dollar legs (insured by Lloyds of London)—has won her way into America's hearts.

Mary Hart was born in Sioux Falls, South Dakota on 8 November 1950, the daughter of a homemaker and an executive with a farm equipment manufacturer. She developed a love for Broadway show tunes and classical music at an early age. While still a young child, Mary and her family moved to Europe, where they lived for 11 years. Upon returning, Mary attended a Lutheran college in Sioux Falls. In 1970, Mary entered and won the Miss South Dakota Beauty Pagent. A few years later, she began her career teaching high school English while teaching piano and doing community theatre on the side. Shortly afterward (while still teaching), she was approached to host a daily talk show on cable television. Her talent was quickly discovered, and she was asked to host a daily program on a network affiliate in Sioux Falls. Moving on, Mary took a position hosting radio and TV shows in Cedar Rapids, Iowa, and later Oklahoma City, where she co-hosted as well as produced the popular daytime talk show "Danny's Day." Continuing to move up the entertainment ladder, Mary became the host of "PM Magazine" in Los Angeles, followed by the nationally televised but short-lived "Regis Philbin Show." By now, her talent was known nationally, and she was asked to join "Entertainment Tonight" as the weekend co-host in 1981. Within weeks she was moved to the daily segment of the show. Her other television credits include the miniseries "Hollywood Wives," "Circus of the Stars," and guest appearances on "Good Morning America" and "David Letterman," in addition to hosting the Tournament of Roses Parade and the Macy's Thanksgiving Day Parade, for both of which she received an Emmy nomination. Mary made her musical debut on ABC's "Dolly," and has since been heard singing the National Anthem at Dodger Stadium, and before a Lakers-Celtics game. In addition Mary has been a headliner dancer and singer, making her Vegas debut in 1988 at the Golden Nugget as well as performing at Resorts International in Atlantic City. Hart is also part owner of the Los Angeles video production company Custom's Last Stand.

Mary Hart wed Burt Sugarman on 8 April 1989. The couple reside in California.

Mariette Hartley

"I am comfortable with my life," Mariette Hartley has said. And well she should be. The Emmy Award-winning actress (for her guest starring role in "The Incredible Hulk") or stage, screen, and television has starred in everything from Shakespeare (*Measure for Measure* for the famed Joseph Papp "Shakespeare Festival in the Park" in New York), to feature films (Peckinpah's *Ride in the Country*), to television (as Claire Morton in the series "Peyton Place"), to stage (*Chemin De Fer*, co-starring Cronyn and Tandy). The multi-dimensional Hartley extended her credits by co-hosting the 1987 "CBS Morning Program", winning three CLIO Advertising Awards in 1979 through 1981 for her Polaroid commercials with James Garner, and singing in a summer stock production of *The King and I*, which led to her autobiographical one woman show, with comedy and music, that Hartley considers to be "a work in progress." In 1987, as a tribute to her various industry contributions, Hartley's star was installed on the Hollywood Walk of Fame.

Born 21 June 1940 in New York City, Hartley was bitten early by the "creative" bug. The pull to the theatre was too irresistible for her to consider doing anything else. At fifteen, Hartley won a full tuition drama scholarship at Carnegie Tech in Pittsburgh. When she was just sixteen, Hartley left school to appear in Chicago in *Merchant of Venice*, then went to New York for *Measure for Measure*, followed by a national tour with the Stratford Shakespeare Festival, which culminated with her first appearance in Los Angeles. Now bitten by the screen bug, Hartley tried Hollywood and Peckinpah signed her for her first film *Ride the High Country* opposite Randolph Scott and Joel McCrea before MGM grabbed her and signed her to a seven-year contract. Television soon followed. After her first exposure as Leslie Nielson's wife on "Peyton Place," Hartley was given her own series "The Hero," which folded after the first thirteen weeks. When she looks back, Hartley states, "It was a lovely series, but we were ten years ahead of our time." That original draw to the theatre was still pulling Hartley, so she returned to the stage in her first comedy, *Happiness Bench*, followed by the French farce *Chemin De Fer*. With her diversified talents it's not surprising that Hartley has a total of six Emmy nominations to her credit for "Rockford Files," two TV movies, and "Goodnight Beantown" plus a Golden Apple Award in 1979 from the Hollywood Woman's Press Club.

Married to French producer and director Patrick Boyriven and the mother of two, Sean (born in 1975) and Justine (born in 1978), Hartley was named the 1984 Outstanding Mother of the Year by the Mother's Day Committee. She is working on her autobiography and has formed her own production company, Maraday Productions, with her manager Arlene L. Dayton. The grandaughter of John B. Watson, internationally renowned psychiatrist who founded the school of psychology known as behaviorism, is also an active and dedicated supporter of a variety of humanitarian organizations (M.A.D.D., SOJURN, and the Children's Museum). Always in demand, Hartley says she is "comfortable with my life."

Lisa Hartman

Her short skirts, tight pants, and lace blouses have set fashion heads turning and men's hearts fluttering. She's played the daughter of a witch, a reincarnated singer, and a district attorney posing as a hooker. The TV and film roles keep rolling in, yet this actress prefers pursuing her dream goal. Lisa Hartman wants to crack the record chart; she would like a hit record. And why not? In 1977 her first album, *Lisa Hartman*, was released on CBS/Kirshner records and *Cash Box* claimed, "Ms. Hartman displays a talent and a poise far beyond her 19 years...." When her second album, *Hold On*, came out in 1979, *Billboard* chose her as a recommended pick, saying "She's a versatile, pleasing vocalist." Both albums established a select group of music fans for Lisa, but not the widespread acceptance she hoped to achieve. In the interim, Hartman struck gold in the TV medium and starred in her own series "Tabitha," her own ABC variety special, a five-hour miniseries of "Valley of the Dolls," and then landed a leading role in the CBS nighttime soap "Knots Landing" (1982) playing a rock-n-roll singer, Ciji Dunne. In this part, she was able to express her acting abilities alongside a record release. She says "the producers agreed to let me do the songs from my *Letterock* album, which had first been released by RCA in 1982. I loved playing Ciji, we both shared the same goal: to have a hit record." The public loved her portrayal of Ciji

Dunne too; when her character was killed off in the storyline, the writers resurrected Lisa in another role on the same show. An unusual TV twist!

Lisa Hartman was born in Houston, Texas on 1 June (circa 1956). Her father was an actor/singer and her mother a producer of television shows. She made her debut at the age of four, in her father's stage act. When she was seven, her family moved to New York City for a two-year period where Lisa was attracted to the Broadway lights. After graduating from the High School of Performing Arts, Lisa put together a nightclub act and was eventually spotted by producer Jeff Barry. Recent TV films include the mini-series "Roses Are for the Rich" (1986), about a woman's obsession for revenge, and "The Sex Tapes" (1988), where Hartman played a mini-skirted district attorney trying to find a murderer involved with homemade sexual video tapes. In 1984 she appeared in the motion picture re-make of *Where the Boys Are.*

Lisa remains single and resides in California, while pursuing her dreams as a singer. Her last album, *Til My Heart Stops* (1988), only dented the airwaves—not enough to satisfy Hartman. As she sang on her 1979 record, "Hold On I'm Comin'," with each release Lisa Hartman is coming closer to her dream.

Orrin Hatch

"I'm conservative and proud of it," declares this Mormon free-enterprise conservative who is one of the fair-haired boys of the New Right. Republican Senator Orrin G. Hatch helped steer Congress to the right on such key social issues as busing, abortion, and school prayer as chairman of the Senate's powerful Labor and Human Resources Committee. He held that position until 1986 when he was replaced by Edward Kennedy. He now holds the title of ranking minority member of Labor and Human Resources. One of the senator's finest moments in Washington came in May 1981, when he chaired hearings on his proposed Constitutional amendment outlawing preferential treatment in hiring. His evenhandedness made him seem less the villainous reactionary. It represented the "new" Hatch who had replaced the aggressive, hard-nosed Senate freshman. Now a recognized leader, Hatch told *Business Week* he realized he should "consider the needs of all kinds of constituents." Senator Hatch has been rated as one of the 10 most effective senators by columnist Jack Anderson. He's also been dubbed "Mr. Free Enterprise," "Guardian of Small Business," and "Mr. Constitution," and is the author of many articles published in general interest magazines and law journals, as well as books.

Born 22 March 1934 in Pittsburgh, Pa., Hatch was reared in a poor, working class neighborhood. Raised as a Mormon, Hatch attended Brigham Young University in Utah and eventually moved to the state to start a law practice. With a zero recognition factor, Hatch decided to run for Congress in 1976—and took the lion's share of the vote. Hatch and his wife, Elaine Hansen of Newton, Utah, have six children and two grandchildren. The senator enjoys sports, music, history, poetry, and literature.

Mark Hatfield

A near-pacifist on defense issues who routinely casts "protest votes" against military spending, this Republican Senator from Oregon was co-sponsor of the Hatfield-McGovern amendment to end the Vietnam War and in 1982 signed on as co-leader of the nuclear weapons freeze campaign in Congress. Clinging tenaciously to views that fly in the face of common opinion, almost alone in the Senate (like Oregon's late great Senate maverick, Wayne Morse), he argues outspokenly that American Mideast policy is tilted too far towards Israel. He moralizes about the importance of human rights as an emphasis in American foreign policy. Yet Hatfield's skill in placing personal friendship above ideological conflict has made him one of the most popular senators among colleagues. (A classic example is his close friendship with hawkish Mississippian John Stennis.) In 1981, Hatfield, the fifth ranking Republican, ascended to the chairmanship of the Senate Appropriations Committee, which carries a long tradition of collegiality and accommodation. A devout Baptist layman of the evangelical social action tradition (which stresses help to the poor and separation of church and state), Hatfield is motivated by his religious convictions. A strong advocate of volunteerism, over the years he has developed a roster of bills to encourage neighborhood-based social programs, and often tells churches that if each of them would take charge of a few poor families, the government welfare burden would almost vanish.

Born in Dallas, Ore., 12 July 1922, the son of a railroad construction blacksmith and a schoolteacher, Mark Hatfield grew up "a small-town kid and convinced isolationist" who was shocked into internationalism by his wartime naval experience at Iwo Jimo and Okinawa. He was a member of the first U.S. military team to enter Hiroshima, a month after the atom bomb demolished the city. Later, he recalls, "I saw men and women dying, literally, of starvation."

After the war, he plunged into politics in the Northwest while teaching political science at his alma mater, Willamette University (A.B., 1943), later collecting a master's degree in political science from Stanford (1948). Enjoying uninterrupted success in Oregon politics, Hatfield served in the state legislature (1951-57), then moved on to secretary of state (1957-59), two-term governor (1959-67), and to the U.S. Senate without one defeat. Senator from Oregon since 1967, he was re-elected in 1972, 1978, and 1984. A constant thorn in the government's defense buildup plans, Hatfield has led the opposition to the neutron bomb and MX missile, and in 1983 introduced an amendment against the militarization of outer space. He is author or coauthor of the books *The Causes of World Hunger* and *Freeze! How You Can Help Prevent Nuclear War* (both in 1982). Hatfield has been married since 1958 to Antoinette Kuzmanich, a former teacher. They have four children.

Goldie Hawn

On "Laugh In" in 1968 she "watched helplessly as her lines seem to flutter out of reach. She embodied the trusting excitement of a baby seeing a cat for the first time. She was a dumb blond, but she was 'learning.' she would surely get it right next time. She was irresistible." So chants Cathleen Schine who interviewed the star for *Vogue* in 1984.

Born Goldie Jean Hawn in Washington, D.C., 2 November 1945, she was named after a late great aunt whom she still regards as a guardian angel. ("I can remember almost all of my childhood, and all the memories are pleasant. There was no conflict, no push, and no competition in my family.") Studying drama at American University, she paid her tuition by operating a dance school. When she reached New York, she landed a job as a can-can dancer at the World's Fair. A depressing interlude of go-go dancing in cages led to a stint as a chorus girl in Las Vegas. ("It was the saddest time of my life. I woke up one morning with a hunch I would do better Los Angeles. I left right away.") She was hired for Rowan and Martin's "Laugh-In" after producer George Schlatter saw her in "Good Morning World," an ABC bomb.

She married Gus Trikonis in 1969 when she was a fledgling dancer in New York City and he a struggling movie-director. Their starving-in-a-garret existence was very romantic but the romance ceased when she was hired for "Laugh-In" and sudden stardom threw the relationship out of kilter. After four years of stresses and strains, the star and the would-be director agreed to divorce. In 1975 she married Bill Hudson of the Hudson Brothers comedy group; the couple had three children, Oliver, Kate, and Garry. That marriage fell apart, and today Goldie is raising her children and living with actor Kurt Russell (one child together, Wyatt, born 10 July 1986). Among her post-*Cactus Flower* (1969; Academy Award for Best Supporting Actress) films are *Butterflies Are Free* (1971), *Shampoo* (1975), *Foul Play* (1978), *Private Benjamin* (1980), *Best Friends* (1982), *Swing Shift* (1984), *Protocol* (1984), *Wildcats* (1986), *Overboard* (1987), and *Last Wish* (1988).

Helen Hayes

Already a legend in her lifetime, with *two* Broadway theatres named after her (when the first, on 46th Street, was razed in 1984 to make way for a new hotel, the second, on 44th Street, was christened immediately to honor "the first lady of the American theatre"), she has been hailed by producer Robert Whitehead as "a great actress because she is a great woman." And with applause ever roaring in her ears, she has said, "The greatest reward of acting is that one moment of miracle when you and the audience get together." Hayes' favorite tribute came from her playwright husband, the late Charles MacArthur. "She has," he said, "a star on her forehead."

Born Helen Hayes Brown in Washington, D.C., 10 October 1900, she attended dancing school to correct pigeon-toes. After *Dear Brutus* (1919) and *Clarence* (1920), she continued playing comedy ingenue roles "until," she sighs, "I was squeezing cuteness out of my greasepaint tubes and scooping charm out of my cold cream jars. It became a compulsion to get away from all that." She then began studying acting seriously ("acting talent is an instinct for understanding the human heart"), and scored enormous successes in *What Every Woman Knows* (1926), *Coquette* (1927), *Mary of Scotland* (1933), and later, *Mrs. McThing*, *The Skin of Our Teeth*, *The Glass Menagerie*, *Time Remembered*, *A Touch of the Poet*, *The Front Page*, and *Harvey*. Films include *The Sin of Madelon Claudet* (1931 Oscar), *Arrowsmith*, *A Farewell to Arms* (1932), *Anastasia* (1956), and *Airport* (1970, another Oscar). Although she won't name her favorite play ("It's like asking a mother which of her children is her favorite"), she has said of *Victoria Regina*, "It was a beautiful friendship." Her interpretation of O'Neill's *Long Day's Journey Into Night* (1971) garnered the following from New York *Times*' critic Walter Kerr: "The standing ovation she received at the performance I saw was in order, and not simply because she has spent a lifetime being Helen Hayes. It was Eugene O'Neil she was working for, first to last."

Since her retirement from the stage in 1971 (because of an allergic reaction to stage dust), Hayes has devoted her time to television, radio, writing and public service. Some of her TV performances include the series, "The Snoop Sisters" (with Mildred Natwick), "A Family Upside Down" (with Fred Astaire), "A Caribbean Mystery," and several documentaries, among them "Miles to Go Before We Sleep" (Peabody Award) and "No Place Like Home." Her books include *A Gift of Joy* (1965), *On Reflection* (1968), *Twice Over Lightly* (1971, in collaboration with Anita Loos), *Loving Life* (1987, with Marion Gladney), and *Where The Truth Lies* (1988).

In 1929 Helen Hayes met the fun-loving Charles MacArthur (*The Front Page*) at a cocktail party. He passed her some peanuts, with the much-quoted remark, "I wish these were emeralds." Their actress daughter, Mary, died of polio in 1949; their adopted son, James, is an actor (TV's "Hawaii Five-O"). Among her many honors was Helen Hayes' salute from the Kennedy Center in Washington for an "Extraordinary Lifetime of Contribution to American Culture Through the Performing Arts." In 1984, the U.S. Mint struck a commemorative gold coin bearing her likeness and in 1987 she was saluted in a special ceremony during which she placed her footprints and signature in cement on the sidewalk outside the theatre on West 44th Street (NYC) named in her honor. In 1988 she was presented with the National Medal of Arts by President Reagan at the White House.

Patty Hearst

"Despite the massive media coverage, people still don't know what actually happened. Enough time has passed that there's an emotional distance from the issues that allows the story to be told," says Patricia Hearst Shaw. The intimate psychological portrait of a young woman under extrordinary pressure, *Patty Hearst* reached the screen in 1988. The powerful film was based on Hearst's book *Every Secret Thing*, written with Alvin Moscow (Doubleday, 1982) and reissued as *Patty Hearst* in Avon paperback. "It's a personal story," says Hearst, "and I hope it will give people the feeling of what happened and how they might react in the same situation. I want people to understand what I experienced." The film, which opens with Patty's kidnapping and concludes prior to her prison sentence being commuted by President Carter, covers as director Paul Schrader says, "the event and the aftermath. Patty had to fight both the terrorists and the political-media establishment." Schrader calls the film "a real journey, an emotional rollercoaster. It's the story of how a person survives, a tribute to the resiliency of the individual."

Patty Hearst was born on 20 February 1954, the middle of five daughters of Randolph Anderson and Catherine Hearst and the granddaughter of William Randolph Hearst, legendary founder of the Hearst newspaper empire. She grew up in her family's house in Hillsborough. After convent schools in Menlo Park and Monterey she transferred to the exclusive Crystal Springs School for Girls in 1970 where she met Steven Weed, a recent graduate of Princeton and one of the school's math teachers. In 1971 she entered Menlo College, graduating with "Highest Honors." After a summer in Europe, she and Weed settled in Berkley where she worked for a semester in an Oakland department store. Plans to be married to Weed on 29 June 1974 were aborted when on 4 February 1974 Patty Hearst was abducted by members of the Symbionese Liberation Army. Over the next five years, she spent nineteen months with her captors, during which time she was emotionally traumatized and transformed into Tania—a self-professed urban guerilla; participated in a bank robbery; witnessed her own death on television; spent over a year as a fugitive in the political underground; was arrested by the FBI; was tried and convicted of bank robbery; and spent nearly 2 years in jail ending with her Presidential commutation on 1 February 1979. In the film the SLA is finally being brought to account, for which she is very pleased. (There was no kidnapping trial because two of her abductors pleaded guilty.) She recently told a reporter: "Finally the SLA has had its day in court. And it seems to me another of the ironies of this whole situation that Hollywood, of all places, did it. They produced an intelligent, artistic, and basically accurate piece of work that is finally my vindication."

Patty Hearst married Bernard Shaw, her former bodyguard, on 1 April 1979. Her friend Trish Tobin, daughter of the owner of the Hibernia Bank that Patty and the SLA robbed, served as her maid of honor. Today, Patricia and Bernard Shaw live with their two young daughters (Gillian Catherine Hearst and Lydia Marie) in Connecticut.

William Randolph Hearst, Jr.

Sixteen years after the death of newspaper mogul William Randolph Hearst, *Forbes* magazine estimated the total assets of his estate as "well over the $500 million mark and approaching $1 billion" in the forseeable future. Hearst named his first son, William Jr., as president of the Hearst Family Trust. The trust holds all the voting stock of the Hearst Corporation. William Randolph Hearst Jr. is a very rich man—but a very different man from his father, the role model for "Citizen Kane." "He's a nice, sweet, thoughtful guy,"

his mother, Millicent, once said. "And if he's not as smart as his father is, it's not his fault." Junior became editor-in-chief of the Hearst papers in 1955, and the tone of the newspapers—traditionally among the yellowist of yellow tabloids—changed dramatically. When he won a Pulitzer prize in 1955, after touring the Soviet Union "because every reporter should get as close as possible to the source of news on a big story," notice was duly served that the old Hearst style was gone forever.

Absent the patriach's adoration for the spotlight, Bill Jr., and the rest of the Hearst clan kept what passes for a multi-millionaire's low low profile—until the celebrated kidnapping of his niece Patty and her re-emergence as the revolutionary Tania of the Symbionese Liberation Army. When the news broke, Bill flew in from the East to warn that the corporate image of the entire Hearst empire was now in danger. He said to hire an Establishment lawyer, fast. His brother Randolph took it from there. The Hearst family's position on the Patty fiasco was perhaps best illustrated by an editorial Bill wrote, prompted by U.N. ambassador Andrew Young's statement that "Patty was a political prisoner." The Hearst editorial agreed fully.

Born in New York City, 27 January 1908, the future publisher first got printer's ink on his fingers as a "fly boy" on the New York *Daily Mirror*. After two years at the University of California he joined his dad's flagship paper, the *New York American*, in 1928 as a cub reporter and became publisher in 1936. During World War II he served as a European correspondent. After two marriages ended in divorce, he wed Austine "Bootsie" McDonnell (1948). He has two children: William Randolph III and John Augustine.

Christie Hefner

Who hasn't dreamed of growing up and becoming an heiress? She's certainly done that, but being the Bunny Heiress in the middle of a long overdue feminist revolution certainly defines the phrase "a hostage to fortune." Nevertheless, Hugh Hefner's very own baby girl (born in Chicago in 1952) has managed to become liberated in the midst of her many fortunes and, by the time she became Playboy Enterprises Chief Operating Officer in 1984, was looking good politically. Of her job, she said: "He handles editorial. I stick to business." Despite cries of nasty nepotism among the Bunny mag's staffers, there was no denying that as a result of the heiress' toilings, papa's company took a much needed healthy upturn after two years of decline.

A summa cum laude English and American literature graduate from Brandeis, Christie Hefner has found the objective correlative, the poetry if you will, in the female flesh trade. "I think [women] are finally realizing that *Playboy* is not the enemy, it's the friend," she has said. "I'm a lot more anxious to change what's going on in *Cosmopolitan* and *Family Circle* magazines than I am in *Playboy*, as far as roles for women are concerned." Her hutch being the business side, among her ventures has been Playboy's successful cable TV channel. When the company lost its British casino license worth $40 million in annual revenues, in 1981, Ms. Hefner provided the guts needed to clean up the company. (One reporter once wrote that interviewing her is like "asking Miss America a question and hearing Lee Iacocca answer.") Respected by the working world, Christie was presented with the Founders Award by the Midwest Women's Center in 1986 and received the Human Rights Award from the American Jewish Commmittee.

Christie was raised, along with her brother David, by her mother, the former Mildred Williams, and her step-father. She saw little of Papa for 14 years after her parents divorced. Father and daughter were reconciled only when she went to work for him. A true blue Yuppie, she doesn't eat red meat, drives a compact automobile, wears *couture* threads by designers like Chloe and Basile, and she never forgets a birthday. She'd like to get married someday and have a "daughter who can take over the company." When she had a live-in boyfriend during her college days, naturally Hef was unphased. He even went on record as saying that it wouldn't bother him in the laest if Christie wanted to do a nude pictorial spread for the glossy. "She's certainly beautiful enough," he said, "but she's found another road that makes me much happier."

Hugh Hefner

Handing the family business down to a son is a fading tradition. But in the case of the far-flung Playboy Enterprises, Hugh Hefner chose to hand his firm over not to his son but to his daughter. "If Christie hadn't existed, our promotion department might want to invent her," he said. "She's rather ideally suited for the role." While more time is needed to evaluate the long-term wisdom of her 1982 promotion, Hef will continue calling the editorial shots, leaving corporate matters to Christie. "It's Christie's job to take us from here to there," he said. As chairman and chief executive officer of the empire he built around his successful magazine, he'll still select Playmates and decide on editorial matters like covers and cartoons. But gone are the weekly forays as late night TV host on "Playboy After Dark" and "Playboy Penthouse." Sold are the gaming operations in Britain and Atlantic City, the publishing company, limousine service, two resort hotels, and other properties. "Our main objective was to stop the dike from spilling water," said one high-ranking Playboy exec, referring to the dwindling profits realized by Playboy Enterprises. There was serious interest in turning the Chicago mansion headquarters into condos and even talk of selling the 5-acre Playboy Mansion West where Hef lives and stars cavort. That prospect was not likely, however. Beside its "unique promotional" value, there was the matter of Hefner's living there. "How do you tell him to move out?" asked a company associate.

You probably don't. Since 1953, when he decided to "publish a magazine that would thumb its nose at all the phony puritan values of the world" in which he'd grown up. Hefner has been his own boss. He was born in Chicago on 9 April 1926, and after high school joined the Army. From there he was on to the University of Illinois, where he majored in psychology, founded a campus humor magazine, and graduated in two-and-a-half-years. He became a publisher after leaving *Esquire*, when they wouldn't give him an additional $5 a week. He mortgaged his furniture twice, borrowed from relatives and friends, and sold $10,000 worth of stock in a magazine called *Stag Party*. When *Stag* magazine objected to Hefner's publication's name, *Playboy* was born. Enough copies of the first issue (October 1953) were sold to finance a second, and the rest is history. Part of recent history has been the feminist movement, and its protest against soft and hard porn. But Hefner responds, "The notion that there is something degrading in pornography relating to women is, I think, just as shallow as the rest of society's attitudes on sex.... Images of sex, no matter how explicit, can be either humanizing or dehumanizing."

Hefner's one marriage was to high school sweetheart Millie Williams in 1949. It lasted ten years and produced son David, and, of course, Christie Ann. After a highly publicized affair with Carrie Leigh, Hefner decided to settle down again and wed playmate Kimberly Conrad in 1989. The couple are expecting a child in 1990.

John Heinz

John Heinz, heir to the H.J. Heinz Company fortune, is one of the most promising young members of the Republican party. A moderate liberal, whose appeal crosses party lines, he first entered politics because he was convinced that "almost all the real vital decisions affecting our lives [were] being made in the public sector." He gained his U.S. Senatorial seat in 1976 after five years in the House of Representatives, and his star grew even brighter when as the nineteenth-ranking member of the Senate's majority party, he won key positions on the Finance, and the Banking, Housing, and Urban Affairs Committees.

He was born Henry John Heinz 3rd on 23 October 1938 in Pittsburgh, Pa., to Henry John Heinz 2nd (chairman of the H.J. Heinz Company founded by the Senator's great-grandfather in 1869) and Joan Diehl Heinz. A graduate of Yale and the Harvard Graduate School of Business Administration, Heinz joined the family firm in 1965. Becoming general manager in 1968, he illustrated his "tried and true" entrepreneurial heritage by introducing 50 new food items. In 1970-1971, he served as a lecturer on the faculty of Carnegie-Mellon University's Graduate School of Industrial Administration in Pittsburgh. Active in local Republican politics throughout the latter half of the '60s, he ran for elective office in 1971 against John E. Connelly on a platform which called for the withdrawal of American troops from Vietnam, a cut in taxes for lower income families, federal assumption of welfare costs, and increased federal aid to education.

Throughout the Nixon presidency, Heinz continued to support these same issues, often criticizing White House positions, demanding progressive social programs, and approving environmental protection legislation. His all-time high with Democrats occurred when Jimmy Carter publicly but mistakenly identified Heinz as a member of his own party. In 1974 when Heinz began to campaign for the Senate, he was an immediate favorite, though he suffered some setback when his foes discovered that he had accepted illegal contributions of $6,000 from Gulf Oil in 1971 and 1972. Donating over 2 million dollars to his own campaign, Heinz won by a small margin and continued in the Senate to support far-reaching social programs, energy conservation, tax reform, veterans assistance programs, and civil rights measures such as the ERA. Reported to be the richest man in the senate, Heinz is a natural athlete who jogs, swims, and plays tennis regularly, and he enjoys his involvement in civic affairs in his home town of Pittsburgh. Married since 1966 to the former Maria Teresa Thierstein Simoes-Ferreira, he has three children and divides his time between Washington and Pennsylvania homes.

Joseph Heller

The "abundantly talented" author of *Catch-22*, *Something Happened*, *Good as Gold* and *God Knows* "has never accepted limits," writes Canadian novelist Mordecai Richler; "neither has he repeated himself. . . . Instead, each time out, he has begun afresh, discovering human folly for the first time: himself amazed, irreverent and charged with appetite." But it hasn't been easy for the American novelist in question: "I'm not a natural writer," he says, "though I do have a writer's imagination. . . . I have very little trouble getting ideas, but I seem to have much work in getting them down on paper."

The idea for *Catch-22* emerged from his World War II service as a bombardier. In that novel, bombardier Yossarian pleads that his is too crazy to fly any more missions, only to learn about the rule of the book's title, which states that anyone rational enough to seek release from hazardous duty is obviously sane and therefore must continue in it. A "well-aimed bomb," in Joseph Epstein's phrase, *Catch-22* sold more than ten million copies to become, Richard Locke wrote, "the great representative document of our era, linking high and low culture." Its title entered the language, and its protagonist, Yossarian, became, according to Jack Schedler, "the fictional talisman to an entire generation."

Thirteen years passed before the appearance of the author's second book, *Something Happened* (1974), based on his experience working in advertising and promotion for *Time*, *Look* and *McCall's* in the '50s. In this exploration of the absurdity and alienation of the American business community, middle-level manager Bob Slocum is haunted, wrote John W. Aldridge, "by the sense that at some time in the past something happened to him, something . . . that changed him [into] a man who aspires to nothing, believes in nothing and no one, least of all himself, who no longer knows if he loves or is loved." During the '60s and early '70s the novelist taught at Yale, the University of Pennsylvania and City College of New York, and in *Good as Gold* (1979) Bruce Gold is a professor of English in public service who yearns to be Secretary of State, and in Leonard Michaels' words, "nearly becomes a Washington non-Jewish Jew, a rich, powerful slave with a tall blonde wife." R.Z. Sheppard called the book "a savage, intemperately funny satire on the assimilation of the Jewish tradition of liberalism into the American main chance."

After 1975 the novelist became a full-time writer, and sure enough, the narrator-protagonist of *God Knows* (1984) is an autobiographical writer who claims to have "the best story in the Bible": 70-year-old King David. To quote Richler again, this book, "as much commentary as novel," is "original, sad, wildly funny and filled with roaring." Recent books include *No Laughing Matter* (1986) and *Picture This* (1988).

Born in Brooklyn 1 May 1923, Heller was married in 1945 after his return from WWII and educated at the University of Southern California, New York University (B.A. 1948), Columbia (M.A. 1949) and Oxford. He has two children. In 1981 he was divorced, and at the end of that year he contracted Guillain-Barre syndrome, an inflammation of the muscle nerves that results in paralysis; he almost died of it but after eight months was able to resume writing. "My characters keep getting older," he told an interviewer, yet they have much in common. All are, he says, "ingenuous, introspective, melancholy, extremely self-conscious, all aware of disease and death." And so, one suspects, is Joseph Heller.

Florence Henderson

She is as versatile as she is talented. Her career has spanned over three decades of work in stage, screen, and television. Florence has done everything from nightclub entertainer, television hostess, country recording artist, and actress to author. The commitment and professionalism she has for her work makes her one of the most respected of today's entertainers.

She was born on 14 February 1934 in Dale, Indiana, and was the daughter of a tobacco sharecropper. Being the youngest of ten, she and her siblings helped raise tobacco in Owensboro, Kentucky, where she spent her childhood. After attending grade school at the St. Francis Academy in Owensboro, she entered New York's prestigious American Academy of Dramatic Arts at age seventeen. While still at the Academy, Florence landed her first part in the Broadway production of *Wish You Were Here* (1952), a Joshua Logan musical. Catching the eye of Rodgers & Hammerstein, she was cast to play the lead part in *Oklahoma* (1952-1953). Following *Oklahoma* she appeared for a brief stint in *The Great Waltz* with the Civic Light Opera of Los Angeles. She then returned to Broadway to perform in the lead role in *Fanny* (1954), which ran for 19 months; *The Sound of Music* (1961); and *The Girl Who Came To Supper* (1963). Following her Broadway performances, she played the lead role in *South Pacific* at the New York State Theater in Lincoln Center (1967). Not limiting herself to stage, her first film, *The Song of Norway* (1970), brought her international exposure. Her television appearances began as a frequent talk show guest, appearing with such talk show hosts as Ed Sullivan, Bing Crosby, Dick Cavett, Merv Griffin and Phil Donahue. Florence was the first woman ever to host the "Tonight Show." She is best known on television, though, as Carol Brady in one of the longest running situation comedies "The Brady Bunch" (1969-1974). Several "Brady Bunch" specials have run over the years, including "The Brady Bunch Hour" (1977) and "A Very Brady Christmas" (1988). She has also made regular appearances on such shows as "Murder, She Wrote," "The Love Boat," "Fantasy Island," and "It's Garry Shandling's Show." Florence also hosts her own program, "Country Kitchen," which has been running for four years on the Nashville Network. The response to her show has been so enthusiastic that it prompted her to write a cookbook entitled *A Little*

Cooking, A Little Talking and a Whole Lotta Fun. Even with her hectic schedule, Florence still finds time to participate in charitable activities including hosting the annual United Cerebral Palsy Telethon, working with the City of Hope, and helping the House Ear Institute.

Florence has four children from her first marriage to Ira Bernstein (married 9 January 1956): Barbara (1956), Joey (1960), Robert Norman (1963), and Elizabeth (1966). The couple later divorced. She remarried John Kappas on 4 August 1987.

Rickey Henderson

It has been said "the best leadoff man in baseball" (in the opinion of Billy Martin) that if you give him first base you've already given him second . . . and third. That assessment drives from Rickey's 78% success rate since coming up to the majors in 1980. An outstanding athlete (born Christmas Day 1958), he was offered more than a dozen football scholarships while attending Oakland's Technical High (as a three-letter man). But his .465 batting average and 30 stolen bases made him an instant draft choice of the Oakland A's shortly after his graduation in 1976, and he was on the way to rewriting baseball's record books while working hard to correct his few weaknesses. (From leading the Northwest League in 1976, then the California League in 1977 in errors, he became a Golden Glover with Oakland in 1981).

When he held one of the legendary positions in baseball (center field) for the New York Yankees, he added "a sixth dimension" to the criteria by which great ballplayers are measured, according to the New York *Times'* Dave Anderson. The extra dimension that set this carefree Chicago-born ballplayer apart is his supreme base-stealing ability (he is the only player in major league history to have stolen 100 bases more than once combined with his superior skills in hitting for average, hitting for power, throwing, catching the ball, and running, which prompted Detroit Tiger skipper Sparky Anderson to proclaim, "I've never seen a player any more exciting than Rickey Henderson." After a disappointing 1987 in pinstripes (began as MVP kind-of-season, finished as "the year of the hammy"), he left the game with a pulled hamstring. This injury demanded the switch to his position as left fielder. In 1988 he made a great comeback—the "man of steal" became the all-time base stealer—followed in 1989 as the lead-off homerun hitter in Major League history. He broke the record on 28 April 1989 when he hit his 36th leadoff homerun.

To the surprise of his many Yankee fans, Henderson was traded back to the Oakland A's in June 1989. Since he's a resident of the Bay area, the move might be convenient for the popular ballplayer. Henderson plans to marry his high school sweetheart, Pamela Palmer; the couple have a young daughter.

Skitch Henderson

He adopted his "bearded boulevardier look" in 1953 and, according to a friend, "it did for him what psychoanalysis does for other persons." Turned mostly to white by 1983, beard and hair meshed perfectly with the white-tie-and-tails he sported on the Carnegie Hall podium as he debuted his long-dreamed-of ("on the drawing board since 1973") New York Pops Orchestra. The conductor-founder sees the aggregation as "a truly all-American orchestra dedicated to presenting the best music by American composers" and it was back in Carnegie for more concerts in 1984.

Born Lyle Russell Cedric Henderson on 27 January 1918 in Birmingham, England, he picked up the nickname "Skitch" after coming to the U.S. at the age of seven. (He never tells how.) He first took piano lessons from a Minnesota aunt who played background music for silent movies and began his musical career in his early teens playing the pipe organ at radio station KFYR in Bismark, N.D. After working as a pianist with various dance bands in the 1930s, he served as a pilot for both the RAF and USAF during World War II and then, after the war, became a conductor for Frank Sinatra and later Bing Crosby on radio. In 1950, he became music director for NBC and moved into the "household name" category when he began leading the band on Steve Allen's original "Tonight" show in the 1950s.

Skitch began his double-life as a concert conductor in the 1950s and appeared with the NBC Symphony at the invitation of Arturo Toscanini. In recent seasons, he has filled the post of music director of the Connecticut Symphony and been a guest conductor with orchestras all over the continent. Reflecting his still-warm affection for pop music, he also has his own syndicated radio show, "The Music Makers."

After his tempestuous seven-year marriage to the late actress Faye Emerson ended in 1957, he married German fashion model Ruth Einsiedel, and they have two adoped children, Heidi (married to actor William Hurt) and Hans Christian.

Beth Henley

"Among today's younger dramatists, Beth Henley possesses a unique talent for combining emotional fragility with robust comedy," observed critic John Beaufort in his 1984 review of *The Miss Firecracker Contest.* "Miss Henley perceives the humor as well as the pathos amid even life's grotesqueries. Her work has been described as Southern-fried Gothic. Kooky Chekhov might also apply." Her first full-length play, *Crimes of the Heart,* written when she was a struggling actress in California, zigzagged its way through regional theatres and an off-Broadway production before opening on Broadway in 1981 to rave reviews ("From time to time a play comes along that restores one's faith in the theatre" gushed drama critic John Simon in one of his rare accolades). She was soon being linked creatively with Eudora Welty, Flannery O'Connor and Tennessee Williams, and in April of that year became the first woman in twenty-three years to win the Pulitzer Prize for drama. In June the New York Drama Critics Circle chose the play as the best American play of the season; in August she received the George Oppenheimer/*Newsday* Playwriting Award for 1980-81.

Born on 8 May 1952 in Jackson, Mississippi, her father was a lawyer who served in both houses of the Mississippi legislature. Growing up she was a lonely "fat kid," asthmatic and susceptible to allergies. "I was real shy when I was little. Spent a lot of time getting shots and laying in bed. At night, Mama'd come into my room and ask me why I was crying. I'd tell her I was pretending to be Heidi." Her attraction to the theatre came from her mother, who acted in amateur productions. Henley studied dramatic arts at Southern Methodist University in Dallas, where she found "veils of the mind lifted; this was alive theatre, someone bringing you in touch with a world you hadn't understood before." She wrote her first play (one-act), *Am I Blue,* in a play-writing course at SMU. Graduating in 1974, she acted with the Dallas Minority Repertory, took graduate work at the University of Illinois, and in 1976 went to Hollywood intending to be an actress, but turned to writing. "I didn't like the feeling of being at everyone's mercy." In 1982 Henley's *Wake of Jamey Foster* and the early *Am I Blue* were produced in New York to less enthusiastic reception than her first play, although Frank Rich of the *Times* wrote of the latter: "We sample Miss Henley's wondrous gift for creating sweet comedy out of Southern eccentricities—as well as her ability to reveal the sad loneliness beneath the spunk."

She's also written screenplays, including the acclaimed film version of *Crimes of the Heart* (nominated for an Academy Award), *The Miss Firecracker Contest, Nobody's Fool* and *Strawberry.* Her play *The Lucky Spot* had its New

York premiere at the Manhattan Theatre Club in the spring of 1987. She has also written a teleplay for the PBS series "Trying Times."

Henley lives in West Hollywood, and her favorite recreations are boxing matches, Dodger baseball games, and jazz sessions. According to interviewers, she has an air of old-fashioned, ladylike delicacy about her; she is modest and self-effacing, speaks with a soft Southern accent and has a predilection for tall tales.

Jim Henson

"When you do puppets," this wizard says, "you can create the whole show yourself. . . . It's a way of saying something. . . . But I don't start out to say things. I try to keep it, first of all, entertaining, and then humorous. Also, puppetry is a good way of hiding." Slender, soft-spoken Henson is "Big Daddy" to Kermit, Cookie Monster, and humanoid Ernie, having created them from foam and plastic and imbued them with such winsome personalities that both young and old have become hooked on these Muppets and their televised shenanigans on "Sesame Street" (since 1969), their own "Muppet show" (since 1976), "Fraggle Rock," and "The Jim Henson Hour" (NBC;1989). Movies include: *The Muppet Movie, The Great Muppet Caper, The Dark Crystal, The Muppets Take Manhattan, Labyrinth,* and *The Witches.*

James Henson was born 24 September 1936 in Greenville, Miss., the son of an agronomist. He took up puppetry almost by accident. "It was the early 1950s and I was between high-school and college, and needed a job. There was this job available for a puppeteer on a local NBC station in Washington, D.C. . . . It served as the best possible training ground for the things I was to do later." After Henson graduated from the University of Maryland in the early '60s, his progeny Rowlf the Dog and other Muppet siblings began appearing on "The Ed Sullivan Show" and other network TV programs. By 1968 he had already produced programming for NET and won the National Educational Television Award for the year's outstanding children's show. His experience in producing would give him the needed know-how to produce "The Muppet Show." The "children" are put together in Henson's New York City headquarters, "an office and a fantasy-like factory housed in two brownstones on East Sixty-Ninth Street." In a smart business move, Henson made a deal with the Disney Company in August, 1989. This phenomenal purchase of the Muppets will initiate unlimited participation of Henson's extended family at Disneyland, Disneyworld, etc. . . . Henson and his wife have five other children and live in Bedford, N.Y. In 1987 he was inducted into the Academy of TV Arts and Sciences Hall of Fame.

Audrey Hepburn

She was a gracefully elfin 22 when the French novelist Colette spied her in Monte Carlo on the set of an English movie and said to herself, "There is Gigi." That afternoon she relayed the information to Gilbert Miller who subsequently offered Hepburn the part in the Broadway play. So the slender Belgian-born ballet student came to New York, charmed everyone she met and was whisked off to Hollywood to become a dainty legend. She collected an Oscar for her first American film, *Roman Holiday* (1953), and wove her "alternately regal and childlike" way through such box-office blockbusters as *Sabrina* (1954), *Funny Face* (1956), *Nun's Story* (1959) and *Breakfast at Tiffany's* (1960) before finding herself in the midst of her only big Hollywood brouhaha for being chosen over Julie Andrews to play Eliza Doolittle in the screen version of *My Fair Lady* (1963). Post Eliza assignments have included *Two for the Road* (1966), *Wait Until Dark* (1967), *Robin and Marion* (1976), *Bloodline* (1979), and *They All Laughed* (1981).

Born Audrey Hepburn-Ruston (her mother was a Dutch Baroness) on 4 May 1929 in Brussels, she grew up in Holland during the German occupation and acted as a courier for the Dutch Resistance during World War II. "When I was a little girl," she recalled later, "my nose wasn't pretty and I was terribly thin. I was sickly too, and quite miserable about my prospects." Nevertheless, she studied ballet in Amsterdam and headed for London in 1948 in search of a stage career. In addition to her 1951 Broadway triumph in *Gigi*, she collected a Tony for her 1954 appearance in the Jean Giraudoux play *Ondine* and later married her co-star Mel Ferrer (a son, Sean, was born in 1960).

Her biography, written by Ian Woodward, was published in 1984 (St. Martins Press). Once the second highest paid actress in films (Elizabeth Taylor being the first), she is now content with a less frenzied lifestyle and lives in Switzerland with her son Luca (born 1970) by her second husband, psychiatrist Andrea Dotti, from whom she is divorced. Named as a Special Ambassador for UNICEF, Hepburn spends her free time devoted to the charity. During the 1986-1987 television season she appeared in the ABC telefilm "Here's a Thief, There's a Thief."

Katharine Hepburn

"I've never written a diary. . . . But there are some happenings you can't forget. There they are. A series of facts—pictures—realities. This happened to me with *The African Queen*. I remember it in minute detail—I can see every second of its making and of me at the time. . . . So here it is . . . thirty-odd years after the fact." So begins the fascinating introduction to Katharine Hepburn's memoir, *The Making of the African Queen; or How I Went to Africa with Bogart, Bacall and Huston and Almost Lost My Mind*. Charged with the adventure of trekking to Africa and the character of the "crazy, psalm-singin' skinny old maid" who cleverly maneuvers the rummy river-boat skipper into action with the WWI German gunboat, Hepburn leaped at the challenge of jockeying the unique giant talents and personalities of director John Huston and actor Humphrey Bogart (both drinking buddies). Her account of daily routines, the magnificence and mystique as well as the muck and mire of Africa are recorded with total recall, and Hepburn's candor and humor (about herself as well as the area and the entourage) make it a rare and winning piece of reportage. It's a fascinating tribute to her colleagues and rip-roaring movies like "they used to be."

She was born Katharine Houghton Hepburn on 8 November 1909 into a hyperactive, unconventional, upper-class Hartford family. ("My parents were much more fascinating people, than I am.") Her father was a urologist and pioneer in social hygiene who insisted that his five youngsters start out every day with a cold shower; her mother was an early women's libber battling for votes and birth control. "They gave me freedom from fear," Hepburn said in a television interview. (She dedicated her book to them.) And about her role in *On Golden Pond:* "The woman reminded me very much of my mother. She was tough, but she was infinitely kind, and brilliant. But she wasn't afraid to say: 'You're a bore.'" It was a surprise to no one when, after Bryn Mawr (and after a brief marriage to a Philadelphian named Ogden Smith), the red haired Hartford hell-raiser headed for Broadway. Her first big success, playing a leggy Amazon in *The Warrior's Husband* (1932), catapulted her west into the arms of RKO, where—starting her film career as John Barrymore's daughter in *Bill of Divorcement* (1932), and continuing it in *Little Women* (1933), *The Little Minister* (1934), *Alice Adams* (1935), *Mary of Scotland* (1936), *Stage Door* (1937), and others—she turned in often brilliant performances but carried on a running battle with autograph hunters and the Hollywood press corps and earned the nickname of "Katherine of Arrogance" for her high handedness off screen. She is the only actress to receive four Academy Awards for Best Performance by an Actress.

Prior to her rebirth as a golden girl in Philip Barry's Hepburn-tailored *Philadelphia Story*, five of her six previous films were losers. Then she starred in *Woman of the Year* (1942), which clinched her comeback and, even more importantly, marked the debut of what was to develop into one of Hollywood's most remarkable associations, her relationship with Spencer Tracy. She describes Tracy as a "brilliant actor." Says Hepburn, "I discovered my hands and he discovered his soul." The two co-starred in eight films in the next twelve years, nearly all of them wonderful: among them, *Without Love* (1945), *State of the Union* (1948), *Adam's Rib* (1949), *Pat and Mike* (1952), and *Desk Set* (1957). Interspersed among these releases was her superb rendition of a proper lady missionary mixed up with Humphrey Bogart in the Congo in *The African Queen* (1951). Busy in the 1950's in Shakespeare and Shaw, (*As You Like It*, *The Millionairess*), she soared to greatness again in 1962 in the film version of Eugene O'Neill's anguished memoir, *Long Day's Journey into Night*, and then entered a quiescent period during which she focused most of her energies on caring for an ailing Tracy. "I have had twenty years of perfect companionship with a man among men," she told a reporter in 1963. "He's a rock and a protection. I've never regretted it." *Guess Who's Coming to Dinner* was her ninth and last film with Tracy. She did not desert the stage and has returned in several productions on Broadway: *Coco*, *A Matter of Gravity*, and *West Side Waltz*.

Hepburn is boundlessly energetic and seemingly indestructible. She's been called the "unchallenged first lady of American cinema." "If you survive you become a legend. I'm a legend because I've survived over a long period of time," she once said. "I'm revered rather like an old building."

Herblock

"My name is Herbert Block. I draw cartoons and sometimes I write books and I'm very glad to meet you." So goes the introduction to Herbert Block's eighth collection of political cartoons culled from his years at the Washington *Post*, where he has been the gem of the editorial page since 1946. The nationally-syndicated cartoonist, who signs his product "Herblock," has won two Pulitzer Prizes: one in 1942 and another in 1954. He is the first living American cartoonist whose work has been purchased for the National Gallery of Arts Foundation.

His eighth cartoon collection, *Herblock On All Fronts*, was published in 1980, and it drew smiles from readers and critics alike. A staff reviewer for the New York *Times Book Review* praised its "sparkle, youth and sense of perpetual indignation." The Herblock formula has remained basically unchanged since he first mastered his style after the war. ("I had to simplify my drawing and be funnier," he explains.) Even his targets would have to agree . . . it works. "An avalanche of slam-bang images so expertly wedded in a chewy, allusive fast-moving text that only one cartoon out of a total of nearly 600 requires a supplementary footnote," marveled the *Times* reviewer.

This shrewd observer of Washington's establishment was born 13 October 1909 in Chicago. He studied at Lake Forest (Ill.) College and took part-time classes at the Art Institute of Chicago before turning professional as a cartoonist with the *Chicago Daily News* (1929). In 1933 he went into the Newspaper Enterprise Association Service, where he won a 1940 National Headliners Club award as well as the Pulitzer Prize. Joining the Army in 1943, he put his pen to the service of the Information and Educational Division. After the war he came to the *Post*, which has been the sanctuary from which he sends the world his daily vision of pointed humor.

Jerry Herman

On the morning of 18 January 1964 entertainment page readers of the New York *Herald Tribune* read that "composer Jerry Herman has torn up a hurdy-gurdy and scattered its tinkling waltzes and mellow quartets and tipsy polkas all over Union Square." Critic Walter Kerr was writing about the slim 30-year-old songwriter's contribution to the instant smash of the season. *Hello Dolly*, whose title song (parodied as "Hello Lyndon") later became the theme of the 1964 Democratic National Convention and, sounded out by the trumpet of Louis Armstrong, an instant pop classic. In May of 1966 Jerry Herman followed up his *Hello Dolly* triumph with another, *Mame*, one memorable hit from the show being "Open a New Window." Earlier in 1961, he'd scored on Broadway with *Milk and Honey*.

Born 10 July 1933 in New York City, Jerry Herman was enticed in the direction of a piano keyboard at the age of six by his mother, who taught both piano and voice. He didn't seriously consider songwriting as a career, however, until he started studying interior decorating at Parsons School of Design, when he wrote a song just for fun and sold it for $200. Encouraged, he switched to a drama major at the University of Miami, wrote a college musical revue, and supported himself after graduation writing special musical material for the likes of Garry Moore, Ray Bolger, and Jane Froman. Off-Broadway revues followed suit, and in a number of years he would be treating theater audiences to *Dear World* (1969) and *Mack and Mable* (1974), neither of which would create the stir that *La Cage Aux Folles*, the 1984 Herman-Harvey Fierstein musical about two male lovers in a French nightclub (based on the film of the same name) did, cleaning up with six Tonys. Accepting the Tony for best score at the 1984 presentation ceremony Herman said, "This award forever shatters a myth. . . . There's been a rumor that the simple, hummable show tune is dead on Broadway. Well, it's alive and well at the Palace" (where *La Cage* was playing). Herman was on a roll in 1985 with the revue *Jerry's Girls* as well as being inducted into the Theatre Hall of Fame. For the 1987-1988 season he supervised the *Mack and Mabel* London production and in 1989 hit the nightclub circuit with "An Evening With Jerry Herman" at the Rainbow & Stars room. When he writes both lyrics and music, he says that he gets most of his musical ideas while strolling the streets of New York. He winks and glibly says, "Someday I'm going to get run over."

Pee-wee Herman

"I had a little one inch harmonica that said 'Pee-wee' on it," Paul Reubens (better known as Pee-Wee Herman) says. "I just loved the way it sounded. . . . Growing up I knew a kid who was extremely obnoxious . . . and his last name was Herman. And the rest is history."

The eldest of Milton and Judy Rubenfeld's three children, Paul was born in Peekskill, New York in July 1952; the family moved to Sarasota, Florida during Paul's childhood years. While Paul entertained friends in his "theater," Milton and Judy operated a retail lamp store. A local production of Herb Gardner's *A Thousand Clowns* enticed eleven-year-old Paul to audition for a major role. By the start of high school, Paul was performing regularly in summer stock at Florida's Apollo State Theater. He attended a program for highly gifted thespians one summer where he set himself apart when his skills earned him the honor of the workshop's best actor after his lead performance in their production of *David and Lisa*. Paul was off to Boston University after graduation. Remaining for only two semesters, he decided to attend an institution of higher education which would further help him develop his talents. Transferring to the California Institute of the Arts at Valencia in 1971, Paul wowed audiences with his versatility in their production of *The Death of Jesse James* in which he portrayed several minor characters. Convinced that southern California was the place where he could accomplish his dream, Paul remained there after his graduation from the institute in 1975. Supporting himself with odd jobs, he changed his surname to Reubens and joined a comedy improvisation troupe called the Groundlings who performed regularly at a small L.A. venue called the Groundling Theater. For his act, Paul developed off-beat characters; one such character was a junk food junkie whose form of communication was uncouthful grunts. During those years he was a frequent contestant on Chuck Barris' "The Gong Show," but he never received the dubious honor of worst act. In 1979 he tried out a character that became the launching pad to stardom. Clad in bow tie and shrunken suit, Paul Reubens evolved into Pee-wee Herman. Originally designed as a five-minute skit which parodied such children's entertainers as Captain Kangaroo and Mister Rogers, Pee-wee was received so enthusiastically that Paul was encouraged to lengthen his repertoire. In 1980 Pee-wee moved to the Roxy Theater in L.A. where his "Pee-wee Herman Party" ran for a year. HBO taped the performance and ran it in 1982. Pee-wee's movie debut came in 1980 as a minor role in *The Blues Brothers*. In 1981 Pee-wee was temporarily shelved and Paul appeared as a punked-out cocaine demon in *Cheech and Chong's Nice Dream*.

On a wider scale, Pee-wee appeared frequently on NBC's "Late Night With David Letterman" and on "The Tonight Show" when Joan Rivers would substitute for Johnny Carson. In 1983 he appeared at the Manhattan comedy club Caroline's where his act was billed as "Paul Reubens Presents Pee-wee Herman." A sold-out performance for "Pee-wee Herman's Party" at Carnegie Hall in New York was the final catylast for the fine line drawn between Paul Reubens and Pee-wee Herman. His 1985 feature film *Pee-wee's Big Adventure* surprisingly became a box office hit among adults as well as children. After that success Pee-wee became the third comic to win the Harvard Lampoon's Elmer Award. In the fall of 1986 Pee-wee created a Saturday morning children's program on CBS-TV "Pee-wee's Playhouse." The expensive venture has set daytime television history by being the only show to receive over twenty Emmy nominations. In it's first year it received twelve nominations and won six Emmys. Having created an environment where children are encouraged to use their creativity, Pee-wee's Playhouse also teaches them that it's okay to be different. *Pee-wee's Big Top* was his second feature film in 1988. In the works for Pee-wee is an album of pop songs featuring some of the music world's top artists and an amusement park appropriately named "Pee-weeland."

Pee-wee Herman loves to visit New York but is dedicated to his home in Los Angeles.

Carolina Herrera

In 1981 when news of her first show began making its way around high fashion circles, ho-hums sounded out. "Who needs another socialite designing a fly-by-night collection?" Then, *violà*, the collection was seen and Herrera was called the most exciting thing to happen to fashion since Velasquez painted the Infanta shimmering in falling empire gazar. "Herrera excels at designing outfits for the glittering lifestyle she no longer has time to lead," commented one reporter. That means lightweight wool luncheon suits that sell for $3,000 (she's not cheap) and evening gowns with exaggerated details—wild sleeves and plunging necklines—the sort of extravagant, elegant style which sparked Diana Vreeland to call the Herrera manner "RRRRRRRRRReeeeeee-mark-able!"

Born 8 January 1939 in Venezuela, she has been fascinated by fashion since she was a little girl designing clothing for her dolls. At 13 she was taken to Paris and introduced, by her grandmother, to Balenciaga. Hers was a charmed life, one of three daughters of Guillermo Pacanins, an officer in the Venezuelan Air Force who later became Caracas' governor. "When I was young," she recalls, "I wanted to wear red and dress like a vamp. But it wasn't allowed and I was very sad." In 1969 she married childhood friend Reinaldo Herrera, the eldest son of wealthy art patron Mimi Herrera, owner of the 65-room "La Vega" the most glamourous house in Caracas (built in 1590). "You have to walk," says the designer, "and that's the exercise I do now daily, walking through the house." Although she'd been designing for herself and for friends, it wasn't until a Venezuelan publishing magnate Armando de Armas offered to back her that she started stitching for a royalist retinue. "Everyone knew me as a social person," she explains. "That was the most difficult thing to prove—that I was not a dilettante." She did quite well in convincing the public. "The clothes are so good," says one of her cohorts on the Best Dressed List Hall of Fame, where she's occupied a niche for more than a decade. "*Chic* is Carolina's passion." In 1988 she was honored at the Casita Maria's "Fiesta '88."

Carolina is a grandmother. She married young and has two grown daughters, Mercedes and Ana Luisa, from her first marriage, and young daughters, Carolina and Patricia, from her marriage to Herrera.

John Hersey

"Palpable 'facts' are mortal," observed John Hersey, who spent most of his writing life touching truth with the magic wand of fiction. "Like certain moths and flying ants, they lay their eggs and die overnight.... The things we remember for longer periods are emotions and impressions and illusions and images and characters: the elements of fiction.... Truth is said to be stranger than fiction; fiction can be stronger than truth."

Born 17 June 1914, in Tientsin, China, where his father and mother served as YMCA "social-gospel" missionaries, Hersey came to the U.S. at ten, speaking Chinese more fluently than English. After Yale, and a year at Cambridge, he became a factotum for Sinclair Lewis, and then a foreign correspondent for *Time* and *Life*. His novel *A Bell for Adano* won a 1945 Pulitzer Prize. It was followed in 1946 by *Hiroshima*, a shattering account of six survivors of the first atomic bomb, a book which achieved the distinction of being given an entire issue of *The New Yorker*. In 1950 in *The Wall*, he wrote of the extermination of the Polish Jews in terms of the fictional "Levinson Archives," a document purported to have been found in the Warsaw ghetto. (*The Wall* was later adapted to television.) More book releases include *The War Lover* (1959), *The Algiers Motel Incident* (1968), *The Conspiracy* (1972), and in 1980 he wrote *Aspects of the Presidency*, portraits of Harry Truman and Gerald R. Ford. His fascination and affinity for his birthplace was revealed in a series of biographical articles in *The New Yorker* in 1982: "I suppose we all lose our childhoods. Before leaving for China, I had told myself that while snapshots in old albums might have anchored a few moments of actuality in my mind, most of my memories had likely softened, I'd doubtless created comforting private myths about Tientsin, I had at times found myself yearning for faraway images that I could not really shape or name.... I suddenly felt, standing there on the porch of the pavilion in the Rec, surveying this ruinous scene, as if my whole childhood had been unfairly and violently snatched away from me." China is the setting of his 1985 novel, *The Call*, about an American Missionary. Recent releases are *Hiroshima* (1986), *Here To Stay* (1988), *The Child Buyer* (1989) and *A Single Pebble* (1989). After an 18-year marriage to Frances Ann Cannon of the Cannon Mills textile family (four children), he was divorced in 1958 and became the third husband of lawyer Barbara Day Addams Kaufman (whose first husband was cartoonist Charles Addams). They have one daughter. An earnest, extremely dedicated man, Hersey makes it clear in all of his books that, as one critic put it, he "cares what humanity does to itself."

Werner Herzog

"Film is not the art of scholars but of illiterates," says the man often considered the leading figure in West Germany's critically acclaimed new wave of cinema. Yet ironically his deeply personal films are frequently impenetrable to viewers. Sometimes painfully slow and vague, his work has nevertheless been acclaimed on the art house and festival circuits for its originality and its visually beautiful, if disturbing, imagery. His characters are usually tortured, aimless and confused, sometimes deformed and grotesque. *Even Dwarfs Started Small* (1970) had a cast consisting totally of midgets and dwarfs. For *Heart of Glass* (1976) he had his entire cast put under hypnosis to achieve a stylized portrayal of hallucination and madness. He's a visionary who explores the essence of humanity by depicting it at its most precarious extremes in some of the world's most exotic, remote locales. His two best-known works are based on bizarre historical incidents. Set in the 16th century, the ironic *Aguirre,the Wrath of God* (1973) is about Pizarro's mutinous, power-mad lieutenant who led a small band of followers to destruction in the Amazon jungles on a futile quest for El Dorado. *The Mystery of Kasper Hauser* (aka *Every Man for Himself and God Against All;* 1974), a parable of innocence destroyed, is based on the story of the 19th-century young man of Nuremberg who became a public oddity after apparently spending his entire youth locked in a cellar. The latter film starred Bruno S., a compelling but emotionally damaged man who had been placed in an asylum for mentally retarded children by his prostitute mother at age three, although he was in no way retarded. He stayed there for ten years, and then spent the next 20 in and out of hospitals, reformatories, and prisons. Although he had never acted, "it didn't take too long for me to convince him to take the part," the director says, "because he understood right away that it was about him, too."

Born Werner H. Stipetic in Munich, Germany 6 September 1942, he was taken a few months later by his mother to a small village about 60 miles away in the Bavarian mountains to escape the Allied bombing of Munich. "I was very much alone in my early childhood," he recalls. "I was quite silent, and wouldn't speak for days. My parents thought I was insane, or retarded. I was very dangerous, my character was peculiar; it was almost as if I had rabies." His parents divorced when he was young and at age 12 he moved back to Munich with his mother and two brothers where they lived in abject poverty sharing a single room. As a teenager he traveled widely, wrote poetry and screenplays, and decided to become a filmmaker. After graduating from school (as a mediocre student) in 1961, he went to the U.S., where he lived in Pittsburgh and supported himself by working in a steel factory, parking cars, and riding in a rodeo. Eventually two of his film shorts—admittedly shot with a stolen 35mm camera—reaped prizes at international festivals. In 1967, in Crete, he directed his first feature, *Sign of Life*. His other films include: *Stroszek* (1977), filmed mostly in Wisconsin, about a trio of born losers—one played by Bruno S.—who leave West Germany with vain hopes for a better life in the U.S.; *Nosferatu* (1979), his remake of Murnau's vampire classic; *Woszeck* (1979), from Buchner's play; *Fitzcarraldo* (1982); and *Cobra Verde* (1988). The last four starred Klaus Kinski, who had played Aguirre so memorably.

Uncompromisingly individualistic in his (generally low budget) filmmaking and a loner by temperament, he has sometimes been described as a nineteenth-century romantic, but he insists that he is closest in spirit and aesthetics to the late Middle Ages. In his teens he had a brief flirtation with Roman Catholicism. His conversion upset his militantly atheistic father. "Since I had become so deeply involved in religion, I have become much more violently against it." He and his wife Martje (married in 1966) are the parents of a son, Rudolph Amos Achmed, whom he calls "Burro" and whom he has instructed to call him "Herzog."

Charlton Heston

Though best known for such larger-than-life roles as Moses (*Ten Commandments*, 1957), Judah (*Ben Hur*, 1959 Best Actor Oscar), and Michelangelo (*The Agony and the Ecstacy*, 1965), this Hollywood veteran of more than 50 films has starred in contemporary dramas as well as historical spectaculars. He says the epic roles taught him humility. "When you're playing Moses, you go to your hotel and try to part the water in the bathtub. When it doesn't part, you feel pretty humble." In recent years, however, with the fervor of a Moses, Heston has become a leading force in Hollywood politics, repeatedly locking horns with ex-Screen Actors Guild president Edward Asner over Asner's public political statements. SAG's board "has no right to set our position on save-the-whales or gun control or Israel," declares Heston, a former six-term guild president who now heads a conservative "watchdog" group called Actors Working for an Actors Guild. While following in the footsteps of several illustrious ex-SAG presidents who have since found a larger political stage (George Murphy, John Gavin, Ronald Reagan), Heston has disclaimed ambitions for a political career. "I've played three presidents, three saints, two geniuses. That should satisfy any man."

Born 4 October 1923 in Evanston, Ill., Chuck Heston was bitten by the acting bug at the tender age of five after appearing in a school play and can't remember ever wanting to be anything but an actor. (Charlton was his mother's maiden name; Heston was his stepfather's name.) "I had what must be a relatively unique childhood for my generation." He recalls "a one room school with 13 pupils in eight grades, three of whom were my cousins." Raised in Michigan timber country in the town of St. Helen (pop. 120), he moved to Winnetka, Ill., and prepared for the stage at Northwestern's School of Speech (classmates included Patricia Neal, Cloris Leachman). After a stint in the Air Corps, he headed for Broadway, first supporting himself as a model and attracting his first major notice as an actor in 1947 with Katharine Cornell in *Antony and Cleopatra*—an auspicious Broadway debut. During the run of the play, he appeared in a number of "live" TV dramas. "It was all set up for us," he recalls. "In the first 16 months of 'Studio One,' I did *Taming of the Shrew, Wuthering Heights, Of Human Bondage, MacBeth, Jane Eyre, Julius Caesar*. Now I submit the actor doesn't exist who can't make an impression in one of those parts." Making an impression on Hollywood, he appeared in Hal Wallis' *Dark City* (1950) and entered the big time in Cecil B. DeMille's big top spectacular, *The Greatest Show on Earth* (1963). Other films include *El Cid, The Greatest Story Ever Told, The President's Lady, Planet of the Apes, Airport,* and *Mother Lode*, which was directed by Heston and written by his son. Returning to TV drama in the 1980s, he starred in CBS's mini-series "Chiefs" and in "Nairobi Affair" (1984). In 1985, he directed and starred in *The Caine Mutiny Court Martial* in London's West End and returned to television as Jason Colby, the patriarch of "Dynasty II: The Colbys of California." In 1978, Heston received the Jean Hersholt Humanitarian Award from the Academy of Motion Picture Arts and Sciences and that same year published *The Actors Life—Journals*, (1956-1976). He's a frequent performer at the Ahmanson Theatre in Los Angeles. He is married to Lydia Clarke, whom he met at Northwestern (two children).

Mary Higgins Clark

This self-described "nice Catholic girl from the Bronx" now keeps the bookstores busy as what an admiring *New Yorker* critic called "truly a mistress of high tension." She was a fortyish widow with five young children when she moved her battered upright typewriter to her suburban New Jersey kitchen table and, working from 5 to 7 a.m. before the kids awakened, wrote her first suspense novel, *Where Are The Children?*, which became a paperback bestseller in 1975. Since then, she's hit the lists with such spinetinglers (as opposed to bloodcurdlers) as 1978's *A Stranger Is Watching* (also a movie), 1980's *The Cradle Will Fall* ("an instant classic," according to the *L.A. Times* and also a movie on TVO, 1983's *A Cry in the Night*, 1984's *Stillwatch*, 1986's *Murder in Manhattan*, and 1987's *Weep No More*. The secret of her success? Her talents as a natural-born storyteller, her disciplined mastery of her mystery-writer's craft and appealing leading characters—always what Mary Clark calls "nice people" and what *Newsweek's* Walter Clemons categorized as "characters to please an aunt of mine who likes to read about 'people I would invite into my own home.'" One further possible success secret might be that all Mary Higgins Clark novels have happy endings. "I love happy endings," says the author. "But only after an ordeal. Life is not 'hark, hark, the lark,' after all!"

Though young Mary Higgins (born on Christmas Eve 1929) prepared herself for the real world by attending secretarial school, she knew early on she wanted to write. After a romantic year flying the world as a Pan Am stewardess, she married her first beau, Warren Clark, and immediately began to fulfill her ambition of "having a large family." Widowed when her five youngsters (Marilyn, Warren, Jr., David, Carol and Patricia) ranged in age from five to thirteen, she decided it was time to follow through on her other ambition: becoming a successful novelist. But her "overnight success" actually came with a couple of decades of preparation. Before hitting the bestseller lists, Mary Higgins Clark had written and sold some three dozen short stories ("My first was rejected forty times"), worked as a radio writer and published a romantic biography of George Washington which sank without a trace. "I recently paid $13 for a copy from a bookhunting service," confides Clark. "When I opened it, it was the autographed copy I'd given my ex-boss."

Hildegarde

When the Plaza celebrated its seventy-fifth anniversary in 1982, the landmark New York City hotel featured special guest Hildegarde at the reception launching its year-long festivities. The "incomparable" had played the hostelry's former Persian Room longer than any other entertainer. The career of our lady of the long gloves, the flowing handkerchief, and the elegant gowns (she was on the ten best dressed list for years) spans more than fifty years. She started as a protégée of Gus Edwards in 1926, and it was he who suggested she use only one name. In the 1940s she became the "service-men's voice back home" through her many recordings, including "Darling, Je Vous Aime Beaucoup" (her theme song), "I'll Be Seeing You," "The Last Time I Saw Paris," "All of a Sudden My Heart Sings," and "Lily Marlene." The original sheet music for these as well as her handkerchief and gloves are now permanently enshrined at the Smithsonian in Washington, D.C.

Born Hildegarde Loretta Sell, 1 Feburary 1906 in Adell, Wisc., she was named from a novel her mother, a church organist, read during her pregnancy. She studied at St. John's Cathedral in Milwaukee and the School of Music at Marquette. In her teens she toured as a pianist in vaudeville and in 1933 won a singing contest to appear at the Cafe de Paris in France. To impresario-songwriter Ann Sosenko she owes her packaging. ("I made her a sensation," says Anna, "before she was a sensation.") In addition to her club appearances, she has presented her one-woman show in London, Paris, Copenhagen, Vienna, and throughout the U.S. and Canada. In 1961 a proclamation issued by Eleanor Roosevelt declared that she would forever be known as "The First Lady of Supper Clubs." She made her Broadway debut in Keep 'Em Laughing co-starring with William Gaxton and Victor Moore. Still active in the '80s, Hildegarde appeared in the revival of The Five O'Clock Girl at the Goodspeed Opera House, toured in The Big Broadcast of 1944 (she actually starred that year in her own NBC radio program "The Raleigh Room," one of the "top ten" for four consecutive years), continues her personal appearances in the Big Apple (she appeared at Carnegie Hall in 1986) and on the road. Her many awards and honors include the AGVA Life Achievement Award, the George M. Cohan award from the Catholic Actor's Guild, and a high papal honor.

George Roy Hill

In defense of his celebrated buddy-buddy films, he asks, "What am I supposed to do—stop the action in an action picture just to drag some women in?" He teamed Paul Newman and Robert Redford in the highly successful *Butch Cassidy and the Sundance Kid* (1969), which brought him his first Oscar nomination as Best Director. He won the Academy Award four years later for *The Sting*, which reunited the two male heartthrobs with equal success.

Born in Minneapolis 20 December 1922, Hill's youthful passions were classical music and aviation. (The latter was paid homage in his 1975 film, *The Great Waldo Pepper*, again with Redford.) At Yale ('43), he studied music, sang with the Whiffenpoofs and headed the Dramat. He served in the Marine Corps during WWII (as a transport pilot in the South Pacific) and in the Korean War with the rank of Captain. In between, he worked briefly for a newspaper in Texas, studied music and literature on the G.I. Bill at Dublin's Trinity College (B. Litt., 1949), made his first professional stage appearance in Dublin and, back in the U.S., acted off-Broadway and in radio soap operas. His first directing (as well as writing and producing) credits were in live television during its so-called Golden Age of dramatic presentations. After winning Emmy Awards for his teleplays, he directed his first Broadway play, *Look Homeward, Angel*, in 1957. He was nearly 40 when he directed his first film, *Period of Adjustment* (Tennessee Williams' only comedy), in 1962, which he had directed earlier on Broadway. His most critically-acclaimed films are *The World of Henry Orient* (1964), *Slaughterhouse Five* (1972; winner of the Special Jury Prize at the Cannes Film Festival), and *The World According to Garp* (1982).

Divorced from his wife, he has two sons and two daughters. Hobbies include flying, playing the piano and reading. "Just as I play nothing but Bach for pleasure," he says, "so do I read nothing but history for pleasure." He directed *Funny Farm* in 1988.

Gregory Hines

"Most people don't know what tap dancing is today. They've never seen it in a contemporary light. The image of a tap dancer is still someone in a top hat and tails dancing up a shiny black lacquer staircase. We need to shake that up." Gregory Hines would like to educate the public on a form of dancing that's been put on the back burner in recent years. His 1989 film, *Tap*, was a dream come true for Hines, co-star Sammy Davis Jr., newcomer Suzzanne Douglas, and a stellar line up of master hoofers from tap's "heyday."

Born on Valentine's Day 1946 in New York City, young Gregory was accessible to the artistic benefits the Big Apple offers. Along with his brother, Maurice, he began his dance instruction under the tutelage of tap teacher Henry LeTang. When Gregory turned 5 years old the two brothers teamed up as the "Hines Kids" (1949-1955) and started performing in nightclubs and theatres around the country. These appearances afforded them the opportunity of watching such dance legends as "Honi" Coles, Sandman Sims, The Nicholas Brothers, and Teddy Hale from an insiders view. As they matured, the brothers renamed themselves the "Hines Brothers" (1955-1963); when Gregory was 18 his father, Maurice joined the act and they became known as "Hines, Hines and Dad" (1963-1973). The family trio toured the U.S. and Europe and were seen on the "Tonight Show." Eventually feeling burned out, Gregory quit the tour and headed for Venice, California where he formed a jazz-rock band "Severance." He stayed on the West Coast for six years, then upon his return to New York he landed a part in *The Last Minstrel Show* (closed in Philadelphia), followed by the lead in *Eubie* on Broadway—a

Judd Hirsch

vehicle earning him a Tony nomination. With his stage acceptance certified, Gregory decided to branch out in other areas of show biz. Some movies include: *Deal of the Century* (1983), *The Cotton Club* (1985), *Running Scared* (1985), and *White Knights* (1985; co-starred with Baryshnikov). Hit Broadway shows include: *Comin' Uptown* (1980), *Sophisticated Ladies* (1981), and *I Love Liberty* (1981-1982). He has accumulated three Tony nominations (1979, 1980, 1981), a Theatre World Award, and an Emmy nomination for an appearance on the "Motown Apollo" TV special. Although he is a diversified showman, Hines insists: "I am a tapper. That's the way I think of myself." In 1988 he released his first album as a solo performer and takes his club act on the road in between new movie roles.

After his first marriage failed (two children), he married Pamela Koslow in 1981. They have one son, Zachary, and this trio happily resides together in New York City.

Judd Hirsch

As a junior engineer, he couldn't hold down a job. Eventually he turned to acting. "I'd started to look around me, to read, to go to plays, and actors fascinated me. Wow! Guys who could, through their work, have some kind of an effect on society. The instant I enrolled in acting school and stepped on a stage to do a scene in front of people, I knew I'd found a home."

Although he was received with acclaim on and off Broadway in shows such as *Barefoot in the Park; Scuba Duba; Knock, Knock* and *The Hot L Baltimore*, Hirsch claims that his big break came as a result of a television movie made in 1974 called "The Law." His performance won him an Emmy and led to further television opportunities. He appeared as a regular on the series "Delvecchio," had a part in the film *King of the Gypsies* and won a second Emmy for a one-shot appearance on "Rhoda." Neil Simon wrote *Chapter Two* for him, and his work as the star of the five-year-running series "Taxi" won him two more Emmys and millions more fans. (That second Emmy for "Taxi" came after the show was cancelled. During Hirsch's acceptance speech he castigated the show's executives who had dropped the guillotine.) His next television series "Dear John" (debut 1988-1989 season) also became an immediate hit. He won an Obie for his performance in Lanford Wilson's play *Talley's Folly* and a Tony Award (Best Actor in a Play, 1986) for his role in *I'm Not Rappaport*. He repeated his performance in *Rappaport* for a thirteen-week Broadway run in 1987. His films include *Ordinary People, Without a Trace, The Goodbye People,* and *Running on Empty.*

Twice married, he is the father of one son. In the early days of his career, he made hundreds of commercials—his face coined the native (born 15 March 1935) New Yorker's image. "I come from a family where self preservation was the only instinct. I was a troublesome kid, a kid who couldn't stop making jokes, a kid who got C's and D's in deportment." Hirsch regularly turns down money parts for better, although frequently less lucrative roles. "If turning down a bad part means it is all over for me tomorrow, as far as fame, riches and all those bad reasons for being an actor goes, well you'll find me back at the Circle Rep, doing some unknown play by an unknown writer. And enjoying it. I don't care what it is, or how big it is, I just want a thing to be good."

Al Hirschfeld

He is the bearded bard who, with his Venus HB pencil, has deftly delineated the casts of Broadway-bound plays for the Sunday New York *Times* since 1925. Graceful, witty, trenchant and tartly amusing, his drawings go beyond just "caricature" to carry, in spare flowing pen-strokes, Hirschfeld's impression of his subject's "character." In 1970 he made the coffee table scene with a noteworthy collection called *The World of Hirschfeld* and in 1973 went a step further with *The Lively Years: 1920-73.*

Born 21 June 1908 in St. Louis, Hirschfeld studied at the Art Students League. His first ventures into caricature were mostly political, and during the 1920s and 30s he was a regular contributor to *New Masses*, working for the left-wing journal without pay. He finally broke with the magazine after an editorial squabble and, he once said, has "ever since been closer to Groucho Marx than to Karl." His first theatrical sketch, which turned up in the New York *Herald Tribune* in the 1920s, was of Sacha Guitry, the French actor. A favorite parlor game of Hirschfeld fans has been to look for the name of the artist's daughter, Nina, hidden in almost every drawing. He adopted this trademark when she was born in 1945. (Her mother, Hirschfeld's second wife, is the actress Dolly Haas.) Though he often includes satiric sketches of himself in crowd scenes, he takes a dim view of other people taking similar liberties. Once, after *Variety* snidely reported that he had "sprouted a hanging garden on his chin," he sued the paper for $300,000. The jury awarded him six cents. Hirschfeld's work is included in the permanent collections of museums across the nation, including the Metropolitan, The Whitney, the Museum of Modern Art, the N.Y. Public Library, and Harvard's Fogg Museum. In 1985 he mounted his first British exhibition at London's National Theatre.

David Hockney

"I'm a rather difficult artist for the serious art world to categorize," says the Yorkshire-accented easel-whiz whose addiction to outsize horn-rimmed glasses and "sexual forth-rightness" make him a sort of Elton John of the art world. In the early 1960s, when he first emerged as a member of Britain's young new wave, he leapt about "from one idiom to another and, in the 1980s, still defying easy pigeonholing, he was alternating between paintings and drawings, stage, ballet and opera sets (e.g., *Le Sacre du Printemps, The Magic Flute*), photography and children's books (e.g. *Six Fairy Tales from the Brothers Grimm*). "I'll tell you the honest truth," he confessed to Roy Bongartz in *ARTnews*, "I just like to make pictures."

David Hockney picked up his first paintbrush as a youngster (born 9 July 1937) in the industrial city of Bradford in the north of England, encouraged by his sign-painter dad. After spending two years of hospital service as a conscientious objector, he collected a gold medal at the Royal College of Art and attracted his first notice in London as much for his gold lamé dinner jacket and dyed thatch of blond hair as his work on canvas. He made his first impact on New York in 1964 with a series at the Museum of Modern Art called "The Rake's Progress," a satirical record of his picaresque adventures on an earlier Manhattan stop-over.

While recognized in the art world as a master especially of the double portrait, Hockney is probably best-known to casual museum visitors for his shimmering swimming-pool paintings which he began after a love-at-first-splash visit to California in 1963. (Before beginning a teaching job in L.A. in 1966, he recalls, "As I got farther and farther west I became more and more excited, imagining my class would be full of young blond surfers. Unfortunately, most of the people who signed on were housewives.") After major shows in such art capitals as London, Paris, Berlin and New York in the 1970s, Hockney became the object of "a sort of international groundswell," with paintings selling for upwards of $50,000. But money isn't what keeps him painting. He once told a friend "I just want to be restaurant rich" meaning to be able to indulge himself in the luxury of eating out anywhere in the world. The observation of a London critic in 1970 still holds true: "The popular image of the golden-haired playboy flitting between California and Europe is a mask to conceal a patient and dedicated craftsman."

Dustin Hoffman

Dustin Hoffman received Academy Award nominations for his performances in *The Graduate, Midnight Cowboy, Lenny, Little Big Man, All The President's Men, Papillon, Marathon Man, Tootsie,* and Oscars for *Kramer vs. Kramer* in 1979 and *Rain Man* in 1989. On his return to the stage in the 1984 Broadway revival of Arthur Miller's *Death of a Salesman* after more than a decade's absence, Hoffman was cited by New York *Times* drama critic Mel Gussow as "one of America's finest and most popular actors. In a career spanning 17 films, playing characters of remarkable diversity, he has given unfailingly good performances—even in his lesser movies. . . . But for all the measurable successes, he remains a man obsessed by his work, craving perfection and driven by private demons in pursuit of his goal, which he considers artistic excellence." The film version of the play was a highlight of the fall 1985 television season.

"Yes, I am very difficult," he admitted to Marie Brenner in *New York* magazine. "If someone is saying to me, 'That's fine, don't worry about it,' well, for me, 'fine' ain't good enough—and tell me if I'm crazy, but it's like in *1984* when they have that kind of double-talk, 'War is Peace.' Now when I'm called a perfectionist, it's like being cursed. Well you bet I'm a pain in the ass." But the audience reaps the rewards. Memorable characters like Ratso Rizzo in *Midnight Cowboy* and Dorothy Michaels in *Tootsie* could only have been created by the performing genius of Dustin Hoffman.

He was born in Los Angeles, 8 August 1937, to a starstruck mother who named him after Dustin Farnum (the silent cowboy star), and a father who wanted to be a film director but wound up a successful designer and salesman of Danish modern furniture. As a child, Hoffman was "pint-sized," wore braces, and had the worst case of acne on the block. Originally his passion was to become a concert pianist, and he studied music at both the Los Angeles Conservatory of Music and Santa Monica City College. Then one spring when he was at his Aunt Pearl's for the Passover feast, he suddenly announced that he was going to become an actor. "You can't," said the astonished Aunt Pearl. "You're not good looking enough." In 1958, a graduate of the Pasadena Playhouse, he packed his bags and left for New York. ("I didn't go out of the house for three weeks. I slept on Gene Hackman's kitchen floor, and every morning at three the refrigerator would have a heart attack and wake me up.") He checked coats at the Longacre Theatre, washed dishes and served as clean-up man at a dance studio. According to Gassow, in one of Hoffman's most convincing acting feats while working in the toy department at Macy's, he "sold" Hackman's 18-month-old son as a life-size doll. ("I did the waiter bit too. Once the boss of a restaurant on Columbus Avenue told me I could eat as much as I wanted to, so one night I ate six steaks, and they fired me.") Remembering those days he told Gussow: "I got on stage whenever I was allowed to. . . . Acting is the only art form I'm aware of in which you cannot practice your craft and be unemployed at the same time. It's so tough to have this ego and not be able to work. A writer can write, a painter can paint, but what can an actor do? He pays the other actors to be the audience and calls it 'class!'" He made his Off Broadway debut as a hunchbacked homosexual in Ronald Ribman's black comedy *Harry, Noon and Night* during the 1964-65 season and won an Obie in 1966 in *The Journey of the Fifth Horse*. In 1968 he appeared on Broadway in Murray Schisgal's *Jimmy Shine*. Mike Nichols spotted him in Alan Arkin's film *Eh?* and flew the young actor out to Hollywood to test for the lead in *The Graduate*. At his first meeting with Joseph E. Levine, the producer mistook the young actor for the window washer. Dustin Hoffman triumphed in the film that widened the generation gap. Divorced from first wife Ann Byrne (two daughters) he is now married to Lisa Gottsegen, a lawyer and the granddaughter of his mother's best friend (four children).

Hal Holbrook

Billowing in white hair, mustaches and cigar smoke, he has transformed himself into Mark Twain on stage *Mark Twain Tonight!* over 2000 times in this country and abroad, making his one man show of the 19th century genius muckraker one of the most successful solo theatrical productions in history. He also played the junior maverick Senator Hays Stowe on TV's "The Bold Ones" but has a hankering to do a farce or western in the future. "You've got to grow as an actor, and change as you grow as a person" he says. "That's . . . the beauty of acting—it's a way of fighting a society that locks you into position."

Born in Cleveland 17 February 1925 and abandoned by his parents at two, he spent "Huck Finnish summers" with "Uncle Sabe and Aunt Ruby." ("I had a tree house with a rope ladder, took long hunting trips with a wooden gun, and I got on fine with Uncle Sabe. He was grumpy but his eyes laughed. There's a lot of Uncle Sabe in my Mark Twain.") He conceived the idea for *Mark Twain Tonight!* as an alternative to selling hats at Macy's when he couldn't get work as an actor. He performed it in 1955 at San Francisco's Purple Onion and later in a Greenwich Village nightclub (while working daytimes in the TV soap opera "The Brighter Day"), and made a hit with it Off-Broadway in 1959, putting together the two-hour show from some nine hours of material. As an actor he has a wide range. On stage he has appeared in *The Glass Menagerie* and *Does a Tiger Wear a Necktie*, as well as various Lincoln Center Repertory productions. His film credits include *The Great White Hope, Wild in the Streets,* followed by *All the President's Men* (1976), *Julia* (1978), *Creepshow* (1981), *The Unholy* (1987), *Wall Street* (1987), and *Fletch* (1989). He appeared in the two television miniseries "North and South: Book II" (1986) and "The Fortunate Pilgrim" (1988). Divorced from Ruby Johnson (two children) and Carol Rossen (one daughter), he tied the nupital knot in spring 1984 to singer-actress Dixie Carter. He joins her on the CBS-TV hit show "Designing Women" in a recurring role.

Fritz Hollings

When a New York *Times* reporter asked this increasingly powerful South Carolina senator if he had formed an exploratory committee to raise money for a possible race for the White House, Ernest F. (Fritz) Hollings replied with his usual candor: "You don't need an exploratory committee when you're a United States Senator. I started exploring from the day I got up here. That's one problem we have in the Senate; we all think at times that we should be President." In 1984, Hollings thought exactly that, testing the campaign waters with his toes only to drop out before the first primary.

The aborted campaign by no means signaled an end to the career of this one-time arch-conservative who, in recent years, has increasingly worked with powerful liberals in fashioning key legislation from Capitol Hill. On his way to the governer's office of South Carolina, back in 1955, Hollings fanned the racial fires by denouncing the NAACP as "against our way of life in the South," urging that the organization be declared "subversive and illegal." Several years later, as governor, he repeatedly made anti-integration comments to the media. Savvy insiders, however, preferred to watch what Hollings did rather than what he said; during his incumbency the public schools of the state were integrated with a minimum of brouhaha. Education in general benefited from his term of office, due in part to his policy of raising teachers' salaries.

Using the governor's post as a springboard to national prominence, Hollings won a Senate seat on a wave of energy, a style that both opponents and admirers labeled the "Fritzkrieg." After his re-election in 1968, Fritz Hollings began to edge towards the political center. He surprised Washington observers by becoming one of the first official leaders of the Deep South to acknowledge the existence of hunger among his constituents. His generally conservative voting record has nevertheless reflected a willingness to be pragmatic; in 1971, for example, he offered a tax relief program for low-income taxpayers, and in 1972 the far right was claiming he had "gone communist" by advocating federal funding for day care centers. His environmental stands have generally received praise by the folks who wear "Save the Whale" buttons. His position as ranking Democrat on the Budget Committee positions him advantageously to influence fiscal proposals.

The senator was born in Charleston, S.C. on New Year's Day 1922, into a family that had fallen out of prosperity and eventually into bankruptcy. With an uncle's money he attended The Citadel, the prestigious Charleston military college. He obtained an L.L.B. degree from the University of South Carolina School of Law in 1947. He is married to a former high school teacher, Rita ("Peatsy") Liddy, and has four children from a previous marriage that ended in divorce.

Celeste Holm

"'My God, young lady,' I replied in astonishment. 'You ask if Celeste Holm takes theatre seriously? She is a star. Do you know what that means?'" Agnes DeMille's spirited response to a thoroughly chastened FBI agent inquiring into the credentials of Celeste Holm for a post with the National Endowment for the Arts is typical of the high regard her colleagues have for the actress who became a Broadway star in 1943 as Ado Annie in *Oklahoma!* (stopping the show each night with her hilarious rendition of "I Can't Say No") and for more than four decades has continued to light up—with her talent, charm and good humor—stage, screen and television. The theatre, however, remains her first love, as attested to by her willingness to risk arrest rather than remove herself from the path of a bulldozer that was about to demolish two venerable Broadway houses to make way for yet another skyscraper. Less spotlighted is Celeste's longtime dedication to a variety of humanitarian causes, most notably UNICEF (her 50¢ an hour autograph charge has netted that organization more than $15,000) and mental health, an interest sparked by her visits to military hospitals during WWII and her experiences while researching her role in the film *The Snake Pit*.

Born 29 April 1919 in New York to an insurance executive and his portrait painter wife, Celeste's education took her from New York to Chicago to Paris, and she made her Broadway acting debut in the Theatre Guild's 1939 production of William Saroyan's Pulitzer Prize winning play, *The Time of Your Life*. Four years later came *Oklahoma!*, then *Bloomer Girl* in 1944, then Hollywood (with frequent trips back for additional Broadway appearances). She won an Oscar early on, as best supporting actress in 1947 for her blistering performance in *Gentlemen's Agreement* (which also led to a lifelong dedication to combating anti-Semitism), and received Academy Award nominations for her roles in *All About Eve* and *Come to the Stable* (for which she won the French Oscar equivalent for her portrayal of a French nun). Other notable films include *The Tender Trap, High Society* and as Aunt Polly in the 1973 version of *Tom Sawyer*. In 1987 she appeared in the popular movie *Three Men And A Baby*. Television has seen her as a continuing character on "Archie Bunker's Place," as the Fairy Godmother in Rodgers & Hammerstein's "Cinderella," as Mrs. Warren G. Harding (Emmy nomination) in "Backstairs at the Whitehouse," in the premiere presentation of the PBS American Playhouse series, John Cheever's "The Shady Hill Kidnapping" and as co-star in 1984 of the series, "Jessie." In 1985 she appeared in several episodes of CBS' "Falcon Crest" as neighboring vintner Anna Rossini. Recent theatrical triumphs include starring roles in the British premiere of *Lady in the Dark* and a 1983 revival of Noel Coward's *Hay Fever* at L.A.'s Ahmanson Theatre. Of Norwegian descent, Celeste was knighted in 1979 by King Olav; in 1982 she was named by President Reagan to the National Arts Council (having long since passed muster for the National Endowment), and in 1983 Governor Kean appointed her Chairman of the New Jersey Motion Picture & Television Development Commission. Although she and her husband, actor Wesley Addy (she has two sons from an earlier marriage), make New York City their principal residence, they spend weekends restoring an 18th-century New Jersey farmhouse.

Larry Holmes

He came along after Muhammad Ali, who'd been boxing's most entertaining (and some say best) heavyweight. Although respected by veteran observers, Holmes' methodical style didn't endear him at first to fight fans who'd grown accustomed to the brash, showboating Ali. But Holmes' consistent winning (three-fourths by knockout) finally added respect to the accomplishments of the terse former street fighter. His philosophy was simple: "I know what I have to do. I have to take my man out."

Larry Holmes was born the seventh of twelve children in Cuthbert, Ga., on 3 November 1949. Parents John and Flossie Holmes were sharecroppers there, but moved to Easton, Pa., when Larry was four. Unable to find work, the father left Flossie and the children to welfare. Larry dropped out of school at thirteen to work and learned boxing at a youth center. At nineteen he decided he "might as well" make boxing his livelihood and after a successful pro beginning, novice promoter Don King brought him into his stable in 1973. Working as both sparring partner to top heavyweights like Ali and Joe Frazier and boxing on fight cards, Holmes moved up in ranking and got a 1978 title shot at World Boxing Council champ Ken Norton. He decisioned Norton, going nine rounds with a shoulder injury, to win the title. As champ, the six-feet-three Holmes fought at 213 pounds, and was noted for a blinding jab, destructive hook and an ability to "clear" or re-orient himself quickly after being stunned to the head. He defended his crown against, among others, Mike Weaver whom he KO'd in twelve, and Earnie Shavers in a rematch. In 1980 he reluctantly TKO'd three-time champ Ali, who was pitifully over-the-hill, but whose financial obligations forced his return. Holmes cried afterwards, asking, "Why did he have to come back? When is [Ali] going to learn the most important things in life are his children and his wife?"

In 1981 he put former (short-term) champ Leon Spinks away in four rounds. (In September 1985 Leon's brother Michael avenged Leon's loss by winning a unanimous decision over Holmes to become the first light heavyweight champion to succeed to the heavyweight championship—and preventing Holmes from equalling Rocky Marciano's 49-0 record.) The next year he met Gerry Cooney, whom he dubbed "white hope for the white dopes." The Irish-American Cooney, a true slugger, enjoyed favorable press for his 26-0 record, with 21 KO's, including one over Ken Norton. Animosity had flared because of negative remarks Cooney gave the press about Holmes. Don King guaranteed each of them $10 million, and the grudge match in an outdoor Los Vegas arena attracted a $50 million live-and-televised gate. Cautious early on, in later rounds Holmes peppered the dangerous, but awkward Cooney until the 13th when the challenger's trainer jumped into the ring and the ref put an end to the beating. The victory marked the point at which Holmes' credibility was permanently established. A boxer-businessman in the new tradition, Holmes owns a restaurant-bar, a parking lot and property in Easton where he lives with wife Diane and two of his four children. He bought a house for his mother there, and opened a fried chicken restaurant named for her.

Benjamin L. Hooks

"Racism in all of its sensitive implications is still part of American life, and we plan to fight that," says this Baptist minister and lawyer, who resigned his post as the first black member of the Federal Communications Commission to become executive director in 1977 of the National Association for the Advancement of Colored People (NAACP). But, he noted, "the battle is much more sophisticated" than in the tumultuous civil rights era of the 1960s, because Americans now face a huge problem "that transcends race—it is employment, education, and a decent welfare system." Member of an elite black Memphis family deeply dedicated to civic service, Hooks was a pioneering civil rights activist in Tennessee and in 1965 became the first black judge appointed in the South since Reconstruction. As chief executive of the NAACP, he set out to revitalize the organization with new programs and alliances and a membership goal of 2 million by 1985. A fiery orator who delivers speeches and sermons in the style of Martin Luther King and other preachers he has admired, Hooks remains close to the church. "The church is my first love and I'll always go back to preaching," he has said. "The church has kept black folks together and I believe it will encourage another civil rights movement, which we need right now."

Benjamin Lawson Hooks was born in Memphis, 31 January 1925, the fifth of seven children of Bessie and Robert B. Hooks Sr. His father, a photographic studio owner, was a stern task master and both parents tried to instill a sense of self-esteem and self-motivation in their children, Hooks recalls. "So many people today have a harum-scarum life, but because of that training I have a fairly disciplined life. That's why I get a lot done." Though the Hooks' were among the black elite, their affluence was only relative, especially during the Depression, and Ben "always wore hand-me-downs, never anything else." But even in the hardest times, "Mother could make things stretch.... We always had something to eat." Although drawn to the ministry, he was influenced by his father (who was cool to organized religion) and turned to a career in law, receiving his J.D. degree in 1948 from DePaul University in Chicago (law schools in Tennessee didn't admit black students at the time). Opportunities were brighter in Chicago, but Hooks returned to Tennessee, vowing to help "break down that segregation, to end those days." He worked as lawyer in Memphis' segregated courts and took part in NAACP's restaurant sit-ins in the late '50s and early '60s. After being elected the first black judge in Shelby County, he served a full eight-year term and gained national recognition with his appointment to the FCC (serving 1972-77). A prominent businessman, he was co-founder and chairman of the Mutual Federal Savings and Loan Association (1955-1969). He serves on numerous boards including the Public Broadcasting Service.

Hooks and Frances Dancy, a teacher, were married in 1951 and have an adopted daughter, Patricia. He is an ordained minister on leave from The Middle Baptist Church in Memphis and The Greater New Mt. Moriah Baptist Church in Detroit.

Bob Hope

He is the most American of comedians, but the superstar with the ski-jump nose and the scooped chin was born in Eltham, Kent, England 29 May 1903. He came to Cleveland, Ohio at age 4 with the name Leslie Townes Hope. He's travelled millions of miles to entertain the troops around the world. He is a friend of Presidents and notables, and once traded ad-libs with the King of England. ("The only time I ever had a King for a straight man.") His 80th birthday in 1983 was celebrated in the Senate and NBC devoted an entire evening's prime time airwaves to a lavish tribute broadcast from the Kennedy Center in Washington. At the time an ecstatic Hope quipped, "Security is so tight in the President's box, one agent checked me for bombs and threw out half my monologue." Describing his brand of humor as "pseudosmart" he says, "I want the audience to enjoy it like I do."

One of the few performers to triumph in five major entertainment media—vaudeville, stage, radio, motion pictures, and television—he was the fifth of his stone-mason father's seven sons. In Cleveland he helped out at home by working as a delivery boy, soda fountain clerk, and shoe salesman before making his vaudeville debut dancing in a Fatty Arbuckle Revue. Known at school as "Les," he says he changed his name to Bob after schoolmates started calling him "Hopeless." Soon after his Cleveland vaudeville debut he also worked as a reporter, a dance instructor, and a prizefighter ("I was the only one they ever carried both ways") after which he soft-shoed his way to Broadway to make his debut in *Sidewalks of New York* in 1927. While working in the musical *Roberta* in 1933, he met and married singer Dolores Reade, still his wife and mother to his four adopted children. A star of his own radio series starting in 1938, he continued on the NBC wireless for a total of 1,145 programs. During WW II he began his tours to entertain the troops. Hope made his film debut in *The Big Broadcast of 1938* and starred in a long parade of big-screen comedies, some of the most popular being the many "road" pictures (*Road to Singapore, Road to Rio* et al) made with his longtime buddy, the late Bing Crosby. He also starred on scores of TV specials and is the author of nine books, including *Road to Hollywood* in 1977 and *Confessions of a Hooker* in 1985.

Hope, who lives in a 25,000 sq. ft. home in Palm Springs, California that's been compared to "Disneyland . . . made to be toured," confesses that he's "slowing down a bit. George Burns, Lawrence Welk and I, for excitement on Saturday night, all sit around and see whose leg falls asleep faster." Every night he heads for the center of Palm Springs for his constitutional walk down the main drag, window shopping and signing autographs. "I still need the laughs and the adulation." He is the recipient of more than a thousand awards and citations for humanitarian and professional efforts including the President's Medal of Freedom and 1985 Kennedy Center Honors for Lifetime Achievement in the Arts. Hope is a dedicated golfer and his annual Bob Hope Desert Classic has produced nearly $10 million dollars for charities in the Palm Springs area. He averages 15 to 20 celebrity golf benefits every year.

Anthony Hopkins

"Acting is a craft. It's common sense. Talent—I don't know what that is. It's knowing the alphabet of one's instrument, knowing the text, and getting on with it." Welshman Anthony Hopkins has been getting on with it on stage, television, and in films, winning in 1973 the Actor of the Year Award from Great Britain's Society of Film & Television Arts for his portrayal of Pierre in the miniseries based on *War and Peace;* in 1976, an Emmy for his impersonation of Bruno Hauptmann in the NBC docu-drama "The Lindbergh Kidnapping Case"; and in 1975 the New York Drama Desk Best Actor Award and the Outer Critics Award for his performance in Peter Shaffer's play *Equus*.

Born on New Year's Eve 1937 in Port Talbot, a small town in South Wales, Hopkins was as a youngster big for his age ("fairly brainless") and his peers hung nicknames of "ox," "ape" and "pig" on him. His father, "a man of little tolerance, was always putting me down." Although his parents "slaved all their lives in a bakery for peanuts," they sent him to an exclusive boarding school, Cowbridge, in nearby Glamorgan. "I loathed it . . . academically, I was an idiot. I wouldn't learn math . . . the only talent I had was for playing the piano and impersonating the schoolmasters. . . . It was a snob school." After a two-year stretch in the army, he studied drama at the Royal Academy of Dramatic Art in London (1961-1963), and made his London stage debut in a 1964 production of *Julius Caesar*. After his second audition for the National Theatre, Laurence Olivier snapped, "I don't think I'm going to lose any sleep tonight, but would you like to join us?" He stayed with the National from 1966-1972, earning the accolade of "most promising actor" in *Variety's* 1970-71 poll of London theatre critics. (He left twice, but returned both times. "I had a marvelous stay there. I had a bad-boy reputation. During the '60s it was fashionable to be very wild and crazy. I was very unsuccessful at it. I couldn't do it with panache. But I had a go at trying to get a bad reputation. . . . It's all forgiven now.") Hopkins was introduced to American audiences in the 1974 production of *Equus*. In 1984 he made an appearance in New York off-Broadway in Harold Pinter's *Old Times* with Jane Alexander and Marsha Mason which was highly praised. He received glowing notices in 1985 for his West End portrayal of Rupert Murdoch-like press lord in *Pravda*. He made his screen debut in 1968 in *The Lion in Winter* with Katharine Hepburn and Peter O'Toole. Other films include: *The Looking Glass War* (1970); *When Eight Bells Toll* (1971); *Young Winston* (1972); *A Doll's House* with Claire Bloom (1973); *Juggernaut* (1974); *Audrey Rose* and *A Bridge Too Far* (9177); *Magic* (1978); *The Elephant Man* and *A Change of Seasons* (1980); *The Bounty* (1984); *84 Charing Cross Road* (1986); *The Good Father* (1987); *The Old Jest* (1987); *A Chorus of Disapproval* (1988); *Three Penny Opera* (1989) and *Great Expectations* (1989). Noteworthy television appearances: "All Creatures Great and Small" (1975); "Dark Victory" (1976); "Kean"; "Mayflower: The Pilgrims' Adventure"; "The Bunker" (he portrayed Adolf Hitler); the miniseries, "QB VII"; "Hollywood Wives"; "Mussolini: The Decline and Fall of Il Duce" (1985); and the Hallmark Hall of Fame presentation "The Tenth Man" (1988).

His first marriage ended in divorce in 1972. He and his second wife, the former Jennifer Layton (a former production secretary on one of his movies, whom he married in 1973), maintain a home in Beverly Hills. He has a daughter by his first wife. His hobbies are astronomy and playing the piano. "I love the stage." says Hopkins. "That's where I obviously want to go back to. But I get the same thrill out of working in television. There's a magical thrill of having words come out of one's mouth in the right order. It's a comic way of making a living, saying lines. But in working it out, the excitement starts. . . . It's easier to work in television and movies. . . . I don't go along with suffering for the sake of art."

Roger Horchow

"The lanky, laid-back catalogue king," says Charlotte Curtis the New York *Times* columnist, has decided that $80 million in gross sales is plenty. 'I don't want to get to too big. If we did, we'd explode out of our warehouse . . . we'd need middle management. I really don't want that.'" Horchow is chairman and owner of the Dallas-based Horchow Collection which is the favorite mail order catalogue for more than 2 million upward income households. Catalogues arrive throughout the year with Roger's best bets, the sort of *tres chic* manna materialist spray for from fun costume jewelry to cozy terrycloth robes by Christian Dior and furs and toys and china and art. Although there's a Carolyn Horchow whose name we see engraved on just about anything engravable in the catalogue, and their three daughters pictures glow in the Collection's frames, he's strictly a one-man show, selecting all the merchandise himself.

Born 3 July 1928 in Cincinnati, he was always a go-getting salesman. He sold magazines and "was a Future Farmer of America. I raised chickens. I was an Eagle Scout. When I went away to the Hill School, they said I'd have to wear a hat. I knew I didn't. The moment I got there, I threw it away . . . everything I've ever done is in what I'm doing now. I always knew I'd be my own boss." After graduating form Yale in 1950 he was an executive in merchandising for several stores including Neiman-Marcus and Federated Department Stores. He was also president of Cambridge, Massachusetts' innovative Design Research. Leaving Neiman-Marcus, where he was the mail order V.P., he founded the Kenton Collection in 1971, bought it from the Kenton Corporation in 1973 and changed the name to Horchow. He is an active fundraiser for charities and the author of two books, *Elephants in Your Mailbox* and *Living in Style*. A Texas resident not the least bit like TV's famous "Dallas" characters, Horchow seems to prefer the nuances of Beacon Hill to "South Fork." He vacations on Nantucket in a grand newly built house on the cliff overlooking the harbor and wears Hawaiian swim trunks to the beach club to "keep from being predictable."

Lena Horne

Still almost as impossibly beautiful as when she was a 16-year old chorine in Harlem's Cotton Club, this personification of the black female entertainment experience found it ironic that she was chosen to be the pioneer that she became. "I was an ingenue, for Christ's sake, you know. I'd suddenly got thrown into this never-never land of Hollywood. . . . I didn't really have the strength to show people how I really was inside." But Lena Horne grew to find that strength, and what's more, at age 63 imparted that quality in her triumphant *Lena Horne: The Lady and Her Music* to world-wide audiences who made it the longest-running one-woman show in history. And what did she make of her rejuvenated career, with its Kennedy Center Honors, two Grammys, special Tony, and NAACP Spingarn Award? "I'm a late bloomer," the glamorous grandmother says. "I hate that I waited so long to let my barriers down. Now you'd have to take a bullet to drive me offstage."

Born "in the better part of Brooklyn" on 30 June 1917, Lena Mary Calhoun Horne had a grandmother who was the child of a black slave woman and her white owner. Lena's numbers-running dad and travelling actress mom were divorced when she was three, so she was passed around as a youngster to the homes of various relatives down South (from whence comes her syrupy Southern inflection). After her debut at the Cotton Club, which at the time catered to whites-only audiences, she was on the move again as a singer with Charlie Barnet's band, and then became the first black woman to ever sign a long-term Hollywood contract. Featured in many films in the 1940's (*Cabin in the Sky, Stormy Weather, Ziegfeld Follies*), she often found herself photographed leaning against a pillar or in some other solo situation so her scenes could be scissored out when the films were shown in the South. But all the while, Lena recalls, "you had to be grateful, grateful, grateful." Married while still in her teens to "incredibly handsome" Louis Jones, she became the mother of two children (daughter Gail is divorced from director Sidney Lumet; son Teddy died in 1970), and was divorced in 1938. In 1947, she was wowing Europeans on her first singing tour of the Continent, she married white musician Lennie Hayton in Paris. "It was cold-blooded and deliberate. I married him because he could get me into places a black man couldn't. But I really learned to love him." When he died after 24 years of marriage, followed closely by the deaths of her father and son in the early '70s, Lena said, "I thought that I was nothing. But the pain of the loss somehow cracked me open, made me feel compassion. Now I'm kinder to myself and to other people."

Her friendship with black actor and activist Paul Robeson clarified her people's history for her, and in Hollywood she was ready to chuck the loneliness of her singular black star status until Count Basie asked her to remain and use the chance for black advancement. She became an ardent civil rights activist early on (supporting Dr. King's marches, and voter registration by speaking throughout the South), as well as giving 30 benefit concerts in Israel in 1952 in support of the fledgling state. She and singer Harry Belafonte gave similar performances in the U.S. for civil rights; all fitting, since in the '40s and '50s she'd had to fight for contracts guaranteeing that blacks could attend her club performances.

In 1979, she said, "the biggest thing that ever happened" to her was Howard University's conferring upon her an honorary doctorate of humane letters. Unlike others she'd rejected, she "was ready to take" that one. The single singer, who says, "Rather than marrying again, I might go as far as hiring somebody to whom I have formed an attachment," lives in a restored olive mill in Santa Barbara, Calif., where she has planted 53 trees, and in an apartment in Washington, D.C. In 1989 she released the record album *The Men in My Life*.

Marilyn Horne

"If the New York *Times* runs a picture and I'm not in it, I'll find you and smack you right in the face, you son of a bitch." That rare bit of temperament, revealed in Marilyn Horne's 1983 autobiography, was directed towards Beverly Sills' press agent whom she caught removing Horne's pictures from a press kit for a La Scala (of Milan) production of *The Siege of Corinth*. Most of the time, the "world's greatest singer" (*Opera News;* Italy's Rossini Foundation, among other proclaimers) is one of opera's most cheerful divas. Long one of the world's most eminent performing artists, Horne's success is the more remarkable because she has achieved it as a mezzo-soprano. Most mezzo parts are either "trouser" roles (originally written for castrati) or roles in support of the soprano. ("To be a mezzo, says Horne, is to be an Avis in a Hertz world.") But the "huggable" singer ("My greatest struggle is not to weigh three hundred pounds!") has tried harder, achieving greatness with a voice "whose richness and technical perfection are matchless" (*People*) and with "the technique, muscianship, vocal range and accuracy of intonation that would have made her a star in any age" (Harold Schonberg in choosing Horne as the all-time mezzo-soprano on his list of great voices of the Metropolitan Opera in 1983 in the New York *Times*). That she is a star in almost *any* language may be attributable to another snippet from *Marilyn Horne: My Life:* I'm not sure Berlitz would admit this, but the best way to learn another language is in bed."

Marilyn Horne's parents decided to move from the small town of Bradford, Pa. (where she was born 16 January 1934) to California for the vocal opportunities it offered her. A scholarship to USC enabled her to study with Lotte Lehmann ("one very tough lady") and become friends with Igor Stravinsky. ("There were so many refugees from Hitler all over . . . I used to have dinner with Stravinsky, Christopher Isherwood, Aldous Huxley.") After making a series of low-budget pop recordings and, at 20, dubbing the singing voice for Dorothy Dandridge in *Carmen Jones,* Jackie (as she is known to friends) moved to Europe in 1956 to launch an operatic career. On the day she returned—2 July 1960—she married black conductor Henry Lewis (she had met him at USC and renewed the friendship in Vienna) whom she divorced in 1979. Of their daughter Angela (born in 1965), Horne says, "she has the voice. . . . The question is whether she has all the other stuff" for a singing career. The diva made her U.S. operatic debut in 1960 in *Wozzeck* with the San Francisco Opera, but it wasn't until her memorable performance with Joan Sutherland at Carnegie Hall in an American Opera Society presentation of *Semiramide* in 1964 that she was launched into the front rank of opera and concert performers. She made a stunning Metropolitan Opera debut as Adalgisa in *Norma* in 1970 (with Sutherland, who says of the duo, "For my money, we can go on singing together until we drop"), but has devoted more and more attention to the baroque repertory, with such trouser roles as *Tancredi* and *Semiramide* and *Rinaldo* (a triumph in the Met's 1983 opener; ditto later that season in Central Park before an audience of a couple of hundred thousand) and the great Rossinian comic heroines like Rosina in *The Barber of Seville.* The recipient of 40 curtain calls in Hamburg in 1980 for her performance in *L'Italiana in Algeri* and "the most unanimous acclaim in the history of Italian opera" after her 1977 debut as *Tancredi* at the Rome Opera, Horne has thus far resisted the temptation to stake out territory in the juicier soprano range. "If I had a dollar for every time people have asked me to sing *Fidelio, Norma,* or *Lady Macbeth,* I'd have a nice piece of change." In 1988 she received the Fidelio Gold Medal Award from the International Association of Opera Directors.

Israel Horovitz

"Art's just slowing down life so we can look at it more closely, that's all it is—whether it's kings or rats, whether my father dies or my foot falls asleep," says this playwright who burst onto the off-Broadway scene the winter of 1967-68 with four hits in four months, including *The Indian Wants the Bronx* in which Al Pacino made his stage debut. Since then, he's written more than 35 plays translated into more than 20 languages. He also wrote the largely autobiographical screenplay for the 1982 Pacino movie *Author! Author!*, a story about a divorced playwright, who, like Horovitz, raises his children alone. Today, he is one of the most frequently produced playwrights in contemporary theatre; on any given night, more than 20 of his plays are produced throughout the world. In his typical self-promoting yet self-mocking style, he calls himself "an internationally known playwright on a very low level." His main trademarks are psychic violence and the use of humor to deal with pain, as in this dialogue from *Author! Author!:* "I joke, you sob—what difference does it make, we're both miserable."

Born in Wakefield, Mass., 31 March 1939, the son of a truck driver, Israel Horovitz was a bright boy with a vivid imagination who, at age 13, wrote a novel called *Steinberg, Sex, and the Saint* and at age 17 wrote his first play, *The Comeback,* and had it produced in Boston. He studied on a fellowship at the Royal Academy of Dramatic Art in London (1961-63) and in 1965 was the first American to be playwright in residence with the Royal Shakespeare Company. His New York debut was *Line* in 1967 at Cafe La MaMa. Among his best-known plays are *Rats, The Primary English Class* (Canada's longest running play which starred Diane Keaton in its New York City premiere) and *The Wakefield Plays* —a Euripides-inspired cycle of seven plays including *Hopscotch, The 75th, Alfred the Great, Our Father's Failing, Alfred Dies, Stage Directions,* and *Spared.* Among his recent plays is *The Widow's Blind Date* (1983) for The Gloucester Stage Company, where he is artistic director, *Today I Am A Fountain Pen* (1985), and *Year of the Duck* (1987). Horovitz first married his high school sweetheart Doris, (three children: Matthew, Rachael, Adam); they were divorced. His film *Author! Author!* reveals some autobiographical details, according to writer Ross Wetzsteaon. Like the playwright in the film, Horovitz jogs obsessively to unwind (running eight to sixteen miles a day), has lied about his age (at different times making himself younger or older), and alternately seeks and scorns critical approval. "Good reviews are like bronchitis, bad reviews are like cancer," he once said. "You know they're going to make you sick, the question is how sick." Horovitz and his second wife, Gillian Adams, a world-class marathoner, divide their time between homes in Gloucester and New York's Greenwich Village.

Vladimir Horowitz

One of classical music's greatest and most durable superstars, this brilliant, mercurial man of the keyboard has frustrated fans with occasional lengthy "sabbaticals" from performing. But Vladimir Horowitz' return is always worth the wait. In 1982, when he went back to London after a 31-year absence for a worldwide television concert at Royal Festival Hall, his dazzling performances of Scarlatti, Chopin and Rachmaninoff were followed by twenty solid minutes of cheering. But, he told Edward Behr of *Newsweek,* "It's the silence that matters, not the applause. Anyone can have applause. But the silence, before and during the playing—that is everything."

Born in Kiev, 1 October 1904, the son of well-to-do Russian-Jewish parents, young Horowitz had ambitions of becoming a composer but was pushed towards the piano. When the Russian Revolution deprived his parents of their possessions, to help his father he began to concertize. Given permission in 1925 to go abroad for purposes of "study," he chose to stay in Europe, appearing in Berlin and other capitals with the orchestras of Bruno Walter, Wilhelm Furtwangler, and other notable conductors. In 1928 he made his debut at Carnegie Hall with the New York Philharmonic and subsequently met Arturo Toscanini while the great Italian maestro was conducting his cycle of Beethoven concerts with the Philharmonic.

Horowitz married Toscanini's daughter Wanda in Milan in 1933; they have a daughter, Sonia. An American citizen now, Horowitz maintains a home in New York, where he gives occasional lessons to a favored few young pianists. His guests are surrounded by paintings by Manet, Rouault and Degas. Unlike some of his contemporaries who yearn nostalgically for the "good old days," the maestro gives high marks to today's audiences. "In the past," he told Edward Behr, "the public did not understand music. But now, through records, cassettes, they know so much, you no longer have to exaggerate. My playing has become simpler, and simplicity is wisdom." In 1988 he received a Grammy for Best Classical Recording (*Horowitz in Moscow*).

Whitney Houston

In the three years since the release of her debut album which bears her name, Whitney Houston has captured numerous awards, long standing records, and made her own indelible mark on music audiences around the world. Called by Stephen Holden in the New York *Times* "a refined belter who wields power by rationing out her enormous resources very carefully," this young, vivacious, 5'8" cover girl, named "Artist of the Year" by *Billboard* Magazine (1986), is the recipient of one Emmy Award (Outstanding Individual Performance in a Variety or Music Program—the 28th Annual Grammy Program), and multiple Grammys and American Music Awards. Whitney's first album could be called the sleeper of the decade, riding on the charts for sixty eight weeks following its February 1985 release before becoming the most successful solo debut album of all time. With sales of more than nine million copies in the United States and over thirteen million worldwide, the album yielded three #1 pop hit singles: "Saving All My Love For You" (which earned Whitney a Grammy), "How Will I Know?" (number two on the dance charts), and "The Greatest Love of All" which Whitney sang for the Statue of Liberty Centennial Celebration to a nationwide TV audience. Her second album, *Whitney,* was released in the spring of 1987 and she became the first female artist (and only the fourth solo artist—behind Elton John, Stevie Wonder and Bruce Springsteen) to have an album debut at the #1 spot on the album charts. *Whitney* spawned such number #1 hits as "I Wanna Dance With Somebody (Who Loves Me)" and "Didn't We Almost Have it All." With the release of her single "Where Do Broken Hearts Go," Whitney Houston is the only artist to achieve an unprecedented seven consecutive #1 hits, surpassing The Beatles, and the Bee Gees, each with six consecutive #1 hits. Like the words in her song, "I Wanna Dance with Somebody," the music world can "feel the heat" of the talented Miss Houston.

Born in Newark, New Jersey on 9 August 1963 to John and Emily "Cissy" Houston, Whitney was raised in a musical environment. Mother Cissy is a veteran gospel and R&B singer who used to sing with her nieces, Dionne and Dee Dee Warwick in a gospel group called the Dinkard Sisters. In the 1960's Cissy was the featured singer in a soul group called Sweet Inspirations who backed up such artists as Aretha Franklin and Elvis Presley. Whitney, who started out singing in the New Hope Baptist Church Junior Choir at age nine, remembers watching rehearsals of her mother and one of her idols Aretha Franklin. "I remember being in the studio and how moving it was to see Aretha work. I decided then that if I was going to sing, I wanted to make people feel the same way about my music." Without pressure from her mother (who expected Whitney to become a teacher), Whitney decided in elementary school that she wanted to be a singer. Once Whitney's mind was made up she turned to her mother to be her "teacher . . . and inspiration." While still in high school, Whitney sang with her mother in nightclubs and in recording studios. At age fifteen, she was doing background vocalist work for Chaka Khan and Lou Rawls when Luther Vandross offered to produce her as a solo artist, but her parents insisted that she finish high school first. At the same time, the tall, lean, and graceful Whitney launched a modeling career, appearing in such magazines as *Vogue, Cosmopolitan,* and a cover of *Seventeen* Magazine when she was only eighteen. After graduating from high school in 1981, Whitney did some advertising jingles and backup on albums for The Nevill Brothers and the funk band, Material. In 1983 she sang "Eternal Love" on the album *Paul Jabara and Friends.* Under the personal wing of Gene Harvey, still her personal manager, Whitney performed in showcases at such places as Sweetwaters (a Manhattan Upper West Side supper club). Seen there by Clive Davis, founder and president of Arista Records, Whitney was soon signed to a recording contract at the age of twenty. Making her national TV debut on "The Merv Griffin Show" singing "Hold On" (a duet with Teddy Pendergrass), Whitney was on her way to fame.

A member of a very close-knit family (her father is her business manager, brother Michael is her road manager, brother Gary sings back-up, and Mom is her coach), Whitney also feels the importance of her religious upbringing. "If you anchor yourself with God, you can resist a lot of temptations." When asked about the future, the soft-spoken, somewhat shy beauty replied, "Tomorrow's not promised. If I'm here, hopefully, I'll still be making good music."

Barbara Howar

Reviewing the 1973 edition of the *Celebrity Register* Liz Smith castigated the editors for excluding this blonde achiever: "How can Willie Morris be more a celebrity than the omitted, admittedly hot, and best-selling Barbara Howar, who is his girlfriend [but is not now] and also wrote a much better book [about herself, in nonfiction] than Willie did in his fictionalized version of her rise and fall in Washington power circles? Have you ever seen Willie on the talk shows? Have you ever *not* seen Barbara?"

Outspoken and feisty on a variety of subjects from politics to sex and marriage. Howar is a native of North Carolina, born 27 September 1934. She was first noticed as the wife of a wealthy Washington, D.C. real estate man; she gave "wild mod parties" and wore fabulous clothes and became the "hostess with the mostes' publicity" in Washington. When she and Ray Howar divorced in 1967 she was granted custody of their two children, a daughter Bader and son Edmond. The former debutante went to work as a TV interviewer and was a hit with the viewers—her brand of enthusiasm, genuine and well-informed instead of Pollyanna-ish, is infectious. Her first book (the aforementioned autobiography) *Laughing All the Way,* billed as "a real insider's guide to Washington," dealt with her transition from astute Southern belle whose main talents were "tea dishing and thank-you-note-writing" to independent woman. A reviewer for the New York *Times* called it "delightful, gossipy and hilarious." It was number one for 26 weeks. She next wrote a novel, *Making Ends Meet,* published in 1976. Howar has been a columnist for the Washington *Post* and television correspondent for CBS News on the prime-time magazine show "Who's Who" in 1976-77. In 1984 and 1985 she became New York correspondent for "Entertainment Tonight." Very much a working woman all the way, her circle of friends form the heart of the New York media scene. She has never remarried. "If there's someone out there who is terrific . . . I would love that. I think it would be marvelous. If there's not, it's not going to be the end of the world. I've never been any good at sleeping around to get what I wanted. If I'd had the ability to do that, you wouldn't have seen me for my dust."

Ron Howard

Only in his thirties, this actor has been a star on TV and in movies, and now he's a major film director. As a little boy he charmed a nation of viewers playing "Opie," that inquisitive little tyke with eyes of chocolate chips, on "The Andy Griffith Show." He was "Winthrop" in the film *The Music Man,* "Steve Bolander" in *American Graffiti* and "Richie" on the teen hit "Happy Days" playing the sweet foil for the randy "Fonz" (Henry Winkler). He has directed the films *Grand Theft, Night Shift, Splash, Cocoon,* and *Gung Ho.* Then, in the truest of Hollywood traditions, he must be, in private, a real creep? A monster? A sleaze?

Forget it. According to all reports, Ron Howard is as good as gold, described by insiders as "homespun . . . down-to-earth . . . modest."

Ron Howard was born 1 March 1953 in Duncan, Oklahoma, and he was raised off-camera in Burbank, California. "I always had a choice about continuing my career," he has recalled. "I remember my mom and dad saying, 'You don't have to do this. If you're not enjoying it, you just have to tell us.'" He met his wife Cheryl when they were in the 11th grade and they have been married since 1975 (they have three daughters, one son).

"I have a lot of patience. I rarely feel betrayed or disgruntled. I don't get revved up," the self-proclaimed workaholic told writer Lisa Birnbach in *Parade* magazine. "Far from reveling in his position," Birnbach writes, "Howard says he regards what he does as simply a job—not, like many of his colleagues, as a 'craft' or 'art.'" Howard confesses: "I've only felt that I was of value to people when I was working. That's the only time I've been useful and interesting." The man whose favorite album is Cat Stevens' *Teaser and the Firecat* believes you can work hard and be good to people, "and it makes me feel good when I see examples of that in life and in the movies. So I tend to want to work that into the stories. . . . I'm always interested in characters who are being told one thing, being told they can't do something—'you can't fall in love with a mermaid'—and turn that around because they don't agree with it." His recent list of movie-making ventures include *No Man's Land* (1987), *Clean and Sober* (1987), *Cowboy Way* (1988), *Willow* (1988), *Dream Team* (1988), and *Bay Window* (1988).

Engelbert Humperdinck

"Show business is a way of life," says the British-born baritone whose virile good looks have been jump-starting women's libidos since his first U.S. concert gig back in 1968. "The moment I stop, I sulk. I don't know what to do with myself. I go crazy. I'm addicted to it. I'm a workaholic." His in-person performances in the early years were characterized, as reporter Alan Niester put it, by "sleaze, innuendo and gossip . . . [with] a seemingly endless parade of middle-aged women willing to sacrifice a lifetime of pride and breeding for the opportunity of a passionate Humper-hug in the glow of the center-stage spotlight." By the 1980s, in some 200 shows a year, he'd developed a more low-key approach. "I don't think you should push the sex symbol thing. Everything you do should be subtle. I don't think it's necessary to go on stage and flaunt it. But it's still there, isn't it."

He was born 2 May 1936 in Madras, India, the ninth of ten children of a British Army captain, and stayed in India, throughout World War II. It was after the family moved to Leicester, England, that he first entered the music business, drawing on six years of saxophone lessons. Then, at 21, he tested his vocal chords in a talent contest on the Isle of Man and won, and a new career was born. The lad christened Arnold George Dorsey at birth went nowhere fast as a singer but shifted into fast-forward when he borrowed a new professional name from Engelbert Humperdinck, composer of the opera *Hansel and Gretel*. His 1966 hit, "Release Me" (still his musical signature) was the first of over a dozen gold records with sales over the 100 million mark. A few of the biggies: "There Goes My Everything," "The Last Waltz," "Am I That Easy to Forget?" In 1983, he returned to the charts with the Nashville-flavored "Til You and Your Lover." Married in 1963 to English sweetheart Patricia Healey (four children), he and his family divide their time between five homes located in Las Vegas, Hawaii, Atlantic City, England and Los Angeles.

Lamar Hunt

"My brother Herbert likes to say, 'Lamar doesn't work. He's in sports,'" says the youngest of the late H.L. Hunt's first family. "I see it differently," Lamar Hunt explains. "I approach sports as a business." And big business it is too in the hands of the stocky Texan who is the owner of the Kansas City Chiefs football team, stockholder in the Chicago Bulls basketball team, part owner of the Tampa Bay Rowdies soccer team, and the man behind World Championship Tennis (WCT for short). Lamar, son of the onetime world's richest man, may not come close to his dad's estimated million-dollar-a-week income, but he's doing very well, indeed. So no one took him seriously when in 1980 after collaborating with brother Bunker, and being stuck with nearly a billion dollars of declining-price silver bullion, he said, "I'm not very good at business." Even with sizable portions of his holdings acting as collateral while the brothers pay back loans on the boondoggle, he's still worth $500 million.

Born 2 August 1932, Hunt, who played football and baseball at Southern Methodist University, is a fairly accomplished golfer, and enjoys tennis so much he has a court at home. As an entrepreneur, he has a reputation as a stayer. Asked some years ago whether his football team, then the Dallas Texans, had lost $1 million in their first season, he replied, "Yeah, and at that rate, I can last just 168 more years." A founder of the American Football League, he was responsible, more than any other individual, for the AFL's survival and its eventual merger with the NFL. Interested in more than financial success, Hunt says, "What attracts me is building something up . . . from scratch . . . into both a financial and an artistic success." The personally frugal scion (he flies coach) is married and has four children.

William Hurt

Tautly handsome and effortlessly charming with a demeanor as cool as a summer's morning in Maine, this ex-prepster, who undoubtedly read Kierkegaard before and after crew practice at Middlesex School, is, according to some critics, a maverick in a major movement in American theatre away from the darkness of stark realism toward romantic yet disciplined drama.

Born 20 March 1950 in Washington D.C., William Hurt spent his early childhood in the South Pacific where his father was director of trust territories for the State Department. When his parents divorced he moved with his mother and two brothers to Manhattan where, in 1960, his mother married Henry Luce III, the son of the founder of Time, Inc. Home became a 22-room duplex in place of a four room Upper Westside flat. Sent off to prep school, Hurt turned inward. "I'd been a street fighter, a little punk kid," he recalls, "and suddenly I was in an Eastern establishment-type school wearing Bass Weejuns, white socks, herringbone jackets and ties, the transition at the time was too great." At Tufts University he graduated magna cum laude, having majored in theology intending to become a minister, but show biz was biting him. "I found myself increasingly interested in theatre. There is a very close relationship between the theatre and theology—both are very concerned about morality and the search for personal values." Three years after intensive training at Juilliard's acting program, his marriage on the rocks, he took off on a cross-country motorcycle tour which ended up in Ashland, Oregon. Appearing there in a production of O'Neill's *Long Day's Journey Into Night*, the light was struck. "I walked onto the stage one day and realized I had some craft. It felt so good." Back in New York his performance in Corinne Jacker's *My Life* won him an Obie.

Hurt went on to win critical acclaim in Lanford Wilson's *Fifth of July;* Albert Innaurato's *Ulysses in Traction; The Runner Stumbles; Childe Byron;* and *Hamlet*, a performance drama critic Clive Barnes called "a marker stone in the career of a great actor." After a successful round of films beginning with *Altered States*, and followed by *Eye Witness, Body Heat, The Big Chill* and *Gorky*

Park, he returned to off-Broadway in 1984 to star in David Rabe's *Hurlyburly*. Subsequent films include *Kiss of the Spider Woman* (1985 Cannes Film Festival Best Actor Award), *Children of a Lesser God*, (1986), *Destiny Alive* (1987), *Broadcast News* (1988-nominated Academy Award for Best Actor, 1989), and *The Accidental Tourist* (1988). In 1988 he won the UCLA Spencer Tracy Award for screen performance and professional achievement.

Divorced from actress Mary Beth Hurt, he had a son with ballet dancer Sandra Jennings. In June 1989, Ms. Jennings took Hurt to court and, under the scrutiny of television cameras in the courtroom, the couple battled whether or not their union was to be considered a common law marriage. However, Hurt married Heidi Henderson (daughter of Skitch Henderson) on 4 March 1989.

Lauren Hutton

She is "the link between the dream and the drugstore. She's the girl next door but she moved away," said top fashion photographer Richard Avedon, whose bold and willowy shots of the gap-toothed blonde made her a supermodel. As a *Vogue* magazine covergirl, and then the glamorous representative of Ultima's line of cosmetics, she remained a whimsical fashion maverick whose throw-away sex appeal epitomized the canny, carefree nature of the contemporary woman.

Mary Laurence Hutton was born in Charleston, S.C. 17 November 1943. Tall and awkward as an adolescent, she painfully recalls bombing out in cheerleader tryouts and attending the prom with a date arranged by a sympathetic teacher. After a year at a Florida university, she worked as a Playboy Bunny before landing her first fashion job in New York at age 21: a $50-a-week gig as house model with Christian Dior. Rejected by nearly every major modeling agency, she finally persuaded top agent Eileen Ford to sign her by agreeing to fix her curved nose and gap-teeth. The adjustments proved unnecessary.

Hutton's career took off with her first *Vogue* cover in 1966, but top model status eluded her until the more casual, accessible look took over fashion in the early 1970s. In 1973, her $200,000 exclusive contract with late cosmetic magnate Charles Revson made her the highest paid model at the time and popularized the notion among advertisers that a model can be more effective if she represents only one product. During her decade with Revlon, Hutton—who made her film debut in the 1968 *Paper Lion*—appeared in *American Gigolo* and *Paternity* (both 1980), *Zorro, The Gay Blade* (1981). *Flagrant Desire*, and *Bulldance*. Released from her modeling duties, she concentrated on her theatrical skill in the gritty, physically demanding off-Broadway play *Extremities*, while continuing to travel extensively in her spare time. She also appeared in the CBS telefilm "Sins."

Lee A. Iacocca

He's easily the auto industry's best-known figure—the corporate superman who turned Chrysler around. With Ford for 32 years, the last 18 as president, he was Motor City's most colorful and celebrated huckster and proud daddy of the Ford Mustang, one of the most heralded cars in automotive history. He took over at Chrysler in 1978 when the company was on the brink of collapse and with "brains, bluster and bravado" set it on the road to recovery. Convinced the cause was just, he negotiated the controversial "Chrysler Bailout," the $1.5 billion loan guarantee from the federal government. To keep Chrysler alive, he cut the company in half, an operation that briefly earned him the label "Ayatollah" Iacocca. A super salesman and manager, he exudes confidence and conviction and is in turn charming and demanding. Iacocca became his company's best pitchman, booming in to the camera for TV commercials, "You can go with Chrysler or you can go with someone else—and take your chances." One Wall Street analyst said, "I wouldn't doubt that people have bought Chrysler because they wanted Lee Iacocca to make it." There have even been bumper stickers declaring IACOCCA FOR PRESIDENT. But Chrysler's chief executive says he's "not interested." Friends say he doesn't have the patience. Comments publisher Keith Crane of *Automotive News:* "Hell, Lee doesn't want to be President; he wants to be appointed Pope."

Lido Anthony (Lee for short) Iacocca was born 15 October 1924 in Allentown, Pa., to a family of Italian immigrants. He is, as one observer put it, "what Willy Loman always wanted to be." His room at the top came from a merger of hard work, tough gut decisions, a talent for executive suite infighting, and an ability to spot marketing trends that borders on the clairvoyant. He decided at 16 he wanted to work at Ford and set forth toward his goal. His stated ambition was to be a vice president by the time he was 35; he missed it by a year, becoming vice president at 36 and president 10 years later. (He graduated from Lehigh in 1945 and from Princeton in 1946 received a master's degree in mechanical engineering.) Fired by Ford in 1978, he was promptly hired by Chrysler. Iacocca found the company in a mess but was spurred on by its new front-wheel drive technology, which allowed for smaller cars without reducing passenger space—exactly what the car market needed. It recharged the dead fiscal batteries of troubled Chrysler and Iacocca's victory symbolized the possibility of a comeback for the whole auto industry. "There are great days in your life. This is certainly one of them," an exuberant Chrysler chairman said in April 1984 as he reported a whopping $705.8 million profit for the first three months of the year, more than Chrysler made before in a total year. Looking forward, he says, "The time has come to restore the confidence of the American car buyer in American technology, American workers, and American cars."

He delights in twitting skeptics who doubt Chrysler's recovery and in giving government officials advice about how to run the economy. Active in numerous charities and civic groups, he was chairman of the Statue of Liberty-Ellis Island Centennial (1986) Commission. Iacocca was widowed in 1983 when his 52-year old wife of 27 years, the former Mary McCleary, died of a stroke and diabetic complications. Their daughters are Kathryn Lisa and Lia Antoinette. His second marriage to Peggy Johnson was short-lived. They were married in April 1986, separated in October of that same year, and finally divorced in 1987. His 1984 bio, *Iacocca*, was a bestseller in 1984 and 1985. He released another book in 1988, *Talking Straight*.

Billy Idol

Billy Idol has been a penetrating presence on the American music scene since 1984 when he had 3 LPs on the charts simultaneously for over 50 weeks straight. Billy Idol's music harnesses the sixties' pop and seventies' big guitars and thunderous drums, plus the "sonic Bauhaus architecture of the new music" of the eighties. Idol's pretty, bad-boy voice is deep, seductive and domineering; his music mixes the energy of raw rock 'n' roll with rockabilly and punk and becomes aggressive street dance music. The 3 albums which earned the British born rocker a secure niche in the U.S.A. were *Billy Idol, Rebel Yell*, and *Don't Stop*. Sales of all three were helped immeasurably by pulsating videos, which were given heavy play on MTV.

Born the son of a traveling salesman in Stanmore, England, in December 1955, he had his first exposure to America when he spent four years of his childhood (ages 3 to 7) in Rockville Centre, Long Island. It was after his family had returned to England that young William Broad (his real name) began to teach himself to play the guitar and think about becoming a pro. Soon after seeing the Sex Pistols perform, he dropped out of school to form his own band, Generation X. He changes his name to Billy Idol, he once explained, because "I can be an idol just by calling myself one, that's how flimsy it all is." He initially considered the name "Billy Idle," he says, because one of his school reports said, "William is idle."

Although Idol more of less disappeared from the performing scene in 1986, he was far from idle. He was, instead, concentrating all his efforts on the album which would become *Whiplash Smile* (1986) followed by *Vital Idol* in 1987. Explaining his long sessions in the recording studio, he observed: "When I'm making a record, I take a long time because I'm thinking of the fans who go out seriously and buy my records....Making a record isn't putting together a product.... Songs are flecks of human fire. Music is emotion. A record is a step into someone's mind. It's one man's heart jump-starting another's. When you make a bad record, you snuff out a little bit of someone's soul." Currently unmarried, Billy's girlfriend Perri Lister, gave birth to their son, Willem Wolf Broad, on 15 June 1988.

Julio Iglesias

"He is the sexiest item to hit the international pop music scene in eons," says one smitten acolyte. The international balladeer touted in *People* magazine as one of its "People to Watch in '83" has prophetically replaced Mick Jagger, Kenny Rogers, even Paul McCartney as the most popular singer in the world according to *Time* magazine, singing songs in six languages. He has earned more than 200 gold and platinum records and his 1983-84 campaign to woo America seemingly panned out. His first American tours saw sell-outs at Radio City, Universal Amphitheatre and the MGM Grand Hotel in Las Vegas. He made strides in Middle America with his *Julio* and *Non Stop* albums selling well, their marketing geared to his tours. His single "To All the Girls I've Loved Before" with Willie Nelson became a chart-topper.

Born 26 September 1941 to a Madrid gynecologist, Iglesias studied law at Cambridge University before joining the Real Madrid soccer team as a goalkeeper. Paralyzed in an auto accident shortly thereafter for nearly two years, Iglesias began writing songs when a nurse gave him a guitar. In 1968 he burst onto the Spanish scene by winning, against all odds, a national song festival. The traumatic end of his first and only marriage in 1979 (by annulment after eight years; three children) propelled him to pursue a glittering array of girlfriends with whom he galavanted globally when not repairing to his $3 million palace near Miami (serviced by spanking clean waiters discreetly passing hors-d'oeuvres to guests flanking one of his three swimming pools.) Iglesias sporting white cotton pants and top quips, "I'm just a skinny guy in a tee-shirt." In 1989 Iglesias was appointed Good Will Ambassador for UNICEF.

INXS

This Australian rock group does not follow tradition, they create it. Formed in 1977 as The Farriss Brothers and renamed INXS in 1979, this group's members have remained unchanged to this day. They possess a kind of unique bond that has grown out of time and hard work. As explained by vocalist Michael Hutchence: "INXS is a unit, and that's our strength. We've never been interested in replacing people, or replacing people with machines. We've grown together in public. We respect each other a lot and we've learned to live with our idiosyncrasies." It is this dedication and commitment towards a common goal that makes INXS one of the best live bands in the world. Toby Creswell of *Rolling Stone* states: "To see INXS on stage is to see one of the last great rock & roll bands, a celebration of physicality and aesthetics."

The members of the band include: Michael Hutchence as vocalist, Andrew Farriss on keyboard and guitar, Kirk Pengilly on guitar, saxophone and vocals, Tim Farriss on guitar, Garry Gary Beers on bass, and John Farriss on drums and percussion. Their first single, "Simple Simon/We Are The Vegetables," was released in Australia in May 1980, and their first album, *INXS*, was released in October of the same year. *Underneath The Colours*, the group's second album, was released in October 1981. In 1983 INXS made their North American debut with the release of the LP *Shabooh Shoobah*, which became the group's third gold album in Australia. Other albums include: *Dekadance* (1983), *The Swing* (1984 certified gold U.S., double platinum Australia), *Listen Like Thieves* (1985 certified gold U.S., triple platinum Australia), and *Kick* (1987).

In addition to five certified gold albums, the group's accomplishments include: winning seven major awards at Australia's annual Countdown Awards (equivalent to U.S. Grammys), being chosen as Australia's representatives for Live Aid at Sydney's Entertainment Centre, performing for "Rockin the Royals," a charity concert for Prince Charles and Princess Diana, and winning Countdown Awards for Most Popular Group, Most Outstanding Achievement, and Most Popular Male (Michael Hutchence).

Eugene Ionesco

Meeting only resounding condemnations at the onset of his career as a playwright, Eugene Ionesco was once asked by a curious interviewer to describe his influences and goals. After all, what kind of playwright would offer dramas that involved three actors and empty chairs as *dramatis personnae?* Ionesco responded: "I'm a bourgeois realist who writes in order to find out what he thinks. My ancestors, as far as my work is concerned, were a mixed bunch: Job, Shakespeare's Richard II, King Solomon, the Marx Brothers, Charlie Chaplin, the Keystone Kops." Ionesco's is a theatre where we laugh for want of a better alternative. "Nothing but humor—rosy or black or cruel—but only humor can give us back our serenity."

For a while it seemed Ionesco would be laughing by himself. The three actors of *The Chairs* played in Paris for an audience of three: the playwright, his wife and their 7-year-old daughter. Since then, Ionesco's avant-garde theatre has become one of the standards by which contemporary dramatists are judged; Ionesco, a Roumanian with French citizenship, has been elected to the French Academy, shocking those who worship a "classicism" that seems incompatible with empty chairs as characters. Ionesco, who prefers to explain himself rather than let critics fumble the task, declares: "I'm all for classicism, for that is what the avant-garde really is. Any true creative artist is classical for he creates archetypes which are always young. We must invent for our time and in being myth-makers we give rise to the kind of sacred, awe-struck theatre which was created by the ancient world." Backing up such lofty ideals, at the age of 70 the playwright made his American acting debut in Virginia Woolf's only play, *Freshwater*, staged farcically by a troupe of New York avant-gardists. Playing the role of Alfred Tennyson, garbed in a St. Nicholas-style beard for the role, Ionesco came to the rueful conclusion that creating myth-making, awe-struck theatre is a young man's job. "I suffered a lot during the rehearsals," admitted the septuagenarian. "I'm no longer as young as I once was."

Born 13 November 1912, he spent the years between the two world wars teaching literature in Bucharest; his first play was not produced until he was 38. Opening in a theatre on the Left Bank in Paris in 1950, *The Bald Soprano* flopped. But Ionesco had the last laugh. The catcalls have turned to cheers for a rich crop of plays, including *The Lesson, Rhinoceros, The Airborne Pedestrian,* and *Exit The King.* In 1988, Grove Press released *The New Tenant, Victims of Duty.*

Jeremy Irons

Britain's Jeremy Irons is equally at home on stage (he was a Tony-winner for *The Real Thing*), in film (e.g. *The French Lieutenant's Woman, The Mission*), and on TV ("Brideshead Revisited"); he also succeeded in another medium: recording. On a London album, released in October 1987, he played the role of Henry Higgins in the Alan Jay Lerner/Frederick Loewe classic *My Fair Lady*. The show album teamed the acting star with opera's Kiri Te Kanawa as Eliza Doolittle and Sir John Gielgud as Colonel Pickering, all performing under the baton of John Mauceri conducting a singing group called London Voices and the London Symphony Orchestra. Although Irons says he had a few qualms about taking on a role so closely associated with the masterful Rex Harrison, "Eventually," he says, "I took it because if I hadn't someone else would have had all the fun."

Jeremy Irons first became a household name, both in the U.K. and U.S., after his portrayal of Charles Ryder in the TV series, "Brideshead Revisited." The stylish, 1920's set series turned out to be so popular that it's been shown on numerous occasions around the world and has become the actor's flagship role. Though he's been in considerable demand by Hollywood in the years since, Irons has opted instead for the more demanding and less financially rewarding path of re-establishing himself as a stage actor, only fitting films in between stage engagements. He was a big hit with summer visitors to England in recent seasons playing in the Royal Shakespeare Company's Stratford productions of *The Winter's Tale* and *Richard II* and on the London stage with Stephanie Beacham in *The Rover*. Recent films include: *A Chorus of Disapproval* (1988), *Dead Ringers* (1988; Best Actor Award from New York Film Critics) and *Danny, Champion of the World* (1989).

Irons suspects the lure of his low-key intensity may be in what he holds back, rather than what he delivers. Says Irons, "I generally don't like giving more than required. If a moment requires A, I won't give A plus 3 just so my technique will dazzle the audience. In fact, I believe that they are moved by the structure of the work, not by an actor going through hoops and dancing on high wires." Indeed, even when ablaze in a scene, the audience looks for what smoulders beneath. Irons married accomplished British stage actress, Sinead Cusack, in 1978; they have two sons: Samuel (born 1979) and Maxmilian (born 1985).

Amy Irving

What a life! She began on Broadway in 1982 playing Mozart's wife in *Amadeus*. She was the sole survivor of Sissy Spacek's bloody revenge in Brian de Palma's *Carrie* and she appeared in other films, usually playing "sweet young things. . . . I suppose it's because I look young and innocent and virginal. Little do they know." Some of her films include: *The Fury, Voices, The Competition, Mickey and Maude*. Reportedly she had affairs with her co-stars Willie Nelson (*Honeysuckle Rose*) and Ben Cross in the television movie "The Far Pavilions." (She insists they were just friends, but has wondered: "Sometimes you think you may as well do it; you have to deal with it anyway.") She did kiss a male garbed Barbra Streisand in *Yentl* and she had Steven Spielberg's baby (Max Samuel born June 1985). Amy married Spielberg in November 1985 and divorced him in April 1989.

Ah, the modern cinema. Amy Irving, born circa 1953, is the daughter of actress Priscilla Pointer (who played her mother in both *Honeysuckle Rose* and *Carrie*) and the late Jules Irving who founded the San Francisco's Actor's Workshop and later became artistic director of New York City's Repertory Theatre of Lincoln Center. Irving, who co-starred with Rex Harrison in Shaw's *Heartbreak House* on Broadway in 1983 and also appeared on Broadway in *The Road to Mecca* in 1988, rejects the money principle of Hollywood filmmaking and prefers theatre as her medium, or so she told *People* magazine writer Andrea Chambers: "You explore every facet of your instrument onstage. When you become one with a character, it's like falling in love. It's that kind of high. . . . If someone said to me, 'You can't do films anymore,' I wouldn't shed a tear." She played the lead role in the light romantic film *Crossing Delancey* (1988).

John Irving

When *The World According to Garp* skyrocketed to best-seller status in 1978, it catapulted an obscure English professor, a moonlighting novelist and wrestling fan named John Irving, into the national spotlight. Finally there appeared a novelist who could be considered a serious man of letters, but whose books virtually jumped off supermarket shelves from White Plains to Oregon. The reading public seemed to turn on instantly to his flaky, unconventional image. "Life is serious. Art is fun," explains the writer, who looks like the Marlboro Man and who has inherited the literary mantle of J.D. Salinger.

Heralded by a paperback publicity campaign "Believe in Garp," Irving's breakthrough novel recounted the often bizarre adventures of a New England family growing up in three different hotels on two continents. The best-seller became a movie, and the next novel. *The Hotel New Hampshire*, did likewise. Predictably, after these back-to-back successes Irving withdrew to his study to write two more novels: *The Cider House Rules* (1988), and *A Prayer for Owen Meany* (1989). "I'm a novelist, and all I want to write right now is another novel," he said not long after *Garp* freed him from the necessity of teaching college English.

The fiction of this New Hampshire-born novelist routinely draws from the facts of Irving's own life, although he insists he does not write autobiography. Readers of "Garp," for instance, know that Irving's hero (or anti-hero) attended elite prep schools, enjoyed European study and travel, and indulged a passion for wrestling, as did Irving. "There is an Irving-clone in nearly everything he writes," charges one critic. But it's not autobiography Irving says he puts on paper, but high melodrama, "artfully disguised soap opera," he confesses. "I mean to make you laugh, to make you cry; these are soap opera intentions all the way."

Irving was born in Exeter 2 March 1942, and educated at Phillips Exeter Academy where his father taught Russian history and managed institutional finances. Irving recalls his childhood: "My father the school teacher and treasurer; my mother, the mother and hospital volunteer; my sister the forklift driver and artist; my brother the nightclub performer and paramedic." Such apparent opposites delight Irving and characterize his fiction. "People do go to extremes, after all," he explains. "It's in the extremes that we often recognize how we truly are." He has two sons from his marriage to Shyla Leary and he lives in Putney, Vermont.

Judith Ivey

"I feel like Cinderella and I hope the ball goes on forever," says the Tony Award-winning (*Steaming*, 1982) actress who generated "beaucoup d'applause" in the 1984 smash hit *Hurlyburly* in which she appeared with William Hurt, Sigourney Weaver, and Christopher Walken and walked off with another Tony for her efforts. It's hard to imagine the magnetic blond was ready to leave the theatre for good in 1981 to become a veterinarian. "It wasn't that she'd failed to get good roles," reported the New York Times, "in fact she'd just won praises for her performances in *Piaf* and *Pastorale*; it was more that she was tired of being poor, tired of waiting in the unemployment lines between shows, and was impatient for success." In *Steaming*, she played many of her scenes in the buff and it didn't seem to bother her as much as she thought it would. "Once I read the play, I realized an integral part of it—this stripping away of layers and all that philosophical stuff."

Born in El Paso, Tex., 4 September 1951, Ivey is the daughter of a college administrator who changed jobs often: her family moved some 15 times before she entered college. She originally wanted to become a painter and it was not until she turned 17 that she discovered her penchant and love for the stage via a high school production of *The Man Who Came to Dinner*. ("Making people laugh: That was the bug.") Following graduation from Illinois State, Ivey wended her way toward Chicago where she worked at the Goodman Theatre. Five years down the road would find her in New York City, where she worked at Joe Papp's Public Theatre and received glowing notices for a one-woman show *Second Lady*. Her movies include *Compromising Positions, The Lonely Guy, Harry and Son, Brighton Beach Memoirs, Hello Again, In Country, Miles from Home* and *Love Hurts*. Recent stage performances include *Precious Sons* (1986), *Blithe Spirit* (1987), and *Mrs. Dally Has A Lover* (1988). She acted as assistant director for the play *The Palace of Amateurs* in 1988. Ivey says she doesn't have to be an actress to feel satisfied. "If someone said 'Tomorrow, actors no longer exist' I'd miss it, but I know I'd find something else that would motivate me as much as acting does." Ivey is single and lives in Manhattan.

Glenda Jackson

For someone who considers enrolling in drama school her "most irrational act," the lady hasn't done too badly. The two-time Oscar winner (*Women in Love; A Touch of Class*) made her initial impression on American audiences on Broadway in 1965 as the mad, murderous Charlotte Corday, who used her floor-length hair as a whip in Peter Brook's *Marat/Sade* with the Royal Shakespeare Company, a play she "really loathed." It's been a mutual admiration society between the former colonials and the laborer's daughter from Birkenhead, Cheshire, ever since. Like her personal heroines—"Bette Davis, Joan Crawford and Katharine Hepburn"—it's been playing forceful females that she's been most successful. On stage, she's scored in *Hamlet, The Three Sisters, Hedda Gabler*, Genet's *The Maids, Rose, Stevie, Antony and Cleopatra*, and in 1984 alone, the demanding roles of *Phedra* and Nina Leeds in Eugene O'Neill's five-hour psychodrama, *Strange Interlude*, which she recreated on Broadway in 1985, looking like (wrote the New York *Times*' Frank Rich) "a cubist portrait of Louise Brooks . . . equally mesmerizing as a Zelda Fitzergeraldesque neurotic, a rotting and spiteful middle-aged matron and, finally, a spent, sphinx-like widow happily embracing extinction." With a career heavily weighted with the classics and historical figures, Jackson feels that "modern playwrights don't find women interesting to write about, except as adjuncts to a male story," adding that she's "not going to hang around waiting for the old lady character parts to come along. . . . When the work isn't interesting, I won't do it," as she told an interviewer for *W* in 1985.

Born 9 March 1936 in Birkenhead, the eldest of four daughters of a bricklayer (which might account for her disdain of "that English obsession with public schools and universities"), Jackson won a two-year scholarship to the Royal Academy of Dramatic Arts, from which—armed with one of its top awards—she embarked on what she calls "the traditional English round: repertory and unemployment." After a half-dozen years in rep, she made her London stage debut in *Alfie* in 1963, and was selected by Peter Brook to play a nude Christine Keeler (a principal in the sex scandal that ruined a cabinet officer) in a Theatre of Cruelty revue. She joined the RSC in 1964, and made her big splash in *Marat/Sade*. "We all felt at one point or another that we were suffering from some kind of mental illness, but by the time I left it, I didn't have to scratch for work any longer." She returned to London—and the RSC—with *Variety's* Most Promising Actress prize, and appeared in *US, The Three Sisters* and *Fanghorn* before making her film debut in 1968 in *Negatives*. A banner year was 1970 when, for her portrayal of Gudrun in Ken Russell's version of D.H. Lawrence's *Women in Love*, she walked off with the Oscar, and the New York Film Critics and National Society of Film Critics awards. Next she played the nymphomaniacal Nina Tchaikovsky in Russell's film biography of the composer, *The Music Lovers*, then the third part of a triangle in John Schlesinger's *Sunday, Bloody Sunday*, sharing the love of a bisexual young artist with a homosexual doctor. She displayed her comic side (and won another Oscar) for *A Touch of Class* in 1973. Other films include *Mary, Queen of Scots* (as Elizabeth vs. Vanessa Redgrave as the doomed Catholic queen), *The Nelson Affair, Stevie, House Calls, Hopscotch, The Return of the Soldier, Turtle Summer, Business as Usual, Castaway, Momento Mori, Beyond Therapy, The Rainbow* and *Salome's Last Dance*. She starred in *Macbeth* (1988) on Broadway, and on television, she won an Emmy for her portrayal of Elizabeth I (aging from 17 to 70) in a BBC six-parter, and in 1985 on HBO as Dr. Elena Bonner to Jason Robards' "Sakharov" ("to tell them they're not alone"). In 1988 Jackson was honored by The Women's Project to receive their Exceptional Achievement Award. Her marriage (1959) to Roy Hodges, who she met in rep and who later became an art gallery owner, ended in 1976. Resolutely mum about her private life, she will say she hopes her son Daniel (born 1969) doesn't become an actor. "It's hard enough to actually go through the process of trying to find work oneself. To watch a child go through it would be torture." She also confesses a fondness for gardening and says she knows "what is meant by the saying, 'You're closest to God in a garden.'"

Janet Jackson

Janet Jackson explains, "A lot has happened to me in the past year and a half since *Dream Street* was released. I've experienced a great deal, and I'm much the wiser for it. I'm making decisions for myself. 'Control' is the song that really relates to my feelings these days, and I didn't pull any punches, on that song or any other."

Janet Jackson was born on 16 May 1966 and has climbed to fame with three highly successful albums. In September 1982 her first album, *Janet Jackson*, proved she was equally deserving of the Jackson fame, showing her own style of musical imagination. In August 1974 *Dream Street* expanded on this budding originality with the considerable help of writers such as Jesse Johnson and Giorgio Moroder and her two famous older brothers, Michael and Marlon Jackson. But in her last and most explosive album, *Control*, she has finally come into her own. Her 1985 marriage to James DeBarge was annulled. It is clear that this experience was both painful and illuminating. From this personal drama grew the need to take back power over her own life, including the artistic creation of her newest album. This time she was not merely content to sing someone else's lyrics. She was intimately involved with every aspect of the record's production. "I was in the studio when every instrumental track was laid. I was in on every decision about how the music would sound, as well as what the lyrics would say." "People will be shocked when they hear *Control* because it's so different from what I've done before. This is a very special record to me—it expresses exactly who I am and how I feel. I've taken control of my life."

Her three albums reflect her life, follow her growth as an individual and mirror her painful disappointments. Art and life in the case of Janet Jackson cannot be separated.

Jesse Jackson

The first black presidential candidate whom America has ever taken seriously explained why he ran for the world's most important job in 1984. "We had to break the dependency syndrome," said the Reverend Jesse Jackson. "We moved from a relationship born of paternalism to one born of power." But when asked if his Rainbow Coalition was actually a black power campaign, he responded, "Of course not. No more than Mondale's or Glenn's [are] white power campaigns.... There is no basis to fear one who has a formula to make the Democratic party win. If blacks, Hispanics, and women are included, the party can't lose. If they're locked out, the party can't win." But the man whom *Black Enterprise* magazine credits with helping to include three million new black voters on registration rolls was himself "locked out" at the 1984 convention, receiving few meaningful concessions in return for turning over his constituency to Democratic nominee Walter Mondale. Party members refused to abide Jackson's demands that they end dual registration and second primaries in state and local elections. And although he left San Francisco having salved wounds opened by his anti-Semitic remarks (calling New York City "Hymietown," etc.) his prediction proved accurate. The "old minorities" whom he said would form "the new majority" ultimately identified the Dems' snub of Jackson as yet another lock-out. Even among those who voted party-loyal on Election Day (in the face of a Reagan landslide), many felt betrayed. "If the party cannot deliver for its membership," Jackson had asked during the primaries, "Why should the membership deliver for the party?"

The six-feet-two Jackson is the same ex-college football player-turned-preacher whom the late Dr. Martin Luther King, Jr., selected to head up the Chicago branch of Operation Breadbasket, the economic arm of the Southern Christian Leadership Conference in 1966. He gripped King's lifeless body moments after the civil rights leader was slain by an assassin's bullet on a Memphis motel balcony in 1968. Jackson went on to become the most influential black power broker in Chicago and then the nation. When he broke with SCLC in 1971, he spent his considerable energies on behalf of Operation PUSH (People United to Save Humanity), an organization dedicated to economic betterment of black communities, and black-owned companies.

Jackson's deep gut knowledge of what it's like to be poor and locked out began when he was born out of wedlock (8 October 1941) and raised in Greenville, SC, among that city's poor blacks. A tough-talking, fast-stepping quarterback at North Carolina A&T (where he met future wife Jacqueline Davis, mother of their five children), his involvement in the sit-in movement brought him to Dr. King's attention, and like his mentor, Jackson became on ordained minister in 1968. His oratorical style remains that of a Baptist preacher, "rich in metaphor and biblical allusions" said the New York *Times*, and he's used it effectively before rallies of thousands, and in controversial one-on-ones with Castro, Arafat and other world leaders. In 1988 Jackson made another bid for the White House as a Democratic presidential candidate. He formally announced his candidacy on 10 October 1987 and won 7 million primary and caucus votes. Although Michael Dukakis became the democratic candidate at the convention, Jackson continues to be a prominent leader. Two recent books focusing on his achievements are *Straight from the Heart* (1987) with thirty-six public speeches and essays, and *Keep Hope Alive* (1989), featuring a collection of speeches and position papers from the 1988 campaign. Jesse Jackson's message for keeping "hope" alive is as follows: "Stop drugs from coming in and jobs from going out; invest in America; invest in our children; fight against crime, economic violence and for common justice."

Kate Jackson

"I loved that voice of hers," recalled Fox talent executive Renee Valente about her interview with Kate Jackson in the early '70s. "It brought to mind Bankhead, Bacall, Hepburn. But I noticed her eyes, those brown eyes that sparkle with such energy ... I told her I thought she could be a major talent if she came to L.A." So the young woman went west and four years later, landed the pivotal role of Sabrina Duncan in the hit television series "Charlie's Angels." After three stormy seasons she made a "I-quit-no-you-can't you're fired" departure. "She brought *class* and *intelligence* to 'Angels,'" stressed Valente, "Sure Jaclyn Smith and Farrah Fawcett were very good, but without Kate—I don't care how much glitter they wrote in—no show. If she was outspoken during the show, she was *bright* and she was *right*."

Born 29 October 1950 in Birmingham, Ala., she first became interested in acting while appearing in high school plays. ("When I was little in Birmingham, I knew I wanted to be an actress, but I didn't tell anybody. I did practice signing my autograph—names like Misty Starlight.") After studying drama at the University of Mississippi and Birmingham U, Jackson enrolled in New York's American Academy of Dramatic Arts, supporting herself selling skis and conducting NBC tours. After graduating in 1971 and having become a successful model ("the hardest work in the world"), she landed her first professional acting job as a regular in the daytime television series "Dark Shadows." ("I was a terrific ghost for nine months. I never spoke, I beckoned. I was 20, and things seemed to be coming on a silver platter. If those folks knew how much of my craft I learned from them, they'd probably slit their throats.") When she hit Hollywood she soon co-starred in "The Rookies" a television series which ran for four years and led to "Angels." After four rocky years and a "series lay-off," in 1984 she bounced back (for two seasons) with another hit series, "Scarecrow and Mrs. King." "Whew. That lady is intense," blurted out a veteran supporting actor in the show. "I love working with her—she pulls it out of you. No *shtick* on this show." Movies made for television include "Satan's School for Girls," "Killer Bees" (with the late Gloria Swanson), "The New Healers," "James at 15," "Thin Ice," "Listen to her Heart" and "Topper." Jackson's feature films: *Limbo, Making Love, Dirty Tricks,* and *Loverboy*. During the 1988-1989 television season she starred in the series "Baby Boom." She often voices her feelings about her two-year marriage to her first husband Andrew Stevens (she filed for divorce on 1 January 1981): "I felt as if my ex-husband drove up to my bank account with a Brinks truck." She didn't have much success with her second husband, David Greenwald; the couple divorced in 1984.

Michael Jackson

1987 was the *Bad* beginning of a two year hit streak. Living up to all pre-hype expectations, Michael Jackson's long-awaited album rocked the record charts and video channels with such hits as "The Way You Make Me Feel," "The Man in The Mirror," "Dirty Diana," and, of course, the title track "Bad." A piece of phenomenal vinyl, the album itself was actually an added touch to Michael's extraordinary career.

Born 29 August 1958 in Gary, Indiana, one of nine children, Michael began singing with his parents and four other brothers as The Jackson Family before the boys went out on their own as The Jackson Five. They were discovered at New York's Apollo Theatre by singer Gladys Knight and pianist Billy Taylor, whose recommendations to Motown Records kingpin Berry Gordy resulted in the group's huge success in the late 1960s and early 1970s when they charted four consecutive #1 singles, "I Want You Back," "ABC," "The Love You Save" and "I'll Be There." The Jackson Five was one of the most amazing success stories in the music biz, with the group selling over an estimated 100 million records, breaking box office records and causing general pandemonium wherever they appeared. Michael's been doing his thing alone, compiling an array of hit singles and albums, since 1971, when he was just a 12-year-old. His fame skyrocketed to incredible heights with the wildly successful *Thriller* album (1983). Aided by the emergence of MTV's 24-hour videos, his singing and dancing in "Beat It" and "Billie Jean" during the summer of 1983 (and later "Thriller" with its narration by Vincent Price) captured the nation's attention. In 1984 Jackson made a sweep of the American Music Awards. He won a total of seven awards (including a special award for merit) which placed him in *The Guinness Book of World Records* for winning the most awards ever at that event. Next came the Grammys where he won another eight awards. The LP "Thriller" held the #1 place on top of *Billboards's* chart for over 30 weeks, and in a more subtle guise, Jackson narrated the bestselling storybook LP of Steven Spielberg's *E.T. The Extraterrestrial*.

1984 was certainly his year, but the thrills and spills of success gave him his moments. Rock singer Prince came along and took some of Jackson's more sophisticated fans away from him, those who'd had it with the hoopla of The Victory Tour and who preferred their rock more raunchy. Then Michael's hair went up in flames during the making of a Pepsi commercial, and although millions were sympathetic, many wondered what he was doing making a Pepsi ad in the first place. Then there were the endless stories about his nose job, his cheek job, his hormone shots and last, but never least, the possibility of his being gay. Against the advice of his manager a press conference was called and a statement was read, its purpose to "once and for all" deny that he was a homosexual. "It saddens me," the statement went, "that many may actually believe the present flurry of false accusations. To this end, and I do mean END!—No! I've never taken hormones to maintain my high voice. No! I've never had my cheekbones altered in any way. No! I've never had cosmetic surgery on my eyes." (The nose went unmentioned.) "YES! One day in the future I plan to get married and have a family. Any statements to the contrary are simply untrue. . . . I love children." On the upside, Michael recorded the *Victory* (1984) album with The Jacksons and a duet with Mick Jagger "State of Shock" climbed to the number three slot on the charts as the LP went double platinum. In November 1984, Michael was honored with his own star on the Hollywood Walk of Fame.

Although 1985 seemed like a relatively quiet year for Michael, he actually accomplished many musical dreams. In January of that year, he wrote "We Are The World" with Lionel Richie as a call to help fight the starvation in Africa. History was made when more than forty of his peers recorded and released the song. In August 1985, the enterprising young man purchased the ATV music catalogue (which includes the Beatles 251-song collection) and became a part of the music publishing world. 1986 saw Michael win a Grammy for Song of the Year ("We Are The World") and the long-awaited release of *Captain Eo* (a 15-minute film collaboration with George Lucas and Francis Coppola which is seen at Disneyland and Disneyworld). Then, the cycle started again. With the release of *Bad* in 1987, the album, videos and tour were all smashes.

Diana Ross, who got to know Jackson well when he appeared as the Scarecrow in 1978's *The Wiz*, singing their duet "Ease on Down the Road," became a mentor to him. "I saw so much of myself as a child in Michael. He was performing all the time. That's the way I was. He could be my son." But unlike Ross who enjoys the limelight *and* the at-home-light, Jackson prefers the isolation of his Encino, Calif., family compound. There amid his electronic toys, his menagerie of exotic animals and his collection of life-size mannequins, he dances unobserved by his adoring fans. On the rare occasion when he leaves the mansion he's likely to be elaborately disguised. Reportedly, he likes to wander about in shopping malls and Disneyland. Otherwise, he may be out on a religious mission: a Jehovah's Witness, he regularly attends prayer meetings and even does door-to-door field service on behalf of the church. He fasts on Sundays and spurns alcohol and drugs. His church frowns upon premarital sex and he is never seen racing around like some Romeo with any old Juliet on Rodeo Drive. In 1988 Michael released his autobiography *Moonwalk* and in 1989 he was the Executive Producer of the astonishing home video "Moonwalker."

Reggie Jackson

He's called "Mr. October" because, while he's hit over 500 homers in the regular season, the talkative, complex, media-loving star is his best when it really counts—in World Series overtime. It's been those times, like the 1977 World Series (when he smashed five Series batting records), that have given him the audacity once to proclaim, "I'm the straw that stirs the drink." Nearing his last years the left-handed slugger said, "I've already had more than my share. I'm gifted and I'm grateful."

Reginald Martinez Jackson was born 18 May 1946 in Wyncote, Pa., a suburb of Philadelphia. He rocketed to stardom in 1969 as a second-year rightfielder for the Oakland A's by holding baseball fans enthralled as he chased Roger Maris' single season record of 61 homers. Jackson finished with 49. The young, talent-laden A's won the World Series in 1973-74-75, and "Jack" won the American League's MVP award in 1973. When he refused to sign a contract with A's owner Charlie Finley he was sent to Baltimore. After that season free agency was installed and he accepted a Yankee offer of almost $3 million less than Montreal's because playing in the Big Apple meant being on a winner, and making far more money off the field. Once there, as he'd predicted, a candy bar was named for him. Divorced, the chipmunk-faced Jackson avoided the late night singles scene, and although he dated lots of women, one o'clock was late for him to be out of his Fifth Avenue apartment. Upon arriving at the Bronx "House That Ruth Built," Jackson was haunted by a news quote in which he'd said that he, not Yank teammate Thurmon Munson, was the team's big stick. "Munson thinks he can be the straw that stirs the drink, but he can only stir it bad," went the quote, and Jackson found himself an outsider in a season marred by dugout tussles with manager Billy Martin. The headline-making chaos didn't hurt their play, however. The 1977-78 Yanks beat the Dodgers in back-to-back Series, and Reggie homered five times in the 1977 classic (three of them on three first pitches in the final game). In 1981 there was more team dissension; at a pennant celebration, the six-feet, 208-pound Jackson traded punches with an equally-capable Graig Nettles, but when, as Jackson said, "[owner] George Steinbrenner came running down the hall, saying, 'Damn it, Jackson. Not again,'" he knew he'd worn out his welcome. Later he'd exclaim, "Everybody wants to play baseball in southern California, and here I am," after the California Angels signed him for nearly a million a year. In the autumn of his playing days, Mr. October is a designated hitter with the goal of cracking the top ten list of homer hitters. A regular TV sports announcer, he's also had success in real estate development. (An avid antique car collector, he lost half of his collection (over $4 million) in a 1988 fire. "I've had some great World Series. . . . My face is known and so is my name. . . . All these are gifts from God," Reggie philosophically allows. In repayment he's been generous to Lou Gehrig's disease research and Big Brothers Incorporated.

Bianca Jagger

"People think I'm arrogant," says this part-time playgirl, part-time mother, part-time actress and most recently, part-time politico. They say, 'When she walks into a room she looks above everybody'—but they never stop to think that maybe 'she's myopic,' which I am very much." The refugee from a much-publicized divorce from the Rolling Stones aging boulder Mick, she has been into the strifetorn and dangerous jungles of her native Nicaragua as well as El Salvador and Honduras, carrying her camera to document the struggles of these troubled peoples. Unprotected by guns, the camera serves just as well, she says,

Mick Jagger (The Rolling Stones)

"We used it as a weapon. I guess they felt that we could do them harm if pictures were shown." The press coverage of Bianca's sojourns in Central America remains cynical, but shuttling back and forth from there to Capitol Hill in Washington where she is an active lobbyist, always wearing her pin that says "Salvador is Spanish for Vietnam," she never shows her irritation with reporters. "Sometimes people have you in a little box and they feel lost when you move out of that box," she explains, "so they react with skepticism."

Born 2 May 1945, the daughter of a wealthy import-export merchant, at 15 she went off to Paris to study political science and by the age of 19 the Jet Set had landed in her lap. She met Mick backstage after a concert in Paris and in the summer of 1971 four-month-pregnant Bianca married the singer in St. Tropez; the very next day after the much publicized event she broke into tears and told Jagger: "You keep your world, your press." Soon enough was she picked up by the fashion press as the butterfly-with-the-mostes' flitting through the Seventies. Jagger's gig with model Jerry Hall, which left Bianca behind with their daughter Jade, helped lift the veil from her caviar black eyes. "It's time for me to grow up. For a while I lived in a fantasy world in which you try to eliminate things that are unpleasant. I expect too much out of marriage. I can spend years without anybody. Sex without love for the sake of sex? I don't need that." Her solo-at-home base is New York City. Utilizing her acting talents, Bianca had a recurring role as "Maya" on the now defunct ABC-TV nighttime soap "The Colbys" (1986-1987).

Mick Jagger (The Rolling Stones)

Time tames all sinners, especially singing ones. Once upon a concert night he'd be wild on the stage, ranting out those dulcet tunes from between his pouting, pendulous lips, begging "Sympathy for the Devil," pleading for some "Brown Sugar." Well, satisfaction's come to Rock 'n' Roll's Peter Pan, whose renegade image of the rebellious bad boy, is worn thin. The allure now is sartorial and sophisticated, but nevertheless, he's still something of the changeling. There's Jagger the mercurial leader of the most bad-ass white band ever; there's Jagger the connoisseur of fine wines and French chateaus (he's painstakingly restoring the 18th Century La Fourchette in the Loire Valley); there's Mick, who like the Chairman of any million dollar board worries over the Stones' every record release and budget sheet, a businessman described by one pal as being "mean, shrewd and sort of sweet." (Despite revenue in the 60s and early 70s that topped $350 million, the band was almost bankrupt after a period of chaotic mismanagement—"not only bad deals," says Jagger, "but not getting the money from bad deals." Now with the help of London's tight fisted wheeler-dealer, Prince Rupert Lowenstein, the Stones are solid.)

Jagger is sophisticated, urbane, well-read. "A man with breadth of interest far beyond his métier," according to record tycoon Ahmet Ertegun. He's a family man, the ex-husband of ultra-chic Bianca, the official live-in of top model Jerry Hall with whom he has a daughter (the third of three) and (in August of 1985) his first son. "He's a lovely bunch of guys," says Stones' guitarist Keith Richards.

"I'm happy eating a nice meal without pressure. To an old fashioned existentialist, that's all that counts," he laughs. "Come on now, I can't possibly be such a complex character," says the once impatient, middle class kid (born 26 July 1943) who sold ice cream cones for pocket money and worked his way into the London School of Economics. "People see more in me than there is. Yeah I've got layers. So does an onion. I'm part of the fun part of rock 'n' roll. And besides, it's all B pictures anyway."

All the other Stones have settled into melodiously domestic grooves. Charlie Watts (born 2 June 1941) lives in a sprawling English country house with his wife and daughter. Bill Wyman (born 24 October 1941) married Mandy Smith in June 1989 and considers himself the new Lord Gedding since purchasing Gedding Hall, a spectacular 15th Century manor house in Suffolk. In 1984 he was responsible for the photos in the book *Chagall's World: Reflections From the Mediterranean* by Andre Verdet. Ron Wood, the newest member of the band (born 1 August 1948) married Jo Howard on 2 January 1985 and his autobiography *Ron Wood by Ron Wood* was released in 1987. Keith Richards (born 18 December 1943) is rehabilitated, off drugs, and shuttling between residences in Ocho Rios and New York with super model wife Patti Hansen (2 daughters: Theodora Dupree, Alexandra Nicole).

Once considered the Dionysian pillagers of polite society, the Stones now couldn't be anything less. Says Wyman: "We're not chucking TV's out of windows anymore. We like to watch them now." Of late, Jagger had a solo album *Primitive Cool* (1987) and he was inducted (along with the Rolling Stones) into the Rock 'n' Roll Hall of Fame in 1989. The group's latest LP is *Steel Wheels* (1989). As they headed out on a long U.S. tour, *Time* magazine remarked, "Just look at these guys. Giants. Golems. Geezers with a quarter-century of history together, 'a long shadow,' as Keith Richards says, 'that we drag around.'"

Byron Janis

The accolades and distinctions conferred on him both at home and abroad are testimony to the maturity and breadth of his keyboard artistry. As one critic summed it up: "Janis offers an experience like no other pianist. He touches the dangerous boundaries of the sublime. . . ." In Russia, said the New York *Times*, "men and women wept." Despite the Cold War, Janis was selected from the multitude of American pianists to represent the U.S. in the first Cultural Exchange with the Soviet Union; his debut there was so forceful in melting the boundaries of political difference that his performances remain the most applauded of any visiting artist. In Paris, said the *Herald Tribune*, he "rendered an elite audience speechless with admiration." And in staid old Boston, said the *Christian Science Monitor*, "he left his Symphony Hall audience in a high state of exhilaration—as a matter of fact at a pitch of shouting enthusiasm." The Pennsylvanian with the flashing fingers began filling his scrapbook with reviews of this rapturous caliber when he performed his first Carnegie Hall piano recital as a 20-year-old back in 1948, and he hasn't stopped since. He's toured the Soviet Union, Western Europe, and South America many times, averaged 50 concerts a year in the U.S., all the while (as one critic put it) "making an artist's private progress from flame to inner glow." He became the first American to win various coveted awards (Grand Prix du Disque, Harriet Cohen Award for his recording of two Beethoven Sonatas, Chevalier dans l'Ordre des Arts et des Lettres, among others), and also was responsible for the discovery of unknown versions of Chopin waltzes. As one of the finest living interpreters of Chopin, Janis filmed a one-hour documentary on the composer in 1975 which has been broadcast in Europe and the U.S.

Born 24 March 1928 in McKeesport, Pennsylvania, Janis took up the piano when a kindergarten teacher discovered he had perfect pitch and an unusual talent. Upon the recommendation that he be taken to New York for more comprehensive training, he eventually studied with Joseph and Rosina Lhevinne, Adele Marcus, and Vladimir Horowitz. He was fifteen when he made his debut with Toscanini's NBC Symphony Orchestra and the concert launched a unique career: that of a brilliant and thought-provoking artist who brings an uncommon immediacy to the quality of his playing. This in the midst of a battle with psoriatic arthritis, which first afflicted him in the early 1970s and which he made public in 1985. As a result, Nancy Reagan appointed him ambassador for the arts for the National Arthritis Foundation. "I thought I might be looked on as a freak," he said at the time he revealed his condition. "I didn't want sympathy. But the thought of helping others became very important. And now I find I'm playing with more ease than ever before. I certainly feel better—and younger-than I have in 20 years."

Married first to June Dickson-Wright (one son, Stefan), he married the former Maria Veronica Cooper, daughter of the late motion picture superstar, Gary Cooper, in 1966. The 1983-84 season marked the 40th anniversary of Janis' debut, and he celebrated with an array of orchestral concerts, recital tours and television appearances. In addition to his performances, he also composed music for the Global Forum of Spiritual and Parliamentary Leaders on Human Survival in 1988.

Tama Janowitz

"It was fantastic. I felt like I was part of a team, something I had never experienced before. Writing the script—with Jim's assistance—watching the production of the movie, from the casting to the locations search, the sets being built—was absolutely the best year of my life." Tama Janowitz was thrilled about participating in the Merchant/Ivory produciton of her story *Slaves of New York*. No wonder, the young writer has come a long way since the banning of her second grade Smith College Day School newspaper.

Born in San Francisco, California, Tama Janowitz grew up in Amherst, Massachusetts. Her early years were unsettled as her family moved around the states. Her father, a psychiatrist, divorced her mother and Tama found solace playing with her animal kingdom—goats, rabbits, a monkey, a chicken, ducks, cats and a racoon. Eventually, she had to say goodbye to her animal friends when Tama's mother moved their family to Israel. By the eighth grade, the future writer was back in Amherst and had adopted a dog; the ninth grade found her moving to Newton, Massachusetts. At long last, she graduated from Lexington High School and went on to attend Barnard College where she majored in creative writing. Upon graduation in 1977 she landed a job as an assistant art director for a Boston advertising agency but her talents did not include drawing, hence, she was fired. Next stop—Hollins College where she was offered a fellowship in order to obtain an M.A. in creative writing. It was at Hollins that she wrote her first novel, *American Dad*, making her a published writer at twenty-three years old. Taking her advance money from the book, she attended the Yale School of Drama to study playwriting. Uninspired, she left the Yale program after one year to become a fellow at the Provincetown Fine Arts Work Center. Having received an award for her fiction, the triumphant Janowitz moved to New York City, completing a couple of novels (never accepted for publication) and winning some grants from the New York State Arts Council. In 1985, *New Yorker* magazine published her first short story which started a chain reaction for other magazines (*Harper's, The Paris Review, The Mississippi Review, Bomb, Between C and D, Spin*) to accept her work. *Slaves of New York* (a collection of short stories) was published in 1986 and immediately became a best seller. In the fall of 1986 the travelling writer moved again—this time to Princeton, New Jersey to be an Alfred Hodder Fellow in the Humanities in fiction at Princeton University. The following year she moved back to Manhattan where she wrote her second novel, *A Cannibal in New York*.

Tama Janowitz, whose works have been translated in approximately eighteen languages has moved from town-to-town for a total of thirty-eight times. She finally settled in New York City with her two Yorkshire terriers, Lulu and Beep-beep. She refuses to cut her long flowing hair because of an incident stretching back to her childhood. Having caught her braids in the chains of a swing, she went to a beauty salon for a trim. In a rare incident, the hairdresser cut her braids at the scalp without ever unbraiding them. So for now, Rapunzel lives on. . . .

Peter Jennings

Amid a controversy concerning the fight for the top in the ratings between the three network evening newscasters, ABC's anchor remarked: "With me, Brokaw and Rather I recognize that there is the factor of three pretty faces. That's an inevitable by-product of television. But if that is what it comes down to in terms of the approach we take, then we will all have made a mistake." When the dapper, urbane and cerebral Jennings assumed the anchorman's post for "ABC's World News Tonight" on 3 September 1983 his career came full circle. Eighteen years earlier, he had captured national attention when he became the youngest person ever to anchor a network newscast. He was branded then a "glamourcaster," left "ABC's Nightly News" three years later and returned to the field as a roving correspondent, establishing a reputation as a top-notch foreign reporter.

Peter Charles Jennings was born 29 July 1938 in Toronto, Canada. His father Charles was a distinguished journalist for the Canadian Broadcasting Corporation; he was considered Canada's equivalent to Edward R. Murrow. Young Peter's first foray behind a microphone was at age 9 hosting "Peter's People," a weekly half-hour CBC radio show of music and news for children. "Bored," he dropped out of prep school without staying for a diploma. Still his career in broadcasting flourished in Canada and in 1964 he moved to New York and was based at ABC's headquarters there. Jennings had been on the job for just a few months when ABC, in an effort to lure younger viewers, put him in the evening anchor seat. He left that throne in 1968 to become ABC's Middle East bureau chief and in 1975 returned to New York to head "Good Morning America's" predecessor "A.M. America." It was cancelled a month later so Jennings took off for London with the video title of Chief Foreign Correspondent. His insightful reports on fast-breaking international crises removed any doubt about him being merely a "glamourcaster." In July of 1983 he returned to Washington, D.C. to fill in for an ailing Frank Reynolds. After Reynolds' death he was picked to replace him on the then revamped news broadcast. Jennings wife is Kati Marton, writer and former bureau chief for ABC News in Bonn, Germany. They have two children, Elizabeth and Christopher.

Waylon Jennings

Repeatedly stifled by Nashville's formula sound, he had an up-and-down career until he finally assumed artistic control of his music. One of country's best-selling performers, he proudly declares that his rock-influenced music "ain't no Nashville Sound. It's my kind of country. It's not Western. It's Waylon." His life roller coastered too, over debts, drugs, and man-killing tour appearances. A 1973 movie, *Payday*, was based on a Jennings-like, self-destructive, country singer.

He was born Waylon Arnold Jennings in Littlefield, Texas, 15 June 1937. "I had the best dad in the world, but he just couldn't ever get it going when it came to money." Jennings said, so the boy dropped out of school by fourteen. As a deejay and guitarist in Lubbock, he joined bandleader Buddy Holly's second "Crickets" group; the first having inspired the Beatles style and even name. Coincidence kept Jennings off the plane that crashed and killed Holly in 1959. In 1965 Jennings went to Nashville and signed with RCA Records under Chet Atkins' direction, and began recording successful, Nashville Sounding hits. "Only Daddy That'll Walk the Line" was number one on country charts in 1968 and in 1969 he won a Grammy for his version of "MacArthur Park." A collaboration with rock star Mick Jagger convinced him he could appeal to more lucrative rock-oriented followings, but since he couldn't do this in his recordings, he booked himself for up to 300 engagements per year. By 1972 he was burnt out with bitterness, excessive touring and hepatitis. He was also about $600,000 in debt. On the brink of disaster he met personal manager Neil Reshen, who also represented Willie Nelson. A Jennings turnabout ensued. They demanded RCA give him musical control and improved promotional support. He produced his own albums by 1974, and was chosen Male Vocalist of 1975 by the Country Music Association. At RCA, Chet Atkins' successor wisely went with the clamor for "country rock" and captured "Nashville outlaw" Jennings, his fourth wife Jessi Colter, and Nelson in a 1976 album, *Wanted: The Outlaws*. It became Country Album of the Year, Nelson's and Jennings' duo was Best of the year, and "Good Hearted Woman" by Jennings was chosen Best Single. He wrote TV's "Dukes of Hazzard" theme and recorded it in 1979. Some recent albums include *Will the Wolf Survive* (1986), *Hangin' Tough* (1987), *A Man Called Joss* (1987) and *Full Circle* (1988).

The tough-looking, bearded Jennings is diabetic. He lives in Old Hickory, Tenn., some 20 miles from Nashville, with wife Jessi and their son. He shuns most publicity and prefers music and family.

Norman Jewison

Norman Frederick Jewison is one of Hollywood's most prolific producer-directors. "I derive inspiration from the nature of the material I am working on, and it is for this reason that I prefer a new subject matter on every film. As a director, I've got to know who and what I'm making a film about, so I have to spend a good deal of time researching the material." A very ambitious and hardworking man, he has not travelled this road because of the lure of success, although his films have been both critical and box-office hits (*The Cincinnati Kid, In the Heat of the Night, The Thomas Crown Affair, Fiddler on the Roof, Rollerball, Moonstruck*). Mr. Jewison is a man of integrity who affirms that "the film you present should preserve your intentions for all time." He is also an outspoken director. Disgusted by the turn of events which transformed American filmmaking into a technical extravaganza, he spoke out during the filming of *Moonstruck*. "Yes, it's a romantic comedy, but it's also a literate piece. Its charm and its power come out of John Patrick Shanley's beautiful dialogue. People will walk out of this film saying, 'I know these characters.' No I know we're into an age where you're not supposed to talk very much in films, because, God forbid, you should bore someone. And as a result, there's not too many people writing, using words anymore. This all started around the time of *Star Wars*, when American films moved into a comic-book era of highly visual movies of endless reels of mindless action. They moved away from the written word. But I think we're moving back to the written word and out of this anti-intellectual period. And I think the Academy Award nominations in the past few years bear me out."

Born 21 July 1926 in Toronto, Canada, his early academic career was colored by the study of music at the Royal Conservatory. This perhaps attuned him to the musicality of language, so important in his films. He eventually earned his bachelor's degree at Toronto's Victoria College. His early professional career was in television. After seven successful years in Canadian television, he accepted an invitation from America to direct "Your Hit Parade." He carried off three Emmy Awards. Nineteen sixty-one marked his debut in feature filmmaking, and in 1965 he took the plunge as an independant filmmaker with *The Cincinnati Kid*, creating a cult classic.

Married for thirty-six years to Margaret Ann Dixon, or "Dixie" as he calls her, he is the father of three. All of his children are involved in filmmaking (a camera assistant, an assistant editor and an actress). After having lived in the United States for nineteen years, he returned to Ontario to make his home there once again. His latest film is *The January Man* (1989). A much-represented producer-director, he has received many accolades from members of his profession, but his greatest tribute will be his cinematic "oeuvre."

Billy Joel

"Any song I write has some kind of love in it. Any human situation has some love in it because you have a feeling for it, you have empathy for it. As far as the personal love songs, I have a hard time describing why they're different or how they got written. You don't really know what it's going to be until you're in the middle of writing it. But I find that describing too much of the writing technique takes away from the mystique of what the song should be. It should be a song for everyone. And if it's too explained or too personalized, then other people can't adapt it to their own life and their situation. So I shy away from really talking about what made a love song get written." Whatever the formula the "piano man" Billy Joel comes up with for composing a song, his records always hit a responsive chord with his fans. With his Grammy Awards, best-selling albums (his second, 1973's *Piano Man* went gold; his fifth and sixth, *The Stranger* of 1977 and *52nd Street* the following year, went platinum) and sold-out concert tours, Joel is an acknowledged melodic master. His vivid song lyrics, morever, range from raunchy to achingly romantic.

Born William Martin Joel in the Bronx, New York on 9 May 1949, Billy Joel and his sister were raised on Long Island by their mother after their father returned to Europe. Although Jewish, Joel says he became "Italian by assimilation" from living in a heavily Italian-American neighborhood. He began playing piano at age two. Recalls his mother: "When we saw that he loved Mozart at four, I took him by the scruff of the neck and dashed off to find him piano lessons." He studied the instrument for 12 years. Joel's teenaged musical gigs interfered with his schoolwork; he never graduated from high school. But he's written dozens of incomparable songs (including "The Entertainer," "N.Y. State of Mind," "Just the Way You Are," "She's Always a Woman") and practically invented a genre: the rock love ballad.

Small in stature (5'8"), Joel (once divorced) and supermodel Christie Brinkley (whom he married in 1985) live with their daughter, Alexa Ray (born 1985), in a Manhattan apartment and on an estate overlooking Long Island Sound. The sports jacket and tie he wears onstage seem slightly at odds with his street-wise persona. "I have a real cynicism about this whole star thing," Joel says. "I don't think I'm so special. I just do what I do." His recent albums include *The Bridge* (1986), *Live in The U.S.S.R.* (1987), and *A Matter of Trust* (1988). In a much publicized 1987 event, Joel put on six sell-out concerts during an unprecedented tour of the Soviet Union. He made an impressive voiceover acting debut in the role of Dodger, "a carefree canine who has a real New York state of mind," in Walt Disney Pictures 27th full-length animated feature *Oliver & Company* (1988). He won the role by auditioning over the phone. "It worked out great," said the director George Scribner. "He could really act, and as he got into the part he defined the character and we started rewriting for him . . . " "Why Should I Worry?" (with words and music by Dan Hartman and Charlie Midnight) is Dodger's theme song. As sung by Billy Joel, it musically expresses that character's carefree philosophy on life. With its animated "canine choreography" and inventive staging, this number is one of the film's visual and audio highlights. Despite the fact that Billy Joel grew up seeing all the Disney classics, it was his daughter that really made this assignment special to him. "I wanted to be a hero to her more than I wanted to be a star in a movie. I knew by the time we were through making it she'd be old enough to see it. It was perfect timing." He adds, "If I do this character well enough and it's a Disney classic, I will last as that dog maybe even longer than my records. Who knows?"

Elton John

"I'm singing better than ever. I regard myself now as a singer who plays piano rather than a piano-player who sings. For the next twenty years, I should be able to sing my ass off. . . . I felt I'm just learning to sing properly now. It took me twenty years to get to this stage, so it's great. I'm at the second starting point." This self described "male Betty Boop" is a free man with dollar signs for veins, singing for his next Rolls-Royce with such top-of-the-chart singles as: "Your Song," "Daniel," "Candle in the Wind," "Benny and the Jets," "Don't Let the Sun Go Down on Me," "Lucy in the Sky with Diamonds," "Crocodile Rock," "Saturday Night's Alright for Fighting," "Goodbye Yellow Brick Road," "I'm Still Standing," and "I Don't Wanna Go On With You Like That," to name a few. By the summer of 1988, he had recorded twenty-eight albums; in 1989 he was inducted into the Songwriters Hall of Fame.

Born Reginald Kenneth Dwight, 2 March 1947 in Middlesex, England, he began playing the piano when he was three. He performed at a music festival when he was 12 and subsequently won a part-time scholarship to the Royal Academy of Music, where he studied for five years. When he was 18, Elton began playing with Bluesology, backing Long John Baldry, until he answered a talent ad in a pop weekly and met Bernie Taupin, a lyricist. It was with Taupin that he created some of his best work such as *Tumbleweed Connection*, and *Madman across the Water*, as well as the 1971 film *Friends*, for which they wrote five songs. Post-Vietnam society's answer to Liberace, John has become known through the years almost as much for his plumage as for his pipes. America's first view of him in 1970 included purple tights, red jumpsuits, velvet capes, stovepipe hats, and bejeweled glasses.

Once a self professed gay, he married German born sound engineer Renata Blauel in 1984 (divorced 1988) and reportedly gave her a large heart-shaped necklace with 26 diamonds to seal their vows. For male companionship he has bankers and plastic surgeons (remember the famous hair transplants?); he's also preoccupied with advancing the fortunes of the Waterford (England) Soccer Club. In January 1987, Elton went under the knife for a throat operation. He said "I lost my falsetto completely after the operation and it took me about five months to get it back. It was just worn out." Fully rested and recovered, the songwriter/singer keeps busy touring, recording and producing. His recent albums include *Too Low for Zero* (1983), *Breaking Hearts* (1984), *Ice on Fire* (1985), *Leather Jackets* (1986), *Elton John Live in Australia with the Melbourne Symphony Orchestra* (1987), and *Reg Strikes Back* (1988). He also wrote and produced Olivia Newton-John's comeback single "The Rumour" in 1988. His latest album, *Sleeping with the Past*, was released in September, 1989.

Jasper Johns

He told reporters he felt "nothing other than amusement" in September, 1980, when his painting, "Three Flags," sold in 1959 for $900 (plus delivery charge) was resold by its owners to the Whitney Museum for $1 million, believed to be the highest price ever paid for the work of a living artist. Though the painter didn't share in the proceeds of the sale, he had the satisfaction of hearing his work hailed by Whitney director Tom Armstrong as a "monument of 20th century art." The movement known as "pop art," of which Johns was a leading light was obviously not (as many critics once predicted) a trend of little importance. In 1984, on the occasion of John's first exhibition of paintings in eight years, Roberta Smith of the *Village Voice* observed that "it proves his ability to surprise and shock, to render the viewer uncomfortable with his latest endeavors, remains undiminished."

Born 15 May 1930, Johns skyrocketed to his position as prophet of pop in an amazingly short time. He arrived in New York City from South Carolina in 1952; by 1958, he had his first sell-out one-man show; by 1964, at only 33, he was honored with a mammoth ten-year retrospective at New York's prestigious Jewish Museum and his paintings were commanding prices in four figures. Johns ("Jap" to his friends) has progressed from the far-out renditions of such everyday objects as American flags, targets, beer cans and lightbulbs which originally made him famous. In the 1970s, his works were patterns that reminded one critic of "the zigzags in a herringbone tweed." The "poetic, suggestive" pieces shown in 1984 were much different, moving "toward a trompe l'oeil illusionism and a very specific, almost literary array of subject." Traditionally one of the most circumspect of painters, the 1984 show at Leo Castelli's Greene Street Gallery unexpectedly revealed him with "his head above ground" with paintings that were clearly autobiographical, albeit (as noted by John Russell of the New York *Times*) "never, never confessional." Russell echoed the enthusiasm of many other gallery-goers when he reported that "what we see here is painting that for an hour or two makes every other sort of painting look superfluous. And if some of the pictures may take a lifetime to unravel—well, that lifetime will be well spent." The reserved artist with the wispy grey hair, a "hero" to John Updike "for his playfulness," lives alone in a house in Rockland County.

Don Johnson

Clad in pastel suits with sleeves pulled up to length and wearing tee shirts underneath, Don Johnson was the forerunner of the casual male chic look. Possessed with a sweet yet sly smile, the dimple-faced hazel green-eyed actor has become the quintessential sex symbol.

Johnson was born 15 December 1949 in Flatt Creek, Missouri. His desire to act was instigated by undesirable circumstances. During a high school business administration class Don fell asleep. Feeling somewhat insulted, his teacher expelled him from the course. This led him to take a drama course in order to fulfill his credit requirements. Discovering his niche, Johnson landed the male lead in the high school production of *West Side Story*. Upon graduation, Johnson was granted a rare full scholarship to the University of Kansas in 1966. He remained there until 1968 when he joined the American Conservatory Theatre in San Francisco. Having spent a year in the Conservatory, he auditioned for and was cast by the late Sal Mineo in the Coronet theatre production of *Fortune & Men's Eyes* (1969). Johnson made his feature film debut in *The Magic Garden of Stanly Sweetheart* (1970). To follow, were the features *Zachariah* (1971), *The Harrod Experiment* (1973), *Return to Macon County* (1975), and *A Boy and His Dog* (1976). Making the transition to television in 1977, Johnson appeared in "Big Hawaii," "Ski Lift to Death," "First You Cry," "Amateur Night at the Dixie Bar and Grill," the mini-series "The Rebels" and "From Here To Eternity—The War Years." Adding yet another mini-series to his credit he appeared in "Beulah Land" in 1980 and the TV movies "The Revenge of the Stepford Wives" and "Elvis and the Beauty Queen" in 1981. It was not until 1984 that Johnson finally received the critical acclaim his abilities deserved. His role as Detective Sonny Crockett in NBC's "Miami Vice" was to be his vehicle to become a household word and receive an Emmy nomination. While his work on the series certainly kept him busy for its five-season run, Johnson still made time for other projects. In 1985 he appeared in the TV movie "The Long Hot Summer." He occasionally directed episodes of "Miami Vice." He displayed his vocal abilities in 1986 with the release of his album *Heart Beat* for Epic Records and executive produced an NBC sitcom pilot "Flip Side." He teamed with Barbra Streisand in 1988 for the duet "Till I Loved You" (the love theme from *Goya*). Johnson was also seen in the feature films *Sweethearts Dance* and *Dead Bang*.

While he has been labeled a ladies man, Johnson had his share of commitment-oriented relationships. A marriage to what was reportedly a high school sweetheart ended in divorce in 1976. On the set of *The Harrod Experiment* he met his second wife, actress Melanie Griffith. That marriage also ended in divorce in 1976. A long term relationship with actress Patti D'Arbanville produced a son, Jesse Wayne, born 7 December 1982. The union between D'Arbanville and Johnson ended in 1986. His fateful reunion with former wife Melanie Griffith led to a trip down the aisle on 6 June 1989 in Aspen, Colorado where they share a home with Jesse and Melanie's son, Alexander. The couple are awaiting the birth of their first child together in the fall of 1989. An avid skier, Johnson also enjoys songwriting, fishing, and a good relaxing game of golf.

John H. Johnson

He is the most prosperous and influential black publisher in the U.S.; his books and magazines (*Ebony* and *Jet*) are read all over the world. "My aim," he once said, "has always been to get myself into a position where I would own the building, not burn it down. I don't want to destroy the system. I want to get in it." The son of a black sawmill worker in rural Arkansas, he has achieved this goal and more, becoming a publisher, businessman and humanitarian. He is Chairman and CEO of Johnson Publishing Company Inc. in Chicago (his daughter, Linda Johnson Rice, is President), chairman and chief executive of Supreme Life Insurance Company, president of

Lady Bird Johnson — CELEBRITY REGISTER 1990

WJPC (Chicago's first black-owned radio station), president of WLOU, in Louisville, Ky., and president of Fashion Fair Cosmetics.

Born 19 January 1918, in Arkansas City, Ark., Johnson's burning drive for success began early in life and continues undiminished. His is a story in the old-fashioned rags-to-riches Horatio Alger tradition. During his early years in Chicago his family was on relief, and the publisher still winces when he remembers the humilitiation he felt wearing shabby clothes to school. When classmates poked fun at the hand-me-downs, Johnson says, "I decided I would show 'em and I did." Exceptional grades in high school won him a job with the Supreme Liberty Life Insurance Company, one of the biggest black-owned firms in the Midwest. He discovered his talent for journalism working on the company magazine, which published as a regular feature a digest of Negro news. He thought such a digest might appeal to a wider audience. In 1942, using his mother's furniture as collateral, he borrowed $500 to start his own magazine, *Negro Digest*. When the magazine caught on, he began *Ebony*, a black version of *Life*, and was well on his way into "the system." His company now publishes books and three magazines, *Ebony*, *Jet*, and *Ebony Jr*. Johnson has numerous philanthropic and civic interests and was a special Ambassador in the early 1960s to independence ceremonies in the Ivory Coast and Kenya. His honors and awards include the Columbia Journalism Award (1974) and Most Outstanding Black Publisher in History (1977). In 1983, he was inducted into Chicago Business Hall of Fame and in 1986 he was honored with the Distinguished Contribution to Journalism Award from the National Press Foundation. Johnson and his wife, Eunice, live in Chicago.

Lady Bird Johnson

During her White House years as First Lady, she made her mark with such projects as daffodils along Pennsylvania Avenue. In the 1980s, she was helping the whole nation burst into bloom. To celebrate her 70th birthday in 1982, she launched the land's first National Wildflower Research Center with the goal of studying the preservation, propagation, as use of wildflowers in public places as well as private backyards. "This does not mean taking over the formal landscape," she said, "but incorporating what the Lord put there," and added: "Wildflowers have always been the stuff in my heart."

Born in an antebellum mansion at the edge of tiny Karnack, Texas, 22 December 1912, the youngest of three, Claudia Alta Taylor was described by a nursemaid, when only two, as being "purty as a ladybird," and Lady Bird she has been ever since. Married to Lyndon B. Johnson in 1934, when her groom was executive secretary to then-Congressman Richard Kleberg, Lady Bird progressed with him through successive stages to the White House, following the assassination of President John F. Kennedy in 1963. Her husband's closest confidante, she is credited with persuading him to run for re-election in 1964 and to step down in '68 and retire to the LBJ ranch, where he died in 1973.

Considered "the real brains" behind the Johnson family's multi-million dollar radio and TV chain, Lady Bird has worked hard to encourage women in business as well as government. A graduate of the U. of Texas, she is the author of *A White House Diary* and *Wildflowers Across America*, plus the mother of daughters Lynda Bird Robb and Luci Nugent Turpin, with a growing brood of grandchildren whom she hopes will love nature as much as she does. "Walking in the woods was one of the first things that I ever did."

Van Johnson

"I was the biggest movie fan you ever saw. What a kick it was to drive through those MGM gates in the smog every morning and see that big Leo the Lion looking down at me . . . and when I'd take my little tin lunch box into the dressing-room building and see those signs on the doors—Clark Gable, Spencer Tracy, Robert Taylor, Lionel Barrymore, Fred Astaire—I'd say to myself, "What are *you* doing here, you schnook?" He arrived in Tinsel Town at the height of its glitter in 1941 and his red-haired, freckle-faced boy-next-door grin soon made him an idol of the bobby-soxers; by 1945, he was one of the industry's top ten box office draws. ("I made my living with my freckles," he once joked. "I get a dollar a freckle.") And demonstrating that the beaming high-wattage Johnson smile hadn't dimmed with the years, he celebrated his fiftieth year in showbiz in June, 1984, still working, alternating mostly between made-for-TV movies and regional theater. In 1985, he returned to Broadway in the role originated by Gene Barry in the musical hit, *La Cage Aux Folles*.

Born 25 August 1916 in Newport, R.I., the son of a plumbing contractor, Van Johnson was starstruck from the start. Heading for New York at 18, he made his debut as a song-and-dance man on stage at the Cherry Lane Theatre in Greenwich Village and later strutted his stuff as a chorus boy on Broadway in *New Faces of 1936*, and *Too Many Girls* and as an understudy to Gene Kelly in *Pal Joey*. On his first venture before the cameras (*Murder in the Big House*, 1941) he attracted little notice, but when he signed on at Metro the magic began. Among his more than 100 films: *Dr. Gillespie's New Assistant* (an early "Dr. Kildare" offering in 1943), *A Guy Named Joe* (1943), *Thirty Seconds Over Tokyo* (his first star vehicle, in 1944), *In the Good Old Summertime* (with Judy Garland in 1949), *Battleground* (1949), *The Caine Mutiny* (1954), *Miracle in the Rain* (1956). Married to (and divorced from) the former Evie Abbott Wynn, he has one daughter, Schuyler. And for collectors of Hollywood trivia: yes, he still wears his trademark of fire-red socks, even with black-tie.

Grace Jones

Now here is the real thing. From her revved-up start in Jamaica, where she was born 12 June 1954, to her archvillainy as the character May Day in the 1985 James Bond film, *A View to a Kill*, Grace Jones embodies the unknown, menace, violence, an enchantress offering unspeakable acts of pleasure in her web of mint-and-mango.

Grace's father was a clergyman and her grand-uncle a bishop. She spent her childhood in Jamaica and was rather strictly raised at home and in parochial schools. At age 12 she and her family moved to Syracuse, N.Y., where Grace began her slow rise to outrageously successful misfit. It is rumored that she was fond of showing off her breasts, loved to swear, and spit blood. Some bore wrote on her report card that the young woman was "socially sick." She tried college for a year (at one time her ambition was to be a Spanish professor; Grace is fluent in several languages) before dropping out. For a brief while she worked as an actress in summer stock and as a model. In the mid-seventies she became famous in the unofficial underworld of Manhattan's club scene because of her outrageous acts and wicked ways with style. American advertisers found her image "too strong" so she sailed to Europe, where, she claims, she was discovered while dancing on a bistro table on Bastille Day. She became a top model in glossies such as French *Vogue* and *Elle* and Germany's *Stern*. And, before she got her first recording contract, so the story goes, a cardinal in Milan fell so fiercely in love with her sensational curiosities that he offered her unofficial marriage. When she refused, they say, he shot himself! Grace's stage act included live black panthers, "white slaves" whom she whipped, and simulated sodomy. As Pat Jordan remembered in *Mademoiselle* in 1982, "often people in the audience would plead with her to whip them. One man hand-cuffed himself to her ankle; when she kicked him with her stiletto-heeled shoes, he loved it." Then she met Jean-Paul Goude who became her lover (they had a son in 1979) and Svengali. He transformed her act into what he called *Tableaux Vivants*, or "living pictures." Some of Jones' album titles are: *Warm Leatherette, Fame, Portfolio,* and *Nightclubbing* with such hit singles as "On Your Knees," and "I Need a Man"—lyrics like "Feeling like a woman, looking like a man," "Pull up to the bumper baby, drive it in between."

These days Jones is going as Hollywood as she can, having appeared in such movies as *Conan* 1984, with Arnold Schwarzenegger), *Siesta* (1987) and *Straight to Hell* (1987). Recent albums include *Inside Story* and *Slave To The Rhythm*.

James Earl Jones

In *The Great White Hope*, James Earl Jones' powerful, Tony Award-winning portrayal of America's first black heavyweight boxing champion Jack Johnson reduced spectators to tears. Some critics called it the most exciting theatre to hit Broadway since Marlon Brando played Stanley Kowalski in *Streetcar Named Desire*. And the *Times* decided that if anyone deserved to become "a star overnight" it was Jones. Later, when he wowed Broadway audiences again in *Fences* (1985-1987; Best Actor Tony and Drama Critics Award), people realized that his success did not come overnight. Behind were years of work in the theatre doing everything from sweeping floors to performing off-Broadway (he won the Obie in 1962) and the great Shakespearean roles.

Jones was born on a farm near Arkabutla, Miss., 17 January 1931. When he was very young, his father left home to become an actor, and the boy grew up on his maternal grandparents' farm in northern Michigan ("a Huck Finn kind of life"). He won a scholarship to the state university, starting as pre-med and ending as a drama major. After a stint in the army, which he came close to making his career ("I wanted to be a Ranger, but I was in with a bunch of Southern boys . . . to them a black man could not be a man"), he joined his father in New York and began the climb that led from experimental plays in the Village to *Othello* in Central Park (his Desdemona, Julienne Marie Hendricks, became Mrs. Jones) to Broadway. He's portrayed the first black U.S. president in the film *The Man* (1972), the singer-actor-activist in the Broadway play *Paul Robeson* (1977), and the author Alex Haley in TV's "Roots: The Second Generation" (1979). Jones' short-lived 1980 TV show, "Paris," about a non-violent detective, whetted his appetite for another series, although he says, "I'm happiest [acting] in shoestring budgets in basements." Nonetheless, he continues to keep busy with interesting work; his rumbling bass voice was heard on Chrysler and other commercials, and he hissed menacingly as the voice of evil Darth Vader in the *Star Wars* films. He starred in the made-for-TV film "The Atlanta Child Murders" (1985) and a variety of major motion pictures, including *Quarterman* (1985), *Soul Man* (1986), *My Little Girl* (1987), *Gardens of Stone* (1987), *Matewan* (1987), *Fugitives* (1988), *Coming to America* (1988), and *Shoeless Joe* (1989). He was inducted into the Theatre Hall of Fame in 1985.

Jones lives in Pawling, N.Y., with "three dogs, three horses, three goats, chickens, and rabbits" and his second wife, the former Cecelia Hart. He voices despair over the roles most often written for black actors. "Most American black characters of my time were written around a basic conflict: the character's problems with the white world—and that frankly gets a little dull. 'Whitey' is often the least of black men's problems."

Quincy Jones

One of the most prolific and versatile forces in both jazz and pop music, he has penned dozens of scores for TV productions and popular movies and produced successful albums for other music superstars, including Michael Jackson, whose album *Thriller* swept the 1984 Grammy Awards. It was Jones who in 1985 kept several dozen recording superstars up for an all-night recording session that produced "We Are The World" for starving Africans.

Quincy Delight Jones, Jr. was born 14 March 1933 on Chicago's South Side. After his large family relocated to Seattle in 1943, Jones met pianist-singer Ray Charles, who introduced him to the world of jazz. "I learned a lot from him about the world and particularly about music. I remember once we were listening to a Billy Eckstine recording. I asked Ray how was it that band members are playing different notes and melodies, but it all fits. Well, he sat down at the piano and showed me. It was like a light came alive in my head. I guess that's what really got me interested in writing, that one little incident."

After graduating from Berklee College of Music in Boston, Jones toured with Dizzy Gillespie as a trumpeter and then formed his own large band for American and European tours in 1960. Named Vice President of Mercury Records in 1964, Jones arranged for the label's artists, while composing scores for such films as *The Pawnbroker* in 1965, and *In Cold Blood* in 1967. His original song and score "Miss Celie's Blues" from *The Color Purple* (1986) was nominated for an Academy Award. On television, he lent his talents to develop the theme songs for the "Bill Cosby Show," "Sanford and Son," and for the 1974 blockbuster "Roots."

Concentrating on his own recording career beginning in 1969, Jones made over ten albums, many of which were both critical and commercial successes. Among his noted albums are, *Body Heat* (1974), *I Heard That* (1976), *Sounds . . . and Stuff Like That* (1978), and *The Dude* (1981). He and his wife Peggy Lipton split in 1986.

Tom Jones

It may be hard to believe, but Tom Jones is a grandfather. The sexy, hipswaying singer's son Mark has two children (Alexander John and Emma Violet) making Tom one of the coolest grandpa's around. Still a contender for selling out nightclubs, Jones also continues to stay on the record charts. In 1987 he performed the title role of "Matador" on a special album project of the same name. The LP consisted of a musical play written by Mike Leander and Eddie Seago, featuring the rags-to-riches story of legendary Spanish bullfighter El Cordobes. The album spawned the single "A Boy from Nowhere" which reached number two on the British charts. The following year (1988), Tom guest-performed with the techno-pop group The Art of Noise and collaborated on a cover of Prince's tune "Kiss"; the record hit the Top Ten charts in Europe as well as the Top Forty in America.

Born Thomas Woodward Jones on 7 June 1940, he went to school only as long as the law required. ("People say the best time of your life is when you're young. I always wanted to grow up, to be a man.") Married to his childhood sweetheart Linda at 16 and the father of a son, Mark, at 17 he supported himself as a construction worker by day and singer at night. Among his 50 gold discs are such songs as "Green, Green Grass of Home," "What's New Pussycat?," "Delilah," and "She's a Lady." In the 1980s, he was a regular on *Billboard's* list of Hot Country LPs. When not on tour, Jones lives in a mansion in Bel Air with a living room that's larger than the entire house in which he grew up. His favorite souvenir: the hometown telephone booth on which, with no phone at home, he had to rely while courting his wife.

"I just wanted to sing, I was thrilled that someone was paying me," says the Welsh coalminer's son about his pub-singing days back home in the town of Pontypridd where, on a good night, he collected one English pound for belting out six songs. Hitting the jackpot in 1964 with his million-seller, two-continent hit, "It's Not Unusual," he's continued on in the musical major leagues and now averages in the $250,000-a-week range during the nine months a year he tours America's performing venues. Famous for his sexy on-stage personal and a bounding gusto which "makes dignified wives and mothers behave the way they've told their daughters not to," he figures he's had a minimum of 5000 room-keys thrown his way during performances, many wrapped in "unmentionables." But the happily married grandfather says he never takes advantage. He's interested in singing, not swinging. "But," he adds, "when I go on stage and they go crazy, I feel terrific."

Erica Jong

"Writing provides intimacy with your secret self, the self that fishes the unconscious, the dreaming self . . . ," says Erica Jong of her craft. The author of the controversial *Fear of Flying*, 1973 (which Henry Miller recognized to be "in some ways . . . the feminine counterpart" of *Tropic of Cancer*) began the journey into herself with two collections of poetry, *Fruits and Vegetables* (1971) and *Half Lives* (1973), recipient of the Alice Faye di Castagnolia Award of the Poetry Society of America and a CAPS (Creative Artists Program Service) award. Her jaunty tales of Isadora Wing's (heroine of *Fear of Flying*) loves continued in Jong's *How to Save Your Own Life* (1977) and *Parachutes and Kisses* (1984). Her latest outing was the 1987 book *Serenissima: A Novel of Venice*.

Born Erica Mann on 26 March 1942, in Manhattan—her father was an importer of fine giftware, her mother, a designer of ceramic objects. Jong describes her childhood (like the upbringing of Isadora Wing) as one "surrounded by books, paintings, all the 'advantages,' which are often not so advantageous. . . . We were smothered with opportunity. . . ." Jong attended the High School of Music and Art and Barnard College (graduated Phi Beta Kappa) where she began in earnest to write poetry. While teaching English at City College of New York, Jong received an M.A. degree in 18th century literature (which she put to practical use in her 1980 novel *Fanny; Being the True History of the Adventures of Fanny Hackabout-Jones*, an 18th century response to John Cleland's erotic *Fanny Hill*). Jong's poetry underwent an evolutionary change after an unpleasant three years in Germany: "My poetry was getting braver. I was no longer writing heroic couplets. . . . I was in psychoanalysis and for the first time was trying to write about my violent feelings about being Jewish in Germany, and my violent feelings about being female in a male-dominated world." In 1975 a third collection of poetry *Loveroot*, was selected as a Book-of-the-Month Club alternate, a distinction that is shared with only two other American poets, Rod McKuen and Robert Frost. *Witches* was Jong's 1981 contribution to her readers; it explores the evolution of witches in art, history and myth. Her 1984 book, *Megan's Book of Divorce* (originally titled *Molly's Book of Divorce* after her daughter, the name was changed when her ex-husband threatened legal action if the child's name remained in the title) was written as a "valentine" for her five year-old daughter. Ironically, the book (told through the eyes of a four year-old) depicts people remaining friends after a divorce.

Jong (thrice divorced) lives in Westport, Connecticut with her daughter. She also has a Manhattan brownstone. She categorizes herself as "a left-leaning feminist" politically; religiously as a "non-practicing Jew"; and in general as "a survivor."

Michael Jordan

"It is hard to keep the recognition in perspective," says this lean, leaping star hoop-hanger of the NBA Chicago Bulls. "I remember one time I was talking to friends and I told them about how Georgetown had doubts that I would take the last shot. I had to clarify myself because it sounded like I was big-headed." That personality flaw Jordan could have easily acquired after his famous shot assured the University of North Carolina the 1982 collegiate basketball championship. But he has also graciously handled other big ego boosts such as being chosen the 1984 College Player of the Year, playing on the winning U.S. Olympic team, and turning pro a year before his college eligibility ran out. On his way to becoming a force in only his first year in the NBA, he was still as unassuming. "I'm not the superstar of this team and I don't want to overshadow anyone, I just want to mingle with the rest of the guys. I need the eleven other guys."

With his 4.3 second speed in the 40-yard dash, Michael Jeffrey Jordan is as fast as most sprinters. Since it often times seems the 6'6" guard forward streaks upcourt that quickly and his career has had a meteoric rise, the whole effect is of someone on the move. Chicago was counting on his all-around play (as so expertly taught by Carolina coach Dean Smith) to extricate the Bulls from the doldrums with even the league's commissioner chiming, "Why am I in Chicago? The same reason everyone else is—to see Michael Jordan." Jordan, born in Brooklyn (17 February 1963) but raised in Wilmington, N.C., came from hard-working parents who instilled healthy skepticism in their talented son. Knowing that his decision to leave school early would be unpopular, he mused, "All these people at the games are here to see me play basketball, not to become a better person. . . . They don't care about . . . how you do in life." With such wit, Jordan is bound to remain modest.

This humble athlete won every major award during the 1987-1988 season, including the league MVP, Defensive Player of the Year, All-NBA First Team and All-Star Slam Dunk Championship. During the 1988 playoffs, Jordan broke NBA and Bulls records. When he's not on the court, he enjoys relaxing with a good game of golf. He says "I'd like to play professional golf . . . [and] win the Masters golf tournament." Still single, he likes to give the following advice to children: "Stay in school and stay off drugs."

Jackie Joyner-Kersee

"I like the heptathlon because it shows what you're made of," states Jackie Joyner-Kersee. Known for being one of the most grueling and varied competitions in women's athletics, Jackie has excelled in it and brought it to the attention of the public as well as the media.

Jacqueline Joyner was born in East St. Louis, Illinois on 3 March 1962. At the insistance of her grandmother, she was named after Jacqueline Kennedy, who was the First Lady at the time. Her grandmother's prediction was that "someday this girl will be the first lady of something." Jackie grew up in an environment of poverty and crime. She was only nine years old when she competed in her first track competition. "I finished last, but I could feel improvement," replies Jackie. Initially her parents were opposed to her participation in track, they felt it inappropriate for a girl, but when Jackie persisted, her parents' attitude began to change. Her first multi-event sport was the five event pentathlon. When she was fourteen she won the first National Junior Pentathlon Championship. In high school, she participated in sports such as track, volleyball and basketball. As committed to studying as she was to sports, Jackie graduated

Lincoln High in 1980 in the top ten percent of her class. After graduating, she received a scholarship in basketball from UCLA. The summer before college, she competed in the United States Olympic trials, but due to a protest against the Soviets, the U.S. pulled out of the competition. Upon entering UCLA, Jackie was discovered by assistant track coach Bob Kersee. Kersee approached the athletic director and threatened to quit unless he waas allowed to coach her, and his ultimatum was met. After heavy persuasion, Jackie finally agreed to take up the heptathlon. In 1983 Jackie and her brother Al were selected to represent the U.S. in the track and field World Championships in Helsinki, Finland. During the competition Jackie suffered a debilitating hamstring injury that prevented her from finishing the meet. A year later Jackie and her brother qualified for the 1984 United States Olympics in Los Angeles. Although favored to win the gold medal, she ended up placing third in the heptathlon. In 1985, Jackie competed in a meet at Zurich, and although she set an American record in the long jump of twenty three feet nine inches, she placed third in the heptathlon. After four years of being strictly her coach, Bob Kersee proposed to Jackie, and they were married on 11 January 1986. That same year Jackie entered four competitions, including the Goodwill Games in Moscow, where she broke a world record and was the first American woman in fifty years to hold a multi-event record, and the United States Olympic Festival in Houston, Texas, where she placed in the top ten Americans in the hurdles, the high jump and the 200 meter run. It was this heptathlete performance, in which she scored 7,000 points, that earned her the 1986 Sullivan Award, the 1986 Jessee Owens Award, and *Track & Field's* "Athlete of the Year" honor. In 1987 Jackie was the women's winner in the Mobil Grand Prix track and field series, and later that year at UCLA she broke the American 100 meter hurdles record. At the 1987 Pan American Games in Indianapolis, Jackie tied the world record in the long jump with one of twenty-four feet, five and one-half inches. In September of that year she won gold medals in both the heptathlon and the open long jump at the Rome World Championships. In addition, in 1987 she was awarded McDonald's Amateur Sports Woman of the Year. In the 1988 Summer Olympics she won two gold medals, one for the long jump competition and one for the heptathlon competition.

Jackie and her husband Bob Kersee, who is currently women's head coach at UCLA, reside in Long Beach, California.

The Judds

"We know we're a one-in-a-million story," Naomi Judd concedes. "You can't get any more normal than we were . . . a nurse and a secretary . . . from blue-collar families." Naomi and Wynonna Judd became an immediate and profound presence in country music upon the release of their first record in 1983. This mother-daughter duo from Kentucky combined their voices to bring listeners the sweet and forlorn shadings of Appalachian folk music, the lilt and drive of classic bluegrass and the sassy assertiveness of jazz.

Naomi Judd (the mother) was born Diana Judd 11 January 1946 in Kentucky. She married while in high school and daughter Wynonna, christened Christina, was born 30 May 1964 during Naomi's high school graduation week. (They chose their stage names from the Bible and the rock song "Route 66," respectively.) The family moved to Los Angeles where another daughter, Ashley, was born some four years later. A divorce occurred when Wynonna was eight and Ashley four. Secretarial and modeling jobs supported the family but poverty and a lack of Kentucky values prompted Naomi to relocate them to a mountaintop house minus a phone and electricity in Morrill, Kentucky. It was there that Wynonna picked up a cheap plastic guitar, and making music to pass the time became all she wanted to do. Eventually, the threesome moved to San Francisco where Naomi earned a nursing degree. They finally relocated to an exurb of Nashville called Franklin, allowing Naomi to take their homemade demo tapes to Nashville producers. Ironically, it was her nursing career that introduced her to the Judds' eventual producer, Brent Maher. His little girl was a patient of Naomi's. When she was released, Naomi gave him a tape which excited him enough that he ultimately gave a rough demo to Joe Galante, RCA Nashville vice-president and general manager. RCA signed them, releasing their first album *The Judds - Wynonna and Naomi* in January 1984. Their first single was "Had a Dream" but the follow-up "Mama He's Crazy" was the first of eight consecutive number one singles, eleven in total on the Billboard country charts. Their next three albums *Why Not Me* (1984), *Rockin' with the Rhythm* (1985) and *Heartland* (1987) were certified platinum and *The Judds Greatest Hits* (1988) was certified gold. Number one singles included "Why Not Me," "Girls Night Out," "Grandpa," "Rockin' with the Rhythm," and "Turn It Loose."

Awards went along with the hit records. The Country Music Association honored them with the Horizon Award in 1984. They earned three consecutive Grammy Awards for Best Country Performance by a Duo or Group with Vocal (1985, 1986, 1987), CMA Vocal Group of the Year (1985, 1986, 1987, 1988), Academy of Country Music Top Vocal Duet (1985, 1986, 1987, 1988) and *Music City News* Award Duet of the Year (1985, 1986, 1987, 1988). They were voted Star of Tomorrow in 1985 by both the *Music City News* and *Performance Magazine* Awards. *Performance* also honored them with the Country Breakout Award (1985) and Country Act of the Year (1988). They also were voted two American Music Awards in 1987 for Favorite Country Video and Single for the song "Grandpa." They've been honored with four International Country Music Awards. *Billboard* named them both Top Country Singles & Albums-Duo and Top New Country Artists-Albums & Singles (1985). "Rockin' with the Rhythm" was named #1 Country Album by *Billboard* and *Cashbox* (1986), and *Cashbox* named them #1 Country Duet-Albums and Singles (1985, 1986, 1987).

Not content to rest on their laurels, the Judds are busy recording a new album, continuing the successful pairing of Wynonna singing lead with Naomi's harmony and countermelodies.

Pauline Kael

"I can't kill anything. Even pictures that I find contemptible are generally pictures that are going to have a big success, and I know it," says famed film critic Pauline Kael, casting aspersion on the power of critics—and the taste of their hapless readership. For there is no subject too dear to be seared by the sharp-edged pen of Kael, the erudite, wasp-tongued film critic for *The New Yorker*, who was once sacked from a magazine early in her career for panning a little family film called *The Sound of Music*.

It was not the first—or likely the last—beloved movie to meet with the harsh words, which, like a paring knife, Kael uses to separate the gifted from the ghastly, the winners from the worthless. Born in Sonoma County, Calif., on 19 June 1919, Kael began her career writing reviews for *The New Republic*, and then joined, and was fired, from the staff of *McCall's*. After that brief setback came her stint as the reigning film critic for *The New Yorker*, making her one of the country's best loved, most hated, and most-read reviewers. Kael's breezy and personal style has been emulated by other, less prominent critics. Says *Newsweek's* David Ansen, "She's the only critic who can make you feel like an asshole for disagreeing with her." The critic takes her preeminence in stride: "You become Queen Victoria if you're around long enough." Among her many books are *I Lost It at the Movies* (1965), *5001 Nights at the Movies* (1984), *The State of the Art* (1986) and *Hooked* (1988).

Madeline Kahn

"I'm not always trying to make people laugh. But they laugh anyway," says the petite redhead. Madeline Kahn considers herself an actress rather than a comedienne, although she's fully aware that she "understands what's funny." Kahn is known to many as the zany and talented leading lady of director Mel Brooks's films. She gave a side-splitting performance as the sexy café singer, Lili von Shtupp, in Brooks' 1974 Western film parody, *Blazing Saddles*. Other memorable Brooks films include *Young Frankenstein*, with Kahn bursting into rapturous song during a "love" scene with the monster. Of her role as Empress Nympho in the 1981 film *The History of the World Part I*, director Brooks commented, "Who but Madeline could look so magnificient, so regal, so stunning, until she spoke and then suddenly metamorphosed into an American princess from Rego Park?"

Born in Boston, 29 September 1942, Madeline won a scholarship to Hofstra University where she studied drama, music and speech therapy. Deciding against teaching, she set out on an acting career and earned her Equity card in a 1965 City Center revival of *Kiss Me Kate*, before capturing a Tony nomination for her sensitive portrayal of Chrissy in David Rabe's *Boom Boom Room*, in 1973. She made her film debut in Peter Bogdanovich's *What's Up Doc*, and as reviewer Vincent Canby noted, played the part "with picture-stealing lunacy." Next followed her Oscar-nominated role as the carnival dancer, Trixie Delight, in Bogdanovich's *Paper Moon*.

According to Kahn, "flexibility is the key." The versatile actress hops from screen to stage, wherever there's a challenging role. In 1978 she starred in the Broadway musical *On the Twentieth Century*, portraying an eccentric movie queen. Television viewers saw her in two series: "O Madeline" (1983), and "Mr. President" (1987-1988). She also appeared in the movie *Clue* (1985) and on Broadway in *Born Yesterday* (1989). Kahn has never been married ("Men don't feel comfortable being romantic with a funny woman.") but doesn't rule out that possibility for the future.

Norma Kamali

"My style is to reverse the standard idea about fashion," says the publicity-shy, New York–born (27 June 1945) fashion designer. "When I decided to do cotton lace sportswear one year, I was tired of the *sameness* around. I wanted to create a jolt! When I think lace, I always think how to bring it to the street level. Fashion today is born in the streets, in my mind, and it must then be made or geared to the streets," she exclaimed to André Leon Talley in *Vogue* in 1984. She has used street-smart findings such as surplus parachutes, sleeping bags, lamé curtains, embroidered Chinese tablecloths and locker room sweat clothes as inspiration. Having graduated from the Fashion Institute of Technology, she opened her first shop in a basement on 53rd Street designing "costumes, not just for performers, but for people who looked like performers . . . it was in the late '60s, so it was easy to mess around and do everything." From her basement boutique she moved uptown to Madison Avenue and after a spell there, and a divorce, she opened her OMO (On My Own) shop and headquarters—it's been the big time ever since.

Some of Kamali's trademark designs include her brightly-colored, oversized, down-filled sleeping bag winter coats, sexy swimming maillots and jogging "sweats" sportswear with football shoulder pads that created a new look in urban wear. As a young woman she picked up her flair from her mother; when she was a teenager she layered her skirts until she had to walk sideways between school desks. "It's a matter of honesty with myself, my work," says the designer, whose clients include Diana Ross, Bette Midler, Raquel Welch and all the members of the former soul group LaBelle. "I have to be and do what I understand. I understand the streets, that's my background. It would be bad, very mediocre at best, if I tried to be somebody who understands castles. . . . It's more challenging to design a good rayon skirt and shirt. Anyone can design a beautiful, expensive dress from a bolt of fabulous French silk. With that, the sky's the limit."

John Kander and Fred Ebb

"If I can make it there, I'd make it anywhere," reads the lyrics in the Kander and Ebb hit song, "New York, New York." Both Kander and Ebb can shout out those lines loud and strong because these two have not only made it big in the Big Apple, but everywhere. They're considered practically court composer and lyricist to Liza Minnelli, as they have written many scores for her that have turned out to be enormously helpful to her career.

Composer John Kander, born in Kansas City, Mo., 18 March 1927, wrote his first scores for the theatre while attending Oberlin College. Graduating in 1951 young Kander went East to get his master's degree at Columbia University (1954). Lyricist Fred Ebb was born in New York City, 8 April 1933, and attended New York and Columbia Universities. Interested in musical theatre as a youth, today Ebb still collects show albums. Since Kander and Ebb started making beautiful music together, their combined musical contributions to the theatre, films, and television have been phenomenal. For the theatre: *A Family Affair; Flora, the Red Menace; Cabaret* (Tony winner); *The Happy Time; 70 Girls 70; Chicago; The Act; Zorba; Woman of the Year* (Tony winner); and *The Rink*. For films: *Cabaret; Norman Rockwell: A Short Subject; Lucky Lady; New York, New York; Funny Lady; A Matter of Time; French Postcards; Something for Everyone; Kramer vs. Kramer; Still of the Night; Blue Skies;* and *Places in the Heart*. In 1974 they received an Emmy award for the television show, "Liza With a Z." In 1989 a new musical revue, *'Round With Kander and Ebb*, was presented at the Whole Theatre starring Karen Mason.

Garson Kanin

It was a meeting with Thornton Wilder that turned him into a writer. "You must learn to ask questions," Wilder told him. "And listen to the answers. And then—pay attention, this is important—write them down." The very next morning 22-year-old Garson Kanin started jotting things down in a notebook, and he's been at it ever since, the result being a parade of highly regarded plays, screenplays, novels, short stories, and the 1971 bestseller *Tracy and Hepburn: An Intimate Memoir*. Not bad for a high school dropout who has also had success with two other careers, acting and directing, and whose "real desire" as a youngster was to be a knock-out saxophonist.

The multi-talented Kanin, born 24 November 1912 in Rochester, N.Y., quit secondary school after one term in the crash year of 1929. He first toiled at Macy's, then as a Western Union messenger, and then, wearing a bright red jacket created by his mother, played sax in his own jazz combo, "Garson Kay and His Red Peppers." Tooting club dates at night and studying by day at the American Academy of Dramatic Arts, he became an actor and did double duty in the 1930s as performer and assistant director (to George Abbott) on a string of comedies that included such classic farces as *Three Men on a Horse, Boy Meets Girl* and *Room Service*. He went to Hollywood in 1937 as a director and became a Boy Wonder with such films as *A Man to Remember* and *My Favorite Wife*, before the World War II draft. In the service, he made documentaries (*The True Glory* was an Oscar winner in 1946), then returned to civilian life to write and direct the four-year running comedy hit *Born Yesterday*. He was married in 1942 to the late actress-writer Ruth Gordon, and the two formed a screen writing team that turned out movies like *A Double Life*, *Adam's Rib* and *The Marrying Kind*. Making his debut at the Met in 1950, he both wrote and directed a new English libretto for *Die Fledermaus*: he later returned to Broadway to direct *The Diary of Anne Frank* (1955) and *Funny Girl* (1964).

His bestseller *Hollywood* was published in 1974, and he has continued to write short fiction and novellas. He's always working on a project, tapping into his left hemisphere, creating. He was inducted into the Theatre Hall of Fame in 1985 and his *Born Yesterday* was revived in a 1989 Broadway production. In March, 1989, Kanin was honored by the Writer's Guild.

Donna Karan

Like most women, she looks into her closet each morning and thinks, "What shall I wear today?" However, unlike most women, the answer Donna Karan comes up with may be the basis of a new fashion idea or a new collection of clothes. For the last 18 years, Karan has assisted in the design of or has designed the women's wardrobe essentials, first with Anne Klein & Company New York and now with her own company, Donna Karan New York. Why New York on the label? "There's a special energy in New York today. It's pulsating and sets the pace for women with style—women in any city or country," says the native New Yorker, Karan. Her collection, based on the needs of a woman's lifestyle, centers around separate pieces designed in simple forms. "The clothes should translate the body language of the woman and enhance her own personal statement," says Karan, who plays with new fabric, often wrapping and tying it around her body to see how the fabric moves and how it relates to the body. Karan's fresh fashion point of view has already received praise and recognition from the industry. In 1977, while she was the Chief Designer for Anne Klein & Company, Karan received the coveted Coty Award. Her second Coty Award was awarded in 1981 while she was collaborating on the Anne Klein Collection with Louis dell'Olio. In 1984, Karan earned the Coty Hall of Fame Citation. As if to reinforce Karan's 1984 decision to start her own company, in 1985 the Council of Fashion Designers of America recognized Karan for her outstanding creative contributions to American fashion.

Born Donna Faske on 2 October 1948 in Forest Hills, New York, to an ex-model mother and a haberdasher father, Donna was raised "eating, sleeping and dreaming" fashion. It's not surprising that her first job, when she was 14, was as a saleslady in a Long Island dress shop (Donna lied about her age to get the job). Hooked on fashion, Donna enrolled in the Parson's School of Design in New York. After her second year, Donna managed to land a summer job with Anne Klein, who convinced her not to return to school in the fall. That was in 1968. Her climb from the summer job reads like a fairy tale: from 1971 to 1974 she was Associate Designer to Anne Klein herself; after Klein's death in 1974 Donna was promoted to Chief Designer and showed the first complete collection for Anne Klein that same year. She was Chief Designer until 1978, and thereafter collaborated with Louis dell'Olio on the collections. In 1982, Donna conceived and designed the Anne Klein II Collection, based on the essentials in a woman's wardrobe. By then Donna knew the timing was right to think about opening her own company. On 3 May 1985, Donna (using her married name) inaugurated the Donna Karan New York label.

The busy designer lives with her second husband, sculptor Stephen Weiss, and her daughter, Gabrielle Karan (from her marriage to Mark Karan) in their Manhattan apartment. Free weekends are spent looking for a country or beach "retreat" where she can ski, play tennis, or sun on the beach.

Casey Kasem

With 18 years of experience behind him, he is the most recognized voice on radio today, and the youngest person ever to be inducted into the Radio Hall of Fame. This fame has also earned him a star on Hollywood Boulevard. In addition to being at the top of his radio profession, Kasem is involved in many social and humanitarian campaigns against smoking, discrimination, drunk driving, alcohol abuse and hunger; he has also co-hosted the Jerry Lewis Muscular Dystrophy Telethon since 1981.

Born Kemal Amin Kasem in Detroit in 1933, the son of Lebanese Druze parents, Kasem dreamed of becoming a baseball player but ended up as a radio sports announcer in high school. He was also a member of his high school's radio club. Upon entering college (Wayne State University), he majored in Speech and English, and landed roles in shows like "The Lone Ranger" and "Sergeant Preston of the Yukon." His college years were cut short when he was called to serve in the U.S. Army in Korea (1952). During his military service, he coordinated and acted in radio drama on the Armed Forces Network. By 1954 Kasem was back in the U.S. as a civilian, and soon became a disc jockey. He landed jobs in Detroit, Cleveland, Buffalo, Oakland, San Fransisco and finally Los Angeles. In 1963, when he moved to Los Angeles, Kasem added TV to his radio work and hosted "Shebang," a dance program produced by Dick Clark. He also branched into film acting and voice-overs, and has done over 2,000 episodes in series such as "Scooby Doo," "Super Friends," "Mister Magoo," and "Transformers," as well as "letters and numbers" on "Sesame Street." His acting continued through the 1970's and 1980's and included such TV series as "Charlie's Angels," "Quincy," "Fantasy Island," "Matt Houston," "Mickey Spillane's Mike Hammer," "America's Top Ten," and the American Video Awards. Kasem also created and hosted the ever-popular "American Top 40," which debuted in July, 1970. In 1989 he presented his countdown show on the Westwood One Network.

Off the air, Kasem is very much involved in philanthropic causes. He is a member of the board of directors for FAIR (Fairness & Accuracy in Reporting), he supports Operation PUSH, which encouraged young people to complete their education, has aided the Great Peace March in the U.S.A., and participated in the American-Soviet Walk To End an Arms Race Nobody Wants, which was held in the U.S.S.R. (1987). His awards include a Distinguished Alumni Award from Wayne State University and the Goodwill Ambassador Award (1987) from the Arab-American Press Guild for his contributions to the Foundation for Mideast Communication.

Kasem and his second wife, Jean (also an actress), live with their three children Kerri, Michael, and Julie, all from his previous marriage.

Elia Kazan

"I've always been crazy for life. As a young kid I wanted to live as much as possible, and now I want to show it—the smell of it, the sound of it, the leap of it. 'Poetic realism' I call it when I'm in an egghead mood." So exults this award-winning stage and film director, novelist, Broadway actor, and co-founder of Actors Studio. Kazan, who once exerted a strong influence on the works of Tennessee Williams and Arthur Miller, can today boast of having directed five plays that won Pulitzer Prizes (two of them, *Death of a Salesman* and *J.B.* won Tonys). He has become a writer himself with solid hits like *America, America* (1962), *The Arrangement* (1967) and his largely autobiographical sixth novel,

Stacy Keach

The Anatolian (1982). His directorial credits include a string of Hollywood film classics such as *East of Eden, Baby Doll, Cat on a Hot Tin Roof, Gentlemen's Agreement* (Oscar, 1947), *On the Waterfront* (Oscar, 1954). He was once described by *Vogue* as "rugged without being tough, opinionated but not obnoxious, charged with energy, perception, and a nice fast shot of humor." Said the late Vivien Leigh, "He's the kind of man who sends a suit out to be cleaned and rumpled."

Born Elia Kazanjoglou 7 September 1909, in Istanbul, Turkey, "Gadge" Kazan first made a name for himself as an acting member of the famous 1930s Group Theatre company, appearing from 1934 to 1941 in such classics as *Waiting for Lefty, Golden Boy* and *Lilliom*. His directing career began in 1942 with *Skin of Our Teeth* for which he won a New York Drama Critics Award. He won four subsequent Drama Critics Awards, among them one for *Streetcar Named Desire* (1947). He has acted in some dozen plays and four movies, and directed more than 40 plays and films. He was co-director of the Repertory Theatre of Lincoln Center (1960-64). His autobiography, *Elia Kazan: A Life* was published in 1988.

Kazan and his first wife, Molly Day Thatcher (who died in 1963) had four children. He married actress-director Barbara Loden in 1967. Following her death in 1980, he married Frances Rudge in 1982. He was a recipient of the Kennedy Center Honors in 1983.

Stacy Keach

This "finest American classic actor since John Barrymore" (in the eyes of Clive Barnes) decided that a classic American hero could also be done well. "I thought that with enough time and flexibility," says Stacy Keach, "I could make [Mike] Hammer as interesting as any Shakespearean character I have ever played." By using "shtick mannerisms," and suits that he'd made to look approximately wrinkled by throwing them into a corner, he made the Mickey Spillane-created detective interesting enough for CBS to launch a series after two TV movies. (The series went on hiatus in 1984 while Keach served a six-month plus jail sentence in Great Britain for cocaine smuggling, and upon his release in June, 1985, he went public about his cocaine addiction). Rather than resume the continuing series, special telefilms of "The New Mike Hammer" pop up once or twice a year with Keach in the starring role. The actor previously gathered bravos, Obies, and Tonys for playing LBJ in the off-Broadway *MacBird*, Buffalo Bill in Broadway's *Indians*, Jamie in *Long Day's Journey Into Night*, and Hamlet in a Central Park production of the New York Shakespeare Festival. He stays busy directing and starring in public or commercial TV movies and in films. In 1989 he filmed *L'Amante* in Paris.

The actor, born Stacy Keach, Jr., in Savannah on 2 June 1941, arrived to actor parents painfully familiar with the hazards of a theatrical career. While they wanted him to become a lawyer, his early acting mentors thought he'd be handicapped by the scar left from four childhood operations for a harelip. "The harelip is me," he said, refusing further corrective surgery. Discouragements notwithstanding, he prepared himself with drama studies at the University of California, Yale Drama School, and the Royal Academy of Dramatic Art in London. In 1964 he started making the rounds in New York. In addition to plays, his film credits include *The Heart is a Lonely Hunter* and *That Championship Season*, and in addition to golfing, sailing, and polo, his athletic skills include tightrope-walking for the 1981 musical, *Barnum*. "Audiences started taking it for granted that my character was an accomplished wire walker and there was thus no suspense in my getting up there and taking the 35-foot walk. So I inserted a fake fall, saving myself by grabbing the wire with my hands. . . . Thing is, when . . . will I ever use that skill again?" Divorced from his third wife, former model Jill Donahue, Keach married actress Malgosia Tomassi in 1986.

Diane Keaton

"I wanted to be more than a nice girl. I felt I wasn't really interesting enough," she says. "I was a California girl—I mean *beach*. I think that's one of the reasons I went into acting." She first became famous playing Al Pacino's wife in Coppola's two *Godfather* films ("background music" is how she dismisses this part) and, more importantly, as the female star of a half dozen Woody Allen films. For her title performance in one of these, *Annie Hall*, she swept the '77 Best Actress honors: the Oscar, Golden Globe, N.Y. Film Critics and National Society of Film Critics Awards. Keaton (which is her mother's maiden name; the actress' own surname is Hall) proved her versatility that year in *Looking for Mr. Goodbar* by playing the intensely dramatic role of a doomed, promiscuous schoolteacher.

Born in L.A. on 5 January 1946, Keaton sang and acted in high school and local theatre productions. After briefly attending two California colleges, she went to N.Y., at 19 to study acting with Sanford Meisner at the Neighborhood Playhouse. She also sang and danced with an obscure rock band. Appearing in the original '68 Broadway production of *Hair*, she eventually assumed the lead role, and the following year starred opposite Allen in his second play, *Play it Again, Sam*, (she repeated the role three years later in her first film with him.) Her initial film appearance was in 1970's *Lovers and Other Strangers*. Her other Allen films are: *Sleeper* ('73), *Love and Death* ('75), *Interiors* ('78, as a death-obsessed poet in his first noncomedy) and *Manhattan* ('79).

Keaton sang at N.Y.'s Reno Sweeney cabaret in 1974 before displaying her singing talent in *Annie Hall*. She is also a photographer and has published books on the subject. In analysis, she says, "In my past I've done an awful lot of apologizing. I always liked to say I'm sorry before anything happened, but I don't do that as much anymore." In the early '80s she romanced Warren Beatty. (Rumors were rife that he was willing to end his lifelong bachelorhood by proposing marriage to her but she refused). Beatty directed and co-starred with her in *Reds* (1981), which earned her a second Oscar nomination. Later movies include *Little Drummer Girl* (1984), *Mrs. Soffel* (1985) *Radio Days* (1987), *Baby Boom* (1987), *The Good Mother* (1988) and *The Lemon Sisters* (1989).

Michael Keaton

He is a successful and talented actor and comedian who has performed in theatre, on television, and in films, both in front of and behind the camera.

He was born and raised Michael Douglas in Pittsburgh, Pennsylvania on 9 September 1951. The youngest of seven children, Michael performed Elvis Presley imitations with Hershey bar wrappers stuck to his ears for sideburns for his family when he was a child. He later spent two years at Kent State University as a speech major, where he also began acting in plays and writing comedy material. After leaving college, he returned home and earned money by driving a taxi, and an ice cream truck. In 1972 he began working for the Pittsburgh PBS station WQED taking a job as a part of the technical crew. Three years later he moved to Los Angeles, where his first job as a singing busboy lasted only two nights. He then became a member of the comedy group Second City in Los Angeles. Soon after that he made his television debut, landing a small part on the show "Maude." Norman Lear liked him so much that he gave him a recurring role as a joke writer on the show "All's Fair," which launched a five year television career that never really quite took off. Other TV appearances include "The Mary Tyler Moore Comedy Hour," "Working Stiffs," "Report To Murphy," and "All in the Family." His film debut was as a morgue attendant in the 1982 comedy *Night Shift*. He was starting to become a recognized actor, so he decided to change his name, since there was already a Michael Douglas. His new name was inspired by a picture of Diane Keaton which he saw in the *Los Angeles Times*. His next film, *Mr. Mom* (1983), was also a comedy. Several other films followed, including *Johnny Dangerously* (1984); *Touch and Go* (1986); *Gung Ho* (1987); *Beetlejuice* (1988); his critically acclaimed performance in *Clean & Sober* (1988) for which he won the best actor prize from the National Society of Film Critics; *The Dream Team* (1989); and the title role in *Batman* (1989), which brought him superstar status.

Michael and Caroline MacWilliams were married in 1982, separated in December of 1988, and were back together in August 1989. They have one son, Sean, who was born in 1983.

Howard Keel

When Clayton Farlow proposed to Miss Ellie on the top-rated TV series, *Dallas*, the entire Ewing family (with the exception of J.R., naturally) and their rich Texas friends approved. Moreover, so did millions of television viewers. From that moment Clayton was "launched," and so was a new TV acting career for singer Howard Keel. Born Harold Keel 13 April 1919, the son of a miner in Gillespie, Ill., he was 17 when his widowed mother moved to Los Angeles. Working as a supervisor at Douglas Aircraft during WWII, he started singing as a hobby until an agent arranged a meeting with Oscar Hammerstein. "Auditions generally were shattering, but singing for Oscar was like singing in the living room for your father." Signed to a 3-year contract, Keel made his stage debut in *Carousel* (1946) followed by *Oklahoma* that same year. "There was very little notoriety when I replaced John Raitt here in *Carousel* and followed Alfred Drake in *Oklahoma*," recalls Keel. "I was making $250 a week, and the Theatre Guild had two hits. Even in London [*Oklahoma*, 1947] our names were nowhere except in the program."

In 1948 he signed for the movie version of *Annie Get Your Gun* followed by a string of "noteworthy" Hollywood musicals—*Seven Brides for Seven Brothers* (his favorite), *Kiss Me Kate*, *Show Boat* and *Rose Marie*. His most frequent co-star in these films was Kathryn Grayson. "She was the most gorgeous girl and she'd been with MGM since she was 13. Oh, she got a little dingy once in a while," chuckles Keel. "We work well together." For several years Keel and Grayson continued their professional pairing in a successful variety act that played Vegas, Miami and Los Angeles clubs. Never staying out-of-tune with the theater during these movie years, Keel appeared in *Saratoga* (1959), *No Strings* (replacing Richard Kiley, 1963), and *The Ambassadors* (1972) on Broadway, as well as touring in many hit musicals. In 1988 he completed a successful concert tour with an entertaining nightclub act. When one of his three children (1 boy, 2 girls) once expressed interest in pursuing an acting career, Keel reflected: "I was one of God's chosen people, doing what I wanted to do in life. If you find your real thing in life, you've got life 90% made."

Ruby Keeler

"It's really amazing. I couldn't act. I had a terrible singing voice and I can see that I wasn't the greatest tap dancer in the world either," says Ruby Keeler, looking back on those zippy, cornball Hollywood extravaganzas (*Forty-Second Street; Gold-Diggers of 1933; Footlight Parade; Dames; Flirtation Walk; Shipmates Forever*) in which she magically captivated audiences during the bleak Depression years. "I'm most impressed with how talented the kids are today. They can do anything."

But in January of 1971, at the age of 61, Keeler stepped onto the stage of New York's 46th Street Theater and broke into a sizzling tap routine. In Busby Berkeley's revival of *No, No, Nanette* she wowed audiences as might a newly-discovered star. "Everytime something opens up for me, I call a family conference," she says, so close is she to her four children and her grandchildren (her late husband, to whom she was married for 27 years, was John H. Lowe, a prominent broker). Yet four years ahead lay a performance she would have no way of negotiating or planning—the struggle to conquer the damaging effects of a stroke. It was while riding in a car with her daughter and son-in-law in Montana that she suffered an abnormally severe headache, and asked to be driven to the nearest hospital. She was operated on for an aneurysm of the brain, and lay comatose for two months; doctors doubted her chances of pulling through and speculated that, if she did, it was doubtful she would ever walk again. She did emerge from the coma, and, with patience and determination, began walking with the aid of a cane. "I can't run or jump or dance," she said, "but, thank God, I'm still here." In 1981, at a gala at Lincoln Center, Ruby Keeler again stepped out on stage singing "I Want to Be Happy" and broke into dance—only a few simple steps with chorus, but enough to bring the house down in a moving finale. "Never give up. That's the worst," she advises everyone.

Born in Halifax, Nova Scotia, 25 August 1910, and brought up on New York's Lower East Side, she was dancing at Texas Guinan's at 13. When the legendary Flo Ziegfeld spotted her in a musical called *Lucky*, he signed Keeler up for *Whoopee* with Eddie Cantor, and sent her on the road. Keeler married Al Jolson in Pittsburgh, lived with him in California, but returned to Broadway to star in his *Showgirl*. Her marriage to Jolson ended in divorce. "I really prefer not talking about my life with Al. It's just that my life since then— my husband, my children—has been so full that what came before seems an entirely different life." She occasionally lectures aboard the Queen Elizabeth II about the old Busby Berkeley days and speaks about her illness. Determination, courage, and honesty are her virtues. She begins each day with a simple prayer, "Please keep me well. I fully depend on you and trust you."

Gene Kelly

"Has anybody here seen Kelly?" He was on view briefly during the TV season of 1971 as part-time host of a short-lived NBC-TV series "The Funny Side," and appeared in the movies *Forty Carats* (1973) and *Xanadu* (1980). As a director he was responsible for the Broadway musical *Flower Drum Song*, the film version of the musical *Hello Dolly* (1970), and the film comedies *A Guide For The Married Man* (1967) and *The Cheyenne Social Club* (1970). One of Hollywood's favorite song and dance men during the 40s and 50s (in such films as *Anchors Aweigh*, *Brigadoon*, *American in Paris*, *On the Town* and *Singin' in the Rain*), Kelly revealed his talent as a choreographer in a *Pas de Deux* for the Paris Opera for which he was made a Chevalier of the Legion of Honor by the French government. In 1982 he was accorded Kennedy Center Honors, in 1985 he was honored with the American Film Institute's Life Achievement Award and in 1988 he received the Campione d'Italia Merit of Achievement Award at the Lake Como Festival.

Born Eugene Curran Kelly on 23 August 1912 in Pittsburgh, he started dancing as a way to impress girls. "It was strictly a case of male ego," he later recalled. "I'd do a buck-and wing and they all thought it was nifty. But I hated it at the time. No, there was no inner impulse. It was just a way to meet girls." After studying economics at Penn State and the University of Pittsburgh, he found himself stuck mid-Depression in filling-station and ditch-digging jobs, decided dancing was easier, and opened up a studio in his basement at home. Almost completely self taught, he did so well he soon had a branch studio in Johnstown, and he did equally well when he decided to pull up stakes and try his luck on Broadway in 1938. Within his first year, he'd won attention as Harry, the hoofer in William Saroyan's *The Time of Your Life*, and in 1941 he danced the lead in *Pal Joey*. After his Hollywood debut with Judy Garland in *For Me and My Gal* (1942) his dancing star status climbed. Wed first to actress Betsy Blair (one daughter, Kerry) he married former dancing assistant Jeane Coyne (now deceased) in 1960 (one son and daughter, Timothy and Bridget). He has only occasional regrets that dance fans sometimes relegate him to the ranks of museum retrospectives and whatever-happened-to? "It's only my ego that says, 'Gee, I wish they knew I do something else.'" He displayed his talents in 1986 during a Liberty Weekend special stage presentation. Kelly provided an introduction to accompany a performance of his choreography from *An American in Paris*, performed by Lesie Caron, Rudolf Nureyev and Mikhail Baryshnikov.

Jack Kemp

"I do not believe there is any future for the Republican party in trying to defeat Democrats. You don't run to fight opponents. You run to promote ideas. Ideas are what rule the world. We, the Republicans, haven't been offering an alternative. We need more positive ideas." Practicing what he preaches, pro-football-star-turned-legislator-turned-candidate for Republican Presidential nomination (1987-88)-turned-cabinet-member Jack Kemp cut his politcal teeth with the backing of Ronald Reagan, holding forth enthusiastically and convincingly on his Cut Taxes-Increase Revenues idea. He promoted this idea so often, in fact, that even supporters dubbed him Jackie One Note. But when his proposal was signed into law by a grinning Ronald Reagan, the "Positive Idea" revolution has scored a touchdown. Next on Kemp's agenda was tax reform, and by 1985 he was well on his way to getting most of what he wanted, especially lower tax rates.

The former Buffalo Bills quarterback (three Eastern division titles and two AFL championships) is one of the most popular and promising standard-bearers of a rejuvenated Republican Party. At self-proclaimed neo-conservative, Kemp nevertheless distinguishes himself as a negotiator and consensus-builder rather than a white-knuckled ideologue. Although an effort to land him a 1980 Vice Presidential nomination fell short, GOP insiders are betting he will be to his party what JFK was for the Democrats in the Sixties. Kemp acknowledges he'd "like to step up the political ladder," and a lot of Republicans as well as neo-conservative, Laffer curvers, gridiron fans—you name it—would like to see him do it.

Born 13 July 1935 in Los Angeles, Kemp's youth was distinguished mostly by his ability to rifle a football into the hands of a receiver. "I got an education (in college) mostly by osmosis," he admits. Small by professional football standards, Kemp's vision of playing pro football seemed quixotic, and for years he hung on marginally. The formation of a second pro league was his opportunity for success, and characteristically he capitalized on it, becoming a standout with the new Los Angeles Chargers of the American Football League before moving to Buffalo. He took a leadership position among his teammates in labor negotiations, and today he is a *rara avis*, a staunchly pro-labor neo-conservative (and his working-class Buffalo constituency has rewarded him with almost automatic re-election each time out). He's also pro-ERA. Keeping a low profile in his early years in the House, Kemp worked hard to learn economic history and to keep expanding his knowledge of contemporary issues. Married to the former Joanne Main, he has four children (one an NFL quarterback), and divides his time between homes in the Washington, D.C. area and upstate New York. An avid fitness buff, a "liquid lunch" for Kemp is a protein drink, which he often quaffs after a quick set of tennis or a downhill run on the slopes.

In 1989 Kemp joined President George Bush's cabinet as Secretary for Housing and Urban Development.

Edward M. Kennedy

"It is admirable, Kennedy's endurance, his lack of self-pity or even of morbidity to which he is so richly entitled. But he cannot be truly serious either, inside this dream, which is so close to nightmare. He has been too often acted upon, too often the vessel for the desire of others, too seldom alone. The irony is down too deep, and to show seriousness one must also show passion. And he dare not show it lest he be overwhelmed by its consequences." Novelist Ward Just (in *The New England Monthly* of October, 1984) aptly describes the toll of shattering events that have contributed to the successes and failures of the surviving son of America's most blessed—and cursed—political family.

It was into a deceptively secure and pampered existence that Edward Moore Kennedy was born 22 February 1932 in Brookline Mass., the ninth and last child of multimillionaire banker and businessman Joseph P. Kennedy and the beautiful and devout Rose Fitzgerald Kennedy. Both parents were third-generation Irish Americans and Mrs. Kennedy was the daughter of "Honey Fitz", legendary Boston mayor. Six-year-old Teddy tagged along to London when FDR named Joe Ambassador to the Court of St. James, and it was in the skies over England during WWII that the family's first public tragedy struck (Rosemary's retardation was a closely held family secret for many years) when oldest son, Joe Jr., went down with his plane in flames during a secret mission. In 1948 sister Kathleen died in a plane crash. Two years later Teddy suffered his first serious reversal when he was expelled from Harvard for cheating, returning to Cambridge only after a two-year Army hitch. Law school followed, and next came his first venture into politics when he managed JFK's 1958 Senate reelection campaign. Two years after JFK ascended to the Presidency, Teddy won election to his brother's old Senate seat (reportedly "held" for him for a year by a family friend until Teddy reached the minimum age of 30). Seven months after JFK's assassination, Teddy's light plane crashed, and he spent the next six months immobilized, winning the election to a full Senate term from a hospital bed. After Robert's assassination in 1968 he maintained a low profile for a time, returning to vigorously oppose the continued U.S. involvement in Vietnam, which he had initially supported when JFK began sending troops there in 1961. In 1969, during a Martha's Vineyard reunion of RFK's "boiler room girls," Teddy drove off a bridge and his car's other occupant, former Kennedy worker Mary Jo Kopechne, remained under water for nine hours before Kennedy reported the accident. After huddles with the Kennedy political coterie, Teddy took to the tube, admitted his "indefensible" conduct, begged forgiveness—and won reelection in 1970. And there he remains—working for arms reduction and an end to hunger (which he sees as the most important international problem; he wept during a 1985 tour of Ethiopia). As for the Presidency, he demurred in 1968 when he probably could have had the nomination for the asking (immediately after his heart-wrenching tribute to RFK at that year's Democratic Convention). Chappaquiddick was still too vivid a memory in 1972; in 1976 Jimmy Carter successfully held him off, and in 1980 he stumbled badly during a television interview with Roger Mudd and was left at the starting gate. He realized the futility of running against Ronald Reagan in 1984. Kennedy voices his concern that "he has to think about running in terms of other people" (his three children, one of whom, Teddy, Jr., lost a leg to cancer; his brother Bobby's ten children, David having succumbed to a drug overdose in 1984; JFK's two children, Caroline and John; and his mother Rose). Yet, this old fashioned liberal may decide, oneday, that he must complete the cycle begun by his brothers, in which case he will take up the banner—with the heretofore suppressed passion but probably without the joy. In the meantime, Ted is now Chairman of the Senate's Labor and Human Resources Committee.

John F. Kennedy, Jr.

"Introducing his uncle from the podium, John F. Kennedy, Jr. was poised, calm and so handsome that Walter Isaacson of *Time*, who was standing next to me, remarked that the roof almost buckled from the sudden drop in air pressure caused by the simultaneous sharp intake of so many thousands of breaths. John Kennedy has none of the slightly edgy boisterousness of his cousin Joe, who backslapped and kissed his way across the convention floor on opening night. John's charm is simpler, quieter, and more modest than his congressman cousin's. But I would guess that his political career, should he choose to pursue one, will ultimately take him further." Hendrik Hertzberg, writer of *The New Republic* was very impressed with the son of our 35th President of the United States. Like his Mom, Jackie Onassis, the dashing young man is followed by photogs wherever he roams. It is only fitting that *People* magazine named him the "Sexiest Man Alive."

Born 25 November 1960, America most remembers "John, John" as a three year old boy standing at his mother's side at his father's tragic funeral on 25 November 1963 (the child's birthday). He has grown up, literally, in the public eye. Like his sister, Caroline, he chose to study law, and everyone watched him graduate from the Phillips Academy in Andover, Mass., then Brown University, and finally from the New York University School of Law in 1989. During the summer of 1988, he worked for a California Law firm, Manatt, Phelps, Rothenberg & Phillips. On 21 August 1989 he was sworn in as an assistant district attorney in Manhattan, where he will be observing trials and arraignments, meet with bureau chiefs, receive lectures on criminal procedures and ethics, plus ride around with cops. According to a spokesperson for Manhattan District Attorney Robert Morgenthau's office, Kennedy will be treated "just like everybody else."

Congenial and warm to the press, John Jr. seems to enjoy publicity. He lives on the upper West Side of Manhattan and prefers to get around the city by bike. Unlike his father and grandfather, he has a reputation for longstanding relationships. One girlfriend, Christina Haag, has known Kennedy since he was fifteen and shares his delight in amateur acting.

Rose Kennedy

"She was the glue," her son John once said, "that held us together." And it is as an indomitable mother, grandmother, and now great-grandmother that she's known all over the world. Once famous as the *grande dame* of a powerful American political dynasty, she now stands as a symbol of durability in the face of disaster and a testament to the renewing power of religious faith. Four of her nine children met violent deaths; one daughter is in a home for the mentally retarded; she nursed her husband through crippling illness for almost a decade. But the observation of hers that is best remembered is one of neither complaint nor sorrow, but the line, "God never sends us a cross that is too heavy to bear."

The mother of the youngest elected President in U.S. history was born Rose Fitzgerald on 22 July 1890, the eldest of six children of one of Massachusetts' most colorful political figures, Boston Mayor John Francis "Honey Fitz" Fitzgerald. Because her mother disliked the limelight, Rose usually stood in for her as "mayoress" at public gatherings, an experience that stood her in good stead in later years when she became an ardent—and expert—campaigner on behalf of her politically minded sons. The "prettiest high school senior in Boston" married Joseph Kennedy when he was a 25-year-old bank president. While he concentrated on building a fortune, she busied herself raising her large family: Joseph, Jr., John, Rosemary, Kathleen, Eunice, Patricia, Robert, Jean, and Edward. Only after F.D.R. appointed the senior Kennedy as his Ambassador to Great Britain did Honey Fitz's daughter return to public life on a grand scale. It has been said that the tone she established during the Kennedy's London years was the inspiration for what became known as "the Kennedy style" in the White House. (In any event, the luminous Molyneux gown she chose to wear when she was presented at court in 1938 was the same one she wore, unaltered, at J.F.K.'s inaugural ball 23 years later.)

The tragedies began in the war years. Eldest son Joe, Jr., was killed on a bombing mission in 1944; daughter Kathleen died in a plane crash in France in 1948. Then the life that Rose Kennedy has said has been full of both "agonies and ecstasies" delivered some of the ecstasies: multitudinous grandchildren, son Jack in the White House married to the exquisite Jacqueline Bouvier, son Robert serving as Attorney General. But during the agonizing 1960s came the assassinations of John and Robert, the long illness of Joe, Sr., and Teddy's ordeal at Chappaquiddick. And modern times could not be kept at bay either. Teddy and his wife Joan were divorced. Grandson Robert, Jr., was arrested twice for drug possession. Grandson David died in a Palm Beach hotel from a drug overdose. Grandson Teddy, Jr., lost a leg to cancer. Through it all her iron will never broke down. In her eighties she was active in her work on behalf of the mentally retarded and remained until recently a shining night person at Palm Beach's charity balls. Her memoirs, *Times to Remember*, were published in 1974. In all her roles—as wife, mother and surrogate stateswoman—she has exhibited a lively sense of humor about herself. At one gathering on behalf of a family charity, her speech began, "I feel a little like old wine. My family keeps me stored away until there's a special occasion."

William Kennedy

Why does this 1984 Pulitzer Prize-winning novelist write about the life of bums, derelicts and gangsters? He told his friend Margaret Croyden in a profile she wrote about him for the *New York Times Magazine* titled "The Sudden Fame of William Kennedy" that: "I'm interested in the human being concealed within a bum's or a gangster's life." The Albany N.Y.,–born (19 January 1928) and –based writer explained further: "When you take a character into his most extreme condition, you get extreme explanations, and you begin to discover what lurks in the far corners of the soul. I really do believe that that's the way a writer finds things out. I love the surrealistic, the mystical elements of life. There is so much mysteriousness going on in everybody's life."

The only child of working-class Irish parents, following a two-year stint in the army he began working at the Albany *Times Union*. Seeking a change, he moved to sunny Puerto Rico where he wrote for an English-language paper, and where he met his wife Ana Daisy, a Puerto Rico–born, New York–raised dancer. (They have three children.) It was Nobel Prize–winning novelist Saul Bellow who urged Kennedy to pursue fiction writing when, as a visiting professor writing at the University of Puerto Rico, Bellow early on recognized Kennedy's talent and encouraged him. Returning to Albany in 1963, Kennedy discovered that his native city was also the inspiration for his work. His relationship with Albany spirited him through twenty years of relative obscurity. Although he worked as free-lance writer, a professor of writing and even published some books, it wasn't until his novel *Ironweed* won the Pulitzer Prize in 1984 that he came to national attention. (He'd been nominated for a Pulitzer in 1965 for a series he wrote on city slums.) His first novel was *The Ink Truck*, followed by his "Albany trilogy" comprised of *Billy Phelan's Greatest Game*, *Legs* and *Ironweed*. One reviewer called *Ironweed* "almost Joycean in the variety of rhetoric it uses to evoke the texture and sociology of Albany in the 1930s," nevertheless it was rejected a total of thirteen times before Saul Bellow scolded Viking Press (Kennedy's publisher) for turning down the book. "These Albany novels will be memorable, a distinguished group of books," Bellow said, adding, "that the author of *Billy Phelan* should have a manuscript kicking around is disgraceful." With Bellows' endorsement, Viking published *Ironweed* and the other Albany books. The rest is the rush to bestow literary laurels. Governor Mario Cuomo has tagged Kennedy "New York State's Homer." The author won the National Book Critics Circle Award for *Ironweed* and was able after his previous novels' good reviews but bad sales to sell his novel *Quinn's Book*, another Albany tale, on the basis of just two chapters. More of his titles include *The Masakado Lesson* (1986), *Charlie Malarkey and the Belly Button Machine* (1986) and *Toy Soldiers* (1988). He wrote the screenplay for *Ironweed;* the movie was released in 1987 starring Jack Nicholson and Meryl Streep. Until his late success, Kennedy, in the words of one friend, had become dragged down by rejection, "like one of his characters, a bum, a literary bum." The desire to succeed was not William Kennedy's salvation. Writing itself was. "I love writing," he says. "I couldn't see any other life for me. I love words. The act of writing, in itself, is a pleasure."

Joanna Kerns

She is tall, blonde, and striking, and as talented as she is versatile. This gymnast turned actress has done everything from dancing, to singing, theatre, television, and writing.

Joanna Kerns was born in San Fransisco, and grew up in Santa Clara, California. At age 13, Joanna, influenced by her older sister, a two time Gold Medal winning 1964 Olympic swimmer, decided to move to Fresno to study gymnastics. In spite of her height (5'8") she ranked 14th out of the 28 competing for the 1968 Olympic gymnastic team. A knee injury ended her gymnastic career, so she turned to dance. She later attended UCLA where she majored in dance. While a student at UCLA, she answered a call for the Broadway bound production of *Clown Around*. She landed a part in the play, but it never got beyond San Fransisco. Next, she took a job at Disneyland as a dancer. Soon following, she landed a part as a singer in Joseph Papp's highly successful *Two Gentlemen of Verona*. It was the positive experience that she had in this musical that led her to make the transition into acting. She then moved to New York and began studying under Lee Strasberg, and soon after found herself performing in the acclaimed Broadway production of *Ulysses in Nighttown*. Wanting to pursue television and film work, Joanna returned to Los Angeles, where she studied with Peggy Feury, Jeff Corey and David Craig. She appeared in numerous television shows including "Hill Street Blues," "Magnum, P.I.," "Quincy," and "Laverne and Shirley," but her first real claim to fame on the tube was as Hollywood stunt woman Pat Devon in the CBS series "The Four Seasons." Simultaneously, she appeared in 18 national commercials. More recent TV work includes "A Bunny's Tale," "The Rape of Richard Beck," and the made for TV movie "The Mistress," and the successful ABC-TV weekly series "Growing Pains," in which she portrays Maggie Seaver who is a mother, wife and professional journalist. Moving on to film, she has been seen in *Love Struck*, which was nominated for a 1987 Oscar for Live Action Short Film, *Street Justice*, and *Cross My Heart*. During the summer of 1989 she was filming the telefilm based on the Robert Chambers/Jennifer Levin story. In addition to acting, Joanna writes. She has co-written an episode of "Growing Pains," in addition to writing a biographical screenpaly entitled *Freestyle*.

Joanne is also active in community organizations and charities. She is National Chairperson of Find the Children, National Chairperson and a member of the Board of Directors of the Institute for the Community as Extended Family in Santa Clara, California. In addition, she has participated in events to benefit such groups as the Muscular Dystrophy Association, Concern II, The Santa Monica Girls Club and The Nancy Reagan Drug Abuse Fund.

Deborah Kerr

"Damn it, I am not the dowager empress," she says "but then, they have seen me play all those ladies-in-pearls, so that one really can't blame them." Even her Karen Holmes, the alcoholic nymphomaniac of *From Here to Eternity* didn't change her image. Before it had been *The Hucksters* and *Young Bess*, and after it, *The King and I, Separate Tables* and *The Arrangement*, in which she was, as she put it, "about as sensual as an oyster." But she is no spiritless dowager empress.

Born Deborah J. Kerr-Trimmer, 30 September 1921, in Helensburgh, Scotland, she recalls being one of "those awful English children with a good bringing up." She won a Sadler's Wells ballet scholarship but doggedly pursued a theatrical and film career. Coming to Hollywood in 1947, she was bogged down in the ladylike-serenity type-casting department ("I came over here to act, but it turned out all I had to do was to be high-minded, long suffering, white-gloved, and decorative"), finally rebelled and wangled her MGM release. She came dramatically to the surface in "*Eternity*" (1953) and scored again with her sensitive portrayal of the housemaster's wife in the Broadway production of *Tea and Sympathy* (1954). Divorced from TV producer Anthony Bartley (two daughters), she married screenwriter/novelist Peter Viertel in 1960. "All the most successful people seem to be neurotic these days," she says. "Perhaps we should stop being sorry for them and start being sorry for me—for being so confounded normal." She describes herself as "really rather like a beautiful Jersey cow, I have the same pathetic droop to the corners of my eyes." Her biography (*Deborah Kerr*) was published in 1978 and she's been seen periodically on television in such telefilms as "Witness for the Prosecution" (1982), "Reunion at Fairborough" (1985), and "A Woman of Substance" (1985). She and Viertel divide their time between homes in Switzerland and Spain.

Richard Kiley

"It's something in my nature, that I don't like groups of any kind—not political or religious groups," says the reticent veteran of such smashes as *The Incomparable Max* and *The Man of La Mancha* (for which he won the 1966 Tony Award for "most distinguished performance in a musical"). Widely known as the creator of the title role in *La Mancha*, he repeated the role with success in London and in January, 1980, concluded a record-breaking tour of the United States. An Irish Catholic schooled by priests, Kiley has earned plaudits as both a musical star and straight actor. He toured in 1983 as Father Tim Farley in *Mass Appeal*, and received awards for his role in the television mini-series "The Thorn Birds" and "A Year in the Life" (1988; Emmy and Golden Globe Award for Best Lead Actor). He also received the American Image Award from the Men's Fashion Association in 1988.

Born in Chicago, 31 March 1922, he attended Catholic schools until he "seceded" at age 18 after "a set-to with a particularly belligerent cleric" at Loyola University. "I decided that in the process of inclusion there's also a process of exclusion, and I don't believe in that," recalled Kiley. He wasn't out of Barlum Dramatic School very long before World War II began. After serving three and a half years as a gunnery instructor in the Navy, he wangled his way into bit parts on radio shows. By 1953, he was ready for his Broadway debut in Shaw's *Misalliance*, followed quickly by *Kismet* (in which he introduced the memorable "Stranger in Paradise"), and eventually for Tony Awards for *Redhead* (1958) and *La Mancha*. He shined on Broadway again in *All My Sons* (1987). As fans began raving about his explosive actor-singer talents, Kiley remarked with amusement, "I think it's ironic that after I've spent over 20 years in the business, some people are just now finding out about me." His television credits include the roles of George Mason in "George Washington," Emperor Claudius in the TV mini-series "A.D.," and Bea Arthur's romantic partner in the telefilm "One More Time" (1988). His films include *The Blackboard Jungle, The Little Prince* and *Looking for Mr. Goodbar*. In 1968, he married Patricia Ferrier. (With ex-wife Mary Wood he has two sons and four daughters.)

James J. Kilpatrick

"Very few of us, I suspect, would like to have our passions and profundities at twenty-eight thrust in our faces at fifty," said conservative columnist James J. Kilpatrick in a *Time* magazine interview in 1970 about the evolution of his views regarding race, admitting that he had "come a long way" from his 1954 denunciation of the landmark *Brown vs. Board of Education* Supreme Court ruling, when he wrote, "These nine men . . . spit upon the Tenth (states' rights) Amendment. . . . If it be said now that the South is flouting the law, let it be said to the high court: *you taught us how.*"

There are those, however, who cannot forgive the nation's most widely circulated political columnist including one critic who holds him "sort of personally responsible for giving intellectual respectability to institutional racism in the fifties." This despite an outraged Kilpatrick's campaign in the early 50s to win a pardon for a black prisoner who had been sentenced to life imprisonment for a murder he didn't commit, and in 1966 dipping into a fund he'd created to purchase copies of *To Kill a Mockingbird* for the children of a suburban Virginia community whose school board had voted to ban the compassionate novel on race relations. Describing himself as "ten miles to the right of Ivan the Terrible" in the eyes of some liberals, Kilpo (as he's known to his colleagues) is to middle-of-the-roader David Broder "about as independent on issues and personalities as anyone I know. . . . And a marvelous writer," To fellow conservative George Will, "He's a Whig and I'm a Tory, which makes it fun."

This "most gifted and eloquent spokesman for the Old South" was born in Oklahoma City, 1 November 1920, learned to read at four, taught himself to type on an old Remington in his lumber-dealer father's office, and from the age of seven was determined to become a newspaperman. He went from editor of his high school paper to the school of journalism at the University of Missouri and ten years later to editor-in-chief of the Richmond (Virginia) *News Leader* in 1951. His stewardship for the next 15 years at the paper was characterized by a colorful and lively style, along with the unusual and highly individualistic combination of idealism and fanciful but pointed humor. The promise of wider exposure and a more influential forum for his views brought him to Washington in 1965 as a syndicated columnist for the capital's former "other paper," the *Star*. He began writing regularly for *National Review, Saturday Review* and *Business Week*, appeared on television vs. Shana Alexander in their weekly "60 Minutes" verbal wrestling matches, and as a regular analyst on "Agronsky and Company." Books include *The Sovereign States, The Smut Peddlers, The Foxes Union, A Political Bestiary* (with Virginia neighbor, former Senator Eugene McCarthy), *The Writer's Art, The Ear Is Human* and *A Bestiary of Bridge*. He has the distinction of having been awarded the prestigious William Allen White Medal for distinguished service to journalism (1979) and having been named in 1973 as sixteenth of the capital's twenty foremost "male chauvinist pigs." He and sculptor Marie Louise Pietri, whom he married 21 September 1942, are the parents of three sons.

Alan King

He's a stage and screen actor, a writer and producer as well as a stand-up comic. "We live," he grouses, "in a suburban town in Long Island. My wife convinced me we were getting our house from an ex-GI. I think it was Benedict Arnold."

Alan King was born in Brooklyn (as Irwin Kniberg) 26 December 1927 and made his professional show biz debut as a 15-year-old when he formed a four-man band and landed a summer job in the Catskills. When he discovered that comics pulled down $400 a week (he was making $10), he shifted gears, names and professions. Before long he was a headlining comic at Manhattan's famed Leon and Eddie's and by the early 1950s was hitting it big with singers Patti Page, Billy Eckstine and Lena Horne, with the really Big Break coming when he closed the first act of Judy Garland's second appearance at New York's Palace Theatre. During the 1960s he made his stage debut as Nathan Detroit in a New York City Center revival of *Guys and Dolls*. He also appeared on Broadway in *The Impossible Years*. He made his screen debut in *Bye Bye Braverman* in 1968 and in the Eighties was seen in *Just Tell Me What You Want, Lovesick, Author Author, Goodnight Moon, Memories of Me* and *Enemies: A Love Story*. His first film-producing venture was *Cattle Annie and Little Britches* (1980). As author, King's credits include *Anyone Who Owns His Own Home Deserves It* and *Help! I'm a Prisoner in a Chinese Bakery*. On balance King has fared well professionally in all his tangential pursuits. He has been married to Jeanette Spring since 1947 and they've reared two sons and a daughter. King has raised millions of dollars in charity benefits around the country but his pet project of them all is the Nassau Center for Emotionally Disturbed Children, a research and rehab complex on Long Island.

Billie Jean King

When she walked off the courts of the women's tour at 40, this winner of 20 Wimbledon titles (singles and doubles), and 13 U.S. Open titles stepped up to the helm of the reborn TEAMTENNIS. The original league, begun in 1973 by her husband Larry and others, folded after five years. What is Commissioner King planning to do differently? "We're going to start small," she said, "and take longer to make it, but we're going to keep losses at a real minimum for the owners (such as L.A.'s Jerry Buss, Oakland's Roy Esenhardt and the Kings themselves, part-owner of the Chicago franchise)." Yet even with a prize money pool as opposed to players' salaries, the league's stars might expect equitable treatment from a commissioner who, in 1970, was largely responsible for making the women's tour independent from the men's. And she still works to better the lot of all women athletes. "What a loss it is," Billie Jean says, "that so many women who excel in team sports cannot follow their dreams and earn a living after (college) because the opportunities aren't there."

Born in Long Beach, Calif., on 22 November 1943, Billie Jean Moffitt—as is often the case with consummate athletes—defied the sterotypical model of a tennis star for the period (late '50s, early '60s) in which she developed. As John Leonard of the *New York Times* observed, "Not only is she little, but her legs are chubby and her eyes are weak—20/400—and she is part Seminole Indian. . . . Imagine being told by a male coach that 'you'll be good because you're ugly'. . . . She grew up lower-middle class; her father was a fireman . . . her mother gave Tupperware parties . . . and she learned to play in the public parks of Long Beach, Calif." Although she first aggressively attacked Wimbledon in 1961, and won its singles title in 1966, it wasn't until 1968 (on the same day she made her first commercial endorsement, for Maxwell House coffee for $1500) that she turned pro.

In 1971 she became the first $100,000-a-year earner in the sport, at a time when *total* annual women's prize money was estimated at $350,000. King says her highly-publicized 1973 challenge win against lovable, wise-cracking old pro Bobby Riggs in the Astrodome put women's tennis on the map. The map prepared, she and players like Rosie Casals, with the help of the president of the Philip Morris company, launched the Virginia Slims circuit, the forerunner of the Women's Tennis Association. King also started *WomenSports* mag (with Larry in 1974), and helped found the Women's Sports Foundation and Women's Hall of Fame. One issue that this two-time president of the WTA pushed was equal pay for equal work (parity with men). She herself made more than almost all other players with up to a half-million dollars in yearly product endorsements. But most of the outside income evaporated with the 1981 "palimony" suit for lifetime support and a Malibu home by King's female secretary and lover. The California judge called it "attempted extortion," and threw the case out. But while her mail and personal appearances showed her that fans were supportive, the tennis star found that "Madison Avenue perpetuates safeness. All athletes have to be milk and honey."

Coretta Scott King

"If it happens," she said, long before her husband's murder, "I think it will be the will of God. If it happens, it would be a great way to give oneself to a great cause. But I pray God nothing happens." After the Reverend Dr. Martin Luther King, Jr., was shot down in a Memphis motel in April, 1968, the dignified, handsome woman, once described as "an island of serenity in the center of a hurricane," put into action her long-standing belief that "for a movement like this to work, the wife must be as dedicated as her husband." She keeps up a busy speaking schedule and maintains a role in black political decision making. She is also president of the Martin Luther King, Jr., Center for Social Change in Atlanta.

Born 27 April 1927 in Marion, Ala., where her father ran a country store, Coretta Scott had to walk five dusty miles every day to the tacky one-room school that served the area's black children. One of her most vivid childhood memories is of the big yellow school bus that passed her each morning filled with white children on their way to school. Graduating from high school with honors, she won a scholarship to Antioch College and, though her first love was music, majored in elementary education. She says her determination to work for social change was reinforced by the school's motto: "Be ashamed to die before you've won something for humanity." She met her husband-to-be when she was taking postgraduate musical studies at Boston's New England Conservatory of Music, and on their first date the brash, young theology student told her, "You're everything I'm looking for in a wife."

They were married 18 months later in 1953 and set up housekeeping in Montgomery, Ala., where King became pastor of the Drexel Avenue Baptist Church and an organizer of the nationally-publicized Montgomery bus boycott. As King's civil rights activities increased, their home was bombed and shot into and they received thousands of phone threats, but the minister's wife never faltered in her faith in the cause. "She has maintained a calmness," her husband said, "that has kept me going . . . and has a unique willingness to sacrifice herself for [the movement's] continuation." Fittingly, Coretta Scott King was at her husband's side in Oslo when he was presented with the Nobel Peace Prize in 1964. In 1969 her story, *My Life with Martin Luther King, Jr.*, was a best-seller. In 1978 she worked for the successful passage of the Humphrey-Hawkins Full Employment Bill, partly by prevailing upon President Carter to pass it. Six years later she endorsed Carter's vice president, Walter Mondale, over her late husband's protégé, Rev. Jesse Jackson, in the 1984 Democratic presidential primaries. She is the mother of four—Yolanda ("Yoki"), Martin Luther III, Dexter, and Bernice.

Don King

"I must go where the wild goose goes," says history's most powerful boxing promoter, and as far as his flamboyant public image goes (insane hairdo, rings on his fingers, bells on his toes) he's no gander to pander to convention. A former "numbers czar" from Cleveland who was once convicted of manslaughter, he became a millionaire two years after his release from prison (1974) promoting such pugilistic extravaganzas as the Ali-Foreman "Rumble in the Jungle," the Ali-Frazier "Thrilla in Manila" et al. Though his entrepreneurial operations are always under investigation (he was once charged with fixed bouts, kickbacks, and exaggerated rankings; when ABC Television suspended a 1977 tournament, King contended he was slandered because of his race; his 1985 indictment for tax fraud produced a King-sized yawn) he has produced many millions for the crème de la crème of prizefighters: Greg Page, Sugar Ray Leonard, Roberto Duran, Leon Spinks, Larry Holmes, and the mighty Mike Tyson. His latest achievement was the Pioneers of Excellence Award, which he received in 1988.

Born 20 August 1932, the fifth of seven children, he found his first job as a chicken runner for Hymie's Chicken Shack, "swiftly delivering live chickens to the slaughterer's knife," and hustling peanuts roasted by the hundreds of pounds by his mother and sister and selling to gamblers in the policy houses. (King would stuff "lucky numbers" into the small sacks of nuts, so that when the numbers happened to match the winners, he'd be due for a tip). To finance his freshman year at Kent State he took over his elder brother's numbers route and by his early twenties emerged as one of the chief numbers operators in Cleveland. When Muhammad Ali, an eighteen-year-old Olympic medalist then known as Cassius Clay, visited a supper club King owned in 1960, the two became buddies and King began to follow the fighter to all his matches across the country, until King was sent to prison after attacking a numbers runner over an unpaid debt. He left the Marion, Ohio, Correctional Institution ("one of my alma maters") "armed with wisdom and knowledge." Soon after, the firm of *Don King Productions* was born. In a 1974 coup, King charted the Ali-Foreman bout in Zaire, Africa, with the unheard-of purse of $5 million for each contender. (With ghetto-jive grandiloquence he convinced the governments officials of Zaire to put up $12.1 million to underwrite the match.) By 1982 he closed a deal with ABC Video Enterprises to produce 15 monthly shows on his own cable system, for about $400,000 for each event. His empire (including D.K. Chemicals) is worth approximately $50 million (not counting the promotional tour he engineered for superstar Michael Jackson in 1984). He escapes from the hubbub to his 400-acre farm in Ohio, where his wife Henrietta raises Black Angus cattle and his daughter and two sons live. It is also where King's fighters receive full medical, including dental, care.

Larry King

"What has ruled my life is my . . . love affair with broadcasting. It's a pleasure, a gift, an honor, to go in front of a microphone and communicate. It's brought me notoriety as well as fame, but always I have felt most alive in front of a microphone, which is something I didn't fully appreciate until it was taken from me." So says America's "unchallenged superstar of the late-night talk show," who was once banished from the air after entanglement in a financial scandal—then made a comeback on radio in 1978 as the "midnight king of the airwaves" on Mutual Broadcasting System's Peabody Award-winning "The Larry King Show" (now heard on more than 250 stations in all 50 states). "Radio is the theater of the mind," he says. "It is anything you want to make it; all you have to do is use your imagination." On his all-night radio show, King chats with guests that include celebrities of all stripes (Mel Brooks, Sophia Loren, Gerald Ford, Walter Mondale, Miss Piggy . . .), then lets the guests take calls from listeners. In the final "Open Phone America" segment, King takes calls "on any and every" subject from listeners across the nation, turning the show into something of a nightly "national town meeting." About a hundred callers get through a night; thousands try. "Our show does get the occasional kook, but for the most part listening to the callers can restore your faith in the quality of the American people."

A Brooklyn native whose childhood chums included Sandy Koufax, the future "hottest talker" on radio was born Lawrence Harvey Zeigler on 19 November 1933, the son of a Russian Jewish immigrant who ran a bar-and-grill. In 1957, at the age of 23, he headed south and began his broadcast career in Miami, rising to the top of his field by the mid-1960s as one of the city's top TV and radio personalities and a newspaper columnist. But in 1972, his disorganized, spendthrift personal life caught up with him, culminating in a widely-publicized financial scandal that toppled his career and banned him from the air-waves for four years. In his 1982 book, *Larry King by Larry King*, he reveals the intimacies of his private life, including his rise and fall in Miami broadcasting, his money problems ($300,000 in debt, he declared bankruptcy to get a fresh start), and his spectacular comeback on the Mutual network. In 1985 he signed on with Cable News Network for a nightly "Larry King Live" interview show (while also signing a new contract with Mutual). He also writes a regular celebrity column for *USA Today*. Twice married, he has a daughter, Chaia, with his first wife Alene, a former Playboy Bunny. King says he's finally overcome the problem that's bedeviled him most of his adult life, "the feeling that I was two people: one Larry King, the consummate professional; one Larry Zeigler, the Brooklyn troublemaker.... I now know that I am living well because I've worked hard to get here." In May, 1989, King was named Broadcaster of the Year.

Stephen King

Living way far away in foggy Maine among the haunted pines and splintering storms, comforted by wife Tabitha and three children—Naomi, Joe Hill and Owen—he makes a fortune writing what he calls "fearsomes," black night, blood-curdling horror tales that have come to capture the imagination of millions of readers and make them his slaves to terror. About the making of a film from one of his many books he said, "simply it is to put people in movie theatres and see if we can scare the hell out of them. I want people crawling under the seats with popcorn and jujubes in their hair." In the early 1980s he was the first writer ever to have three books at one time haunt the highest rafters of the *New York Times* Bestseller List. In his autobiographical *Danse Macabre*, he wrote about the popularity of all things grim and horrific: "the dream of horror is in itself an out-letting and a lancing... and it may well be that the mass media dream of horror can sometimes become a nationwide analyst's couch."

As a child, King, born 21 September 1947, cast aside the milk bottle for long, nourishing afternoons in Portland, Maine, movie theatres drinking in horror and science fiction films. "Their chief value," he postulates, "is an ability to form a liaison between our fantasy fears and our real fears." His father, a merchant seaman, deserted the family and King's mother struggled to support the children. Years later, King found some stories his father had written. They were, like the son's own endeavors, horror stories. Tough times haunted King's wallet until Doubleday decided to publish his novel *Carrie* in 1974. Filmmaker Brian dePalma made an engrossing genre classic from the book, a story about Carrie's loneliness and resulting telekinetic revenge upon the "bottomless conservatism and bigotry of high school life." In King's words, "the movie made the book and the book made me." The Broadway musical based on the story, however, was slashed by bad reviews. Some of King's other tales of fear and revenge include *Salem's Lot*, *Christine*, *The Shining*, *The Dead Zone*, *Cujo*, *Pet Semitary*, *Cycle of the Werewolf*, *The Eyes of the Dragon*, *Skeleton Crew*, *Misery* and *Maximum Overdrive*.

Ben Kingsley

"I knew that I was playing a star, and that I wasn't one," says Ben Kingsley of the film role that ended nearly 20 years of obscurity as a classically-trained actor on the British stage. "And the more I learned about Gandhi, the more I felt genuinely ennobled by my task." Kingsley's only previous screen appearance had been a decade earlier in a British adventure film flop, but his portrayal of the title role in Richard Attenborough's controversial, internationally popular *Gandhi* earned him a slew of awards, culminating in an Oscar (beating out no less than Dustin Hoffman, Jack Lemmon, Paul Newman, and Peter O'Toole).

Kingsley was born Krishna Bhanji 31 December 1943 in a Yorkshire village, the son of an Indian physician who emigrated from South Africa to England to study and a British fashion model/actress. As associate artist of the Royal Shakespeare Co., Kingsley was in the original cast of *Nicholas Nickleby* and has also performed at London's National Theatre and on British telvision. He confirmed his versatility with his portrayal of an intense, articulate cuckold in the post-*Gandhi* film version of Harold Pinter's play *Betrayal*. Later films include *Harem* (with Natassja Kinski), *Turtle Diary* (with Glenda Jackson), *Pascali's Island* (a suspense drama based on the Barry Unsworth novel), *Secret of the Sahara*, *Without a Clue* and *Testimony*. He also starred in the 1988 HBO production "Murderers Among Us: The Simon Wiesenthal Story."

Kingsley is committed to "good modern writers who encourage a degree of thought and consciousness about society." But, he claims, "Shakespeare's my great love. If I play other parts I get withdrawal symptoms—chemical longings in my veins." Kingsley's one-man show, *Edmund Kean* (in which he evoked the 19th century tragedian's legendary Shakespearean interpretations), was a New York hit in fall of 1983. It was directed by his second wife (since 1978), Alison Sutcliffe, with whom Kingsley and their son Edmund (named for Kean) live in a rambling old house in a village eight miles from Stratford-upon-Avon. Kingsley also has two children from his former marriage to actress Angela Morant.

Nastassja Kinski

"I guess I have been the creature of the director's imagination. You see, I want to get a glimpse of his eyes searching things out inside me. I want to go to heaven and hell for him. I want to make his dreams come true," says the woman who some say is most likely to succeed as Garbo's ethereal replacement in the late 20th Century. "You live and love twice as deeply in the movies. I always fall in love when I'm working on a film. Then you slip out of it, like a snakeskin and you're cold and naked. What worries me is that when these loves die, they hardly leave a trace on me. I wonder why I don't suffer?"

Maybe no suffering, but all that living and loving did leave its trace. Nastassja, born 24 January 1961, the daughter of the German film star Klaus Kinski, was pregnant in 1984 and reluctant to name the lucky father. This sparked a lot of gossip. (The German magazine *Bunte* printed the names and photos of eight of the film star's possible baby-maker boyfriends. They included Wim Wenders, and actors Gerard Depardieu and Dudley Moore. A son was born July, 1984, and mummy was mum until the baby was named (Aljosha) and a father/fiance produced as well (Ibrahim Moussa, the Egyptian-born talent agent–producer). At least the international media calmed down, especially when the couple finally wed in September of 1984. The couple have another child, Sonia, born in 1986.

Discovered in a Munich rock and roll club when she was in her early teens, Kinski made her film debut in the German-made *The Right Move*. Introduced by her mother, who also doubled as best friend, to Roman Polanski, the actress and the director made *Tess* together, a painstaking evocation of 19th Century English countryside life based on a Thomas Hardy novel. After receiving the Polanski polish, she alighted tender and dewy, a true camera animal in films such as *Cat People*, *One From the Heart*, *Exposed*, *Hotel New Hampshire*, *Paris-(Texas)*, *Revolution*, *D'Amour*, *L'Intervista*, *Silent Night, Crystal or Ash*, *Torrents of Spring* and *Up to Date*. Of all her films, it was *Tess* that lighted the fuse. Richard Avedon's 1981 nude photograph of Kinski melding with a sprawling python straight from Central Casting's Garden-of-Eden bin became an international sell-out poster, boosting her notoriety. It said: "Nastassja is nasty, but so very divine."

Gelsey Kirkland

"Speed was her natural pace and air her habitat," wrote one beguiled critic. Another exulted, "She could turn on a dime, stand on one point forever, all slim curves like a Brancusi." Clive Barnes wrote in 1975 that her *Giselle* was "the coming together of a dancer and a role that had been made for each other . . . the fairy tale debut little girls dream about." But some dreams are also nightmares, and not a few of them have punctuated Gelsey Kirkland's career. She was a principal dancer with the New York City Ballet when in 1974 she defected to American Ballet Theatre, reputedly at the behest of another defector, Mikhail Baryshnikov. Their partnership was hailed as "the meeting of two of our dance world's greatest legacies—balletic detente." Two years later the dancer who had been "too scared to collapse" did just that, as a result of nervous exhaustion and a potassium deficiency. Her months' long illness prevented her from starring with Baryshnikov in the hit film *The Turning Point*. She recovered in time to score a dual triumph—as a moving Clara in Baryshnikov's version of *The Nutcracker*, which has become a perennial holiday television treat, and in 1978 she reached the pinnacle of her profession as Kitri in a new production of *Don Quixote*. But in the spring of 1981 she was fired for coming late (or not at all) to rehearsals and for generally unprofessional behavior, which she later admitted was due to a drug problem. Rehired in the fall of 1982, she danced the straight and narrow until May of 1984 when, two days after dancing the leading female role in Antony Tudor's *The Leaves Are Fading* (created for her in 1975), she quit the company.

Born 29 December 1952 in Bethlehem, Pennsylvania, to playwright Jack Kirkland (*Tobacco Road*; the stage adaptation of *The Man With the Golden Arm*) and his former actress wife, Gelsey lived briefly with her older sister and younger brother on a Bucks County farm before relocating to New York, where at eight she followed her sister Johnna (also a principal dancer) to classes at the New York City Ballet's School of American Ballet. At 15 she joined the company's corps de ballet and at 17 was promoted to soloist. NYCB's resident genius George Balanchine selected her to dance the title role in his new production of *Firebird* in 1970, declaring, "I didn't want a woman. I wanted a bird, one of God's creatures." Herbert Saal wrote in *Newsweek* of her performance "This Firebird is not Rima the bird-girl, but an honest-to-goodness magical bird, stripped of sentiment, grateful for freedom, always in flight except when the Prince cunningly and gently traps her." Inspired by Kirkland's exceptional prowess (former NYCB principal dancer Edward Villella described her "steel-like legs that are doing the most fantastic technical feats while the upper body is soft and lovely as though nothing were going on underneath"), other choreographers created works for her to add to the Balanchine repertory. She explained her departure in 1974 (two years after becoming a principal dancer with NYCB) for the more classically oriented American Ballet Theatre: "I was twenty-one, a pivotal time. Ballets like *Giselle* need acting technique and concepts I haven't learned." Typical of the critical response to her first appearance with Baryshnikov was, "Spurred by [Baryshnikov's] bravado, she's taken on a new daring and ostentation. Her dancing didn't just shine, it radiated. Now she looks and poses and moves like the star she has become." Her roles with ABT included Nikiya in *La Bayadere*, Swanilda in *Coppelia*, Lise in *La Fille Mal Gardee*, Princess Aurora in *Sleeping Beauty*, Odette/Odile in *Swan Lake*, the Sylph in *La Sylphide*, the Sleepwalker in *La Sonnambula*, the ballerina in *Theme and Variations* and the leading female role in *Voluntaries*. Armchair analysts may detect in a 1971 interview in *Seventeen* magazine a clue to her later behavior. "I'm a dancer. The rest I'd rather keep to myself. My ideas change day to day. I don't want to tell people who I am, what I feel, why I do things. If I couldn't dance, I don't know what I would do." Since leaving the American Ballet Theatre in 1984, Kirkland has been a guest performer with several European companies. Her book, *Dancing on My Grave* (1986), was a bestseller and the once-married (now divorced) prima ballerina is currently writing another book.

Jeane J. Kirkpatrick

A political science scholar wrote a magazine article in 1979 that contained a phrase many found controversial. The author urged more tolerance for "moderately repressive regimes." The piece—and the phrase—found its way into the hands of President Ronald Reagan, who decided that just such an attitude should distinguish the next U.S. Ambassador to the United Nations. Thus did a professor at Georgetown University named Jeane Kirkpatrick find herself in the international spotlight in just that job in 1981. The spotlight shone brightest, if not always most favorably when Kirkpatrick used the position to advance her own views. She was the first woman to serve as chief United States representative to the world body—and a cabinet member as well.

Her style did not win her many admirers among establishment types, but she soon became the undisputed darling of the neo-conservatives. Cartoonists depicted her as a witch, a dreary scold, a schoolmarm. All of this was thinly-veiled misogyny, she said, and held her ground. "Henry Kissinger is called professorial—yet, I'm called schoolmarmish." An early battle with Secretary of State Alexander Haig ended, to the surprise of Washington insiders, with Haig sending his resumé around and Kirkpatrick still in the polyglottal U.N. After a stormy beginning, Kirkpatrick was finally enjoying more respect—and success and celebrity have followed her even as the "permanent representative" post became past history. (She resigned shortly after Reagan's second term began.)

Born in Duncan, Okla., 19 November 1926, Stephens-Barnard-Columbia-educated Jeane Jordan was an active Democrat whose qualifications for the U.N. post include speaking Spanish and French. The Ambassador is wedded to Evron M. Kirkpatrick, a fellow poli-sci professor. The couple has three sons, and Kirkpatrick says raising them was her best credential for serving at the factitious U.N. She also is a prolific writer and has produced, in addition to her numerous articles, many books, among them: *Dictatorships and Double Standards; Rationalism and Reason in Politics* (1982); *Leader and Vanguard in Mass Society: A Study of Peronist Argentina* (1971); and *Legitimacy and Force: National and International Dimensions* (1988). On 1 April 1985, Kirkpatrick resumed her position as Leavey Professor at Georgetown University and as Senior Fellow at the American Enterprise Institute (AEI). In May, 1985, she was awarded the Medal of Freedom by the President of the United States, in addition to other honors including the French Prix Politique for political courage, the Gold Medal of the Veterans of Foreign Wars and the Harry S. Truman Good Neighbor Award. Her book in progress centers on the U.S. role at the United Nations. She is presently lecturing throughout the country on America's role in the world.

Henry Kissinger

"There are many occasions in diplomacy when dedication is measured by the ability to pretend indifference when every fiber strains for getting to the point." This was the Henry Kissinger, America's first immigrant Secretary of State, who in the waning years of the Nixon administration became a kind of "substitute President" (his words), a powerbroker who operated like a Metternich reborn in the age of telecommunications and global shuttle diplomacy. This was the Henry Kissinger who was awarded a Nobel Peace Prize even as anti-war protesters were denouncing him as the Butcher of Cambodia. A German-born (27 May 1923) Jewish refugee and Harvard professor, Kissinger presided over U.S. foreign affairs at a time of deep and seemingly unbridgeable differences among Americans. The issue that divided the country, of course, was U.S. military involvement in Southeast Asia, and Henry Kissinger was the chief architect of that policy. "If he were renamed Secretary of State tomorrow," speculates *New York* magazine, "the stock market would probably shoot up a dozen points. This, despite the criticism, despite Cambodia, Iran, the wiretaps, the fawning over Nixon . . . Kissinger seems to levitate above everything, and there are many reasons for this: his brilliance, his personality, the charm he can exude."

Harvard did not welcome Kissinger back after his White House years, and so the controversial "Super K" remained in New York with wife, Nancy, running a lucrative consulting firm out of his townhouse, lecturing at $15,000 per appearance, and writing his memoirs. The first two volumes, *The White House Years* and *Years of Upheaval*, became instant required reading for students of political science and diplomacy.

The other side to Dr. Henry Kissinger is that of the glib socialite. He and Nancy are considered *de rigeur* at any serious Manhattan dinner party, and the former Secretary obliges an average of five hostesses each week. Leaving Washington has meant freedom from official dinner parties, and he has replaced those obligatory soirees with the best Manhattan has to offer. He still finds time for all his work because he has long survived on only four hours of sleep a night. "The light goes out at two and he's up at six," a close friend confides. Currently, he is Chairman of Kissinger Associates, Inc., an international consulting firm. Kissinger is a member of the Boards of Directors of American Express Company, R.H. Macy and Company, a Trustee for the Rockefeller Brothers Fund and a Contributing Analyst for ABC News. The recipient of many awards, he was awarded the Medal of Liberty in 1986.

My childhood is probably the reason I feel more deeply about America than some homegrown intellectuals who focus on its failings," says the refugee who fled Germany with his family just before Kristallnacht. "I am very conscious of what hope America gave me when I was a boy in Germany." Kissinger is the father of two grown sons from his first marriage.

Darci Kistler

"Balanchine told me three things. 'Be in the moment. Be yourself. Don't act.' I've held on to those things off the stage even more than on." The Principal Dancer of the New York City Ballet is sincere about her success. She has danced leading roles in many Balanchine ballets, including *Brahms-Schoenberg Quartet*, *Symphony in C* (Second Movement), *Variations Pour Une Porte Et Un Soupir*, *Vienna Waltzes*, *Walpurgisnacht Ballet*, *Apollo*, *Mozartiana* and *The Nutcracker* (as the Dewdrop and Sugar Plum Fairy), while earning the respect of her audiences and critics. When a foot injury, requiring two operations, halted her rising career in 1983, her comeback in 1985 was well received. Elizabeth Kendall, dance critic of *Vogue* exclaimed in her June 1986 article "Kistler's comeback is as important as her earlier dazzling appearance when Balanchine was alive. It proves she has found somthing inside herself to replace the encouragement of the master."

Darci Kistler was born circa 1964, in Riverside, California; the only girl in a family with five children. Her younger years were filled with sports activities—she enjoyed skiing, waterskiing, swimming, tennis, football and even dirtbiking. An all-american-type girl she also played the clarinet in her school band. Discovering her flexible dance ability, she began studying at age twelve with Irinia Kosmouska in Los Angeles. That same year she enrolled in a summer session at the School of American Ballet, the official school of the New York City Ballet. At fourteen she was given a full scholarship to study dance at the school while pursuing her academic studies at the Professional Children's School. She trained intensely with Balanchine for three invaluable years and became a soloist at sixteen and principal Dancer at seventeen. She participated in two School of American Ballet workshops; the first in 1979 with a principal role in Jean-Pierre Bonnefoux's *Haydn Concerto* and for the second she danced the *pas de deux* from the opera *William Tell*. The following year she performed the principal role in Balanchine's second act *Swan Lake*.

Describing a recent performance of Kistler's, Arlene Croce of *The New Yorker* magazine stated "She was in full bloom . . . I'll not soon forget the sight of her. . . . Kistler herself is 'different' in a very special and potentially eventful way. Whether she will bring about the next large-scale development in ballerina style is a question the company has yet to face."

Calvin Klein

"I think fantasies are for the birds; anything I wanted to do, I did. If there's something I want, nothing stops me!" So states the Seventh Avenue tycoon whose blue jeans alone ("Nothing comes between me and my Calvins," cooed Brooke Shields in one of his many controversial ads) gross over $250 million annually. And indeed this boyish, sandy-haired, dermatologically-perfect man has espoused his mercantile dreams to a youth-crazed consumer society through a variety of risque images: a dozing, golden young man on the beach against the blue sky wearing a scant pair of all-American white Calvin Klein briefs; a pretty model is given a name and a one minute story and poured into a pair of jeans. Her attitude says it all. Klein himself takes to plastering himself full page and bare-torsoed in the glossies. His ads are 1980s icons: the American mind religiously lost in a star-spangled body.

Born 19 November 1942, the Bronx boy spent his youth fashion sketching, sewing and hanging out at Loehmann's, a high-fashion discount store where he'd study the designs of Norman Norell and the like. After attending the Fashion Institute of Technology, he went into business with childhood pal Barry Schwartz in 1968. His first big hit was a trench coat that grossed $1 million its first year on the racks. His 1973 sportswear won him the prestigious Coty award for fashion. In the mid-70s he fathered the unconstructed look. "Fashion for me," he said in 1976, "is not moving in an ethnic direction. It has to be what you consider clean," Bernadine Morris, the fashion critic, says Klein's year-after-year success is because "he makes clothes women like to wear." His designs for men are just as popular.

Divorced in 1974 from his wife Jayne, Klein has one daughter, Marci, who, in 1978, was kidnapped by a former baby-sitter, but ransomed by her father and released unharmed. On 26 September 1986, Klein married his design assistant, Kelly Rector, in Rome, Italy. He and Kelly now live in a stark, palatial apartment overlooking Manhattan's Central Park and maintain a weekend house on Fire Island.

Robert Klein

His parents wanted him to go into medicine but as he explains, "things got in the way, like chemistry and physics." Instead, Robert Klein went on to become a multimedia personality as a comedian and actor. From clubs to Broadway, records to home video, television to movie appearances, Klein has done it all successfully.

Robert Klein was born 8 February 1942 in the Bronx, New York, to Ben and Frieda Klein. The family, including Klein's sister Rhoda, filled the house with singing and laughter but no show business aspirations. The closest Klein got to it was when at the age of fourteen, he appeared with the Teen Tones, a singing group, on the "Ted Mack Amateur Hour." They lost

Kevin Kline

to a one-armed piano player. The Dewitt Clinton High School graduate entered Alfred (New York) University as a pre-med student but graduated in 1962 with a B.A. in political science and history. Klein had joined the school's acting company, whose drama teachers encouraged him to enter the Yale University School of Drama. He spent a year there after graduation. Regarding his Yale experience, Klein said, "Drama coach Connie Welch . . . didn't give me a very good advice, but she did say one thing that rang in my ears. 'Klein,' she said in front of Drama 22, 'You ought to do a one-man show.'" Klein supported himself as a substitute teacher in the Mount Vernon, N.Y., school system while making his foray into stand-up comedy. He performed at Greenwich Village coffeehouses like Cafe Wha? and Bitter End. Initially a hit, Klein began to feel like a "bomb," so he auditioned for the Second City Improvisational Troupe in Chicago, which he joined in March, of 1965. "I learned everything. Discipline, improvisation, and the art of working a comedy routine. It matured me as a performer, and gave me a feeling of control." Klein returned to N.Y. in 1966 with the troupe's revue and was cast in the Broadway musical *The Apple Tree* directed by Mike Nichols. Other Broadway appearances included *New Faces of 1968* and *Morning, Noon and Night* (1968-1969). Carnegie Hall welcomed him in 1973 with "The First Annual Robert Klein Reunion." The show's successors still sell out annually. Klein's Broadway triumph came in 1979 with the musical *They're Playing Our Song*, for which he was nominated for a Tony Award as Best Actor and awarded the L. A. Drama Critics Award. Broadway led to film roles: *The Landlord* (1970), *The Owl and the Pussycat* (1970), *The Pursuit of Happiness* (1971) and *Rivals* (1972). He has also performed in *Hooper, The Bell Jar, Nobody's Perfect* and the animated *The Last Unicorn* (voice over). Television also called, with a 1968 appearance on "The Ed Sullivan Show." He hosted the 1970 CBS series "Comedy Tonight," and made countless appearances on "The Tonight Show Starring Johnny Carson" (as a guest and guest host), "Late Night With David Letterman" and as a regular on NBC's "Bloopers and Practical Jokes." He acted in the new "Twilight Zone" series as well as television movies such as "Summer Switch," "This Wife for Hire," "Poison Ivy" and "Your Place or Mine?" Cable TV has carried five of Klein's one-man shows on HBO and his special "Robert Klein at Yale" (1982) has become a permanent part of the Museum of Broadcasting collection. He also acted in HBO's "Table Settings" and Showtime's "Pajama Tops" and starred in two home videos, "Robert Klein: Child of the 50's, Man of the 80's" (1984) and "Robert Klein on Broadway" (1986). Klein hosts the USA Network show "Robert Klein Time," which debuted in October, 1986. Two of Klein's comedy albums, *Child of the Fifties* (1973) and *Mind Over Matter*, earned him Grammy nominations and from 1979 to 1981 he hosted "The Robert Klein Radio Show," a syndicated comedy/rock show.

Klein resides with his wife, opera singer Brenda Boozer, and their son, Alexander Stewart, in Manhattan. He relaxes in his spare time by traveling throughout the country appearing at colleges, universities, and theaters as well as Atlantic City.

Kevin Kline

"Acting humanizes me. When I saw a movie and was moved or allowed to feel something deeply that transcended the mundane, it was very exciting. Music for me was transcendental, it made me feel more alive. It was a peak experience. And when I was moved by acting, it was the same kind of celebratory experience. Actually, when I first did it I was attracted to it because it was impossible to do. I stank when I first started acting. I was really wretched. Very stiff, repressed, inhibited. Acting was a release for me. I'm much more expressive of emotion now than I used to be. Eventually, I found that simpering emotional wreck that I really am. I feel actors are very fortunate because they can get this stuff out. You get to explore those things in yourself. When I was moved by an acting performance, I'd think, 'I'd like to do that for somebody. I'd like to make people feel alive.' I love sensation. . . . I'm just a cheap sensationalist, is what it comes down to."

Born 24 October 1947 in St. Louis to a Jewish father who owned a record store, sang opera, and played the piano, and a Catholic mother, Kline attended Catholic schools run by Benedictine monks. After discovering acting in college, he moved to New York to attend the drama division of Juilliard and was on hand when John Houseman formed The Acting Company. "It was a cushy introduction to acting profession," he explains. "I didn't have to bang on doors and try to sneak into Equity auditions. We were given our Equity cards and about 47 weeks of employment a year, along with the opportunity to play great roles in the classical repertory as well as modern. It was a great training ground."

After four years touring with the company, this "1980's Errol Flynn" (*Vanity Fair*) returned to New York's theatre scene and, as quick as you can say. "The envelope, please," he won two Tony Awards—one for *On the Twentieth Century*, a second for *Privates of Penzance*.

In 1985, Kline appeared on Broadway in a revival of Shaw's *Arms and the Man* as well as the Off-Broadway production of *Hamlet*. He made a brilliant film debut as a schizophrenic opposite Meryl Streep in *Sophie's Choice* and went on to film fame in the cinema version of *Pirates, The Big Chill, Silverado, Cry Freedom, The January Man, A Fish Called Wanda* (for which he won the Academy Award for Best Supporting Actor) and *I Love You to Death*. Noting his "come-hither charm" and his "cavalier-cad" quality, *Vanity Fair* borrowed a line from *Sophie's Choice* and called him "utterly, fatally glamorous." The dashing actor left the single scene in 1989 when he married actress Phoebe Cates.

Bobby Knight

The only man ever to play for, then go on to coach a NCAA basketball championship team, this iron-willed head of Indiana's Hoosiers is absolutely outspoken (saying he'd like his epitaph to say, "He was honest and he didn't kiss anybody's ass"). He is too good a teacher of the game and too much a winner to be dismissed as a boorish jock, which is why the U.S. chose him to coach its 1984 Olympic team and its 1979 Pan-American Games squad, both of which won gold medals. He remains an anomaly to bewildered sports fans who are confused by how one man can be so villified by the press yet given such glowing praise from his players.

Born in Massillon, Ohio, on 25 October 1940, Robert Montgomery Knight was the only child of a railroad man and an elementary school teacher. He was a basketball, baseball, and football player in high school who went on to become a sixth man on Ohio State University's 1960 national championship basketball team, where he played behind future NBA stars John Havlicek, Jerry Lucas and Larry Siegfried. After coaching at West Point for six years, and reversing that Academy's basketball fortunes (102-50), he went to Indiana University in 1971. Known for their relentless man-to-man defenses and methodical scoring, the Hoosiers of 1976 went 32-0 and won the collegiate crown. In 1979, as coach of the Pan-Am team, Knight endured an acrimonious tournament in Puerto Rico to lead the U.S. to victory; he showed an unattractive side as he got into a fight with and was arrested by a San Juan policemen, was threatened with expulsion from the game for verbally abusing the officials and ended his visit by saying, "The only thing they know how to do is grow bananas." A Puerto Rican offical termed him an "ugly American."

Back in the States, Knight's Hoosiers led by the then fancy-passing Chicago youngster named Isaiah Thomas won its second national title. Knight, who reveres older coaches, is the youngest to win 300 games. His on-court style is punctuated by loud profanities hurled at officials and players during time-outs, and he became infamous after a 1976 incident in which he yanked a player off the court by his jersey because of a mistake (later the boy's mother said she'd have snatched her son off too). He calls journalism "slipshod" and remarks that while everyone learns to write by the time they're in the second grade, most people move into other (and apparently, higher) callings. His stern discipline may have some root in his study of militiary history and tacticians, of whom Ulysses S. Grant, not Patton, is his favorite. "First of all," says the six-feet-five mentor, "you have to understand that before anything, I'm a teacher. I can do [a lot] for a kid in terms of discipline, keeping him going in the right direction." He is vehemently opposed to college recruiting excesses, and has a higher player-graduation rate than most universities. He has proposed a plan whereby colleges would have to graduate ballplayers before issuing new scholarships to replacements (but despairs of it being instituted). At the Los Angeles Olympics he was his volatile old self—accused of taking all of the fun out of the Games for the young men, and racking up technical fouls for berating officials. Playing without the presence of the Soviet team (which they'd probably have beaten) the Americans used Knight's forward-oriented "motion" offense to make routs of most of their games and to defeat Spain in the gold medal game.

Knight has seen his team win the NCAA Championships several times (1976, 1981, 1987) and has been named "Coach of the Year." He is described as having a "street-corner-guy appearance." Knight lives in Bloomington, Indiana, with his wife Nancy and two sons.

Edward I. Koch

Perhaps somewhere there exists a more archetypical New Yorker than Edward I. Koch. Then again, maybe not. "It's me!" he yells at the border guards of the somber Berlin Wall. "It's Mayor Koch! I'm here!" Here, it seems, is everywhere for this Bronx-born, former Greenwich Village lawyer whose confrontational, brassy tactics have made him the city's most popular mayor in years. His election in 1978, and his smashing re-election victories in 1982 and 1986 have capped a career that began with an idealistic corruption-buster campaign against an entrenched, unresponsive Tammany Hall. In his first term of office his familiar "How am I doing?" motto became a daily part of New York life, from blue-collar Staten Island to mid-town Manhattan.

Bouncing back from an ill-conceived attempt to move from mayor to governor ("I must have been nuts to want to leave New York," he now insists), Koch found himself in the surprising position of being both mayor of the Big Apple and author of a bestseller, titled—less surprisingly—*Mayor*. Koch's 357-page *opus de gripe* came filled with abuse, attacks and more plain kvetching than you'd find at a Catskills card game. The Mayor's old supporters at the *Village Voice* found that Koch "went out of his way to criticize and hurt." The street-wise mayor proved himself a sure-fire book personality. "He is the publicity director's dream," sighs his publisher's PR rep. "He understands the value of publicity, shows up on time and delivers."

Born 12 December 1924 in the Bronx, Edward Irving Koch is the second of three children of Polish immigrants. During the Depression the family moved to Newark, N.J. where New York's future mayor worked part-time jobs around his classwork, frequently lending his father a hand with a hat-check concession at a catering hall. He sold shoes while attending City College, then fought overseas during WW II, earning two battle stars for service in Northern France and in the Rhineland. He was discharged with the rank of sergeant in 1946, and returned to New York where he attended New York University Law School. By the end of the decade he had set up a law practice in Greenwich Village, which he maintained along with a City Council seat until elected to Congress in 1968. He lives alone, either in the mayoral digs uptown at Gracie Mansion or at the one-bedroom rent-controlled Village flat he's never relinquished. He customarily shoots down questions about his private life, claiming it's not a public's concern. *Mayor* was the inspiration in 1985 for a smash hit off-Broadway revue by Charles Strouse.

C. Everett Koop

In 1981, when C. Everett Koop, a retired pediatric surgeon, moved to Washington, D.C., from Philadelphia, what he expected was a brief confirmation hearing—instead he had a long and stormy nine-month battle to win the post of 13th Surgeon General of the United States. As if to celebrate, and give a new decorum to his office, he donned the official gold-trimmed uniform of the U.S. Public Health Service and went out to battle, and this he did for eight long years. He has left a legacy of conviction and courage by his controversial stance on many touchy political health issues.

Born in 1917, and growing up in New York, Koop knew at the age of five he wanted to be a doctor. At 15, he would take the subway in to Columbia-Presbyterian Hospital in Manhattan, "borrow" a white medical coat and sit mesmerized before complicated operations in the balcony of the operating rooms. He was, however, an all-around student, excelled in sports (wrestling, football and baseball) and was editor of his school paper. His higher education was most impressive; first Dartmouth, then Cornell University Medical College and finally, University of Pennsylvania. His specialty was pediatric surgery, very unusual at that time (1947). "Children weren't getting a fair shake in surgery, getting giant incisions like their grandfather's and being sewn up like a football when a tiny hole would do—I saw a chance to make a difference." At the time there were perhaps only five such surgeons in the country, so his training was elementary (now there are at least 500 pediatric surgeons). He studied at Boston's Children's Hospital, then returned to Philadelphia to estabish his practice. He was named Surgeon in Chief at Children's Hospital in 1948, and was renowned for his surgical techniques. He separated Siamese twins, and he established this country's first neonatal unit. He was revered by both his patients and the young dedicated doctors who had the privilege to train under him. In 1968, he experienced great personal tragedy. He lost his youngest son, David, in a mountain-climbing accident. He and his wife have 3 surviving children and 7 grandchildren. He has recently celebrated 50 years of marriage.

When he assumed office in 1981, he took several controversial stances. He defied powerful corporations (tobacco companies) and very influential political groups (pro-choice groups). For example, he categorically called smoking an addiction that could kill. Despite a climate of moral "laissez faire," he advocated sex only in marriage, and if need be, condoms to prevent the spread of AIDS. He was dogmatically opposed to abortion and cried out for help to save deformed newborns. In spite of this intimate belief, in March 1988 he confirmed in a report that he couldn't find any evidence showing that abortion is more damaging to a woman's mental hygiene than actually having the baby. This was dramatic proof of Koop's underlying objectivity and honesty. And in a 712-page nutrition report, the first ever by a U.S. Surgeon General, he attacked Americans' excessive intake of saturated fat.

He was opinionated, outspoken, but entirely dedicated to his office—a man of considerable moral courage. And at 72, Koop, who has drawn heavy criticism even from fellow conservatives, has stepped down from his podium; he informed the president of his early retirement as of July 1989. He is a tough act to follow.

Ted Koppel

"I love doing 'Nightline,'" he says. "If someone said, 'Create for yourself a program that is the quintessence of what you would like to do—a program with a budget sufficient to do anything in the world, with a cachet such that

Ted Koppel

anyone would want to appear on it, staffed by the finest people in the business that we can get, with access to state-of-the-art technology'—a program in which I have a significant amount of input—I would have a hard time coming up with anything more than I have." In 1983 Roone Arledge obliquely offered him the much-coveted anchor slot of ABC's "World News Tonight." "He is more than an anchor," wrote *Esquire* in 1984, "he's a ringmaster and a catalyst, a moderator, an interviewer and a cross examiner. In another life he might have been a trial lawyer."

Born in Lancashire, England, in 1940, he spent the first thirteen years of his life in England where his German Jewish parents had fled to escape the Nazis. He arrived with them in New York in 1953 and sailed through the McBurney School in three years (getting his diploma at 16) and went on to Syracuse University and Stanford. He joined ABC in 1963 and has stayed ever since, serving as anchor for the Saturday night news from 1975-77 before coming to "Nightline," where half the mail he gets from viewers is about his hair: people wanting to know if its a wig (no) and who does it (Salon Roi, Inc.). "Some of them send elaborate diagrams of how it should be restyled." His hair was even a topic of conversation in a 1989 episode of CBS's "Murphy Brown," in which the young producer fears that his new haircut resembles the Ted Koppel "look." Despite the fact that Koppel knows, as one journalist put it, that "in the values of television, everything is toothpaste," he takes his job seriously and is no welterweight when it comes to interviewing. When deposed President Ferdinand Marcos of the Phillipines appeared on "Nightline" denying charges that human rights were being violated during riots in Manila (despite Koppel's videotape depicting troops shooting civilians), he admonished, "With all due respect, Mr. President, we just saw the videotape." Koppel has three daughters and one son and lives in Potomac, Md. His thriller, *In the National Interest,* written with Marvin Kalb, was published in 1977. He's also something of a poet. In 1982, when he was awarded the George Polk Award for Best Television News Reporting, he wrote:

"No matter how an anchor tries
His function is to symbolize,
To spice the viewer's evening meal
With equal parts of sex appeal
And evidence that we are free—
By oozing credibility."

Michael Korda

"I suppppose, more than anything else, I love fame," says this aggressive, flamboyant editor-writer who is one of the most productive and successful entrepreneurs in publishing. Editor-in-chief of Simon & Shuster since 1968, he edits some 25 to 35 books a year and has a reputation for turning out commercial successes. Not content with just editing bestsellers ("I was suffering from an overdose of anonymity"), he's published more than 100 magazine articles and his sixth book, *Queenie* (based loosely, he doesn't mind admitting, on the life and loves of his former aunt-in-law, Merle Oberon), in 1985, was a runaway winner. The book was made into a successful ABC-TV miniseries in 1987 starring Mia Sara. Korda says he gets his ambition and provocative behavior from his distinguished family, the movie-making Kordas. (The late British film mogul, Sir Alexander Korda, was his uncle.) "I come from a family that was very strong, very successful, very bizarre and terrifically exciting," says Korda. An Oxford graduate who speaks four languages, he has unabashedly downplayed literary quality and with meticulous zeal goes for what his instincts tell him will sell and make money. "I'm a closet educated person," he observes. "My instinct is to submerge my own notion of what's good. As an editor, I want to publish successful books and interesting ones—and occasionally take a wild flyer."

Born in London, England, 8 October 1933, of Hungarian ancestry, Michael Korda was educated in Berverly Hills, New York, and Switzerland. After serving two years in the Royal Air Force, he went to Oxford, interrupting his last year of university to participate in the 1956 Hungarian revolution. He moved to the U.S. after graduating, worked briefly for CBS, then got a low-level job at Simon & Shuster through family connections, rising swiftly up the hierarchy on his own talents to become editor-and-chief at age 36. His early successes include editing Irving Wallace's first novel, *The Chapman Report*, and Jacqueline Susann's *The Love Mavchine*. Among other authors he's published are Graham Greene, Harold Robbins and Mary Higgins Clark. Korda became a bestselling author himself with a book on *Male Chauvinism*, two "how-tos" on *Power* and *Success* (which were panned by critics as exploitive) and a novel, *Worldly Goods*. A biography about his family, *Charmed Lives*, received critical respect. "Success was always critical to me," says Korda. "What it meant was winning enough praise and external admiration that I could feel myself to be a logical extension of my Uncle Alex, Uncle Zoli (a director) and my father (art director), in that order. . . . Being a Korda is something I regard as special."

Twice married, Korda, is presently married to Margaret, a former model. He considers himself a "deliberate outsider" who "by and large" never joins groups "and when I do it is something that tends to irritate people by being bizarre." He is a member of the National Rifle Association and is also involved in a motorcycle club, the Blue Knights. "Korda is a scholar who decided to exploit his talents almost to the detriment of what he could have done," noted Peter Schwed, former publisher of Simon & Shuster. Says Korda, "I am confident it's right to do what seems interesting and exciting and worth doing and to take the consequences. Do what you really want to do, every single time, no matter how hard work it is. And no matter what other people say, pay no attention to it whatsoever."

Jerzy Kosinski

Take One: The *New York Times* ran a glowing story on the Polish-born author in its 22 February 1982 Sunday *Magazine*. The cover shows the author naked to the waist but otherwise dressed for polo. He's leaning against a stable wall looking hurt and mildly menacing. Anything can happen. The article suggests he has a dark, romantic life, deliberately mysterious, all of which informs his fiction. (He is the author of *The Painted Bird, Being There, The Devil Tree, Cockpit, Blind Date, Passion Play, Pinball*. His *Steps* won the National Book Award. He has also received the American Academy and National Institute of Arts and Letters Award in Literature and served two-terms as the President of American P.E.N., the international association of writers and editors.)

Take two: 22 June 1982. New York's *Village Voice* runs a front-page article entitled "Jerzy Kosinski's Tainted Words." Among other things he is accused of having received an unusual amount of editorial assistance on most of his books from freelance assistants whom he had employed.

Take Three: Kosinski denies the allegations, although he is on record in the mid-1960s telling an interviewer that he taught himself English by memorizing words from an English-Russian dictionary, listening to the radio, going to the same movies repeatedly, and memorizing poems when he arrived in New York in 1957 to take his doctorate in political sociology at Columbia University. When he began to write fiction, he wrote in English. When he had a syntax question he would resort to dialing "0" on the telephone to consult with the operator. "Late at night you have no one to ask. . . . I got incredible advice. I did it hundreds of times."

Take Four: The *Village Voice* stands by its story with the statement: "The point is that Kosinski has always insisted it was all him. Basically the story is that it isn't all him."

Take Five: *The New York Times* publishes a nearly 6,000-word piece in its

Arts and Leisure section of a Sunday edition in November. Its principle theory, according to a *Publisher's Weekly* editorial, that "Kosinski had been repeatedly under attack from his native country almost from the time he left it, and that charges, repeated in the *Voice*, that the C.I.A. had something to do with the publication of his early books, originated there."

And so it goes. The winner? Is Jerzy Kosinski sham or lamb? Whatever the answer, Kosinski is the ultimate survivor. *The Painted Bird* is a mythic rendering of his nightmarish childhood during the Holocaust. Born an only child in Lodz in central Poland on 14 June 1933, he was sent by his parents into the countryside for refuge during the war. Contrary to rumor, he was not orphaned although many of his relatives died and after the war he was lucky enough to be reunited with his mother and father, which gave him the chance to catch up with his schooling. He worked as a ski instructor and photographer while studying for his Master's degrees in history and political science in 1953 and 1955 respectively at the University of Lodz. He made his film acting debut portraying the Russian revolutionary leader Grigori Zinoviev in *Reds*, and he wrote the screenplay adaptation of his novel *Being There* (starring Peter Sellers) in 1978. A regular on New York's party circuit, he was married for several years to Mary Hayward Weir, widow of an American steel magnate. She died in 1968. He married the lively Baroness Kiki von Fraunhofer on 15 February 1987. His latest book, *The Hermit of Sixty-Ninth Street: The Working Papers of Norbett Kosky*, was released in 1988.

Stanley Kramer

"When I was a young man," says this independent film producer and director, "I stopped at a drive-in on Highland Avenue and for some reason decided to go inside and sit at the counter. Two fellows were there, going over a racing form, and I eavesdropped and learned there was a bookie across the street. I went across to it with $26 in my pocket." To make a long story short, he came back with $4,200. "That really made my life," says Kramer, "because I could afford to wait for the kind of job I wanted."

He made his first film shortly after World War II. "I formed my own independent company," he says. "Then, fantasy entered my life, just as it had when I went into the bookie place." Known as a man who gambles with idea in film, he has broken the rules when the spirit moves him. A flashback of the Kramer filmmaking story reveals some spectacular hits, a few failures and near-misses, and volumes of critical comment from lavish praise to vitrioloc abuse. Hitting his first Oscar jackpot with the multi-award-winning *High Noon* in 1952, he has collected 15 Oscars (and 85 nominations) for his films, among them *Judgment at Nuremberg* (1961) and *Guess Who's Coming to Dinner* (1967). Perhaps reflecting himself, Kramer has defined the independent producer as "a self-styled originator and quadruple-threat man who can move in several directions at the same time and wind up the day's work by expertly sweeping up the studio after everyone else has gone home."

Born 29 September 1913 in New York, Stanley Kramer began his film career as a carpenter on a hot movie lot in 1933 and worked his way up to film editing before turning producer. Starting with *Champion* (1949), he began turning out what came to be known as "Kramer's think pieces"—*Home of the Brave* (1949), *The Men* (1950), *Death of a Salesman* (1951) and *High Noon*. Then, after being hailed as the white hope of low-budget independent producers in the David Goliath struggle against the mammoth Hollywood studios, Kramer began making the big-star blockbusters he once disdained: *Not as a Stranger* (1955), *The Pride and the Passion* (1957), *On the Beach* (1959). "When I was young and arrogant", Kramer says, "I felt I could go on my own and do things as I wished . . . and stood in peril of being washed out." Realizing "that if I want to play ball with the entrenched people who control the industry, I have to play in their ball park," he learned "which rules to keep, as well as which ones I can break." In 1962, he was saluted by his peers with the Irving Thalberg Merorial Award of the Academy of Motion Picture Arts and Science. Kramer's film *The Runner Stumbles* (1979) was shot in his new home state, Washington. His latest film, *Polonaise*, was released in 1988.

Stanley Kramer and his former-actress wife, Karen Sharpe, have two daughters. He also has two children by a former marriage.

Judith Krantz

"Verbal popcorn—light, addictive, not exactly nourishing but not really bad for you either," is *Newsweek's* description of her romantic epics. The author of such blockbusters as *Scruples* and *Princess Daisy* takes no offense: "I am aware that I'm asking for it when I have a golden haired princess, or a California blond, blue-eyed young god. But I don't care. I do it 'cause its fun for me. . . . When Daisy drives off, on the last page, in a troika with three white horses—talk about clichéd endings! But it makes everyone so happy. What do they want her to do—trudge in the snow?"

She was born Judith Tarcher on 9 January 1928 in New York City. The offspring of an advertising executive and an attorney, she was an avid reader by age five. After graduation from Wellesley College, she became fashion accessories editor for *Good Housekeeping* magazine, but abandoned her job soon after marrying TV producer Steven Krantz in 1954. While raising two sons, she freelanced nonfiction articles for many leading magazines, and penned the controversial piece, "The Myth of the Multiple Orgasm." Her husband persuaded her to try fiction, insisting that her eye for detail and vivid imagination made her a natural novelist. *Scruples*, her 1978 ugly duckling-to-swan story of an aristocrat's daughter who conquers Beverly Hills as owner of a boutique called "Scruples," loomed atop the *New York Times* bestseller list for almost a year and spawned a three-part CBS miniseries in 1980. She repeated her success with the 1980 *Princess Daisy*, brought to TV in 1983, and with *Mistral's Daughter*, the story of "three passionate heroines whose shared legacy is their love for one dominating, tempestuous man—the great painter Julien Mistral. "The 1984 miniseries was produced by her husband. Although the Krantzes lived an opulent lifestyle in Paris until their return to the States in 1985, she insists that unlike some of the heroines she's created, "my values are with my parents, poor, self-made immigrants." Krantz's novels had many exotic European settings. Her next two books, *I'll Take Manhattan* (1985) and *Till We Meet Again* (1988), continued her string of bestsellers, followed by successful television miniseries.

Mathilde Krim

Referred to as "the one person who knows more than anyone who exists about AIDS" (Aline Frazen in *Manhattan* Magazine), Dr. Mathilde Krim is in the forefront of this country's efforts to try to find a cure for acquired immune deficiency syndrome—AIDS—the killer disease that has reached epidemic proportions both here in the United States (it's estimated that 80,000 Americans have been diagnosed as having AIDS while another 1 to 1.5 million are assumed infected) and abroad.

Born and raised in Switzerland, Mathilde Galland was educated in Geneva where she received her Ph.D. in genetics in 1953. After graduating, she went to work at the Weizmann Institute of Science in Israel where she stayed until 1959. Focusing on human genetics—she was a member of the team that first determined the sex of an unborn child—Mathilde later switched to researching cancer-causing viruses. After her December, 1958, marriage to the well-know picture executive and New York attorney Arthur B. Krim, Mathilde moved to his homeland where she pursued her research at Cornell University Medical School. In the early 1970's the mother of one daughter (Daphna) took an active interest in interferon research and its potential uses in the treatment of viral infections, chronic diseases, and cancer. In 1976 she became the head of the newly formed Interferon Laboratory at Sloan-Kettering Institute for Cancer Research. Krim also organized two international meetings on the research; one in 1975 and the other in 1979. Shortly after the first case of AIDS was identified in 1981, Krim became involved, recognizing the challenging scientific and medical questions involved. As interferon treatment proved to be effective in a form of cancer common in AIDS patients, Krim stepped forward, founding the AIDS Medical Foundation in 1983. Two years later her foundation combined with a similar California-based organization to form the American Foundation for AIDS Research ("AmFAR"), the only national organization devoted entirely to research and education on AIDS. AmFAR has awarded $11 million in start-up grants to more than 170 research teams.

Currently, the indefatigable Krim, who travels around the world to study the different forms of the AIDS epidemic, is at once a Founding Co-Chair (along with Dr. Michael Gottlieb) of AmFAR and a member of both its Board of Directors and Scientific Advisory Committee. She also holds the position of Associate Research Scientist at the College of Physicians and Surgeons, Columbia University, and at St. Luke's-Roosevelt Hospital Center in New York. Along with her husband, Krim has been active in a number of educational and philanthropic organizations dealing with health and civil rights. It's not surprising that this dedicated doctor has been honored for her achievements by the French Government in the 1988 "France Salutes Manhattan's Women of Charity."

Kris Kristofferson

Probably the only Rhodes Scholar ever to use his Oxford educational opportunity to pen American country music, Kristofferson writes lambently literate lyrics that have become more soul-baringly autobiographical than ever. His songs haven't been recorded by more than 450 crooners without good reason, and the man Willie Nelson referred to as the most prolific contemporary songwriter ("If he could sing, he'd be a threat to me.") used his disappointments as material for even more hits. Afterwards, he says, "Everybody was welcoming me back to the record business when I'd never been gone. God knows, I've been on tour every year almost, but I was the world's best-kept secret."

The tough-but-tender screen and recording star who has been able to command $1 million per role also draws down half a million a year for song royalties. Son of an Army general (now retired), Kris Kristofferson spent most of his boyhood in Brownsville, Texas (born 22 June 1936), and became a fan of late country singer Hank Snow. An aspiring songwriter at age eleven, he was the winner of four *Atlantic Monthly* fiction prizes, and as a football player and boxer at Pomona College won a Rhodes scholarship in 1958. While deep in the classics at Oxford, Kristofferson was approached by a British promoter who tried to transform him into a rock idol, but the experience almost turned him away from the music business entirely. "They renamed me Kris Carson and my friends were calling me the Golden Throated Thrush," he says. After collecting his degree he "bailed out, got married, and went into the army," and there picked up the songwriting habit again. When he was assigned to teach English at West Point, he spent all his leaves in Nashville. ("I got so excited I wrote ten songs the first week I was there.") He tended bar part-time and was a janitor in the same studios where Johnny Cash was plying his trade. His 1965 hit, "Vietnam Blues" set him up for a bigger blues smash, "Me and Bobby McGee," which made him a full-time performer-songwriter. He made his debut as an actor in 1972 in *Cisco Pike*, and has been in evidence since in *Pat Garrett and Billy the Kid* (1973), *Bring Me the Head of Alfredo Garcia* (1974), *Alice Doesn't Live Here Anymore* (1974), *The Sailor Who Fell from Grace with the Sea* (1976), the 1976 unkindly-received remake of *A Star Is Born*, *Heaven's Gate* (1981), *Rollover* (1981), *Songwriter* (co-starring Willie Nelson, 1985), *Trouble in Mind* (1986), *Dead or Alive* (1988), *Helena* (1988), *Big Top Pee-Wee* (1988), *Millennium* (with Cheryl Ladd, 1989), *Welcome Home* (1989) and *Ryder* (1989). He also appeared in the CBS miniseries "Blood and Orchids" in 1985. The lithe, square-jawed, twice-divorced balladeer said after his break-up with singer Rita Coolidge (divorced, 1979), "I don't feel any anxiety about my solo condition. I ain't gonna be a hard case, but the next one will have to be carrying notes from the Pope." Nevertheless, in 1983 he married attorney Lisa Meyers. The couple have a son John Robert (born 15 May 1987); Kristofferson has three children (Tracy, Kris, Casey) from his previous marriages. During an interview with the *Gavin Report* he comments on his optimistic point of view. "If I didn't have hope, I wouldn't get out of bed. I feel like a person can make a difference and that it matters to try and make a difference."

Elisabeth Kübler-Ross

Initially recognized for her additions to the body of knowledge and techniques of thanatology, the study of death, through her pioneering work in counseling terminally ill patients, she emerged as a leading advocate of the "death awareness" movement with her book *On Death and Dying* (1969), a best-selling account of a seminar on the process of dying conducted at Chicago's Billings Hospital. Her reputation as a scientist of courage and compassion continued with the later books *Living With Death and Dying*, *Questions and Answers on Death and Dying* (1972), *Death: The Final Stage of Growth* (1975) and *AIDS: The Ultimate Challenge* (1988). Although there is still public approval of her methods of caring for the dying, there has been growing skepticism—particularly from her medical colleagues—since she announced, in 1975, "I know for a fact that there is life after death." Her controversial spiritualistic investigations and the establishment of centers that appear to glorify the "near-death experience" have led to increased speculation about the "Queen of Death" and her four personal spirit guides, or attending "entities," whom she identified in 1980 as "Mario," "Anka," "Salem" and "Willie."

The first born of triplets, Elisabeth Kübler weighed only two pounds at birth on 8 July 1926, in Zurich, Switzerland. "It is hard to say if my precarious introduction to life was the first 'instigator' to going into this field." She studied medicine at the University of Zurich, obtaining her M.D. in 1957 and, after an internship and residencies in the New York City area, accepted a fellowship in psychiatry at the University of Colorado School of Medicine. In 1965 she became assistant professor of psychiatry and assistant director of psychiatric consultation and liaison service at the University of Chicago Medical School, where she began the work which brought her to prominence. She and her colleagues were able to identify five main stages that terminally ill patients pass through in reacting to the knowledge of their own deaths: denial (not me!), anger (why me?), bargaining (why now?), depression (self-grief), and acceptance (a passive state of awareness in which there is a sense of detachment). It is the fifth step, in which death may be viewed as a favored stage of life, that has given rise to such phenomena as "creative suicide" and innumerable spiritualistic speculations, investigations and possible scams, an alarming number of which seem to have had more than tacit support from Kübler-Ross.

On 7 February, 1958, she married Dr. Emanuel Robert Ross, a Swiss neuropathologist with a practice in Illinois. They divorced after 11 years and two children. She is currently based at Shanti Nilaya ("Home of Peace" in Sanskrit), near Escondido, California, which she hopes "will be the first of a worldwide network of similar 'retreats' to expound her theories of survival of the spirit after death in the form of a living 'entity.'" The recipient of some 20 honorary degrees, she travels over 250,000 miles a year and has taught, in her estimation, over 125,000 death-and-dying courses in colleges, seminaries, medical schools, hospitals and social-services institutions.

Stanley Kubrick

"The most powerful level on which a film works on the audience is on the subconscious," he says. "On this level we are all equally perceptive and equally blind. Watching a film is really like taking part in a controlled dream." Director Stanley Kubrick controlled the dreamy imagery for us in his futuristic epic, *2001 A Space Odyssey* (1968), in the disturbing 1971 opus, *A Clockwork Orange,* and in *Sparatacus* (1960), *Dr. Stangelove* (1964), *Barry Lyndon* (1975) and *The Shining* (1979).

Born 26 July 1928 in New York, he started out as a photojournalist (on *Look,* among other publications), did documentary films, and crested as a much-heralded New Wave director with his stark 1958 anti-war film, *The Paths of Glory.* Explaining that he operates 'three-quarters on intuition," he considers the most important part of filmmaking what he calls "the C.R.P.—crucial rehearsing period." ("Shooting is the part of filmmaking I enjoy the least. I don't particularly enjoy working with a lot of people. I'm just not an extrovert.") But he is a perfectionist who has been known to call for more than 100 retakes, and who not only oversees every aspect of filming and post-production, but even promotion.

Twice married and divorced, he's now wed to painter Suzanne Christiane Harlan (three daughters), with whom he lives outside London. He owns a wardrobe consisting almost exclusively of blue blazers, gray trousers, black shoes and socks (thereby eliminating tough decisions about what to wear). The admitted safety nut won't ride in a car going faster then 30 mph unless he's behind the wheel, nor will he fly in planes. And he thinks moviegoers ought to see films more than once to absorb them. "The thing I really hate," Kubrick says, "is to explain why the film works, what I had in mind, and so forth." In 1988, Kubrick received the Luchino Visconti Award in Italy.

Irv Kupcinet

Kup's Column in the *Chicago Sun-Times* runneth over with more than gossip about the Windy City; it has a heart and civic conscience too. (For four decades Kup's been the old master pilot behind the Purple Heart Cruise, an annual lake outing for vets.) Kup, of course, is Chicago's Irv Kupcinet, who hosted the Emmy-winning television program "Kup's Show" from 1959-1986. He has become as much a Chicago institution as the Loop itself; in 1986 the Wabash Avenue Bridge in Chicago was renamed the Irv Kupcinet Bridge. When "Rupe the Scoop" Murdoch bought the *Sun-Times,* Kup remained faithful and didn't leave. (The two other journalists of stature in Chicago, Studs Terkel and Mike Royko, disparaged the purchase and defected. "No self-respecting fish would want to be wrapped in a newspaper published by Rupert Murdoch," said Royko.)

One of Kup's favorite off-hour sports is de-mything his hometown. In his book, *Kup's Chicago,* he says it's not the nation's chief "Hog Butcher" (Kansas City and Omaha are ahead), and neither is it the Windy City ("18 other cities are windier"). Some say Kup's real forte is writing about celebs. (Saul Bellow put Kup in *Humboldt's Gift* as the gossip columnist Mike Schneiderman, whose cuff links glint among the stars.) Let Kup take on the glitterati—as long as he comes home to Chicago—since in his own words, "I've come to love this American giant, viewing it as the most misunderstood, most underrated city in the world."

Born in Chicago, 31 July 1912, the son of a bakery driver, Kup visited journalism class on his first day in high school and the die was cast. A football star at Northwestern and North Dakota, he was given a pro contract, but a shoulder injury stopped his career. Married to Essee Solomon, he has one son who is a television director; his daughter Karyn, was the victim of a brutal Hollywood murder in 1963. Kupcinet's tell-all *Kup: An Autobiography* (written with Paul Neimark) was published in 1988.

Charles Kuralt

"Drive across the country and you find that hardly anybody makes anything anymore," mused Kuralt, who logged more than a million miles as CBS's roving lifestyles reporter. His "On the Road" reports—first aired as a CBS news segment and later as a half-hour feature program—championed the nobility of average Americans, and earned the former foreign correspondent a loyal viewing audience. He developed a CBS radio series, "Dateline, America," beginning in 1972, and anchored his own TV specials, documentaries, and probing examinations of social trends. The positive audience response led to his job of anchoring the ninety-minute weekly program, "Sunday Morning." For his fine efforts, Kuralt has won many Emmy Awards (1969, 1978, 1981, 1986, 1987) and was named Broadcaster of the Year (1985) by the International Radio and Television Society. Also an accomplished author, his recent books include *Southerners, North Carolina Is My Home* and *On the Road.*

Charles Bishop Kuralt was born 10 September 1934 in Wilmington, N.C. As a high school student, Kuralt won the American Legion essay contest and a trip to Washington to meet President Truman. After graduation from the University of North Carolina, where he edited the campus newspaper, he was hired by CBS news in 1957. Replaced by Walter Cronkite as host of a weekly public affairs program in 1959, Kuralt remained on general assignment until 1967, when he persuaded the network to give his "On the Road" idea a three-month trial. Setting off on his backroads journey in a second-hand camper, he encountered such characters as an Iowa farmer who constructed a fifty-eight-foot yacht, a black Samaritan who provides free bicycles to kids who can't afford them, and a 78-year-old man who spent 20 years building a road single-handed. "Reporters flying from one city to another on assignment never have time to learn anything about those little clusters of lights in between." The affable, countrified Kuralt served as a sort of visiting uncle for more than a decade, with his five-minute news segments.

Kuralt, a private person who contends that "newsmen ought not to go about aggrandizing themselves," married Suzanna Folsom in 1962. He has two daughters from an earlier marriage.

Swoosie Kurtz

Named after "the Swoose", a B17 bomber flown by her father Colonel Frank Kurtz (the most decorated pilot of World War II), she had her first taste of Broadway stardom playing a pill-popping heiress in *The Fifth of July* (1981), and soon thereafter walked off with a Tony, a Drama Desk Award and an Outer Critics Circle Award. "I think what made me a good actress is the fact that as an Army officer's daughter, I was always on the move. I attended seventeen different grammar schools and was constantly assaulted with traumas. I had to keep adjusting. Thank God for my wonderful parents. If it hadn't been for them, I might be deeply disturbed instead of only mildly disturbed."

Born in 1944 Swoosie (rhymes with Lucy, not woozy) Kurtz describes herself as a "late bloomer." After aspiring to be a ballerina and a writer, she instead chose acting and, following high school, attended the London Academy of Music and Dramatic Art. Arriving back in the U.S., she experienced the usual slings and arrows of an unknown actress trying to become known but when things finally started to happen, she found her two years in London hadn't been wasted: "I learned to get right on with it in rehearsal, to simply 'have a bash'. So that's what I do, with total commitment. And then I work backward to figure out why things happen." The '77-'78 theater season was a crucial one for Kurtz. She appeared in *Tartuffe* (Tony nomination) and *Uncommon Women and Others* (Obie and Drama Desk Award nominations). Nearly stealing the show for her performance in the latter production, Swoosie says that it was *Uncommon Women* that really "did it" for her. Since then she has cruised at high altitude—a 1980 role with the Yale Repertory Company as Honey in *Who's Afraid of Virgina Woolf?* was "one of the greatest experiences in my life." After trying her television wings on the shortlived "Mary Tyler Moore Variety Show," she spent two seasons on the tube (opposite Tony Randall) on NBC's "Love Sidney" and was twice nominated for an Emmy Award. Her film credits include *Slap Shot*, *The World According to Garp*, *Against All Odds*, *Wildcats*, *Vice Versa*, *Bright Lights, Big City*, *Dangerous Liasons*, and *Letters*.

and the Live AID Benefit Concert. Patti's versatility shows in her dramatic performance in the film, *Unnatural Causes* with John Ritter and as the only female in the film *A Soldier's Story*. Patti's album *Winner* turned platinum and became the third highest album on the pop charts (behind Whitney Houston and Janet Jackson). Patti performed her third one-woman show, within a year and a half, on Broadway. Patti's tours, including the summer 1988 tour to Japan, have been complete sell-outs, attesting to her magnetic voice and rapport with her audiences.

When not performing, Patti finds a few hours to manage her boutique, "LaBelle Amie," in Philadelphia. Married since 1969, Patti and husband Armstead Edwards reside in her native Philadelphia and are the parents of three sons: Dodd and Stanley, adopted after their mother, a neighbor, died, and Zuri, born in 1973. Patti, who doesn't smoke, take drugs, drive or swim, supports a number of charities to aid children.

Patti LaBelle

She has been called the "Judy Garland of pop-soul" (New York *Times*), the "high priestess of good vibrations" (New York *Times*) and "Pop's Queen of Soul"(*People*). Now, after more than 25 years of singing, Patti LaBelle has reached the height of popularity. Singer on the 1986 platinum album *Winner in You*, Patti has "crooned, screamed, muttered, cooed and roared her songs" (*Philadelphia Inquirer*) to audiences in sold-out houses in and out of the United States. The flamboyant performer, known for her indulgences in theatrical excess, was the first to sport the sexy "spacequeen' costumes which were later adopted by such male groups as Kiss. Patti's unofficial trademark—her out-of-this world hairstyle—changes with each outfit, sometimes looking as if she stuck her finger in an electric socket and her hair half froze in that position. Husband-manager Armstead Edwards says, "On stage I see a completely uninhibited person. Thank goodness I don't have to live with Patti LaBelle the performer."

Born Patricia Holt on 4 October 1944 in Philadelphia, Patti at seven told her father (a railroad worker) that she was going to be a star. At age thirteen Patti began her career by singing with the church choir and glee clubs. The 1960's saw the formation of Patti LaBelle and the BlueBells with its first hit "Sold my Heart to the Junkman" in 1962. The three-women group, dressed identically and demurely, sang harmonies. In 1966, while touring England, the group was accompanied by a piano player, Reginald Dwight, who later went on to become famous in his own right under the name of Elton John. The 1970's brought a change of name and image: LaBelle became the first all-woman, all-black rock ensemble. Wearing glitter and space suits, the group sang an amalgamation of rock, soul and disco such as the 1974 hit song "Lady Marmalade." LaBelle opened for The Who on its first tour and became the first rock group to perform at the Metropolitan Opera House.

1977 saw the last transformation as Patti went solo and captured the middle-of-the-road pop fans with her rousing live shows that seemed a cross between a Las Vegas show and a revival meeting. "What I do comes from the soul," Patti says. "I let all my emotions out." Patti likens her spiritual version of 'Over the Rainbow," which has been part of her repertoire for over twenty years, to her long quest for recognition. She has four Grammy nominations, two Emmy nominations and an assortment of awards ranging fron B'nai B'rith Creative Achievement Award, NAACP Image Award for musical excellence, Congressional Black Caucus Medallion, the 1986 NAACP Entertainer of the Year Award, to the 1986 Special Citation from President Reagan. Her credits include her own CBS-TV special with Bill Cosby and Cyndi Lauper (who remarked, "Singing with Patti is like being in heaven."), an HBO special "Sisters in the Name of Love," the 1986 closing ceremonies for the Statue of Liberty Celebration, and her showstopping performances in "Motown Returns to the Apollo"

Cheryl Ladd

In 1977 Cheryl Ladd became a household name. Joining the cast of the hit TV series "Charlie's Angels" as Kris Munroe, the petite blonde actress succeeded in pulling in viewers after Farrah Fawcett split from the show. Naturally, Ladd had a respectable resume before her huge national exposure ("Police Woman," "Happy Days." "Switch," "Policy Story"), but it was her role as an "Angel" that set her career in flight. Today, Ladd is still riding in the sky with her latest motion picture release, *Millenium* (in which she costars with Kris Kristofferson). Taking on the role of Louise Baltimore, a mysterious airline employee with a special knowledge of midair collisions, this "contemporary time-travel-thriller" was released in 1989.

Cheryl Stoppelmoor was born in Huron, South Dakota, on 2 July 1951. She made her dance-recital debut at age seven and sang and danced throughout elementary and high school. In her teens, she joined a local band as a way to get to Hollywood. Landing in Los Angeles, she set out on her own after the band's breakup (two members were injured in an automobile accident) and won the audition to become the voice of Melody in Hanna-Barbera's animated TV series "Josie and the Pussy Cats." Guest appearances on television series followed, plus commercials, including a major campaign for Max Factor. Then came "Charlie's Angels". . .

Resisting the tititlating typecast, Ladd thrived on presenting her musical talents on various television specials ("Ben Vereen . . . His Roots," "General Electric's All-Star Anniversary," "John Denver and the Ladies"), eventually headlining her own: "Cheryl Ladd" (1979), "Cheryl Ladd—Souvenirs" (1980), "Cheryl Ladd, Scene from a Special" (1982) Simultaneously, Ladd cut two record albums, *Cheryl Ladd* (1978) and *Dance Forever* (1979), which produced four gold singles. Dramatic telefilms became her next step as she dirtied up to work in the coal mines ("Kentucky Woman," 1983), then slicked up one month later to play the late Grace Kelly in ABC-TV's biopic "Grace Kelly." Later telefilms include "When She Was Bad . . ." (1979), "Romance on the Orient Express" (with Sir Laurence Olivier in 1985), "Deadly Care" (1986), and the upcoming "Fulfillment" (1990). Her miniseries include: "A Death in California" (1985), "Crossings" (1986) and "Bluegrass" (1988). She made her motion picture debut in *Now and Forever*, and in that same year starred in *Purple Hearts* with Ken Wahl.

After a brief first marriage, Cheryl married David Ladd in May 1973 (one daughter, Jordan Elizabeth, born 14 January 1975). The couple divorced in July 1980, and Cheryl married Brian Russell in 1981 (one stepdaughter, Lindsay). On a continual push to succeed, she says, "I want to stretch myself and do a range of projects that run the gamut—musical comedy, farce, serious dramatic roles, everything. . . . And I won't quit until I do."

Arthur Laffer

"As a professor, I shiver at the thought of making public policy. You should never let a professor run your country. But you should listen to what he has to say"; this, from the California economics prof and "prophet of supply-side economics" whose name has come into the language as the originator of "the Laffer Curve," a bell-shaped model illustrating the relative revenue results of different sizes of tax rates. He earned his first fame (or as John Brooks put it in *The New Yorker*, "in some cases, infamy") in the 1970s when "attention was forcibly called to his specialty, tax cuts, and their advantages, by California's passage of Proposition Thirteen." Although he was not officially a member of the Reagan team (his only formal connection was membership on the President's Economic Policy Advisory Board), he's credited with being one of the "high priests of the faith" who helped bring about such aspects of "Reaganomics" as the much-publicized tax cuts. He was a member of the Policy Committee and the Board of Directors of the American Council for Capital Formation in Washington, D.C., and he is presently a contributing editor of the *Conservative Digest*. He is also associated with the editorial page of the *Wall Street Journal*.

Born in Youngstown, Ohio, in 1940, Arthur Laffer progressed, first to Cleveland, and then to the more affluent suburbs of Shaker Heights and Lyndhurst as his businessman father moved up the corporate ladder. He did poorly at first as a Yale undergraduate ("I was involved in all kinds of goof-off activities") but after a year studying in Munich, he came back and graduated in 1963 with high honors in economics. He later picked up an M.B.A. and Ph.D. degree, each from Stanford, taught there and at the University of Chicago and, in 1970, went to Washington to be chief economist of the Office of Management and Budget in the Nixon Administration. There he soon caused something of a brouhaha when a forecast credited to him about the 1971 gross national product seemed impossibly high. As things turned out, the forecast was reasonably correct, but by the time Laffer could have had his last laugh, most of his critics had forgotten the whole affair. The economist moved out to the University of Southern California's Los Angeles campus in 1976 as a full professor and still teaches there, while operating a consulting service and doing considerable lecturing on the side. Laffer and his wife, Patricia, separated in 1979 and he is raising his four children, with the help of a governess, in a Los Angeles suburb. John Brooks, interviewing him in 1982, found him "so undogmatic and modest in his claims as to be somewhat disconcerting." "My role," the supply-side guru told Brooks, "is to be balanced and eclectic."

Karl Lagerfeld

"In the old days of fashion, ready-to-wear only copied couture. Now fashion is created by young stylists and is in the air where it is picked up again by *haute couture*—whose only function is as a catalyst. *Haute couture* picked up all the themes that were in the streets: shorts, pop, high heels," says European fashion dynamo Karl Lagerfeld whose method of contriving his life as artfully as his fashions caused *Newsweek* to dub him "the bad boy of high fashion." "I would like to be a one-man multinational fashion phenomenon," he has said and so he has become, dating back to the 1962 ready-to-wear revolution pioneered in Paris by former Balenciaga model Emmanuelle Khành. "It's life that has changed," Lagerfeld says, explaining the movement that brought him to prominence. "Before, one used to dress to go out in the evening. Now, one needs clothes for a variety of occasions—sports, beach, travel. The couturiers have one big defect. They always do the same thing. I do what I feel like doing. . . . But I don't do anything because of others."

A decade or so ago he pranced around Paris dressed as a kind of 18th century seigneur pumped up in gold brocades and dancing slippers, a throw-back to his youth when he took delight in illustrating the historical books he read. ("If what I drew happened in 1753 I can assure you that people were not dressed like that in 1763 or 1749," he says, pointing out his obsession with authenticity.) He now describes himself as "a working class person," then adds, "Working with class." Born 10 September 1938 Lagerfeld is the German-born son of a Swedish dairy tycoon and he was raised on a 19th-century estate near Hamburg that was undisturbed during the era of Hitler and World War II, allowing the little boy—as he loves to relate—to demand a valet as a present on his fourth birthday. (No valet was given.) At 14 he went away to school in Paris and two years later won the prestigious prize for best coat design from the International Wool Fashion office. (During the same competition a youngster from Algeria named Yves Saint Laurent won the top prize for dresses.)

Pierre Balmain was so impressed by the teenager, he made him his assistant. Lagerfeld, besides designing street and evening clothes, also had the chance to design for film via Balmain, and some of the stars he wardrobed include Sophia Loren, Rita Hayworth and Gina Lollabrigida. After three years he moved to Patou, but bored with high *couture*, dropped out and "spent two years mostly on beaches—I guess I studied life." Then he returned to Paris and the pret-a-porter scene. In 1964 he signed on with Chloe (and signed off in 1985), in 1966 with Fendi for furs and in 1983 became the head couturier for the house of Chanel, which has since undergone an inspired rejuvenation. ("I'm like a computer," he said in 1984, "who for the moment is plugged in at the House of Chanel.") He also has had his own label since 1984. "He designs much in the way he talks," describes the fashion gazette *W*, ". . . rapidly, mercurially and with generous lacings of sharp wit." He is credited with revolutionizing the way clothing is constructed by simplifying it. He introduced scarf dressing, perfected the art of layering, and encouraged women to create their own look and not maintain strict fealty to one couture house. A loner at heart, he still manages many nights "out" all around the world sporting his Figaro-style ponytail. "I may live in an ivory tower," he says, "but I have good glasses to look out. I see the world . . . from every century. I read. I read. I read." In 1986 he released his detailed book *Lagerfeld's Sketchbook*.

Cleo Laine

The versatile Cleo Laine prefers to be known simply as a "singer of songs" rather than in the variety of roles to which her versatility entitles her. She is the only singer ever to be nominated in the Female Popular, Classical and Jazz categories of America's prestigious Grammy Awards. She has achieved extraordinary success in the fields of opera, drama and musical comedy, as well as appearing as soloist in concerts with major orchestras throughout the world.

Born Clemintine Dinah Campbell 28 October 1927 in Southall, Middlesex, England, today's Cleo Laine began performing at the age of three and became a bandsinger with the Dankworth Seven (later the John Dankworth Big Band) touring dance halls throughout England. Shortly after marrying Dankworth in 1958, Laine left the band to begin a career in the theatre, her first role being the lead in *Flesh To a Tiger*, a play directed by Tony Richardson at the Royal Court Theatre. For the next decade she divided her time between singing and theatre. She appeared in *A Midsummer Night's Dream*, *Valmouth*, *Women of Troy* and in the title role of *Hedda Gabler*. She was also performing in lieder recitals with the Scottish National Orchestra and London Philharmonic and appearing in cabaret (where Dudley Moore was often her pianist). After her enormous success as Julie in the 1971 revival of *Show Boat* (the longest running production of the musical in its history), she and Dankworth rejoined forces for a tour of Australia. They first appeared in New York at Alice Tully Hall in 1972, followed by many sell-out concerts at Carnegie Hall. The special "10th Anniversary Concert" in 1983 was recorded, and the album, *Cleo at Carnegie* was nominated for a Grammy award. Since then the team has toured extensively throughout North America, New Zealand, Australia, Japan, Hong Kong as well as Europe and Britain, and Laine has appeared singly here and abroad in musical stage productions. In 1985 she made her first New York stage appearance in the musical adaption of Charles Dickens' *The Mystery of Edwin Drood* at Central Park's Delacorte Theatre, and moved with the show to Broadway that fall.

Her single recording sales have earned her gold and platinum awards. She has also recorded an album with Dudley Moore entitled *Smilin' Through*. She's made numerous appearances on British television specials, was a featured performer on "That Was The Week That Was", and a guest on every major English variety program. She has appeared frequently in the U.S., including "The Muppet Show," with the Boston Pops in "An Evening at the Pops with Cleo Laine," "Cleo Laine: Live at Wolftrap," and as a guest on all the talk shows. She has received an O.B.E. from Queen Elizabeth II and was named Variety Club's 1977 Show Business Personality of the Year (jointly with John). The Dankworths have a 17-acre estate in England they call home where every summer a musical festival takes place.

Burt Lancaster

One-time acrobat, veteran of the tank-town carnival circuit, and a former floor-walker in Marshall Field's ladies lingerie department, Burt Lancaster vaulted to filmdom's center ring only after—so the Hollywood legend goes—he was discovered in an elevator by Harold Hecht. "Movies," Lancaster is supposed to have said to Hecht with whom he later formed a successful production company (1957), "I'm not interested." Clearly he changed his mind, exploding onto the screen in 1946 in *The Killers* and later appearing in such films as *Brute Force, All My Sons, Come Back Little Sheeba, From Here to Eternity, Sweet Smell of Success, Separate Tables, Elmer Gantry* (an Oscar in 1960), *Bird Man of Alcatraz* (Best Actor, Venice Film Festival), *The Train, The Swimmer, Airport, The Leopard, Atlantic City, The Goldsmith Shop, The Suspect, The Betrothed, Rocket Gilbraltar,* and *Shoeless Joe*. As New York Times' critic Vincent Canby has pointed out, Lancaster began evidencing a pattern in the late 1950s. "For each mass-market entertainment film he made, there was always one comparatively risky, 'artistic' venture." At about the same time, columnist Roberta Ashley suggested Lancaster was acting with his hair, meaning when his hair looked "leading-mannish" in stills one could bet the movie would be on the order of *I Walk Alone* or *Ten Tall Men* as opposed to his more "serious" films (*Sheeba, Judgment at Nuremburg, The Leopard*) which portrayed him wearing a bowl-shaped cut, plastering his hair down, or parting it in the middle. On TV he acted as the host-narrator of the highly praised series on the life and music of Verdi.

Born Burton Stephen Lancaster 2 November 1913, he was the two fisted baby of a large Irish family in Manhattan's East Harlem. "If you want to know love," his mother is said to have counseled, "stay in the house with me. But if you want to know life, go out in the streets." Little Burt opted for the streets, because an accomplished scrapper, and won a scholarship to New York University, where he stayed just two years before hitting the tanbark trail in tandem with a partner improbably named Nick Cravat. "I'd always wanted to be an acrobat," he explains (and he played one in *Trapeze*). At some point amid the somersaulting, Lancaster began to itch to do some acting and so left Cravat and went on his first audition. (He "wasn't nervous. . . . I said to myself, 'What can happen to me? I can miss a line, but I can't get hurt.'" Except by the critics, of course.)

Married first to a woman trapeze artist (it "did not work out"), his second wife was Norma Anderson, whom he met overseas during World War II and from whom he divorced more than two decades and five children later. He is known for his love of animals, for his short temper (he once walked off a Mike Wallace interview. When the "Big Temper" blows, one columnist wrote, he chews out like "an angry dockworker") and for his consistent refusal to adhere to filmtown standards. "The streak of nonconformity appeared early," a friend says. As a kid, "he was supposed to be an angel in the Christmas pageant . . . the audience roared. I looked up and there was Burt peeling the chewing gum off the sole of his shoe."

Ann Landers

"Before her divorce in 1981," according to veteran celebrity watcher Frances Sacerdote, "she was for marriage, motherhood and a hot lunch for orphans." Now this vastly read advice columnist has become the hip voice of wit and practicality in a woolly world where what was once considered profane is not humdrum, and even the humdrum isn't what it used to be.

"I know you didn't ask for any advice," she wisecracks to "No Hang-ups" in Stanford, "but I just happen to have some lying around." When she's not waging her one-woman war against an all-too-spiritually-bereft and nattering nation, she's offering someone advice from an expert such as the Secretary of the Treasury, or providing something philosophical from Kierkegaard addressed, "Confidential to Losing Battle with Grief:'Despair is never ultimately over the external object, but always over ourselves. A girl loses her sweetheart and she despairs. It is not over the lost sweetheart that she mourns, but for what life can be without him. . . . If you can understand and accept this, you will have made the first step of a long and difficult journey.'"

The A-to-Z advisor was born Esther "Eppie" Pauline Friedman 4 July 1918 in Sioux City, Iowa (as was her rivalrous, 17-minutes younger twin, Pauline "Popo" Friedman, aka Dear Abby). "People often came to my parents for advice," she recalls. "Mother always had somebody saying to her, 'Becky, I don't know what to do.' 'Be a *mensch*,' she'd say. 'Be a real person.' Integrity was ground into us." She dropped out of college in her senior year to marry Jules Lederer, an in debt salesman who later went on to found Budget Rent-a-Car (one daughter, Margo—mother of three and wife of actor Ken Howard). The Lederers moved to Chicago in 1954 where Eppie became intrigued by a newspaper column called "Ann Landers." She phoned an executive friend at the newspaper to see about becoming Landers' assistant and was told: "Fascinating you should call. She died last week." She auditioned against 28 professionals and got the job. Her seven-day-a-week column is syndicated in over 1,000 newspapers from her home base in the Chicago *Sun-Times* building. She employs eight secretaries to sort her mail—"not *screening* it though, I see most everything"—which means upwards of 300,000 letters.

She was vehemently anti-divorce until one night in 1975 when her husband, during dinner, announced he was in love with another woman—a 28-year-old English nurse. In her 1 July 1975 column she broke the news to her readers: "The lady with all the answers does not know the answer to this one," she wrote and closed by leaving four inches of blank space "as a memorial to one of the world's best marriages that didn't make it to the finish line." The romantic columnist, famous among her friends for her all-consuming love of ballroom dancing, prevailed like roses in paradise. "Hate, jealousy, envy, they eat you up," she told one interviewer. "They're exhausting and corrosive. They make you look old."

Michael Landon

"If Michael Landon bombs, I don't want anybody else to have to take the blame but Michael Landon." Few stars have managed to influence the total production of a television series with the authority he wielded over "Little House on the Prairie." As executive producer and lead, as well as frequent director and writer, he imbued the wholesome program with his ideologies about faith and family. Soon after the show's demise, he returned to the tube in 1984 with a new series, "Highway to Heaven." The show ran through 1989, with the possibility of resurrecting the cast for yearly telefilms.

He was born Eugene Maurice Orowitz 1 October 1936; his mother was the former Broadway comedienne Peggy O'Neill. Raised in Collingswood, N.J., he was one of two Jewish children at his school and painfully recalls suffering anti-Semitic taunting from his classmates. At home, his parents waged a silent cold war. "My parents never spoke much to each other and didn't even argue. We never hugged or showed any emotion. Basically, I was a loner.... I'm a driven man because from the time I was a kid, I wanted to show myself and others I was somebody." He found solace in athletics, earning honors in the javelin throw and winning a sports scholarship to the University of Southern California.

Picking his stage name out of the Los Angeles phone book, he pursued acting roles while working odd jobs, and was cast as little Joe Cartwright, the upstart son of a ranching patriarch on "Bonanza." During a popular 14-year run, it held the number one ratings position for seven consecutive seasons and was aired in 87 countries. While growing up before the cameras, he worked behind the scenes as a scriptwriter, and occasional director. However, his growing expertise made him critical of the show's scripts, leading to friction on the set. With "Bonanza" finished in 1973, he looked for an opportunity that would allow him to make a greater contribution and decided on NBC's answer to "The Waltons," "Little House on the Prairie," an adaption of Laura Ingalls Wilder's children's classic about an American frontier family. Again, Landon battled his associates over the direction of the storyline, favoring greater deviation from the original book series. He prevailed and provided the network with almost a decade of well-rated, noncontroversial programming. "People still say I'm arrogant. They just don't say I'm insecure anymore."

After an early marriage ended in divorce. Landon married model Lynn Noe in 1963, and they have five children. Their divorce, in 1982, which received much attention in the gossip press, was quickly followed by Landon's marriage to a young make-up artist, Cindy Clerico. They have a daughter and a son.

Kenneth Jay Lane

"If I wore 'fake' jewelry," quipped one New York-based socialite, "I'd wear his of course." Well, when she had her emeralds lifted after dinner one night, the next day Lane, no stranger to society's children, received a phone call. Sooner or later everyone wears Kenneth Jay Lane's frankly fake gewgaws, and his devotees find both paste and peripatetic pastemaker as dandy as candy.

Born in Detroit, 22 April 1932, Lane came to jewelry after a ten-year stint designing shoes for Delman and Dior. The baubles-bangles-and-beads potentate's new career emerged at the same time as the social phenomenon known as the Beautiful People. He caught on immediately. ("I really didn't know what the weather was like for two whole years. I worked 18 hours a day, seven days a week.") By designing handbags, scarves, sunglasses, gloves, sleepwear, hosiery, and even hairpieces, Lane has become a wealthy man. For a while in the 1970s the taste for paste waned, but it returned with a vengeance in the early 1980s and, of course, Lane went right to the top with boutiques in Paris, London and New York's Trump Tower for example; he opened a boutique on ritzy Rodeo Drive in 1986. He married Nicola Waymouth in London (1975), but the couple were later divorced.

Jessica Lange

The daughter of a traveling salesman, she moved 18 times as a youngster. "I just know that how I survived all those family years was my ability to withdraw and live in a dream world," she says. "It's not that it was horrendous—it was my way of removing myself." Although this onetime dreamer began her film career inauspiciously in 1976 via the Fay Wray part in a second-best remake of *King Kong*, her contrasting roles in two films released at Christmastime, 1982— *Frances* and *Tootsie* — clinched her reputation. Her performance in the latter as a romantically victimized soap opera actress earned Lange several supporting actress awards: from the New York Film Critics, National Society of Film Critics and, ultimately, the Oscar.

Born in rural Minnesota on 20 April 1949. Lange was an 'A' student in high school and won an art scholarship to the University of Minnesota. She soon dropped out, however, and, while still a teenager, married Spanish photographer Paco Grande, with whom she traveled the U.S. extensively, living in an old truck. They later divorced. After spending about two years in Paris studying mime with Marcel Marceau's teacher and dancing at the Opera Comique, Lange moved to New York, where she studied acting and worked as a waitress and model. Following her *King Kong* debut, her career languished for three years—during which she resumed acting lessons—until her friend Bob Fosse offered her a small part in his autobiographical film, *All That Jazz*. The following year, 1980, marked Lange's first professional stage appearance in summer stock in North Carolina. She was praised for her sexually-charged performance in another disappointing film remake, *The Postman Always Rings Twice* .

Making *Frances* "devastated" her. Lange told *Newsweek*. "I was really hell to be around. I took on the characteristic of Frances [Farmer, the talented but troubled actress] that was elemental in her demise—battling every little thing that came along." Kim Stanley, who played her mother in *Frances*, advised Lange: "Make a comedy as fast as you can." Hence *Tootsie*.

Keeping her single status, Lange has one daughter Alexandra by ballet superstar Mikhail Baryshnikov, whom she never married and two children Hannah and Samuel by present live-in boyfriend, playwright Sam Shepard. Lange leads a nomadic existence: apartments in New York and Los Angeles, a lakefront cabin (on 120 acres she owns) near her parents' home in Minnesota, another retreat near Taos, N.M., to which this self-described "loner" might "just retire and paint." As a young girl, Lange couldn't wait to escape from northern Minnesota; now when she's "in trouble," that's where she retreats, to "get my head clear.... All those midwestern traits—honesty, simplicity, lack of ambition—those virtues I used to see as dull. I now see as admirable." Her films include *Country* (1984, she also produced and co-starred with Shepard), *Sweet Dreams* (1985), *Crimes of the Heart* (1986), *Far North* (1988), *Everybody's All-American* (1988) and *Men Don't Leave* (1989). She also starred in a television remake of "Cat on a Hot Tin Roof," in which she scored as a smouldering and clawing Maggie the Cat.

Frank Langella

"I'm bred for the theatre." Frank Langella told writer Judy Klemesrud, "I'm sensory. I love to touch, feel, smell, love, kiss, hug, and that's what happens when you're in front of an audience every night." The gamut of his stage lives stretches from a sea lizard named Leslie to Count Dracula, the Prince of Homburg, Cyrano, Salieri in *Amadeus*, to the explorer of the erotic in *Passion* and one of the capricious trio in the 1984 revival of Noel Coward's *Design For Living*. That same year his portrayal of Quentin in the revival of Arthur Miller's *After the Fall* ("... absorbing is Mr. Langella's driving performance in the marathon role") added another dimension to his keenly crafted career. In 1987 he mesmerized the Broadway audiences again in *Sherlock's Last Case*.

Born in Bayonne, New Jersey, New Year's Day 1940, the son of the president of the Bayonne Barrel and Drum Company was nourished as a child by a close-knit Italian-American family. He realized early that the theatre was the life for him, "the combined passions of the kitchen table and the Catholic Church" instilling in him "a great love of majesty and size, heroism and grandeur." In his early years, a "funny looking kid with glasses who competed for attention with a beautiful sister and a brilliant brother by standing upon restaurant tables and reciting poems," he imitated John Gielgud's Shakespearean recordings in a concentrated effort to get rid of his New Jersey accent. He attended Columbia High School in Maplewood, N.J., Syracuse University, and after apprenticing at the Pocono Playhouse, made his official New York debut in a revival of *The Immoralist*. Off-Broadway Obie-award performances for three consecutive years (*The Old Glory, Good Day* and *The White Devil*). were followed by Lincoln Center Repertory appearances in *Yerma* and *A Cry of Players* and a Circle in the Square production of *Iphigenia in Aulis*. He made his Tony-winning debut on Broadway in 1975 with painted face and wearing a tail in the bizarre role of a talkative sea lizard in Edward Albee's Pulitzer Prize-winning play, *Seascape*. Following the brief off-Broadway run of *The Prince of Homburg*, he opened again on Broadway in 1977 in a virtuoso portrayal of *Dracula*. Langella's movie debut was the 1970 *The Twelve Chairs* with Mel Brooks, followed by *The Diary of a Mad Housewife* for which he received the National Society of Film Critics award. Other films: *The Deadly Trap, The Wrath of God, Dracula*, a remake of *Invasion of the Body Snatchers, Sphinx, The Men's Club*, and *Masters of the Universe*. Television roles include: "Eccentricities of a Nightingale," "The Sea Gull," "The Prince of Homburg," "Sherlock Holmes," and a series based on the life of George Washington. Married in 1977 to the former Ruth Weil, they live in a handsome Manhattan apartment. Not content to rest on his laurels, Langella says:"I would rather have a sixty-year span as a good, fine actor than have five hot years as a superstar, become rich and then disappear. My work is my life, and I want my work to last the length of all my lifetime."

Lester Lanin

Dubbed both "The Debutantes' Delight" and "The Dowagers' Darling," this society maestro has been producing his sparkling dance music at society shindigs long enough for many to two-step right from the first category and glissade gracefully towards the latter. The pert patriarch of the posh podium opened with his own band at Palm Beach's Normandy Hotel in June 1926, months short of his sixteenth birthday, and was soon playing for the comely up-and-coming, the coming-out and coming-backs from Hyannis to Shaker Heights, Grosse Pointe and Nob Hill. When the competition for his services became too keen (the birth of a daughter in social circles was frequently quickly followed by a booking for a date 16 years later), he moved his headquaters to New York and began booking multiple bands. This way he has been able to fulfill engagements for over 10,000 weddings, 3,000 debutante parties, 1,500 proms and countless cotillions, assemblies, balls and private parties. Today, with some 4,500 musicians on call throughout the nation, there may be as many as 40 bands working in different cities on a given night. Whether it's a lone accordionist, a trio or a full 18-piece orchestra, with or without Lanin himself,"it's guaranteed Lester Lanin music." Wiry, dapper and as smooth as his music, he likens his many bands to a can of soup: "If you open it up in one place, it has to be the same soup when you open it anywhere else." The ingredient that makes each occasion special is Lanin's "adaptability . . . meeting the specific requirements" which tailor the music for the audience and the locale. Steeped in the Lanin style and repertoire ("If you play it straight . . . it's always the same"), his musicians switch tunes or keys at the flick of the baton.

His grandfather was a bandleader in Europe and his father carried on the tradition in Philadelphia, where Lester Lanin was born 26 August 1910, the youngest of nine sons, all musicians. He married Texas socialite Marilyn Weiss, a former Miss Texas, in 1958, but their separate careers ended the union 12 years later. A friend to politicians and royalty as well, Lanin has played every inaugural ball from Eisenhower on (save Carter's) and provided the dance music for Prince Charles and Lady Di at both the engagement party and the wedding party at Claridges. Although Queen Elizabeth II personally told Lanin that she thought everyone would be too tired to dance past eleven that evening, he recalls that she didn't leave the dance floor until 11:30 and "they were still calling for more when we stopped playing at 3:30 in the morning." He first serenaded First Lady Nancy Reagan in her days at Smith College and his long-standing friendship with the late Princess Grace of Monaco began many years ago when he played in Philadelphia for her father, John Kelly. "I could retire," he has mused, "but to retire without a wife or a hobby is dangerous."

Angela Lansbury

When mystery writer Jessica Fletcher became involved in the solving of a murder in the inital episode in 1984 of the hit television series, "Murder, She Wrote," Angela Lansbury began another phase of her phenomenal career. "My sense is that Jessica Fletcher also embodies many of the qualities which are quintessentially American," she asserted in a New York *Times* interview about the series. "She's very open, resilient and brave, a woman of very strong moral character. But she's never a bore."

The London-born (16 October 1925) daughter of the respected Irish actress Moyan Macgill and Edgar Lansbury, an English lumber merchant and mayor of Poplar in the East End of London, Angela Lansbury first studied acting and singing as a teen-ager. "I had a make-believe life that I would be like the characters in the movies I saw," she recalls. "I had a whole secret life and used to sit on buses, staring out the window and looking as though I had T.B., always playing someone other than myself. I thought a lot about America, but I never thought of myself as an actress playing these roles. I was going to go to America and walk down those golden sidewalks, step into a club and meet Boston Blackie on the corner. That was my Make Believe Mountain." She was only 15 when World War II changed her whole way of life. She and her mother were evacuated from London and she came to New York to continue her theatrical studies. She first became a favorite of American movie audiences in 1944 (after a move to Hollywood) when she played the Cockney maidservant in *Gaslight* for which she was nominated for a "Best Supporting Actress" Academy Award. ("One day I was making $28 a week at Bullock's department store and the next day I was up to $500 a week at MGM.") She received a second nomination the following year for *The Picture of Dorian Gray*. Subsequently, she appeared in more than seventy films, most often in character roles of either hussies or heavies. "There's nothing like a good villainess," Lansbury confesses. "You can go to town and chew on great chunks of scenery." Her favorite film portrayal was the monstrously malevolent mother in *The Manchurian Candidate*.

Lansbury launched what she calls "Phase II" of her career in 1957, making her Broadway debut as the object of the adulturous affections of Bert Lahr in *Hotel Paradise*. Audiences on Broadway have cheered her in *A Taste of Honey*; the Stephen Sondheim musical, *Anyone Can Whistle; Mame*; her portrayal of the seventy-five-year old Madwoman of Chaillot in *Dear World;* the persona of Mama Rose in a revival of *Gypsy;* and as the fiendish piemaker, Mrs. Lovett, in Sondheim's *Sweeney Todd*. She won Tony Awards for all four of the latter shows and, in 1982, was inducted into the Theatre Hall of Fame. Her love for the theatre and her professional charm makes Angela a favorite host of the yearly Tony Awards.

Before settling into her series, Lansbury zigzagged between movies and television. Recent films included *The Mirror Crack'd, Death On The Nile, Bedknobs and Broomsticks, and Pirates of Penzance*. On television, she's starred in : "Little Gloria . . . Happy at Last" (1982), "A Gift of Love" (1984), "A

Talent for Murder" (1984), "Rage of Angels: The Story Continues" (1986) and "One More Time" (1988). On the home video scene, she released "Angela Lansbury's Positive Moves" in 1989.

In 1949, Lansbury married American Peter Shaw, who manages her career. "We decided long ago to make it a tandem operation," she says. They have a son, Anthony, a daughter, Deirdre, a stepson, David, plus grandchildren. When asked if she would ever consider giving up her career, Lansbury quickly replied, "No, I need it desperately. I need that outlet in my life. I need to perform very much or I'm just not happy. I often try to describe what it is that I want to share with the audience. I want to achieve those high, screaming moments in theatre which you can't always hit, but which, when you do, there's no experience in the world that can match it."

Lewis H. Lapham

"*Harper's* is the oldest of America's monthly magazines for the oldest of American reasons—because it has had the good luck to retain an instinct for survival, a willingness to experiment, and the wit to change with the times and make a new deal in a new line of country," says the editor who's guided the destinies of this venerable (but financially shaky) "magazine of ideas" off and on since 1975. In March, 1984, he presided over the periodical's radical break from tradition to emerge in a new format which Lewis H. Lapham calls "a synopticon of fact and opinion" and which some skeptics dubbed "a highbrow *Reader's Digest*." Operating in a non-profit status with funds from the MacArthur Foundation, *Harper's* seemed to many a much different magazine from the monthly which first published *Moby Dick* and the Lincoln-Douglas debates. But its editor still sees it as "a barometer of the social and intellectual weather of the times" and hopes for the best.

Born 8 January 1935 in San Francisco ("I come from a background that was not big rich, but it was certainly affluent"), Lewis Lapham came to *Harper's* via Hotchkiss, Yale and Cambridge, reporting stints on the San Francisco *Examiner* (1957-60) and New York *Herald-Tribune*(1960-62), and five years as a contributing writer for the *Saturday Evening Post* (1963-67). He signed on with *Harper's* as managing editor in 1971 and during his first term in the editor's chair (1975-81) demonstrated what's been called his "neoconservative perspective" in his ruminating monthly column, "Easy Chair," as well as the table of contents. Though, as *Publisher's Weekly* once pointed out, "an undercurrent of dismay is perceptible in the essays, "Lapham considers himself "a writer more optimistic than gloomy [but] if what you write comes out like Pollyanna, people won't believe it." "In 1980, a worsening financial picture forced *Harper's* to announce it would cease publication and Lapham departed in 1981 until he was called back to reshape the magazine in 1983. "Much of the media," he said shortly thereafter, "has become an institutional Wizard of Oz.... *Harper's*... undertakes to ask questions, not to provide ready-made answers, to say, in effect, look at this, see how much more beautiful and strange and full of possibility is the world than can be imagined by the mythographers at *Time* or NBC."

In addition to his monthly *Harper's* column, Lapham writes a fortnightly newspaper piece for the Washington *Post* and other papers, and a collection of his past articles was published in 1980 under the title, *Fortune's Child*. His book *Money and Class in America; Notes and Observation on Our Civil Religion* was released in 1988. He has been married since 1972 to the former Joan Brooke Reeves and they have a son and daughter.

Estée Lauder

"I love life, I love love, I love my children, I love my friends, I love clothes," exclaims the last of the great beauty tycoons, Estée Lauder who, like her predecessors Elizabeth Arden, Helena Rubenstein, and Charles Revson has made millions and millions of dollars painting faces.

She was born Josephine Estée Menczer in early July to a Czech-German father and a Viennese-Hungarian mother in the Flushing section of Queens, New York. After the birth of her two sons Leonard and Ronald, she and her husband Joe—her close and constant companion for nearly 50 years until his death in 1983—started their cosmetics business with a formula for face cream that had belonged to an uncle in Vienna. Business boomed when the Lauder magic cleared up the skin of the teenager daughter of a Saks Fifth Avenue buyer. When asked about her beginnings Lauder is terse: "I will tell you how I got started; not by dreaming or wishing about it, but by working for it. That's how I got started." Although her empire now boasts several scents and various cosmetics for women and men, it was the launching of "Youth-Dew Bath Oil" that sent sales skyrocketing. With her financial success came her success as an international hostess whose parties, replete with international types from the Duke and Duchess of Windsor to various heads of state, are like last vestiges of turn-of-the century splendor: fabulous food, waiters wearing white gloves so as to not smudge the silver, and always gypsy music in the background. She maintains homes in New York, London, Wainscott, Palm Beach, and the South of France.

The recipient of numerous prestigious awards including Outstanding Mother of the Year in 1984, France's highest award given for outstanding service to that country, the insignia of Chevalier of the Legion of Honor, and the city of Pairs' Gold Medal, Lauder, whose company is ranked as the third largest cosmetics and perfume company in the nation is also, via the Lauder Foundation, one of the nations most generous givers. Since 1962 she had funded creative playgrounds for New York City as well as social agencies, museums, medical research and education, totalling approximately $500,000 annually. A $10 million gift to the University of Pennsylvania established an institute for management and international studies in 1984.

She has, what one calls, an "eye." She says, "I love everything shiny and clean, there's nothing nicer, it shows you care." Around the town she is wardrobed as if she were the last of the great ladies, striking in her hat and gloves, her hazel eyes and honey colored hair. She has looked one age for twenty years, somewhere between thirty and sable. She has decorated her own homes and once, as reported in *W*, she was showing a well-known decorator up the winding staircase of her New York townhouse when he turned and said enthusiastically, "I could do wonders with this." She patted his jowls and replied, "I could do wonders with these." Although she stands a mere 5 feet 4 inches, she is a fulfillment of one of America's tallest dreams. Her autobiography, *Estée: A Success Story* was released in 1985. She told WWD's Jane Lane, "Every day means an awful lot to me. It's not easy. I want you to know it's not easy. If you think it's easy, you're wrong. I don't feel I'm successful. I always worry. Anybody who doesn't worry, it's all over. It's one thing becoming successful but it's hard to stay that way."

Cyndi Lauper

"My work isn't just about me being famous. It's about opening up new avenues for new kinds of singers, for new songwriters. I've been very lucky: Every time I've lost sight of my real purpose, I've met people who brought me back to it." Cyndi Lauper reflects on her reasons for success, believing that her latest album *A Night To Remember* (1989) will bring her back to the top of the pop charts. She says. "These songs are all about love, love won and love lost. It's a common denominator, something all of us feel. I write from experience—unfortunately, I've lived through most of this record!"

In the midst of Madonna mania, this madcap vocalist, whom *Newsweek* has called "the Gracie Allen of rock," sweeped onto the music scene with hair that was buzz-shaved to her scalp on one side of her head while the other side was long, dyed day-glo something and teased into ribbons. Although Cyndi is reluctant to give her birthday ("I'm not a car. It doesn't matter"), She was born in Brooklyn 20 June 1953 and was raised in Queens. And such a misfit was she that, according to *Newsweek*, her mother would light candles for her to St. Jude, the patron saint of desperate cases. "No matter how hard I tried to look normal, there was always something that wasn't right," she says. "I'd put on false eyelashes and one would always curl up." She dropped out of high school and, following the inspiration of her all-time hero Vincent van Gogh, tried to become a painter. She has worked as a "hot walker," walking horses at Belmont racetrack (her sports' patronage these days favors wrestlers), was a singing Geisha in a New York-Japanese piano bar and sang Janis Joplin songs in clubs around Manhattan. For a while she played with a rockabilly band, the Blue Angel, but it wasn't until her solo song about the fun loving girls, aided by heavy rotation on MTV, that she became America's wacko darling. As a star she's risen to the occasion. She's joked with Rodney Dangerfield as the presenter of the Grammy Awards, and when she appeared on the "Tonight Show" Johnny Carson dug her so much that he devoted half his show to her adorable deadpanning. The key to her success is the P.E.G. Principle. She explains: "See the P.E.G. principle stands for politeness, etiquette and grooming." Lauper, whose other hits have included "Time After Time," "She Bop" and "All Through the Night," told rock columnist Lisa Robinson that she pursued a music career "after I tried everything else. Every time I would start to sing, people would say, 'Oh Cyndi, don't sing, you don't sing that good.' Or I'd sing a lot and they'd say, 'Please Cyndi, please, I can't take it anymore.' When I started singing, however, I always felt better; I felt like I wasn't in this body. The human voice is a great healer. I also thought I had this guardian angel. To this day I think that. After all someone up there must be smiling." During the 1985 Grammy Awards telecast she was chosen Best New Artist. That same year she was honored as one of *Ms.* magazine's Women of the Year. Taking her comedic talents to the big screen she had a leading role as a psychic opposite Jeff Goldblum and Peter Falk in *Vibes* (1988) and appeared in *Steel Magnolias* (1988).

Acclaimed for her unique live concerts, Lauper embarked on a massive "True Colors" world tour, following the release of the *True Colors* album in 1986. Highlights of her appearance in Paris were taped for the CBS home video "Cyndi Lauper in Paris." The past few years, she's been nurturing her craft. In 1988 she stayed for two weeks in Russia as part of a collaboration attempt between American and Soviet songwriters. She explains, "I met a lot of people, a lot of great writers—the trip gave me renewed inspiration at a time when I was really down. *Vibes* and my single 'Hole in My Heart' had both gone south, and I was about ready to move to Siberia!" In June 1988, she finally graduated from Richmond Hill High School and was presented with an honorary diploma in a ceremony at Queens College. Also in 1988 she became a spokesperson for Sapporo Japanese beer "Dentsu" in Japan. The girl with a gimmick has high hopes that her 1989 album will reinstate her fans. She admits, "I know that what I do is looked on as a 'product,' but I can't just look at it that way. The music has to give you the chills or tickle your funny bone."

Ralph Lauren

His fantastically successful fashion empire preys upon nostalgia—worshipping Old Money and reinventing, from neckties to home furnishings (with such fully coordinated themes [or schemes?] as "Log Cabin," "New England," "Thoroughbred," "University" and "Ski Lodge,") the supposed luxuries of inherited wealth. "I am thankful I don't have to work anymore," declared famed fashion photographer Louise Dahl-Wolfe in 1984. "Designers are not first rate anymore. All they do is take a man's suit and dress a woman like a man." Citing Ralph Lauren among several others, she said, "they're commercial manufacturers, not designers." The ascent of this modern-age Silas Lapham reached its apex in 1985 when it was announced that Ralph Lauren/Polo had acquired one of New York City's most handsome landmarks, the Rhinelander Mansion on the corner of 72nd Street and Madison Avenue. Buying out the leases of the shops already established on the ground floor, Lauren turned the mansion into a retail shop for his wares. The diminutive Ralph Lauren, a former necktie salesman born Ralph Lifshitz in the Bronx, New York, 14 October 1939, had come full circle from outsider to insider. His renovation of the former glamorous home of the Rhinelanders seemed akin to building a period attraction in Disneyland, a place for selling High Society souvenirs to the perpetually status seeking consumer.

As a young man he was active in sports, but he was also addicted to movies and the novels of F. Scoot Fitzgerald. He first became interested in clothes when he was in seventh grade. "My friends were the hoods wearing motorcycle jackets, but I was wearing tweeds, bermudas and button down shirts." Throughout high school he worked as a part time stockboy at Alexander's, saving his salary for weeks so he could buy a Brooks Brothers suit. After graduating he worked fulltime as a salesman at Alexander's before serving in the Army. He planned to break into designing, but no one would have him. "I had no portfolio and no sketches. All I had was taste." In 1967, he started the Polo neckwear division of Beau Brummet neckties. His was a wide tie, expensive and opulent. Polo ties soon became status ties and the "wide tie revolution" soon caused a much broader fashion revolution in men's wear. Over the next few years he added the Polo line of shirts, suits, knitwear, coats and on and on. Having designed his wife Ricky's clothes (the couple have three sons, Andrew, David, Dylan), he launched his first women's collection in 1971—small-collared, man-tailored shirts in soft cotton handkerchief linen. ("I didn't think it was necessary for a woman to dress like a vamp, like Jean Harlow or Marilyn Monroe.") Called "Polo" for its connotation of class and elegance, he once explained: "All I want is the Old Money look. I want the same kind of thing that Abercrombie and Fitch used to have or that Brooks Broithers should have gone on to." In 1974 he designed the menswear for the film *The Great Gatsby*. Diane Keaton was said to have used the "Polo" look to put her "look" together for *Annie Hall*. Clad in denims redolent with faded glory, he appears in magazine spreads advertising his Western apparel. The winner of half a dozen Coty Awards avoids socializing, preferring his upper Fifth Avenue duplex, house on the beach in East Hampton, 300-acre ranch in Colorado or Jamaican island hideaway. He has a network of shops worldwide, even in London where many lords and ladies rarely pass up a chance to laugh at the way Ralph Lauren seems to be showing them how best to dress. Nevertheless, they buy. And that's what counts in a world in which, to coin a phrase from the TV show "Lifestyles of the Rich and Famous"—"fortune is the final frontier."

Steve Lawrence

He is first and foremost a singer who also acts (made his debut in a summer revival of *Pal Joey*). ("Here I was doing what every red-blooded young man really wants to do—be a rotten mean character with women.") Married to songstress Eydie Gorme in 1957, the couple had two children. Their youngest, Michael Robert died in 1986 from a heart attack. Steve & Eydie have been a ticket (personally and professionally) setting house records at clubs, theatres and concert halls throughout the U.S. The pair have also fared well on vinyl, earning a Grammy with the song "We Got Us" in 1960. The TV special, "Steve and Eydie Celebrate Irving Berlin" collected seven Emmy Awards and "Our Love Is Here to Stay," their TV tribute to George and Ira Gershwin, won two more. They have also received the Award of Excellence from the Film Advisory Board for their tribute to Cole Porter entitled "From This Moment On." In 1984 Lawrence co-hosted (with Don Rickles) TV's "Foul-Ups, Bleeps & Blunders."

Lawrence, born 8 July 1935, nee Sidney Liebowitz, sang in his father's choir until he was 11 and after a three-year hiatus while his voice changed, began singing again at his synagogue and for public functions. In 1953 he became a regular on Steve Allen's Tonight show, where he met Eydie, and when the two co-starred as Allen's summer replacements, they were reviewed as "the musical little league Lunts."

Joe Layton

He's passed muster directing such Broadway extravaganzas as *On the Town, The Sound of Music, No Strings, George M, Dear World, Two by Two, Barnum,* and *Woman of the Year* (with Lauren Bacall), garnering a crop of Tonys in the process, and the roster of successful concert tours he's staged (Lionel Ritchie, Kenny Rogers, Diana Ross, Julio Iglesias, and Jeffrey Osborne) speaks its own praises. His three TV specials for Barbra Streisand ("My Name Is Barbra" won him his first Emmy) put him in the catbird seat and quicker than you can hum a scale earned him directing gigs with Joel Grey, Cher, Olivia Newton-John, and Diana Ross. Movie credits include directing *Richard Pryor: Live on the Sunset Strip* (1982) and producing *Annie* (1981).

Born Joseph Lichtman in New York City, 3 May 1931, he grew up in the Crown Heights section of Brooklyn, where his parents operated a luncheonette. At the age of 12 he was tap-dancing up a storm and later studied ballet and Spanish dance with Joseph Levinoff. After graduating from Manhattan's High School of Music and Art in 1948, he was a chorus boy in such Broadway shows as *Oklahoma, Gentlemen Prefer Blondes,* and *Wonderful Town.* In 1952 the tall (six-feet-three), lanky Layton entered military service and was assigned to U.S. Army Special Services as a choreographer-director. Upon his discharge in 1954, he associated himself with the "Ballet Ho de George Reich" in Paris and Cannes and subsequently returned to the U.S. to do his brief thing as a nightclub singer ("I was trying to be the Jewish Yves Montand"). In 1960 he married former tap dancer Evelyn Russell (now deceased, one son, Jeb James). He summers on Roanoke Island in North Carolina where he has worked with the Waterside Theatre for the past twenty years.

Irving Lazar

"I'm not an *agent*. . . . I'm something *other* than an agent," declares this implish, bossy, lone-wolf, gregarious, five-foot-three, colossal deal maker who's the most renowned literary agent in the world. His fast deals as a Hollywood superagent earned him the nickname "Swifty"—coined by his client-friend Humphry Bogart the day Lazar, on a dare, made five deals in five hours for the star. Lazar deals with world class superstars in the various arts and is "always annoyed" by the "misnomer" of being called a *Hollywood* agent. "I am a lit'ry agent," asserts Lazar, who likes to use British pronunciations in conversation. "You can't be a *Hollywood* agent and handle Moss Hart, Teddy White, Arthur Schlesinger, Roald Dahl, Noel Coward, Francoise Sagan, Georges Clouzot." His celebrity clients agree that Lazar is something more than an agent. He's made millions of dollars for them, but he's also their friend. Said *New York* magazine, "Lazar loves it that his clients know that he will spend the time and money just to see them, loves knowing that he coddles them with his attention and affection. He is incapable of separating business from pleasure, professional from personal."

Born Irving Paul Lazar, 28 March 1907, he grew up in the tough Brownsville section of Brooklyn but rarely talks about his childhood, causing one of his friends to remark, "Like all godlike creatures, Irving was probably born in the bulrushes." Richard Brooks, a client director who's known Lazar for more than 35 years, says: "Irving wasn't born until he became an agent. I don't think he was ever born. He was probably quarried. It occurs to me that I've never known anything about his family." Says Lazar, "I was born in a jungle, and I'm still in a jungle—a little classier, but it's still a jungle." He credits his father, a bread-and-butter wholesale broker and "a good friend," for his own drive. Lazar knew from boyhood that he wanted to be in show business and soon after graduating form Brooklyn Law School in 1930 became an agent at the Music Corporation of America. For 10 years he booked bands and acts around the country (Ted Lewis, Eddie Cantor, Sophie Tucker, Fred Allen. . .).

While in the Army during World War II, he pulled off a deal for a smash revue, *Winged Victory,* featuring the talents of Moss Hart, Red Buttons, Mario Lanza and others— propelling Lazar into the role of Hollywood agent. Prompted by Hart, he became a literary agent ("Moss anointed me"). Hart made Lazar believe he could be a different kind of agent who could hobnob with writers, educated people, witty people who dressed for dinner. Since the late 1960s, Lazar's presence has been felt more in New York than in Hollywood, but he's continued the same frenetic style—giving and going to endless rounds of parties, globe-trotting, acquiring culture, and always making deals. For his twenty-odd clients, he earned $10 million in 1982, says one report. Friends can't imagine him without a phone receiver in his ear. "Someday, he'll have to have an operation and get it removed," says client friend Garson Kanin.

He is married to tall, striking, former model Mary Van Nuys. Their apartment in Manhattan and their Beverly Hills home are hung with paintings by Chagall, Utrillo, Picasso, and Degas. As energetic as ever, he says, "Tomorrow is the best time."

David Lean

"Good films can be made only by a crew of dedicated maniacs," declares this "Michelangelo" of film directors whose credits include such classics as *The Bridge on the River Kwai, Lawrence of Arabia, Dr. Zhivago,* and *A Passage to India.* A man with a tremendous sense of environment, a photographer's eye for composition, a musician's feel for rhythm, Lean immerses himself completely in his work. The hardest part of filmmaking is finding a story to fall in love with says Lean, confessing that it's love stories that he's always enjoyed most of all. "I like telling stories," he says. "I want to direct films where the audiences come out discussing the characters they've just been watching. . . ." Since 1955, when he depicted an unforgettable image of Venice, as seen through the eyes of Katherine Hepburn in *Summertime,* he's shown a fascination for locations. The essence of places has continually pervaded Lean's cinema, whether barren and exotic as the desert in *Lawrence* or verdent and storm-tossed like the west coast of Ireland in *Ryan's Daughter.*

Born into a Quaker family in Croyden, England, 25 March 1908, David Lean was educated in a local Quaker school. His father wanted him to be an accountant, but David decided he wanted to work in films. A top film cutter by the 1930s, he also had a complete grounding in newsreel making. ("It's essential to learn to use the tools of the trade, then it's up to talent.") Noel Coward gave Lean his first chance to direct with *In Which We Serve* (1942). Lean formed his own company, Cineguild, the next year, and followed with such notable Coward pictures as *This Happy Breed, Blithe Spirit,* and *Brief Encounter.* ("I learned a lot from working with Noel. A lot about handling actors . . . tactful as anything, encouraging to frightened rabbits, tough when necessary.") After the Coward films, Lean made *Oliver Twist* and the unforgettable *Great Expectations.* Three of his films (*Dr. Zhivago,* 1965; *Lawrence of Arabia,* 1962; *The Bridge on the River Kwai,* 1957) collected a total of 19 Oscars and Lean won the award for best director on the latter two. *Ryan's Daughter* (1970)—which he viewed as his most realized work but was condemned by most critics as his worst—was Lean's last film until *Passage to India,* the long-awaited movie based on E.M. Forster's great 1924 novel.

Norman Lear

"*Passage* is a very special subject." says Lean. "There are six wonderful characters, which is a rare thing in a movie. . . . There are a lot of loose ends just as there are in real life. You meet people, you understand certain aspects of them, but others are hidden and you have to guess what they are. This kind of interplay intrigues me enormously." Producer Anthony Havelock-Allan once said of this master filmmaker: "David is a marvellous storyteller, not only of the main scene but of each scene in a story. In another age, he would have sat around a fire and told stores." In February 1989, the revered and legendary film director participated in a starstudded presentation of the eagerly-awaited restoration of *Lawrence of Arabia*. Lean has been through three divorces (Kay Walsh, Ann Todd, Leila Devi), and he tied the knot with his fourth wife, Sandra Hotz, in 1985.

Norman Lear

In a quip that succinctly described this ridiculously-successful TV and film producer-director-writer's Midas touch, host Johnny Carson re-greeted viewers in the 1972 Emmy Awards show with "welcome to an evening with Norman Lear." That night, Lear's "All in the Family" comedy series received seven awards, only a fraction of the total that his profitable sitcom stable of "Sanford & Son," "Maude," "Good Times," "Mary Hartman, Mary Hartman," "The Jeffersons," and "One Day at a Time" has piled up. Writer Paddy Chayefsky credited Lear with taking "television away from dopey (TV character) wives and dumb fathers, from the pimps, hookers, hustlers, private eyes, junkies, cowboys and rustlers that constituted television chaos and in their place he put the American people. . . . He took the audience and he put them on the set." Norman Milton Lear himself (born in New Haven on 27 July 1922), "I want to entertain but I gravitate to subjects that matter and people worth caring about."

The WWII Air Corps radioman-turned-publicity agent-turned-salesman got his biggest breaks by collaborating with his cousin's husband on comedy routines that they sold to L.A. comedians, and, in particular, to Danny Thomas. Lear obtained access to Thomas by contacting the funnyman's agent, and, on the pretext that he was from the New York *Times*, got Thomas' personal phone number. After Danny-Boy bought the sketch for "five bills," David Susskind saw it and asked Lear and his partner to write for "The Ford Star Review," a TV series. In quick succession, Lear was spinning gags for other 1950s shows starring Dean Martin and Jerry Lewis, Matha Raye, Tennessee Ernie Ford and George Gobel. As a partner in Tandem Productions, he put on TV specials and feature films (*Come Blow Your Horn*, 1963; *The Night They Raided Minsky's*, 1968) but really struck paydirt when he decided to adapt a British TV comedy series to U.S. sensibilities. "My father and I fought all those battles," Lear said of the bigot in the BBC show, and he borrowed his own dad's admonitions that Mrs. Lear "stifle herself" in launching "All in the Family" in pilot form in the late 1960s, ABC steered clear of the show, but in 1971 CBS went with it, "vulgarity," "irreverence" and all, and Archie Bunker became the nation's lambastador or laughing stock, depending on a viewer's values. Spin-offs proliferated at an amazing clip. Lear, criticized by fundamentalist and/or ethnic groups for making light of subjects they consider serious matters, helped found People for the American Way, a star-studded organization, to encourage freedom of expression. The award-winning creative mastermind has far too many productions under his belt to name. He has received numerous awards and was inducted into the TV Hall of Fame in 1984. His marriage to Frances Loeb produced three children. Since their divorce in 1986, Frances struck gold by launching *Lear's* magazine and Norman remarried Lynn Davis in 1987. The couple have one son, Benjamin Davis. Lear was also the Executive Producer for the feature film *The Princess Bride* (1987).

Timothy Leary

Back in the Sixties, when the age of psychedelia was first blossoming, Timothy Leary was the most glorious guru of the "blow your mind" generation, an iconoclastic Harvard psychologist who was to LSD trips what Jimi Hendrix was to sonic guitar distortion, what Abbie Hoffman was to politics, and what Haight-Ashbury was to psychedelic street corners. Today, his epigrams from those days ("Tune in, turn on, drop out!") seem about as timely as a pair of groovy, tie-died bellbottoms. But he is still preaching the hallucinogenic gospel. These days his podium is supplied by an entertainment booking agency that has him touring the country's college campuses with another figure from yesteryear's headlines, Watergate culprit Gordon Liddy. Lear's alleged use of undergrads in drug experiments led to his being sacked by Harvard; twenty years later he got a second chance to tell his side to Cambridge, this time to a new generation. "Harvard is the big league of chemical psychedelic experimentation," he declared to a full house at Memorial Hall. Leary, a psychological researcher, was first hired as a lecturer at Harvard in 1959. The following year he discovered the hallucinogenic properties of Mexican mushrooms and launched a lengthy personal investigation. It's his contention now that, "The problem was the world wasn't ready for us. [But] I have never felt any rancor against Harvard," a school he calls "the mainline of American transcendental thinking."

Born 22 October 1920 in Springfield, Mass., the so-called "Messiah of LSD" was in and out of jail in the 1970s on drug-related charges. He went underground in Switzerland for a while and returned to California only to be found guilty of prison escape. Having paid his dues to society, Leary was deemed free to return to the podium, which he has done with the same old flamboyant style. Thrice married, last in 1978 to Barbara Chase, he has two children, Susan and John, from his first marriage. He is the president and producer of Futique Inc, an electronic book company, and written may books. His latest include *Flashbacks: An Autobiography* (1983, with G. Gordon Liddy), *Infopsychology* (1987), and *The Cybernetic Societies of the 21st Century* (1987).

Fran Lebowitz

When *Metropolitan Life*, a collection of her astringent and ingenious essays of existence first published in *Mademoiselle* and *Interview*, came out in 1978, New York *Times* book critic John Leonard described her as "an unlikely and perhaps alarming combination of Mary Hartman and Mary McCarthy . . . to a dose of Huck Finn add some Lenny Bruce, Oscar Wilde and Alexis de Tocqueville, a dash of cabdriver, an assortment of puns, minced jargon and top it off with smarty pants." Edmund White, reviewing for the Washington *Post* affirmed: "Fran Lebowitz is the funniest woman in America." Despite her publisher's doubts that her urbane tone would appeal to the Beluga-less masses, *Metrolitan Life* sold more than 100,000 copies in hardback alone and made Fran a national celebrity. The 1988 paperback version kept her name in the public eye. *Social Studies*, published in 1981, was the worthy successor to her first book and it dealt with her transformation from poor New York scribbler into media personality. "Owing to some rather favorable publicity," she wrote, "I came into what is know as a little money. . . ."

"Coming from a family where literary tradition runs largely toward the picture postcard, it is not surprising that I have never really succeeded in explaining to my grandmother exactly what it is that I do. . . . My beginnings are humble of course, but I am not ashamed of them. I started with a humor pushcart on Delancey Street—comic essays, forty cents a piece, four for a dollar. It was tough out there on the street; competition was cutthroat, but it was the best education in the world because on Delancey 'mildly amusing' was not enough—you had to be funny."

For the record: Ms. Lebowitz was born 27 October 1950 in Morristown, New Jersey, where her prosperous parents own a furniture store nearby. She dropped out of high school, got a high school equivalency diploma, and did not go to college. She worked for Head Start in Poughkeepsie for six months before she came to New York to be a struggling poet. She had some very odd jobs including ice cream parlor waitress, taxi driver and apartment cleaner—"I specialized in venetian blinds." She worked at *Changes*, a countercultural music-oriented magazine before going to Andy Warhol's *Interview* in the early 1970s where she wrote monthly movie screen reviews under the heading "The Best of the Worst." Later, when producers banned her from screenings, she started writing her column "I Cover the Waterfront."

A gadfly who covers the waterfront from its most literary of coasts to its most affluent vistas, she is always spotted wearing her regulation Fran Lebowitz *haute couture*—no couture. Straight leg Levi bluejeans, penny loafers, a boy's Brooks Brothers shirt and a sweater on her five-foot bookworm frame *avec* cigarette. She lives to smoke and is the media's favorite spokesperson for the right-to-smoke movement, all the more inflamed after she lit up inside an East Hampton, Long Island cinema amidst cries of protest which ended in a court appearance to face charges. Although she insists she hates writing, she enjoys the English language to its fullest; furthermore she is a highly visible supporter of other writers. Time—it takes time to sculpt those perfect aphorisms at which she excels. (She was fired from writing her column at *Mademoiselle* because she missed her deadline.) Here's a Lebowitz sampler: "Always a godmother never a god . . . Calling a taxi in Texas is like calling a Rabbi in Iraq. . . . Women who insist upon having the same options as men would do well to consider the option of the strong silent type who wants to go back to the land; I am the type who wants to go back to the hotel. . . . Don't bother discussing sex with small children. They rarely have anything to add. . . .Sleep is death without the responsibility."

John Le Carré

Which celebrated writer in the espionage genre once taught Latin and French at Eton College? Give up? The answer is John Le Carré, who frequently taps his bookish background in devising his best-selling espionage tales. He also knows the scene firsthand, having worked a stint in British intelligence following World War II and lurked around Bonn and Hamburg for Her Majesty's Foreign Service in the early 1960s. Le Carré wears his erudition brightly; unlike his fellow writers of "this-bowtie-is-really-a camera" school, his heroes thrive in a milieu of "grubby realism and moral squalor," as one critic observed. His most famous character, George Smiley, is described by the author: "His fear makes him servile." Fear and servility, decidedly out of place in James Bond circles, nevertheless have enabled Le Carré's characters to seize the imagination of high-brow spy-novel readers. It all crested for LeCarré with the blockbuster 1964 success of *The Spy Who Came in from the Cold*, which soon became a popular movie starring Richard Burton.

Le Carré immediately began making plans to skirt the formula for success he had only just created. "I am not going to plod like an old athlete around the same track because it makes money," he informed one interviewer. That makes the author a decided rarity among genre writers. As dour and cynical as any of his characters, Le Carré identifies with their role in life. Like the spy, the writer/artist also wants to "come in from the cold," he believes. "The artist," he observes, "is also outside city walls." As to his own financial success, Le Carré says, "I am only slightly less happy than I was before it happened." Born 19 October 1931 in Poole, Dorsetshire, England, Le Carré—legal name David Cornwell—was wedded to the former Alison Ann Sharp (sons Simon, Stephen, Timothy) and, since 1972 to Valerie Jane Eustace (one son, Nicholas). He is an Oxford graduate. His other books include *Tinker, Tailor, Soldier, Spy* (1974), *Honourable Schoolboy* (1977), *Smiley's People* (1979), *The Little Drummer Girl* (1983; later became a movie starring Diane Keaton), *The Looking Glass War* (1984), and *A Perfect Spy* (1986). His book, *The Russia House* (1989) is being considered for a movie deal.

Michele Lee

"Apart from the notable strength, the sheer likability of Michele Lee is infectious," T.E. Kalem once said in *Time* Magazine, speaking of the perky, highly energetic singer, dancer and actress who stars as Karen Fairgate Mackenzie in the hit TV series, "Knots Landing." In recognition of her talents, Michele was named "The Best Actress of the Year" (1981) by Gannett Newspapers, was nominated for an Emmy Award (1982), and won the 1988 Soap Opera Digest Awards for "Best Actress" and "Super Couple" with Kevin Dobson. Aside from the series, Michele was also seen on the small screen in three TV movies: "Dark Victory," "Bud and Lou," and the 1985 version of "A Letter to Three Wives." However, TV is not this active star's only forte. Aside from a highly successful Broadway background—two years in the hit musical, *How to Succeed in Business Without Even Trying* and *Seesaw*, earned Michele the Drama Desk Award, the Outer Circle Award, the Outer Circle Critics Award and a Tony nomination—Michele also won acclaim for her role in the film version of *How To Succeed In Business Without Even Trying*, when she received the Motion Picture Exhibitors of US and Canada's 1967 "Fame" Award as the country's most promising new actress. The multitalented Michele showed her versatility by recording a hit album, *A Taste of the Fantastic*, a hit single, "L. David Sloane," and preparing her nightclub act.

Born Michele Dusick on 24 June 1942 in Los Angeles, California, Michele knew almost from the beginning that she wanted to be a performer. Her parents Sylvia and Jack (a make-up artist based primarily at MGM studios, which is now Lorimar TelePictures, the studio which films "Knots Landing") watched Michele as she sang in school assemblies in junior and senior high school. At sixteen she was a semi-professional, singing with a local society band. After graduating from high school, Michele learned of an open audition for a musical review set to play in Hollywood. Thinking that their seventeen-year-old daughter Michele would not get the part because the director would want someone more mature, her parents let her try out. She sang "You Make Me Feel So Young" and landed the part. The show, *Vintage 60* went from Los Angeles to Broadway eight months after opening. Although it closed soon after its move to the east, Michele had made it to Broadway on her first audition. Back in Los Angeles, the energetic teenager landed starring spots in two more reviews, *Parade* and *Point of View*. Hearing about an audition in New York for the ingenue lead in a new musical called *Bravo Giovanni*, Michele borrowed money from her father and flew to New York to give it a shot. The eighteen-year-old auditioned and won the role. While the musical only ran for three months, it was long enough for Michele to be seen and be signed to star opposite Robert Morse in *How to Succeed*, which ran from 1962-1964, followed by the film version in 1967. After a variety of television appearances, an album, and a dazzling nightclub act which played in both New York City and Las Vegas, the busy Michele made two motion pictures, *The Love Bug* (1969) and *The Comic* (1969), which showed her strength as a dramatic actress.

Michele is a private person who places family, close friends and principles first. She, along with second husband CBS Vice President Fred Rappoport (married 27 September 1987) and her son, David Farentino (son of James Farentino whom Michele divorced in April 1981, live in West Los Angeles. She keeps over forty photo albums containing four generations of her family. Michele also finds time to serve as Vice-Chair of the Entertainment Industries Council, Inc. (for a Drug-Free Society) and Chairperson of California's Action for Youth. For her public service work, she has been honored by a number of groups, including the California Women's Council on Alcoholism and The Anit-Defamation League of New York.

Peggy Lee

When a band with whom she was singing hit a clinker, Peggy Lee turned to the conductor and said, "I don't think we are in the same key. I'm in tune with the infinite, so you figure out where that leaves you." Jazz critic Leonard Feather has called her "Miss Standing Ovation," and she's won them in the lushest supper clubs in the land. She's also made her mark on records (well over 500 of them), on TV, in movies, on the stage; and when she's not singing, she writes songs, arranges them, and also paints pictures ("my favorite color is plaid") and sculpts. In the era of fast-changing musical fashions, polished perfectionist Peggy has not only survived but triumphed. "What she has," said a fan in *The New Yorker*, "is a good voice, a good ear, good time, great taste, a wonderful way with ballads, a sure feeling for jazz-oriented and blues-oriented material, and an actress' ability with lyrics."

Born Norma Deloris Engstrom, 26 May 1920 in Jamestown, N.D., she worked as a milkmaid as a youngster to help boost sagging family finances, and became singer "Peggy Lee" via a radio show in nearby Fargo. Benny Goodman tapped her for a band singer, and she zoomed to stardom when they cut the hit record " Why Don't You Do Right?" On her own ever since, her big-big-big hits include "Lover," "Fever," "Golden Earrings," and "Is That All There Is?" In 1956 she won an Oscar nomination for her portrayal of a boozy singer in *Pete Kelly's Blues*. In 1943 she married guitarist Dave Barbour, and the couple collaborated on such hits as "Mañana," "It's a Good Day," and "I Don't Know Enough About You," and also a daughter, Nikki, before a 1951 divorce. Afterward came marriages to (and divorces from) actors Brad Dexter and Dewey Martin, and in 1964 a marriage to bongo player Jack Del Rio (she described him as "an Argentinian percussionist"). In an interview before the opening of her autobiographical musical, *Peg*, on Broadway (1983), Lee said, " We're going to treat this all with a light hand, but it's really about survival." Unfortunately, the musical didn't survive. However, the "I-love-Peggy" crowd cheered her, and one critic rhapsodized: "The lady and her music unfurled a platinum mound of glowing artistry . . . the theatre may never again witness such magic." Her autobiography, *Miss Peggy Lee*, was released in 1989 as she continues to perform in nightclubs. A whole new generation has fallen in love with Ms. Lee as Walt Disney put out the home video of *Lady and The Tramp*. Although the tape was originally released without her permission, she became determined to receive her rightful share of the profits; the video is one of the top videocassettes of the 1980's.

Spike Lee

"One of the biggest lies going is that no matter what race, creed, or religion you are, it doesn't matter: we're all Americans. . . . I want people to feel the horror at the end of the movie. I want people to know that if we don't talk about the problems and deal with them head on, they're going to get much worse," states Spike Lee.

Spike Lee is the producer, writer, director, and star of the 40 Acres and a Mule Filmworks Production of the film *Do the Right Thing*. The purpose of this picture is to combine humor and drama to expose the absurdity of racism, and to explore social realism. In the movie, he combines music with a heavy dose of social commentary. The inspiration for this film was derived from racial incidents.

Spike was born in Atlanta, Georgia, but grew up in Brooklyn. His film career began while he was a graduate student in Film School at New York University. His thesis film *Joe's Bed-Stuy Barbershop: We Cut Heads* won the Student Academy Award from the Academy of Motion Picture Arts and Sciences. His next film was about bicycle messengers and wasn't successful. Determined to make it, he went on to write, direct, and co-star in *She's Gotta Have It,* which won the Best New Director award at the Cannes Film Festival. His second feature film, the $6 million musical *School Daze,* which he also wrote, directed, and co-starred in, was Columbia's most profitable picture in 1988.

Ursula Le Guin

"She is probably the best writer of speculative fabulation working in the country today," writes critic Robert Scholes. Her extraordinary tales are quests into uncharted territory both in outer space and "the Inner Lands." Ursula Le Guin is riding the crest of a wave hitherto dominated by men—science fiction.

Born in California 21 October 1929 (father anthropologist; mother children's writer), she was introduced to the tradition of fantasy through her father's retelling of Indian legends and was later influenced by the "open and intuitive way" of Chinese philosopher Lao Tsu. Le Guin began writing stories when she was nine but was so dismayed after submitting her first piece to *Amazing Stories*, and having it rejected, that she shied from aiming for publication for 10 years. She studied the classics at Radcliffe (B.A.) and then went to Columbia (M.A.). The following year she received a Fulbright grant (1953). She had, of course, been writing all this time, but it wasn't until she resumed reading sci-fi in 1960 that she discovered the literary niche that was to make her famous. When first trying her hand at sci-fi, she knew too little of science to employ it as a framework, and so wrote what she describes as "fairytales decked out in space suits." The first of these tales to appear in print was *April in Paris* (1962). She has since written numerous books which "have enlivened the hardware-oriented genre with emotional immediacy much as Ray Bradbury's haunting tales once brought Midwest folksiness to the future," observes *Time's* J.D. Reed. *The Left Hand of Darkness* (1969) won both Hugo and Nebula prizes (sc-fi's Pulitzers). Le Guin also won the National Book Award for her children's novel *The Farthest Shore* in 1972. Her recent books include *Always Coming Home* (1985), *Buffalo Gals and Other Animal Presences* (1987), *Catwings* (1988), *Dreams Must Explain Themselves* (1988), *The Tombs of Atwan* (children's series; 1988) and *Dancing at the Edge of the World: Thoughts on Words, Women, Places* (1989). Le Guin, who lives in Portland, Oregon with her husband (a history professor) and three children, does not consider herself a dilettante as regards to her work. She made the decision early in her life to make fiction her career. "It's like music. Are you going to play the piano in the basement, or is it for real?"

Jim Lehrer

"Our heads told us there would be some negative response," he says about the decision to turn the multi-award-winning PBS "The MacNeil-Lehrer Report" into an hour-long prime time program. "But our hearts were saying they'll all jump up and down with enthusiasm saying, 'You're neat guys. Let's go wherever you want.'" Some programmers feared the team media critic Alexander Cockburn called "the tedium twins" might be boring at a sixty-minute length ("'The MacNeil-Lehrer Report' is going to be an hour?" commented one station manager. "I thought it was already"). The much-bally-hooed "The MacNeil/Lehrer NewsHour" made its debut in September, 1983, and its even-handed combination of hard and soft news was, to many, a welcome and rare example of "news for adults."

Lehrer, who serves as associate editor and Washington anchor of TMLN, first teamed up with newsman Robert MacNeil to provide continuous "live" coverage of 1974's spellbinding Senate Watergate hearings for the National Public Afairs Center for Television. He became half of the unique, one-story-a-night "MacNeil-Lehrer Report" in 1975. Born 19 May 1934 in Wichita, Kansas, he was a 1956 grad of the University of Missouri and a veteran print reporter (Dallas *Morning News*; Dallas *Times-Herald*) before entering broadcast journalism via Dallas's KERA-TV. In addition to his nightly on-camera duties, the newsman finds time to write; his books include: *We Were Dreamers, Viva Max,* and *Kick The Can*. He and his wife, Kate, are the parents of three daughters—Jamie, Lucy, and Amanda. Recovered from a 1984 heart attack, he filmed a TV documentary on the event in 1985.

Jack Lemmon

"Happiness is discovering that your daughter is in love with an older man—J.Paul Getty. Happiness is having a doctor who smokes four packs a day. Happiness is working with Jack Lemmon." So says director Billy Wilder of one of Hollywood's hardest working, best liked and most "bankable" stars. For over three decades the actor with the jittery but jaunty air has been generating giggles in such screen comedies as *Mister Roberts* (for which he won an Oscar in 1955), *Some Like It Hot, The Apartment, The Fortune Cookie* and *The Odd Couple*. Nor has this engaging man failed to receive critical kudos for his serious dramatic roles in such films as *Days of Wine and Roses, Save the Tiger, Missing* and *Mass Appeal* (1984). "He has that very fortunate Mr. Everyman face and it's very difficult not to believe him," says director Stuart Rosenberg.

He was born John Uhler Lemmon III, 8 February 1925 at the Newton-Wellesley Hospital in Massachusettes—in the elevator. (His mother had been playing bridge and had ignored the labor pains. "I was born two months premature, with a testicle that refused to drop and acute jaundice—and the nurse quipped, 'My, look at the yellow Lemon.' At least that's what my mother told me.") He was educated at Phillips Andover and Harvard, where in his senior year he was elected president of the Hasty Pudding Club. He had his pick of Back Bay Businesses but chose the theatre and New York. Over the next five years, Lemmon did about 500 parts on television and by 1953 had a Columbia contract and the male lead in *It Should Happen to You*. After two more films, Lemmon played Ensign Pulver to Henry Fonda's *Mr. Roberts* and became a star. Lemmon's first marriage (which ended in divorce in 1956)produced one son Chris (1954). Actress Felicia ("Farfel" as he calls her) Farr became his second wife (one daughter Courtney). One of his favorite pastimes is composing and playing the piano and he always keeps one near studio sets to while away the periods between takes: "For me, a piano can make an hour and a half seem like five minutes—it's a joy—and a terrific outlet." Seen on Broadway in 1978 in *Tribute*, in 1985 he returned to the New York stage in a revival of Eugene O'Neill's *Long Day's Journey into Night*, directed by Jonathan Miller. Other films include *The China Syndrome, That's Life,* and *Dad*. He also appeared in the NBC television miniseries "The Ballad of Mary Phagan" in 1987.

Greg LeMond

He is one of the most talented athletes to ever compete in professional cycling. His rigorous training includes riding his bicycle approximately 30,000 miles per year, and his training techniques are said to be among the most advanced in the sport.

Greg was born circa 1961 in Lakewood, California, and grew up in Reno, Nevada. He developed his passion for cycling when he was a teenager and was determined to turn professional. In order to gain the experience necessary to become a pro, he moved to Europe. Shortly after his move, he won the World Championship in 1983. More victories followed. In 1985 he placed fourth in Paris-Roubaix, he came in second place in Tour De France, and finished first in Giro d'Italia, the Coors Classic and the Lac Vassiviere Stage Race. Greg was also named "Cyclist of the Year" by *Bicycling* magazine in 1985. In 1986, however, he achieved what every professional cyclist dreams of; he won the Tour De France, which is the most important event in cycling. He was the first American to win the race in its 83 years of existence. His other accomplishments for that year included coming in second place in the Milan-San Remo and Paris-Nice races, and being named the fifth place "Ultra Athlete of the Year" by *UltraSport* magazine. For the future, Greg has two goals. The first is to make cycling a major spectator sport in the United States. He states his second goal as: "I have another five or six years to be at the top of the sport. I really do feel I can win the Tour de France several more times, and once you have that in your mind, nothing really should hold you back."

Married in 1981, he and his wife Kathy have two children.

Ivan Lendl

"What do you hate being asked the most?" "Everything." This exchange between a television reporter and Ivan Lendl did much to contribute to the Czech tennis superstar's public image as a model of Garboesque remoteness ("Mr. Grim on the court, Mr. Glare in press conference," snapped sports-scribe Vic Ziegel in *New York* magazine). It also expressed the frustration Lendl felt at never winning Wimbledon. Although he has won big matches (including the 1989 Australian Open) he says, "I've won I don't know how many tournaments in my career and I would give them all away for a Wimbledon." Lendl shouldn't feel too bad. He was the first male player to surpass $13 million in career prize money and was the all-time leading prize money winner in men's tennis. He was the ATP Player of the Year in 1985, 1986 and 1987 and the Most Improved Player in 1980. His best career rank was in February 1983 and he owns the second-longest match winning streak in the Open Era, 44, set between October 1981 and January 1983. Lendl only played ten tournaments in 1988; he underwent shoulder surgery in September of that year.

Born 7 March 1960 in Ostrava, Czechoslovakia, the son of a tennis playing attorney and his wife who had once been ranked second nationally, Ivan (ee-VAHN) saw his first tennis court at the age of two when his mother brought him along to her tennis club (and tied him to a net post to keep him from wandering). At six he became a ball boy, at 13 he bested his father and a year later his mother. ("She had very good ground strokes," he recalls.) His fierce competitive spirit developed early. At eight, after losing a game of table soccer to his father, he seethed, then practiced for ten straight hours in anticipation of a rematch. He was the world's top junior player in 1978, winning at Wimbledon, at the Orange Bowl, and the Italian and French titles, and in 1979 he turned pro, winning $583,000 in prize money (third highest among men players) and being named *Tennis Magazine's* Rookie of the Year. In 1980 he teamed with Tomas Smid to win for Czechoslovakia its first ever Davis Cup. In 1981 he was the only player to beat Bjorn Borg twice. His array of court weapons, according to Herbert Warren Wind in the *New Yorker*, include a "Tildenesque" cannonball serve, ground strokes ("the foundation of his fame") that are "as hard as any player since Lew Hoad (the Australian star of the '50s) and "a whistling forehand or backhand down the line (that brings to mind that savage hitter of the '30s, Ellsworth Vines)."

Providing his fans with a view of his career, he wrote his autobiography *From My Side of the Net* (1986) with George Mendoza. Fluent in six languages,

Lendl's reading matter runs along the lines of books about the German development of the V-1 and V-2 rockets, with time out for such diversions as Rubik's Cube, which he solves in two and a half minutes. ("It requires concentration and a certain type of mind," he explains.) His other playthings, purchased with his astronomical earnings (after sending twenty percent to the Czech Tennis Federation; the rest is protected by Monte Carlo residency and Netherlands Antilles incorporation), includes six cars, a house in Connecticut, a Boca West (Flordia) condo and a $4.2 million Palm Beach estate with 18 bedrooms, 19 baths, a wine vault, a greenhouse and a tennis court seating 300. He works with the Foundation for Children with Learning Disabilities. His friends insist that he has a good sense of humor, although even he admits "the jokes are hidden pretty well." Another explains the apparent aloofness: "He comes [from an Eastern European country] to America and suddenly everything's free and easy. That's not his nature. His nature is to wonder what's going to happen bad to him next."

Jay Leno

"I would rather make fun of the corporation or whatever it is that dehumanizes people than make fun of the people themselves," says the stand-up comedian Jay Leno whose forte is using a common-sense point of view to satarize America's consumer culture. Unlike some of his contemporaries, Leno refuses to tell sexist, racial or ethnic jokes stating, "I find I get more laughs working clean." With such targets as all-night gas stations or minimarts ("This way criminals don't have to drive around all night wasting gas") or gratuitous violence in horror films ("Woman opens refrigerator and gets her head split open by an axe. Now there's a common household accident, huh?"), the burly six-foot tall Leno has been called a "natural"—a genuinely funny man who does not need gimmicks to get laughs—by his fellow comedians. Since his first appearance on the "Tonight Show" in 1977, Leno's star has been rising. He began making the rounds of talk variety shows, was a warm-up act for such entertainers as Johnny Mathis, John Denver and Tom Jones and hones his act on the road, playing everything from shopping mallls to Las Vegas casinos. When asked about being named as one of the two permanent guest hosts of the "Tonight Show," (1986) Leno replied, "I host most Mondays and a bunch of weeks a year, except for sweeps week or weeks without vowels in them or something." Despite his commitment to the "Tonight Show," Leno (who in 1986 also played a sold out engagement in Carnegie Hall, had his first hour-long comedy special and signed an exclusive multiyear contract with NBC) continues to spend much of his time on the road where he finds inspiration for many of his routines. "I love to travel the country and identify the absurd."

Born James Douglas Muir Leno on 28 April 1950 in New Rochelle, New York, Leno came by his quick wit naturally. His father, Angelo, an Italian-American insurance salesman, made jokes at sales meetings and served as master of ceremony at company banquets. Leno, an indifferent student in grade school, was known for his "boyish" pranks—flushing tennis balls down a toilet and hiding a dog in a locker. His fifth grade teacher unknowingly predicted the future when stating on his report card, "If Jay spent as much time studying as he does trying to be a comedian, he'd be a big star." While attending Emerson College in Boston, Leno often emceed campus talent shows. To help pay for school, Leno tried doing stand-up comedy at some of the local Boston night spots. His first agent booked Leno into the Boston Civic Center and then tried to convince the six-foot one-hundred-eighty-pounder to become a "funny wrestler." Over the next few years, he entertained at birthday parties, in nursing homes, and at bar mitzvahs and served at the opening act for local strip clubs. After graduating with a speech degree, he took a part-time job as a mechanic/auto delivery man for a shop that specialized in luxury cars (one of his future passions). When delivering cars to New York City, Leno took advantage of the opportunity and began making the rounds of comedy clubs, becoming friendly with Robert Klein and David Brenner. After landing a job writing for Jimmie Walker in the TV hit "Good Times," Leno helped another aspiring comic David Letterman by introducing him to Walker, who hired Letterman as a gag writer for the show. Although Leno went on to make numerous appearances on the "Tonight Show," he feels it was his frequent appearances on "Late Night with David Letterman" that brought him more national attention. Letterman, a long-time fan of Leno, says he's "the funniest comedian working today."

Married since 1980 to Mavis Nicholson, a scriptwriter, the couple enjoys seeing the country while living out of a suitcase. When not traveling, Leno and wife settle into their large home in Beverly Hills where he maintains his growing collection of "Kinetic Art"—more than a dozen motorcycles and a half-dozen vintage cars.

Sugar Ray Leonard

"I don't consider myself a fighter," said the impishly appealing former welterweight champion. "I'm a personality." His assessment was accurate. After winning Americans' hearts with his 1976 Olympic gold medal performance he was rudely awakened that it didn't lead to lucrative commercial endorsements (as it had for decathlete Bruce Jenner in the same year). So he postponed his plan to become the first college man in the family and relaced the gloves he'd promised his mother and future wife he'd put down. His first pro bout was unlike that of most beginning pugilists, however; it was a televised main event. He won a 1979 title match against Wilfredo Benitez for the welterweight crown the for 2 years blasted a path through the field of contenders with his lightning-fast hand speed and merciless combination punching. His one loss in 33 fights came at the "stone hands" of former lightweight champ Roberto Duran in 1980, but five months later in their rematch in New Orleans' Superdome, Duran said, "No mas!" ("No more!") in the eighth round and quit. Leonard was called a "pocket-sized (Muhammand) Ali" as his footwork and sense of shownmanship conjured memories of the great heavyweight. The endorsements now came, as did the TV boxing commentating, the speaking engagements, and the huge paydays. After winning a junior welterweight crown, he sought to unify his other title, welterweight champ of the World Boxing Council, by meeting WBA king Thomas (Hit Man) Hearns. The five-feet-ten Leonard was at great disadvantage against the taller Hearns who tatooed Leonard's eye almost shut by the eleventh round. Finding a hole in Hearns' defense in the thirteenth, Leonard battered his opponent's head with uppercuts and sent him through the ropes, but Hearns was saved by the bell. Knowing he was behind on points with only two rounds left, Leonard went to his corner and stared without blinking at Hearns as trainer Angelo Dundee shouted to him he needed a knockout to win. At the start of Round 14 Leonard bolted out of his corner and, having set up Hearns with a crunching left hook, rained almost two minutes of unanswered blows against him. The referee had to stop it; Leonard had done what he had to do. But after the gladiator-like showing, the eye Hearns had beaten closed finally showed it; the retina detached eight months later. After successful surgery Leonard announced his retirement from boxing. He had made over $35 million in winnings. Save for one winning return match almost a year later, Leonard became the rarest of men, a boxer who left while on top. But, as the saying goes, "you can't keep a good man down." Leonard stepped into the ring again in 1987 and won the WBC Middleweight Championship. A 1989 rematch with Hearns ended in a draw.

Born Ray Charles Leonard in Wilmington, N.C. on 17 May 1956, young Ray grew up in the community of Palmer Park, Md., near Washington, D.C. While he showed interest in gymnastics and wrestling, he also became interested in hitting the speed bags, at the Palmer Park Recreation Center. When he went to Montreal in '76 he wore a picture of his girlfriend in his boxing shoes for all to see. She'd supported their son while he devoted himself to training. When she had to go on welfare to feed Ray, Jr., the requisite paternity suit hurt Leonard's image. He hadn't denied the child was his; he just couldn't support him. Those days are far behind now as

Leonard has boasted he is his state's largest taxpayer. After buying Juanita (whom he married on her birthday in 1980) three homes in four years of married life, they've settled into a million dollar six-bedroom house in Maryland. The newest Leonard was born June, 1984—a son, Jarrell.

Richard Lester

"I used to make films in a kind of smash and grab manner, working on my nerves, trying to get a burst of exuberance or panic or hysteria going among the crew, the actors, myself, literally dragging everyone else along. That's fine when you are doing a four or six week shoot and you are thirty, but I'm over fifty now and I don't know how long I would be able to keep that up. I have had to learn to work in a more straghtforward, craftsmanlike way." So says the American-born but decidedly British-accented director who gained instant industry recognition for the sightgag-filled Beatles' flicks, *A Hard Day's Night* and *Help* back in the 1960s. He vividly turned other films like *A Funny Thing Happened on the Way to the Forum* and *The Knack* (both 1965) into magical experiences with his own knack for non sequiturs and Marx Brothers bedlam. But it is his savagely anti-war *How I Won the War* (1967) which outraged audiences by breaking down sacrosanct war myths with ridicule and shock that he is most proud of. (Others consider 1968's *Petulia* his best, albeit most underrated, film. Then came a string of misfortunes: a murdered screenwriter, poor film promotions, his own financing of a film that led to his bankruptcy, and, more importantly, mediocre movies, that made Lester not much in demand in the film industry. "And the pictures I was offered . . . were not things I felt I wanted to touch. I made commercials . . . and did very well financially" but didn't direct features from 1969 to 1973. He got back in the swing with *The Three Musketeer*, then *The Four Musketeers*, and has since been involved with the "prequel" *Butch and Sundance—The Early Days* and all three *Superman* movies. Sticking with a good idea, Lester directed the latest Musketeer adventure, *The Return of the Three Musketeers* (1989).

Born on 19 January 1932 just north of Philadelphia, Richard Lester received his clinical psych B.S. from Penn at the tender age of 18. He went to work at a local TV station and in five months became a director. ("It became clear to me that I could settle down, make a lot of money, buy a house in the suburbs, get a deep freeze, and have lots of filet mignon. But I didn't want to live like that.") So he trekked off to Europe and became a roving correspondent, a jazz pianist, and a money runner. ("You could get a few pesetas more on your money in Tangiers, so I'd load up my pockets on the Spanish side and take the boat over and unload in Tangiers.") In London he submitted a comedy script and directed TV shows including a comedy series modeled on *The Goon Show* of British radio fame, and in 1962 he made his first feature film, *It's Trad, Dad*. The father of two lives with his wife, former choreographer Deirdre Vivian Smith, and his brood near London. In 1984 he received a special award from Music TV for his early Beatles visualizations.

James Levine

"Every year my life gets better," reflects James Levine, the most powerful opera conductor in America. "It's all sort of like a dream." As principal conductor (since 1973) and de facto artistic director (officially assumed the title in 1986) of the Metropolitan Opera, Levine must do a good deal more than brilliantly wield his baton. The strikingly versatile musician is still active as a pianist—in chamber music, accompanying singers and performing concertos (particularly Bach and Mozart). He spends a portion of his summers at the Salzburg Festival in Austria and conducted the 100th anniversary production of *Parsifal* at the Beyreuth Festival. A hectic recording schedule not to mention his film debut as conductor of Franco Zeffirelli's staging of *La Traviata* tops off the maestro's demanding musical life. Some critics have attempted to burst Levine's bubble claiming that his authoritarian administrative manner and ego have superseded the Met's best interests. Irving Kolodin in *Saturday Review* ("Is James Levine Wrecking the Met?") suggested that Levine has failed to forge the company into a cohesive ensemble, has neglected, alienated or misused some of today's ablest singers, and allowed his ambitions to cloud his judgement." Retorts Levine, with unaccustomed harshness: "I'm doing my damnedest to make the Met as good as I can. Every decision I make is to try to do that and I can't help it if I'm wrong or sometimes I'm no good. That's just the way it is."

Born in Cincinnati, 23 June 1943, toddler Jimmy Levine (rhymes with devine) astounded his father (a former bandleader) when he spotted the rhythm of "Mary Had a Little Lamb" when it was idly drummed on a tabletop. Piano lessons came at four, recitals at six, and in 1953 he debuted with the Cincinnati Symphony. Studying under Walter Levin (then principal violinist of the LaSalle Quartet), Levine struggled through the rudimentary levels of music—"I realized that you had to work your way through the frustrating, boring phases of music, and that unless you got on with it, you didn't get to the treasure at the end." Levine discovered the treasure after more studies—summers at the Marlboro Music Festival in Vermont and the Aspen Festival (thirteen summers) and more schooling at Juilliard. As apprentice conductor for six years under the legendary George Szell (Cleveland Orchestra) Levine founded the University Circle Ensemble and with it began what has come to be regarded as an outstanding interpretation of the works of Gustav Mahler.

Levine lives on Central Park West in Manhattan and at a forty-one acre farm in upstate New York. Unwinding with plenty of fruit juice, diet soda and candy bars, Levine prefers studying musical scores to sleep. His relationship to his music is total—"If I am walking in the woods, I am hearing music in my head; if I am in a boat I may be going over scores in my mind. For me, music is like eating, breathing or sleeping." The musician is the recipient of the Smetana medal in 1987, among many other honors. In 1989, Levine announced his intentions to phase out of his position at the Met by 1990.

Allan Levy

On bended knees and with outstretched arms, they come to this man from all over the world for his expertise. A pioneer in Sports Medicine, Dr. Allan Levy is the active team physician for the Football Giants. In addition, he is the chief of Pascack Valley Hospital's Department of Sports Medicine plus the innovator of a program called "Safe Sports." Dr. Levy explains, "One of the biggest problems facing high school athletes is injuries, especially in football. We can do much to reduce these injuries through education and individual athletic fitness evaluations."

The "Doc" who sports a fur coat on the sidelines, was born on 28 May 1927. He grew up in Saranac Lake, New York, graduated Columbia University in 1947, then went on to graduate from Cornell University Medical School in 1951. Believing "Do what you can do," he is an advocate of an early return to sports rather than support the old fashioned view of long rest periods after injury. With the foresight to see the need for specialized physicians in the sports arenas, Dr. Levy took a gamble and left his comfortable productive internal medicine practice to concentrate on helping athletes. He was the Team physician for the Newark Bears Football Club (1964-1965), the Brooklyn Dodgers Football Club (1966), the Westchester-Long Island Bulls (1967-1970), the New York Islanders (1972), the New Jersey Nets (1967-1983 and 1987-present), and

Huey Lewis (Huey Lewis and the News)

of course, the Football Giants (1976-present). In 1986, the "Doc" was honored with a testimonial dinner attended by Governor Thomas Kean of New Jersey and packed with Sports personalities from all fields. A huge full page "thank you" was placed in *The Record* newspaper stating, "No one in this area is better known for his work with athletes young, old, professional and amateur than is Allan Levy, or Doc, as he is called by his friends. . . . Doc has always been there!" Levy is an Honorary Member of the National Athletic Trainers Association, a Member of the American College of Sports Medicine and on the Medical Committee of Garden State Games. He is the author of several articles, including "When a Pro Athlete's E C G Mimics Heart Disease" (1974), "What's Causing the Athlete's Leg Pain?" (1988), and the book *Conditioning for the High School Athlete* (1979).

Dr. Levy lives in Mahwah, New Jersey with his wife, Gail. They have three children: Deborah, Lisa and Paul. He is also the proud grandfather of Robin.

Huey Lewis (Huey Lewis and the News)

In 1978, Huey Lewis formed the News (Sean Hopper on keyboard, Chris Hayes on guitar, Johnny Colla on guitar and saxophone, Mario Cipollina on bass and Bill Gibson on drums) and made it safe for white collar workers over 25 to rock out. They rose to prominence using witty videos on MTV to showcase their "music without makeup" style with Huey as the frontman. With a voice he has described as "a cross between Phyllis Diller's and the Spinners," Huey led this San Francisco-based rock and roll band to the top creating cutting yet tuneful music. Huey feels; "Just because a band's stance is politically valid and they're sincere about what they're saying, doesn't mean that they have to sing out of tune. I don't insist on my music being unlistenable for its validity." Fans and critics agree, rewarding the group with hit singles and albums as well as a Grammy, several American Music Awards and BAMMIES galore.

Huey Lewis was born Hugh Anthony Cregg III on 5 July 1951 in New York City. His family moved to Marin City (County), California, one of the few white families in a predominantly black neighborhood. His mother, Magda was an artist who joined the 1950's beat movement and introduced Huey to her friends poet Alan Ginsberg and jazz great Dizzy Gillespie. She introduced him musically to the Grateful Dead and Bob Dylan, while his father, Hugh Jr, a former jazz drummer in Les Brown's band turned radiologist, played Dixieland jazz, swing and Benny Goodman. Huey rebelled by listening to Otis Redding, James Brown, Wilson Pickett and Sam Cooke. At age 12 his parents divorced and Huey elected to go away to the Lawrenceville School, a prep school in Princeton, New Jersey, where he hung out with the greasers. His aptitude for math led him to 18 months of engineering classes at Cornell University, but only after he spent a year travelling throughout Europe and North Africa at his father's insistence. Backpacking across Europe, he earned money by playing harmonica in London's tube (subway) stations and at odd jobs. A paying harmonica gig in Seville, Spain convinced him rock and roll and *not* engineering was his future. He formed several cover groups in college and eventually joined the San Francisco group, Clover (with future Newsman Sean Hopper). They produced two unsuccessful albums in 1977 and disbanded. Soon after, Huey formed the News from several bar bands who played at Uncle Charlie's bar and the group signed with Chrysalis Records three months later. Their first album, *Huey Lewis and The News* (1980), was a promising but unsuccessful debut initially selling only 30,000 copies. The followup *Picture This* (1982) earned them a Grammy nomination and yielded their first hit "Do You Believe in Love." It reached #7, taking the gold album to #13 on Billboard. Two more hits including "Workin for a Livin" came off the album. It was *Sports* (1983) that made them a household name. The #1 album sold 9 million copies and yielded five hit singles including "Heart and Soul," "I Want a New Drug," and "Heart of Rock and Roll." The group wrote and recorded two songs for the film *Back to the Future* with "Power of Love"

CELEBRITY REGISTER 1990

earning them an Academy Award nomination. Huey even had a cameo in the film as a nerdy teacher. Under pressure to follow up *Sports*, they scored with *Fore* (1986) which sold over 6 million copies with four hit singles including "Hip to Be Square" and "Jacob's Ladder." The News' 1988 album *Small World* was a musical departure, expanding upon their signature sound with cross currents of jazz and reggae plus guest performances by Stan Getz and Bruce Hornsby.

Lewis married the former Sidney Conroy in 1983. They have a daughter Kelly and a son Austin and reside in Mill Valley, California. A world tour followed the latest album. "We love to play live. It's how we began and what keeps it fresh for us," Lewis states.

Jerry Lewis

Don't look for Jerry Lewis at the poolside of his palatial mansion. Philosopher, clown and movie tycoon, Jerry believes that guys who sit by the pool long enough, wake up one morning to find it isn't there. A comedian who can make you laugh or cry. Lewis is "the Pied Piper of the business" according to Leo McCrary, "the heir to the mantle of Charlie Chaplin and Harold Lloyd." Born Joseph Levich, 16 March 1926 in Newark, N.J., he busted into showbiz as a teenager with a record act on the Borscht circuit and, joining singer Dean Martin in Atlantic City in 1946, was half of the hottest entertainment act in the country by the time he was 20. His ten year stint with Martin ended with their spectacular split in 1956. Regarding his film career, Lewis not only starred in such international hits as *The Geisha Boy*, *The Bellhop*, *Cinderfella* and *The Nutty Professor*, but in many instances also served as director, producer and co-author. He later made his dramatic debut with Robert DeNiro in *The King of Comedy*.

Lewis as a child was wracked by feelings of abandonment. "I'm nobody," he complained as a lowly urchin, when his showbiz parents left him with his grandmother. Married and divorced to singer Patti Palmer, Lewis has six sons. After his second marriage to Sandee Pitnick in 1983 he moved to Paris. The couple were expecting to have a child together in 1989. Anyone bumping into him might notice that under his vicuna coat he wears a tiny red strip of ribbon on his collar. "That signifies that I have the Legion of Merit," Lewis says beaming. He was awarded the medal by President Francois Mitterrand of France where Lewis is a hero because of his films. "Look at the company I'm in. There's a guy named Pasteur and there's Albert Schweitzer, John F. Kennedy, Emile Zola, General Pershing and Alfred Hitchcock. Not bad, huh?"

He was nominated for the Nobel Peace Prize in 1978 for his work on behalf of a number of charitable causes, most notably his telethons which have raised upwards of $200 million for the Muscular Dystrophy Association. Lewis underwent open heart surgery in 1983 and since then has been working out and watching his cholesterol. "Listen, when you have your chest opened with a Black and Decker chain saw, you begin to think. My scar runs from my throat all the way down to Hoboken."

Richard Lewis

Affectionately referred to as the comedian from hell with bad posture, Richard Lewis is regarded by his peers as a true "comic's comic." He claims that he could have marketed a signature line of bad-posture clothing had he not spent almost a quarter-million dollars to date on therapy. His neurosis, however, has become a part of our language ("I had a date from Hell") and his warped sense of humor is very much in demand. It is so in demand that he appears on *GQ*'s list of the 20th Century's Most Influential Humorists.

Lewis was "born and lowered," as he refers to it, in New Jersey on 29

June. His first attempt at a career was in advertising in New Jersey. Not satisfied, he created a stand-up routine and began performing at the Improvisation in New York, which marked the beginning of his successful career as a comic. Since then, his credits include more than 40 appearances on "The David Letterman Show," featured performances on HBO's "Salute to The Improv," "Comic Relief I & III," "No Life To Live," the concert special "Richard Lewis: I'm Exhausted," the Showtime special "I'm In Pain," the cult film *Diary of a Young Comic* (which Lewis also co-wrote), a co-starring role on the ABC-TV series "Harry," and a co-starring role with Jamie Lee Curtis on ABC-TV's series "Anything But Love." In addition to television performances, he has co-headlined at Caesars Palace in Las Vegas and The Sands in Atlantic City.

Although Lewis remains single, he states: "I think by the turn of the century I will make a good husband. I just pray that I don't wind up having to marry myself in drag and sell the screen rights to De Palma. I'll call it 'Myself, My Bride.'"

Shari Lewis

Described by *Boston Globe* critic Carol Stocker as ". . . a five-foot monument to positive thinking," and as a "diminutive fireball of a performer whose talents have universal appeal" by another reviewer, Shari Lewis possesses a combination of exceptional talent, versatility and imagination. Her many talents include: actress, dancer, musician, ventriloquist, puppeteer, author and symphony conductor.

Shari was born 17 January 1934 in New York City into a family where her father was a magician and always had magicians and ventriloquists around the house. One day Shari's father heard her sister screaming to be let out of a closet. When he opened the door, the closet was empty! To his surprise, Shari had thrown her voice into the closet and made it appear as though her sister was inside. Her father was so impressed with this that he gave her some books on ventriloquism, along with an old dummy (named Buttercup). Her father said, "If Mary has a little lamb, why shouldn't Shari have a little lamb?" The rest is history. She began studying music at a young age and attended Music and Art High School. Later she studied acting with Sanford Meisner and also worked with Lee Strasberg. Her first television appearance was on the "Captain Kangaroo Show," where Lamb Chop made her debut. They were so well received that NBC gave Shari her own Sunday morning show in New York City called "The Shari Lewis Show." A year later, the show was on six days a week, and the following year it went national. In the years that followed, Shari and Lamb Chop had a weekly TV series on the BBC in London (1969-1973) and a weekly show in Great Britain (1970). She wrote, produced and starred in the NBC special "A Picture of Us" (1971). Starting in 1977, she conducted and performed in over 100 orchestras. Shari has also given three Command Performances for the Queen of England (1970, 1973, 1978). Television appearances include hour-long specials on the Disney Channel, "The Shari Show" on the Nickelodeon Channel, and "Shari's Christmas Concert" which was aired Christmas 1988 and 1989. She has written several books, some of which include: *One Minute Bedtime Stories* (1986), *101 Things for Kids to Do* (1987), and *101 Magic Tricks for Kids to Do* (1986). Some of her videos are: *One Minute Bedtime Stories, Kooky Classics, 101 Things for Kids to Do, Shari's Christmas Concert* (1988), and *Lamb Chop's Sing-Along, Play-Along* (1988).

Among Shari's numerous awards are five Emmys, a Peabody Award, a Monte Carlo TV Award for the World's Best Variety Show (1961), the Kennedy Center Award for Excellence and Creativity in the Arts (1983), the Girl Scout Grace Award, The Video Choice Award for *101 Things for Kids to Do* (1988), and the American Video Conference Award for *Lamb Chop's Sing-Along, Play-Along* (1988). She was selected to *V* Magazine's "Video Hall of Fame," and she was selected as one of the Ten Most Influential Women in America.

Shari and her publisher husband Jeremy Tarcher (married 15 March 1958) live in Beverly Hills. They have one daughter, Mallory.

Roy Lichtenstein

"It's true that when I looked at what I was doing, it offended my own sense of taste. I mean, I realize that taste develops as you work. . . . And so I kept doing these paintings, I couldn't work in any other way . . . they stood around my studio, and they were just too insistent. Actually, I didn't think anyone would be interested in them and I didn't really care. That part wasn't important. What was important was that I was doing them." Though one art critic called Roy Lichtenstein "the worst artist in the country," people were and remained interested in his work (his pieces command six figures) and he continues as (according to a more appreciative critic) "Pop art's most classic and enduring exponent." The Whitney Museum's 1984 blockbuster show, "BLAM! The Explosion of Pop, Minimalism, and Performance, 1958-64," took its attention-getting title from Lichtenstein's 1962 painting of a fighter plane shot down in battle which he titled "Blam."

Says Manhattan born Lichtenstein (27 October 1923), "As a child, I had no idea what I wanted to do." "But from age fifteen he studied art and did drawings. His formal art education took place at Ohio State University where he received his bachelor's degree and, after a stint in the Army during World War II, his master's. Lichtenstein spent the following seventeen years, teaching at various colleges in the east. It was in 1960 while teaching at Rutgers University that he met Allan Kaprow, Robert Watts, and Claes Oldenburg and found himself "in an entirely new and exciting creative outlook." Best known for the brash, provocative comic strip paintings (which he began in the 1960s) that established his reputation, Lichtenstein has also explored, through his paintings, drawings, prints and sculpture, such modern art movements as Cubism, Purism, Art Deco, Surrealism, German Expressionism and Futurism and come up with a number of ways to examine critically the values embodied in these styles. Though still controversial, his mock cartoons with crashing colors are looked upon by more and more critics and collectors as the perfect vehicle for capturing the essence of this larger-than-life era in Western cultural history. In 1986 his book *Landscape Sketches 1984-1985* was released displaying Lichtenstein's works. His art to date has developed in many directions and it is difficult to tell what will come next, but as one critic put it, "whatever its tendencies, the look of his work is uniquely his own." Roy Lichtenstein and his wife Dorothy live year round in Southampton, Long Island (he has two sons by a former marriage).

Anne Morrow Lindbergh

"I've always been interested in looking for meanings in life." This gentle, sensitive poet (*The Unicorn & Other Poems*, 1956) has, in her lifetime, flown to great adventure, romance and literary success. "I believe," Anne Morrow Lindbergh once wrote, "that what woman resents is not so much giving herself in pieces as giving herself purposelessly."

Born in Englewood, New Jersey in 1906, she was the daughter of Dwight Morrow, who was U.S. Ambassador to Mexico when the shy, handsome flying hero Charles Lindbergh visited there on a goodwill tour in 1929, shortly after his historic solo transatlantic flight. Despite her dislike of "that odious name," Lindy, she fell in love with him. "All my life," she confided to her diary, "in fact my world—my little embroidered beribboned world—is smashed." The horrible, fantastic, absurd publicity" which surrounded their courtship, engagement and subsequent marriage drove her to seek privacy in the sky, where, under her husband's "wings," she soon qualified for a pilot's license. Says Anne,"You had the freedom to escape from the earth, but in a sense you were always in touch with it." The tragic kidnapping and murder of the Lindberghs' first son in 1932 sent them into the skies again, and subsequent shared aviation adventures led to her writing of such books as *North to the Orient* (1935) and *Listen! the Wind* (1938). "What a commentary on our civilzation," she wrote in a later book, *Gift from the Sea*, in 1955, "when being alone is considered suspect; when one has to apologize for it, hide the fact that one practices it—like a secret vice."

Now a mother of five (Jon, Land, Anne, Scott, Reeve), she has also published *Dearly Beloved* (1962), *Bring Me a Unicorn* (1972), a volume of her earliest diaries and letters, continuing in 1973 with *Hour of Gold, Hour of Lead*. She was the focus of a 1984 segment of the TV series *Smithsonian World* titled "Crossing the Distance."

Recent books include *The Worry Week* (1985), *The Shadow on the Dial* (1987), *Nobody's Orphan* (1987), and *The Prisoner of Pineapple Place* (1988).

Hal Linden

He was the inimitable Barney Miller for 170 episodes in the late 1970s until he finally closed the door of the 12th Precinct of which he was the lovable captain for eight television seasons. Before that, he was awarded the Tony for best musical actor in 1970 as Mayer in *The Rothschilds*. ("This is for you, too." he shouted to the Palace Theatre balcony. "All you veterans of the Saturday morning understudy rehearsals. I'm a sticker. Don't give up.") Up until his big splash, Linden had indeed been the King of the Stickers. He had understudied more luminaries (Keith Andes, Louis Jourdan, Arthur Hill, Sydney Chaplin) than Shubert Alley has closed doors for young hopefuls.

Born 20 March 1931 into a traditionally Jewish family, he left P.S. 98 to attend the High School of Music and Art and later Queens College. After the Korean war (where he had been a member of the U.S. Army Band and also been involved in revues) he realized he had found his metier—acting. Following his discharge, Linden enrolled at New York's American Theatre wing and for six years he worked until he got his big break in 1958 in *Bells are Ringing*. Following *Bells: On a Clear Day, Wildcat, Something More, I'm Not Rappaport, Man of LaMancha*, etc. He was also the host of "FYI," ABC's Emmy award-winning public sevice program. On the big screen, he starred with Ann-Margret and Alan Alda in 1987's *A New Life*.

Married to Frances Martin (four children), the Lindens live in Los Angeles. Of his marriage he says: "Living with anyone for 25 years is hard and I'm not being facetious. I don't think that man was *meant* to live with a woman for that many years." Despite the candid testimony, Hal is proud of the way the relationship has weathered the vicissitudes of married life compounded by the added pressures of a show business career.

John V. Lindsay

This former two-term mayor of New York City still attracts more than his share of the limelight, and says, "I continue to run into people from all walks of life who say that (my mayoralty) was the time the city was exciting and together and somehow cities were being noticed for the first time. I have a sense that they think of me more and more as a statesman, and that's a very good feeling," Lindsay's good vibes were often disrupted, however, by latter-day Mayor Ed Koch. "John Lindsay mortgaged the city's future," Koch pouted, and added that while Abe Beame (Lindsay's immediate successor) was also to blame for New York's near-bankruptcy (a decidedly minority view) in the mid-1970s, Lindsay was considered more accountable because "there's a certain arrogance there—he didn't want to accept responsibility." Lindsay countered that Koch's accusations were cop-outs for his own failings in not reducing crime, fixing the subways, cleaning up the city, or keeping the city from becoming polarized. Aside from such occasional unwanted publicity as the Koch allegations and his son's conviction of selling less than a gram of cocaine, the highly photogenic, six-feet-three international lawyer warrants newsprint as an arts administrator and trade promoter. In 1984 he was named chairman and would-be savior of Lincoln Center's six-year-darkened Vivian Beaumont Theater based on his long-time dedication to theatre and arts development. "Lincoln Center does not need another Broadway theatre of booking operation," he said at the outset. "It needs a company with a character . . . of its own." Holding this position for over five years, Lindsay still reigns as the Chairman of the Lincoln Centre Theater.

John Vliet Lindsay was born in New York City, 24 November 1921, and was called to public office at 34, as executive assistant to U.S. Attorney General Herbert Brownell. In three terms as Republican congressman from the posh 17th "Silk Stocking" congressional district, Lindsay was considered a liberal who promoted immigration reform, public housing, and civil rights legislation. The Mayor became a familiar figure in Harlem and was credited with keeping the city "cool" through the long, hot summers of 1966 and 1967, when riots rocked major cities from nearby Newark to Los Angeles.

Many observers said Lindsay began running for president when he became New York mayor so his 1972 candidacy for Democratic (his new party) nominee came as no surprise. In 1973, after eight wearying years in the City Hall hot seat, he chose not to seek reelection, although he ran unsuccessfully in 1980 for the U.S. Senate after anemic campaign coffers and a bicycle injury to his shoulder limited his campaigning effectiveness. The Yale Law grad and Navy man demonstrated his love for the arts by his congressional legislation creating the National Endowment for the Arts, and mayoral birthing of New York City's Cultural Affairs Department. Often appearing on TV news shows, and to a lesser extent at banquets, he sings, dances and tells jokes (often on himself), and has even been in a Broadway musical, *Seesaw*, and a movie. He and wife Mary live in an Upper West Side apartment.

Art Linkletter

"I cannot sing or dance and I was never much of an actor," says this frequently off-the-cuff link between the common man and microphones. "My art", asserts Art, "is getting other people to perform. If I had talent I'd probably be unbearable." Born Arthur Gordon Kelley, 17 July 1912 in Moose Jaw, Saskatchewan, he was deserted by his own parents as an infant and adopted by a family named Linkletter, the patriarch of which was a one-legged itinerant evangelical preacher who held side-walk meetings at which young Art clanged the triangle. Parlaying "a microphone, a natural curiosity, and a gush of words," into a radio career, starting in San Diego in 1934, he made a national name for himself on both radio and TV with such hardy audience participation perennials as "People Are Funny," "House Party" (Emmy Award-winner), and "Life with Linkletter." He has also written a number of books (*Kids Say the Darndest Things*—one of the top 15 best sellers in

American publishing history, it was #1 for two straight years in the non-fiction list; his latest *Old Age Is Not for Sissies: Choices For Senior Americans*) and is involved in multitudinous business interests ranging from Peruvian copper mines to a sheep ranch in Australia, not to mention a few oil wells. "Some of them," he says modestly, "wouldn't give enough to oil my lawn mower." His chief interest today is his work in the crusade against drug abuse. He writes, speaks and broadcasts from coast to coast in the fight against the drug epidemic threatening our nation. (Daughter Diane committed suicide in 1969 after a bad LSD trip.)

He married the former Lois Foerster in 1935; his eldest son, Jack, has been following along in dad's ad-libs on various TV game shows since he was 20. He also has a son, Robert, and two daughters, Dawn and Sharon. A caustic *Time* critic once described Linkletter as "a toothy paragon of commercial insincerity," but most associates seem to feel the genial MC really believes in what he's doing, both off-screen and on. His autobiography, in any case, is entitled *Confessions of a Happy Man*.

John Lithgow

With almost twenty years of professional acting experience under his belt, John Lithgow's talents are of great stature and diversity. He demonstrates his tremendous depth and range as an actor through such diverse roles as Roberta Muldoon in *The World According to Garp* (Academy Award nomination), his Tony Award-Winning performance in *The Changing Room*, the psychopathic murder in *Blow Out*, and a panic stricken airline passenger in a segment of "Twilight Zone."

Born in Rochester, New York, he was destined to be in theatre. His father, Arthur, was one-time head of Princeton's McCarthur Theatre. When Lithgow was an infant, the family moved to Ohio where his father began running Shakespeare Festivals throughout the state. It was in one of his father's productions that Lithgow made his stage debut. He appeared in *Henry VI, Part 3* when he was only six years old. Later, upon receiving a Fulbright scholarship, Lithgow traveled to England to study at the London Academy of Music and Dramatic Art. While in England, he interned with the Royal Shakespeare Company and The Royal Court Theatre. After finishing his internship, he returned to the U.S. and moved to New York to pursue a career on Broadway. Some of his stage performances include: *My Fat Friend, Comedians, A Memory of Two Mondays, Secret Service, Anna Christie, Once in a Lifetime, Spokesong, Division Street, Beyond Therapy, Kaufman at Large, The Front Page* and *M. Butterfly*. His performance in the latter show not only burned up the boards but brought superlative reviews. Frank Rich of the *Times* proclaimed that in *M. Butterfly* Lithgow "projects intelligence and wit, and his unflagging energy drives and helps unify the evening." Clive Barnes, in the *Post*, cites the star's exquisite sketching of his character's "tortured bafflement and wimpish determination" and concludes, "Lithgow has never been better." His off-Broadway appearances include the New York Shakespeare Festival production of *Hamlet, Trelawny of the Wells*, and *Salt Lake City Skyline*. In addition to numerous stage credits, Lithgow has also appeared in several films. He received an Academy Award nomination for Best Supporting Actor for *Terms of Endearment* and held leading roles in *Footloose, Buckaroo Bonzai, 2001, All That Jazz, Obsession, Rich Kids*, and the critically acclaimed *The Manhattan Project*. Although he has been devoting most of his time to theatre and films, Lithgow has found time for television. Some of his roles include: the part of John Waters in an episode of "Amazing Stories" (for which he won an Emmy), "The Oldest Living Graduate," "Big Blond," and the television movie "The Day After" (nominated for an Emmy).

Lithgow resides in Los Angeles with his wife Mary, their daughter Phoebe, and their son Nathan George. He also has a fifteen-year-old son, Ian, from a previous marriage.

Rich Little

"I think the voices I do best are the people I admire the most," Rich Little, man of 1,000 voices, has said. Yet Little is perhaps best known for seeing the nation through the sticky Watergate era with his dog-faced, peace-signing harpoonery of Richard Nixon, making "one thing perfectly clear."

Richard Caruthers Little was born 26 November 1938 in Ottawa, Ontario to a wealthy Canadian family. After gaining confidence from impromptu schoolyard performances and dinner shows for local civic groups, Little's developing skill for banter landed him a disc jockey job in Ontario in 1957. His impressions became a popular nightclub act and a 1963 album, *My Fellow Canadians*, made record sales history. That same year, Judy Garland imported him as a featured guest on her variety show, and spots on other leading programs followed. He became a regular on a short-lived 1966 series, "Love on a Rooftop," leading to frequent appearances on the "Tonight Show" and finally his own variety program, "The Rich Little Show" on NBC in 1975.

Little, whose uncannily accurate impressions are often five years in preparation, makes three-dimensional cartoons of his subjects, with vocal mimicry so exact he has dubbed dialogue for both Peter Sellers and David Niven when they became too ill to complete films. "You don't have to be letter-perfect. In fact, the best impressions depend on exaggeration," he says, admitting that the essence of some personalities he would like to imitate still eludes him. Always on alert for new material, Little manages to perform for the political scene as he sizes up his next imitatable candidate. In April 1989, he was Master of Ceremonies at the Association of White House News Photographers annual dinner honoring the President and his wife.

Little married Jeanne Worden in 1971, and they have one daughter.

Little Richard

The most flamboyant of rock 'n' roll's founding fathers, he's now an evangelistic preacher who calls the music he spawned satanic. But it was also highly profitable . . . mostly for others. He filed a $115 million lawsuit to recover some of the money he said three record companies (not to mention the Beatles, Elvis, Mick Jagger and others) made from his music while he received almost no royalties. Little Richard was actually the first crossover artist, although his sound was called "race music" in the 1950s and later "ryhthm and blues." Already a blatantly outrageous homosexual when he first shouted, "A Wop Bop Alu Bop A Wop Bam Boom!" in his 1955 hit, "Tutti-Frutti," his eyelashes, mascara, and marcelled six-inch high pompadour made him a non-threatening, acceptable black male. "But when my band members would get near white girls," he recalls, "other whites would say, 'Alright now, watch out, boys.'"

Little Richard was born Richard Penniman in 1932. Growing up in Macon, Ga., he was not yet "The Handsomest Man in Rock 'n' Roll," he says. "I had this great big head and little body, and I had one big eye and one little eye." His shorter right leg made him walk with a twist that kids misconstrued as effeminacy. Gradually he modelled himself after his mother, whom he adored, and he applied to himself her powder and rose water. "I always felt like a girl," he says. Although he wanted to be a preacher, and sang with his family in contests and churches, early trouble as a teen prompted him to join Dr. Hudson's Medicine Show where his singing helped the not-so-good doctor sell snake oil. He later spent weekends singing in Atlanta theatres preceding top billers like B.B. King. After signing a rigged contract (as most black artists then had to), he sold the rights to "Tutti-Frutti" for fifty dollars. "We knew then, to make money, we had to go on the road, and it had to be the best show in the U.S." (It turned out to be exciting enough; during a show in Baltimore, dozens of young women flung their panties onto the stage.) Typical of his former life was his involvement with a beautiful, buxom groupie who travelled with the band and was available to "please" him and friends. While he loved Angel, he said in his autobiography, *The Life and Times of Little Richard, The Quasar of Rock*, she was used as a magnet for a "lot of handsome guys" Richard wanted. In the midst of making hits like "Long Tall Sally," "Good Golly, Miss Molly," and "Slipping and Slidin'" he says he let people shoot dope into his veins, and he later became a cocaine addict. "My nose was big enough to suck up diesel trucks," he says. When his brother Tony died of a heart attack, Penniman decided that events pointed clearly for him to stop just reading the Bible, but to heed its injunction about repenting. His conversion in the late 1970s wasn't the last his fans heard from him, however. In addition to recordings (*Lifetime Friend;* 1986), Richard appeared in the films *Down & Out in Beverly Hills* (1985) and *Purple People Eater* (1988). He also had a role in NBC-TV's "The Goddess of Love" (1988). In 1986 he converted to Judaism. Little Richard travels, sings gospel, preaches, and tells young folks, "The grass may look greener on the other side, but it's just as hard to cut."

Andrew Lloyd Webber

Andrew Lloyd Webber is as serious about his composing as he is prolific. When *Jesus Christ Superstar* became a "cult item," he was as much annoyed as he was gratified. "With all those ludicrous pro and con reactions people had, it's taken a long time for some to realize I'm serious about composing."

Andrew Lloyd Webber was born 22 March 1948 into a musical clan. His father William is a composer and the director of the London College of Music. His mother Jean is a piano teacher and his brother John is an accomplished celist. He was raised to believe that "music was just music and that the only division was between good music or bad music." His fascination with musical theatre began when, at age 8, he staged productions of American shows in a toy theatre in his home. His "absolute idol" was Richard Rodgers. At age 9 he published a suite of his own composition. He spent a year at Oxford University's Magdalen College before transferring to the Royal Academy of Music. Then working with Tim Rice as lyricist, Lloyd Webber wrote *Joseph and the Amazing Technicolor Dreamcoat*, first produced in England in 1968. They followed *Joseph* with the controversial rock opera, *Jesus Christ Superstar* in 1970, which chimed right into the melding of Christian revivalism and the American hippie movement to become a huge success. By the end of the 1970s its revenues—including recordings, concerts, stage productions and a motion picture—were in excess of $150 million. In 1976, the duo unleashed the successful musical about Argentina's legendary first lady, *Evita*, and in 1981, *Cats*, a musical set to T.S. Eliot's book of children's verse. *Old Possum's Book of Practical Cats*, opened in London and later New York. The composer also created the music for the award-winning *Tell Me on Sunday* and the gold album, *Variations*. In 1974 he composed the music for *Jeeves* based upon the P.G. Wodehouse character with lyrics by Alan Ayckbourn.

Lloyd Webber married Sarah Tudor Hughill in 1971. They have two children, a son Nicholas and a daughter Imogen. He married Sarah Brightman in 1984, three hours before his new musical *Starlight Express* opened in London. His *Requiem* premiered in New York City's St. Thomas' Church in 1985, and later that year, the musical *Song and Dance*, opened on Broadway with Bernadette Peters in the lead role. His monopoly on Broadway increased when *Starlight Express* opened at the Gershwin Theatre in 1987, followed by the box-office phenomenon *The Phantom of the Opera* in 1988. Not only did *Phantom* win the Tony Award for Best Musical, but the show's merchandise (T-shirts, sweatshirts, masks, watches, towels, etc. . .) has helped support Broadway's resumed popularity. Andrew's musical *Aspects of Love* premiered in London in 1989 with future plans for a 1990 New York City production. The story is based on a novel by David Garnett, which focuses on the sexual and romantic intertwinings of four principal characters.

Kenny Loggins

Since attaining stardom as a member of Loggins and Messina, Kenny Loggins' career has been one of artistic and commercial success. The singer/songwriter's music has yielded hits for Kenny and other superstars while earning him accolades and awards.

Kenny Loggins was born 7 January 1948 in Everett, Washington. He moved to Los Angeles when he was very young. The city's local club circuit provided a place for him to hone his skills as an artist and writer. While playing with a late incarnation of the Electric Prunes, he was hired as a staff writer by ABC/Wingate Publishing earning $100 a week. In 1970, Kenny met Jim Messina who was highly impressed by several Loggins tunes recorded by the Nitty Gritty Dirt Band. Later that year, the two formed a band which would create two platinum and five gold albums over the ensuing six years. Their classic hits included "Danny's Song," "House at Pooh Corner." "Love Song," and "Your Momma Don't Dance". The duo disbanded in 1976 to pursue solo careers, and Loggins soon established himself as a solo star. His first three albums, *Celebrate Me Home, Nightwatch* and *Keep the Fire* were certified platinum. He scored with hit singles including "Celebrate Me Home," "Whenever I Call You 'Friend,'" "This Is It," and "Forever." Other releases included a live double album *Alive*, which captured his exciting stage personality and performance, and the self produced *Vox Humana* (1985), which went gold. The film industry recognized Loggins' talent, and he soon found a second career contributing to movie soundtracks. It started in 1980 when he hit with "I'm Alright" from the film *Caddyshack*. This was followed in 1984 by the #1 title track from *Footloose*, which also earned him an Academy Award nomination in 1985. Other movie hits were the #2 song "Danger Zone" from *Top Gun*, the Top 5 "Meet Me Halfway" from *Over the Top* and "Nobody's Fool" from *Caddyshack II*. The last two songs were featured on his first solo album in three years *Back To Avalon* (1988). Loggins can also be heard on "Double or Nothing" with Gladys Knight on the *Rocky IV* soundtrack. After conquering radio and film Loggins headed for Broadway. He headlined *Kenny Loggins on Broadway*, live concerts on the "Back to Avalon" tour at the Neil Simon Theater in early November 1988. It showcased his music and afforded his fans an intimacy never achieved in coliseums, as he chatted with them, telling jokes and taking requests. Throughout Loggins' career, his efforts have been rewarded with a multitude of awards including two Grammys (1980 Song of The Year for "What A Fool Believes" and 1981 Best Pop Vocal for "This Is It") and Japan's 1984 International Artists Award. Other career highlights include his participation in the "We Are the World" recording session and his performance at "the end of the line" in Long Beach, California for the 1986 charity Hands Across America. He takes his social responsibilities as an artist seriously. "Being able to influence issues like world hunger, or raise money for causes I believe in, is the main benefit of being successful."

Despite all his remarkable success, Kenny Loggins is still basically a songwriter. "I've started to redefine my borders and see that I can't be the workaholic I used to be," he notes with a smile. He continues to craft some of today's best songs from the Santa Barbara, California home he shares with his wife and children.

Nancy Lopez

The lady of the links whose extraordinary rookie year catapulted women's golf to greater national prominence says golf is "why God put me on the earth. . . . I feel like I'm making people believe in a lot of things. I'm not a Jesus person. I don't preach to anybody, but I believe there's a lot of power in the Lord." While she doesn't attend church regularly, the young Mexican-American's faith may have aided her in becoming the sport's all-time rookie money winner—male or female. Since that phenomenal 1978 season she's had her share of trials but has managed to remain one of the tours' best-liked competitors.

Nancy Marie Lopez, born in Torrance, Calif. on 6 January 1957, developed her amazing 240-yard drive (one of women's golf's longest) from a first lesson at age seven from her father when he told her, "Just put the ball on the ground and . . . hit it into the hole down there." Growing up in Roswell, N.M., where her father owned an auto body shop, little Nancy found strong familial support in her efforts to better her game. She was exempt from housework and dishes because her hands had loftier duties. She became so good at the game her parents had played on public courses that she led the Goddard High *boys'* team to the state championship. "Mama, she got to wear braces," Mr. Lopez told his wife, because "our Nancy's gonna be a public figure." The family put off a new house and washing machine to pay for the dental work and to send the future celebrity to far-off tourneys. In 1975 the two-time national junior girls' champ went to the University of Tulsa and turned pro after her sophomore season in which she won the women's pro tournament in memory of her mother, who'd just died after an operation. She won five straight tourneys in 1978, nine in all that year, and a record $189,813 in winnings.

Calling herself a "sucker for good looks" and revealing that it had become a goal to capture him, she married a Pennsylvania TV sportscaster, Tim Melton, in 1979. Later she said, "I think that . . . I wanted my marriage to be so good that I stopped being Nancy Lopes," and the two parted in 1982. But while she trimmed down from 170 pounds to 135, the five-feet-four, dark-eyed Lopez soon added another love to her life, N.Y. Mets' third baseman Ray Knight. They were married in 1983, and have two children (Ashley Knight and Arinn Shea).

In 1987 Lopez was inducted into the Ladies Pro Golf Association's Hall of Fame. The all-around athlete tries not to be sterotyped as a sexy lady golfer. She says, "Playing good golf is more important than being a beauty queen out there. I want to be feminine, but having friends and the gallery rooting for me because I'm me and not just beautiful is what counts."

Shirley Lord

Writer Shirley Lord, Director of Beauty at *Vogue* for the past ten years, places her third novel *Faces* (1989) in the world she knows intimately, "the world of fashion magazines, modeling—and plastic surgery." When Teri, a former supermodel, is told by her philandering husband that he is going to trade her in "for a younger model," she secretly checks into The Fountain, a clinic just outside L.A., in a desperate attempt to save both her marriage and her career. What happens to Teri at this non-accredited but highly touted "rejuvenation" clinic sets the terrifying plot of *Faces* into motion. When Teri's daughters, Jo and Alexa, become involved in the strange proceedings and the unravelling of what happened to their mother and why, Shirley Lord's novel becomes a gripping "page-turner."

Born in London 28 August, Shirley Lord, the "cockney sparrow with Bow Bells in her ears," first "put her foot in the door" at the *Daily Mail* as a typist in the typing pool and strode on to become one of the best know and most successful journalists in England. Beginning at age 17 as a reporter on London's *Street of Ink* and *Fleet Street*, Ms. Lord rose to fiction editor of England's largest women's magazine, and then, in turn, women's editor of all three London evening newspapers, first the *Star*, then the evening *Standard*, and finally the evening *News*. After coming to America in 1971, Ms. Lord became Beauty Editor of *Harper's Bazaar* and later moved over to Helena Rubenstein where she zoomed to corporate vice president. In 1980 she went to *Vogue* as Director of Special Projects, Beauty and Fitness.

The author of three non-fiction books—*Beer at Claridges*, *The Easy Way to Good Looks*, and *You Are Beautiful and How to Prove It*—she turned to fiction in 1982 with her first novel *Golden Hill*, which became a tremendous success. Her second novel, *One Of My Very Best Friends*, was published in the fall of 1985, and became a Literary Guild selection.

Shirley has been married four times, first to James Hussey by whom she had a son Mark, then to millionaire textile magnate Cyril Lord (another son, Richard), third to David Anderson, who died in 1983, and she is presently married to A.M. Rosenthal.

Sophia Loren

"To have perfect beauty is not so special. To have a special look, one must have irregularities, otherwise you look like everyone else," says Italian superstar and author (*In the Kitchen with Love; Sophia: Living & Loving; women & Beauty*) Sophia Loren. The high cheekbones, generous mouth and voluptuous figure have made her into a worldwide legend. Says Sophia: "My nose is too long, my chin too short, my hips too broad. But together, all these irregularities seem to work. On second thought, I rather like the way I look." Her autobiography, *Sophia: Living & Loving* (1979), was made into a TV movie a year later—with Sophia in an unusual dual role playing her mother and herself (ages 20-40). In 1981, she teamed up with the Coty Cosmetics Company and launched a new fragrance line named especially for her—"Sophia."

Born out of wedlock in a Rome charity hospital as Sofia (Villani) Scicolone, 20 September 1934, she was reared by her grandparents amidst the poverty of wartime Italy in Pozzuoli, on the Bay of Naples. After winning second place in a beauty contest at the age of 15, she headed with her star-struck mother for the movie studios in Rome, seeking work as an extra under the name of Sofia Lazarro. Producer Carlo Ponti (one of the contest judges) took notice of her, changed her name to Sophia Loren, and took control of her career. "I believe in luck," she says, "but I also believe one has to know how to grab at luck, to seize the moment. Otherwise opportunities can slip through one's fingers. "In 1954 with *The Gold of Naples*, she came to the world's attention. Her career now spans over 70 films (her favorites: *Yesterday, Today, and Tomorrow; Marriage, Italian Style;* and *Two Women*, for which she won an Oscar in 1961 as best actress). She was reunited with frequent co-star Marcello Mastroianni in 1985 in *Saturday, Sunday, Monday.* she followed that movie with the telefilm "Mother Courage" on CBS in 1986. For her next project, Loren dropped her customary sex-symbol persona to play a gutsy Italian emigre mother in the NBC blockbuster five-hour miniseries, "Mario Puzo's The Fortunate Pilgrim" in 1988.

Choosing between Cary Grant and Carlo Ponti, she declined Cary Grants' proposal of marriage ("I would cherish forever what Cary brought into my life"), married Carlo Ponti by proxy in Mexico in 1957 (he subsequently became a French citizen to avoid a bigamy suit pending against him in Italy), and in 1966 remarried Ponti in France. After suffering four miscarriages, Sophia took to bed nine months in a Swiss clinic. Carlo, Jr. ("Cipi") was born in 1968; Edoardo ("Eli") in 1972. In July 1980, Italy's highest appeals court ordered her to serve a 30-day jail term for failure to pay $180,000 in supplementary taxes in 1963-64. Arriving at Rome airport in May, 1982, she was taken to Giudidiario Prison in Caserta, north of Naples. She told reporters: "I am content to go and serve this sentence because I want to see my mother, sister, my friends, my country . . . my roots," and claimed that she was incorrectly advised in not declaring the income she earned outside Italy in 1963. She served 17 days in prison until a Naples court granted her leave. "My jail sentence was not in vain. It's something I will never forget. It was the ugliest experience of my life."

Lucille Lortel

"The Queen of Off-Broadway" was born on Manhattan's Riverside Drive, circa 1910. She was sent by her garment-industry papa to study in Berlin with American drama teacher Arnold Korf and returned to make her debut on Broadway in the 1920s Theatre Guild production of Shaw's *Caesar and Cleopatra*. The doe-eyed, dark-haired actress played in other Broadway shows and took the lead in *The Man Who Laughed Last* on stage and in the screen version. Her acting career ended when she married the marvelously rich chemical engineer Louis Schweitzer aboard the great oceanliner *S.S. Leviathan*. During WW II she bought a big white barn and moved it to the Schweitzers' 18-acre estate in Westport, Conn. Supposedly, the barn was purchased for horses, but Lortel convinced her husband to let it be turned into a theatre. The White Barn opened its doors in 1947 with a series of weekend play readings, attended by the cream of New York's theatre world. (The first play was *The Painted Wagon*.) But it soon became more than a small-town summer stock showcase. Eva Le Gallienne taught there (actor Peter Falk spoke his first words of Shakespeare in one of her classes) and among the shows which have premiered there are: Eugene Ionesco's *The Chairs*, Sean O'Casey's *Red Roses for Me*, Murray Schisgal's *The Typist* and Paul Zindel's *The Effect of Gamma Rays on Man-in-the-Moon Marigolds*.

Next, for their 24th wedding anniversary, her husband bought Lucille a small theatre on Christopher Street, the Theatre de Lys, and immediately produced the Brecht/Weil musical *The Threepenny Opera* which ran to full houses from 1955 to 1962. The stature of off-Broadway thus elevated, some say off-Broadway was born in the Theatre de Lys. Lortel began producing a Tuesday matinee series in the theatre. Godfrey Cambridge appeared in an all-black production of Langston Hughes's *Soul Gone Home* and *Shakespeare in Harlem;* Richard Burton read poetry with Cathleen Nesbitt. In the early 1980s the theatre (renamed the Lucille Lortel Theatre in 1982) was home to Tommy Tune's brilliant direction of Caryl Churchill's *Cloud 9*.

Lortel has been honored by many theatre organizations and a gallery was named after her at the Museum of the City of New York. Now a widow, she says "I know that I keep saying that I am going to retire . . . people keep approaching me with projects. Before I know it, I've said 'yes' again. I guess you could say I'm too busy to retire. Off-Broadway has always seemed a more appropriate place for the kind of theatre I like—new playwrights, revivals of classics, adaptations of poetry, and things which are slightly offbeat." In 1985 Lortel was the first recipient of the Lee Strasberg Award for Lifetime Achievement in the Theatre, and in 1986 she received three more awards: Exceptional Achievement Award (Women's Project Am. Pl. Theatre), George M. Cohan Award (Catholic Actors Guild) and First Citation Mus. Am. Theatre in New Haven.

Dorothy Loudon

Once upon a less than merry time, Broadway's most glamorous, endearing giggle—who'd rather be known "as an actress who does comedy than a comedienne,"—said: "I'm not the most secure person in the world. In the past, it seemed that I was headed for disaster. My first Broadway show, *Nowhere To Go But Up*, in 1962, was the first show where the backers picketed the theatre. They wanted to close it . . . and I've closed so many clubs. They burn down, a club in Cleveland, a club in Montreal. . . ."

All that changed after she copped a Tony award for her performance as the deliciously wicked Miss Hannigan in the musical *Annie*. From there she starred in Michael Bennett's short-lived extravaganza *Ballroom* (her favorite part of all), Stephen Sondheim's *Sweeney Todd*, played opposite Katharine Hepburn in *The West Side Waltz*, and stopped the show in the hilarious British farce *Noises Off*—plus, squeezed in a TV sitcom "Dorothy" and made her film debut in *Garbo Talks*, reuniting her with Sidney Lumet, who directed *Nowhere to Go But Up*. "I bought a new mink coat with the money I'm making from the movie. And I named it Sidney." In 1985 she starred in *Jerry's Girls*, a revue featuring the words and music of Jerry Herman. Capturing her vocal ability on disc, Loudon recorded the album *Broadway Baby* in 1986. It was announced in 1989 that she would reprise her role as "Miss Hannigan" in the 1990 Broadway musical *Annie II: Miss Hannigan's Revenge*.

The lady, whom columnist Liz Smith calls "irrepressible . . . even when going too far she gives the theatre world's chain a humorous jerk," was born 17 September 1933 in Boston. Her father worked in advertising and her mother played organ at Filene's Salad Bowl. She got her first break in show business in 1954 working as a saloon singer at Jimmy Ryan's East Side in Manhattan and "Julius Monk saw me there and got me up on my feet and into comedy." In 1962-63, she was seen by millions when she replaced Carol Burnett on "The Gary Moore Show."

Loudon lives in a rambling seven-room Upper West Side New York co-op. She makes her own clothes calling them "Dorothy Loudon dresses . . . if you notice, they all look like Kitty Foyle with little collars. I'm always ready to sit in court and testify." She is decidedly domestic and does all her own housework. "I adore it. There's only one thing I hate: doing dishes. If the dishwasher ever breaks down, I'm moving." Her husband, Norman Paris, died in 1977. "I have no thoughts on 'my life' that do not include my late husband. He loved the theatre, as do I, and was my reason for being and my constant inspiration to perservere. I will devote my life to the justification of the faith he had in me and to the faith of all those everywhere who love the theatre."

Greg Louganis

Ladies and gentlemen—Neptune. Arisen from the chlorine of the 1984 Summer Olympic Games where he was the first man in fifty-six years to capture gold medals in both springboard and platform diving competitions. Five feet nine inches tall, 150 pounds of relentless muscle, his body contains an uncommonly-low seven percent body fat. Super-Neptune. "I was scared going into that last dive," he recalls of standing on the platform, psyching himself up as he customarily does, by singing the song from the musical *The Wiz*, "Believe in Yourself," and then, leaping into the air, curling his body into a tight globe, spinning three-and-a-half somersaults, straightening, spotting his entry point into the water, and descending and winning, becoming the first diver to exceed 700 points in the history of the sport, (710.92, but who is counting?) "You're up there thirty-three feet above the water, with not a whole lot on, and seven people judging you, and it's a very vulnerable position." Two days before the event, he had turned in six nearly flawless optional dives. Virtually unchallenged on the springboard, he has taken first place in every major national and international event since 1981. As the world watched in wonder during the 1988 Olympics in Seoul, Louganis gave another spectacular performance. After scalping his head on the diving board he recovered enough to take the gold medal again in springboard/platform diving. Sports commentator Phil Boggs put it best: "There are people who get into the water cleaner . . . like some of the Chinese divers. But there's nobody who combines all the elements like Greg does—power, grace, and that catlike awareness of his body that enables him to stay almost always straight up and down in the air. He's the state of the art in diving."

The aquatic hero, born of Samoan and northern European ancestry, was adopted shortly after his birth in 1960 by Peter and Francis Louganis. His father was a bookkeeper for a marine company in San Diego who later became a tuna-boat controller, and, as Greg tells it, his mother enrolled him and his sister into a dance class when they were little more than toddlers because "mom didn't want any klutzes." Soon brother and sister were a winning combo at local recitals. Greg learned in dance class the concentration that later proved crucial to his development as a championship diver—visualizing the dance routine from beginning to end. " I didn't leave the room until I could do the routine flawlessly in my head," Teased because he had a reading disability, Louganis spent his time in the dance studio or in the gymnasium. (Gymnastics had been suggested as a way of increasing his lung capacity so as to cure his childhood asthma.) When his father saw him practicing his acrobatics on the diving board in the family's backyard pool, he knew Greg should take swimming lessons and within two years, Greg Louganis was skilled enough to score "a perfect ten" at the 1971 AAU Junior Olympics. It was there that he was spotted by 1948 and 1952 Olympic diving gold medalist Dr. Sammy Lee, who eventually became his coach, and the rest is history—a tale with a certain mythic appeal. In 1985 Greg won the Sullivan Award as the nation's outstanding amateur athlete, finishing first in national voting by about 2,500 participants—a group that included the media, past winners, the sponsoring Amateur Athletic Union and representatives of the U.S. Olympic Committee. A 1983 graduate of the University of California, Greg received his bachelor's degree in theatre with a minor in dance. " I'd much rather be in a studio and dance my heart out than go to the gym and pump iron," he has said. Louganis has retired from competitive diving to pursue an acting career.

Iris Love

"Frankly, I have always preferred to be a pagan," confides the socialite-turned archeologist whose flamboyant role in popularizing her arcane subject has made her (according to *People*) "a sort of Carl Sagan of archeology." Sniffed at by some of her fellow diggers, who consider her style "brash and unscholarly," Iris Love nevertheless ranks as one of the most visible and beguiling practitioners of the excavator's art and certainly the most popular on the lecture circuit. Wrote Natalie Angier in *Discover* in 1982: "Iris Love racks up marvelous discoveries the way most people accumulate debts. She is a dedicated archeologist and a natural actress, for whom any patch of barren soil is both a potential treasure chest and a makeshift stage." Iris Love's most heralded discovery to date, front page news in the New York *Times* in 1969, was the long-buried Temple of Aphrodite at Knidos, on the southwest coast of Turkey. Media types were understandably responsive to the fact that this spot sacred to the Greek goddess of love was unearthed by someone *named* Love, who also happened to be highly photogenic in a mini-skirt.

The daughter of a socially-prominent New York stockbroker and a great-niece of mining magnate Solomon Guggenheim, Iris Cornelia Love (born 1 August circa 1938) was called by her late celebrated cousin, artist/art collector Peggy Guggenheim, "the foremost Guggenheim of her generation." Originally guided to Greek mythology by an English governess ("I was brainwashed by Homer"), Love was educated further in the classics at prep schools like Brearley and Madeira, and became a magnet for controversy early on. She did her first major ruffling of feathers when, as an undergraduate at Smith, she wrote a paper exposing the Metropolitan Museum's celebrated terra-cotta Etruscan Warrior group as fakes. (She was right, and Met officals later removed them from display.) When she first headed for Knidos, where she ultimately excavated for twelve seasons, it was assumed to have been thoroughly "dug out" by Britain's Sir Charles Newton who, in the mid-19th century, sent back to the Brish Museum 384 crates of objects which he'd found there. There were many red faces after her discovery of the Aphrodite Temple, and even more when she declared in 1970 that one of Newton's early finds, relegated for nearly a century in the Museum's basement, labeled simply Head 1314, was the long-looked-for head of the most celebrated statue of antiquity, the Aphrodite of Praxiteles. (British Museum officials who don't agree with Iris's assessment, have not been on speaking terms with her since.) Barred from further digging at Knidos when the Turkish government turned the area into a military zone in 1977, the "appositely-named apostle of Aphrodite" has been seeking additional artifacts of her favorite goddess in Italy, Greece and Crete.

Iris Love's "brainwashing" by Homer as a child has obviously had a lasting influence. The four-times-engaged-but-still-unmarried "last of the romantic archeologists" makes a regular habit of pouring wine on the floor "as a libation to the gods" before beginning a meal, refuses to eat *foie gras* because geese were sacred to Aphrodite, and always wears something blue, "the color that the ancients believed warded off evil spirits."

Rob Lowe

After completing the movie *Class* in June 1983 Rob Lowe told *Seventeen* magazine: "I like the fact that I come from the Midwest. . . . I like the people I know who come from there; it's not that the Midwest is better than anywhere else, but it's like real life. And you grow up with a good sense of values." Those *values* were tested in May 1989 when the mother of a teenage girl sued Lowe for having sex with her daughter and recording the event on videotape. The case also brought Atlanta's district attorney into the investigation. Although the handsome actor had originally refused to speak to the press about the accusations, the media had a heyday exploiting the tale. After making a deal to perform 20 hours of community service over a period of two years, Lowe finally spoke his mind on the "Today" Show. He said, "There was never anything wrong with my ethics, there were things wrong with my judgment."

Rob Lowe does have a special screen presence—that *je ne sais quoi*. His figure looms large on the screen, magnetism radiates from the finely sculpted features and those eyes, oh those eyes. . . . With just the lift of an eyebrow, tilt of the head, hearts are sent fluttering. "People are always making such a big deal about the way I look," he says, a little wearily. Warren Beatty and Robert Redford are the actors he admires most—"for overcoming their faces."

Born 17 March 1964 in Dayton, Ohio, Lowe has been acting since he was 8, contracting the bug after seeing the musical *Oliver*. His parents divorced when he was only four years old; when his mother and stepfather relocated to Los Angeles, Rob and younger brother, Chad, received the opportunity to grow up in California. Lowe began making the rounds as an actor while still an undergraduate at Santa Monica High. He made his small screen debut on two After School Specials, "A Matter of Time" and "Schoolboy Father." He also appeared with Eileen Brennan in the ABC-TV series, "A New Kind of Family." About that time, Lowe's career hopes began to fizzle. "I was washed up at 17," he says. He was losing teenage roles to rivals who were over 18 and thus not subject to child labor laws. His agent persuaded him to ride the tide till he was "legal." And as luck would have it, it was a worthwhile hiatus. Labeled as an 1980's screen idol, he hit big in several major films—*The Outsiders* (his feature film debut), *Class*, *The Hotel New Hampshire*, *Oxford Blues*, *Youngblood*, and *St. Elmo's Fire*. Surrounding himself with his co-stars at night and at Hollywood parties, he became a member of the "brat-pack." Presently, he lives in Malibu and is adjusting to his star-status. "I hope I can still do the things I like to do. I know now that I can't go to a theatre in Westwood and stand in line," aware that he'd be immediately pursued by swarms of young girls. As for romance and girls—"I've always been in love with them," he says. He has been linked variously to actress Melissa Gilbert (those rumors ended when she married another actor) and sultry beauty Nastassja Kinski. His recent movies include: *Youngblood* (1986), *Square Dance* (1986), *About Last Night* (1986), *Illegally Yours* (1988), and *Masquerade* (1988). Lowe seems finally to be comfortable with his leading-man status, whether it be on screen or off.

Myrna Loy

"I don't know how it started—the 'perfect wife' label—but I saved more marriages than you can imagine," laughs Movie Queen Myrna Loy who, playing William Powell's wife in a film that only took 21 days of shooting in 1934 —*The Thin Man*—earned a lifelong tag of the "perfect wife" (meaning married but attractive; sexy but humorous; romantic but fun). "I was the perfect American wife—which I wasn't. It was so funny." (Offscreen, she was married and divorced four times; Arthur Hornblow, Jr., John Hertz, Jr., Gene Markey, and Howland Sargeant.) "All anyone seemed to care about was my marriage. I can't see what that has to do with my work. I think carrying on a life that is meant to be private in public is a breach of taste, common sense, and mental hygiene. I made my mistakes, paid for them, recovered from them, and did it all in privacy. And I'm glad."

Born Myrna Williams 2 August 1905 in Helena, Montana, her first appearance in front of a camera was opposite Rudolph Valentino in a screen test for *Corba*. Typecast into portraying sinuous Oriental sirens and vamps (*Noah's Ark*, 1929; *The Squall*, 1929; *The Mask of Fu Manchu*, 1932), it was director W.S. Van Dyke who recognized her true potential, accomplished her metamorphosis from "homewrecker" to "homemaker" with *Penthouse* (1933), then "perfectly" cast her opposite William Powell in *The Thin Man*. Her career sky-rocketed, and to movie audiences the name Loy became linked with Powell, with whom she co-starred in *Manhattan Melodrama*, 1934, *The Great Ziefeld*, 1936, *Libeled Lady*, 1936; and the classic *Thin Man* series (six in total), and with Clark Gable, for *Night Flight*, 1933, *Manhattan Melodrama*, 1934, and *Test Pilot*, 1938. She was Franklin Roosevelt's favorite actress. John Dillinger was so enthralled with her screen images that he let himself be lured to see her in *Manhattan Melodrama*, only to be gunned down by G-men's bullets outside Chicago's Clark Theater. And in 1937, through a national newspaper poll, Myrna Loy and Clark Gable were officially crowned "'King' and 'Queen' of the Movies," with a coronation ceremony in Hollywood. "I made so many marvelous pictures, but I suppose *The Best Years of Our Lives* is *the* one. When I see those movies now I just sit and cry." A veteran actress, Myrna Loy turned to the stage in 1962 with *There Must Be a Pony*, subsequently toured with Neil Simon's *Barefoot in the Park*, and on Broadway appeared in a revival of *The Women*. After WW II, Myrna Loy became active in the fledgling United Nations ("I'm an actress but not such a dedicated one that I'm not concerned with other things"); she has a rarely given UNESCO medal for her work. With a career spanning seven decades in movie making, Myrna Loy appeared in the first European-American co-production (the silent *Ben-Hur*); the first film with a score (*Don Juan*); the first talkie (*The Jazz Singer*); and the first filmed operetta (*The Desert Song*). In 1985 the Academy of Motion Picture Arts and Sciences paid special tribute to her at a gala evening at Carnegie Hall. She was also honored by the Kennedy Center Honors in 1988 and her autobiography *Myrna Loy: On Being and Becoming* was released in 1987.

George Lucas

George Lucas's career is a demonstration of how far a film school graduate can go. He claims to have made his second film, 1973's beloved *American Graffiti*, for 16-year-olds, and his third, *Star Wars* (one of the all-time box-office champions), "for kids of all ages." The latter film's huge success has enabled Lucas—regrettably perhaps—to retire early (temporarily?) as a director and concentrate instead on producing other blockbusters, like Spielberg's *Raiders of the Lost Ark*, and on providing financial assistance to fledgling filmmakers.

Born on 14 May 1944, in Modesto, Calif. (and raised nearby on his father's walnut ranch), Lucas "barely squeaked through high school," aspiring to be a motor car racer until, days before his graduation, a near-fatal accident in his souped-up Fiat crushed his lungs and sent him to the hospital for three months. His second career choice was art, but cinematographer Haskell Wexler encouraged his filmmaking and helped him gain admittance to the University of Southern California's film department. While there, he made a science fiction short which—with Francis Coppola's help—he expanded into his first feature, 1971's *THX-1138*. Starring Robert Duvall and set in the 25th century, the film's white-on-white visual texture belies its grim undercurrents.

By contrast, the ebullient *American Graffiti*, set on one summer night in 1962, is based on Lucas' own coming of age in Modesto (where it was filmed on a shoestring budget in 28 days). "It all happened to me, but I sort of glamorized it," the directors says. Divorced from film editor (*Taxi Driver*) Marcia Griffin Lucas (whom he married in 1969), the short, slightly-built Lucas lives near San Francisco and, for fun, enjoys "flicking out" in movie theatres. His religious faith, developed while recuperating from his car accident, is based on a belief in a power roughly similar to the concept of *Star Wars'* "The Force." His continual drive has kept him busy throughout the 1980's. He was the executive producer for *The Land Before Time*, *Tucker, The Man and His Dream*, *Willow*, and *Indiana Jones and the Last Crusade*.

Susan Lucci

A little bit of trivia.... What famous soap opera actress has been passed over by the Emmy Awards for eight years in a row? Susan Lucci, resident villainess on daytime's "All My Children" has millions of fans but has never received the prestigious award presented by the National Academy of Television Arts and Sciences. But this petite actress who's had precious few other credits says, "It's fun to play Erica. It's a way to express a part of my personality that's there and to give people insight into why they behave the way they do." The abominable behavior that her TV character has engaged in since Susan Lucci got the part of the rotten high school tease in 1969 has included having affairs, divorcing, aborting her baby, and breaking up marriages. Lucci's personal life is apparently quite different. Born 23 December 1950, she's the product of a strict Catholic, Garden City, Long Island family. (Dad, a building contractor, "would wait for me when I went on dates," she admits.) Bitten early by the acting bug, a flubbed Broadway tryout at 19 sent her into serious training and she was ready for the Erica part when it happened along later that year. With only a couple of TV and movie roles under her small belt (she's five-feet-two, and 95 pounds), she hints she'd like more. "Frankly, when I started they weren't making all these movies where the leads were young girls.... I thought... 'If I leave "All My Children," what will I play—someone's daughter or girlfriend?' Now I'm grown up and there are a lot of grown-up parts for me to play and I feel I'm ready." Home life is said to be sedate, unlike the TV persona that brings her a half million a year, with Austrian-born restaurant impresario hubby Helmut Huber. Still living in Garden City, Lucci commutes into Manhattan every dawn to go to work. "I always thought that being on a daytime show was the only way I could combine being a full-time mother and a full-time actress," says she, the mother of Susan. In 1985 she starred in "Mafia Princess," an NBC movie for TV. Joining in on the fragrance wars, Lucci became the new Revlon Woman in 1986. She is promoting the aptly titled perfume "Scoundrel."

Robert Ludlum

"The reader is never moved or enchanted by Ludlum's writing, but he is never bored," said one reviewer. He has "an unerring sense of when to push a reader, when to stop and when—wham, bang—to get him going again," said *Newsweek*. After more than 20 years as an actor and producer, he took a mid-life career gamble to try his luck as a novelist. The result was a string of bestsellers of international intrigue (beginning with 1971's *The Scarlatti Inheritance*), which hooked readers with intricate plots, exotic locations, and payoff endings in which heroes laugh last. The author himself laughed all the way to the bank with "more money than I thought was in Saudi Arabia. I really had no idea I'd make a living at writing."

Even as a youth, Ludlum was hungry for adventure. Born 25 May 1927 and raised in New Jersey, he shook off the trappings of his sedate, suburban upbringing and set off to pursue acting at age 16. He auditioned for and—to his astonishment—won a role on Broadway in *Junior Miss*. Still restless, he tried to enlist in the Canadian Air Force but was rejected for being too young. He served two years in the U.S. Marines before earning a theatre degree at Wesleyan University. Weary of playing "homicidal maniacs and lawyers" in such television dramas as "Studio One" and "Kraft Television Theatre," he moved into producing in 1957 at a Fort Lee, N.J. playhouse and later established in Paramus, N.J. the first major year-round theatre in a suburban shopping center. The theatre flourished by drawing in appreciative audiences with bigname stars, but Ludlum, almost 40, was itchy for a new challenge and resigned his producer's post to tackle his typewriter. "The theatre is marvelous training for a novelist. You learn to hold the attention of an audience. You must capture and maintain the crowd's interest or you'll close the next Saturday night. It's a very disciplined craft. You learn what I call the 'architecture of scenes'—building of suspense, conflict of character. You learn not to bore an audience."

The Scarlatti Inheritance quickly became a best-seller and a Book-of-the-Month-Club selection upon its release. His other popular novels include *The Osterman Weekend* (1972), *The Rhinemann Exchange* (1974), *The Matarese Circle* (1979), *The Parsifal Mosaic* (1982), *The Aquitaine Progression* (1984), *The Bourne Supremacy* (1986), and *The Icarus Agenda* (1988).

Ludlum married former actress Mary Ryde in 1951. They have three children.

Richard Lugar

At a time when most big city mayors were more or less permanently positioned on their hands and knees begging Washington for money to keep their cities solvent, this Indianapolis intellectual was busy devising and implementing a plan to make Federal aid unnecessary. He called his plan Unigov; amidst fevered debate ("I was described as a Hitler, Mussolini and Stalin combined") he consolidated the city of Indianapolis with the surrounding suburbs. Explained Richard G. Lugar: "Unigov will be large and wealthy enough to meet everyone's needs. And it will avoid the plight of most cities—being strangled by a ring of rich suburbs that draw wealth out but put very little back in. The real city must become real in actuality as well as philosophy." Widely praised for his successful urban management, this self-described "moderate conservative" took his professorial style national in 1976 when he was elected Senator.

Once known as "Richard Nixon's favorite mayor," the scholarly Lugar survived the Watergate fall-out and in the eighties threw in with the New Right, though perhaps it would be more accurate to say he was thrown in. He is allied with the New Right on most issues, although he reaches his conclusions very differently. According to one political pundit, "Lugar sees himself as one of the people who, in the natural course of events, run things, and who will succeed in stamping their imprint on history in the long run." Lugar has become a major Republican spokesman on both foreign and domestic affairs, assuming the Chairmanship of the Senate Foreign Relations Committee from 1985 to 1986. Liberals should not assume that because he is bright he is sympathetic to their positions. Quite the contrary. He believes in more defense spending and a more aggressive confrontation with the Soviets on a variety of issues, especially human rights."

Richard Green Lugar, a fourth generation Hoosier, was born 4 April 1932 to a family prominent in Indianapolis community service. His youth was marked by high achievement, ranging from the attainment of the rank Eagle Scout in the Boy Scouts to a Rhodes scholarship to Oxford. (The only American in the school, his classmates voted him student body president.) Returning stateside, he showed a Midas touch with two ailing family businesses, and in 1964 entered community sevice himself as vice president of the Indianapolis school board. He got the political bug and jumped into electoral politics in 1967, campaigning against the incumbent mayor and defeating him to become the first Republican mayor in two decades. Married to Charlene Smeltzer in 1956, the couple has four sons. The senator keeps trim by jogging, and his diversions include performing classical music on cello and piano.

Sidney Lumet

A directorial dynamo who's happiest "working at white heat," Sidney Lumet first warmed the cockles of critical hearts during TV's Golden Age. Back in the 1950s when the name of the game was "live," his dramas for such shows as "Kraft Television Theatre" and "Studio One" stamped him as a promising comer; by the time he collected an Emmy for his 1960 TV production of "The Iceman Cometh," he definitely had arrived. Switching from little screen to big, he chalked up another O'Neill triumph with the darkly brooding *Long Day's Journey into Night* (1962) and subsequently attracted notice with *The Pawnbroker* (1965), *The Group* (1966), *Child's Play* (1972), *Serpico* (1974), *Murder On the Orient Express* (1974), *Prince of the City* (1981), *Deathtrap* and *The Verdict* (1982), *Daniel* (1983), *Garbo Talks* (1984), *Power* (1985), *The Morning After* (1987), *Running on Empty* (1988), *Family Business* (1989), and *Q&A* (1989).

He was born in Philadelphia 25 June 1924, moved with his family to New York when he was two, and working with his actor father, Baruch, was a greasepaint veteran of the Yiddish Art Theater by the time he was four. Then, studying at the Professional Children's School by day, he labored on Broadway at night, progressing from a tough East Side *Dead End* kid in 1935 to the young Jesus in Maxwell Anderson's *Journey to Jerusalem* in 1940. After performing as a radar man in another sort of theater (the CBI) during World War II, he began working as a director off-Broadway and joined CBS-TV in 1950, quickly establishing himself as a whirlwind of energy and talented innovator. Among the more than 200 plays he directed for TV was "Twelve Angry Men," the drama which later marked his film debbut (1957). He was married first to actress Rita Gam, then to Gloria Vanderbilt, then to Gail Jones (daughter of Lena Horne), then to Piedie Gimbel (1980). He moves through wives like he moves through movies, covering a lot of ground. "I believe in continuity. All I want to do is get better, and quantity can help me to solve problems."

Joan Lunden

She is one of America's most visible women on television today. She co-hosts ABC-TV's "Good Morning America," is the spokesperson for Beechnut Baby Foods, Revlon's Care For Kids line of baby products, the American Lung Association's smoking and pregnancy campaign, and has done several public service announcements for the California Highway

Alison Lurie

Patrol urging parents to use child safety seats when driving with young children.

The future television co-anchor was born 19 September 1950 as Joan Blunden. She started her broadcasting career in Sacramento, California at KCRA-TV and radio as co-anchor and producer of the daily noon television news program. In 1975 she joined WABC-TV Eyewitness News and within a year became co-anchor on the weekend newscasts. She began co-hosting "Good Morning America" in 1980 and has since covered such events as the 1984 Winter Olympics in Yugoslavia, the Royal Weddings in London, and both of Ronald Reagan's Presidential Inaugurations. Joan has also become a nationally known author. Her books include: *Good Morning*, *I'm Joan Lunden*, *Mother's Minutes*, and *Your Newborn Baby*. In addition to writing, Joan has been busy hosting several television programs relating to child rearing. In 1987, she hosted the ABC special, "Our Kids and the Best of Everything," the ACE Award winning cable series "Mother's Day," and "Mother's Minutes," a daily series of TV spots. She also hosted a video entitled "Your Newborn Baby: Everything You Need to Know," which was named Best Parenting Video of the Year by *TV Guide* magazine. She is currently the host of a syndicated talk show, "Everyday."

In addition to her numerous professional achievements, Joan has attained several civic honors and awards, which include the Spirit of Achievement Award from Albert Einstein College of Yeshiva University, YWCA Outstanding Woman's Award Speaker, National Women's Political Caucus Award, New Jersey Division on Civil Rights Award, and Baylor University Outstanding Woman of the Year. She was also selected by the National Mother's Day Committee as Outstanding Mother of the Year in 1982-1983.

Joan and her producer husband Michael Krauss have three children, Jamie Beryl, Lindsay Leigh, and Sarah Emily.

Alison Lurie

Gore Vidal heralded her as "the Queen Herod of modern fiction," and other eminent writers have also sung praises for Alison Lurie's work. Said John Fowles; "I am convinced that Alison Lurie's fiction will long outlast that of many currently more fashionable names. There is no American writer I have read with more constant pleasure and sympathy over the years." Penetrating, sensitive and witty, Lurie is not only a master of her craft, she's an unabashed fan as well—"I find writing great fun, though I know you're not supposed to say that. You're supposed to suffer." The road to the top was not such a smooth one however; during the first fourteen years of hard work at the typewriter, Lurie received countless rejection slips: "The attitude of my friends and family was, 'It's too bad Alison is exhausting herself trying to do this thing. She is obviously not very well equipped. Why doesn't she give up?' But I had already decided that I would go on even if I were never published. My life felt empty if I wasn't writing." Her first novel was published in 1962 but she didn't make a name for herself till her 1974 commercial success *The War Between the Tates*, which tells a story of a failing marriage of the '60s. (It sold nearly a million paperback copies and was filmed for television.) Her 1984 Pulitzer Prize-winning novel *Foreign Affairs* was praised by critics, followed by *Imaginary Friends* (1986), *Nowhere City* (1986), and *The Truth about Lorin Jones* (1988). Lurie has published two works of nonfiction: *V.R. Lang* (1975), a memoir of a Cambridge friend who was one of the founders of the Poet's Theatre, and *The Language of Clothes* (1981), a lavishly illustrated whimsical social history of fashion.

Born 3 September 1926 in Chicago, Lurie was raised in the New York suburb of White Plains. As a child, she recalls, "I was underweight and very bad at games. So from the age of six, I concentrated on reading and telling stories and drawing." Graduating from Radcliffe (1947), she married the following year and very soon was the mother of two. After a year off from writing, she resumed her work, had another child and went on successfully to author over half a dozen books. Lurie is the recipient of an award in literature from the American Academy of Arts and Letters and of several fellowships (Yaddo Foundation fellow, 1963, 1964, 1966, Guggenheim fellow, 1965; Rockefeller Foundation fellow, 1967). She is divorced from her husband and currently resides in Ithaca, New York. She spends each January in London and heads for her Key West cottage the following month, where she writes undisturbed until summer.

Loretta Lynn

"I sing stories from life," says this Appalachian coal miner's daughter who rose from a tar paper shack to the pinnacle of international stardom. "I just speak with my heart and scribble verses on whatever is near," she says. "Heck, I've written songs on paper bags and napkins." She cut a record back in 1962 called "Success" and that's been her story ever since. Her major hits, ("You Ain't Woman Enough," "Coal Miner's Daughter," "The Pill," "Don't Come Home A-Drinkin'") are rooted in her unique life experiences. Her autobiographical best seller *Coal Miner's Daughter* (1977) was made into a film in 1980 with Sissy Spacek in the title role. A favorite on television specials, she has one of the highest TV-Q ratings and ranks among the most admired women in the world in Gallup Poll listings. The "First Lady of Country Music" has continued to transcend boundaries in the 1980s but insists she's not a star: " I am not hanging way up there shining. I am right down here, a-grinding with the rest of them. Her album *Just A Woman* (1985) was a prime example of how "the first female Country artist to be certified gold" is sustaining her reputation.

Born Loretta Webb in Butcher Hollow, Ky., 14 April 1935, the second of eight children of a coal miner and his wife, she was raised in the bleakest rural poverty of the Depression. Loretta remembers dining on bread dipped in gravy and a rare luxury, "miner's steak"—baloney. But the Webb family had "love-a-plenty," grit, and the gift of music. Loretta loved to sing and made her debut at age 13 at a school social, an event which changed her life. That night, she sang to the crowd, won a beauty contest, and sold a homemade pie to a brash young man from a nearby "holler," who later became her husband. After a month-long courtship, she married O.V. "Mooney" (for moonshine). Lynn, just shy of her 14th birthday and was a mother of four at age 18 and a grandmother at 32. Loretta's career began when she was 24 while she and Mooney were living in Custer, Washington, supporting their children by picking fruit in season and doing odd jobs; he working in construction and logging and she as a cleaning lady. But she continued her singing. One day, Mooney came home with a Sears and Roebuck guitar and persuaded her to learn to play it. Later, he pushed her on a local stage to perform. She wrote and recorded "A Honky Tonk Girl," which zoomed up the charts and became her ticket to a Decca (now MCA) contract and a debut on the Grand Ole Opry. She's since released more than 30 albums and was the first woman to receive the Country Music Association's prestigious "Entertainer of the Year" award. Loretta maintains a hectic touring schedule to keep close to her fans, many of whom are hard-working folk like herself. The girl from Butcher "Holler" now owns a 5,000-acre farm in Tennessee which includes an entire town (Hurricane Mills, population 250) and a tourist attraction, the Loretta Lynn Dude Ranch. She owns a chain of western wear clothing stores. Loretta and Mooney (six children) are still together, and keep working hard, but they suffered deep heartache in 1984 when their son Jack lost his life in an accidental drowning. She says of her lifestyle, music and values, which are sometimes called old-fashioned: "I don't know why people call these things old-fashioned. The Bible never grows old. Love never grows old. It's people that grow old. Their love don't."

Yo-Yo Ma

"Yo-Yo Ma has an enviable quality not often encountered among musicians, For as long as he is playing, it becomes very difficult for any listener to think that any cellist today could possibly surpass him," a New York *Times* critic once said about one of the youngest instrumental "legends" on the scene today. His boundless enthusiasm and cheerful equanimity, his prankish sense of humor and sincere efforts to share the limelight with lesser-known instrumentalists, have made him a favorite with professional musicians the world over. He's *always* been a hit with audiences. Known for his effortless technique, his ravishing tone, and the extraordinary breadth of his interpretive power, it is his ability to project his compelling personality to an audience that makes Ma an exceptional artist. "The desire to communicate with an audience [is] the main reason I've chosen to perform music—the *only* reason, as opposed to being a music lover," he says.

Born 7 October 1955 in Paris to a musicologist-violinist-composer from Shanghai and a mezzo-soprano from Hong Kong, Ma successfully combines his father's "analytical, technical and intellectual" approach with his mother's "more emotional" direction. His father improvised a cello (using a viola with an endpin) for his four-year old son and carefully supervised his early training, utilizing a pedagogical approach of short stints of concentrated work rather than long hours of practice. At five Ma knew three Bach cello suites and at six made his recital debut in Paris, before moving with the family to New York, where his father accepted a teaching job at a school for musically gifted children. Two of his pupils were the children of Isaac Stern, who dropped by one day and heard Yo-Yo play. Stern recommended him to Leonard Rose at Juilliard, and Yo-Yo studied there from the age of nine to sixteen. Meanwhile Pablo Casals heard the seven-year old prodigy and insisted that Leonard Bernstein employ him for one of his TV specials. He graduated from high school at fifteen and left home for the first time that summer to attend music camp. He recalls that he "went just wild . . . never showed up at rehearsals . . . left my cello out in the rain, beer bottles all over the room . . . midnight escapades . . . just about everything." He found his bearings at Harvard. "Seeing all the possibilities in life" made him "less neurotic" and equipped him to do other things. "It's not that I'm stuck playing the cello because it's the only thing I can do," he told Richard Thorne for a *Saturday Review* profile.

Since graduating from Harvard with a degree in the humanities, Ma averages 150 concerts a year. In 1978 he was the sole recipient of the prestigious Avery Fisher Prize. That same year he married Harvard German literature instructor Jill Horner, who sometimes accompanies him on tour but more often stays home in Winchester, Massachusetts. Yo-Yo Ma has an extensive discography. The New York *Times* called his 1983 three-disk set of *Bach's Six Suites for Unaccompanied Cello* "truly magical performances in which the young cellist transcends the characteristics and limitations of his instrument and creates textures that are—unbelievably—nearly orchestral." But it is in live performance that Yo-Yo Ma is most impressive. In a review headlined "The Performance of a Lifetime," the Boston *Globe* exclaimed, "There is no cellist at all, and indeed hardly any virtuoso of *any* instrument, who is as complete, profound, passionate and humane as Ma." For the future he'd like to commission new works "to make fantastic connections others haven't made before." Yo-Yo is not only the recipient of multiple Grammy Awards, he also received the Edison Award.

Andie MacDowell

"Every time I meet someone for a reading, I'm aware they know my work, know I'm a model—it's this fact. And there's a stigma," claims Andie. She has managed to dispel the myth that models are dumb, and has overcome the obstacles that models often come up against while auditioning for a part in a film. She has made the transition from successful model to successful actress.

Andie MacDowell was born Anderson MacDowell in the small town of Gaffney, South Carolina. When she was only six years old her parents divorced. Growing up in a broken family with an alcoholic mother, she had to take on a lot of responsibility at an early age. Because she was so busy having to take care of her mother as well as herself, she never did well in school. In her second year of college, she decided to drop out to pursue a career in modeling. She started out in newspaper ads for a department store, and soon began working for the Elite Modeling Agency. Since then, she has modeled in commercials for Calvin Klein jeans and L'Oreal. Her studies in acting include training with Shakespeare and Company, as well as being a student of the Meisner technique. Andie made her film debut in 1984 playing the role of Jane in *Greystoke; The Legend of Tarzan, Lord of the Apes*. Following that she appeared in *St. Elmo's Fire*. In Europe, she played the role of Anthea in "Sahara's Secret," which was the highest rated mini-series on RAI Italian television in 1988. Her latest film, *sex, lies and videotape* (1989), in which she starred as Ann, was the winner of both the Best Film Prize and the Best Actor Award (for James Spader) at the Cannes Film Festival.

Andie is married to model Paul Qualley and is the mother of two boys, Justin and Rainey.

Bob Mackie

Can you imagine TV and the 1970s without Cher's navel in living color? Thank this man. He did it: made color TV worth the price just to see his weekly shimmering and gossamer confections dripping with rhinestones and beads. Not since Sally Rand first appeared on stage with only her ostrich feathers have clothes—or lack of them—created as big a sensation as did his costumes for Cher's variety show (with and without her erstwhile partner, Sonny). You may recall a certain famed "nude feather dress." It is to Cher's image what the crown is to Elizabeth II. And besides Cher, there are the costumes he designed for one of Mitzi Gaynor's nightclub acts, which caused Joe Hamilton, then Carol Burnett's husband and producer of her variety show, to hire Mackie to design *her* entire TV show wardrobe. (Burnett now has a studio closet crammed with over 1,500 Mackie originals.) As a matter of fact, his client list reads like this book's contents—"Raquel," "Ann-Margret," "Diana Ross," "Angie Dickinson," "Streisand." One of his sequined creations provided the clue to a *TV Guide* scandal when a cover photo featured Ann-Margret's body supporting Oprah Winfrey's head.

Born 24 March 1940, Mackie, a native Californian, confesses to having had "a beatnik stage where I dyed my varsity sweater black." He received his formal training in costume design at Los Angeles' Chouinard Art Institute and began his career as a sketch artist for designer Jean Louis. After working on several films with Louis, he went to work for Edith Head at Paramount. In 1963 he had just recently been divorced (one son, Robin) when he was hired as Ray Aghayan's assistant on TV's "Judy Garland Show." They soon established a partnership, and Mackie's first solo showcase was designing for "The King Family Show." "It was a comedown, but it was my very own." Mackie modestly attributes his early success to the mid-1960s "youthquake—if you were under 25, you were considered brilliant and got hired a lot. I even lied about my age." The four-time Emmy Award winner and three-time Academy Award nominee decided to settle his stitch into fashion's Seventh Avenue in 1982 by designing a collection of ready-to-wear clothing for women. His film credits include *Pennies From Heaven, Lady Sings the Blues, Funny Lady*, and *Max Dugan Returns*. He also designed the gowns for the "Cher" doll and wrote *Dressing for Glamour* in 1979.

Shirley MacLaine

"I've wondered for 26 years what this would feel like," the redheaded singer, actress, dancer, writer and spiritual crusader said in her 1984 Oscar acceptance speech. "Thank you so much for terminating the suspense." The award was for her portrayal of Aurora Greenway, "a feisty, frustrated Houston widow," in the film *Terms of Endearment*. The film shows Aurora's relationship with her defiant daughter, played by Debra Winger, over a period of thirty years. The Oscar followed four previous nominations—as best actress in *Some Came Running* (1958), *Irma La Douce* (1963), and *The Turning Point* (1977); a documentary feature which she produced, *The Other Half of the Sky: A China Memoir*, was also nominated for an Academy Award in 1975. For her forty-ninth birthday she'd retreated into the Rockies to "project," as she calls it, three wishful visualizations: that she'd win an Oscar (she did), that her book on spiritualism and reincarnation *Out On a Limb*, in which a nice WASP lady-liberal discovers her Karmic thread, would become a bestseller (did it ever; it became a 1986 TV miniseries with its author as the star), and finally that her nightclub act would score big on Broadway (and it did at the Gershwin). Proud, inspired, elegant, joyous, a globetrotting Renaissance woman (and author of bestsellers: the autobiographical *Don't Fall Off the Mountain* (1970) and *You Can Get There From Here* (1975) in which she discussed her involvement with American politics and her reaction to the Chinese Revolution), MacLaine is her own best emblem. "I basically think of myself as a dancer," she explains. "It's the first thing I learned to do." Her recent literary offerings include *Dancing in the Light* (1985), *It's All in the Playing* (1987), and *Going Within* (1989).

Born on 24 April 1934, Shirley MacLaine Beaty (brother Warren added the second "t" later) was raised in Arlington, Virginia, and was a whiz in ballet slippers by the time she was three. When her legs grew too long for ballet, she was heartbroken. At sixteen she shifted to musical comedy and went to New York and got a part in a regional touring production of *Oklahoma*. Two years later, having completed high school, she moved back to New York. When she was not yet twenty she got her first break when, while understudying Carol Haney in *The Pajama Game* on Broadway, Haney sprained her ankle three days after the show opened and Shirley went on for her. MacLaine was spotted by Hollywood producer Hal Wallis and within months she was signed to star in her first picture, Alfred Hitchcock's *The Trouble with Harry*. By 1969 she was one of Hollywood's highest-paid performers, getting as much as $800,000 for a film.

"My strongest personality trait is the way I keep unsettling my life when most other people are settling down." Indeed this is key in mapping her many ways, be it as a wife and mother (to Steve Parker, divorced in 1982, one daughter Sachi), to running with the Hollywood Rat Pack, meditating in the Himalayas, campaigning for McGovern and keeping to the left romantically with the likes of Pete Hamill and Soviet director Andrei Mikhalkov-Konchalovsky. "I have mostly used relationships to learn, and when that process is over, so is the relationship." She remained Parker's wife for nearly thirty years, although they lived separately from the time he moved to Japan soon after they were married. One observer described her relationship with her brother Warren as the "most explosive in her life." Warren has said: "As for what goes on between Shirley and me, you can safely call it complicated." Shirley once remembered that the two had "sat for twenty years, warily watching each other grow up. . . . He knows me and I know him. . . . I think in terms of black and white . . . he's a respecter of gray."

Borrowing a line from her pal Gloria Steinem when she turned fifty MacLaine said: "This is what fifty looks like. . . . I love the idea of fifty because the best is yet to come. I am going to live to be one hundred, because I want to, and I am going to go on learning." MacLaine is working as hard as ever. Her recent movies include *Madame Sousatzka* (1988), and *Steel Magnolias* (1989). Sharing some of her longevity secrets, she released a home video "Shirley MacLaine's Inner Workout" in 1989.

Robert MacNeil

Believing that today's TV news has "bred a form of journalism that often leaves the public very poorly served," Robert MacNeil has blazed—with co-anchor Jim Lehrer—a new journalistic trail marked by a hype-free, impartial (critics say to a fault) style of in-depth news coverage. In 1975, they pioneered an award-winning half-hour "one-issue-per-show" news format for PBS, which expanded in 1983 into the "The MacNeil/Lehrer NewsHour"—America's first hour-long national evening news program. "We started MacNeil/Lehrer under the assumption that it's very easy to produce heat on TV but very difficult to produce light," said executive editor MacNeil. They were on target. While the public grew to mistrust journalists in general, MacNeil/Lehrer became two of the most respected television news personalities in the country. Their balanced, factual reporting and dispassionate analysis won the program journalistic awards—and some barbs such as "the tedium twins." MacNeil, who considers himself a liberal, asserts: "In my twenties and thirties I had a more committed view. But that usually came from ignorance. Our evenhandedness is one reason why people like us."

The son of a Canadian naval officer, Robert (called Robin) MacNeil was born 19 January 1931 in Montreal. He was an aspiring actor and playwright before turning to journalism in 1955 as a rewrite man for Reuters News Agency in London. He joined NBC as a London correspondent in 1960 and transferred to NBC's Washington office in 1963, covering such pivotal events of the 1960s as the Berlin Crisis and President Kennedy's assassination. He has also worked with the BBC. He first teamed with Jim Lehrer to cover the Watergate hearings for PBS. A graduate of Carleton University in Ottawa, he is author of the autobiographical *The Right Place at the Right Time* and *The People Machine*, which criticizes commercial television's preoccupation with entertainment.

MacNeil lives alone in a brownstone in Manhattan, divorced from his second wife. He has four children. While he didn't follow his father into the navy, a love of the sea runs in the family. His younger brother, Hugh, became a commander of NATO's Atlantic standing naval force, and MacNeil's own extracurricular passion is sailing.

Elle Macpherson

Australian-born model Elle Macpherson is known for her repeat-appearance covers of the "swimsuit issues" of *Sports Illustrated*. Traditionally, the winter fun-in-the-sun number is always a blockbuster seller, and having the honor of a "repeat performance" places the statuesque six-foot star of the Ford modeling stable in the same prestigious league as such covergirl superstars as Christie Brinkley and Cheryl Tiegs (both of whom filled out swimsuits for *Sports Illustrated* on three separate occasions). Elle's third appearance in 1988 earned her spot of honor in the Ford Models *Sports Illustrated* Hall of Fame.

A native of Sydney, Elle was the recipient at Killara High School of an assortment of awards in swimming, basketball, and public speaking. She was also scheduled to start Law School before she embarked on her successful glamourous career. Since departing the southern hemisphere to make her way in New York City environs, she has shown up on numerous *Elle* magazine covers and, in the field of cosmetics, is the exclusive model for Biotherm. The striking brown-haired, brown-eyed Aussie has been warming up male hearts by wearing the stunning Gotex bathing suit in the ads visible in many bus shelters. Her television commercials include Impulse body fragrance, Sea Breeze, Miller Lite, and Diet Coke. She's also appeared on "Late Night with Letterman," "The Tonight Show," "The Oprah Winfrey Show," and "Good Morning America."

Elle is married to fashion photographer Gilles Bensimon. When she's not in front of the cameras, the fit young lady likes working out and running. To relax, Elle enjoys gourmet cooking.

Madonna

"Madonna is a video vamp, her trademark a coyly exposed navel, and her only apparent desire, to drive all the boys crazy," wrote *Newsweek* magazine. "People like her give people like us a hard way to go. She doesn't help anybody take women seriously. But you know what? I love the record," said Gina Schock in *Rolling Stone* about the popular singer who, at the age of twenty-five in 1985, emerged with the top selling LPs *Madonna* and *Like A Virgin*, a string of hit singles including "Material Girl," (which spent three weeks in the Number One slot of *Billboard's* Hot 100), and a starring role in a motion picture, *Desperately Seeking Susan*, with Rosanna Arquette. In an age of music videos broadcast twenty-four hours-a-day to record consumers, she livened up the medium with her state-of-the-art titillations and became video's Number One female artist by appearing partially clothed, wearing a belt tag that said Boy Toy. ("Spelling out the most hackneyed male erotic fantasies," said *Newsweek*, "she's like Veronica of the Ronettes without the tenderness, the vulnerability or the clothes.") Maintaining her popularity throughout her consecutive hair colors (brown to blonde to brown to auburn to blonde again) and movie hits and misses, she continues to turn out the commercial stuff that expands her superstar status.

The *Time* (June 1985) covergirl and indifferent *Penthouse* and *Playboy* (both September 1985) layout girl was born Madonna Louise Ciccone in Bay City, Michigan, 16 August 1960, one of eight children. When she was six her mother (after whom she was named) died, and Madonna was raised by her father, by relatives and eventually by her step-mother ("a real disciplinarian"). "From the time that I was very young I just knew that being a girl and being charming in a feminine sort of way could get me a lot things, and I milked it for everything I could," she recalls. She devoted herself to ballet as a teenager because her junior-high teacher "told me I had a beautiful ancient Roman face. No one had ever talked to me like that before. I latched onto him like a leech and took everything I could from him." After a year at the University of Michigan, she headed for musical Manhattan, where she learned to play the guitar and studied briefly at the Alvin Ailey Dance Theater. Boyfriends introduced her to the club world and she cultivated her look of strategically torn lace and mostly religious-themed junk jewelry. To get a deejay to play a cassette of her song "Everybody," she danced in front of the music booth and requested a lot of tunes. When the deejay finally played it the disco's patrons loved her music. So did Sire Records, which signed her in 1983. The single "Holiday" made it as one of that summer's big hits.

"I get so much bad press for being overtly sexual," says she. Her first film was an underground ditty called *A Certain Sacrifice* (1979 in which she played a dominatrix with three slaves). She described the film as "not hard-core porn—it's mostly just weird." Following her success in *Desperately Seeking Susan*, she flopped with *Shanghai Surprise* (1986) and *Who's That Girl* (1987), although she scored with the soundtrack from the latter film and the LP from *Vision Quest*. Against all odds, she made her Broadway stage debut in *Speed-The Plow* (1988) which packed the house each night. Later that year she appeared in the movie *Bloodhounds of Broadway*, and her next feature is the screen adaptation of the comic strip *Dick Tracy*. Her recent LPs include *True Blue* (1986), *You Can Dance* (1987) and *Like A Prayer* (1989). The last album spawned the hit singles "Like A Prayer" and "Express Yourself." Although the title song was to be a promotional vehicle tied in with Pepsi, the deal was canned when the advertising people viewed her controversial video scenes. In August 1985, Madonna married temperamental actor Sean Penn and their rocky relationship became fair game for tabloid headlines. In 1989 the couple filed for divorce.

Norman Mailer

Whether or not he ever is actually awarded the Nobel Prize for Literature which he briefly thought he'd won in 1969 (a garbled message from Stockholm mixed him up with close-but-no-cigar nominee Andre Malraux), this novelist, journalist, poet, playwright, filmmaker, philosopher, lover and onetime pugilist manqué has a secure niche as the most written about of all America's writers and surely the most argued about by critics, readers and even, on occasion, the man in the street. Among the 1980s whirlwinds of controversy: Norman Mailer's refusal to turn his back on the convict writer Jack Abbott (*In the Belly of the Beast*) even after his protégé committed murder; and his predominant theme of "bugger the victim" in *Ancient Evenings*, his 1983 "big novel" about the palace life in Egypt in the 13th century B.C. Representative opinions of the latter ranged from one critic's "nasty, brutish" to a *Publisher's Weekly* sigh that the graphically-described mass rape of battle-weary prisoners by a pharoah's victorious army was "one of the most memorable scenes in this magnificent novel." Stanley Kauffman's long-ago observation that "comment on Norman Mailer has become an active subsidiary in the U.S. literary industry" is equally valid today.

Where, indeed, is one to file him? His preoccupations are enormous: nothing less (as recounted by Mailerophile Richard Poirier) than "technology, fascism, dialectics, apocalypse, Being, cancer, obscenity, dread, existentialism, drugs, violence, totalitarianism, waste, orgy, God and the Devil, paranoia, revolution, sex, and time." And his talents are as prodigious as his themes. James Wolcott notes Mailer's genius "for being attuned to the faintest quiver of mood and inflection, and then using the springboard of his senses to make an imaginative intuitive leap." Benjamin DeMott admires his "surprising perspective—the leap offering instant release from bondage to cliche." And Jack Richardson singles out the fact that Mailer has "enlarged the territories of language, something the very best writers have always done for us." So it goes. "To ignore Mailer," someone once remarked, "is like ignoring China."

The human male Vesuvius who is Norman Mailer erupted on 31 January 1923 in the town of Long Branch, New Jersey, but the Eastern Parkway section of Brooklyn was where he grew up and where the lava started to flow. Then came Harvard, a prizewinning Hemingwayesque entry in *Story* Magazine and eighteen months as a rifleman in the WWII Pacific, the inspirational spark for his first novel, *The Naked and the Dead*. "The greatest writer to come out of this generation," proclaimed Sinclair Lewis, the spokesman for an earlier one. (Said Norman, four decades later: "Early success, that was the worst damn thing that could have happened to me.") Sure enough, 1951's *Barbary Shore* and, in 1955, disillusioned-with-Hollywood novel *The Deer Park*, induced most critical thumbs to turn down. It's been like that—raves alternating with raps; praise with pouts—throughout one of the most "important, notorious, and mercurial careers in postwar American literature."

A few years before becoming inextricably enveloped in what Mailer has called "the sarcophagus of his image," the author wed, in 1944, the New York intellectual Beatrice Silverman (three daughters; divorced, 1952). He made headlines in 1960 when, drunkenly wielding a penknife, he stabbed his second wife, the Spanish-Peruvian artist Adele Morales, later receiving a suspended sentence when she refused to press charges. Personally, these were the bad years ("for the first time, my hangovers in the morning were steeped in dread") but, typically, they were not unproductive. Mailer's now-historic essay, "The White Negro," appeared in *Dissent* in 1957; *Advertisements for Myself*, the opening jig of what Wilfred Sheed called Mailer's "one-man dance marathon" was published in 1959; the much-praised "Superman Comes to the Supermarket," a report on the Los Angeles Democratic Convention at which John F. Kennedy became the candidate, came out in *Esquire* in 1960. There was a book of poems in 1962 (together with more headlines when he married Lady Jeanne Campbell, granddaughter of British press titan, Lord Beaverbrook; one daughter); *Presidential Papers* appeared in 1963 (as did news stories of his divorce from Lady Jean and marriage to actress Beverly Bentley; two sons) and in 1964, after ten non-novel-writing years, he undertook to write a novel (*American Dream*) against monthly deadlines in *Esquire*.

The years of the second great Norman Conquest began in 1969 when, breaking new ground in the genre of personal journalism, he published an account of a 1967 peace march on the Pentagon (*Armies of the Night*) and received both a National Book Award and a Pulitzer Prize. But characteristically, the restless philosophical rover did not rest long on his laurels, and Mailer-watchers soon had new grist for their mills. In 1969, he recorded his impressions of the Republican and Democratic political conventions in *Miami and the Siege of Chicago*. In 1969, on a "Vote the Rascals In" ticket with Jimmy Breslin, he campaigned (unsuccessfully) for the job of mayor of New York City, and also covered the first U.S. moon landing, his account of it published as *A Fire on the Moon*. In 1971, he precipitated a cirsis at *Harper's* (editor Willie Morris and a large portion of the staff quit) and raised a rumpus among feminists with his nonfictional monologue, *A Prisoner of Sex*. And tucked in between these activities were (a) another divorce, and marriage to actress Carol Stevens (one daughter), (b) several cinema verité movies in which he served as producer, director, author and leading actor (e.g. *Maidstone*) and (c) several fisticuff encounters which he either reported on (Ali vs. Frazier in *The Fight*) or engaged in personally (Mailer vs. *Maidstone* actor Rip Torn) not to mention reports—on the 1972 political conventions—published as *St. George and the Godfather*. Always a writer who seems to "flourish in tumult," Mailer made waves again in 1973 with the first of his two books about Marilyn Monroe (*Marilyn;* and in 1980, *Of Women and Their Elegance*) and with his "butting" of Gore Vidal at a party. His personal life calmed down considerably with his marriage, in 1975, to his sixth wife, artist Norris Church (one son, with the distinctive name of John Buffalo) but his career hit another high with the publication of his chilling 1979 "True Life Novel," *The Executioner's Song* (Mailer's second Pulitzer Prize-winner), about the Utah killer Gary Gilmore, who insisted upon his own execution by a firing squad in 1977. The "impish inconoclast" took time out from the typewriter in the early 1980s to play a bemused Stanford White in Milos Forman's *Ragtime*, but was back at work in time to finally complete the long awaited *Ancient Evenings*, ten years in the writing. (In addition to its preoccupation with buggering, the 709-page novel dealt exhaustively with reincarnation, mental telepathy and dung, not necessarily in that order.) Mailer made the book pages once again in 1984 with his murder mystery pot-boiler, *Tough Guys Don't Dance;* he wrote the screenplay and directed the 1987 movie based on the book. His next endeavor was to appear in the film *King Lear* (1988). Mailer was elected to the prestigious post of president of the author's organization PEN, and in 1985 he was the subject of Peter Manso's biography *Mailer: His Life and Times*.

Mailer has been called many names. "Don Quixote," "Don Juan," "Walt Whitman." "A contemporary, choleric Virgil." Or, in the 1980s, proud patriarch and favored Manhattan dinner-party guest. Or, as he once put it, "the one personality he found insupportable—the nice Jewish boy from Brooklyn—a man early accustomed to mother-love." His mind, it has been said, "is one of our greatest natural resources." Mailer himself has observed: "I've been accused of having frittered many talents away, of having taken on too many activities, of having worked too self-consciously at being a celebrity, of having performed at the edges and, indeed, at the center of my own public legend." In actual fact, "I'm really simple, honest, hardworking . . . as close to Abe Lincoln as Arthur Miller is." And, pricking his own balloon, he told Marie Brenner in 1983: "Years ago, Lillian Ross did a profile of me, and when I read it, I called her up and said, 'Lillian, where's the twinkle?' People don't understand that a great deal of the time I'm just kidding."

Natalia Makarova

Her Headline-making "leap into the West" in 1970 made her the most spectacular cultural defector from the U.S.S.R. since Nureyev. Heading for New York, and American Ballet Theatre, she danced from the wings as *Giselle* with "that heartstopping quality of a great dancer," executed the series of dazzling turns, and was subsiding into a bow—the simplest of maneuvers—when she slipped and very nearly fell on her face. As *Time* observed, it was "like a man who had scaled Mount Everest slipping in his shower." For the rest of the opening night performance, Makarova was "remarkable, superb," an "earth-bound mortal . . . incredible creature of some other air." The raves multiplied during her two years with Ballet Theatre and continued while she was dancing as a guest artist with most of the world's great companies.

Born in Leningrad, 28 November 1940, she was nicknamed "The Giraffe" in her student days at ballet school where she sailed through a nine-year course of study in six. She pirouetted her way into the famed Kirov troupe with a performance of *Giselle*, a role many balletomanes thought she brought to perfection with another Westward-leaper, Mikhail Baryshnikov, in the 1970s. It was while dancing in *Giselle* in London, that, "frustrated as an artist," she decided to remain in the West. She has also found critical favor in such major classical ballets as *Swan Lake* and *Sleeping Beauty* and in contemporary works choreographed especially for her by the likes of Bejart, Tetley, Ashton and Robbins. In 1985 Roland Petit created *The Blue Angel* for her (using the original story, not the film).

What Jack Kroll of *Newsweek* called "the second coming of Makarova" occurred in 1983 when she dazzled Broadway audiences with her sexy dancing of "Slaughter on Tenth Avenue" in a revival of the 1936 Rodgers and Hart musical, *On Your Toes* (for which she received a Tony Award), later encored in London's West End. She wowed them also with what *People* called "her delicious display of comic talent and timing" emerging as "a veritable Slavic Lucille Ball." In 1988 she performed with the National Ballet of Canada in *Onegin*.

When she departed from Leningrad, Makarova ("Natasha" to friends) left behind a mother, brother, stepfather and two former husbands, the first a dancer, the second a film director. With millionaire industrialist Edward Karkar, whom she married in 1976, she has a son, Andrei Michel, born in 1978, whom she calls "my greatest achievement."

Karl Malden

It's another night in front of the TV. You haven't been anywhere outside Poughkeepsie in three years. Then he appears, watchdog-extraordinaire, in his trench coat and he says, in the last voice of authority you are likely to hear that night, "Don't leave home without them—American Express Travelers' Checks." You wake up a bit. You see the sad folks in the foreign country who've lost their everything and now they're stranded, so you dive into a sack of potato chips and decide never to leave home again, but if you do, he's right. You'll do anything Karl Malden says to stay safe in treacherous Abu Dhabi, Lyford Cay, Biarritz . . . anyplace beyond your driveway's delta.

"Work," he says, "is one of the greatest things I do, and if I'm not working, I get terribly depressed." Through the years he's kept busy on Broadway in such stage successes as *A Streetcar Named Desire*, *Desperate Hours* and *Desire Under the Elms*, and in Hollywood in film versions of the first two (he won an Oscar for *Streetcar*) plus *On the Waterfront*, *Birdman of Alcatraz*, *Nevada Smith*, *Gypsy*, *Patton*, *Billy Galvin* and *Nuts*. TV, he once said, was "too hectic" for him. "Do you want to make a violin in a week or do you want to make a Stradivarius? I always try to make a Stradivarius." He succumbed to the tube, however, with the series "The Streets of San Francisco," in 1972-77, and the short-lived "Skag." His telefilm appearances include leading roles in "Alice in Wonderland" (1985) and "My Father, My Son" (1988).

Born to Yugoslav parents in Chicago, 22 March 1913, as Malden Sekulovich, he grew up in Gary, Indiana, where he worked in the steel mills, dug ditches, and delivered milk, but through it all, "I knew I'd be an actor. My father was an actor in Yugoslavia." In 1938, after dramatic training in Chicago, he moved to New York, began working on Broadway and, after time out for Army service in World War II, tried acting before the cameras. Married to actress Mona Graham (two daughters), whom he met in 1938 while he was appearing in a production of Tolstoy's *Redemption* at Chicago's Goodman Theater, he occasionally conducts acting seminars in colleges.

John Malkovich

"When I originally saw John in *True West*, I figured that either a psycopath was up on that stage, or he was one of the great actors of our times," recalled Robert Benton, writer-director of *Places in the Heart*, the 1984 film in which the protean actor-director made his film debut. The "childlike ... trivial ... circus freak," who is both "funny [and] odd" (all self-described traits) from the Windy City's adventurous Steppenwolf repertory company set off-Broadway ablaze in 1983 as the loutish and beefy slob in Sam Shepard's *True West* (for which he won an Obie while evoking memories of early Brando), traveled uptown to share the stage with Dustin Hoffman in the 1984 revival of Arthur Miller's *Death of a Salesman*, portraying Biff, the sensitive, neurotic and inspired son of Willie Loman who is trapped in the imposed role of simple-minded jock (the play was filmed for TV in the fall of 1985). Malkovich responded to Hollywood's call to play a blind man in *Places in the Heart* (Oscar nomination). For research he "went to the Dallas Lighthouse to observe blind people (he told Marjorie Rosen for a New York *Daily News* profile) ... but I try never to do any more research than is absolutely necessary ... I became an actor to exercise my imagination, not my research skills." His follow-up film (for which he also earned an Oscar nomination) was *The Killing Fields* (1984), and in 1985 he filmed *Eleni*, playing Nicholas Gage (a former New York *Times* reporter) in his search for the killer of his mother in the Greek Civil War.

"We weren't really trainable," Malkovich recalled for Rosen of his growing up with four siblings in Benton, Illinois, where he was born 9 December 1953, and where his grandmother founded and still runs the Benton *Evening News*. "Although my parents were bright and articulate and well-mannered, something just went awry. We had a lot of freedom, too much freedom, it was always chaos." A loner who read a lot as a child, Malkovich entered Illinois State University with the intention of becoming a conservationist like his father, but soon switched to acting. After graduation he joined the newly-formed Steppenwolf company in Chicago. It was there that he met his wife (married 2 August 1982), Glenne Headley ("She's very odd ... a funny mix ... a city kid") whom he directed in 1984 off-Broadway in Lanford Wilson's *Balm in Gilead* and in 1985 in a Broadway revival of Shaw's *Arms and the Man*. His next hit was the critically acclaimed Broadway play *Burn This* which opened in October 1987. Malkovich's recent movies include *Making Mr. Right* (1986), *Empire of the Sun* (1987), *The Glass Menagerie* (1987), and *Dangerous Liasons* (1988), and he was also the co-executive producer of *The Accidental Tourist* (1988). When asked how he keeps so much acclaim in perspective, he replies, "Well, I count on my good friends to treat me as they always do—like dirt."

Louis Malle

"It's not that I see things others don't," said the French director living and working in America, "but I'm curious about things that, probably if I were born here, I would take for granted." He was speaking of his critically acclaimed 1980 movie *Atlantic City*. Starring Burt Lancaster, *Atlantic City* is about frantic efforts to create hope in a crumbling environment, and several reviewers noted that the director's perceptions as a foreigner added something fresh and vital to John Guare's insightful screenplay. For his next feature he picked what almost anyone else would consider a hopelessly uncinematic subject: two middle aged friends, intellectuals, conversing in a restaurant for an hour and a half. To his astonishment, *My Dinner with Andre*, shot in less than three weeks for $450,000, turned out to be the sleeper of the year 1981, breaking house records in big cities from coast to coast.

With these two solid successes Malle achieved recognition as one of the most accomplished and innovative filmmakers at work in the U.S. While his subsequent releases—e.g., *Crackers* (1984), which the *Village Voice* called "something of a fiasco and clearly a labor of love"—did not come up to the great expectations aroused by *Atlantic City* and *Andre*, his record suggested that he would soon score big again, given his audacity and versatility. ("The only quality common to the films of Louis Malle," critic Pauline Kael has written, "is the restless intelligence one senses in them.") He did succeed again in 1988 as the director and screenwriter for the film *Au Revoir, Les Enfants* which received an Academy Award nomination for best foreign language film. Next up is a social comedy *May Fools* in 1989.

Born 30 October 1932 in Thumieres, in the department of Nord, France, Malle is the seventh and youngest child of a sugar heiress and her onetime naval officer husband. After a standard Catholic secondary education he was destined for a degree in political science, but switched from the Sorbonne to the Institut des Hautes Etudes Cinematographiques, then left to become an assistant to underwater explorer Jacque-Yves Cousteau, filming marine life in the Red Sea, Persian Gulf, and Indian Ocean. The feature-length documentary *Silent World* (1956) won top honors at Cannes and became a classic. In 1957 Malle was Jacques Tati's cameraman on *Mon Oncle*, and later that year completed his first feature, released here as both *Elevator to the Gallows* and *Frantic*. His most notable films include *Zazie* (1960, about an 11-year-old *gamine*), *The Fire Within* (1964, about a suicide), *Phantom India* (1968), *Murmur of the Heart* (1970, about mother-son incest), *Lacombe, Lucien* (1974, about a French collaborator with the Nazis) and his first American film, *Pretty Baby* (1978, about a child prostitute, played by Brooke Shields).

The director has two children born out of wedlock to separate women. In 1980 he married Candice Bergen, and since then, he says, "My life has become much more important than my work." The couple have a daugher Chloe born 8 November 1985.

David Mamet

"The American Dream gone bad" is how David Mamet dexcribes the subject of some of his plays. "In *Glengarry Glen Ross*, it's worse than bad," said the New York *Times'* Arthur Holmberg, "and Mr. Mamet proves himself the master of dramatizing the rip-off society." Mamet's 1984 real estate rouser won the year's Pulitzer Prize for Best American Play and the Drama Critics' Circle Award (having previously won plaudits in England where, the play was staged before coming to Broadway). Reared in regional theatre, Mamet was "Chicago's own" (he was named playwright in residence and associate director of the Goodman Theatre there) until the Broadway opening in 1977 of *American Buffalo*, which won the Drama Critics' Circle Award, after winning an off-Broadway "Obie" the previous year. (Since that time Al Pacino hopscotched the controversial play between Broadway and off.) The *Times'* Walter Kerr was fascinated by Mamet's sharp ear for "everyday language" and the "cadence of loneliness" and his uncanny ability to find "a rough kind of poetry" in the raw and raunchy street language. His turning of ordinary conversations into unique stage dialogues has been called "one of the relative wonders of the present theatre." Some critics carp at his sacrificing plot and character development for words, but many, like *The New Yorker's* Edith Oliver in her review of *Duck Variations*, feel he "cherishes characters even more" than he "cherishes words." "If it's not poetic on the stage, forget it," Mamet, who admits he has "a certain flair for dialogue," told Mark Zweigler of *After Dark*. "If it's solely serving the interest of the plot, I'm not interested. As a consequence, I go overboard the other way."

David Alan Mamet was born 30 November 1947 in Chicago, Illinois, and grew up on the city's South Side. After his parents' divorce in the late 1950s, his secondary education was split between schools in suburban Olympia Fields and the city itself. He attributes tuning his ear to the "music of language" to his father (an attorney and "amateur semanticist"), his piano lessons, and being a busboy at Second City, Chicago's improvisational cabaret. He attended the experimental Goddard College in Vermont with time off during his graduate work studying acting at New York's Neighborhood Playhouse where he says he was "terrible." He subsequently returned to Goddard as Artist in Residence and drama instructor and started the St. Nicholas Theatre Company. After "settling into" playwrighting, he introduced a 1975 double bill, *Duck Variations* and *Sexual Perversity in Chicago*, which *Time* magazine placed on its list of ten best plays of 1976. His other plays include: *A Life in the Theatre, Mr. Happiness, The Water Engine, Prairie du Chien, The Sanctity of Marriage, Squirrels, Lone Canoe, Reunion, Lakeboat, The Space Pandas, Donny March* and *Speed-the-Plow*. He wrote the screenplays for the remake of *The Postman Always Rings Twice, The Verdict, The Untouchables, Things Change, House of Games* and *We're No Angels*. He's also written two children's books: *Warm and Cold* (with his wife) and *The Owl* as well as being an Associate Professor of film at Columbia University.

Mamet married actress Lindsay Crouse in 1977 (two daughters) and, although he admits to feeling "claustrophobic in New York," they have a Manhattan apartment. They also have a country place in Vermont.

Melissa Manchester

"Please, don't let this feeling end; it's everything I am, everything I want to be . . . I can see what's mine now, finding out what's true . . . Since I found you—looking through the eyes of love . . ." sings one of the queens of movie soundtracks; her distinctive voice shines on the theme from *Ice Castles*. Melissa was born and raised in the Bronx (15 February 1951); her mother was a clothing designer and her father a bassoonist with the Metropolitan Opera. His practicing at home gave Melissa her first exposure to music. ("A bassoon out of context is a rare thing to grow up on," she laughs. "Maybe it does something to your brain.") After graduating from New York's prestigious High School for the Performing Arts and serving a brief stint at New York University where she studied acting, she learned songwriting in a class taught by singer-composer Paul Simon. She composed and sang commercial jingles for products like Coppertone and Kentucky Fried Chicken; she also began performing at coffeehouses and clubs around the town. At one commercial gig she met Barry Manilow, who introduced her to Bette Midler. Midler asked her if she'd like to be her back-up singer and Manchester answered, "No, I'd like to sing *instead* of you." Nevertheless, she was one of the raunch-and-rolling Harlettes for six months.

With the proceeds of her first album in 1973 she moved to Los Angeles, where she rented Liberace's house and fell into "the complete California life—chronic barbecuing." "Midnight Blue," recorded on her third album, sold more than a million copies. In 1974 she was picked as *Cashbox's* best new female vocalist. Meanwhile superstars like Johnny Mathis, Aretha Franklin and the Captain and Tennille were singing her songs. In 1978 she co-wrote with Kenny Loggins his hit with Stevie Nicks, "Whenever I Call You 'Friend.'" A year and a half after backing Midler up at Carnegie Hall, Manchester was back there as a headliner. She has collaborated with many of the top names in contemporary music, among them Marilyn and Alan Bergman, Carole Bayer Sager and Bernie Taupin. Her other hit singles include "Come in From the Rain," and "Don't Cry Out Loud." In 1985 she released the albums *Mathematics* and *Water From The Moon* along with the video "Energy." In 1986 she sang the film *Out of Africa's* theme, entitled "The Music of Goodbye," and the following year she shifted her focus to theatre when she starred in the Andrew Lloyd Webber musical *Song and Dance*.

Manchester divorced her first husband and former manager, Larry Brezner, after seven years of marriage. In 1982 she married Kevin De Remer, her tour coordinator, and the couple have a son, Nathan.

Henry Mancini

Composer-arranger-conductor Henry Mancini collects sculpture. He has pieces by Rodin and more by a sculptor whose name is not so well known but whose statues, designed for the Academy of Motion Picture Arts and Sciences, are recognized all over the world. Mancini's Rodins and Oscars now share space in his California home with his multiple Grammy Awards, countless Gold Albums, and an assortment of scrolls and certificates signaling practically every other honor the music industry can bestow. Mancini's music for the film *Breakfast at Tiffany's* won him his first two Oscars back in 1961 for best original score and best song, "Moon River" (with Johnny Mercer). His third Oscar came the following year for the song "Days of Wine and Roses" (also with Mercer) from the film of the same name.

Born 16 April 1924, Mancini inherited his musical proclivities from his steelworker father who played the flute in the Aliquippa, Pennsylvania Sons of Italy band. Eight-year-old Henry's first instrument was the piccolo, then came the flute, finally the piano. He served his musical apprenticeship working as pianist and arranger for the post-World War II Glenn Miller band headed by Tex Beneke. He found a bride at the same time—the former Ginny O'Conner, who sang with the Mellowlarks (three children: a son and twin girls). He started working in Hollywood at Universal-International in 1952, and in six years wrote the scores for over 100 films, among them, fittingly, *The Glenn Miller Story*. Mancini's home base is California, but conducting assignments often take him away from it. Still busy with movie work, he wrote the score for *Victor/Victoria* (1982), *Santa Claus: The Movie* (1985) and *Physical Evidence* (1989). He recorded the album *The Hollywood Musicals* with Johnny Mathis (1986) and he was honored by the Friars in 1988.

Barbara Mandrell

She calls herself "a hopeless ham and an occasional show-off" but Barbara Mandrell can just as easily be dubbed "the human dynamo." The five feet, two inch, 100 pound blue-eyed blond celebrated her twenty-fifth anniversary in show business in 1985. She lives her goal of "Always reach a little bit higher".

Barbara Ann Mandrell was born 25 December 1948 in Houston, Texas. Her father, Irby, owned a music store and made sure Barbara had her pick of the instruments. Her mother, Mary, herself an avid musician and teacher taught Barbara to play the accordion. Mandrell read music before she could read the English language. The five year old made her first public appearance playing the one gospel song she knew on her accordion at her uncle's church. When she was eleven her father took her from their California home to a music trade show in Chicago, where she made her first professional performance demonstrating various musical instruments. By now she had mastered the accordion, steel guitar and saxophone, and her appearance impressed "Uncle" Joe Maphis enough to earn her an invitation to join his Las Vegas show. She soon became a regular on a local Los Angeles TV show "Town Hall Party," and at age twelve made her network debut on Red Foley's ABC-TV show "Five Star Jubilee". Concert tours followed at age thirteen as she toured with the Johnny Cash Show, featuring Patsy Cline and George Jones. The Mandrells, a group consisting of Barbara, her parents and three non-family members (including Barbara's future husband, Ken Dudney) were formed shortly thereafter, and they toured the West Coast and eighteen foreign countries entertaining the military community and various civic groups. Ken and Barbara were married 28 May 1967 after Ken received his wings as a naval pilot. Mandrell retired to be a Navy wife, but the lure of the Grand Ole Opry proved too strong. In 1969, she signed with CBS Records, and her first release was a cover of Otis Redding's "I've Been Loving You Too Long". She recorded a collection of country hit singles, scoring her first Number One with "Midnight Oil" in 1973. Switching to ABC (eventually MCA) Records she scored with hits like "Married, But Not To Each Other", "Woman To Woman" and crossover hits "Sleeping Single In A Double Bed" and "If Loving You Is Wrong (I Don't Want To Be Right)". In 1982 her albums *The Best of Barbara Mandrell* and *Barbara Mandrell Live* went gold. Mandrell also enjoyed duet success with a variety of partners, including Lee Greenwood.

Mandrell's accomplishments have earned her over sixty awards. She is the first artist to ever win the CMA "Entertainer of the Year" Award two consecutive years (1980, 1981). Other awards include CMA Female Vocalist of the Year (1979, 1981); Academy of Country Music Female Vocalist (1981); nine People's Choice Awards, including six consecutive honors as "Favorite All-Around Female Entertainer" (1982-1987); six American Music Awards as "Favorite Female Country Vocalist" (1980-1986); nine Music City Awards, including the Living Legend Award; and an 1983 Grammy for "Best Inspirational Performance" for the LP "He Set My Life To Music," which also earned her a Dove Award for Gospel Album of the Year. She has also earned numerous *Billboard, Cashbox*, and *Record World* honors.

Television success came with "Barbara Mandrell and the Mandrell Sisters", an NBC hit from 1980 to 1982, and specials like "Barbara Mandrell—Something Special" (1985). The shows showcased her musical ability: She played bass, banjo, guitar, mandolin, pedal steel, saxophone and dobro. Her transition to acting occurred with the lead role on the CBS telefilm "Burning Rage" (1984). In addition to other specials, she made over thirty guest appearances on award and talk shows.

Her election in 1982 to the Tennessee Sports Hall of Fame highlighted her committment to sports and physical fitness. Her interests include sponsoring a celebrity softball tournament in Nashville, a golf tournament for the Alabama Sheriff's Girl and Boy Ranches, a youth hockey league team, and a Nashville women's city league softball team. Mandrell herself is an avid golfer and skier and attends family fishing trips as frequently as possible.

On 11 September 1984 Mandrell and her two oldest children were involved in a serious car crash. She was severely injured, escaping death only because she had suggested, just minutes earlier, that the three wear their seat belts. She had not been a seat belt user previously but the incident made her a seat belt advocate. She has completed a public service announcement urging people to "Please, buckle up. You may never get another chance."

Mandrell's life and career has been chronicled at "Barbara Mandrell Country," the museum she opened in May 1984 in Nashville. She arranged the displays and wrote the explanatory plaques featuring items special and dear to her from her personal and professional life. Inducted as a Grand Ole Opry member in 1972, Mandrell resides in Tennessee with her husband and their three children, sons Matthew and Nathaniel and daughter Jamie. She has recorded over twenty albums. Her latest *I'll Be Your Jukebox Tonight* (1988), featuring the hit single "I Wish That I Could Fall In Love Today," assures us Mandrell is a force who will be reckoned with for quite possibly another twenty-five years.

Manhattan Transfer

They are one of the most popular groups in contemporary music today. With their creative flair, versatility, and ability to master new forms of expression, the Manhattan Transfer regularly travel around the country performing in concert to standing-room-only audiences. So far they have released eleven albums in the 17 years they have been together.

The Manhattan Transfer was formed in 1972, the brainchild of member Tim Hauser. He wanted to form a vocal harmony group featuring vocal parts around a Count Basie saxophone section. Original members of the group were Tim Hauser, who at the time was everything from an executive at a large ad agency, to a New York City cab driver; Janis Siegel, who was singing in an all-girl band called Laurel Canyon; Alan Paul, who was on Broadway in *Grease;* and Laurel Masse, who was a waitress. In 1979 Laurel was replaced by Cheryl Bentyne. After rehearsing for six months, the band began performing in cabarets. Their debut album was *The Manhattan Transfer*, and was released in 1975 on Atlantic records. Several LP's followed, including *Coming Out* (1976), *Pastiche* (1978), *Manhattan Transfer Live* (1981), *Mecca for Moderns* (1981), *The Best of the Manhattan Transfer* (1981), *Bodies and Soul* (1983), *Bop Doo Wop* (1984), *Vocalese* (Grammy Award winner, 1985), *The Manhattan Transfer Live* (1987), *Brasil* (1987), *Vocalese Live 1986* (1987). In keeping up with their high standards of performance, it is only natural that they are the recipients of numerous Grammy Awards. In 1980 the group won a Grammy for Best Vocal Arrangement, as well as Best Jazz Fusion Performance for "Birdland." Several followed, including Best Pop Performance for "Boy from New York City," Best Vocal Arrangement for "A Nightingale Sang in Berkeley Square," and Best Vocal Jazz Performance By A Duo or Group for "Until I Met You" (Corner Pocket) all in (1981); Best Jazz Vocal Performance for "Route 66" (1982); Best Jazz Vocal Performance for "Why Not" (1983); and Best Jazz Vocal Performance for *Vocalese*, Best Male Jazz Performance and Best Vocal Arrangement For Two or More Voices for "Another Night in Tunisia" (1985). The group also received a Grammy in 1989 for Best Pop Vocal Duo Group.

Barry Manilow

"I just never got into the rock & roll thing as much as other people did. I know a lot of people will hang me for saying that, but being the musical snob that I am, I can take just so much of four chords." So states Barry Manilow during an interview with *US* magazine. "People see this picture of a guy in a silly Copacabana jacket and they think that is me. But if I am unhappy about that perception, it is up to me to do something about that." Throughout his career, Barry Manilow has been trying to please his fans and win over the critics. He has acquired a stable of tear-flowing female music lovers, and during his 1989 Broadway powerhouse presentation *Barry Manilow At The Gershwin* he lassoed in rave reviews from his long-term nonbelievers. The show, although intimate, pulled out all theatre stops, utilizing state-of-the-art theatrical devices such as the "magic screen" as well as the latest concert technology, videos and choreography. The evening was filled with anecdotes and stories from Manilow's career, interpreted through music and humorous sketches, and included a show-stopping thirty-minute medley highlighting his greatest hits. It also included material from his latest album *Barry Manilow* (1989).

Born 17 June 1946 in Brooklyn, he began music lessons at seven, ending up at Juilliard (while working in CBS' mailroom to defray school expenses). His first break came when a CBS director asked him to arrange some public domain songs for a musicalized version of *The Drunkard*. (He wrote an entire musical score for it, and the play ran off-Broadway for eight years.) By 1967

TV and radio commercials were his mainstay, and who would have guessed that a chance encounter with Bette Midler in 1972 would change the course of both their careers. In effect, Manilow became her musical director/arranger/pianist, contributing significantly to her Grammy-winning LP, *The Divine Miss M*. After sharing the bill with Midler on her first big national tour, Manilow went on his own solo tour in 1974. That tour was to become the springboard of his fame to come. By 1983 he would conclude his "Around the World in 80 Dates" (which included an all-time record for Broadway ticket sales: *Barry Manilow on Broadway*) with a gala charity concert at Royal Festival Hall in London in support of the Royal College of Music and the British Fund for World Jewish Relief, hosted by the Prince and Princess of Wales. His unprecedented string of hits include "Mandy," "Could It Be Magic," "I Write The Songs," "Tryin' to Get the Feeling," "It's A Miracle," "At The Copa," "Can't Smile Without You," "Weekend in New England," and "I Made It Through The Rain." Among his biggest album blockbusters are 1979's *One Voice* (double platinum); 1975's *Tryin' To Get The Feeling* (triple platinum) and 1978's *Greatest Hits - Volume 1* (quadruple platinum). Record sales to date exceed fifty million worldwide. Manilow picked up an Emmy in 1977 for his first special on ABC-TV. He earned a Tony for his first Broadway run. His Grammy (for best pop male vocal performance) came for "At The Copa," and it was in a CBS-TV film "Copacabana" that he made his dramatic acting debut in 1985. In 1987 he talked up his autobiography *Sweet Life: Adventures on the Way to Paradise* with a national book tour, which was followed by a creative album *Swing Street* and a CBS-TV special "Barry Manilow: Big Fun on Swing Street."

Manilow was once married to a former girlfriend from Brooklyn, but he is currently living in Los Angeles next door to Nancy and Ronald Reagan. His constant companion is Linda Allen, and he told *US*, "I don't know how I have changed her life, but she has made me more solid and given me much more security." When he's not making music, Manilow likes to catch up and read the Top 10 books on The *New York Times* bestseller lists or think about Paris. He says, "You know, if I hadn't become a pop singer, I would have been happy playing the piano in some bistro in Paris."

Dinah Manoff

"Look at me . . . the real me, the cheerleader from hell!" Riding the rave reviews of the 1989 hit TV sitcom "Empty Nest," Dinah Manoff insists she's not exactly like the character, Carol, that she portrays on the show. But she's also quick to note that it has been wonderful working with such a fine group of players, including Richard Mulligan, Kristy McNichol, Park Overall and David Leisure.

The talented Tony winning actress was born in New York City circa 1957 to playwright Arnold Manoff and actress Lee Grant. Dinah lived in the Big Apple until she was seven, then in Malibu for awhile, then back to New York again when her Mom's career forced them to return to the east coast. She told *TV Guide* in June 1989, "My rhythm is New York. My inside clock ticks New York. I get on the subway and feel serene. I've been in every New York neighborhood at every time of night, and I have no fear. I just blend in." Manoff attended public schools on both coasts, and she later discovered she didn't blend in; she proved her acting talents to be outstanding in her early productions. After appearing in the films *Grease* (1977), *Ordinary People*, (1979), the TV sitcom "Soap" (1977-1978), and the telefilms "High Terror" (1977), "The Possessed" (1977), and "Raid on Entebbe" (1977), she won the role of the spunky daughter in Neil Simon's Broadway play *I Ought To Be In Pictures* (1980) which earned her a Tony Award and a Theatre World Award. More roles followed, including another Broadway show, *Leader of the Pack* (1984-1985 with Patrick Cassidy), telefilms "Flight 90" (1984), "A Matter of Sex" (1984), "The Seduction of Gina" (1984), and "Classified Love" (1986), plus the NBC miniseries "Celebrity" (1984) and the movies *I Ought To Be In Pictures* (1981), *Backfire* (1987), and *Childsplay* (1988). Her latest film, *Boy's Life* (1989) was directed by her mother. Of their relationship, Dinah says, "It's hard when Mommy is directing. Very Hard. I instantly become the rebellious teenager. I want to please her, but I don't want her to tell me what to do. I know that isn't logical. When I can separate her giving me direction from her telling me to make my bed in the morning, we do very well."

Manoff's marriage to French designer Jean-Marc Joubert lasted only five years. Now living alone in a house in Laurel Canyon, California, she prefers her privacy.

Marcel Marceau

"In the womb of my mother I was already a mime. I was born to be a mime as a fish is born to be in water." The fragile-looking Frenchman reigned as the premier pantomime artist worldwide even before his American debut in 1955. In his trademark role of Bip, the doleful white-faced clown, Marceau was the embodiment of all mortals buffeted by life's dilemmas. As one critic put it, he "serves as a sort of Everyman, pitting himself against strong winds and recalcitrant ladders and the invisible cages in which life traps us all."

He was born Marcel Mandel in Strasbourg, France on 22 March 1923, the son of a Kosher butcher. After his father was taken to Auschwitz during the German occupation of France, he fled with his mother to Limoges and in 1944 joined his older brother in the French Underground. During service in the French army he entertained the troops with mime. A fan of Charlie Chaplin and Buster Keaton, Marceau (he renamed himself after a young general of the French Revolution) enrolled in Charles Dullin's School of Dramatic Art in Paris to study under the great mime master Etienne Decroux in 1946. He created his Bip character after joining the theatre company of Jean-Louis Barrault and became, almost overnight, a favorite of Left Bank intellectuals. Of his summation of the ages of man in the famous, "Youth, Maturity, Old Age, and Death," one critic said, "He accomplishes in less than two minutes what most novelists cannot do in a volume." Appearances on television both here and abroad helped him attract a wide audience. With assistance from the French government, Marceau operates the International School of Mime, which trains students from across the world. Marceau is married to a former actress, Huguette, and they have two sons.

Dan Marino

The football quarterback "who swaggers even when he is standing still" signed a six-year, $9 million contract (with an extra $100,000 per year in bonuses) with the Miami Dolphins in 1986. That high salary was arrived at for Dan Marino after bringing his team to the Superbowl two years in a row (1984 and 1985) and staging a thirty-seven-day walk-out against the owner of the team when contract talks hit a stalemate.

Daniel Marino, Jr., born 15 September 1961 in Pittsburgh, Pennsylvania, grew up five blocks from the University of Pittsburgh campus where he later was to star. The blue-collar neighborhood, like industrial Pittsburgh itself, molded young Danny's down-to-earth personality; notes sent to him by his father helped affirm his impressive talents. "You are the most dominating player in college football," Dan Sr. jotted. "Remember nobody does it better." Having led his team to one of the nations' best college records in the three years he was a starter, Marino was often favorably compared to such former Pitt All-

Americans as Tony Dorsett, whose jerseys he kept in his room. Miami coach Don Shula, who'd guided Johnny Unitas and Bob Griese, brought him to the NFL Dolphins. "I expected him to do well," Shula said after the rookie's sterling year, "but nobody could have expected this much from Dan. Wet or dry, against blitzes or zones, nothing bothers him." Although the 1986 and 1987 seasons were not as rewarding for the Miami Dolphins, Marino still kept his strong image. In 1986 he led the conference in passing, and the following year he led the AFC in completions and touchdown passes. Marino married his hometown sweetheart, Claire Veazey, in Januray 1985 and the couple have two sons, Daniel Charles and Michael Joseph. They live in Ft. Lauderdale, Florida, and when Marino's not tossing the pigskin he enjoys playing golf, catching up on movies and eating Italian food. Lending his notability to good causes, he supports the Leukemia Fund and has appeared on posters for the American Library Association.

Marisol

The Spanish name "Marisol" can be translated in English into the words "sea and sun." But to the contemporary art world, Marisol has another meaning. To habitués of such institutions as New York's Museum of Modern Art, the Whitney, and Chicago's Art Institute, it has become since the 1960s synonymous with a new genus of sculpture created by a dark, enigmatic Venezuelan who bears a close resemblance to the beautiful witch in the early Charles Addams cartoons. A "Marisol," in most instances, is a life-size wooden human-like figure (or group of them) "as compelling, often as charming, as her name." In the early years, Marisol pieces were often topped off with the gaunt Garboesque face of their creator, but no longer. "I gave up," the artist says, "because there's no end. You can never find out who you are."

The original flesh and blood Marisol was born on 22 May 1930 in Paris to a wealthy and nomadic Venezuelan couple named Escobar. As a child she lived on and off in France, South America, and California, and dived for the first time into the turbulent New York art pool in 1950. She studied painting for several years with the noted abstract expressionist Hans Hoffman and then moved off on a tangent of her own into a new, often whimsical dimension. Inspired in part by the stylized figures of pre-Columbian folk art, she began peopling her work with the toylike totems that have become her trademark. Given her first solo exhibition in 1958 by gallery giant Leo Castelli, she is now represented in collections as far afield as the Wallraf-Richartz Museum in Cologne, Germany, and the Hakone Open Air Museum in Japan. Long attracted by the challenge of carving sculptural versions of famous paintings, the artist is especially fond of the works of Leonardo da Vinci. In 1978, she exhibited her idiosyncratic tableaux of his "Madonna and Child with St. Anne and St. John" and in 1984, presented a plywood-plaster-stone version of "The Last Supper". *New York* Magazine critic Kay Larson speculated of the latter piece that some viewers might be outraged at the notion of "a Pop artist making a Pop homage out of a High Renaissance masterpiece." "But," she quickly added "Deep affection has always been one of Marisol's strong points, and deep affection is what you find here. Your outrage instantly disappears, and what remains is pure, uncomplicated pleasure at her feat of gentle audacity."

Branford Marsalis

"When I realized how much of a contribution jazz music and jazz musicians have made to the world, that's when I decided I really wanted to be a jazz musician," says the multiple Grammy nominee in the category of best jazz instrumental performance, soloist. After touring the world with rock star Sting's Blue Turtle Band; performing at such widely watched concerts as Live-Aid and Freedomfest; lending his talents to a wealth of recording artists, including The Duke Ellington Brass Band Orchestra ("Digital Duke"), Miles Davis ("Decoy"), Teena Marie ("Emerald City"), Tina Turner ("Break Every Rule") and the movie soundtrack of Spike Lee's "School Daze"; and being a band member of such illustrious groups as Art Blakey & the Jazz Messengers, Herbie Hancock's B.S.O.P. II Quartet and The Wynton Marsalis Quintet, the smooth-playing saxophonist has formed his own group and come into his own spotlight. "The classic tunes and straight ahead swing showed off his warm sound and mercurial phrasing to perfection," wrote Robert Palmer in the *New York Times*. "On record... he has sounded something like a Coletrane or Shorter copycat. At (the club), he sounded like himself." But jazz is not the only medium of expression for the talented musician who has released four jazz albums. He also crossed over and recorded a classical album, "Romances for Saxophone" with the English Chamber Orchestra, which was top five on the *Billboard* classical chart for over two months. Not limiting himself to music, Marsalis has also hosted VH-1's "New Vison" and acted in feature films "Throw Momma From the Train" and "School Daze."

Born 26 August, 1960 as one of six sons of Delores and Ellis, Branford was greatly influenced by his parents. Their father, a renowned jazz pianist, became the boys' mentor and educator, exposing them to music. Branford's first instrument was a piano at age four, followed by the clarinet two or three years later ("so I could play in the school band"). At fifteen, he was given an alto saxophone because his father thought it was the hardest sax to play. Branford admits, "I didn't want to play tenor because everybody else was playing tenor." In high school, Branford played football and ran track, but "I always knew I could be a musician, it was easy for me." Singing with "funk bands," Branford wanted to be a "media superstar. But the more I practiced and listened to records and tapes, the more I got into jazz." At sixteen, Branford was asked by his younger brother, Wynton, to join his band. "There wasn't one second's hesitation. I wanted to play in Wynton's band because I knew it was going to be the best band around." In 1978, Branford started at Southern University in Baton Rouge, where he studied with clarinetist Alvin Batiste, who convinced the budding talent to try a music school. The following year, Branford attended Berklee School of Music in Boston. During the summer of 1980, the music student was playing baritone sax in Art Blakey's band touring Europe. During Christmas break, Branford played for two weeks with the Lionel Hampton Orchestra after winning an audition by sight-reading the band's charts. Returning to Berklee in 1981, Branford secured a four month job playing with the Clark Terry Band, studying Wayne Shorter ("my guru at the time"), Ben Webster and Sonny Rollins before accepting an offer to play with the Blakey Band and brother Wynton. The brothers traveled and performed together with Blakey and Hancock. In 1985, Branford met Sting and toured with his band, taking time out to record his classical album. 1986 saw the start of Branford's own band and the release of his second jazz album, "Royal Garden Blues," which brought Branford a Grammy nomination. Now the father of his own son, Reese, (born 29 June 1987) he says "I'm confident of my ability, but I'm not ready to break new ground right now; I still want to do classical and pop records."

Wynton Marsalis

"I do not entertain and I will not entertain. I'm a musician. I studied the music and my music should be presented that way. I'm serious about what I'm doing ... I took the route the record company doesn't think is commercially viable. But the record companies aren't musicians, they're great businessmen. I don't tell them how to run a record company. They don't tell me how to play music." It may be just this music-for-music's-sake attitude that has allowed Marsalis to develop his pure and extraordinary talent, and the recognition of his peers. He was the winner of the 1981 *Down Beat* Critics Poll for talent deserving wider recognition. *Stereo Review* granted him the Record of the Year Award in 1982. In 1984 he won the *Down Beat* Reader's Poll as "Best Trumpeter' and "Jazz Musician of the Year" both for the second year in a row, as well as back-to-back Grammy's as "Best Jazz soloist" *and* "Best Classical soloist with an Orchestra" (the first artist to have made that crossover in Grammy history). In 1988 he walked away with another Grammy as Best Jazz Instrumental Performance by a group for his album *Marsalis Standard Time, Vol. 1.*

Wynton Marsalis, born 18 October 1961 in New Orleans, is the son of renowned pianist Ellis Marsalis, who played in the band of jazz giant Al Hirt. In fact, it was Hirt, recognizing Wynton's talent, who gave the boy his first horn at age six. Marsalis began serious music study in high school, and before graduation had earned the chance to perform with professional symphonies at the Eastern Music Festival in North Carolina and at Tanglewood, a rare honor for someone not yet eighteen. After beginning classical study at Juilliard School, he performed with the Brooklyn Philharmonic and was a soloist with the Mexico City Symphony. His first jazz album—*Wynton Marsalis*—was released by Columbia in 1982 to wide acclaim. Although his classical finishing school education has opened heavy doors, Marsalis prefers the jazz schooling he received on the road studying and performing with such jazz heavyweights as Art Blakey an Herbie Hancock. It may be a matter of family heritage: "I'm doing what I want to do. I'm playing jazz, period. And if I get squashed—and it could happen—I just get squashed. But I'm functioning on the premise that this is good music and deserves to be heard. And I am a jazz musician . . . my father was a jazz musician. I play jazz." His recent LPs include: *J. Mood* (1986), *Blues Alley* (1988) and *The Majesty of the Blues* (1989).

E.G. Marshall

"There's a saying among actors that goes, 'who's E.G. Marshall, get me E.G. Marshall, get me an E.G. Marshall type and who's E.G. Marshall?' I used to go anywhere and people would . . . know me from my television shows," the actor says, referring to his two longtime TV hits, "The Bold Ones" and the "Defenders" for which he won two Emmys. "Now there's a group of people who have grown up and don't know me at all." But perhaps the best thing to have happened with age to this actor, whom Orson Wells once called "one of the only three actors to think while he was acting" (the other two were Garbo and Chaplin) is what Marshall calls "the era of the character actor. At one point everything was going to all the young studs, like Brando and Dean. But things go through phases and now it's turning around and the character actor is really coming into his own."

Born 18 June 1910 in the small Minnesota farming community of Owatonna, E.G. Marshall once considered becoming a Protestant minister. He settled on an acting career and started out in 1933 performing with a Shakespearean company in the South and Southwest, moved with it to Chicago for four years, and then headed for Broadway. He debuted in 1942 in *Jason* and received critical acclaim in such landmark productions as Eugene O'Neill's *The Iceman Cometh*, Thornton Wilder's *The Skin of Our Teeth* and Samuel Beckett's *Waiting for Godot*. Demonstrating his skill at comedy as well as drama, he was a standout in Neil Simon's *Plaza Suite* and replacing Hume Cronyn opposite Jessica Tandy in the Pulitzer Prize-winning *The Gin Game*. His many film roles have included *Twelve Angry Men, The Caine Mutiny, Compulsion, My Chauffer* and *The Power*. He also played the President of the United States in the film *Superman*, and the father in Woody Allen's *Interiors*. He appeared in a 1983 revival of the Broadway hit *Mass Appeal* and the two television miniseries "At Mother's Request" (1986) and "War and Remembrance" (1988).

Garry Marshall

During the past twenty five years he has distinguished himself as a master of contemporary comedy. Not only has he created, written, directed, and produced some of the biggest hits on TV, but he has also proven his talent in feature films as well. Garry has directed five motion pictures, in addition to writing and producing over 1,000 television shows.

Garry Marshall was born 13 November 1934 in New York City. His formal education included Northwestern's Medill School of Journalism. Upon graduating, he left for the Army where he pursued his interest in jazz by playing the drums with his own jazz group. After his commitment to the Army was completed, he went on to become a reporter for the *New York Daily News.z* Soon following, he began writing scripts for television shows. He entered into the world of television as a writer for Jack Paar's "Tonight Show" in 1960, and later for the "Joey Bishop Show." While in California, Garry met Jerry Belson, and together they became one of the most prolific writing teams ever. The two are responsible for such popular television sitcoms as "The Danny Thomas Show," "The Lucy Show," the "Dick Van Dyke Show" which won an Emmy, and "I Spy." They also created and wrote their first series "Hey Landlord" in 1966. In 1969, the team brought Neil Simon's "The Odd Couple" to TV, in which Garry served as the executive producer for five years. Their first experience with motion pictures came soon after when they were contracted to write and produce the comedy *How Sweet It Is*, followed by a drama entitled *The Grasshopper*. Deciding to go solo, he created and produced several successful comedy shows including "Happy Days," "Laverne and Shirley," "Mork and Mindy," and "Blansky's Beauties," as well as directing the films *Young Doctors in Love, The Flamingo Kid, Nothing In Common, Overboard*, and his most recent endeavor, the hit drama *Beaches*. Not limiting himself to writing, creating, and producing, Garry made the move to the other side of the camera performing in the films *Lost in America*, and *Jumping Jack Flash*, which was directed by his sister Penny Marshall.

Garry and his wife Barbara reside in California and have three children.

Penny Marshall

She has a special talent for making people laugh. Penny has appeared in numerous television sitcoms, made-for-TV movies, and films, as well as directing two hit movies.

Penny was born on 15 October 1944 in New York City. She spent her childhood (from age three) tap dancing at her mother's dancing school, and it was her dancing that introduced her to the world of show business. She and a group of friends competed on and won "Ted Mack's Amateur Hour" at fourteen, and then went on to perform on the "Jackie Gleason Show." After attending the University of New Mexico in Albuquerque, and spending six years there, she left for Hollywood and made her television debut in California on "The Danny Thomas Hour." Other TV appearances include: "The Odd Couple" (1972-1974), "Chico and the Man" (1975), "The Mary Tyler Moore Show" (1975), "Saturday Night Live" (1975-1977), "Happy Days" (1975), "The Tonight Show" (1976-1977), and "Laverne and Shirley" (1976-1983). She made appearances in the TV movies *More Than Friends* (1978), and *Love Thy Neighbor* (1984). She also performed in the films *How Sweet It is* (1967), *The Grasshopper* (1970), and *1941* (1979). Proving that she is as versatile as she is funny, she has directed two hit movies, *Jumpin' Jack Flash* (1986) and *Big* (1988).

Penny has been married two times; the first time to Michael Henry, with whom she had her daughter Tracy, and the second time to Rob Reiner, married 10 April 1971 and divorced in 1979. She is currently single and resides in Los Angeles.

Thurgood Marshall

When Lyndon Johnson named Thurgood Marshall as his selection for a vacant Supreme Court seat, he knew he was both making history and nominating a brilliant judicial thinker. Marshall, the great-grandson of a freed slave, was born Thoroughgood Marshall in Baltimore, 2 July 1908; he is the first black man to don Supreme Court robes. But perhaps his greatest impact came some 13 years before his 1967 appointment, when—as the nation's foremost civil rights attorney—he brought the *Brown v. Topeka Board of Education* case to the Court. His pleading resulted in the unanimous decision by which the Court overturned the longstanding "separate but equal" doctrine of racial segregation in public schools. The decision crowned his history of winning 29 of the 32 cases he argued before that body.

Head of his class at Howard Law School (1933), Marshall graduated and began practicing law in his home town, where much of his practice was devoted to civil rights cases. He was invited to join the legal staff of the NAACP, and by 1938 was leading that organization's assault on state segregation laws, particularly in the field of education. For more than 27 years he was chief counsel to the NAACP. President Kennedy appointed him to the Second Circuit Court of Appeals, and in 1965 President Johnson told Marshall he was naming him Solicitor General. Marshall hesitated. Johnson snapped: "I want folks to walk down the hall at the Justice Department and look in the door and see a nigger sitting there." Johnson never knew what Marshall was thinking: that as a boy his father had insisted he fight any boy who called him that name. This jovial, cigar-chomping joke-teller (when he's off the bench) has two sons by his first wife, Vivian G. ("Buster") Burey. Following her death he wed the former Cecilia Suyat.

Billy Martin

Either as a player or manager, the man once known as "Billy the Kid" has been an outlaw for over three decades in the game he so loves. The three-time American League Manager of the Year (1974 with the Texas Rangers, and 1980 and '81 with the Oakland A's) has skippered five clubs to improved records, pennants and/or a World Series crown. The five-feet-eleven, 170 pounder is known as "baseball's street fighter" for an ever-threatening temper that's led him to punch out players, sportswriters, and team execs. "They talk about my temper," Martin says. "Well I haven't seen a good race horse yet who wasn't high strung. . . . Jesus Christ took a whip to the money changers, right? Well, that's a temper and that's not a bad guy to follow. The way I see it, my temper is a great ally. It is what has pushed Billy Martin."

Born on 16 May 1928 in Berkeley, Calif., Alfred Manuel Martin's push started early. He was raised by his Italian grandparents, and was so spunky and competitive that he was able to play with major leaguers in their off-season when he was only fifteen years old. He was in the minors at eighteen, and when he played for Oakland's Oaks he became a favorite of manager Casey Stengel, who brought Martin up when he took over the Yankee helm. Termed "the best little player" Stengel ever had, the infielder's fighting reputation began when he was released after a nightclub fracas in 1957. He bounced around the league and then into managing, leaving a trail of fisticuffed unfortunates in his wake. When in 1975, he finally got his dream job as Yanks manager, he soon reversed the twelve-year decline of the once proud pinstripers. After a dugout shove-match with Reggie Jackson and headaches galore en route to a World Series win in 1977 he quit in mid-season of 1978 only to be rehired the next year, after which he and Yankee bossman George Steinbrenner fell out again and he was fired. Not one, apparently, to hold a grudge, George hired Billy to manage the Yankees again in 1985 after they got off to a slow start under Yogi Berra. By the time June 1988 came around, Martin had been fired from the Yankees for the fifth time. However, he remains with the team as a "Special Advisor." The author of two books, *Number One* and *Billyball* he is also the owner of a western boot store on Madison Avenue. Martin married his third wife, Jill Guiver on 25 January 1987.

Dean Martin

The basic ingratiating ingredients of this card-shark-turned-actor and crooning superstar has been said to be five parts gin to one part forsooth. In any case, he wryly insists, "I drink only moderately. I've got a case of Moderately in my dressing room."

Born Dino Crocetti, 17 June 1917 in Steubenville, Ohio, into the family of a barber, he toiled as a gas station attendant, boxer and croupier before turning to singing. "There wasn't much else for a kid to do," he remembers genially, "except a little stealing, of course. Why, even today when I go into a fancy haberdashery and spend $500, I always steal a necktie or something." When he switched to singing in Steubenville night spots, he was surprised by the low pay. ("When the guy offered $50 a week, I thought he was crazy. I was makin' more than that just palmin' silver dollars.") Eventually he warbled his way up to the $750-a-week bracket at Atlantic City's 500 club where, in 1946, he shared the bill with a gangly, long-jawed comedian named Jerry Lewis. When their scripted show brought no laughs, they turned to ad-libbing and became one of the most popular teams in show business, in clubs, and on TV. The team made a total of sixteen films together before severing the partnership with raging animosity. (Their reunion in the late 1970s on one of Lewis' annual Muscular Dystrophy telethons was an A-level tearjerker.) "It was wonderful," Martin says of his days with Lewis, "we did all the crazy things I'd always wanted to do. Hearing a whole audience laugh is just like getting drunk." He admits that the general consensus was "I'd drown without Jerry," but the singer famous for his sly winks, double entendres and boozer image made it even bigger on his own. After making a less-than-impressive solo film debut in a clinker called *10,000 Bedrooms*, he began to be taken seriously as an actor when he landed the juicy role of the draft dodger in *The Young Lions* in 1958. Since then, he's alternated between serious roles (*Rio Bravo*, *Airport*,) with those featuring light comedy and music (e.g. *Bells Are Ringing*). In the recording studios, Martin has made his gold and/or platinum mark with such hits as "That's Amore" and "Memories Are Made of This." He has been associated with NBC-TV since 1948 ("Actually, it's the only network I know how to get to") where, among a number of innovations (including sliding down a brass pole in his mock bachelor pad by way of making his entrance on his variety show) is his having transformed "the roast" into a fresh new entertainment art form. The thrice-married six-footer (to Betty McDonald, Jeanne Biggers and Catherine Mae Hawn) is the father of seven (he also adopted his third wife's daughter). His talented actor/singer son, Dean Paul Martin, was killed in 1987 in a crash near the Air Force Base where he served as an Air National Guard Captain.

Judith Martin

Gentle reader . . . "The ancient Greek code of hsopitality," writes America's best-loved etiquette-etc-expert, "is the one to which Miss Manners still subscribes. You may never murder a guest while he is in your house. It is so

Mary Martin

much more polite to get him off the premises first, by sending him on an impossible mission from which you are certain he cannot return alive." This is just a wee-little-bit of her witty advice which is syndicated throughout the country and featured in the *Washington Post*. She provides comprehensive information on everything from birth to death. For instance: Parties ("at dinner parties, married couples must be separated because they tell the same stories and tell them differently"), Advice ("First, ask the person for advice on everything . . . then ignore the advice"), and What to say when introduced to a homosexual couple ("How do you do; how do you do").

Judith Martin, daughter of a United Nations diplomat, was born in Washington ca. 1938 and received her B.A. from Wellesley, where she majored in Gracious Living (and took a B.A. in English). She has worked for the *Washington Post* for over twenty years and, in addition to her witty "Miss Manners" offerings, she serves as a drama and film critic. She has made journalism news a number of times, most notably for her review of Tricia Nixon's White House tour for television (which resulted in her being banned from the First Daughter's White House wedding), her remarks on Amy Carter being allowed to read at a state dinner ("If the book was better than the table conversation . . . why can't everyone bring one?") and her frequent comments on the style of the Reagans. The writer whom *Publishers Weekly* calls "a winning combination of Dear Abby, Amy Vanderbilt and Fran Lebowitz," is also the author of several books: *The Name on the White House Floor*, a collection of essays on White House and diplomatic life; *Gilbert*, a comic-novel of manners; *Miss Manner's Guide to Excruciatingly Correct Behavior* and *Miss Manner's Guide to Rearing Perfect Children*. Her latest titles include: *Common Courtesy* (1985), *Style and Substance* (1986) and *Everybody Everybody* (1987). She lives graciously in Washington with her husband Robert, a scientist in biochemical genetics, and their children, Nicholas and Jacobina.

"To Miss Manners," wrote a reviewer for *New York* magazine, "etiquette is a thrilling battle waged by the mature against the large children disguised as adults. . . . Miss Manners doesn't think it's polite to remain silent and smiling when a visitor's child tries to put your cat in the freezer. . . . She knows that the only thing necessary for the triumph of evil is that people of etiquette do nothing." Dear Miss Manners.

Mary Martin

"Mary Martin flew like Peter Pan again last night, sprinkling magic dust over the audience" marvelled the reviewer about her October, 1984, performance benefitting the trauma center (now renamed the Mary Martin Trauma Center) at San Francisco General Hospital. "Last night she said she wanted to do 'something nice' for the hospital that saved her life after a San Francisco traffic accident in 1982" (claiming the life of her manager and seriously injuring the now-late actress, Janet Gaynor, and her husband, Paul Gregory).

She was born on 1 December 1913 in Weatherford, Tex., the town in which she made her singing debut at five at the local fireman's ball. In 1938, on Broadway, after she sang "My Heart Belongs to Daddy" in the musical *Leave It to Me*, audiences' hearts belonged to her. Because of her performance, Paramount offered her a 10-picture deal, so she "returned" to Hollywood (she had been there for two years earlier with no luck in landing a job—"I tried so hard that people in Hollywood nicknamed me 'Audition Mary'"). She made half a dozen pictures (*The Great Victor Herbert* and *Rhythm on the River* among them), but she hated the countless retakes, the lack of spontaneity ("It was all so boring, so wasteful, so enervating"). Under the guidance of Richard Halliday, a tall, dignified story editor at Paramount whom she married in 1940, she returned to Broadway and a string of musical hits including *One Touch of Venus*, *Lute Song*, the touring *Annie Get Your Gun*, *South Pacific*, *The Sound of Music* (Tony) and the perennial *Peter Pan* (Tony). (She says that *Peter Pan* is "absolutely" her favorite of all the shows she's performed.) Stricken with a serious illness after the long run in *I Do, I Do* (1968) she and Halliday took a four-year sabbatical at Nossa Fazenda, their ranch in Brazil. He died in 1973.

Martin first appeared on TV in 1953 when she co-starred with Ethel Merman, live, in the famed Ford 50s Anniversary Show. She then co-starred, again live, with Noel Coward, in a 90-minute dual sing-along, a program which *Time* magazine said proved that "talent has no need for production numbers." Other productions (also live) were "Annie Get Your Gun," "Peter Pan" and (after touring 3 months in 87 cities from Texas to Alaska) "Music with Mary" *and* "Magic with Mary Martin" on the afternoon and evening of Easter Sunday, 1959. Recent television projects include her first TV movie, "Valentine" (1979) which received a Peabody award, and "Over Easy," the 1981-1983 PBS-TV series, which she co-hosted with Jim Hartz. In 1969 Martin published her first book, *Mary Martin's Needlepoint* ("I read books and did needlepoint to save my sound whenever I did a show. Since Richard's been gone, I haven't stopped.") The first edition of her autobiography, *My Heart Belongs* was published in 1976, and the second edition in 1984. For three years she was associated with Fieldcrest Mills, both as a designer and their roving ambassadress.

These days, she is in residence (but seldom indoors) in a new house in Rancho Mirage near Palm Springs. She meditates, swims, and (of course) needlepoints. Will she return to the stage? (Her last Broadway appearance was in *So You Turn Somersaults* (1977). "I don't wish to do eight shows a week and go back into my cocoon," she confesses, "I'm having such a lovely life with my children, and my six grandchildren ('they're all so gorgeous') and my friends." From an early Texas marriage she is the mother of actor Larry Hagman, the infamous J.R. Ewing on television's long-running "Dallas" ("he's a *fabulous* actor," boasts his mother). Her daughter, Heller, (so named because "prenatally she kicked like mad") is the child of her second marriage to Halliday ("she's a *fabulous* mother," boasts Martin). Hagman says of his mother: "She has magic. Olivier has it. Brando has it—that 'other' thing that makes us want to look at her on stage." Although she may not return to stage, we will see her in other media. "Never stop working" she advised readers in a 1983 New York *Times* interview. "Keep active. I've been practicing what I preach. I tend to think I'm 19. I'm sort of retarded that way . . . I always have a good time. I really love living. I love every second of it. I guess it's my stubborn Texas determination to continue to the last breath." TV viewers experienced a special treat in 1989 when "Peter Pan" was rebroadcast after a long hiatus from the small screen.

Steve Martin

His motto: "Be courteous, kind and forgiving . . . be oblong and have your knees removed. Be tasteless, rude and offensive." Irreverent, for sure. "Well, excuuuuuuse me. It's blow your brains out time." The comedian blows on, "I'm so mad at my mother. She's 102 years old and she calls up wanting to borrow ten dollars for some food. I told her, heyyy, what is this bull? I work for a living!" Described as "Jekyll and Hyde alternating between frenzy and sobriety," he offers this bit of self analysis: "I think ultimately, when I'm at my best, it's a total presentation of a human being, on-stage, being vulnerable, being afraid, being confident, fooling myself, you know lying to myself . . . the different little jokes and things are held together by an attitude of that personality."

Steve Martin was born in Waco, Texas in either 1945 or 1946. His birthdate is his mystery. At three he became stagestruck, the result of seeing a Jerry Lewis film, and at age five he began his career as a comedian. "I'd watch the skits on the Ed Sullivan show, memorize them and then go to school and headline them during Show and Tell." When the family moved to Garden Grove, California, the ten-year-old Martin took a job selling twenty-five cent guidebooks to Disneyland just two miles down the road.

Throughout his teen years he performed in those special Disneyland clean-and-safe revues, then spread his Dumbo ears and flew through Long Beach State College majoring in philosophy. He appeared in local comedy clubs and received his big break writing gags for the "Smothers Brothers Comedy Hour." Then in big demand with other comedy performers he wrote for them for a while but stopped. "Comedy comes down to a split second and by the time it leaves the typewriter and gets to the director or the star, it's gone." Success was slow in coming. On the road for years, he vowed to quit performing until in 1975 his despair actually transformed his act. Close to the edge, he changed his routine by allowing the outrageous to blossom into his trademark shtick—self-styled absurdity. Television appearances on nationwide talk and variety shows lead to regular appearances on NBC's popular "Saturday Night Live" and his "wild and crazy guy" routine became as popular overnight as the hula hoop. Suddenly Martin was the new pop of the American funnybone. His mood swung, back to Hollywood where he appeared in films such as *The Jerk*, 1979, the musical *Pennies From Heaven*, 1981, and comedies such as *Dead Men Don't Wear Plaid*, *The Man with Two Brains*, *The Lonely Guy*, *All of Me* in 1984 (for which he received Best Actor honors from the N.Y. Film Critics), the film version of *Little Shop of Horrors* (1986), *The Three Amigos* (1986), *Planes, Trains and Automobiles* (1987), *Roxanne* (1987; won award from National Film Critics) and *Dirty Rotten Scoundrels* (1989). He expanded his horizons to live theatre and appeared in the Lincoln Center production of *Waiting for Godot* in 1988. Martin is also the author of the autobiographical *Cruel Shoes*, published in 1979. Having guested more than fifty times on NBC's "Tonight Show," he has commented, "It's rumored that Johnny Carson moved to the West Coast to be closer to me." After sharing some live-in chuckles with the likes of Bernadette Peters, the comedian married actress Victoria Tennant on 20 November 1986 in Rome.

Richard Marx

Richard Marx embarked on his second international concert tour which began in August 1989. Tokyo was the first of 200 stops across the world, with other appearances in Japan, Australia, and the U.S. In addition, he has performed in various night clubs throughout the U.S. including Los Angeles, New York, and his hometown of Chicago.

The Chicago-born singer, composer, and musician began his singing career as a child. An 18-year veteran of the business, he began singing professionally at age five, and began writing his own rock music at age seventeen. Initially, he was trying to make it as a songwriter. "That meant doing a lot of legwork and anything else I could do to make a living and to position myself in the right place at the right time. I worked as a background singer, arranger, and keyboardist on record projects. Ultimately, that led to my first song being cut by Kenny Rogers," states Richard. Five years later he signed on with Manhattan Records to produce his hit debut album, *Richard Marx*, which was released in 1987. Moving rapidly up the charts, *Richard Marx* soon went double platinum, containing such enormous hits as "Don't Mean Nothing," "Should've Known Better," "Endless Summer Nights," and "Hold On to the Nights," all of which made top three on the charts. "Hold On to the Nights" became his first number one hit. Because of the overwhelming success of this album, Richard became the first male solo artist ever to have released a debut album with four top three songs. His second album, *Repeat Offender*, was co-produced by him, as well as being written by him while on his first tour. A lyricist's milestone, the emphasis is on a rock and roll sound, and is filled with rock classics. "The new album is harder edged than the songs on the first record. All the way through, it's more rock and roll," Richard says, describing his latest LP. The premiere single "Satisfied" has already hit number one after only seven weeks on the charts. In addition to writing his own songs, he has written and produced songs for such groups and artists as Vixen, Animotion, Poco, Ann Wilson, and Kevin Cronin. A Grammy nominee, Richard was voted Best Male New Singer of 1987 in *Rolling Stone's* Reader's Poll, and placed in the top five in the 1988 Poll. He was also named one of the ten sexiest men in rock and roll by *Playgirl* magazine.

Richard is married to singer Cynthia Rhodes who is a member of the group Animotion.

Marsha Mason

"I believe there's a certin amount of luck in everybody's life. Director Elia Kazan once said that an actor gets about three lucky breaks. You have to be ready for them. Everybody has some luck. It's a question of whether or not you take advantage of it." It may have been one such lucky break that brought Mason together with leading playwright Neil Simon. During their decade-long marriage (1973-1983), Simon created several films, including *The Goodbye Girl*, that showcased Mason as an appealing but emotionally tattered woman squaring off against life and men.

Mason was born in St. Louis, Mo., 3 April 1942. Star-struck as a child, Mason did not let her strict upbringing and education deter her from pursuing the Bohemian life of a struggling actress in New York. She debuted off-Broadway in *The Deer Park* and soaped some suds on "Love of Life," before making it to Broadway in 1970 in *Happy Birthday, Wanda June*, based on the Kurt Vonnegut satire. After extensive performances with the San Francisco-based American Conservatory Theater, she drew critical notice on film as a troubled prostitute in the 1973 film *Cinderella Liberty*. "If you play a down-and-out loser part, they send you down-and-out loser parts," she noted. She sidestepped typecasting roles and auditioned, instead, for *The Good Doctor* Simon's Chekhov inspired production. She got the part, met Simon, and three weeks later, they were married. Mason's high key performance opposite Richard Dreyfuss in *The Goodbye Girl*, which Simon rescripted for them, helped make the upbeat story of loathing-turned-to-love one of 1977's most heralded movies. In Simon's 1979 autobiographical tale, *Chapter Two*, Mason had the rare opportunity to play a character based on herself.

She was a study of charm and vulnerability in *Only When I Laugh*, Simon's 1981 remake of his 1970 play, *The Gingerbread Lady*. Although the movie, like the play, earned lukewarm response from critics, Mason was applauded for her portrayal of an actress battling alcoholism to win a second chance with her teenage daughter. Noted one reviewer, "Mason handles her bravura moments superbly; she gives you great technique and fierce emotional honesty." Her other film credits include Simon's 1978 comedy, *The Cheap Detective*, Simon's 1983 *Max Dugan Returns*, and the non-Simon movies *Promises in the Dark* (1979), *Heartbreak Ridge* (1986) and *Stella* (1989). She starred in the CBS-TV Schoolbreak special "Little Miss Perfect" (1986) and the telefilm "Trapped in Silence" (1985) as well as appeared on stage in a New York Theatre Workshop limited run of *The Big Live* (1988) and a one-time-only performance in the A.R. Gurney play *Love Letters* in April 1989.

Masters and Johnson

Their landmark medical texts *Human Sexual Response* (1966) and *Human Sexual Inadequacy* (1970) revolutionized the discipline of sex therapy and established this husband-wife team as the pioneering "first family" of sexology. "If you can't communicate in bed, you probably can't communicate in marriage," asserted Dr. William Masters, who with his wife, Virginia Johnson, researched and developed unprecedented clinical prescriptions for treating such sexual hang-ups as frigidity, impotency, and premature ejaculation. They set up the St. Louis-based Reproductive Biology Research

Foundation (now called Masters & Johnson Institute), published nine books and more than 100 scientific papers, appeared on hundreds of television and radio shows, and wrote a monthly column in *Redbook* magazine for several years. However, in the early 1980s, sexology's first family was put on the defensive. their heretofore hallowed reputation was challenged by critics who claimed Masters and Johnson used vague criteria for measuring successful sex therapy and that their research was slipshod. Deflecting the attacks, Masters and Johnson in 1983 released their standards for successful treatment, which included: three erections in every four attempts in cases of impotence and two orgasms in every four tries for anorganismic women.

Born 27 December 1915, it was an internship in obstetrics and gynecology in St. Louis that reinforced Masters' conviction that sex was the last important biological function still largely unexplored. In 1954 he began a research program in sexual physiology that evolved into the Foundation. While looking for a female research associate, he met Johnson in 1956. Born 11 February 1925, Johnson says of her childhood on a Missouri farm, "There was a very rigid rejection of anything sexual. You didn't talk about it." Becoming a team in 1957, they developed a therapy model based on a male-female team treating the sexual problems of couples, rather than each one separately. This is the model currently used at Masters & Johnson Institute (where he is board chairman, she is director). "If you're going into sex research it is apparent that both sexes should be represented," commented Masters, who received his M.D. in 1943 from University of Rochester School of Medicine. Johnson is a certified sex therapist. Both are lecturers in human sexuality and recipients of numerous honors and awards including the Modern Medical Award for Distinguished Achievement and World Association for Sexology Biomedical Research Award. Their latest publications include *Human Sexuality* (1982), and *Crisis: Heterosexual Behavior in the Age of AIDS* (1988).

Marcello Mastroianni

"Method acting is pure nonsense. All an actor must do is cultivate intelligence. For instance, if you have to play someone who's mad, there's no use going to an asylum to watch a madman. The madness you see is his, the gestures, the looks are his, not yours. To play a madman as I did in (Pirandello's) *Henry IV*, you must search within yourself, above all, invent." Ever since *La Dolce Vita* (1961) Mastroianni has been an emblem of romantic Latin fascination. ("I can't understand why this label has stuck to me.... In pictures I've been a homosexual, impotent, and in one I was pregnant, but never a seducer. The label is even more unreasonable now that I am sixty.") Whatever the reason, he is indeed, highly sought after: (After *Henry IV* closed in Paris in 1983, Mastroianni underwent thirty-eight interviews in seven hours in Italian, French and English.)

Born 28 September 1924 in Fontana Liri, Italy, the son of a carpenter, he moved with his family to Turin at age five, and then to Rome. After WWII he attended the University of Rome and did some collegiate theatre, meeting and acting with Federico Fellini and Giulietta Masina in the process. Hired in 1948 by Luchino Visconti, who headed Italy's leading theatrical troupe, he worked with heavyweights like Vittorio Gassman and Rina Morelli. His first major screen-role was in *Una Domentica d'Agosto* (1949); *La Notte, Divorce Italian Style* and *The Priest's Wife* followed. Of cinema he says, "[It's] a pure lie, and the actor is a liar, the most ancient seller of smoke who finds satisfaction in simulation. Yet some say acting is complicated, a torment. Come on. Complaining when it's enjoyable. Acting is a pleasure like making love. No, wait a minute, not always; lovemaking is often an ordeal." He harbors a penchant for beautiful blonds, be they wife (former actress Flora Carabella, one daughter) or mistress (Faye Dunnaway, who ditched him in 1971 for another man), or Catherine Deneuve, (his co-star in the tearjerker *It Only Happens to Others* and mother of his second daughter). His films include: *Wifemistress* (1979), Fellini's *City of Women* (1981), *La Nuit de Varennes* (1983), a film version of *Henry IV* (1985), a reunion with frequent co-star Sophia Loren in *Saturday, Sunday, Monday* (1985), *Ginger and Fred* (1985), *Marconi* (1985), *The Two Lives of Mattia Pascal* (1985), *Miss Arizo* (1987) and *L'Intervista* (1987). He received an Academy Award nomination as best actor for his striking performance in *Dark Eyes* (1987).

Johnny Mathis

"A lot of people who grew up listening to me now have their children listening to my music," says the mellow Mathis. His ballad-belting career has been "Wonderful, Wonderful" ever since his first blockbuster single of that title back in 1955. He's accumulated more that fifty gold and platinum albums and singles, representing over 100 million record sales worldwide. He also holds the unchallenged record of having one album, "Johnny's Greatest Hits," on *Billboard's* pop charts for an incredible 480 weeks—nine and one half years!

Born John Royce Mathis, 30 September 1935, he was the fourth of seven children of a vaudeville song-and-dance man who, to support his family, teamed up with his wife in a chauffer-butler-cook combination. Young Johnny caught the showbiz bug from his dad and started studying singing at 13. But when he became a champion jumper in high school and was invited to the Olympic trials, he decided to pursue a career as a physical education teacher. The switch from sports back to singing came when he joined a musical jam session with friends at a San Francisco club and was heard by a Columbia Records exec who immediately signed him up. Among the many still-requested Mathis mega-hits: "It's Not for Me to Say," "Chances Are," "The Twelfth of Never," and "Small World." Through the eras of Elvis Presley, the Beatles, New Wave and disco, the balladeer's records have never stopped selling. How come? One theory: "Mathis sings primarily of love and love is never out of fashion."

Fulfilling a life-long wish, Mathis had the distinction of hosting his own PGA golf tournament, The Johnny Mathis Seniors Classic, for two years (1985-1986) at his home course of Mountain Gate Country Club in Bel Air, California. When the crooner's not singing, he likes to cook. He recently rebuilt his entire kitchen, utilizing the latest cooking aids on the market. Some of his favorite home-made recipes include: Western style beef stew, Mustard Greens, and Wild Duck à la Johnny Mathis. On his latest album, *The Hollywood Musicals*, he provides a special salute to songs from movie musicals.

Marlee Matlin

Marlee Matlin once spoke of her spiritual mentor, Henry Winkler. "I actually live with his family and they are so wonderful, so giving, so loving and so funny. I met Henry at a benefit in Chicago when I was just twelve years old. I was doing a play and just before I went on stage he tapped me on the shoulder at the curtain and said 'I love you' in sign language. Once I got on stage, I gave the audience all I had. I told Henry I wanted to be an actress and he said, 'Believe in yourself and you'll do what you want.' I can honestly say I wouldn't be here if it weren't for him. He still knows best." And this fine young actress went on to prove Mr. Winkler's words true.

In 1987, at the age of 21, she became the youngest recipient of the Best Actress Oscar for her outstanding debut film performance in *Children of a Lesser God*. Although she won this prestigious Award at a very early age, she had already been acting for fifteen years!

Marlee Beth Matlin, born in 1965 in Morton Grove, a Chicago suburb, was a normal, happy child. "I had roseola when I was 18 months old. My grandmother's best friend was babysitting and told my parents there was something wrong with my hearing." She began to act as an outlet for her immense frustration. Her mother, Libby Matlin, a powerhouse in her own right, took her to the Center for Deafness in Chicago and she immediately won the role of Dorothy in *The Wizard of Oz*. "I stayed seven or eight years. We did plays all over Illinois, Nebraska and Indiana." Eventually, she got a minor role in a stage production of *Children of a Lesser God*. She was spotted by a talent agent and the rest is history.

Marlee is determined to build on this first success and have a long and varied career. She has spoken publicly, as a presenter at the 1988 Academy Awards, and continues to improve her speech with the aid of voice coach Lillian Glass. She has become the spokeswoman for the hearing impaired who are also potential film lovers and hopes to convince movie studios and televison networks to automatically "close caption" their movies and programs. She desperately wants them to understand how frustrating it is "to be denied access to the world's most powerful communication media."

Walter Matthau

"Anybody with a bulbous nose and beady eyes looks like me," the superstar once remarked. "It's a fairly ordinary physiognomical phenomenon. In the ghetto, you develop facial muscles in order to survive, and they can serve you well as an actor." People who expect him to be like the beer-swilling Little League coach he played in the film *Bad News Bears*, or the vaudevillian of the *Sunshine Boys*, or the happy-go-nowhere slob, Oscar Madison, in the *Odd Couple*, are taken back by his elegance in speech and sartorial manner. He sprinkles his conversation with bits of French and German, does the *New York Times* Sunday crossword in 20 minutes (using a pen) and, reportedly, on one of his very first dates with his wife, Carol, arrived with a puzzle and asked her, "What's a three-letter word for beverage?" And she, not used to the game, replied, "7-Up." Matthau fell in love with her immediately. They'd met first when they both appeared in the play *Will Success Spoil Rock Hunter?* He married the former Carol Wellington-Smythe Marcus Saroyan (she was a debutante pal of Gloria Vanderbilt and Oona Chaplin as well as wife of the late playwright William Saroyan) in 1959. He had two children, David and Jenny from his first marriage to Grace Johnson. She had two children from her marriage to Saroyan. Together they have a son, Charles.

"Social adversity frustrates you. You need a place to express yourself. Had I grown up in a palace, I doubt I would have made much of an actor." Born 1 October 1920 on the lower East Side of New York, he was raised on potato soup and the Yiddish Theater. "I was in a religious festival play when I was four," he remembers. "I knew that I liked to get up in front of people and do things." As a teenager he locked himself in the bathroom to read Shakespeare aloud because he "liked the sound." In 1942 he enlisted in the Army Air Corps, saw action in Europe, and after his discharge studied at the New School's Dramatic Workshop on the G.I. Bill. Though constantly employed on Broadway and television, he never got his name above the title until Neil Simon picked him to play Oscar Madison in his play *The Odd Couple*. At first Matthau wanted to play the part of finicky Felix Unger because he felt it would be too easy to play Oscar. ("That part I can phone in," he told Simon.) But the playwright had his way and the *Odd Couple* ran on Broadway for two years and made Matthau a star at age 45. He once said he preferred to act on stage rather than films, but after a severe heart attack while making *The Fortune Cookie*, he settled down to a regular California life of two films a year and weekends in the Desert. He's appeared in many films, such as *First Monday in Octoer; Buddy, Buddy; Hopscotch; California Suite; House Calls; Movers and Shakers, Pirates*, and *The Couch Trip*.

At a meeting with studio executives during the filming of *Hopscotch*, Matthau walked in somberly, aware that everyone was concerned about his serious heart condition, since he had just had surgery. In one cold beat he said, "My doctor has just given me six months to live," The executives were stunned. "And when he found out I couldn't afford to pay his bill—he gave me another six months."

Don Mattingly

In 1987, Don Mattingly set the record for an incredible six grand slam home runs in one season. The following year he signed a $6.7 million, three year guaranteed contract with the New York Yankees. The Gold Glove first baseman has been a growing legend to baseball since his first full season in the majors when he won the 1984 American League batting championship. The achievement added plausibility to his N.Y. Yankees' team owner George Steinbrenner's boast that Mattingly is "the best young player in baseball today," one who wouldn't be considered trade bait for even crosstown superstar Darryl Strawberry of the Mets. The rather single-minded first baseman started his great season just hoping to be played in former Yankee manager Yogi Berra's daily line-up instead of being used as a utility player. "To establish consistency you've got to play every day. If you don't you don't see the ball as well, and there's all sorts of extra pressure to perform." Mattingly says. By season's end extra pressure was generated by the league-leading-batting-average race he and teammate Dave Winfield were having. In the last game of the season, Mattingly pulled away from Winfield by getting four hits to the big power hitter's one, thus winning the title by three percentage points with a .343 average. He became the first Yank to win the honor since Mickey Mantle in 1956, and he and Winfield were the first 1-2 batting finishers on the same team since Rod Carew and Lyman Bostock of the Angels did it in 1977. His formula was simple: "Basically I wanted to get a hit every time up." His formula also works. Mattingly was chosen for five years in a row (1984-1988) for the American League All-Star Team, hit a home run in eight consecutive games (ten HR total) in 1987, and received the Rawlings A.L. Gold Glove Award (best fielding by a first baseman) for four years (1985-1988).

"Baseball's a more demanding job than people realize," says Donald Arthur Mattingly. "You really need to take the time every night to think about how you did your job—or didn't do it." The Evansville, Indiana-born (20 April 1961) infielder spent four minor league years in modest surroundings with wife Kim Sexton while honing his concentration at bat and in the field. Taken in the nineteenth round of 1979s baseball draft, he's proven to be an exceptional gloveman as well as spray hitter. The five-feet-eleven, 185-pounder would rather spend time at home with his wife than out in the Big Apple. "I don't think I'm a New York personality," he says. "God's a very important part of my life. I don't think God is out there helping me to hit the ball," says the so-called "hard-nosed" Mattingly who's described as a manager's dream player. "But I do think he helps me stay calm, stay concentrated." Off the field, Mattingly owns a successful restaurant "Mattingly's 23" in Evansville, Indiana. He and his wife reside in Teaneck, New Jersey, with their two sons, Taylor Patrick (born 17 March 1985) and Preston Michael (born 28 August 1987).

Bill Mauldin

"You know blankety well you're not drawing an accurate representation of the American soldier!" bellowed a beribboned General Patton to the scrawny American sergeant midway through World War II. "You make them look like blinkety bums!" The perky pint-sized noncom paid the general no mind and continued to regale G.I. readers with the wartime adventures of his scruffy, sloppy, sardonic and skeptical cartoon soldiers, Willie and Joe. The *Up Front* drawings won him a vast audience, and, in 1944 at the age of 23, his first Pulitzer Prize. Still at the top of his field in editorial cartooning, he collected a second Pultizer in 1959.

The drawing-board daddy of Willie and Joe was born 29 October 1921 in Mountain Park, N.M. and family legend has it that he could draw before he could talk. Moving from school to school as his father moved from job to job around the Southwest, young Bill never managed to graduate, but he did manage to squeeze in a year's worth of art lessons at the Chicago Academy of Fine Arts. Hard pressed for funds, he recalled later "it was some time before I got smart enough to spend my money on hamburgers, steal my pen points from the post office, and scrounge my pencils from the nearest secretary." Finding the going tough for cartoonists, Mauldin joined the National Guard. When his infantry division was "Federalized" 15 months before Pearl Harbor, the 18-year-old greenhorn found himself a buck private in the Army. Looking back on his childhood in his 1971 autobiography, *The Brass Ring*, Mauldin says, "Whenever I was bored, or felt unnoticed . . . I felt compelled to irritate whoever was in charge." He's been doing it ever since, as a *Stars and Stripes* cartoonist all through the war, and on into civilian life. After a stint on the St. Louis *Post-Dispatch*, he became in 1962 "cartoon commentator" for the Chicago *Sun-Times*. Divorced from Norma Humphries (two sons), he married Natalie Evans (killed in an auto accident in 1971; four sons) and Christine Lund (one daughter). The feisty, foe-of-the-fatuous cartoonist has also produced more that a dozen books, ranging from *Star Spangled Banner* in 1941 to *Mud and Guts* in 1978 to *Let's Declare Ourselves Winners . . . & Get The Hell Out* in 1985.

Robert Maynard

An apt headline for his own newspaper could have read, "Trib Publisher Becomes First Black Owner of a Major White Daily." And the 1983 acquisition of *The* (Oakland, Calif.) *Tribune* by editor and publisher Robert Maynard was also financial page news. The Gannett communications empire was so eager to sell its losing proposition in Oakland that it lent him $17 million of the $22 million necessary, thus also making him the first editor of a major daily ever to buy out his own paper.

While Maynard's immediate sphere of influence is the *Trib's* 174,000 readers, that number equals only a few ice cubes off the iceberg. The Booklyn-born (17 June 1937) scribe was founder, with journalist wife Nancy Hicks, of the Institute for Journalism Education, a Cal-Berkeley-based effort to pump more trained, non-white newspersons into the industry. Add to this others whom he helped aboard while he was affirmative action consultant for the ubiquitous Gannett Newspaper group, not to mention his widely-read reportage as correspondent for the Washington *Post*, and *Black Enterprise* magazine, and Maynard's news sense has touched many readers indeed. In 1961, thrilled by the prospect of reporting to the rather small circulation of the (York, Pa.) *Gazette and Daily*, the novice newsman "was so damned excited that [he] walked into the newsroom, was shown [his] desk and typewriter and promptly got [his] first nosebleed since childhood." The one-time Nieman Fellow at Harvard has been able to control his blood pressure since then and has been a judge for the Pulitzer Prize. His judgment is also valued on the boards of such diverse organizations as The African-American Institute and The Rockefeller Foundation. But his biggest decisions are those that must turn around the foundering, formerly-conservative journal based in blue-collar, no-white Oakland, which needs suburban, white readers to survive. "We will just continue fine-tuning the product and making it stronger," Maynard asserts.

Willie Mays

If the late Jackie Robinson brought grace and nobility to the game of baseball, Willie Howard Mays Jr., with his unworldly skills and affecting insouciance, brought soul. When the basket-catching center fielder, whom many claim is the nation's best-ever player, hung up his spikes after 23 years, he ranked behind only Babe Ruth in home-runs. (Hank Aaron, has, of course, surpassed both.) *Sporting News* Player of the 1960s hit 660 homers, while accumulating a .302 average at the plate. He beamed brightly upon his induction into the Hall of Fame in 1979, but "The Say Hey Kid" would be ostracized from Major League Baseball after Commissioner Kuhn decided Willie's job as a greeter at an Atlantic City casino was bad imagery. That decision was reversed by new Commissioner Peter Ueberroth who restored Willie (and Mickey Mantle, also a toiler in the casino world) to baseball's good graces.

Born 6 May 1931 in Fairfield, Ala., Willie recalls, "We'd play on the street, and there would be Dr. Drake, driving up in his big white Cadillac . . . right there and then I started dreaming." By 1948 he was an outfielder for the Black Barons of the Negro League (his father had starred for them), and two years later the N.Y. Giants bought his contract. As the only black minor leaguer in the Interstate League he once had to play in Maryland. "On a Friday," Willie explains, "they were cheering me." Said manager Leo Durocher, "You're going to be the Giants center fielder forever."

But sophisticated Bay area fans didn't show the same affection for Mays as had Polo Grounds aficionados when the Giants moved to Frisco in 1958. He also ran into financial and marital difficulties there. But Mays enjoyed more of his 18 All-Star seasons in Frisco, and won the second of his two MVP Awards there. In 1972 he was given the chance to return to New York as a member of the Mets. As for his temporary absence from the game he so loved, Willie was philosophical, "How can anyone think I'm bitter? The game will go on. There will always be great stars *because that's baseball.*" Fans were able to get an inside view of their sports hero when his book *The Autobiography of Willie Mays* was released in 1988.

Paul Mazursky

"There are two kinds of movies: movies made out of passion and movies made to make money. They're both authentic, but the pictures I've loved were made out of passion," says the writer-director-actor-producer whom Pauline Kael has called "the manic poet of the middle class quirk." Mazursky's 1978 production, *An Unmarried Woman*, garnered an Oscar nomination for Best Picture and earned him a slew of critics' awards for the screenplay. But regarding passion, how closely can a man identifiy with a woman (Jill Clayburgh) whose husband leaves her? According to the man in question, very easily: asked where he got the material for his intimate exploration of his title character's emotional evolution, he replied, "Can't you tell I'm the Unmarried Woman?"

As Mazursky has said, he writes (and directs) "personal comedies about very serious subjects." During the 70s his best movies—*Bob & Carol & Ted & Alice, Blume in Love* and *An Unmarried Woman*—were, in the records of one reviewer, "bulletins from a combat zone," i.e., affluent urban America in the throes of sexual revolution, "that document the changing mores of an exasperating decade." In 1982 he tried his method on a classic, Shakespeare's *The Tempest*, but the outcome got negative reviews. Andrew Sarris called it "a disaster of sufficient magnitude to require the services less of a critic that a coroner." Subsequently, however, he won plaudits for an original comedy (co-authored by Leon Capetanos) *Moscow on the Hudson*, about a Soviet visitor to Manhattan (Robin Williams) who defects to the consumer society in—where else?—Bloomingdale's.

Born Irwin Mazursky in Brooklyn, 25 April 1930, he acted off-Broadway while at Brooklyn College, had bit parts in movies and bigger ones in television plays, and after moving to Los Angeles in 1959 was a writer on the CBS-TV "Danny Kaye Show," finally teaming up with Larry Tucker to write and produce *I Love You, Alice B. Toklas*. Their next collaboration was *Bob & Carol*. His more recent projects include *Down and Out in Beverly Hills* (1986) and *Moon Over Parador* (1988). From his more domestic collaboration with the former Betsy Purdy, whom he married in 1953, he has two daughters, Meg and Jill.

Anthony T. Mazzola

"Women today want it all and every issue of the *Bazaar* is dedicated to making sure they get it all," says the alluring monthly magazine's editor-in-chief. He has been *Bazaar's* top dog since 1972, before that he was editor-in-chief of *Town & Country* from 1965. Known in the society and magazine world as a super-pro editor, Tony was born 13 June 1923 in Passaic, and graduated from Cooper Union Art School. He joined the Hearst publishing empire at the behest of former *Town & Country* editor-in-chief Henry Sell, as the magazine's art director in 1948.

Of Sicilian heritage, he was decorated by Italy with the Knight Officer of the Order of Merit. The father of two sons by his first marriage, he has a daughter by his present wife, the former Michele Elsinore.

Andrew McCarthy

He has starred in ten feature films since his 1983 film debut opposite Jacqueline Bisset and Rob Lowe in *Class*. In addition to films, this versatile, talented actor has performed in the theatre, and both off and on Broadway.

Andrew McCarthy was born in 1962 in Westfield, New Jersey, where he attended Pingry School before going on to New York University where he majored in theatre. It was in high school, though, when Andrew decided to go into acting. "I decided on acting in high school when I was cut from the basketball team," he states. While attending NYU, a fellow classmate told him about the casting for the upcoming movie *Class*. Andrew auditioned and won a starring role in the film. Still attending NYU, he studied acting at Circle in the Square, and appeared in the off-Broadway productions of *Life Under Water*, *Marion's Camera*, *Been Taken*, and *Herself as Lust*. Other stage performances include the *Festival '88* of the Arts in New York, the Ensemble Studio Theatre's production of *Neptune's Hip*, and on Broadway, he co-starred with Matt Dillon in the drama *Boys of Winter*. Returning to films, he starred in several movies after *Class*, including *Heaven Help Us*, *St. Elmo's Fire*, *Pretty in Pink*, and *Mannequin*. Although *Mannequin* turned out to be one of the biggest sleepers of 1987, it was his biggest personal box office smash. Following that film, he took a supporting role in the American Playhouse production of *Waiting for the Moon* in France. Upon his return to the U.S., he appeared at Lincoln Center in the theatre presentation of *Bodies, Rest & Motion*, and took the lead roles in the films *Less Than Zero*, *Kansas*, *Fresh Horses*, and *Weekend at Bernies*. After filming *Weekend at Bernies*, Andrew was off to Paris again to appear in the film *Quiet Days in Clichy*.

Andrew, an avid Yankee fan and golf enthusiast, currently resides in the Greenwich Village section of New York.

Mary McCarthy

The writer singled out as "possibly the cleverest woman America has ever produced" is not enthusiastic about the emerging Women's Movement. Feminism, she says, "just does not say Hello to me at all.... I've always liked being a woman. And it seems to me that one of the problems of a lot of feminists is that they don't like being women." Like it or not, being a woman has done nothing to keep Mary McCarthy from her place (as *Publisher's Weekly* put it in 1984) "in the forefront of intellectual life for more than forty years." She first emerged into the consciousness of American highbrows in the 1930s, composing book reviews for the *Nation* and the *New Republic* and theatre criticism for *Partisan Review*. She created a further stir with her first novel, *The Company She Keeps*, in 1942, and has been roiling the literary waters ever since with such novels as *The Groves of Academe*, *A Charmed Life*, *The Group*, *Birds of America* and *Cannibals and Missionaries*, as well as such observations of the political scene as *Vietnam*, *Hanoi* and *The Mask of State: Watergate Portraits Including a Postscript on the Pardons, 1975*, and two books about Italy, *The Stones of Florence* and *Venice*. Twenty-one essays, reviews, etc., appeared in her 1985 collection, *Occasional Prose*.

Mary Therese McCarthy was born 21 June 1912 in Seattle, and she and younger brothers, Kevin (the actor), Preston and Sheridan, orphaned by the 1918 flu epidemic, became pawns in a familiar tug-of-war exacerbated by the interreligious aspects of her parents' marriage (her mother was a half-Jewish, half-Protestant convert to Catholicism). Their wealthy paternal grandparents farmed Mary out to a great aunt and her monstrous husband, who beat ten-year-old Mary to keep her humble when she won a state essay contest. Eventually, she was rescued by her other grandparents, who sent her to be educated as a Catholic in Minneapolis parochial schools—which she thoroughly enjoyed while at the same time losing her faith. She wrote about this at length in her *Memories of a Catholic Girlhood*. Emerging with a B.A. from Vassar in 1933, she moved to New York, Married actor Harold Johnsrud and, although Stalinism was fashionable in intellectual circles, became an avid Trotskyite, explaining that Trotsky "possessed those intellectual traits of wit, lucidity and indignation which I still regard as a touchstone." She solidified her status in the world of letters when she married critic Edmund Wilson in 1938. ("He was a terrible bully and a tyrant," she told Carole Brightman in 1980, "but in terms of work he was marvelous. He made me write. I would never have written fiction, I think, if if hadn't been for him.") They had one son, Reuel, now an expert on Slavic literature. In 1946, McCarthy married writer-teacher Bowden Broadwater and in 1961 wed husband number four, overseas government official James R. West. Developing " a kind of horror of the sort of tinniness of New York intellectual and literary life," she made her home for many years in Paris, except for summers spent in a house in Maine on Penobscot Bay. In the 1980s, she made the book-page headlines by being awarded the National Medal for Literature and being sued by playwright Lillian Hellman for $2.5 million for comments she'd made on "The Dick Cavett Show." (Hellman, MacCarthy told Cavett, was "over-rated, a bad writer and a dishonest writer ... I said once in some interview that every word she writes is a lie, including 'and' and 'the'.") With Hellman's death in 1984, the case remained unresolved. McCarthy's latest release is the illustrated paperback book *How I Grew* (1988).

Paul McCartney

Maybe "Money Can't Buy You Love," but let us borrow a phrase (penned by writer David Harrop in *People*) from one of the Beatles' earliest hits, "Roll over Rockefeller, and tell J. Paul Getty the news." Ex-Beatle McCartney is one of the richest men in the world and history's most commercially successful musician.

Here's a wee sampling of his tally: He has sold more that 60 million gold singles in musical money-making with the Beatles, Stevie Wonder, his

Rue McClanahan

group Wings, and Michael Jackson (helped by the video of the two as snake-oil charmer in "Say Say Say"); Wings' album *Band on the Run* sold 6 million copies—all in all he's sold more than 100 million albums. Assisted by his wife Linda's dad, prominent show-biz lawyer Lee Eastman, Paul created MPL Communications, which includes ownership of numerous musical copyrights on properties such as *Grease*, *A Chorus Line*, *Annie*, *La Cage aux Folles*, the songs of Buddy Holly and ten thousand others, including "Stormy Weather," and "Sentimental Journey." What it does not own are the copyrights on the Beatles' songs which were lost when their publishing company was acquired by Lord Lew Grade. This is a source of great pain to McCartney now, especially after Grade refused to sell them back to him and turned around and sold them to an Australian. Biographer Peter Brown says Paul "wants to own his children"—meaning the Beatles portfolio.

Born James Paul McCartney near Liverpool, 18 June 1942, he was the son of a district nurse and a cotton salesman. ("My dad played the piano and the trumpet too, until his teeth fell out.") He joined the group that was to become the Beatles in his late teens, and he is the only ex–Boy Scout of the famous quartet. Maintaining an A-level in literature in high school, he could have gone on to a university. ("I didn't quite know what to do then. When the time came to decide, we had a chance to go to a date in Hamburg, so it was either a matter of going to Hamburg with the fellows or going into teacher's training. I had thought about that but I had no big ambition.") In October 1961 the group was discovered by Liverpool record-shop owner Brian Epstein, and the rest is rock-and-roll history. The Beatles have been honored, celebrated in films, in print, on record and in the memories of a generation. In 1984 Sothebys, the auction house, made a killing selling thousands of pieces of Beatle memorabilia. *Time* magazine once said the group "distilled the mood of their time. Gilbert and Sullivan frolics limned the pomposities of the Victorian British 'Empah'; Cole Porter's urbanities were tonics for the hung-over 30s; Rodgers and Hamerstein's ballads reflected the sentiment and seriousness of the World War II era. The Beatles' cunning collages pieced together scraps of tension between the generations, the loneliness of the dislocated 60s and the bitter sweets of young love in any age."

McCartney has lived down various ridiculous rumors, one of which was that he had mysteriously died and been quickly replaced by a double, and if you played their song "Revolution #9" backwards you were meant to be able to hear John sing, "Paul is dead." The Beatles split up in 1971. McCartney's output, which was awarded the unique "Triple Superlative Award" by *The Guiness Book of Records*, shows no signs of flagging. Even his latest album, *Flower in the Dirt* (1989), drew immediate attention as it spawned a new hit song, "My Brave Face." The father of four (Heather, by Linda's previous marriage, Mary, Stella and James) starred in the film *Give My Regards to Broad Street*, which he describes as "a sort of *Hard Day's Night* of me, solo, a parody of me now." The idea for the film came about when he was busted in Japan for "marijuana and was held in jail for nine days. I knew I had to write it down to remember the incident, and in the end I'd written 20,000 words." The "cute one" of the fabulous four is now sporting a bit of a tummy, crinkling eyes and wisps of graying hair. He says he does miss the Beatles, "But I don't miss it as much as I would have if I were a 28-year-old bachelor. One of the great things about my life is that I don't have too many regrets. As far as women are concerned, I don't lust after them now 'cause I sowed a lot of wild oats. Me and Linda got a lot done, y'know, in the sixties. We got a lot out of our systems. Which is good for now, because it allows you to sort of settle back and be content with just kind of an ordinary life. That's how we feel. We don't feel like we missed anything."

Rue McClanahan

Cast in the role of Blanche, a southern belle who owns the Miami Beach home which she occupies along with three other older women, Rue McClanahan is not only winning acclaim for "The Golden Girls," she's also enjoying herself. "I'm playing a man-crazy, self-centered widow, and I'm having a lot of fun doing it," says the 1987 Emmy Award winner for best actress in a comedy series. The show has also been a reunion for some of the cast. "I'm very lucky and thrilled to be back with Bea (Arthur) and Betty (White), two fantastic actresses I've worked with before." The five-foot-four, blue-eyed actress played Vivian Cavender Harmon in the award-winning TV series "Maude," starring Bea Arthur, which ran from 1972 through 1978. Rue starred with Betty White in NBC-TV's "Mama's Family" (1983), playing Aunt Fran.

Born on 21 February, in Headtown, Oklahoma, Rue was educated at the University of Tulsa. Coming to New York City, she studied with Uta Hagen and Harold Clurman before going on to become a veteran of theater, film, TV and commercials. Rue was seen on Broadway in "Father's Day," while her off-Broadway credits include "Who's Happy Now?," "Secret Life of Walter Mitty" and "Dark of the Moon." Traveling to California, Rue did regional and stock theater, such as "The House of Blue Leaves" in Pasadena and "Picnic" in Denver and California. With a love for the small screen, Rue has appeared as a guest star on "Trapper John, M.D.," "The Love Boat," and "The Lou Grant Show." Her TV movies include "The Day the Bubble Burst" and "The Little Match Girl." The smiling belle most recently completed three made-for-TV movies: "My Darling Daughters" (NBC), "The Man in the Brown Suit" (CBS) and "Liberace" (ABC), in which she plays the virtuoso's mother.

A resident of the San Fernando Valley, Rue, six times married, shares her home with five dogs and two cats.

Alec McCowen

"If you're hankering to hear one of England's best actors, Alec McCowen, speak the words of one of England's second-best writers, you'll enjoy *Kipling* . . . it's a flawless performance," kudoed *New York Times* critic Frank Rich in his 11 October 1984 review. The English actor had not been on Broadway since 1981 when he appeared in his solo performance of *St. Mark's Gospel*. "I really did *St. Mark's Gospel* because I didn't have a hobby," admits McCowen, "Most actors, it seems to me, are happiest working. I have no outside interests, no hobbies. I live and breathe show business."

Born Alexander Duncan McCowen in Tunbridge Wells, England, 26 May 1925, he confesses he was a secretive little boy. "I was the little boy who smiled too much. I found real life either dull or overwhelming. Real life was something I didn't want to participate in." He attended London's Royal Academy of Dramatic Art and subsequently joined a repertory company in which he was often assigned the roles of doddering old men. Graduating to small parts in London's West End, he soon became a member of the Old Vic and later the Royal Shakespeare Company, In 1967 he had the leading role in *After the Rain*, an allegorical something-or-other which was accorded an indifferent reception in both London and New York. "McCowen's performance deserves all the praise it's been given," rhapsodized a critic of *Hadrian VII* (1969), for which he received a Drama League of New York best-acting award. New Yorkers were also treated to his virtuoso performance in *The Philanthropist* (1971). And he also did a brief stint as the doubt-ridden psychiatrist in *Equus* in the New York company (he really claims it as his role since he originated it in London). As a learned critic has said about McCowen, "He is one of those actors who energetically fashion their domination over the stage instead of bringing it with them in the form of fame, physique, or vocal splendor." McCowen lives a comfortable bachelor life in his London flat, and although he claims he has no outside interests, he enjoys writing (his autobiography *Young Gemini* appeared in 1979 and *Double Bill* in 1980) and "bashing out show tunes" on his upright piano. His most recent stint on the London stage was in the play *The Heiress* (1989).

John McEnroe

His first million and men's tennis top ranking were only partly responsible for the brattish behavior. Speaking of his childhood, he said, "I don't think I was spoiled. Except I always had what I wanted. Isn't everybody spoiled?" Whether it was deriding linesmen with profanities or resorting to histrionics like feigning prostration on the court after questionable line calls, or tossing sawdust at a fan who jeered him, McEnroe joins his fellow tennis bad boys Ilie Nastase and Jimmy Connors with his antics on the court. "I've got to stand up for my rights," he says. Nevertheless, by age twenty-five he'd won four U.S. Opens, including three straight (1979-1981) and a multiwinner at Wimbledon. Reacting to recent observations that he was behaving (marginally) better, "Mac" responded, "My concentration improved when I decided not to let things bother me on the court. Others don't seem to see the things I do. But I can see that lady in the fiftieth row who is standing up, or hear that conversation in the stands. I guess I'm a stickler for details.... Some people can block those things out; I can't. But I'm not as bad as I used to be."

Whichever of his variety of temperaments John Patrick McEnroe, Jr. (born in Wiesbaden, West Germany, on 16 February 1959), chooses to display, his textbook-perfect court work made him the dominant men's player in the game. No less an authority than former champ John Newcombe wrote in his *New York Post* column, "There can be no argument that . . . McEnroe is the best combined singles and doubles competitor ever." Known as a touch vs. power player, the son of a Douglaston, Queens, N.Y., self-made corporate-securities lawyer needed only a year of competitive tuning at Stanford (NCAA team and singles victor) before turning pro in 1978. Said one Stanford teammate, "He's such a jerk, we're glad he's leaving school." But Palo Alto's loss was soon to lead to losses for his singles, doubles, and Davis Cup opponents. The young rebel found a cause in 1982 when he joined other players in criticizing the pro tour's "must-play" tournament regulation. He played with a slight injury and his interest flagged. His challengers waved white flags, though, in his white hot year of 1984, when he burned Jimmy Connors in straight sets for titles at Wimbledon and Flushing Meadows, after going 64-2 in the year's previous matches. In an article written by Billie Jean King in a June 1989 issue of *TV Guide*, a comparison is made between "The Best Shots in Tennis." King says, "Lately, John McEnroe has been serving with renewed confidence. He has such variety to his serve because he can hit it flat, with topspin or with a slice, and his left-handed delivery makes it doubly hard to return."

An active participant at charity benefits, he not only plays tennis for such worthwhile causes as the Cystic Fybrosis Foundation, but he's also been seen playing acoustic guitar. McEnroe married actress Tatum O'Neal on 1 August 1986 and the couple have two children, Kevin Jack and Sean Timothy.

Mary McFadden

From the New York Social Register to stardom on Seventh Avenue is a big leap, but she made it. "When I was very young my mother took me with her to a psychiatrist. I never forgot what he said—that contemporary humans do not use nearly all the power with which they have been endowed, and I have tried to expand." As a result she has not stopped at being a fashion designer, but she has become an intellectual, a student of ancient civilizations, a sculptor whose work has been exhibited, and an expert businesswoman.

Born 1 October 1938, daughter of a wealthy and prominent North Shore Long Island family, she studied at the very social Foxcroft School in Virginia, the Traphagen School, L'Ecole Lubec in Paris, Columbia University and the New School for Social Research, where she specialized in sociology. Her father, Alexander McFadden, was killed by an avalanche on a skiing holiday in Aspen. After several years directing public relations at Christian Dior's New York office, McFadden married Philip Harrari and went to live with him in South Africa, where her daugher Justine was born. After her divorce from Harrari, she married William McEwen, director of a museum in Rhodesia. Their marriage was brief and in 1970 Mary returned to New York. During her African years Mary collected all kinds of unique and exquisite fabrics from China as well as Africa. As Projects Editor for *Vogue*, she was able to make a collection of quilted jackets and long tunics over wide pants, a new look at the time. In 1976, Patrick Lannan (who died in 1983), a second generation Irish investor and collector of sculptures and other objects from ancient civilizations, gave Mary financial advice on how to set up her own dress business. In a few years she had won three awards that put her in the Fashion Hall of Fame. "My clothes are feminine," says McFadden. "They are very soft, very architectural, very pared down and very sculptural. *They are not for everyone.*" She is currently married to Kohle Yohannan.

Bobby McFerrin

"If I can bring joy into the world, if I can get people to stop thinking about their pain for a moment, or the fact that tomorrow morning they're going to get up and tell their boss off or write a nasty note to their girlfriend or something; if I can delay that for a moment and bring a little joy into that spot and help them to see things a little bit differently, then I'll be successful." So states the runaway winner at the 1989 Grammy Awards. His joyful ditty "Don't Worry, Be Happy" captured both Song of the Year and Record of the Year honors, plus it was the vehicle for earning him Best Pop Vocal Performance, Male. He also won Best Jazz Vocal Performance for "Brothers." All told, Bobby McFerrin has collected nine Grammy Awards (five previous awards in the last few years) leaving very little room for him ever to worry....

Born in New York on 11 March 1950 to classical singers Robert and Sara McFerrin, young Bobby began studying music theory at the age of six. His father, a baritone with the Metropolitan Opera, moved the family to Los Angeles in 1958, where, among his other theatrical work, he dubbed Sidney Poitier's singing voice in *Porgy and Bess*. In his teens, McFerrin studied piano and created a quartet. A few years later (1970) he heard a Miles Davis album, *Britches Brew*, which opened his ears to a new direction. He studied at Sacramento State University and Cerritos College and took his talents on the road to work with lounge bands. In 1977 he heard a voice inside him push for the singer-in-him to emerge and he found a gig as a singer/pianist at the Salt Lake City Hilton piano bar. Attempting to settle down, he and his wife, Debbie (married 1975), tried New Orleans, then migrated to San Francisco. He hooked up with former jazz singer Linda Goldstein as his manager; she became the producer of his albums as well as a guiding light in his career.

Bridging the gap between jazz and pop, McFerrin fused the two genres together for his hit album *Simple Pleasures* (1988). His easy voice is not only heard on recordings, but he has also become a television personality. On the tube he's brightened up the Oceanspray commercials, he's sung the "Cosby Show" theme song, he's lent his vocals to the "Levi's 501" blues and he's appeared on "Sesame Street." He has also been involved with several children's projects, such as costarring with Kelly McGillis in "Santabear" and performing on the soundtrack of Rudyard Kipling's *The Elephant Child* and *The Just So Stories* with Jack Nicholson. However, he insists, "I don't

Kelly McGillis

perform for kids. They don't need me. I'd be an adult teaching kids to be kids, and wouldn't that be silly." His other recent pop/jazz recordings include *The Voice* (1985) and *Spontaneous Inventions* (1986). Lending his talents to the literary field, he penned a fun book, titled of course, *Don't Worry, Be Happy* (1989). The happy fellow resides with his wife, Debbie, in San Francisco.

Kelly McGillis

"I've always been rebellious," she acknowledges. "I must say I grew up in a very perfect way." Although this feisty Irish beauty has been compared to Grace Kelly, Lauren Bacall, and Ingrid Bergman, she is still insecure about her talent as well as her looks. In response to how she feels being compared to these legends, she sums up her feelings by replying, "How can anybody live up to all that?"

Kelly McGillis was born in 1958 in Newport Beach, California, the eldest daughter of a housewife and a doctor. Although she grew up in a comfortable home, she had a weight problem (she weighed 210 pounds at one time) and she was a bit of a rebel. Her first ambition was to become a doctor like her father, but that all came to an end when she went on a house call with her father. He went to the aid of a man who had torn off his thumb. The man was crying, and seeing him in pain caused Kelly to cry as well. It was then she realized that she was too sensitive to become a doctor. A few years later, when Kelly was 15 years old, she won an acting award for her role in her high school production of *The Serpent*. When she was sixteen, she became consumed with acting, and when she was seventeen, just six months before she was to graduate high school, she dropped out to become an actress. "I was a pretty wild girl," states Kelly. "My outlets were acting. I decided not to do anything else. I didn't like anything else." Soon after, she packed her bags and headed for the Pacific Conservatory of Performing Arts in Santa Maria, where she studied for three years. She then was accepted into the Juilliard School of Drama in New York City. While she was attending Juilliard, Kelly appeared in theatre productions of *Three Sisters*, *Love for Love*, *Six Characters in Search of an Author*, and *The Winter's Tale*. While she was still attending Juilliard, she was doing summer work in Shakespeare in the Park, where she was discovered by producer Philip Epstein. He was the author of the film *Reuben, Reuben*, in which she made her debut in 1983. Other films to follow include *Witness* (1985), *Top Gun* (1985), *Made In Heaven* (1987), *Promised Land* (1987), *The House on Carroll Street* (1988), *Dreamers* (1988), *The Accused* (1988), *The Winter People* (1989), *Down with the Lions* (1989), and *Cat Chaser* (1989).

Kelly has been married three times; to writer Boyd Black, actor Barry Tubb and currently, to yacht broker Fred Tillman (married January 1989).

Elizabeth McGovern

What the *New York Times* headlined as "the Swift, Magical Rise of Elizabeth McGovern" began when Robert Redford, in his film-directing debut, cast her as Timothy Hutton's high-school girlfriend in *Ordinary People*. The picture won an Oscar in 1981 (so did Redford and Hutton), and the blue-eyed nineteen-year old was off and running to her own first Oscar nomination for her subsequent portrayal of the bird-in-a-gilded cage beauty, Evelyn Nesbit, in Milos Forman's *Ragtime*. "I was shocked," she said afterward. "I mean, I was very pleased, but at the same time, I didn't think I'd got to the point where I deserved it." Which may give a clue as to why a second feature story in the *Times* about McGovern was headlined "How to Succeed by Being Talented, Ambitious and Nice." "How ambitious?" asked writer Chris Case. The star, in rapid succession, of *Lovesick* with Dudley Moore, *Once upon a Time in America* with Robert DeNiro and *Racing with the Wind* with Sean Penn, allowed that it was probably "relative. I suppose, compared to Joan Crawford, I'm a sweet little cotton puff." More films followed, including *Native Son* (1986), *The Bedroom Window* (1986), *She's Having a Baby* (1987), *The Handmaid's Tale* (1989) and *Johnny Handsome* (1989).

A middle child of a middle-class family in the Midwest, McGovern (born in 1962) grew up in Evanston, Illinois, where her father was a law professor at Northwestern and her mother taught high school. When her dad switched classrooms to UCLA, Elizabeth transferred to a North Hollywood high school and, after toying with notions of becoming a veterinarian, a painter or a ballerina ("that died because I never could do a pirouette"), she "started to do plays, and it felt right, so I thought, maybe I'll be an actress." It was after an agent spotted her in a school production of *Lysistrata* that she auditioned for Redford and the "swift, magical rise" began. McGovern has alternated film roles with a number of stints off-Broadway including Lorraine Hansberry's *To Be Young, Gifted and Black*, Wallace Shawn's *The Hotel Play*, an Obie Award–winning production of *My Sister in This House*, *Painting Churches*, *A Map of the World*, *The Two Gentlemen of Verona* and the New York Shakespeare production of *A Midsummer Night's Dream*. "Acting makes me feel alive and thinking," says the versatile young woman whom Walter Kerr placed in his category of "actresses of special grace." "When I go see a play and my imagination is stimulated, it just makes the sky wider."

Maureen McGovern

The singer of the Academy Award songs "The Morning After" and "We May Never Love Like This Again" has an extraordinary four-octave range. Whether making records, performing live, or appearing on television or in a motion picture, Maureen McGovern demonstrates her unique and moving way of interpreting a song.

The daughter of James Terrence and Mary Rita (Welsh), Maureen was born in Youngstown, Ohio, on 27 July 1949. Although she was interested in music, the future singer started her career in the business world as an executive secretary for the Youngstown Cartage Company (1968-1969). Finding her forte was singing folk songs, she eventually stretched her vocal ability to perform jazz and soft rock. McGovern first invaded the public consciousness via her million-seller recording of 1972's Oscar-winning "The Morning After," followed by an appearance in *The Towering Inferno*, singing another Oscar winner, "We May Never Love Like This Again" (1974). On a streak, she scored again with the theme from *Superman*, entitled "Can You Read My Mind?" (1978). That tune reached #1 on the *Billboard* chart. Spreading her wings, McGovern tried acting again and landed the role of a guitar-playing nun in the spoof *Airplane!* (1980). In the eighties, in an effort to break out of the mold of easy musical categorization, she branched out into theater, making her debut in the Pittsburgh Civic Light Opera's 1981 production of *The Sound of Music*. Joseph Papp gave the singer her first Broadway role (replacing Linda Ronstadt) in *The Pirates of Penzance*, and she followed by playing the sultry Luisa Contini in *Nine* (replacing Karen Akers). She has also appeared in touring productions of *South Pacific*, *Guys and Dolls*, and *I Do, I Do*. McGovern has performed at all the major clubs from coast to coast, and she made her solo Carnegie Hall debut in May 1989. Among her many albums are *Maureen McGovern* (1979), *Another Woman in Love* (1987), *State of the Heart* (1988) and *Naughty Baby* (1989). She has won many gold records and awards, among them the Gold Leaf Award (1973), the Australian Gold Award (1975) and the Grand Prize at the Tokyo Music Festival (1975). A much-admired participant in such presentations as the Kool Jazz Festival, she has also, since making her concert debut with the Honolulu Symphony, sung with the Boston Pops, New York Pops and other concert orchestras.

Jay McInerney

"We don't believe in anything we can't put in our wallets. I would love to find a way beyond that," said novelist Jay McInerney, talking about the theme of misplaced community figures so prominent in his first two novels, *Bright Lights, Big City* and *Ransom*. "There's a nostalgia, but also a great skepticism, among well-to-do upper-middle-class Easterners for these values," he said in an interview with the *Christian Science Moniter*. The good natured McInerney, who claims to abhor identification with trendiness but dresses in perfect preppie style, shot to fame with his first novel, *Bright Lights, Big City*, the sobering odyssey of a cocaine-snorting preppie coming to terms with failure. The story's young protagonist, a would-be author, narrates the story in the second-person singular. Based loosely on the author's own experiences in Manhattan between 1979 and 1981, the book is, in McInerney's own words, "a satire about the mindless fashion following of the 1980's," "yuppie" trendiness, drugs, such as "Bolivian marching powder," and "even nutrition." Published by Random House in 1984, the book quickly attracted a cult readership among young, upwardly mobile urbanites and it was made into a motion picture, released in April 1988. In 1985, McInerney's second novel, *Ransom*, was published. Dealing with a young man who has "lost his bearing spiritually," McInerney sends his character to Japan "to reclaim himself" by becoming "morally taut" through the discipline of karate. While the book sold well, it also met with mixed reviews. The reviewer for *Publisher's Weekly* found "more substance" in *Ransom* than in *Bright Lights*. Galen Strawson, reviewer for the *Times Literary Supplement*, wrote of the author, "He is not a natural story-teller. He is an accumulator of moments, small-scale set pieces, and he has to work hard to provide a narrative vehicle for them. He has worked hard (in *Ransom*). He has tried to write a "proper" novel. And in a stiff and formal way, he has succeeded."

Born 13 January 1955 in Hartford, Connecticut, to an international sales executive father, McInerney grew up in a series of cities before settling in Pittsfield, Massachusetts, where he remained long enough to attend high school and Williams College. After graduating with a philosophy degree, McInerney and his best friend, Gary Fisketjon, bought a used car and traveled across the United States. Aiming at a writing career, McInerney worked in a number of jobs, from mink-farm worker to weekly-newspaper employee, to broaden his experience. In 1977, he went to Japan on a Princeton in Asia Fellowship, taking courses at the Institute for International Studies, studying Samurai self-discipline and teaching at Kyoto University. Two years later he returned to New York City and worked for a few months as a fact checker at *New Yorker* magazine before becoming a reader at Random House. McInerney's traveling buddy, Fisketjon, was now an editor at Random and he introduced McInerney to the poet Raymond Carver, who was teaching at Syracuse. Carver advised McInerney to concentrate on his writing by taking the Ph.D. program at Syracuse. Leaving behind the downtown nightclub life and a failed marriage to a fashion model, McInerney followed this advice and went to Syracuse in 1981 on a literary fellowship. There he met his second wife, Merry Reymond, a Ph.D. candidate in philosophy who became a stabilizing force in his life. "All my serious writing dates from the time I met my wife," McInerney states. The following year his short story "It's Six A.M. Do You Know Where You Are?" was published, and it became the beginning of his first novel. Other published short stories include "Reunion" (Esquire, 3/87), "Smoke" (Atlantic, 3/87) and "Story of My Life" (Esquire, 8/87), which became the beginning of his third novel of the same name, published in 1988 by Atlantic Monthly Press. The quick-witted writer and his wife Merry (married June 1984) maintain homes in Michigan and New York City.

Jim McKay

"I live in a permanent state of jet-lag," says this globe-trotting sportscaster. "I guess I will slow down someday, but I can't see retiring completely. I'll always want to cover a *few* things. Some golf. The horse racing. And, yes, maybe even the Olympics." It was in the '72 Games that McKay rose to his finest demonstration of instant analysis as he held forth for nineteen straight hours in describing the Black September abduction of nine Israeli athletes and coaches. The tragic drama ended with McKay being the first to tell the American viewing millions, "They're all gone," when he was informed through his headset of the aborted rescue attempt that cost fifteen lives. That Munich, Germany, coverage was the sad occasion for one of his six Emmys. Usually not faced with such serious assignments, McKay says, "My job, in addition to being a reporter, is being a storyteller.... The real drama is seeing exceptionally difficult feats done exceptionally well. That's what viewers remember; that's the story I want to tell."

McKay is really Jim McManus, born in Philadelphia on 24 September 1921. Raised in Baltimore, he attended Loyola College there, and was off to World War II after graduation as captain on a Navy minesweeper. The postwar Baltimore *Evening Sun* reporter had only to look across the newsroom for his future wife, Margaret, but had to be drafted into service as a television reporter when the *Sun* bought a TV station, "I said, 'Why me?' and they said, 'You were president of the dramatic society in school, weren't you? Well, that's good enough.'" McKay was a news and sports commentator in Baltimore from 1947 to 1950, then moved north to CBS in New York, where he anchored the Rome Olympics of 1960. "That was before the satellite. What I did was sit in a studio and narrate tapes as they came off the plane." Since then he's covered the Summer and Winter Games for ABC, where he made his debut on "Wide World of Sports" in 1961. The smallish, avuncular witness to "the thrill of victory, and the agony of defeat" wasn't much of an athlete himself, never advancing beyond JV in college. He and Margaret have their 1830 Bellefield Farm in Maryland, and three racing horses. When he's not on the road, he calls his Westport, Connecticut, semicolonial manse, home.

Ian McKellen

"Ian McKellen is perhaps the most respected classical actor of his generation in England," noted *Time's* Richard Schickel in his 1984 review of the actor's return to Broadway after thirteen years, "but an adolescent's enthusiasm and wonder animate every moment of *Ian McKellen Acting Shakespeare*. The cheerful energy this approach releases in McKellen and the air of confidentiality it gives his evening are entrancing." The monumental McKellen mastery (he was named a Commander of the British Empire in 1979) first became apparent in 1969 at the Edinburgh Festival, when he doubled, to universal acclaim, in the roles of *Edward II* and *Richard II* (a theatrical feat not performed in repertory since 1903). Since then his portrayals in dozens of British productions, principally for the Royal Shakespeare Company, have garnered many awards, including an unprecedented three consecutive Society of West End Theatre awards for *Pillars of the Community* in 1977, *The Alchemist* in 1978, and *Bent* in 1979. ("In this play alone, his range is immense," wrote the reviewer of *Bent* in *Plays & Players*. "He swoops through Coward-like control of comedy to all the pain of a destroyed human being. It should now be clear that McKellen is a great actor.") Although he has appeared less frequently in the U.S., he won the 1981 Tony for his portrayal of Salieri in Peter Shaffer's *Amadeus*. He scored in 1984 in London as *Coriolanus*, playing Shakespeare's strutting antihero in a leather trench coat and jumpsuit. In 1986 he appeared on Broadway again in *Wild Honey* and during 1987 he toured throughout London and the U.S. in his one-man show *Acting Shakespeare*.

Born Ian Murray McKellen in Burnley, England, on 25 May 1939, he moved at the age of twelve to Bolton, where his father was borough engineer and surveyor. As a boy he haunted the local variety theatres and attended performances at Stratford-upon-Avon. "Daft about the theatre" even then, his "stumblings about the amateur stage" began at Wigan Grammar School and Bolton School and continued when he enrolled at St. Catharine's College, Cambridge, where he received critical accolades ("It was like being told you were beautiful when you always thought you had big ears"). Graduating in 1961, he made his professional debut as Roper in Robert Bolt's *A Man for All Seasons*. In 1964 he won a Clarence Derwent Award for the most promising newcomer of the year (*A Scent of Flowers*), and in 1966 was again named most promising actor for *A Lily in Little India* by *Plays & Players*. The following year he appeared on Broadway in *The Promise*, a critical success in London but not in New York. In 1974 he joined the Royal Shakespeare Company and in 1976 was named best actor by *Plays & Players* for his bold performance as *Macbeth*. "As an actor one is allowed to get in touch with all the things that human beings are capable of—very deep emotion, or murder, or suicide—and step over that dangerous line which most of us pull away from," said McKellen. *Ian McKellen Acting Shakespeare* was televised in the U.S. in 1982. His other television credits include "Ross," "Hedda Gabler," "David Copperfield," "The Scarlet Pimpernel," "Dying Day," "Walter," and the telefilm "Windmills of the Gods." Films include *Alfred the Great, Thank You All Very Much,* and *Priest of Love*.

McKellen enjoys cooking, writing, and puttering around his eighteenth-century, book-and-painting-filled London house. Modest, shy and unpretentious offstage, he enjoys interviews, especially when the conversation turns to the relationship between art and society in general. In 1988 he received the Elliot Norton Award in Boston.

Rod McKuen

What Walt Disney was able to do for mice, this handsome, sandy-haired fellow has done for words, and he has enjoyed a rhapsodist's following of millions of fans. Poet, composer, singer, entrepreneur, he's published dozens of books, appeared in numerous films, on TV and in concerts, composed motion-picture scores (nominated twice for Academy Awards for *The Prime of Miss Jean Brodie* and *A Boy Named Charlie Brown*), been nominated for a Pulitzer Prize in music for composing "The City" for the Louisville Orchestra, recorded more than 200 albums, has more than 40 million books in print and is the only author ever to have three books on *Publisher's Weekly*'s year-end bestseller list. In 1978 he received the Carl Sandburg Award as "The People's Poet, for making poetry so much a part of our daily lives." His most recent books include *The Sound of Solitude* (1983) and *Valentines* (1985).

"I'm a total product of this time and this age," says Rod McKuen, born 29 April 1933. He spent his youth drifting with his sometime waitress mother from town to town in the Far West. He never knew his father, and in every town he went to with his mother he'd look in the phone book under the name McKuen to see if his dad was there. At age forty-three, his search came to an end when one of his readers sent him a picture of her own brother, and, as it turned out, the man was Rod's father. He was also dead. "In a way, I felt complete, because the search was over and I knew who I was. But at the same time I felt cheated, because the man lying under the stone would never be known to me. I just stood there for a long time," he wrote in *Finding My Father: One Man's Search for Identity* (1976). As a result of his experience he became a major proponent of adoptee rights. He was known first as a New York–Hollywood singer-composer, but when he put his poem "Stanyan Street" to music for a Glen Yarbrough album, RCA phoned him about the source of the poem. "It's from a book of mine, *Stanyan Street and Other Sorrows*," said Rod, a knowledgeable self-promoter. There was no such book, but there easily could be. When RCA wanted to include information on Yarbrough's album-liner notes, Rod asked them to list a box number where the book might be obtained. Then he wrote the book, published it himself and, working out of his Hollywood Hills home, sold 65,000 copies. In the spring of 1967 he came to the attention of super-editor Nan Talese, then working at Random House. She took over *Stanyan Street* and launched McKuen as Everyman's Homer.

"I've worked on the railroad, split logs and danced log jams free on the river out of the lumber camps. I've dug ditches and dug graves, worked in a cookie factory, been a shoe salesman, a theatre doorman, a disc jockey; broke both legs in the rodeo, again in the army, and a third time in the backyard horsing around. I've held jobs that don't exist anymore. Lived through half a dozen depressions without even knowing it, watched radio turn to television, television to video, found myself smack in the middle of the electronics revolution. And if out of all that I couldn't be observant enough to write a couple thousand songs, make 200 albums, write 35 books and give a few thousand concerts that mirrored how people during my lifetime felt and lived, I wouldn't have much to show for all those earlier years of preparation.... Poetry is not a luxury; it's a necessity. The poetry in our lives separates sanity from savagery.... By poetry I mean gentleness, understanding, truth and illumination.... Poetry is transportation, taking us out of ourselves. It need not be a vehicle, but it is definitely transportation."

Diana McLellan

"Everyone, even the caterer and the servants, is sworn to secrecy about every detail—and it always gets out," laughs this "outrageously well-informed" surveyor of such Washington, D.C., social institutions as "the Nancy lunch," about which, she says, "hostesses go through paranoid fits because they're not inviting their best friends; they're inviting people they hope will impress Nancy Reagan." One of the most quoted writers in the capital with her worldly-wise and witty column, "The Ear," English-born Diana McLellan first surfaced in the Washington *Star;* when that paper folded, she moved on to the *Post* and eventually landed at the Washington *Times*. Adept at collecting lore of both the high jinks and low jinks of Capitol Hill and White House movers and shakers, she put it all between hard covers in 1981 in the book *Ear on Washington*. Upon her retirement from the *Post* in September 1985 she joined the staff of *Washingtonian* magazine, where she writes her column "Diana's Washington."

Born in Leicester, 22 September 1937, Diana Dicken first came to the U.S. in 1957 when her father, an RAF Air Commodore, was appointed Defense Attache for the British Embassy in Washington. In her early years in the capital, she supported herself as a poodle portraitist, dress designer, writer-producer of radio and TV commercials, phone operator and both a fashion and society reporter. She began her career as a professional gossip in 1975. Married to historian Richard McLellan, she was working with him in the early 1980s on a biography of Jenny Marx, whom she identifies as "Karl's wife, not Groucho's." They have a married daughter, Fiona.

Ed McMahon

"H-e-e-e-r-r-e-'s Johnny!" TV's reigning second banana, superpitchman, and talk-show foil booms out five times a week, heralding the start of another "Tonight" show starring Johnny Carson. Big (6'4", 225 lbs.), jovial, and quick to guffaw at Johnny's jokes ("He's been accused of laughing too much," Carson once said, "but I think he really thinks I'm funny"), Edward Leo McMahon, born 6 March 1923 in Detroit, was the son of a onetime minstral-show interlocutor who turned pro fund-raiser. He worked his way through Catholic University by, among other things, selling pots and pans door-to-door and hawking vegetable slicers on the Boardwalk of Atlantic City. He broke into bigtime

TV in 1954 as Carson's sidekick on a daytime quiz show called "Who Do You Trust?" and has since gone on to host "Star Search" (the popular national TV talent forum which premiered in '83) and co-host NBC-TV's runaway hit "TV Bloopers and Practical Jokes" (which also premiered in '83). Over the years, he has moved more and more into acting, with a list of credits that includes the movie *Butterfly* ('81) and the telefilm "The Golden Moment." He also appeared on Broadway in the comedy, *The Impossible Years*. For many years he has also served as co-host of Jerry Lewis's annual Muscular Dystrophy Telethon. He is one of America's top TV salesmen, as evidenced by his long association with Budweiser, Alpo, and Chris Craft Boats. Ed and his wife Victoria separated in 1989 (one baby girl, Katherine Mary). He is the father of four by his first marriage, which ended in divorce. In 1988 McMahon was awarded an Honorary Doctorate in Communications from his Alma Mater, Catholic University of America. One of McMahon's proudest achievements was receiving the prestigious "Horatio Alger Award," an honor he shares with former Presidents Eisenhower and Ford as well as Reagan. He is also the author of two books, *The Art of Public Speaking* (1986) and *Selling* (1989).

Terrence McNally

"McNally can create amusing situations and write funny lines, and there are some of the former and quite a few of the latter floating around," observed John Simon in his *New York* review of *The Rink* (1984). That critique of the book for the musical was quite a different tune from Howard Taubman's summation of *And Things That Go Bump in the Night* (McNally's first play) in his *New York Times* review a couple of decades earlier (1965). "It is sick, sick, sick." Terrence McNally's zigzaggy career on-and-off Broadway, marked by on-and-off critical reviews, has always generated enthusiasm and admiration in the theatrical community. (Norman Mailer and Alan Schneider were great champions of his first play, *Bump*, and were supportive in his winning a Guggenheim fellowship in 1967.)

Born in St. Petersburg, Florida, 3 November 1939 and raised in Corpus Christi, Texas, McNally attended the Columbia School of Journalism, where he tried his hand at penning the senior-year varsity show. When he won a $6,000 grant he took the money, ran off to Mexico, and settled down to some serious writing.

Prior to *The Rink*, McNally was represented on the New York stage by *It's Only a Play* at the Manhattan Punch Theatre. His other credits include *Frankie and Johnny in the Clair de Lune, The Lisbon Traviata, The Ritz, Bad Habits, Noon, Where Has Tommy Flowers Gone, Next, Sweet Eros/Witness*, and *Whiskey*. He also created the film version of *The Ritz* and a number of plays for PBS. McNally has received an Obie Award and a citation from the American Academy of Arts and Letters. He was elected Vice-President of the Dramatists Guild in 1981.

"As an Eisenhower baby I was raised to believe life was eminently fair. The fact that my first play could be treated as badly, nothing had prepared me for it. I guess I'd expected the reviews to say, 'This is a talented young man who bit off more than he could chew.' What I got was more like, 'This kid should be killed,'" observed McNally in a *New York Times* interview. "I don't think I'll ever get crazy with a play again. I feel ready to have a wonderful middle age and a wonderful old age in the theatre." McNally divides his time between an apartment in Greenwich Village and a house in Bridgehampton.

Julia Meade

A glamorous survivor of the frenetic days (and nights) of live television, this titan-haired actress/pitchlady (and, offstage and off-camera, one of the zestiest joke tellers around) still regularly adds her dazzle to the New York party scene and is a draw in regional theater. The marble mantelpiece in her Fifth Avenue apartment boasts Chicago's prestigious Sarah Siddons Award, which she won during the year she packed them in in the Windy City playing the title role in *Mary, Mary*. (She also played the role on Broadway.) She's indulged her passion for traveling on sea as well as on land, showing up as star entertainer on cruise ships sailing everywhere from Montevideo and South Africa to Japan and Alaska. Among her other passions: cats, ice-skating (she has served as chairman of Superskates for the U.S. Olympic Fund) and baseball.

Once dubbed "Miss Lady of Television" (because she eschewed too-revealing low-cut gowns), Julia Meade made her debut in the real world on 17 December, circa 1930, in Boston, where her actress mother, Caroline Meade, took time out from Playing Roxanne to Walter Hampden's Cyrano in repertory to give birth to her first daughter. Raised in Ridgewood, New Jersey, and treading the boards in school plays from the age of seven, Julia grew up, she says, thinking "all little girls just automatically grew up to be actresses." She prepared for her own greasepaint activities at the Yale Drama School.

After serving a grueling apprenticeship on a daytime audience-participation show called "Okay, Mother" on live television, she "reluctantly" did a commercial on the "Ed Sullivan Show" and wound up as a soft-selling regular for nine lucrative years. Intermingled with the huckstering have been multitudinous stage appearances in and out of New York, a few movies (*Pillow Talk; Tammy, Tell Me True*), her own cable TV series, and a role in the CBS telefilm "One More Time" (1988). Married and divorced from Studio 54 biggie Worsham Rudd, the two are still live-in friends and the parents of two daughters, Caroline and Alice. Julia's cliff-top house on the Maine coast near Ogunquit is as much a source of local tourist interest as the town's tasty offshore lobsters.

Zubin Mehta

The music director of the New York Philharmonic is a prime product of the jet-age's impact on the classical music world. Zubin Mehta soared to international renown on the music scene by substituting for celebrated maestros throughout the world, receiving critical acclaim wherever he went. Assessing his success in the early 1960s, he said, "I made half my career by jumping in at the last moment. I sometimes think my success was due almost entirely to the misfortunes of my elderly colleagues." Boundless energy and the fact that he is an intensely serious and involved musician did, of course, play their part. His ability to conduct virtually the entire standard repertoire from memory is instrumental in his continued success, as is his now-legendary baton technique. "No one could ask for a more vital and loving collaborator," says violinist Isaac Stern, a close musical friend of many years, who feels that Mehta provides "an orchestral partner with a powerful concept." Stern calls Mehta "the classical example of a conductor who combines clarity of beat with a total knowledge of the score and a sheer ecstasy for the music."

Born in Bombay, India, 29 April 1936, Mehta is the descendant of Zoroastrian Parsees. His father, Mehli Mehta, who taught himself violin with phonograph records, founded the Bombay String Quartet and, later, the Bombay Symphony. Taught piano and violin from age seven, Mehta was conducting full orchestra rehearsals in Bombay at age sixteen. After two years of medical school, he enrolled in Vienna's state music academy, where he studied composition and conducting. Only a year after receiving his conducting diploma in 1957, at age twenty-one, he won first prize at Liverpool (England) International Conductor's Competition, which included a year's contract as associate conductor of the Royal Liverpool

Philharmonic. Soon after, a second prize at a competition in Tanglewood, Massachusetts, brought him to the attention of Charles Munch of the Boston Symphony. During his glob-trotting guest appearances in 1960 and 1961, he made his New York Philharmonic debut on 26 July 1960 with an outdoor concert at Lewisohn Stadium. Following a guest conductorship in Montreal arranged by Munch, Mehta was appointed musical director of the Montreal Symphony in January 1961. Exactly one year later, he began his first season as musical director of the Los Angeles Philharmonic; at twenty-six, he was the youngest person ever to hold that title and the first one to direct two North American symphony orchestras at the same time. Within five years, he had revamped the formerly style-less Los Angeles organization to produce the "Vienna sound" of his student days. Active in the Israeli Philharmonic since he first guest-conducted there in 1961, Mehta dropped the Montreal directorship in 1967 to make the Israeli group his new "second home." In turn, Los Angeles was left behind when he was engaged to lead the New York Philharmonic with the 1978 season. A decade later, Mehta opened the 147th season of the New York Philharmonic at Avery Fisher Hall. With his contract coming due, the acclaimed musical director has decided to resign as of the 1990/1991 season.

Handsome and flamboyant, Mehta spent years as part of the Hollywood social swirl. With his vibrant television appearances, he has become something of a cultural matinee idol. First married to Canadian singer Carmen Lasky (one son, one daughter), he was married for the second time in 1969, to actress Nancy Kovack.

Richard Meier

"Romantic Modernist Wins a Plum From the Getty," ran the *New York Times* headline. In what has been called the architectural commission of the century, the J. Paul Getty Trust finally decided who they wanted to design and build their new arts complex in the Brentwood section of Los Angeles. The two-year quest began with a list of thirty-three contenders, was narrowed down to seven semifinalists and at last, in the fall of 1984, to New York architect Richard Meier. The Getty board praised Meier as "a confirmed modernist, but a very personal kind of one; his work is at once romantic and highly disciplined, and it is exceptionally pristine and elegant." He is also an architect of international stature, the youngest recipient of his profession's highest accolade, the Pritzker Architecture Prize (viewed by many as his field's equivalent of the Nobel Prize), and only the sixth architect in the world to be so honored. Meier was cited by the jury "for his single-minded pursuit of new directions in contemporary architecture . . . [with] works which are personal, vigorous, original . . . [and] have enriched our imaging."

What makes these facts all the more remarkable is that it was just twenty-five years ago that Meier really committed himself to an architectural career. Born 12 October 1934 in Newark, N.J., he received a Bachelor's in architecture from Cornell University and apprenticed at a couple of New York architectural firms as well as with Marcel Breuer. But Meier's professional "epiphany" did not happen until a night in 1963 when he visited the opening of an exhibition at the Museum of Modern Art. The exhibit was of models and drawings by the French master Le Corbusier and "marked a turning point in my life. To me, he was the greatest architect of the century." Citing the other influences on him (Frank Lloyd Wright, Alvar Aalto), Meier says, "Architecture is a tradition, a long continuum. Whether we break with tradition or enhance it, we are still connected to the past. We evolve." Part of his own evolution came from painting large expressionist canvases and making intricate collages which Meier feels keep "the eye and hand in training; it is in effect, my work-out." The result has been the production of outstanding working drawings and exhibitions which have been seen in museums around the world.

In 1963, Meier established his private practice and launched the business with a commission from his parents, a residence in Essex Falls, N.J. His progression to the present firm, Richard Meier & Partners, has been steady. In 1965, one of his early residential commissions, Smith House in Darien, Conn., brought him national prominence. His Bronx Development Center for the mentally retarded has been called one of the most significant architectural accomplishments of the decade. In 1979, after devoting nearly five years of work, Meier completed The Atheneum (orientation headquarters for the restoration community of New Harmony, Indiana), which as the *New York Times* reported, advances "conventional modernist practice provocatively beyond established limits." On an even grander scale was his much praised High Museum of Art in Atlanta, Georgia, completed in 1983. He is also responsible for a major museum in Frankfurt, West Germany, and the Des Moines Art Center in Iowa. Meier also designs tableware and furniture. He enjoys lecturing and teaching, and has done both in this country and abroad. His work has been published in several books and periodicals, and this past year he was elected to the American Academy and Institute of Arts and Letters. Married to Katherine Gormley in 1978, they have a son and a daughter.

John Cougar Mellencamp

He is a down-to-earth midwestern-born singer/songwriter who has not forgotten his roots. They are reflected in the lyrics of his songs as well as in the visuals of his videos. Not only does he identify with the common people, he has organized and participated in several live concerts to benefit such stricken groups as the farmers.

John Mellencamp was born on 7 October 1951 in Seymour, Indiana. He attended the University of Vincennes in Indiana before beginning his singing career. His first album, *Chestnut Street Incident*, was released in 1976. Since his debut album, he has released LP's which include *A Biography* (1978), *John Cougar* (1979), *Nothing Matters and What if It Did* (1980), *The Kid Inside* (1982), *American Fool* (1982), *Uh-Huh* (1983), *Scarecrow* (1985), *The Lonesome Jubilee* (1987) and *Big Daddy* (1989). His accomplishments go far beyond recording albums. Each of his last four LP's has generated at least three top 20 and two top 10 singles. In addition, his other outstanding accomplishments include sales records—*American Fool* was the biggest selling album in 1982; *American Fool*, *Scarecrow*, and *The Lonesome Jubilee* each spent an average of six months in the *Billboard* top 10; in 1987-88 the only other male performer to have an album in the top 10 longer than John Cougar Mellencamp was Michael Jackson, and Mellencamp and John Lennon were the only male artist to have a number one album and two top 10 singles on the charts concurrently. His work has earned him several awards, such as a Grammy for Best Male Performance for "Hurts So Good," Grammy nominations for Album of the Year for *American Fool* (1982), Best Male Rock Performance for *American Fool* (1982), Best Rock Performance for "Pink Houses" (1984), Best Performance Music Video for *The Lonesome Jubilee* (1987), a Special NARAS Award in 1988 for "Check It Out," the President's Merit Award for Farm Aid (1986), and the American Music Award for Favorite Pop Male (1982). Additional *Billboard* awards include Best Conceptual Video for "Rain on the Scarecrow" (1986). *Cash Box* awards include: Number One Artist of the Year (1982), Number One Male Pop Album Artist (1982), Number One Male Pop Singles Artist (1982). In addition, he has received an ASCAP Award for Most Performed Songs for "R.O.C.K. in the U.S.A." and "Small Town," and the NARM Award for Best Selling LP by a Male Artist for *American Fool* (1982). The singer/songwriter is also a humanitarian. He has volunteered his time and talents to help those less fortunate than himself. John Cougar Mellencamp, along with Willie Nelson and Neil Young, organized and performed in Farm Aid I, II, and III (1985-87). In 1986, he made an appearance at the Farmer's Home Administration in Missouri, performing on the back of a flatbed truck in order to call attention to the plight of the American farmer. In addition, in December 1987 he performed two free concerts in Chillicothe, Ohio, as a present to the town.

John and his wife Vicky (separated August 1989) have three children, Michelle, Teddy Joe, and Justice. One for the record books, Mellencamp became a grandfather in August 1989 when his daughter, Michelle, gave birth to Elexis Suzanne Peach.

Gian Carlo Menotti

The most performed of contemporary opera composers, Italian-born Gian Carlo Menotti stands alone on the American scene. "It is not opinion but fact," states fellow composer Ned Rorem, "that Menotti singlehandedly revitalized the concept of living opera for Americans. . . . Menotti violently altered the nature of lyric theatre here, and by extension, throughout the world." His fame as a composer has been confirmed by two naturalistic, Pulitzer Prize–winning operas, *The Consul* (1950) and *The Saint of Bleecker Street* (which also won the Drama Critics Circle Award in 1955), both powerful and tragic works. This reputation has also been enhanced by his creation of TV's poetic Christmas show *Amahl and the Night Visitors*.

Born in Cadegliano, Italy, 7 July 1911, the sixth of ten musical young Menottis who played their own chamber music each evening, Gian Carlo started to compose at six, and at eleven wrote an opera, *The Death of Pierrot*. By the time he was seventeen, he had become a spoiled prodigy, lionized in the salons of the local elite. His mother eventually took him to America in 1928 and enrolled him at the Curtis Institute of Music in Philadelphia, where he studied on a scholarship with Rosario Scalero and also wrote pieces for orchestra and piano and selections for children as part of his homework in composition. He enjoyed his first operatic success at age twenty-two with the ebullient opera buffa *Amelia Goes to the Ball*, given in 1936 at Philadelphia's Academy of Music, and went on to produce a body of work that is unique—and awesome. He was the first to produce an original opera successfully on Broadway with the 1947 hit double-bill presentation of *The Medium* and *The Telephone*. Menotti has also enriched the artistic world with his ballets, including *Sebastian*, *Errand into the Maze*, and *The Unicorn, the Gorgon and the Manticore*, orchestral works (*Apocalypse*), cantatas, songs, librettos, plays and another first—the opera *The Labyrinth*, written exclusively for TV in 1963. In 1979, his contemporary creation *Juana, La Loca*, with Beverly Sills in the title role, was one of the soprano's last operatic performances.

Menotti lives a peripatetic existence; as an involved creator, he constantly travels the world to direct his own operas and those of other composers; acts as stage director "in spite of myself"; produces his operas in many languages, collaborating on the translations; and consistently edits/revises his compositions for a publishing project. In addition, he is involved in fundraising and leadership for the two extraordinary festivals that he founded: the Festival of Two Worlds in Spoleto, Italy—an international event that brings together performing artists from the old world and the new—and America's "Spoleto" in Charleston, S.C. With all these projects in the fire, retirement to his neoclassical mansion in Scotland does not appear to be in the cards just yet. Among his recent compositions is an opera, written for tenor Placido Domingo, about the great Spanish artist Goya. "My life is full of disorder, but I love order," he says wistfully.

Yehudi Menuhin

At the age of eleven, after playing a concert of Bach, Beethoven and Brahms in Berlin, the young violinist was kissed and lifted high by a bushy-haired stranger. "Yehudi," said Albert Einstein, "now I know that there is a God in heaven." A few months before, on 25 November 1927, "the most prodigious of prodigies" had ignited the New York music world at Carnegie Hall with an interpretation of the Beethoven Violin Concerto that displayed not only technical brilliance but also a deep emotional and intellectual insight. In the ensuing years, he has broadened the scope of his musicianship and invested enormous energy in the training and guiding of talented youngsters toward professional careers. Still ranked as one of the world's top violinists, he now devotes a major portion of his career to guest conducting. President of The Royal Philharmonic in London, he toured North America for the first time with that orchestra in the 1984-85 season as conductor. He recently received the prestigious Buber-Rosenzweig Medal.

Born 22 April 1916 in New York of Russian parents, he began to play violin at age three and was given lessons at five. He made his debut with the San Francisco Orchestra at seven and has concertized to rave reviews ever since, making the transition from child prodigy to leonine adult virtuoso without difficulty. In 1933, he and his late sister Hephzibah gave the first of their piano and violin sonata evenings, which were memorable highlights of concert seasons for many years. His younger sister Yaltah is also an accomplished pianist, as is his youngest son, Jeremy, who performs with his father in concert and on recordings. Menuhin has been married twice, first to Nola Nicholas (two children), then to former dancer-actress Diana Gould (two children). For more than 500 concerts in military hospitals during World War II, he received the French Legion of Honor and, from de Gaulle himself, the Cross of Lorraine. Forty-nine other honors and awards include an Honorary Knighthood by Queen Elizabeth II in 1966, which became official in 1985 when he was granted British citizenship (to go with his U.S. and Swiss citizenship), and a doctorate from the Sorbonne in Paris; he was the first musician ever so honored in the 723-year history of the university. In 1956, he founded the famous Gstaad Festival in Switzerland and was for years the guiding force behind the annual festivals at Bath and Windsor, England. In 1963, he founded the Yehudi Menuhin School at Stoke d'Abernon, Surrey, to provide special training for promising musicians from age six to sixteen and has served two terms as president of the International Music Council of UNESCO. Other humanitarian activities include membership in some 250 organizations covering fields as far-flung as ecology and music therapy. Largely responsible for popularizing Indian music in the West, he made a number of best-selling records with sitar player Ravi Shankar, and is now investigating the world of jazz violin.

Menuhin has published a number of books, including an autobiography, *Unfinished Journey*, *The Music of Man* (with Curtis W. Davis, 1979), based on his television series of that name, several textbooks and, in 1972, *The Violin—Six Lessons with Yehudi Menuhin* and *Theme and Variations*, in which he philosophizes, "Man's peculiar privilege is walking erect on two feet and thereby being forced to stretch his hands upwards to heaven. This conquering of gravity, space and height, as well as of horizon, is essential in violin playing."

Merchant/Ivory

Film producer Ismail Merchant and director, James Ivory, made it into the *Guiness Book of Records* as the longest-running producer/director team in film history. In 1988 they released a two-record set spotlighting original soundtrack highlights from their twenty-five years of filmmaking. The two LPs released under the title: *Merchant Ivory Productions: Twenty-Fifth Anniversary (1962-1987)* includes excerpts from such recent successes as *Maurice*, *A Room with a View*, and *The Bostonians* all the way back to the partner's debut production, *The Householder*, from 1963. The record release was the first of many activities in connection with the

Melina Mercouri

twenty-five-year milestone. The two men were also honored with major anniversary screenings at The Kennedy Center in Washington, D.C., as well as the New York and Toronto Film Festivals.

Bombay-born Ismail Merchant and California-born James Ivory had their historic initial meeting in 1961 en route to the Cannes Film Festival, where Merchant's first film—a theatrical short called *The Creation of Woman*— was an official U.S. entry. Merchant Ivory Productions had its launching soon thereafter, with the goal of making English language features in India for the international market. It was not only the vast visual resources of the Asian subcontinent that attracted the filmmakers, but also the opportunity to finance releases with funds from the frozen rupee account of major American distributors. These accounts contained distribution income which the Indian government would not allow to be repatriated, but which could be utilized under an agreement to make films in India. MIP's first feature, *The Householder*, based on an early novel by Ruth Prawer Jhabvala, was the first Indian film to be distributed worldwide by a major American company, Columbia Pictures. Jhabvala, who wrote the screenplay for this film, also wrote the screen adaptation for the partner's filmization of E.M Forster's novel *Maurice*, written in 1914 but because of its controversial autobiographical elements, not published until 1971, after the author's death.

The award winning team's latest release was *Slaves of New York*, starring Bernadette Peters. James Ivory says: "Lately I'd been wanting to make a film about 'smart society' in fin de siècle New York—only not about smart society at the end of the last century, as a lot of people might suppose, but instead at the end of my own. Tama Janowitz's stories about the downtown art scene seemed to offer me an avenue to do that."

Melina Mercouri

In 1955, she was Greece's most famous stage actress. In 1967, her passport revoked by the new dictatorial government ("a group of ridiculous colonels." she sniffed), she was stateless. In the 1980s, she was back home again, serving as a highly visible Minister of Culture of the Socialist government of Prime Minister Andreas Papandreou. Her special crusade: campaigning for the return from the British Museum of the world-famous Elgin Marbles, removed from the Athenian Acropolis circa 1804. "Because they are the symbol and the blood and the soul of the Greek people. Because we have fought and died for the Parthenon and the Acropolis. Because when we are born, they talk to us about all this great history that makes Greekness. . . . Because the marbles were taken by an aristocrat like Lord Elgin for his own pleasure. Because this is our cultural history and belongs . . . to this country and this temple."

Born 18 October 1925 into one of the most prominent families in Greece (her father was a longtime member of Parliament; her grandfather, the mayor of Athens for thirty years), she was christened Maria Amalia Mercouri. Melina is a nickname from her granddad, based on the Greek word "meli," meaning "honey." Strong-willed and smoldering even as a young woman, she was thrown out of several private schools and, at the age of seventeen, married an older Greek businessman. Her first great stage success was in an Athens production of Eugene O'Neill's *Mourning Becomes Electra*, and her initial movie triumph came in Michael Cacoyannis' 1955 film, *Stella*, an instant international hit. While taking in the Cannes Film Festival, she met the American-born director Jules Dassin and, soon inseparable both on and off screen, they made many films together, notably *He Who Must Die, Never on Sunday, Phaedra* and *Topkapi*. After disentangling themselves from their respective spouses, the two were married in 1966. A year later, Melina starred on Broadway in a musical version of the "Sunday" film, renamed *Ilya, Darling*. She also made a Broadway stopover in *Lysistrata* in 1972, a year after the publication of her outspoken autobiography, *I Was Born Greek*.

David Merrick

Dubbed "the abominable showman" by *Time* in his heyday as a pre-eminent Broadway producer, he was still represented on The Great White Way midway through the eighties by *42nd Street*, his eighty-fourth Broadway show and the Tony Award winner as Best Musical of 1981. When the *New York Times* gave the show mixed reviews, the abrasive impresario (also the show's sole financial backer) responded by trying to place a front-page ad in the *Times* soliciting arsonists to burn down the newspaper. The show has since generated a London production and two national companies. Certainly, he built his $50-million theatrical empire by promoting his own efforts; by getting a girl to jump onto the stage during the third act of *Look Back in Anger* and slap an actor's face, he is said to have added about eight months to the play's run and helped sell the subsequent tour. Assessing such antics by "the meanest man on Schubert Alley," David Susskind once allowed, "If means to ends are justified, he is the greatest product of our times."

Born David Margulies, 27 November 1912 in St. Louis, he was stage-struck while still in his teens and made his debut on Broadway by walking into a producer's office and offering $5,000 to back a play; he got a job. His first effort (*Clutterbuck*, 1949) was a miss, but *Fanny* (1954) was a hit. In the very busy thirty years that followed, he was responsible for such blockbusters as *Hello Dolly; Carnival; Gypsy; Oliver!; Promises, Promises; Sugar; Very Good Eddie; Play It Again, Sam; Regina; Luther; Becket; Marat/Sade; Rosencrantz and Guildenstern Are Dead; The Milk Train Doesn't Stop Here Anymore;* and *Private Lives*. Twice honored with special Tony Awards for distinguished achievement in the theater, he is also one of the few producers inducted into the Theater Hall of Fame in New York City. Of his five marriages, Merrick's first, to Lenore Beck, had the longest run (1939-1962). This was followed by Jeannie Gilbert (one daughter), writer Etan Aronson (1969-1976, one daughter) and former *42nd Street* star Karen Prunczik, whom he married July 1, 1982. As played, the script for this stormy, ten month marriage was worthy of one of his Woody Allen productions; he married his star, retired her, later sent her out in a road company, fired her from the show and then, seriously ill, was confined by her in a rehab when, according to the fourth Mrs. Merrick, "he escaped . . . in a wheelchair . . . in the pouring rain without a coat. He was ultimately picked up by the police in a Korean noodle factory." The fifth marriage was a revival; he remarried Etan again in August, 1983. However, this was a short revival, ending again in divorce. Although he has turned in recent years to producing movies—*The Great Gatsby* (1974), *Semi-Tough* (1977) and *Rough-Cut* (1980)—he has unfinished business on Broadway. Because of his enduring sensitivity to "scatter-brained" criticism, he has promised one day to have the pleasure of throwing critic Clive Barnes' "fat Limey posterior out in the street." Merrick's latest production took place in London—a new show entitled *Emerald City* (1988).

Dina Merrill

"Dina Merrill," once enthused an admirer, "is glamour—with both feet on the ground." Although she grew up in more of a castle than a home (her bedroom was decorated to look like the Sleeping Beauty's; the door-knobs were silver squirrels, and a specially designed rug told the whole story) and could have slept through her whole life, she wasn't the type. "I always wanted to stand on my own feet and be somebody," says the granddaughter of the inventor of Postum, named Nedenia for her stockbroker father, Ned Hutton (Barbara Hutton was her cousin). "Besides," added Dina, "I come from hard-working pioneer stock and was brought up with the work ethic."

As a child (born 29 December 1925) Dina used to sit on her mother's lap and watch her make up and comb her hair. At six, she already knew she wanted to act. Although her parents, Marjorie Merriweather Post and Edward F. Hutton, were not in favor of their daughter joining the acting profession, after a year at George Washington University, Dina enrolled at the American Academy of Dramatic Arts while working as a fashion model to support herself. "It never occurred to me to ask my parents to pay for something they didn't believe in. I wouldn't, so why should they? They could have stopped me but they didn't; they were sure I'd never stay with it," After summer stock, she made her Broadway debut in *The Mermaids Are Singing*. But in 1946 she married Stanley Rumbaugh, Jr., and for the next ten years led an active Long Island North Shore social life centered around a home in Locust Valley and her three children, Nina, Stanley and David (who later died in a boating accident). In 1952 she took time out to appear on television with Dick Powell, and in 1957 made her film debut.

Her motion pictures include *Catch as Catch Can*, *Butterfield 8*, *Operation Petticoat*, Robert Altman's *A Wedding* and *Just Tell Me What You Want*. Her television performances include "The Tenth Month" (1979) co-starring Carol Burnett, "Anna to the Infinite Power," a cable-TV movie, "The Brass Ring," a series, "Hot Pursuit" (1984) and numerous guest appearances. Broadway stage appearances included *Angel Street* (1976), *Are You Now or Have You Ever Been . . .* (reading Lillian Hellman's letter to the House Un-American Activities Committee, 1979) and *On Your Toes* (1983).

After a divorce from Rumbaugh in 1964, Dina married actor Cliff Robertson in 1966 (one daughter, Heather). They separated in 1985 and their divorce was finalized in 1989.

Robert Merrill

In the spring of 1973 this baritone celebrated his 500th performance with the Metropolitan Opera. He still appears regularly at Yankee Stadium to sing the National Anthem at Yankee opening games. The "Star Spangled Baritone" once confessed he would "like to be a comedian, but their material wears out so fast. . . . I've got the best writers in the world—guys like Verdi, Puccini, and Bizet."

Born Morris Miller (later changed to Merrill Miller, then to Robert Merrill), 4 June 1919 in Brooklyn, he played small clubs and the Borscht Belt and sang opera in such exotic locales as Hoboken and Newark before taking off with a Major Bowes Amateur Hour company. Major Bowes was "a thrifty man," he remembers. "Once he asked me to sing at a special affair. . . . I sang my head off, about ten songs. As I left, he slipped me a bill . . . ten dollars, or a dollar a song."

In 1945 Merrill won recognition on the "Metropolitan Opera Auditions of the Air"; later the same year, he made his Met debut as the elder Germont in *La Traviata*. "A big jump," he says, "from the New Utrecht High School kid playing baseball, to singing all these Italian operas." Subsequent roles have included Valentin in *Faust*, Amonasro in *Aida*, Escamillo in *Carmen*, and Iago in *Otello*. He was married first to singer Roberta Peters, then to Marion Machno (two children). Colorful on stage and off, he is dead serious about his craft. ("The big mistake some singers make is forgetting that their voices are the most important thing.") He conquered the world of musical theater for the first time in 1970 when he starred in *Fiddler on the Roof*, which toured the country. In 1983 he sang for President Reagan, the latest in a long list of presidents—Truman, Eisenhower, Kennedy and Johnson—who have invited him to sing at the White House. In 1970 the then mayor John Lindsay presented him with the Handel Medallion, NYC's highest cultural award.

He is also a published author: *Once More from the Beginning* (an autobiography), *Between Acts* (1976) and *Divas* (1978). Met marvel but a down-home man, he recalls, "I did *La Traviata* in Brooklyn. . . . Some of the guys that didn't know from opera came and saw me in the long beard. They yelled . . . 'Hey Moishe! Whattayuh wit'ta beard, hey Moishe, hey Merrill, hey Morris, yuh gotta be kiddin!' It was," Merrill says, "one of the great days of my life."

George Michael

He has faith—faith in himself as well as faith in pop music. "The happiest moments for me are on stage. That feeling when you know a crowd is going absolutely crazy and had a great time can't be beaten," says pop star George Michael. *Rolling Stone* magazine described George Michael as "an unquestionably gifted songwriter in a field of otherwise dismal hacks," and the *London Times* declared him "The new Paul McCartney." With the debut of his solo album *Faith*, George has emerged as one of the biggest pop stars of the eighties.

Born George Panayiotou in England on 25 June 1963, he had a passion for pop music and American R & B at a young age. His first band, The Executive, was formed with his childhood friend Andrew Ridgley. Later, they were signed to Innervision Records, and they renamed the band Wham! Starting in 1982, Wham! had four back-to-back hits from their debut LP *Fantastic*. Their second hit album, *Make It Big*, produced three number-one singles in the U.S., including "Wake Me Up Before You Go-Go," "Careless Whisper," and "Everything She Wants." In 1985, Wham! received worldwide acclaim when they became the first Western pop band ever to perform in the People's Republic of China. Following this, Wham! produced their final album, *Music from the Edge of Heaven*, which contained three hit singles.

Ready to take on a career as a solo artist, George and his Wham! partner Andrew Ridgley went their separate ways in June of 1985. His first project as a solo artist was a duet with Aretha Franklin entitled "I Knew You Were Waiting (for Me)," which was a number-one hit worldwide. He began producing and writing his first solo LP, which took two years to complete. Released on 2 November 1987, *Faith* became the number-one album in the U.S., producing such top-of-the-chart hits as the controversial "I Want Your Sex," "Faith," "Father Figure," "One More Try," "Monkey," and "Kissing a Fool." In 1988 George won a Grammy for Best Vocal Performance Duo R & B for the single "I Knew You Were Waiting (for Me)," along with the BPI (British Phonography Industry) award for Best British Male Artist of the Year. In addition, in 1989 George won a Grammy as well as an American Music Award for his album *Faith*.

James Michener

"I make my living by writing and guessing," says Pulitzer Prize (*Tales of the South Pacific*) recipient James Michener. His "guesses" have been quite accurate, right on target it seems—his thirty-odd books have been translated into over fifty languages, several hitting the top of the best-seller charts (*Chesapeake*, *Centennial*, *The Covenant*, *Space*—#1 for over six months). He has written nine movies, four TV shows, and one Rodgers and Hammerstein hit musical. Other books include *Sayonara*, *The Source*, *Iberia*, *Caravans* and *Poland*.

Born 3 February 1907 of unknown parents, James Albert Michener was raised in Doylestown, Pennsylvania, under the care of Mabel Michener, a kind-hearted widow who took him in as a foundling, along with other abandoned children. A brilliant student, even from high school, Michener was awarded the first four-year scholarship given by Swarthmore College (he repaid the $2,000 "loan" in 1984 along with $1,998,000 of "interest"). His passion for reading

(Dickens, Keats, the Bible, Wordsworth) and travel (by high-school graduation he had visited forty-eight states) have immensely influenced his writing. A longing for the Pacific was relieved when the U.S. Navy transported him there during World War II; he later succeeded in vividly recreating the wartime South Pacific for countless readers. This theme was to set the course for books to come—he would write of different cultures, religions and life-styles. One critic describes Michener's novels as "not really novels and not really history, not genuine art nor awful kitsch," but "docudramas." Those works are made up of enormous amounts of research, travel to far away places, and a good deal of time spent with natives, (Michener has a way of making people feel at ease and reveal much about themselves.) Michener's most recent undertakings include a saga based in *Texas*, a place Michener has a special passion for, and a tome on *Alaska*. In addition to his immense narratives, Michener has written texts for five art books. A lifelong Quaker, he has devoted a great deal of his time to public service; he has served as cultural ambassador to a number of countries. He is a strong supporter of budding writers and has established an endowment to award fellowships to graduates of the Iowa Writers Workshop. In 1983 President Reagan honored Michener at a White House ceremony for the tremendous support he's given to the arts. Thirty leading universities have awarded Michener honorary doctorates in five fields. He was awarded the nation's highest civilian award, the Medal of Freedom, in 1977. From 1979 to 1983 he served on NASA's Advisory Council. Since 1978, he has served on the committee that advises the U.S. Postal Service on which stamps the government should print, and this has allowed him to pursue the interest in travel which he has had since childhood.

James Michener and his wife Mari Yoriko Sabusawa (a second-generation Japanese American) maintain homes in Pipersville, Pennsylvania, and St. Michaels, Maryland. A diligent worker with a fear of poverty that has always remained with him, Michener was still going strong in his eighties. "I love the expansiveness of this world, I can hardly wait to get up in the morning and see it all. I've never been bored." Nor, obviously, have his loyal readers.

Bette Midler

"I may put several thousand feet of tulle around it, but my message is that people should feel hope, overcome fear and stand on their own. Of course I'm discreet about it *in my way* ... but I think of it as a grand thing, almost as a mission," explains this entertainer whose special blend of talent, vocal versatility, high-speed locomotion, camp sophistication and wide-eyed innocence has earned her devoted fans, gold records and several box-office breakthroughs. Her 1975 sell out revue *Clams on the Half Shell* grossed more than $1.8 million. She's also won one Grammy—for her 1972 debut album, "The Divine Miss M," a special Tony award in 1973, an Oscar nomination for her portrayal of a self-destructive hard-rock singer in *the Rose*, and an Emmy for her 1978 TV special "Ol' Red Hair is Back."

She was appalled recently when an admiring fan asked her, "How does it feel to be an institution?" Her reply: "Don't *say* that! I'm too young to be an institution. Besides, I'd rather be a bank!" She was born 1 December 1945, named after Bette Davis (but pronounced *Bet*) and raised in Hawaii in the family of a transplanted New Jersey housepainter. She spent a year at the University of Hawaii studying drama, then dropped out to work in a pineapple cannery until she was hired to play a missionary's wife in the film *Hawaii*. (Despite dropping out of school, Midler is an avid and eclectic reader. According to *People* magazine's Andrea Chambers, "volumes of Shakespeare and Molière are lined up on a bookshelf near a pair of rhinestone platform heels, a gift from Cher," in her New York loft.)

The part in *Hawaii* paid her $350 and took her to Los Angeles for final shooting. With her life's savings she went to New York and worked as a go-go dancer, a glove saleswoman at Stern's and a typist at Columbia University, until she landed a part in the chorus of *Fiddler on the Roof,* eventually graduating to the principal role of Tzeitel, Tevye's eldest daughter, which she played for three years. About that time, she saw a production of the Theater for the Ridiculous. "There was this character, Waterfront Woman. . . . I'll never forget her. I wanted to be just like her." That, perhaps, formed the early nucleus for her "Divine Miss M" persona.

Midler's career breakthrough came in the winter of 1971, when she beguiled the sybarites at the all-male Continental Baths with her "rock and raunch blend of music and action." She became an overnight cult figure and word of mouth quickly brought her to the attention of Ahmet Ertegun, who-signed her to a recording contract at Atlantic Records. It's been "Venus de Midler" ever since, hoopla and Hollywood, mostly highs, but some lows, such as *Jinxed* (1981, a movie that most certainly was well named) and management troubles in 1979. Married in December, 1984, to business consultant–musician Martin von Haselberg, she is the author of two books, *A View from a Broad* and *The Saga of Baby Divine*. In 1985 she released the album *Mud Will Be Flung Tonight*, and the video and single entitled "Wind Beneath My Wings," from her film *Beaches*, became a smash hit in 1989. Her other movies include *Down and Out in Beverly Hills* (1986), *Ruthless People* (1986), *Outrageous Fortune* (1986), *Big Business* (1987) and *Stella* (1989). She also did the voice-over for the animated 1988 feature *Oliver and Company*.

Julia Migenes

"Julia Migenes Johnson [she dropped the Johnson after her divorce] has the full potential to be, in her very different fashion, the greatest actress/singer since Callas," said New York *Post* drama critic Clive Barnes. That high compliment and others like it are echoed throughout the opera world today. Her highly acclaimed title-role performance in the 1984 film of Bizet's *Carmen* with Placido Domingo is a significant achievement. (She was nominated in both France and Italy as best actress in a dramatic role.) Her next two films, *Berlin Blues* (1987) and *Three Penny Opera* (1989), also displayed her extraordinary talents. In addition, her performance in *Lulu* at the Met in 1985 gained more critics' praise.

Born of Greek and Puerto Rican–Irish descent in New York City circa 1946, she made her first stage appearance at three-and-a-half in *Madame Butterfly*. At the age of four, she and her older brother and sister began performing in an RCA show at Macy's, and on other stages and stores around New York. Julia attended the Moser Academy (for performing children) and at the age of six was chosen for a role in the touring company of the Rodgers and Hammerstein classic *South Pacific*. She continued her vocal and dance studies at the High School of Music and Art and during her junior year was chosen by Leonard Bernstein as a soloist for a "Young People's Concert." On Broadway, Julia appeared in the revival of *West Side Story* and in the original-cast production of *Fiddler on the Roof*. While in *Fiddler*, Migenes found time to perform with the New York City Opera. Performing around the world, the diva gained recognition in many roles at the Vienna Volksoper and in television appearances in a variety of European countries. She has been honored with numerous awards, among them the Golden Bambi (the most coveted award in the German-speaking countries) and the prestigious Golden Lion of Luxembourg for her work in television. In 1985 Migenes participated in the Grammy Award ceremonies as both performer and award winner for her vocal performance in *Carmen*. Having demonstrated superior ability to sing both the popular and operatic repertoire as well as dance and act, Migenes has remained a prominent fixture in opera, popular music and film. She was the subject of a lively "60 Minutes" segment in 1985.

Divorced from her husband, Julia lives with her two daughters on Long Island, New York.

Ann Miller

Moira Hodgson in the *New York Times* described the Technicolor tap dancer thus: "Ann Miller . . . a genuine old-fashioned movie star. At 13, with a forged birth certificate, she put poverty behind her and became a star at a top Hollywood studio. . . . Now, years, later, remembering her struggles as a child, she keeps a jar of candy and bubble gum by her bed. She also saves all her old clothes, just in case. Her bedroom in her Beverly Hills mansion has ancient Egyptian decor, right down to a Tutankhamen-style throne, because she believes in reincarnation and is convinced she lived in Egypt in an earlier life."

Born Lucy Ann Collier 12 April 1923 in Chireno, Texas, she started ballet lessons at the age of five to cure knock-knees and weak legs, the result of rickets. She did so well that her mother took her backstage one day to meet Bill (Bojangles) Robinson and show him how the kid could dance. He responded by giving Miller her first tap lesson. After her parents divorced when she was ten, she supported her mother by tapping at Rotary luncheons until she won a local "personality" contest and, soon thereafter, a seven-year contract at RKO, making her debut in *New Faces of 1937*. Her father forged her birth certificate so that the young teenager would meet the legal requirements of being eighteen. ("It was the only kind thing he ever did for me," she says.) She took small parts in *Room Service, Stage Door*, and *You Can't Take It with You*, with a brief term on Broadway in *George White's Scandals of 1939*. Ultimately she played supporting roles and second leads in over forty musical films, most notably *Easter Parade, Kissing Bandit, On the Town, Two Tickets to Broadway* and *Kiss Me Kate*. In 1979, she signed on to return to Broadway in the burlesque-inspired *Sugar Babies* with Mickey Rooney. In rehearsals for the super-hit she was about to throw in the towel when made to feel like a chorus girl, but pal Mickey threatened to leave with her. "I said, 'I am a star from MGM and the public expects glamour.' They finally gave me some showstoppers." And stop the show she did. Miller continues to please her audiences by appearing in revised *Sugar Babies* productions. Her latest opening was in London (September 1988).

She has been married (briefly) three times: first to playboy Reese Milner, heir to Consolidated Steel; next to William Moss; and lastly to Arthur Cameron. The latter two were wealthy Texas oilmen.

"I have worked like a dog all my life, honey," she told Rex Reed in 1979. "Dancing, as Fred Astaire said, is next to ditch-digging. You sweat and you slave and the audience doesn't think you've got a brain in your head. So every time a good-looking millionaire came along chasing me with cars and jewels, I married him because he promised I'd never have to dance again." These days her two long-haired poodles, Cinderella and Jasmine, are her companions. Once a year she visits her jewels in their bank vault. "I look at all the pretty things sparkling and it makes me feel good. Yet they are nothing but pieces of earth."

Arthur Miller

The day after Bernard Gimbel attended the opening night of *Death of a Salesman* on Broadway in January, 1949, he sent a memo to every executive that no one was to be fired because he was growing old. Arthur Miller, the young playwright who had written this morality play about a failed travelling salesman who strives for dignity and sees life passing him by, was thunderstruck. "I had no idea people would take it so god-damned personally," he says in his raspy, Brooklyn-accented voice. "I was quite shocked. You know," he continues, "'craft' has two meanings, and one of them is 'sinister.' When people came out staggering, I felt guilty about it."

The play was Miller's stepping stone into the top echelon of the American theater. In 1984 the Kennedy Center named him one of four recipients of its Lifetime Achievement in the Arts Award. Not that his career as America's Playwright—the voice of the average man—has been all peaks and no valleys. *Salesman* has remained a gem of the American stage, and enjoyed a revival on Broadway in 1983 starring Dustin Hoffman. It made its People's Republic of China premiere in 1984 and was presented with the Broadway cast on TV in the fall of 1985. The play has been translated into twenty-nine languages and is required reading in high schools and colleges. And 1955's *View from the Bridge* (also an eighties revival on Broadway), a kind of Greek tragedy transplanted to Brooklyn, has become a modern classic. Miller at that time was hauled before the House Committee on Un-American Activities, refused to name names, and suddenly became a political celebrity. Several weeks later he married Marilyn Monroe and was suddenly more famous for his politics and boudoir life than for his scripts. Ironically, his critical stock began to plummet. His life with Marilyn was the thinly veiled material for his next play, *After the Fall* (performed in 1964 after her death), and the critics turned thumbs down. He didn't attend her 1962 funeral and today won't discuss that marriage "unless some stupid jerk brings it up." His relationship with Broadway producers has been touch-and-go; although his plays fill theaters, Miller's decidedly lofty stance and tendency to preach have kept him at arm's distance from certain moguls of the Great White Way. Give him a moment and he'll tell you that serious theater on Broadway is dead, killed off by "high priced soap-bubble entertainment. Now it's all *Dreamgirls*." His latest Broadway endeavor was 1987's *All My Sons*, and he wrote the screenplay for the 1989 film *Everybody Wins*. His autobiography *Timebends: A Life* was published in 1987.

Born 17 October 1915 in New York City, Miller takes a "Brooklyn boy's delight in land ownership," noted Jennifer Allen of *New York* magazine after visiting the playwright and his wife, photographer Inge Morath, in their big eighteenth-century white frame farmhouse on a hillside in Roxbury, Connecticut. Miller, an amateur carpenter, built himself a one-room studio some yards from the house and does his writing here. The couple have a daughter, Rebecca.

Jonathan Miller

This Cambridge-educated medical doctor, iconoclast and renaissance man has carved a unique role in the arts as a comedian, author, and eclectic stage and film director. He has also evoked cheers and jeers on both sides of the Atlantic with his stinging wit (he once called Broadway "a sewer") and controversial interpretation of the classics. (The Miller staging of *Rigoletto* for the English National Opera moved the Verdi opera from sixteenth-century Mantua to New York's Little Italy in the 1950s.) "Simply to have an automatic update is mindless, but no more mindless than simply leaving a work in its place. . . . Works of . do not remain the same," he proclaims, asserting that it's sometimes only by departing from the "definitive" that a work recaptures the spirit of the original source. Miller first gained international attention in the early 1960s as co-writer and one of the four stars of the comedy *Beyond the Fringe*. (Dudley Moore was one of his laugh-getting stage colleagues.) Since then, he has flitted among the arts, directing the classics on stage, staging operas, and mounting both on television, on which he has also hosted the widely acclaimed series "The Body in Question," in which he utilized his medical expertise.

Born 21 July 1934 in London, Jonathan Miller was educated at Cambridge and graduated as a doctor of medicine from University College Hospital Medical School. Having made his first stage appearance in 1954 in a Cambridge Footlights Club Revue, his professional debut came in 1961 in London in *Beyond the Fringe*, and he first came to New York in 1962 with the company. Miller's directorial stage credits include productions for Britain's National Theatre (*The Merchant of Venice*, Beaumarchais's *The Marriage of Figaro*. . .), *Hamlet* in London's West End and *A Midsummer Night's Dream* for the Vienna Bergtheater. As Associate Artist of the English National Opera, he has directed *The Marriage of Figaro, The Turn of the Screw, Arabella* and *Othello*. He announced his retirement from the arts after his 1985 production of *Don Giovanni*, to return full-time to medicine, but he soon returned to the stage. He directed Jack Lemmon on Broadway in 1985 in a revival of O'Neill's *Long Day's Journey into Night*.

In the fall of 1986 he presented an English National Opera production of *The Mikado*, and his book on working in the theatre, *Subsequent Performance*, was also published that year. The following year, he directed a London production of *Taming of the Shrew* at the Royal Shakespeare Theatre. Some of his other books include *The Body in Question* (a companion volume to the TV series), *The Human Body Book* and *The Facts of Life* (pop-up books) and *States of Mind*. He married Helen Rachel Collet in 1956 and they have two grown sons and a daughter. The happy couple live in London's Camden Town.

Mitch Miller

It was a stately and hirsute portrait of the Emir Feisal (from T.E. Laurence's *Seven Pillars of Wisdom*) that inspired his now celebrated Vandyke, and he's been sporting it since 1940. It has accompanied him through a multitude of careers in the music business: as a highly respected classical oboist, as a well-known A and R man in the record business, and as the TV conductor who urged a nation on "Sing Along with Mitch." More recently, the ubiquitous beard has been in evidence on a series of conducting tours of symphony orchestras all over the U.S., Canada and Mexico (he made his Italian debut in 1983—in an all-Gershwin program) and in the last decade has raised more than a half-million dollars for symphony orchestras in financial straits.

The music man was born on Independence Day 1911 in Rochester, New York, and took up the oboe as a twelve-year-old when, turning up late for a school band tryout, he discovered that all the most popular instruments had been spoken for. Within a few years he was tripling as first oboe with both the Syracuse and Eastman Symphonies and second oboe with the Rochester Philharmonic. In New York City, starting in 1932, he alternated between pop and classical fare and was good enough to move Virgil Thomson to rhapsodize: "There is no oboe playing like that of Mr. Miller. The tone of it, which is round without being greasy, is woody and rich. Warm and laughing, sensuous and faun-like . . . and the rhythm of its speech is both faultless and free."

Married to Frances Alexander in 1935 (three children), Mitch switched careers in 1947 and became a pop artist and repertory man (first at Mercury, later at Columbia). He masterminded the million-seller platter careers of the likes of Frankie Laine, Tony Bennett, Rosemary Clooney, Jo Stafford, and Doris Day, and later moved up to the job of director of all Columbia's pop productions. He became the country's most sung-along-with choirmaster in the early sixties and has recorded at least nineteen "Sing Along" albums, which have sold over sixteen million copies. His most recent LP is entitled *The Gershwin Album* (1988). A prominent critic observed, "there's probably none in this country who hasn't been touched in one way or another by Mitch Miller's music."

Donna Mills

"I decided to leave 'Knots Landing' for reasons that seem right to an actress: I had been playing Abby for nine seasons on CBS, and I had reached a point where I needed new roles and new challenges. I could have played her forever, but it was just time to let her go and say goodbye." Sultry nighttime soap vixen Donna Mills wrote an article entitled "My Life as a Troublemaker" for *TV Guide* in 1989 explaining her sudden departure from the popular show. She adds. "But, being entirely honest, I'm looking forward to the new projects I have lined up and to having a personal life again."

Donna Miller (she changed her name to Mills when she discovered Actor's Equity already had a Miller) was born in Chicago on 11 December 1943 and she began to study dance at an early age. After graduating from the University of Illinois, she first appeared in local theater productions as a dancer, then eventually acted in three plays in Chicago's Drury Theatre before settling in New York City. Breaking in with commercials, Donna landed a three-year run on the daytime soap "Love is a Many Splendored Thing." Her next role was as a regular on Burt Reynolds' TV series "Dan August," followed by her performance on the big screen as Clint Eastwood's almost-murdered girlfriend in *Play Misty for Me*. When approached about the part of Abby on "Knots Landing," the spunky actress demanded not to be considered for it on her past credits, but to read for the role and prove she could be the woman viewers love to hate. Although Donna is not as ruthless as Abby, they do share a desire to be "independent of the influences of others; marching to the beat of your own drummer, with the courage to identify what you really want and go for it: win, lose or draw. It takes a lot of courage and determination, but everything has more value when you earn it yourself."

"No girl on TV has ever been raped, strangled, assaulted, kidnapped, beaten or killed more than I," she insists. Some of her past credits include the daytime soap "The Secret Storm," a TV series with Larry Hagman— "The Good Life" (1971-72)—a Broadway part in *Don't Drink the Water*, the TV films "Waikiki," "Doctor's Private Lives," "Superdome," "The Hunted Lady," "Woman on the Run," "Fire," "The Bait," "Alice in Wonderland," "Outback Bound," plus two miniseries, "Hanging by a Thread" and "Bare Essence." Among other distinctions, she won the Soap Opera Award for Best Villainess. In a sincere attempt to share her beauty secrets, Donna released the home video "The Eyes Have It" in 1986. The actress loves to practice ballet or play tennis in her spare time. She says, "I couldn't possibly accomplish all of my goals without the benefit of good health." Never married, she enjoys her self-decorated home: "My surroundings are extremely important, since it is my place to rejuvenate."

Sherrill Milnes

"Music has always been an integral part of my life," says the good-looking, blue-eyed baritone Sherrill Milnes. Renowned for his mastery of the Verdi roles, Milnes was awarded the title of Commander of the Order of Merit of the Republic of Italy in recognition of his love and dedication to Italian music (1983). One of the most recorded American opera stars, Milnes has made over thirty complete recordings, including *La Traviata*, which won the Grand Prix de Paris; *Cosi Fan Tutte*, winner of the NARAS award for best opera recording; and *Il Tabbaro*, winner of the Premio della Critica Discografica Italia. As the host of a syndicated radio program, "A New World of Music," he was dedicated to sharing the diverse heritage of American music. In 1988 he celebrated the twentieth anniversary of his appearance in Verdi's *Luisa Miller* at the Met and he starred in the PBS television special "Richard Tucker—the American Caruso."

American-born, 10 January 1935 in Downers Grove, Illinois, Milnes is the second son of James Milnes, a methodist-minister-turned-farmer, and Thelma Roe, a singer, pianist, choir director and conductor. Though his music studies began early (with piano, violin, viola, tuba, and voice) his childhood was filled with the concerns of a typical farm boy (rising early, milking cows, etc.) rather than the rigorous demands often placed on a young musician. Milnes began college as a pre med student, switching later to music and voice. "I didn't like the sound of my voice in high school but in college it was different. It all seemed to come together somehow." The meshing took time, nevertheless. Milnes' early work included TV and radio voice overs and jingles, and brief stints as pianist, string bassist and violinist with dance bands. After an audition for Boris Goldovsky, Milnes' career began to bloom—the maestro immediately signed him for a tour as Masetto in *Don Giovanni*. In 1964 he joined the New York City Opera company and in 1965 Milnes made his debut at the Metropolitan Opera; that performance was hailed as spectacular by every critic in New York. Milnes' 1972 performance as Iago in Franco Zeffirelli's production of *Otello* won him more laudatory comments—"Sherrill Milnes is simply the finest Iago I have ever heard or seen . . . ," said one admiring critic. The "made in America" baritone (named American Man of Music—1982—by the Phi Mu Alpha Sinfonia) has brought down the house in many of the world's greatest opera centers. Married (for the second time) to soprano Nancy Stokes, Milnes and his wife make their home in New York (with their son Shawn). Milnes has two other children by his first wife.

Ronnie Milsap

"I have played and can play any kind of music, but you must do what your heart feels is right. And to me, that's country," says Ronnie Milsap. Blind since birth, Milsap is comfortable with musical styles ranging from classical to country, and from R & B to rock and roll. He was a violin virtuoso at seven, played the piano at eight, and mastered the guitar at twelve. Now Milsap plays nearly every keyboard, stringed, percussion and woodwind instrument there is. Nevertheless, he has settled for a successful career in country music, although his singles and albums regularly cross over the pop and adult contemporary charts. "If you're going to make advances in your life," says Milsap, "you're going to have to take chances." The advances that have come so far include gold and platinum albums, Country Music Association Album of the Year awards, CMA Male Vocalist of the Year awards, CMA Entertainer of the Year (1977) and multiple Grammy Awards (Best male country vocalist - 1974, 1976, 1981, 1985; Best Country Vocal Duet - 1987).

Born in Robinsville, North Carolina, 16 January and raised by his grandparents, Ronnie Milsap was kicked out of music class at the Governor Morehead School for the Blind in Raleigh for playing rock and roll instead of classical music. After attending Young-Harris Junior College near Atlanta, Georgia, for two years, he turned down a scholarship to Emory University School of Law in favor of playing music for a living. He moved to Atlanta in 1965, the year he married Frances Joyce Reeves (one son) and signed with the New York–based Scepter Records as an R & B artist. His first single, "Never Had It So Good," was a top-five R & B hit, but he never had another big record for the rest of the decade.

In 1972, Milsap, troubled with management problems and without a record label, moved to Nashville, Tennessee. "When I first came to Nashville, I was at the lowest point in my life," says Milsap. "It was almost like a last chance: 'Do this, and if you blow it, you're probably going to have to get out of the business and go back to law school.' So I came into the whole thing—in some ways—very desperate." He eventually became a success in a Nashville club, and went on to sign a recording contract with RCA. He established himself solidly in the country-music field and rapidly acquired a loyal legion of fans with hits like "Daydreams about Night Things" and "(I'm a) Stand by My Woman Man." Some of his recent albums are *Keyed Up* (1985), *Believe It* (1986), *Lost in the Fifties Tonight* (1986; Grammy Award), *Christmas with Ronnie Milsap* (1987), *Heart and Soul* (1988), and *Stranger Things Have Happened* (1989).

As for his blindness, Milsap says he doesn't really think about it that much. "I'm not going to make light of it. I think I make it look so easy that people sometimes think it is easy."

Nathan Milstein

Performing on a violin (circa 1716) from Stradivarius's golden period, Nathan Milstein himself is a master of his instrument—"a dazzling technician" and "a most individual interpreter," say music aficionados. The fiery-tempered musician is now a firmly disciplined one. At the age of five, "wild young Nathan" was forced to take violin lessons in order to keep him out of trouble. "At the time it was very unpleasant for me." But, when he was eleven, he played for the great violinist Leopold Auer, who, reported one newspaper, promptly fainted, and several years later he played for Eugene Ysaye, who just as promptly said, "Go—there is nothing I can teach you."

Born in Odessa, Russia, 31 December 1904, Milstein studied at the Odessa Music School and the St. Petersburg Conservatory. He initially supported himself by concertizing in Russia with Vladimir Horowitz and by the time he was twenty, had not only conquered his native Russia, but all the music capitals of Western Europe. Milstein is admired for his "combination of technical perfection with emotional freshness and resilience." His 1929 American debut with the Philadelphia Orchestra was widely praised, as were subsequent performances with other major American orchestras. His 1984 tour, for instance, included performances with the Cleveland Orchestra, the San Francisco Symphony, the National Symphony Orchestra and the Vancouver Symphony.

Married to Theresa Weldon (one daughter), and a man of wide-ranging interests (philosophy, painting, politics and literature), he is also the holder of a prize collection of Tourte, Pecatte and Voirin bows. The recipient of many honors internationally (rank of Commander of the Legion of Honour from the French government and the Grand Cross of Honour, First Class, from Australia), Milstein won a Grammy Award for his recording for Deutsche Grammophon of the Bach *Partitas and Sonatas for Violin Solo*. In 1987 he was presented with the Kennedy Center Award for Lifetime Achievement. "Of course I have grown," he once said of himself. "You try to refresh and enrich what you do every time you play. . . . My great gain, I suspect, is that I have learned to project what I had in my mind and heart."

Liza Minnelli

With her days at the Betty Ford Clinic behind her, Liza Minnelli has been doing what she does best—performing in concert, appearing on television and in films, plus giving her all to the entertainment industry. The recipient of three Tony awards, one Oscar, and one Emmy is happy to be on the right track. "I like my life. It feels good to be on the move and surefooted. Drugs are a banana peel—why fall down when you don't have to?" The famous singer/actress has gone through some big highs and lows in her personal and professional life. Her first two marriages (Peter Allen, Jack Haley, Jr.) failed as her career wavered between "comebacks." "Her life," one observer says, "has seemed both flight from and fulfillment of the Garland legacy."

Born 12 March 1946 in Los Angeles to Judy Garland and Vincente Minnelli, she was a student at sixteen different schools on both sides of the Atlantic before she reached the age of sixteen. Still, she claimed hers was not an "unhappy childhood, my mother wasn't always in Europe, and I didn't have a nanny. I lived at the Plaza Hotel. . . . A lot of kids lived there, and I really wasn't any different—it was like everybody poured water down the mail chute." Liza made her first public appearance at seven where her mother, who was playing at the Palace, called her onstage to dance. The eldest of Judy's three children, Liza left home before her sixteenth birthday: "Mama went on a kick every now and then where she used to kick me out of the house. Usually, I'd stand outside the door and pretty soon she'd open it and we'd fall into each other's arms, crying and carrying on. But one day she did it and I took her up on it. I went to New York; I had my plane fare and $100 and I've never taken a penny since." (Unlike her mother, who was often broke, Liza had invested astutely.) Before her money ran out she got work in summer stock and a part in an off-Broadway revivial of *Best Foot Forward* and cut her first record, "You Are For Loving," that same year (1963). The following year her mother asked her to share the bill at the London Palladium, and the year after Liza won a Tony for the title role in *Flora, the Red Menace* and also made her nightclub debut at the Shoreham Hotel in Washington, D.C. In short order she was appearing on the top TV variety shows and in the leading nightclubs in the U.S. and Europe.

Minnelli's first film was *Charlie Bubbles* followed by her Oscar-nominated portrayal of a mixed-up college student in *The Sterile Cuckoo*, and next, as the victim of a battery-acid attack, in the touching *Tell Me That You Love Me, Junie Moon*. Her fourth film, *Cabaret*, brought her the Oscar for best actress, something even Garland never accomplished. That same year (1972) she won an Emmy for her TV special "Liza with a Z." Some of her other credits include: narrating *The Owl and the Pussycat* for the Martha Graham Dance Company at the Metropolitan Opera House; movies *New York, New York, Arthur, Rent-a-Cop*, and *Arthur On The Rocks*; the TV special "Baryshnikov on Broadway," and in 1984, on Broadway, *The Rink*. She starred in the NBC telefilm, "A Time to Live" (1985) as the mother of a terminally ill son; the role brought her a Golden Glove Award. In 1987 she appeared on stage at Carnegie Hall and released a two-album recording of the event. Also in 1987 she hosted a PBS documentary "Minnelli on Minnelli: Liza Remembers Vincente." The following year she made a unique ABC-TV special "Liza Minnelli in Sam Found Out: A Triple Play."

After her cure at the Betty Ford Clinic, she and third husband, theatrical producer Mark Gero, put their lives on the back burner so that Liza could take a year off from all activity. Finally feeling fit, she embarked on a six-month, twenty-seven-city concert tour in the summer of 1985, reportedly sounding "better than ever." With two earlier broken marriages, assuming responsibility for her mother's debts, two miscarriages, a fire in her Manhattan apartment, hospitalizations for lung infections and exhaustion—as well as heartbreaking romances with Martin Scorsese, Desi Arnaz, Jr., and Peter Sellers, the actress-singer-dancer, who once said: "I believe in grabbing at happiness . . . if you have to pay later for a decision you've made, that's all right," is off gathering new forces, recovering herself and no longer grabbing. Making her claim in the Pop field, Minnelli released a new album, *Results* in September 1989.

Grace Mirabella

During the years when what was in *Vogue* was determined by super-editor Diana Vreeland, the venerable journal of *haute couture* was, like the woman in charge, "shatteringly chic," skittish, ebullient and loaded with pizzazz. When Grace Mirabella moved to the editor's *chaise* in 1972, the magazine went from its "think-pink-shy-don't-you" past to become sharper and more "feet-on-the-ground" (albeit *très cher* footing in fancy shoes), a sort of tap dance with the women's movement. The *Vogue* personality was personified by its then editor-in-chief, the willowy, Hall of Fame Best Dressed wife of surgeon William G. Cahan. She said at the outset of her editorial reign, "We want to round her (the reader of *Vogue*) out and intensify her." She certainly strengthened her. *Vogue* averaged so many advertising pages each month it resembled the Sears Catalogue and required Wonder Woman strength to hold. Carrying her expertise one step further, the enterprising lady left *Vogue* in 1988 and became the publication director of her namesake magazine, *Mirabella*, which debuted on the stands in June 1989.

Good right arm to Mrs. Vreeland for eight years, Mirabella was described by her former boss as "a marvelous with it girl." She got her feet wet in the fashion waters by working at Saks Fifth Avenue and Macy's following her graduation from Skidmore and her earlier years in Maplewood, New Jersey, where she was born 10 June 1929. She started as *Vogue's* shopping editor in 1952 and inked her way to associate editor in 1965. She has endured in a field where fashions changed at a rate equal to pages in a brisk wind. Grace Mirabella has received many honors and awards throughout her career, including the Susan G. Komen Foundation Award for Excellence in Media (1987) and the 1988 Child Care Organization "Fabulous Family" Award.

Joni Mitchell

"As a songwriter," a critic once said, "she plays Yang to Bob Dylan's Yin." Among her song titles are "Woodstock," "Both Sides Now," "Free Man in Paris," "Help Me," "Chelsea Morning," "Ladies of the Canyon," "Blue," "Lessons in Survival," and "Big Yellow Taxi." Toting a guitar and a pocketful of folk songs, she came down out of Saskatoon, Saskatchewan, in the mid-60s and emerged from the shadowy brewings in the New York coffee house scene as (according to the *New York Times*) "one of the most genuinely gifted composers North America has yet developed."

Known first for the sensitive lyrical inventions she provided for such singers as Judy Collins, she started recording her own songs in 1968 with an album called *Song to a Seagull*. At first she was not given to a comfortable performing style on stage, but she learned. A reviewer for the London *Guardian* said of her concert at Festival Hall: ". . . Never have I experienced such a close communion between a singer and an audience." And Mitchell once silenced a persistent fan who kept yelling out the name of his favorite song hoping she would sing it by saying, "There's one thing that's always been a difference between the performing arts and being a painter. A painter does a painting and it hangs on a wall somewhere and that's it. . . . Nobody ever said to Van Gogh, 'Paint *A Starry Night* again, man!'"

Born Roberta Joan Anderson on 7 November 1943 in a little town of McLeod, Alberta, Canada, the tall, willowy singer with an exquisitely chiseled face, soft blue eyes, prominent cheekbones and yellow-blonde hair, had her eye on a career in commercial art when she was a schoolgirl. But when she packed up for the Alberta College of Art she found she could pick up extra money by performing in a local coffeehouse. She left school and moved to Toronto to try her luck as a folk singer. There she met fellow folksinger Chuck Mitchell and the two were married in 1965, just 36 hours after they had met. They moved to Detroit but within a year the marriage broke up and Joni moved to New York to sing solo. (In New York she wrote a song about her failed marriage, "I Had a King." The lyrics included: "I had a king dressed in drip-dry and paisley. Lately he's taken to saying I'm crazy and blind . . . I had a king in a salt-rusted carriage/Who carried me off to his country for marriage too soon.") Although it did not top the charts, her first album offered an alternative to the sounds of the Doors, the Grateful Dead and Jefferson Airplane. She has written well over 100 songs and in 1977 Alfred Knopf published *Joni Mitchell Complete*, a book of her songs. In 1979 she branched out and recorded *Mingus*, an album of the music of the jazz great Charlie Mingus. Some of her last albums include *Dog Eat Dog* (1985) and *Chalk Mark in a Rainstorm* (1988).

Pop music reporters found it fun to write about her famous boyfriends who seemed to have been chosen from the music industry, however, Joni finally settled down and married Larry Klein in November 1982. She is an accomplished and exhibited painter (many of her album covers are her paintings) and although she rarely performs formally, some lucky Los Angeles folk have been at the Nucleus Nuance when she's felt comfortable enough to jam with the musicians.

Robert Mitchum

He lived for years with the image of Hollywood Bad Boy mostly because, in 1948, long before pot-smoking came into vogue, he was arrested for marijuana possession and served six months in a work camp. When asked what it was like, he reported, "Just like Palm Springs. Without the riffraff, of course." Asked in court to give his occupation, he dryly stated, "Ex-actor," figuring the negative publicity would ruin his career. Instead, he found himself bigger than ever and he's remained a "bankable" star ever since.

He was born Robert Charles Duran Mitchum, 6 August 1917 in Bridgeport, Conn. As a Depression Kid he spent most of his teens traveling the country on the bum (with time out for a short stretch on a Georgia chain gang for vagrancy). Landing in California, he went to work at Lockheed Aircraft until overexposure to noisy machinery began to take its toll and a doctor suggested he change his line of work. He signed up as a film extra, brushed up on his horsemanship, and appeared in eight Hopalong Cassidy movies before becoming a big-league movie star in 1945 with *The Story of G.I. Joe*. Since then the actor with the battered, belligerent face ("I agree with the guy who wrote that I looked like a shark with a broken nose") has been a standout in such films as *Crossfire* (1947), *Night of the Hunter* (1955), *The Sundowners* (1960), *Ryan's Daughter* (1970), *The Friends of Eddie Coyle* (1973), *The Big Sleep* (playing the Bogart role in a 1978 remake of the 1946 Raymond Chandler detective thriller) and *That Championship Season* (1982). More recent films include *Maria's Lovers* (1985), *The Conspiracy* (1986), *Mr. North* (1988), *Scrooged* (1988), and *Presume Dangereux* (1989). In 1983, he had a high-rated week on ABC-TV starring in Herman Wouk's novel-for-television, "Winds of War." The sequel "War and Remembrance" in 1988 did not fair as well in the ratings. He also appeared in NBC's "The Brotherhood of the Rose" (1988) and "Family Man" (1989).

Though Mitchum became the center of a cause celebre at the 1954 Cannes Film Festival when he was photographed with a bare-bosomed starlet, and has made on-screen love to some of the most glamorous females in Hollywood (Elizabeth Taylor, Rita Hayworth, Ava Gardner, Susan Hayward), he's been married since 1940 to the former Dorothy Spence, mother of his three children. Both of his sons, James and Christopher, are now film actors. Why is the laconic Robert Mitchum of the somnolent eyes so very "definitely a survivor" (as one critic called him) when so many other '40s faces have fallen by the wayside? "When I first went to work," he recalls, "I'd go into casting offices and they'd say, 'What's he do?' Or, 'Did you ever think about getting your nose fixed or changing your name?' Later, not too much later, they'd say, 'We need a Mitchum type.'. . . I turned out to be the only one, which ensured my longevity."

Issey Miyake

Opposed to the rigid formality of *haute couture*, he tried to find "the limits of clothing" and has made his signature with "intriguingly textured fabrics, unusual knits, draped skirts and distinctively combined layers—a blend of Oriental inventiveness and Western tailoring," as *W* explained. When the fashion press and the big-city department stores ushered, with loud accolades, the inventive new Japanese designers into their respective nests, Miyake rebelled, not wanting to be pigeonholed in one group. "I've been working in New York and Paris for fifteen years," he said in 1984 when he refused to be part of a Bloomingdale's Japanese promotion. "Suddenly Japanese designers are trendy and they put me into this trendy group. I want to stay calm."

Born in Hiroshima in 1938, he knew as a teenager he wanted to design clothes. After four years of art training in Tokyo he went to Paris to study with Givenchy and Guy Laroche. "My idea was to become an American designer," he recalls of his ambitions in 1969 when he moved to New York to study at Columbia University while working as Geoffrey Beene's assistant. "I was fascinated by the blue-jeans revolution," he recalls. "It changed traditional thinking everywhere." Eventually the New York high-life got to him and he became ill and returned to Japan in 1970. A two-month exhibition at the San Francisco Museum of Modern Art in 1983 was intended "to display my thinking . . . not to sell." In Japan he creates books and is involved in that country's intellectual and artistic life. All for androgyny, he declared before a group of art students, "Sexiness is finished." Writing in *Newsweek*, correspondent Douglas David commented, "Roland Barthes once argued that the 'fashion system' has become, in this century, an instantaneous language of coded symbols. Miyake uses this language like a poet—reaching an audience that is intensely literate."

Matthew Modine

"It's nice to be able to slip through because that's how you get your material—in the streets," says this versatile young actor of his relative anonymity among celebrity watchers. The only advantage of movie stardom (he opts for movie "actordom"), says Matthew Modine, is "the ability to work with people that you want to work with. . . . I don't give a hoot about the money and stuff." Unless he takes a vow of poverty and assumes a Brando/Garbo attitude, it's unlikely he'll escape for long the "money and stuff" destined to come his way as he rides the crest of the wave of youth-oriented movies that were becoming standard cinema fare in the mid-1980s. What makes Modine different is his unwillingness to go the pin-up poster and fan-magazine cover route that might prevent "teen-idol Modine" from being cast in the offbeat roles that have brought him screen prominence, ranging from the sexually-ambivalent soldier knifed to death in the screen version of David Rabe's play, *Streamers* (1983 best actor award at the Venice Film Festival), to the title role in the film adaptation of William Wharton's cult novel, *Birdy*, in which the central character thinks he's a bird.

The youngest of seven children, Matthew Modine (born 22 March 1959) in Loma Linda, California) grew up with the movies as his baby-sitter—his father managed drive-in theatres in California and Utah. At 18, he went to New York to pursue a stage career, studying with Stella Adler, doing commercials and eventually landing a role on the TV soap opera "Texas." John Sayles tapped him for a bit part in *Baby, It's You* in and that four minutes on the screen convinced Harold Becker, director of his 1985-starrer, *Vision Quest*, that "he's a natural. . . . I've always used the term for him . . . there are no rough edges on him." The sex romp *Private School*, helped his career only to the extent that it displayed his versatility when viewed in conjunction with his next film, the shattering *Streamers*, about which he recalls, "I was terrified of that part . . . I don't think I stopped sweating that entire film." He agreed to do *Hotel New Hampshire* because "I got to play two different people—Ernst and Chipper Dove."

In *Mrs. Soffel* he had the opportunity to work with one of his idols, Mel Gibson who played his jailbird brother. Modine also had a chance to "listen to the kind of range I didn't even know Diane [Keaton] and Mel had". His most acclaimed performance to date is *Birdy*. "I never auditioned," he says. "I didn't think I was appropriate. . . . It's hard to talk about how I became the bird. You have to be there physically, but not mentally. It sounds inane, but you just do it." More Modine movies include Stanley Kubrick's *Full Metal Jacket* (1987), *Orphans* (1987), *Married to the Mob* (1987) and *La Partita* (1988). Naturally, this pursuer of the offbeat could not have met his wife, Carrie, in a conventional way. Instead, he engaged her on a New York City street in 1982 and offered to carry her packages, then took her to a movie, dinner, and finally Central Park, where they talked—about the importance of friendship—until 4 A.M. Offbeat.

Anna Moffo

Acclaimed at the height of her career as one of the greatest singing actresses, she's been called the last of the real prima donnas. "You may not like what I do, baby, but you can't say I'm dull," asserts the raven-haired cobbler's daughter who not only attracted sellout houses at the Met and Carnegie Hall, but whose nude love scene in the movie *Una Storia d'Amore* had her sued in Italy for indecent exposure. "It is impossible to discuss Anna Moffo without continually referring to one or another of the senses," said one critic. "She is beautiful to look upon and her voice is a constant ravishment to the ear."

Born 26 June 1935 in Wayne, Pennsylvania of humble, hard working Italo-American parents, Anna Moffo was a near-champion tennis player, a basketball star, and captain of her school field-hockey team before she concentrated on exercising her vocal chords at the Curtis Institute in Philadelphia. Going to Italy on a Fulbright for further vocal studies, she studied Italian by living alone with a widow who spoke no other language. Both singing and language studies paid off in 1956 when impresario Mario Lanfranchi chose her to star in an Italian TV production of *Madama Butterfly*, which made her literally a star overnight and, not long afterward, Mrs. Mario Lanfranchi. She's maintained her celebrity status and become a pioneer among leading opera singers in bringing her versatile talents to the public through a variety of media. In addition to singing more than twenty-five major roles at the Met, she's starred at leading opera houses worldwide and has been a success in concerts, TV (she had her own show on Italian TV), recordings, and motion pictures. Moffo looks upon her star status as the result of concentrated hard work: "Everything I did contributed to my career. It's very hard to get to the top, it's even harder to stay there once you've made it." Since 1974, she has been married to erstwhile broadcasting tycoon Robert Sarnoff.

Monaco Royal Family

His Serene Highness Prince Rainier III of Monaco was born on 31 May 1923 in Monaco, the son of Her Serene Highness Princess Charlotte Louise Juliette, Duchess of Valentinois, and His Serene Highness Prince Pierre Marie Xavier Antoine Melchior, Count of Polignac (who became a Grimaldi in 1920). Prince Rainier III studied in England, then attended the College of the Chateau of Rosey in Rolle, Switzerland. Continuing his studies, he obtained a Bachelor of Arts degree at Montpellier and took courses in the School of Political Science in Paris. On 28 September 1944 he joined the French Army as a volunteer. He was soon promoted to second lieutenant and because of his service was awarded the Military Cross with Bronze Star. He was promoted several more times, and in 1954 he was awarded the rank of colonel. On 9 May 1949, Prince Rainier III succeeded his grandfather Prince Louis II to the Throne. Prince Rainier III's most significant contribution has been in renovating, modernizing and enlarging the state of Monaco. He has so far increased the principality surface area by one fifth. His Royal Highness accomplished this by re-establishing the port area and rebuilding the underground railway line. In addition, he built three platforms that took one fifth of the total surface area from the sea. Prince Rainier III has taken over or founded Monaco organizations such as the International Commission for the Scientific Exploration of the Mediterranean, the First Scientific Conference on the Elimination of Radioactive Waste, the Monaco Scientific Centre, the Rainier III Foundation for Paleontological Research, the Monaco Underwater Reserve, and the Prince Pierre of Monaco Foundation, which is awarded for progress in culture and the arts, and he gave Monaco a ballet company. Prince Rainier III has also served the disadvantaged and less fortunate by providing them with services such as temporary allowances, hospital and medical care, housing allowances, and public assistance for those without work. In addition, he has set up the Autonomous Fund for Retired Self Employed Workers, as well as the Labour Medical Service that regulates general hygiene in industry. Prince Rainier III has had numerous honors bestowed upon him, including Grand Master of the Order of Saint Charles, Grand Master of the Order of the Crown, Grand Master of the Order of the Grimaldi, the Collar of Merit of the Sovereign Military Order of Malta, the Italian Military Cross, the French Military Cross, and the Grand Decoration of the Order of Leopold of Belgium. His Royal Highness Prince Rainier III married actress Grace Kelly on 18 April 1956, but became a widower when she died a tragic death on 14 September 1982. The Royal couple had three children together: Princess Caroline, Prince Albert, Princess Stephanie.

He was born Prince Albert, Alexandre, Pierre, Marquis des Baux on 14 March 1958 in the Palais Princier Monaco-Ville in Monaco to His Serene Highness Prince Rainier III and Her Serene Highness Princess Grace. His Serene Highness Prince Albert of Monaco is the Heir to the Throne of Monaco. His formal education includes attending Amherst College, where he received a Bachelor of Arts. Upon graduating, he served as ensign 2nd class in the French Navy, touring around the world in the helicopter carrier "Jeanne d'Arc." He then gained experience by working as a trainee at Morgan Guaranty Trust Company in New York, the law firm of Rogers and Wells in New York, and the Moet-Hennessy Company in Paris. Among the honors bestowed upon the Prince are the distinctions of Grand Officer of the Legion Honor of France and the Grand Officer of the National Order of the Lion of Senegal. His Serene Highness Prince Albert also has several responsibilities of state within Monaco, including acting as president of the Monaco Red Cross and vice-president of the Princess Grace Foundation. He is also president of the Monaco Swimming Federation, the Monaco Yacht Club, and the Athletic Federation of Monaco, and he was elected to serve as a member of the International Olympic Committee. In his spare time, Prince Albert enjoys swimming, soccer, tennis, volleyball, track and field, judo, rowing, team handball and auto racing.

Princess Caroline Louise Marguerite was born on 23 January 1957 in the Royal Palace in Monaco, the daughter of Prince Rainier III and Princess Grace Kelly. She attended the Ecole Libre des Sciences Politiques (School of Political Science) in Paris in 1975, and obtained a psychology degree. Three years later, on 29 June 1978 she married the French businessman Philippe Junot. Two years later, in October 1980, they divorced. Princess Caroline then decided to put her energy into writing rather than another marriage. She wanted to create her own identity and discover her real potential. To achieve this, at twenty years old, she decided to go to London to study and live with a friend, but her request was denied by her mother Princess Grace. Soon after, Princess Caroline married the Italian industrialist Stefano Casiraghi. Together they had three children, Andrea Albert Peirre, born on 8 June 1984, Charlotte Marie Pomeline, born on 3 August 1986; and Pierre Stefano Rainier, born on 5 September 1987. Princess Caroline has also recently become involved in the founding and organizing of the Monte Carlo Ballet.

Princess Stephanie Marie Elisabeth de Grimaldi of Monaco was born on 1 February 1965 in the Palais Princier, in Monaco Ville. While growing up Princess Stephanie enjoyed drawing and painting and was a committed ballet student. She also excelled in sports, participating in gymnastics, and swimming and won her first competition in swimming when she was only six. Her education consisted of private tutoring at home from age four, followed by formal education at the local convent school, Les Dames de St. Maur on the Rock. Following, she attended several secondary schools in Paris. She was expelled from St. Dominique's Catholic finishing school for breaking the school's rules of conduct, and left another school only months later. It wasn't until her enrollment into Charles de Foucauld School that she began to take her studies seriously. She finally received her baccalaureat in 1982. Fighting her Princess status and the media attention fiercely, Princess Stephanie proclaimed, "I want to be an ordinary girl. I can't stand for my friends to call me Princess." On 13 September 1982, Princess Stephanie and her mother Princess Grace were traveling when their car lost control and went over an embankment. Princess Grace was killed, and

Princess Stephanie sustained an injury to her spine. Although in time she physically recovered, she was deeply scarred emotionally. At her fathers' request she returned to Paris in January 1983 to study fashion design, but soon quit. Shortly after she joined Christian Dior, with some of her designs making it into his 1985 coture collection. In January she represented La Prairie cosmetics, and soon after began modeling with Paul Hagnauer's First. By 1985, Princess Stephanie was recruited by Wilhelmina in New York, but due to an illness she never went through with it. Later that year, in August 1985, she and a friend from Dior started up a swimwear company called Nautic, which manufactured their Pool Positions line. Princess Stephanie became her countries first "working girl" princess. Their line made it over to the U.S., and were purchased by Rich's, Macy's and Bloomingdales. Princess Stephanie currently resides in both Monaco and Paris, and she likes to vacation in Mauritius.

Meredith Monk

What distinguishes her from other "Next Wave" multi-media performance artists is that she is a devout non-self-promoter. So when she celebrated her 25th season as a leading innovator in her field with a musical retrospective of her works at Carnegie Hall in 1985, it was very much a private triumph—one that was shared by all her fans who had followed her career from its beginnings, with the now legendary Judson Dance Theater, to the present. "Enormous leaps from cozy coloratura to keening wails, hollers and sighs, "is how the *Christian Science Monitor* summed up what Monk's chameleonlike art is, all about: "a cry from the heart refined by a busy intellect and expressed with shivering immediacy." The dance critic Deborah Jowitt has described Monk's work as a "textured backdrop for daydreams." Monk once told an interviewer: "I'm trying to approach a vocal music that's both primordial and futuristic. Maybe there won't be language differentiation in the future."

Born 20 November 1942 in Lima, Peru, where her mother, a singer, was performing, she grew up in New York City in a musical household. "I sang before I talked and read music before I read words—at three." She studied the technique of Swiss composer Emile Jacques-Dalcroze before attending Sarah Lawrence College where she "was able to combine movement with music and words, all coming from a single source . . . a total experience." In 1964 she joined the Judson Dance Theater, a troupe dedicated to exploring and expanding the confines of dance. Her style of combining all sorts of instruments, voices, projections and films, began in her 1966 piece "16mm Earrings." Until the 1980s, she was better known in Europe than she was in the U.S. Traveling abroad with her communal group of singers and dancers known as "the House," her best known pieces include: "Barbershop" (1969), "Dedicated to Dinosaurs" (1969), "NeedleBrain Lloyd and the Systems Kid" (1970), "Juice" (1969), "Vessel" (1972), "Our Lady of Late" (1974), "Songs from the Hill" (1979), "Quarry" (1976), "Dolmen Music" (1981), "Turtle Dreams" and "Specimen Days" (1981), "The Games" (1983), as well as the film, *Ellis Island*, which was seen on WNET-TV and won major prizes at the Atlanta and San Francisco film festivals. She was awarded the German Critics Prize for best records in 1981 and 1986 as well as the National Music Theatre Award in 1986.

Monk has been likened, in appearance, to a Modigliani painting. She is slender, about five feet two inches tall, has large eyes and long brown hair which she wears most often in a ponytail. She lives in New York.

Ricardo Montalban

He is set apart from the prototypical Hollywood fold by virtue (and the sentence could end right there as his strong religious conviction carries over into his life) of the facts: he is not a social gadfly, has been married only once and is still married to Georgiana Young (youngest sister of Loretta Young), and believes an actor is never an actor unless he is working (this includes bad roles.) "Gene [Lockhart] once told me always take the best of three roles offered, but if only one offer came along, take it, no matter what I think of it."

Mr. Roarke, the man who made dreams come true (from 1978-84) for a price on ABC's "Fantasy Island" was born in Mexico City, 25 November 1920, the youngest of four children. After finishing grade school in Northern Mexico he was brought to the United States by an older brother and entered Fairfax High in Hollywood, soon attracting the attention of a studio scout. Shunning an MGM screen test, he wended his way toward New York to try his luck in legit theatre. His first break came when he was cast in a small part with Tallulah Bankhead in *Her Cardboard Lover* after which he appeared in several plays, returning to Mexico in 1941 to make 13 Spanish language films in four years. When he re-surfaced on Yankee turf it was to make his American feature film debut in *Fiesta*. *Neptune's Daughter*, *Latin Lovers*, *Battleground* and *Sombrero* followed. Later films include *Sweet Charity* (1968) and *Return to Planet of the Apes* (1972). Today he does his share of TV guest spots, periodically returning to the stage. (He played on tour *Don Juan in Hell* in the early 70s under the respective direction of Agnes Moorehead and John Houseman playing 138 cities to good notices). As spokesman, he has chanted the amenities of the Chrysler Cordoba, Maxwell House Coffee, and Bulova Watches but what he is especially proud of is the publication of his autobiography *Reflections: A Life in Two Worlds* (1980). His most recent projects included a continuing role on the nighttime "Dynasty" spin-off "The Colby's" (1986-1987) and a starring role in the film *The Naked Gun* (1988). For his contributions to film and Latin culture, Montalban has been awarded many honors in Mexico City. He and Georgiana (four children) live in the Hollywood hills.

Claude Montana

People in the know in Paris and New York say that this designer "with a range of imagination that makes him, many fashion observers feel, capable of virtually anything he wants to do as a designer," (noted *WWD* writer Ben Brantley) is the heir apparent to the reigning king of French couture—Yves Saint Laurent. Young Paris can't wait. Montana, the brazen radical who rose to prominence by designing leather costumes with booming-runway shoulders wild enough to tame Grace Jones's closet is worshipped there and the seasonal showings of his collections are the *hot* tickets, the *hot-hot* tickets among the fashion crazed.

Born in 1949 he says that he only knew that "I didn't want to do long studies or any of the things my father intended for me." At 17, he ran away from his bourgeois family to work as an extra at the Paris Opéra and at 22 he began designing and selling papier-maché jewelry. Worried about working without legal permission in Great Britain, he returned to Paris at the suggestion of a friend and took a job as a design assistant at MacDouglas, one of the better fashion leather houses there. He learned the basics of designing and, more importantly, discovered that he was a natural with a needle and a sketching pen. "Suddenly I realized that there was no other choice for me, that this was something I should stick to." Eventually he found financial backing from an Italian fashion manufacturer; in 1983 his fashion empire, including licensees and designs for men, earned, in volume, over $35 million. When Bloomingdale's put Montana fashions *en mannequin* in their windows, thieves broke through the glass to steal a Montana original; his competition should be so unlucky. Montana's 1984 collection reflected a maturity of his vision, the campiness was gone but the inspiration expanded. Saks Fifth Avenue's top fashion planner Ellin Saltzman, usually reticent with the big kudos, declared: "The clothes in his shows used to look like costumes. Now they look sensational on the stage and people's backs. He's a creative genius and I don't use the words loosely." Brantley described

Montana as a "strikingly vulnerable man having a profound fear of failure," and says that he is the combination of "several mythic personalities" including "the cowboy, the regal crown prince of fashion . . ." reflected in his home decor: " . . . there's a stately dining room with red-cushioned gold chairs and Empire antiques and his study is split into perfect mind-body dichotomy, with a neatly arranged, homey desk on one side and a wall of serious-looking weightlifting equipment."

Joe Montana

He's a different kind of quarterback, one who's said, "I'm not the kind of guy to be telling somebody what they're doing wrong all the time." This tactful field tactician still found words to guide the San Francisco 49ers to their first National Football League championship in his third year as a pro. His poise, not his noise, set him apart as a leader the Niners could believe in. Always a flinger who could pull games out in the last minutes, he became a national superstar for doing just that when, against the favored Dallas Cowboys, he won the 1981 NFC title game with a throw that arched above the Candlestick Park astroturf and down into the waiting hands of Dwight Clark at the back of the end zone. The 49ers went on to victory in the Super Bowl that season, an achievement they repeated in Super Bowl XIX in 1985. It could have been 1979 and Notre Dame all over again, when the nearly frostbitten Montana beat Houston in the Cotton Bowl by tossing a touchdown with no time left. While Montana describes himself as laid-back, 49er field boss Bill Walsh says, "He is one of the coolest competitors, one of the greatest instinctive players this game has ever seen and I think he's just getting started." In 1986 he was selected by his teammates as the "Len Eshmont Award" winner, for his "courageous and inspirational play." The following year he won the first NFL Passing Title of his career as he led the entire league, and in 1988 he threw for a Super Bowl record 357 yards. All told, Montana has thrown for 656 yards in three Super Bowls!

Joseph C. Montana (originally spelled "Montagna" in Italy) began life and a sports career on 11 June 1956 in New Eagle, Pa., a region that produced pro passers Joe Namath, Johnny Unitas, and George Blanda. Having been notified that Notre Dame would give him a football scholarship, he cancelled plans to play basketball at North Carolina State. Montana began at South Bend as a seventh-string freshman QB, and he missed a year due to injuries. But "the Comeback Kid" brought the Fighting Irish back from defeat no less than six times, and in 1977 they finished as national champs. At San Francisco he'd defer to the take-charge attitude of his friend and rival quarterback, Steve DeBerg, and it was not until coach Walsh had inserted and replaced Montana in all kinds of situations that he revealed that DeBerg was expendable now that Montana was ready. The insecure team leader gradually gained confidence to go with his growing patience. Subsequently, he was able to find deeper receivers, and better stats. In 1982 he set an NFL record by passing for over 300 yards in five straight games.

Montana and his third wife, Jennifer Wallace, reside in California with their two daughters (Alexandra and Elizabeth); they expect to have a third child sometime in the future. Lending his fame to charity, the football player works with the "Make-A-Wish" foundation in the Bay Area. For each touchdown pass he threw in 1987 and 1988, Montana and his wife donated $200 to the Crippled Children's Society of Santa Clara County.

Yves Montand

Hollywood wasted him in such light romantic bromides as *Let's Make Love* (with Marilyn Monroe in 1960) and *On a Clear Day You Can See Forever* (with Barbra Streisand in 1970). Europe let him demonstrate his full dramatic mettle in Clouzot's classic, *Wages of Fear* (1955), Costa-Gavras's *Z* (Best Foreign Picture Oscar in 1970) and many more. A hit on Broadway in 1959 with his one-man show ("If Trenet has 'the sound,'" wrote a critic, "and Chevalier 'the charm,' it is Montand who has 'the soul'"), he returned in 1982 (after a triumphant "comeback" tour of Europe) to become the first popular entertainer ever to be presented on the stage of New York's Metropolitan Opera House—to an ecstatic reception. His most recent films *Jean de Florette* (1987) and *Manon of the Springs* (1987) were both critical successes and he was honored by the Film Society of Lincoln Center at their annual Spring gala.

Though viewed by many as the quintessential Frenchman, Yves Montand was actually born Ivo Livi in Monsummano, Italy, 13 October 1921, the youngest child of a peasant family. When he was two, his socialist father fled from Mussolini's fascism to France and the tough harbor district of Marseilles. Forced to leave school at 11 ("It was a time of real misery"), he found a job in a spaghetti factory and worked successively as a waiter, barman, and apprentice hairdresser before displaying his talents as a singer in the local public square which was an incubator for fledgling entertainers. He made his first professional bow at 18 at the Alcazar in Marseilles, was "discovered" by Edith Piaf in Paris and proceeded to become one of France's favorite Music Hall *chanteurs populaires*.

Touring in 1949, he met actress Simone Signoret and married her in 1950. (She died 30 September 1985.) The "sex symbol nonpareil" also had much publicized affairs along the way with both Piaf and Monroe. He's presently living with his young secretary, Carole Amiel, and the couple have a child Valentin Gioanni Jacques (born 31 December 1988). He also has one granddaughter, Clementine. Once considered as a candidate for the 1988 French Presidential elections, he denied the opportunity in favor of working on a movie musical about his life.

Moody Blues

"We agreed then, and shook hands on it, that we would just play what we wanted to play, make music for ourselves, and trust our own judgment. We've done that ever since. We haven't been influenced by fashions or trends, and because of that we've seen a lot of other things come and go—and we're still here." Those mystical, magical, musical Moody Blues have sustained their place in pop history with a career spanning over twenty years. Justin Hayward (guitar), John Lodge (bass), Graeme Edge (drums), Ray Thomas (flute), and Patrick Moraz (who replaced original member Mike Pinder on keyboards) make up the group.

Remember the 60s and you'll find yourself humming a Moody Blues song. While Richard Nixon ran against Nelson Rockefeller for the GOP's presidential nomination and Robert F. Kennedy chose to seek the Democratic nomination, the group's album *Days of Future Passed* (1968) received a Pop Pick in *Cash Box* magazine. At that time no one could have predicted that this LP, with the hit single "Nights In White Satin" would remain on the *Billboard* charts for two years. Although their stardom seemed to skyrocket out of nowhere, these men from Birmingham had only touched the surface in previous efforts. It wasn't until they were thrown together with a Decca Records staff producer, Tony Clarke, that the chemistry clicked. The band cemented their success with their live concerts (touring with Cream and Canned Heat). Eventually forming their own record label, Threshold, they were able to control their creative work. More hit albums followed including *In Search of the Lost Chord* (1968), and *On the Threshold of a Dream* (1969). After discovering a shift in creative juices, the group decided to split up in 1972. As John Lodge said, "I remember us all sitting down one day and saying, 'I don't think we want to do this anymore, not for now, anyway. Let's put it away, and find some breathing space.' So we decided to do other things and form new relationships which, in the end, only came back to the Moody Blues and made us stronger." After solo efforts, they reunited six years later to record the *Octave* album (1978). Although producer Tony Clarke and keyboardist Mike Pinder left in the middle of the sessions, the combined efforts paid off down the road. Three years later, they recorded *Long Distance Voyager* (1981) which brought their chart position to Number 1 (their first chart-topper since *Seventh Sojourn* in 1972). This outing added former Yes keyboard player Patrick Moraz (replacing Pinder) to the group. Justin Hayward claims that "Patrick brought a new spirit, a new energy to the band. . . . It was something we never knew we needed until it happened. His contribution has been that enthusiasm, as much as his playing."

Today the Moody Blues are performing to a new generation of fans in addition to maintaining their initial "moodies." Recent albums include *The Other Side Of Life* (1986) and *Sur La Mer* (1988), which spawned the hit singles "Your Wildest Dreams" and the haunting "I Know You're Out There Somewhere."

Dudley Moore

"I think my own desire to be loved is really what makes me sexually attractive. It stands out so blatantly in me," he says, expounding on his theory of how he became Hollywood's unlikely romantic hero. Short of stature and long of nose, his bawdy sense of humor and teddy-bear appeal have made him a box-office magic in the cinematic world of tall, dark and handsome.

Dudley Stuart John Moore, born 19 April 1935, recalls a childhood in the gray town of Dagenham, Essex, made lonely and painfully self-conscious by stunted growth and a club foot. Humor was his only defense. "I got funny so I wouldn't get beaten up anymore."

He graduated from schoolyard performances to the English pub circuit with *Beyond the Fringe*, a satirical revue he formed with Alan Bennett, Peter Cook and Jonathan Miller in 1960. Its risqué, dark-humored flavor caught on, leading Moore to star in a weekly English series, "Not Only . . . but Also." "I have a very ribald sense of humor, which is conventionally known as obscene," he has said. American audiences found him hysterical as the midlife bumbler who lusts after Bo Derek in *10*, and the 1981 *Arthur* provided Moore with the perfect vehicle for his deadpanning and raucous laughter. He came across as the perfect lovable drunk, bringing out the maternal in women and comradeship in men. However, he didn't fair as well with the critics in the 1988 sequel *Arthur on the Rocks*. Other film credits include *Six Weeks* and *Lovesick*, both in 1983, *Unfaithfully Yours* in 1984, *Santa Claus - the Movie* in 1985, *Like Father Like Son* in 1987 and *Crazy People* in 1989. He is also an accomplished jazz pianist and composer.

Divorced twice—from British actress Suzy Kendall and actress Tuesday Weld (a son, Patrick)—Moore married his third wife, Brogan Lane, in February 1988.

Mary Tyler Moore

"I'm not an actress who can create a character. I play me," said she, when still a pixie comedienne, known first as the beautiful but slightly birdbrained wife on "The Dick Van Dyke Show," and then as perky Mary Richards, heroine of "The Mary Tyler Show." She, and the critics, would wish to retract that assessment later in her career, when she delivered powerful performances on screen and Broadway. She said of the transition, "As a comedienne, I'm an observer of life and people. That's what enables one to do dramatic work. I didn't have to study or train for it. It was there."

Moore, born in Brooklyn, N.Y., on 29 December 1937, debuted in show business as a singing spokeswoman for Hotpoint Appliances, and sported her legs as a telephone operator in the 1957 detective series "Richard Diamond." She was likeable in "The Dick Van Dyke Show," as Laura Petrie, suburban housewife who responded to strife with a quivering upper lip and heavy sigh, "Oh, Rob." But it was with the premiere of "The Mary Tyler Moore Show" in 1970, a sitcom set in a television newsroom, that Moore reached her comedic prime. Said one reviewer, "Much, justifiably, has been made of Miss Moore's extravagant gestures, superb sense of timing, comic instinct, repertoire of tricks."

When the hit show finally went off the air in 1977, Moore tackled challenging dramatic projects, including "First You Cry," a somber TV movie on breast cancer, which won her an Emmy. *Whose Life Is It Anyway*, an emotionally grueling play about a paraplegic, earned her a Tony. Her stark, controlled performance in the 1980 film *Ordinary People*, the story of a family torn apart by the accidental death of a son, came the same year as the loss of her own son, Richard, who committed suicide. Said Moore, "I've grown to know myself better, to trust myself. I am still a person who enjoys having control. But I know there are some things over which you have no control, and you just have to accept that."

Divorced twice, the second time from NBC television chief Grant Tinker, Moore married Dr. Robert Levine in 1984, with the press playing up their age differences: she was 45 and he was 30. Her stay at the Betty Ford Clinic in 1984 was, she admitted, to rid her of a "social drinking" habit that threatened her health, already impaired by diabetes. She returned to the televison world again with an HBO film, *Finnegan Begin Again* (1985), a story about two people mismatched, but in love. Her next project was the NBC miniseries "Gore Vidal's Lincoln" (1987), in which she played Mary Todd Lincoln, a role which earned her another Emmy nomination. Giving another weekly television series a shot, she developed "Annie McGuire" for CBS's 1988-1989 season, but it never clicked. Other recent projects have included the Broadway show *Sweet Sue* (1987) and the film *Just between Friends* (1986).

Roger Moore

The sleek British actor, who starred for seven years as "The Saint," was well experienced in playing sweatless heroes when he was picked to portray the most sweatless of them all, James Bond. Taking over the role from Sean Connery, Moore brought an aristocratic charm to Bond, shaking off danger with a martini and expressing emotion with the raising of an eyebrow.

Moore was born 14 October 1927, the son of a London policeman. He left school at age 15 to become an artist but failed to demonstrate any impressive talent until he found his way to the Royal Academy of Dramatic Art. Again, Moore found himself out of place around serious students, as he was given to a lighthearted attitude and a flair for self-effacing humor. After service in the army and sporadic performances in the London theatre, Moore moved to New York and signed with MGM. A series of mostly unimpressive film performances followed, including, in 1954, *The Last Time I Saw Paris*, and in 1956, *Diane*, in which his name appeared above the title for the first time. Even so, Moore recalls that a reviewer for *Time* magazine noted that "he invariably wears the expression of a peevish raisin."

But as James Bond, Moore's lack of dramatic abilities hardly seemed to matter. Audiences alike generally agreed that the dapper Moore, with his slim, athletic build, blue eyes, and ample light brown hair, fit the bill. Some said Moore came closer to the character as originally conceived in Ian Fleming's novels than did Connery. Moore played Bond beginning in 1973 with *Live and Let Die*, then in *The Man with the Golden Gun* (1974), *The Spy Who Loved Me* (1977), *Moonraker* (1979), *For Your Eyes Only* (1981), and *Octopussy* (1983). His last 007 role was in *A View to a Kill* (1985) as he passed the torch to Timothy Dalton as the new Bond. Early in 1989 he attempted musical theatre with Andrew Lloyd Webber's London production of *Aspects of Love*, but he withdrew from the show. Divorced twice, Moore married Italian actress Luisa Mattioli in 1968 and has three children.

Esai Morales

Esai Morales knows how to turn his ethnicity to his own advantage: "It allows more people to identify with me and puts me in a unique position to help bridge gaps in human understanding."

Brooklyn born, he grew up as a ward of the state and a foster child. He attended the much-celebrated New York High School of Performing Arts, and at seventeen he originated the title role in *El Hermano* at New York's Ensemble Studio Theater. Joseph Papp recognized his talent and cast him along with Raul Julia in a production of William Shakespeare's *The Tempest*. But it was his electrifying performance opposite Sean Penn in *Bad Boys* (1983) which finally attracted the attention this fine young actor deserved.

His next poignant role was that of Ritchie Valens' troubled brother in *La Bamba* (1987). In this performance he made a weak and jealous brother seem both pathetic and touching and took the evil out of the villain. In 1987 he also appeared in a less successful film called *The Principal*.

His acting career has been varied, and his frequent appearances on television have added to his visibility. He participated in the Emmy Award-winning "Afterschool Special" *The Great Experiment* as well as making guest star appearances on "Miami Vice," "The Equalizer" and "Fame." He is perhaps most remembered on television for his portrayal of Rashid, the Iranian hero of the NBC miniseries "On Wings of Eagles," starring Burt Lancaster.

His brave and positive outlook on life permeates all of his work. He has received several awards for his contribution to Latin culture. He was applauded as the Most Promising Actor at the NOSOTROS Golden Eagle Awards, named Entertainer of the Year by the organization Latino Playwrights and won the New York Image Award. He has also become a spokesperson for New York City's Foster Care Program, and because of his commitment to fighting major problems facing runaways and homeless youths and his vocal support in the fight against AIDS, he is as much in demand as a speaker addressing students and community groups as he is as an up-and-coming young actor. Clearly, he has taken seriously the responsibility his fame has brought him.

Jeanne Moreau

"I act and I direct. I sing and I record and I cook and I do different things. Why not? They're complementary," says Jeanne Moreau ("La Moreau," as French audiences call her), who changes moods and emotions faster than a chameleon changes color. Witness any Moreau film (*Frantic*, 1958; *La Notte* and *Jules et Jim*, 1961; *The Bride Wore Black*, 1968; *Chimes at Midnight*, 1967; *Going Places*, 1974; *The Trout*, 1982; *Querelle*, 1982) and invariably she is of blinding intensity—dark eyes seducing an audience. "While I'm doing a role, I'm the part. I'm the person. But once I'm finished, I'm me." She has worked for Renoir, Truffaut, Buñuel, Antonioni, Fassbinder, Orson Welles, Joseph Losey, Louis Malle, Peter Brooks, Paul Mazursky. She chooses a role for its director, not for its character.

Born in Paris, 23 January 1928, her mother an English dancer and her father a Monmartre restaurateur, Moreau spent her early years in England, gained recognition as a member of France's famed Comédie Française in 1949, and rose to international stardom after appearing in Louis Malle's *The Lovers* in 1959. "I'm not successful by accident," she says firmly. "I've worked hard. I'm passionate and my world is cinema, acting, theatre, creativity, art, painting, books, music, sculpture, landscapes, movements of the people in the streets. Everything!"

Three times married and divorced: in 1949 to Jean-Louis Richard, one son, divorced 1951; in 1966 to Teodora Rubanis, divorced; and in 1977 to director William Friedkin (*The French Connection, The Brink's Job, The Exorcist*), whom she divorced in 1980. Moreau says: "It's very moving to be loved and hard to resist."

Having worked only with the finest directors, Moreau herself turned director in 1976 with *Lumière* (which she wrote and also starred in) and followed her directorial success with *L'Adolescente* in 1979. She recalls that some directors were shocked or resentful at the prospect of her decision to direct, except Orson Welles, "who was," she says, "the first person to whom I spoke about directing, and the only one who wasn't protective about it." Today she finds herself in the flattering position of being approached by newcomers for advice on the craft. On this she remarks: "There's room for everybody." She appeared on Broadway in the 1985 revival of Tennessee Williams' *The Night of the Iguana* and appeared on stage at the Atelier theatre in Paris in *The Servant Zerline* (1987).

Rita Moreno

She's listed as the only performer to receive the four highest entertainment awards—the Tony, the Oscar, the Emmy, the Grammy. "My photo is in the Guinness Book of Records," Rita Moreno chuckles, "I'm right there in the book with Kermit the Frog." For years she was cast as the beautiful little Injun that could, and, after her outspoken refusal to take any more such roles, her next role was a Latin halfbreed. When in 1972 she turned up on daytime children's public TV in "The Electric Company" (her Grammy Award for Best Children's Recording in 1973) aimed at seven-to-ten-year-old children trying to improve their reading skills, she stated: "I represent all the Hispanic peoples in America . . . because I have a mother who does not read English fluently. . . . I am Latin and know what it is to feel alone and ignored because you are different [they called her Pierced Ears and Gold Teeth when she was a kid]. . . . I was for six years in analysis in Hollywood. The ethnic problems galvanize some people into action. Me, they paralyzed."

Born Rosita Dolores Alverio, 11 December 1931 in Humacao, Puerto Rico, she was brought to New York at the age of four (her mother had come the year before, worked as a seamstress, saved her money, and returned to bring her daughter to America). She made her nightclub debut the very next year and was singing and dancing in clubs when she was 13, "ducking the juvenile officers." At 13 she did her first Broadway show, and at 17 joined MGM's starlet stable for a string of B movies in which she was required merely to "flare my nostrils, gnash my teeth, and look spirited." But a fine job of acting in *The King and I* led to her role as Anita in the film *West Side Story* and the 1962 Oscar, firmly implanting her in the mind of Hollywood as "the Latin girl." "It's not that I mind playing Latins," said Moreno in 1981. "They have to be the real ones, not that you-stole-my-people's-gold crap. I've been lucky for five years now. Ethnic considerations don't come up any more." Later movies include *Marlowe, Popi, Carnal Knowledge, The Ritz, Happy Birthday Gemini, The Boss's Son*, and *The Four Seasons*. Her Broadway credits include *The Sign in Sidney Brustein's Window* (1964), *Gantry* (1969), *The Last of the Red Hot Lovers* (1970), *The National Health* (1974), *The Ritz*, for which she won the 1975 Tony Award, and *Wally's Cafe* (1981). Neil Simon reworked *The Odd Couple* for a female duo, and she appeared in it on Broadway in 1985 with Sally Struthers. After winning two Emmys for performances on television, she starred in the 1982 "9 to 5" TV series.

Married to New York physician Dr. Leonard I. Gordon (1965), Moreno lives in Manhattan and spends weekends at their house in upstate New York. They have a daughter, Fernanda. The lady shows no sign of tiring. Of her nightclub act she said, "I dance my butt off and sing my lungs out."

Robert Morley

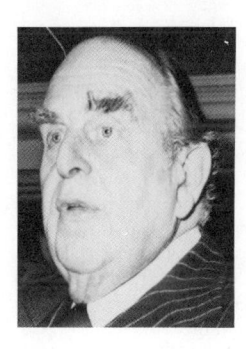

While perhaps not a household word, his is a most familiar face, best recognized for his juicy cameo/camp roles as well as commercials for British Airways. Often cast as an aristocratic bumbler or pompous ass, he has created a variety of memorable character roles (e.g., the missionary brother of Katharine Hepburn in the John Huston classic *African Queen*, the unfortunate father of Laurence Harvey in *The Good Die Young*), and whether the films were examples of "unbelievable awfulness" or top-notch, he invariably managed to be a scene stealer. When critics sigh, "Not even Robert Morley can save it," one knows a film is unsalvageable.

Actually, Morley's most sturdy success has come from his stage career. He was born into a moneyed family on 26 May 1908 in Wiltshire, England, but most of the fortune was gambled away by his father, an army officer. Due to rather "chequered finances," Morley's education was a bit uneven, but he eventually was accepted at the Royal Academy of Dramatic Arts in London. His first full-fledged stage appearance was in *Treasure Island* in 1929. He spent several subsequent years with a repertory company, trouping through the provinces and appearing in a grab-bag of plays, finally achieving London success in 1936 with the title role in *Portrait of Oscar Wilde*. The following year he appeared as Henry Higgins in *Pygmalion* and was spotted by an MGM exec looking for a "Charles Laughton type" for the role of Louis XVI opposite Norma Shearer in *Marie Antoinette* (1938). Morley then had a busy film career in Britain, including *Major Barbara* (1941), while showing up on stage in such long-runners as *The Man Who Came to Dinner* and *Edward My Son* (which he co-authored). In 1960, he reprised his stage role in a film version of *Oscar Wilde*. While Morley's career continued to be colorful, it was also unpredictable. He remained the bright spot in many pictures (*Take Her She's Mine, Of Human Bondage, Topkapi, Genghis Khan, Those Magnificent Men in Their Flying Machines*) but then film interest in Morley waned for a time. After the 1966 publication of his spritely autobiography, *Robert Morley Responsible Gentleman*, his popularity picked up again and he appeared in the films *Someone Is Killing the Great Chefs of Europe* (1978), *The Wind* (1986) and *Little Dorrit* (1986). He also appeared in the U.S. TV version of "Great Expectations" (1974), CBS-TV's "Alice In Wonderland" (1986), the ABC miniseries "War and Remembrance" (1988) and CBS's "The Lady and the Highwayman" (1989). Morley is married to Joan Buckmaster, daughter of actress Gladys Cooper, and they have three children. Son Sheridan is a prolific London theatre and arts critic (*Punch*, etc.) and a biographer of Noel Coward, Katharine Hepburn and David Niven.

Gary Morris

To label Gary Morris as "just a country singer" would be erroneous and incomplete. He has spanned the performing arts, taking chances and triumphing on the country charts, in concert, in legitimate theater and on television.

Gary Morris was born in Fort Worth, Texas. His musical roots reach back to his paternal grandfather, a musician who could "play anything with strings on it" and his maternal grandfather, a traveling minister of music who wrote several songs in his Baptist hymnal. Morris's father was a big country-music fan who kept the radio tuned to Fort Worth radio station WBAP, but it was his mother who instilled in him the desire to sing, encouraging singalongs on family vacations. While a high-school sophomore, Morris sang and played guitar with a local band. He even appeared with a friend on "Ted Mack's Amateur Hour," but it was athletics that attracted him. He excelled, lettering in four sports and winning a college scholarship in football. "Athletics altered the way I do things and what I've chosen to do with my life," says Morris. "I was always inspired to do well in sports. Winning is not everything, but losing is nothing. That translates to my career in show business as well." Traveling to Colorado during his college summer break, he entertained in clubs throughout the state and gained valuable studio experience singing and writing jingles for corporations like Coors Beer and Frontier Airlines. He decided against continuing in academia, going instead to Nashville. Norro Wilson, then A & R Director with Warner Brothers, had seen Morris and his trio perform at the White House under the Carter administration and after listening to a tape of his original songs immediately offered him a contract. His 1982 debut album, *Gary Morris*, and his first single, "Sweet Red Wine," were immediate hits. The album contained three smash singles, "Headed for A Heartache," "Don't Look Back" and "Dreams Die Hard." *Billboard* named him New Male Singles Artist of the Year. His followup album, *Why, Lady Why* (1983), yielded three more hits, including the Academy of Country Music and Country Music Association Song of the Year, 1984, "The Wind Beneath My Wings." His third album, *Faded Blue* (1984), launched another three hits, including the #1 singles "Baby Bye Bye." He also had a Top Ten hit with "Lasso the Moon" off the *Rustler's Rhapsody* film soundtrack.

A *"first"* occurred in late 1984 when Morris was cast as Rodolfo in Joseph Papp's New York Shakespeare Festival production of *La Bohème*. His acting debut marked the first appearance of a country star in a legitimate NYC stage production. The two-month run led to a recurring role as blind country singer Wayne Masterson on ABC-TV's "The Colbys" (1985-1986) as well as guest stints on NBC-TV's "Another World," performing the Top Ten title song with Crystal Gayle. Morris's fourth album, *Anything Goes* (1985), contained two more #1 singles, "I'll Never Stop Loving You" and "100% Chance of Rain" and reached #1 on the *Billboard* chart. He also scored a #1 hit with "Makin' Up for Lost Time," with Crystal Gayle, off their duet album, *What If We Fall in Love*. Producing himself for the first time, *Plain Brown Wrapper* reached the Top Ten as both an album and a single featured the #1 single "Leave Me Lonely." His 1987 album, *Hits* featured his greatest hits as well as the self-produced aria from *La Bohème* (recorded at the Grand Ole Opry) and two new releases. 1988 saw Morris return to Broadway, replacing Colm Wilkinson in the role of Jean Valjean in *Les Misérables*. He enjoyed a successful run before returning to the Nashville scene. With such a varied background, Morris's options for the future seem endless.

Toni Morrison

Novelist Toni Morrison has written five critically acclaimed books: *The Bluest Eye* (1969), *Sula* (1973), *Song of Solomon* (1977), *Tar Baby* (1981) and *Beloved* (1987). *Song of Solomon* was the first novel by a black writer to be chosen as a main selection of the Book of the Month Club since Richard Wright's *Native Son* in 1940. It also won the National Book Critics Circle Award. In 1988, Morrison was the winner of the Pulitzer Prize for *Beloved*. The well-respected author has taught at Yale and Bard, lectured extensively and worked as an editor at Random House "rewriting and editing a messy world, imagining a better one."

When *Newsweek* put her on the cover in March of 1981, it marked the first time a black writer has been so honored (in fact, few writers had ever appeared on the cover, regardless of color). Morrison remarked, "The day you put a middle-aged, gray-haired colored lady on the magazine ... the revolution is over!"

Morrison is her own revolution. Pacing her prose with the magic and precision of one creating myth, her subjects—black family life and relationships—come alive and speak powerfully to all people. "There's a quality of not having any past—not just for blacks, just people in the country. Nobody is from anywhere. This is a country of orphans and immigrants and people who just refuse to think about the Old World. ... The insistence on no past, the cult of the young, and the insistence on 'innocence' that means 'eternally stupid' is one of the characteristics of this country."

She was born Chloe Anthony Wofford 18 February 1931 in Lorain, Ohio, a steel town 25 miles west of Cleveland. Her father did whatever jobs he could during the worst of the Depression, while her mother, described as a "feisty, determined woman," handled the home. "If there were maggots in our flour," recalled Morrison, "she wrote a letter to Franklin Roosevelt. My mother believed something should be done about inhuman situations." Graduating with honors from high school, Morrison received her B.A. from Howard University and her M.A. in English from Cornell. After two years of teaching at Texas Southern University in Houston, she taught at Howard until 1964. While there, she met and married Jamaican architect Harold Morrison. Uncomfortable in her marriage, which produced two sons, she began to write fiction in the early 1960s. "It was as though I had nothing left but imagination. ... I had no will, no judgement, no perspective, no power, no authority, no self—just this brutal sense of irony, melancholy and a trembling respect for the world. I wrote like someone with a dirty habit. Secretly. Compulsively. Slyly." In 1964 she and her sons moved to Syracuse, New York where she found a position as a textbook editor for a division of Random House. She wrote *The Bluest Eye* after work and after her sons had gone to sleep. *Sula* was written while she was editing (mostly black) fiction at her new position as senior editor for Random House in its Manhattan office. Her next two books received wide recognition, and Morrison appeared on interview shows nationwide. PBS devoted an entire segment of "Writers in America" to her. In 1984 she received an honorary doctorate from Columbia University.

Morrison's favorite pastime is gardening, which she does at her home in Nyack, New York. She resents being labeled "a black writer" when "it appears as though I am a star within a diminishing world; on the other hand I am very much a black writer, that is very much a part of what I do ... sometimes I get my hackles up either way, but that's my problem."

Robert Motherwell

He's one of the last of the founding fathers of Abstract Expressionism. Together with such leading lights as the late Mark Rothko and Jackson Pollock, he helped forge the postwar art movement that, in the 1950s, "assured an artistically provincial country that it was a cultural superpower" and "provided American intellectuals with a ... chance to celebrate a 'heroic' age in American painting." As a mammoth retrospective of his life work toured the U.S. in 1984, *Time* hailed him as "deservedly a celebrated figure" and "a man respected not only for his art but also for his writings, scholarship and personal presence."

Born in Aberdeen, Wash., 24 January 1915, Robert Burns Motherwell III (of Scotch and Irish lineage) polished his scholar-philosopher role as an undergraduate at Harvard and later applied his studies of logic and aesthetics to his art. ("It has helped me in the foundation of a defense of the paintings my colleagues and I do.") His own oil and water color paintings have been called "incendiary meetings of emotion and gesture," and although many of his canvases are in stark black and white, he has some very strong ideas about color. "The 'pure' red of which certain abstractionists speak does not exist," he once observed. "Any red is rooted in blood, glass, wine, hunters' caps, and a thousand other concrete phenomena. Otherwise we should have no feeling toward red and its relations, and it would be useless as an artistic element." Divorced from artist Helen Frankenthaler (he has two daughters by a prior marriage), he married photographer Renate Ponsold in 1972. Of his writing, teaching, and editing activities, he has said, "It's my way of being social, rather than going to cocktail parties. It's also," he told critic Robert Hughes, "an excellent relief from the anguish of painting—an attempt to regain my social equilibrium and to give back to society something of what it has so generously given me: education, respect, dignity, artistic freedom." Motherwell is the 1985 recipient of the MacDowell Colony Medal, and he was elected to the American Academy of Arts and Letters in December 1986.

Tommy Mottola

What do Daryl Hall and John Oates, Carly Simon, and John Cougar Mellencamp have in common? Not only hit records, but the input of a dynamic man who has guided their careers to superstar status. Today, Tommy Mottola is the president of CBS Records, a division of CBS Records Inc. His responsibilities include overseeing the direction of the CBS Records labels in the United States (Columbia, Epic, Portrait, CBS Associated) as well as talent acquisition, development, business affairs, and marketing.

Born in New York City on July 14, Mottola began his career as a professional musician. He later perfected his listening skills for six years as the head of Chappell Music's Contemporary Music Division. Eventually making the connections, in 1974 he formed his own company, Champion Entertainment, where he nurtured Dr. Buzzard's Original Savannah Band, Kid Creole and the Coconuts, Split Enz, and Odyssey, in addition to the above mentioned celebrities. When the position opened for the head of CBS, the young mogul jumped at the chance to run the huge company.

Music-making Mottola is spreading his wings to conquer another *"M"* category—movies. He acted as music supervisor for Bette Midler's *Ruthless People* (1986) and Michael J. Fox's *The Secret of My Success* (1987). He has also produced some made-for-TV movies and music specials for cable television.

Bill Moyers

"The past is a great ocean, and what we've done is dip our bucket into it 20 times," said this award-winning TV journalist about his PBS series "A Walk Through the Twentieth Century." (The show was named the outstanding information series of the year in 1987 by the National Academy of Television Arts and Sciences.) "It's important to know that the events of today begin in the past," he says. "The stories in the news today have a root, a history. ... But I think television has helped to sever our society from what Lincoln called 'the mystic cords of memory.' Our sole criterion of thought and action is what is happening at this moment, this hour, this day. We suffer from an historical amnesia ... a severance from all previous ties and identities so that the person is left in a state of confusion about where in time and space and place he belongs." Master of what's been called "personality journalism," Moyers brings both immediacy and depth to his subjects. A sense of identity has always been important to Moyers, a small town boy who first became a "somebody" at age 15 as a cub reporter, and went on to fame: deputy director of the Peace Corps under President Kennedy, a member of President Johnson's inner circle and press secretary, publisher of *Newsday*. Since entering broadcast journalism in 1971, he's been executive editor and correspondent at CBS and public television, becoming one of the most respected journalist in the industry.

Born 5 June 1934 in Hugo, Oklahoma, Bill Moyers grew up in Marshall, Texas, and began his career as a cub reporter for the Marshall *News Messenger*. ("That job gave me an identity and a role in the town when I was too small to play football and too unattractive to be a lady's man and too skinny to win in neighborhood fights.") After graduating in 1956 from the University of Texas, he studied at the University of Edinburgh in Scotland on a fellowship, then attended Southwestern Theological Seminary, graduating in 1959. He went to Washington in 1960 as an aide to Sen. Lyndon B. Johnson, later winning posts in the Kennedy and Johnson administrations. In 1968, he left government to become publisher of the Long Island newspaper, *Newsday*, which won 33 major awards including two Pulitzers during his tenure. Resigning from *Newsday* in 1970, he traveled throughout the country for *Harper's* magazine, the journey resulting in the best-seller *Listening to America*. As a TV journalist, he was executive editor of the PBS series *Bill Moyer's Journal* and *Creativity*. As a CBS news correspondent and senior news analyst for "CBS Evening News," Moyers worked on "CBS Reports" and "Our Times." He's received almost every major award, including 18 Emmy Awards for excellence and the Dupont-Columbia University Award for "contribution to the highest standards and well-being of broadcast journalism generally."

Mr. Moyers is married to Judith, a vice-chair of the board of trustees of the State University of New York and an educational specialist who serves on several corporate boards, and President of their production company, Public Affairs Television, Inc. They have three grown children. Says Moyers former English teacher Inez Hatley Hughes: "Everybody at school loved Bill. He was very affable, very boyish. Just exactly as you see him now. He hasn't changed a bit. He gets very serious looking on TV sometimes, but when you see him carefree, he's just like he always was."

Daniel Patrick Moynihan

"Pat Moynihan would be a splendid President," muses a colleague in the Capitol. "Only he's overqualified. The man's too intelligent." His admirers see him as another Churchill, writes a Washington journalist: ". . . literate, original, patriotic and fervent. But Churchill was not summoned to the top office until his nation was on the brink of ruin and [there] was no other choice." Admired for the originality and breadth of his thinking, Senator Daniel Patrick Moynihan has been put to work by both Democratic and Republican presidents. Employed by Kennedy, Johnson, Nixon, and Ford, he became the only person in American history to officially serve four successive administrations. He has been the U.S. ambassador to India, and our U.N. representative. He has served on numerous trouble-shooting committees concerned with issues of war and peace, both domestic and international. He has been a college professor and a stevedore. And his famous arched eyebrows make him a delight of the political cartoonists.

The 6'5" senior U.S. senator from New York got his start in politics as a gubernatorial aide in the late 1950s. He has since shuttled between politics and campuses, often town-and-gowning it simultaneously. He has taught government studies at Harvard, headed the Joint Center for Urban Studies at MIT, and taught education and urban politics at Harvard on a graduate level. He is the author, co-author, or editor of fourteen books; his study on the deterioration of the black family unit, titled *Beyond the Melting Pot*, won him major awards as well as the continual enmity of black activists. His most recent work is *Came the Revolution: Argument in the Reagan Era*, and he is on the publication committee of *The Public Interest*. The garrulous Moynihan is a compulsive joiner of organizations and supporter of causes, both political and scholarly. He is chairman of the Subcommittee on Social Security and Family Policy of the Committee on Finance, and of the Subcommittee on Water Resources, Transportation and Infrastructure of the Committee on Environment and Public Works. He is a member of the Committee on Foreign Relations, the Committee on Rules and Administration, and the Joint Committee on Taxation, as well as a member of the Senate Arms Control Observer Group. Academics see him as one of their own, a scholar *manqué* who's just playing with politics (albeit for over three decades).

Born 16 March 1927 in Tulsa, Oklahoma, the grandson of an Irish immigrant, Moynihan was soon supporting himself shining shoes on Times Square in New York, where his family had moved. In 1943 he headed his class at City College while working on the docks. After naval service he received a B.A. from Tufts University and, in 1949, an M.A. from the Fletcher School of Law and Diplomacy. He attended the London School of Economics on a Fulbright Scholarship. With his wife Elizabeth Brennan and three children, his favorite retreat is a 300-acre farm in upstate New York.

Richard Mulligan

Richard Mulligan must have made the most hilarious corpse in cinematic history in the wonderful sleeper, *S.O.B*. Well, the funny man has come back to life, and so much so, that his new TV series "Empty Nest" was one of the 1988-1989 season's biggest hits. For his role, he won a Best Actor Emmy in September 1989. You may remember his quirky face from "Soap," another very successful television series which also brought him a 1980 Emmy.

Born 13 November 1932 in New York City, he is the son of a policeman. One of five sons, he grew up in the Bronx and was a serious student at Cardinal Hayes High School, and later Maryknoll Junior Seminary where he thought of becoming a priest. He changed his mind a year later when he discovered a certain affection for playwriting at Columbia University. After a stint in the Navy as a crash rescue man in Pensacola, Florida, Mulligan landed his first acting role. While driving to Miami, his car had a flat tire right in front of a local theatre. Hoping to sell a play, he entered the theatre, but ended up auditioning for a role in Eugene O'Neill's play *Beyond the Horizon*. With good reviews rolling in, Mulligan went back to New York and wound up performing in more plays. He appeared in productions of *All the Way Home*, *Never Too Late*, *Nobody Loves an Albatross* and *The Mating Game*. Branching out into television, he won roles on "The Defenders," "Route 66," "The Dupont Show of the Month," and the "Armstrong Circle Theater." In 1977 he cracked up TV land with his portrayal of Burt Campbell on "Soap" which made him an overnight household name. Being chosen by Blake Edwards for the films *S.O.B.*, *Trail of the Pink Panther*, *Micki & Maude*, and *A Fine Mess*, added to Mulligan's popularity.

Other recent performances include the CBS-TV film "Poker Alice" with Elizabeth Taylor and the theatrical release of *Babes in Toyland*. Divorced from Patricia Jones and Joan Hackett, Mulligan was separated from his third wife, Lenore Stevens in 1989.

Brian Mulroney

The Right Honourable Brian Mulroney, Canada's prime minister since 1984, is the first Conservative leader to emerge from the province of Quebec in ninety-two years and also the first Tory ever to come to Conservative leadership directly from the private sector (former president of the Iron Ore Company of Canada). The sweeping victory by Mulroney and the Progressive Conservatives restored the Tories to majority power for the first time in twenty-six years.

Martin Brian Mulroney was born on 20 March 1939 in Baie Comeau, a pulp and paper maunfacturing town on the St. Lawrence River north of Quebec City. His early aspiration was to be manager of the Quebec paper mill where his father toiled. "It was almost in some ways an idyllic community," Mulroney said of the paper-mill town in which he grew up, "except for the fact that nobody had any money; but nobody needed very much." Set on educating their son, his parents scraped together enough money to send him to St. Thomas College, a boys' boarding school. Mulroney worked his way through college and law school; he was one of the first Anglo-Canadians to take his law degree entirely in French, and later he made his mark as a lawyer handling difficult labor negotiations. In 1974, after rebellious workers damaged a construction site for a hydroelectric dam on James Bay to the tune of $35 million, Mulroney was appointed to a three-man Royal Commission on Inquiry into Union Freedom. Uncovering a network of corruption, the commission was the focus of much publicity. Mulroney's role left him open to death threats, but also kept his name in the press. In 1976 Mulroney sought control of the Troy party. After an unsuccessful campaign, he joined the Iron Ore Company of Canada as president for corporate affairs; one year later he became its president. Focusing on service endeavors, Mulroney enhanced his civic stature and helped collect funds for several universities. In 1983, he resigned from his position and sought, and this time won, the party's leadership. In order to win a seat from Nova Scotia, Mulroney moved himself and his family to a log cabin, adopting the lifestyle of the blue-collar workers. Mulroney promised improved ties with the United States and appealed to voters using American-style tactics.

The strikingly handsome six-footer is married to the former Mila Pivnicki. They have three children—Caroline Ann, Benedict Martin and Robert Mark. He unwinds from work, coffee and cigarettes with a game of tennis.

Patrice Munsel

At the age of seventeen, still a bobby-soxer, Patrice Munsel startled the music world in 1943 with her debut at the Metropolitan Opera. "It wasn't quite the miracle it sounds," she maintains. "I happened to have been born with a good natural instrument and I knew at the age of 12 that I wanted to be an opera singer. I had come to New York with my mother and had worked eight hours a day studying voice, piano, theory, harmony and acting. I knew French, Italian and nine operas." A Metropolitan Opera star for fifteen years, she concentrated on coloratura roles in such operas as *The Tales of Hoffman, Rigoletto,* and *Lucia de Lammermoor*. Many careers have followed: she was featured on CBS radio's "Family Hour," made her film debut in Sam Spiegel's (Nellie) *Melba*, broke all box-office records in the Lincoln Center production of the *Merry Widow* and was featured for two seasons on TV with her own show, "The Patrice Munsel Hour," via ABC. On the musical-comedy stage she has toured the country in *Kiss Me Kate, Can Can, The Sound of Music, Applause,* and *A Musical Jubilee,* besides concerts and Las Vegas engagements. In 1988 she toured with Rex Smith and Stephanie Zimbalist in the Rodgers and Hammerstein musical *Carousel*.

Born 14 May 1926 in Spokane, Washington, the only child of Dr. Audley J. and Eunice Munsil, she married Robert Schuler in 1952 and they have four children, Heidi, Rhett, Scott and Nicole. "Fortunately, I never missed a season with all those pregnancies," she said. "My timing was great. One year, I was doing *Fledermaus* and Rudolf Bing came to me and said it was time to retire for the season, because he couldn't tell whether my bustle was in the front or back."

Rupert Murdoch

A 1977 *Newsweek* article entitled "Killer Bee Reaches New York: The Sensational History of Rupert Murdoch" posed the question, "Is this the future?" Over a decade later, the answer comes through loud and clear. A glance at a newsstand, or a turn of a channel proves Murdoch's influence on mass media. The newspaper publisher declares, "The role of a newspaper is to inform, but in such a way that people buy," and the public continues to purchase his publications on a consistent basis. At last count, Murdoch's running list of magazines include: *Automobile, European Travel & Life, New Woman, New York, Premiere, Soap Opera Digest, Star, Mirabella, TV Guide* and *Seventeen*. His newspapers are: *The Sun* (London), *The Australian,* both the London *Times* and Sunday London *Times, The Daily Racing Form,* the *San Antonio Express-News* and *The Herald* (Boston). In other areas of communications, his News Corp. owns 20th-Century Fox Film Corp., the Fox Broadcasting Company, and seven Fox Television stations (including WNYW in New York and WTTG in Washington, D.C.).

The real life "Citizen Kane" was born 11 March 1931 to Sir Keith Murdoch, a celebrated World War One correspondent turned publishing executive, and Dame Elisabeth Murdoch, who was made a Dame of the British Empire for her welfare work. Young Murdoch attended the Australian counterpart to Eton, and then Oxford, where he was active in Labor politics and was nicknamed "Red" (he's much more conservative now). Some people close to the scene speculate that Murdoch considered it his challenge to exceed his father at the newspaper game, especially in the eyes of his mother. He wings around the world checking on his many newspapers and other communications enterprises, and says of himself: "I'm a bit dull and humorless. Not the sort of person who makes social friends easily." He claims his best asset is his lovely wife, Anna, whom he married in 1967; they have three children, Elisabeth, Lachlan and James. By a previous marriage he has a daughter, Prudence. He lives mostly in New York in a Fifth Avenue duplex, decorated with English antiques and Australian modern art. To keep fit he swims, plays tennis, rides; and skis. Once a man who bet on the ponies, he now confines his gambling to publishing—a "life," he says, "full of calculated risks." In 1985 he became an American citizen, a prerequisite for his purchase of Metromedia and its package of TV stations. At that point, he was required to sell his newspapers in New York *(The Post)* and Chicago *(Sun Times)* when the deal was completed. As the *New York Times* said in 1983, "There is an element in Rupert Murdoch that can only be sensed. He acts as if he is trying to get even for something. He loves to show contempt for journalists, believing that he can always find some to buy and sell. So far he has been right about that."

Dale Murphy

This devout Mormon says, "My church has 30,000 missionaries worldwide. I expect to do that someday." While he remained stateside he made it worth his while by becoming only the fourth baseball player to win back-to-back Most Valuable Player honors in the National League. The big (six-feet-five, 215 pounds), brown-haired rightfielder (switched from centerfield in 1987) has a sterling reputation as a man of moral integrity, and it's said he can and does deflect almost any praise. The congenial Murphy, who was considered an outside possibility for a third straight MVP, realized how he got to be the bleacher-reaching power slugger he is today; it was through hard, consistent work. So what did he do during the off-season after his first MVP award in 1982? He went to the Instructional League to improve on his hitting.

310

Although Dale Bryan Murphy now has a Gold Glove for his centerfielding, he was a migrant to the outfield. Born 12 March 1956 in Portland, Ore., he was a hot catching prospect whom the Atlanta Braves drafted out of high school. Their selection caused him to abandon his plans to play for Arizona State University. In the minors he became a Mormon (after a close friend and teammate sparked his Presbyterian-influenced mind) and he even attended the church's Brigham Young University for a short time. It was there that he met his future wife, Nancy. When Murphy went to Atlanta to stay in 1978, he was still working behind the plate, but his throws from there to the pitcher and to second base proved wayward, and the problem affected his batsmanship. A shift to first base didn't improve the situation, but when the Braves put him in center, he became an All-Star pasture master. One of the few homer hitters who can steal bases as well, his speed makes him a threat to have a 50-home-run season some year since he plays in small Atlanta Stadium. Meanwhile this tithing prospective missionary signed a new free agent three-year contact in 1987, which ought to come in handy for his wife and five children (Chad, Travis, Shawn, Tyson Davis, Tyler).

Eddie Murphy

"His friends call him Money. He looks like money, like $40 million, if perchance one speculates. He looks crisp, controlled. He is twenty-eight yet not terribly youthful; he fancies himself much older, more world-weary. He stares straight ahead and seems to notice no one, but he sees all and hears even more. Unless he's erupting into his deft repertoire of character voices, his presence is shy, inscrutable. Usually he is sullen, almost somber—but this creates a quiet aura of power. You feel him before you see him; first you see his men. He is insulated by bodies, a cleaving pack of old friends and relations on the payroll. These are Eddie's Boys. . ." An apt description by Bill Zehmen in the 24 August 1989 issue of *Rolling Stone*. Labeled as a king of the box office, Eddie Murphy has secured his standing as one of the world's most popular movie, television, concert, and recording artists. However, Murphy tries to remain humble about his surroundings. He insisted to *People* magazine, "I don't have an entourage . . . I don't have bodyguards. I don't have anybody to, like, choke you and say, 'Get away from this man!' My cousin Ray, he takes care of all my little stuff. Kenneth Frith, who we call Fruitie—he went to school with me—he's a production assistant now. And Larry [Johnson] is an assistant. They're big guys. People see them and it's like, 'Oh. Bodyguards.'"

Murphy was born 3 April 1961 in the Bushwick section of Brooklyn. His father was a New York City cop and amateur comedian who died when Murphy was eight. Murphy, his brother, and stepbrother were raised by his mother and stepfather in suburban Long Island in comfortable, middle class surroundings. His energetic good looks and contagious, wide-brimmed smile made him stand out immediately from the pack of young comedians hired for NBC's revamped late-night comedy show, "Saturday Night Live" in 1980. He proved himself both charismatic and versatile with his characterizations of such unsavory fellows as Velvet Jones, the pimp who hard sells how-to books; Tyrone Green, the illiterate convict who becomes a celebrated poet; and Buckwheat from the old serial, "Our Gang." In that skit, Murphy, hair braided and standing on end, explained, "I have a sister named Shredded Wheat, a sister who's a prostitute named Trix, an older brother who's gay, Lucky Charms, and a mentally retarded brother, Special K." Audiences loved his uncanny impressions of Stevie Wonder, Mr. Rogers, Bill Cosby, James Brown and Richard Simmons.

Teamed with Nick Nolte in 1982 in *48 Hours*, Murphy was engaging as a smart-aleck convict. In 1983, he teamed with SNL veteran Dan Aykroyd, playing a begger who strikes it rich in *Trading Places*. Other films include *The Best Defense* (1984), *Beverly Hills Cop* (1985), *Golden Child* (1986), *Beverly Hills Cop II* (1987), *Coming to America* (1988) and *Beverly Hills Cop III* (1989). There have been a slew of Eddie Murphy comedy albums, two singing albums, a cable TV special that is more than a bit raunchy, and *The Unofficial Eddie Murphy Scrapbook*, published in 1984.

Still single, he says his film *Coming to America* parallels his own personal situation. He told *Ebony* magazine, "I think everybody who doesn't have somebody is looking for someone to call their own, even though they might say they want to be single. . . . When I'm talking to my friends, I say the same thing about wanting to be single, but if I met the bomb tomorrow. . . . I don't care who you are, what you have or what you did, there's always a woman out there who can bring you down to one knee. I can be brought to one knee, but the woman would have to have a helluva punch. I've been wobbled a couple of times already, but I haven't been to one knee."

Anne Murray

"An Anne Murray audience doesn't come for surprises; they come to fit into an old comfy slipper," said one reviewer. The apple-cheeked, Canadian singer ascended gently on the Country and Pop charts while remaining—to the chagrin of her promoters—as folksy and serene as her music itself.

Born Morna Anne Murray on 20 June 1945 in the coal-mining town of Springhill, Nova Scotia, she grew up in an environment not unlike the rural American South—which may help to explain the ease with which she's made the successful cross-over from pop to the country charts. Musically gifted from childhood, her parents encouraged her with years of piano and voice lessons, but she rejected a professional career, believing singing was "something you did in the bathtub and around bonfires." She opted for a career in physical education and began singing in local clubs only to supplement her meagre salary as a gym teacher. Hired as a featured singer on a Canadian television program, "Sing-Along-Jamboree," in 1967, she gained recognition as a fresh, distinctive talent, before taking the U.S. charts by storm. The Anne Murray hit parade began twenty years ago with the 1970 single "Snowbird," which earned her the first gold record ever awarded to a solo female Canadian artist. She toured the U.S. extensively, while a string of managers sought to glamorize her image to spice up her career. "I was on the road eight months a year, playing to 400 people in 3,000 seat auditoriums . . . I just had to stop. I knew there had to be more to life than suitcases and hotels and rotten food and not enough sleep. I found out there was—a lot more to life." After a mid-1970s respite—during which she wed former "Sing Along" host Bill Langstroth and started a family (two children)—she began to exercise greater control over her career. Concentrating on recording and intimate concert settings she produced the hit single, "Broken Hearted Me," followed by "You Needed Me," which netted Canada's Juno award and a 1978 Grammy for Best Female Pop Vocalist. Her third Grammy came for "Could I Have This Dance?" from the soundtrack of the 1980 movie, *Urban Cowboy*. Her album credits include *Highly Prized Possession* (1975), *Let's Keep It That Way* (1978), *The Other Side of Anne Murray* (1980), *The Hottest Night of the Year* (1982), *Now and Forever (You and Me)* (1986), *Harmony* (1987) and *As I Am* (1988).

Presently, Murray lives in Toronto with her family, hitting the road for around a hundred concert dates a year, and always on the look-out for new material. How does she zero in on her chart-busters? "It's a gut reaction," explains the singer, "combined with experience. It's really very simple."

Bill Murray

He is (according to David Edelstein of *The Village Voice*) "the most serenely corrupt comic actor since W.C. Fields with a "whiff of Cary Grant's unflappability." Pauline Kael of the *New Yorker* sees him as "a master of show business insincerity. . . . Part of him is always in hiding, and there's a wild strain loose inside the doughy handsomeness which saves him from predictability. He looks capable of anything, yet he isn't threatening; he'd just do something crazy." After four comic seasons on NBC's "Saturday

Night Live," Bill Murray made an effortless transition to movies and, in short order, became what one reporter called "a young people's star of major proportions." That fact was verified by his 1984 box office smash, *Ghostbusters* ranking as one of the biggest movie moneymakers of all time and reinforced by *Ghostbusters II* in 1989.

Born 21 September 1950 in the Chicago suburb of Wilmette, Bill Murray was one of nine spirited youngsters in the home of a lumber salesman and the family dinner table was, traditionally, "bedlam." Bill started out with the notion of perhaps becoming a doctor or pro baseball player but dropped out after only a year at tiny Jesuit-run Regis College in Denver, entered a hippie phase and became the self-described "family black sheep." After an uninspiring series of odd jobs, ranging from hauling concrete blocks to cooking pizzas in a window, Murray decided to try emulating his older brother, Brian, who was getting paid for improvising in the comedy company, Second City. (Bill still insists that Brian—who now uses the name Brian-Doyle Murray—is the more talented of the two.) First learning the ropes in Second City's workshop for novices, he was at last signed on to join such future cohorts as John Belushi, Gilda Radner and Dan Aykroyd and he followed them to New York in 1975 to perform on "The National Lampoon Radio Show" and later, in the cabaret revue *The National Lampoon Show*. (Murray credits Belushi for his early breaks. "He was like my big brother. . . . He made this whole thing possible for me.") At the time of the historic launching of the frenetic NBC comedy show, "Saturday Night Live" in 1975, Murray went with his old Second City buddies to audition but was turned down the first time at bat and the show premiered without him. It wasn't until Chevy Chase departed from the line-up of the Not Ready for Prime Time Players in January, 1977, that Murray got his chance (Brian ended up on the show too) and, after a slow start, was one of the SNL superstars by the 1978-79 season. He made his big-screen debut in the 1979 comedy *Meatballs* and subsequent films include *Caddy Shack* (1980), *Stripes* (1981), *Tootsie* (1982), *The Razor's Edge* (1984), *Scrooged* (1988) and *Quick Change* (1989).

Murray's feelings about stardom, fame, riches and all that jazz? When he was getting his first heavy sampling of it, he was a bit ambivalent. He told a *Rolling Stone* reporter: "No one is raised by their parents to be prepared for what happens when you become famous." But, he concluded, "It's bullshit to hear people whine and complain about their success, and I don't like to hear about it." The deadpan comic is married to Mickey Kelley and the couple have a son, Homer.

Riccardo Muti

"A conductor must be king," asserts Riccardo Muti, a musician of enormous integrity and uncompromising principle. As conductor of the Philadelphia Orchestra, Muti's search for musical truth requires him " to perform the score as the composer left it, without cuts and without interpolations. . . . In my theatre . . . and everywhere . . . I conduct, the composer is the star." Says one devoted member of his orchestra, "Muti is unquestionably the most important conductor of his generation. He embodies a perfect blend of absolute professional musicianship and intelligence. Muti's given the orchestra a new personality and he's charismatic." Since his appointment as Music Director of the Philadelphia Orchestra in 1980, succeeding legendary maestro Eugene Ormandy, he has brought new life and versatility to their concerts.

The Italian wonderboy (born in Naples 28 July 1941) was surrounded by a family of music born lovers (five brothers, each of whom studied a different instrument). Encouraged by his father, a doctor with a tenor voice, Muti studied violin and piano at an early age. Graduating with highest honors in piano from the San Pietro a Maiella Conservatory and in philosophy from the University of Naples, he then received degrees in composition and conducting (also with highest honors) from the Verdi Conservatory. He launched his international career in 1968 after winning the Guido Cantelli International Competition for conductors. Muti's posts have included permanent conductor of the Maggio Musicale Fiorentino, the Teatro Communale and principal conductor of the London Philharmonia. Presently (along with his commitment to Philadelphia) he guest conducts for the Berlin Philharmonic, the Orchestre de France, and the Amsterdam Concertgebouw. Muti has the capability of freezing an entire orchestra with his "death ray" glare; his iron will and enormously disciplined work habits are tempered by the ebullience displayed when rehearsals and performances go well.

Muti, his wife Cristina (a retired opera singer) and their three children live in Ravenna. He spends sixteen weeks a year with the Philadelphia Orchestra (at a salary of $400,000) living in a luxurious condo purchased for him by the orchestra. "No matter how much time I spend away from my family, I like to think that my official bed is in Italy." The modest, likeable conductor says of his passion, "Music is so big. Even if you study all your life, you reach just a small part."

Ralph Nader

Question: Can you name the one nationally known resident of Washington, D.C., for whom a wild night on the town means driving recklessly (that is, without buckling his seatbelt) to a take-out restaurant, ordering a roast-beef sandwich and cola, then stopping off at a shoe store and choosing a pair of loafers? Answer: Ralph Nader.

The spartan lifestyle of Ralph Nader, consumer advocate, has long impressed his devotees and amazed his adversaries in corporate America. When General Motors hired a private eye to tail him after his 1965 Detroit exposé, *Unsafe at Any Speed*, became a bestseller, the snoop turned up information like: "Last car owned—1949 Studebaker . . . Diet—eats no red meat . . . Luxuries—nonexistent. For example, his feet are clad in the eleventh pair of low-cut army dress shoes he bought for six bucks apiece in 1959 at the PX. At the bottom of the closet of his one-room efficiency apartment off DuPont Circle, the twelfth pair awaits him. Beau Brummel he isn't. This no-frills lifestyle is largely accountable, many feel, for the mammoth success in the 60s and 70s of his consumerism movement, which raised national public support for legislation and mechanisms that could give the consumer a voice regarding the safety, cost and value of the goods and services on the market. Moving with the dedication and righteousness of a free-lance saint, Nader proselytised for his movement with a sincerity and evangelical fervor that could not be doubted. Few were the distractions that infiltrated his monkish life. Today, Nader's firebrand ideology is out of fashion in a nation that once again salutes Horatio Alger. But his intense brand of consumerism is far from moribund. The substantial fees he collects for writing and lecturing support the Center for Study of Responsive Law, the traditional "guerrilla base" for Nader's Raiders. Other Nader creations, including the well-reputed Public Interest Research Groups, have spun off and keep the Nader fires burning. He also wrote a book, *The Big Boys: Portraits of Corporate Power*, which was published in 1986.

Nader was born 27 February 1934 to a hard-working Lebanese immigrant couple who turned a dilapidated diner in Winsted, Conn., into a successful bakery and restaurant. Because his background was closer to greasy spoon than silver spoon, Nader seemed a bit different from his classmates at Princeton and later Harvard. As a student he developed a stubborn streak of nonconformity that became his greatest asset as a reform leader. "If he had been born with a silver spoon in his mouth," one associate suggests, "his first investigation would have been to analyze the chemical content of its coating."

Joe Namath

In the course of his ascent to stardom a Houston columnist wrote of him, " It is truly amazing how quickly an innocent, unsophisticated country lad can acquire the gracious manner of a great star." Putting in an appearance at a local sportsmen's club, hairdo rippling down the back of his bull neck, he showed up in a lace-front dress suit. He pinched snuff out of a silver container and talked in soft languid tones. He was obviously worried about his throat, because he frequently gargled with a special golden-colored mouthwash he'd brought along in a tumbler." Author (*My Spartan Life,* 1969 and *Football for Young Players and Parents,* 1986) as well as esteemed superstar at large, he has been damned by critics as "spoiled and immature," yet for all their invective, he was the New York Jets' and possibly the country's greatest quarterback (best arm anyway), leading the then underdog Jets to the AFL's first Super Bowl victory over the powerful Baltimore Colts in 1969. (He is the only player in pro-football history to pass for more than 4,000 yards in one season.)

His success as an actor is equally impressive. Namath's charm eased the switch from football to acting once he retired from the former in 1978. He made his dramatic stage debut in 1979 with the Kenley Players of Ohio in the starring role of Hal Carter in Inge's *Picnic,* went on to tour in the title role of the musical *L'il Abner* and as Sky Masterson in *Guys and Dolls.* In 1981 he played Joe Hardy in *Damn Yankees* at Jones Beach, but his theatrical coup, according to most critics, came by way of his portrayal of Lt. Maryk in Circle in the Square's *Caine Mutiny Court Martial.* His film work includes *C.C. and Co.* with Ann-Margret, *Norwood, The Last Rebel* and *Avalanche Express.*

Joe Willie was cast perfectly for image making. Born on the wrong side of the tracks in Beaver Falls, Pa., 31 May 1943, the son of a steelworker, he went from the University of Alabama and a dollar-an-hour job tending the baseball field to the bright lights. He could quip, "As a kid I wanted to go to Maryland or Notre Dame, but I couldn't pass Maryland's entrance exams and I found Notre Dame was all boys."

A popular guest star through the years on many top variety shows and sitcoms, Joe's string of TV credits includes the guest-host spot on the Johnny Carson Show, not to mention his own syndicated talk show (1969-72). In the fall of 1985 he joined the broadcasting team of Frank Gifford and O.J. Simpson on ABC's "Monday Night Football." An altruist by nature, he has, for many years, operated a football camp for youngsters with former Jet teammate John Dockery.

After years as one of showbiz' most sought-after bachelors, Joe Willie finally took himself a wife in 1984, in the person of sweet young thing Deborah Lynn Mays. The couple have a daughter, Jessica Grace, born 12 October 1985. In the summer of '85 the peerless passer was inducted into the Pro Football Hall of Fame.

Martina Navratilova

Billie Jean King on Martina Navratilova: "I think that Navratilova's problem these days is her brain. Physically she can do it all, but I just think she's burned out." However, in an article in *TV Guide* (1989) King goes on to say that "As evidenced by her versatility, Navratilova is a natural athlete who's trained hard to refine her inherent skills." The eight-time Wimbledon champion, Navratilova is a tough opponent to beat. She's the rarest of tennis birds, a Grand Slam winner, meaning she was consecutively victorious at the 1983 Australian, 1984 French and U.S. Opens and at Wimbledon. This Czechoslovakian-born net pro was the first to crack the $4 million mark in career prize money, walking off with over $1 million in 1982 alone, and was presented with a $1 million check as bounty for her Big Four wins. She is the richest earner in tennis history, regardless of sex. "I play tennis the way it should be played, whether by a man or woman," says Martina Navratilova.

Born in Prague 18 October 1956, Navratilova made international headlines in 1975 when she announced her defection from Czechoslovakia to the U.S. Born into a family of tennis buffs, she played her first tournament at eight, had her first national title at 14, and reigned as national champion from 1972-75. Her mighty topspin forehand and punishing volleys won her a host of fans when she made her debut visit to the U.S. in 1975. She achieved international stardom when, teaming up with Chris Evert, she won the Wimbledon doubles in '76. She's been the singles winner there at center court in 1978 and '79, and for a streak from 1982 through 1985 (the first woman in 55 years to win fourth straight). But the athlete whose rhinestone-studded tennis dresses and man-sized muscles as well as her cannonball serves have made her famous has also endured more than her share of personal turmoil. In addition to the wrenching departure from her home country and her lesbian affair-turned-sour with gay novelist Rita Mae Brown, there was her parents' disgruntlement with her new lifestyle when they gave American life a try. Once known as "The Great Wide Hope," she loaded a hefty 167 pounds onto five-feet-seven inches as a result of packing in American junk foods and desserts. But when she lost the 1983 French Open to a No. 33-ranked player, she fired her famous transsexual coach, Dr. Renee Richards, and took on former player Mike Estrep in her place. She also added women's pro basketball star Nancy Lieberman as fitness conditioner. "I've told Martina that confidence is not a new car, a diamond ring, or another house," Lieberman says of her once-notoriously binge-buying roomie. "When I first met her, I couldn't believe how unconfident she was. I expected this great athlete, this tennis superstar, to be like me—cocky." Indeed, as *Newsweek* described, "... through all her reincarnations, swept along in a dizzying whirl of new hair dyes and diets, Navratilova ... developed into one of the most complex and fascinating of modern sports figures." Prodded by the competitive hoop star, Lieberman and her coach, she steadied herself in the early '80s, finally captured the elusive U.S. Open title in '83, and with relentless weight training, reflex drills, and practice, practice, practice, became the game's dominant player, and the prototype New Woman Athlete. Chris Evert Lloyd's assessment that "you can be good and still respect other players—but Martina doesn't" may be valid, but her evaluation that Navratilova wasn't "in the same league ... as me or even Billie Jean [King] as far as being mentally tough," has certainly been disproved. Now a fit 145 pounds, Navratilova endorses Porsches, Computerland, and other companies' products, and lives in Fort Worth, Texas. No longer a tantrum-thrower or sore loser on the court, she nevertheless still speaks her mind. "Are you not supposed to have any opinions?" she askes. "Are you supposed to be a nun? What's ordinary? Where's the happy medium?" Her exceedingly candid autobiography—*Martina*—was published in 1985. Losing out to a younger generation, Navratilova was beaten by Steffi Graf at the 1989 US Open.

Patricia Neal

"Courage? It isn't something you are born with. It comes to you with experience. I've learned that," says actress Patricia Neal in the honey-and-sandpaper voice famous on stage and in Hollywood. Despite a brilliant career [acting credits included a Tony Award in 1946—the first year the award was given—for her Broadway debut in *Another Part of the Forest;* an Oscar in 1963 for *Hud;* accolades in such plays as *The Children's House,* 1952; *Cat on a Hot Tin Roof,* 1956; *The Miracle Worker,* 1960], Patricia Neal is probably best known for her extraordinary recovery from the damaging effects of a massive stroke suffered in 1965. Unable to speak, read, write, or walk, she underwent extensive therapy and emerged three years later to deliver a stunning performance in the film *The Subject Was Roses,* bringing her an Academy Award nomination.

Born 20 January 1926 in Packard, Kentucky, the daughter of a coal company bookkeeper, she studied at the University of Tennessee and Northwestern. "I first got the bright notion of becoming an actress when I was in the sixth grade. Have had a one-track mind ever since." With the shooting of her second film, *The Fountainhead* in 1948, a publicized romance with co-star Gary Cooper lasted four years. When Cooper would not divorce his wife, she resigned herself to leaving Hollywood for New York. There she married British writer Roald Dahl in 1953. They faced tragedy. In 1960, a Manhattan taxicab hit the pram of their 4-month-old son. The child survived after remaining in critical condition two years, having undergone five brain operations. Two years later their 7-year-old daughter died of measles. In 1965, six months pregnant, Patricia Neal was crippled with a stroke. "In everyone's life a lot of bad things happen," she remarks. "I just seemed to have had a larger dose of the bad things."

Her fortitude, coupled with her husband's devotion and dogged encouragement, was the subject of "The Patricia Neal Story," a television film aired in 1981 (script written by playwright Robert Anderson, starring roles played by Glenda Jackson and Dirk Bogarde). Ironically, in 1983, after 30 years of marriage, she found herself divorced. (Roald left her for a wardrobe woman she had befriended while filming a TV commercial for Maxim coffee.) "It's as if the worst dream I can think of has happened," she acknowledges sadly. "But my husband did a lot, I've got to give him credit. He's really the one who pushed me to get well, and he pushed me back into acting. I'm so very glad he did because now it's all I've got." A pioneer of strength, she travels extensively on lecture tours for the handicapped; a rehabilitation center was named for her in Atlanta. Her autobiography, *As I Am* was published in 1988.

James Nederlander

"I guess I've done practically everything in the theatre line," says this theatrical executive, "except act." Chairman of the Board of the Nederlander Organization, he is a scion of a family prominent for three generations in management and operation of theaters and the production of shows. Nederlander owns and/or operates 10 Broadway theaters in New York City and a chain of legitimate theaters across the nation and in London. His more than 25 Broadway productions include, most recently, *The Life and Adventures of Nicholas Nickleby*, *The Dresser*, *Nine*, *Merlin*, *Annie*, *La Cage Aux Folles*, *Strange Interlude*, *Arsenic and Old Lace* and *Breaking the Code*. Nederlander's multiple hats have made him a figure of unquestionable importance in American theater. But as an individual, he seems to prefer obscurity, cultivating little of the flair and fanfare of the stereotypical Broadway entrepreneur.

Born 31 March 1922 in Detroit, Jimmy Nederlander like his four brothers, served his apprenticeship at the Shubert Theatre in Detroit, the city where their father, David T. Nederlander, unfurled the family banner, buying a 99-year lease on the old Detroit Opera House at the turn of the century. Although Jimmy entered the Detroit Institute of Technology with the intention of studying law, World War II landed him right back into show business when the Air Force assigned him to Moss Hart's production of *Winged Victory*. Bowing to the inevitable, James Morton Nederlander went into press agentry and theater management and rejoined the family chain when old D.T. decided it was time to ease up on his normal 15-hour working day. New York theatres in the Nederlander chain include the Biltmore, Lunt-Fontanne, Brooks Atkinson, Mark Hellinger, Minskoff, Nederlander, Neil Simon, Palace, and Gershwin (formerly the Uris), which houses the Theater Hall of Fame. Other Nederlander legit houses are in Los Angeles, Detroit, San Francisco, Boston, San Diego, Chicago, and London. There are also a half dozen outdoor theatres. Jimmy got into producing after his brother, Joseph, and associate Gerard Oestreicher set an objective of filling 30,000 seats a night. Other Broadway productions include *Seesaw*, *Applause*, and revivals of *Hello, Dolly!*, *Oklahoma*, *The Music Man*, and *Peter Pan*. He's produced *Otherwise Engaged*, *Woman of the Year* with Lauren Bacall, *Lena Horne: The Lady and Her Music*, and *Shirley Bassey*.

He married Charlene Saunders in 1969; they have three children; James L., Sharon, Kristina. Nederlander nominally makes his home in New York City, but claims it's more accurately aboard American Airlines.

Kate Nelligan

When she appeared in David Hare's *Plenty* critics ran out of superlatives. Hers has been a career blessed with instant, deserved recognition and opportunity, beginning with her 1974 London stage debut in Hare's *Knuckle* and including star parts in John Schlesinger's London revival of Shaw's *Heartbreak House*, playing Josie in the American Rep's 1984 revivial of O'Neill's *Moon for the Misbegotten*, and an exceptional performance in 1988's *Spoils of War*. In films, she's appeared in *Without a Trace*, *Dracula*, *Eye of the Needle* and *Eleni*. On television, she starred in the 1989 miniseries "Love & Hate: The Story of Colin and Joann Thatcher."

"I'm often hired to play from the eyebrows up," she has commented. Born 16 March 1951 in London, Ontario, she says one of the keys to her success is her "tremendous self-confidence. There were six children, but my mother always made me feel that I would do something important, which stood me in good stead." At age 16, she entered the University of Toronto and discovered the theater and of her first time on stage she says, "I didn't feel elated or ecstatic—just at home. From that day forward I never thought I would do anything else. Acting satisfied something very deep in me, and I suppose it still does." At the end of her second year, she traveled south to audition at Yale University and became one of two from among hundreds of North American drama students to be selected to attend London's prestigious Central School of Speech and Drama. Once there she ran into a problem: finances. "I sat down at the typewriter and wrote to people I'd been told were interested in the theater: 'I'm poor. You are rich. Give me money.'" The money came. Her next hurdle was her Canadian accent and she decided not only to sound British but to become British in every possible sense of the word. "I did what was necessary. Once I made the decision to adopt that speech, it became mine." After graduating from the Central School, she joined the Bristol Old Vic Company. "I was in seventeen plays and in fourteen of them I was bad. In *Private Lives* I was so bad I actually cried on stage . . . it's so agonizing to be bad in public. But the Bristol experience gave me five year's experience in twelve months." She is so adored as an artist that when she ruptured a vocal cord during a performance of *Moon for the Misbegotten* (her mouth had filled up with blood; although she carried on with the show, the next day she was unable to speak), her recuperation was watched hawkishly by her fans and reported daily in the papers.

Her stage triumphs haven't yet been matched in films. Nowadays, she is very much based in America, "In retrospect, I'm not sure I should have gone to the lengths I did in becoming English," she confesses, "I gave up too much, I sacrificed relaxation, humor, kindness, classlessness, democracy." At long last love, Nelligan married arranger/pianist Robert Reale on 19 February 1989.

Willie Nelson

The bedraggled outlaw of country music reached the pinnacle of commercial success by way of backwoods bars and dance halls across Texas. He never relinquished the scraggly beard, baggy pants, and red bandanna befitting a rebel, even after his remarkably tender voice came to dominate country charts. Nelson is credited for forging a progressive movement toward a purer country sound, expanding the tastes of country and pop music fans.

Born 30 April 1933, Nelson grew up in a small Texas town hit hard by the Great Depression. While he garnered some success as a songwriter early in his career, his first recording efforts hit a sour note. The Nashville music industry was intimidated by the popularity of the British rock invasion of the 1960s, and Nelson's honky-tonk style violated the twangy, orchestrated formula considered commercially viable for Country and Western. He did score a big hit for the late Patsy Cline with "Crazy" in 1961, but it wasn't until 1973 that Nelson, having left Nashville for Austin, recorded his first hit album, *Shotgun Willie.* In the next decade, his rambler laments, such as "Mama Don't Let Your Babies Grow Up to be Cowboys," and "On the Road Again," and his ballads of love unfulfilled, such as "Always on My Mind," became country standards. His rich, sweet voice was instantly recognizable.

Nelson acted in the 1979 movie, *The Electric Horseman,* starred as a Willie-like character in the 1980 *Honeysuckle Rose,* co-starred with Kris Kristofferson in 1985's *Songwriter,* and played in the CBS-TV movie "Where the Hell's that Gold" in 1988. He also released his autobiography *Willie: An Autobiography* in 1988.

His personal life appeared to be the stuff love ballads are made of, until he separated from his third wife, Connie in 1987. All told, Nelson has five children from his three marriages.

Peter Nero

His career at the keyboard has taken him from the clinking glasses and clanking silverware of the bar and club circuit into recording studios (over 20 albums; two Grammy Awards) and, more recently, into the nation's concert halls. Musical director and maestro of the Philly Pops Orchestra since its establishment in 1979, he also serves in the same double capacity with the Denver, Edmonton (Alberta), and Tulsa Pops Orchestras. In 1986 he was honored by the International Society of the Performing Arts Administrators.

He started out as Bernie Nierow on 22 May 1934 in Brooklyn, the son of a social worker. Groomed for a classical career, he won a Juilliard scholarship and well remembers the subway trek to get to class—31 stops from Broadway to the upper reaches of Manhattan. Drawn to jazz, he spent six years playing in various smoke-filled rooms before cutting his first album, which became a hit. In 1961, he collected his first Grammy as Best New Artist of the Year and in 1962, picked up another in the Best Instrumental Performance category for his LP, "The Colorful Peter Nero." In 1963, he was nominated for a Golden Globe for his score and title song for the Jane Fonda comedy, *Sunday in New York,* in which he also appeared. Even more ambitious were his compositions, "Anne Frank: The Diary of a Young Girl" and "His World." The latter, a three-movement piece for piano, rhythm section, full orchestra and rock group has been performed by a number of major orchestras under Nero's baton. Nero and his first wife, Marcia (wed 1956), had two children. He and his present wife, Peggy (wed 1977), live in Los Angeles, where the pianist-conductor-composer-arranger spends his free time playing chess and backgammon and watching Dodger games. He has a full recording studio in his home and his interest and expertise in the mystique of computers puts him on a par with many pros.

Bob Newhart

His sober low-key comedy style is "so diffident," says one critic, "that he can bite the hand that feeds him and make it feel like a manicure." He rose to popularity almost overnight early in the 1960s with a comedy album called "The Button Down Mind of Bob Newhart" and has been on and off the air-waves and in and out of clubs ever since. His first regular TV series (1961-62 season) won a Peabody and an Emmy, but was a casualty of the ratings war. After a decade of guest spots, he launched a new "Bob Newhart Show" in 1972 (six seasons). In 1982 CBS reinstated him, this time simply as "Newhart."

Born George Robert Newhart in Chicago on 5 September 1929, he took law courses at Loyola and began his working career as an accountant. "But I was a bum one," he said after cheerfully escaping from business life. "I always figured that if you came within six or eight bucks of it, you were going to be OK." The album that served as his showbiz passport, a satiric epic of split-second timing, aimed gentle darts at the everyday working man: bus drivers, real estate salesmen, and 50-year employees ("I had to get half gassed to get down to this crummy joint every day"), plus a Madison Avenue braintruster who, on the eve of the Gettysburg Address offers advice to Abe Lincoln on how to polish up his image. His film credits include *Catch-22* (1970), *Little Miss Marker* (1980) and *The First Family* (1980). Married to the former Virginia Quinn, he's the father of two sons and two daughters.

Anthony Newley

Composer of such well-known songs as "Candy Man," "What Kind of Fool Am I?" and "Who Can I Turn To?," he became an international hero in the antiheroic 1960s with his smash hit musical, *Stop the World, I Want to Get Off,* and its successor, *The Roar of the Greasepaint, The Smell of the Crowd.* Says this singer-composer-actor-playwright-mime, "I'm not a trained musician or singer—but I can turn out a song." He's turned out so many pop classics that audiences now remark, "I didn't know he wrote that, too." Ironically, most of his songs were turned into hit records by other singers (Sammy Davis Jr., Andy Williams, Tony Bennett . . .), but Newley says good-naturedly, "Their records sell in the millions; when I do it, it just trickles. But for the composer and lyricist there's a tidy bit to be made that way, too, so I don't really mind." But Newley has continued to have his own following, and his distinctive accent has filled the air waves as well as night spots. During a 1984 U.S. tour he shared the stage and spotlight with Sarah Vaughn.

A cockney Jew born in the east end of London 24 September 1931, he dropped out of school at age 14 and played in children's films, including (in the role of the Artful Dodger) *Oliver Twist.* He made some 40 minor films before fame touched him. Portraying a rock-and-roll singer in the film, *Idle on Parade,* one song he sang ("I've Waited So Long") made him an overnight idol of British teenagers. Then in 1961 at age 30, he ignited west end and Broadway with his impersonation of "Littlechap" fighting the establishment in *Stop the World.* In collaboration with Leslie Bricusse, he created and starred in a number of musicals which dealt with the plight of the "little man," but he isn't an angry rebel. ("I don't hate anybody or anything. But I do expect to make statements about the problems of being a human being.") One of his most successful songs, "What Kind of Fool Am I?," featured in *Stop the World,* had blanketed the U.S. even before the musical reached New York and some 75 vocalists eventually recorded it, among them Tony Bennett and Ella Fitzgerald. Newley's own recording contained the word "damn," which bothered some radio stations. So London Records, which first issued the song, put out a damn-less version for disc jockeys. In 1973, he recorded an album of his original songs titled "Ain't It Funny?" In between songs, Newley has made some American films (*Dr. Doolittle, Garbage Pail Kids*) and also appeared on television. He was inducted into the Songwriters Hall of Fame in 1989. He ex-wife is "Dynasty" star Joan Collins; they have two children, Tara (born 1963) and Alexander (born 1965). By a former airline hostess, he has another daughter, Shelby Pandora (born 1973). He married for a third time, Dareth, in April 1989.

Edwin Newman

Veteran televison journalist Edwin Newman, occasionally described as "the only host of 'Saturday Night Live' ever to moderate a presidential debate," emerged from his "NBC voluntary retirement" in 1988 as the narrator for "Television," the panoramic PBS series which spotlighted the high points of sixty years of television broadcasting. The eight-part series, focused on some of the spectacular "live" events covered on the tube over past decades.

Newman was a perfect choice to serve as spokesman on the ambitious video project. It's been estimated that he has taken part in more documentaries than anyone else in television history and he has received numerous awards for reporting from abroad, news commentary, interviewing, and even drama criticism on the tube. Since retiring from NBC News early in 1984, Newman has continued to be active in television, anchoring numerous programs on PBS, including the series, "Congress: We the People." His two books on English usage, *Strictly Speaking* and *A Civil Tongue*, were both national best sellers.

Born 25 January 1919 in New York City, Newman majored in political science at the University of Wisconsin and began his journalism career in 1941 with the Washington bureau of INS. After service as a Navy communications officer during World War II, he wound up, in 1949, as NBC's man in London, Rome and Paris, compiling what he later described as "a spotless record of being in the wrong place at the wrong time." By the time he departed NBC, he'd reported from a total of 35 different countries, in addition to covering seven sets of national political conventions in the U.S. (In 1976, he also served as moderator of the first Ford-Carter TV debate.) Newman has earned Emmy Awards for his drama criticism, his literate television interview series, "Speaking Freely," and (in 1983) his special report on "Kids, Drugs and Alcohol." He and his wife Rigel have one daughter, Nancy.

Paul Newman

Star of stage, screen and supermarket, and likewise a winning auto racer, Paul Newman is, according to one writer, "almost universally a catalyst of moist and turbulent emotions. Men's eyes mist over, and women's knees go wobbly." A very private person, with "a moat and a drawbridge which he lets down occasionally," he writhes under the screenland sex symbol image and refuses to play celebrity. He avoids being the public "Paul Newman" as much as possible; even in his films, he takes pains to look as gruesome as possible when the scene can use it. Scriptwriter William (*Harper* and *Butch Cassidy*) Goldman says that the star "could be called a victim of the Cary Grant syndrome. He makes it look so easy, and he looks so wonderful, that everybody assumes he isn't acting." A serious actor who believes "an actor should act" when the scripts are right, he "is very sensitive to writing, and is the best director of actors I know," states writer Stewart (*Rachel, Rachel*) Stern, who explains "I think there's less impediment between his talent and its expression when he's directing. That's probably because, as in racing, 'Paul Newman' doesn't have to be there."

Newman grew up in Cleveland Heights, a comfortable suburb of Cleveland, where he was born Paul Leonard Newman on 26 January 1925. The son of a prosperous Jewish businessman, Newman refers to himself as a Jew ("because it's more of a challenge"), although his mother was a Catholic of Hungarian descent. He did a lot of acting in children's groups and high school. When the brilliant blue eyes turned out to be partially color blind, he was dropped from flight training and spent World War II as a radioman in bombers in the Pacific Campaign. After acting his way through Kenyon College (graduated 1949), he spent two years doing stock and married actress Jacqueline Witte (one son, two daughters). His father's death recalled him to the family business, but 18 months later he enrolled in Yale's Drama School. "I wasn't driven to acting by any inner compulsion," he recalls, "I was running away from the sporting goods business." Within months, he was in New York, where he did television bits before opening on Broadway in *Picnic* (1953) to excellent notices. During *Picnic*, he joined the Actors Studio, landed a long-term Warners contract and met *Picnic* understudy Joanne Woodward, whom he married five years later (three daughters). His film debut was in *The Silver Chalice*, "The Worst Picture Ever Made" (a Newman family consensus). In this 1954 religious costume drama, he was garbed in a "cocktail dress," and the parts left exposed gave rise to the affectionate family sobriquet "Old Skinny Legs." He fled back to Broadway for *The Desperate Hours*, and didn't make another film for two years, returning only for *Somebody Up There Likes Me* (1956). He garnered his first Best Actor Oscar nomination for *Cat on a Hot Tin Roof* (1958) and Best Actor nominations followed for *The Hustler* (1961), *Hud* (1963) and *Cool Hand Luke* (1967), in which he created a trio of miscreant antiheroes so fallible and faulted that the American public has willed them into the national character, along with his other lovable loser, *Harper* (1966). Newman ended the sixties with his hedonistic romp through *Butch Cassidy and the Sundance Kid* ("too bad they got killed at the end, 'cause those two guys could have gone on in films forever") and *Winning*, which he later called a "pretty good story about racing." Sports car racing has since become an integral part of his life; from April to October, he does not make movies, seeking instead the anonymity of P.L. Newman, amateur sports car driver. He has twice been a national champion in his class.

In the seventies, Newman made such films as *Sometimes a Great Notion* (1971), *The Life and Times of Judge Roy Bean* (1972) and *The Sting* (1973). Of *Sting's* famous scene in which Newman and Robert Shaw cheat each other at draw poker, director George Roy Hill said "one of the best pieces of comedic acting I've ever seen. I defy any actor to play the scene better." There followed: *The Towering Inferno* (1974), *Buffalo Bill and the Indians* (1976) and *Slap Shot* (1977). Oscar nominations came for *Absence of Malice* (1981) and *The Verdict* (1982). ("It was such a relief to let it all hang out in the movie—blemishes and all.") Co-writer and co-producer of *Harry and Son* (1984), he also directed and starred "for the last time. Never again—you can't do both." Frequently Oscar-nominated for tasks other than acting, Newman made his directorial debut with Oscar-nominated *Rachel, Rachel* (1968), starring Woodward, and has since directed her in film versions of the plays, *The Effect of Gamma Rays on Man-in-the-Moon Marigolds* (1972), with daugher Nell, "The Shadow Box," made for ABC-TV (1980), and *The Glass Menagerie* (1987).

Up until 1986, Newman had never received an Academy Award. That year, he became the recipient of an honorary Academy Award for career achievement. However, in typical Hollywood style, Newman won the Best Actor Oscar the following year for his performance in *The Color of Money*.

A daily runner, sailor, fisherman and general cut-up, he maintains an athletic 145 pounds on his 5'10" frame, but is under family pressure to give up auto racing. A life-long liberal, he speaks out on civil rights, the nuclear freeze, gay rights and seat belts. His various charities include the Scott Newman Foundation, an anti-drug campaign in the film industry named in honor of Paul's late son who died in 1978 of an overdose of painkillers and alcohol at age 28. The Foundation and his other charities are partially funded by profits from his "Newman's Own" brand of olive oil and vinegar dressing, which forced the actor and writer-pal A.E. Hotchner (*Papa Hemingway*) "out of the basement" and into marketing of their blend, and "Newman's Own Industrial Strength Spaghetti Sauce," also on grocers' shelves. Although the Newmans maintain an apartment in Manhattan and a house in Beverly Hills, they have been happily exiled from celebrity in Westport, Connecticut for many years.

Wayne Newton

"Wayne Newton is not a joke anymore. If you know Las Vegas . . . you know he is more than the Midnight Idol, more than Mr. Excitement in Vegas, he's the center of a veritable *cult* in the town. . . . If you don't know Vegas, you might be tempted to class him with Tiny Tim as a brief freakish aberration in the evolution of pop music, a phenomenon preserved . . . as the occasional butt of jokes in Johnny Carson's monologue. . . . But Johnny doesn't tell Wayne Newton jokes anymore. Not since a hulking six-foot-three-inch, black-belt karate expert named Wayne Newton walked into his office, flexed the muscles he's pumped up with Steve (*Hercules*) Reeves and all but threatened to thrash the comedian if he didn't cut out the ridicule of Newton's formerly fat and effeminate image. '"He was making fag jokes about me' is the way Wayne explained it to me," wrote Ron Rosenbaum in an *Esquire* magazine piece on the star.

This once-upon-a-time lounge singer transformed himself into the giant of the more-macho-than-macho singers with the surprising endorsement of Howard Hughes, won over Las Vegas, turned it into his dream oasis by surpassing both Frank Sinatra and Elvis Presley as Vegas' highest grossing entertainer. He squeezes over $1,000,000 a month from ticket sales into his piggy bank. As Merv Griffin puts it: "Las Vegas without Wayne Newton is like Disneyland without Mickey Mouse."

Born 3 April 1942, he's come a long way from his humble Virginia boyhood to the Circus Maximus Showroom of Caesar's Palace, his current performing base. The son of two half-American Indians, he still hurts from the racial ridicule he received as a youngster. "During your formative years, when you're as far out in left field as I was, being an Indian . . . it left its lessons with me. I think I'll always carry those scars." He broke into the business singing Country and Western songs for school and church gatherings and achieved his first success as a "singing, strumming, high-pitched paragon of wholesome virtue whose cherubic behavior on stage earned him a reputation as a sort of Andy Hardy of Las Vegas." "Danke Schoen," his first big record hit (sung in a "strange, sexually indecipherable tone" led some people to think that the vocalist was a German fräulein).

Newton lives in a Southern style mansion named Case de Shenandoan that "combines influences of the White House's north portico and the main entrance to Caesar's Palace." He also breeds exquisite Arabian horses on a 52-acre Nevada ranch, pilots his own helicopter and keeps a fleet of perfectly restored Dusenbergs and other antique cars. In 1985 he divorced his wife of 19 years, Elaine, with whom he has a daughter, Erin. When he's not singing in Vegas, or checking on his investments, Newton pops up on television. He's hosted the New York segment of the "Weekend with the Stars Telethon for Cerebral Palsy" and he appeared in the ABC-TV miniseries, "North and South, Book II." In 1989 he appeared in the James Bond flick *License to Kill*.

Olivia Newton-John

"When it came time to do this album, I'd gone through some new experiences," says Olivia as she talks about *The Rumour* (1988). "I'd been raising my daughter Chloe, and had come to see things differently. I wanted the album to reflect that, and I co-wrote many of the songs myself. There's songs about ecology, AIDS, single parenting and role reversal in marriage—different kinds of subjects from what I'd done before." The sweet, pretty blonde girl has matured into a musical mainstay as well as a model mother. Her first single was a recording of Bob Dylan's "If Not for You" and next came the ballad "Let Me Be There" which established her first U.S. beachhead in 1973 and won her the best country vocalist Grammy. She donned a new, sharper-focus image when she teamed up with John Travolta to rock-and-roll in spike heels and black leather in the film version of *Grease* (1978)—the all-time highest grossing movie musical. After playing a romantic enchantress in the musical film *Xanadu* (it barely said "howdy-do" at the box office, but she met her 10-years-younger husband-to-be Matt Lattanzi—they were married in 1984), she sent music video watchers in 1981 for a spin with her sexy, sweaty hit "Let's Get Physical" and "Heart Attack" (1982). Some of her other hit titles have been: 'I Honestly Love You," "Have You Never Been Mellow," and from the *Grease* score, "You're the One That I Want." From sweetheart to temptress makes a Pop Goddess grow, but to know her, one suspects, is to know a home-loving, animal-loving, easy-going woman who has been able to teach quite a few cash registers to play her tune.

Born 26 September 1948 in Cambridge, England, the daughter of a Welsh university don and a German mother, her maternal grandfather was Max Born, a Nobel laureate in physics. The family moved to Australia when she was five and it was there she launched her singing career. At 15, she won a talent contest that took her back to England, and by 1971 she'd been voted Best British Girl Singer, an honor she received two years in a row. Since winning her first Grammy (1973) for "Let Me Be There," her awards have multiplied and her total record sales are in the millions. In 1983 she teamed up with Travolta again and made the film *Two of a Kind*. The film received mixed reviews but the song "Twist of Fate" became a hit record.

Touring gives her sleepless nights and butterflies in her stomach, although she did manage to cap an SRO tour of the U.S. in the mid-seventies with a solo concert at New York's Metropolitan Opera House. "I don't have the desire I think a lot of performers feel," she told George Christy in 1983, "to get the applause. It's not life and death to me. I like to sing, and I love doing what I'm doing, but it's not a dire need."

Craving things Australian, she and her ex-singing pal, Pat Farrar, opened the Koala Blue boutique in West Hollywood in 1984. Going with this winning idea, there are now over fifteen stores in a chain of outlets across the US and Canada, plus plans for a Koala Blue to open in Japan. Keeping her heart in Australia, she produced a HBO special about the Aussies in 1988 to coincide with the release of *The Rumour* album. In a surprise move, Olivia left her record company of eighteen years, MCA, to go with Geffen records in 1989. Her first project will be an album for children. Olivia lives on a three-acre ranch in Malibu with what she calls her "zoo," a household filled with many animals she adores (five cats, seven dogs, five horses). She said as a youngster she wanted to become a veterinarian. When she's not working, the singer likes to spend time with her handsome actor-husband Lattanzi, and their daughter Chloe Rose (born 17 January 1986).

Mike Nichols

"Having fame is wonderful, if you can control its tendency 'to make you feel like a baby,'" says director Mike Nichols, who feels he can most effectively deal with actors from the other end of the spectrum; to him, the process of his craft "is in some ways like being an ideal parent." Jeremy Irons, star of *The Real Thing* (1984), which earned Nichols his sixth Tony award for directing, has said "Mike creates a very protective environment. He's like the best of lovers; he makes you feel he's only for you." Sigourney Weaver, assessing Nichols' technique with the disparate training and professional backgrounds of her fellow actors in *Hurlyburly* (1984), affirmed that he "worked with each actor and part individually," but noted that "the end result was ensemble playing." In a play, as in movies, Nichols relentlessly strives to convey what is "really going on," so that the audience will perceive "real people living their lives." According to playwright Neil Simon, Nichols' guidance enables him to "get the actor to physically express what the author gives only clues to" and thereby, achieve Nichols' event, the moment(s) of arch truth that illuminates the author's meaning in each scene. Nichols has attributed the concept of the hidden event to his years of improvisation with Elaine May. Doing improvisation, he says, "You learned to damn well pick something that would happen in the scene—an event . . . as long as something is happening, you can continue." An author's script is made to unfold within this content. Apparently, Nichols' success is in identifying each event, working mechanically within it and, most importantly, leaving it unstated.

Born Michael Igor Perschkowsky in Berlin, 6 November 1931, he is the elder son of a Russian who fled his homeland in 1917, became a physician and married a Jewish girl. His father Anglicized his patronymic, Nicholaiyevitch, when he left Germany during the rise of Hitler and requalified as a physician in the U.S. Nichols was reunited with his father in New York on 4 May 1939. A "little bald kid" from age four due to an adverse reaction to a whooping cough injection, Nichols bounded through boarding schools even after his father's death when he was 12. After studying pre-med at the University of Chicago and acting with Lee Strasberg in New York, he returned to Chicago where he connected with the Compass troupe which became the Second City company. He then teamed with Elaine May in a satiric comedy improvisation act that captivated nightclub and television audiences, made three records and spent a year on Broadway with *An Evening with Mike Nichols and Elaine May* (1960). The play *A Matter of Position*, written by May and starring Nichols, upset the teetering balance between the two and, closing the play out of town, they split personally and professionally in 1962. "When Elaine and I split up—that was a shattering year for me. . . . I was the leftover half of something." Within months, Neil Simon tapped him to direct *Barefoot in the Park* (1963) for which he won his first Tony. He has since directed three more Simon plays, *The Odd Couple* (1965), *Plaza Suite* (1968) and *The Prisoner of Second Avenue* (1971), and each has earned him a Tony. Numbers five and six were for *Luv* (1964) and *The Real Thing*. Nichol's most successful serious play was David Rabe's *Strangers* (1976); the duo teamed again in *Hurlyburly*, a tragicomedy. Nichols' approach to all plays is the same ("I don't think comedy is an escape from tragedy. They are both *life*.") In 1986 he directed Marlo Thomas on Broadway in *Social Security*.

First married to Pat Scot, a singer, Nichols had just married Margot Callas (one daughter) when he undertook his directorial debut with *Barefoot*. He used revelation of his own experience to enhance his actor's consciousness, a tool which he continues to utilize with great success. His third marriage is to Annabel Davis-Goff, a screenwriter-turned-novelist (one son, one daughter). He married his fourth wife, "60 Minutes" anchorwoman Diane Sawyer on 29 April 1988. Hollywood has tapped his directorial dexterity for such films as: *Who's Afraid of Virginia Woolf?* (1966), *The Graduate* (1967) for which he won an Oscar; *Catch-22* (1969), *Carnal Knowledge* (1971), *Heartburn* (1986), *Biloxi Blues* (1987) and the Academy Award nominated *Working Girl* (1988).

Jack Nicholson

"What is it that makes people think you're this high-living maniac of Herculean proportions?" asked Martin Torgoff of this two-time Oscar winner (*One Flew Over the Cuckoo's Nest* and *Terms of Endearment*) whose star appeal Pauline Kael once called "a satirical approach to macho." The avuncular anti-hero responded: "I don't do anything about shaping my public image. I'm also very protective of my private life—you could come through [my] house and not find out a thing about me. Therefore, into this vacuum come other impressions from the little bit that people do know about me from my background—plus the roles I've played, of course . . . my friends know that I don't drink that much, and when I do get loaded—twice in my life, *I think*—I've fallen down. But more generally I don't do anything like that. Chase girls? Certainly, as all men have—[His first marriage to actress Sandra Knight (one daughter) ended in divorce; he's lived for many years with Anjelica Huston in Hollywood Hills and Aspen, Colorado]—if it's a chase, it's too long. I didn't always feel that way . . . I did believe that candid was what you should be . . . it's only misused. I can't really know what my reputation is, but I can tell you from what I hear that it's extremely distorted."

Born 28 April 1937 in Neptune, New Jersey, he's always had a sense of destiny about being involved in films. Initially, he thought about directing. He moved to California at age 17 and worked for 15 years in television ("Daytime Divorce Court", "Matinee Theater") and made nearly 20 B films for producer Roger Corman, including *Hell's Angels on Wheels* and *Back Door to Hell*. "I always sort of stunk of TV. At the time Roger was the only guy who would employ me as a professional." At age 32, he became a star by replacing Rip Torn in *Easy Rider* (1969) starring opposite Peter Fonda in the counter-culture cycle romp. Since then he has starred in films such as: *Five Easy Pieces, On a Clear Day You Can See Forever, Carnal Knowledge, King of Marvin Gardens, A Safe Place, The Last Detail*, Roman Polanski's *Chinatown*, Antonioni's *The Passenger, The Fortune, Goin' South* (which he directed), *Reds, The Shining* and *The Postman Always Rings Twice*. His latest pics are 1985's *Prizzi's Honor* (Academy Award Best Actor nomination), *Heartburn* (1986), *The Witches of Eastwick* (1987), *Ironweed* (1987, Academy Award Best Actor nomination), *Broadcast News* (1987), *Batman* (1989) and he directed as well as appeared in *The Two Jakes* (1989). Blending his talents to another medium, he recorded the album *The Elephant's Child* with Bobby McFerrin for which he received a Grammy for Best Recording for Children in 1987.

"I've always felt that I could come at the work from first principles. Start from zero, take by take. That's been where my enthusiasm comes from. I've never felt obligated to my talent—in other words, I dont' have the impression that anyone would give a shit if I didn't make another movie . . . you can always retire. To sum it up, I like making beautiful things. That's really my desire in life."

Jack Nicklaus

When he was ten years old, a chubby and cherubic-looking Jack Nicklaus discovered golf. When he was 12, golf discovered him. Neither has been the same since. When he was approaching his thirties, the "Golden Bear" had already established himself as the supreme golfer of his era and, by the next decade, was recognized as not only the best dimpled-ball smacker of all time, but the most dominant athlete for the longest period in any American sport. His record 19 major titles were won starting when he was a 22-year old U.S. Open victor in 1962. Having stayed near the top of his game for two decades, he silenced growing speculation that he was too old to be competitive by winning the U.S. Open and the PGA Championship in 1980. Though it may disappoint his followers in "Jack's Pack" he now concentrates on the major events on the tour, prompting one observer to quip, "Nicklaus has become a legend in his spare time." Golfdom's top money-winner (more that $4.5 million), his Golden Bear Enterprises grosses almost $300 million annually.

Born in Columbus, Ohio, 21 January 1940, Jack was ten when his drugstore chain-owning father asked his son to join him for a round because he didn't want to hinder his golf buddies while hobbling around the course on a recently-injured ankle. Jack won the U.S. Amateur title while attending Ohio State (having abandoned his father's dream of seeing his beef of a boy playing for a Woody Hayes Buckeye football team). In 1960, he married Ohio State beauty queen Barbara Bash and turned pro four months later. ("It was the only way I knew how to keep playing golf and make a living too.") A devoted father of five (one of whom he named for friend, Gary Player), he pilots his own plane back home to North Palm Beach right after tournaments to be with his family, with occasional fishing trips to his Bahamian home in Great Harbour Cay.

Alwin Nikolais

So distinctive is the style of Alwin Nikolais that he alone among modern dance pioneers does not have a direct line of descendants, like a Graham, a Balanchine or a Cunningham. Those who try to copy the master of "the original gesture" risk being accused of plagiarism, their work labelled "Bad Nikolais." What young choreographers of the 1980s *are* doing is approaching Nikolais' "total theatre" concept with new and original aesthetics. The Nikolais style is a combination of the creative vision of one man in every aspect of a dance work and the placement of the dancer as part of his environment, rather than as a controlling force over it. Unlike other dance companies whose works are collaborative efforts among designer, composer and choreographer, the Nikolais company dances the Nikolais music, wearing Nikolais costumes, against Nikolais backdrops, lighted by Nikolais designs. He uses his dancers as a dynamic function of the entire creation, so that although part of the work, they are not necessarily "featured." To charges that his concept necessarily dehumanizes the dancers and strips them of emotional content, Nikolais replies, "Man is a fellow traveler within the total universal mechanism. I have explored the idea of dance not entirely as a kinetic art but as more entire, looked-at, visual art."

Born into a large German-Russian family in Southington, Conn., 25 November 1912, Nikolais began his performing career as an organist in a Westport movie house and became a puppeteer in 1936. ("I learned a lot from those puppets. They are all motion and no nerves. I found out that art is motion, not emotion.") While attending summer classes at the Bennington School of the Dance, where the great figures of American modern dance were forging their art, he met Hanya Holm, who became his most influential teacher. He began his long-time association with the Henry Street Playhouse in 1948, and gained national attention in the late fifties through the successes of his dance company at the American Dance Festival. International acclaim grew out of an early success at the Spoleto Festival of Two Worlds, followed by a 1968 Paris season with a typically Gallic reception: boos, fights, and followed by a blast of bravos, wild foot stomping and an ecstatic celebration at Maxim's. Always a French favorite, in 1978 he was invited to form the Centre National de Danse Contemporaine in Angers; in 1980 his 99th choreographic work, *Schema*, was created for the Paris Opéra, and in 1983 he was made a Chevalier of the Legion of d'Honneur. His other honors include the *Dance Magazine* Award, the Grand Prix de Paris International Festival de Danse, an Emmy citation (for contributions to dance on television), the Capezio Award for Career Excellence, two Guggenheim fellowships, the 1985 Samuel H. Scripps American Dance Festival Award, the Kennedy Center Alliance Award (1987), the American Dance Guild Award (1987), and the National Medal of Arts Award (1987). "It goes without saying that Mr. Nikolais is a very special choreographer," said Anna Kisselgoff in the *New York Times*. "The proof is that no one has succeeded in doing what he does."

Leonard Nimoy

Every Trekkie knows the story behind the U.S.S. *Enterprise*, its galactic mission: "to seek out new life and civilizations, to go boldly where no man has gone before." And every Trekkie knows the Vulcan's survival was based on the decision to extirpate emotionalism from their race. Logic would rule supreme. Ears are pointed. And every Trekkie worth his TV is enraptured by the famous Vulcan hybrid Mr. Spock, in whom exists a very special mixture of space age tensions. The logic and emotional suppression of the Vulcan people through his father Sarek, in conflict with the emotional and humanistic traits inherited from his human mother Amanda, a scientist.

"For three years, twelve hours a day, five days a week, approximately ten months a year," he says, "I functioned as an extraterrestrial and years later I am still affected by the character of Spock. Of course the role has changed my career. Or rather, gave me one. It made me wealthy by most standards and opened up vast opportunities. It also affected me deeply. To this day I sense Vulcan speech patterns, Vulcan social attitudes and even Vulcan patterns of logic and emotional suppression in my behavior. What started out as a welcome job to a hungry actor has become a constant and ongoing influence in my thinking and lifestyle."

Born in Boston, 26 March 1931, the intense actor was passed over by all the pretty girls in high school in favor of the more popular jocks. Nimoy vowed to get his revenge by becoming a famous actor and with $600 in his pocket, set out for California's Pasadena Playhouse. He struggled towards success for years. Endeavoring to rid himself of his Boston accent, he intentionally developed a temporary stutter. In 1954 he married actress Sandi Zober (divorced, 2 children). He worked a variety of menial jobs and wanted to quit acting but Sandi changed his mind. In the early '60s, he began to get regular work on television and in 1966, cast in the part of Mr. Spock, his star was fixed in the Hollywood firmament. After "Star Trek" Nimoy went on to appear for two years on TV's "Mission Impossible" and then to expand into other fields. As a writer he has published three volumes of poetry—*You and I* (1973), *I Think of You* (1974), and *We Are All Children Searching for Love* (1977). His autobiography, *I Am Not Spock*, was published in 1975. Nimoy has also cut several albums (*Leonard Nimoy Presents Mr. Spock's Music from Outer Space*, etc.) and has toured the country appearing in serious theatrical works, including a tremendous success on Broadway in *Equus* (1977), and in a one-man-show *Vincent* about the painter Vincent Van Gogh. Turning his talents to directing he's gone behind the camera for some of the *Star Trek* movie sequels as well as directing the popular *Three Men And A Baby* (1987) and *The Good Mother* (1988). His film parts include *Invasion of the Body Snatchers, Star Trek—The Motion Picture, Star Trek II: The Wrath of Khan, Star Trek III: The Search for Spock* (he also directed), *Star Trek IV: The Voyage* and *Star Trek V: The Final Frontier*. In 1989, he married Susan Bay.

Richard Nixon

On August 9, 1974, a helicopter carried its passengers—including the most disgraced President in United States history—to Andrews Air Force Base, where the party boarded a jetliner. The destination was California . . . and oblivion. A decade later, the man who rivaled Bernhardt in farewell appearances and Rocky in comebacks emerged at 71 as an elder statesman, comentator on foreign and domestic affairs, a multimillionaire (reputed wealth of more than $3 million) and a successful author and lecturer addressing audiences at home and abroad. The most convincing proof of the extent of Richard Nixon's resurgence was the response to his appearance in May 1984 before the American Society of Newspaper Editors (it had *always* been the press which was the most implacable of his real and imagined enemies, the ones whom he had assured in 1962 that they "wouldn't have Nixon to kick around any more"). The New York *Daily News* reported that "he was cheered lustily, congratulated for his sweeping, authoritative view of world affairs, admired for his quick repartee and held in some measure of awe by many of the same people who were crying for his scalp when he was in office."

The odyssey of victory, crisis, defeat, revival, triumph, ruin and finally, resurrection began on a lemon farm in Yorba Linda, California, where Richard Nixon was born 9 January 1913. Then began the steady climb. Student body president at Whittier College; student body president at Duke University Law School; law practice in Whittier; marriage 21 June 1940 to Thelma Patricia (Pat) Ryan (two daughters, Tricia Cox and Julie Eisenhower; four grandchildren); Naval Service in World War II (returning as a Lieutenant Commander); victory over Jerry Voorhees for Congress in 1946;

the Alger Hiss case in 1948; election to the Senate in 1950 in a bruising battle with Helen Gahagan Douglas; election in 1952 and in 1956 as Ike's Vice President; the "kitchen debate" with Kruschev in 1959. Then the defeats: 1960's razor-thin loss to JFK for the presidency; 1962's defeat by Pat Brown for governor of California, which set the stage for his morning after "last press conference."

New York and the financial rewards of a partnership in a Wall Street law firm beckoned, and Richard Nixon settled down for what appeared to be a life of comfort and ease. But, as he wrote in *Six Crises* (1962), "the greatest magnet of all is that those who have known great crisis—its challenge and tension, its victory and defeat—can never become adjusted to a more leisurely and orderly pace." Sensing an LBJ victory in 1964, he sat tight. He was rewarded for his patience and in 1968 became the beneficiary of the tumultuous and tragic Democratic primary campaign that saw the assassination of Robert Kennedy and a tug of war between Eugene McCarthy and Hubert Humphrey, with the latter gaining a Pyrrhic victory at the convention and suffering defeat at Nixon's hands in the general election. His first term, domestically predictable, produced not a few surprises in foreign affairs, which he has always considered his forte. A trip to Russia in 1972 to sign Strategic Arms Limitation Treaties was followed by a journey to China where startled TV audiences watched the former scourge of "Red China" exchange pleasantries with Chairman Mao and toast Premier Chou En-lai, while a Peoples Republic of China band played, "Home On the Range." George McGovern, the Democrats' 1972 standard bearer, tried to capitalize on an inept break-in at the Democratic Party campaign headquarters in the posh Watergate complex by people tied to CREEP (Committee for the Re-Election of the President), but the White House was able to dismiss it at the time as a "two bit burglary." After the election, however, what has become known in political history as Watergate—coverups, illegal wiretaps, additional break-ins, use of the FBI and CIA to harass opponents, illegal campaign contributions, etc.—erupted, resulting in jail terms for nineteen officials and campaign workers. With the House Judiciary Committee proceeding along the impeachment route and Federal prosecutors preparing indictments, Richard Nixon on that historic August day sent a one-sentence letter to the Secretary of State, "I hereby resign the Office of the President of the United States," and delivered to the group assembled in the White House that afternoon a rambling statement which ended, "I am not a crook." He was pardoned by President Ford a month later. In April 1984, he was asked during an interview on "60 Minutes" (for which he received $500,000), whether he thought he should apologize for Watergate. The phoenix of American politics responded, "There's no way that you could apologize that is more eloquent, more decisive, more finite, which would exceed resigning the Presidency of the United States. That said it all." His books include *Memoirs* (1978); *The Real War* (1980), *Leaders* (1982), *No More Vietnams* (1985), and *1999: Victory Without War* (1988).

Nick Nolte

"You've got to be attached to both the piece and the character, so that your commitment to them eventually transcends your critical faculties. What we're all trying to do is get to where we're totally without self-consciousness as the characters before the cameras roll." The blond-haired, brawny actor trashes the 1977 underwater thriller *The Deep*. "I wasn't attached to it, so doing it was an alienating and isolating experience." It may have alienated Nolte, but movie-goers loved it, and it established him as a box office draw.

Born in 1942 in Omaha, Nebraska, Nolte recalls a rebellious childhood that may have molded his Brando-like appeal. After portraying shady characters on television episodes of popular shows and made-for-TV movies, Nolte made that long leap to film with the 1975 release, *Return to Macon County*. It was back to the small screen in 1976 for the ABC landmark mini-series, "Rich Man, Poor Man," based on Irwin Shaw's best-selling novel. As the down-and-out brother of a wealthy businessman, Nolte raised blood pressures with shirtless scenes of passion and earned an Emmy nomination. Nolte's other film credits include *Who'll Stop the Rain* (1978), a somber effort dealing with the Vietnam war; *North Dallas Forty*, a 1979 football farce; *Cannery Row* (1982); *48 Hours* (1983) with comedian Eddie Murphy and *Teachers* (1984). In 1985, he co-starred with Katharine Hepburn in *Grace Quigley* and filmed *Down and Out in Beverly Hills* with Bette Midler and Richard Dreyfuss. His recent movies include *Weeds* (1987), *New York Stories* (1988), *Three Fugitives* (1989), *Farewell to the King* (1989), *Everybody Wins* (1989) and *Q & A* (1989).

Nolte is known by his peers for going to strenuous lengths to prepare for his roles. He worked out four hours a day and wore a back brace for one, and gained 40 pounds for another. Nolte is also known for his stormy personal life, including three marriages and a palimony suit by former girlfriend, Karen Louise Eklund. He married Becky Linger in 1984, and they have one child.

Jessye Norman

The *New York Times* calls her "... an artist of extraordinary technical confidence and interpretive magnetism." Another critic declared her voice "one of the wonders of the world," and *Life* magazine wrote that Jessye Norman "stands on the threshold of domestic fame." After singing in most of Europe's most famous opera houses and concert halls, the soprano from Georgia finally made her long-awaited U.S. opera debut with the Opera Company of Philadelphia in 1982 which paired Stravinsky's dramatic opera-oratorio *Oedipus Rex* with Purcell's *Dido and Aeneas*. What *Newsweek* praised as her "blazing gem" of a performance laid the groundwork for her 1983 Metropolitan Opera debut on the opening night of the Met's centennial anniversary season. As Cassandra in Berlioz's monumental *Les Troyens*, the *New York Times* proclaimed Jessye Norman "a soprano of magnificent presence who commanded the stage at every moment." Next came a triumphant New Year's Eve performance (again at the Met) in the title role of Strauss's *Ariadne auf Naxos*. Norman's artistry and musicality encompass a wide variety of styles and moods. "I'm not interested in so-called mainstream repertory.... The fact is I adore the unusual. But more importantly, I must be fully involved in everything I do. For me, it's the only way." The "dyed-in-the-wool Democrat" sang at President Reagan's swearing-in ceremony in January 1985.

Born 15 September 1945 in Augusta, Georgia, Norman trained at Howard University, Baltimore's Peabody Conservatory and the University of Michigan. Finding her earliest success abroad (in 1968 she was awarded first prize in the International Music Competition of the German Broadcasting Corporation in Munich and in 1969 Norman made her operatic debut at the prestigious Deutscher Opera in Berlin as Elisabeth in Wagner's *Tannhauser*), Norman made London her home base. From 1975 to 1980 she sang only orchestral engagements and lieder recitals. "I wanted to fully develop my voice," said the diva. "To galvanize myself into a performance, I must be left totally alone. I must have solitude in order to concentrate—which I consider a form of prayer.... Composers know very well what they are doing and sometimes we don't trust them as much as we should. But if you look carefully at the words and absorb them, you're halfway home already. The rest is honesty—honesty of feeling, honesty of involvement.... Of course, love is the thing that propels us all. It's what carries us along—that's the fuel."

Home is London's fashionable Belgravia section where she enjoys its "small town feeling," and noted that her resident town "is very civilized." Norman's schedule is packed with performances and recording dates (she has over 30 records to her credit) but she still "of course" has time for a very private personal life. "All I will say is that I'm very happy, perhaps a bit spoiled and unmarried. I will also say that I'm a religious person and I hope this fact can be sensed and felt through my work."

Marsha Norman

"I have never been on the point of committing suicide," says Marsha Norman, "but I have thought about it. To think about it is to think about life as a possession to do with as you see fit." The playwright's *'night Mother,* winner of the 1983 Pulitzer Prize, was a controversial hit. The two-character intermissionless drama concerns a suicide-bent woman calmly putting her affairs in order—including attempting to explain the reasons for her impending act to her understandably distraught mother. Norman doesn't feel *'night, Mother* endorses suicide, an act she considers "merely the business of the person who commits it." The play was made into a film in 1986.

Born Marsha Williams (circa 1947), the eldest of four in a Louisville, Kentucky fundamentalist family, Norman grew up cautious about expressing her own more liberal views. She took refuge in books and essay writing, and majored in philosophy—a subject she still pursues—at Agnes Scott College in Decatur, Georgia. While there she volunteered in an Atlanta hospital's pediatric burn unit and later worked with mentally ill children in Kentucky. She also wrote a children's column for the *Louisville Times.* "People were always hiring me to do things I did not know how to do," Norman says modestly. In 1977 Jon Jory invited her to write her first play for his Actors Theatre in Louisville. The result, *Getting Out,* became an off-Broadway hit in 1979.

Divorced in 1974 from English teacher Michael Norman (after 4 years of marriage), her second husband is Louisville department store heir Dan Byck, who left the family business to produce *'night, Mother.* They enjoy playing piano-clarinet duets. The petite, affable Norman collects antique quilts, Indian rugs and ceramics, and knits when nervous. Of *'night, Mother,* she says, "I thought this was a play that no one would ever want to see, so there were no compromises to be made." The play, though not without humor, is grim. But Norman doesn't believe people go to the theater just to be entertained. "There are a lot of other sources of entertainment—cheaper and quicker. . . . People come to the theatre for conformation of their views of the human condition." Other works include a musical, *Shakers,* and a book *The Fortune Teller* (1987).

Chuck Norris

"Do what has to be done without complaint and think only postively. Don't allow yourself to think negatively," says movie tough guy Chuck Norris, known for his action-thriller movies and his knowledge of the martial-arts. In 1987, he toured the talk shows and chatted up his autobiography hardcover, *The Secret of Inner Strength: My Story.* This paean to the power of positive thinking, co-written with Hollywood veteran Joe Hyams, gives the lowdown on how the author progressed from collecting kudos for his karate skills to become a popular box office hitmaker. The biographical details are interspersed with philosophical nuggets and conclude with a two-page listing of "Chuck Norris's Code of Ethics." "A true champion can deal with his failures and losses as well as with his successes, and he learns from both."

Born, equal parts Irish and Cherokee Indian, in Ryan, Oklahoma in 1940, the youngster christened Carlos Ray Norris dates his life's true beginning to the early 60's when he joined the Air Force and was sent to Korea. It was during this overseas stint that he became interested in the martial arts and when he obtained his Black Belt in karate; it "changed my entire outlook on life. I realized there was nothing I couldn't achieve if I just had the determination and persistence." After his discharge, Norris began to pursue karate professionally and, in 1968, became the World Middleweight Champion, a title he held until his retirement from competition in 1974. "A combination of discipline and learning leads to confidence. Remember that everyone is a beginner at some point in his life; even your teacher was once a pupil."

Operating a karate school in Los Angeles, Norris soon attracted a number of celebrity pupils (including the entire Osmond family) and it was Steve McQueen who pointed him toward an acting career. After making his movie debut with another friend, Bruce Lee, in *Return of the Dragon,* he appeared in several martial-arts action releases. The karate whiz graduated to the status of action hero in the Clint Eastwood/Charles Bronson mold in 1984, when he first portrayed the battle-scarred Vietnam vet, Colonel James Braddock, in the hit, *Missing in Action.* He later reprised the role in a "prequel" called *Missing in Action 2: The Beginning,* and other Norris-starrers have been *The Delta Force, Invasion, U.S.A., Braddock: Missing in Action III,* and *Hero and the Terror.* With his wife Dianne, he has two children.

William Norwich

"A lot of people have worked for Mr. Blackwell, including yours truly . . . I had just gotten a graduate degree in poetry, of all things, when Amy Penn hooked penniless me up with Mr. Blackwell. I spent the next year writing biographical sketches for the 1986 *Celebrity Register;*" William Norwich reminisced in his *Daily News* column on 5 May 1989. Less than four years later, Norwich has stepped into the main body of the book as a celebrity.

The only child of elderly parents, William Goldberg was born on 18 July 1954 in Norwich, Connecticut. He attended Pomfret School with the Kennedy clan and went on to the exclusive Hampshire College. By the time he came to New York in his twenties, his trust fund had run dry forcing the aspiring writer to hold various jobs—teaching, writing for a punk rock magazine, and selling books at Fiorucci. He finally sold a film script which brought in the cash for creative writing courses at Columbia. Changing his name to Norwich (as he notes, "Now it's Billy Norwich from Goldberg, CT.), he began to move in the right circles. After earning his M.F.A. from Columbia University, he worked briefly for Eugenia Sheppard.

When Suzy left the *Daily News* in 1985 for the *Post,* columnist Liz Smith recommended Norwich for the position. He began his five-day-a-week column in November of that year with enthusiasm. As society columnist about town, he reports the goings-on of the wealthy set. Called the "Gilding Contractor" by *Harper's & Queen,* he "expands on arguably the most extravagant, richest group of people on earth." He is at ease talking about the famous group:

"Supposedly acting on advice from Queen Elizabeth, Diana, Princess of Wales, has had the metal fillings in her gleaming gnashers replaced with ceramic composite ones."

"The latest from Monaco's madcap summer scene concerns Prince Albert's newest pastime. The heir apparent has taken up bronco riding at his family's farm."

"Lots of other Americans were in London. Robert and Blaine Trump were there doing the polo circuit, Kitty Carlisle Hart was catching up on all the hot plays. . . "

"Oh, what a beautiful morning it is for billionaires, their second wives, and noted chief executive officers fated for Malcolm Forbes' million-dollar magic carpet ride to Tangier."

Humble and honest, the writer works comfortably from his New York apartment—complete with a screen hooked up to his editor, Margaret Farley at the *Daily News.* In 1989 he started writing a monthly column about America for *Harper's & Queen* (the British monthly magazine). Adding another dimension to his career, his revealing caricatures of some of the town's wealthy set were featured in a *New York* magazine article "Billy's Pen Pals" in April 1989. With pen in hand, William Norwich has the flair to write on.

Rudolf Nureyev

"I possess a certain quality, a mastery over what I do. It would be a crime to hide a precious thing," was the response in 1984 to the mere suggestion that it might be time for him to hang up his dancing slippers. Rudolf Nureyev won't hear of it—or perhaps like the ballerina in *The Red Shoes*, he simply can't stop dancing. "From the age of eight I can truthfully say I was possessed," he wrote in his biography and years later, he admits the "blind passion" for the dance is still there. If anything, he has increased his workload, staging new productions of the great classical repertory for companies throughout the world, and guiding the fortunes of the Paris Opera Ballet, of which he was made director in 1983. Just as Petipa the Frenchman elevated Russia to the ballet capital of the world, so this Tartar has been charged with restoring the French company to its former glory. In 1988 he was honored by the New York City Ballet in "Nureyev: A Celebration."

The Paris man about town, habitué of Maxim's, and owner of an apartment overlooking the Seine, was born 17 March 1938 on a train carrying his soldier father to Vladivostok. Raised in cruel poverty in the Tartar village of Ufa in the Urals, Nureyev's one solace from "always being hungry and cold" was to listen to music by the hour. He saw his first ballet at eight, and from that moment on, he recalls, "I had to dance—there was nothing else." Although a talented folk dancer, he didn't get to audition for the school of Leningrad's famed Kirov Ballet until the relatively advanced age of 17, but soon became the school's most gifted (and incorrigible) student. Three years later he won the national classical ballet contest in Moscow and was offered a soloist's position with both the Bolshoi and the Kirov, choosing the Kirov over the Bolshoi's "mere athletes, record breakers with marvelous muscles of steel but no heart." Another three years were to pass before the "Kirov's cosmonaut," as he was dubbed by French critics during the company's European tour in 1961, performed his grandest jeté over a fence at Paris' LeBourget airport and defected to the West. Since that day, neither he nor the West has been the same. Whether alone or in tandem with Margot Fonteyn in the "celestial accident" of their famous partnership, Nureyev set the ballet world on its collective ear. His Dinoysian qualities, his self-described Tartar mixture of "brutality and tenderness," his unquenchable ego, the force that was Nureyev could not be contained withing the confines of one ballet company or one dance form. He experimented with modern dance. He made motion pictures—*The Bible* (1964); *The Dancer* (1970); *Exposed* (1982). He traveled with the jet set. He was a media favorite. He could name his price for appearances in the four corners of the world. But everywhere he went, as he told John Gruen in a *New York Times* interview, "I am an intruder. I am an intruder in the West. I am an intruder in every company. Always, I intrude and always I am made to feel this. It is not a pleasant sensation." Perhaps it can never be pleasant for someone who, in the words of ballet writer Alexander Brand, is "not just one more dancer of first class talent. He is something much more rare. He is one of those strange, haunted artists that ballet throws up from time to time, dancers through whom some intense urgent message seems to be passing. Such individual performers are not always the easiest to fit into organizations, or even into society. But what they have to contribute is unique."

The Oak Ridge Boys

The history of the Oak Ridge Boys has been one of progression and change since their 1945 inception as a country/gospel group in Knoxville, Tennessee. They've had over 40 members while segueing from a successful albeit controversial gospel group (winning 12 Dove Awards between 1969 and 1973 and 4 Grammy Awards for Best Vocal Performance 1971-1979) to the present day popular country quartet comprised of lead singer Duane Allen, bass Richard Sterban, tenor Joe Bonsall and, its newest member, baritone Steve Sanders.

The group's senior member, joining in May 1966, is Duane David Allen, born 29 April 1943 in Taylortown, Texas. Allen started singing at age four with his family in church. He had formal operatic and quartet school training before becoming a professional singer. From 1963-65 while juggling the roles of DJ/Music Director and ad salesman for KPLT Radio in Paris, Texas, Allen earned a B.S. in Music from East Texas University (1965). In addition to singing, 6' brown-haired, blue-eyed Allen plays guitar and piano. Aside from music, he has co-authored *The History of Gospel Music* (1971) and his role as the group's business leader kept the Oaks out of bankruptcy during their transitional period from gospel to country in the 1970's.

Richard Anthony Sterban was born 24 April 1943 in Camden, New Jersey. Prior to joining the Oaks in 1972, Sterban belonged to several gospel groups, most notably *The Stamps* who backed up Elvis Presley. Besides his vocal contributions, especially on platinum single "Elvira" and the gold single "Bobbie Sue", Sterban plays a variety of musical instruments—the trumpet, baritone horn, french horn and E-flat sousaphone. The 5'10" brown-haired, blue-eyed Sterban is noted for his fashionable style and is often called upon to model. He also has an avid interest in sports and is a partner in two minor league teams, the Nashville Sounds and the Greensboro Hornets.

Joseph Sloan Bonsall, Jr. was born 18 May 1948 in Philadelphia, Pennsylvania. He made his public debut at age six on a local amateur TV show the "Horn & Hardart Hour." A member of the Keystone Quartet 1966-1973 (where he sang briefly with Richard Sterban), he joined the Oaks in 1973. The 5'11" brown-haired, brown-eyed Bonsall's energetic personality and unique tenor sound have become Oaks trademarks. He plays the piano and is developing his songwriting ability, contributing two songs to the *Christmas Again* (1986) album.

The Oaks newest member, replacing William Lee Golden in spring 1987, Steve Sanders was born 17 September circa 1952 in Richland, Georgia. "Little Stevie Sanders" began a solo career at age five, belting out gospel songs on the professional circuit. He landed the starring role on Broadway in *The Yearling* at age twelve, enjoying a two-year run. It was followed by a role in Otto Preminger's 1967 film *Hurry, Sundown* and TV appearances including "Gunsmoke." By age sixteen, Sanders realized that there was a lack of good acting roles. He returned to the gospel circuit, but he became disenchanted with it and at age nineteen he formed a pop group with Mylon Lefevre. They went to England where they worked with acts like Steve Winwood's *Traffic* and *The Who*. Songwriting ambitions eventually brought him to Nashville, where he later joined the Oaks band as lead singer during featured portions of their stage show and as rhythm guitarist for five years. The 5'11" blond, blue-eyed Sanders brings a soulful quality to the Oaks sound. Besides guitar, he also plays the piano.

Since signing with MCA records in 1977 as a country group, the Oaks have released over 30 singles and 17 albums. Nine of the albums from their first one *Y'All Come Back Saloon* (1977, winner of Academy of Country Music Best Album), *Together* (1980), *Bobbie Sue* (1982), *Oak Ridge Boys Christmas* (1982), *Greatest Hits 2* (1984) and four others have been certified gold; two, *Greatest Hits* (1980) and *Fancy Free* (1981) were certified platinum. They were named the Academy of Country Music's Best Vocal Group (1977, 1979), CMA Vocal Group of the Year (1978), American Music Award Country Group of the Year (1982) as well as Best Country Group by AGVA (1981), Disc Jockey Awards (1980), Juke Box Operators of America (1980), Radio & Records Country Music Poll (1978-1980), Radio Programmers Choice (1981), Performance Magazine Readers Poll (1981), and The Nashville Network (1988) among others. "Elvira" was named Best Single or Song of the Year by the CMA and it was also the most performed song of 1981, earning it the BMI award. It brought the Oaks the Grammy in 1982 for Best Vocal Performance Country Group or Duo. *Billboard* awarded them the Breakthrough Award (1977) and named them #1 Country Group (1978, 1980) and #1 Country Group—Singles and Albums (1980). Cashbox named them Country Vocal Group Singles (1978, 1979, 1980) and Albums

(1979, 1981), Country Crossover Group Pop singles & albums ('81) and Country Crossover Group Singles ('83).

All of the Oak Ridge Boys reside near Hendersonville, Tennessee in the greater Nashville area. In his spare time, Allen collects antique automobiles housed in the "Ace On Wheels" museum, loves gardening, sports and hopes to own a private zoo. He is married with two children. Bonsall, married with a daughter, enjoys bicycling, water skiing and pro sports. Sanders fishes and scuba dives and Sterban, recently married, pursues his sports and fashion interests.

Joyce Carol Oates

"Writing is an absolutely fascinating activity, an immersion in drama, language and vision," says this master storyteller. Joyce Carol Oates has enthralled her readers in over a dozen novels, several collections of short stories, poetry, plays and literary criticism. Oates has been a frequent recipient of the prestigious O. Henry Award and her novel *them* (1969) received a National Book Award. Also a member of the American Academy and Institute of Arts and Letters, Oates was hailed by one critic as ". . . the finest American novelist, man or woman since Faulkner. . . ." Some of her books include: *Bellefleur* (1980), *A Bloodsmoor Romance* (1982), *Last Days* (1984), *Solstice* (1985), *Mysteries of Winterthurn* (1985), *Marya: A Life* (1986), *On Boxing* (1987), *You Must Remember This* (1987), *Woman Writer: Occasions & Opportunities* (1988) and *American Appetites* (1989). Along with the notable accolades has come some harsh criticism centering on what critics call Oates' preoccupation with violence and gore. Oates defends her manner of writing insisting that her art is a reflection of American life—"Why should a novelist be criticized for writing about what she sees? . . . When people say there is too much violence in Oates, what they are saying is there is too much reality in life." The Princeton professor explains simply her philosophy on writing—"Good writing comes from interior commitment. First comes the emotional and the spiritual need to write . . . and as one gets older, the mind turns to publishing as an extension of the artistic impulse. . . . If you are a writer, you locate yourself behind a wall of silence and no matter what you are doing, driving a car or walking or doing housework . . . you can still be writing because you have that space."

Born in Lockport, New York, 16 June 1938, she dismisses her childhood as "dull, ordinary, nothing people would be interested in." Yet one gets from her works the weird impression that, far from being dull and ordinary, her youth may have been marred by incidents she chooses not to recall—or reveal. "A great deal frightened me," she adds cryptically. At Syracuse University, which she entered in 1956 under a New York State Regents' Scholarship, she majored in English. She obtained her M.A. in English from the University of Wisconsin, where she studied under a Knapp Scholarship in 1961. Earlier in that year she married Raymond Smith, and shortly after, Oates produced her first novel *With Shuddering Fall*. The couple taught at the University of Detroit (1962-1967) and the University of Windsor (1967-1978, during which time Oates published twenty-seven books) and in 1978 moved to Princeton. "She is quiet, almost timorous," wrote *Newsweek*, "occasionally remote in self-defense when asked questions that invade her carefully guarded inner life. She endures interviews, her eyes staring away like some trapped bird unable to focus on the enemy. Her diffident, controlled exterior conceals a fiery intensity. Only the pen unleashes it." Oates and her husband (a professor of 18th century literature) reside on the outskirts of Princeton where they also run a small book-publishing press (an offshoot of "The Ontario Review" a literary journal they founded in 1974).

Billy Ocean

Although a quiet man who shuns publicity, Billy Ocean is making waves on at least two continents with his music. Since 1976 when his second single "Love Really Hurts without You," climbed to number two in the U.K. and to number twelve on the American Pop Chart, Ocean has continued to have worldwide hits. When he is not singing his own songs, Ocean is writing them. Along with Trinidad-born Keith Diamond, Ocean wrote and recorded the album *Suddenly* which was completed in early 1984. It's first single, "Caribbean Queen," became a hit across the world reaching number one in the U.S. on Pop, Dance and Black Charts, and was certified Gold. It reached number six (silver status) in the U.K. Two other singles from the *Suddenly* album, "Loverboy" and "Suddenly," both soared to the single digit spots on the charts in both countries. The album itself spent more than one year on the American Pop Album Chart. The Grammy Award winner (for the single "Caribbean Queen") has also had his works performed by the Nolans, Latoya Jackson, The Dells and Lenny Williams.

Ocean, born in Trinidad in 1952, discovered music at an early age and when a friend of his mother bought him a blue ukulele he joined in, playing with his musical family. His rich calypsonian heritage was to come out later in his music. At the age of seven, the family moved to London's East End where Ocean was exposed to the pop music of The Beatles and The Rolling Stones. He also discovered American soul singers such as Otis Redding and Sam Cooke who influenced Ocean's future style. After spending more time in the music room at school instead of the classroom, Ocean left school and took a job as an apprentice cutter in the tailoring world. Fortunately, Ocean's employer saw other budding skills and loaned Ocean thirty pounds to buy his first piano. Ocean stayed in tailoring only until the release of his first single in 1974, under the pseudonym "Scorched Earth." Ocean's first release under his own name was in 1975. Although it wasn't very successful, the songs showed enough promise and there was sufficient interest in it for the record company to allow Ocean to record "Love Really Hurts Without You" the following year. Ocean and his manager, Laurie Jay, raised their own financing to record the single "Feel Like Getting Down" after his record company rejected the song. It rose to number five on the American R&B Charts in 1982, and the track was included on Jane Fonda's Work-out album. Still breaking records, Ocean's recording of the theme from *Jewel of the Nile* reached number one in the U.S. and stayed number one in the U.K. for four weeks.

Still a resident of England, Ocean's 1986 U.K. tour, his third tour since 1985, was sold out. Popularity has come to the quiet man from Trinidad. With seven hits in a row in the U.S., six in the Top 10 Pop Charts and the popularity of his album *Love Zone*, Ocean may have to change his feelings about publicity.

Carroll O'Connor

His ten-season run as the beer-drinking, bigoted Archie Bunker—beefy, middle-aged, and lower-middle-class, with about as much room for "them-not-his-own-kind"—on the TV show "All in the Family" and then, later, "Archie Bunker's Place," was the quintessence of characterization, an American archetype of all seasons. "I'm not playing him to make people hate him for his attitude," he said of Archie, "or to make them like him, either. I'm just playing his attitude as truthfully as I know how." O'Connor won an Emmy as best comedy actor in the 1971-72 season and was nominated many more times for the same award.

A veteran of nearly 30 feature films and more than 100 TV programs, this New York born actor, 2 August 1924, was spotted in a college production at the National University of Dublin, where he was studying for his B.A., and offered a part in a play at the Gate Theater. He stayed with The Gate for three years, then went on to act in plays in London, Paris, Edinburgh and New York. Of people who now connect his name with his face, he says, "I was in a very old-fashioned department store and two elderly ladies spotted me. 'We always watch you, Mr. O'Connor,' they said. 'We don't always like you, but we always watch you.'"

When Archie went the way of worldwide re-runs a la "I Love Lucy," O'Connor who is a licensed English teacher, went on to write and star in a 1973 televison version of "The Last Hurrah," publish an autobiography in 1981, play in and direct *Brothers* on Broadway in 1983 and return to the Great White Way in 1984 in James Duff's *The War at Home*. In 1985 he starred in the CBS-TV series "Brass". Although the actor underwent heart bypass surgery at Emory University Hospital in March 1989, he continues to be active in the industry. His NBC-TV show "In the Heat of the Night" was a favorite for the 1988-1989 season.

John Cardinal O'Connor

John Cardinal O'Connor, archbishop of New York: "The people plead for bread; we must not give them stones. . . . The pulpit is not the place for theological speculation. Our people are crying for fundamentals. They hear too many uncertain trumpets, are misled by too many pied pipers."

When Pope John Paul appointed the bishop of Scranton, Pennsylvania, as spiritual overseer of the 1.8 million Catholics in the rich, grand archdiocese of New York, few—including O'Connor—were prepared. At 64, O'Connor was considered old for the position. A third of the diocese's faithful speak Spanish as their first language; O'Connor promised to start learning the tongue (and he did). And most of his experience as an administrator had been military. He spent 30 years as a Navy and Marine Corps chaplain, retiring from the Navy with the rank of Rear Admiral. But O'Connor could not hide his sense of humor. "I've been a devout Catholic all my life, and never once did I ever question the Holy Father's decision's—until now," he said of his appointment. He was named a prince of the Church in May 1985.

Those who fear that the church has become too liberal have rejoiced at the archbishop's positions, particularly on abortion. He was responsible for toning down the language of the national bishops' committee statement concerning nuclear war; he challenged the position of the Democratic Vice Presidential candidate Geraldine Ferraro that a Catholic could personally oppose abortion yet vote for legislation that would allow others this choice. The cardinal wears an ever-present red rose on his lapel, a symbol of the Right-To-Life movement. One Catholic journalist called O'Connor "a mirror image of the pope: they're both masculine, active guys. The Pope skis; O'Connor plays golf. They are both strongly anti-Communist, pretty liberal on social justice, and very conservative on family life issues."

Born 15 January 1920 to a working class family in Philadelphia, young John's family had mixed feelings about his decision to enter the priesthood. "The discipline was constant; you were never sure you were going to make it," he recalls of the St. Charles Borromeo Seminary in Overbrook, Pennsylvania, which ordained him in 1945. He spent his first few years as a priest teaching high school and working towards a master's degree in clinical psychology and then a doctorate in political science at Georgetown. When Cardinal O'Hara of Philadelphia encouraged his priests to become military chaplains during the Korean War, O'Connor volunteered. "I served on almost everything-destroyers, cruisers, carriers-and truly enjoyed the duty," he told the New York *Daily News* soon after he was appointed archbishop. With the help of Nat Hentoff, O'Connor wrote the book *John Cardinal O'Connor: At the Storm Center of a Changing American Catholic Church in 1988*.

Sandra Day O'Connor

"Ah, the tombstone question," smiled Sandra Day O'Connor after members of the Senate Judiciary Committee asked during her confirmation hearings in September 1981 as Associate Justice, how she wished to be remembered. She retorted: "I hope it says, 'Here lies a good judge!'" Then she added; "I hope I am remembered as the first woman who served on the Supreme Court." With such grace, intuition and smarts, the Arizona-born lawyer has managed to be at once the conservative's champion and the feminists' choice. On 21 September 1981 she was appointed unanimously as the first woman in the 191-year history of the Supreme Court. Writing of her appointment, the *New York Times* said: "Of the ways in which Sandra O'Coonor is different from the other Justices, her political savvy, relative youth, and continued openness to the world at large are at least as significant as gender. Sex may turn out to be the least important difference of all." Yet to no one's surprise, much speculation has been raised on how the first justice to wear a skirt sees the important social issues of today. She votes for the most part with the court's conservatives. Yet she does not fear to dissent. Discrimination against women was a major concern of Mrs. O'Connor as an Arizona state legislator and state appeals judge. She has put judicial muscle behind the state's rights movement. She finds abortion "personally repugnant," but doesn't equate her own view with how the law should limit what feminists call "reproductive freedom."

Born 26 March 1930 in El Paso, Texas, Sandra Day and her two younger brothers grew up on a ranch that lacked electricity and dated back to the 1880s. She learned to ride horseback, to round up cattle, although she hesitated to do "all the things that boys did." She admits though, that she did "fix windmills and repair fences." Her parents thought she was too bright for rural schooling; a private education led to Stanford University, where she majored in economics and continued at law school. She met John Jay O'Connor 3rd on the Stanford *Law Review*. They married in 1952. The couple (they have three sons), is firmly ensconsed on the "A" list of Washington hostesses.

Claes Oldenburg

He established his reputation as a wildly inventive creator during the Pop Art era with his larger-than-life, unorthodox sculptures—banana sundaes; gooey wedges of pecan pie; hamburgers; cheeseburgers; soggy, baggy toilets and washstands. Now his attention has turned to visionary drawings for huge urban monuments, many of which have become a reality: "Flashlight," a 38-foot-high flashlight in Las Vegas; a 45-foot-high clothespin erected across from Philadelphia's city hall; "Batcolumn," a 101-foot-tall baseball bat placed in front of Chicago's new Social Security Building, a monument to baseball and industry which began as a study of classical columns and "Hat in Three Stages of Landing," placed in a grassy field in front of the Salinas Community Center in California. Oldenburg collaborates on his sculptures with his second wife, Cossje Bruggen, a Dutch art historian.

Born 28 January 1929 in Stockholm, Oldenburg had his first exposure to what he views as the American preoccupation with snack food and plumbing when his father was appointed Swedish Consul General in Chicago. He attended school in the Midwest and then went east to Yale, but it was while working as a summer dishwasher at Provincetown on Cape Cod that he began to consider dishes of food as art objects. He set up shop in New York in the early 1960s and began producing the high-calorie models that thrust him into the vanguard of the burgeoning Pop Art movement. In 1977 a new creative process was emerging for Oldenburg—that year he began his partnership with his wife (they met in 1970 when an Oldenburg retrospective traveled to an Amsterdam museum where she was assistant curator). Two years in Holland gave Oldenburg a new perspective on his art. "I rediscovered the seriousness about life that I associated with Europe. I became more interested in politics and ideas and more critical of my production. The early 70s began to look a bit formalistic, escapist." His contemporary icons begin in the studio as scale models—they are then taken to Lippincott in New Haven, Connecticut where engineers translate them into mechanical drawings. A large project may take Oldenburg and his wife two years to complete so there are always several in the works at once. A recent piece has fueled much controversy in Vail, Colorado where local residents attempted to "un-Vail" Oldenburg's proposal for a giant fishing pole and tin can. Outcome: the pole, complete with taut line and tin can, was OK'd.

Oldenburg, Cossje and her two children live quietly on Manhattan's Lower West Side in two adjoining loft buildings.

Richard Oldenburg

His brother Claes is the one whose floppy, flabby sculptural forms are in such high favor with collectors. Richard is the one who minds the museum. Taking over as director of New York's Museum of Modern Art in 1972, he's guided that tempest-tossed institution during the period of its greatest expansion. MOMA's striking new home (in planning for seven years; in actual construction for five, and dedicated in May 1984) is, according to Paul Goldberger, architectural critic of the *New York Times,* "of great importance for the cultural life not only of New York but of the world." It also represents "the largest and perhaps the final, step in the gradual movement of modernism from the role of outsider in our culture to that of insider.... Now, both modern art and modern architecture have become the establishment...."

Born 21 September 1933 in Stockholm, Richard Oldenburg came to the U.S. with his family at the age of three when his consular officer father was posted to Chicago. Influenced in part by brother Claes's disenchantment with Yale, he chose to go to Harvard, spent a year of Army service "vigorously defending the border in El Paso as a battery clerk," and then came to New York to pursue a career in publishing. Married in 1960 to the former Lisa Turnure, he worked at Doubleday and Macmillan before joining MOMA in 1969 as director of publications, overseeing the largest publishing program of any museum in the world. Despite its grand new size, he still sees his museum as being unusually accessible—"a place where you can see the whole development of the modern movement, but which you feel you can still capture, at least remotely, on a single visit."

Jacqueline Onassis

What's better than a rainbow in Manhattan? Spotting Jackie O somewhere. Most New Yorkers have a story, recalled with photographic detail. "I'd been to the Metropolitan. It was a Tuesday afternoon, I'd taken off early from work to see the Vatican show.... I stopped at a coffee shop on Madison. Just a coffee shop, a greasy hamburger joint and, then, she came in. She walked in. To eat! At the counter! With a copy of *New York* magazine. I mean everything just stopped, even the burgers ceased their sizzling. She ate a burger, wearing a tan raincoat and black pants and she had, I think it was, a Gucci shoulder bag and a Cartier tank watch and..."

Yes, America, Jackie O eats hamburgers too. The woman who was revered as John F. Kennedy's widow and denounced for marrying the late shipping tycoon Aristotle Onassis, is on her own, a woman of the '80s, a master of detachment, a private citizen, loyal relative and friend, a working editor, a successful mother (notes one insider: "Jackie's an amazing mother. She cares. She's always been there for those kids and regardless of what those kids have been through they are fabulous people, a bit shy, wouldn't you be, but not in the least bit tricky"), and still, when it comes to celebrity she is the reigning star. She's also the proud grandmother to Caroline and Edwin Schlossberg's darling daughter, Rose Kennedy Schlossberg (born 25 June 1988). Her son, John, Jr. graduated law school in 1989.

America has experienced the depths and heights of tragedy with her. Jacqueline Onassis' story is legendary. Born 28 July 1929 in East Hampton, Long Island, she was named after her stockbroker father, John ("Black Jack") Bouvier. She attended Chapin, Vassar and graduated from George Washington University. The young beauty came out in 1947; columnist Cholly Knickerbocker called her "Queen Deb of the Year." When mother Janet divorced Bouvier, Jackie and sister Lee (Princess Radziwill) lived with mom and their new stepfather Hugh Auchincloss in Newport and Washington. As the "Inquiring Camera Girl" on the *Washington Times Herald* in 1952 she earned $42.50 a week, interviewing people like Richard Nixon and John F. Kennedy. Her 1953 wedding to Kennedy in Newport was the "Wedding of the Year." As First Lady she spent $2 million renovating the White House, rode an elephant in India, and so fascinated the world that her husband introduced himself in France as, "the man who accompanied Jacqueline Kennedy to Paris." Her bouffant hairdo and pillbox hats were her trademark. She miscarried in 1955. In 1956, a child was stillborn; an infant son named Patrick died 39 hours after birth in 1963. Then, 1,000 days of Camelot later, assassin's bullets on 22 November 1963 ended the idyll.

She stayed on at The White House because she had "no place to go," she commented at that time. "My major effort must be devoted to my children," she told a reporter. "If Caroline and John turn out badly, nothing I could do in the public eye would have any meaning." Four months after Robert F. Kennedy was killed in June 1968, she married Aristotle Onassis on his private island of Skorpios. Instantly she became the Empress of the Jet Set. The American public and press openly disapproved of her marriage. "You know, nobody could understand why I married Ari," she reportedly told a friend of her children. "I just couldn't live anymore as the Kennedy widow. It was a release, freedom from the oppressive obsession with me and the children." Most of their marriage was spent apart. When he died he left the bulk of his vast fortune to his daughter Christina. Jackie fought for—and got—more. Six months later she went to work as a $200-a-week consulting editor at Viking Press. She now works at Doubleday and divides her time between Peapack, New Jersey, where she hunts on weekends with the Essex Hounds, her secluded place on Martha's Vineyard and her Fifth Avenue apartment. Her public appearances are calculated to promote a cause of her choosing, such as saving a landmark building or drawing attention to one of her book projects.

Ryan O'Neal

What can you say about a Hollywood boy with freckles? That he is built like the best of Malibu studs; that he's got the girl all America wants (Farrah Fawcett, one son, Redmond); that he makes about one film each year (included are *Paper Moon, Love Story, The Games, What's up Doc?, Barry Lyndon, Nickelodeon, A Bridge Too Far, Oliver's Story, The Main Event, Irreconcilable Differences, Fever Pitch, Tough Guys Don't Dance* and *Chances Are*) and that he has fallen arches and wears rose-colored foot supports to prove it.

Born in Los Angeles 20 April 1941, the son of playwright-novelist Charles O'Neal and actress Patricia O'Callaghan, Ryan O'Neal grew up roving with his family in Mexico, the West Indies and England, but went to high school in Los Angeles. In 1959, while the family was in Germany, the blond with a boxer's alter-ego (he competed in the Los Angeles Golden Gloves of 1956 and 1957), he got a job as a stunt man on the TV series "Tales of the Vikings." When the series ended he went to Hollywood, worked for a while as a busboy, lined up an agent and began appearing on such TV shows as "Bachelor Father," "The Untouchables," and "My Three Sons." As Rodney Harrington, the good-looking bad boy on television's first prime-time soap, "Peyton Place," he became the nation's leading weekly heartthrob.

Roving photographers and assorted others must not come too close or they are likely to receive an O'Neal autograph: below-the-belt epithets or a sharp right. Ryan served 51 days in a Lincoln Heights, California, pesthouse for assault and battery on an unfriendly stranger at a 1960s New Year's Eve party. In 1964, he took out a New Orleans entertainment writer with one punch. In 1983 he removed his son Griffin's two front teeth in an altercation over some missing stereo equipment. Soon after, the son was sent off to a drug rehabilitation center in Hawaii. Griffin is his son from his first marriage to Joanna Moore. He starred with their daughter Tatum in *Paper Moon*. She got the Oscar. His second wife was the beauteous Leigh Taylor-Young; one son Patrick.

Lately he asserts a calmer facade. "Farrah pulled the rug out from under me," he says. "For the first time in my life, something took precedence over myself."

Tatum O'Neal

Since her blast-off in *Paper Moon* (1975), she's no longer "Ryan's daughter." She was only 10 years old when director Peter Bogdanovich told Ryan, "If you don't let her play it (Addie Loggins in *Paper Moon*), I don't want you for the picture." Ryan had been reluctant because he didn't know if she could act or even if she wanted to be an actress; as it turned out she was overjoyed at the offer but later admitted she didn't know making a picture was hard work. "If I knew after a week on location, I wouldn't have taken the job." (She thought since you see a movie in a day, it should be finished in a day.) In her next two films, *Bad News Bears* (1976) and *Nickelodeon* (1976), she did nothing more than play herself. "A brat." *International Velvet* (sequel to the original *National Velvet* that shot 12-year-old Elizabeth Taylor to stardom) was made when Tatum was 14 and "was really Tatum's first crack at acting" according to one critic. Interviewed during the shoot she explained, " . . . I also get to wear nice clothes. I have a boyfriend and you'll see my very first screen kiss. There is no sex or even heavy petting in 'Velvet.'" She pulled off *Velvet* and the ensuing *Little Darlings* (in which she and Kristy McNichol wager which one will be the first to lose her virginity at summer camp) and *Circle of Two* (both 1979 releases).

Born 5 November 1963, she was named after her mother's (Joanna Moore) grandmother. ("I'd rather be named Elizabeth.") Neither parent pushed her toward acting. Said Ryan, "She will not become an adult with a bankrupt childhood." In fact she never had an acting lesson. Her ambition at one time was to be a great actress or a secretary, *Time* reported, and she's continued her screen appearances into the 80s (*Captured*, 1981; *Certain Fury*, 1985). She has lived with her father in the past but in 1984 set up housekeeping in Malibu with tennis ace John McEnroe. The couple married in Oyster Bay, Long Island on 1 August 1986 and have two sons (Kevin Jack and Sean Timothy). She has a brother, Griffin, two years her junior, a stepbrother Patrick, five years her junior (from Ryan's second wife, Leigh Taylor-Young) and another stepbrother, Redmond, whose mother is Farrah Fawcett.

Jennifer O'Neill

This cover-girl-turned-actress experienced one of her most memorable career highs in 1971 in a part in which she was visible on screen for only eleven minutes, but for which she received rave notices. The film was the quintessentially "nostalgic, first-teenage-love" picture, *The Summer of '42*, in which she played a luminously beautiful young war widow, subject of an adolescent's crush. Even today many men, hearing Michel Legrand's Oscar-winning title song from the movie, automatically dream of girls who look like Jennifer O'Neill. O'Neill herself, in fact, may have some nostalgic yearnings for her "summer" days. Both her career and her life, since then, have had a number of plunging downs. One of the worst was when Jon-Erik Hexum, her co-star on the 1984-85 CBS-TV series, "Cover-Up," accidentally shot himself to death on the set. The tragedy was a grim parallel to her own "accidental" self-inflicted gunshot wound to the stomach in 1982, which led to a headline-making trial and a divorce and also kept her away from the cameras for some time. "A pattern of mine used to be terrific highs and lows," the actress once said. "Now I operate more in the middle. You sacrifice some fantastic highs, but you get rid of the lows."

Jennifer Lee O'Neill was born in Rio de Janeiro on 20 February 1948, and raised in the suburban expanses north of New York City. As a young girl she cleaned out stables to pay for her own horse and, in her teens, became a trophy-winning equestrienne. Also in her teens she became a top model ("The money was terrific, but I didn't enjoy the work, and at the end, it wasn't a challenge") and also a wife at age 17 and a mother of a baby girl two years later. But she was still able to snare the small movie parts which led up to *The Summer of '42*.

Although she says she once feared she was accident-prone, she realized later that "I was letting . . . things happen to me." Some may still view her three car accidents, serious riding fall (all resulting in a bad back) and gunshot incident more than coincidence. O'Neill's refusal to do nude scenes lost her many parts, she says. She later decided to begin a sportswear line, which fizzled, and a production company, which also failed to take flight. Divorced by the 1980s a total of five times, she married her sixth husband, Richard Alan Brown in 1986 (filed for divorce in 1989). All toll she has three children. Some of her recent movies include *I Love New York* (1986), *Committed* (1988), *Keys to Freedom* (1989) and the CBS-TV telefilm "The Red Spider" (1988).

Thomas P. O'Neill

"It was at Harvard University in 1927 that I first decided to go into politics," begins Thomas (Tip) O'Neill Jr.'s extremely candid and fascinating book, *Man of the House: The Life and Political Memoirs of Speaker Tip O'Neill* written with William Novak and published in 1987. (Mind you, O'Neill did not attend Harvard; he was mowing the lawn there, eavesdropping on the chatter of the commencement class and it convinced him he had to do something.) When one of the most extraordinary political careers of our century came to a close in 1986, O'Neill had completed 34 years as a member of Congress and a decade as Speaker of the House. In his book he shares inside stories of American politics over the past five decades.

O'Neill was married in 1941 to his high school sweetheart, Mildred Anne Miller, and their five children include Tom III, who followed his father in Bay State politics. The son of a "two-boat" (the two-boaters were those emigrants who had money enough only for passage to Nova Scotia and had to work to save up enough for the second leg to Massachusetts) bricklayer from County Cork, Tom II was born in Cambridge 9 December 1912. He was nicknamed "Tip" after an 1880s ballplayer named O'Neill who had a habit of tipping foul balls. After graduation from Boston College in 1936 he entered the insurance business and the Massachusetts Legislature, where he became, in 1948, the first Democratic Speaker of the Massachusetts House. He remained that until 1952, when he ran for the U.S. House seat being vacated by John F. Kennedy. Even his most severe critics praise his unaffected style. "It's difficult to imagine life in Washington without Thomas P. O'Neill," muses a *Nation* critic.

O'Neill's frankness and humor surfaces throughout his book. While he was writing it, he said: "What I'm trying to do is give a picture of what life is like in the United States, the power of local politics, and the fact that two thirds of the people were poor back in the 30's, and it all changed during the New Deal and President Roosevelt, and we saw the growth of the middle class . . . I wanted people to read it. So I enjoyed writing it."

Yoko Ono

"When John died, I thought it was the worst thing that could ever happen," this avant-garde artist and widow of Beatle John Lennon declared in 1984. "But that was just the beginning." Since Lennon was shot down in front of his Dakota apartment in December 1980, Yoko Ono has received sporadic death threats, her apartment was burglarized and electronically bugged, an employee stole personal papers to write a book and she lost a six-figure lawsuit. But there were bright spots, too. Her solo albums released after John's death did extremely well. In early 1984, she took son Sean on a happy sentimental journey to Liverpool to visit Lennon's youthful haunts. Also in 1984, Yoko and Sean presided over the groundbreaking for a $1 million 2.5 acre memorial garden to John Lennon in his beloved Central Park. The garden, to be planted with 25,000 strawberry plants, bears the name Strawberry Fields, after one of the Beatle's most popular songs. Inheriting John's $150 million estate, she now presides over the Lennon-Ono enterprises, giving generously to charity through the Spirit Foundation they founded and continuing the tradition she started with John of promoting world peace through newspaper ads.

Born 18 February 1933 in Tokyo, Yoko Ono moved with her affluent parents to Scarsdale, New York, when she was 19 and inhaled her first deep breath of the local art and literary atmosphere as a student at Sarah Lawrence. Supporting herself as a building superintendent and waiting tables at a macrobiotic restaurant, she became a familiar figure in gatherings of the New York avant-garde, staging "events" and giving concerts with, among others, John Cage and David Tudor. Her work includes paintings, sculpture, notational poetic writings, and what Yoko terms "Pieces," many of which require the participation of the viewer. (Sample: a row of empty flowerpots entitled "Imagine the Flowers.") Also a filmmaker of underground renown, she created such films as *Fly* (in which a housefly, in closeup, crawls across a woman's body for 23 minutes) and *Legs* (which zeros in on 331 pairs of legs). Shortly before his death, John and Yoko recorded the album *Double Fantasy* and since then, she's turned out solo albums that have won over some mainstream critics. Well known for her spiritual leanings, she takes a minutely detailed interest in her records, to the extent of using numerology to decide the number of seconds between tracks.

Previously married to film producer Anthony Cox (one daughter), Yoko met John Lennon in 1966 at a London gallery and wed him in 1969. During John's reclusive period, Yoko ran his business empire (music company, real estate, copyrights, cattle, etc.), making him the world's richest house husband. Now Yoko's ranked among the richest in the *Forbes 400* list. She considers business an extension of her art. Asked why she continues living at the Dakota, she told *People* magazine: "This is where John and I built a beautiful life for ourselves, and being here is almost like still being with John. There are still a lot of things from the life we had together that are unfinished. You just can't walk away from them."

Jerry Orbach

To his cueball pals from the pool hall—Brooklyn Joey, Johnny Eyebrows, and Hundred Ball Blackie—he is known as Jerry the Actor. But to New York's greasepaint set he is a player of no mean talent who bounced from pocket to pocket on and off Broadway for more than a decade before scoring a solid hit as the key-lending hero of *Promises, Promises* in 1968 (which netted him a Tony Award). "It's like 'Wow,'" Jerry Orbach crowed when the verdict was in. "'By gosh, you're a star!' It goes on and on 24 hours a day and it's a lot of fun . . . people get used to it. . . . I'm getting used to it." At times in the past things had been different. "Like when a television name who everybody knew was really terrible would get the lead in a big Broadway show that I wanted desperately. . . . A lot of things that went on in the business used to make me brook." But not enough to make him quit.

The son of a restaurant manager (who had once tried vaudeville himself and did not object when his son began to lean towards the stage), Jerry was born 20 October 1935 in the Bronx, and grew up in Waukegan, Illinois. He studied drama at Northwestern, worked in summer stock, and after graduation made straight for New York, where he and a friend shared a shabby flat. Pounding the pavement looking for jobs, he remembers, "we got by on peanut butter, beer and whatever food my friend brought back from parties." The Orbach star began to rise when Joel Grey's wife helped Jerry get a job as an understudy in *The Threepenny Opera* in 1955. He worked his way through seven parts to the starring role (in the process marrying Marta Curro, another understudy, and raising two sons). He married again in 1979 (Elaine Cancilla). After *Threepenny Opera*, Orbach went on to play in *The Fantasticks* (1960; he introduced the haunting "Try to Remember"), *Carnival, Scuba-Duba, Promises, Promises, 6 Rms Riv Vu, Chicago* (Tony nomination), and *42nd Street* (1980). He made a stunning screen debut in 1981 in *Prince of the City*, directed by Sidney Lumet. His recent movie credits include: *F/X* (1985), *I Love New York* (1986), *Someone to Watch Over Me* (1987), *Dirty Dancing* (1987), and *Last Exit to Brooklyn* (1989). He also starred in the CBS-TV series "The Law and Harry McGraw" (1987). The climb to the top "seems short" Orbach insists. "I was never forced into a job I didn't want. . . . I've had a good time on the way." He has also learned his craft. "I found out that real acting takes a great deal of energy and an attitude slightly bigger than life," he once explained. "Over the years this washed and washed over me. Do you see," he asks rather gently, "how a star is born overnight?"

Brian Orser

He is one of the greatest competitors in the history of figure skating. Brian has been ranked the number one free-style skater in the world since 1984.

Brian Orser was born on 18 December 1961 in Penetanguishine, Ontario. He began skating at the age of five, and within four short years he was discovered by Coach Doug Leigh. Soon following, he won the Canadian Novice Championship and the Canadian Junior Championship, as well as capturing the Canadian National Championships for a record 8 straight years. In 1978 Brian was the first man to land the Triple Axel correctly, and for the next four years he was the only skater to do so, thus it became his signature move. In 1984 Brian participated in the Winter Olympics at Sarajevo, Yugoslavia, competing against the phenomenal Scott Hamilton. Although he lost out to Scott, it was a close match. In 1985 Scott retired, giving way to a new competitor, Brian Boitano, and the two Brians have been engaged in one of

Donny Osmond

sport's great rivalries ever since. In just about every competition they have dominated the first and second place. In 1987 Brian Orser won the World Championship. Although Orser had a 7-3 edge going into the 1988 Olympics, Boitano won the Gold Medal by a slim margin, with Orser right behind placing close second, winning the Silver Medal. At the 1988 World Championship in Budapest, Orser won the long program, as well as scoring three 6.0 scores for artistic impression. The 1988 World Championship was his last amateur competition. Brian entered the realm of professional skating as the reigning World Freestyle Skating Champion. When he's not skating, Brian oversees his three Culture restaurants located in Toronto. In addition, he is the national corporate spokesperson for NutraSweet and Campbell Soup Company. Brian has received the Order of Canada (C.M.) which is the most prestigious civilian award in Canada.

Brian is single and resides in Ontario, Canada.

Donny Osmond

He sings, "I am willing to fight ... I'm a Soldier of Love," as he struggles to travel up the pop charts. In April 1989, Donny Osmond finally found the vehicle to launch his dormant career. With the release of his album *Donny Osmond* (1989) he found the perfect combination of style and songs to capture new fans and resurrect the old standbys. Ironically, it is his name, rather than his musical talent, which placed the stigma on the handsome Osmond. When "Soldier of Love" was introduced in the U.S. on New York radio station WPLJ, the programmers gave the record a spin without revealing the singer's identity. It wasn't until a personal appearance by Donny, on-the-air, that the secret vocalist was revealed. His follow-up single (with video), "Sacred Emotion," established the fact that Osmond is holding his ground, even after the public discovered that he is the name behind the songs.

Donald Clark Osmond was born in Ogden, Utah, on 9 December 1957. The seventh of nine children to George and Olive Osmond, he spent his first five years in Ogden before the family moved on to Arleta, California, then to Westwood, California, and eventually back to Utah, to reside in Provo. Joining his brothers Alan, Wayne, Merrill and Jay (the original members of the Osmond Brothers quartet), he immediately grabbed attention as the precocious member of the group. He was only four years old when he debuted on "The Andy Williams Show," on which he did an imitation of Andy singing "You Are My Sunshine." As he grew in size, so did his popularity in the pop field. As well as working with his brothers, he branched out on his own and made twelve gold albums. One of his biggest hits was the remake of "Puppy Love." When his sister, Marie, was ready to step in front of the cameras after her country hit "Paper Roses," the "Donny & Marie" TV variety program was launched to wonderful reviews. While she sang "a little bit country," he remained "a little bit rock 'n' roll." Not only did the TV show take off, but there were duet record albums, movies *(Goin' Coconuts)*, and nightclub tours. On his own, he landed on Broadway in the short-lived *Little Johnny Jones* (1982) and continued to pursue his solo career. Undaunted by the fact that peer Michael Jackson was monopolizing the airwaves, he continued to search for his next project. In 1987, Osmond met Peter Gabriel while both were participating in a UNICEF show in New York City. When Gabriel said to Donny, "I've always been intrigued with what you were going to do next with your career," Osmond followed up their conversation with a trip to Bath, England, to work with Gabriel's musicians. The result was a signing with Virgin Records UK, followed by Capitol records in the states; hence, "Soldier of Love."

Donny broke many a teenage girls heart on 8 May 1978 when he married Debra Glenn in Salt Lake City, Utah. They have one son, Donald Clark, born on 25 January 1985.

Marie Osmond

"I love country," says the famous female Osmond. "When we had the variety series ... I did a lot of different kinds of music. But long before that, I had decided country was for me. I love music. I love the people and lifestyle. And I like the fact that women can be successful in country music, and that there's some longevity to a country singer's career. That's really wonderful. It says a lot about the people, the fans, and it says a lot about the music." After exploring all types of music, Marie has settled into a comfortable country setting. Her albums *I Only Wanted You*, 1986 and *All In Love*, 1988 were both successful records, spawning hit country singles. In 1989, the chart-climbing album *Steppin' Stone* was released.

Born to Olive and George Osmond on 13 October 1959 in Ogden, Utah, she found her way into show business at age three, appearing on the "Andy Williams Show," with her brothers' singing group. "I will always cherish the way I grew up. I think I've survived without the problems lots of other child entertainers have had because I was surrounded by an incredible ten-person support system—my parents and eight brothers." She cut her first record, "Paper Roses," at age 13, and performed with the family in Las Vegas and on the "Mike Douglas Show." "The Donny and Marie Show," a hodgepodge of gag skits and music, with a little ice skating thrown in, ran from 1976 to 1979. She's hosted her own short-lived variety show and starred in a few choice television projects. Her home video "Marie Osmond's Exercises for Mothers to Be" was released in 1985. She is known for her charitble contributions, most notably as the board member of the Osmond Foundation and co-founder/chairman of the Children's Miracle Network Telethon which airs the first weekend every June. The charity raises millions of dollars for children's hospitals across the United States, Canada, Mexico, Australia and Jamaica.

Marie married Steven Craig, a former basketball player, in a well publicized wedding in 1982. After several attempts at holding their marriage together, and one son, Stephen James, the couple divorced in 1985. A year later, she married Brian Blosil (two daughters). As for the "little bit country" Osmond says, "I feel very fortunate because I can work in a business that I grew up in and love. And my career also allows me the freedom to be a mom. Since I work at night, I can be with my children during the day—all day. I feel like I have the best of all worlds."

Peter O'Toole

"From the age of sixteen, I couldn't put my foot wrong no matter how hard I tried. And I tried. I had a lot of bumps. I look at it now, and it's almost as if it were inevitable," says the actor. At age 40 he retreated to some family property in the west of Ireland, where he did nothing but plant trees for a year. After this sabbatical, he performed an assembly of plays at the Bristol Old Vic; refreshed, he found "the work was better than ever." In 1975, however, the life of ease collapsed when doctors discovered in his stomach "a sort of form of malignancy." Battling the illness which, "proved inconvenient to a few people, but there you go," he had other battles to confront. Although his two daughters and his mother-in-law continued to live with him, he and his wife of many years, actress Sian Phillips, divorced. And both his parents died. His luck changed when *My Favorite Year* was released in 1982. In it he played Alan Swann, an elegant, boozy, swashbuckling star. Critics began comparing O'Toole to John Barrymore.

Born Seamus O'Toole in County Galway, Ireland, 2 August 1933, the son of a roving bookie who finally settled with his family in the London slums, he was sent to St. Anne's in Leeds, where the nuns tried to beat discipline into him. ("I was just left-handed and, Lord how they whipped me just trying to get me to write with my other hand. Today I have no religion as such.") Quitting school at 13, he got a job in a warehouse wrapping cartons, then landed a job as a copy boy with the Yorkshire *Evening News*. ("It was a jump from being a poor slum kid to meeting people," he said.) In a 1982 *Rolling Stone* interview he amended his background. "The one thing I am *not* is working class." It's just that his father was the black sheep of an Irish Catholic family. His mother was from an aristocratic Protestant Irish family, and both met at the running of the 1929 Epson Derby in England. Still, Leeds was tough. "The bravest thing I ever did in my life was to walk through that district at the age of 11, when I was Little Lord Fauntleroy in a kilt." Following a two-year hitch with the Royal Navy, he won a scholarship to the Royal Academy of Dramatic Art in London. ("I thought I'd died and gone to heaven when I went into RADA.") Having spent three and half years with the Bristol Old Vic, he was appearing on-stage in a London production of *The Long and the Short and the Tall*, when Katharine Hepburn, having seen his performance, recommended the young actor to movie producer Sam Spiegel. O'Toole had been named 1959's Actor of the Year in London and was invited by Spiegel to test for *Lawrence of Arabia*. O'Toole arrived on the set reeking of a grog "ordinarily used to remove rust from old car bumpers," and when a pint of scotch fell out of his hip pocket, Spiegel gasped, flung his hands into the air, and rasped, "Never!" However, at the insistence of director David Lean, O'Toole got the part. Some of O'Toole's other films include *What's New Pussycat?*, *Goodbye Mr. Chips*, *Under Milkwood*, *Man of La Mancha*, cult favorite *The Ruling Class*, which was re-released in the early 1980s, *Becket*, *The Stunt Man*, *Creator* and, with Hepburn, *Lion in Winter*. Other films include *Club Paradise* (1985), *Banshee* (1985), *The Last Emperor* (1987) and *Helena* (1988). He also appeared on Broadway in *Pygmalion* (1987).

About all those stories of his legendary carousing with Richard Harris and the late Peter Finch and Richard Burton, O'Toole, who in 1983 had a son with Karen Brown, recalls: "Our hours as actors are absurd, be it stage or cinema. It's impossible to be drunk or stoned and perform at high definition. It's impossible. So the carousers that I knew—Fincy, Bob Shaw, Richard, any of them—were practically monkish during the week. Then came what we used to call collier's night out. And we went *whoopee*. And if we weren't working, we went *whoopee, whoopee, whoopee*. Yes, we had a ball."

Al Pacino

Both a bankable movie star and serious stage actor—a rare breed—unlike others who might feel acting is somehow akin to prostitution, he honors his calling as a most noble endeavor. "What can you say," he asks, "about a profession where you can be anybody and do anything?" *New York Times* critic Mel Gussow described the Pacino cast of characters as " ... misfits, people out of the mainstream, besieged by and battling society's expectations of conformity. The essential Pacino character is a loner—isolated, but with a burning intensity. Within this framework, Pacino's range is extraordinary. The characters are, by turns, extroverted and withdrawn, articulate and barely literate, assertive and acquiescent."

He made his film debut as a manipulative junkie in *The Panic in Needle Park* and soon cornered the market on deadly effective anti-heroes. Next he portrayed the implacable Mafia don, Michael Corleone, in *The Godfather* and *The Godfather II*. These were followed up by more Pacino successes such as *Serpico* and *Dog Day Afternoon* and the more notorious *Cruising* and *Scarface*. Such anti-social characters are in direct contrast to Pacino's tradition-bound upbringing in the Bronx where he was born 25 April 1940 of Sicilian descent. Lonely, bright and bored, Pacino spent much of his time at the movies and afterwards would act out for his family and friends the stories he'd seen. "Every time I came home, I fell down as if I were dead. I *always* made an entrance into my house." He quit the High School of Performing Arts after the first two years—the end of his formal education. Since then all he has studied is acting. While attending the Herbert Berghof Studio, he met Charles Laughton who volunteered to work with Pacino on his craft. Encouraged by the veteran, he auditioned for off off-Broadway parts. His first appearance was in William Saroyan's *Hello Out There* at the Cafe Cino. Aside from the classroom this was his first time acting in front of an audience. The experience was so unnerving he refused to perform in public for one year. He was admitted after a second try to Lee Strasberg's Actor's Studio. It was there that he received most of his training. He began auditioning again and, in time, became involved in Israel Horovitz' *The Indian Wants the Bronx* and won an Obie in 1968 for his performance as a drunken hood. His "discovery" led him to Broadway where he won a Tony for his part as a psychotic in 1969's *Does a Tiger Wear a Necktie?* He won a second Tony in 1977 for *The Basic Training of Pavol Hummel*. In 1983 he struck a critical stride in the revival of David Mamet's *American Buffalo*. Other films include *Revolution* (1986) with Nastassja Kinski, Martin Bregman's *Sea of Love* (1989), and *Carlitto's Way* (1989). Pacino lives in New York and guards his privacy so much that columnist Earl Wilson once dubbed the actor "the male Greta Garbo."

Bob Packwood

"In a nation dedicated to democratic ideals, it is an anomaly for the Senate to elevate men to key positions of leadership without regard to any qualification except length of service.... Long service does not necessarily produce expertise. Natural ability, devoted interest, and detailed study do." Speaking of anomaly, meet Oregon's junior senator Bob Packwood (and the author of that heretical statement). A surprise dark horse winner in 1968 when he took his Senate seat at the age of 32, Packwood is now a fixture in the Senate and a burr in the sides of his party's mainstream. His opinions and style have made him the Democrat's Republican: he favors environmentalism and is pro-choice on the abortion issue, opposes Washington's encouragement of get-along-go-along politics, and wants the Republican party to reach out to minorities.

Born 11 September 1932, Packwood is a Portland boy, son of a professional political lobbyist and great-grandson of an Oregon pioneer. After majoring in political science and participating in campus politics at Willamette University in Salem, Oregon, he went east and got a law degree from NYU, where he was the law school's student body president. He returned to Oregon and worked as a law clerk briefly, then as a lawyer with local law firms, forming his own firm with several associates in 1965. He became active in state politics through the Republican party, and in 1962 decided to run for state legislature, enchanting middle-class voters of both parties with his own Pacific Northwest brand of progressivism. He was re-elected twice, and by 1965 had organized the first of his unofficial party conferences. Packwood began setting his sights on national office and in 1968 challenged and beat—by a hair's breadth—popular four-term incumbent maverick Wayne Morse, becoming the youngest member of the Senate. One journalist describes him as "an athletic six-footer with green eyes and sandy brown hair [who] keeps his weight at about 180 pounds by swimming and pitching for his staff's softball team." A classical music enthusiast, he and wife Georgia Ann (Oberteuffer) live in Bethesda, Maryland, with their two children, William Henderson and Shyla.

Nam June Paik

"The automobile dominated this century, and TV will dominate the next," observes this pioneer of the video art movement. Paik uses the cathode ray tube as his canvas, rendering scenes on multiple TV screens which together create "electronic paintings." Initially associated with neo-dadaistic "happenings," he gained notoriety during the '60s with his "action concerts," characterized by a kitchen sink variety of visual and sound effects, including a giant robot, a cellist in a bikini of electric lights, and nudity, for which he was once arrested. Today, Paik's compositions are equally inventive, and are so recognized by art curators and collectors worldwide.

Born 20 July 1932 in Seoul, Korea, Paik was one of five children in an upper-middle class family who left Korea as refugees at the outbreak of the Korean war. Between 1950 and 1962, Paik studied aesthetics and music at the Universities of Tokyo, Munich, and Cologne, and at the Freiburg Conservatory, where he developed interest in electronic music. In 1958, a meeting with composer John Cage changed his life, and when he made his first trip to the United Sates in 1964, he was ready for his infamous collaboration with classically trained cellist Charlotte Moorman. With her, he produced such showpieces as *Variations of a Theme by Saint-Sains* during which she wore a mere sheet of cellophane, and while in concert, immersed herself in an oil drum filled with water. Undaunted by outraged critics, Paik staged numerous shows, received a Rockefeller grant, did a stint as artist in residence at SUNY Stony Brook, and joined other video artists in the screen breaking production of *The Medium is the Medium*, the first showing of video art for home TV. The height of his honors so far was a 1982 Whitney Museum show, which was the first major retrospective of a video artist. He was also acclaimed for presenting a live interactive ninety-minute video special on the 1986 Asian Games in Seoul called "Bye Bye Kipling."

Paik is small and self-effacing; he wears rumpled clothes and rubber boots to protect him from possible electrical shock as he works. His English is still hard to understand, though he is eloquent on the subject of video art. A citizen since 1976, he lives in Soho with his wife, Japanese video artist Shigeko Kubota.

Alan Pakula

His particular strength as a director is handling difficult actors or is it better to say actors in difficult parts? Under his direction, Jane Fonda (for *Klute*), Jason Robards (for *All the President's Men*), and Meryl Streep (for *Sophie's Choice*) won Academy Awards. Liza Minnelli (*The Sterile Cuckoo*), Jane Alexander (*All the President's Men*), Jill Clayburgh and Candice Bergen (*Starting Over*) and Richard Farnsworth (*Comes a Horseman*) all received Oscar nominations. "If a director has one job with actors," he explains, "it's to make them feel safe and to try to dare. The reason I became a director was that I've always loved actors. The very first time I worked with actors on stage, while I was still at Yale, I got this very exulted feeling that I was finally a part of the universe, in the adolescent, Thomas Wolfian sense. I remember leaving the theatre that night and leaping, goat-like all the way home, full of the arrogant belief that those actors had done something they could never have done without me. Now I'm not so sure."

Born of Polish-Jewish parentage, 7 April 1928, Pakula penned plays at Pennsylvania's prep palace, The Hill School, before his ivy days as a drama major at Yale. The summer before his studies in New Haven, he responded to a want-ad and wound up the office boy to the late, great agent Leland Hayward. His job was to deliver scripts to directors, producers and actors, but instead he would take the scripts home at night, read them, and then deliver them in the morning. He gunned his way to success in Hollywood after college, first as an assistant to the head of cartoons at Warner Brothers, then at age 23 when his mentor at Hollywood's arty Circle Theatre, Don Hartman was made head of production at Paramount Pictures, Pakula went with him. In 1955 he got the green light to produce *Fear Strikes Out* about a baseball player's struggle with mental illness, starring Anthony Perkins. Joining forces with fellow director Richard Mulligan, soon Pakula-Mulligan Productions was popping out box office hit after hit. Among them were *To Kill a Mockingbird*; *Love with a Proper Stranger*; *Baby, the Rain Must Fall*; *Inside Daisy Clover* and *Up the Down Staircase*.

He began directing in 1968 with *The Sterile Cuckoo*. "I was interviewing lots of directors for the job. Suddenly I realized it was something I wanted to do myself. I'd always wanted to direct, not produce." He had a major turning point with the film of William Styron's *Sophie's Choice* in 1983. Although it was his ninth film as director, it was his first as a screenwriter and he received an Oscar nomination for best screenplay adaptation. Other endeavors include *See You in the Morning* (co-produced/screenplay) and *Orphans* (produced/directed).

Once married to actress Hope Lange, in 1973 he married the former Hannah Cohn Boorstin. (Her 1985 biography about Queen Marie of Rumania—*The Last Romantic*—drew critical raves.) They reside in New York.

Arnold Palmer

Although he hasn't won a major tourney since his fourth Masters victory in 1964, nor a PGA gathering since the 1973 Bob Hope Desert Classic, just the hint of a Palmer success is the only whiff needed to swell the last-day attendance at tournaments with thousands in "Arnie's Army." He's one of golf's all-time money-winners (in what seems like eons ago he became the first man ever to win $100,000 in a year—1963), and he is seemingly at peace as he continues to play in national meets, court adoring fans and admiring press, and travel with his wife, friend, and business partner, Winnie.

Born 10 September 1929 in Youngstown, Pennsylvania, Arnold Palmer spent his boyhood in Latrobe, Pennsylvania, where his father was a golf pro, and where he was a golf tyro ("I taught him to hold a club when he was three," recalled his pop years later) before he went to kindergarten. He won two conference titles as a Wake Forest student, took time out to serve in the Coast Guard, then came back to take the U.S. Amateur Championship in 1954. That same year, having married Winifred Walzer (two daughters), he turned pro. "My God, I wanted to win," he says of the early, unsuccessful years. Then the temper tantrums which had marred his early tournaments diminished considerably. "I learned concentration," he said, but Mrs. Palmer went further. "Arnie's father saw him throw a club once," she explained. "He told Arnie that golf was a gentleman's game and that if he ever did it again, he wouldn't get to play." Added the sand trapper himself, "That did it."

Now a prosperous businessman (Arnold Palmer Golf Clubs, among other interests), and a products endorser ad infinitum, as a tournamenteer Palmer hasn't lost the gritty determination that gave him his U.S. Open win in 1960, or that made him the Associate Press' Athlete of the Decade in 1969. At age 53, he was leading at the Masters after 16 holes when rain stopped play. But he poo-poohed well-wishers' hopes for an early cancellation so that he could become the oldest golfer to win a major. "It's a physical game," said the man whose talent and charisma "turned America on to golf." "If a guy can't go out and play," he continued, "then he shouldn't win a tournament." Sharing some of his tips, he wrote the book *Play Great Golf: Mastering the Fundamentals of Your Game* in 1987.

Joseph Papp

He is an indefatigable champion and indisputably a force behind some of the best American theatre in the past fifteen years. Almost thirty seasons since he put his first *Julius Caesar* into the East River Amphitheater, his New York

Shakespeare Festival has produced over 400 works. These include: the original production of *Hair*, which, in 1967, opened the Festival's year-round home, the converted landmark Astor Library (it is actually five theatres under one roof); *No Place to Be Somebody, Two Gentlemen of Verona, Sticks and Bones, That Championship Season, Streamers, A Chorus Line, Miss Margarida's Way, For Colored Girls Who Have Considered Suicide When the Rainbow Is Enuf, I'm Getting My Act Together and Taking It on the Road, Plenty, The Pirates of Penzance, La Boheme*, starring Linda Ronstadt and *The Normal Heart*. From 1973 to 1977, the NYSF served as the theatre constituent at Lincoln Center where its productions included *Threepenny Opera, The Cherry Orchard* and *Streamers*. On 29 September 1983, *A Chorus Line* became the longest running show in the history of Broadway when it gave its 3,389th performance at the Shubert Theatre. As of 1984, NYSF productions had collectively won 23 Tony awards (including three special Tonys), 76 Obies, 19 Drama Desk Awards, 6 New York Drama Critics Awards and three Pulitzer prizes. In 1962 Papp built the Delacorte Theatre in Central Park and in 1964 developed a mobile theatre to tour city parks and playgrounds. A list of Papp's credits is immeasurable as is the list of the many battles he has waged in the name of art. In 1988, he was honored by the Vietnam Veterans Ensemble Theatre Company at their second annual Vetty Awards.

Born Joseph Papirofsky in the Williamsburg section of Brooklyn 22 June 1921, he discoverd Shakespeare when he was 12 years old. "Shakespeare," he says, "was tied into a lot of things.... I learned one of Mark Antony's speeches. Then I went into Manhattan to a place on 14th Street that made recorded discs, and I recorded myself reading it with Stravinsky's 'Firebird Suite' in the background.... I love the sound of the English language because we spoke only Yiddish at home. To have a guy get up like Mark Antony and talk to a crowd and have him change their minds . . . that was very persuasive." Papp staged his first productions while in the Navy during WW II. After his discharge in 1946 he studied acting and directing at the Actors Lab in Los Angeles on the G.I. Bill. Back in New York in the 1950s, he worked as a stage manager at CBS. He first realized his vision of the New York Shakespeare Festival in a church on East 6th Street after he convinced the minister that the church resembled the Globe Theatre of William Shakespeare's day. Papp is both a nurturer of talent and a ruthlessly competitive businessman and fundraiser. Once after *New York Times* critic Walter Kerr gave one of his productions a bad review, Papp screamed at him the next time they met at the Public: "Keep out. I don't want you here. You are incapable of judging and evaluating new works."

These days the NYSF is rich and its masterbuilder, after four marriages (his fourth and present wife is Gail Merrifield, a longtime NYSF staffer) and five children (from the first three marriages) is ready for even bigger shows and tougher battles. "I wouldn't mind being called upon by the government to do something of a cultural nature . . . if the U.S. government appointed me to be cultural ambassador-at-large, I would be interested."

Bill Parcells

The coach who lead the Football Giants to their first Super Bowl championship in club history was also named as the NFL Coach of the Year. He was the hero that fans were longing for—the miracle man who brought the athletes out of their slump. When he joined the ballclub as the 12th head coach of the team on the 15 December 1982, he went through a dramatic first season. A slew of injuries hit the players (25 men on the injured reserve list) and with the sudden death of backfield coach Bob Ledbetter during the season, followed by the passing of former running back Doug Kotar, this strong head coach was plagued with problems. Not one to worry, Parcells kept his chin up and worked long hours to bring the Giants back in the running.

Bill Parcells was born in Englewood, New Jersey on 22 August 1941. He played scholastic football at River Dell High School in Oradell, New Jersey and went on to be a linebacker at Wichita State University where he was an All Missouri Valley Conference selection. Tough on the field, he was drafted No. 7 by the Detroit Lions, but rather than accept an immediate start he chose a job on the coaching field for Hastings College in Nebraska. The following year he returned to Wichita State as an assistant coach for Army (three seasons). His experience continued as he became defensive coordinator for Florida State (three years), Vanderbilt (two seasons) and Texas Tech (three seasons). He was named Head Coach at the Air Force Academy in 1978, then was given a defensive job with the New York Giants in 1979 (he resigned to enter private business). By 1980 he had reentered the sports arena as linebacker coach of the New England Patriots. In 1981 he made his way back to the Giants to become a defensive coordinator. He was responsible for the 3-4 defense and the revamping of the secondary, producing a No. 3 ranked defensive team in the NFL (up from No. 25). Since the team's Super Bowl victory in 1986, the Giants have had their ups and downs, but under Parcell's direction there is a team spirit which keeps them kicking.

Residing in Upper Saddle River, New Jersey, with his wife, Judy, they have three daughters—Suzy, Jill and Dallas.

Estelle Parsons

"I hate the theatre. That whole thing about the theatre being sacred is ridiculous," says the energetic and outspoken actress. "It's full of boring, unimaginative, third-rate people. Every good actor I know has moved to Hollywood." She walked off with an Oscar as best supporting actress in 1967 for her portrayal of the knee-knocking gangster's moll in *Bonnie and Clyde*. Her favorite part was in the film, *I Never Sang for My Father*, in which she played "the only woman who is brighter than I am. The part lasted 14 minutes on the screen. I come in at the end, tell everybody off, and leave." Other films include *Rachel, Rachel* with Joanne Woodward, *Don't Drink the Water* ("I learned more from Jackie Gleason than any actor I've ever worked with") and *The Night the Sun Came Out* ("I play a woman who wakes up one morning and discovers her husband has turned into Godfrey Cambridge"). Commenting on her film career Parsons says, "I get scripts and my agent gets scripts, continually for film roles, but I haven't found one worth doing recently."

Born in Lynn, Massachusetts, 20 November 1927, she holds a B.A. in political science from Connecticut College for Women and attended Boston University Law School. She landed her first job as a reporter and production assistant on the old Dave Garraway "Today" show, and then made her way into the theatre, playing a small part in the 1957 Ethel Merman musical *Happy Hunting*, followed by *Skin of Our Teeth* for Arthur Penn. Other stage appearances include *Miss Margarida's Way*, for which she won a Drama Desk Award in 1977 as a wacky, authoritarian schoolteacher, and *The Pirates of Penzance* in which she appeared as the aging nursemaid. "I always like to do something new," says the actress. In 1983 she starred in the one-woman show, *Adulto Orgasmo Escapes from the Zoo*, a series of sketches on the subjugation of women which Parsons says, "fall in the crack between cabaret and theatre. I love them more than anything I've ever done." She hit the stage again in 1989's *The Unguided Missile*.

Divorced from the late magazine writer Richard Gehman in 1953 (twin daughters), Parsons has since married Peter Zimroth, a trial lawyer. The couple adopted a baby boy in 1983—a surprise to some, but not to Estelle's

28-year-old daughter, Abbie—"There's nothing Mom would do that would stun me." chuckles Parton. "They know I'm going to come out with every spangled thing I can get on. It's a joke we share."

Dolly Parton

"Her visual trademark is not far from that of Diamond Lil: a mountainous, curlicued bleach-blonde wig, lots of make-up, and outfits that accentuate her quite astonishing hour-glass figure," was John Rockwell's *New York Times* observation when Dolly Parton opened at New York's Felt Forum in 1974 with the newly-formed Travelin' Family Band (two brothers, two sisters, an uncle and a cousin). "But Miss Parton is no artificial dumb blonde. Her thin little soprano and girlish way of talking suggest something childlike, but one quickly realizes both that it is genuine and that she is a striking talent." The leading lady of country music who became a pop-rock superstar surfaced in Nashville as the protégée of the legendary Porter Wagoner. She struck out on her own in 1974, was chosen Best Female Singer of the Country Music Association in 1975 and 1976, blazed into pop with her rockish backup band Gypsy Fever in 1977 (her touring van was a whopper studio-and-home-on-wheels with a closet for twenty gowns and four wigs, and sleeping accommodations for eleven), and by the '80s had become a multi-faceted entertainer in concert, on records, television and films.

Dolly Rebecca Parton was born 19 January 1946 in a two-room wooden shack in Locust Ridge, near Sevierville, Tennessee. As the fourth of twelve children of a struggling dirt farmer and a preacher's daughter (her mixed ancestry is Dutch, Irish, and Cherokee Indian), she helped raise her younger brothers and sisters. "We had absolutely nothin'. We wore rags. . . . For make-up we used merthiolate and mercurochrome . . . flour for powder. I was fascinated even then with make-up and stuff. Course they never allowed us to wear lipstick. My daddy would whip me . . . but the whippin' was worth it for a few days with a red mouth." She had "the best mama and daddy in the world" and she and her brothers and sisters had "fun . . . love . . . music." Parton's first love was gospel music ("my grandaddy bein' the preacher, we didn't feel ashamed to sing and play our git-tars. We believed in makin' a joyful noise unto the Lord.") At six her first musical instrument was a "busted-up mandolin"; at eight her uncle gave her a guitar and at eleven she had radio bookings in Knoxville. The day after her high school graduation in 1964 (she played the snare drum in the marching band), she took off for Nashville. In 1967 she joined Porter Wagoner's band, the Wagon Masters, and with him for the next seven years she sang at the Grand Ole Opry, wrote and recorded songs, and eventually co-founded the Owepar Publishing Company in Nashville. (She was later sued by Wagoner for $3 million in back fees and royalties; it was settled out of court.) From being a frequent guest on prime-time television shows, she went on to star in her own specials (a 1984 Christmas special with Kenny Rogers was followed by a recording with him and writing the title tune "Christmas In America" for Kenny's 1989 album), concerts, and records. She is a prolific lyric writer (many have been recorded and "thousands" fill trunks and boxes in her home). She writes, or sings, into a tape recorder, up to twenty sets of lyrics a day. "A strange feeling usually comes over me; almost like being in a trance. When you're talented I think much of the inspiration is spiritual—from God." Parton's film career leaves her with definite opinions: *9 to 5*, with Jane Fonda and Lily Tomlin, "the best experience I could have had;" *The Best Little Whorehouse in Texas*, with Burt Reynolds, "the worst;" *Rhinestone*, with Sylvester Stallone, "my favorite." (Many critics, on the other hand, put the latter on their "Ten Worst Films" list in 1984.) She also appeared in 1989's *Steel Magnolias*.

A woman with many of her dreams fulfilled, she opened Dollywood (a theme park tourist attraction) in 1986. She runs Dolly Parton Enterprises, making her own decisions on investments and charitable contributions and has homes in Hawaii, Hollywood, New York and Nashville, all of which she shares with her husband, Carl Dean. "I enjoy the way I look, but it's a joke,"

Joe Paterno

This spectacled full professor is also chief coordinator of the extra-curricular fall activity that draws up to 86,000 members of the Penn State University community for Saturday enjoyment. He says, "I don't like to put myself up as a do-gooder, but I am. We have an obligation to make these athletes better people. If a kid goes through here, and can't read and write but can knock people down, is that good? We've got more of an obliagation than that." Thus the scholarly Brooklyn-born (21 December 1926) Joseph Vincent Paterno continues to go on record as saying that not only should colleges' soft, special and often unethical treatment of athletes be stopped, but that schools which put academics first (like Penn State) can still produce national champions in football. And although "The Grand Experiment" sounded like an idea whose time had come, it wasn't until Paterno's 17th season that his student-athletes could hold up degrees in one hand *and* display the Number One index finger with the other.

While holding that there's more to college than football and more to football than winning, Paterno's Nittany Lions still did plenty of the latter. In 1968, '69 and '73 they were undefeated, all of which worked to give this running-oriented mentor the second-best winning percentage (80% plus) among active college coaches. But while he was grudgingly swelling the rosters of the NFL, with scads of players (Penn State is nicknamed "Linebacker U."), the Experiment remained an incomplete equation; it hadn't led to a national championship. Finally, in 1982, Paterno, who'd been a quarterback at Brown, was blessed with the shot-slinging arm of Todd Blackledge, and the ground-galloping legs of Curt Warner, and this balanced offense proved to be the ingredient that enabled the Lions to beat No. 1-ranked Georgia (starring Herschel Walker) in the Sugar Bowl to finish in the top spot. Still not interested in leaving College Park despite annual pro offers to coach, he turns down seven-figure contracts because "I have five kids [with wife Suzanne] and this is the perfect place to raise them." But he realizes he is far from being perfect. "I hate the freshman-eligible rule [allowing newcomers to play varsity]," Paterno says. "If I had enough guts I'd say that . . . regardless, freshmen aren't going to play here. But that's how I'm hypocritical. I don't say that because it would hurt our recruiting." In 1989 he shared his coaching tips in the book *Paterno: By the Book*, written with Bernard Asbell.

Mandy Patinkin

"To say that Mandy Patinkin became inhabited by the ghost of George Seurat, the 19th century artist, is hardly an exaggeration," said the *New York Times'* Nan Robertson about his performance in Stephen Sondheim's controversial musical *Sunday in the Park with George*, "At least Mr. Patinkin thinks so, at the risk of sounding 'pretentious, corny and a fool.'" Pointing out that he was 31 and that Seurat died at the age of 31 in 1891, Patinkin added: "I even look like the guy, too. I get a little freaked about how much I looked like him." Raised in Chicago, Patinkin "grew up" with the painting which has hung in the Art Institute there for years, and before the show started workshop rehearsals (later moving to Broadway) he made several trips to Chicago and sat for a total of seven hours in front of the painting that inspired the musical—"Sunday Afternoon on the Island of La Grande Jette."

Mandel (everybody has called him "Mandy" since babyhood) Patinkin was born 30 November 1952 in Chicago. After attending the University of Kansas he came to New York and studied at the Juilliard School. From 1975 to 1981 he appeared frequently with the New York Shakespeare Festival as well as the Hudson Guild Theatre. His Broadway appearances include *Shadow Box;* an outstanding portrayal of Che Guevara in *Evita,* for which he won a 1980 Tony Award; *George* (nominated for a 1984 Tony) and the two-day concert version of *Follies*. In 1989 he starred on Broadway in a one-man show *Mandy Patinkin In Concert: Dress Casual*. He also appeared in 1987's *The Knife*. His films include *The Big Fix, French Postcards, The Last Embrace, Night of the Juggler, Ragtime, Yentl, Daniel, Free Spirit Maxie, Heartburn, The House on Carroll Street, Alien Nation* and *Dick Tracy*.

His vocal acrobatics have won accolades from music critics, including Sondheim who calls Patinkin's voice "brilliant—a gift from God. That's in addition to his terrific stage presence and acting skill." The actor has "wide tessitura, both top and bottom," continues Sondheim, "a working two-octave range, up and down to G-sharp." Reacting to those remarks, Patinkin said: "If I knew what that meant, it would really scare me. I don't read music. I read the words. I just know when it goes up and down." He married actress Kathryn Grody in 1980 and they live in Manhattan's West Side (two sons, Isaac and Gideon).

Jane Pauley

Wholesome and surprisingly demure for a newcomer, she was a fast-rising star in television news. Appearing on the horizon at the advent of a major push toward women broadcasters, her crisp, Midwestern delivery propelled her from hometown cub reporter to co-host of a national morning wake-up program.

Born in Indianapolis, 31 October 1950, she graduated from Indiana University at Bloomington, and showed no interest in journalism until a long-shot interview with the local CBS affiliate won her a reporting job. She advanced to WMAQ-TV, the NBC Chicago affiliate, as co-anchor in 1975. Skeptical of her youth and lean experience, critics labeled her a lightweight. One Chicago TV reviewer ventured that she appeared to have "the IQ of a cantaloupe."

Pauley was characteristically irreverent about her good fortune and limited abilities. "It was a terrible rating gimmick to have a girl doing the news. I'm a hell of a news reader, and that's a talent. I'm not naive. I know I'll never have the experience of being on the road as a correspondent."

But in 1976, she beat out—by audience testing—250 candidates for the co-host job on NBC's durable "Today" show, vacated by Barbara Walters, and came to anchor the network's Sunday night news program, as well. Initially distinguished only for her school-marm hairstyle and resemblance to a younger version of her popular predecessor, Pauley grew on early-morning audiences, slowly revealing a wry, spontaneous humor and a more cosmopolitan style. "I'm a lot more cynical than I appear and I'm always a little chagrined to see myself described as 'prim and Midwestern.' I am Midwestern, I can't deny that, but prim? I'm not a prim person." For her constant "concern for the well-being of our men and women in uniform, and their families at home and abroad, through on-site visits to ships at sea and military bases in the U.S. and overseas," Pauley was selected as the USO of Metropolitan New York's "Woman of the Year" in 1987.

The "Today" star married "Doonesbury" cartoonist/playwright Garry Trudeau in 1980. The couple have three children (twins: Richard Ross and Rachel Grandison, and son: Thomas Moore).

Paulina

Actress/model Paulina Porizkova made her film debut as the wily actress in the 1987 film *Anna*, but she is better know as Paulina (the world-famous fashion model who has appeared on the covers of more than 300 international magazines). She starred as the beautiful and mysterious Nina Ionescu, who is accused of murder in the 1989 comedy-thriller *Her Alibi* and was the first choice of both director Bruce Beresford and producer Keith Barish, who felt she could be comedic yet mysteriously alluring. Once Ms. Porizkova received the script, she said: "I read it and thought it sounded good. The interplay between Phillip (Tom Selleck) and Nina (Porizkova) reminded me of Cary Grant's romantic comedies, which are my all-time favorites. And it wasn't a heavy, dramatic movie. This movie has light, fun moments, while 'Anna' was dark. . . . Nina is an American prototype of the mysterious Eastern European woman. And that's where I come in."

Born in Prostejov, Czechoslovakia, in 1965, Paulina Porizkova was left in her grandmother's care in 1968 when her parents escaped Czechoslovakia during the Russian invasion. Her parents settled in Sweden and began efforts to free her. Using the media to their advantage, and employing tactics ranging from hunger strikes to supplying the press with photographs of their young daughter hugging a teddy bear, the world was alerted to their plight. In 1971, Ms. Porizkova's mother tried to smuggle her daughter out of the country but was arrested in the process and jailed for several months before being sentenced to three years under house arrest. As a result of massive political pressure from Sweden, mother and daughter were released in 1974. After reuniting with her father in Sweden, Ms Porizkova was discovered by the Elite Modeling Agency, who sent her to Paris at age 13. Following three successful years there, she moved to New York and became one of the world's most popular models. Paulina currently represents the Estee Lauder Company as a spokeswoman for the firm's entire line of products.

Luciano Pavarotti

"I'm an ordinary man," insists this extraordinary tenor who made operatic history in a production of *La Fille du Regiment*, hitting all nine high C's in the aria "Quel destin" perfectly. He's been the cause of what one critic calls "Pavarotti Pandemonium" among music lovers since his La Scala debut in 1966. Hailed by *Newsweek* as "opera's greatest turn-on," Luciano Pavarotti has drawn throngs to the world of classical music with his ebullient manner and superb voice via "live" televised broadcasts, his appearance in the film *Yes, Giorgio* (which was panned by the critics) and the publication of his autobiography, *Pavarotti, My Own Story* (a national bestseller). In addition, his recordings have made it to the top of both classical and pop charts and he's appeared on numerous talk shows (often giving cooking demos) and on TV commercials for American Express. His latest recording was *Pavarotti at Carnegie Hall* in 1988.

Born in Modena, Italy, 12 October 1935, Pavarotti was indoctrinated into the music world by his father, a baker who sang with a local choral group. The Pavarotti phenomenon began in this country in 1965 when the tenor gave several performances of *Lucia di Lammermoor* in Miami with Joan Sutherland and exploded with full force after his Metropolitan Opera debut in *La Boheme* in November 1968. Since then his fame and popularity have spread like wildfire. Lately, however, "opera's golden tenor" has been disappointing audiences with last minute cancellations and in 1983 he was booed and whistled at in *Lucia di Lammermoor* (which once had brought him standing ovations) because of a sudden weakening of his voice. More recently, he was banned from the Lyric Opera of Chicago for backing out of a performance in 1989. This was the twenty-sixth time he had cancelled an appearance at the Lyric during this decade. Pavarotti tries not to think about the day he'll have to give up singing. "We don't have time to pause and see where we are. If someone asks an old singer how he is feeling he will either say he doesn't know or lie. Because every moment of every day is a new experience to be conquered. People my age don't ask who and why and what is it like to be great—we just do, and be the best we can. I love people. I genuinely love everybody," says the equally lovable, singer who never fails to bring enthusiasm and sheer delight to his performances. His hectic performing schedule keeps him on the road ten months a year and he puts in time to conduct master classes and appear in documentary films. When he does make it home—one month each year—to Rimini, Italy, he spends the time with his wife Adua and their three daughters. Pavarotti also keeps a Manhattan apartment, the scene of many late night poker games with fellow singers and musicians.

Gregory Peck

His screen credits provide a cross-section of some of Hollywood's finest cinematic contributions, including *Twelve O'Clock High, Spellbound, The Gunfighter, Roman Holiday,* and *The Guns of Navarone.* But it was his classic portrayal of the Lincolnesque southern lawyer, Arthur Finch in the widely-hailed *To Kill a Mockingbird* that won him an Academy Award in 1962.

The legendary Peck (born Eldred Gregory Peck in La Jolla, California, 5 April 1916) was a pre-med student at the University of California at Berkeley when the compulsion to act overrode his interest in medicine. A back injury, which had previously caused him to drop out from the university rowing team, also barred him from military service in World War II. After a drama scholarship and short-run appearances on Broadway, he attained instant stardom in RKO's *Days of Glory,* followed by *The Keys to the Kingdom* (which won him one of four Oscar nominations he would receive). In due time he would produce features as well, one of which, *The Trial of the Catonsville Nine* was a "labor of love," a militant, anti-war movie based on Father Dan Berrigan's play. "We made it," says Peck, who also helped underwrite the costs, "because we wanted to get it said." In making *Catonsville* (1972), Peck could not bring himself to endorse civil disobedience to the extent propounded by author Berrigan. At the same time he and his associates felt that the picture itself was their way of saying *no* to war. Peck has also produced or co-produced: *Pork Chop Hill, Cape Fear, Behold a Pale Horse, The Dove and Dodsworth* (1983). Other screen credits include *Sea Wolves* (1981), *Amazing Grace and Chuck* (1986) and *The Old Gringo* (1989).

Peck was first married to Greta Rice, from whom he was divorced in 1954 (three sons, one of whom committed suicide in 1975). In 1955 he married the French newspaper writer Veronique Passani (two children). His significant distinctions include The Medal of Freedom in 1969 and an appointment as National Chairman of the American Cancer Society in 1966. From 1967-70 he was President of the Academy of Motion Picture Arts and Sciences, and in 1968 he was reappointed for a six-year term as a member of the National Council on the Arts. He is a member of the Board of Trustees of the American Film Institute.

I.M. Pei

"The form that a building takes has to be emotionally satisfying. Geometry can be expressive, not sterile," says this modern architect and city planner who's been called the master builder of the '70s, 80s and 90s. Typical of his graceful jewel-like structures dominated by geometric shapes are the John F. Kennedy Library in Boston and the East Building of the National Gallery of Art in Washington. D.C. At a time when many of his contemporaries have turned decisively against modernism, Pei apparently stands firm and is viewed by some as "the last modernist." Yet, he's not a conventional modernist and insists he's never been addicted to the motion that "form follows function." Part of the "function" they talk about is psychological, he says. Pei's destiny is to discover the "middle way" between extremes—a balance between rigid geometry and deep psychological needs, between modernism and tradition. And "when he succeeds, the results are worth the struggle," says *Newsweek*.

Ieoh Ming Pei was born in Canton, China, 26 April 1917, the son of a prominent banker and economist. His early years were spent in Shanghai, Hong Kong and Suzhou, his family's ancestral home. After attending St. John's Middle School in Shanghai, he went to the United States in 1935 for his professional education, enrolling first at MIT (Bachelor of Architecture, 1940) and later at Harvard Graduate School of Design (Master of Architecture, 1946). He studied with Walter Gropius and Marcel Breuer at Harvard and was a member of the faculty from 1945-48. Joining William Zeckendorf's Webb & Knapp real estate development firm in 1948 as director of architecture, Pei became a leading expert in urban multi-story designing and city planning. Brooklyn's Bedford-Stuyvesant renewal project is among the many redevelopments he's helped plan in American cities. In 1955, he formed I.M. Pei & Associates, which became I.M. Pei & Partners in 1966. His firm has designed more than 100 projects in the United States and abroad, including 42 award winners.

Pei's one great disaster came in the early 1970s when the doublepaned windows of the spectacular 60-story John Hancock Tower in Boston, designed by a Pei partner, began mysteriously to fall out. For a while, the tower was a national laughingstock and Pei, as the frontline name, shared the blame. The problem was corrected and knowledgeable observers now fault the manufacturer. Pei's myriad honors pile as high as his drafting board. His designs have been hailed as incorporating "beauty and common sense" and relating "sympathetically to the background, whether it is natural landscape or neighboring buildings."

Pei likes to define architecture as the "art of the possible." His Fragrant Hill Hotel in Peking was a blend of East and West, built around a dozen luxuriant garden courts, each designed by a living Chinese master. In 1942, he married Eileen Loo (three sons, one daughter). They became American citizens in 1954.

Sean Penn

If *Time* magazine is correct in calling them the "sons of De Niro," referring to the new breed of intense, young matinee idols, then this consummate pro is the heir-apparent, the likeliest-to-succeed of the lot. His realistic portrayals of a diverse group of characters in movies such as *Racing with the Moon* and *The Falcon and the Snowman* have won him plenty of praise. "I like to spend my time researching my parts, the people I play, because I feel a need and a responsibility to the people who *live* the life I'm portraying, so that they're not disappointed or feel misrepresented when they see the film. So they recognize something real," says Sean Penn about whom director Louis Malle recalls: "I'd see him in *Fast Times at Ridgemont High* and I thought he was brilliant as the stoned surfer—to the point that I didn't think it was a characterization at all. When he came to my office to interview for *Crackers*, I nearly fell off my chair because in front of me was someone who had nothing to do with that character; this young man, lean, not very tall, good looking, very shy, very quiet. Sean has exceptional talent for absorbing all sorts of different characters." His most challenging role may have been the one he assumed in August 1985 when he married Madonna. After continual on-again-off-again battles, they filed for divorce in January 1989.

He was born 17 August 1960 in Santa Monica, California, the middle son of a show biz family: Pop Leo is a TV director; mom Eileen Ryan is a former New York stage actress and younger brother Chris also acts. Just a bebopper with a surfboard when he decided to skip college to work at the Los Angeles Repertory Theatre, his parents had reservations. "They said, 'You've got to have something solid, some solid profession to fall back on.' I said, 'I won't fall back!'" His professional debut came in the TV series "Barnaby Jones" in 1979 and he made his Broadway debut in Kevin Heeland's *Heartland*, and from there starred in the film *Taps*. He returned to Broadway in *Slab Boys* with a perfect Scottish accent and next blew into his film part in *Bad Boys* with long hair, a tattooed arm and a few weeks' experience hanging out with Chicago Street gangs. For the part of the Texan musician in *Crackers* he went down to Austin and Dallas and brought back two real-life Lone Star musicians to hang around with—authenticity is everything, you see. However, about to have his near-perfect teeth filed down and capped with "grubby looking covers, maybe a few cracked ones as well" his mother, the daughter of a dentist, vetoed that idea with a firm parental no. "Ruining perfectly good teeth is definitely going too far," she told her hot-in-Hollywood son. Other movies include: *At Close Range* (1985), *Shanghai Express*, (1986), *Colors* (1987), *Judgement in Berlin* (1988), *State of Grace* (1989), *We're no Angels* (1989) and *Casualties of War* (1989).

George Peppard

Just 16 days into filming the pilot for TV's super hit soapsud, "Dynasty", he was replaced by John Forsythe in the part of Blake Carrington, Denver's multi-millionaire. Rumors were he was trying to run the show; he says he resented the notes on his acting from the producers. In any case, he worried that the rest of his dollars would have to be made on the obscure route of dinner theatres across the land. "I was about to lose the only asset I had, which was a house." he says, "and what I was saying in my prayers and to my friends was, 'I'm sure the good Lord will find work for his humble servant,' and there it was, the "A-Team," one of the best roles in my career." Despite raising the umbrage level of the National Coalition on Television Violence to ultra high frequency (they found a record breaking 34 offensive acts per hour, versus seven on other prime time offenders), the tall, handsome and now silver haired Peppard justifies the "A-Team's" huge success with its viewers this way: "What matters is what the show, as an excuse in escapism and entertainment, means in terms of service to people."

Success is no stranger to this veteran method actor whose good looks have been the madness and the method behind a variety of movies (*Breakfast at Tiffany's*, *How the West Was Won*, *The Carpetbaggers*, and the *Executioner*), television shows ("Banacek," "Doctor's Hospital," and "The Sam Sheppard Murder Trial"), and four broken marriages, the first to Helen Davies, two marriages to wildcat Elizabeth Ashley, and the third to Sherry Boucher. He gave matrimony another try in 1984 when he wed artist Alexis Adams.

Peppard was born in Detroit on 1 October 1928, son of a building contractor and mother who sang light opera. After studies at Purdue and Carnegie Tech, he worked at odd jobs on Wall Street and drove a taxi so he could afford to study with Lee Strasberg. He was so confident of immediate Broadway success that he demanded an unlisted telephone number, but nobody called for a long time until bit parts led to increasingly important roles in New York television dramas, such as "Little Moon of Alban" with Julie Harris. His starmaking role in films was MGM's *Home from the Hill*. Peppard's most recent film is *Silence Like Glass* (1989).

The actor is said to be moody but to have an irreverent and whimsical sense of humor. He has three children—Bradford and Julie from his first marriage, and a son Christian from his marriage to Elizabeth Ashley.

Frank Perdue

"If your husband is a breast or a leg man, ask for my chicken parts." he advises housewives on television. Thanks to Madison Avenue marketing and the most modern methods for producing broilers and roasters, Frank Perdue has full-feathered his nest with astonishing speed. To go from a small family chicken farm to the 4th largest integrated poultry processor in the country is indeed something to crow about. Today, as chairman of the board of Perdue Farms, Incorporated, he boasts a business that employs over 7,000 people and processes over 5 million chickens each week, all shipped *fresh* from the plants to poultry wholesalers and chain supermarket warehouses from Boston to Norfolk.

Franklin Parsons Perdue was born in 1920 on the Delmarva Peninsula, a strip of land east of the Chesapeake Bay. It includes parts of DELaware, MARyland, and VirginiA, and is one of the country's major poultry production areas. That same year Arthur Perdue, Frank's father, bought 50 Leghorn chickens for five dollars and was in the egg business. At the age of ten Frank's parents presented him with his own 50 chickens to tend and collect the egg money (ten to fifteen dollars a month). A shy country boy, Frank attended one-room rural schools until Salisbury High School, in Maryland, followed by two years at Salisbury State College. A mediocre student, he seemed to excel primarily in table tennis (was it like hitting an egg?). So, in 1939, deciding the egg business wasn't so rotten after all, he left college and returned to the folks, the farm, and his feathered friends.

Except for several frivolous flights outside of the poultry business, Frank has stayed very close to the nest. Other ventures included a nightclub, an oyster business, and an Ocean City resort. He admits failures in these ventures made him a shrewd businessman. "The prime ingredient of success is fear," he has said, "I'm talking about the kind of fear that made me thorough. You should have enough fear to always second-guess yourself." And he admits in one of his many television promotion spots that it takes a tough man to make a tender chicken. Perdue's work schedule doesn't leave much time for non-business activities. He still enjoys playing table tennis and is an avid sports fan. The divorced father of four children—a son and three daughters, married investment banker Kathleen Markey in May of 1985, they divorced in 1988. Perdue married Mitzi Henderson Ayala in 1988.

Anthony Perkins

With his blend of boyish charm and haunted intensity, he is "Hollywood's perennial pubescent" and brilliant portrayer of "psycho" personalities and inner conflict. Most widely known as the classic manic inkeeper Norman Bates in Hitchcock's 1960 gothic thriller *Psycho* and the sequels, Perkins excels in projects and roles rich in psychological complexities, injecting depth and realism to bizarre situations. (He played the mentally unstable baseball player Jim Piersall in *Fear Strikes Out*, a war-torn Army chaplain in Mike Nichols' *Catch-22*, a megalomaniacal scientist in *Winter Kills*, a tormented psychiatrist in the Broadway hit *Equus* and a sadistic minister in *Crimes of Passion*.) Perkins' insight is rooted in his own tormented childhood, growing up under a smothering widowed mother. He became an actor to escape himself. "There was nothing about *me* I wanted to be," he once recalled, "but I felt wonderfully happy about being somebody else. I made up my mind to be a great actor, greater than my father" (stage and film actor Osgood Perkins). He did just that, and also happily overcame his personal obsessions.

A veteran of three dozen movies and many Broadway productions, Anthony Perkins was born 4 April 1932 in New York City to Janet Rane and

Osgood Perkins, a suave actor of proper Boston origin who died when Tony was only five. After private schooling in Cambridge, Massachusetts, and half-hearted college attempts at Rollins and Columbia, he turned to acting with quick success. Following an impressive film debut as the juvenile lead in *The Actress* with Jean Simmons and Spencer Tracy, he hit Broadway in 1954 in *Tea and Sympathy*. Returning to Hollywood to play Gary Cooper's son in *Friendly Persuasion*, he became a star. Following *Psycho* he made films in Europe, winning the Cannes International Film Festival's best actor award for his role in *Goodbye Again* opposite Ingrid Bergman. Other films include *Pretty Poison, Murder on the Orient Express, Mahogany, Destroyer,* and *Lucky Stiff*. Other Broadway appearances include *Steambath* (which he also directed) and *Look Homeward Angel* (his favorite role). On television, he starred in the movie "Les Miserables" and with Mary Tyler Moore in "First You Cry." He collaborated with Stephen Sondheim on the screenplay for the suspense film *The Last of Sheila*.

He is married to Berry Berenson, granddaughter of Elsa Schiaparelli, kid sister of actress Marisa Berenson. They have two sons, Osgood and Elvis.

Itzhak Perlman

"His talent is utterly limitless," says fellow musician Isaac Stern. "Nobody comes anywhere near him in what he can physically do with the violin." The consummate virtuoso's performances radiate with the sheer delight he expresses with his instrument and more than once have caused listeners to weep. Billed by *Newsweek* (whose cover he graced in 1980) as "Top Fiddle," Itzhak Perlman is a classical music superstar; his concerts are nearly always sold out and his recordings often reach the top of the charts and have won him numerous Grammy awards. "He has everything," says Victor Aitay, concertmaster of the Chicago Symphony. "An impeccable memory, coordination, musicianship and technique that are absolutely top-notch. He's a perfectionist." In addition to the classical violin repertory, Perlman has explored jazz violin, producing three recordings (among them *Joplin: The Easy Winners* with Andre Previn and *It's a Breeze*). Perlman even sang a bit part in *Tosca* at a televised gala event in New York. A darling of the talk show circuit—"I've been on the 'Tonight,' 'Tomorrow,' 'Today,' 'Yesterday' and 'A Little Bit Later' shows"—he's reached new audiences with his spirited sense of humor and zest for life. Struck with polio at the age of four, Perlman has become an outspoken advocate for the handicapped.

Born in Tel Aviv, 31 August in 1945, Perlman began studying violin at the age of four. At the Tel Aviv Academy of Music he studied under violinist Rivka Goldgart and gave his first recital at age ten. In 1958 after having been selected to appear on the *Ed Sullivan Caravan of Stars*, Perlman set out for the United States and international fame. He moved to New York, won a scholarship to Juilliard and made his Carnegie Hall debut at age seventeen. At the prestigious Leventritt Competition the following year (which he won), the young violinist's 200-year-old borrowed Gaurnieri was stolen. It turned up the next day in a Times Square pawnshop—where it had been pawned for $15.00. Perlman now plays a 1714 Stradivarius.

Perlman spends nine or ten months a year travelling and performs more than one hundred concerts a year in the United States, Europe and the Far East. He resides with his wife Toby (a former violinist) and their five children in a Manhattan apartment and a weekend home in upstate New York which they have named "Ritardano" (a musical term for slowing down). A family man, Perlman is an excellent cook (especially of Chinese food), a Knicks and Yankees fan, and an avid poker player.

Ron Perlman

"I was one of these actors who landed wonderfully artistic projects once a year and then just sat around because nobody ever thought of me as a commercial property." Ron Perlman, star of the critically acclaimed CBS series "Beauty and the Beast," has made a career of being unrecognizable in quality roles. His greatest success, portraying Vincent, the half-man/half-beast, keeps him covered under layers of make-up requiring four and a half hours of application. Hesitant at first to accept the part, having previously been hidden in make-up for the film roles of Salvatore, the hunchback, in *The Name of the Rose* and a prehistoric man in *Quest for Fire*, Perlman relented because "Vincent is so romantic, it's like playing Hamlet every week. This may be the greatest role of my life."

Perlman was born 13 April 1950 in Manhattan, the son of a jazz drummer who played with Artie Shaw's band before giving up music as a profession. He began performing on stage while still in high school, first as a comedian, then as an actor. He continued to appear in theater productions as a student at the City University of New York and while earning a Master of Fine Arts degree at the University of Minnesota. On his return to New York he joined the Classic Stage Company where he performed the works of Shakespeare, Chekhov, O'Neill, Ibsen, and Pinter for almost two years. Director Tom O'Horgan then cast Perlman as the Emperor in the Off-Broadway production of *The Architect and the Emperor of Assyria*, which later toured Europe. Perlman also starred in the Broadway production *American Heroes, The Resistable Rise of Arturo Ui* Off-Broadway, and in the regional tour of *Pal Joey* with Joel Grey and Alexis Smith, all of which O'Horgan directed. Other stage appearances in New York and regional theater included *Tartuffe, Two Gentlemen of Verona, House of Blue Leaves* and *The Iceman Cometh*. Perlman also appeared on Broadway with F. Murray Abraham in Isaac Bashevis Singer's *Tiebele and Her Demon*. After appearing in the MGM film *Ice Pirates* with Anjelica Huston, Perlman returned to New York for Peter Brook's production of *La Tragedie De Carmen* at Lincoln Center.

"Beauty and the Beast" has brought Perlman awards as well as praise. He received 1988 and 1989 Emmy nominations as Outstanding Lead Actor in a Drama Series and a People's Choice Award nomination as Favorite Male Performer in a New Television Program. In 1989, a Golden Globe Award for Best Actor followed. Perlman was voted Best Actor in a Quality Drama by the Viewers for Quality Television. He was honored by the Hollywood Women's Press Club with their 48th Annual Golden Apple Award as Male Discovery of the Year in 1988.

Since "Beauty and the Beast," Perlman has also appeared in the telefilm "A Stoning in Fulham County." He resides in Los Angeles with his wife, fashion designer Opal Stone, and their daughter Blake Amanda. Now that he is receiving attention as Vincent, Perlman feels as if his career is actually beginning. "If things go the way they should, I see myself ending up as perhaps the next antihero—like Jack Nicholson. . . . That will be the ultimate experiment—to see if anyone is interested in my face."

H. Ross Perot

In the case of Henry Ross Perot, wrote a columnist for the Dallas *Times Herald*, you have "one of our better right-wing billionaires." That writer was referring to the manner in which Perot has convinced his home state of Texas that its economy would be bolstered by graduating high schoolers versed, not in football and marching band, but in math, science, and literature. But this computer company-founder has also shown a propensity for putting his own money where his patriotism is. When the North Vietnamese wouldn't take money for U.S. prisoners of war, Perot tried to get 28 tons of airlifted food and gifts to them. While that didn't work, he had learned a little something so that by 1979, when he needed to spring two of his employees from a Teheran, Iran prison, he knew how to go about it. Perot had spies bribe the warden with $1.5 million, and thereby initiated a prison break of his two people . . . as well as 11,000 other inmates.

Born 27 June 1930, in Texarkana, Texas, the chairman of Electronic Data Systems is a former IBM salesman who started EDS in 1962 with $1,000 start-up capital. He provided data-processing services for companies by leasing other companies' computers. Twenty-two years later, General Motors paid $2.5 billion for the Dallas-based operation. In advance of that fiscal coup, however, the smallish man with the Texas-sized dreams became the first person ever to lose a billion dollars, at least on paper, when in 1969 the once-bullish EDS stock fell off. "My stock was just the pawn in a fool's game," Perot said. It took him 13 years to recoup the loss, but he was still generous enough to give to ghetto youth programs and to the Texans War on Drugs in the meantime. When the Naval Academy grad made his recommendations to reform public schools (he'd been made the special committee's chairman by the governor) he was criticized because his kids went to private schools. While that's true, the father of five is giving away his money because Perot says, "The saddest thing that could happen to me is to raise weak children as a result of my financial success."

Becoming the first businessman to receive the prestigious Winston Churchill Award, Perot was presented with this honor in 1986 by Prince Charles of Great Britain. That same year he also received the Jefferson Award for Public Service by a Private Citizen. In 1987, Perot's accomplishments were recognized again when he was given the Raoul Wallenberg Award for a lifetime of service that embodies the spirit, courage, and dedication of Raoul Wallenberg, the Swedish diplomat who saved thousands of Hungarian Jews from the Nazis in World War II.

Bernadette Peters

"I've done it all. I'm doing it all—except circus acrobatics," says Bernadette Peters, whose childhood acting career has left no visible marks on her porcelain, doll-like beauty. She is at home on stage, screen, television, nightclubs, and recording studios, and wears all five career hats with a distinctive flair.

Born Bernadette Lazzara in Ozone Park, Queens, in New York City, 28 February 1948, her father, a first generation Italian-American, drove a bread truck. Thanks to her mother, a stage-struck housewife, she was taking tap dancing lessons at the age of three and singing sessions soon after. ("Mom . . . always wanted to become an actress herself. When I was a kid, she fulfilled herself through me.") At five, while attending kindergarten at P.S. 58, Peters made her professional debut as a regular on TV's "Horn and Hardart Children's Hour," and won $800 on "Name That Tune." At nine she joined Actors Equity; at ten she changed her name to Peters, and at eleven appeared in the New York City Center revival of *The Most Happy Fella* (1959). Two years later she won her first major role, as Baby June in a road tour of *Gypsy* (accompanied by her mother). As a teenager she stopped performing ("The words are sticking in my mouth and all I could think about was how I looked"), and she attended Quintano's School for Young Professionals in Manhattan. "I used to get home from high school in time for the 4:30 movie, and I got to see all those great old pictures. I developed a real love for Ruby Keeler and Rita Hayworth and Mary Martin. . . . I have a photographic mind, and I remember exactly how they were sometimes when I sing." In 1967 she appeared off Broadway in *Curley McDimple*, a musical parody of Shirley Temple movies, the next year on Broadway in *George M* and later that year (1968) off-Broadway again in *Dames at Sea*. (*New York Times* critic Walter Kerr was captivated by Peters, who he found "especially interesting in relation to her feet: she dances as if they'd stuck to her and she were frantically trying to get rid of them.") Other Broadway appearances include a musical production of *La Strada*, a revival of *On the Town*, *Mack & Mabel* (1974), *Sally and Marsha* (1982) at the Manhattan Theatre Club (*New York Post's* critic Clive Barnes rhapsodized: "Miss Peters has become a virtuoso actress with flying saucer eyes, a sincerity as tangible as her nose, and a transparent inner range for feeling made all the more poignant by her manic doll-like exterior"), and Stephen Sondheim's Pulitzer Prizewinning *Sunday in the Park with George* (1984) ("I've never worked with anyone I like working with more than Bernadette," said Sondheim in *Life*. "She tells you exactly what's on her mind.") Other professionals agree on her directness, efficiency, and competence. She returned to Broadway again in 1985 as the star of Andrew Lloyd Webber's *Song & Dance* for which she received the Tony Award. In 1987 she played the witch in another Sondheim show, *Into the Woods*.

Her movies include *The Longest Yard* (1974), Mel Brooks' *Silent Movie* (1976), *The Jerk* (1979), the innovative *Pennies From Heaven* with Steve Martin (1981), *Tulips* (1981), *Heartbeeps* (1981), *Annie* (1982), *Slaves of New York* (1989) and *Pink Cadillac* (1989). Peters' many appearances on television were climaxed with her own series in 1976, a Norman Lear sitcom, "All's Fair" in which she co-starred with Richard Crenna. She's recorded two albums, *Bernadette Peters* (1980) and *Now Playing* (1981). Peters tours with her nightclub act and in 1980 received the first annual "Best of Las Vegas" Award. "It's very good practice to sing the same songs and get just as involved in them every time; it feeds my craft".

Roberta Peters

"I'd be lying if I told you I could give up singing tomorrow and not care," says this *soprano acutissima* (a coloratura capable of reaching the highest notes—high G in public, high A in private). "I couldn't be happy without it." And, she might add, after a lifetime of rigid self-imposed musical discipline, she could hardly throw over stardom for, say, a lifetime of tennis in Scarsdale.

Born 4 May 1930 in the Bronx, she left school at 13. ("I was pushed right into an adult world and expected to share adult values. . . . Now . . . I realized I missed many things.") Still, she "had always wanted to be an opera singer." And with that goal in mind, she studied Italian and German ("I wanted to speak it naturally and not just wait for cues"), as well as music (under a "really great teacher, William Herman. . . . Good teachers are extremely hard to find . . . a poor one can ruin a young singer's voice"). That likelihood was reduced in Roberta's case by the constant influence of Met tenor Jan Peerce, "a friend of our family [who] advised me not to become a child prodigy, not to sing in public until I was ready." Rudolf Bing decided she was ready sometime around noon one day in November 1950, when he discovered that Nadine Connor, scheduled to sing the role of Zerlina in *Don Giovanni* that night, had fallen ill. Roberta went on (wearing Miss Connor's shoes), made a dazzling debut, and before the night was out, a new star, age 20, had arrived. "Her fine preparation should be a lesson to other young American singers," said conductor Fritz Reiner. Divorced from Robert Merrill and married since 1955 to hotel magnate Bertram Fields (two sons), Peters subsequently found herself qualified to write a book called, what else, *A Debut at the Met*. She has represented her country abroad on two visits to the Soviet Union, the first in 1960 only two days following the downing by the Soviet of a U-2 spy plane, and the second during a state visit by the then-President Nixon when she became the first American-born artist to receive the coveted Bolshoi Medal.

Since then, she has traveled to the People's Republic of China for recitals and master classes, and to Israel, where she sang a benefit concert for the Robert Peters Scholarship Fund of Hebrew University. Her 35th consecutive season with the Met in 1985 marked a record unequaled by any other coloratura in the company's history and her discography is varied and extensive. Although opera stands at the center of her artistic life, Peters has expanded her field of endeavor to become a stage actress. In 1973 she did a four week tour in *The King and I* and the following season in Noel Coward's *Bittersweet*. As for TV acting, she once did a coffee commercial and "that," she told one columnist, "made me more widely recognized than all my years in music." The same thing happened in the 1980s when she sounded forth on a commercial for American Express.

Oscar Peterson

"I could never think of giving up what I'm doing," says this fleet-fingered technocrat of the keyboard, much to the delight of his appreciative fans in all parts of the globe. British jazz critic Benny Green echoes the sentiments of aficionados as far afield as Russia, Africa and the Far East when he asserts that Oscar Emmanual Peterson "today stands as one of the greatest soloists of all time, a player whose technique never obscures the lucidity of his thoughts or the wonderful buoyancy of his execution."

"Start early—and stay with it," says the piano-organ-clavichord whiz who as a youngster used to practice more than eight hours a day. Born 15 August 1925 in Montreal, Quebec, he's the son of a Canadian Pacific railway porter whose five youngsters had formed their own family band. Oscar took up the trumpet at the age of five, but after a bout with TB (hospitalized a year), switched to the piano and had his own radio show by the time he was in his mid-teens. He scored his first U.S. triumph when jazz impresario Norman Granz brought him to New York's Carnegie Hall in 1949 for a Jazz at the Philharmonic concert. *Down Beat* reported then that Peterson "stopped the concert dead in its tracks" and that's been the pattern of Peterson performances (both with and without his trio) ever since. Still associated with Granz's Pablo Records, he is probably the most recorded jazz pianist of all time, having often performed in tandem with the likes of Ella Fitzgerald, Count Basie, Roy Eldridge and Dizzy Gillespie.

Known in recent years for his composing as well as his virtuoso pianistics, Peterson created a suite to celebrate the Royal Wedding of England's Prince Charles and Princess Diana. His best know work is "Canadian Suite," each movement of which commemorates a different area of his native Canada. Married (five children), the award-winning jazzman (12 consecutive years as *Down Beat's* "Best Jazz Pianist") still practices tirelessly. "The only musician I ever heard of who didn't need to practice," he says, "is a fellow named Gabriel. But he has wings."

Richard Petty

The greatest stock-car racer in the world is a good ol' boy from Level Cross, North Carolina, by the name of Richard Petty. Born 2 July 1937 to Elizabeth and Lee Petty (one of the early stock-car racing greats), not-so-little (6'2", 195 lbs) Richard ("If my mother had wanted to call me Dick, she would have named me Dick") has won more NASCAR Grand National titles than any other driver, making him the "undisputed 'king' of stock-car racing."

Petty contends that he is only 25% responsible for his victories, that his car (once a Plymouth Roadrunner, more recently a Ford or Chevrolet) deserves 50%, and his pit crew 25% of the credit. Not that his cars appear out of the blue; they are put in top shape by his brother Maurice and cousin Dale Inman at the huge (35-plus employees) Petty Enterprises garage in Level Cross. Says Richard of his pit crew: "We average about 22 seconds per stop. Other guys take 25 seconds. The difference is worth between half a lap and a full lap, depending upon the size of the track." Always concerned about safety, the Pettys were the first stock-car competitors to use a roll-bar, a nylon window screen, and a helmet-cooler, and have employed the use of two-way radios for communication with the pit. His cars are painted blue and red with the number 43 (Lee Petty's number was 42) on the side.

Married in 1958, Richard and Lynda have four children, Kyle (also a NASCAR racer), Sharon, Lisa and Rebecca. The family resides in Level Cross, a few miles from Lee Petty's house and the family business. In 1986 his book was released *King Richard I: The Autobiography of America's Greatest Auto Racer* and in 1989 he appeared on screen in the film *Speed Zone*.

Regis Philbin

Regis Philbin, co-star of "Live with Regis and Kathie Lee" (the ABC morning show which went national in 1988) traveled a long hard road until he finally found "his" show.

Born in New York on August 25th and raised in a strict Catholic family it was quite a leap for him to turn towards show business. He caught "the bug" in 1958 during a stint as an NBC page on Steve Allen's "Tonight" program. It was this particular form of entertainment (talk show host) which appealed to him, so he packed his bags and did whatever he could (he was a stage hand, a truck driver) until he eventually landed a job in San Diego as a news broadcaster and talk show emcee. His first big break came in 1964 when he caught the eye of comedian Joey Bishop who had his own talk show. Regis was hired and played a marvelous second fiddle to Bishop's dry and depressed sense of humor. Their relationship was grand. "Regis Philbin is like a son to me. He's one of the nicest persons I've ever met," said Joey of his announcer. The show eventually failed and in 1981, NBC gave him a shot at his own show, but this one did not succeed.

However, his new format with Kathie Lee Gifford, provides just the right chemistry. Jeff Jarvis, critic of *People* magazine, describes his unique ability to play with people and not offend them. "He may seem like a game show host with no prizes. . . . Sure he's pleasant and charming but don't hold that against him. He's also witty, if harmlessly so. He can insult guests and get away with it. He can talk about mundane frustrations in his own life . . . and not put us back to sleep." This is an art which very few can master. Accordingly, he is very popular with his fans.

Occasionally, you can see him appearing with his present wife, Joy, (he was first married to Catherine Faylen, a former TV actress, and has two children from this marriage) when Kathie Lee is on vacation. He is wonderfully irascible, describing his daily exasperations at life in the Big Apple. Everyone knows he has two more teenage daughters that drive him batty and that he doesn't own a car, but prefers to rent "clunkers." Why buy a car when these rentals provide him with such marvelous material for his show? He is a fine craftsman, for he makes his work appear effortless, the sign of a true professional.

Lou Diamond Phillips

Initially thought of as the "kid who got a lucky break," Lou Diamond Phillips has proven himself to be an actor worthy of impressive roles. Born 17 February 1962 in Arlington, Texas, Phillips developed a yearning to act in the sixth grade. Carrying his interest through his school years he studied the dramatic arts while attending the University of Texas. Displaying an insatiable appetite to learn and perfect his craft, Phillips studied film technique vigorously with Adam Rourke. Having appeared in numerous theater productions, among them *Whose Life Is It Anyway?*, *P.S. Your Cat Is Dead*, and *Hamlet*, Phillips moved into television with spots on CBS-TV's "Dallas", NBC'S "Miami Vice" and an NBC Movie of the Week "Time Bomb". Although experienced and somewhat recognized, Phillips was basically unknown until that fateful day when he was cast in the role of Richie Valens in the Columbia feature *La Bamba* (1987). The film, which Lou is deeply indebted to and proud of, propelled him into the throes of stardom. Since his "lucky break," Phillips has starred in the Warner Brothers feature *Stand and Deliver*. ("Miami Vice" co-star Edward James Olmos suggested the young Phillips after having been impressed with his work on "Vice") and Twentieth Century's *Young Guns* (1988) with Emilio Estevez and Kiefer Sutherland. Although he has launched a successful and popular film career, Lou still manages to find time to engage in television production. He appeared in the ABC-TV movie "The Three Kings" (1989) in which he portrayed an insane asylum inmate whose delusions of grandeur, after being involved in a Christmas play, lead him to believe he is one of the three wisemen. With his workaholic film schedule, Lou has completed two more feature films: Universal's *Renegades* (again placing him side by side with Kiefer Sutherland) and Disney's *The Bank Job*.

"Although I consider myself an actor," says Lou, "my other interests excite me too. Writing, directing, producing and teaching all help me to be a better actor." Already having guest-lectured at the prestigious American Film Institute, Phillips hopes to be able to reach more aspiring thespians by committing himself to open an extension of the Film Actors Lab in Los Angeles.

Many may embark on an acting career for money or fame, but for Lou Diamond Phillips acting is something spiritual. "It gives me the opportunity to say things about love, courage, and conviction that I feel need to be said. We in the film industry have an obligation: people should leave a movie having learned something about themselves, about others, and about life."

Lou lives in Hollywood Hills with his actress wife Julie Cypher.

Paloma Picasso

Asked what she'd salvage were she caught in a sudden fire, she answered, "My memories." In her case, those are certainly the second half of the family jewels. The other half is having had Pablo Picasso as her father. She's been described as having "her padre's burning black eyes and a proud señorita's carriage." Her mother, Francoise Gilot (now married to Dr. Jonas Salk), lived with the painter for 11 years. Picasso was 67 when baby Paloma was born in April of 1949. Her parents separated when she was four and summers were spent with her father and his mistress Jacqueline Roque. "We got up at noon," Paloma remembers, "had lunch at two which lasted 'til four. Then we often went to the beach. This was a person who knew how to live. He worked in a frenzy," she says, explaining her father's work habits. He left behind 38,000 paintings and other works. "There isn't another painter who did so much in a lifetime. At the same time he found an equilibrium." From among her father's famous friends she was most fascinated by Cocteau whose "house was like his paintings." The artist's last mistress prevented Paloma from attending Picasso's funeral in 1973. There was a long period of bad blood among the master's kin after his death. Eventually, when matters were settled in the courts, her inheritance amounted to an estimated $30 million from her share of her father's works of art. The amount meant more to Paloma watchers than it did to her. "It hasn't changed my life or the people in my life. Others can't understand that I'm the same person as before." (She married Argentine playwright Rafael Lopez-Sanchez in 1978).

"Style evolves," says the industrious jewelry designer (she sells at Tiffany), *parfum* endorsee (her scent is dispensed by Warner Communications), and leather designer (Paloma Picasso for Lopez-Cambil). She has declared New York "the capital of the world." Paloma and Rafael are considered two of the hottest seasonings among the big-money, late-night set where one observer noted that, "they are aware of everything from the decaying Buddhist temples of Borobudur to the ritual of cocktails at poolside at the Beverly Hills Hotel." When she is not in New York or sampling the exotic in little known faraway places, she concentrates her energies in Paris at the Foundation Picasso which she established with her brother to centralize research about their father. It is also in that city that she must "remember to take a *flacon* when we go to the theatre to spray the air around us with Guerlain or some other scent. Paris is old," she sighs.

T. Boone Pickens

The canny corporate-takeover tactics of this maverick Texas oilman have led some observers to liken him to such long-ago financial sharpies as Jay Gould and Jim Fisk, but a more contemporary parallel might be (the television show) "Dallas" wily wheeler-dealer J.R. Ewing. When *Time* put him on its cover in March 1985, T. (for Thomas) Boone Pickens, fresh from challenges to such petroleum giants as Gulf and Phillips, had earned an estimated three-quarters of a billion dollars for his own Mesa Petroleum and, in the process, enriched millions of smaller shareholders. Entrenched corporate execs see Pickens as a "pirate raider," out for blood; the stockholders who've profited from his exquisitely-organized Wall Street ventures consider him a "modern David" going after the Goliath of Big Oil. Long before the headlined raid on Phillips of 1985, *Fortune* called Pickens "a rebellious populist" who "identifies his own interest . . . with what he claims is the interest of a downtrodden constituency, the stockholders of other oil companies." Although he has never actually acquired a major corporation, Pickens' has caused considerable lost sleep for wary CEO's who wonder where his fancy might turn next. In July 1989 he was challenging corporate officers of Koito Manufacturing, a Tokyo-based automotive-lighting maker, against Japanese investment barriers. Standing tall in his crusade to have a seat with two colleagues on Koito's board, he questioned their policy. "Do you treat all owners this way? Or is it just American shareholders?"

Born 22 May 1928, the only son of an inveterate gambler dad and his practical-minded wife, the Master of Merger Mania considers himself "very fortunate in my gene mix. The gambling instincts I inherited from my father were matched by my mother's gift for analysis." From his birthplace of Holdenville, Oklahoma, the family moved to Amarillo, where the entrepreneur now lives ("like an Indian prince," according to one friend) on a 14,000 acre spread. Graduating with a degree in geology from Oklahoma State, Pickens spent four years toiling as a geologist for Phillips Petroleum before losing patience with what he considered the company's lack of receptivity to new ideas. One day, frustrated and fed up, he quit, and using the $1300 he received in severance pay, set off sniffling around oilwell sites on his own. By the early 1970s, he had parlayed his "mother's gift for analysis," his geological know-how and a bit of luck into his first million and the pile is now significantly higher.

Married and divorced from first wife Lynn O'Brien (four children), his second wife, the former Beatrice Carr (after whom he named a 1975 North Sea oil strike) has helped make his life what he calls "a perfect deal." In addition to their Amarillo digs, they own an Oklahoma cattle ranch and a vacation hideaway in Palm Springs. But the workaholic Pickens, who averages twelve-hour work days, seldom goes on holiday. When not planning one of his corporate raids from high in a Manhattan hotel, he's apt to be speechifying around the country on the need for shareholder uprisings against mediocre corporate management. In 1988 his book *Boone* was released.

Joe Piscopo

Whether he's Frank Sinatra leading a band of heavy metal rockers, or Joan Rivers sporting a five o'clock shadow, Joe Piscopo is a multifaceted entertainer who's always "on target." The talented Piscopo was born to a Passaic, New Jersey couple on 17 June 1951. Raised in Essex County, the middle child of his family, he led a happy childhood playing little league baseball and catching the waves at Bruce Springsteen's beloved Jersey Shore. Not particularly swayed by homework, Piscopo was somewhat rebellious during his high school tenure. Caught smoking and cutting classes, he was suspended from school on at least eight occasions. However, it was during high school that Joe discovered he had a home on the stage. Performing in high school productions not only whet his appetite for the performing arts but also bestowed him with the honor of being a recipient of the Lincoln Center Student Arts award. Being limited in his choices of which college to attend, Piscopo made his decision based on what any young student would consider the essential factor—better surf! With surfboard under arm he headed south to Jones College in Jacksonville, Florida where he majored in broadcast management. To better prepare himself for what he does best, he chose community theater and worked at the school's four radio stations. Graduation led him back to New Jersey where he found employment at a radio station in Trenton, and continued his participation in community theater. Ripe with experience at twenty-five, he decided it was time to give acting his undivided attention. Between 1976 and 1980 he had the fortune of being cast in commercials endorsing a wide range of products from automobiles to soft drinks. During these years he also conceived a stand-up routine which he performed at some of the most notorious comedy clubs in New York. It was in 1980 when he achieved his "big break." Joining the cast of NBC's "Saturday Night Live" he remained with the program until the 1983 season.

The show was Piscopo's vehicle in evolving new characters such as the "Sports Guy," Solomon and Pudge, and spoofs on David Letterman, David Hartman and Joan Rivers. Says Piscopo as an alumnus of the late night comedy show, "it was up to me to create a lot of the original characters for the show. I'll always be indebted to 'Saturday Night Live' because it taught me so much." His departure from "Saturday Night Live" introduced him to the world of feature films. Portraying Danny Vermin in the 20th Century Fox gangster spoof *Johnny Dangerously* with Michael Keaton in 1984, he later co-starred with Danny DeVito and Captain Lou Albano in Brian DePalma's *Wise Guys* in 1985. His new found film career did not, however, take him away from television. On 22 September 1984, Piscopo starred in an HBO cable special. The sixty-minute program was a great project for his "ultimate tribute to my hero" Frank Sinatra. May 1986 brought another Piscopo special this time airing on ABC-TV titled the "Joe Piscopo New Jersey Special." In late 1986 the two-time ACE award recipient added to his repertoire of characters "Python Piscopo," "Bruce Piscopo" (his Springsteen spoof) and "Rappin Fats Piscopo," characters which he developed for his Miller Lite Beer endorsements. In 1987 he returned to HBO with the special "The Joe Piscopo Halloween Party" and a role in the feature film *Dead Heat*. In addition to on-camera activities, Piscopo penned a book, *The Joe Piscopo Tapes* with co-author Pam Norris. Having released a single "The Honeymooner's Rap" with Eddie Murphy, plus an album on Columbia Records *New Jersey*, Piscopo has added recording artist to his already impressive resume.

Piscopo and his wife Nancy were divorced in 1988 after 15 years of marriage. He is attentive to his young son Joey; he was named Father of the Year by the National Father's Day Committee in 1983.

Suzanne Pleshette

"I don't sit back and wait for great parts. I love being an actress, and I'll probably be one until I'm 72, standing around the back lot doing 'Gunsmokes'." The throaty-voiced, sultry actress, credited by some as having the most riveting hazel eyes this side of Elizabeth Taylor, has enjoyed a versatile career in film, stage, and television. She is perhaps best recognized as Emily Hartley, subdued wife of mild-mannered Bob Hartley on the popular sitcom, "The Bob Newhart Show," which ran from 1972 until 1978. A followup series, 1983's "The Suzanne Pleshette Show," failed to make the grade. Neither did her most recent series, "Nightingales" (1989).

The only child of a ballerina and a theatre manager, Pleshette, born 31 January 1937 in Brooklyn, New York, was weaned on show business through exposure to her father's colorful friends in the entertainment industry. After graduating from the High School of Performing Arts and studying at the Neighborhood Playhouse, she appeared in a production of *A Streetcar Named Desire* with Peter Falk and debuted on Broadway in the drama, *Compulsion*. Jerry Lewis enticed her to Hollywood to co-star in his film, *The Geisha Boy*. Some thirty other film roles followed, including *A Rage to Live* and *If It's Tuesday This Must Be Belgium*. Audiences remember her as the love-spurned school teacher who got pecked to death in Alfred Hitchcock's 1963 thriller, *The Birds*. Recent TV appearances include CBS's "Bridges to Cross" and "Command in Hell."

Pleshette, who acknowledges that she is "hopelessly middle class" in her values, was divorced after an early marriage to actor Troy Donahue. She married businessman Tom Gallagher in 1968.

George Plimpton

This quintessential Harvard man does things most folks only dream about, like playing quarterback for the Detroit Lions (*Paper Lion*, 1966), pitching for the New York Yankees (*Out of My League*, (1961), playing hockey for the Boston Bruins, performing in the percussion section of the New York Philharmonic, photographing centerfolds for *Playboy*, and flying on a trapeze for the Clyde Beatty-Cole Brothers Circus. He's a respected writer and an innovative editor of other people's lives, notably of the book *Edie*, biography of Edie Sedgewick (co-edited with Jean Stein) and *D.V.*, the oral histoire of the one and only Diane Vreeland. He is also the founding editor of the sophisticated literary quarterly *The Paris Review*. "In my opinion," he says, "to write accurately and vividly one must know first hand one's subject matter." A *New Yorker* cartoon had the late Lyndon Johnson saying of his mail, "Letter from George Plimpton. He wants to be president for the day."

Born in New York City, 18 March 1927, the son of the late Francis Plimpton, lawyer and a deputy ambassador to the United Nations, George attended—besides Harvard—Exeter and Cambridge universities. He founded *The Paris Review* in 1953, and in 1968 married the former Freddy Espy with whom he has two children, Medora and Taylor. Once the big bang in New York's social high life, things seem to be tapering off in the 80's due to his many projects including numerous lectures and commercial endorsements, all in his capacity as an adventurer, America's participatory journalist, often referred to as the country's best-known "jack of all trades, master of none."

He claims as his two favorite hobbies, bird watching and fireworks (the title of a 1984 book), an odious combo for the birds no doubt. As New York City's Fireworks Commissioner, Plimpton has been responsible for a renaissance of the colorful flashes and sparks—his duties included planning the now famous display celebrating the Brooklyn Bridge Centennial in 1983. "It's been my observation," he told *People*, "that writers have a particular affinity with fireworks. It's because fireworks, especially those he sets off himself, bursting spectacularly in the night sky, do everything hoped for but rarely achieved with words on a page—beauty, drama and oohs and aahs from an audience. The only reaction one gets from words on a page is an occasional low hmmm." Plimpton's other books are *Open Net* (1985) and *The Curious Case of Sidd Finch* (1987).

Amanda Plummer

"The only other actress I've ever seen make a debut this weirdly lyrical was Katharine Hepburn," wrote Pauline Kael about Amanda Plummer's performance in her first film, *Cattle Annie and Little Britches* in 1980. For her later Tony award winning performance in Broadway's *Agnes of God*, *New York Times* critic Frank Rich practically elevated her to sainthood: "as close to an angel as we're ever likely to see on Broadway." She is not the conventional ingenue, nor is she at all glamorous. Slightly built, with a long slender neck, she has large expressive eyes, short dark hair, and a thin wide mouth. Jack Kroll of *Newsweek* says: "There's an air of suspense about Plummer's acting; you sense that she's creating her character and herself at the same time." Another observer notes: "Even when she is still, she can make her immobility the most eloquent thing onstage."

She was born on Bank Street in New York City's Greenwich Village in 1957, the child of two star performers and strong personalities, Christopher Plummer ("My father—wow—I love him. I adore him. But I don't really know him . . . he's the privatest man I know in the world"), and Tammy Grimes ("It wasn't easy being her daughter, she was travelling all the time. . . . I saw very little of her. . . . When I was older I began to miss her. . . . We've talked about it. We understand"). An only child, she became a one-parent child at the age of 4 when her parents broke up (her father lived abroad for thirteen years). "I was terribly relieved," says her father, "I didn't want to have anything to do with the upbringing of a child. . . . Children are not of great interest to me until they form their own personalities in their teenage years." When Amanda was 18, having led a fantasy childhood ("I made up different characters: some were boys, some were girls, some were animals. Going into these characters freed me. I could do anything"), she told her mother she wanted to be an actress. ("She said fine. . . . It was our coming together.") After two and a half years at Middlebury College in Vermont, she studied at the Neighborhood Playhouse, and then joined the Williamstown Theater Festival's second company. In 1979, she made her New York theatre debut in *Artichoke* at the Manhattan Theater Club. In 1980, she appeared with her mother in a Roundabout production of Turgenev's *A Month in the Country* (for which she had auditioned without knowing her mother had the lead). She made her Broadway debut as Jo in the 1981 revival of *A Taste of Honey* (Tony nomination) and won the Tony for best supporting actress of 1982 for *Agnes of God*. In 1983, she was Laura Wingfield to Jessica Tandy's Amanda in the Broadway revival of Tennessee Williams' *The Glass Menagerie*. In 1985 she appeared in Sam Shepard's *A Lie of the Mind*, and in 1987 *Pygmalion*. Her other films include *The World According to Garp*, *Hotel New Hampshire*, *Daniel*, *Riders to the Sea* and *Drugstore Cowboy*. She also made the NBC television pilot "Truck One" in 1989. "Life and the stage are not separate," philosophized Plummer, "Those two hours are not separate from your night and day. The people you're working with are flesh and blood, and there's always danger involved. It's exciting."

Christopher Plummer

In America he's considered an English actor, in England he is looked upon as an American actor. Born in Canada, 13 December 1927 in Toronto, he is active on both sides of the Atlantic, with a reputation for testy independence, for doing roles he enjoys rather than those that promote his career. If he is not an international movie star, it is by his choice. "My position in films is more difficult because I do both theatre and films. . . . I've chosen a much harder path, trying to keep my position in both. Perhaps I'm a renaissance man," he has said. "I'm bored with questions about acting. There's more to life than acting. Talking about acting is murder for the artist. Most actors I know are sophisticated, charming, informed people who, contrary to popular opinion, know a good deal about other things. You don't have to sweat about it."

Plummer's first important role was as D'Arcy in a high school production of *Pride and Prejudice*. He turned pro at 17 and in the following five years appeared in over 75 plays in both French and English, ranging from Shakespeare to Tennessee Williams. Hailed by critic Brooks Atkinson at age 26 as, "a Shakespearean actor of first rank," he has played the works of the Bard in London, New York and all three Stratfords: Avon, Ontario and Connecticut. He has also starred on Broadway in Archibald MacLeish's verse play, *J.B.*, Christopher Fry's *The Dark is Light Enough* (with the late Katharine Cornell), *The Lark*, *The Royal Hunt of the Sun*, *Arturo Ui*, E.L. Doctorow's *Drinks Before Dinner*, as Iago to James Earl Jones's, *Othello*, and *Macbeth*. His most popular film role was that of Captain von Trapp in 1965's *The Sound of Music*. Recent films include *Dragnet 1987* (1987), *Souvenir* (1987) and *Deadly Surveillance* (1989). A winner of many prestigious theatrical awards, Plummer's notable contribution to theatre history is his daughter from his first marriage to Tammy Grimes, Amanda Plummer. Divorced from Grimes, he is married to Elaine Taylor with whom he resides in Connecticut.

Sidney Poitier

At 18 he saw an ad in a Negro paper saying, "Actors Wanted." "I didn't know it was any different from 'Dishwashers Wanted' or 'Porters Wanted,'" he recalled, "So I walked into this little theatre place in Harlem and I said to the man there, 'I want one of your actor jobs.' The man put me on a stool and had me read a part. I'd read about four lines in my West Indian accent when he stopped me. 'Now, look, boy,' he said, 'You can't even talk. Why don't you get a job as a porter?'"

His Bahamian patois long behind him, the actor from Cat Island has proven himself an actor many times over in such films as *The Blackboard Jungle*, *In the Heat of the Night*, *A Raisin in the Sun* (also on Broadway), *Guess Who's Coming to Dinner* and *Lilies of the Field*, which in 1963 provided him with the vehicle to become the first black actor ever awarded an Oscar. In 1972 he passed muster as a director (as well as co-starring with Harry Belefonte) in *Buck and the Preacher*.

Raised on his father's tomato farm in the Bahamas, Poitier was born in Miami (20 February 1924), when his parents took a trip there to sell their produce. He had only a year and a half of formal schooling during what one reporter described as "a growing-up absurd that makes the usual theatrical hard luck story sound like a blithe bedtime fable." Odd-jobbing, he returned to Miami as a teenager and, brazenly defying the color line, worked his way up to New York where, sleeping on rooftops in the summer and in public toilets in the winter, he met the casting director of the American Negro Theater. He had his first taste of success on Broadway in *Anna Lucasta* in 1948 and within a decade had become the first Black matinee idol. He has been married twice and has six daughters. He published his autobiography in 1980 and since then has continued to direct and appear in the movies: *China Blues*, *Traces*, *Shootout*, *Fast Forward*, *Hard Knox*, *Little Nikita* and *Shoot to Kill*. In 1989 he was honored by the American Museum of Moving Image.

Roman Polanski

Life and its capacity for paradox still stalks this haunted cinema artist who created such macabre spine-tinglers as *Knife in the Water* (1962), commercial Hollywood vehicles such as *Rosemary's Baby* (1968), and *Chinatown* (1974), as well as the romantic epic, *Tess* (1979). The Polish-born director was the toast of Tinseltown before 1969 when Charles Manson directed a demented band of drug-bent disciples to break into Polanski's L.A. home where they butchered his wife, Sharon Tate, 26, and three other friends. What police found—Tate, who was nine months pregnant, had been indiscriminately slashed as she and the others fought for their lives, and an X had been cut on her stomach—so traumatized Polanski, who was in London at the time, that for five grief-stricken days he couldn't walk without assistance. Ironically,

Maury Povich

he says, both public and the press seemed to deduce that the victims and Polanski had been involved in drugs, illicit sex, and satanic rites which had brought on the murders. Later, the director's own deeds led to his own demise—residentially at least—in the U.S. After his widely publicized affair with then 15-year-old actress Nastassja Kinski in Europe, he was convicted in California in 1977 of bedding a 13-year-old girl at Jack Nicholson's pad. Having already spent a month-and-a-half in Chino prison and facing a longer term, Polanski fled before sentencing to France where he can't be extradited. "I know in my heart of hearts," he says, "that the spirit of laughter has deserted me. It isn't just that success has left me jaded or that I've been soured by tragedy and by my own follies. (But) I seem to be toiling to no discernible purpose."

The little man (five-feet-four) whose fictionalized screen nightmares have been nothing as compared to his life, was born in Paris, 18 August 1933. Polanski is the son of a Jewish mother who died in a concentration camp, and a father who survived one. Roman became a member of the Polish Crakow theater troupe at the age of 14 ("The stage was just, for me, one way to get to films"), and later studied film directing at the world-renowned National Film Academy at Lodz in 1954. His first wife was Polish film actress Barbara Kwiatkowska, and he met and married actress Sharon Tate when he directed her in his film, *The Vampire Killers* (1966). Polanski wrote *Roman*, his autobiographical tome, in 1984. In 1985 he directed *Pirates*, and in 1987 wrote the screenplay and directed *Frantic*.

Maury Povich

He is a polished broadcaster as well as a skillful interviewer. A 20-plus-year veteran of television, Povich began his career in broadcasting as a sportscaster at a local Washington, D.C. station, and has worked his way up to being the host of a highly acclaimed and controversial syndicated investigative magazine series.

Maury Povich was born the son of Shirley Povich, the prominent sports editor of the *Washington Post*, circa 1939 in Washington, D.C. He attended the University of Pennsylvania where he was placed on academic suspension due to poor grades. Eventually, he re-entered and graduated at age 23. Upon graduating, Povich married his college sweetheart Phyllis Minkoff. His first job in television was as a broadcaster with WTTG Channel 5 in Washington, D.C. In 1969, he became the host of the popular midday talk show "Panorama," also on WTTG. In 1973, in addition to hosting "Panorama" he also became weekend anchor. Ready for bigger and better things, in 1976 Povich accepted a position as news anchor and talk show host with the NBC affiliate WNAQ in Chicago. A few short months later, he quit following a bitter contract dispute. His next job was with the CBS affiliate KNXT in Los Angeles. Within four months he was fired due to low ratings. "I was shattered to the core," replied Maury. "I began wondering whether I should be selling shoes." At the same time, his marriage was floundering. Soon after his job in Los Angeles he took a job with KGO, an ABC station in San Francisco, where he became close friends with who was to become his future wife Connie Chung. "Connie nurtured me," said Maury, "and kept telling me that I should not question my talent." And what words of wisdom they were. In 1983 Maury went from San Francisco, to Philadelphia, to Washington, D.C. where he resumed hosting "Panorama." and co-anchored the "10 O'Clock News." Both shows received Emmys as well as other prestigious awards from the broadcasting industry, and in 1984 Maury received an Emmy for Best Co-Anchor. As he became more stable, thoughts of marriage became more frequent. Finally on 2 December 1984, Maury and Connie tied the knot, although they didn't actually live under the same roof until 1986, when Maury was offered a position with the controversial tabloid talk show "A Current Affair." Maury has been the host of the Fox television nightly talk show since its inception in July 1986. The show has been both praised and criticized. According to Maury, "I have as much fun defending the show as I have doing it. I'm only sad the critics take it so seriously. . . ." In addition, he also co-anchors the 7 P.M. news on Fox 5 in New York.

Maury and Connie reside in New York City, but spend their weekends at their 1840 manor house in New Jersey.

Jane Powell

Can a soprano, one with a two-and-a-half-octave voice be acceptable in the pop music world? The answer, was yes—if the soprano had the versatility of Jane Powell. A petite 5 foot 1, blue eyed, blonde charmer, Jane Powell captured audiences and made her shot to stardom while in her teens. Throughout her career, she has worked in radio, films, television, summer stock, night clubs, recording studios and on Broadway. If that isn't enough, she graced the shelves of bookstores with an autobiography, *The Girl Next Door . . . And How She Grew*.

Jane Powell grew up in Portland, Oregon, where her parents, Paul (baby food salesman and apartment building manager) and Eileen Bruce lived in a modest three-room apartment. She was born Suzanne Bruce on 1 April 1929, and at the young age of two began singing on a local children's radio program. Impressed by the quality of her voice, neighbors urged the Bruces to enroll her in singing classes. Her exceptional singing talents at eleven years old prompted her teacher to introduce her to radio station KOIN in Portland. Suzanne soon had her own radio show and became Oregon's Victory girl by appearing at patriotic rallies to promote United States war bonds. It was a holiday trip to Southern California with her parents that changed the course of the singer's life. While in Los Angeles, the Bruces took their daughter to Stars Over Hollywood (a broadcast talent show) and as a contestant she sang an aria from Georges Bizet's opera *Carmen* that caught the attention of Metro-Goldwyn-Mayer talent scouts. A contract followed, and in 1944 (while on loan to United Artists) she had her first picture *Song of the Open Road*. In this film she played a character named Jane Powell—she kept it. Her first MGM musical was *Holiday in Mexico* (1946), which starred Walter Pidgeon, Illona Massey, and Roddy McDowall. A string of pictures followed, including *Date with Judy, Royal Wedding, Small Town Girl, Seven Brides for Seven Brothers, Hit the Deck,* and *Girl Most Likely*. When she left MGM, Jane Powell's career won a new generation of fans. She concentrated on Las Vegas Revues, Nite Clubs, Broadway *(Irene)*, and, most recently, television (soap opera: "Loving" and recurring role on "Growing Pains"). She also released the home video "Jane Powell's Fight Back With Fitness."

Powell's early days at the studio were not easy. The MGM school was packed with such famous students as Elizabeth Taylor, Margaret O'Brien, Debbie Reynolds and Judy Garland, and according to a *Life* article, when asked about the social scene, Jane said, "I'm too young for the old ones, and too old for the young ones." It was in 1949 she married Geary Steffen (children: Geary, Suzanne) and after a divorce in 1953 she married Pat Nierney in 1954 (one child, Lindsey), only to be divorced in 1963. Jane Powell tried again in 1965 with Jim Fitzgerald who produced her revue "Just Twenty—Plus Me." She married longtime beau, Dick Moore on 21 May 1988; they have homes in Connecticut and Manhattan. Powell observes as an epigraph to her autobiography, "Life is a ladder that we all ascend in a different way. Sometimes we run up too fast and miss a few rungs." In her spare time, Jane enjoys cooking and gardening.

Lewis Powell

For Lewis Franklin Powell Jr., appointment to the Supreme Court was not exactly the thrill of a lifetime. When Nixon's attorney general John Mitchell phoned Powell with the news, Powell, then an attorney in private practice in his native Virginia, turned Mitchell down flat. At age 64, he felt he was too old to begin a new career. Nixon's men were scrambling to find a candidate for the Court after the Senate had turned thumbs down on two other Nixon choices, but Powell had already served as president of the American Bar Association and felt he had had enough of the national spotlight. That night, when he returned home from a day at his office, the phone rang. It was Nixon himself, making a hard sell pitch. Powell had a "duty" to accept—a duty to the South, to the law, the Court, the President, the country, Nixon said. Powell, a Democrat, became the last member of his party to become one of the "brethren" of the nation's top court.

By the time Nixon picked him for the Supreme Court, Powell generally was recognized as a first-rate attorney and a political moderate. His views had been shaped by decades of law practice in Richmond, years of active participation in the American Bar Association, and deep involvement in efforts to desegregate the public schools of Virginia, where he had earlier served as president of the state board of education. Powell helped keep the schools open despite widespread pressure to close them in a show of resistance to desegregation.

Born in Suffolk, Va., 19 September 1907, Powell has happily kept within his state's borders (or within shouting distance, as the nation's capital is virtually carved out of the state's terrain) all of his life. Higher education commenced at Washington and Lee University, where he graduated Phi Beta Kappa in 1929, then Washington and Lee University Law School, from which he graduated 1931; he advanced his law studies at Harvard for a year and then returned to Virginia where he joined one of the state's oldest and most prestigious law firms. Powell eventually became a senior partner, continuing his association with the firm until his nomination to the Court. He married the former Josephine M. Rucker in 1936; the couple has three daughters and one son.

Stefanie Powers

A sophisticated beauty with a breezy and painlessly seductive air, Hollywood raised her in the style to which she always seemed accustomed. Stefanie Powers, born in Hollywood on 2 November 1942, grew up with the likes of Natalie Wood and Jill St. John, taking ballet, going to the movies, and plotting her invasion of the high studio walls that loom so large throughout Los Angeles. She slipped through once at age 15 by lying about her age to snare a bit part in *West Side Story*, but she was discovered and trounced out. After graduation from Hollywood High she commanded small, and soon larger roles in television series until she was cast in her first lead with the mid-1960s adventure entry, "The Girl from U.N.C.L.E." A spinoff from the popular "The Man from U.N.C.L.E.," expectations ran high, but the show fizzled in the ratings and the "Girl" in question found herself back at casting calls. Top billing generally eluded her until old pal Robert Wagner suggested she play his wife in the 1979 romantic-action show, "Hart to Hart." The slick and entertaining vehicle about two fabulously rich and gloriously well-wed people who find love at home and murder at every cocktail party, was a ratings hit for most of its five-year run. Many feminists praised Power's character, Jennifer Hart, as a positive role model for women. Ms. Hart was equal to her husband, smart, brave, and kind *in addition* to being fabulously rich and gloriously well-wed.

The show's demise has allowed its beautiful star to do more made-for-TV movies and such mini-series as Judith Krantz' "Mistral's Daughter." She starred in 1985 in the film *The Second Lady* and in the 1986 CBS-TV show "Maggie." Ultra-fit Powers shared her prowess in the 1985 book *Stefanie Powers Superlife* and her 1989 video *Stefanie Powers: Introduction to Horseback Riding and Horse Care.*

But for the actress herself, life has been a bit more trying. Her lengthy and bitter estrangement from her father, noted photographer M.B. Paul, has received considerable—and unwanted—publicity. "The reason I don't talk about growing up is that I have a lot of unresolved conflicts and anger." An early marriage to Gary Lockwood ended in divorce, and her relationship with longtime companion William Holden ended tragically with the actor's alcohol-related accidental death. Powers maintains an active involvement in wildlife preservation, which she developed during her extensive travels with Holden.

Priscilla Presley

She has successfully balanced her life as a wife, mother, business woman, and actress. She has done everything from modeling, to designing clothing, to owning a boutique that catered to celebrities, not to mention marrying one of the most infamous, loved and remembered celebrities of all time. She was born Priscilla Beaulieu, on 24 May 1945 in Brooklyn, New York, the daughter of an Air Force officer. Although born in New York, and raised in Connecticut, she traveled extensively throughout the U.S. and Europe due to the nature of her father's profession. She attended high school in Weisbaden, Germany, which is also where she had her first experience in professional modeling. Later she moved to Memphis to pursue her modeling career, which is where she met her future husband, the legendary king of rock and roll, Elvis Presley. They wed on 1 May 1967 in Las Vegas, and a year later the couple had their first, and only child together, Lisa Marie, on 1 February 1968. Five years later, in 1973, Priscilla and Elvis divorced.

Deciding to go into business, Priscilla and her personal dress designer opened up a boutique which carried their exclusive designs, and catered to such stars as Cher, Barbra Streisand, and Natalie Wood. She later sold out to her partner. From there, she went to television, making her debut in 1979 in ABC's "Those Amazing Animals," She also began appearing in prime time commercials, endorsing Wella Balsam hair products nationally. Other television credits include hosting "the 14th Annual Country Music Awards," appearing on "Good Morning America," "Night of 100 Stars II," the nighttime soap series "Dallas," and the television special "Life with Elvis." Moving on to film, she made her debut in motion pictures with *Comeback*, followed by *The Naked Gun* (1988). In addition to being a celebrity of TV and film, Priscilla is also a writer, and wrote a novel entitled *Elvis and Me*, (1984). In 1986, she moved in with Brazilian Marco Garibaldi. A year later on 1 March 1987, Priscilla gave birth to their son Navarone Anthony Garibaldi. In her spare time Priscilla enjoys practicing the ancient art of karate and overseeing the growth of Graceland as a successful tourist attraction.

Frances Preston

Frances Williams Preston is a woman's woman. Her list of accomplishments could fill a small volume. Presently, she is President and Chief Executive Officer of B.M.I. (Broadcast Music Inc.), but she has been with B.M.I. since 1958. Broadcast Music Incorporated is a not-for-profit organization formed by some 460 broadcasters in 1940. In 1986, B.M.I. collected just under $200,000,000 in licensing fees which it distributed to over 85,000 songwriters/composers and music publishers. Without her organization's backing she is convinced that "a group of songwriters trying to negotiate with a large television organization would have a difficult time. They just won't have the clout or the power to do it." These are two things this lady does not lack.

She was born in Nashville and attended George Peabody College from 1946 to 1949, but there is very little information relative to her age. "The music industry is very young. Once your age is in print, years get added on and added on. The next thing you hear is 'she'll be retiring soon.' Not likely!" How did this all begin? Her first contact with the music and recording business can be traced back to 1950 when she began as a receptionist at WSM-AM-TV, Nashville. What started off as a summer job, ended up becoming her life's passion. "It looked like an exciting place to work at the time. . . . At the station I met movie stars, musicians and songwriters that came to Nashville from New York and Los Angeles to record . . . I also met a number of music publishers who came by to pitch songs." Mrs. Preston's duties at the station grew. At one point she was both marketing new television programs and hosting her own fashion show. Is it any wonder that in 1955 when she met B.M.I.'s vice president Robert Burton, that he offered her the job of forming a new bastion for B.M.I. in Nashville? She took up this challenge and for the next twenty-seven years built her division to where a two-person staff which represented one state grew to a staff of 35, representing sixteen states. Her rise to power in B.M.I.'s organization was as steady as it was dramatic. She is a force to be reckoned with in the music industry. She spends every waking moment working. Even her evenings are devoted to catching the latest act at local clubs either in L.A., New York or Nashville. She is credited with having discovered Willie Nelson, Waylon Jennings and Kris Kristofferson. "I've always been interested in the development of new writers and new talent. . . . Often, when we find bands, they are completely unknown. They don't have a publisher, agents haven't heard them, nor have record companies. We act as a conduit between that new writer and the rest of the music industry so they will have an opportunity to be heard." It is for her courage and immense sense of dedication that she has been recognized by her own company and by the American business community as well. She is politically alert and deeply involved in the fight against "source licensing" bills which have been reintroduced in both the Senate and the House. Finally, she was named one of the "50 Most Fascinating Business People" in 1987 by *Fortune* Magazine with just cause. Her three sons, Kirk, David and Donald, who she managed to raise in the midst of this hectic career, and her husband, E.J. Preston, can be proud.

André Previn

"What you get for Mahler is not what you get for Sandra Dee," said André Previn explaining the huge dip his income took as a result of his decision to leave Hollywood (and some 60 original film scores) and take up the conductor's baton in the early sixties. When he returned to Lotus Land in 1986, it was to succeed Carlo Maria Giulini as music director of the Los Angeles Philharmonic, not quite so alliterative as "Previn and the Pittsburgh" (the orchestra he led from '76 to '86) nor so international as the London Symphony (which he headed for 13 years), but nice just the same. The fact that he won four Oscars in the award-conscious town shouldn't hurt the box office either.

Born 6 April 1929 in Berlin, the son of a prominent Jewish lawyer and judge, his family fled the Nazis and lived briefly in Paris before taking up U.S. citizenship in 1943. A child prodigy who had entered the Berlin Conservatory at four, Previn wrote his first full film score at 18. ("The first movie I scored had a cast like a sick joke: Jeanette MacDonald, Lassie and Lloyd Nolan.") But he always hankered to be a conductor, so after studying for two years with Pierre Monteux, he set off to practice his trade "in the sticks with semi-pro orchestras, where the members all have other jobs." Then in 1967 he became chief conductor of the Houston Symphony and a year later was hired by the musicians of the self-governing London Symphony. In 1982 after three years of "self-scrutiny" (having divorced Mia Farrow in 1979), he married Heather Hales, a 33-year-old divorcee with two young sons. Previn has two daughters, now adults, from his first marriage to Betty Bennett, a jazz singer. There were no children from his second marriage to lyricist Dory Langdon. With Mia he had twins (a boy and a girl), and adopted three Oriental girls. (He is amazed at Alan J. Lerner marrying for the eighth time; he thinks divorce is life's most painful experience.)

His four Oscar-winning movie adaptations are *Gigi*, *My Fair Lady*, *Porgy and Bess* and *Irma La Douce*. He recorded 13 albums with the Pittsburgh and hosted the PBS series, "Previn and the Pittsburgh" (giving the steel town's football Steelers and baseball Pirates competition for publicity). It's violin virtuoso Isaac Stern's belief that former jazz pianist Previn is "the most underrated great conductor of our time."

Leontyne Price

Hailed as the "diva di tutte le dive" by the New York *Times* in 1981 when she sang arias by Verdi, Richard Strauss and Puccini "with resplendent warmth and freshness" at the 100th Anniversary Gala of the Boston Symphony Orchestra, Price has described herself as "a lyric soprano . . . a juicy lyric, yes, but I've never said I was a dramatic soprano." Born Mary Violet Leontine (*i* to *y* later) Price on 10 February 1927, in Laurel, Miss., she was a star of the choir of St. Paul's Methodist Church there. She first catapulted to worldwide prominence in a production of Gershwin's *Porgy and Bess* which toured international music capitals for 25 months beginning in 1952, the year she made her Paris debut in Virgil Thomson's *Four Saints in Three Acts*. After a Town Hall debut recital in 1954 which included the first performance of Samuel Barber's *Hermit Songs* with the composer at the piano, she debuted with the NBC-TV Opera Company's 1955 production of *Tosca* ("I learned about Tosca from singing Bess . . . they're both strumpets"). Although there were no black opera stars at the time, and few Americans, in 1958 Herbert von Karajan invited her to appear at the Vienna State Opera in the title role of *Aida* under the maestro's direction. When she repeated the role at La Scala, one critic wrote "our great Verdi would have found her the ideal Aida." Just the sixth black headliner ever to tread the boards at the Old House, she made her Metropolitan Opera debut as Leonora in *Il Trovatore* to a wildly enthusiastic audience (42-minute ovation) and sang seven different roles with the company that year. Although she had once attended a teacher's college in Ohio to assure her survival should she fail in the music world, whe was chosen to open the new Met at New York's Lincoln Center on 16 September 1966 as the lead in the world premier of Samuel Barber's *Antony and Cleopatra*. She later related that it was the "most grueling" experience of her life, one that left her "almost traumatized for two and one-half years." Price earned the accolade prima donna *assoluta* for career-long glittering performances as Donna Anna in *Don Giovanni*, as Verdi's two Leonoras (in *La Forza del Destine* and *Il Trovatore*) and playing the title roles in *Tosca* and *Aida*. Her recordings have been recognized for excellence with 18 Grammy awards and her third Emmy award (1984) was awarded for her appearance as hostess for the PBS-TV series *In Performance at the White House*. Awarded the nations' highest civilian honor, the Presidential Medal of Freedom, in 1965, she is often a performing guest at 1600 Pennsylvania Avenue. In 1980 she was recipient of the Kennedy Center Honors in recognition of "great achievement in the performing arts." In 1985 she received the Handel Medallion from the City of New York. Although a confessed egomaniac, she began describing her instrument as at "the maturest stage of vocal maturity" in the early 1980s and, with a triumphant televised performance of *Aida* at the Met on 3 January 1985, marched away from the opera stage, "leaving behind one phase" of her career. "It is thrilling to be asked why I am retiring, rather than why not." Solid bookings for concerts and recital tours, her "first love," are allowing her to indulge her joy in presenting works by contemporary composers, many of them American, spirituals and interpretations of Lieder and French art songs.

Her Porgy, baritone William C. Warfield, became her husband during the tour of *Porgy and Bess*, but the couple divorced in 1973 after several years of separation. A three-story, 12-room Federal house in New York's Greenwich Village is home and haven for the soprano, who tends to avoid all but the most necessary public functions. "I don't like making entrance unless I'm *in* costume, at 8:00 o'clock on stage."

Vincent Price

"I sometimes feel that I'm impersonating the dark unconscious of the whole human race," he says of his wily and villainous roles in such memorable horror films as *The Masque of the Red Death* and *House of Wax*. "I know this sounds sick but I love it." And the versatile Vincent is equally enamoured of his role as a cultural connoisseur. For Sears Roebuck's Vincent Price Collection, he personally bought over 10,000 pictures, ranging from Rembrandt to the drawings of a talented 13-year-old. ("My taste has become, over the years, more and more catholic. I've been through so many phases and fads that I've come out at the other end liking almost everything.")

Born 27 May 1911 in St. Louis and educated at Yale (B.A. 1933) and the University of London, Price was for years mistakenly labeled an Englishman because of his cultivated diction. He did spend some time in London during his early acting days, but after appearing as Prince Albert in a West End production of *Victoria Regina*, he returned to America in 1935 to make his debut in the same role opposite Helen Hayes, followed by such hits as *Outward Bound* (1939) and the chilling *Angel Street* (1941). He made his movie debut in 1937. Formerly married to actress Edith Barrett (one son), and costume designer Mary Grant (one daughter), he is currently wed to actress Coral Browne. He started collecting art when he was 12 years old and, on a 50 cents a week allowance, bought a Rembrandt etching for $34.50 on the installment plan. Now his collection is housed in a residence that has become a mecca for Hollywood tours. His book *I Like What I Know* tells the story, as he puts it, of "what I've seen in my life, not what I've done." He has continued to do voice-over work (*I Go Pogo*, *The Monster Club:* 1980) but it was his V/O work on the phenomenally successful "Thriller" (1983, sung by Michael Jackson) that won due (multiple Grammys) acclaim. He has served as host for the syndicated PBS series "Mystery" and his latest list of films include *Dead Heat* (1987), *The Offspring* (1987), *Whales of August* (1987), *Backtrack* (1988) and *Blood Bath at the House of Death* (1988).

Charley Pride

As a child in Sledge, Miss., Charley Pride listened to the Saturday night broadcasts of the "Grand Ole Opry" from Nashville and sang along with the country singers. Little did he know that one day he would be a star on the program and the only black superstar in the overwhelmingly white field of country music.

As a stage performer, he is one of the hottest tickets in country music, drawing sell-out audiences in the United States, Europe, Australia, New Zealand and Japan. Pride has won many awards, including the prestigious Country Music Association Entertainer of the Year and twice winning the Best Male Vocalist award. In addition, he has won Grammy Awards for Best Country Male Performance for the album *Songs of Love* and Best Sacred Performance for the album *Did You Think to Pray*. "We give them the lyric, the story of the man and the woman, the feeling of life and love itself. That's what I try to communicate in the most sincere way I can. It's the way I live."

Born 18 March 1939 into a family of 11 children, Pride thought "the way out of the cotton fields was baseball." He left Sledge and started playing the Negro American League before going to the majors in 1961 with the Los Angeles Angels. He still goes to spring training with the Texas Rangers, where he works out with the team. An avid golfer as well, he plays in a number of celebrity programs, including his own Charley Pride Golf Fiesta, a PGA Tournament Players Series held in Albuquerque, N.M. His wife, Rozene, is his business partner, and they have three children.

Prince

He is a gifted musician, who, by writing and arranging and playing most all the instruments himself on his albums, has been compared to Little Richard, Jimi Hendrix and mostly Stevie Wonder. He's succeeded at fusing the 69 flavors of soul, gospel, rock, funk and punk into one sweet cone, and the most popular buzz about the busy bee is his keynote position vis-a-vis the high voltage issue of androgyny among rock stars, and particularly Prince's ambisexual eroticism. In "Controversy" he sings: "Am I white or black/Am I straight or gay/Was I what you wanted me to be?" His songs, according to New York *Times* writer Michiko Kakutani, "preach a kind of sexual evangelism—redemption achieved through erotic release." He is rhapsodic when he sings about fellatio ("Head") or incest ("Sister") or masturbation or nuclear holocaust in "1999" (". . .If I gotta die/I'm going to listen to/My body tonight. . . . Everybody's got a bomb/We could all die any day/But before I'll let that happen/I'll dance my life away.") He appears in garb that swings from raunch to dandy-*riche*, anything from just a pair of genital-hugging silk bikini briefs and high-heeled boots to brocaded velvet "Little Boy Blue" suits (usually in purple, his favorite shade). With his ebony curls and "I-remember Sid-Vicious-pout" he's like a cross between a shadow in an X-rated movie house and Rita Moreno in *West Side Story*, appealing to his fans as a welcome release from societally-imposed repressive attitudes towards race, gender and sexual preference.

Born 7 June 1962 to a black jazz musician father and Mediterranean mother, in Minneapolis, his 1984 super-hit *Purple Rain*—film and soundtrack—made mythical his own alienated childhood. His parents split up when he was seven and in his early teens, perhaps haunted by his father's failed-musician image, he turned to music as a safe escape from the pressures of his father versus his mother and step-father. He moved into a friend's basement and formed his first band, and taught himself to play over 20 instruments. "My brain was free of everything. I didn't have anything to worry about. I knew it was okay to explore whatever I wanted down there in the basement because things weren't forbidden anymore. That's when I realized that music could express what you were feeling it started coming out in my songs—loneliness and poverty and sex." After graduating from high school at 17 he went to New York to try the music scene there. Three companies offered him recording contracts, but none offered him complete control. He returned to Minneapolis and shortly thereafter was given a contract in excess of $1 million by Warner Brothers which granted him complete control in the studio. "For You," his first album debuted in 1978, followed by "Dirty Mind," "Controversy," "1999," *Purple Rain, Under The Cherry Moon, Sign O' The Times* (from movie of the same name), and *Lovesexy*. His hit single from *Purple Rain*, "When the Doves Cry" rivalled Michael Jackson's top seller "Billie Jean." In 1989, Prince performed the uneven beated theme from the film *Batman*. One reviewer has said that to their adoring masses, "Jackson was like Peter Pan and Prince was like the seductive Pied Piper."

Harold Prince

"What I've had all my life are patrons, right out of those nice Elizabethan times," Harold Prince told writer Marilyn Stasio in 1983 while discussing "new money" in the theatre, "But these people are corporations and conglomerates, not patrons. They're interested in investing in something that will turn a buck. They are not in it for the pleasure a patron gets out of watching an artist grow, experiment, and learn." The patrons of Prince's past are "principally" responsible for his achieving the distinction of having produced more "best show" Tony Award winners than any other Broadway producer: *The Pajama Game, Damn Yankees, Fiorello* (Pulitzer Prize winner), *A Funny Thing Happened on the Way To the Forum, Fiddler on the Roof, Cabaret, Company, A Little Night Music* and *Candide*. As a theatre director, he has won Tonys for *Cabaret, Company, Follies, Candide, Sweeney Todd, Evita* and *The Phantom of the Opera*. He received a special Tony in 1972 for *Fiddler* when it was, up to that time, the longest running musical in Broadway history. All told, the talented man has received a record sixteen Tonys. His recent directorial duties surfaced for *Grind* (1985), the 1987 revival of *Cabaret*, the 1987 musical *Roza* and, of course, the London and New York productions of *Phantom*. Steering in a slightly different direction, Prince staged his first bona fide opera in New York, *Don Giovanni* for the New York City Opera's 1989 season.

A native New Yorker, born 30 January 1928, Harold Smith Prince was the only child of Milton Prince, who was a member of the New York Stock Exchange, while his theatre-loving mother Blanche encouraged his early enthusiasm for the stage. "Theatre was always part of my life," says Prince, "and Saturday matinees and second balconies were a passionate hobby all through my school days." Graduated from the University of Pennsylvania in 1948, Prince was what he calls, "an extra-curricular student, writing and directing plays, starting a radio station, and showing profit by broadcasting the football games." After 2 years of Army service (and writing *Where a G.I. Should Go in Europe*), he returned to civilian life, teamed up with the late Frederick Brisson and Robert Griffith to produce the 1954 musical *The Pajama Game*. In the next six years Griffith and Prince produced six consecutive musical hits on Broadway, including *West Side Story*.

The death of Bobby Griffith in 1961 marked Prince's debut as solo producer with the hit comedy *Take Her, She's Mine*, followed by *Forum* and *She Loves Me*, which he directed and produced in New York and London, subsequent productions which he has produced and/or directed include *Cabaret, Follies, Night Music, Baker Street, Superman, Pacific Overtures, On the 20th Century, Sweeney Todd* and *Evita*. Prince has learned to come to terms with an occasional failure. He says *A Family Affair* was his first flop ("I walked down the street, and you know what, people talked to me. It made me feel better to know I could cope with a flop."). *Merrily We Roll Along* (1981-82 season) closed after 16 performances and *A Doll's Life*, a 1983 $4-million musical, closed in 4 nights after spectacularly bad notices. Prince's recent directorial efforts include *Play Memory, End of the World, Diamonds*, an off-Broadway revue (1984) and *Grind* (1985). He directed the film *Something for Everyone* and *A Little Night Music*. He has moved into another area—opera, staging works from Houston to Vienna, including New York, Chicago, and San Francisco. The operas include *Madame Butterfly, La Fanciula del West, Willie Stark, Ashmedai* and *Silverlake*. Prince is married to the former Judith Chaplin, daughter of composer-producer Saul Chaplin. His recreations are walking, playing tennis, and swimming. He has a house on Manhattan's East Side and a home in Majorca. Prince makes a convincing case that audiences themselves are a great part of today's theatre problem ("Too easy to please" with flamboyant production gimmickry . . . "what is so damned awesome about a lot of feathers?").

Paul Prudhomme

Real men may not eat quiche, but they sure hanker after blackened redfish, rabbit tenderloin with oyster sauce, crayfish pie, chicken and seafood jambalaya, guinea hen and andouille gumbo, sweet potato-pie and all the other hot and spicy and mysterious Cajun wonders served up by the man called by many the most creative chef in America. The *New York Times'* Craig Claiborne calls Paul Prudhomme "a celebrated, internationally known chef who just happens to have been born in the United States." In 1980, he became the first American chef to receive the coveted *Mérite Agricole* from the French government. His K-Paul's Louisiana Kitchen is a gastronomic mecca. "I feel that food is a celebration of life," says Prudhomme. "It's a universal thing: shared need and experiences. But there's more to it. Watching people eat something that they didn't believe could *be* that good, watching their eyes and their whole expressions change, and even their attitude toward the cook change—that's what keeps me cooking."

It was into a 200-year heritage of French cooking in Acadian country south of Opelousas, Louisiana, that Paul Prudhomme was born 13 July 1940. The youngest of 13 children, he began cooking at seven with his mother. "We didn't have electricity," he recalls, "so we didn't have refrigeration. This meant we used only what was fresh. I know that fresh ingredients are the msot important factor in preparing exceptional food." After 12 years on the road, apprenticing under chefs of every professional and ethnic background, he returned to Louisiana ("the place for creative cooking in the United States") to focus on Creole and Cajun cooking. He served as Corporate Chef for the Brennan family (of New Orleans style cooking fame) from 1975 until 1979, when he and his wife K. (she's the "K" in K-Paul) Hinrichs Prudhomme opened their restaurant on Chartres Street in the French Quarter of New Orleans. Intended originally as a small, unassuming place to serve the local populace, the delectations purveyed therein soon became known nationwide and throughout the world, so that today the long waiting lines usually associated with New Orleans' older established culinary emporiums are a daily scene at K-Paul's. The recipient of numerous awards and a fixture on national and international televison (including two films for the BBC), this wizard of the kitchen in 1984 published *Chef Paul Prudhomme's Louisiana Kitchen*, containing recipes for his Cajun and Creole (more citified) creations. In 1987 he created *The Prudhomme Family Cookbook*.

Richard Pryor

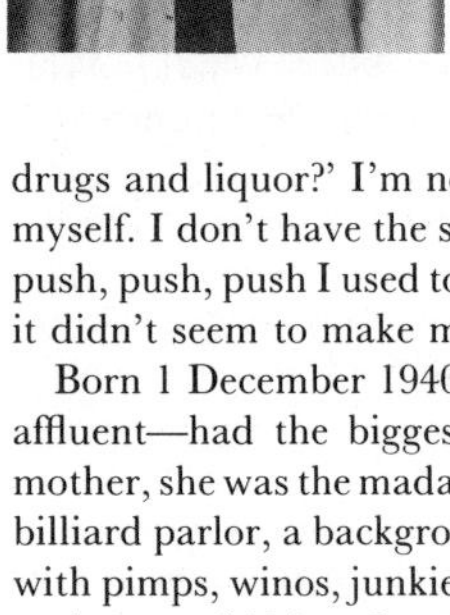

In 1980 while he was preparing "freebase," a highly inflammable mixture of cocaine and ether, he accidentally set himself on fire, and received third degree burns over half his body. He was not expected to survive. The "accident" did not lack a metaphor. Richard Pryor was, before his accident, an explosive comedian, controversial and ferociously satirical. Some faulted him for mellowing after the accident, others applauded his maturity. "People call me up and say, 'You're not like you used to be.' I say to them, 'That's right but do you know what I was really like then? Do you know what kind of insanity I was into, with drugs and liquor?' I'm not going to do that again. I'm going to be nice to myself. I don't have the same desire to succeed anymore. I don't have that push, push, push I used to have. I think I had it until I burned up. After that it didn't seem to make much sense."

Born 1 December 1940 in Peoria, Ill., Pryor says facetiously, "We were affluent—had the biggest whorehouse in the neighborhood. My grandmother, she was the madam." He grew up there and also in his grandfather's billiard parlor, a background well represented in his night club act peopled with pimps, winos, junkies and the like. All this a far cry from his debut role at the age of 12 in a Peoria community center production of *Rumpelstiltskin*. After dropping out of school at age 14, Pryor worked a slew of menial jobs and, after spending two years overseas with the Army in Germany, began his performing career in Peoria's Harold's Club. Inspired by the success of Bill Cosby, he moved to New York in 1963, and soon became a regular at all the comedy clubs. Then, via an appearance in 1966 on the "Ed Sullivan Show," he became a national celebrity and began appearing on many other television shows and soon had his own Las Vegas show. For his sixth film part, playing the Piano Man opposite Diana Ross in the 1972 *Lady Sings the Blues*, he received an Oscar nomination. Next came the comedy classic *Blazing Saddles* which he co-wrote with Mel Brooks and which earned him an American Writers Guild Award. Other screen comedies were *Car Wash*, *Silver Streak*, and *California Suite*. Pryor's most popular hits were scored after recuperating from his accident when he threw himself frantically back into his film work. "I had to make certain amounts of money to pay some bills, so I went to work fast. Also, I guess, I worked so hard because I wanted to prove I was all right." These hits include *Stir Crazy*, *Bustin' Loose*, *Superman III*, *Some Kind of a Hero*, *Richard Pryor Live on the Sunset Strip*, *JoJo Dancer*, *Your Life is Calling*, *Critical Condition*, *Moving*, *See No Evil, Hear No Evil* and *Harlem Nights*. "Things are real good for me," he says, but adds with realistic consideration, "but if I walk out on the street to try to get a taxi in New York, they go right by me. They think I'm going to Harlem and they ain't taking me. So what's changed?"

Married and divorced five times, Pryor has several children. In 1987 he had another son with actress Geraldine Mason. He lives in Beverly Hills.

Keshia Knight Pulliam

Learning to read lines is not an easy feat for any actor, but it's even harder when you haven't yet learned to read. Cute little five-year-old Keshia not only learned her lines for her role as Rudy, the youngest child in the Huxtable family on the NBC hit sitcom "The Bill Cosby Show," she also earned a reputation on the set for rarely flubbing her lines. Now in her fifth year on the show, Keshia's ability to learn quickly is more than evident. Her TV father, Cosby, says "We are taking the baby out of her character and asking for more maturity." Winner of the 1988 People's Choice Award for Best Young TV Performer, the adorable Keshia has become adept at trading quips with Cosby during the show's tapings. One of her favorite things to do is to steal the microphone and the limelight from her TV dad and to tell jokes to the audience.

Born 9 April 1979 in Newark, New Jersey, Keshia has been in show business almost all of her life. At eight months of age she appeared in her first print ad for baby powder followed by numerous print ads and TV commercials. In 1984, at age 5, Keshia landed the role of Rudy. Her parents, James and Denise Pulliam, took turns teaching Keshia her lines and helping her memorize them. Since then, Keshia has starred in such TV specials as "Back to Next Saturday" (NBC), "Andy Williams and NBC Kids Search for Santa," "NBC's 60th Anniversary Celebration" and in the title role in "The Little Match Girl" (1988). Keshia also appeared in "Night of 100 Stars II," "Motown Returns to the Apollo," several segments of "Sesame Street," and in the feature film *The Last Dragon*.

Although thoroughly enjoying her budding acting career, the pixy has other plans for her adult life. Wanting to be a doctor, the little heartbreaker and showstopper says, "I want to be able to help all people and make them feel good."

Dennis Quaid

Hollywood-comer Dennis Quaid, who played astronaut Gordon Cooper in *The Right Stuff*, a space pilot from Earth in Wolfgang Petersen's *Enemy Mine*, an incorrigible, hell-raising ex-navy pilot in *Innerspace*, and a law enforcer in *The Big Easy*, topped his career in 1989 by playing Jerry Lee Lewis in *Great Balls of Fire*. Commended for his high energy performance, Quaid portrays the rock 'n' roll great who sang such hits as "Whole Lotta Shakin' Goin' On," and "Breathless." The movie which was filmed mainly in Memphis, with some filming in Arkansas, Mississippi and London as well, gave Quaid the opportunity to expand his acting capabilities and project a man whose life was filled with turmoil and tragedy.

Dennis Quaid was born on 9 April 1954 in Houston, Texas. Although he initially wanted to be a musician, he discoverd acting while in high school and was inspired to perfect his craft by his older brother, Randy, now a well-established figure on movie screens and the stage. Dennis's first major break in films came a year to the day after his arrival in Hollywood, when director Jim Bridges signed him for a role in the film about the death of James Dean, *9/30/55*. Dennis first captured wide notice from both critics and fans playing a rebellious young Indianian in Peter Yates' 1979 coming-of-age picture, *Breaking Away*. In his next role, Walter Hills's saga of the James Brothers, *The Long Riders*, he co-starred not only with his own brother Randy but with two additional sets of acting brothers, David, Keith and Robert Carradine and James and Stacy Keach. Also on his list of Hollywood credits are *Crazy Mama*, *Our Winning Season*, *Gorp*, *Dreamscape*, *Suspect* (opposite Cher), *D.O.A.*, and *Everybody's All American*. On television, viewers may remember him in NBC's Emmy-winning Movie of the Week, "Bill," co-starring Mickey Rooney. He also received glowing reviews for his strong dramatic appearances in both the Off Broadway and L.A. Stage Company's productions of Sam Shepard's play, t*True West*. Currently single, his steady date is actress Meg Ryan.

Dan Quayle

The youngest person ever elected to the U.S. Senate from the state of Indiana was sworn in as the 44th vice-president of the United States on 20 January 1989. As he admitted in a television interview before the inauguration, he is "a huge question mark" to most people. *Time* magazine reported that his "cram course—just in case" was taught by such political luminaries as Richard Darman for Economics, Henry Kissinger and Jeane Kirkpatrick for Advanced Foreign Policy, plus Richard Nixon and Walter Mondale for Modern Vice-President Problems. Even with the advice of these tutors, Quayle's exams will have to be taken on his own. One person interviewed in *Time* observed that "If Dan Quayle can act as an address for the right wing of the party and make them feel included, that's all for the best. At the very least, maybe they won't be bothering the President as much as they might otherwise."

James Danforth Quayle was born on 4 February 1947 in Indianapolis, Indiana, to James C. Quayle and Corinne (Pulliam) Quayle. The oldest of four children (two brothers, one sister), he was named after James Danforth, a Quayle family friend who was killed in World War II. When Quayle's father, who sold advertising for Pulliam's *Huntington Herald-Press*, was transferred to the *Arizona Republic* and the *Phoenix Gazette* in 1955, the family moved to Phoenix. Eight years later, they returned to Indiana, where Dan's father became the publisher of the *Huntington Herald-Press*. During this period of time, Dan graduated from Huntington High School in Huntington, Indiana (1965), and then matriculated at DePauw University, where he received his B.A. degree in political science (1969). According to a former political science professor, Michael Lawrence, Quayle "was not a serious student. . . . He did mediocre work. He was just a charming, nice guy" (*Chicago Tribune*). Upon graduation, Quayle joined Indiana National Guard and served from 1969-1975. He earned a law degree from the Indiana University in 1974. His resume matured when he entered the family business as associate publisher/general manager of the *Huntington Herald-*

Marilyn Quayle

Press. His career as a newspaperman was supressed by two underlying factors: his marriage to Marilyn Quayle (November 1972) and the beginning of their law firm, Quayle & Quayle; and his fascination with the Robert Redford film *The Candidate* (1972). The movie "made a tremendous impression on Quayle, according to friends. . . ." His next springboard was in 1976, when he was elected to the U.S. Congress from Indiana's Fourth Congressional District, followed by a reelection in 1978. In 1980 he defeated three-term incumbent Democrat Birch Bayh for the Indiana senate, and he was reelected in 1986 with the "largest margin ever achieved to that date by a candidate in a statewide Indiana race." His reputation grew as he became known for his legislative work and services on the Armed Services Committee, the Budget Committee and the Labor and Human Resources Committee. It was in August 1988 that Quayle was thrown into the national arena, as George Bush requested that he be his running mate.

As vice-president of the United States, he is also the first chairman of the National Space Council. He has some pie-in-the-sky dreams to fulfill, and he revealed an ambitious U.S. space program in July 1989, encompassing plans for a flight to Mars by 2010. Quayle also serves as president of the United States Senate, is a statutory member of the National Security Council, and on 9 February 1989 was named by President Bush as the head of the Competitiveness Council. Dan and Marilyn Quayle have three children (Tucker, Benjamin, Corinne). In his spare hours, he likes to play golf, tennis, and basketball. He enjoys horseback riding, skiing, fly fishing and reading.

Marilyn Quayle

"Behind her demure shirtwaist dresses and her trademark Mary Tyler Moore flip hairdo there was a strong-minded, intelligent woman who wished to be viewed as Quayle's 'senior advisor'." A 1989 *Time* magazine article went on to say "At a Christmas party, a reporter told her jokingly that as the Vice President's wife she could set her own style. Marilyn smiled saucily and replied, 'That's right—the flip is back'." Some politicians protest, however, that a flip-deal is a more appropriate phrase; she is the shining force behind her husband. When Quayle first ran for Congress in Indiana, Marilyn admitted "I made all the decisions."

The current Second Lady of the land was born Marilyn Tucker on 29 July 1949 in Indianapolis, Indiana. Both her parents, Warren S. and Mary Alice were doctors. She and her five siblings were raised in a Christian household; she attended School Number 84 in Indianapolis and graduated in 1967 from Broad Ripple High School, then later from Purdue University in 1971 with a degree in Political Science. While attending Indiana University law school she met Dan Quayle and, after a ten week romance, married him. By the time of her bar exam, she had to induce the delivery of their first child in order to take the test. Sharing a law practice, the couple worked together until the birth of their second child and Dan's election to Congress in 1976. Ever since, she has been a supportive housewife and dedicated mother.

Assuming the role model as wife of the Vice-President, she is careful on her views. She opposes abortion and the ERA. In addition, she's active in her children's schools and civic affairs. The Quayles made the move from McLean, Virginia, to Washington and Marilyn raised funds to renovate the Vice-Presidential residence for her family (three children: Tucker, born 1974; Benjamin, born 1976; Corinne, born 1978). Her friend Joanne Kemp says, "She understands the role, but if she can find a way to do it differently that is proper, she will."

Anthony Quinn

"I *am* Zorba," says this versatile actor cum artist whose zest for life parallels that of his favorite character. The once dark-haired, high-cheek-boned, vaguely sinister-looking Quinn—actually Irish and Mexican—declared of the second time he played Zorba on Broadway in 1984, "Before I had to paint my hair white. Now I'm just right." And while theatre audiences agree, it was not always so easy. Quinn tells of arriving in Hollywood "in the era of the golden boys" when the only parts he got was playing Indians. Since that time he has played a Mexican revolutionary in *Viva Zapata!* (for which he won an Academy Award), Paul Gauguin in *Lust for Life* (another Oscar), a Russian Pope, the *Hunchback of Notre Dame*, a prize-fighter (*Requiem for a Heavyweight*), an Arab (*Lawrence of Arabia*), an Italian strongman (*La Strada*), and a Greek in *The Guns of Navarone* and *Zorba*. "To me," he once said, "acting . . . [is] living. I love to live, so I live. I love to act, so I act. I gotta have vitality." The actor hasn't been short of his ambition. His latest films include *Stradivarius* (1988), *Revenge* (1989), *Ghosts Can't Do It* (1989), and *A Man of Passion* (1989). On the television screen, he's starred in ABC's "Richest Man in the World: Story of Onassis" (1988) and Hemingway's "The Old Man And The Sea" (1989).

Born "in a hail of bullets" 21 April 1915 in Chihuahua, the son of a Mexican mother and an Irish-American soldier of fortune fighting in the bloody revolution then in progress, he was smuggled out of the country "hidden in a wagon under a pile of coal. . . . I nearly choked to death." He went to work in Los Angeles at the age of five ("The truant officer caught me"), later toiled as a cement mixer, dress cutter, amateur boxer, and fruit picker. He did some little-theater parts, formed an acting company at 15 "solely so I could have access to the wardrobe department, because I had no clothes," made his professional stage debut in a Mae West clinker called *Clean Beds*, bummed around the country "with my Bible, pajamas and play notices," and at 21 returned to Hollywood, "It was *horrible* breaking into pictures," he recalls. "It's a miracle that any of us survive." Quinn held on long enough to screen-test for Cecil B. De Mille, who approved him as an actor but not, when he married daughter Katherine De Mille after a brief courtship, as a son-in-law. "I think," Quinn explained, "he kind of thought I was an Indian from some reservation and was always terrified that the tribe would gather around his house some night for a war dance." Quinn's tribe came to include four children by Miss De Mille (a fifth drowned in W.C. Field's pool at the age of three), from whom he was divorced after nearly three decades of marriage.

In 1966 he wed Iolanda Addolori, an Italian teacher turned wardrobe girl (on the *La Strada* set), who had borne him two sons prior to their marriage and was carrying the third at the time of their wedding. They live in a villa near Rome, where Quinn first met Iolanda while making *Barabbas*. On a health regimen, he jogs and swims, and most days he paints and sculpts, often working on several pieces at once. "I'm like a guy playing a horn," he once said. "There's a note I hear inside me but I can't play it yet. Some day I'm going to hit that note."

David Rabe

"Much of the early struggle in writing is with what I call 'The Censor,' the voice that says 'It's no good' or wants to know what the third line will be before you've written the first one," confessed David Rabe to New York *Times'* writer Helen Dudar. "The voice is very, very untalented, and when I really get going, it just vanishes." After he "got going," Rabe won his playwright's wings in the 70s with a trilogy of dramas about the Vietnam War—*The Basic Training of Pavlo Hummel*, *Sticks and Bones* (1972 Tony award), and *Streamers*. His controversial 1984 powerhouse play *Hurlyburly* is a far battle cry from the earlier plays and wages its sexual war on the Hollywood front. "A lot of what's dark in the play doesn't come from California," says Rabe. "It comes from being in the world today, being barraged with information—philosophies that aren't philosophies, answers that aren't answers, one pharmaceutical solution after another." To people who say the play is anti-woman, Rabe declares: "I don't think that's true. It's about the price some guys pay to be men." It was producer Joseph Papp who launched Rabe with *Hummel* and within three years had presented on-and-off Broadway productions of three additional Rabe plays—*Sticks and Bones*, *The Orphan*, and *In the Boom Boom Room*. Due to differences about the Lincoln Center production of the latter, Papp and Rabe came to a professional split (widened in 1982 when *Goose and Tom* opened against Rabe's wishes and got poor reviews). "I would never deny the real feeling I had and still have for him," admits Rabe. Although sorry they can no longer work together, Papp still feels Rabe is "the most powerful new playwright we've ever produced." Rabe moved to Hollywood for a few months in 1974 in search of work that would support his playwriting habit. His first marriage had ended in divorce, and he tackled screenwriting. "I had an insane terror of the place . . . I think I had some notion that a writer could make more of an impact on a script than he can." (His screenplays include *I'm Dancing as Fast as I Can*, *Streamers* and *Casualties of War*—based on a true story by Daniel Lang).

David William Rabe was born 3 October 1940 in Dubuque, Iowa, the son of a teacher who became a meat packer to better his income. Raised in the Catholic religion, he was a devout follower until he attended Loras College and found himself disagreeing with a priest who taught ethics. (Rabe admits that leaving the faith, though liberating, was frightening. "Whether consciously or not, he has searched for a replacement ever since," says one critic.) Rabe spent much of his time in the movie houses and had very little contact with "live" theatre. He remembers seeing a production of *Show Boat* when he was in his early teens and was "very moved and excited by the whole thing." The character that lingered with him was Julie, the "outcast" of the story. "There's always somebody in my plays who's trying to get into some closed society," says Rabe, "The essential dynamic of *Show Boat* is very close to a lot of my work."

Married to his second wife, actress Jill Clayburgh, Rabe has two children, a son by his first marriage, and a daughter by Clayburgh, born in 1982. "Choosing to write a play is some kind of surrender," Rabe confided to *Times'* writer Samuel G. Freedman. "I sit and work and suddenly the door opens and out it comes. I used to be scared of it. And what I've learned over the years is not to try to shape it or control it. . . . But it's better for the writing to burst out that way, rather than torturing yourself by holding it in."

Robert Rafelson

Robert Rafelson is considered a skillful filmmaker who approaches his work with an intense emotional commitment both to detail and the ideas he conveys to his movie audiences. He's been the subject of some controversy in Hollywood; it is said that Rafelson was fired from *Brubaker* after throwing a chair at a Twentieth Century-Fox exec who was pleading with Rafelson for commercial concessions and an accelerated shooting pace. After exhaustive hours of research (two years of scouting dangerous locations in Panama, which resulted in the deaths of two guides assisting him) for Peter Matthiessen's *At Play in the Fields of the Lord*, the project was shelved. Recently Rafelson directed and co-wrote the screenplay for *Mountains of the Moon* (1989) which followed his *Black Widow* (1986) and the remake of James M. Cain's classic novel *The Postman Always Rings Twice* (which was generally not favored by the critics). The mood on Rafelson's sets is often emotionally charged, sometimes almost violent. Says associate producer (*Postman*) Michael Barlow: "Bob recapitulates the emotion of the scene. The mood on the set is the same as the scene. He sucks everybody into the moment. . . . He goes for the highs. . . ."

Born in New York City in 1934, Rafelson as a teenager was riding in rodeos and breaking horses (and his back) in Arizona. At 17 he shipped out on a liner to and from Europe. At 18 he played in a jazz combo in Acapulco "faking the drums and bass and hitting up rich tourists for drinks and a place to sleep." In fact, he says, "One night I woke up aboard a huge schooner and wound up crewing on a mad expedition to Panama." During this period he studied philosophy at Dartmouth College where he became especially interested in existentialism. Rafelson considers Sartre to be "his guiding light." Ultimately, he found his way into television and film. His first TV work was on "Play of the Week", for which he wrote 34 adaptations. Films include *Head* (based on the Monkees), 1968; *Five Easy Pieces*, 1970; *The King of Marvin Gardens*, 1972 and *Stay Hungry*, 1976. He also directed Lionel Richie's famed 1984 video "All Night Long."

Raffi

The line encircling Carnegie Hall with expectant ticket holders for a summer 1989 Raffi concert was longer than a line-up of pop fans. The only difference was that most of these women waiting were expectant mothers, wheeling around their tiny offspring. Raffi really reels them in—he is the Barry Manilow of the toddler set. According to the *L.A. Times*, the singer is "something of a phenomenon, this mild, neatly bearded Canadian with soft brown eyes." Raffi says: "My music respects its audience. By understanding that children are whole people with important feelings and concerns, we give them the best chance of becoming healthy, loving adults."

This minstrel man was a child once himself. He was born in Cairo, Egypt, on 8 July 1948. In 1968 his family moved to Canada, and by 1970 he had started his career as a Toronto-based singer/songwriter. In 1974 he discovered his talent of performing for young children when his mother-in-law asked him to play his guitar and sing with the children in her Toronto nursery school. He remembers, "those first 'performances' were quite daunting. I didn't know any North American children's songs until my wife [Debi Pike—a kindergarten teacher at the time] taught me 'Eensy Weensy Spider' and 'Baa Baa Black Sheep.' I sat on the floor with a few children, and hoped they would sing along." And la, la, la, they sang as Raffi poured his talents into recordings. With the help of his wife, some close friends and a coproducer, Ken Whiteley, he recorded *Singable Songs for the Very Young* (1976). Over thirteen years later, that album remains Raffi's best selling LP (went triple-platinum in Canada).

These days, Raffi is an enterprise. There are Raffi record albums, Raffi books, Raffi concerts, Raffi videos, Raffi songbooks, etc. Some of his hit songs include "Baby Beluga," "Rise and Shine," "He's Got the Whole World in His Hands," "The Wheels on the Bus," and "Shake Your Sillies Out." *People* magazine notes, "It's a cinch this is no David Lee Roth concert, where you couldn't hear a bomb blast through the roar. The man in the spotlight is a 37-year-old Toronto-based singer named Raffi (he never used his surname), and as soon as he speaks, the fans hush like a pack of preschoolers. In fact most of them are. Ranging in age from 2 to 8, the kids remain standing so that they can see the stage."

Raffi and his wife live in Canada; they do not have any children of their own at the moment. However, he does like to show people pictures of his 12-year-old mongrel, Bundles. As a pioneer in producing exceptional music for children, Raffi has been bestowed with numerous awards. The title of his 1987 Grammy-nominated album perhaps states his goal best: *Everything Grows!*

Deborah Raffin

"There are a lot of nice people in this business, but there are also people who are insecure and so wrapped up in themselves that they aren't anxious to help someone who is just starting out." Raffin was lucky to have had the generous support of Liv Ullmann in the budding stages of her career (Ullmann played her mother in Raffin's first movie, *Forty Carats*) and Milton

Katselas (director of same) as well. Since then she has starred in *The Dove* and *Once Is Not Enough*, taking a hiatus after the latter to do theater exclusively, honing her craft in the process. (" . . . I wasn't happy with the direction my career was taking. I knew I had a great deal to learn about acting, and things were happening too quickly. I was nineteen when I made *Forty Carats* . . .") She worked her way up to playing Ophelia in *Hamlet* with the National Theatre in England, then returned to Hollywood to star in the ABC-TV movie "Nightmare in Badham County" (1977) which won her an Emmy nomination. A slew of films followed: *Touched By Love* (which she made in China and which became quite popular there) and the made-for-TV "Haywire," "The Last Convertible," "Running Out" and "Dance of the Dwarfs" all in the early 1980s. Other TV starrers include "Lace II" (1985), a made-for-TV movie based on the life and lucrative loves of a Mayflower Madam-type called "Dinner Date," and the NBC miniseries of John Clavell's "Noble House." She appeared with Charles Bronson in 1986's *Death Wish III*.

Born in L.A., 13 March 1954, Raffin started studying drama at 15. At 30 she felt things were finally clicking into place. ("I'm very happy to be thirty because I think the roles are more interesting.") Asked to define some of the terms by which the public defines actors and actresses she says, "'Starlet' is a term which is often used, but I don't like the image it conveys. I always associate the term with some empty-headed, sort of fuzzy little girl who wants to be famous more than she wants to create excellent films. I think it's sad when people aspire to be 'stars' when they should aspire to be actors and actresses." Raffin lives with her husband, producer/manager Michael Viner, and five dogs in homes in Beverly Hills and Vermont. Together with her husband they formed Dove, Inc.—a books-on-tape concept utlizing celebrities to read books aloud to the public. In 1989, Deborah released her own book *The Presence of Christmas*.

Samuel Ramey

"This is a voice with a future," proclaimed *Opera News* in 1976. "This is the stuff of which opera legends are made," posited the New York Post. "Samuel Ramey is hot. He epitomizes a new breed of stars that has emerged in the past decade. . . . In addition to a pair of gymnastic vocal chords that can span two octaves, he has the lanky (6') lithe shape of a male sex symbol," declared *People*. These laudatory notes were reserved for a modestly mannered midwesterner who in 1984 made a tremendous impression in his Metropolitan opera debut in Handel's *Rinaldo*. Prior to that, Samuel Ramey had been stamped a star in (as *Newsweek* put it) the "diabolical and diabolically difficult" title role in Boito's *Mefistofele*. Since then he's been dubbed one of the greatest interpreters of the role (he also played *all four* villains in Offenbach's *Tales of Hoffman*). Success for Ramey, who believes opera stars could learn a few things from Broadway ("When someone simply stands there and sings, I'm bored to death. Drama is 50% of opera.") rests largely on his versatility. His voice has the weight to sustain heavier roles (Verdian) and the grace and flexibility needed in the operas of Handel, Mozart and Bellini.

Born 28 March 1942 in Colby, Kansas, Ramey's father was a meat cutter and his mother an amateur singer. The self-professed small-town boy grew up on baseball and the music of Pat Boone and began singing in elementary school. With the intention of becoming a music teacher, Ramey studied first at Kansas State University (on-and-off due to financial setbacks) and then at Wichita State University (with Arthur Newman), where his courses included ballet, voice and drama. Apprenticing with the Central City Opera in Colorado, Ramey heard Norman Triegle as Mozart's *Don Giovanni*. The experience ignited his desire to be an opera star—"I went there on a lark and suddenly I was fascinated by the whole thing. . . . I was in awe."

A finalist in the Metropolitan Opera's National Council Auditions in 1972, Ramey made his New York City Opera debut the next year as Zuniga in *Carmen* and has been on that roster ever since. The most recorded American-born bass now spends about 75% of his time abroad. The golden-throated Ramey can be heard on the soundtrack of Peter Shaffer's *Amadeus* and is seen frequently on television ("Live from Lincoln Center," PBS's "Gala of the Stars" and abroad, on the BBC). In 1987 he recorded *Carousel* with Barbara Cook. Ramey and his wife, Carrie Tenante, make their permanent home Manhattan. When not on the road together they spend time hiking and camping in upstate New York.

Jean-Pierre Rampal

"You must sing. The flute is the closest instrument to the human voice. You must listen to opera and to everything in music except your instrument. If you listen only to the flute you will lose the humanity of the music." The man with the "golden flute" has enjoyed success worldwide and even sang the role of *Don Giovanni* on an "extraordinary" tape of the duet "La ci darem la mano." Jean-Pierre Rampal's music is created in a seemingly effortless style which is at once both seductive and tender. Words like "brilliant," "silvery," "golden," "sweet and pure" are used by critics to characterize Rampal's playing. He is one of the most recorded classical instrumentalists today and, in addition to all of the well-known pieces for flute, he has recorded English folk songs, Japanese classics, Indian music, duos, trios, quartets and woodwind quintets. His jazz album "Suite for Flute and Jazz Piano" (with Claude Bolling) quickly went gold and his recording of Tellemann's "Twelve Fantasies for Unaccompanied Flute" was the first digital recording released in America.

Rampal (born in Marseille, 7 January 1922) was first introduced to the flute by his father, Joseph Rampal. After starting out to study medicine he switched to the Paris Conservatory (where he was later appointed professor) and from 1947–51 played in the orchestra of the Vichy Opera. Founder of the Quintette a Vent Francais and the Ensemble Baroque, Rampal was also first flutist at the Paris Opera. Though 18th century music is Rampal's great love, he will (according to another flutist) "play 'Ease on Down the Road' on *The Muppet Show* with the same zest with which he'll approach a Mozart concerto. [He] knows all of Fred Astaire's movies by heart and can sing Don Giovanni *and* Zerlina."

Now at the pinnacle of his career, Rampal has coupled his worldwide tours as a soloist with some teaching activities. Says a former student who has recorded and concertized with him, "The sun just comes pouring through when he plays." Rampal has also explored conducting. Several French composers have written special works for him and though some critics have suggested that at times he seems to "rest on his own considerable laurels," one still reads reviews which certify that Rampal is still a master: "He has it in him to make slight music seem . . . so charming and dapper that one dines without complaint on the musical hors d'oeuvre and the dessert he prefers to serve. He creates a magic that goes beyond mere superlative performing into a kind of trance spinning . . . " His story *Music, My Love: An Autobiography* was published in 1989.

Tony Randall

"Comedy's a serious business," says this rich and busy master of it. "You've got to be true and funny, and not look as though you're trying. You have to feel funny inside." In 1970, TV's "Odd Couple" premiered, with Randall doing his schtick as Felix, the ash-tray emptying, pillow-fluffing, obsessive-compulsive half of a very funny duo, but his theatrical background includes such straight characterizations as Marchbanks in Shaw's *Candida* and as the stuttering brother in *The Barretts of Wimpole Street*. It's still his dream to go back to the classics. "No one is really more suited to certain roles in Chekhov, Shaw or Shakespeare," he says modestly. "Benedick in *Much Ado*, for example."

Born on 26 February 1920 in Tulsa, young Anthony Randall left the oil capital "as soon as it was humanly possible" and was refining himself as an actor under the guidance of acting coach Sanford Meisner by the time he was 19. After the war and several Broadway flops, he was cast as Harvey Weskit on the *Mr. Peepers* TV show in 1952, and amid guffaws shot to national prominence. Randall has since made numerous movie appearances, starred in the Broadway musical *Oh Captain* and toured as the Mencken-like reporter in *Inherit the Wind*. He starred in "Love Sidney" which premiered on TV in the early 1980s. In 1988 he starred in *Two Into One* at the Paper Mill Playhouse.

Bachelor though he is in "The Odd Couple," he is happily married to Florence Gibbs (his childhood sweetheart). He collects records, antiques, and paintings. "I love classical music with the same passion with which I despise rock and roll," he declares. Reflecting his passion for opera, he has served as a regular on Texaco's "Opera Quiz" and as intermission commentator on TV's "Live From Lincoln Center." A man of many opinions, Randall says, "There's only one thing worse than a man who doesn't have strong likes and dislikes and that's a man who has strong likes and dislikes without the courage to voice them."

Sally Jessy Raphael

"I'm trying to reach one person. There isn't a crowd out there. There's just one other human being and we're trying to figure out life together", says Sally Jessy Raphael, host of her own talk show which is now rated as the Number 3 daytime syndicated TV show in the U.S. The "Sally Jessy Raphael Show" started broadcasting over KSDK in St. Louis in 1983 each weekday. However, because of the overwhelming response, the show became syndicated only six months later. Now the petite blond with the expressive eyes, partially hidden behind those big red eyeglass frames that have become her trademark, can be seen in over 130 cities in the U.S., as well as in Canada and England. This 1989 Emmy award winner for Outstanding Talk Show Host also has the distinction of being the first nationally syndicated female TV talk show host. With an approach that's been described as "like a friendly neighbor over for coffee. Homey advice for women", Raphael focuses on what interests her viewers, choosing almost 75% of the show's topics from viewer mail and phone calls. Because of her strong belief in follow-up, Raphael also offers some of her guests post-show additional guidance and return visits to the show so the guests can share their progress with the audience. Taping her TV show isn't enough to keep the energetic broadcaster busy. Raphael has also broadcasted her live three-hour radio show, NBC-TALKNET, from Manhattan each weekday evening since 1982. Between her daytime TV show and her nighttime radio show, this remarkable dynamo logs 18 hours on-air time; that's more than any other broadcaster. Even with this schedule Raphael found time to write a book *Finding Love: Practical Advice for Men and Women* (1984) and she is planning its sequel, *Keeping Love*. When asked about the success that has earned her the 1985 Bronze Medal from the International Film and Television Festival of New York, Raphael responds, "I'm a plodder, a very slow builder, who has had a chance to grow."

Born on 25 February 1943 in Easton, Pennsylvania, Sally Jessy grew up in Westchester County and in Puerto Rico where her father had a rum exporting business. It was during one of her stays in Puerto Rico that Jessy started using her mother's maiden name, Raphael, since "down there everyone has three names." She attended Carnegie Mellon in Pittsburgh and the University of Puerto Rico before obtaining her BFA from Columbia in New York City. Getting into the broadcasting business early, Jessy hosted "Junior High News" on WFAS radio in White Plains, New York. Her career had its ups and downs with Raphael holding numerous jobs including rock-and-roll disc jockey, TV news anchor with WPIX-TV in New York, host of a cooking show in Puerto Rico (on WAPA-TV from 1965–1967), news correspondent with the Associated Press in the Caribbean, TV anchor and host of a radio interview show in Miami (1969–1974). As sideliners, Raphael was a part-time owner of a perfume factory (1964–1968), an owner of an art gallery (1964–1969) and an owner of "The Wine Press", a wine bar in New York City (1979–1983). After being fired from 18 jobs and spending almost 20 years of her career in Mexico, Paris and Aruba, Raphael's broadcasting career settled down in 1976 when she took the job as anchor on WMCA-radio in New York, staying until 1981. The next year, Raphael began to host NBC-radio's "Talknet." The following year, in 1983, she began hosting her own show in St. Louis. But life was hectic as Raphael commuted from her New York home, husband, children and animals to St. Louis for four years. It wasn't until June 1987 that the show's production was moved to WTNH-TV in New Haven, CT. and then to New York City in 1989, in order to make life a little easier for Raphael.

Residing in a house in the woods in upstate New York with her second husband, Karl Soderlund (who was a local station manager in Puerto Rico when Raphael met and married him in 1963), 8 children (2 from her first marriage-Allison and Andrea, 2 of Karl's, Robby-their adopted son, and 3 foster children) and an assortment of dogs, cats, a snake and a bird, the untiring Raphael spends her spare time dabbling in her hobby—Japanese dolls, writing another book—this time on broadcast yarns—and running a bed and breakfast business.

Ahmad Rashad

A feature reporter and commentator on NBC, he has covered everything from live NFL sports events to the 1988 Summer Olympics in Seoul, Korea.

Ahmad Rashad was born in Portland, Oregon, and later attended the University of Oregon, where he was involved in sports. He received all-American honors as a running back, as well as competing as a varsity basketball player and high jumper. Ahmad began his professional sports career in 1972, when he was a first-round draft choice of the St. Louis Cardinals football team and played for Buffalo and Seattle. In 1976 he joined the Minnesota Vikings: he spent seven seasons with the team, and became Minnesota's all-time career-reception and receiving-yardage leader. His career in broadcasting began in Minneapolis on KMSP-TV when he hosted a "Monday Night Football" preview show. In 1978, he joined WCCO-TV in Minnesota as a full-time sports reporter. A few years later, NBC offered Ahmad a position, and in 1982, at the conclusion of his NFL playing career, Ahmad accepted their offer. He began by covering the AFC championship game, as well as contributing to the pregame show for Super Bowl XVII. In 1983, he alternated between being a game analyst and a commentator for the pregame show. More recent assignments have included being a feature reporter and studio commentator on NBC's pregame show "NFL Live!" In addition, he has covered several events on NBC's "Sports World" and was the afternoon anchor for NBC's exclusive coverage of the 1988 Summer Olympics in Seoul. Other television appearances include hosting NBC's "Friday Night Videos," "Entertainment Tonight," and "NBC News at Sunrise."

Ahmad and his actress wife Phylicia Rashad (married in 1986) live in New York with their daughter, Condola Phylea. Ahmad also has three children from a previous marriage.

Phylicia Rashad

She is a beautiful, intelligent, versatile, multi-talented actress and singer. Phylicia Rashad has been seen on the successful weekly series "The Cosby Show," as well as on Broadway in the starring role of *Into the Woods*.

She was born Phylicia Ayers-Allen in Houston, Texas. Born into a creative and talented family, it only seems natural that she follow in their footsteps. Her sister is actress/singer/dancer, Debbie Allen; her mother, Vivian Ayers, is a poet and scholar, whose first published works *Spice of Dawns*, earned her a nomination for the Pulitzer Prize; and her brother, Tex Allen, is an accomplished jazz musician. Phylicia began her acting studies while still in elementary school. Her musical training began at age 5, when her mother taught her to read music and play the piano. While in elementary school, she performed in assemblies and in amateur operettas. In high school she joined the Merry-Go-Round Theatre, which was a training program for talented children sponsored by Houston's Alley Theatre. After graduating from high school, Phylicia attended Howard University, where she majored in theatre and graduated magna cum laude. Her professional theatre debut came while she was still at Howard, appearing in the production of *Sons and Fathers of Sons* presented by the Negro Ensemble Company. Other NEC productions include *Weep Not for Me*, *In an Upstate Motel*, and *Zoo Man and the Sign*. After graduating college, she moved to New York and appeared in *To Be Young, Gifted and Black*. Even though she didn't have an agent at the time, she managed to have fairly steady work, filling the employment gaps with temporary typing jobs. Soon after moving to New York, she got her first big break by being cast in the ensemble in the Broadway production of *The Wiz*. She was with the show for three years, and played a variety of roles including a Munchkin, Fieldmouse, and an Emerald City swing dancer. Other Broadway performances include *Ain't Supposed to Die a Natural Death* and *Dreamgirls*. Phylicia made her television debut in a series of national commercials, but made her dramatic debut on the daytime soap "One Life to Live." She has also been seen on the small screen on the CBS series "Delvecchio," the PBS program "Watch Your Mouth," and on several Bob Hope specials. In 1987 she made her TV film debut in *Uncle Tom's Cabin*. But it was her role as Clair Huxtable on the "Cosby Show" that brought her real recognition and fame. She credits her real life experience as a mother rather than her acting for landing the role. "There's a certain rhythm to motherhood," states Phylicia, "an understanding that's unspoken, but it's felt; it's just there." She also explains, "I was always somebody's mother, and I couldn't understand why that kept happening. Then I realized that I was often acting out a scene on stage that I had played for real in my living room. I guess the truth of that just came through." In addition to theatre, Broadway and television, she also has a musical side to her. She has headlined in Atlantic City, the Concord Hotel, and with the Dallas Symphony. In 1988, she returned to Broadway for the first time in four years to take on the lead role of Grindl the Good Witch in the musical *Into the Woods*.

Phylicia and her husband Ahmad Rashad married in 1986, after his on-air proposal during a Thanksgiving Day broadcast. The couple have a daughter, Condola Phylea, and Phylicia has a son William Bowles from a previous marriage, while Ahmad has three children from a previous marriage. The Rashads reside in New York.

Dan Rather

"Ever since I can remember, I never wanted to be anything but a reporter," says Dan Rather. "But I never thought of myself as a broadcaster. Performing doesn't turn me on. It's an egomaniac business, filled with prima donnas—including this one." When CBS's inner circle elevated the Texas-born, award-winning correspondent into Walter Cronkite's chair as managing editor and anchorman of CBS News in 1981, Rather inherited broadcast journalism's most visible hot seat as well as the almost-saintly reputation of his predecessor. Over the years Cronkite had come to personify fair TV news reporting to the American viewer.

If Rather was intimidated, he didn't show it. He shot off a respectful salute to Cronkite, paired him off admiringly with broadcasting pioneer Edward R. Murrow, then cooly and swiftly grabbed the reins. And he did it his way. Never comfortable in Cronkite's grandfatherly role, Rather's hard-hitting style has made him enemies. A city in Indiana opposed his assignment even before his first broadcast, based on a report he had once experimented with heroin. (It was 25 years earlier, under strict police supervision for a magazine story.) In 1984 a phalanx of New Right leaders launched a grass roots campaign encouraging conservatives to buy up CBS stock and thus "become Dan Rather's boss"—thereby ending what they saw as his biased reporting. Never stooping to accept criticism, his career boomed. Not only the Anchor and Managing Editor of the CBS Evening News, he now hosts "48 Hours" (premiered 19 January 1988) making him the only network journalist ever to anchor an evening news broadcast and a primetime news program at the same time.

He was born 31 October 1931 in Wharton, Texas. His father was a pipeliner, and his mother a waitress. When he was about eight Rather started attending Democratic party precinct meetings with his father, and learned the rough-and-tumble Texas-style politicking. A football scholarship got him into Sam Houston State College. He had to drop out after losing the scholarship, but he returned and completed a journalism degree in 1953 while working part-time at local radio station KSAM. After college he taught journalism, worked for UPI and the Houston *Chronicle*, then moved into radio journalism with CBS's radio affiliate in Houston. Covering President Kennedy's tragic visit to Dallas in 1963, Rather skillfully coordinated CBS's round-the-clock coverage of the assassination. Throughout four sleepless nights and days, Rather impressed viewers with his cool professionalism. "We were very careful all along to check and double-check everything for accuracy," he explained afterward. "I think this is what sold the nation—including many former critics—on electronic journalism." His marriage to the former Jean Goebel has produced two children, Dawn Robin and Daniel Martin.

Robert Rauschenberg

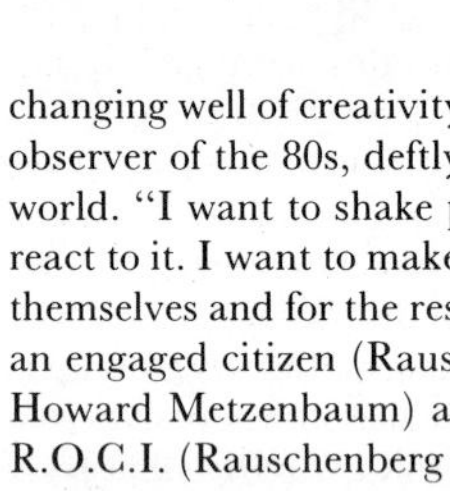

The essence of the creative impulse is awesome to the artist Robert Rauschenberg. "It's like a crystal, clear and hard inside, and light hits it from somewhere. From where? Somewhere in outer space, maybe, that we haven't explored yet. And what comes out is just a reflection of that light, from the unknown source." Rauschenberg considers himself more journalist than artist, having recently delved into photography as art. "I never wanted to be an artist. There wasn't even a choice. I just spontaneously or organically found out that the best way I could communicate with anybody was visually." An unending and ever changing well of creativity, the *enfant terrible* of the 60s has become the social observer of the 80s, deftly commenting on the horrors and beauties of our world. "I want to shake people awake. I want to look at the material and react to it. I want to make them aware of individual responsibility, both for themselves and for the rest of the human race." The artist-journalist is also an engaged citizen (Rauschenberg has raised funds for Ted Kennedy and Howard Metzenbaum) and a roving ambassador for the arts. His project R.O.C.I. (Rauschenberg Overseas Culture Interchanges—named after his pet turtle) is a five-year traveling exhibition which began in 1985. He creates a new work in each of the 22 countries where he collaborates with the local artists. The final exhibition will end up at the National Gallery of Art in Washington sometime in 1990.

Since he captured first prize in the Venice Biennale in 1964, Rauschenberg has influenced the course of art history—beginning with his all-white and all-black canvases of the 50s, then with his "combines" (collages using every imaginable common object—from clocks, radios and neckties to stuffed chickens and goats). The late seventies were marked by a slowdown of Rauschenberg's creative energies and a cooldown of the art world's once laudatory comments. Then finally after two giant retrospectives (at MOMA and in Berlin) Rauschenberg revealed "new variations on his almost infinitely expandable aesthetic, created with methods he has invented for the occasion, and produced on a scale more ambitious than any he has attempted," observed *New York* magazine. His "Quarter Mile Piece" created in the 80s has been called "a retrospective of a whole life in art." Fond of collaborations (with the dance companies of Merce Cunningham and Trisha Brown and performance artists John Cage and Laurie Anderson), Rauschenberg recently combined cultures and technologies, incorporating age-old materials and techniques ("1,000 year" paper and clay "guaranteed not to change organically for 3,000 years" in China and Japan, respectively) resulting in his most ambitious projects to date.

Born in 1925 in the Gulf Coast refinery town of Port Arthur, Texas, Rauschenberg enjoyed drawing as a youngster but didn't seriously consider a career in art until he was in the Navy and saw his first Old Master in a California museum. Divorced and the father of one son, Christopher (a photographer), he now lives on Captiva Island, Florida, a sun-kissed paradise. He remains exuberant about his work—"Art can change life . . ."

Lou Rawls

The buttery baritone of this soul "fusion" singer is one of the most recognizable voices in pop music. With gold and platinum albums to his credit, he has received three Grammys from the NARAS for best male rhythm and blues vocalist. Among his Grammy nominations was one for his gold single "You'll Never Find (Another Love Like Mine)."

Born 1 December 1936 on Chicago's South Side to a Baptist minister and a factory-worker mother, Lou was raised by his grandmother in what he calls a "tough" part of town. "Everything happened in my neighborhood. I learned about people. I just sing about them, that's all." He did a brief stint in the Army after which he toured churches across the United States with the Pilgrim Travelers. Rawls made the transition from gospel halls to nightclubs and by 1959 he had performed on a Dick Clark show at the Hollywood Bowl and had had non-singing roles in ABC-TV's "Bourbon Street Beat" and "77 Sunset Strip." Capitol Records signed Rawls in 1961, apparently intending to groom him as a possible successor to Nat King Cole. In 1966 he broke attendance records at the Village Gate and the following year won the *Down Beat* poll for favorite male vocalist, displacing the perennial winner of that poll, Frank Sinatra. By the mid-1970s he was a familiar figure on the television shows of Johnny Carson, Mike Douglas, Merv Griffin et al., and his concert and club engagements included such prestigious names as the Newport Jazz Festival, the Palmer House, and the MGM Grand Hotel. In recent years he has become the chief fundraiser for the United Negro College Fund, for which he hosts an annual telethon, and the chief commercial spokesman for Anheuser-Busch, the brewers of Budweiser beer. After an eleven-year marriage, in 1973 he and Lana Jean Rawls were divorced. Rawls spends ten months of each year on the road and the other two months he lives in central Los Angeles with his two children.

Nancy Reagan

Ronald Reagan, when asked to describe his wife, responded misty-eyed: "How do you describe someone who makes your life like coming into a warm room?" On the other hand, one of his staff members feeling not so warm in her presence said of the ex-First Lady: "She's an anachronism who lives in the 1950s when it was a man's world and women were there to be perfect wives . . . issues of the day . . . have never been in her sphere of life." On a biographical form MGM asked her to fill out in 1949 she wrote that her pet peeves were: "superficiality, vulgarity (especially in women), untidiness of mind and person, and cigars." Her childhood ambition was "to be an actress" and her greatest ambition was "to have a happy, successful marriage."

Born 6 July 1923, she explained to a reporter in the L.A. *Herald Examiner* that, "I never was really a career girl. I majored in drama at Smith and I became an actress because I didn't want to go back to Chicago and lead the life of a post-debutante. I wanted to do something until I found the man I wanted to marry." Her longing for security may have something to do with her unhappy early years. Anne Frances Robbins, nicknamed "Nancy" at birth, was the daughter of actress Edith "DeeDee" Luckett and a New Jersey car salesman who left her mother shortly after Nancy was born; she was then turned over to an aunt in Maryland to be raised while her mother returned to the stage in order to pay the bills. Five years later when "DeeDee" married Dr. Loyal Davis, a prominent, politically conservative neurosurgeon in Chicago, Nancy's life circumstances changed considerably. At age 14 she was legally adopted by her step-father.

The highlight of her New York stage career was in *Lute Song*, a musical starring Mary Martin and Yul Brynner. A film scout from MGM spotted her in a television play and offered her a screen test which family friend Spencer Tracy made sure was conducted under the most favorable circumstances. Signed to a seven year contract, she got good notices in her mostly B films (of her film debut in *Shadow on the Wall*, the critic for the New York *Times* wrote: "Nancy Davis is beautiful and convincing"). But a year after arriving in Hollywood her name turned up on a list of Communist sympathizers. Knowing that there must be an error, Mervin LeRoy referred her to Ronald Reagan, then president of the Screen Actor's Guild. At a meeting he explained that there was another Nancy Davis. The young woman in front of him was no Communist. Love led to marriage. The Reagans have two children, Patti and Ron. Jr. Together, before appearing in the Governor's Mansion in Sacramento and in The White House, the Reagan's appeared in one film, *Hellcats of the Navy* and a TV show, "Money and the Minister."

During her White House years, Nancy Reagan became crusader against the use of drugs and alcohol among the nation's youth, and she served as a strong advocate of the Foster Grandparents Program, with which she has long been associated. ("If I can make a difference in those areas, I will be happy.") Perhaps the greatest public turnabout came in the aftermath of the President's cancer surgery when she was praised for her grace and courage by many of the same people who had earlier dismissed her absolute devotion to her husband as anachronistic. Her autobiography, *My Turn: Memoirs of Nancy Reagan*, was published in 1989.

Ronald Reagan

"He took one more sweeping look around the room where he had exercised the globe's greatest power so long and so exuberantly, slowly squared his shoulders and walked out to the sun-streaked colonade that links the office with the mansion. White House staff members crowded against the glass doors and windows, some of them openly weeping." A touching scene as described by *Time* magazine in January 1989 for a President who touched us all. Riding out to the hills as winner, he broke the line of his four immediate predecessors Lyndon Johnson, Richard Nixon, Gerald Ford and Jimmy Carter who never managed two full terms in office. Tip O'Neill pretty much summed up the attitude in Washington in 1985 when he said "They all laughed when he sat down in the Oval Office..." It's his partisans who are laughing now. The others, the ones who spent a political lifetime underestimating "the Gipper," never will learn. They've forgotten that the American people—after twenty years of assassinations, of scandals, of humiliation in the jungles of Vietnam, and gun-toting Iranian "students" taking Americans hostage in their own U.S. Embassy—desperately wanted someone in whom they could believe, someone who enunciated their concerns simply (some would say simplistically) and clearly, someone who believed in something himself—and they got that in Ronald Reagan. They would forgive him his campaign and press conference gaffes (replete with sometimes surrealistic facts and figures), his potentially dangerous red-baiting ("the evil empire"), his frequent vacations "back at the ranch"—even Nancy's Galanos knickers at the Elysee Palace, for goodness sake—Revolution with the 1984 promise, "You ain't seen nothin', yet," had proved that America is governable—a notion that until his inauguration in 1981 had very few supporters. His place in history is guaranteed.

The ninth chief executive of the United States of Irish ancestry was born in Tampico, Illinois, 6 February 1911, the son of an itinerant (and alcoholic) shoe salesman, "Jack" Reagan, and theatre-lover and general do-gooder, Nelle Reagan, on whom his father's "cynicism never made the slightest impression... while I suspect her sweetness often undermined his practical view of the world," their son recalled in his 1965 autobiography, *Where's the Rest of Me?* Supplementing his partial scholarship to Eureka (Illinois) College by working as a lifeguard, a swimming coach and dishwasher in his fraternity house, Reagan got his first taste of politics in his freshman year when he acted as spokesman for a student strike committee and discovered "that an audience has a feel to it and, in the parlance of the theatre, that audience and I were together." After college and a job as a sports announcer in Des Moines, where he broadcast the Chicago Cubs' games, he was spotted by a Warner Brothers agent while covering the Cubs' spring training in Catalina Island and made his motion picture debut—as a crusading radio announcer—in 1937 in *Love Is On the Air*. In all, he made some 52 films, the most notable of which were *Knute Rockne—All American* (1940), in which he played legendary Notre Dame running back George Gipp, whose deathbed plea, "Win one for the Gipper," inspired many Reagan followers to extend the mandate beyond the gridiron; *King's Row* (1941), playing an amputee, whose plaintive post-operative cry became the title of his autobiography; and for casting notes only, *Bedtime for Bonzo* (oppostie a chimp; 1951) and *Hellcats of the Navy* (opposite future wife, Nancy Davis; 1957). His love for horses led him to sign up in the pre-war U.S. Army cavalry reserve, but when he was called up to active days in 1942, his nearsightedness disqualified him for combat and he spent the war years as an officer making air force training films. His first wife, actress Jane Wyman (doyenne of TV's "Falcon Crest"), divorced him in 1948 (citing his obsession with politics among the reasons for her disenchantment), and he and Nancy wed in 1952. From his first marriage, he has a daughter Maureen and a son, Michael, and from his present union a daughter, Patti (who, in 1984, married her yoga instructor) and a son, Ron, who left Yale to become a ballet dancer, then a writer, now a TV entertainment reporter. Reagan signed on with the General Electric Company in 1952 and stayed with them as a spokesman for a decade, eight years as host of television's "General Electric Theater." The one-time FDR idolator, a self-described "hemophiliac" liberal, began to turn rightward politically during his tenure as president of the Screen Actors Guild (1947-52) when he became disenchanted with the rule-or-ruin tactics of Communists in Hollywood unionism. Although he cooperated with the Hollywood blacklist, he refused to "name names" before J. Parnell Thomas' Committee on Un-American Activities, which he viewed as a "pretty venal bunch" themselves.

He came to the attention—via a campaign speech for Barry Goldwater in 1964 (known forever after as THE SPEECH)—of a group of California industrialists who urged him to run for Governor in 1966. He beat incumbent Pat Brown by a million votes (Brown's quip that "an actor killed Lincoln" backfired disastrously for the first of the Reagan underestimators) and won re-election four years later. He was poised to make a run for the presidency in 1976—expecting the field to be open at the end of Nixon's second term. He hadn't counted on Watergate and a Ford incumbency, so he bided his time until 1980. Easily overcoming the age issue by the vigor and stamina of his campaigning, he bested Carter (who seemed to be campaigning against a nightly backdrop of blindfolded American hostages) in their debate ("There you go, again," etc.) and swamped the Georgian at the polls.

Two months later after taking office, he took a bullet to the chest, and his good humor ("I forgot to duck, honey"), his grace and his remarkably resilient recovery only increased the good will the American people had sent his way in November, permitting him to get his revolutionary tax-cutting program through an all but prostrate Congress. The fierce activism of his first six months in office bore favorable comparisons with FDR's "first hundred days."

The proud leader now resides with his wife, Nancy, in Californa as a private citizen. He has written a book *Speaking My Mind (Selected Speeches)* published in 1989. As he believes, "A revolution of ideas became a revolution of governance on January 30, 1981."

Harry Reasoner

Pro athletes were doing it. High-powered execs were too. And in 1970 this CBS "60 Minutes" correspondent joined the types of professionals who were flying their employers' coops. "I had long wanted a chance to anchor," says Reasoner, "and even though I'd often substituted for Walter Cronkite when he was unavailable, there was little likelihood that he'd be run over by a truck, and no assurance that if he was I'd succeed him. So I became to the television news business what [pitcher] Andy Messersmith was to baseball. It was the first time a senior correspondent had jumped from one network to another simply for a new job and better pay." He felt for competitor ABC. The seven-and-a-half year hiatus began fizzling when ABC added highly-paid and promoted Barbara Walters to the anchor desk Reasoner thought was his alone. Their scarcely-veiled dislike for each other prompted Reasoner to jump back to CBS, where he resumed his commentary on election night results, narrating occasional documentaries, and working on the highly-rated "60 Minutes" TV newsmagazine.

Described as "dry and affable" as well as "stern ... [and] tight-mouthed," Reasoner says he likes to believe "that if the happy ending doesn't exist, it ought to." Born 17 April 1923 in Dakota City, Iowa, the son of teachers, he was orphaned while still in his teens. He studied journalism at Stanford and the University of Minnesota, worked as reporter, and later as a broadcaster, in Minneapolis. At 23 he published his first novel, *Tell Me About Women*. ("I didn't sell to well," Reasoner recalls.) In 1981 his memoirs *Before the Colors Fade* did considerably better. The sardonically irreverent newsman whom Mike Wallace describes as "middle America... honest and compassionate" is divorced from the former Kathleen Carroll, with whom he had eight children. He remarried in May 1988 Lois Harriet Weber in Humboldt, Iowa. Although he's won Emmys for reports about the Sicilian Mafia, and President Nixon's trip to China, he calls one of his lighter pieces, a tribute to the Bergman-Bogart classic film, *Casablanca*, one of his favorites. He allowed that real people, Reasoner included, often didn't get the girl just as Bogart had not at the conclusion. "You never forget who you first saw it with. I wonder if she remembers. If she does, here's looking at you, kid."

Robert Redford

Newsweek writer David Ansen concluded his 1984 profile "American Adonis" with the following anecdote the actor told about himself. It took place when he was nineteen. "It is New Year's Eve in Rome, and the young art student Redford is staying in a youth hostel and feeling lonely and in need of revelry. He makes a reservation at Bricktop's for midnight, but first stops in at the American bar next door. More and more depressed as he sits drinking alone in the back of the room, he's suddenly aware of a commotion at the door. In walks Ava Gardner with five Italian escorts. She seems the most gorgeous creature Redford has ever seen, and he builds up the drunken resolve: come midnight, he's going to walk over and kiss her. Twelve o'clock strikes, Redford stands up and 'all courage went out of me like steam from a valve. I could hardly walk. I got all the way to her table and lost everything. Nerve, courage, memory, vocabulary. I just stood there like a dope in front of her.' The escorts looked alarmed, sensing trouble. He stands there paralyzed. And Ava Gardner looks up at the nineteen-year-old Redford and says, 'Happy New Year, soldier.' And then reaches up, grabs his hand, pulls him down and kisses the poor boy on the lips. . . . It was his fate, even then, to be *Robert Redford.*"

Being the king of American dreamboats is a mixed blessing for the actor. Born in Santa Monica, Calif. 18 August 1937, the son of a milkman who later became a Standard Oil accountant, he attended the University of Colorado on a baseball scholarship, although in his earlier years he preferred having a sentimental education to a formal one. ("I never learned as much in the classroom as I did staring out a window and imagining things.") His mother died his freshman year, and he spent most of his time coping by drinking or skiing; his "dark side" (both parents were of Scottish-Irish descent) as he calls it, surfacing and alienating him from his peers. He dropped out and went to Europe to study painting. ("I had a sidewalk showing of my paintings in Florence. Made $200. Enough to return to New York.") Thinking first that he would become an art director, he instead found his way into classes at the American Academy of Dramatic Arts. In 1959, he got his first acting job, a small part in *Tall Story* on Broadway. Roles in major New York television dramas followed and he made his first film, the low-budgeted *War Hunt*. Redford made his name on Broadway, first in *Sunday in New York*, and then (directed by Mike Nichols) in *Barefoot in the Park*. His success in the latter sent him to Hollywood where he worked non-stop in *Inside Daisy Clover, The Chase* and *This Property is Condemned*. Teamed with Jane Fonda in the film version of *Barefoot in the Park* he achieved soon-to-be-a-star recognition. His films include: *Butch Cassidy and the Sundance Kid; Downhill Racer; Little Fauss, Big Halsey; Jeremiah Johnson* (his personal favorite); *The Way We Were; The Sting; The Great Gatsby; Three Days of the Condor; All The President's Men; A Bridge Too Far, The Natural, Out of Africa* and *Legal Eagles*. He won an Oscar for directing 1980's *Ordinary People*, his directorial debut. In 1986 he directed *The Milagro Beanfield War*. A political and environmental activist, he is the owner of the Sundance Resort in Utah, the founder of the prestigious Sundance Institute for independent filmmaking and the funding source of the environmental Institute Resource Management.

Describing Redford as a mature screen star, Ansen writes, ". . . . It's as if he has arrived at the face that he had intended all along: a little wary, a little haunted, a gorgeous battlefield that can be suddenly transformed by the legendary flash of pearly white—into pure sunlight. . . . He is the master of the close-up. A slight squint of the eye, a sideways movement of the jaw tells all: his features are like microchips, carrying a startling load of information." Redford says that acting requires that one "live your character. It's like skiing. You can't be thinking too much. When you get on the hill, your skis are doing the work. You'd better just hang on. Acting is a bit the same way. You've got to submit to what's going on around you and be able to do that fully. You've got to behave as the character. A lot of what acting is paying attention." Separated from his wife, Lola, they have three children.

Lynn Redgrave

She's the formerly "plump duckling" of Britain's famous theatrical family of swans. But having been Oscar- and Tony-nominated, she's proven herself worthy of the Redgrave mantle. Born in London on 8 March 1943, Lynn Redgrave almost bucked three previous generations of tradition by planning to become an equestrienne or a cook. But Sir Michael her distinguished actor dad (who died in 1985) won the day (and shaped a career) when he persuaded her to dump gourmet cooking at Polytechnic College and enter the Central School of Speech and Drama. "Being so big," Lynn recalls, "I frequently played male roles. I was a late developer, and at 18, I looked like a giant 12-year old." But in 1966, four years after taking up the art as livelihood, she snared the klutzy title role in the hit movie, *Georgy Girl*. "Looking up at my horrible, ugly bulk on that huge screen was the turning point of my life," she says now, and she shed pounds to become a svelte five-foot-ten, 138-pound swan herself. The Academy Award-nominated performance led to Broadway, Hollywood, and TV roles, and curiously, game show appearances. Despite her almost-hallowed background, Redgrave had no compunctions against pitching her latest play amidst the inanities of "Hollywood Squares" or "The $20,000 Pyramid." The strategy helped her pack 'em in when she toured places like Tallahassee and Skowhegan, and strengthened her conviction to "not be boxed into any category of any sort." To prove her unsnobbish approach to show biz, she hosted a so-called "pseudo-serious syndicated chat show" for a couple of years, did a TV sitcom, "House Calls," for a couple more, and in 1984 was starring on "Weight Watcher's Magazine," the cable TV show of that organization. Presently, she stars in their "This is living" commercials.

Her reputation as a substantial actress, however, was earned in Shakespearean plays for the National Theatre Company of Great Britain, in Broadway plays including *California Suite*, in films, among them *Everything You Always Wanted to Know About Sex* (1972) and in the miniseries *Centennial* on the tube. Unlike her politically active thespian siblings, Vanessa and Corin, Lynn is a confirmed capitalist. Since 1967 she's been married to British-born producer-director John Clark, who besides being the father of her brood of three - Benjamin, Kelly, and Annabel - was at one time her manager as well as her director in several stage productions. Pleased to have escaped the pitfall of constant type-casting, Michael Redgrave's daughter once observed, "It has reached the point where I am offered most interesting work - far more interesting than I ever was - simply because nobody can say, 'Oh, but she can't do that becuase she only does this sort of thing.' They can't label me." She co-starred on Broadway in 1985 with Claudette Colbert and Rex Harrison in *Aren't We All* and in 1987 with Mary Tyler Moore in *Sweet Sue*. Her latest films include *Midnight* (1988) and *Getting It Right* (1989) and her book *This Is Living: An Inspirational Guide To Freedom* was published in 1988. She currently co-stars with Jackie Mason in the TV sitcom "Chicken Soup."

Vanessa Redgrave

"I give myself to my parts as to a lover," she explains. "It's the only way." Italian film director Michelangelo Antonioni thought so too, and requested that she strip to the waist in 1966 for her role in the eerie *Blow-Up*. Cutting an elegant, aristocratic and daring figure, some said the cause-oriented Vanessa had practically offered to "walk stark naked down Piccadilly for Antonioni," though she denies it.

The crown princess of a transatlantic show business royal family, Vanessa is the eldest child (born 30 January 1937 in London) of a family steeped in theatrical tradition.

Younger sister Lynn is an accomplished actress (*Georgy Girl, Black Comedy* and the the television series "Chicken Soup"); brother Corin is also an actor. And of course, the patriarch of this renowned, talented pack is Sir Michael Redgrave, the late great actor known to pose for family portraits in costume and who once said of his first-born: "She'll never be an actress, we're having her do languages. That way she can always get a job with an airline or something." Naturally, as Vanessa's reputation grew, Sir Michael accommodated: "She's mad," he said, "I mean, divinely mad . . . an inspired actress." "Mod Goddess," an American magazine trumpeted. "A rainwashed daffodil in a fire-green Sussex meadow . . . Eleanor of Aquitaine in a miniskirt."

Vanessa launched her career after graduating from the Central School of Speech and Drama in 1958, making her debut performance in London in N.C. Hunter's *A Touch of the Sun*, as the daughter of the schoolmaster played by her father. In 1959 she joined the Stratford-upon-Avon Theatre Company, working in productions directed by the illustrious likes of Tony Richardson, Sir Tyrone Guthrie and Sir Peter Hall. She continued impressively in classics at the Royal Shakespeare Company. Gracefully moving into a film career, her performances included the startling *Isadora* (Duncan), under the direction of Karel Reisz, *A Suitable Case* (for which she won the Best Actress Award at the Cannes Film Festival, 1965), *Camelot*, *The Trojan Women*, Ken Russel's *The Devil*, *Mary Queen of Scots*, *Yanks* and *Julia*, for which she won an Academy Award as Best Supporting Actress in 1977. She's also starred in *Second Serve*, *Steaming*, *Consuming Passions* and *Prick Up Your Ears* (received Best Supporting Actress Award from NY Film Critics in 1988), as well as appeared on television in "Playing for Time" (receiving an Emmy Award as Best Actress), in the Shelly Duvall Faerie Tale Theatre production of "Snow While and the Seven Dwarfs" (as the Wicked Queen), in 1985 in "Three Sovereigns for Sarah," a three-part dramatization of the Salem witch trials for PBS's "American Playhouse" series and in 1986 a nine-hour miniseries, "Peter the Great." In 1985, she appeared in the film *Wetherby* with daughter Joely and on stage in London in *The Sea Gull* with daughter Natasha. Her recent theatre productions include *A Touch of the Poet* in London and *Orpheus Descending* on Broadway.

A controversial individual in both her personal and political lives, Vanessa admits, "I have a tremendous use for passionate statement." She has supported a variety of causes including pacifism and ban-the-bomb, in addition to the Palestine Liberation Organization. This association led to a 1984 lawsuit with Vanessa filing a complaint against the Boston Symphony Orchestra for cancelling her performance as narrator of *Oedipus Rex* for what she called "political reasons" and in violation of her civil rights. (A Federal jury awarded her $100,000 in damages for breach of contract, but rejected her claim about the BSO's motives.) In the process of issuing passionate statements, Vanessa herself has been arrested four times. But in the mother country they say it has all come about because she is an incurable romantic. "It's a kinky part of my nature—to meddle," she says. Divorced from director Tony Richardson in 1967, she has daughters Joely and Natasha from that marriage. In 1969 Vanessa gave birth to Carlo Gabriel, son of Franco Nero, her Lancelot in *Camelot*. Her latest lover is the new 007, Timothy Dalton.

Rex Reed

"I have never set out to destroy anybody," he has said. "If I see somebody is basically a s.o.b., but underneath is real, then I say they're a nice s.o.b. But if some jackass picks his nose, I'm going to write it." Rex Reed is a film critic, raconteur, and sometime actor. (Films: *Myra Breckenridge*, *Inchon*, *Superman*, *Irreconcilable Differences*; legit: *Rope*; books: *Do You Sleep in the Nude*, *Conversations in the Raw*, *Big Screen, Little Screen*, *People Are Crazy Here*, *Valentines and Vitriol*, *Personal Effects*.) Many of his critics feel he is a "master of the celebrity interview." "The old broads are the ones who interest me most," admits Reed. "Nothing bores me more than these . . . girls with nothing on their minds. . . . For years people didn't know celebrities went to the bathroom. . . . The public won't settle for pap any more. . . . It wants its copy bitchy." His style of film reviewing gets a lot of flack from fellow reviewers and writers. He currently is a syndicated film critic for the NY *Post* and the star of the TV show "At The Movies."

Born in Fort Worth 2 October 1939, the son of a Texas oil company supervisor, he spent his formative years in the South traveling from oil boom to oil boom (13 schools, straight As, a degree in journalism from LSU). As a boy Reed was awe-struck by Hollywood. "From what I saw on the movie screen I knew that people were living a better life than we did in the South. I wanted to live like them; to eat wonderful food and go to plays and walk through Madison Avenue at midnight. I didn't want just to trudge along dusty country roads and eat fried chicken." He dabbled in acting and jazz singing before he broke into print in 1965 with a brace of unsolicited interviews (Jean Paul Belmondo, Buster Keaton) in the *New York Times* and the late Herald Tribune's *New York* magazine. In a review of one of Reed's collections, New York *Times's* Richard R. Lingeman concluded: "Mr. Reed is the rhinestone cowboy of journalism. If he's a bit world-weary now, he's still the small-town kid from Louisiana dazzled by marquees. Deep inside his subconscious there's an old radio still playing 'Grand Central Station,' 'Mr. First Nighter,' and Jimmy Fiddler. As long as there's a Rex Reed, there'll always be a Broadway—and a Hollywood."

Christopher Reeve

The Adonis-built actor brought Superman alive on the big screen for a new generation of hero seekers. With wavy brown hair, sculpted features, and a hulky virility, he was cartoon-perfect for the coveted role as The Man of Steel. However, he was far from the producers first choice. In fact, over 200 other actors were considered—including the producer's wife's dentist—before they settled on Reeve, an extraordinarily handsome but little-known actor. His humanizing, lighthearted interpretation of the role was largely credited for making the 1978 *Superman* and its 1980, 1983 and 1987 sequels huge box office hits. "I wanted to show a character who's warm, who isn't aloof, who cares, a hero secure enough to have a sense of humor," he said.

Born 25 September 1952 in Manhattan, the son of a writer and an English professor who divorced when he was young, Reeve saw the theatre as a haven from turmoil and growing pains. "If you look at pictures of me when I was a kid I never cracked a smile. Really grim. Acting was a way to help me loosen up, expose myself, relax, and I think I've made some progress. But I also think it takes twenty years to make an actor. I'm halfway there." His reverence for acting as a fine craft has kept him dedicated to talent-stretching roles in sometimes risky vehicles and away from lucrative, hero type-casting parts he could command.

Reeve began his theatrical career in summer theatres and continued to study acting in college until his Cornell University education was interrupted by a two-year stint on the soap opera, "Love of Life." His Broadway stage debut in 1976 in *A Matter of Gravity*, which starred Katharine Hepburn, received mixed reviews. He fared better with the critics as the embittered paraplegic casualty of the Vietnam War in Lanford Wilson's *Fifth of July* in 1980 and on the London stage in 1984 with Wendy Hiller and Vanessa Redgrave in *The Aspern Papers*. Other films include Ira Levin's *Deathtrap* and *Monsignor* (1982), *The Bostonians* (1984), *Street Smart* and *Switching Channels* (1987). In 1985 he played Vronsky in a television version of "Anna Karenina" opposite Jacqueline Bisset and in 1988 starred in the NBC telefilm "The Great Escape." A critic of the institution of marriage (stemming no doubt from early memories of marital discord between his parents) he lived with Gae Exton (two children: Matthew and Alexandra). The couple separated in 1987. He appeared on stage again in 1989 for the NY Public Theatre production of *The Winter's Tale*.

Regine

The "Death-to-Disco" movement has its influence these days, but this international Queen of the Night will have none of it. "There is great competition between discos. But I will stay. For me it is a career. And not only that. Look, I come from the streets. I like the glamour, the sophistication, the sexiness."

Born Regine Zylberberg in Belgium, 26 December 1929, she refers to her childhood as a *chasse au père* (hunt for father). After he was taken into a detention camp, Regine, just a youngster, hid from the Nazis in such places as the Catholic convent where the other girls beat her because she was a Jew. When her father escaped she was found and taken hostage by the Gestapo. "Anguish is my best friend," she says now, adding that because of her past, "I need insecurity, that is how I create." There are still scars and hostilities. "When I saw Rita Hayworth and Aly Khan the focus of all the eyes at the best table in a chic Deauville restaurant, I vowed one day to sit where they were." Her first husband (one son, Lionel, raised by his grandmother) sent her to a psychiatrist for a year because he found her boasts about how one day she'd have a night club in which she'd receive the world, so bizarre. After she peddled brassieres on the street and worked as a dancer and a chanteuse, she became a hatcheck girl and dancer at Paris's Whiskey-a-Go-Go where her little eccentricities— wearing rings over her gloves, dancing with a champagne glass in her hair—brought her the midnight friendships of such swell gents as Jean-Paul Belmondo, Alain Delon and the late Porfirio Rubirosa. With their help she opened her first club by sitting in Chez Regine for a month with a sign on the door that said "Full" and by the time she took down the white lie of a sign, the public was hungry for admittance. In they came in droves, barefoot and bohemian, chic and princely and all together they learned the "Twist." Regine has clubs all over the globe, and as one of France's recording artists her biggest hit was scored with the song "La Grande Zoa" (the tale of a man who is an antiquarian by day and a transvestite by night). In 1989 she opened a new restaurant in Paris, "Ledoyen." That same year she was named "Woman of the Year" by the National Woman's Division of Jerusalem Shaare Zadek's Medical Center.

As much as she is the Queen of the Night she is also its slave. Married to Roger Choukroun since 1969, she is always on the move. Globetrotting is hard, her nights are by and large sleepless. To help her, she travels with a large staff including a make-up person and a psychic medium. "Disco has a whole psychology," she says, "when people say it is expensive, I make the prices more. I'm in my full glory, I'm not having a sale."

William Rehnquist

His owlish face framed by long black sideburns and hair uncharacteristically long for a judge, William H. Rehnquist emerges from formal portraits of the Justices as the "baby" of the bunch—and he is. Wearing his tortoise shell glasses, he likes to relax in chambers and conduct meetings with his clerks with his feet up on the conference table, his penny loafers surrounded by legal briefs. "Ultraconservative" by his own estimate, he is nevertheless the Court's most casual Justice. Washington insiders Bob Woodward and Scott Armstrong describe Rehnquist's informal manners, which fly in the face of the Court's buttoned-down tradition: "During the nice weather, he and his clerks sometimes ate lunch [outdoors]. They brought their food in paper bags and simply enjoyed the sun and the outdoors. As they were picnicking in shirtsleeves one day, Burger's messenger [began] setting up a small table with silver service and a white linen tablecloth. Moments later, Burger came out with his clerks [and] jacket on, poured the wine. . . . As they gazed on the solemnity of the Burger table, Rehnquist's laughter grew almost uncontrollable. He and his clerks had to dash inside."

Rehnquist's appointment to the Court followed his service to the Nixon administration, where his widely-admired legal craftsmanship helped keep a thumb in the dike of the Watergated administration. He dug deeply into legal archives to uncover rationales for such Nixonian antics as governmental wiretapping, surveillance of civilians, and pretrial detention. Nixon's pledge to make the Court conservative again seemed closer to fulfillment in January 1972 when William Hubbs Rehnquist of Milwaukee was sworn in as Associate Justice.

Born on 1 October 1924, Rehnquist first earned a reputation as a razor-sharp superbrain when he was Phi Beta at Stanford. He received a B.A. in Political Science from Harvard and went on to graduate first in his class at Stanford Law (1952). While clerking for Supreme Court Justice Robert Jackson, he married Natalie Cornell (three children). Later, in private practice in Phoenix, he became a Republican to be reckoned with. He is noted for his preference of law and order over first amendment rights, and— true to his Nixonian background—has anchored the Court firmly from the right. In a speech in October of 1984, Rehnquist said that, although "there is no reason in the world" for a President not to try to "pack" the Supreme Court with Justices who agree with him, he predicted that unexpected legal developments, personal antagonisms, the Court's tradition of independence as well as "blind chance" all tend to frustrate a President's ability to predict the performance of Supreme Court nominees.

Tim Reid

Mediocrity is a state which holds no place in the world of handsome actor Tim Reid. His strive for perfection manifests itself in his versatility. Track athlete, stand-up comedian, business man and anti-drug activist compose the essence of the masterful Reid.

While Reid has managed to accomplish much in his life, his beginnings were humble. He was born in Norfolk, Virginia, on 19 December 1944. His family was poor; the lack of money forcing them to live a somewhat nomadic life ("We did a lot of moving, especially around the time rent was due"). Tim settled down from his wandering days at the age of nine when he was sent to live with his grandmother. The move delighted Tim, but something happened during Tim's teen years. He fell prey to a normal stage of rebellion. Doing poorly in school and running around with the wrong crowd, his father (living in Chesapeake, Virginia) decided to send for his son and detour him from the path of destruction. Although meager in financial resources, Tim's life was affluent in love. The love and devotion displayed by his father placed Tim on the correct path of life. No longer under the influence of the "Bad crowd" Tim did a turn-around—a star on the high school track team, vice president of the student council and an editor on the high school yearbook staff. It was these early experiences which led Tim to adopt the belief: "That old cliché about all a child needs is love is true." Upon graduating high school, Tim decided to join the Air Force. Enroute to the recruitment office, he stopped through ritzy Virginia Beach and placed the Air Force idea on hold while taking a job as a waiter in a swanky seasonal restaurant. The money he earned while waiting tables enabled him to enroll in the all-black Norfolk State College. Although a business marketing major, Reid also studied drama during his college tenure. He auditioned for a major role in the college's production of *Oedipus Rex*, landed the role and was bit by the acting bug.

During his years in marketing Tim hooked up with an insurance agent, Tom Dreesen. Similar in their anti-drug beliefs, Reid and Dreesen decided to do their part to deter drug use with an anti-drug presentation geared towards grade-school kids. Imbued with a comedic nature, they began catching on like wild fire. "Tim and Tom" began making headway—they once followed Stevie Wonder, appeared on David Frost and Merv Griffin. In 1975 "Tim and Tom" decided they had come to the end of their alliance and Reid went solo. He toured with Della Reese as her opening act. It was not long afterwards that Tim would move into television. He started with a recurring role on a CBS replacement series "Easy Does It" and a role on the "Richard Pryor Show." Doing the usual rounds of guest appearances on various sitcoms, it was not until he landed a job as a regular on "WKRP" that he became a celebrity. The Supercool DJ "Venus Flytrap" was Reid's ticket to stardom. He remained with "WKRP" for four years. Roles which followed included a CBS-TV movie "You Can't Take It With You," a

357

Carl Reiner

regular stint on the short-lived "Teachers Only", the role of undercover police lieutenant "Downtown Brown" on "Simon & Simon" followed by his very own CBS series "Frank's Place." His acting career may keep him busy but Reid still finds time to spread the word of drug abstinence. "Stop the Madness" was a music video Tim created and produced in 1986. Reid's anti-drug activities have also taken him to Senate hearings in Washington, D.C., where he has testified before a Senate Subcommittee on Special Investigations. A talented writer, Reid has penned television scripts and, as an avid amateur photographer, he has compiled a book of his poetry (illustrated by his photographs) titled *As I Feel It*.

Probably the most important and precious role in his life is that of husband to actress Daphne Maxwell Reid whom he wed on 4 December 1982. They have three children: Tim Jr., daughter Tori (from Tim's first marriage) and Christopher (from Daphne's first marriage). The Reids live in Encino, California, where Tim can be found dabbling in his herb and vegetable garden.

Carl Reiner

"The comedian will flourish as long as the world stays complicated and cockeyed," says this actor-raconteur-writer-producer-director who's been called a veritable "conglomerate of comedy." Launching his TV career in the late 1940s as second banana to Sid Caesar and Imogene Coca on the landmark laugh series, "Your Show of Shows," he's gone on to conceive and write the long-running (1961-1966) sitcom, "The Dick Van Dyke Show," and to appear in and/or direct and/or write an impressive succession of big screen comedy offerings. The record albums he created with Mel Brooks (as the 2000-year-old man) stand as comedy classics.

Born on 20 March 1922, Reiner grew up in an Italian-Jewish section of the Bronx and was attracted to laugh-getting as a means of self-defense. "I was what I call a charming coward," he told TV columnist Kay Gardella. "It was one of those neighborhoods where if you fought back you had to be good. So to get attention I'd turn to comedy. I'm more and more convinced that *all* comedians are charming cowards." Reiner turned to performing after studies at the WPA Dramatic Workshop (the launching pad for countless fine talents during the Depression) and, during World War II, toured the South Pacific with Major Maurice Evans's Special Services Unit, which entertained servicemen. Appropriately, Reiner's first major postwar effort was in a road company production of the back-to-civvies musical, *Call Me Mister*. His nine years on "Your Show of Shows" served as what he now calls his "writing college," laying the groundwork for all his future TV and film work. Among his screen acting credits: *It's a Mad, Mad, Mad, Mad World* (1963), *The Russians Are Coming* (1966). He made his directorial debut in 1967 with *Enter Laughing*, the movie version of his own play of that title based on his early acting experiences. Subsequent directing efforts include *The Comic* (1968), *Where's Poppa?* (1970), and three Steve Martin comedies *The Jerk* (1979), *Dead Men Don't Wear Plaid* (the ingenious 1982 spoof of 1940s thrillers), and *All of Me* (1984). His recent works include *Summer Rental* (1985), *Summer School* and *Bert Rigby, You're A Fool* (1988).

Married in 1943 to the former Estelle (Stella) Lobost, Reiner is the father of three children, Rob, Sylvia Ann and Lucas. Rob, following in his dad's Merry Andrew footsteps, achieved TV immortality of a sort playing the indomitable Meathead on "All in the Family," and has several praiseworthy directorial film credits.

Rob Reiner

He is a multi-talented actor, writer, director, and producer. In addition to appearing on television, in films, and on stage, he has written for several comics, directed numerous hit films and is part-owner of Castle Rock Entertainment.

Rob Reiner was born on 6 March 1945 in New York City, the son of actor/director Carl Reiner. He attended U.C.L.A., and he began his showbiz career by acting with regional theatres and improv troupes. Starting out writing scripts, he wrote for such shows as "Halls of Anger" (1970), "Where's Poppa?" (1970), "Summertree" (1971), the summer series "The Super" (1972), "Fire Sale" (1977) and "The Smothers Brothers Comedy Hour." His big break came when he appeared as a guest star on a comedy show for which he was the story editor. This appearance led to his role as Michael "Meathead" Stivic on the long-running hit comedy series "All in the Family," which ran from 1971-1978 and earned Rob two Emmy Awards. Other television appearances include "Free Country" (1978), "The Beverly Hillbillies" (for which he also received an Emmy), "Thursday's Game" (1974) and "More Than Friends" (1978). Although he was successful in front of the camera, his real goal was to be behind it, directing and producing. The first film to be directed by Rob was the rockumentary *This Is Spinal Tap* (1984), which received widespread acclaim and established him as a filmmaker with a unique talent. He has directed several other films since then, such as *The Sure Thing* (1985), *Stand By Me* (1986), *The Princess Bride* (1987), and *When Harry Met Sally* (1989).

Rob and actress Penny Marshall were married in April 1971 and divorced ten years later. He is currently married to Michele Singer (married May 1989), and the couple reside in California.

Lee Remick

"Television is making the movies that Hollywood made during the 1940s and 50s," observed Lee Remick while making the 1982 TV version of Somerset Maugham's *The Letter*. Since 1975 she has plucked and pitted some of the small-screen plums: "Jennie, Lady Randolph Churchill" (Best Actress Award by the British Society of Film and TV Arts), "Torn Between Two Lovers," "Haywire," and the miniseries, "Wheels," "Ike," "Mistral's Daughter," "The Gift of Love: A Christmas Story," "Lena: My Hundred Children," and "Jesse." ("The pace is a lot quicker than feature films," says Remick). The sultry blonde with the begging-blue eyes knows whereof she speaks: she twirled her way onto the big movie screen in 1956 as the sexy drum majorette in Elia Kazan's *A Face in the Crowd* and has been cheered on ever since. Other taunt-and-tease movie performances of that decade include *The Long Hot Summer*, *Anatomy of a Murder*, and *Wild River*. Since 1960 she has sizzled, snapped, seduced and has been seduced in such movies as *Sanctuary*, *Experiment in Terror*, *Days of Wine and Roses*, *The Wheeler Dealers*, *No Way to Treat a Lady*, *The Detective*, *Hard Contract*, *Loot*, *A Delicate Balance*, *Hennessy*, *The Omen*, *Telefon*, and *The Europeans*. She "wrapped" three movies in five months in 1980—*The Women's Room*, *The Competition*, and *Tribute* (Remick admits the rigorous filming paid for a new house in Brentwood, California, after eleven years in London, but "I wouldn't recommend a schedule like that to anyone"). In 1988 she was seen in *The Vision*.

Born 14 December 1935 in Quincy, Mass., (her father owns Remick's Department Store), her divorced mother took her to Manhattan when she was 7. After attending Miss Hewitt's and Barnard College, Remick made her Broadway debut in *Be Your Age* in 1953 and didn't return until 1964 in Stephen Sondheim's musical *Anyone Can Whistle*. In 1966 she starred in the stage version of *Wait Until Dark*, in 1985 in the concert version of Sondheim's *Follies*, and in 1989 she performed in A.R. Gurney's *Love Letters*.

Divorced in 1969 after eleven years from TV producer-director William Colleran (two children, Kate and Matthew), Remick married English producer William ("Kip") Gowans in 1970. In addition to the Brentwood home, they have a summer place at Cape Cod where they go clamming and sail their 16-foot boat. "... I think she's one of the most important actresses working in America today—no, working *anywhere*," says Gowans. "It would be nice to make films for grown-ups again," sighs Remick, "and when they decide to start filming them, I'll start acting in them."

Burt Reynolds

Given his musclebound power to shatter box-office records, it seems likely that this screen idol who hunked his way to stardom overnight in 1972 (in the screen adaptation of James Dickey's *Deliverance* and a nude, living color centerfold in *Cosmopolitan* magazine) will triumph as the hairy chest most likely to prevail in dollar-conscious Hollywood. Reynolds' take from *Smokey and the Bandit Part I* was 20 per cent of a gross in excess of 100 million dollars. Add to that similar percentages for other recent flicks like *Smokey and the Bandit Part II, Cannonball I & II, Paternity, Sharky's Machine, Best Friends, Stick, The Bourne Identity, Rent-A-Cop, Switching Channels* and you may have to recharge your calculator.

Early in his career, Reynolds played bit parts on Broadway and in TV series such as "Gunsmoke," "Mod Squad," and "Hawk," then starred in the title role in ABC's "Dan August." His early movies included *100 Rifles, Skullduggery, Fuzz, Shamus, The Man Who Loved Cat Dancing* and Woody Allen's *Everything You Always Wanted To Know About Sex*, in which he played the part of a sperm. With his own special combination of modesty and egocentricity, Johnny Carson wisecracked at a Friar's Club roast of Reynolds: "We are gathered here ... for one purpose. To watch Burt Reynolds give the finest performance of his career—being humble. Generous. Warm. Loving. Charitable ... and to become the world's number 1 box office star without possessing any of those qualities is quite an achievement...." He credits his stardom to television talk shows. ("They're the best thing that ever happened to me; they changed everything overnight.") The publicity he got by dating Dinah Shore, whom he met while appearing on her daytime show, also helped.

Burt was born 11 February 1936 in Waycross, Georgia and grew up in Palm Beach, Fla., where his father was the Chief-of-Police. He attended Florida State for a brief spell before signing up to play football with the Baltimore Colts, but an automobile accident took him off the tackle line and into acting classes at Palm Beach Junior College. ("I read two words and they gave me a lead.") During an apprenticeship at the Hyde Park Theatre in New York, he met Joanne Woodward, who was instrumental in his early career. She introduced him to her agent who got Reynolds his first stage and TV work. Deciding that he'd never make it as a "talented New York actor," he went to Hollywood. It was slow at first trying to get himself noticed. During one interview, in which he was asked to deliver a dramatic monologue, the phone rang. Reynolds, furious with the interruption, reached over and grabbed the phone, pulling it so hard the wire ripped right out of the wall. "You have to do something to get their attention," he told a friend at the time. Sure enough the next day he got a call from one of the agents. "That was the most exciting thing I've seen all week," she told Burt.

When he's not making a film, he's supervising the Burt Reynolds Dinner Theatre which he built in Florida in 1979. Divorced from actress Judy Carne, Reynolds tried marriage again in 1988 by taking actress Loni Anderson as his wife. The couple adopted a son, Quinton Anderson, in August of that year. Reynolds' recent pictures include *Breaking In* (1989) and *All Dogs Go To Heaven* (1989, voice-over).

Debbie Reynolds

Once dubbed by Hollywood cynics "the iron butterfly," she floated high for well over a decade on her ball-of-fluff image of apple pie America. Then, proving herself unsubmergible in more ways than one, she rose from the ignominy of being the bride Eddie Fisher traded in for Elizabeth Taylor, to score personal triumphs in *The Unsinkable Molly Brown* (1964), a revival of *Irene* (1973) and *Woman of the Year* (1983) (replacing Lauren Bacall and Raquel Welch, and earning $30,000 a week.)

She was born Mary Francis Reynolds in El Paso, Texas, an April Fool's Day baby of 1932. Her longtime Girl Scout image comes naturally; she earned a total of 48 merit badges during her years in the green uniform. Reynolds' show business career began after the family moved to California, where she won the title of Miss Burbank of 1948 doing an imitation of Betty Hutton. Spotted by a Warner talent scout, she was signed for $65 a week, and her first role was in *The Daughter of Rosie O'Grady*. She then switched to MGM and played Helen Kane, the boop-boop-a-doop girl, in *Three Little Words* (1950). Going the way of the ingenue, she soared ever upward in such films as *Singin' in the Rain* (1952), *Tammy and the Bachelor* (1957) and *The Singing Nun* (1966).

She married Eddie Fisher in 1955 (2 children, Todd and Carrie; Todd is a born-again Christian minister and Carrie an actress in her own right). In 1960 she married shoe tycoon Harry Karl, who lost $15 million of her money as well as his own fortune when his shoe business failed. "I resented it very much," she says recalling that she signed anything he asked her to. When he went bankrupt, she was responsible for another $2 million of his debts. "The banks took everything—the Beverly Hills house, the beach house, all my jewelry and art," she says. Finally out of debt in the early 80s she says, "I'm starting to build my life again. If you have faith—and a sense of humor—you can survive anything." Married in 1984 to Richard Hamlett of Miami Beach, Debbie came out in 1985 with a successful home video of aerobic exercises called "Do It Debbie's Way," followed by another home exercise program "Couples (Do It Debbie's Way)" in 1988. Her tell-all autobiography *Debbie: My Life* was released in October 1988. Always of interest to the public, Debbie supplied her readers with Hollywood scandals and stories, while providing an insightful look on how that little girl from El Paso became a movie star.

Lionel Richie

"All blacks don't sing the blues.... There are many different sides of me and I've really enjoyed exploring them all." As lead singer of The Commodores, and as a solo artist, his rich, melancholy love songs dominated the charts, making him the "pop-soul ballad king" of his era. Said *Rolling Stone* magazine; "The appeal of these songs lies in their utter lack of sophistication.... Ballads like this require a singer's absolute conviction and Richie delivers them with an understated fervor that suggests a pop-soul equivalent to the late Nat King Cole."

If the music of Lionel Richie (born 1950) lacks even a trace of ethnic rage, it may be due to his sheltered and cultured upbringing on the campus of Alabama's historic Tuskeegee Institute, where his grandfather worked. He learned to play piano by ear, and discovering he was "too small to play football, too short to play basketball and too slow to run track," he fell in with a group of musicians with high ambitions. "I would love to say I went to Julliard, then went to Berkeley to get my master's degree and that someone discovered me writing music. But that's not the way it happened. Two days after I began attending classes at Tuskeegee, I ran into a guy named Thomas McClary who wanted me to join a group. Soon, there were six little guys sitting in my grandmother's house talking about taking over the world. We wanted to be bigger than the Beatles."

The group moved to New York, played gigs on ocean liners, and eventually became the opening act for the Jackson Five. The Commodores produced 11 albums, beginning in 1974 with "Machine Gun," and including the 1978 "Natural High," and the 1979 "Midnight Magic." Their chart-toppers included the singles, "Easy," "Still," and "Three Times a Lady."

Going solo in 1981, he had the number one song with the title track for Brooke Shields' movie, *Endless Love*, sung with Diana Ross. His award-winning resume includes: The ballad "Truly" (1982, Grammy for Best Pop Male Performance); the song "We Are The World" (won Grammy for Best Song and Record of the Year in 1986); the single "Hello" (won two American Music Awards in 1985) and the song "Say You, Say Me" from the film *White Nights* (won both the Oscar and Golden Globe for Best Song in 1986). In addition, he has written and produced several hits for Kenny Rogers. Although Richie has been successful on the music scene, his home front was floundering when he and his wife, Brenda separated in 1988.

Don Rickles

What can you say about a man who comes onstage and screams, "Hello dummy"? It's funny, but don't tell Sigmund. "I'm the guy who tells off the boss at the office party and still has a job on Monday," brags this king of the show-biz putdown. He says he has a "sixth sense" that keeps him from digging too deep with his verbal jabs at the paying customers. "My style is to rib people I like. If there is anger in it, it isn't funny."

Born 8 May 1926, the only child of a Queens, N.Y., insurance salesman ("He was always on the rib. . . . I learned a lot from him."), Rickles broke into show business while still in high school as an entertainment director at a resort in the Catskills. ("I played bingo with the guests . . . if it rained, I was supposed to go out and make it stop.") After Navy service in World War II ("I grew up in the Navy . . . it was better than summer camp") he put together a nightclub act and shot straight to oblivion ("I was cancelled out of a great many places, including the worst strip joint in Boston") before his gently abrasive jibes earned him a reputation as a "comic's comic." A success on the Miami-Vegas-Manhattan nightclub circuit in the late 1950s, Rickles nonetheless "frightened" TV executives, until Johnny Carson gave him his big break on the night of 7 October 1965. Rickles' free-wheeling performance was the next day's "Topic A" of the industry, and prompted nationwide reaction. His next break was the chance to do his bit weekly on the "Dean Martin Show," followed by numerous TV shows and nightclub appearances including "The Don Rickles Show" in 1971 and as a Navy petty officer in "C.P.O. Sharkey" (1976). In 1984 he was co-host of "Foul-Ups, Bleeps & Blunders"—the show that sugarcoats the slip-ups of the stars for the benefit of those who love to watch their favorites flop. Rickles is a major headliner at the Las Vegas Sahara and Riviera Hotels, Resorts International in Atlantic City and Harrah's Clubs in Reno and Lake Tahoe.

Rickles' wife Barbara (one daughter, one son), whom he married in 1965 (she was at one time his agent's secretary), and his mother have asked him why he insults people. "It buys you jewels," he told his wife. Insults "got you your beautiful apartment," he told his mother. "You know what they said then?" he asked rhetorically. "'You're right. Insult people.'"

Diana Rigg

She has played an amazing variety of dramatic roles over the years, ranging from James Bond's wife to King Lear's daughter, from a TV crimefighter to Lady Macbeth, from slinky sex objects to nuns. But this leggy Yorkshire beauty (she admits to five feet eight and a half) is best known to Americans as Emma Peel, the karate-chopping widow and cult heroine of TV's stylish 1965-67 spy spoof "The Avengers," which returned in the 1980s as reruns on cable television. She also starred in the 1973 shortlived TV series, "Diana," in which she played a footloose British fashion designer adrift in the garment district. Off the stage or the movie screen, some critics have called her "brutally frank." ("I should say that for the most part, 'brutally frank' is applied to me, but why they say 'brutally' I don't know. I'd say 'frank'" she concedes.) One of Rigg's highly publicized "frank" comments came in 1973 on the "Tonight" Show when she said: "American men are boring companions and bad lovers."

The daughter of a British government official, Rigg was born in Yorkshire, England, on 20 July 1938, and grew up in India. She returned home from India to train at the Royal Academy of Dramatic Art. "I used to look at myself in the mirror when I was thirteen or fourteen and know what I saw wasn't me. It was curious seeing the chrysalis, finding it insufficient and yet knowing that something inside there was going to pop out, was going to be better," she says. The next step in Rigg's career was a short stint as a model, then an apprenticeship with The Chesterfield Repertory Company in the British Midlands, where she earned $17 a week doing a variety of jobs from hunting props to acting. Finally she auditioned for The Royal Shakespeare Company and was admitted in 1959. In 1972, she joined the National Theatre where Laurence Olivier was director. The actress over the years has appeared on Broadway as a sometimes-nude Heloise in *Abelard and Heloise*, and in Molière's *The Misanthrope*, in which she played Celimente, the accommodating but sharp-tongued love of Alceste, a rigidly unaccommodating man. Her latest movies include *Evil Under the Sun* (1982), *The Great Muppet Caper* (1981), *Madame Colette* (1982), *Snow White* (1986) and *A Hazard of Hearts* (1987). Married in 1973 to the Israeli artist Manachem Gueffen (one daughter, Rachel, born in 1977) she has been, since 1982, the wife of Archibald (Archie) Stirling, a former Scots Guards officer.

Molly Ringwald

This multi-talented star of television, stage, and screen, is perhaps the most publicized member of the teenage actors who became popular in the mid-1980's.

Molly Ringwald was born in Roseville, California on 18 February 1968, and grew up in a musical environment. Her father, who was blind since childhood, is a pianist who leads the Great Pacific Jazz Band. Molly quickly learned the songs that the band performed and would sing along while her father practiced. "I was singing before I can remember, to the cats, to the swings,"recalls Molly. By the time she was four, she was appearing regularly with the Great Pacific Jazz Band, singing such old-time favorites as "Oh Daddy," and "I Wanna Be Loved by You." Those songs, along with several others comprised *Molly Sings*, an album she recorded with the band in 1974. When she was five, she was enrolled in singing, dancing, and acting classes, which led to her performance with the local community theatre in the amateur production of *The Glass Harp*. She made her professional television debut in 1977, as a guest on the "New Mickey Mouse Club," and her professional stage debut in 1978 in the West Coast production of the hit musical *Annie*. A few months later, she was cast in the TV sitcom series "The Facts of Life," (1979) but after just one season, her character was written out of the script. "I was devastated. But my mom kept saying it was for the best, and she was right. I didn't work for a year, which gave me a chance to grow up a lot." One year later, she made her theatrical film debut in Shakespeare's *The Tempest*, followed by *Spacehunter: Adventures in the Forbidden Zone* (1983). It wasn't until her appearance in the very successful *Sixteen Candles* (1984) that her career really began to take off. Soon following, she landed roles in the several other hit movies including *The Breakfast Club* (1985), *Pretty in Pink* (1986), *The Pick-Up Artist* (1988), *For Keeps* (1988) and *Fresh Horses* (1989). Molly has also appeared in the made-for-television movies "Surviving," "Packin' It In," and "P.K. and the Kid."

In her spare time, Molly enjoys shopping in neighborhood malls, listening to rock music, and singing with her father's band. She is single and lives with her parents in the San Fernando Valley in California.

John Ritter

"If I had grown up with just dad, I'd have become a good ol' boy and probably been a trucker. And if I'd been raised by mother, I'd be an interior designer. Between the two, I have a nice balance." John Ritter is the offspring of the white hat star of 78 Westerns and the warbler of various Country-style hits, the late "You Are My Sunshine" Tex Ritter, and Dorothy Fay, now official greeter at Nashville's Grand Ole Opry. Luck on a stick pointed the way for this former Hollywood High Student Council President and lapsed 1960s idealist to find his star as a TV actor. On "Three's Company" he played Jack Tripper, a beguiling Santa Monican who pretends to be homosexual in order to beat the heat from vexed parents and landlords when, due to limited funds, he bunked in with two lady roommates. The sexy situation never got beyond titillation, but it afforded lots of chances for the girls to "flit around in their nighties" while poor Jack struggled to keep his heterosexual plumes from shooting out and ruining the gay facade and losing the lease. The show's theme was altered in 1984. Jack came out from behind the guise and the show was renamed "Three's A Crowd." Not as successful as the original premise, the sitcom was cancelled after one season. Making a quick comeback, Ritter became the star of a new series, "Hooperman". This show propelled his receiving the People's Choice Award for Best Male Performance in a New TV Program in 1988.

Born 17 September 1948 in Burbank, Calif., Ritter planned on being a psychology major at the University of Southern California but switched to acting after a successful stint at the Edinburgh Festival in Scotland. At age 20 he discovered acting was better than shrinking. Following his college graduation, Ritter did many summer stock productions across the country and made his television debut in a 1971 episode of "Dan August." He went on to appear in numerous TV shows including the semi-regular part of Reverend Matthew Frowick on "The Waltons." "Three's Company" debuted in 1977. His films include 1980's *Hero at Large*, and *Unnatural Causes* (1986). Behind-the-scenes he was the co-executive producer of the ABC-TV comedy "Have Faith" (1989).

Ritter married actress Nancy Morgan in 1977. They live in California with their three children.

Chita Rivera

"Packing thirty years of Broadway savvy into the frame of a vivacious teenager, the fifty-one-year-old entertainer could by now sell a song to the deaf," said Richard Corliss in *Time* about Chita Rivera's 1984 Tony Award-winning performance as Anna in *The Rink* (she commanded the audience like "a lion tamer with a whip snap in her walk"). She had previously racked up a string of Tony nominations for memorable roles on Broadway: Anita in *West Side Story* (1957), Rose in *Bye Bye Birdie* (1960), Anyanka in *Bajour* (1964) and Velma in *Chicago* (1975). In addition to all her work on stage and on television, the former "gypsy" played Nickie in the 1969 movie version of *Sweet Charity* (hailed by Judith Crist as one of the "freshest and most gifted of song-and-dance newcomers to the screen"), and "exploded like a rocket" with what is widely regarded as one of the best cabaret acts in show business. In 1980 she received the National Academy of Concert and Cabaret Arts award for the best variety performance.

She was born Dolores Conchita Figuero del Rivero in Washington, D.C., on 23 January 1933. Her father, who played clarinet and saxophone with the U.S. Navy Band, "sat in" with Harry James's band, and was a member of the pit orchestra for the 1924-25 Broadway musical *Lady Be Good*. When she was 7, Rivera's father died, and her mother went to work as a government clerk. She was "brought up very strictly, in the old fashioned Latin way." She describes herself as a hyperenergetic tomboy who "could run faster than a whippet and beat all the boys." Her mother enrolled her in singing, piano and ballet classes; the dance became her passion. She won a scholarship to George Balanchine's School of American Ballet in N.Y.C. while attending Taft High School in the Bronx (graduated in 1951). Answering an open call for dancers for the touring company of *Call Me Madam*, she was hired. After the tour she replaced Onna White on Broadway in *Guys and Dolls*, stepped into the chorus of *Can Can*, and in 1954 became a full-fledged triple-threat performer in Ben Bagley's off-Broadway *Shoestring Revue*. After a brief run in *Seventh Heaven* (1955) and the role of Rita Romano in *Mr. Wonderful*, with the exception of a couple of "short runs" along the way, the rest is "Tony-time" history. Her marriage (to Anthony Mordente from *West Side Story* days) ended in divorce. Their daughter, Lisa Mordente, is now herself an actress in the musical theatre and on television. Rivera lives in Westchester County, plays tennis, bowls, rides horseback, and is rumored to be an expert at cooking and needlepoint. Just before winning the Tony in 1984, Rivera said: "My mother passed away before *The Rink* opened. We were devoted. We were as one. I'm only an extension of my mother. I look like her. Think like her. Every step I do on that stage is for her. I'm dancing for her. If I win this Tony, I'm winning for her. For me this is all a master plan." She returned to Broadway in 1985 in *Jerry's Girls*, a revue featuring the words and music of Jerry Herman and she joined the Rockettes in a national tour of *Can-Can* in 1988 and 1989.

Geraldo Rivera

"I'm not smarter, or better looking than Phil, Oprah, Johnny or David, but am different.... These mid-life eyes have witnessed the full range of the human experience: from exhilaration and triumph to the pits of misery and despair.... This program will have action, emotion, style, old-fashioned values and contemporary ideas. I want it to be an alternative for people afflicted by game show saturation and the talk show blahs." Geraldo speaks about "Geraldo"—the nationally syndicated daily one-hour talk show (topics include: "Prostitution," "Cross-dressing," "Sexually Transmitted Diseases," "Teen Sex," "Chappaquiddick Incident") which has shot up in the ratings to become a favorite choice of viewers. Since the young journalist came to television in 1970, more than 100 awards have been brought to him including a Peabody, national and local Emmys, plus Associated Press kudos as a "special kind of individualist in a medium which too often breeds the plastic newsman." Rivera came to daytime with years of investigative reporting under his belt. Since turning to syndicated television, he has hosted and produced "Sons of Scarface: The New Mafia," a live two-hour investigation into organized crime; "American Vice: The Doping of a Nation" about narcotics trafficking; "Innocence Lost: The Erosion of American Childhood," and the highest rated syndicated show ever: "The Mystery of Al Capone's Vaults," during which the alleged vaults of the Chicago vice lord were blasted open. The program received a 34.2 national rating.

Born in Manhattan on 4 July 1943, Rivera was raised in the Williamsburg section of Brooklyn. Coming from a Puerto Rican family, he maintains strong ties with the Puerto Rican community in New York, and was an empathetic spokesman for the Young Lords, a Spanish-speaking youth organization devoted to "revolutionary action" (some of whose members have later done quite well themselves as TV reporters). After leaving Brooklyn, he sailed as a merchant seaman and bummed around (for a while as semi-pro soccer player) before attending the University of Arizona and Brooklyn Law School. Then, just when he was learning the hard way that "it was impossible for me to change the destinies of anyone as a poverty lawyer," TV reporter Gloria Rojas told him that New York station WABC was looking for a bilingual reporter. With his shocking reports on the Willowbrook State School for the Mentally Retarded, he established a reputation as one of TV's most passionate newsmen. Having obtained a key to one of the institution's buildings, he let himself and a camera crew in one morning to film the patients without authorization. "This is what it looked like," Rivera told the TV audience. "This is what it sounded like. But how can I tell you about the way it smelled?" As a result of the exposé, Gov. Rockefeller reinstated $20 million that had been cut from Willowbrook's budget, and elsewhere some 50 other news reports were done on prison-like mental hospitals. But, he also came under industry-wide fire for what was perceived as trigger-happy, indicting reports against the suspected "Son of Sam" killer. (By way of contrast, his 1984 report on convicted Atlanta murderer Wayne Williams, after whose capture the mass child killings ceased in that southern city, left doubts in some viewers' minds as to Williams' guilt.) While covering some of his more than 2000 other stories (award winners like his reports on the new heroin epidemic, or those leading to investigations like that on organized crime's food stamp fraud), he's also reported for "Good Morning, America," and hosted segments of "Good Night, America" from 1974-78. As the senior producer-correspondent of the "20/20" prime time newsmagazine, he conceded "I make no pretense of objectivity. But I'm not in the business of making people cry. I'm in the business of change." He scored record-breaking ratings with his segment "The Elvis Cover-up," a special report on the circumstances surrounding Elvis Presley's death on "20/20."

Away from the camera, he's found time to write four books: *Puerto Rico: Island of Contrast; Miguel Robles: So Far; A Special Kind of Courage* and *Willowbrook*. In 1987 he married his fourth wife, C.C. Dyer.

Joan Rivers

"Oh grow-up!" The lady rasps, her finger wagging at the audience. And they just love having Joan Rivers explain "it" all to them. Says she: "Nancy Reagan . . . a great lady. Sure. We're very close. She never swears. She told me to go reproduce myself . . . oh sure. . . . Elizabeth Taylor? Ugh, can we talk here, I feel very close to you. I think she's a pig. Oh please. She pierced her ears and gravy came out . . . oh grow-up, mosquitos see her and scream 'buffet!' She has more chins than a Chinese phonebook. Please, can we talk? Look, I'm a very sensitive person. I only go after the ones who are big enough to take it. Bo Derek, so dumb she studies for a Pap test. Oh sure. Sophia Loren, an old tramp from World War II. I threw a Hershey bar into her dressing room and she laid down. Willie Nelson, he's so dirty he wears a Roach Motel around his neck. I am telling the truth in a very angry age. I succeed by saying what everyone else is thinking. Queen Elizabeth. A dog. Oh please. I mean, if you're Queen of England, Scotland and Ireland, the least you can do is shave your legs. Don't tell me beauty doesn't count, I don't wanna hear it," says the Brooklyn-born (8 June 1933), Barnard educated doctor's daughter whose real name is Joan Molinsky. "Oh sure, beauty is power. If you don't want the diamond, send it to me. My body is sagging so fast my gynecologist wears a hardhat. Oh grow-up. On my wedding night Edgar (Edgar Rosenberg, her late husband—one daughter, Melissa. A first and much earlier marriage to department store tycoon James Sanger lasted less than a year. "If God wanted me to cook and clean, my hands would be aluminum.") said: 'Let me undo your buttons.' I was naked at the time. Oh please. . . ."

For the woman Liz Smith adulated as the "most brilliant comic mind of all, a woman for our own skeptical times, a kind of gadfly and social goad, a phenomenon of today's entertainment industry rapidly becoming a multi-millionaire superstar thanks to the things only she dares to say," recognition was a long time coming. She defied her parents and "starved" as a Greenwich Village comic and writer and blew her big chance when she appeared on "The Jack Paar Show" because he hated her act. Her agent advised her to quit just the week before, when, in 1965 (after eight previous attempts to do so) she made it onto "The Johnny Carson Show" and was an instant hit. "He was Moses. He parted the seas and took me home. Carson was the one who stood up and said 'she's funny.'" Since then she's hosted the "Tonight Show" more than any other personality and, in 1983, became Carson's sole replacement—doing so one week each month. She tried her hand at hosting her own "The Late Show" in 1986-87, but the ratings didn't fly. Instead, she spread her acting wings and joined the cast of the Neil Simon play *Broadway Bound* and became a regular center square on the "New Hollywood Squares." Her other credits include the 1974 best-seller *Having A Baby Can Be A Scream*, the 1984 best-seller (about Rivers's mythical high school nemesis) *The Life and Hard Times of Heidi Abramowitz*, 1986's *Enter Talking*; a Broadway comedy (flop), *Fun City*, co-authored with Edgar; the LP, *What Becomes a Semi-Legend Most?* and the film comedy *Rabbit Test*, which she directed and co-scripted. She also appeared in the 1987 film *Spaceballs*. Her new syndicated talk show "The Joan Rivers Show" debuted in the fall of 1989.

Jason Robards

Frequently described as "cadaverous-looking," he himself thinks he looks "stepped on." Whatever the adjective, his appearance seems perfectly matched to the tragic, disturbed characters he has so often portrayed in plays such as Eugene O'Neil's *The Iceman Cometh* and *Long Day's Journey Into Night*, Lillian Hellman's *Toys in the Attic*, and Arthur Miller's *After the Fall*. "I've always played disintegrated characters," he once said. "I don't know much about acting, but I can play those kinds of characters."

The son of Jason Robards, a well-known Broadway and Hollywood actor of the 1920s, Jason, Jr., (he no longer uses the Jr., in his billing) was born on 26 July 1922 in Chicago, grew up in Hollywood, and served seven years in the Navy before coming to New York to try for an acting career. A late bloomer, it wasn't until 1956 that he garnered major critical hosannas for his playing of the salesman, Hickey, in O'Neill's *Iceman*. ("I didn't know at the time I got Hickey what it would lead to. I just thought it was an off-Broadway show which I hoped would have a good run, and my family and I would all eat.") Actually, the O'Neill play propelled him into being one of the steadiest workers on Broadway, (and into the Theater Hall of Fame) not to mention movies and TV. Among the more memorable Robards films; *Tender is the Night* (1962); *A Thousand Clowns* (1966 film version of his 1962 B'way comedy hit); *Isadora* (1969); *All the President's Men* (1976 Oscar-winner for Best Supporting Actor); and *Melvin and Howard* (1979). "A Day in the Life of Ivan Denisovitch" and Eugene O'Neils "Hughie" were both blockbusters on TV, as was 1983's much-publized "The Day After." He won an Emmy in 1988 as Lead Actor in a miniseries for his role in NBC's "Inherit The Wind." In 1983, Robards returned to Broadway in another comedy, a revival of *You Can't Take It With You*, in 1985 he reprised the role of Hickey in *The Iceman Cometh*, 29 years after his original triumph, and in 1989 he appeared in A.R. Gurney's *Love Letters*. Recent films include *Square Dance* (1986), *Bright Lights, Big City* (1987), *The Good Mother* (1988) and *Quick Change* (1989).

Married first to the former Eleanor Pitman (Jason III, Sarah, Louise, David), he married for the second time, Rachel Taylor; for the third, actress Lauren Bacall (one son, Sam); for the fourth, producer Lois O'Connor. He and the present Mrs. Robards have one daughter, Shannon, born in 1971 via natural childbirth, with the father's active on-the-scene participation, and one son, Jake.

Harold Robbins

"What is my philosophy of life? I'm not dead yet—that's my philosophy.... I have enough books in my head to go on writing until the end of my life."

Not even one of Robbins's rags-to-riches heroes has made so great a leap from abject poverty to the zenith of success as this author has. He was born Francis Kane on 21 May 1916 in New York and spent his early days in a Catholic orphanage in Hell's Kitchen. He left the care of his foster family at age 15, borrowing their name Rudin, which later changed to Robbins. (He still supports his foster family a half century later). At 15 he began a long succession of jobs which included soda jerk, cashier, ice cream peddler, and bookies runner. Then he invested in commodities futures, made a fortune—and lost over a million dollars before he was 21. Robbins went back to odd jobs, this time on the West Coast in 1940. He began as a shipping clerk at Universal Studios, rose to become a budget and planning executive and in his spare time began to write. His first novel, *Never Love a Stranger*, became an immediate success, a pattern followed by nearly every Robbins book. Among the biggies: *The Dream Merchants*, *A Stone for Danny Fisher*, *The Carpetbaggers* and *The Betsy*. Robbins books are sold in 63 countries and each has been in continuous printing from the day of original publishing. Nine of the novels have been made into movies and Robbins's publishers estimate that more than 40,000 people worldwide buy a Robbins product every single day. Robbins and his wife Grace divide their time between homes in Beverly Hills, Acapulco and Cannes on the Cote d'Azur. They have one daughter named Adreanna. From his first marriage, Robbins had another daughter named Caryn.

Jerome Robbins

Renowned master choreographer and stage director Jerome Robbins, who made the giant leap from ballet to Broadway, became the big 1989 Tony Award winner for the magical nostalgic potpourri of his Broadway musicals *Jerome Robbins' Broadway* which opened on 26 February 1988. The musical contains excerpts from the shows he directed and/or choreographed on Broadway "from 1944 to 1964, from *On The Town* to *Fiddler On the Roof*—eleven of which are represented in this production." Robbins, a former dancer himself, is a hard taskmaster, a doer, and a driver, and makes his dancers (who revere his talent) toe the mark (often creating love/hate work relationships). "I am a perfectionist," says Mr. Robbins in a recent *New York Times* interview. "I wear that badge proudly. I think that's what art is about—trying to make it as good as you possibly can.... People gripe. They gripe, I can't help what they say. I don't think it's anyone's business how I work. I'm not in the profession to show people how I work. My idea is to do a show and make it as good as I can and as good as I think it should be."

Born 11 October 1918 in New York City to Russian immigrant parents, Harry and Lena Rabinowitz, Jerome Robbins grew up in Weehawken, New Jersey, where he graduated from Woodrow Wilson High School. Dropping out of NYU after a year he followed his sister Sonya into dance classes and was advised by his teacher (Gluck Sandor) to "study ballet, it's going to come back." "I used to come to New York and audition for shows," recalled Mr. Robbins in the recent *Times* interview, "and not get them and go back to Jersey and look back at New York from the Palisades and say, 'Well, I'll be back tomorrow and study some more, and maybe I'll get in a show sometime." Which he did, as we know—*Great Lady*, *Stars In Your Eyes*, *Straw Hat Revue*, with summers at Tamiment, an adult camp in Pennsylvania, where, as a dancer, he also choreographed a few ballets. In 1940 with Ballet Theatre (now American Ballet Theater) he danced as Petrouchka in Lichine's *Helen of Troy* and de Mille's *Three Virgins and a Devil*. In 1944 he created *Fancy Free* (the first ballet he choreographed for Ballet Theatre) which mushroomed into his first Broadway hit show, *On The Town*. Others followed: *Billion Dollar Baby*, *High Button Shoes* (Tony Award), *Call Me Madam*, *The King and I*, *Peter Pan* (Emmy Award), *The Pajama Game*, *Bells Are Ringing*, *West Side Story*, (Tony Award) and *Fiddler On The Roof* (2 Tonys—choreography/direction). Robbins also won 2 Oscars for the film of *West Side Story* (choreography/direction.) He left Broadway after *Fiddler* to concentrate on his activities with the City Ballet where he was Associate Artistic Director with George Balanchine (today he is Ballet Master in Chief with Peter Martins). He has created more than 50 ballets, including *Afternoon of a Faun* (1953), *The Concert* (1956), *Dances At a Gathering* (1969), *The Four Seasons* (1979), *Glass Pieces* (1983), *Ives, Songs* (1988). His many awards are an endless list, including the National Medal of Art presented by President Reagan.

Will Jerome Robbins ever do a "brand-new" Broadway musical again? "It depends," he said in a recent interview, "If material came along that interested me enough I would do it.... It's got to be something in which the creative part of me will be satisfied."

Cliff Robertson

Predictions were he'd "never work again" after he blew the whistle on what columnists called "Hollywood-gate," the pressure to hush up an embezzlement scandal involving David Begelman, then powerful president of Columbia Pictures. But Robertson, shocked to discover that Begelman had forged his signature on a $10,000 studio check, notified both the police and the FBI, the papers got wind of the tale (later told at length in the 1982 David McClintick bestseller, *Indecent Exposure*) and Robertson found himself *persona non grata* in the movie capital. ("I got phone calls from powerful people who said, 'You've been very fortunate in this business—I'm sure you wouldn't want all this to come to an end.'") It took him nearly four years to get a job, but in 1984 he clicked with playing a neurosurgeon on TV's "Falcon Crest," and serving as commercial spokesman for AT&T. He also began making movies, too.

Born Clifford Parker Robertson in LaJolla, Calif., on 9 September 1925, he had an even more dramatic "comeback" before he ever inaugurated his acting career. At the time of Pearl Harbor he was a 16-year-old seaman aboard a merchant ship in the Pacific; when the ship was bombed, word got back to LaJolla that he was a casualty, and his house carried the town's first Gold Star—until the young tar, very much alive, returned home. After studying at Antioch College in Ohio, Robertson's first professional acting job was with a Catskills troupe for five dollars a week plus room and board. Then came Broadway (*The Wisteria Trees*, Tennessee Williams's *Orpheus Descending*) and a long apprenticeship as one of Hollywood's faceless craftsmen, "confused in name with Dale Robertson and in appearance with a dozen other actors." After many movies (e.g. *Picnic*, *Autumn Leaves*, *The Best Man*) and more than 100 dramatic shows on the tube, he won TV's Emmy for his performance in a drama called "The Game" (1956-66 season) and three years later collected an Oscar for his film portrayal of *Charly*. His latest endeavors include the film *Malone* (1987) and the Robert Halmi 40-hour miniseries "Ford: The Man and His Machine" (1987). In 1989 he received the Campione d'Italia Merit of Achievement Award in Italy.

Married first to Cynthia Stone (who was earlier married to Jack Lemmon), mother of his daughter Stephanie, he wed actress/heiress Dina Merrill in 1966 and now has a second daughter, Heather. The couple separated in 1985; their divorce was final in 1989. A flying buff since his teens, he chose a contemporary model when he flew a mercy mission to Biafra, but his particular passion is his collection of vintage biplanes. "One man, one plane," he rhapsodizes. "There was *glamour* to those birds."

James D. Robertson, III

"The next 25 years will be a much tougher environment for corporate management. You've almost got to reinvest the entrepreneurial spirit," he told Jack Egan in *New York* magazine in 1982. His courtly southern manner (which comes naturally to this scion of an old and wealthy Atlanta family) belies the force with which the chairman and chief executive officer of American Express Company has pursued his goal of making the company into the nation's premier provider of personal financial services. And it is *Business Week*'s contention (in April 1984) that "if AmEx can exhibit the same flair in managing its diverse parts that it has in acquiring them, it could well emerge as the world's preeminent financial services company." To that end, since 1980 "the plastic card company" has acquired investment firms (Shearson, Lehman Bros., etc.), insurance companies (Fireman's Fund, IDS), has ventured into cable television, and those diversifications combined with their crown jewel—its credit card and check business—will, if Robinson's vision holds true, enable the company to "sell you everything from stocks and commodities to insurance, mutual funds and traveler's checks, finance your purchases, plan your vacations, and let you take care of all your business through a computer system hooked by cable to your TV—and all of it will be paid for with your American Express card," according to *Business Week*.

Born 19 November 1935 in Atlanta (where both his father and grandfather had been chairman of the First National Bank of Atlanta), Robinson graduated from Georgia Tech in 1957 and after two years as an officer in the U.S. Naval Supply Corps, entered Harvard Business School, from which he received an M.B.A. in 1961. From 1961 to 1970 he held a variety of executive positions in investment banking and in 1970 joined American Express as Executive Vice President (aware that its longtime chairman Howard Clark was planning to take an early retirement). He became president in 1975 and chairman and CEO two years later. If further proof were needed that work "is my avocation," Robertson provided it after realizing every duffer's dream by sinking a 20-yard chip shot over a trap (for a birdie) at the final hole of the 1983 Bing Crosby Pro-Am golf tournament in front of a nationwide television audience, when he allowed (albeit with a wink), "You know, I've got to say that buying Shearson was better."

Robinson serves on the boards of such companies as Bristol-Myers, Coca-Cola (which, along with *Gone With the Wind*, put Atlanta on the map) and Union Pacific. He's chairman of Memorial Hospital for Cancer and Allied Diseases, and is a member of The Business Roundtable, and on the board of The Brookings Institution, the Council on Foreign Relations, The Economic Club of New York and The Rockefeller University Council. Of the future, he tried in 1981 to calm the misgivings of those who foresaw a totally computerized society by making his own prediction: "Total automation and dehumanization of financial services will not occur in the Eighties. Perhaps it never will. However, the coming decade will bring to all of us the opportunity to seize control of our electronic destiny. Let us protect the individual's right to privacy . . . and embrace the multiple choice society. Let us do so promptly, and wisely." The father of a daughter by a previous marriage, he married Linda Gosden, a senior vice president of Warner Communications, 27 July 1984.

David Rockefeller

One afternoon more than a half century ago, three boys were playing in the vast confines of a billionaire's estate. The estate's owner was the boys' grandpa, John Davison Rockefeller. Although they were to become—with the possible exception of the Kennedys—the most watched siblings in American history, that day there was no adult supervision of the trio (two others were absent). David was leisurely shooting arrows with his bow when he suddenly felt himself being drenched. When asked why they had turned a hose on their youngest brother, Nelson and Winthrop replied, "Because he is fat and lazy and we want to keep him moving." Whether or not it was his brothers' action that got David Rockefeller moving, there's no question but that he proceeded to move—and in a big way.

Today, David Rockefeller's wealth may well exceed that of his fabled grandfather. The last-born of John D. Rockefeller, Jr., in New York City (12 June 1915), David may well also be the brainiest. He earned the family's only Ph. D. (in economics—what else?—from the University of Chicago, just one of the many institutions founded with grandpa's oil money), having taken his undergraduate degree from Harvard. Long before his ascendancy to "not only [Chase's] chairman but the untitled chairman of the American establishment" (according to financial scribe Adam Smith), David paid his dues as a humble secretary in the administration of Mayor Fiorello LaGuardia. After WWII, he took an entry level management position at Chase (the family's bank; they also have their own law firm, etc., etc.) as assistant manager of the foreign department, he soon headed up Latin American operations, and when the bank merged with the Bank of Manhattan Company, Rockefeller became executive vice president (1955), then president and chairman of the executive committee of the board of directors (1961) until his retirement in 1981 (he retains the title of chairman of the international advisory committee).

The walls of David Rockefeller's office in the 60-story chromium and glass Chase headquarters in lower Manhattan (he was responsible in a major way for the area's revival) reflect his eclectic and informed taste in African art, gems from the Orient, pottery from classical Greece, etc. Less in evidence is his lifelong obesion with beetles, which began when as a boy he visited the forests of Yellowstone Park. (As an adult he sometimes stops speaking, pulls a vial out of his breast pocket and traps a beetle he has spotted on the floor, corks the vial and proceeds as if nothing unusual had happened.) Entomologists, in acknowledgment of his enduring financial support, have named two species of beetle after him—Armaeodera Rockefelleri and Cicindela Rockefelleri.

Philanthropist, former president of the Museum of Modern Art (the family's museum), developer, investor and moneyman—David Rockefeller (only he and the late Nelson of the five were able to collect the $2500 their father had promised to give them if at 21 they had never smoked nor drank) is married to the former Margaret McGrath, and is the father of two sons and four daughters and assorted grandchildren.

John D. Rockefeller IV

As a new generation of Rockefellers elbows its way into the public spotlight, America may yet learn how much a Rockefeller will spend to be elected President. In 1980 John D. Rockefeller IV—great grandson of the oil billionaire—waged the costliest nonpresidential political campaign in U.S. history to become second-term governor of West Virginia. Jay, as he is better known, won in a landslide . . . and it only cost $12 million. "I have no problem at all," he declared afterwards, "in spending that kind of money in an election. The name of the game in campaigns is media, getting your message across." Four years later he breezed into the Senate, putting him that much nearer the White House—which is where he might be living in not too many years.

Jay Rockefeller blew into the Appalachian town of Emmons, West Virginia, in 1964, as a young staffer with a federal youth program. He expected the locals might be a little suspicious, and he was right. He quickly called a community meeting, reports *People* magazine "and entertained the crowd with a slide show of scenes like the Rockefeller clan gathered around the family Christmas tree." Somehow it worked. Despite an appearance and manner that could get him elected as Preppie of the Year—without a necktie he gets uncomfortable, even when touring a coal mine—Jay's admirers report he has a folksy charm that eventually wins over skeptics.

Born 18 June 1937 in New York, Jay Rockefeller attended Exeter then went to college in Japan. He finally graduated from Harvard, after a brief stop-over at Yale. He first broke into Mountain State politics in 1966 representing Kanawha County in the House of Delegates, and served as Secretary of State for four years before first running for Governor (and losing) in 1972. He bade his time as president of West Virginia Wesleyan College and finally made it to the governor's mansion in 1976, winning by the largest margin of victory in the history of the state.

He married the daughter of former Illinois Senator Charles Percy, Sharon, in 1967. "But [being Mrs. Rockefeller] is not a full time job," she points out. She is also former board chairperson at the Corporation for Public Broadcasting (and current board member). The couple's four children were all born and raised in the state and they attend public schools. Citing David Rockefeller as the quintet's exemplar "of progressive finance," historian William Manchester concluded about the family: "Modern society is getting everything it wants from the Rockefeller brothers. They are not only as devoted to it as their father was. They are comfortable with it. . . . [They are] men attuned to the rhythm of their own time . . . and are determined not to miss a beat."

Peter Rodino

"This was greater than one man . . . it was our system being tested, [and] it was my responsibility . . . to proceed, no matter what," says the congressman whose Judiciary Committee voted to impeach President Richard Nixon. Afterwards, he says, he asked his staff to leave his office, phoned his wife, then "just broke down." One place where he seldom lets his guard down is the House committee he's chaired since before those Watergate days, a committee the *Wall Street Journal* calls "a congressional Bermuda Triangle for . . . conservative social legislation." But Peter Rodino answers criticism that he bottles up legislation against school busing, abortions, and tougher crime laws, while blitzing through liberal bills, by saying that keeping his finger in the dike is his job. "You just don't tamper with the Constitution," adds the New Jersey Democrat.

Peter W. Rodino, Jr., whose name adorns a federal office building in his native Newark, N.J., is the Garden State's toughest perennial. The Italian-American septuagenarian (born 7 June 1909) has bloomed consistently in every two-year voting cycle since 1949, and authored the bill that made Columbus Day a national holiday, while working to extend the 1965 Voting Rights Act and to make fair housing mandatory. Rodino occasionally leads Judiciary in devising laws which supersede Supreme Court decisions as he did during President Reagan's first term. He overturned the finding that only departments in colleges and other institutions that get federal dollars could be subject to anti-discrimination laws, a move that pleased his now predominantly black Newark constituency. "Despite the Reagan Administration," said a colleague, "we not only preserved civil rights laws, we strengthened them." But the televised impeachment inquiry of 1973 remains Rodino's main claim to fame. He expected Nixon aides to use any potentially damaging information they could dig up about him. So did other congressmen. At one point, one of them walked up to him and confessed, "God, I just hope you're clean." More than 17 university boards have since found him to be just that, and have given the Rutgers-educated lawyer honorary degrees. Congressman Rodino, who was decorated as an Army captain in North Africa in World War II, has been married since 1941 to the former Marianna Stango, the mother of his two children.

Fred Rogers

"I think I'm just somebody who comes to visit, who knows who he is, is accepting of feelings, and is prepared to talk about them honestly." For millions of children bombarded with education-oriented television programming, his "Mister Roger's Neighborhood," provides a respite from the cerebral. Emotional support is his stock and trade. "You are my friend, you are special," he chimes before introducing some subject close to the hearts of the very young and restless. His languid, earnest delivery amuses adults, and Rogers has become a subject of parody to comedians ranging from Johnny Carson to "Saturday Night Live." But children revere him.

Fred Rogers, born 20 March 1928, is a man of diverse interests. Religious even as a child, he planned to devote his life to the ministry but was sidetracked by a love of music. After graduation from Rollins College, he tried to make it as a songwriter but was rebuffed. A job as a clerk at WNBC-TV in New York evolved into the position of network floor manager. It was then that Rogers, who was ordained a Presbyterian minister in 1963, became aware of the lack of quality television programming for children. Volunteering time at children's centers, he developed a deeper understanding of their needs. "I spent hours and hours observing and listening, and little by little something wonderful began to happen: I remembered how it felt to be a child myself. I remembered the bewilderments, the sadnesses, the joys, the lonely times, the angers." He jumped at the chance to put his ideas to practice on WQED-TV in Pittsburgh, the nation's first educational station. Picked up by PBS in 1970, the program was carried on over 250 stations, with a viewership of some 8 million. Rogers published *Mister Rogers Talks with Parents* in 1983 plus two adults books *Mr. Rogers Talks with Families about Divorce* (1987) and *How Families Grow* (1988). Rogers and his wife, Joanne, a concert pianist, have two children. As testimony to his position in the American consciousness, the Smithsonian Institution in Washington, D.C., added one of his sweaters to its collection in 1984.

Ginger Rogers

When asked in a 1984 interview for the *Christian Science Monitor* her opinion about breakdancing, Rogers replied firmly: "I think dancing is something that's graceful, charming, lyrical. But not this. You can't dance on your back, on your derrière, on your neck, on your head. It's like flying a plane on the ground. You can't do it. It's ersatz." From Charleston champ of Texas, she danced her way to screen superstardom in such a glittering garland of superhits that in 1945 she reigned as the highest paid performer in Hollywood and one of the top ten salary earners in the entire U.S. (In 1980 when she starred with the Rockettes at New York's Radio City Music Hall, she had appeared on its movie screen more than any other actress in its 48-year history—in 21 films, from *Professional Sweetheart* to *Weekend at the Waldorf*.) Among her more than 70 films (many as dancing partner to Fred Astaire) were such gems of glamour and glide as *Flying Down to Rio* (1933), *Top Hat* (1935), *The Gay Divorcee* (1934), *Roberta* (1935), *Swing Time* (1936), *Shall We Dance?* (1937) and *The Story of Vernon and Irene Castle* (1939). (Fans remember the effortless perfection of their dancing; Rogers remembers dancing "to the farther shores of weariness"—dancing until her "feet bled.") Off the dance floor she made her mark in films like *Stage Door* (1937), *Kitty Foyle* (Academy Award, 1940), and *Lady in the Dark* (1944). And proving herself to be enduring as well as adorable, she dazzled fans on Broadway in 1965 in *Hello Dolly*.

Born Virginia Katherine McMath, on 16 July 1911 in Independence,

Mo., she acquired the nickname "Ginger" as a moppet, combined it with "Rogers" when her mother (the driving force behind her career) moved to Texas and remarried. In a 1980 *People* interview she admitted her mother was the most influential person in her life. "She was *not* a stage mother; she was a very dignified woman." Hoofing on the vaudeville circuit in 1928, Ginger met and married Edward Culpepper (stage name, Jack Pepper), has since been married to actor Lew Ayres (1933), Jack Briggs (1944), Jacques Bergerac (1953), and William Marshall (1961) and was on her own again as of 1972. When asked in a recent interview if she would consider marrying again, Rogers answered: "Certainly. It's my nature. The only civilized way is marriage; the rest is chaos. No one believes in it more than I do. Trouble is, in my profession you must have a very secure male or the relationship is doomed. That was my problem." Bringing her shapely 19-year-old gams to the Main Stem in 1930 as star of George Gershwin's *Girl Crazy* (in which she introduced the song "Embraceable You"), she made her presence felt that same year in her very first film, *Young Man of Manhattan*, with the line "Cigarette me, big boy," which soon swept the country. Untarnished by time, the golden girl of the 1930s was busy in the 1970s serving as fashion consultant for J.C. Penney.

Although Rogers has a ranch on Oregon's Rogue River and a house near Palm Springs, she spends many months a year on the road performing in nightclubs from Las Vegas to Paris. In an interview with *People* she spoke frankly about today's movies and stage musicals. The movies: "We have fallen into the trap of trying to outdo each other with graphic sex and violence." And Hollywood: "It's Sodom and Gomorrah. The drugs, the corruption drag down an industry—and a nation. They're not going to get my money to see the junk that's being made today. No way." The musical theatre: "I don't like these shows where everybody gets undressed and does a war dance. The performers are there, but where are the Gershwins, the Berlins, the Richard Rodgerses—the creative geniuses?" Rogers admits she's no nostalgia nut. "Who wants to live in the past? I don't." In 1986 she received the first George M. Cohan Memorial Award from the 42nd Street River to River Committee.

Kenny Rogers

Outside his Georgia mansion, a jet-powered helicopter awaits his every move ready to whisk him away from his wife, son and multi-million dollar estate, as it did when he made his first feature film, *Sixpack* (1982). First and foremost a country singer, he gives upwards of a 100 concerts a year and with the income from his record sales, TV/movie production ventures and real estate holdings, this onetime resident of a Houston public housing project takes in as much as $2 million a month. He won *People* magazine's Most Popular Male Singer Award for three years in a row ('81-'83), for songs like "Lucille" and "The Gambler" which he parlayed into 35 million LP's and a pair of Grammys. Other memorable melodies include his 1980 duet with Kim Carnes, "Don't Fall in Love with a Dreamer" and "Lady."

Rogers was born in Houston, Texas, 21 August 1938. The first member of his family ever to complete high school, he joined an avant-garde jazz band (with whom he played bass fiddle) shortly after graduation in 1960—and stayed with the group for six years. In 1966 he merged with the New Christy Minstrels but defected a year later with three other members to form the First Edition, soon billed as Kenny Rogers and the First Edition. The group starred in its own TV series ("Rollin"), and made more than 70 guest appearances on other TV programs. Rogers's personal appearances keep him working most of the year in arenas, state fairs and Nevada showrooms. He has also starred in TV variety specials that have pulled top ratings for CBS as well as a telefilm based on his hit song "The Gambler". His latest albums include *I Prefer the Moonlight* (1987) and the new *Christmas in America* (1989). In 1986 he published a photographic book *Kenny Rogers's America*.

Rogers has been married four times, most recently to Marianne Gordon, a former regular on TV's "Hee Haw." They have one child, Christopher Cody, born in 1981. Rogers also has two children (now grown), Carol and Kenny, Jr., from a previous marriage. Despite his success, he harbors some doubt about the future. "Right now me and Willie Nelson are pretty much at the top of things. The question is, how long can I continue?"

Rosemary Rogers

Rosemary Rogers gets right to the heart of the matter in her best-selling historical romance novels (thirty million books in print in more than a dozen countries). The former Air-Force secretary (salaried at $4,200 per year) launched this romantic business in 1974 with her best-seller *Sweet Savage Love*, and has since sent nine more books to the top of the charts.

Born Rosemary Jansz (circa 1927) in Ceylon to a wealthy educator and his wife, her girlhood was spent much like a heroine from one of her novels—a pampered childhood, including summers in London at the home of an uncle. While studying English Literature at the University of Ceylon in 1953, she married Summa Navarantnam (a local track and rugby star) and bore him two children (Rosanne and Sharon). But alas, the romance died after five years. Rogers frolicked with the European jet set after her divorce and shortly thereafter married an American G.I., Leroy Rogers. With two more children in tow (Michael and Adam), again the flame of love was extinguished. In 1985 she married for the third time, Christopher Kadison.

Rogers's books are recognizable for their turgid literary style spiced with scenes that can be termed "once more into the breeches." As one critic put it: "She has perfected the soft-edge sex scene... sadomasochism in costume is a Rogers's specialty." Beginning work at midnight, setting the mood for each scene with music ("My books come to me in mind movies. I see the action in Technicolor on a wide screen in my head, and I hear the characters speak every line before I write it") she composes on a word processor, working through to the next day. Relaxation means yoga and meditation. "I've done yoga for years. It got me through the worst times... meditation gives me the feeling of being part of the universe." Does this promoter of the romantic revolution pine for a daring, supersexed hero? She admits to a "huge crush" on box office giant Clint Eastwood and used him as a model for her hero Steve Morgan. (They've met exactly once, when she interviewed him on special assignment for *Ladies Home Journal*.) Rogers attempts to "handle the cold, rarified air of success" by being contented with who she is inside and not confusing her role as super-writer with reality. "I write for myself and I write to entertain because people like and need to be entertained." In addition to her home in Carmel, Rogers maintains a Big Sur beach house and a three-bedroom Manhattan apartment.

Roy Rogers

Bedecked in a ten-gallon hat and astride his beloved palomino, he was the cowboy hero of more than 90 motion pictures, a radio broadcast, and a long running television program. Retired from the saddle, he is best known to recent generations as the smiling image behind a large chain of fast-food restaurants.

He was born Leonard Franklin Slye on 5 November 1911 in Cincinnati. Beset with poverty during the depression, the family headed for California in search of work. "There are parts of [*The Grapes of Wrath*] that made me wonder if maybe Mr. Steinbeck wasn't looking over the shoulder of the Slye Family." He mastered guitar and singing to earn money in his travels. After recording Western songs with a band called Sons of the Pioneers, he was riding high as

Gene Autry's replacement in the 1938 film, *Under Western Stars*. Among his noted films for Republic Studios were *Billy the Kid Returns* in 1938, King of the Cowboys in 1943 (the title of which became his trademark), and the 1947 *Springtime in the Sierras*. Rogers made 35 films with Dale Evans, beginning in 1944 with *The Cowboy and the Senorita*. The popular co-stars married three years later, after the sudden death of his first wife, Arlene. In 1948, they starred in "The Roy Rogers Show," on radio, and transferred the concept to television in 1951 for a six year run.

By his first wife, he has two children and an adopted daughter. A deeply religious man, he turned to the Billy Graham Crusade for strength when he and Evans suffered the loss of their child to Mongolism in 1953, and the death of two adopted children in separate accidents. They have reared several other adopted children of different nationalities.

The more than 500 Roy Rogers Family Restaurants are owned by Marriott Corp., of which he is a stockholder. He also owns real estate, a music publishing company, and a Museum in California. He was honored in 1988 with the International Galaxy of Fame Award from the Angel Foundation for his work with children.

Felix Rohatyn

"I spent our last night in a hotel room stuffing gold coins into toothpaste tubes. Ever since, I've had the feeling that the only permanent wealth is what you carry around in your head," recalls one of the world's most distinguished investment bankers and the man who helped save Wall Street and New York City from fiscal catastrophe, about his family's flight from Nazi-occupied Paris in 1942 and the formation of the principles that have elevated him to the summit of the world of international fiance.

Felix George Rohatyn (ROE-uh-t'n; the name is of Tartar origin) was born 29 May 1928 in Vienna into a prosperous Jewish banking and brewery family. His parents were divorced in the early 30s, and in 1934 he, his mother and stepfather were forced to flee Vienna in the face of the increasing Nazi menace. Their route from Paris in 1942 took them to Spain, Casablanca and Rio before depositing them in New York in time for Felix to begin high school. He studied English so assiduously that today he carries no trace of a foreign accent. At Middlebury College (which he chose partly for its skiing opportunities), He "never took a course in economics," did take advantage of the school's "extremely rigorous intellectual process" and joined a non-Jewish fraternity, which promptly lost its national charter.

With Andre Meyer, the legendary tyrannical head of the international banking firm of Lazard Freres as his mentor, Rohatyn worked in the company's Paris office (with time out for U.S. Army service during the Korean War) before returning to New York in 1955 to specialize in corporate finance and restructuring. So accomplished did he become and so successful were the results of his efforts ("He is better than the teacher," Meyer once admitted) that when Wall Street faced financial disaster in 1970 it was to Rohatyn that it turned. Working round the clock as the head of the New York Stock Exchange's Crisis Committee, sometimes making more than 150 telephone calls a day to keep some companies from folding and resuscitating others, he arranged the deals and mergers that restored confidence to the nation's financial capital. Five years later, when New York City teetered on the edge of bankruptcy with default a real possibility, Rohatyn again was called. Likening default to "someone stepping into a tepid bath and slashing his wrists—you might not feel yourself dying but that's what would happen," he helped set in motion a plan whereby government and private financial services would help the city survive fiscally. The plan's centerpiece was a new state agency, the Municipal Assistance Corporation, "Big Mac" ("my indulgence"), which would have the responsibility of borrowing money for the city to cover its "cash-flow" interruption so that it could pay its enormous debts. While awaiting the next "S.O.S." Rohatyn tends to his blue-chip clients at Lazard Freres ("The day I don't put my business first is the day I'll be out of business"). His influence does not stop at the water's edge. It's not unusual for him to lunch with the likes of French President Francois Mitterand. ("It amuses him to have an American who speaks French. . . . I guess I'm a sort of sounding board for him on what's happening in the U.S. and the world.")

The father of three sons—Pierre, Michael and Nicolas—by a previous marriage, Rohatyn married the former Elizabeth Vagliano on 31 May 1979, and the couple share a Park Avenue duplex and a Southampton weekend house. A collection of his articles on industrial policy (which he may someday be able to put into practice as Secretary of the Treasury in a Democrat administration) was published in early 1984 as *The Twenty-Year Century: Essays on Economics and Public Finance*. He is chairman of the International Council of the Israel Museum in Jerusalem and in New York ("I am rather sentimental about New York because it took me in"), he is a director of the New York City Heart Association, the Alvin Ailey Dance Company and Independence House, a job and counselling center for juvenile offenders.

Linda Ronstadt

After showing the world that her mastery of rock, country, folk, country-rock, pop, punk, standard big-band ballads and Gilbert and Sullivan could rock the charts, she turned classical *diva* in 1984 in Joe Papp's contemporary version of Puccini's *La Boheme*. How does she manage to be so versatile? It's a combination of intelligence, curiosity and most of all talent. Said musical arranger Nelson Riddle (his 47-piece orchestra backed Linda's super-popular album "What's New" a medley of standard hits from the '20s, '30s and '40s): "She's got a strong, beautiful voice and really unbelievable power." Ronstadt is shrewd about business and aloof about the sensation caused by her dating the likes of California's former governor Jerry Brown, comedian Steve Martin and film producer-director George Lucas. Her attitude towards "performing" says it all: "Performing is not my gift. I always feel the songs speak the most eloquently for themselves. The more simply they can be presented, the better they are."

Born 15 July 1946 in Tucson, her father, who loved to sing, pronounced his daughter a soprano at age four and that was that: she wanted to become a singer. She attended Catholic schools and was surrounded by her father's vast interest in all kinds of music. "He always said there's great music in everything. One of the most influential records my father bought was the Ella Fitzgerald and Louis Armstrong duet album," she recalls. "I was about 8 and I listened all day long. I had this little baby voice and I'd sing along." After one semester at the University of Arizona she hit the road and in Los Angeles formed the Stone Poneys, a folk-country band that had one hit, "Different Drum." In 1969, Ronstadt struck out on her own and released her first solo album, "Hand Sown, Home Grown." Her second album, "Silk Purse," released in 1970, included her first hit, "Long, Long Time"; it also earned her her first Grammy nomination. After two more albums, "Linda Ronstadt" and "Don't Cry Now," she teamed up with Peter Asher who became her producer and manager, and her career really took off. She released "Heart like a Wheel," and the single from that album "You're No Good," sprinted up the charts to number one. Her version of the Hank Williams's song "I Can't Help It (If I'm Still In Love With You")" won her her first Grammy. Next came her superhit, "Blue Bayou," and the 1978 album, "Living in the USA," further showed the famous Ronstadt versatility. She made her stage debut in the revival of *The Pirates of Penzance* in 1980 and her movie debut in the film of that show, also starring Kevin Kline and Angela Lansbury, in 1983. She followed her successful 1983 album with Nelson Riddle with a second: "Lush Life," in 1984. Ronstadt's ever-widening range prompted *Time* to ask: "What next, Gregorian chant for soprano?" One critic described her as "the sweetest creature this side of Little Bo-Peep." Her fans didn't have to wait too long to see Ronstadt's next move. After her albums *'Round Midnight* (1986) and *For Sentimental Reasons* (1986) she recorded the album *Canciones de Mi Padre* (1987) as well as touring in concert. She says, "These songs are a tradition both of my family and of a country which has made a profound and important contribution to the world of music. They also comprise a living memory of heartfelt experience." Ronstadt also sang the Academy Award winning song "Somewhere Out There" with James Ingram. In 1988 she made her London musical debut in *Sugar Babies.*

When the shepherdess is home in L.A., she shares her house with two friends. I like companionship," she says. "I can be alone if I want to be. I close my door. If I want friendship I go into the kitchen. If I've got a date and want to sit on the couch and neck, I ask everyone to beat it for the night and they will." In the 1970s she belted out "You're No Good," "When Will I Be Loved?" and "Heat Wave." Why the cool-out in her choice of tunes in the 1980s? Ronstadt's cards are on the table. She's a hopeless romantic. "I just want to make people dream," she says, "make them slow dance around the living room, sit down on the couch and make out."

Andy Rooney

In 1970 Andy Rooney wrote an angry piece about Vietnam called "Essay On War." It was to be for "60 Minutes," but was canned and Rooney quit the network. He decided to bring "Essay on War" to the airwaves via public television, but there was one hitch; he'd have to read the essay himself. Rooney, who had always been *the writer* since breaking into television in 1949 with Arthur Godfrey, suddenly had to brave the cameras. He almost got cold feet—but not quite. The essay, however controversial, helped him win his third Writer's Guild of America Award. Soon an advertising agency called to offer Rooney a speaking role in a headache commercial, "Told me a lot about my voice," he quipped.

Times have changed. Andy Rooney's days as a rebel are over. These days he puts his considerable writing talents to use exploring subjects near and dear to the heart of mainstream America. After returning to "60 Minutes," his role as raconteur of middle class life was expanded to include a series of light-hearted specials. (The 1988/1989 season marked his eleventh season with the show.) Typical of this highly popular series was "Mr. Rooney Goes to Dinner," in which the pixieish Rooney takes a high-calorie look at American noshing habits. Sitting at his 1920 Underwood typewriter ("I distrust a typewriter smarter than I am") he ventilates the minor mishaps that vex John and Mary Public. His themes are socks that don't match, working breakfasts in which he suspects the participants have already "had a little something" previously, and whether or not the President minds living "above the store." A philosopher for the shopping malls, a Whitman for a complacent era, Rooney knows just how far—or how short—metaphysics will take you between commercials.

Critics may deride him as a lightweight, but his fellow TV writers know he is expert in his craft. Six times he has won the Writer's Guild Award for Best Script of the Year. He wrote his first signature piece—the chuckle filled look at obscure commonplaces—back in 1964. Since then the personalized television essay has become institutionalized and very closely associated with him, to the extent that his "60 Minutes" essays have become grist for "Saturday Night Live's" satire mill. His periodic hour-long broadcasts are paced with "just the limited amount of good writing that people will take on TV," he admits. On his Underwood he has also tapped out eight books (his latest *Word For Word,* 1986), scores of magazines articles, and an every-other-day newspaper column that's carried by more than 300 newspapers. Born 14 January 1919 in Albany, NY, Rooney attended Colgate University, worked as a newspaper copyboy, then was drafted in 1941. In the army he worked on *Stars & Stripes,* the G.I.'s newspaper, covering such major stories as the Battle of the Bulge. He and his wife, the former Marguerite Howard (married in 1942) live in Rowayton, Conn., in the house in which they raised four children. "Writing is always hard work," says the man who appears as a "personality" rather than a scribe to American viewers. He adds: "That's why it's dying out. But I still enjoy closing the door and fighting it out."

Mickey Rooney

"I've been through four publics. I've been coming back like a rubber ball for years, but I never had aspirations to remain a star—that would have been rougher," admitted Rooney a few years ago. "I just want to be a professional. I couldn't live without acting." Outshining even such supergiants as Gable and Tracy, he was Hollywood's No. 1 box-office idol back in 1939, '40, and '41. Now, after 8 trips to the altar, several career slumps and one journey to bankruptcy court, the perennial Andy Hardy is balding, but unbowed, busy and back on top. Appearing on Broadway in 1979 in the smash hit *Sugar Babies* (with Ann Miller) made him a "hot ticket" once again and put him back "in the chips." Everybody's tickled pink, especially "the Mick." He likes to be seen in the present productions of *Sugar Babies* (London, 1988), as well as try other roles. In 1987 he appeared on Broadway in the Stephen Sondheim musical *A Funny Thing Happened On The Way To The Forum* and in 1988 he starred in the CBS telefilm "Bluegrass." His latest feature film is *Erik the Viking* (1989).

Born Joe Yule, Jr., on 23 September 1920 in Brooklyn, a few blocks from the theatre in which his showbiz parents were appearing, he wandered out on stage for the first time in 1921 as Baby New Year. A few months later he made his "formal" debut as a midget, wearing a tuxedo and smoking a rubber cigar, and he went on to play a midget in his first movie, a silent called *Not to Be Trusted.* A star, at six, of innumerable *Mickey (Himself) McGuire* comedy shorts, he became Mickey Rooney (not Mickey Looney, as his mother first suggested) in such golden oldies as *Boys Town, Babes in Arms,* and *Captains Courageous,* and made his first Andy Hardy picture (*A Family Affair*) in 1937. The eight marriages (producing almost as many children) started with Ava Gardner, proceeded through Betty Jane Rase, Martha Vickers, Eileen Mahnken, Barbara Ann Thomasen, Margie Dane, Carolyn Hockett, to Jan Chamberlin, the present Mrs. Rooney.

After a bunch of "typical" Rooney performances in *Breakfast at Tiffany's, It's a Mad, Mad, Mad, Mad World, How to Stuff a Wild Bikini* (movies) and a couple of short-lived TV series ("Mickey" and "One of the Boys"), his superb television portrayals in "The Comedian," "Eddie," "Somebody's Waiting," "Bill" (1982 Emmy award) "Bill: On His Own" and his acclaimed film acting in *Black Stallion* have recently exposed the in-depth dramatic talent of the mite-but-mighty Mickey. In the late '60s Rooney joined the Church of Religious Science and says he has found a deeper, richer meaning to living. "All of the muddy waters of my life cleared up when I gave myself to Christ," declares Rooney. In 1983 Rooney was given an honorary Oscar for "50 years of versatility in a variety of memorable film performances" (he received a special miniature statue in 1938 at the height of his career as a juvenile film performer). In a 1980 *Life* magazine interview, Rooney assessed his philosophy about work and his career: "Listen, you never reach an apex in life. If you think you do, then you become effete, something starts to decay very fast. See, I'm this 59-year-old-guy who's going on 34. There may be a little snow on the mountain, but there's a lot of fire in the furnace. I'm still learning, and, of course, I'll never stop paying my dues. I'd be happy carrying a spear, saying: 'Your horse waits without.'" Rooney's autobiography *The Beginning And The Middle* was released in 1985.

Ned Rorem

"I like glory and I like fame," says 1976's Pulitzer Prize-winning composer (*Air Music*), Ned Rorem. Once called "the best composer of art songs now living," Rorem's celebrity status now rests primarily on his personal life, much of which he has candidly exposed in a series of published "diaries," notably *The Paris Diary of Ned Rorem* ("I published my first book, a diary, in 1966 and in the six months that followed I had more reaction from strangers than I have had in twenty years as a professional composer.") *The New York Diary* (1967), *The Final Diary* (1974), *Setting the Tone: Essays and A Diary* (1984) and *The Nantucket Diary* (1987). Rorem's musical compositions—words (often well-known poets' works) put to music; orchestral scores;

ballet scores; symphonies—are noted for "their astringent lyricism and exotic instrumental combinations," according to New York Times's critic John Gruen. There exists an almost magical interplay and exchange between the music Rorem writes and his telling self revelations—"... that prose began to take on the aspects of my music, becoming ever more pristine, clear, direct, pure, and above all objective, while the music, like Dr. Hyde, grew gradually more virile, more violent, and, I hope, more ugly—for all art must contain ugliness within its beauty. These two aspects of myself crossed each other, as though I were entering a mirror, or like two amoebas merging, then separating."

Born 23 October 1923, in Richmond, Ind., he was raised in "an upper-class, semi-bohemian milieu, but with a strong Quaker emphasis." Seemingly predestined to exploit his creative talents, Rorem once remarked, "I was an artist since birth." Actually, it was his introduction to Ravel and Debussy at age ten that set the resolve in motion to become a composer and to live in France. His training included the Music School of Northwestern University, the Curtis Institute of Music (under Gian-Carlo Menotti), Juilliard (composition under Bernard Wagenaar), the Berkshire Music Center in Tanglewood (under Aaron Copland) and orchestration lessons under Virgil Thomson (in return for which Rorem became Thomson's copyist). Winner of the coveted Lili Boulanger Award, Rorem's most notable works include *Lions*, *To a Young Girl*, *Eagles* and *Eleven Studies for Eleven Players*. Rorem's gifts reach further to the theater—he has written the music for many plays, among them, *Cock-A-Doodle* (1949), *Suddenly Last Summer* (1958), *Motel* (1960), *Lady of the Camelias* (1963) and *The Milk Train Doesn't Stop Here Anymore* (1964).

Rorem resides in New York City. He views his art as all important and all encompassing. "No one else is making what I need. Success is forever transient, frozen, dead. What it represents may live on, but the maker collapses ... without daily reassurance (in the form of performances and recognition, good or bad) I could not persist. ... Anyone can be drunk, anyone can be in love, anyone can waste time and weep, but only I can pen my songs in the few remaining years or minutes. The sponge is always there but where would I throw it? Where could I go?"

Pete Rose

When *Los Angeles Times* sportswriter Jim Murray described 1984 Olympic gold-medal gymnast Mary Lou Retton as "Pete Rose in a leotard," no further amplification was needed. So firmly implanted in America's sports consciousness are the qualities of "Charlie Hustle" that his name has become a virtual synonym for the toughness and fierce competitive spirit so often missing in athletes blessed with greater natural gifts. It came as no surprise, then, when in August of 1984, Peter Edward Rose was recalled from a five-year exile to take over the fortunes of the baseball team whose reputation as the Big Red Machine had more recently taken on the image of a broken Tinker Toy. His task as player-manager of the Cincinnati Reds was complicated somewhat by his personal pursuit of Ty Cobb's all-time hit mark of 4,191. He surpassed Cobb's singles record in 1984 when he hit his 3,053rd off Steve Carlton. Then on 11 September 1985 before an overflow Cincinnati crowd, he connected No. 4,192, surpassing Cobb as the premier hit producer in baseball history. His past few years have been full of controversial incidents. In 1988 he was suspended for thirty days for pushing umpire Dave Pallone. The following year was filled with gambling accusations which prompted Rose to travel to Federal Court, claiming that Major League Baseball was not giving him a fair trial. A compromise was reached when the late Commissioner of Baseball A. Bartlett Giamatti declared Rose banned from baseball for life effective 24 August 1989. The announcement did not declare him guilty of betting on baseball games and he can apply for reinstatement in one year.

It was at the age of two that Pete Rose (born 14 April 1942 in Cincinnati) began playing catch with his father. "Each Christmas I would get a new glove or a new basketball," he recalls. "Once, Mom sent Dad downtown to buy a pair of shoes for my sister. Instead, he came back with a pair of boxing gloves for me." At nine, he played organized ball for the first time (with Cincinnati's Little League equivalent) but only after his father had extracted from the team's manager a promise to let the boy switch hit (with the ultimate result that Rose became the most accomplished switch-hitter in baseball). Only his spirit and hustle (head first dives, running to first base after receiving a base on balls, etc.,) saved him from baseball oblivion after an unimpressive minor league debut in the Reds organization, with which he signed out of high school. His steady improvement, however, provided a ticket to the majors in 1963 when he became the Reds's second baseman and was named the league's Rookie of the Year. In 1970 and 1972, he led the team to National League pennants, and in 1975 and 1976 to World Series victories. The National League's Most Valuable Player in 1973, Rose won three batting titles and led the league in hits six times. His surprise departure from the Reds in 1979 was the result as much of a falling out with the team's front office (precipitated by a headlined paternity suit and a messy divorce) as of his desire to enhance his bank account with the generous contract he signed with the Philadelphia Phillies. He is the father of a daughter, Fawn Renee, and a son, Peter Edward II (Petey), by his marriage to the former Karolyn Ann Englehardt. He married Carol Woliung in 1984 (a son, Ty, was born the same year; their daughter, Cara Chae was born 22 August 1989). An autobiography, *Charlie Hustle* (a name given to him by former Yankee pitcher Whitey Ford), was published in 1975, and *The Official Pete Rose Scrapbook* came out in 1978.

Diana Ross

"I'd like to think one of my greatest accomplishments musically is to take the music of a specific community, put my own spin in it, and take it out to the world. I'm aware of the great gift I've been given in having a voice and a style that seem to cut across boundaries of race, age and nations. To be able to turn people onto new sounds, new ideas ... to make them move and dance and feel excitement about living," states the Diva of Pop. The Supremes's singular siren is a celebrity who has captured the sounds of the times and bridged generation gaps. Head of her own management and film production companies, she thoughtfully plans her life by writing down her priorities, thoughts for the day, and "mind-maps." The actress-singer-fashion designer has sold more No. 1 hits—from among over 50 albums—than anyone except the Beatles and Elvis Presley, and *Billboard* called her Female Entertainer of the Century. The release of her most recent album *Workin' Overtime* (1989) cemented her slot as a continual chart buster.

Born in Detroit, 26 March 1944, she sang in the choir of a Baptist church and learned secular music from a cousin who was known as "the girl with the golden voice." After graduating from high school, Diana and her friends Florence Ballard and Mary Wilson auditioned for Detroit's Motown Records. They were soon enrolled in Berry Gordy's specially-commissioned daily "artist's development" lessons, which included how to speak, sit, shake hands properly, and climb up on a piano. After their ditty called "Where Did Our Love Go?" hit it big they were to become the most successful of all American record-sellers in the music-filled '60s. Soon they were Diana Ross and the Supremes. In 1970 Diana went solo, but with the solid backing of Motown mogul Gordy. He took the record company into movie-making and personally supervised screen vehicles for Ross. She was nominated for a Best Actress Oscar for her portrayal of Billie Holiday in *Lady Sings the Blues*, designed the clothes for her role as a model in *Mahogany* (as well as singing the Oscar-nominated theme song), and recreated Judy

Garland's Dorothy in the all-black *The Wiz*. On the drawing board as her film company's first production: a bio of the chanteuse Josephine Baker.

The divorced mother of three daughters, Diana said officially in 1983, "I'm a dreamer . . . I dreamed of building a playground in the park for some time, and now that playground is going to be a reality." The free outdoor concert she put on for that end was disastrous, however; when thunder and rain doused the 350,000 who came out for the Great Lawn event, it was postponed a day. That date was marred by gangs of hoods who thought it was a thugfest instead of a songfest. Finally, after Ross and Paramount Video, co-producer and televiser of the show, handed the city the bill, there was not only nothing left for a playground, but New Yorkers were out of $650,000 in security and cleanup. All was mended, however, when the diva, who claimed she had had to cough up almost three hundred thousand in expenses, presented Mayor Ed Koch with a check for a quarter of a million several months later, anyway. Hizzoner presented her with garb she could have used way back when: a rain slicker. Very much in love, Diana married her second husband, Arne Naess, Jr., in two ceremonies (23 October 1985 in New York; 1 February 1986 in Geneva). All told she has five children (three daughters from her previous marriage and two sons with Arne).

Philip Roth

"I'm not a public entertainer," says novelist Philip Roth, "other than as a writer." Few would argue that his novels are not entertaining: lewd, crude, self-indulgent, and maybe not "good for the Jews," but they are certainly entertainment. Having started out as a kind of "Jewish Henry James," according to writer Albert Goldman, Roth's 1969 priapic novel of the artist as a randy young man made the author of *Portnoy's Complaint* a household name. Epic in its wet-palmed way, the book has been called the "*Moby Dick* of masturbation."

Portnoy's creator has moved on from that celebrated *succès de scandale*, although the raunch quotient in his books has dropped hardly an iota. From his 190-year old clapboard farmhouse in Connecticut, Roth has remained a prolific wordsmith, inspired by the presence of his live-in love, British actress Claire Bloom. The author of 16 books, as well as numerous screenplays, short stories and magazine articles, Roth recently completed the last installment of his trilogy describing the life and times of Nathan Zuckerman. Zuckerman, who, like Roth, is literary, Newark-born (19 March 1933) and Jewish, has been publicly separated from his creator; Roth always takes pains to declare his work to be fiction and not dressed-up confessionals. The trilogy came to a head with *The Anatomy Lesson*, in the wake of *Zuckerman Unbound* (1981) and *The Ghost Writer* (1979). (The three, with an epilogue, were published in a single 1985 volume, *Zuckerman Bound*.) His latest books are *The Counterlife* (1987) and *The Facts: A Novelist's Autobiography* (1988).

Jacqueline Susann said once to Johnny Carson, "I'd adore meeting Philip Roth," but added that she would be reluctant to shake his hand. Fortunately for Roth, whose first marriage he does not discuss, his relationship with Claire Bloom goes far beyond hand-shaking. They met at an East Hampton soirée in 1965, and the British actress decided Roth was "stunningly good looking." Both romantically involved with others, they went their separate ways. But a chance meeting on a Manhattan sidewalk renewed their friendship. Neither talks optimistically of marriage, while fiercely guarding their right to privacy on the subject. "Marriage," Claire says breezily, "gets vulgar after the second time."

Mike Royko

"No self-respecting fish would want to be wrapped in newspaper published by Rupert Murdoch," sniffed this Windy City columnist when the Australian presslord bought up his journalistic home base, the Chicago *Sun-Times*, in December, 1982. Mike Royko's column, "must" reading for Chicagoans since 1963, was, according to one observer, "one of the principal assets Murdoch thought he was buying" so he took a dim view when the writer decamped for the rival *Tribune* (which had the added advantage of giving him a New York City outlet in the Trib-owned *Daily News*). When Murdoch sued, Royko handily beat the suit and, basking in all the publicity the fuss caused, was bigger than ever. Says good friend Studs Terkel, another Chicago institution, "Everyone is reading Royko's column . . . it's the first thing they turn to."

The Chicago-born (19 September 1932) Royko hasn't gotten very far in terms of geographical career trekking. He started as a reporter for the Chicago North Side newspapers in 1956, was an assistant city editor at *City News* for three years, reported and wrote a column for Chicago *Daily News* from '59-'78, then settled on the south side of the Chicago River with the *Sun-Times* before crossing the stream to his present *Tribune* desk. Through most of his travels he's taken his fictitious "Slats Grobnik," a lower-middle class Everyman, who is suspicious of the powers-that-be as are many residents of the city of stockyards and stock trading. His simple, straightforward observations on people and events in America's Second City are usually delivered with all the tact of a miffed waitress spilling coffee in one's lap. For instance, Royko claimed that neighboring state Indiana is "the most miserable in the union" and that Indianapolis is "the dullest large city in the U.S." Protesting Hoosiers wrote him by the droves. To which Royko cracked, "I was amazed how many people from Indiana could write. [But] most of the letters were done in crayon." Adhering to his inimitable style, he released his book *Dr. Kookie, You're Right* in 1989.

Pete Rozelle

This lanky and elegant Californian was dubbed "The Child Commissioner" in 1960 when he became the czar of the National Football League. He's since been derogated as "Pete Doughsmell" for what his critics consider his too-consuming passion for financial success, has been nicknamed "St. Peter" for his supercop stance on the matter of pro football morals, and has been praised as "Peter the Great" for his uncanny acumen in "litigation, amalgamation, legislation, communication, negotiation, and administrative prestidigitation." The key to his "let's think league" transformation of a band of 12 feifdoms into today's multi-billion dollar 28-club fraternity is his deferential power of persuasion. His contributions to the NFL were recognized in 1985 when he was elected to the Pro Football Hall of Fame.

Alvin Ray Rozelle, born 1 March 1926 in South Gate, Calif., was a shy, unathletic schoolboy growing up in Lynwood and Compton, where he was shoved around on playgrounds until a wise and sympathetic uncle changed his name from Alvin to Pete and toughened him up. Still, the fact he played tennis in school instead of football nettled some future colleagues. He started out on the night sports desk of the Long Beach *Press-Telegram*, then became a press agent for the L.A. Rams and later the team's general manager. Considered something of a mouse when he took over the NFL chief's job, he soon proved to be a mouse who could roar. Of his genius at snaring lucrative TV deals, a CBS exec once said, "Rozelle is always thinking a couple of steps ahead of any negotiation, but no matter how closely you study him, he never lets you know it's happened." In 1983 he witnessed the erosion of his biggest coup, however, when the legislation he'd persuaded Congress to pass making football immune from anti-trust laws was successfully challenged. Rozelle's enemy, Raider owner Al Davis, won $35 million in a lawsuit which sharply accused Rozelle of master-minding the league's blockage of his team's move to Los Angeles.

He and second wife Carrie "weren't wedded, they were welded" says a friend of his decade-plus marriage. A British-educated Canadian, Mrs. Rozelle had three learning disabled sons from her first marriage. With Pete's prodding, she set up the Foundation for Children with Learning Disabilities. The self-contained "man with a mask" picked Howard Hughes for his model on how to be reticent though rich. There's no mystery, however, about his overall grand design: keeping the sport of professional football very big business indeed.

John Rubinstein

"I lacked the digital dexterity and I couldn't sightread music . . . I hated to practice and playing classical music was a chore. Acting, on the other hand, was not." So the son of the late great concert pianist Arthur Rubinstein (born when his father was 57) opted for a career on stage rather than at the keyboard. In 1972, he was chosen over 400 other auditioners for the title role of the musical *Pippin* and his performance as Charlemagne's son launched him on a career that's still going strong. He earned a Best Actor Tony in 1980 for his demanding role of a teacher of the deaf in the Tony Award-winning Best Play, *Children of a Lesser God*.

Born in Beverly Hills (8 December 1946), John Rubinstein remembers his famous father as "an inspiring, lovely man. His commanding personality and the demands of his career certainly at times affected our family life. But, nevertheless, it was a very happy household." Moving with his parents to New York when he was seven, he discovered the joys of acting at St. Bernard's School where, at 13, still with a high voice and braces on his teeth, he played Macbeth. ("I can't vouch for the quality of my Macbeth, but it made me realize that acting was to become an important part of my life.") In tandem with his now-prospering acting career, the pianist's son has become a successful composer of film scores (e.g. Robert Redford's *Jeremiah Johnson* and *The Candidate;* the Jane Fonda TV movie, "The Dollmaker."). He also plays a mean barroom piano. Married to actress Judi West (two children: Michael and Jessica) he has a further passion for baseball and in the 1980s was playing leftfield for the Broadway Show League in Central Park. On the little screen, he scored in the critically well-received CBS-TV series, "Crazy Like a Fox" (which debuted in 1984) co-starring Jack Warden, the NBC miniseries "The Two Mrs. Grenvilles" (1986) and the ABC telefilm "Liberace" (1988). On 20 February 1989 he replaced David Dukes on Broadway in *M. Butterfly* as well as appearing in the A.R. Gurney play *Love Letters*.

Run-DMC

"Punks, runts, chumps, we're yoking
News is crews are choking
Out like that? Not going!
In like men, we're growing
Chance to dance, not blowing
Got to show dough flowing . . ."

Rapping away, Run-DMC have made a name for themselves as the most popular rap act around and one of the hottest music acts of any description. Their name stems from the nicknames of two of the rappers, Joseph "Run" Simmons and Darryl "DMC" McDaniels. They and Jason "Jam Master Jay" Mizzell all attended the same Catholic high school, St. Pascal's, and they made their first record shortly after graduating in 1982. Within two years, the lads had made their first gold album and, in the process, became the first black rap group to crack *Billboard's* Top 100 and thus enter the musical mainstream. Run himself says, "We've made it work not by softening up, but by being tougher than leather." Their albums include *Run-DMC* (1984) and *Raising Hell* (1986); they were the first rap act to have their videos aired on MTV, the first to appear on "American Bandstand," and the first on the cover of *Rolling Stone* magazine. In 1987 they headlined the Together Forever tour with the Beastie Boys and by 1989 had released four albums to date. They also released a film, *Tougher Than Leather* (same title as their 1988 album), which was financed independently. Jam Master Jay said the movie " . . . is not Hollywood, it's *Hollis*wood!"

Ken Russell

"I know my films upset people. I want to upset people," says the veteran director of such R-rated but X-ceedingly erotic pictures as *Women in Love* (1969), *The Devils* (1971) and *Crimes of Passion* (1984). "People are simply not prepared. I do hit them below the belt and they react to being exposed." So do some critics, who "would rather be bored than shocked. All good art," the great upsetter asserts categorically, "all good entertainment, shocks people."

Born in Southampton, England, 3 July 1927, Russell served in Britain's merchant marine at the close of World War II, then attended an art school and finally enrolled at the International Ballet School, where "an 80-year-old Russian martinet . . . taught us to jump very high by shouting in blasphemous Russian and beating us about the legs with a stick." After performing with the Norwegian Ballet and in the chorus of an English touring company of *Annie Get Your Gun*, he switched to acting, but finding that life too insecure, took up photography and became a successful lensman. This led to an interest in motion pictures, and before long he had shot and edited three shorts—a fantasy, a drama, and a documentary—on budgets of around £150 each; one came to the attention of a highly placed BBC producer, who commissioned Russell to make what turned out to be the first of a series of documentaries.

Russell quickly became noted—and notorious—for his unconventional methods of dealing with films of this type: "My way of directing documentaries," he declared, "finally cleared the air of the word 'documentary' and all that is dreary, reverential and schoolmastery that the word entails." (One newspaper dubbed him "the wild man of the BBC and England's most accomplished and imaginative director.") He has profiled on film, among other celebrated figures, Bela Bartok, Claude Debussy, Peter Ilyitch Tchaikovsky, Frederick Delius, Edward Elgar, Gustav Mahler, Richard Strauss and Isadora Duncan. He completed his first theatrical feature, *French Dressing*, in 1964, and his second, *Billion Dollar Brain*, in 1967, but it was his third big picture, *Women in Love*, that brought him international attention. Though controversial, his succeeding films were, on the whole, quite respectfully received until *Altered States* (1980), which Pauline Kael characterized as "probably the most aggressively silly picture since *The Exorcist*." While awaiting his next film project he directed operas in Florence, Lyon, Charleston (S.C.) and Spoleto.

By his first wife, Shirley, whom he married in 1957, Russell has five children: Xavier, James, Alexander, Victoria and Toby; he already had another daughter, Molly, by Vivian Jolly by the time he married that lady on 10 June 1984 aboard the old *Queen Mary* in Long Beach, Calif., with actor Anthony Perkins, an ordained minister, officiating. With *Crimes of Passion* in the can he turned to directing *La Boheme* in Italy. "After so many years making movies," he says, "I find directing operas . . . a great deal more fun. They don't take too long to direct—just a month—and they're exciting." And controversial. The climax of his recent *Madame Butterfly* was the dropping of the A-bomb on Hiroshima and his *La Boheme* had Mimi experimenting with drugs of the non-prescription kind. His recent bunch of films include *Gothic* (1987), *The Lair of the White Worm* (1988) *Salome's Last Dance* (1988) and *The Rainbow* (1989).

Meg Ryan

"It's hard to pin someone with Ryan's range down to a short phrase.... If the roles are diverse, there's one constant: Men are bowled over by her. When describing Ryan, grown journalists—men who interview glamorous starlets all the time—resort to romance-novel words like 'breezy sexuality' and make note of her 'slow, sexy smile,'" raves an article in *Mademoiselle*. Meg Ryan is hot! Although her screen cameo in *Top Gun* brought her into the Hollywood mainstream, she doesn't feel that particular film launched her career. She insists, "I guess I never felt like it did. It's not like I walk down the street and people say, 'Oh, there's the girl from *Top Gun*....' I was more famous when I was on 'As the World Turns.'"

Ryan was born in 1963 in Fairfield, Connecticut. While studying journalism at New York University, she supported herself by making commercials. Those big round blue eyes and sensuous smirk landed the young actress her feature film debut as Candice Bergen's daughter in George Cukor's *Rich and Famous* (1981). Her theatrical resume blossomed when she landed the role as Betsy on the daytime soap "As the World Turns" (1983-1985), followed by her appearances in *Amityville III: The Demon, Armed and Dangerous, Top Gun, Innerspace, D.O.A.* and *The Presidio*. She also starred in a critically acclaimed independent feature *Promised Land* (executive producer, Robert Redford). Her performance as a tough drifter won her a Best Actress Award in Europe and a nomination for Best Actress from the I.F.P. However, it was her role as Sally Albright opposite Billy Crystal in the 1989 film *When Harry Met Sally* that made Meg Ryan a household name with star billing on the marquee. In the film, her character "brings contemporary relationship problems out into the open." It is Meg's interpretation of a woman having an orgasm (in front of amazed onlookers in a restaurant) that set film audiences roaring in their seats. Next up, Meg will appear with Tom Hanks in the 1990 movie *Joe Versus the Volcano*.

Stepping up the ladder of success, Meg has some additional goals. She observes that good scripts are hard to find and hopes to write one herself, someday. "I just love words," she offers. "I love when a writer says something that you've thought way back in your subconscious. When it becomes a conscious thought, you're like, wooooow." Still single, she makes a steady habit of seeing her actor/boyfriend Dennis Quaid.

Sade

"I thought my songs wouldn't sit well on the charts," Sade admitted in *People*. But the opposite seems to be true. The sultry-voiced singer and all-male band have taken the pop-music world by storm since the 1984 release of their first album, *Diamond Life*. "So alluring is Sade, so cool and seductive her sound, poised and subtly sexual her presence—so right the whole package—that her rise to greater popular acclaim can surely be only a matter of time." The words in Mick Brown's review in the *Guardian* were prophetic. *Diamond Life* became the best-selling debut album by *any* British female artist and had already topped the U.K. and European charts before its January 1985 release in the U.S. The album, the sound of Sade the singer and Sade the band—jazz-infused music blending pop melodies with supple African and Brazilian rhythms—were immediately accepted by the U.S. music audience. *Diamond Life* went gold within two months of release and multi-platinum by the end of that year. The album also spawned three hit singles, "Hang on to Your Love," "Smooth Operator" (which rose to the Top 5 on the pop chart), and "Your Love is King" (which made the Top 20.) Before the clamor died down, Sade released a second album, *Promise,* spawning two hit singles ("Sweetest Taboo" and "Never as Good as the First Time") and outselling *Diamond Life* two-to-one. Aside from providing that distinctive, smokey alto voice, Sade also co-wrote, with Stuart Matthewman (guitarist-saxophonist for the group), most of the songs on both albums. It's not surprising that Sade won the Grammy for Best New Artist of 1985 and was named New Artist of the Year by the British Phonographic Institute.

Born late in 1959 in Ibadan, Nigeria, as Helen Folasade Abu, Sade (an affectionate, diminutive form of her middle name) was the second child of a Nigerian schoolteacher and his English wife whom he had met when he was a student at the London School of Economics. Sade's parents separated when she was four, and she moved with her mother and brother to London's North End. After another move around age ten, Sade found herself in Clacton-on-Sea. At age fourteen, Sade discovered jazz, funk, soul music and peers with her passion for dancing. She listened to her mother's records—Sinatra, Basie and Dinah Washington—but really fell for American soul music—Aretha Franklin, Al Green, Smokey Robinson and Marvin Gaye—even though, as she told the *Washington Post*, "I had no great burning desire to be a singer." When she was seventeen, Sade moved to London to attend St. Martin's College, studying fashion design for three years. She created her own line of menswear after graduation, some of which made it to the U.S. in conjunction with the first U.S. appearance of the British rock band Spandau Ballet. After the fashion career failed, Sade tried a number of jobs to support herself, including waitressing, bicycle messengering, and modeling. However, the coffee-and-cream colored beauty, with her dramatic high forehead, arched eyebrows, almond eyes and sensual mouth, did not enjoy modeling clothes and let the career die naturally.

Although still devoted to dancing, Sade jumped at the invitation to audition for a jazz-funk group as a back-up singer. Asked to audition because of her exotic looks and chosen because the band failed to find a more suitable vocalist, the untrained Sade entered the music world with the band Pride. Soon Sade was collaborating on writing songs with Pride's saxophonist-guitarist Stuart Matthewman. When Pride disbanded, the splintered group, fronted by Sade and Matthewman, already had a cult following. Sade the band, comprised of Sade, Matthewman, Paul Denman (bass) and Andrew Hale (keyboards), emerged, playing at the Institute of Contemporary Arts in 1983. Playing a unique blend of soft soul, jazz and light Latin sounds, the band brought additional form and color to Sade's words and melodies.

Sade's talents have continued to develop. She produced the group's third album, *Stronger Than Pride*, released in 1988, with her lyrics set to music composed by the members of the band. Worldwide, this talented group of British performers has sold more than twenty million albums and singles. Meanwhile, Sade, named by *Elle* magazine as one of the ten most elegant women in the world in 1985, continues to expand her own horizon. In 1986 she appeared in her first movie *Absolute Beginners*, which also featured David Bowie, as a nightclub chanteuse singing a torch ballad. Such a role is not surprising for a singer who has been dubbed the "reluctant siren" by *People*. When not singing or touring, Sade escapes to her flat in the quiet North London section of Highbury to write music and prepare for the next song that will probably sit well on the charts.

Morley Safer

The urbane, subtly scrutinizing co-editor of the CBS highly rated news magazine, "60 Minutes," first made his mark as a foreign correspondent for Canadian, then American television. His nightly reports from Vietnam for CBS graphically exposed the brutality of the war and its toll on the villagers. He is largely credited for ushering in the era of the "living-room war."

Safer was born 8 November 1931 in Toronto. An average student, he "just scraped through" the University of Western Ontario before becoming a Canadian newspaper man. As a foreign correspondent for the Canadian Broadcasting Corp., he was stolen away by CBS's London office in 1964 and transferred to Vietnam to head the network's Saigon bureau. "Jungle bashing" with the troops, he turned up stories that angered the administrations of two presidents, causing pressure on CBS to tone down his reports. He incorporated his footage in a 1967 special, "Morley Safer's Vietnam—A Personal Diary." When Harry Reasoner left "60 Minutes" in 1970 to co-anchor the ABC nightly news, the network replaced him with Safer. Safer's witty tours de force, on everything from the game of croquet to a coin collector's rip-off scheme, were a welcome contrast to the hard-hitting interrogation pieces supplied by his associates. He prefers the essay-style, "in the sense that the reporter's observed this or that, and interviews don't get in the way. You observe. Of course, you talk to people—but you don't take up good television time talking to them."

Safer married Jane Fearer, whom he met in 1968, while she was a doctoral student at Oxford. They have a daughter, Sarah. Although they live in Manhattan, he remains a Canadian citizen.

Carole Bayer Sager

This petite, L.A.—based songwriter's lyrics have become such an important part of the contemporary music scene that one record trade publication proclaimed a new album unique simply because it did not contain one Carole Bayer Sager song. From Frank Sinatra to Bette Midler, Sager's tunes sing where the music is sweetest: on top of the chart, where million-dollar earnings hit the highest notes.

Born in New York City 8 March 1947, Carole finds songwriting her most reliable form of communication. She first began writing poems to her parents as a child. Her music career began when she was 15 and a student at New York City's High School of Music and Art. She began writing music professionally as soon as she graduated from New York University, where she studied speech, English and dramatic arts.

Credits? She's got plenty. As half of one of the world's most successful contemporary songwriting teams she and husband Burt Bacharach (one child) won the Academy Award for Best Song for *Arthur* in 1981. Her credits on films include the songs for *Making Love*, three songs for *Night Shift* and the Neil Diamond smash "Heartlight" (*E.T.* inspired). Carole's songs also include "Midnight Blue," "A Groovy Kind of Love," "Don't Cry Out Loud," "Nobody Does it Better," which was a Carly Simon super-hit, "On My Own," and, in collaboration with Marvin Hamlisch, the Broadway-blessed score for *They're Playing Our Song*. A singer as well as a writer, she has three albums with her songs: *Carole Bayer Sager*, *Carole Bayer Sager . . . Too*, and *Sometimes Late at Night*, which she co-wrote with Burt Bacharach. In 1985, her first novel, *Extravagant Gestures*, was published.

It is relationships, in all their many guises, that are the subjects of her music. "Fortunately, there is not a simple definition of what 'love' really is," she says. "If there were, I would not have any songs to write."

Susan Saint James

Ever since she built her acting career on six thespian lessons, and then (as legend has it) barged into a Hollywood casting office demanding to be given a reading, this offbeat former model has not only stayed in TV roles, but has garnered an Emmy and nominations for at least seven others. Born Susie Jane Miller in the City of Angels on 14 August 1946, she grew up in Rockford, Ill., where her dad was chairman of Testor Corp., company that makes model planes. She spent one high-school year in a French exchange-student program, "came back wriggling like Brigitte Bardot," and shortly thereafter altered her parents' agenda for her education at Connecticut College for Women by splitting after a week and hightailing it for New York with the French-inspired name Susan Saint James. Soon she left for Paris, where she modeled and "goferred" in Charles Aznavour's entourage, then in 1966 she headed for Hollywood, where her spunk impressed a Universal Studios veep. One of the last of the seven-year contract actors, she played in a TV movie that became the "Name of the Game" series, co-starring Gene Barry, Tony Franciosa, and Robert Stack. After winning an Emmy in her first season, she stayed with the show for its duration, then landed the part of Rock Hudson's wacky spouse in another NBC series, "McMillan & Wife," on the air from 1971-76. After some uninspired movies and some memorable comedic and dramatic video flicks, she returned regularly to the tube in 1984 in the smash-hit sitcom "Kate & Allie," opposite comedienne Jane Curtin.

The thrice-married, former vegetarian is now ensconced in matrimony and motherhood with erstwhile "Saturday Night Live" producer Dick Ebersol and three little ones. She even narrated the children's story *Peter and the Wolf* at two New York Pops concerts conducted by Skitch Henderson in 1988. Once an anti-Vietnam War activist, she says, "Having kids de-radicalizes you a bit. I had a falling out with the Catholic Church in my radical days, but now I realize I can do more being active in the church. Plus it's the only way I know to pray. That gives a deeper sense to life."

Yves Saint Laurent

"'The magnificent and pitiful family of the hypersensitive,' Proust wrote, 'is the salt of the earth. It is they, not the others, who have founded religions and produced masterpieces.' That family is my second family, and whatever I have achieved that might approach a masterpiece I owe to that affiliation." So said the "King of Couture," whom Diana Vreeland, at the time of the retrospective exhibition she organized at the Costume Institute at New York's Metropolitan Museum in 1983, called "the Pied Piper of fashion—whatever he does, women of all ages, from all over the world, follow." Saint Laurent was referring to his shyness, an affliction so severe it made his school years hell and later caused him to have a nervous breakdown and to be discharged from the French Army. But he was already famous by then. Christian Dior called him "my Dauphin," and when Dior died in 1957, the frail, gangling 21-year-old was chosen to take over his $20-million-a-year House of Dior designing empire. Saint Laurent made headlines in 1958 as the daring young man with the flying trapeze, but it all came to a halt when he was drafted in 1960.

"At the time of my early torment, and later when I lay flattened by drugs, anguish, and fear in a military hospital, I did not perceive of mental suffering as a gift. Nor does it seem so each time I begin a collection, even now, four times a year—each time in anguish of not being up to the expectations of the critics, and, more important, not being equal to the task itself, not being able to create, waiting for three weeks out of four for the click that sets my fantasies in motion toward their appointment with the physical world. It doesn't seem a gift, but I know it is. A gift, or a vaccine. I think creative people react to suffering the way they fight death, making the illusions of immortality we call art."

He was born in Oran, Algeria, 1 August 1936, and headed for Paris at the age of 17. Christian Dior hired him as an assistant soon after his arrival. Although he had ascended to the top of the House of Dior, after his discharge from the army he found himself replaced by Marc Bohan, the welcome mat withdrawn, and nowhere to go but up. Backed by American dollars, he opened his own establishment on the elegant Rue Spontini in 1962 and now designs everything from belts to sable coats. His business empire, fashioned by his partner Pierre Berge, includes a worldwide chain of posh ready-to-wear salons known as Saint Laurent Rive Gauche Boutiques.

Says *W:* "At his best—which is better than anyone—he soars into realms of fantasy that may initially shock, but, on second glance, prove to be sublimely sensible . . . a man who has come to represent what modern style and elegance mean. He has always insisted that clothes be, above all, simply wearable, but he also knows that fashion without fantasy is merely a uniform."

What inspires him? Many things in the past—the Ballet Russe, Proust, Picasso, Mondrian—but mostly, he says, it is his models. "They are the bulls and I am the toreador. Their bodies either live or die when they wear a dress for the first time," he observes. "If the dress isn't good, the body underneath doesn't seem to exist. If the dress is right, the girl finds the exact gesture to signify that it is right, that the style is right." Additional inspiration is provided by lavish residences in Morocco, Deauville, and Paris, each displaying the elegance of days gone by. "My heart has always been divided between the vestals of constancy and the avatars of change." This French national treasure was made a Chevalier of the Legion d'Honneur in March 1985.

Pat Sajak

He's an enigma. He is professional and witty, and can carry on a conversation with ordinary people in a manner that puts them totally at ease. Pat is seen by millions of people every night on his incredibly successful nighttime game show "Wheel of Fortune." When asked about all this fame, he simply replies, "I'm lucky." Pat has been the host of the "Wheel of Fortune" since it's debut in 1982. "I enjoy my work for 'Wheel' very much. It's been a tremendous opportunity for me in so many ways. The contestants are a lot of fun, the staff is terrific and it really is a great game show."

Pat Sajak was born in 1947 in Chicago, Illinois. He attended Columbia College, and from there, began his show biz career as a newscaster for WEDC, a radio station in Chicago. However, in 1968 he was drafted to serve his country in the U.S. Army in Vietnam. From 1968 to 1972 Pat was a disc jockey with Armed Forces Vietnam in Saigon. Following his discharge, he moved to Nashville and made the switch to television, working for WSM-TV, where he was the weatherman as well as host of the station's public affairs program. In 1977 he moved to Los Angeles, also working as a weatherman, for KNBC-TV. Later, he was given the position of hosting "The Sunday Show," which was a public affairs program. It was his position as host of "The Sunday Show" which gave him the exposure that caused him to be discovered and land the role of the host of "Wheel of Fortune." Pat attributes the show's phenomenal success to the fact that the viewers at home can play along. He explains, "If you're sitting at home watching, it's a challenge to try and figure out the puzzle. It gives you the feeling of satisfaction if you can get it faster or just get it right. Plus there's that vicarious thrill of winning." In addition to the "Wheel," Pat also hosts the CBS late night talk show "The Pat Sajak Show" which debuted in 1988. He has been seen on several other television shows, including the "Merv Griffin Show," "The Tonight Show," "Late Night with David Letterman," "Hour Magazine," and "Gimme a Break." Extending his talents, Pat has hosted the Macy's Thanksgiving Day Parade and made his film debut in the feature film *Airplane II*.

In his spare time he likes to play tennis and racquetball, and is an avid fan of the Chicago Cubs. Pat resides in Los Angeles and is engaged to marry fashion model Lesly Brown.

J.D. Salinger

His last interview was granted more than thirty-five years ago, in 1953, and that to a 16-year-old for her high-school newspaper. He lives with three watchdogs on his property in tiny Cornish, New Hampshire, where he has built a tunnel entrance to his house. He clearly does not wish to be disturbed. The hermit receives thousands of advances from fans of all ages—please, let me touch you, please rub off on me, they seem to be saying. But nothing. The older flower children were reading him under their desks in the late 1950s and early '60s when they were in high school. What so attracted the young to *Catcher in the Rye* (1951) and his other books, *9 Stories* (1953), *Franny and Zooey* (1961), *Raise High the Roofbeam Carpenters* and *Seymour: An Introduction* (1962), was the curious ethic they proposed—deprecating the phoniness of our great American society as seen through ingenuous eyes, and embracing a faddist interpretation of Zen they helped create. Salinger's use of language—a manner of speaking whose strength has been evidenced in its gradual incorporation into American idiomatic speech—is regularly discussed in English classes nationwide, where his *Catcher* is now required reading.

Born Jerome David Salinger on New Year's Day in 1919 in New York, he suffered through his days at the Valley Forge Military Academy much as Holden Caulfield endured the fictional Pencey. Without graduating from any of them, he attended three colleges including Columbia, where he studied short-story writing with Whit Burnett. In 1937, between colleges, he apprenticed himself to a master pig slaughterer in Bydogoszcz, Poland. Writing since he was 15, his first short story was published by *Story* magazine in 1940. In 1953 he married Claire Douglas, divorced in 1967; they had two children—a daughter Peggy and a son Matthew (an actor).

In 1978 he was harassed by a Canadian police reporter, an ardent fan who wanted to meet him. He came to Cornish and waited in ambush for the writer at the end of his driveway. (Later this writer would sell his report of his encounter with Salinger as a three-part series to the New York *Times*.) Salinger addressed his interloper: "I've gone through this so many times. There's no gracious way to tell you to leave. I'm becoming embittered. The words are a little different each time. People with problems, people needing to communicate, people wanting help for their careers. They've collared me in elevators, on the street, even here. I get stacks of mail and questions every day. But there are no generalizations. I'm not a teacher or a seer. I pose questions a little differently, perhaps. But I don't pretend to know the answers. When I started in this business, I had no idea this was going to happen. In ways, I regret ever having been published. I'm a private person. Why can't my life be my own? I never asked for this and have done absolutely nothing to deserve it."

Harrison Salisbury

Harrison E. Salisbury, one of the most distinguished postwar foreign correspondents for the New York *Times*, realized early on that he "was to be a reporter of events, not a participator in them." Telling the truth, he says, is a difficult business—because truth tends to be inconvenient as well as dangerous. Having mastered the fine art of pulling the truth, or at least shades of it, from the Kremlin and the intrigue that surrounds it, Salisbury also learned a thing or two about power. Leaving the Moscow bureau in 1954 after five long years, he returned to New York and quickly shot up the *Times* career ladder. Once when a subordinate leaned down to pick up a paper that had dropped from his desk, Salisbury snapped: "When I drop a piece of paper to the floor, that's where I want it to stay."

Born 14 November 1908 in Minneapolis, he became a reporter for the Minneapolis *Journal* in college (U. of Minnesota). He then joined United Press International, which sent him to London to cover World War II. In 1964 he returned stateside and married Charlotte Rand. He has two sons from his first marriage (to Mary Hollis).

Salisbury has been a newsman all his adult life, and became an author in 1946 (*Russia on the Way*). This account of his extensive travels through the Soviet Union depicted life in regions long sealed off to Western journalists, including Siberia, the sub-Arctic, Central Asia, and the Ukraine. His *Times* series, "Russia Re-Viewed," won the 1955 Pulitzer Prize. Other books include *A Journey for Our Times*, an autobiography, and *Without Fear or Favor: An Uncompromising Look at the New York Times*. His most recent writings are *The Long March* (1985), *A Time of Change* (1988) and *The Great Black Dragon Fire* (1989). His numerous volumes on the Soviet Union has established him as dean of Kremlin-watchers. In recent years, though, he has widened his sights. After retiring from the New York *Times*, where he has nurtured the Op Ed page from the concept stage into a nationwide forum of informed opinion, he has concentrated on his book writing. He explored China in *To Peking and Beyond;* his homeland in *Travels around America;* his own life story, and the history of the *Times*. Former colleagues describe him as "ambitious"; and indeed, "ambition" is the reason he gives to explain why his first marriage crumbled.

Jonas Salk

"The time has arrived in which we have to realize that we are all parts of a single organism and develop some new kinds of responses and relationships," says this medical pioneer who developed the first polio vaccine in 1955. At that time, he regarded research as "one way to get at reasonableness and logic." Since his heralded discovery, Salk has illustrated his more catholic interests not only through the research he directs at the Salk Institute for Biological Studies, but also through his philosophical explorations of human genetics, scientific ethics, and the evolution of man. Over the past decade, his four books have established him as a highly original and insightful thinker.

Born 28 October 1914 in New York City, Jonas Edward Salk, a garment worker's son, was headed early for the law. Switching to medicine, he discovered an improved influenza vaccine by 1946 and began research on polio in 1949. "It was just another job to be done in a field in which I was interested," he has said. Later, when asked who owned the vaccine's patent, he answered quietly, "The people.... Could you patent the sun?" By 1963, on land donated by the people of San Diego and with the assistance of the National Foundation–March of Dimes, the research center was completed. Now, under Salk's direction, it is a leading center of research in immunology and cellular and molecular biology, staffed by over 400 scientists and technicians. For the last 15 years, a major portion of his time has been devoted to a philosophy of ideas based on biological principles ("a bill of responsibility written on behalf of the species as well as for the individual") which are the focus of his four books: *Man Unfolding; the Survival of the Wisest; World Population and Human Values: A New Reality* and *Anatomy of Reality: Merging of Intuition and Reason.*

Divorced from his first wife (three sons), he married Francoise Gilot (longtime mistress of Pablo Picasso) in 1970, and they live near San Diego on a cliff 600 feet above the Pacific.

Susan Sarandon

She works "from the gut. I've never learned to make this vein here pop out or to cry on cue. But, you know, in film you've only got to get it right once and you've got all day to do it.... Anybody can act. It's no big deal." The raven-haired actress with the Bette Davis eyes is somewhat of an anomaly in an industry beseiged with acting schools: She is a natural. Having never taken an acting lesson, she was cast in her first major film role less than a week after arriving in New York.

She was born Susan Tomaling on 4 October 1946, the oldest of nine children in a Catholic family in Edison, N.J. She stumbled into acting quite by accident when, as a freshman in college, her husband's agent offered to sign her. She debuted in the 1970 movie *Joe*. Her marriage to actor Chris Sarandon eventually failed but the acting bug remained. She was cast as Brooke Shields's prostitute mother in *Pretty Baby,* directed by Louis Malle, with whom she became romantically involved. Her performance in Malle's 1982 *Atlantic City* drew critical acclaim. Some of her less memorable film work has included the soapy disaster *The Other Side of Midnight, King of the Gypsies,* and *The Great Waldo Pepper.* Picking roles for their potential to "stretch" her talents, rather than to advance her career, she has appeared in some offbeat vehicles. "One of the reasons I've done the roles that I've done is that they freighten me so much." She appeared in the cultish *Rocky Horror Picture Show,* the grim off-Broadway play about rape and revenge, *Extremities,* and the movie *The Hunger,* in which she played a graphic love scene with Catherine Deneuve. She starred in one of 1985's more popular films, *Compromising Positions,* followed by *The Witches of Eastwick* (1987), *Sweetheart's Dance* (1988), *Bull Durham* (1988), *The January Man* (1988), *A Dry White Season* (1989) and *Erik the Viking* (1989).

Off-screen, Sarandon is active in the movement for a nuclear freeze and is outspoken in her liberally oriented political views. In 1985 she gave birth to a daughter fathered by Italian screenwriter Franco Amurri, and in 1989 she had a son with actor Tim Robbins.

Vidal Sassoon

It's been more than two decades since he flipped the wigs of the fashion and cosmetics industry with his new-wave hairstyles such as the "Asymmetric" (one side short, one side long), the "Five Point" (two points at the sides, three at the back), the "Eye-Eye" (hair over one eye), and the "Greek Goddess" (short permanent-waved all-over curls). America gasped when he was flown over from London and paid $5,000 to cut Mia Farrow's hair for her part in *Rosemary's Baby*. But soon America was "Sassooning" itself and the hairdresser had become an empire of beauty parlors, beauty schools, hair care products for men and women, and clothing. (Not those trendy Sasson jeans, the "Ooh-la-la" ones that Vidal sued for misappropriation of his name. The jeans company countersued. Both won, or lost, depending on your point of view. Vidal must call all his products "Vidal Sassoon." The jeanery must pronounce its name "Sassohn.")

"I became a businessman to survive. There's no money in being a hairdresser. Products are where the money is," says this son of a Jewish carpet salesman from Istanbul who spent eight years during the Depression in a London orphanage. Born 17 January 1928, he dropped out of school at age 14 and went to work in a beauty parlor at his mum's suggestion. "Her feeling was that I didn't have the intelligence to pick a trade myself." He fought for the Israel Army in its 1948 War of Independence, then returned to London where he opened his first shop on Bond Street. He made his first fashion headline when he gave designer Mary Quant a haircut with the back cut short and the sides left long, and her models introduced the cut with her 1963 collection. In May of 1983 Richardson-Vicks bought Vidal Sassoon, Inc. Today he is spokesman for the company. He travels around the globe and is the principal stockholder. The company grosses $100 million-plus annually, so his take makes him not the sort of man most women would want to wash out of their hair. Nevertheless, he and his wife Beverly split in 1980, but they remain congenial and share custody of their four children. Politically ambitious, he is also the founder and active president of the Vidal Sassoon Foundation. He is the co-author of *A Year of Beauty and Health*, written in 1976 with Beverly.

Telly Savalas

Bald-headed and fleshy-faced, his appeal was the surprise of the 1970s. Ugly was he? Only for a few weeks when his super-hit TV series "Kojak" debuted in 1973. As soon as the world came around to his gruffer-than-thou-side, the once-ugly became the decidedly sexy. "This street-smart tough egg also has a soft and thoughtful center," wrote *Time*. "'Kojak' shows New York City in all its roach and racketeering misery. The directors neatly capture the alternately plodding and explosive rhythm of policework. But ultimately the show is a one-man operation." It was Telly Savalas's idea to suck on lollipops while trying to give up cigars, offer the suckers to the local stooges, and wear three-piece suits. "Men watch Kojak," said *Time*, "because they see a guy they'd like to be. And women see a guy who's strong but still wounded a little bit, tough but not too tough, full of compassion."

Born Aristotles Savalas in Garden City, Long Island, New York, on 21 January in years that have been reported anywhere from 1921 to 1927, his father was, by Telly's description, "a millionaire five times and a pauper six," and his mother was a former Miss Greece. After military service in World War II, Telly got his B.A. in psychology and was trying to get into medical school when, through his brother, he got a job writing for the U.S. Department of State Information Services. He eventually was promoted to assistant director for the Near East, South Asia and Africa. In 1955 he left government service and got a job as ABC-TV's news and special events senior director. It was while he was teaching a night course that an agent asked him if he could find someone with a European accent to play an old judge in the television play "Bring Home a Baby." Savalas auditioned and got the part. He appeared on several TV series and in movies, including *Bird Man of Alcatraz*, for which he was nominated for a Best Supporting Actor Academy Award in 1962. He first shaved his head to play Pontius Pilate in 1965's *The Greatest Story Ever Told* and kept it for *The Dirty Dozen* in 1967. Based on the success of a TV-movie with "Kojak" in 1984, Savalas returned to playing the cop in "The Belarius File" in 1985; the "Kojak" series was resurrected in 1989 on ABC. He has been divorced three times, and married his fourth wife, Julie Hovland, in 1985. The couple added two more children (Christian and Ariana) to his four kids from previous marriages.

Diane Sawyer

The former White House press aide and confidante of Richard Nixon raised the hackles of news reporting heavyweights when she made the uneasy transition to broadcast journalism. But the creamy and cerebral Sawyer soon earned a reputation for skilled reporting, as well as ratings credibility, as co-anchor of the "CBS Morning News." Her sunny disposition and forceful delivery helped edge the network's offering closer to its rivals in the Neilsen race for morning viewers. "This job is so seductive. It really is the decathlon of news. When you're finished each morning, you feel like you deserve to be hosed down and given a gold medal." Teamed initially with Charles Kuralt on the "CBS Morning News" show, she survived a rehaul of the program and was matched with Bill Kurtis until the fall of 1984, when she left the show to become the first woman on "60 Minutes." She made headlines herself in 1989 when she signed a multi-year (high salary) contract with ABC-TV News. Sawyer currently co-hosts "Prime Time Live" with Sam Donaldson which premiered in the Fall 1989.

The daughter of a Kentucky judge and a schoolteacher, Sawyer, born 22 December 1945, was a model student. "I was terribly extracurricular. I lived for overextension, and there are those who think I still do. I edited the yearbook, did a little basketball, was a junior varsity cheerleader, joined every club, all of which I took inordinately seriously." She won the America's Junior Miss contest in 1963. After graduation from Wellesley College she worked as a reporter in her native Louisville before family connections landed her a job on the staff of Presidential Press Secretary Ron Ziegler. After Nixon's resignation, Sawyer went to San Clemente to help the former president with his memoirs. She later said she did so out of "loyalty" to a man who had boosted her career and given her a "ringside seat" for a turbulent time in history. Her move to CBS in 1978 as a Washington correspondent was met with strenuous objections from the likes of Dan Rather, who cited her background as a potential compromise of journalistic objectivity. Undaunted, she mastered grubby assignments nobody wanted and worked feverishly during the Iranian hostage crisis, eventually converting Rather and convincing others at CBS she had the right stuff.

On the personal side, Sawyer married producer/director Mike Nichols on 29 April 1988.

John Sayles

"If storytelling has a positive function it's to put us in touch with other people's lives, to help us connect and draw strength or knowledge from people we'll never meet, to help us see beyond our experiences." Director/screenwriter and occasional actor John Sayles has his own thoughts on filmmaking. One of his recent cinematic products, *Eight Men Out* (1988) is the story of the 1919 World Series, when eight members of the Chicago White Sox connived with gamblers to throw the Series to the Cincinnati Reds. Sayles not only wrote and directed the picture, but he also appeared in it as the sportswriter Ring Lardner, who covered the White Sox for years before the success of his *You Know Me Al* stories made him famous. Sayles has also been represented on the big screen with *Matewan*, his 1987 saga of a 1920 coal miners' strike in Matewan, West Virginia. He started his film career in 1978, with only $60,000 (money he earned from screenwriting), with *Return of the Secaucus Seven*, the story of a reunion of a group of sixties student activists. The picture was an unexpected success, won the Best Screenplay Award from the Los Angeles Screen Critics and gained international distribution after being shown at film festivals. Later Sayles pics were *Lianna* (1983); *Baby, It's You* (1983); and *The Brother From Another Planet* (1984).

Born 28 September 1950 in Schenectady, NY. Sayles found his calling as a scribbler while a student at ivy-bordered Williams College in Massachusetts, where he majored in "intramural sports and foreign movies." By the time he graduated in 1972 he had a 1,000-page novel stashed in a suitcase. He rambled around the East Coast finding bits and pieces for jobs, and for the next two years he received only rejections from magazines. Luck changed with a short story called *1—80 Nebraska, M. 490—M.205*. Published in the *Atlantic Monthly*, it won an O. Henry Short Story Award and set fire to Sayles's ambitions and talent. He expanded a short story, *Men*, into the novel *Pride of the Bimbos* (1975) and the critics rejoiced. He won another O. Henry Short Story Award in 1977 and his novel of that year, *Union Dues*, won a National Book Award nomination and led him to Hollywood, where he was hired by Roger Corman to doctor the script for the 1978 sci-fi thriller *Piranha*. "My whole job," says Sayles, "was to contrive a reason why people, once they hear there are piranhas in the river, don't just stay out of the river but end up getting eaten."

"Writing isn't easy, but it sure beats working for a living," he's been known to say. For all of his output he won a genius grant from the MacArthur Foundation—$30,000 a year, tax-free, for five years, which ended in 1988. In 1985, further expanding his horizons, he created Bruce Springsteen's "Glory Days" video. More of his films include *Wild Thing* (1987) and *Breaking In* (1989). The filmmaker has appeared in cameo roles in all but one of his earlier films and, on stage, picked up good reviews for his portrayal of Tom in *The Glass Menagerie* in a production in Williamstown co-starring Joanne Woodward and Karen Allen. Sayles has also published a book about his moviemaking philosophy entitled, *Thinking in Pictures: The Making of the Movie 'Matewan.'*

An atypical celebrity, he lives in Hoboken, New Jersey, with his companion since college, Maggie Renzi, and rides the bus into Manhattan where he keeps an office.

Arnold Scaasi

"I believe I'm the best dressmaker in the United States today," Arnold Scaasi modestly said in a 1984 interview. He added, "I'm also the only made-to-order designer of clothes across the country." Scaasi, whose exotic name is simply Isaacs spelled backwards, was born 8 May circa 1930 in Montreal, where his father was a well-to-do furrier. After finishing high school and college, with a brief stay in New York between, he took off for Australia, where he lived with his aunt. She was a social Auntie Mame type, and the glitter of feathers and furs that she wore had a lasting effect on his career. Returning to Montreal, he spent a year in a school of fashion design, and then went to Paris, where he worked for some of the top designers. It was Dior who advised him, "Go back to America. The future of fashion is there." Scaasi took his advice and for several years worked on Seventh Avenue. Finally, encouraged by Charles James (one of America's famous fashion designers of pre-World War II) and by Norman Norell, he opened his own firm in 1964.

In the beginning Scaasi tried to be both made-to-order and ready-to-wear but soon found that he preferred to do custom work with embroideries, laces and fabrics he bought in France, Italy and Switzerland. He also enjoyed the contact with his clients, many of whom became his friends. "When a designer finds a look that he feels is right for him and his clients, he should keep it and not keep changing." No matter whether Milan goes mannish or the Paris clothes look like Japanese kites, Scaasi has kept his word. The menu is always basically the same with different fabrics and colors but always based on glamor, glitter and sex.

Francesco Scavullo

Hasselblad in hand, photographing yet another model or movie star, he is fashion's preeminent photographer, the man behind hundreds of *Vogue* and *Cosmo* covers, not to mention three books of his own: *Scavullo on Beauty, Scavullo on Men, Scavullo Women*. So divinely adept at making women beautiful in photographs ("He could make a warthog look like Victoria Principal"), his talents command a minimum fee of $6,500 per session for a black and white "shoot."

The court painter of our time was born 16 January 1929 to a comfortable Staten Island family that made its money from a banqueting and cooking utensil business, and began his career by shooting teenagers for *Seventeen* in the early '50s ("I got into trouble with the editors.... I used Vaseline on their lips instead of lipstick, and I loved straight hair. Toni home permanents were a major advertiser, and the editors were afraid Toni would pull out...."). A renegade who was mold-breaking even then, Scavullo doesn't like to talk about correct exposure, *f*-stops and all that. "It's too boring... I don't know anything about exposures, I always use two assistants." On the subject of his past he says, "Being raised a Roman Catholic and yet thinking everyone should be free to do what they want creates problems. Being the only one of five children who didn't go into the hotel business creates problems. When I told my father I was going to be a photographer, he didn't speak to me anymore. But the moment he saw my pictures in *Seventeen* magazine he said, 'What can I do for you?' And so he bought me my house." He continues, "I think people like the pictures I take of them. It's like gathering moss. The models liked what I did for them and now I do personalities. When I did Helen Reddy—I got all these stars. Like when I did Janis Joplin—she was fabulous! Beautiful! I didn't see her bad skin, the chin, anything. I saw something beautiful in that girl! Vulnerable!... Lester Persky, the producer of *Equus*, he calls me one Sunday, and wants me to do a picture of him for the New York *Times*. Well I didn't have a camera—'No Camera?!?' It was a Sunday. I never carry a camera." Topical shift to marriage. "Yes, I was married once. I married a model, but we were divorced after four years. You know, you can't be a photographer and be married. I'm always looking for The New Girl.... You know I once said that with men—well I photograph men standing up—and I do it in 15 minutes. But women—I put them on the floor. It takes the whole afternoon. And I kneel."

William Donald Schaefer

"He had taken the city into him. He was its flesh, its incarnation, its own much-wounded ego. It was his life, so the city must have its life in him." This reverential plaudit from a 1984 *Esquire* article is among many bestowed upon the man whom George Will called "the best [mayor] in America." William Donald Schaefer has been called "the genius mayor" by Howard Cosell, and his accomplishments and boosts to the city of Baltimore are numerous. "This point is," said *Esquire*, "it's his city hall... he rebuilt it... it's his highway system: he built five interstates after five mayors before him couldn't manage a mile apiece. It's his subway: he got the money when there was no money.... It's his homesteading: he sold the houses and shops for a dollar apiece after they'd sat abondoned.... It's his aquarium, his world trade center, his symphony hall, his convention center, his half dozen new hotels, his millions of square feet of office space...."

Neither talker nor charmer, Schaefer is sometimes ruthless in his quest to make Baltimore the best. But, if results are the name of the game, Schaefer plays to win—he has made Baltimore his life in his obsessive pursuit to transform it into "the city that works."

Baltimore-born on 2 November 1921, Schaefer is the son of William Henry and Tululu Irene Schaefer (Schaefer lived with his mother until her death in 1984). He began his career—after three years in the United States Army—as a lawyer and was elected to the Baltimore City Council in 1955. (In 1955 Schaefer was chairman of the Ways and Means Committee.) From 1959-1967 he served as vice president of the City Council; chairman, Ways and Means Committee; and chairman, Judiciary Committee. In 1967 he was elected president of the City Council, and in 1971 was elected mayor of the city of Baltimore. He was re-elected in 1975, 1979 and 1983. Amidst the chaotic, frenzied pace, Schaefer finds time for his only hobbies—making candles and nurturing African violets. Unmarried, his constant close companion is Hilda Mae Snoops.

Roy Scheider

"There are, I think, three essential attributes every actor should have," says the actor whose parts in *The French Connection* and *Jaws* have made him a household name. "One is intelligence, but not too much; just enough to

Charles Schulz — CELEBRITY REGISTER 1990

make good choices. The audience wants to see the actor's emotions, not his intellect. Second, is a certain physical grace, regardless of character, and third, an enormous child-like belief in the 'make-believe.' To be all those different people, to live out all those different lifetimes is a little like being God. You may even choreograph your own death many times."

Born 10 November 1935, this half-Irish, half-German Protestant never thought he'd have a life on stage or in films. Between the Depression and World War II his father sold gasoline and ran a service station. Rheumatic fever attacks at age six, ten and fifteen kept him apart from children his age. An "enormously fat" teenager, he was forbidden to play sports and he daydreamed about "being somebody else . . . I started to read . . . all my life writers have been my real heroes." As soon as he could after leaving his sickbed, Scheider started to swim every day, played baseball and even entered the New Jersey Diamond Gloves as an amateur welterweight in 1951. After graduation from Pennsylvania's Franklin and Marshall College and three years in the air force, he began his career in regional and Off-Broadway theater in shows such as *Sergeant Musgrove's Dance* and *The Alchemist*. (In 1968 he won an Obie Award for his performance in *Stephen D*. Later, in 1980, he won the Drama League of New York award for his performance on Broadway in Harold Pinter's *Betrayal*.)

Scheider has appeared in many films, some of which have been among the highest-earning pictures in Hollywood. His screen credits include *Klute, The French Connection, Jaws I* and *Jaws II, Blue Thunder, Marathon Man, All That Jazz, Across the River and into the Trees, Mismatch, Night Game* and *Listen To Me*. He beat out Edward Asner and Richard Burton to play the outspoken newspaper publisher Jacobo Timerman in the television movie based on Timerman's memoir *Prisoner Without a Name, Cell without a Number* in 1983.

Although married to his wife Cynthia for more than 20 years (one daughter, Maximillia), they recently divorced, and he took up with Brenda King. Scheider is a part-owner of Joe Allen's restaurants in Paris and L.A., and he admits liking to drop in occasionally to see who's around. "That way," he quips, "I know who my friends are." Scheider also finds himself more involved politically now than he was in the early 1970s. "I don't think it's because Roy Scheider has become politically conscious. It's because Roy Scheider, like most citizens in this country, has been forced to take a look at [the] issues."

Charles Schulz

He is famous for having created the popular comic strip *Peanuts* which is read by more than one hundred million people daily in some two thousand newspapers in thirty-four countries. His cast of cartoon characters—Charlie Brown, Lucy, Schroeder, Linus, Peppermint Patty, and Snoopy—will celebrate their fortieth anniversary in 1990. They are popular folk heroes whose animated antics inspire a seemingly endless spate of profitable spin-offs: stationery, sweatshirts, ashtrays, a Broadway play, and books, books, books (two hundred million volumes published). The *Peanuts* characters have appeared on network television since 1965, the first special being "A Charlie Brown Christmas" which earned Schulz an Emmy, as did "A Charlie Brown Thanksgiving" in 1973. There have also been feature films, the first of which, *A Boy Named Charlie Brown*, received an Oscar nomination in 1969. "I don't mind how the *Peanuts* idea is used," Schulz has said, "as long as I feel it has come directly from my head." Schulz regards Charlie Brown as "a victim of his own weaknesses. . . . He's wishy-washy—but that doesn't mean I don't like him." Lucy, Schulz says, is "not as smart as she thinks she is." Beneath her facade "there's something tender, but perhaps if you scratched deeper, you'd find she's even worse than she seems."

Born 26 November 1922 in Minneapolis, Charles Monroe Schulz was nicknamed "Sparky," after the Barney Google comic-strip horse, flunked every subject in the eighth grade plus four more in high school, and always wanted to draw cartoons, though "there were no artists in the family," only "a lot of funny people." Schultz has won many awards: the coveted Reuben Award (comic art's highest honor), the International Cartoonist of the Year Award (1978), the Elzie Segar Award, the Lester Patrick Award, et al. Split from Joyce Halverson (five children—one Charles, Jr., no Lucys), Schulz now lives in Northern California with his wife Jeannie.

Stephen Schwartz

"If there was any composer-lyricist who seemed to be leading a new generation to Broadway in the seventies, it was Stephen Schwartz. Until he failed with two shows, everything he did had been a hit. Indeed, for most of 1974 through 1977, his *Godspell*, *Pippin* and *The Magic Show* were running simultaneously." Chronicled in Martin Gottfried's huge glossy text, *Broadway Musicals*, Schwartz has made a place for himself in theatre history. Although this fourth-generation composer/lyricist has been criticized for his simplistic melodies and use of gimmicks, he's managed to pile up two Grammys and three Drama Desk Awards.

Born 6 March 1948 and raised in a non-showbiz household in Roslyn, N.Y., Stephen Schwartz saw his first Broadway musical at six and "knew immediately I was going to be involved in theatre." After classes at Juilliard in composition and piano, he headed for Carnegie Tech's drama school, where he had his original inspiration for *Pippin* in his sophomore year and saw it produced as an undergraduate musical. In New York, after graduation, he failed at first to spark any producer's interest in his musical saga of Charlemagne's son but he did manage an assignment to write the title song for *Butterflies Are Free*. Drawing on the New Testament for *Godspell* (based on the Gospel of St. Matthew) he also found inspiration in the Bible for his collaboration with Leonard Bernstein on the lyrics for his *Mass*, which opened the Kennedy Center in Washington, D.C. in 1971. Is his reliance on the Good Book on these two occasions merely coincidence or something more significant? "Just a coincidence," says Schwartz. He adapted, directed, and contributed four songs to *Working* (1978) and collaborated with composer Charles Strouse on the musical *Rags* (1986). In 1988 he freshened up *Godspell* with some modern jokes for a successful off-Broadway production. His latest project is a production of *The Baker's Wife* (1989) in Ipswich and then on to the West End.

In addition to his Broadway endeavors, he wrote a children's book, *The Perfect Peach*. He lives with his wife, Carole, and their two children in Connecticut. When he's not composing, he likes adding to "his tiny but growing handful of tennis trophies."

Arnold Schwarzenegger

The prize-winning bodybuilder retired from competition in 1975 to pursue a film career, but he left an imprint both on techniques for muscle development and on the public's perception of the sport of body sculpting.

Born 30 July 1947 in Graz, Austria, to a family that stressed physical discipline, Schwarzenegger discovered bodybuilding at age 15 as a means of training for other sports. "I learned up about the body, how it works, how each muscle can be worked. I felt like Leonardo da Vinci; I was a sculptor shaping the body," he has said.

After competing successfully in junior championships in Austria and Europe and completing a year of military service, Schwarzenegger won the National Bodybuilding Association's Mr. Universe professional title for the first time in 1969. He continued on as a judges' favorite, winning more than 10 major championships. In addition to his handsome, Nordic looks and sleek muscle definition, audiences took to his engaging personality. To a public that largely viewed bodybuilding as a freakish exhibition, Schwarzenegger, who was featured in the 1977 bodybuilding documentary *Pumping Iron*, was a disarmingly intelligent spokesman for the sport (or art) of body sculpting. He was known as an aggressive competitor with a penchant for chiding his rivals with a quick wit, but always recognized as a good sportsman. Satisfying a longtime desire to be an actor, he debuted in the 1976 *Stay Hungry* to favorable reviews. His performance in the 1983 *Conan the Barbarian*, a prehistoric fantasy film based on the cartoon character, delighted the cultish devotees of action sci-fi and grossed well, as did *The Terminator* and *Red Sonya*. More films followed, including *Commando* (1985), *Raw Deal* (1986), *Predator* (1986), *The Running Man* (1987), *Red Heat* (1987), *Twins* (1988) and *Total Recall* (1989).

Schwarzenegger has stated a preference for women who are, "dark haired, pretty intelligent, witty, and very charming," an apt description of his wife, Maria Shriver (married 26 April 1986).

Martin Scorsese

"My friends used to say, 'jeez Marty, do you really believe all that stuff the priests tell you?' Well I did believe it, every word of it. I wouldn't touch meat on Friday and I believed I would go to hell if I missed Mass on Sunday. As a matter of fact, I went into the seminary after school, but they threw me out at the end of my first year for rough-housing during prayers. They thought I was a thug." So did the critics after his sleeper hit *Mean Streets* caught on in 1973. It was about the wild side of New York's Little Italy, shown with a violence and realism that was often painful to watch.

Born 17 November 1942, Scorsese grew up a frail and asthmatic youth who was himself a product of Little Italy. As a youngster he fantasized himself a priest but stopped attending Mass when he heard a priest endorse the Vietnam War as a holy cause. Filmmaking became his sacred intention when he was a student at NYU. "There's a great similarity in the way I look at reality and the things I saw in the musicals and the dark 'noir' films of the '40s," he said, "my reality and film reality are interchangeable. They blend." Student films won grants from foundations, and his first big mark was the documentary of the pop-musical happening of the century, *Woodstock*. Other musical films included *Elvis on Tour* and *Medicine Ball Express*, films that followed his *Knocking at My Door* and preceded his first major studio film, *Boxcar Bertha*, starring David Carradine and Barbara Hershey. Ellen Burstyn won an Oscar for her performance in his *Alice Doesn't Live Here Anymore* in 1974. Robert de Niro starred in his shatteringly explicit and critically controversial *Taxi Driver* as well as the bittersweet romance *New York, New York*, which also starred Liza Minnelli. "My light frothy musical turned out to be my most personal film," said Scorsese. "It's about that period in your life when you're about to make it; you know you're talented, but you just don't quite make it for another four or five years. It is that period when your first marriage breaks up, when people who are crazy in love with each other can't live with each other." Scorsese has found Robert de Niro to be his essential representative in his films. The actor won an Academy Award in *Raging Bull* and also starred in *King of Comedy*, a film the director describes as "... an examination of American values, values that give us the wrong goals to go for." Recent films include *After Hours* (1985), the picketed *Last Temptation of Christ* (1988), and *Wise Guy* (1989). He also directed one segment of *New York Stories* (1989).

Scorsese's first three marriages have all ended up on the cutting room floor. First married to Laraine Brennan, he has a daughter Catherine. From his marriage to writer Julia Cameron, he has a daughter Domenica. His 1979 marriage to Isabella Rossellini, daughter of the late actress Ingrid Bergman and the late director Roberto Rossellini, was a very short feature. He married his fourth wife, Barbara DeFina, on 9 February 1985. His autobiography, *Scorsese on Scorsese*, was released in October 1989.

George C. Scott

After his Oscar-winning *Patton* in 1970, and subsequent no-show at what he called the Academy's "annual orgy of self-adulation," he became one of the stage's most memorable Willie Lomans as well as director of the 1975 Broadway revival of *Death of a Salesman*. For a time hailed by critics as among the foremost contemporary actors, George C. Scott, of the no-sell-out persona, says, "Even after being successful... there's dozens... of well-known people in this business who have met less than auspicious ends. You start feeling like a survivor. But I'm only a survivor up to this point; tomorrow I may not be."

Born in Wise, Va., 18 October 1927, he attended the University of Missouri and studied journalism until he "realized acting paid much better. I became an actor to escape my own personality. Acting is the most therapeutic thing in the world. I think all the courage that I may lack personally I have as an actor. There are ruts we get into in life that we don't have the courage to shake ourselves out of." But shake himself out he did. After two unsuccessful marriages (Carolyn Hughes, Patricia Reed), many drunken brawls, and five fractured noses, he "came to" in 1957 when his *Richard III* (with the New York Shakespeare Festival) won sudden acclaim. His "stunningly venomous" performance led to a flurry of offers from Hollywood and TV, which in turn led him to comment, "I'm getting older, mellow, and lovable."

Marriage (and remarriage) to actress Colleen Dewhurst was stormy, but it produced two sons. Scott has three other children from his previous marriages. In late 1972 he married actress Trish Van Devere. Both actresses have played on-stage opposite the man whose face critic Kenneth Tynan describes as resembling "a victorious bottle opener." Scott says, "I make movies for financial reasons and this allows me the luxury of acting on Broadway... (where) I lose money." Thus, for the loot, he's been in *The Hustler* (1961), *Dr. Strangelove* (1964), *Hospital* (1971), *The New Centurions* (1972), *Taps* (1981), and *A Fine Mess* (1986). Indulging his luxury, he's been in *Children of Darkness*, *The Merchant of Venice*, *Desire Under the Elms*, *Present Laughter* (which he also directed) and *The Boys of Autumn*. He appeared in the TV adaptation of Dickens's "A Christmas Carol" in 1984 and starred in the NBC-TV miniseries "Mussolini: The Untold Story" in 1986. He struck out with the 1987 TV series "Mr. President." His latest project was filming *The Exorcist: 1990*.

Willard Scott

If anyone can find the sunny side of acid rain—Willard Scott can. NBC-TV's "Today Show" weatherman and pastry-bellied gadfly made broadcasting history on a hot August morning in 1983, when he appeared on the show dressed as Carmen Miranda in an effort to raise $1,000 for the U.S.O. He then performed an original musical number with two guitarists and later walked on platform shoes to the weather map, where he proceeded to deliver the morning's weather report! That's how Willard's shtick works: outrageous clowning around with a teasing tongue (he's always knocking the competition or his own producer; he flirts with anchor-woman Jane Pauley and bursts Bryant Gumbel's you-heard-it here-first balloon with risable regularity). And a heart as big as his weather map! He announces droughts and country fairs, blizzards and hospital fund raisers, earthquakes and the 100th birthdays and 75th anniversaries of his senior citizen viewers.

He was born 7 March 1934 in Alexandria, Va., and began his career in 1950 at NBC's WRC Radio. A 1955 graduate of American University in Washington, where he majored in philosophy and religion (ah, that explains his happy Buddha approach to weather), he formed, with Ed Walker, one of DC's most popular broadcast teams ever, "The Joy Boys." He did weather on WRC from 1959 through 1972 and joined the "Today Show" in 1980. He was named Washingtonian of the Year by *Washingtonian* magazine in 1979, and 1984 he was voted one of *Playgirl* magazine's 10 sexiest men. Oh sure, you either love him or you hate him, and to love him is reason enough to rise in the morning. The father of two (he is married to the former Mary Dwyer) is the author of a 1980 autobiography. *The Joy of Living, Willard Scott's Down-Home Stories* (1984), *Willard Scott's All-American Cookbook* (1986) and *America Is My Neighborhood* (1987). In 1987 he played the recurring character of Peter Poole on NBC's "The Hogan Family."

Renata Scotto

One of the most highly prized divas of the Metropolitan Opera has been called (by Washington *Post* critic Paul Hume) "the greatest singing actress in the world." Says Renata Scotto, "When I'm onstage I take care to phrase, communicate and give emotion to the audience." The prima donna boasts a repertoire of extraordinary range and diversity (more than sixty roles) and continues to gain the attention and acclaim of the international music world. While plaudits and sparkling critiques are customary, critics have begun to suggest that her voice shows signs of strain and that she is suffering from overexposure. But critics and fans alike delighted in her frank and revealing autobiography, *Scotto/More Than a Diva*.

She was born in Savona, Italy, 24 February 1934, to a policeman and "a real Italian housewife." At four, Scotto sang to her neighbors from her balcony ("Every moment I wanted to be a star, a prima donna . . . ") and began dreaming of an operatic career. At sixteen, after studying voice, piano and violin in Savona, she moved to Milan to further her voice studies. Her first operatic appearance (age twenty) was in the role of Violetta in *La Traviata* (at Milan's Teatro Nuovo), and although it brought Scotto considerable critical acclaim, it literally cost her the roof over her head—"I had been living with nuns at a local convent. They didn't approve of my debut role so I had to move out." After Scotto's La Scala debut *Opera* magazine correctly predicted that she "was destined to go to the first rank of operatic singers." At twenty-three Scotta substituted for Maria Callas (with three days' notice) in Bellini's *La Sonnambula*—"I came to Edinburgh unknown and I left it known all over the world. I had my magic moment." Many more magical moments were to follow and so would a rivalry between Scotto and Callas (Scotto launched a much-publicized attack against Callas for upstaging her at La Scala in 1971). Another onstage flap with Pavarotti (in 1979) caught the attention of the public and the TV cameras when, refusing to take a final bow after Pavarotti had upstaged her in San Francisco with an extra solo bow, Scotto's "petty tantrum" was captured on film by PBS. (She later won an Emmy for that performance.) Television was to play an important role in her rise to stardom—she inaugurated the first "Live from the Met" PBS telecast as Mimi in *La Boheme* (and shed forty pounds after seeing herself in that 1977 telecast) and was the subject of a PBS documentary feature, "Renata Scotto, Prima Donna."

Scotto's hectic touring (London's Covent Garden, the Vienna State Opera, the Paris Opera, Moscow's Boshoi) and recording schedules permit her little time for relaxation, but she makes it clear that her family (husband Lorenzo Anselmi, former concertmaster for the La Scala Orchestra; children, Laura and Filippi) comes first. They have apartments in London, Paris, Italy and New York and a sprawling house in Westchester. America is clearly home for Scotto—"In this country, I found Renata Scotto. Here I am free, like a butterfly without the pin, to work hard every day, to find the best way to express my artistry."

Pete Seeger

A hero of the New Left during the 1960s (as he'd been of the Old Left in the 40s and 50s), singing out at peace rallies and civil-rights demonstrations, he wrote one of the Woodstock generations's favorite songs, "Where Have All the Flowers Gone?" (1961), and bridged the generation gap still again in Arlo Guthrie's 1969 film, *Alice's Restaurant*. Today, he sings for the anti-nuclear movement of the 1980s, for world peace, for jobs for all people, his songs expressing hope for a better world. In concert, Seeger displays his special talent for bringing people together in song, drawing out the entire audience to raise their voices in harmony and become singing partners with him. When not touring the country and world with his songs, the man Carl Sandburg placed "in the first rank of American folk singers" is engaged in ecology and environmental causes—giving a lot of time to the Hudson River *Clearwater*, organizing to clean up the polluted waterway.

A self-styled "banjo picker," Peter Seeger was born in New York City on 3 May 1919, the son of musicologist Charles Seeger (kinfolk Peggy, Penny and Mike also pluck a mean guitar) and violinist Constance Edson Seeger. It wasn't long before Peter picked up the five-string banjo, guitar or any instrument lying around. After two years at Harvard studying sociology and journalism, he dropped out, gave up his career goal of becoming a newspaperman, and turned to studying the likes of Leadbelly and other songsters from the back country. After assisting Alan Lomax for a year at the Library of Congress Archive of Folk Song, Seeger formed the Almanac Singers with, among others, Woody Guthrie, Lee Hays and Millard Lampell. Later, Seeger and Guthrie traveled the country playing union halls and migrant farm worker camps. After serving overseas in the army during World War II, Seeger and Hays formed *People's Songs, Inc.*, forerunner of *Sing Out!* magazine. In 1949, Seeger, Hays, Ronnie Gilbert and Fred Hellerman formed the Weavers, which by 1952 had sold more than 4 million records and helped popularize topical and folk songs. Among their early hits was "Goodnight Irene." They staged an emotional and joy-filled reunion on the stage of Carnegie Hall in 1980 before a house packed with fans old and new.

The Weavers were blacklisted from commercial work during the McCarthy era, and Seeger was held in contempt of Congress but continued singing at schools and colleges. Seeger was blacklisted first for his outspoken opposition to McCarthyism and later because of his refusal in 1955 to answer questions in a House Un-American Activities Committee investigation of communism in entertainment. Convicted in 1961 on 10 counts of contempt of Congress, he was sentenced to a year's imprisonment, but the conviction was unanimously reversed in 1962 by a Federal Court of Appeals. His 17-year performance ban on TV was finally lifted via a much publicized appearance in 1967 on "The Smothers Brothers Comedy Hour." He later went on singing tours with his family, including wife Toshi and three children. In 1968, he wrote "Peace," the theme song of the Mexican Olympic Games.

George Segal

He was one of the first in a new school of film stars who, bereft of movie-idol looks and slightly frumpled in appearance, offered comic appeal and heavy doses of personality. Born in New York City on 13 February 1936, he was raised in suburban N.Y., where he began a fledgling showbiz career at age eight, entertaining at children's parties with a magic act. After graduation from Columbia University, he dabbled in a music career as a banjo player (he still plays a number of club dates each year), formed a nightclub act, and joined an improvisational revue before making his film debut in *The Young Doctors* in 1961. A string of movies followed during the early 1960s, including the 1964 *Invitation to a Gun Fighter* and the 1965 *Ship of Fools*. Segal was praised for his strong performance in *Who's Afraid of Virginia Woolf*, the 1966 screen version of Edward Albee's acclaimed play, and he appeared as Biff, son of Willy Loman, in the 1966 television production of *Death of Salesman*.

Although one of the busiest actors in Hollywood during the late 1960s, it took the 1970 hit comedy *The Owl and the Pussycat*, with Barbra Streisand, to solidify his bankability as a romantic lead. His gentle comedic touch was perfectly matched with Glenda Jackson's prickly performance in *A Touch of Class*, a stylish comedy about an extramarital affair and one of 1973s most popular movies. Segal dallied with Jane Fonda in the satirical *Fun With Dick and Jane* in 1977, with Jacqueline Bisset in *Who is Killing the Great Chefs of Europe?* and with Natalie Wood in 1980 in *The Last Married Couple in America*. Not known for discriminating taste in movie projects, Segal made the tasteless racial satire, *Carbon Copy*, in 1981. His latest efforts include the films *Daddy's Home* (1988) and *All's Fair* (1988), plus the CBS-TV telefilm "Take Five" (1987).

Segal is divorced from former television editor Marion Sobel, whom he married in 1956 (two daughters). In 1984 he married Linda Rogoff, onetime manager of the Pointer Sisters, who presently manages his career.

Tom Selleck

Macho televison and film star Tom Selleck chalked up another "special delivery" male film portrait as Phillip Blackwood in his fifth film, *Her Alibi* in 1989. It was important to Selleck that his latest character (a successful mystery writer, whose wife had abandoned him for a literary reviewer) did not resemble any of his former roles. "Phillip Blackwood is a guy unlike Magnum or Peter Mitchell [his character in *Three Men And A Baby*]. He's a man who has created all the action in his life through his writing. For example, he hasn't been in a fistfight since he was six years old. Now he must face reality with the new woman in his life. During the course of this movie he realizes that he must take action. At times he fails, but that gives the film its conflict."

Born 29 January 1945 in Detroit, Tom Selleck's investment executive father and his mother nurtured "traditional values" in their four children. The whole family had moved to Sherman Oaks some time before his 21st birthday when Tom, like the other siblings, "received a gold Rolex watch for having successfully steered clear of swearing, drinking, and smoking." He won a basketball scholarship to USC (played baseball and football) but on the advice of a drama teacher decided to try modeling. After loads of commercials and bit parts in movies, he found steady work on the soap opera "The Young and the Restless." Selleck's first big break was in the made-for-TV movie "Returning Home," (a remake of the "The Best Years of Our Lives.") Then, a role in "The Rockford Files" and "The Sacketts," a miniseries based on the Louis L'Amour stories. Under contract to Universal Studios, Selleck turned out a bunch of television pilots before being cast as "Magnum, P.I.". . . . The series was an immediate hit, and during its eight-year run, he won an Emmy and a Golden Globe Award for Best Actor. Other television credits include the movies: "Divorce Wars," and "The Shadow Riders." Big Tom's appearances on the "big screen include *High Road to China*, a 1940's jewel thief coerced into espionage in *Lassiter* (1984) and the science-fiction thriller *Runaway*. His film *Three Men And A Baby* in which he co-starred with Ted Danson and Steve Guttenberg, was one of the most popular film comedies of the decade. Upcoming he will star in the character drama *Hard Rain*.

Divorced from his first wife, Selleck married Jillie Mack *(Cats)* in 1987. They have a daugher together—Hannah Margaret Mack Selleck born in 1988—and he has a stepson, Kevin. A restauranteur on-the-side, he owns The Black Orchid in Hawaii with fellow actor Larry Manetti.

Dr. Seuss

"Children are a tough audience," says the creator of such smallfry classics as *How the Grinch Stole Christmas*, *If I Ran the Zoo* and *The Cat in the Hat*. "You can fool an adult audience with persiflage or purple prose, but a kid can tell if you're faking immediately." Since venturing into the field of children's literature, the author-illustrator who calls himself "Dr. Seuss" has published 44 books with sales topping 100 million worldwide. He celebrated his 80th birthday in 1984 with *The Butter Battle Book*, a fable about two superpowers girding for nuclear war. "I don't know if this is an adult book for children or a children's book for adults," he observed. "But unlike most of my other books, this does not have a guaranteed happy ending." In 1987 he published *The Seven Lady Godivas*.

Theodor Seuss Geisel was born 2 March 1904 in Springfield, Mass., and started sketching animals on visits to the local zoo with his father, whose job as city superintendent included the running of it. "I've always drawn," he says, "but I never learned how." After graduating from Dartmouth in 1925, Ted Geisel studied literature at Oxford and first made a living at his drawing board with an ad campaign for an insecticide called Flit. His buggy cartoons, with their "Quick, Henry! The Flit!" slogan, went on for 17 years and attracted as many fans as, years later, his Oscar-winning movie portrait of *Gerald McBoing Boing*. His chief assistant and critic for many years was his wife, Helen; after her death in 1967, he married Audrey Stone. He has no children of his own, but has very firm ideas about writing for them. "They don't want to feel you're trying to push something down their throats. So when I have a moral, I try to tell it sideways." In 1984, the body of his work earned him a special Pulitzer Prize.

Jane Seymour

She was a shy, reserved child whose only concerns were sewing and dancing. Her dream was to be a prima ballerina. But little did she know at that time she would become a well-known star of stage and screen.

She was born Joyce Frankenberg in Hillingdon, Middlesex, England on 15 February 1951. Because of her love for dance, she began taking ballet lessons at the age of two, and made her professional debut with the London Festival Ballet at thirteen in *The Nutcracker Suite*. In 1964, Jane transferred from her high school, Wimbledon High, to the Arts Educational Trust, where she trained in dance, music, and theatre. Her performance in *Cinderella* with the Kirov Ballet in 1967 turned out to be her last because of knee problems. So instead of dancing, Jane turned to acting at sixteen. She took her stage name from the most obscure of Henry VIII's six wives, Jane Seymour. She made her film debut in 1968 in the controversial *Oh! What a Lovely War*. Following her film debut, she decided that the stage would provide the best training, and soon after was cast in everything from Shakespeare to Ibsen to Christie. At the same time she was also performing radio dramas on the BBC. Although her next film role was in *The Only Way* (1968), it was her performance in *Young Winston* (1969) that caught the eye of one of England's most powerful casting directors. Among the roles she landed as a result of her performance include the BBC-TV series "The Onedin Line," and "The Strauss Family." Jane's next film appearance was in the James Bond thriller *Live and Let Die* (1971). To keep from being typecast, she joined the English repertory theatres. Two years later, she landed a role in the film *Sinbad and the Eye of the Tiger* (1973). Three years later she moved to the U.S. to pursue her acting career, and upon the advice of Hollywood producers, she worked diligently to lose her British accent. Soon after, she appeared in *Battlestar Galactica*. Several other films followed including *Somewhere in Time* (1979), *Oh Heavenly Dog* (1979), *Lassiter* (1984), *The Tunnel* (1988), and *Keys to Freedom* (1989). She has also been seen in numerous made for TV movies and miniseries such as "Frankenstein, the True Story" (1972), "Our Mutual Friend" (1975), "Captains and Kings," for which she received an Emmy nomination (1976), "7th Avenue" (1976), "The Awakening Land" (1977), "The Four Feathers" (1977), "Jamaica Inn" (1982), "The Haunting Passion" (1983), "Sun also Rises" (1984), "Crossings" (1986), "East of Eden" for which she won a Golden Globe (1980), "Obsessed with a Married Woman" (1988), "War and Remembrance" (1988), "The Woman He Loved" (1988), "The Richest Man in the World," for which she received an Emmy for Best Supporting Actress (1988), and "Jack the Ripper" (1989). Jane appeared on Broadway for one season in the production of *Amadeus* (1980). This accomplished actress has also written a book entitled *Jane Seymour's Guide to Romantic Living* which was released in 1986.

Jane, her husband David Flynn, (married 18 July 1981) and their two children Katie and Sean, reside in Santa Barbara, California. The couple own an estate just outside of Bath, England.

Gene Shalit

"No one has accused Gene Shalit of being another pretty face," recorded a *Newsweek* reporter. "His lumpy visage is crowned by an aureole of bushy black hair and slashed with quizzical eyebrows and a 5-inch-wide mustache, conjuring up a cross between Jerry Colonna and a startled bullfrog." NBC-TV has stated that market-research data supports the "Colonna/bullfrog" as the most popular film critic in the U.S. Shalit has been on the NBC News' "Today Show" on a permanent basis since January 1973. In addition to his off-the-cuff "Shalitisms," funny and punny, he reviews the arts daily during his "Critic's Corner" segment, and conducts interviews (chortling all the way) with a variety of guests. His movie reviews are syndicated to many stations affiliated with the NBC television network, and he has a daily feature broadcast on the NBC radio network.

Born in New York City in 1932, Shalit grew up in Morristown, N.J. (his father was a pharmacist), where he started his career as editor of his fourth-grade newspaper, *The Forlorn News*. After studying journalism at the University of Illinois, he became a partner in a public relations firm (Scrooge & Marley) specializing in irreverent promotions for magazines. That led to his column in the *Ladies' Home Journal* and, eventually, to book reviews on the "Today Show." Former NBC News president Reuven Frank, who in 1973 added Shalit to "Today's" permanent cast, recalls that network executives expressed "doubts about my sanity. But the fact that he looked different struck me as a plus." The "clown-in-critic's-clothing" knocks himself out delivering his own material and delights in his review "gimmicks" (which he claims he slips in only when he is outraged). He used a fly swatter to demonstrate what he thought about the movie *Superfly*. His review of *The Great Gatsby* consisted of shaking his head (side-to-side) as the "great" in the title was changed to "good," "fair," and "poor." When it finally reached "yecch" he nodded assent. While presumably amusing his millions of viewers, he is infuriating "industryites" who have nicknamed him "Gene Shallow." "Publicists find it difficult to get him to screenings," growled an article in the trades, "an annoyance lessened by his seemingly constitutional inability to remain still and seated at those showings he does elect to attend." When he was asked to narrate *Peter and the Wolf* with the Boston Pops at Tanglewood, *Variety* reported: "Shalit, who likes to be on the scene, also popped up visually in several other portions of the programs, topped by waving an American flag during the closing 'Stars and Stripes Forever.' Arthur Fiedler was also at the concert." The walrus-moustached king-pun of the "Today Show" has commented on his sashaying around New York City getting his ego fan-fed: "Cops in squad cars pull over to say they like me. Little old ladies get out of limousines to shake my hand and black guys in garbage trucks shout, 'Right on.'" His book *Laughing Matters: A Celebration of American Humor* was published in 1987.

William Shatner

"If I do nothing else in life, I've made a contribution. Between 'Star Trek' on TV and in films, if Captain Kirk has become part of the consciousness of a generation, that's not a bad thing to be remembered by," he said after the demise of the sci-fi series. But Shatner was beamed back to earth for more hero doings in the 1981 cop show "T.J. Hooker." His galaxy may have changed, but his swagger remained the same, demonstrating that his machismo traveled well and did not falter with age and a toupee.

William Shatner was born in Montreal on 22 March 1931. Intent on acting from an early age, he ignored his parent's prodding to join the family clothing business and devoted his time to regional theater and repertory companies in Canada. After relocating to New York, he appeared on Broadway and on the "Defenders" and "Studio One," among other leading TV programs. He reportedly turned down the lead on the megahit "Dr. Kildare," deeming series television work to be a trap for a "serious" actor. He changed his mind when offered the helm of the starship *Enterprise*. Intrigued by the program's ambitious concept and scripts, he relocated to Los Angeles, anxious over the fate of such creative fare in the ratings game. The drama about a futuristic exploratory space mission guided by a virile captain and his stolid Vulcan sidekick survived a three-year search for a mainstream audience, and was cancelled in 1969. But the show's youthful and fiercely loyal fans, called "Trekkies," kept the 79 episodes alive in reruns and flocked to the five movies based on the space saga, beginning with the 1979 *Star Trek*, all the way through to *Star Trek V* in 1989. Shatner married actress Marcie Lafferty in 1973. He has three children from an earlier marriage to Gloria Rand. His latest endeavor is his creation of the science-fiction book, *Tekwar* (1989).

Artie Shaw

His hit recordings of "Begin the Beguine," "Dancing in the Dark," "Frenesi," et al, made him a legend-in-his-own-time back in the Big Band Era of the 1940s and are still selling in re-issue albums. In 1983 "Beguine" made a list of "the most played recordings of all time." And that same year, the clarinetist-bandleader answered the often-asked question, "Will Artie Shaw ever play again?" with an ambiguous affirmative. An All-New Artie Shaw Band (under the baton of Massachusetts jazzman Dick Johnson) played a much-publicized debut gig at the old Big Band stomping ground, the Glen Island Casino. Shaw didn't perform himself, but personally supervised the orchestra's revival.

Born Arthur Arshowsky ("I was this strange kind of creature called 'Jew'") 23 May 1910 on New York's lower East Side, he grew up a shy introspective lad who liked to read but forced himself to flunk out of school at 15 so he could start playing sax with a band; by the age of 21, he was an arranger as well. Beginning in 1936, and for the next 18 years (until his retirement from the music biz in 1954), there were a series of Artie Shaw orchestras-small bands (e.g., the celebrated Gramercy Five), swing bands, symphonic bands and, during World War II, a service orchestra which toured the frontline battles areas of the Pacific. Among the vocalists who recorded hits with Shaw musical ensembles were Billie Holiday, Helen Forrest, Tony Pastor, Georgia Gibbs and Hot Lips Page. Known in his heyday as "the intellectual of the swing band maestros," Shaw was famous not only for his music but as an author and often-married man-about-town. Among the most notable of his eight wives were actress Lana Turner, Ava Gardner and Evelyn Keyes; he also wed novelist Kathleen (*Forever Amber*) Windsor. In addition to his 1952 autobiography, *The Trouble with Cinderella*, he penned a novel, *I Love You, I Hate You, Drop Dead*. A special *Documentary on Artie Shaw* film won an Academy Award in 1986.

George Shearing

"George Shearing plays with a lifetime of soul," marvels Canadian bass player Don Thompson, who often accompanies the London-born jazz pianist at live concerts or recording sessions. Shearing is that rarity; the jazz musician who can be at once entertaining and musically provocative, commercially successful yet a favorite of jazz connoisseurs. During the 1950s, his quintet records for Capitol (the standard trio enhanced by guitar and vibes) became best-sellers. The Shearing style has been much imitated: dramatic two-handed chords that suddenly give way to lilting single-note runs, the single notes protracted ever so slightly.

His elegant appearance in tuxedo, dark glasses and carefully coiffed hairstyle very much matches his music. Yet most patrons, savoring his sounds within fancy boites in fashionable neighborhoods, would never suspect that behind Shearing's courtly charm lies a boyhood spent in cockney slums. Born 13 August 1919, he was one of eight children of a Battersea coalman. Finding himself drawn to the piano, he seized an opportunity to study the instrument at the Lincoln Lodge School for the Blind in London. His proficiency won him jobs playing London pubs; he won so many he had to turn down a university scholarship. Many years later, after becoming a U.S. citizen (1956), he took a sabbatical to study classical music.

His best-selling quintet years behind him, the versatile pianist has nevertheless adapted to changing musical tastes. He has recorded with superstar vocalist Mel Torme, in the company of a bassist and drummer, as a solo artist, and, increasingly, as half of a piano duet. "When two musicians agree on the harmony of a ballad, it's wonderful; the music just plays itself," he says modestly. The modesty is misleading; when Marian McPartland—also a naturalized British-American pianist—formed her own record label, one of the first artists she contracted was George Shearing. He is especially popular among other musicians. From his early London days (he once played piano with the Claude Bampton Orchestra, an all-blind band) to today, he has never stopped composing. His hits include "Lullaby of Birdland," the royalties from which alone are enough to keep George and wife, the former Trixie Bayes, well supplied in Twinings tea for many years to come. Adding to his list of wonderful albums, Shearing recorded *An Elegant Evening* with Mel Torme in 1986.

Charlie Sheen

In only three short years, he has been seen in an amazing 18 films, as well as attaining stardom status in the world of show business.

Charlie Sheen was born Carlos Estevez in Los Angeles on 3 September 1965, and grew up in a family of entertainers. His father is the multi-talented actor, Ramon Estevez, a/k/a Martin Sheen, and his brother, actor Emilio Estevez. Charlie made his television debut at age nine in the CBS feature "The Execution of Private Slovik," which starred his father. Eight years later, he made his film debut in *Grizzly II—The Predator*. He has also appeared in *Red Dawn*, *The Boys Next Door*, *Lucas*, *The Wraith*, *Ferris Buehler's Day Off*, *Platoon*, *Three for the Road*, *No Man's Land*, *Never on a Tuesday*, *Eight Men Out*, *Wall Street*, *Johnny Utah*, *Young Guns* with his brother Emilio, *Beverly Hills Brats*, *Backtrack* and *Major League*. He has also been seen on television in the CBS made-for-TV movie "Silence of the Heart," the ABC special "Jack London's California," and on Steven Spielberg's "Amazing Stories." In addition to acting, he is interested in writing, producing, and directing. He has already written, produced and directed a 35mm short entitled "R.P.G. II," as well as a collection of poems entitled "A Piece of My Mind," An avid sports lover, Charlie spent several of his summers at the Mickey Owen Baseball School in Springfield, Missouri. "If I weren't an actor, I would definitely be playing college baseball at this time," says Charlie.

In his spare time Charlie's hobbies include music and filmmaking. Still single, he resides in Malibu, California.

Martin Sheen

Tabbed "an actor's actor" for his powerful and uncompromising performances on film and Broadway, Sheen's experience during the political turmoil of the 1960s led him to tackle portrayals of major political figures, including John Kennedy in a 1983 television production, and John Dean in the TV version of his post-Watergate biography, *Blind Ambition*.

Sheen was born Ramon Estevez in Dayton, Ohio, on 3 August 1940, the seventh child of a poor family of ten. He earned pocket money caddying at a local golf course while dreaming of becoming a pro like his childhood idol, Arnold Palmer. But Sheen was sidetracked into acting when he won first prize—a trip to New York—in a talent show. "I let my hair grow long, listened to a lot of music and was very aware of the times. There were two big influences on me, James Dean and Elvis Presley, and no one who had that kind of effect came along until Bob Dylan." Sheen (he changed his name to avoid ethnic typecasting) first came to critics' attention in the 1964 play *The Subject Was Roses* after an apprenticeship with the Living Theater. He appeared in productions of Joseph Papp's N.Y. Shakespeare Festival, and in episodic television, before making his first feature film, *The Incident*, in 1967, playing a hood who terrorized subway riders. He played a killer in the 1973 low-budget movie *Badlands*, and appeared on TV in "The Execution of Private Slovik."

Surviving a heart attack he suffered during the grueling filming for Francis Ford Coppola's *Apocalypse Now* in 1979, Sheen, who played Robert Kennedy in the 1974 "The Missiles of October," took on the role of John Kennedy in a seven-hour dramatization, "Kennedy." Although the project was dismissed by some as a whitewash, the longtime admirer of the Kennedys said, "He was no less human than any of us, but he was far more courageous. That's really what a hero is. Courage is the first virtue." Recent films include *Wall Street* (1987), *Judgment In Berlin* (1988), *Da* (1988; he was co-executive producer/star) and *Personal Choice* (1989). He also appeared in a Turner Network Television film, "Nightbreaker" (1988). Sheen married his wife, Janet, in 1961, and they have four children. His sons, Emilio Estevez and Charlie Sheen, are popular young actors.

Sidney Sheldon

"In real life, women are not stereotyped, nor are men. So I also write about women who are ruthless, domineering, nymphomaniacs, frigid, and about

Sam Shepard

men who are weak, ruthless, satyriasts and homosexuals. The world is a complex place, filled with complex characters: a feast for writers," Sheldon has said. The versatile writer served up best-selling novels, more than 30 motion pictures, eight Broadway plays, and more than 250 television scripts, spiced to suit the taste of the public if not always the critics.

Born in Chicago on 11 February 1917, Sheldon abandoned a semi-successful career as a composer for a chance to become a writer. In the 1940s, Sheldon penned musical comedies and screenplays, some memorable, many forgettable. His work was often damned by critics for having the substance of cotton candy. *The Bachelor and the Bobby-soxer*, a 1947 Shirley Temple vehicle, won Sheldon an Oscar for best original screenplay. Under contract to MGM, he wrote the 1948 box-office smash *Easter Parade*, and made his directorial debut in 1953 with *Dream Wife*. "The Patty Duke Show," a 1963 sitcom about the adolescent antics of two lookalike cousins (both played by Duke), was his first television product, followed by "I Dream of Jeannie," in 1965. Several of Sheldon's lusty novels have been profitable as melodramatic epic movies. *The Other Side of Midnight*, the 1975 rags-to-riches story of a woman scorned, adapted from his second novel, established his pattern of concurrent book/movie releases, such as *Bloodline*, published in 1978, and the 1980 *Rage of Angels*. He served as executive producer of the NBC miniseries "Rage of Angels: Story Continues" (1987). His latest quick page-turners are *If Tomorrow Comes* (1985), *Windmills of the Gods* (1987) and *The Sands of Time* (1988).

Sheldon married former actress Jorja Curtwright in 1951, and they have a daughter, Mary, who is an actress and writer. Long a supporter of the Freedom to Read foundation, which seeks to sustain constitutional protections for reading choice, Sheldon is a national spokesman for the Coalition for Literacy.

Sam Shepard

Sam Shepard, playwright (*Cowboy Mouth*, 1971; *The Tooth of Crime*, 1972; *Curse of the Starving Class*, 1977; *Buried Child*, *True West* and *Fool for Love*, 1978; and *A Lie of the Mind*, 1985), musician (the Holy Modal Rounders) and actor (*Days of Heaven*, 1978; *Frances*, 1982; *The Right Stuff*, 1983; *Country*, 1984; *The Fever*, 1985; *Crimes of the Heart*, 1986; *Baby Boom*, 1987; and *Steel Magnolias*, 1988), has made his mark on the theatre as one of its most multi-faceted artists and has gained for himself a reputation as "a genuine American original."

Sam Shepard was born in Fort Sheridan, Ill., on 5 November 1943, to Jane and Samuel Shepard. As his father was a career army man, the family moved around when Sam was young, and eventually settled in Duarte, Calif., where Sam finished high school. He started his career in the theater with a church drama group and eventually moved to New York City. While working as a waiter at the Village Gate, he met the founder of Theatre Genesis, and his career in Off-Off-Broadway was launched. Shepard worked in theatres like Cafe La MaMa, the Open Theatre, Cafe Cino and the American Place Theatre. He settled in England for a few years, where his work was well-received. After his return, he went with Bob Dylan on tour with the Rolling Thunder Revue in 1975, and wrote the *Rolling Thunder Logbook* in 1977, an account of the tour. Most of Shepard's themes deal with the displacement and stifling of the artist's creative spirit and many have western/cowboy lead characters. His writing ("his language reminds us of Pinter, his landscape of Beckett") has earned him several Obie awards and the Pulitzer Prize for Drama (*Buried Child*). Screenwriting credits include the 1984 film *Paris, Texas*, and *Far North* (1988). Described as "soft-spoken and unaffected," Shepard, who has received critical praise for his acting (especially in *Frances* and *The Right Stuff*), maintains homes in the Middle West, Marin County, and a farm in Nova Scotia. Shepard has a son, Jesse Mojo, from his marriage to actress O-Lan Johnson Dark. His current companion is his *Frances* and *Country* co-star Jessica Lange; the couple have a son and a daughter.

Nicollette Sheridan

According to *TV Guide*, she "seems to be the quintessential siren of the younger set. Drop-dead gorgeous, with movie-star eyes and legs that last for days, Nicollette recalls Grace Kelly—icy, regal, even aloof. As Paige, Sheridan blends the freshness of youth with the sensibilities of a well-heeled fashion expert; her clothes may be daring for some, but with her panache, she brings it off without a hitch. For the adventurer in all of us, she's the one to watch."

Born 21 November in Sussex, England, Nicollette relocated with her parents to Los Angeles at ten years old. In a ping-pong progression, she first attended the Isabel Buckley Elementary School in California, then she returned to England where she attended the Milford School at Somerset. Setting her sights on acting, she came back to the United States and was signed by New York's Elite Modeling Agency. On a chance meeting while auditioning for a TV commercial, Nicollette caught the eye of the famous photographer Francesco Scavullo who was instrumental in helping her make the February 1984 prestigious spot as cover girl for *Cosmopolitan*. Nicollette remained a model but branched her talents to television and silver screen. Her credits include the telefilm "Agatha Christie's Dead Man's Folly," the T.V. series "Paper Dolls" and the movie *The Sure Thing*. Her biggest claim to fame is playing Paige Matheson on "Knots Landing." As the glamourous daughter of the leading male (played by Kevin Dobson), Paige cuts her weekly appearances in the nighttime soap in a way that has given her a household name. The 1989 cliffhanger saw Paige running deliriously in the rain, frightened about whether her lover (played by William Devane) or a press agent was a murderer.

Nicollette Sheridan is not married and has homes in New York and Los Angeles. She enjoys traveling, painting, reading, and outdoor sports such as motorcycle riding, horseback riding and snow skiing.

Brooke Shields

"Her beauty, her smile, that's what works," says Scavullo. Another observer asks, "Yeah, but where's the tragic flaw?" Joan Rivers, known for her sixth-sense ability to find the pea in the celebrity mattress, turned to Brooke Shields one night having nearly completed her interview with the then dewy teenager on the "Tonight" Show, took her hand and said, in effect, you're a sweet kid, don't blow it. Brooke is the apple that inspires the American pie. She's as sweet as they grow, and now Brooke Shields & Co., Inc., is as rich as she is ripe. The photogenic/model also has a bright head on her shoulders. She graduated from Princeton University in 1987 with a knowledge of French literature. Shields also took many psychology courses to enrich her education. During an interview on "Entertainment Tonight" in 1989, she explained how she is applying the sense of facts she learned in school to future parts. She says her goal is to do "all different roles I can sink my teeth into."

Born 31 May 1965 in New York, her father is six-foot-seven socialite and businessman Frank Shields (whose father was Francis X. Shields, an American tennis champion of the 1930s, and mother the Princess Marina Torlonia of Rome.) Brooke's mom, Teri, came from a poor, devoutly Roman

Catholic family in Newark who worked in the cosmetics field and was a part-time Seventh Avenue model. Teri was managing a Manhattan restaurant when she met Brooke's father; the marriage lasted for less than a year. Teri launched Brooke's career almost inadvertantly one day when fashion photographer and friend "Scavullo called me up," she recalls. "He was sitting in a studio with 300 screaming kids and he had to shoot an Ivory Soap commercial . . . so he asked me to bring Brookie over—he knew her—and we made $35." A few months later, legend has it, Teri was wheeling Brooke down 52nd Street when they came upon Greta Garbo, who stopped to pat the child and admire her.

Brooke became Eileen Ford's very first child model. For three years she was Avedon's model for the Colgate toothpaste ads, and for nearly as long was a lustrous Breck Shampoo girl. (It was also during this time that Teri consented to let Brooke be photographed in some nude "art" photographs which proved embarassing years later when the photographer decided to publish them. A teary Brooke and Teri tried unsuccessfully to get a court order to halt publication.) Brooke made her TV debut sitting in Christopher Plummer's lap in Arthur Miller's "After the Fall" and became a national celebrity in 1977 playing a twelve-year old prostitute in Louis Malle's film *Pretty Baby*, set mostly in a New Oreleans brothel. As Violet, *Time* magazine observed she was "a child model of astounding beauty . . . also a natural actress . . . a volatile mixture of both innocence and carnality . . . she makes the audience feel that anything can happen when she is around." Still, it was risque, and the *Washington Post* wondered what the film would do to its child star: "At the end of *Pretty Baby*, you're more intrigued by what the future holds for Brooke Shields than what it held for Violet." Brooke admitted in *New York* magazine, "Sure, I knew what was going on with the sex scenes and everything in New Orleans. I just didn't say so. I very often pretend I don't know what's going on. It works better for me."

Among her many films and projects have been *The Blue Lagoon* opposite Christopher Atkins, *Endless Love, King of the Gypsies, Tilt, Wanda Nevada, Sahara, Just You and Me Kid,* and *Alice, Sweet Alice* (a/k/a *Communion*). Her latest films are *Brenda Starr* and *Backstreet Strays*. On the little screen, she has appeared in the telefilms "Wet Gold" and "The Diamond Trap." Anyone living on this planet has seen Brooke's face grace the covers of fashion magazines; *Time* deemed her the official "Face of 1980s". The public has a never-ending fascination with her, as her nearly 2,000 pieces of fan mail a week reveal. Will success spoil Miss Shields? It's a bit like asking a bird how she feels about the air. Brooke's always been a star, still she answers the question demurely: "Sometimes it's hard to take in that *Brooke Shields* who everybody seems to be talking about is me. . . ."

Dinah Shore

Her Sunday night "Dinah Shore Show" was a TV staple (and five-time Emmy winner) back in the 1950s and she was TV's reigning Southern songbird for years (earning nine gold records). She resurfaced doing more talking than singing in 1970 on "Dinah's Place," a gabfest on NBC that covered everything from cooking and child rearing to contour sheets. "Dinah" (CBS-TV, 1974), another daily talk-variety show, followed suit. In 1989 she was at it again with "A Conversation With Dinah" on the TNN cable network.

Be that as it may, for most of Frances ("Fanny") Rose Shore's years (born 1 March 1917 in Winchester, Tenn.) the music came first. "Dinah" (from the time she had her own radio show in Nashville) established her adopted name in New York teaming with another young singer, Frank Sinatra, on radio station WNEW. She cut some records with Xavier Cugat, sang out with radio's Chamber Music Society of Lower Basin Street, and found national popularity during a three-year hitch on Eddie Cantor's weekly program on NBC radio. A World War II favorite at camp shows all over the globe, she had only a so-so film career ("I bombed as a movie star") but found greater glory as the "Mumm-wah" Chevy girl on TV. In the 1960s, she bowed out of her 18-year marriage with George Montgomery, filled her time rearing their two children, appeared in an occasional TV special and engaged in a short-lived marriage to Maurice Smith, all the while playing lots of tennis. In 1971 the sweetly smiling singer-turned-talker became a writer with the book *Someone's in the Kitchen with Dinah.* (Her second book, *The Dinah Shore Cookbook*, was published by Doubleday in 1983.) In 1972 she popped up regularly in the gossip columns as the date of Burt Reynolds, famous then for posing as the first male nude centerfold in *Cosmopolitan*. Dinah has garnered ten Emmys all told and was the first woman to be awarded the Babe Zaharias Award from the Metropolitan Golf Writers Association. She was also the first woman to receive the Silver Hope Chest Award of the Multiple Sclerosis Dinner of Champions for her contributions to sports (the Dinah Shore Open is a top women's golf tournament) and to receive the Entertainer of the Year Award from the All American Collegiate Golf Foundation.

Bobby Short

In May of 1968, on the occasion of his now-historic Town Hall concert with the late legendary Mabel Mercer, the Boston *Globe's* Kevin Kelly (only one of many who traveled in from all coasts for the occasion) gratefully noted that this "jaunty" and "nattily trim" singer-pianist exhibited an "ultra-charm hard to come by in these blaring days of bearded rocks and loud manners." Were the critic to stop by Bobby Short's customary domain of New York's Hotel Carlyle or have an aisle seat at one of Short's many guest appearances with symphony orchestras around the country, he'd be happy to discover that nothing's changed. The debonair performer who sings and plays the supersophisticated songs of Porter, Kern, Gershwin, Weill, Coward, Sondheim et al. as nobody else can is still the unchallenged king of the cafe troubadours. At last count he had some 100,000 lyrical words at his command, and he has enunciated them in all their wit and splendor on innumerable record albums (the latest include: *50 by Bobby Short*, 1986; and *Guess Who's in Town*, 1987) as well as in precincts like Town and Carnegie Halls. Wherever he is, Bobby Short (to quote Rex Reed) "polishes off the sadly fading art of the popular song with the regal aplomb of a dispossessed duke."

Born far from Manhattan's madding crowd in the Midwestern town of Danville, Ill., on 15 September 1926, the bright-eyed, button-nosed Robert Waltrip Short toddled to the family upright and taught himself to play jazz when he was still in Dr. Dentons. He journeyed on the vaudeville circuit as the "Midget King of Swing," returned home to finish high school, and made his adult debut as a singer-pianist at the Chase Hotel in St. Louis in 1944. Hollywood, Paris and New York followed, and by his mid-twenties he was securely established as (in composer Vernon Duke's words) "the Pied Piper of Plushier Saloons." Famous for his prodigious repertoire, he has performed noble service for pop-music lovers by salvaging long-forgotten gems from obscurity and giving them elegant and/or effervescent airings (e.g., "The Motion Picture Ball" and the rowdy Bessie Smith shouter "Gimme a Pigfoot and a Bottle of Beer"). Renowned also for his deep respect for the meaning of a lyric, Bobby confesses that it was not always thus. As a youngster, he says, he invariably began his rendition of "Cocktails for Two" as "In some secluded rondaydoo." Turning to words without music in 1971, he published the autobiographical *Black and White Baby*. A not-yet-written chapter might contain mention of his chichi summer home, Villa Manhattan, in Mougins in the south of France, and the fabled who's-who-of-chicdom parties he throws in his ditto West 57th Street spring-fall-and-winter digs.

Eunice Kennedy Shriver

Second-oldest sister in the primary Kennedy clan, her tough-minded, independent spirit has led some to observe that in many ways, she is the most qualified family member to run for the Oval Office. Reminiscent of her brother Jack and closest to her mother Rose, she is also a wife, mother and very traditional public activist. Considering her background, abilities and eloquence, it is no surprise that in 1976 Senator Edward Kennedy (her youngest brother) stated, "I've declared that I am not supporting any democratic candidate before the convention. But, if my sister Eunice should decide to run, I might have to reconsider." Four months pregnant when JFK was assassinated in 1963 (she was purportedly closer to him than any other member of the tightly knit clan), and despite the fact that brother Robert also was the victim of an assassin, Eunice has remained an unfailing public servant, fervently involved in sociopolitical issues and crusading for legislation (e.g., alternatives to abortion). She enthusiastically supported her husband Sargent Shriver's unsuccessful bid for the 1976 Democratic presidential nomination, proving to be one of his most valuable political assets.

Widely regarded as the most compassionate of the Kennedys, Eunice combines a deep sense of empathy—developed as a child by taking care of her retarded sister Rosemary—with volcanic drive towards "improving the lot of the powerless." Born 10 July 1920, the fifth of Joseph and Rose Kennedy's nine children, she quickly showed what her mother remembers as "particularly marked" feeling for others. In addition to her inherent sensitivity, she also acquired her father's tremendous drive. Always an unconventional woman, as a teenager her idol was Amelia Earhart, whom she admired for her "courage and toughness in a male world, and as an explorer of the unknown." Eunice's own professional career began in 1943 upon receiving a bachelor's degree from Stanford University. Working as a junior staff member of the State Department Special War Problems Division, she subsequently became coordinator of the Justice Department National Conference on the Prevention and Control of Juvenile Delinquency. During this period she lived in Washington and played hostess for JFK, who was in his first term in the House of Representatives (she was also active in his congressional and presidential campaigns, 1948-1960). In 1950, she became a social worker at the Penitentiary for Women in Alderson, West Virginia.

In 1947, a mutual admiration had developed between Eunice and a young *Newsweek* editor named Robert Sargent Shriver, whom she met at a New York party and soon recommended to her father, who hired him to run the Kennedy-owned Chicago Merchandise Mart. They married in 1953. Marriage did not, however, diminish Eunice's drive to improve the lot of the helpless. "I don't so much want to straighten people out as I want to create opportunities for them." She didn't find her true calling until 1963, when she was invited to join the board of the Menninger Foundation dealing with problems of the mentally ill. Alarmed to discover that no government or private organization existed to provide adequate financial aid for research into the development of resources for the retarded, Eunice launched an all-out campaign. With the help of her husband, other family members and sponsorship of the Joseph P. Kennedy, Jr. Foundation (of which she has been executive vice president since 1950), funding began for programs at prominent teaching hospitals affiliated with universities. It was the first time that mental retardation was defined as an important medical research problem worthy of time and effort. She also encouraged JFK to establish the President's Panel on Mental Retardation. As a direct result of work done by the panel, he later signed into law the Mental Retardation Facilities Construction Act of 1963, providing for the first time federal funds to help the nation's six million retarded. Throughout, Eunice acted as a consultant, working persuasively and tirelessly for the program. "Her knowledge of how to get legislation passed is awesome," said one associate. Since directing the Kennedy Foundation's efforts toward mental retardation, she has been responsible for many of its most innovative programs, including the 1968 inception of the Special Olympics, the world's largest sports and recreation program for the mentally retarded, now involving close to a million youngsters internationally. For this work, Eunice received the Medal of Freedom from President Reagan in 1984. Public service activist, model wife and mother (five children), she is what Art Buchwald calls "a get-it-done dame," and what Ethel Kennedy calls "One of the great originals."

Don Shula

"He hates to lose," revealed Mary Shula about her son, who is also the NFL's most consistently winning coach. "When he was eight years old," she continued, "he would play cards with his grandmother. If he lost, he would tear up the cards and hide under the porch." But it took a Miami Dolphins victory in the 1973 Super Bowl, capping an unprecedented NFL season of 17 victories and no losses, to dispel his image as a coach who couldn't win the big one. Even though he'd been named Coach of the Year five times in his first ten years (during which he won more than 100 games), he still said, "You don't like to hear yourself introduced at a banquet as a guy who lost two Super Bowls."

Donald Francis Shula was born on 4 January 1930 in Grand River, Ohio, to an immigrant Hungarian nurseryman and dock worker and a housewife. "As a kid," he recalls,, "I was the one who organized the games—in high school I knew what everyone was supposed to do and I corrected their mistakes." The meticulous mentor was first a player (a defensive back) for John Carroll University who later played for the Browns, the Colts and the Redskins. Admittedly patterning his precisionist approach to football after Paul Brown, he became a college coach, then in 1963 got the head tactician job for the Baltimore Colts. Their 1969 Super Bowl loss to the New York Jets displeased the team's owner, so a year later Shula moved to Miami as head coach and vice president. Said former Dolphin quarterback Bob Griese, "We were ready to go, but needed someone to take us." Shula, an offensive mastermind, took them to regular American Football Conference Eastern division titles behind personnel known as "No-Names" and "Killer Bees." A strong, silent type, he once told Dolphins' owner Joe Robbie, "Yell at me again and I'll knock you on your ass." Rather than test his dare, Robbie eventually made him the highest-paid NFL coach, because in spite of everything—poor draft picks, bad trades, an erratic front office—"Shoes" finds a way to win. With wife Dorothy and their five children, he now basks in Miami sunshine and the glow of unqualified success.

Beverly Sills

"If you want to think of the Met in terms of glamour, then think of the City Opera in terms of adventure," said Beverly Sills in 1979 when she crowned her 25 years as the latter company's reigning coloratura soprano by assuming its directorship. As an opera star she was revolutionary "because I proved that one can have a great career without the Met and in this country, without European approval." From 1979 to 1989 she held the prestigious position of general director of the New York City Opera Company (situated in the New York State Theater across the Lincoln Center plaza from the Metropolitan Opera House).

Beverly Miriam Silverman was born on 25 May 1929 in Brooklyn "with a bubble in her mouth. That was something to do with God," her mother recalled in 1979. "Bubbly" (which was soon to evolve into the present "Bubbles"), after attending another famous coloratura's concert as a preschooler, declared to her mother, "Momma, I want to sing like Lily Pons." Launched in the early '30s on WOR's "Uncle Bob's Rainbow House," Bubbles soon became a regular on "Major Bowes' Capital Family" ("I'm seven years old and I can sing 23 arias"), did one of the first singing commercials (the immortal Rinso White bird call) and by the time she was 15 had mastered 20 operatic roles (under the tutelage of Estelle Liebling, her only vocal coach, beginning in 1936). In 1945, Sills began a full-time singing career as a member of a Gilbert and Sullivan touring company, and a year later was performing leading roles in operettas. After eight auditions for City Opera, she was finally signed and in 1955 made her debut as Rosalinde in *Die Fledermaus*. Three years later her performance as Baby in the New York premiere of *The Ballad of Baby Doe* established her as a soprano to watch. Meanwhile, in 1956 she had married Peter Greenough, the wealthy associate editor of his family-owned Cleveland *Plain Dealer*. When tests proved that their daughter Muffy (born 1959) was deaf and their son Bucky (born 1961) was mentally retarded, it took all of City Opera general manager Julius Rudel's persistence and Greenough's supportiveness to enable Sills to overcome the bitterness and self-pity that drove her initially to declare, "I can't sing anymore."

Throughout the mid-60's, she scored in such roles as Queen of the Night in *The Magic Flute*, all three female leads in *The Tales of Hoffman*, the fiendishly difficult role of Cleopatra in Handel's *Julius Caesar* ("the turning point of my career"), the title role of Massenet's *Manon* and as Lucia in *Lucia di Lammermoor*. "If I were recommending the wonder of New York to a tourist," proclaimed Winthrop Sargeant in the *New Yorker* in 1969, "I would place Beverly Sills at the top of the list—way ahead of such things as the Statue of Liberty and the Empire State Building." There followed conquests of La Scala, Covent Garden, Berlin's Deutsche Opera, the Vienna Opera—and in a long overdue debut at the Met, an 18-minute ovation greeted her performance in April of 1975 as Pamira in Rossini's *Siege of Corinth*. Other outstanding performances were in *The Daughter of the Regiment*, *Lucretia Borgia*, *Anna Bolena* and *Thais*. To close out an Emmy and Grammy-winning career, this 1980 Medal of Freedom awardee appeared in 30 nationwide fund-rising performances topped off by a Lincoln Center gala in 1980 that was televised nationally, thereby giving the diva-turned-director (according to the Los Angeles *Times*) "one last opportunity to kick up her heels, to flash those fabled dimples, to wear improbable gowns with almost absurd assurance, to toy with the creaky banalities of plot and to dip into the melodic riches of the score." In further recognition of her extraordinary contributions to the arts, Sills was a Kennedy Center Honoree in 1985. Her autobiography, *Beverly*, was published in 1987, and she hosted "The Beverly Sills Show" in 1988.

Ron Silver

This accomplished actor has graced us with his presence on the stage as well as on the screen. Although his initial interest was in the field of Chinese studies, he went on to become well known in the field of acting.

He was born Ron Zimelman on 2 July 1946 in New York City. He attended the University of Buffalo, where he received his bachelor's degree, then continued his studies, obtaining a master's in Chinese from St. John's University and the College of Chinese Culture in Taiwan. Upon his return to New York several years later he began his acting training at the Herbert Berghof Studios, the Actors Studio, Uta Hagen and Lee Strassberg. He made his stage debut in *Kaspar* and *Public Insult* in 1971. Several theatre performances followed, including *El Grande de Coca-Cola* (1972), *More Than You Deserve* (1973), *Angel City* (1977), *In the Boom Boom Room* (1979), and on Broadway in *Hurly Burly* (1984-85), *Social Security* (1986), and *Speed the Plow*, with Madonna (1988), which won him both a Tony and a Drama Desk Award. Ron made his television debut in 1976 in the sitcom "Rhoda" as her upstairs neighbor, and remained with the show for two seasons. Other television credits include "The Mac Davis Show," "Hill Street Blues," "Betrayal," and "Billionaire Boys Club." Moving on to film, he appeared in his first film, *Semi-Tough*, in 1977, followed by *The Entity*, *Silkwood*, *Garbo Talks*, *Eat and Run*, *Oh God! You Devil*, and *Blue Steel*.

Ron and his wife, Lynne Miller, have been married since 24 December 1975.

Jean Simmons

The *Great Expectations* (1946) of an 18-year-old dancer who had disliked Shakespeare in school could hardly have included playing Ophelia to Sir Laurence Olivier's *Hamlet* (1948). One reviewer commented, "She has an oblique, individual beauty and a trained dancer's continuous grace. Compared with most of the members of the cast, she is obviously just a talented beginner. But she is the only person in the picture who gives every one of her lines the bloom of poetry and the immediacy of ordinary life." She has received the highest film-acting awards from Italy, Belgium, Switzerland, and Ireland. She was voted Britain's most popular star of 1950 at the age of 21. In the fall of that year she rocketed to Hollywood to launch her American career.

Born Jean Merilyn Simmons on 31 January 1929 in London, she was 14 when she was plucked from dancing school for *Give Us the Moon* (1942). Her first Hollywood film was *Androcles and the Lion* (1952). She has also appeared in *Young Bess*, *The Robe*, *Desiree*, *Guys and Dolls*, *Spartacus* (all in the 1950s), *Elmer Gantry* (1960), *All the Way Home* (1963) and *The Happy Ending* (1969). Divorced from British-born actor Stewart Granger (one daughter), she married film director Richard Brooks (one daughter). Although she has announced retirement on several occasions, the hazel-eyed Ophelia seems unlikely ever to take the plunge. In 1983 she appeared in the televised version of "The Thorn Birds," and in 1988 she was in a miniseries for the Disney Channel, "Great Expectations." On the big screen she starred in the 1988 film *The Old Jest*.

Richard Simmons

Transforming himself from a chubby kid into TV's "Clown Prince of Fitness," the spritely exercise guru knows firsthand that losing weight is no picnic. Simmons dropped over 100 lbs., and in the process gained great compassion for the fat and frumpy. "We have saints for everything, but not a weight saint. That's why I'm here," he explained.

Simmons was born on 12 July 1948 in New Orleans, a city dedicated to fattening food. Despite a constant weight problem—he hit the scales at 200 lbs. by age 15—he became a highly paid actor with over 250 TV commercials to his credit. He learned to diet correctly through extensive research and testing after a crash diet in 1968 left him listless. "I ended up looking like a thin Glad Bag. My hair fell out, my skin dropped, my breath was foul, and my mood matched."

Applying his acquired expertise to free enterprise, he opened an eatery and exercise spa in Beverly Hills in 1975. A devout following among the famous—it became the "in" place to drop a celebrated ton—led to a 1979 featured role on "General Hospital," ABC's popular daytime drama. "The Richard Simmons Show" went into national syndication in 1980, and was picked up by more than 100 markets. As host and entertainment, he was a flurry of body contortions, irreverent truisms about "pigging out," and heapings of positive encouragement delivered affectionately to his predominantly female audience. He led exercises to uplifting music and delivered skits featuring such characters as "the cop from Slob Squad" and "Reverend Pounds, a man of the cloth, the tablecloth," which helped him do the unlikely: make exercise entertaining. Always, while cajoling away the pounds, he avoided using the word "diet," saying, "The first syllable is die. Now is that any way to inspire anyone?" Simmons is the author of many bestsellers, including *The Never Say Diet Book* (1981) and *Reach For Fitness: A Special Book of Exercises for the Physically Challenged* (1986; with a forward by Sylvester Stallone). In 1987 he created a syndicated television show, "Slim Cooking," and in 1989 was busy promoting his line of low-cal salad

387

dressings, "Richard Simmons' Salad Spray." Always on the lookout for unique ways to shed pounds, Simmons invented "Deal-A-Meal." The program utilizes a special video workout entitled "Sweatin' to the Oldies" (includes such hits as "Great Balls of Fire," "It's My Party") combined with good eating habits ruled by a deck of color-coded playing cards.

Phil Simms

He caused quite a stir during the summer of 1989 by holding out for top dollar while his fans held their breath waiting for him to show up to practice. Alas, in mid-August, he accepted a multi-million dollar/multi-year contract. Quoted in the New York *Post* on how he was feeling after his first day back doing drills, the athlete replied, "I had no complaints. I'm happy." Actually, Simms should be ecstatic. He's come a long way since he arrived from itty-bitty Morehead State University in Kentucky (the seventh player taken in the 1979 National Football League draft). He's no longer "Phil who?", but rather the leader of the 1986 Super Bowl Football Giants.

A Kentucky native, Phil Simms was born 3 November 1956. In the beginning, putting on a Giants' uniform had drawbacks. Having been the salvation of a losing college football program, his skills enticed pro scouts from 20 of the NFL's 28 teams for personal visits. When he was drafted by the Giants, it was expected he could help the troubled team. Unfotunately, repeated injuries early on delayed his expected blossoming. Called a confident, "macho" team leader, the six-feet-three, 216 pounder did the only thing he could do under the circumstances; he watched and tried to learn from the sidelines. The vicarious experience of watching other Giants' flingers had a maturing effect on Simms. "Once, I got satisfaction doing things physically. Now I get just as much satisfaction by making the right play, even if I drop off a pass to a back for a 2-yard gain."

The maturity has paid off in gleaming stats; by his sixth year Simms was one of the National Conference's highest yardage-collecting passers with lots of TD's and few interceptions. The Giants offense became in a position to catch up to its vaunted defense, and thus reversed the team's 20 years of mediocrity. In 1987 his book *Simms to McConkey* shared some interesting notes on his athletic ability. Wife Diana and son Christopher David are Simms' most devoted fans at home in New Jersey.

Carly Simon

The singer/songwriter with unrelenting stage fright came out of her shell in the latter part of the 1980's. With a solid track record of hits behind her, Simon emerged as a popular artist on music videos as she received renewed enthusiasm from her present record label, Arista. Clive Davis says, "Carly's magic as an artist has always been an uncommon ability to tap emotions believably, to make every listener feel as though he or she is hearing a point of view that is simultaneously intimate and universal." That appeal shined through during the 1989 Academy Awards show when she excitedly accepted the Oscar for Best Song, "Let the River Run" from *Working Girl*. The sensuous songstress began her career crooning such emotional and insightful ballads as "That's the Way I Always Heard It Should Be" in the early 1970s, and continued on for more than a decade, delivering numerous stylish pop hits about love and contemporary struggles. Her rocky ten-year marriage to singer/songwriter James Taylor, beginning in 1972, provided her with sufficient angst for hit material. She's sung of passion and disappointment (the couple divorced), peaking public interest in her marital woes. Her risque album covers, featuring her tall, lanky figure, tousled hair and provocative features have heightened her popularity.

Born 25 June 1945 to a wealthy, musical family—her father is co-founder of the publishing giant Simon and Schuster—she began singing and composing with her two sisters, Lucy and Joanna (the latter is an opera singer). With only her second major album, *Anticipation*, she received a Grammy Award as best new artist of 1971, and the 1972 durable hit "You're So Vain" (is it about Mick Jagger?) propelled her to superstardom. Taking refuge from publicity on the Cape Cod island of Martha's Vineyard, Simon and Taylor raised two children and largely bucked the tour-behind-the-album theory for commercial success. Simon attributed her reluctance to perform to her stage fright and a desire to maintain a "normal" home environment for her children. She also rejected voice lessons, preferring the untrained, unbridled quality of her natural voice. "Sometimes I wish I had studied voice, because I would have more control and fewer problems with my vocal chords, but I think voice can reduce singers to a common denominator." Recent projects include her score for *Heartburn*, a children's book called *Amy the Dancing Bear*, and the albums *Spoiled Girl, Coming Around Again, Greatest Hits Live* and *City Streets*. She married James Hart on Christmas day in 1987. In her own words, Carly admits, "I am a complicated compound of paradoxes. My life is a jigsaw puzzle where the pieces have been scrambled and I've just started to piece together the outside edges. The inside pieces are still turned on the floor."

John Simon

"The main purpose of criticism is not to make its readers agree, nice as that is, but to make them, by whatever orthodox or unorthodox methods, think," states John Simon, one of the most controversial of the New York theatre and film critics. Even his fellow writers have taken Simon to task for his reviews, but, on the other hand, he has been known to cry when moved by a play.

Born in Subotica, Yugoslavia, 12 May 1925, Simon came to the U.S. in 1941. After securing his A.B. at Harvard in 1946, he proceeded to finish his M.A. in 1948, study in Paris under a Fulbright Fellowship (1949-50) and complete his Ph.D. in 1959. After years of teaching at several universities—including Harvard, MIT and Bard—Simon embarked on his career as a drama critic in 1960 with the *Hudson Review*. He has been represented in the *New Leader, Commonweal* and on WNET-TV. As a film critic, he can be read in *Esquire* and the *National Review*. Since 1968, Simon has been the theatre critic for *New York Magazine*, which has been the outlet for most of his controversy. In recognition of his work, John Simon has been the recipient of the George Jean Nathan Award for Dramatic Criticism (1969-70) and is the author of several books on film. His latest publication is *The Sheep From the Goats: Selected Literary Essays* (1989).

Simon, who lives in New York City, has been known to be quite opinionated, even to the point of devoting an entire column to addressing the criticism leveled at him by his readers. Never one to stifle an opinion, he has also been known to remark about such topics as the lack of beauty in the theatre and the lack of understanding of theatre by his fellow critics.

Neil Simon

"The theme is me. My outlook on life. If you spread it out like a map you can chart my emotional life. More so in the plays than the movies. The films . . . show the little boy side of me." So says "the top money-making playwright of all time," who is also a successful screenwriter. "The plays," he adds, "are all about things that have happened to me, are happening to me, or will happen to me." And they and the movies are nearly all comedies, straight and musical.

Born on Independence Day 1927, in the Bronx, the son of a man who sold piece goods to dress manufacturers, young Neil aspired to a medical career, and so earned the nickname "Doc" by which his close friends still call him. On graduating from high school in 1945 he joined the Army Air Corps, and after being discharged attended New York University for a spell, quitting when CBS radio producer Goodman Ace hired him and his big brother Danny as comedy writers. Danny eventually became a director, but Neil spent the '50s writing material for comics like Phil Silvers, Sid Caesar and Jackie Gleason. Finally, in 1961, his first play, *Come Blow Your Horn*, was produced; it would run on Broadway for two years. In 1962 he adapted a comic novel by Patrick Dennis into a musical, *Little Me*, and the following year his second original play, *Barefoot in the Park*, opened; it was still playing three years later, by which time three more hits of his were also on Broadway: *Sweet Charity*, *The Star-Spangled Girl* and his biggest hit of all, *The Odd Couple*. Incidentally, *Barefoot* and *The Odd Couple* were just the first of a string of his plays to be transferred to the screen—with screenplays by you know who. (He has also authored several *original* screenplays.) Simon's roster of hits—plays, movies, and both—continues to lengthen. It includes *Plaza Suite* (1968), *The Last of the Red Hot Lovers* (1969), *The Prisoner of Second Avenue* (1971, "about an uncle of mine who couldn't get a job"), *The Sunshine Boys* (1972, "cathartic because it dealt with the death of my father and taking care of my mother"), *California Suite* (1976), *Chapter Two* (1977), *Max Dugan Returns* (movie, 1983), *Brighton Beach Memoirs* (1983, nine years in gestation, but "It doesn't necessarily mean you're thinking about it all the time, it means it's thinking about itself"; movie 1986), *The Slugger's Wife* (movie, 1984), *Biloxi Blues* (1984; movie, 1987), *The Odd Couple* (1985, female version), *Broadway Bound* (1986) and *Rumors* (1988). Additional honors came his way in 1984 when a Broadway theatre was named for him.

Simon lost his first wife, dancer Joan Baim, to cancer in 1973, and three months later married actress Marsha Mason, from whom he parted in 1983. He has two daughters by his first wife, Ellen and Nancy. In 1987 he married Diane Lander, but the couple filed for divorce in 1988. Asked about his "message," if any, he says, "I try to give a sense of hope in most of my plays. Through my own experience, I'm just trying to tell people to stick with it." In 1985, 25 years after his first hit play, he finally won a Tony Award for Best Play of the Year for *Biloxi Blues*.

Paul Simon

"It is rare . . . to find a singer-songwriter who was a center of the Sixties' cultural explosion—indeed, who was a musical influence in that culture—creating new and original music in the Eighties. By these criteria alone, Paul Simon may be one of the most successful composers and performers in the history of pop music." This *Playboy* precis offers an accurate snapshot of Simon as he hops from one to yet another success. Continuing to write crowd-acclaimed songs, the artist now owns at least 15 Grammys and has sold upwards of 40 million albums. "I'm embarrassed to say I burst into tears when I wrote and first sang the line "Like a bridge over troubled waters, I will lay me down," Simon says. "Now it's been sung so many times I have no feeling whatsoever for it." His feeling now goes into new music; since his 1971 breakup with Art Garfunkel his hits have included "Fifty Ways to Leave Your Lover," "Late in the Evening," "Still Crazy After All These Years," "You Can Call Me Al," and "Graceland." The formula for good fortune was so wholly his that none of his albums have sold less than a half-million copies. In 1981 he and Garfunkel reunited for an outdoor Central Park concert that drew 500,000 fans, and sold a video and album from the date that prompted them to take their act on the road. That the worldwide tour was a success is an understatement; it's said in Paris they drew 130,000, but had to refuse 400,000 ticket requests and their 15-year-old hit "Mrs. Robinson" returned to No. 1 in France shortly afterwards.

Born in Newark on 13 October 1941, Simon has also been in three feature films, including *One-Trick Pony*, which he wrote, scored, and starred in. Simon, a Queens, New York, teacher's son, and his neighbor Garfunkel discovered their mutual enthusiasm for rock 'n' roll in the sixth grade. They performed as a team in high school, then went their separate ways to college (Paul was an English-lit major at Queens). Teaming up again later in Europe, they began to record Simon's songs, which led them to their chart-topping popularity. Still not on completely amicable terms with Garfunkel, Simon also broke up with actress Carrie Fisher, his second wife (rumors surface every now and again of their renewed friendship). The busy writer lives in a duplex apartment overlooking New York's Central Park. "The whole world was big Simon and Garfunkel fans," Simon says rather immodestly. "But I wasn't. We were a folk act and I'm a rock 'n' roll kid . . . what we did was too sweet, too serious. When I began making my albums, the songs became funkier. They were more about the streets." His latest LP was a recollection of his music, *Negotiations and Love Songs (1971-88)*, in 1988. His African concert, "Paul Simon's Graceland," was aired on Showtime in 1987; the album *Graceland* won the Grammy as Album of the Year in 1986.

O.J. Simpson

"I wanted people to say, 'Hey there's O.J.' I wanted to be creative, to be liked. I knew the money came with it." Such motivation nudged classic athlete-turned-media-celebrity Orenthal James Simpson to become the first man ever to pack pigskins for 2,000 yards in a season (friend and former fellow Trojan Marcus Allen later matched the feat in college). This son of a bank custodian was born on 9 July 1947 in the slums of San Francisco. (Orange) "Juice" exploded onto the national scene in 1967 as a transfer-student junior tailback. He carried the ball 70 percent of the time for Southern Cal as he led it to the national championship that year and won the Heisman Trophy for himself in 1968. He also scatted on a world-record quarter-mile relay team. As he'd wanted to be, he was "somebody." Then came the money; after an eleven-year pro career he would retire as football's highest-paid player. But in his first three years at Buffalo, his formidable talent was squandered as offensive linemen were being used to protect aging quarterback (now Congressman) Jack Kemp. It was in a pre-game chapel service, upon hearing about workaholics without goals, that he set his goal to stutterstep his way to record yardage. Under new coach Lou Saban, who told his wide receivers to block for O.J. or be traded, Simpson ran for 200 yards in 1973's final game in the Shea Stadium snow to finish with 2,003. In 1979 he retired with his hometown '49ers as the game's second-leading turf tallier. In 1985 he was elected to the Pro Football Hall of Fame.

But long before he became a gridiron retiree he began supplementing his income with commercials, sportscasting, acting and his film production company. Known as a spokesman for Hertz rental cars and for broadcasting with Frank Gifford on "Monday Night Football", O.J. became the co-host of "NFL Live" in 1989. He also appeared in the 1988 film *The Naked Gun* with Priscilla Presley. Divorced from Marguerite in 1979 (three children; one of whom drowned at age 23 months), O.J. married Nicole in 1985.

Frank Sinatra

"In today's trend-crazed world of pop music, Frank Sinatra is not simply the ultimate survivor but the ultimate victor," wrote New York *Times* pop-music critic Stephen Holden. On 23 May 1985 a double victory of sorts came to this musical legend: at a luncheon in the White House, he was given the nation's highest civilian honor, the Medal of Freedom; and later in the day he received an honorary engineering degree from Stevens Institute of Technology in his hometown of Hoboken, N.J. Remaining an active performer, Sinatra still packs the house as he did on "The Ultimate Tour" (1988) with Sammy Davis, Jr., and Liza Minnelli.

Ol' Blue Eyes was born Francis Albert Sinatra on 12 December 1915, the son of a prizefighter-turned-fire captain (who once told his son singing was "for sissies") and a dynamic mother (Dolly) who was active in Democratic politics. After high school, Sinatra worked for a time as a copy boy on the *Hudson Observer*—an interesting beginning given his later well-known love/hate relationship with the press. Then he organized a singing group, the Hoboken Four ("I wanted to be like Bing Crosby"). He won first prize on the Major Bowes' Radio Amateur Hour, singing "Night and Day," and was sent on a Bowes tour. Other jobs followed, and one night while Sinatra was acting as a singing emcee at a small club, Harry James caught him and signed him to sing with his band at $75 a week. During an engagement in Los Angeles, Tommy Dorsey saw him and offered $150. With Dorsey, Sinatra sang with the Pied Pipers and later as a soloist. In 1942 he went out on his own and began attracting national attention with his own radio show; by 1943, he was starring on "Your Hit Parade." When teenagers began to scream and swoon, he was booked into New York's Paramount Theatre at $7500 a week, and when a girl who had stood in line for seven hours and sat through several shows fainted from hunger, the "swooning over Frankie" fad began. Headlines blazed: "5000 Girls Fight to Get View of Frank Sinatra." He was mobbed by the attention-hungry wartime teenagers (Sinatra himself was 4-F because of a punctured ear drum). Ultimately, he became a top box-office draw in films such as *Anchors Aweigh* (1945), *On The Town* (1949) and *Pal Joey* (1957).

He has been married four times; his first wife was Nancy Barbato, with whom he had three children—Nancy, Frank, Jr., and Tina. His second marriage was to screen temptress Ava Gardner, then Mia Farrow and the former Barbara Marx. After his marriage to Gardner in the early 1950s crumbled, he toppled off the top of the Hollywood heap. His vocal chords hemorrhaged, and MCA, the colossal talent agency, unsymphathetically dropped him. Eventually he was able to sell himself to Columbia for an insulting $8000 to play the Italian GI Maggio in *From Here to Eternity*, a role which brought him his now-legendary comeback when he won the Best Supporting Actor Academy Award. He has made other popular films, including *High Society, Guys and Dolls, The Manchurian Candidate, The Detective* and *The Man with the Golden Arm*. He won an earlier Oscar in 1945 for the documentary *The House I Live In*, a plea for an end to prejudice.

He was once the top tail in the Rat Pack, and although Marlene Dietrich dubbed him "The Mercedes Benz of Men," he hasn't always been known for his smooth drive and purring motor. His *causes célèbres* are legendary—among them: hissing, "Get your hand off the suit, creep" to Speaker of the House Sam Rayburn at the 1956 Democratic Convention when Rayburn placed his hand on Sinatra's sleeve and requested he sing "The Yellow Rose of Texas." More recently his activity has been filled with prodigious activity in recordings, concerts, awards (he was the recipient of the prestigious Kennedy Center Honors in 1983 and the Jean Hersholt Award of the Motion Picture Academy in 1971) and he has garnered a whole new group of fans—young people. Critic Holden has written that Sinatra's albums and songs are "heroic feats of self-generation, of finding more with less and gaining in the struggle a reason for going on." (Sinatra says his greatest inspiration is Billie Holiday.) *Newsweek*'s Jim Miller wrote in 1982: "Age has softened his sinister aura—the petty feuds and hair-trigger temper, his association with reputed underworld figures. . . . He presents himself as a champion of charity, an apostle of the American Way." One thing is certain: he has refuted his father's contention that singing was for sissies.

Siskel & Ebert

They are America's favorite film-critic team. Between the two of them, they have received a Pulitzer, two Emmys and the IRIS Award, and have been inducted into a hall of fame.

Roger Ebert was born on 18 June 1942, in Urbana, Illinois, where he later attended the University of Illinois and was the editor of the *Daily Illini*. He began his career as a film critic in 1967 writing a column for the *Chicago Sun Times*. In 1975 he won a Pulitzer Prize for his distinguished criticism in the *Chicago Sun Times*, and to date he is the only film critic to have ever received the prestigious award. Since then, Roger has also written several books, including *A Kiss Is Still A Kiss* (1984), *Roger Ebert's Movie Home Companion* (1985), he co-authored *The Perfect London Walk* (1986), and *Two Weeks In The Midday Sun* (1989). In addition, Ebert is also film critic for *The New York Post* as well as for WLS-TV, the ABC affiliate in Chicago, and teaches at the University of Chicago in the Fine Arts Program.

Gene Siskel was born on 26 January 1946, in Chicago, Illinois. He attended Yale, and graduated with a B.A. in Philosophy. He began his career in 1967 as a film critic with Roger Ebert in "At The Movies." Two years later he became a newspaper reporter for the *Chicago Tribune* and within seven months he became the papers film critic. In 1974, Siskel became the film critic for the CBS affiliate in Chicago, WBBM-TV, where he still reviews movies on the evening news. In 1978 Siskel won an Emmy Award for hosting "Nightwatch," which was an experimental monthly series featuring the independent film and video works.

The duo began performing together in 1967 as film critics on the show "Sneak Previews," which was the highest rated weekly half hour program in the history of the Public Broadcasting System. In 1979, the team won an Emmy Award for their excellent reviews on "Sneak Previews." In 1982 they joined Tribune Entertainment which produced the nationally syndicated "At the Movies," and in 1986 they teamed up again for another film show simply called "Siskel & Ebert." They were one of the initial performers to be inducted into the NATPE Hall of Fame, and received the IRIS Award for successfully moving from local to national syndicated television.

Leonard Slatkin

The St. Louis sound is in his blood. His father Felix was once concertmaster of the St. Louis Symphony Orchestra, and Leonard Slatkin moved up the ranks of assistant conductor, associate, associate principal, principal guest conductor, to the top, where he stands now as one of the few American-born music directors and conductors of a major U.S. orchestra. According to *People*, Slatkin "has transformed the St. Louis Symphony from a ho-hum ensemble into an acclaimed musical powerhouse." Known for his imaginative programming and, as per a *Time* critique, "performances marked by precision and a command of musical architecture," Slatkin is a true artist at the podium: "I use my hands like a sculptor, to mold and shape the sound I want to clarify." In 1982 he made music-page headlines conducting the American premiere of a newly discovered symphony of Mozart written when Mozart was only nine. But Slatkin's extensive repertoire is not limited to the classics; he has a penchant for contemporary music, and, like his father (former conductor and arranger for a major movie studio), he has had a relationship with Hollywood. He conducted the score of *The Exorcist*, recorded the soundtrack for *Unfaithfully Yours* and conducted the original symphonic version of *Jesus Christ Superstar*.

Leonard Slatkin was born 1 September 1944 into a musical family. "Our family was unbelievable. All musicians. How many people grow up with a resident string quartet? Every night we heard Beethoven, Brahms and Bartok." Slatkin's violinist father and cellist mother founded the Hollywood String Quartet, and musicians like Stravinsky and Schoenberg were frequent guests. Slatkin's musical training began at age three with the violin; at eleven he took up the piano, and at fifteen studied viola. Slatkin studied conducting as a teenager, first with his father and then with Walter Susskind, and by night played piano at a cocktail bar in La Brea. After one semester at the University of Indiana (Slatkin refused to participate in compulsory ROTC training—"I am a lifelong pacifist") he returned to California and attended LA City College, majoring in English. It was only after his father's death that he made the decision to make a career of conducting. "I do not think that I ever would have become a conductor if my father had lived. I could never have challenged him in that way." Slatkin has led the world's finest symphony orchestras; he has performed at the White House, and his recordings with the St. Louis Symphony have thrice been nominated for Grammy Awards—in 1985 they had a winner with their recording of Prokofiev's Symphony No. 5.

His two marriages ended in divorce. "I've come to the conclusion that a long, personal relationship is next to impossible." Slatkin lives fifteen minutes from his work in a spacious old house filled with penguin replicas—glass, scuptured, stuffed. A teetotaler, he prefers to indulge in ice cream or root beer. A film buff and sports fan, Slatkin has been known to announce baseball scores during concerts. He's also a devotee of writer Stephen King, but it's his music that consumes him—"I simply do not know what I could do if I could no longer conduct. This is my life. I don't consider it work—I consider it an honor. It's almost entirely pleasurable—even the problems. Music nourishes, it fulfills."

Jaclyn Smith

"I don't regret 'Charlie's Angels,'" says this chestnut-haired beauty whose flawless skin, luminous eyes, sensitive mouth, and clipped Texas-accented voice helped make the detective series one of the most successful television programs in history. Along with Farrah Fawcett and Kate Jackson, "we did get hyped and thought of as slick, empty-headed girls. Step by step we are all living it down."

Smith always knew she wanted to be an actress and she started studying ballet and acting as a child in her native Houston, where she was born 24 October 1947. After studying drama at Trinity University she peformed with regional theater groups in Boston and New York. Eventually she appeared in productions of *West Side Story, Gentlemen Prefer Blondes, Bye Bye Birdie* and *Peg*. But Smith didn't really start breaking hearts until she was signed as the Breck shampoo girl, a success which led her to Hollywood, to television and stardom's sunshine on "Charlie's Angels" in 1976.

Life after "Charlie" continues to be glamorous for the thrice-married beauty. (Her third husband is British filmmaker Tony Richmond, whom she married in 1981; they separated in 1989. A son, Gaston Anthony, was born in March 1982 and a daughter, Spencer Margaret, was born in December 1985.) She has starred in top-rated TV miniseries such as "Jacqueline Bouvier Kennedy"; Sidney Sheldon's "Rage of Angels" (1986) plus the sequel, "The Story Continues"; as Sally Fairfax in "George Washington"; "The Nightingale Saga"; "Windmills of the Gods" (1987); "The Bourne Identity" (1988); and "Blood Knot" (1989). In addition to her acting work, Smith appears in many commercials—in fact, she is likely to show up whenever a call goes out for beauty. Naturally, she wrote *The Jaclyn Smith Beauty Book* for Simon and Schuster in 1985, and she premiered a new fragrance by Max Factor, "Jaclyn Smith's California," in 1989. Once asked if she thought she would be as much in demand if it weren't for her fabulous looks, Smith leveled her interviewer with a demure and modest response: "I really can't answer that." Her latest project, untitled at the moment is to star in the ABC Mystery-wheel series as a San Francisco attorney who specializes in representing wealthy clients.

Liz Smith

"Gossip is news in a red satin dress."—Liz Smith

The Texas-born "good ole gal" whom *Town and Country* singles out as "Manhattan's, if not the nation's, most influential personality reporter" has been "today's Delphic Oracle of inside information" since February 1976, when she signed on with the New York *Daily News* and helped spearhead the gossip renaissance which has made people-writing one of the hottest fields in contemporary journalism. Now "the nation's second most famous Liz" (she often gets scoops directly from the violet-eyed No. 1, Liz Taylor), Liz Smith is (according to *US* magazine) "that rarity, a beloved gossip, probably because she dispenses it with Southern sweetness that makes it both palatable and delicious." She has remarkably few enemies, one outspoken exception being Frank Sinatra, who has made anti-Smith comments even from such high-toned precincts as the stage of Carnegie Hall. But people such as William Buckley, Jr., have saluted her "mordant wit," and most of the famous find her unreasonably fair. Her wide popularity also might stem from the fact that, when not at her typewriter, Liz says that, personally, she has very little interest in gossip. "My idea of a really good time," says the columnist, "is to curl up with *Peter the Great*."

A product of a cotton-broker father and "a beautiful Mississippi belle," Mary Elizabeth Smith was born on Ground Hog's Day (2 February) 1923, in Fort Worth, and still hasn't lost her Lone Star way of speaking. (Nor her taste for chili and chicken-fried steak.) Despite her strict Baptist upbringing, she was a starstruck movie fan as a child, and despite her frequent hobnobbing with today's hottest stars, she still dreams of one day meeting her idol, Fred Astaire. She had her first taste of column-writing on the student newspaper of the University of Texas at Austin after a 5-year marriage to a World War II air force bombadier. She headed north to New York in 1949.

Landing on the staff of *Modern Screen*, Liz went on to work for Mike Wallace at CBS radio and, after a producing stint at NBC-TV, cut her gossip teeth ghostwriting the Cholly Knickerbocker column during its first five years under Hearstling Igor Cassini. Subsequent movie reviews she wrote for *Cosmopolitan* were quoted so often in ads that her name was familiar to entertainment insiders even before she established herself as one of the busier free-lancers around. But it's been her exposure as a *Daily News* columnist (syndicated to a total of some fifty million readers) that has provided her present clout, a state of affairs about which she's eminently realistic. "Listen, if I didn't have this column, I would fade from sight and memory faster than Pia Zadora's last movie." She's also realistic about her gossipy subject matter, the demand for which, she believes, runs in cycles. "Gossip," says Liz Smith, "reflects the time, the luxury, the inclination, the joy, the pettiness, the gaiety of life. But we live in a perilous age. If something terrible ever happens, then, like Nixon, we won't have gossip to kick around any more." In the meantime, however, Smith says of her frenetic pace: "A column is like riding a tiger. You can't get off." Nevertheless, Smith has found the time to produce an unlikely sounding tome for a gossip columnist, *The Mother Book* ("a compendium of trivia and grandeur about mothers, motherhood and maternity"), which has enjoyed a number of incarnations here and abroad. She also is active in her two favorite causes, Literacy Volunteers of New York and the New York Public Library. Asked to define her job, Liz calls it, "Making a molehill out of mountains of trivia, rumor, gossip and crap." Along with her other endeavors, Liz Smith wrote the

Steven Soderbergh

wonderful introduction "Thank God for the Celebrity Register" for the 1986 edition.

Steven Soderbergh

He began making films when he was a mere 13 years old. His first experience with filmmaking was in an animation class offered by Louisiana State University. Realizing that it involved "far too much work for far too little result," says Steven, he switched from animation to live action.

Steven Soderbergh was born circa 1963 in Georgia. Shortly after he was born, his family made several moves, the last of which was to Baton Rouge, Louisiana, where Soderbergh began high school. Acquainting himself with students from Louisiana State University had made it possible for easy access to all sorts of film equipment. He spent the next four years making a series of Super 8 short films. After graduating from high school, he followed his dreams and moved to Los Angeles. He stayed there a year and a half, during which time he landed his first job as an editor for a program that was quickly cancelled. Realizing that he needed more experience in the field, Soderbergh picked up and moved back to Baton Rouge to further develop his skills as writer and director. Upon returning to Louisiana, he spent two years as a coin attendant at a video arcade, where he aggressively worked on scripts. He later worked at a local video production house where he would produce occasional commercials for friends. A friend from LSU gave him work salvaging programs for "Showtime," for which he would fly out to LA, recut the footage and return home. His break came when someone working in management for the rock group Yes called "Showtime" to see if they knew anyone who could go on the road with the band to shoot an in-house documentary, and they recommended Soderbergh. Yes was so impressed with his work that they later hired him to direct the feature-length concert movied 9012 Live. In the spring of 1986, the film premiered on MTV, and later was nominated for a Grammy Award for Best Music Video, Long Form. Soon following this successful concert movie, he signed on with an agent, and was hired to write a TV movie and a musical. Neither of these were made. Outlaw Productions had faith in Steven and his talent, and the outcome of this was *sex, lies, and videotape*, winner of both the Best Film Prize and the Best Actor Award at the 1989 Cannes Film Festival. *sex, lies, and videotape* is the first full length feature film to be written by Soderbergh. Not only did he write the film, but he also edited and directed it. He wrote the script in eight days in 1987 on his way from Baton Rouge to Los Angeles. When describing the film, Steven states, "The film deals with people not coming out and saying exactly what they're thinking or feeling. Sex, lies, and videotape are what the film is about and a lot of the country revolves around: the selling of sex, the telling of lies and the inundation of video."

Aleksandr Solzhenitsyn

An insightful look at Russian novelist and dissident Aleksandr Solzhenitsyn appears in the preface of *The Gulag Archipelago*, his monumental account of Soviet repression under Lenin and Stalin, a repression he claims took 66 million Russian lives. The preface, written by late German novelist Heinrich Boll, observes: "What surprises me most in Solzhenitsyn is the calm that he emanates—he who has been threatened and fought over more than any other man on earth. Nothing, it seems, can destroy his serenity, neither the terrible insults to which he has been exposed to in his own country nor the banishment—the 'one-way ticket'—which he has been offered. . . . At the same time, Solzhenitsyn's calm is not at all that of a gilded Olympian monument but that of a living man, concerned and involved with the course of human events."

While his literary denunciation of Soviet policies won him a strong American following, his readers and supporters in this country took a surprised step back in the early 1980s when he suddenly lashed out at life in the good ol' U.S.A. Making a rare public appearance outside his remote New England home-in-exile, the most recognizable author in the world gripped an Ivy League podium and let forth a stream of invective towards the West. It turns out Solzhenitsyn dismisses the Western powers as "weak and effete" and claims that the "United States has a weak and undeveloped national consciousness." If his homeland is a political wasteland, the author suggested, his adopted nation is a moral wasteland. When the dust cleared, William Buckley was still to be found in the Solzhenitsyn cheering section; around him, though, were some vacant seats.

Solzhenitsyn is the son of an army officer for the Czar who died a few months before his birth on 11 December 1918. Aleksandr was a brilliant student, particularly in mathematics and science. He also became an active and fervent member of the Komsomol, the young Communist organization, and a firm Soviet champion. His faith was shaken in the 1930s during the purges under Stalin, and his doubts intensified during the war. Serving as a captain in the Red Army, he wrote a letter with critical views to a friend serving on another front; that letter began eight years of interrogation and punishment that he has described in depth in *The Gulag Archipelago*. His novel *One Day in the Life of Ivan Denisovich*, describes in graphic detail the life of a political prisoner in a hard-labor concentration camp in Siberia. Published with Krushchev's blessings, the story turned out to be his last work sanctioned officially in the Soviet Union. Solzhenitsyn, of course, kept writing and distributing his works through the underground publishing network. He writes from a Christian point of view, depicting the suffering of the innocent world where good and evil vie for the human soul.

In his personal life, his first wife divorced him, at his request, during his imprisonment; they were remarried in 1956, and divorced in 1972. He married Natalya Svetlova, a mathematics teacher, in April 1973. He has three sons from his first marriage and one stepson. He and his family became U.S. citizens in 1985. Residing in Cavendish, Vermont, Solzhenitsyn spends his time writing sequels to his 1986 book *August 1914*. The new collection, which is titled *Krasnoe Koleso (The Red Wheel)*, includes the volumes *October 1916* and *March 1917*.

Suzanne Somers

Nude photos in the December 1984 *Playboy* brought the soft-porn public back to her favor, although she denied she posed for the glossy spread because her career was sagging. "The pictures that were published in *Playboy* [before] were test shots used without my approval. I was in awful shape. I'd just had a baby and I still had baby fat. This time I had complete control and I'm in very good shape. Besides, the things I've done that were supposed to be 'good' for my career—movies with Donald Sutherland and Ian McShane—turned out to be disasters. The things that I've done that were supposed to be 'bad'—like playing Chrissie on 'Three's Company' and taking my act to Las Vegas—turned out to be the best things I've ever done. So now I just follow my instincts."

Blue-eyed, blond-haired Suzanne Somers (real name Mahoney) was born on 16 October 1947 in San Bruno, Calif. and attended schools in San Francisco. She worked as a nurse's aide giving psychological tests for a year before she became a model. While working on "Mantrap," a syndicated show in the Bay Area, she met late writer Jacqueline Susann, who encouraged her to find a publisher for her first volume of poetry, *Touch Me*. It sold well and was followed by another volume, quite naturally, *Touch Me Again*. She then wrote a self-help volume, *Some People Live More Than Others*. She married Bruce Somers, now a lawyer and psychologist, when he was 19 and she 17. (She'd been expelled from a Catholic convent school when she was caught writing detailed love letters to him.) Quite soon afterwards she became pregnant. Everything about the marriage, especially morning neighborhood coffee klatches, scared her. "I just panicked," Suzanne recalls. "I knew I couldn't stay in that marriage." Out from it she went, determined to become an actress via modeling, but by her own description she was "the worst model in San Francisco." She had a young child to care for and times were tough, but when she met and married Alan Hamel she began to get parts in TV commercials, summer stock, and when she won the part of Chrissie on "Three's Company" (beating out 299 other blond sexpots), she became an instant overnight star in the Farrah Fawcett mode. Since leaving the show in a salary dispute in 1980, Somers has had another child, worked in Vegas (named Las Vegas Female Entertainer of the Year in 1986), and made the TV version of Jackie Collins's super-sleaze sizzler "Hollywood Wives," playing back stabbing actress Gina Germaine. She currently stars in the television syndicated sitcom "She's the Sheriff" and has become the honorary chairperson for the National Association of Children of Alcoholics. To top it all off, her latest book, *Keeping Secrets*, was published in 1988. In her spare time, Suzanne likes to cook or stroll around the desert.

Stephen Sondheim

The Broadway musical's most innovative horizon-widener, composer/lyricist Stephen Sondheim, who (according to the *Times's* Frank Rich) "won his largest victory yet in his struggle to expand the... theatre to the size of his own artistic ambitions" in 1984 with *Sunday in the Park with George*, topped his career with the 1987 opening of *Into the Woods*, on which he collaborated once again with author/director James Lapine. The musical gave a melodic new life to the tales of such familiar fairy-tale characters as Cinderella, Little Red Riding Hood, Rapunzel, and Jack of beanstalk fame. Stephen Sondheim has been making his very distinctive mark on the musical stage since the 1950's, when he contributed the lyrics to the landmark hits *West Side Story* (1957) and *Gypsy* (1959). He provided both words and music for such later successes as *A Funny Thing Happened on the Way to the Forum* (1962), *Company* (1970), the operetta *A Little Night Music* (1973) and the even more operatic *Sweeney Todd* (1979). Other inventive Sondheim productions have included *Follies* (on B'way in 1971 and a hit in London), *Pacific Overtures* (1976) and *Merrily We Roll Along* (1981). A musical potpourri of Sondheim compositions, *Side by Side by Sondheim*, was another favorite of Main Stem audiences. He has won many Tony Awards and a Pulitzer Prize, the latter with Lapine in 1985 for *Sunday in the Park*.

Born in New York on 22 March 1930, Stephen Joshua Sondheim was educated at the George School and Williams College. The son of a successful dress manufacturer, Sondheim moved to Pennsylvania with his mother following his parents' divorce. There he found a surrogate father in Oscar Hammerstein II and was soon the lyricist's piano protégé. Sondheim reflects. "The first influence I had was a highly professional, highly rule-conscious man. He didn't say obey the rules, he just pointed them out." Sondheim acquired an enduring taste for classical music in college. Of his fellowship with avant-garde composer Milton Babbitt after graduation, he has said: "What I was learning from Milton was basic grammar—sophisticated grammar, but grammar. It was a language, whereas what I learned from Oscar was what to do with language." He debuted as lyricist for *West Side Story*, followed by *Gypsy*, and first wrote both music and lyrics for *Forum*. Sondheim's lyrics are written in character ("I like writing within parameters") and his accomplishments in that oeuvre stand him, as an author, in the forefront of contemporary playwrights. He immerses himself in each character and emerges with some distinctive nuance about each that can be conveyed in his lyrics. To Sondheim, "the telling detail is the essence of playwriting, of all writing." Knowledge of each cast member's vocal capabilities and copious notes, both musical and lyrical, help him establish the musical atmosphere for each song. This, in turn, is the provenance of melodic ideas ("they're not related to a conscious lyrical phrase, but it gives you a basic melodic rhythm that can spring into other things").

Sondheim lives in a town house in Manhattan's Turtle Bay section, and despite his huge successes he merrily remains a virtually faceless celebrity. Interested in mathematics, he loves puzzles of all kinds, including crosswords. He regularly competes in the word games in the *New York Times*, the *London Times* and the *Nation* magazine, and some of his inventions have appeared in *New York* magazine. He has fondly referred to lyric writing as "an elegant kind of puzzle." Puzzles and plot twists were also the meat of the screenplay of the mystery movie *The Last of Sheila* (1973), which he cowrote with actor-friend Anthony Perkins. A lover of order, he is ill-at-ease with improvisation in any form, be it Method acting or jazz music.

Sissy Spacek

"The only thing I can figure is that I had so many of the basics," responded Sissy Spacek when asked where she got her fearlessness. "I always had a secure life, always had such support from my family, so much love from them... maybe that makes it easier to focus on what you want. You can go farther out on a limb, because you know if you don't make it, it doesn't really matter. Someone will be there when you fall." Going out on limbs has paid off for Spacek, who has played a drugged orphan in *Prime Cut*, her first professional film (1972), a naive friend of a psychotic boy on an interstate crime spree in *Badlands* (1974), a weird teenager who unleashes her telekinetic powers in Brian de Palma's *Carrie* (1976), a way-out young maid who housecleans in the nude and hustles on the side in *Welcome to L.A.* (1977) and a young Texas wanderer who steals her roommate's personality in *Three Women* (1977). But it took her strong, non-kooky portrayal of Loretta Lynn in *The Coal Miner's Daughter* to win the 1980 Academy Award ("I was Loretta's choice. She was looking through a pile of pictures, and when she came to one of me, she said, 'that's the coal miner's daughter'"). She received Oscar nominations for *Carrie*, *Missing*, *The River* and in 1987 for *Crimes of the Heart*.

Mary Elizabeth Spacek was born Christmas Day, 1949, in Quitman, Texas. Her older brothers called her "Sissy," and the name stuck. She was adored by her family and friends, twirled a baton and led cheers, and was a homecoming queen for the Quitman Bulldogs ("... after my brother Robbie died of leukemia I was elected homecoming queen, probably for sympathy reasons... I felt really cradled by that town"). Her high school dream was to become a singer-musician (she sang with a choral group and taught guitar for fifty cents an hour); after graduation she packed her guitar and went to New York and lived for several months with her cousin, Rip Torn, and his wife, Geraldine Page ("It gave me strength being Rip's cousin"). She enrolled in Lee Strasberg's acting class, and after a few months took off for California and a film career. Other films include *Heart Beat* (1980), *Raggedy Man*, directed by her husband (1981). *Marie* (1985) and *'night, Mother* (1986). Television appearances include Tennessee Williams's "The Migrants" (1973), "Katherine" (1975), and "Verna: USO Girl" (1978).

Spacek married Jack Fisk, an art director, in 1974, in "an eensy, sweet little chapel near the beach" in Santa Monica with Fisk's Hungarian sheepdog their only witness. Between films they take off for Quitman with their children to enjoy piney woods, rolling hills and fishing. "She enjoys getting back to grass roots," says her mother. "After she finishes a movie, she can come back there, relax and remember who she really is."

James Spader

He is a young and upcoming superstar who has appeared in theatre, television, and film. He has co-starred with everyone from brat packers

Aaron Spelling — CELEBRITY REGISTER 1990

Andrew McCarthy and Charlie Sheen to the distinguished and established Robert Mitchum and Diane Keaton.

James Spader was born in Boston, Massachusetts in 1961 into a family of educators. After attending the prestigious Phillips Academy, he moved to New York City to pursue a career in acting, where he trained in theatre at the Michael Chekov Studio. To support himself during his studies, Spader loaded railroad cars, drove trucks and worked as a stable boy at the Claremont Riding Academy. He made his film debut in 1981 in *Endless Love*. Since then he has appeared in *The New Kids*, *Tuff Turf*, *Pretty in Pink* in which he portrayed Andrew McCarthy's best friend, *Mannequin*, *Wall Street*, in which he played Charlie Sheen's lawyer friend, *Less Than Zero*, *Baby Boom* in which he starred as Diane Keaton's rival at work, *Jack's Back* with a critically acclaimed performance of a portrayal of twins, *sex, lies, and videotape*, in which he plays Graham, a man in search of truth and his inner self, *The Rachel Papers*, and *Bad Influence*. He made his TV debut in 1983 in *The Family Tree*. Other television credits include the ABC science fiction film "Starcrossed," "Diner," and the made-for-TV movies "A Killer in the Family," and "Cocaine: One Man's Seduction." James's theatre work includes productions of *Equus*, and *Veronica's Room*. He also appeared in xSundown Beach for the Actor's Studio in New York.

James and his wife are bi-coastal, residing in both Los Angeles and New York.

Aaron Spelling

Television's most prolific producer has dazzled millions with what he considers "escapist medicine," in the form of shows like "Hotel," "Charlie's Angels," "Dynasty," "Starsky and Hutch," "Fantasy Island," "The Love Boat," and "The Colbys." Aaron Spelling's philosophy is: "When someone works all day with his hands as my father did, he comes home and uses the TV set as a paint brush to paint over the horrors of the day, to forget what real life is. I am giving people a happy pill in the nicest sense of the word." With a track record as impressive as Spelling's, most would consider the future a breeze. But the producer confides: "I live in terrible fear of failure. There is pain and there is joy. If a show fails, 70 people are out of work. You take that responsibility to heart. And certainly this string of hits will stop or slow down. I can't expect to have seven shows on the air [as he did in 1984-85] every season.' Spelling hit a slump during the 1989 season when his angels-of-the-nursing-staff show "Nightingales" didn't fly in the ratings.

Born in Dallas to a Russian Jewish immigrant tailor on 22 April 1928, Aaron Spelling knows from experience how to give the viewing public what it wants. At Southern Methodist University, which he attended on his post-World War II G.I. Bill, he won two Eugene O'Neill Awards for writing one-act plays. In 1953 he started out as an actor in Hollywood, meanwhile writing 27 scripts that went nowhere until Dick Powell picked one up for his "Zane Grey Theater." In time, Spelling became the show's producer, and later supplied Four Star Studios with eight weekly series at once, highlighting Powell, Lloyd Bridges, June Allyson and others. Spelling's been teamed with Danny Thomas, and later, Leonard Goldberg, in production profusion, and is now in Aaron Spelling Productions with Douglas S. Cramer and E. Duke Vincent. The small, large-nosed, white-haired Spelling has a fear of flying (meaning he almost never gets Back East), and is so reclusive he rarely visits his Malibu beach house even though he, second wife, Carole, a.k.a. Candy (his first was late actress Carolyn Jones), and their two children live in L.A.'s Holmby Hills. The Spellings also have a penthouse hideaway in Las Vegas. With more than 100 TV movies to his credit, and more than a score of series, "television's hottest producer" has never won an Emmy. "I regret that the critics don't like my work more," Spelling says. "I think I relate to the people better. . . . They get a little joy for an hour."

Steven Spielberg

"I never believed in anything before I believed in movies," states this extraordinary young filmmaker whom Hollywood big chief Michael Eisner called "the highest paid human being for performing a service in the history of the world," referring to such phenomenally popular and profitable box office hits as *Jaws*, *E.T.*, *Raiders of the Lost Ark*, *Poltergeist*, *Close Encounters of the Third Kind*, *Indiana Jones and the Temple of Doom*, *Gremlins*, the *Goonies*, *Back to the Future*, *An American Tail*, *The Color Purple*, *The Land Before Time*, *The Empire of the Sun*, *Who Framed Roger Rabbit*, *Indiana Jones and The Last Crusade*, *Gremlins II*, and the upcoming *Always* in 1989. He made his TV debut in the fall of 1985 hosting an anthology series on NBC "Steven Spielberg's Amazing Stories."

Born 18 December 1947, he moved all over the country with his father, an electrical engineer, and his concert pianist mother until his parents separated when he was a teenager. ("Divorce was the first scary word I remember hearing.") So involved was he in movies and television and filmmaking (Richard Dreyfuss, the actor, said of him: "He's a big kid who at 12 years old decided to make movies, and he's still 12 years old") that he claims not to have noticed any of the social-political upheaval of the 1960s. "*Poltergeist* reflects a lot of the fears I had at night—scary shadows that could simply be bunched up dirty clothes or a shadow like Godzilla cast by the hall light. In *E.T.* I'm reacting to a situation in my life. When my father left, I went from tormentor to protector with my family. I'd never assumed responsibility for anything except making my home movies—my sisters were constantly getting killed off in my little 8-mm extravanganzas. Suddenly here was real life knocking at my door. I had to become the man of the house. The first scary thing I learned to do was turn off the lights. But I also knew that light was something to make things beautiful. To me light is a magnet—it can veil something wondrous or, as in the flashlights in *E.T.*, something terrifying."

His high school grades weren't good enough for him to be accepted at any of the major film schools, so as an English major at California State College he regularly fibbed his way onto movie studio lots to observe directors such as Hitchcock and Franklin Schaffner in action. His 22 minute *Amblin'*, which he describes as an "attack of crass commercialism," won awards at both the Atlanta and Venice Film Festivals and was distributed as a featured short with *Love Story* in 1970 by Universal. At age 20 the wunderkind was signed to a seven-year directing contract at that studio. His first assignment was directing Joan Crawford in Rod Serling's "Night Gallery" on TV. Directing episodes of TV shows such as "Marcus Welby M.D.," "Columbo," and "The Name of the Game" was his "diploma to feature films," the first being *Duel*, starring Dennis Weaver as a mild-mannered traveling salesman chased down a lonesome freeway by a driverless truck. Shot in just 16 days for $350,000, it grossed over $5 million in Europe and Japan. His next feature was the critically acclaimed *The Sugarland Express*, made in 1974, before his mega-hit *Jaws* (1975) netted millions from a toothsome, terrifying deep blue sea.

Home for this celluloid Croesus (whom a 1985 *Time* cover story labelled "Magician of the Movies") includes an adobe mansion-office headquarters for himself and staff of 15 on Universal's Hollywood lot and top drawer satellites in Bel-Air, Malibu and high in the sky in Manhattan's Trump Tower. Friends say he's as darling as Peter Pan and not unlike the fabled ageless boy. After the birth of his son, Max, Spielberg married actress Amy Irving in 1985. They were divorced in 1989.

Mickey Spillane

"I've been around, my fine foreign friend. . . . Only right now I still have the little goodie that makes me an unpenetrated virgin and I'm going to keep it that way." So said the virgin in Spillane's *The Erection Set* (which was sold to MGM in 1973). And on the Dick Cavett Show the boyish host gaped at the book jacket and gasped something like, "That can't be Mickey's wife!" But Sherri Spillane, the second Mrs. S., who lives alone in New York when Mickey is down in South Carolina writing, replied, "I told him I wanted to be naked on the cover of his next book." And she was.

Frank Morrison Spillane was born on 9 March 1918 in Brooklyn, and after he dropped out of Fort Hayes State College and a couple of post-Depression era jobs, he created the hard-boiled private eye Mike Hammer. Spillane wrote Hammer's first vehicle, *I, The Jury*, in three weeks; it hit the sex-and-violence aficionados like a solid right to the gut, and they gobbled up his subsequent thrillers as fast as he could turn them out—to the tune of a probable 130 million copies printed since 1947. Then there was a long hiatus while the author was busy being a Jehovah's Witness after a member convinced him the theory of evolution was wrong. (Although Spillane asserted, "I'm clean inside. I've always been clean inside," he later said, "I was christened in two churches and neither took.") Although he wrote and acted in TV and movies, it wasn't until 1961 that he returned to novels with *The Deep*, and a generation of avid TV viewers, who may never have opened one of his many books, finally had a chance to see their hero's creator via a series of Miller Lite beer commercials. Former readers were delighted when the 1983 television season brought with it the series, "Mickey Spillane's Mike Hammer," followed by special movies-of-the-week.

Benjamin Spock

"I never thought of myself as changing society," he says, "I was not a sculptor, looking to make the ideal person of the future." Nevertheless, the Reverend Norman Vincent Peale in 1968 denounced the pediatrician-author of *The Common Sense Book of Baby and Child Care* as being responsible for "the most undisciplined age in history." And Harry Stein, in a 1983 *Esquire* spot-lighting "Fifty Who Made a Difference," made the point that "Benjamin Spock, more than any other individual of his time, was able to reshape the process by which human beings are formed in this country." His "Baby Bible," first published in 1946, is the most successful book ever written in the U.S.

While marching for peace during the Vietnam War, often surrounded by the hirsute young of the 1960s, Spock was often blamed for a generation of drop-outs, drug freaks, and other by-products of the youthquake because of his supposed advocacy of a loosely disciplined upbringing. Actually, his famous tome's keynote was reassurance, which was misinterpreted as "permissiveness." The book's opening message to parents, "You know more than you think you do," has proved to be, according to one advisor, as memorable as any since Melville's immortal, "Call me Ishmael." No dogmatic crank in his advice-giving, Spock emphasizes that child rearing is a problem that has to be revised from generation to generation as the life around the problem changes.

The lanky, craggy-faced baby doctor was born in New Haven, Conn., 2 May 1903. While at Yale he was an oarsman on the university crew that won in the 1924 Olympics in Paris. After Yale Medical School he began his practice in New York in 1933. He served in the U.S. Navy from 1944-46, during which time—at night—he wrote the book for parents which was eventually translated into some 30 languages and made him known around the world. He retired as supervising pediatrician of Western Reserve University's Family Clinic in 1967 to devote all his time to anti-war activities. ("What's the sense of physicians like myself trying to help parents to bring up healthy and happy children to have them killed in such numbers for a cause that is ignoble?") At his trial in Boston in 1968 for "conspiracy" to foment resistance to military conscription, he was found guilty, but the conviction was overturned by a court of appeals. ("My opposition to the war," he now says, "and my defiance of Lyndon Johnson were, in a sense, a delayed adolescent rebellion. I certainly never rebelled against my parents at home.") In what was called a folly of a move, he ran for president in 1972 and managed to come in fourth with 78,801 votes. In the 1980s, his anti-war sentiments were directed into work on behalf of nuclear disarmament.

Spock married Jane Davenport Cheney, a silk heiress, in 1927 (two sons: Michael and John) and they were divorced after forty-nine years. In 1976, when he was seventy-three, he married Mary Morgan Wright, a businesswoman in her thirties. About the influence of the "Baby Bible," which still sells worldwide close to a million copies a year, Spock shrugs, "People don't read the book for its political content, they use it for when the kid has colic." In 1988 he released *Dr. Spock on Parenting*, and the following year he wrote the book *Spock on Spock*.

Bruce Springsteen

Initially regarded as the "new Bob Dylan," he exploded on the music scene as a kind of rock messiah: a pied piper to restless suburban youths who caught the tail-end of the 1960s rock-and-rebellion era and were hungry for more. Belting out hard-driving ballads of life on the seedy side of town, he built an enthusiastic following in the early 1970s. His rambling lyrics spurted colorful, poignant (although, some said, pretentious) images. "We gotta get out of here while we're young 'cause tramps like us, baby were born to run," he bellowed in the title song of his 1975 hit album, *Born to Run*. Strutting, swaggering, and groping toward the audience, he could whip his concert fans into a unified frenzy of foot-stomping and chanting. His energy was boundless. "Some guy bought his ticket, and there's a promise made between the musician and the audience. I've got a lot of energy naturally, but when I get on stage, and I'm running on empty, I just think of the promise to the guy or girl who's down there. . . . It's no different than if you stood with this person and shook his hand."

Bruce Springsteen was born on 23 September 1949 in the working-class town of Freehold, N.J. Restless and burdened by feelings of isolation, he turned to music, mastering a second-hand guitar, harmonica, and piano by age 14. "If I hadn't found music, I don't know what I would have done." He became a local celebrity fronting hard-rock bands that toured the club circuit along the Jersey coast. In 1972, he was signed by a Columbia executive who heard him sing two of his early songs, "Blinded by the Light," and "It's Hard To Be a Saint in the City." He made a tame recording debut with his 1973 album, *Greetings from Asbury Park*, but returned to his barroom-rocker roots the next year with *The Wild, The Innocent and the E Street Shuffle*. The critics were enthralled. Said one Boston reviewer, "I saw rock and roll future and its name is Bruce Springsteen." Heartened by the accolades, Columbia embarked on a massive promotion of *Born to Run*, which zoomed to the top of the album charts and boosted sales of his previous records. In October 1975, Springsteen graced the covers of *Time* and *Newsweek* simultaneously, a feat referred to as a "staggering triumph for the public relations men." Other album credits include the 1978 *Darkness on the Edge of Town* and *The River* in 1980. After a three-year absence from the rock scene, the Boss returned triumphantly in 1983 with the superhit album *Born in the U.S.A.* It was number one on the charts for some time, as was the LP's first single release, "Dancing in the Dark." Without glitter, gloves, garlands or groupies, he went on tour. Tickets to see his nearly four-hour show were half the price of those to see Michael Jackson's Victory tour. "Born in the U.S.A." was an anthem for the blue-collar worker, the disenfranchised, who, despite lots of hard knocks, could still rock and roll, singing: "I'm a cool rocking daddy in the U.S.A." Ronald Reagan tried to tell the voters that election-year summer that he was a big fan of Springsteen's, but Bruce finessed the "mutual endorsement," proclaiming his independence. After all, he was the Boss. One of the few performers who can go out into his audience knowing that his fans will protect him from harm, his politics were not sharply defined. "To me, the idea is to get a band, write some songs and go out to people's towns. It's my favorite thing. It's like a circus. You just kind of roll on, walk into somebody's town and bang! It's heart to heart. Something can happen to you; something can happen to them. You feel you can make a difference in somebody's life. All I'm trying to do is wake up people's senses and do the same thing for myself. I want to make their bodies tingle. Make their blood run. Make them scream . . . mainly, all my records try to do is offer some sort of survival course. Maybe you can't dream the same dreams when you're 34 that you did when you were 24, you know, but you can still dream something." The Boss took himself a wife in May of 1985—model and actress Julianne Phillips—in a Catholic wedding ceremony in her home state of Oregon. Their union dissolved into divorce (1989) and Bruce took up with his back-up singer Patti Scialfa. He continues to sell out concerts in Europe and the U.S. as his songs and videos hit the airwaves. (His music video "Glory Days" was directed by John Sayles.) His current LPs include *Bruce Springsteen & The E Street Band Live* (1986), *Tunnel of Love* (won Grammy for Best Rock Performance in 1988) and *Chimes of Freedom* (1988).

Robert Stack

It took 20 years and 30 movies for this handsome, athletic actor to hit pay dirt as Elliot Ness in TV's outrageously successful "The Untouchables." The series ran for four years, made him a superstar, won him an Emmy, made him the most popular star on French TV and led to a flood of offers from European producers who wanted him in their films. A versatile actor who began his career in the Jack Benny comedy film *To Be or Not to Be*, in recent years Stack has starred in both comedy roles (*Airplane!; 1941*) and heavy dramatics (*Uncommon Valor*). However, TV remains his favorite medium. He's one of the few actors to star in four major television series, and the only one with so many shows dealing with crime. Starting with the Prohibition-era series "The Untouchables," he went on to portray the editor of *Crime* magazine in "Name of the Game," followed by his third and fourth series, "Most Wanted" and "Strike Force," both police action shows.

Born 13 January 1919 in Los Angeles, he's a fifth-generation Californian whose ancestors were among first U.S. families to settle in the little pueblo now known as L.A. He grew up among motion picture, concert, opera and radio favorites, many of whom were guests at his home during his childhood years. (His grandmother was the renowned singer Marina Perrini; his father was the millionaire adman who dreamed up the slogan, "The Beer That Made Milwaukee Famous.") Raised for six years in Europe as a young child, he learned French and Spanish before he knew English. Returning to the states, he became a champion skeet shooter at age 16 (holding two world records) and later, at USC, "majored in polo." Turning to an acting career, he entered the Henry Duffy School of the Theatre, was soon scouted by a Universal Studios talent scout, and made his film debut giving Deanna Durbin her first kiss in *First Love*. He scored in such films as *Written on the Wind* (Oscar nomination) and *The High and the Mighty* (his favorite role), but his career was mired in largely mediocre films for years. Bob joined the navy during World War II, graduating at the top of his class from the Naval Air Base at Pensacola and serving as an aerial gunnery instructor. Among his postwar films were *A Date with Judy*, with Elizabeth Taylor and Jane Powell, and *Mr. Music*, with Bing Crosby.

Offscreen, he was known as one of Hollywood's more flamboyant playboy types until his marriage in 1956 to starlet Rosemarie Bowe (two children). "Since Rosemarie got married it's OK to say she's well stacked," he once joked. Their fragrance and fashion ventures are being managed through Rosemarie Stack Ltd., a division of the Stacks' St. Pierre production company formed in April 1984, of which she is chairman and he is president. Stack remains very active in the business. He's starred in CBS-TV's "Falcon Crest" and remains the host of "Unsolved Mysteries." Recent films are *Glory Days, Blood Relations, Dangerous Curves* and *Caddyshack II*.

Lesley Stahl

"I think women, over the last ten years, even though we're not in the boardroom have had an enormous influence on what we cover and how we cover the news," Lesley Stahl said in an interview after she was asked to be anchor for the revamped Sunday-morning showcase of journalism "Face the Nation" in September 1983. Long a CBS News White House correspondent, Stahl has come up with some brilliantly exciting news coups (like the Sunday morning of 23 October 1983, when Stahl had already lined up the Syrian Ambassador and other officials for an update on Lebanon—one of the earliest reports on the U.S. Marine massacre in Beirut which had occurred that morning.)

Born in Lynn, Mass., 16 December 1941, she received her B.A. cum laude from Wheaton College. She was assistant speechwriter in Mayor John V. Linday's office in New York City from 1966 to 1967 and was with NBC News from 1967 to 1969. From 1970 to 1972 she was producer/reporter on WHDH-TV, Boston, and then became a news correspondent for CBS News in Washington in 1972. She is a trustee of Wheaton College and the recipient of the Texas Headliners Award of 1973.

Stahl is married to writer Aaron Latham; they have a daughter, Taylor. How does she manage career and marriage? "About the same way anyone in the frenetic news business manages it—with patience, hard work and zest." Stahl has said her daughter probably will not follow in her mother's footsteps. "My daughter is writing a book," said the journalist, "I have a feeling she takes after her father more than she takes after me. The book is a much more fanciful kind of book than it is a reporter's journal or diary. I won't push her. I want her to taste everything, then make a decision." What effect does Stahl think the women's movement has had on television? "All the media have been enormously influenced by the women's movement, although to be pragmatic and open-minded about it, it has a lot to do with demographics. There are lot more women in this country than there are men."

Sylvester Stallone

"The champion represents the ultimate warrior—the nearest thing to being immortal while mortal. The champion lives on forever. The championship belongs to a single person who because of the nature of what he does, has the respect of everyone on the face of the earth." Thus spoke the most famous muscle man in Hollywood ("Pacific Palisades Pecs," they call him) and, in 1985, the highest-paid actor in Hollywood.

Born on 6 July 1946 in New York's Hell's Kitchen and raised in Philadelphia after his parent's divorce, the multi-muscled talent remembers: "I was told by my teachers that my brain was dormant, and I took it to heart and channeled a tremendous amount of energy into my physical development." An appearance in a school production of *Death of a Salesman* made him determined to make it in New York's acting world. In the peculiar early 1970s, he caged up in a fleabag hotel and practiced his craft in front of the mirror between jobs working as a food demonstrator, a sweeper in the lion's cages at the Central

Park Zoo and as an usher at the Baronet Movie Theatre (where he met his wife, Sasha, also an usher). It was during this time that he became determined to create heroes for the common man and, having seen the film *Easy Rider* in 1969, convinced himself that "I couldn't write any worse." He wrote two novels that were never published and made minor appearances in several films, his first important role being Stanley in *The Lords of Flatbush* (critics singled him out.) Inspired by a prizefight between heavyweight champion Muhammed Ali and an obscure New Jersey fighter named Chuck Wepner who managed to go almost the full 15 rounds before being knocked out, Stallone got the idea for *Rocky*. He dictated the script to his wife in a mere 86 hours, shooting lines at her and rejoicing, "This is it, this is it!" It certainly was. The film made Stallone not just a star but a hero. His life changed. *Rocky* won a 1977 Academy Award as Best Picture and give birth to *Rocky II, III,* and *IV,* all blockbuster hits. He has also revived the character he played in *First Blood* and spawned a line of (machine-gun toting?) dolls with *Rambo: First Blood II in 1985 and Rambo III* in 1988. Besides these films, Stallone starred in *F.I.S.T.*, wrote a successful novel, *Paradise Alley*, and produced, directed and coauthored the sequel to *Saturday Night Fever-Staying Alive*—which starred a waxed and shining John Travolta. In 1986 he starred in two more movies, *Cobra* and *Over the Top*. His latest film is 1989's *Lock Up*.

Success spoiled Mr. Stallone, too. His marriage faltered and for a while he went around the ring of life without his wife and two children, Sage Moonblood and Sergio. "There are no perfect people," he said, "only perfect moments. Our separation has brought us closer together." Not for long. They split permanently in 1985, and Sly took up with decidedly non-melancholy Dane Brigitte Nielson. Bad casting from the beginning, the couple had a brief marriage (1985-1988).

The tough guy also has a soft side. Always concerned for his fellow man, Stallone was the 1988 honorary chairman for the New York March of Dimes. His character on the screen reflects to his personal life: "Just the other day I got on the subway to remind myself what it was like. I took the 59th Street BMT. I only went one stop because, being recognized, there was quite a lot of shoving, with guys yelling, 'Hey my man, you're Rock, my rock! Come over here and kiss my sister.' That's the real wealth - it's not the money but the communication."

Barbara Stanwyck

"Attention embarrasses me. I don't like to be on display," says the striking screen legend who is sometimes characterized as a "loner" because she does not attend big social events ("I never did care for big parties. You don't get to talk to anybody. I prefer groups of six or eight people"). And so it was with great reluctance that she consented to be feted by the Film Society of Lincoln Center in 1981. "It was a terrible shock. But a splendid shock," she later admitted. After this honor, Stanwyck was not as stage shy; in 1986 she was the recipient of the Cecil B. DeMille Award at the 43rd Annual Golden Globe Awards, and in 1989 she was given the American Film Institute Award.

The youngest of five children, she was born Ruby Stevens in Brooklyn, 16 July 1907. She was orphaned at four and, for a time, was brought up by an older sister, Mildred. "But we were very poor so we were all skipped off to foster homes. Growing up with nobody, I had to cope with loneliness at a very early age. Now the psychoanalysts tell you to be your own best friend. I had to master that earlier than most people." At fifteen she worked as a night-club dancer, landed a bit with Ziegfeld's *Follies* in 1922, and subsequently worked as a chorine until 1926. Under the name of Barbara Stanwyck (taking her name from an old playbill listing Jane Stanwyck as Barbara Frietchie), she bowed as a dramatic actress in Willard Mack's play *The Moose*. Her first film was *The Locked Door* (1928), but it was with Frank Capra's *Ladies of Leisure* (1930) that she became a star. She has given many unforgettable performances (her favorites: *The Lady Eve*, 1941; *Double Indemnity*, 1944; *Sorry, Wrong Number*, (1948) and four times was nominated for an Academy Award (for *Stella Dallas*, 1937; *Ball of Fire*, 1941; *Double Indemnity* and *Sorry, Wrong Number*). Not until 1982 did the Academy of Motion Picture Arts and Sciences finally bestow upon her their award—a special Oscar for a long and distinguished career. "People talk about my 'career' but 'career' is too pompous a word. It was a job, and I always have felt privileged to be paid for doing what I love doing." Among the Stanwyck traits of honesty, generosity, punctuality ("I'd rather wait for people than have them wait for me") ranks fearlessness. She has never used a double, and in a fight scene in *Clash By Night* she was accidentally shoved againt a hot projection machine. Blood dripping from her arm would not deter her from finishing the scene, hiding her injury from the camera. She still has a scar. Never demanding, she was known to the crew as "Missy" an endearment that became her nickname.

Her first marriage in 1928 (one adopted son) to Broadway comedian Frank Faye ended in divorce in 1935, and in 1939 she married Robert Taylor. After a decade, that marriage ended in painful divorce and she never remarried ("Nobody ever asked me, and that's the truth"). "Bob and I didn't stay friends. We became friends again," and in 1965 they costarred in *The Night Walker*. An Emmy Award winner for her TV series "The Big Valley" (1965-68). Barbara Stanwyck emerged in 1983 to appear in the mini-series "The Thorn Birds"; her performance considered among the best of her career, she won an Emmy as Best Actress in a Dramatic Special. She returned to the series scene from 1985-1987 as the family matriarch in "The Colbys." "I have no intention of being the old lady in a purple shawl in my rocking chair looking at my old scrapbooks," she states firmly. "I'm not a yesterday's woman. I'm a tomorrow's woman."

Maureen Stapleton

"The actor has to hang out his ego on the line for everyone to see and weigh. He better hang it on a good line." The unglamorous but glowing and immensely talented Maureen Stapleton ("I'm kind of nondescript-looking"), who is just as likely to wear a hooded Army surplus jacket as a mink, has hung her ego on such lines as *The Rose Tattoo* (1950, her first Tony), *Toys in the Attic* (1960), *Plaza Suite* (1969), *The Gingerbread Lady* (1970, her second "best actress" Tony, for which she won a *Times* accolade—"As variegated and dazzling a performance as New York has ever seen"), and the 1981 Broadway revival of *The Little Foxes* (starring Elizabeth Taylor).

Born on 21 June 1925 in Troy, N.Y., her parents separated when she was very young. She grew up "nice, fat, and unhappy," and her escapes were eating and going to the movies. ("My real ambition, from the age of 6, was to be Jean Harlow—but alive of course. I always thought if I became an actress, I'd automatically look like her.") Stapleton arrived in New York at age 17 weighing 170 pounds and with $100 dollars in her purse. Her first Broadway part was in *Playboy of the Western World*. That led to Tennessee Williams's *Rose Tattoo*, after which the stage became her playing field. In 1958 Stapleton appeared in her first film, *Miss Lonelyhearts*, for which she received an Oscar nomination. After 11 years on the stage, film acting didn't come easy ("I kept telling myself, you learn three acts in plays, why can't you remember one little passage?"). Since that time she has appeared in many films, including *Bye Bye Birdie, Plaza Suite, Airport,* Woody Allen's *Interiors, The Fan, Reds* (1982, for which she won an Oscar playing the anarchist Emma Goldman), *Heartburn*, (1986), *My Little Girl* (1986), *Nuts* (1987), *Sweet Lorraine* (1987) and *Cocoon: The Return* (1988). Acclaimed television performances include "Among the Paths to Eden" (1967 Emmy), "Queen of the Stardust Ballroom," "The Gathering," "Family Secrets," and "The Thorns." Recently Stapleton admitted film is her favorite medium: "It's easier. They pay you more money. And you get two days off a week, and that's nice."

Divorced from Max Allentuck (two children) and David Rayfiel, she insists: "My children are the most exciting thing that's ever happened to me. I know that sounds Pollyanna-ish, but it happens to be true." And does she have a preference in performing comedy or drama? "Sorry to sound so crass, but whatever job pays is the one I want. . . . It doesn't sound very artistic, but I have a granddaughter now, and all I'm thinking about is money for her teeth, for her school, maybe for a little house for her. . . ."

Ray Stark

This onetime literary and film agent has been wheeling and dealing and producing some of Hollywood's biggest hits for almost 40 years. No longer identified parenthetically as "Fanny Brice's son-in-law" (his wife is her daughter Fran; two children, one of whom is deceased), his 1968 blockbuster, *Funny Girl*, earned Barbra Streisand a Best Actress Oscar playing the late comedienne. Ray Stark was one of Columbia Pictures' largest stockholders before it was sold to Coca-Cola, and is one of the richest men around Tinseltown.

Stark, born circa 1917, got into the movie industry as a publicity writer for Warner Brothers. After WW II he represented his former Rutgers University prof in selling Red Ryder radio scripts, and became agent to writers such as Raymond Chandler, and actors such as Kirk Douglas and Richard Burton. In 1957, he co-founded Seven Star Productions, then spun off several other successful companies using variations of his Midas-touch name. (Rastar Productions, and Rastar Films were both bought by Columbia in 1980, and preceded Ray Stark Productions). He has personally produced more than 20 movies including *Night of the Iguana* (1964), and *The Way We Were* (1973), and his companies have done more than 250, e.g. the film remake of the comic strip-inspired Broadway musical, *Annie* (1981). Some of his latest films are *Brighton Beach Memoirs* (1985), *Private Affairs* (1986), *Biloxi Blues* (1987), *Steel Magnolias* (1989) and *Revenge* (1989). While he has enjoyed long-term working relationships with Streisand and writer Neil simon, other artists like director Sydney Pollack and actor Robert Redford have preferred not to work with him again, citing creative control problems. "No one who's worked for him has escaped his generosity," says a former employee; Stark likes giving associates expensive baskets of Italian wine, lasagna, and sausages, or gifts of chocolates, but following a power struggle at Columbia after "Hollywoodgate," heads rolled while he and insiders locked horns. But the crafty, quiet Stark, whose gigantic Holmby Hills, California home once belonged to Humphrey Bogart, downplays talk of himself as a mogul. "[In Hollywood] there is no such thing as power. There is selling, salesmanship, and influence based on your record." Stark's record was sufficiently influential for the Academy of Motion Pictures, Arts & Sciences to give him its Thalberg Award in 1980 for lifetime achievement.

Ringo Starr

He's only 18 inches tall and he's as popular with the offspring of the baby boomers as he was when he banged the drums for the Beatles. Playing the miniature, magical, Mr. Conductor on public television's children's series "Shining Time Station," Ringo Starr is back in the limelight. Not only are the accolades pointing in his direction for his work on the delightful program (Daytime Emmy nomination in 1989), but Starr's crossing back over to the adult world with the formation of his All-Starr band. The group began a 25-city U.S. and Canada tour sponsored by Diet Pepsi in July 1989.

Born Richard Starkey on a poor street in Dingle (outside of Liverpool), 7 July 1940, an only child of a barmaid and a house painter, he was plagued as a child with peritonitis and a mass of broken pelvic bones after a year on his back with pleurisy. ("Three times they told my mother I'd be dead, but here I am. Maybe that's why I'm not a particularly wild fellow.") Having quit school at 14 he toiled at several jobs until his mother bought him his first drums and he decided to play for money. He replaced original Beatles' drummer Pete Best in 1960 while enduring audiences shouting their disapproval: "Ringo never, Pete forever."

Performing with history's most successful music group, Starr showed a comic bent in the Beatles' movies that made up for his lack of songwriting input. "I just happened to be the one who enjoyed movies the most. I used to get to the set early and I'd say, 'Put me on camera, man! Put me in front of it. I have a good time here!'" A nonconformist, possibly because of missing so much school time as a sickly child, he says he learns more from doing, like acting with the late Richard Burton and Peter Sellers, just as he had learned drums from playing in bands. His movies include *Lisztomania*, *Candy*, and *Caveman*, but the twice-wed skins-beater also learned he doesn't like producing after his ne'er-released loser, *The Son of Dracula*. But he says, "I'm most creative as a drummer. I'm probably the best rock and roll drummer on earth. I say that now because I used to be embarrassed to speak up for myself." He is currently married to actress—and onetime James Bond girl—Barbara Bach. In 1985 he made us all feel older as he became the first Beatle grandpa via son Zack.

Danielle Steel

The steamy fictional creations of this "reigning queen of the romance writers" are avidly read on Caribbean beaches, in crowded Manhattan delis at noon, and on buses, planes and trains anywhere in the world. Published in 22 countries in 18 languages, Danielle Steel has sold approximately 50 million copies of her books worldwide. In 1984 she had a double whammy; her novel *Full Circle* topped the *New York Times* list of hardcover bestsellers at the same time her *Crossings* topped the paperback chart. Some of her books include: *Passion's Promises, Now and Forever, The Promise, Season of Passion, To Love Again, Remembrance, A Perfect Stranger, Family Album, Secrets, Finer Things, Kaleidoscope,* and *Zoya*.

Published stories about the woman-behind-the-bestsellers tend to follow the starry-eyed formula of Steel's prose. "She was born to wealthy, cultured parents," throbbed the *National Equirer* in 1984. "Her father was a dashing rake, her mother an international beauty. She crisscrossed the Atlantic on luxury liners between their homes in Paris and New York City and attended posh European boarding schools. But, she has confided, 'It was a lonely, heartbreaking, no-one-wanted-me kind of growing up.'"

Born in 1948, educated mostly abroad, Steel returned to New York at 15 and simultaneously attended NYU and the Parson's School of Design. She first earned her keep running a public relations firm but, since deciding to try her hand at writing, she's never looked back. Though critics are often ambivalent (". . . cliches abound, characters come and go just as quickly, but the lively plot and fast romp . . . make the book a good read"), readers adore her. Demonstrative of her standing in the competitive romance-writing market is the fact that in a single month (September) in 1982, she was responsible for the top seven titles in the mass market romance paperback category.

Steel's childhood may have been miserable but (according to the *Enquirer*) the writer has finally found true happiness in her fourth marriage to shipping magnate John Traina . . . "divinely handsome, tall slim elegant and the nicest person I know." They share a San Francisco house with their children from previous marriages and ones they have had together. Despite these distractions, Danielle Steel manages to grind out an average of two books a year "in which handsome men fall in love at first sight with exotic beauties and in which people without money at the outset end up with buckets of it at the end."

Mary Steenburgen

Although this Oscar-winning player states, "If there's one thing I loathe about what happened to the American theatre after Brando, it's these actors who show you how much they're acting," she doesn't yearn for the torn T-shirt-and-mumble days either. "If you want naturalism in acting, you go film the butcher. For me, the whole point of acting is to 'sail' a little and give a view of what's wonderful from a few feet off the ground." It would be trite, but right, to point out that hers have been more than a few feet off the ground since her rocket-rapid rise in filmdom. The press agent's-sounding story goes that she was audition-interviewing by day and waiting tables by night when, after nearly six years in Manhattan, she read for and wowed actor-director Jack Nicholson, and he slotted her as the leading lady in his 1978 flick, *Goin' South*. She's been going strong ever since, and went on to a 1980 Best Supporting Actress performance in *Melvin and Howard*. "I try to retain my sanity. Life is too short for me to be tortured by my roles. I hope that doesn't make me less of an actress," Mary Steenbergen says. "But if it does—tough luck."

Speaking of luck, Steenburgen (pronounced steen-berjen) has employed the paying-your-dues variety. Born in 1953, the daughter of a railroad conductor based in Newport, Arkansas, she first studied drama at her home state's Hendricks College, where her professor suggested she drop out and study acting in New York. At 19, she enrolled at the Neighborhood Playhouse to study with Sanford Meisner, supporting herself during her studies mostly by waitressing. In the years before her first paid performing job in *Goin' South*, she worked with an improv comedy troupe. Following her first movie, once again over formidable competition, she was cast as time-travelling H.G. Wells' San Francisco lady-love in the offbeat romance, *Time After Time*, opposite Malcolm McDowell. (Not long after finishing the film, she and her co-star were married, and are now the New York and Hollywood-residing parents of two.) She has also been seen in *Ragime*, Woody Allen's *A Midsummer Night's Sex Comedy*, *Romantic Comedy* (opposite Dudley Moore) and as author Marjorie Kinnan Rawlings in 1983's *Cross Creek*. Her other movies include *Dead of Winter* (1987), *End of the Line* (1988), *Miss Firecracker* (1989), and *Parenthood* (1989). Mary has dropped the distinctive Arkansas accent of her youth. "Ah tawked lahk thay-ut!" Steenburgen recalls. She also starred in the TV miniseries "Tender is the Night" and "The Attic: The Hiding of Anne Frank."

Rod Steiger

In more than half-a-hundred films and TV presentations, he's played some of history's most notable personalities: Napoleon, Mussolini, W.C. Fields, Al Capone, Pontius Pilate. While doing them, Steiger has made (film) history himself, sharing in some of the screen's best efforts: *On the Waterfront*, *Oklahoma*, *the Pawnbroker*, *Dr. Zhivago* and *In the Heat of the Night* (for which he won the 1968 Best Actor Oscar). Little wonder, then, that he peers with disdain at the New Hollywood. "The motion picture business is in bad shape," Steiger says. "All they want to do is to . . . make sequels and . . . a lot of money. All art is lost, out the window." When reminded, however, that occasional Steiger-starring showings (such as *The Amityville Horror*) have been deemed less than artistic, he admits, "Well, it was bad, I guess, but I needed the job. I want to act." But his transgressions, unlike Pontius Pilate's, are minor and infrequent. "I think of acting as an immediate reward and an immediate death," he says. "The greater the moment on stage, the longer the mourning." Some of his other films include *Catch the Heat* (1987), *American Gothic* (1987), *The January Man* (1988), and *Tennessee Waltz* (1989).

Born Rodney Steven Steiger 14 April 1925 in Westhampton, N.Y., he joined the wartime Navy at the age of 16, whiled away Pacific hours by broadcasting "Shadow" stories over his ship's intercom. "Shadow!" the captain once interrupted, "this is Phantom. Get the hell off that line and pipe down!" After the war he joined a drama group at the Vet's Administration, "because that's where all the girls were." Advised to take his acting seriously, he built a solid reputation as evidenced by his winning the 1953 Sylvania Award as one of the best five TV performers of the year. The thrice-divorced Malibu resident wants to direct movies next. "I don't want to end up playing grandpa," Steiger says. "That would be hard." His ex-wives include Sally Gracie, Claire Bloom (one daughter), and Sherry Nelson.

George Steinbrenner

"I'm the heavy. I don't like it, but I don't know how to change it," laments the mercurial principal (55%) owner of the New York Yankees (since 1973). Thanks to his aggressive penetration of baseball's free agent market with promises of dollars and the pride of wearing Yankee pinstripes, the Yankees of the late 70's resembled the mythic teams of yesteryear. By making millionaires of such stellar diamond performers as Catfish Hunter, Reggie Jackson, Goose Gossage and Dave Winfield, George Steinbrenner produced four American League championships and two World Series triumphs in his first decade with the team. By the mid-80s there were, however, indications that George's imperious ways and temperamental outbursts towards his players and series of managers (his hiring and firing of fiery manager Billy Martin seemed to be an annual ritual) were taking their toll on a team which didn't appreciate its boss' philosophy of winning through intimidation. But Steinbrenner, who views the Yankees as the essence of America like "apple pie and hot dogs," and believes they are—like America—to be revered and respected, insists on doing it his way, accepting the judgment that he is tough, but asking that it be qualified by "but fair." A close friend sees him as an "empire builder" who came along a little too late, when "most of the world has already been parceled out."

Perhaps the fireworks that have punctuated his public life are merely an echo of the ones that accompanied his birth (4 July 1930 in Rocky River, Ohio) to a mother of Irish descent who, he says, imbued in him compassion for the underdog (his charitable works are legion) and a father of German ancestry who instilled in him a perfectionist's will-to-win. Armchair shrinks may trace his later outbursts against Yankee players to George's memory of his collegiate-hurdling champion father's charge to his 12-year old son who had failed to win a track meet. "What the hell happened? How'd you let that guy beat you?" (In 1978 Steinbrenner told an interviewer, "Anything I ever accomplish I owe to him.") At Culver Military Academy and at Williams College, he ran hurdles on the track team, was president of the glee club, and studied voice along with his academic studies. After army service, he became an assistant football coach at the high school level, progressing quickly to assistant's spots at Northwestern and Purdue. In 1957 he put sports temporarily aside when his father asked him to join the family's Great Lakes' shipping business, which ultimately became a subsidiary of American Ship Building Company, of which he's been chairman since 1967.

In 1973 Steinbrenner headed the group that bought the Yankees from CBS for $10 million, and began the trading and free-agent-luring spree that produced the team's first pennant in 12 years in 1976 and in 1977 its first World Series' championship in 15 years. With the pleasure came the pain of a two-year (1974-76) suspension from baseball which Commissioner Bowie Kuhn imposed on Democrat Steinbrenner for violating federal campaign contribution laws by donating funds illegally to the Nixon re-election campaign. Married 12 May 1956 to the former Elizabeth Zieg, he is the father of two daughters and two sons, and makes his home in Tampa, Florida, where his company has a major facility. Near his stud farm in Ocala and Florida Downs, he races his thoroughbreds. When in New York overseeing the Yankees' fortunes, he takes in the theatre (he co-produced

Applause and *Two for the Seesaw*), ballet and opera. The recipient of many humanitarian awards (most of his good works are unpublicized at his request), the holder of a host of honorary degrees, a member of the U.S. Olympic Committee and part owner of the Chicago Bulls basketball team, Steinbrenner was selected in 1970 as one of *Fortune* magazine's "Twelve Movers and Shakers in the U.S.A." His hirings and firings added a new twist in 1985—a few weeks after letting Yogi Berra go (after a slow Yankee start) and re-hiring tempestuous Billy Martin as field general, he promptly fired the jockey who failed to win—or even make a respectable showing—in the Kentucky Derby on one of George's mounts. Shortly thereafter he acknowledged a preference for his four-legged charges because "they can't talk to sportwriters." In an unusual happening in 1989, a West side watering hole in New York City launched a campaign to oust Steinbrenner. A petition was formed for each signee to make a minimum contribution of one dollar toward a "people's purchase" of the Yankees.

Gloria Steinem

Why is the world still fascinated by Marilyn Monroe more than two decades after her death? According to feminist writer/editor Gloria Steinem, "One reason is true for all public people who die prematurely—if a story is not brought to its own logical, or illogical conclusion, our imaginations are compelled to carry it on. That's why we hear more about James Dean than Gary Cooper, or about Jack Kennedy than Roosevelt. We are deprived of the natural end of a story, so our imaginations supply it." Steinem explores this question and others relating to the trouble-plagued, Hollywood super-siren in a thoughtful book *Marilyn: Norma Jeane* (1986) from Henry Holt & Co. The book features photographs of Monroe taken in the last summer of her life by George Barris, with whom she was collaborating an autobiographical work at the time of her death in 1962. Using Barris's interview notes and both color and black and white photographs as a central theme, Steinem has interwoven research, direct quotes, and insight to provide an unusual portrait of the private woman inside the public image, "the real but unknown girl named Norma Jeane who looked out of Marilyn's eyes."

One of the cofounders of *Ms.* magazine back in 1971, Steinem actually met Marilyn only once. The occasion was a session at the Actor's Studio where, present as a student observer, the writer was surprised to see the Hollywood sex symbol as a shy and uncertain woman who was the object of condescension by many Studio regulars. Later, when Steinem wrote a short essay, "Marilyn Monroe: The Woman Who Died Too Soon," for *Ms.*, she was astonished by the number of letters the article evoked. The essay attracted attention again in 1983 when it was reprinted in Steinem's first book, *Outrageous Acts and Everyday Rebellions*, and this encouraged her to pursue the subject in even greater depth. *Marilyn: Norma Jeane* takes the form of seven essays, each one complete in itself but also part of a whole portrait.

Born in Toledo, Ohio, 25 March 1934, the second daughter of an itinerant Jewish antique dealer and a former newspaperwoman, she lived after her parents' divorce with her ailing mother in a rat-filled East Toledo tenement. At fifteen she moved to better quarters with her sister, ten years her senior, in Washington, D.C. Despite poor grades, she fared so well on the entrance exam she was accepted to Smith, where she earned her degree in political science, graduating magna cum laude. She continued her studies in India, where she caught fire politically. "I discovered that I'd been ghettoed as a white person. I came home with this crusading zeal." Following a stint with the National Student Association and writing several unsigned magazine pieces, an essay called "The Moral Disarmament of Betty Co-ed" about the pill, appeared in *Esquire* in 1961. She went on to profile Paul Newman, James Baldwin, and Barbara Streisand. Best known among her early works was the 1963 expose, "I was a Playboy Bunny" (she'd infiltrated a hutch) for *Show* magazine. She helped begin *New York* magazine and was its political columnist until 1971. Her feminist consciousness was galvanized, she says, in 1969 when she attended an abortion hearing and in the first issue of *Ms.*,

she added her name to a list of well-known women who'd had abortions. Steinem was an active campaigner for Eugene McCarthy, Bella Abzug, George McGovern, Cesar Chavez's United Farm Workers, Shirley Chisholm, Norman Mailer's bid to become the mayor of New York City, and John and Robert Kennedy. In 1984, for the sixth consecutive year, she was named One of the 25 Most Influential Women in America.

In addition to her continuing work for *Ms.*, Steinem travels widely as a lecturer and feminist organizer and appears frequently on television and radio as a spokeswoman on issues of sexual equality. In addition, she serves as a contributing correspondent to NBC's "Today Show."

Isaac Stern

One of the most renowned and recorded violinists in the world, Isaac Stern was once described by *Time* magazine as "a natural force not to be explained." Said Zubin Mehta of his close friend and colleague, "We do not know how many hours Isaac lives in a day, we only know it must be more than twenty-four." When the master fiddler turned sixty in 1980, the music world celebrated along with him during "Isaac Stern season" and Stern himself stepped up his travel and performance schedule "to a pitch guaranteed to induce terminal jet lag," according to *High Fidelity* magazine. Called ubiquitous, irresistible and impossible (by *Time*), Stern is an exhausting hardworking musician. It is the "ubiquitous" Stern who doesn't miss a beat in his performance schedule but still finds time to act, in all but title, as a minister of culture: during the Cold War, Stern was the first American instrumentalist to visit the Soviet Union; he traveled to China to advise on the integration of its musical life (all but terminated during the cultural revolution) with that of the West (during that trip, Stern made the Oscar-winning 1981 documentary *From Mao to Mozart: Isaac Stern in China*) and he also serves as a patriarch of Israeli musical life, having helped launch the careers of several talented musicians, among them Itzhak Perlman and Pinchas Zukerman. Following the Six Day War of 1967, Stern performed a memorial concert atop Mt. Scopus which was made into the film *A Journey to Jerusalem*. Another film project was his violin solo on the Oscar-winning soundtrack for *Fiddler on the Roof* in 1971. It was the "irresistible" Stern who persuaded the City of New York and various patrons of the arts to save Carnegie Hall. (Stern now wants to use the great institution as a base for developing "a graduate institute of the most rigorous and ruthless quality.") And it is the "impossible" Stern who chooses not to choose between music and his dozens of other activities. "I practice more than most people think. With more experience over the years, your palette becomes more varied."

Born in Kreminiecz, Russia 21 July 1920, Stern was taken to California as a baby. Making his debut with the San Francisco Symphony at age 11, he went from youthful prodigy to youthful virtuoso at Carnegie Hall in 1943, when he "rocketed into the sparsely populated heavens of first-rate violinists." In addition to his solo flights, Stern for many years performed with pianist Eugene Istomin and the late cellist Leonard Rose in a chamber ensemble. Stern and his second wife, Vera (who is Chairman of the Friends of Carnegie Hall) have three children. An avid tennis buff, he once played Jimmy Connors a locker room solo. "Music is not an acquired culture, not something you learn instead of something else," he says. "It is an active part of natural life." His multitudinous awards include the Kennedy Center Honors in 1984.

John Paul Stevens

For a member of the world's most exclusive judicial fellowship, the United States Supreme Court, Justice John Paul Stevens holds some decidedly unlikely views. "Neither the Bill of Rights nor the laws of sovereign states create the liberty which the due process clause protects.... Of course, law is essential to the exercise and enjoyment of individual liberty in a complex society. But it is not the source of liberty, and surely not the exclusive source." John Paul Stevens is direct, down-to-earth and consistently open-minded regarding the issues that survive the tortuous trail to the Supreme Court. This makes Stevens, a master at constitutional line-drawing, the least predictable member of the august panel. Justice Stevens did not take his seat until just before Christmas 1975, but quickly hit his stride... and his stride includes a saucy willingness to criticize the very history and traditions of the bench. In typical manner, Stevens offered an elegantly-structured dissenting opinion that displayed his characteristic position as (according to New York Times court watcher Linda Greenhouse) "enigmatic, maverick, loner... a wildcard." Stevens began his memorable opinion with this sentence: "This case has illuminated the character of an institution." The institution at issue seemed to be an eastern university, but by the time Stevens ended the opinion—repeating the identical sentence—Washingtonians realized Stevens was wagging his finger at his own brethren.

Born 20 April 1920 in Chicago, Stevens married Elizabeth Jane Sheeren June 1942 (divorced). Four years after becoming an Associate Justice on the Supreme Court, he married again—this time to Maryan Mulholland Simon. He has one son, John Joseph, and three daughters: Kathryn Stevens Jedlicka, Elizabeth Jane and Susan Roberta.

Shadoe Stevens

The man with the leather pants and deep, sexy voice, was also a square. A "Hollywood Square". The announcer/actor whose "hawkishly handsome" good looks have earned him press attention also replaced longtime radio king, Casey Kasem, as the host of the radio countdown show "American Top 40." The booming-voiced performer has achieved almost cult status in California as Fred Rated, wild-and-crazy pitchman for the Federated Group, an electronics chain. His production company, Shadoevision, has put together more than 900 of the zany spots in the past few years ("Rabid frogs ate our warehouse, so we're passing the savings on to you"), helping to build a 14-link chain into 48 stores and upping sales a reported 1000 percent. As one L.A. paper put it, "Fred Rated is to spiel-o-matic forebears like Mad Man Muntz as "Miami Vice" is to "Dragnet."

Stevens—real name: Terry Ingstad-first hit the airwaves with his own radio show, broadcast (at aged 11) from his North Dakota bedroom. Later, he toiled as an on-mike pro in Arizona, Boston and Los Angeles, but invariably ruffled the feathers of upper management and was invited to move on. At the height of his radio career (at KMET in L.A.), he was named Billboard's "radio personality of the year." Stevens debuted on "Hollywood Squares" as an announcer, then he was occasionally asked to appear as one of the celebrity squares. When fan mail surged after each such appearance, the producers promoted him to a permanent square of his own. When the program was broadcast on location from Radio City Music Hall, Stevens made the Hollywood Reporter after "female fans nearly caused a riot and began chanting his name when he tried to exit the stage door." Police officials reported, "It was just like a rock concert."

Among the suave one's recent extracurricular career activities have been a comedy special on Cinemax ("sort of like Ernie Kovacs meets Monty Python meets Salvador Dali") and a feature film, Traxx. He is presently married to a model, Beverly Cunningham (daughter, Amber) and has a son from a previous marriage.

James Stewart

"Sometimes," drawls Hollywood's original Mr. Aw-Shucks, "I wonder if I'm doing a Jimmy Stewart imitation myself. I'm a lazy person. By nature I would have planned a quieter life, I don't act. I react." Since his arrival in Hollywood as a blushing, bumbling beanpole of a boy back in 1935, he's "reacted" in more than 70 films, among them such American classics as *You Can't Take It With You* (1938), *Mr. Smith Goes to Washington* (1939), *The Philadelphia Story* (1940); Oscar), *Harvey* (1950; later also on Broadway and TV), *Rear Window* (1954) and *The Spirit of St. Louis* (1957).

In recognition of all this he was the recipient in 1980 of the American Film Institute's Lifetime Acheivement Award, in 1983 of the Kennedy Center Honors and in 1985 of the Medal of Freedom, America's highest civilian honor (which also acknowledged his military contributions. In 1989 he wowed the literary set with his book *Jimmy Stewart and His Poems*.

Born James Maitland Stewart, 20 May 1908, in Indiana, Pa., he was the son of a Scottish hardware store owner and grew to lanky manhood with no thoughts of being a thespian. "But then at Princeton two things happened," he explains, "I was studying engineering and I flunked math. And I took part in a Triangle show." When school chum Josh Logan suggested a summer with a stock company on Cape Cod, he packed up his accordian ("People would not only talk right through my act; they would also sometimes say 'Shut up'") and emerged in the fall as an actor on Broadway. In New York he appeared in numerous flops, acquiring an unenviable reputation for occasional malaprops. On one opening night, he recalls, "I tugged so violently at a door which wouldn't open that I lifted the whole scenery wall. It came down on my head. When I finally got it fixed again, the door creaked open by itself. So I rushed over and shut it. It creaked open again and I rushed over and shut it again. Finally it creaked open a third time and a disembodied hand from backstage appeared and held it shut. We closed the second night." Later the doors opened for him when a movie scout saw him in *Yellow Jacket* (1934), and he set off for Hollywood.

Early in his picture career he played in *Wife Versus Secretary* as a gone-to-hayseed swain. "Jean Harlow had to kiss me," he later remembered nostalgically, "and it was then I knew that I'd never been kissed before. By the time we were ready to shoot the scene, my psychology was all wrinkled." But his first MGM contract enabled him to give vent to another love—flying. He bought his first real plane. "It's something that you never forget, never tire of. It's a freedom—it's true." Many planes—bigger and better—followed, but when he got to marriage, only one was for him. After a long tenure as the movie colony's most resolute bachelor, he married the once-divorced big-game huntress Gloria McLean in 1949, and often has gone with her on safaris. (He does most of his shooting with a camera, deciding "to leave the other part to Gloria.") Mrs. Stewart had two sons by a previous marriage, Michael and Ronald (who was killed in action in Vietnam); the Stewarts also have twin daughters, Judy and Kelly.

Noteworthy for many years as the highest-ranking movie star in the military, Stewart was an Air Force Reserve brigadier general before his retirement in 1968. One of the first stars to enlist in World War II, he rose from private to bomber pilot and squadron commander, participating in more than 20 missions over Bremen, Frankfurt, and Berlin. "I always prayed," says Stewart, "but I really didn't pray for my life or for the lives of other men. I prayed that I wouldn't make a mistake." He was a much-decorated colonel by war's end. Shortly after his appointment to brigadier general in 1959 (after some Congressional hassling), he ran into engine trouble while flying a tour of duty, but managed to bring his plane to a safe landing. "All I could think of was not my personal safety," he said later, "but what Senator Margaret Chase Smith (who was then Chairman of the Senate Armed Services Committee) would say if I crashed such an expensive plane."

Rod Stewart

"I really think that if you're gonna make rock and roll, you've got to live the lifestyle." One of rock music's reigning male sex symbols, he is as distinguished for his bawdy flamboyance and womanizing ways as he is for his raspy, soulful sound.

Roderick David Stewart, born in North London on 10 January 1945, abandoned a professional soccer contract to make music with his wayward teenage buddies, who later became members of the Kinks. Stewart fronted several bands in England—most notably the Jeff Beck Group, which became popular in the U.S.—before forming The Faces, with Ron Wood, in 1969. The seven albums the group made before its split in 1976 garnered such hits as "You Wear it Well," "Reason to Believe," and "Maggie May," and they popularized Stewart's emotionally-laden vocals, described by one critic as, "an unmistakably original expression . . . crackling [with] masculine authority." Going solo, he had a big hit off his 1976 "A Night on the Town," album, with the single, "Tonight's the Night," a sultry sexual innuendo number featuring a backup track of ecstatic moaning by girlfriend Britt Ekland. She later sued him in a celebrated palimony case, which was settled out of court for a reported $500,000 in property value. When his 1979 "Blondes Have More Fun," album was released, featuring "Mod Rod" with a mop of bleached blond hair, some rock critics—with whom Stewart himself later agreed—faulted the singer for an attack of vanity, suggesting that he had gazed too often into Narcissus' pond and finally fell in. But the throbbing disco cut; "Do Ya Think I'm Sexy?" became the fastest selling single in Warner Bros. history. His other hit singles in the 80s include "Young Turks," "Infatuation," "Lost in You," Forever Young," and "Crazy About Her." His LPs are *Footloose and Fancy Free*, *Tonight I'm Yours*, *Security Device* and *Out of Order*.

The singer, who says his passions are "soccer, drinking, and women, in that order," married Alana Hamilton, the former wife of actor George Hamilton in 1979; they later divorced in 1984 (two children). He had a child, Ruby, with Kelly Emberg in 1987.

Stiller and Meara

"We felt we'd made it when we saw our picture on the wall at the local dry cleaner," answered Anne Meara with a twinkle in her Irish eye when asked when she and Jerry Stiller first knew they were a success. Today the red-headed Irish Rose, "tall, bubbly, and beautiful," from Brooklyn, and the nice Jewish boy, "short, pensive, and retiring," from the lower East Side, are now the best known husband and wife comedy team in show business since Burns and Allen. They first met in an agent's office where they swear the agent chased each of them around his desk during separate interviews. Neither one got the job, but they found each other (which turned out to be a long booking).

Stiller, born 8 June, attended the lower East Side's Seward Park High (other alumni: Tony Curtis, Walter Matthau, Zero Mostel). He went on to Syracuse University, majoring in drama. After acting in various theater groups in New York City and across the country, he met Anne Meara "making the rounds." Meara, born in Brooklyn 20 September, was brought up on Long Island. After high school, she appeared in summer stock in Southold, L.I., and Woodstock, N.Y., studied at the Herbert Berghof studio, won an Equity award for *Maedchen in Uniform*, did some television, and then met Jerry Stiller "making the rounds." Married 14 September 1954, they joined Joseph Papp's newly-formed Shakespeare-in-the-Park. "In those days we didn't have a stage in Central Park," Stiller recalls. "So, in the middle of a play you'd have a guy yelling from the grass, 'Eh, Romeo! Give it to her! Give it to her!'" Meara adds: "The lines stayed the same, but our scenes got longer and longer." The actual formation of the comedy team was in the mid 1960s, as "an act of desperation." They had decided to have a baby and were forced to find another way to make some money. They played New York clubs like Phase Two, Village Gate, Village Vanguard, Bon Soir, a record-breaking 14-week engagement at The Blue Angel, the Royal Roost, and the Persian Room of the Plaza. An appearance on Merv Griffin's afternoon talent show led to the first major break with a guest shot on the Ed Sullivan show (resulting in a contract for 6 shows a year). Today they are constantly in demand for their tandem talents. (They now create and produce prize-winning radio and TV commercials for such clients as Blue Nun, Amalgamated Bank, GTE, United Van Lines and Harrah's, via their own production company.) And, while continuing as "the team" each has had phenomenal successful "turns" on their own. Anne created the role of Bunny in John Guare's award-winning *The House of Blue Leaves*. On television she appeared on "Medical Center," "The Male Menopause," was a regular on the "Corner Bar," "Archie Bunker's Place" and "Rhoda" series, and starred on her own show, "Kate McShane." Her films include *Boys from Brazil*, Neil Simon's *The Out-Of-Towners*, *Lovers and Other Strangers* and *Fame*. She received personal praise for her appearance in Harvey Fierstein's short-lived 1984 *Spookhouse* on the stage. She recently won the Writers Guild Award for "The Other Women." a TV movie which she co-scripted with Lila Garrett (Meara co-starred with Stiller and Hal Linden).

Stiller was "indecently funny" in the 1984 blockbuster David Rabe hit *Hurlyburly*. He previously starred on Broadway in *Unexpected Guest*, *The Ritz* (also the movie) and *Passione*. He created the role of Launce in Joseph Papp's production of Shakespeare's *Two Gentlemen of Verona*. Other movie appearances: *The Taking of Pelham One, Two, Three*; *Airport '75* and *Those Lips, Those Eyes*. He also was co-star of the television series "Joe and Sons." Stiller and Meara live in Manhattan (2 children, Benjamin and Amy) and are devoted to the city. For years Stiller has been an active member of his West Side block association. And with Meara he has made TV commercials promoting block associations and an "I Love a Clean New York" spot for radio.

Sting

"Why does tradition locate our emotional center at the heart and not somewhere in the brain? Why is the most common image in popular music the broken heart? I don't know. . ."

"I once asked my history teacher how we were expected to learn anything useful from his subject, when it seemed to me to be nothing but a monotonous and sordid succession of robber baron scumbags devoid of any admirable human qualities. I failed History."

"A great uncle of mine who was a seafaring man once gave me the following advice 'Never board a ship unless you know where it's going.' Sometimes it's hard to tell the game shows from the TV evangelists."

The former Gordon Matthew Sumner, erstwhile leader of the British rock group, The Police, has "no intention of becoming a victim of the whole rock myth." Not blending into the mainstream, his music is a combination of reggae and pop with lyrics that make you think. . . .

Having become something of a movie sensation-in films such as *Brimstone and Treacle;* a five-minute appearance wearing a leather jockstrap in *Dune;* in *Plenty* as the working-class black marketeer whom Meryl Streep asks to father her child; in *The Bride*, starring opposite Jennifer "Flashdance" Beals; a cameo in *The Adventures of Baron Munchausen* and roles in *Julia and Julia* plus *The Side*—he speaks defiantly about his independence from the trio that made his career: "The mistake that people always make about music groups," he told John Duka in a New York *Times* interview, "is they assume that if you're successful, the group becomes a way of life. For me, the band is only a tool in which I express my ideas, not a way of life. As soon as it becomes limited in expressing my ideas, then it's over. I can transcend it and use it to accomplish other things. Why should I have to make music with the same two people the rest of my life?" (The group disbanded in 1985, the year Sting made his first solo album—*The Dream of the Blue Turtles*.) He expanded his career one step further as he headed the cast of *The 3 Penny Opera* on Broadway in 1989.

Born 2 October 1952 in Newcastle, England, the son of a milkman and a hairdresser, he was given his nickname because of a black and yellow jersey he wore with the frequency of a second skin. By the time The Police formed in 1977 Sting was already married, a father, and the veteran of seven British television commercials, as well as having made his screen debut in the Who's film *Quadrophenia*. The almost instant success of The Police had many comparing them to the Beatles. (Their concert at Shea Stadium topped the attendance figures set a decade earlier by the long-haired foursome.) Lisa Robinson, the syndicated rock columnist, had said that Sting is "an incredibly talented songwriter.... But it's strange. When the Beatles came along they affected an entire generation in terms of dress and politics. Everyone grew their hair and changed clothes. Sting has not affected people that way. I hate to say this, but Sting has become enormously successful because he is safe and knows how to sell." His music is some of the most intellectually conceived, well-crafted pop music around. Speaking about The Police's 1983 superhit album "Synchronicity," Duka wrote that Sting had become "the intellectual Dark Prince of Sadness, his persona mingling menace and melancholy." Sting agreed. "I'm very melancholic, but I'm lucky in that I have a mode of expression that rewards melancholy. I express it in song. It's heard by other people and makes them sad and melancholic. And then you have a success on your hands."

With his first wife, Frances Tomelty, he had two children, Kate and Joe. He shares his house outside London in posh Hampstead with Trudie Styler, with whom he also has kids. "My children are very important to me," he says. "I see them all the time." Sting claims to prefer classical music to rock, calling rock "a sort of wonderful mongrel that takes from everywhere. That's its genius." In recognition of other artists making music, Sting formed his own label, Pangaea Records, with Miles Copeland. The label concentrates on esoteric music rather than pop.

"It is part of his anachronistic appeal that, physically, Sting is a bit of a throwback to the old-time, Hollywood type of glamour: tall, blonde and handsome, a classic heartthrob, perfectly proportioned," John Duka observed, "and able to tear his shirt off during concerts with the best of them." In 1988 he was voted the best Male Pop Vocalist by NARAS, as he received the Grammy for "Bring on the Night."

Oliver Stone

Twice-wounded Vietnam veteran Oliver Stone also has a matching pair of Oscars. The decorated Purple Heart with Oak Leaf cluster director was acclaimed by the Academy for both *Midnight Express* and *Platoon*. His followup film, *Wall Street* added more praises to the already established man of the cinema.

Oliver Stone was born in New York City on 15 September 1946. He attended Yale University and New York University, and served in the U.S. Infantry (1967-1968) fighting in Vietnam. Stone was only 21 when he and the rest of his 25th Infantry Division were shipped to War Zone C in the Hobo Woods not far from Vietnam's Cambodian border. Wounded during a night ambush in his first few days in the field, the filmmaker created a similar ambush for *Platoon* and the movie's final battle that took place on New Year's Day, 1968. "I wrote the script seven years after I'd come back," says the vet. "It took me that long to come to terms with the reality of what happened there." *Platoon* was Stone's fourth directorial effort. It came on the heels of the highly acclaimed (albeit controversial) *Salvador*, another exploration of grim contemporary reality, this time in Central America. He made his directorial debut as a 25-year-old with the low-budget film, *Seizure*, made from his own screenplay. For his second outing as a director, he made the thriller, *The Hand*, with a screenplay he adapted from the novel, *The Lizard's Tale*. The 1981 release starred Michael Caine.

Stone's reputation as a screenwriter hit its first peak in 1978 when *Midnight Express* (about an American jailed in Turkey) not only won the Oscar but the Writers Guild of America Award. In recent seasons, Stone co-authored the script for *Conan the Barbarian*, wrote the screenplay for *Scarface* and collaborated (with Michael Cimino) on the script for *Year of the Dragon*. In what can be viewed as the unassailable rights of a writer-director, Stone appeared in *Platoon* as a major who is blown up in his bunker at the end of the film. A far cry from the lowly rank of "grunt" over twenty years ago.

Tom Stoppard

The Tony Award winning author of such plays as *Rosencrantz and Guildenstern Are Dead, Jumpers, Travesties, Night and Day, The Real Inspector Hound, The Real Thing, Every Boy Deserves Favor*, and *Hapgood* as well as TV plays and scripts for movies like *The Human Factor, Empire of the Sun*, and *The Romantic Englishwoman*, established himself, in the words of one critic, as "the modern stage's star acrobat of language and ideas."

"One writes about human beings under stress, whether it is about losing one's trousers or being nailed to the cross," says the playwright, born Thomas Straussler 3 July 1937 in Czechoslovakia, son of a doctor. When the Nazis occupied his native country the Strausslers fled to Singapore, but when the Japanese took over the English naval base his mother and brother were evacuated to India. Dr. Straussler died in captivity. Describing himself as "a bounced Czech" he says; "my first language was Czech but it was baby Czech. The first proper school I went to was an American school in India. By the time I was six, English was my first real language." After his mother remarried an English officer named Stoppard, the family moved to England. "I went to prep school in Nottinghamshire and to public school in Yorkshire. I became a reporter in Bristol, England when I was 17. My ambitions were exclusively journalistic. A big-name roving reporter. My first ambition was to be lying on the floor of an African airport while machine gun bullets zoomed over my typewriter. But I wasn't much use as a reporter. I felt I didn't have the right to ask people questions. For me it was like knocking on the door, wearing a reporter's peaked cap and saying 'hello, I'm from journalism. I've come to inspect you. Take off your clothes and lie down.' I wrote a lot about the Bristol theater which was flourishing and I knew people in it. I became quite hooked on it and I wrote a play, *A Walk on the Water*, that was produced on TV in England in 1963. In 1966 I wrote *Rosencrantz and Guildenstern*."

From his first marriage to Jose Ingle he has two sons, Oliver and Barnaby. He is now married to a dermatologist and top British TV personality, Dr. Miriam Moore-Robinson with whom he has two sons. So fond is he of cricket that his country house sports a special lawn for the game and in *The Real Thing* he compared the artistic process to cricket. "My feeling is that in the theatre the emotions should be gratified as well as the intellect. Theatre is an event, not a text. I respond to spectacle. Ambushing the audience is what the theatre is all about."

George Strait

The "new traditionalist" movement in country music was pioneered by a Texas tenor noted for white cowboy hats, pressed jeans and buttondown shirts accenting his trim, athletic appearance. His name was George Strait (as in arrow). Strait brought pure country, heavy on southwestern swing and Texas twang, to then *crossover* pop-oriented country charts. His first single "Unwound" (1981) revealed a voice that was clear, cool and in command, capable of everything from broken-hearted ballads to Bob Wills blues. Strait and his "Ace In The Hole Band" revitalized the respect for and contemporary interpretation of traditional roots country. His clean-cut matinee idol looks (5'10", 160 lbs, green eyes, brown hair) elicit screams and gifts from a legion of female fans. Strait's reaction to the fanfare: "It surprises me. People are so generous. . . . I just go out and do my songs and don't tell jokes or do a lot of talking."

George Strait was born 18 May 1952 in Pearsall, Texas, the son of a junior high school math teacher who was also a part-time rancher. Strait grew up a rock and roll fan. During an Army stint following high school, Strait taught himself to play guitar by reading Hank Williams songbooks. Singing in a military country band, he decided he wanted to be a country recording star. After the Army, Strait earned a degree in agriculture from Southwest Texas State University in San Marcos. The Ace in the Hole Band was formed from a campus bulletin board ad—three original band members remain. They played small bars and clubs all over Texas, even when Strait went to work as a rancher. Foreman of a 1,000 head cattle ranch for two years, he continued to sing at night. Two self-financed albums went unnoticed. Failing to land a recording contract, Strait took a fulltime job designing barns and other ranch facilities. Deciding to give music one more try, he was discovered by then MCA executive Erv Woolsey and signed with MCA Records in Nashville in 1981. Strait was an immediate hit.

George Strait was named *Billboard* Magazine's New Male LP Artist of the Year and *Record World* New Male Artist of the Year in 1981. All nine of his albums (not including a 1986 Christmas album) went gold with two, *Greatest Hits Vol. I* and *Ocean Front Property* certified platinum. *Ocean Front Property* made history when it debuted at Number One on *Billboard's* Country Album chart, where it stayed for six consecutive weeks spawning three Number One singles. Strait has enjoyed nearly two dozen Number One records and a multitude of awards. He was named *Billboard* Male Singles Artist of the Year (1983), Academy of Country Music Male Vocalist (1984, 1985), CMA Male Vocalist of the Year (1985, 1986), CMA & Academy of Country Music- Albums of the year (1985), *Music City News* Male Vocalist of the Year (1986), *Billboard* Overall Top Artist and *Billboard* Top Male Artist (1986) and *Billboard* Number One Top Country Artist of the Year (1987). In January 1987, he set a new record when the Astrodome sold out 48,000 seats for a February concert in less than 24 hours. At the concert itself, 49,246 fans crammed into the Houston Livestock Show and Rodeo for a new attendance record.

Strait resides in San Marcos, Texas, with his wife, Norma, and their son George, Jr. ("Bubba"). When Strait is not performing he enjoys steer-roping, hunting, fishing, skiing, and golf. His musical success and good looks have prompted movie offers which he has considered but great music remains a priority. "I have always gone into the studio to make it better than the last one. Each time, I feel I have."

Roger W. Straus, Jr.

He's built a publishing house that puts out the books of a glittering list of authors including Nobel laureates Knut Hamsun, Herman Hesse, Francois Mauriac, Nelly Sachs and Aleksandr Solzhenitsyn. In the desperate bargaining for the Solzhenitsyn book *August 1914* (1972), the author's Western agent chose Straus's house because of its "dedication to literary quality and their past regard for the work of Solzhenitsyn." The firm also published his *Stories and Prose Poems* in 1971.

Born 3 January 1917 in New York City, the son of Roger W. Straus, president of the American Smelting and Refining Company, he dropped out of high school to work for the White Plains, N.Y. *Daily Reporter*. He persuaded Hamilton College to accept him without a high school diploma but left there also, finally getting his degree at the University of Missouri School of Journalism. After a reporting stint at the Columbia *Missourian*, he worked as an editor at *Current History* and at G.P. Putnam's before entering the Navy in 1942. In 1945, he and John Farrar (formerly of Farrar & Rhinehart) founded the firm of Farrar, Straus & Company, which since 1964 has been Farrar, Straus, Giroux, Inc. The firm has made a number of acquisitions including Creative Age Press and L.C. Page & Company in the 1950s, Noonday Press and Octagon Book in the 1960s and Hill and Wang in 1971. Straus is president and chief executive officer of Farrar, Straus and Giroux, and president of Octagon Books and Hill and Wang. Straus is married to Dorothea Leibmann, a former childhood friend. They have one child, Roger III. Though he's headed his company since its founding, Straus is quick to credit his success to others, especially Robert Giroux, who joined the firm in 1955. "The single most important thing to happen was the arrival of Bob Giroux," says Straus. "He's a great editor, probably the best in the United States."

Darryl Strawberry

The 1988 National League home run champ has found there is much expected of him. Born Darryl Strawberry in Los Angeles on 12 March 1962 and raised in a broken home with four brothers and sisters, he was the best young prospect in America after playing at Crenshaw High. Chosen by the New York Mets in 1980 (the same year brother Michael went to the Dodgers) Strawberry was the recipient of a large bonus and an inordinate amount of publicity. The minor league town of Kingsport, Tenn., held a press conference for the awestruck 18-year old when he arrived. He had to overcome a lonely, fishbowl-like existence and the resultant pressure to perform (as well as extraordinary back-home phone bills) on his way to the bigs. "I was thinking of so many things: girlfriend (at the time, USC women's basketball star, Paula McGee), family, being in the big leagues, going from city to city, new pitchers. . . . It hit me all at one time." After a weak start with the Mets in 1983 he began to spend long pre-game sessions talking with Mets' batting coach Jim Frey who mellowed him with advice like, "A lot of good things are going to happen to you if you put in the work. . . . Study pitchers and get a feel for what each is trying to do." The advice settled him, Strawberry says, and he finished with 26 homers and 74 RBI's in less than a full season at Shea Stadium. He was also named 1983's National League Rookie of the Year. By the next year the fans voted him an All-Star (he is the first NL'er picked for All-Star Game for five full seasons).

Strawberry's personal life hasn't been as stable as his career with the Mets. He married Lisa Andrews, a former model and Pasadena bank employee, in January 1985 (two children), but they were divorcing in 1989. Another foul ball took flight in 1989 when he was charged with a paternity suit by Lisa Clayton of Missouri. His experiences were to be detailed in the 1990 autobiography *Hard Learnin': The Coming of Age of a Major League Baseball Star* written with Don Gold.

Meryl Streep

"She has an incredible piece of working life ahead of her," says Dustin Hoffman of his co-star in *Kramer Vs. Kramer*. "She's going to be the Eleanor Roosevelt of acting." By the 1980s, she was unquestionably America's premier dramatic screen actress. In addition to her Oscar as 1979's Best Supporting Actress for *Kramer*, she won another Academy Award as Best Actress of '82 for her moving performance in the title role of *Sophie's Choice*. Coincidentally her '78 Emmy Award for the TV mini-series *Holocaust* was for her portrayal of a woman like Sophie: a Gentile victimized by the Nazis. But still, the radiant actress says, referring to her childhood: "I thought no one liked me. Besides that, I was ugly."

Born Mary Louise Streep (Meryl was her mother's nickname) on 22 June 1949 in Summit, N.J., she was raised with two younger siblings in that state's affluent suburbs. Possessing an operatic soprano voice, she studied singing with Beverly Sills' teacher. Bossy and obsessed with her looks, Streep transformed herself into "the perfect *Seventeen* magazine knockout"—a high school cheerleader, swimmer and homecoming queen. She graduated from Vassar College in '71, and attended Yale Drama School where, prior to her '75 graduation, she attained near-legendary status playing over 40 roles, some at the Yale Repertory Theatre. She went on to perform extensively at New York's Phoenix Theatre and Joseph Papp's N.Y. Shakespeare Festival, winning both a Tony nomination and an Outer Critics Circle Award in Tennessee Williams' *27 Wagons Full of Cotton*. Other New York stage highlights: her Lincoln Center performances in *Trelawny of the "Wells"* and Andre Serban's production of *The Cherry Orchard;* demonstrating her singing talent in Brecht-Weill's *Happy End* and Elizabeth Swados' *Alice in Wonderland*. Her '77 film debut in *Julia* led to a larger part the next year in *The Deer Hunter;* her supporting role won an Oscar nomination. Other supporting parts in '79's *Manhattan* and *The Seduction of Joe Tynan* preceded leads in *The French Lieutenant's Woman* ('81) and *Silkwood* ('83), both of which earned her additional Oscar nominations. The busy actress went on to star with Robert DeNiro in *Falling in Love* (1984), with Charles Dance and Sting in *Plenty* (1985), with Robert Redford in *Out of Africa* (1985; Los Angeles Film Critics Award for Best Actress), and with Jack Nicholson in *Heartburn* (1985), and *Ironweed* (1987). She received another Academy Award nomination for Best Actress for her moving performance in *A Cry in The Dark* (1988) and her next scheduled films are *She-Devil* (1989) and *Postcards From the Edge* (1990).

When someone urged Streep to change her last name to "Street," she defended her own as "a perfectly good Dutch name, like Rockefeller." She nursed her cancer-ridden *Deer Hunter* co-star and lover John Cazale through his terminal illness. After his death she married sculptor Donald Gummer in 1978. With their three children (Henry, Mary Willa, Grace), they live in Connecticut. Robert Benton, *Kramer's* writer-director, who allowed Streep to write her own lines for the film's court-custody fight scene, says of her, "She's one of the most sensible, well adjusted people I've ever met."

Barbra Streisand

The Hollywood jackals in their Armani suits had their triumph when she was denied any of 1983's Oscar nominations for her 16-years-in-the-planning musical *Yentl*, based on Isaac Balshevis Singer's tale about a Jewish girl in turn-of-the-century Poland who disguises herself as a boy so she can study Talmud at a Yeshiva. So what, she has a reputation for being a bitch? What else is a female perfectionist called, a perfectionist whose standards for herself result in a record of concurrent popularity in both pop music and movies that exceed such greats as Presley, Sinatra and Crosby? But such a snob? She wrote the *Yentl* screenplay (with Jack Rosenthal) produced, headlined, directed, sang all nine songs and recorded the album. The reviews ran from a low "Barbra Streisand wears a pillbox-contoured designer yarmulke ... technical sloppiness is evident throughout," to Steven (E.T.) Spielberg calling it "the best directing debut since *Citizen Kane*."

"That so-called designer yarmulke is an authentic one of the period," she retorted. "It's mostly the women reviewers who are attacking me. Can't they stand to see another woman succeed?" But it wasn't just the women, it was all of Hollywood. Nevertheless, the film did very good business at the box office—despite Oscar's snub, and making it proved to be a breakthrough in the emotional life of the superstar who first burst into public notice at age 19 with her big nose and "delicatessen accent" in Broadway's *I Can Get It For You Wholesale*. Born in Brooklyn, 24 April 1942, she was 15 months old when her high school English teacher father died suddenly. "Emotionally, my mother left me at the same time—she was in her own trauma.... I didn't have any toys to play with, all I had was a hot water bottle with a little sweater on it. That was my doll.... Growing up I used to wonder—what did I have to do to get attention? When I started to sing I got attention."

When her mother discounted her as an actress because she wasn't pretty enough, and said she should skip singing because her voice was too weak—suggesting instead that she become a secretary—Barbra grew her nails so long as to render the suggestion moot. At age 18, she won an amateur talent contest at a Greenwich Village bar—her remuneration was $50 a week and free meals. She studied the great voices of pop music past and latched onto material that lent itself to emotional interpretation. She discovered comedy when at one audition she "forgot I had gum in my mouth, and I took it out and stuck it on the microphone. It got a big howl." Her manager begged her to change her name, fix her nose and sing more conventional songs. Theatrical manager Marty Erlichman sought her out when her star was rising at *Club Le Soir*—he wanted to represent her. She asked him if he thought she should change anything about herself. Erlichman answered no and became her manager.

Her stage debut was in the ill-fated off-Broadway *Another Evening With Harry Stones* in 1961. In rehearsals for *I Can Get It For You Wholesale*, Producer David Merrick thought she was unattractive. When the show opened, the critics changed his mind. The other novice in the play was actor Elliott Gould. The two fell in love, were married and had one son, Jason. Gould and she divorced in 1971. Streisand's career includes countless gold and platinum albums, memorable TV specials and films such as *Funny Girl*, for which she won an Oscar, *Hello Dolly*, *On A Clear Day You Can See Forever*, *The Owl and The Pussycat*, *What's Up Doc?*, *Up the Sandbox*, *The Way We Were*, with Robert Redford, *The Main Event* and *A Star is Born*.

In 1986 she produced and appeared in the film *Nuts* with Richard Dreyfuss, but was snubbed again by the Oscars. To the delight of her fans, she recorded *The Broadway Album* in 1985, followed by *One Voice* in 1987. The latter LP's proceeds went to the Streisand Foundation which supports organizations committed to the preservation of the environment. In 1988 she recorded *Till I Love You*, a thematic album about "love in a relationship, finding it, questioning it, losing it, and finding it again." Her latest album, *A Collection: Greatest Hits & More* (1989), produced the single, "We're Not Making Love Anymore."

Elaine Stritch

When Elaine Stritch returned to New York in 1981 after eleven years in London ("Now that an actor is President it was time for me to come home"), Earl Wilson asked her if she was aware of the new doggy bag custom in the posh restaurants since she had been away. "I'm taking not only the steak, but the bottle of wine, too," she bellowed. "My doggy doesn't even drink." A convent-bred sometime bartender who once took a delivery boy from the grocery store to a party for Princess Margaret, the breezy blonde actress has observed somewhat ruefully: "The only time I've ever gotten great publicity is when I've done something other than my work." Not quite. It is true that she has made news for occasionally slipping behind a bar in New York or London. ("Everybody says 'What's *that* all about?'") One writer described her as "a sort of Grosse Pointe Texas Guinan having a helluva time." But it is equally true that critics and public have cottoned to her brassy brand of song and dance in vehicles like *Pal Joey, Call Me Madam, Goldilocks, Sail Away, Company* and the 1985 concert version of *Follies*, and to her dramatic performances in *Bus Stop* and *Who's Afraid of Virginia Woolf?* And English audiences cheered her stage and television performances while she resided there (very nicely, thank you, at the Savoy Hotel).

Charles Strouse

Born 2 February 1982 in Detroit, the youngest daughter of a rubber company executive (and a cousin of the late Samuel Cardinal Stritch), she decided early on a theatrical career and went to New York after high school. At her parents' insistence, she first lived at Manhattan's uptown Convent of the Sacred Heart (the same order had been her Michigan mentors), while attending a Greenwich Village actors' studio, where Marlon Brando was a classmate. "Between Mr. B and the Mother Superior," she said. "I didn't miss a thing." "I know what I'm doing." she says of her work, "and I love what I'm doing . . . the theatre . . . it's Pygmalion City. You can walk down Third Avenue in a pair of blue jeans for three days . . . then come on stage in white fox. And that's what it's all about. An actress is being someone else, but taking exactly what you've got in the blue jeans into the white fox."

Since her return to the United States she lives in New York City. Her husband, Irish actor John Bay, who she married in 1973, died in 1982. She loves cooking and entertaining her close friends. When she learned she had diabetes (she was living in London), she quipped: "Listen, I'm just looking forward to the day they catch me in the ladies' room at the Connaught Hotel 'shooting up.' Boy, am I going to have the last laugh." In 1984, she authored *Am I Blue*, an account of her coming to terms with diabetes. She had a role on the short-lived "Ellen Burstyn show" in 1986 and appeared in Woody Allen's film *September* in 1987, followed by a role in Ron Howard's *Cocoon II: The Return* in 1988. Working again in the theatre, she performed on Broadway in A.R. Gurney's revolving cast play *Love Letters* (1989). Rarin' to go, Stritch was being considered for some new London and U.S. productions for 1990.

Charles Strouse

Once Upon A Time, One Boy, who was *Honestly Sincere*, decided *Tomorrow* that everyone should *Put On A Happy Face*. *This is the Life* of composer, Charles *(A Lot of Livin' To Do)* Strouse. His melodic gift has made him a stand-out of the third generation of musical writers for theatre. He told *Songwriter* magazine, "I went to shows early on with my parents, and it was the glamor that hit me. . . . That's what musicals were about then, and still are, to a certain degree."

Strouse was born 7 June 1928 in Manhattan. His father was a tobacco merchant and his mother was a jazz pianist. A serious music student, he graduated from the Eastman School of Music in Rochester. He supplemented his education by studying privately with composer Aaron Copland and won a summer scholarship to study with Nadia Boulanger in Paris. Looking to break into the business while supporting himself, he played jazz piano for Butterfly McQueen and Sally Blair throughout the South, plus accompanied dance classes. In 1949, Strouse met his longterm lyricist and friend Lee Adams at a party for a mutual acquaintance. Together, they teamed up to write a revue each week for an in-spot in the Adirondacks called Green Mansions. Their special material was performed by such up and comings as Carol Burnett, Dick Shawn and Don Adams. As their reputation grew, the two men were approached by a producer to work on a show—*Bye Bye Birdie* was born. The musical launched Strouse's career on Broadway in 1959, earned him a Tony Award, and paved the way for future shows. *All-American* opened in 1962 based on a story about a slavic professor (starring Ray Bolger) who comes to America for all the reasons Americans detest—the vulgarity, brashness and spirit. Next, *Golden Boy* (1964) starred Sammy Davis, Jr., in the title role of a boxer. Strouse related to Al Kasha and Joel Hirschorn in the book *Notes On Broadway*, "Oh, I'll tell you, the most personal song in all of my shows is probably 'Night Song' from *Golden Boy*. That's the song about a lonely young man in Central Park—in this case he was on a rooftop—looking over the city. I remember being very lonesome and standing out in the park, looking toward perhaps this building . . . that was me as a kid; I had the same feelings." In March 1966, *It's A Bird, It's A Plane, It's Superman* was received with less vigor, but *Applause* (1970), starring Lauren Bacall, won a Tony Award for Best Musical. Other notable shows are *Charlie and Algernon* and *Dance A Little Closer*.

Moving on to another era, Strouse collaborated with other lyricists. He worked with Martin Charnin on *Annie* (1977), which brought him another Tony Award, with Stephen Schwartz on *Rags*, (1986) which gave him a Tony nomination, and with Sammy Cahn on *Bojangles*. He says, "Lee and I have never formally broken up. . . . We are still good friends. It's that our working habits grew different . . . he moved to the country, and already that was a big change."

Martin Gottfried in *Broadway Musicals* notes that "the comparison to [Leonard] Bernstein is appropriate because few among Broadway's third generation of composers rival Strouse's musical background." Serious music still retains a hold on Strouse. He has written piano concertos and operas, among them *Singers* (premiered with the Michigan State Opera Company), *Nightingale* (had its first performance in London in 1983), and *The Future of the American Musical Theatre*. He also succeeded solo (wrote both music & lyrics) with the score for the 1985 off-Broadway to Broadway show, *Mayor*, based on New York City's irrepressible Edward I. Koch. Adding another dimension to his theatrical career, he wrote the scores for the films *Bonnie and Clyde*, *The Night They Raided Minsky's*, and *Just Tell Me What You Want*, plus the theme song for TV's "All In The Family." The movie adaptation of *Bye Bye Birdie* starring Ann-Margret is a popular favorite, as well as the John Huston-directed movie version of *Annie*. Upcoming Broadway projects include *Annie II: Miss Hannigan's Revenge*, *Nick and Nora* (based on the *Thin Man* stories), and *Madame La Gimp*. He completed the film score for the animated film *All Dogs Go To Heaven* (1989) which featured the voices of Loni Anderson and Burt Reynolds.

The native New Yorker married Barbara Siman in 1962 and is the father of four children: Benjamin, Nicholas (an actor in the stage version of *Brighton Beach Memoirs* and the film *Doin' Time On Planet Earth*), Victoria, and William. The member of the Songwriter's Hall of Fame and Director of the annual ASCAP Musical Theatre Workshop, emotes, "I have a fantasy about a show that is hard to put in words. At the finish I would like to hear the sound of children. I'm after a feeling of great human warmth."

Jule Styne

Toiling as a Hollywood vocal coach for the likes of Alice Faye, Linda Darnell, and Shirley Temple, he took time out back in 1942 to try his hand at songwriting. Results? "I Don't Want to Walk Without You" (introduced in the film *Sweater Girl*), followed by a steady stream of song hits: "Make Someone Happy," "Three Coins in a Fountain," (Oscar 1954) "The Party's Over," et al. Says the whirligig music man about this ASCAP Comstock Lode: "I like to think about the tens of thousands of persons all over the world who whistle the songs I wrote. They don't know me from the Cardiff Giant, but they know the tunes."

Born 31 December 1905 in London as Julius Stein (he changed his name many years later to avoid being confused with MCA's Jules Stein), he came to Chicago with his family (also musical) as a child, and emerged as a bona fide child prodigy by the age of eight, playing as piano soloist with both the Detroit and Chicago symphony orchestras. In the twenties he renounced "serious" music to organize his own successful dance band and eventually landed in Hollywood. After making a musical name for himself with his film scores (*Anchors Away*, *Two Tickets to Broadway*, *My Sister Eileen*), he transferred his tunesmithing to Broadway in *High Button Shoes* (1947), *Gentlemen Prefer Blondes* (1949), *Bells Are Ringing* (1956), *Gypsy* (1959), *Funny Girl* (1964), *Hallelujah, Baby* (Tony, 1968), and *Sugar* (1972). As a producer his credits include *Pal Joey*, (Donaldson Award, Drama Critics Award), *Hazel Flagg*, *Peter Pan* and *Will Success Spoil Rock Hunter?* He won Grammy awards for both *Gypsy* and *Funny Girl* and has been inducted into the Theatre Hall of Fame as well as the Songwriter's Hall of Fame. Styne has been twice married, first to Ethel Rubenstein in 1927 and second to actress Maggie Brown in 1962, and is the father of four children, two from each marriage. In an interview with Lee Morrow in 1984, Styne mused, "Looking way back, the theatre used to be healthy. I mean healthy, where people said, 'I'm going to the theatre tonight.' They didn't say the name of the show. They're going to the *theatre*. If they couldn't get a ticket for one show they went to another. But they went. Now they go to *shows*. One particular show or nothing. The theatre is just rambling, floating." On the *format* of The Musical he states " . . . it may seem that musicals are very stylized today, but they always were. From the very beginning, back in the days when a fellow walked out and said, "Tennis, anyone?"—even that was a kind of style. You must remember that a musical is a crazy form. It violates every form of dramatics. It really does." While enjoying a renewed popularity of his *Peter Pan*, Mr. Styne received the Achievement in Arts Award in 1988.

William Styron

Sophie's Choice, a novel of our age's central horrors, the unmapped regions of heaven and hell that constitute the true 20th century, is imbued with the heavy air of Auschwitz as the intense story (nominally set in Brooklyn) reveals that violence, insanity and Nazism are not isolated horrors but slow poisons in our society. Queried about why he set his imagination loose in this area, William Styron said ". . . I was attracted to Auschwitz as a theme partly because no American writer, to my knowledge, seems to be able to deal with it as an imaginative situation. . . . I think that possibly a book gains by its writer *not* having been through the experience. . . . Experience itself doesn't authenticate good writing." Sophie Zawistowska, a survivor of Auschwitz, is blond, Catholic, polyglot and sexual, while her lover, Nathan Landau, is a masterful, brilliant, unbalanced New York Jew. (In the 1982 film version, the parts were played by Meryl Streep and Kevin Kline.) Their lives become intertwined with that of Stingo, the story's narrator, a 22-year old Southern boy fresh out of the Marines who has come to New York in 1947 to become a writer. Styron/Stingo uses his 30-year perspective to make excursions backward and forward in time to weave the central tragedy into history and into the life of the reader. While detailing the events of the story, he seduces the reader in to the grim drama of our own times. Present events unfold and past truths come to light, and the three lives, which represent three radically different histories, interpenetrate.

Like Stingo, Styron was born in the South (Newport News, Va. 11 June 1925) and grew up among its cultivated people. Styron attended Davidson College in North Carolina and saw active service as a Marine lieutenant before graduating from Duke University and settling in New York in 1947, determined to write. After a brief stint at McGraw-Hill, he studied writing at the New School and began his first novel, *Lie Down in Darkness*, which he finished in 1951. Receiving the Prix de Rome for this promising work, he went to Europe, where he met and married (4 May 1953) Rose Burgunder, mother of his four children. Returning to the U.S., he planted himself in Roxbury, Conn. in 1957. *The Long March* (1953) was based on his experience in 1950 when, back in the Marines, a martinet ordered a 36-mile forced march for his men. Then came *Set This House on Fire* (1960), an account of American degeneracy abroad. With *The Confessions of Nat Turner* (1967), he stirred up controversy and landed a Pulitzer Prize (1968) for his attempt to fuse the points of view of the master and the black in Nat's telling of a long, vivid account of the way it felt to be a slave in 1831. In *Time's* assessment, "Styron's narrative power, lucidity and understanding of the epoch of slavery achieve a new peak in the literature of the South." After *Nat Turner*, Styron's body of work, including his play (*In the Clap Shack*, 1972), was frequently compared to that of Faulkner. In 1988 Styron was inducted into the American Academy of Arts and Letters.

Danny Sullivan

"His racing whim"—as Danny Sullivan's parents once called their son's interest in the high speed sport—has catapulted him from ex-taxi driver, part-time model and sometimes waiter into the superstar, glamour boy of Formula One racing. The winner of the Indy 500 (after surviving a harrowing 360 degree spin, Sullivan went on to defeat Mario Andretti) "will do for racing," according to producer Jerry Weintraub (who signed Danny to star in the racing film *Yankee Lady*) 'what Ali did for boxing, Palmer did for golf and Connors did for tennis. . . . He's the first to come along in 20 years who is not going to be just a name but a face as well." The supercharged world of auto racing attracts as spectators the glitterati as well as the grease monkeys. Among those who keep on top of Sullivan's races are Christie Brinkley, Victoria Principal and Prince Albert of Monaco. In 1988 Sullivan received the American Image Award from the Men's Fashion Institute.

Born 9 March 1950 in Louisville, Ky., Sullivan established his fast pace early. Though scheduled to take over the construction company that belonged to his father, Sullivan didn't exactly take to the business environment, preferring fast cars and fast women. After a year at the University of Kentucky, where he "majored in partying." Sullivan moved to New York and began driving—a cab, that is. An old family friend concerned about the directionless youth agreed to pay for an eight-day course at the Jim Russell School of Driving in England providing Sullivan return to college if he didn't show the necessary skill as a driver. There, Danny not only was one of the best pupils the school had ever taught, he "fell in love" with the world of racing. Sullivan spent the next seven seasons competing in races from Monte Carlo to New Zealand and in 1978 returned to the United States to participate in the North American Formula Atlantic Championship. His career gained speed in the early '80s.

The racer admits, "I am a lucky guy. I know this isn't a rehearsal and that every day can't be lived again. They all count and I'm out to enjoy them." Danny divides his time between L.A., Aspen and New York City.

Kathleen Sullivan

Her climb to the top of the broadcast ladder has been filled with criticism, but Kathleen Sullivan has become one of the outstanding ladies on the television screen. As co-host of the CBS Morning Show, she's holding her own as a competitive AM anchor. When she was on ABC's "World News This Morning" the executive producer of the program said, "You can relate to her [on the air]. She is able to translate what she is thinking into real communication with the viewer. It's kind of magic." On the other hand, a former colleague of Sullivan's remarked, "Kathleen looks great on camera and is a wonderful performer, but she's a weak writer and a weaker reporter." All criticism aside, Sullivan remains at the top with a reportedly high salary.

Born circa 1953 in Pasadena, California, Sullivan studied business administration and speech communication at the University of Southern California. An all around athlete, she made the varsity tennis team, and after graduation interned in the sports department at a Los Angeles station. In 1978 she went to work as co-anchor for KTVX-TV an ABC affiliate in Salt Lake City and two years later she joined Atlanta's Cable News Network (CNN) as co-anchor of "Prime News" (Sullivan was the first anchor hired by CNN.) She was paired with ABC's Frank Gifford to cover the 1984 Summer Olympics. *Newsweek* magazine noted that she "could have used a bit more homework." Interviewing former Olympic sprinter Wilma Rudolph, Kathleen asked how she felt while carrying the Olympic flag during Saturday's opening ceremonies. Replied Rudolph: "Oh that wasn't me. That was Wyomia Tyus. We're always being confused."

Kathleen tried the married life with Mike Kiner in 1986; the couple had separated in June 1988.

Arthur Ochs Sulzberger

When Arthur Ochs Sulzberger was named publisher of the New York *Times*, one of the first things he did was shut down the newspaper's floundering West Coast edition. The corridors on West 43rd Street buzzed with the second-guessing of *Times* editors. One warned Sulzberger: "You can't close down the edition, Punch," he said, using the nickname favored by everyone but Sulzberger's wife. "We must save face." The reply came instantly: "We're loaded with face. It's a bad paper. Let's get rid of it."

The move, calculated to displease key *Times*men, established the ninth publisher as a man to be reckoned with. A publisher by inheritance, after his brother-in-law, his father, and his grandfather before him, Punch suddenly was calling the shots over the heads of people who still remembered him as a youngster cavorting in the corridors outside the executive desks of senior editors. Many also remembered his lackluster student years, where discipline and achievement eluded him until a Marine drill instructor finally made him shape up. Yet he never developed the ace reporter's killer instinct. During his apprenticeship at the *Times* Paris bureau in 1955, he attended the LeMans auto race and watched in horror as a car jumped the road and plowed into the stands. But he didn't write the story, or even call the office.

Yet he was no slouch as publisher. *Times* chronicler Gay Talese praised his familiarity with the "modern techniques that might help run the *Times* more effectively and economically. Sulzberger wanted to experiment with modern systems and to learn more about them; his newspaper could not merely follow the formulas of his father or grandfather." For a newspaper so steeped in tradition, this was the equivalent of coming to an embassy soiree wearing a psychedelic tie. Punch himself remains very much the friendly, unostentatious man who always says hello in the elevator. Without any trace of the rigidity that characterized his predecessors, he has let some fresh air into the *Times* executive suites—whatever fresh air there is, that is, in Times Square.

Born 5 February 1926 in New York City, his first marriage to Barbara Winslow Grant ended after eight years, during his Paris assignment. Back home he met and married Carol Fox Fuhrman, (two children from his first marriage, one child with his present wife, and an adopted child from his present wife's first marriage).

Donna Summer

At the point where people were asking, "What ever happened to Disco Queen, Donna Summer?", she came out of oblivion with a new hit record in 1989. "It's called *Another Place and Time* because it was recorded in another place, known as London. We had a song by that name on the record, and it just fit with the idea of the album." It spawned the danceable single "This Time I Know It's For Real." A refreshing new comeback for the woman who sang "Love to Love You Baby," complete with openly ecstatic orgasms.

Born 31 December 1948 in Boston, LaDonna Andrea Gaines was one of seven children. After singing solos in Boston churches and also with a white rock group called Crow, ("get it, I was the only black person?") she won a part in a German production of the rock musical *Hair* and, against her family's wishes, set off in 1967. She remained in Europe for 8 years modeling and singing in Vienna Volksoper productions of *Showboat* and *Porgy and Bess* as well as *Godspell* and *The Me Nobody Knows*. In Vienna she married her now ex-husband, Helmut Sommer (her professional name comes from a record label misspelling). They moved to Italy and soon she was pregnant with her daughter Mimi. "It was the spaghetti. You get so lazy you just lie there." After the spaghetti, she met composer Giorgio Moroder and Pete Belloter and in Munich she began writing and recording her own songs.

"I told my mother I would never come home to live in America until I was famous." When she did return she was astounded by her popularity. After hits such as "I Feel Love," "MacArthur Park," "Bad Girls," "Hot Stuff," "On The Radio," "Last Dance," "Dim All The Lights," some of which won her Grammy awards, all of which have been top grossing songs in pop music history, she's been able to weather all the changes in a fickle record business to make her own style of singing (a sort of seething storytelling you can dance to with gyrating abandon) special and ever-desirable. No longer the hyped up sexpot of her "Love To Love You Baby" days, she's anti-drug and devoutly religious—she reads a Bible before going on stage to perform. Home in Los Angeles is a 25 room mansion where she enjoys being close with her family (three daughters). "I think inside of me there's a farmer, a person who lives to be around green things and the dirt. It's the peace-producing quality I've needed in my life all along."

Donald Sutherland

"I don't see myself as a Cary Grant or a Clark Gable," says the lanky, 6'6" Canadian who's become a favorite of film directors on both sides of the Atlantic. "I see myself playing roles where you can say, 'That's perfect for him'—not as a character actor, but as an actor performing a character which is close to one's self." Among the many perfect-for-him roles since his turning point casting as the iconoclastic surgeon Hawkeye Pierce in *M*A*S*H* in 1970: the sensitive detective who saves Jane Fonda from a homicidal maniac in *Klute* (1971); the father haunted by the vision of his drowning daughter in *Don't Look Now* (1973); the conscientious health inspector in the 1978 remake of *Invasion of the Body Snatchers* and the troubled father in the Oscar-winning *Ordinary People* in 1980. His recent films are *Revolution* (1985), *Lock Up* (1989), and *Lost Angels* (1989).

Born in St. John, New Brunswick, 17 July 1934, Sutherland was raised in Nova Scotia, attended the University of Toronto, and studied at London's Academy of Music and Dramatic Art. As an average obscure repertory actor who lived a hand-to-mouth existence, he once occupied a basement room for $2 a week. ("It was an excellent deal. I lived right next to the hot-water heater and was warmer than anyone else in the building.") He now works with an almost ferocious intensity in films, being featured in anywhere from three to five a year and courted by such European directorial luminaries as Federico Fellini, Bernardo Bertolucci, and Nicolas Roeg as well as Americans such as Alan Pakula and Robert Altman. He sees the relationship between actor and director as much like a love affair. "I become a director's plaything," he says, "something he can manipulate but upon which he must bestow a certain amount of affection. I've either loved directors or hated them. There hasn't been much in between." The twice-married, twice-divorced actor has lived since 1974 with French-Canadian actress and sometime co-star Francine Racette. They are the parents of two sons, both of whom they delivered themselves. Kiefer, his look-alike son from an early marriage to Canadian actress Shirley Douglas, is also a movie actor. A self-described workaholic who often values the creative process more than the completed film, Sutherland doesn't mind that many of his fifty pictures have not been commercially successful. "I work so much because I like to," he says, "There isn't any game plan. I'm very happy being an actor."

Joan Sutherland

The Australian super soprano credited with teaching Luciano Pavarotti correct breathing first came to the attention of music lovers Down Under when she won the *Sun* Aria Contest sponsored by the continent's largest newspaper. In another competition the following year she was named "Australia's best singer." "La Stupenda," as she is nicknamed (it is also the title of her 1983 biography) can rest assured that she made the right choice in music when she left her position as a private secretary years ago. "Unparalleled in the flamboyant bel canto roles" (raved the New York Times), Dame Joan Sutherland (she became a Commander of the British Empire in 1979) continues to jet between the world's major opera houses and concert halls.

Born in Sydney, Australia, 7 November 1926, Sutherland's first teacher was her mother, an amateur singer. After capturing several singing awards in Australia she attended London's Royal College of Music. In 1952 she began her career with the Royal Opera and in 1959 at Covent Garden in *Lucia di Lammermoor* Sutherland was catapulted to stardom. Thirty years later on the very same day, she celebrated her Royal Opera House Anniversary. Though some say time has taken its toll on her voice, Sutherland was still going strong as she approached 60. She insists she has improved her poor diction (always a sore spot with critics) and admits her bad memory cost her a few roles. She now concentrates more on nuance and detail rather than aiming for sheer vocal perfection—"If I crack or miss a top note, I don't worry, I'm only human. But I have a more philisophical attitude. I never come off the stage feeling I've done all I wanted to do." She credits husband Richard Bonynge (musical director of the Australian Opera) with guiding and shaping her art and her forerunner Nellie Melba for "inspiring me to have the guts to go overseas." Though for several years Sutherland was conspicuously absent from New York's Metropolitan Opera House because of a "grand old row" over repertory, she returned to her adoring New York public in 1982. She enjoyed continued success in the late 1980's with a re-recording of Bellini's *Norma* and several stage appearances in the same work. Joan and her husband (they are the parents of a son), from whom she is seldom separated (musically or mentally) spend five months of the year in Australia and make their legal residence in Montreux, Switzerland. The unpretentious, cheerful Sutherland is a talented gardener, a lover of Swiss cooking and food (twice a year she goes on the Scarsdale diet). It seems the end of Sutherland's operatic days are a long way off—"I've always thought I'd like to dabble in my garden, but if I continue at this rate, I'll be too old to bend down."

Keifer Sutherland

In the seven years he has been acting, London-born Keifer Sutherland has made quite an impression in both film and television. He has appeared in 12 films as well as on stage and TV. When asked about his father's influence on his success, Kiefer adds, "I've worked for seven years. I've only been living in a house for two. I'm not even going to say I'm famous, but any kind of public attention I've achieved, I've achieved on my own. If my father helped me to acquire that, it's one thing; if I put myself in a position to sustain it, that's different." "Be polite. Smile. Be nice," is reportedly the only advice about showbusiness Donald Sutherland has ever given to his son Keifer.

Keifer was born in London, England on 21 December 1966, the son of Canadian actress Shirley Douglas and actor Donald Sutherland. Knowing at an early age that he wanted to act, he debuted at age nine in the Los Angeles Odyssey Theatre production of *Throne of Straw*. Following his parents divorce, he and his mother moved to Toronto when he was ten. At age twelve, he was sent to a "quasi-military" Canadian boarding school, where he was a bit undisciplined, and not into studying. By the time he reached 15, he was ready to quit school, leave the family and become an actor. "The last six months before I left home, the feeling got stronger and stronger, and then I said, 'I'm going to do this.' And I left," stated Keifer. Soon after leaving, he performed with several local workshops which later led to his first acting break and film debut. He was cast in a starring role in the Canadian feature film *The Bay Boy* (1984), for which he won the Genie Award, which is the Canadian equivalent of our Academy Award. Soon after, Keifer made his television debut in the made-for-TV movie "Trapped in Silence" (1986), followed by the telefilm "Brotherhood of Silence." On stage he has been seen in *Minnesota Moon* and *America Modern*. He has given many memorable performances in such feature films as *At Close Range, Crazy Moon, Stand By Me, The Lost Boys, The Killing Time, Bright Lights, Big City, 1969, Promised Land, Young Guns, Lakota,* and *Renegades*.

Keifer and actress Camelia Kath were married on 12 September 1987, and separated in September 1988. They have two daughters, Sarah, born in February of 1988, and an eleven-year-old daughter from Camelia's previous marriage.

Suzy

"Why should anyone apologize for writing gossip—or reading it? Gossip is from the front page of the paper to the back of the paper. There's gossip on the sport's page, gossip on the business page, gossip about politicians . . . gossip and speculation. Gossip is just talking about people. Anytime you talk about people you are gosiping," exclaims the sassy, glamourous Mrs. Mehle (or Aileen if you're "in"). Her five-times-a-week column is syndicated to over 100 newspapers and read by approximately 30 million people who couldn't possibly have a clue to some of the people about whom they are reading. Why *dio mio*, the column is deliciously peppered with foreign phrases and *entre nous* coos from the inner recesses of the *haute* and *demi-mondes!* But people eat it up, from Presidents (and their wives) to plumbers and secretaries going home on the subway. Suzy is a confection. "What they care about," she says, "is getting a good laugh."

Born Aileen Elder in El Paso, Texas 10 June, she got her start in gossip writing by complaining to the publisher of the *Miami Daily News* about the inaccuracies of the columnist in the rival paper. Since the publisher needed a columnist, he dared her to try to do better. She accepted, provided no one know who she was—choosing for her byline the name of her stepdaughter, Suzy. "It was a lark," she says, recalling her 1952 column, "I'd be with friends and we'd be talking about Suzy's column and they never knew I was Suzy." She chronicled society in Miami for a year before she and her husband, Admiral Roger Mehle (one son, Roger Jr.) moved to Washington, D.C. and divorced. (She was married a second time and divorced from the late Kenneth Frank.) Persuaded by the publisher of the New York *Mirror* to move to New York as its society scribbler, she wrote for the *Mirror* and several Hearst newspapers before taking over Igor Cassini's Cholly Knickerbocker column in the *Journal American*, henceforth renamed, "Suzy Knickerbocker." In June of 1967 she and her merry followers moved to the New York *Daily News* and in September 1985 to the New York *Post*. Witty and pretty (her face has been on the covers of *Harper's Bazaar* and *Ladies Home Journal*), she lives a life citing as those she writes about. (In a writing style, we might add, that is unique, as if a jazzy chanteuse was bubbling in the Court of Louis XIV.) "All doors are open to me," she says, "not just in New York, but Washington, Newport, Southampton, Paris, London, Greece—everywhere," Feisty, especially when it concerns her competition, she reportedly once said: "I hate all the press." Like any public figure she too is chatted about. Unmarried now, she's been linked romantically to such luminous stars as Frank Sinatra, Aristotle Onassis and Walter Wanger, but you knew that. "Everyone loves publicity. It says you are somebody," she says, discussing why people would go to Mars and back to be mentioned just once in her glittering daily list. "Clare Booth Luce once said: 'Aileen, they don't realize they are born, married or dead until you write it.'"

Elizabeth Swados

"I'm just a regular gal," says Elizabeth Swados. This original and prolific jill-of-all-trades is better classified as a veritable gypsy of talent. An eclectic composer who has continually captivated New York theatre audiences with her powerful, innovative musical scores for plays, Swados is also a writer and director. Born in Buffalo, New York on 5 February 1951, she possessed a heritage rich in creativity, descended from a long line of actors, writers and musicians (among them Kurt Weill)—eccentric and gifted characters. At five Swados played the piano, progressing to the guitar by ten, and was soon composing on both instruments. By twelve she performed as a folksinger and in her teens began submitting short stories to the *New Yorker*. When her mother committed suicide in 1974, Swados found in such tragedy a "source of enormous energy and inspiration." Inspired she has always been. At Bennington College she became intrigued with Far Eastern music and composed a symphony resplendent with 30 performers imitating a band of Balinese monkeys.

Swados first received recognition off-Broadway at La MaMa Experimental Theatre in the early seventies, creating widely acclaimed adaptations of Greek classics with her cohort, the director Andrei Serban. Incorporating dramatic sound effects into her scores, Swados won her first Obie award at the age of twenty for her 1972 *Medea*. She received admiring reviews, citing the exotic and effective musical influences she'd developed through travel, artistic adventures and a naturally discriminating ear. Mel Gussow of the New York *Times* wrote: " . . . the songs have a Weill touch, but also their own sweet 'n' sour flavor—sounding something like an Oriental version of American jazz." In 1977, Swados ventured out on her own to launch an entertaining cabaret revue called *Nightclub Cantata*. For this she won a second Obie and the Outer Critics Circle Award. She subsequently oversaw the Broadway production of her *Runaways*, a musical collage based in part on her own turbulent childhood and adolescence, and she became the first person ever to receive five Tony nominations for a single show. In 1980, she reworked a musical version of Lewis Carroll's *Alice in Wonderland* which starred Meryl Streep. Swados collaborated with Garry Trudeau in transforming his famous comic strip *Doonesbury*—accompanied by her "rollicking" rock tunes—to the Broadway stage in 1983. They subsequently concocted a video and theatrical revue complete with satirical songs on President Reagan, entitled *Rap Master Ronnie*. Her latest works include an original score *Popular Science* (1986), a musical *Esther: A Vaudeville Megillah* (1988), and an Off-Broadway production *The Red Sneaks* (1989).

Sometime faculty member at several colleges and author of both the children's book *The Girl With the Incredible Feeling* and the instructional *Listening Out Loud: Being A Composer*, Swados is also a woman of divergent moods, potently energetic and productive with a self-satirical and artistic temperament. "I want to do a lot of things. . . . The way to survive is to work and to live entirely in the moment."

Patrick Swayze

As Dalton, the rough-and-tumble bouncer who's the best in the business, actor/dancer Patrick Swayze gave another memorable film portrait in *Road House* (1989). Set amidst the sex, drugs and rock 'n' roll of the Double Deuce, a rural Missouri nightclub, *Road House* is the story of Dalton's "righteous battle against a brutal town patriarch whose lust for power barely overshadows his lewd and lascivious greed." Dalton's motto is: "It's my way or the highway." The Double Deuce is "a joint featuring chicken wire surrounding the stage, passed out bodies littering the dance floor and semi-coherent power drinkers pawing the weary waitresses. At closing, the blood is mopped up, the bar is wiped down, and another day is over." A bit of a different role for Swayze who had just hung up his dancing duds from his star-making part in *Dirty Dancing* (1987). The film was set in 1963, in a summer resort in the Catskills. Patrick plays the resort dance instructor, "an enigmatic amalgam of Brando and Astaire," who comes to understand his place in a changing world through his relationship with the young guest who becomes his dancing partner. The teenager is played by Jennifer Grey.

The son of a choreographer, Patsy Swayze, he made his debut into the world on 18 August 1954 in Houston, Texas. He began his career as a dancer under his mother's tutelage. After studying with the Harkness Ballet Company and the Joffrey Ballet, he became a principal with the Eliot Feld Dance Company. He also danced on Broadway in *Good Time Charley* (Opposite Jennifer's father, Joel Grey), a revival of *West Side Story*, and, for two years, the lead role in *Grease*. Swayze made his feature film debut in the comedy, *Skatetown, U.S.A.* and went on to act in such films as Francis Ford Coppola's *The Outsiders*, the action adventure *Uncommon Valor*, *Youngblood*, John Milius' controversial war film *Red Dawn*, *Tiger Warsaw* and *Steel Dawn* in which his wife, Lisa Niemi, co-starred. In 1987 Swayze was nominated for a Golden Globe award as Best Actor for his portrayal of Johnny Castle in *Dirty Dancing*. After *Road House* he was set to star as a Chicago cop in *Next of Kin*.

In addition to his starring role in the television miniseries "North and South," Swayze has appeared in several television movies, "The Comeback Kid" with John Ritter, "Return of the Rebels" and "The New Season." He starred in "The Renegades" which ultimately became a series. Swayze received excellent reviews for his dramatic portrayal of a soldier dying of leukemia in an episode of "M*A*S*H" and also starred in an "Amazing Stories" episode entitled "Life on Death Row." A special added note: he is the composer/performer of "She's Like The Wind," a hit song from *Dirty Dancing*.

Jessica Tandy

She's played obedient daughters, crazed nymphomaniacs and fierce matrons. She is praised across the board as one of Broadway's greats. She first sparked the public's attention as Blanche Dubois in Tennessee Williams' *A Streetcar Named Desire* in 1947 and 36 years later played the pivotal role of Amanda Wingfield in another Williams' classic, *The Glass Managerie*. In 1988 she won the Emmy (Lead Actress in a miniseries/special) for her performance in the television version of "Foxfire."

Born in London, 7 June 1909, Tandy made her first stage appearance in the West End in 1927 and on Broadway a year later. She has won Tonys for her roles in *Streetcar* (opposite Brando), *The Gin Game* (1977), and in the musical play *Foxfire* (1983). In between she has stirred audiences in such plays as *Five Finger Exercise*, Edward Albee's *A Delicate Balance*, and David Storey's *Home*. Her repertoire is to a large extent classical with a heavy helping of Shakespeare and Chekhov. She is no stranger to the screen: (*The Birds, Butley, The World According to Garp, Cocoon, The House On Sullivan Street, Batteries Not Included, Cocoon II: The Return*) but her stellar contribution to the arts lies in the realm of theatre and in 1979 Tandy was elected to the Theater Hall of Fame. In 1985 she appeared off-Broadway in *Solonik* and in 1986 with Cronyn on Broadway in *The Petition*. In April 1988 she was honored by the American Academy of Dramatic Arts.

Her marriage to Hume Cronyn has proved as glistening as their professional work together. Wed since 1942, the pair have shared the Broadway stage together 11 times and raised three children in the process. "When you know and understand each other as well as Hume and I do, then you can be critical in rehearsal and there's no threat." She adds, "I think he's a very good actor, I know that I've got to pull my socks up if I'm going to keep up."

CELEBRITY REGISTER 1990

Elizabeth Taylor

Back in the 1940s, Universal Studios in Hollywood dropped one of its child players from the payroll because the powers-that-be decided that the little girl, who'd been cast in bit parts for a year, could never be a star. She didn't have dimples like Shirley Temple. She couldn't sing like Judy Garland, nor dance like some other child stars. And, the casting director felt, her violet eyes were "too old." MGM thought other wise, and so, in 1944, 13-year-old Elizabeth Taylor was cast in the starring role of *National Velvet*. She's been a star ever since, a star whose luster has been alternately gilded and gouged by the comet-turns of her celebrity.

Born Elizabeth Frances Taylor in London, on 27 February 1932, as a teenager at MGM her parts expressed a childish shyness and onscreen sweetness. Offscreen she was intrigued by glamourous stars like Lana Turner and Ava Gardner and her biggest dream was to stimulate the same kind of response. At 15, her dream came true when columnist Hedda Hopper became the first of many who have proclaimed Elizabeth "the most beautiful woman in the world." But at home, she read comic books, devoured stories in fan magazines about other, older movie stars and dreamed romantic dreams. She once confided to a chum that she "practiced kissing" with a pillow every night. At 18 she married first husband Nicky Hilton and ever since then, as legend and newspaper headlines have it, there always seems to be someone waiting on Elizabeth's pillow. Six more marriages followed the first: Michael Wilding (two sons), Mike Todd, killed in a plane crash (one daughter), Eddie Fisher, the late Richard Burton (twice; one adopted daughter), and Senator John Warner.

Her fans are among the most devout worshippers in filmdom, fascinated by her every new role, jewel, house, fur, child, husband, lover or illness. Taylor's films include *Little Women, Father of the Bride, A Place in the Sun, Ivanhoe, Giant, Raintree Country, Cat on a Hot Tin Roof, Suddenly Last Summer, The Taming of the Shrew, The Blue Bird, Ash Wednesday* and *Cleopatra*. She has won two Oscars, for *Butterfield 8* in 1960 and *Who's Afraid of Virginia Woolf* in 1966. In 1981, she delighted her followers undertaking her first Broadway play, Lillian Hellman's *The Little Foxes*. In 1983, she teamed up with Burton on Broadway for a revival of Noel Coward's *Private Lives*. It proved to be a general embarrassment for everyone involved—in retrospect the show foretold even greater difficulties. A lifetime of illness, near deaths and overindulgence would take its toll unless Elizabeth pulled herself together. She'd become the brunt of Joan Rivers's pointed commentary. "She's so fat," the comedienne rasped on the Carson Show, "mosquitos see her and scream: 'buffet!'" When Rivers's comic routines failed to intervene in Taylor's downward course, her family took over and the star checked into the Betty Ford Rehabilitation Center near Palm Springs and re-emerged a svelte size 8. In the months that followed her rehabilitation many crises arose that challenged her sobriety, especially when Richard Burton died late in the fall of 1984. She carried on. "Elizabeth Taylor is Elizabeth Taylor again," noted one friend, adding: "Of all the contributions she's made to people, I don't think anything counts as much as this. Elizabeth is thin and pretty again and finally sober. She's saying, 'Look, if I can do something about the quality of my life, so can you Mr. and Mrs. America.' Stars have often shown us how to self-destruct. Too few show us how to prevail."

Her most recent acting credits are on television, filling superstar slots on "General Hospital," "Hotel," with Carol Burnett in the Hallmark special "Return Engagement," portraying Louella Parsons in the TV movie "Malice in Wonderland", starring in the 1986 miniseries, John Jake's "North and South," and CBS-TV's "Poker Alice" in 1987. Next up is NBC's "Sweet Bird of Youth." In 1988 she was on the big screen in the film *Young Toscanni*.

Carrying her celebrityhood one step further, she used the power of her name and attention of her friends to help raise funds to fight AIDS. In 1985 she announced the formation of The American Foundation for AIDS Research (AmFAR) and as the National Chairman she devotes her free time to fundraising. Miss Taylor also shared some of her beauty secrets in her 1988 book, *Elizabeth Takes Off - On Weight Gain, Weight Loss, Self Esteem & Self Image*. This tome on her philosophy of dieting, etc. was preceded by her entrance into the Fragrance industry. In September 1987 she launched "Elizabeth Taylor's Passion" in conjunction with the Parfums International Division of Chesebrough-Pond's Inc. The product was so successful that in 1989 she introduced a new men's cologne, naturally titled "Elizabeth Taylor's Passion for Men." Always acknowledged for her contributions to the theatrical world, she received an extra honor in September 1985 when she traveled to Paris to be given the prestigious French title of Commander of Arts and Letters.

James Taylor

This master of the "ordinary guy" philosophy sings, he says, "because I don't know how to talk." Although he's not the only singing Taylor (his brothers, Alex and Livingston, and his sister Kate all have launched individual careers), James is the moody introvert of the family. He hates giving interviews; he is embarrassed by the superstar trip; even though he's been on *Time* mag's cover, he doesn't like posing for pics ("I feel as if a piece of my soul is lost every time a picture is taken") and he hates to talk about his work. ("The whole reason you write a song is so you don't have to talk about it.") Not as popular in the 1980s as when he painted the darkly personal, musical ideas of the post-1960s youth, he has of recent years become involved in the move for nuclear disarmament. "I'm a . . . man with two children. Before [them], I was perfectly happy to think of human beings as another race of dinosaurs. But now I can't look at it the same way."

Born into a well-established Boston family on 12 March 1948, James Taylor openly admits to a troubled youth. Three years at strait-laced and demanding Milton Academy brought him to near suicide, and at 17 he signed himself into a mental institution. He began to reflect upon what it takes to survive. "In a euphoric society," he explains, "it certainly is necessary to have buffers like Christianity. To me Jesus is a metaphor, but also a manifestation of needs and feelings people have deep within themselves." After nine months he packed up and headed for New York, where he formed a new band, the Flying Machine, which never got off the ground. He also started using drugs heavily, especially heroin.

Needing an escape, he left for London, where Beatle Paul McCartney discovered him, and signed him for his first album. But his career beginning didn't end his personal battle to live with himself, and before the 1970 album that catapulted Taylor to the top of rock music charts, *Sweet Baby James*, as well as after, he returned to a mental hospital and fought bouts of depression. His music, an innovative force for "soft and gentle" rock, has been deftly described as a "fusion of the three black and white mainstreams of pop: the lonely twang of country, the pithy narrative of folk, and the rhythmic melancholy of blues." He was a doubly-Grammy winner in 1977 (Best Pop Vocalist and Best Performance by a Male) for his single, "Handy Man." CBS Records produced his 1981 album, *Dad Loves His Work*. His recent albums include *That's Why I'm Here* (1985) and *Never Die Young* (1988); the latter produced the hit single "Baby Boom Baby." Taylor's ten-year marriage to fellow entertainer Carly Simon, leggy singer of the slick-folk school, and offspring of the publishing Simon (& Schuster), ended in 1982. He married actress Kathryn Walker in 1985.

Lawrence Taylor

A marauding personification of football violence, this roving linebacker earned NFL Defensive Player of the Year honors in each of his first three seasons. "The guy loves to hit people," says teammate Harry Carson. As the league's best offense-stopper, he loves to win. Playing with the Football Giants (so called since their move to New Jersey deprived them of their "New York" designation), he says, "I want to be known for being on a

Paul Taylor

winning team." If not, he'll at least be recognized as the prototype "new wave" linebacker of the 80s. Although he was forced to sit out the first four games of the 1988 season (because of league suspension), Taylor still managed to earn his eighth straight Pro Bowl and the All-NFL designation with 73 total tackles and 15 QB sacks.

In 1978 the NFL tried to make pro football more exciting (for higher TV ratings) by changing rules to favor passing plays. Defensive coaches countered the trend by keeping more men downfield to harass or intercept from receivers. To that end the Giants spent their No. 1 draft choice in 1981 (and No. 2 overall league selection) to obtain Taylor from the University of North Carolina. Born 4 February 1959 in Williamsburg, Va., he had little more than a semester to go to graduate. The perfectly-built, six-feet-three, 237 pounder was a mean, fleet tackler with a reputation for being in or near almost every play, and in his first training camp the Giants's defensive coordinator said, "All we had to do was to get him in tune and get out of his way." His rookie year exploits (chasing down the fleet Tony Dorsett, traumatizing quarterbacks and downfield receivers alike) helped New York to its first play-off spot in 18 years. But after two more All-Pro seasons he signed with the Manhattan developer's New Jersey Generals of the USFL, causing woes for the Giants until he let them buy back his contract.

Somehow the anemic Giants still leave him cold. He admires Al Davis and says he'd like to retire as one of Davis's L.A. Raiders. In the meantime "L.T." works off his $7.3 million, seven-year Giants's contract. His wife Linda (three children) in Upper Saddle River, N.J., keeps him warm.

Paul Taylor

From the mid-1950s when his audiences were "mostly beatniks" to 1984 when Robet Jacobson of *Ballet News* called him "one of the authentic geniuses in the world of dance," Paul Taylor, once headlined by *Time* magazine as "The Tolkien of Choreographers" has emerged as a dominant figure of 20th century dance and as one of the finest theatre fantasy minds this country has produced. Although his career has been a journey of exploring new territories, he has, according to Jacobson, "that uncanny Janus-like ability to look at past and future at the same time, while enlivening the present with a directness and completeness of vision that is invigorated by such duality. This lends his work that texture of dimension, that awareness of dance's past and its future, which he registers as limitless."

Self-described as of "American mongrel descent," Paul Belville Taylor, whose father was a physicist, was born 29 July 1930 in Allegheny, Pa., and grew up in the environs of Washington, D.C. An art major on a swimming scholarship to Syracuse University ("I loved competitions which is already part of the theatre"), his life changed after the Ballet Russe came through town. Leaving Syracuse, he traveled to New York and studied wherever he could—at Juilliard, with Martha Graham, Antony Tudor and Merce Cunningham—and joined Cunningham's company in 1953. Then in 1955 he joined the Graham company where he would remain for six years (collecting impressive notices for his "brilliant dancing and penetrating characterizations"), and that same year founded his own small company and began choreographing. "Paul Taylor . . . seemed determined to drive his viewers right out of their minds (or out of the theatre)," was an early Walter Terry assessment in the *Herald Tribune*, but four years later that same dance critic called Taylor "one of the most fascinating, intriguing, gifted and, at times, infuriating of modern dance performers-choreographers." The reviews—for work ranging from such "pure dance" offerings as *Esplanade* and *Airs* to such enigmatic creations as *Images*, *Runes* and *Cloven Kingdom* and finally to dark, troubling pieces like *Big Bertha*, *Nightshade*, *Byzantium* and *Last Look*—have grown more enthusiastic over the three decades of Taylor's creative output. "Every so often the stunningly great performance rolls around," wrote Anna Kisselgoff in the New York *Times* of Taylor's 1981 "gift to his dancers," *Arden Court*. "Any major ballet company or modern dance company, no matter how excellent . . . will have its work cut out . . . to match the supreme level of dancing of the Taylor dancers. . . . It is the kind of performance that rises above routine greatness. . . . Here is instant Taylor at a glance, impossible to be mistaken for anyone else's work." Among Paul Taylor's honors are "Dancer of the Year" by London's *Dance and Dancers* magazine in 1965 (he retired as a dancer in 1975); bestowal of Knighthood by the French government in 1969; the International Award for Choreography by the Festival of Nations, three Guggenheim Fellowships for Choreography, the Capezio Dance Award in 1967, the *Dance Magazine* Award in 1980, the Samuel H. Scripps/American Dance Festival Award in 1983 and in 1985 a MacArthur Foundation award, one of only two choreographers (Merce Cunningham is the other) to be accorded that honor. His autobiography, *Private Domain*, was released in 1987.

Kiri Te Kanawa

"When I heard Kiri was interested in doing Maria, I was just thrilled," recalled Leonard Bernstein, composer of *West Side Story* and conductor of the 1985 recording of his landmark musical with an all-star opera cast (including Jose Carreras, who had to lose his native Spanish accent to play the leading Anglo in the cast). To Dame Kiri Te Kanawa, it was just another job, disdaining as she does the word "career." "Its ostentatious . . . I may use it when I'm fifty. Right now it's a job." Not since the heyday of Lisa della Casa and Elizabeth Schwarzkopf has a soprano graced the world's operatic stages with so potent a combination of vocal and physical beauty, prompting critics to use the word "gorgeous" to describe both her voice and her face. Dame Kiri is relatively unfazed by all the hoopla, recalling well the day before her sensational Covent Garden debut as one on which "the press didn't want to know me, agents didn't want to know me." The anonymity came to a happy end 1 December 1971 when Te Kanawa triumphed as the Countess Almaviva in Mozart's *The Marriage of Figaro*, producing hosannas ranging from Andrew Porter (in the London *Financial Times*) who called her characterization "such a Countess as I have never heard before, not at Covent Garden, nor in Salzburg or Vienna," to Peter Heyworth (*The Observer*): "The radiant tenderness with which this Rosina finally forgave her erring spouse was evidence enough that Covent Garden here has a pearl of great price." That early appreciation of her combined singing and acting efforts indicates that she is well advanced towards her life goal of being a singing actress, and who looks upon the incomparable Dame Janet Baker as her "ideal of the world."

Born 6 March 1944 in Gisborne, New Zealand, to a Maori (the Polynesian natives who inhabited New Zealand for centuries before the arrival of Europeans) building contractor and his Anglo-Irish wife (a descendant of Sir Arthur Sullivan of Gilbert and Sullivan fame), the future Dame Commander of the British Empire (so created in 1982) decided "when I was three" to be a singer, and at 12 began her operatic training to the exclusion of everything else. ("I did not want to be a shorthand typist.") With $10,000 in prize money from the Melbourne *Sun's* aria competition, she moved with her mother to London to complete her vocal studies. She kept her "Maori cool" during a dispute with her first teacher at the London Opera Centre by remembering that "we used to eat people like you." Conductor Richard Bonynge told the young mezzo that she was really a soprano after hearing her in a master class (he'd done the same with his wife Joan Sutherland), and her voice began to ascend. After her 1971 Covent Garden triumph, she annexed to her repertory such roles as Desdemona in *Otello* (in which she debuted at the Met on three hours' notice in 1974 to a chorus of "bravas"), Mimi in *La Boheme*, Marguerite in *Faust*, Donna Elvira in *Don Giovanni* (encoring in the Joseph Losey film), Tatiana in *Eugene Onegin*, Amelia in

Simon Boccanegra, Pamina in *The Magic Flute,* The Marschallin in *Der Rosenkavalier* and Rosalinde in *Die Fledermaus* (a hit via live worldwide television transmission from Covent Garden New Year's Eve of 1977). Of all soprano roles, few seem more suitable for the special combination of physical and vocal beauty of Kiri Te Kanawa than the title role of Richard Strauss's *Arabella*. That suspicion was gloriously confirmed in Houston in 1977 and at the Met in 1984, when *Newsweek* hailed Dame Kiri as "the quintessential Arabella—dancing girlishly around the room one minute, singing wistfully of the future the next, all the while the picture of elegant beauty. Her voice, a royal blend of shining high notes and creamy low ones, soars effortlessly over the orchestra. No wonder Prince Charles asked her to sing at his wedding: she's a born aristocrat onstage." Offstage, in their homes outside London and in Oyster Bay, N.Y., she's the wife of Australian mining engineer Desmond Park, whom she married 30 August 1967 six weeks after meeting on a blind date. Te Kanawa has two adopted children. She is the subject of the 1984 biography by David Fingleton, *Kiri*. Her latest recordings include an album of popular (Cole Porter et al) songs with Nelson Riddle (1985), *South Pacific* (1986), *Kiri Sings Gershwin* (1987) and *My Fair Lady* (with Jeremy Irons in 1987).

Studs Terkel

Only Chicago's "From the People" tradition of Carl Sandburg could produce this gifted interviewer, lecturer, and journalist, known for his best-selling oral histories, *Working: People Talk about What They Do All Day and How They Fell About What They Do,* and *Hard Times: An Oral History of the Great Depression.* From interview after interview with hundreds of Americans, Terkel has compiled in these works the average person's ideas, emotions, opinions, hopes, and dreams, which have called forth a variety of mixed reviews. Regardless, public opinion credits him with siring America's oral history fixation, and since his 1984 book *The Good War* (a 1985 Pulitzer Prize winner), a record of memories and opinions of World War II veterans, Studs Terkel has been appropriately hailed as "America's troubadour of the unsung."

Born Louis Terkel in the Bronx section of New York City on 16 May 1912, he was the third son of working-class parents. At eleven, he moved with his family to Chicago, where he has for the most part remained. His youthful experiences included evenings spent in the Wells-Grand Hotel on Chicago's North Side, a hotel run by his mother which catered to blue-collar workers, mechanics, and craftsmen. He saw there the roistering workers who got drunk every Saturday night until the Great Depression, and on Chicago's West Side where he attended school, he became acquainted with the city's gangster element during Prohibition. A graduate of the University of Chicago, he continued for three more "traumatic" years at the U. of C. Law School (he says he entered "dreaming of Clarence Darrow—and woke up to see Julius Hoffman"), only to fail his bar exam after obtaining his J.D. degree in 1934. After a few tedious government jobs, and one stage success (as villain Shad Larue in *It Can't Happen Here*), Terkel joined the Federal Writer's Project in 1935, and with Richard Wright and Nelson Algren, wrote weekly radio shows for WGN. He acted in radio soaps ("Ma Perkins" and "Road of Life") where he usually played an actor who came to a sudden and violent end. It was in the late '30s when he returned himself to the stage with the Chicago Repertory Theatre, that he renamed himself Studs after Chicago novelist James T. Farrell's proletarian protagonist Studs Lonigan. The '40s saw Terkel as an established voice of Chicago radio who became best known during the '50s for his diversified programs during which he engaged people in spontaneous interviews. His first TV show "Studs' Place" was full of banter with the regulars and distinguished guests who just happened to "drop in." A man of many talents and interests, he wrote a jazz column for the Chicago *Sun-Times,* made numerous stage appearances both in Chicago and in summer stock, wrote a book on American jazz, lectured, narrated documentary films, hosted music and folk festivals, won a number of coveted awards, and wrote one play—all during one decade.

Since 1967, Terkel has produced four volumes—all explorations of average, everyday people—that bring together the best of his talents. *Division Street: America* (1967), *Hard Times* (1970), *Working* (1974), and *The Good War* (1984), were all best-sellers, and were translated into every major Western language, as well as Hungarian and Chinese. His latest book was *Chicago* (1986). Interviewers have commented on Terkel's vitality, restlessness, and youthful attitude, but those he has interviewed remember his empathy, sensitivity, and compelling vulnerability to time and circumstance. Terkel considers his ultimate test of journalism yet to come—some "tough" book that will be his "Everest." Since 1939, he has been married to Ida Goldberg, a social worker from Wisconsin whom he met when they were both members of the Chicago Repertory Theatre. They have one son, Paul. Aside from his literary endeavors, Terkel had a role in the 1988 film *Eight Men Out.*

Twyla Tharp

"So many people, when they think of ballet, think of *Giselle* and *Swan Lake*, but those ballets are exceptions—they represent ballet at a certain period of its history. Ballet isn't *waft*, it's something taut and rigorous," says the hottest choreographer on the scene today and an articulate spokesperson for the New American Classicism in the dance. Her schedule in one recent year alone—1983-1984—testifies to her astonishing versatility: she resumed dancing with her own company, which she then took on tour throughout the U.S., South America, England, Germany and on Broadway for a two-week stint. She choreographed the operatic scenes for the film *Amadeus* on location in Prague and created new choreography for Mikhail Baryshnikov's film *White Nights* on location in Finland. She created *The Little Ballet, Sinatra Suite* (a shortened version of her *Nine Sinatra Songs*) and *The Bach Partita* for Baryshnikov and American Ballet Theatre and saw the fulfillment of a 20-year old dream that she would "be good enough to make a dance on The New York City Ballet," with the ballet *Brahms/Handel* (co-choreographed with Jerome Robbins). She directed a PBS Ballet special. She was planning a full-length ballet "in Europe where they understand how to do full-length ballets." In 1985 she directed and choreographed *Singin' In the Rain* on Broadway, which critics compared unfavorably to the screen classic on which it was based. "I'm just going to keep working until I reach my real creative time," she says, "which should start somewhere around the age of 55."

Twyla Tharp was born on 1 July 1941 in Portland, Ind., where she began piano lessons at two and dance training at four. After moving with her family to California, she added the violin and viola to her instrumental studies, and supplemented these with classes in music theory, harmony and composition. While majoring in art history at Barnard College in New York, she studied ballet with a variety of teachers and modern dance with Martha Graham, Merce Cunningham ("the *master* teacher"), Alwin Nikolais and Erick Hawkins. After graduation she spent a year dancing with the then small but adventurous Paul Taylor Dance Company, and left a promising career there to form her own company in 1965, the year of her choreographic debut with *Tank Dive,* set to Petula Clark's recording of "Downtown." Of that earliest work Clive Barnes said in the *New York Times* that it was "too bland, too gently naive"and of her dancing, "She is a very good performer, and cool almost to the point of frigidity." Succeeding early works were performed on a bare stage without music ("People watching dance with music responded primarily to the music, so I tried to discover what you could do with dance alone"). Her series of jazz or "pop" ballets marked her return to choreography set to music: *Eight Jelly Rolls* (using the music of Jelly Roll Morton), *The Bix Pieces* (the music of Bix Beiderbecke) and *The Raggedly Dances* (combining Scott Joplin rags with Mozart variations), which Clive Barnes praised as "quintessentially American in its laconic ease and deliberately underplayed bravado." In 1973 she received her first outside commission from the Joffrey Ballet, for which she created *Deuce Coupe* (using a dozen of the Beach Boys' surfer rock hits). Critic John Rockwell declared that "the work marked the emergence of Miss Tharp from avant-garde cultism into an artist who could bridge the seemingly contradictory worlds of modern dance experimentation, pop and ballet." Other works include *After All* and *Three Fanfares* for ice dancer John Curry, *Dance Is A Man's Sport, Too* for New York City Ballet's Peter Martins and the Pittsburgh Steelers's wide receiver Lynn Swann; choreography for the films *Hair* (1978) and *Ragtime* (1980) and a number of television specials, including "The Catherine Wheel," for which she received an Emmy nomination in 1983. The recipient of the 1981 *Dance Magazine* Award, she is the holder of five Honorary Doctorate degrees in the performing arts. She and her former husband Robert Huot are the parents of a son, Jesse, born 3 March 1971.

Taki Theodoracopulos

"There are two kinds of gossip," he says, "the puerile kind which is time-wasting by halfwits, and the other, which informs and helps to define the age. When I read history, I always find that it's the gossip that gives the flavor, and, often the substance, of who people were and what life was like. Without writers who peek through keyholes, politics and history would be dull stuff." This is Taki talking "one of the hottest tickets in British journalism," according to Tom Wolfe. Erstwhile columnist for the London *Spectator* and *Esquire*, and author of *Princes, Playboys and High-Class Tarts*, Taki tells all from a pedigree perspective that distinguishes him from the garden variety of celebrity chroniclers. Taki differentiates between the "truly rich" and the "merely rich"; those with veritable style and those imitators of it, all the while examining a crop of "upper-crust concerns."

Born in Greece, 11 August 1937, into a wealthy and socially prominent family (father, $400 million dollar shipping magnate; grandfather, Greece's prime minister), Taki flitted from prep school to prep school in the U.S. until he relinquished his formal schooling in favor of the "lessons of life" (jet setting being the curriculum). Soon after, he capitalized on his athletic skill and earned world rank as a tennis player (competing for the Davis Cup), won positions on the best polo teams in England and France, raced as a skier for Greece in the Olympics and secured a black belt in karate. In the 60's he served as a war correspondent in Jordan for the *Athens Acropolis* and was a (photo) journalist for the *National Review* and *Newsweek*. In 1984 he began writing for *Vanity Fair*.

Taki's first wife was Parisian socialite Christina de Caraman. He married Princess Alexandra Schoenburg in 1981, and they have a son and a daughter. Based in New York, he divides his time between a townhouse in Manhattan, and homes in London, Athens, Gstaad and, briefly and reluctantly in 1984, a London jail cell after being arrested for cocaine possession at Heathrow Airport. His lawyer explained that coke was consumed like wine at the kind of dinner parties the columnist attended.

Alan Thicke

Since the hit television situation comedy, "Growing Pains" premiered in the fall of 1985, its star has been propelled into, like his name, the thick of American popularity. However, Canadian-born Alan Thicke is no stranger to popularity and success. The multi-talented compulsive achiever has been working as a TV writer, producer, performer and host on both sides of the border for almost two decades. During the 1970's, Thicke wrote for a long list of comedy and musical series and specials in the U.S. including Flip Wilson, Sammy Davis, Jr., Sandy Duncan, Glen Campbell and Richard Pryor. In the 1980's, Thicke's writing included specials for Frank Mills and Anne Murray. His writings captured Thicke two Emmy Awards, including one for a Barry Manilow Special in 1977. As a producer/writer, Thicke's talents were not to be overlooked by his adopted homeland. The 1977 parody talk show series "Fernwood 2-Night," predecessor to the shortlived 1978 "America 2-Night," earned Thicke two Emmy nominations. Thicke, the writer, has written more than thirty compositions for TV, composed theme music for such sitcoms as "Diff'rent Strokes" and "Facts of Life," and game shows such as the hit "Wheel of Fortune," "Celebrity Sweepstakes" and "The Joker's Wild," as well as composed singles for artists Lou Rawls, David Foster and ex-wife, Gloria Loring. Changing hats again, the untiring Thicke returned to his homeland to host the TV game show "First Impressions" and the "Alan Thicke Show," a talk-variety program, which received the highest ratings of any program in the history of Canadian daytime TV. But success sometimes can be fickle. The Canadian hit was followed by the 1983 American flop "Thicke of the Night" which was cancelled at the end of its first season. While the late night variety show emphasizing music and comedy was not well received by the critics, Robert MacKenzie, writing in *TV Guide*, said, "When Thicke gets away from all this backup and wings his way through a real situation, he's charming."

The facile and funny Thicke again switched hats and recorded the show's theme song, which he composed before moving on to act in "Love Boat" episodes and in the 1985 TV movie "The Calendar Girl Murders." Pointed out to Michael Sullivan, Executive Producer, Thicke landed the role of Dr. Jason Seaver, psychiatrist and father in "Growing Pains" which, in its second season, was the tenth most popular series on the air.

Born Alan Jeffery on 1 March 1948, in a small mining town named Kirkland Lake, Ontario, Alan jokes about his hometown. ("There were two ways a guy could get out of town: play hockey or get a girl pregnant. I wasn't good at either.") His parents divorced when Alan was six and mom remarried a physician whose surname Alan and his brother, Todd (now a TV producer and director) adopted. Stepfather Thicke taught the boys a lot about drive and ambition. Alan became a good hockey player and entertained his schoolmates with imitations of the Beatles. He also developed his musical and verbal skills. "I gave sermons in the local United Church of Canada at the same time I was president of Catholic Youth Organization." To please his stepfather, Thicke took pre-med courses at the University of Western Ontario, but then auditioned with the Canadian Broadcasting Corp., (CBC) in Toronto, singing to his own guitar accompaniment and doing a comic monologue. Hired by CBC as a "gofer" Thicke began to contribute material for shows while he was chauffeuring personalities and fetching coffee. His 1960's credits include "Good Company Show," "Tommy Hunter Show," and "Johnny Cash Special." In 1970, at the age of twenty two, Thicke came to Los Angeles and was introduced to show business people by some of his professional hockey friends. His first major credits on this side of the border were in 1974 as a writer for Flip Wilson's comedy specials. Since his new series, Thicke has found himself constantly in demand. He's acted in "Not Quite Human," a TV movie, "Hit and Run" a feature film with Colleen Dewhurst and the soon to be released film *Return of the Kiwis* where Thicke plays a member of a rock and roll band making a comeback after twenty years. One of the most sought after hosts-for-hire in the country, Thicke has hosted the ABC Christmas Special, Disney's Easter Parade and the Olympic Kick-Off Gala. When asked about his many offers, the witty Thicke jokingly explains, "I get all the television appearances and banquet gigs that Bill Cosby can't do."

The father of two sons, Brennan and Robin, Thicke shares custody with his ex-wife, Gloria Loring (divorced in 1984), and the three men reside on Toluca Lake in the San Fernando Valley. "I still feel Canadian," Thicke told Bill Mann of the *Toronto Globe and Mail*, "and am certainly going to keep my citizenship." Named "Father of the Year" by the Father's Day Council in Los Angeles, Muscular Dystrophy, and The Juvenile Diabetes Foundation (for which he is the spokesperson), Thicke hosts ABC's educational comedy show, "Animal Crack-Ups," which is rated number one in its time slot. With his "easy, naturalistic style" (*Variety*) and wit, the good-looking, slightly built man who prefers to dress informally, but drives a Porsche, has a lot of insecurities. "I worry about things like, Am I Handsome enough? Smart enough? Witty enough?," Thicke confessed. "And that's just for a dinner date, much less putting yourself in front of a national audience."

Danny Thomas

Television's pet paterfamilias for a fantastic 11 straight seasons (1953-64), he's been "retiring" off and on since the middle 1960s. But the beak-nosed comic who persuaded the nation to "Make Room for Daddy" still turns up two or three times a year in Vegas, on commercials, and/or in the plush offices of his prosperous production complex, and there isn't much doubting that this restless, volatile Thomas will stick around in show biz for a long, long time. His latest projects include a short-lived series "One Big Family" (1986-1987) and the CBS-TV movie "Side by Side" (1988). The majority of his time is taken up with St. Jude's Children's Hospital in Memphis. At a desperate point in his career many years ago, Thomas knelt before the statue of St. Jude (patron saint of the hopeless) and begged for a sign. Should he or should he not remain in show business? He promised to erect a shrine to St. Jude if he should succeed in the business he loved above all others - and the rest is show-biz history.

A high school dropout who caught the grease-paint virus while laboring as a candy butcher in a burlesque house, he was born Amos Muzyad Jacobs (or Jahoob), of Lebanese immigrant parents in Deerfield, Mich., on 6 January 1914. He considers his "second birthday" to be 12 August 1940, the day he stood up on stage at the 5100 Club in Chicago and, borrowing the names of two of his brothers, introduced himself for the first time as Danny Thomas. "Discovered" on radio in 1945 on the "Baby Snooks Show," he's made movies (*Call Me Mister, The Jazz Singer*) and has been a nightclub headliner as well as a regular on TV. "Make Room for Daddy" won 5 Emmys. Following in daddy's footsteps, daughter Marlo made a hit in another TV sitcom, "That Girl." The National Conference of Christians and Jews selected Danny "Man of the Year" and the American Medical Association presented him with its Layman's Award, the highest it can bestow on a non-medical man. Thomas was nominated for the Nobel Prize in 1981. He received a "Doctor of Humane Letters" degree from the Medical College of Toledo in 1989. Unabashedly religious, the funnyman with the epic schnozz ("If you're going to have a nose, you ought to have a real one"), is also unabashedly sentimental. "They say I'm a sentimentalist. And I am. Why, I'm so sentimental I cry at basketball games." The mother of his three children is the former Rose Marie Cassaniti, whom he married in 1936.

Debi Thomas

The long hours of training and practicing have definitely paid off for this young figure skater. In just four years of professional skating she has received three special awards and has placed first in seven national as well as international events.

Debi Thomas was born on 25 March 1967 in Poughkeepsie, New York. She began skating professionally in 1985. Within that same year, she had already received the Figure Skater of the Year Award, as well as competing in six events. She placed first in three competitions, the Skate America International in St. Paul, Minnesota; the St. Ivel International in London, England; and the National Sports Festival VI in Baton Rouge, Louisiana. In the U.S. National Championships in Kansas City, Missouri, she placed second, as well as the Pacific Coast Sectional in Berkeley, California. Winding up the year, she placed fifth in the World Championships which were held in Tokyo, Japan. The year 1986 proved to be even better, with Debi winning the 1986 Wide World of Sports Athlete of the Year Award, in addition to the 1986 Amateur Female Athlete of the Year Award, as well as placing first in both of the competitions she participated in. These events were the World Championships in Geneva, Switzerland, and the U.S. National Championships in Long Island, New York. In 1987 she came in second place in two more skating competitions, the World Championships in Cincinnati, Ohio and in the U.S. National Championships in Tacoma, Washington. Continuing her busy schedule, she competed in three more events in 1988, including the Olympics. In the World Championships in Budapest, Hungary, she placed third, in the Women's Figure Skating division in Winter Olympics she took the Bronze medal, and in the U.S. National Championships in Denver, Colorado, Debi earned an impressive first place. Taking a break from the pressures of competition, she guest stars on weekends with Discover Card's Stars on Ice and Benson and Hedges' On Ice Tours. She has also made her television debut on ABC's Ice Capades TV special.

When she's not practicing, performing, or competing, Debi is a pre-med student studying and attending classes full-time at Stanford University. Debi and her husband, Brian Vanden Hogen (married in March 1988), reside in San Jose, California.

Isiah Thomas

The six-foot-one guard with the Old Testament moniker has inevitably had to endure biblical metaphors from fans and press alike. As his teams' playmaker, the sentiment most visible on sheets during his apprenticeship at Indiana University, and used by writers during his spectacular early pro seasons was "And a little child shall lead them," from, of course, the Book of Isaiah.

The "little" floor leader is the youngest of nine children of a trucker and a housing authority worker. Born in Chicago on 30 April 1961, Isiah Lord Thomas III was four when his father left the family. He saw several of his brothers drift into heroin use and street hustling. But he became an honor roll student and All-American at St. Joseph High, and chose Indiana for the abrasive but effective discipline administered by coach Bobby Knight; later Thomas may have regretted the choice as Knight berated him well into his second year. Their conflict abated when Knight allowed Thomas to be his natural floor leader, a role that brought the Hoosiers the 1981 collegiate championship. By then NBA teams had been convinced that Isiah, child or not, and his thread-the-needle passing could lead their offenses. A $400,000-a-year offer by the Detroit Pistons lured him out of his pre-law studies after his sophomore year, although mom Mary made him sign a written promise to complete his education. He thanked her with a new Chicago house. "I haven't lost sight of my goal of becoming a criminal lawyer," he told her. "I realized I can always get an education.... But I can't always get the cash." Astonished by the difference the cash made (". . . one day you can't buy a pair of shoes and the next day you can buy anything in the whole world"), his instant team leadership astonished the league and thrilled beleaguered Piston fans. The All-Star game's MVP in 1984, he ranks among the NBA's steals and assists leaders. Perhaps the high point of his career so far came in the 1989 NBA playoffs, when his Pistons stuffed the L.A. Lakers, defending champs, in four straight to assume the basketball crown.

Thomas's dimpled countenance and wholesome characteristics have brought out the maternal instincts in women, young and old, who want to "watch over" the modest, handsome, well-built, and rich young bachelor.

Marlo Thomas

She was "That Girl" on the air waves for five years, not just any girl, mind you, but the spunky brunette who subsequently created and starred in the much lauded "Free To Be You and Me" (which won her three of her four Emmys) and who is known in the business as someone who "wants things done right."

Born in Detroit, on 21 November 1938, the daughter of veteran entertainer Danny Thomas ("Sometimes inherited fame from a superstar father can be tough on second generation talent. It opens the doors, but you must fight to keep them from slamming shut"), she attended Beverly Hills Catholic Grammar School, Marymount High School, and the University of Southern California, where she studied for her B.A. in education. But her thespian itch would not be quashed and so she "pounded the pavement in New York and L.A. Everybody just about gave up on me." Enter Mike Nichols and Neil Simon. Offered the lead in the London production of *Barefoot in the Park* she became, as it were, an "overnight sensation." "A great new comic actress hit London last night," wrote one critic. "Hit it? She almost demolished it." After eight months of blitzing London, she returned to America to star in TV's "That Girl." Since then she has starred with Alan Alda in the feature film *Jenny* and has appeared in both the Broadway and motion picture productions of *Thieves* (1975). Her first TV special "Acts of Love and Other Comedies" (1973) was at the time the highest rated comedy special in ABC history. Ten years later, apparently still interested in domestic tug-of-war she appeared in "Love, Sex . . . And Marriage" (ABC-TV). Her latest projects include the 1986 telefilm "Nobody's Child" (Emmy Award), a lead role in the Broadway play *Social Security* (1986) and a sequel to her *Free To Be . . .* album, called *Free To Be . . . A Family* (1988). Thomas is married to Phil Donahue and serves on the boards of the Ms. Foundation, the National Women's Political Caucus, and St. Jude's Children Research Hospital, founded by her father.

Richard Thomas

"I was one of those born-in-a-trunk babies," Richard Thomas proudly reveals. "My parents were extremely happy in the theatre and saw no reason why I shouldn't be." Their positive attitude resulted in the 1973 Emmy winner's (for his portrayal of John-Boy in the television series "The Walton's") successful three-fold career on television, stage and films.

Born in New York City, 13 June 1951, the son of ballet dancers Richard Thomas III and Barbara (Fallis) Thomas (later owners and operators of the New York School of Ballet), he spent his early years touring with his parents. "I had the discipline of having watched them work since I was young." He attended Allen-Stevenson School, McBurney School and Columbia (switching from an English major to study Chinese). His Broadway career began when he played John Roosevelt in *Sunrise at Campobello* "It was the first time I knew I was a real actor because I did it all myself. I was seven.") In 1963 he played the son in the Actor's Studio revival of Eugene O'Neill's *Strange Interlude*. Other early appearances were in *The Playroom* and Edward Albee's *Everything in the Garden*. After an absense of 15 years, Thomas returned to Broadway in the 1981 critically-acclaimed *The Fifth of July* (later televised). In 1983 he received good personal notices for the Circle Rep's production of *The Sea Gull*, proving he was one of the few actors "who had refined rather than forgotten his craft during a long career in television." That wedge of his performing pie began in the late 50s with the roles on the early live shows and soap operas ("I was always dying and I love to die, because then I knew the audience would feel sorry for me"). In 1971 he appeared in Earl Hammer's "The Homecoming" on which the 1972 Walton series was based (it ran for 5 years). His many films for television include "The Red Badge of Courage," "The Silence," "Roots: The Second Generation," "No Other Love," "All Quiet on the Western Front," "To Find My Son," "Berlin Tunnel: 21," "Barefoot in the Park," "Johnny Belinda," "The Hank Williams Jr. Story," "Hobson's Choice," "The Master of Ballantrae" and "Go Towards The Light." He also appeared in the 1988 HBO miniseries, "Glory, Glory!" Devoting the latter part of the 80s to theatre, Thomas starred in eight plays back-to-back (beginning in 1986). These include: *The Barbarians* and *Hawthorne Country* (at Williamstown); *Two Figures in Dense Violet Light* (at Kennedy Center); *The Front Page* (Lincoln Center); *Citizen Tom Paine* (Philadelphia Company); plus *Hamlet* and *Peer Gynt* (at the Hartford Stage). He made his film debut in 1969 as Paul Newman and Joanne Woodward's son in *Winning*. Other film roles include *Last Summer, Red Sky at Morning, Cactus in the Snow, 9/30/55*, and Roger Corman's *Battle Beyond the Stars*. Three volumes of Thomas's poetry have been published, the most recent in 1985.

Richard now lives in Los Angeles with his wife, the former Alma Gonzales, whom he married on Valentine's Day, 1975. They have a son, Richard Francisco, and in 1981 became parents of triplets - Barbara, Gwyneth and Pilar. "I get up every morning and thank God I have three beautiful little girls and a wonderful son," beams Thomas. As a humanitarian, the actor was elected National Chairman of the Better Hearing Institute, serving in that position through 1988. Also in 1988, he spent the spring touring colleges around the country on behalf of the Kennedy Center's Education Program where he offered guidance on theatre and acting.

John Thompson

He says he tried to create a disciplined program at mostly-white Georgetown University because predominantly-black teams are often accused of "being big and fast . . . who can leap like kangaroos" but who "can't play as a team . . . and choke under pressure." His teams certainly didn't blow many in the 1983-84 season as the Hoyas enabled the six-feet-ten, 300-pound Thompson to become the first black coach to guide a Division 1 team to an NCAA basketball title. Having been criticized by the press for overseeing all his players' interviews, he won tangible proof of the utility of old-style father-image coaching. "I'm the director . . . they're the actors . . . I don't want anyone putting on their own act," he says.

Native Washingtonian John Thompson, born 1 September 1941, was All-American at D.C.'s John Carroll high school, then went on to Providence College before becoming a backup center to the Boston Celtics' Bill Russell. In 1967 the newly-married Thompson turned down offers from the Chicago Bulls and ABA teams to play because, he said, "I didn't like that lifestyle, living on planes and in hotels, the high life." He earned a master's degree in youth counseling, then became director of Washington, D.C.'s 4-H program and coach of the highly-successful Saint Anthony's high school. After a 3-23 record in 1971-72, Georgetown's coach resigned and Thompson took the advice of a friend by applying for the opening. The oldest Catholic university in the U.S., Georgetown made a determined effort to attract black students in the wake of the 1968 D.C. riots. Although the school's president said his hiring committee didn't make a conscious decision to pick a black coach to work in predominantly-black Washington, when it encountered "an intelligent black man, with a clear idea of what he wanted," Thompson was hired. Soon he changed the makeup of the squad that usually used one or two black "token" players. While guiding his teams to post-season tournaments almost every year and compiling a .700 winning average, he brought several teams to the NCAA Final Four. Having taken the pressure of handling the press off his seven-foot All-American center Patrick Ewing, the Hoya coach led Georgetown to the 1984 championship game. With Ewing concentrating on defending Houston University's Nigerian giant Akeem Olajuwon, freshman Reggie Williams was able to sear the nets with his outside jumper. Georgetown won 84-75. (The following year the Hoyas bowed to scrappy underdog Villanova in the NCAA finals.)

To keep their valuable asset, Georgetown alumni bought a $350,000 house in Washington where Thompson, wife Gwen and their two teenaged sons live, and pay a nominal rent. Graduating nearly 85% of his players, the imposing former youth counselor says, "I don't think [dummies] can learn my system. . . . I can coach a kid who [in school] had decided it *is* possible to learn things."

Strom Thurmond

Former Dixiecrat Strom Thurmond rules with an iron hand as head of the Minority Staff for the Judiciary Committee (since 1986), obviously someone to be reckoned with on Capitol Hill. (He was previously the Chairman of the Judiciary Committee from 1980-1986). An old hand on the Hill—he still holds the filibuster record (24 hours 18 minutes against civil rights, 1957)—he remains the get-along-go-along powerbroker despite an ongoing flirtation with the New Right. Other Senators make sure to get along with him, at least most of the time.

A physical fitness enthusiast who hoists barbells in his back office, he threw his political weight toward Nixon in 1968 and helped him win over the Southern states. Although he placed numerous South Carolinians in key Nixon posts, his man for the Supreme Court, Clement Haynsworth, didn't pass Senate scrutiny. Striding down legislative halls, his erect carriage declares his military training; he holds a two-star general's reserve commission in the Army. Thurmond's Senate facade is rather cold and austere. Wintry of eye, he has spring in his heart; the Senator has made it a habit to wed Miss Carolinas, the first Mrs. Thurmond (now deceased) was 21 when she moved into the governor's mansion in 1947, the youngest first lady in state history. Bride No. 2, Nancy Moore, also a former Miss Carolina, became Mrs. Thurmond at 22. Explains the Senator: "I prefer the smell of perfume to the smell of linament." When the couple's first child was born in 1971, it produced the first U.S. Senate baby shower.

This stony-faced Southern strategist was born 5 December 1902 in Edgefield, S.C. He took a correspondence course in law, became a county attorney, state senator, and in 1938 the youngest circuit court judge in the state. In 1947 he was elected governor and the following year, when the States' Rights Democrats bolted from the party convention, he was nominated for the presidency and carried four states. Nevertheless, once, during a governor's conference, he complained Governor R. Gregg Cherry carried a grudge against him. "Shucks, I like you well enough, Strom. I'm just no damn fool about you." Thurmond's political career is distinguished by the fact that he first won office on the basis of a write-in-vote, in 1954. He threw in with the GOP in 1964.

Cheryl Tiegs

The quintessential California girl and one of the cosmetic industry's most durable models, her quick rise to cover-girl status in 1966 beckoned in a new era of beauty: healthy, breezy, and blonde. The look was an abrupt departure from the stark, high-fashion trend epitomized by Twiggy; and Tiegs, with her lanky 5'10" frame and natural glow, championed the new standard. Talent agent Nina Blanchard has said, "If you could design a face for this business, a face everyone wants, it would be Cheryl's. She can sell anything from sable coats to candy."

Born 25 September 1947 into a Minnesota farm family of German descent, Tiegs began modeling in high school, after relocating to Alhambra, Calif., but was boosted into the big money after a move to New York and the famed Ford Agency. More than 100 magazine covers followed, including *Time* (1978) and *Sports Illustrated*, and long, lucrative contracts with Cover Girl, Clairol, and Olympus Camera. Tiegs branched out as a beauty commentator on ABC's "Good Morning America" in 1978, and the next year as a narrator of a special on African wildlife with photographer Peter Beard, whom she married in 1981 (since divorced), directly after a much publicized divorce from film director Stan Dragoti. She is partners in a Sears Roebuck sportswear line bearing her name, and a nationally distributed line of women's eyeglass frames.

When gossip magazines barked details of her unraveling personal life, Tiegs remained focused on staying healthy and staying on top. She believes an honest life makes for honestly good looks. "I like to represent healthy sex. I think the most unsexy thing you can do is try to be sexy. It's all in the attitude."

Grant Tinker

The former Chief Executive Officer of NBC (1981-1986) began his job by saying, "If in two or three years my efforts aren't rewarded (by increased ratings), they should let someone else try." After a five-year reign he hadn't extricated the peacock network from the bottom of the heap and said, "I was underestimating the difficulties then. If, by the end of five years, we haven't come a far piece, they should pasture me out." He lamented that "to the bulk of the audience, bad programming may not be a problem," and was so apprehensive about a turnabout that he later stated that in 15 years he'd be living in France regardless of what happened. What happened is that Tinker left NBC and formed his own company GTG Entertainment in 1987.

Before Grant A. Tinker, born in Stamford, Conn., 11 January 1926, made his return to the web headquarters at Rockefeller Center, he'd been president of MTM Enterprise for eleven years. That production company, named for his then-wife Mary Tyler Moore, crafted such highly-regarded shows as "The Mary Tyler Moore Show," "Lou Grant," "The White Shadow," "Hill Street Blues," and "WKRP in Cincinnati." With credentials unsurpassed as a producer, he was expected to elevate the level of programming tastes, but in time found himself resorting to the pragmatic choices of the television executive. "I had to watch a pilot of a new program a while ago," Tinker said. "And we made the decision: It's a little too good . . . it just didn't work." He acquired his TV savvy at NBC as a management trainee after graduation from Dartmouth in 1949. After climbing to become head of the radio network, he took off to work for Radio Free Europe. In the '50s he headed television programming departments of ad agencies McCann-Erickson and Benton & Bowles in the days of advertiser-developed shows. For most of the '60s he was a V.P. in NBC's programming department, then was off to Hollywood to work in TV divisions of Universal and Twentieth Century-Fox before starting MTM in 1970. Tanned, white-haired and urbane, the youthfully-handsome Tinker abandons his Manhattan hotel on weekends for his L.A. home. A bachelor since his 1981 divorce from Moore, he personifies the type of creative mind he wants to recruit for NBC's shows. "I call them the 'A Group.' They have a different mind-set than the second-raters. They avoid the cheap sex joke and the easy use of violence to climax a scene. For want of a better word, you might call them literate."

Lily Tomlin

She sprang forth from "Laugh-In" with her delightful camp creations of Ernestine (the love-starved telephone operator), and Edith Ann to become a top-caliber performer in films as well as TV. Lily Tomlin has won Emmys for her comedy specials, a Grammy for an LP, a Tony for her one-woman Broadway show, and in her film debut (*Nashville* in 1975) she was nominated for a Supporting Actress Oscar. For her screen credits, which include *Moment to Moment, Nine to Five, The Incredible Shrinking Woman* and *All of Me*, she is held in high esteem by the industry which profoundly affected her as a teenager ("To say movies had a big influence on me is an epic understatement. They devoured me whole and vice versa. Like a dame in distress in a B-grade Carole Mathews swamp movie, I was caught in movieland's magical muck of fantasy quicksand.").

Born in Detroit, 1 September 1936, she studied English at Wayne State University and subsequently became a secretary to a New York casting director, performing in a revue at the Gotham nightspot, "Upstairs at the Downstairs," and appearing off-Broadway as the lead in *Arf and the Great Airplane Snatch*. After a taste of television regularity on "The Gary Moore Show," she headed West and landed in the show, "Laugh-In," then a national craze. Now calling herself a bi-coastal person (California and New York), she owes much of her success to her ability as a people-watcher. "At school, you could almost divide girls into two groups. The squares who acted like the girls in the fun 'n surf movies and the hipper, cooler set who were like the girls in woman's prison movies. I didn't know much about feminism, but I knew it forced me to make a choice; I would rather be Ruby Gentry who wrecked a whole town, than be Sandra Dee and be wrecked by a whole bunch of surfers." Tomlin returned to Broadway in 1985 with her solo *The Search for Signs of Intelligent Life in the Universe*. Her latest screen outing was with Bette Midler in *Big Business* (1987).

Mel Torme

Singing for his (and his family's) supper since the age of four, he's successfully survived the slings and arrows of changing musical tastes and emerged from his "Velvet Fog" period (hecklers called it "Frog") to make himself tunefully at home on the contemporary supper club scene despite the fits and starts along the way.

He was born Melvin Howard Torme, 13 September 1925, to Russian-Jewish immigrants in Chicago, where his father was the owner of a dry-goods store and a butter-and-eggs business conducted in his Model-A Ford. This songster's early talent was triggered by three musical sources: his mother Betty who demonstrated sheet music at Woolworth's and taught him the new songs as they came out; the radio, which Torme claims he "was addicted to"; and Alberta, a 300-pound woman who not only raised him but who, on weekends, played barrel house piano in an all-girl band at the Savoy. At the age of four, Torme made his singing debut at the Blackhawk Restaurant for $15 a session. By six, he was in vaudeville, and became, until his voice changed, one of the busiest child actors on network radio. At Hyde Park high school on Chicago's South Side, he played drums in a band that included Steve Allen on piano. He composed his first song when he was 15, "Lament for Love," which he sang in audition for the Harry James Band, and though he failed the audition, Harry James recorded the song, which became a juke-box hit. He left high school to play drums in Chico Marx's band in California, and was soon hailed as the crooner most likely to succeed Sinatra and Crosby. This visibility gained him his first part in the movie *Higher and Higher* (1943) with Frank Sinatra and Jack Haley, which began a string of screen credits. By 1947, Torme was followed by waves of raving bobby-soxers, but got little excitement from the audiences at the Copacabana, and his backstage attitude had won him few friends. One underwhelmed observer described him as "a sour-faced man whose glance wilts a flower." After his stint at the Copa, Dorothy Kilgallen called him "an egotistical little amateur." Torme fled to England where he found his most loyal audiences.

During the '50s, Torme sang jazz, on a day-time talk show that lasted for seven years, walked away with an Emmy for a part on CBS's Playhouse 90, made more movies but never became the matinee idol of his youthful dreams. The '60s saw him hit the charts, and author such memorable and loved songs as "The Christmas Song" ("Chestnuts roasting on an open fire . . .") and such TV scripts as "Run for Your Life" and "The Virginian." He also wrote a memoir having to do with his work as writer for Judy Garland's TV series. The book, entitled *The Other Side of the Dawn with Judy Garland on the Dawn Patrol*, was poorly received mainly because of its treatment of Garland. The '70s and '80s found him at Carnegie Hall, the Newport Jazz Festival, European festivals, often in London and New York, and home-based in Las Vegas. He has a repertoire of some 5,000 songs ranging through name composers, and his voice has become rich and pure in tone. He has become a superb vocal known for his laidback improvisational technique. He recorded the album *Gone With The Wind* in 1986 and published his memoirs *It Wasn't All Velvet* in 1988. Married four times (five children), Torme is a collector of nostalgic items, a licensed pilot, and an aviation buff who attributes his easier voice to healthier sleeping habits.

Randy Travis

If awards are any measure of success and accomplishments, then Randy Travis has proven that he's no one-hit wonder. The patented Travis blend of tradition and innovation coupled with his winning personality and distinctive vocal style has made him the heir apparent to country superstars like George Jones, Merle Haggard and others. The talented singer and songwriter's music reflects the deep and enduring roots of his upbringing in the heartland. It has garnered him audience loyalty, two double platinum albums with the third album following suit, and over thirty awards in just two years.

Randy Travis was born Randy Traywick on 4 May 1959 in Marshville, North Carolina. He began playing guitar and singing at age eight. By the age of ten, he and his brother Ricky had put together their own duo, playing throughout the South at fiddler's conventions, private parties, VFW halls—anywhere they could draw a crowd. Relocating to Charlotte, N.C., at age sixteen, Travis entered a talent show hosted by the club Country City, U.S.A. as a solo performer and won. The club's owner, Lib Hatcher, invited him to play regularly at the nightspot. Travis performed there for five years, first on weekends and eventually fulltime. Hatcher became his manager and in the 1970's, Travis recorded two singles for Paula Records, "Dreamin" and "She's My Woman." In 1981, Travis relocated to Nashville, where he wrote songs and became acquainted with the Nashville scene while commuting to Charlotte to perform at Country City, U.S.A. Eventually, Hatcher began managing the Nashville Palace where Travis became a popular attraction as well as a short order cook. Signed to Warner Bros., Records in 1985, Travis's first single for WB was "Prairie Rose" on the *Rustler's Rhapsody* movie soundtrack. It was followed by the singles "On The Other Hand" (his first major hit and the 1987 Academy of Country Music Song of the Year and ACM & Music City News Single of the Year) and "1982". In early 1986 Travis's debut album *Storms of Life* went to the top of the charts, remaining in the Top Twenty two years after its release. Travis was awarded the 1986 CMA Horizon Award as most promising new artist and the album was awarded the 1987 ACM & Music City News Album of the Year. Extensive concert appearances followed. His follow-up album *Always & Forever* (1987) joined *Storms of Life* in reaching double platinum-plus numbers and remained number 1 on *Billboard* Country charts for forty-three weeks. This album was voted 1987 CMA & American Music Award as well as the 1988 Music City News and Nashville Network Viewers Choice Awards as Album of the Year. It generated the smash hit "Forever & Ever, Amen" which won 1987 CMA, AMA, 1988 ACM and TNN Single of the Year as well as ACM Song of the Year honors. The song's video won the

1987 AMA and TNN (1988) favorite video award. The song was also picked the 1987 AMOA Jukebox Best Country Record. Travis himself was honored as the Top Male Vocalist in 1987 & 1988 by the ACM, MCN, CMA, in 1988 by TNN and won the 1987 Grammy for Best Country Vocal Performance - Male. He was also the 1987 MCN Star of Tomorrow and the 1988 TNN and MCN Entertainer of the Year. 1988 also marked Travis's induction into the Grand Ole Opry, as the youngest male member ever. His third album *Old 8 X 10* has continued his successful pattern with the hit singles "Honky Tonk Moon" and the Number 1 "Deeper Than The Holler". Aside from recording, Travis filmed a bit part in the film *Young Guns* (which was edited out of the final cut) and performed for President Bush at an inaugural special, as well as appearing on "Saturday Night Live" and "Late Night With David Letterman." He continues to tour extensively and seems destined for a long and brillant career.

John Travolta

"Man, nobody pushed me into show business. I was aching for it," Travolta says. The ache first began to pay off in the mid-70s, when he achieved his initial fame on television as Vinnie Barbarino in "Welcome Back Kotter." That character—a cocky, dimwitted but endearing punk—wasn't so unlike that of Tony Manero, which made him an instant movie star at the end of 1977 with the release of *Saturday Night Fever*. The disco music film, and particularly its star, created a sensation. He was named the year's best actor by the National Board of Review and received an Oscar nomination for his performance.

Born in Englewood, N.J. on 18 February 1954, John Travolta was the youngest of six—all involved in the performing arts. He studied acting with his late mother (who, along with one of his sisters, had a bit role in *Fever*), began his performing career at age nine in a summer stock production of *Bye Bye Birdie*, and left school at 16 for the stage. In 1974 he made his Broadway debut in *Over Here!*, the Andrews Sisters musical. At 18 he joined the original Broadway production of *Grease* in a minor part. He was acclaimed for his title role in the 1976 TV film "The Boy in the Plastic Bubble." Co-starring as his mother was Diana Hyland, who became his lover, and whose death from cancer at 41 early the next year devastated Travolta, who left the *Fever* set to be with her. A small part in *Carrie* led to *Fever*, which was soon followed by the hugely popular film version of *Grease*. *Urban Cowboy* (based, like *Fever*, on a true *New York* magazine story) was another hit, and the critically roasted *Two of a Kind* reunited him with his *Grease* leading lady, Olivia Newton-John. He recreated his role of Tony in the *Fever* sequel, *Staying Alive*, directed by Sylvester Stallone. For the film, the *Rocky* star put Travolta on an intensive body-building regime. "I'm in awe of it," he says of his new body. He was named Man of the Year in 1981 by Harvard University's Hasty Pudding Club.

Mixing his pumped-up body with a dancercise score and Jamie Lee Curtis, Travolta played a reporter in the less-than-perfect film *Perfect* (1985). Seeking a successful vehicle, he was directed by Robert Altman in Harold Pinter's play "The Dumb Waiter" for ABC-TV (1987). John appeared on the big screen in *The Tender* (1988) as a father of a young daughter involved with Chicago's underworld. His latest feature, a comedy entitled *The Experts*, was filmed in Ontario for a 1989 national release.

Travolta lives on a 17-acre Santa Barbara ranch, and his hobby is flying. He pilots a $1.7 million jet. Formerly in psychotherapy, he has become a devotee of Scientology. Despite his fortune and popularity, he's a recluse who claims, "I am really a very modest man."

Lee Trevino

Like a Southwest dustbowl sandstorm swirling through the insular ranks of professional golf, "Super Max" merrily chipped and putted his way to golf superstardom and into the hearts of his devoted "Lee's Fleas" (so named in good-natured parody of Mr. Palmer's "Arnie's Army"), whose chorus of "Olés" followed his every shot. When, in 1982, NBC hired him as their expert golf analyst and color commentator (he re-signed a multi-year agreement with NBC as an analyst in 1988), no one who had followed Lee Trevino's colorful career was surprised. The most talkative pro on the tour—with a running stream of jokes and repartee with the galleries and press alike—Trevino once admitted, "I even had to quit smoking on the golf course because I nearly choked to death while I was talking." It is on the golf course, however, that Trevino's major triumphs have been recorded, where his astonishing consistency accounted for at least one major tournament victory per year for 14 consecutive years, beginning with his victory after only two years on the tour at the U.S. Open in 1968. He was elevated to the American Golf Hall of Fame in 1979.

Lee Buck Trevino was born on 1 December 1939 near Dallas, the son of Mexican-American parents who separated when he was two. He grew up in the care of his grandfather, a gravedigger, in a house with no running water or electricity. "Rent-free and we even had a lake behind the house," he cheerfully recalls. Next to the lake was the fairway of the Glen Lakes Country Club, where Lee made a penny or two ("I cleared maybe $10 a day") selling stray balls back to erratic duffers. At six, he cut down to size a discarded club ("If you were rich enough to play golf you were rich enough to throw clubs away") and began to emulate club members by playing on a two-hole course he dug in his backyard. In teaching himself, he developed a style that has been decribed as "a horrendously flat baseball swing." He quit school after the seventh grade to become an assistant greens keeper, and shot a 77 the first time he played a full 18 holes at the age of 15. Lying about his age, he joined the Marines for a four-year hitch ("I made sergeant by swinging my clubs with the colonels"), then returned to Dallas as a pro at a par-three pitch-and-putt course. To supplement his meager earnings, he "hustled" strangers by offering to play them using an ostensibly disadvantageous club whose head was a taped-on Dr. Pepper bottle. "I can hit a ball 100 yards with a Dr. Pepper bottle," he was later to confess. Horizon Hills Country Club outside of El Paso, where he worked as an assistant pro, paid his way to his first U.S. Open in 1966, where he finished tied for 54th. Discouraged but undeterred, he finished fifth in the 1967 U.S. Open and triumphed in 1968 with a score of 275, thereby tying Jack Nicklaus for the lowest score in U.S. Open history. In 1971 he became the only golfer to win the game's "Triple Crown"—the U.S. Open, the British Open and the Canadian Open, with its appropriate rewards: PGA Player of the Year; *Golf* magazine's Player of the Year; *Sports Illustrated*'s Sportsman of the Year; the Hickok Belt (as top professional athlete); Associated Press' Male Athlete of the Year; the *Sporting News*' Sports Man of the Year; and the British Broadcasting Association's International Sports Personality of the Year. The "undershirt guy (who was) just what the buttoned down world of professional golf has needed for some time" rarely leaves the scene of a tournament victory without first writing a check to a local charity. He is the author of *How to Groove a Better Golf Swing* (1976) and the autobiographical *They Call Me Super Mex* (1983), the same year the twice-divorced father of three married Claudia Bove. It's she whom he credits for keeping him in the game. "She's the one kept whipping me, kept telling me I could win," he says.

Pauline Trigère

"A designer can't relax," says this French-born "American" fashion doyenne. "I'm a tyrant. I have a temper, and can be an impossible perfectionist. We work on a collection until the first model hits the runway." In the years since Pauline Trigère hocked a diamond brooch and two jeweled clips to open her first shop, this perfectionism has paid off in patrons, prizes and prestige. Three-time winner of the Coty American Fashion Critics Award and the first living woman to be named to Fashion's Hall of Fame, Trigère is still at the top of her form. "You're only as good as your next collection," she says. "You can't live on your last."

Born a block away from Place Pigalle in Paris on 4 November 1912, Trigère learned to cut and fit in her father's tailoring shop and arrived in New York with her tailor husband and two small sons on Christmas Day, 1936. When the marriage broke up and she found herself with a family to support, she went to work as an assistant designer to Hattie Carnegie. Establishing her own label in 1942, she soon was in the forefront of American couture. The Trigère hallmark has remained, as one critic put it, "A deceptive look of simplicity which emerges from artistic, intricate cut."

A self-confessed workaholic, Trigère uses working in her country garden as "therapy." "I plant in November," laughs the designer, "and no matter how much I cajole, rant and rage, those damn daffodils never bloom 'til spring."

Calvin Trillin

"He's the kind of writer," wrote reviewer Gene Lyons in *Newsweek*, "who gets nothing but favorable reviews, and for perfectly good reasons. No professional writer could fail to admire his virtues. Whether he's holding forth on the joys of spaghetti carbonara, poking fun at newsmagazine journalists (as in his novel *Floater*) or reporting on the violent deaths of a cross section of his fellow Americans (*Killings*), Trillin's wit, even-tempered curiosity and admirable brevity are always on display."

He was born on 5 December 1935 in Kansas City, Mo. After graduating from Yale and serving in the army, "Bud," as he is known, worked for *Time* before becoming a staff writer for the *New Yorker* in 1963. From 1967 to 1982, he did a series of articles called "U.S. Journal" which earned him the descriptive tag of "the Marco Polo of Junk Food." His pieces on eating have been collected in books such as *American Fried - The Adventures of a Happy Eater*. (1974), *Alice, Let's Eat* (1978), and *Third Helpings* (1983). He has also written *An Education in Georgia* (1964), an account of the experience of the first two black undergraduates at the University of Georgia; *Barnett Frummer Is an Unbloomed Flower* (1969), a series of short stories about trendiness in the sixties; *U.S. Journal* (1971), the first three years of his column; and *Uncivil Liberties* (1982), a collection of pieces he's written for the *Nation*. His latest book is *If You Can't Say Something Nice* (1987).

Husband to Alice, father to two daughters, he considers himself a magazine writer rather than a book writer. Plot seems to be a problem for him. "Let me tell you," he said of his novel *Floater*, it took 20 strong men to pull the plot in from the wings, all sweating and cursing and mumbling about overtime, so I simply put them to work a bit longer."

Tatiana Troyanos

"I always felt drawn, extremely drawn, to music and it has held me together. It spoke to my soul and spirit, the communication I had with it. I felt I was another person when involved with music, but there was difficulty in identification . . . my intensity comes from this. . . ." A singer of extraordinary versatility, Tatiana Troyanos is able to portray with equal credibility a sultry, sensual beauty or an impish young man. She built her repertory and her solid reputation as leading mezzo of the Hamburg Staatsoper (for a decade). Home is now the New York Metropolitan Opera, where Troyanos debuted in 1976 and which she "adores" because of the supportive, family-like environment there—"It's what I've wanted all my life . . . not to run around. . . ." Troyanos made operatic history in her La Scala debut as the only American in the first worldwide live telecast and radio broadcast of an opera, appearing as Adalgisa opposite the *Norma* of Montserrat Caballe in 1977.

Born in New York on 12 September 1938 to a "temperamentally combustible" Greek father and German mother, she was placed in the Brooklyn Home for Children at the age of seven. There she had her first taste of music, studying piano with a former bassoonist from the Met Orchestra. A scholarship to the Brooklyn Music School was followed by another to the Juillard Preparatory School, and after a brief stint with the New York City Opera, Troyanos took off for Hamburg and got herself a contract with the Staatsoper. Returning to the United States, she joined the Met family with whom she has performed over 14 roles. Troyanos resides in a New York City co-op and a country home and has chosen to put her career above all else—"If you have a talent it needs to be nurtured. You have to stick to it and that's tough. . . . I have given myself totally to my career but not without question marks. . . . I've needed to be single-minded about my career or I wouldn't have come as far as I have." She was heard in the role of Anita in the 1985 recording of *West Side Story*, conducted by its composer, Leonard Bernstein.

Garry Trudeau

"It is usually understood by both reader and editor that the comics are a special kind of territory, the sacred part of the paper, unantagonizing, unconfronting, almost tranquilizing," he says. "This is the way many readers like it and this is the way many editors try to keep it. The particular sociological outlook of 'Doonesbury' is specific enough to leave more than a few readers irate."

Called "the J.D. Salinger of cartooning" because of his penchant for privacy ("If I have anything of interest to say, I say it in the strip"), cartoonist Garry Trudeau, born in New York City in 1948, grew up in Saranac Lake, the offspring of a well-to-do, well-connected Social Register family. He made his debut as a cartoonist while still an undergraduate at Yale, creating a strip for the *Yale Daily News* entitled "Bull Tales." Featured in the strip was the character of Mike Doonesbury, whose last name derived from "Doone," a Yalie term for a good-natured fool, plus the second half of Pillsbury, a college roommate of the artist's. Launched off campus in 1970 by the fledgling Universal Press Syndicate, "Doonesbury"'s wryly biting exploration of such real-life current events as the massacre at Kent State soon attracted a small counter-cultural cult following which, through the years, grew to a regular readership in the neighborhood of 60 million in over 700 newspapers. Collections of his work have sold over 6 million copies worldwide, and his animated film, *A Doonesbury Special*, was nominated for an Academy Award. Trudeau, who was the first non-editorial page artist to win the prestigious Pulitzer Prize for cartooning, suspended the strip for a sabbatical from his seven-day-a-week (12 years running) characters in 1982. During this hiatus he worked with composer Elizabeth Swados to bring a musical to Broadway called *Doonesbury*, and he wrote a screenplay for Orion Pictures about the White House Press Corps. Trudeau said it was time for Doonesbury and his friends—Congresswoman Lacey Davenport, struggling to sort out her canvassers from her maids; megaphone radical Mark Slackmeyer; Zonker Harris; and Joanie Caucus, the liberted woman—to make the transition from the 1960s to the 1980s, "from draft beer and mixers to cocaine and herpes," he explained. "My characters are understandably confused and out of sorts. It's time to give them some haircuts, graduate them and move them out into the larger world of grown-up concerns." His recent books include *Death of a Party Animal* (1986) and *Downtown Doonesbury* (1987).

The shy artist is married to someone who is seen more frequently in the morning than is the sun—NBC's "Today Show" hostess, Jane Pauley. They have twins, Richard and Rachel, born in 1983, and a son, Thomas Moore, born in 1986.

Margaret Truman

"The way to this old man's heart," the ex-President once confided, "is to be nice to his daughter." Thus, when music critic Paul Hume wrote in 1950, "Miss Truman cannot sing with anything approaching professional finish . . . she communicates almost nothing of the music she presents," Dad got mad. "Someday I hope to meet you," an irate Harry wrote to Hume. "When that happens you'll need a new nose, a lot of beefsteak for black eyes, and perhaps a supporter below." Said Margaret: "Hume's a very fine critic. He has a right to write what he pleases." But admitting that, like her father, she had a "low boiling point," she had her own annoyances. "People have hinted that after my father became President I took the opportunity to launch myself on a career to make money while the iron was hot. This is singly untrue." Criticized for receiving more money as an entertainer than her father as President, she cracked, "Naturally an artist receives more than her accompanist."

A Missourian, she was born Mary Margaret Truman in Independence (where her father was a county judge) on 17 February 1924, and has described her upbringing as "Midwestern, mid-Victorian." An only child, she was ten when the family moved to Washington, D.C., where she later attended George Washington University, majoring in history and international relations. She made her debut as a professional singer in 1947, and during the 1950s made a number of guest appearances on radio and TV shows. She gave up her singing career after her marriage in 1956 to then *New York Times* editor Clifton Daniel. Said Daniel about their first meeting: "I looked down the neck of that Fontana dress and I haven't looked back since." She continued, however, to act in summer and/or winter stock, had a radio program on New York's WOR, and along the way had four sons. In 1973, Mrs. Daniel joined the ranks of best-selling authors with her biography of—who else but—Harry S. Truman, and since has written nine other books, including five murder mysteries set in some of Washington's most venerable institutions. Her string of books with such titles as *Murder in the White House, Murder in the Supreme Court, Murder in the Smithsonian, Murder At The F.B.I., Murder In Georgetown, Murder in the C.I.A.* and *Murder at the Kennedy Center* seems to provide endless possibilities. She also serves on numerous boards and committees, and is trustee of her alma mater.

Donald Trump

The man *Time* described as the "Flashy Symbol of an Acquistive Age" in their 1989 cover story is a handsome, rich entrepreneur who can proclaim, "Who has done as much as I have? No one has done more in New York than me." He's "mad and wonderful," says architect Philip Johnson. His pastor, the Reverend Norman Vincent Peale, positively avows he's "kindly and courageous . . . and has a profound streak of honest humility." His wife calls him "an all-American boy." His father admitted "he was a pretty rough fellow when he was small." His critics charge that he is a raving egomaniac, bent on putting his name on every inanimate object in the city, ". . . a rogue billionaire like some sort of movie monster . . . ready to transform Midtown Manhattan into another glass-and-glitz downtown Houston, with Central Park for parking." Says the object of these mixed reviews, who transformed his father's $40 million Brooklyn-Queens real-estate empire into the billion-dollar Manhattan-based Trump Organization, "I don't like to lose." As one of the nation's wealthiest businessmen, this lone wolf (Trump does not syndicate his deals—"I don't have to") has successfully used his mastery of the three L's of real estate—leverage, luck and location ("I have the best diamonds in the city of New York as far as location")—to make the name Trump an internationally recognized symbol of New York City as the mecca for the world's rich and famous. Centerpiece of Donald Trump's empire is the 68-story Trump Tower on Fifth Avenue, with its six-story atrium and $1 million waterfall, and doormen dressed in imported uniforms that would put Buckingham Palace to shame. Hailed by architectural critics from Ada Louise Huxtable ("a dramatically handsome structure") to Paul Goldberger ("warm, luxurious and even exhilarating"), it houses some of the most exclusive shops in the world and famous celebrities. A few blocks east is Trump Plaza, with more famous tenants. Recently completed, Trump Parc is a super-luxury condominium with breathtaking views of Central Park. He also sold the St. Moritz hotel and purchased the landmark Plaza Hotel, where his wife, Ivana, runs the show. He holds real estate in Florida (Palm Beach Estate, Trump Plaza) and Atlantic City (Trump Plaza and Casino; he sold the Taj Majal Casino-Hotel to Merv Griffin). As most people know, he completed the Wollman Skating Rink in Central park (took more than six years at more than $12 million), and he owns the world's largest yacht (the 282-foot Trump Princess). Of the future, Trump will only say, "We've built up a lot of cash [to use] not necessarily in this business. I'm not married to this business."

An early interest in the business was evidenced when a very small Donald John Trump (born 14 June 1946 in Jamaica Estates, Queens, New York) glued together all the toy blocks he could find into one giant skyscraper. A period of adolescent mischief-making ended when his father packed him off to military school. At the University of Pennsylvania's Wharton School of Finance, Trump was bored because the real estate courses emphasized single-family houses instead of major projects. ("Donald always used to talk about changing the Manhattan skyline," a college friend remembers.) After graduation, Trump joined his father in Brooklyn, kept on buying and building, and entered the Manhattan real-estate market during the 1974-75 low point in the city's fiscal fortunes. Along the way, he discarded his former attire (matching maroon suits and shoes, etc.) for more conservative dress, moved from the trendy Hamptons to a $10 million waterfront estate in Greenwich, Connecticut, began to dine at "21" and the Reagan White House. He married Ivana, now in charge of the Plaza Hotel and former Czech Olympic skier and fashion model, in 1977 (three children). In 1988, Trump released his enlightening autobiography, *The Art of the Deal*, followed by a fun adult game based on the book. Never one to stop trying to scale all heights he has his own air travel service, Trump Air.

Ivana Trump

She has set new standards of excellence in the hotel industry, and she is one of the most powerful and influential figures in the country today. Ivana has gone from being the only daughter of a homemaker and an electrical engineer to the wife of the real estate mogul and multimillionaire Donald Trump, and the president of one of the most exclusive and famous hotels in the world, The Plaza.

Ivana Winkelmayr was born in Czechoslovakia, where she attended public schools and received a Master's Degree in Physical Education from Charles University in Prague. During her college years, she was chosen as an alternate for the 1972 Czechoslovakian Women's Olympic Ski Team. Shortly after, she emigrated to Canada where she was a successful fashion model working exclusively for the Audrey Morris Agency in Montreal. It was in 1976 that she met her future husband Donald Trump at the Montreal Summer Olympics. Ten months later, in April 1977, the couple wed and Ivana moved to the U.S. In 1984, she started her career with The Trump Organization as the vice-president in charge of design for the Trump Plaza

Tanya Tucker

Casino Hotel in Atlantic City, for which she personally supervised all of the interior decorating. Ivana was also responsible for the interior decorating of Trump Tower as well. Following her success as vice president for the Trump Plaza Casino Hotel, Ivana was appointed as chief executive officer of Trump's Castle Hotel & Casino, where her responsibilities included directing an eight member team of employees. Since her appointment as CEO in 1985, the casino has set such impressive revenue records that the facility moved into the upper half of the market in just five months. In addition, Ivana serves as vice-chairman of Trump Hotels, for which she has the responsibility of overseeing the activities of their three Atlantic City based casino hotels. In 1988 Ivana was named president of the world renowned, luxurious Plaza Hotel. Under her direction are a seven member executive committee as well as 1,200 full time employees. She attributes her participation in sports as an important factor in her overwhelming success. "Sports gave me the competitiveness and discipline that have been important for my success," states Ivana. In addition to her career, Ivana is active in several community and charitable organizaitons. She has co-chaired and been a committee member of the New York City Ballet, the School of American Ballet, United Cerebral Palsy, the March of Dimes, American Cancer Society, the New York Philharmonic, and the Boys Town of Italy.

Ivana and Donald currently reside on a water front estate in Greenwich, Connecticut, with their three children, Donald Jr., Ivanka, and Eric. They also own an estate in Palm Beach, Florida.

Tanya Tucker

From child prodigy to adult country superstar, Tanya Tucker has proven she has staying power. Her successful Capitol album *Strong Enough to Bend* aptly describes her fortitude in weathering a life full of personal and professional challenges. She became an instant star at the age of thirteen with the release of the single "Delta Dawn" and remained in the spotlight throughout her highly publicized turbulent twenties. After a brief try as a rock star, Tanya returned to her country music roots, where she thrived with over twenty top ten records.

Tanya Denise Tucker was born on 10 October 1958 in Seminole, Texas. The youngest of three children, she was encouraged by her parents, Boe and Juanita Tucker, from a very early age to pursue her musical interest. By the time Tanya turned nine, her parents were convinced that she had a future as an entertainer. They took her to an audition for the film *Jeremiah Johnson*, and she landed a small role. Encouraged, her parents paid for a demo tape of Tanya singing, which eventually found its way to record producer Billy Sherrill, who had helped shape the careers of Tammy Wynette and George Jones. He suggested that she record "Happiest Girl in the Whole U.S.A." (eventually a number one hit for Donna Fargo), but Tanya opted for "Delta Dawn," which also became a number 1 hit. It was followed by a double-sided hit single, "Jamestown Ferry" and "Love's the Answer". She became a regular on the "Lew King Show." Television appearances included "A Country Christmas" (1979), "The Georgia Peaches" (1980) and a part in the mini-series "The Rebels" (1979). Albums include *Tanya Tucker* (1975), *Greatest Hits* (1978), *TNT* (1978), *Tear Me Apart* (1979), *Changes* (1982), *Girls Like Me* (1986), *Love Me Like You Used To* (1987), and *Strong Enough to Bend* (1988). Of her over twenty records that reached the top ten, at least nine reached the number one spot. With the release of the Capitol records "Girls Like Me" and "Love Me Like You Used To," she added to her list of seven top ten singles in a row. Three of these, "Just Another Love," "I Won't Take Less Than Your Love" and "If It Don't Come Easy" reached the number one spot. "Strong Enough to Bend" continued the streak. Nominated for numerous awards over the years, the 5'5" blond singer received American Music Award nominations in 1989 and a Grammy nomination for Best Female Country Vocal Performance in 1989. Two successful music videos for "Love Me Like You Used To" and "Strong Enough To Bend," recent television appearances and a strenuous touring schedule are evidence of a career well underway and full of promise. An additional joy came Tanya's way on 5 July 1989 when she gave birth to her daughter, Presley Tanita Tucker. The father of the little girl is a well-kept secret.

Alice Tully

Best known as the donor and guiding light of Alice Tully Hall at New York's Lincoln Center, she is the consummate music lover, patron of music and the arts par excellence, and a former professional singer who capitivated audiences for 14 years as a sensitive dramatic soprano. Granddaughter of Corning Glass Works founder Amory Houghton, Jr., Alice shocked her family by breaking away from their routine to follow her own purpose in life, which was music. ("I existed only for my music and my voice. . . .") Since the late 1940s, she has directed her creative energies and resources to the support of good music and other causes. Mark A. Shubert, director of the Lincoln Center Institute, described her as a "professional in the arts" who "brings to philanthropy not only generosity, but a real understanding of what she is helping." *Town and Country*, in its 1983 list of the Most Generous Living Americans, cited Alice Tully as "a leading patroness of the performing arts and countless other causes."

Alice Bigelow Tully was born on 11 September 1902 in Corning, NY, to William J. Tully, a state senator and lawyer. Corning founder Amory Houghton was her maternal grandfather. Katharine Hepburn is a second cousin. She made her professional debut at a Paris concert in 1927, earning high marks for her readings of dramatic songs in performances across the Continent and America. Her career change to philanthropy began in World War II when she became a Red Cross nurse's aide, thinking she would be of "more use." Since then, her philanthropic works have been vast. She provided most of the funds for Alice Tully Hall, called by some the "perfect concert hall," and for its organ. The hall was formerly opened on her birthday in 1969. Her other charities include the Alliance Francaise, Maison Francaise, New York University Medical Center and various wildlife groups. But "that's only the tip of the iceberg. . . ." The regal, publicity-shy heiress has never married. She lives in an apartment near Lincoln Center and attends almost every concert at Alice Tully Hall.

Tommy Tune

The first song he sang on Broadway was "It's Not Where You Start," and his career has proven the song correct. It is where you end up, and he certainly has ended up on top. A Manhattan resident, in the summertime he is Fire Island's early morning sight, often mistaken for a multi-gaited unicorn as he runs along the shore. His soft spiritual approach to show biz and life is contrasted by his down-home-in-Texas ambitions, but the spurs on his boots are stars. "I like to get an image in my head of something—just about anything— the slow gait of a five-gaited horse, a giraffe running over a plain, a rubber band being stretched—and I let the image work through my body," says this lanky, six-foot-six-inch phenom who has been described as "an exquisitely animated beanpole as well as a gracefully sinuous vine." The creative savior of many a show asinking, he says about his own special vision, "I think that I on purpose present a distortion of reality in order to show a new way of viewing it. We don't have to buy a ticket to see reality."

Thomas James Tune, who is one third Shawnee Indian and the rest English, was born on 28 February 1939 in Wichita Falls, Texas. Dad Jim serviced oil rigs and as a sideline trained Tennessee Walking Horses. The Tunes were amateur ballroom dancers, and, in hopes of finding an outlet for their son's tremendous energies, they enrolled him in a dance class when he was five. He loved it. But when he began to grow so fast and so painful were his growing pains, doctors feared he had poliomyelitis, and he abandoned the idea of ever becoming a *premier danseur* in an international ballet company. Having at about that time seen a road company production of Rodgers and Hammerstein's *King and I*, he said, "from that moment on . . . it had to be musical comedy." Held back at the gates of the University of Texas drama department, as soon as he graduated he charged into New York and landed his first gypsy dancing spot in a 1965 production of *Baker Street*. He would wear all black so he wouldn't stick out at auditions because he was so much taller than all the other dancers, and he took to wearing red shoes so that the casting people would be sure to look down rather than look up to all that height. His big break came with the musical *Seesaw*, for which he won a Tony. By helping Michael Bennett out with a show in Chicago, Tune discovered his skills as a director. In New York he directed Eve Merriam's *Club*, then choreographed and directed *The Best Little Whorehouse in Texas*, *A Day in Hollywood—A Night in the Ukraine*, followed by the multi-generational and multi-sexual (non-musical) *Cloud 9*, written by Caryl Churchill. All hits. After getting the musical *Nine* off the ground and into the black, he returned to the stage as a performer after a ten-year absence in *My One and Only*, a reworking of George and Ira Gershwin's 1927 musical *Funny Face*. Starring with Twiggy, the former model—they met when they made Ken Russell's *Boyfriend* together—he won two Tony Awards for his performance and his choreography. His latest directorial effort is the upcoming show *Grand Hotel*, scheduled to open on Broadway in October 1990.

Kathleen Turner

The actress *Time* magazine called the "kind of treasure everyone in Hollywood should be filching the map to discover" seems a throwback to the great stars of the past—a real Hollywood leading lady—by virtue of the beauty, presence and versatility she has displayed in her films since her debut in 1981, steaming and sizzling her way through the defenses of William Hurt in *Body Heat*. Compared to Lauren Bacall in her sultry good looks, resonantly husky voice and willful spirit, and to Katharine Hepburn in her stern individualism and outspokenness, Kathleen Turner nevertheless insists that "all this is still a learning process for me. I don't know yet what I'm best at. What I want, ideally, is acting that's a jump. You can prepare as best you can, then jump—emotionally, physically or in whatever way is required." The leaps she's made thus far include murder in *Body Heat;* a satirical characterization of a nefarious screen seductress in *The Man with Two Brains* (with Steve Martin, 1983); a lonely Appalachian woman in *A Breed Apart* (1984); a repressed and frumpy writer who was scratched and bruised running through the jungle, dropped into ice-cold water, sprayed with mud and thrown down a hill in the 1984 blockbuster *Romancing the Stone* (co-star and producer Michael Douglas says, "Assuming she lives, Kathleen will come out of this a big star, and deservedly so"); a fashion designer by day and hooker by night involved in bondage and mock-rape in Ken Russell's controversial *Crimes of Passion* (1984); and in 1985 a "hit man" in John Houston's *Prizzi's Honor* (co-starring Jack Nicholson). In 1985 she filmed the sequel to *Romancing the Stone—The Jewel of the Nile*. She starred in Coppola's *Peggy Sue Got Married* in 1986, followed by *Switching Channels* (1987), *Julia and Julia* (1987), *The Accidental Tourist* (1988) and *The War of the Roses* (1989). She was also the seductive voice of "Jessica" in the animated blockbuster *Who Framed Roger Rabbit* (1988). Offscreen, Turner is one of the few stars who are openly critical of the gladhanding and pretense that often passes for friendship and talent in the film industry.

The Missouri-born actress (19 July 1954 in Springfield) graduated from the University of Maryland's dramatic arts program in 1977 and moved to New York, where she substituted on off-off-Broadway parts before landing a continuing role on the NBC soaper "The Doctors." She kept her theatre credentials in order by appearing in regional theatre in roles ranging from Titania in *A Midsummer Night's Dream* at the Arena Stage in Washington, D.C., to Nina in *The Seagull* at the Manitoba Theatre Center in Winnipeg, Canada. On Broadway she appeared in *Gemini*. Although she auditioned for numerous film roles (she lost the female lead in *Oliver's Story* to Candice Bergen), she wasn't tapped for Hollywood until screenwriter and novice director Lawrence Kasdan cast her as Matty Walker in *Body Heat* against the advice of various casting directors and studio executives. When asked during a 1984 interview in *Moviegoer* magazine if she saw a danger in playing roles so varied that people "can't get a handle on Kathleen Turner," the actress replied, "Yes. But there is another sort of problem, in which you become so good as a type that people *have* to have you for a certain kind of role." In August of 1984, she relinquished her single status by marrying realtor Jay Weiss (one daughter, Rachel Ann).

Lana Turner

Hollywood's pre-eminent Sweater Girl of the 1940's joined the ranks of celebrity authors in 1982, declaring, "I refuse to leave this earth with that pile of movie-magazine trash, scandal and slander, as my epitaph." Setting the record straight in *Lana*, she told the story of her life from her birth (as Julia Jean Mildred Frances Turner) on 8 February 1920 in the mining town of Wallace, Idaho, to her "discovery" in a Los Angeles soda fountain (*not* Schwab's) and on through her years as one of MGM's most alluring box office attractions. From her first small part in 1937's *They Won't Forget* ("I was just a 15-year-old kid with a bosom and a backside strolling across the screen"), she quickly rose to superstar status, steaming up the screen especially (with John Garfield) in *The Postman Always Rings Twice* in 1946. Her more than fifty other films include *The Bad and the Beautiful* (1952), *Peyton Place* (1957) and a remake of *Imitation of Life* (1959).

Turner made headlines with her seven marriages (to, among others, bandleader Artie Shaw, millionaire Bob Topping, movie-Tarzan Lex Barker, restaurateur Stephen Crane) and one of "the most nightmarish of all Hollywood scandals" when her daughter Cheryl Crane, then 14, murdered her lover, smalltime hood Johnny Stompanato. Later, she suffered bouts with both alcohol and depression, but, in 1980, with the help of a holistic physician, she became "very close to God" and in the 1982-83 TV season proved herself once again an audience draw in the cast of the nighttime soap "Falcon Crest." Waxing philosophical about the lights and shadows in her life, she observes in *Lana:* "I love sunshine; who doesn't feel terrific when the sun is shining and warming you? But I also love rain. Real, pouring rain, not the drizzling kind. If it's going to rain, then rain. Don't just futz around."

Ted Turner

Although he's often called "The Mouth from the South," it's his many cable TV enterprises which now spew news, sports, and movies 24 hours a day from his Atlanta headquarters. And while Ted Turner has also been dubbed "Captain Outrageous," this winner of the 1977 America's Cup yacht race and four-time Yachtsman of the Year in his *Courageous* put on the manager's uniform of his Atlanta Braves mostly as a publicity stunt. He took it off before a second game after being told to do so by baseball hierarchy. "Why can't you be like everybody else?" Bowie Kuhn asked him. The Big Three networks may also have liked to ask that; his all-out war against their "trash-pumping, show biz" newscasts a moderate success, he has continued to install "stark terror" in them with threats of forming a fourth commercial network on VHF stations. "Whenever there is an opportunity, you take advantage of it," Turner says. "Everybody who is successful does that."

Robert Edward Turner III, born on 19 November 1938 in Cincinnati, was introduced to success at an early age by his strict, driven, billboard business-owning father. He was shipped off to military academies until college age, when he failed to convince his father he should go to the Naval Academy. Instead he went to Brown, where he drew paternal ire for majoring in Greek classics. Wrote dad: "I am a practical man, and for the life of me I cannot understand why . . . [you're majoring in classics] I think you are rapidly becoming a jackass." With such de-motivation, Ted left school after two suspensions for girls-related infractions. Going into business with his millionaire dad (after bumming around Florida), young Turner had to assume the helm when his father shot himself in 1963. He stopped a previously arranged sale of the Atlanta-based company with fast talk and nerve, and made it bigger than ever. With his profits he competed in big-league sailing (a longtime interest of his), then bought a struggling UHF station in 1970 which became Superstation WTBS.

Now the nationally cabled originator of the superstation concept reaches more than 21 million homes and is the progenitor of Cable News Network, CNN2, CNNRadio, the Cable Music Channel, as well as satellite-transmitted programming that's sent to Japan and other nations. The hard-cussing, hard-drinking owner of the Atlanta Braves, part-owner of the Atlanta Hawks NBA team, and rifleman (who hunted ducks in Cuba with Castro in 1982) is the husband of Jane Turner and father of five (two are his from a previous marriage). With a 5,000-acre planatation in Jacksonboro, S.C., and an Atlanta home, he still acts out a role as eternal underdog and regular guy. Ever quotable, he's big on family values, the shortcomings of the networks, the need to stop violence in society, and, of course, Ted Turner. "I am the right man in the right place at the right time, not me alone, but all the people who think the world can be brought together by telecommunications."

Tina Turner

"In ballads or rockers, she's still an indomitable singer and an indefatigable dancer . . . there's no doubt that after nearly thirty years on the road, Ms. Turner could rock for the next three decades," states John Pareles of the *New York Times*. The powerhouse singer, before breaking into her legendary song "Proud Mary" (1970), explains: "We never, ever, do nothin' nice and easy . . . So we're gonna do it nice—and *rough*." That not only sums up the musical style of the Ike and Tina Turner Revue, it also describes the demise of their nearly 16 year union. Although Tina had been the most visible asset in the duo's successful act (by 1969 it included 15 albums and 60 singles to its credit), it was Ike who directed every facet of the act. Tina's share of the earnings, it has been said, was less like a share or even a salary, but more like an allowance. "I was living a life of death; I didn't exist," she said of that period. She finally left Ike when, in Dallas, Texas, in the summer of 1976, he physically beat her shortly after arriving for a concert date. With almost no money and just one credit card, Tina flew to L.A. to begin her new life, sans Ike. "I felt proud, I felt strong. I felt like Martin Luther King." And she had hard times with the hundreds of thousands of dollars of debt that resulted from the Turner broken concert dates. Tina did everything to pay her way, including singing at McDonalds's sales conventions. "It looked like bad times from the orthodox way of thinking, but the times without a record have been great for me." In 1984 her solo album *Private Dancer* soared to the top of the charts, and Tina Turner was rediscovered. Sexy, hot, liberated and on her own, she became part of a *McCall's* magazine ad campaign tongue-in-cheekily showing her as one of its "drab homebodies" readers, and her videos on MTV (such as "What's Love Got To Do With It") heralded the resurrection of this sultry "jungle Aphrodite." She has won multiple Grammy Awards, as well as the MTV Video Award. Her latest albums include *Break Every Rule, Tina Live in Europe*, and *Foriegn Affair*. Her biography, *I, Tina: My Life Story*, was released in 1986.

Born Annie Mae Bullock in Nutbush, Tennessee, on 25 November 1941 (some sources say 1938), she grew up in Knoxville singing in the church choir and in the cotton fields, where she and her friends "sang harmony as we worked." At 17, she joined up in St. Louis with bandleader Ike, a minister's son. One day, when he was slated to record, the scheduled girl singer failed to show up, so Tina filled in, and the resulting disc, "A Fool for Love," was a breakthrough hit in 1962, selling over a million copies and establishing the duo's popularity with all sorts of listeners, not just soul. Before long they had "ascended from the black steps of one night stands down South to the vestibules of recognition in St. Louis and finally to frontroom success in New York"—and the world. Some of their hits were "It's Gonna Work Out Fine," "River Deep, Mountain High", and "Honky Tonk Woman." Several times they were the opening act for the Rolling Stones, and Tina was the far-out and electrifying "Acid Queen" in *Tommy*, the 1975 motion-picture rock opera.

God gave Tina Turner two of the best legs in history, and she uses them to sexual-revolutionary perfection. In the words of one observer Tina pounces onstage "in midscream with both legs pumping, hips grinding, long mane whirling with her mouth wrapped around some of the sexiest sounds ever set to music." Awarded a *Ms.* magazine citation in 1984, she played "Entity," the proprietress of a post-apocalyptic Dodge City, in one of George Miller's *Mad Max* movies with Mel Gibson before she embarked on a world-wide tour in 1985. In 1989 she was signed to star in the Chrysler television commercials. She has raised four sons and now lives alone in Sherman Oaks, Calif.

Twiggy

"People are still surprised to find that I don't look like I did at 16," she blurted during the run of her 1983 hit musical, *My One and Only*. "I used to have 31-inch hips. Now I have *massive* 35-inch ones." The model-turned-performer, famous in the '60s for her gawky charm, who (as Sidney Skolsky once put it) "turned the world flat [chested] during the reign of such busty queens as Taylor, Loren, Lollobrigida and Welsh," now weighs 20 pounds more, has "dancer's legs" instead of the former "hairpin" ones. But Twiggy bowled over the Broadway critics with her singing and dancing in her show; "instantly winning," cooed Frank Rich in the *New York Times*, while Clive Barnes of the *New York Post* dubbed her "a genuine star."

Christened Lesley Hornby when she was born on 19 September 1949 in Neasden, a working-class district in London (the daughter of a scenery builder), Twiggy was just another skinny English schoolgirl when, in her early teens, she found a Saturday job shampooing at the House of Leonard hairdressers. Her fantasy was to be a model, and thanks to an out-of-work shampooer, Nigel Davies, who changed his name to the aristocratic-sounding Justin de Villeneuve, her wish came true. Lesley became Twiggy, she got a boyish haircut, her mousy hair was dyed bright Harlow blonde, and she sported triple rows of eyelashes. Spotted by the *London Daily Express* fashion editor and saluted as the paper's "Girl of the Year," the Cockney miss with the "see-through" body became the symbolic model of the '60s. Photographer Richard Avedon enthused: "This little girl is not a Cockney phenomenon. For us at *Vogue*, she represents beauty, her inner security." Her security apparently made her decide to abandon her $240-an-hour modeling career for a fling at films. Ken Russell, the director of her first starring film, *The Boyfriend* (1971), is the one she credits for her acting success. Other films include *The Blues Brothers*, with the late John Belushi and Dan Aykroyd; a forgettable film, *W* (in which she starred with her late husband, American actor-writer Michael Whitney); and she played Jenny in *Madame Sousatzka*. In 1988 she starred in the CBS telefilm "The Diamond Trap." On London's West End, she won critical acclaim on the stage for

Cinderella and Captain Beaky, and she was praised as Eliza Doolittle in an English television production of Pygmalion. Other films include The Doctor and the Devils and Club Paradise.

In 1988, Twiggy married Leigh Lawson. Her career fantasy is to do a "wonderful" film. And soon. "I'm not worried about aging, but obviously in 10 years I won't look like this."

Conway Twitty

"Perhaps there has never been a harder working artist in Country music than Conway Twitty," Country Music magazine once said of this Tennessee-based singer-strummer. But Conway Twitty works just as hard outside the entertainment arena. Besides being a Country-music star, he is a successful businessman whose ventures include a restaurant, a travel agency, music publishing companies and a booking agency. Twitty also is a major stockholder in two minor-league baseball teams, one of which is the Nashville Sounds, the most successful minor-league team in America. In June 1982, the performer unveiled his Twitty City, a nine-acre complex in Nashville where Twitty presently resides, not far from Conway's Showcase, an entertainment center that tells his life story through sound, lights and visual displays. Twitty also has a reputation as a humanitarian, often singing at the bedside of sick children or helping friends get started on their careers. "If you do right," says Twitty, "it'll come back to you." And, indeed, it has all come back to him in the form of an incredible 38 number one hits, more than anyone else in popular music.

Born in Friars Point, Miss., on 1 September 1933, Twitty's father, a riverboat pilot, taught him his first chords on a small guitar when he was four years old. When Twitty was 10, the family moved to Helena, Ark., and he started his first band, the Phillips Country Ramblers. Two years later, he had his own radio show every Saturday morning on a local station. Twitty had an offer to play baseball with the Philadelphia Phillies in 1954, but Uncle Sam drafted him in the army before he could attend spring training. After his discharge from the army, Twitty heard a jukebox record of Elvis Presley's "Mystery Train." "Although I loved Country music, I didn't think I was good enough to compete with my idols—people like Hank Williams, Ray Price and Roy Acuff. But I did think I could play Elvis' style of music." He had a brief period of success with rock and roll, starting in 1958 with an eight million seller, "It's Only Make Believe." He recalls he didn't make much money from his rock hits, adding that, "I was just a kid and when they stuck something in front of me and said 'Sign this,' I signed it." Twitty was singing in clubs in the Southwest and Midwest when a promoter called him about singing Country music. "One night I was singing rock, and the next night Country." The first Country song was "Together Forever and Always," and he followed it with "Guess My Eyes are Bigger Than My Heart." His albums include Chasin' Rainbows (1985), Fallin' for You for Years (1986), Conway Twitty—Songwriter (1986), Borderline (1987) and Still in Your Dreams (1988). Twitty's real name is Harold Jenkins, but while on the road, he decided to change his name and go by the names of the next two towns he drove through (Conway, Arkansas, and Twitty, Texas). Divorced from his first wife, Mickey (four children), he married Dee Henry in February 1987.

Cicely Tyson

"I had to make a choice and I decided I could not afford the luxury of just being an actress. I had very definite statements to make. It was my way of picketing." A statement resounded from the roles she selected, all of which paid powerful homage to the dignity of black women, including her double-Emmy portrayal of a 110-year-old former slave in the 1974 TV movie "The Diary of Miss Jane Pittman."

She was born on 19 December circa 1933 in East Harlem, the daughter of immigrants from Nevis, a small Caribbean island. Head-strong by nature, she bucked her strict upbringing—and her mother's insistence that the theatre was a "den of iniquity"—and ditched her secretarial job to pursue acting. Ejected from her home by her mother (with whom she later reconciled and enjoyed a close relationship), she debuted off-Broadway as a prostitute in Genet's The Blacks in 1961-63. Her career really took off when she played a sharecropper's wife in the 1972 film Sounder. Her other credits include Kunte Kinta's mother in the TV blockbuster "Roots," Coretta Scott King in the mini-series "King," and Harriet Tubman in the 1978 NBC movie "A Woman Called Moses." Other telefilms include "Samaritan" (CBS, 1986) and "Women of Brewster Place" (ABC, 1989). Her Broadway performances include The Corn is Green. A leading advocate in the struggle for racial equality in the arts, she is a cofounder and vice-president of the Dance Theatre of Harlem. A stunning, statuesque woman with a bold sense of style, she is largely credited with popularizing the "natural hairstyle" for American black women, and introducing into high fashion the corn row hairdo made famous by Bo Derek in 10. Married since 1981 to jazz great Miles Davis, their relationship has been rocky (filed for divorce in 1988). She is known to be reticent, even mysterious, about her personal life, yet she describes herself as an active romantic. "The only way I can give of myself emotionally is for me to have emotions, and certainly one must express one's emotions. That's what acting is all about. How can you interpret a life if you have not lived."

Mike Tyson

He has risen from the rough ghettos of Bedford Stuyvesant, Brooklyn where he has gone from being a painfully shy boy, to a convicted felon, to the youngest heavyweight boxing champion ever.

Mike Tyson was born on 30 June 1966 in Bedford-Stuyvesant, Brooklyn. When he was ten, he, his two brothers, and his mother (he never knew his father) moved to the slums of Brownsville, Brooklyn. His mother was very gentle, and didn't like violence. "My mother didn't believe in violence. She detested it," states Tyson, which might have caused his initial shyness. "I was very shy, almost effeminate." he replies. In his earlier days, the neighborhood boys used to beat him up, and steal his personal belongings. Tyson finally fought back one day when an older boy tried to steal one of the pigeons he was raising, and that turned out to be the start of his days as a fighter. Almost overnight he turned from a shy victim to an aggressive victimizer. He began pickpocketing, mugging, purse snatching, and robbing stores. In 1979, the deeply troubled Tyson was sent to the Tyron School for Boys, which is a reformatory in New York. His third grade reading level and violent temper led some of the staff members to believe that he was retarded. Eventually he assaulted another inmate, and was sent to the Elmwood Cottage, a reformatory reserved for the most out of control prisoners. As it turned out, Bobby Steward, a light heavyweight champion was a staff member. When Tyson asked Steward to teach him to box, Steward brought Tyson to the attention of Cus D'Amato, and this was the beginning of a boxing legend. D'Amato took custody of Tyson when he was 13, and moved him from the reform school to his Catskill home to pursue training. In 1981 D'Amato became Tyson's legal guardian when his mother was dying of cancer. In 1982 Mrs. Tyson died, and four years later D'Amato himself died. Jim Jacobs and Bill Cayton became D'Amato's successors. Tyson developed an aggressive knock-out style. In

U2

1983 he was an alternate for the United States Olympics, and in 1985 Tyson turned professional after only 26 amateur fights. On 6 March 1985, in his first professional fight, Tyson knocked out Hector Mercedes in his first round. That same year, Tyson fought fifteen other opponents knocking 11 of them out in the first round. It wasn't until the 1986 fight against Mitch Green that an opponent went the distance with him. Green lasted ten rounds. Later that same year, Tyson entered the heavyweight championship "unification" tournament organized by HBO and Don King. Matches to follow included Alonso Ratliff, and Trevor Berbick, for which he was triumphant in both. Commenting on the Berbick fight, Tyson states that he had come "to destroy" Berbick, and that "every punch had a murderous intention." In 1987, he won over James Smith in a 12 round fight. Soon following, he fought Pinklon Thomas, flooring him for the first time in his career. In another fight sponsored by Don King and HBO, Tyson defeated Tony Tucker in in a 12 round bout. In 1987, Tyson defended his undisputed triple crown against Tyrell Biggs in Atlantic City, in a bout which lasted six rounds before Tyson knocked him through the ropes. Among those not impressed with Tyson's style was Larry Holmes trainer Richie Giachetti, "He doesn't take anybody out with finesse. A good fighter wears his guy down and takes him down in style. This guy plays bully. He bullies him into submission with dirty tricks." In 1988 Tyson faced Larry Holmes (He had never been KO'd in his career), flooring him three times in round four. Later that same year, Tyson fought against the undefeated Michael Spinks, beating him in 91 seconds. In March of 1988, one of his co-managers, Jim Jacobs, died, leaving Bill Cayton to take over as his sole manager.

Mike Tyron married actress Robin Givens on 7 February 1988. Soon after the marriage, there were stories of domestic violence, and physical abuse. After one argument with Robin, Tyson reportedly threatened to kill her and then take his own life, and he proceeded to drive her car into a tree which knocked her unconscious. Tyson was described by Givens on national TV as a physically abusive sufferer of "manic depression." Shortly after this incident they were divorced.

Leslie Uggams

She progressed from her first flash of fame as a cheery subdeb regular on the "Sing Along with Mitch" TV series in the 1960s to become, in the 1970s and 80s, an accomplished dramatic actress and sleek cabaret star known for her "large, smooth and pliable" singing voice. In 1977, she was a standout in the cast of ABC's blockbuster TV miniseries of *Roots*, Alex Haley's saga of American blacks.

Of her own black childhood, she has said, "I never really had it that rough. Not that it was so ritzy where we used to live. I see that now, but it was all right. I don't think unhappiness is a necessity. I don't think it adds soul."

Born in Washington Heights section of New York City, 25 May 1943, she learned about the performing life from both her dad, a onetime member of the famed Hall Johnson Choir, and her mother, a veteran of the Cotton Club chorus line. Leslie made her own debut—as an actress—at the age of six, appearing as Ethel Waters's niece on the "Beulah" TV series. She began singing at 7 on local TV and her vocalizing came to full flower as a 15-year-old contestant on TV's "Name That Tune," where Columbia Records' Mitch Miller spotted her and signed her to a recording contract and for his TV show. She won a Tony her first time out on Broadway in 1967 in *Hallelujah, Baby;* went on to host her own TV series and appear in guest spots on countless specials. She and her Australian husband, Graham Pratt, have two adopted children, a daughter and a son. She spent much of 1984 and 1985 on tour in *Jerry's Girls*, a revue featuring the words and music of Jerry Herman, which opened on Broadway in the fall of 1985. In March 1989, she replaced Patti LuPone on the hit show *Anything Goes* and in the Fall 1989 she starred in concert on Broadway.

U2

Referred to as "the band of the eighties" by *Rolling Stone* magazine and "Rock's Hottest Ticket" by *Time* magazine, U2 is one of the hottest bands in existence today. They have performed in sold-out concerts from New Zealand to Ireland to Arizona.

U2 was formed in 1978 in Dublin, with The Edge on guitars, piano, and vocals; Bono on vocals and guitar; Larry Muller, Jr., on drums; and Adam Clayton on bass. In December 1979 the group held their first London concerts in places like Hope and Anchor with an audience of nine, but by 1980 they were signed to the Island record label. A few months later, their first album, *Boy*, was released, and they embarked on their first American tour. Other albums include *October* (1981), *War* (1982), *The Joshua Tree* (1987) and *Rattle and Hum* (1988), from which the rockumentary *U2 Rattle and Hum* evolved. In addition to recording albums and making worldwide tours, the group has also performed in several benefit concerts, such as Live Aid at Wembly Stadium (1985); Self Air, an all-day concert in Dublin for Ireland's unemployed (1986); and six shows for Amnesty International (1986). U2 has received several awards for their outstanding achievements, including being voted Band of the Year by the *Rolling Stone* critics poll in 1983, the Best Band and Best Live Aid Performance in *Rolling Stone's* readers poll, a Grammy for Album of the Year for *The Joshua Tree* in 1988, and a Grammy for Best Performance by a Group/Vocals for *The Joshua Tree* in 1988.

Tracey Ullman

Tracey Ullman has taken America by storm this decade. Her introduction to the states triggered the same impact as many of the notorious "Saturday Night Live" talents. With an uncanny ability to take an ordinary situation and expose a humorous side, she is a versatile performer who is also an accomplished dramatic actress and a trained dancer and singer.

Her father emigrated from Poland to Slough, England (near London), where he and his wife, an England native, brought Tracey into the world on 30 December 1959. When she was six years old, tragedy struck the Ullman family: her father passed away, leaving Tracey's mother with the duty of single parenthood. Even at that tender age, Tracey displayed a knack for performing, which was supported and encouraged by her mother. By the time she was twelve years old, Tracey had matured so well in her craft that she received a scholarship to stage school. Her first professional appearance was as a dancer in the Berlin production of *Gigi*, at sixteen years old. She then returned to her native England, where she further pursued a career in dance with the well-known Second Generation dance troupe. It was at this point in time when Tracey began appearing on television variety programs. Acting as a stepping stone, it was these programs which ultimately led Tracey to perform in West End theater musicals. Among her West End credits: the role of a backup singer in *Elvis;* Frenchy in *Grease;* and the cult favorite *The Rocky Horror Picture Show*, in which she portrayed Dr. Frank N. Furter's rival for the perfect man's attentions, Janet. Tracey proved herself more than able in straight theater when she landed the leading role in *Talent* at the Everyman's Playhouse. The role which displayed Tracey's talents at their optimal level was her characterization of Beverly, a bizarre club singer, in the improvised play *Four in a Million*. So entralled were they by her performance, the London Theater Critics awarded her the honored title of Most Promising New Actress of 1981. England's ingenue was now back on television variety programs with top billing in the BBC comedy series "Three of a Kind" and "A Kick up the Eighties." In 1983, she was awarded Best Light Entertainment Performance for her television portrayals by the British Academy (the equivalent of the U.S. Emmy Award for best comedienne in a sitcom). The theatre rejoiced in her return in *She Stoops to Conquer* and then in the workshop production of the musical *Starlight Express*. Tracey has tried her hand at feature films, too, with her debut in Paul McCartney's *Give My Regards to Broad Street*. A second feature film placed her opposite Meryl Streep in *Plenty*. Departing from her usual endeavors, Miss Ullman has also dabbled as a recording artist—the result: four top ten singles on the British pop charts, and an album, *You Broke My Heart in Seventeen Places* (certified gold). In April 1987, Tracey came to America with the inception of "Tracey Ullman Show," for which she won a Golden Globe Award for Best Comedic Actress.

The "Jack-of-all-trades" lives with her British television producer/husband, Allan McKeown, and their young daughter, Mable Ellen (born 2 April 1986), in homes in London and Los Angeles.

Liv Ullmann

Shortly after the filming of Ingmar Bergman's *Personna* (in which she played the role of a highly disturbed actress; 1966), the rumors began. The acclaimed Scandinavian actress Liv (pronounced Leave) and Bergman released the news that they shared an "extraordinarily fine relationship." Soon she and her psychiatrist husband Gappe Stang divorced, and with daughter Linn (by Bergman), moved into his posh Sheep Island retreat, the setting of his anti-war film *Shame* (1968). "As in photography, Liv is a complete commentary unto herself," said the then-spellbound Bergman. From their creative love-nest came *Hour of the Wolf* (1968), *The Passion of Anna* (1969), and *Cries and Whispers* (1972). Her non-Bergman films include *The Night Visitor* (1970), *Pope Joan* (1972), *Lost Horizon* (her first Hollywood venture, a faltering musical version of the Shangri-La story with Peter Finch), the lively and charming *Forty Carats*, *Zandy's Bride* with Gene Hackman, Ibsens' *The Wild Duck* co-starring Jeremy Irons, and *Bay Boy*. For NBC-TV she appeared in her first American television movie, "Prisoner Without a Name . . . Cell Without a Number" based on the Jacobo Timerman book. Playing opposite Roy Scheider, she was the personal choice of Timerman to play his wife.

Born in Tokyo, 16 December 1939, of Norwegian parents, Liv Ullmann accompanied her family to Canada during the war years and returned with her mother (her engineer father had died in the interim) to Norway. She remembers wanting all her life to become an actress and with her heart set on an acting career, dropped out of high-school and set off for Oslo to enter the National Theatre School there. Refused admission, she stubbornly turned to London, acquired intensive dramatic training, and sailed home to become a member of the prestigious National Theatre of Norway, debuting with the title role in *The Diary of Anne Frank*. While there she played, possibly in anticipation of her somber screen characterizations, "only serious roles—Shakespeare, Ibsen, Brecht." Following several Norwegian film appearances, Liv participated in her first Swedish film, *Pan*, with close pal Bibi Anderson, who soon introduced her to Bergman. Liv was the first non-Swedish actress to work in one of his films; since the break-up, they've remained close friends and have continued to make movies together: *Scenes from a Marriage*, *The Serpent's Egg* and the moving *Autumn Sonata*, the story of a troubled mother-daughter bond in which Liv and her co-star, Ingrid Bergman, gave stunning performances. In reference to her hunch that she ought to perform in comedies instead of the heavy dramas that have made her an international star, she says: "Bergman has promised me a role in which I'll be neither neurotic nor suicidal. I can hardly wait." She's also won kudos for her work in *The Emigrants*, a film project about the immigration of Swedish farmers to America which featured Max von Sydow. She first captured Broadway theatre audiences in a 1975 New York Shakespeare Festival production of *A Doll's House*. Again on Broadway in O'Neill's *Anna Christie* (1977) and for the 1979 musical update of *I Remember Mama*, she has subsequently appeared as another Ibsen leading lady in *Ghosts* and starred in a highly acclaimed PBS television special of Cocteau's *The Human Voice*. Winner of several best actress awards from both the New York Film Critics and National Society of Film Critics, she has received two Acadamy Award nominations and was the first female recipient of Norway's Peer Gynt Award. Liv also wrote and directed a short film, *Parting*, in 1981.

A vibrant woman of substance, an actress who possesses phenomenal range and depth, it is no surprise that her substantial and heart-warming reflections would culminate in the best-selling autobiography *Changing* (1978). *Without Makeup* came out in 1979, and a third, *Choices*, followed in 1985. Her work with the International Rescue Committee has been extensive and in 1980 she was appointed a UNICEF Ambassador of Goodwill, making a series of fact-finding visits to Latin America, Lebanon, Africa, and the Middle East. In Rome in September 1985 Ullmann married Boston real estate man Richard Saunders. During that year she toured in Pinter's *Old Times* and filmed *Let's Hope It's a Girl*. Other films include *Gaby* (1987), *Time of Indifference* (1987), and *Girlfriend* (1988). In December 1986, Ullmann was presented the first Great Artist Award by New York University.

John Updike

"I've had a generous share of the good things, money, prizes. . . . I lack for nothing. What I would like to do in the time I have left is deliver my best self," admitted the prolific and masterful prose stylist (in a 1982 *Time* cover story). His exquisitely wrought novels, short stories, poetry collections, and innumerable essays and book reviews make him a worthy candidate for designation as America's foremost man of letters, and one of its most percipient observers of the manners and mores of its middle-class landscape. If *Rabbit, Run*, the 1960 novel that made John Updike famous, explores the vapid world of suburbia and the protracted adolescence of some of its male occupants, and if the steamy *Couples* (1968) probes the complications and implictions of life in America's "post-Pill paradise," then might not *The Witches of Eastwick* (1984)—"witty, ironic, engrossing and punctuated by transports of spectacular prose" though it may be—also represent the author's hunch that a counterfeminist movement is in the works? Is Updike, as Leslie Fiedler once alleged, merely the author of "essentially 19th century novels . . . irrelevant?" Or does he, as Donald J. Greiner cautions in *The Other John Updike* (1981), use his obvious humor to mask "serious intent."

Sole offspring ("I'm sure that my capacity to fantasize . . . relates to being an only child") of a high school math teacher and a mother with literary ambitions, Updike (born on 8 March 1932 in Shillington, Pa.) began submitting stories to the *New Yorker* while still in high school. But it wasn't until he was out of Harvard (as a scholarship student) and studying on a fellowship at Oxford that Mrs. E.B. White, a *New Yorker* editor, offered him a job at the magazine that "since boyhood . . . I always wanted to work for." Another youthful wish was that he might someday live in New York, but in spite of his early success at the *New Yorker*, earning praise for his light verse, his "Talk of the Town" vignettes, and his short stories, he soon decided that "New York was not going to let me unpack my shadowy message," and he departed for the more congenial surroundings of Ipswich, Massachusetts—with Mary Pennington, whom he married while they were both undergraduates (four children). His first novel, *The Poorhouse Fair* (1959), won the 1960 Rosenthal Foundation Award of the National Institute of Arts and Letters, and established its author as an exceptionally promising novelist. *Rabbit, Run* (1960) introduced Henry "Rabbit" Angstrom to America (he returned in 1971 in *Rabbit Redux* and in 1981 in *Rabbit is Rich*, which won the National Book Critics Circle Award, the American Book Award, and the Pulitzer Prize). Some critics discern in Rabbit, a high school basketball star who never regains his teenage glory, Updike's *doppelganger*, "the one who didn't leave Shillington, go to Harvard, become a dazzling novelist." Updike admitted in 1981 that "Harry was invented as sort of a real alter-ego." The citation for the National Book Award *The Centaur* won in 1963 called it "a courageous and brilliant account of a conflict in gifts between an inarticulate American father and his highly articulate son." Updike described the book as "a monument, however inadequate" to his father. *Couples* was alternatively dismissed as a "sex novel" and praised as an examination of "the moral disease which is eating at the soft vitals of the American middle class." Updike's Bech novels—*Bech: A Book* (1970) and *Bech is Back* (1982)—were created "to show that I was really a Jewish writer also" to the literary establishment and therefore entitled to the kind of attention it had lavished on such prominent Jewish writers as Saul Bellow, Bernard Malamud, Philip Roth, and J.D. Salinger. Ohter novels include *A Month of Sundays* (1975), *Marry Me: A Romance* (1976) and *The Coup* (1978). *Too Far To Go: The Maples Stories*, the 1979 collection of stories chronicling the slow dissolution of a marriage, follows by two years the end of the Updikes' marriage. He remarried the same year (1977), to Martha R. Bernhard.

In an appearance on the PBS series "First Edition," Updike, with characteristic grace, put it all in perspective: "Tolstoy is always going to be the champ, and you can't out-Proustify Proust." The prolific author's latest books are: *Roger's Version* (1986), *S* (1988), *Self Consciousness* and *Just Looking: Essays On Art* (1989).

Leon and Jill Uris

In 1975, master storyteller Leon Uris took on a partner in his attempt to relate the divergent features (the beauty and the horror) of a troubled Ireland.

That associate was his wife Jill (married since 1970), and the fruit of their labor is *Ireland: A Terrible Beauty*—Leon wrote the text; Jill took the photographs (studied photography at Colorado College, Harvard, and New York University). A similar arrangement in 1981 brought *Jerusalem: Song of Songs*, a pictorial history of Jerusalem from ancient times to the present. Since then Jill has assembled her own book, *Ireland Revisited* (1982), with her photographs accompanied by quotes from famed Irish writers as well as talespinners from outside the Emerald Isle (her husband being one of them). Leon is best known for his "nonfiction" novels (*Exodus*, 1958; *Mila 18*, 1961; *Armageddon*, 1964; *QB VII*, 1970; *Trinity*, 1976; and another which received the scorn of critics—*The Haj*, 1984). Uris devotes an enormous amount of time to the research of his historically complex novels (he read some 300 books, travelled 12,000 miles inside Israel and interviewed over 1,200 people to write *Exodus*, his most famous work). Though critics are divided in their assessment of Uris's literary skills, there is no question about the impact his books have had. Questions one critic, "There remains the riddle of why these books by themselves have seemed to accomplish what years of persuasion, arguments, appeals and knowledge of events have failed to do— why people have claimed to be converted ... uplifted, thrilled, [and] enthralled by them." A recent publications is *The Mital Pass* (1988).

An ex-marine who emerged from the corps with a wife (he married his sergeant; three children), Leon Uris was born in Baltimore, 3 August 1924, stumbled onto the best-selling scene in 1952 with his tale of the South Pacific war, *Battle Cry*, and, despite lack of encouragement from the critics, established himself as a successful novelist and screenwriter *(Gunfight at the O.K. Corral)*. In 1964 he was involved in a much publicized court case in England, when Dr. Wladislav Dering, portrayed in *Exodus* as having committed atrocities at Auschwitz, turned out to be alive and sued Uris for libel. Referred to in the press as "England's War Crime Trial," it lasted for a spectacular month and was conducted in Greek, Polish, Hebrew, English, German, and French, with witnesses from all over the world. Result: Dering was awarded one halfpenny in contemptuous damages and ordered to pay the court costs of both sides. (Uris's 1970 novel, *QB VII*, was a fictionalized version of the proceedings.) Uris divorced his first wife in 1968 and married Marjorie Edwards (deceased) before teaming up with his present lifetime collaborator, Jill Peabody. The couple relaxes by skiing in the mountains around their Aspen home and climbing the mountain trails by motorcycle.

Peter Ustinov

This actor, producer, director, novelist, and playwright has won two Oscars for Best Supporting Actor (*Spartacus*, 1961, and *Topkapi*, 1964), a Grammy for his inventive rendition of *Peter and the Wolf*, and the New York Critics Award for his play *The Love of Four Colonels* (1953). Regarded as one of the wittiest raconteurs in recent memory, he speaks more than a half-dozen languages and has been described as "the greatest good party insurance." He travels widely and has a grand cosmopolitan air. "I live like an Englishman, think like a Frenchman, and write like a Russian," he once said.

Born in London, 16 April 1921, of gifted parents (his father, Iona, was a famed journalist known as "Klop," his mother, Nadia, was a painter), Peter Ustinov is part Russian, German, French, and Italian. He has relatives in many parts of the world and a number of ancestors were proficient in the arts. Educated at Mr. Cibbs Preparatory School for Boys, he was punished for writing plays instead of doing homework. He began his writing career at age 14 when he sold a satirical magazine piece about a classmate who happened to be the son of Hitler's foreign minister Joachim von Ribbentrop, nearly causing an international incident. Dropping out of school at age 16, he joined the London Theatre Studio (now part of Old Vic) and made his London stage debut at age 18, appearing in a number of his own sketches. "All old people with fascinating make-ups," he reminisces, "I always played old men in the beginning. The older I get, the younger my parts get, so I'm always in the make-up chair longer than necessary." Ustinov was a playwright by age 19 and a producer by 20,. Since making his first American film *(The Egyptian)* in 1954, he's demonstrated his considerable talents on these shores on a regular basis. Among his noteworthy screen credits are Agatha Christie's *Evil Under the Sun* and *Death on the Nile* (playing the canny detective Hercule Poirot), *Billy Budd*, *Quo Vadis*, and his *Romanoff and Juliet*. Among his other works are a light comedy, *Beethoven's Tenth* (1984), in which he starred as a lecherous Ludwig van Beethoven, *Appointment With Death* (1987), and *King Lear* (1988). He also starred in the television miniseries "Around the World in 80 Days" (1989). How does he manage so many careers? "One relaxes me from the others," he replies. For diversion, he writes articles on the theatre, travel and political subjects.

Married twice before meeting his present wife, Helene du Lau d'Allemans, he has four children. (His two ex-wives are Isolda Denham, sister of Angela Lansbury, and French-Canadian actress Suzanne Cloutier.) Peter and Helene, married in 1972, live in a Paris apartment and have a country chalet in Switzerland. Ustinov collects rare prints and original drawings and has a collection of 6,000 classical music records. He also has time to serve as an ambassador for UNICEF and each year produces 4,000 bottles of a fine white wine from his vineyards. He admits that the only conspicuous failure in his life has been an inability to play the flute because of an unusually protuberant upper lip.

Jack Valenti

This former special assistant to President Lyndon Johnson reigns as Hollywood's "man in Washington," the motion-picture industry's chief arm twister in Congressional corridors. As president of the Motion Picture Association of America (which includes the nine major film companies), his major lobbying efforts of the 1980s involved spearheading a million-dollar campaign against unrestricted videotaping. "The future of creative entertainment of the American family is what's at stake here," he told anyone who would listen. "If you don't license the VCR it will become a wild animal out there, devouring everything." A lesser battle—which he lost—was his opposition to adding a new classification to the film-rating system to protect children against "overly violent" movies. Despite Valenti's "Who can draw that line? Who is smart enough to say what is permissible for a 13-year-old and not for a 12-year-old?" The PG-13 rating went into effect in 1984.

Born in Houston, 5 September 1921, Jack Valenti picked up a B.A. from the U. of Houston (1946) and an M.B.A. from Harvard (1948) and was in business with an advertising and political-consulting agency (which he cofounded) before climbing aboard the LBJ bandwagon in 1963. He served as special assistant in the White House until he took on his movie job in 1966, and he wrote about his old boss in *A Very Human President* in 1977. In addition to his present Washington duties on behalf of American films, he serves as president of the Motion Picture Export Association, traveling the world over to negotiate film treaties on behalf of member companies. Married, with one daughter, he is also a member of the board of the JFK Center for the Performing Arts and the American Film Institute.

Valentino

A quintessential Italian with an unabashed, zesty appetite for elegance, he was born Valentino Garavani just outside of Milan 11 May 1932. At the age of 17 he abandoned his studies and left for Paris to pursue a career in fashion. Within six months he was working for Jean Desses, one of the top *couture* houses of the time. He remained there for the next six years, perfecting his talents as a designer. When Desses's assistant, Guy Laroche, left to open his own salon, Valentino accompanied him as his assistant for the next two years. In 1960 he left Paris for Rome to open his own house on the Via Gregoriana—and within a few years he became one of the world's top designers, made famous by the ladies who trotted around the globe glittering in his sleek, feminine clothes. The ladies included such society-page headliners as Princess Luciana Pignatelli, Cristina Ford, Vicomtesse Jacqueline de Ribes, Marie-Helene de Rothschild and most significantly, Jacqueline Onassis, who seemed to prefer Valentino designs for the finest hours of her jours et soirs.

According to *Women's Wear Daily*, Valentino is "the linchpin of a fashion business that [in 1983] does $600 million a year." The money has been spent lavishly—a house in Gstaad, a Moorish palace on Capri, a 95-foot yacht called the *T.M. Blue*, and a 28-room villa on the Via Appia feathered with opulence such as flamingos by the man-made pond, gold fixtures, white-gloved servants and almost as many bodyguards as the Pope. His long-term pal and business partner Giancarlo Giammetti calls him "the world's biggest dreamer," and the richness of his vision has always shown up in his designs. In the beginning they were elaborate and ornate, abounding in ruffles and flourishes; of late everything's been brought tightly together and simplified in an equation of elegance and confidence—but thoroughly *elegante, molto elgante*.

What makes Valentino sew? It's his response to an inelegant world. "I was born like that," he says, "wanting to dress nicely and to see beauty all around me. . . . Life is very difficult. We have lots of problems today. We are all a little nervous, a little hysterical. Not me. I am calm. . . . I pretend a lot. I pretend perfection, professionality, a good education and lots of experience." When he threw a party for himself at the Metropolitan Museum of Art in New York at a cost of approximately $700,000—that was confidence (and also a social success). Perhaps he is a bit disenchanted when he says that "there are no more muses for me. I am proud when these ladies wear my clothes, but today when I dream about somebody, I look to my models and try to create a mirror for my ladies. Besides, the ladies today are so fickle. They wear a Saint Laurent blouse with an Ungaro skirt and somebody else's shoes." In 1985 he was made a great Officer of the Honor of Merit of the Italian Republic, his nation's highest honor.

Joan Van Ark

Extending herself beyond acting, this star of stage and screen utilizes her spare time participating in philanthropic and humanitarian work. In addition to professional awards, Joan has received recognition for her personal contributions as well. She was voted Best Actress in a Leading Role on a Nighttime Soap in both 1986 and 1988 for her outstanding performance as Valene Ewing on "Knots Landing," and was also the UCLA Cancer Research Institute's Person of the Year.

Joan Van Ark was born in New York City, but her family moved to Boulder, Colorado, when she was only three. She began her theatrical studies at the Yale School of Drama. Her first acting break came when she moved back to New York to appear in *Barefoot in the Park*, where she joined the show's national theatre company and went on to perform in London. Since then, she has given excellent performances on Broadway in *The School for Wives*, which earned her a Tony nomination, and *The Rules of the Game*, for which she won a Theatre World Award. In Los Angeles, she appeared in *Cyrano de Bergerac* with Richard Chamberlain, *Ring Around the Moon* with Michael York, *Heartbreak House*, and *Chemin De Fer*. Adding to her award-winning performances, she won a Los Angeles Drama Critics Award for her "Distinguished Performance" in the Los Angeles Shakespeare Festival's production of *As You Like It*. Although she is best known for her work on the Broadway stage, Joan has made several television appearances as well. Her television debut was two appearances on the popular nighttime soap "Dallas." Audience response to her was so positive that she was cast in the successful spin-off series "Knots Landing," in which she plays the role of Valene Ewing, the sweet, innocent, single parent of twins and author. She has also appeared in numerous made-for-TV movies, including "Red Flag," "The Ultimate Game," "A Testimony of Two Men," "The Last Dinosaur," "Big Rose," "The Bionic Boy," "The Judge and Jake Wyler," "Shakedown on Sunset Strip," and "My First Love." Her guest appearances include "The Love Boat," "Quincy," "Vegas," and "The Rockford Files." In addition to acting, Joan has endorsed products from Estee Lauder, Kodak, Carnation, and Hallmark.

An accomplished marathon runner, Joan trains for such events as the Boston Marathon in her spare time. Joan and her husband, NBC newsman John Marshall, have one daughter, Vanessa.

Abigail Van Buren

Dear Abby is so popular that a Texas judge once grew alarmed and huffed, "She is as much an expert on human relations as I am on how to play polo—and I have never sat on a polo horse in my life!" Abby greeted the judge's remark with equanimity: "I agree," she said, "it is a sad commentary on our times when our young must seek advice and counsel from Dear Abby instead of going to Mom and Dad." Then, borrowing a well-worn phrase, she turned the problem back to him: "Judge not," she said, "that ye not be judged."

Born Pauline Esther (Popo) Friedman, 4

July 1918 in Sioux City, Iowa, she is the twin sister and rival of her fiercest competitior—Ann Landers (née Eppie Friedman), who began her column a few months before Abby. (Actually what happened was, as soon as Eppie landed the Ann Landers gig, Popo paid her twin a visit. Grasping the enormity of the opportunity ahead of Eppie, Popo proposed herself to the San Francisco *Chronicle*, where she first launched her column in 1956 without telling Eppie. This caused some long-term sisterly rivalry, which Ann Landers says wasn't as bitter as the gossip mill says it was: "There was a problem at first—she didn't tell me and I was quite surprised and disappointed—but I soon forgot about it. There are plenty of papers for both of us and she does a very good job. We're very close. She comes and stays with me. She's an extremely warm, loving, funny, darling woman. Yet today people still ask why I don't speak to my sister!" A hard-driving, well-organized career woman, Abby hardly needs the cash ("Talking about money offends me") as she is the wife (since 1939—two children) of millionaire Morton Phillips. Yet she rushes all over the country visting editors and drumming up business for her column, which now appears in more than 800 newspapers throughout the world. From 1963 until 1975 she was heard six days a week on CBS radio. She is the author of several books, including *The Best of Dear Abby* (1981), in which she offers all sorts of advice on all sorts of problems, always with wit and humor—her putdowns are pointed and punny: Dear Abby: I've been going with a girl for two years and can't get her to say yes. What should I do? Joe. Dear Joe: What's the question?

Gloria Vanderbilt

"There's something paradoxical about her—a sureness and a shyness- that's absolutely remarkable," says Bill Blass of the porcelain-faced heiress. "As public as she is, she remains an enigma." The woman who has been a poet, an actress, painter, designer, wife, mother, and business entrepreneur credits her late mother (after a long period of estrangement) as being the inspiration for her self-imagined empire, a world of darlings, where beauty is "something that exists in fantasy." Her ideal "is a woman who is straight up and down, very stylized and also very remote. A woman with a sense of mystery, something you can't quite catch."

Gloria Laura Morgan Vanderbilt was born in New York on 20 February 1924, daughter of Lady Thelma Furness's beautiful twin Gloria, and 43-year-old sportsman-diplomat Reginald Vanderbilt, a charming wastrel who managed to run through $25 million in 14 years. He died when "Little Gloria" was only 18 months old. As Barbara Goldsmith's 1970 bestseller and subsequent TV mini-series "Little Gloria . . . Happy at Last" reminded everyone, a highly publicized custody battle was waged and won by her paternal aunt Gertrude Vanderbilt Whitney, the sculptress and American art patron, against the 10-year-old's mother, whom Gertrude accused of being a sybarite with an indiscriminate libido. The 1934 trial racked up more than 7,000 pages of testimony and uncovered some unsavory sorts among the "high tea" set. Since America's notion of indoor sports is following the travails of the rich, Gloria has been followed with fascination her whole life. Given how many suds there were in the soap, as one observer says, "It's a testament to her resilience that she ended up stitching her signature on millions of trendy derrières rather than brandishing a holdup gun on the evening news," the stitching referring to her svelte jeans and sportswear line. The marketing of Gloria Vanderbilt is one of the high points in the history of hype. "Vanderbilt jeans hit all the best places," went one of many advertisements. "Your waist. Your hips. Your rear." Sometimes Gloria would speak her throaty "our-class-darling" drawl—"It's a million dollar look"; all for blue jeans, the uniform of the working class. From 1977 to 1985, the jeans had sold more than 10 million pairs a year. In 1988 she introduced a new fragrance, "Glorious."

Gloria's marriage at age 17 to actor's agent Pat De Cicco was an "act of defiance"; she divorced him three years later and eloped to Mexico to wed the then 63-year-old Leopold Stokowski, and the following year married director Sideny Lumet. Analysis had stimulated her interest in acting, and though their marriage was doomed, Lumet gave his wife support. (The swan insignia on her fashion came "from my favorite role, in my favorite play, Molnar's *The Swan*.")

She married writer Wyatt Cooper in 1963 and had two sons. Cooper, a writer, died in 1978, and her son Carter Vanderbilt committed suicide in 1988. Her friendship with black singer Bobby Short in the early 1980s is thought to be the reason she was prohibited from buying an apartment at the exclusive River House in New York; instead she found some equally spectacular digs on Gracie Square. The author of two earlier books (*You're Never Fully Dressed Without a Smile* and *Gloria Vanderbilt's Book of Collage*), in the spring of 1985 she published the first of six planned volumes of her autobiography, *Once Upon a Time/A True Story*. In 1987 *Black Knight, White Knight* was published. Despite the fact that her life had already been hashed over ad infinitum in the gossip press, Vanderbilt was able to write her memoirs because she "tried never to read any of the things written about me. I tried to keep my own person, my own vision."

Dick Van Dyke

Writer-producer Carl Reiner once said about this gifted comedic-actor: "He's made me the happiest bald-headed producer in Hollywood." Quite understandable. Van Dyke won five Emmy Awards for his 1960s sitcom, "The Dick Van Dyke Show," co-starring with Mary Tyler Moore, and gained wide acclaim in the Broadway musical *Bye Bye Birdie*, as well as the films *Mary Poppins, Divorce American Style, Chitty Chitty Bang Bang, The Comic, The Runner Stumbles*, and on TV's American Playhouse in "Breakfast with Les and Bes." His popular hit sitcom ran from 1961 until 1966, and went off the air after 157 episodes not because of low ratings but, in Van Dyke's words, "to quit while we're proud of it." Van Dyke tried again in 1971 with "The New Dick Van Dyke Show," but it didn't live up to the old. For a while he costarred with Carol Burnett on her prime-time variety show, and then left series-making for televison movies and commercials. He tried another "The Dick Van Dyke Show" with CBS in 1988; again it didn't last the season. He appeared in the telefilm "Ghost of a Chance" (1987) and the motion picture *Dick Tracy* (1990).

Born in West Plains, Mo., 13 December 1925, he grew up in a home in Danville, Ill., that, from all the evidence, must have been as cheerfully nourishing as his salesman father's product, Sunshine Biscuits. ("I guess you could say I had a Penrodian childhood; barefoot boy with cheek of tan and all.") Schooled in announcing on the local radio station, he did mike duty at an Oklahoma army base during World War II, and after his discharge, toured with a buddy and a trunkful of Spike Jones records as half of a pantomime lip-sync act called the Merry Mutes. He went through such a lean period professionally that in 1948, when he sent for his high school sweetheart, Marjorie Millett, to come get married, they had to do it on the radio show "Bride and Groom" in order to afford a ring and a honeymoon. It was a nomad's life until the Van Dykes settled in Manhattan in 1956. It was four more years before he got his break in the musical *Bye Bye Birdie*. He and wife Marjorie have four children. A lifelong fan of Stan Laurel, Van Dyke delivered the eulogy at the late comic's funeral. Stan Laurel's sad face was one Van Dyke could easily relate to. Everyone's clown and funny man, the times haven't always been filled with laughter. Dick is a participant in a program for recovering alcoholics, a problem he has been open about for quite some time.

Van Halen

They are America's premiere rock and roll band who have redefined no-holds-barred rock music. They have successfully survived band member changes, changes in fashion trends, as well as thousands of high-energy, unrestrained, high-velocity concerts. The band has a high standard for their performances which the members of the band proudly call "the Van Halen tradition."

The band was formed in 1974. It's original members included Eddie Van Halen on lead guitar, his brother Alex Van Halen on drums, David Lee Roth as lead vocalist, and Michael Anthony on bass guitar. Their first album together, *Van Halen*, was recorded in 1978. The follow-up to that LP was *Van Halen II*, which was released a year later, in 1979. Several albums followed, including *Women and Children First* (1980), *Fair Warning* (1981), *Diver Down* (1982), *1984* (1984), and *The Wild Life* (1985), which was the last album to feature David Lee Roth as lead singer. In August of 1985 Roth left the band to pursue a solo career, and was replaced by singer Sammy Hagar. Soon after his joining the band, they cut the hit album *5150* in April 1986. That LP sold five million copies worldwide, and was a chart topper in twelve countries. In 1988, the group released their second album with Hagar doing lead vocals, entitled *OU812*. Van Halen believes that this is their best album to date. According to the band, "We took our time putting this one together." "We've gotten to know each other a lot better and feel completely comfortable with the writing and recording process." "At least we think it's our best album, but it's up to our audience to decide." The release of the dynamic album was kicked off with the "Van Halen's Monsters of Rock" tour, which was the biggest musical event of the summer of 1988, attracting over two million fans. Planning to keep on rocking for years to come, the band is successfully carrying their high-energy concert performances into a second decade.

Sarah Vaughan

Ella Fitzgerald once described her as "the greatest singing talent in the world." Internationally known to jazz fans as "The Divine One," she started her career as a toothy, skinny, 16-year-old choir singer who in April of 1942 entered an amateur contest at Harlem's Apollo Theater on a dare. Singing "Body and Soul," she won the contest and found herself "discovered" by Earl "Fatha" Hines, who invited her to sing with his band. ("She just came out there, cool as a cucumber, never moved a muscle, just sang.") Soon thereafter, "Sassy" Vaughan became a favorite of the pop set via records, TV, nightclubs, and jazz concerts and still ranks today as one of music's all-time greats.

Sarah Lois Vaughan was born on 27 March 1924 in Newark, the daughter of a carpenter who sang for the fun of it. She started studying piano and organ when she was eight and by the time she turned 12 was the organist at the Mount Zion Baptist Church. Jazz critic Leonard Feather salutes her for having "brought to jazz an unprecedented combination of attractive characteristics: a rich beautifully controlled tone and vibrato; an ear for the chord structure of songs, enabling her to change the melody as an instrument might; a coy, sometimes archly naive quality alternating with a sense of great sophistication." Divorced three times: Jazz trumpeter George Treadwell, footballer Clyde Atkins (one adopted child), and restaurant owner Marshall Fisher, she wed Waymon Reed in 1978 (another trumpeter). Though she is known as a jazz and pop artist, her stature is such that in recent years, she has made guest appearances with such presitgious orchestras as the Boston Pops, National Symphony, and the Los Angeles Philharmonic. In 1989 she appeared on stage at Carnegie Hall as part of the JVC Jazz Festival.

Gwen Verdon

"A kaleidoscopic combination of Chaplin, Garbo, and a Picasso harlequin," this geranium-tressed hoofer with the "superior posterior" highkicked her way to Broadway stardom in 1953 in Cole Porter's *Can Can*. In 1955, *Damn Yankees* ("Whatever Lola Wants, Lola Gets") made her a superstar, and *New Girl in Town* (1957), *Redhead* (1959), and *Sweet Charity* (1966), with their multitude of Tony Awards, placed her, as one critic put it, "in that class of performers Who Can Do No Wrong."

Born in Culver City, Calif., on 13 January 1925, the daughter of a movie studio electrician and a dancing teacher, little Gwyneth Verdon says she grew up thinking that "all mothers and daughters danced and all fathers carried lunch boxes to the studio." Actually, dancing in her case was a matter of Determination over Disaster. A series of childhood illnesses threatened her with the possibility of being crippled for life and only a rigorous regimen of exercise (and steel braces on her legs) made it possible for her to follow in her mother's dancing footsteps. Half of a ballroom dancing act at 14, she "retired" at 16 to elope with James Hanaghan, a Hollywood reporter twice her age (one son, who has made her a grandma), and didn't resume her career again until the divorce five years later. Only after dancing for six more years with Jack Cole and serving as his backstage assistant on various Hollywood assignments (including coaching Marilyn Monroe to walk less sexily and Jane Russell to walk more so) did she finally, at the age of 28, become an "overnight success" on Broadway. Married in 1960 to late dancemaster/director Bob Fosse (who did the choreography for four of the five Verdon musical hits), she became a mother again in 1963 (Nicole, a dancer who can be seen in the 1986 film *A Chorus Line*). In 1982 Verdon substituted for Carol Burnett on ABC's "All My Children" and appeared in the made-for-TV movie "Legs" in 1983. She's appeared in the films *Nadine* (1987) and *Cocoon II: The Return* (1988). In 1989 she received the NYS Governor's Arts Award presented by Governor and Mrs. Cuomo. Once described as a "mobile without a conscience," she does not consider her dancing, or for that matter her personal appearance, sexually provocative; "Sex in a dance is in the eyes of the beholder. I never thought my dances sexy. I suppose that's because I see myself with my face washed, and to me I look like a rabbit."

Ben Vereen

From appearances on Broadway in *Sweet Charity*, *Hair*, and *Jesus Christ Superstar*, he channeled his highly charged talent into *Pippin* (1972) which won him both the *Tony* and the *Drama Desk Awards*. Thriving on the electricity of a live audience, his talent won him "Entertainer of the Year," "Rising Star," and "Song and Dance Star" in 1978 from the American Guild of Variety Artists. (He's the first simultaneous winnter of these AGVA awards.) He gives full credit for his success to his mother: "Mom was born in Louisiana and she remembers how the entertainers would come and sing in the fields during the lunch breaks on the plantation. . . . And Mom can sing the blues too—boy, can she ever sing the blues. . . . I'll tell you the kind of woman Mom is. She's the kind of woman who finds a pregnant girl in the park, takes her home until the baby is born, and then keeps the baby."

The Miami-born (10 October 1946) super-entertainer moved as a child to Brooklyn, where his father worked in a paint factory and his mother labored as a maid. His first performance was at the age of four singing solo in the Baptist church where his father was a deacon. Discovering, after graduation from the High School of Performing Arts, no open doors in either the dance or theatre, he entered Manhattan's Pentecostal Theological

Seminary, where it took him six months to find out he was not cut out to be a man of the cloth. After a few years with dance and stock companies, he landed a part in 1968 in the Los Angeles production of *Hair,* and in 1971 he joined the Broadway cast of *Jesus Christ Superstar,* eventually moving up to the Judas role. The former seminarian (divorced from his first wife and the father of her son; currenly wed to Nancy Brunner; four daughters) was reluctant at first to remove his clothes for the finale of *Hair.* When he finally did take them off he admitted, ". . . . It felt good. I took off a heavy layer, a burden." In television as well, he has made several notable contributions: Chicken George in the Emmy Award-winning mini-series "Roots" and his own network special: "Ben Vereen—His Roots" which won seven Emmy awards. In 1984 Vereen was signed as Uncle Philip on the ABC comedy series "Webster." Moviegoers saw him in *Funny Lady* and *All That Jazz.* He returned to Broadway in 1985 in *Grind* and later that year made the TV movie "Lost in London." In addition to his accomplishments as a performer, Vereen has also been honored for his humanitarian activities. In 1978, he was the recipient of Israel's Cultural Award; in 1979, Israel's Humanitarian Award, and in 1983 the Eleanor Roosevelt Humanitarian Award. He is currently planning the funding and organization for a drug rehabilitation center in his old neighborhood of Bedford-Stuyvesant in Brooklyn that will offer assistance to needy youths. It will be named in honor of his daughter Naja, who was killed in an automobile accident in 1987. Mr. Vereen presently serves as a Celebrity Spokesperson for "Big Brothers" and is the National Celebrity Spokesperson for "A Drug-Free America."

Shirley Verrett

A former mezzo-soprano, in her mid-40s she undertook the risky task of transforming herself into a soprano without benefit of a voice coach. Having made the grade there too, she's now a successful switch-hitter, i.e., she's a hit at the Metropolitan Opera in roles for either voice. Shirley Verrett made the addition after years of holding to the advice of her Juilliard teacher, who persuaded her to discontinue soprano exercises. "If you vant to be a soprano," her Old World instructor told her, "I will be the first to help you find a new teacher. But it vill brreaak my heart." Uncomfortable as Shirley was at suppressing her natural sound, she acquiesced. Now she uses her insturment to sing the *piano* high notes in opera houses around the world.

Born in New Orleans, 31 May 1931, she grew up in Los Angeles, one of six children of a successful building contractor. Her Seventh Day Adventist family expressed some dismay over her interest in opera. To them, *Aida* and the like fell somewhere on the frivolity scale between the tootlings of jazz and the banalities of Broadway. Shirley's dad commandingly suggested she earn a business degree at L.A. State, and while she did that too, then briefly became a licensed real-estate agent, music was a consuming interest. She won first prize on an "Arthur Godfrey Talent Scouts" TV show in 1955, which led to a Marian Anderson Scholarship to Juilliard. "At Juilliard, I entered every contest that came along, and won them all. I had to. I started late. I needed the money which I plowed into extra coaching." Blocked to a certain extent by racial prejudice, for seven years she traveled the opera and concert festival route from such exotic locales as Fish Creek, Wis., to the Bolshoi, Spoleto, and finally New York City's Lincoln Center. The Met was her goal, but twice she rejected Rudolf Bing's offer of less than major roles in Verdi and Wagner productions. She would bow as *Carmen* or not at all. In 1968 Bing capitulated, and Miss Verrett's "sexily undulating" debut as Bizet's Spanish gypsy left audiences cheering and critics raving. Alternating, as she often does, on Met productions with colleague Grace Bumbry, another winner of a Marian Anderson Scholarship, she is openly grateful to American opera's first black diva. Verrett and Bumbry gave a joint performance in 1982 in honor of Anderson, who, in her 80s, was present at the Carnegie Hall event. Now in her second marriage (since 1963), to Italian painter Louis LoMonance, Verrett approached roles by asking, "How would this person carry herself . . . I begin with the walk." In 1986 she appeared in the PBS television special "Shirley Verrett and the Mormon Tabernacle Choir."

Gore Vidal

When notified he'd been selected for membership in the prestigious American Academy of Arts and Letters, he rejected it with a cordial note: "Thank you, but I already belong to the Diners Club," for which the late John Cheever scolded the iconoclastic naysayer, "Gore, why couldn't you have said Carte Blanche? Diners Club is so tacky."

"What I like least about myself is my belligerence. I just love fighting. I'd have thought it would have been better, all in all, for my blood pressure were I less awash in adrenalin," says the writer whom *Time* considers along with Norman Mailer, "the only two writers of the World War II generation who have combined the talent, versatility, nerve, style and combative instincts to make it in the great, big American way that joins the oak leaf cluster of durable celebrity to money."

Vidal was born 3 October 1925 in West Point, New York, at the U.S. Military Academy where his father was an instructor of aeronautics (they say the young Gore could pilot a plane at age ten). After his parents split (he and Jacqueline Onassis had, on separate occasions, Hugh Auchincloss as a stepfather) he spent a great deal of his time with his grandfather, the blind Senator Gore of Oklahoma, guiding the elder stateman around Washington and reading to him from the *Congressional Record.* Politics at a high level were a key part of his daily life. "If you're brought up to that sort of thing, it's all you really care about." After attending Exeter he served in World War II from 1943 to 1946. His first novel, *Williwaw,* attracted attention when it was published in 1946 when the author was only twenty. A most prolific writer of novels, plays (including *The Best Man* and *Visit to a Small Planet*—both of which played on Broadway for two seasons each) and essays; some of his works include the bestsellers: *Julian* (1964), *Washington, D.C.* (1967), *Myra Breckenridge* (1968), *Burr* (1973), *1876* (1976), *Lincoln* (1984), *Empire* (1987), *Vidal in Venice* (1987), and *At Home: Essays 1982-88* (1988). Upcoming is *Hollywood* (1990). In 1989 his "Gore Vidal's Billy The Kid" was featured on the TNT Network. Vidal, defined by critics as a cynic whose weapon is "a keen, corkscrew mind," and labelled "a gentleman bitch," divides his time between homes in Southern California and Ravello, Italy, 1200 feet high on the Amalfi Coast, where he's known as *lo scrittore,* the writer.

He's made two bids for public office. In 1960 he ran for Congress from Upstate New York and, although he lost, received more votes in the traditional Republican stronghold than any other Democrat in half a century. In 1982, he ran in the Democratic primary for the U.S. Senate in California and in a field of eleven, came in second with close to half a million votes. The literary gadfly made outrageousness a campaign asset, with unmerciful attacks on the Republicans, especially Ronald Reagan, about whom Vidal often repeated: "I know for a fact that Reagan is not clear about the difference between the Medici and Gucci. He only knows that Nancy wears one of them." Discussing his political blood, he once said, ". . . I so romanticize the American people. They are not stupid. I know that goes against the wisdom of the three networks and every newspaper. The public is just 'tuned out'—anesthetized. Nearly 50% did not vote in that last presidential election. I'm longing for the moment only 45% vote. That will make the election illegitimate. Then something can happen.

Edward Villella

"It takes more strength to get through a six-minute *pas de deux* than four rounds of boxing," says Edward Villella, who ought to know. His *alma mater*'s welterweight boxing champion also happens to be the American dancer who (along with Jacques D'Amboise) is often credited with persuading his countrymen that male dancers are as virile as any athlete, a proposition he resoundingly proved during his twenty years as a principal dancer with America's foremost ballet company, the New York City Ballet. The only American dancer (who pursued his career in America) to be named to the "Hall of Fame" in the 1984 book *Men Dancing* etched his unforgettable presence in America's dance consciousness in such roles as the boy in Jerome Robbins' *Afternoon of a Faun* (only two weeks after joining NYCB's corps), and in the Balanchine canon the title role of *The Prodigal Son*, the male leads in *Tarantella*, *Bugaku*, the Rubies section of *Jewels*, *Harlequinade* and as Oberon in *A Midsummer Night's Dream*, among many others. So impressed were the Russians with "his leaps, his technique, his stage presence," that members of a visting Kirov troupe came backstage demanding to meet "the Prodigal Son." During an overseas tour in the 60s, he was forced to break a City Ballet rule against encores on the stage of Moscow's Bolshoi Theatre; in Copenhagen, he became the first non-Danish male to guest-star with the Royal Danish Ballet, and in London his tripple triumph was complete. "He can go up in the air like a bird, seem to pose there and flash a friendly grin at the gaping audience," exulted one critic, while another called him "easily the most comfortable male artist of great accomplishment we have seen. . . . " Back home, his dark and dynamic presence as host of PBS dance specials helped create a lively nationwide interest in the supposedly elite performing art; in 1968, this "beer drinker in the champagne world of ballet" was the subject—via "Man Who Dances"—of the "Telephone Hour's" first televison special on classical dance, and in 1976 the compact virtuoso won an Emmy Award for his CBS television children's ballet, *Harlequin*. Onetime chairman of the New York Commission for Cultural Affairs, today Villella is the Artistic Director of the Miami City Ballet, as he continues to inspire new generations of male dancers, many of whom regard "Eddie" as a major influence on their careers. In 1989 he received the 38th Annual Capezio Dance Award.

It was an unlikely turn of events that produced America's first native-born male dance superstar. Born 1 October 1936, Edward Villella spent most of the spare time of his Italian-American Queens, New York, boyhood playing sandlot baseball and sharing his pals' view that dancing was strictly for girls. After a beaning at the age of 10 his concerned mother sent him to dance classes with his sister, where he soon discovered that he loved the leaping and jumping ("moving, that's it, you are moving in space and time with full freedom and full control"). Five years later, his parents, concerned that dance was too precarious a career for a young man, vetoed further lessons. He stopped dancing until his sophomore year at the New York Maritime Academy, when a night on the town resulted in a serious concussion—and secret resumption of dancing during his recuperation. He joined City Ballet in 1957 (he later completed his college credits and got his degree in 1959), impressed all involved with an extraordinary technical virtuosity, complemented in time by his development into an actor with a powerful stage presence and sensitivity towards his partners. Decidedly unlike "some dancers [who] live as if they were locked in a box," Villella also gained a reputation as a man about town, in part due to a financial interest in the trendy disco Arthur, a predilection for fast sports cars, and a busted marriage (one child; he's currently married to a former member of the Ice Capades—one daughter/one stepdaughter). But dance was—and remains—his passion. A *Dance Magazine* citation hailed his "exceptional prowess . . . enhanced by magnetism, musical awareness . . . and a passionate search for the inner truth of the role."

Jon Voight

"His performance in *Coming Home* is closer to the truth than you'll ever see again on screen," said the film's producer, Jerome Hellman, of Jon Voight's role as a paraplegic Vietnam vet. Managing to talk himself into the part when both Jack Nicholson and Al Pacino became unavailable, Voight gave a performance (opposite Jane Fonda) that earned him honors throughout the world, including the 1979 Academy Award as Best Actor, the New York and Los Angeles Film Critics Awards and the Cannes Film Festival Award. The blond actor with the body of a college fullback prepared himself for the part by spending eleven weeks in a wheelchair living with paraplegics at Rancho Los Amigos Hospital in California. But it was the illness of his father, a Westchester golf pro who later died in an auto accident, which added the sentimental substance to his part. "Health was the number one thing with him because he suffered so much pain. Maybe that's why I acclimated myself so easily to the role of the paraplegic in *Coming Home*. I knew the difficulties, the anger, the frustration, and the heroism too."

Despite such cinematic successes as *Coming Home*, 1972's *Deliverance* and 1974's *The Odessa File*, Voight has experienced financial difficulties and an inability to attract directors' attention for major roles on a regular basis. During the casting of the 1979 remake of *The Champ*, he was the fourth actor approached for the role of the down-and-out boxer originally played by Wallace Beery. And in *Midnight Cowboy*, the 1969 film in which he first moved into the front ranks of Hollywood's leading men, he earned a meager $17,000 (his co-star Dustin Hoffman reportedly got $700,000) for his on-screen performance as a New York hustler which won him the New York Film Critics' Best Actor Award and an Oscar nomination. "Before I did *The Champ*," he told an interviewer, "I was flat broke, right at the bottom."

Born 29 December 1938, one of three brothers, Jon Voight seemed headed at first for the life of a pro golfer like his dad. "For a while I played in the low 70s, but I was a rebel," he recalls. "Then I played an 80-year-old man in a high-school play . . . acting was all I wanted to do after that." He has had two busted marriages, with actresses Lauri Peters and Marcheline Haven. The father of two children by Haven, Voight coproduced and starred in 1982 in *Table for Five*, the story of a divorced father trying to re-enter the lives of his kids. "In the film," he explains, "I'm trying to say something about myself." Most critics scoffed at the film's sentiment, causing Voight to make an uncharacteristically strong promotional effort to turn it around. "How do I handle a review?" he asks. "I don't handle it very well. I get hurt. That's about all. I get rejected because you've been rejected—your work is rejected." Recent films include *Runaway Train* (1985) and *Desert Bloom* (1986). Upcoming in 1990 is *The Eternity*.

Nicholas von Hoffman

"I think you're mad," he says, "if you come into journalism with the idea that you're going to change things for the better. I write because I enjoy it. I sincerely believe in what I write and I get a kick out of getting those Washington mossbacks angry. If I can provoke people into getting angry, I've made a contribution to journalism." Applying these standards, Nicholas von Hoffman has made a considerable journalistic contribution, for at feather ruffling this columnist has proven very adept. (He once described Richard Nixon as looking "like he's got lip cramps and a Charley horse in the cheek.") Some readers describe his writing style as "shooting from the hip," and he sees himself as meeting a "need to cut through the crap and write about reality." During the early seventies he shared the lively Point-Counterpoint segment on CBS's "60 Minutes" with conservative James J. Kilpatrick.

Born in New York City, 16 October 1929, the son of an immigrant Russian cavalry officer and pioneering woman dentist, von Hoffman taught himself to write and report while working for nine years in the Chicago ghettoes as a community organizer for "the professional radical," Saul Alinsky. ("The experience of trying to organize black and Puerto Rican groups taught me how important it was to cut through the bull.") He moved to Washington after working at the *Chicago Daily News* and emerged on the groups taught me how important it was to cut through the bull.") He moved to Washington after working at the *Chicago Daily News* and emerged on the *Washington Post* as an expert on the hip youth underworld; from that period came the book *We Are the People Our Parents Warned Us About*. His formerly thrice-weekly columns in the *Post* moved to King Features Syndicate exclusively in 1972. Von Hoffman pooh-poohs detractors who decry his lack of objectivity. "The illusion of objectivity is that there are two sides to an argument and both must be reported. This defies the reality of today, where there are 30 or 40 sides to a story," Volumes in which he's presented *his* side are *Fireside Watergate* (1973) and *Tales from the Margaret Mead Taproom* (1976), both with Garry Trudeau, *Make Believe Presidents: Illusions of Power from McKinley to Carter* (1978) and the novel *Organized Crimes* (1984). His 1988 book *Citizen Cohn: The Life and Times of Roy Cohn* told the inside story of the fallen-from-grace lawyer.

Frederica von Stade

"I love bel canto. This is the core of what singing is about," says the internationally admired mezzo-soprano. "Part of performing is just blind faith. You want to do something and you just do it. . . . You have to have that sense of abandon. . . . My best [performances] are when I'm just totally concentrated on what I'm doing, when there's no space to think. . ." Since her international debut (1973) in Paris as Cherubino in *The Marriage of Figaro*, critics have praised her voice as "creamy," "luscious," "smooth," "sensuous" and like that of an angel. Fellow mezzo Marilyn Horne describes von Stade thusly—"She has a 'tear' as we say in her voice, a built-in pathos." The seemingly unaffected mezzo-soprano is modest about her talent, constantly striving to enrich her characters and her gift. "You are what you are and that's good enough. The art comes in making as much of it as you can. Music isn't about perfection. . . . It's about humility and process and more than that it's about humanity."

Von Stade practices what she preaches and her superstar reputation is balanced by her professionalism. She has sung in every major opera house in Europe and the United States and her 1982 recording of "Chants d'Auvergne" won her a Grand Prix du Disque.

Born 1 June 1945 in Somerville, New Jersey, into a distinguished family of huntsmen and polo players, "Flicka," nicknamed after one of her father's polo ponies, attended a convent school in Connecticut and moved to Paris upon graduation. She immediately enrolled in piano classes and supported herself alternately as a barmaid, housekeeper, and nanny. Returning to the U.S., von Stade found a job at Tiffany's, taking a secretarial course at night. For a time she worked as a secretary to the American Shakespeare Festival in Connecticut, but dissatisfied, she was again drawn to music and began voice study at the Mannes School. It was not until her second year there that Flicka finally realized her calling, when ". . . Sebastian Engelberg, my vocal teacher, pushed all the right buttons." A prizewinner in the Metropolitan Opera National Council auditions, von Stade was offered a contract with the Met by Rudolf Bing. Her career blossomed as did her voice. Said one conductor, "There's something so seemingly fragile about it that you can't believe it really exists. It's like a perfect flower." Von Stade regularly appears with the Chamber Music Society of Lincoln Center, of which she is the only vocal artist member. Some of the roles she has triumphed in include Rosina in *Il Barbiere de Siviglia*, Adalgisa in *Norma*, Elena in *La Donna Del Lago* and the title role of *La Cenerentola* and she was the subject of a BBC film, "Call Me Flicka." In 1988 she was on stage at Carnegie Hall in "An Evening with Marilyn Horne And friends." Von Stade resides in Long Island with her husband and voice coach, Peter Elkus, and their two children, Jennifer and Lisa. For von Stade "singing is a direct line to the soul."

Max von Sydow

"Max von Sydow," points out the *New Yorker*, "has the longest face in movies since Stan Laurel." But unlike Laurel, "he has never played his face for laughs. Indeed, ever since . . . he appeared in Ingmar Bergman's *The Seventh Seal* as a knight returned from the Crusades, von Sydow has been film's most reliable totem of dignity, gravity and a king of lonely wisdom." His credits are truly awesome: stage classics, from Molière to Tennessee Williams, fifty-odd numbers ranging from the Bergman collection to *The Exorcist* and *Flash Gordon*. With that long face which mirrors every nuance of emotion, he is one of the screen's most sensitive, versatile, and powerful actors. Tall (six feet four), lean, and impressive, the talented Swede is one of the few, the very few, actors who has never been unemployed. Since high school, he's never worked at anything else.

Born Carl Adolf von Sydow in the university town of Lund in southern Sweden on 10 July 1929, his father was a professor of Scandinavian and Irish folklore. In high school, he and a pal established their own theatre group and began to put on plays by Strindberg and Lagerkvist. Subsequently, von Sydow attended the elite Royal Dramatic Academy of Stockholm from 1948-51, and after graduation, honed his craft in provincial theatres, performing in plays like Ibsen's *Peer Gynt*, Pirandello's *Henry IV*, Moliere's *The Misanthrope* and Goethe's *Faust*. During his membership at the municipal theatre of Malmö in 1955, he met the then unknown director Ingmar Bergman and he worked with Bergman for the thirteen years, doing plays in the winter, movies in the summer. Their first film together, *The Seventh Seal* (1956), brought them both worldwide fame when von Sydow was only 27. As the famous director's pet actor, he also emoted in such classics as *Wild Strawberries*, *The Magician*, *The Virgin Spring*, *Hour of the Wolf*, *Shame*, *The Passion of Anna*, *Through a Glass Darkly* and *Winter Light*, often playing opposite Bergman's favorite leading lady, Liv Ullmann. He also starred with Ullmann in Jan Troell's *The Emigrants* (1972) and *The New Land* (1973). While 1963's *The Greatest Story Ever Told* was not a classic, von Sydow's portrayal of Jesus was considered "probably the finest we have in the long history of cinematic, biblical epics." His recent film work is a lesson in diversity: Father Merin in *The Exorcist*, 1973; *Three Days of the Condor*, 1975; the non-Nazi ship's captain in *Voyage of the Damned*, 1976; as the menacing Ming in *Flash Gordon*, 1980; *Conan the Barbarian*, 1981; *Never Say Never Again*, *Dune* in 1984, *Hannah and Her Sisters* (1985), *The Second Victory* (1986), *Duet For One* (1986), *Wolf at the Door* (1987), *Katinka* (1987), *Roadside* (1987) and *Pelle the Conqueror* (1988).

Married for over thirty years to actress Kerstin Olin (two sons), Sydow works hard at his craft and still performs in repertory in his native Sweden. When not involved in acting, he is at home in Rome or, in summer, an old farmhouse in Gotlan, an island in the Baltic where he cultivates his passion for gardening and indulges his leisure interest—natural history. Of acting, he says: "There are some moments when the chemistry is absolutely right. The laws of nature cease. It is like levitation and you and the audience rise in the theatre."

Lindsay Wagner

Best known for her role as "the bionic woman" on a show bearing the same name, this diversified actress has also appeared in numerous made-for-TV movies and several films. She has a video and book out—plus the dynamic lady sings!

Lindsay Wagner was born on 22 June 1949 in Los Angeles. When she was 13 she began studying dance with Jody Best, but when that didn't pan out, she switched to acting. She took very well to acting, and performed in several plays in high school. While performing in the play *This Property Is Condemned*, she was discovered by an MGM scout who offered her a part in a series, which she turned down. Soon after that incident, she became a model for Nina Blanchard. While in her senior year in high school, she and her family moved to Portland, Oregon. It was there that she decided to make a commitment to acting as a profession. After graduating, she attended college for a brief period before she began singing with a professional rock group. In 1968, determined to pursue an acting career, Lindsay moved back to Los Angeles. She made her television debut on "Marcus Welby, M.D.," which was followed by an exclusive contract from Universal in 1971. Several television shows followed, including "The FBI," "Owen Marshall," "Night Gallery," "The Six Million Dollar Man," the Emmy Award-winning series "The Bionic Woman" (1976-78), the series "Jessie" and "The Fall Guy." Her latest series, "Peaceable Kingdom" debuted in September 1989. In addition, she has tackled many diverse, dramatic and critically acclaimed made-for-TV movies, such as "The Two Worlds of Jeanie Logan" (1979), "The Incredible Journey of Dr. Meg Laurel" (1979), the highly successful miniseries "Scruples" (1980), "I Want To Live" (1983), "Two Kinds of Love" (1983), "Princess Daisy" (1983), "Callie and Son" (1983), "Passion" (1984), "This Child Is Mine" (1985) "The Other Lover" (1985), "Nightmare at Bitter Creek" (1988), "The Taking of Flight 847" (1988), "Evil in Clear Water" (1988) and "Voices of the Heart" (1989). Her film credits include *Two People* (1972), *The Paper Chase* (1973), *Second Wind* (1976), *Nighthawks* (1981) and *Martin's Day* (1984). Expanding beyond TV and film, she created a video and book entitled *Lindsay Wagner's New Beauty: The Acupressure Facelift*.

Married and divorced three times, Lindsay is currently single and resides in Los Angeles with her two sons, Dorian and Alex. When not working, she likes to spend time with her sons at Salmon River near Mt. Hood, Oregon.

Robert Wagner

The deep voice quells like velvet over a storm-beaten rock. The twinkle in his eyes is sad-happy, but bright as a night in Paris. Dapper, suave, seductive as an emerald in a rich man's hand, he smiles now—and then he winks. Very subtle. He's the Cary Grant of the television medium, the armchair object of desire whether he's on "It Takes a Thief," "Switch," or "Hart to Hart"—his three superhits. He returned to the tube in the fall of 1985 with a short-lived adventure series, "Lime Street," followed by additional TV appearances in "Here's a Thief, There's a Thief" (ABC, 1986), "There Must Be a Pony" (ABC, 1986) and "Indiscreet" (CBS, 1988).

Born on 10 February 1930 in Detroit, he grew up in California's San Fernando Valley and at 17 brazened his way into a casting office to read for a part, only to flub his lines and flee. By age 20 he was under contract to 20th Century-Fox, at Darryl F. Zanuch's urging. His one-minute appearance as a crippled soldier in *With a Song in My Heart* (tears pouring from his eyes as he listened to the singing of Susan Hayward's Jane Froman) launched him. Soon thereafter Spencer Tracy singled him out in *Beneath the Twelve Mile Reef*, and Wagner appeared in two films with Tracy: *Broken Lance* and *The Mountain*. From there it was all systems go. He has appeared in more than 30 movies. His most noteworthy casting triumph was when Laurence Olivier personally selected him to play Brick in a TV adaptation of Tennessee Williams's *Cat on a Hot Tin Roof* in the late 1970s. Maggie was played by Natalie Wood, his wife, who died tragically when she accidentally drowned near their 60-foot yacht *Splendour* in 1981.

Wagner married Natalie in 1957, but they divorced after she fell in love with Warren Beatty during the making of *Splendor in the Grass*. After a marriage to Marion Marshall (one daughter), he married Natalie again in 1970. (The Wood-Wagner marriage provided a nest for three daughters—hers from a marriage to Richard Gregson; his, and theirs: Courtney.) After Wood's death, Wagner and actress Jill St. John often made the columns as a duo. Said St. John about him: "I can't think of anyone who is more of a Superdad." He still finds it hard to talk about Natalie's death. "Sometimes," he admits, "it is a struggle to make it through a day. . . . I was made a single father by a tremendous tragedy, but one thing I was very fortunate about was that Natalie was a great mother. It's just a matter of sustaining the goodness and love she put there. Thank God they had her as long as they did."

Ken Wahl

He is as talented as he is good looking. This versatile actor, who began his acting career in a feature film in 1978 with virtually no prior acting experience, is now the star of a successful weekly television series.

Ken Wahl was born in Chicago, Illinois, on 14 February 1960. He began acting in 1978, when he debuted in the role of Richie in the film *The Wanderers*. Successfully pulling the performance off without a hitch, he was cast in another feature film, entitled *Running Scared* (1979). Others to follow include *Fort Apache, the Bronx* (1980), *Race for the Yankee Zephyr* (1981), *Jinxed* (1981), *The Soldier* (1982), and *Purple Hearts* (1984). In addition to films, Ken has been seen on several popular television shows and series, such as "The Dirty Dozen: The Next Mission," "Double Dare," and "The Gladiator." He can also be seen every week on CBS in his successful television series "Wiseguy," which earned him an Emmy nomination and has been on the air since 1987. In the show he plays the role of Vinnie Terranova, an undercover agent for the Organized Crime Bureau. When asked what he thinks is the main contributing factor to the show's success, he replies, "The television business in general is based not so much on the hope of success, but the fear of failure—and that's one fear we just don't have."

Ken and his wife Corinne have two children.

The Prince and Princess of Wales

The stuff of dreams? The Honorable (Lady) Diana Frances Spencer was born on 1 July 1961 on the royal estate of Sandringham in Norfolk, which neighbors the Queen's holiday home. The Spencers are not a "royal" family, but they are more than sufficiently "top drawer." Diana's father, the 8th Earl Spencer, dates his wealth back to the early 16th century; it comes from extensive sheep farming and many advantageous marriages. Diana's mother is now married to the wallpaper heir Peter Shand-Kydd. (Diana's parents divorced in 1969.) Mrs. Shand-Kydd was born the Honourable Frances Roche, daughter of the 4th Baron Fermoy and of Ruth, Lady Fermoy, a close personal friend to Queen Elizabeth, the Queen Mother. Earl Spencer is now married to Raine, the former Countess of Dartmouth and daughter of romance novelist Barbara Cartland, who couldn't have written the story of her step-granddaughter any better than history already has.

As a youngster, Diana's chums were Prince Andrew and Prince Edward, who would swim in the Spencer's heated swimming pool whenever they were in residence at Sandringham. Diana did not know Charles until she was 16 and home from school for a weekend pheasant shoot. The guest of honor at the Spencer's was His Royal Highness, who at the time was dating Diana's elder sister Sarah. What did the sweet sixteen-year-old think of the future king of England? She thought him "pretty amazing." But the romance did not bloom until 1980. Diana attended the Chateau d'Oex School in Montreaux, Switzerland, and then returned to London where her parents had gotten her an apartment near Sloane Square. The future Queen of the British Empire worked briefly as a part-time cook, a nanny, and as governess for an American family before she found work as a kindergarten teacher. Diana's contact with the royal family was renewed during visits to her sister Lady Jane, who, as assistant secretary to the Queen, had a apartment in Kensington Palace. The court set was smitten by the charming couple as they tried to keep their affection for each other an international secret. Diana told friends she was dating a Charles Renfrew; Baron Renfrew is one of Prince Charles's titles. She tried to keep it all hush-hush but her love sparkled like a diamond crown under a thousand camera flashes.

Soon after his romance with Diana was being talked of, Charles said: "I've fallen in love with all sort of girls, and I fully intend to go on doing so." Born in 1948, the eldest son of Queen Elizabeth II and Prince Philip, Duke of Edinburgh, he is thusly titled: Charles Philip Arthur George the Prince of Wales and Earl of Chester, Duke of Cornwall and Rothesay, Earl of Carrick and Baron Renfrew, Lord of the Isles and Great Stewart of Scotland. On his meeting Diana when she was 16, he recalled her as "very jolly and amusing and attractive." Royalty watcher Robert Lacey (author of *Majesty*) has said that Charles (whose favorite actress is Marilyn Monroe, whose film *Some Like It Hot* he often screened in Balmoral's private cinema) wasn't ready to settle down with anyone, but that the British press was determined he do so. "[Prince Charles's] image as an adventurous young bachelor sowing his wild oats was getting worn out. It was the opinion of Fleet Street that he should settle down and do his duty. The press pushed Diana as a girlfriend beyond the reality of the situation in the early stages," Lacey told *Time* magazine in 1983. He would have been crucified had he been anything less than tender with the greatest British confection since the Beatles.

So it was the love Charles and Diana continue to share that the press romanced with their constant attention. Headlines called her "Lady Di" and photographers followed her everywhere she went. The Royal Wedding on 29 July 1981 was an extravaganza of tear-provoking pomp and circumstance viewed by nearly 600 million people worldwide, a true commune of starry-eyed dreamers, the biggest ever held, thanks to the television satellite.

During Charles and Diana's engagement, the world got to know the bride-to-be. Charles just sat back contentedly. He had done his greatest service to history-to-date: he gave us a star named Diana. For her part, she suffered the embarrassment of publicity quite well as the shy, pretty young thing went from high-collared schoolgirl to ripe-on-the-vine rose, a femme fatale who stunned British society by appearing at a staid charity event wearing a black strapless gown. Buckingham Palace was not amused; the public was delighted.

Diana had moved into Clarence House, home of the Queen Mother, for lessons in royal conduct. While she was being tutored, souvenir manufacturers turned out Charles and Diana coffee mugs and bath towels and other commemorative bits, *ad infinitum*. Gold-embossed, hand-addressed wedding invitations were received by a lucky 2500 British subjects and world royals. ("The Lord Chamberlain is Commanded by the Queen and the Duke of Edinburgh to invite . . . " they began.) Lady Diana arrived at St. Paul's Cathedral in her David and Elizabeth Emmanuel wedding gown with its supremely lengthy train. (Five copies of the gown were made in case of emergency.) Soprano Kiri Te Kanawa sang a selection from Handel, and Prince Charles had personally selected Jeremiah Clarke's "Trumpet Voluntary" for the bridal procession. Diana arrived at the church in a 1910 glass coach; she left as the Princess of Wales in a 1902 royal Landau adorned with gold and upholstered in crimson satin.

Charles promised Diana that the press fervor would abate as soon as their honeymoon was over. It hasn't. She has had to realize that as the future Queen of England her lifelong commitment is to the international press. Besides, Fleet Street credits itself with the discovery of her star in all relevant firmaments. Since her marriage she has given birth to two royal heirs—William Arthur Philip (on 21 June 1982), known as Prince William of Wales, and Henry Charles Albert David (on 15 September 1984), known as Prince Henry of Wales. Diana has become the most publicized member of the royal family and perhaps the most watched celebrity in the world today.

The Prince and Princess of Wales are "a man and a woman deeply in love," says London journalist Ian Walker. Most publicity is by nature pejorative and the world's image of the Prince and Princess has been forged on, as Walker says, "such mind-blowing trivia" as how many dresses Diana buys and the purchasing of a piggy bank for Prince William. Their good works, and especially the Prince's, have "second billing to trivia."

Robert Lacey feels that journalists do tell too much about the monarchy in general. "One must not reveal too much of the mystery because the royals have faults, dishonesties, nastinesses like anyone else. A lot of us happen to think that the illusions and idealizations which surround this family is quite a healthy thing. Everyone needs vehicles for their social dreams."

Long live the dream, then.

Alice Walker

"*The Color Purple*," declared writer Carole Bovoso in *Essence* magazine, "is one of the great books of our time. The *Nation* said in its review that the novel placed Walker "in the company of Faulkner." It remained on the *New York Times* best-seller list for over 25 weeks, and, in 1983, it was awarded the Pulitzer Prize for fiction, the first ever so given to a black woman novelist. The novel was transferred to the screen in 1985 as a starring vehicle for Whoopi Goldberg under the direction of Steven Spielberg and was nominated for an Academy Award in 1985 as Best Film.

Alice Malsenior Walker was born 9 February 1944 in Eatonton, Georgia, the youngest of eight children born to a sharecropper and a maid, both of whom were lively storytellers. Alice began writing her thoughts and poems down in a journal when she was just eight. In 1952 she was blinded in one eye by a BB gun fired by her brother. Because the family had no access to an automobile, it was a week before she saw a doctor. A disfiguring layer of scar tissue formed over the eye and Alice withdrew from her playful world. She was fourteen when the scar tissue was surgically removed and although she went on to graduate valedictorian from her high school, winning a scholarship to Spelman College in Atlanta, the injury left other sorts of scars. It also taught her to "really see people and things, really to notice relationships and to learn to be patient enough to care about how they turned out."

Walker transferred from Spelman to Sarah Lawrence where she was given a scholarship. In the summer of 1964 she traveled to Africa and returned to college only to discover she was pregnant. She decided to have an abortion and for the week immediately afterwards she wrote poems nonstop and when they were completed she slipped them under the door of her writing teacher, poet Muriel Rukeyser. Rukeyser in turn passed them on to her literary agent and a collection of Walker's poems was sold to Harcourt Brace and published four years later.

After receiving her B.A. in 1965, Walker worked in New York City's Welfare Department and wrote at night. During the summer of 1966 she joined the civil rights movement in Mississippi where she met and married Melvyn Leventhal, a young Jewish civil rights lawyer (one daughter, Rebecca). After a year in Manhattan, the Leventhals settled in Jackson, Miss., in 1967 and became the city's first legally married interracial couple. They remained there for several years during which time Walker wrote and taught, there and in Massachusetts. Her first novel *The Third Life of Grange Copeland* was published in 1970. Walker's other books include: *Revolutionary Petunias and Other Poems* (1973); a collection of short fiction, *In Love and Trouble: Stories of Black Women* (1973), her second novel *Meridian* (1976) and *You Can't Keep a Good Woman Down* (1981). In 1983, a collection of the essays she'd written since 1966 were published, *In Search of Our Mother's Gardens: Womanist Prose*. Her most recent books are *Living by the Word* (1988) and *The Temple of My Familiar* (1989).

Divorced from Leventhal in 1976, Walker lives in San Francisco where she is a "long-distance" editor for *Ms.* Her "cherished companion" is Robert Allen, editor of the *Black Scholar*. "If you're silent for a long time," she once told Gloria Steinem, "people just arrive in your mind." Celie, whose letters are the basis of *The Color Purple*, "is the voice of my step-grandmother,

Rachel. I tried very hard to record her voice for America because America doesn't really hear Rachel's voice."

Now it has been heard.

Irving Wallace

"As soon as an author becomes popular—I mean by that, that he is widely read—he becomes suspect," says novelist Irving Wallace. "The seriousness of his works is questioned; his literary intentions and motivations are put in doubt, however, these suspicions do not stem from the public but from serious critics." One of the most popular writers of this century, Wallace has been rewarded by the public with sales exceeding 182 million and several bestsellers. Cited in a recent issue of *Saturday Review* as "one of the five most widely read authors of the world today," he has (collaborating with various members of his family) created a number of reference books—*The People's Almanac* (#1, #2, and #3), *The Book of Lists* (#1, #2 and #3) and *The Intimate Sex Lives of Famous People*. But it is the novel which has brought this storyteller fame; among the titles are *The Chapman Report, The Prize, The Three Sirens, The Man, The Seven Minutes, The Plot, The Miracle* and *The Seventh Secret*. His most recent books are *The Celestial Bed* (1987) and *The Guest of Honor* (1989). Most of his novels have been bought for motion pictures and television. He is also believed (by his readers) to possess foreknowledge of future events. Wallace acknowledges that he has "some kind of undeveloped psychic streak." Said one reader/author, "In fact, his 1962 novel, *The Prize*, was strangely prophetic. It might even be called, in part at least, psychic itself."

Born in Chicago, 19 March 1916, but raised in Kenosha, Wisconsin, he claims to have "never not written books," although his earliest efforts didn't find him a publisher. He began making it into print in 1931 when he sold his first article, "The Horse Laugh," to *Horse and Jockey* magazine for $5. While in the Army during WW II (with Lt. Ronald Reagan) he made his breakthrough as a screenwriter and continued in Hollywood after the war. Following the worldwide success of *The Chapman Report*, he decided to write books and nothing else. He has been back with a new book every 18 months, as regularly as the swallows of San Juan Capistrano.

Wallace married the former Sylvia Kahn in 1941 because "she was young, she was pretty, and most of all, she admired me." They have two children, David and Amy (both writers). The senior Wallaces divide their time between houses in Brentwood, Malibu, and on the island of Minorca.

Mike Wallace

"I've got the best job in television journalism, bar none," says this TV veteran whose arched-in-disbelief eyebrows and prosecutorial manner ("He can ask somebody 'Where did you go to college?' and make it sound like an indictment," E. J. Kahn, Jr., once observed) have made him a linchpin of CBS's blockbuster "60 Minutes." Starting with the program on its debut broadcast on 24 September 1968, he has contributed significantly to its slow-but-sure rise from the ratings basement to the Number One spot (first reached in 1978) and to become (in the proud words of CBS doyen William S. Paley) "the most successful news series in television history."

Born 9 May 1918 in Brookline, Mass., Mike Wallace attended the University of Michigan and made his early radio-TV reputation in Chicago. He exploded on the Manhattan TV scene in 1956 with a program called "Night Beat," in which his battering cross-examinations of interviewees gave the term "mike fright" a new nerve-shattering dimension. Looked upon by some as a sadistic grand inquisitor and by others as "the most courageous voice in TV," he was the talk of New York, but when he widened his operations to a full network (ABC), the talk subsided to a whisper. "The Mike Wallace Interview" became a defunct TV art form and the newsman's career briefly slipped into limbo before, gradually, the Wallace star began to rise again. Though still considered a tough interviewer, he is also admired as one of the Good Guys. "People will come out of the woodwork for '60 Minutes,'" says his confrere Harry Reasoner, "partly out of their belief that if there's something wrong in their life Mike Wallace can fix it." The list of luminaries Wallace has questioned include: Menachem Begin ("He was very difficult because he did not like to be reminded of his terrorist beginnings. As far as he was concerned, he was a freedom fighter and only the other side were terrorists. . . ."), Anwar Sadat (". . . you could ask Sadat almost anything. He was a professional. . . . When I asked him about corruption with which he and his family had been charged, he handled the question in a straightforward way and we went on to the next") and Ronald and Nancy Reagan (" . . . Presidents by and large are not all that interesting for an American audience. A Shah of Iran—about whom we do not know as much—is really a more interesting interview.").

Married first to Norma Kaplan, second to Buff Cobb, and third to painter Lorraine Perrigord, his son Chris is also a TV newsman (for NBC). He married his fourth and present wife, Mary Yates, in June 1986.

Eli Wallach

"Acting is the most delicious experience in life," he says. "When I'm supposed to be feeling despair on the stage, what I really feel is that I'm sitting on top of the world." One of the most eloquent advertisements for the Actors Studio (he's a charter member), he first blazed into stardom on Broadway as the Sicilian truckdriver (one of his favorite roles) in Tennessee Williams's *The Rose Tattoo* (Tony Award, 1951). He has since enhanced the playwriting fortunes not only of Williams but Eugene Ionesco and Murray Schisgal by making hit fare of *Camino Real* and *Baby Doll* (film version), *The Chairs* and *Rhinoceros, The Typist and the Tiger, Luv,* and *Twice Around the Park*.

Born 7 December 1915 in Brooklyn ("In the Red Hook section, known as little Italy . . . we were the only Jews in a sea of Italians"), Eli Wallach graduated from high school in 1932 ("one of the worst years of the Depression") and planned at first on a teaching career, although his heart belonged to the stage. Rather happy at flunking the New York City teachers' exam ("I felt free to do what I wanted to do . . . I was a little guy and I knew the odds were against me, but I was determined anyway"), he signed up for studies at the Neighborhood Playhouse and, indicative of what was to come, one of his first jobs was in an Equity Library Theater production of Tennessee Williams's *This Property is Condemned*. There was only one other character in the play," he recalls, "a girl named Annie Jackson. We had a few arguments about how the roles should be played and settled it all by getting married." They now have three children, not to mention a long, distinguished list of co-star credits. In 1977-78 they had a real family triumph off-Broadway in *The Diary of Anne Frank*, (which also starred their two actress daughters, Roberta and Katherine Wallach). In 1984 the critics cheered their performances in Joseph Papp's N.Y. Shakespeare Festival production of *Nest of the Woodgrouse*.

Although Wallach prefers the theatre to film ("Movies, by comparison to the stage, are like calendar art next to great paintings"), he's applied his remarkable talent to, among others, *How the West Was Won; The Magnificent Seven; The Misfits; Lord Jim; The Moonspinners; The Good, The Bad, and the Ugly; The Deep; Cinderella Liberty; Movie, Movie; The Hunter, Girlfriends, Nuts* and *Funny*. He has appeared on the screen with Jackson in *How to Save a Marriage* and *Ruin Your Life, Zigzag,* and *The Tiger Makes Out*. He has appeared on television in the specials "I, Don Quixote," "For Whom the Bell Tolls" with Jason Robards, "Skokie" with Danny Kaye, "The Wall," Norman Mailer's

"The Executioner's Song" and "Christopher Columbus." He made his series debut in 1985 in "Family Honor." His latest accomplishments at the theatre include his acclaimed performance in *Cafe Crown* and his induction into the Theatre Hall of Fame in 1988.

Wallach's passions off-stage are tennis, photography, clock collecting and architecture. However, he is still enthusiastic about his profession. "Acting is the most alive thing I can do, and the most joyous."

Barbara Walters

The incomparable ABC News Correspondent and interviewer-par-excellence, Barbara Walters, assembled portions of her very special "Specials" for "The 50th Barbara Walters Special" which aired in December 1988, with "the best, most unforgettable moments from twelve years of unique interviews." In the brilliant two-hour presentation celebrating the Emmy Award-winning "The Barbara Walters Specials," Ms. Walters shared her impressions of the personalities she has interviewed, as well as what was occurring before and after the cameras rolled. She disclosed intimate personal details about each interview, her impressions, her likes and dislikes, and what was most surprising to her. Ms. Walters's informative and bull's-eye interviews are blockbusters; she has zeroed in on political figures, entertainment figures, entertainment biggies, controversial subjects and those involved in issues topping the news, and, with her usual grace and brilliance, has made each one a gem. Since their preview on 14 December 1976, "The Barbara Walters Specials" have become the number one primetime television interview specials in history. One longed to see each one replayed in its entirety. "Nobody thought they would last," Barbara Walters recalled. "We worried so about that very first program with Barbra Streisand and then President-elect and Mrs. Carter. But the audience was with us all the way and, lo and behold, we're still here fifty Specials later."

Born in Boston on 25 September 1931, the daughter of nightclub impresario Lou Walters, the original owner of the Latin Quarter, she moved to New York after graduating from Sarah Lawrence College. She worked for an advertising agency for awhile and then wrote material for Dick Van Dyke, Jack Parr, Anita Colby and the NBC News bureau before joining the "Today Show." In 1970 her book *How To Talk to Practically Anybody About Practically Anything* was a bestseller. Reflecting on her career and its success, she says: "I've missed all the corny stuff, I've missed smelling the flowers. . . . I'm always on the phone saying, 'I'll make this fast.' Just once I'd like to get on the phone and say, 'Let's make it slow, I have no place to go.' A long time ago there was so much about myself I didn't like and so much I couldn't do. I remember going to a therapist and saying, 'But you know I can't do any of the things other women can do.' It was Thanksgiving and I said: 'I can't make a turkey, I'm such a klutz,' and the doctor said: 'Do you know what you do if you want to make a turkey? You go home and make a turkey,' and I thought that was so wise . . . but I still can't make a turkey. The difference is, now I don't want to make a turkey." She also had her own highly popular syndicated series, "Not for Women Only," which lasted five years. Ms. Walters joined ABC News in 1976. "20/20" aired the first Barbara Walters segment in July 1979 and she joined Hugh Downs as host of the broadcast in 1984.

From her first marriage to Lee Guber, she has a daughter Jacqueline. In 1986 she married Merv Adelson. Ms. Walters's many awards, accolades, and honorary degrees have established her as one of the most respected and admired women in America.

Joseph Wambaugh

Fourteen years with the Los Angeles Police Department taught him all he needed to know about the pummeled emotional lives of cops on the urban beat. He re-enacted his vivid memories in a series of best-selling novels about men in blue wrestling with moral dilemmas and nonsensical realities.

A police officer's son, Joseph Wambaugh Jr., was born in East Pittsburgh, Pa, on 22 January 1937, and raised in Los Angeles. After service in the Marines, he followed his father into the force, while pursuing an undergraduate, and then graduate English degree at night. Assigned by the LAPD to East Los Angeles, a predominantly minority neighborhood, he became embroiled in the futile effort to quell the riots in Watts during the midsixties. He recalled the mayhem in vivid detail in *The New Centurions*, his first novel (1971). "I had drawers full of notes, scraps of paper that I saved over the years with all my ideas, thoughts, observations, and so forth as a policeman. I had years of that stacked up in a drawer which I pulled out when I started putting the books together." The story of three fictional LAPD officers was initially rejected by a score of publishers before it saw print and became a best-seller and Book-of-the-Month Club offering. Wambaugh was displeased with the film version of the novel, as he is with most dramatizations of his work. His disputes with film and television executives have led to frequent litigation. About the movie version of his 1975 novel, *The Choirboys*, he said. "It was vile and simpleminded slime from the first frame to the last. . . . The settlement—for which I got a lot of money and my name off the picture—had one condition: silence from me for a year." His 1972 novel, *The Blue Knight*, the story of officer Bumper Morgan, became a 1973 NBC mini-series and a 1975 CBS series. Wambaugh also battled his associates as consultant to NBC's "Police Story." After suing Columbia Pictures to regain the rights to his 1973 novel, *The Onion Field*, he used personal finances to produce the movie version. Called "gripping" and "disturbing" by critics, it was applauded as one of the outstanding films of 1979.

After retiring from police work with the rank of detective sergeant, he penned *The Black Marble*, *The Glitter Dome* (a title suggested by his wife, Dee Altsup, with whom he has two adopted sons), *The Secrets of Harry Bright*, *Echoes in the Darkness*, and a true story, *The Blooding*.

Dionne Warwick

Her 1979 album, *Dionne*, put her back in the music industry's little black book of hot artists after a dip in popularity. But having snared a host slot on "Solid Gold," the weekly showcase of Top 40 artists, she was fired, some say, because of her temper. She disagreed about the cause. "I am *not* a temperamental bitch," she told reporters. "Look at Barbra Streisand. When she's working she won't stand for less than the best. She's only interested in perfection. What's wrong with that? How often do blacks get a chance to host a TV show? When blacks were on my show I wanted them to be presented in the best possible way. . . . Why shouldn't I?" Since her well-trained, clear voice first pierced the public ether over twenty years ago, she's remained beautiful, a couture-wearing clothes horse, and although smolderingly cool of manner, not about to be put down by anyone.

Christened Marie Dionne Warwick (she added a final "e" for a time for numerological reasons) on 12 December 1940 into a gospel-oriented family in Orange, N.J., Dionne first sang in public as an occasional member of the famous Drinkard Singers, a church choir group managed by her mother. As a teen-ager, she joined up with her sister Dee Dee and a cousin to form her own trio, The Gospelaires, while studying at the Hart School of Music in Connecticut. Her career as a soloist began to take off when, in 1960, she caught the ear of then-fledgling composer Burt Bacharach and began cutting demos for the songs that he and lyricist Hal David were trying to sell. The threesome wound up with a Top Ten hit, "Don't Make Me Over," in 1962, and continued on with a long string of big sellers, including Dionne's first Grammy-winning single, "Do You Know the Way to San Jose?" Grammy number two came in 1970 for her album, "I'll Never Fall in Love Again," also comprised of Bacharach/David creations. Trying to maintain her pop standing, Warwick has worked with other producers (including Barry Manilow) and continues to come across with hit products. Her 1986 "That's What Friends Are For" kept the singer on top of the charts. Nowadays, she finds herself competing against her award-winning vocalist niece, Whitney Houston.

The singer married former drummer Bill Elliott in 1967, divorced him, married him again and divorced him again. They have two sons. She is involved contributing her talent and name to help fight AIDS and has established the Warwick Foundation.

Lew Wasserman

"In those days agents wore plaid suits and purple shirts. I changed all that to grey flannel," recalls the flesh-peddler-turned-tycoon who now heads up MCA, Inc., one of the entertainment industry's sprawlingest corporate empires (Univeral Pictures, Decca Records, et al). Tapped in 1982 as one of The Forbes Four Hundred ("His 1.9 million shares worth over $115 million"), he also made *Town & Country's* 1983 list of "The Most Generous Living Americans." His largesse extends from the Los Angeles Music Center and the Kennedy Center for the Performing Arts to the California Institute of Technology and the Jet Propulsion Laboratory. In acknowledgement of all this he was honored in 1973 with the Jean Hersholt Humanitarian Award of the Academy of Motion Picture Arts and Sciences.

Born in Cleveland on 15 March 1913, Lew Wasserman's first job in show business was as a movie usher on the 3 p.m. to midnight shift. Married to the former Edith Beckerman (one daughter), he joined MCA in 1936, the era when it was still a talent agency. (In the 1940s, it represented nearly one third of the stars in Hollywood). Ten years later, when founder Jules Stein moved up to chairman of the board, he was given presidential billing. He now serves as chairman of the board himself, as well as Chief Executive Officer. Wasserman was the man at the helm during MCA's most cataclysmic changes, when, in 1962, the federal government filed an anti-trust suit forcing it to divest itself of the talent agency portion of its activities. Said he at the time: "We did what other agencies did . . . only we did it better." Regarded with a mixture of fear, admiration and animosity by competitors as well as the people he hires and fires, the MCA mogul surrounds himself with an air of mystery almost as dark as the suits he once decreed to be the mandatory uniform of all MCA male employees. "There is probably," according to one Tinseltown observer, "no man in show business of whom so much is said and so little known."

Wendy Wasserstein

"This is hard work," she pronounced. "My mother tells me I shouldn't work so hard. I'm a girl, my mother says, and girls shouldn't work so hard." Wendy laughs. But behind the laughter is a serious concern for society, for people, and for a decent quality of life.

Wendy Wasserstein was born in Brooklyn and raised in Manhattan where she attended the private Calhoun School. Following her graduation there, she attended college at Mt. Holyoke. After turning thumbs down on "the so-called respectable professions like law or medicine," she took off for Yale Drama School.

Since then, Wendy has written and co-written several off-Broadway plays, her latest of which was the acclaimed Tony Award winning comedy *The Heidi Chronicles*. She has also authored *Isn't It Romantic*, which had a long run off-Broadway. Other credits include *Any Woman Can't*, *Montpelier Pa-Zazz*, *Uncommon Women and Others* and *Miami*, which was a workshop of a musical. In addition, Wendy has contributed scenes for *Urban Blight* and has written the one acts *Tender Offer* and *The Man in Case*. Her screenplays include adaptations of *The House of Husbands*, which was co-authored with Christopher Durang, and *The Object of My Affection*. Her PBS contributions have been "Uncommon Women and Others," "The Sorrows of Gin," and "Drive She Said." Wendy has taught at Columbia and New York Universities. She is also a contributing editor of *New York Woman* Magazine and the author of *Bachelor Girl*, a collection of essays published by Knopf. Wendy is a recipient of a Guggenheim Fellowship and an NEA playwright grant, and has also been awarded The Susan Smith Blackburn Prize for *The Heidi Chronicles*. She serves on the council of the Dramatists Guild and is one of nine resident writers who form Playwrights Horizons' Artistic Board. Wendy states that she enjoys being a playwright, and enjoys being able to say she's one. "Can you think of any other job where you can work all day in a flannel nightshirt and slippers?"

Tom Watson

The verdict was the same, it was only a question of probability. "You can hit that chip [shot] a hundred times," said one golf pro, "and you couldn't get it close to the pin, much less in the hole." "A thousand times," Jack Nicklaus dryly offered. The shot in subjective dispute was the one made by golf's Tom Sawyer look-alike, Tom Watson. His 16-foot chip, from ankle-deep grass, onto the green and then into the cup at the 1982 U.S. Open's 17th hole amazed Nicklaus because it beat him, after he'd almost assured himself a victory. But Watson said, "I've practiced that shot for hours, days, months and years." Such dedication has made him the PGA's second-ranking career money winner.

On 4 September 1949 Thomas Sturges Watson (born in Kansas City, Mo.,) arrived as the future playing partner to his father, Ray "Hook" Watson. Teaching Tom to play with a shortened putting club at age six, he later made a caddy of his son for his weekend golf games with friends at Kansas City Country Club. While practicing, practicing, practicing his swing, stance, and other elements of the game, he had enough time to develop into an all-around athlete (unusual for a golfer) by playing varsity basketball and quarterbacking his football team to a conference championship in high school. Of sturdy build at five-feet-nine and 160 pounds, with enormous forearms, he became a powerful fairway driver, as well as golf's best putter. After walking on Stanford University's team without a scholarship (he'd been an honor student in high school and wanted to become an insurance man) he had a rather undistinguished college golf career. But his father and dad's golfing buddies still pooled their money to back him for four years upon his decision to turn pro after his 1971 graduation. The intelligent, modest redhead took a wife after two years on tour; she'd turned him down twice before since they began dating in high school, but later Linda said, "If I'd known how great the tour was going to be, I'd have married him in college."

He's a multiple winner of the British Open, and all the other major tournaments, leaving many observers to conclude that he may well become one of the greatest golfers ever to play the game. His more than $3 million in prize money is downplayed, and he prefers to center conversations about money to the good that his annual "Children's Mercy Hospital Golf Classic" can do with the quarter of a million dollars it raises each June for Kansas City kids. The well-ordered, well-read Watson takes his wife and two small children on tour with him. They live near Kansas City. "I'm somebody who takes fame as a disruption of a normal way of living. . . . Doing what I do for a living well is important to me. . . . Most of all, I treasure being a normal person."

André Watts

"Pull out the adjectives, men! The performance was: electrifying, sensational, daring, colorful, imaginative, powerful. I not only never heard the *Todtentanz* played better, I cannot even imagine it played better." So trumpeted *New York Times* music critic Harold C. Schonberg about the handsome prodigy who exploded into a super-nova at 16 when Leonard Bernstein introduced him to a national television audience via a New York Philharmonic "Young People's Concert." Three weeks later Bernstein called him to sit in as a last-minute substitution for the ailing Glenn Gould on a regular Philharmonic subscription night. Now Watts performs up to 100 concerts a year all over the world and earns an income that keeps him well-supplied with his favorite indulgences—imported cigars and caviar, ("Bad caviar is no fun.")

Born in Nuremberg, Germany, 20 June 1946, the son of a Hungarian-born mother and a black American career soldier, André Watts lived in Europe, mostly around Army posts, until he was eight. His mother, a good pianist herself, gave him his first piano lessons, spurring his interest in practicing with stories of the accomplishments of her countryman, Franz Liszt. (Fittingly, it was with Liszt's demanding *E-flat Concerto* that he scored his Philharmonic success in 1963.) By age nine, his family had settled in Philadelphia and young André felt so at home at the keyboard that he played a Haydn concerto at a Philadelphia Orchestra Children's Concert; when (after studies at the Philadelphia Academy of Music) he auditioned for Bernstein at 16, the maestro, by his own description, "flipped." Says André of his now-historic debut, "Bernstein actually made me play better than I would have ordinarily." He started on the European circuit in 1966 and keeps in shape for his heavy practice and performing schedule by doing yoga (including headstands), maintains his eligible-young-bachelor status with a fairly monastic social life (he considers parties "a great waste of life force"), and says, "My music comes before everything else and I am never bored by it. . . . Performing is my way of being part of humanity—of sharing." In 1982, the National Society of Arts and Letters presented one of its prestigious Gold Medals of Merit to Watts.

Sigourney Weaver

"I never went to a co-ed school, so to me it's like being put in a class with the awful boys, who spend all their time throwing spitballs and dunking your braids into the inkwell. It's a streak of masochism in me. I find it wonderful." Sigourney Weaver comments on her return as Dana Barrett in *Ghostbusters II* (1989). The dynamic actress has captured the cream-of-the-crop roles of the '80s; she played Dian Fossey in Universal's *Gorillas In The Mist* (Golden Globe Best Actress, Academy Award nomination for Best Actress) and Tess, the "beautiful, treacherous boss," in *Working Girl* (Golden Globe Best Supporting Actress, Academy Award nomination for Best Supporting Actress).

She was born Susan Weaver in 1949 in New York City, the daughter of former NBC President Sylvester Weaver and British actress Elizabeth Inglis. Early in her teen age years, she picked the name Sigourney which was inspired from the name of a character in the F. Scott Fitzgerald classic *The Great Gatsby*. She began studying acting as an undergrad at Yale Drama School, and went on to receive her M.A. Her first acting job was as an understudy in Sir John Gielgud's production of *The Constant Wife*. Her off-Broadway debut was in *The Nature and Purpose of the Universe*, a play that was written by a friend from drama school. Sigourney also co-starred and co-wrote *Das Lusitania Songspiel* and *Naked Lunch*, as well as appearing in *Titanic* and *Beyond Therapy*. For her debut in the Broadway production of *Hurlyburly*, she received a Tony nomination. Although she made her film debut in a bit part in *Annie Hall*, it was the 1979 sci-fi thriller *Alien* that made her a star. She returned in her role of Warrent Officer Ripley in the sequel *Aliens*, for which she received an Oscar nomination. Other film credits include *Eyewitness, The Year of Living Dangerously, Half Moon Street, One Woman or Two, Deal of the Century,* and *Ghostbusters.*

In 1984, she wed Jim Simpson, a director she met at the Williamstown, Mass., Playhouse.

Jimmy Webb

Eleven-time Grammy-winning singer/songwriter Jimmy Webb, the only musical artist ever to collect Grammys for music, lyrics *and* orchestration, began his cabaret debut in 1987—to the delight of his fans. Though Webb is best known for the instant classics he has provided for the likes of the Fifth Dimenson ("Up, Up, and Away"), Richard Harris ("MacArthur Park," "Didn't We") and Glen Campbell ("By the Time I Get to Phoenix"), he has released many albums of his own, including *And So On*, cited in 1971 by *Stereo Review* as Album of the Year, and the popular *Angel Heart* from 1982.

The son of a Baptist minister in Elk City, Oklahoma, (born 15 August 1946), Webb burst on the pop music scene at 20 with "Up, Up and Away," written in exactly 35 minutes. Not one to rest on past laurels, Webb has continued to turn out hits—most notably in recent years, "The Highwayman," which made it to the number one spot, won Webb a Grammy for Best Country Song of the Year and a CMA Award for Single of the Year. (It was recorded by Waylon Jennings, Willie Nelson, Johnny Cash, *and* Kris Kristofferson.) Other memorable Webb breakthroughs: his "All I know" launched Art Garfunkel's solo career in 1973; Linda Ronstadt reached the Top Ten with her haunting rendition of Webb's "Easy for You to Say." Webb has involved himself since the sixties in film and television projects, among them his dazzling 1982 score for the animated film, *The Last Unicorn*, which became Germany's second-highest grossing picture that year. His most recent film project was the score for a number of series, including "E/R," "Amazing Stories" and the "Cinderella" episode of Shelley Duvall's Faerie Tale Theatre. Amy Grant's Christmas special in 1986 spotlighted songs from the Jimmy Webb cantata, "The Animals' Christmas" (performed on record by Art Garfunkel, Grant and the London Symphony). Four of his songs are featured on Linda Ronstadt's latest album, John Denver recently recorded a comeback single of his song "Wish You Were Here" and Webb is working with Ray Bradbury on a musical version of *Dandelion Wine* to bring to Broadway.

Webb married Barry Sullivan's daughter, Birgitta Patricia Sullivan ("Patsy"), on 14 July 1974 in Ojai, California. The couple have three children. He has written a memoir about the Hollywood rock star set during the late-'60s-early-'70s for his offspring, *Future Letters to My Children*. Not content to rest on his sizeable royalties, he says, "I was very lucky. One morning, when I was twenty, I woke up with a million dollars. I could do anything I wanted, and so, of course, I ran amok."

John Weitz

"Clothes do not make the man. Brains make the man. Charm makes the man. Achievement makes the man." This from the international menswear designer, John Weitz. Said one friend of the movie-star handsome man for all seasons "Weitz is like a real life James Bond." He's also the writer of novels: *The Value of Nothing* (1970) and *Friends in High Places* (1982); of the non-fiction *Man in Charge* (1974); and a photographer whose first project, "Manhattan Faces" was exhibited at the Museum of the City of New York in 1984.

He was born in Berlin on 25 May 1923, the only son of a wealthy Jewish businessman, educated at St. Paul's in London and migrated to New York in 1940. As a member of the OSS in WW II, he parachuted behind enemy lines and was part of the group that liberated the Dachau concentration camp survivors. He has been a top-notch amateur race driver and yachtsman, a winner of the coveted Coty Award and the Cartier Design Award, and is a member of the men's International Best Dressed List Hall of Fame. Weitz is also seen as the model in print and television advertisements for his wares. He summers aboard his 50-foot-yacht "Milagros" which is berthed at Sag Harbor, and winters in Palm Beach. Weitz has two children from his first marriage and two from his second to former actress Susan Kohner whom he married in 1964.

Raquel Welch

"My body is just there," she sighs, "like Mt. Rushmore." If you have that sex-symbol image, "they try to cut you off at the knees if you want to be anything else." How delighted she was, then, when she replaced Lauren Bacall in the Broadway musical *Woman of the Year* in 1982 and met with raves and rahs from the critics. Howard Kissel, writing in *WWD*, said that she "gives the dreary musical a wonderful new energy and freshness." She said she was "shell-shocked" from all the praise. She'd come a long way from her national debut in a poster from her 1967 film *One Million Years B.C.* wearing a fur bikini, long legs spread wide, encouraging the caveman in everyman to stand up and grunt with desire. "I finally get a chance to prove in the flesh what I've said all along," she exulted, "I'm a better actress than anyone knows."

After enough shelling in such films as *The Three Musketeers* (for which she won the Golden Globe Best Actress Award), *Kansas City Bomber, Myra Breckenridge, Bedazzled,* and *The Four Musketeers,* she'd finally won some respect. The mother of two grown children (from her marriage to childhood sweetheart Jim Welch) is one of America's most popular and enduring beauties. The how-to of it all was told in her book *Raquel: The Raquel Welch Total Beauty and Fitness Program* published in 1984 with an accompanying videotape. In 1987, she made her recording debut on Columbia Records with "This Girl's Back in Town," a throbbing anthem of female survival which the glamorous one considers "a combination of strength and vulnerability—which is where I'm coming from." Her fitness video was released the same year "A Week with Raquel" was a top videocassette seller on the *Billboard* chart. Raquel's latest telefilms include "Scandal in a Small Town" (1988) and "The Education of Leda Beth Vincent" (1988).

Born Raquel Tejada in Chicago, 5 September 1940, she studied ballet for ten years, modeled, won beauty contests and studied drama. Her studies were interrupted by the birth of her son Damon and daughter Tahnee (who made her film debut in 1985 as an exquisite space creature in *Cocoon*). When her marriage to Welch dissolved she headed for Hollywood, arriving broke and not knowing anyone. The billboard girl on TV's "Hollywood Palace," she was getting nowhere until she met Patrick Curtis, a former press agent, who became her manager. ("He is to me what the Colonel is to Elvis," she said before their four-year union dissolved in 1971.) When Twentieth Century-Fox put her under contract she became a star almost overnight, and she began making the more than 35 movies that made her known to film fans worldwide. In addition to her film and television work, which also include French-made *L'Animal,* co-starring Jean Paul Belmondo, and one of ABC's highest rated TV specials ever—"From Raquel With Love," her nightclub act is performed to capacity audiences from Las Vegas to Rio de Janeiro, and in Paris she broke the box office record at the famed Palais des Congres.

Raquel married Andre Weinfeld on 5 July 1980, but the couple had split up in 1989.

Lawrence Welk

Lawrence Welk's Honolulu Fruit Gum Chewing Orchestra (circa 1934—originally the Hotsy Totsy Boys) may sound like the Beatle's Sergeant Pepper's Lonely Hearts Club Band, but the similarity in name is the only similarity you'll find. The favorite band leader of Middle America, using an infectious blend of champagne music and a bubble machine straight out of a polyester nightmare, is likely to live on forever in pop culture. Why, it's even been suggested that "latter-day historians and sociologists in their expeditions into the heartland of America will do well to search out the tapes of the 'Lawrence Welk Program.'" Even when Welk was dropped by ABC in 1971, he retrieved the loss by personally lining up more than 200 independent stations for his syndicated music fest which now plays the rerun circuit.

"It's a bad hurt when you're brought face to face with the fact you're being held up to ridicule," says the oft-parodied Welk ("A one-and-a two"). But if he is made jest of, he is also warmly regarded by the millions who were his fans during his 16-year tenure on prime-time TV. They bought millions of his albums and wrote thousands of concerned letters about his TV "family." Welk is also consoled by the bubbling personal fortune he's amassed, including a music recording and publishing empire, the Lawrence Welk Country Club Village (motel and mobile homes), the Lawrence Welk Union Bank building, and more. He followed his bestselling 1971 autobiography *Wunnerful, Wunnerful* with *Ah-One, Ah-Two: Life with My Musical Family* (1974) and *My America, Your America* (1976).

Born in Strasburg, N.D., 11 March 1903, of Alsatian immigrant parents, Welk dropped out of school in the fourth grade and was 21 years-old before he spoke English—an accomplishment some critics still debate: "In some sentence constructions he would make Weber and Fields sound like a pair of early Noel Cowards." He married Fern Renner, a former nurse, in 1931, and she bore him three children. His commitment to wholesomeness on the tube was quite genuine. He once fired a female performer—in the days before the miniskirt—for showing too much knee. "She tried to be too sexy," he said.

Lina Wertmuller

Some say that *Seven Beauties* (generally considered everyone's "personally discovered masterpiece") is the best film since *Citizen Kane;* others that it is "fascist trash." The critic John Simon (uncharacteristically) called it a "milestone," adding, "A couple more films like *Seven Beauties,* and Lina Wertmuller will take her rightful place among the grand masters of cinema: the Fellinis and Bergmans, the Antonionis and Renoirs." A provocative and gifted writer-director, this Italian *auteur* is responsible for a number of heady, entertaining but challenging films like *Love and Anarchy* (1973), *The Seduction of Mimi* (1972), and *Swept Away* (1975) which have found international success and blazed new trails in the difficult terrain between feminism and film. Wertmuller features have helped rattle and revise the myth of male supremacy in the world of celluloid. Of her American debut, *Newsweek* raved about "the most exciting woman director on the international scene and the most remarkable new talent from the Continent since Bernardo Bertolucci."

Born in Rome between 1926 and 1928 (she's mum), she is of aristocratic Swiss ancestry. Passionately Italian by nature, she refers to herself as the product of "boiling blood." Wertmuller's father was a well-to-do lawyer, but the parents had a stormy relationship and her childhood was marked by early rebellion. A prankster, she was "thrown out of fifteen schools" and counteracted her rigorous Roman Catholic upbringing and educational restrictions by sneaking off to see American films. Dramatically inclined, she took like a duck to water at the Academy of Theatre in Rome. For the next fifteen years, Wertmuller had a hodge-podge of occupations: actress, stage manager, set designer, publicist, and writer for commercial Italian radio, TV and theatre. Then she met Fellini and was recruited as his assistant on *8*. She said of the association: "It was one of those experiences that open new dimensions of life. I was totally enlightened by his personality . . . you *can* learn . . . the freedom of art." That exposure to Fellini's effective spontaneity and imaginative juices inspired Wertmuller to become a film director on her own. A customized "bitter-sentimental/grotesque-erotic" humor came into expression. In the year following, she financed her debut film *The Lizards* (first prize at the 1963 Locarno Film Festival) and then in 1966, *Let's Talk About Men;* neither was shown commercially in U.S. Next, a young matinee idol, Giancarlo Giannini came under her professional wing and starred in *The Seduction of Mimi* (1972) which won a Best Director Award at the 1972 Cannes Film Festival. Of its opening in New York, a *Time* critic said: "Here is the perfect summer tonic: a brainy, rowdy comedy." True fame happened in 1975 with her most far-reaching comedy, the smash hit *Swept Away*. Called "a kind of witty, slapdash Marxist comedy that owes as much to Groucho as to Karl," it captivated critics and large audiences alike. In 1978, she made *A Night Full of Rain* with Candice Bergen as the leading lady opposite that "meltable Mimi," Giancarlo, and in 1984 attracted attention with *A Joke of Destiny*. Her latest films include *Notte D'Estate* (1986), *Summer Night* (1987), and *Crystal or Ash* (1989). She received the First Friendship Award of National Organization of Italian-American Women in 1987.

Short and slight with signature white-rimmed eyeglasses and a barrage of jewelry, she looks (in her own words) "like a crazy gypsy." Since their marriage in 1968, sculptor and scenic designer Enrico Job has served as the art director on all of his wife's pictures. The last laugh? Of international opportunities she complains: "I learn that English has no funny dirty words."

Ruth Westheimer

"What's wrong with peanut butter or new uses for onion rings as long as there's a relationship?" asks pioneer media therapist Dr. Ruth Westheimer to a listener calling in with a question about kinky sex. Although she is not precisely the first therapist to treat her "clients" on the airwaves instead of the couch, she is certainly unique. A trained psychotherapist and former kindergarten teacher, she dispenses quickie advice in her instantly-recognizable German accent and is relentlessly upbeat about the problems that perturb her listeners. Frigidity? Premature ejaculation? "You're going to be fine, you betcha," she chirps.

Her Sunday night program over a New York radio station stirred up a hornet's nest of controversy, leading almost inevitably to even greater exposure on the "Tonight" show and to her receiving that indisputable badge of media celebrityhood: being spoofed on "Saturday Night Live." "Some critics think she is frivolous, some call her irresponsible and others say her candor is positively indecent," winked *Newsweek*. "Have good sex!" she exhorts her listeners at the close of each program, a decidedly original twist on "Have a nice day." Two years after she hung out her shingle on the Big Apple airwaves, the cable health channel "Lifetime" guided her 4 feet 7 inch frame in front of their cameras and the couchless counselor had her own TV show. Actors portray the sexually-troubled people whose problems in the sack get aired on a program titled—what else?—"Good Sex."

Born in Germany in 1928 and orphaned by the second world war, Westheimer lived in Switzerland, Israel and France (where she studied psychology at the Sorbonne) before emigrating to New York at 28. Enrolling at Columbia she earned first a master's in sociology ("Americans are the only [nationality] to worry much about armpits") and then a doctorate in family studies. But it is not her academic credentials that have made her something of a cult heroine among high school and college students, who rib her for her accent, age and stature (*Newsweek:* "She looks more like a retired jockey than an expert in psychosexual therapy") and yet tune in to her program attentively. "I don't come across as a sex symbol," she recognizes. "People trust me because I'm not a put-on." The walking talking sex lady is the author of five books to date: *Dr. Ruth's Guide to Good Sex, First Love, Dr. Ruth's Guide for Married Lovers, Sex and Morality: Who is Teaching Our Sex Standards*, and *All In A Lifetime* (her autobiography). She writes a syndicated advice column, *Ask Dr. Ruth*, and is a contributing editor to *Redbook* Magazine. Her latest book will be co-authored with Dr. Louis Lieberman, entitled *A Guide to Sexual Self-Help and Skills*. In addition, she has marketed a board game, "Dr. Ruth's Game of Good Sex" with Victory Games, and she had a role in the Sigourney Weaver French film *One Woman Or Two*. "The All New Dr. Ruth Show" won an Ace Award in 1988.

Dr. Westheimer has two children and resides with her husband in New York City.

Betty White

All the charm, humor, sincerity and love that has captivated television audiences everywhere shines throughout Betty White's second book, *Betty White: In Person* (1987). Television's snappy Sue Anne Nivins of "The Mary Tyler Moore Show" and the endearing Rose of the current "The Golden Girls" revealed her innermost thoughts and feelings with wit and wisdom on such varied subjects as anger, jealousy, sex, superstition, love, marriage, competition, fear, and aging. She sprinkles these short pieces with anecdotes about her colleagues and friends—Bea Arthur, Carol Burnett, Carol Channing, Fred Astaire, Rue McClanahan, Mary Tyler Moore, Grant Tinker, Connie Chung, Mel Brooks, Burt Reynolds, and, of course, her late husband, Allen Ludden. "Having been a dedicated closet writer, I have been jotting down thoughts and ideas for as along as I can remember. So that is the book I assumed I would be working on—random observations—nothing personal. What I discovered was there is no way to report about on your feelings without getting personal," says White. "As a result, there's a lot about the people who have been closest to me . . . Allen Ludden, my parents, the people I work with, my friends . . . and superfriends. You will hear about what makes me laugh . . . and what makes me cry . . . what I hate . . . what I love."

Born on 17 January 1922 in Oak Park, Illinois, Betty White moved with her parents to Los Angeles when she was two years old. After graduating from Beverly Hills High School and performing with the Bliss-Hayden Little Theatre Group, she appeared on several radio series: "Blondie," "The Great Gildersleeve," and "This is Your FBI." By the early fifties she had become the host of an L.A. television talk show. White formed a production company with producer Don Fedderson and writer George Tibbles; they produced a daytime talk-variety show and two situation comedies, including "Life With Elizabeth," which won her an Emmy in 1952. Since then she has copped more Emmy awards for "The Mary Tyler Moore Show" (as Sue Anne Nivins), one for "Just Men" as the Best Daytime Game Show Host, and for her current role (Rose) on "The Golden Girls." She pops up often on numerous game shows and TV interview programs. White has been parade hostess for the Pasadena Tournament of Roses Parade on network television for 20 years and the Macy's Thanksgiving Day Parade for 10 years. In 1976 she was awarded the Pacific Pioneers in Broadcasting "Golden Ike" for outstanding achievements in television, and in 1977 the Southern California chapter of American Women's Genii award for her extensive contributions to all facets of the industry. White's love for animals led her to create "The Pet Set" TV series and the daily radio show "Betty White on Animals." She has hosted the Patsy Awards for performing animals and their trainers since 1971. Her first book *Betty White's Pet Love* is now out in paperback. In 1987, she was given the AVMA Humane Award for her continual caring work with animals.

Vanna White

"Her first name was 'Vanya' or 'Savannah' or something like that. I mean, who ever heard of a 'Vanna'? And she was nervous; I mean nervous. Her upper lip quivered and her tiny voice trembled. She was gorgeous and seemed very sweet, but who would hire a bundle of nerves with a name no one could even remember? Merv Griffin, that's who. The rest, as someone (probably Merv) once said, is history." So writes Pat Sajak in the foreword of the letter flipper's 1987 autobiography *Vanna Speaks*. She tells her story in a frank, comfortable style, supporting the fact that there's more to her than meets the eye. She answers the ultimate question at the start: "Do I really speak? Sure. After all, I couldn't fill very many pages with just 'hi's and 'bye-bye's, could I?"

In her own words: "It was my father's twenty-eighth birthday—and Momma was just barely twenty-one—when I was born on Monday, 18 February 1957, at 2:35 P.M. There was no maternity hospital along the Grand Stand, the sixty-mile strip of beach that includes North Myrtle Beach, so I was born at the Conway Hospital, in Conway, South Carolina, about a half hour's drive away.... They named me Vanna Marie Rosich. The 'Marie' was after my mother's middle name, and 'Vanna' was after my grandmother's godchild... Momma added the second *n* just to make it different." Her mother and father split up before her first birthday; Vanna's father moved to New York, while her mother moved to Miami. In the interim, the baby was raised by her grandparents. Later that year, Vanna's Mom met her new "daddy", Herbert Stackley White, Jr., to whom she credits her upbringing and full name today, Vanna White. She attended school, but her favorite subject was studying members of the opposite sex. "I was absolutely boy crazy.... I was shy around boys, but that didn't stop me from having 'boyfriends' from the first grade on." Coincidentally, her other favorite subject was spelling; she was an excellent speller. "I had a photographic memory, so I didn't have to study that hard to get good grades." She credits her parents, mostly her mother, in instilling important values in her and younger brother, Chip. "Most important, they always encouraged us to go after dreams, no matter how impossible they seemed."

Vanna's teen-age years were filled with rewarding fun; she was a finalist in the Sun Fun Festival bubble gum-blowing contest. After graduating from high school, she went on to the Atlanta School of Fashion and Design, although she felt "I could have learned much of this either on my own or at a finishing school." Instead of intense study, she fell back to her favorite pastime—boys. She went out at night to clubs and eventually met a man, Gordy Watson, who was about fifteen years older. It was a relationship which lasted for over four years, while she pursued agent hunting. She signed with Atlanta Models and Talent, Inc., where the aspiring model received various assignments—a part in an industrial film, local commercials, print and catalog work, etc. By 1978, she was not just a local girl and was hired in other locales. Vanna entered the Miss Georgia Universe Beauty Pageant and came in fourth runner-up. In 1980, she moved to Los Angeles with a friend, to try and make it in Hollywood. Having the late actor Christopher George as a family acquaintance helped Vanna stay on steady ground. George's wife, Lynda Day, gave her a list of reputable agents, until she signed with a known commercial agent. She received small parts in the films *Looker, Graduation Day* and *The Burning*. Later, she landed a job on the game show "Pot of Gold." Around that same time period, she fell in love with actor/Chippendale dancer John Gibson ("The Young and the Restless"). In 1982, she discovered that Susan Stafford, the hostess of "Wheel of Fortune," was leaving the show and, with her gameshow background, she auditioned. TV land knows the rest..

Vanna White remains single; her main love, John Gibson, died in a plane crash in 1986. She philosophizes that things happen sometimes faster than one can absorb them, "but you always have to just keep going and never lose sight of who you are or your dreams."

Margaret Whiting

She grew up with such legendary songwriting giants as the Gershwins, Jerome Kern, Jule Styne and Frank Loesser dropping in for dinner; (after all, her father, Richard Whiting,—"Ain't We Got Fun," "Sleepy Time Gal," "Beyond the Blue Horizon," etc.,—was no slouch in the songwriting department, and these were his peers.) No coincidence then, this thrush was meant to warble—and warble she has, most recently in *4 Girls 4* (an early 80s tour with Rosemary Clooney, Rose Marie, and Helen O'Connell) and *Maggie and Friends*. Elected to honorary membership in the Songwriters' Hall of Fame, she is a veteran album artist, who has appeared with the St. Louis Symphony, and made her off-Broadway theatrical debut in *Taking My Turn* in New York in 1983 during a brief interlude between club dates.

Born 22 July 1924, she grew up in Hollywood during the golden age of the movie musical. Tutored by her father in the rich legacy of American popular music, she began singing professionally at age 16, making her first record for Capitol (headed by her mentor Johnny Mercer) singing material written by her father ("My Ideal" sold over a million copies). By the fifties she had a string of over a dozen million-selling records (including "It Might As Well Be Spring," "Far Away Places," etc.,) and was headlining in major nightclubs. She then became a twice-a-week regular on "The Jack Smith Show" and resident vocalist on "The Bob Hope Show." Her theatrical career started in a touring company of *Girl Crazy* which propelled her to starring roles in rep productions of *Wildcat, Mr. President, I Married An Angel, Call Me Madam, Pal Joey* and *Plain and Fancy*. Her "Mama Rose" role in *Gypsy* caused Gypsy Rose Lee to salute her as the best actress ever to play the part. She has one daughter, Deborah by second husband Lou Busch (first husband was Hubbell Robinson, third husband was John Moore; all ended in divorce) and resides in New York City. Her autobiography, *It Might As Well Be Spring*, was released in 1987. Asked once if she had ever received a bad review, she paused and said, "No, I guess not."

Marylou and Cornelius Vanderbilt Whitney

Although he's made millions from investments, he says the best one he ever made was the two-dollar marriage license he bought so he could marry the former Marie Louise Hosford on 24 January 1958 in Scottsdale, Arizona. "It was God's will that made me fall in love with her. I never thought I could fall in love with a woman who could cook.... Mary (as he calls her) is the best cook in the country," he insists. According to Marylou, "we sparked each other up. We were very, very low at that time. I was very discouraged, working, struggling along in the middle of a divorce with four children. I needed to be perked up, but I had no time for men and dates."

Sonny Whitney had been married three times before and was already the father of four children. Combined with Marylou's flock, this particular strain of Whitneys is in a good deal less danger of running out of heirs than it is of them running out of anything to inherit. Sonny has, however, been quite good about replenishing the reported $194 million he inherited as the principal beneficiary of his father Harry Payne Whitney's estate. Born 20 February 1899 in Roslyn, Long Island, Sonny is also the son of the famous art patron and sculptress Gertrude Vanderbilt Whitney who waged a successful custody battled for her brother Reginald's little daughter Gloria. One of the "democratic" Vanderbilts, Cornelius Vanderbilt Whitney felt impelled as a youth to go his parents one better. A bid for Congress on the Democratic ticket having failed, he became the founder of Pan American Airways, and later Marineland in Florida. For countless society fans his escapades with international playgirls and starlets were breathlessly chronicled from Hollywood to Broadway. His presence was felt in the former, where he co-produced *Gone with the Wind* and was instrumental in making *A Star is Born* and *Rebecca*.

In the wake of Pearl Harbor, Sonny unloaded his share of Pan Am to join the Army Air Corps, as he had during World War I. Returning at war's end a much decorated colonel, he was appointed by President Truman First Assistant Secretary of the newly independent U.S. Air Force and was subsequently named Undersecretary of Commerce. A graduate of Groton and Yale (where he was not tapped for a Senior Socity because of unseemly publicity attached to his growing reputation as a playboy), he was sued for breach of promise by a former Ziegfeld Follies dancer who lost not only the suit but was forced to pay court costs of $131. His marriage to Marylou marked a settling down time. It did, however, cause a North Shore scandal, since his divorce from the former Eleanor Searle had not been recognized by the State of New York. The Whitney name "is magic," says Marylou, "and I do feel an obligation to the name and the family." As a result, she has developed a wide variety of projects that bear the Whitney name to revitalize places like Saratoga and an international list of the couple's other concerns.

As is often reported in the gossip columns, the peregrinating Whitneys have seven residences around the globe (reportedly because Confucius said man should have a house for every day of the week). There's the Fifth Avenue "flat" in Manhattan; a home in Lake Placid; Marineland in Florida; Whitney Park's 100,000 acres in the Adirondacks; Majorca—and, reflecting a lifelong interest in horseracing, homesteads in Saratoga and Lexington, Kentucky. (In 1985, in what Sonny describes as "the most moving event of my life," he was given the coveted Eclipse Award as "the person who has done the most for thoroughbred horseracing in this century.") Says Marylou: "The marvelous thing about moving from house to house, although I sometimes do forget where my clothes are, is that I never get into squabbles or arguments with people. People say, 'How could I have so-and-so and so-and-so together at a dinner party?' I say, 'Well six months ago they were friends. . . . ' I don't stay in one place long enough to know the funny things that go on." In 1975 Marylou published *Cornelius Vanderbilt Whitney's Dollhouse*. Sonny quietly published his autobiography, *High Peaks*, in 1977.

Tom Wicker

"Don't be afraid to be wrong," says longtime *New York Times* columnist about his philosophy of taking editorial stands. He has become best known to the general public for his role as liaison between inmates and state officials during the 1971 Attica prisoner takeover, what *Wall Street Journal* writer Lark Starr called "a classic American tragedy where institutions and their trappings took priority over human lives." The tragedy, of course, was that neither Wicker (summoned from Washington by the prisoners becasue of his literary fairness to the oppressed) nor attorney William Kunstler, Black Panther Bobby Seale, or the New York prisons commissioner could prevent Governor Nelson Rockefeller's dispatch of state troopers to the scene—and its bloody outcome. In 1980, a TV movie was based on Wicker's searching 1975 book, *A Time to Die*, about the incident, in which 39 people were killed, most in the blaze of gunfire as troopers retook the prison yard.

Born 18 June 1926, Wicker's first train trip to the nation's capital, from his birthplace of Hamlet, N.C., was free, since his dad worked for the railroad. "In the summer when I was nine years old my parents gathered up what cash the Depression had left them and took my sister and me to Washington. I never got over it." Thus began Wicker's long love affair with the City of Monuments. He would work his way back there by way of a journalism degree from the University of North Carolina and stints on such papers as the *Sandhill Citizen* (Aberdeen, S.C.), the Winston-Salem *Journal*, and the Nashville *Tennessean*. The tall Southerner, a Harvard Nieman Fellow, joined up with the *Times* D.C. bureau in 1960 and was taken under the wing of veteran James Restong. Wrote *Times* chronicler Gay Talese, "Wicker was the sort of man, Reston believed, who could be driving down a country road during a political campaign, could jump over a fence and learn what a farmer was really thinking, and could then go back to town, change into a tuxedo, and be equally at home at an embassy party." At 34 he succeeded Reston as D.C. bureau chief and was an associate editor from 1968 to 1985 (when the *Times* changed its policy, not its high opinion of Wicker). Finding lots not to like in the halls of Congress, in Foggy Bottom, the Pentagon and thereabouts, he illuminated federal goings-on and also penned at least a half dozen novels and nonfiction books, either under a penname or his own moniker. Having moved to New York, where he writes his twice-weekly "In the Nation" column, he lives in a Manhattan brownstone with his second wife, Pamela Hill, top-notch TV documentary producer and an ABC News vice president. Some journalistic colleagues have recently questioned Wicker's zeal. "He's a classic populist writer," says Robert Healy, "but to be a populist you've got to know what the hell's going on with the populace." But the *Boston Globe's* Thomas Winship feels that "Tom is getting livelier . . . he began to do some legwork and got better." His latest books include *Nixon Bio* (1987) and *One of Us: The Age of Richard Nixon* (1990).

Mats Wilander

He's been an anomaly in the formerly genteel—but recently rude and crude—sport of men's tennis. His arrestingly different sense of good sportsmanship has led him actually to ask umpires to replay points on behalf of the other guy. On the way to winning the French Open at age 17, the youngest ever to win a Grand Slam tournament, he demonstrated just such an appreciation of fairness; coupled with his unflappable demeanor, he prompted the French sports newspaper, *L'Equipe*, to say, "What a joy to discover an angel under that impenetrable armor!" In 1985 and 1988, he had his second and third French Open victories; he also won Australian Open championships in 1983, 1984 and 1988.

Mats Wilander (VEE-lan-der) from the southern Swedish, wood-and-furniture town of Vaxjo (born 22 August 1964), somewhat reticently accepted the enormously burdensome mantle of his country's previous tennis great, Bjorn Borg. The comparisons were inevitable and many; the two are blond and handsome and started beating world-class champs at the same age. In fact, however, while Borg was on his way to becoming a national hero, young Mats was already hard at work refining the aspects of a future No. 1 seed's game. "I start with two-handed backhand even before Bjorn was getting famous," said the eight-years-younger upstart. That backhand would make *him* famous in 1982 as he beat an unbelievalbe line up in Paris: Vitas Gerulaitis, Jose-Luis Clerc, Guillermo Vilas, and finally Ivan Lendl for the French victory, only a year after having won the French Juniors title. Despite his youth, he's all business, according to an opponents' coach. "Wilander's mind is a weapon," he said. "Let's put it this way: This is an *old* kid."

The handsome athlete married model Sonia Mulholland in South Africa in 1987. When he's not playing tennis, he likes strumming his guitar or fencing.

Billy Wilder

"As far as I'm concerned, this ballgame is not over," vowed Billy Wilder when he was honored in 1982 by the Film Society of Lincoln Center for his work, spanning half a century. "There are still a few hits left in me." The renowned filmmaker has received six writing and/or directing Oscars (and twenty Oscar nominations) since coming to Hollywood from Europe in the 1930s. Wilder is the first filmmaker ever to win three Academy Awards in one year (Best Director, Best Story and Screenplay and Best Picture for *The Apartment* in 1960). His other three Oscars were for direction and screenplay (with Charles Brackett) for *The Lost Weekend* (1945) and for story and screenplay (with Brackett and D.H. Marshman) of *Sunset Boulevard* (1950). The nominations were for *Double Indemnity* and *Some Like It Hot* (writing and directing), *A Foreign Affair* and *The Big Carnival* (writing), and *Stalag 17*, *Sabrina*, and *Witness for the Prosecution* (directing). In 1988 he was the proud recipient of the Irving G. Thalberg Memorial Award at the sixtieth Annual Academy Awards.

Billy Wilder was born Samuel Wilder on 22 June 1906 in the town of Sucha in Galicia, a section of Poland that was then part of the Austro-Hungarian Empire. His father ran a chain of railway cafes, imported watches, and operated a trout hatchery. His mother had spent several years in the U.S. in her youth (she died in Auschwitz during World War II) and nicknamed her younger son Billy because of her fascination with the legendary American hero Buffalo Bill. In 1926 Wilder's interests led him to a publicity job with the American bandleader Paul Whiteman in Berlin, where he also worked on newspapers and "ghosted" scenarios for silent films. In 1929 he collaborated with Fred Zinnemann and others in making *People on Sunday*. In 1933, he fled to Paris and directed his first film, *Bad Seed*, a juvenile crime thriller starring Danielle Darrieux. Summoned to Hollywood in 1934, he eventually teamed up with Brackett, and helped write such hits as *Ninotchka*, *Hold Back the Dawn*, and *Ball of Fire* (all of which earned Oscar nominations). His first American directorial assignment was *The Major and the Minor* (1942).

In 1936 Wilder married Judith Coppicus Iribe (divorced, 1947, one daughter). He married his second wife, starlet and singer Audrey Young, in 1949. He lives in an elegant Hollywood apartment filled with part of his modern art collection, one of the largest in private hands in the world. The master storyteller is often quoted about the liveliness of his films: "I sleep an awful lot in movie houses and I try to stop others from doing it"; on considering working for TV: "I wouldn't drink the water in television"; on meeting his second wife who lived in East Beverly Hills: "I'd worship the ground you walked on, if you lived in a better neighborhood."

Gene Wilder

His unique whimsy is the marriage of his classical acting training and his love of motion pictures, bringing to the screen a series of madcap period spoofs that filmgoers tended either to delight in or find totally inane, depending on their comedic tastes. Although fond of elaborate costumes and settings, Wilder films are distinguished more for their devotion to romance and slapstick than to authenticity.

Born 11 June 1934 or 1935 in Milwaukee, Wis., Jerome Silberman, a bug-eyed and curly-topped kid, found that being funny was the best medicine for his semi-invalid mother. After studying at the Old Vic Theater School in Bristol, England, and the Lee Strasberg Studio in New York, he made his screen debut with a small but memorable role as a nervous undertaker in the 1967 winner, *Bonnie and Clyde*. Meanwhile, Mel Brooks was preparing to make *The Producers* and created a part for Wilder, this time as a nervous accountant. A series of genre spoofs followed, beginning with *Start the Revolution without Me* in 1970, a farce on the twins-switched-at-birth theme, and marking for Wilder a break from character roles into romantic comedy leads. Wilder parodied Hollywood westerns in Brooks' *Blazing Saddles* (a 1974 loosely plotted film of questionable taste) and horror films in Brooks' *Young Frankenstein* that same year. Detective movies got the Wilder treatment in the 1975 *The Adventure of Sherlock Holmes' Smarter Brother*, which he wrote and directed. In 1977, he paid tribute to Charlie Chaplin in *The World's Greatest Lover*, adding producer to his credits. He teamed with Richard Pryor in 1980 for the hit movie *Stir Crazy* and with Gilda Radner (whom he married in 1984) for *Hanky Panky* in 1982; in 1986 the couple costarred in *Haunted Honeymoon*. His recent movies include *The Man with One Red Shoe* and *See No Evil, Hear No Evil*, for which he also cowrote the screenplay. A private person who avoids interviews like the plague, Wilder is mum about his two failed marriages, first to playwright Mary Mercier and then to Mary Joan Schutz. His third wife, Gilda Radner, died in 1989 after a long struggle with cancer.

George F. Will

"George is unquestionably the biggest man since Lippmann, mainly because of his televison omnipresence. The column [twice weekly in more than 400 papers] is fine, the *Newsweek* is fine, but, boy, what makes him a big deal is that he's on the bloody tube all the time," grumbled fellow columnist Robert Novak in a 1984 *Vanity Fair* survey of "The Op-Ed Set." Those readers intellectually disinclined to read George Will's graceful, erudite, Pulitzer Prize-winning (1977) philosophical essays (frequently larded with references to T.S. Eliot, Dante *et al*) can catch the scrubbed, bespectacled, and intimidating conservative thinker on the ABC televison network—either dispensing commentary on the regular evening news, acting as a panelist on Sunday's "This Week with David Brinkley" or offering the view from the right on the frequently contentious "Nightline." That Will has reached the pinnacle of his profession little more than a decade after departing the halls of academe and a Senate staffer's quarters, has made him, according to Novak, "very, very unpopular in the press corps. In the first place, he's not a reporter. George is a superb writer, but he didn't earn his way up, which is very important to people in my business." His colleagues' opinions notwithstanding. Will was voted in a 1983 poll by the Washington *Journalism Review* the journalist most admired by senators, congressman and their staffs. Of his reputed clout, he insists, "On a list of one hundred things that determine a congressman's behavior, I'd bet that the most influential columnist comes in about eighty-third, right below sunspots."

The son of educators, George Frederick Will, born in 1941 in Chicago, was more interested in National League baseball than cerebral matters during his first three years at Trinity College in Hartford, Conn. (He has facetiously attributed his conservatism, with it accompanying bleak view of mankind, to the persistent failures of his beloved Chicago Cubs.) As cochairman of Trinity Student for Kennedy in 1960, he left Hartford a liberal, but at Oxford, where he continued his studies, he was gradually drawn to free-market economic principles. At Princeton, where he received a Ph.D. in political science in 1964, he moved away from strict laissez-faire conservatism towards a philosophy that held that political institutions have a crucial function because the free play of market forces does not necessarily insure justice. To William F. Buckley, Jr., this is typical of "the crotchet or two he cultivates to separate himself from the more identified conservatives in America." To Neil Grauer, writing in *Wits & Sages*, it reflects Will's "rare talent to feel the insecurity, fear and distress of others." From 1964 to 1970, he taught political science, then moved to Washington, which he found "terrific" because "bad times are always fun." After the senator (Gordon Allott of Colorado) whose staff he joined was defeated for re-election, Will became Washington editor of Buckley's *National Review* and began writing columns for the *Washington Post*, adding *Newsweek* to his outlets in 1976. Books include *Statecraft as Soulcraft* (a compilation of lectures delivered in

1981) and two volumes of his collected columns, *The Pursuit of Happiness and Other Sobering Thoughts* (1978) and *The Pursuit of Virtue and Other Tory Notions* (1982). His latest books are *The Morning After* (1987) and *The New Season: A Spectator's Guide to the 1988 Elections* (1987). Married since 1947 to Madeleine C. Marion (two sons; one daughter, moderately retarded, about whom he's written movingly), Will once said, "I do not produce grade-B columns. I write in longhand, and I work until I get it right. It was Auden, I think, who said a poem is never finished, it's abandoned. But I don't abandon columns. I finish them."

Billy Dee Williams

Once billed as the "black Clark Gable," he nevertheless insists he is part of an innovative force making producers project black actors in other than stereotypical roles. While saying he tires of talking about race ("It totally, absolutely bores me"), or himself, Billy Dee Williams perpetuates his sex idol status by conceding he never tires of female fan adulation. His interviews are sometimes spiced by remarks that "nothing else in the world competes with making love" for relaxation or self-expression and that he's even better in bed than his fans assume.

Williams and his twin sister, Loretta, were born in Harlem, New York City, on 6 April 1937. His father worked three jobs and his mother operated an elevator at a Broadway theatre. His artistic avocation was given early impetus by her (a former opera student) and his maternal grandmother who encouraged the twins in cultural pursuits. Both became adept at drawing and Bill studied fashion illustration at New York's School of Fine Arts after high school. His acting career having started as a walk-on at age seven, Billy dabbled at the craft in high school, and later while in art school, in bit parts on CBS network TV shows. He studied "method" acting from Sidney Poitier and Paul Mann, and in 1959 co-starred with Paul Muni in *The Last Angry Man*. After a well-received Broadway performance in *A Taste of Honey*, Williams couldn't land another decent part until 1963, and plummeted to emotional depths from which a former prostitute who taught him Eastern philosophy eventually helped him to emerge. His big break came with his 1971 Emmy-nominated portrayal of football star Gayle Sayers in "Brian's Song." A year later, Motown chief Berry Gordy inked him to a seven-year contract, and a major role in "Lady Sings the Blues" opposite Diana Ross. His performance as the caddish but high voltage lady killer brought in 8,000 letters a week from adoring female fans. "A star is what everybody wants to be, even presidents," he said at the time. He co-starred in a TV series, "Double Dare," in 1985.

But from among all his roles (Martin Luther King, Jr.; composer Scott Joplin), Williams says the turning point of his career came in 1980 with his playing a space pirate in sequels to the wildly-successful *Star Wars*. The part, like he, embodied a "universal person." His latest movies include *Deadly Illusion* (1987) and *Batman* (1989). He also appeared on Broadway, replacing James Earl Jones, in *Fences* (1988).

The six-footer with the sly smile and wavy curls says he looks forward to colorless, romantic roles. Thrice-married, but a serious family man, he and Japanese-American wife, Teruko, live in Beverly Hills with her daughter Miyako, his son Corey Dee, and their daughter Hanako. A quiet man offscreen, he says his pursuit of faith led him from Buddhism to Jung. "The only way to education is to find masters in life. I feel surrounded by good, positive spirits in my private, silent moments."

John Williams

A master of a wide range of musical styles as a composer and conductor, he seemed the ideal candidate to fill the shoes of the late Arthur Fiedler on the podium of the commercially successful Boston Pops Orchestra. But in 1984, after five years of service, John Williams resigned from his position as conductor of the Pops, citing "artistic and creative differences with the orchestra." Two months after that announcement Williams withdrew his resignation and worked to establish the rapport that now exists between the conductor and his orchestra. "My sole motive is musical—to keep the continuity of a great orchestra having a great tradition, and vitalize it as much as I can. I would frankly do it for nothing." His recent compostions include the instrumental "Olympic Fanfare and Theme" and the film scores for *The Witches of Eastwick* (1987), *Empire of the Sun* (1987) and *The Accidental Tourist* (1988). He is also the composer of NBC's long-playing "Today" and "Nightly News" themes.

Born 8 February 1932 in New York City to a musical family—his father, Johnny Williams, was one of the original members of the Raymond Scott Quintet—Williams mastered piano, trombone and trumpet while still in high school. Drafted in 1952, he conducted and arranged for service bands and upon his discharge financed his Juilliard education by performing in nightclubs. His lucrative career as a composer of film scores began with the 1960 movie *Because They're Young*. During the next twenty-five years, he penned scores for such blockbusters as 1977's *Close Encounters of the Third Kind* (which won him a Grammy), *Superman* and *Raiders of the Lost Ark*. He is also a four-time Oscar winner for his arrangement in 1972 of *Fiddler on the Roof*, his haunting accompaniment for *Jaws* in 1975, his 1977 *Star Wars* music and the magical score for *E.T.* in 1982. His fifty other film-score credits include the 1979 *Dracula*, the *Star Wars* sequel *The Empire Strikes Back* in 1980, and the 1970s disaster flicks *Earthquake*, *The Towering Inferno*, and *The Poseidon Adventure*. For television, he contributed the music for "Gilligan's Island" and "Playhouse 90," among other programs. Before coming to the Pops in 1980, he conducted light classical music with symphonies across the country.

Widowed after his first wife, Barbara, died in 1974, Williams married Samantha Winslow, a photographer, in 1980. He has three children from his first marriage.

Robin Williams

Brilliantly bubbling and babbling, television/club/screen pixie personality (and ad-libber par excellence), Robin Williams made his professional stage debut in the eagerly awaited Mike Nichols's production of Samuel Beckett't *Waiting for Godot* in 1988. The powerhouse cast also included Bill Irwin and Steve Martin. Taking his career another notch higher, his latest film, *Dead Poet's Society* (1989), opened to critical acclaim. Not bad for the comedian who had just received an Academy Award nomination for Best Actor (*Good Morning, Vietnam*).

Born in Chicago on 21 July 1952, to an upper-middle-class family, Robin Williams's lovable lunacy and high school antics got him voted "Most Humorous" and "Least Likely to Succeed" by his peers. He didn't succeed initially in impressing a producer who saw his act in a Los Angeles comedy club, but his continued clowning on comedy shows led him to an audition for the role of the famous Orkean in "Mork and Mindy" (1978). Asked to sit like an alien, Williams immediately turned on his head, and got the part. His Chaplinesque antics and ad-libbingwas greatly responsible for the show being a hit. It was a "triumph of Mork over medium", quipped one critic. His other television appearances have included: "Laugh In" (the revival), "Happy Days", "Saturday Night Live," and "Seize the Day", Mr. Williams's television dramatic debut. The Williams television comedy specials include: "Robin Williams Live at the Met," "Comic Relief" (Ace Award), "Carol, Carl, Whoopi and Robin" (Emmy Award), and "A Royal Gala," (Emmy Award). His film appearances include: *Popeye*, *The World According to Garp*, and *Moscow on the Hudson*.

Although he did not win the Academy Award, he won the Golden Globe Award for his leading role in *Good Morning, Vietnam*. Upcoming films are *Cadillac Man* (1989), *The Adventures of Baron Munchausen* (1989) and *Awakenings* (1990). Williams's best-selling recordings: *Reality . . . What A Concept* (Grammy Award), *Throbbing Python of Love* (Grammy nomination) and *Robin Williams: An Evening at the Met* (Grammy Award).

Williams speaks candidly about the lure of life in the fast lane, "Cocaine is God's way of saying you're making too much money," and unabashedly advocates fits of craziness. "You're only given a little spark of madness," he has said. "You mustn't lose that madness." Williams married former dancer Valerie Velardi in 1978; they divorced ten years later (one child, Zachary Williams). He married Marsha Garces on 30 April 1989; they have a child together, Zelda (born 31 July 1989).

Treat Williams

This handsome, hairy-browed thespian with the Welch monicker stays in demand (and in roles) both on Broadway and in Hollywood. A descendant of a singer of the Declaration of Independence, Richard Treat Williams was born in 1951 in affluent Rowayton, Conn., and discovered by Broadway-connected friends of the family while in a college play. After being taken under the famous wing of the William Morris agency in 1973, within a week Williams was an understudy of John Travolta in the New York version of *Grease*. Later, he didn't use much grease and underwent a painful hair weave to play an unkempt pied piper of flower children in the film *Hair*. "I've had a taste of celebrity," Williams said after the experience. "And it left a bad taste. I got a lot of invitations (to star-studded galas) after *Hair*, but after the film flopped, the invitations stopped." After another celluloid flop he temporarily changed careers and flew planes for a living. "I felt so out of control I wasn't working with people I wanted to work with. I was very frustrated. Eventually the director Sidney Lumet called to ask him to play the lead in the true story of a New York City cop, Detective Robert Leuci, who helped the government nab 52 corrupt fellow narcotics detectives. Williams learned his role—how to treat junkies, lawyers and judges the way cops actually treat them—by spending a month hanging around a New York precinct, going on drug busts, and living with the cop who inspired his 1981 hit movie, *Prince of the City*. Since then, Williams, who sings tenor, has continued to appear in three genres: scampering around live onstage (once in the musical *Pirates of Penzance*), on TV (as Jack Dempsey in a filmed bio of the ring legend and Stanley Kowalski in *A Streetcar Named Desire*), and of course in movies (his latest: *Sweet Lies, Dead Heat, Heartbreak Hotel;* currently filming opposite Jill Clayburg in *Beyond the Ocean*). What's left for Treat to try? "I always felt it was limiting to do what you could do easily. I'm beginning to want to do some light comedy and a little more normal people. . . . I'm not avoiding playing classical leading men anymore."

Vanessa Williams

It was just one of those things. Soon after she was crowned Miss America 1984, she received a congratulatory phone call from President Reagan, who told her, "Your selection is not only a wonderful thing for you, it's a wonderful thing for our nation." On 14 September 1983 she won the swimsuit competition at the Miss America Pageant in Atlantic City, New Jersey. Two nights later she was first in the talent trials, singing the "Happy Days Are Here Again" number that had helped her become Miss New York State in 1983. In the heat of the pageant some compared her singing to Streisand's. She compared herself to Lena Horne. "I'm a stylistic singer," she explained. Then that next night, that all-important next night, she was crowned Miss America. The first *black* Miss America in the pageant's 62-year history. She received a $25,000 scholarship and some $100,000 in personal appearances. She dined at the White House. She fed George Burns a piece of birthday cake. She appeared with the Guy Lombardo band and Lionel Hampton at the United Nations. She made a cameo appearance on "The Love Boat." There she was, "Miss America," when *Penthouse* magazine publisher Bob Guccione printed nude photographs of her which *Playboy* had refused. She tried to defend herself, and everyone wanted to believe her. She said she was just a young and naive kid when she allowed herself to be photographed nude. She said she never signed the photo release form Guccione claimed to have had authenticated before he ran the nasty pics. Copies of the flesh mag sold like lottery tickets. Most expected a demure series of the dear one, perhaps a bit of T and a hint of A. But the photos were decidedly adult, and steamily Sapphic. On 23 July 1984 Vanessa Williams resigned as Miss America. "I am not a slut and I am not a lesbian," she said. Nevertheless she disappeared from the cereal boxes; the mayor to Talladega, Alabama, demanded she return the key to that fair city; she was attended to by round-the-clock shrinks, while teenagers in her hometown of Millwood, N.Y., yelled dirty words as they cruised by her parents' simple home.

For Vanessa Williams (born 18 March 1963) 1984 was not a year fit to treasure in a little gold box. However, as time became a healing factor, Vanessa started to make a comeback in 1986 by appearing the film *Pickup Artist*. Her big move came in 1988 when she released her record album *The Right Stuff*, which cemented the ex-Miss America's career as a performer. In 1987, she married her manager, Ramon Harvey, and the happy couple have two children: Melanie Lynne (born 30 June 1987) and Jillian Kristin (19 June 1989).

Nicol Williamson

As multifaceted a Scotsman as Macbeth, he's been described as "intimidating, temperamental, bristling, and uninhibited," motivated to be chronically outspoken, he says, from "a belief in what your're doing." Because of his sinister smile and ability to create sympathetic villains, Nicol Williamson is often cast as the heavy, but feels light comedy is really his strong suit. With a reputation as an explosive actor, he's also noted for a toro-like temperament, once sloshing a glass of beer at producer David Merrick and then rapping him in the face during an out-of-town tryout of John Osborne's *Inadmissible Evidence* in 1965. "I'm a person violence just happens to," he once explained. (He's been known to chastise audiences for "rudeness," and stop a performance until latecomers were seated.) Williamson attempts to live life to its utmost, spending little time sleeping or eating and choosing only the most demanding parts because he is afraid "to waste six months of my life."

Born in Hamilton, Scotland, 14 September 1938, Nicol left home against his father's wishes, to begin his acting career in 1960 with the Dundee Repertory Theatre. He soon made a name for himself as a "highly accomplished and versatile actor" at the Royal Court Theatre and with the Royal Shakespeare Company in such productions as *A Midsummer Night's Dream*, *The Lower Depths*, *The Ginger Man*, and *Waiting for Godot*. But it was not until the role of Bill Maitland in *Inadmissible Evidence* in 1964 that he won fame. London and New York critics were unanimus in weighing his performance as a theatrical event that well deserved the best actor awards on both sides of the Atlantic. His controversial production of *Hamlet*, directed by Tony Richardson (filmed, 1969), was called "the most exciting, intelligent, and straightforward *Hamlet* for a very long time." Williamson explained that, "All I wanted was a *Hamlet* who was alive, who was real." He's since done *Plaza Suite* (1969) for New York theatregoers, and performed a rousing, fiery interpretation of the title role in *Macbeth* (which he directed for the stage and presented on television for the PBS series, "The Shakespeare Plays"). All the classical acting has prompted Williamson to comment, "When you've played *Hamlet*, *Macbeth*, and *Coriolanus* by your mid-thirties, you're in danger of becoming a pillar of the English theatre." Not one to be pigeonholed, he's appeared in such films as *The Seven Per Cent Solution* (1975); *The Cheap Detective* (1978); *The Goodbye Girl* (1977); *Robin and Marion* (1977); *Venom* (1980); and *I'm Dancing as Fast as I Can* (1981). His latest films are: *Black Widow* (1986), *Apt Pupil* (1987), and *Berlin Blues* (1987). In a slightly different move, he performed in a one-man show *Nicol Williamson: An Evening With A Man And His Band* at the Hollywood Playhouse in California in August 1986. The stage and screen equally fascinate Williamson, and he attributes his success as an actor in both mediums to his perceptiveness and a gift for communication. "I can understand people's pain, passion, fear, hurt, mirth, and I can mirror it and set it up for them to look at."

Once married to American actress Jill Townsend, Williamson enjoys quoting a favorite maxim: "Life isn't all you want, but it's all you got, so stick a geranium in your hat and be happy."

Bruce Willis

He has risen from the depths of New York City's Hell's Kitchen to the glitz and glamour of star studded Hollywood, California. Like most actors, he started out bartending. In the evening, he worked at the New York nightclub, Kamikaze, while during the day he made commercials for Levi's 501 jeans.

Walter Bruce Willis was born on 19 March 1955 in Germany. When he was only two years old, his family moved to the U.S. to New Jersey, where Bruce attended high school. After graduating, he worked briefly at a DuPont plant in a nearby town. His first entertainment work was playing the harmonica with a band called Loose Goose. Bruce attended Montclair State University where he studied acting, and made his first stage appearance in *Cat on a Hot Tin Roof*. Soon after he made his New York stage debut in the off-Broadway production of *Heaven and Earth*, followed by the lead role in *Fool For Love* (1984). Later that year Bruce decided to take a trip to Los Angeles to watch the Olympics. While he was there, he auditioned for the role of a private eye David Addison in the television series "Moonlighting," (1984-1987) which he ultimately landed. Other television credits include appearances in the series "Hart to Hart," and "Miami Vice." In 1986 he made his movie debut in the comedy *Blind Date*. Films that followed include *Sunset* (1987), *Die Hard* (1988) and *In Country* (1989). In addition to acting, Bruce has a knack for singing. He has recorded two albums, *The Return of Bruno* (1987), and *If It Don't Kill You, It Just Makes You Stronger* (1989).

Bruce and actress Demi Moore were married in Las Vegas on 21 November 1987, and have one son—Rumer Glenn, who was born on 16 August 1988. Although the successful, happy family resides in Hollywood, Bruce still has the lease to the apartment in Hell's Kitchen.

Julie Wilson

Julie Wilson's return to the New York supper club scene in 1984 after eight years' absence marked a return as well of the kind of glamour and excitement that once routinely characterized New York nightlife. In her skin tight beaded gowns, her signature gardenia tucked beguilingly into her slicked-back chignon (the more to call attention to an exquisitely chiseled profile), Julie "has established herself as the most elegant and fiercely expressive singer-actress on New York's cabaret circuit ... [displaying] a kill, unmatched by her peers, at lending classic theatre songs an intense psychological immediacy that is independent of the material's original context," according to Stephen Holden in the *New York Times*. Whether performing in the sleek Cafe Carlyle on the East Side or the West Side's fable Algonquin Oak Room (of Round Table fame), Julie insists this time around there'll be no premature retirement. "I'm going to die working," she promises.

Born 21 October 1924 in Omaha, Julie Wilson first attracted more than local notice when she was crowned Miss Nebraska at the age of 17. Signing on with a touring company of *Earl Carroll's Vanities* a year later, she left the troupe in Hollywood to embark on a solo career. Of the various media in which she has appeared, Julie prefers clubs and theatre for the opportunity to continue her lifelong love affair with live audiences. Julie's triumphant New York supper club debut at the St. Regis gave an important boost to her career, and she soon became a regular at such legendary places as the Mocambo, Copacabana, Desert Inn, Ciro's, the Copley Plaza, and in London at the Bagatelle and Talk of the Town. Her club work has always been influenced by her theatrical experience—she calls herself an "actress first, singer second." On Broadway she has appeared in *Three to Make Ready*, *Kismet*, *The Pajama Game*, *Jimmy* (about NYC's colorful mayor Walker) and *Park*. Having replaced Lisa Kirk as Bianca in *Kiss Me, Kate* on Broadway, she made the role her own by originating it in the show's London production and on television. Other West End starring roles include *South Pacific* and *Bells Are Ringing*. (She returned to London in early 1986, after an absence of 20 years, for an engagement at the Ritz.) On television, she appeared on all the major variety shows as well as in dramatic roles, including "The Strange One" and "This Must Be the Night." A mainstay of regional, repertory, stock, and national touring companies, Julie has starred in *Follies*, *Company*, *A Little Night Music*, *The Country Girl*, *Babes in Arms*, *Two for the Seesaw* and as Mama Rose in four separate productions of *Gypsy*. Although the Broadway show *Legs Diamond* (1989) was negatively received by many critics, Julie still received a Tony nomination for holding the audience.

Married first to Hollywood agent ad producer Barron Polan, she has two sons—Holt and Michael—from her second marriage.

Lanford Wilson

"I don't like it when they haven't understood what I've done," Lanford Wilson replied softly when asked what it was about Broadway that bothered him. "I go a lot to my plays and I listen to people in the lobby during intermission and hear them say, 'Do you want to go, Harry?', when I know damn well the production's gone brilliantly that day." Wilson's plays show "a proliferative sense of peopleness," wrote Arthur Sainer in *Contemporary Dramatists*, but you are convinced that he "loves the theatre, loves the play, and over and over again he veers from the concerns of his people to the attitudes of theatrical frolics." Loaded with labels like "the populist playwright," "America's poet of loss and endurance," "the bard of lyric-realism," the prolific writer is a founder and number-on playwright of Circle Repertory company (which received a special off-Broadway "Obie" for sustained achievement), located off New York's Sheridan Square. In operation since 1969, the company boasts a collaboration between Wilson and another company founder, director Marshall Mason, for more than 30 productions, a link perhaps unmatched in the American theatre. Wilson's work at Circle Rep includes: *The Family Continues* (1972), *The Hot L Baltimore* (1973), *The Mound Builders* (1975), *Serenading Louie* (1976), *The 5th of July* (1978), *Talley's Folly* (which won the 1980 Pulitzer Prize for Drama and the New York Drama Critics' Award), *A Tale Told* (1981), *Angels Fall* (1982), all directed by Mason, and the one-act plays *Brontosaurus* (1977) and *Thymus Vulgaris* (19982). The final play of the Talley trilogy—*Talley & Son*—was presented in 1985-86. His other plays include; *Balm in Gilead* (1965), later revived in 1984 at the Circle, *Rimers*

(1967), *Lemon Sky* (1969) and over twenty produced one-act plays. He has also written the libretto for Lee Holby's opera of Tennessee Williams' *Summer and Smoke* (1972) and two television plays, "The Migrants" (1974), in collaboration with Tennessee Williams, and "Taxi!" (1978). In 1975 there was a short-lived TV series based on his play *Baltimore* which he did not write ("They would have been much better off it they'd remembered it was about urban decay instead of prostitutes and queers"). He made a big showing on Broadway in 1987 with his play *Burn This*, starring John Malkovich. In April 1989, he was working on an off-Broadway presentaiton of his translation of Chekhov's *The Three Sisters*.

Lanford Eugene Wilson was born 13 April 1937 in Lebanon, Mo. "It's a very small, dusty little town with nice people and some frankly uninteresting frank kind of architecture." (It was the locale of *The Fifth of July*.) "I don't think of myself as a Southern writer at all. The rhythm is very different. Missouri's dead center." Divorced when Wilson was five, his mother remarried and moved to Ozark, Mo. where he attended high school, spent a short time at Southwest Missouri State College and in 1955 moved to San Diego where he studied art at the state college. From there he went to Chicago for six years, during which time he worked at an ad agency. ("Through observing the continual wear and tear on creative people and seeing their work turned into chicken shit.... My goal was to be a really super playwright.") In 1962 he headed for Manhattan and by choice became involved with the off-off-Broadway world of Caffe Cino and La Mama until he joined the Circle Rep.

Wilson's recreations are gardening and reading, which he enjoys at his renovated house in Sag Harbor, Long Island, his home away from his Greenwich Village apartment. Although he says he is not incorruptible ("If it were something absolutely wonderful I'd do it. I certainly listen to all options"), he has no intention of doing a movie. ("I like movies from time to time—very much—I just don't want to do 'em.") Does he have a religion? "I was saved at the Black Baptist Church in Lebanon, Missouri. I guess I must have been a fast 11-year-old—anyway, it was the church I felt most comfortable in. I was good proselytizing material, ready to be saved."

Dave Winfield

His nearly $25 million pact with the Yankees would have been just another record-breaking athletic contract expect that several millions were allocated to programs for underprivileged youngsters. "The reason I do this, and nobody seems to understand," the articulate rightfielder says, "is that I never got anywhere by myself. I had a lot of people helping me. Now I want to return that favor and help the kids." An all-around athlete (at six-feet-six he was drafted in three sports), he conquered Yankee Stadium by adjusting his batting style and perenially ranks with the American League's leaders in homers, RBI's, and game-winning hits.

David Mark Winfield was born in St. Paul, Minn., on 3 October 1951, the second of two boys. His father, a dining car waiter, and mother separated when he was three. After going All-State in two high school sports, baseball and basketball, he rejected an offer from the Red Sox because he didn't want to invite traditionally-racist treatment at some minor league outpost. He instead chose to play at the University of Minnesota where he maintained a B-average in co-majors political science and Afro-American culture. He was a 1973 college All-American in baseball, and a good second-string basketball forward, so baseball's San Diego Padres had competition from two pro basketball leagues as well as football's Minnesota Vikings for his services. In 1977 at San Diego he founded the David M. Winfield Foundation; in the beginning it meant he paid kids' way into games. By the time he decided to become a Yankee, however, support of the organization's grants to hospitals, nutrition programs, and Christmas gift-giving had become a contract stipulation. Upon signing with the Yanks as a free agent he was under enormous pressure to produce. Playing in teammate Reggie Jackson's rather long shadow, Winfield responded with "total concentration" and had a fine season. But in the '81 World Series he couldn't buy hits and his relationship with owner George Steinbrenner soured. The next year he sued, saying the owner hadn't met agreed-upon Foundation payments; later Steinbrenner accused him of mismanaging the fund. He may have been the first ballplayer arrested in the line of duty when, in a 1983 game in Toronto, a ball he threw in warm-ups brained a seagull. Police there booked him (although later dropped the charges) for willful, unnecessary cruelty to animals. "It's the first time he's hit the cut-off man all year," quipped manager Billy Martin. In 1988, his book *Winfield: A Player's Life* was released with some interesting tidbits about baseball. Once a bachelor with a long-time "main lady" (ruled in 1989 as a "common-law wife"), Winfield married Tonya Turner on 18 February 1988 in New Orleans. He has a daughter, Lauren Shanel, with Sandra Renfro. On the side, Winfield also designs his own clothes. One of his favorite TV shows is "Wall Street Week." "I don't blow money," the multimillionaire says.

Oprah Winfrey

This young black woman with a megawatt smile, sparkling hazel eyes, and an unusual first name took the television world by storm in January 1984. She began hosting a local Chicago talk show which was struggling to stay afloat opposite the "Phil Donahue Show"; within two months "AM Chicago" was beating "Donahue" in the Chicago ratings. In 1985, the show's name was changed to "The Oprah Winfrey Show" as the program hit national syndication by September 1986. In just three years since her arrival in Chicago, Oprah had become a nationally-known personality, host of the third most popular syndicated show overall (behind "Jeopardy" and "Wheel of Fortune") and a millionaire by the age of thirty two. Her hosting style combines "plainspoken curiosity, robust humor and, above all, empathy" (*Time*) and propelled the show, in its first year of eligibility, to capture three Daytime Emmys for Outstanding Host, Outstanding Direction, and Outstanding Talk/Service Program. With her track record, it's not surprising that syndicator King World has extended the agreement with Oprah to host the show through 1993.

Born 29 January 1954 in Kosciusko, Mississippi, Oprah has come a long way. She was raised under her grandmother's protective wing on a Mississippi farm when her parents left her in search of separate dreams. Oprah learned to read early and made her first speech in church at age three. When she turned six, she left the sheltered farm life and went to live with her mother Vernita Lee in Milwaukee, where she was sexually abused at age nine by an older cousin and later by a family "friend." Oprah acted out her frustrations and angers by becoming a runaway at age thirteen. As a last resort before detention home, the young girl was sent to live with her father, (a barber, a businessman, and a city councilman) Vernon, in Nashville, Tennessee. Living here, Oprah's life obtained structure and security. Seeking outlets for her talents, Oprah eventually became an honor student, joined the drama club, and at sixteen won an oratorical contest, along with a $1,000 scholarship which helped her pay her tuition at Tennessee State University. While in college, in 1972, Oprah was hired by local station WVOL as a reporter, and later by CBS affiliate WTVF-TV. By 1976, the twenty-two-year-old Oprah was in Baltimore working for WJZ-TV as a feature reporter and co-anchor of the six o'clock news. Unfortunately, Oprah was dumped as co-anchorwoman. Looking back, Oprah philosophizes, "I had no business anchoring the news in a major market." What most felt to be a demotion, being moved to co-host the station's morning show proved a blessing for Oprah. She had found her niche. The show's ratings zoomed, and based upon her performance she was offered the slot for "AM Chicago." Having to wait four months to finish her contract in Nashville, Oprah started to eat ... and eat ... losing her beauty-queen figure (Miss Black Tennessee, 1971). This sudden gain of weight produced her debut style; overweight, sexy, and elegant, with a drop-dead wardrobe. Today, Oprah is a remarkable fifty-five pounds lighter while she still maintains that special winning style.

In addition to her talk show ability, Oprah has become an accomplished actress. Her portrayal of Sofia in Spielberg's film *The Color Purple* won her both Academy Award and Golden Globe nominations for Best Supporting Actress. She also appeared in the film adaptation of Richard Wright's *Native Son*. Her third acting role was in the TV miniseries "Women of Brewster Place" which was co-produced by her company Harpo Productions ("Oprah" spelled backwards). The production company also owns the movie rights to *Kaffir Boy* and Toni Morrison's Pultizer Prize winning novel, *Beloved*. In 1988, Harpo assumed ownership and all production responsibilities for "The Oprah Winfrey Show" making Oprah the first woman in history to own and produce her own talk show. The subsequent purchase of an 88,000 square foot movie studio and TV production complex in Chicago, renamed Harpo Studios, made Oprah the first black individual and only the third woman (behind Mary Pickford and Lucille Ball) to own such a studio.

Living by herself in a three bedroom Chicago apartment with a panoramic view of Lake Michigan, Oprah carries on a long distance relationship with boyfriend, Stedman Graham, former basketball player now based in a North Carolina public relations firm. Remembering her roots, each year she endows her alma mater with ten full scholarships in her father's name, aside from her other philanthropic endeavors. "My mission is to use this position, power, and money to create opportunities for other people," she says. Renowned for her lavish gifts to friends and staff (in 1989 she hosted a television special on friendship), Oprah who reads a Bible verse every morning, believes she is guided by a higher calling. "I believe in the God-force that lives inside all of us, and once you tap into that you can do anything." Oprah is doing everything she wants to, doing it well. In 1988 she received the "Broadcaster of the Year Award" from the International Radio & TV Society, making her the youngest person and only the fifth woman to ever receive this honor in the Society's twenty-five year history. In 1989, "The Oprah Winfrey Show" won the Daytime Emmy Award as Outstanding Talk/Service Program.

Debra Winger

Pauline Kael wrote in the *New Yorker*, "Debra Winger has the vividness of those we call 'born' performers. She makes you feel that there's something humming inside her." Jack Nicholson, who costarred with her in perhaps her most important film to date, *Terms of Endearment* (1983), felt she was "a metamorphic actress, this girl. I think she's a great actress—a genius." Perhaps Winger thinks she is just lucky to be alive, let alone successful. Born Mary Debra Winger in Cleveland, Ohio, 17 May 1955 and raised in Sepulveda, Calif., she was employed at the Magic Mountain amusement park in 1973 when on New Year's Eve she was thrown from a truck and nearly died of a cerbral hemorrhage. She was left partially paralyzed and blind in one eye for several months. "Poetically, I look at my accident as a huge hunk of grace, which propelled me into doing what I wanted to do."

After high-school graduation, Winger went to Israel, where she lived and worked on a kibbutz. She applied for citizenship there and even served three months with the Israeli Army before heading back to the States. She enrolled at California State University at Northridge and planned on becoming a socio-criminologist until she realized that she was a "juvenile delinquent," at least in spirit. Then came the accident, after which she studied acting and began making television commercials, which led to parts of programs including "Police Woman" and a featured part as Drusilla the Wonder Girl, Lynda Carter's younger sister, in ABC-TV's "Wonder Woman." Her film debut was in *Thank God It's Friday* (1978), which was followed by a more noteworthy part in *French Postcards* (1979). Her real breakthrough came when she won out over 200 other hopefuls and was cast opposite John Travolta in *Urban Cowboy* (1980). She stole the show with her extraordinary ride on a bucking mechanical bronc that included eye rolling and other orgasmic notions. She was the voice of *E.T.*, won an Oscar nomination as Richard Gere's homegrown sweetheart in *An Officer and a Gentleman* (1982) and a second nomination for her portrayal of Emma in *Terms of Endearment*. As Shirley MacLaine's fictional daughter, her part spanned a period of 14 years, in which she goes from a teenager in bobby sox to become a mother herself and a young victim of cancer. All the while she "plays cello to her mother's trumpet," as described by *People* magazine, which also said that Winger "at every stage of the story is simply and translucently Emma, inhabiting her character as naturally as red inhabits a rose." Winger, who also appeared in TV's "Cannery Row" (1982) and in *Mike's Murder* (1984), said that the attention-getting film *Terms* was for "the mothers of young children, the middle-class mother . . . that's who the film was for inside of me. I've always had this deep resentment of how the middle class is treated. I mean the lower class, it's obvious what they catch, you know, life is rough. But the true crime, some of the worst psychic abuse, is on the middle-class. So here was this perfectly middle-class girl who turned into a housewife with children, and I really felt the responsibility, it was very important to me to make a hero out of this class of woman." Her most recent films have produced assorted reviews. She was acclaimed for her role as a lawyer opposite Robert Redford in *Legal Eagles* (1986) and almost ignored for her role in *Betrayed* (1988). Upcoming films include *Tea in the Desert*, *Everybody Wins* and Bertolucci's *The Sheltering Sky*.

Winger married actor Timothy Hutton on 16 March 1986; the couple separated in June 1988 (one son, Emmanuel Noah).

Henry Winkler

"There are a staggering number of people in the country who appear to be ready to do anything for me, women I've never met who want to mother my children, elderly ladies who stand for hours in the hope of touching my hand. It's easy to say these people are all unbalanced, or lonely beyond recall, but there are a lot of them and I have some sort of obligation to them, even if it's just to tell them to relax." His performance as a pseudo-hood with a heart of gold in the durable, wholesome comedy, "Happy Days," erupted in a rash of Fonzie fever, making Winkler one of the most popular personalities in television history.

Winkler's real-life scenario is a far cry from that of his blue-collar, motorcycle-riding TV alter-ego. Born 30 October 1945 in New York to German-Jewish refugees, he suffered through a prep-school adolescence spent in an unsuccessful quest for "cool." "I was so self-effacing it makes me sick. Every year I'd go to the really cool guys in school and say, 'Listen, this year I'm different. I've changed.' . . . I was willing to be whoever anyone wanted me to be." To his parents' dismay, he rejected the family lumber business to pursue acting at Emerson College and Yale. He performed with the Yale Repertory Theatre Company and appeared in television commercials before trying his luck in Hollywood. Within a year, he was cast as the one colorful character in the innocent comedy about a Milwaukee family during the 1950s. Featured initially as a minor character, Winkler quickly came to dominate the show as thunderous viewer response indicated the nation was hungry for a bigger role for "The Fonz." He was the big brother many kids dream about. Seeming taller than his five-foot-seven frame, he was slick, forceful, and always there in a pinch. As the show progressed (it lasted just over a decade), Fonzie grew up but never grew out of his ever-present leather jacket, or his uncanny ability to snap women to attention or start a juke box with a tap of his fist.

Despite Winkler's desire to avoid typecasting, his film attempts have failed to set hearts—or critics' pens—aflutter. His film credits include *The Lords of Flatbush*, *Heroes* and *Night Shift*, and the made-for-TV 1979 "American Christmas Carol," in which he played Scrooge. Nowadays, he spends most of his time behind the camera. He is the producer of the popular television show "MacGyver," and he directed the Alan King film *Memories of Me* (1988). Winkler has become an advocate for children's welfare, and in 1984 he created a videocassette on the subject of child abuse entitled "Strong Kids, Safe Kids." He married the former Stacey Weitzman in 1978 and is father to her son, Jed, from a previous marriage, and their daughter Zoe and son Max.

Jonathan Winters

This orotund comic with a genius for mimicry is a veritable album of characters, small town and otherwise. You might see Jonathan Winters portraying anybody from an old grandmother to a filling-station attendant, or, as a whole new generation of fans has come to know him, the man who advertises the trash bags on television. He explains that his brand of humor holds up a mirror in which people either see themselves or their friends. Another rare talent is his way with sound effects. He can, he insists, make 5000 different sounds with his mouth.

Born 11 November 1925 in Dayton, Ohio, he planned on becoming a commercial artist, but a lost watch changed the course of his life. A local talent contest offered a watch to its top prize winner and Winters entered the contest hoping to win a new timepiece. He did win and soon was offered a job as a disc jockey by a local radio station; this gave him plenty of opportunity to perfect his monologues and voice tricks. He headed to New York and performed at a series of clubs. His big break came when he appeared on TV's "Jack Paar Show" and was selected as a regular substitute host for Paar. The comedy-obsessed workaholic had a breakdown in 1959 and was sent to a place that has always been a mainstay in his routine—a place he refers to as the "funny farm." He recovered swiftly and has spent the past 25 years appearing on televison, including his own CBS show, ABC's "Good Morning America," many variety shows and television movies and in films (e.g. the comedy classic *It's a Mad, Mad, Mad, Mad World*, *The Loved One* and *The Russians Are Coming*). In 1987 he released the enlightening book *Winter's Tales* (1987) and was filming *The Teddy Bear Habit* in 1989.

Director Stanley Kramer once called Winters, "the only genius I know" because of the comedian's ability to create characters out of thin air. Winters, who is married and has two children, credits his talent to his school days. "I was the class clown. Other guys had more security, steady dates and all that ... I didn't. The only thing that kept me together was my comedy. We'd all go to a tavern called O'Brien's and I would do impressions of the Indianapolis Speedway."

Shelley Winters

Her new 1989 autobiography *Shelley II: The Middle of My Century* picks up where she left off. . . . "America's most irrepressible star takes us on a wild ride through the Hollywood of the 1950s and early 1960s, with side trips to Broadway, the Actors Studio, and around the world." She freely talks bout her associations with fellow celebrity friends: Marilyn Monroe, "her Hollywood roommate, who is perfect in front of the camera but helpless in the kitchen," Sean Connery, "a young Scottish actor who romances Shelley in his chilly London flat", and Tony Franciosa whom she states, "If there had been an Olympic sex team that year, Tony would have been the captain."

Brash and stormy ("I admit I'm not all sweetness and light, but when I speak my mind, it usually clears the air"), Shelley Winters, nee Shirley Shrift, took her first not-so-tentative steps toward an acting career when, at fourteen, she showed up at a Manhattan talent agency and announced in her best Southern (and Brooklynese) accent, "Ah'm heah to play Scarlett O'Hara." That didn't work, but she did make a significant inroad on screen stardom in 1948 complicating one of the lives of Ronald Colman in his Academy Award-winning role in *A Double Life*. She had her own first taste of an Oscar nomination after she played Montgomery Clift's inconvenient lower-class girlfriend in *A Place in the Sun* in 1951 and later won two Supporting Actress Oscars for *Diary of Anne Frank* (1959) and *A Patch of Blue* (1965). Winter's was nominated in that category again for *The Poseidon Adventure* in 1972 and later in the decade, picked up a "David," the Italian version of the Oscar, for her bravura performance playing a mute in the Italian-made film *An Average Little Man*. She has made more than a dozen films in Italy and, according to one Rome-based director, has "filled the gap left by Anna Magnani." Says Shelley about her enormous popularity in pastaland: "I think in another life I *was* Italian."

She was born into *this* life on 18 August 1922 in St. Louis, moved to Brooklyn as a child and has made her presence felt in New York acting circles as well as Hollywood's. More secure in her craft after adopting The Method at the Actor's Studio, she has observed: "Money can be devalued or taken away from you. The only real security is talent. If you have that, you'll always have work." In recent years, she has taken to the typewriter with mixed results. After seeing her 1971 play, *One Night Stands of a Noisy Passenger*, critic Richard Watts decided that she was a "simply dreadful dramatist." But her 1980 autobiography, *Shelley, Also Known as Shirley*, was a bestseller, possibly because of her frankness in describing affairs she had with the likes of Errol Flynn, Burt Lancaster, and others, before, between and after her marriages to and/or divorces from Mack Paul Mayer, Vittorio Gassman (one daughter) and Anthony Franciosa. ("Of course, I didn't have all that many men in my life," says Shelley. "Considering today's Women's Lib attitudes, I was a piker.") How can anyone resist someone who relates: "You know, I went out with Clark Gable. When he picked me up, my mother, that most moral lady, whispered in my ear. 'Don't be careful!'"

Steve Winwood

Almost 25 years after his debut as the sixteen-year-old lead singer for the Spencer Davis Group, Steve Winwood's voice is as phenomenal as ever, and his talent for songwriting and producing has never been better.

Steve was born in Birmingham, England, 12 May 1948. He was first introduced to the music world in 1964 when he was the lead singer for the Spencer Davis Group, which had originally evolved from his brother's Muff Wood's Jazz Band. The members from this band got together with the members of another English band and their first record, *Dimples*, was released in 1964. The band released several more singles, including "Keep on Running" (their first number one hit in England), "Gimme Some Lovin'" and "I'm a Man" (1967). By this time, Steve was ready to move in a new direction with his career. He wanted to incorporate jazz, classical, and folk with the rhythm and blues he had already been so used to playing. He teamed up with Jim Capaldi, Dave Mason, and Chris Wood and formed Traffic. Their first single, "Paper Sun," was released in 1967, and reached Top 5 on the British charts. By the end of the year, the group's first album, *Mr. Fantasy*, was released. Traffic released their second album entitled *Traffic* in 1968. In 1969, Steve made yet another change. He joined Eric Clapton, Ginger Baker, and Rick Grech and formed the band Blind Faith. The band was an enormous success and soon acquired the identity as a "supergroup", one of music's first. After one extraordinarily successful album, *Blind Faith*, a concert in London, and a lengthy tour in America, Blind Faith disbanded. Winwood then returned to Traffic, and the group released the album *John Barleycorn Must Die* in 1970. The group released three more albums, the last of which was *When the Eagle Flies* in 1974. Steve spent the next three years recouperating from the pressures and demands that touring and working with a band presented. It was in 1977 that he started putting together his first solo album, *Steve Winwood*. Several albums followed including: *Arc of a Diver* (1980); *Talking Back to the Night* (1982); *Back in the High Life* (1986), which was nominated for six Grammy's in 1986, won three, and won Record of the Year for *Higher*

Love; Chronicles (1987); and *Roll with It* (1988), which is his first number one album. His achievements include fourteen Gold Record Awards, three Platinum Record Awards, and two Grammy Awards.

He married Eugenia Crafton on 17 January 1987 in New York.

Tom Wolfe

Liz Smith described his meteoric rise to prominence in the free-spirited sixties as having caused "severe jealousy and outrage pangs throughout the U.S. literary establishment when he sprang right out of Pop Culture's forehead to become a star practically overnight. His subject matter often trembled like Jello about to collapse . . . but there was no one who could touch him." His 1965 *The Kandy-Kolored Tangerine-Flake Streamline Baby* is considered the grandpa of the New Journalism. His books include *The Electric Kool-Aid Acid Test* about time spent with writer Ken Kesey and his Merry Pranksters; *Radical Chic and Mau-Mauing the Flak Catchers* about limousine liberals; *The Painted Word*, concerning arbiters of artistic fashion; *From Bauhaus to Our House*, a study of glass-box architecture and *The Right Stuff* about the U.S. Space Program (the film version was nominated for a Best Picture Academy Award). All the books have that certain Wolfian bite, but as time went on and the New Journalism became part of the mainstream, the question arose (in *GEO* magazine): Was the bite "timely lampoons of what is foolish in American culture or merely polemical expression of an archconservative's point of view?" Other publications were 1987's *Country Carving: Hound Dogs, Racoon, Coon Hunter* and *The Bonfire of the Vanities*.

No relation to the North Carolina Tom, Thomas Kennerly Wolfe was born in Richmond, 2 March 1931, the son of a former Virginia Polytechnic Institute professor. After receiving a Ph. D. in American Studies at Yale in 1957, Wolfe went to work as a reporter on the Springfield (Mass.) *Union* and the *Washington Post*. With his flair for drawing sketches, he got a job doubling as an artist and reporter for the New York *Herald Tribune* and its Sunday supplement, which survived the *Trib's* demise and became *New York* magazine. Most of his early books appeared first in either *New York* or *Esquire*. In the summer of 1984 *Rolling Stone* began publishing excerpts from a novel-in-progress called *Vanities*.

The sartorially splendent writer (his cloths are as dandy as his prose—"Since you always have the things on, I thought I might as well shake people up a bit") is married to wife Sheila, an art director. They have one daughter, Alexandra, and live in Manhattan and Southampton. The controversy about his politics is due to the fact that it is considered "heretical" to make fun of the left orthodoxy, as he did in the 1960s. "There was one crazy piece written about me in *The New Republic* that said—and not metaphorically—that while at Yale I had been brainwashed by the Establishment, with a large *E*, presumably by Allen Dulles, who was then head of the CIA, and then sent forth to assassinate liberal culture. This thing was serious." When *GEO* asked if he wrote mainly for recognition, Wolfe recalled being asked that same question while giving a college lecture. He could not think of an answer until the Presbyterian catechism, which he hadn't looked at since he was seven years old, came to his mind. "The first question in the catechism is 'Who created heaven and earth?' And the answer is 'God.' The second question is 'Why did he do it?' And looking back on it, the answer fascinates me: 'For his own glory.' That's quite an answer. That was the answer I came up with, so maybe that's it."

Stevie Wonder

He grew up impoverished in Detroit during the infancy of the Motown sound, "Little Stevie Wonder" had his first hit song at 13, a jumping harmonica number called "Fingertips Part 2." There was a period in time where anyone nominated against Wonder would go home empty-handed at an Awards show; he has won over a dozen Grammy Awards and has had numerous Top Ten Singles in a career spanning three decades. "Little" has long been dropped from his name, but his prolific talent still produces wonders in the world of music.

The songwriting of Steveland Judkins Morris, born blind on 13 May 1950 in Saginaw, Mich., was recognized early by the then-forming Motown label. Wonder created a string of smash hits under the record company's tight reins, including, "I Was Made to Love Her," "For Once in My Life," and "My Cherie Amour," before breaking free to experiment with a less orthodox black sound.

The results were phenomenal. Using a million dollars that had been held in trust by Motown, he produced the 1972 album, "Music of My Mind." Returning to Motown with more clout and a contract allowing him complete control over the production of his records—a rarity in a nervous industry—he produced "Talking Book" that same year, featuring the blockbuster songs, "Superstition" and "You are the Sunshine of My Life." His next album, "Innervisions," was the Grammy's 1974 Best Album of the Year. His release in 1985 was "In Square Circle." In addition to the rock/soul fusion beat that drives his music up the charts, fans are moved by Wonder's poignant outrage, evident in such songs as "You Haven't Done Nothing," in which he chides the white political system for ignoring minorities. His other dynamic record releases surfaced on the albums *In Square Circle* (1985) and *Characters* (1987). In 1988 he was inducted into the Rock and Roll Hall of Fame and in 1989 he wowed audiences during his "Peace and Freedom World Tour."

B.D. Wong

He is a multi-talented actor, singer, dancer, and choreographer. He has appeared in the feature film *The Karate Kid* and the Broadway production of *M. Butterfly*.

Wong studied acting with Don Hotton, and in addition was a Casting Society of America Minority Committee Acting Seminar Participant. His vocal training was under Ruth Cooper, as well as Roger Love with the Seth Riggs Studio. He also studied tap under Tony Wing. His screen appearances include the feature film *The Karate Kid II* and *No Big Deal*. He has been seen on numerous television shows as well, such as "Driver's Ed," "Double Switch," "Sweet Surrender," "Shell Game," "Hard Copy," "Blackes Magic," the weekly series "Simon and Simon," "TV's Bloopers & Practical Jokes," and the "New Love American Style." Wong has also given several outstanding theatre performances in *La Cage Aux Folles, See Below Middle Sea, The Gifts of the Magi, A Salute to Sondheim, Part II, Mail* and *M. Butterfly*. In addtiion to being an accomplished actor, Wong is an excellent singer, possessing a high baritone and a superior falsetto.

In his spare time Wong enjoys designing, drawing, crafting and bowling.

Edward Woodward

Once hailed by Sir Laurence Olivier as one of the best actors in England, Edward Woodward has lived up to that statement. Woodward's thirty-five-year career span has secured his presence as a stage actor, star of feature films and television, musician, and vocalist.

Born 1 June 1930 in Croyden, Surrey England to Edward and Violet Woodward, Edward's primary career interest was in journalism. While attending Kingston College, Woodward discovered his niche after appearing in several of the college's theatrical productions and later attended England's notorious Royal Academy of Dramatic Arts. His 1954 stage debut in London's West End production of *Where There's a Will*, started a slew of successful theatrical appearances across the globe from Shakespearean tours in India, Ceylon, and Australia to New York's honored Broadway stage. The successful Broadway production *Rattle of a Simple Mind* in 1962 bestowed him with the New York Theatre Critics Award. Noel Coward's Broadway musical *High Spirits* was Woodward's vehicle to combine his acting and vocal talents. Among Woodward's theatrical credits are *Romeo & Juliet* (1985), *Hamlet* (1958), *Richard III*, *Cyrano de Bergerac* (1971), *The White Devil* (1971), *The Wolfe* (1973), *Male of the Species* (1975), *On Approval* (1976), *The Dark Horse Comedy* (1978), *The Beggar's Opera* in 1980 which he also directed, *Private Lives* (1980), and *The Assassin* (1982).

Successful in the transition from stage to film, Woodward has completed over a dozen feature films. Among them the starring role in 1980's *Breaker Morant*. He also appeared in *The File on the Golden Goose* (1968), *Young Winston* (1974), and *The Wicker Man* (1974). The 1980's saw Woodward in *Who Dares Wins* (1982) and *King David* (1986).

Woodward is best known to American audiences for his portrayal of Robert McCall in CBS-TV's critically acclaimed dramatic series "The Equalizer" which began in 1985. His brilliant portrayal of the mysterious benevolent avenger has earned him Emmy nominations for best lead actor in a dramatic series (1986, 1989) and a Golden Globe (1987). British television audiences adored him in the successful series "Callan" and "Winston Churchill: The Wilderness Years." Telefilm credits include his performance as "Simon Legree" in the cable production of "Uncle Tom's Cabin," HBO mini-series "Code Name Kyril," CBS-TV's "Arthur the King," and "A Christmas Carol." Blessed with musical talent as well, Woodward is a renowned vocalist in England and Australia having recorded fourteen albums for which he has acquired several gold discs. During his hiatus in the Spring of 1988 he engaged in a twelve-city tour in England. With a passion for the written word, he has also recorded albums of dramatic poetry readings, prose, and Shakespeare.

A decorated officer of the Order of the British Empire, Woodward has been married twice. His first marriage in 1952 was to Venetia Mary Collet (divorced 1986; three children—Timothy, Peter, and Sarah, all pursuing acting careers). In one episode of the "Equalizer," son Timothy portrayed his dad "McCall" as a young man in a flashback sequence. Remarried in 1987 to Michelle Dotrice, herself an actress (daughter of fellow thespian Roy Dotrice), Woodward and Dotrice have found themselves working side by side in various theatrical productions and an episode of the "Equalizer." By far their proudest collaboration is daughter Emily Beth born in 1983. An avid collector of antique swords, rock and mineral specimens, plus antique and Jacobean furniture, his hobbies include boating, photography, and reading on such topics as American history and politics. The Woodwards have homes in New York City, upstate New York, and England.

Joanne Woodward

"Given the right parts, she is a great actress. She can find so many different facets of herself to play," explains husband Paul Newman. "That is magic." Indeed, at 27, Joanne Woodward stunned the film industry when, in her third film, she delineated the troubled *Three Faces of Eve* (1957), giving Oscar-winning depth to each characterization. Despite her range ("I've never been the same person twice on the screen"), demonstrated in such highly regarded films as *The Sound and the Fury* (1959), *The Fugitive Kind* (1960), *From the Terrace* (1960), *The Stripper* (1963), and *A Fine Madness* (1965), she finally decided "Hollywood never really knew what to do with me." Declaring "I'm not a movie star anyway," she avoided the film capital until she found the script that was to become *Rachel, Rachel* ("I was determined I'd rather do nothing than just work for the sake of having a job"). After completion of the critically acclaimed *Rachel, Rachel* (1968), directed by Newman, she concluded she would "never do anything again unless I felt strongly about it." Newman has since directed her in three major vehicles, the films *The Effect of Gamma Rays on Man-in-the-Moon Marigolds* (1972), *The Glass Menagerie* (1987), plus "The Shadow Bow" (1980) for ABC-TV. In 1985, Woodward gave a touching performance as a victim of Alzheimer's disease in the TV movie, "Do You Remember Love?" (Her own mother is afflicted with the disease.)

Born 27 February 1930 in Thomasville, Ga., Joanne Gignilliat Woodward was raised in Greenville, S.C. and first studied acting at Louisana State University before switching to New York's Neighborhood Playhouse. While working steadily in early TV, she understudied both Kim Stanley and Janice Rule in *Picnic* (1953), playing each role about 50 times in the play's 477 performances on Broadway. She also met fellow understudy Newman, whom she married 29 January 1958, shortly after making *The Long Hot Summer* (1958), their first movie together (1984's *Harry and Son* marked their tenth). Newman had three young children (one boy, two girls) and the couple produced three more daughters. Subjugating her career to Newman's superstardom and raising the family created problems ("my tendency is to shriek and throw things, being childish myself, as most actors are"). Woodward necessarily turned down interesting offers, "and, being a total actress—I really like to act morning, noon, and night, that was another problem our girls had to suffer with, because, not always being allowed to act on stage or screen, I was giving brilliant performances at home." Home was mainly converted old buildings on rambling acres of apple tress in Westport, Conn., supplemented by "Mommie's Tree House," off-limits to those under 16. Their brownstone in New York sports a bedroom Tennessee Williams once pronounced "the finest example of Southern decadence I have ever seen" and there is the obligatory house in Brentwood, Calif. ("I've been knocking Hollywood so long it's a joke.") In addition to occasional films, she has made specials for all three television networks, including "Lady Chatterly's Lover" (1978), "See How She Runs" (1978), and "Passions" (1985). On Broadway, her appearance in the title role in *Candida* opened the 1982 season for Circle in the Square.

Her children rekindled Woodward's interest in the dance, to which she devotes time, practice, artistic energy, and financial support. In the mid-1970s, she became Chairman of the Board and chief financial backer for "Dancers," a New York–based company formed by Dennis Wayne. With the family mostly grown and more time for herself, Woodward has said "I do what I like to do now, which is to act, and that does not necessarily mean in movies. But, when I do act in movies, I do it mostly for the money, because it's very expensive supporting a ballet company."

Herman Wouk

Novelist and playwright Herman Wouk (pronounced woke) received the 1952 Pulitzer Prize in fiction for *The Caine Mutiny: A Novel of World War II*, and has since published other bestsellers, including *The Winds of War* and *War and Remembrance*. A compelling narrator, Wouk remains, according to one critic, "an unembarrassed believer in such 'discredited' forms of commitment as valor, gallantry, leadership, [and] patriotism." Wouk has enjoyed a wide readership and, more recently, an enormous viewing audience; the premiere segment of an ABC-TV adaptation of *The Winds of War* was seen by over 80 million viewers. The follow-up TV version of "War and Remembrance" didn't fare as well in the ratings. Said *Time* magazine of his 1985 novel *Inside Outside*, "Wouk plays his own inside-outside game ... the surreptitious satisfaction of the autobiographical urge through a fictional character ... the novel is patterned on the life and times of Herman Wouk." In 1988, he wrote the screenplay for the CBS-TV adaptation of "The Caine Mutiny Courtmartial."

Born 27 May 1915, in New York City, Wouk began his professional writing career as a scriptwriter for radio personalities, among them the late Fred Allen. Following a year's stint writing and producing plays to promote war bond sales, he spent four years with the United States Navy, later using his experience aboard ship as background for his third novel, *The Caine Mutiny*. (Wouk later wrote a play based on a sequence from the novel, *The Caine Mutiny Courtmartial*.) In 1943 Wouk began writing fiction and upon his release from the navy he began in earnest the career of novelist. From 1953-57 Wouk held a teaching post (visiting professor) at Yeshiva University and was to remain linked to academia for the next two decades. His fourth novel, *Marjorie Morningstar* drew wide critical acclaim. Wouk interrupted his career (as novelist) to write *This Is My God* (his own personal account of the Jewish faith) which he dedicated to his grandfather (a rabbi) and it became a best-seller.

Wouk is known for careful attention to detail: while researching his two massive war novels, he traveled to England, Germany, Italy, France, Poland, Czechoslovakia, Iran, Israel, and the Soviet Union. "Since both have been best-sellers, it is likely that more Americans have learned about, or remembered the war through Wouk's account than from any other single source in the last decade," claims one Wouk admirer. Wouk is most proud of his 1980 honor—the Alexander Hamilton Medal awarded annually by the Columbia College Alumni Association of Columbia University to a living alumnus or former member of the faculty for "recognition of distinguished service and accomplishment in any field of human endeavor."

Wouk and his wife (and agent) live in Washington, D.C. and in Middleburg, Va. Very much a family man, Wouk is also an active supporter of wildlife preservation.

Andrew Wyeth

Dubbed by his detractors as "the rich man's Norman Rockwell," and by his fans as "the Robert Frost of the paintbrush," he ignored the art world's leanings toward abstract expressionism, earning the highest prices ever paid for the work of a living American artist. The reason behind his popularity? "I think," he said at the time of his mammoth 1967 retrospective at New York's Whitney Museum, "it's because I happen to paint things that reflect the basic truths of life: sky, earth, friends, the intimate things. People are drawn to my work by common feelings that go beyond art." One critic admitted, "His sharp-focus technique is reassuring to people who like 'seeing something their six-year-old child couldn't do.'"

Born 12 July 1917 at Chadds Ford, Pa., (where he still lives and works), Andrew Wyeth was the son of famous illustrator N.C. Wyeth. He began exhibiting at 20 and from that point on, positioned himself apart from the avant-gardists: "My aim is to escape from the medium with which I work. To leave no residue of technical mannerism to stand between my expression and the observer. . . . Not to exhibit craft but rather to submerge it; and make it rightfully the handmaiden of beauty, power, and emotional content." Married to Betsy Merle James in 1940, he has two sons, Nicholas and Jamie, the latter a popular painter in his own right. Snubbed by some critics, Wyeth is likened by others to the noted Flemish masters, although they painted in oils and he works in tempera and water colors. Since his people and landscapes often seem to evoke another era, he was asked in 1967 if he thought his painting was pertinent to the times. "I don't know," he said after a pause, "it's pertinent to me." Probably his most famous painting is "Christina's World," picturing a young woman lying in a field, straining toward the top of a hill. "Christina's a close friend of mine and crippled," he once explained. "Every day she drags herself across the field . . . to visit the graves of her family. People might call that a gloomy thing to paint, but I don't look at it that way."

In 1987 his book *The Helga Pictures* was released.

Jamie Wyeth

"When he looks at a painting of mine, the father-and-son thing goes out the window," says artist James Browning Wyeth about his relationship with artist Andrew Wyeth. "It's one artist talking to another." At six, decked out in his favorite Davy Crockett coonskin, Jamie posed for one of his father's most reproduced portraits, "Faraway" (1952). But since the 1960s, Andrew Wyeth's son has been working on the other side of the easel. When at 20 he had his first one-man show at the Knoedler Gallery in New York City, he was hailed as "the finest American portrait painter since the death of John Singer Sargent." Another critic not so awed, complained that Jamie's debut "had occasioned a trumpeting of dynastic piety that would have been excessive to mark the coming of age of British royal heir."

The Chadds Ford, Pa., artistic dynasty into which Jamie Wyeth was born 6 July 1946 began with his grandfather, N.C. Wyeth, famous as an illustrator of children's books. His father, Andrew, is one of the most popular artists in America. His uncle, Peter Hurd, is a well-known Texas portrait painter (his most celebrated subject: Lyndon Johnson, who didn't like his portrait one bit). Jamie quit school at 11 to follow in the family tradition; he was tutored privately in the mornings, studied painting in the afternoons with his father's older sister, Carolyn. He learned so fast that the gallery director at his first one-man show was only half-joking when he called it a "retrospective." Wyeth is a super-realist who takes great pains with his portraits. To get the proper "feel" for the posthumous portrait he painted of John F. Kennedy (now in the Kennedy Memorial Library) he spent two weekends at Hyannis Port soaking up atmosphere and watching films of the assassination repeatedly, familiarizing himself with Kennedy's appearance through photographs, and talks with people who knew him. "To paint a person, I practically go to bed with him. Through osmosis I become the object. I just stay with a person, I follow him around for days. . . . A portrait is a distillation of different kinds of moods." Wyeth shrugs off comparisons between his style and his father's. "If someone wants to compare us, fine. I couldn't care less. I'm just interested in painting and that's all I want to do." In 1968 he married Phyllis O. Mills. Exhibitions include a show he had in tandem with Andy Warhol at the Hotel de Paris in Monte Carlo (1980) and a show at the Coe Kerr Gallery in New York to benefit Sloan-Kettering (1984). Jamie lives on a farm in Wilmington, Del., and spends summers on Mohegan Island, Maine.

Jane Wyman

As "Falcon Crest's" wine tycooness extraordinaire she's tougher than a plug in a bottle of champagne and bitchier than sour grapes. She is reclusive, she dislikes interviews and in the words of one of her co-stars, "Falcon Crest is *her* set." From a flighty snub-nosed bit player to a mature, assured leading lady, Jane Wyman has built her career with care and shrewdness, using better and more challenging roles to reach the top ranks of her craft.

Born Sarah Jane Fulks, 4 January 1914 in St. Joseph, Mo., her father was mayor for a time and her mother entertained ambitions for little Sarah Jane to be the first Shirley Temple. At the age of 8, she made her first trip to Hollywood with her mother to break into the movie biz, but they returned to St. Joseph, daunted. After graduating from the University of Missouri she worked as a manicurist and switchboard operator until, under the name "Jane Durrell," she got a job singing on the radio. A next attempt in the movies succeeded—somewhat. She was given bit parts, chorus girl roles, some publicity, and her present name. ("I posed in bathing suits with Santa Claus, the Easter

Bunny, and the Thanksgiving turkey.") In 1936 she appeared in *My Man Godfrey* and following that, worked steadily as a tow-headed ingenue in comedies like *Cain and Mabel* (1936). "I was the Joan Blondell of the B's." Married in 1937 to Myron Futterman, she divorced him in 1938, the year she starred opposite her soon-to-be second husband, Ronald Reagan, in the film *Brother Rat*. Wyman and Reagan were married from 1940 until 1948; they had one daughter Maureen and adopted a son, Michael. With *Lost Weekend* in 1945 her acting had matured and she was established as a Hollywood actress. Better and better roles followed; she became more and more the Noble Heroine and less and less the Featherbrained Flirt. In 1947 she won an Oscar nomination as the mother in *The Yearling* and in 1948 she won the award for *Johnny Belinda*, playing a deaf mute. When a second daughter, born prematurely, died, the Wyman-Reagan ticket split apart. "He's very political," she said, "and I'm not." Louella Parsons lamented that "it was the saddest break-up of Hollywood's most seemingly ideal couple since Douglas Fairbanks and Mary Pickford." Reagan thought the death of the newborn and Wyman's Oscar winning characterization had been too much of a strain and quipped at the time that the only correspondent in his ailing marriage "was Johnny Belinda."

The star of later films such as *The Glass Menagerie* (1950), *Magnificent Obsession* (1954), *Miracle in the Rain* (1956), and a successful TV series in the 1950s bears the distinction of being the only ex-wife of a United States president in history—a fact that hardly impresses her. She walks away from interviews if Ronald Reagan's name is mentioned, feeling, in the words of one observer on the "Falcon Crest" set, "that all that ended 35 years ago and has no relevance to her life now." A third and fourth marriage to Fred Karger ended in divorce. Now single she says, "I recommend marriage very highly, for everyone but me."

Tammy Wynette

The "First Lady of Country Music" whose recording of "Stand By Your Man" is the biggest selling single in the history of Country Music, is both songwriter and singer. Having co-written many of her own hits and written for other artists as well, Wynette sees composing as "a form of therapy, the best way I know of getting something off my chest." Also the title of her autobiography, "Stand By Your Man" was transformed into a CBS-TV movie special in 1981. It is a rags-to-riches saga, a poignant tale of Wynette's arduous climb to the top. Her debut single of 1966, "Apt. #9," was an instant hit and her next 11 albums went on to number one on the charts. Three years later she won her first Grammy and was twice named Female Vocalist of the Year by the Country Music Association. She's gone on to sell more than 30 million records and her LPs and/or singles have made the top spot on the charts some 35 times. In 1976 Wynette was named Number One Female Vocalist in Great Britain. Some of her latest albums include: *Sometimes When We Touch* (1985), *Higher Ground* (1987), and *Next to You* (1989).

Born Virginia Wynette Pugh on 5 May 1942, on her grandfather's cotton farm in Itawamba County, Mississippi, she began crooning and dreaming of stardom as a very young girl. She was raised by her grandparents and began working in the cotton fields by the age of 7—"hoeing, chopping, picking, and hating every minute of it." Her father's legacy—a piano, a guitar, and the dream that his daughter would make music her life—became her only escape from the dull, toilsome routine of farm life. As a means to escape the farm, Wynette married while still in her teens and produced two children. Shackled in an unhappy marriage and worn out from the drudgery of her life, she borrowed enough money to enroll in beauty school, moved to Birmingham and had a third child. Her marriage crumbled and Wynette moved to Nashville determined to make an all-out, do-or-die effort to break into the business. The rest is country music history. Wynette is most comfortable singing, sharing her innermost feelings in song as she mesmerizes her audiences with a tearful vocal style that has become her trademark.

"I like what I'm doing because I sing about things that happen in real people's lives. We don't hide what we're saying behind fancy language."

Wynette (four times divorced) has an estate in Nashville and a beach house in Jupiter, Florida. She is the mother of four children and clings to a fervent belief in love and marriage—"I'm not sorry I tried to find happiness in marriage, I'm just sorry the failures had to be so public." A rare combination of girlish vulnerability, both on stage and off, not only makes her one of the greatest song stylists performing today, but one of the most fascinating women as well.

Cale Yarborough

This five-time Southern 500 Winner and multi-time Grand National stock car champion says he means business when he's behind the wheel and on the racing tracks of America. Otherwise, he says, "I could be back on the farm, poking around on my combine." He was a long way from South Carolina, and seemingly out of his element, when in 1981 he entered the grueling 24 Hours of Le Mans in France. There, amidst sleek Porches and Ferraris he gunned his American-made modified Chevrolet Camaro down the Mulsanne Straight until a wall claimed it (but left him unharmed). Yarborough is the owner of virtually all speed records in stock car racing, having taken up where former NASCAR king Richard Petty left off.

William Caleb Yarborough, born 23 March 1939 in Timmonsville, South Carolina, has most of the qualities required of stereotypical "good ol' Southern boys." The offspring of a tobacco farmer, he's now a folk hero around the community where he's remained since he gave up turkey farming after scrounging up $10.37 to get to a race in Savannah, Ga. The race car blew its engine on the warm up lap and he had to borrow $20 to get back home. The former all-state fullback and two-time Golden Gloves welterweight champ is much too macho to use such recently introduced amenities as water-cooled suits, relief drivers, or centrifugal force-countering neck straps. But although he's been flipped upside down in cars at Atlanta and Darlington, he's still tender enough to be called a generous, caring man. Yarborough raced in four Indianapolis 500s to earn a living after the Ford Motor Company dropped racer sponsoring. But the difference in the flat Indy-car tracks and the banked curves of the stock car ovals were considerable. Wife Betty Jo recalls "back when we were just starting out, living in a house trailer and really scratching, many a night Cale cried to me, 'Momma (her nickname), I just don't know if I can make it.'" He's done quite well, and realizing his slump in 1985 and 1986, he began fielding his own team, the Race Hill Farms Organization in 1987.

The Yarboroughs own three dry cleaners, a carpet factory, a 1,300-acre farm, a Honda/Mazda dealership, and seven Hardee restaurants. They live on a huge farm in Sardis, South Carolina, (3 children). Yarborough wrote his autobiography *Cale: The Hazardous Life and Times of the World's Greatest Stock Car Driver* in 1987 with William Neely.

Carl Yastrzemski

When this diamond leader trotted off the Fenway Park turf for the last time in 1983, he was finally able to do what a note taped in his locker reminded him to do: "Relax." Consciously abating pressure had been almost as much an effort during Yaz's 23 Red Sox seasons as making "hard contact" with baseballs. Called up from the minors in 1961 to step into the slugging shoes of the retired Ted Williams, Yastrzemski suffered from the shakes at the notion of trying to replace the man he idolized as "the greatest hitter who ever lived." In his first few seasons, he gulped down a tranquilizer before every game. When he didn't live up to the premature ballyhoo, and was criticized as another of the lackluster "Fenway Millionaires," he downplayed it and forgave. "They booed me," Yaz says of the home fans, "but they didn't really mean it. . . . When you have been told at 20 that you will replace Ted Williams, nothing after that is pressure." Earning the Triple Crown by winning the 1967 American League batting, RBI, and homer titles while also sparking the Sox to their first pennant in two decades helped relieve the pressure, and gave Yaz what he sought. "I never cared about being a superstar. I just wanted respect." The no-longer-sluggish slugger received that in the way of being chosen the league's MVP.

Yastrzemski (pronounced Yeh-*strem*-ski) seemed destined for this designation almost from the day he was born, 22 August 1939. His father, a Long Island potato farmer, had played semi-pro ball (as Carl would) and gave Carl his first batting lesson almost as soon as he could walk. He was a white-hot high school hitter, and was at the University of Notre Dame when Boston signed him as the seemingly perfect choice for Williams' eventual replacement. Amid much fanfare, he broke in for the 1961 season, slumped along for six-seasons, then made the big breakthrough with help of special coaching lessons from the Splendid Splinter himself, who later managed Boston. The future Hall of Famer went on to become an 18-time All Star, one of only four swatters to get 3,000 hits *and* 400 homers, and he made no bones about the work that it took. But "you pay a price. At home too." (His 23-year marriage was near divorce on several occasions). "I've gotten everything out of me that I had," he said while still an active player. "So the day I retire, it's going to be a good feeling." Like his father before him, he can now sit back and watch the development of his son Mike, a major league prospect. He and wife Carol Ann have two other children. In 1989 he received the highest of his honors as he was inducted into the Baseball Hall of Fame.

Dwight Yoakam

Dwight Yoakam is one of the most conspicuously mythical figures among country music's new traditionalists. Yoakam responded to his label: "Every few years there has to be an artist that addresses the basic, austere, raw elements of the form. But I don't see the music as conservative. I've been considered more of a rebel than a conformist." The rebel image was enhanced by Yoakam's appearance. With his cowboy hat brim (so low his eyes remained in ominous shadow), studded jeans, and jackets whose elaborate designs he created, Yoakam appeared a lean, charismatic figure.

Born 23 October 1956 in southeast rural Kentucky, he grew up in Columbus, Ohio. He spent some time attending Ohio State University, then went to Los Angeles looking for a recording contract. Instead, he found work as a trucker for six years. "Driving for a living gives you a lot of time to think and be alone. . . . I enjoy being alone and find a great deal of creative energy in solitude." He developed a cult following in Los Angeles before landing a recording contract. His outspoken support for a less commercial style of country music has led him into hot water and for a time Yoakam and the Nashville powers in the country music industry were at odds. Yoakam saw the music as a genuine form of expression, emotional and political, and maintained creative control over his music. The release of Reprise Records *Guitars, Cadillacs Etc. Etc.* in 1986 started Yoakam on his successful career with hits like "Honky Tonk Man" and "Guitars, Cadillacs." His second album *Hillbilly Deluxe* was dedicated to his idol, one of the originators of the Bakersfield sound, Buck Owens. It continued the stylistic pattern of the first album and led to the thematic third album *Buenas Noches from a Lonely Room* which hit the number one spot on *Billboard*. The first two albums have been certified gold with *Noches* sure to follow suit. Side one follows a relationship from romantic buoyancy to the girl's murder by the jilted lover. "I made the statement I wanted to make on side one. Side one's really dark, deadly dark. But it was a catharsis for me to write and sing these feelings. Side two is to inhale again, to breathe." It features Yoakam's hit duet with Buck Owens "Streets of Bakersfield." It contains the chorus "You don't know me but you don't like me, you say you care less what I feel" seemingly tailored for Yoakam's perceived persona of the reputation he had in the industry. The album gave Yoakam the credibility he had been denied, earning rave reviews and reestablishing Owens' career as well. Yoakam earned a 1989 Grammy nomination as Best Vocal Performance Male Country for the album and enjoyed a successful ninety-city tour with Buck Owens appearing at some of the stops.

Yoakam seems to have won his struggle with the industry over his self-described "Hillbilly" music. The combination of bluegrass, road-house honky-tonk, tragic troubadourian ballads, and folk ballads from the banks of the Ohio, enhanced by the spirit and soul of the Kentucky county where Yoakam spent much of his youth visiting grandparents, is firmly ensconced on the country charts, occasionally crossing over to rock charts. Yoakam's plans for the future are simple. "I have songs written that I haven't recorded yet, but I don't believe in forcing anything—you just have to keep doing it. I do what I'm doing because I want to—I didn't sit down and decide it was the right time to be a country artist. My plan is to continue to make my music. That's where I go . . ."

The Duke and Duchess of York

Sarah Margaret Ferguson was born on 15 October 1959, the second daughter of Major Ronald Ferguson and his former wife Mrs. Hector Barrantes. She spent her early years at her parents' home in Sunninghill near Ascot, and was educated at two local boarding schools, Daneshill and Hurst Lodge. Upon finishing her education there, she went on to attend a secretarial college in South Kensington. Following her training, she landed a job with a public relations firm. This position led to a job with an art gallery in Covenent Gardens, and later, a position with the London office of a fine-art publishing company, of which she was in charge at the time of her marriage to Prince Andrew. Utilizing her publishing experience, the Duchess of York has written—an autobiography entitled *Duchess: An Intimate Portrait of Sarah, Duchess of York*, which was published in 1989.

The Royal Duchess of York's father served in the Life Guards from 1949 to 1968 and commanded the Sovereign's Escort of the Household Cavalry. He is currently deputy chairman of the Guards Polo Club at Windsor. Her parents divorced, and her mother, Susan, moved to Argentina. Her father has remarried and lives with his wife at Dummer Down House near Basingstoke. Her Royal Highness has an older sister who lives in Australia, as well as a half-brother and two half-sisters. The ancestry of the Royal Duchess can be traced back to the Royal House of Stuart, even though her grandmother Lady Elmhirst is a member of the family of Duke of Buccleuch.

The Duchess of York is a patron to many organizations including the Chemical Dependency Centre, the Carr Gomm Society, the Tate Gallery Foundation, Winchester Cathedral Trust and Blue Cross Animal Welfare. She also holds presidencies in the Anastasia Trust for the Deaf, Action Research for the Crippled Child, and the Royal Commonwealth Society. In addition, she is continuing her publishing work. In her spare time, she enjoys riding, skiing, tennis and flying (in February 1987 she received her private pilot's licence, and in December her private helicpoter licence).

Andrew Albert Christian Edward Edinburgh was born on 19 February 1960 in Buckingham Palace. He was named Andrew after Prince Philip's father and Albert after King George VI. After his initial education by a governess, he left for the Heatherdown Preparatory School near Ascot at the age of eight. Five years later, he went on to attend the Gordonstoun School in Scotland where he studied English, history, economics and political science. During his time there, His Royal Highness spent two terms at Lakefield College School in Ontario, as well as some time in France. The Duke of York was, and still is, very athletic, participating in such sports as rugby football, cricket, squash, skiing and sailing, and glider flying (he received his parachutist's badge from the Royal Air Force in 1978). The Duke of York joined the Royal Navy on 12 September 1979 for a short service commission as a seaman officer specializing as a helicopter pilot. Soon after, he entered the Britannia Royal Naval College Dartmouth where he joined the HMS *Hermes* (a training ship) for a short period of professional training. Upon his return to the U.K., His Royal Highness took a course for Royal Marine young officers which qualified him for his green beret. Returning to Dartmouth, he graduated at the Lord High Admiral's Divisions. His Royal Highness then started his flying training in RAF Leeming in North Yorkshire with the Royal Navy Elementary Flying Training Squadron. He then went on to the Royal Naval Air Station in Cornwell in 1980 for helicopter flying training. In April 1981, he received his wings from the Duke of Edinburgh. In October 1981, the Duke of York joined the 820 Squadron on HMS *Invincible* and sailed throughout the Falkland Islands, as well as flying as second pilot in *Sea King*. Two years later, he was appointed to 702 Naval Air Squadron in Portland, Dorset, to undertake a Lynx helicopter conversion course. On 1 February 1984 His Royal Highness was promoted to lieutenant, and the Queen appointed him a Personal Aide-de-Camp. He continued his flight studies, taking courses at the Royal Naval College, and the Royal Naval Air Station Yeovilton. A few years later, in 1987, His Royal Highness was appointed to 702 Naval Air Squadron at Portland as Helicopter Warfare Instructor, followed by his joining the HMS *Edinburgh* in 1988. When the Duke of York turned 21 in 1981, he became eligible to act as Counsellor of State. His first official public-speaking engagement was in 1981 at the celebratory dinner for the rugby match between Oxford and Cambridge.

His Royal Highness is patron of the British Schools Exploring Society and the SS Great Britain Appeal, as well as the Jubilee Sailing Trust and Aycliffe School. In addition, since 1986 he has been the Governor of Gordonstoun School. In his spare time, the Duke of York is a photographer. In 1983 a few of his photographs were selected to be exhibited at the Hamilton Gallery in London. In addition, he had a book published in 1985 entitled *Photographs By HRH The Prince Andrew*. In 1986 yet another exhibition of his photos was held in the Royal Albert Hall.

Princess Sarah and Prince Andrew were married on 23 July 1986 in Westminster Abbey. On that same day, the Prince had been created Duke of York, Earl of Iverness and Baron Killyleagh. The royal couple spent their honeymoon upon the Royal Yacht in the Azores. They have made several overseas visits together since their marriage. Their first voyage was to the Netherlands in 1986 to join in the opening of the Scheldt Barrier. Following visits include the Bordeaux region of France (1987), Canada, which was their first official joint visit (1987), and Mauritius for British Week. They have one child, Beatrice Elizabeth Mary, who was born 8 August 1988.

Michael York

He looks like a blond lightweight pugilist (his nose has been broken twice), yet his accent is very much Oxford, his style cleverly subdued. Though he received critical acclaim in such films as *Accident, Romeo and Juliet, Justine, Something for Everyone* and *Zeppelin*, it wasn't until his highly sensitive performance as a scholarly bisexual in *Cabaret* that his stock became unassailably blue chip. Recent films include: *The White Lions* (1979), *Final Assignment* (1979), *For Those I Loved* (1983), *Success is the Best Revenge* (1983), *Casablanca Express* (1989), and *The Return of the Three Musketeers* (1989). He did a season stint as the ex-boyfriend of Abbye Ewing, on the popular nighttime soap, "Knots Landing" in 1987. He also appeared in the CBS telefilm "The Lady and the Highwayman" (1988).

Born in Fulmer, England, 27 March 1942, he was admitted to Britain's National Theatre after graduating from Oxford. ("I stayed there two years and I felt I was actually getting down to the ground roots of acting.... Everyone takes the same classes—movement, voice, fencing—so you suddenly find yourself doing knee bends next to Sir Laurence.") A minor role in Franco Zeffirelli's National Theatre production of *Much Ado about Nothing* proved to be the big opportunity. When Zeffirelli got around to casting his film version of *The Taming of the Shrew* in 1966, he remembered Michael, and gave him the part of the lovestruck *Lucentio*. Later that year he reached a turning point in his career as the doomed blueblood in Joseph Losey's *Accident*. Broadway credits include *Bent* (1980) and the musical version of *The Little Prince* (1982).

His wife is American Patricia McCallum, a former *Glamour* magazine photographer, whom he married in 1968.

Andrew Young

His election as the first black mayor of Atlanta in 1981 occurred just two years after he had been embarrassingly ousted as Jimmy Carter's UN ambassador for having met with a representative of the PLO. For Young, it was a political resurrection. For blacks, it was a major boost to the growing minority power base nation-wide. Born in New Orleans on 12 March 1932, Andrew Young learned to negotiate growing up black in an Italian and Irish middle-class neighborhood. "I was taught to fight when people called me Nigger, and that's when I learned negotiating was better than fighting." That lesson stood him in good stead years later, when marching beside Martin Luther King, Jr. during historic civil rights demonstrations.

Young's first career inclinations were far more pragmatic. He planned to follow his father into dental practice, but was sidetracked by an interest in the ministry. After attending Howard University, he entered a seminary in Connecticut, and was ordained in 1955 by the United Church of Christ, a predominantly white denomination. Young pastored churches throughout the South and, through his congregations, spearheaded a voter registration drive. As a member of the Southern Christian Leadership Conference, the largest civil rights group, Young helped draft the Civil Rights Act of 1964 and the Voting Rights Act of 1965, and directed the massive non-violent assault against segregation in Birmingham. Resigning form the SCLC as Vice-president in 1970, Young set his sights on the U.S. House seat from Georgia's mainly white fifth district, but lost the racially charged campaign against Republican incumbent Fletcher Thompson. He ran for Congress again two years later against Republican Rodney Cook and won. Young retained his seat in landslide victories in 1974 and 1976. In Congress Young opposed the Vietnam war and increases in military spending. He fought for increased aid to the poor and generally voted the liberal line.

Largely credited for helping deliver the black vote for Carter, Young was rewarded with the post of U.S. Ambassador to the U.N. But his outspoken nature and tendency to act independently led to embarrassments for the Administration; his meeting with the PLO forced Young's resignation. "It is very difficult to do the things that I think are in the interest of the country and also maintain the standards of protocol and diplomacy," he said. "I really don't feel a bit sorry for anything that I have done." And with that, Young returned to Atlanta to win the mayoral race. Young married Jean Childs, a teacher, in 1954, and they have four children. He is currently in his last term as mayor.

Loretta Young

Tall, slender, stylishly dressed, she swirled through a distant doorway into living rooms all across America back in the 1950s on her own "Loretta Young Show." Twenty years later, much to her chagrin, she was swirling again, via reruns, in foreign countries all over the world—tall, slender, but dressed out of style. In 1972 the actress with the "luminously virginal quality" showed her "steel butterfly" side in Los Angeles Superior Court. Suing NBC for $1,300,000 for circulating the old shows without her permission, she said, "I wanted to present myself as a well-dressed fashionable woman." The judge saw it her way.

Loretta was born 6 January 1913 in Salt Lake City. When her father abandoned his family early on, her mother packed up her pretty daughters, headed for Los Angeles, and soon had all of the girls working regularly in the movies. Polly Ann, Betty, Jane, and Georgianna eventually went on to other things (Georgianna married Ricardo Montalban) but four-year-old Gretchen, later renamed Loretta, stuck it out. She was the star of close to a hundred big screen features (she won an Oscar for *The Farmer's Daughter* in 1947, and Oscar nomination for her own favorite, *Come to the Stable*, the following year) and dramas by the score on the little screen (two Emmys as best actress in a continuing series) and won a Golden Globe Award for her role in the NBC-TV special "Christmas Eve," in 1987.

After eloping at 17 with Grant Withers (the marriage was annulled after less than a year), she married (and divorced in 1969) Thomas Lewis, father of her three children. A Catholic and unabashed Puritan, famous in her TV days for the swear box she kept on the set (anyone caught cursing had to contribute a fine to St. Ann's Home for Unwed Mothers), she believes in the merits of stern self-discipline and hard work—qualities she touts highly in her autobiography, *The Things I Had to Learn*. A believer also in the old proverb about cleanliness being next to godliness she offers a special reminder in the book's section on beauty regarding the advantages of washing one's neck.

Robert Young

"Metro was going through the motions of testing a producer's girlfriend. I fed her the lines. She was so terrible they kept shooting over her shoulders at me," laughs actor Robert Young, musing on the beginnings of a long and distinguished career—his first screen test with Metro in 1931. "I was signed and she wasn't." When he went home to announce the news, his mother, brothers, and sister joined hands and danced around the kitchen table. His name conjures up three careers. First he played the prototypical thirties man—smooth-faced in cable-knit sweaters and Oxford bags or changing into white tie and tails, elegantly lighting Joan Crawford's cigarettes. Second the mature forties actor played Boston Brahmin in *H. M. Pulham, Esq.*, scarred war veteran in *The Enchanted Cottage*, and David to Dorothy McGuire's classic *Claudia*. Third, Young played the all-American father figure, starring for six years on television as Jim Anderson, harrassed dad in "Father Knows Best" (which originated as a network radio show in 1949 before moving to television in 1954), and finally from 1969-1976 as the benevolent Dr. Welby in "Marcus Welby, M.D.," achieving the highest Nielsen ratings. This role sequence of dad and doctor earned Young three Emmys.

Robert Young was born 22 February 1907 in Chicago, but raised in Seattle and Los Angeles. The family barely had enough to eat and he recalls having to work from the age of eight selling newspapers. After his father's final desertion of home when he was ten, the constant struggle for survival preyed upon him. "As far back as I can remember, I was afraid—of some imagined disaster that never did eventuate. When I was a child, I used to hide in the crooks of trees, just to be alone." (His high school teacher coaxed him to act at the Pasadena Playhouse, helping him escape his harrowing shyness.) "When I became an actor I constantly felt I wasn't worthy, that I had no right to be a star. All those years at Metro, and even later, on "Father Knows Best," I hid a black terror behind a cheerful face. Naturally, I tried to find a way out. Alcoholism was the inevitable result," he confides. "It took me thirty years to realize I was poisoning myself to death. It was an immensely slow, difficult process, but after slipping back again and again, I at last made a kind of giant step and I was across the threshold to sanity and health." Coupled with the help and understanding of a sympathetic wife (married only once, he wed his high school sweetheart, Betty Henderson, in 1933 and has four daughters), Alcoholics Anonymous aided him, and he has worked on their behalf, lecturing and arranging meetings.

His indelible image—warm, wise, benevolent, understanding, and compassionate—culminated in many a television commercial for "Sanka Brand Decaffeinated Coffee," when Young was asked to play himself in a long series of commercials revolving around his presence. And in 1984 ABC brought Dr. Welby out of retirement after eight years away from his practice, with a two-hour TV-movie titled "The Return of Marcus Welby, M.D."—and Robert Young emerged, as always, dapper and dignified. In 1988 he filmed another continuation of the medical man, "Dr. Marcus Welby in Paris." Other recent television appearances include the telefilms "Mercy or Murder?" (1987) and "Conspiracy of Love" (1987).

Henny Youngman

His "Take my wife—please!" is surely the the most famous four-word joke in the language and, as the *New Yorker* once pointed out, "it's a joke so compact it has a punch *word* instead of a punch line." That pared-to-the-bone precision is typical of the comic Walter Winchell heralded as "The King of the One-Liners," who regularly manages to deliver an incredible 250 jokes in a single 40-minute routine. Says Henny: "For me, every joke is really a cartoon—you can see it." Another Youngman classic is a perfect example of this: "She was bowlegged, he was knock-kneed. When they stood together, they spelled 'OX.'"

Born in London, about the time of his jokes (circa 1907), Henry Youngman was brought to Brooklyn as an infant by his Russian-born parents. His opera-loving dad gave him fiddle lessons in the hope that he'd wind up in the Metropolitan Opera orchestra but instead, at 18, he formed his own band. One night, when a comedy act failed to show up, a club owner asked Henny (by now billed as Youngman) to go on and tell some of the jokes he'd been cracking during band rehearsals. He went over big and was on his way. From a two-year stint on Kate Smith's radio show, Henny progressed to night clubs and, still using his fiddle for a prop ("Would you believe it, I used to play at Carnegie Hall—till the cops chased me away"), moved into the rarefied inner circle of "comic's comics," adored as much by other joke-peddlers as audiences. (Says Milton Berle: "His *mind* has a funny bone.") The six-feet-two Henny averaged 200 shows a year and never missed a performance. And, as pointed out by Tony Hiss in Youngman's *New Yorker* profile, "he doesn't do nasty material; he never attacks people . . . and he stay away from all X-rated material; he stays clean."

Henny's wife, Sadie Cohen, whom he met when she was working in the sheet music department of Kresge's and he had a concession in the store printing business cards for actors, died in March 1987. She had once assured everyone that she never took personally her husband's famous one-liner about her—nor any of the others which have become staples of his act. Youngman appeared in the 1987 film *Amazon Women on the Moon* and his autobiography, *Take My Life, Please* was published in 1988.

Richard Zanuck

A competitor of this granite-jawed son of a movie mogul once said of Richard Zanuck: "He wants to win at all costs." Since being forced to resign in 1971 as president of Twentieth Century-Fox while his father watched with cool detachment, the younger Zanuck has gone on to co-produce revenue-winning films like *The Sting* (1973), *Jaws* (1975), *Cocoon* (1985), and outstanding features like *The Verdict* (1980) with Paul Newman. It's a far cry from the day when he was literally led out of Fox's offices through the boiler room, and figuratively thrown on his ear. "I remember going down Hollywood Boulevard," Zanuck says, "and wondering, will they take my star away from in front of the restaurant."

Born in Beverly Hills, 13 December 1934, the combative Richard spent most of his life one step behind his father, Darryl. He began working at Fox during summer holidays from military school. After graduating from Stanford, and military service, he joined his dad as story and production assistant on such films as *Island in the Sun* and *The Sun Also Rises*. At 22, he became vice president of the independent Darryl Zanuck Productions where, in 1959, he filled in for his already-occupied elder and produced *Compulsion*, which won awards at Cannes. When his father returned to Fox, Richard went with him to become a V.P. of the Hollywood studio, then was sent to New York.

The Zanucks were partly responsible for hits like *Patton* (1970), *M.A.S.H.* (1970), *Butch Cassidy and the Sundance Kid* (1969), and *The Sound of Music* (1965; co-produced by Richard's present partner, David Brown). But after high-budgeted bombs like *Hello, Dolly!* and *Doctor Dolittle*, the ax fell on Zanuck the younger. When Zanuck and Brown (who was also fired), lost their subsequent jobs at competitor Warner Bros., they formed Zanuck/Brown Productions. With *The Sting*, the pair have a Best Picture Oscar on their mantle, and *The Verdict* received five Academy nominations. Richard Darryl Zanuck and his partner tried to sue Fox and the elder Zanuck for $22 million shortly after their dismissal. With the death of Darryl in 1979, and two of the biggest box office draws in movie history (*Jaws* and *The Sting*) behind him, Richard may finally have matched his father's formidable achievements. In 1988 Zanuck split from Brown to go solo. His most recent productions include *Cocoon II* (1988) and *Driving Miss Daisy* (1989). Divorced from Lili Gentle (two girls), and Linda Harrison (two sons), he is now married to the former Lili Fini.

Franco Zeffirelli

"To be despised by critics but loved by the audience," writes Corby Kummer in *Horizon*, is all right with Franco Zeffirelli. The director, who has made a name for florid showmanship in theatre, opera, and film, doesn't much mind if critics accuse him of churning out trash disguised with thick coats of varnish. His audiences say his films move them deeply, and that's enough for him." His favorite entertainment medium is opera, to which "nothing else in the arts can come near," but on the other hand he has called motion pictures "a fascinating medium which gives many opportunities that the others don't give." About his own contribution to these and other media he can be disarming with interviews: "As a director I'm so-so," he told the *New York Times* in 1983, "but as a designer I'm the best."

Born in Florence, Italy, 12 February 1923, the only child of a young couple in modest circumstances, little Franco was packed off at six to live with an aunt when his parents divorced, the latter a most unusual occurrence in prewar Italy. As a youth he studied architecture at the University of Florence and, when Italy became the scene of fighting between Germans and invading Allies, he joined up with some partisans and then with British troops. When peace came he returned to Florence and took up acting, on stage and in films, but a meeting with Luchino Visconti in 1949 led to his designing sets for several of that director's productions, including *A Streetcar Named Desire* and *The Three Sisters;* this in turn led to his designing and directing operas for La Scala of Milan. In 1959 he was invited to Covent Garden to stage a production of *Lucia di Lammermoor* starring Joan Sutherland. Thereafter, he put on numerous operas in Milan, London, New York, Paris, and Vienna. Simultaneously he has directed plays since 1960 and films and television shows since 1966.

Zeffirelli's most ambitious film is the epic *Jesus of Nazareth* (1975-76). Of *The Champ*, his 1979 remake of a 1931 tear-jerker that touched him profoundly as a child, Pauline Kael wrote that he "directed as if he had never met a human being." But the director, warned that no mass market existed for Shakespeare, also had the satisfaction of seeing his *Romeo and Juliet* gross $52 million. As a passionate opera-lover he takes special delight in recording on film live performances of great operatic works, with the world's leading singers, and he has, to date, filmed several, including *Cavalleria Rusticana*, *I Pagliacci*, and *La Traviata* (1983, starring Teresa Stratas and Placido Domingo). At the Metropolitan Opera he has designed and staged—with notable success—a sumptuous *La Boheme* and *Tosca*. In 1985 he turned his considerable talents to ballet, staging *Swan Lake* with two ballerinas (one as Odette, the other as Odile) instead of the traditional single ballerina essaying both roles, and in 1988, he directed the film *Young Toscanini*.

Stephanie Zimbalist

"I like my name. I like the rhythm. Besides, I've never had the problems that everybody assumes children of well-known people are supposed to have," says the actress-daughter of longtime TV perennial Efrem Zimbalist, Jr. ("The FBI," 1965-74) and grand-daughter of the world-famous violinist Efrem Zimbalist and opera diva Alma Gluck. As Laura Holt on TV's "Remington Steele" (1982-1987), she operated her detective agency under a fictitious male name, but Stephanie Zimbalist herself "never really seriously considered" changing her own. Zimbalist's "sexually-charged on-camera battles" with series co-star Pierce Brosnan kept viewers entranced enough for the show to last for five seasons, and then to be resurrected again in two-hour telefilms after the series was cancelled. The show established the pert, down-to-earth, frecklefaced actress as one of the hotter young performers on the prime time line-up.

Manhattan-born, 8 October circa 1958, Stephanie is not only from a famous family but of preppy Foxcroft in Virginia and, among other acting studies, she spent a year at the theatre division of Juilliard. At the end of her first term there, the powers-that-be released her with the suggestion that she'd led too sheltered a life and needed to "experience the world." "It was a devastating moment," Stephanie recalled to Michael Leahy of *TV Guide*. "I began contemplating things. Maybe I should take LSD or become a hooker." Instead, she headed for Hollywood and managed to find work on two TV movies—as a kidnap victim in "Yesterday's Child" on NBC and a high school girl in love on CBS's "Forever." Not long afterward she was asked to do the pilot for "Remington Steele" and has since appeared in films (*The Awakening; The Magic of Lassie*), assorted mini-series on TV ("Centennial"), telefilms ("Love on the Run," "The Man in the Brown Suit"), and theatre projects (e.g. *The Cherry Orchard*, *My One and Only*, and *Carousel*).

Pinchas Zukerman

"The most versatile of all major musicians," according to the *Washington Post*, is violinist/violist/conductor Pinchas Zukerman. A musician of amazing virtuosity and personal charm, Zukerman (as violinist) is "absolutely without peer" said the London *Times* and (as violist) "probably the best living." "For me to do these three things—to play the violin and viola

Pinchas Zukerman

and to conduct," explains Zukerman, "is a way of gathering more information.... Conducting improves your playing. You see and hear more.... But I have a feeling inside of me that without playing—producing my own sound—I'm lost, I need to do it. It's like sex, I can't live without the fiddle. Maybe when I'm 74. But it's my friend, my companion. I was born to play it."

He was born 16 July 1948 in Israel where Zukerman was given his early musical education via the recorder, clarinet, and a half-sized violin by his father. At the age of eight, he was enrolled at the Israel Conservatory and Academy of Music under Ilona Fedler, where as a child prodigy, his arrogance (the spoils of early adultation) was apparent—"It was put in my head that I was good and, of course, after a while you start believing it. I didn't have the emotional support to know there was so much I had to learn." With the encouragement of Isaac Stern and Pablo Casals, Zukerman was brought to the United States as a thirteen-year-old for studies at Juilliard. "It was a lonely time, a very lonely time. I didn't know a word of English.... I played a lot of hooky. I haunted the pool halls and almost got into trouble. When Isaac Stern found out . . . he got me to see that music isn't a profession, it's a way of life. I was 16. There was still time, thank God." "Pinky," as Zukerman is known to his friends, used the time well and entered the spotlight of a brilliant, world-wide career after he captured first prize (1967) in the Levintritt Foundation International Competition. From there he performed to great critical acclaim in recitals and festivals the world over. In 1970 Zukerman debuted as conductor with the English Chamber Orchestra, the country's only full-time professional chamber orchestra. The superstar (who usually conducts without the "barrier" of a score) is humbled by the awesomeness of music at its best; "It can transform you somewhere beyond ordinary reality.... You move and the orchestra goes with you." Zukerman still gets an "incredible hot flash of blood to the head" when the music begins with the first downbeat of the baton. "There is always that moment of silence and apprehension before you go on-stage to perform. This is an amazing feeling, this silence."

Zukerman is divorced from his flutist/writer first wife, Eugenia (two children). He married actress Tuesday Weld in October 1985. An avid tennis enthusiast, Zukerman also rides horses and enjoys spectator sports. His commitment to his music is a total one—"It's like walking in a desert and all of a sudden you need water. If you can transmit this to the audience, this wonderful need for music, well, that is what you are always trying to do. . . . "

CUMULATIVE INDEX

Celebrities listed in this index have appeared in one or more volumes of CELEBRITY REGISTER. After each listee's name, the volume(s) in which he or she appeared are indicated by number:

1 — 1959
2 — 1963
3 — 1973
4 — 1986
5 — 1990

If the celebrity is deceased, the death date is provided after the individual's name in the order of month, day, year.

A

AARON, Hank **1,2,3,4,5**
ABBOTT, Bud (d.4/24/74) **1**
ABBOTT, George **1,2,3,4,5**
ABDUL-JABBAR, Kareem **3,4**
ABDULLAH, Sheik of Kuwait (d.11/24/65) **1**
ABERNATHY, Ralph **3**
ABERNETHY, Roy (d.2/28/77) **2**
ABRAMS, Creighton (d.9/4/74) **3**
ABZUG, Bella **3,4**
ACE, Goodman (d.3/25/82) **1,2,3**
ACHESON, Dean (d.10/12/71) **1,2**
ACKERMAN, Fred **2**
ADAMS, Cedric (d.2/18/61) **1**
ADAMS, Charles Francis (d.9/29/88) **2**
ADAMS, Edie **1,2**
ADAMS, Eva **2**
ADAMS, J. Donald **2**
ADAMS, Franklin P. (d.3/23/60) **1**
ADAMS, Joey and Cindy **4,5** (see also ADAMS, Joey, **2,3**)
ADAMS, Sherman (d.10/27/86) **1,2**
ADDAMS, Charles **1,2,3,4**
ADDAMS, Dawn (d.5/7/85) **1**
ADDERLY, Julian "Cannonball" (d.8/8/75) **3**
ADENAUER, Konrad (d.1/19/67) **1**
ADLER, Buddy (d.7/12/60) **1**
ADLER, Larry **1,2**
ADLER, Luther (d.12/8/84) **1**
ADLER, Mortimer **1,2,4**
ADLER, Polly (d.6/9/61) **1**
ADLER, Richard **2**
ADOLFO **3,4,5**
ADRIAN (d.8/4/77) **1**
AGAR, Herbert (d.11/24/80) **1**
AGASSI, Andre **5**
AGNEW, Spiro **3**
AGRONSKY, Martin **1,2,4**
AHERNE, Brian (d.2/10/86) **1,2**
AIKEN, Conrad (d.8/17/73) **1,2**
AIKEN, George (d.11/19/84) **1,2,3**
AILEY, Alvin **3,4,5**
AKIHITO, Crown Prince of Japan **1**
ALABAMA **4,5**
ALAJALOV, Constantin **1,2**
ALBANESE, Licia **1,2**
ALBEE, Edward **2,3,4,5**
ALBERGHETTI, Anna Maria **1,2**
ALBERT, Carl **2,3**
ALBERT, Eddie **1,2,3,4,5**
ALBERT, Edward **3**
ALBRIGHT, Tenley **1**
ALDA, Alan **4,5**
ALDRICH, Larry **2**
ALDRICH, Richard (d.3/31/86) **1,2**
ALDRICH, Winthrop (d.2/25/74) **1,2**
ALDRIN, Edwin "Buzz" **3**

ALESSANDRONI, Eugene **2**
ALEXANDER, Henry (d.12/14/69) **2**
ALEXANDER OF TUNIS, Earl (d.6/16/69) **1**
ALEXANDER, Jane **4,5**
ALEXANDER, Shana **4,5**
ALEXANDRA, Princess **1**
ALEXANDRA, Queen **1**
ALEXIS, Kim **5**
ALGREN, Nelson (d.5/9/81) **1,2**
ALI, Muhammad **3,4,5** (see also CLAY, Cassius, **2**)
ALLEN, Charles **2**
ALLEN, Dick **3**
ALLEN, George **3**
ALLEN, George E. (d.4/23/73) **1,2**
ALLEN, George V. (d.7/11/70) **1,2**
ALLEN, Gracie (d.8/28/64) **1,2**
ALLEN, Ivan, Jr. **3**
ALLEN, Marcus **4,5**
ALLEN, Mel **1,2**
ALLEN, Peter **4,5**
ALLEN, Steve **1,2,3,4,5**
ALLEN, William **2**
ALLEN, Woody **2,3,4,5**
ALLERS, Franz **3**
ALLILUYEVA, Svetlana **3**
ALLYSON, June **1,2**
ALMOND, J. Lindsay **1,2**
ALONSO, Alicia **1**
ALPERT, Herb **3,4,5**
ALPHAND, Hervé **1**
ALSOP, John **2**
ALSOP, Joseph (d.8/28/89) **1,2,3,4**
ALSOP, Stewart (d.5/26/84) **1,2,3**
ALSTON, Walter (d.10/1/84) **1,2,3**
ALTMAN, Robert **3,4,5**
ALVAREZ, Luis **1,2,3**
AMADO, Jorge **3**
AMBERG, Richard (d.9/3/67) **2**
AMBLER, Eric **1**
AMECHE, Don **1,2**
AMIES, Hardy **3,4,5**
AMORY, Cleveland **1,2,3,4,5**
AMSTERDAM, Morey **2**
ANASTASIA, (d.2/84) **1**
ANDERSON, Clinton (d.11/11/75) **1,2**
ANDERSON, Eugenie **2**
ANDERSON, Jack **3,4,5**
ANDERSON, John **2**
ANDERSON, Judith **1,2,3,4**
ANDERSON, Laurie **4**
ANDERSON, Leroy (d.5/18/75) **1,2**
ANDERSON, Loni **4,5**
ANDERSON, Marian **1,2,3,4**
ANDERSON, Paul **1**
ANDERSON, Richard Dean **5**
ANDERSON, Robert **1,2,3,4**
ANDERSON, Robert B. **1,2**
ANDERSON, William R. **1,2**
ANDERSSON, Bibi **3**

ANDRESS, Ursula **3**
ANDRETTI, Mario **3,4,5**
ANDREWS, Dana **1,2**
ANDREWS, Julie **1,2,3,4,5**
ANDREWS SISTERS La Verne (d.5/8/57), Maxine, Patti **1,2**
ANDREWS, T. Coleman (d.10/83) **1**
ANGELES, Victoria De Los **1**
ANGELI, Pier (d.9/10/71) **1**
ANGLE, Paul (d.5/11/75) **2**
ANKA, Paul **2,3,4,5**
ANNABELLA **1**
ANNE, Princess **1**
ANNENBERG, Walter **1,2,3,4,5**
ANN-MARGRET **2,3,4,5**
ANOUILH, Jean **1**
ANSERMET, Ernest (d.2/20/69) **1**
ANTHONY, Joseph **2**
ANTOINE (d.6/76) **1**
ANTONIONI, Michelangelo **3**
ARAGON, Louis (d.12/24/82) **1**
ARCARO, Eddie **1,2,3**
ARCHER, Anne **5**
ARCHIBALD, Nate **3**
ARCHIPENKO, Alexander (d.2/25/64) **1,2**
ARDEN, Elizabeth (d.10/18/66) **1,2**
ARDEN, Eve **1,2**
ARDREY, Robert (d.1/14/80) **2,3**
ARENDS, Leslie C. (d.7/16/85) **1,2**
ARENDT, Hannah (d.12/4/75) **3**
ARGERICH, Martha **4**
ARGUELLO, Alexis **4**
ARKIN, Alan **3**
ARLEDGE, Roone **4,5**
ARLEN, Harold (d.4/23/86) **1,2,3,4**
ARLETTY **1**
ARMANI, Giorgio **4,5**
ARMOUR, Richard (d.2/28/89) **2**
ARMOUR, Tommy (d.9/12/68) **1,2**
ARMSTRONG, Anne **3**
ARMSTRONG, Hamilton Fish (d.4/24/73) **1,2**
ARMSTRONG, Louis (d.7/6/71) **1,2**
ARMSTRONG, Neil **3,4**
ARNALI, Ellis **1,2**
ARNAZ, Desi (d.12/2/86) **1,2**
ARNESS, James **1,2,3,4,5**
ARNO, Peter (d.2/22/68) **1,2**
ARNOLD, Eddy **3,4,5**
ARNOLD, Thurman (d.11/69) **1,2**
ARNOUL, Francoise **1**
ARONSON, Boris (d.11/16/80) **3**
ARON, Raymond C.F. (d.10/17/83) **1**
ARP, Jean (Hans) (d.6/7/66) **1**
ARQUETTE, Cliff (d.9/23/74) **1**
ARQUETTE, Rosanna **4,5**
ARRAU, Claudio **1,2,3,4,5**
ARRUZA, Carlos (d.5/20/66) **1**
ARTHUR, Bea **3,4,5**
ARTHUR, Jean **1**
ARTZYBASHEFF, Boris (d.7/18/65) **1**

461

Cumulative Index

ASCOLI, Max (d.1/1/78) **1,2**
ASH, Mary Kay **4,5**
ASH, Roy L. **3**
ASHCROFT, Peggy **4,5**
ASHE, Arthur, Jr. **3,4,5**
ASHKENAZY, Vladimir **4,5**
ASHLEY, Lady Sylvia (d.6/30/77) **1**
ASHLEY, Merrill **4,5**
ASHMORE, Harry **1,2**
ASHTON, Frederick (d.8/18/88) **1,4**
ASIMOV, Isaac **1,2,3,4,5**
ASNER, Ed **4,5**
ASTAIRE, Adele (d.1/25/81) **2**
ASTAIRE, Fred (d.6/22/87) **1,2,3,4**
ASTLEY, Rick **5**
ASTOR, Brooke **4,5**
ASTOR, John Jacob (d.7/19/71) **1,2**
ASTOR, Lady (LANGHORNE, Nancy Witcher) (d.5/2/64) **1,2**
ASTOR, Mary (d.9/25/87) **1,2,3,4**
ASTRID, Princess of Norway (INGEBORG, Maud) **1**
ATKINS, Chet **3,4,5**
ATKINS, Christopher **4**
ATKINSON, Brooks (d.1/13/84) **1,2,3**
ATKINSON, Ted **1,2**
ATLAS, Charles (d.12/23/72) **1**
ATLEE, Clement (d.10/8/67) **1**
ATTENBOROUGH, Richard **3,4,5**
AUBREY, James **2,3**
AUCHINCLOSS, Mrs. Hugh (d.7/22/89) **2**
AUCHINCLOSS, Louis **2,3,4,5**
AUDEN, W.H. (d.9/28/73) **1,2,3**
AUERBACH, Arnold "Red" **3,4,5**
AUMONT, Jean-Pierre **1**
AURIOL, Jacqueline **1**
AURIOL, Vincent (d.1/1/66) **1**
AUSTIN, J. Paul **3**
AUSTIN, Warren R. (d.4/1/63) **1**
AUTRY, Gene **1,2**
AVALON, Frankie **2**
AVEDON, Richard **1,2,3,4,5**
AX, Emanuel **4,5**
AXELROD, George **1,2,3**
AYKROYD, Dan **4,5**
AYRES, Lew **1,2**
AZNAVOUR, Charles **3,4**
AZUMA, Tokuho **1**

B

BABIN, Victor (d.3/1/72) **2**
BABSON, Roger W. (d.3/5/67) **1,2**
BACALL, Lauren **1,2,3,4,5**
BACHARACH, Bert (d.9/15/83) **1,2,3**
BACHARACH, Burt **3,4,5**
BACHAUER, Gina (d.8/22/76) **3**
BACHRACH, Bradford and Fabian **2**
BACKHAUS, Wilhelm (d.7/5/69) **1**
BACKUS, Jim **1,2,3**
BACON, Mrs. Robert Low **2**
BADILLO, Herman **3**
BAER, Arthur "Bugs" (d.5/17/69) **1,2**
BAER, Max **1**
BAEZ, Joan **2,3,4,5**
BAGNOLD, Enid (d.3/31/81) **1**
BAILEY, F. Lee **3,4,5**
BAILEY, Jack (d.2/1/80) **2**
BAILEY, John (d.4/10/75) **2**
BAILEY, Pearl **1,2,3,4,5**
BAIRD, Bil and Cora (Cora—d.6/12/67) **2** (see also BAIRD, Bil **3**)
BAKER, Anita **5**
BAKER, Carroll **1,2**

BAKER, James **4,5**
BAKER, Janet **4,5**
BAKER, Josephine (d.4/12/75) **1,2,3**
BAKER, Milton (d.8/7/76) **2**
BAKER, Russell **3,4,5**
BALABAN, Barney (d.3/7/71) **1,2**
BALANCHINE, George (d.4/30/83) **1,2,3**
BALDRIGE, "Tish" **2**
BALDRIGE, Malcolm (d.7/25/87) **4**
BALDWIN, Faith (d.3/18/78) **1,2**
BALDWIN, Hanson **2**
BALDWIN, James (d.12/1/87) **2,3,4**
BALDWIN, Roger (d.8/26/81) **3**
BALDWIN, William (Billy) (d.11/26/83) **2,3**
BALENCIAGA (d.3/23/72) **1**
BALIN, Ina **2**
BALL, George **2**
BALL, Lucille (d.4/26/89) **1,2,3,4**
BALLARD, Kaye **2,3,4**
BALLESTEROS, Severiano **4,5**
BALMAIN, Pierre (d.6/29/82) **1,3**
BALSAM, Martin **2,3,4**
BALSAN, Consuelo Vanderbilt (d.12/6/64) **1,2**
BAMPTON, Rose **1**
BANCROFT, Anne **1,2,3,4,5**
BANKHEAD, Tallulah (d.12/12/68) **1,2**
BANKS, Ernie **2**
BANNING, Margaret Culkin (d.1/4/82) **2**
BANNISTER, Roger **1**
BAO DAI **1**
BARAKA, Imamu Amiri (JONES, Leroi) **3,4**
BARBER, Red **1,2**
BARBER, Samuel (d.1/23/81) **1,2,3**
BARBERA, Joe (see also HANNA & BARBERA) **4**
BARBIERI, Fedora **1**
BARBIROLLI, Sir John (d.7/29/70) **1**
BARDOT, Brigitte **1,3,4**
BARENBOIM, Daniel **3,4,5**
BARKER, Lex (d.5/12/73) **1**
BARKIN, Ben **2**
BARNARD, Christiaan **3,4,5**
BARNES, Clive **3,4,5**
BARNES, Henry (d.9/16/68) **2**
BARNET, Charlie **1**
BARNETT, Ross **2**
BARR, Alfred Hamilton, Jr. (d.8/15/81) **2**
BARR, Stringfellow (d.2/2/82) **1,2**
BARRAULT, Jean-Louis **1**
BARRETT, William (d.9/14/86) **2**
BARRIE, Wendy (d.2/2/78) **1**
BARRON, William **2**
BARRY, Gene **2,4**
BARRY, Harold **2**
BARRY, Jack (d.5/2/84) **1**
BARRY, Rick **3**
BARRYMORE, Diana (d.1/25/60) **2**
BARTHELME, Donald **3,4,5**
BARTHOLOMEW, Frank (d.3/85) **2**
BARTLETT, E.L. (d.12/11/68) **2**
BARTOK, Eva **1**
BARTON, Alfred (d.3/15/80) **2**
BARTON, Betsey (d.12/62) **1**
BARTON, Bruce (d.7/5/67) **2**
BARUCH, Bernard (d.6/20/65) **1,2**
BARYSHNIKOV, Mikhail **4,5**
BARZUN, Jacques **1,2,3,4**
BASEHART, Richard (d.9/17/84) **1,2**
BASIE, Count (d.4/26/84) **1,2,3**
BASILIO, Carmen **1**
BASINGER, Kim **5**
BASSEY, Shirley **3,4**
BATEMAN, Jason **5**

BATEMAN, Justine **5**
BATES, Alan **3,4,5**
BATISTA, Fulgencio (d.8/6/73) **1**
BATTELLE, Phyllis **2**
BATTLE, Hinton **4**
BATTLE, Kathleen **4,5**
BAUDOUIN I **1**
BAUM, Vicki (d.8/29/60) **1**
BAXTER, Anne (d.12/12/85) **1,2,3,4**
BAXTER, Dr. Frank **2**
BAXTER-BIRNEY, Meredith **5**
BAY, Mrs. Charles Ulrick (d.9/62) **1**
BAYH, Birch **2,3**
BEACH BOYS, The **4,5**
BEADLE, George **2**
BEALE, Betty **2,3,4**
BEALL, J. Glen **2**
BEAN, Orson **1,2**
BEARD, James (d.1/23/85) **3**
BEATON, Cecil (d.1/18/80) **3**
BEATTIE, Ann **4,5**
BEATTY, Warren **2,3,4,5**
BEAUVOIR, Simone De (d.4/14/86) **1,3,4**
BEAVERBROOK, Lord (d.6/9/64) **1**
BECK, Julian (d.9/14/85), and MALINA, Judith **3**
BECKER, Boris **4,5**
BECKETT, Samuel **1,3,4,5**
BEDFORD, Brian **3**
BEDFORD, Duke of **1**
BEEBE, Lucius (d.2/4/66) **1,2**
BEEBE, William (6/6/62) **1**
BEECHAM, Sir Thomas (d.3/9/61) **1**
BEENE, Geoffrey **3,4,5**
BEGLEY, Ed (d.4/28/70) **1,2**
BEHRENS, Hildegarde **4,5**
BEHRMAN, S.N. (d.9/9/73) **1,2**
BEISE, S. Clark **2**
BÉJART, Maurice **4**
BELAFONTE, Harry **1,2,3,4,5**
BELAFONTE, Shari **5**
BEL GEDDES, Barbara **1,2,3,4,5**
BELINSKY, Bo **2**
BELL, Bert (d.10/11/59) **1**
BELL, David **2**
BELLAMY, Ralph **1,2,3**
BELLI, Melvin **2,3,4,5**
BELLMON, Henry **2**
BELLOW, Saul **1,2,4,5**
BELLUSCHI, Pietro **2**
BELMONDO, Jean-Paul **3,4,5**
BELMONT, Mrs. August (d.10/24/79) **1**
BEMELMANS, Ludwig (d.10/1/62) **1**
BENATAR, Pat **4,5**
BENCH, Johnny **3,4,5**
BENCHLEY, Nathaniel (d.12/14/81) **1,2,3**
BENDIX, William (d.12/14/64) **1,2**
BEN-GURION, David (d.12/1/73) **1**
BENJAMIN, Richard **3,4,5**
BENNETT, Constance (d.7/24/65) **1,2**
BENNETT, Joan **1,2,3,4**
BENNETT, Michael (d.7/2/87) **4**
BENNETT, Robert Russell (d.8/18/81) **2,3**
BENNETT, Tony **1,2,3,4,5**
BENNY, Jack (d.12/27/74) **1,2,3**
BENSON, Ezra Taft **1,2**
BENSON, George **4,5**
BENTLEY, Eric **3,4**
BENTON, Robert **4**
BENTON, Thomas Hart (d.1/19/75) **1,2,3**
BENTON, William (d.3/18/73) **1,2**
BENZELL, Mimi (d.12/23/70) **1,2**
BERENGER, Tom **5**
BERENSON, Bernard (d.10/6/59) **1**
BERG, Gertrude (d.9/14/66) **1,2**

CELEBRITY REGISTER 1990 — Cumulative Index

BERG, Patty **1,2**
BERGEN, Candice **3,4,5**
BERGEN, Edgar (d.9/30/78) **1,2**
BERGEN, Polly **1,2,3,4,5**
BERGMAN, Ingmar **1,3,4,5**
BERGMAN, Ingrid (d.8/29/82) **1,2,3**
BERLE, A.A. (d.2/17/71) **1**
BERLE, Adolph (d.2/18/71) **2**
BERLE, Milton **1,2,3,4,5**
BERLIN, Irving (d.9/22/89) **1,2,3,4,5**
BERLIN, Richard E. **1,2,3**
BERLITZ, Charles **2**
BERMAN, Eugene (d.12/15/72) **1,2**
BERMAN, Shelley **2**
BERNARDI, Herschel **3**
BERNAYS, Edward **1,2**
BERNHARD, Prince **1**
BERNSEN, Corbin **5**
BERNSTEIN, Carl **4**
BERNSTEIN, Elmer **2,3**
BERNSTEIN, Leonard **1,2,3,4,5**
BERRA, Yogi **1,2,3,4,5**
BERRIGAN, Daniel and Philip **3**
BERTOLUCCI, Bernardo **3,4,5**
BEST, Edna (d.9/18/74) **1**
BETTELHEIM, Bruno **3,4,5**
BETTIS, Valerie (d.9/26/82) **1,2**
BEVAN, Aneurin (d.7/6/60) **1**
BEVERIDGE, Don **2**
BEVERIDGE, Sir William (d.4/1/63) **1**
BIBB, Leon **2**
BIBLE, Alan (d.9/12/88) **2**
BIBLE, Dana X. **1**
BIDAULT, Georges (d.1/27/83) **1**
BIDDLE, Francis (d.10/4/68) **2**
BIFFLE, Leslie (d.4/6/66) **2**
BIGART, Homer **1,2**
BIGGS, E. Power (d.3/1/77) **1,2**
BIJAN **4,5**
BIKEL, Theodore **2**
BILLINGSLEY, Sherman (d.10/4/66) **1,2**
BIMSON, Walter **2**
BING, Rudolph **1,2,3**
BINGHAM, Barry **1,2**
BIONDI, Matt **5**
BIRD, Larry **4**
BIRMINGHAM, Stephen **3,4,5**
BISHOP, Elizabeth (d.10/6/79) **3**
BISHOP, Jim (d.7/26/87) **1,2,3**
BISHOP, Joey **2,3**
BISSELL, Richard (d.5/4/77) **1,2**
BISSET, Jacqueline **3,4,5**
BJOERLING, Jussi (d.9/9/60) **1**
BLACK, Eugene **1,2**
BLACK, Hugo (d.9/25/71) **1,2**
BLACK, James **2**
BLACK, Karen **3,4,5**
BLACK, Shirley Temple **1,2** (see also BLACK, Shirley **3,4,5**)
BLACK, William (d.3/7/83) **2**
BLACKMER, Sidney (d.10/6/73) **1,2**
BLACKMUN, Harry A. **3,4,5**
BLACKWELL, Betsy Talbot (d.2/5/85) **2**
BLACKWELL, Earl **2,3,4,5**
BLAIK, Earl **1**
BLAINE, Vivian **1,2**
BLAIR, Clay, Jr. **2**
BLAIR, Frank **2,3**
BLAIR, Janet **1,2**
BLAIR, William McCormick, Jr. **2,3**
BLAKE, Amanda (d.8/16/89) **2,3**
BLAKE, Eugene Carson **2,3**
BLANDING, Sarah Gibson (d.3/3/85) **2**
BLASS, Bill **3,4,5**
BLISS, Anthony **2**

BLITZSTEIN, Marc (d.1/22/64) **1,2**
BLOCK, Joseph (d.11/76) **2**
BLOCK, Martin (d.9/19/67) **1,2**
BLONDELL, Joan (d.12/25/79) **1,2,3**
BLOOM, Claire **1,2,3,4,5**
BLOOMGARDEN, Kermit (d.9/20/76) **1,2**
BLOOMINGDALE, Alfred (d.8/20/82) **1,2,3**
BLOOMINGDALE, Betsy **4,5**
BLOUGH, Roger **1,2**
BLUE, Vida **3**
BLUFORD, Guy **4**
BLUM, Daniel (d.2/24/65) **2**
BLYTH, Anne **1**
BOB (ELLIOTT) & RAY (GOULDING) (see also ELLIOTT and GOULDING) **2,3,4**
BOBST, Tom **2**
BOCK, Jerry **3,4**
BOESKY, Ivan **4**
BOGAN, Louise (d.2/4/70) **1,2**
BOGARDE, Dirk **1,3,4,5**
BOGDANOVICH, Peter **3,4,5**
BOGGS, Hale (d.10/16/72) **2**
BOGGS, J. Caleb **2**
BOGGS, Wade **5**
BOHAN, Marc **3,4**
BOHLEN, Charles (d.1/1/74) **1,2**
BÖHM, Karl (d.8/14/81) **3**
BOHR, Niels (d.11/19/62) **1**
BOITANO, Brian **5**
BOK, Curtis **1**
BOK, Derek Curtis **3,4,5**
BOLGER, Ray (d.4/15/87) **1,2**
BÖLL, Heinrich (d.7/85) **3**
BOLLING, Richard **2**
BOLT, Robert **3**
BOLT, Tommy **1,2**
BOLTON, Frances P. (d.3/9/77) **1,2**
BOLTON, Oliver (d.12/13/72) **2**
BOMBECK, Erma **4,5**
BOND, Alice Dixon **2**
BOND, Julian **3,4**
BOND, Ward **1**
BON JOVI **5**
BONO, Sonny **5** (see also SONNY & CHER **3**)
BOONE, Debby **5**
BOONE, Pat **1,2,3,4,5**
BOONE, Richard (d.1/10/81) **1,2,3**
BOORSTIN, Daniel **4**
BOOTH, Shirley **1,2,3**
BORG, Bjorn **4,5**
BORGE, Victor **1,2,3,4,5**
BORGES, Jorge Luis (d.6/14/86) **3,4**
BORGNINE, Ernest **1,2,3**, (see also BORGNINE, Ernest & Tovah **4**)
BORKH, Inge **1**
BORLAUG, Norman **3**
BORMAN, Frank **4,5**
BOROS, Julius **1,2**
BOSLEY, Tom **2**
BOSSY, Mike **4**
BOSTON, Ralph **2**
BOSTWICK, Pete **2**
BOSWORTH, Brian **5**
BOTVINNIK, Mikhail **1**
BOUDREAU, Lou **2**
BOULANGER, Nadia (d.10/22/79) **1**
BOULEZ, Pierre **3,4,5**
BOURGUIBA, Habib **1**
BOURKE-WHITE, Margaret (d.8/27/71) **1,2**
BOUTON, Jim **3**
BOW, Clara (d.9/27/66) **1**
BOWEN, Catherine Drinker (d.11/1/73) **1,2**

BOWEN, Elizabeth (d.2/22/73) **1**
BOWIE, David **4,5**
BOWLES, Chester **1,2,3**
BOWLES, Paul **1**
BOY GEORGE (Culture Club) **4,5**
BOYD, Bill (d.9/12/72) **2**
BOYD, Malcolm **3**
BOYD, William (d.8/12/72) **1,2**
BOYER, Charles (d.8/26/78) **1,2,3**
BOYINGTON, Pappy **1,2**
BOYLE, KAY **1,2**
BRACKETT, Charles (d.3/8/69) **1,2**
BRADBURY, Norris **2**
BRADBURY, Ray **1,2,3,4,5**
BRADDOCK, James J. (d.11/29/74) **1**
BRADEN, Spruille (d.1/10/78) **1,2**
BRADFORD, Barbara Taylor **5**
BRADLEE, Ben **4,5**
BRADLEY, Bill **3,4,5**
BRADLEY, Ed **4,5**
BRADLEY, Omar (d.4/8/81) **1,2,3**
BRADLEY, Tom **4,5**
BRADSHAW, Terry **3,4,5**
BRADY, James **3,4,5**
BRADY, Scott (d.4/85) **2**
BRAILOWSKY, Alexander (d.4/25/76) **1,2**
BRAND, Oscar **2**
BRANDO, Marlon **1,2,3,4,5**
BRANDT, Willy **1,3**
BRAQUE, Georges (d.9/1/63) **1**
BRAUTIGAN, Richard (d.10/25/84) **3**
BRAZZI, Rossano **1,2**
BREECH, Ernest (d.7/3/78) **2**
BREL, Jacques (d.10/9/78) **3**
BRENNAN, Ella **2**
BRENNAN, Peter J. **3**
BRENNAN, Walter (d.9/21/74) **1,2,3**
BRENNAN, William J., Jr. **1,2,3,4,5**
BRENNER, Eleanor **5**
BRENT, George (d.5/26/79) **1,2**
BRENT, Stuart **2**
BRESLIN, Jimmy **3,4,5**
BRETON, Andre (d.9/28/66) **1**
BRETT, George **4,5**
BREUER, Marcel (d.7/1/81) **2,3**
BREWER, Theresa **1,2**
BREWSTER, Kingman **3**
BRICKER, John W. **1,2**
BRICKHOUSE, Jack **2**
BRICKTOP (d.1/3/84) **1,2**
BRIDGES, Beau **3,4**
BRIDGES, Harry **1,2,3**
BRIDGES, Jeff **4,5**
BRIDGES, Lloyd **1,2,3,4,5**
BRIDGES, Styles (d.11/26/61) **1**
BRIDGMAN, P.W. (d.8/20/61) **1**
BRINKLEY, Christie **4,5**
BRINKLEY, David **1,2,3,4,5**
BRIONI **3**
BRISCOE, Robert (d.5/30/69) **1**
BRISSON, Frederick (d.10/8/84) **2,3**
BRITT, May **2**
BRITTEN, Benjamin (d.12/4/76) **1,3**
BROCKHURST, Gerald (d.5/4/78) **1**
BROCKINGTON, John **3**
BRODER, David S. **4,5**
BRODERICK, Matthew **4,5**
BRODY, Jerome **2**
BROKAW, Tom **4,5**
BROLIN, James **4,5**
BRONFMAN, Edgar **2**
BRONSON, Charles **3,4,5**
BROOK, Alexander (d.2/26/80) **1,2**
BROOK, Peter **3,4,5**
BROOKE, Edward **3**

Cumulative Index — CELEBRITY REGISTER 1990

BROOKS, Donald **2,3,4,5**
BROOKS, Gwendolyn **2,3,4,5**
BROOKS, Mel **4,5**
BROOKS, Richard **2,3,4**
BROOKS, Van Wyck (d.5/2/63) **1**
BROPHY, Frank **2**
BROSNAN, Jim **2**
BROSNAN, Pierce **4,5**
BROTHERS, Dr. Joyce **1,2,3,4,5**
BROUGH, Louise **1**
BROWDER, Earl (d.6/27/73) **1**
BROWER, Charles **1**
BROWER, David **3,4,5**
BROWN, Harrison **1,2**
BROWN, Helen Gurley **2,3,4,5**
BROWN, J. Carter **4,5**
BROWN, James **3,4**
BROWN, Jerry **4**
BROWN, Jim (Jimmy) **1,2,3,4,5**
BROWN, Joe E. (d.7/6/73) **1,2**
BROWN, John Mason (d.3/16/69) **1,2**
BROWN, Larry **3**
BROWN, Pamela (d.9/18/75) **1**
BROWN, Pat **1,2**
BROWN, Paul **1,2,3**
BROWN, Tina **4,5**
BROWN, Tony **4,5**
BROWNE, Burton **2**
BROWNE, Jackson **5**
BROWNELL, Herbert **1,2**
BROWNING, John **3,4,5**
BROWNMILLER, Susan **4,5**
BRUBECK, Dave **1,2,3,4,5**
BRUCE, David (d.12/5/77) **1,2**
BRUCE, Lenny (d.8/3/66) **2**
BRUCKER, Herbert (d.4/77) **2**
BRUCKER, Wilber M. **1,2**
BRUHN, Erik (d.4/1/86) **3,4**
BRUNDAGE, Avery (d.5/8/75) **1,2,3**
BRUSTEIN, Robert **3,4,5**
BRYAN, Tennant **2**
BRYANT, C. Farris **2**
BRYANT, Paul "Bear" (d.1/26/83) **3**
BRYNNER, Yul (d.10/10/85) **1,2,3,4**
BRYSON, Lyman L. (d.11/24/59) **1**
BUBER, Martin (d.6/14/65) **1**
BUCHANAN, Wiley T. **1,2**
BUCHMAN, Frank (d.8/9/61) **1**
BUCHWALD, Art **1,2,3,4,5**
BUCK, Pearl (d.3/6/73) **1,2**
BUCKLEY, James **3**
BUCKLEY, William F., Jr. **2,3,4,5**
BUDGE, Don **1,2**
BUETOW, Herbert (d.1/8/72) **2**
BUFFET, Bernard **1**
BUFFET, Jimmy **5**
BUJOLD, Genevive **3,4,5**
BUJONES, Fernando **4,5**
BULGANIN, Nicolai (d.2/24/75) **1**
BUMBRY, Grace **3,4,5**
BUNCHE, Ralph (d.12/9/71) **1,2**
BUNDY, McGeorge **2,3**
BUNDY, William **3**
BUNKER, George M. **2**
BUNTING, Mary **2**
BUÑUEL, Luis (d.7/29/83) **3**
BURCH, Dean **3**
BURDEN, Carter **3**
BURDETTE, Lew **1**
BURDICK, Eugene (d.7/26/65) **2**
BURGER, Warren E. **3,4,5**
BURGESS, Anthony **3,4,5**
BURGESS, Thornton (d.6/5/65) **2**
BURKE, Albert **2**
BURKE, Arleigh **1,2**

BURKE, Billie (d.5/14/70) **1,2**
BURKE, Jack **1**
BURKE, Michael **3**
BURMAN, Ben Lucien (d.11/12/84) **2**
BURNETT, Carol **2,3,4,5**
BURNETT, Leo (d.6/7/71) **2**
BURNS, Arthur F. **3**
BURNS, George **1,2,3,4,5**
BURNS, Haydon **1**
BURNS, James MacGregor **2,3,4,5**
BURNS, John (d.4/5/75) **2**
BURPEE, David (d.6/24/80) **1,2**
BURR, Raymond **2,3**
BURROUGHS, William **3,4**
BURROWS, Abe **1,2,3**
BURSTYN, Ellen **4,5**
BURTON, Richard (d.8/5/84) **1,2,3**
BUSCAGLIA, Leo F. **4**
BUSCH, August, Jr. **1,2,3,4**
BUSH, Barbara **5**
BUSH, George **3,4,5**
BUSH, Melinda **5**
BUSH, Prescott S. (d.10/8/72) **1,2**
BUSH, Vannevar (d.6/28/74) **1,2,3**
BUSHKIN, Joey **1,2**
BUSHMAN, Francis X. (d.8/23/66) **1**
BUTCHER, Fanny **2**
BUTKUS, Dick **3**
BUTLER, John Marshall (d.3/16/78) **1**
BUTLER, Michael **3**
BUTLER, Paul (d.6/24/81) **1,2**
BUTLER, "RAB" (Richard Austin) (d.3/9/82) **1**
BUTTON, Dick **1,2,3,4**
BUTTONS, Red **1,2**
BUZZI, Ruth **3**
BYINGTON, Spring (d.9/7/71) **1,2**
BYRD, Harry (d.10/20/66) **1,2,3**
BYRD, Robert C. **2,4,5**
BYRNE, David **4,5**
BYRNES, Edd **2**
BYRNES, James (d.4/9/72) **1,2**

C

CAAN, James **3,4,5**
CABALLÉ, Montserrat **4,5**
CABOT, John Moors (d.2/23/81) **2**
CABOT, Paul **2**
CABOT, Sebastian (d.8/23/77) **3**
CACCIA, Sir Harold A. **1**
CACOYANNIS, Michael **3**
CADMUS, Paul **1,2,3,4,5**
CAEN, Herb **1,2,3,4,5**
CAESAR, Sid **1,2,3,4,5**
CAFRITZ, Gwen (d.11/29/88) **1,2**
CAGE, John **3,4**
CAGE, Nicolas **5**
CAGNEY, James (d.3/30/86) **1,2,3,4**
CAHN, Sammy **2,3,4,5**
CAIN, James M. (d.10/27/77) **1,2,3**
CAINE, Michael **3,4,5**
CALDER, Alexander (d.11/11/76) **1,2,3**
CALDICOTT, Helen **4**
CALDWELL, Erskine (d.4/11/87) **1,2,3,4**
CALDWELL, Millard **2**
CALDWELL, Sarah **4,5**
CALDWELL, Taylor (d.8/30/85) **1,2,3**
CALDWELL, Zoë **3,4,5**
CALHOUN, David **2**
CALHOUN, Rory **1,2**
CALISHER, Hortense **3**
CALLAS, Maria (d.9/16/77) **1,2,3**
CALLOWAY, Cab **1,2,3,4,5**

CALVET, Corinne **1**
CAMBRIDGE, Godfrey (d.11/29/76) **3**
CAMERON, Kirk **5**
CAMPANELLA, Roy **1,2,3**
CAMPBELL, Donald **1**
CAMPBELL, Glen **3,4,5**
CAMUS, Albert (d.1/4/60) **1**
CANADAY, John (d.7/19/85) **2,3**
CANDY, John **4,5**
CANFIELD, Cass **1,2**
CANHAM, Erwin (d.1/3/82) **1,2,3**
CANIFF, Milton (d.4/3/88) **1,2,3,4**
CANNON, Charles **2**
CANNON, Clarence (d.5/13/64) **1,2**
CANNON, Dyan **4,5**
CANNON, Howard **2**
CANNON, Jimmy (d.12/5/73) **2**
CANNON, Poppy (d.4/1/75) **2**
CANOVA, Judy (d.8/5/83) **1**
CANSECO, Jose **5**
CANTERBURY, Archbishop of (FISHER, Dr. Geoffrey Francis) **1**
CANTINFLAS **1**
CANTOR, Eddie (d.10/10/64) **1,2**
CANTRELL, Lana **3**
CAPEHART, Homer (d.9/3/79) **1,2**
CAPLIN, Mortimer **2**
CAPOTE, Truman (d.8/25/84) **1,2,3**
CAPP, Al (d.11/5/79) **1,2,3**
CAPRA, Frank **1,2,3,4**
CARBINE, Patricia **3**
CARDIN, Pierre **3,4,5**
CARERE, Christine **1**
CAREY, James B. (d.9/11/73) **1,2**
CARLE, Frankie **1**
CARLIN, George **4,5**
CARLISLE, Kitty **1,2,3** (see also HART, Kitty Carlisle **4**),**5**
CARLSON, Frank **2**
CARLSON, Richard (d.11/25/77) **1**
CARLTON, Steve **3,4**
CARMEN, Eric **5**
CARMER, Carl (d.9/11/76) **1,2**
CARMICHAEL, Hoagy (d.12/27/81) **1,2,3**
CARMICHAEL, John **2**
CARMICHAEL, Leonard (d.9/16/73) **2**
CARNERA, Primo (d.6/29/67) **1**
CARNES, Kim **5**
CARNEY, Art **1,2,3,4,5**
CARNOVSKY, Morris **1,2**
CAROL, Martine (d.2/6/67) **1**
CARON, Leslie **1,3,4,5**
CARPENTER, Bob **2**
CARPENTER, John **4,5**
CARPENTER, Mrs. Leslie (Liz) **2**
CARPENTER, Scott **2,3**
CARR, Allan **4,5**
CARR, John Dickson (d.2/27/77) **1**
CARR, Lawrence (d.1/17/69) **1**
CARRADINE, John **1**
CARRERAS, José **4,5**
CARROLL, Diahann **2,3,4,5**
CARROLL, Leo G. (d.10/16/72) **1,2**
CARROLL, Madeleine **1,2**
CARSON, Jack (d.1/2/63) **1**
CARSON, Johnny **2,3,4,5**
CARSON, Mindy **1,2**
CARSON, Rachel (d.4/14/64) **1,2**
CARTER, Amon, Jr. (d.7/24/82) **2**
CARTER, Elliott **4,5**
CARTER, Hodding (d.4/4/72) **1,2**
CARTER, Hodding III **4,5**
CARTER, Jimmy **4,5**
CARTER, Lyndia **4,5**
CARTER, Nell **4,5**

CELEBRITY REGISTER 1990 — Cumulative Index

CARTIER-BRESSON, Henri **1**
CARTLAND, Barbara **4,5**
CARVER, Raymond (d.8/2/88) **4**
CARY, W. Sterling **3**
CASADESUS, Robert (d.9/19/72) **1,2**
CASALS, Pablo (d.10/22/73) **1,2,3**
CASE, Clifford P. (d.3/6/82) **1,2**
CASH, Johnny **1,2,3,4,5**
CASH, Norm **2**
CASH, Pat **5**
CASHIN, Bonnie **2**
CASPER, Billy **1,2,3**
CASS, Peggy **2,3**
CASSAVETES, John (d.2/3/89) **3,4**
CASSIDY, Claudia **1,2,3,4**
CASSIDY, David **3,4**
CASSINI, Igor **1,2**
CASSINI, Oleg **1,2,3,4,5**
CASTELLANO, Richard **3,4**
CASTELLI, Leo **4**
CASTLE, Irene (d.1/25/69) **1,2**
CASTRO, Fidel **1**
CATTON, Bruce (d.8/28/78) **1,2,3**
CAUTHEN, Steve **4**
CAVALLARO, Carmen **1,2**
CAVETT, Dick **3,4,5**
CECIL, Lord David **1**
CELEBREZZE, Anthony **2**
CELLER, Emanuel (d.1/15/81) **1,2,3**
CEPEDA, Orlando **2**
CERF, Bennett (d.8/27/71) **1,2**
CETERA, Peter **5**
CHABROL, Claude **3**
CHADWICK, Florence **1**
CHAFEE, John **2**
CHAGALL, Marc (d.3/28/85) **1,3**
CHAKIRIS, George **2**
CHAMBERLAIN, John **2**
CHAMBERLAIN, Richard **2,3,4,5**
CHAMBERLAIN, Wilt **1,2,3,4,5**
CHAMBERS, Anne Cox **4,5**
CHAMBERS, Whittaker (d.6/9/61) **1**
CHAMPION, George **2**
CHAMPION, Gower (d.8/25/80) **1,2,3;** w/Marge **1**
CHANCELLOR, John **2,3,4,5**
CHANDLER, Happy **1,2**
CHANDLER, Jeff (d.6/17/61) **1**
CHANDLER, Norman (d.10/20/73) **1,2**
CHANDLER, Mrs. Norman **2,3**
CHANDLER, Otis **3,4,5**
CHANEL, Coco (d.1/10/71) **1**
CHANEY, Lon, Jr. (d.7/12/73) **1,2**
CHANNING, Carol **1,2,3,4,5**
CHAPLIN, Charlie (d.3/20/68) **1,2,3**
CHAPLIN, Sydney **1,2**
CHAPMAN, Ceil (d.7/13/79) **1,2**
CHAPMAN, John (d.1/19/72) **2**
CHAPMAN, Tracy **5**
CHARISSE, Cyd **1,2**
CHARLES, Ezzard (d.5/28/75) **1**
CHARLES, Prince of Wales **1** (see also WALES, The Prince & Princess of **4**)
CHARLES, Ray **2,3,4,5**
CHARNIN, Martin **4,5**
CHASE, Barrie **2**
CHASE, Chevy **4,5**
CHASE, Ilka (d.2/15/78) **1,2,3**
CHASE, Lucia **1,2,3**
CHASE, Mary (d.10/29/81) **1**
CHASE, Stuart **1,2**
CHATTERTON, Ruth (d.11/25/61) **1**
CHAVEZ, Cesar **3,4**
CHAVEZ, Dennis (d.11/19/62) **1**
CHAYEFSKY, Paddy (d.8/1/81) **1,2,3**

CHEATHAM, Owen (d.10/24/70) **2**
CHECKER, Chubby **2**
CHEEVER, John (d.6/18/82) **1,2,3**
CHER **4,5** (see also SONNY & CHER **3**)
CHERNE, Leo **2,3,4,5**
CHESHIRE, Maxine **3**
CHEVALIER, Maurice (d.1/1/72) **1,2**
CHIANG KAI-SHEK, Generalissimo (d.4/5/75) **1**
CHIANG KAI-SHEK, Madame **1**
CHICAGO, Judy **4,5**
CHILD, Julia **3,4**
CHILDS, Marquis **1,2,3**
CHIRICO, Giorgio De (d.11/20/78) **1**
CHISHOLM, Shirley **3**
CHOATE, Robert **2**
CHOMSKY, Noam **3,4,5**
CHOU EN-LAI (d.1/7/76) **1**
CHRISTIAN, Linda **1,2**
CHRISTIE, Agatha (d.1/12/76) **1,3**
CHRISTIE, Julie **3,4,5**
CHRISTO **3,4**
CHRISTOPHER, George **2**
CHRISTY, Marian **4**
CHRYSLER, Walter P. **2**
CHUNG, Connie **5**
CHURCH, Frank (d.4/7/84) **1,2,3**
CHURCH, Sandra **2**
CHURCHILL, Randolph (d.6/5/68) **1**
CHURCHILL, Reba and Bonnie **2**
CHURCHILL, Sarah (d.9/24/82) **1**
CHURCHILL, Sir Winston (d.1/24/65) **1,2**
CHUTE, Marchette **2**
CIARDI, John **1,2,3**
CLAIBORNE, Craig **4,5**
CLAIRE, Ina (d.2/21/85) **1,2**
CLAPTON, Eric **3,4,5**
CLARK, Alicia Purdom **2**
CLARK, Bobby (d.2/12/60) **1**
CLARK, Dane **1,2**
CLARK, Deena **2**
CLARK, Dick **1,2,4,5**
CLARK, Grenville (d.1/13/67) **2**
CLARK, Joseph S., Jr. **1,2**
CLARK, Kenneth B. **3,4**
CLARK, Mark (d.4/17/84) **1,2,3**
CLARK, Mary Higgins **4,5**
CLARK, Petula **3**
CLARK, Ramsey **3,4**
CLARK, Tom (d.6/13/77) **1,2**
CLARKE, Arthur C. **1,3,4,5**
CLAVELL, James **4,5**
CLAY, Cassius **2** (see also ALI Muhammad **3,4,5**)
CLAYBURGH, Jill **4,5**
CLEAVER, Eldridge **3,4**
CLEMENS, Roger **5**
CLEMENT, Frank (d.11/4/69) **2**
CLEVELAND, Harlan **2**
CLIBURN, Van **1,2,3,4,5**
CLIFFORD, Clark **2,3,4**
CLIFT, Montgomery (d.7/23/66) **1,2**
CLOETE, Stuart (d.3/20/76) **1**
CLOONEY, Rosemary **1,2,4,5**
CLOSE, Glenn **4,5**
CLURMAN, Harold (d.9/9/80) **1,2**
COBB, Jerrie **2**
COBB, Lee J. (d.2/11/76) **1,2,3**
COBB, Ty (d.7/17/61) **1**
COBURN, Charles (d.8/30/61) **1**
COBURN, James **3,4**
COCA, Imogene **1,2**
COCHRAN, Jacqueline (d.8/9/80) **1,2**
COCHRAN, Ron **2**
COCHRAN, Steve (d.6/15/65) **1,2**

COCO, James (d.2/25/87) **3,4**
COCTEAU, Jean (d.10/11/63) **1**
COE, Fred (d.4/29/79) **1,2**
COFFIN, William Sloan **2**
COHEN, Alexander H. **2,3,4,5**
COHEN, Leonard **3**
COHEN, Myron (d.3/10/86) **2**
COHN, Roy (d.8/2/86) **4**
COIT, Margaret **2**
COLAVITO, Rocky **2**
COLBERT, Claudette **1,2,3,4,5**
COLBERT, Tex **1**
COLBY, Anita **1,2**
COLE, Edward N. (d.5/2/77) **3**
COLE, Nat "King" (d.2/15/65) **1,2**
COLE, Natalie **5**
COLEMAN, Cy **2,3,4,5**
COLEMAN, Dabney **4,5**
COLEMAN, Emil (d.1/26/65) **1,2**
COLEMAN, Gary **4**
COLEMAN, John R. **4**
COLEMAN, Ornette **4,5**
COLES, Robert **3,4,5**
COLLINGWOOD, Charles (d.10/3/85) **1,2,3**
COLLINS, Dorothy **1**
COLLINS, Jackie **5**
COLLINS, Joan **1,2,4,5**
COLLINS, John F. **2**
COLLINS, Judy **3,4,5**
COLLINS, Larry **3**
COLLINS, Leroy **1,2**
COLLINS, Martha Layne **4**
COLLINS, Michael **3**
COLLINS, Phil **4,5**
COLLYER, Bud (d.9/8/69) **1,2**
COLONNA, Jerry **1,2**
COMDEN, Betty **1,2,3,4,5**
COMFORT, Harold **2**
COMINSKY, J.R. **2**
COMMAGER, Henry Steele **1,2**
COMMONER, Barry **3,4**
COMO, Perry **1,2,3,4,5**
COMPTON, Arthur Holly (d.3/15/62) **1**
COMPTON-BURNETT, Ivy (d.8/27/69) **1**
CONANT, James B. (d.2/11/78) **1,2**
CONDON, David **2**
CONDON, Eddie (d.8/4/73) **1,2**
CONDON, Richard **2**
CONE, Fairfax (d.6/20/77) **2**
CONERLY, Charlie **2**
CONNALLY, John **2,3,4**
CONNALLY, Tom **1,2**
CONNELLY, Marc (d.12/21/80) **1,2**
CONNERY, Sean **3,4,5**
CONNIFF, Frank (d.5/25/71) **2**
CONNOLLY, Cyril (d.11/26/74) **1**
CONNOLLY, Maureen (d.6/21/69) **1**
CONNOLLY, Mike (d.11/18/66) **2**
CONNOLLY, Sybil **1**
CONNORS, Chuck **2**
CONNORS, Jimmy **4,5**
CONNORS, Mike **3**
CONOVER, Harry (d.7/25/65) **1**
CONRAD, Barnaby **1,2,3**
CONRAD, Paul **4**
CONRAD, William **3**
CONREID, Hans (d.1/5/82) **2**
CONSIDINE, Bob (d.9/25/75) **1,2,3**
CONTE, Richard (d.4/15/75) **1,2**
CONWAY, Shirl **2**
COOGAN, Jackie (d.3/1/84) **1,2**
COOK, Barbara **2,4,5**
COOK, Donald (d.10/1/61) **1**
COOKE, Alistair **1,2,3,4,5**

Cumulative Index — CELEBRITY REGISTER 1990

COOLEY, Denton **3,4,5**
COONEY, Joan Ganz **3,4,5**
COOPER, Alice **3**
COOPER, Ashley **1**
COOPER, Lady Diana (d.6/16/86) **1**
COOPER, Gary (d.5/13/61) **1**
COOPER, Gladys (d.11/17/71) **1**
COOPER, Jackie **1,2**
COOPER, John Sherman **1,2**
COOPER, L. Gordon **2**
COPELAND, Jo (d.3/20/82) **1,2**
COPELAND, Lammot Du Pont (d.7/83) **2**
COPLAND, Aaron **1,2,3,4,5**
COPLEY, James **2**
COPPERFIELD, David **5**
COPPOLA, Francis Ford **3,4,5**
CORD, Alex **3**
CORDERO, Angel **4,5**
CORDINER, Ralph J. **1,2**
CORELLI, Franco **3,4**
COREY, Wendell (d.11/8/68) **2**
CORIO, Ann **2,3**
CORMAN, Roger **4,5**
CORNELL, Katharine (d.6/9/74) **1,2,3**
CORRIGAN, Leo (d.6/75) **2**
CORWIN, Norman **1,2**
COSBY, Bill **3,4,5**
COSELL, Howard **3,4,5**
COSTA-GAVRAS **4,5** (see also GAVRAS, Costa **3**)
COSTAIN, Thomas B. (d.10/8/65) **1,2**
COSTAS, Bob **5**
COSTNER, Kevin **5**
COTT, Ted (d.6/12/73) **2**
COTTEN, Joseph **1,2**
COTTON, Norris **2**
COTY, René (d.11/22/62) **1**
COURT, Margaret Smith **3**
COURTENAY, Tom **3,4**
COURTRIGHT, Hernando (d.2/24/86) **2,4**
COUSINS, Norman **1,2,3,4,5**
COUSTEAU, Jacques **1,3,4,5**
COUSY, Bob **1,2,3**
COUVE DE MURVILLE, Maurice **1**
COWAN, Louis G. (d.11/18/76) **1,2**
COWARD, Noel (d.3/26/73) **1,2**
COWELL, Henry (d.12/10/65) **2**
COWLES, Fleur **1,2**
COWLES, Gardner (d.7/15/85) **1,2,3**
COWLES, John (d.7/8/85) **1,2**
COWLEY, Malcolm **1,2,3,4**
COX, Archibald **2,4**
COX, James M., Jr. (d.10/74) **2**
COX, Wally (d.2/15/73) **1,2**
COZZENS, James Gould (d.8/9/78) **1,2**
CRABBE, Buster (d.4/23/83) **1**
CRAIG, Marjorie **3**
CRAIG, May (d.2/8/72) **1,2**
CRAWFORD, Broderick **1,2,3**
CRAWFORD, Cheryl **1,2**
CRAWFORD, Joan (d.5/13/77) **1,2,3**
CRAWFORD, John **1,2**
CRAWFORD, Michael **5**
CRENSHAW, Ben **4,5**
CRICHTON, Michael **3,4,5**
CRICK, Francis **3,4,5**
CRISLER, Fritz (d.8/19/82) **1**
CRISP, Donald (d.5/25/74) **1**
CRIST, Judith **3,4**
CROMIE, Robert **2**
CRONIN, A.J. (d.1/6/81) **1,2**
CRONKITE, Walter **1,2,3,4,5**
CRONYN, Hume **1,2,3,4,5**
CROSBY, Bing (d.10/14/77) **1,2,3**
CROSBY, Bob **1,2**

CROSBY, Gary **2**
CROSBY, John **1,2**
CROSS, Milton (d.1/3/75) **1,2,3**
CROUSE, Russel (d.4/3/66) **1,2**
CROWLEY, Mart **3**
CROWN, Henry **2**
CROWTHER, Bosley (d.3/7/81) **1,2**
CRUISE, Tom **5**
CRYSTAL, Billy **5**
CSONKA, Larry **3**
CUGAT, Xavier **1,2,3**
CUKOR, George (d.1/24/83) **1,2,3**
CULLEN, Bill **1,2**
CULLIGAN, Matthew **2**
CULLMAN, Howard (d.6/29/72) **1,2**
CULLMAN, Marguerite **2**
CULP, Robert **3,4**
CUMMINGS, E.E. (d.9/3/62) **1**
CUMMINGS, Nathan (d.2/19/85) **2,3**
CUMMINGS, Robert **1,2** (see also CUMMINGS, Bob **3**)
CUNNINGHAM, Briggs **1,2**
CUNNINGHAM, Merce **4,5**
CUOMO, Mario **4,5**
CURRAN, Joseph (d.8/14/81) **2**
CURRY, John **4**
CURTICE, Harlow H. (d.11/3/62) **1**
CURTIN, Jane **4,5**
CURTIS, Charlotte **3**
CURTIS, Jamie Lee **4,5**
CURTIS, Thomas **2**
CURTIS, Tony **1,2,3,4,5**
CUSHING, Alec **2**
CUSHING, Cardinal Richard (d.11/2/70) **1,2**
CUSHMAN, Austin (d.6/12/78) **2**

D

DABNEY, Virginia **1,2**
DACHÉ, Lilly **1,2**
DA COSTA, Morton (d.1/29/89) **1,2**
DAGMAR **1,2**
DAHL, Arlene **1,2,3,4,5**
DAHLBERG, Edward (d.2/27/77) **3**
DALAI LAMA (Jetson Jampel Ngawang Labsang Yishey Tenzing Gyatso) **1**
DALE, Jim **5**
DALEY, Richard (d.12/20/76) **2,3**
DALI, Salvador (d.1/23/89) **1,2,3,4**
DALLESANDRO, Joe **3**
DALRYMPLE, Jean **1,2**
DALTON, John **2**
DALTON, Timothy **5**
DALY, John **1,2**
DALY, Timothy **5**
DALY, Tyne **4,5**
D'AMATO, Alfonse **4,5**
D'AMBOISE, Jacques **2,3,4,5**
DAMONE, Vic **1,2**
DANCE, Charles **4**
DANCER, Stanley **1,2,3**
DANDRIDGE, Dorothy (d.9/8/65) **1,2**
DANGERFIELD, Rodney **4,5**
DANIEL, Clifton **2**
DANIEL, Price **1,2**
DANIELS, Bebe (d.3/16/71) **1,2**
DANIELS, Jonathan (d.11/6/81) **1,2**
DANILOVA, Alexandra **1,2**
DANNER, Blythe **4,5**
DANSON, Ted **4,5**
DANZA, Tony **5**
DARCEL, Denise **2**
DARIN, Bobby (d.12/20/73) **2**

DARK, Alvin **2**
DARNELL, Linda (d.4/10/65) **1,2**
DARRIEUX, Danielle **1**
DARROW, Whitney, Jr. (d.8/27/70) **1,2**
DART, Justin (d.1/26/84) **2**
DASSIN, Jules **1,2**
DAUPHIN, Claude (d.11/16/78) **1**
DAVENPORT, Marcia **1,2**
DAVID, Hal **3,4,5**
DAVIES, Marion (d.9/22/61) **1**
DAVIES, Paul **2**
DAVIS, Adelle (d.5/31/74) **3**
DAVIS, Al **4,5**
DAVIS, Angela **3**
DAVIS, Arthur Vining **1**
DAVIS, Bette **1,2,3,4,5**
DAVIS, Gary (d.5/5/72) **2**
DAVIS, Geena **5**
DAVIS, Jimmie **2**
DAVIS, Marvin **4,5**
DAVIS, Meyer (d.4/5/76) **1,2,3**
DAVIS, Miles **2,3,4,5**
DAVIS, Ossie **2,3,4,5**
DAVIS, Sammy, Jr. **1,2,3,4,5**
DAVIS, Stuart (d.6/24/64) **2**
DAVIS, Tommy **2**
DAWBER, Pam **5**
DAWKINS, Darryl **4**
DAWSON, Richard **4**
DAY, Dennis (d.6/22/88) **2**
DAY, Doris **1,2,3,4,5**
DAY, Dorothy (d.11/29/80) **3**
DAY, James Edward **2**
DAY, Laraine **1,2**
DAYAN, Moshe (d.10/16/81) **3**
DEALEY, E.M. **2**
DEAN, Arthur **2**
DEAN, Dizzy (d.7/17/74) **1,2**
DEAN, Jimmy **1,2**
DEAN, Gen. William **1,2**
DEANE, Martha (d.12/9/73) **2,3**
DE BAKEY, Michael **3,4,5**
DEBRÉ, Michel **1**
DE BUSSCHERE, Dave **3**
DE CARLO, Yvonne **1,2,3**
DECKER SLANEY, Mary **4,5**
DECTER, Midge **4,5**
DE CUEVAS, Marquis (d.2/22/61) **1**
DEDMON, Emmett (d.9/83) **2**
DEE, Ruby **2,3,4,5**
DEE, Sandra **2**
DE FORE, Don **2**
DE FOREST, Lee (d.7/2/61) **1**
DE GAULLE, Charles (d.11/9/70) **1**
DE GIVENCHY, Hubert **1**
DE HARTOG, Jan **1**
DE HAVILLAND, Olivia **1,2,3,4,5**
DE KOONING, Willem **1,2,3,4,5**
DE KRUIF, Paul (d.7/28/71) **1,2**
DELACORTE, George **2,3,4**
DELANY, Ron **1**
DELAPLANE, Stan **2,3**
DE LA RENTA, Oscar **3,4,5**
DE LARROCHA, Alicia **4,5**
DE LAURENTIIS, Dino **4,5**
DE LIAGRE, Alfred, Jr. **1,2**
DELLA FEMINA, Jerry **3**
DELLO JOIO, Norman **1,2,3**
DELLUMS, Ron **4,5**
DEL MONACO, Mario (d.10/16/82) **1**
DELON, Alain **3,4**
DEL RIO, Dolores (d.4/11/83) **1,2,3**
DEMARET, Jimmy (d.12/28/83) **1**
DE MILLE, Agnes **1,2,3,4,5**
DE MONTEBELLO, Philippe **4,5**

CELEBRITY REGISTER 1990 — Cumulative Index

DEMPSEY, Jack (d.5/31/83) **1,2,3**
DEMPSEY, John N. **2**
DENEUVE, Catherine **3,4,5**
DE NIRO, Robert **4,5**
DENNIS, Patrick (d.11/6/76) **1,2**
DENNIS, Sandy **3,4,5**
DENT, Frederick B. **3**
DENVER, John **4,5**
DE ORSEY, Leo **2**
DE PALMA, Brian **4,5**
DEPARDIEU, Gerard **4,5**
DEREK, Bo **4**
DE RIBES, Jacqueline **4,5**
DERLETH, August (d.7/4/71) **2**
DE ROCHEMONT, Louis (d.12/23/78) **1,2**
DE SAPIO, Carmine **1**
DE SICA, Vittorio (d.11/13/74) **1,3**
DESMOND, Johnny **1,2**
DEUKMEJIAN, George, Jr. **4,5**
DEUTSCH, Hermann **2**
DEVANE, William **5**
DE VALERA, Eamon (d.8/29/75) **1**
DE VALOIS, Ninette **1**
DEVER, Joseph X. **2,3**
DEVITO, Danny **5**
DEVLIN, Bernadette **3**
DE VRIES, Peter **1,2,3,4**
DE VRIES, William **4,5**
DEWEY, Thomas E. (d.3/16/71) **1,2**
DEWHURST, Colleen **3,4,5**
DE WILDE, Brandon (d.7/6/72) **1,2**
DEY, Susan **5**
D'HARNONCOURT, René (d.8/13/68) **2**
DIAL, Morse (d.10/4/82) **1,2**
DIAMOND, Neil **3,4,5**
DICHTER, Ernest **1,2,3**
DICK, John Henry **2**
DICKERSON, Eric **4,5**
DICKEY, James **4,5**
DICKEY, John Sloan **1,2**
DICKINSON, Angie **3,4,5**
DIDION, Joan **4,5**
DIEBOLD, John **2**
DIEFENBAKER, John (d.8/16/79) **1**
DIEM, Ngo-Dinh (d.11/2/63) **1**
DIETRICH, Marlene **1,2,3,4,5**
DIETZ, Howard (d.7/30/83) **1,2,3**
DIETZEL, Paul **2**
DILLER, Phyllis **2,3,4,5**
DILLMAN, Bradford **2**
DILLON, C. Douglas **1,2,3**
DILLION, Matt **4,5**
DILWORTH, Richardson (d.1/23/74) **2**
DI MAGGIO, Joe **1,2,3,4,5**
DINE, Jim **3,4**
DINESEN, Isak (d.9/7/62) **1**
DINKLER, Carling, Jr. (d.) **2**
DIRKSEN, Everett M. (d.9/7/69) **1,2**
DI SALLE, Michael (d.9/15/81) **1,2**
DISNEY, Walt (d.12/15/66) **1,2**
DIXON, George **2**
DIXON, Jeane **3,4**
DIXON, Sir Pierson (d.4/21/65) **1**
DJILAS, Milovan **1**
DMITRI, Ivan (d.4/25/68) **1,2**
DOAN, Herbert **2**
DOBBS, Mattiwilda **1,2**
DOBIE, J. Frank (d.9/19/64) **1,2**
DOBSON, Kevin **5**
DOCTOROW, E.L. **4,5**
DODD, Christopher **4,5**
DODD, Thomas (d.5/24/71) **2**
DODGE, Gregg **2**
DOHNANYI, Christoph von **4,5**
DOLE, Elizabeth Hanford **4,5**

DOLE, Bob (Robert Joseph) **3,4,5**
DOLIN, Anton (d.11/25/83) **1**
DOMINGO, Placido **3,4,5**
DOMINICK, Peter (d.3/18/81) **2**
DONAHUE, Phil **4,5**
DONAHUE, Troy **2**
DONALDSON, Sam **5**
DONEGAN, Horace W.B. (Rt. Rev.) **1,2**
DONEHUE, Vincent (d.1/17/65) **2**
DONLEVY, Brian (d.4/5/72) **1**
DONNER, Frederic G. (d.2/28/87) **1,2**
DONOVAN, Carrie **3**
DONOVAN, James (d.1/70) **2**
DOOLITTLE, James **1,2,3,4**
DORATI, Anta **1**
DORNE, Albert (d.12/15/65) **2**
DORS, Diana (d.5/4/85) **1**
DORSETT, Tony **4**
DOS PASSOS, John (d.9/28/70) **1,2**
DOUBLEDAY, Nelson **4,5**
DOUGLAS, Donald W. (d.2/1/81) **1,2**
DOUGLAS, Donna **2**
DOUGLAS, Helen Gahagan (d.6/27/80) **1**
DOUGLAS, Jack (d.1/31/89) **2**
DOUGLAS, James H., Jr. **1**
DOUGLAS, Kirk **1,2,3,4,5**
DOUGLAS, Lewis (d.3/7/74) **1,2**
DOUGLAS, Melvyn (d.8/4/81) **1,2,3**
DOUGLAS, Michael **4,5**
DOUGLAS, Mike **2,3**
DOUGLAS, Paul (d.9/11/59) **1**
DOUGLAS, Paul H. **1,2**
DOUGLAS, William O. (d.1/19/80) **2,3**
DOVIMA **1**
DOWELL, Anthony **4**
DOWLING, Eddie (d.2/18/76) **1,2**
DOWLING, Robert W. (d.8/28/73) **1,2**
DOWNEY, Morton **1,2**
DOWNEY, Robert, Jr. **5**
DOWNS, Hugh **2,3,4,5**
DRAKE, Alfred **1,2,3,4**
DRAKE, Debbie **2**
DRAKE, Galen **1,2**
DRAPER, Dorothy (d.3/10/69) **2**
DRAPER, Paul **1,2**
DREIER, Alex **2**
DRESSEN, Chuck (d.8/10/66) **1**
DREYFUSS, Richard **4,5**
DRU, Joanne **2**
DRUCKER, Peter (d.3/6/70) **2**
DRUMMOND, Roscoe (d.9/30/83) **1,2**
DRURY, Allen **2,3,4,5**
DRYSDALE, Don **2**
DUBINSKY, David (d.9/17/82) **1,2**
DUBOS, René (d.2/20/82) **3**
DU BRIDGE, Lee **1,2**
DUCHAMP, Marcel (d.10/1/68) **1,2**
DUCHIN, Peter **2,3,4,5**
DUFFY, Patrick **4,5**
DUGAN, Alan **2**
DUKAKIS, Michael **5**
DUKAKIS, Olympia **5**
DUKE, Angier Biddle **2,3,4,5**
DUKE, Doris **1,2,3,4,5**
DUKE, Patty **2,3,4,5**
DUKE, Vernon (d.1/17/69) **1**
DUKES, David **5**
DULLEA, Keir **3,4,5**
DULLES, Allen (d.1/29/69) **1,2**
DU MAURIER, Daphne **1**
DU MONT, Allen (d.11/15/65) **1,2**
DUNAWAY, Faye **3,4,5**
DUNCAN, Sandy **5**
DUNCAN, Todd **1**
DUNHAM, Katherine **1,2**

DUNNE, Dominic **5**
DUNNE, Irene **1,2,3,4**
DUNNINGER (d.3/9/75) **1,2**
DUNNOCK, Mildred **1,2,3,4**
DUPOND, Patrick **4**
DU PONT, Irénée **1,2**
DURAN DURAN **4,5**
DURANT, Will (d.11/7/81) **1,2**
  (w/Ariel **3**)
DURANTE, Jimmy (d.1/29/80) **1,2,3**
DURBIN, Deanna **1**
DUROCHER, Leo **1,2,3**
DURYEA, Dan (d.6/7/68) **1**
DUVALL, Robert **4,5**
DYER-BENNET, Richard **1**
DYKES, Jimmy (d.6/15/76) **1**
DYLAN, Bob **3,4,5**

E

EAGLETON, Thomas **3,4**
EASTLAND, James O. **1,2,3**
EASTMAN, Max (d.3/25/69) **1,2**
EASTON, Sheena **5**
EASTWOOD, Clint **3,4,5**
EATON, Cyrus (d.5/9/79) **1,2,3**
EBAN, Abba **1**
EBB, Fred (see KANDER & EBB **4**)
ECKSTINE, Billy **1,2**
EDDY, Nelson (d.3/6/67) **1,2**
EDDY, Roger **2**
EDEL, Leon **2**
EDEN, Sir Anthony (d.1/4/77) **1**
EDERLE, Gertrude **1**
EDMONDSON, J. Howard **2**
EDWARDS, Blake **4,5**
EDWARDS, Douglas **1,2**
EDWARDS, India **1**
EDWARDS, Ralph **1,2,3,4,5**
EDWARDS, Vincent **2**
EGAN, William (d.5/6/84) **2**
EGGAR, Samantha **3**
EGBERT, Sherwood (d.7/30/69) **2**
EGLEVSKY, André (d.12/4/77) **1,2**
EHRENBOURG, Ilya (d.9/1/67) **1**
EICHELBERGER, Robert L. **1**
EISELEY, Loren **2,3**
EISENHOWER, Dwight D.
  (d.3/28/69) **1,2**
EISENHOWER, Mamie Doud (d.11/1/79)
  1,2,3
EISENHOWER, Milton (d.5/2/85) **1,2,3**
EKBERG, Anita **1,2**
ELAINE **3,4,5**
ELDRIDGE, Florence **1,2**
ELIAS, Rosalind **2,3**
ELIOT, George Fielding (d.4/21/71) **1,2**
ELIOT, T.S. (d.1/4/65) **1,2**
ELIZABETH II, Queen **1**
ELIZABETH, Queen Mother of England **1**
ELKINS, Hillard **3**
ELLENDER, Allen J. (d.7/27/72) **1,2**
ELLINGTON, Duke (d.5/24/74) **1,2,3**
ELLIOT, Cass (d.7/29/74) **3**
ELLIOTT, Bob **2,3** (see also BOB & RAY **4**)
ELLIOTT, Herb **1**
ELLIS, Albert **2**
ELLIS, Perry (d.5/30/86) **4**
ELMAN, Mischa (d.4/5/67) **1,2**
ELSON, Bob **2**
ELWAY, John **4**
EMERSON, Faye (d.3/9/83) **1,2**
EMERY, John (d.11/16/64) **1**
ENGLE, Clair (d.7/30/64) **2**

Cumulative Index — CELEBRITY REGISTER 1990

ENGLE, Paul 2
ENGSTROM, Elmer 2
ENTERS, Angna 2
EPHRON, Nora 4
ERHARD, Ludwig (d.5/5/77) 1
ERHARD, Werner 1
ERIKSON, Erik 3,4
ERNST, Max (d.4/1/76) 1,2,3
ERNST, Morris (d.5/21/76) 1,2
ERTEGUN, Ahmet 3,4
ERVIN, Sam (d.4/23/85) 2,3
ERVING, Julius 4,5
ESTEFAN, Gloria (Miami Sound Machine) 5
ESTEVEZ, Emilio 5
ETHERINGTON, Edwin D. 2
ETHRIDGE, Mark (d.4/5/81) 2
ETTINGER, Richard (d.2/24/71) 2
EVANS, Bergen (d.2/4/78) 1,2,3
EVANS, Dale 1
EVANS, Dame Edith (d.10/14/76) 1,3
EVANS, Linda 4,5
EVANS, Maurice 1,2
EVANS, Robert 3
EVANS, Rowland & Robert NOVAK 3,4,5
EVELYN, Judith (d.5/7/67) 1
EVERST, Lt. Col. Frank K., Jr. 1
EVERT LLOYD, Chris 3,4,5
EVERETT, Chad 3
EVERS, Charles 3
EWBANK, Webb 3
EWELL, Tom 1,2
EWING, Patrick 4

F

FABIAN 2
FABIAN, Françoise 3
FABRAY, Nanette 1,2
FADIMAN, Clifton 1,2,3,4
FAIRBANKS, Douglas, Jr. 1,2,3,4,5
FAIRCHILD, John, Jr. 2,3,4,5
FAIRCHILD, Morgan 4
FAIRCHILD, Sherman (d.3/28/71) 2
FAIRLESS, Benjamin (d.1/2/62) 1
FAITH, Percy (d.2/9/76) 2
FALK, Peter 2,3,4,5
FALKENBURG, Jinx 1,2
FALLACI, Oriana 4
FALWELL, Jerry 4
FANNING, Katherine 4
FARAGO, Ladislas (d.10/15/80) 3
FARBER, Barry 2
FARLEY, James A. (d.6/9/76) 1,2,3
FAROUK I, King (d.3/18/65) 1
FARRAR, Geraldine (d.3/11/67) 1
FARRELL, Eileen 1,2,3,
FARRELL, Frank (d.3/21/83) 2
FARRELL, James T. (d.8/22/79) 1,2
FARRELL, Suzanne 4,5
FARROW, Mia 3,4,5
FAST, Howard 1,2
FAUBUS, Orval 1,2
FAULK, John Henry 2
FAULKNER, William (d.7/6/62) 1
FAURE, Edgar (d.3/30/88) 1
FAWCETT, Farrah 4,5
FAY, Frank (d.9/26/61) 1
FAYE, Alice 1,2,3
FEATHER, William 2
FEIFFER, Jules 2,3,4
FEINSTEIN, Dianne 4
FEINSTEIN, Michael 5
FELD, Irvin (d.9/6/84) 3
FELICIANO, José 3,4

FELKER, Clay S. 3,4
FELLER, Bob 1,2
FELLINI, Federico 3,4,5
FELT, Harry 2
FELT, Irving Mitchell 3
FERBER, Edna (d.4/16/68) 1,2
FERGER, Roger (d.4/8/74) 2
FERKAUF, Eugene 2
FERLINGHETTI, Lawrence 3
FERMI, Laura 2
FERNANDEL (d.2/26/71) 1
FERRARO, Geraldine 4
FERRER, José 1,2,3,4,5
FERRER, Mel 1,2
FERRIL, Thomas Hornsby 2
FEUER, Cy 2,3,4
FICKETT, Mary 2
FIDLER, Jimmie 2
FIEDLER, Arthur (d.7/10/79) 1,2,3
FIEDLER, Leslie 3
FIELD, Betty (d.9/13/73) 1,2
FIELD, Marshall, Jr. (d.9/18/65) 1,2
FIELD, Marshall V. 3
FIELD, Sally 4,5
FIELDING, Temple (d.5/18/83) 1,2,3
FIELDS, Dorothy (d.3/28/74) 1,3
FIELDS, Gracie (d.9/27/79) 1
FIELDS, Joseph (d.3/4/66) 1
FIERSTEIN, Harvey 4,5
THE 5TH DIMENSION 3
FINE, Dr. Benjamin 2
FINE, William 3
FINLETTER, Thomas K. (d.4/24/80) 1,2
FINLEY, Charles O. 2,3
FINLEY, David (d.2/1/77) 2
FINNEY, Albert 3,4,5
FIRESTONE, Harvey S., Jr. (d.6/1/73) 1,2,3
FIRESTONE, Leonard 2
FIRESTONE, Raymond 2,3
FIRESTONE, Russell 2
FISCHER, Bobby 1,2,3,4,5
FISCHER, John (d.8/18/78) 2
FISCHER-DIESKAU, Dietrich 3,4
FISH, Hamilton 2
FISHBEIN, Morris (d.9/27/76) 1
FISHER, Avery 4,5
FISHER, Carrie 4,5
FISHER, Eddie 1,2
FISHER, Dr. Geoffrey Francis (see CANTERBURY, Archbishop of) 1
FITZGERALD, Barry (d.1/4/61) 1
FITZGERALD, Ed (d.3/21/82) & Pegeen 1,2
FITZGERALD, Ella 1,2,3,4,5
FITZGERALD, Geraldine 1,4
FITZSIMMONS, Frank (d.5/6/81) 3
FITZSIMMONS, Jim (d.3/11/66) 1,2
FLACK, Roberta 4,5
FLAGSTAD, Kirsten (d.4/1/63) 1
FLANDERS, Ralph 1,2
FLANNER, Janet (d.11/7/78) 1,2,3
FLEESON, Doris 2
FLEISCHMAN, Lawrence 2
FLEISHER, Leon 2
FLEMING, Peggy 3,4
FLEMING, Rhonda 1,2
FLEMING, Robert 2
FLEMMING, Arthur S. 1,2
FLETCHER, James Chipman 3
FLUTIE, Doug 4
FLYNN, Errol (d.10/4/59) 1
FLYNN, Sean (d.1970?) 2
FLYNT, Larry 4
FOCH, Nina 1,2

FOGARTY, Anne (d.1/15/80) 1,2
FOLSOM, Frank (d.1/12/70) 1
FOLSOM, James 2
FONDA, Henry (d.8/12/82) 1,2,3
FONDA, Jane 2,3,4,5
FONDA, Peter 2,3,4,5
FONG, Hiram 2,3
FONSSAGRIVES, Lisa 1
FONTAINE, Frank (d.8/4/78) 2
FONTAINE, Joan 1,2,3,4,5
FONTAINE, Pat (d.8/24/77) 2
FONTANNE, Lynn (d.7/30/83) 1,2,3
FONTEYN, Margot 1,2,3,4,5
FORBES, Malcolm 2,3,4,5
FORD, Art 1
FORD, Benson (d.7/27/78) 2
FORD, Betty 4,5
FORD, Corey 1,2
FORD, Doug 1
FORD, Mrs. Edsel (d.10/19/76) 2
FORD, Eileen & Jerry 4,5
FORD, Ernie 1
FORD, Gerald 2,3,4,5
FORD, Glenn 1,2,3
FORD, Harrison 4,5
FORD, Henry II (d.9/29/87) 1,2,3,4
FORD, John (d.8/31/73) 1,2
FORD, Paul (d.4/12/76) 2
FORD, Ruth 2,3,4
FORD, Tennessee Ernie 2
FORD, Walter Buhl 2
FORD, Whitey 1,2
FORD, William Clay 2
FOREMAN, George 3
FORESTER, C.S. (d.4/2/66) 1
FORMAN, Milos 4,5
FORSTER, E.M. 1
FORSYTH, Frederick 4,5
FORSYTHE, John 1,2,3,4,5
FORTUNE, Michele 5
FOSDICK, Harry Emerson (d.10/5/69) 1,2
FOSS, Joe 2
FOSS, Lukas 2
FOSSE, Bob (d.9/23/87) 2,3,4
FOSTER, Jodie 4,5
FOUTS, Dan 4
FOWLER, Gene (d.7/2/60) 1
FOWLES, John 3,4
FOX, Michael J. 4,5
FOX, Nellie (d.12/1/75) 2
FOXX, Redd 3,4
FOYT, A.J. 3,4
FRANCESCATTI, Zino 1,2
FRANCIOSA, Anthony 1,2
FRANCIS, Arlene 1,2,3,4,5
FRANCIS, Connie 2
FRANCIS, Dick 4,5
FRANCO, Generalissimo Francisco (d.11/20/75) 1
FRANK, Gerold 1,2
FRANKENHEIMER, Jonn 2
FRANKENTHALER, Helen 3,4,5
FRANKFURTER, Felix (d.2/23/65) 1,2
FRANKLIN, Aretha 3,4,5
FRANKLIN, Bonnie 4
FRASER, Antonia 4,5
FRAZIER, Brenda (d.5/2/82) 1
FRAZIER, George 2
FRAZIER, Joe 3,4,5
FRAZIER, Walt 3
FREBERG, Stan 2
FREDERICK, Pauline 2,3
FREDERICKS, Marshall 2
FREDERIK IX, King of Denmark (d.1/14/72) 1

468

FREDERIKA, Queen (d.2/6/81) **1**
FREED, Alan (d.1/20/65) **1**
FREED, Arthur (d.4/12/73) **1,2**
FREEMAN, Orville **2**
FREEMAN, Y. Frank (d.2/5/69) **2**
FRENI, Mirella **4,5**
FRESHEL, Curtis **2**
FRICK, Ford (d.4/9/78) **1,2**
FRIEDAN, Betty **3,4,5**
FRIEDKIN, William **3,4,5**
FRIEDMAN, Milton **3,4**
FRIENDLY, Fred **2**
FRINGS, Ketti (d.2/11/81) **1**
FROMAN, Jane (d.4/22/80) **1**
FROMM, Erich (d.3/18/80) **1,2**
FRONDIZI, Arturo **1**
FROST, David **3,4,5**
FROST, Robert (d.1/29/63) **1**
FRY, Christopher **1**
FRYER, Robert **1**
FUCHS, Joseph **2**
FUCHS, Sir Vivian **1**
FUGARD, Athol **4,5**
FULBRIGHT, William **1,2,3,4**
FULLER, Alfred Carl (d.12/4/73) **1,2**
FULLER, Clement (d.10/19/75) **3**
FULLER, R. Buckminster (d.7/1/83) **3**
FUNK, Wilfred (d.6/2/65) **1,2**
FUNSTON, Keith **1,2**
FUNT, Allen **2**
FURCOLO, Foster **1**
FURNESS, Betty **1,2,3,4,5**
FURSTENBERG, Diane Von **3,4,5**
FURSTENBERG, Egon Von **3,4**

G

G. KENNY **5**
GABEL, Martin (d.5/22/86) **1,2**
GABIN, JEAN (d.11/15/86) **1**
GABLE, Clark (d.11/17/60)
GABOR, Eva **1,2,3,4,5**
GABOR, Jolie **1,2**
GABOR, Magda **1,2**
GABOR, Zsa Zsa **1,2,3,4,5**
GABRIEL, Peter **5**
GAITSKELL, Hugh (d.1/19/63) **1**
GALANOS, James **2,3,4**
GALBRAITH, J. Kenneth **1,2,3,4**
GALBREATH, John **2,5**
GALLAGHER, Helen **3**
GALLICO, Paul (d.7/16/76) **1,2**
GALLUP, George (d.7/26/84) **1,2,3**
GALWAY, James **4,5**
GAM, Rita **1,2**
GAMBLING, John B. (d.11/21/74) **1**
GARAGIOLA, Joe **2,3,4,5**
GARBO, Greta **1,2,3,4,5**
GARCIA, Carlos P. (d.6/14/71) **1**
GARCIA-MÁRQUEZ, Gabriel **4,5**
GARDEN, Mary (d.1/3/67) **1**
GARDINER, Reginald (d.7/7/80) **1,2**
GARDNER, Ava **1,2,3,4,5**
GARDNER, Ed (d.8/17/63) **1**
GARDNER, Erle Stanley (d.3/11/70) **1,2**
GARDNER, Herb **2**
GARDNER, Hy (d.6/17/89) **1,2**
GARDNER, John **2,3**
GARFUNKEL, Art **3,4,5**
GARLAND, Judy (d.6/22/69) **1,2**
GARNER, Erroll (d.1/2/77) **1,2,3**
GARNER, James **1,2,3,4,5**
GARNER, John Nance (d.11/7/67) **1,2**
GARRETT, Paul **1,2**

GARROWAY, Dave (d.7/21/82) **1,2,3**
GARSON, Greer **1,2**
GARY, Romain (d.12/2/80) **1**
GASTINEAU, Mark **4**
GATES, Thomas (d.3/25/83) **2**
GAUTIER, Felisa Rincon De **1,2**
GAVIN, James M. **1,2**
GAVRAS, Costa **3** (see also COSTA-GAVRAS **4**)
GAYLE, Crystal **5**
GAYLORD, E.K. **2**
GAYNOR, Janet (d.9/14/84) **1,2**
GAYNOR, Mitzi **1,2**
GAZZARA, Ben **1,2,3,4**
GEARY, Tony **4**
GEBEL-WILLIAMS, Günther **3,4**
GEFFEN, David **4,5**
GEIS, Bernard **2**
GELL-MANN, Murray **3**
GENEEN, Harold **2**
GENET, Jean (d.4/14/86) **3,4**
GENEVIEVE **1,2**
GENNARO, Peter **2,3**
GEORGE, Chief Dan (d.9/23/81) **3**
GEORGE, Phyllis **4,5**
GERE, Richard **4,5**
GERNREICH, Rudi (d.4/21/85) **3**
GERSHWIN, Ira (d.8/17/83) **1,2,3**
GERULAITIS, Vitas **5**
GETTY, Estelle **5**
GETTY, Gordon **4,5**
GETTY, J. Paul (d.6/6/76) **1,2,3**
GHIAUROV, Nicolai **4**
GIBBS, Georgia **1,2**
GIBSON, Althea **1,2**
GIBSON, Charles **5**
GIBSON, Kenneth **3,4**
GIBSON, Mel **4,5**
GIELGUD, John **1,3,4,5**
GIESLER, Jerry (d.9/27/62) **1**
GIFFORD, Frank **2,3,4,5**
GIFFORD, Kathi Lee **5**
GIL, Jean-Charles **4**
GILBERT, Carl **2**
GILBERT, Lewis **2**
GILBERT, Melissa **5**
GILBRETH, Frank, Jr. **2**
GILELS, Emil (d.10/14/85) **1,4**
GILES, Warren (d.2/7/79) **2**
GILLESPIE, Dizzy **1,2,3,4,5**
GILPATRIC, Roswell **2**
GIMBEL, Benedict, Jr. (d.2/5/71) **2**
GIMBEL, Bernard (d.9/29/66) **1,2**
GIMBEL, Peter (d.7/12/87) **3,4**
GIMBEL, Sophie (d.11/28/81) **2**
GINGOLD, Hermione (d.4/30/87) **1,2,3,4**
GINGRICH, Arnold (d.6/9/76) **2,3**
GINGRICH, Newt **4,5**
GINSBERG, Allen **2,3,4,5**
GIOVANNI, Nikki **3,4,5**
GISH, Dorothy (d.6/4/68) **1,2**
GISH, Lillian **1,2,3,4,5**
GIULIANI, Rudolph **5**
GIVENCHY, Hubert de **4,5**
GLASS, Philip **4,5**
GLEASON, Jackie (d.6/24/87) **1,2,3,4**
GLENN, John **2,3,4,5**
GLENVILLE, Peter **1,2,3**
GOBEL, George **1,2**
GODARD, Jean-Luc **3,4**
GODDARD, Paulette **1,2,3,4**
GODDEN, Rumer **1**
GODFREY, Arthur (d.3/15/83) **1,2,3**
GODUNOV, Alexander **4,5**
GOETZ, William (d.8/15/69) **2**

GOHEEN, Robert **1,2**
GOLD, Herbert **2**
GOLDBERG, Arthur **2,3**
GOLDBERG, Leonard **4**
GOLDBERG, Rube (d.12/7/70) **1,2**
GOLDBERG, Whoopi **4,5**
GOLDBLATT, Joel **2**
GOLDBLUM, Jeff **5**
GOLDEN, Harry (d.10/2/81) **1,2,3**
GOLDENSON, Leonard **1,2,3**
GOLDING, William **4**
GOLDMAN, Eric **2**
GOLDMAN, Nahum (d.8/29/82) **2**
GOLDSBORO, Bobby **3**
GOLDSTEIN, Ruby (d.4/22/84) **2**
GOLDWATER, Barry **1,2,3,4**
GOLDWYN, Samuel (d.1/31/74) **1,2,3**
GOMULKA, Wladyslaw (d.9/1/82) **1**
GONZALES, Pancho **1,2,3**
GOODEN, Dwight **4,5**
GOODMAN, Andrew **2**
GOODMAN, Benny (d.6/13/86) **1,2,3,4**
GOODMAN, Dody **1**
GOODMAN, Linda **3**
GOODPASTER, Andrew J. **3**
GOODSON, Mark **2**
GOOLAGONG, Evonne **3**
GORDON, Dorothy **2**
GORDON, Ellen **5**
GORDON, John **2**
GORDON, Kermit **2**
GORDON, Max (d.11/2/78) **2**
GORDON, Ruth (d.8/28/85) **1,2,3**
GORDY, Berry, Jr. **3,4,5**
GORE, Albert **1,2**
GOREN, Charles **1,2,3**
GORMAN, Cliff **3**
GORMÉ, Eydie **1,2,3,4,5**
GOSDEN, Freeman (d.12/10/82) **2**
GOSSETT, Louis, Jr. **4,5**
GOULD, Bruce **1**
GOULD, Chester **1,2,3**
GOULD, Elliot **3,4,5**
GOULD, Glenn (d.10/4/82) **1**
GOULD, Jack **2**
GOULD, Morton **1,2**
GOULD, Shane **3**
GOULDING, Ray **2,3** (see also BOB & RAY **4**)
GOULET, Robert **2,3,4,5**
GOWDY, Curt **3**
GRABLE, Betty (d.7/2/73) **1,2,3**
GRACE, Eugene G. **1**
GRACE, Joseph Peter, Jr. **1,2**
GRAHAM, Billy **1,2,3,4,5**
GRAHAM, Katharine **3,4,5**
GRAHAM, Martha **1,2,3,4,5**
GRAHAM, Otto **2**
GRAHAM, Philip (d.8/3/63) **1**
GRAHAM, Sheilah **1,2,3**
GRAHAM, Virginia **2,3**
GRAND FUNK RAILROAD **3**
GRANGER, Farley **1**
GRANGER, Stewart **1,2**
GRANT, Amy **5**
GRANT, Cary (d.11/29/86) **1,2,3,4**
GRANT, Kathy (Kathryn) **1,2**
GRANT, Lee **4,5**
GRANZ, Norman **2**
GRASS, Günter **3,4,5**
GRATEFUL DEAD **3**
GRAUER, Ben (d.5/31/77) **1,2**
GRAVEL, Mike **3**
GRAVES, Peter **3**
GRAVES, Robert **1**

Cumulative Index — CELEBRITY REGISTER 1990

GRAY, Barry **2,3,4,5**
GRAY, Dolores **1,2**
GRAY, Gilda (d.12/22/59) **1**
GRAY, Gordon **1**
GRAY, Harold (d.5/9/68) **1,2**
GRAY, Linda **4,5**
GRAYSON, Kathryn **2**
GRAZIANO, Rocky **1,2,3,4,5**
GRECO, José **1,2,3,4**
GREELEY, Andrew **4,5**
GREEN, Abel (d.5/10/73) **1,2,3**
GREEN, Adolph **1,2,3,4,5**
GREEN, Johnny **1**
GREEN, Martyn (d.2/8/75) **1,2**
GREEN, Paul (d.5/4/81) **1,2**
GREEN, Theodore Francis (d.5/19/66) 1,2
GREENBERG, Hank **1,2**
GREENE, Graham **1,3,4**
GREENE, Lorne (d.9/11/87) **3,4**
GREENEWALT, Crawford H. **1,2**
GREER, Germaine **3,4**
GREER, Michael (d.4/19/76) **2,3**
GREGORY, Cynthia **4,5**
GREGORY, Dick **2,3,4**
GREGORY, Paul **1,2**
GRENFELL, Joyce (d.11/30/79) **1**
GRENNAN, Jacqueline (see also WEXLER, Jacqueline Grennan **3,4**)
GRETZKY, Wayne **4,5**
GREY, Jennifer **5**
GREY, Joel **3,4,5**
GRIESE, Bob **3**
GRIFFIN, Marvin (d.6/13/82) **1**
GRIFFIN, Merv **2,3,4,5**
GRIFFIS, Stanton (d.8/29/74) **2**
GRIFFITH, Andy **1,2,3,4**
GRIFFITH, Melanie **5**
GRIFFITH, Robert (d.6/7/61) **1**
GRIFFITH-JOYNER, Florence **5**
GRIFFITHS, Martha **2**
GRIMES, Tammy **2,3,4,5**
GRISSOM, Virgil (d.1/27/67) **2**
GRISWOLD, A. Whitney (d.4/19/63) **1**
GRIZZARD, George **2**
GRODIN, Charles **3,4,5**
GROFÉ, Ferde (d.4/3/72) **1**
GROMYKO, Andrei **1**
GRONCHI, Giovanni (d.10/17/78) **1**
GROOMS, Red **4**
GROPIUS, Walter (d.7/5/69) **1,2**
GROSSINGER, Jennie (d.11/20/72) **1,2**
GROSVENOR, Gilbert **2**
GROSVENOR, Melville Bell (d.4/22/82) **3**
GROTEWOHL, Otto (d.9/22/64) **1**
GROVES, Leslie R. (d.7/13/70) **1,2**
GRUBER, Lewis (d.4/71) **1,2**
GRUENING, Ernest (d.6/26/74) **2**
GRUENTHER, Alfred M. (d.5/30/83) **1,2**
GRUNWALD, Henry **4**
GUARE, John **3,4,5**
GUBBRUD, Archie **2**
GUCCI, Aldo **3,4,5**
GUCCIONE, Bob **3,4,5**
GUEDEN, Hilde **1**
GUEST, Mrs. Winston (C.Z.) **1,2,4,5**
GUGGENHEIM, Harry **2**
GUGGENHEIM, Peggy (d.12/22/79) **2,3**
GUILLAUME, Robert **4**
GUINNESS, Alec **1,2,3,4,5**
GUINZBURG, Thomas **2**
GUMBEL, Bryant **4,5**
GUNTHER, John (d.5/29/70) **1,2**
GUSTAV VI, King Of Sweden (d.9/15/73) **1**
GUTHRIE, A.B., Jr. **1,2**

GUTHRIE, Arlo **3,4,5**
GUTHRIE, Tyrone (d.5/15/71) **1,2**
GUTHRIE, Woody (d.10/3/67) **2**
GUY, William **2**

H

HABER, Joyce **3**
HACKETT, Buddy **1,2,3,4**
HACKMAN, Gene **3,4,5**
HAGEN, Uta **1,2**
HAGEN, Walter (d.10/5/69) **2**
HAGERTY, James (d.4/11/81) **1,2**
HAGGARD, Merle **3,4,5**
HAGLER, Marvelous Marvin **4**
HAGMAN, Larry **4,5**
HAHN, Emily **1,2**
HAIG, Alexander **4**
HAILE SELASSIE (d.8/27/75) **1**
HAILEY, Arthur **4**
HAJI-SHEIKH, Ali **4**
HALABY, Najeeb **2**
HALAS, George (d.12/16/79) **2,3**
HALBERSTAM, David **3,4,5**
HALE, Frank (d.12/20/72) **1,2**
HALE, Nancy **2**
HALE, Prentis Cobb **2,3,4**
HALL, Arsenio **5**
HALL, Daryl and John OATES **4,5**
HALL, Jerry **5**
HALL, Joseph **2**
HALL, Joyce (d.10/29/82) **1,2,3**
HALL, Juanita (d.2/29/68) **1,2**
HALL, Leonard W. (d.6/2/79) **1,2**
HALL, Monty **3,4**
HALL, Peter **4**
HALLECK, Charles **1,2**
HALSEY, William **2**
HALSTON **3,4,5**
HAMILL, Dorothy **4**
HAMILL, Mark **4,5**
HAMILL, Pete **3,4,5**
HAMILTON, Chico **2**
HAMILTON, Edith (d.5/31/63) **1**
HAMILTON, George **2,3,4,5**
HAMILTON, Linda **5**
HAMILTON, Scott **4**
HAMLISCH, Marvin **4,5**
HAMMARSKJOLD, Dag (d.9/18/61) **1**
HAMMER, Armand **4,5**
HAMMERSTEIN, Oscar II (d.8/22/60) **1**
HAMMETT, Dashiell (d.1/10/61) **1**
HAMMOND, Caleb **2,3**
HAMMOND, John Hays, Jr. (d.2/12/65) **2**
HAMPSHIRE, Susan **3**
HAMPTON, Hope (d.1/23/82) **2**
HAMPTON, Lionel **1,2,3,4,5**
HAND, Learned (d.8/18/61) **1**
HANEY, Carol (d.5/10/64) **1,2**
HANEY, Fred **1**
HANKS, Tom **5**
HANNA, Bill & Joe BARBERA **4,5**
HANNAH, Daryl **5**
HANSBERRY, Lorraine (d.1/12/65) **2**
HANSEN, Clifford **2**
HANSON, Duane **4**
HANSON, Howard (d.2/26/81) **1**
HARBURG, E.Y. "Yip" (d.2/5/81) **3**
HARD, Darlene **2**
HARDWICK, Elizabeth **4**
HARDWICKE, Sir Cedric (d.8/6/64) **1,2**
HARGIS, Billy James **3**
HARGROVE, Marion **1,2**
HARING, Keith **4,5**

HARKNESS, Rebekah (d.6/17/82) **3**
HARKNESS, Richard **2**
HARLAN, John Marshall (d.12/29/71) **1,2**
HARMON, Mark **5**
HARNICK, Sheldon **3,4,5**
HARPER, Marion **2**
HARPER, Valerie **5**
HARRIMAN, Averell (d.7/26/86) **1,2,3,4**
HARRINGTON, Michael **3,4,5**
HARRIS, Barbara **2,3**
HARRIS, Bucky (d.11/8/77) **1**
HARRIS, Franco **3**
HARRIS, Jed (d.11/15/79) **1,2**
HARRIS, Julie **1,2,3,4,5**
HARRIS, Louis **3,4**
HARRIS, Phil **1,2**
HARRIS, Radie **4**
HARRIS, Richard **3,4,5**
HARRIS, Roy **1,2**
HARRIS, Sydney (d.12/7/86) **2**
HARRISON, Albertis **2**
HARRISON, George **3,4,5**
HARRISON, Gilbert **2**
HARRISON, Gregory **4**
HARRISON, Rex **1,2,3,4,5**
HARRISON, Wallace K. (d.12/2/81) **1,2**
HART, Gary **4**
HART, Kitty Carlisle **4** (see also CARLISLE, Kitty **1,2,3,5**)
HART, Moss (d.12/20/61) **1**
HART, Philip (d.12/26/76) **2**
HARTACK, Willie **1,2**
HARTFORD, Huntington **1,2,3**
HARTKE, Vance **2**
HARTLEY, Mariette **5**
HARTMAN, David **4**
HARTMAN, Lisa **5**
HARTSFIELD, William (d.2/22/71) **2**
HARVEY, Laurence (d.11/25/73) **1,2**
HARVEY, Paul **3,4**
HATCH, Orrin **4,5**
HATFIELD, Mark **2,3,4,5**
HAUPT, Enid **2**
HAUSER, Gayelord (d.12/26/84) **2,3**
HAVOC, June **1,2**
HAWKINS, Coleman (d.5/19/69) **1,2**
HAWKINS, Jack (d.7/18/73) **1**
HAWKS, Howard (d.12/29/77) **2**
HAWN, Goldie **3,4,5**
HAYAKAWA, Sessue (d.11/24/73) **1**
HAYAKAWA, S.I. **3**
HAYDÉE, Marcia **3,4**
HAYDEN, Carl (d.1/25/72) **1,2**
HAYDEN, Melissa **1,2**
HAYDEN, Sterling **1,2**
HAYDN, Hiram (d.12/2/73) **2**
HAYES, Helen **1,2,3,4,5**
HAYES, Isaac **3**
HAYES, Peter Lind and Mary HEALY **1,2**
HAYES, Roland (d.12/31/76) **2**
HAYES, Woody **2,3**
HAYMES, Dick **1,2**
HAYS, Brooks (d.10/11/81) **1,2**
HAYWARD, Leland (d.3/18/71) **1,2**
HAYWARD, Susan (d.3/14/75) **1,2**
HAYWORTH, Rita (d.5/15/87) **1,2,3,4**
HEAD, Edith (d.10/24/81) **1,2,3**
HEALD, Henry Townley (d.11/23/75) **1,2**
HEALY, George, Jr. **2**
HEARN, George **4**
HEARST, Patty **4,5**
HEARST, Randolph **2**
HEARST, William Randolph, Jr. **1,2,3,4,5**
HEATTER, Gabriel (d.3/30/72) **1**
HECHT, Ben (d.4/18/64) **1,2**

HECKART, Eileen **3**
HECKSCHER, August **2**
HEFFNER, Richard **2**
HEFLIN, Van (d.7/23/71) **1,2**
HEFNER, Christie **4,5**
HEFNER, Hugh **2,3,4,5**
HEIFETZ, Jascha (d.2/11/87) **1,2,3,4**
HEINZ, H.J. **2,3**
HEINZ, John **4,5**
HEISENBERG, Werner (d.2/1/76) **1**
HEISS, Carol **1,2**
HELLER, Joseph **2,4,5**
HELLER, Walter (d.6/15/87) **2,3,4**
HELLMAN, Geoffrey (d.9/26/77) **2**
HELLMAN, Lillian (d.6/30/84) **1,2,3**
HELMS, Jesse **4**
HELMS, Richard **3**
HELMSLEY, Leona & Harry **4**
HELOISE (d.12/28/77) **2**
HELPMANN, Robert **1**
HEMINGWAY, Ernest (d.7/2/61) **1**
HEMMINGS, David **3**
HENDERSON, Ernest (d.9/6/67) **1,2**
HENDERSON, Florence **2,5**
HENDERSON, Ricky **4,5**
HENDERSON, Skitch **1,2,3,4,5**
HENIE, Sonja (d.10/12/69) **1,2**
HENLE, Ray (d.1/21/74) **2**
HENLEY, Beth **4,5**
HENNING, Doug **4**
HENRIED, Paul **1,2**
HENSON, Jim **4,5**
HEPBURN, Audrey **1,2,3,4,5**
HEPBURN, Katharine **1,2,3,4,5**
HERBERT, Frank (d.2/11/86) **4**
HERBLOCK **1,2,3,4,5**
HERLIHY, James Leo **3**
HERMAN, Jerry **3,4,5**
HERMAN, Pee Wee **5**
HERMAN, Woody (d.10/29/87) **1,2**
HERRERA, Carolina **4,5**
HERSEY, John **1,2,3,4,5**
HERSHEY, Lewis B. (d.5/20/77) **1,2**
HERSHFIELD, Harry (d.12/15/74) **2**
HERTER, Christian (d.12/30/66) **1,2**
HERZOG, Werner **4,5**
HESBURGH, Theodore **2,3,4**
HESS, Dame Myra (d.11/25/65) **1**
HESTON, Charlton **1,2,3,4,5**
HEYERDAHL, Thor **1,2,3,4**
HIBBS, Ben (d.3/29/75) **1**
HICKENLOOPER, Bourke (d.9/4/71) **1,2**
HICKMAN, Dwayne **2**
HICKS, Granville (d.6/18/82) **2**
HIGGINS, Marguerite (d.1/1/66) **1,2**
HIGHET, Gilbert (d.1/20/78) **1,2,3**
HILDEGARDE **1,2,3,4,5**
HILL, George Roy **4,5**
HILL, Lister (d.12/84) **1,2**
HILL, Phil **2**
HILLARY, Sir Edmund **1**
HILLER, Wendy **1**
HILLS, Lee **2**
HILTON, Conrad (d.1/3/79) **1,2,3**
HINDEMITH, Paul (d.12/29/63) **1**
HINES, Gregory **5**
HINES, Jerome **2**
HIROHITO (d.1/7/89) **1**
HIRSCH, Judd **4,5**
HIRSCHFELD, Al **1,2,3,4,5**
HISS, Alger **1,2**
HITCHCOCK, Alfred (d.4/29/80) **1,2,3**
HOAD, Lewis A., Jr. **1**
HOBBY, Oveta Culp **1,2**
HOBLITZELLE, Karl (d.3/8/67) **2**

HOCKNEY, David **4,5**
HODGES, Gil (d.4/2/72) **1,2**
HODGES, Luther (d.10/6/74) **2**
HOFF, Philip **2**
HOFFA, Jimmy/James (d.7/30/75?) **2,3**
HOFFER, Eric (d.5/22/83) **2,3**
HOFFMAN, Abbie (d.4/12/89) **3**
HOFFMAN, Dustin **3,4,5**
HOFFMAN, Malvina **2**
HOFFMAN, Paul (d.10/8/74) **1,2**
HOFHEINZ, Roy (d.11/21/82) **3**
HOFMANN, Hans (d.2/17/66) **1,2**
HOGAN, Ben **1,2,3**
HOGAN, Frank (d.4/2/74) **1,2**
HOLBROOK, Hal **2,3,4,5**
HOLBROOK, Stewart **2**
HOLDEN, William (d.11/16/81) **1,2,3**
HOLDER, Geoffrey **2**
HOLLAND, Spessard (d.11/6/71) **2**
HOLLIDAY, Judy (d.6/7/65) **1,2**
HOLLIMAN, Earl **2**
HOLLINGS, Ernest/Fritz **2,4,5**
HOLLOWAY, Stanley (d.1/30/82) **1**
HOLM, Celeste **1,2,4,5**
HOLM, Hanya **4,5**
HOLM, Jeanne **3**
HOLMAN, Eugene (d.8/12/62) **1**
HOLMAN, Libby (d.6/18/71) **1,2**
HOLMES, Larry **4,5**
HOMER, Arthur (d.6/18/72) **2**
HOMOLKA, Oscar (d.1/28/78) **2**
HOOK, Sydney **2,3,4**
HOOKS, Benjamin **4,5**
HOOVER, Herbert (d.10/20/64) **1,2**
HOOVER, Herbert, Jr. (d.7/9/69) **1,2**
HOOVER, J. Edgar (d.5/2/72) **1,2**
HOPE, Bob **1,2,3,4,5**
HOPKINS, Anthony **4,5**
HOPKINS, Miriam (d.10/9/72) **1**
HOPPER, Dennis **3**
HOPPER, Edward (d.5/15/67) **1,2**
HOPPER, Hedda (d.2/1/66) **1,2**
HORCHOW, Roger **4,5**
HORGAN, Paul **2**
HORNE, Lena **1,2,3,4,5**
HORNE, Marilyn **3,4,5**
HORNUNG, Paul **2**
HOROVITZ, Israel **3,4,5**
HOROWITZ, Vladimir **1,2,3,4,5**
HORTON, Edward Everett (d.9/30/70) **2**
HORTON, Robert **2**
HOTTELET, Richard C. **2**
HOUGHTON, Amory (d.2/21/81) **1,2**
HOUK, Ralph **2,3**
HOUSEMAN, John (d.10/31/88) **1,2,3,4**
HOUSTON, Whitney **5**
HOVDE, Frederick **2**
HOVING, Thomas P.F. **3,4**
HOVING, Walter **1,2,3,4**
HOWAR, Barbara **4,5**
HOWARD, Jack **2,3**
HOWARD, Ron **4,5**
HOWARD, Roy (d.11/20/64) **1,2**
HOWARD, Trevor (d.1/7/88) **1,3,4**
HOWE, Quincy (d.2/17/77) **2**
HOWES, Sally Ann **2**
HOYT, Palmer (d.6/25/79) **2**
HUDSON, Joseph **2**
HUDSON, Rock (d.10/2/85) **1,2,3,4**
HUFF, Sam **2**
HUGHES, Emmet (d.9/19/82) **2**
HUGHES, Howard (d.4/5/76) **1,2,3**
HUGHES, Langston (d.5/22/67) **1,2**
HUGHES, Richard (d.4/28/76) **2**
HULL, Bobby **3**

HUMPERDINCK, Engelbert **3,4,5**
HUMPHREY, George (d.1/20/70) **1,2**
HUMPHREY, Hubert (d.1/13/78) **1,2,3**
HUNT, H.L. (d.11/30/74) **1,2,3**
HUNT, Lamar **2,3,4,5**
HUNT, Linda **4**
HUNTER, Kim **1,2**
HUNTER, Ross **2,3,4**
HUNTER-GAULT, Charlayne **4**
HUNTER, Tab **1,2**
HUNTLEY, Chet (d.3/20/74) **1,2,3**
HURLEY, Neil **2**
HURLEY, Roy (d.10/31/71) **1,2**
HUROK, S. (d.3/5/74) **1,2,3**
HURST, Fannie (d.2/23/68) **1,2**
HURT, William **4,5**
HUSING, Ted (d.8/10/62) **1**
HUSSEIN I, King **1**
HUSTON, John (d.8/28/88) **1,2,3,4**
HUTCHINS, Robert (d.5/14/77) **1,2,3**
HUTTON, Barbara (d.5/11/79) **1,2,3**
HUTTON, Betty **1,2**
HUTTON, Lauren **4,5**
HUTTON, Timothy **4**
HUXLEY, Aldous (d.11/22/63) **1,2**
HUXLEY, Julian (d.2/14/75) **1**
HUXTABLE, Ada Louise **3,4**
HYAMS, Joe **2**

I

IACOCCA, Lee A. **3,4,5**
IDOL, Billy **4,5**
IGLESIAS, Julio **4,5**
INDIANA, Robert **3,4**
INGE, WILLIAM (d.6/10/73) **1,2**
INGERSOLL, R. Sturgis (d.5/20/76) **2**
INNIS, ROY **3**
INOUYE, Daniel **2,3**
INXS **5**
IONESCO, Eugene **1,3,4,5**
IRONS, Jeremy **4,5**
IRVING, Amy **4,5**
IRVING, John **4,5**
ISHERWOOD, Christopher (d.1/4/86) **1,2,3,4**
ITURBI, José (d.6/28/80) **1,2,3**
IVANEK, Zeljko **4**
IVES, Burl **1,2**
IVEY, Judith **4,5**
IVORY, James (see MERCHANT/IVORY) **5**

J

JACK, Homer **2**
JACKSON, Anne **2**
JACKSON, Charles (d.9/21/68) **1,2**
JACKSON, C.D. (d.9/18/64) **2**
JACKSON 5 **3** (see also JACKSON, Michael **4,5**)
JACKSON, Glenda **3,4,5**
JACKSON, Henry M. (d.9/1/83) **1,2,3**
JACKSON, Janet **5**
JACKSON, Jesse **3,4,5**
JACKSON, Kate **4,5**
JACKSON, Mahalia (d.1/27/72) **1,2**
JACKSON, Michael **4,5** (see also JACKSON 5 **3**)
JACKSON, Reggie **4,5**
JACKSON, Shirley (d.8/8/65) **2**
JACOBS, Jody **4**
JACOBS, Walter **1,2**

Cumulative Index — CELEBRITY REGISTER 1990

JACOBSSON, Per (d.8/22/82) **1**
JACOBY, Oswald (d.6/27/84) **1,2**
JAFFE, Rona **1,2**
JAFFE, Sam (d.2/8/85) **2**
JAGGER, Bianca **4,5**
JAGGER, Mick **4** (see also ROLLING STONES **3,5**)
JAMES, Harry (d.7/5/83) **1,2**
JAMES, Joni **1,2**
JANEWAY, Elizabeth **1,2**
JANIS, Byron **2,3,4,5**
JANOWITZ, Tama **5**
JARMAN, Maxey **2**
JARRELL, Randall (d.10/14/65) **2**
JAVITS, Jacob (d.3/7/86) **1,2,3,4**
JEANMAIRE, Renée **1**
JEFFERS, Robinson (d.1/20/62) **1**
JEFFERSON AIRPLANE **3** (see also SLICK, Grace **4**)
JEFFERSON, Floyd **2**
JENNER, Bruce **4**
JENNER, William **1**
JENNINGS, Peter **4,5**
JENNINGS, Waylon **4,5**
JESSEL, George (d.5/24/81) **1,2,3**
JEWISON, Norman **5**
JIMMY THE GREEK (SNYDER, Jimmy) **3,4**
JOBS, Steven **4**
JOEL, Billy **4,5**
JOFFREY, Robert (d.3/25/88) **4**
JOHANSSON, Ingemar **1**
JOHN, Augustus (d.10/31/61) **1**
JOHN, Elton **3,4,5**
JOHN, Mr. **1,2**
JOHN, XXIII, Pope (d.6/3/63) **1**
JOHNS, Jasper **3,4,5**
JOHNSON, Dean Hewlett (d.10/22/66) **1**
JOHNSON, Don **5**
JOHNSON, Earvin "Magic" **4**
JOHNSON, Gerald W. (d.3/23/80) **1,2**
JOHNSON, Herbert (d.12/13/78) **2**
JOHNSON, Howard (Sr.) (d.6/20/77) **2**
JOHNSON, Howard B. (Jr.) **3**
JOHNSON, John H. **3,4,5**
JOHNSON, Lady Bird **2,3,4,5**
JOHNSON, Lyndon (d.1/22/73) **1,2**
JOHNSON, Nicholas **3**
JOHNSON, Nunnally (d.3/25/77) **1,2**
JOHNSON, Philip **3,4**
JOHNSON, Rafer **2,3**
JOHNSON, Robert Wood (d.1/30/68) **2**
JOHNSON, Van **1,2,3,4,5**
JOHNSON, Virginia (see MASTERS & JOHNSON) **3,4**
JOHNSTON, Eric (d.8/22/63) **1**
JOHNSTON, Jill **3**
JOHNSTON, Olin (d.4/18/65) **2**
JONES, Bobby (d.12/18/71) **1,2**
JONES, Christopher **3**
JONES, Grace **4,5**
JONES, Jack **3**
JONES, James (d.5/9/77) **1,2,3**
JONES, James Earl **3,4,5**
JONES, Jenkin Lloyd **2**
JONES, Jennifer **1,2**
JONES, Leroi (see BARAKA, Imamu Amiri) **3,4**
JONES, Quincy **4,5**
JONES, Robert Trent **2**
JONES, Shirley **2**
JONES, Spike (d.5/1/65) **1,2**
JONES, Tom **3,4,5**
JONG, Erica **4,5**
JORDAN, Dr. Sara (d.11/21/59) **1**

JORDAN, Michael **4,5**
JORGENSEN, Christine (d.5/3/89) **1**
JOSEPH, Richard **2,3**
JOURDAN, Louis **1,2**
JOYNER-KERSEE, Jackie **5**
JUAN, CARLOS (Principe de Asturias) **1**
JUDD, Walter **2**
JUDDS, The **5**
JULIANA, Queen **1**
JUNG, C.G. (d.6/6/61) **1**
JURGENS, Curt (d.6/18/82) **1**

K

KADAR, Jan (d.6/1/79) **3**
KADAR, Janos **1**
KAEL, Pauline **3,4,5**
KAHANE, Melanie **2**
KAHN, Herman (d.7/7/83) **3**
KAHN, Louis (d.3/17/74) **3**
KAHN, Madeline **4,5**
KAISER, Edgar (d.12/11/81) **2**
KAISER, Henry J. (d.8/24/67) **1,2**
KALINE, Al **1,2,3**
KALTENBORN, H.V. (d.6/14/65) **1,2**
KAMALI, Norma **4,5**
KAMEN, Milt (d.2/24/77) **2**
KANDER, John & Fred EBB **4,5**
KANE, Harnett **2**
KANGAROO, Captain (Keeshan, Bob) **2**
KANIN, Garson **1,2,3,4,5**
KANTOR, Mackinlay (d.10/11/77) **1,2**
KAPPEL, Frederick **1,2**
KARAJAN, Herbert Von **3,4** (see also VON KARAJAN **1,5**)
KARLOFF, Boris (d.2/2/69) **1,2**
KARAN, Donna **5**
KARSH, Yousuf **1**
KASSEBAUM, Nancy Landon **4,5**
KAUFMAN, George **4**
KAUFMAN, George S. (d.6/2/61) **1**
KAYE, Danny (d.3/3/87) **1,2,3,4**
KAYE, Nora **1,2**
KAYE, Sammy **1,2**
KAZAN, Elia **1,2,3,4,5**
KAZAN, Lainie **3**
KAZIN, Alfred **2,3,4**
KEACH, Stacy **3,4,5**
KEATING, Kenneth (d.5/5/75) **1,2**
KEATON, Buster (d.2/1/66) **1**
KEATON, Diane **4,5**
KEATON, Michael **5**
KEEDICK, Robert **2**
KEEL, Howard **1,2,4,5**
KEELER, Ruby **3,4,5**
KEESHAN, Bob (see Captain KANGAROO) **2**
KEFAUVER, Estes (d.8/10/63) **1**
KELL, Reginald **1**
KELLAND, Clarence Budington (d.2/18/64) **1,2**
KELLER, Greta (d.11/4/77) **3**
KELLER, Helen (d.6/1/68) **1,2**
KELLY, Emmett (d.3/28/79) **1,2**
KELLY, Gene **1,2,3,4,5**
KELLY, Grace (d.9/14/82) **1,2** (see Princess GRACE of Monaco **3**)
KELLY, John B., Jr. (d.3/2/85) **2,3**
KELLY, Nancy **1,2**
KELLY, Patsy (d.9/24/81) **3**
KELLY, Walt (d.10/18/73) **1,2,3**
KELSEY, Frances **2**
KEMP, Jack **4,5**
KEMPTON, Murray **2,3,4**

KENNAN, George F. **1,2,3,4**
KENNEDY, Arthur **1,2**
KENNEDY, Edward **2,3,4,5**
KENNEDY, Ethel **2,3**
KENNEDY, Jacqueline **2** (see also ONASSIS, Jacqueline **3,4,5**)
KENNEDY, Joan **3**
KENNEDY, John F. (d.11/22/63) **1,2**
KENNEDY, John Jr. **5**
KENNEDY, Joseph P. (d.11/18/69) **1,2**
KENNEDY, Robert F. (d.6/6/68) **1,2**
KENNEDY, Rose **2,3,4,5**
KENNEDY, William **4,5**
KENNETH, Mr. **2,3**
KENNY, Nick (d.12/1/75) **2**
KENT, Duchess of (Marina) **1**
KENT, Duke of (Edward) **1**
KENT, Rockwell (d.3/13/71) **1,2**
KENTON, Stan (d.8/25/79) **1,2**
KEPPEL, Francis **2**
KERKORIAN, Kirk **4**
KERNER, Otto (d.5/9/76) **2**
KERNS, Joanna **5**
KEROUAC, Jack (d.10/21/69) **1,2**
KERR, Clark **2**
KERR, Deborah **1,2,3,4,5**
KERR, Jean **1,2,3**
KERR, John **1,2**
KERR, Robert (d.1/1/63) **1**
KERR, Walter **1,2,3,4**
KESTNBAUM, Meyer (d.12/14/60) **1**
KETCHAM, Hank **2**
KEYES, Frances Parkinson **1,2,3**
KEYS, Ancel **2**
KEYSERLING, Leon **2**
KHACHATURIAN, Aram (d.5/1/78) **1**
KHAN, Aga (Prince Karim) **1**
KHAN, Aly (d.5/13/60) **1**
KHAN, Begum Aga (Yvette Labrousse) **1**
KHRUSHCHEV, Nikita (d.9/11/71) **1**
KIDD, Michael **1,2,3**
KIERAN, John (d.12/10/81) **1,2**
KIERNAN, Walter (d.1/8/71) **2**
KIEWIT, Peter **2**
KILEY, Richard **3,4,5**
KILGALLEN, Dorothy (d.11/8/65) **1,2**
KILGORE, Bernard (d.11/14/67) **2**
KILLEBREW, Harmon **1,2**
KILLIAN, James **1,2**
KILLION, George **2**
KIILLY, Jean-Claude **3**
KILMER, Bill **3**
KILPATRICK, James J. **4,5**
KIMBROUGH, Emily **1,2**
KING, Alan **2,3,4,5**
KING, Alexander (d.11/16/65) **1,2**
KING, Bernard **4**
KING, Billie Jean **3,4,5**
KING, Carole **2**
KING, Coretta **3,4,5**
KING, Dennis (d.5/21/71) **1,2**
KING, Don **4,5**
KING, John (d.7/8/79) **2**
KING, Larry **4,5**
KING, Larry L. **4**
KING, Martin Luther, Jr. (d.4/4/68) **1,2**
KING, Stephen **4,5**
KINGMAN, Dave **4**
KINGMAN, Dong **2,3**
KINGSBURY-SMITH, Joseph **2,3**
KINGSLEY, Ben **4,5**
KINGSLEY, Sidney **4,5**
KINSKI, Nastassja **4,5**
KINTNER, Robert (d.12/20/80) **2**
KIPLINGER, W.M. (d.8/6/67) **1,2**

KIRBY, Allan P. (d.5/2/73) **1,2**
KIRBY, Durward **2**
KIRK, Grayson **1,2**
KIRK, Lisa **1,2**
KIRK, Phyllis **1**
KIRK, Russell **2**
KIRKLAND, Gelsey **4,5**
KIRKPATRICK, Jeane **4,5**
KIRKWOOD, James **4**
KIRSTEIN, Lincoln **1,2,4**
KIRSTEN, Dorothy **1,2**
KISHI, Nobusuke **1**
KISSINGER, Henry A. **1,2,3,4,5**
KISTLER, Darci **5**
KITT, Eartha **1,2,3,4**
KLEBERG, Robert J. (d.10/13/74) **1,2**
KLEIN, Calvin **4,5**
KLEIN, Robert **5**
KLEMPERER, Otto (d.7/7/73) **1**
KLEMPERER, Werner **3**
KLINE, Kevin **4,5**
KLUGE, John **3,4**
KLUGMAN, Jack **4**
KLUSZEWSKI, Ted **1**
KNAUER, Virginia **3**
KNEBEL, Fletcher **2**
KNEF, Hildegarde **3**
KNIEVEL, Evel **3**
KNIGHT, Bobby **4,5**
KNIGHT, Frances **2,3**
KNIGHT, Gladys & The Pips **4**
KNIGHT, Goodwin (d.5/22/70) **1,2**
KNIGHT, John **1,2**
KNIGHT, Ted (d.8/26/86) **4**
KNOPF, Alfred A. **1,2,3**
KNORR, Nathan H. (d.6/8/77) **1,2**
KNOWLAND, William (d.2/23/74) **1,2**
KNOX, Seymour **2**
KOCH, Edward I. **4,5**
KOFOED, Jack **2**
KOESTLER, Arthur (d.3/3/83) **1**
KOLLEK, Teddy **4**
KOOP, Charles Everett **5**
KOPIT, Arthur **2,4**
KOPPEL, Ted **4,5**
KORDA, Michael **4,5**
KORTH, Fred **2**
KOSINSKI, Jerzy **4,5**
KOSTELANETZ, André (d.1/13/80) **1,2**
KOUFAX, Sandy **2,3**
KOVACS, Ernie (d.1/13/62) **1**
KOZOL, Jonathan **3**
KRAFT, Joseph **4**
KRAMER, Jack **1,2**
KRAMER, Stanley **1,2,3,4,5**
KRANTZ, Judith **4,5**
KREISLER, Fritz (d.1/29/62) **1**
KRESGE, S.S. (d.10/18/66) **1,2**
KRICK, Irving **2**
KRIENDLER, Mac (d.8/7/73), Bob (d.8/15/74), Pete **1,2,3**
KRIM, Mathilde **5**
KRIPS, Josef (d.10/12/74) **2**
KRISHNA MENON, V.K. (d.10/6/74) **1**
KRISTOFFERSON, Kris **3,4,5**
KROCH, Carl **2**
KROCK, Arthur (d.4/12/74) **1,2,3**
KRONENBERGER, Louis (d.4/30/80) **1,2**
KRUGER, Otto (d.9/6/74) **1**
KRUPA, Gene (d.10/16/73) **1,2**
KRUPP, Alfried (d.7/30/67) **1**
KRUTCH, Joseph Wood (d.5/22/70) **1,2**
KUBITSCHEK, Juscelino (d.8/22/76) **1**
KUBLER-ROSS, Elisabeth **4,5**
KUBRICK, Stanley **2,3,4,5**

KUCHEL, Thomas H. **1,2**
KUHN, Bowie **3**
KUHN, Maggie **4**
KUNSTLER, William **3,4**
KUPCINET, Irv **2,3,4,5**
KURALT, Charles **4,5**
KURNITZ, Harry (d.3/19/68) **1,2**
KURTZ, Swoosie **4,5**
KUWATLY, Shukri Al (d.6/30/67) **1**
KWAN, Nancy **2**
KYLIAN, Jiri **4**

L

LABELLE, Patti **5**
LADD, Alan (d.1/29/64) **1,2**
LADD, Cherly **5**
LA FARGE, John, S.J. (d.11/24/63) **1**
LA FARGE, Oliver (d.8/3/63) **1**
LAFFER, Arthur **4,5**
LAGERFIELD, Karl **4,5**
LAHR, Bert (d.12/4/67) **1,2**
LAINE, Cleo **4,5**
LAINE, Frankie **1,2**
LAING, R.D. **3**
LAIRD, Melvin **3**
LAMARR, Hedy **1,2,3**
LAMAS, Fernando (d.10/8/82) **1,2**
LAMBERT, Gerard B. **1,2**
LAMOUR, Dorothy **1,2**
L'AMOUR, Louis **4**
LANCASTER, Burt **1,2,3,4,5**
LANCHESTER, Elsa **1,2,3**
LAND, Edwin **1,2,3,4**
LANDERS, Ann **1,2,3,4,5**
LANDON, Alf **2**
LANDON, Michael **4,5**
LANDRY, Tom **4**
LANE, Abbe **1,2**
LANE, Frank **1,2**
LANE, Kenneth Jay **3,4,5**
LANE, Mills **2**
LANGE, Hope **2**
LANGE, Jessica **4,5**
LANGELLA, Frank **4,5**
LANGER, William (d.11/8/59) **1**
LANGLEY, Jane Pickens **3**
LANGNER, Lawrence (d.12/26/62) **1**
LANIN, Lester **2,3,4,5**
LANSBURY, Angela **2,3,4,5**
LANZA, Mario (d.10/7/59) **1**
LAPHAM, Lewis **4,5**
LAPIDUS, Morris **2**
LAPIERRE, Dominique **3**
LARDNER, John **1**
LA ROSA, Julius **1,2**
LARSEN, Don **1**
LARSEN, Roy (d.9/9/79) **2,3**
LARSON, Arthur **1,2**
LASKER, Mary **2,3,4**
LASKY, Victor **2,3,4**
LATTIMORE, Owen **2**
LAUDER, Estée **3,4,5**
LAUGHTON, Charles (d.12/15/62) **1**
LAUPER, Cyndi **4,5**
LAUREN, Ralph **4,5**
LAURENCE, William I. (d.3/19/77) **2**
LAURENTS, Arthur **1,2**
LAURIE, Piper **2**
LAUSCHE, Frank **1,2**
LAVER, Rod **1,2**
LAVERY, Sean **4**
LAW, John Phillip **3**
LAWFORD, Peter (d.12/24/84) **1,2,3**

LAWRENCE, Carol **2**
LAWRENCE, David (d.2/11/73) **1,2**
LAWRENCE, David L. **1,2**
LAWRENCE, Harding **3**
LAWRENCE, Mary Wells (see also WELLS, Mary) **3,4**
LAWRENCE, Steve **1,2,3,4,5**
LAXALT, Paul **4**
LAYTON, Joe **3,4,5**
LAZAR, Irving **1,2,3,4,5**
LAZARUS, Fred, Jr. (d.5/29/73) **2**
LEA, Tom **1,2**
LEAF, Munro (d.12/21/76) **1,2**
LEAN, David **1,3,4,5**
LEAR, Bill (d.5/14/78) **3**
LEAR, Frances **5**
LEAR, Norman **4,5**
LEARNED, Michael **4**
LEARY, Timothy **3,4,5**
LEBOWITZ, Fran **4,5**
LE CARRÉ, John **4,5**
LE CLERCQ, Tanaquil **1**
LE CORBUSIER (d.8/27/65) **1**
LEDERER, William **2**
LEE, Brenda **2**
LEE, Gypsy Rose (d.4/26/70) **1,2**
LEE, Michele **5**
LEE, Peggy **1,2,3,4,5**
LEE, Spike **5**
LEEK, Sybil (d.10/26/82) **3**
LE GALLIENNE, Eva **1,2**
LEGHORN, Richard **1,2**
LE GUIN, Ursula **4,5**
LEHMAN, Herbert (d.3/8/76) **1,2**
LEHMAN, Orin **3**
LEHMAN, Robert (d.8/9/69) **1,2**
LEHMANN, Lotte (d.8/26/76) **1,2**
LEHRER, Jim **4,5**
LEIGH, Dorian **1,2**
LEIGH, Douglas **2,3,4**
LEIGH, Janet **1,2**
LEIGH, Vivien (d.7/8/67) **1,2**
LEIGH, W.Colston **2,3,4,5**
LEIGHTON, Margaret (d.1/13/76) **1,2**
LEINSDORF, Erich **2,3,4**
LEMAY, Curtis **1,2**
LEMMON, Jack **1,2,3,4,5**
LEMNITZER, Lyman L. **1,2**
Le MONDE, Gregg **5**
LENDL, Ivan **4,5**
LENNON, John (d.12/8/80) **3**
LENO, Jay **5**
LENYA, Lotte (d.11/27/81) **1,2,3**
LEONARD, Bill **2**
LEONARD, Jack E. (d.5/9/73) **2**
LEONARD, Sugar Ray **4,5**
LEOPOLD OF BELGIUM (d.9/25/83)
LERNER, Alan Jay (d.6/14/86) **1,2,3,4**
LERNER, Max **1,2,3**
LE ROY, Mervyn **1,2**
LESCOULIE, Jack **2**
LESER, Tina **1,2**
LESLIE, Frank **2**
LESTER, Richard **3,4,5**
LE TOURNEAU, Robert (d.6/1/69) **2**
LETTERMAN, David **4,5**
LEVANT, Oscar (d.8/14/72) **1,2**
LEVENE, Sam (d.12/26/80) **1,2,3**
LEVENSON, Sam (d.8/27/80) **1,2,3**
LEVIN, Herman **1,2**
LEVIN, Meyer (d.7/9/81) **1,2,3**
LEVINE, James **4,5**
LEVINE, Joseph E. **2,3,4**
LEVITT, William J. **1,2,3,4**
LEVY, Allan **5**

Cumulative Index — CELEBRITY REGISTER 1990

LEWIS, Anthony 4
LEWIS, Carl 4
LEWIS, Emmanuel 4
LEWIS, Fulton, Jr. (d.8/21/66) **1,2**
LEWIS, Huey 5
LEWIS, Jerry **1,2,3,4,5**
LEWIS, Joe E. (d.6/4/71) **1,2**
LEWIS, John **2,3**
LEWIS, John L. (d.6/11/69) **1,2**
LEWIS, Richard 5
LEWIS, Robert 1
LEWIS, Robert Q. **1,2**
LEWIS, Shari **2,5**
LEWIS, Ted (d.8/25/71) **1,2**
LEY, Willy (d.6/24/69) **1,2**
LHEVINNE, Rosina (d.11/9/76) **2,3**
LIBBY, W.F. (Willard) (d.9/7/80) **1,2,3**
LIBERACE (d.2/4/87) **1,2,3,4**
LICHTENBERGER, Arthur (d.9/2/68) **2**
LICHTENSTEIN, Roy **3,4,5**
LICHTY, George (d.7/83) **2**
LIDDY, G. Gordon **4**
LIE, Trygve (d.12/30/68) **1**
LIEBERSON, Goddard (d.5/27/77) **3**
LIEBLING, A.J. (d.12/28/63) **1,2**
LIGHT, Judith **5**
LILIENTHAL, David E. (d.1/15/81) **2,3**
LILLIE, Beatrice **1,2,3**
LILLY, Doris **2,3**
LILLY, John **2,3**
LIMON, José (d.12/2/72) **2**
LINCOLN, Abbey **3**
LINCOLN, Murray (d.11/7/66) **2**
LINDBERGH, Anne Morrow **1,2,3,4**
LINDBERGH, Charles (d.8/26/74) **1,2,3**
LINDEN, Hal **3,4,5**
LINDFORS, Viveca **1**
LINDSAY, Howard (d.2/11/68) **1,2**
LINDSAY, John **2,3,4,5**
LINDSTROM, Pia **3**
LING, James **2**
LINKLETTER, Art **1,2,3,4,5**
LINN, Bambi **2**
LIN YUTANG (d.3/26/76) **1**
LIPCHITZ, Jacques (d.5/26/73) **1,2,3**
LIPPMANN, Walter (d.12/13/74) **1,2,3**
LIPPOLD, Richard **2,3,4**
LIQUORI, Marty **3**
LISTON, Sonny (d.1/5/71) **2**
LITHGOW, John **5**
LITTLE, Clarence Cook (d.12/22/71) **2**
LITTLE, Lou (d.5/28/79) **1**
LITTLE, Rich **4,5**
LITTLE, Sally **4**
LITVAK, Anatole (d.12/15/74) **2**
LLOYD, Chris Evert (see EVERT LLOYD) **3,4**
LLOYD, Harold (d.6/9/71) **1,2**
LLOYD, Selwyn **1**
LLOYD WEBBER, Andrew **4,5**
LOBO, Julio **1**
LOCKHART, June **2**
LODEN, Barbara (d.9/5/80) **3**
LODGE, George **2**
LODGE, Henry Cabot, Jr. **1,2,3**
LODGE, John Davis **1,2**
LOEB, Gerald (d.4/74) **1,2**
LOESSER, Frank (d.7/28/69) **1,2**
LOEWE, Frederick (d.2/14/88) **1,2,3,4**
LOEWY, Raymond **1,2,3**
LOGAN, Joshua (d.7/12/88) **1,2,3,4**
LOGGINS, Kenny **5**
LOLLOBRIGIDA, Gina **1,2**
LOMBARDI, Vince (d.9/30/70) **2**
LOMBARDO, Guy (d.11/5/77) **1,2,3**

LONDON, George (d.3/24/85) **1,2**
LONDON, Julie **1,2**
LONG, Augustus **2**
LONG, Earl (d.9/5/60) **1**
LONG, Edward (d.11/6/72) **2**
LONG, Oren (d.5/6/65) **2**
LONG, Russell **1,2,3,4**
LONGDEN, Johnny **1**
LONGWORTH, Alice Roosevelt (d.2/20/80) **1,2,3**
LOOS, Anita (d.8/18/81) **1,2,3**
LOPER, Don (d.11/22/72) **2**
LOPEZ, Al **1,2**
LOPEZ, Nancy **4,5**
LOPEZ, Trini **3**
LOPEZ, Vincent (d.9/20/75) **1,2**
LOPEZ MATEOS, Adolfo (d.9/22/69) **1**
LORANT, Stefan **2**
LORD, Jack **3**
LORD, Shirley **4,5**
LORD, W.G. **2**
LOREN, Sophia **1,2,3,4,5**
LORENGAR, Pilar **3**
LORRE, Peter (d.3/23/64) **1,2**
LORTEL, Lucille **4,5**
LOSEY, Joseph (d.6/22/84) **3**
LOUCHHEIM, Kathleen **2**
LOUDON, Dorothy **4,5**
LOUGANIS, Greg **4,5**
LOUIS, Jean **3**
LOUIS, Joe (d.4/12/81) **1,2,3**
LOUISE, Tina **1,2**
LOVE, Iris **4,5**
LOVE, John **2**
LOW, David (d.9/19/63) **1**
LOWE, Rob **4,5**
LOWELL, Ralph (d.5/78) **2**
LOWELL, Robert (d.9/12/77) **1,2,3**
LOWENSTEIN, Leon (d.4/76) **1,2**
LOY, Myrna **1,2,3,4,5**
LUBELL, Sam **2**
LUCAS, George **4,5**
LUCCI, Susan **4,5**
LUCE, Claire **1**
LUCE, Claire Boothe (d.10/9/87) **1,2,3,4**
LUCE, Henry (d.2/28/67) **1,2**
LUCE, Henry, III **3**
LUCEY, Robert **2**
LUCKMAN, Charles **2**
LUDDEN, Allen (d.6/9/81) **2**
LUDLUM, Robert **4,5**
LUDWIG, Christa **3**
LUDWIG, D.K. **4**
LUGAR, Richard **4,5**
LUKAS, Paul (d.8/15/71) **1,2**
LUMET, Sidney **2,3,4,5**
LUNDEN, Joan **5**
LUNT, Alfred (d.8/3/77) **1,2,3**
LUPESCU "Magda" (d.6/29/77) **1**
LUPINO, Ida **1,2**
LURIE, Alison **4,5**
LURIE, Louis (d.9/6/72) **2**
LYNES, Russell **1,2,3**
LYNLEY, Carol **2**
LYNN, Diana (d.12/17/71) **2**
LYNN, Loretta **3,4,5**
LYON, Herb (d.8/6/68) **2**
LYON, Sue **2**
LYONS, Leonard (d.10/7/76) **1,2,3**
LYONS, Ruth **2**
LYSENKO, Trofim D. (d.11/20/76) **1**

M

MA, Yo Yo **4**

MAAZEL, Lorin **4**
MacARTHUR, Douglas (d.4/5/64) **1,2**
MacARTHUR, Douglas II **1,2**
MacARTHUR, James **2**
MacARTHUR, John (d.11/5/78) **2**
MacDERMOT, Galt **3**
MacDONALD, Dwight (d.12/19/82) **2,3**
MacDONALD, E.F. **2**
MacDONALD, Jeanette (d.1/14/65) **1,2**
MacDOWELL, Andie **5**
MacGRATH, Leueen **2**
MacGRAW, Ali **3,4**
MacINTYRE, Malcolm **2**
MACK, Ted, (d.9/26/75) **1,2**
MacKENZIE, Gisele **1,2**
MACKIE, Bob **4,5**
MacLAINE, Shirley **1,2,3,4**
MacLEISH, Archibald (d.4/20/82) **1,2,3**
MacLEOD, Gavin **4**
MACMILLAN, Harold **1**
MacMURRAY, Fred **1,2,3**
MacNEIL, Robert **4**
MACPHERSON, Elle **5**
MacRAE, Gordon and Sheila **1,2**
MADONNA **4,5**
MADDOX, Lester **3**
MADISON, Guy **1,2**
MAGNANI, Anna (d.9/16/73) **1**
MAGNIN, Cyril **2**
MAGNUSON, Warren **2**
MAGOWAN, Robert **2**
MAHARIS, George **2**
MAHONEY, David **4**
MAHONEY, Tom (d.7/13/82) **2**
MAILER, Norman **1,2,3,4,5**
MAINBOCHER (d.12/27/76) **1,2**
MAJORS, Lee **4**
MAKARIOS III, Archbishop (Mouskos, Michael Christedoulos) (d.8/3/77) **1**
MAKAROVA, Natalia **3,4,5**
MALAMUD, Bernard **3,4**
MALCOLM, Wilbur **2**
MALDEN, Karl **1,2,3,4,5**
MALFITANO, Catherine **4**
MALIK, Charles **2**
MALINA, Judith (see BECK & MALINA) **3**
MALKOVICH, John **4,5**
MALLE, Louis **4,5**
MALONE, Moses **4**
MALONE, Ted **1**
MALRAUX, André (d.11/23/76) **1**
MANCHESTER, Melissa **4,5**
MANCHESTER, William **3,4**
MANCINI, Henry **3,4,5**
MANDEL, Carola **2**
MANDLIKOVA, Hana **4**
MANDRELL, Barbara **4,5**
MANEY, Richard (d.7/1/68) **1,2**
MANHATTAN TRANSFER **5**
MANILOW, Barry **4,5**
MANKIEWICZ, Joseph L. **1,2,3,4**
MANNERS, Dorothy **3**
MANNES, Marya **1,2,3**
MANSFIELD, Jayne (d.6/29/67) **1,2**
MANSFIELD, Mike **1,2,3,4**
MANTLE, Mickey **1,2**
MANVILLE, Tommy (d.10/8/67) **1,2**
MAO TSE-TUNG (d.9/9/76) **1**
MARA, Wellington **2,3**
MARAIS, Josef (d.4/27/78) and Miranda **2**
MARAVICH, Pete **3**
MARCEAU, Marcel **1,4,5**
MARCH, Fredric (d.4/14/75) **1,2,3**
MARCH, Hal (d.1/19/70) **2**

CELEBRITY REGISTER 1990 — Cumulative Index

MARCIANO, Rocky (d.8/31/69) **1,2**
MARCUS, Stanley **1,2,3,4**
MARCUSE, Herbert (d.7/29/79) **3**
MARGARET, Princess **1**
MARINO, Dan **4,5**
MARIS, Roger **2**
MARISOL **3,4,5**
MARITAIN, Jacques (d.4/28/73) **1**
MARKEL, Lester (d.10/13/77) **2**
MARKOVA, Alicia **1**
MARQUAND, J.P. **1**
MARRINER, Neville **4**
MARSALIS, Branford **5**
MARSALIS, Wynton **4,5**
MARSH, Ngaio (d.2/18/82) **1**
MARSHALL, Catharine (d.3/18/83) **1**
MARSHALL, E.G. **2,3,4,5**
MARSHALL, Garry **5**
MARSHALL, George C. (d.2/17/75) **1**
MARSHALL, George Preston (d.8/9/69) **2**
MARSHALL, Penny **5**
MARSHALL, Thurgood **1,2,3,4,5**
MARTIN, Billy **4,5**
MARTIN, Dean **1,2,3,4,5**
MARTIN, Dick (see ROWAN & MARTIN) **3**
MARTIN, Ernest **2,3** (see also FEUER & MARTIN **4**)
MARTIN, Joseph W., Jr.(Joe) (d.3/6/68) **1,2**
MARTIN, Judith **4,5**
MARTIN, Mary **1,2,3,4,5**
MARTIN, Steve **4,5**
MARTIN, Tony **1,2**
MARTIN, William McChesney, Jr. **1,2**
MARTINDELL, Jackson **2**
MARTINS, Peter **4**
MARUSIA (d.3/13/82) **2**
MARVIN, Lee (d.8/29/87) **3,4**
MARX, Chico (d.10/11/61) **1**
MARX, Groucho (d.8/19/77) **1,2,3**
MARX, Harpo (d.9/28/64) **1,2**
MARX, Louis (d.2/5/82) **1,2**
MARX, Richard **5**
MASEFIELD, John (d.5/12/67) **1**
MASINA, Giulietta **1**
MASON, F. Van Wyck (d.8/28/78) **1,2**
MASON, Jackie **2**
MASON, James (d.7/27/84) **1,2,3**
MASON, Marsha **4,5**
MASSELOS, William **3**
MASSEY, Raymond (d.7/27/83) **1,2**
MASSEY, Vincent (d.12/30/67) **1**
MASSINE, Leonide (d.3/16/79) **1**
MASTERS, Dexter **2**
MASTERS & JOHNSON **3,4,5**
MASTROIANNI, Marcello **3,4,5**
MATHEWS, Eddie **1,2**
MATHEWS, William **2**
MATHIS, Johnny **1,2,3,4,5**
MATLIN, Marlee **5**
MATTHAU, Walter **2,3,4,5**
MATTHEWS, Herbert (d.7/30/77) **2**
MATTHEWS, T.S. **2**
MATTINGLY, Don **4,5**
MATURE, Victor **1,2**
MAUGHAM, Somerset (d.12/16/65) **1**
MAULDIN, Bill **1,2,3,4,5**
MAURIAC, François (d.9/1/70) **1**
MAUROIS, André (d.10/9/67) **1**
MAXWELL, Elsa (d.11/1/63) **1,2**
MAXWELL, Marilyn (d.3/20/72) **1,2**
MAXWELL, W. Don (d.5/22/75) **2**
MAY, Elaine **2,3**
MAY, Mrs. Marjorie Merriweather Post (d.9/12/73) **2** (see also POST **3**)

MAY, Morton (d.4/13/83) **2**
MAY, Rollo **3,4**
MAYES, Herbert **2**
MAYNARD, Robert **4**
MAYO, Charles (d.7/28/68) **1,2**
MAYS, Willie **1,2,3,4**
MAYTAG, Lewis, Jr. **2,3**
MAZURSKY, Paul **3,4**
MAZZOLA, Anthony T. **3,4,5**
McBRIDE, Mary Margaret (d.4/7/76) **1,2**
McBRIDE, Patricia **4**
McCAREY, Leo (d.7/5/69) **1,2**
McCARTHY, Andrew **5**
McCARTHY, Eugene **2,3,4**
McCARTHY, Glenn **1,2**
McCARTHY, Mary **1,2,3,4,5**
McCARTNEY, Paul **3,4,5**
McCLANAHAN, Rue **5**
McCLELLAN, John L. (d.11/28/77) **1,2,3**
McCLENDON, Sarah **2,3**
McCLINTIC, Guthrie (d.10/29/61) **1**
McCLINTOCK, Barbara **4**
McCLOSKEY, Matthew **2**
McCLOSKEY, Paul **3**
McCLOY, John **1,2**
McCLUSKEY, Ellen (d.10/21/84) **2,3**
McCONE, John A. **1,2**
McCORMACK, Edward, Jr. **2**
McCORMACK, John W. (d.11/22/80) **1,2**
McCORMACK, Myron (D.7/30/62) **1**
McCOWEN, Alec **3,4,5**
McCRARY, Tex **1,2**
McCULLERS, Carson (d.9/29/67) **1,2**
McDONALD, David 8/8/79) **1,2**
McDONALD, Marie (d.10/21/65) **1,2**
McDONNELL, Jim (d.8/22/80) **2,3**
McDOWALL, Roddy **1,2**
McELROY, Neil (d.11/30/72) **1,2**
McENROE, John **4,5**
McFADDEN, Mary **4,5**
McFERRIN, Bobby **5**
McGEE, Frank (d.4/17/74) **2,3**
McGHEE, George **2**
McGILL, Ralph (d.2/3/69) **1,2**
McGILLIS, Kelly **5**
McGINLEY, Phyllis (d.2/22/78) **1,2**
McGOVERN, Elizabeth **4,5**
McGOVERN, George **2,3,4**
McGOVERN, Maureen **5**
McGRORY, Mary **4**
McGUIRE, Dorothy **1,2**
McGUIRE SISTERS **1,2**
McINERNEY, Jay **5**
McINTOSH, Millicent **1,2**
McINTYRE, Thomas **2**
McKAY, Gardner **2**
McKAY, Jim **4,5**
McKAY, John **3**
McKEEN, John (d.2/23/78) **2**
McKELDIN, Theodore (d.8/10/74) **2**
McKELLEN, Ian **4,5**
McKELWAY, Benjamin (d.8/30/76) **2**
McKENNA, Siobhan **1,2,3**
McKINLEY, Chuck **2**
McKUEN, Rod **3,4**
McLAGLEN, Victor (d.11/7/59) **1**
McLEAN, Robert (d.12/5/80) **2**
McLELLAN, Diana **4**
McLUHAN, Marshall (d.12/31/80) **3**
McMAHON, Ed **3,4,5**
McNALLY, Andrew **2**
McNALLY, Terrence **3,4,5**
McNAMARA, Pat **1,2**
McNAMARA, Robert **2,3,4**
McNEIL, Claudia **2**

McNEILL, Don **1,2**
McNELLIS, Maggi **2**
McQUEEN, Steve (d.11/7/80) **2,3**
McWILLIAMS, Carey (d.6/27/80) **2,3**
MEAD, Margaret (d.11/15/78) **1,2,3**
MEAD, SHEPHERD **2**
MEADE, Julia **2,3,4,5**
MEADER, Vaughn **2**
MEADOWS, Audrey **1,2**
MEADOWS, Jayne **1,2**
MEANY, George (d.1/10/80) **1,2,3**
MEANY, Tom **2**
MEARA, Anne (see Stiller & Meara) **4**
MECHEM, Edwin **2**
MEDARIS, John **1,2**
MEDINA, Harold **1,2**
MEESE, Edwin **4**
MEHLE, Aileen (see SUZY) **2,3,4**
MEHTA, Zubin **3,4,5**
MEIER, Richard **4,5**
MEIR, Golda (d.12/8/78) **1,3**
MELCHIOR, Lauritz (d.3/18/73) **1,2**
MELLENCAMP, John Cougar **5**
MELIS, Jose **2**
MELLON, Paul **1,2,3,4**
MELLON, Richard King (d.6/3/70) **2**
MELTON, James (d.4/21/61) **1**
MENDERES, Adnan **1**
MENDÈS-FRANCE, Pierre (d.10/18/22) **1**
MENEN, Aubrey **1**
MENJOU, Adolphe (d.10/29/63) **1,2**
MENKEN, Helen (d.3/27/66) **2**
MENNIN, Peter (d.6/17/83) **2,3**
MENNINGER, Karl **1,2,3,4**
MENNINGER, William (d.9/6/66) **1,2**
MENOTTI, Gian-Carlo **1,2,3,4,5**
MENSHIKOV, Mikhail (d.7/21/76) **1**
MENUDO **4**
MENUHIN, Yehudi **1,2,3,4,5**
MENZIES, Robert G. (d.5/14/78) **1**
MERCER, Johnny (d.6/25/76) **1,2,3**
MERCER, Mabel (d.4/20/84) **3**
MERCHANT, Ismail (see MERCHANT/IVORY) **5**
MERCHANT/IVORY **5**
MERCHANT, Livingston (d.5/15/76) **2**
MERCOURI, Melina **3,4,5**
MEREDITH, Burgess **1,2**
MEREDITH, James **2**
MERIWETHER, Lee **2**
MERMAN, Ethel (d.2/15/84) **1,2,3**
MERRICK, David **1,2,3,4,5**
MERRILL, Dina **1,2,3,4,5**
MERRILL, Robert **1,2,3,4,5**
MERTON, Thomas (d.12/10/68) **1,2**
MESSIAEN, Olivier **4**
MESTA, Perla (d.3/16/75) **1,2,3**
METALIOUS, Grace (d.2/25/64) **1,2**
MEYNER, Robert **1,2**
MIAMI SOUND MACHINE (see ESTEFAN, Gloria) **5**
MICHAEL, George **5**
MICHEL, Robert **4**
MICHENER, James **1,2,3,4,5**
MIDDLECOFF, Cary **1**
MIDLER, Bette **3,4,5**
MIELZINER, Jo (d.3/15/76) **1,2,3**
MIES VAN DER ROHE, Ludwig (d.8/17/69) **1,2**
MIGENES JOHNSON, Julia **4,5**
MIKOYAN, Anastas (d.10/22/78)1
MILANOV, Zinka **1**
MILES, Sarah **3**
MILES, Sylvia **3**

Cumulative Index — CELEBRITY REGISTER 1990

MILFORD-HAVEN, Marquess of (Mountbatten, David Michael) (d.4/14/70) **1**
MILHAUD, Darius (d.6/22/74) **1,2,3**
MILLAND, Ray **1,2,3**
MILLER, Ann **1,2,3,4,5**
MILLER, Arjay **2**
MILLER, Arnold (D.7/85) **3**
MILLER, Arthur **1,2,3,4,5**
MILLER, Gilbert (d.1/2/69) **1,2**
MILLER, Henry (d.6/7/80) **1,2,3**
MILLER, Hope Ridings **2**
MILLER, Jack (d.1/12/80) **2**
MILLER, Jason **3**
MILLER, Jonathan **4,5**
MILLER, Merle **3**
MILLER, Mitch **1,2,3,4,5**
MILLER, Paul **2**
MILLER, Robert **2**
MILLER, William **2**
MILLETT, Kate **3**
MILLIKEN, Roger **2**
MILLIS, Walter (d.3/17/68) **2**
MILLS, Donna **4,5**
MILLS, Hayley **2,3**
MILLS, John **3**
MILLS, Marjorie **2**
MILLS, Wilbur **2,3**
MILNES, Sherril **4,5**
MILSAP, Ronnie **4,5**
MILSTEIN, Nathan **1,2,3,4,5**
MIMIEUX, Yvette **2**
MINDSZENTY, Joseph Cardinal (d.5/6/75) **1**
MINEO, Sal (d.2/12/76) **1,2**
MINER, Worthington (d.12/11/82) **2**
MINK, Patsy **3**
MINNELLI, Liza **3,4,5**
MINNELLI, Vincente (d.7/25/86) **1,2,3,4**
MINOSO, Orestes **2**
MINOW, Newton **2**
MIRABELLA, Grace **3,4,5**
MIRÓ, Joan (d.12/25/83) **1,3**
MR. T **4**
MITCHELL, Arthur **4**
MITCHELL, Howard **2**
MITCHELL, James P. (d.10/19/64) **1,2**
MITCHELL, Jan **2**
MITCHELL, Joni **3,4,5**
MITCHELL, Joseph **2**
MITCHELL, Martha (d.5/31/76) **3**
MITCHELL, Thomas (d.12/17/62) **1**
MITCHUM, Robert **1,2,3,4,5**
MITFORD, Nancy (d.6/30/73) **1**
MITROPOLOS, Dimitri (d.11/2/60) **1**
MIYAKE, Issey **4,5**
MODINE, Matthew **4,5**
MOFFO, Anna **2,3,4,5**
MOHAMMED REZA SHAH PAHLEVI (d.7/27/80) **1**
MOLEY, Raymond (d.2/18/75) **2**
MOLLET, Guy (d.10/3/75) **1**
MOLLOY, Paul **2**
MOLOTOV, Vyacheslav **1**
MONACO, The Royal Family (PRINCE RAINIE III, PRINCE ALBERT, PRINCESS STEPHANIE, PRINCESS CAROLINE) **5**
MONDALE, Walter **4**
MONK, Julius **2**
MONK, Meredith **4,5**
MONK, Thelonious (d.2/17/85) **2,3**
MONROE, Lucy **1,2**
MONROE, Marilyn (d.8/5/62) **1**
MONROE, Vaughn (d.5/21/73) **1,2**

MONRONEY, Mike (d.2/13/80) **1,2**
MONTAGU, Ashley **1,2,3,4**
MONTALBAN, Ricardo **2,4,5**
MONTANA, Claude **4,5**
MONTANA, Joe **4,5**
MONTAND, Yves **1,3,4,5**
MONTEUX, Pierre (d.7/1/64) **1,2**
MONTGOMERY, George **1,2**
MONTGOMERY, Robert (d.9/27/81) **1,2**
MONTGOMERY, Ruth **4**
MONTGOMERY, Viscount of Alamein (d.3/24/76) **1**
MONTOYA, Carlos **2,3,4**
MOODY BLUES, The **5**
MOON, Rev. Sun Myung **4**
MOORE, Archie **1,2**
MOORE, Douglas (d.7/25/69) **2**
MOORE, Dudley **4,5**
MOORE, Garry **1,2,3**
MOORE, Henry **1,4**
MOORE, Marianne (d.2/5/72) **1,2**
MOORE, Mary Tyler **2,3,4,5**
MOORE, Melba **3**
MOORE, Robin **3**
MOORE, Roger **3,4,5**
MOORE, Terry **1,2**
MOORE, Victor (d.7/23/62) **1**
MOOREHEAD, Agnes (d.4/30/74) **1,2,3**
MOORER, Thomas **3**
MORALES, Esai **5**
MORAN, Jim **2**
MORAVIA, Alberto **1**
MOREAU, Jeanne **3,4,5**
MORENO, Rita **2,3,4,5**
MORGAN, Al **2**
MORGAN, Edward P. **2**
MORGAN, Henry **1,2**
MORGAN, Jane **1,2**
MORGAN, Michele **1**
MORINI, Erica **1**
MORISON, Patricia **1**
MORISON, Samuel Eliot (d.5/15/76) **2,3**
MORLEY, Robert **1,4,5**
MORRIS, Desmond **3**
MORRIS, Gary **5**
MORRIS, Willie **3,4**
MORRISON, deLESSEPS (d.5/22/64) **2**
MORRISON, Frank **2**
MORRISON, Toni **4,5**
MORRISSEY, Paul **3**
MORSE, Robert **2,3**
MORSE, S.F.B. (d.5/10/69) **2**
MORSE, Wayne (d.7/22/74) **1,2**
MORTIMER, Charles (d.12/25/78) **2**
MORTON, Thruston (d.8/14/82) **1,2**
MOSBACHER, Emil (Bus) **2,3**
MOSCONI, Willie **2,3,4**
MOSCOSO, José Tedoro **2**
MOSELY, Philip E. (d.1/13/72) **2**
MOSES, Edwin **4**
MOSES, Grandma (d.12/13/61) **1**
MOSES, Robert (d.7/29/81) **1,2,3**
MOSHER, Samuel **2**
MOSS, Stirling **1**
MOSTEL, Zero (d.9/8/77) **2,3**
MOTHERWELL, Robert **2,3,4,5**
MOTLEY, Willard (d.3/4/65) **1,2**
MOTTOLA, Tommy **5**
MOUNTBATTEN, Lord (d.8/27/79) **1**
MOYERS, Bill **4,5**
MOYNIHAN, Daniel Patrick **3,4,5**
MUDD, Roger **3**
MUELLER, Merrill (d.11/30/83) **2**
MUGGERIDGE, Malcolm **1**

MUHAMMAD ALI (see also ALI, **3,4;** CLAY **2**)
MUHAMMAD, Elijah (d.2/25/75) **3**
MULCAHY, Leo **2**
MULHOLLAND, John (d.2/25/70) **2**
MULLIGAN, Gerry **2**
MULLIGAN, Richard **5**
MULRONEY, Brian **4,5**
MUMFORD, Lewis **1,2,3,4**
MUNCH, Charles (d.11/5/68) **1,2**
MUNDT, Karl (d.8/16/74) **1,2**
MUNI, Paul (d.8/25/67) **1,2**
MUÑOZ MARIN, Luis (d.4/30/80) **1,2**
MUNSEL, Patrice **1,2,4,5**
MURCHISON, Clint **1,2**
MURDOCH, Rupert **4,5**
MURPHY, Audie (d.5/28/71) **1,2**
MURPHY, Dale **4,5**
MURPHY, Eddie **4,5**
MURPHY, George (d.9/28/73) **1,2,3**
MURPHY ROCKFELLER, Happy **2**
MURPHY, Robert (d.3/19/73) **1,2**
MURRAY, Anne **4,5**
MURRAY, Arthur **1,2**
MURRAY, Bill **4,5**
MURRAY, Don **2**
MURRAY, Eddie **4**
MURRAY, Jan **2**
MURRAY, Mae (d.3/23/65) **1**
MURROW, Edward R. (d.4/27/65) **1,2**
MUSBURGER, Brent **4**
MUSIAL, Stan **1,2**
MUSKIE, Edmund **1,2,3**
MUTI, Riccardo **4,5**
MYDANS, Carl **1**
MYERS, Fred **2**
MYERSON, Bess **2,3,4**

N

NABOKOV, Vladimir (d.7/2/77) **1,2,3**
NABORS, Jim **3**
NADER, Ralph **3,4,5**
NAMATH, Joe **3,4,5**
NASH, Ogden (d.5/19/71) **1,2**
NASH, Philleo **2**
NASSER, Gamal Abdel (d.9/28/70) **1**
NASTASE, Ilie **3**
NATHAN, Robert (d.5/25/85) **1,2**
NAVRATILOVA, Martina **4,5**
NEAL, Patricia **1,2,3,4,5**
NEBEL, Long John (d.4/10/78) **2,3**
NEDERLANDER, James **3,4,5**
NEHRU, Jawaharlal (d.5/27/64) **1**
NELLIGAN, Kate **4,5**
NELSON, Barry **2**
NELSON, Gaylord **2,3**
NELSON, Lindsey **3**
NELSON, Ozzie (d.6/3/75) **1,2**
NELSON, Ricky **1,2**
NELSON, Willie **4,5**
NERO, Peter **2,3,4,5**
NERUDA, Pablo (d.9/23/73) **3**
NESBITT, Cathleen (d.8/1/82) **1,2**
NEUBERGER, Maurine **1**
NEUBERGER, Richard L. **1**
NEVELSON, Louise (d.4/17/88) **3,4**
NEVINS, Allan (d.3/5/71) **1,2**
NEWCOMBE, Don **1**
NEWHART, Robert (Bob) **2,3,4,5**
NEWHOUSE, Sam (d.8/29/79) **1,2**
NEWHOUSE, S.I., Jr. **4**
NEWLEY, Anthony **3,4,5**
NEWMAN, Edwin **2,3,4,5**

CELEBRITY REGISTER 1990 — Cumulative Index

NEWMAN, Paul **1,2,3,4,5**
NEWMAN, Phyllis **2**
NEWMAR, Julie **2**
NEWTON, Huey **3**
NEWTON, Wayne **3,4,5**
NEWTON-JOHN, Olivia **4,5**
NIARCHOS, Stavros **1,3**
NICHOLS, Mike **2,3,4,5**
NICHOLS, William **2**
NICHOLSON, Jack **3,4,5**
NICKERSON, Albert **2**
NICKLAUS, Jack **2,3,4,5**
NIEBUHR, Reinhold (d.6/1/71) **1,2**
NIELSEN, Arthur (d.6/1/80) **2,3**
NIER, Alfred **2**
NIKOLAIS, Alwin **3,4**
NILSSON, Birgit **3,4**
NIMITZ, Chester W. (d.2/20/66) **1,2**
NIMOY, Leonard **4,5**
NITZE, Paul **2**
NIVEN, David (d.7/29/83) **1,2,3**
NIXON, Pat **3**
NIXON, Richard **1,2,3,4,5**
NIZER, Louis **2,3,4**
NKRUMAH, Kwame (d.4/27/72) **1**
NOAH, Yannick **4**
NOGUCHI, Isamu (d.12/30/88) **2,3,4**
NOLAN, Lloyd (d.9/27/85) **1,2**
NOLTE, Nick **4,5**
NORELL, Norman (d.10/25/72) **2**
NORMAN, Jessye **4,5**
NORMAN, Marsha **4,5**
NORRIS, Chuck **5**
NORRIS, Kathleen (d.1/18/66) **1,2**
NORSTAD, Lauris **1,2**
NORTH, Jay **2**
NORTH, John Ringling (d.6/4/85) **1,2**
NORTH, Sheree **2**
NORTHSHIELD, Robert **2**
NORTON, Elliot **2,3**
NORWICH, William **5**
NOVACK, Ben **2**
NOVAK, Kim **1,2**
NOVAK, Robert (see EVANS & NOVAK) **3,4**
NOYES, Newbold **2**
NUREYEV, Rudolf **3,4,5**
NUTTING, Anthony **1**
NUYEN, France **1,2**
NYRO, Laura **3**

O

OAK RIDGE BOYS **5**
OATES, Joyce Carol **3,4,5**
OBERON, Merle (d.11/23/79) **1,2,3**
OBOLENSKY, Serge (d.9/29/78) **1,2,3**
O'BRIAN, Hugh **1,2,3**
O'BRIEN, Edmond (d.5/7/85) **2**
O'BRIEN, Lawrence **2**
O'BRIEN, Margaret **1,2**
O'BRIEN, Pat (d.10/15/83) **1,2**
O'CASEY, Sean (d.9/18/64) **1**
OCEAN, Billy **5**
O'CONNOR, Carroll **3,4,5**
O'CONNOR, Donald **1,2**
O'CONNOR, Edwin (d.3/23/68) **2**
O'CONNOR, John Cardinal **4,5**
O'CONNOR, Sandra Day **4,5**
O'DAY, Anita **2**
ODETS, Clifford (d.8/14/63) **1**
ODETTA **2**
ODLUM, Floyd (d.6/17/76) **1,2**
O'DWYER, William (d.11/24/64) **1,2**

OELMAN, Robert **2**
OENSLAGER, Donald (d.6/21/75) **1,2**
OGILVY, David **2**
O'HARA, John (d.4/11/70) **1,2**
O'HARA, Maureen (d.9/21/78) **1,2**
O'HORGAN, Tom **3**
OISTRAKH, David (d.10/24/74) **1**
O'KEEFE, Dennis (d.8/31/68) **1,2**
O'KEEFFE, Georgia (d.3/6/86) **2,3,4**
OLAJUWON, Akeem **4**
OLAV V, King **1**
OLDENBURG, Claes **3,4,5**
OLDENBURG, Richard **3,4,5**
OLIVEIRA, Elmar **4**
OLIVIER, Sir Laurence (d 7/11/89) **1,2,3,4**
OLLENHAUER, Erich (d.12/14/63) **1**
OLMEDO, Alex **1**
O'MALLEY, Walter (d.8/9/79) **1,2**
ONASSIS, Aristotle (d.3/15/75) **1,3**
ONASSIS, Christina (d.11/19/88) **4**
ONASSIS, Jacqueline **3,4,5** (see also KENNEDY, Jacqueline **2**)
O'NEAL, Ryan **3,4,5**
O'NEAL, Tatum **4,5**
O'NEILL, Jennifer **4,5**
O'NEILL, Thomas P. **3,4,5**
ONO, Yoko **3,4,5**
OPPENHEIMER, Harry **1**
OPPENHEIMER, Robert (d.2/18/67) **1,2**
ORBACH, Jerry **3,4,5**
ORDONEZ, Antonio **1**
ORMANDY, Eugene (d.3/12/85) **1,2,3**
ORR, Bobby **3**
ORSER, Brian **5**
OSBORN, Fairfield **2**
OSBORNE, John **1,3,4**
OSMOND, Donny **5**
OSMOND, Marie **4,5**
O'SULLIVAN, Maureen **1,2**
O'TOOLE, Peter **3,4,5**
OVERSTREET, Harry (d.8/17/70) **1,2**
OWENS, Buck **3**
OWENS, Jesse (d.3/31/80) **1**
OZAWA, Seiji **4**

P

PAAR, Jack **1,2,3,4**
PACE, Frank (d.1/8/88) **1,2**
PACINO, Al **3,4,5**
PACKARD, Vance **1,2,3**
PACKWOOD, Bob **4,5**
PADDLEFORD, Clementine (d.11/13/67) **2**
PAEPCKE, Walter (d.4/13/60) **1**
PAGE, Geraldine (d.6/13/87) **1,2,3,4**
PAGE, Patti **1,2,3**
PAGET, Debra **1,2**
PAGLIAI, Bruno (d.4/83) **2**
PAHLMANN, William **1,2**
PAIGE, Janis (d.3/3/76) **2**
PAIGE, Leroy Satchel (d.6/8/82) **2,3**
PAIK, Nam June **4,5**
PAKULA, Alan **4,5**
PALANCE, Jack **1,2**
PALEY, William **1,2,3,4**
PALEY, Mrs. William (d.7/6/78) **1,2**
PALMER, Arnold **1,2,3,4**
PALMER, Betsy **2**
PALMER, Bud **2,3**
PALMER, Jim **4**
PALMER, Lilli (d.1/27/86) **1,4**
PANDIT, Vijaya Lakshmi **1**
PANITT, Merrill **2**
PAOLOZZI, Christina **2**

PAPAS, Irene **3**
PAPP, Joseph **2,3,4,5**
PARCELLS, Bill **5**
PARK, Rosemary **2**
PARKER, Dave **4**
PARKER, Dorothy (d.6/67) **1,2**
PARKER, Fess **2**
PARKER, Suzy (d.12/15/65) **1,2**
PARKINSON, Norman **4**
PARKS, Bert **1,2**
PARKS, Gordon **3,4**
PARNIS, Mollie **2,3**
PARSONS, Estelle **3,4,5**
PARSONS, Louella (d.12/8/72) **1,2**
PARTCH, Virgil (d.8/10/84) **1,2**
PARTON, Dolly **4,5**
PARTON, James **1,2**
PASSMAN, Otto **2**
PASTERNAK, Boris (d.5/28/60) **1**
PASTERNAK, Joe **1,2**)
PASTORE, John **2,3**
PATCEVITCH, Iva **1,2**
PATERNO, Joe **4,5**
PATINKIN, Mandy **4,5**
PATMAN, Wright (d.3/7/76) **2,3**
PATON, Alan **1**
PATRICK, John **1,2**
PATRICK, Ted **1,2**
PATTERSON, Alicia (d.7/2/63) **1**
PATTERSON, Floyd **1,2**
PATTERSON, John **2**
PATTERSON, William (d.6/13/80) **1,2**
PAUL I, King (d.3/6/64) **1**
PAUL, Les and Mary FORD **2**
PAULEY, Ed (d.7/21/81) **2**
PAULEY, Jane **4,5**
PAULINA **5**
PAULING, Linus **1,2,3,4**
PAVAROTTI, Luciano **4,5**
PAYNE, Les **4**
PAYSON, Joan (d.10/4/75) **2,3**
PAYTON, Walter **4**
PEABODY, Endicott **2**
PEALE, Norman Vincent **1,2,3,4**
PEARCE, Alice (d.3/3/66) **2**
PEARL, Minnie **3,4**
PEARSON, Billy **1,2**
PEARSON, Drew (d.9/1/69) **1,2**
PEARSON, Lester (d.12/27/72) **1**
PECK, Gregory **1,2,3,4,5**
PECK, Joseph **2**
PECKINPAH, Sam (d.12/28/84) **3**
PEERCE, Jan (d.12/15/84) **1,2,3**
PEGLER, Westbrook (d.6/24/69) **1,2**
PEI, I.M. **3,4,5**
PELÉ, **3,4**
PELL, Claiborne **2**
PENN, Arthur **2,3,4**
PENN, Irving **1,2,4**
PENN, Sean **4,5**
PENNEY, James C. (d.2/12/71) **1,2**
PEPPARD, George **3,4,5**
PEPPER, Claude (d.5/30/89) **2,4**
PERAHIA, Murray **4**
PERCY, Charles **2,3**
PERDUE, Frank **4,5**
PERELMAN, S.J. (d.10/17/79) **1,2,3**
PEREZ, Leander (d.3/19/69) **2**
PERKINS, Anthony **1,2,4,5**
PERKINS, Frances (d.5/14/65) **2**
PERKINS, Marlin **2**
PERLMAN, Alfred E. (d.4/30/83) **1,2**
PERLMAN, Itzhak **4,5**
PERLMAN, J. Samuel **1**
PERLMAN, Ron **5**

477

PERON, Juan (d.7/1/74) **1**
PEROT, H. Ross **4,5**
PERRY, John **2**
PETER II, of Yugoslavia (Karageorgeovitch, Peter) (d.11/4/70) **1**
PETERS, Bernadette **4,5**
PETERS, Roberta **1,2,3,4,5**
PETERSON, Oscar **2,3,4,5**
PETERSON, Robert **2**
PETERSON, Roger Tory **2,3,4**
PETERSON, Virgilia (d.12/24/66) **1,2**
PETIT, Roland **1,4**
PETRILLO, James Caesar (d.10/23/84) **1,2**
PETTY, Richard **3,4,5**
PEW, Joseph (d.4/9/63) **1**
PHILBIN, Regis **5**
PHILIP, Prince **1**
PHILIPE, Gerard (d.11/27/59) **1**
PHILLIPS, Lou Diamond **5**
PIAF, Edith (d.10/11/63) **1**
PIATIGORSKY, Gregor (d.8/6/76) **2,3**
PICASSO, Pablo (d.4/8/73) **1**
PICASSO, Paloma **4,5**
PICK, Albert, Jr. **2**
PICKENS LANGLEY, Jane (see Langley) **3**
PICKENS, T. Boone **4,5**
PICKFORD, Mary (d.5/29/79) **1,2,3**
PICON, Molly **2**
PIDGEON, Walter (d.9/25/84) **1,2**
PIEL, Gerard **2**
PIERSALL, Jimmy **2**
PIGNATARI, Baby (d.10/27/77) **1**
PIKE, James A. (d.9/7/69) **1,2**
PILLSBURY, John (d.1/31/68) **2**
PINCAY, Lafitt, Jr. **4**
PINEAU, Christian **1**
PINKERTON, Robert (d.10/11/67) **2**
PINTER, Harold **3,4**
PIPER, Bill (d./1/15/70) **2**
PISCOPO, Joe **5**
PISTON, Walter (d.11/12/76) **1,2,3**
PITTMAN, Steuart **2**
PITTS, Zasu (d.6/7/63) **1**
PLAYER, Gary **3**
PLESHETTE, Suzanne **2,4,5**
PLIMPTON, Francis T.P. (d.7/30/83) **2**
PLIMPTON, George **3,4,5**
PLUMMER, Amanda **4,5**
PLUMMER, Christopher **1,2,3,4,5**
PLUNKETT, Jim **3,4**
PODHORETZ, Norman **3,4**
POITIER, Sidney **1,2,3,4,5**
POLANSKI, Roman **3,4,5**
POLING, Daniel (d.2/7/68) **2**
POLLINI, Maurizio **4**
PONS, Lily (d.2/13/76) **1,2**
PONTI, Carlo **3,4**
PORTER, Cole (d.10/15/64) **1,2**
PORTER, Katherine Anne (d.9/18/80) **1,2,3**
PORTER, Sylvia **1,2,3,4**
PORTERFIELD, Robert (d.10/28/71) **2**
PORTMAN, Eric (d.12/7/69) **1**
PORTMAN, John **4**
POST, Emily (d.9/25/60) **1**
POST, Marjorie Merriweather (see also MAY) (d.9/12/73) **2,3**
POST, Troy **2,3**
POSTON, Tom **2**
POTTER, Philip **3**
POTTER, Stephen (d.12/2/69) **1**
POULENC, Francis (d.1/30/63) **1**
POUND, Ezra (d.11/1/72) **1,2**
POVICH, Maury **5**
POWELL, Adam Clayton, Jr. (d.4/4/72) **1,2**
POWELL, Dick (d.1/2/63) **1**

POWELL, Eleanor (d.2/11/82) **2**
POWELL, Jane **1,5**
POWELL, Lewis, Jr. **3,4,5**
POWELL, Wesley (d.1/6/81) **2**
POWELL, William (d.3/5/84) **1,2**
POWER, Donald C. (d.3/11/79) **2**
POWERS, Betram **2**
POWERS, Francis Gary (d.8/1/77) **2**
POWERS, J.F. **2**
POWERS, Shorty **2**
POWERS, Stefanie **4,5**
PRATT, Theodore (d.12/69) **2**
PREMINGER, Otto (d.4/23/86) **1,2,3,4**
PRENTISS, Paula **2**
PRESCOTT, Orville **1,2**
PRESLEY, Elvis (d.8/16/77) **1,2,3**
PRESLEY, Priscilla **5**
PRESSER, Jackie (d.7/9/88) **4**
PRESTON, Frances **5**
PRESTON, Robert (d.3/21/87) **1,2,3,4**
PREVIN, André **2,3,4,5**
PRICE, George **1,2**
PRICE, Leontyne **2,3,4,5**
PRICE, Roger **2**
PRICE, Vincent **1,2,3,4,5**
PRIDE, Charley **3,4,5**
PRIEST, Ivy Baker (d.6/23/75) **1,2**
PRIESTLEY, J.B. (d.8/15/84) **1**
PRIMA, Louis (d.8/24/78) **1,2**
PRIMUS, Pearl **1,2**
PRINCE **4,5**
PRINCE, Harold **1,2,3,4,5**
PRINCIPAL, Victoria **4**
PRINGLE, John **2**
PROVINE, Dorothy **2**
PROWSE, Juliet **2**
PROXMIRE, William **1,2,3,4**
PRUDHOMME, Paul **4,5**
PRYOR, Richard **4,5**
PUCCI, Emilio **3**
PULITZER, Joseph, Jr. **2,3**
PULLIAM, Eugene (d.6/23/75) **2**
PULLIAM, Keisha Knight **5**
PUSEY, Nathan **1,2**
PUTNAM, Roger Lowell **2**
PUZO, Mario **3**
PYNCHON, Thomas **4**

Q

QUAID, Dennis **5**
QUAYLE, Anthony **1,3**
QUAYLE, Dan **5**
QUAYLE, Marilyn **5**
QUEEN, Ellery (Manfred B. Lee [d.4/2/70], Frederic Dannay [d.9/3/82]) **2,3**
QUEENY, Edgar Monsanto (d.7/7/68) **2**
QUESADA, Elwood **1,2**
QUILL, Michael (d.1/28/66) **1,2**
QUINN, Anthony **1,2,3,4,5**
QUINN, William F. **2**
QUINTERO, José **1,2**
QUIRK, James (d.1/12/71) **2**

R

RABE, David **4,5**
RABORN, William **2**
RADER, Dotson **3**
RADFORD, Arthur W. (d.8/17/73) **1,2**
RADNER, Gilda (d.5/22/89) **4**
RADZIWILL, Lee **2**
RAFELSON, Robert **3,4,5**

RAFFI **5**
RAFFIN, Deborah **4,5**
RAFT, George (d.11/24/80) **1,2**
RAINIER, Prince **1**
RAINS, Claude (d.5/30/67) **1,2**
RAITT, John **1,2**
RAMEY, Samuel **4**
RAMPAL, Jean-Pierre **4,5**
RAMA RAU, Santha **1,2** (see also Rau, Santha Rama **3**)
RAND, Ayn (d.3/6/82) **1,2,3**
RAND, James (d.6/3/68) **2**
RAND, Sally (d.8/31/79) **1,2**
RAND, William **2**
RANDALL, Clarence (d.8/4/67) **1,2**
RANDALL, Tony **2,3,4,5**
RANDOLPH, A. Philip (d.5/16/79) **2,3**
RANDOLPH, Jennings **2**
RANDOLPH, Nancy (d.12/29/74) **2**
RANK, J. Arthur (d.3/29/72) **1**
RANSOM, Harry **2**
RANSOM, John Crowe (d.7/3/74) **2,3**
RAPHAEL, Sally Jesse **5**
RASHAD, Ahmad **5**
RASHAD, Phylicia **5**
RATHBONE, Basil (d.7/21/67) **1,2**
RATHBONE, Monroe (d.8/2/76) **2**
RATHBONE, Perry **2,3**
RATHER, Dan **4,5**
RATTIGAN, Terence (d.11/30/77) **1**
RAU, Santha RAMA **3** (see also Rama Rau, Santha **1,2**)
RAUSCHENBERG, Robert **3,4,5**
RAVDIN, Isidor (d.4/28/72) **2**
RAWLINGS, Edwin **2**
RAWLS, Lou **3,4,5**
RAY, Aldo **1**
RAY, Dixy Lee **2,3**
RAY, Johnnie **1,2**
RAYBURN, Sam (d.11/16/61) **1**
RAYE, Martha **1,2,4**
RAYMOND, Gene **1,2**
REAGAN, Nancy **4,5**
REAGAN, Ronald **1,2,3,4,5**
REASONER, Harry **2,3,4,5**
REDDY, Helen **4**
REDER, Bernard **2**
REDFORD, Robert **3,4,5**
REDGRAVE, Lynn **4,5**
REDGRAVE, Sir Michael (d.3/21/85) **1**
REDGRAVE, Vanessa **3,4,5**
REED, Sir Carol (d.4/25/76) **1**
REED, Donna **1,2**
REED, John **2**
REED, Oliver **3**
REED, Ralph (d.1/21/68) **1**
REED, Rex **3,4,5**
REED, Whitney **2**
REEVE, Christopher **4,5**
REEVES, Rosser (d.1/84) **2**
REEVES, Steve **2**
REGINE **4,5**
REGAN, Donald **4**
REHNQUIST, William **3,4,5**
REICH, Steve **4**
REID, Elliott (d.11/28/79) **2**
REID, Ogden **1,2**
REID, Tim **5**
REID, Whitelaw **1**
REIK, Theodor (d.12/3/70) **1,2**
REINER, Carl **2,3,4,5**
REINER, Rob **5**
REINER, Fritz (d.11/15/63) **1,2**
REISCHAUER, Edwin **2**
REISINI, Nicolas **2**

REMARQUE, Erich Maria (d.9/25/70) **1,2**
REMICK, Lee **1,2,4,5**
RENAULT, Mary (d.12/13/83) **1**
RENOiR, Jean (d.2/12/79) **1**
RENSE, Paige **4**
RESNIK, Regina **3**
RESTON, James **1,2,3,4**
RETTON, Mary Lou **4**
REUBEN, David **3**
REUTHER, Walter (d.5/10/70) **1,2**
REVENTLOW, Lance (d.7/25/72) **2**
REVSON, Charles (d.8/24/75) **1,2,3**
REVSON, Peter (d.3/22/74) **3**
REXROTH, Kenneth (d.6/6/82) **3**
REYNOLDS, Allie **2**
REYNOLDS, Burt **3,4,5**
REYNOLDS, Debbie **1,2,3,4,5**
REYNOLDS, Quentin (d.3/17/65) **1,2**
REYNOLDS, Richard J. (d.12/14/64) **2**
REYNOLDS, Richard S. (d.10/5/80) **2,3**
RHEE, Syngman (d.7/19/65) **1**
RHINE, J.B. **1**
RHODES, James **2**
RHODES, Zandra **4**
RIBICOFF, Abraham (d.4/12/72) **1,2,3**
RICE, Elmer (d.5/8/67) **1,2**
RICE, Jim **4**
RICH, Richard **2**
RICHARD, Maurice **1**
RICHARDS, Paul (d.12/10/74) **2**
RICHARDS, Renee **4**
RICHARDS, Rev. Robert E. **1**
RICHARDSON, Elliot **3,4**
RICHARDSON, Sir Ralph (d.10/10/83) **1,2,3**
RICHIE, Lionel **4,5**
RICHTER, Charles (d.9/30/85) **3,4**
RICKENBACKER, Eddie (d.7/23/73) **1,2,3**
RICKEY, Branch (d.12/9/65) **1,2**
RICKLES, Don **3,4,5**
RICKOVER, Hyman G. (d.7/8/86) **1,2,3,4**
RIDE, Sally **4**
RIDGWAY, Matthew B. **1,2**
RIESEL, Victor **1,2**
RIESMAN, David **1,2**
RIGG, Diana **3,4,5**
RIGGINS, John **4**
RIGHTER, Carroll (d.4/30/88) **2,3,4**
RIGNEY, Bill **1**
RINGWALD, Molly **5**
RIPKEN, Cal, Jr. **4**
RIPLEY, S. Dillon **2,3**
RITCHARD, Cyril (d.12/18/77) **1,2**
RITTER, John **4,5**
RITTER, Thelma (d.2/5/69) **1,2**
RIVERA, Chita **2,4,5**
RIVERA, Geraldo **3,4,5**
RIVERS, Joan **3,4,5**
RIVERS, Larry **3,4**
RIVLIN, Alice **4**
RIZZO, Frank **3**
RIZZUTO, Phil **1,2**
ROBARDS, Jason, Jr. **1,2,3,4,5**
ROBB, Inez (d.4/4/79) **1,2**
ROBBINS, Harold **2,3,4,5**
ROBBINS, Jerome **1,2,3,4,5**
ROBERTS, Oral **2,3,4**
ROBERTS, Pernell **4**
ROBERTS, Rachel (d.11/25/80) **3**
ROBERTS, Robin **1,2**
ROBERTS, Roy (d.5/28/75) **1,2**
ROBERTSON, A. Willis (d.11/1/71) **2**
ROBERTSON, Cliff **2,3,4,5**
ROBERTSON, Dale **2**
ROBERTSON, Oscar **2,3**

ROBERTSON, Pat **4**
ROBESON, Paul (d.1/23/76) **1,2,3**
ROBINSON, Brooks **3**
ROBINSON, Edward G. (d.1/26/73) **1,2**
ROBINSON, Emmett **2**
ROBINSON, Francis (d.5/14/80) **2**
ROBINSON, Frank **2,3**
ROBINSON, Hubbell (d.9/4/74) **2**
ROBINSON, Jackie (d.10/24/72) **1,2**
ROBINSON, James D. III **4,5**
ROBINSON, Sugar Ray (d.4/12/89) **1,2,3**
ROCCA, Antonino (d.3/15/77) **1,2**
ROCK, John (d.12/84) **2,3**
ROCKEFELLER, "Bobo" **1,2**
ROCKEFELLER, David **1,2,3,4,5**
ROCKEFELLER, John D., Jr. (d.5/11/60) **1**
ROCKEFELLER, John D., III (d.7/10/78) **1,2,3**
ROCKEFELLER, John D., IV **3,4,5**
ROCKEFELLER, Laurance **1,2,3,4**
ROCKEFELLER, Nelson (d.1/26/79) **1,2,3**
ROCKEFELLER, Winthrop (d.2/22/73) **1,2**
ROCKWELL, George Lincoln (d.8/25/67) **2**
ROCKWELL, Norman (d.11/8/78) **1,2,3**
RODALE, J.I. (d.6/7/71) **2**
RODGERS, Bill **4**
RODGERS, Jimmie **1,2**
RODGERS, Mary **2**
RODGERS, Richard (d.12/30/79) **1,2,3**
RODINO, Peter, Jr. **4,5**
ROEBLING, Mary **1,2,3,4**
ROGERS, Fred **4,5**
ROGERS, Ginger **1,2,3,4,5**
ROGERS, Kenny **4,5**
ROGERS, Rosemary **4,5**
ROGERS, Roy **1,4**
ROGERS, Wayne **4**
ROGERS, Will, Jr. **1,2**
ROGERS, William P. **1,2,3**
ROHATYN, Felix **4,5**
ROHMER, Eric **3,4**
ROLAND, Gilbert **1**
ROLLING STONES, The **3** (see also JAGGER, Mick **4**)
ROLLINS, Howard, Jr. **4**
ROMAINS, Jules (d.8/14/72) **1**
ROMANOFF, Mike (d.9/1/71) **1,2**
ROME, Harold **1,2,3,4**
ROMERO, Cesar **1,2**
ROMNEY, George **1,2,3**
ROMULO, Carlos **1**
RONSTADT, Linda **4,5**
ROONEY, Andy **4,5**
ROONEY, Mickey **1,2,3,4,5**
ROOP, Guy **1,2**
ROOSEVELT, Eleanor (d.11/7/62) **1**
ROOSEVELT, Elliott **1,2**
ROOSEVELT, Franklin D., Jr. **1,2,3**
ROOSEVELT, James **1,2**
ROOSEVELT, John (d.4/27/81) **1,2**
ROPER, Elmo (d.4/30/71) **1,2**
ROREM, Ned **4,5**
RORIMER, James (d.5/11/66) **2**
ROSE, Alex (d.12/28/76) **3**
ROSE, Billy (d.2/10/65) **1,2**
ROSE, Pete **4,5**
ROSE, Reginald **2**
ROSELLINI, Albert **2**
ROSENBERG, Anna (d.5/9/83) **2**
ROSENBLOOM, Slapsie-Maxi (d.3/6/76) **1**
ROSENQUIST, James **3,4**
ROSENSTEIN, Nettie (d.3/13/80) **1**
ROSENSTIEL, Lewis (d.1/21/76) **2**

ROSEWALL, Kenneth **1,3**
ROSS, Barney (d.1/18/67) **1**
ROSS, Diana **3,4,5**
ROSS, Lanny **1,2**
ROSS, Nancy Wilson **2**
ROSS, Nellie Tayloe (d.12/19/77) **2**
ROSS, Norman **2**
ROSSELLINI, Roberto (d.5/3/72) **1**
ROSSET, Barney **3**
ROSTEN, Leo **2**
ROSTENKOWSKI, Dan **4**
ROSTOW, W.W. **2**
ROSTROPOVICH, Mstislav **4**
ROTH, Lillian (d.5/12/80) **1,2**
ROTH, Philip **3,4,5**
ROTHKO, Mark (d.2/25/70) **2**
ROUNDTREE, Richard **3**
ROUNTREE, Martha **2**
ROVERE, Richard (d.11/23/79) **2,3**
ROWAN, Carl **2,4**
ROWAN and MARTIN **3**
ROYKO, Mike **4,5**
ROYSTER, Vermont **1,2**
ROZELLE, Pete **2,3,4,5**
RUARK, Robert (d.7/1/65) **1,2**
RUBICAM, Ray (d.5/8/78) **2**
RUBINSTEIN, Artur (d.12/20/82) **1,2,3**
RUBINSTEIN, Helena (d.4/1/65) **1,2**
RUBINSTEIN, John **3,4,5**
RUBIROSA, Porfirio (d.7/5/65) **1**
RUBY, Harry (d.2/23/74) **2**
RUDEL, Julius **3,4**
RUDOLPH, Wilma **2**
RUGGLES, Charles (d.12/23/70) **1,2**
RULE, Janice **2**
RUN DMC **5**
RUSK, Dean **2,3**
RUSK, Dr. Howard **1,2,3**
RUSSELL, Anna **1**
RUSSELL, Bertrand (d.2/2/70) **1**
RUSSELL, Bill **3,4**
RUSSELL, Jane **1,2,3**
RUSSELL, Ken **3,4,5**
RUSSELL, Nipsey **3,4**
RUSSELL, Pee Wee (d.2/15/69) **2**
RUSSELL, Richard B. (d.1/21/71) **1,2**
RUSSELL, Rosalind (d.11/28/76) **1,2**
RUTHERFORD, Margaret (d.5/22/72) **1**
RYAN, Cornelius (d.11/23/74) **2,3**
RYAN, Meg **5**
RYAN, Nolan **4**
RYAN, Robert (d.7/11/73) **1,2,3**
RYSANEK, Leonie **1,2**
RYUN, Jim **3**

S

SAARINEN, Aline (d.7/14/72) **2**
SAARINEN, Eero (d.9/1/61) **1**
SABIN, Albert **2,3,4**
SABLON, Jean **1**
SACKVILLE-WEST, Victoria (d.6/2/62) **1**
SADE **5**
SAFER, Morley **4,5**
SAFIRE, William **4**
SAGAN, Carl **4**
SAGAN, Françoise **1**
SAGENDORPH, Robb **2**
SAGER, Carole Bayer **4,5**
SAHL, Mort **1,2**
SAINT, Eva Marie **1,2**
SAINT JAMES, Susan **4,5**
SAINT LAURENT, Yves **1,3,4,5**
SAINT-SUBBER, Arnold **3**

ST. CYR, Lili (d.3/14/74) **1,2**
ST. DENIS, Ruth (d.6/21/68) **1,2**
ST. GEORGE, Katharine (d.5/2/83) **2**
ST. JOHN, Jill **2,3**
ST. JOHN, Robert **2**
ST. JOHNS, Adela Rogers **2,3**
ST. LEWIS, Roy **2**
SAJAK, Pat **5**
SALAZAR, Alberto **4**
SALAZAR, Antonio De Oliveira (d.7/27/7?) **1**
SALINGER, J.D. **1,2,3,4,5**
SALINGER, Pierre **2,4**
SALISBURY, Harrison **1,2,3,4,5**
SALK, Jonas **1,2,3,4,5**
SALTONSTALL, Leverett (d.6/17/79) **1,2**
SALTONSTALL, William **2**
SAMPSON, Ralph **4**
SAMUELS, Howard (d.10/26/84) **3**
SAMUELSON, Paul **3,4**
SANDA, Dominique **3**
SANDBURG, Carl (d.7/22/67) **1,2**
SANDERS, George (d.4/25/72) **1,2**
SANDERS, Colonel Harland (d.12/16/80) **3**
SANDERSON, Ivan (d.2/19/73) **2**
SANDS, Diana (d.9/22/73) **3**
SANDS, Tommy **1**
SANDOZ, Mari (d.3/10/66) **2**
SANDYS, Duncan **1**
SANFORD, Isabel **4**
SANFORD, Terry **2**
SANGER, Margaret (d.9/6/66) **1,2**
SANT'ANGELO, Giorgio di **3**
SARANDON, Susan **4,5**
SARDI, Vincent, Jr. **2,3,4**
SARNOFF, David (d.12/12/71) **1,2**
SARNOFF, Robert **1,2,3**
SAROYAN, William (d.5/18/81) **1,2,3**
SARTRE, Jean-Paul (d.4/15/80) **1,3**
SASOON, Vidal **3,4,5**
SAUD, King (Saud ibn Abdul-Aziz ibn Abdul-Rahman al Faisal al Saud) (d.2/23/69) **1**
SAUDEK, Robert **2**
SAVALAS, Telly **4,5**
SAVOY, Maggie **2**
SAWYER, Diane **4,5**
SAWYER, Grant **2**
SAYLES, John **4,5**
SCAASI, Arnold **3,4,5**
SCALI, John (d.7/7/85) **2,3**
SCAVULLO, Francesco **4,5**
SCHACHT, Al (d.7/14/84) **2**
SCHAEFER, George **2**
SCHAEFER, William Donald **4,5**
SCHAFER, Harold **2**
SCHARY, Dore (d.7/7/80) **1,2**
SCHEIDER, Roy **4,5**
SCHELL, Maria **1,2**
SCHELL, Maximilian **3,4**
SCHERCHEN, Herman (d.6/7/66) **1**
SCHERMAN, Harry (d.11/12/69) **2**
SCHERMAN, Thomas (d.5/14/79) **2**
SCHIAPARELLI, Elsa (d.11/13/73) **1,3**
SCHIFF, Dorothy **1,2,3**
SCHILDKRAUT, Joseph (d.1/21/64) **1,2**
SCHIPPERS, Thomas (d.12/16/77) **2,3**
SCHIRRA, Walter **2**
SCHISGAL, Murray **3,4**
SCHLAFLY, Phyllis **4**
SCHLEE, George (d.10/3/64) **2**
SCHLESINGER, Arthur, Jr. **1,2,3,4**
SCHLESINGER, James R. **3**
SCHLUMBERGER, Jean **2,3**
SCHNABEL, Julian

SCHNEIDER, Alan (d.5/3/84) **3**
SCHOENBRUN, David **2**
SCHRIEVER, Bernard A. **1,2**
SCHULBERG, Budd **1,2,3,4**
SCHULLER, Robert **4**
SCHULZ, Charles **2,3,4,5**
SCHUMAN, Robert (d.9/4/63) **1**
SCHUMAN, William **2**
SCHUSTER, M. Lincoln (d.12/20/70) **1**
SCHWAB, Jack **2**
SCHWARTZ, Arthur (d.9/3/84) **1,2**
SCHWARTZ, Maurice (d.5/10/60) **1**
SCHWARTZ, Stephen **3,4,5**
SCHWARZENEGGER, Arnold **4,5**
SCHWARZKOPF, Elizabeth **1**
SCHWEITZER, Albert (d.9/4/65) **1**
SCHYGULLA, Hanna **4**
SCORE, Herb **2**
SCORSESE, Martin **4,5**
SCOTT, George C. **3,4,5**
SCOTT, Hazel (d.10/2/81) **1,2**
SCOTT, Hugh **2,3**
SCOTT, Martha **1,2**
SCOTT, Randolph **1,2**
SCOTT, Willard **4,5**
SCOTT, Winfield Townley **2**
SCOTT, Zachary (d.10/3/65) **1,2**
SCOTTO, Renata **4,5**
SCRANTON, William **2**
SCRIBNER, Charles, Jr. **2,3**
SCRIPPS, Charles **2,3**
SEABORG, Glenn **2**
SEAGRAVE, Dr. Gordon (d.3/28/65) **2**
SEALE, Bobby **3**
SEATON, Fred (d.1/16/74) **1,2**
SEAVER, Tom **3,4**
SEBERG, Jean (d.9/8/79) **1,2**
SEEGER, Pete **2,3,4,5**
SEGAL, Erich **3**
SEGAL, George (actor) **4,5**
SEGAL, George (sculptor) **3,4**
SEGNI, Antonio (d.12/1/72) **1**
SEGOVIA, Andres (d.6/2/87) **1,2,3,4**
SEGURA, Pancho **1**
SELDES, Gilbert (d.9/29/70) **1,2**
SELL, Henry (d.10/23/74) **2,3**
SELLARS, Peter **4**
SELLECK, Tom **4,5**
SELLERS, Peter (d.7/23/80) **2,3**
SELTZER, Louis (d.4/2/80) **1,2**
SELYE, Hans (d.10/16/82) **1**
SELZNICK, David O. (d.6/22/65) **1,2**
SELZNICK, Irene **1,2**
SEMENEKO, Serge (d.4/24/80) **1,2**
SERKIN, Rudolf **1,2,3,4**
SERLING, Rod (d.6/28/75) **1,2,3**
SESSIONS, Roger (d.3/16/85) **2,3**
SETON, Anya **2**
SEUSS, Dr (Geisel, Theodor Seuss) **2,3,4,5**
SEVEREID, Eric **1,2,3**
SEVERSKY, Alexander De (d.8/24/74) **1,2,3**
SEYMOUR, Jane **5**
SEYMOUR, Whitney North **2**
SHAHN, Ben (d.3/14/69) **1,2**
SHALIT, Gene **4,5**
SHANKAR, Ravi **3,4**
SHANKS, Carrol **1,2**
SHAPIRO, Karl **1,2,3**
SHAPLEY, Harlow (d.10/20/72) **1,2**
SHARIF, Omar **3**
SHATNER, William **4,5**
SHAW, Artie **1,2,3,4,5**
SHAW, Carolyn **2,3**
SHAW, Irwin (d.5/16/84) **1,2,3**

SHAW, Robert (d.8/28/78) **1,2,3**
SHAWN, Ted (d.1/9/72) **1,2**
SHAWN, William **3,4**
SHAY, Dorothy (d.10/22/78) **2**
SHEARER, Moira **1**
SHEARER, Norma (d.6/12/83) **1,2**
SHEARING, George **1,2,3,4,5**
SHEEAN, Vincent (d.3/15/75) **1,2**
SHEEN, Bishop Fulton (d.12/9/79) **1,2,3**
SHEEN, Charlie **5**
SHEEN, Martin **4,5**
SHELDON, Sidney **4,5**
SHEPARD, Alan **2,3**
SHEPARD, Sam **4,5**
SHEPHERD, Jean **2,3**
SHEPLEY, Ehtan (d.6/75) **2**
SHEPPARD, Eugenia (d.11/11/84) **2,3**
SHERIDAN, Ann (d.1/21/67) **1,2**
SHERIDAN, Nicollette **5**
SHERMAN, Allie **2**
SHERWOOD, Roberta **1,2**
SHIELDS, Brooke **4,5**
SHIRER, William L. **1,2**
SHNAYERSON, Robert **3**
SHOEMAKER, Willie **1,2,3,4,5**
SHOR, Toots (d.1/23/77) **1,2**
SHORE, Dinah **1,2,3,4,5**
SHORT, Bobby **2,3,4,5**
SHOSTAKOVICH, Dmitri (d.8/9/75) **1**
SHOTWELL, James (d.7/15/65) **2**
SHOUP, David (d.1/13/83) **2**
SHRINER, Herb (d.4/23/70) **1,2**
SHRIVER, Eunice Kennedy **4,5**
SHRIVER, Pam **4**
SHRIVER, Sargent **2,3**
SHULA, Don **3,4,5**
SHULMAN, Max **1,2**
SHULTZ, George **3,4**
SHUMLIN, Herman (d.6/14/79) **1,2**
SHURLOCK, Geoffrey (d.4/26/76) **2**
SHUTE, Nevil (d.1/12/60) **1**
SIDNEY, Sylvia **1,3,4**
SIEGEL, Don **3**
SIEGEL, Sol (d.12/29/82) **1**
SIEPI, Cesare **1,2,3**
SIGNORET, Simone (d.9/30/85) **3,4**
SIKORSKY, Igor **1,2**
SILBER, John **4**
SILLMAN, Leonard (d.7/23/82) **2**
SILLS, Beverly **3,4,5**
SILONE, Ignazio (d.8/22/78) **1**
SILVER, Ron **5**
SILVERS, Phil **1,2,3**
SIM, Alastair (d.8/19/76) **1**
SIMENON, Georges **1,4**
SIMMONS, Jean **1,2,3,4,5**
SIMMONS, Richard **4,5**
SIMMS, Phil **4,5**
SIMON, Carly **3,4,5**
SIMON, John **4,5**
SIMON, Neil **3,4,5**
SIMON, Norton **2,3,4**
SIMON, Paul **3,4,5**
SIMONE, Nina **3**
SIMONS, David G. **1**
SIMPSON, Adele **3**
SIMPSON, O.J. **3,4,5**
SIMPSON, Valerie **3**
SIMS, Billy **4**
SINATRA, Frank **1,2,3,4,5**
SINATRA, Nancy **3**
SINCLAIR, Upton (d.11/25/68) **1,2**
SINGER, Isaac Bashevis **3,4**
SIQUEIROS, David Alfaro (d.1/6/74) **1**
SISKEL & EBERT **5**

CELEBRITY REGISTER 1990 — Cumulative Index

SITWELL, Dame Edith (d.12/9/64) **1**
SITWELL, Sir Osbert (d.5/4/69) **1**
SIX, Robert **2**
SKELTON, Red **1,2,3,4**
SKINNER, B.F. **3,4**
SKINNER, Cornelia Otis (d.7/9/79) **1,2,3**
SKOLSKY, Sidney (d.5/3/83) **2,3**
SKOURAS, Spyros (d.8/15/71) **1,2**
SKROWACZEWSKI, Stanislaw **2,3**
SLATKIN, Leonard **4,5**
SLAYTON, Donald **2,3**
SLENCZYNSKA, Ruth **1**
SLEZAK, Walter **1,2,3**
SLICK, Grace **4** (see also Jefferson Airplane **3**)
SLOAN, Alfred P., Jr. (d.2/17/66) **1,2**
SMATHERS, George A. **1,2**
SMEAL, Eleanor **4**
SMITH, Alexis **3,4**
SMITH, Betty (d.1/17/72) **1,2**
SMITH, Cecil **2**
SMITH, C.R. **1,2**
SMITH, Earl E.T. **2,3**
SMITH, H. Allen (d.2/24/76) **1,2,3**
SMITH, Howard K. (d.10/3/76) **1,3**
SMITH, Howard Worth **2**
SMITH, Jaclyn **4,5**
SMITH, Kate **1,2**
SMITH, Keely **2**
SMITH, Lillian (d.9/28/66) **1,2**
SMITH, Liz **4,5**
SMITH, Maggie **3,4**
SMITH, Margaret Chase **1,2,3**
SMITH, Merriman (d.4/13/70) **2**
SMITH, Oliver **1,2,3,4**
SMITH, Red (d.1/15/82) **1,2,3**
SMITH, Robert Paul **1,2**
SMITH, Stan **3**
SMITH, Stephen **2**
SMITH, Walter Bedell (d.8/9/61) **1**
SMOTHERS BROTHERS **3**
SNEAD, Sam **1,2,3,4**
SNIDER, Duke **1,2**
SNODGRESS, Carrie **3**
SNOW, Carmel (d.5/7/61) **1**
SNOW, C.P. (d.7/1/80) **1**
SNOW, Edgar (d.2/15/72) **2**
SNYDER, Jimmy (JIMMY THE GREEK) **3,4**
SOBOL, Louis (d.2/9/86) **1,2**
SOBOLEV, Arkady A. (d.12/1/64) **1**
SOKOLSKY, George (d.12/12/62) **1**
SOLERI, Paolo **3,4**
SOLTI, Georg **3,4**
SOLZHENITSYN, Aleksandr **4,5**
SOMERS, Suzanne **4,5**
SOMMER, Elke **3**
SONDHEIM, Stephen **1,2,3,4,5**
SONNABEND, A.M. (d.2/11/64) **1,2**
SONNENBERG, Benjamin (d.9/16/78) **1,2**
SONNY & CHER **3** (see also CHER **4**)
SONTAG, Susan **3,4**
SORAYA, Princess **1**
SORENSEN, Theodore C. **2**
SOROKIN, Pitirim (d.2/10/68) **1**
SOTHERN, Ann **1,2**
SOULE, Henri (d.1/27/66) **2**
SOUSTELLE, Jacques **1**
SOYER, Moses (d.9/2/74) **3**
SOYER, Raphael (d.11/4/87) **2,3,4**
SPAAK, Paul-Henri (d.7/31/72) **1**
SPAATZ, Carl (d.7/14/74) **1,2**
SPACEK, Sissy **4,5**
SPADER, James **5**
SPAETH, Sigmund (d.11/11/65) **1,2**
SPAHN, Warren **1,2,3**

SPARKMAN, John J. **1,2**
SPELLING, Aaron **4,5**
SPELLMAN, Francis Cardinal (d.12/2/67) **1,2**
SPENDER, Stephen **1**
SPEWACK, Sam (d.10/14/71) and Bella **1,2**
SPIEGEL, Sam (d.2/31/85) **1,2,3,4**
SPIELBERG, Steven **4,5**
SPILLANE, Mickey **1,2,3,4,5**
SPINKS, Michael **4**
SPITZ, Mark **3**
SPIVAK, Lawrence **1,2,3**
SPOCK, Benjamin **1,2,3,4,5**
SPRAGUE, Marshall **2**
SPRAGUE, Robert **2**
SPRINGFIELD, Rick **4**
SPRINGS, Elliott (d.10/15/59) **1**
SPRINGSTEEN, Bruce **4,5**
STACK, Robert **1,2,3,4,5**
STAFFORD, Jean (d.3/26/79) **1,2**
STAFFORD, Jo **1,2**
STAHL, Lesley **4,5**
STALLONE, Sylvester **4,5**
STANLEY, Kim **1,2**
STANTON, Frank **1,2,3**
STANWYCK, Barbara **1,2,3,4,5**
STAPLETON, Jean **3,4**
STAPLETON, Maureen **1,2,3,4,5**
STARK, Ray **4,5**
STARNES, Richard **2**
STARR, Kay **1**
STARR, Ringo **3,4,5**
STASSEN, Harold **1,2**
STAUBACH, Roger **3,4**
STAUFFER, Oscar **2**
STEBER, Eleanor **1,2**
STEEL, Danielle **4,5**
STEENBERGEN, Mary **4,5**
STEGNER, Wallace **2**
STEICHEN, Edward (d.3/25/73) **1,2**
STEIG, William **1,2,3,4**
STEIGER, Rod **1,2,3,4,5**
STEIN, Jules (d.4/29/81) **1,2,3**
STEINBECK, John (d.12/21/68) **1,2**
STEINBERG, David **1**
STEINBERG, Saul **1,2,3,4**
STEINBERG, William (d.5/16/78) **2,3**
STEINBRENNER, George **4,5**
STEINEM, Gloria **3,4,5**
STEINER, Max (d.12/28/71) **1**
STELLA, Frank **4**
STENGEL, Casey (d.9/29/75) **1,2,3**
STENNIS, John **2**
STEPHENSON, Jan **4**
STERLING, Jan **1,2**
STERLING, Robert **1**
STERLING, Wallace **2**
STERN, Bill (d.11/19/71) **1**
STERN, Issac **1,2,3,4,5**
STEVENS, Christine **2**
STEVENS, Connie **2**
STEVENS, George (d.3/8/75) **1,2,3**
STEVENS, George, Jr. **3,4**
STEVENS, Inger (d.4/30/70) **2**
STEVENS, John Paul **4,5**
STEVENS, Risë **1,2**
STEVENS, Robert T. (d.1/30/83) **1,2**
STEVENS, Roger L. **1,2,3,4**
STEVENS, Shadoe **5**
STEVENSON, Adlai (d.7/14/65) **1,2**
STEVENSON, Adlai, III **3**
STEWART, Ellen **3,4**
STEWART, James **1,2,3,4,5**
STEWART, Potter **1,2**

STEWART, Rod **4,5**
STICKNEY, Dorothy **1,2**
STILL, Clyfford (d.6/23/80) **3**
STILLER & MEARA **4,5**
STING **4,5**
STODDARD, Haila **2**
STOKES, Carl **3**
STOKOWSKI, Leopold (d.9/13/77) **1,2,3**
STONE, Edward Durell (d.8/6/78) **1,2,3**
STONE, I.F. (d.6/18/89) **3,4**
STONE, Irving (d.8/26/89) **1,2,3,4**
STONE, Oliver **5**
STONE, Tobias **1,2**
STONEHAM, Horace **1,2**
STOPPARD, Tom **4,5**
STORKE, Thomas (d.10/12/71) **2**
STORM, Gale **1,2**
STOUT, Rex (d.10/27/75) **1,2,3**
STRAIT, George **5**
STRASBERG, Lee (d.2/17/82) **2,3**
STRASBERG, Susan **1,2**
STRATTON, Julius **2**
STRAUS, Jack (d.9/19/85) **2,3**
STRAUSS, Roger W., Jr. **3,4,5**
STRAUSS, Franz Josef (d.10/3/88) **1**
STRAUSS, Lewis (d.1/21/74) **1,2**
STRAUSS, Robert **3,4**
STRAVINSKY, Igor (d.4/6/71) **1,2**
STRAWBERRY, Darryl **4,5**
STREEP, Meryl **4,5**
STREETER, Edward (d.3/31/76) **2**
STREISAND, Barbra **2,3,4,5**
STRELSIN, Alfred (d.2/25/76) **2,3**
STRICK, Joseph **3**
STRITCH, Elaine **1,2,3,4,5**
STRODE, Woody **3**
STROESSNER, Alfredo **1**
STROUSE, Charles **4,5**
STRUTHERS, Sally **3,4**
STUART, Jesse (d.2/17/84) **1,2**
STUART, Lyle **3**
STUTZ, Geraldine **2,3,4**
STYNE, Julie **1,2,3,4,5**
STYRON, William **3,4,5**
SUKARNO (d.6/21/70) **1**
SULLAVAN, Margaret (d.1/1/60) **1**
SULLIVAN, Barry **1,2**
SULLIVAN, Danny **4,5**
SULLIVAN, Ed (d.10/13/74) **1,2,3**
SULLIVAN, Frank (d.2/19/76) **2**
SULLIVAN, Kathleen **4,5**
SULZBERGER, Arthur Hays (d.12/11/68) **1,2**
SULZBERGER, Arthur Ochs **3,4,5**
SULZBERGER, C.L. **1,2,3**
SUMAC, Yma **1,2**
SUMMER, Donna **4,5**
SUMMERFIELD, Arthur E. (d.4/26/72) **1**
SUSANN, Jacqueline (d.9/21/74) **3**
SUSMAN, Karen **1**
SUSSKIND, David (d.2/22/87) **1,2,3,4**
SUTHERLAND, Donald **3,4,5**
SUTHERLAND, Joan **2,3,4,5**
SUTHERLAND, Keifer **5**
SUTTON, Horace **1,2,3,4**
SUZUKI, Pat **1,2**
SUZY **2,3,4,5**
SVERDRUP, Leif **2**
SWADOS, Elizabeth **4,5**
SWAGGERT, Jimmy **4**
SWANSON, Gloria (d.4/4/83) **1,2,3**
SWARTHOUT, Gladys (d.7/7/69) **1,2**
SWAYZE, John Cameron **1,2**
SWAYZE, Patrick **5**
SYLVESTER, Arthur (d.10/11/69) **2**

Cumulative Index

SYLVESTER, Robert (d.2/9/75) **2**
SYMINGTON, Stuart **1,2,3**
SZELL, George (d.7/30/70) **1,2**
SZIGETI, Joseph (d.2/19/73) **1**
SZILARD, Leo (d.5/30/64) **2**

T

T, Mr. (see MR. T) **4**
TAFT, Charles P. (d.6/24/83) **1,2**
TAFT, Robert, Jr. **2,3**
TAGLIAVINI, Ferruccio **1**
TALBERT, William **1**
TALLCHIEF, Maria **1,2**
TALLEY, Lee **2**
TALMADGE, Herman **1,2**
TALMEY, Allene **2**
TAMAYO, Rufino **1**
TANDY, Jessica **1,2,3,4,5**
TANKERSLEY, Mrs. Garvin **2**
TANKOOS, Joseph (d.9/21/76) **2**
TANNY, Vic **2**
TARKENTON, Fran **3**
TATE, Allen (d.2/9/79) **2**
TATI, Jacques (d.11/5/82) **1**
TAWES, J. Millard (d.6/25/79) **21**
TAYLOR, Deems (d.7/3/66) **1,2**
TAYLOR, Elizabeth **1,2,3,4,5**
TAYLOR, Harold **1,2**
TAYLOR, Henry J. (d.2/26/84) **1,2,3**
TAYLOR, James **3,4,5**
TAYLOR, Jim **2**
TAYLOR, Lawrence **4,5**
TAYLOR, Maxwell **1,2**
TAYLOR, Paul **4,5**
TAYLOR, Robert (d.6/8/69) **1,2**
TAYLOR, Rod **2,3**
TEAGARDEN, Jack (d.1/15/64) **1**
TEBALDI, Renata **1,2**
TEBBETTS, Birdie **1,2**
TE KANAWA, Kiri **4,5**
TELLER, Edward **1,2,3,4**
TEMPLE, Shirley **1,2** (see also BLACK, Shirley Temple **3,4**)
TEMPLETON, Alec (d.3/28/63) **1**
TERKEL, Studs **4,5**
TERRY, Luthur **2**
TEYTE, Maggie (d.5/26/76) **1**
THARP, Twyla **4,5**
THEBOM, Blanche **1,2**
THEISMANN, Joe **4**
THEODORACOPULOS, Taki **4,5**
THICKE, Alan **5**
THOMAS, Danny **1,2,3,4,5**
THOMAS, Debi **5**
THOMAS, Isaiah **4,5**
THOMAS, John Charles **1**
THOMAS, Lewis **4**
THOMAS, Lowell (d.8/29/81) **1,2,3**
THOMAS, Marlo **3,4,5**
THOMAS, Michael **3**
THOMAS, Michael Tilson **3,4**
THOMAS, Norman (d.12/19/68) **1,2**
THOMAS, Richard **4,5**
THOMPSON, Dorothy (d.1/30/61) **1**
THOMPSON, John **4,5**
THOMPSON, Kay **1,2,3**
THOMPSON, Llewellyn E., Jr. (d.2/6/72) **1,2**
THOMSON, Virgil **1,2,3,4**
THORNDIKE, Dame Sybil (d.6/9/76) **1**
THORNTON, Charles Bates/Tex (d.11/24/81) **2,3**
THULIN, Ingrid **3**

THURBER, James (d.11/2/61) **1**
THURMOND, J. Strom **1,2,3,4,5**
TIBBETT, Lawrence (d.7/17/60) **1**
TIEGS, Cheryl **4,5**
TIERNEY, Gene **1**
TIFFIN, Pamela **2**
TIGER, Dick (d.12/13/71) **2**
TILLICH, Paul (d.10/22/65) **1,2**
TILLINGHAST, Charles **2,3**
TILLSTROM, Burr **2,3**
TINKER, Grant **4,5**
TINY TIM **3**
TIOMKIN, Dimitri (d.11/11/79) **1,2,3**
TISCH, Laurence and Robert **2**
TITO (BROZ, Josip) (d.5/4/80) **1**
TITTLE, Y.A. **2**
TOBEY, Mark (d.4/24/76) **2,3**
TODD, Ann **1**
TODD, Mike, Jr. **2**
TODMAN, William (d.7/28/79) **2**
TOGLIATTI, Palmiro (d.8/21/64) **1**
TOKLAS, Alice B. (d.3/7/67) **1,2**
TOLKIEN, J.R.R. (d.9/2/73) **3**
TOMLIN, Lily **3,4,5**
TONE, Franchot (d.9/18/68) **1,2**
TONGG, Rudy **2**
TOPPING, Dan (d.5/18/74) **1,2**
TORMÉ, Mel **2,3,4,5**
TORN, Rip **2**
TORRE, Marie **1,2**
TORS, Ivan (d.6/4/83) **3**
TORVILL & DEAN **4**
TOUREL, Jennie (d.11/23/73) **2**
TOWER, John **2,3**
TOWNSEND, Lynn **2**
TOWNSEND, Peter **1**
TOWNSEND, Robert **3,4**
TOYNBEE, Arnold (d.10/22/75) **1**
TOZZI, Georgio **2,3,4**
TRABERT, Tony **1**
TRACY, Spencer (d.6/10/67) **1,2**
TRAMMELL, Alan **4**
TRAMMELL, Niles (d.3/28/73) **2**
TRAPP, Maria **2**
TRAUBEL, Helen (d.7/30/72) **1,2**
TRAVANITI, Daniel J. **4**
TRAVELL, Janet **2**
TRAVIS, Randy **5**
TRAVOLTA, John **4,5**
TREACHER, Arthur (d.12/14/75) **1,2,3**
TREADWAY, Richard **1,2**
TREE, Marietta **2**
TRESH, Tom **2**
TREVINO, Lee **3,4,5**
TREVOR-ROPER, H.R. **1**
TRIGÉRE, Pauline **1,2,3,4,5**
TRILLIN, Calvin **4,5**
TRILLING, Lionel (d.11/5/75) **1,2,3**
TRINTIGNANT, Jean-Louis **3**
TRIPPE, Juan (d.4/3/81) **1,2**
TROUT, Robert **1,2,3**
TROYANOS, Tatiana **4,5**
TRUDEAU, Arthur **2**
TRUDEAU, Garry **4,5**
TRUDEAU, Pierre Elliott **3,4**
TRUFFAUT, François (d.10/21/84) **3**
TRUJILLO, Rafael (d.5/30/61) **1**
TRUJILLO, Rafael, Jr. **1**
TRUMAN, Harry S. (d.12/26/72) **1,2**
TRUMAN, Margaret **1,2,3,4,5**
TRUMP, Donald **4,5**
TRUMP, Ivana **5**
TRYON, Thomas **3**
TUCHMAN, Barbara (d.2/6/89) **3,4**
TUCKER, Richard (d.1/8/75) **1,2,3**

CELEBRITY REGISTER 1990

TUCKER, Sophie (d.2/9/66) **1,2**
TUCKER, Tanya **5**
TUDOR, Anthony (d.4/20/87) **1**
TULLY, Alice **4,5**
TUNE, Tommy **4,5**
TUNNEY, Gene (d.11/7/78) **1,2,3**
TUNNEY, John **3**
TURECK, Rosalyn **4**
TURNER, Glenn W. **3**
TURNER, Ike & Tina **3** (see also TURNER, Tina **4**)
TURNER, Kathleen **4,5**
TURNER, Lana **1,2,3,4,5**
TURNER, Ted **4,5**
TURNER, Tina **4,5** (see also TURNER, Ike & Tina **3**)
TURNURE, Pamela **2**
TWIGGY **3,4,5**
TWINING, Nathan (d.3/29/82) **1,2**
TWITTY, Conway **4,5**
TYSON, Cicely **4,5**
TYSON, Mike **5**

U

UDALL, Stewart **2**
UEBERROTH, Peter V. **4**
UGGAMS, Leslie **3,4,5**
UIHLEIN, Robert (d.11/12/76) **2**
ULANOVA, Galina **1**
ULBRICHT, Walter (d.8/1/73) **1**
ULLMAN, James Ramsey (d.6/20/71) **1,2**
ULLMAN, Tracey **5**
ULLMANN, Liv **3,4,5**
UMEKI, Miyoshi **1,2**
UNITAS, John **2,3**
UNSER, Al **3,4**
UNSER, Bobby **3,4**
UNTERMEYER, Louis (d.12/18/77) **1,2,3**
U NU **1**
UPDIKE, John **2,3,4,5**
UREY, Harold (d.1/5/81) **1,2,3**
URIS, Leon **1,2,3,5** (see also URIS, Leon and Jill **4**)
USTINOV, Peter **1,2,3,4,5**

V

VACCARO, Brenda **3,4**
VAIL, Thomas **2**
VALENTI, Jack **3,4,5**
VALENTINA **2**
VALENTINO **3,4,5**
VALENZUELA, Fernando **4**
VALLEE, Rudy (d.7/3/86) **1,2**
VAN ACKER, Achille (d.7/10/75) **1**
VAN ALLEN, James A. **1,2,3,4**
VAN BUREN, Abigail ("Abby") **1,2,3,4,5**
VANCE, Cyrus **2**
VANDERBILT, Alfred Gwynne **1,2,3,4**
VANDERBILT, Amy (d.12/27/74) **1,2,3**
VANDERBILT, Cornelius, Jr. (d.7/7/74) **1,2**
VANDERBILT, Gloria **1,2,3,4,5**
VANDERBILT, Harold (d.7/4/70) **1,2**
VANDERCOOK, John W. (d.1/6/63) **1**
VANDIVER, Ernest **2**
VAN DOREN, Charles **1,2**
VAN DOREN, Mamie **1,2**
VAN DOREN, Mark (d.12/10/72) **1,2**
VAN DYKE, Dick **2,3,4,5**
VANESS, Carol **4**
VAN FLEET, James A. **1,2**

CELEBRITY REGISTER 1990 — Cumulative Index

VAN FLEET, Jo **1,2**
VAN HALEN **5**
VAN HEUSEN, Jimmy **2,3,4**
VAN HORNE, Harriet **2,3**
VANIER, George **1**
VANOCUR, Sander **2**
VAN PAASSEN, Pierre (d.1/8/68) **1,2**
VAN PEEBLES, Melvin **3**
VAN VECHTEN, Carl (d.12/21/64) **1,2**
VAN VOOREN, Monique **1,2**
VARSI, Diane **1**
VAUGHAN, Sarah **2,3,4,5**
VAUGHAN, William **2**
VEECK, Bill **1,2**
VENETOULIS, Ted **4**
VENTURI, Robert **3,4**
VERA-ELLEN (d.8/30/81) **1**
VERDON, Gwen **1,2,3,4,5**
VEREEN, Ben **3,4,5**
VERRETT, Shirley **3,4,5**
VIC, Trader **2**
VICTOR, Sally (d.5/14/77) **1,2**
VIDAL, Gore **1,2,3,4,5**
VIDOR, King (d.11/1/82) **1**
VIERECK, Peter **1,2**
VIGUERIE, Richard **4**
VILA, George **2**
VILLA-LOBOS, Hector (d.11/17/59) **1**
VILLELLA, Edward **3,4,5**
VINSON, Carl (d.6/1/81) **1,2**
VISCONTI, Luchino (d.3/17/76) **3**
VOIGHT, Jon **3,4,5**
VOLPE, John **3**
VON BEKESY, Georg (d.6/13/72) **2**
VON BRAUN, Wernher (d.6/77) **1,2,3**
VON FURSTENBERG, Betsy **1,2,3**
VON HOFFMAN, Nicholas **3,4,5**
VON KARAJAN, Herbert (d.7/20/89) **1**
 (see also KARAJAN **3,4**)
VONNEGUT, Kurt, Jr. **3,4**
VON STADE, Frederica **4,5**
VON SYDOW, Max **3,4,5**
VOROSHILOV, Klementii (d.12/2/69) **1**
VREELAND, Diana (d.8/22/89) **2,3,4**

W

WADSWORTH, James (d.3/13/84) **2**
WAGNER, Lindsay **5**
WAGNER, Robert **1,2,4,5**
WAGNER, Robert F. **1,2**
WAKSMAN, Selman A. (d.8/16/73) **1,2,3**
WALCOTT, Jersey Joe **1**
WALD, Jerry (d.7/13/62) **1**
WALDHEIM, Kurt **3**
WALES, The Prince & Princess of **4** (see also PRINCE CHARLES **1,5**)
WALKER, Alice **4,5**
WALKER, Danton (d.8/8/60) **1**
WALKER, Edwin **1**
WALKER, Herchel **4**
WALKER, Nancy **1,2**
WALLACE, Dewitt (d.3/30/81) **1,2** (see also VERA WALLACE, Dewitt & Lila **3**)
WALLACE, George C. **2,3,4**
WALLACE, Henry (d.11/18/65) **1,2**
WALLACE, Irving **3,4,5**
WALLACE, Mike **1,2,3,4,5**
WALLACH, Eli **1,2,3,4,5**
WALLENDA, Karl (d.3/22/78) **2**
WALLENSTEIN, Alfred (d.3/22/78) **1,2**
WALLIS, Hal (d.10/5/86) **1**
WALSH, Bill **4**
WALTARI, Mika (d.8/26/79) **1**

WALTER, Bruno (d.2/17/65) **1**
WALTER, Francis (d.5/31/63) **1,2**
WALTERS, Barbara **3,4,5**
WALTERS, Charles (d.8/14/82) **2**
WALTERS, Vernon **4**
WALTON, Sir William (d.3/8/83) **1**
WAMBAUGH, Joseph **4,5**
WANG, An **4**
WANGER, Walter (d.11/18/68) **1,2**
WANNISKI, Jude **4**
WARHOL, Andy (d.2/22/87) **3,4**
WARING, Fred (d.7/29/84) **1,2**
WARMATH, Murray **2**
WARNER, Curt **4**
WARNER, Jack (d.9/9/78) **1,2,3**
WARNER, Robert F. **1,2**
WARREN, Earl (d.7/9/74) **1,2,3**
WARREN, Leonard (d.3/4/60) **1**
WARREN, Robert Penn **1,2**
WARWICK, Dionne **3,4,5**
WASHINGTON, Dinah (d.12/14/63) **2**
WASHINGTON, Harold **4**
WASHINGTON, Walter **3**
WASSERMAN, Lew **2,3,4,5**
WASSERSTEIN, Wendy **5**
WATERS, Ethel (d.9/1/77) **1,2,3**
WATKINS, Franklin **2**
WATSON, James **3,4**
WATSON, Thomas J., Jr. **1,2**
WATSON, Tom **4,5**
WATTS, Alan (d.11/16/73) **3**
WATTS, André **3,4,5**
WAUGH, Alec (d.9/3/81) **1,2**
WAUGH, Evelyn (d.4/10/66) **1**
WAYNE, David **1,2**
WAYNE, John (d.6/11/79) **1,2,3**
WEAVER, Dennis **2**
WEAVER, Earl **4**
WEAVER, Robert **2**
WEAVER, Sigourney **4,5**
WEAVER, Sylvester ("Pat") **1,2**
WEBB, Clifton (d.10/13/66) **1,2**
WEBB, David **3**
WEBB, Del (d.7/4/74) **1,2**
WEBB, Jack (d.12/23/82) **1,2**
WEBB, James **2**
WEBB, Jimmy **3,4,5**
WEBER, Bruce **4**
WEBSTER, Margaret (d.11/13/72) **1,2**
WECHSBERG, Joseph (d.4/10/83) **2**
WECHSLER, James (d.9/11/83) **1,2,3**
WEDEMEYER, Albert C. **1**
WEEDE, Robert (d.7/9/72) **1,2**
WEEKS, Edward **1,2**
WEEKS, Sinclair (d.1/27/72) **1,2**
WEICKER, Lowell **4**
WEIDMAN, Jerome **1,2**
WEIN, George **2**
WEINBERG, Sidney J. (d.7/23/69) **1,2**
WEINBERGER, Caspar **4**
WEISS, George (d.8/13/72) **1,2**
WEISS, Seymour **2**
WEISSBERGER, L. Arnold (d.2/27/81) **2**
WEISSMULLER, Johnny (d.1/20/84) **1**
WEITZ, John **3,4,5**
WELCH, Joseph (d.10/6/60) **1**
WELCH, Leo (d.10/22/78) **2**
WELCH, Raquel **3,4,5**
WELCH, Robert (d.9/19/69) **2,3**
WELD, Tuesday **2,3**
WELK, Lawrence **1,2,3,4,5**
WELLES, Orson (d.10/10/85) **1,2,3,4**
WELLS, Mary (see LAWRENCE, Mary Wells) **3,4**
WELSH, Matthew **2**

WELTY, Eudora **1,2,3,4,5**
WERNER, Oskar (d.10/23/84) **3**
WERTHAM, Fredric (d.11/18/81) **1,2**
WERTMULLER, Lina **4,5**
WEST, Jerry **3**
WEST, Jessamyn (d.2/23/84) **1,2**
WEST, Mae (d.11/22/80) **1,2,3**
WEST, Rebecca (d.3/15/83) **1**
WESTHEIMER, Ruth **4,5**
WEXLER, Jacqueline Grennan **3,4**
WHALEN, Grover (d.4/20/62) **1**
WHITCOMB, Jon **1,2**
WHITE, Betty **4**
WHITE, Byron (Whizzer) **2,3,4**
WHITE, E.B. (d.9/30/85) **1,2,3,4**
WHITE, Josh (d.9/6/69) **1,2**
WHITE, Miles **2**
WHITE, Nancy **2**
WHITE, Paul Dudley (d.10/31/73) **1,2**
WHITE, Robert **2**
WHITE, T.H. (d.1/18/64) **1**
WHITE, Theodore H. (d.5/16/86) **1,2,3,4**
WHITE, Thomas (d.12/22/65) **1,2**
WHITE, William L. (d.7/26/73) **1,2**
WHITE, William S. **2**
WHITEHEAD, Edward (d.4/16/78) **1,2,3**
WHITEMAN, Paul (d.12/29/67) **1,2**
WHITING, Margaret **1,4,5**
WHITNEY, C.V. ("Sonny") **1,2,3** (see also WHITNEY, Cornelius Vanderbilt and Marylou **4**)
WHITNEY, John Hay ("Jock") (d.2/8/82) **1,2,3**
WHITTAKER, Charles Evans (d.11/26/73) **1,2**
WHITWORTH, Kathy **3,4**
WHORF, Richard (d.12/14/66) **1,2**
WHYTE, William H. **1,2,3**
WICKER, Tom **3,4,5**
WIDMARK, Richard **1,2**
WIENER, Norbert (d.3/18/64) **1,2**
WIESENBERGER, Arthur **2**
WIESNER, Jerome **3**
WILANDER, Mat **4,5**
WILDE, Cornell **1,2**
WILDE, Frazar **2**
WILDER, Billy **1,2,3,4,5**
WILDER, Gene **4,5**
WILDER, Thornton (d.12/7/75) **1,2,3**
WILDING, Michael (d.7/9/79) **1**
WILEY, Alexander (d.10/26/67) **1,2**
WILKINS, Roy (d.9/8/81) **2,3**
WILKINSON, Bud **1,2**
WILL, George **4,5**
WILLIAMS, Andy **2,3,4**
WILLIAMS, Billy Dee **4,5**
WILLIAMS, Cara **2**
WILLIAMS, Edward Bennett (d.8/13/88) **2,3,4**
WILLIAMS, Emlyn **1,2**
WILLIAMS, Esther **1,2**
WILLIAMS, G. Mennen **1,2**
WILLIAMS, Harrison **1,2**
WILLIAMS, John **2,4,5**
WILLIAMS, Robin **4,5**
WILLIAMS, Ted **1,2,3,4**
WILLIAMS, Tennessee (d.2/25/83) **1,2,3**
WILLIAMS, Treat **4,5**
WILLIAMS, Vanessa **4,5**
WILLIAMS, William Carlos (d.3/4/63) **1**
WILLIAMSON, Nicol **3,4,5**
WILLIS, Bruce **5**
WILLS, Maury **2**
WILLSON, Meredith (d.6/15/84) **1,2**

483

WILSON, Charles E. ("Electric") (d.1/31/72) **1**
WILSON, Charles E. ("Engine") **1**
WILSON, Colin **1**
WILSON, Don (d.4/25/82) **1,2**
WILSON, Earl (d.1/16/87) **1,2,34**
WILSON, Edmund (d.6/12/72) **1,2**
WILSON, Flip **3,4**
WILSON, Joseph (d,3/76) **2**
WILSON, Julie **1,2,4,5**
WILSON, Kemmons **3**
WILSON, Kendrick **2**
WILSON, Lanford **4,5**
WILSON, Marie (d.11/23/72) **1,2**
WILSON, Nancy **3**
WILSON, O.W. **2**
WILSON, Robert **4**
WILSON, Sloan **1,2**
WINCHELL, Paul **1,2**
WINCHELL, Walter (d.2/5/70) **1,2**
WINDSOR, Duchess of (d.4/24/86) **1,2,3,4**
WINDSOR, Duke of (d.5/28/72) **1**
WINDSOR, Kathleen **1**
WINFIELD, Dave **4,5**
WINFREY, Oprah **5**
WINGER, Debra **4,5**
WINKLER, Henry **4,5**
WINSTON, Harry (d.12/8/78) **1,2**
WINSTON, Norman (d.10/16/77) **1,2**
WINTERS, Jonathan **1,2,3,4,5**
WINTERS, Shelley **1,2,3,4,5**
WINWOOD, Estelle (d.6/20/84) **1**
WINWOOD, Steve **5**
WIRTZ, Willard **2**
WODEHOUSE, P.G. (d.2/14/75) **1,2,3**
WOLFE, Tom **3,4**
WOLFSON, Louis (d.10/11/79) **1,2**
WONDER, Stevie **4,5**
WONG, Anna May (d.2/3/61) **1**
WONG, B.D. **5**
WOOD, Natalie (d.11/29/81) **1,2,3**
WOOD, Peggy (d.3/18/78) **1,2**
WOOD, Robert (d.11/6/69) **1**
WOOD, Sidney **1,2**
WOODCOCK, Leonard **3**

WOODEN, John **3**
WOODFILL, W. Stewart (d.3/7/84) **1,2**
WOODLAWN, Holly **3**
WOODRUFF, Judy **4**
WOODRUFF, Robert (d.3/85) **2**
WOODS, George **2**
WOODWARD, Bob **4**
WOODWARD, Edward **5**
WOODWARD, Joanne **1,2,3,4,5**
WOOLDRIDGE, Dean **2**
WOOLLEY, Monty (d.5/6/63) **1**
WOOLMAN, C.E. (d.9/11/66) **2**
WOUK, Herman **1,2,4,5**
WOZNIAK, Stephen **4**
WRIGHT, Cobina (d.4/9/70) **1,2**
WRIGHT, Jim **4**
WRIGHT, Martha **2**
WRIGHT, Richard (d.11/28/60) **1**
WRIGHT, Teresa **1,2**
WRIGHTSMAN, C.B. **2,3**
WRIGLEY, P.D. (Philip) (d.4/12/77) **1,2,3**
WYATT, Jane **1,2**
WYETH, Andrew **1,2,3,4,5**
WYETH, Jamie **3,4,5**
WYLER, William (d.7/27/71) **1,2,3**
WYLIE, Philip (d.10/25/71) **1,2**
WYMAN, Jane **1,2,4**
WYNETTE, Tammy **4,5**
WYNN, Early **2**
WYNN, Ed (d.6/19/66) **1,2**
WYNN, Keenan (d.10/14/86) **1,2**
WYNTER, Dana **1**

X

X, Malcolm (d.2/21/65) **2**

Y

YAMASAKI, Minoru **2,3,4**
YANKELOVICH, Daniel **4**
YARBOROUGH, Cale **4,5**
YARBOROUGH, Ralph **2**
YASTREZEMSKI, Carl **3,4,5**

YAWKEY, Tom (d.7/9/76) **2,3**
YCAZA, Manuel **2**
YERBY, Frank **1,2**
YOAKIM, Dwight **5**
YORK, Duke & Duchess **5**
YORK, Michael **3,4,5**
YORK, Susannah **3**
YORTY, Samuel **2**
YOUNG, Alan **2**
YOUNG, Andrew **4,5**
YOUNG, Chic (d.3/14/73) **1,2**
YOUNG, Gig (d.10/19/78) **3**
YOUNG, Loretta **1,2,3,4,5**
YOUNG, Robert **1,2,3,4,5**
YOUNG, Stephen **2**
YOUNG, Steve **4**
YOUNGMAN, Henny **2,3,4,5**
YOUNT, Robin **4**
YOUSKEVITCH, Igor **1,2**
YURICK, Sol **3**

Z

ZACKERLY **1**
ZANOVA, Aja **2**
ZANUCK, Darryl (d.12/22/79) **1,2,3**
ZANUCK, Richard **3,4,5**
ZAPPA, Frank **3**
ZAUDERER, George (d.12/22/80) **2**
ZECKENDORF, William (d.9/30/76) **1,2,3**
ZEFFIRELLI, Franco **3,4,5**
ZELLERBACH, J.D. (d.8/3/63) **1**
ZERBE, Jerome (d.8/19/88) **1,2,3**
ZHUKOV, Georgi (d.6/18/74) **1**
ZIMBALIST, Efrem **1,2,3**
ZIMBALIST, Stephanie **4,5**
ZINDEL, Paul **3**
ZINNEMAN, Fred **1,2**
ZIOLKOWSKI, Korczak (d.10/20/82) **2,3**
ZOLOTOW, Maurice **1,2**
ZORINA, Vera **1,2**
ZUCKERMAN, Mortimer **4,5**
ZUKERMAN, Pinchas **4,5**
ZUKOR, Adolph (d.6/10/76) **2,3**